LITERATURE

LITERATURE

A Contemporary Introduction

James Hurt

University of Illinois

Macmillan College Publishing Company

New York

Editor: D. Anthony English
Production Supervisor: Jane O'Neill
Production Manager: Lynn Pearlman
Cover Designer: Robert Freese
Cover illustration: Giacomo Balla. *Street Light.* 1909. Oil on canvas. 68¾ in. × 45¼ in. (174.7 × 114.7 cm.). The Museum of Modern Art, New York. Hillman Periodicals Fund.

This book was set in Baskerville by Americomp
and was printed and bound by Rand McNally and Co.
The cover was printed by New England Book Components, Inc.

Macmillan College Publishing Company
866 Third Avenue, New York, New York 10022

Macmillan College Publishing Company is part of
the Maxwell Communication Group of Companies.

Maxwell Macmillan Canada, Inc.
1200 Eglinton Avenue East
Suite 200
Don Mills, Ontario M3C 3N1

Library of Congress Cataloging-in-Publication Data
Literature: a contemporary introduction / edited by James Hurt.
    p. cm.
   Includes index.
   ISBN 0-02-359011-4.
   1. Literature—Collections. I. Hurt, James, 1934–
  PN6014.L57 1994   93-12570
  808—dc20   CIP

Printing: 1 2 3 4 5 6 7   Year: 4 5 6 7 8 9 0

Acknowledgments appear on pages 1479–1489, which constitute a continuation of the copyright page.

PREFACE

༄ 𓃬 ༅

Literature: A Contemporary Introduction has been designed to offer something new in the crowded field of college introductions to literature. About 80 percent of its contents are drawn from contemporary American fiction, poetry, and drama. Men and women writers are represented roughly equally, and there are a number of selections by gay and lesbian writers. African-American, Asian-American, Euro-American, Hispanic-American, and Native American writers are also represented fairly equally. The book is arranged by traditional genres—fiction, poetry, and drama; other forms, such as nonfiction prose, are not represented, although a number of critical commentaries are included.

The arguments for making *Literature: A Contemporary Introduction* a largely contemporary, American, culturally diverse book were compelling enough to outweigh the arguments against it. The first, most basic one is based on a simple pedagogical principle: the most successful learning begins in the familiar and then moves out into the unfamiliar. If the student can master literary interpretations of his or her own culture, it will be easier to understand other literatures far removed in space and time, literatures more appropriately studied further along the educational pathway.

Restricting the bulk of the volume to the contemporary and the American also made it possible to achieve a richness and depth often lacking in books of this kind. If one attempts to give a sampling of literature from the beginning to the present and from every part of the globe, the coverage is bound to be quite thin, with the Middle Ages, say, represented by a couple of folk ballads and Africa perhaps represented by a single short story. This thinness of coverage is the reason that the contents of so many introductory books seem so abstract and unreal. A text from Periclean Greece stands next to one from twentieth-century Mississippi; John Donne rubs shoulders with Emily Dickinson; Geoffrey Chaucer and Kate

v

Chopin are thrown into the same pot. This is a version of "literature" unknown outside the classroom: a literature ripped out of its time and place and reassembled into a synthetic construction whose connection to any lived experience is mysterious and unexamined.

Literature: A Contemporary Introduction, by contrast, presents a body of literature that refers to the culture we know best—our own. No single book, of course, can fairly represent the range of contemporary American writing, but by concentrating on one time and one place the book is able to achieve a depth of reference impossible when texts are presented independent of their historical and cultural contexts.

The emphasis on contexts is the other reason this book has claim to be called "a contemporary introduction." The transcendent work of art, existing in some space outside history, is a phenomenon hard to believe in anymore. This book, far from presenting its selections as pure or autonomous, takes every opportunity to set them within their times and places. Introductions, notes, and study questions are intended not only to help readers apprehend the form of the literary work but also to alert them to its place within a culture. Each section of the book develops a distinction among three "registers" of literary study—reading, interpretation, and criticism—adapted from the work of the well-known critic and theorist Robert Scholes. "Criticism" is defined as the process of placing the literary work within its historical and cultural context, and the book offers the student as much help as possible in achieving this difficult goal.

The decision to retain the traditional organization of introductory literature books by genre was less a matter of principle than of pragmatics: the courses that use these books are overwhelmingly organized by genre. Also arguing in favor of this organization was the fact that acknowledgment of genre represented another kind of contextualization, that of literary tradition, which has habitually divided the kingdom of literature into the provinces of stories, poems, and plays.

Only one person's name appears on the book's title page, but many people have made important contributions to it. Four colleagues at the University of Illinois read and critiqued my proposal for the book at an early stage and made valuable suggestions: Alice Deck, Cary Nelson, Robert Dale Parker, and Michael Shapiro. Julie Longhofer read the completed version of the drama section and made many useful comments, which I have acted on whenever possible. A year spent teaching at St. Patrick's College in Dublin just before beginning work on the book directed my attention to a number of questions of literary pedagogy which have shaped my thinking on this book. I am very grateful to the staff of the English department there: Patrick Burke, Brenna Clarke, Michael Clarke, Tom Halpin, Celia Keenan, and John Killeen. Zohreh T. Sullivan has followed the progress of the manuscript from the beginning and has been a great source of ideas as well as inspiration.

A number of colleagues at other institutions have contributed to the book in a more formal way, by serving as press reviewers of the manuscript. They include Professor Judith Mattson Bean, Texas A & M University; Professor Sherill Cobb, Collin Community College; Professor Irene R. Fairley, Northeastern University; Professor Ruth A. Gerik; Professor Jane Helm Maddock, Western Montana College; Professor David Smit, Kansas State University; and Professor Lynn West, Spokane Community College.

At Macmillan, D. Anthony English initiated the project and provided wise and generous guidance through its realization. Bernice Margulies and Eric Newman copyedited a bulky manuscript skillfully and efficiently. Jane O'Neill, as production supervisor, kept a complex publishing job on track with unfailing energy and good humor. My fervent thanks to all of them.

CONTENTS

჻ᎧᎧᎧ჻

ix

II POETRY

From Reading to Interpretation and Criticism   607

Writing About Poetry   610

Poems for Further Reading   614

III DRAMA

Introduction

ঝৎ ৵৵

Literature: A Contemporary Introduction, as a text for a college introductory literature class, is very much like a number of other books. It is arranged by genre—fiction, poetry, and drama—and it makes available, conveniently and inexpensively, a great many short stories, poems, and plays for reading and study. *Literature,* again like comparable books, also contains a great deal of material designed to help you improve your skills of reading and interpreting literature: biographical introductions to the various authors, questions on each work for discussion and writing, and analytic introductions to the elements of fiction, poetry, and drama designed to help you focus your study on the component parts of the works you read.

But *Literature* has some unusual features, too, that set it apart from other introductions to literature and justify its claim to be called a *"contemporary* introduction." The first is that the overwhelming majority of its selections in all three genres are contemporary and American. There are a couple of reasons for this feature. Most introductory anthologies try to include texts from as wide a range of periods and places as possible—for example, the Middle Ages as well as the twentieth century, Africa as well as New York. As a result, nothing is represented very well. A handful of lyric poems ends up standing for the Middle Ages, and a single short story ends up representing, say, Africa. *Literature* sacrifices breadth for depth. By not trying to include the entire world for 3,000 years, *Literature* is able to represent our own time and place with some depth and "thickness." (No single book, of course, can include the entire range of contemporary American writing.)

The other reason for *Literature*'s emphasis on the familiar and the near-at-hand is that the most successful learning begins with what we know and gradually moves into what we do not know. Most of the stories, poems, and plays in *Literature* deal with contemporary American life. If we are to be well read, we will eventually want to read works that deal with other times and places (*not* American, *not* contemporary). But we will be better equipped to understand the less familiar if we have mastered the familiar.

1

The emphasis in *Literature* is on the contemporary American work, but that is not to say that older literature is excluded. Each section begins with a selection of older works, chosen mainly to illustrate the traditions out of which contemporary writing has grown. Fiction writers, after all, cannot write as if Chekhov never lived; the precedents of Shakespeare and Wordsworth are equally powerful for play-wrights and poets. Shakespeare (and Chekhov and Wordsworth) is truly our con-temporary, in several senses, and correspondingly has a place here.

Literature is a "contemporary" introduction to literature in another sense as well, and that is in its pervasive emphasis upon the historical and cultural contexts of literature. Until fairly recently, the study of literature in schools and colleges was dominated by the "New Criticism," which insisted that anything "outside" the literary work was irrelevant, even the author's name and the date of compo-sition. There were good reasons for this insistence—it made readers pay close attention to what was "inside" the story or poem—but it went against readers' natural curiosity about writers and the circumstances under which they wrote. In recent years the prohibition against consideration of contexts has fallen, and literary critics of all kinds rely heavily on contexts—historical, social, cultural—to build their interpretations of literary works. *Literature* emphasizes contexts throughout—in biographical author introductions, in the suggestions for discus-sion and writing, and in the sections on reading fiction, poetry, and drama. At the same time, close formal analysis is not neglected. The best reading combines close attention to form and structure with equal attentiveness to contexts. This is the sort of reading that *Literature* seeks to encourage.

Finally, *Literature* is designed to demystify literary interpretation as much as possible. Understanding stories, poems, and plays is mostly common sense; it does not differ fundamentally from understanding anything else—newspapers and magazines, television, even one's friends. Even the term "introduction to litera-ture," which colleges and universities and textbooks, including this one, use, is dubious. By the time you get to college, you have had many introductions to literature—from being read to as a baby, from watching television, from taking grade school and high school classes. Your college introduction to literature may be a little more systematic and sophisticated than these earlier introductions, but it is no different in kind. It pushes a little further skills you learned to use long ago, to interpret not only your reading but also movies and television shows as well as the events of everyday life. We are never "introduced" to literature once and for all. Ideally, we should continue to sharpen our interpretive skills, to be "intro-duced" to literature over and over all our lives. *Literature* is nothing more than a tool for use on one part of that journey. The editor hopes it will be a helpful and enjoyable one.

I

FICTION

Reading Fiction Critically

ॐ ୧

The most common way of classifying literature divides it into poetry, fiction, and drama. These genres ("types") correspond roughly to the "modes" of literature recognized by the ancient Greeks: the lyric, the narrative, and the dramatic. Distinctions between the modes turn upon the relationship between speaker and subject. In the lyric mode (a lyric poem is an example), the speaker takes his or her own experiences and feelings as the subject. In the narrative mode (say, a novel), the speaker describes and reports the doings of characters other than himself or herself. In the dramatic mode (a play or movie), the speaker vanishes, and the characters speak and act directly to us and to one another.

Neither the division into the genres of poetry, fiction, and drama nor the related division into the modes of lyric, narrative, and dramatic does justice to the complexity of literature. Poetry can be narrative and even dramatic as well as lyrical. A much wider range of narrative stances is available to the writer of fiction than the idea of modes suggests, and drama can have lyrical and narrative elements in it. Nevertheless, dividing literature into poetry, fiction, and drama has the virtue of simplicity as well as that of corresponding to the way writers, publishers, and readers ordinarily conceive of their work. Genres may be mixed freely, but we still organize the world of literature into poems, novels and short stories, and plays.

We call novels and short stories *fiction*, a word we usually use to set off the imaginary from the factual. The emphasis in the word *fiction*, however, was originally not on falseness but on artfulness; it comes from the Latin verb that means "to form." "Truth" and "art" are both difficult concepts. Just as it is hard to imagine a narrative that is all true or all false (most fiction is probably autobiographical or historical on some level), so it is difficult to imagine a narrative that is "unformed," told without any art at all. Indeed, some of the most factual, artless, utilitarian narratives (news items, obituaries, court testimony) have the most rigid and obvious forms. The crucial difference between fictional and non-

5

fictional narrative is not that one is false and the other true or that one is "formed" and the other "unformed" but that fiction is formed in such a way as to generate the most provocative and interesting interpretations. A newspaper account of an automobile accident may be quite artfully told, but it is written in such a way as to convey precise information. A fictional account of an accident may be no more artfully told, but it will be told in such a way as to generate speculation, ambiguity, interpretation. We might call the newspaper account interpretively "thin," and the fictional account "thick." Whatever the mix of truth and falsehood in each, we will value the newspaper account for the information it gives us about the real world and the piece of fiction for its suggestiveness, its power to stimulate thought.

Interpretation, the reader's response, is therefore crucial to fiction. We might even go so far as to say that a novel or a short story does not fully exist as long as it remains words on printed pages; it is fully realized only in the interactive process of reading and interpretation. The interpretation of fiction can, on one level, be quite simple, consisting simply of the intuitive, commonsense recognition of what a story "means," that is, what area of experience it deals with and what it has to say about that experience. We might call this kind of initial, global response "synthetic" because it intuitively makes a synthesis of the various elements of the story and makes provisional sense of their relationship. This kind of initial response is very valuable and should be remembered in later stages of study in order to test later perceptions against that first "gut feeling."

If one is to test, refine, and enrich that first reaction to a narrative, however, one has to go beyond synthesis to analysis, breaking the story into its parts and examining each part separately. In the following pages, six elements of fiction are discussed—plot and structure, point of view and focalization, character, setting, metaphor, and theme—each in connection with a particular story. To end the process of interpretation, however, with the elements of the story all separate would be like finishing a job of auto repair with all the engine parts scattered around the shop. The process of analysis has to come full circle back to synthesis, back to a holistic reading that sets each element in its proper relation to the others and results in an overall reading similar to the first reaction but enriched and deepened by the intervening analysis. So this section ends with an interpretation of Talat Abbasi's short story "Sari Petticoats" that not only takes into account the story's formal elements but also arrives at a synthesis of those elements in a rich, contextualized interpretation of the story.

Read the following story, James Alan McPherson's "A Loaf of Bread," as preparation for a discussion of plot and structure.

James Alan McPherson

James Alan McPherson (b. 1943) grew up in Georgia. After receiving a law degree at Harvard, he turned to writing. He has published two collections of short stories, *Hue and Cry* (1969) and *Elbow Room* (1977). *Elbow Room* won a Pulitzer Prize for fiction in 1978. He teaches writing at the University of Iowa Writer's Workshop.

A LOAF OF BREAD

It was one of those obscene situations, pedestrian to most people, but invested with meaning for a few poor folk whose lives are usually spent outside the imaginations of their fellow citizens. A grocer named Harold Green was caught red-handed selling to one group of people the very same goods he sold at lower prices at similar outlets in better neighborhoods. He had been doing this for many years, and at first he could not understand the outrage heaped upon him. He acted only from habit, he insisted, and had nothing personal against the people whom he served. They were his neighbors. Many of them he had carried on the cuff during hard times. Yet, through some mysterious access to a television station, the poor folk were now empowered to make grand denunciations of the grocer. Green's children now saw their father's business being picketed on the Monday evening news.

No one could question the fact that the grocer had been overcharging the people. On the news even the reporter grimaced distastefully while reading the statistics. His expression said, "It is my job to report the news, but sometimes even I must disassociate myself from it to protect my honor." This, at least, was the impression the grocer's children seemed to bring away from the television. Their father's name had not been mentioned, but there was a close-up of his store with angry black people and a few outraged whites marching in groups of three in front of it. There was also a close-up of his name. After seeing this, they were in no mood to watch cartoons. At the dinner table, disturbed by his children's silence, Harold Green felt compelled to say, "I am not a dishonest man." Then he felt ashamed. The children, a boy and his older sister, immediately left the table, leaving Green alone with his wife. "Ruth, I am not dishonest," he repeated to her.

Ruth Green did not say anything. She knew, and her husband did not, that the outraged people had also picketed the school attended by their children. They had threatened to return each day until Green lowered his prices. When they called her at home to report this, she had promised she would talk with him. Since she could not tell him this, she waited for an opening. She looked at her husband across the table.

"I did not make the world," Green began, recognizing at once the seriousness in her stare. "My father came to this country with nothing but his shirt. He was exploited for as long as he couldn't help himself. He did not protest or picket. He put himself in a position to play by the rules he had learned." He waited for his wife to answer, and when she did not, he tried again. "I did not make this world," he repeated. "I only make my way in it. Such people as these, they do not know enough to not be exploited. If not me, there would be a Greek, a Chinaman, maybe an Arab or a smart one of their own kind. Believe me, I deal with them. There is something in their style that lacks the patience to run a concern such as mine. If I closed down, take my word on it, someone else would do what has to be done.''

But Ruth Green was not thinking of his leaving. Her mind was on other matters. Her children had cried when they came home early from school. She had no special feeling for the people who picketed, but she did not like to see her children cry. She had kissed them generously, then sworn them to silence. "One day this week," she told her husband, "you will give free, for eight hours, anything your customers come in to buy. There will be no publicity, except what they spread by word of mouth. No matter what they say to you, no matter what they take, you will remain silent." She stared deeply into him for what she knew was there. "If you refuse, you have seen the last of your children and myself."

Her husband grunted. Then he leaned toward her. "I will not knuckle under," he said. "I will *not* give!"

"We shall see," his wife told him.

The black pickets, for the most part, had at first been frightened by the audacity of their undertaking. They were peasants whose minds had long before become resigned to their fate as victims. None of them, before now, had thought to challenge this. But now, when they watched themselves on television, they hardly recognized the faces they saw beneath the hoisted banners and placards. Instead of reflecting the meekness they all felt, the faces looked angry. The close-ups looked especially intimidating. Several of the first pickets, maids who worked in the suburbs, reported that their employers, seeing the activity on the afternoon news, had begun treating them with new respect. One woman, midway through the weather report, called around the neighborhood to disclose that her employer had that very day given her a new china plate for her meals. The paper plates, on which all previous meals had been served, had been thrown into the wastebasket. One recipient of this call, a middle-aged woman known for her bashfulness and humility, rejoined that her husband, a sheet-metal worker, had only a few hours before been called "Mister" by his supervisor, a white man with a passionate hatred of color. She added the tale of a neighbor down the street, a widow woman named Murphy, who had at first been reluctant to join the picket; this woman now was insisting it should be made a daily event. Such talk as this circulated among the people who had been instrumental in raising the issue. As news of their victory leaked into the ears of others who had not participated, they received all through the night calls from strangers requesting verification, offering advice, and vowing support. Such strangers listened and then volunteered stories about indignities inflicted on them by city officials, policemen, other grocers. In this way, over a period of hours, the community became even more incensed and restless than it had been at the time of the initial picket.

Soon the man who had set events in motion found himself a hero. His name was Nelson Reed, and all his adult life he had been employed as an assembly-line worker. He was a steady husband, the father of three children, and a deacon in the Baptist church. All his life he had trusted in God and gotten along. But now something in him capitulated to the reality that came suddenly into focus. "I was wrong," he told people who called him. "The onliest thing that matters in this world is *money*. And when was the last time you seen a picture of Jesus on a dollar bill?" This line, which he repeated over and over, caused a few callers to laugh nervously, but not without some affirmation that this was indeed the way things were. Many said they had known it all along. Others argued that although it was certainly true, it was one thing to live without money and quite another to live without faith. But still most callers laughed and said, "You right. You *know* I know you right. Ain't it the truth, though?" Only a few people, among them Nelson Reed's wife, said nothing and looked very sad.

Why they looked sad, however, they would not communicate. And anyone observing their troubled faces would have to trust his own intuition. It is known that Reed's wife, Betty, measured all events against the fullness of her own experience. She was skeptical of everything. Brought to the church after a number of years of living openly with a jazz musician, she had embraced religion when she married Nelson Reed. But though she no longer believed completely in the world, she nonetheless had not fully embraced God. There was something in the nature of Christ's swift rise that had always bothered her, and something in the blood and vengeance of the Old Testament that was mellowing and refreshing. But she had never communicated these thoughts to anyone, especially her husband. Instead, she smiled vacantly while others professed leaps of faith, remained silent when friends spoke fiercely of their convictions. The presence of this vacuum in her contributed to her personal mystery; people said she was beautiful, although she was not outwardly so. Perhaps it was because she wished to protect this inner beauty that she did not smile now, and looked extremely sad, listening to her husband on the telephone.

Nelson Reed had no reason to be sad. He seemed to grow more energized and talkative as the days passed. He was invited by an alderman, on the Tuesday after the initial picket, to tell his story on a local television talk show. He sweated heavily under the hot white lights and attempted to be philosophical. "I notice," the host said to him, "that you are not angry at this exploitative treatment. What, Mr. Reed, is the source of your calm?" The assembly-line worker looked unabashedly into the camera and said, "I have always believed in *Justice* with a capital *J.* I was raised up from a baby believin' that God ain't gonna let nobody go *too* far. See, in *my* mind God is in charge of *all* the capital letters in the alphabet of this world. It say in the Scripture He is Alpha and Omega, the first and the last. He is just about the *onliest* capitalizer they is." Both Reed and the alderman laughed. "Now, when *men* start to capitalize, they gets *greedy.* The put a little *j* in *joy* and a littler one in *justice.* They raise up a big *G* in *Greed* and a big *E* in *Evil.* Well, soon as they commence to put a little *g* in *god,* you can expect some kind of reaction. The Savior will just raise up the *H* in *Hell* and go on from there. And that's just what I'm doin', giving these sharpies *HELL* with a big *H.*" The talk show host laughed along with Nelson Reed and the alderman. After the taping they drank coffee in the back room of the studio and talked about the sad shape of the world.

Three days before he was to comply with his wife's request, Green, the grocer, saw this talk show on television while at home. The words of Nelson Reed sent a chill through him. Though Reed had attempted to be philosophical, Green did not perceive the statement in this light. Instead, he saw a vindictive-looking black man seated between an ambitious alderman and a smug talk-show host. He saw them chatting comfortably about the nature of evil. The cameraman had shot mostly close-ups, and Green could see the set in Nelson Reed's jaw. The color of Reed's face was maddening. When his children came into the den, the grocer was in a sweat. Before he could think, he had shouted at them and struck the button turning off the set. The two children rushed from the room screaming. Ruth Green ran in from the kitchen. She knew why he was upset because she had received a call about the show, but she said nothing and pretended ignorance. Her children's school had been picketed that day, as it had the day before. But both children were still forbidden to speak of this to their father.

"Where do they get so much power?" Green said to his wife. "Two days ago nobody would have cared. Now everywhere, even in my home, I am condemned as a rascal. And what do I own? An airline? A multinational? Half of South America? *No!* I own three stores, one of which happens to be in a certain neighborhood inhabited by people who cost me money to run it." He sighed and sat upright on the sofa, his chubby legs spread wide. "A cabdriver has a meter that clicks as he goes along. I pay extra for insurance, iron bars, pilfering by customers and employees. Nothing clicks. But when I add a little overhead to my prices, suddenly everything clicks. But for someone else. When was there last such a world?" He pressed the palms of both hands to his temples, suggesting a bombardment of brain-stinging sounds.

This gesture evoked no response from Ruth Green. She remained standing by the door, looking steadily at him. She said, "To protect yourself, I would not stock any more fresh cuts of meat in the store until after the giveaway on Saturday. Also, I would not tell it to the employees until after the first customer of the day has begun to check out. But I would urge you to hire several security guards to close the door promptly at seven-thirty, as is usual." She wanted to say much more than this, but did not. Instead she watched him. He was looking at the blank gray television screen, his palms still pressed against his ears. "In case you need to hear again," she continued in a weighty tone of voice, "I said two days ago, and I say again now, that if you fail to do this you will not see your children again for many years."

He twisted his head and looked up at her. "What is the color of these people?" he asked.

"Black," his wife said.

"And what is the name of my children?"

"Green."

The grocer smiled. "There is your answer," he told his wife. "Green is the only color I am interested in."

His wife did not smile. "Insufficient," she said.

"The world is mad!" he moaned. "But it is a point of sanity with me to not bend. I will not bend." He crossed his legs and pressed one hand firmly atop his knee. *"I will not bend,"* he said.

"We will see," his wife said.

Nelson Reed, after the television interview, became the acknowledged leader of the disgruntled neighbors. At first a number of them met in the kitchen at his house; then, as space was lacking for curious newcomers, a mass meeting was held on Thursday in an abandoned theater. His wife and three children sat in the front row. Behind them sat the widow Murphy, Lloyd Dukes, Tyrone Brown, Les Jones—those who had joined him on the first picket line. Behind these sat people who bought occasionally at the store, people who lived on the fringes of the neighborhood, people from other neighborhoods come to investigate the problem, and the merely curious. The middle rows were occupied by a few people from the suburbs, those who had seen the talk show and whose outrage at the grocer proved much more powerful than their fear of black people. In the rear of the theater crowded aging, old-style leftists, somber students, cynical young black men with angry grudges to explain with inarticulate gestures. Leaning against the walls, huddled near the doors at the rear, tape-recorder-bearing social scientists looked as detached and serene as bookies at the track. Here and there, in this diverse crowd, a politician stationed himself, pumping hands vigorously and pressing his palms gently against the shoulders of elderly people. Other visitors passed out leaflets, buttons, glossy color prints of men who promoted causes, the familiar and obscure. There was a hubbub of voices, a blend of the strident and the playful, the outraged and the reverent, lending an undercurrent of ominous energy to the assembly.

Nelson Reed spoke from a platform on the stage, standing before a yellowed, shredded screen that had once reflected the images of matinee idols. "I don't mind sayin' that I have always been a sucker," he told the crowd. "All my life I have been a sucker for the words of Jesus. Being a natural-born fool, I just ain't never had the *sense* to learn no better. Even right today, while the whole world is saying' wrong is right and up is down, I'm so dumb I'm *still* steady believin' what is wrote in the Good Book. . . ."

From the audience, especially the front rows, came a chorus singing, "Preach!"

"I have no doubt," he continued in a low baritone, "that it's true what is writ in the Good Book: 'The last shall be first and the first shall be last.' I don't know about y'all, but I have *always* been the last. I never wanted to be the first, but sometimes it look like the world get so bad that them that's holdin' onto the tree of life is the onliest ones left when God commence to blowin' dead leafs off the branches."

"Now you preaching," someone called.

In the rear of the theater a white student shouted an awkward "Amen."

Nelson Reed began walking across the stage to occupy the major part of his nervous energy. But to those in the audience, who now hung on his every word, it looked as though he strutted. "All my life," he said, "I have claimed to be a man without earnin' the right to call myself that. You know, the *average* man ain't really a man. The average man is a *bootlicker*. In fact, the *average* man would *run away* if he found hisself standing alone facin' down a adversary. I have done that *too many a time* in my life! But *not no more*. Better to be *once* was than *never* was a man. I will tell you tonight, there is somethin' *wrong* in being average. *I intend to stand up!* Now, if your average man that ain't really a man stand up, two things gonna happen: *one,* he gon bust through all the weights that been place on his head, and, *two,* he gon feel a lot of pain. But that same hurt is what make things fall in place. That, and gettin' your hands on one of these slick four-flushers tight enough so's you can squeeze him and say, *'No more!'* You do that, you g'on hurt some, *but you won't be average no more. . . .*"

"No *more!*" a few people in the front rows repeated.

"I say *no more!*" Nelson Reed shouted.

"No more! No more! No more!" The chant rustled through the crowd like the rhythm of an autumn wind against a shedding tree.

Then people laughed and chattered in celebration.

As for the grocer, from the evening of the television interview he had begun to make plans. Unknown to his wife, he cloistered himself several times with his brother-in-law, an insurance salesman, and plotted a course. He had no intention of tossing steaks to the crowd. "And why should I, Tommy?" he asked his wife's brother, a lean, bald-headed man named Thomas. "I don't cheat anyone. I have never cheated anyone. The businesses I run are always on the up-and- up. So why should I pay?"

"Quite so," the brother-in-law said, chewing an unlit cigarillo. "The world has gone crazy. Next they will say that people in my business are responsible for prolonging life. I have found that people who refuse to believe in death refuse also to believe in the harshness of life. I sell well by saying that death is a long happiness. I show people the realities of life and compare this to a funeral with dignity, *and* the promise of a bundle for every loved one salted away. When they look around hard at life, they usually buy."

So?" asked Green. Thomas was a college graduate with a penchant for philosophy.

"So," Thomas answered. "You must fight to show these people the reality of both your situation and theirs. How would it be if you visited one of their meetings and chalked out, on a blackboard, the dollars and cents of your operation? Explain your overhead, your security fees, all the additional expenses. If you treat them with respect, they might understand."

Green frowned. "That I would never do," he said. "It would be admission of a certain guilt."

The brother-in-law smiled, but only with one corner of his mouth. "Then you have something to feel guilty about?" he asked.

The grocer frowned at him. *"Nothing!"* he said with great emphasis.

"So?" Thomas said.

This first meeting between the grocer and his brother-in-law took place on Thursday, in a crowded barroom.

At the second meeting, in a luncheonette, it was agreed that the grocer should speak privately with the leader of the group, Nelson Reed. The meeting at which this was agreed took place on Friday afternoon. After accepting this advice from Thomas, the grocer resigned himself to explain to Reed, in as finite detail as possible, the economic structure of his operation. He vowed to suppress no information. He would explain everything: inventories, markups, sale items, inflation, balance sheets, specialty items, overhead, and that mysterious item called profit. This last item, promising to be the most difficult to explain, Green and his brother-in-law debated over for several hours. They agreed first of all that a man should not work for free, then they agreed that it was unethical to ruthlessly exploit. From these parameters, they staked out an area between fifteen and forty percent, and agreed that someplace between these two borders lay an amount of return that could be called fair. This was easy, but then Thomas introduced the factor of circumstance. He questioned whether the fact that one serviced a risky area justified the earning of profits, closer to the forty-percent edge of the scale. Green was unsure. Thomas smiled. "Here is a case that will point out an analogy," he said, licking a cigarillo. "I read in the papers that a family wants to sell an electric stove. I call the home and the man says fifty dollars. I ask to come out and inspect the merchandise. When I arrive I see they are poor, have already bought a new stove that is connected, and are selling the old one for fifty dollars because they want it out of the place. The electric stove is in good condition, worth much more than fifty. But because I see what I see I offer forty-five."

Green, for some reason, wrote down this figure on the back of the sales slip for the coffee they were drinking.

The brother-in-law smiled. He chewed his cigarillo. "The man agrees to take forty-five dollars, saying he has had no other calls. I look at the stove again and see a spot of rust. I say I will give him forty dollars. He agrees to this, on condition that I myself haul it away. I say I will haul it away if he comes down to thirty. You, of course, see where I am going."

The grocer nodded. "The circumstances of his situation, his need to get rid of the stove quickly, placed him in a position where he has little room to bargain?"

"Yes," Thomas answered. "So? Is it ethical, Harry?"

Harold Green frowned. He had never liked his brother-in-law, and now he thought the insurance agent was being crafty. "But," he answered, "this man does not *have* to sell! It is his choice whether to wait for other calls. It is not the fault of the buyer that the seller is in a hurry. It is the right of the buyer to get what he wants at the lowest price possible. That is the rule. That has *always* been the rule. And the reverse of it applies to the seller as well."

"Yes," Thomas said, sipping coffee from the Styrofoam cup. "But suppose that in addition to his hurry to sell, the owner was also of a weak soul. There are, after all, many such people." He smiled. "Suppose he placed no value on the money?"

"Then," Green answered, "your example is academic. Here we are not talking about real life. One man lives by the code, one man does not. Who is there free enough to make a judgment?" He laughed. "Now you see," he told his brother-in-law. "Much more than a few dollars are at stake. If this one buyer is to be condemned, then so are most people in the history of the world. An examination of history provides the only answer to your question. This code will be here tomorrow, long after the ones who do not honor it are not."

They argued fiercely late into the afternoon, the brother-in-law leaning heavily on his readings. When they parted, a little before five o'clock, nothing had been resolved.

Neither was much resolved during the meeting between Green and Nelson Reed. Reached at home by the grocer in the early evening, the leader of the group spoke coldly at first, but consented finally to meet his adversary at a nearby drugstore for coffee and a talk. They met at the lunch counter, shook hands awkwardly, and sat for a few minutes discussing the weather. Then the grocer pulled two gray ledgers from his briefcase. "You have for years come into my place," he told the man. "In my memory I have always treated you well. Now our relationship has come to this." He slid the books along the counter until they touched Nelson Reed's arm.

Reed opened the top book and flipped the thick green pages with his thumb. He did not examine the figures. "All I know," he said, "is over at your place a can of soup cost me fifty-five cents, and two miles away at your other store for white folks you chargin' thirty-nine cents." He said this with the calm authority of an outraged soul. A quality of condescension tinged with pity crept into his gaze.

The grocer drummed his fingers on the counter top. He twisted his head and looked away, toward shelves containing cosmetics, laxatives, toothpaste. His eyes lingered on a poster of a woman's apple-red lips and milk-white teeth. The rest of the face was missing.

"Ain't no use to hide," Nelson Reed said, as to a child. "*I* know you wrong, *you* know you wrong, and before I finish, *everybody in this city* g'on know you wrong. God don't *like* ugly." He closed his eyes and gripped the cup of coffee. Then he swung his head suddenly and faced the grocer again. "Man, why you want to *do* people that way?" he asked. "We human, same as you."

"Before *God!*" Green exclaimed, looking squarely into the face of Nelson Reed. "Before *God!*" he said again. "*I am not an evil man!*" These last words sounded more like a moan as he tightened the muscles in his throat to lower the sound of his voice. He tossed his left shoulder as if adjusting the sleeve of his coat, or as if throwing off some unwanted weight. Then he peered along the counter top. No one was watching. At the end of the counter the waitress was scrubbing the coffee urn. "Look at these figures, please," he said to Reed.

The man did not drop his gaze. His eyes remained fixed on the grocer's face.

"All right," Green said. "Don't look. I'll tell you what is in these books, believe me if you want. I work twelve hours a day, one day off per week, running my business in three stores. I am not a wealthy person. In one place, in the area you call white, I get by barely by smiling lustily at old ladies, stocking gourmet stuff on the chance I will build a reputation as a quality store. The two clerks there cheat me; there is nothing I can do. In this business you must be friendly with everybody. The second place is on the other side of town, in a neighborhood as poor as this one. I get out there seldom. The profits are not worth the gas. I use the loss there as a write-off against some other properties," he paused. "Do you understand write-off?" he asked Nelson Reed.

"Naw," the man said.

Harold Green laughed. "What does it matter?" he said in a tone of voice intended for himself alone. "In this area I will admit I make a profit, but it is not so much as you think. But I do not make a profit here because the people are black. I make a profit because a profit is here to be made. I invest more here in window bars, theft losses, insurance, spoilage; I deserve to make more here than at the other places." He looked, almost imploringly, at the man seated next to him. "You don't accept this as the right of a man in business?"

Reed grunted. "Did the bear shit in the woods?" he said.

Again Green laughed. He gulped his coffee awkwardly, as if eager to go. Yet his motions slowed once he had set his coffee cup down on the blue plastic saucer. "Place yourself in *my* situation," he said, his voice high and tentative. "If *you* were running my store in this neighborhood, what would be *your* position? Say on a profit scale of fifteen to forty percent, at what point in between would you draw the line?"

Nelson Reed thought. He sipped his coffee and seemed to chew the liquid. "Fifteen to forty?" he repeated.

"Yes."

"I'm a churchgoin' man," he said. "Closer to fifteen than to forty."

"How close?"

Nelson Reed thought. "In church you tithe ten percent."

"In restaurants you tip fifteen," the grocer said quickly.

"All right," Reed said. "Over fifteen."

"How much over?"

Nelson Reed thought.

"Twenty, thirty, thirty-five?" Green chanted, leaning closer to Reed.

Still the man thought.

"Forty? Maybe even forty-five or fifty?" the grocer breathed in Reed's ear. "In the supermarkets, you know, they have more subtle ways of accomplishing such feats."

Reed slapped his coffee cup with the back of his right hand. The brown liquid swirled across the counter top, wetting the books. *"Damn this!"* he shouted.

Startled, Green rose from his stool.

Nelson Reed was trembling. "I ain't *you*," he said in a deep baritone. "I ain't the *supermarket* neither. All I is is a poor man that works *too* hard to see his pay slip through his fingers like rainwater. All I know is you done *cheat* me, you done *cheat* everybody in the neighborhood, and we organized now to get some of it *back!*" Then he stood and faced the grocer. "My daddy sharecropped down in Mississippi and bought in the company store. He owed them twenty-three years when he died. I paid off five of them years and then run away to up here. Now, I'm a deacon in the Baptist church. I raised my kids the way my daddy raise me and don't bother nobody. Now come to find out, after all my runnin', they done lift that *same company store* up out of Mississippi and slip it down on us here! Well, my daddy was a *fighter*, and if he hadn't owed all them years he would of raise him some hell. Me, I'm steady my daddy's child, plus I got seniority in my union. I'm a free man. Buddy, don't you know *I'm gonna raise me some hell!*"

Harold Green reached for a paper napkin to sop the coffee soaking into his books.

Nelson Reed threw a dollar on top of the books and walked away.

"I will not do it!" Harold Green said to his wife that same evening. They were in the bathroom of their home. Bending over the face bowl, she was washing her hair with a towel draped around her neck. The grocer stood by the door, looking in at her. "I will not bankrupt myself tomorrow," he said.

"I've been thinking about it, too," Ruth Green said, shaking her wet hair. "You'll do it, Harry."

"Why should I?" he asked. "You won't leave. You know it was a bluff. I've waited this long for you to calm down. Tomorrow is Saturday. This week has been a hard one. Tonight let's be realistic."

"Of course you'll do it," Ruth Green said. She said it the way she would say "Have some toast." She said, "You'll do it because you want to see your children grow up."

"And for what other reason?" he asked.

She pulled the towel tighter around her neck. "Because you are at heart a moral man."

He grinned painfully. "If I am, why should I have to prove it to *them?*"

"Not them," Ruth Green said, freezing her movements and looking in the mirror. "Certainly not them. By no means them. They have absolutely nothing to do with this."

"Who, then?" he asked, moving from the door into the room. "Who else should I prove something to?"

His wife was crying. But her entire face was wet. The tears moved secretly down her face.

"Who else?" Harold Green asked.

It was almost eleven P.M. and the children were in bed. They had also cried when they came home from school. Ruth Green said, "For yourself, Harry. For the love that lives inside your heart."

All night the grocer thought about this.

Nelson Reed also slept little that Friday night. When he returned home from the drugstore, he reported to his wife as much of the conversation as he could remember. At first he had joked about the exchange between himself and the grocer, but as more details returned in his conscious mind he grew solemn and then bitter. "He ask me to put myself in *his* place," Reed told his wife. "Can you imagine that kind of gumption? I never cheated nobody in my life. All my life I have lived on Bible principles. I am a deacon in the church. I have work all my life for other folks and I don't even own the house I live in." He paced up and down the kitchen, his big arms flapping loosely at his sides. Betty Reed sat at the table, watching. "This here's a low-down, ass-kicking world," he said. "I swear to God it is! All my life I have lived on principle and I ain't got a dime in the bank. Betty,'' he turned suddenly toward her, "don't you think I'm a fool?"

"Mr. Reed," she said. "Let's go on to bed."

But he would not go to bed. Instead, he took the fifth of bourbon from the cabinet under the sink and poured himself a shot. His wife refused to join him. Reed drained the glass of whiskey, and then another, while he resumed pacing the kitchen floor. He slapped his hands against his sides. "*I* think I'm a fool," he said. "Ain't got a dime in the bank, ain't got a pot to *pee* in or a wall to pitch it over, and that there *cheat* ask me to put myself inside *his* shoes. Hell, I can't even *afford* the kind of shoes he wears." He stopped pacing and looked at his wife.

"Mr. Reed," she whispered, "tomorrow ain't a work day. Let's go to bed."

Nelson Reed laughed, the bitterness in his voice rattling his wife. "The *hell* I will!" he said.

He strode to the yellow telephone on the wall beside the sink and began to dial. The first call was to Lloyd Dukes, a neighbor two blocks away and a lieutenant in the organization. Dukes was not at home. The second call was to McElroy's Bar on the corner of Sixty-fifth and Carroll, where Stanley Harper, another of the lieutenants, worked as a bartender. It was Harper who spread the word, among those men at the bar, that the organization would picket the grocer's store the following morning. And all through the night, in the bedroom of their house, Betty Reed was awakened by telephone calls coming from Lester Jones, Nat Lucas, Mrs. Tyrone Brown, the widow-woman named Murphy, all coordinating the time when they would march in a group against the store owned by Harold Green. Betty Reed's heart beat loudly beneath the covers as she listened to the bitterness and rage in her husband's voice. On several occasions, hearing him declare himself a fool, she pressed the pillow against her eyes and cried.

The grocer opened later than usual this Saturday morning, but still it was early enough to make him one of the first walkers in the neighborhood. He parked his car one block from the store and strolled to work. There were no birds singing. The sky in this area was not blue. It was smog-smutted and gray, seeming on the verge of a light rain. The street, as always, was littered with cans, papers, bits of broken glass. As always the garbage cans overflowed. The morning breeze plastered a sheet of newspaper playfully around the sides of a rusted garbage can. For some reason, using his right foot, he loosened the paper and stood watching it slide into the street and down the block. The movement made him feel good. He whistled while unlocking the bars shielding the windows and door of his store. When he had unlocked the main door he stepped in quickly and threw a switch to the right of the jamb, before the shrill sound of the alarm could shatter his mood. Then he switched on the lights. Everything was as it had been the night before. He had already telephoned his two employees and given them the day off. He busied himself doing the usual things—hauling milk and vegetables from the cooler, putting cash in the till—not thinking about the silence of his wife, or the look in her eyes, only an hour before when he left home. He had determined, at some point while driving through the city, that today it would be business as usual. But he expected very few customers.

The first customer of the day was Mrs. Nelson Reed. She came in around nine-thirty A.M. and wandered about the store. He watched her from the checkout counter. She seemed uncertain of what she wanted to buy. She kept glancing at him down the center aisle. His suspicions aroused, he said finally, "Yes, may I help you, Mrs. Reed?" His words caused her to jerk, as if some devious thought had been perceived going through her mind. She reached over quickly and lifted a loaf of whole wheat bread from the rack and walked with it to the counter. She looked at him and smiled. The smile was a broad, shy one, that rare kind of smile one sees on virgin girls when they first confess love to themselves. Betty Reed was a woman of about forty-five. For some reason he could not comprehend, this gesture touched him. When she pulled a dollar from her purse and laid it on the counter, an impulse, from no place he could locate with his mind, seized control of his tongue. "Free," he told Betty Reed. She paused, then pushed the dollar toward him with a firm and determined thrust of her arm. "Free," he heard himself saying strongly, his right palm spread and meeting her thrust with absolute force. She clutched the loaf of bread and walked out of his store.

The next customer, a little girl, arriving well after ten-thirty A.M., selected a candy bar from the rack beside the counter. "Free," Green said cheerfully. The little girl left the candy on the counter and ran out of the store.

At eleven-fifteen A.M. a wino came in looking desperate enough to sell his soul. The grocer watched him only for an instant. Then he went to the wine counter and selected a half-gallon of medium-grade red wine. He shoved the jug into the belly of the wino, the man's sour breath bathing his face. "Free," the grocer said. "But you must not drink it in here."

He felt good about the entire world, watching the wino through the window gulping the wine and looking guiltily around.

At eleven twenty-five A.M. the pickets arrived.

Two dozen people, men and women, young and old, crowded the pavement in front of his store. Their signs, placards, and voices denounced him as a parasite. The grocer laughed inside himself. He felt lighthearted and wild, like a man drugged. He rushed to the meat counter and pulled a long roll of brown wrapping paper from the rack, tearing it neatly with a quick shift of his body resembling a dance step practiced fervently in his youth. He laid the paper on the chopping block and with the black-inked, felt-tipped marker scrawled, in giant letters, the word FREE. This he took to the window and pasted in place with many strands of Scotch tape. He was laughing wildly. "Free!" he shouted from behind the brown paper. "Free! Free! Free! Free! Free! Free!" He rushed to the door, pushed his head out, and screamed to the confused crowd, *"Free!"* Then he ran back to the counter and stood behind it, like a soldier at attention.

They came in slowly.

Nelson Reed entered first, working his right foot across the dirty tile as if tracking a squiggling worm. The others followed: Lloyd Dukes dragging a placard, Mr. and Mrs. Tyrone Brown, Stanley Harper walking with his fists clenched, Lester Jones with three of his children, Nat Lucas looking sheepish and detached, a clutch of winos, several bashful nuns, ironic-smiling teenagers and a few students. Bringing up the rear was a bearded social scientist holding a tape recorder to his chest. "Free!" the grocer screamed. He threw up his arms in a gesture that embraced, or dismissed, the entire store. *"All free!"* he shouted. He was grinning with the grace of a madman.

The winos began grabbing first. They stripped the shelf of wine in a matter of seconds. Then they fled, dropping bottles on the tile in their wake. The others, stepping quickly through this liquid, soon congealed it into a sticky, bloodlike consistency. The young men went for the cigarettes and luncheon meats and beer. One of them had the prescience to grab a sack from the counter, while the others loaded their arms swiftly, hugging cartons and packages of cold cuts like long-lost friends. The students joined them, less for greed than for the thrill of the experience. The two nuns backed toward the door. As for the older people, men and women, they stood at first as if stuck to the wine-smeared floor. Then Stanley Harper, the bartender, shouted, "The man said *free*, y'all heard him." He paused. "Didn't you say *free* now?" he called to the grocer.

"I said free," Harold Green answered, his temples pounding.

A cheer went up. The older people began grabbing, as if the secret lusts of a lifetime had suddenly seized command of their arms and eyes. They grabbed toilet tissue, cold cuts, pickles, sardines, boxes of raisins, boxes of starch, cans of soup, tins of tuna fish and salmon, bottles of spices, cans of boned chicken, slippery cans of olive oil. Here a man, Lester Jones, burdened himself with several heads of lettuce, while his wife, in another aisle, shouted for him to drop those small items and concentrate on the gourmet section. She herself took imported sardines, wheat crackers, bottles of candied pickles, herring, anchovies, imported olives, French wafers, an ancient, half-rusted can of paté, stocked, by mistake, from the inventory of another store. Others packed their arms with detergents, hams, chocolate-coated cereal, whole chickens with hanging asses, wedges of bologna and salami like squashed footballs, chunks of cheeses, yellow and white, shriveled onions, and green peppers. Mrs. Tyrone Brown hung a curve of pepperoni around her neck and seemed to take on instant dignity, much like a person of noble birth in possession now of a long sought-after gem. Another woman, the widow Murphy, stuffed tomatoes into her bosom, holding a half-chewed lemon in her mouth. The more enterprising fought desperately over the three rusted shopping carts, and the victors wheeled these along the narrow aisles, sweeping into them bulk items— beer in six-packs, sacks of sugar, flour, glass bottles of syrup, toilet cleanser, sugar cookies, prune, apple and tomato juices—while others endeavored to snatch the carts from them. There were several fistfights and much cursing. The grocer, standing behind the counter, hummed and rang his cash register like a madman.

Nelson Reed, the first into the store, followed the nuns out, empty-handed.

In less than half an hour the others had stripped the store and vanished in many directions up and down the block. But still more people came, those late in hearing the news. And when they saw the shelves were bare, they cursed soberly and chased those few stragglers still bearing away goods. Soon only the grocer and the social scientist remained, the latter stationed at the door with his tape recorder sucking in leftover sounds. Then he, too, slipped away up the block.

By twelve-ten P.M. the grocer was leaning against the counter, trying to make his mind slow down. Not a man given to drink during work hours, he nonetheless took a swallow from a bottle of wine, a dusty bottle from beneath the wine shelf, somehow overlooked by the winos. Somewhat recovered, he was preparing to remember what he should do next when he glanced toward a figure at the door. Nelson Reed was standing there, watching him.

"All gone," Harold Green said. "My friend, Mr. Reed, there is no more." Still the man stood in the doorway, peering into the store.

The grocer waved his arms about the empty room. Not a display case had a single item standing. "All gone," he said again, as if addressing a stupid child. "There is nothing left to get. You, my friend, have come back too late for a second load. I am cleaned out."

Nelson Reed stepped into the store and strode toward the counter. He moved through wine-stained flour, lettuce leaves, red, green, and blue labels, bits and pieces of broken glass. He walked toward the counter.

"All day," the grocer laughed, not quite hysterically now, "all day long I have not made a single cent of profit. The entire day was a loss. This store, like the others, is *bleeding* me." He waved his arms about the room in a magnificent gesture of uncaring loss. "Now do you understand?" he said. "Now will you put yourself in my shoes? I have nothing here. Come, now, Mr. Reed, would it not be so bad a thing to walk in my shoes?"

"Mr. Green," Nelson Reed said coldly. "My wife bought a loaf of bread in here this mornin'. She forgot to pay you. I, myself, have come here to pay you your money."

"Oh," the grocer said.

"I think it was brown bread. Don't that cost more than white?"

The two men looked away from each other, but not at anything in the store.

"In my store, yes," Harold Green said. He rang the register with the most casual movement of his finger. The register read fifty-five cents.

Nelson Reed held out a dollar.

"And two cents tax," the grocer said.

The man held out the dollar.

"After all," Harold Green said. "We are all, after all, Mr. Reed, in debt to the government."

He rang the register again. It read fifty-seven cents.

Nelson Reed held out a dollar.

PLOT AND STRUCTURE

Perhaps the most obvious feature of any piece of fiction is its plot. When a book or movie is being discussed and people ask, "What is it about?" they are much more likely to get a plot summary than a character description or a thematic analysis: "It's about a detective who tracks down the crooks who killed his partner," or "It's about some ranchers who try to keep some farmers from fencing in their land." Such statements accomplish what they are intended to do—give a general idea of subject matter—but plot is much more interesting and complex than this. Close analysis of plot can reveal a lot about the writer's craft.

A good starting point for the study of the plot of a story is just a list of the scenes in the story. Every story has a *scenic structure*—a sequence of events, some dramatized in detail, some merely summarized, by which the story is told. Here is a list of the scenes, for example, in James Alan McPherson's "A Loaf of Bread."

1. *Exposition.* In the first two paragraphs, the opening situation is summed up.

2. *Dinner scene.* Harold Green has to deal with his children's hostility and discusses the situation with his wife, who threatens to leave him if he does not make reparation.

3. *The protesters.* After the first white space, the focus shifts to the black protesters. After a paragraph of typical actions, Nelson Reed is introduced.

4. *Television studio.* After the description of Reed, he is given a scene on a television talk show.

5. *Green's home.* After another white space, another scene with Green follows, in which he reacts to Reed's television appearance.

6. *Rally in theater.* A short scene is next devoted to the protesters and a meeting at which Nelson Reed gives an effective speech.

7. *Barroom and luncheonette.* Two scenes follow, in a barroom and a luncheonette, in which Green discusses the situation with his brother-in-law, Thomas.

8. *Drugstore.* Green and Reed meet at a drugstore lunch counter to discuss their differences but part after quarreling.

9. *Bathroom.* In the bathroom of their home, Green's wife insists to Green that he give away groceries for one day.

10. *Reed's house.* In a scene closely parallel with the preceding scene with Green and his wife, Reed discusses the situation with his wife and, drinking heavily, arranges picketing of Green's store for the following day.

11. *Grocery.* The rest of the story is essentially one extended, complex scene set in Green's grocery. It begins with his walk to the store and continues with his giving a loaf of bread to Reed's wife, the arrival of the pickets, the stripping of the store, and the final encounter between Green and Reed, in which Reed pays Green for the loaf of bread.

One thing that an exercise of this kind should make clear is the essentially artificial, constructed nature of the plot. A distinction between *story* and *plot* is useful here. The *story* of "A Loaf of Bread" might be defined as the entire implied narrative of the grocery protest, whereas its *plot* is just those scenes by which McPherson chose to tell the story. To make this distinction clear, it might be useful to outline an altogether different plot that might be constructed out of the story. Is it necessary or inevitable, for example, that Green and Reed be the main characters? What if the story were told from the points of view of the two wives, and the climactic scenes were between them rather than the men? Would it be possible to tell the story by a series of scenes all in the grocery store? An exercise like this helps us recognize the amount of choice a writer has in making a plot out of a story and to inquire into the reasons for the choices made.

This scenic analysis also throws into relief the role of *conflict* in the making of plots. "A Loaf of Bread" is actually quite classical in the way it sets up and develops conflict. A *protagonist* (Green) comes into conflict with an *antagonist* (Reed). The conflict develops in stages. First there is the *exposition,* in which the conflict is announced (in this case the argument over Green's pricing policies). Then there is the *development* or *rising action,* in which protagonist and antagonist clash increasingly violently but without a clear winner; in this case sections 2 through 10 are devoted to development. Then comes the *climax,* in which protagonist and antagonist clash decisively and one wins over the other, and the *dénouement* or *falling action,* which suggests the resolution following the climax. In this case the climax is clearly the confrontation between Green and Reed at the very end of the story. This climax is very interesting because of the ambiguity of who wins. The preceding part of the scene in which the store is stripped is also quite ambiguous. Green has been defeated in one sense; he is giving in to his wife's demands and making retribution. Yet in the process he seems to be trying to show up the other side as crude and greedy, as he has imagined them to be, in a kind of self-fulfilling prophecy. The appearance of Nelson Reed and his demand to pay for the loaf of bread, along with Harold Green's willingness to take the money, reestablishes the dignity and the mutual respect of the two men. The story is finally one of reconciliation, then, rather than of one side defeating the other.

The scenic structure of a piece of fiction can be examined not just for the overall climactic structure but also for *ordering principles* along the way. As the scene list suggested, "A Loaf of Bread" is a network of parallels between Green and Reed. The scenes tend to alternate between the two men. Scene 2 with Green is balanced by scene 4 with Reed. Scene 5 (Green) is balanced by scene 6 (Reed). Scenes 9 and 10 show the two men in order reacting to their hostile meeting at the lunch counter. Each is shown interacting with his wife, who is shown in each case as a moderating influence. By the end of the story, we are prepared to see the two men as parallel and, in some ways, quite similar characters, each the understandable product of certain experiences and influences. The plot and structure of the story have led us to this conclusion.

Of course, not all plots are as straightforward as that of "A Loaf of Bread." The chronological arrangement of scenes, the clear-cut climax, and the rather simple parallelisms of the episodes are all characteristic of the realistic style to which "A Loaf of Bread" adheres. More elaborate or experimental fictions will have more complex structures. We will point these out in the next few stories, even when the emphasis is upon different elements. In the meantime, though, a reading of Diana Chang's story "The Oriental Contingent" will prepare us for a study of point of view and of focalization.

Diana Chang

Diana Chang (b. 1934) has had an outstanding career as both a novelist and a poet. Among her six novels are *The Frontiers of Love* (1956), *A Passion for Life* (1961), and *A Perfect Love* (1978). Her poetry collections include *The Horizon Is Definitely Speaking* (1982). An accomplished painter as well as a writer, she teaches at Barnard College.

THE ORIENTAL CONTINGENT

Connie couldn't remember whose party it was, whose house. She had an impression of kerosene lamps on brown wicker tables, of shapes talking in doorways. It was summer, almost the only time Connie has run into her since, too, and someone was saying, "You must know Lisa Mallory."

"I don't think so."

"She's here. You must know her."

Later in the evening, it was someone else who introduced her to a figure perched on the balustrade of the steps leading to the lawn where more shapes milled. In stretching out a hand to shake Connie's, the figure almost fell off sideways. Connie pushed her back upright onto her perch and, peering, took in the fact that Lisa Mallory had a Chinese face. For a long instant, she felt nonplussed, and was rendered speechless.

But Lisa Mallory was filling in the silence. "Well, now, Connie Sung," she said, not enthusiastically but with a kind of sophisticated interest. "I'm not in music myself, but Paul Wu's my cousin. Guilt by association!" She laughed. "No-tone music, I call his. He studied with John Cage, Varese, and so forth."

Surprised that Lisa knew she was a violinist, Connie murmured something friendly, wondering if she should simply ask outright, "I'm sure I should know, but what do you do?" but she hesitated, taking in her appearance instead, while Lisa went on with, "It's world-class composing. Nothing's wrong with the level. But it's hard going for the layman, believe me."

Lisa Mallory wore a one-of-a-kind kimono dress, but it didn't make her look Japanese at all, and her hair was drawn back tightly in a braid which stood out from close to the top of her head horizontally. You could probably lift her off her feet by grasping it, like the handle of a pot.

"You should give a concert here, Connie," she said, using her first name right away, Connie noticed, like any American. "Lots of culturati around." Even when she wasn't actually speaking, she pursued her own line of thought actively and seemed to find herself mildly amusing.

"I'm new to the area," Connie said, deprecatingly. "I've just been a weekend guest, actually, till a month ago."

"It's easy to be part of it. Nothing to it. I should know. You'll see."

"I wish it wasn't so dark," Connie found herself saying, waving her hand in front of her eyes as if the night were a veil to brush aside. She recognized in herself that intense need to see, to see into fellow Orientals, to fathom them. So far, Lisa Mallory had not given her enough clues, and the darkness itself seemed to be interfering.

Lisa dropped off her perch. "It's important to be true to oneself," she said. "Keep the modern stuff out of your repertory. Be romantic. Don't look like that! You're best at the romantics. Anyhow, take it from me. I know. And *I* like what I like."

Released by her outspokenness, Connie laughed and asked, "I'm sure I should know, but what is it that you do?" She was certain Lisa would say something like, "I'm with a public relations firm." "I'm in city services."

But she replied, "What do all Chinese excel at?" Not as if she'd asked a rhetorical question, she waited, then answered herself. "Well, aren't we all physicists, musicians, architects, or in software?"

At that point a voice broke in, followed by a large body who put his arms around both women, "The Oriental contingent! I've got to break this up."

Turning, Lisa kissed him roundly, and said over her shoulder to Connie, "I'll take him away before he tells us we look alike!"

They melted into the steps below, and Connie, feeling put off balance and somehow slow-witted, was left to think over her new acquaintance.

"Hello, Lisa Mallory," Connie Sung always said on the infrequent occasions when they ran into one another. She always said "Hello, Lisa Mallory," with a shyness she did not understand in herself. It was strange, but they had no mutual friends except for Paul Wu, and Connie had not seen him in ages. Connie had no one of whom to ask her questions. But sometime soon, she'd be told Lisa's maiden name. Sometime she'd simply call her Lisa. Sometime what Lisa did with her life would be answered.

Three, four years passed, with their running into one another at receptions and openings, and still Lisa Mallory remained an enigma. Mildly amused herself, Connie wondered if other people, as well, found her inscrutable. But none of her American friends (though, of course, Lisa and she were Americans, too, she had to remind herself), none of their Caucasian friends seemed curious about backgrounds. In their accepting way, they did not wonder about Lisa's background, or about Connie's or Paul Wu's. Perhaps they assumed they were all cut from the same cloth. But to Connie, the Orientals she met were unread books, books she never had the right occasion or time to fully pursue.

She didn't even see the humor in her situation—it was such an issue with her. The fact was she felt less, much less, sure of herself when she was with real Chinese.

As she was realizing this, the truth suddenly dawned on her. Lisa Mallory never referred to her own background because it was more Chinese than Connie's, and therefore of a higher order. She was tact incarnate. All along, she had been going out of her way not to embarrass Connie. Yes, yes. Her assurance was definitely uppercrust (perhaps her father had been in the diplomatic service), and her offhand didacticness, her lack of self-doubt, was indeed characteristically Chinese-Chinese. Connie was not only impressed by these traits, but also put on the defensive because of them.

Connie let out a sigh—a sigh that follows the solution to a nagging problem . . . Lisa's mysteriousness. But now Connie knew only too clearly that her own background made her decidedly inferior. Her father was a second-generation gynecologist who spoke hardly any Chinese. Yes, inferior and totally without recourse.

Of course, at one of the gatherings, Connie met Bill Mallory, too. He was simply American, maybe Catholic, possibly lapsed. She was not put off balance by him at all. But most of the time he was away on business, and Lisa cropped up at functions as single as Connie.

Then one day, Lisa had a man in tow—wiry and tall, he looked Chinese from the Shantung area, or perhaps from Beijing, and his styled hair made him appear vaguely artistic.

"Connie, I'd like you to meet Eric Li. He got out at the beginning of the *detente*, went to Berkeley, and is assimilating a mile-a-minute," Lisa said, with her usual irony. "Bill found him and is grooming him, though he came with his own charisma."

Eric waved her remark aside. "Lisa has missed her calling. She was born to be in PR," he said, with an accent.

"Is that what she does?" Connie put in at once, looking only at him. "Is that her profession?"

"You don't know?" he asked, with surprise.

Though she was greeting someone else, Lisa turned and answered, "I'm a fabrics tycoon, I think I can say without immodesty." She moved away and continued her conversation with the other friend.

Behind his hand, he said, playfully, as though letting Connie in on a secret, "Factories in Hongkong and Taipei, and now he's—Bill, that is—is exploring them on the mainland."

"With her fabulous contacts over there!" Connie exclaimed, now seeing it all. "Of course, what a wonderful business combination they must make."

Eric was about to utter something, but stopped, and said flatly, "I have all the mainland contacts, even though I was only twenty when I left, but my parents . . ."

"How interesting," Connie murmured lamely. "I see," preoccupied as she was with trying to put two and two together.

Lisa was back and said without an introduction, continuing her line of thought, "You two look good together, if I have to say so myself. Why don't you ask him to one of your concerts? And you, Eric, you're in America now, so don't stand on ceremony, or you'll be out in left field." She walked away with someone for another drink.

Looking uncomfortable, but recovering himself with a smile, Eric said, "Lisa makes me feel more Chinese than I am becoming—it is her directness, I suspect. In China, we'd say she is too much like a man."

At which Connie found herself saying, "She makes me feel *less* Chinese."

"Less!"

"Less Chinese than she is."

"That is not possible," Eric said, with a shade of contempt—for whom? Lisa or Connie? He barely suppressed a laugh, cold as Chinese laughter could be.

Connie blurted out, "I'm a failed Chinese. Yes, and it's to you that I need to say it." She paused and repeated emphatically, "I am a failed Chinese." Her heart was beating quicker, but she was glad to have got that out, a confession and a definition that might begin to free her. "Do you know you make me feel that, too? You've been here only about ten years, right?"

"Right, and I'm thirty-one."

"You know what I think? I think it's harder for a Chinese to do two things."

At that moment, an American moved in closer, looking pleased somehow to be with them.

She continued, "It's harder for us to become American than, say for a German, and it's also harder not to remain residually Chinese, even if you are third generation."

Eric said blandly, "Don't take yourself so seriously. You can't help being an American product."

Trying to be comforting, the American interjected with, "The young lady is not a product, an object. She is a human being, and there is no difference among peoples that I can see."

"I judge myself both as a Chinese and as an American," Connie said.

"You worry too much," Eric said, impatiently. Then he looked around and though she wasn't in sight, he lowered his voice. "She is what she is. I know what she is. But she avoids going to Hongkong. She avoids it."

Connie felt turned around. "Avoids it?"

"Bill's in Beijing right now. She's here. How come?"

"I don't know," Connie replied, as though an answer had been required of her.

"She makes up many excuses, reasons. Ask her. Ask her yourself," he said, pointedly.

"Oh, I couldn't do that. By the way, I'm going on a concert tour next year in three cities—Shanghai, Beijing and Nanking," Connie said. "It'll be my first time in China."

"Really! You must be very talented to be touring at your age," he said, genuinely interested for the first time. Because she was going to China, or because she now came across as an over-achiever, even though Chinese-American?

"I'm just about your age," she said, realizing then that maybe Lisa Mallory had left them alone purposely.

"You could both pass as teenagers!" the American exclaimed.

～∭ ♪♪～

Two months later, she ran into Lisa again. As usual, Lisa began in the middle of her own thoughts. "Did he call?"

"Who? Oh. No, no."

"Well, it's true he's been in China the last three weeks with Bill. They'll be back this weekend."

Connie saw her opportunity. "Are you planning to go to China yourself?"

For the first time, Lisa seemed at a loss for words. She raised her shoulders, then let them drop. Too airily, she said, "You know, there's always Paris. I can't bear not to go to Paris, if I'm to take a trip."

"But you're Chinese. You *have* been to China, you came from China originally, didn't you?"

"I could go to Paris twice a year, I love it so," Lisa said. "And then there's London, Florence, Venice."

"But—but your business contacts?"

"*My* contacts? Bill, he's the businessman who makes the contacts. Always has. I take care of the New York office, which is a considerable job. We have a staff of eighty-five."

Connie said, "I told Eric I'll be giving a tour in China. I'm taking Chinese lessons right now."

Lisa Mallory laughed. "Save your time. They'll still be disdainful over there. See, *they* don't care," and she waved her hand at the crowd. "Some of them have been born in Buffalo, too! It's the Chinese you can't fool. They know you're not the genuine article—you and I."

Her face was suddenly heightened in color, and she was breathing as if ready to flee from something. "Yes, you heard right. I was born in Buffalo."

"You were!" Connie exclaimed before she could control her amazement.

"Well, what about you?" Lisa retorted. She was actually shaking and trying to hide it by making sudden gestures.

"Westchester."

"But your parents at least were Chinese."

"Well, so were, so are, yours!"

"I was adopted by Americans. My full name is Lisa Warren Mallory."

Incredulous, Connie said, "I'm more Chinese than you!"

"Who isn't?" She laughed, unhappily. "Having Chinese parents makes all the difference. We're worlds apart."

"And all the time I thought . . . never mind what I thought."

"You have it over me. It's written all over you. I could tell even in the dark that night."

"Oh, Lisa," Connie said to comfort her, "none of this matters to anybody except us. Really and truly. They're too busy with their own problems."

"The only time I feel Chinese is when I'm embarrassed I'm not more Chinese— which is a totally Chinese reflex I'd give anything to be rid of!"

"I know what you mean."

"And as for Eric looking down his nose at me, he's knocking himself out to be so American, *but as a secure Chinese!* What's so genuine about that article?"

Both of them struck their heads laughing, but their eyes were not merry.

"Say it again," Connie asked of her, "say it again that my being more Chinese is written all over me."

"Consider it said," Lisa said. "My natural mother happened to be there at the time—I can't help being born in Buffalo."

"I know, I know," Connie said with feeling. "If only you had had some say in the matter."

"It's only Orientals who haunt me!" Lisa stamped her foot. "Only them!"

"I'm so sorry," Connie Sung said, for all of them. "It's all so turned around."

"So I'm made in America, so there!" Lisa Mallory declared, making a sniffing sound, and seemed to be recovering her sangfroid.

Connie felt tired—as if she'd traveled—but a lot had been settled on the way.

POINT OF VIEW AND FOCALIZATION

As central as plot to the meaning of a piece of fiction is *point of view;* indeed, they are inextricably related, as we suggested when we imagined a version of "A Loaf of Bread" told from the point of view of the two wives. Like plot, the concept of point of view is very simple and yet capable of very complex variations and developments in practice, all of which affect the meaning of a story.

Basically, point of view refers to the narrator's relationship to or involvement in the events of the story, and it is expressed in terms of grammatical person:

First person ("I")

1. The main character tells his or her story
2. A minor character tells the main character's story

Second person ("You")
   (Second-person narratives are quite rare, because of the ambiguity of trying to involve the reader ["you"] in an imaginary action.)

Third person ("he," "she")

1. *Omniscient.* An "all-knowing" narrator can be everywhere in the story at once and has unlimited access to the thoughts and feelings of the characters.

2. *Limited-omniscient.* The narrator has access to the thoughts and feelings of only some of the characters.
3. *Objective.* The narrator has no access to the characters' thoughts and feelings and reports only what could be observed externally.

This scheme for analyzing point of view does not take into account a number of possible variations. The distinction between "major" and "minor" characters in first-person narratives does not distinguish between minor characters who are personally involved in the action and ones who are only observers, although this might be important. And the category of "limited-omniscient third-person point of view" does not distinguish between various kinds of limitations. Is the narrator limited to access to the mind of one character? Does he or she enter the minds of several characters but not others? Accordingly, some critics of fiction have created many more categories. No matter how many categories are used, however, the reader still has to be attentive to the variations in point of view in any particular story. So it is probably best to keep the categories few in number and keep in mind the possibility of variations.

For illustrations of various narrative points of view, we might look at the various stories in this section. "A Loaf of Bread," for example, is written from an omniscient third-person point of view. The narrator can tell us at any point what any of the characters are thinking—Harold Green, for instance:

> At the dinner table, disturbed by his children's silence, Harold Green felt compelled to say, "I am not a dishonest man." Then he felt ashamed. The children, a boy and his older sister, immediately left the table, leaving Green alone with his wife. "Ruth, I am not dishonest," he repeated to her.

The narrator can also enter the minds of secondary characters:

> Ruth Green did not say anything. She knew, and her husband did not, that the outraged people had also picketed the school attended by their children.

Other third-person points of view in these stories appear in "The Oriental Contingent," "Bop," and "China." All three of these points of view are "limited-omniscient," that is, the narrators are able to report the thoughts and feelings of only some of the characters. In "The Oriental Contingent," the narrator's omniscience is limited to the mind of Connie Sung, in "Bop," to the mind of Oleg Lum, and in "China" to the mind of Evelyn Jackson. There are reasons for these differences, of course. In "A Loaf of Bread," an important theme is that we can understand the attitudes even of people who violently disagree if we know their background and experiences. So the narrator enters the minds of both Harold Green and Nelson Reed to help us understand them better. "The Oriental Contingent," "Bop," and "China" all turn in various ways on a character's trying to figure out somebody else who remains essentially mysterious or enigmatic. Thus we enter the mind of Connie Sung but not that of Lisa Mallory, of Oleg Lum but not of Claire Remm, and of Evelyn Jackson but not of Rudolph Jackson.

The three first-person narratives in this section also differ considerably. In both "Johnny Ray" and "Rock River," the first-person narrator is a secondary character who is telling the story of the major character. In "Johnny Ray," the nameless young narrator is describing his eccentric classmate Johnny Ray, and in "Rock River," the equally nameless narrator is remembering his "hopeless" friend Rick, now a suicide. In "Sari Petticoats," too, the first-person narrator is thinking of someone else, her ex-husband, but she, rather than the ex-husband, seems to be the main character. The line between "major" and "minor" character is not clear-cut, however. It could be argued that the narrator's remembering Johnny Ray is more important than Johnny Ray's violent resistance to the seniors and that he is therefore the main character. The same thing could be said of the narrator's memory of Rick in "Rock River." Rigid categories are less important than careful analysis of how the points of view of individual stories work.

Another ambiguity in the concept of point of view lies in the fact that limited-omniscient third-person narratives are very similar in effect to first-person narratives, much more similar than they are to omniscient third-person narratives. "The Oriental Contingent," "Bop," and "China" could be said to be told from the points of view of Connie Sung, Oleg Lum, and Evelyn Jackson, despite the fact that they are formally and grammatically in the first person; all three stories stick closely to what their main characters experience and think. This feature of the narrative structure can be accounted for with the concept of *focus*. "The Oriental Contingent," we might say, is told from a limited-omniscient third-person point of view, but it is *focalized* through the figure of Connie Sung. Or we might say that "A Loaf of Bread" is told by an omniscient third-person narrator and focalized through that same narrator, who is sympathetic, unbiased, and insightful. (Even anonymous, omniscient third-person narrators can have personalities.)

As a final way of exploring the ideas of *point of view* and *focalization*, we might think some more about "The Oriental Contingent" and imagine it told from various points of view. In its actual form, its limited-omniscient third-person point of view and focalization through the character of Connie are evident from the very beginning:

> Connie couldn't remember whose party it was, whose house. She had an impression of kerosene lamps on brown wicker tables, of shapes talking in doorways. It was summer, almost the only time Connie has run into her since, too, and someone was saying, "You must know Lisa Mallory."

If we wanted to recast the story as an omniscient third-person story, we might follow this opening paragraph with one from Lisa Mallory's point of view, as James Alan McPherson moves between the points of view of Harold Green and Nelson Reed in "A Loaf of Bread." Of if we wanted to tell the story as a third-person dramatic narrative, we would have to take out all references to Connie's perceptions and include only what could be observed: "It was summer, and a party was going on. Someone said to Connie, 'You must know Lisa Mallory.' "

The story, as a limited-omniscient third-person narrative, sticks so closely to Connie's mind that turning it into a first-person narrative requires little more than changing the pronouns:

> I can't remember whose party it was, whose house. I have an impression of kerosene lamps on brown wicker tables, of shapes talking in doorways. It was summer, almost the only time I have run into her since, too, and someone was saying, "You must know Lisa Mallory."

Making the first-person narrator someone other than Connie—Lisa Mallory, for instance, or the minor character who said, "You must know Lisa Mallory"—would involve much more extensive rewriting and would change the emphasis of the story radically.

Any such changes in point of view would make "The Oriental Contingent" a very different story. For point of view, though a technical matter, is never only technical. It is one of the principal ways by which writers show us how meaning is produced out of the diverse and conflicting voices of society. A common device for managing point of view is the frame story, a story which gives the circumstances for the telling of an embedded story. In a frame story, the writer might set up conflicting values by contrasting the voice of the narrator with that of the protagonist who tells the tale. But in any story, frame story or not, the teller is as important as the tale—indeed, *is* the tale in many cases.

The next story, "Johnny Ray," by Alberto Alvaro Rios, will prepare us for a discussion of character in fiction.

Alberto Alvaro Rios

Alberto Alvaro Rios (b. 1952) was born and grew up in Nogales, Arizona, on the border between Mexico and the United States; his father was Mexican, his mother English. Both a poet and a fiction writer, he has published the poetry collection *Whispering to Fool the Wind* (1982) and the short-story collection *The Iguana Killer: Twelve Stories of the Heart* (1984), as well as *Five Indiscretions* (1985) and *Teodora Luna's Two Kisses* (1990). He teaches at the University of Arizona, Tempe.

JOHNNY RAY

Let me tell you that when any of the boys used to talk to him they would call him HEY Johnny RAY just to watch his cheeks turn red, nice big fat ones, and of course he was always the boy who blushed so red he was nothing but clown cheeks. I guess he came into his own sometime around about junior high school when the story was going around about his sister Patsy. Now Patsy was a story in herself, but she went off to school somewhere and nobody knew exactly where that was, but then, nobody exactly cared, either. She had some sort of bladder infection or something and one day she just kinda let loose in class and pretty soon there was a regular old Mississippi—remember the old bouncing ball cartoon that showed you how to spell that? Well there was a regular old Mis-sis-sippi shooting right off one of the legs of her desk. Of course everybody started laughing and Mrs. Snow got pretty angry and sent everyone out of the room. I say angry cause Mrs. Snow was the one in our school who always used to say that only dogs got mad. Anyway, it was too late to keep anybody from knowing what happened cause kids are pretty quick when something exciting is going on.

I guess it was just after that when Patsy didn't come back to school anymore. I suppose we were pretty mean to Patsy, school kids are sometimes, but we didn't try to be, not on purpose. We just wanted to see what was going on, and what was going on was mighty funny. Us Mexican kids, who were in the majority then, started laughing in Spanish and the rest laughed just as hard in what I guess you'd call English. Funny is funny, I guess. That's another thing about Johnny Ray and his family. They just seemed misplaced. Everyone round these parts was Mexican save his family and maybe one or two other missionary families. We all just sort of fit in and got to gettin along except those Tisons. They just kinda stuck out like books in a house. They were, well I don't know for sure, Seventh Day Adventists or somesuch and were just too pushy for the Mexicans, so them Tisons sort of had to take to being ignored, a lot, even with all the help my papa and the rest try to give 'em. I don't suppose they ever changed, though, just moved around from place to place, to this day I'd guess.

Well, suppose it was because I lived next to him that Johnny Ray and me sort of got thrown together by fate or something. Those Tisons came from the missionary families who kinda treated us Mexicans different, like we had to be changed or something, like we didn't do stuff right, and this is probably why we treated them different. Of course our families still got along, talking and all that, but it was different. Johnny Ray's father always had that big left eye on you no matter what you was saying. Me and Johnny Ray, though, we got to know each other pretty well when his father wasn't around. After all, we were the last ones to get off the school bus. Maybe we got to know each other too well for my liking. I mean, you just *knew*

Johnny Ray was gonna grow up to be just like his father. Not yet, but he would. He wouldn't get no smarter or anything than his father, but he would just still be a missionary. One that did exactly the same stuff. I guess he was just like my father, too, and the rest of the missionaries and the rest of the Mexicans when they were all small. I hate to talk about my father that way, comparing him to Johnny Ray and all, but it's probably pretty true. I don't want you to think I'm saying I thought us Mexicans were all that much better cause I didn't, not all the time. But I did always figger there had to be some kinda island in the middle, you know what I mean? Like a playground we could all get dirty in. Nobody else seemed to, not even Johnny Ray when we talked about it. That's why I thought he'd grow up just like his papa and mine. Fathers said funny things about other fathers.

Now I used to go over to Johnny Ray's a lot cause I figgered there was hope for everybody. But it seemed like every time I got there he was making bread. That isn't so bad except you just *knew* he was a guy who would make bread even though he wasn't sissy or anything like that as far as I could tell. I guess I don't blame him though. I mean those Tisons didn't have no TV or anything. Johnny Ray used to read for fun, if you can imagine that. I guess if I was having fun like that I would consider giving it up to make bread, too, or baskets or something. I mean I probably would have even taken up something like sewing, you know what I mean? It wasn't till later I found out Johnny Ray sewed, too. I figger I was just always afraid to ask him cause I was afraid for the worst. I could of bet on it, though, and I would of except that I don't think none of the guys would of taken the bet.

Well, I thought I knew Johnny Ray pretty well by this time, both personal and story-wise. I even knew the latest story, something about his picking his nose then sticking his finger in his mouth. Some even said he used to swallow. One day we even organized, and took turns watching all day. I never said nothing, either, to Johnny Ray about these stories, and I guess that's just as well. I think it's better that he didn't know. And besides, I was kinda afraid of the worst after I found out about his sewing.

By this time I had found out lots of things about Johnny Ray which is why I still remember him and why probably everybody else does too. You could likely describe almost everything about him without even knowing him. I mean stuff like that he always wore glasses with black rims and had them since I think second grade. And he always wore green jeans. And he always read science-fiction, and probably believed it. And his father always read science-fiction, and probably believed it. And his father always gave him haircuts with his mother helping out like a back seat driver even though he had short hair to begin with. And he always brought one of those big can openers to school in his sack lunch so that he had to carry it around with him the rest of the day. He always stuck it in the same pocket as his lunch bag, which he always folded and saved. I think in one school year he probably didn't use more than two bags. And he always wore a big watch with a worn black band. And he always did his homework even if he didn't always do it well. He wasn't real smart all the time but he tried real hard. And his bread. You can't help mentioning his bread every time you talk about Johnny Ray. I guess the list could go on forever, but you get the idea. I think you could know him real well without really knowing him. Thing is, I did know him.

Now like I said, nobody hardly talked to Johnny Ray, just about him. I guess in this he was a little bit lucky cause he never had to worry about getting beat up or anything, like I did. Everybody just plain left him alone. It was kinda magic sometimes, I think, and that's how come I used to hang around him a lot of the time.

Of course it was because of all this that I guess I shouldn't have been surprised at what happened that day in class, but I was. It was *El Día del Vaquero,* cowboy day, you know, and everybody was supposed to come to school dressed up like a cowboy or Indian. It was real popular in this town cause everybody seemed to come from a ranch sometime along the way and they enjoyed dressing up. Cap guns and stuff like that were real popular, too. The school had a special assembly in the morning—remember assemblies?—just for skits and things and then they gave us a two-hour lunch period, and to top that off we got to leave school early. You can imagine. It was a real perfect holiday.

Well, it was that day in school and everybody came dressed up pretty good. Some of the richer kids even came with real rawhide chaps and everybody was making a real fuss over them, and there were lots of Indians with real stuff, and Mexican in-between things. Then the school bus came, and of course, Johnny Ray rode the school bus. I did, too, but that's different. You just could of guessed he did. Johnny Ray also came dressed as if this was any other day. He had his green jeans on which was all right, but he also had on his white shirt—more or less white—his black surplus shoes, his red socks, and his watch. Now Johnny Ray was *really* out of place. Neon, if you know what I mean.

Now you know of course this was no big crime or nothing like that but Johnny Ray knew as well as any other person in that school what the seniors did at lunch time if you didn't have at least three western things on. And those seniors, let me give you a clue, weren't above anything or anybody. I must of had on ten or twenty things just to be absolutely sure. Of course that would be at lunch time, so Johnny Ray could get along okay until at least eleven-thirty, which is when they started.

Exactly what it was these seniors did every year was, first of all, build a jail out of plywood and put it up where everybody could see it for about two days before the festivities. Then on the *Día del Vaquero* they would come around to all the classes at about eleven and look for people who weren't dressed up. Then they'd put a rope around whoever wasn't and haul them off to jail. Now these people would have to stay in jail until twelve-thirty or so when they could pay a fifty-cent fine and get out. But, whoever didn't want to pay the fine got taken in a pick-up about five miles out of town and had to walk back. It was all done in fun and mostly nobody got mad or nothing, just mostly drunk though the principal would never say so. This had been going on for just about as long as the school had been built, which was a considerable piece of time.

So, like I said, Johnny Ray could get by till then, eleven or eleven-thirty, and he did. Nobody said nothing to him and he didn't say anything to anybody about it, except me cause I asked him. I was kinda curious and I had him for American history or somesuch at ten so I went up to him and I asked him if he knew what he was in for and he said he didn't care. Then I asked him why he didn't dress up cause I knew he had enough cowboy-looking clothes to pass, or I could even lend him some, and he said he just didn't want to, that's all. I figgered I had learned enough, which really wasn't nothing but it was enough considering it was Johnny Ray I had been talking to. I was just mighty glad I had dressed up enough. Mighty glad.

Everybody else was having a grand time of it shooting cap guns and showing off and of course nobody was paying much attention to school work. It was probably one of the best school days we had that year, even with what happened later.

At about eleven-fifteen or so, we could hear the vigilante posse of seniors roping and tying up a few kids who weren't dressed up. Most of them were juniors and probably didn't dress up on purpose. They were hollering and carrying on so much we had a hard time hearing the teacher, not that anybody was straining. It wouldn't be long before they got to our class. Johnny Ray was the only one who was gonna get carried off. We were all pretty anxious cause it was gonna be mighty funny to see Johnny Ray turn red and get carried off and all.

Well, when they finally did get to our room, about five of those seniors jangled in all dressed up so there wasn't a lick of regular person in them. They were all dressed up as Mexican *vaqueros,* and a couple of them reminded me of the pictures I had seen of Zapata when he had those two gun belts wrapped around his chest and looked hard tough. They was making all kinds of fuss and finally one of them stands up front and yells out, "We have come for anybody not dressed up like a *vaquero!*" You could tell right off by the way he said *vaquero* that he was one of us. It was a funny thing, but it sounded just like it should and just like none of those missionaries ever could say it no matter how long they tried. The teacher sat back and enjoyed the scene pretty much. Miss James was all right. Now all these seniors started to shooting off their cap guns and rifles and started to looking around. Of course, they all headed for Johnny Ray just about right off but he didn't look up. It was about this time that everything seemed to sort of slow down like it was taking years or something. You ever been in an accident? Well it always happens right before important things and so that was right off a sign of what was to come.

When those five seniors got to Johnny Ray it was like setting off a firecracker before you're ready and they was all too close. I swear I never seen nothing like it and I never thought Johnny Ray would be the one to show me. It was TV, pure and simple. Of course Johnny Ray couldn't have known that, but he was a natural. Johnny Ray got the hand of the first guy who touched him and threw it as if he was throwing a football. The guy nearly twirled around right where he was standing. Then Johnny Ray got his whole big notebook, that gray-blue kind, you know? and threw it the length of the room. I swear it was a pretty sight when all the papers flew out all over the place and it hit a desk right up in front. It nearly caught the boy sitting there right square in his open mouth, the kind of open mouths fathers always say are gonna catch flies. Now all this was happening while Johnny Ray was still sitting down.

By this time all the seniors had backed off quite a piece and I think two of them were hiding in the big closet back there. Anyway, it gave Johnny Ray room to stand up, and jeez he was in such a hurry to stand up that he brought his desk with him so it fell over and all his books kinda slid down the aisle. Now by this time, Miss James, who was usually all right like I said, was sorta screaming her head off and everybody else was just watching and talking as if this was Saturday morning at the movies or something. Better, even. Nobody was getting up to go to the bathroom.

Now everybody, by this time, had noticed something kinda queer about the whole situation and that was that Johnny Ray wasn't saying nothing like you'd probably expect. I mean he was as red in the face as I'd ever seen him and his eyes were streaming water down his round cheeks so they was dripping but he wasn't saying nothing, just holding his breath I think. Of course everybody else pretty much made up for it cause they were all jabbering and Miss James was still yelling louder and louder so she could be heard, "Johnny Ray! Johnny Ray Tison you stop that this instant! Johnny Ray you listen to me and stop that! Johnny Ray!"

It didn't do much good. By this time he had stood up and had kicked his desk over to the window and had picked up a book and threw it at one of the seniors. Now Miss James came marching as mad as gray cats down the aisle and she grabbed Johnny Ray by the arm which was lucky cause she couldn't get hit but

Johnny Ray kicked her instead. Johnny Ray still had nothing to say but he was crying and all red now like his head was gonna bust open like a stepped-on tomato. "Johnny Ray, I'm taking you straight to the principal's office!" Johnny Ray had calmed down a little by the time she said this, since all the seniors had got out of this town after one got kicked. Miss James stomped out with Johnny Ray and we were all left just watching.

Well we had an awful lot of talking and comparing to do so you can imagine the state the classroom was in by now. I swear five languages was being spoken all at once and I could understand all of them. Of course it wasn't too long before another teacher came in and dismissed the class, which made the whole thing even better cause it was only twenty till twelve and so we felt kinda special after all this happening.

I guess you can still hear this story lots of different ways like that Johnny Ray really did hit somebody with his notebook or that when he kicked Miss James there was blood spilling out all over the place but I don't remember it that way. Still, this is my favorite story about him, good ole Johnny Ray. I heard later that he didn't get into too much trouble or anything cause those seniors didn't really have any right or anything to take him out if he didn't want to go, and I guess he showed that all right. His folks came down to the principal's office and there was a pretty big fuss and everything, but like I said, he didn't get into too much trouble. Of course he didn't talk to nobody again, not even me. And that was his last year at that school, too. I guess he went away to where his sister Patsy was but nobody cared enough to find out for sure. It was sorta like when Patsy left, I think. Come to think of it, that might've been the year his whole family moved away but I can't remember if it was that way for sure.

Now I gotta say to this day, and I hate to admit it, but his bread was awful good to taste. I just kinda wish now I had asked him how to make it before he left. Now I mean I wouldn't have took up sewing or anything like that, but I just gotta say that his bread was probably, no, it was the best I ever tasted when that honey got to dripping down the sides and I had a little butter, real stuff. Yeah, good old Johnny Ray. He made the butter too, and had bees.

CHARACTER

Character is probably the element of fiction that appeals most to readers. We may read for the plot, to find out what happens next, but even plots cannot be divorced from the characters involved in them. Even in such comparatively plot-centered forms as suspense stories and mysteries, we tend to care less about what happens than about what happens to whom, in events as they affect the lives of interesting characters.

Characters in most fiction, certainly in realistic fiction, are usually intended to be credible, to seem like living people. They have understandable feelings and ideas, and they react to their experiences in ways that we can understand and identify with. In a story like "A Loaf of Bread," for example, most of the story turns around the characters of Harold Green and Nelson Reed, and when it seems that we have arrived at a good understanding of their respective values and feelings, the story ends. Some psychoanalytic critics even go so far in equating fictional characters with real people that they construct hypothetical experiences for them that do not appear in the story (a practice that can be defended with some kinds of fiction).

But just as important as the ways that characters in fiction are like living people are the ways in which they are not. One is that fictional characters tend to be either *major* or *minor* characters, whereas in real life everyone is presumably of equal value and importance. Or maybe it's a matter of perspective. Just as in real life, certain people at certain times are at the center of our attention and other people recede into the background, so in fiction certain characters are in the foreground, other, secondary characters are behind them in a sort of middle ground, and a third group of rather shadowy figures forms the background. In real life, foreground and background are constantly changing, whereas in fiction (or at least in short fiction) major characters tend to remain major and minor ones minor for the duration of the story. Thus in "A Loaf of Bread," Green and Reed are clearly foregrounded, their wives form a less clearly focused middle ground, and a number of minor characters (the demonstrators, the customers) form the background.

A second distinction much more important for fictional characters than for real people is that between *dynamic* and *static* characters, between characters who change in the course of their stories and those who do not. It could be argued that there are no static real people; some people resist change more than others, but everybody eventually changes in response to the processes of life. It is important that characters not be evaluated by whether they change or not; in fiction, at least, staying put is as good as changing. But they belong in different kinds of stories. Dynamic characters tend to undergo initiations and other sorts of maturing and learning experiences; it is important to recognize such experiences and their effects.

Finally, fictional characters, more than real people, tend to exist not in isolation but as part of a *system,* a network of repetitions designed to provide an entry into an issue or problem. If the protagonist of a story is having trouble with her mother, then it is likely that she is part of a system in which other characters are also having trouble with their mothers. (If a character seems to be included only as a contrast to the main character on some issue, we call him or her a *foil* character.) Harold Green and Nelson Reed in "A Loaf of Bread" seem to exist within a system of attitudes toward the subject of profit, a system that includes also even the minor background characters, like the protestors. Perhaps this is a matter of fictional focus as well; Green and Reed may have feelings and ideas on any number of other subjects, but they are brought together on this single one.

All of these points may be illustrated by Alberto Alvaros Rios's story "Johnny Ray." The title is significant. Just as "A Loaf of Bread" is named after its central symbol, and "The Oriental Contingent" ironically quotes a phrase that suggests the theme of the story, so the title "Johnny Ray" suggests the centrality of character by naming the principal figure in the story.

But is Johnny Ray the principal figure? The first-person narrator is so powerful a presence in the story and is so clearly contrasted to Johnny Ray that he seems as important in the story as Johnny Ray himself. Despite the very different organization and point of view of "Johnny Ray," it seems very similar to "A Loaf of Bread" in one respect: It is the story of two complementary people and of their relationship and interaction.

What methods of *characterization* does Rios use in "Johnny Ray"? We have two sets of methods in the story. One is the methods the narrator uses to characterize his friend Johnny Ray, and the other is the way he unconsciously characterizes himself. The narrator characterizes Johnny Ray in two ways: by direct description and, indirectly, by reporting what he says and does. He begins by telling us that

Johnny Ray blushed easily, turning into "nothing but clown cheeks." Later in the story he describes Johnny Ray's appearance and habits more fully:

> You could likely describe almost everything about him without even knowing him. I mean stuff like that he always wore glasses with black rims and had them since I think second grade. And he always wore green jeans. And he always read science-fiction, and probably believed it. . . . I think you could know him real well without really knowing him. Thing is, I did know him.

One of the curious things about this and similar passages is that the narrator describes Johnny Ray while declaring that such "describing" is not really "knowing." Clearly the narrator finds something puzzling and incomplete in his memories of Johnny Ray.

If the narrator tells us about Johnny Ray through direct description, he also shows us what Johnny Ray is like by reporting his sudden, unexpected resistance to the senior *vaqueros* on cowboy day. Even the narrator, who has told us that he really did know Johnny Ray, is surprised by his violence: "I swear I never seen nothing like it and I never thought Johnny Ray would be the one to show me."

At the same time that the narrator is characterizing Johnny Ray, he is, less consciously, characterizing himself. Most obviously, the narrator identifies himself as Mexican, as opposed to Johnny Ray, who comes from an Anglo, "missionary" family. That is, the narrator is ostensibly a member of the dominant, majority group whereas Johnny Ray is part of the subordinate, minority group:

> Everyone round these parts was Mexican save his family and maybe one or two other missionary families. We all just sort of fit in and got to gettin along except those Tisons.

As the story unfolds, though, the narrator's comfortable status as insider is undercut, and he comes to seem something of an outsider himself:

> Now like I said, nobody hardly talked to Johnny Ray, just about him. I guess in this he was a little bit lucky cause he never had to worry about getting beat up or anything, like I did. Everybody just plain left him alone. It was kinda magic sometimes, I think, and that's how come I used to hang around him a lot of the time.

The narrator and Johnny Ray are a part of a system; both are characterized in terms of their relation to a system of social tyranny by the majority. If the narrator were completely unaware of this, we might call him an *obtuse narrator,* one who does not realize the significance of what he is communicating. But this narrator is struggling to understand. The story begins with an ugly incident in which Johnny Ray's sister is humiliated and driven from school when she soils her pants in class. The narrator has joined in this but feels uncomfortable about it: "I suppose we were pretty mean to Patsy, school kids are sometimes, but we didn't try to be, not on purpose." Throughout the story, the narrator struggles to understand Johnny Ray, even when he most shocks teenage male expectations by baking bread, sewing, and (as we learn in the last line) keeping bees. Is the narrator, then, a dynamic character—one who changes? Does he learn something about conformity and nonconformity through his experience with Johnny Ray and thereby change? It is a difficult question to answer. The narrator does seem to have tried to come to terms with the memory of Johnny Ray. On the other hand, Johnny is isolated from the group (like his sister) at the end of the story—"he didn't talk to nobody again, not even me"—and the narrator is left with the dominant group. The judgment of him as dynamic or static depends upon one's evaluation of his insight at the end of the story. Whatever one's conclusions on these issues, it is clear that they are only a small part of a larger strategy that shapes and constructs characters to develop the narrative as a whole.

To prepare for a discussion of setting in fiction, read the following story, Maxine Chernoff's "Bop."

Maxine Chernoff

Maxine Chernoff published five volumes of poetry before turning to fiction with her short-story collection *Bop* (1987). She has since published a novel, *Plain Grief* (1991). A native of Chicago, she teaches in the Chicago City Colleges and co-edits, with Paul Hoover, the periodical *New American Writing*.

BOP

The machine would not cooperate. It photographed his original, but when Oleg looked in the metal pan, the duplicate was zebra-striped and wordless. Three more times he inserted the grocery ad. He got back stripes leaning toward each other and crossing in the middle like insane skate blades.

"Please, if you will."

It was obvious that the woman wasn't interested in her job. You could tell by the way she handled the paper. Her nails tore the pleasant green wrapping that reminded him of larger American money. Her eyes never met the machine that perhaps needed ink, fluid, straightening, or encouragement. Her behavior wouldn't be tolerated if he ran the place.

"Can I ask you something?" she said.

"It is free country. One may ask what one wishes."

"You come here every day with something different. I know I'm not supposed to look, but here you are again Xeroxing garbage and your machine is acting up. Why do you make me so busy?"

"Please, I will tell you. The duplication of materials is of great interest to me. Since I came to this country, for three years now, I make copies of everything. If I could, I would copy my hair, my clothing, my food, and my bowels."

She had walked away. He left the office carrying the perfect finished copies of the grocery ads. These went into the large books stamped *Souvenirs* purchased from Woolworth's. He had filled fourteen already.

Now he was back in his small apartment, whose attitude toward America was one of total acceptance. Plastic-molded coral and gold-flecked seats blended with torn leather. A portrait of a sailboat edged up to a Degas dancer. A Cubs schedule followed. Family photos marched along in the parade. A wall clock resembling an owl's face kept the beat. And leading the line was a caricature that a street artist had done at a fair. Since he already thought he resembled a red-haired Pinocchio, the artist didn't need to use much imagination. His eyes were blue points, his mouth a slit, his ears question marks, and his nose pointed aggressively, like a blind man's white cane. His hair was unruly. He was never going to get on a beauty pageant, but maybe his odd array of features would not be discouraged on the quiz shows he loved to watch.

"Please," he'd say to the check-out girl, "what city has the highest ratio of pets to people?" If she didn't know it was Los Angeles, he'd tell her right out. But he wouldn't embarrass her. He'd say it gently, as if he were providing her with a blessing. One check-out woman, whose badge read *Marta*, seemed especially eager to see him on market days. "There's Mr. Know-It-All," she told her bag boy. They both laughed. Americans were very pleasant.

Upstairs the jesters were at it again. That's not what they were called, but he could never remember the name for what they were. How could two men practicing the art of silence make so much noise? Was it the rope pull or the human washing machine they were doing? Were they sizzling down to the floor like angry bacon, or were they sentimental clowns on an invisible tightrope? He hated what they did. It reminded him of loneliness, of which he already had enough evidence. He had taken to tapping the ceiling with a broom lately. The jesters had taken to giving him free tickets to their performances.

He went to the kitchen, poured lukewarm tea into a *Star Wars* glass, and went back to the letter he'd left that morning. "I am sorry to say," he continued, "that there is a proliferation of bad ideas here. It reminds one, if you please, of the duplication industry. For a nickel, which is very small, a man can copy anything, including his ears. However, who is it that needs four ears? The same with ideas. Everyone in America has the opinions. I read a paper and there is opinion on where dogs should leave their excrement, there is opinion on homosexuals adopting infants, there is opinion on facial hair and robins. There is opinion on cooking cabbage without odor. A child even has opinions. He thinks the governor is fat. Here is large black cat in ad choosing one cat food. If you please, why is every goddamned thing discussed in America?"

He would leave the "goddamned" out when he sent it to the "Personal View" column of the paper. If it was printed, which it wouldn't be with cursing, he'd receive five hundred dollars. But for now it exhilarated him to curse. He pounded the table for emphasis. The red Formica was unresponsive.

He worked every night from nine until five in the morning. His job was to sit at a switchboard that was hooked into store alarms. If an alarm rang, his switchboard would wail, and he would call the police, giving them a code, and call the store owner with the news. In his eleven months of employment, there'd been only twenty-seven alarms, and most of those were due to faulty wiring. He was able to spend most of his time sleeping, just as Mr. Kaplan had suggested upon hiring him. Mr. Kaplan had been insanely happy to give him a job. Just sixty years ago, Mr. Kaplan's own father had come over here, untrained, illiterate, and if it weren't for a *landsman,* he would have perished. Mr. Kaplan got very emotional then and swiped at his eyes with a big hanky and hugged Oleg Lum stiffly and told him, "Welcome, brother." Oleg thought Kaplan might burst into an American spiritual song. Although his job paid minimum wage, he had his days free to do as he wished. Usually he wished to go to the library.

The influx of Russian immigrants to the Rogers Park area had altered its environment. Russian shoemakers hung shingles on every block. Several Russian delicatessens displayed gleaming samovars next to pickled fish in windows, and the library had begun to carry a good amount of Russian-language books but mostly the classics. He had already read those books in Russian, which he had once taught. Now he wanted to read American books rich in history: Sacco and Vanzetti, Sally Rand, Nat Turner, and Howard Hughes. And when he flashed his neat green library card at the girl, who even in summer required a sweater, she always smiled at him. Maybe she, like Mr. Kaplan, assumed he was uneducated, a pretender to the American shelves. She never spoke, but once when he'd asked for a book on the process of photocopying, she had looked worried, as if her patron might be a spy.

He liked sitting at the blond wooden tables with the other patrons. Though protocol barred speech, there was good spirit to share in silent reading. He liked watching the old men who moved their lips as they read. Maybe their false teeth read words differently, trying to trick them. And children, he noticed, read in the same way. For the last week he'd observed a girl about eleven years old who had been sitting across from him. She always used encyclopedias and took notes. She was plump and had hair that wouldn't cooperate. It deserted its braids and bristled in front like cactus. Maybe even American plants had opinions, he suddenly thought.

"Have a pen? Mine's out of ink."

"Please, for you to keep." He handed a ball-point to the girl. Americans were generous, and so he wished to practice in small ways. He kept pens and paper clips and rubber bands and note paper in his pockets for such occasions.

"Thanks," she said and began copying again.

He was rereading the part in *The Grapes of Wrath* in which the turtle slowly, slowly crosses the road. The passage is marked by adversity, he'd have told a classroom of students. At one point the turtle is intentionally hit by a sadistic driver, yet it survives. In fact, the driver speeds the turtle across the road with the force of his cruelty. Oleg had arrived in America in the same way: the crueler his government had become, the more reason he had to leave. He would write an article entitled "The Cruel Kick," as soon as he had a chance.

"What's your name?" she was asking.

"I am Oleg Lum."

"Nice to meet you, Mr. Glum. I'm Carrie Remm. Where're you from?"

The other people at the table were eyeing them. He suggested with a nod that they move outside. Taking her spiral, she followed.

"I am from Moscow," he said, once outside. "And you?"

"Chicago. I'm ten years old, and my parents are divorced. My mother always looks sad because she had an operation. Now she can't have children, but since she's divorced, I'm not sure it matters that she can't have children. I just think the operation was the last straw. Anyway, I like to get out of the house. She makes me nervous."

"Please, what means *last straw?*"

"It means *curtains, cut, that's it, I've had it.*"

"And your mother is alone then all the time?"

"Oh, she calls her friends. But she never goes out. When my dad comes to pick me up on Sundays, she looks a little better."

Cars whizzed by, as Lum smoked a cigarette. He liked the bold bull's-eye of Lucky Strikes.

"You would like a cigarette?" He kept an extra pack at all times for his generosity training.

"No thanks. Kids don't smoke here."

"You would like maybe ice cream?"

They walked silently to the Thirty-One Flavors, took a corner booth, and talked all afternoon.

They decided on dinner for Saturday night, his night off. On Saturday night Mr. Kaplan's son Denny answered the phones for time and a half. Once when Denny had had a tooth extracted, Oleg had taken his place.

He was worried about Mrs. Remm's grief. Losing one's reproductive ability, he imagined, was tragic for a thirty-four year old woman. He might buy her a get-well card, but he didn't know that she was really ill. Maybe a sympathy card was in order, and flowers, but they'd have to wait for Saturday.

"Please, if you may help," he asked a small wizened woman who looked like a lemur he'd seen at Brookfield Zoo. When one got old, hair and face turned gray together, and fine down started growing everywhere. The woman's cheeks, chin, and ears were furry. She looked as if someone had spun a web over her.

"Yes?"

"If you please, a dozen flowers."

"We have roses, carnations, combos, mixed in-season, zinnias, peonies, Hawaiian, birds-of-paradise, honeymoon bouquets, orchids, the woodsy spray, and dried. Can you be more specific?"

"The woman has lost her reproductive abilities. I wish to supply her with flowers."

"How about roses?"

They cost him fourteen dollars and ninety-five cents, and accompanying them was a card with etched blue hands folded in prayer. Inside, the card read, "With *extreme* sympathy upon your loss." He signed it Oleg, hoping for the intimacy of first names. No one called him Oleg anymore, except an old friend from Moscow he saw now and then at The Washing Well. Sometimes it was hard to remember that Oleg was his name. "In *extreme* sympathy," he repeated, liking especially how the word *extreme* looked in italics. They were a marvelous invention. He hoped for an entire evening of wavy italic emotion. When he caught his reflection in shop windows, his nose appeared optimistically upturned, and the bouquet he held, wrapped in paper depicting a trellis of ivy and roses, waved like a banner.

"Get the door," he heard through the wood after he'd been buzzed into Claire Remm's apartment-building hallway. Claire was a lovely name. It reminded him of water.

When Carrie opened the door, she appeared cross. "You're on time. I thought you were the pizza. I was hoping it'd come first."

"I am not pizza. However, it is good to be here." He hoped she wouldn't assume the flowers were for her. He hid them behind his back. Since she didn't ask what he was holding, he knew she understood.

"Mom, it's Mr. Glum."

"Who?" She sounded confused, but her voice was melodic, a song, a tribute.

"My friend, Mr. Glum."

Never, he thought, had so much natural beauty been wasted on such a negligent caretaker. Not on the American side of Niagara Falls, not in those Tennessee caves where stalagmites and stalactites are overwhelmed by tepees and imitation Indian blankets. Claire Remm had blue eyes, shiny black hair one usually saw on Japanese women, and a complexion somewhere in the range of infant pink. She wore furry slippers, blue jeans, a sweat shirt that said SPEED WAGON, and no make-up. Her hair wasn't combed but stuck over one ear as if it had been glued there. Her eyes looked dried up, like African drinking holes.

"For you, Mrs. Remm, with thanks." Oleg extended the flowers in a shaky hand.

"Who are you?" she asked, peering over the flowers. She had the look of someone who doesn't care she's being observed, a look he'd seen on sleepers and drunks.

"I am Oleg Lum, friend of Carrie."

"I thought . . . Well, I'm sorry, Mr. Lum. I thought Carrie had invited a child."

"It is no problem. I eat very little. Like a child." He smiled so hard he thought his face might crumble.

"You don't understand, Mr. Lum. I've ordered a pizza. I assumed you two would eat and watch TV while I read a book." Her thin neck wobbled.

"The plans can exist. And may I ask, what book is engaging you?"

"*Pride and Prejudice.* I haven't read it since college."

"Is tale of civil-rights movement or of women's movement?"

Claire laughed and called Carrie. "Why didn't you explain, Care?" Carrie shrugged her shoulders and left the room again.

He pointed the flowers in Claire's direction, and she finally took them. "Please," he said, "if problem, I can exit."

"No, Mr. Lum. The pizza should arrive soon. Would you like a beer?" She had put the flowers on a silver radiator.

"May we plant the flowers?" Oleg asked.

"Oh," she said and told Carrie to get a vase and water. Lum wasn't certain, but he thought maybe she was smiling ever so slightly like someone who is trying not to laugh at a joke.

While Carrie and Claire sat on the couch, Lum sat in an oversized tan corduroy chair that made him feel fat. He assumed that the chair was Mr. Remm's and that Mr. Remm was a large man with bristly hair like Carrie's. He wondered if it made Carrie sad that he was sitting in her father's chair. He would have asked, but Claire and Carrie were watching *Dance Fever*. They concentrated on it like scholars at the Moscow Institute of Technology.

"Is good for fashion education."

"You bet," Carrie assured him. Claire watched the television and absent-mindedly dissected the pizza, which sat in the middle of the floor. Carrie had placed the roses next to the pizza in a green vase that hid their stems. He wondered whether Claire might reach for pizza and come up with a rose. The room appeared freshly painted, meaning that everything had been taken down and the walls whitewashed. No decorations had been rehung where picture hooks and curtain rods waited. It looked as if a civilization had perished there. The place made him feel foolish. It was not the first American home he'd visited. Mrs. Kaplan's was, with its plastic-covered everything and miniature dog statues and candelabra. But hers could have been the aberration. Suppose Americans were more like Danes in character than he'd imagined: melancholic, spare, and joyless.

During a commercial he spoke. "Mrs. Remm, your daughter is very clever girl and hard worker at library. She tells me about you. She is sorry for you."

"She is?" The voice was shrill, a verbal grimace.

"She is sad that you are not able, may I say, to reproduce."

"Carrie, why did you tell him *that*?" The entire room vibrated with new energy. He imagined lamps crashing to the floor. Carrie shrugged her nonchalant shoulders.

"I am sorry, Mrs. Remm, to cause this trouble. She is loving you and wanting to be of help."

Now Claire was smiling and Carrie exhaling. It couldn't have been his explanation. Some signals, he imagined, like those third-base coaches use to coax on their runners, must have been exchanged in the blink of an eye. The blink must have been invented for such a purpose. What had happened in the invisible moment was a détente. Finally Carrie spoke. "Mom, he's okay to tell things to. Who do you think he knows?"

Lum smiled. He knew he'd been insulted, but the insult was harmless. Besides, it had made Claire smile again.

"Mr. Lum," she began, "I expected a little Russian boy. You know. Pointy ears.

Fat cheeks. Shorts. Sandals. Instead, you walk in knowing everything about me, bringing me flowers. I guess I must be very glum!''

They all laughed. It was a moment of joy, one he'd recall along with his first erection and leaving Russia. A triptych of pleasure. Claire kept laughing even after he and Carrie had finished. Quacking and quacking like a beautiful blue-eyed duck until she said, "I haven't read the card. Let's read the card." She opened it with high drama and stared at Lum's hopeful smile. More signals were exchanged with Carrie, who, after reading the card aloud, stared at Lum too. Mother and daughter then slapped hands palm to palm, and Claire suggested that they all take a walk.

"Better yet," Oleg said, "a trick is up the sleeve. I have procured tickets for an event of pantomime to begin in twenty minutes. We should begin our arrival now."

Claire excused herself. He and Carrie stood in the doorway at nervous attention. He could look beyond Carrie and see down the hallway to the roses opening in the vase next to the pizza cardboard. "Let's go," Claire was saying as she joined them, "or we'll be late." She was dressed as an Indian princess.

Dear Readers of Chicago:

It strikes me as new American that much is made of largeness in your country. Examine, if you please, the Mount Rushmore. Here are the great stone faces of the profound leaders of men. But here is a man also. He is cleaning the stone faces. Up the nostril of Abraham Lincoln, freer of slaves, the cleaner climbs, as a fly, without notice. Or, let us say, a family on vacation takes his photo. There is the great stone Lincoln. There is the tiny man with huge brush for nostril cleaning. Thus is humor because the size of man is made small by large design of beauty.

In America I hear many jokes. Some are about women whose husbands cannot meet their desires, which are too large. In others, several members of Polish nation are trying to accomplish small goal, the removing of light bulb. Their effort is too large for smallness of task.

On a certain Sunday I was driving with American acquaintance down the Madison Street. My American said, "You'll never believe what we waste our money on here," and it is true that in Soviet Union largeness is always minor premise of grandeur. There are large monuments to workers, huge squares to fill with people cheering for politics, heads of Lenin the size of cathedrals, and many women with large breasts, who are called stately by the Russian men. Now on American Sunday I look to right, and there stands a huge bat of metal. It stands, perhaps, fifty feet tall like apartment building. I say to my friend, "The baseball is grand American entertainment. The baseball is your Lenin." "No," says American friend, "the bat is joke about wasting money. It has nothing to do with baseball."

The bat is then humorous. I believe words of my friend, who is businessman. In poor or undemocratic countries there is no humorous public art. History is the only public art. The huge stone pyramids are not meant as joke. In America the bat of abundance is cynic's joke. Same cynic points at huge genitals of corpse. He makes public monument to frozen bat. The lover of art points to the living genitals or makes the beautiful statue like Michelangelo's *David*.

As the huge Gulliver was tied down by the little citizens for possible harm done, so the public shows the disdain for size, even with its power. Thus is opposite, humor from largeness. The bully is, yes, strong, but he is also fool. He is laborer digging in dirt. His brain is mushroom producing no truths. Largeness is victory and also defeat. To largeness we prostrate ourselves and then up our sleeves die laughing.

Thank you,
Oleg Lum

Since it was Sunday and Carrie would be away, he thought of calling Claire and arranging a private visit. The evening before had been a success, the pantomimists having done a version of *Antony and Cleopatra* in which the larger, bearded Cleopatra swooned into the compact Antony's arms. Carrie quacked like her mother. Claire cried when she was happy. Both mother and daughter had walked him home, kissed him good night, and said they'd treat him to lunch on Monday.

If he called her now, the spell might be broken. She'd infer the obscene length of his nose in his altered phone voice. She'd laugh at his misuse of articles. He'd not flirt with ruin. The beach beckoned with its Sunday collage of summer bodies.

"What is your name, little boy?" Lum asked the child who sat next to his towel squeezing sand between his toes. He wore a seersucker sunsuit and a bulging diaper. His cheeks were fat, but he was not tan. In fact, he was pale and resembled Nikita Khrushchev with his spikes of just emerging white-blond hair. He was no older than a year and a half, though Lum might be wrong, having had no experience with babies.

"Do you know your name?" Lum asked again. The sun was behind them, and he felt his skin radiating heat. He'd fallen asleep in the afternoon, and, judging by the sun's angle, he'd slept two or three hours. It was evening. People were beginning to pack up for the day. The lifeguard, who had made a white triangle of cream on his nose, looked bored. Not enough people were swimming, Lum observed, much less drowning, to give his life definition.

Lum offered the child a piece of banana, which he greedily accepted. He mashed it in his hand and pressed pieces slowly into his mouth.

"Bop," said the boy.

"Pleased to meet you. I am Oleg Lum." The child looked at Lum's extended hand.

"Of course, babies do not understand the handshake," he explained. "Tell me, little Bop, is your mama here?"

Bop stood on tiptoe in the sand, wobbled, and tumbled to Lum's towel. A cascade of sand followed him.

Lum pointed at a young couple loading cans of Coke into a cooler. "Do you know these people, little Bop?"

Bop ignored all questions, sharing Lum's blanket, kicking his feet in the air, and humming, "Gee-dah, Gee-dah."

After an hour of Bop's company, Lum thought of asking the lifeguard about a lost-and-found service. He was afraid, though, that the lifeguard would call the police and scare the boy, who looked at Lum with such peaceful eyes, who joyously accepted crackers, and who laughed at the seagulls' W-shaped assaults, at bugs he found in the sand, and at Lum cooing, "little Bop, little Bop."

Bop had fallen asleep at the edge of Lum's towel, sucking the corner he held in his fist. Lum folded another triangle over his back to protect it from the waning sun.

When the lifeguard was tying up his boat and the sun had changed to a forgiving twilight, in which couples twisted together on blankets or faced each other with their legs folded Indian-style to share a joint, Lum realized there were no families left to step forward and claim Bop. It was clear in this instant that he would either have to call the authorities, men whose hands shot lead at robbers, who poked sticks into kidneys, or keep the child with him. The law would not recommend that decision, he was sure, but parents who'd forgotten a child at the beach, in the way he might leave an umbrella on a bench, weren't worthy of a search.

He'd carry the child home with him. In the morning he'd read the paper, hoping for news. And if news didn't materialize, there was Claire waiting, arms open, bereft of the ability to reproduce. She had said the night before, admiring Carrie's impressions of the mimes, that she'd have liked to have had one more child, a son. Then she'd wrinkled her nose, frowned, smiled, looked away, asked for a cigarette, and shrugged. Every emotion could be observed as it changed direction like a sailboat wobbling to shore in cross winds. She'd thank him for the child. It was clear the police weren't needed.

The lifeguard had left the beach, surrendering the safety of its inhabitants to Lum. He'd not disappoint the lifeguard. He put his book and wallet and keys in his back pockets, slid into his sandals, gathered the child up in his towel, and began walking, Bop snoring soundly in his arms.

He'd never thought of having a child himself. He had spent his years getting out of Russia, while other men searched for lovers or wives. Now, diapering the boy with the clean supplies he had bought at midnight last night when the need presented itself, it seemed he had never done anything more natural. Lum soothed Bop's rash with Vaseline, powdered his plump half-moons, and watched in awe as Bop cooed and pulled his pink penis, doubling over it, snail-like, and curling around his softer part. At least the parents had fed the poor child and not in any way hurt him. He was mottled pink, plump, and clean in all places but the creases, which were easy to overlook even if one was diligent.

The seersucker sunsuit was drying in the washroom. The child had eaten crackers, cheese, a peach, and milk already. Bop pronounced "milk," "shoe," "dog," and "bird." Lum pronounced, "Little Bop is very clever." Bop pointed at Lum, wordless. The morning passed quickly.

Walking to Claire's, he hoped that Bop would not soil himself on Lum's new shirt. He had even given Bop a bath for the occasion and combed his sparse hair so it stood in neat little rows, like toy farm crops. He wanted to meet Claire upstairs with the child rather than on the street, where her reaction might be too private for display. Suppose she thanked him with tears or fell into his arms, a crest of emotion filling her chest. Suppose she suggested marriage on the spot, Oleg Lum the father of little Bop, she the mother, Carrie the big sister, a home on a quiet street, maybe a dog, lots of American television to cool his rapid-fire brain. He carried Bop, who mostly smiled. Lum smiled too. It might be his wedding day.

"Just a minute," he heard through the door. As he'd hoped, Claire answered. But she didn't meet him with sobs or whispers of praise.

"What, Oleg!"

"Is boy I found at beach. Is he not handsome?"

"You found him at the beach? Didn't he have parents?"

"Parents could not be located. I wait until beach closes and only drug takers remain. Then I take him home."

"He spent the night with you? You didn't call the police?"

"I do not want government thug with stick in belt to take child and frighten him. I want you to take him."

"Me, Oleg?"

Lum looked hopeful. Bop offered Claire a sucked-on cracker.

"Oleg, let's sit down." They walked into the front room. Carrie was not home. Bop sat on the floor and busied himself by dismembering a magazine. "I know you mean well, Oleg, but laws are strict. If a child is lost, he must be given to the authorities. They'll find his parents."

"Parents dump child on beach like trash. They leave him there. Why should such parents have themselves found?"

"It's true, Oleg, but there are laws. I wouldn't be surprised if his damned Easter picture weren't being flashed on every newscast."

"Is no damned flashing. I watch last night and news today."

"Oleg," Claire continued, "you could be considered a criminal."

"Is no crime to help little Bop and to hope that you will also help."

"How do you know his name?"

"I ask him, 'Baby, what is your name?' He says, 'Bop.'"

"Oleg, Bop isn't an American name. Bop isn't any kind of name. Babies make sounds."

"Bop is not name. Parents are not caring. Police are not called. What should I do? Take baby back to beach? Leave him in rowboat like Moses?"

"No, Oleg. I'll call the police. They'll come for him and find his parents or relatives. You were very kind to care for him. Bop is lucky to have found you, Oleg." She kissed the crown of his head.

"Please, before police, let us sit together and watch Bop."

Claire sat down next to him, and he took her hand. Bop was pretending to water some violets with an empty watering can. Then he sat down opposite Oleg and insisted, plainly, on milk. Claire got a small glass and offered it to Bop.

"He is needing help," Oleg suggested and held the glass for him.

They sat hand in hand for an hour, Oleg enjoying the most mundane fantasy. They were at an American pediatrician's, taking their child for a checkup. She was the bride he'd met in college, and she still wore her modest wedding ring, though he'd have liked to have been more extravagant. She didn't have to talk, his wife of many years, just sit and admire their little son.

"Police are not needing to be called."

"I'll call them now, Oleg. I'll explain. You go home, and I'll phone you after they've left."

Lum felt large tears forming under his lids. He watched Bop shredding the interior-design magazine. The blurry room lost its sofa, its draperies, its rug. Everything was in pieces. This was not to be his wedding day.

Dear Personal View:

Everything in America gets lost, sometimes stolen. I lose my umbrella on el train. It is never returned. Meanwhile, baby is left on beach to weather, danger, criminals, drug takers, God knows. Parents come to police. Say they are sorry, so baby is returned. Why in America is easier to find lost baby than umbrella costing nine dollars? But I worry most for sandy American baby who is found on beach like walking rubbish heap called Bop. He is dirty, hungry little immigrant. I give him new life visa, which police revoke.

The switchboard was howling. An alarm had gone off at Cusper Motors, but Lum closed his eyes and listened as the howling continued. He was not going to call the police. Let the thieves do as they wished to Cusper's Fords. The police were worse than criminals. They were blind men, liars, fools. Lum disconnected the phone, and in the sudden silence, he willed his eyes closed and tried to fall asleep. He would sleep until his shift ended, until all Mr. Cusper's Fords were taken, until the police were running over the whole city in search of car thieves and drug takers and lost babies.

SETTING

In our earlier analyses of plot, point of view, and character, we have seen that these aspects of fiction represent an arrangement and a heightening of aspects of real life in the interest of meaning. The same thing is true of settings. All stories have settings, no matter how neutral or indefinite, and on one level they merely provide a realistic grounding for the action. But it is hard to imagine a story in which the setting has no more significance than that, and many stories seem to be *about* their settings, interpretations of place.

Take the stories we have read so far in this section, for example. It is surprising that the setting for "A Loaf of Bread," perhaps the earthiest, most realistic story we have read so far, is left unspecified. It takes place in the black section of a large American city at a time near the present, but we are never told which city. On the other hand, although the actual city is left unnamed, the individual locations at which the story unfolds are quite specific: an abandoned theater, a barroom, a luncheonette, a drugstore lunch counter, Green's grocery. It is as if McPherson were suggesting that the particular city is not important, that his story could take place anywhere where such conditions exist.

The settings of "The Oriental Contingent" are vague and multiple. The story starts at a vaguely described, half-remembered party: "Connie couldn't remember whose party it was, whose house. She had an impression of kerosene lamps on brown wicker tables, of shapes talking in doorways." Even in this first paragraph, the setting melts into a later, similar one: "It was summer, almost the only time Connie has run into her since, too," and later the recurrent action (running into Lisa) is placed in a series of vague, similar settings: "Three, four years passed, with their running into each other at receptions and openings." The vague, serial settings do convey an atmosphere of wealth and privilege—these are well-to-do people—but the vagueness and similarity of the settings may be even more important than their suggestion of money. Connie and Lisa do not have a very strong or significant relationship to their American homes. Their preoccupation with China and degrees of "Chineseness" makes their actual location pale into insignificance. The best way to define the setting of the story may be negative—"not-China," rather than any particular place.

If we check the setting of "Johnny Ray," again, as with "A Loaf of Bread," we find a curious combination of the vague and nameless and the concrete and detailed. The small town where the school is located is never named, and even the part of the country is never stipulated. And yet at the same time the social structure and ethnic balance are described in enough detail that we can locate the small town in the southwestern United States near the Mexican border. The narrator is young and naïve enough that it never occurs to him to locate his little town; to him, it is the whole world. And yet from the reader's perspective, the society of the story is upside down. The Mexican-Americans who are the oppressive majority in this little town are an oppressed minority in the larger society. It is almost as if the author were suggesting that it doesn't matter who the majority is; the mere fact of its being in the majority makes it oppressive.

The role of setting is somewhat different in Maxine Chernoff's story "Bop." The setting is very explicit, for one thing; it is contemporary Chicago, but Chicago seen as representative of contemporary America. The protagonist, Oleg Lum, is engaged in a study of American life as exemplified in Chicago. He fills scrapbooks with American trivia, and his apartment, stuffed with American kitsch, expresses an attitude toward America of "total acceptance." And yet he carries on a running critique of American ways in the letters he writes to the "Personal View" column of the newspaper. He finds a "proliferation of bad ideas" in American pop culture, he criticizes Americans' love of size for its own sake, and he finally protests the police handling of the lost baby Bop.

What is the Chicago of "Bop" like? To pick just one of many possible answers, it is full of surprises: mimes who make lots of noise, babies inexplicably abandoned on the beach, and characters like Oleg Lum. American culture, in "Bop," is an open, indeterminate society full of possibilities, not the polarized battleground of a story like "A Loaf of Bread." In the world of "Bop," people can establish human ties and even a rudimentary family in the atomized, depersonalized city.

As we have noticed before, there is something very artificial about isolating only one element in a story and examining only that. "Bop" has a very interesting plot structure, with Bop himself not introduced until the last third of the story. It would be illuminating to examine how the various plot pieces of the story go together. Character, too, is obviously central to the story, and to look closely at the complementary relationship between Oleg Lum and Claire Remm would be to learn a good bit about the story. But these dimensions are strongly reinforced by the story's invention of a comic, surprising Chicago.

A reading of the following story, Charles Johnson's "China," will prepare us for a discussion of metaphor in fiction.

Charles Johnson

Charles Johnson (b. 1948) grew up in Evanston, Illinois, and was educated at Southern Illinois University and the State University of New York at Stony Brook. His first novel was *Faith and the Good Thing* (1974). It was followed by *Oxherding Tale* (1982) and *Middle Passage* (1990), for which he received the National Book Award. He has also published a collection of short stories, *The Sorcerer's Apprentice* (1986), from which "China" is taken; two collections of drawings, *Black Humor* (1970) and *Half-Past Nation-Time* (1972); and a book of literary criticism, *Being and Race: Black Writing Since 1970* (1988). He is on the faculty of the University of Washington in Seattle.

CHINA

If one man conquer in battle a thousand men, and if another conquers himself, he is the greatest of conquerors.
— *The Dharmapada*

Evelyn's problems with her husband, Rudolph, began one evening in early March—a dreary winter evening in Seattle—when he complained after a heavy meal of pig's feet and mashed potatoes of shortness of breath, an allergy to something she put in his food perhaps, or brought on by the first signs of wild flowers around them. She suggested they get out of the house for the evening, go to a movie. He was fifty-four, a postman for thirty-three years now, with high blood pressure, emphysema, flat feet, and, as Evelyn told her friend Shelberdine Lewis, the lingering fear that he had cancer. Getting old, he was also getting hard to live with. He told her never to salt his dinners, to keep their Lincoln Continental at a crawl, and never run her fingers along his inner thigh when they sat in Reverend William Merrill's church, because anything, even sex, or laughing too loud—Rudolph was serious—might bring on heart failure.

So she chose for their Saturday night outing a peaceful movie, a mildly funny comedy a *Seattle Times* reviewer said was fit only for titters and nasal snorts, a low-key satire that made Rudolph's eyelids droop as he shoveled down unbuttered popcorn in the darkened, half-empty theater. Sticky fluids cemented Evelyn's feet to the floor. A man in the last row laughed at all the wrong places. She kept the popcorn on her lap, though she hated the unsalted stuff and wouldn't touch it, sighing as Rudolph pawed across her to shove his fingers inside the cup.

She followed the film as best she could, but occasionally her eyes frosted over, flashed white. She went blind like this now and then. The fibers of her eyes were failing; her retinas were tearing like soft tissue. At these times the world was a canvas with whiteout spilling from the far left corner toward the center; it was the sudden shock of an empty frame in a series of slides. Someday, she knew, the snow on her eyes would stay. Winter eternally: her eyes split like her walking stick. She groped along the fractured surface, waiting for her sight to thaw, listening to the film she couldn't see. Her only comfort was knowing that, despite her infirmity, her Rudolph was in even worse health.

He slid back and forth from sleep during the film (she elbowed him occasionally, or pinched his leg), then came full awake, sitting up suddenly when the movie ended and a "Coming Attractions" trailer began. It was some sort of

49

gladiator movie, Evelyn thought, blinking, and it was pretty trashy stuff at that. The plot's revenge theme was a poor excuse for Chinese actors or Japanese (she couldn't tell those people apart) to flail the air with their hands and feet, take on fifty costumed extras at once, and leap twenty feet through the air in perfect defiance of gravity. Rudolph's mouth hung open.

"Can people really do that?" He did not take his eyes off the screen, but talked at her from the right side of his mouth. "Leap that high?"

"It's a *movie*," sighed Evelyn. "A *bad* movie."

He nodded, then asked again, "But can they?"

"Oh, Rudolph, for God's sake!" She stood up to leave, her seat slapping back loudly. "They're on *trampolines!* You can see them in the corner—there!—if you open your eyes!"

He did see them, once Evelyn twisted his head to the lower left corner of the screen, and it seemed to her that her husband looked disappointed—looked, in fact, the way he did the afternoon Dr. Guylee told Rudolph he'd developed an extrasystolic reaction, a faint, moaning sound from his heart whenever it relaxed. He said no more and, after the trailer finished, stood—there was chewing gum stuck to his trouser seat—dragged on his heavy coat with her help, and followed Evelyn up the long, carpeted aisle, through the exit of the Coronet Theater, and to their car. He said nothing as she chattered on the way home, reminding him that he could not stay up all night puttering in his basement shop because the next evening they were to attend the church's revival meeting.

Rudolph, however, did not attend the revival. He complained after lunch of a light, dancing pain in his chest, which he had conveniently whenever Mount Zion Baptist Church held revivals, and she went alone, sitting with her friend Shelberdine, a beautician. She was forty-one; Evelyn, fifty-two. That evening Evelyn wore spotless white gloves, tan therapeutic stockings for the swelling in her ankles, and a white dress that brought out nicely the brown color of her skin, the most beautiful cedar brown, Rudolph said when they were courting thirty-five years ago in South Carolina. But then Evelyn had worn a matching checkered skirt and coat to meeting. With her jet-black hair pinned behind her neck by a simple wooden comb, she looked as if she might have been Andrew Wyeth's starkly beautiful model for *Day of the Fair*. Rudolph, she remembered, wore black business suits, black ties, black wing tips, but he also wore white gloves because he was a senior usher—this was how she first noticed him. He was one of four young men dressed like deacons (or blackbirds), their left hands tucked into the hollow of their backs, their right carrying silver plates for the offering as they marched in almost military fashion down each aisle: Christian soldiers, she'd thought, the cream of black manhood, and to get his attention she placed not her white envelope or coins in Rudolph's plate but instead a note that said: "You have a beautiful smile." It was, for all her innocence, a daring thing to do, according to Evelyn's mother—flirting with a randy young man like Rudolph Lee Jackson, but he did have nice, tigerish teeth. A killer smile, people called it, like all the boys in the Jackson family: a killer smile and good hair that needed no more than one stroke of his palm to bring out Quo Vadis rows pomaded sweetly with the scent of Murray's.

And, of course, Rudolph was no dummy. Not a total dummy, at least. He pretended nothing extraordinary had happened as the congregation left the little whitewashed church. He stood, the youngest son, between his father and mother, and let old Deacon Adcock remark, "Oh, how strong he's looking now," which was a lie. Rudolph was the weakest of the Jackson boys, the pale, bookish, spiritual child born when his parents were well past forty. His brothers played football, they went into the navy; Rudolph lived in Scripture, was labeled 4-F, and hoped to attend Moody Bible Institute in Chicago, if he could ever find the money. Evelyn could tell Rudolph knew exactly where she was in the crowd, that he could feel her as she and her sister, Debbie, waited for their father to bring his DeSoto—the family prize—closer to the front steps. When the crowd thinned, he shambled over in his slow, ministerial walk, introduced himself, and unfolded her note.

"You write this?" he asked. "It's not right to play with the Lord's money, you know."

"I like to play," she said.

"You do, huh?" He never looked directly at people. Women, she guessed, terrified him. Or, to be exact, the powerful emotions they caused in him terrified Rudolph. He was a pud puller if she ever saw one. He kept his eyes on a spot left of her face. "You're Joe Montgomery's daughter, aren't you?"

"Maybe," teased Evelyn.

He trousered the note and stood marking the ground with his toe. "And just what you expect to get, Miss Playful, by fooling with people during collection time?"

She waited, let him look away, and, when the back-and-forth swing of his gaze crossed her again, said in her most melic, soft-breathing voice: *"You."*

Up front, portly Reverend Merrill concluded his sermon. Evelyn tipped her head slightly, smiling into memory; her hand reached left to pat Rudolph's leg gently; then she remembered it was Shelberdine beside her, and lifted her hand to the seat in front of her. She said a prayer for Rudolph's health, but mainly it was for herself, a hedge against her fear that their childless years had slipped by like wind, that she might return home one day and find him—as she had found her father—on the floor, bellied up, one arm twisted behind him where he fell, alone, his fingers locked against his chest. Rudolph had begun to run down, Evelyn decided, the minute he was turned down by Moody Bible Institute. They moved to Seattle in 1956—his brother Eli was stationed nearby and said Boeing was hiring black men. But they didn't hire Rudolph. He had kidney trouble on and off before he landed the job at the Post Office. Whenever he bent forward, he felt dizzy. Liver, heart, and lungs—they'd worn down gradually as his belly grew, but none of this was as bad as what he called "the Problem." His pecker shrank to no bigger than a pencil eraser each time he saw her undress. Or when Evelyn, as was her habit when talking, touched his arm. Was she the cause of this? Well, she knew she wasn't much to look at anymore. She'd seen the bottom of a few too many candy wrappers. Evelyn was nothing to make a man pant and jump her bones, pulling her fully clothed onto the davenport, as Rudolph had done years before, but wasn't sex something else you surrendered with age? It never seemed all that good to her anyway. And besides, he'd wanted oral sex, which Evelyn—if she knew nothing else—thought was a nasty, unsanitary thing to do with your mouth. She glanced up from under her spring hat past the pulpit, past the choir of black and brown faces to the agonized beauty of a bearded white carpenter impaled on a rood, and in this timeless image she felt comforted that suffering was inescapable, the loss of vitality inevitable, even a good thing maybe, and that she had to steel herself—yes—for someday opening her bedroom door and finding her Rudolph facedown in his breakfast oatmeal. He would die before her, she knew that in her bones.

And so, after service, Sanka, and a slice of meat pie with Shelberdine downstairs in the brightly lit church basement, Evelyn returned home to tell her husband how lovely the Griffin girls had sung that day, that their neighbor Rod Kenner had been saved, and to listen, if necessary, to Rudolph's fear that the lump on his shoulder was an early-warning sign of something evil. As it turned out, Evelyn found that except for their cat, Mr. Miller, the little A-frame house was empty. She looked in his bedroom. No Rudolph. The unnaturally still house made Evelyn uneasy, and she took the excruciatingly painful twenty stairs into the basement to peer into a workroom littered with power tools, planks of wood, and the blue-prints her husband used to make bookshelves and cabinets. No Rudolph. Fright-ened, Evelyn called the eight hospitals in Seattle, but no one had a Rudolph Lee Jackson on his books. After her last call the starburst clock in the living room read twelve-thirty. Putting down the wall phone, she felt a familiar pain in her abdo-men. Another attack of Hershey squirts, probably from the meat pie. She hurried into the bathroom, lifted her skirt, and lowered her underwear around her ankles, but kept the door wide open, something impossible to do if Rudolph was home. Actually, it felt good not to have him underfoot, a little like he was dead already. But the last thing Evelyn wanted was that or, as she lay down against her lumpy backrest, to fall asleep, though she did, nodding off and dreaming until some-thing shifted down her weight on the side of her bed away from the wall.

"Evelyn," said Rudolph, "look at this." She blinked back sleep and squinted at the cover of a magazine called *Inside Kung-Fu,* which Rudolph waved under her nose. On the cover a man stood bowlegged, one hand cocked under his armpit, the other corkscrewing straight at Evelyn's nose.

"Rudolph!" She batted the magazine aside, then swung her eyes toward the cluttered nightstand, focusing on the electric clock beside her water glass from McDonald's, Preparation H suppositories, and Harlequin romances. "It's morn-ing!" Now she was mad. At least working at it. "Where have you been?"

Her husband inhaled, a wheezing, whistlelike breath. He rolled the magazine into a cylinder and, as he spoke, struck his left palm with it. "That movie we saw advertised? You remember—it was called *The Five Fingers of Death.* I just saw that and one called *Deep Thrust.*"

"Wonderful." Evelyn screwed up her lips. "I'm calling hospitals and you're at a Hong Kong double feature."

"Listen," said Rudolph. "You don't understand." He seemed at that moment as if he did not understand either. "It was a Seattle movie premiere. The North-west is crawling with fighters. It has something to do with all the Asians out here. Before they showed the movie, four students from a kwoon in Chinatown went onstage—"

"A what?" asked Evelyn.

"A kwoon—it's a place to study fighting, a meditation hall." He looked at her but was really watching, Evelyn realized, something exciting she had missed. "They did a demonstration to drum up their membership. They broke boards and bricks, Evelyn. They went through what's called kata and kumite and ..." He stopped again to breathe. "I've never seen anything so beautiful. The reason I'm late is because I wanted to talk with them after the movie."

Evelyn, suspicious, took a Valium and waited.

"I signed up for lessons," he said.

She gave a glacial look at Rudolph, then at his magazine, and said in the voice she had used five years ago when he wanted to take a vacation to Upper Volta or, before that, invest in a British car she knew they couldn't afford:

"You're fifty-*four* years old, Rudolph."

"I know that."

"You're no Muhammad Ali."

"I know that," he said.

"You're no Bruce Lee. Do you want to be Bruce Lee? Do you know where he is now, Rudolph? He's dead—dead here in a Seattle cemetery and buried up on Capitol Hill."

His shoulders slumped a little. Silently Rudolph began undressing, his beefy backside turned toward her, slipping his pajama bottoms on before taking off his shirt so his scrawny lower body would not be fully exposed. He picked up his magazine, said, "I'm sorry if I worried you," and huffed upstairs to his bedroom. Evelyn clicked off the mushroom-shaped lamp on her nightstand. She lay on her side, listening to his slow footsteps strike the stairs, then heard his mattress creak above her—his bedroom was directly above hers—but she did not hear him click off his own light. From time to time she heard his shifting weight squeak the mattress springs. He was reading that foolish magazine, she guessed; then she grew tired and gave this impossible man up to God. With a copy of *The Thorn Birds* open on her lap, Evelyn fell heavily asleep again.

At breakfast the next morning any mention of the lessons gave Rudolph lock-jaw. He kissed her forehead, as always, before going to work, and simply said he might be home late. Climbing the stairs to his bedroom was painful for Evelyn, but she hauled herself up, pausing at each step to huff, then sat on his bed and looked over his copy of *Inside Kung-Fu*. There were articles on empty-hand combat, soft-focus photos of ferocious-looking men in funny suits, parables about legendary Zen masters, an interview with someone named Bernie Bernheim, who began to study karate at age fifty-seven and became a black belt at age sixty-one, and page after page of advertisements for exotic Asian weapons: nunchaku, shuriken, sai swords, tonfa, bo staffs, training bags of all sorts, a wooden dummy shaped like a man and called a Mook Jong, and weights. Rudolph had circled them all. He had torn the order form from the last page of the magazine. The total cost of the things he'd circled—Evelyn added them furiously, rounding off the figures—was $800.

Two minutes later she was on the telephone to Shelberdine.

"Let him tire of it," said her friend. "Didn't you tell me Rudolph had Lower Lombard Strain?"

Evelyn's nose clogged with tears.

"Why is he doing this? Is it me, do you think?"

"It's the Problem," said Shelberdine. "He wants his manhood back. Before he died, Arthur did the same. Someone at the plant told him he could get it back if he did twenty-yard sprints. He went into convulsions while running around the lake."

Evelyn felt something turn in her chest. "You don't think he'll hurt himself, do you?"

"Of course not."

"Do you think he'll hurt *me*?"

Her friend reassured Evelyn that Mid-Life Crisis brought out these shenanigans in men. Evelyn replied that she thought Mid-Life Crisis started around age forty, to which Shelberdine said, "Honey, I don't mean no harm, but Rudolph always was a little on the slow side," and Evelyn agreed. She would wait until he worked this thing out of his system, until Nature defeated him and he surrendered, as any right-thinking person would, to the breakdown of the body, the brutal fact of decay, which could only be blunted, it seemed to her, by decaying *with* someone, the comfort every Negro couple felt when, aging, they knew enough to let things wind down.

Her patience was rewarded in the beginning. Rudolph crawled home from his first lesson, hunched over, hardly able to stand, afraid he had permanently ruptured something. He collapsed facedown on the living room sofa, his feet on the floor. She helped him change into his pajamas and fingered Ben-Gay into his back muscles. Evelyn had never seen her husband so close to tears.

"I can't *do* push-ups," he moaned. "Or sit-ups. I'm so stiff—I don't know my body." He lifted his head, looking up pitifully, his eyes pleading. "Call Dr. Guylee. Make an appointment for Thursday, okay?"

"Yes, dear." Evelyn hid her smile with one hand. "You shouldn't push yourself so hard."

At that, he sat up, bare-chested, his stomach bubbling over his pajama bottoms. "That's what it means. *Gung-fu* means 'hard work' in Chinese. Evelyn"—he lowered his voice—"I don't think I've ever really done hard work in my life. Not like this, something that asks me to give *every*thing, body and soul, spirit and flesh. I've always felt ..." He looked down, his dark hands dangling between his thighs. "I've never been able to give *every*thing to *any*thing. The world never let me. It won't let me pull all of myself into play. Do you know what I'm saying? Every job I've ever had, everything I've ever done, it only demanded part of me. It was like there was so much *more* of me that went unused after the job was over. I get that feeling in church sometimes." He lay back down, talking now into the sofa cushion. "Sometimes I get that feeling with you."

Her hand stopped on his shoulder. She wasn't sure she'd heard him right, his voice was so muffled. "That I've never used all of you?"

Rudolph nodded, rubbing his right knuckle where, at the kwoon, he'd lost a stretch of skin on a speed bag. "There's still part of me left over. You never tried to touch all of me, to take everything. Maybe you can't. Maybe no one can. But sometimes I get the feeling that the unused part—the unlived life—*spoils*, that you get cancer because it sits like fruit on the ground and rots." Rudolph shook his head; he'd said too much and knew it, perhaps had not even put it the way he felt inside. Stiffly, he got to his feet. "Don't ask me to stop training." His eyebrows spread inward. "If I stop, I'll die."

Evelyn twisted the cap back onto the Ben-Gay. She held out her hand, which Rudolph took. Veins on the back of his hand burgeoned abnormally like dough. Once when she was shopping at the Public Market she'd seen monstrous plastic gloves shaped like hands in a magic store window. His hand looked like that. It belonged on Lon Chaney. Her voice shook a little, panicky. "I'll call Dr. Guylee in the morning."

Evelyn knew—or thought she knew—his trouble. He'd never come to terms with the disagreeableness of things. Rudolph had always been too serious for some people, even in South Carolina. It was the thing, strange to say, that drew her to him, this crimped-browed tendency in Rudolph to listen with every atom of his life when their minister in Hodges, quoting Marcus Aurelius to give his sermon flash, said, "Live with the gods," or later in Seattle, the habit of working himself up over Reverend Merrill's reading from Ecclesiastes 9:10: "Whatsoever thy hand findeth to do, do it with thy might." Now, he didn't *really* mean that, Evelyn knew. Nothing in the world could be taken that seriously; that's *why* this was the world. And, as all Mount Zion knew, Reverend Merrill had a weakness for high-yellow choir girls and gin, and was forever complaining that his salary was too small for his family. People made compromises, nodded at spiritual commonplaces—the high seriousness of Biblical verses that demanded nearly superhuman duty and self-denial—and laughed off their lapses into sloth, envy, and the other deadly sins. It was what made living so enjoyably *human:* this built-in inability of man to square his performance with perfection. People were naturally soft on themselves. But not her Rudolph.

Of course, he seldom complained. It was not in his nature to complain when, looking for "gods," he found only ruin and wreckage. What did he expect? Evelyn wondered. Man was evil—she'd told him that a thousand times—or, if not evil, hopelessly flawed. Everything failed; it was some sort of law. But at least there was laughter, and lovers clinging to one another against the cliff; there were novels—wonderful tales of how things should be—and perfection promised in the after-world. He'd sit and listen, her Rudolph, when she put things this way, nodding because he knew that in his persistent hunger for perfection in the here and now he was, at best, in the minority. He kept his dissatisfaction to himself, but occasionally Evelyn would glimpse in his eyes that look, that distant, pained expression that asked: *Is this all?* She saw it after her first miscarriage, then her second; saw it when he stopped searching the want ads and settled on the Post Office as the fulfillment of his potential in the marketplace. It was always there, that look, after he turned forty, and no new, lavishly praised novel from the Book-of-the-Month Club, no feature-length movie, prayer meeting, or meal she fixed for him wiped it from Rudolph's eyes. He was, at least, this sort of man before he saw that martial-arts B movie. It was a dark vision, Evelyn decided, a dangerous vision, and in it she whiffed something that might destroy her. What that was she couldn't say, but she knew her Rudolph better than he knew himself. He would see the error—the waste of time—in his new hobby, and she was sure he would mend his ways.

In the weeks, then months, that followed, Evelyn waited, watching her husband for a flag of surrender. There was no such sign. He became worse than before. He cooked his own meals, called her heavy soul-food dishes "too acidic," lived on raw vegetables, seaweed, nuts, and fruit to make his body "more alkaline," and fasted on Sundays. He ordered books on something called Shaolin fighting and meditation from a store in California, and when his equipment arrived UPS from Dolan's Sports in New Jersey, he ordered more—in consternation, Evelyn read the list—leg stretchers, makiwara boards, air shields, hand grips, bokken, focus mitts, a full-length mirror (for Heaven's sake) so he could correct his form, and protective equipment. For proper use of his headgear and gloves, however, he said he needed a sparring partner—an opponent—he said, to help him instinctively understand "combat strategy," how to "flow" and "close the Gap" between himself and an adversary, how to create by his movements a negative space in which the other would be neutralized.

"Well," crabbed Evelyn, "if you need a punching bag, don't look at *me.*"

He sat across the kitchen table from her, doing dynamic-tension exercises as she read a new magazine called *Self.* "Did I ever tell you what a black belt means?" he asked.

"You told me."

"Sifu Chan doesn't use belts for ranking. They were introduced seventy years ago because Westerners were impatient, you know, needed signposts and all that."

"You told me," said Evelyn.

"Originally, all you got was a white belt. It symbolized innocence. Virginity." His face was immensely serious, like a preacher's. "As you worked, it got darker, dirtier, and turned brown. Then black. You were a master then. With even more work, the belt became frayed, the threads came loose, you see, and the belt showed white again."

"Rudolph, I've heard this before!" Evelyn picked up her magazine and took it into her bedroom. From there, with her legs drawn up under the blankets, she shouted: "I *won't* be your punching bag!"

So he brought friends from his kwoon, friends she wanted nothing to do with. There was something unsettling about them. Some were street fighters. Young. They wore tank-top shirts and motorcycle jackets. After drinking racks of Rainier beer on the front porch, they tossed their crumpled empties next door into Rod Kenner's yard. Together, two of Rudolph's new friends—Truck and Tuco— weighed a quarter of a ton. Evelyn kept a rolling pin under her pillow when they came, but she knew they could eat that along with her. But some of his new friends were students at the University of Washington. Truck, a Vietnamese only two years in America, planned to apply to the Police Academy once his training ended; and Tuco, who was Puerto Rican, had been fighting since he could make a fist; but a delicate young man named Andrea, a blue sash, was an actor in the drama department at the university. His kwoon training, he said, was less for self-defense than helping him understand his movements onstage—how, for example, to convincingly explode across a room in anger. Her husband liked them, Evelyn realized in horror. And they liked him. They were separated by money, background, and religion, but something she could not identify made them seem, those nights on the porch after his class, like a single body. They called Rudolph "Older Brother" or, less politely, "Pop."

His sifu, a short, smooth-figured boy named Douglas Chan, who, Evelyn figured, couldn't be over eighteen, sat like the Dalai Lama in their tiny kitchen as if he owned it, sipping her tea, which Rudolph laced with Korean ginseng. Her husband lit Chan's cigarettes as if he were President Carter come to visit the common man. He recommended that Rudolph study T'ai Chi, "soft" fighting systems, ki, and something called Tao. He told him to study, as well, Newton's three laws of physics and apply them to his own body during kumite. What she remembered most about Chan were his wrist braces, ornamental weapons that had three straps and, along the black leather, highly polished studs like those worn by Steve Reeves in a movie she'd seen about Hercules. In a voice she thought girlish, he spoke of eye gouges and groin-tearing techniques, exercises called the Delayed Touch of Death and Dim Mak, with the casualness she and Shelberdine talked about bargains at Thriftway. And then they suited up, the boyish Sifu, who looked like Maharaj-ji's rougher brother, and her clumsy husband; they went out back, pushed aside the aluminum lawn furniture, and pommeled each other for half an hour. More precisely, her Rudolph was on the receiving end of hook kicks, spinning back fists faster than thought, and foot sweeps that left his body purpled for weeks. A sensible man would have known enough to drive to Swedish Hospital pronto. Rudolph, never known as a profound thinker, pushed on after Sifu Chan left, practicing his flying kicks by leaping to ground level from a four-foot hole he'd dug by their cyclone fence.

Evelyn, nibbling a Van de Kamp's pastry from Safeway—she was always nibbling, these days—watched from the kitchen window until twilight, then brought out the Ben-Gay, a cold beer, and rubbing alcohol on a tray. She figured he needed it. Instead, Rudolph, stretching under the far-reaching cedar in the backyard, politely refused, pushed the tray aside, and rubbed himself with Dit-Da-Jow, "iron-hitting wine," which smelled like the open door of an opium factory on a hot summer day. Yet this ancient potion not only instantly healed his wounds (said Rudolph) but prevented arthritis as well. She was tempted to see if it healed brain damage by pouring it into Rudolph's ears, but apparently he was doing something right. Dr. Guylee's examination had been glowing; he said Rudolph's muscle tone, whatever that was, was better. His cardiovascular system was healthier. His erections were outstanding—or upstanding—though lately he seemed to have no interest in sex. Evelyn, even she, saw in the crepuscular light changes in Rudolph's upper body as he stretched: Muscles like globes of light rippled along his shoulders; larval currents moved on his belly. The language of his new, developing body eluded her. He was not always like this. After a cold shower and sleep his muscles shrank back a little. It was only after his workouts, his weight lifting, that his body expanded like baking bread, filling out in a way that obliterated the soft Rudolph-body she knew. This new flesh had the contours of the silhouetted figures on medical charts: the body as it must be in the mind of God. Glistening with perspiration, his muscles took on the properties of the free weights he pumped relentlessly. They were profoundly tragic, too, because their beauty was earthbound. It would vanish with the world. You are ugly, his new muscles said to Evelyn; old and ugly. His self-punishment made her feel sick. She was afraid of his hard, cold weights. She hated them. Yet she wanted them, too. They had a certain monastic beauty. She thought: He's doing this to hurt me. She wondered: What was it like to be powerful? Was clever cynicism—even comedy—the byproduct of bulging bellies, weak nerves, bad posture? Her only defense against the dumbbells that stood between them—she meant both his weights and his friends—was, as always, her acid Southern tongue:

"They're all fairies, right?"

Rudolph looked dreamily her way. These post-workout periods made him feel, he said, as if there were no interval between himself and what he saw. His face was vacant, his eyes—like smoke. In this afterglow (he said) he saw without judging. Without judgment, there were no distinctions. Without distinctions, there was no desire. Without desire . . .

He smiled sideways at her. "Who?"

"The people in your kwoon." Evelyn crossed her arms. "I read somewhere that most body builders are homosexual."

He refused to answer her.

"If they're not gay, then maybe I should take lessons. It's been good for you, right?" Her voice grew sharp. "I mean, isn't that what you're saying? That you and your friends are better'n everybody else?"

Rudolph's head dropped; he drew a long breath. Lately his responses to her took the form of quietly clearing his lungs.

"You should do what you *have* to, Evelyn. You don't have to do what anybody else does." He stood up, touched his toes, then brought his forehead straight down against his unbent knees, which was physically impossible, Evelyn would have said—and faintly obscene.

It was a nightmare to watch him each evening after dinner. He walked around the house in Everlast leg weights, tried push-ups on his fingertips and wrists, and, as she sat trying to watch "The Jeffersons," stood in a ready stance before the flickering screen, throwing punches each time the scene, or shot, changed to improve his timing. It took the fun out of watching TV, him doing that—she preferred him falling asleep in his chair beside her, as he used to. But what truly frightened Evelyn was his "doing nothing." Sitting in meditation, planted cross-legged in a full lotus on their front porch, with Mr. Miller blissfully curled on his lap, a bodhisattva in the middle of houseplants she set out for the sun. Looking at him, you'd have thought he was dead. The whole thing smelled like self-hypnosis. He breathed too slowly, in Evelyn's view—only three breaths per minute, he claimed. He wore his gi, splotchy with dried blood and sweat, his callused hands on his knees, the forefingers on each tipped against his thumbs, his eyes screwed shut.

During his eighth month at the kwoon, she stood watching him as he sat, wondering over the vivid changes in his body, the grim firmness where before there was jolly fat, the disquieting steadiness of his posture, where before Rudolph could not sit still in church for five minutes without fidgeting. Now he sat in zazen for forty-five minutes a day, fifteen when he awoke, fifteen (he said) at work in the mailroom during his lunch break, fifteen before going to bed. He called this withdrawal (how she hated his fancy language) similar to the necessary silences in music, "a stillness that prepared him for busyness and sound." He'd never breathed before, he told her. Not once. Not clear to the floor of himself. Never breathed and emptied himself as he did now, picturing himself sitting on the bottom of Lake Washington: himself, Rudolph Lee Jackson, at the center of the universe; for if the universe was infinite, any point where he stood would be at its center—it would shift and move with him. (That saying, Evelyn knew, was minted in Douglas Chan's mind. No Negro preacher worth the name would speak that way.) He told her that in zazen, at the bottom of the lake, he worked to discipline his mind and maintain one point of concentration; each thought, each feeling that overcame him he saw as a fragile bubble, which he could inspect passionlessly from all sides; then he let it float gently to the surface, and soon—as he slipped deeper into the vortices of himself, into the Void—even the image of himself on the lake floor vanished.

Evelyn stifled a scream.

Was she one of Rudolph's bubbles, something to detach himself from? On the porch Evelyn watched him narrowly, sitting in a rain-whitened chair, her chin on her left fist. She snapped the fingers on her right hand under his nose. Nothing. She knocked her knuckles lightly on his forehead. Nothing. (Faker, she thought.) For another five minutes he sat and breathed, sat and breathed, then opened his eyes slowly as if he'd slept as long as Rip Van Winkle. "It's dark," he said, stunned. When he began, it was twilight. Evelyn realized something new: he was not living time as she was, not even that anymore. Things, she saw, were slower for him; to him she must seem like a woman stuck in fast-forward. She asked:

"What do you see when you go in there?"

Rudolph rubbed his eyes. "Nothing."

"Then *why* do you do it? The world's out here!"

He seemed unable to say, as if the question were senseless. His eye angled up, like a child's, toward her face. "Nothing is peaceful sometimes. The emptiness is full. I'm not afraid of it now."

"You empty yourself?" she asked. "Of me, too?"

"Yes."

Evelyn's hand shot up to cover her face. She let fly with a whimper. Rudolph rose instantly—he sent Mr. Miller flying—then fell back hard on his buttocks; the lotus cut off blood to his lower body—which provided more to his brain, he claimed—and it always took him a few seconds before he could stand again. He reached up, pulled her hand down, and stroked it.

"What've I done?"

"That's it," sobbed Evelyn. "I don't know what you're doing." She lifted the end of her bathrobe, blew her nose, then looked at him through streaming, unseeing eyes. "And you don't either. I wish you'd never seen that movie. I'm sick of all your weights and workouts—sick of them, do you hear? Rudolph, I want you back the way you were: *sick.*" No sooner than she said this Evelyn was sorry. But she'd done no harm. Rudolph, she saw, didn't want anything; everything, Evelyn included, delighted him, but as far as Rudolph was concerned, it was all shadows in a phantom history. He was humbler now, more patient, but he'd lost touch with everything she knew was normal in people: weakness, fear, guilt, self-doubt, the very things that gave the world thickness and made people do things. She *did* want him to desire her. No, she didn't. Not if it meant oral sex. Evelyn didn't know, really, what she wanted anymore. She felt, suddenly, as if she might dissolve before his eyes. "Rudolph, if you're 'empty,' like you say, you don't know who—or what—is talking to you. If you said you were praying, I'd understand. It would be God talking to you. But this way . . ." She pounded her fist four, five times on her thigh. "It could be *evil* spirits, you know! There *are* evil spirits, Rudolph. It could be the Devil."

Rudolph thought for a second. His chest lowered after another long breath. "Evelyn, this is going to sound funny, but I don't believe in the Devil."

Evelyn swallowed. It had come to that.

"Or God—unless we are gods."

She could tell he was at pains to pick his words carefully, afraid he might offend. Since joining the kwoon and studying ways to kill, he seemed particularly careful to avoid her own most effective weapon: the wry, cutting remark, the put-down, the direct, ego-deflating slash. Oh, he was becoming a real saint. At times it made her want to hit him.

"Whatever is just *is*," he said. "That's all I know. Instead of worrying about whether it's good or bad, God or the Devil, I just want to be quiet, work on myself, and interfere with things as little as possible. Evelyn," he asked suddenly, "how can there be *two* things?" His brow wrinkled; he chewed his lip. "You think what I'm saying is evil, don't you?"

"I think it's strange! Rudolph, you didn't grow up in China," she said. "They can't breathe in China! I saw that today on the news. They burn soft coal, which gets into the air and turns into acid rain. They wear face masks over there, like the ones we bought when Mount St. Helens blew up. They all ride bicycles, for Christ's sake! They want what we have." Evelyn heard Rod Kenner step onto his screened porch, perhaps to listen from his rocker. She dropped her voice a little. "You grew up in Hodges, South Carolina, same as me, in a right and proper colored church. If you'd *been* to China, maybe I'd understand."

"I can only be what I've been?" This he asked softly, but his voice trembled. "Only what I was in Hodges?"

"You can't be Chinese."

"I don't want to be Chinese!" The thought made Rudolph smile and shake his head. Because she did not understand, and because he was tired of talking, Rudolph stepped back a few feet from her, stretching again, always stretching. "I only want to be what I *can* be, which isn't the greatest fighter in the world, only the fighter *I* can be. Lord knows, I'll probably get creamed in the tournament this Saturday." He added, before she could reply, "Doug asked me if I'd like to compete this weekend in full-contact matches with some people from the kwoon. I have to." He opened the screen door. "I will."

"You'll be killed—you know that, Rudolph." She dug her fingernails into her bathrobe, and dug this into him: "You know, you never were very strong. Six months ago you couldn't open a pickle jar for me."

He did not seem to hear her. "I bought a ticket for you." He held the screen door open, waiting for her to come inside. "I'll fight better if you're there."

She spent the better part of that week at Shelberdine's mornings and Reverend

Merrill's church evenings, rinsing her mouth with prayer, sitting most often alone in the front row so she would not have to hear Rudolph talking to himself from the musty basement as he pounded out bench presses, skipped rope for thirty minutes in the backyard, or shadowboxed in preparation for a fight made inevitable by his new muscles. She had married a fool, that was clear, and if he expected her to sit on a bench at the Kingdome while some equally stupid brute spilled the rest of his brains—probably not enough left now to fill a teaspoon—then he was wrong. How could he see the world as "perfect"? That was his claim. There were poverty, unemployment, twenty-one children dying every minute, every day, every year from hunger and malnutrition, more than twenty murdered in Atlanta; there were sixty thousand nuclear weapons in the world, which was dreadful, what with Seattle so close to Boeing; there were far-right Republicans in the White House: *good* reasons, Evelyn thought, to be "negative and life-denying," as Rudolph would put it. It was almost sin to see harmony in an earthly hell, and in a fit of spleen she prayed God would dislocate his shoulder, do some minor damage to humble him, bring him home, and remind him that the body was vanity, a violation of every verse in the Bible. But Evelyn could not sustain her thoughts as long as he could. Not for more than a few seconds. Her mind never settled, never rested, and finally on Saturday morning, when she awoke on Shelberdine's sofa, it would not stay away from the image of her Rudolph dead before hundreds of indifferent spectators, paramedics pounding on his chest, bursting his rib cage in an effort to keep him alive.

From Shelberdine's house she called a taxi and, in the steady rain that northwesterners love, arrived at the Kingdome by noon. It's over already, Evelyn thought, walking the circular stairs to her seat, clamping shut her wet umbrella. She heard cheers, booing, an Asian voice with an accent over a microphone. The tournament began at ten, which was enough time for her white belt husband to be in the emergency ward at Harborview Hospital by now, but she had to see. At first, as she stepped down to her seat through the crowd, she could only hear—her mind grappled for the word, then remembered—kiais, or "spirit shouts," from the great floor of the stadium, many shouts, for contests were progressing in three rings simultaneously. It felt like a circus. It smelled like a locker room. Here two children stood toe to toe until one landed a front kick that sent the other child flying fifteen feet. There two lean-muscled female black belts were interlocked in a delicate ballet, like dance or a chess game, of continual motion. They had a kind of sense, these women—she noticed it immediately—a feel for space and their place in it. (Evelyn hated them immediately.) And in the farthest circle she saw, or rather felt, Rudolph, the oldest thing on the deck, who, sparring in the adult division, was squared off with another white belt, not a boy who might hurt him—the other man was middle-aged, graying, maybe only a few years younger than Rudolph—but they were sparring just the same.

Yet it was not truly him that Evelyn, sitting down, saw. Acoustics in the Kingdome whirlpooled the noise of the crowd, a rivering of voices that affected her, suddenly, like the pitch and roll of voices during service. It affected the way she watched Rudolph. She wondered: who are these people? She caught her breath when, miscalculating his distance from his opponent, her husband stepped sideways into a roundhouse kick with lots of snap—she heard the cloth of his opponent's gi crack like a gunshot when he threw the technique. She leaned forward, gripping the huge purse on her lap when Rudolph recovered and retreated from the killing to the neutral zone, and then, in a wide stance, rethought strategy. This was not the man she'd slept with for twenty years. Not her hypochondriac Rudolph who had to rest and run cold water on his wrists after walking from the front stairs to the fence to pick up the *Seattle Times*. She did not know him, perhaps had never known him, and now she never would, for the man on the floor, the man splashed with sweat, rising on the ball of his rear foot for a flying kick—was he so foolish he still thought he could fly?—would outlive her; he'd stand healthy and strong and think of her in a bubble, one hand on her headstone, and it was all right, she thought, weeping uncontrollably, it was all right that Rudolph would return home after visiting her wet grave, clean out her bedroom, the pillboxes and paperback books, and throw open her windows to let her sour, rotting smell escape, then move a younger woman's things onto the floor space darkened by her color television, her porcelain chamber pot, her antique sewing machine. And then Evelyn was on her feet, unsure why, but the crowd had stood suddenly to clap, and Evelyn clapped, too, though for an instant she pounded her gloved hands together instinctively until her vision cleared, the momentary flash of retinal blindness giving way to a frame of her husband, the postman, twenty feet off the ground in a perfect flying kick that floored his opponent and made a Japanese judge who looked like Oddjob shout "ippon"—one point—and the fighting in the farthest ring, in herself, perhaps in all the world, was over.

METAPHOR

Metaphor is sometimes thought of as an ornament of speech in which a term is transferred from an object to which it is ordinarily applied ("the roses in my garden," "the autumn of the year") to an object to which it can be applied only through an implicit comparison or analogy ("the roses in her cheeks," "the autumn of life"). As verbal ornament, metaphor is no more significant in fiction than it is in ordinary speech. But conceived slightly differently, as a comparison or analogy that underlies an entire narrative, it is not incidental but perhaps the essence of literature. A work of literature, after all, asks us to regard a particular action as representative of (or "analogous to," or "a metaphor for") some aspect of the real world.

Take "A Loaf of Bread" again. Would we be justified in regarding the loaf of bread as a metaphor? And how would we decide what it is a metaphor for? Writers, if they want their work to be read metaphorically, often lay particular stress upon metaphorical elements. McPherson, for example, names his story "A Loaf of Bread," and the final, climactic scene turns around Nelson Reed paying Harold Green for the bread. Apparently he wants us to pay particular attention to the loaf of bread and to interpret it as especially meaningful. How do we decide what the bread "stands for"? The answer is that we try several possibilities and select the one that most closely corresponds to our experience of the story and that seems most in harmony with the rest of the story. What happens in that final scene which turns around that loaf of bread? Harold Green and Nelson Reed, who have been antagonists throughout the story, in this scene meet on common ground and treat each other with some degree of mutual understanding and respect. Green treats Reed like someone who will pay his bills, rather than in the contemptuous way he treated the protesters, and Reed treats Green as someone who deserves fair payment for his goods. We might say that the loaf of bread comes to be a metaphor for this small ground of respect and understanding.

(Some might call the bread a *symbol* rather than a *metaphor*. There would be nothing wrong with this. The difference between a symbol and a metaphor is usually defined in terms of multiplicity of meanings. A symbol suggests a number of associations, even incompatible ones, simultaneously, whereas a metaphor is likely to suggest only one or two. But the distinction is a matter of interpretation. If someone were able to make a case that McPherson's bread means a number of things on different levels—the essential foodstuff or the basis of survival, for instance—he or she would be justified in calling it a symbol.)

To move to a very different example, would it be illuminating to interpret *El Día del Vaquero,* "cowboy day," in "Johnny Ray" metaphorically? Notice that cowboy day reproduces precisely in the form of a game or a festival the social structures of the community itself. The Mexican majority proclaims its identity through cowboy clothing and tyrannizes anyone who does not conform to its rules. The narrator's attitude toward the game is the same as his attitude toward the larger divisions of the school. He insists that it was all in good fun, "one of the best school days we had that year," and yet he is afraid of the seniors:

> And those seniors, let me give you a clue, weren't above anything or anybody. I must have had on ten or twenty things just to be absolutely sure.

Johnny Ray's rebellion against cowboy day, then, becomes a rebellion against the entire social structure of the school, a rebellion that the rather timid narrator can admire without actually joining.

The titular baby of "Bop" may also be read as a metaphor. As in "A Loaf of Bread," the metaphoric element is highlighted by being cited in the title and featured in the climatic scene of the story. Baby Bop is of course a literal element in the story, and his presence stirs many parental feelings in both Oleg and Claire. But in the story, he also becomes a sort of blank screen (enigmatically saying "Bop") upon which Oleg and Claire project their wishes and needs. For Oleg, he represents the family he has missed having: "He had spent his years getting out of Russia, while other men searched for lovers or wives." And for Claire, he represents the son that she will never have, after her hysterectomy: "She had said the night before, admiring Carrie's impressions of the mimes, that she'd have liked to have had one more child, a son."

"China," though, is the clearest example of a story that turns around a central metaphor. "I think it's strange!" says Evelyn Jackson to her husband who at the age of fifty-four has become obsessed with martial arts.

> "Rudolph, you didn't grow up in China," she said. "They can't breathe in China! I saw that today on the news. They burn soft coal, which gets into the air and turns into acid rain. They wear face masks over there, like the ones we bought when Mount St. Helens blew up. They all ride bicycles, for Christ's sake! They want what we have. . . . You grew up in Hodges, South Carolina, same as me, in a right and proper colored church. If you'd *been* to China, maybe I'd understand."

Clearly, Evelyn is having some trouble understanding a metaphor. She reads Rudolph's enthusiasm for the Chinese martial arts with an absurd literalness, while the appeal is metaphoric to him, as he explains: "I don't want to be Chinese! . . . I only want to be what I *can* be, which isn't the greatest fighter in the world, only the fighter *I* can be." Rudolph explains in detail in the story what his training means to him, the chance to put all of himself into something, the chance "to be quiet, work on myself, and interfere with things as little as possible."

The irony is that Evelyn responds to "China" as a metaphor just as much as

Rudolph does, although she doesn't realize it. In her desperate speech to Rudolph about not being Chinese, she sets up two metaphoric worlds of values: China and South Carolina. China, for her as for Rudolph, means living fully for once, realizing one's abilities, and fighting against aging and mortality. But the challenge frightens her, and she is more comfortable with the sort of surrender to physical decline and the compromises with life that she associates with South Carolina: "She would wait until he worked this thing out of his system, until Nature defeated him and he surrendered, as any right-thinking person would, to the breakdown of the body, the brutal fact of decay, which could only be blunted, it seemed to her, by decaying *with* someone, the comfort every Negro couple felt when, aging, they knew enough to let things wind down."

China, of course, figures heavily in "The Oriental Contingent" as well as in "China," and it might be interesting to compare the way it is used in the two stories. It might be argued that China is used literally in "The Oriental Contingent" and metaphorically in "China." Connie Sung and Lisa Mallory in "The Oriental Contingent" were both born in the United States but wryly acknowledge that they feel, against all logic, that there is virtue in being as Chinese as possible. "The only time I feel Chinese," says Lisa, "is when I'm embarrassed I'm not more Chinese—which is a totally Chinese reflex I'd give anything to be rid of!" China is as charged with personal meaning in "The Oriental Contingent" as it is in "China." But in "The Oriental Contingent" the meaning is literal—it is the real China they are talking about—whereas in "China" China has become primarily a metaphor for some highly personal values for the characters.

All of the elements of fiction—plot, point of view, character, setting, and metaphor—contribute to our understanding of theme. We can prepare for a study of theme by reading John Edgar Wideman's "Rock River."

John Edgar Wideman

John Edgar Wideman (b. 1941) grew up in Homewood, a predominantly black suburb of Pittsburgh, Pennsylvania, and the setting for his Homewood Trilogy: *Damballah* (1981), *Hiding Place* (1981), and *Sent for You Yesterday* (1983). Other novels include *A Glance Away* (1967), *Hurry Home* (1970), *The Lynchers* (1973), *Reuben* (1987), and *Philadelphia Fire* (1990). *The Stories of John Edgar Wideman* appeared in 1992. John Edgar Wideman teaches at the University of Massachusetts, Amherst.

ROCK RIVER

Main Street out of Rock River narrows abruptly into a two-lane and in twenty-five minutes you are in the middle of nowhere. Past a couple clumps of buildings that used to be towns and one that might still be, then a railroad embankment's on your left for a while till it veers off over the plains, a spine of mountains to the right, blue in the distance, miles of weather-cracked wasteland stretching to foothills hunkered like a pack of gray dogs at the base of the mountains. Moonscape till you turn off at the Bar H gate on the dirt track under the power line and follow it through a pass, along a ridge and then things get brown, green some, not exactly a welcome mat rolled out but country you could deal with, as long as you don't decide to stay. Trees can tunnel out of thickets of boulders, grass can root in sand and shale, the river you can't find most summers in its seamed bed manages to irrigate a row of dwarf cottonwoods whose tops, situated as they are, higher than anything else around, black-green silhouettes orderly on the horizon, remind you that even the huge sky gives way to something, sometimes, that its weight can be accommodated by this hard ground, that the rooster tail of dust behind your pickup will dissipate, rise and settle.

The road twists and bumps and climbs, curves back on itself, almost disappears totally in a circus of ruts, gouges and tire-size stones, dropping steadily while it does whatever else it's doing, shaking the pickup to pieces, steering it, tossing it up and catching it like a kid warming up a baseball. No seat belt and your head would squash on the roof of the cab. Last few miles the steepest. Then this fold of land levels, meadows and thick pine woods, sudden outcroppings of aspen, hillocks, miniravines, deer country, a greenness and sweet smell of water cutting the sage, a place nothing most of the trip here would have suggested you'd find.

I am alone. My job is to clean up Rick's truck, get it ready to bring back to town. They said that would be all right now. The police have finished their investigation. Tomorrow I'll come back with Stevenson. He can drive my truck and I'll drive Rick's. But today I want to do what I have to do by myself. I expect it will be a mess. He stood outside, but the blast carried backwards to the open window of the truck. They warned me, then they said the gas is OK. Better take jumper cables, though, Quinson said. As if any fool wouldn't know that. Cops were making arrangements to tow it to town. I thought I'd rather drive it. Clean it up first. Then me and Stevenson come out and I'll bring it in.

I have old towels. Two five-gallon cans of water. Upholstery cleaner. Brillo. Spot remover. Mr. Clean, sponges, rags, Windex, all the tools on my knife, heavier gear like shovel, ax, and rope that's always stowed in the truck box. I think I have enough. Mary Ellen said, Take this, holding out a can of Pine-Sol spray deodorant.

I hadn't thought of that and was surprised she did and didn't know what to say when she held it out to me.

I shook my head no, but she didn't take it back. Didn't push it on me but she didn't pull it away either.

I think to myself. Can't hurt, can it? There's room. So I took it.

She nodded. Rick got on her nerves. He liked her. He reminded her of her father. Hopeless. Hopeless. Hopeless. You had to smile and be nice to him he was so hopeless. She'd never neglect the small kindnesses to him she said because you'd never want him to feel you'd given up on him. But he could try your patience. Try a saint's. He couldn't count the times she'd said in private she'd given up on Rick. Don't bring him around here anymore, she'd say. I'm sick and tired of that man, she'd say. But then she'd always hug Rick or cry on his shoulder or say something awful and provoking to let him know she was very well aware of how hopeless he was, and let him know he'd never force her to give up on him.

Mary Ellen.

It's been a week. They probably locked it and shut the windows to keep out the rain. They'd want to protect a brand-new vehicle like that.

Almost new.

Looked new. He was so cockeyed proud of it.

I doubt Sarah will want to keep it. Either way if it's cleaned up, that's one thing she won't have to bother with.

Will you be all right?

There's room. Won't hurt to take it. They probably did close up the windows.

⁓⁓⁓

I have Rick's extra set of keys. Went by his house to get them. Here's what I saw.

A tall woman. Sarah, Rick's wife. In blue jeans sitting at a table with a look I'd seen somewhere before, a picture of a Sioux Indian in a long line of Indians staring at the camera and it was hard to tell whether male or female, the photo was old and brown, the face I remembered round and the hood of dark hair could be a woman or a long-haired Indian man.

Sarah never wore blue jeans. Dresses almost always. If pants, they were slacks with sewn-in creases. You could never guess what she might say or do but her clothes wasn't the place that she showed she was different. I liked her a whole lot less than I liked Rick. Nobody talked more than Rick once he'd had his few drinks but you knew Rick didn't mean anything by it. When Rick talked you could tell he was talking just to keep himself from sinking down. If he stopped talking, he'd be in trouble, worse trouble than anything he might say would get him in. He needed to keep talking so he could sit there with you and play liar's poker or watch a campfire burn or just drink on Friday afternoon at the Redbird where we all did to forget the week that was. He'd made people mad who didn't know him because he was subject to say anything about anybody, but after a while, if you were around Rick any amount of time at all you knew it was foolish to take what he said seriously, personally. Rick was just riding along on this stream of words, merrily, merrily riding along and you could ride it too or pay it no mind, cause he wasn't really either.

Sarah on the other hand couldn't be any way but personal. She couldn't say Howdy-do without an edge to it. Like she's reminding you she had spoke first, giving you a lesson in manners and too bad you weren't raised right. I think the woman just couldn't help it. Something about growing up in too holy a house.

Like the best anybody could do would never be good enough. And somebody had
to take the job of reminding people of that fact. So here's Sarah. Eagle eyed and
cat quick to pounce on universal slovenliness and your particular personal pec-
cadilloes any hour of night or day. In blue jeans. Looking, as you might suspect,
as if she's sleeping poorly or not at all, on the losing side force-marched by cavalry
back to the reservation and mug shot. A drink on the kitchen table and offering
me one even though we both know it's barely ten o'clock in the morning and
that's not what I came for, reminding me, her lips pursed tight, that I'm in no
position to judge her, in fact just the opposite case, because when she stares up at
me red eyed there's just a little silliness, a little judgmentalness, a little I-know-
better-than-you this is not the right thing to be doing but we've both started
drinking earlier of a morning, you many more mornings than I, and you with Rick
nonstop so morning, afternoon or night left far behind.

I better not stop now.

Didn't think you would.

Better get this done while I'm feeling up to it.

Why don't you let the police handle it?

It's just something I thought I could do. Ease a little of the burden.

You've done enough already. We're all grateful for what you've done for us.

They were going to tow it. Makes more sense to drive it. They said if it was all
right with you, it was all right with them. I'm happy to help out if it's OK with you.

There the keys are on the table.

I won't be bringing it back today. Thought I'd just go up today and see what had
to be done. Get it ready and tomorrow Stevenson said he would ride up with me
and drive my truck back.

Don't bring it here.

You want me to park it at my place?

I don't care where you park it. It's Rick's truck. He won't be needing it. His
brains were all over the seat. He drove away from us in that cute little shiny red
truck and I don't care if I never see it again.

It's almost new. Rick talked himself up on a real bargain. Probably get most of
what he paid if you sell it.

You've been a great help. Keep the truck. He'd want you to have it.

I couldn't do that.

I have some other stuff of his you might want as well. To remember him by. You
can have his shotgun if the cops return it.

If you want me to take care of selling the truck I'd be happy to try. I'm sure it
will bring a good price. From the outside it seemed in decent shape. Police sealed
it and roped off the clearing where it was parked but as far as I could tell from
where they kept us standing, everything was fine. Quinson told me it has plenty of
gas, that I should bring cables just in case. I guess he thought I was born yesterday.

Simon?

Yes.

Do you miss him?

I'm real sorry. My heart goes out to you and your fine boys.

I can't miss him. He was gone too long.

Still in a state of shock, I guess. I sat there at the funeral still hoping Rick would
change his mind.

He left while I was sleeping. I didn't get worried till the third day. I woke up
early, early that morning and decided I'd call you. Ask if you'd seen him. Begin
the whole humiliating routine. Has anybody seen my husband wandering around

town? Blue eyes, blond, slightly balding, eyeglasses, middle-aged but boyish face, till he's acutely sloshed, then he resembles his grandfather's corpse. Tame when sober, answers to the name Rick. Please call 545-6217 if you've seen this individual. No reward. Except knowing you've saved a happy home. I'd made up my mind to begin phoning around and you of course were at the top of the list, but the cops called me first.

What I saw was she looked like parts of this town, skimpy as it is, I haven't seen for years. Below Second Street, near the railroad tracks where there are storage bins for rent. It's a ragtag, helter-skelter whole lot of nothing dead end. Nobody lives there. Nobody's ever going to or ever has. You can hear sixteen-wheelers humping on the interstate, trains rattle across the overpass. It's the kind of hard-scrabble little patch of concrete and gravel and cinders and corrugated tin-roofed sheds that will always be at the edge of towns on the prairie and outlast the rest—downtown, the nice neighborhoods—be here when no one's left to listen to coyotes howling, the sage running, wind at night screaming in as many voices as there's stars.

What I saw was her eyes on a level only slightly below mine, fixing me, daring me to ignore them. The last party at their house is what I saw. Rick was chef. Spaghetti sauce from ground antelope. Elk liver pâté. Neatly wrapped packages from his game locker that I'd seen thawing, blooding in his refrigerator when I'd popped in for a Bud the afternoon before. Sarah's eyes told me Rick probably hadn't been to bed or stopped drinking before he started up for this party. He'd been telling the story of how he'd tracked the wily elk whose liver was being nibbled as an hors d'oeuvre on Ritz crackers. No one was listening so Rick was telling it softly, slouched down in an armchair, telling again what he'd related at least three times to every single one of us that evening, mumbled quietly, one more time, his gestures slow motion as somebody underwater, his eyes invisible behind his bifocals, his drink glass abiding on the chair's mashed-potato arm, sunken as deeply, as permanent as Rick is in its lap. You pass by and think that man's not moving soon, nor his drink, and wonder how they ended up that way and wonder if they'd ever get unstuck from the tacky fruit-and-flower print slip-cover that couldn't hide the fact that easy chair had seen better days.

Eye to eye with Sarah and she winks at me, even though both of us long past having fun at this party. But she's sloshed and I'm two sheets and that's why we both came so I wink back and hear the banjo and fiddle and whiny hill voices from the next room, the slapping of knees, whooping and stomping. It's getting good to itself in there. Dancing usually means wee hours before you can squeeze everybody out the door. It's what we've come for. To stay late. To holler a little bit and grab ass and thump a little on one another. I look back but Sarah's gray eyes are gone in the direction of the music, but music's not what's in them. I know by the set of her jaw what's in them. If I was close enough so her breath would ripple my lashes, that close but invisible so I wouldn't spoil her view, what I'd see would be two little Ricks, one in each gray globe of her eyes, two Ricks the stereo in her brain turns to one in three dimensions, real as things get in a kitchen at 11:00 P.M. when a full-scale party's raging.

Sure enough what I see is him stumbling into the kitchen this morning, hitting both sides of the doorframe before he gets through. He tries one more step. More lurch than step. As if his dancing partner has fooled him. He reaches for her hand and she whirls away laughing and he's caught with his weight on the wrong foot and almost falls on his nose after her. But he respects the quickness, the cunning, the spinning sexy grace in her, and forgives and catches himself with a little clumsy half skip, half shuffle, do-si-do, it's just a thing that happens. Hi. Hi. Hi. All. He catches me red-handed sliding the keys off the vinyl tablecloth. There are too many to close in my fist. She didn't separate the truck keys from the rest, twelve, thirteen, fifteen keys in my fist. I could shake them and make a mighty noise, shake them to the beat of that dancing music from the next room.

Where are you going with ma keys, Simon? Simon-Simon. What you doing wit ma fucking keys, boyo? Ho. Ho. Don't touch that dial.

He glides in slow. The tempo has changed. He clamps one hand on Sarah's shoulder. Twirls her so she lands smack up against his chest. Then they are both gliding cheek to cheek and the song is waltz time, but they two-step it, hitch around the kitchen graceful as Arthur Murray and Ginger Rogers on stilts. Don't stop when Rick's elbow chops a whole row of empty beer bottles off the counter and they tumble and break and scatter and the worst godawful racket in the world does not attract one interested or curious face from the party in the other room.

THEME

A literary *theme* is the central idea of a literary work stated as a generalization about human experience. It is an answer to the question "What is this story about?" It should be distinguished from both *subject* and *plot*. If someone asked what "A Loaf of Bread" was about and the reply were, "It's about a strike by African-Americans against a neighborhood grocery store," the question would have been answered in terms of *subject*, not theme. If the answer were, "It's about a white grocer and a black leader of a protest against him and how they come to respect each other," the question would have been answered in terms of *plot*. But if the answer is, "It is about how human decency and respect can help people rise above social and racial differences," then the question has been answered in terms of *theme*. Notice that statements of subject tend to take the form of noun phrases, whereas statements of plot tend to be summarized stories. But statements of theme tend to be cast in complete sentences that allude to general principles rather than to the particular details of the story.

Form aside, though, is "Human decency and respect can help people rise above social and racial differences" a good statement of the theme of "A Loaf of Bread"? It does seem to capture the meaning of the climactic last scene. On the other hand, it may sound rather more optimistic than the story does. What is going to happen after Nelson Reed pays for his loaf of bread? Is everyone going to live happily ever after? Or do basic conflicts remain to be resolved? One can experiment with other thematic statements: "Emotional experience is more important than logic in social and racial conflicts," "Economics underlies social and racial conflicts," or "Men are more prone than women to turn disagreements into self-righteous crusades."

There is something to be said for each of these thematic statements. None is positively wrong, and each can help illuminate at least part of the story. When we create hypothetical themes, test them against the details of the story, and then discard or refine them, we are engaging in an act of *interpretation*. The process tends to confirm the widely held belief in contemporary criticism that meaning in literature is not something fully existing within the text but is partially created in the interplay between the text and the individual reader's mind.

"Human decency and respect can help people rise above social and racial differences" is not only a very tentative and provisional thematic statement, it is also something of a vague truism. Not that its commonplace quality is an argument against it as a theme. Fiction is not good or bad because of the complexity or profundity of its themes. Many great literary works sound hackneyed and moralistic when reduced to their basic themes. We value literary works for their concrete development of characters, events, and ideas, not for the reductive "themes" around which they turn.

To explore the idea of theme in a rather more complex story than "A Loaf of Bread," let us look at John Edgar Wideman's "Rock River." "Rock River" is a subtle and oblique story that takes more than a little unraveling. To begin, we can look at the separate elements in the story, all of which can provide material for definition of theme.

PLOT. The plot of "Rock River" is interesting because it includes no action in the ordinary sense. Simon, the narrator, is going to clean up the pickup truck where his friend Rick shot himself and bring the pickup back to town. But he doesn't do this in the story. Instead, the story consists of only two scenes, Simon getting equipment and supplies together for the job and discussing it with his friend Mary Ellen, and then a visit with Sarah, Rick's widow, to get the keys to the truck. (This second scene may have taken place before the first, as it is recounted as a memory by Simon.) The story ends with a memory-fantasy of Rick still alive and dancing with Sarah. This structure takes the emphasis off the job of cleaning the truck and places it on Simon's perceptions of Rick and Sarah and their relationship.

POINT OF VIEW. Simon's perceptions are emphasized even more by the story's being told from his point of view in the first person. He is an outsider in the story of Rick and Sarah's relationship and of Rick's suicide, and so we have the familiar situation of a minor or observer character telling the story of a major one. But we should not overemphasize Simon's insignificance. The fact that the story follows his consciousness and his thinking about Rick and Sarah makes him an important character. In a sense, his thinking is the principal action of the story, more than the suicide or the cleaning of the truck.

CHARACTER, SETTING, AND METAPHOR. These elements of "Rock River" are so closely intertwined that they can best be treated together. We might begin with the title. Why is the story called "Rock River"? Notice not only the title but the fact that the story begins with a lengthy landscape description of the route out of Rock River to the place where Rick killed himself. The road leads through a wasteland, over a ridge, and then down a rough road to a beautiful and fertile section. This sort of highlighting of landscape suggests that it is being given a metaphoric meaning, a suggestion that is strengthened when we notice that Sarah is identified with the town of Rock River:

> What I saw was she looked like parts of this town, skimpy as it is, I haven't seen for years.

The parts of town that Sarah reminds Simon of are the poorer, more desolate parts, "the kind of hardscrabble little patch of concrete and gravel and cinders and corrugated tin-roofed sheds that will always be at the edge of towns on the prairie and outlast the rest." So Sarah is identified with the sterile town and Rick with the country, difficult of access but beautiful and fertile.

This contrast is only one of several between husband and wife, suggested if not developed in this poetic, elliptical story. The narrator obviously has liked Rick, as has Mary Ellen, despite her judgment of him as "hopeless," like her father:

> Don't bring him around here anymore, she'd say. I'm sick and tired of that man, she'd say. But then she'd always hug Rick or cry on his shoulder or say something awful and provoking to let him know she was very well aware of how hopeless he was, and let him know he'd never force her to give up on him.

Simon says of Sarah, "I liked her a whole lot less than I liked Rick," and describes her as narrow, rigid, and judgmental:

> Sarah on the other hand couldn't be any way but personal. She couldn't say Howdy-do without an edge to it. Like she's reminding you she had spoke first, giving you a lesson in manners and too bad you weren't raised right.

Rick and Sarah as Wideman economically sketches them in are as opposite as oil and water in almost every way. He is talkative, she is reticent; he is easy-going, she is rigid and judgmental; he is an out-of-control drunk, she controls her drinking; he is male, she is female; he is country, she is town. And yet the story ends with Simon's vision of the couple dancing gracefully and ecstatically, a memory of their last party blending with the present.

Having analyzed the various other elements in the story, can we pull together what we have observed into a coherent statement of the theme of "Rock River"? We need a subject and a predicate, a statement of the topic Wideman is dealing with and what he has to say about it. The subject would seem to be "love," the relationship between Rick and Sarah as Simon has observed it and tried to understand it. And the story seems to suggest that love is essentially mysterious and can survive the deepest divisions and conflicts. Once having arrived at this tentative statement of theme, we will want to go back to the story and test the statement against every detail and modify it to make it fit as closely as possible.

We have considered a number of elements of fiction: plot and structure, point of view and focalization, character, setting, metaphor, and theme. We are now ready to work on integrating these elements in a holistic reading of a short story. To prepare to do this, read Talat Abbasi's "Sari Petticoats."

Talat Abbasi

Talat Abbasi was born in 1942 in Lucknow, India; her Muslim family moved to Karachi, Pakistan, when India was partitioned in 1947. She was educated at St. Joseph's Convent School in Karachi, Kinnaird College of Punjab University, and the London School of Economics. She moved to the United States in 1977. She lives in New York, where she works for the United Nations and publishes short stories in various periodicals.

SARI PETTICOATS

I received a letter from my ex-husband. My almost late ex-husband because he says he's dying. Not that it'll affect me at all since I'm hard as iron. Imagine a house burning, everything turns to ashes. The fire escape alone remains standing. That's me. He's always envied me this quality because he himself is sensitive. That's why he's dying before his time. It's not his kidneys, lungs, liver, that's killing him. It's his heart. It palpitates so. He feels everything. Felt it when I said six years ago, "All right go!" He didn't mind the parting. But there's a standard way of doing these things. Tears and pleading on my part, firm refusal on his. Instead I took the initiative away from him as if I were the man. And it's not as though I'm an American woman born and bred. Not that he knows anything about American women or any other for that matter because he's a decent man.

And it's this tendency to forget I'm a woman that brought down all our misfortunes upon us. A tendency he detected in me even when he was living in my father's house as the orphan nephew who had to be fed and clothed and educated. Being a decent man he's grateful, though it was all done out of a sense of duty, not affection. He sensed that. A nuisance, a poor relation. He was only ten and I was sixteen when he was orphaned. Suddenly they both died in an accident, his parents, sitting together in a horse-drawn *tonga* on a stormy winter night in Lahore. The truck driver said how could he see the *tonga* when there wasn't even a lantern dangling from it? That wasn't true because they found the shattered lantern by the three bodies. The *tongawallah* died too. Four if you count the horse which had to be shot too. What chance does a *tonga* have against a truck?

... a question he asked himself throughout the period of our marriage—a rhetorical question of course, because he always knew the answer. But he was fatalistic, so he agreed to marry me. Now they all tell him he never should have, but how could he have said no? Consider the scene. My father lay on his death bed. I lay on the shelf. He pretended not to see. But then from his death bed my father begged. She's twenty-five, he called out. The anguish in that cry. In all decency then, the offer had to be made. How was he to know that my father would survive another ten years and run through his fortune himself? Or that when he brought me down from shelf to bed he'd turn the other way. Dark, shapeless and hairy. He slept for years on his left side and dreamt of buffaloes.

Still, he was young then. He came to America with such high hopes thinking that the streets were paved with gold. He discovered that the street in Brooklyn where we lived was riddled with bullets instead. He's sure to this day those were bullet holes. So he stayed in the studio. About the size of a servant's quarter at home, without a bathroom, rats, roaches, flies, even mosquitoes, everything the lower classes there are used to. Plus neighbors worse than ever he'd imagined,

71

junkies all, he was sure. While I, having nothing to fear from bullets, lost no time, jumped on a subway to seek my fortune, got off at a station chosen at random. There I stood astonished. Naturally. Because Jackson Heights in New York City is like the smell of sandalwood coming from an apple tree. My senses whirled even faster than the *saris* on high-heeled *chappals*. Oiled plaits swung like pendulums against bare midriffs. Gold earrings tinkled, glass bangles jingled. Netted beards and saffron turbans. Hindi, Urdu, Punjabi, Bengali, English, too, in thick accents. And of course the smell of sandalwood. Then suddenly the spinning stopped and in my head I clearly heard a whirring sound.

And imagine his amazement when peeping anxiously through the window (where in his waking hours he kept constant watch with the blinds drawn down, of course) he saw me come home that same evening. I was lugging a sewing machine which I proceeded to open as soon as I entered. Without a word of explanation I sat down crossed-legged (a common tailor sitting by a roadside sewing *shalwars* for laborers immediately came to his sensitive mind) and started sewing *sari* petticoats. He paced the floor for months exclaiming tragically, "A Master's in Persian poetry from Punjab University is sewing *sari* petticoats!" I could not see the tragedy for the dollar bills which Sardarji of Sari Mahal paid me regularly. But the green of the dollar bills which I flaunted at him so shamelessly made him so bilious he had to leave the country, went back to Lahore. There, he writes, it's all patronage and he's discovered he isn't a landowner's son. We're first cousins he reminds me in the next sentence. That's a relationship which can never be severed. Americanized as I am, that's surely something I still understand. The doctor's bills, he repeats . . .

Two thousand four hundred *rupees,* two thousand—I drum my fingers on my mahogany desk and look out of the picture window. It's not all that much he's asking. He's doesn't know how my view's improved since I bought out Sardarji. I can see every one of the tall ships which will pass by today on the East River on their way to Miss Liberty to celebrate her centenary. I've waited all week for this moment. But now it's here all I can hear is hooves and wheels clattering down cobbled streets, the *tonga* and the truck. How I love that bit! The stroke of genius I can't resist! Perhaps I shouldn't but my weakness is still poetry. So I give in, take out my cheque book. Besides, suppose he's really dying. It's true about the first cousin anyway. And, as he points out, two thousand four hundred *rupees* at twelve *rupees* to the dollar equals only two hundred dollars. I pick up my pen then put it down immediately. He's not dying, it's a lie! The *rupee* is seventeen to the dollar in the black market. Over my dead body.

"Come and see," calls out my neighbor from her balcony.

I step out. It is indeed a fantastic sight, the East River. It's filled with *tongas*.

I go in and take out my calculator. At seventeen to the dollar two thousand four hundred *rupees* equal . . .

From Reading to Interpretation and Criticism

𝔰𝔞 𝔞𝔠

So far in our study of fiction we have concentrated on the "elements" of fiction, isolating plot, point of view, character, setting, metaphor, and theme and analyzing each closely. But this sort of fragmented analysis will not necessarily result in a balanced general interpretation of a work of fiction. For that we must put back together what we have taken apart, define how each element interacts with all the others, and arrive at a method for overall interpretation.

In doing this, we may think of the reading process as moving from *reading* to *interpretation* and finally to *criticism,* rather than from one element of the story to another. In the *reading* stage, we ask ourselves, "What does the story say?" In this stage, we read the story as carefully as possible, looking up difficult words, identifying allusions, and analyzing such formal elements as plot structure, point of view and focalization, character development, setting, and governing metaphors. In the *interpretation* stage, we ask ourselves, "What does the story mean?" or, to put it another way, "What is the story's theme?" In practice, of course, reading and interpretation cannot be so neatly separated. Our analyses of plot, character, and other narrative elements will determine the way we articulate the theme. But on the other hand, the way we define the theme will often lead us to go back and modify our analyses of other elements. This back-and-forth movement between the general and the particular is characteristic of the process of interpretation.

In the stages of reading and interpretation, we should identify ourselves as closely as possible with the story and its author. It is in these stages that we sometimes say that we are "lost in a book." We try to move inside the world of the story or the novel imaginatively and see the world through the eyes of the writer or the characters. Meaning, in the stages of reading and interpretation, is the meaning the author seems to have intended. (Intention is hard to gauge, of course, but the point is empathic identification with the author.)

Criticism is different. Here we separate ourselves from the story and its author to regain our objectivity as much as possible. Then we measure the values and meanings of the story against our own ideas, not necessarily to reject new ideas, but to place them within our own moral and intellectual world. In terms of the psychology of reading, if in reading and interpretation we are being carried "out of ourselves," then criticism carries us back into ourselves where our experience of new ideas is integrated with our previous experiences and attitudes. One of the most important ways of placing the themes of a story in relation to our own beliefs is *contextualization*, working out the historical, geographic, or philosophical contexts of a story. A story written a hundred years ago is unlikely to be based on exactly the same assumptions a contemporary reader would bring to it. A story written in contemporary Japan is unlikely to reflect the same beliefs an American reader would hold. A secular, skeptical reader would not necessarily automatically agree with the ideas of a conservative Catholic writer. A popular theory of literature holds that such differences should be minimized in favor of the "universal" themes that everyone shares. It is hard, though, to see why we should pay attention to things we all have in common and neglect the things that separate us. Perhaps the best reading is that which does justice to both similarities and differences.

To illustrate criticism, in the sense we have defined it here, we might go back to the story we have drawn on so often for illustration, McPherson's "A Loaf of Bread." In the section on theme, we suggested that the theme of "A Loaf of Bread" might be formulated thus: "Human decency and respect can help people rise above social and racial differences." Assuming that we agree that this is at least a roughly acceptable statement of a major theme in the story, how can we move beyond the interpretation it formulates to a criticism of the story? We might begin by imagining different endings for the story. What if Nelson Reed did not come into the store to pay for the loaf of bread? What if he came in but engaged in a hostile confrontation with Harold Green? (If you have seen Spike Lee's film *Do the Right Thing*, which has a subject similar to that of "A Loaf of Bread," you will be able to compare the radically different endings of the film and of the short story.) Notice that McPherson's ending reflects a rather optimistic liberalism. Individual character matters more in the story than economic forces, and a conflict can have a "happy ending" if people are individually decent. This is a generous and attractive point of view, but it is not the only one possible. One might equally argue that changing the conditions under which Green does business is more important than paying for one loaf of bread and that McPherson's final emphasis upon individual good will sweeps too many issues under the rug. Or one might argue on McPherson's side. The point in not whether we agree or disagree with McPherson, but that we see his ideas in context.

For another example of the movement from reading to interpretation to criticism, we might look at Talat Abbasi's short but skillful "Sari Petticoats."

READING. "Sari Petticoats" is a first-person narrative by a Pakistani woman now living in New York. She has received a letter from her ex-husband, who writes that he is dying and asks her for two thousand *rupees* for medical bills. She reviews their life together. The scenic structure of the story is very simple; although the narrator does organize her narrative into scenes, they are presented in brief, summarized form without dramatic development: the death of the husband's parents in an accident when he was ten, the engagement in response to her father's plea from his supposed deathbed, the move to New York, the husband's fearful agoraphobia and the narrator's daring entrepreneurship in making *sari* petticoats, and the husband's return to Pakistan. By the time of the action, the narrator has prospered: She has bought the *sari* business and has an apartment overlooking the East River.

"Sari Petticoats" is, then, a memory story. The present action is very slight, and almost the entire story consists of memories. The narrative voice is very important in this story, especially for the way the narrator characterizes herself and her husband. She is strong and he is weak, and the husband has compared their relationship to the collision between a truck and a *tonga* (a light carriage) that killed his parents. The narrator does not disagree.

INTERPRETATION. The line between reading and interpretation is indistinct, but we are crossing it when we move from what a story *says* to what it *means*. What are we to make of the narrator's story? The first paragraph in a story or novel is often very important, announcing the main issues of the narrative, and that is the case here. The narrator tells us that she is "hard as iron," whereas her ex-husband is "sensitive." As illustration, she described their parting:

> He didn't mind the parting. But there's a standard way of doing these things. Tears and pleading on my part, firm refusal on his. Instead I took the initiative away from him as if I were the man.

This emphasis upon the reversal of gender roles runs throughout the story. The husband has noticed the narrator's "tendency to forget I'm a woman" when he was growing up, an orphan nephew, in her father's house.

The ending of the story, like the beginning, is especially striking, and here it gives an ironic metaphoric twist to the story of the narrator and her husband. It is the hundredth anniversary of the Statue of Liberty, which is to be celebrated by the "tall ships" sailing up the East River to the statue. The narrator looks out at the ships and sees a river full of *tongas*. The Statue of Liberty celebrates the immigrant experience ("Give me your tired, your poor"), and the narrator sees in the allusion to the Statue in the centenary pageant a reference to her own experience and that of her husband.

At this point, we may try to formulate a statement of theme for "Sari Petticoats." Drawing upon our first, intuitive reaction to the story and adding to it our observations about separate elements in the story as they confirm or not that first reaction, we may arrive at something like this: "Gender roles that are regarded as inevitable and 'natural' in one culture may seem fragile and artificial in another culture." Such a thematic statement, of course, implies a judgment about what is most important in the story. It is intended to capture the central irony that the woman, subordinate and "on the shelf" in Pakistan, is not only assertive but also wildly successful in America, whereas the husband, privileged by his gender and class in Pakistan, does not succeed in America. Other emphases would produce other statements of theme.

CRITICISM. The movement from interpretation to criticism, from identifying a theme to placing that theme in a larger context, is sometimes harder the closer the story is to the present. We may find it comparatively easy to say that an older literary work reflects a "romantic" or a "naturalistic" world view. But when we are reading a contemporary work based on assumptions that we share, we may make the mistake that the husband in "Sari Petticoats" makes and not recognize those assumptions as assumptions at all but merely as "human nature."

The first step in arriving at a critique of a story is to think about the assumptions or beliefs upon which the story rests. We are after the *author's* assumptions, not the character's. So far we have been interested in the narrator's beliefs, but now we must ask ourselves such questions as these: "Why would the author be interested in writing a story about such a character?" and "Given the theme of this story, in whose interest is it that the theme be established?" We must sometimes draw upon instinct and gut feelings here. How can we know for sure the extent to which a fictional character represents an author? We may sense that the narrator in "Sari Petticoats" expresses opinions and feelings very close to those of Talat Abbasi and point, as evidence, to the generally sympathetic treatment of the narrator and the absence of irony directed against her. But whether we can prove it or not, we need to form some sense of where the author stands behind the text of the story.

Notice that the conflict in the story is between two value systems, represented by husband and wife. The husband holds views that we might call "traditionalist." He organizes his life by hierarchies of family, class, and gender. Notice that growing up for him does not include going to work and that his way of "making money" is to marry into a wealthy family; he is shocked that "a Master's in Persian poetry" should stoop so low as to sew *sari* petticoats; and he cannot reconcile himself to a woman's being more successful than he is. The narrator, on the other hand, embraces a belief system that we might call "modernist-individualist." She ignores the roles imposed by family, class, and gender and puts her faith in individual effort. These opposing world views are echoed in the many oppositions in the story: Pakistan and America, male and female, husband and wife, unearned income and earned income. They are also internalized as a conflict within the wife herself. She begins the story by saying that her ex-husband's death will not affect her at all, because she's as "hard as iron." But she goes on to describe him very sympathetically, twice calling him "a decent man." And at the end of the story, she is still torn between sending him the money he has asked for and not. "He's not dying. It's a lie!" she says. "Over my dead body." But almost immediately she changes her mind and starts planning how to send the money: "I go in and take out my calculator. At seventeen to the dollar two thousand four hundred *rupees* equal . . ."

Despite this ambivalence, the narrator—and apparently Talat Abbasi—comes down firmly on the side of modernist-individualism. We, if we have grown up in modern, individualist, capitalist America, are likely to be much more sympathetic with the narrator than with her traditionalist husband; we may feel that her beliefs are "natural." Part of the purpose of criticism, as a stage in the interpretive process, is to "denaturalize" such beliefs, to come to see how beliefs, however natural they may seem, are socially constructed and that others may reasonably hold other beliefs. This, too, is a goal of criticism: to define an area of disagreement. If we see in literature only what is "universal," what everyone agrees with, we see only a part of literature; the other and more exciting part is that which expresses disagreement and debate over basic beliefs.

Writing About Fiction

In the course of your study of fiction, your instructor will undoubtedly ask you to write about one or more of the stories you have read. Indeed, it is hard to imagine a study of fiction that does not involve some writing. With a course that emphasizes the acquisition of facts, a short-answer or objective test may be enough for you to check your progress. But with a study that emphasizes interpretation, as the study of literature does, mastery can be demonstrated only by engaging in interpretation. And that usually means writing essays, producing texts upon texts.

It could even be argued (and was argued in the introduction to fiction) that "literature" does not exist—that the literary transaction is not complete—until the literary text has been responded to, until the message sent by the author-sender has been received and processed by the reader-receiver. The response need not be written and it may be as simple as "Wow!" but the literary act is not completed until a textual response closes the circuit.

In principle, a response-text to a literary text could be purely an expression of emotion (whether "Wow!" or something more elaborate) or could even be non-verbal (a drawing or a piece of music that "responds" in some way to the literary work). In practice, though, responses in a formal literature course usually take the form of critical–analytical essays on some part of the reading. The skills needed to write such an essay are for the most part the skills needed to write well about anything: the ability to articulate a strong central idea; to develop it concretely and convincingly; to organize shapely, well-developed paragraphs; to construct interesting and varied sentences; and to command a large and precise vocabulary. Fiction offers its own challenges to these skills, though, and we will concentrate here on those challenges.

CHOOSING A TOPIC. Your instructor may assign a specific topic. In this case, an important and often difficult first step has been taken for you. But even so, you need to think through the topic and make sure that you see the various possibilities for developing it. Suppose, for example, your instructor has asked you to write about "Cultural Conflict in 'Bop.' " The first thing you need to resolve is what "cultural conflict" is. There are many conflicts in the story, but not all of them can be rightly called "cultural." Some of them are purely individual and idiosyncratic. Defining key terms in the assignment is a good first step in thinking through its possibilities.

If your instructor does not assign a specific topic, you have the challenge of selecting one yourself. Often, class discussion will have generated a number of good topics for papers, and all you have to do is look through your class notes and select a topic that interests you and that you think you would have something to say about that would go beyond class discussion. If nothing presents itself as a good topic, you might try the simple exercise of selecting a story that you'd like to write about and analyzing it in terms of one of the "elements of fiction." This would generate a list like "Plot Structure in 'A Loaf of Bread,' " "Focalization in 'A Loaf of Bread,' " "Characterization in 'A Loaf of Bread,' " and so forth. Most of these topics will strike you as dull and mechanical, but some may strike you as promising topics. One hint, though: Always mentally add "and theme" to your topic—"Plot Structure and Theme . . . " or "Focalization and Theme . . . " in "A Loaf of Bread." Formal analysis can get very tedious if it is not connected to meaning; showing how a formal element helps advance the meaning of the story gives your paper a more obvious sense of purpose.

COLLECTING MATERIAL. Once you have selected a topic, or narrowed the possibilities down to two or three, the next step is to collect materials you can use in developing it. And here is one of the differences between writing about literature and writing about most other topics. With other topics you would have to collect facts from reference books and other sources. With literature, your data are within the literary work itself. And so the crucial next step is to reread the story carefully with your topic in mind, combing the text for details relevant to your topic. It is best at this stage to keep an open mind about your thesis. If you make up your mind prematurely about your topic, there is a temptation to read the text with blinders on, seizing on any detail that can support your thesis and ignoring any contrary details. If you are looking at the function of setting in "Rock River," for instance, it is best to just note all the references to setting and wait to fit them into a pattern until you have them all in front of you.

What is the best form to use in collecting these details? One of the best is marginal annotations. Injunctions against writing in books were never meant for serious students of literature, and underlinings and marginal notes can help you throw relevant details into relief. Highlighting with special pens can do the same, though marginal notes are probably still needed; highlighters sometimes have the experience of not remembering what struck them as notable about a passage they have highlighted earlier. It is often useful to write out on a piece of paper passages that bear on the tentative topic. Outlining is probably premature at this stage, but a "web" outline may be useful in seeing patterns and connections. For example, you could start off with the two major settings of "Rock River"—the town and the country—in the center of the page and build out from there, connecting relevant images and details to one or the other. Connections with other elements could be indicated with connecting lines until you have a "map" of the various relationships in the story. Whatever the mechanics of this stage of prewriting, here you are laying the groundwork for a concrete, well-supported argument.

FRAMING A THESIS SENTENCE. When you have collected your material (say, all the references to setting in "Rock River"), you are ready to decide on a thesis. Your thesis—the generalization you are prepared to defend—is crucial to your paper and will probably be adjusted and refined several times in the course of writing. If your thesis is too vague or general ("Setting is used very effectively in 'Rock River' "), your essay is likely to be dull and diffuse. If it is overstated or strained (" 'Rock River' is really about the Western landscape"), the essay is likely to be unconvincing. The best thesis is one that makes the boldest and most unexpected claim that can be persuasively developed ("The contrast between Rick and Sarah is partially expressed in the settings associated with each").

ORGANIZING THE ARGUMENT.   Once you have a tentative thesis and notes on specific passages you can use to support your argument, you are ready to decide on a pattern of organization for your essay. Would it be best to have two sections, one devoted to Rick and his setting, the other to Sarah and her setting? Or would it be better to deal first with what we know about Rick and Sarah's relationship and then move to the settings? What other possibilities are there? If you are comfortable working with outlines, this is the point at which you might experiment with several outlines, searching for what promises to be the most natural and convincing way to develop your point. Some people are more comfortable with only the most general kind of plan; the words "Rick" and "Sarah" on a piece of scratch paper and some notes about development of these two parts and about paragraph organization may be the only outline needed. Whatever the process, it is desirable at this stage to think through the possibilities for organization and not rely completely on intuition when you begin to write.

WRITING A FIRST DRAFT.   Now you are ready to write the first version of your essay. There are no rules for doing this; everyone has his or her own method of composition. Some people like to dash off a rough first draft as quickly as possible, so as to catch the spontaneous quality of speech. (And some people like actually to speak their first draft into a tape recorder and transcribe it later.) Others are slower and more painstaking; they like to have each section as polished as possible before going on to the next section. They tend to do a good bit of revising even in the process of writing a first draft. Whatever your habits, the goal here is to get down an initial version of the essay that can serve as the basis of revision.

REVISING THE ESSAY.   Unfortunately, a lot of academic writing stops right there. The first draft becomes the only draft, and it is turned in to the instructor, perhaps retyped and tidied up a bit. It is true that sometimes a piece of writing clicks the first time through and needs no revision. Usually, though, even professional writers find that they can improve a first draft considerably. The first step in successful revision is seeing *how* the first draft can be improved. We sometimes get so involved in our own phraseology that we cannot see any alternatives. In such cases, we need to attain a critical distance from our own work so that we can see how it could be improved. Sometimes the mere passage of time will help; a draft that seemed terrific at midnight may seem somewhat less than that the next morning. Reading a draft aloud, to a friend or even just to yourself, can show up awkwardnesses, gaps in logic, and other opportunities for improvement.

Once you arrive at a good self-evaluation, the next challenge is to make the needed changes. If you are using a computer to write, even so small a choice as whether to revise on a printout or directly on the screen may be important. Computers make revision mechanically easy compared with the old days when the prospect of repeated retyping discouraged much revision. But the ease of making changes on computers is sometimes deceptive and may lead us to glide too easily over problematic passages. Reading a hard printout of your essay may be different enough from reading it on screen to provide needed distance and objectivity. Some people do their best revisions with an old-fashioned pencil on a printout; others can revise just as well on screen. Whatever the mechanics, the goal here is to see the possibilities for revision as clearly as possible and to revise accordingly.

PREPARING THE FINAL MANUSCRIPT.   Your instructor will probably give you directions for the form of the essay to be turned in. It should ordinarily be double-spaced, with ample margins for instructor's comments. You should hold yourself to the highest standard of mechanical correctness. Quotations should be checked and rechecked, doubtful words should be looked up in the dictionary, and awkward grammar and diction should be corrected. Care in the small things suggests care in larger matters as well, and the instructor's time is better spent in engaging and evaluating your ideas than in correcting spelling and grammar. You should always keep a copy of your work; papers can go astray, and computers and photocopy machines make copies so easily that there is no excuse for not making use of them.

There is no formula for writing well about literature. The best writing about literature, as about anything else, grows out of urgency and commitment, of having something to say. But there are ways of discovering what it is you have to say, through an orderly process of exploration and discovery. The rewards are great; ideally a writing assignment should not only lead you to formulate a better understanding of a text you have read but should also be a source of pride in the formulation of a new text upon that text, a piece of work that makes your reading fully yours.

Stories for Further Reading

❧ ❧ ❧

Nathaniel Hawthorne

Nathaniel Hawthorne (1804–64) was one of the major figures in the American Renaissance, the great flowering of New England literature in the mid–nineteenth century. Born in Salem, Massachusetts, the descendant of a judge in the Salem witchcraft trials, Hawthorne was fascinated by the power of the past, especially the Puritan past, over the present and by the workings of the mind, especially those involving pride, isolation, and guilt. His novels include *The Scarlet Letter* (1850), *The House of the Seven Gables* (1851), *The Blithedale Romance* (1852), and *The Marble Faun* (1860). Collections of short stories include *Twice-Told Tales* (1837) and *Mosses from an Old Manse* (1846), which included "Young Goodman Brown."

YOUNG GOODMAN BROWN

Young Goodman Brown came forth at sunset, into the street of Salem village, but put his head back, after crossing the threshold, to exchange a parting kiss with his young wife. And Faith, as the wife was aptly named, thrust her own pretty head into the street, letting the wind play with the pink ribbons of her cap, while she called to Goodman Brown.

"Dearest heart," whispered she, softly and rather sadly, when her lips were close to his ear, "prithee, put off your journey until sunrise, and sleep in your own bed to-night. A lone woman is troubled with such dreams and such thoughts, that she's afeard of herself, sometimes. Pray, tarry with me this night, dear husband, of all nights in the year!"

"My love and my Faith," replied young Goodman Brown, "of all nights in the year, this one night I must tarry away from thee. My journey, as thou callest it, forth and back again, must needs be done 'twixt now and sunrise. What, my sweet, pretty wife, dost thou doubt me already, and we but three months married!"

"Then God bless you!" said Faith with the pink ribbons, "and may you find all well, when you come back."

"Amen!" cried Goodman Brown. "Say thy prayers, dear Faith, and go to bed at dusk, and no harm will come to thee."

So they parted; and the young man pursued his way, until, being about to turn the corner by the meeting-house, he looked back and saw the head of Faith still peeping after him, with a melancholy air, in spite of her pink ribbons.

"Poor little Faith!" thought he, for his heart smote him. "What a wretch am I, to leave her on such an errand! She talks of dreams, too. Methought, as she spoke, there was trouble in her face, as if a dream had warned her what work is to be done to-night. But no, no! 't would kill her to think it. Well; she's a blessed angel on earth; and after this one night, I'll cling to her skirts and follow her to Heaven."

With this excellent resolve for the future, Goodman Brown felt himself justified in making more haste on his present evil purpose. He had taken a dreary road, darkened by all the gloomiest trees of the forest, which barely stood aside to let the narrow path creep through, and closed immediately behind. It was as lonely as could be; and there is this peculiarity in such a solitude, that the traveller knows not who may be concealed by the innumerable trunks and the thick boughs overhead; so that, with lonely footsteps, he may yet be passing through an unseen multitude.

"There may be a devilish Indian behind every tree," said Goodman Brown to himself; and he glanced fearfully behind him, as he added, "What if the devil himself should be at my very elbow!"

His head being turned back, he passed a crook of the road, and looking forward again, beheld the figure of a man, in grave and decent attire, seated at the foot of an old tree. He arose at Goodman Brown's approach, and walked onward, side by side with him.

"You are late, Goodman Brown," said he. "The clock of the Old South was striking, as I came through Boston; and that is full fifteen minutes agone."

"Faith kept me back awhile," replied the young man, with a tremor in his voice, caused by the sudden appearance of his companion, though not wholly unexpected.

It was now deep dusk in the forest, and deepest in that part of it where these two were journeying. As nearly as could be discerned, the second traveller was about fifty years old, apparently in the same rank of life as Goodman Brown, and bearing a considerable resemblance to him, though perhaps more in expression than features. Still, they might have been taken for father and son. And yet, though the elder person was as simply clad as the younger, and as simple in manner too, he had an indescribable air of one who knew the world, and would not have felt abashed at the governor's dinner-table, or in King William's court, were it possible that his affairs should call him thither. But the only thing about him that could be fixed upon as remarkable, was his staff, which bore the likeness of a great black snake, so curiously wrought, that it might almost be seen to twist and wriggle itself like a living serpent. This, of course, must have been an ocular deception, assisted by the uncertain light.

"Come, Goodman Brown!" cried his fellow-traveller, "this is a dull pace for the beginning of a journey. Take my staff, if you are so soon weary."

"Friend," said the other, exchanging his slow pace for a full stop, "having kept covenant by meeting thee here, it is my purpose now to return whence I came. I have scruples, touching the matter thou wot'st of."

"Sayest thou so?" replied he of the serpent, smiling apart. "Let us walk on, nevertheless, reasoning as we go, and if I convince thee not, thou shalt turn back. We are but a little way in the forest, yet."

"Too far, too far!" exclaimed the goodman, unconsciously resuming his walk. "My father never went into the woods on such an errand, nor his father before him. We have been a race of honest men and good Christians, since the days of the martyrs. And shall I be the first of the name of Brown that ever took this path and kept—"

"Such company, thou wouldst say," observed the elder person, interrupting his pause. "Well said, Goodman Brown! I have been as well acquainted with your family as with ever a one among the Puritans; and that's no trifle to say. I helped your grandfather, the constable, when he lashed the Quaker woman so smartly through the streets of Salem. And it was I that brought your father a pitch-pine knot, kindled at my own hearth, to set fire to an Indian village, in King Philip's war. They were my good friends, both; and many a pleasant walk have we had along this path, and returned merrily after midnight. I would fain be friends with you, for their sake."

"If it be as thou sayest," replied Goodman Brown, "I marvel they never spoke of these matters. Or, verily, I marvel not, seeing that the least rumor of the sort would have driven them from New England. We are a people of prayer, and good works to boot, and abide no such wickedness."

"Wickedness or not," said the traveller with the twisted staff, "I have a very general acquaintance here in New England. The deacons of many a church have drunk the communion wine with me; the selectmen, of divers towns, make me their chairman; and a majority of the Great and General Court are firm supporters of my interest. The governor and I, too—but these are state secrets.''

"Can this be so!" cried Goodman Brown, with a stare of amazement at his undisturbed companion. "Howbeit, I have nothing to do with the governor and council; they have their own ways, and are no rule for a simple husbandman like me. But, were I to go on with thee, how should I meet the eye of that good old man, our minister, at Salem village? Oh, his voice would make me tremble, both Sabbath-day and lecture-day!''

Thus far, the elder traveller had listened with due gravity, but now burst into a fit of irrepressible mirth, shaking himself so violently, that his snakelike staff actually seemed to wriggle in sympathy.

"Ha, ha, ha!" shouted he, again and again; then composing himself, "Well, go on, Goodman Brown, go on; but, prithee, don't kill me with laughing!''

"Well, then, to end the matter at once," said Goodman Brown, considerably nettled, "there is my wife, Faith. It would break her dear little heart; and I'd rather break my own!''

"Nay, if that be the case," answered the other, "e'en go thy ways, Goodman Brown. I would not, for twenty old women like the one hobbling before us, that Faith should come to any harm.''

As he spoke, he pointed his staff at a female figure on the path, in whom Goodman Brown recognized a very pious and exemplary dame, who had taught him his catechism in youth, and was still his moral and spiritual adviser, jointly with the minister and Deacon Gookin.

"A marvel, truly, that Goody Cloyse should be so far in the wilderness, at nightfall!" said he. "But, with your leave, friend, I shall take a cut through the woods, until we have left this Christian woman behind. Being a stranger to you, she might ask whom I was consorting with, and whither I was going.''

"Be it so," said his fellow-traveller. "Betake you to the woods, and let me keep the path.''

Accordingly, the young man turned aside, but took care to watch his companion, who advanced softly along the road, until he had come within a staff's length of the old dame. She, meanwhile, was making the best of her way, with singular speed for so aged a woman, and mumbling some indistinct words, a prayer, doubtless, as she went. The traveller put forth his staff, and touched her withered neck with what seemed the serpent's tail.

"The devil!" screamed the pious old lady.

"Then Goody Cloyse knows her old friend?" observed the traveller, confronting her, and leaning on his writhing stick.

"Ah, forsooth, and is it your worship, indeed?" cried the good dame. "Yea, truly is it, and in the very image of my old gossip, Goodman Brown, the grandfather of the silly fellow that now is. But, would your worship believe it? my broomstick hath strangely disappeared, stolen, as I suspect, by that unhanged witch, Goody Cory, and that, too, when I was all anointed with the juice of smallage and cinque-foil and wolf's-bane—''

"Mingled with fine wheat and the fat of a new-born babe," said the shape of old Goodman Brown.

"Ah, your worship knows the recipe," cried the old lady, cackling aloud. "So, as I was saying, being all ready for the meeting, and no horse to ride on, I made up my mind to foot it; for they tell me there is a nice young man to be taken into communion to-night. But now your good worship will lend me your arm, and we shall be there in a twinkling."

"That can hardly be," answered her friend. "I may not spare you my arm, Goody Cloyse, but here is my staff, if you will."

So saying, he threw it down at her feet, where, perhaps, it assumed life, being one of the rods which its owner had formerly lent to the Egyptian Magi. Of this fact, however, Goodman Brown could not take cognizance. He had cast his eyes in astonishment, and looking down again, beheld neither Goody Cloyse nor the serpentine staff, but his fellow-traveller alone, who waited for him as calmly as if nothing had happened.

"That old woman taught me my catechism!" said the young man; and there was a world of meaning in this simple comment.

They continued to walk onward, while the elder traveller exhorted his companion to make good speed and persevere in the path, discoursing so aptly, that his arguments seemed rather to spring up in the bosom of his auditor, than to be suggested by himself. As they went he plucked a branch of maple, to serve for a walking-stick, and began to strip it of the twigs and little boughs, which were wet with evening dew. The moment his fingers touched them, they became strangely withered and dried up, as with a week's sunshine. Thus the pair proceeded, at a good free pace, until suddenly, in a gloomy hollow of the road, Goodman Brown sat himself down on the stump of a tree, and refused to go any farther.

"Friend," said he, stubbornly, "my mind is made up. Not another step will I budge on this errand. What if a wretched old woman do choose to go to the devil, when I thought she was going to Heaven! Is that any reason why I should quit my dear Faith, and go after her?"

"You will think better of this by and by," said his acquaintance, composedly. "Sit here and rest yourself awhile; and when you feel like moving again, there is my staff to help you along."

Without more words, he threw his companion the maple stick, and was as speedily out of sight as if he had vanished into the deepening gloom. The young man sat a few moments by the roadside, applauding himself greatly, and thinking with how clear a conscience he should meet the minister, in his morning walk, nor shrink from the eye of good old Deacon Gookin. And what calm sleep would be his, that very night, which was to have been spent so wickedly, but purely and sweetly now, in the arms of Faith! Amidst these pleasant and praiseworthy meditations, Goodman Brown heard the tramp of horses along the road, and deemed it advisable to conceal himself within the verge of the forest, conscious of the guilty purpose that had brought him thither, though now so happily turned from it.

On came the hoof-tramps and the voices of the riders, two grave old voices, conversing soberly as they drew near. These mingled sounds appeared to pass along the road, within a few yards of the young man's hiding-place; but owing, doubtless, to the depth of the gloom, at that particular spot, neither the travellers nor their steeds were visible. Though their figures brushed the small boughs by the wayside, it could not be seen that they intercepted, even for a moment, the faint gleam from the strip of bright sky, athwart which they must have passed. Goodman Brown alternately crouched and stood on tiptoe, pulling aside the branches, and thrusting forth his head as far as he durst, without discerning so much as a shadow. It vexed him the more, because he could have sworn, were such a thing possible, that he recognized the voices of the minister and Deacon Gookin, jogging along quietly, as they were wont to do, when bound to some ordination or ecclesiastical council. While yet within hearing, one of the riders stopped to pluck a switch.

"Of the two, reverend Sir," said the voice like the deacon's, "I had rather miss an ordination dinner than to-night's meeting. They tell me that some of our community are to be here from Falmouth and beyond, and others from Connecticut and Rhode Island; besides several of the Indian powwows, who, after their fashion, know almost as much deviltry as the best of us. Moreover, there is a goodly young woman to be taken into communion."

"Mighty well, Deacon Gookin!" replied the solemn old tones of the minister. "Spur up, or we shall be late. Nothing can be done, you know, until I get on the ground."

The hoofs clattered again, and the voices, talking so strangely in the empty air, passed on through the forest, where no church had ever been gathered, nor solitary Christian prayed. Whither, then, could these holy men be journeying, so deep into the heathen wilderness? Young Goodman Brown caught hold of a tree, for support, being ready to sink down on the ground, faint and over-burthened with the heavy sickness of his heart. He looked up to the sky, doubting whether there really was a Heaven above him. Yet, there was a blue arch, and the stars brightening in it.

"With Heaven above, and Faith below, I will yet stand firm against the devil!" cried Goodman Brown.

While he still gazed upward, into the deep arch of the firmament, and had lifted his hands to pray, a cloud, though no wind was stirring, hurried across the zenith, and hid the brightening stars. The blue sky was still visible, except directly overhead, where this black mass of cloud was sweeping swiftly northward. Aloft in the air, as if from the depths of the cloud, came a confused and doubtful sound of voices. Once, the listener fancied that he could distinguish the accents of townspeople of his own, men and women, both pious and ungodly, many of whom he had met at the communion-table, and had seen others rioting at the tavern. The next moment, so indistinct were the sounds, he doubted whether he had heard aught but the murmur of the old forest, whispering without a wind. Then came a stronger swell of those familiar tones, heard daily in the sunshine, at Salem village, but never, until now, from a cloud at night. There was one voice, of a young woman, uttering lamentations, yet with an uncertain sorrow, and entreating for some favor, which, perhaps, it would grieve her to obtain. And all the unseen multitude, both saints and sinners, seemed to encourage her onward.

"Faith!" shouted Goodman Brown, in a voice of agony and desperation; and the echoes of the forest mocked him, crying—"Faith! Faith!" as if bewildered wretches were seeking her, all through the wilderness.

The cry of grief, rage, and terror was yet piercing the night, when the unhappy husband held his breath for a response. There was a scream, drowned immediately in a louder murmur of voices fading into far-off laughter, as the dark cloud swept away, leaving the clear and silent sky above Goodman Brown. But something fluttered lightly down through the air, and caught on the branch of a tree. The young man seized it and beheld a pink ribbon.

"My Faith is gone!" cried he, after one stupefied moment. "There is no good on earth, and sin is but a name. Come, devil! for to thee is this world given."

And maddened with despair, so that he laughed loud and long, did Goodman Brown grasp his staff and set forth again, at such a rate, that he seemed to fly along the forest path, rather than to walk or run. The road grew wilder and drearier, and more faintly traced, and vanished at length, leaving him in the heart of the dark wilderness, still rushing onward, with the instinct that guides mortal man to evil. The whole forest was peopled with frightful sounds: the creaking of trees, the howling of wild beasts, and the yell of Indians; while, sometimes, the wind tolled like a distant church bell, and sometimes gave a broad roar around the traveller, as if all Nature was laughing him to scorn. But he was himself the chief horror of the scene, and shrank not from its other horrors.

"Ha! ha! ha!" roared Goodman Brown, when the wind laughed at him. "Let us hear which will laugh loudest! Think not to frighten me with your deviltry! Come witch, come wizard, come Indian powwow, come devil himself! and here comes Goodman Brown. You may as well fear him as he fear you!"

In truth, all through the haunted forest, there could be nothing more frightful than the figure of Goodman Brown. On he flew, among the black pines, brandishing his staff with frenzied gestures, now giving vent to an inspiration of horrid blasphemy, and now shouting forth such laughter, as set all the echoes of the forest laughing like demons around him. The fiend in his own shape is less hideous, than when he rages in the breast of man. Thus sped the demoniac on his course, until, quivering among the trees, he saw a red light before him, as when the felled trunks and branches of a clearing have been set on fire, and throw up their lurid blaze against the sky, at the hour of midnight. He paused, in a lull of the tempest that had driven him onward, and heard the swell of what seemed a hymn, rolling solemnly from a distance, with the weight of many voices. He knew the tune. It was a familiar one in the choir of the village meeting-house. The verse died heavily away, and was lengthened by a chorus, not of human voices, but of all the sounds of the benighted wilderness, pealing in awful harmony together. Goodman Brown cried out; and his cry was lost to his own ear, by its unison with the cry of the desert.

In the interval of silence, he stole forward, until the light glared full upon his eyes. At one extremity of an open space, hemmed in by the dark wall of the forest, arose a rock, bearing some rude, natural resemblance either to an altar or a pulpit, and surrounded by four blazing pines, their tops aflame, their stems untouched, like candles at an evening meeting. The mass of foliage, that had overgrown the summit of the rock, was all on fire, blazing high into the night, and fitfully illuminating the whole field. Each pendent twig and leafy festoon was in a blaze. As the red light arose and fell, a numerous congregation alternately shone forth, then disappeared in shadow, and again grew, as it were, out of the darkness, peopling the heart of the solitary woods at once.

"A grave and dark-clad company!" quoth Goodman Brown.

In truth, they were such. Among them, quivering to-and-fro, between gloom and splendor, appeared faces that would be seen, next day, at the council-board of the province, and others which, Sabbath after Sabbath, looked devoutly heavenward, and benignantly over the crowded pews, from the holiest pulpits in the land. Some affirm, that the lady of the governor was there. At least, there were high dames well known to her, and wives of honored husbands, and widows a great multitude, and ancient maidens, all of excellent repute, and fair young girls, who trembled lest their mothers should espy them. Either the sudden gleams of light, flashing over the obscure field, bedazzled Goodman Brown, or he recognized a score of the church members of Salem village, famous for their especial sanctity. Good old Deacon Gookin had arrived, and waited at the skirts of that venerable saint, his reverend pastor. But, irreverently consorting with these grave, reputable, and pious people, these elders of the church, these chaste dames and dewy virgins, there were men of dissolute lives and women of spotted fame, wretches given over to all mean and filthy vice, and suspected even of horrid crimes. It was strange to see, that the good shrank not from the wicked, nor were the sinners abashed by the saints. Scattered, also, among their pale-faced enemies, were the Indian priests, or powwows, who had often scared their native forest with more hideous incantations than any known to English witchcraft.

"But, where is Faith?" thought Goodman Brown; and, as hope came into his heart, he trembled.

Another verse of the hymn arose, a slow and mournful strain, such as the pious love, but joined to words which expressed all that our nature can conceive of sin, and darkly hinted at far more. Unfathomable to mere mortals is the lore of fiends. Verse after verse was sung, and still the chorus of the desert swelled between, like the deepest tone of a mighty organ. And, with the final peal of that dreadful anthem, there came a sound, as if the roaring wind, the rushing streams, the howling beasts, and every other voice of the unconverted wilderness were mingling and according with the voice of guilty man, in homage to the prince of all. The four blazing pines threw up a loftier flame, and obscurely discovered shapes and visages of horror on the smoke-wreaths, above the impious assembly. At the same moment, the fire on the rock shot redly forth, and formed a glowing arch above its base, where now appeared a figure. With reverence be it spoken, the apparition bore no slight similitude, both in garb and manner, to some grave divine of the New England churches.

"Bring forth the converts!" cried a voice, that echoed through the field and rolled into the forest.

At the word, Goodman Brown stepped forth from the shadow of the trees, and approached the congregation, with whom he felt a loathful brotherhood, by the sympathy of all that was wicked in his heart. He could have well-nigh sworn, that the shape of his own dead father beckoned him to advance, looking downward from a smoke-wreath, while a woman, with dim features of despair, threw out her hand to warn him back. Was it his mother? But he had no power to retreat one step, nor to resist, even in thought, when the minister and good old Deacon Gookin seized his arms, and led him to the blazing rock. Thither came also the slender form of a veiled female, led between Goody Cloyse, that pious teacher of the catechism, and Martha Carrier, who had received the devil's promise to be queen of hell. A rampant hag was she! And there stood the proselytes, beneath the canopy of fire.

"Welcome, my children," said the dark figure, "to the communion of your race! Ye have found, thus young, your nature and your destiny. My children, look behind you!"

They turned; and flashing forth, as it were, in a sheet of flame, the fiend-worshippers were seen; the smile of welcome gleamed darkly on every visage.

"There," resumed the sable form, "are all whom ye have reverenced from youth. Ye deemed them holier than yourselves, and shrank from your own sin, contrasting it with their lives of righteousness and prayerful aspirations heavenward. Yet, here are they all, in my worshipping assembly! This night it shall be granted you to know their secret deeds; how hoary-bearded elders of the church have whispered wanton words to the young maids of their households; how many a woman, eager for widow's weeds, has given her husband a drink at bedtime, and let him sleep his last sleep in her bosom; how beardless youths have made haste to inherit their father's wealth; and how fair damsels—blush not, sweet ones!—have dug little graves in the garden, and bidden me, the sole guest, to an infant's funeral. By the sympathy of your human hearts for sin, ye shall scent out all the places—whether in church, bedchamber, street, field, or forest—where crime has been committed, and shall exult to behold the whole earth one stain of guilt, one mighty blood-spot. Far more than this! It shall be yours to penetrate, in every bosom, the deep mystery of sin, the fountain of all wicked arts, and which inexhaustibly supplies more evil impulses than human power—than my power, at its utmost!—can make manifest in deeds. And now, my children, look upon each other."

They did so; and, by the blaze of the hell-kindled torches, the wretched man beheld his Faith, and the wife her husband, trembling before that unhallowed altar.

"Lo! there ye stand, my children," said the figure, in a deep and solemn tone, almost sad, with its despairing awfulness, as if his once angelic nature could yet mourn for our miserable race. "Depending upon one another's hearts, ye had still hoped that virtue were not all a dream! Now are ye undeceived!—Evil is the nature of mankind. Evil must be your only happiness. Welcome, again, my children, to the communion of your race!"

"Welcome!" repeated the fiend-worshippers, in one cry of despair and triumph.

And there they stood, the only pair, as it seemed, who were yet hesitating on the verge of wickedness, in this dark world. A basin was hollowed, naturally, in the rock. Did it contain water, reddened by the lurid light? or was it blood? or, perchance, a liquid flame? Herein did the Shape of Evil dip his hand, and prepare to lay the mark of baptism upon their foreheads, that they might be partakers of the mystery of sin, more conscious of the secret guilt of others, both in deed and thought, than they could now be of their own. The husband cast one look at his pale wife, and Faith at him. What polluted wretches would the next glance show them to each other, shuddering alike at what they disclosed and what they saw!

"Faith! Faith!" cried the husband. "Look up to Heaven, and resist the Wicked One!"

Whether Faith obeyed, he knew not. Hardly had he spoken, when he found himself amid calm night and solitude, listening to a roar of the wind, which died heavily away through the forest. He staggered against the rock, and felt it chill and damp, while a hanging twig, that had been all on fire, besprinkled his cheek with the coldest dew.

The next morning, young Goodman Brown came slowly into the street of Salem village staring around him like a bewildered man. The good old minister was taking a walk along the grave-yard, to get an appetite for breakfast and meditate his sermon, and bestowed a blessing, as he passed, on Goodman Brown. He shrank from the venerable saint, as if to avoid an anathema. Old Deacon Gookin was at domestic worship, and the holy words of his prayer were heard through the open window. "What God doth the wizard pray to?" quoth Goodman Brown. Goody Cloyse, that excellent old Christian, stood in the early sunshine, at her own lattice, catechising a little girl, who had brought her a pint of morning's milk. Goodman Brown snatched away the child, as from the grasp of the fiend himself. Turning the corner by the meeting-house, he spied the head of Faith, with the pink ribbons, gazing anxiously forth, and bursting into such joy at sight of him that she skipt along the street, and almost kissed her husband before the whole village. But Goodman Brown looked sternly and sadly into her face, and passed on without a greeting.

Had Goodman Brown fallen asleep in the forest, and only dreamed a wild dream of a witch-meeting?

Be it so, if you will. But, alas! it was a dream of evil omen for young Goodman Brown. A stern, a sad, a darkly meditative, a distrustful, if not a desperate man did he become, from the night of that fearful dream. On the Sabbath day, when the congregation were singing a holy psalm, he could not listen, because an anthem of sin rushed loudly upon his ear, and drowned all the blessed strain. When the minister spoke from the pulpit, with power and fervid eloquence, and with his hand on the open Bible, of the sacred truths of our religion, and of saint-like lives and triumphant deaths, and of future bliss or misery unutterable, then did Goodman Brown turn pale, dreading lest the roof should thunder down upon the gray blasphemer and his hearers. Often, awaking suddenly at midnight, he shrank from the bosom of Faith, and at morning or eventide, when the family knelt down at prayer, he scowled, and muttered to himself, and gazed sternly at his wife, and turned away. And when he had lived long, and was borne to his grave, a hoary corpse, followed by Faith, an aged woman, and children and grand-children, a goodly procession, besides neighbors not a few, they carved no hopeful verse upon his tombstone; for his dying hour was gloom.

QUESTIONS FOR DISCUSSION AND WRITING

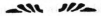

1.   How would you characterize the narrator in "Young Goodman Brown"? Is the narrative voice wholly neutral and objective, or does it take a particular stance toward the tale it tells?

2.   "Young Goodman Brown" is presented as a fantasy or dream-story with allegorical overtones. (Note the ambiguity of the names "Goodman" and "Faith," for example.) Can it be read psychologically, as an account of an inner rather than an outer experience? What has happened to young Goodman Brown?

3.   What stance does the story take toward the Puritan past? Note that young Goodman Brown idealizes his ancestors: "We have been a race of honest men and good Christians, since the days of the martyrs." But the demonic "elder person" suggests that they were friends of the devil: "I have been well acquainted with your family as with ever a one among the Puritans, and that's no trifle to say." Is Hawthorne suggesting that Brown sees things as black or white, that he swings from idealization to demonizing with nothing in between? Discuss.

4.   Examine the way Hawthorne describes his forest setting. How does he make it simultaneously a credible, realistic setting and an allegorical one?

Herman Melville

Herman Melville (1819–91) sailed on a whaler for the South Seas in 1841, when he was twenty-one years old. Three years later, his career as a sailor ended, after a desertion in the Marquesas, participation in a mutiny, and beachcombing in Tahiti. He was to draw upon his sea experiences as a writer for the rest of his life, first in the novels *Typee* (1846), *Omoo* (1847), *Mardi* (1849), *Redburn* (1849), and *White-Jacket* (1850) and later in his masterpiece *Moby-Dick* (1851). After the failure of *Pierre* (1852), Melville turned to writing short stories, which after magazine publication he collected as *The Piazza Tales* (1856), the volume that contained "Benito Cereno." Melville spent his later years as a deputy inspector of customs in New York City and writing poetry, most notably a book-length poem named *Clarel* (1876). When he died in 1891, he left among his papers the novella *Billy Budd, Sailor,* which became one of his best-known works after it was published in the 1920s.

BENITO CERENO

In the year 1799, Captain Amasa Delano, of Duxbury in Massachusetts, commanding a large sealer and general trader, lay at anchor with a valuable cargo in the harbor of St. Maria—a small, desert, uninhabited island toward the southern extremity of the long coast of Chile. There he had touched for water.

On the second day, not long after dawn, while lying in his berth, his mate came below, informing him that a strange sail was coming into the bay. Ships were then not so plenty in those waters as now. He rose, dressed, and went on deck.

The morning was one peculiar to that coast. Everything was mute and calm; everything gray. The sea, though undulated into long roods of swells, seemed fixed, and was sleeked at the surface like waved lead that has cooled and set in the smelter's mold. The sky seemed a gray surtout. Flights of troubled gray fowl, kith and kin with flights of troubled gray vapors among which they were mixed, skimmed low and fitfully over the waters, as swallows over meadows before storms. Shadows present, foreshadowing deeper shadows to come.

To Captain Delano's surprise, the stranger, viewed through the glass, showed no colors, though to do so upon entering a haven, however uninhabited in its shores, where but a single other ship might be lying, was the custom among peaceful seamen of all nations. Considering the lawlessness and loneliness of the spot, and the sort of stories at that day associated with those seas, Captain Delano's surprise might have deepened into some uneasiness had he not been a person of a singularly undistrustful good nature, not liable except on extraordinary and repeated incentives, and hardly then, to indulge in personal alarms any way involving the imputation of malign evil in man. Whether, in view of what humanity is capable, such a trait implies, along with a benevolent heart, more than ordinary quickness and accuracy of intellectual perception, may be left to the wise to determine.

But whatever misgivings might have obtruded on first seeing the stranger would almost, in any seaman's mind, have been dissipated by observing that the ship, in navigating into the harbor, was drawing too near the land, a sunken reef making out off her bow. This seemed to prove her a stranger, indeed, not only to the sealer, but the island; consequently she could be no wonted freebooter on that ocean. With no small interest Captain Delano continued to watch her—a proceeding not much facilitated by the vapors partly mantling the hull, through which the far matin light from her cabin streamed equivocally enough; much like the sun—by this time hemisphered on the rim of the horizon, and, apparently, in company with the strange ship entering the harbor—which, wimpled by the same low, creeping clouds, showed not unlike a Lima intrigante's one sinister eye peering across the Plaza from the Indian loophole of her dusk *saya-y-manta.*

It might have been but a deception of the vapors, but the longer the stranger was watched the more singular appeared her maneuvers. Erelong it seemed hard to decide whether she meant to come in or no—what she wanted, or what she was about. The wind, which had breezed up a little during the night, was now extremely light and baffling, which the more increased the apparent uncertainty of her movements.

Surmising at last that it might be a ship in distress, Captain Delano ordered his whaleboat to be dropped, and, much to the wary opposition of his mate, prepared to board her, and, at the least, pilot her in. On the night previous, a fishing party of the seamen had gone a long distance to some detached rocks out of sight from the sealer, and, an hour or two before daybreak, had returned, having met with no small success. Presuming that the stranger might have been long off soundings, the good captain put several baskets of the fish, for presents, into his boat, and so pulled away. From her continuing too near the sunken reef deeming her in danger, calling to his men he made all haste to apprise those on board of their situation. But, some time ere the boat came up, the wind, light though it was, having shifted, had headed the vessel off, as well as partly broken the vapors from about her.

Upon gaining a less remote view, the ship, when made signally visible on the verge of the leaden-hued swells, with the shreds of fog here and there raggedly furring her, appeared like a whitewashed monastery after a thunderstorm, seen perched upon some dun cliff among the Pyrenees. But it was no purely fanciful resemblance which now, for a moment, almost led Captain Delano to think that nothing less than a shipload of monks was before him. Peering over the bulwarks were what really seemed, in the hazy distance, throngs of dark cowls; while, fitfully revealed through the open portholes, other dark moving figures were dimly described, as of Black Friars pacing the cloisters.

Upon a still nigher approach, this appearance was modified, and the true character of the vessel was plain—a Spanish merchantman of the first class, carrying Negro slaves, amongst other valuable freight, from one colonial port to another. A very large, and, in its time, a very fine vessel, such as in those days were at intervals encountered along that main; sometimes superseded Acapulco treasure ships, or retired frigates of the Spanish king's navy, which, like superannuated Italian palaces, still, under a decline of masters, preserved signs of former state.

As the whaleboat drew more and more nigh, the cause of the peculiar pipe-clayed aspect of the stranger was seen in the slovenly neglect pervading her. The spars, ropes, and great part of the bulwarks looked woolly from long unacquaintance with the scraper, tar, and the brush. Her keel seemed laid, her ribs put together, and she launched, from Ezekiel's Valley of Dry Bones.

In the present business in which she was engaged, the ship's general model and rig appeared to have undergone no material change from their original warlike and Froissart pattern. However, no guns were seen.

The tops were large, and were railed about with what had once been octagonal network, all now in sad disrepair. These tops hung overhead like three ruinous aviaries, in one of which was seen perched, on a ratline, a white noddy, a strange fowl so called from its lethargic, somnambulistic character, being frequently caught by hand at sea. Battered and moldy, the castellated forecastle seemed some ancient turret long ago taken by assault, and then left to decay. Toward the stern, two high-raised quarter galleries—the balustrades here and there covered with dry tindery sea moss—opening out from the unoccupied state cabin, whose deadlights, for all the mild weather, were hermetically closed and calked—these tenantless balconies hung over the sea as if it were the grand Venetian canal. But the principal relic of faded grandeur was the ample oval of the shieldlike stern-piece, intricately carved with the arms of Castile and Leon, medallioned about by groups of mythological or symbolical devices, uppermost and central of which was a dark satyr in a mask holding his foot on the prostrate neck of a writhing figure, likewise masked.

Whether the ship had a figurehead, or only a plain beak, was not quite certain, owing to canvas wrapped about that part, either to protect it while undergoing a refurbishing, or else decently to hide its decay. Rudely painted or chalked, as in a sailor freak, along the forward side of a sort of pedestal below the canvas, was the sentence, SEGUID VUESTRO JEFE ("follow your leader"); while upon the tarnished headboards near by appeared, in stately capitals, once gilt, the ship's name *SAN DOMINICK*, each letter streakingly corroded with tricklings of copper-spike rust; while, like mourning weeds, dark festoons of sea grass slimily swept to and fro over the name with every hearselike roll of the hull.

As, at last, the boat was hooked from the bow along toward the gangway amid-ship, its keel, while yet some inches separated from the hull, harshly grated as on a sunken coral reef. It proved a huge bunch of conglobated barnacles adhering below the water to the side like a wen—a token of baffling airs and long calms passed somewhere in those seas.

Climbing the side, the visitor was at once surrounded by a clamorous throng of whites and blacks, but the latter outnumbering the former more than could have been expected, Negro transportation ship as the stranger in port was. But, in one language, and as with one voice, all poured out a common tale of suffering; in which the Negresses, of whom there were not a few, exceeded the others in their dolorous vehemence. The scurvy, together with the fever, had swept off a great part of their number, more especially the Spaniards. Off Cape Horn they had narrowly escaped shipwreck; then, for days together, they had lain tranced with-out winds; their provisions were low; their water next to none; their lips that moment were baked.

While Captain Delano was thus made the mark of all eager tongues, his one eager glance took in all faces, with every other object about him.

Always upon first boarding a large and populous ship at sea, especially a foreign one, with a nondescript crew such as Lascars or Manila men, the impression varies in a peculiar way from that produced by first entering a strange house with strange inmates in a strange land. Both house and ship—the one by its walls and blinds, the other by its high bulwarks like ramparts—hoard from view their interiors till the last moment, but in the case of the ship there is this addition: that the living spectacle it contains, upon its sudden and complete disclosure, has, in contrast with the blank ocean which zones it, something of the effect of enchantment. The ship seems unreal; these strange costumes, gestures, and faces but a shadowy tableau just emerged from the deep, which directly must receive back what it gave.

Perhaps it was some such influence, as above is attempted to be described, which, in Captain Delano's mind heightened whatever, upon a staid scrutiny, might have seemed unusual, especially the conspicuous figures of four elderly grizzled Negroes, their heads like black, doddered willow tops, who, in venerable contrast to the tumult below them, were couched, sphinxlike, one on the starboard cathead, another on the larboard, and the remaining pair face to face on the opposite bulwarks above the mainchains. They each had bits of unstranded old junk in their hands, and, with a sort of stoical self-content, were picking the junk into oakum, a small heap of which lay by their sides. They accompanied the task with a continuous, low, monotonous chant, droning and druling away like so many gray-headed bagpipers playing a funeral march.

The quarter-deck rose into an ample elevated poop, upon the forward verge of which, lifted, like the oakum-pickers, some eight feet above the general throng, sat along in a row, separated by regular spaces, the cross-legged figures of six other blacks, each with a rusty hatchet in his hand, which, with a bit of brick and a rag, he was engaged like a scullion in scouring, while between each two was a small sack of hatchets, their rusted edges turned forward awaiting a like operation. Though occasionally the four oakum-pickers would briefly address some person or persons in the crowd below, yet the six hatchet-polishers neither spoke to others nor breathed a whisper among themselves, but sat intent upon their task, except at intervals, when, with the peculiar love in Negroes of uniting industry with pastime, two and two they sideways clashed their hatchets together, like cymbals, with a barbarous din. All six, unlike the generality, had the raw aspect of unsophisticated Africans.

But that first comprehensive glance which took in those ten figures, with scores less conspicuous, rested but an instant upon them, as, impatient of the hubbub of voices, the visitor turned in quest of whomsoever it might be that commanded the ship.

But as if not unwilling to let nature make known her own case among his suffering charge, or else in despair of restraining it for the time, the Spanish captain, a gentlemanly, reserved-looking, and rather young man to a stranger's eye, dressed with singular richness but bearing plain traces of recent sleepless cares and disquietudes, stood passively by, leaning against the mainmast, at one moment casting a dreary, spiritless look upon his excited people, at the next an unhappy glance toward his visitor. By his side stood a black of small stature, in whose rude face, as occasionally, like a shepherd's dog, he mutely turned it up into the Spaniard's, sorrow and affection were equally blended.

Struggling through the throng, the American advanced to the Spaniard, assuring him of his sympathies, and offering to render whatever assistance might be in his power. To which the Spaniard returned for the present but grave and ceremonious acknowledgments, his national formality dusked by the saturnine mood of ill-health.

But losing no time in more compliments, Captain Delano, returning to the gangway, had his basket of fish brought up, and as the wind still continued light, so that some hours at least must elapse ere the ship could be brought to the anchorage, he bade his men return to the sealer and fetch back as much water as the whaleboat could carry, with whatever soft bread the steward might have, all the remaining pumpkins on board, with a box of sugar and a dozen of his private bottles of cider.

Not many minutes after the boat's pushing off, to the vexation of all, the wind entirely died away, and, the tide turning, began drifting back the ship helplessly seaward. But trusting this would not long last, Captain Delano sought, with good hopes, to cheer up the strangers, feeling no small satisfaction that, with persons in their condition, he could—thanks to his frequent voyages along the Spanish Main—converse with some freedom in their native tongue.

While left alone with them, he was not long in observing some things tending to heighten his first impressions; but surprise was lost in pity, both for the Spaniards and blacks, alike evidently reduced from scarcity of water and provisions, while long-continued suffering seemed to have brought out the less good-natured qualities of the Negroes, besides at the same time impairing the Spaniard's authority over them. But, under the circumstances, precisely this condition of things was to have been anticipated. In armies, navies, cities, or families, in nature herself, nothing more relaxes good order than misery. Still, Captain Delano was not without the idea that had Benito Cereno been a man of greater energy, misrule would hardly have come to the present pass. But the debility, constitutional or induced by hardships bodily and mental, of the Spanish captain was too obvious to be overlooked. A prey to settled dejection, as if long mocked with hope he would not now indulge it even when it had ceased to be a mock, the prospect of that day, or evening at furthest, lying at anchor, with plenty of water for his people, and a brother captain to counsel and befriend, seemed in no perceptible degree to encourage him. His mind appeared unstrung, if not still more seriously affected. Shut up in these oaken walls, chained to one dull round of command whose unconditionality cloyed him, like some hypochondriac abbot he moved slowly about, at times suddenly pausing, starting, or staring, biting his lip, biting his fingernail, flushing, paling, twitching his beard, with other symptoms of an absent or moody mind. This distempered spirit was lodged, as before hinted, in as distempered a frame. He was rather tall, but seemed never to have been robust, and now with nervous suffering was almost worn to a skeleton. A tendency to some pulmonary complaint appeared to have been lately confirmed. His voice was like that of one with lungs half gone—hoarsely suppressed, a husky whisper. No wonder that, as in this state he tottered about, his private servant apprehensively followed him. Sometimes the Negro gave his master his arm, or took his handkerchief out of his pocket for him; performing these and similar offices with that affectionate zeal which transmutes into something filial or fraternal acts in themselves but menial, and which has gained for the Negro the repute of making the most pleasing body servant in the world; one, too, whom a master need to be on no stiffly superior terms with, but may treat with familiar trust—less a servant than a devoted companion.

Marking the noisy indocility of the blacks in general, as well as what seemed the sullen inefficiency of the whites, it was not without humane satisfaction that Captain Delano witnessed the steady good conduct of Babo.

But the good conduct of Babo, hardly more than the ill-behavior of others, seemed to withdraw the half-lunatic Don Benito from his cloudy languor. Not that such precisely was the impression made by the Spaniard on the mind of his visitor. The Spaniard's individual unrest was, for the present, but noted as a conspicuous feature in the ship's general affliction. Still, Captain Delano was not a little concerned at what he could not help taking for the time to be Don Benito's unfriendly indifference towards himself. The Spaniard's manner, too, conveyed a sort of sour and gloomy disdain, which he seemed at no pains to disguise. But this the American in charity ascribed to the harassing effects of sickness, since, in former instances, he had noted that there are peculiar natures on whom prolonged physical suffering seems to cancel every social instinct of kindness, as if, forced to black bread themselves, they deemed it but equity that each person coming nigh them should, indirectly, by some slight or affront, be made to partake of their fare.

But erelong Captain Delano bethought him that, indulgent as he was at the first in judging the Spaniard, he might not after all have exercised charity enough. At bottom it was Don Benito's reserve which displeased him, but the same reserve was shown towards all but his faithful personal attendant. Even the formal reports which, according to sea usage, were, at stated times, made to him by some petty underling, either a white, mulatto, or black, he hardly had patience enough to listen to without betraying contemptuous aversion. His manner upon such occasions was, in its degree, not unlike that which might be supposed to have been his imperial countryman's, Charles V, just previous to the anchoritish retirement of the monarch from the throne.

This splenetic disrelish of his place was evinced in almost every function pertaining to it. Proud as he was moody, he condescended to no personal mandate. Whatever special orders were necessary, their delivery was delegated to his body servant, who in turn transferred them to their ultimate destination, through runners, alert Spanish boys or slave boys, like pages or pilot fish within easy call continually hovering round Don Benito. So that to have beheld this undemonstrative invalid gliding about, apathetic and mute, no landsman could have dreamed that in him was lodged a dictatorship beyond which, while at sea, there was no earthly appeal.

Thus the Spaniard, regarded in his reserve, seemed the involuntary victim of mental disorder. But, in fact, his reserve might, in some degree, have proceeded from design. If so, then here was evinced the unhealthy climax of that icy though conscientious policy more or less adopted by all commanders of large ships, which, except in signal emergencies, obliterates alike the manifestation of sway with every trace of sociality, transforming the man into a block, or rather into a loaded cannon, which, until there is call for thunder, has nothing to say.

Viewing him in this light, it seemed but a natural token of the perverse habit induced by a long course of such hard self-restraint that, notwithstanding the present condition of his ship, the Spaniard should still persist in a demeanor which, however harmless or, it may be, appropriate, in a well-appointed vessel, such as the *San Dominick* might have been at the outset of the voyage, was anything but judicious now. But the Spaniard, perhaps, thought that it was with captains as with gods: reserve, under all events, must still be their cue. But probably this appearance of slumbering dominion might have been but an attempted disguise to conscious imbecility—not deep policy, but shallow device. But be all this as it might, whether Don Benito's manner was designed or not, the more Captain Delano noted its pervading reserve, the less he felt uneasiness at any particular manifestation of that reserve towards himself.

Neither were his thoughts taken up by the captain alone. Wonted to the quiet orderliness of the sealer's comfortable family of a crew, the noisy confusion of the *San Dominick*'s suffering host repeatedly challenged his eye. Some prominent breaches, not only of discipline but of decency, were observed. These Captain Delano could not but ascribe, in the main, to the absence of those subordinated deck officers to whom, along with higher duties, is intrusted what may be styled the police department of a populous ship. True, the old oakum-pickers appeared at times to act the part of monitorial constables to their countrymen, the blacks, but though occasionally succeeding in slaying trifling outbreaks now and then between man and man, they could do little or nothing toward establishing general quiet. the *San Dominick* was in the condition of a transatlantic emigrant ship, among whose multitude of living freight are some individuals, doubtless, as little troublesome as crates and bales, but the friendly remonstrances of such with their ruder companions are of not so much avail as the unfriendly arm of the mate. What the *San Dominick* wanted was, what the emigrant ship has, stern superior officers. But on these decks not so much as a fourth mate was to be seen.

The visitor's curiosity was roused to learn the particulars of those mishaps which had brought about such absenteeism, with its consequences, because, though deriving some inkling of the voyage from the wails which at the first moment had greeted him, yet of the details no clear understanding had been had. The best account would, doubtless, be given by the captain. Yet at first the visitor was loath to ask it, unwilling to provoke some distant rebuff. But, plucking up courage, he at last accosted Don Benito, renewing the expression of his benevolent interest, adding that, did he (Captain Delano) but know the particulars of the ship's misfortunes, he would, perhaps, be better able in the end to relieve them. Would Don Benito favor him with the whole story?

Don Benito faltered, then, like some somnambulist suddenly interfered with, vacantly stared at his visitor, and ended by looking down on the deck. He maintained this posture so long that Captain Delano, almost equally disconcerted, and involuntarily almost as rude, turned suddenly from him, walking forward to accost one of the Spanish seamen for the desired information. But he had hardly gone five paces, when, with a sort of eagerness, Don Benito invited him back, regretting his momentary absence of mind, and professing readiness to gratify him.

While most part of the story was being given, the two captains stood on the after part of the main deck, a privileged spot, no one being near but the servant.

"It is now a hundred and ninety days," began the Spaniard, in his husky whisper, "that this ship, well officered and well manned, with several cabin passengers—some fifty Spaniards, in all—sailed from Buenos Ayres bound to Lima, with a general cargo, hardware, Paraguay tea and the like—and," pointing forward, "that parcel of Negroes, now not more than a hundred and fifty, as you see, but then numbering over three hundred souls. Off Cape Horn we had heavy gales. In one moment, by night, three of my best officers, with fifteen sailors, were lost, with the mainyard, the spar snapping under them in the slings as they sought, with heavers, to beat down the icy sail. To lighten the hull, the heavier sacks of maté were thrown into the sea, with most of the water pipes lashed on deck at the time. And this last necessity it was, combined with the prolonged detentions afterwards experienced, which eventually brought about our chief causes of suffering. When———"

Here there was a sudden fainting attack of his cough, brought on, no doubt, by his mental distress. His servant sustained him, and, drawing a cordial from his pocket, placed it to his lips. He a little revived. But, unwilling to leave him unsupported while yet imperfectly restored, the black with one arm still encircled his master, at the same time keeping his eye fixed on his face, as if to watch for the first sign of complete restoration, or relapse, as the event might prove.

The Spaniard proceeded, but brokenly and obscurely, as one in a dream.

—"Oh, my God! rather than pass through what I have, with joy I would have hailed the most terrible gales; but———"

His cough returned and with increased violence; this subsiding, with reddened lips and closed eyes he fell heavily against his supporter.

"His mind wanders. He was thinking of the plague that followed the gales," plaintively sighed the servant; "my poor, poor master!" wringing one hand, and with the other wiping the mouth. "But be patient, *señor*," again turning to Captain Delano, "these fits do not last long; master will soon be himself."

Don Benito reviving, went on; but, as this portion of the story was very brokenly delivered, the substance only will here be set down.

It appeared that after the ship had been many days tossed in storms off the Cape, the scurvy broke out, carrying off numbers of the whites and blacks. When at last they had worked round into the Pacific, their spars and sails were so damaged, and so inadequately handled by the surviving mariners, most of whom were become invalids that, unable to lay her northerly course by the wind, which was powerful, the unmanageable ship for successive days and nights was blown northwestward, where the breeze suddenly deserted her, in unknown waters to sultry calms. The absence of the water pipes now proved as fatal to life as before their presence had menaced it. Induced, or at least aggravated, by the more than scanty allowance of water, a malignant fever followed the scurvy, with the excessive heat of the lengthened calm making such short work of it as to sweep away, as by billows, whole families of the Africans, and a yet larger number, proportionally, of the Spaniards, including, by a luckless fatality, every remaining officer on board. Consequently, in the smart west winds eventually following the calm, the already rent sails, having to be simply dropped, not furled, at need, had been gradually reduced to the beggars' rags they were now. To procure substitutes for his lost sailors, as well as supplies of water and sails, the captain, at the earliest opportunity, had made for Baldivia, the southernmost civilized port of Chile and South America, but upon nearing the coast the thick weather had prevented him from so much as sighting that harbor. Since which period, almost without a crew, and almost without canvas and almost without water, and at intervals giving its added dead to the sea, the *San Dominick* had been battledored about by contrary winds, inveigled by currents, or grown weedy in calms. Like a man lost in woods, more than once she had doubled upon her own track.

"But throughout these calamities," huskily continued Don Benito, painfully turning in the half-embrace of his servant, "I have to thank those Negroes you see, who, though to your inexperienced eyes appearing unruly, have, indeed, conducted themselves with less of restlessness than even their owner could have thought possible under such circumstances."

Here he again fell faintly back. Again his mind wandered, but he rallied, and less obscurely proceeded.

"Yes, their owner was quite right in assuring me that no fetters would be needed with his blacks; so that while, as is wont in his transportation, those Negroes have always remained upon deck—not thrust below, as in the Guineamen—they have, also, from the beginning, been freely permitted to range within given bounds at their pleasure."

Once more the faintness returned—his mind roved—but, recovering, he resumed:

"But it is Babo here to whom, under God, I owe not only my own preservation, but likewise to him, chiefly, the merit is due of pacifying his more ignorant brethren, when at intervals tempted to murmurings."

"Ah, master," sighed the black, bowing his face, "don't speak of me; Babo is nothing; what Babo has done was but duty."

"Faithful fellow!" cried Captain Delano. "Don Benito, I envy you such a friend; slave I cannot call him."

As master and man stood before him, the black upholding the white, Captain Delano could not but bethink him of the beauty of that relationship which could present such a spectacle of fidelity on the one hand and confidence on the other. The scene was heightened by the contrast in dress, denoting their relative positions. The Spaniard wore a loose Chile jacket of dark velvet; white smallclothes and stockings, with silver buckles at the knee and instep; a high-crowned sombrero of fine grass; a slender sword, silver mounted, hung from a knot in his sash—the last being an almost invariable adjunct, more for utility than ornament, of a South American gentleman's dress to this hour. Excepting when his occasional nervous contortions brought about disarray, there was a certain precision in his attire curiously at variance with the unsightly disorder around, especially in the belittered ghetto, forward of the mainmast, wholly occupied by the blacks.

The servant wore nothing but wide trousers, apparently, from their coarseness and patches, made out of some old topsail; they were clean, and confined at the waist by a bit of unstranded rope, which, with his composed, deprecatory air at times, made him look something like a begging friar of St. Francis.

However unsuitable for the time and place, at least in the blunt-thinking American's eyes, and however strangely surviving in the midst of all his afflictions, the toilette of Don Benito might not, in fashion at least, have gone beyond the style of the day among South Americans of his class. Though on the present voyage sailing from Buenos Ayres, he had avowed himself a native and resident of Chile, whose inhabitants had not so generally adopted the plain coat and once plebeian pantaloons, but, with a becoming modification, adhered to their provincial costume, picturesque as any in the world. Still, relatively to the pale history of the voyage, and his own pale face, there seemed something so incongruous in the Spaniard's apparel as almost to suggest the image of an invalid courtier tottering about London streets in the time of the plague.

The portion of the narrative which perhaps most excited interest, as well as some surprise, considering the latitudes in question, was the long calms spoken of, and more particularly the ship's so long drifting about. Without communicating the opinion, of course, the American could not but impute at least part of the detentions both to clumsy seamanship and faulty navigation. Eying Don Benito's small, yellow hands, he easily inferred that the young captain had not got into command at the hawsehole, but the cabin window; and if so, why wonder at incompetence, in youth, sickness, and gentility united?

But, drowning criticism in compassion, after a fresh repetition of his sympathies, Captain Delano, having heard out his story, not only engaged, as in the first place, to see Don Benito and his people supplied in their immediate bodily needs, but, also now further promised to assist him in procuring a large permanent supply of water, as well as some sails and rigging; and, though it would involve no small embarrassment to himself, yet he would spare three of his best seamen for temporary deck officers, so that without delay the ship might proceed to Conception, there fully to refit for Lima, her destined port.

Such generosity was not without its effect, even upon the invalid. His face lighted up; eager and hectic, he met the honest glance of his visitor. With gratitude he seemed overcome.

"This excitement is bad for master," whispered the servant, taking his arm, and with soothing words gently drawing him aside.

When Don Benito returned, the American was pained to observe that his hopefulness, like the sudden kindling in his cheek, was but febrile and transient.

Erelong, with a joyless mien, looking up towards the poop, the host invited his guest to accompany him there, for the benefit of what little breath of wind might be stirring.

As, during the telling of the story, Captain Delano had once or twice started at the occasional cymbaling of the hatchet-polishers, wondering why such an interruption should be allowed, especially in that part of the ship, and in the ears of an invalid; and moreover, as the hatchets had anything but an attractive look, and the handlers of them still less so, it was, therefore, to tell the truth, not without some lurking reluctance, or even shrinking, it may be, that Captain Delano, with apparent complaisance, acquiesced in his host's invitation. The more so since, with an untimely caprice of punctilio, rendered distressing by his cadaverous aspect, Don Benito, with Castilian bows, solemnly insisted upon his guest's preceding him up the ladder leading to the elevation, where, one on each side of the last step, sat for armorial supporters and sentries two of the ominous file. Gingerly enough stepped good Captain Delano between them, and in the instant of leaving them behind, like one running the gantlet, he felt an apprehensive twitch in the calves of his legs.

But when, facing about, he saw the whole file, like so many organ-grinders, still stupidly intent on their work, unmindful of everything beside, he could not but smile at his late fidgety panic.

Presently, while standing with his host looking forward upon the decks below, he was struck by one of those instances of insubordination previously alluded to. Three black boys, with two Spanish boys, were sitting together on the hatches, scraping a rude wooden platter in which some scanty mess had recently been cooked. Suddenly one of the black boys, enraged at a word dropped by one of his white companions, seized a knife, and, though called to forbear by one of the oakum-pickers, struck the lad over the head, inflicting a gash from which blood flowed.

In amazement, Captain Delano inquired what this meant. To which the pale Don Benito dully muttered that it was merely the sport of the lad.

"Pretty serious sport, truly," rejoined Captain Delano. "Had such a thing happened on board the *Bachelor's Delight*, instant punishment would have followed."

At these words the Spaniard turned upon the American one of his sudden, staring, half-lunatic looks, then, relapsing into his torpor, answered, "Doubtless, doubtless, *señor*."

Is it, thought Captain Delano, that this hapless man is one of those paper captains I've known, who by policy wink at what by power they cannot put down? I know no sadder sight than a commander who has little of command but the name.

"I should think, Don Benito," he now said, glancing toward the oakum-picker who had sought to interfere with the boys, "that you would find it advantageous to keep all your blacks employed, especially the younger ones, no matter at what useless task, and no matter what happens to the ship. Why, even with my little band, I find such a course indispensable. I once kept a crew on my quarter-deck thrumming mats for my cabin, when, for three days, I had given up my ship—mats, men, and all—for a speedy loss, owing to the violence of a gale, in which we could do nothing but helplessly drive before it."

"Doubtless, doubtless," muttered Don Benito.

"But," continued Captain Delano, again glancing upon the oakum-pickers and then at the hatchet-polishers, near by, "I see you keep some, at least, of your host employed."

"Yes," was again the vacant response.

"Those old men there, shaking their pows from their pulpits," continued Captain Delano, pointing to the oakum-pickers, "seem to act the part of old dominies to the rest, little heeded as their admonitions are at times. Is this voluntary on their part, Don Benito, or have you appointed them shepherds to your flock of black sheep?"

"What posts they fill, I appointed them," rejoined the Spaniard, in an acrid tone, as if resenting some supposed satiric reflection.

"And these others, these Ashantee conjurers here," continued Captain Delano, rather uneasily eying the brandished steel of the hatchet-polishers, where in spots, it had been brought to a shine, "this seems a curious business they are at, Don Benito?"

"In the gales we met," answered the Spaniard, "what of our general cargo was not thrown overboard was much damaged by the brine. Since coming into calm weather, I have had several cases of knives and hatchets daily brought up for overhauling and cleaning."

"A prudent idea, Don Benito. You are part owner of ship and cargo, I presume; but none of the slaves, perhaps?"

"I am owner of all you see," impatiently returned Don Benito, "except the main company of blacks, who belonged to my late friend, Alexandro Aranda."

As he mentioned this name, his air was heartbroken; his knees shook; his servant supported him.

Thinking he divined the cause of such unusual emotion, to confirm his surmise Captain Delano after a pause said: "And may I ask, Don Benito, whether—since awhile ago you spoke of some cabin passengers—the friend, whose loss so afflicts you, at the outset of the voyage accompanied his blacks?"

"Yes."

"But died of the fever?"

"Died of the fever. Oh, could I but———"

Again quivering, the Spaniard paused.

"Pardon me," said Captain Delano, lowly, "but I think that, by a sympathetic experience, I conjecture, Don Benito, what it is that gives the keener edge to your grief. It was once my hard fortune to lose, at sea, a dear friend, my own brother, then supercargo. Assured of the welfare of his spirit, its departure I could have borne like a man, but that honest eye, that honest hand—both of which had so often met mine—and that warm heart—all, all—like scraps to the dogs—to throw all to the sharks! It was then I vowed never to have for fellow voyager a man I loved, unless, unbeknown to him, I have provided every requisite, in case of a fatality, for embalming his mortal part for interment on shore. Were your friend's remains now on board this ship, Don Benito, not thus strangely would the mention of his name affect you."

"On board this ship?" echoed the Spaniard. Then, with horrified gestures, as directed against some specter, he unconsciously fell into the ready arms of his attendant, who, with a silent appeal toward Captain Delano, seemed beseeching him not again to broach a theme so unspeakably distressing to his master.

This poor fellow now, thought the pained American, is the victim of that sad superstition which associates goblins with the deserted body of man, as ghosts with an abandoned house. How unlike are we made! what to me, in like case, would have been a solemn satisfaction, the bare suggestion, even, terrifies the Spaniard into this trance. Poor Alexandro Aranda! what would you say could you here see your friend—who on former voyages, when you for months were left behind, has,

I dare say, often longed and longed for one peep at you—not transported with terror at the least thought of having you anyway nigh him.

At this moment, with a dreary graveyard toll betokening a flaw, the ship's forecastle bell, smote by one of the grizzled oakum-pickers, proclaimed ten o'clock through the leaden calm, when Captain Delano's attention was caught by the moving figure of a gigantic black emerging from the general crowd below and slowly advancing towards the elevated poop. An iron collar was about his neck, from which depended a chain thrice wound round his body, the terminating link padlocked together at a broad band of iron, his girdle.

"How like a mute Atufal moves," murmured the servant.

The black mounted the steps of the poop, and, like a brave prisoner brought up to receive sentence, stood in unquailing muteness before Don Benito, now recovered from his attack.

At the first glimpse of his approach, Don Benito had started; a resentful shadow swept over his face, and, as with the sudden memory of bootless rage, his white lips glued together.

This is some mulish mutineer, thought Captain Delano, surveying, not without a mixture of admiration, the colossal form of the Negro.

"See, he waits your question, master," said the servant.

Thus reminded, Don Benito, nervously averting his glance as if shunning, by anticipation, some rebellious response, in a disconcerted voice, thus spoke:

"Atufal, will you ask my pardon now?"

The black was silent.

"Again, master," murmured the servant, with bitter upbraiding eying his countryman; "Again, master; he will bend to master yet."

"Answer," said Don Benito, still averting his glance, "say but the one word, *pardon*, and your chains shall be off."

Upon this, the black, slowly raising both arms, let them lifelessly fall, his links clanking, his head bowed; as much as to say, "No, I am content."

"Go," said Don Benito, with inkept and unknown emotion.

Deliberately as he had come, the black obeyed.

"Excuse me, Don Benito," said Captain Delano, "but this scene surprises me; what means it, pray?"

"It means that that Negro alone, of all the band, has given me peculiar cause of offense. I have put him in chains; I———"

Here he paused; his hand to his head, as if there were a swimming there, or a sudden bewilderment of memory had come over him; but meeting his servant's kindly glance seemed reassured, and proceeded:

"I could not scourge such a form. But I told him he must ask my pardon. As yet he has not. At my command, every two hours he stands before me."

"And how long has this been?"

"Some sixty days."

"And obedient in all else? And respectful?"

"Yes."

"Upon my conscience, then," exclaimed Captain Delano, impulsively, "he has a royal spirit in him, this fellow."

"He may have some right to it," bitterly returned Don Benito, "he says he was king in his own land."

"Yes," said the servant, entering a word, "those slits in Atufal's ears once held wedges of gold; but poor Babo here, in his own land, was only a poor slave; a black man's slave was Babo, who now is the white's."

Somewhat annoyed by these conversational familiarities, Captain Delano turned curiously upon the attendant, then glanced inquiringly at his master; but, as if long wonted to these little informalities, neither master nor man seemed to understand him.

"What, pray, was Atufal's offense, Don Benito?" asked Captain Delano; "if it was not something very serious, take a fool's advice, and, in view of his general docility, as well as in some natural respect for his spirit, remit him his penalty."

"No, no, master will ever do that," here murmured the servant to himself, "proud Atufal must first ask master's pardon. The slave there carries the padlock, but master here carries the key."

His attention thus directed, Captain Delano now noticed for the first time that, suspended by a slender silken cord from Don Benito's neck, hung a key. At once, from the servant's muttered syllables, divining the key's purpose, he smiled and said: "So, Don Benito—padlock and key—significant symbols, truly."

Biting his lip, Don Benito faltered.

Though the remark of Captain Delano, a man of such native simplicty as to be incapable of satire or irony, had been dropped in playful allusion to the Spaniard's singularly evidenced lordship over the black, yet the hypochondriac seemed some way to have taken it as a malicious reflection upon his confessed inability thus far to break down, at least on a verbal summons, the entrenched will of the slave. Deploring this supposed misconception, yet despairing of correcting it, Captain Delano shifted the subject; but finding his companion more than ever withdrawn, as if still sourly digesting the lees of the presumed affront above mentioned, by and by Captain Delano likewise became less talkative, oppressed, against his own will, by what seemed the secret vindictiveness of the morbidly sensitive Spaniard. But the good sailor, himself of a quite contrary disposition, refrained on his part alike from the appearance as from the feeling of resentment, and if silent, was only so from contagion.

Presently the Spaniard, assisted by his servant, somewhat discourteously crossed over from his guest, a procedure which, sensibly enough, might have been allowed to pass for idle caprice of ill-humor had not master and man, lingering round the corner of the elevated skylight, began whispering together in low voices. This was unpleasing. And more: the moody air of the Spaniard, which at times had not been without a sort of valetudinarian stateliness, now seemed anything but dignified, while the menial familiarity of the servant lost its original charm of simplehearted attachment.

In his embarrassment, the visitor turned his face to the other side of the ship. By so doing, his glance accidentally fell on a young Spanish sailor, a coil of rope in his hand, just stepped from the deck to the first round of the mizzen rigging. Perhaps the man would not have been particularly noticed were it not that, during his ascent to one of the yards, he, with a sort of covert intentness, kept his eye fixed on Captain Delano, from whom, presently, it passed, as if by a natural sequence, to the two whisperers.

His own attention thus redirected to that quarter, Captain Delano gave a slight start. From something in Don Benito's manner just then, it seemed as if the visitor had, at least partly, been the subject of the withdrawn consultation going on—a conjecture as little agreeable to the guest as it was flattering to the host.

The singular alternations of courtesy and ill-breeding in the Spanish captain were unaccountable, except on one of two suppositions—innocent lunacy, or wicked imposture.

But the first idea, though it might naturally have occurred to an indifferent observer, and, in some respect, had not hitherto been wholly a stranger to Captain Delano's mind, yet, now that, in an incipient way, he began to regard the stranger's conduct something in the light of an intentional affront, of course the idea of lunacy was virtually vacated. But if not a lunatic, what then? Under the circumstances, would a gentleman, nay, any honest boor, act the part now acted by his host? The man was an impostor. Some low-born adventurer, masquerading as an oceanic grandee, yet so ignorant of the first requisites of mere gentlemanhood as to be betrayed into the present remarkable indecorum. That strange ceremoniousness, too, at other times evinced, seemed not uncharacteristic of one playing a part above his real level. Benito Cereno—Don Benito Cereno—a sounding name. One, too, at that period, not unknown, in the surname, to supercargoes and sea captains trading along the Spanish Main, as belonging to one of the most enterprising and extensive mercantile families in all those provinces, several members of it having titles; a sort of Castilian Rothschild, with a noble brother, or cousin, in every great trading town of South America. The alleged Don Benito was in early manhood, about twenty-nine or thirty. To assume a sort of roving cadetship in the maritime affairs of such a house, what more likely scheme for a young knave of talent and spirit? But the Spaniard was a pale invalid. Never mind. For even to the degree of simulating mortal disease, the craft of some tricksters had been known to attain. To think that, under the aspect of infantile weakness, the most savage energies might be couched—those velvets of the Spaniard but the silky paw to his fangs.

From no train of thought did these fancies come; not from within, but from without; suddenly, too, and in one thing, like hoarfrost, yet as soon to vanish, as the mild sun of Captain Delano's good nature regained its meridian.

Glancing over once more towards his host—whose side face, revealed above the skylight, was now turned towards him—he was struck by the profile, whose clearness of cut was refined by the thinness incident to ill-health, as well as ennobled about the chin by the beard. Away with suspicion. He was a true offshoot of a true hidalgo Cereno.

Relieved by these and other better thoughts, the visitor, lightly humming a tune, now began indifferently pacing the poop, so as not to betray to Don Benito that he had at all mistrusted incivility, much less duplicity; for such mistrust would yet be proved illusory, and by the event, though, for the present, the circumstance which had provoked that distrust remained unexplained. But when that little mystery should have been cleared up, Captain Delano thought he might extremely regret it did he allow Don Benito to become aware that he had indulged in ungenerous surmises. In short, to the Spaniard's black-letter text, it was best, for a while, to leave open margin.

Presently, his pale face twitching and overcast, the Spaniard, still supported by his attendant, moved over towards his guest, when, with even more than his usual embarrassment, and a strange sort of intriguing intonation in his husky whisper, the following conversation began:

"*Señor*, may I ask how long you have lain at this isle?"

"Oh, but a day or two, Don Benito."

"And from what port are you last?"

"Canton."

"And there, *señor*, you exchanged your sealskins for teas and silks, I think you said?"

"Yes. Silks, mostly."

"And the balance you took in specie, perhaps?"

Captain Delano, fidgeting a little, answered, "Yes; some silver; not a very great deal, though."

"Ah—well. May I ask how many men have you, *señor?*"

Captain Delano slightly started, but answered, "About five-and-twenty, all told."

"And at present, *señor*, all on board, I suppose?"

"All on board, Don Benito," replied the Captain, now with satisfaction.

"And will be tonight, *señor?*"

At this last question, following so many pertinacious ones, for the soul of him Captain Delano could not but look very earnestly at the questioner, who, instead of meeting the glance, with every token of craven discomposure dropped his eyes to the deck; presenting an unworthy contrast to his servant, who, just then, was kneeling at his feet, adjusting a loose shoe buckle, his disengaged face meantime, with humble curiosity, turned openly up into his master's downcast one.

The Spaniard, still with a guilty shuffle, repeated his question:

"And—and will be tonight, *señor?*"

"Yes, for aught I know," returned Captain Delano—"but nay," rallying himself into fearless truth, "some of them talked of going off on another fishing party about midnight."

"Your ships generally go—go more or less armed, I believe, *señor?*"

"Oh, a six-pounder or two, in case of emergency," was the intrepidly indifferent reply, "with a small stock of muskets, sealing spears, and cutlasses, you know."

As he thus responded, Captain Delano again glanced at Don Benito, but the latter's eyes were averted, while, abruptly and awkwardly shifting the subject, he made some peevish allusion to the calm, and then, without apology, once more, with his attendant, withdrew to the opposite bulwarks, where the whispering was resumed.

At this moment, and ere Captain Delano could cast a cool thought upon what had just passed, the young Spanish sailor before mentioned was seen descending from the rigging. In act of stooping over to spring inboard to the deck, his voluminous, unconfined frock, or shirt, of coarse woolen, much spotted with tar, opened out far down the chest, revealing a soiled undergarment of what seemed the finest linen, edged, about the neck, with a narrow blue ribbon, sadly faded and worn. At this moment the young sailor's eye was again fixed on the whisperers, and Captain Delano thought he observed a lurking significance in it, as if silent signs, of some Freemason sort, had that instant been interchanged.

This once more impelled his own glance in the direction of Don Benito, and, as before, he could not but infer that himself formed the subject of the conference. He paused. The sound of the hatchet-polishing fell on his ears. He cast another swift side look at the two. They had the air of conspirators. In connection with the late questionings, and the incident of the young sailor, these things now begat such return of involuntary suspicion that the singular guilelessness of the American could not endure it. Plucking up a gay and humorous expression, he crossed over to the two rapidly, saying: "Ha, Don Benito, your black here seems high in your trust, a sort of privy councilor, in fact."

Upon this, the servant looked up with a good-natured grin, but the master started as from a venomous bite. It was a moment or two before the Spaniard sufficiently recovered himself to reply; which he did at last, with cold constraint: "Yes, *señor*, I have trust in Babo."

Here Babo, changing his previous grin of mere animal humor into an intelligent smile, not ungratefully eyed his master.

Finding that the Spaniard now stood silent and reserved, as if involuntarily, or purposely giving hint that his guest's proximity was inconvenient just then, Captain Delano, unwilling to appear uncivil even to incivility itself, made some trivial remark and moved off, again and again turning over in his mind the mysterious demeanor of Don Benito Cereno.

He had descended from the poop, and, wrapped in thought, was passing near a dark hatchway leading down into the steerage, when, perceiving motion there, he looked to see what moved. The same instant there was a sparkle in the shadowy hatchway and he saw one of the Spanish sailors, prowling there, hurriedly placing his hand in the bosom of his frock, as if hiding something. Before the man could have been certain who it was that was passing, he slunk below out of sight. But enough was seen of him to make it sure that he was the same young sailor before noticed in the rigging.

What was that which so sparkled? thought Captain Delano. It was no lamp—no match—no live coal. Could it have been a jewel? But how come sailors with jewels?—or with silk-trimmed undershirts either? Has he been robbing the trunks of the dead cabin passengers? But if so he would hardly wear one of the stolen articles on board ship here. Ah, ah—if, now, that was indeed, a secret sign I saw passing between this suspicious fellow and his captain awhile since; if I could only be certain that, in my uneasiness, my senses did not deceive me, then————

Here, passing from one suspicious thing to another, his mind revolved the strange questions put to him concerning his ship.

By a curious coincidence, as each point was recalled, the black wizards of Ashantee would strike up with their hatchets, as in ominous comment on the white stranger's thoughts. Pressed by such enigmas and portents, it would have been almost against nature had not, even into the least distrustful heart, some ugly misgivings obtruded.

Observing the ship, now helplessly fallen into a current, with enchanted sails drifting with increased rapidity seaward, and noting that, from a lately intercepted projection of the land, the sealer was hidden, the stout mariner began to quake at thoughts which he barely durst confess to himself. Above all, he began to feel a ghostly dread of Don Benito. And yet, when he roused himself, dilated his chest, felt himself strong on his legs, and coolly considered it—what did all these phantoms amount to?

Had the Spaniard any sinister scheme, it must have reference not so much to him (Captain Delano) as to his ship (the *Bachelor's Delight*). Hence the present drifting away of the one ship from the other, instead of favoring any such possible scheme, was, for the time at least, opposed to it. Clearly any suspicion combining such contradictions must need to be delusive. Beside, was it not absurd to think of a vessel in distress—a vessel by sickness almost dismanned of her crew—a vessel whose inmates were parched for water—was it not a thousand times absurd that such a craft should, at present, be of a piratical character; or her commander, either for himself or those under him, cherish any desire but for speedy relief and refreshment? But, then, might not general distress, and thirst in particular, be affected? And might not that same undiminished Spanish crew, alleged to have perished off to a remnant, be at that very moment lurking in the hold? On heartbroken pretense of entreating a cup of cold water, fiends in human form had got into lonely dwellings, nor retired until a dark deed had been done. And among the Malay pirates it was no unusual thing to lure ships after them into their treacherous harbors, or entice boarders from a declared enemy at sea, by the spectacle of thinly manned or vacant decks, beneath which prowled a hundred spears with yellow arms ready to upthrust them through the mats. Not that Captain Delano had entirely credited such things. He had heard of them—and now, as stories, they recurred. The present destination of the ship was the anchorage. There she would be near his own vessel. Upon gaining that vicinity, might not the *San Dominick*, like a slumbering volcano, suddenly let loose energies now hid?

He recalled the Spaniard's manner while telling his story. There was a gloomy hesitancy and subterfuge about it. It was just the manner of one making up his tale for evil purposes, as he goes. But if that story was not true, what was the truth? That the ship had unlawfully come into the Spaniard's possession? But in many of its details, especially in reference to the more calamitous parts, such as the fatalities among the seamen, the consequent prolonged beating about, the past sufferings from obstinate calms and still continued suffering from thirst; in all these points, as well as others, Don Benito's story had collaborated not only the wailing ejaculations of the indiscriminate multitude, white and black, but likewise—what seemed impossible to be counterfeit—by the very expression and play of every human feature which Captain Delano saw. If Don Benito's story was throughout an invention, then every soul on board, down to the youngest Negress, was his carefully drilled recruit in the plot: an incredible inference. And yet, if there was ground for mistrusting his veracity, that inference was a legitimate one.

But those questions of the Spaniard. There, indeed, one might pause. Did they not seem put with much the same object with which the burglar or assassin, by daytime, reconnoiters the walls of a house? But, with ill purposes to solicit such information openly of the chief person endangered, and so, in effect, setting him on his guard—how unlikely a procedure was that? Absurd, then, to suppose that those questions had been prompted by evil designs. Thus, the same conduct which in this instance had raised the alarm, served to dispel. It short, scarce any suspicion or uneasiness, however apparently reasonable at the time, which was not now with equal apparent reason dismissed.

At last he began to laugh at his former forebodings, and laugh at the strange ship for, in its aspect, someway siding with them, as it were; and laugh, too, at the odd-looking blacks, particularly those old scissors-grinders, the Ashantees; and those bed-ridden old knitting women, the oakum-pickers; and almost at the dark Spaniard himself, the central hobgoblin of all.

For the rest, whatever in a serious way seemed enigmatical was now good-naturedly explained away by the thought that, for the most part, the poor invalid scarcely knew what he was about; either sulking in black vapors, or putting idle questions without sense or object. Evidently, for the present the man was not fit to be intrusted with the ship. On some benevolent plea withdrawing the command from him, Captain Delano would yet have to send her to Conception, in charge of his second mate, a worthy person and good navigator—a plan not more convenient for the *San Dominick* than for Don Benito; for, relieved from all anxiety, keeping wholly to his cabin, the sick man, under the good nursing of his servant, would, probably, by the end of the passage, be in a measure restored to health, and with that he should also be restored to authority.

Such were the American's thoughts. They were tranquilizing. There was a difference between the idea of Don Benito's darkly preordaining Captain Delano's fate and Captain Delano's lightly arranging Don Benito's. Nevertheless, it was not without something of relief that the good seaman presently perceived his whaleboat in the distance. Its absence had been prolonged by unexpected detention at the sealer's side, as well as its returning trip lengthened by the continual recession of the goal.

The advancing speck was observed by the blacks. Their shouts attracted the attention of Don Benito, who, with a return of courtesy approaching Captain Delano, expressed satisfaction at the coming of some supplies, slight and temporary as they must necessarily prove.

Captain Delano responded, but while doing so, his attention was drawn to something passing on the deck below: among the crowd climbing the landward bulwarks, anxiously watching the coming boat, two blacks, to all appearances accidentally incommoded by one of the sailors, violently pushed him aside, which the sailor someway resenting, they dashed him to the deck, despite the earnest cries of the oakum-pickers.

"Don Benito," said Captain Delano quickly, "do you see what is going on there? Look!"

But, seized by his cough, the Spaniard staggered, with both hands to his face, on the point of falling. Captain Delano would have supported him, but the servant was more alert, who, with one hand sustaining his master, with the other applied the cordial. Don Benito restored, the black withdrew his support, slipping aside a little, but dutifully remaining within call of a whisper. Such discretion was here evinced as quite wiped away, in the visitor's eyes, any blemish of impropriety which might have attached to the attendant from the indecorous conferences before mentioned, showing, too, that if the servant were to blame it might be more the master's fault than his own, since, when left to himself, he could conduct thus well.

His glance called away from the spectacle of disorder to the more pleasing one before him, Captain Delano could not avoid again congratulating his host upon possessing such a servant, who, though perhaps a little too forward now and then, must upon the whole be invaluable to one in the invalid's situation.

"Tell me, Don Benito," he added, with a smile—"I should like to have your man here myself—what will you take for him? Would fifty doubloons be any object?"

"Master wouldn't part with Babo for a thousand doubloons," murmured the black, overhearing the offer, and taking it in earnest, and, with the strange vanity of a faithful slave appreciated by his master, scorning to hear so paltry a valuation put upon him by a stranger. But Don Benito, apparently hardly yet completely restored, and again interrupted by his cough, made but some broken reply.

Soon his physical distress became so great, affecting his mind, too, apparently, that, as if to screen the sad spectacle, the servant gently conducted his master below.

Left to himself, the American, to while away the time till his boat should arrive, would have pleasantly accosted some one of the few Spanish seamen he saw, but recalling something that Don Benito had said touching their ill conduct, he refrained, as a shipmaster indisposed to countenance cowardice or unfaithfulness in seamen.

While, with these thoughts, standing with eye directed forward towards that handful of sailors, suddenly he thought that one or two of them returned the glance and with a sort of meaning. He rubbed his eyes and looked again, but again seemed to see the same thing. Under a new form, but more obscure than any previous one, the old suspicions recurred, but, in the absence of Don Benito, with less of panic than before. Despite the bad account given of the sailors, Captain Delano resolved forthwith to accost one of them. Descending the poop, he made his way through the blacks, his movement drawing a queer cry from the oakum-pickers, prompted by whom, the Negroes, twitching each other aside, divided before him, but, as if curious to see what was the object of this deliberate visit to their ghetto, closing in behind in tolerable order, followed the white stranger up. His progress thus proclaimed as by mounted kings-at-arms, and escorted as by a Kaffir guard of honor, Captain Delano, assuming a good-humored, off-handed air, continued to advance; now and then saying a blithe word to the Negroes, and his eye curiously surveying the white faces, here and there sparsely mixed in with the blacks, like stray white pawns venturously involved in the ranks of the chess-men opposed.

While thinking which of them to select for his purposes, he chanced to observe a sailor seated on the deck engaged in tarring the strap of a large block, a circle of blacks squatted round him inquisitively eying the process.

The mean employment of the man was in contrast with something superior in his figure. His hand, black with continually thrusting it into the tarpot held for him by a Negro, seemed not naturally allied to his face, a face which would have been a very fine one but for its haggardness. Whether this haggardness had aught to do with criminality could not be determined, since, as intense heat and cold, though unlike, produce like sensations, so innocence and guilt, when, through casual association with mental pain stamping any visible impress, use one seal—a hacked one.

Not again that this reflection occurred to Captain Delano at the time, charitable man as he was. Rather another idea. Because observing so singular a haggardness combined with a dark eye, averted as in trouble and shame, and then again recalling Don Benito's confessed ill opinion of his crew, insensible, he was oper-ated upon by certain general notions which, while disconnecting pain and abash-ment from virtue, invariably link them with vice.

If, indeed, there be any wickedness on board this ship, thought Captain Delano, be sure that man there has fouled his hand in it, even as now he fouls it in the pitch. I don't like to accost him. I will speak to this other, this old Jack here on the windlass.

He advanced to an old Barcelona tar, in ragged red breeches and dirty night-cap, cheeks trenched and bronzed, whiskers dense as thorn hedges. Seated be-tween two sleepy-looking Africans, this mariner, like his younger shipmate, was employed upon some rigging—splicing a cable—the sleepy-looking blacks per-forming the inferior function of holding the outer parts of the ropes for him.

Upon Captain Delano's approach, the man at once hung his head below its previous level; the one necessary for business. It appeared as if he desired to be thought absorbed with more than common fidelity in his task. Being addressed, he glanced up, but with what seemed a furtive, diffident air, which sat strangely enough on his weather-beaten visage, much as if a grizzly bear, instead of growling and biting, should simper and cast sheep's eyes. He was asked several questions concerning the voyage—questions purposely referring to several particulars in Don Benito's narrative, not previously corroborated by those impulsive cries greet-ing the visitor on first coming on board. The questions were briefly answered, confirming all that remained to be confirmed of the story. The Negroes about the windlass joined in with the old sailor, but, as they became talkative, he by degrees became mute, and at length quite glum, seemed morosely unwilling to answer more questions, and yet, all the while, this ursine air was somehow mixed with his sheepish one.

Despairing of getting into unembarrassed talk with such a centaur, Captain Delano, after glancing round for a more promising countenance but seeing none, spoke pleasantly to the blacks to make way for him, and so, amid various grins and grimaces, returned to the poop, feeling a little strange at first, he could hardly tell why, but upon the whole with regained confidence in Benito Cereno.

How plainly, thought he, did that old whiskerando yonder betray a conscious-ness of ill desert. No doubt when he saw me coming he dreaded lest I, apprised by his captain of the crew's general misbehavior, came with sharp words for him, and so down with his head. And yet—and yet, now that I think of it, that very old fellow, if I err not, was one of those who seemed so earnestly eying me here awhile since. Ah, these currents spin one's head round almost as much as they do the ship. Ha, there now's a pleasant sort of sunny sight; quite sociable, too.

His attention had been drawn to a slumbering Negress, partly disclosed through the lacework of some rigging, lying, with youthful limbs carelessly disposed, under the lee of the bulwarks, like a doe in the shade of a woodland rock. Sprawling at her lapped breasts was her wide-awake fawn, stark naked, its black little body half lifted from the deck, crosswise with its dam's; its hands, like two paws, clambering upon her; its mouth and nose ineffectually rooting to get at the mark; and mean-time giving a vexatious half-grunt, blending with the composed snore of the Negress.

The uncommon vigor of the child at length roused the mother. She started up, at a distance facing Captain Delano. But as if not at all concerned at the attitude in which she had been caught, delightedly she caught the child up, with maternal transports, covering it with kisses.

There's naked nature, now, pure tenderness and love, thought Captain Delano, well pleased.

This incident prompted him to remark the other Negresses more particularly than before. He was gratified with their manners: like most uncivilized women, they seemed at once tender of heart and tough of constitution, equally ready to die for their infants or fight for them. Unsophisticated as leopardesses, loving as doves. Ah! thought Captain Delano, these, perhaps, are some of the very women whom Ledyard saw in Africa, and gave such a noble account of.

These natural sights somehow insensibly deepened his confidence and ease. At last he looked to see how his boat was getting on, but it was still pretty remote. He turned to see if Don Benito had returned, but he had not.

To change the scene, as well as to please himself with a leisurely observation of the coming boat, stepping over into the mizzen-chains, he clambered his way into the starboard quarter-gallery—one of those abandoned Venetian-looking water balconies previously mentioned—retreats cut off from the deck. As his foot pressed the half-damp, half-dry sea mosses matting the place, and a chance phan-tom cat's-paw—an islet of breeze, unheralded, unfollowed—as if this ghostly cat's-paw came fanning his cheek; as his glance fell upon the row of small, round, deadlights—all closed like coppered eyes of the coffined—and the state-cabin door, once connecting with the gallery, even as the deadlights had once looked out upon it, but now calked fast like a sarcophagus lid; and to a purple-black, tarred-over panel, threshold, and post; and he bethought him of the time when the state cabin and this state balcony had heard the voices of the Spanish king's officers, and the forms of the Lima viceroy's daughters had perhaps leaned where he stood—as these and other images flitted through his mind as the cat's-paw through the calm, gradually he felt rising a dreamy inquietude, like that of one who alone on the prairie feels unrest from the repose of the noon.

He leaned against the carved balustrade, again looking off toward his boat, but found his eye falling upon the ribbon grass, trailing along the ship's water line, straight as a border of green box, and parterres of seaweed, broad ovals and crescents, floating nigh and far, with what seemed long formal alleys between, crossing the terraces of swells, and sweeping round as if leading to the grottoes below. And overhanging all was the balustrade by his arm, which, partly stained with pitch and partly embossed with moss, seemed the charred ruin of some summerhouse in a grand garden long running to waste.

Trying to break one charm, he was but becharmed anew. Though upon the wide sea, he seemed in some far inland country, prisoner in some deserted château, left to stare at empty grounds and peer out at vague roads where never wagon or wayfarer passed.

But these enchantments were a little disenchanted as his eye fell on the corroded mainchains. Of an ancient style, massy and rusty in link, shackle, and bolt, they seemed even more fit for the ship's present business than the one for which she had been built.

Presently he thought something moved nigh the chains. He rubbed his eyes, and looked hard. Groves of rigging were about the chains; and there, peering from behind a great stay, like an Indian from behind a hemlock, a Spanish sailor, a marlingspike in his hand, was seen, who made what seemed an imperfect gesture towards the balcony, but immediately, as if alarmed by some advancing step along the deck within, vanished into the recesses of the hempen forest like a poacher.

What meant this? Something the man had sought to communicate, unbeknown to anyone, even to his captain. Did the secret involve aught unfavorable to his captain? Were those previous misgivings of Captain Delano's about to be verified? Or, in his haunted mood at the moment, had some random, unintentional motion of the man, while busy with the stay as if repairing it, been mistaken for a significant beckoning?

Not unbewildered, again he gazed off for his boat. But it was temporarily hidden by a rocky spur of the isle. As with some eagerness he bent forward, watching for the first shooting view of its beak, the balustrade gave way before him like charcoal. Had he not clutched an outreaching rope he would have fallen into the sea. The crash, though feeble, and the fall, though hollow, of the rotten fragments, must have been overheard. He glanced up. With sober curiosity peering down upon him was one of the old oakum-pickers, slipped from his perch to an outside boom, while below the old Negro, and, invisible to him, reconnoitering from a porthole like a fox from the mouth of its den, crouched the Spanish sailor again. From something suddenly suggested by the man's air, the mad idea now darted into Captain Delano's mind that Don Benito's plea of indisposition, in withdrawing below, was but a pretense: that he was engaged there maturing his plot, of which the sailor, by some means gaining an inkling, had a mind to warn the stranger against, incited, it may be, by gratitude for a kind word on first boarding the ship. Was it from foreseeing some possible interference like this that Don Benito had, beforehand, given such a bad character of his sailors, while praising the Negroes, though, indeed, the former seemed as docile as the latter the contrary? The whites, too, by nature, were the shrewder race. A man with some evil design, would he not be likely to speak well of that stupidity which was blind to his depravity, and malign that intelligence from which it might not be hidden? Not unlikely, perhaps. But if the whites had dark secrets concerning Don Benito, could then Don Benito be any way in complicity with the blacks? But they were too stupid. Besides, who ever heard of a white so far a renegade as to apostatize from his very species almost, by leaguing in against it with Negroes? These difficulties recalled former ones. Lost in their mazes, Captain Delano, who had now regained the deck, was uneasily advancing along it when he observed a new face; an aged sailor seated cross-legged near the main hatchway. His skin was shrunk up with wrinkles like a pelican's empty pouch, his hair frosted, his countenance grave and composed. His hands were full of ropes, which he was working into a large knot. Some blacks were about him obligingly dipping the strands for him, here and there, as the exigencies of the operation demanded.

Captain Delano crossed over to him and stood in silence surveying the knot, his mind, by a not uncongenial transition, passing from its own entanglements to those of the hemp. For intricacy, such a knot he had never seen in an American ship, nor indeed any other. The old man looked like an Egyptian priest making Gordian knots for the temple of Ammon. The knot seemed a combination of double-bowline-knot, treble-crown-knot, back-handed-well-knot, knot-in-and-out-knot, and jamming knot.

At last, puzzled to comprehend the meaning of such a knot, Captain Delano addressed the knotter: "What are you knotting there, my man?"

"The knot," was the brief reply, without looking up.

"So it seems; but what is it for?"

"For someone else to undo," muttered back the old man, plying his fingers harder than ever, the knot being now nearly completed.

While Captain Delano stood watching him, suddenly the old man threw the knot towards him, saying in broken English—the first heard in the ship—something to this effect: "Undo it, cut it, quick." It was said lowly, but with such condensation of rapidity, that the long, slow words in Spanish, which had preceded and followed, almost operated as covers to the brief English between.

For a moment, knot in hand, and knot in head, Captain Delano stood mute, while, without further heeding him, the old man was now intent upon other ropes. Presently there was a slight stir behind Captain Delano. Turning, he saw the chained Negro, Atufal, standing quietly there. The next moment the old sailor rose, muttering, and, followed by his subordinate Negroes, removed to the forward part of the ship, where in the crowd he disappeared.

An elderly Negro, in a clout like an infant's, and with a pepper-and-salt head and a kind of attorney air, now approached Captain Delano. In tolerable Spanish, and with a good-natured, knowing wink, he informed him that the old knotter was simple-witted, but harmless, often playing his odd tricks. The Negro concluded by begging the knot, for of course the stranger would not care to be troubled with it. Unconsciously, it was handed to him. With a sort of *congé*, the Negro received it, and, turning his back, ferreted into it like a detective custom-house officer after smuggled laces. Soon, with some African words equivalent to pshaw, he tossed the knot overboard.

All this is very queer, thought Captain Delano, with a qualmish sort of emotion; but, as one feeling incipient seasickness, he strove, by ignoring the symptoms, to get rid of the malady. Once more he looked off for his boat. To his delight, it was now again in view, leaving the rocky spur astern.

The sensation here experienced, after at first relieving his uneasiness, with unforeseen efficacy soon began to remove it. The less distant sight of that well-known boat—showing it, not as before, half blended with the haze but with outline defined, so that its individuality, like a man's, was manifest; that boat, *Rover* by name, which, though now in strange seas, had often pressed the beach of Captain Delano's home, and, brought to its threshold for repairs, had familiarly lain there, as a Newfoundland dog; the sight of that household boat evoked a thousand trustful associations, which, contrasted with previous suspicions, filled him not only with lightsome confidence, but somehow with half humorous self-reproaches at his former lack of it.

"What, I, Amasa Delano—Jack of the Beach, as they called me when a lad—I, Amasa, the same that, duck-satchel in hand, used to paddle along the waterside to the schoolhouse made from the old hulk—I, little Jack of the Beach, that used to go berrying with cousin Nat and the rest—I to be murdered here at the ends of the earth on board a haunted pirate ship by a horrible Spaniard? Too nonsensical to think of! Who would murder Amasa Delano? His conscience is clean. There is someone above. Fie, fie, Jack of the Beach! you are a child indeed; a child of the second childhood, old boy; you are beginning to dote and drool, I'm afraid."

Light of heart and foot, he stepped aft, and there was met by Don Benito's servant, who, with a pleasing expression responsive to his own present feelings, informed him that his master had recovered from the effects of his coughing fit, and had just ordered him to go present his compliments to his good guest, Don Amasa, and say that he (Don Benito) would soon have the happiness to re-join him.

There now, do you mark that? again thought Captain Delano, walking the poop. What a donkey I was. This kind gentleman who here sends me his kind compliments, he, but ten minutes ago, dark-lantern in hand, was dodging round some old grindstone in the hold, sharpening a hatchet for me, I thought. Well, well; these long calms have a morbid effect on the mind, I've often heard, though I never believed it before. Ha! glancing towards the boat, there's *Rover*, a good dog, a white bone in her mouth. A pretty big bone though, seems to me—What? Yes, she has fallen afoul of the bubbling tide rip there. It sets her the other way, too, for the time. Patience.

It was now about noon, though, from the grayness of everything, it seemed to be getting towards dusk.

The calm was confirmed. In the far distance, away from the influence of land, the leaden ocean seemed laid out and leaded up, its course finished, soul gone, defunct. But the current from landward, where the ship was, increased, silently sweeping her further and further towards the tranced waters beyond.

Still, from his knowledge of those latitudes, cherishing hopes of a breeze, and a fair and fresh one, at any moment, Captain Delano, despite present prospects, buoyantly counted upon bringing the *San Dominick* safely to anchor ere night. The distance swept over was nothing, since, with a good wind, ten minutes' sailing would retrace more than sixty minutes' drifting. Meantime, one moment turning to mark *Rover* fighting the tide rip and the next to see Don Benito approaching, he continued walking the poop.

Gradually he felt a vexation arising from the delay of his boat; this soon emerged into uneasiness, and at last—his eye falling continually, as from a stage box into the pit, upon the strange crowd before and below him, and by and by recognizing there the face, now composed to indifference, of the Spanish sailor who had seemed to beckon from the mainchains—something of his old trepidations returned.

Ah, thought he, gravely enough, this is like the ague: because it went off, it follows not that it won't come back.

Though ashamed of the relapse, he could not altogether subdue it; and so, exerting his good nature to the utmost, insensibly he came to a compromise.

Yes, this is a strange craft, a strange history, too, and strange folks on board. But—nothing more.

By way of keeping his mind out of mischief till the boat should arrive, he tried to occupy it with turning over and over, in a purely speculative sort of way, some lesser peculiarities of the captain and crew. Among others, four curious points recurred:

First, the affair of the Spanish lad assailed with a knife by the slave boy; an act winked at by Don Benito. Second, the tyranny in Don Benito's treatment of Atufal, the black, as if a child should lead a bull of the Nile by the ring in his nose. Third, the trampling of the sailor by the two Negroes, a piece of insolence passed over without so much as a reprimand. Fourth, the cringing submission to their master of all the ship's underlings, mostly blacks, as if by the least inadvertence they feared to draw down his despotic displeasure.

Coupling these points, they seemed somewhat contradictory. But what then, thought Captain Delano, glancing towards his now nearing boat—what then? Why, Don Benito is a very capricious commander. But he is not the first of the sort I have seen, though it's true he rather exceeds any other. But as a nation—continued he in his reveries—these Spaniards are all an odd set; the very word Spaniard has a curious, conspirator, Guy-Fawkish twang to it. And yet I dare say Spaniards in the main are as good folks as any in Duxbury, Massachusetts. Ah good! At last *Rover* has come.

As, with its welcome freight, the boat touched the side, the oakum-pickers, with venerable gestures, sought to restrain the blacks, who, at the sight of three gurried water casks in its bottom and a pile of wilted pumpkins in its bow, hung over the bulwarks in disorderly raptures.

Don Benito, with his servant, now appeared, his coming, perhaps, hastened by hearing the noise. Of him Captain Delano sought permission to serve out the water, so that all might share alike, and none injure themselves by unfair excess. But sensible, and, on Don Benito's account, kind as this offer was, it was received with what seemed impatience; as if aware that he lacked energy as a commander, Don Benito, with the true jealousy of weakness, resented as an affront any interference. So, at least, Captain Delano inferred.

In another moment the casks were being hoisted in, when some of the eager Negroes accidentally jostled Captain Delano where he stood by the gangway, so that, unmindful of Don Benito, yielding to the impulse of the moment, with good-natured authority he bade the black stand back, to enforce his words making use of a half-mirthful, half-menacing gesture. Instantly the blacks paused, just where they were, each Negro and Negress suspended in his or her posture, exactly as the word had found them—for a few seconds continuing so—while, as between the responsive posts of a telegraph, an unknown syllable ran from man to man among the perched oakum-pickers. While the visitor's attention was fixed by this scene, suddenly the hatchet-polishers half rose, and a rapid cry came from Don Benito.

Thinking that at the signal of the Spaniard he was about to be massacred, Captain Delano would have sprung for his boat, but paused, as the oakum-pickers, dropping down into the crowd with earnest exclamations, forced every white and every Negro back, at the same moment, with gestures friendly and familiar, almost jocose, bidding him, in substance, not be a fool. Simultaneously the hatchet-polishers resumed their seats, quietly as so many tailors, and at once, as if nothing had happened, the work of hoisting in the casks was resumed, white and blacks singing at the tackle.

Captain Delano glanced towards Don Benito. As he saw his meager form in the act of recovering itself from reclining in the servant's arms, into which the agitated invalid had fallen, he could not but marvel at the panic by which himself had been surprised, on the darting supposition that such a commander, who, upon a legitimate occasion, so trivial too, as it now appeared, could lose all self-command, was, with energetic iniquity, going to bring about his murder.

The casks being on deck, Captain Delano was handed a number of jars and cups by one of the steward's aids, who, in the name of his captain, entreated him to do as he had proposed—dole out the water. He complied, with republican impartiality as to this republican element, which always seeks one level, serving the oldest white no better than the youngest black, excepting, indeed, poor Don Benito, whose condition, if not rank, demanded an extra allowance. To him, in the first place, Captain Delano presented a fair pitcher of the fluid, but, thirsting as he was for it, the Spaniard quaffed not a drop until after several grave bows and salutes, a reciprocation of courtesies which the sight-loving Africans hailed with clapping of hands.

Two of the less wilted pumpkins being reserved for the cabin table, the residue were minced up on the spot for the general regalement. But the soft bread, sugar, and bottled cider Captain Delano would have given the whites alone, and in chief Don Benito, but the latter objected; which disinterestedness not a little pleased the American; and so mouthfuls all around were given alike to whites and blacks, excepting one bottle of cider, which Babo insisted upon setting aside for his master.

Here it may be observed that as, on the first visit of the boat, the American had not permitted his men to board the ship, neither did he now, being unwilling to add to the confusion of the decks.

Not uninfluenced by the peculiar good humor at present prevailing, and for the time oblivious of any but benevolent thought, Captain Delano, who from recent indications counted upon a breeze within an hour or two at furthest, dispatched the boat back to the sealer, with others for all the hands that could be spared immediately to set about rafting casks to the watering place and filling them. Likewise he bade word be carried to his chief officer that if, against present expectation, the ship was not brought to anchor by sunset, he need be under no concern; for as there was to be a full moon that night, he (Captain Delano) would remain on board ready to play the pilot, come the wind soon or late.

As the two Captains stood together observing the departing boat—the servant, as it happened, having just spied a spot on his master's velvet sleeve, and silently engaged rubbing it out—the American expressed his regrets that the *San Dominick* had no boats, none, at least, but the unseaworthy old hulk of the longboat, which, warped as a camel's skeleton in the desert and almost as bleached, lay pot-wise inverted amidships, one side a little tipped, furnishing a subterraneous sort of den for family groups of the blacks, mostly women and small children, who, squatting on old mats below, or perched above in the dark dome on the elevated seats, were described, some distance within, like a social circle of bats sheltering in some friendly cave, at intervals, ebon flights of naked boys and girls three or four years old darting in and out of the den's mouth.

"Had you three or four boats now, Don Benito," said Captain Delano, "I think that, by tugging at the oars, your Negroes here might help along matters some. Did you sail from port without boats, Don Benito?"

"They were stove in the gales, *señor*."

"That was bad. Many men, too, you lost then. Boats and men. Those must have been hard gales, Don Benito."

"Past all speech," cringed the Spaniard.

"Tell me, Don Benito," continued his companion with increased interest, "tell me, were these gales immediately off the pitch of Cape Horn?"

"Cape Horn?—who spoke of Cape Horn?"

"Yourself did, when giving me an account of your voyage," answered Captain Delano, with almost equal astonishment at this eating of his own words, even as he ever seemed eating his own heart, on the part of the Spaniard. "You yourself, Don Benito, spoke of Cape Horn," he emphatically repeated.

The Spaniard turned, in a sort of stooping posture, pausing an instant as one about to make a plunging exchange of elements, as from air to water.

At this moment a messenger boy, a white, hurried by, in the regular performance of his function carrying the last expired half-hour forward to the forecastle from the cabin timepiece, to have it struck at the ship's large bell.

"Master," said the servant, discontinuing his work on the coat sleeve and addressing the rapt Spaniard with a sort of timid apprehensiveness, as one charged with a duty the discharge of which, it was foreseen, would prove irksome to the very person who had imposed it and for whose benefit it was intended, "master told me never mind where he was, or how engaged, always to remind him, to a minute, when shaving-time comes. Miguel has gone to strike the half-hour afternoon. It is *now*, master. Will master go into the cuddy?"

"Ah—yes," answered the Spaniard, starting, as from dreams into realities, then, turning upon Captain Delano, he said that erelong he would resume the conversation.

"Then if master means to talk more to Don Amasa," said the servant, "why not let Don Amasa sit by master in the cuddy, and master can talk, and Don Amasa can listen while Babo here lathers and strops."

"Yes," said Captain Delano, not unpleased with this sociable plan, "yes, Don Benito, unless you had rather not, I will go with you."

"Be it so, *señor.*"

As the three passed aft, the American could not but think it another strange instance of his host's capriciousness, this being shaved with such uncommon punctuality in the middle of the day. But he deemed it more than likely that the servant's anxious fidelity had something to do with the matter, inasmuch as the timely interruption served to rally his master from the mood which had evidently been coming upon him.

The place called the cuddy was a light deck cabin formed by the poop, a sort of attic to the large cabin below. Part of it had formerly been the quarters of the officers, but since their death all the partitionings had been thrown down and the whole interior converted into one spacious and airy marine hall; for absence of fine furniture and picturesque disarray of odd appurtenances, somewhat answering to the wide, cluttered hall of some eccentric bachelor squire in the country, who hangs his shooting jacket and tobacco pouch on deer antlers, and keeps his fishing rod, tongs, and walking stick in the same corner.

The similitude was heightened, if not originally suggested, by glimpses of the surrounding sea, since, in one aspect, the country and the ocean seem cousins-german.

The floor of the cuddy was matted. Overhead, four or five old muskets were stuck into horizontal holes along the beams. On one side was a claw-footed old table lashed to the deck, a thumbed missal on it, and over it, a small, meager crucifix attached to the bulkhead. Under the table lay a dented cutlass or two with a hacked harpoon, among some melancholy old rigging, like a heap of poor friars' girdles. There were also two long, sharp-ribbed settees of Malacca cane, black with age, and uncomfortable to look at as inquisitors' racks, with a large, misshapen armchair, which, furnished with a rude barber's crotch at the back, working with a screw, seemed some grotesque engine of torment. A flag locker was in one corner, open, exposing various colored buntings, some rolled up, others half unrolled, still others tumbled. Opposite was a cumbrous washstand of black mahogany, all of one block, with a pedestal like a font, and over it a railed shelf, containing combs, brushes, and other implements of the toilet. A torn hammock of stained grass swung near, the sheets tossed, and the pillow wrinkled up like a brow, as if whoever slept here slept but illy, with alternate visitations of sad thoughts and bad dreams.

The further extremity of the cuddy, overhanging the ship's stern, was pierced with three openings, windows or portholes, according as men or cannon might peer, socially or unsocially, out of them. At present neither men nor cannon were seen, though huge ringbolts and other rusty iron fixtures of the woodwork hinted of twenty-four-pounders.

Glancing towards the hammock as he entered, Captain Delano said, "You sleep here, Don Benito?"

"Yes, *señor*, since we got into mild weather."

"This seems a sort of dormitory, sitting room, sail loft, chapel, armory, and private closet all together, Don Benito," added Captain Delano, looking round.

"Yes, *señor*, events have not been favorable to much order in my arrangements."

Here the servant, napkin on arm, made a motion as if waiting his master's good pleasure. Don Benito signified his readiness, when, seating him in the Malacca armchair, and for the guest's convenience drawing opposite one of the settees, the servant commenced operations by throwing back his master's collar and loosening his cravat.

There is something in the Negro which, in a peculiar way, fits him for avocations about one's person. Most Negroes are natural valets and hairdressers, taking to the comb and brush congenially as to the castinets, and flourishing them apparently with almost equal satisfaction. There is, too, a smooth tact about them in this employment, with a marvelous, noiseless, gliding briskness, not ungraceful in its way, singularly pleasing to behold, and still more so to be the manipulated subject of. And above all is the great gift of good humor. Not the mere grin or laugh is here meant. Those were unsuitable. But a certain easy cheerfulness, harmonious in every glance and gesture, as though God had set the whole Negro to some pleasant tune.

When to this is added the docility arising from the unaspiring contentment of a limited mind, and that susceptibility of blind attachment sometimes inhering in indisputable inferiors, one readily perceives why those hypochondriacs, Johnson and Byron—it may be, something like the hypochondriac Benito Cereno—took to their hearts, almost to the exclusion of the entire white race, their servingmen, the Negroes, Barber and Fletcher. But if there be that in the Negro which exempts him from the inflicted sourness of the morbid or cynical mind, how, in his most prepossessing aspects, must he appear to a benevolent one? When at ease with respect to exterior things, Captain Delano's nature was not only benign, but familiarly and humorously so. At home, he had often taken rare satisfaction in sitting in his door, watching some free man of color at his work or play. If on a voyage he chanced to have a black sailor, invariably he was on chatty and halfgamesome terms with him. In fact, like most men of a good, blithe heart, Captain Delano took to Negroes, not philanthropically, but genially, just as other men to Newfoundland dogs.

Hitherto, the circumstances in which he found the *San Dominick* had repressed the tendency. But in the cuddy, relieved from his former uneasiness, and, for various reasons, more sociably inclined than at any previous period of the day, and seeing the colored servant, napkin on arm, so debonair about his master, in a business so familiar as that of shaving too, all his old weakness for Negroes returned.

Among other things, he was amused with an odd instance of the African love of bright colors and fine shows, in the black's informally taking from the flag locker a great piece of bunting of all hues and lavishly tucking it under his master's chin for an apron.

The mode of shaving among the Spaniards is a little different from what it is with other nations. They have a basin, specifically called a barber's basin, which on one side is scooped out, so as accurately to receive the chin, against which it is closely held in lathering, which is done, not with a brush, but with soap dipped in the water of the basin and rubbed on the face.

In the present instance salt water was used for lack of better, and the parts lathered were only the upper lip and low down under the throat, all the rest being cultivated beard.

The preliminaries being somewhat novel to Captain Delano, he sat curiously eying them, so that no conversation took place, nor, for the present, did Don Benito appear disposed to renew any.

Setting down his basin, the Negro searched among the razors, as for the sharpest, and, having found it, gave it an additional edge by expertly stropping it on the firm, smooth, oily skin of his open palm; he then made a gesture as if to begin, but midway stood suspended for an instant, one hand elevating the razor, the other professionally dabbling among the bubbling suds on the Spaniard's lank neck. Not unaffected by the close sight of the gleaming steel, Don Benito nervously shuddered; his usual ghastliness was heightened by the lather, which lather, again, was intensified in its hue by the contrasting sootiness of the Negro's body. Altogether the scene was somewhat peculiar, at least to Captain Delano, nor, as he saw the two thus postured, could he resist the vagary that in the black he saw a headsman, and in the white a man at the block. But this was one of those antic conceits, appearing and vanishing in a breath, from which, perhaps, the best-regulated mind is not always free.

Meantime the agitation of the Spaniard had a little loosened the bunting from around him, so that one broad fold swept curtainlike over the chair arm to the floor, revealing, amid a profusion of armorial bars and ground colors—black, blue, and yellow—a closed castle in a blood-red field diagonal with a lion rampant in a white.

"The castle and the lion," exclaimed Captain Delano—"why, Don Benito, this is the flag of Spain you use here. It's well it's only I, and not the King, that sees this," he added, with a smile, "but"—turning towards the black—"it's all one, I suppose, so the colors be gay"; which playful remark did not fail somewhat to tickle the Negro.

"Now, master," he said, readjusting the flag, and pressing the head gently further back into the crotch of the chair, "now, master," and the steel glanced nigh the throat.

Again Don Benito faintly shuddered.

"You must not shake so, master. See, Don Amasa, master always shakes when I shave him. And yet master knows I never yet have drawn blood, though it's true if master will shake so I may some of these times. Now master," he continued. "And now, Don Amasa, please go on with your talk about the gale, and all that; master can hear, and between times, master can answer."

"Ah yes, these gales," said Captain Delano; "but the more I think of your voyage, Don Benito, the more I wonder, not at the gales, terrible as they must have been, but at the disastrous interval following them. For here, by your account, have you been these two months and more getting from Cape Horn to St. Maria, a distance which I myself, with a good wind, have sailed in a few days. True, you had calms, and long ones, but to be becalmed for two months, that is, at least, unusual. Why, Don Benito, had almost any other gentleman told me such a story, I should have been half disposed to a little incredulity."

Here an involuntary expression came over the Spaniard, similar to that just before on the deck, and whether it was the start he gave, or a sudden gawky roll of the hull in the calm, or a momentary unsteadiness of the servant's hand, however it was, just then the razor drew blood, spots of which stained the creamy lather under the throat; immediately the black barber drew back his steel, and, remaining in his professional attitude, back to Captain Delano, and face to Don Benito, held up the trickling razor, saying, with a sort of half humorous sorrow, "See, master—you shook so—here's Babo's first blood."

No sword drawn before James the First of England, no assassination in that timid king's presence, could have produced a more terrified aspect than was now presented by Don Benito.

Poor fellow, thought Captain Delano, so nervous he can't even bear the sight of barber's blood; and this unstrung, sick man, is it credible that I should have imagined he meant to spill all my blood, who can't endure the sight of one little drop of his own? Surely, Amasa Delano, you have been beside yourself this day. Tell it not when you get home, sappy Amasa. Well, well, he looks like a murderer, doesn't he? More like as if himself were to be done for. Well, well, this day's experience shall be a good lesson.

Meantime, while these things were running through the honest seaman's mind, the servant had taken the napkin from his arm, and to Don Benito had said—"But answer Don Amasa, please, master, while I wipe this ugly stuff off the razor, and strop it again."

As he said the words, his face was turned half round, so as to be alike visible to the Spaniard and the American, and seemed, by its expression, to hint that he was desirous, by getting his master to go on with the conversation, considerately to withdraw his attention from the recent annoying accident. As if glad to snatch the offered relief, Don Benito resumed, rehearsing to Captain Delano that, not only were the calms of unusual duration, but the ship had fallen in with obstinate currents, and other things he added, some of which were but repetitions of former statements, to explain how it came to pass that the passage from Cape Horn to St. Maria had been so exceedingly long, now and then mingling with his words incidental praises, less qualified than before, to the blacks, for their general good conduct. These particulars were not given consecutively, the servant, at convenient times, using his razor, and so, between the intervals of shaving, the story and panegyric went on with more than usual huskiness.

To Captain Delano's imagination, now again not wholly at rest, there was something so hollow in the Spaniard's manner, with apparently some reciprocal hollowness in the servant's dusky comment of silence, that the idea flashed across him that possibly master and man, for some unknown purpose, were acting out, both in word and deed, nay, to the very tremor of Don Benito's limbs, some juggling play before him. Neither did the suspicion of collusion lack apparent support, from the fact of those whispered conferences before mentioned. But then, what could be the object of enacting this play of the barber before him? At last, regarding the notion as a whimsey, insensibly suggested, perhaps, by the theatrical aspect of Don Benito in his harlequin ensign, Captain Delano speedily banished it.

The shaving over, the servant bestirred himself with a small bottle of scented waters, pouring a few drops on the head, and then diligently rubbing, the vehemence of the exercise causing the muscles of his face to twitch rather strangely.

His next operation was with comb, scissors, and brush, going round and round, smoothing a curl here, clipping an unruly whisker hair there, giving a graceful sweep to the temple lock, with other impromptu touches evincing the hand of a master, while, like any resigned gentleman in barber's hands, Don Benito bore all much less uneasily, at least, than he had done the razoring; indeed, he sat so pale and rigid now that the Negro seemed a Nubian sculptor finishing off a white statue head.

All being over at last, the standard of Spain removed, tumbled up, and tossed back into the flag locker, the Negro's warm breath blowing away any stray hair which might have lodged down his master's neck, collar and cravat readjusted, a speck of lint whisked off the velvet lapel—all this being done, backing off a little space, and pausing with an expression of subdued self-complacency, the servant for a moment surveyed his master, as, in toilette at least, the creature of his own tasteful hands.

Captain Delano playfully complimented him upon his achievement, at the same time congratulating Don Benito.

But neither sweet waters, nor shampooing, nor fidelity, nor sociality, delighted the Spaniard. Seeing him relapsing into forbidding gloom, and still remaining seated, Captain Delano, thinking that his presence was undesired just then, withdrew, on pretense of seeing whether, as he had prophesied, any signs of a breeze were visible.

Walking forward to the mainmast, he stood awhile thinking over the scene, and not without some undefined misgivings, when he heard a noise near the cuddy, and, turning, saw the Negro, his hand to his cheek. Advancing, Captain Delano perceived that the cheek was bleeding. He was about to ask the cause, when the Negro's wailing soliloquy enlightened him.

"Ah, when will master get better from his sickness; only the sour heart that sour sickness breeds made him serve Babo so, cutting Babo with the razor because, only by accident, Babo had given master one little scratch, and for the first time in so many a day, too. Ah, ah, ah," holding his hand to his face.

Is it possible, thought Captain Delano; was it to wreak in private his Spanish spite against this poor friend of his that Don Benito, by his sullen manner, impelled me to withdraw? Ah this slavery breeds ugly passions in man.—Poor fellow!

He was about to speak in sympathy to the Negro, but with a timid reluctance he now re-entered the cuddy.

Presently master and man came forth, Don Benito leaning on his servant as if nothing had happened.

But a sort of love quarrel, after all, thought Captain Delano.

He accosted Don Benito, and they slowly walked together. They had gone but a few paces, when the steward—a tall, rajah-looking mulatto, Orientally set off with a pagoda turban formed by three or four Madras handkerchiefs wound about his head, tier on tier—approaching with a saalam, announced lunch in the cabin.

On their way thither, the two captains were preceded by the mulatto, who, turning round as he advanced, with continual smiles and bows, ushered them on, a display of elegance which quite completed the insignificance of the small bare-headed Babo, who, as if not unconscious of inferiority, eyed askance the graceful steward. But, in part, Captain Delano imputed his jealous watchfulness to that peculiar feeling which the full-blooded African entertains for the adulterated one. As for the steward, his manner, if not bespeaking much dignity of self-respect, yet evidenced his extreme desire to please, which is doubly meritorious, as at once Christian and Chesterfieldian.

Captain Delano observed with interest that while the complexion of the mulatto was hybrid, his physiognomy was European—classically so.

"Don Benito," whispered he, "I am glad to see this usher-of-the-golden-rod of yours; the sight refutes an ugly remark once made to me by a Barbados planter, that when a mulatto has a regular European face, look out for him; he is a devil. But see, your steward here has features more regular than King George's of England, and yet there he nods, and bows, and smiles, a king, indeed—the king of kind hearts and polite fellows. What a pleasant voice he has, too."

"He has, *señor.*"

"But tell me, has he not, so far as you have known him, always proved a good, worthy fellow?" said Captain Delano, pausing, while with a final genuflexion the steward disappeared into the cabin; "come, for the reason just mentioned, I am curious to know."

"Francesco is a good man," rather sluggishly responded Don Benito, like a phlegmatic appreciator, who would neither find fault nor flatter.

"Ah, I thought so. For it were strange indeed, and not very creditable to us whiteskins, if a little of our blood mixed with the African's should, far from improving the latter's quality, have the sad effect of pouring vitriolic acid into black broth—improving the hue, perhaps, but not the wholesomeness."

"Doubtless, doubtless, *señor,* but"—glancing at Babo—"not to speak of Negroes, your planter's remark I have heard applied to the Spanish and Indian intermixtures in our provinces. But I know nothing about the matter," he listlessly added.

And here they entered the cabin.

The lunch was a frugal one. Some of Captain Delano's fresh fish and pumpkins, biscuit and salt beef, the reserved bottle of cider, and the *San Dominick*'s last bottle of Canary.

As they entered, Francesco, with two or three colored aids, was hovering over the table giving the last adjustments. Upon perceiving their master they withdrew, Francesco making a smiling *congé,* and the Spaniard, without condescending to notice it, fastidiously remarking to his companion that he relished not superfluous attendance.

Without companions, host and guest sat down, like a childless married couple, at opposite ends of the table, Don Benito waving Captain Delano to his place, and, weak as he was, insisting upon that gentleman being seated before himself.

The Negro placed a rug under Don Benito's feet, and a cushion behind his back, and then stood behind, not his master's chair, but Captain Delano's. At first, this a little surprised the latter. But it was soon evident that, in taking his position, the black was still true to his master, since by facing him he could the more readily anticipate his slightest want.

"This is an uncommonly intelligent fellow of yours, Don Benito," whispered Captain Delano across the table.

"You say true, *señor*."

During the repast, the guest again reverted to parts of Don Benito's story, begging further particulars here and there. He inquired how it was that the scurvy and fever should have committed such wholesale havoc upon the whites, while destroying less than half of the blacks. As if this question reproduced the whole scene of plague before the Spaniard's eyes, miserably reminding him of his solitude in a cabin where before he had had so many friends and officers round him, his hand shook, his face became hueless, broken words escaped; but directly the same memory of the past seemed replaced by insane terrors of the present. With starting eyes he stared before him at vacancy. For nothing was to be seen but the hand of his servant pushing the Canary over towards him. At length a few sips served partially to restore him. He made random reference to the different constitution of races, enabling one to offer more resistance to certain maladies than another. The thought was new to his companion.

Presently Captain Delano, intending to say something to his host concerning the pecuniary part of the business he had undertaken for him, especially— since he was strictly accountable to his owners—with reference to the new suit of sails, and other things of that sort, and naturally preferring to conduct such affairs in private, was desirous that the servant should withdraw, imagining that Don Benito for a few minutes could dispense with his attendance. He, however, waited awhile, thinking that, as the conversation proceeded, Don Benito, without being prompted, would perceive the propriety of the step.

But it was otherwise. At last catching his host's eye, Captain Delano, with a slight backward gesture of his thumb, whispered, "Don Benito, pardon me, but there is an interference with the full expression of what I have to say to you."

Upon this the Spaniard changed countenance, which was imputed to his resenting the hint, as in some way a reflection upon his servant. After a moment's pause, he assured his guest that the black's remaining with them could be of no disservice; because since losing his officers he had made Babo (whose original office, it now appeared, had been captain of the slaves) not only his constant attendant and companion, but in all things his confidant.

After this, nothing more could be said; though indeed Captain Delano could hardly avoid some little tinge of irritation upon being left ungratified in so inconsiderable a wish, by one, too, for whom he intended such solid services. But it is only his querulousness, thought he, and so, filling his glass, he proceeded to business.

The price of the sails and other matters was fixed upon. But while this was being done, the American observed that, though his original offer of assistance had been hailed with hectic animation, yet now when it was reduced to a business transaction, indifference and apathy were betrayed. Don Benito, in fact, appeared to submit to hearing the details more out of regard to common propriety than from any impression that weighty benefit to himself and his voyage was involved.

Soon his manner became still more reserved. The effort was vain to seek to draw him into social talk. Gnawed by his splenetic mood, he sat twitching his beard, while to little purpose the hand of his servant, mute as that on the wall, slowly pushed over the Canary.

Lunch being over, they sat down on the cushioned transom, the servant placing a pillow behind his master. The long continuance of the calm had now affected the atmosphere. Don Benito sighed heavily, as if for breath.

"Why not adjourn to the cuddy," said Captain Delano; "there is more air there." But the host sat silent and motionless.

Meantime his servant knelt before him with a large fan of feathers. And Francesco, coming in on tiptoes, handed the Negro a little cup of aromatic waters, with which at intervals he chafed his master's brow, smoothing the hair along the temples as a nurse does a child's. He spoke no word. He only rested his eye on his master's, as if, amid all Don Benito's distress, a little to refresh his spirit by the silent sight of fidelity.

Presently the ship's bell sounded two o'clock, and through the cabin windows a slight rippling of the sea was discerned, and from the desired direction.

"There," exclaimed Captain Delano, "I told you so, Don Benito, look!"

He had risen to his feet, speaking in a very animated tone, with a view the more to rouse his companion. But though the crimson curtain of the stern window near him that moment fluttered against his pale cheek, Don Benito seemed to have even less welcome for the breeze than the calm.

Poor fellow, thought Captain Delano, bitter experience has taught him that one ripple does not make a wind, any more than one swallow a summer. But he is mistaken for once. I will get his ship in for him, and prove it.

Briefly alluding to his weak condition, he urged his host to remain quietly where he was, since he (Captain Delano) would with pleasure take upon himself the responsibility of making the best use of the wind.

Upon gaining the deck, Captain Delano started at the unexpected figure of Atufal, monumentally fixed at the threshold, like one of those sculptured porters of black marble guarding the porches of Egyptian tombs.

But this time the start was, perhaps, purely physical. Atufal's presence, singularly attesting docility even in sullenness, was contrasted with that of the hatchet-polishers, who in patience evinced their industry; while both spectacles showed that, lax as Don Benito's general authority might be, still, whenever he chose to exert it, no man so savage or colossal but must, more or less, bow.

Snatching a trumpet which hung from the bulwarks, with a free step Captain Delano advanced to the forward edge of the poop, issuing his orders in his best Spanish. The few sailors and many Negroes, all equally pleased, obediently set about heading the ship towards the harbor.

While giving some directions about setting a lower stunsail, suddenly Captain Delano heard a voice faithfully repeating his orders. Turning, he saw Babo, now for the time acting, under the pilot, his original part of captain of the slaves. This assistance proved valuable. Tattered sails and warped yards were soon brought into some trim. And no brace or halyard was pulled but to the blithe songs of the inspirited Negroes.

Good fellows, thought Captain Delano, a little training would make fine sailors of them. Why see, the very women pull and sing too. These must be some of those Ashantee Negresses that make such capital soldiers, I've heard. But who's at the helm? I must have a good hand there.

He went to see.

The *San Dominick* steered with a cumbrous tiller, with large horizontal pulleys attached. At each pulley end stood a subordinate black, and between them, at the tillerhead, the responsible post, a Spanish seaman, whose countenance evinced his due share in the general hopefulness and confidence at the coming of the breeze.

He proved the same man who had behaved with so shamefaced an air on the windlass.

"Ah—it is you, my man," exclaimed Captain Delano— "Well, no more sheep's-eyes now; look straight forward and keep the ship so. Good hand, I trust? And want to get into the harbor, don't you?"

The man assented with an inward chuckle, grasping the tillerhead firmly. Upon this, unperceived by the American, the two blacks eyed the sailor intently.

Finding all right at the helm, the pilot went forward to the forecastle to see how matters stood there.

The ship now had way enough to breast the current. With the approach of evening, the breeze would be sure to freshen.

Having done all that was needed for the present, Captain Delano, giving his last orders to the sailors, turned aft to report affairs to Don Benito in the cabin, perhaps additionally incited to rejoin him by the hope of snatching a moment's private chat while the servant was engaged upon deck.

From opposite sides, there were, beneath the poop, two approaches to the cabin, one further forward than the other, and consequently communicating with a longer passage. Marking the servant still above, Captain Delano, taking the nighest entrance—the one last named, and at whose porch Atufal still stood— hurried on his way, till, arrived at the cabin threshold, he paused an instant, a little to recover from his eagerness. Then, with the words of his intended business upon his lips, he entered. As he advanced toward the seated Spaniard, he heard another footstep, keeping time with his. From the opposite door, a salver in hand, the servant was likewise advancing.

"Confound the faithful fellow," thought Captain Delano; "what a vexatious coincidence."

Possibly the vexation might have been something different, were it not for the brisk confidence inspired by the breeze. But even as it was he felt a slight twinge, from a sudden indefinite association in his mind of Babo with Atufal.

"Don Benito," said he, "I give you joy; the breeze will hold, and will increase. By the way, your tall man and timepiece, Atufal, stands without. By your order, of course?"

Don Benito recoiled, as if at some bland satirical touch delivered with such adroit garnish of apparent good breeding as to present no handle for retort.

He is like one flayed alive, thought Captain Delano; where may one touch him without causing a shrink?

The servant moved before his master, adjusting a cushion; recalled to civility, the Spaniard stiffly replied: "You are right. The slave appears where you saw him, according to my command, which is that if at the given hour I am below he must take his stand and abide my coming."

"Ah now, pardon me, but that is treating the poor fellow like an ex-king indeed. Ah, Don Benito," smiling, "for all the license you permit in some things, I fear lest, at bottom, you are a bitter hard master."

Again Don Benito shrank, and this time, as the good sailor thought, from a genuine twinge of his conscience.

Again conversation became constrained. In vain Captain Delano called attention to the now perceptible motion of the keel gently cleaving the sea; with lackluster eye, Don Benito returned words few and reserved.

By and by, the wind having steadily risen, and still blowing right into the harbor, bore the *San Dominick* swiftly on. Rounding a point of land, the sealer at distance came into open view.

Meantime Captain Delano had again repaired to the deck, remaining there some time. Having at last altered the ship's course so as to give the reef a wide berth, he returned for a few moments below.

I will cheer up my poor friend this time, thought he.

"Better and better, Don Benito," he cried as he blithely re-entered: "there will soon be an end to your cares, at least for a while. For when, after a long, sad voyage, you know, the anchor drops into the haven, all its vast weight seems lifted from the captain's heart. We are getting on famously, Don Benito. My ship is in sight. Look through this side light here; there she is, all a-taunt-o! The *Bachelor's Delight*, my good friend. Ah, how this wind braces one up. Come, you must take a cup of coffee with me this evening. My old steward will give you as fine a cup as ever any sultan tasted. What say you, Don Benito, will you?"

At first, the Spaniard glanced feverishly up, casting a longing look towards the sealer, while, with mute concern his servant gazed into his face. Suddenly the old ague of coldness returned, and dropping back to his cushions he was silent.

"You do not answer. Come, all day you have been my host; would you have hospitality all on one side?"

"I cannot go," was the response.

"What? it will not fatigue you. The ships will lie together as near as they can without swinging foul. It will be little more than stepping from deck to deck, which is but as from room to room. Come, come, you must not refuse me."

"I cannot go," decisively and repulsively repeated Don Benito.

Renouncing all but the last appearance of courtesy, with a sort of cadaverous sullenness, and biting his thin nails to the quick, he glanced, almost glared, at his guest, as if impatient that a stranger's presence should interfere with the full indulgence of his morbid hour. Meantime the sound of the parted waters came more and more gurglingly and merrily in at the windows; as reproaching him for his dark spleen, as telling him that, sulk as he might, and go mad with it, nature cared not a jot, since whose fault was it, pray?

But the foul mood was now at its depth, as the fair wind at its height.

There was something in the man so far beyond any mere unsociality or sourness previously evinced that even the forbearing good nature of his guest could not longer endure it. Wholly at a loss to account for such demeanor, and deeming sickness with eccentricity, however extreme, no adequate excuse, well satisfied, too, that nothing in his own conduct could justify it, Captain Delano's pride began to be roused. Himself became reserved. But all seemed one to the Spaniard. Quitting him, therefore, Captain Delano once more went to the deck.

The ship was now within less than two miles of the sealer. The whaleboat was seen darting over the interval.

To be brief, the two vessels, thanks to the pilot's skill, erelong in neighborly style lay anchored together.

Before returning to his own vessel, Captain Delano had intended communicating to Don Benito the smaller details of the proposed services to be rendered. But as it was, unwilling anew to subject himself to rebuffs, he resolved, now that he had seen the *San Dominick* safely moored, immediately to quit her, without further allusion to hospitality or business. Indefinitely postponing his ulterior plans, he would regulate his future actions according to future circumstances. His boat was ready to receive him; but his host still tarried below. Well, thought Captain Delano, if he has little breeding, the more need to show mine. He descended to the cabin to bid a ceremonious, and, it may be, tacitly rebukeful adieu. But to his great satisfaction, Don Benito, as if he began to feel the weight of that treatment with which his slighted guest had, not indecorously, retaliated upon him, how, supported by his servant, rose to his feet, and grasping Captain Delano's hand, stood tremulous, too much agitated to speak. But the good augury hence drawn was suddenly dashed by his resuming all his previous reserve with augmented gloom, as, with half-averted eyes, he silently reseated himself on his cushions. With a corresponding return of his own chilled feelings, Captain Delano bowed and withdrew.

He was hardly midway in the narrow corridor, dim as a tunnel, leading from the cabin to the stairs, when a sound, as of the tolling for execution in some jailyard, fell on his ears. It was the echo of the ship's flawed bell striking the hour, drearily reverberated in this subterranean vault. Instantly, by a fatality not to be withstood, his mind, responsive to the portent, swarmed with superstitious suspicions. He paused. In images far swifter than these sentences, the minutest details of all his former distrusts swept through him.

Hitherto, credulous good nature had been too ready to furnish excuses for reasonable fears. Why was the Spaniard, so superfluously punctilious at times, now heedless of common propriety in not accompanying to the side his departing guest? Did indisposition forbid? Indisposition had not forbidden more irksome exertion that day. His last equivocal demeanor recurred. He had risen to his feet, grasped his guest's hand, motioned toward his hat; then, in an instant, all was eclipsed in sinister muteness and gloom. Did this imply one brief repentant relenting at the final moment from some iniquitous plot, followed by remorseless return to it? His last glance seemed to express a calamitous yet acquiescent farewell to Captain Delano forever. Why decline the invitation to visit the sealer that evening? Or was the Spaniard less hardened than the Jew, who refrained not from supping at the board of him whom the same night he meant to betray? What imported all those daylong enigmas and contradictions, except they were intended to mystify, preliminary to some stealthy blow? Atufal, the pretended rebel but punctual shadow, that moment lurked by the threshold without. He seemed a sentry, and more. Who, by his own confession, had stationed him there? Was the Negro now lying in wait?

The Spaniard behind—his creature before: to rush from darkness to light was the involuntary choice.

The next moment, with clenched jaw and hand, he passed Atufal, and stood unharmed in the light. As he saw his trim ship lying peacefully at anchor and almost within ordinary call; as he saw his household boat, with familiar faces in it, patiently rising and falling on the short waves by the *San Dominick*'s side; and then, glancing about the decks where he stood, saw the oakum-pickers still gravely plying their fingers, and heard the low, buzzing whistle and industrious hum of the hatchet-polishers still bestirring themselves over their endless occupation; and more than all, as he saw the benign aspect of nature taking her innocent repose in the evening, the screened sun in the quiet camp of the west shining out like the mild light from Abraham's tent—as charmed eye and ear took in all these, with the chained figure of the black, clenched jaw and hand relaxed. Once again he smiled at the phantoms which had mocked him, and felt something like a tinge of remorse that, by harboring them even for a moment, he should by implication have betrayed an atheist doubt of the ever-watchful Providence above.

There was a few minutes' delay, while, in obedience to his orders, the boat was being hooked along to the gangway. During this interval, a sort of saddened satisfaction stole over Captain Delano at thinking of the kindly offices he had that day discharged for a stranger. Ah, thought he, after good actions one's conscience is never ungrateful, however much so the benefited party may be.

Presently his foot, in the first act of descent into the boat, pressed the first round of the side ladder, his face presented inward upon the deck. In the same moment he heard his name courteously sounded, and, to his pleased surprise, saw Don Benito advancing—an unwonted energy in his air, as if, at the last moment, intent upon making amends for his recent discourtesy. With instinctive good feeling, Captain Delano, withdrawing his foot, turned and reciprocally advanced. As he did so, the Spaniard's nervous eagerness increased, but his vital energy failed, so that, the better to support him, the servant, placing his master's hand on his naked shoulder, and gently holding it there, formed himself into a sort of crutch.

When the two captains met, the Spaniard again fervently took the hand of the American, at the same time casting an earnest glance into his eyes, but, as before, too much overcome to speak.

I have done him wrong, self-reproachfully thought Captain Delano; his apparent coldness has deceived me; in no instance has he meant to offend.

Meantime, as if fearful that the continuance of the scene might too much unstring his master, the servant seemed anxious to terminate it. And so, still presenting himself as a crutch, and walking between the two captains, he advanced with them towards the gangway; while still, as if full of kindly contrition, Don Benito would not let go the hand of Captain Delano but retained it in his, across the black's body.

Soon they were standing by the side, looking over into the boat, whose crew turned up their curious eyes. Waiting a moment for the Spaniard to relinquish his hold, the now embarrassed Captain Delano lifted his foot to overstep the threshold of the open gangway, but still Don Benito would not let go his hand. And yet, with an agitated tone, he said, "I can go no further; here I must bid you adieu. Adieu, my dear, dear Don Amasa. Go—go!" suddenly tearing his hand loose, "go, and God guard you better than me, my best friend."

Not unaffected, Captain Delano would now have lingered, but, catching the meekly admonitory eye of the servant, with a hasty farewell he descended into his boat, followed by the continual adieus of Don Benito, standing rooted in the gangway.

Seating himself in the stern, Captain Delano, making a last salute, ordered the boat shoved off. The crew had their oars on end. The bowsmen pushed the boat a sufficient distance for the oars to be lengthwise dropped. The instant that was done, Don Benito sprang over the bulwarks, falling at the feet of Captain Delano; at the same time calling towards his ship, but in tones so frenzied that none in the boat could understand him. But, as if not equally obtuse, three sailors, from three different and distant parts of the ship, splashed into the sea, swimming after their captain, as if intent upon his rescue.

The dismayed officer of the boat eagerly asked what this meant. To which Captain Delano, turning a disdainful smile upon the unaccountable Spaniard, answered that, for his part, he neither knew nor cared; but it seemed as if Don Benito had taken it into his head to produce the impression among his people that the boat wanted to kidnap him. "Or else—give way for your lives," he wildly added, starting at a clattering hubbub in the ship, above which rang the tocsin of the hatchet-polishers, and seizing Don Benito by the throat he added, "this plotting pirate means murder!" Here, in apparent verification of the words, the servant, a dagger in his hand, was seen on the rail overhead, poised, in the act of leaping, as if with desperate fidelity to befriend his master to the last; while, seemingly to aid the black, the three white sailors were trying to clamber into the hampered bow. Meantime, the whole host of Negroes, as if inflamed at the sight of their jeopardized captain, impended in one sooty avalanche over the bulwarks.

All this, with what preceded and what followed, occurred with such involutions of rapidity that past, present, and future seemed one.

Seeing the Negro coming, Captain Delano had flung the Spaniard aside, almost in the very act of clutching him, and, by the unconscious recoil shifting his place, with arms thrown up so promptly grappled the servant in his descent, that with dagger presented at Captain Delano's heart, the black seemed of purpose to have leaped there as to his mark. But the weapon was wrenched away, and the assailant dashed down into the bottom of the boat, which now, with disentangled oars, began to speed through the sea.

At this juncture, the left hand of Captain Delano, on one side, again clutched the half-reclined Don Benito, heedless that he was in a speechless faint, while his right foot, on the other side, ground the prostrate Negro, and his right arm pressed for added speed on the after oar, his eye bent forward, encouraging his men to their utmost.

But here the officer of the boat, who had at last succeeded in beating off the towing sailors, and was now, with face turned aft, assisting the bowsman at his oar, suddenly called to Captain Delano to see what the black was about, while a Portuguese oarsman shouted to him to give heed to what the Spaniard was saying.

Glancing down at his feet, Captain Delano saw the free hand of the servant aiming with a second dagger—a small one, before concealed in his wool—with this he was snakishly writhing up from the boat's bottom at the heart of his master, his countenance lividly vindictive, expressing the centered purpose of his soul; while the Spaniard, half-choked, was vainly shrinking away, with husky words, incoherent to all but the Portuguese.

That moment, across the long-benighted mind of Captain Delano, a flash of revelation swept, illuminating, in unanticipated clearness, his host's whole mysterious demeanor, with every enigmatic event of the day, as well as the entire past voyage of the *San Dominick*. He smote Babo's hand down, but his own heart smote him harder. With infinite pity he withdrew his hold from Don Benito. Not Captain Delano, but Don Benito, the black, in leaping into the boat, had intended to stab.

Both the black's hands were held, as, glancing up towards the *San Dominick*, Captain Delano, now with scales dropped from his eyes, saw the Negroes, not in misrule, not in tumult, not as if frantically concerned for Don Benito, but, with mask torn away, flourishing hatchets and knives in ferocious piratical revolt. Like delirious black dervishes, the six Ashantees danced on the poop. Prevented by their foes from springing into the water, the Spanish boys were hurrying up to the topmost spars, while such of a few Spanish sailors not already in the sea, less alert, were described, helplessly mixed in, on deck with the blacks.

Meantime Captain Delano hailed his own vessel, ordering the ports up, and the guns run out. But by this time the cable of the *San Dominick* had been cut, and the fag end, in lashing out, whipped away the canvas shroud about the beak, suddenly revealing, as the bleached hull swung round towards the open ocean, death for the figurehead, in a human skeleton, chalky comment on the chalked words below, FOLLOW YOUR LEADER.

At the sight, Don Benito, covering his face, wailed out:

" 'Tis he, Aranda! my murdered, unburied friend!"

Upon reaching the sealer, calling for ropes, Captain Delano bound the Negro, who made no resistance, and had him hoisted to the deck. He would then have assisted the now almost helpless Don Benito up the side; but Don Benito, wan as he was, refused to move, or be moved, until the Negro should have been first put below out of view. When, presently assured that it was done, he no more shrank from the ascent.

The boat was immediately dispatched back to pick up the three swimming sailors. Meantime, the guns were in readiness, though, owing to the *San Dominick* having glided somewhat astern of the sealer, only the aftermost one could be brought to bear. With this, they fired six times, thinking to cripple the fugitive ship by bringing down her spars, but only a few inconsiderable ropes were shot away. Soon the ship was beyond the gun's range, steering broad out of the bay, the blacks thickly clustering round the bowsprit, one moment with taunting cries towards the whites, the next with upthrown gestures hailing the now dusky moors of ocean—cawing crows escaped from the hand of the fowler.

The first impulse was to slip the cables and give chase. But, upon second thoughts, to pursue with whaleboat and yawl seemed more promising.

Upon inquiring of Don Benito what firearms they had on board the *San Dominick*, Captain Delano was answered that they had none that could be used, because, in the earlier stages of the mutiny, a cabin passenger, since dead, had secretly put out of order the locks of what few muskets there were. But with all his remaining strength Don Benito entreated the Americans not to give chase, either with ship or boat, for the Negroes had already proved themselves such desperadoes that, in case of a present assault, nothing but a total massacre of the whites could be looked for. But, regarding this warning as coming from one whose spirit had been crushed by misery, the American did not give up his design.

The boats were got ready and armed. Captain Delano ordered his men into them. He was going himself when Don Benito grasped his arm.

"What! have you saved my life, *señor*, and are you now going to throw away your own?"

The officers also, for reasons connected with their interests and those of the voyage, and a duty owing to the owners, strongly objected against their commander's going. Weighing their remonstrances a moment, Captain Delano felt bound to remain; appointing his chief mate—an athletic and resolute man, who had been a privateer's-man—to head the party. The more to encourage the sailors, they were told that the Spanish captain considered his ship good as lost; that she and her cargo, including some gold and silver, were worth more than a thousand doubloons. Take her, and no small part should be theirs. The sailors replied with a shout.

The fugitives had now almost gained an offing. It was nearly night, but the moon was rising. After hard, prolonged pulling, the boats came up on the ship's quarters, at a suitable distance laying upon their oars to discharge their muskets. Having no bullets to return, the Negroes sent their yells. But upon the second volley, Indianlike, they hurtled their hatchets. One took off a sailor's fingers. Another struck the whaleboat's bow, cutting off the rope there, and remaining stuck in the gunwale like a woodman's ax. Snatching it, quivering, from its lodgment, the mate hurled it back. The returned gauntlet now stuck in the ship's broken quarter-gallery, and so remained.

The Negroes giving too hot a reception, the whites kept a more respectful distance. Hovering now just out of reach of the hurtling hatchets, they, with a view to the close encounter which must soon come, sought to decoy the blacks into entirely disarming themselves of their most murderous weapons in a hand-to-hand fight, by foolishly flinging them, as missiles, short of the mark, into the sea. But, erelong perceiving the stratagem, the Negroes desisted, though not before many of them had to replace their lost hatchets with handspikes, an exchange which, as counted upon, proved, in the end, favorable to the assailants.

Meantime, with a strong wind the ship still clove the water, the boats alternately falling behind and pulling up to discharge fresh volleys.

The fire was mostly directed towards the stern, since there, chiefly, the Negroes at present were clustering. But to kill or maim the Negroes was not the object. To take them, with the ship, was the object. To do it, the ship must be boarded, which could not be done by boats while she was sailing so fast.

A thought now struck the mate. Observing the Spanish boys still aloft, high as they could get, he called to them to descend to the yards, and cut adrift the sails. It was done. About this time, owing to causes hereafter to be shown, two Spaniards, in the dress of sailors and conspicuously showing themselves, were killed, not by volleys, but by deliberate marksman's shots; while, as it afterwards appeared, by one of the general discharges Atufal, the black, and the Spaniard at the helm likewise were killed. What, now, with the loss of the sails and loss of leaders, the ship became unmanageable to the Negroes.

With creaking masts, she came heavily round to the wind, the prow slowly swinging into view of the boats, its skeleton gleaming in the horizontal moonlight and casting a gigantic ribbed shadow upon the water. One extended arm of the ghost seemed beckoning the whites to avenge it.

"Follow your leader!" cried the mate; and, one on each bow, the boats boarded. Sealing-spears and cutlasses crossed hatchets and handspikes. Huddled upon the longboat amidships, the Negresses raised a wailing chant, whose chorus was the clash of the steel.

For a time, the attack wavered, the Negroes wedging themselves to beat it back, the half-repelled sailors, as yet unable to gain a footing, fighting as troopers in the saddle, one leg sideways flung over the bulwark and one without, plying their cutlasses like carters' whips. But in vain. They were almost overborne, when, rallying themselves into a squad as one man, with a huzzah they sprang inboard, where, entangled, they involuntarily separated again. For a few breaths' space there was a vague, muffled, inner sound, as of submerged swordfish rushing hither and thither through shoals of blackfish. Soon, in a reunited band, and joined by the Spanish seamen, the whites came to the surface, irresistibly driving the Negroes toward the stern. But a barricade of casks and sacks, from side to side, had been thrown up by the mainmast. Here the Negroes faced about, and though scorning peace or truce, yet fain would have had respite. But, without pause overleaping the barrier, the unflagging sailors again closed. Exhausted, the blacks now fought in despair. Their red tongues lolled, wolflike, from their black mouths. But the pale sailors' teeth were set; not a word was spoken, and, in five minutes more, the ship was won.

Nearly a score of the Negroes were killed. Exclusive of those by the balls, many were mangled; their wounds—mostly inflicted by the long-edged sealing-spears, resembling those shaven ones of the English at Preston Pans, made by the poled scythes of the Highlanders. On the other side, none were killed, though several were wounded, some severely, including the mate. The surviving Negroes were temporarily secured, and the ship, towed back into the harbor at midnight, once more lay anchored.

Omitting the incidents and arrangements ensuing, suffice it that, after two days spent in refitting, the ships sailed in company for Conception, in Chile, and thence for Lima, in Peru; where, before the viceregal courts, the whole affair, from the beginning, underwent investigation.

Though, midway on the passage, the ill-fated Spaniard, relaxed from constraint, showed some signs of regaining health with free-will, yet, agreeably to his own foreboding, shortly before arriving at Lima, he relapsed, finally becoming so reduced as to be carried ashore in arms. Hearing of his story and plight, one of the many religious institutions of the City of Kings opened an hospitable refuge to him, where both physician and priest were his nurses, and a member of the order volunteered to be his one special guardian and consoler, by night and by day.

The following extracts, translated from one of the official Spanish documents, will, it is hoped, shed light on the preceding narrative, as well as, in the first place, reveal the true port of departure and true history of the *San Dominick*'s voyage, down to the time of her touching at the island of St. Maria.

But ere the extracts come it may be well to preface them with a remark.

The document selected, from among many others, for partial translation, contains the deposition of Benito Cereno, the first taken in the case. Some disclosures therein were at the time held dubious, for both learned and natural reasons. The tribunal inclined to the opinion that the deponent, not undisturbed in his mind by recent events, raved of some things which could never have happened. But subsequent depositions of the surviving sailors, bearing out the revelations of their captain in several of the strangest particulars, gave credence to the rest. So that the tribunal, in its final decision, rested its capital sentences upon statements which, had they lacked confirmation, it would have deemed it but duty to reject.

I, DON JOSÉ DE ABOS AND PADILLA, His Majesty's Notary for the Royal Revenue, and Register of this Province, and Notary Public of the Holy Crusade of this Bishopric, etc.

Do certify and declare, as much as is requisite in law, that, in the criminal cause commenced the twenty-fourth of the month of September, in the year seventeen hundred and ninety-nine, against the Negroes of the ship *San Dominick*, the following declaration before me was made:

Declaration of the first witness, DON BENITO CERENO.

The same day, and month, and year, His Honor, Doctor Juan Martínez de Rozas, Councilor of the Royal Audience of this Kingdom, and learned in the law of this Intendency, ordered the captain of the ship *San Dominick*, Don Benito Cereno, to appear, which he did in his litter, attended by the monk Infelez, of whom he received the oath, which he took by God, our Lord, and a sign of the Cross, under which he promised to tell the truth of whatever he should know and should be asked; and being interrogated agreeably to the tenor of the act commencing the process, he said that, on the twentieth of May last, he set sail with his ship from the port of Valparaiso, bound to that of Callao, loaded with the produce of the country beside thirty cases of hardware and one hundred and sixty blacks of both sexes, mostly belonging to Don Alexandro Aranda, gentleman, of the city of Mendoza; that the crew of the ship consisted of thirty-six men beside the persons who went as passengers; that the Negroes were in part as follows:

[*Here, in the original, follows a list of some fifty names, descriptions, and ages, compiled from certain recovered documents of Aranda's, and also from recollections of the deponent, from which portions only are extracted.*]

—One, from about eighteen to nineteen years, named José and this was the man that waited upon his master, Don Alexandro, and who speaks well the Spanish, having served him four or five years; *** a mulatto, named

Francesco, the cabin steward, of a good person and voice, having sung in the Valparaiso churches, native of the province of Buenos Ayres, aged about thirty-five years. *** A smart Negro, named Dago, who had been for many years a gravedigger among the Spaniards, aged forty-six years. *** Four old Negroes, born in Africa, from sixty to seventy, but sound, calkers by trade, whose names are as follows: the first was named Muri, and he was killed (as was also his son named Diamelo); the second, Nacta; the third, Yola, likewise killed; the fourth, Ghofan; and six full-grown Negroes, aged from thirty to forty-five, all raw, and born among the Ashantees—Matiluqui, Yan, Lecbe, Mapenda, Yambaio, Akim; four of whom were killed; *** a powerful Negro named Atufal, who being supposed to have been a chief in Africa, his owner set great store by him. *** And a small Negro of Senegal, but some years among the Spaniards, aged about thirty, which Negro's name was Babo; *** that he does not remember the names of the others, but that still expecting the residue of Don Alexandro's papers will be found, will then take due account of them all, and remit to the court; *** and thirty-nine women and children of all ages.

[*The catalogue over, the deposition goes on*]

*** That all the Negroes slept upon deck, as is customary in this navigation, and none wore fetters, because the owner, his friend Aranda, told him that they were all tractable; *** that on the seventh day after leaving port, at three o'clock in the morning, all the Spaniards being asleep except the two officers on the watch, who were the boatswain, Juan Robles, and the carpenter, Juan Bautista Gayete, and the helmsman and his boy, the Negroes revolted suddenly, wounded dangerously the boatswain and the carpenter, and successively killed eighteen men of those who were sleeping upon deck, some with handspikes and hatchets, and others by throwing them alive overboard, after tying them; that of the Spaniards upon deck they left about seven, as he thinks, alive and tied, to maneuver the ship, and three or four more, who hid themselves, remained also alive. Although in the act of revolt the Negroes made themselves masters of the hatchway, six or seven wounded went through it to the cockpit, without any hindrance on their part; that during the act of revolt the mate and another person, whose name he does not recollect, attempted to come up through the hatchway, but, being quickly wounded, were obliged to return to the cabin; that the deponent resolved at break of day to come up the companionway, where the Negro Babo was, being the ringleader, and Atufal, who assisted him, and having spoken to them, exhorted them to cease committing such atrocities, asking them, at the same time what they wanted and intended to do, offering, himself, to obey their commands; that notwithstanding this, they threw, in his presence, three men, alive and tied, overboard; that they told the deponent to come up and that they would not kill him; which having done, the Negro Babo asked him whether there were in those seas any Negro countries where they might be carried, and he answered them, No; that the Negro Babo afterwards told him to carry them to Senegal, or to the neighboring islands of St. Nicholas, and he answered that this was impossible on account of the great distance, the necessity involved of rounding Cape Horn, the bad condition of the vessel, the want of provisions, sails, and water; but that the Negro Babo replied to him he must carry them in anyway, that they would do and conform themselves to everything the deponent should require as to eating and drinking; that after a long conference, being absolutely compelled to please them, for they threatened to kill all the whites if they were not, at all events, carried to Senegal, he told them that what was most wanting for the voyage was water, that they would go near the coast to take it, and thence they would proceed on their course; that the Negro Babo agreed to it, and the deponent steered towards the intermediate ports, hoping to meet some Spanish or foreign vessel that would save them; that within ten or eleven days they saw the land, and continued their course by it in the vicinity of Nasca; that the deponent observed that the Negroes were now restless and mutinous because he did not effect the taking in of water, the Negro Babo having required, with threats, that it should be done, without fail, the following day; he told him he saw plainly that the coast was steep, and the rivers designated in the maps were not to be found, with other reasons suitable to the circumstances, that the best way would be to go to the island of Santa Maria, where they might water easily, it being a solitary island, as the foreigners did; that the deponent did not go to Pisco, that was near, nor make any other port of the coast, because the Negro Babo had intimated to him several times that he would kill all the whites the very moment he should perceive any city, town, or settlement of any kind on the shores to which they should be carried; that having determined to go to the island of Santa Maria, as the deponent had planned, for the purpose of trying whether, on the passage or near the island itself, they could find any vessel that should favor them, or whether he could escape from it in a boat to the neighboring coast of Arruco, to adopt the necessary means he immediately changed his course, steering for the island; that the Negroes Babo and Atufal held daily conferences, in which they discussed what was necessary for their design of returning to Senegal, whether they were to kill all the Spaniards, and particularly the deponent; that eight days after parting from the coast of Nasca, the deponent being on the watch a little after daybreak, and soon after the Negroes had their meeting, the Negro Babo came to the place where the deponent was and told him that he had determined to kill his master, Don Alexandro Aranda, both because he and his companions could not otherwise be sure of their liberty, and that, to keep the seamen in subjection, he wanted to prepare a warning of what road they should be made to take did they or any of them oppose him, and that, by means of the death of Don Alexandro, that warning would best be given, but that what this last meant the deponent did not at the time comprehend, nor could not, further than that the death of Don Alexandro was intended; and moreover the Negro Babo proposed to the deponent to call the mate Raneds, who was sleeping in the cabin, before the thing was done, for fear, as the deponent understood it, that the mate, who was a good navigator, should be killed with Don Alexandro and the rest; that the deponent, who was the friend from youth of Don Alexandro, prayed and conjured, but all was useless, for the Negro Babo answered him that the thing could not be prevented, and that all the Spaniards risked their death if they should attempt to frustrate his will in this matter or any other; that, in this conflict, the deponent called the mate, Raneds, who was forced to go apart, and immediately the Negro Babo commanded the Ashantee Martinqui and the Ashantee Lecbe to go and commit the murder; that these two went down with hatchets to the berth of Don Alexandro, that, yet half alive and mangled, they dragged him on deck; that they were going to throw him overboard in that state, but

the Negro Babo stopped them, bidding the murder be completed on the
deck before him, which was done, when, by his orders, the body was carried
below, forward; that nothing more was seen of it by the deponent for three
days; *** that Don Alonzo Sidonia, an old man, long resident at Valparaiso,
and lately appointed to a civil office in Peru, whither he had taken passage,
was at the time sleeping in the berth opposite Don Alexandro's; that awakening at his cries, surprised by them, and at the sight of the Negroes with
their bloody hatchets in their hands, he threw himself into the sea through
a window which was near him, and was drowned, without it being in the
power of the deponent to assist or take him up; *** that a short time after
killing Aranda, they brought upon deck his german-cousin, of middle-age,
Don Francisco Masa, of Mendoza, and the young Don Joaquín, Marqués de
Aramboalaza, then lately from Spain, with his Spanish servant Ponce, and the
three young clerks of Aranda, José Mozairi, Lorenzo Bargas, and Hermenegildo Gandix, all of Cádiz; that Don Joaquín and Hermenegildo Gandix,
the Negro Babo, for purposes hereafter to appear, preserved alive, but Don
Francisco Masa, José Mozairi, and Lorenzo Bargas, with Ponce the servant,
beside the boatswain, Juan Robles, the boatswain's mates, Manuel Viscaya and
Roderigo Hurta, and four of the sailors the Negro Babo ordered to be thrown
alive into the sea, although they made no resistance nor begged for anything
else but mercy; that the boatswain, Juan Robles, who knew how to swim, kept
the longest above water, making acts of contrition, and, in the last words he
uttered, charged this deponent to cause mass to be said for his soul to our
Lady of Succor; *** that, during the three days which followed, the deponent,
uncertain what fate had befallen the remains of Don Alexandro, frequently
asked the Negro Babo where they were, and, if still on board, whether they
were to be preserved for interment ashore, entreating him so to order it, that
the Negro Babo answered nothing till the fourth day, when, at sunrise, the
deponent coming on deck, the Negro Babo showed him a skeleton, which
had been substituted for the ship's proper figurehead—the image of Christopher Colón, the discoverer of the New World; that the Negro Babo asked
him whose skeleton that was, and whether, from its whiteness, he should not
think it a white's, that, upon discovering his face, the Negro Babo, coming
close, said words to this effect: "Keep faith with the blacks from here to
Senegal, or you shall in spirit, as now in body, follow your leader," pointing
to the prow; *** that the same morning the Negro Babo took by succession
each Spaniard forward, and asked him whose skeleton that was, and whether,
from its whiteness, he should not think it a white's; that each Spaniard covered his face; that then to each the Negro Babo repeated the words in the first
place said to the deponent; *** that they (the Spaniards), being then assembled aft, the Negro Babo harangued them, saying that he had now done all;
that the deponent (as navigator for the Negroes) might pursue his course,
warning him and all of them that they should, soul and body, go the way of
Don Alexandro if he saw them (the Spaniards) speak or plot anything against
them (the Negroes)—a threat which was repeated every day; that, before the
events last mentioned, they had tied the cook to throw him overboard, for it
is not known what thing they heard him speak, but finally the Negro Babo
spared his life, at the request of the deponent; that a few days after, the
deponent, endeavoring not to omit any means to preserve the lives of the
remaining whites, spoke to the Negroes of peace and tranquility, and agreed
to draw up a paper, signed by the deponent and the sailors who could write,

as also by the Negro Babo, for himself and all the blacks, in which the deponent obliged himself to carry them to Senegal, and they not to kill any more, and he formally to make over to them the ship, with the cargo, with which they were for that time satisfied and quieted. *** But the next day, the more surely to guard against the sailors' escape, the Negro Babo commanded all the boats to be destroyed but the longboat, which was unseaworthy, and another, a cutter in good condition, which, knowing it would yet be wanted for towing the water casks, he had it lowered down into the hold.

* * * * * *

[*Various particulars of the prolonged and perplexed navigation ensuing here follow, with incidents of a calamitous calm, from which portion one passage is extracted, to wit:*]

—That on the fifth day of the calm, all on board suffering much from the heat and want of water, and five having died in fits, and mad, the Negroes became irritable, and for a chance gesture, which they deemed suspicious— though it was harmless—made by the mate, Raneds, to the deponent in the act of handling a quadrant, they killed him; but that for this they afterwards were sorry, the mate being the only remaining navigator on board, except the deponent.

* * * * * *

—That omitting other events which daily happened, and which can only serve uselessly to recall past misfortunes and conflicts, after seventy-three day's navigation, reckoned from the time they sailed from Nasca, during which they navigated under a scanty allowance of water, and were afflicted with the calms before mentioned, they at last arrived at the island of Santa Maria, on the seventeenth of the month of August, at about six o'clock in the afternoon, at which hour they cast anchor very near the American ship *Bachelor's Delight*, which lay in the same bay, commanded by the generous Captain Amasa Delano; but at six o'clock in the morning they had already descried the port, and the Negroes became uneasy, as soon as at distance they saw the ship, not having expected to see one there; that the Negro Babo pacified them, assuring them that no fear need be had; that straight- way he ordered the figure on the bow to be covered with canvas, as for repairs, and had the decks a little set in order; that for a time the Negro Babo and the Negro Atufal conferred; that the Negro Atufal was for sailing away but the Negro Babo would not, and, by himself, cast about what to do; that at last he came to the deponent, proposing to him to say and do all that the deponent declares to have said and done to the American captain; * * * * * * * that the Negro Babo warned him that if he varied in the least, or uttered any word, or gave any look that should give the least intimation of the past events or present state, he would instantly kill him, with all his companions, showing a dagger which he carried hid, saying something which, as he understood it, meant that the dagger would be alert as his eye; that the Negro Babo then announced the plan to all his companions, which pleased them; that he then, the better to disguise the truth, devised many expedients, in some of them uniting deceit and defense; that of this sort was the device of the six Ashantees before named, who were his bravoes; that them he stationed on the break of the poop, as if to clean certain hatchets (in cases, which were part of the cargo), but in reality to use them, and distribute them at need, and at a given word he told them; that, among other devices, was the device of presenting Atufal, his right-hand man, as chained, though in a moment the chains could be dropped; that in every particular he informed the deponent what part he was expected to enact in every device, and what story he was to tell on every occasion, always threatening him with instant death if he varied in the least: that, conscious that many of the Negroes would be turbulent, the Negro Babo appointed the four aged Negroes, who were calkers, to keep what domestic order they could on the decks; that again and again he harangued the Spaniards and his companions, informing them of his intent and of his devices, and of the invented story that this deponent was to tell, charging them lest any of them varied from that story; that these arrangements were made and matured during the interval of two or three hours between their first sighting the ship and the arrival on board of Captain Amasa Delano coming in his boat, and all gladly receiving him; that the deponent, as well as he could force himself, acting then the part of principal owner and a free captain of the ship, told Captain Amasa Delano, when called upon, that he came from Buenos Ayres, bound to Lima, with three hundred Negroes; that off Cape Horn, and in a subsequent fever, many Negroes had died; that also, by similar casualties, all the sea officers and the greatest part of the crew had died.

* * * * * *

[*And so the deposition goes on, circumstantially recounting the fictitious story dictated to the deponent by Babo, and through the deponent imposed upon Captain Delano, and also recounting the friendly offers of Captain Delano, with other things, but all of which is here omitted. After the fictitious story, etc., the deposition proceeds:*]

* * * * * *

—That the generous Captain Amasa Delano remained on board all the day, till he left the ship anchored at six o'clock in the evening, deponent speaking to him always of his pretended misfortunes, under the fore-mentioned principles, without having had it in his power to tell a single word or give him the least hint, that he might know the truth and state of things, because the Negro Babo, performing the office of an officious servant with all the appearance of submission of the humble slave, did not leave the deponent one moment; that this was in order to observe the deponent's actions and words, for the Negro Babo understands well the Spanish, and besides, there were thereabout some others who were constantly on the watch, and likewise understood the Spanish; *** that upon one occasion, while deponent was standing on the deck conversing with Amasa Delano, by a secret sign the Negro Babo drew him (the deponent) aside, the act appearing as if originating with the deponent; that then, he being drawn aside, the Negro Babo proposed to him to gain from Amasa Delano full particulars about his ship, and crew, and arms; that the deponent asked "For what?" that, the Negro Babo answered he might conceive; that, grieved at the prospect of what might overtake the generous Captain Amasa Delano, the deponent at first refused to ask the desired questions, and used every argument to induce the Negro Babo to give up this new design; that the Negro Babo showed the point of his dagger; that after the information had been obtained the Negro Babo again drew him aside, telling him that that very night he (the deponent) would be captain of two ships, instead of one, for that, great part of the American's ship's crew being to be absent fishing, the six Ashantees, without anyone else, would easily take it; that at this time he said other things to the same purpose; that no entreaties availed; that, before Amasa Delano's coming on board, no hint had been given touching the capture of the American ship; that to prevent this project the deponent was powerless; ***—that in some things his memory is confused, he cannot distinctly recall every event; ***—that as soon as they had cast anchor at six of the clock in the evening, as has before been stated, the American captain took leave, to return to his vessel; that upon a sudden impulse, which the deponent believes to have come from God and his angels, he, after the farewell had been said, followed the generous Captain Amasa Delano as far as the gunwale, where he stayed, under pretense of taking leave, until Amasa Delano should have been seated in his boat; that, on shoving off, the deponent sprang from the gunwale into the boat, and fell into it, he knows not how, God guarding him; that—

[*Here, in the original, follows the account of what further happened at the escape, and how the* San Dominick *was retaken, and of the passage to the coast; including in the recital many expressions of "eternal gratitude" to the "generous Captain Amasa Delano." The deposition then proceeds with recapitulatory remarks, and a partial renumeration of the Negroes, making record of their individual part in the past events, with a view to furnishing, according to command of the court, the data whereon to found the criminal sentences to be pronounced. From this portion is the following:*]

—That he believes that all the Negroes, though not in the first place knowing to the design of revolt, when it was accomplished, approved it. *** That the Negro José, eighteen years old, and in the personal service of Don Alexandro, was the one who communicated the information to the Negro Babo about the state of things in the cabin, before the revolt; that this is known, because, in the preceding midnight, he used to come from his berth, which was under his master's, in the cabin, to the deck where the ringleader and his associates were, and had secret conversations with the Negro Babo, in which he was several times seen by the mate; that, one night, the mate drove him away twice; ** that this same Negro José was the one who, without being commanded to do so by the Negro Babo, as Lecbe and Martinqui were, stabbed his master, Don Alexandro, after he had been dragged half-lifeless to the deck; ** that the mulatto steward, Francesco, was of the first band of revolters, that he was, in all things, the creature and tool of the Negro Babo; that, to make his court, he, just before a repast in the cabin, proposed to the Negro Babo poisoning a dish for the generous Captain Amasa Delano; this is known and believed, because the Negroes have said it; but that the Negro Babo, having another design, forbade Francesco; ** that the Ashantee Lecbe was one of the worst of them, for that, on the day the ship was retaken, he assisted in the defense of her with a hatchet in each hand, with one of which he wounded in the breast the chief mate of Amasa Delano, in the first act of boarding; this all knew; that, in sight of the deponent, Lecbe struck with a hatchet, Don Francisco Masa, when, by the Negro Babo's orders, he was carrying him to throw him overboard alive, beside participating in the murder, before mentioned, of Don Alexandro Aranda and others of the cabin passengers; that, owing to the fury with which the Ashantees fought in the engagement with the boats, but this Lecbe and Yan survived; that Yan was bad as Lecbe; that Yan was the man who, by Babo's command, willingly prepared the skeleton of Don Alexandro, in a way the Negroes afterwards told the deponent, but which he, so long as reason is left him, can never divulge; that Yan and Leche were the two who, in a calm by night, riveted the skeleton to the bow; this also the Negroes told him; that the Negro Babo was he who traced the inscription below it; that the Negro Babo was the plotter from first to last; he ordered every murder, and was the helm and keel of the revolt; that Atufal was his lieutenant in all, but Atufal with his own hand committed no murder, nor did the Negro Babo; ** that Atufal was shot, being killed in the fight with the boats, ere boarding; ** that the Negresses, of age, were knowing to the revolt, and testified themselves satisfied at the death of their master, Don Alexandro; that, had the Negroes not restrained them, they would have tortured to death, instead of simply killing, the Spaniards slain by command of the Negro Babo; that the Negresses used their utmost influence to have the deponent made away with; that, in the various acts of murder, they sang songs and danced—not gaily, but solemnly, and before the engagement with the boats, as well as during the action, they sang melancholy songs to the Negroes, and that this melancholy tone was more inflaming than a different one would have been, and was so intended; that all this is believed, because the Negroes have said it. ***—that of the thirty-six men of the crew, exclusive of the passengers (all of whom are now dead), which the deponent had knowledge of, six only remained alive, with four cabin boys and ship boys, not included with the crew; ***—that the Negroes broke an arm of one of the cabin boys and gave him strokes with hatchets.

[*Then follow various random disclosures referring to various periods of time. The following are extracted;*]

—That during the presence of Captain Amasa Delano on board, some attempts were made by the sailors, and one by Hermenegildo Gandix, to convey hints to him of the true state of affairs, but that these attempts were ineffectual, owing to fear of incurring death, and, furthermore, owing to the devices which offered contradictions to the true state of affairs, as well as owing to the generosity and piety of Amasa Delano incapable of sounding such wickedness; *** that Luys Galgo, a sailor about sixty years of age, and formerly of the king's navy, was one of those who sought to convey tokens to Captain Amasa Delano; but his intent, though undiscovered, being suspected, he was, on a pretense, made to retire out of sight, and at last into the hold, and there was made away with. This the Negroes have since said; *** that one of the ship boys feeling, from Captain Amasa Delano's presence, some hopes of release, and not having enough prudence, dropped some chance word respecting his expectations, which being overheard and understood by a slave boy with whom he was eating at the time, the latter struck him on the head with a knife, inflicting a bad wound, but of which the boy is now healing; that likewise, not long before the ship was brought to anchor, one of the seamen steering at the time endangered himself by letting the blacks remark some expression in his countenance, arising from a cause similar to the above, but this sailor, by his heedful after conduct, escaped; *** that these statements are made to show the court that from the beginning to the end of the revolt it was impossible for the deponent and his men to act otherwise than they did; ***—that the third clerk, Hermenegildo Gandix, who before had been forced to live among the seamen, wearing a seaman's habit, and in all respects appearing to be one for the time, he, Gandix, was killed by a musket ball fired through mistake from the boats before boarding; having in his fright run up the mizzen rigging, calling to the boats—"don't board," lest upon their boarding the Negroes should kill him; that this inducing the Americans to believe he some way favored the cause of the Negroes, they fired two balls at him, so that he fell wounded from the rigging, and was drowned in the sea; ***—that the young Don Joaquín, Marqués de Aramboalaza, like Hermenegildo Gandix, the third clerk, was degraded to the office and appearance of a common seaman; that upon one occasion when Don Joaquín shrank, the Negro Babo commanded the Ashantee Lecbe to take tar and heat it, and pour it upon Don Joaquín's hands; ***—that Don Joaquín was killed owing to another mistake of the Americans, but one impossible to be avoided, as, upon the approach of the boats, Don Joaquín, with a hatchet tied edge out and upright to his hand, was made by the Negroes to appear on the bulwarks; whereupon, seen with arms in his hands and in a questionable attitude, he was shot for a renegade seaman;***—that on the person of Don Joaquín was found secreted a jewel, which, by papers that were discovered, proved to have been meant for the shrine of our Lady of Mercy in Lima, a votive offering, beforehand prepared and guarded, to attest his gratitude when he should have landed in Peru, his last destination, for the safe conclusion of his entire voyage from Spain; ***—that the jewel, with the other effects of the late Don Joaquín, is in the custody of the brethren of the Hospital de Sacerdotes, awaiting the disposition of the honorable court; ***—that, owing to the condition of the deponent, as well as the haste in which the boats departed for the attack, the Americans were not forewarned that there were, among the apparent crew, a passenger and one of the clerks disguised by the Negro Babo;***—that, beside the Negroes killed in action, some were killed after the capture and reanchoring at night, when shackled to the ringbolts on deck; that these deaths were committed by the sailors, ere they could be prevented. That so soon as informed of it, Captain Amasa Delano used all his authority, and in particular with his own hand struck down Martínez Gola, who having found a razor in the pocket of an old jacket of his which one of the shackled Negroes had on, was aiming it at the Negro's throat; that the noble Captain Amasa Delano also wrenched from the hand of Bartholomew Barlo a dagger, secreted at the time of the massacre of the whites, with which he was in the act of stabbing a shackled Negro, who, the same day, with another Negro, had thrown him down and jumped upon him; ***—that, for all the events, befalling through so long a time, during which the ship was in the hands of the Negro Babo, he cannot here give account, but that what he has said is the most substantial of what occurs to him at present, and is the truth under the oath which he has taken; which declaration he affirmed and ratified, after hearing it read to him.

He said that he is twenty-nine years of age, and broken in body and mind; that when finally dismissed by the court, he shall not return home to Chile but betake himself to the monastery of Mount Agonia without; and signed with his honor, and crossed himself, and, for the time, departed as he came, in his litter, with the monk Infelez, to the Hospital de Sacerdotes.

BENITO CERENO.

DOCTOR ROZAS.

If the deposition have served as the key to fit into the lock of the complications which precede it, then, as a vault whose door has been flung back, the *San Dominick*'s hull lies open today.

Hitherto the nature of this narrative, besides rendering the intricacies in the beginning unavoidable, has more or less required that many things, instead of being set down in the order of occurrence, should be retrospectively or irregularly given; this last is the case with the following passages, which will conclude the account:

During the long, mild voyage to Lima, there was, as before hinted, a period during which the sufferer a little recovered his health, or, at least in some degree, his tranquility. Ere the decided relapse which came, the two captains had many cordial conversations—their fraternal unreserve in singular contrast with former withdrawments.

Again and again it was repeated how hard it had been to enact the part forced on the Spaniard by Babo.

"Ah, my dear friend," Don Benito once said, "at those very times when you thought me so morose and ungrateful, nay, when, as you now admit, you half thought of me plotting your murder, at those very times my heart was frozen; I could not look at you, thinking of what, both on board this ship and your own, hung, from other hands, over my kind benefactor. And as God lives, Don Amasa, I know not whether desire for my own safety alone could have nerved me to that leap into your boat, had it not been for the thought that, did you, unenlightened, return to your ship, you, my best friend, with all who might be with you, stolen upon that night in your hammocks, would never in this world have wakened again. Do but think how you walked this deck, how you sat in this cabin, every inch of ground mined into honeycombs under you. Had I dropped the least hint, made the least advance towards an understanding between us, death, explosive death— yours as mine—would have ended the scene."

"True, true," cried Captain Delano, starting, "you have saved my life, Don Benito, more than I yours; saved it, too, against my knowledge and will."

"Nay, my friend," rejoined the Spaniard, courteous even to the point of religion, "God charmed your life, but you saved mine. To think of some things you did—those smilings and chattings, rash pointings and gesturings. For less than these, they slew my mate, Raneds; but you had the Prince of Heaven's safe conduct through all ambuscades."

"Yes, all is owing to Providence, I know: but the temper of my mind that morning was more than commonly pleasant, while the sight of so much suffering, more apparent than real, added to my good-nature, compassion, and charity, happily interweaving the three. Had it been otherwise, doubtless, as you hint, some of my interferences might have ended unhappily enough. Besides, those feelings I spoke of enabled me to get the better of momentary distrust, at times when acuteness might have cost me my life, without saving another's. Only at the end did my suspicions get the better of me, and you know how wide of the mark they then proved."

"Wide, indeed," said Don Benito, sadly; "you were with me all day; stood with me, sat with me, talked with me, looked at me, ate with me, drank with me; and yet, your last act was to clutch for a monster, not only an innocent man, but the most pitiable of all men. To such degree may malign machinations and deceptions impose. So far may even the best man err in judging the conduct of one with the recesses of whose condition he is not acquainted. But you were forced to it, and you were in time undeceived. Would that, in both respects, it was so ever, and with all men."

"You generalize, Don Benito; and mournfully enough. But the past is passed; why moralize upon it? Forget it. See, yon bright sun has forgotten it all, and the blue sea, and the blue sky; these have turned over new leaves."

"Because they have no memory," he dejectedly replied; "because they are not human."

"But these mild trades that now fan your cheek, do they not come with a human-like healing to you? Warm friends, steadfast friends are the trades."

"With their steadfastness they but waft me to my tomb, *señor*," was the foreboding response.

"You are saved," cried Captain Delano, more and more astonished and pained; "you are saved: what has cast such a shadow upon you?"

"The Negro."

There was silence, while the moody man sat, slowly and unconsciously gathering his mantle about him, as if it were a pall.

There was no more conversation that day.

But if the Spaniard's melancholy sometimes ended in muteness upon topics like the above, there were others upon which he never spoke at all; on which, indeed all his old reserves were piled. Pass over the worst, and, only to elucidate, let an item or two of these be cited. The dress, so precise and costly, worn by him on the day whose events have been narrated, had not willingly been put on. And that silver-mounted sword, apparent symbol of despotic command, was not, indeed, a sword, but the ghost of one. The scabbard, artificially stiffened, was empty.

As for the black—whose brain, not body, had schemed and led the revolt, with the plot—his slight frame, inadequate to that which it held, had at once yielded to the superior muscular strength of his captor, in the boat. Seeing all was over, he uttered no sound, and could not be forced to. His aspect seemed to say: since I cannot do deeds, I will not speak words. Put in irons in the hold with the rest, he was carried to Lima. During the passage, Don Benito did not visit him. Nor then, nor at any time after, would he look at him. Before the tribunal he refused. When pressed by the judges he fainted. On the testimony of the sailors alone rested the legal identity of Babo.

Some months after, dragged to the gibbet at the tail of a mule, the black met his voiceless end. The body was burned to ashes; but for many days, the head, that hive of subtlety, fixed on a pole in the plaza, met, unabashed, the gazes of the whites, and across the Plaza looked towards St. Bartholomew's church, in whose vaults slept then, as now, the recovered bones of Aranda, and across the Rimac bridge looked towards the monastery, on Mount Agonia without; where, three months after being dismissed by the court, Benito Cereno, borne on the bier, did, indeed, follow his leader.

QUESTIONS FOR DISCUSSION AND WRITING

1. Describe the narrative voice in "Benito Cereno." What is the narrator like? What is the relationship between him and the focal character, Captain Delano? What is the effect of shifting, late in the story, to Benito Cereno's deposition before the court in Lima?

2. By presenting the story twice, first from the point of view of Delano and then again in the deposition from the viewpoint of Cereno, Melville makes the story a study in interpretation—the difficulty of determining the truth behind what we see and hear. Is it significant that the viewpoint of the third major character, Babo, is never represented?

3. Would we be justified in considering the two captains, Delano and Cereno, as foils? How are they alike? How do they differ?

4. Early readers of "Benito Cereno" regarded it as a racist story that caricatured Babo and celebrated his victim Benito Cereno. More recently, critics have read it as a devastatingly ironic attack on slavery and racism. What is the evidence for each reading?

5. Ships have often been used as microcosms: models of the larger world. Is there any suggestion that Melville would like us to interpret the *San Dominick* in this way? Notice that the original figurehead of the ship is Columbus, "discoverer" of the New World, and that "Follow Your Leader" can be taken as referring to him. Do other details support the interpretation of the *San Dominick* as microcosmic?

Leo Tolstoy

Count Leo Tolstoy (1828–1910) was born into a wealthy, aristocratic Russian family and grew up on the family estate at Yasnaya Polyana, about one hundred miles south of Moscow. He began to write in his twenties while serving as a soldier. When he left the army, he returned to manage the family estate; there he wrote his two great masterpieces *War and Peace* (1869) and *Anna Karenina* (1877). Soon after writing the second novel, Tolstoy underwent a radical personal transformation. Adopting a creed of Christian anarchy, he gave up such luxuries as meat, tobacco, and alcohol, dressed as a peasant, and spent his days in manual labor. Most of his works after 1879 develop his ascetic creed: *What Then Must We Do?* (1886), "The Death of Ivan Ilyitch" (1886), "The Kreutzer Sonata" (1891), *Resurrection* (1899), and the play *The Power of Darkness* (1888). Tolstoy, alienated from most of his family, fled his home in 1910, at the age of eighty-two, and died in a railway station a few days later.

THE DEATH OF IVAN ILYITCH*

I

Inside the great building of the Law Courts, during the interval in the hearing of the Melvinsky case, the members of the judicial council and the public prosecutor were gathered together in the private room of Ivan Yegorovitch Shebek, and the conversation turned upon the celebrated Krasovsky case. Fyodor Vassilievitch hotly maintained that the case was not in the jurisdiction of the court. Yegor Ivanovitch stood up for his own view; but from the first Pyotr Ivanovitch, who had not entered into the discussion, took no interest in it, but was looking through the newspapers which had just been brought in.

"Gentlemen!" he said, "Ivan Ilyitch is dead!"

"You don't say so!"

"Here, read it," he said to Fyodor Vassilievitch, handing him the fresh still damp-smelling paper.

Within a black margin was printed: "Praskovya Fyodorovna Golovin with heart-felt affliction informs friends and relatives of the decease of her beloved husband, member of the Court of Justice, Ivan Ilyitch Golovin, who passed away on the 4th of February. The funeral will take place on Thursday at one o'clock."

Ivan Ilyitch was a colleague of the gentlemen present, and all liked him. It was some weeks now since he had been taken ill; his illness had been said to be incurable. His post had been kept open for him, but it had been thought that in case of his death Alexyeev might receive his appointment, and either Vinnikov or Shtabel would succeed to Alexyeev's. So that on hearing of Ivan Ilyitch's death, the first thought of each of the gentlemen in the room was of the effect this death might have on the transfer or promotion of themselves or their friends.

"Now I am sure of getting Shtabel's place or Vinnikov's," thought Fyodor Vassilievitch. "It was promised me long ago, and the promotion means eight hundred rubles additional income, besides the grants for office expenses."

---

*Translated by Constance Garnett

"Now I shall have to petition for my brother-in-law to be transferred from Kaluga," thought Pyotr Ivanovitch. "My wife will be very glad. She won't be able to say now that I've never done anything for her family."

"I thought somehow that he'd never get up from his bed again," Pyotr Ivanovitch said aloud. "I'm sorry!"

"But what was it exactly was wrong with him?"

"The doctors could not decide. That's to say, they did decide, but differently. When I saw him last, I thought he would get over it."

"Well, I positively haven't called there ever since the holidays. I've kept meaning to go."

"Had he any property?"

"I think there's something, very small, of his wife's. But something quite trifling."

"Yes, one will have to go and call. They live such a terribly long way off."

"A long way from you, you mean. Everything's a long way from your place."

"There, he can never forgive me for living the other side of the river," said Pyotr Ivanovitch, smiling at Shebek. And they began to talk of the great distances between different parts of town, and went back into the court.

Besides the reflections upon the changes and promotions in the service likely to ensue from this death, the very fact of the death of an intimate acquaintance excited in every one who heard of it, as such a fact always does, a feeling of relief that "it is he that is dead, and not I."

"Only think! he is dead, but here am I all right," each one thought or felt. The more intimate acquaintances, the so-called friends of Ivan Ilyitch, could not help thinking too that now they had the exceedingly tiresome social duties to perform of going to the funeral service and paying the widow a visit of condolence.

The most intimately acquainted with their late colleague were Fyodor Vassilievitch and Pyotr Ivanovitch.

Pyotr Ivanovitch had been a comrade of his at the school of jurisprudence, and considered himself under obligations to Ivan Ilyitch.

Telling his wife at dinner of the news of Ivan Ilyitch's death and his reflections as to the possibility of getting her brother transferred into their circuit, Pyotr Ivanovitch, without lying down for his usual nap, put on his frockcoat and drove to Ivan Ilyitch's.

At the entrance before Ivan Ilyitch's flat stood a carriage and two hired flies.[1] Downstairs in the entry near the hat-stand there was leaning against the wall a coffin-lid with tassels and braiding freshly rubbed up with pipeclay. Two ladies were taking off their cloaks. One of them he knew, the sister of Ivan Ilyitch; the other was a lady he did not know. Pyotr Ivanovitch's colleague, Shvarts, was coming down; and from the top stair, seeing who it was coming in, he stopped and winked at him, as though to say: "Ivan Ilyitch has made a mess of it; it's a very different matter with you and me."

Shvarts's face, with his English whiskers[2] and all his thin figure in his frockcoat, had, as it always had, an air of elegant solemnity; and this solemnity, always such a contrast to Shvarts's playful character, had a special piquancy here. So thought Pyotr Ivanovitch.

Pyotr Ivanovitch let the ladies pass on in front of him, and walked slowly up the stairs after them. Shvarts had not come down, but was waiting at the top. Pyotr

[1] Light, covered, horse-drawn cabs.
[2] Long, flowing side whiskers.

Ivanovitch knew what for; he wanted obviously to settle up with him where their game of *vint*[3] was to be that evening. The ladies went up to the widow's room; while Shvarts, with his lips tightly and gravely shut and amusement in his eyes, with a twitch of his eyebrows motioned Pyotr Ivanovitch to the right, to the room where the dead man was.

Pyotr Ivanovitch went in, as people always do on such occasions, in uncertainty as to what he would have to do there. One thing he felt sure of—that crossing oneself never comes amiss on such occasions. As to whether it was necessary to bow down while doing so, he did not feel quite sure, and so chose a middle course. On entering the room he began crossing himself, and made a slight sort of bow. So far as the movements of his hands and head permitted him, he glanced while doing so about the room. Two young men, one a high school boy, nephews probably, were going out of the room, crossing themselves. An old lady was standing motionless; and a lady, with her eyebrows queerly lifted, was saying something to her in a whisper. A deacon in a frockcoat, resolute and hearty, was reading something aloud with an expression that precluded all possibility of contradiction. A younger peasant who used to wait at table, Gerasim, walking with light footsteps in front of Pyotr Ivanovitch, was sprinkling something on the floor. Seeing this, Pyotr Ivanovitch was at once aware of the faint odor of the decomposing corpse. On his last visit to Ivan Ilyitch Pyotr Ivanovitch had seen this peasant in his room; he was performing the duties of a sicknurse, and Ivan Ilyitch liked him particularly. Pyotr Ivanovitch continued crossing himself and bowing in a direction intermediate between the coffin, the deacon, and the holy pictures on the table in the corner. Then when this action of making the sign of the cross with his hand seemed to him to have been unduly prolonged, he stood still and began to scrutinize the dead man.

The dead man lay, as dead men always do lie, in a peculiarly heavy dead way, his stiffened limbs sunk in the cushions of the coffin, and his head bent back forever on the pillow, and thrust up, as dead men always do, his yellow waxen forehead with bald spots on the sunken temples, and his nose that stood out sharply and, as it were, squeezed on the upper lip. He was much changed, even thinner since Pyotr Ivanovitch had seen him, but his face—as always with the dead—was more handsome, and, above all, more impressive than it had been when he was alive. On the face was an expression of what had to be done having been done, and rightly done. Besides this, there was too in that expression a reproach or a reminder for the living. This reminder seemed to Pyotr Ivanovitch uncalled for, or, at least, to have nothing to do with him. He felt something unpleasant; and so Pyotr Ivanovitch once more crossed himself hurriedly, and, as it struck him, too hurriedly, not quite in accordance with the proprieties, turned and went to the door. Shvarts was waiting for him in the adjoining room, standing with his legs apart and both hands behind his back playing with his top hat. A single glance at the playful, sleek, and elegant figure of Shvarts revived Pyotr Ivanovitch. He felt that he, Shvarts, was above it, and would not give way to depressing impressions. The mere sight of him said plainly: the incident of the service over the body of Ivan Ilyitch cannot possibly constitute a sufficient ground for recognizing the business of the session suspended,—in other words, in no way can it hinder us from shuffling and cutting a pack of cards this evening, while the footman sets four unsanctified candles on the table for us; in fact, there is no ground for supposing that this incident could prevent us from spending the evening agree-

---

[3] A game similar to auction bridge.

ably. He said as much indeed to Pyotr Ivanovitch as he came out, proposing that the party should meet at Fyodor Vassilievitch's. But apparently it was Pyotr Ivanovitch's destiny not to play *vint* that evening. Praskovya Fyodorovna, a short, fat woman who, in spite of all efforts in a contrary direction, was steadily broader from her shoulders downwards, all in black, with lace on her head and her eyebrows as queerly arched as those of the lady standing beside her coffin, came out of her own apartments with some other ladies, and conducting them to the dead man's room, said: "The service will take place immediately; come in."

Shvarts, making an indefinite bow, stood still, obviously neither accepting nor declining this invitation. Praskovya Fyodorovna, recognizing Pyotr Ivanovitch, sighed, went right up to him, took his hand, and said, "I know that you were a true friend of Ivan Ilyitch's . . ." and looked at him, expecting from him the suitable action in response to these words. Pyotr Ivanovitch knew that, just as before he had to cross himself, now what he had to do was to press her hand, to sigh and to say, "Ah, I was indeed!" And he did so. And as he did so, he felt that the desired result had been attained; that he was touched, and she was touched.

"Come, since it's not begun yet, I have something I want to say to you," said the widow. "Give me your arm."

Pyotr Ivanovitch gave her his arm, and they moved towards the inner rooms, passing Shvarts, who winked gloomily at Pyotr Ivanovitch.

"So much for our *vint!* Don't complain if we find another partner. You can make a fifth when you do get away," said his humorous glance.

Pyotr Ivanovitch sighed still more deeply and despondently, and Praskovya Fyodorovna pressed his hand gratefully. Going into her drawing-room, which was upholstered with pink cretonne and lighted by a dismal-looking lamp, they sat down at the table, she on a sofa and Pyotr Ivanovitch on a low ottoman with deranged springs which yielded spasmodically under his weight. Praskovya Fyodorovna was about to warn him to sit on another seat, and changed her mind. Sitting down on the ottoman, Pyotr Ivanovitch remembered how Ivan Ilyitch had arranged this drawing-room, and had consulted him about this very pink cretonne with green leaves. Seating herself on the sofa, and pushing by the table (the whole drawing-room was crowded with furniture and things), the widow caught the lace of her black fichu[4] in the carving of the table. Pyotr Ivanovitch got up to disentangle it for her; and the ottoman, freed from his weight, began bobbing up spasmodically under him. The widow began unhooking her lace herself, and Pyotr Ivanovitch again sat down, suppressing the mutinous ottoman springs under him. But the widow could not quite free herself, and Pyotr Ivanovitch rose again, and again the ottoman became mutinous and popped up with a positive snap. When this was all over, she took out a clean cambric handkerchief and began weeping. Pyotr Ivanovitch had been chilled off by the incident with the lace and the struggle with the ottoman springs, and he sat looking sullen. This awkward position was cut short by the entrance of Sokolov, Ivan Ilyitch's butler, who came in to announce that the place in the cemetery fixed on by Praskovya Fyodorovna would cost two hundred rubles. She left off weeping, and with the air of a victim glancing at Pyotr Ivanovitch, said in French that it was very terrible for her. Pyotr Ivanovitch made a silent gesture signifying his unhesitating conviction that it must indeed be so.

"Please, smoke," she said in a magnanimous, and at the same time, crushed

[4] Shawl or scarf draped over the shoulders and fastened in front to hide a low neckline.

voice, and she began discussing with Sokolov the question of the price for the site for the grave.

Pyotr Ivanovitch, lighting a cigarette, listened to her very circumstantial inquiries as to the various prices of sites and her decision as to the one to be selected. Having settled on the site for the grave, she made arrangements also about the choristers. Sokolov went away.

"I see to everything myself," she said to Pyotr Ivanovitch, moving on one side the albums that lay on the table; and noticing that the table was in danger from the cigarette-ash, she promptly passed an ash-tray to Pyotr Ivanovitch, and said: "I consider it affectation to pretend that my grief prevents me from looking after practical matters. On the contrary, if anything could—not console me ... but distract me, it is seeing after everything for him." She took out her handkerchief again, as though preparing to weep again; and suddenly, as though struggling with herself, she shook herself, and began speaking calmly: "But I've business to talk about with you."

Pyotr Ivanovitch bowed, carefully keeping in check the springs of the ottoman, which had at once begun quivering under him.

"The last few days his sufferings were awful."

"Did he suffer very much?" asked Pyotr Ivanovitch.

"Oh, awfully! For the last moments, hours indeed, he never left off screaming. For three days and nights in succession he screamed incessantly. It was insufferable. I can't understand how I bore it; one could hear it through three closed doors. Ah, what I suffered!"

"And was he really conscious?" asked Pyotr Ivanovitch.

"Yes," she whispered, "up to the last minute. He said good-bye to us a quarter of an hour before his death, and asked Volodya to be taken away too."

The thought of the sufferings of a man he had known so intimately, at first as a light-hearted boy, a schoolboy, then grown up as a partner in whist, in spite of the unpleasant consciousness of his own and this woman's hypocrisy, suddenly horrified Pyotr Ivanovitch. He saw again that forehead, the nose that seemed squeezing the lip, and he felt frightened for himself. "Three days and nights of awful suffering and death. Why, that may at once, any minute, come upon me too," he thought, and he felt for an instant terrified. But immediately, he could not himself have said how, there came to his support the customary reflection that this had happened to Ivan Ilyitch and not to him, and that to him this must not and could not happen; that in thinking thus he was giving way to depression, which was not the right thing to do, as was evident from Shvarts's expression of face. And making these reflections, Pyotr Ivanovitch felt reassured, and began with interest inquiring details about Ivan Ilyitch's end, as though death were a mischance peculiar to Ivan Ilyitch, but not at all incidental to himself.

After various observations about the details of the truly awful physical sufferings endured by Ivan Ilyitch (these details Pyotr Ivanovitch learned only through the effect Ivan Ilyitch's agonies had had on the nerves of Praskovya Fyodorovna), the widow apparently thought it time to get to business.

"Ah, Pyotr Ivanovitch, how hard it is, how awfully, awfully hard!" and she began to cry again.

Pyotr Ivanovitch sighed, and waited for her to blow her nose. When she had done so, he said, "Indeed it is," and again she began to talk, and brought out what was evidently the business she wished to discuss with him; that business consisted in the inquiry as to how on the occasion of her husband's death she was to obtain a grant from the government. She made a show of asking Pyotr Ivanovitch's advice about a pension. But he perceived that she knew already to the minutest details, what he did not know himself indeed, everything that could be got out of the government on the ground of his death; but that what she wanted to find out was, whether there were not any means of obtaining a little more? Pyotr Ivanovitch tried to imagine such means; but after pondering a little, and out of politeness abusing the government for its stinginess, he said that he believed that it was impossible to obtain more. Then she sighed and began unmistakably looking about for an excuse for getting rid of her visitor. He perceived this, put out his cigarette, got up, pressed her hand, and went out into the passage.

In the dining-room, where was the bric-à-brac clock that Ivan Ilyitch had been so delighted at buying, Pyotr Ivanovitch met the priest and several people he knew who had come to the service for the dead, and saw too Ivan Ilyitch's daughter, a handsome young lady. She was all in black. Her very slender figure looked even slenderer than usual. She had a gloomy, determined, almost wrathful expression. She bowed to Pyotr Ivanovitch as though he were to blame in some way. Behind the daughter, with the same offended air on his face, stood a rich young man, whom Pyotr Ivanovitch knew, too, an examining magistrate, the young lady's *fiancé*, as he had heard. He bowed dejectedly to him, and would have gone on into the dead man's room, when from the staircase there appeared the figure of the son, the high school boy, extraordinarily like Ivan Ilyitch. He was the little Ivan Ilyitch all over again as Pyotr Ivanovitch remembered him at school. His eyes were red with crying, and had that look often seen in unclean boys of thirteen or fourteen.[5] The boy, seeing Pyotr Ivanovitch, scowled morosely and bashfully. Pyotr Ivanovitch nodded to him and went into the dead man's room. The service for the dead began—candles, groans, incense, tears, sobs. Pyotr Ivanovitch stood frowning, staring at his feet in front of him. He did not once glance at the dead man, and right through to the end did not once give way to depressing influences, and was one of the first to walk out. In the hall there was no one. Gerasim, the young peasant, darted out of the dead man's room, tossed over with his strong hand all the fur cloaks to find Pyotr Ivanovitch's, and gave it him.

"Well, Gerasim, my boy?" said Pyotr Ivanovitch, so as to say something. "A sad business, isn't it?"

"It's God's will. We shall come to the same," said Gerasim, showing his white, even, peasant teeth in a smile, and, like a man in a rush of extra work, he briskly opened the door, called up the coachman, saw Pyotr Ivanovitch into the carriage, and darted back to the steps as though bethinking himself of what he had to do next.

Pyotr Ivanovitch had a special pleasure in the fresh air after the smell of incense, of the corpse, and of carbolic acid.

"Where to?" asked the coachman.

"It's not too late, I'll still go round to Fyodor Vassilievitch's."

And Pyotr Ivanovitch drove there. And he did, in fact, find them just finishing the first rubber, so that he came just at the right time to take a hand.

II

The previous history of Ivan Ilyitch was the simplest, the most ordinary, and the most awful.

---

[5] Tolstoy apparently means that the boy engages in masturbation.

Ivan Ilyitch died at the age of forty-five, a member of the Judicial Council. He was the son of an official, whose career in Petersburg through various ministries and departments had been such as leads people into that position in which, though it is distinctly obvious that they are unfit to perform any kind of real duty, they yet cannot, owing to their long past service and their official rank, be dismissed; and they therefore receive a specially created fictitious post, and by no means fictitious thousands—from six to ten—on which they go on living till extreme old age. Such was the privy councilor, the superfluous member of various superfluous institutions, Ilya Efimovitch Golovin.

He had three sons. Ivan Ilyitch was the second son. The eldest son's career was exactly like his father's, only in a different department, and he was by now close upon that stage in the service in which the same sinecure would be reached. The third son was the unsuccessful one. He had in various positions always made a mess of things, and was now employed in the railway department. And his father and his brothers, and still more their wives, did not merely dislike meeting him, but avoided, except in extreme necessity, recollecting his existence. His sister had married Baron Greff, a Petersburg official of the same stamp as his father-in-law. Ivan Ilyitch was *le phénix de la famille*,[6] as people said. He was not so frigid and precise as the eldest son, nor so wild as the youngest. He was the happy man between them—a shrewd, lively, pleasant, and well-bred man. He had been educated with his younger brother at the school of jurisprudence. The younger brother had not finished the school course, but was expelled when in the fifth class. Ivan Ilyitch completed the course successfully. At school he was just the same as he was later on all his life—an intelligent fellow, highly good-humored and sociable, but strict in doing what he considered to be his duty. His duty he considered whatever was so considered by those persons who were set in authority over him. He was not a toady as a boy, nor later on as a grown-up person; but from his earliest years he was attracted, as a fly to the light, to persons of good standing in the world, assimilated their manners and their views of life, and established friendly relations with them. All the enthusiasms of childhood and youth passed, leaving no great traces in him; he gave way to sensuality and to vanity, and latterly when in the higher classes at school to liberalism, but always keeping within certain limits which were unfailingly marked out for him by his instincts.

At school he had committed actions which had struck him beforehand as great vileness, and gave him a feeling of loathing for himself at the very time he was committing them. But later on, perceiving that such actions were committed also by men of good position, and were not regarded by them as base, he was able, not to regard them as good, but to forget about them completely, and was never mortified by recollections of them.

Leaving the school of jurisprudence in the tenth class, and receiving from his father a sum of money for his outfit, Ivan Ilyitch ordered his clothes at Sharmer's, hung on his watchchain a medallion inscribed *respice finem*,[7] said good-bye to the prince who was the principal of his school, had a farewell dinner with his comrades at Donon's, and with all his new fashionable belongings—traveling trunk, linen, suits of clothes, shaving and toilet appurtenances, and traveling rug, all ordered and purchased at the very best shops—set off to take the post of secretary on special commissions for the governor of a province, a post which had been obtained for him by his father.

[6] *Le phénix de la famille.* "The phoenix of the family," a paragon (French).
[7] "Look to the end" (Latin).

In the province Ivan Ilyitch without loss of time made himself a position as easy and agreeable as his position had been in the school of jurisprudence. He did his work, made his career, and at the same time led a life of well-bred social gaiety. Occasionally he visited various districts on official duty, behaved with dignity both with his superiors and his inferiors; and with exactitude and an incorruptible honesty of which he could not help feeling proud, performed the duties with which he was entrusted, principally having to do with the dissenters.[8] When engaged in official work he was, in spite of his youth and taste for frivolous amusement, exceedingly reserved, official, and even severe. But in social life he was often amusing and witty, and always good-natured, well-bred, and *bon enfant*,[9] as was said of him by his chief and his chief's wife, with whom he was like one of the family.

In the province there was, too, a connection with one of the ladies who obtruded their charms on the stylish young lawyer. There was a dressmaker, too, and there were drinking bouts with smart officers visiting the neighborhood, and visits to a certain outlying street after supper; there was a rather cringing obsequiousness in his behavior, too, with his chief, and even his chief's wife. But all this was accompanied with such a tone of the highest breeding, that it could not be called by harsh names; it all came under the rubric of the French saying, *Il faut que la jeunesse se passe.*[10] Everything was done with clean hands, in clean shirts, with French phrases, and, what was of most importance, in the highest society, and consequently with the approval of people of rank.

Such was Ivan Ilyitch's career for five years, and then came a change in his official life. New methods of judicial procedure were established; new men were wanted to carry them out. And Ivan Ilyitch became such a new man. Ivan Ilyitch was offered the post of examining magistrate, and he accepted it in spite of the fact that his post was in another province, and he would have to break off all the ties he had formed and form new ones. Ivan Ilyitch's friends met together to see him off, had their photographs taken in a group, presented him with a silver cigarette-case, and he set off to his new post.

As an examining magistrate, Ivan Ilyitch was as *comme il faut*,[11] as well-bred, as adroit in keeping official duties apart from private life, and as successful in gaining universal respect, as he had been as secretary of private commissions. The duties of his new office were in themselves of far greater interest and attractiveness for Ivan Ilyitch. In his former post it had been pleasant to pass in his smart uniform from Sharmer's through the crowd of petitioners and officials waiting timorously and envying him, and to march with his easy swagger straight into the governor's private room, there to sit down with him to tea and cigarettes. But the persons directly subject to his authority were few. The only such persons were the district police superintendents and the dissenters, when he was serving on special commissions. And he liked treating such persons affably, almost like comrades; liked to make them feel that he, able to annihilate them, was behaving in this simple, friendly way with them. But such people were then few in number. Now as an examining magistrate Ivan Ilyitch felt that every one—every one without exception—the most dignified, the most self-satisfied people, all were in his hands, and

---

[8] The Old Believers, members of a sect broken off from the Russian Orthodox Church in the seventeenth century and subjects of a number of legal restrictions.
[9] Literally, "good child"; congenial (French).
[10] French for "Youth must pass" (That's the way young people are).
[11] "As it should be"; proper (French).

that he had but to write certain words on a sheet of paper with a printed heading, and this dignified self-satisfied person would be brought before him in the capacity of a defendant or a witness; and if he did not care to make him sit down, he would have to stand up before him and answer his questions. Ivan Ilyitch never abused this authority of his; on the contrary, he tried to soften the expression of it. But the consciousness of this power and the possibility of softening its effect constituted for him the chief interest and attractiveness of his new position. In the work itself, in the preliminary inquiries, that is, Ivan Ilyitch very rapidly acquired the art of setting aside every consideration irrelevant to the official aspect of the case, and of reducing every case, however complex, to that form in which it could in a purely external fashion be put on paper, completely excluding his personal view of the matter, and what was of paramount importance, observing all the necessary formalities. All this work was new. And he was one of the first men who put into practical working the reforms in judicial procedure enacted in 1864.[12]

On settling in a new town in his position as examining magistrate, Ivan Ilyitch made new acquaintances, formed new ties, took up a new line, and adopted a rather different attitude. He took up an attitude of somewhat dignified aloofness towards the provincial authorities, while he picked out the best circle among the legal gentlemen and wealthy gentry living in the town, and adopted a tone of slight dissatisfaction with the government, moderate liberalism, and lofty civic virtue. With this, while making no change in the elegance of his get-up, Ivan Ilyitch in his new office gave up shaving, and left his beard free to grow as it liked. Ivan Ilyitch's existence in the new town proved to be very agreeable; the society which took the line of opposition to the governor was friendly and good; his income was larger, and he found a source of increased enjoyment in whist, at which he began to play at this time; and having a faculty for playing cards good-humoredly, and being rapid and exact in his calculations, he was as a rule on the winning side.

After living two years in the new town, Ivan Ilyitch met his future wife. Praskovya Fyodorovna Mihel was the most attractive, clever, and brilliant girl in the set in which Ivan Ilyitch moved. Among other amusements and recreations after his labors as a magistrate, Ivan Ilyitch started a light, playful flirtation with Praskovya Fyodorovna.

Ivan Ilyitch when he was an assistant secretary had danced as a rule; as an examining magistrate he danced only as an exception. He danced now as it were under protest, as though to show "that though I am serving on the new reformed legal code, and am of the fifth class in official rank, still if it comes to a question of dancing, in that line, too, I can do better than others." In this spirit he danced now and then towards the end of the evening with Praskovya Fyodorovna, and it was principally during these dances that he won the heart of Praskovya Fyodorovna. She fell in love with him. Ivan Ilyitch had no clearly defined intention of marrying; but when the girl fell in love with him, he put the question to himself: "After all, why not get married?"

The young lady, Praskovya Fyodorovna, was of good family, nice-looking. There was a little bit of property. Ivan Ilyitch might have reckoned on a more brilliant match, but this was a good match. Ivan Ilyitch had his salary; she, he hoped, would have as much of her own. It was a good family; she was a sweet, pretty, and perfectly *comme il faut* young woman. To say that Ivan Ilyitch got married because he fell in love with his wife and found in her sympathy with his views of life, would

---

[12] Russian law was reformed in 1864, following the emancipation of the serfs in 1861.

be as untrue as to say that he got married because the people of his world approved of the match. Ivan Ilyitch was influenced by both considerations; he was doing what was agreeable to himself in securing such a wife, and at the same time doing what persons of high standing looked upon as the correct thing.

And Ivan Ilyitch got married.

The process itself of getting married and the early period of married life, with the conjugal caresses, the new furniture, the new crockery, the new house linen, all up to the time of his wife's pregnancy, went off very well; so that Ivan Ilyitch had already begun to think that so far from marriage breaking up that kind of frivolous, agreeable, lighthearted life, always decorous and always approved by society, which he regarded as the normal life, it would even increase its agreeableness. But at that point, in the early months of his wife's pregnancy, there came in a new element, unexpected, unpleasant, tiresome and unseemly, which could never have been anticipated, and from which there was no escape.

His wife, without any kind of reason, it seemed to Ivan Ilyitch, *de gaieté de coeur*,[13] as he expressed it, began to disturb the agreeableness and decorum of their life. She began without any sort of justification to be jealous, exacting in her demands on his attention, squabbled over everything, and treated him to the coarsest and most unpleasant scenes.

At first Ivan Ilyitch hoped to escape from the unpleasantness of this position by taking up the same frivolous and well-bred line that had served him well on other occasions of difficulty. He endeavored to ignore his wife's ill-humor, went on living lightheartedly and agreeably as before, invited friends to play cards, tried to get away himself to the club or to his friends. But his wife began on one occasion with such energy, abusing him in such coarse language, and so obstinately persisted in her abuse of him every time he failed in carrying out her demands, obviously having made up her mind firmly to persist till he gave way, that is, stayed at home and was as dull as she was, that Ivan Ilyitch took alarm. He perceived that matrimony, at least with his wife, was not invariably conducive to the pleasures and proprieties of life; but, on the contrary, often destructive of them, and that it was therefore essential to erect some barrier to protect himself from these disturbances. And Ivan Ilyitch began to look about for such means of protecting himself. His official duties were the only thing that impressed Praskovya Fyodorovna, and Ivan Ilyitch began to use his official position and the duties arising from it in his struggle with his wife to fence off his own independent world apart.

With the birth of the baby, the attempts at nursing it, and the various unsuccessful experiments with food, with the illnesses, real and imaginary, of the infant and its mother, in which Ivan Ilyitch was expected to sympathize, though he never had the slightest idea about them, the need for him to fence off a world apart for himself outside his family life became still more imperative. As his wife grew more irritable and exacting, so did Ivan Ilyitch more and more transfer the center of gravity of his life to his official work. He became fonder and fonder of official life, and more ambitious than he had been.

Very quickly, not more than a year after his wedding, Ivan Ilyitch had become aware that conjugal life, though providing certain comforts, was in reality a very intricate and difficult business towards which one must, if one is to do one's duty, that is, lead the decorous life approved by society, work out for oneself a definite line, just as in the government service.

---

[13] "Out of gaiety of heart"; willfully or arbitrarily (French).

And such a line Ivan Ilyitch did work out for himself in his married life. He expected from his home life only those comforts—of dinner at home, of house-keeper and bed—which it could give him, and above all, that perfect propriety in external observances required by public opinion. For the rest, he looked for good-humored pleasantness, and if he found it he was very thankful. If he met with antagonism and querulousness, he promptly retreated into the separate world he had shut off for himself in his official life, and there he found solace.

Ivan Ilyitch was prized as a good official, and three years later he was made assistant public prosecutor. The new duties of this position, their dignity, the possibility of bringing any one to trial and putting any one in prison, the publicity of the speeches and the success Ivan Ilyitch had in that part of his work,—all this made his official work still more attractive to him.

Children were born to him. His wife became steadily more querulous and ill-tempered, but the line Ivan Ilyitch had taken up for himself in home life put him almost out of reach of her grumbling.

After seven years of service in the same town, Ivan Ilyitch was transferred to an-other province with the post of public prosecutor. They moved, money was short, and his wife did not like the place they had moved to. The salary was indeed a little higher than before, but their expenses were larger. Besides, a couple of children died, and home life consequently became even less agreeable for Ivan Ilyitch.

For every mischance that occurred in their new place of residence, Praskovya Fyodorovna blamed her husband. The greater number of subjects of conversation between husband and wife, especially the education of the children, led to ques-tions which were associated with previous quarrels, and quarrels were ready to break out at every instant. There remained only those rare periods of being in love which did indeed come upon them, but never lasted long. These were the islands at which they put in for a time, but they soon set off again upon the ocean of concealed hostility, that was made manifest in their aloofness from one another. This aloofness might have distressed Ivan Ilyitch if he had believed that this ought not to be so, but by now he regarded this position as perfectly normal, and it was indeed the goal towards which he worked in his home life. His aim was to make himself more and more free from the unpleasant aspects of domestic life and to render them harmless and decorous. And he attained this aim by spending less and less time with his family; and when he was forced to be at home, he endeav-ored to secure his tranquillity by the presence of outsiders. The great thing for Ivan Ilyitch was having his office. In the official world all the interest of life was concentrated for him. And this interest absorbed him. The sense of his own power, the consciousness of being able to ruin any one he wanted to ruin, even the external dignity of his office, when he made his entry into the court or met subordinate officials, his success in the eyes of his superiors and his subordinates, and, above all, his masterly handling of cases, of which he was conscious,—all this delighted him and, together with chats with his colleagues, dining out, and whist, filled his life. So that, on the whole, Ivan Ilyitch's life still went on in the way he thought it should go—agreeably, decorously.

So he lived for another seven years. His eldest daughter was already sixteen, another child had died, and there was left only one other, a boy at the high school, a subject of dissension. Ivan Ilyitch wanted to send him to the school of jurispru-dence, while Praskovya Fyodorovna to spite him sent him to the high school. The daughter had been educated at home, and had turned out well; the boy too did fairly well at his lessons.

III

Such was Ivan Ilyitch's life for seventeen years after his marriage. He had been prosecutor a long while by now, and had refused several appointments offered him, looking out for a more desirable post, when there occurred an unexpected incident which utterly destroyed his peace of mind. Ivan Ilyitch had been expecting to be appointed presiding judge in a university town, but a certain Goppe somehow stole a march on him and secured the appointment. Ivan Ilyitch took offense, began upbraiding him, and quarrelled with him and with his own superiors. A coolness was felt towards him, and on the next appointment that was made he was again passed over.

This was in the year 1880. That year was the most painful one in Ivan Ilyitch's life. During that year it became evident on the one hand that his pay was insufficient for his expenses; on the other hand, that he had been forgotten by every one, and that what seemed to him the most monstrous, the cruelest injustice, appeared to other people as a quite commonplace fact. Even his father felt no obligation to assist him. He felt that every one had deserted him, and that every one regarded his position with an income of three thousand five hundred rubles as a quite normal and even fortunate one. He alone, with a sense of the injustice done him, and the everlasting nagging of his wife and the debts he had begun to accumulate, living beyond his means, knew that his position was far from being normal.

The summer of that year, to cut down his expenses, he took a holiday and went with his wife to spend the summer in the country at her brother's.

In the country, with no official duties to occupy him, Ivan Ilyitch was for the first time a prey not to simple boredom, but to intolerable depression; and he made up his mind that things could not go on like that, and that it was absolutely necessary to take some decisive steps.

After a sleepless night spent by Ivan Ilyitch walking up and down the terrace, he determined to go to Petersburg to take active steps and to get transferred to some other department, so as to revenge himself on *them*, the people, that is, who had not known how to appreciate him.

Next day, in spite of all the efforts of his wife and his mother-in-law to dissuade him, he set off to Petersburg.

He went with a single object before him—to obtain a post with an income of five thousand. He was ready now to be satisfied with a post in any department, of any tendency, with any kind of work. He must only have a post—a post with five thousand, in the executive department, the banks, the railways, the Empress Marya's institutions,[14] even in the customs duties—what was essential was five thousand, and essential it was, too, to get out of the department in which they had failed to appreciate his value.

And, behold, this quest of Ivan Ilyitch's was crowned with wonderful, unexpected success. At Kursk there got into the same first-class carriage F. S. Ilyin, an acquaintance, who told him of a telegram just received by the governor of Kursk, announcing a change about to take place in the ministry—Pyotr Ivanovitch was to be superseded by Ivan Semyonovitch.

The proposed change, apart from its significance for Russia, had special significance for Ivan Ilyitch from the fact that by bringing to the front a new person, Pyotr Petrovitch, and obviously, therefore, his friend Zahar Ivanovitch, it was in

---

[14] The Empress Marya, wife of Paul I, founded a number of charitable institutions.

the highest degree propitious to Ivan Ilyitch's own plans. Zahar Ivanovitch was a friend and school-fellow of Ivan Ilyitch's.

At Moscow the news was confirmed. On arriving at Petersburg, Ivan Ilyitch looked up Zahar Ivanovitch, and received a positive promise of an appointment in his former department—that of justice.

A week later he telegraphed to his wife: *"Zahar Miller's place. At first report I receive appointment."*

Thanks to these changes, Ivan Ilyitch unexpectedly obtained, in the same department as before, an appointment which placed him two stages higher than his former colleagues, and gave him an income of five thousand, together with the official allowance of three thousand five hundred for traveling expenses. All his ill-humor with his former enemies and the whole department was forgotten, and Ivan Ilyitch was completely happy.

Ivan Ilyitch went back to the country more lighthearted and good-tempered than he had been for a very long while. Praskovya Fyodorovna was in better spirits, too, and peace was patched up between them. Ivan Ilyitch described what respect every one had shown him in Petersburg; how all those who had been his enemies had been put to shame, and were cringing now before him; how envious they were of his appointment, and still more of the high favor in which he stood at Petersburg.

Praskovya Fyodorovna listened to this, and pretended to believe it, and did not contradict him in anything, but confined herself to making plans for her new arrangements in the town to which they would be moving. And Ivan Ilyitch saw with delight that these plans were his plans; that they were agreed; and that his life after this disturbing hitch in its progress was about to regain its true, normal character of lighthearted agreeableness and propriety.

Ivan Ilyitch had come back to the country for a short stay only. He had to enter upon the duties of his new office on the 10th of September; and besides, he needed some time to settle in a new place, to move all his belongings from the other province, to purchase and order many things in addition; in short, to arrange things as settled in his own mind, and almost exactly as settled in the heart too of Praskovya Fyodorovna.

And now when everything was so successfully arranged, and when he and his wife were agreed in their aim, and were, besides, so little together, they got on with one another as they had not got on together since the early years of their married life. Ivan Ilyitch had thought of taking his family away with him at once; but his sister and his brother-in-law, who had suddenly become extremely cordial and intimate with him and his family, were so pressing in urging them to stay that he set off alone.

Ivan Ilyitch started off; and the lighthearted temper produced by his success, and his good understanding with his wife, one thing backing up another, did not desert him all the time. He found a charming set of apartments, the very thing both husband and wife had dreamed of. Spacious, lofty reception-rooms in the old style, a comfortable, dignified-looking study for him, rooms for his wife and daughter, a schoolroom for his son, everything as though planned on purpose for them. Ivan Ilyitch himself looked after the furnishing of them, chose the wallpapers, bought furniture, by preference antique furniture, which had a peculiar *comme-il-faut* style to his mind, and it all grew up and grew up, and really attained the ideal he had set before himself. When he had half finished arranging the house, his arrangement surpassed his own expectations. He saw the *comme-il-faut* character, elegant and free from vulgarity, that the whole would have when it was all ready. As he fell asleep he pictured to himself the reception-room as it would be. Looking at the drawing-room, not yet finished, he could see the hearth, the screen, the *étagère*,[15] and the little chairs dotted here and there, the plates and dishes on the wall, and the bronzes as they would be when they were all put in their places. He was delighted with the thought of how he would impress Praskovya and Lizanka, who had taste too in this line. They would never expect anything like it. He was particularly successful in coming across and buying cheap old pieces of furniture, which gave a peculiarly aristocratic air to the whole. In his letters he purposely disparaged everything so as to surprise them. All this so absorbed him that the duties of his new office, though he was so fond of his official work, interested him less than he had expected. During sittings of the court he had moments of inattention; he pondered the question which sort of cornices to have on the window-blinds, straight or fluted. He was so interested in this business that he often set to work with his own hands, moved a piece of furniture, or hung up curtains himself. One day he went up a ladder to show a workman, who did not understand, how he wanted some hangings draped, made a false step and slipped; but, like a strong and nimble person, he clung on, and only knocked his side against the corner of a frame. The bruised place ached, but it soon passed off. Ivan Ilyitch felt all this time particularly good-humored and well. He wrote: "I feel fifteen years younger." He thought his house-furnishing would be finished in September, but it dragged on to the middle of October. But then the effect was charming; not he only said so, but every one who saw it told him so too.

In reality, it was all just what is commonly seen in the houses of people who are not exactly wealthy but want to look like wealthy people, and so succeed only in being like one another—hangings, dark wood, flowers, rugs and bronzes, everything dark and highly polished, everything that all people of a certain class have so as to be like all people of a certain class. And in his case it was all so like that it made no impression at all; but it all seemed to him somehow special. When he met his family at the railway station and brought them to his newly furnished rooms, all lighted up in readiness, and a footman in a white tie opened the door into an entry decorated with flowers, and then they walked into the drawing-room and the study, uttering cries of delight, he was very happy, conducted them everywhere, eagerly drinking in their praises, and beaming with satisfaction. The same evening, while they talked about various things at tea, Praskovya Fyodorovna inquired about his fall, and he laughed and showed them how he had gone flying, and how he had frightened the upholsterer.

"It's as well I'm something of an athlete. Another man might have been killed, and I got nothing worse than a blow here; when it's touched it hurts, but it's going off already; just a bruise."

And they began to live in their new abode, which, as is always the case, when they had got thoroughly settled in they found to be short of just one room, and with their new income, which, as always, was only a little—some five hundred rubles—too little, and everything went very well. Things went particularly well at first, before everything was quite finally arranged, and there was still something to do to the place—something to buy, something to order, something to move, something to make to fit. Though there were indeed several disputes between husband and wife, both were so well satisfied, and there was so much to do, that it all went off without serious quarrels. When there was nothing left to arrange, it

---

[15] Cabinet with a tier of open shelves; bookcase (French).

became a little dull, and something seemed to be lacking, but by then they were making acquaintances and forming habits, and life was filled up again.

Ivan Ilyitch, after spending the morning in the court, returned home to dinner, and at first he was generally in a good humor, although this was apt to be upset a little, and precisely on account of the new abode. Every spot on the table-cloth, on the hangings, the string of a window blind broken, irritated him. He had devoted so much trouble to the arrangement of the rooms that any disturbance of their order distressed him. But, on the whole, the life of Ivan Ilyitch ran its course as, according to his conviction, life ought to do—easily, agreeably, and decorously. He got up at nine, drank his coffee, read the newspaper, then put on his official uniform, and went to the court. There the routine of the daily work was ready mapped out for him, and he stepped into it at once. People with petitions, inquiries in the office, the office itself, the sittings—public and preliminary. In all this the great thing necessary was to exclude everything with the sap of life in it, which always disturbs the regular course of official business, not to admit any sort of relations with people except the official relations; the motive of all intercourse had to be simply the official motive, and the intercourse itself to be only official. A man would come, for instance, anxious for certain information. Ivan Ilyitch, not being the functionary on duty, would have nothing whatever to do with such a man. But if this man's relation to him as a member of the court is such as can be formulated on official stamped paper—within the limits of such a relation Ivan Ilyitch would do everything, positively everything he could, and in doing so would observe the semblance of human friendly relations, that is, the courtesies of social life. But where the official relation ended, there everything else stopped too. This art of keeping the official aspect of things apart from his real life, Ivan Ilyitch possessed in the highest degree; and through long practice and natural aptitude, he had brought it to such a pitch of perfection that he even permitted himself at times, like a skilled specialist as it were in jest, to let the human and official relations mingle. He allowed himself this liberty just because he felt he had the power at any moment if he wished it to take up the purely official line again and to drop the human relation. This thing was not simply easy, agreeable, and decorous; in Ivan Ilyitch's hands it attained a positively artistic character. In the intervals of business he smoked, drank tea, chatted a little about politics, a little about public affairs, a little about cards, but most of all about appointments in the service. And tired, but feeling like some artist who has skillfully played his part in the performance, one of the first violins in the orchestra, he returned home. At home his daughter and her mother had been paying calls somewhere, or else some one had been calling on them; the son had been at school, had been preparing his lessons with his teachers, and duly learning correctly what was taught at the high school. Everything was as it should be. After dinner, if there were no visitors, Ivan Ilyitch sometimes read some book of which people were talking, and in the evening sat down to work, that is, read official papers, compared them with the laws, sorted depositions, and put them under the laws. This he found neither tiresome nor entertaining. It was tiresome when he might have been playing *vint;* but if there were no *vint* going on, it was better anyway than sitting alone or with his wife. Ivan Ilyitch's pleasures were little dinners, to which he invited ladies and gentlemen of good social position, and such methods of passing the time with them as were usual with such persons, so that his drawing-room might be like all other drawing-rooms.

Once they even gave a party—a dance. And Ivan Ilyitch enjoyed it, and everything was very successful, except that it led to a violent quarrel with his wife over the tarts and sweetmeats. Praskovya Fyodorovna had her own plan; while Ivan Ilyitch insisted on getting everything from an expensive pastry-cook, and ordered a great many tarts, and the quarrel was because these tarts were left over the pasty-cook's bill came to forty-five rubles. The quarrel was a violent and unpleasant one, so much so that Praskovya Fyodorovna called him "Fool, imbecile." And he clutched at his head, and in his anger made some allusion to a divorce. But the party itself was enjoyable. There were all the best people, and Ivan Ilyitch danced with Princess Trufanov, the sister of the one so well known in connection with the charitable association called "Bear my Burden." His official pleasures lay in the gratification of his pride; his social pleasures lay in the gratification of his vanity. But Ivan Ilyitch's most real pleasure was the pleasure of playing *vint*. He admitted to himself that, after all, after whatever unpleasant incidents there had been in his life, the pleasure which burned like a candle before all others was sitting with good players, and not noisy partners, at *vint;* and, of course, a four-hand game (playing with five was never a success, though one pretends to like it particularly), and with good cards, to play a shrewd, serious game, then supper and a glass of wine. And after *vint,* especially after winning some small stakes (winning large sums was unpleasant), Ivan Ilyitch went to bed in a particularly happy frame of mind.

So they lived. They moved in the very best circle, and were visited by people of consequence and young people.

In their views of their circle of acquaintances, the husband, the wife, and the daughter were in complete accord; and without any expressed agreement on the subject, they all acted alike in dropping and shaking off various friends and relations, shabby persons who swooped down upon them in their drawing-room with Japanese plates on the walls, and pressed their civilities on them. Soon these shabby persons ceased fluttering about them, and none but the very best society was seen at the Golovins. Young men began to pay attention to Lizanka; and Petrishtchev, the son of Dmitry Ivanovitch Petrishtchev, and the sole heir of his fortune, an examining magistrate, began to be so attentive to Lizanka, that Ivan Ilyitch had raised the question with his wife whether it would not be as well to arrange a sledge drive for them, or to get up some theatricals. So they lived. And everything went on in this way without change, and everything was very nice.

IV

All were in good health. One could not use the word ill-health in connection with the symptoms Ivan Ilyitch sometimes complained of, namely, a queer taste in his mouth and a sort of uncomfortable feeling on the left side of the stomach.

But it came to pass that this uncomfortable feeling kept increasing, and became not exactly a pain, but a continual sense of weight in his side and the cause of an irritable temper. This irritable temper, continually growing, began at last to mar the agreeable easiness and decorum that had reigned in the Golovin household. Quarrels between the husband and wife became more and more frequent, and soon all the easiness and amenity of life had fallen away, and mere propriety was maintained with difficulty. Scenes became again more frequent. Again there were only islands in the sea of contention—and but few of these—at which the husband and wife could meet without an outbreak. And Praskovya Fyodorovna said now, not without grounds, that her husband had a trying temper. With her characteristic exaggeration, she said he had always had this awful temper, and she had needed all her sweetness to put up with it for twenty years. It was true that it was he now who began the quarrels. His gusts of temper always broke out just before dinner, and often just as he was beginning to eat, at the soup. He would notice that some piece of crockery had been chipped, or that the food was not nice, or that his son put his elbow on the table, or his daughter's hair was not arranged as he liked it. And whatever it was, he laid the blame of it on Praskovya Fyodorovna. Praskovya Fyodorovna had at first retorted in the same strain, and said all sorts of horrid things to him; but on two occasions, just at the beginning of dinner, he had flown into such a frenzy that she perceived that it was due to physical derangement, and was brought on by taking food, and she controlled herself; she did not reply, but simply made haste to get dinner over. Praskovya Fyodorovna took great credit to herself for this exercise of self-control. Making up her mind that her husband had a fearful temper, and made her life miserable, she began to feel sorry for herself. And the more she felt for herself, the more she hated her husband. She began to wish he were dead; yet could not wish it, because then there would be no income. And this exasperated her against him even more. She considered herself dreadfully unfortunate, precisely because even his death could not save her, and she felt irritated and concealed it, and this hidden irritation on her side increased his irritability.

After one violent scene, in which Ivan Ilyitch had been particularly unjust, and after which he had said in explanation that he certainly was irritable, but that it was due to illness, she said that if he were ill he ought to take steps, and insisted on his going to see a celebrated doctor.

He went. Everything was as he had expected; everything was as it always is. The waiting and the assumption of dignity, that professional dignity he knew so well, exactly as he assumed it himself in court, and the sounding and listening and questions that called for answers that were foregone conclusions and obviously superfluous, and the significant air that seemed to insinuate—you only leave it all to us, and we will arrange everything, for us it is certain and incontestable how to arrange everything, everything in one way for every man of every sort. It was all exactly as in his court of justice. Exactly the same air as he put on in dealing with a man brought up for judgment, the doctor put on for him.

The doctor said: This and that proves that you have such-and-such a thing wrong inside you; but if that is not confirmed by analysis of this and that, then we must assume this and that. If we assume this and that, then—and so on. To Ivan Ilyitch there was only one question of consequence, Was his condition dangerous or not? But the doctor ignored that irrelevant inquiry. From the doctor's point of view this was a side issue, not the subject under consideration; the only real question was the balance of probabilities between a loose kidney, chronic catarrh, and appendicitis. It was not a question of the life of Ivan Ilyitch, but the question between the loose kidney and the intestinal appendix. And this question, as it seemed to Ivan Ilyitch, the doctor solved in a brilliant manner in favor of the appendix, with the reservation that analysis of the water[16] might give a fresh clue, and that then the aspect of the case would be altered. All this was point for point identical with what Ivan Ilyitch had himself done in brilliant fashion a thousand times over in dealing with some man on his trial. Just as brilliantly the doctor made his summing-up, and triumphantly, gaily even, glanced over his spectacles at the prisoner in the dock. From the doctor's summing-up Ivan Ilyitch deduced the conclusion—that things looked bad, and that he, the doctor, and most likely every one else, did not care, but that things looked bad for him. And this con-

[16] Urine.

clusion impressed Ivan Ilyitch morbidly, arousing in him a great feeling of pity for himself, of great anger against this doctor who could be unconcerned about a matter of such importance.

But he said nothing of that. He got up, and, laying the fee on the table, he said, with a sigh, "We sick people often ask inconvenient questions. Tell me, is this generally a dangerous illness or not?"

The doctor glanced severely at him with one eye through his spectacles, as though to say: "Prisoner at the bar, if you will not keep within the limits of the questions allowed you, I shall be compelled to take measures for your removal from the precincts of the court." "I have told you what I thought necessary and suitable already," said the doctor; "the analysis will show anything further." And the doctor bowed him out.

Ivan Ilyitch went out slowly and dejectedly, got into his sledge, and drove home. All the way home he was incessantly going over all the doctor had said, trying to translate all these complicated, obscure, scientific phrases into simple language, and to read in them an answer to the question, Is it bad—is it very bad, or nothing much as yet? And it seemed to him that the upshot of all the doctor had said was that it was very bad. Everything seemed dismal to Ivan Ilyitch in the streets. The sledge-drivers were dismal, the houses were dismal, the people passing, and the shops were dismal. This ache, this dull gnawing ache, that never ceased for a second, seemed, when connected with the doctor's obscure utterances, to have gained a new, more serious significance. With a new sense of misery Ivan Ilyitch kept watch on it now.

He reached home and began to tell his wife about it. His wife listened; but in the middle of his account his daughter came in with her hat on, ready to go out with her mother. Reluctantly she half sat down to listen to these tedious details, but she could not stand it for long, and her mother did not hear his story to the end.

"Well, I'm very glad," said his wife; "now you must be sure and take the medicine regularly. Give me the prescriptions; I'll send Gerasim to the chemist's!" And she went to get ready to go out.

He had not taken a breath while she was in the room, and he heaved a deep sigh when she was gone.

"Well," he said, "may be it really is nothing as yet."

He began to take the medicine, to carry out the doctor's directions, which were changed after the analysis of the water. But it was just at this point that some confusion arose, either in the analysis or in what ought to have followed from it. The doctor himself, of course, could not be blamed for it, but it turned out that things had not gone as the doctor had told him. Either he had forgotten or told a lie, or was hiding something from him.

But Ivan Ilyitch still went on just as exactly carrying out the doctor's direction, and in doing so he found comfort at first.

From the time of his visit to the doctor Ivan Ilyitch's principal occupation became the exact observance of the doctor's prescriptions as regards hygiene and medicine and the careful observation of his ailment in all the functions of his organism. Ivan Ilyitch's principal interest came to be people's ailments and people's health. When anything was said in his presence about sick people, about deaths and recoveries, especially in the case of an illness resembling his own, he listened, trying to conceal his excitement, asked questions, and applied what he heard to his own trouble.

The ache did not grow less; but Ivan Ilyitch made great efforts to force himself to believe that he was better. And he succeeded in deceiving himself so long as nothing happened to disturb him. But as soon as he had a mischance, some unpleasant words with his wife, a failure in his official work, an unlucky hand at *vint*, he was at once acutely sensible of his illness. In former days he had borne with such mishaps, hoping soon to retrieve the mistake, to make a struggle, to reach success later, to have a lucky hand. But now he was cast down by every mischance and reduced to despair. He would say to himself: "Here I'm only just beginning to get better, and the medicine has begun to take effect, and now this mischance or disappointment." And he was furious against the mischance or the people who were causing him the disappointment and killing him, and he felt that this fury was killing him, but could not check it. One would have thought that it should have been clear to him that this exasperation against circumstances and people was aggravating his disease, and that therefore he ought not to pay attention to the unpleasant incidents. But his reasoning took quite the opposite direction. He said that he needed peace, and was on the watch for everything that disturbed his peace, and at the slightest disturbance of it he flew into a rage. What made his position worse was that he read medical books and consulted doctors. He got worse so gradually that he might have deceived himself, comparing one day with another, the difference was so slight. But when he consulted the doctors, then it seemed to him that he was getting worse, and very rapidly so indeed. And in spite of this, he was continually consulting the doctors.

That month he called on another celebrated doctor. The second celebrity said almost the same as the first, but put his questions differently; and the interview with this celebrity only redoubled the doubts and terrors of Ivan Ilyitch. A friend of a friend of his, a very good doctor, diagnosed the disease quite differently; and in spite of the fact that he guaranteed recovery, by his questions and his suppositions he confused Ivan Ilyitch even more and strengthened his suspicions. A homeopath[17] gave yet another diagnosis of the complaint, and prescribed medicine, which Ivan Ilyitch took secretly for a week; but after a week of the homeopathic medicine he felt no relief, and losing faith both in the other doctor's treatment and in this, he fell into even deeper depression. One day a lady of his acquaintance talked to him of the healing wrought by the holy pictures. Ivan Ilyitch caught himself listening attentively and believing in the reality of the facts alleged. This incident alarmed him. "Can I have degenerated to such a point of intellectual feebleness?" he said to himself. "Nonsense! it's all rubbish. I must not give way to nervous fears, but fixing on one doctor, adhere strictly to his treatment. That's what I will do. Now it's settled. I won't think about it, but till next summer I will stick to the treatment, and then I shall see. Now I'll put a stop to this wavering!" It was easy to say this, but impossible to carry it out. The pain in his side was always dragging at him, seeming to grow more acute and ever more incessant; it seemed to him that the taste in his mouth was queerer, and there was a loathsome smell even from his breath, and his appetite and strength kept dwindling. There was no deceiving himself; something terrible, new, and so important that nothing more important had ever been in Ivan Ilyitch's life, was taking place in him, and he alone knew of it. All about him did not or would not understand, and believed that everything in the world was going on as before. This was what tortured Ivan Ilyitch more than anything. Those of his own household, most of all his wife and daughter, who were absorbed in a perfect whirl of visits, did not, he

---

[17] Practitioner of homeopathy, a system of medicine that treats illnesses by administering minute doses of substances that, in healthy persons, would produce symptoms of the disease treated.

saw, comprehend it at all, and were annoyed that he was so depressed and exacting, as though he were to blame for it. Though they tried indeed to disguise it, he saw he was a nuisance to them; but that his wife had taken up a definite line of her own in regard to his illness, and stuck to it regardless of what he might say and do. This line was expressed thus: "You know," she would say to acquaintances, "Ivan Ilyitch cannot, like all other simple-hearted folks, keep to the treatment prescribed him. One day he'll take his drops and eat what he's ordered, and go to bed in good time; the next day, if I don't see to it, he'll suddenly forget to take his medicine, eat sturgeon (which is forbidden by the doctors), yes, and sit up at *vint* till past midnight."

"Why, when did I do that?" Ivan Ilyitch asked in vexation one day at Pyotr Ivanovitch's.

"Why, yesterday, with Shebek."

"It makes no difference. I couldn't sleep for pain."

"Well, it doesn't matter what you do it for, only you'll never get well like that, and you make us wretched."

Praskovya Fyodorovna's external attitude to her husband's illness, openly expressed to others and to himself, was that Ivan Ilyitch was to blame in the matter of his illness, and that the whole illness was another injury he was doing to his wife. Ivan Ilyitch felt that the expression of this dropped from her unconsciously, but that made it no easier for him.

In his official life, too, Ivan Ilyitch noticed, or fancied he noticed, a strange attitude to him. At one time it seemed to him that people were looking inquisitively at him, as a man who would shortly have to vacate his position; at another time his friends would suddenly begin chaffing him in a friendly way over his nervous fears, as though that awful and horrible, unheard-of thing that was going on within him, incessantly gnawing at him, and irresistibly dragging him away somewhere, were the most agreeable subject for joking. Shvarts especially, with his jocoseness, his liveliness, and his *comme-il-faut* tone, exasperated Ivan Ilyitch by reminding him of himself ten years ago.

Friends came sometimes to play cards. They sat down to the card-table; they shuffled and dealt the new cards. Diamonds were led and followed by diamonds, the seven. His partner said, "Can't trump," and played the two of diamonds. What then? Why, delightful, capital, it should have been—he had a trump hand. And suddenly Ivan Ilyitch feels that gnawing ache, that taste in his mouth, and it strikes him as something grotesque that with that he could be glad of a trump hand.

He looks at Mihail Mihailovitch, his partner, how he taps on the table with his red hand, and affably and indulgently abstains from snatching up the trick, and pushes the cards towards Ivan Ilyitch so as to give him the pleasure of taking them up, without any trouble, without even stretching out his hand. "What, does he suppose that I'm so weak that I can't stretch out my hand?" thinks Ivan Ilyitch, and he forgets the trumps, and trumps his partner's cards, and plays his trump hand without making three tricks; and what's the most awful thing of all is that he sees how upset Mihail Mihailovitch is about it, while he doesn't care a bit, and it's awful for him to think why he doesn't care.

They all see that he's in pain, and say to him, "We can stop if you're tired. You go and lie down." Lie down? No, he's not in the least tired; they will play the rubber. All are gloomy and silent. Ivan Ilyitch feels that it is he who has brought this gloom upon them, and he cannot disperse it. They have supper, and the party breaks up, and Ivan Ilyitch is left alone with the consciousness that his life is poisoned for him and poisons the life of others, and that this poison is not losing its force, but is continually penetrating more and more deeply into his whole existence.

And with the consciousness of this, and with the physical pain in addition, and the terror in addition to that, he must lie in his bed, often not able to sleep for pain the greater part of the night; and in the morning he must get up again, dress, go to the law-court, speak, write, or, if he does not go out, stay at home for all the four-and-twenty hours of the day and night, of which each one is a torture. And he had to live thus on the edge of the precipice alone, without one man who would understand and feel for him.

V

In this way one month, then a second, passed by. Just before the New Year his brother-in-law arrived in the town on a visit to them. Ivan Ilyitch was at the court when he arrived. Praskovya Fyodorovna had gone out shopping. Coming home and going into his study, he found there his brother-in-law, a healthy, florid man, engaged in unpacking his trunk. He raised his head, hearing Ivan Ilyitch's step, and for a second stared at him without a word. That stare told Ivan Ilyitch everything. His brother-in-law opened his mouth to utter an "Oh!" of surprise, but checked himself. That confirmed it all.

"What! have I changed?"

"Yes, there is a change."

And all Ivan Ilyitch's efforts to draw him into talking of his appearance his brother-in-law met with obstinate silence. Praskovya Fyodorovna came in; the brother-in-law went to see her. Ivan Ilyitch locked his door and began gazing at himself in the looking-glass, first full face, then in profile. He took up his photograph, taken with his wife, and compared the portrait with what he saw in the looking-glass. The change was immense. Then he bared his arm to the elbow, looked at it, pulled the sleeve down again, sat down on an ottoman and felt blacker than night.

"I mustn't, I mustn't," he said to himself, jumped up, went to the table, opened some official paper, tried to read it, but could not. He opened the door, went into the drawing-room. The door into the drawing-room was closed. He went up to it on tiptoe and listened.

"No, you're exaggerating," Praskovya Fyodorovna was saying.

"Exaggerating? You can't see it. Why, he's a dead man. Look at his eyes—there's no light in them. But what's wrong with him?"

"No one can tell. Nikolaev" (that was another doctor) "said something, but I don't know, Leshtchetitsky" (this was the celebrated doctor) "said the opposite."

Ivan Ilyitch walked away, went to his own room, lay down, and fell to musing. "A kidney—a loose kidney." He remembered all the doctors had told him, how it had been detached, and how it was loose; and by an effort of imagination he tried to catch that kidney and to stop it, to strengthen it. So little was needed, he fancied. "No, I'll go again to Pyotr Ivanovitch" (this was the friend who had a friend a doctor). He rang, ordered the horse to be put in, and got ready to go out.

"Where are you off to, Jean?" [18] asked his wife with a peculiarly melancholy and exceptionally kind expression.

This exceptionally kind expression exasperated him. He looked darkly at her.

"I want to see Pyotr Ivanovitch."

---

[18] French form of "Ivan."

He went to the friend who had a friend a doctor. And with him to the doctor's. He found him in, and had a long conversation with him.

Reviewing the anatomical and physiological details of what, according to the doctor's view, was taking place within him, he understood it all. It was just one thing—a little thing wrong with the intestinal appendix. It might all come right. Only strengthen one sluggish organ, and decrease the undue activity of another, and absorption would take place, and all would be set right. He was a little late for dinner. He ate his dinner, talked cheerfully, but it was a long while before he could go to his own room to work. At last he went to his study, and at once sat down to work. He read his legal documents and did his work, but the consciousness never left him of having a matter of importance very near to his heart which he had put off, but would look into later. When he had finished his work, he remembered that the matter near his heart was thinking about the intestinal appendix. But he did not give himself up to it; he went into the drawing-room to tea. There were visitors; and there was talking, playing on the piano, and singing; there was the young examining magistrate, the desirable match for the daughter. Ivan Ilyitch spent the evening, as Praskovya Fyodorovna observed, in better spirits than any of them; but he never forgot for an instant that he had the important matter of the intestinal appendix put off for consideration later. At eleven o'clock he said good night and went to his own room. He had slept alone since his illness in a little room adjoining his study. He went in, undressed, and took up a novel of Zola,[19] but did not read it; he fell to thinking. And in his imagination the desired recovery of the intestinal appendix had taken place. There had been absorption, rejection, re-establishment of the regular action.

"Why, it's all simply that," he said to himself. "One only wants to assist nature." He remembered the medicine, got up, took it, lay down on his back, watching for the medicine to act beneficially and overcome the pain. "It's only to take it regularly and avoid injurious influences; why, already I feel rather better, much better." He began to feel his side; it was not painful to the touch. "Yes, I don't feel it—really, much better already." He put out the candle and lay on his side. "The appendix is getting better, absorption." Suddenly he felt the familiar, odd, dull, gnawing ache, persistent, quiet, in earnest. In his mouth the same familiar loathsome taste. His heart sank, and his brain felt dim, misty. "My God, my God!" he said, "again, again, and it will never cease." And suddenly the whole thing rose before him in quite a different aspect. "Intestinal appendix! kidney!" he said to himself. "It's not a question of the appendix, not a question of the kidney, but of life and . . . death. Yes, life has been and now it's going, going away, and I cannot stop it. Yes. Why deceive myself? Isn't it obvious to every one, except me, that I'm dying, and it's only a question of weeks, of days—at once perhaps. There was a light, and now there is darkness. I was here, and now I am going! Where?" A cold chill ran over him, his breath stopped. He heard nothing but the throbbing of his heart.

"I shall be no more, then what will there be? There'll be nothing. Where then shall I be when I'm no more? Can this be dying? No; I don't want to!" He jumped up, tried to light the candle; and fumbling with trembling hands, he dropped the candle and the candlestick on the floor and fell back again on the pillow. "Why trouble? it doesn't matter," he said to himself, staring with open eyes into the darkness. "Death. Yes, death. And they—all of them—don't understand, and don't want to understand, and feel no pity. They are playing." (He caught through

---

[19] Émile Zola, contemporary French naturalist writer. Tolstoy disliked Zola's work and regarded it as indecent and demoralizing.

the closed doors the far-away cadence of a voice and the accompaniment.) "They don't care, but they will die too. Fools! Me sooner and them later; but it will be the same for them. And they are merry. The beasts!" Anger stifled him. And he was agonizingly, insufferably miserable. "It cannot be that all men always have been doomed to this awful horror!" He raised himself.

"There is something wrong in it; I must be calm. I must think it all over from the beginning." And then he began to consider. "Yes, the beginning of my illness. I knocked my side, and I was just the same, that day and the days after it; it ached a little, then more, then doctors, then depression, misery, and again doctors; and I've gone on getting closer and closer to the abyss. Strength growing less. Nearer and nearer. And here I am, wasting away, no light in my eyes. I think of how to cure the appendix, but this is death. Can it be death?" Again a horror came over him; gasping for breath, he bent over, began feeling for the matches, and knocked his elbow against the bedside table. It was in his way and hurt him; he felt furious with it, in his anger knocked against it more violently, and upset it. And in despair, breathless, he fell back on his spine waiting for death to come that instant.

The visitors were leaving at that time. Praskovya Fyodorovna was seeing them out. She heard something fall, and came in.

"What is it?"

"Nothing. I dropped something by accident."

She went out, brought a candle. He was lying, breathing hard and fast, like a man who has run a mile, and staring with fixed eyes at her.

"What is it, Jean?"

"No—othing, I say. I dropped something."—"Why speak? She won't understand," he thought.

She certainly did not understand. She picked up the candle, lighted it for him, and went out hastily. She had to say good-bye to a departing guest. When she came back, he was lying in the same position on his back, looking upwards.

"How are you—worse?"

"Yes."

She shook her head, sat down.

"Do you know what, Jean?" I wonder if we hadn't better send for Leshtchetitsky to see you here?"

This meant calling in the celebrated doctor, regardless of expense. He smiled malignantly, and said no. She sat a moment longer, went up to him, and kissed him on the forehead.

He hated her with all the force of his soul when she was kissing him, and had to make an effort not to push her away.

"Good night. Please God, you'll sleep."

"Yes."

VI

Ivan Ilyitch saw that he was dying, and was in continual despair.

At the bottom of his heart Ivan Ilyitch knew that he was dying; but so far from growing used to this idea, he simply did not grasp it—he was utterly unable to grasp it.

The example of the syllogism that he had learned in Kiseveter's logic[20]—Caius is a man, men are mortal, therefore Caius is mortal—had seemed to him all his life correct only as regards Caius, but not at all as regards himself. In that case it was

[20] Ivan is remembering a school textbook, *Outline of Logic* (1796), by the German Karl Kiesewetter.

a question of Caius, a man, an abstract man, and it was perfectly true, but he was not Caius, and was not an abstract man; he had always been a creature quite, quite different from all others; he had been little Vanya with a mamma and papa, and Mitya and Volodya, with playthings and a coachman and a nurse; afterwards with Katenka, with all the joys and griefs and ecstasies of childhood, boyhood, and youth. What did Caius know of the smell of the leathern ball Vanya had been so fond of? Had Caius kissed his mother's hand like that? Caius had not heard the silk rustle of his mother's skirts. He had not made a riot at school over the pudding. Had Caius been in love like that? Could Caius preside over the sittings of the court?

And Caius certainly was mortal, and it was right for him to die; but for me, little Vanya, Ivan Ilyitch, with all my feelings and ideas—for me it's a different matter. And it cannot be that I ought to die. That would be too awful.

That was his feeling.

"If I had to die like Caius, I should have known it was so, some inner voice would have told me so. But there was nothing of the sort in me. And I and all my friends, we felt that it was not at all the same as with Caius. And now here it is!" he said to himself. "It can't be! It can't be, but it is! How is it? How's one to understand it?" And he could not conceive it, and tried to drive away this idea as false, incorrect, and morbid, and to supplant it by other, correct, healthy ideas. But this idea, not as an idea merely, but as it were an actual fact, came back again and stood confronting him.

And to replace this thought he called up other thoughts, one after another, in the hope of finding support in them. He tried to get back into former trains of thought, which in old days had screened off the thought of death. But, strange to say, all that had in old days covered up, obliterated the sense of death, could not now produce the same effect. Latterly, Ivan Ilyitch spent the greater part of his time in these efforts to restore his old trains of thought which had shut off death. At one time he would say to himself, "I'll put myself into my official work; why, I used to live in it." And he would go to the law-courts, banishing every doubt. He would enter into conversation with his colleagues, and would sit carelessly, as his old habit was, scanning the crowd below dreamily, and with both his wasted hands he would lean on the arms of the oak arm-chair just as he always did; and bending over to a colleague, pass the papers to him and whisper to him, then suddenly dropping his eyes and sitting up straight, he would pronounce the familiar words that opened the proceedings. But suddenly in the middle, the pain in his side, utterly regardless of the stage he had reached in his conduct of the case, began its work. It riveted Ivan Ilyitch's attention. He drove away the thought of it, but it still did its work, and then *It* came and stood confronting him and looked at him, and he felt turned to stone, and the light died away in his eyes, and he began to ask himself again, "Can it be that It is the only truth?" And his colleagues and his subordinates saw with surprise and distress that he, the brilliant, subtle judge, was losing the thread of his speech, was making blunders. He shook himself, tried to regain his self-control, and got somehow to the end of the sitting, and went home with the painful sense that his judicial labors could not as of old hide from him what he wanted to hide; that he could not by means of his official work escape from *It*. And the worst of it was that It drew him to itself not for him to do anything in particular, but simply for him to look at It straight in the face, to look at It and, doing nothing, suffer unspeakably.

And to save himself from this, Ivan Ilyitch sought amusements, other screens, and these screens he found, and for a little while they did seem to save him; but soon again they were not so much broken down as let the light through, as though It pierced through everything, and there was nothing that could shut It off.

Sometimes during those days he would go into the drawing-room he had furnished, that drawing-room where he had fallen, for which—how bitterly ludicrous it was for him to think of it!—for the decoration of which he had sacrificed his life, for he knew that it was that bruise that had started his illness. He went in and saw that the polished table had been scratched by something. He looked for the cause, and found it in the bronze clasps of the album, which had been twisted on one side. He took up the album, a costly one, which he had himself arranged with loving care, and was vexed at the carelessness of his daughter and her friends. Here a page was torn, here the photographs had been shifted out of their place. He carefully put it to rights again and bent the clasp back.

Then the idea occurred to him to move all this setting up of the albums to another corner where the flowers stood. He called the footman; or his daughter or his wife came to help him. They did not agree with him, contradicted him; he argued, got angry. But all that was very well, since he did not think of It; It was not in sight.

But then his wife would say, as he moved something himself, "Do let the servants do it, you'll hurt yourself again," and all at once It peeped through the screen; he caught a glimpse of It. He caught a glimpse of It, but still he hoped It would hide itself. Involuntarily, though, he kept watch on his side; there it is just the same still, aching still, and now he cannot forget it, and *It* is staring openly at him from behind the flowers. What's the use of it all?

"And it's the fact that here, at that curtain, as if it had been storming a fort, I lost my life. Is it possible? How awful and how silly! It cannot be! It cannot be, and it is."

He went into his own room, lay down, and was again alone with It. Face to face with It, and nothing to be done with It. Nothing but to look at It and shiver.

VII

How it came to pass during the third month of Ivan Ilyitch's illness, it would be impossible to say, for it happened little by little, imperceptibly, but it had come to pass that his wife and his daughter and his son and their servants and their acquaintances, and the doctors, and, most of all, he himself—all were aware that all interest in him for other people consisted now in the question of how soon he would leave his place empty, free the living from the constraint of his presence, and be set free himself from his sufferings.

He slept less and less; they gave him opium, and began to inject morphine. But this did not relieve him. The dull pain he experienced in the half-asleep condition at first only relieved him as a change, but then it became as bad, or even more agonizing, than the open pain. He had special things to eat prepared for him according to the doctor's prescriptions; but these dishes became more and more distasteful, more and more revolting to him.

Special arrangements, too, had to be made for his other physical needs, and this was a continual misery to him. Misery from the uncleanliness, the unseemliness, and the stench, from the feeling of another person having to assist in it.

But just from this most unpleasant side of his illness there came comfort to Ivan Ilyitch. There always came into his room on these occasions to clear up for him the peasant who waited on the table, Gerasim.

Gerasim was a clean, fresh, young peasant, who had grown stout and hearty on the good fare in town. Always cheerful and bright. At first the sight of this lad, always cleanly dressed in the Russian style, engaged in this revolting task, embarrassed Ivan Ilyitch.

One day, getting up from the night-stool,[21] too weak to replace his clothes, he dropped on to a soft low chair and looked with horror at his bare, powerless thighs, with the muscles so sharply standing out on them.

Then there came in with light, strong steps Gerasim, in his thick boots, diffusing a pleasant smell of tar from his boots, and bringing in the freshness of the winter air. Wearing a clean hempen apron, and a clean cotton shirt, with his sleeves tucked up on his strong, bare young arms, without looking at Ivan Ilyitch, obviously trying to check the radiant happiness in his face so as not to hurt the sick man, he went up to the night-stool.

"Gerasim," said Ivan Ilyitch faintly.

Gerasim started, clearly afraid that he had done something amiss, and with a rapid movement turned towards the sick man his fresh, good-natured, simple young face, just beginning to be downy with the first growth of beard.

"Yes, your honor."

"I'm afraid this is very disagreeable for you. You must excuse me. I can't help it."

"Why, upon my word, sir!" And Gerasim's eyes beamed, and he showed his white young teeth in a smile. "What's a little trouble? It's a case of illness with you, sir."

And with his deft, strong arms he performed his habitual task, and went out, stepping lightly. And five minutes later, treading just as lightly, he came back. Ivan Ilyitch was still sitting in the same way in the arm-chair.

"Gerasim," he said, when the latter had replaced the night-stool all sweet and clean, "please help me; come here." Gerasim went up to him. "Lift me up. It's difficult for me alone, and I've sent Dmitry away."

Gerasim went up to him; as lightly as he stepped he put his strong arms round him, deftly and gently lifted and supported him, with the other hand pulled up his trousers, and would have set him down again. But Ivan Ilyitch asked him to carry him to the sofa. Gerasim, without effort, carefully not squeezing him, led him, almost carrying him, to the sofa, and settled him there.

"Thank you; how neatly and well . . . you do everything."

Gerasim smiled again, and would have gone away. But Ivan Ilyitch felt his presence such a comfort that he was reluctant to let him go.

"Oh, move that chair near me, please. No, that one, under my legs. I feel easier when my legs are higher."

Gerasim picked up the chair, and without letting it knock, set it gently down on the ground just at the right place, and lifted Ivan Ilyitch's legs on to it. It seemed to Ivan Ilyitch that he was easier just at the moment when Gerasim lifted his legs higher.

"I'm better when my legs are higher," said Ivan Ilyitch. "Put that cushion under me."

Gerasim did so. Again he lifted his legs to put the cushion under them. Again it seemed to Ivan Ilyitch that he was easier at that moment when Gerasim held his legs raised. When he laid them down again, he felt worse.

"Gerasim," he said to him, "are you busy just now?"

---

[21] Commode; seat over a chamber pot.

"Not at all, sir," said Gerasim, who had learned among the town-bred servants how to speak to gentlefolks.

"What have you left to do?"

"Why, what have I to do? I've done everything, there's only the wood to chop for to-morrow."

"Then hold my legs up like that—can you?"

"To be sure, I can." Gerasim lifted the legs up. And it seemed to Ivan Ilyitch that in that position he did not feel the pain at all.

"But how about the wood?"

"Don't you trouble about that, sir. We shall have time enough."

Ivan Ilyitch made Gerasim sit and hold his legs, and began to talk to him. And, strange to say, he fancied he felt better while Gerasim had hold of his legs.

From that time forward Ivan Ilyitch would sometimes call Gerasim, and get him to hold his legs on his shoulders, and he liked talking with him. Gerasim did this easily, readily, simply, and with a good-nature that touched Ivan Ilyitch. Health, strength, and heartiness in all other people were offensive to Ivan Ilyitch; but the strength and heartiness of Gerasim did not mortify him, but soothed him.

Ivan Ilyitch's great misery was due to the deception that for some reason or other every one kept up with him—that he was simply ill, and not dying, and that he need only keep quiet and follow the doctor's orders, and then some great change for the better would be the result. He knew that whatever they might do, there would be no result except more agonizing sufferings and death. And he was made miserable by this lie, made miserable at their refusing to acknowledge what they all knew and he knew, by their persisting in lying to him about his awful position, and in forcing him too to take part in this lie. Lying, lying, this lying carried on over him on the eve of his death, and destined to bring that terrible, solemn act of his death down to the level of all their visits, curtains, sturgeons for dinner . . . was a horrible agony for Ivan Ilyitch. And, strange to say, many times when they had been going through the regular performance over him, he had been within a hair's breadth of screaming at them: "Cease your lying! You know, and I know, that I'm dying; so do, at least, give over lying!" But he had never had the spirit to do this. The terrible, awful act of his dying was, he saw, by all those about him, brought down to the level of a casual, unpleasant, and to some extent indecorous, incident (somewhat as they would behave with a person who should enter a drawing-room smelling unpleasant). It was brought down to this level by that very decorum to which he had been enslaved all his life. He saw that no one felt for him, because no one would even grasp his position. Gerasim was the only person who recognized the position, and felt sorry for him. And that was why Ivan Ilyitch was only at ease with Gerasim. He felt comforted when Gerasim sometimes supported his legs for whole nights at a stretch, and would not go away to bed, saying, "Don't you worry yourself, Ivan Ilyitch, I'll get sleep enough yet," or when suddenly dropping into the familiar peasant forms of speech, he added: "If thou weren't sick, but as 'tis, 'twould be strange if I didn't wait on thee." Gerasim alone did not lie; everything showed clearly that he alone understood what it meant, and saw no necessity to disguise it, and simply felt sorry for his sick, wasting master. He even said this once straight out, when Ivan Ilyitch was sending him away.

"We shall all die. So what's a little trouble?" he said, meaning by this to express that he did not complain of the trouble just because he was taking this trouble for a dying man, and he hoped that for him too some one would be willing to take the same trouble when his time came.

Apart from this deception, or in consequence of it, what made the greatest misery for Ivan Ilyitch was that no one felt for him as he would have liked them to feel for him. At certain moments, after prolonged suffering, Ivan Ilyitch, ashamed as he would have been to own it, longed more than anything for some one to feel sorry for him, as for a sick child. He longed to be petted, kissed, and wept over, as children are petted and comforted. He knew that he was an important member of the law-courts, that he had a beard turning grey, and that therefore it was impossible. But still he longed for it. And in his relations with Gerasim there was something approaching to that. And that was why being with Gerasim was a comfort to him. Ivan Ilyitch longs to weep, longs to be petted and wept over, and then there comes in a colleague, Shebek; and instead of weeping and being petted, Ivan Ilyitch puts on his serious, severe, earnest face, and from mere inertia gives his views on the effect of the last decision in the Court of Appeal, and obstinately insists upon them. This falsity around him and within him did more than anything to poison Ivan Ilyitch's last days.

VIII

It was morning. All that made it morning for Ivan Ilyitch was that Gerasim had gone away, and Pyotr the footman had come in; he had put out the candles, opened one of the curtains, and begun surreptitiously setting the room to rights. Whether it were morning or evening, Friday or Sunday, it all made no difference; it was always just the same thing. Gnawing, agonizing pain never ceasing for an instant; the hopeless sense of life always ebbing away, but still not yet gone; always swooping down on him that fearful, hated death, which was the only reality, and always the same falsity. What were days, or weeks, or hours of the day to him?

"Will you have tea, sir?"

"He wants things done in their regular order. In the morning the family should have tea," he thought, and only said—

"No."

"Would you care to move on to the sofa?"

"He wants to make the room tidy, and I'm in his way. I'm uncleanness, disorder," he thought, and only said—

"No, leave me alone."

The servant still moved busily about his work. Ivan Ilyitch stretched out his hand. Pyotr went up to offer his services.

"What can I get you?"

"My watch."

Pyotr got out the watch, which lay just under his hand, and gave it to him.

"Half-past eight. Are they up?"

"Not yet, sir. Vladimir Ivanovitch" (that was his son) "has gone to the high school, and Praskovya Fyodorovna gave orders that she was to be waked if you asked for her. Shall I send word?"

"No, no need." Should I try some tea? he thought. "Yes, tea . . . bring it."

Pyotr was on his way out. Ivan Ilyitch felt frightened of being left alone. "How keep him? Oh, the medicine. Pyotr, give me my medicine. Oh well, may be, medicine may still be some good." He took the spoon, drank it. "No, it does no good. It's all rubbish, deception," he decided, as soon as he tasted the familiar, mawkish, hopeless taste. "No, I can't believe it now. But the pain, why this pain?

If it would only cease for a minute." And he groaned. Pyotr turned round. "No, go on. Bring the tea."

Pyotr went away. Ivan Ilyitch, left alone, moaned, not so much from the pain, awful as it was, as from misery. Always the same thing and again, all these endless days and nights. If it would only be quicker. Quicker to what? Death, darkness. No, no. Anything better than death!

When Pyotr came in with the tea on a tray, Ivan Ilyitch stared for some time absent-mindedly at him, not grasping who he was and what he wanted. Pyotr was disconcerted by this stare. And when he showed he was disconcerted, Ivan Ilyitch came to himself.

"Oh yes," he said, "tea, good, set it down. Only help me to wash and put on a clean shirt."

And Ivan Ilyitch began his washing. He washed his hands slowly, and then his face, cleaned his teeth, combed his hair, and looked in the looking-glass. He felt frightened at what he saw, especially at the way his hair clung limply to his pale forehead. When his shirt was being changed, he knew he would be still more terrified if he glanced at his body, and he avoided looking at himself. But at last it was all over. He put on his dressing-gown, covered himself with a rug, and sat in the armchair to drink his tea. For one moment he felt refreshed; but as soon as he began to drink the tea, again there was the same taste, the same pain. He forced himself to finish it, and lay down, stretched out his legs. He lay down and dismissed Pyotr.

Always the same. A gleam of hope flashes for a moment, then again the sea of despair roars about him again, and always pain, always pain, always heartache, and always the same thing. Alone it is awfully dreary; he longs to call some one, but he knows beforehand that with others present it will be worse. "Morphine again— only to forget again. I'll tell him, the doctor, that he must think of something else. It can't go on; it can't go on like this."

One hour, two hours pass like this. Then there is a ring at the front door. The doctor, perhaps. Yes, it is the doctor, fresh, hearty, fat, and cheerful, wearing that expression that seems to say, "You there are in a panic about something, but we'll soon set things right for you." The doctor is aware that this expression is hardly fitting here, but he has put it on once and for all, and can't take it off, like a man who has put on a frockcoat to pay a round of calls.

In a hearty, reassuring manner the doctor rubs his hands.

"I'm cold. It's a sharp frost. Just let me warm myself," he says with an expression, as though it's only a matter of waiting a little till he's warm, and as soon as he's warm he'll set everything to rights.

"Well, now, how are you?"

Ivan Ilyitch feels that the doctor would like to say, "How's the little trouble?" but that he feels that he can't talk like that, and says, "How did you pass the night?"

Ivan Ilyitch looks at the doctor with an expression that asks—

"Is it possible you're never ashamed of lying?"

But the doctor does not care to understand this look.

And Ivan Ilyitch says—

"It's always just as awful. The pain never leaves me, never ceases. If only there were something!"

"Ah, you're all like that, all sick people say that. Come, now, I do believe I'm thawed; even Praskovya Fyodorovna, who's so particular, could find no fault with my temperature. Well, now I can say good morning." And the doctor shakes hands.

And dropping his former levity, the doctor, with a serious face, proceeds to examine the patient, feeling his pulse, to take his temperature, and then the tappings and soundings begin.

Ivan Ilyitch knows positively and indubitably that it's all nonsense and empty deception; but when the doctor, kneeling down, stretches over him, putting his ear first higher, then lower, and goes through various gymnastic evolutions over him with a serious face, Ivan Ilyitch is affected by this, as he used sometimes to be affected by the speeches of the lawyers in court, though he was perfectly well aware that they were telling lies all the while and why they were telling lies.

The doctor, kneeling on the sofa, was still sounding him, when there was the rustle of Praskovya Fyodorovna's silk dress in the doorway, and she was heard scolding Pyotr for not having let her know that the doctor had come.

She comes in, kisses her husband, and at once begins to explain that she has been up a long while, and that it was only through a misunderstanding that she was not there when the doctor came.

Ivan Ilyitch looks at her, scans her all over, and sets down against her her whiteness and plumpness, and the cleanness of her hands and neck, and the glossiness of her hair, and the gleam full of life in her eyes. With all the force of his soul he hates her. And when she touches him it makes him suffer from the thrill of hatred he feels for her.

Her attitude to him and his illness is still the same. Just as the doctor had taken up a certain line with the patients which he was not now able to drop, so she too had taken up a line with him—that he was not doing something he ought to do, and was himself to blame, and she was lovingly reproaching him for his neglect, and she could not now get out of this attitude.

"Why, you know, he won't listen to me; he doesn't take his medicine at the right times. And what's worse still, he insists on lying in a position that surely must be bad for him—with his legs in the air."

She described how he made Gerasim hold his legs up.

The doctor smiled with kindly condescension that said, "Oh well, it can't be helped, these sick people do take up such foolish fancies; but we must forgive them."

When the examination was over, the doctor looked at his watch, and then Praskovya Fyodorovna informed Ivan Ilyitch that it must, of course, be as he liked, but she had sent to-day for a celebrated doctor, and that he would examine him, and have a consultation with Mihail Danilovitch (that was the name of their regular doctor).

"Don't oppose it now, please. This I'm doing entirely for my own sake," she said ironically, meaning it to be understood that she was doing it all for his sake, and was only saying this to give him no right to refuse her request. He lay silent, knitting his brows. He felt that he was hemmed in by such a tangle of falsity that it was hard to disentangle anything from it.

Everything she did for him was entirely for her own sake, and she told him she was doing for her own sake what she actually was doing for her own sake as something so incredible that he would take it as meaning the opposite.

At half-past eleven the celebrated doctor came. Again came the sounding, and then grave conversation in his presence and in the other room about the kidney and the appendix, and questions and answers, with such an air of significance, that again, instead of the real question of life and death, which was now the only one that confronted him, the question that came uppermost was of the kidney and the appendix, which were doing something not as they ought to do, and were for that reason being attacked by Mihail Danilovitch and the celebrated doctor, and forced to mend their ways.

The celebrated doctor took leave of him with a serious, but not a hopeless face. And to the timid question that Ivan Ilyitch addressed to him while he lifted his eyes, shining with terror and hope, up towards him, Was there a chance of recovery? he answered that he could not answer for it, but that there was a chance. The look of hope with which Ivan Ilyitch watched the doctor out was so piteous that, seeing it, Praskovya Fyodorovna positively burst into tears, as she went out of the door to hand the celebrated doctor his fee in the next room.

The gleam of hope kindled by the doctor's assurance did not last long. Again the same room, the same pictures, the curtains, the wallpaper, the medicine-bottles, and ever the same, his aching suffering body. And Ivan Ilyitch began to moan; they gave him injections, and he sank into oblivion. When he waked up it was getting dark; they brought him in his dinner. He forced himself to eat some broth; and again everything the same, and again the coming night.

After dinner at seven o'clock Praskovya Fyodorovna came into his room, dressed as though to go to a *soirée*,[22] with her full bosom laced in tight, and traces of powder on her face. She had in the morning mentioned to him that they were going to the theatre. Sarah Bernhardt[23] was visiting the town, and they had a box, which he had insisted on their taking. By now he had forgotten about it, and her smart attire was an offense to him. But he concealed this feeling when he recollected that he had himself insisted on their taking a box and going, because it was an aesthetic pleasure, beneficial and instructive for the children.

Praskovya Fyodorovna came in satisfied with herself, but yet with something of a guilty air. She sat down, asked how he was, as he saw, simply for the sake of asking, and not for the sake of learning anything, knowing indeed that there was nothing to learn, and began telling him how absolutely necessary it was; how she would not have gone for anything, but the box had been taken, and Liza, their daughter, and Petrishtchev (the examining lawyer, the daughter's suitor) were going, and that it was out of the question to let them go alone. But that she would have liked much better to stay with him. If only he would be sure to follow the doctor's prescription while she was away.

"Oh, and Fyodor Dmitryevitch" (the suitor) "would like to come in. May he? And Liza?"

"Yes, let them come in."

The daughter came in, in evening clothes, her fresh young body showing, while his body made him suffer so. But she made a show of it; she was strong, healthy, obviously in love, and impatient of the illness, suffering, and death that hindered her happiness.

Fyodor Dmitryevitch came in too in evening dress, his hair curled *à la Capoul*,[24] with his long sinewy neck tightly fenced round by a white collar, with his vast expanse of white chest and strong thighs displayed in narrow black trousers, with one white glove in his hand and a crush opera hat.

Behind him crept in unnoticed the little high school boy in his new uniform,

---

[22] Evening affair.

[23] Immensely popular French actress (1844–1923), who toured widely in Europe, the United States, and Russia.

[24] In the fashionable Capoul style (French).

poor fellow, in gloves, and with those awful blue rings under his eyes that Ivan Ilyitch knew the meaning of.

He always felt sorry for his son. And pitiable indeed was his scared face of sympathetic suffering. Except Gerasim, Ivan Ilyitch fancied that Volodya was the only one that understood and was sorry.

They all sat down; again they asked how he was. A silence followed. Liza asked her mother about the opera-glass. An altercation ensued between the mother and daughter as to who had taken it, and where it had been put. It turned into an unpleasant squabble.

Fyodor Dmitryevitch asked Ivan Ilyitch whether he had seen Sarah Bernhardt? Ivan Ilyitch could not at first catch the question that was asked him, but then he said, "No, have you seen her before?"

"Yes, in *Adrienne Lecouvreur*."[25]

Praskovya Fyodorovna observed that she was particularly good in that part. The daughter made some reply. A conversation sprang up about the art and naturalness of her acting, that conversation that is continually repeated and always the same.

In the middle of the conversation Fyodor Dmitryevitch glanced at Ivan Ilyitch and relapsed into silence. The others looked at him and became mute, too. Ivan Ilyitch was staring with glittering eyes straight before him, obviously furious with them. This had to be set right, but it could not anyhow be set right. This silence had somehow to be broken. No one would venture on breaking it, and all began to feel alarmed that the decorous deception was somehow breaking down, and the facts would be exposed to all. Liza was the first to pluck up courage. She broke the silence. She tried to cover up what they were all feeling, but inadvertently she gave it utterance.

"*If we are going,* though, it's time to start," she said, glancing at her watch, a gift from her father; and with a scarcely perceptible meaning smile to the young man, referring to something only known to themselves, she got up with a rustle of her skirts.

They all got up, said good-bye, and went away. When they were gone, Ivan Ilyitch fancied he was easier; there was no falsity—that had gone away with them, but the pain remained. That continual pain, that continual terror, made nothing harder, nothing easier. It was always worse.

Again came minute after minute, hour after hour, still the same and still no end, and ever more terrible the inevitable end.

"Yes, send Gerasim," he said in answer to Pyotr's question.

IX

Late at night his wife came back. She came in on tiptoe, but he heard her, opened his eyes, and made haste to close them again. She wanted to send away Gerasim and sit up with him herself instead. He opened his eyes and said, "No, go away."

"Are you in great pain?"

"Always the same."

"Take some opium."

He agreed, and drank it. She went away.

Till three o'clock he slept in a miserable sleep. It seemed to him that he and his

[25] A light, commercial play by the immensely prolific French playwright Eugène Scribe. Tolstoy disliked his work.

pain were being thrust somewhere into a narrow, deep, black sack, and they kept pushing him further and further in, and still could not thrust him to the bottom. And this operation was awful to him, and was accompanied with agony. And he was afraid, and yet wanted to fall into it, and struggled and yet tried to get into it. And all of a sudden he slipped and fell and woke up. Gerasim, still the same, is sitting at the foot of the bed half-dozing peacefully, patient. And he is lying with his wasted legs clad in stockings, raised on Gerasim's shoulders, the same candle burning in the alcove, and the same interminable pain.

"Go away, Gerasim," he whispered.

"It's all right, sir. I'll stay a bit longer."

"No, go away."

He took his legs down, lay sideways on his arm, and he felt very sorry for himself. He only waited till Gerasim had gone away into the next room; he could restrain himself no longer, and cried like a child. He cried at his own helplessness, at his awful loneliness, at the cruelty of people, at the cruelty of God, at the absence of God.

"Why hast Thou done all this? What brought me to this? Why, why torture me so horribly?"

He did not expect an answer, and wept indeed that there was and could be no answer. The pain grew more acute again, but he did not stir, did not call.

He said to himself, "Come, more then; come, strike me! But what for? What have I done to Thee? what for?"

Then he was still, ceased weeping, held his breath, and was all attention; he listened, as it were, not to a voice uttering sounds, but to the voice of his soul, to the current of thoughts that rose up within him.

"What is it you want?" was the first clear idea capable of putting into words that he grasped.

"What? Not to suffer, to live," he answered.

And again he was utterly plunged into attention so intense that even the pain did not distract him.

"To live? Live how?" the voice of his soul was asking.

"Why, live as I used to live before—happily and pleasantly."

"As you used to live before—happily and pleasantly?" queried the voice. And he began going over in his imagination the best moments of his pleasant life. But strange to say, all these best moments of his pleasant life seemed now not at all what they had seemed then. All—except the first memories of childhood—there, in his childhood there had been something really pleasant in which one could have lived if it had come back. But the creature who had this pleasant experience was no more; it was like a memory of some one else.

As soon as he reached the beginning of what had resulted in him as he was now, Ivan Ilyitch, all that had seemed joys to him then now melted away before his eyes and were transformed into something trivial, and often disgusting.

And the further he went from childhood, the nearer to the actual present, the more worthless and uncertain were the joys. It began with life at the school of jurisprudence. Then there had still been something genuinely good; then there had been gaiety; then there had been friendship; then there had been hopes. But in the higher classes these good moments were already becoming rarer. Later on, during the first period of his official life, at the governor's, good moments appeared; but it was all mixed, and less and less of it was good. And further on even less was good, and the further he went the less good there was.

His marriage . . . as gratuitous as the disillusion of it and the smell of his wife's breath and the sensuality, the hypocrisy! And that deadly official life, and anxiety about money, and so for one year, and two, and ten, and twenty, and always the same thing. And the further he went, the more deadly it became. "As though I had been going steadily downhill, imagining that I was going uphill. So it was in fact. In public opinion I was going uphill, and steadily as I got up it, life was ebbing away from me.... And now the work's done, there's nothing left but to die.

"But what is this? What for? It cannot be! It cannot be that life has been so senseless, so loathsome? And if it really was so loathsome and senseless, then why die, and die in agony? There's something wrong.

"Can it be I have not lived as one ought?" suddenly came into his head. "But how not so, when I've done everything as it should be done?" he said, and at once dismissed this only solution of all the enigma of life and death as something utterly out of the question.

"What do you want now? To live? Live how? Live as you live at the courts when the usher booms out: 'The Judge is coming!' ... The judge is coming, the judge is coming," he repeated to himself. "Here he is, the judge! But I'm not to blame!" he shrieked in fury. "What's it for?" And he left off crying, and turning with his face to the wall, fell to pondering always on the same question, "What for, why all this horror?"

But however much he pondered, he could not find an answer. And whenever the idea struck him, as it often did, that it all came of his never having lived as he ought, he thought of all the correctness of his life and dismissed the strange idea.

X

Another fortnight had passed. Ivan Ilyitch could not now get up from the sofa. He did not like lying in bed, and lay on the sofa. And lying almost all the time facing the wall, in loneliness he suffered all the inexplicable agonies, and in loneliness pondered always that inexplicable question, "What is it? Can it be true that it's death?" And an inner voice answered, "Yes, it is true." "Why these agonies?" and a voice answered. "For no reason." Beyond and besides this there was nothing.

From the very beginning of his illness, ever since Ivan Ilyitch first went to the doctor's, his life had been split up into two contradictory moods, which were continually alternating—one was despair and the anticipation of an uncomprehended and awful death; the other was hope and an absorbed watching over the actual condition of his body. First there was nothing confronting him but a kidney or intestine which had temporarily declined to perform its duties, then there was nothing but unknown awful death, which there was no escaping.

These two moods had alternated from the very beginning of the illness; but the further the illness progressed, the more doubtful and fantastic became the conception of the kidney, and the more real the sense of approaching death.

He had but to reflect on what he had been three months before and what he was now, to reflect how steadily he had been going downhill, for every possibility of hope to be shattered.

Of late, in the loneliness in which he found himself, lying with his face to the back of the sofa, a loneliness in the middle of a populous town and of his numerous acquaintances and his family, a loneliness than which none more complete could be found anywhere—not at the bottom of the sea, not deep down in the earth;—of late in this fearful loneliness Ivan Ilyitch had lived only in imagination in the past. One by one the pictures of his past rose up before him. It always began from what was nearest in time and went back to the most remote, to childhood, and rested there. If Ivan Ilyitch thought of the stewed prunes that had been offered him for dinner that day, his mind went back to the damp, wrinkled French plum of his childhood, of its peculiar taste and the flow of saliva when the stone was sucked; and along with this memory of a taste there rose up a whole series of memories of that period—his nurse, his brother, his playthings. "I mustn't . . . it's too painful," Ivan Ilyitch said to himself, and he brought himself back to the present. The button on the back of the sofa and the creases in the morocco.[26] "Morocco's dear, and doesn't wear well; there was a quarrel over it. But the morocco was different, and different too the quarrel when we tore father's portfolio and were punished, and mamma bought us the tarts." And again his mind rested on his childhood, and again it was painful, and he tried to drive it away and think of something else.

And again at that point, together with that chain of associations, quite another chain of memories came into his heart, of how his illness had grown up and become more acute. It was the same there, the further back the more life there had been. There had been both more that was good in life and more of life itself. And the two began to melt into one. "Just as the pain goes on getting worse and worse, so has my whole life gone on getting worse and worse," he thought. One light spot was there at the back, at the beginning of life, and then it kept getting blacker and blacker, and going faster and faster. "In inverse ratio to the square of the distance from death," thought Ivan Ilyitch. And the image of a stone falling downwards with increasing velocity sank into his soul. Life, a series of increasing sufferings, falls more and more swiftly to the end, the most fearful sufferings. "I am falling." He shuddered, shifted himself, would have resisted, but he knew beforehand that he could not resist; and again, with eyes weary with gazing at it, but unable not to gaze at what was before him, he stared at the back of the sofa and waited, waited expecting that fearful fall and shock and dissolution. "Resistance is impossible," he said to himself. "But if one could at least comprehend what it's for? Even that's impossible. It could be explained if one were to say that I hadn't lived as I ought. But that can't be alleged," he said to himself, thinking of all the regularity, correctness, and propriety of his life. "That really can't be admitted," he said to himself, his lips smiling ironically as though some one could see his smile and be deceived by it. "No explanation! Agony, death. . . . What for?"

XI

So passed a fortnight. During that fortnight an event occurred that had been desired by Ivan Ilyitch and his wife. Petrishtchev made a formal proposal. This took place in the evening. Next day Praskovya Fyodorovna went in to her husband, resolving in her mind how to inform him of Fyodor Dmitryevitch's proposal, but that night there had been a change for the worse in Ivan Ilyitch. Praskovya Fyodorovna found him on the same sofa, but in a different position. He was lying on his face, groaning, and staring straight before him with a fixed gaze.

She began talking of remedies. He turned his stare on her. She did not finish what she had begun saying; such hatred of her in particular was expressed in that stare.

"For Christ's sake, let me die in peace," he said.

She would have gone away, but at that moment the daughter came in and went

---

[26] A fine leather made from goatskin, often used as a furniture-covering in the nineteenth century.

up to say good morning to him. He looked at his daughter just as at his wife, and to her inquiries how he was, he told her drily that they would soon all be rid of him. Both were silent, sat a little while, and went out.

"How are we to blame?" said Liza to her mother. "As though we had done it! I'm sorry for papa, but why punish us?"

At the usual hour the doctor came. Ivan Ilyitch answered, "Yes, no," never taking his exasperated stare from him, and towards the end he said, "Why, you know that you can do nothing, so let me be."

"We can relieve your suffering," said the doctor.

"Even that you can't do; let me be."

The doctor went into the drawing-room and told Praskovya Fyodorovna that it was very serious, and that the only resource left them was opium to relieve his sufferings, which must be terrible. The doctor said his physical sufferings were terrible, and that was true; but even more terrible than his physical sufferings were his mental sufferings, and in that lay his chief misery.

His moral sufferings were due to the fact that during that night, as he looked at the sleepy, good-natured, broad-cheeked face of Gerasim, the thought had suddenly come into his head, "What if in reality all my life, my conscious life, has been not the right thing?" The thought struck him that what he had regarded before as an utter impossibility, that he had spent his life not as he ought, might be the truth. It struck him that those scarcely detected impulses of struggle within him against what was considered good by persons of higher position, scarcely detected impulses which he had dismissed, that they might be the real thing, and everything else might be not the right thing. And his official work, and his ordering of his daily life and of his family, and these social and official interests,—all that might be not the right thing. He tried to defend it all to himself. And suddenly he felt all the weakness of what he was defending. And it was useless to defend it.

"But if it's so," he said to himself, "and I am leaving life with the consciousness that I have lost all that was given me, and there's no correcting it, then what?" He lay on his back and began going over his whole life entirely anew. When he saw the footman in the morning, then his wife, then his daughter, then the doctor, every movement they made, every word they uttered, confirmed for him the terrible truth that had been revealed to him in the night. In them he saw himself, saw all in which he had lived, and saw distinctly that it was all not the right thing; it was a horrible, vast deception that concealed both life and death. This consciousness intensified his physical agonies, multiplied them tenfold. He groaned and tossed from side to side and pulled at the covering over him. It seemed to him that it was stifling him and weighing him down. And for that he hated them.

They gave him a big dose of opium; he sank into unconsciousness; but at dinner-time the same thing began again. He drove them all away, and tossed from side to side.

His wife came to him and said, "Jean, darling, do this for my sake" (for my sake?). "It can't do harm, and it often does good. Why, it's nothing. And often in health people———"

He opened his eyes wide.

"What? Take the sacrament? What for? No. Besides . . ."

She began to cry.

"Yes, my dear. I'll send for our priest, he's so nice."

"All right, very well," he said.

When the priest came and confessed him he was softened, felt as it were a relief from his doubts, and consequently from his sufferings, and there came a moment of hope. He began once more thinking of the intestinal appendix and the possibility of curing it. He took the sacrament with tears in his eyes.

When they laid him down again after the sacrament for a minute, he felt comfortable, and again the hope of life sprang up. He began to think about the operation which had been suggested to him. "To live, I want to live," he said to himself. His wife came in to congratulate him; she uttered the customary words and added—

"It's quite true, isn't it, that you're better?"

Without looking at her, he said, "Yes."

Her dress, her figure, the expression of her face, the tone of her voice—all told him the same: "Not the right thing. All that in which you lived and are living is lying, deceit, hiding life and death away from you." And as soon as he had formed that thought, hatred sprang up in him, and with that hatred agonizing physical sufferings, and with these sufferings the sense of inevitable, approaching ruin. Something new was happening; there were screwing and shooting pains, and a tightness in his breathing.

The expression of his face as he uttered that "Yes" was terrible. After uttering that "Yes," looking her straight in the face, he turned on to his face, with a rapidity extraordinary in his weakness, and shrieked—

"Go away, go away, let me be!"

XII

From that moment there began the scream that never ceased for three days, and was so awful that through two closed doors one could not hear it without horror. At the moment when he answered his wife he grasped that he had fallen, that there was no return, that the end had come, quite the end, while doubt was still as unsolved, but remained doubt.

"Oo! Oo—o! Oo!" he screamed in varying intonations. He had begun screaming, "I don't want to!" and so had gone on screaming on the same vowel sound— oo!

All those three days, during which time did not exist for him, he was struggling in that black sack into which he was being thrust by an unseen resistless force. He struggled as the man condemned to death struggles in the hands of the executioner, knowing that he cannot save himself. And every moment he felt that in spite of all his efforts to struggle against it, he was getting nearer and nearer to what terrified him. He felt that his agony was due both to his being thrust into this black hole and still more to his not being able to get right into it. What hindered him from getting into it was the claim that his life had been good. That justification of his life held him fast and would not let him get forward, and it caused him more agony than all.

All at once some force struck him in the chest, in the side, and stifled his breathing more than ever; he rolled forward into the hole, and there at the end there was some sort of light. It had happened with him, as it had sometimes happened to him in a railway carriage, when he had thought he was going forward while he was going back, and all of a sudden recognized his real direction.

"Yes, it has all been not the right thing," he said to himself, "but that's no matter." He could, he could do the right thing. "What is the right thing?" he asked himself, and suddenly he became quiet.

This was at the end of the third day, two hours before his death. At that very moment the schoolboy had stealthily crept into his father's room and gone to his bedside. The dying man was screaming and waving his arms. His hand fell on the schoolboy's head. The boy snatched it, pressed it to his lips, and burst into tears.

At that very moment Ivan Ilyitch had rolled into the hole, and caught sight of the light, and it was revealed to him that his life had not been what it ought to have been, but that that could still be set right. He asked himself, "What is the right thing?"—and became quiet, listening. Then he felt some one was kissing his hand. He opened his eyes and glanced at his son. He felt sorry for him. His wife went up to him. He glanced at her. She was gazing at him with open mouth, the tears unwiped streaming over her nose and cheeks, a look of despair on her face. He felt sorry for her.

"Yes, I'm making them miserable," he thought. "They're sorry, but it will be better for them when I die." He would have said this, but had not the strength to utter it. "Besides, why speak, I must act," he thought. With a glance to his wife he pointed to his son and said—

"Take away . . . sorry for him. . . . And you too . . ." He tried to say "forgive," but said "forgo" . . . and too weak to correct himself, shook his hand, knowing that He would understand Whose understanding mattered.

And all at once it became clear to him that what had tortured him and would not leave him was suddenly dropping away all at once on both sides and on ten sides and on all sides. He was sorry for them, must act so that they might not suffer. Set them free and be free himself of those agonies. "How right and how simple!" he thought. "And the pain?" he asked himself. "Where's it gone? Eh, where are you, pain?"

He began to watch for it.

"Yes, here it is. Well, what of it, let the pain be.

"And death. Where is it?"

He looked for his old accustomed terror of death, and did not find it. "Where is it? What death?" There was no terror, because death was not either.

In the place of death there was light.

"So this is it!" he suddenly exclaimed aloud.

"What joy!"

To him all this passed in a single instant, and the meaning of that instant suffered no change after. For those present his agony lasted another two hours. There was a rattle in his throat, a twitching in his wasted body. Then the rattle and the gasping came at longer and longer intervals.

"It is over!" some one said over him.

He caught those words and repeated them in his soul.

"Death is over," he said to himself. "It's no more."

He drew in a breath, stopped midway in the breath, stretched and died.

QUESTIONS FOR DISCUSSION AND WRITING

1. *The Death of Ivan Ilyitch* is a straightforward, chronological account of the life of Ivan Ilyitch except for Part I, which takes place after Ivan Ilyitch's death. What is the function of this "prologue"?

2. "Ivan Ilyitch" is a very ordinary Russian name, the rough equivalent of the American "John Smith." What does this suggest about his story?

3. Faced with death, Ivan Ilyitch wonders, "What if in reality all my life, my conscious life, has been not the right thing?" What does "not the right thing" mean? What does Ivan Ilyitch come to feel has been missing in his life?

4. Who tells Ivan Ilyitch's story? What is the narrative voice like? Notice especially such expressions as the first sentence of Part II.

5. Ivan's wife, Praskovya Fyodorovna, is the chief secondary character in the story. How is she characterized? Is she a foil to Ivan Ilyitch, a sort of female version of him?

6. What is the role of the peasant Gerasim in the story? Why does Ivan become so attached to him?

Sarah Orne Jewett

Sarah Orne Jewett (1849–1909) was one of the best of the American "regionalist" writers who drew their material from specific parts of the country in the second half of the nineteenth century. She was born in 1849 in the small inland port town of South Berwick, Maine, the town to which she was later to give the fictional name "Deephaven." The daughter of a doctor (whom she was to celebrate in the novel *A Country Doctor,* 1884), she began writing when she was still in her teens. Encouraged by the novelist and editor William Dean Howells, who accepted one of her earliest pieces for the *Atlantic Monthly,* she wrote *Deephaven* (1877), a volume of stories and sketches about her part of Maine. Later collections included *A White Heron and Other Stories* (1886), *The King of Folly Island* (1888), *A Native of Winby* (1893), *The Life of Nancy* (1895), and her best-known book, *The Country of the Pointed Firs* (1896).

A WHITE HERON

I

The woods were already filled with shadows one June evening, just before eight o'clock, though a bright sunset still glimmered faintly among the trunks of the trees. A little girl was driving home her cow, a plodding, dilatory, provoking creature in her behavior, but a valued companion for all that. They were going away from the western light, and striking deep into the dark woods, but their feet were familiar with the path, and it was no matter whether their eyes could see it or not.

There was hardly a night the summer through when the old cow could be found waiting at the pasture bars; on the contrary, it was her greatest pleasure to hide herself away among the high huckleberry bushes, and though she wore a loud bell she had made the discovery that if one stood perfectly still it would not ring. So Sylvia had to hunt for her until she found her, and call Co'! Co'! with never an answering Moo, until her childish patience was quite spent. If the creature had not given good milk and plenty of it, the case would have seemed very different to her owners. Besides, Sylvia had all the time there was, and very little use to make of it. Sometimes in pleasant weather it was a consolation to look upon the cow's pranks as an intelligent attempt to play hide and seek, and as the child had no playmates she lent herself to this amusement with a good deal of zest. Though this chase had been so long that the wary animal herself had given an unusual signal of her whereabouts, Sylvia had only laughed when she came upon Mistress Moolly at the swamp-side, and urged her affectionately homeward with a twig of birch leaves. The old cow was not inclined to wander farther, she even turned in the right direction for once as they left the pasture, and stepped along the road at a good pace. She was quite ready to be milked now, and seldom stopped to browse. Sylvia wondered what her grandmother would say because they were so late. It was a great while since she had left home at half past five o'clock, but everybody knew the difficulty of making this errand a short one. Mrs. Tilley had chased the horned torment too many summer evenings herself to blame any one else for lingering, and was only thankful as she waited that she had Sylvia, nowadays, to give such valuable assistance. The good woman suspected that Sylvia loitered occasionally on her own account; there never was such a child for straying about out-of-doors since the world was made! Everybody said that it was a good change for a little maid who had tried to grow for eight years in a crowded manufacturing town, but, as for Sylvia herself, it seemed as if she never had been alive at all before she came to live at the farm. She thought often with wistful compassion of a wretched dry geranium that belonged to a town neighbor.

" 'Afraid of folks,' " old Mrs. Tilley said to herself, with a smile, after she had made the unlikely choice of Sylvia from her daughter's houseful of children, and was returning to the farm. " 'Afraid of folks,' they said! I guess she won't be troubled no great with 'em up to the old place!" When they reached the door of the lonely house and stopped to unlock it, and the cat came to purr loudly, and rub against them, a deserted pussy, indeed, but fat with young robins, Sylvia whispered that this was a beautiful place to live in, and she never should wish to go home.

The companions followed the shady woodroad, the cow taking slow steps, and the child very fast ones. The cow stopped long at the brook to drink, as if the pasture were not half a swamp, and Sylvia stood still and waited, letting her bare feet cool themselves in the shoal water, while the great twilight moths struck softly against her. She waded on through the brook as the cow moved away, and listened to the thrushes with a heart that beat fast with pleasure. There was a stirring in the great boughs overhead. They were full of little birds and beasts that seemed to be wide-awake, and going about their world, or else saying good-night to each other in sleepy twitters. Sylvia herself felt sleepy as she walked along. However, it was not much farther to the house, and the air was soft and sweet. She was not often in the woods so late as this, and it made her feel as if she were a part of the gray shadows and the moving leaves. She was just thinking how long it seemed since she first came to the farm a year ago, and wondering if everything went on in the noisy town just the same as when she was there; the thought of the great red-faced boy who used to chase and frighten her made her hurry along the path to escape from the shadow of the trees.

Suddenly this little woods-girl is horror-stricken to hear a clear whistle not very far away. Not a bird's whistle, which would have a sort of friendliness, but a boy's whistle, determined, and somewhat aggressive. Sylvia left the cow to whatever sad fate might await her, and stepped discreetly aside into the bushes, but she was just too late. The enemy had discovered her, and called out in a very cheerful and persuasive tone, "Halloa, little girl, how far is it to the road?" and trembling Sylvia answered almost inaudibly. "A good ways."

She did not dare to look boldly at the tall young man, who carried a gun over his shoulder, but she came out of her bush and again followed the cow, while he walked alongside.

"I have been hunting for some birds," the stranger said kindly, "and I have lost my way, and need a friend very much. Don't be afraid," he added gallantly. "Speak up and tell me what your name is, and whether you think I can spend the night at your house, and go out gunning early in the morning."

Sylvia was more alarmed than before. Would not her grandmother consider her much to blame? But who could have foreseen such an accident as this? It did not appear to be her fault, and she hung her head as if the stem of it were broken, but managed to answer "Sylvy," with much effort when her companion again asked her name.

Mrs. Tilley was standing in the doorway when the trio came into view. The cow gave a moo by way of explanation.

"Yes, you'd better speak up for yourself, you old trial! Where'd she tucked herself away this time, Sylvy?" Sylvia kept an awed silence; she knew by instinct that her grandmother did not comprehend the gravity of the situation. She must be mistaking the stranger for one of the farmer-lads of the region.

The young man stood his gun beside the door, and dropped a heavy game-bag beside it; then he bade Mrs. Tilley good-evening, and repeated his wayfarer's story, and asked if he could have a night's lodging.

"Put me anywhere you like," he said. "I must be off early in the morning, before day; but I am very hungry, indeed. You can give me some milk at any rate, that's plain."

"Dear sakes, yes," responded the hostess, whose long slumbering hospitality seemed to be easily awakened. "You might fare better if you went out on the main road a mile or so, but you're welcome to what we've got. I'll milk right off, and you make yourself at home. You can sleep on husks or feathers," she proffered graciously. "I raised them all myself. There's good pasturing for geese just below here towards the ma'sh. Now step round and set a plate for the gentleman, Sylvy!" And Sylvia promptly stepped. She was glad to have something to do, and she was hungry herself.

It was a surprise to find so clean and comfortable a little dwelling in this New England wilderness. The young man had known the horrors of its most primitive housekeeping, and the dreary squalor of that level of society which does not rebel at the companionship of hens. This was the best thrift of an old-fashioned farmstead, though on such a small scale that it seemed like a hermitage. He listened eagerly to the old woman's quaint talk, he watched Sylvia's pale face and shining gray eyes with ever growing enthusiasm, and insisted that this was the best supper he had eaten for a month; then, afterward, the new-made friends sat down in the doorway together while the moon came up.

Soon it would be berry-time, and Sylvia was a great help at picking. The cow was a good milker, though a plaguy thing to keep track of, the hostess gossiped frankly, adding presently that she had buried four children, so that Sylvia's mother and a son (who might be dead) in California were all the children she had left. "Dan, my boy, was a great hand to go gunning," she explained sadly. "I never wanted for pa'tridges or gray squer'ls while he was to home. He's been a great wand'rer, I expect, and he's no hand to write letters. There, I don't blame him, I'd ha' seen the world myself if it had been so I could.

"Sylvia takes after him," the grandmother continued affectionately, after a minute's pause. "There ain't a foot o' ground she don't know her way over, and the wild creatur's counts her one o' themselves. Squer'ls she'll tame to come an' feed right out o' her hands, and all sorts o' birds. Last winter she got the jay-birds to bangeing here, and I believe she'd 'a' scanted herself of her own meals to have plenty to throw out amongst 'em, if I had n't kep' watch. Anything but crows, I tell her, I'm willin' to help support,—though Dan he went an' tamed one o' them that did seem to have reason same as folks. It was round here a good spell after he went away. Dan an' his father they did n't hitch,—but he never held up his head ag'in after Dan had dared him an' gone off."

The guest did not notice this hint of family sorrows in his eager interest in something else.

"So Sylvy knows all about birds, does she?" he exclaimed, as he looked round at the little girl who sat, very demure but increasingly sleepy, in the moonlight. "I am making a collection of birds myself. I have been at it ever since I was a boy." (Mrs. Tilley smiled.) "There are two or three very rare ones I have been hunting for these five years. I mean to get them on my own ground if they can be found."

"Do you cage 'em up?" asked Mrs. Tilley doubtfully, in response to this enthusiastic announcement.

"Oh, no, they're stuffed and preserved, dozens and dozens of them," said the ornithologist, "and I have shot or snared every one myself. I caught a glimpse of a white heron three miles from here on Saturday, and I have followed it in this direction. They have never been found in this district at all. The little white heron, it is," and he turned again to look at Sylvia with the hope of discovering that the rare bird was one of her acquaintances.

But Sylvia was watching a hop-toad in the narrow footpath.

"You would know the heron if you saw it," the stranger continued eagerly. "A queer tall white bird with soft feathers and long thin legs. And it would have a nest perhaps in the top of a high tree, made of sticks, something like a hawk's nest."

Sylvia's heart gave a wild beat; she knew that strange white bird, and had once stolen softly near where it stood in some bright green swamp grass, away over at the other side of the woods. There was an open place where the sunshine always seemed strangely yellow and hot, where tall, nodding rushes grew, and her grandmother had warned her that she might sink in the soft black mud underneath and never be heard of more. Not far beyond were the salt marshes and beyond those was the sea, the sea which Sylvia wondered and dreamed about, but never had looked upon, though its great voice could often be heard above the noise of the woods on stormy nights.

"I can't think of anything I should like so much as to find that heron's nest," the handsome stranger was saying. "I would give ten dollars to anybody who could show it to me," he added desperately, "and I mean to spend my whole vacation hunting for it if need be. Perhaps it was only migrating, or had been chased out of its own region by some bird of prey."

Mrs. Tilley gave amazed attention to all this, but Sylvia still watched the toad, not divining, as she might have done at some calmer time, that the creature wished to get to its hole under the doorstep, and was much hindered by the unusual spectators at that hour of the evening. No amount of thought, that night, could decide how many wished-for treasures the ten dollars, so lightly spoken of, would buy.

The next day the young sportsman hovered about the woods, and Sylvia kept him company, having lost her first fear of the friendly lad, who proved to be most kind and sympathetic. He told her many things about the birds and what they knew and where they lived and what they did with themselves. And he gave her a jackknife, which she thought as great a treasure as if she were a desert-islander. All day long he did not once make her troubled or afraid except when he brought down some unsuspecting singing creature from its bough. Sylvia would have liked him vastly better without his gun; she could not understand why he killed the very birds he seemed to like so much. But as the day waned, Sylvia still watched the young man with loving admiration. She had never seen anybody so charming and delightful; the woman's heart, asleep in the child, was vaguely thrilled by a dream of love. Some premonition of that great power stirred and swayed these young foresters who traversed the solemn woodlands with soft-footed silent care. They stopped to listen to a bird's song; they pressed forward again eagerly, parting the branches,—speaking to each other rarely and in whispers; the young man going first and Sylvia following, fascinated, a few steps behind, with her gray eyes dark with excitement.

She grieved because the longed-for white heron was elusive, but she did not lead the guest, she only followed, and there was no such thing as speaking first. The sound of her own unquestioned voice would have terrified her,—it was hard enough to answer yes or no when there was need of that. At last evening began to fall, and they drove the cow home together, and Sylvia smiled with pleasure when they came to the place where she heard the whistle and was afraid only the night before.

II

Half a mile from home, at the farther edge of the woods, where the land was highest, a great pine-tree stood, the last of its generation. Whether it was left for a boundary mark, or for what reason, no one could say; the woodchoppers who had felled its mates were dead and gone long ago, and a whole forest of sturdy trees, pines and oaks and maples, had grown again. But the stately head of this old pine towered above them all and made a landmark for sea and shore miles and miles away. Sylvia knew it well. She had always believed that whoever climbed to the top of it could see the ocean; and the little girl had often laid her hand on the great rough trunk and looked up wistfully at those dark boughs that the wind always stirred, no matter how hot and still the air might be below. Now she thought of the tree with a new excitement, for why, if one climbed it at break of day, could not one see all the world, and easily discover whence the white heron flew, and mark the place, and find the hidden nest?

What a spirit of adventure, what wild ambition! What fancied triumph and delight and glory for the later morning when she could make known the secret! It was almost too real and too great for the childish heart to bear.

All night the door of the little house stood open, and the whippoorwills came and sang upon the very step. The young sportsman and his old hostess were sound asleep, but Sylvia's great design kept her broad awake and watching. She forgot to think of sleep. The short summer night seemed as long as the winter darkness, and at last when the whippoorwills ceased, and she was afraid the morning would after all come too soon, she stole out of the house and followed the pasture path through the woods, hastening toward the open ground beyond, listening with a sense of comfort and companionship to the drowsy twitter of a half-awakened bird, whose perch she had jarred in passing. Alas, if the great wave of human interest which flooded for the first time this dull little life should sweep away the satisfactions of an existence heart to heart with nature and the dumb life of the forest!

There was the huge tree asleep yet in the paling moonlight, and small and hopeful Sylvia began with utmost bravery to mount to the top of it, with tingling, eager blood coursing the channels of her whole frame, with her bare feet and fingers, that pinched and held like bird's claws to the monstrous ladder reaching up, up almost to the sky itself. First she must mount the white oak tree that grew alongside, where she was almost lost among the dark branches and the green leaves heavy and wet with dew; a bird fluttered off its nest, and a red squirrel ran to and fro and scolded pettishly at the harmless housebreaker. Sylvia felt her way easily. She had often climbed there, and knew that higher still one of the oak's upper branches chafed against the pine trunk, just where its lower boughs were set close together. There, when she made the dangerous pass from one tree to the other, the great enterprise would really begin.

She crept out along the swaying oak limb at last, and took the daring step across into the old pine-tree. The way was harder than she thought; she must reach far and hold fast, the sharp dry twigs caught and held her and scratched her like angry talons, the pitch made her thin little fingers clumsy and stiff as she went round and round the tree's great stem, higher and higher upward. The sparrows and robins in the woods below were beginning to wake and twitter to the dawn, yet it seemed much lighter there aloft in the pine-tree, and the child knew that she must hurry if her project were to be of any use.

The tree seemed to lengthen itself out as she went up, and to reach farther and farther upward. It was like a great main-mast to the voyaging earth; it must truly have been amazed that morning through all its ponderous frame as it felt this determined spark of human spirit creeping and climbing from higher branch to branch. Who knows how steadily the least twigs held themselves to advantage this light, weak creature on her way! The old pine must have loved his new dependent. More than all the hawks, and bats, and moths, and even the sweet-voiced thrushes, was the brave, beating heart of the solitary gray-eyed child. And the tree stood still and held away the winds that June morning while the dawn grew bright in the east.

Sylvia's face was like a pale star, if one had seen it from the ground, when the last thorny bough was past, and she stood trembling and tired but wholly triumphant, high in the tree-top. Yes, there was the sea with the dawning sun making a golden dazzle over it, and toward that glorious east flew two hawks with slow-moving pinions. How low they looked in the air from that height when before one had only seen them far up, and dark against the blue sky. Their gray feathers were as soft as moths; they seemed only a little way from the tree, and Sylvia felt as if she too could go flying away among the clouds. Westward, the woodlands and farms reached miles and miles into the distance; here and there were church steeples, and white villages; truly it was a vast and awesome world.

The birds sang louder and louder. At last the sun came up bewilderingly bright. Sylvia could see the white sails of ships out at sea, and the clouds that were purple and rose-colored and yellow at first began to fade away. Where was the white heron's nest in the sea of green branches, and was this wonderful sight and pageant of the world the only reward for having climbed to such a giddy height? Now look down again, Sylvia, where the green marsh is set among the shining birches and dark hemlocks; there where you saw the white heron once you will see him again; look, look! a white spot of him like a single floating feather comes up from the dead hemlock and grows larger, and rises, and comes close at last, and goes by the landmark pine with steady sweep of wing and outstretched slender neck and crested head. And wait! wait! do not move a foot or a finger, little girl, do not send an arrow of light and consciousness from your two eager eyes, for the heron has perched on a pine bough not far beyond yours, and cries back to his mate on the nest, and plumes his feathers for the new day!

The child gives a long sigh a minute later when a company of shouting cat-birds comes also to the tree, and vexed by their fluttering and lawlessness the solemn heron goes away. She knows his secret now, the wild, light, slender bird that floats and wavers, and goes back like an arrow presently to his home in the green world beneath. Then Sylvia, well satisfied, makes her perilous way down again, not daring to look far below the branch she stands on, ready to cry sometimes because her fingers ache and her lamed feet slip. Wondering over and over again what the stranger would say to her, and what he would think when she told him how to find his way straight to the heron's nest.

"Sylvy, Sylvy!" called the busy old grandmother again and again, but nobody answered, and the small husk bed was empty, and Sylvia had disappeared.

The guest waked from a dream, and remembering his day's pleasure hurried to dress himself that it might sooner begin. He was sure from the way the shy little girl looked once or twice yesterday that she had at least seen the white heron, and now she must really be persuaded to tell. Here she comes now, paler than ever, and her worn old frock is torn and tattered, and smeared with pine pitch. The grandmother and the sportsman stand in the door together and question her, and the splendid moment has come to speak of the dead hemlock-tree by the green marsh.

But Sylvia does not speak after all, though the old grandmother fretfully rebukes her, and the young man's kind appealing eyes are looking straight in her own. He can make them rich with money; he has promised it, and they are poor now. He is so well worth making happy, and he waits to hear the story she can tell.

No, she must keep silence! What is it that suddenly forbids her and makes her dumb? Has she been nine years growing, and now, when the great world for the first time puts out a hand to her, must she thrust it aside for a bird's sake? The murmur of the pine's green branches in her ears, she remembers how the white heron came flying through the golden air and how they watched the sea and the morning together, and Sylvia cannot speak; she cannot tell the heron's secret and give its life away.

Dear loyalty, that suffered a sharp pang as the guest went away disappointed later in the day, that could have served and followed him and loved him as a dog loves! Many a night Sylvia heard the echo of his whistle haunting the pasture path as she came home with the loitering cow. She forgot even her sorrow at the sharp report of his gun and the piteous sight of thrushes and sparrows dropping silent to the ground, their songs hushed and their pretty feathers stained and wet with blood. Were the birds better friends than their hunter might have been,—who can tell? Whatever treasures were lost to her, woodlands and summer-time, remember! Bring your gifts and graces and tell your secrets to this lonely country child!

QUESTIONS FOR DISCUSSION AND WRITING

1.   Jewett throws special emphasis upon the heron by naming the story after it. Is it a symbol? If so, what is it a symbol of? What does it seem to mean to Sylvia?

2.   The nine-year-old Sylvia is being reared by her grandmother, who took her from her home the year before, apparently because Sylvia's mother could not care for all her children. Does Sylvia seem to bear any psychological signs of her loss of parents and siblings and her move from town into the country?

3.   Analyze the narrative voice. Look especially at the final paragraph. What stance does the narrator take toward the material?

4.   Why does Sylvia not tell the young man where the heron's nest is?

Kate Chopin

Kate Chopin (1851–1904) was born Katherine O'Flaherty in St. Louis. When she was twenty, she married a businessman named Oscar Chopin and moved with him to New Orleans. Oscar Chopin died suddenly in 1883, and Kate Chopin moved with her six children back to St. Louis, where she began to write to support her family. *At Fault,* a weak, rather didactic novel, was published in 1890. Much more successful was *Bayou Folk* (1894), a collection of Louisiana "local color" stories. It was followed by a second collection, *A Night in Acadie,* in 1897. Chopin's masterpiece, however, was a novel, *The Awakening* (1899). The story of a young married woman's awakening to her own sensuality and sense of self, the novel provoked a scandal. Chopin died five years after the novel was published; her work was largely forgotten for half a century but was "rediscovered" in the 1960s and occupies a high place in American literary history.

THE STORY OF AN HOUR

Knowing that Mrs. Mallard was afflicted with a heart trouble, great care was taken to break to her as gently as possible the news of her husband's death.

It was her sister Josephine who told her, in broken sentences; veiled hints that revealed in half concealing. Her husband's friend Richards was there, too, near her. It was he who had been in the newspaper office when intelligence of the railroad disaster was received, with Brently Mallard's name leading the list of "killed." He had only taken the time to assure himself of its truth by a second telegram, and had hastened to forestall any less careful, less tender friend in bearing the sad message.

She did not hear the story as many women have heard the same, with a paralyzed inability to accept its significance. She wept at once, with sudden, wild abandonment, in her sister's arms. When the storm of grief had spent itself she went away to her room alone. She would have no one follow her.

There stood, facing the open window, a comfortable, roomy armchair. Into this she sank, pressed down by a physical exhaustion that haunted her body and seemed to reach into her soul.

She could see in the open square before her house the tops of trees that were all aquiver with the new spring life. The delicious breath of rain was in the air. In the street below a peddler was crying his wares. The notes of a distant song which some one was singing reached her faintly, and countless sparrows were twittering in the eaves.

There were patches of blue sky showing here and there through the clouds that had met and piled one above the other in the west facing her window.

She sat with her head thrown back upon the cushion of the chair, quite motionless, except when a sob came up into her throat and shook her, as a child who has cried itself to sleep continues to sob in its dreams.

She was young, with a fair, calm face, whose lines bespoke repression and even a certain strength. But now there was a dull stare in her eyes, whose gaze was fixed away off yonder on one of those patches of blue sky. It was not a glance of reflection, but rather indicated a suspension of intelligent thought.

There was something coming to her and she was waiting for it, fearfully. What was it? She did not know; it was too subtle and elusive to name. But she felt it, creeping out of the sky, reaching toward her through the sounds, the scents, the color that filled the air.

Now her bosom rose and fell tumultuously. She was beginning to recognize this thing that was approaching to possess her, and she was striving to beat it back with her will—as powerless as her two white slender hands would have been.

When she abandoned herself a little whispered word escaped her slightly parted lips. She said it over and over under her breath: "free, free, free!" The vacant stare and the look of terror that had followed it went from her eyes. They stayed keen and bright. Her pulses beat fast, and the coursing blood warmed and relaxed every inch of her body.

She did not stop to ask if it were or were not a monstrous joy that held her. A clear and exalted perception enabled her to dismiss the suggestion as trivial.

She knew that she would weep again when she saw the kind, tender hands folded in death; the face that had never looked save with love upon her, fixed and gray and dead. But she saw beyond that bitter moment a long procession of years to come that would belong to her absolutely. And she opened and spread her arms out to them in welcome.

There would be no one to live for her during those coming years; she would live for herself. There would be no powerful will bending hers in that blind persistence with which men and women believe they have a right to impose a private will upon a fellow-creature. A kind intention or a cruel intention made the act seem no less a crime as she looked upon it in that brief moment of illumination.

And yet she had loved him—sometimes. Often she had not. What did it matter! What could love, the unsolved mystery, count for in face of this possession of self-assertion which she suddenly recognized as the strongest impulse of her being!

"Free! Body and soul free!" she kept whispering.

Josephine was kneeling before the closed door with her lips to the keyhole, imploring for admission. "Louise, open the door! I beg; open the door—you will make yourself ill. What are you doing, Louise? For heaven's sake open the door."

"Go away. I am not making myself ill." No; she was drinking in a very elixir of life through that open window.

Her fancy was running riot along those days ahead of her. Spring days, and summer days, and all sorts of days that would be her own. She breathed a quick prayer that life might be long. It was only yesterday she had thought with a shudder that life might be long.

She arose at length and opened the door to her sister's importunities. There was a feverish triumph in her eyes, and she carried herself unwittingly like a goddess of Victory. She clasped her sister's waist, and together they descended the stairs. Richards stood waiting for them at the bottom.

Some one was opening the front door with a latchkey. It was Brently Mallard who entered, a little travel-stained, composedly carrying his grip-sack and umbrella. He had been far from the scene of accident, and did not even know there had been one. He stood amazed at Josephine's piercing cry; at Richards' quick motion to screen him from the view of his wife.

But Richards was too late.

When the doctors came they said she had died of heart disease—of joy that kills.

QUESTIONS FOR DISCUSSION AND WRITING

1.   "The Story of an Hour" is, as the title would suggest, a very short story. And yet it has three clear scenes: a long scene with Louise Mallard alone in her upstairs room, preceded by a short scene downstairs, in which she receives news of her husband's death, and followed by a brief scene, back downstairs, in which she learns that the husband is still alive. How does Chopin use this structure to set up ironies in the story?

2.   The Mallards do not seem to have had a bad marriage; indeed, Louise acknowledges that she loved Brently, at least "sometimes." How does this fact bear upon the story's critique of marriage from a woman's point of view?

3.   How does Chopin convey Louise's state of mind during the hour that she spends in her room? Notice that she is not "thinking," in the ordinary sense; we are told that her eyes reflect "a suspension of intelligent thought."

Mary E. Wilkins Freeman

Mary E. Wilkins Freeman (1852–1930), like her close contemporary Sarah Orne Jewett, was a regionalist who took as her subject the life of her native area. In Freeman's case, the area was the Vermont countryside, as it had been Maine in Jewett's work. Freeman was born in Randolph, Massachusetts, just south of Boston; her father moved the family to Brattleboro, Vermont, when Freeman was fifteen. By the time her parents died—her mother in 1880, her father three years later—Freeman had begun to publish magazine stories. Her first collection of stories was *A Humble Romance* (1887); it was followed by *A New England Nun and Other Stories* (1891). Through her long career, Freeman published a number of other story collections and a number of novels, notably *Pembroke* (1894) and *The Shoulders of Atlas* (1908). She is best remembered, however, for her early Vermont short stories and sketches.

THE REVOLT OF "MOTHER"

"Father!"

"What is it?"

"What are them men diggin' over there in the field for?"

There was a sudden dropping and enlarging of the lower part of the old man's face, as if some heavy weight had settled therein; he shut his mouth tight, and went on harnessing the great bay mare. He hustled the collar on to her neck with a jerk.

"Father!"

The old man slapped the saddle upon the mare's back.

"Look here, father, I want to know what them men are diggin' over in the field for, an' I'm goin' to know."

"I wish you'd go into the house, mother, an' 'tend to your own affairs," the old man said then. He ran his words together, and his speech was almost as inarticulate as a growl.

But the woman understood; it was her most native tongue. "I ain't goin' into the house till you tell me what them men are doin' over there in the field," she said.

Then she stood waiting. She was a small woman, short and straight-waisted like a child in her brown cotton gown. Her forehead was mild and benevolent between the smooth curves of gray hair; there were meek downward lines about her nose and mouth; but her eyes, fixed upon the old man, looked as if the meekness had been the result of her own will, never of the will of another.

They were in the barn, standing before the wide open doors. The spring air, full of the smell of growing grass and unseen blossoms, came in their faces. The deep yard in front was littered with farm wagons and piles of wood; on the edges, close to the fence and the house, the grass was a vivid green, and there were some dandelions.

The old man glanced doggedly at his wife as he tightened the last buckles on the harness. She looked as immovable to him as one of the rocks in his pastureland, bound to the earth with generations of blackberry vines. He slapped the reins over the horse, and started forth from the barn.

"*Father!*" said she.

The old man pulled up. "What is it?"

"I want to know what them men are diggin' over there in the field for."

"They're diggin' a cellar, I s'pose, if you've got to know."

"A cellar for what?"

"A barn."

"A barn? You ain't goin' to build a barn over there where we was goin' to have a house, father?"

The old man said not another word. He hurried the horse into the farm wagon, and clattered out of the yard, jouncing as sturdily on his seat as a boy.

The woman stood a moment looking after him, then she went out of the barn across a corner of the yard to the house. The house, standing at right angles with the great barn and a long reach of sheds and out-buildings, was infinitesimal compared with them. It was scarcely as commodious for people as the little boxes under the barn eaves were for doves.

A pretty girl's face, pink and delicate as a flower, was looking out of one of the house windows. She was watching three men who were digging over in the field which bounded the yard near the road line. She turned quietly when the woman entered.

"What are they digging for, mother?" said she. "Did he tell you?"

"They're diggin' for—a cellar for a new barn."

"Oh, mother, he ain't going to build another barn?"

"That's what he says."

A boy stood before the kitchen glass combing his hair. He combed slowly and painstakingly, arranging his brown hair in a smooth hillock over his forehead. He did not seem to pay any attention to the conversation.

"Sammy, did you know your father was going to build a new barn?" asked the girl.

The boy combed assiduously.

"Sammy!"

He turned, and showed a face like his father's under his smooth crest of hair. "Yes, I s'pose I did," he said, reluctantly.

"How long have you known it?" asked his mother.

"'Bout three months, I guess."

"Why didn't you tell of it?"

"Didn't think 'twould do no good."

"I don't see what father wants another barn for," said the girl, in her sweet, slow voice. She turned again to the window, and stared out at the digging men in the field. Her tender, sweet face was full of a gentle distress. Her forehead was as bald and innocent as a baby's, with the light hair strained back from it in a row of curl-papers. She was quite large, but her soft curls did not look as if they covered muscles.

Her mother looked sternly at the boy. "Is he goin' to buy more cows?" said she.

The boy did not reply; he was tying his shoes.

"Sammy, I want you to tell me if he's goin' to buy more cows."

"I s'pose he is."

"How many?"

"Four, I guess."

His mother said nothing more. She went to the pantry, and there was a clatter of dishes. The boy got his cap from a nail behind the door, took an old arithmetic from the shelf, and started for school. He was lightly built, but clumsy. He went out of the yard with a curious spring in the hips, that made his loose home-made jacket tilt up in the rear.

The girl went to the sink, and began to wash dishes that were piled up there. Her mother came promptly out of the pantry, and shoved her aside. "You wipe 'em," said she; "I'll wash. There's a good many this mornin'."

The mother plunged her hands vigorously into the water, the girl wiped the plates slowly and dreamily. "Mother," said she, "don't you think it's too bad father's going to build that new barn, much as we need a decent house to live in?"

Her mother scrubbed a dish fiercely. "You ain't found out yet we're women-folks, Nanny Penn," said she. "You ain't seen enough of men-folks yet to. One of these days you'll find it out, an' then you'll know that we know only what men-folks think we do, so far as any use of it goes, an' how we'd ought to reckon men-folks in with Providence, an' not complain of what they do any more than we do of the weather."

"I don't care; I don't believe George is anything like that, anyhow," said Nanny. Her delicate face flushed pink, her lips pouted softly, as if she were going to cry.

"You wait an' see. I guess George Eastman ain't no better than other men. You hadn't ought to judge father, though. He can't help it, 'cause he don't look at things jest the way we do. An' we've been pretty comfortable here, after all. The roof don't leak—ain't never but once—that's one thing. Father's kept it shingled right up."

"I do wish we had a parlor."

"I guess it won't hurt George Eastman any to come to see you in a nice clean kitchen. I guess a good many girls don't have as good a place as this. Nobody's ever heard me complain."

"I ain't complained either, mother."

"Well, I don't think you'd better, a good father an' a good home as you've got. S'pose your father made you go out an' work for your livin'? Lots of girls have to that ain't no stronger an' better able to than you be."

Sarah Penn washed the frying-pan with a conclusive air. She scrubbed the outside of it as faithfully as the inside. She was a masterly keeper of her box of a house. Her one living-room never seemed to have in it any of the dust which the friction of life with inanimate matter produces. She swept, and there seemed to be no dirt to go before the broom; she cleaned, and one could see no difference. She was like an artist so perfect that he has apparently no art. To-day she got out a mixing bowl and a board, and rolled some pies, and there was no more flour upon her than upon her daughter who was doing finer work. Nanny was to be married in the fall, and she was sewing on some white cambric and embroidery. She sewed industriously while her mother cooked, her soft milk-white hands and wrists showed whiter than her delicate work.

"We must have the stove moved out in the shed before long," said Mrs. Penn. "Talk about not havin' things, it's been a real blessin' to be able to put a stove up in that shed in hot weather. Father did one good thing when he fixed that stove-pipe out there."

Sarah Penn's face as she rolled her pies had that expression of meek vigor which might have characterized one of the New Testament saints. She was making mince-pies. Her husband, Adoniram Penn, liked them better than any other kind. She baked twice a week. Adoniram often liked a piece of pie between meals. She hurried this morning. It had been later than usual when she began, and she wanted to have a pie baked for dinner. However deep a resentment she might be forced to hold against her husband, she would never fail in sedulous attention to his wants.

Nobility of character manifests itself as loop-holes when it is not provided with large doors. Sarah Penn's showed itself to-day in flaky dishes of pastry. So she made the pies faithfully, while across the table she could see, when she glanced up from her work, the sight that rankled in her patient and steadfast soul—the digging of the cellar of the new barn in the place where Adoniram forty years ago had promised her their new house should stand.

The pies were done for dinner. Adoniram and Sammy were home a few minutes after twelve o'clock. The dinner was eaten with serious haste. There was never much conversation at the table in the Penn family. Adoniram asked a blessing, and they ate promptly, then rose up and went about their work.

Sammy went back to school, taking soft sly lopes out of the yard like a rabbit. He wanted a game of marbles before school, and feared his father would give him some chores to do. Adoniram hastened to the door and called after him, but he was out of sight.

"I don't see what you let him go for, mother," said he. "I wanted him to help me unload that wood."

Adoniram went to work out in the yard unloading wood from the wagon. Sarah put away the dinner dishes, while Nanny took down her curl-papers and changed her dress. She was going down to the store to buy some more embroidery and thread.

When Nanny was gone, Mrs. Penn went to the door. "Father!" she called.

"Well, what is it!"

"I want to see you jest a minute."

"I can't leave this wood nohow. I've got to git it unloaded an' go for a load of gravel afore two o'clock. Sammy had ought to helped me. You hadn't ought to let him go to school so early."

"I want to see you jest a minute."

"I tell ye I can't, nohow, mother."

"Father, you come here." Sarah Penn stood in the door like a queen; she held her head as if it bore a crown; there was that patience which makes authority royal in her voice. Adoniram went.

Mrs. Penn led the way into the kitchen, and pointed to a chair. "Sit down, father," said she; "I've got somethin' I want to say to you."

He sat down heavily; his face was quite stolid, but he looked at her with restive eyes. "Well, what is it, mother?"

"I want to know what you're buildin' that new barn for, father?"

"I ain't got nothin' to say about it,"

"It can't be you think you need another barn?"

"I tell ye I ain't got nothin' to say about it, mother; an' I ain't goin' to say nothin'."

"Be you goin' to buy more cows?"

Adoniram did not reply; he shut his mouth tight.

"I know you be, as well as I want to. Now, father, look here"—Sarah Penn had not sat down;' she stood before her husband in the humble fashion of a Scripture woman—"I'm goin' to talk real plain to you; I never have sence I married you, but I'm goin' to now. I ain't never complained, an' I ain't goin' to complain now, but I'm goin' to talk plain. You see this room here, father; you look at it well. You see there ain't no carpet on the floor, an' you see the paper is all dirty, an' droppin' off the walls. We ain't had no new paper on it for ten year, an' then I put it on myself, an' it didn't cost but ninepence a roll. You see this room, father; it's all the one I've had to work in an' eat in an' sit in sence we was married. There ain't another woman in the whole town whose husband ain't got half the means you have but what's got better. It's all the room Nanny's got to have her company in; an' there ain't one of her mates but what's got better, an' their fathers not so able as hers is. It's all the room she'll have to be married in. What would you have thought, father, if we had had our weddin' in a room no better than this? I was married in my mother's parlor, with a carpet on the floor, an' stuffed furniture, an' a mahogany card-table. An' this is all the room my daughter will have to be married in. Look here, father!"

Sarah Penn went across the room as though it were a tragic stage. She flung open a door and disclosed a tiny bedroom, only large enough for a bed and bureau, with a path between. "There, father," said she—"there's all the room I've had to sleep in forty year. All my children were born there—the two that died, an' the two that's livin'. I was sick with a fever there."

She stepped into another door and opened it. It led into a small ill-lighted pantry. "Here," said she, "is all the buttery I've got—every place I've got for my dishes, to set away my victuals in, an' to keep my milk-pans in. Father, I've been takin' care of the milk of six cows in this place, an' now you're goin' to build a new barn, an' keep more cows, an' give me more to do in it."

She threw open another door. A narrow crooked flight of stairs wound upward from it. "There, father," said she. "I want you to look at the stairs that go up to them two unfinished chambers that are all the places our son an' daughter have had to sleep in all their lives. There ain't a prettier girl in town nor a more ladylike one than Nanny, an' that's the place she has to sleep in. It ain't so good as your horse's stall; it ain't so warm an' tight."

Sarah Penn went back and stood before her husband. "Now, father," said she, "I want to know if you think you're doin' right an' accordin' to what you profess. Here, when we was married, forty year ago, you promised me faithful that we should have a new house built in that lot over in the field before the year was out. You said you had money enough, an' you wouldn't ask me to live in no such place as this. It is forty year now, an' you've been makin' more money, an' I've been savin' of it for you ever since, an' you ain't built no house yet. You've built sheds an' cow-houses an' one new barn, an' now you're goin' to build another. Father, I want to know if you think it's right. You're lodgin' your dumb beasts better than you are your own flesh an' blood. I want to know if you think it's right."

"I ain't got nothin' to say."

"You can't say nothin' without ownin' it ain't right, father. An' there's another thing—I ain't complained; I've got along forty year, an' I s'pose I should forty more, if it wa'n't for that—if we don't have another house. Nanny she can't live with us after she's married. She'll have to go somewheres else to live away from us, an' it don't seem as if I could have it so, noways, father. She wa'n't ever strong. She's got considerable color, but there wa'n't never any backbone to her. I've always took the heft of everything off her, an' she ain't fit to keep house an' do everything herself. She'll be all worn out inside of a year. Think of her doin' all the washin' an' ironin' an' bakin' with them soft white hands an' arms, an' sweepin'! I can't have it so, noways, father."

Mrs. Penn's face was burning; her mild eyes gleamed. She had pleaded her little cause like a Webster; she had ranged from severity to pathos; but her opponent employed that obstinate silence which makes eloquence futile with mocking echoes. Adoniram arose clumsily.

"Father, ain't you got nothin' to say?" said Mrs. Penn.

"I've got to go off after that load of gravel. I can't stan' here talkin' all day."

"Father, won't you think it over, an' have a house built there instead of a barn?"

"I ain't got nothin' to say."

Adoniram shuffled out. Mrs. Penn went into her bedroom. When she came out, her eyes were red. She had a roll of unbleached cotton cloth. She spread it out on the kitchen table, and began cutting out some shirts for her husband. The men over in the field had a team to help them this afternoon; she could hear their halloos. She had a scanty pattern for the shirts; she had to plan and piece the sleeves.

Nanny came home with her embroidery, and sat down with her needlework. She had taken down her curl-papers, and there was a soft roll of fair hair like an aureole over her forehead; her face was as delicately fine and clear as porcelain. Suddenly she looked up, and the tender red flamed all over her face and neck. "Mother," she said.

"What say?"

"I've been thinking—I don't see how we're goin' to have any—wedding in this room. I'd be ashamed to have his folks come if we didn't have anybody else."

"Mebbe we can have some new paper before then; I can put it on. I guess you won't have no call to be ashamed of your belongin's."

"We might have the wedding in the new barn," said Nanny, with gentle pettishness. "Why, mother, what makes you look so?"

Mrs. Penn had started, and was staring at her with a curious expression. She turned again to her work, and spread out a pattern carefully on the cloth. "Nothin'," said she.

Presently Adoniram clattered out of the yard in his two-wheeled dump cart, standing as proudly upright as a Roman charioteer. Mrs. Penn opened the door and stood there a minute looking out; the halloos of the men sounded louder.

It seemed to her all through the spring months that she heard nothing but the halloos and the noises of saws and hammers. The new barn grew fast. It was a fine edifice for this little village. Men came on pleasant Sundays, in their meeting suits and clean shirt bosoms, and stood around it admiringly. Mrs. Penn did not speak of it, and Adoniram did not mention it to her, although sometimes, upon a return from inspecting it, he bore himself with injured dignity.

"It's a strange thing how your mother feels about the new barn," he said, confidentially, to Sammy one day.

Sammy only grunted after an odd fashion for a boy; he had learned it from his father.

The barn was all completed ready for use by the third week in July. Adoniram had planned to move his stock in on Wednesday; on Tuesday he received a letter which changed his plans. He came in with it early in the morning. "Sammy's been to the post-office," said he, "an' I've got a letter from Hiram." Hiram was Mrs. Penn's brother, who lived in Vermont.

"Well," said Mrs. Penn, "what does he say about the folks?"

"I guess they're all right. He says he thinks if I come up country right off there's a chance to buy jest the kind of a horse I want." He stared reflectively out of the window at the new barn.

Mrs. Penn was making pies. She went on clapping the rolling-pin into the crust, although she was very pale, and her heart beat loudly.

"I dun' know but what I'd better go," said Adoniram. "I hate to go off jest now, right in the midst of hayin', but the ten-acre lot's cut, an' I guess Rufus an' the others can git along without me three or four days. I can't get a horse round here to suit me, nohow, an' I've got to have another for all that wood-haulin' in the fall. I told Hiram to watch out, an' if he got wind of a good horse to let me know. I guess I'd better go."

"I'll get your clean shirt an' collar," said Mrs. Penn calmly.

She laid out Adoniram's Sunday suit and his clean clothes on the bed in the little bedroom. She got his shaving-water and razor ready. At last she buttoned on his collar and fastened his black cravat.

Adoniram never wore his collar and cravat except on extra occasions. He held his head high, with a rasped dignity. When he was all ready, with his coat and hat brushed, and a lunch of pie and cheese in a paper bag, he hesitated on the threshold of the door. He looked at his wife, and his manner was defiantly apologetic. "*If* them cows come to-day, Sammy can drive 'em into the new barn," said he; "an' when they bring the hay up, they can pitch it in there."

"Well," replied Mrs. Penn.

Adoniram set his shaven face ahead and started. When he had cleared the door-step, he turned and looked back with a kind of nervous solemnity. "I shall be back by Saturday if nothin' happens," said he.

"Do be careful, father," returned his wife.

She stood at the door with Nanny at her elbow and watched him out of sight. Her eyes had a strange, doubtful expression in them; her peaceful forehead was contracted. She went in, and about her baking again. Nanny sat sewing. Her wedding-day was drawing nearer, and she was getting pale and thin with her steady sewing. Her mother kept glancing at her.

"Have you got that pain in your side this mornin'?" she asked.

"A little."

Mrs. Penn's face, as she worked, changed, her perplexed forehead smoothed, her eyes were steady, her lips firmly set. She formed a maxim for herself, although incoherently with her unlettered thoughts. "Unsolicited opportunities are the guide-posts of the Lord to the new roads of life," she repeated in effect, and she made up her mind to her course of action.

"S'posin' I *had* wrote to Hiram," she muttered once, when she was in the pantry—"s'posin' I had wrote, an' asked him if he knew of any horse? But I didn't, an' father's goin' wa'n't none of my doin'. It looks like a providence." Her voice rang out quite loud at last.

"What are you talkin' about, mother?" called Nanny.

"Nothin'."

Mrs. Penn hurried her baking; at eleven o'clock it was all done. The load of hay from the west field came slowly down the cart track, and drew up to the new barn. Mrs. Penn ran out. "Stop!" she screamed—"stop!"

The men stopped and looked; Sammy upreared from the top of the load, and stared at his mother.

"Stop!" she cried out again. "Don't you put the hay in that barn; put it in the old one."

"Why, he said to put it in here," returned one of the haymakers, wonderingly. He was a young man, a neighbor's son, whom Adoniram hired by the year to help on the farm.

"Don't you put the hay in the new barn; there's room enough in the old one, aint there?" said Mrs. Penn.

"Room enough," returned the hired man, in his thick, rustic tones. "Didn't need the new barn, nohow, far as room's concerned. Well, I s'pose he changed his mind." He took hold of the horses' bridles.

Mrs. Penn went back to the house. Soon the kitchen windows were darkened, and a fragrance like warm honey came into the room.

Nanny laid down her work. "I thought father wanted them to put the hay into the new barn?" she said wonderingly.

"It's all right," replied her mother.

Sammy slid down from the load of hay, and came in to see if dinner was ready.

"I ain't goin' to get a regular dinner to-day, as long as father's gone," said his mother. "I've let the fire go out. You can have some bread an' milk an' pie. I thought we could get along." She set out some bowls of milk, some bread, and a pie on the kitchen table. "You'd better eat your dinner now," she said. "You might jest as well get through with it. I want you to help me afterward."

Nanny and Sammy stared at each other. There was something strange in their mother's manner. Mrs. Penn did not eat anything herself. She went into the pantry, and they heard her moving dishes while they ate. Presently she came out with a pile of plates. She got the clothes-basket out of the shed, and packed them in it. Nanny and Sammy watched. She brought out cups and saucers, and put them in with the plates.

"What you goin' to do, mother?" inquired Nanny, in a timid voice. A sense of something unusual made her tremble, as if it were a ghost. Sammy rolled his eyes over his pie.

"You'll see what I'm goin' to do," replied Mrs. Penn. "If you're through, Nanny, I want you to go upstairs an' pack up your things; an' I want you, Sammy, to help me take down the bed in the bedroom."

"Oh, mother, what for?" gasped Nanny.

"You'll see."

During the next few hours a feat was performed by this simple, pious New England mother which was equal in its way to Wolfe's storming of the Heights of Abraham. It took no more genius and audacity of bravery for Wolfe to cheer his wondering soldiers up those steep precipices, under the sleeping eyes of the enemy, than for Sarah Penn, at the head of her children, to move all their little household goods into the new barn while her husband was away.

Nanny and Sammy followed their mother's instructions without a murmur; indeed, they were overawed. There is a certain uncanny and superhuman quality about all such purely original undertakings as their mother's was to them. Nanny went back and forth with her light loads, and Sammy tugged with sober energy.

At five o'clock in the afternoon the little house in which the Penns had lived for forty years had emptied itself into the new barn.

Every builder builds somewhat for unknown purposes, and is in a measure a prophet. The architect of Adoniram Penn's barn, while he designed it for the comfort of four-footed animals, had planned better than he knew for the comfort of humans. Sarah Penn saw at a glance its possibilities. Those great box-stalls, with quilts hung before them, would make better bedrooms than the one she had occupied for forty years, and there was a tight carriage-room. The harness-room, with its chimney and shelves, would make a kitchen of her dreams. The great middle space would make a parlor, by-and-by, fit for a palace. Upstairs there was as much room as down. With partitions and windows, what a house would there be! Sarah looked at the row of stanchions before the allotted space for cows, and reflected that she would have her front entry there.

At six o'clock the stove was up in the harness-room, the kettle was boiling, and the table set for tea. It looked almost as home-like as the abandoned house across the yard had ever done. The young hired man milked, and Sarah directed him calmly to bring the milk to the new barn. He came gaping, dropping little blots of foam from the brimming pails on the grass. Before the next morning he had spread the story of Adoniram Penn's wife moving into the barn all over the little village. Men assembled in the store and talked it over, women with shawls over their heads scuttled into each other's houses before their work was done. Any deviation from the ordinary course of life in this quiet town was enough to stop all progress in it. Everybody paused to look at the staid, independent figure on the side track. There was a difference of opinion with regard to her. Some held her to be insane; some, of a lawless and rebellious spirit.

Friday the minister went to see her. It was in the forenoon, and she was at the barn door shelling pease for dinner. She looked up and returned his salutation with dignity, then she went on with her work. She did not invite him in. The saintly expression on her face remained fixed, but there was an angry flush over it.

The minister stood awkwardly before her, and talked. She handled the pease as if they were bullets. At last she looked up, and her eyes showed the spirit that her meek front had covered for a lifetime.

"There ain't no use talkin', Mr. Hersey," she said. "I've thought it all over an' over, an' I believe I'm doin' what's right. I've made it the subject of prayer, an' it's betwixt me an' the Lord an' Adoniram. There ain't no call for anybody else to worry about it."

"Well, of course, if you have brought it to the Lord in prayer, and feel satisfied that you are doing right, Mrs. Penn," said the minister, helplessly. His thin gray-bearded face was pathetic. He was a sickly man; his youthful confidence had cooled; he had to scourge himself up to some of his pastoral duties as relentlessly as a Catholic ascetic, and then he was prostrated by the smart.

"I think it's right jest as much as I think it was right for our forefathers to come over from the old country 'cause they didn't have what belonged to 'em," said Mrs. Penn. She arose. The barn threshold might have been Plymouth Rock from her bearing. "I don't doubt you mean well, Mr. Hersey," said she, "but there are things people hadn't ought to interfere with. I've been a member of the church for over forty year. I've got my own mind an' my own feet, an' I'm goin' to think my own thoughts an' go my own ways, an' nobody but the Lord is goin' to dictate to me unless I've a mind to have him. Won't you come in an' set down? How is Mis' Hersey?"

"She is well, I thank you," replied the minister. He added some more perplexed apologetic remarks; then he retreated.

He could expound the intricacies of every character study in the Scriptures, he was competent to grasp the Pilgrim Fathers and all historical innovators, but Sarah Penn was beyond him. He could deal with primal causes, but parallel ones worsted him. But, after all, although it was aside from his province, he wondered more how Adoniram Penn would deal with his wife than how the Lord would. Everybody shared the wonder. When Adoniram's four new cows arrived, Sarah ordered three to be put in the old barn, the other in the house shed where the cooking-stove had stood. That added to the excitement. It was whispered that all four cows were domiciled in the house.

Towards sunset on Saturday, when Adoniram was expected home, there was a knot of men in the road near the new barn. The hired man had milked, but he still hung around the premises. Sarah Penn had supper all ready. There were brown-bread and baked beans and a custard pie; it was the supper that Adoniram loved on a Saturday night. She had on a clean calico, and she bore herself imperturbably. Nanny and Sammy kept close at her heels. Their eyes were large, and Nanny was full of nervous tremors. Still there was to them more pleasant excitement than anything else. An inborn confidence in their mother over their father asserted itself.

Sammy looked out of the harness-room window. "There he is," he announced, in an awed whisper. He and Nanny peeped around the casing. Mrs. Penn kept on about her work. The children watched Adoniram leave the new horse standing in the drive while he went to the house door. It was fastened. Then he went around to the shed. That door was seldom locked, even when the family was away. The thought how her father would be confronted by the cow flashed upon Nanny. There was a hysterical sob in her throat. Adoniram emerged from the shed and stood looking about in a dazed fashion. His lips moved; he was saying something, but they could not hear what it was. The hired man was peeping around a corner of the old barn, but nobody saw him.

Adoniram took the new horse by the bridle and led him across the yard to the new barn. Nanny and Sammy slunk close to their mother. The barn doors rolled back, and there stood Adoniram, with the long mild face of the great Canadian farm horse looking over his shoulder.

Nanny kept behind her mother, but Sammy stepped suddenly forward, and stood in front of her.

Adoniram stared at the group. "What on airth you all down here for?" said he. "What's the matter over to the house?"

"We've come here to live, father," said Sammy. His shrill voice quavered out bravely.

"What"—Adoniram sniffed—"what is it smells like cooking?" said he. He stepped forward and looked in the open door of the harness-room. Then he turned to his wife. His old bristling face was pale and frightened. "What on airth does this mean, mother?" he gasped.

"You come in here, father," said Sarah. She led the way into the harness-room and shut the door. "Now, father," said she, "you needn't be scared. I ain't crazy. There ain't nothin' to be upset over. But we've come here to live, an' we're goin' to live here. We've got jest as good a right here as new horses an' cows. The house wa'n't fit for us to live in any longer, an' I made up my mind I wa'n't goin' to stay there. I've done my duty by you forty year, an' I'm goin' to do it now; but I'm goin' to live here. You've got to put in some windows and partitions; an' you'll have to buy some furniture."

"Why, mother!" the old man gasped.

"You'd better take your coat off an' get washed—there's the wash-basin—an' then we'll have supper."

"Why, mother!"

Sammy went past the window, leading the new horse to the old barn. The old man saw him, and shook his head speechlessly. He tried to take off his coat, but his arms seemed to lack the power. His wife helped him. She poured some water into the tin basin, and put in a piece of soap. She got the comb and brush, and smoothed his thin gray hair after he had washed. Then she put the beans, hot bread, and tea on the table. Sammy came in, and the family drew up. Adoniram sat looking dazedly at his plate, and they waited.

"Ain't you goin' to ask a blessin', father?" said Sarah.

And the old man bent his head and mumbled.

All through the meal he stopped eating at intervals, and stared furtively at his wife; but he ate well. The home food tasted good to him, and his old frame was too sturdily healthy to be affected by his mind. But after supper he went out, and sat down on the step of the smaller door at the right of the barn, through which he had meant his Jerseys to pass in stately file, but which Sarah designed for her front house door, and he leaned his head on his hands.

After the supper dishes were cleared away and the milk-pans washed, Sarah went out to him. The twilight was deepening. There was a clear green glow in the sky. Before them stretched the smooth level of field; in the distance was a cluster of hay-stacks like the huts of a village; the air was very cool and calm and sweet. The landscape might have been an ideal one of peace.

Sarah bent over and touched her husband on one of his thin, sinewy shoulders. "Father!"

The old man's shoulders heaved: he was weeping.

"Why, don't do so, father," said Sarah.

"I'll—put up the—partitions, an'—everything you—want, mother."

Sarah put her apron up to her face; she was overcome by her own triumph. Adoniram was like a fortress whose walls had no active resistance, and went down the instant the right besieging tools were used. "Why, mother," he said, hoarsely, "I hadn't no idee you was so set on't as all this comes to."

QUESTIONS FOR DISCUSSION AND WRITING

1. Analyze the scenic structure of "The Revolt of 'Mother.'" Notice how clear each setting is and how much dialogue Freeman uses, almost as if the story were a play or film. What is the effect of these dramatic devices?

2. Sarah Penn and Adoniram Penn have proper names, but they usually refer to each other as "Mother" and "Father." What does this suggest about their relationship?

3. Try thinking of the story as an anthropologist might. By what rules do the Penns live? How is power divided? What are the rights and obligations of men and women, respectively?

4. What values are in conflict behind the overt disagreement of Sarah and Adoniram Penn? How is the conflict resolved?

Anton Chekhov

Anton Chekhov (1860–1904) is often credited with inventing the modern short story. That may be an overstatement, but certainly the loosely knit, novelistic tales that predominated in earlier short fiction bore little resemblance to Chekhov's compressed, oblique, psychologically revealing short stories. Chekhov was born in the southern Russian seaport town of Taganrog; the family moved to Moscow when Chekhov was sixteen. There he studied medicine, supporting both himself and his penurious family by writing comic sketches for humor magazines. After he began to practice medicine in 1884, his writing became more serious and ambitious. His finest achievement in fiction consists of about fifty stories written between 1888 and his death in 1904. During his last years, Chekhov also became a playwright, his plays forming the basic repertoire of the famous Moscow Art Theatre: *The Seagull* (1898), *Uncle Vanya* (1899), *The Three Sisters* (1901), and *The Cherry Orchard* (1904). He died, tragically prematurely, of tuberculosis at the age of forty-five.

THE LADY WITH THE DOG*

I

People were telling one another that a newcomer had been seen on the promenade—a lady with a dog. Dmitri Dmitrich Gurov had been a fortnight in Yalta, and was accustomed to its ways, and he, too, had begun to take an interest in fresh arrivals. From his seat in Vernet's outdoor café, he caught sight of a young woman in a toque, passing along the promenade; she was fair and not very tall; after her trotted a white pomeranian.

Later he encountered her in the municipal park, and in the square, several times a day. She was always alone, wearing the same toque, and the pomeranian always trotted at her side. Nobody knew who she was, and people referred to her simply as "the lady with the dog."

"If she's here without her husband, and without any friends," thought Gurov, "it wouldn't be a bad idea to make her acquaintance."

He was not yet forty, but had a twelve-year-old daughter and two schoolboy sons. He had been talked into marrying in his second year at college, and his wife now looked nearly twice as old as he was. She was a tall, black-browed woman, erect, dignified, imposing, and, as she said of herself, a "thinker." She was a great reader, omitted the "hard sign"[1] at the end of words in her letters, and called her husband "Dimitri" instead of Dmitri; and though he secretly considered her shallow, narrowminded, and dowdy, he stood in awe of her, and disliked being at home. It was long since he had first begun deceiving her and he was now constantly unfaithful to her, and this was no doubt why he spoke slightingly of women, to whom he referred as *the lower race.*

He considered that the ample lessons he had received from bitter experience entitled him to call them whatever he liked, but without this "lower race" he

* *Translated by Constance Garnett*
[1] Certain progressive intellectuals omitted the hard sign after consonants in writing, thus anticipating the reform in the Russian alphabet introduced later on.—*Tr.*

could not have existed a single day. He was bored and ill-at-ease in the company
of men, with whom he was always cold and reserved, but felt quite at home among
women, and knew exactly what to say to them, and how to behave; he could even
be silent in their company without feeling the slightest awkwardness. There was an
elusive charm in his appearance and disposition which attracted women and
caught their sympathies. He knew this and was himself attracted to them by some
invisible force.

Repeated and bitter experience had taught him that every fresh intimacy, while
at first introducing such pleasant variety into everyday life, and offering itself as a
charming, light adventure, inevitably developed, among decent people (especially
in Moscow, where they are so irresolute and slow to move), into a problem of
excessive complication leading to an intolerably irksome situation. But every time
he encountered an attractive woman he forgot all about this experience, the
desire for life surged up in him, and everything suddenly seemed simple and
amusing.

One evening, then, while he was dining at the restaurant in the park, the lady
in the toque came strolling up and took a seat at a neighboring table. Her
expression, gait, dress, coiffure, all told him that she was from the upper classes,
that she was married, that she was in Yalta for the first time, alone and bored. . . .
The accounts of the laxity of morals among visitors to Yalta are greatly exaggerated, and he paid no heed to them, knowing that for the most part they were
invented by people who would gladly have transgressed themselves, had they
known how to set about it. But when the lady sat down at a neighboring table a few
yards away from him, these stories of easy conquests, of excursions to the mountains, came back to him, and the seductive idea of a brisk transitory liaison, an
affair with a woman whose very name he did not know, suddenly took possession
of his mind.

He snapped his fingers at the pomeranian, and when it trotted up to him, shook
his forefinger at it. The pomeranian growled. Gurov shook his finger again.

The lady glanced at him and instantly lowered her eyes.

"He doesn't bite," she said, and blushed.

"May I give him a bone?" he asked, and on her nod of consent added in
friendly tones: "Have you been long in Yalta?"

"About five days."

"And I am dragging out my second week here."

Neither spoke for a few minutes.

"The days pass quickly, and yet one is so bored here," she said, not looking at
him.

"It's the thing to say it's boring here. People never complain of boredom in
God-forsaken holes like Belyev or Zhizdra, but when they get here it's: 'Oh, the
dullness! Oh, the dust!' You'd think they'd come from Grenada to say the least of
it."

She laughed. Then they both went on eating in silence, like complete strangers.
But after dinner they left the restaurant together, and embarked upon the light,
jesting talk of people free and contented, for whom it is all the same where they
go, or what they talk about. They strolled along, remarking on the strange light
over the sea. The water was a warm, tender purple, the moonlight lay on its surface
in a golden strip. They said how close it was, after the hot day. Gurov told her he
was from Moscow, that he was really a philologist, but worked in a bank; that he
had at one time trained himself to sing in a private opera company, but had given
up the idea; that he owned two houses in Moscow. . . . And from her he learned

that she had grown up in Petersburg, but had got married in the town of S., where she had been living two years, that she would stay another month in Yalta, and that perhaps her husband, who also needed a rest, would join her. She was quite unable to explain whether her husband was a member of the gubernia council, or on the board of the Zemstvo, and was greatly amused at herself for this. Further, Gurov learned that her name was Anna Sergeyevna.

Back in his own room he thought about her, and felt sure he would meet her the next day. It was inevitable. As he went to bed he reminded himself that only a very short time ago she had been a schoolgirl, like his own daughter, learning her lessons, he remembered how much there was of shyness and constraint in her laughter, in her way of conversing with a stranger—it was probably the first time in her life that she found herself alone, and in a situation in which men could follow her and watch her, and speak to her, all the time with a secret aim she could not fail to divine. He recalled her slender, delicate neck, her fine grey eyes.

"And yet there's something pathetic about her," he thought to himself as he fell asleep.

II

A week had passed since the beginning of their acquaintance. It was a holiday. Indoors it was stuffy, but the dust rose in clouds out of doors, and people's hats blew off. It was a thirsty day and Gurov kept going to the outdoor café for fruit-drinks and ices to offer Anna Sergeyevna. The heat was overpowering.

In the evening, when the wind had dropped, they walked to the pier to see the steamer in. There were a great many people strolling about the landing-place; some, bunches of flowers in their hands, were meeting friends. Two peculiarities of the smart Yalta crowd stood out distinctly—the elderly ladies all tried to dress very young, and there seemed to be an inordinate number of generals about.

Owing to the roughness of the sea the steamer arrived late, after the sun had gone down, and it had to manoeuvre for some time before it could get alongside the pier. Anna Sergeyevna scanned the steamer and passengers through her lorgnette, as if looking for someone she knew, and when she turned to Gurov her eyes were glistening. She talked a great deal, firing off abrupt questions and forgetting immediately what it was she had wanted to know. Then she lost her lorgnette in the crush.

The smart crowd began dispersing, features could no longer be made out, the wind had quite dropped, and Gurov and Anna Sergeyevna stood there as if waiting for someone else to come off the steamer. Anna Sergeyevna had fallen silent, every now and then smelling her flowers, but not looking at Gurov.

"It's turning out a fine evening," he said. "What shall we do? We might go for a drive."

She made no reply.

He looked steadily at her and suddenly took her in his arms and kissed her lips, and the fragrance and dampness of the flowers closed round him, but the next moment he looked behind him in alarm—had anyone seen them?

"Let's go to your room," he murmured.

And they walked off together, very quickly.

Her room was stuffy and smelt of some scent she had bought in the Japanese shop. Gurov looked at her, thinking to himself: "How full of strange encounters life is!" He could remember carefree, good-natured women who were exhilarated by love-making and grateful to him for the happiness he gave them, however short-lived; and there had been others—his wife among them—whose caresses were insincere, affected, hysterical, mixed up with a great deal of quite unnecessary talk, and whose expression seemed to say that all this was not just love-making or passion, but something much more significant; then there had been two or three beautiful, cold women, over whose features flitted a predatory expression, betraying a determination to wring from life more than it could give, women no longer in their first youth, capricious, irrational, despotic, brainless, and when Gurov had cooled to these, their beauty aroused in him nothing but repulsion, and the lace trimming on their underclothes reminded him of fish-scales.

But here the timidity and awkwardness of youth and inexperience were still apparent; and there was a feeling of embarrassment in the atmosphere, as if someone had just knocked at the door. Anna Sergeyevna, "the lady with the dog," seemed to regard the affair as something very special, very serious, as if she had become a fallen woman, an attitude he found odd and disconcerting. Her features lengthened and drooped, and her long hair hung mournfully on either side of her face. She assumed a pose of dismal meditation, like a repentant sinner in some classical painting.

"It isn't right," she said. "You will never respect me any more."

On the table was a water-melon. Gurov cut himself a slice from it and began slowly eating it. At least half an hour passed in silence.

Anna Sergeyevna was very touching, revealing the purity of a decent, naive woman who had seen very little of life. The solitary candle burning on the table scarcely lit up her face, but it was obvious that her heart was heavy.

"Why should I stop respecting you?" asked Gurov. "You don't know what you're saying."

"May God forgive me!" she exclaimed, and her eyes filled with tears. "It's terrible."

"No need to seek to justify yourself."

"How can I justify myself? I'm a wicked, fallen woman, I despise myself and have not the least thought of self-justification. It isn't my husband I have deceived, it's myself. And not only now, I have been deceiving myself for ever so long. My husband is no doubt an honest, worthy man, but he's a flunkey. I don't know what it is he does at his office, but I know he's a flunkey. I was only twenty when I married him, and I was devoured by curiosity, I wanted something higher. I told myself that there must be a different kind of life. I wanted to live, to live. . . . I was burning with curiosity . . . you'll never understand that, but I swear to God I could no longer control myself, nothing could hold me back, I told my husband I was ill, and I came here. . . . And I started going about like one possessed, like a madwoman . . . and now I have become an ordinary, worthless woman, and everyone has the right to despise me."

Gurov listened to her, bored to death. The naive accents, the remorse, all was so unexpected, so out of place. But for the tears in her eyes, she might have been jesting or play-acting.

"I don't understand," he said gently. "What is it you want?"

She hid her face against his breast and pressed closer to him.

"Do believe me, I implore you to believe me," she said. "I love all that is honest and pure in life, vice is revolting to me. I don't know what I'm doing. The common people say they are snared by the devil. And now I can say that I have been snared by the devil, too."

"Come, come," he murmured.

He gazed into her fixed, terrified eyes, kissed her, and soothed her with gentle affectionate words, and gradually she calmed down and regained her cheerfulness. Soon they were laughing together again.

When, a little later, they went out, there was not a soul on the promenade, the town and its cypresses looked dead, but the sea was still roaring as it dashed against the beach. A solitary fishing-boat tossed on the waves, its lamp blinking sleepily.

They found a droshky and drove to Oreanda.

"I discovered your name in the hall, just now," said Gurov, "written up on the board. Von Diederitz. Is your husband a German?"

"No. His grandfather was, I think, but he belongs to the Orthodox church himself."

When they got out of the droshky at Oreanda they sat down on a bench not far from the church, and looked at the sea, without talking. Yalta could be dimly discerned through the morning mist, and white clouds rested motionless on the summits of the mountains. Not a leaf stirred, the grasshoppers chirruped, and the monotonous hollow roar of the sea came up to them, speaking of peace, of the eternal sleep lying in wait for us all. The sea had roared like this long before there was any Yalta or Oreanda, it was roaring now, and it would go on roaring, just as indifferently and hollowly, when he had passed away. And it may be that in this continuity, this utter indifference to life and death, lies the secret of our ultimate salvation, of the stream of life on our planet, and of its never-ceasing movement towards perfection.

Side by side with a young woman, who looked so exquisite in the early light, soothed and enchanted by the sight of all this magical beauty—sea, mountains, clouds and the vast expanse of the sky—Gurov told himself that, when you came to think of it, everything in the world is beautiful really, everything but our own thoughts and actions, when we lose sight of the higher aims of life, and of our dignity as human beings.

Someone approached them—a watchman, probably—looked at them and went away. And there was something mysterious and beautiful even in this. The steamer from Feodosia could be seen coming towards the pier, lit up by the dawn, its lamps out.

"There's dew on the grass," said Anna Sergeyevna, breaking the silence.

"Yes. Time to go home."

They went back to the town.

After this they met every day at noon on the promenade, lunching and dining together, going for walks, and admiring the sea. She complained of sleeplessness, of palpitations, asked the same questions over and over again, alternately surrendering to jealousy and the fear that he did not really respect her. And often, when there was nobody in sight in the square or the park, he would draw her to him and kiss her passionately. The utter idleness, these kisses in broad daylight, accompanied by furtive glances and the fear of discovery, the heat, the smell of the sea, and the idle, smart, well-fed people continually crossing their field of vision, seemed to have given him a new lease on life. He told Anna Sergeyevna she was beautiful and seductive, made love to her with impetuous passion, and never left her side, while she was always pensive, always trying to force from him the admission that he did not respect her, that he did not love her a bit, and considered her just an ordinary woman. Almost every night they drove out of town, to Oreanda, the waterfall, or some other beauty-spot. And these excursions were invariably a success, each contributing fresh impressions of majestic beauty.

All this time they kept expecting her husband to arrive. But a letter came in which he told his wife that he was having trouble with his eyes, and implored her to come home as soon as possible. Anna Sergeyevna made hasty preparations for leaving.

"It's a good thing I'm going," she said to Gurov. "It's the intervention of fate."

She left Yalta in a carriage, and he went with her as far as the railway station. The drive took nearly a whole day. When she got into the express train, after the second bell had been rung, she said:

"Let me have one more look at you. . . . One last look. That's right."

She did not weep, but was mournful, and seemed ill, the muscles of her cheeks twitching.

"I shall think of you . . . I shall think of you all the time," she said. "God bless you! Think kindly of me. We are parting for ever, it must be so, because we ought never to have met. Good-bye—God bless you."

The train steamed rapidly out of the station, its lights soon disappearing, and a minute later even the sound it made was silenced, as if everything were conspiring to bring this sweet oblivion, this madness, to an end as quickly as possible. And Gurov, standing alone on the platform and gazing into the dark distance, listened to the shrilling of the grasshoppers and the humming of the telegraph wire, with a feeling that he had only just waked up. And he told himself that this had been just one more of the many adventures in his life, and that it, too, was over, leaving nothing but a memory. . . . He was moved and sad, and felt a slight remorse. After all, this young woman whom he would never again see had not been really happy with him. He had been friendly and affectionate with her, but in his whole behavior, in the tones of his voice, in his very caresses, there had been a shade of irony, the insulting indulgence of the fortunate male, who was, moreover, almost twice her age. She had insisted in calling him good, remarkable, high-minded. Evidently he had appeared to her different from his real self, in a word he had involuntarily deceived her. . . .

There was an autumnal feeling in the air, and the evening was chilly.

"It's time for me to be going north," thought Gurov, as he walked away from the platform. "High time!"

III

When he got back to Moscow it was beginning to look like winter, the stoves were heated every day, and it was still dark when the children got up to go to school and drank their tea, so that the nurse had to light the lamp for a short time. Frost had set in. When the first snow falls, and one goes for one's first sleigh-ride, it is pleasant to see the white ground, the white roofs; one breathes freely and lightly, and remembers the days of one's youth. The ancient lime-trees and birches, white with rime, have a good-natured look, they are closer to the heart than cypresses and palms, and beneath their branches one is no longer haunted by the memory of mountains and the sea.

Gurov had always lived in Moscow, and he returned to Moscow on a fine frosty day, and when he put on his fur-lined overcoat and thick gloves, and sauntered down Petrovka Street, and when, on Saturday evening, he heard the church bells ringing, his recent journey and the places he had visited lost their charm for him. He became gradually immersed in Moscow life, reading with avidity three newspapers a day, while declaring he never read Moscow newspapers on principle. Once more he was caught up in a whirl of restaurants, clubs, banquets, and celebrations, once more glowed with the flattering consciousness that well-known lawyers and actors came to his house, that he played cards in the Medical Club opposite a professor.

He had believed that in a month's time, Anna Sergeyevna would be nothing but a wistful memory, and that hereafter, with her wistful smile, she would only occasionally appear to him in dreams, like others before her. But the month was now well over and winter was in full swing, and all was as clear in his memory as if he had only parted with Anna Sergeyevna the day before. And his recollections grew ever more insistent. When the voices of his children at their lessons reached him in his study through the evening stillness, when he heard a song, or the sounds of a musical-box in a restaurant, when the wind howled in the chimney, it all came back to him: early morning on the pier, the misty mountains, the steamer from Feodosia, the kisses. He would pace up and down his room for a long time, smiling at his memories, and then memory turned into dreaming, and what had happened mingled in his imagination with what was going to happen. Anna Sergeyevna did not come to him in his dreams, she accompanied him everywhere, like his shadow, following him everywhere he went. When he closed his eyes, she seemed to stand before him in the flesh, still lovelier, younger, tenderer than she had really been, and looking back, he saw himself, too, as better than he had been in Yalta. In the evenings she looked out at him from the bookshelves, the fireplace, the corner, he could hear her breathing, the sweet rustle of her skirts. In the streets he followed women with his eyes, to see if there were any like her. . . .

He began to feel an overwhelming desire to share his memories with someone. But he could not speak of his love at home, and outside his home who was there for him to confide in? Not the tenants living in his house, and certainly not his colleagues at the bank. And what was there to tell? Was it love that he had felt? Had there been anything exquisite, poetic, anything instructive or even amusing about his relations with Anna Sergeyevna? He had to content himself with uttering vague generalizations about love and women, and nobody guessed what he meant, though his wife's dark eyebrows twitched as she said:

"The role of a coxcomb doesn't suit you a bit, Dimitri."

One evening, leaving the Medical Club with one of his card-partners, a government official, he could not refrain from remarking:

"If you only knew what a charming woman I met in Yalta!"

The official got into his sleigh, and just before driving off turned and called out:

"Dmitri Dmitrich!"

"Yes?"

"You were quite right, you know—the sturgeon was just a *leetle* off."

These words, in themselves so commonplace, for some reason infuriated Gurov, seemed to him humiliating, gross. What savage manners, what people! What wasted evenings, what tedious, empty days! Frantic card-playing, gluttony, drunkenness, perpetual talk always about the same thing. The greater part of one's time and energy went on business that was no use to anyone, and on discussing the same thing over and over again, and there was nothing to show for it all but a stunted, earth-bound existence and a round of trivialities, and there was nowhere to escape to, you might as well be in a mad-house or a convict settlement.

Gurov lay awake all night, raging, and went about the whole of the next day with a headache. He slept badly on the succeeding nights, too, sitting up in bed, thinking, or pacing the floor of his room. He was sick of his children, sick of the bank, felt not the slightest desire to go anywhere or talk about anything.

When the Christmas holidays came, he packed his things, telling his wife he had to go to Petersburg in the interests of a certain young man, and set off for the town of S. To what end? He hardly knew himself. He only knew that he must see Anna Sergeyevna, must speak to her, arrange a meeting, if possible.

He arrived at S. in the morning and engaged the best room in the hotel, which had a carpet of gray military frieze, and a dusty ink-pot on the table, surmounted by a headless rider, holding his hat in his raised hand. The hall porter told him what he wanted to know: von Diederitz had a house of his own in Staro-Goncharnaya Street. It wasn't far from the hotel, he lived on a grand scale, luxuriously, kept carriage-horses, the whole town knew him. The hall porter pronounced the name "Drideritz."

Gurov strolled over to Staro-Goncharnaya Street and discovered the house. In front of it was a long gray fence with inverted nails hammered into the tops of the palings.

"A fence like that is enough to make anyone want to run away," thought Gurov, looking at the windows of the house and the fence.

He reasoned that since it was a holiday, her husband would probably be at home. In any case it would be tactless to embarrass her by calling at the house. And a note might fall into the hands of the husband, and bring about catastrophe. The best thing would be to wait about on the chance of seeing her. And he walked up and down the street, hovering in the vicinity of the fence, watching for his chance. A beggar entered the gate, only to be attacked by dogs, then, an hour later, the faint, vague sounds of a piano reached his ears. That would be Anna Sergeyevna playing. Suddenly the front door opened and an old woman came out, followed by a familiar white pomeranian. Gurov tried to call to it, but his heart beat violently, and in his agitation he could not remember its name.

He walked on, hating the gray fence more and more, and now ready to tell himself irately that Anna Sergeyevna had forgotten him, had already, perhaps, found distraction in another—what could be more natural in a young woman who had to look at this accursed fence from morning to night? He went back to his hotel and sat on the sofa in his room for some time, not knowing what to do, then he ordered dinner, and after dinner, had a long sleep.

"What a foolish, restless business," he thought, waking up and looking towards the dark window-panes. It was evening by now. "Well, I've had my sleep out. And what am I to do in the night?"

He sat up in bed, covered by the cheap gray quilt, which reminded him of a hospital blanket, and in his vexation he fell to taunting himself.

"You and your lady with a dog . . . there's adventure for you! See what you get for your pains."

On his arrival at the station that morning he had noticed a poster announcing in enormous letters the first performance at the local theatre of *The Geisha*. Remembering this, he got up and made for the theatre.

"It's highly probable that she goes to first-nights," he told himself.

The theatre was full. It was a typical provincial theatre, with a mist collecting over the chandeliers, and the crowd in the gallery fidgeting noisily. In the first row of the stalls the local dandies stood waiting for the curtain to go up, their hands clasped behind them. There, in the front seat of the Governor's box, sat the Governor's daughter, wearing a boa, the Governor himself hiding modestly behind the drapes, so that only his hands were visible. The curtain stirred, the orchestra took a long time tuning up their instruments. Gurov's eyes roamed eagerly over the audience as they filed in and occupied their seats.

Anna Sergeyevna came in, too. She seated herself in the third row of the stalls, and when Gurov's glance fell on her, his heart seemed to stop, and he knew in a flash that the whole world contained no one nearer or dearer to him, no one more important to his happiness. This little woman, lost in the provincial crowd, in no way remarkable, holding a silly lorgnette in her hand, now filled his whole life, was his grief, his joy, all that he desired. Lulled by the sounds coming from the wretched orchestra, with its feeble, amateurish violinists, he thought how beautiful she was ... thought and dreamed. ...

Anna Sergeyevna was accompanied by a tall, round-shouldered young man with small whiskers, who nodded at every step before taking the seat beside her and seemed to be continually bowing to someone. This must be her husband, whom, in a fit of bitterness, at Yalta, she had called a "flunkey." And there really was something of the lackey's servility in his lanky figure, his side-whiskers, and the little bald spot on the top of his head. And he smiled sweetly, and the badge of some scientific society gleaming in his buttonhole was like the number on a footman's livery.

The husband went out to smoke in the first interval, and she was left alone in her seat. Gurov, who had taken a seat in the stalls, went up to her and said in a trembling voice, with a forced smile: "How d'you do?"

She glanced up at him and turned pale, then looked at him again in alarm, unable to believe her eyes, squeezing her fan and lorgnette in one hand, evidently struggling to overcome a feeling of faintness. Neither of them said a word. She sat there, and he stood beside her, disconcerted by her embarrassment, and not daring to sit down. The violins and flutes sang out as they were tuned, and there was a tense sensation in the atmosphere, as if they were being watched from all the boxes. At last she got up and moved rapidly towards one of the exits. He followed her and they wandered aimlessly along corridors, up and down stairs; figures flashed by in the uniforms of legal officials, high-school teachers and civil servants, all wearing badges; ladies, coats hanging from pegs flashed by; there was a sharp draught, bringing with it an odor of cigarette-stubs. And Gurov, whose heart was beating violently, thought:

"What on earth are all these people, this orchestra for? ..."

The next minute he suddenly remembered how, after seeing Anna Sergeyevna off that evening at the station, he had told himself that all was over, and they would never meet again. And how far away the end seemed to be now!

She stopped on a dark narrow staircase over which was a notice bearing the inscription "To the upper circle."

"How you frightened me!" she said, breathing heavily, still pale and half-stunned. "Oh, how you frightened me! I'm almost dead! Why did you come? Oh, why?"

"But, Anna," he said, in a low, hasty tones. "But, Anna. ... Try to understand ... do try. ..."

She cast him a glance of fear, entreaty, love, and then gazed at him steadily, as if to fix his features firmly in her memory.

"I've been so unhappy," she continued, taking no notice of his words. "I could think of nothing but you the whole time, I lived on the thoughts of you. I tried to forget—why, oh, why did you come?"

On the landing above them were two schoolboys, smoking and looking down, but Gurov did not care, and, drawing Anna Sergeyevna towards him, began kissing her face, her lips, her hands.

"What are you doing, oh, what are you doing?" she said in horror, drawing back. "We have both gone mad. Go away this very night, this moment. ... By all that is sacred, I implore you. ... Somebody is coming."

Someone was ascending the stairs.

"You must go away," went on Anna Sergeyevna in a whisper. "D'you hear me, Dmitri Dmitrich? I'll come to you in Moscow. I have never been happy, I am unhappy now, and I shall never be happy—never! Do not make me suffer still more! I will come to you in Moscow, I swear it! And now we must part! My dear one, my kind one, my darling, we must part."

She pressed his hand and hurried down the stairs, looking back at him continually, and her eyes showed that she was in truth unhappy. Gurov stood where he was for a short time, listening, and when all was quiet went to look for his coat, and left the theatre.

IV

And Anna Sergeyevna began going to Moscow to see him. Every two or three months she left the town of S., telling her husband that she was going to consult a specialist on female diseases, and her husband believed her and did not believe her. In Moscow she always stayed at the "Slavyanski Bazaar," sending a man in a red cap to Gurov the moment she arrived. Gurov went to her, and no one in Moscow knew anything about it.

One winter morning he went to see her as usual (the messenger had been to him the evening before, but had not found him at home). His daughter was with him for her school was on the way, and he thought he might as well see her to it.

"It is three degrees above zero," said Gurov to his daughter, "and yet it is snowing. You see it is only above zero close to the ground, the temperature in the upper layers of the atmosphere is quite different."

"Why doesn't it ever thunder in winter, Papa?"

He explained this, too. As he was speaking, he kept reminding himself that he was going to a rendezvous and that not a living soul knew about it, or, probably, ever would. He led a double life—one in public, in sight of all whom it concerned, full of conventional truth and conventional deception, exactly like the lives of his friends and acquaintances, and another which flowed in secret. And, owing to some strange, possibly quite accidental chain of circumstances, everything that was important, interesting, essential, everything about which he was sincere and never deceived himself, everything that composed the kernel of his life, went on in secret, while everything that was false in him, everything that composed the husk in which he hid himself and the truth which was in him—his work at the bank, discussions at the club, his "lower race," his attendance at anniversary celebrations with his wife—was on the surface. He began to judge others by himself, no longer believing what he saw, and always assuming that the real, the only interesting life of every individual goes on as under cover of night, secretly. Every individual existence revolves around mystery, and perhaps that is the chief reason that all cultivated individuals insisted so strongly on the respect due to personal secrets.

After leaving his daughter at the door of her school Gurov set off for the "Slavyanski Bazaar." Taking off his overcoat in the lobby, he went upstairs and knocked softly on the door. Anna Sergeyevna, wearing the gray dress he liked most, exhausted by her journey and by suspense, had been expecting him since the evening before. She was pale and looked at him without smiling, but was in his arms almost before he was fairly in the room. Their kiss was lingering, prolonged, as if they had not met for years.

"Well, how are you?" he asked. "Anything new?"

"Wait, I'll tell you in a minute. . . . I can't. . . ."

She could not speak, because she was crying. Turning away, she held her handkerchief to her eyes.

"I'll wait till she's had her cry out," he thought, and sank into a chair.

He rang for tea, and a little later, while he was drinking it, she was still standing there, her face to the window. She wept from emotion, from her bitter consciousness of the sadness of their life; they could only see one another in secret, hiding from people, as if they were thieves. Was not their life a broken one?

"Don't cry," he said.

It was quite obvious to him that this love of theirs would not soon come to an end, and that no one could say when this end would be. Anna Sergeyevna loved him ever more fondly, worshipped him, and there would have been no point in telling her that one day it must end. Indeed, she would not have believed him.

He moved over and took her by the shoulders, intending to fondle her with light words, but suddenly he caught sight of himself in the looking-glass.

His hair was already beginning to turn gray. It struck him as strange that he should have aged so much in the last few years. The shoulders on which his hands lay were warm and quivering. He felt a pity for this life, still so warm and exquisite, but probably soon to fade and droop like his own. Why did she love him so? Women had always believed him different from what he really was, had loved in him not himself but the man their imagination pictured him, a man they had sought for eagerly all their lives. And afterwards when they discovered their mistake, they went on loving him just the same. And not one of them had ever been happy with him. Time had passed, he had met one woman after another, become intimate with each, parted with each, but had never loved. There had been all sorts of things between them, but never love.

And only now, when he was gray-haired, had he fallen in love properly, thoroughly, for the first time in his life.

He and Anna Sergeyevna loved one another as people who are very close and intimate, as husband and wife, as dear friends love one another. It seemed to them that fate had intended them for one another, and they could not understand why she should have a husband, and he a wife. They were like two migrating birds, the male and the female, who had been caught and put into separate cages. They forgave one another all that they were ashamed of in the past, in their present, and felt that this love of theirs had changed them both.

Formerly, in moments of melancholy, he had consoled himself by the first argument that came into his head, but now arguments were nothing to him, he felt profound pity, desired to be sincere, tender.

"Stop crying, my dearest," he said. "You've had your cry, now stop. . . . Now let us have a talk, let us try and think what we are to do."

Then they discussed their situation for a long time, trying to think how they could get rid of the necessity for hiding, deception, living in different towns, being so long without meeting. How were they to shake off these intolerable fetters?

"How? How?" he repeated, clutching his head. "How?"

And it seemed to them that they were within an inch of arriving at a decision, and that then a new, beautiful life would begin. And they both realized that the end was still far, far away, and that the hardest, the most complicated part was only just beginning.

QUESTIONS FOR DISCUSSION AND WRITING

1. "The Lady with the Dog" is focalized through Gurov, but the narrator is quite distinct from Gurov. What sorts of judgments does the narrator make about Gurov that Gurov would be unable to make about himself, especially in Part I?

2. How does the focus on Gurov rather than on Anna Sergeyevna affect the story? How might the story be different if Anna were in the foreground?

3. Gurov changes in the course of the story, from the shallow, cynical, rather misogynistic man of Part I to something altogether different at the end. Describe the change and its causes.

4. A passage in Part II seems to be an important thematic statement: "The sea had roared like this long before there was any Yalta or Oreanda, it was roaring now, and it would go on roaring, just as indifferently and hollowly, when we had passed away. And it may be that in this continuity, this utter indifference to life and death, lies the secret of our ultimate salvation, of the stream of life on our planet, and of its never-ceasing movement towards perfection." What do you make of this passage? Is it a thought attributed to Gurov and/or Anna? Can you relate it to the rest of the story?

5. Chekhov ends "The Lady with the Dog" at a point you may find surprising, without revealing how the love affair came out. What is likely to happen, given the situation and the characters of the lovers? Will they get divorces and end up together? Will they end their love affair? What does Chekhov gain by ending the story where he does?

James Joyce

James Joyce (1882–1941) was born in Dublin into a family once prosperous but by the time of his birth in precipitous decline. He attended Jesuit schools and University College, Dublin, graduating in 1902. Two years later, he left Ireland in the company of Nora Barnacle and never returned there to live. The couple lived in Trieste, then in Zurich, then in Paris, and then again briefly in Zurich, after France fell to the Nazis in 1940. Joyce's reputation rests largely on four books, each longer and more complex than the one before: *Dubliners* (1914), a collection of fifteen short stories of Dublin life; *A Portrait of the Artist as a Young Man* (1916); *Ulysses* (1922), a comic-epic account of one day, June 16, 1904, in the life of a Dublin advertising salesman; and *Finnegans Wake* (1939), a massive "book of the night," written in a distorted form of English invented for it. Joyce died in Zurich in 1941.

THE BOARDING HOUSE

Mrs Mooney was a butcher's daughter. She was a woman who was quite able to keep things to herself: a determined woman. She had married her father's foreman and opened a butcher's shop near Spring Gardens. But as soon as his father-in-law was dead Mr Mooney began to go to the devil. He drank, plundered the till, ran headlong into debt. It was no use making him take the pledge: he was sure to break out again a few days after. By fighting his wife in the presence of customers and by buying bad meat he ruined his business. One night he went for his wife with the cleaver and she had to sleep in a neighbour's house.

After that they lived apart. She went to the priest and got a separation from him with care of the children. She would give him neither money nor food nor house-room; and so he was obliged to enlist himself as a sheriff's man. He was a shabby stooped little drunkard with a white face and a white moustache and white eyebrows, pencilled above his little eyes, which were pink-veined and raw; and all day long he sat in the bailiff's room, waiting to be put on a job. Mrs Mooney, who had taken what remained of her money out of the butcher business and set up a boarding house in Hardwicke Street, was a big imposing woman. Her house had a floating population made up of tourists from Liverpool and the Isle of Man and, occasionally, *artistes* from the music halls. Its resident population was made up of clerks from the city. She governed her house cunningly and firmly, knew when to give credit, when to be stern and when to let things pass. All the resident young men spoke of her as *The Madam*.

Mrs Mooney's young men paid fifteen shillings a week for board and lodgings (beer or stout at dinner excluded). They shared in common tastes and occupations and for this reason they were very chummy with one another. They discussed with one another the chances of favourites and outsiders. Jack Mooney, the Madam's son, who was clerk to a commission agent in Fleet Street, had the reputation of being a hard case. He was fond of using soldiers' obscenities: usually he came home in the small hours. When he met his friends he had always a good one to tell them and he was always sure to be on to a good thing—that is to say, a likely horse or a likely *artiste*. He was also handy with the mits and sang comic songs. On Sunday nights there would often be a reunion in Mrs Mooney's front drawing-room. The music-hall *artistes* would oblige; and Sheridan played waltzes and pol-

kas and vamped accompaniments. Polly Mooney, the Madam's daughter, would
also sing. She sang:

> I'm a ... naughty girl.
> You needn't sham:
> You know I am.

Polly was a slim girl of nineteen; she had light soft hair and a small full mouth.
Her eyes, which were grey with a shade of green through them, had a habit of
glancing upwards when she spoke with anyone, which made her look like a little
perverse madonna. Mrs Mooney had first sent her daughter to be a typist in a
corn-factor's office but, as a disreputable sheriff's man used to come every other
day to the office, asking to be allowed to say a word to his daughter, she had taken
her daughter home again and set her to do housework. As Polly was very lively the
intention was to give her the run of the young men. Besides, young men like to
feel that there is a young woman not very far away. Polly, of course, flirted with the
young men but Mrs Mooney, who was a shrewd judge, knew that the young men
were only passing the time away: none of them meant business. Things went on so
for a long time and Mrs Mooney began to think of sending Polly back to type-
writing when she noticed that something was going on between Polly and one of
the young men. She watched the pair and kept her own counsel.

Polly knew that she was being watched, but still her mother's persistent silence
could not be misunderstood. There had been no open complicity between mother
and daughter, no open understanding but, though people in the house began to
talk of the affair, still Mrs Mooney did not intervene. Polly began to grow a little
strange in her manner and the young man was evidently perturbed. At last, when
she judged it to be the right moment, Mrs Mooney intervened. She dealt with
moral problems as a cleaver deals with meat: and in this case she had made up her
mind.

It was a bright Sunday morning of early summer, promising heat, but with a
fresh breeze blowing. All the windows of the boarding house were open and the
lace curtains ballooned gently toward the street beneath the raised sashes. The
belfry of George's Church sent out constant peals and worshippers, singly or in
groups, traversed the little circus before the church, revealing their purpose by
their self-contained demeanour no less than by the little volumes in their gloved
hands. Breakfast was over in the boarding house and the table of the breakfast-
room was covered with plates on which lay yellow streaks of eggs with morsels of
bacon-fat and bacon-rind. Mrs Mooney sat in the straw arm-chair and watched the
servant Mary remove the breakfast things. She made Mary collect the crusts and
pieces of broken bread to help to make Tuesday's bread-pudding. When the table
was cleared, the broken bread collected, the sugar and butter safe under lock and
key, she began to reconstruct the interview which she had had the night before
with Polly. Things were as she had suspected: she had been frank in her questions
and Polly had been frank in her answers. Both had been somewhat awkward, of
course. She had been made awkward by her not wishing to receive the news in too
cavalier a fashion or to seem to have connived and Polly had been made awkward
not merely because allusions of that kind always made her awkward but also
because she did not wish it to be thought that in her wise innocence she had
divined the intention behind her mother's tolerance.

Mrs Mooney glanced instinctively at the little gilt clock on the mantelpiece as
soon as she had become aware through her revery that the bells on George's

Church had stopped ringing. It was seventeen minutes past eleven: she would have lots of time to have the matter out with Mr Doran and then catch short twelve at Marlborough Street. She was sure she would win. To begin with she had all the weight of social opinion on her side: she was an outraged mother. She had allowed him to live beneath her roof, assuming that he was a man of honour, and he had simply abused her hospitality. He was thirty-four or thirty-five years of age, so that youth could not be pleaded as his excuse; nor could ignorance be his excuse since he was a man who had seen something of the world. He had simply taken advantage of Polly's youth and inexperience: that was evident. The question was: What reparation would he make?

There must be reparation made in such cases. It is all very well for the man: he can go his ways as if nothing had happened, having had his moment of pleasure, but the girl has to bear the brunt. Some mothers would be content to patch up such an affair for a sum of money; she had known cases of it. But she would not do so. For her only one reparation could make up for the loss of her daughter's honour: marriage.

She counted all her cards again before sending Mary up to Mr Doran's room to say that she wished to speak with him. She felt sure she would win. He was a serious young man, not rakish or loud-voiced like the others. If it had been Mr Sheridan or Mr Meade or Bantam Lyons her task would have been much harder. She did not think he would face publicity. All the lodgers in the house knew something of the affair; details had been invented by some. Besides, he had been employed for thirteen years in a great Catholic wine-merchant's office and publicity would mean for him, perhaps, the loss of his sit. Whereas if he agreed all might be well. She knew he had a good screw for one thing and she suspected he had a bit of stuff put by.

Nearly the half-hour! She stood up and surveyed herself in the pier-glass. The decisive expression of her great florid face satisfied her and she thought of some mothers she knew who could not get their daughters off their hands.

Mr Doran was very anxious indeed this Sunday morning. He had made two attempts to shave but his hand had been so unsteady that he had been obliged to desist. Three days' reddish beard fringed his jaws and every two or three minutes a mist gathered on his glasses so that he had to take them off and polish them with his pocket-handkerchief. The recollection of his confession of the night before was a cause of acute pain to him; the priest had drawn out every ridiculous detail of the affair and in the end had so magnified his sin that he was almost thankful at being afforded a loophole of reparation. The harm was done. What could he do now but marry her or run away? He could not brazen it out. The affair would be sure to be talked of and his employer would be certain to hear of it. Dublin is such a small city: everyone knows everyone else's business. He felt his heart leap warmly in his throat as he heard in his excited imagination old Mr Leonard calling out in his rasping voice: *Send Mr Doran here, please.*

All his long years of service gone for nothing! All his industry and diligence thrown away! As a young man he had sown his wild oats, of course; he had boasted of his free-thinking and denied the existence of God to his companions in public-houses. But that was all passed and done with . . . nearly. He still bought a copy of *Reynolds's Newspaper* every week but he attended to his religious duties and for nine-tenths of the year lived a regular life. He had money enough to settle down on; it was not that. But the family would look down on her. First of all there was her disreputable father and then her mother's boarding house was beginning to get a certain fame. He had a notion that he was being had. He could imagine his friends talking of the affair and laughing. She *was* a little vulgar; sometimes she said *I seen* and *If I had've known*. But what would grammar matter if he really loved her? He could not make up his mind whether to like her or despise her for what she had done. Of course, he had done it too. His instinct urged him to remain free, not to marry. Once you are married you are done for, it said.

While he was sitting helplessly on the side of the bed in shirt and trousers she tapped lightly at his door and entered. She told him all, that she had made a clean breast of it to her mother and that her mother would speak with him that morning. She cried and threw her arms round his neck, saying:

—O, Bob! Bob! What am I to do? What am I to do at all?

She would put an end to herself, she said.

He comforted her feebly, telling her not to cry, that it would be all right, never fear. He felt against his shirt the agitation of her bosom.

It was not altogether his fault that it had happened. He remembered well, with the curious patient memory of the celibate, the first casual caresses her dress, her breath, her fingers had given him. Then late one night as he was undressing for bed she had tapped at his door, timidly. She wanted to relight her candle at his for hers had been blown out by a gust. It was her bath night. She wore a loose open combing-jacket of printed flannel. Her white instep shone in the opening of her furry slippers and the blood glowed warmly behind her perfumed skin. From her hands and wrists too as she lit and steadied her candle a faint perfume arose.

On nights when he came in very late it was she who warmed up his dinner. He scarcely knew what he was eating, feeling her beside him alone, at night, in the sleeping house. And her thoughtfulness! If the night was anyway cold or wet or windy there was sure to be a little tumbler of punch ready for him. Perhaps they could be happy together. . . .

They used to go upstairs together on tiptoe, each with a candle, and on the third landing exchange reluctant goodnights. They used to kiss. He remembered well her eyes, the touch of her hand and his delirium. . . .

But delirium passes. He echoed her phrase, applying it to himself: *What am I to do?* The instinct of the celibate warned him to hold back. But the sin was there; even his sense of honour told him that reparation must be made for such a sin.

While he was sitting with her on the side of the bed Mary came to the door and said that the missus wanted to see him in the parlour. He stood up to put on his coat and waistcoat, more helpless than ever. When he was dressed he went over to her to comfort her. It would be all right, never fear. He left her crying on the bed and moaning softly: *O my God!*

Going down the stairs his glasses became so dimmed with moisture that he had to take them off and polish them. He longed to ascend through the roof and fly away to another country where he would never hear again of his trouble, and yet a force pushed him downstairs step by step. The implacable faces of his employer and of the Madam stared upon his discomfiture. On the last flight of stairs he passed Jack Mooney who was coming up from the pantry nursing two bottles of *Bass*. They saluted coldly; and the lover's eyes rested for a second or two on a thick bulldog face and a pair of thick short arms. When he reached the foot of the staircase he glanced up and saw Jack regarding him from the door of the return-room.

Suddenly he remembered the night when one of the music-hall *artistes*, a little blond Londoner, had made a rather free allusion to Polly. The reunion had been almost broken up on account of Jack's violence. Everyone tried to quiet him. The music-hall *artiste*, a little paler than usual, kept smiling and saying that there was no harm meant: but Jack kept shouting at him that if any fellow tried that sort of a game on with *his* sister he'd bloody well put his teeth down his throat, so he would.

. . . .

Polly sat for a little time on the side of the bed, crying. Then she dried her eyes and went over to the looking-glass. She dipped the end of the towel in the water-jug and refreshed her eyes with the cool water. She looked at herself in profile and readjusted a hairpin above her ear. Then she went back to the bed again and sat at the foot. She regarded the pillows for a long time and the sight of them awakened in her mind secret amiable memories. She rested the nape of her neck against the cool iron bed-rail and fell into a revery. There was no longer any perturbation visible on her face.

She waited on patiently, almost cheerfully, without alarm, her memories gradually giving place to hopes and visions of the future. Her hopes and visions were so intricate that she no longer saw the white pillows on which her gaze was fixed or remembered that she was waiting for anything.

At last she heard her mother calling. She started to her feet and ran to the banisters.

—Polly! Polly!

—Yes, mamma?

—Come down, dear. Mr Doran wants to speak to you.

Then she remembered what she had been waiting for.

QUESTIONS FOR DISCUSSION AND WRITING

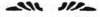

1. Joyce said that his purpose in *Dubliners* was to reveal the paralysis at the heart of life in Dublin. What are the sources of paralysis in "The Boarding House"? What social forces combine to entrap Bob Doran?

2. Examine the scenic structure of "The Boarding House." Notice that the first third or so of the story is devoted to exposition or summarized action. The dramatized scenes begin with the paragraph that starts, "It was a bright Sunday morning of early summer. . . ." From this point on, the narrative is focalized through, successively, Mrs. Mooney, Bob Doran, and Polly Mooney. What ironies are involved in this divided perspective?

3. Mrs. Mooney's boarding house is described throughout the story in terms that suggest a house of prostitution. Trace these references.

4. How would you characterize the narrator's *tone* in "The Boarding House"? Note especially such expressions as Mrs. Mooney "dealt with moral problems as a cleaver deals with meat." Is Bob Doran's sad story being presented tragically or as a dark, sardonic comedy?

Virginia Woolf

Virginia Woolf (1882–1941) was born in London, the daughter of Sir Leslie Stephen, a distinguished man of letters, and Julia Pattle Stephen, a famous beauty and literary hostess. After the death of their parents, Virginia and her brothers Thoby and Adrian moved to the London area of Bloomsbury, where they formed the nucleus of the so-called "Bloomsbury Group," a circle of artists and intellectuals that eventually included the biographer Lytton Strachey, the economist J. M. Keynes, the art critic Roger Fry, and the novelist E. M. Forster, among others.

Virginia Stephen married Leonard Woolf, a journalist and political writer, in 1912. The following year, her first novel, *The Voyage Out*, was published. A second novel, *Night and Day*, appeared in 1919. In a collection of stories, *Monday or Tuesday* (1920), Woolf began to experiment with a flowing, subjective style that tried to capture the moment-to-moment consciousness of her characters, a style used in her great novels of the 1920s: *Jacob's Room* (1922), *Mrs. Dalloway* (1925), and *To the Lighthouse* (1927). In addition to her imaginative writing, Woolf was a prolific literary critic and feminist social critic, in such books as *A Room of One's Own* (1929) and *Three Guineas* (1938). Recurringly haunted by clinical depressions throughout her life, Woolf took her own life in 1941.

AN UNWRITTEN NOVEL

Such an expression of unhappiness was enough by itself to make one's eyes slide above the paper's edge to the poor woman's face—insignificant without that look, almost a symbol of human destiny with it. Life's what you see in people's eyes; life's what they learn, and, having learnt it, never, though they seek to hide it, cease to be aware of—what? That life's like that, it seems. Five faces opposite—five mature faces—and the knowledge in each face. Strange, though, how people want to conceal it! Marks of reticence are on all those faces: lips shut, eyes shaded, each one of the five doing something to hide or stultify his knowledge. One smokes; another reads; a third checks entries in a pocket book; a fourth stares at the map of the line framed opposite; and the fifth—the terrible thing about the fifth is that she does nothing at all. She looks at life. Ah, but my poor, unfortunate woman, do play the game—do, for all our sakes, conceal it!

As if she heard me, she looked up, shifted slightly in her seat and sighed. She seemed to apologize and at the same time to say to me, "If only you knew!" Then she looked at life again. "But I do know," I answered silently, glancing at the *Times* for manners' sake. "I know the whole business. 'Peace between Germany and the Allied Powers was yesterday officially ushered in at Paris—Signor Nitti, the Italian Prime Minister—a passenger train at Doncaster was in collision with a goods train. . . ' We all know—the *Times* knows—but we pretend we don't." My eyes had once more crept over the paper's rim. She shuddered, twitched her arm queerly to the middle of her back and shook her head. Again I dipped into my great reservoir of life. "Take what you like," I continued, "births, deaths, marriages, Court Circular, the habits of birds, Leonardo da Vinci, the Sandhills murder, high wages and the cost of living—oh, take what you like," I repeated, "it's all in the *Times*!" Again with infinite weariness she moved her head from side to side until, like a top exhausted with spinning, it settled on her neck.

The *Times* was no protection against such sorrow as hers. But other human beings forbade intercourse. The best thing to do against life was to fold the paper so that it made a perfect square, crisp, thick, impervious even to life. This done, I glanced up quickly, armed with a shield of my own. She pierced through my shield; she gazed into my eyes as if searching any sediment of courage at the depths of them and damping it to clay. Her twitch alone denied all hope, discounted all illusion.

So we rattled through Surrey and across the border into Sussex. But with my eyes upon life I did not see that the other travellers had left, one by one, till, save for the man who read, we were alone together. Here was Three Bridges station. We drew slowly down the platform and stopped. Was he going to leave us? I prayed both ways—I prayed last that he might stay. At that instant he roused himself, crumpled his paper contemptuously, like a thing done with, burst open the door, and left us alone.

The unhappy woman, leaning a little forward, palely and colourlessly addressed me—talked of stations and holidays, of brothers at Eastbourne, and the time of year, which was, I forget now, early or late. But at last looking from the window and seeing, I knew, only life, she breathed, "Staying away—that's the drawback of it—" Ah, now we approached the catastrophe. "My sister-in-law"—the bitterness of her tone was like lemon on cold steel, and speaking, not to me, but to herself, she muttered, "nonsense, she would say—that's what they all say," and while she spoke she fidgeted as though the skin on her back were as a plucked fowl's in a poulterer's shop-window.

"Oh, that cow!" she broke off nervously, as though the great wooden cow in the meadow had shocked her and saved her from some indiscretion. Then she shuddered, and then she made the awkward angular movement that I had seen before, as if, after the spasm, some spot between the shoulders burnt or itched. Then again she looked the most unhappy woman in the world, and I once more reproached her, though not with the same conviction, for if there were a reason, if I knew the reason, the stigma was removed from life.

"Sisters-in-law," I said—

Her lips pursed as if to spit venom at the word; pursed they remained. All she did was to take her glove and rub hard at a spot on the window-pane. She rubbed as if she would rub something out for ever—some stain, some indelible contamination. Indeed, the spot remained for all her rubbing, and back she sank with the shudder and the clutch of the arm I had come to expect. Something impelled me to take my glove and rub my window. There, too, was a little speck on the glass. For all my rubbing it remained. And then the spasm went through me; I crooked my arm and plucked at the middle of my back. My skin, too, felt like the damp chicken's skin in the poulterer's shop-window; one spot between the shoulders itched and irritated, felt clammy, felt raw. Could I reach it? Surreptitiously I tried. She saw me. A smile of infinite irony, infinite sorrow, flitted and faded from her face. But she had communicated, shared her secret, passed her poison; she would speak no more. Leaning back in my corner, shielding my eyes from her eyes, seeing only the slopes and hollows, greys and purples, of the winter's landscape, I read her message, deciphered her secret, reading it beneath her gaze.

Hilda's the sister-in-law. Hilda? Hilda? Hilda Marsh—Hilda the blooming, the full bosomed, the matronly. Hilda stands at the door as the cab draws up, holding a coin. "Poor Minnie, more of a grasshopper than ever—old cloak she had last year. Well, well, with two children these days one can't do more. No, Minnie, I've got it; here you are, cabby—none of your ways with me. Come in, Minnie. Oh, I could carry *you*, let alone your basket!" So they go into the dining-room. "Aunt Minnie, children."

Slowly the knives and forks sink from the upright. Down they get (Bob and Barbara), hold out hands stiffly; back again to their chairs, staring between the resumed mouthfuls. [But this we'll skip; ornaments, curtains, trefoil china plate, yellow oblongs of cheese, white squares of biscuit—skip, oh, but wait! Halfway through luncheon one of those shivers; Bob stares at her, spoon in mouth. "Get on with your pudding, Bob"; but Hilda disapproves. "Why *should* she twitch?" Skip, skip, till we reach the landing on the upper floor; stairs brass-bound; linoleum worn; oh, yes! little bedroom looking out over the roofs of Eastbourne— zigzagging roofs like the spines of caterpillars, this way, that way, striped red and yellow, with blue-black slating.] Now, Minnie, the door's shut; Hilda heavily descends to the basement; you unstrap the straps of your basket, lay on the bed a meagre nightgown, stand side by side furred felt slippers. The looking-glass—no, you avoid the looking-glass. Some methodical disposition of hat-pins. Perhaps the shell box has something in it? You shake it; it's the pearl stud there was last year—that's all. And then the sniff, the sigh, the sitting by the window. Three o'clock on a December afternoon; the rain drizzling! one light low in the skylight of a drapery emporium; another high in a servant's bedroom—this one goes out. That gives her nothing to look at. A moment's blankness—then, what are you thinking? (Let me peep across at her opposite; she's asleep or pretending it; so what would she think about sitting at the window at three o'clock in the afternoon? Health, money, hills, her God?) Yes, sitting on the very edge of the chair looking over the roofs of Eastbourne, Minnie Marsh prays to God. That's all very well; and she may rub the pane too, as though to see God better; but what God does she see? Who's the God of Minnie Marsh, the God of the back streets of Eastbourne, the God of three o'clock in the afternoon? I, too, see roofs, I see sky; but, oh, dear—this seeing of Gods! More like President Kruger than Prince Albert—that's the best I can do for him; and I see him on a chair, in a black frock-coat, not so very high up either; I can manage a cloud or two for him to sit on; and then his hand trailing in the cloud holds a rod, a truncheon is it?—black, thick, thorned—a brutal old bully—Minnie's God! Did he send the itch and the patch and the twitch? Is that why she prays? What she rubs on the window is the stain of sin. Oh, she committed some crime!

I have my choice of crimes. The woods flit and fly—in summer there are bluebells; in the opening there, when spring comes, primroses. A parting, was it, twenty years ago? Vows broken? Not Minnie's! . . . She was faithful. How she nursed her mother! All her savings on the tombstone—wreaths under glass— daffodils in jars. But I'm off the track. A crime. . . . They would say she kept her sorrow, suppressed her secret—her sex, they'd say—the scientific people. But what flummery to saddle *her* with sex! No—more like this. Passing down the streets of Croydon twenty years ago, the violet loops of ribbon in the draper's window spangled in the electric light catch her eye. She lingers—past six. Still by running she can reach home. She pushed through the glass wing door. It's sale-time. Shallow trays brim with ribbons. She pauses, pulls this, fingers that with the raised roses on it—no need to choose, no need to buy, and each tray with its surprises. "We don't shut till seven," and it *is* seven. She runs, she rushes, home she reaches, but too late. Neighbours—the doctor—baby brother—the kettle—scalded—hospital—dead—or only the shock of it, the blame? Ah, but the detail matters nothing! It's what she carries with her; the spot, the crime, the thing to expiate, always there between her shoulders. "Yes," she seems to nod to me, "it's the thing I did."

Whether you did, or what you did, I don't mind; it's not the thing I want. The draper's window looped with violet—that'll do; a little cheap perhaps, a little commonplace—since one has a choice of crimes, but then so many (let me peep across again—still sleeping, or pretending sleep! white, worn, the mouth closed—a touch of obstinacy, more than one would think—no hint of sex)—so many crimes aren't *your* crime; your crime was cheap, only the retribution solemn; for now the church door opens, the hard wooden pew receives her; on the brown tiles she kneels; every day, winter, summer, dusk, dawn (here she's at it) prays. All her sins fall, fall, for ever fall. The spot receives them. It's raised, it's red, it's burning. Next she twitches. Small boys point. "Bob at lunch today"—But elderly women are the worst.

Indeed now you can't sit praying any longer. Kruger's sunk beneath the clouds—washed over as with a painter's brush of liquid grey, to which he adds a tinge of black—even the tip of the truncheon gone now. That's what always happens! Just as you've seen him, felt him, someone interrupts. It's Hilda now.

How you hate her! She'll even lock the bathroom door overnight, too, though it's only cold water you want, and sometimes when the night's been bad it seems as if washing helped. And John at breakfast—the children—meals are worst, and sometimes there are friends—ferns don't altogether hide 'em—they guess, too; so out you go along the front, where the waves are grey, and the papers blow, and the glass shelters green and draughty, and the chairs cost tuppence—too much—for there must be preachers along the sands. Ah, that's a nigger—that's a funny man—that's a man with parakeets—poor little creatures! Is there no one here who thinks of God?—just up there, over the pier, with his rod—but no—there's nothing but grey in the sky or if it's blue the white clouds hide him, and the music—it's military music—and what they are fishing for? Do they catch them? How the children stare! Well, then home a back way—"Home a back way!" The words have meaning; might have been spoken by the old man with whiskers—no, no, he didn't really speak; but everything has meaning—placards leaning against doorways—names above shop-windows—red fruit in baskets—women's heads in the hairdresser's—all say "Minnie Marsh!" But here's a jerk. "Eggs are cheaper!" That's what always happens! I was heading her over the waterfall, straight for madness, when, like a flock of dream sheep, she turns t'other way and runs between my fingers. Eggs are cheaper. Tethered to the shores of the world, none of the crimes, sorrows, rhapsodies, or insanities for poor Minnie Marsh; never late for luncheon; never caught in a storm without a mackintosh; never utterly unconscious of the cheapness of eggs. So she reaches home—scrapes her boots.

Have I read you right? But the human face—the human face at the top of the fullest sheet of print holds more, withholds more. Now, eyes open, she looks out; and in the human eye—how d'you define it?—there's a break—a division—so that when you've grasped the stem the butterfly's off—the moth that hangs in the evening over the yellow flower—move, raise your hand, off, high, away. I won't raise my hand. Hang still, then, quiver, life, soul, spirit, whatever you are of Minnie Marsh—I, too, on my flower—the hawk over the down—alone, or what were the worth of life? To rise; hang still in the evening, in the midday; hang still over the down. The flicker of a hand—off, up! then poised again. Alone, unseen; seeing all so still down there, all so lovely. None seeing, none caring. The eyes of others our prisons; their thoughts our cages. Air above, air below. And the moon and immortality. . . . Oh, but I drop to the turf! Are you down too, you in the corner, what's your name—woman—Minnie Marsh; some such name as that? There she is, tight to her blossom; opening her hand-bag, from which she takes a hollow shell—an egg—who was saying that eggs were cheaper? You or I? Oh, it was you who said it on the way home, you remember, when the old gentleman, suddenly opening his umbrella—or sneezing was it? Anyhow, Kruger went, and you came "home a back way," and scraped your boots. Yes. And now you lay across your knees a pocket-handkerchief into which drop little angular fragments of egg-shell—fragments of a map—a puzzle. I wish I could piece them together! If you would only sit still. She's moved her knees—the map's in bits again. Down the slopes of the Andes the white blocks of marble go bounding and hurtling, crushing to death a whole troop of Spanish muleteers, with their convoy—Drake's booty, gold and silver. But to return—

To what, to where? She opened the door, and, putting her umbrella in the stand—that goes without saying; so, too, the whiff of beef from the basement; dot, dot, dot. But what I cannot thus eliminate, what I must, head down, eyes shut, with the courage of a battalion and the blindness of a bull, charge and disperse are, indubitably, the figures behind the ferns, commercial travellers. There, I've hidden them all this time in the hope that somehow they'd disappear, or better still emerge, as indeed they must, if the story's to go on gathering richness and rotundity, destiny and tragedy, as stories should, rolling along with it two, if not three, commercial travellers and a whole grove of aspidistra. "The fronds of the aspidistra only partly concealed the commercial traveller—" Rhododendrons would conceal him utterly, and into the bargain give me my fling of red and white, for which I starve and strive; but rhododendrons in Eastbourne—in December—on the Marshes' table—no, no, I dare not; it's all a matter of crusts and cruets, frills and ferns. Perhaps there'll be a moment later by the sea. Moreover, I feel, pleasantly pricking through the green fretwork and over the glacis of cut glass, a desire to peer and peep at the man opposite—one's as much as I can manage. James Moggridge is it, whom the Marshes call Jimmy? [Minnie, you must promise not to twitch till I've got this straight.] James Moggridge travels in—shall we say buttons?—but the time's not come for bringing *them* in—the big and the little on the long cards, some peacock-eyed, others dull gold; cairngorms some, and others coral sprays—but I say the time's not come. He travels, and on Thursdays, his Eastbourne day, takes his meals with the Marshes. His red face, his little steady eyes—by no means altogether commonplace—his enormous appetite (that's safe; he won't look at Minnie till the bread's swamped the gravy dry), napkin tucked diamond-wise—but this is primitive, and, whatever it may do the reader, don't take me in. Let's dodge to the Moggridge household, set that in motion. Well, the family boots are mended on Sundays by James himself. He reads *Truth*. But his passion? Roses—and his wife a retired hospital nurse—interesting—for God's sake let me have one woman with a name I like! But no; she's of the unborn children of the mind, illicit, none the less loved, like my rhododendrons. How many die in every novel that's written—the best, the dearest, while Moggridge lives. It's life's fault. Here's Minnie eating her egg at the moment opposite and at t'other end of the line—are we past Lewes?—there must be Jimmy—what's her twitch for?

There must be Moggridge—life's fault. Life imposes her laws; life blocks the way; life's behind the fern; life's the tyrant; oh, but not the bully! No, for I assure you I come willingly; I come wooed by Heaven knows what compulsion across ferns and cruets, table splashed and bottles smeared. I come irresistibly to lodge myself somewhere on the firm flesh, in the robust spine, wherever I can penetrate or find foothold on the person, in the soul, of Moggridge the man. The enormous stability of the fabric; the spine tough as whalebone, straight as oaktree; the ribs radiating branches; the flesh taut tarpaulin; the red hollows; the suck and regurgitation of the heart; while from above meat falls in brown cubes and beer gushes to be churned to blood again—and so we reach the eyes. Behind the aspidistra they see something: black, white, dismal; now the plate again; behind the aspidistra they see elderly woman; "Marsh's sister, Hilda's more my sort"; the tablecloth now. "Marsh would know what's wrong with Morrises . . ." talk that over; cheese has come; the plate again; turn it round—the enormous fingers; now the woman opposite. "Marsh's sister—not a bit like Marsh; wretched, elderly female. . . . You should feed your hens. . . . God's truth, what's set her twitching? Not what *I* said? Dear, dear, dear! these elderly women. Dear, dear!"

[Yes, Minnie; I know you've twitched, but one moment—James Moggridge.]

"Dear, dear, dear!" How beautiful the sound is! like the knock of a mallet on seasoned timber, like the throb of the heart of an ancient whaler when the seas press thick and the green is clouded. "Dear, dear!" what a passing bell for the souls of the fretful to soothe them and solace them, lap them in linen, saying, "So long. Good luck to you!" and then, "What's your pleasure?" for though Moggridge would pluck his rose for her, that's done, that's over. Now what's the next thing? "Madam, you'll miss your train," for they don't linger.

That's the man's way; that's the sound that reverberates; that's St. Paul's and the motor-omnibuses. But we're brushing the crumbs off. Oh, Moggridge, you won't stay? You must be off? Are you driving through Eastbourne this afternoon in one of those little carriages? Are you the man who's walled in green cardboard boxes, and sometimes sits so solemn staring like a sphinx; and always there's a look of the sepulchral, something of the undertaker, the coffin, and the dusk about horse and driver? Do tell me—but the doors slammed. We shall never meet again. Moggridge, farewell!

Yes, yes, I'm coming. Right up to the top of the house. One moment I'll linger. How the mud goes round in the mind—what a swirl these monsters leave, the waters rocking, the weeds waving and green here, black there, striking to the sand, till by degrees the atoms reassemble, the deposit sifts itself, and again through the eyes one sees clear and still, and there comes to the lips some prayer for the departed, some obsequy for the souls of those one nods to, the people one never meets again.

James Moggridge is dead now, gone for ever. Well, Minnie—"I can face it no longer." If she said that—(Let me look at her. She is brushing the eggshell into deep declivities). She said it certainly, leaning against the wall of the bedroom, and plucking at the little balls which edge the claret-coloured curtain. But when the self speaks to the self, who is speaking?—the entombed soul, the spirit driven in, in, into the central catacomb; the self that took the veil and left the world—a coward perhaps, yet somehow beautiful, as it flits with its lantern restlessly up and down the dark corridors. "I can bear it no longer," her spirit says. "That man at lunch—Hilda—the children." Oh, heavens, her sob! It's the spirit wailing its destiny, the spirit driven hither, thither, lodging on the diminishing carpets—meagre footholds—shrunken shreds of all the vanishing universe—love, life, faith, husband, children, I know not what splendours and pageantries glimpsed in girlhood. "Not for me—not for me."

But then—the muffins, the bald elderly dog? Bead mats I should fancy and the consolation of underlinen. If Minnie Marsh were run over and taken to hospital, nurses and doctors themselves would exclaim. . . . There's the vista and the vision—there's the distance—the blue blot at the end of the avenue, while, after all, the tea is rich, the muffin hot, and the dog—"Benny, to your basket, sir, and see what mother's brought you!" So, taking the glove with the worn thumb, defying once more the encroaching demon of what's called going in holes, you renew the fortifications, threading the grey wool, running it in and out.

Running it in and out, across and over, spinning a web through which God himself—hush, don't think of God! How firm the stitches are! You must be proud of your darning. Let nothing disturb her. Let the light fall gently, and the clouds show an inner vest of the first green leaf. Let the sparrow perch on the twig and shake the raindrop hanging to the twig's elbow. . . . Why look up? Was it a sound, a thought? Oh, heavens! Back again to the thing you did, the plate glass with the violet loops? But Hilda will come. Ignominies, humiliations, oh! Close the breach.

Having mended her glove, Minnie Marsh lays it in the drawer. She shuts the drawer with decision. I catch sight of her face in the glass. Lips are pursed. Chin held high. Next she laces her shoes. Then she touches her throat. What's your brooch? Mistletoe or merrythought? And what is happening? Unless I'm much mistaken, the pulse's quickened, the moment's coming, the threads are racing, Niagara's ahead. Here's the crisis! Heaven be with you! Down she goes. Courage, courage! Face it, be it! For God's sake don't wait on the mat now! There's the door! I'm on your side. Speak! Confront her, confound her soul!

"Oh, I beg your pardon! Yes, this is Eastbourne. I'll reach it down for you. Let me try the handle." [But Minnie, though we keep up pretences, I've read you right—I'm with you now.]

"That's all your luggage?"

"Much obliged, I'm sure."

(But why do you look about you? Hilda won't come to the station, nor John; and Moggridge is driving at the far side of Eastbourne.)

"I'll wait by my bag, ma'am, that's safest. He said he'd meet me. . . . Oh, there he is! That's my son."

So they walk off together.

Well, but I'm confounded. . . . Surely, Minnie, you know better! A strange young man. . . . Stop! I'll tell him—Minnie!—Miss Marsh!—I don't know though. There's something queer in her cloak as it blows. Oh, but it's untrue, it's indecent. . . . Look how he bends as they reach the gateway. She finds her ticket. What's the joke? Off they go, down the road, side by side. . . . Well, my world's done for! What do I stand on? What do I know? That's not Minnie. There never was Moggridge. Who am I? Life's bare as bone.

And yet the last look of them—he stepping from the kerb and she following him round the edge of the big building brims me with wonder—floods me anew. Mysterious figures! Mother and son. Who are you? Why do you walk down the street? Where tonight will you sleep, and then, tomorrow? Oh, how it whirls and surges—floats me afresh! I start after them. People drive this way and that. The white light splutters and pours. Plate-glass windows. Carnations; chrysanthemums. Ivy in dark gardens. Milk carts at the door. Wherever I go, mysterious figures, I see you, turning the corner, mothers and sons; you, you, you. I hasten, I follow. This, I fancy, must be the sea. Grey is the landscape; dim as ashes; the water murmurs and moves. If I fall on my knees, if I go through the ritual, the ancient antics, it's you, unknown figures, you I adore; if I open my arms, it's you I embrace, you I draw to me—adorable world!

QUESTIONS FOR DISCUSSION AND WRITING

1. "An Unwritten Novel" is a reverie or daydream by a woman sitting in a train compartment watching a fellow passenger. What actually goes on in the compartment that inspires the narrator's "unwritten novel"?

2. The narrator's imaginary history of her fellow traveler reveals nothing accurate about the traveler but a great deal about herself. What are her preoccupations?

3. A basic conflict in Woolf's work is between the fragmentation of everyday life and a transcendental unity that lies behind the surface of life, a unity we can apprehend in pure "moments of being." Identify passages in "An Unwritten Novel" in which this conflict is apparent.

4. Woolf's friend the novelist E. M. Forster noted her reordering of the values of fiction: "She does not tell a story or weave a plot—can she create character?" If not plot or character, what do you find interesting or rewarding (if anything) about "An Unwritten Novel"?

D. H. Lawrence

D. H. Lawrence (1885–1930)—the initials stand for David Herbert—was born in Eastwood in the middle of the Nottinghamshire coal-mining country. His father was a miner, his mother a cultivated ex-schoolteacher who felt that she had married beneath her. Their conflicts are recorded in *Sons and Lovers* and other of their son's works. Lawrence studied to become a schoolteacher at University College, Nottingham, and briefly taught at a school in South London. His first novel, *The White Peacock,* appeared in 1911.

In 1912, he fell in love with Frieda van Richthofen Weekley, the wife of one of his professors at Nottingham. The two moved to the continent; they returned to England and married in 1914. Lawrence's passionate, conflicted relationship with Frieda was to form the veiled theme of much of his fiction, a theme expressed in *Women in Love* as the school inspector Birkin's ideal of "star equilibrium": "not meeting and mingling, but an equilibrium, a pure balance of two single beings:—as the stars balance each other." Of his more than sixty-five books, among the most notable are the novels *Sons and Lovers* (1913), *The Rainbow* (1916), and *Women in Love* (1921) and his five collections of short stories. Lawrence died of tuberculosis in 1930, at the age of forty-four.

THE HORSE DEALER'S DAUGHTER

"Well, Mabel, and what are you going to do with yourself?" asked Joe, with foolish flippancy. He felt quite safe himself. Without listening for an answer, he turned aside, worked a grain of tobacco to the tip of his tongue, and spat it out. He did not care about anything, since he felt safe himself.

The three brothers and the sister sat round the desolate breakfast-table, attempting some sort of desultory consultation. The morning's post had given the final tap to the family fortunes, and all was over. The dreary dining-room itself, with its heavy mahogany furniture, looked as if it were waiting to be done away with.

But the consultation amounted to nothing. There was a strange air of ineffectuality about the three men, as they sprawled at table, smoking and reflecting vaguely on their own condition. The girl was alone, a rather short, sullen-looking young woman of twenty-seven. She did not share the same life as her brothers. She would have been good-looking, save for the impassive fixity of her face, "bulldog," as her brothers called it.

There was a confused tramping of horses' feet outside. The three men all sprawled round in their chairs to watch. Beyond the dark holly bushes that separated the strip of lawn from the high-road, they could see a cavalcade of shire horses swinging out of their own yard, being taken for exercise. This was the last time. These were the last horses that would go through their hands. The young men watched with critical, callous look. They were all frightened at the collapse of their lives, and the sense of disaster in which they were involved left them no inner freedom.

Yet they were three fine, well-set fellows enough. Joe, the eldest, was a man of thirty-three, broad and handsome in a hot, flushed way. His face was red, he twisted his black moustache over a thick finger, his eyes were shallow and restless. He had a sensual way of uncovering his teeth when he laughed, and his bearing was stupid. Now he watched the horses with a glazed look of helplessness in his eyes, a certain stupor of downfall.

The great draught-horses swung past. They were tied head to tail, four of them, and they heaved along to where a lane branched off from the high-road, planting their great hoofs floutingly in the fine black mud, swinging their great rounded haunches sumptuously, and trotting a few sudden steps as they were led into the lane, round the corner. Every movement showed a massive, slumbrous strength, and a stupidity which held them in subjection. The groom at the head looked back, jerking the leading rope. And the cavalcade moved out of sight up the lane, the tail of the last horse, bobbed up tight and stiff, held out taut from the swinging great haunches as they rocked behind the hedges in motion-like sleep.

Joe watched with glazed hopeless eyes. The horses were almost like his own body to him. He felt he was done for now. Luckily he was engaged to a woman as old as himself, and therefore her father, who was steward of a neighbouring estate, would provide him with a job. He would marry and go into harness. His life was over, he would be a subject animal now.

He turned uneasily aside, the retreating steps of the horses echoing in his ears. Then, with foolish restlessness, he reached for the scraps of bacon-rind from the plates, and making a faint whistling sound, flung them to the terrier that lay against the fender. He watched the dog swallow them, and waited till the creature looked into his eyes. Then a faint grin came on his face, and in a high, foolish voice he said:

"You won't get much more bacon, shall you, you little b———?"

The dog faintly and dismally wagged its tail, then lowered its haunches, circled round, and lay down again.

There was another helpless silence at the table. Joe sprawled uneasily in his seat, not willing to go till the family conclave was dissolved. Fred Henry, the second brother, was erect, clean-limbed, alert. He had watched the passing of the horses with more *sang-froid*. If he was an animal, like Joe, he was an animal which controls, not one which is controlled. He was master of any horse, and he carried himself with a well-tempered air of mastery. But he was not master of the situations of life. He pushed his coarse brown moustache upwards, off his lip, and glanced irritably at his sister, who sat impassive and inscrutable.

"You'll go and stop with Lucy for a bit, shan't you?" he asked. The girl did not answer.

"I don't see what else you can do," persisted Fred Henry.

"Go as a skivvy," Joe interpolated laconically.

The girl did not move a muscle.

"If I was her, I should go in for training for a nurse," said Malcolm, the youngest of them all. He was the baby of the family, a young man of twenty-two, with a fresh, jaunty *museau*.

But Mabel did not take any notice of him. They had talked at her and round her for so many years, that she hardly heard them at all.

The marble clock on the mantelpiece softly chimed the half-hour, the dog rose uneasily from the hearth-rug and looked at the party at the breakfast-table. But still they sat in an ineffectual conclave.

"Oh, all right," said Joe suddenly, apropos of nothing. "I'll get a move on."

He pushed back his chair, straddled his knees with a downward jerk, to get them free, in horsey fashion, and went to the fire. Still he did not go out of the room; he was curious to know what the others would do or say. He began to charge his pipe, looking down at the dog and saying in a high, affected voice:

"Going wi' me? Going wi' me are ter? Tha'rt goin' further than tha counts on just now, dost hear?"

The dog faintly wagged his tail, the man stuck out his jaw and covered his pipe with his hands, and puffed intently, losing himself in the tobacco, looking down all the while at the dog with an absent brown eye. The dog looked up at him in mournful distrust. Joe stood with his knees stuck out, in real horsey fashion.

"Have you had a letter from Lucy?" Fred Henry asked of his sister.

"Last week," came the neutral reply.

"And what does she say?"

There was no answer.

"Does she *ask* you to go and stop there?" persisted Fred Henry.

"She says I can if I like."

"Well, then, you'd better. Tell her you'll come on Monday."

This was received in silence.

"That's what you'll do then, is it?" said Fred Henry, in some exasperation.

But she made no answer. There was a silence of futility and irritation in the room. Malcolm grinned fatuously.

"You'll have to make up your mind between now and next Wednesday," said Joe loudly, "or else find yourself lodgings on the kerbstone."

The face of the young woman darkened, but she sat on immutable.

"Here's Jack Ferguson!" exclaimed Malcolm, who was looking aimlessly out of the window.

"Where?" exclaimed Joe loudly.

"Just gone past."

"Coming in?"

Malcolm craned his neck to see the gate.

"Yes," he said.

There was a silence. Mabel sat on like one condemned, at the head of the table. Then a whistle was heard from the kitchen. The dog got up and barked sharply. Joe opened the door and shouted:

"Come on."

After a moment a young man entered. He was muffled up in an overcoat and a purple woollen scarf, and his tweed cap, which he did not remove, was pulled down on his head. He was of medium height, his face was rather long and pale, his eyes looked tired.

"Hello, Jack! Well, Jack!" exclaimed Malcolm and Joe. Fred Henry merely said: "Jack."

"What's doing?" asked the newcomer, evidently addressing Fred Henry.

"Same. We've got to be out by Wednesday. Got a cold?"

"I have—got it bad, too."

"Why don't you stop in?"

"*Me* stop in? When I can't stand on my legs, perhaps I shall have a chance." The young man spoke huskily. He had a slight Scotch accent.

"It's a knock-out, isn't it," said Joe, boisterously, "if a doctor goes round croaking with a cold. Looks bad for the patients, doesn't it?"

The young doctor looked at him slowly.

"Anything the matter with *you*, then?" he asked sarcastically.

"Not as I know of. Damn your eyes, I hope not. Why?"

"I thought you were very concerned about the patients, wondered if you might be one yourself."

"Damn it, no, I've never been patient to no flaming doctor, and hope I never shall be," returned Joe.

At this point Mabel rose from the table, and they all seemed to become aware of her existence. She began putting the dishes together. The young doctor looked at her, but did not address her. He had not greeted her. She went out of the room with the tray, her face impassive and unchanged.

"When are you off then, all of you?" asked the doctor.

"I'm catching the eleven-forty," replied Malcolm. "Are you goin' down wi' th' trap, Joe?"

"Yes, I've told you I'm going down wi' th' trap, haven't I?"

"We'd better be getting her in then. So long Jack, if I don't see you before I go," said Malcolm, shaking hands.

He went out, followed by Joe, who seemed to have his tail between his legs.

"Well, this is the devil's own," exclaimed the doctor, when he was left alone with Fred Henry. "Going before Wednesday, are you?"

"That's the orders," replied the other.

"Where, to Northampton?"

"That's it."

"The devil!" exclaimed Ferguson, with quiet chagrin.

And there was silence between the two.

"All settled up, are you?" asked Ferguson.

"About."

There was another pause.

"Well, I shall miss yer, Freddy, boy," said the young doctor.

"And I shall miss thee, Jack," returned the other.

"Miss you like hell," mused the doctor.

Fred Henry turned aside. There was nothing to say. Mabel came in again, to finish clearing the table.

"What are *you* going to do, then, Miss Pervin?" asked Ferguson. "Going to your sister's, are you?"

Mabel looked at him with her steady, dangerous eyes, that always made him uncomfortable, unsettling his superficial ease.

"No," she said.

"Well, what in the name of fortune *are* you going to do? Say what you mean to do," cried Fred Henry, with futile intensity.

But she only averted her head, and continued her work. She folded the white table-cloth, and put on the chenille cloth.

"The sulkiest bitch that ever trod!" muttered her brother.

But she finished her task with perfectly impassive face, the young doctor watching her interestedly all the while. Then she went out.

Fred Henry stared after her, clenching his lips, his blue eyes fixing in sharp antagonism, as he made a grimace of sour exasperation.

"You could bray her into bits, and that's all you'd get out of her," he said, in a small, narrowed tone.

The doctor smiled faintly.

"What's she *going* to do, then?" he asked.

"Strike me if *I* know!" returned the other.

There was a pause. Then the doctor stirred.

"I'll be seeing you tonight, shall I?" he said to his friend.

"Ay—where's it to be? Are we going over to Jessdale?"

"I don't know. I've got such a cold on me. I'll come round to the 'Moon and Stars', anyway."

"Let Lizzie and May miss their night for once, eh?"

"That's it—if I feel as I do now."

"All's one————"

The two young men went through the passage and down to the back door together. The house was large, but it was servantless now, and desolate. At the back was a small brick house-yard and beyond that a big square, graveled fine and red, and having stables on two sides. Sloping, dank, winter-dark fields stretched away on the open sides.

But the stables were empty. Joseph Pervin, the father of the family, had been a man of no education, who had become a fairly large horse dealer. The stables had been full of horses, there was a great turmoil and come-and-go of horses and of dealers and grooms. Then the kitchen was full of servants. But of late things had declined. The old man had married a second time, to retrieve his fortunes. Now he was dead and everything was gone to the dogs, there was nothing but debt and threatening.

For months, Mabel had been servantless in the big house, keeping the home together in penury for her ineffectual brothers. She had kept house for ten years. But previously it was with unstinted means. Then, however brutal and coarse everything was, the sense of money had kept her proud, confident. The men might be foul-mouthed, the women in the kitchen might have bad reputations, her brothers might have illegitimate children. But so long as there was money, the girl felt herself established, and brutally proud, reserved.

No company came to the house, save dealers and coarse men. Mabel had no associates of her own sex, after her sister went away. But she did not mind. She went regularly to church, she attended to her father. And she lived in the memory of her mother, who had died when she was fourteen, and whom she had loved. She had loved her father, too, in a different way, depending upon him, and feeling secure in him, until at the age of fifty-four he married again. And then she had set hard against him. Now he had died and left them all hopelessly in debt.

She had suffered badly during the period of poverty. Nothing, however, could shake the curious, sullen, animal pride that dominated each member of the family. Now, for Mabel, the end had come. Still she would not cast about her. She would follow her own way just the same. She would always hold the keys of her own situation. Mindless and persistent, she endured from day to day. Why should she think? Why should she answer anybody? It was enough that this was the end, and there was no way out. She need not pass any more darkly along the main street of the small town, avoiding every eye. She need not demean herself any more, going into the shops and buying the cheapest food. This was at an end. She thought of nobody, not even of herself. Mindless and persistent, she seemed in a sort of ecstasy to be coming nearer to her fulfillment, her own glorification, approaching her dead mother, who was glorified.

In the afternoon, she took a little bag, with shears and sponge and a small scrubbing-brush, and went out. It was a grey, wintry day, with soddened, dark green fields and an atmosphere blackened by the smoke of foundries not far off. She went quickly, darkly along the causeway, heeding nobody, through the town to the churchyard.

There she always felt secure, as if no one could see her, although as a matter of fact she was exposed to the stare of everyone who passed along under the church-yard wall. Nevertheless, once under the shadow of the great looming church, among the graves, she felt immune from the world, reserved within the thick churchyard wall as in another country.

Carefully she clipped the grass from the grave, and arranged the pinky white, small chrysanthemums in the tin cross. When this was done, she took an empty jar from a neighboring grave, brought water, and carefully, most scrupulously sponged the marble headstone and the coping-stone.

It gave her sincere satisfaction to do this. She felt in immediate contact with the world of her mother. She took minute pains, went through the park in a state bordering on pure happiness, as if in performing this task she came into a subtle, intimate connection with her mother. For the life she followed here in the world was far less real than the world of death she inherited from her mother.

The doctor's house was just by the church. Ferguson, being a mere hired assistant, was slave to the country-side. As he hurried now to attend to the out-patients in the surgery, glancing across the graveyard with his quick eye, he saw the girl at her task at the grave. She seemed so intent and remote, it was like looking into another world. Some mystical element was touched in him. He slowed down as he walked, watching her as if spellbound.

She lifted her eyes, feeling him looking. Their eyes met. And each looked away again at once, each feeling, in some way, found out by the other. He lifted his cap and passed on down the road. There remained distinct in his consciousness, like a vision, the memory of her face, lifted from the tombstone in the churchyard, and looking at him with slow, large, portentous eyes. It *was* portentous, her face. It seemed to mesmerize him. There was a heavy power in her eyes which laid hold of his whole being, as if he had drunk some powerful drug. He had been feeling weak and done before. Now the life came back into him, he felt delivered from his own fretted, daily self.

He finished his duties at the surgery as quickly as might be, hastily filling up the bottles of the waiting people with cheap drugs. Then, in perpetual haste, he set off again to visit several cases in another part of his round, before tea-time. At all times he preferred to walk if he could, but particularly when he was not well. He fancied the motion restored him.

The afternoon was falling. It was grey, deadened, and wintry, with a slow, moist, heavy coldness sinking in and deadening all the faculties. But why should he think or notice? He hastily climbed the hill and turned across the dark green fields, following the black cindertrack. In the distance, across a shallow dip in the country, the small town was clustered like smouldering ash, a tower, a spire, a heap of low, raw, extinct houses. And on the nearest fringe of the town, sloping into the dip, was Oldmeadow, the Pervins' house. He could see the stables and the out-buildings distinctly, as they lay towards him on the slope. Well, he would not go there many more times! Another resource would be lost to him, another place gone: the only company he cared for in the alien, ugly little town he was losing. Nothing but work, drudgery, constant hastening from dwelling to dwelling among the colliers and the iron-workers. It wore him out, but at the same time he had a craving for it. It was a stimulant to him to be in the homes of the working people, moving, as it were, through the innermost body of their life. His nerves were excited and gratified. He could come so near, into the very lives of the rough, inarticulate, powerfully emotional men and women. He grumbled, he said he hated the hellish hole. But as a matter of fact it excited him, the contact with the rough, strongly-feeling people was a stimulant applied direct to his nerves.

Below Oldmeadow, in the green, shallow, soddened hollow of fields, lay a square, deep pond. Roving across the landscape, the doctor's quick eye detected a figure in black passing through the gate of the field, down towards the pond. He looked again. It would be Mabel Pervin. His mind suddenly became alive and attentive.

Why was she going down there? He pulled up on the path on the slope above, and stood staring. He could just make sure of the small black figure moving in the hollow of the failing day. He seemed to see her in the midst of such obscurity, that he was like a clairvoyant, seeing rather with the mind's eye than with ordinary sight. Yet he could see her positively enough, whilst he kept his eye attentive. He felt, if he looked away from her, in the thick, ugly falling dusk, he would lose her altogether.

He followed her minutely as she moved, direct and intent, like something transmitted rather than stirring in voluntary activity, straight down the field towards the pond. There she stood on the bank for a moment. She never raised her head. Then she waded slowly into the water.

He stood motionless as the small black figure walked slowly and deliberately towards the center of the pond, very slowly, gradually moving deeper into the motionless water, and still moving forward as the water got up to her breast. Then he could see her no more in the dusk of the dead afternoon.

"There!" he exclaimed. "Would you believe it?"

And he hastened straight down, running over the wet, soddened fields, pushing through the hedges, down into the depression of callous wintry obscurity. It took him several minutes to come to the pond. He stood on the bank, breathing heavily. He could see nothing. His eyes seemed to penetrate the dead water. Yes, perhaps that was the dark shadow of her black clothing beneath the surface of the water.

He slowly ventured into the pond. The bottom was deep, soft clay, he sank in, and the water clasped dead cold round his legs. As he stirred he could smell the cold, rotten clay that fouled up into the water. It was objectionable in his lungs. Still, repelled and yet not heeding, he moved deeper into the pond. The cold water rose over his thighs, over his loins, upon his abdomen. The lower part of his body was all sunk in the hideous cold element. And the bottom was so deeply soft and uncertain, he was afraid of pitching with his mouth underneath. He could not swim, and was afraid.

He crouched a little, spreading his hands under the water and moving them round, trying to feel for her. The dead cold pond swayed upon his chest. He moved again, a little deeper, and again, with his hands underneath, he felt all around under the water. And he touched her clothing. But it evaded his fingers. He made a desperate effort to grasp it.

And so doing he lost his balance and went under, horribly, suffocating in the foul earthy water, struggling madly for a few moments. At last, after what seemed an eternity, he got his footing, rose again into the air and looked around. He gasped, and knew he was in the world. Then he looked at the water. She had risen near him. He grasped her clothing, and drawing her nearer, turned to take his way to land again.

He went very slowly, carefully, absorbed in the slow progress. He rose higher, climbing out of the pond. The water was now only about his legs; he was thankful, full of relief to be out of the clutches of the pond. He lifted her and staggered onto the bank, out of the horror of wet, grey clay.

He laid her down on the bank. She was quite unconscious and running with water. He made the water come from her mouth, he worked to restore her. He did not have to work very long before he could feel the breathing begin again in her; she was breathing naturally. He worked a little longer. He could feel her live beneath his hands; she was coming back. He wiped her face, wrapped her in his overcoat, looked round into the dim, dark grey world, then lifted her and staggered down the bank and across the fields.

It seemed an unthinkably long way, and his burden so heavy he felt he would never get to the house. But at last he was in the stableyard, and then in the house-yard. He opened the door and went into the house. In the kitchen he laid her down on the hearth-rug and called. The house was empty. But the fire was burning in the grate.

Then again he kneeled to attend to her. She was breathing regularly, her eyes were wide open and as if conscious, but there seemed something missing in her look. She was conscious in herself, but unconscious of her surroundings.

He ran upstairs, took blankets from a bed, and put them before the fire to warm. Then he removed her saturated, earthy-smelling clothing, rubbed her dry with a towel, and wrapped her naked in the blankets. Then he went into the dining-room, to look for spirits. There was a little whiskey. He drank a gulp himself, and put some into her mouth.

The effect was instantaneous. She looked full into his face, as if she had been seeing him for some time, and yet had only just become conscious of him.

"Dr. Ferguson?" she said.

"What?" he answered.

He was divesting himself of his coat, intending to find some dry clothing upstairs. He could not bear the smell of the dead, clayey water, and he was mortally afraid for his own health.

"What did I do?" she asked.

"Walked into the pond," he replied. He had begun to shudder like one sick, and could hardly attend to her. Her eyes remained full on him, he seemed to be going dark in his mind, looking back at her helplessly. The shuddering became quieter in him, his life came back to him, dark and unknowing, but strong again.

"Was I out of my mind?" she asked, while her eyes were fixed on him all the time.

"Maybe, for the moment," he replied. He felt quiet, because his strength had come back. The strange fretful strain had left him.

"Am I out of my mind now?" she asked.

"Are you?" he reflected a moment. "No," he answered truthfully. "I don't see that you are." He turned his face aside. He was afraid now, because he felt dazed, and felt dimly that her power was stronger than his, in this issue. And she continued to look at him fixedly all the time. "Can you tell me where I shall find some dry things to put on?" he asked.

"Did you dive into the pond for me?" she asked.

"No," he answered. "I walked in. But I went in over head as well."

There was silence for a moment. He hesitated. He very much wanted to go upstairs to get into dry clothing. But there was another desire in him. And she seemed to hold him. His will seemed to have gone to sleep, and left him, standing there slack before her. But he felt warm inside himself. He did not shudder at all, though his clothes were sodden on him.

"Why did you?" she asked.

"Because I didn't want you to do such a foolish thing," he said.

"It wasn't foolish," she said, still gazing at him as she lay on the floor, with a sofa cushion under her head. "It was the right thing to do. *I* knew best, then."

"I'll go and shift these wet things," he said. But still he had not the power to move out of her presence, until she sent him. It was as if she had the life of his body in her hands, and he could not extricate himself. Or perhaps he did not want to.

Suddenly she sat up. Then she became aware of her own immediate condition.

She felt the blankets about her, she knew her own limbs. For a moment it seemed as if her reason were going. She looked round, with wild eye, as if seeking something. He stood still with fear. She saw her clothing lying scattered.

"Who undressed me?" she asked, her eyes resting full and inevitable on his face.

"I did," he replied, "to bring you round."

For some moments she sat and gazed at him awfully, her lips parted.

"Do you love me, then?" she asked.

He only stood and stared at her, fascinated. His soul seemed to melt.

She shuffled forward on her knees, and put her arms round him, round his legs, as he stood there, pressing her breasts against his knees and thighs, clutching him with strange, convulsive certainty, pressing his thighs against her, drawing him to her face, her throat, as she looked up at him with flaring, humble eyes of transfiguration, triumphant in first possession.

"You love me," she murmured, in strange transport, yearning and triumphant and confident. "You love me. I know you love me, I know."

And she was passionately kissing his knees, through the wet clothing, passionately and indiscriminately kissing his knees, his legs, as if unaware of everything.

He looked down at the tangled wet hair, the wild, bare, animal shoulders. He was amazed, bewildered, and afraid. He had never thought of loving her. He had never wanted to love her. When he rescued her and restored her, he was a doctor, and she was a patient. He had had no single personal thought of her. Nay, this introduction of the personal element was very distasteful to him, a violation of his professional honour. It was horrible to have her there embracing his knees. It was horrible. He revolted from it, violently. And yet—and yet—he had not the power to break away.

She looked at him again, with the same supplication of powerful love, and that same transcendent, frightening light of triumph. In view of the delicate flame which seemed to come from her face like a light, he was powerless. And yet he had never intended to love her. He had never intended. And something stubborn in him could not give way.

"You love me," she repeated, in a murmur of deep, rhapsodic assurance. "You love me."

Her hands were drawing him, drawing him down to her. He was afraid, even a little horrified. For he had, really, no intention of loving her. Yet her hands were drawing him towards her. He put out his hand quickly to steady himself, and grasped her bare shoulder. A flame seemed to burn the hand that grasped her soft shoulder. He had no intention of loving her: his whole will was against his yielding. It was horrible. And yet wonderful was the touch of her shoulders, beautiful the shining of her face. Was she perhaps mad? He had a horror of yielding to her. Yet something in him ached also.

He had been staring away at the door, away from her. But his hand remained on her shoulder. She had gone suddenly very still. He looked down at her. Her eyes were now wide with fear, with doubt, the light was dying from her face, a shadow of terrible greyness was returning. He could not bear the touch of her eyes' question upon him, and the look of death behind the question.

With an inward groan he gave way, and let his heart yield towards her. A sudden gentle smile came on his face. And her eyes, which never left his face, slowly, slowly filled with tears. He watched the strange water rise in her eyes, like some slow fountain coming up. And his heart seemed to burn and melt away in his breast.

He could not bear to look at her any more. He dropped on his knees and caught her head with his arms and pressed her face against his throat. She was very still. His heart, which seemed to have broken, was burning with a kind of agony in his breast. And he felt her slow, hot tears wetting his throat. But he could not move.

He felt the hot tears wet his neck and the hollows of his neck, and he remained motionless, suspended through one of man's eternities. Only now it had become indispensable to him to have her face pressed close to him; he could never let her go again. He could never let her head go away from the close clutch of his arm. He wanted to remain like that for ever, with his heart hurting him in a pain that was also life to him. Without knowing, he was looking down on her damp, soft brown hair.

Then, as it were suddenly, he smelt the horrid stagnant smell of that water. And at the same moment she drew away from him and looked at him. Her eyes were wistful and unfathomable. He was afraid of them, and he fell to kissing her, not knowing what he was doing. He wanted her eyes not to have that terrible, wistful, unfathomable look.

When she turned her face to him again, a faint delicate flush was flowing, and there was again dawning that terrible shining of joy in her eyes, which really terrified him, and yet which he now wanted to see, because he feared the look of doubt still more.

"You love me?" she said, rather faltering.

"Yes." The word cost him a painful effort. Not because it wasn't true. But because it was too newly true, the *saying* seemed to tear open again his newly-torn heart. And he hardly wanted it to be true, even now.

She lifted her face to him, and he bent forward and kissed her on the mouth, gently, with the one kiss that is an eternal pledge. And as he kissed her his heart strained again in his breast. He never intended to love her. But now it was over. He had crossed over the gulf to her, and all that he had left behind had shrivelled and become void.

After the kiss, her eyes again slowly filled with tears. She sat still, away from him, with her face drooped aside, and her hands folded in her lap. The tears fell very slowly. There was complete silence. He too sat there motionless and silent on the hearth-rug. The strange pain of his heart that was broken seemed to consume him. That he should love her? That this was love! That he should be ripped open in this way! Him, a doctor! How they would all jeer if they knew! It was agony to him to think they might know.

In the curious naked pain of the thought he looked again to her. She was sitting there drooped into a muse. He saw a tear fall, and his heart flared hot. He saw for the first time that one of her shoulders was quite uncovered, one arm bare, he could see one of her small breasts; dimly, because it had become almost dark in the room.

"Why are you crying?" he asked, in an altered voice.

She looked up at him, and behind her tears the consciousness of her situation for the first time brought a dark look of shame to her eyes.

"I'm not crying, really," she said, watching him, half frightened.

He reached his hand, and softly closed it on her bare arm.

"I love you! I love you!" he said in a soft, low vibrating voice, unlike himself.

She shrank and dropped her head. The soft, penetrating grip of his hand on her arm distressed her. She looked up at him.

"I want to go," she said. "I want to go and get you some dry things."

"Why?" he said. "I'm all right."

"But I want to go," she said. "And I want you to change your things."

He released her arm, and she wrapped herself in the blanket, looking at him rather frightened. And still she did not rise.

"Kiss me," she said wistfully.

He kissed her, but briefly, half in anger.

Then, after a second, she rose nervously, all mixed up in the blanket. He watched her in her confusion as she tried to extricate herself and wrap herself up so that she could walk. He watched her relentlessly, as she knew. And as she went, the blanket trailing, and as he saw a glimpse of her feet and her white leg, he tried to remember her as she was when he had wrapped her in the blanket. But then he didn't want to remember, because she had been nothing to him then, and his nature revolted from remembering her as she was when she was nothing to him.

A tumbling, muffled noise from within the dark house startled him. Then he heard her voice: "There are clothes." He rose and went to the foot of the stairs, and gathered up the garments she had thrown down. Then he came back to the fire, to rub himself down and dress. He grinned at his own appearance when he had finished.

The fire was sinking, so he put on coal. The house was now quite dark, save for the light of a street-lamp that shone in faintly from beyond the holly trees. He lit the gas with matches he found on the mantelpiece. Then he emptied the pockets of his own clothes, and threw all his wet things in a heap into the scullery. After which he gathered up her sodden clothes, gently, and put them in a separate heap on the copper-top in the scullery.

It was six o'clock on the clock. His own watch had stopped. He ought to go back to the surgery. He waited, and still she did not come down. So he went to the foot of the stairs and called:

"I shall have to go."

Almost immediately he heard her coming down. She had on her best dress of black voile, and her hair was tidy, but still damp. She looked at him—and in spite of herself, smiled.

"I don't like you in those clothes," she said.

"Do I look a sight?" he answered.

They were shy of one another.

"I'll make you some tea," she said.

"No, I must go."

"Must you?" And she looked at him again with the wide, strained, doubtful eyes. And again, from the pain of his breast, he knew how he loved her. He went and bent to kiss her, gently, passionately, with his heart's painful kiss.

"And my hair smells so horrible," she murmured in distraction. "And I'm so awful, I'm so awful! Oh no, I'm too awful." And she broke into bitter, heart-broken sobbing. "You can't want to love me, I'm horrible."

"Don't be silly, don't be silly," he said, trying to comfort her, kissing her, holding her in his arms. "I want you, I want to marry you, we're going to be married, quickly, quickly—to-morrow if I can."

But she only sobbed terribly, and cried:

"I feel awful. I feel awful. I feel I'm horrible to you."

"No, I want you, I want you," was all he answered, blindly, with that terrible intonation which frightened her almost more than her horror lest he should *not* want her.

QUESTIONS FOR DISCUSSION AND WRITING

1. The third-person narrator of "The Horse Dealer's Daughter" adopts several points of view in succession. Trace them and discuss their effect.

2. The horses are described in some detail as they are led off. Why the emphasis? Are they used as symbols?

3. We are told that Ferguson, "being a mere hired assistant, was slave to the country-side." Mabel and her brothers were also represented as enslaved in various ways. Discuss the motifs of slavery and freedom in the story.

4. The experience of Mabel and Jack in the pond is clearly symbolic. Examine the imagery of the pond in detail; what does it symbolize?

William Faulkner

William Faulkner (1897–1962) grew up in Oxford, Mississippi. A high-school dropout, he held a series of jobs as a young man, including a three-year stint as postmaster of the University of Mississippi post office. His first novels were *Soldiers' Pay* (1926) and *Mosquitoes* (1927). *Sartoris* and *The Sound and the Fury* (both 1929) inaugurated the Yoknapatawpha cycle, a series of interrelated novels and stories that told the history of the imaginary Yoknapatawpha County, Mississippi. The principal novels in the cycle are, besides *Sartoris* and *The Sound and the Fury, As I Lay Dying* (1930), *Sanctuary* (1931), *Light in August* (1932), *Absalom, Absalom!* (1936), *The Unvanquished* (1938), *The Wild Palms* (1939), *The Hamlet* (1940), and *Go Down, Moses* (1942). *The Town* (1957) and *The Mansion* (1959) complete the "Snopes trilogy" begun with *The Hamlet,* a trio of novels about the rise of a vulgar, unscrupulous family, a story also told in short stories such as "Barn Burning." Faulkner won the Nobel Prize for literature in 1949.

BARN BURNING

The store in which the Justice of the Peace's court was sitting smelled of cheese. The boy, crouched on his nail keg at the back of the crowded room, knew he smelled cheese, and more: from where he sat he could see the ranked shelves close-packed with the solid, squat, dynamic shapes of tin cans whose labels his stomach read, not from the lettering which meant nothing to his mind but from the scarlet devils and the silver curve of fish—this, the cheese which he knew he smelled and the hermetic meat which his intestines believed he smelled coming in intermittent gusts momentary and brief between the other constant one, the smell and sense just a little of fear because mostly of despair and grief, the old fierce pull of blood. He could not see the table where the Justice sat and before which his father and his father's enemy (*our enemy* he thought in that despair: *ourn! mine and hisn both! He's my father!*) stood, but he could hear them, the two of them that is, because his father had said no word yet:

"But what proof have you, Mr. Harris?"

"I told you. The hog got into my corn. I caught it up and sent it back to him. He had no fence that would hold it. I told him so, warned him. The next time I put the hog in my pen. When he came to get it I gave him enough wire to patch up his pen. The next time I put the hog up and kept it. I rode down to his house and saw the wire I gave him still rolled onto the spool in his yard. I told him he could have the hog when he paid me a dollar pound fee. That evening a nigger came with the dollar and got the hog. He was a strange nigger. He said, 'He say to tell you wood and hay kin burn.' I said, 'What?' 'That whut he say to tell you,' the nigger said. 'Wood and hay kin burn.' That night my barn burned. I got the stock out but I lost the barn."

"Where is the nigger? Have you got him?"

"He was a strange nigger, I tell you. I don't know what became of him."

"But that's not proof. Don't you see that's not proof?"

"Get that boy up here. He knows." For a moment the boy thought too that the man meant his older brother until Harris said, "Not him. The little one. The boy," and, crouching, small for his age, small and wiry like his father, in patched and faded jeans even too small for him, with straight, uncombed, brown hair and eyes gray and wild as storm scud, he saw the men between himself and the table part and become a lane of grim faces, at the end of which he saw the Justice, a shabby, collarless, graying man in spectacles, beckoning him. He felt no floor under his bare feet; he seemed to walk beneath the palpable weight of the grim turning faces. His father, stiff in his black Sunday coat donned not for the trial but for the moving, did not even look at him. *He aims for me to lie,* he thought, again with that frantic grief, and despair. *And I will have to do hit.*

"What's your name, boy?" the Justice said.

"Colonel Sartoris Snopes," the boy whispered.

"Hey?" the Justice said. "Talk louder. Colonel Sartoris? I reckon anybody named for Colonel Sartoris in this country can't help but tell the truth, can they?" The boy said nothing. *Enemy! Enemy!* he thought; for a moment he could not even see, could not see that the Justice's face was kindly nor discern that his voice was troubled when he spoke to the man named Harris: "Do you want me to question this boy?" But he could hear, and during those subsequent long seconds while there was absolutely no sound in the crowded little room save that of quiet and intent breathing it was as if he had swung outward at the end of a grape vine, over a ravine, and at the top of the swing had been caught in a prolonged instant of mesmerized gravity, weightless in time.

"No!" Harris said violently, explosively. "Damnation! Send him out of here!" Now time, the fluid world, rushed beneath him again, the voices coming to him again through the smell of cheese and sealed meat, the fear and despair and the old grief of blood:

"This case is closed. I can't find against you, Snopes, but I can give you advice. Leave this country and don't come back to it."

His father spoke for the first time, his voice cold and harsh, level, without emphasis: "I aim to. I don't figure to stay in a country among people who . . ." he said something unprintable and vile, addressed to no one.

"That'll do," the Justice said. "Take your wagon and get out of this country before dark. Case dismissed."

His father turned, and he followed the stiff black coat, the wiry figure walking a little stiffly from where a Confederate provost's man's musket ball had taken him in the heel on a stolen horse thirty years ago, followed the two backs now, since his older brother had appeared from somewhere in the crowd, no taller than the father but thicker, chewing tobacco steadily, between the two lines of grim-faced men and out of the store and across the worn gallery and down the sagging steps, and among the dogs and half-grown boys in the mild May dust, where as he passed a voice hissed:

"Barn burner!"

Again he could not see, whirling; there was a face in a red haze, moonlike, bigger than the full moon, the owner of it half again his size, he leaping in the red haze toward the face, feeling no blow, feeling no shock when his head struck the earth, scrabbling up and leaping again, feeling no blow this time either and tasting no blood, scrabbling up to see the other boy in full flight and himself already leaping into pursuit as his father's hand jerked him back, the harsh, cold voice speaking above him: "Go get in the wagon."

It stood in a grove of locusts and mulberries across the road. His two hulking sisters in their Sunday dresses and his mother and her sister in calico and sun-bonnets were already in it, sitting on and among the sorry residue of the dozen and more movings which even the boy could remember—the battered stove, the broken beds and chairs, the clock inlaid with mother-of-pearl, which would not run, stopped at some fourteen minutes past two o'clock of a dead and forgotten day and time, which had been his mother's dowry. She was crying, though when she saw him she drew her sleeve across her face and began to descend from the wagon. "Get back," the father said.

"He's hurt. I got to get some water and wash his . . ."

"Get back in the wagon," his father said. He got in too, over the tail-gate. His father mounted to the seat where the older brother already sat and struck the gaunt mules two savage blows with the peeled willow, but without heat. It was not even sadistic; it was exactly that same quality which in later years would cause his descendants to over-run the engine before putting a motor car into motion, striking and reining back in the same movement. The wagon went on, the store with its quiet crowd of grimly watching men dropped behind; a curve in the road hid it. *Forever* he thought. *Maybe he's done satisfied now, now that he has . . .* stopping himself, not to say it aloud even to himself. His mother's hand touched his shoulder.

"Does hit hurt?" she said.

"Naw," he said. "Hit don't hurt. Lemme be."

"Can't you wipe some of the blood off before hit dries?"

"I'll wash to-night," he said. "Lemme be, I tell you."

The wagon went on. He did not know where they were going. None of them ever did or ever asked, because it was always somewhere, always a house of sorts waiting for them a day or two days or even three days away. Likely his father had already arranged to make a crop on another farm before he . . . Again he had to stop himself. He (the father) always did. There was something about his wolflike independence and even courage when the advantage was at least neutral which impressed strangers, as if they got from his latent ravening ferocity not so much a sense of dependability as a feeling that his ferocious conviction in the rightness of his own actions would be of advantage of all whose interest lay with his.

That night they camped, in a grove of oaks and beeches where a spring ran. The nights were still cool and they had a fire against it, of a rail lifted from a nearby fence and cut into lengths—a small fire, neat, niggard almost, a shrewd fire; such fires were his father's habit and custom always, even in freezing weather. Older, the boy might have remarked this and wondered why not a big one; why should not a man who had not only seen the waste and extravagance of war, but who had in his blood an inherent voracious prodigality with material not his own, have burned everything in sight? Then he might have gone a step farther and thought that that was the reason: that niggard blaze was the living fruit of nights passed during those four years in the woods hiding from all men, blue or gray, with his strings of horses (captured horses, he called them). And older still, he might have divined the true reason: that the element of fire spoke to some deep mainspring of his father's being, as the element of steel or of powder spoke to other men, as the one weapon for the preservation of integrity, else breath were not worth the breathing, and hence to be regarded with respect and used with discretion.

But he did not think this now and he had seen those same niggard blazes all his life. He merely ate his supper beside it and was already half asleep over his iron plate when his father called him, and once more he followed the stiff back, the stiff and ruthless limp, up the slope and onto the starlit road where, turning, he could see his father against the stars but without face or depth—a shape black, flat, and bloodless as though cut from tin in the iron folds of the frockcoat which had not been made for him, the voice harsh like tin and without heat like tin:

"You were fixing to tell them. You would have told him." He didn't answer. His father struck him with the flat of his hand on the side of the head, hard but without heat, exactly as he had struck the two mules at the store, exactly as he would strike either of them with any stick in order to kill a horse fly, his voice still without heat or anger: "You're getting to be a man. You got to learn. You got to learn to stick to your own blood or you ain't going to have any blood to stick to you. Do you think either of them, any man there this morning, would? Don't you know all they wanted was a chance to get at me because they knew I had them beat? Eh?" Later, twenty years later, he was to tell himself, "If I had said they wanted only truth, justice, he would have hit me again." But now he said nothing. He was not crying. He just stood there. "Answer me," his father said.

"Yes," he whispered. His father turned.

"Get on to bed. We'll be there to-morrow."

To-morrow they were there. In the early afternoon the wagon stopped before a paintless two-room house identical almost with the dozen others it had stopped before even in the boy's ten years, and again, as on the other dozen occasions, his mother and aunt got down and began to unload the wagon, although his two sisters and his father and brother had not moved.

"Likely hit ain't fitten for hawgs," one of the sisters said.

"Nevertheless, fit it will and you'll hog it and like it," his father said. "Get out of them chairs and help your Ma unload."

The two sisters got down, big, bovine, in a flutter of cheap ribbons; one of them drew from the jumbled wagon bed a battered lantern, the other a worn broom. His father handed the reins to the older son and began to climb stiffly over the wheel. "When they get unloaded, take the team to the barn and feed them." Then he said, and at first the boy thought he was still speaking to his brother: "Come with me."

"Me?" he said.

"Yes," his father said. "You."

"Abner," his mother said. His father paused and looked back—the harsh level stare beneath the shaggy, graying, irascible brows.

"I reckon I'll have a word with the man that aims to begin tomorrow owning me body and soul for the next eight months."

They went back up the road. A week ago—or before last night, that is—he would have asked where they were going, but not now. His father had struck him before last night but never before had he paused afterward to explain why; it was as if the blow and the following calm, outrageous voice still rang, repercussed, divulging nothing to him save the terrible handicap of being young, the light weight of his few years, just heavy enough to prevent his soaring free of the world as it seemed to be ordered but not heavy enough to keep him footed solid in it, to resist it and try to change the course of its events.

Presently he could see the grove of oaks and cedars and the other flowering trees and shrubs where the house would be, though not the house yet. They walked beside a fence massed with honeysuckle and Cherokee roses and came to a gate swinging open between two brick pillars, and now, beyond a sweep of drive, he saw the house for the first time and at that instant he forgot his father and the terror and despair both, and even when he remembered his father again (who had not stopped) the terror and despair did not return. Because, for all the twelve movings, they had sojourned until now in a poor country, a land of small farms and fields and houses, and he had never seen a house like this before. *Hit's big as a courthouse* he thought quietly, with a surge of peace and joy whose reason he could not have thought into words, being too young for that: *They are safe from him. People whose lives are a part of this peace and dignity are beyond his touch, he no more to them than a buzzing wasp: capable of stinging for a little moment but that's all; the spell of this peace and dignity rendering even the barns and stable and cribs which belong to it impervious to the puny flames he might contrive* . . . this, the peace and joy, ebbing for an instant as he looked again at the stiff black back, the stiff and implacable limp of the figure which was not dwarfed by the house, for the reason that it had never looked big anywhere and which now, against the serene columned backdrop, had more than ever that impervious quality of something cut ruthlessly from tin, depthless, as though, sidewise to the sun, it would cast no shadow. Watching him, the boy remarked the absolutely undeviating course which his father held and saw the stiff foot come squarely down in a pile of fresh droppings where a horse had stood in the drive and which his father could have avoided by a simple change of stride. But it ebbed only for a moment, though he could not have thought this into words either, walking on in the spell of the house, which he could even want but without envy, without sorrow, certainly never with that ravening and jealous rage which unknown to him walked in the ironlike black coat before him: *Maybe he will feel it too. Maybe it will even change him now from what maybe he couldn't help but be.*

They crossed the portico. Now he could hear his father's stiff foot as it came down on the boards with clocklike finality, a sound out of all proportion to the displacement of the body it bore and which was not dwarfed either by the white door before it, as though it had attained to a sort of vicious and ravening minimum not to be dwarfed by anything—the flat, wide, black hat, the former coat of broadcloth which had once been black but which had now that friction-glazed greenish cast of the bodies of old house flies, the lifted sleeve which was too large, the lifted hand like a curled claw. The door opened so promptly that the boy knew the Negro must have been watching them all the time, an old man with neat grizzled hair, in a linen jacket, who stood barring the door with his body, saying, "Wipe yo foots, white man, fo you come in here. Major ain't home nohow."

"Get out of my way, nigger," his father said, without heat too, flinging the door back and the Negro also and entering, his hat still on his head. And now the boy saw the prints of the stiff foot on the doorjamb and saw them appear on the pale rug behind the machinelike deliberation of the foot which seemed to bear (or transmit) twice the weight which the body compassed. The Negro was shouting "Miss Lula! Miss Lula!" somewhere behind them, then the boy, deluged as though by a warm wave by a suave turn of carpeted stair and a pendant glitter of chandeliers and a mute gleam of gold frames, heard the swift feet and saw her too, a lady—perhaps he had never seen her like before either—in a gray, smooth gown with lace at the throat and an apron tied at the waist and the sleeves turned back, wiping cake or biscuit dough from her hands with a towel as she came up the hall, looking not at his father at all but at the tracks on the blond rug with an expression of incredulous amazement.

"I tried," the Negro cried. "I tole him to . . ."

"Will you please go away?" she said in a shaking voice. "Major de Spain is not at home. Will you please go away?"

His father had not spoken again. He did not speak again. He did not even look at her. He just stood stiff in the center of the rug, in his hat, the shaggy iron-gray brows twitching slightly above the pebble-colored eyes as he appeared to examine the house with brief deliberation. Then with the same deliberation he turned; the boy watched him pivot on the good leg and saw the stiff foot drag round the arc of the turning, leaving a final long and fading smear. His father never looked at it, he never once looked down at the rug. The Negro held the door. It closed behind them, upon the hysteric and indistinguishable woman-wail. His father stopped at the top of the steps and scraped his boot clean on the edge of it. At the gate he stopped again. He stood for a moment, planted stiffly on the stiff foot, looking back at the house. "Pretty and white, ain't it?" he said. "That's sweat. Nigger sweat. Maybe it ain't white enough yet to suit him. Maybe he wants to mix some white sweat with it."

Two hours later the boy was chopping wood behind the house within which his mother and aunt and the two sisters (the mother and aunt, not the two girls, he knew that; even at this distance and muffled by walls the flat loud voices of the two girls emanated an incorrigible idle inertia) were setting up the stove to prepare a meal, when he heard the hooves and saw the linen-clad man on a fine sorrel mare, whom he recognized even before he saw the rolled rug in front of the Negro youth following on a fat bay carriage horse—a suffused, angry face vanishing, still at full gallop, beyond the corner of the house where his father and brother were sitting in the two tilted chairs; and a moment later, almost before he could have put the axe down, he heard the hooves again and watched the sorrel mare go back out of the yard, already galloping again. Then his father began to shout one of the sisters' names, who presently emerged backward from the kitchen door dragging the rolled rug along the ground by one end while the other sister walked behind it.

"If you ain't going to tote, go on and set up the wash pot," the first said.

"You, Sarty!" the second shouted. "Set up the wash pot!" His father appeared at the door, framed against that shabbiness, as he had been against that other bland perfection, impervious to either, the mother's anxious face at his shoulder.

"Go on," the father said, "Pick it up." The two sisters stooped, broad, lethargic; stooping, they presented an incredible expanse of pale cloth and a flutter of tawdry ribbons.

"If I thought enough of a rug to have to git hit all the way from France I wouldn't keep hit where folks coming in would have to tromp on hit," the first said. They raised the rug.

"Abner," the mother said. "Let me do it."

"You go back and git dinner," his father said. "I'll tend to this."

From the woodpile through the rest of the afternoon the boy watched them, the rug spread flat in the dust beside the bubbling wash-pot, the two sisters stooping over it with that profound and lethargic reluctance, while the father stood over them in turn, implacable and grim, driving them though never raising his voice again. He could smell the harsh homemade lye they were using; he saw his mother come to the door once and look toward them with an expression not anxious now but very like despair; he saw his father turn, and he fell to with the axe and saw from the corner of his eye his father raise from the ground a flattish fragment of field stone and examine it and return to the pot, and this time his mother actually spoke: "Abner. Abner. Please don't. Please, Abner."

Then he was done too. It was dusk; the whippoorwills had already begun. He could smell coffee from the room where they would presently eat the cold food remaining from the mid-afternoon meal, though when he entered the house he realized they were having coffee again probably because there was a fire on the hearth, before which the rug now lay spread over the backs of the two chairs. The tracks of his father's foot were gone. Where they had been were now long, water-cloudy scoriations resembling the sporadic course of a lilliputian mowing machine.

It still hung there while they ate the cold food and then went to bed, scattered without order or claim up and down the two rooms, his mother in one bed, where his father would later lie, the older brother in the other, himself, the aunt, and the two sisters on pallets on the floor. But his father was not in bed yet. The last thing the boy remembered was the depthless, harsh silhouette of the hat and coat bending over the rug and it seemed to him that he had not even closed his eyes when the silhouette was standing over him, the fire almost dead behind it, the stiff foot prodding him awake. "Catch up the mule," his father said.

When he returned with the mule his father was standing in the black door, the rolled rug over his shoulder. "Ain't you going to ride?" he said.

"No. Give me your foot."

He bent his knee into his father's hand, the wiry, surprising power flowed smoothly, rising, he rising with it, on to the mule's bare back (they had owned a saddle once; the boy could remember it though not when or where) and with the same effortlessness his father swung the rug up in front of him. Now in the starlight they retraced the afternoon's path, up the dusty road rife with honey-suckle, through the gate and up the black tunnel of the drive to the lightless house, where he sat on the mule and felt the rough warp of the rug drag across his thighs and vanish.

"Don't you want me to help?" he whispered. His father did not answer and now he heard again that stiff foot striking the hollow portico with that wooden and clocklike deliberation, that outrageous overstatement of the weight it carried. The rug, hunched, not flung (the boy could tell that even in the darkness) from his father's shoulder struck the angle of wall and floor with a sound unbelievably loud, thunderous, then the foot again, unhurried and enormous; a light came on in the house and the boy sat, tense, breathing steadily and quietly and just a little fast, though the foot itself did not increase its beat at all, descending the steps now; now the boy could see him.

"Don't you want to ride now?" he whispered. "We kin both ride now," the light within the house altering now, flaring up and sinking. *He's coming down the stairs now,* he thought. He had already ridden the mule up beside the horse block; presently his father was up behind him and he doubled the reins over and slashed the mule across the neck, but before the animal could begin to trot the hard, thin arm came round him, the hard, knotted hand jerking the mule back to a walk.

In the first red rays of the sun they were in the lot, putting plow gear on the mules. This time the sorrel mare was in the lot before he heard it at all, the rider collarless and even bareheaded, trembling, speaking in a shaking voice as the woman in the house had done. His father merely looking up once before stooping again to the hame he was buckling, so that the man on the mare spoke to his stooping back:

"You must realize you have ruined that rug. Wasn't there anybody here, any of your women . . ." he ceased, shaking, the boy watching, the older brother leaning now in the stable door, chewing, blinking slowly and steadily at nothing appar-ently. "It cost a hundred dollars. But you never had a hundred dollars. You never will. So I'm going to charge you twenty bushels of corn against your crop. I'll add it in your contract and when you come to the commissary you can sign it. That won't keep Mrs. de Spain quiet but maybe it will teach you to wipe your feet off before you enter her house again."

Then he was gone. The boy looked at his father who still had not spoken or even looked up again, who was now adjusting the loggerhead in the hame.

"Pap," he said. His father looked at him—the inscrutable face, the shaggy brows beneath which the gray eyes glinted coldly. Suddenly the boy went toward him, fast, stopping as suddenly. "You done the best you could!" he cried. "If he wanted hit done different why didn't he wait and tell you how? He won't git no twenty bushels! He won't git none! We'll gether hit and hide hit! I kin watch . . ."

"Did you put the cutter back in that straight stock like I told you?"

"No, sir," he said.

"Then go do it."

That was Wednesday. During the rest of that week he worked steadily, at what was within his scope and some which was beyond it, with an industry that did not need to be driven nor even commanded twice; he had this from his mother, with the difference that some at least of what he did he liked to do, such as splitting wood with the half-size axe which his mother and aunt had it earned, or saved money somehow, to present him with at Christmas. In company with the two older women (and on one afternoon, even one of the sisters), he built pens for the shoat and the cow which were a part of his father's contract with the landlord, and one afternoon, his father being absent, gone somewhere on one of the mules, he went to the field.

They were running a middle buster now, his brother holding the plow straight while he handled the reins, and walking beside the straining mule, the rich black soil shearing cool and damp against her bare ankles, he thought *Maybe this is the end of it. Maybe even that twenty bushels that seems hard to have to pay for just a rug will be a cheap price for him to stop forever and always from being what he used to be;* thinking, dreaming now, so that his brother had to speak sharply to him to mind the mule: *Maybe he even won't collect the twenty bushels. Maybe it will all add up and balance and vanish—corn, rug, fire; the terror and grief, the being pulled two ways like between two teams of horses—gone, done with for ever and ever.*

Then it was Saturday; he looked up from beneath the mule he was harnessing and saw his father in the black coat and hat. "Not that," his father said. "The wagon gear." And then, two hours later, sitting in the wagon bed behind his father and brother on the seat, the wagon accomplished a final curve, and he saw the weathered paintless store with its tattered tobacco- and patent-medicine posters and the tethered wagons and saddle animals below the gallery. He mounted the gnawed steps behind his father and brother, and there again was the lane of quiet, watching faces for the three of them to walk through. He saw the man in spectacles sitting at the plank table and he did not need to be told this was a Justice of the Peace; he sent one glare of fierce, exultant, partisan defiance at the man in collar and cravat now, whom he had seen but twice before in his life, and that on a galloping horse, who now wore on his face an expression not of rage but of amazed unbelief which the boy could not have known was at the incredible circumstance of being sued by one of his own tenants, and came and stood against his father and cried at the Justice: "He ain't done it! He ain't burnt . . ."

"Go back to the wagon," his father said.

"Burnt?" the Justice said. "Do I understand this rug was burned too?"

"Does anybody here claim it was?" his father said. "Go back to the wagon." But he did not, he merely retreated to the rear of the room, crowded as that other had been, but not to sit down this time, instead, to stand pressing among the motionless bodies, listening to the voices:

"And you claim twenty bushels of corn is too high for the damage you did to the rug?"

"He brought the rug to me and said he wanted the tracks washed out of it. I washed the tracks out and took the rug back to him."

"But you didn't carry the rug back to him in the same condition it was in before you made the tracks on it."

His father did not answer, and now for perhaps half a minute there was no sound at all save that of breathing, the faint, steady suspiration of complete and intent listening.

"You decline to answer that, Mr. Snopes?"Again his father did not answer. "I'm going to find against you, Mr. Snopes. I'm going to find that you were responsible for the injury to Major de Spain's rug and hold you liable for it. But twenty bushels of corn seems a little high for a man in your circumstances to have to pay. Major de Spain claims it cost a hundred dollars. October corn will be worth about fifty cents. I figure that if Major de Spain can stand a ninety-five dollar loss on something he paid cash for, you can stand a five-dollar loss you haven't earned yet. I hold you in damages to Major de Spain to the amount of ten bushels of corn over and above your contract with him to be paid to him out of your crop at gathering time. Court adjourned."

It had taken no time hardly, the morning was but half begun. He thought they would return home and perhaps back to the field, since they were late, far behind all other farmers. But instead his father passed on behind the wagon, merely indicating with his hand for the older brother to follow with it, and crossed the road toward the blacksmith shop opposite, pressing on after his father, overtaking him, speaking, whispering up at the harsh, calm face beneath the weathered hat: "He won't git no ten bushels neither. He won't git one. We'll . . ." until his father glanced for an instant down at him, the face absolutely calm, the grizzled eyebrows tangled above the cold eyes, the voice almost pleasant, almost gentle:

"You think so? Well, we'll wait till October anyway."

The matter of the wagon—the setting of a spoke or two and the tightening of the tires—did not take long either, the business of the tires accomplished by driving the wagon into the spring branch behind the shop and letting it stand there, the mules nuzzling into the water from time to time, and the boy on the seat with the idle reins, looking up the slope and through the sooty tunnel of the shed where the slow hammer rang and where his father sat on an upended cypress bolt, easily, either talking or listening, still sitting there when the boy brought the dripping wagon up out of the branch and halted it before the door.

"Take them on to the shade and hitch," his father said. He did so and returned. His father and the smith and a third man squatting on his heels inside the door were talking, about crops and animals; the boy, squatting too in the ammoniac dust and hoof-parings and scales of rust, heard his father tell a long and unhurried story out of the time before the birth of the older brother even when he had been a professional horsetrader. And then his father came up beside him where he stood before a tattered last year's circus poster on the other side of the store, gazing rapt and quiet at the scarlet horses, the incredible poisings and convolutions of tulle and tights and the painted leers of comedians, and said, "It's time to eat."

But not at home. Squatting beside his brother against the front wall, he watched his father emerge from the store and produce from a paper sack a segment of cheese and divide it carefully and deliberately into three with his pocket knife and produce crackers from the same sack. They all three squatted on the gallery and ate, slowly, without talking; then in the store again, they drank from a tin dipper tepid water smelling of the cedar bucket and of living beech trees. And still they did not go home. It was a horse lot this time, a tall rail fence upon and along which men stood and sat and out of which one by one horses were led, to be walked and trotted and then cantered back and forth along the road while the slow swapping and buying went on and the sun began to slant westward, they—the three of them—watching and listening, the older brother with his muddy eyes and his steady, inevitable tobacco, the father commenting now and then on certain of the animals, to no one in particular.

It was after sundown when they reached home. They ate supper by lamplight, then, sitting on the doorstep, the boy watched the night fully accomplish, listening to the whippoorwills and the frogs, when he heard his mother's voice: "Abner! No! No! Oh, God. Oh, God. Abner!" and he rose, whirled, and saw the altered light through the door where a candle stub now burned in a bottle neck on the table and his father, still in the hat and coat, at once formal and burlesque as though dressed carefully for some shabby and ceremonial violence, emptying the reservoir of the lamp back into the five-gallon kerosene can from which it had been filled, while the mother tugged at his arm until he shifted the lamp to the other hand and flung her back, not savagely or viciously, just hard, into the wall, her hands flung out against the wall for balance, her mouth open and in her face the same quality of hopeless despair as had been in her voice. Then his father saw him standing in the door.

"Go to the barn and get that can of oil we were oiling the wagon with," he said. The boy did not move. Then he could speak.

"What . . ." he cried. "What are you . . ."

"Go get that oil," his father said. "Go."

Then he was moving, running, outside the house, toward the stable: this the old habit, the old blood which he had not been permitted to choose for himself, which had been bequeathed him willy nilly and which had run for so long (and who knew where, battening on what of outrage and savagery and lust) before it came to him. *I could keep on,* he thought. *I could run on and on and never look back, never need to see his face again. Only I can't. I can't,* the rusted can in his hand now, the liquid sploshing in it as he ran back to the house and into it, into the sound of his mother's weeping in the next room, and handed the can to his father.

"Ain't you going to even send a nigger?" he cried. "At least you sent a nigger before!"

This time his father didn't strike him. The hand came even faster than the blow had, the same hand which had set the can on the table with almost excruciating care flashing from the can toward him too quick for him to follow it, gripping him by the back of his shirt and on to tiptoe before he had seen it quit the can, the face stooping at him in breathless and frozen ferocity, the cold, dead voice speaking over him to the older brother who leaned against the table, chewing with that steady, curious, sidewise motion of cows:

"Empty the can into the big one and go on. I'll catch up with you."

"Better tie him up to the bedpost," the brother said.

"Do like I told you," the father said. Then the boy was moving, his bunched shirt and the hard, bony hand between his shoulder-blades, his toes just touching the floor, across the room and into the other one, past the sisters sitting with spread heavy thighs in the two chairs over the cold hearth, and to where his mother and aunt sat side by side on the bed, the aunt's arms about his mother's shoulders.

"Hold him," the father said. The aunt made a startled movement. "Not you," the father said. "Lennie. Take hold of him. I want to see you do it." His mother took him by the wrist. "You'll hold him better than that. If he gets loose don't you know what he is going to do? He will go up yonder." He jerked his head toward the road. "Maybe I'd better tie him."

"I'll hold him," his mother whispered.

"See you do then." Then his father was gone, the stiff foot heavy and measured upon the boards, ceasing at last.

Then he began to struggle. His mother caught him in both arms, he jerking and wrenching at them. He would be stronger in the end, he knew that. But he had no time to wait for it. "Lemme go!" he cried. "I don't want to have to hit you!"

"Let him go!" the aunt said. "If he don't go, before God, I am going up there myself!"

"Don't you see I can't?" his mother cried. "Sarty! Sarty! No! No! Help me, Lizzie!"

Then he was free. His aunt grasped at him but it was too late. He whirled, running, his mother stumbled forward on to her knees behind him, crying to the nearer sister: "Catch him, Net! Catch him!" But that was too late too, the sister (the sisters were twins, born at the same time, yet either of them now gave the impression of being, encompassing as much living meat and volume and weight as any other two of the family) not yet having begun to rise from the chair, her head, face, alone merely turned, presenting to him in the flying instant an astonishing expanse of young female features untroubled by any surprise even, wearing only an expression of bovine interest. Then he was out of the room, out of the house, in the mild dust of the starlit road and the heavy rifeness of honeysuckle, the pale ribbon unspooling with terrific slowness under his running feet, reaching the gate at last and turning in, running, his heart and lungs drumming, on up the drive toward the lighted house, the lighted door. He did not knock, he burst in, sobbing for breath, incapable for the moment of speech; he saw the astonished face of the Negro in the linen jacket without knowing when the Negro had appeared.

"De Spain!" he cried, panted. "Where's . . ." then he saw the white man too emerging from a white door down the hall. "Barn!" he cried. "Barn!"

"What?" the white man said. "Barn?"

"Yes!" the boy cried. "Barn!"

"Catch him!" the white man shouted.

But it was too late this time too. The Negro grasped his shirt, but the entire sleeve, rotten with washing, carried away, and he was out that door too and in the drive again, and had actually never ceased to run even while he was screaming into the white man's face.

Behind him the white man was shouting, "My horse! Fetch my horse!" and he thought for an instant of cutting across the park and climbing the fence into the road, but he did not know the park nor how high the vine-massed fence might be and he dared not risk it. So he ran on down the drive, blood and breath roaring; presently he was in the road again though he could not see it. He could not hear either: the galloping mare was almost upon him before he heard her, and even then he held his course, as if the very urgency of his wild grief and need must in a moment more find him wings, waiting until the ultimate instant to hurl himself aside and into the weed-choked roadside ditch as the horse thundered past and on, for an instant in furious silhouette against the stars, the tranquil early summer night sky which, even before the shape of the horse and rider vanished, stained abruptly and violently upward: a long, swirling roar incredible and soundless, blotting the stars, and he springing up and into the road again, running again, knowing it was too late yet still running even after he heard the shot and, an instant later, two shots, pausing now without knowing he had ceased to run, crying

"Pap! Pap!", running again before he knew he had begun to run, stumbling, tripping over something and scrabbling up again without ceasing to run, looking backward over his shoulder at the glare as he got up, running on among the invisible trees, panting, sobbing, "Father! Father!"

At midnight he was sitting on the crest of a hill. He did not know it was midnight and he did not know how far he had come. But there was no glare behind him now and he sat now, his back toward what he had called home for four days anyhow, his face toward the dark woods which he would enter when breath was strong again, small, shaking steadily in the chill darkness, hugging himself into the remainder of his thin, rotten shirt, the grief and despair now no longer terror and fear but just grief and despair. *Father. My father,* he thought. "He was brave!" He cried suddenly, aloud but not loud, no more than a whisper: "He was! He was in the war! He was in Colonel Sartoris' cav'ry!" not knowing that his father had gone to that war a private in the fine old European sense, wearing no uniform, admitting the authority of and giving fidelity to no man or army or flag, going to war as Malbrouck himself did: for booty—it meant nothing and less than nothing to him if it were enemy booty or his own.

The slow constellations wheeled on. It would be dawn and then sun-up after a while and he would be hungry. But that would be to-morrow and now he was only cold, and walking would cure that. His breathing was easier now and he decided to get up and go on, and then he found that he had been asleep because he knew it was almost dawn, the night almost over. He could tell that from the whippoorwills. They were everywhere now among the dark trees below him, constant and inflectioned and ceaseless, so that, as the instant for giving over to the day birds drew nearer and nearer, there was no interval at all between them. He got up. He was a little stiff, but walking would cure that too as it would the cold, and soon there would be the sun. He went on down the hill, toward the dark woods within which the liquid silver voices of the birds called unceasing—the rapid and urgent beating of the urgent and quiring heart of the late spring night. He did not look back.

QUESTIONS FOR DISCUSSION AND WRITING

1. Describe the narrative voice in "Barn Burning." What is its relationship to Sarty Snopes? Notice that when Sarty first sees Major de Spain's house, the narrator gives Sarty's reaction in words that he says Sarty could not have used: *"Hit's big as a courthouse* he thought quietly, with a surge of peace and joy whose reason he could not have thought into words, being too young for that. . . ."

2. What is the conflict in this story? Abner Snopes and Major de Spain seem to represent two codes or sets of values, and Sarty seems to be torn between the two. Define the values on each side and show how they appear in Sarty.

3. What happens at the end of the story? What does Faulkner gain by not making it explicit?

4. When does "Barn Burning" take place? (Notice that Abner had been shot in the Civil War "thirty years ago.") What evidence does the story give of social and economic conditions in the South at this time?

Ernest Hemingway

Ernest Hemingway (1899–1961) grew up in Oak Park, Illinois. When the United States entered World War I, the eighteen-year-old Hemingway joined the ambulance corps; he was almost immediately wounded by shrapnel and was decorated for heroism for carrying to safety a comrade more seriously wounded than he. Back home, he married Hadley Richardson and went with her to live in Paris, where they became part of a circle of American expatriates that included Gertrude Stein, F. Scott Fitzgerald, Sherwood Anderson, and Ezra Pound. Here Hemingway won international acclaim for a series of books: *In Our Time* (1925), a collection of short stories that drew on his boyhood vacation experiences in the Michigan woods; *The Sun Also Rises* (1926), a novel about a "lost generation" of American expatriates in Paris; *Men Without Women* (1927), a second collection of short stories; and *A Farewell to Arms* (1929), a novel about the love of Fredrick Henry, an American officer in World War I, and Katherine Barkely, an English nurse. His successes in the 1920s gave Hemingway celebrity status for the rest of his life. His writing suffered as his life became more public, although he had some later successes, including *For Whom the Bell Tolls* (1940) and *The Old Man and the Sea* (1952). He was awarded the Nobel Prize in 1954. Despondent over health problems, he killed himself at his home in Idaho in 1961.

THE SNOWS OF KILIMANJARO

Kilimanjaro is a snow covered mountain 19,710 feet high, and is said to be the highest mountain in Africa. Its western summit is called the Masai "Ngàje Ngài," the House of God. Close to the western summit there is the dried and frozen carcass of a leopard. No one has explained what the leopard was seeking at that altitude.

"The marvellous thing is that it's painless," he said. "That's how you know when it starts."

"Is it really?"

"Absolutely. I'm awfully sorry about the odor though. That must bother you."

"Don't! Please don't."

"Look at them," he said. "Now is it sight or is it scent that brings them like that?"

The cot the man lay on was in the wide shade of a mimosa tree and as he looked out past the shade onto the glare of the plain there were three of the big birds squatted obscenely, while in the sky a dozen more sailed, making quick-moving shadows as they passed.

"They've been there since the day the truck broke down," he said. "Today's the first time any have lit on the ground. I watched the way they sailed very carefully at first in case I ever wanted to use them in a story. That's funny now."

"I wish you wouldn't," she said.

"I'm only talking," he said. "It's much easier if I talk. But I don't want to bother you."

"You know it doesn't bother me," she said. "It's that I've gotten so very nervous not being able to do anything. I think we might make it as easy as we can until the plane comes."

"Or until the plane doesn't come."

"Please tell me what I can do. There must be something I can do."

252

"You can take the leg off and that might stop it, though I doubt it. Or you can shoot me. You're a good shot now. I taught you to shoot didn't I?"

"Please don't talk that way. Couldn't I read to you?"

"Read what?"

"Anything in the book bag that we haven't read."

"I can't listen to it," he said. "Talking is the easiest. We quarrel and that makes the time pass."

"I don't quarrel. I never want to quarrel. Let's not quarrel any more. No matter how nervous we get. Maybe they will be back with another truck today. Maybe the plane will come."

"I don't want to move," the man said. "There is no sense in moving now except to make it easier for you."

"That's cowardly."

"Can't you let a man die as comfortably as he can without calling him names? What's the use of slanging me?"

"You're not going to die."

"Don't be silly. I'm dying now. Ask those bastards." He looked over to where the huge, filthy birds sat, their naked heads sunk in the hunched feathers. A fourth planed down, to run quick-legged and then waddle slowly toward the others.

"They are around every camp. You never notice them. You can't die if you don't give up."

"Where did you read that? You're such a bloody fool."

"You might think about some one else."

"For Christ's sake," he said, "That's been my trade."

He lay then and was quiet for a while and looked across the heat shimmer of the plain to the edge of the bush. There were a few Tommies that showed minute and white against the yellow and, far off, he saw a herd of zebra, white against the green of the bush. This was a pleasant camp under big trees against a hill, with good water, and close by, a nearly dry water hole where sand grouse flighted in the mornings.

"Wouldn't you like me to read?" she asked. She was sitting on a canvas chair beside his cot. "There's a breeze coming up."

"No thanks."

"Maybe the truck will come."

"I don't give a damn about the truck."

"I do."

"You give a damn about so many things that I don't."

"Not so many, Harry."

"What about a drink?"

"It's supposed to be bad for you. It said in Black's to avoid all alcohol. You shouldn't drink."

"Molo!" he shouted.

"Yes Bwana."

"Bring whiskey-soda."

"Yes Bwana."

"You shouldn't," she said. "That's what I mean by giving up. It says it's bad for you. I know it's bad for you."

"No," he said. "It's good for me."

So now it was all over, he thought. So now he would never have a chance to finish it. So this was the way it ended in a bickering over a drink. Since the gangrene started in his right leg he had no pain and with the pain the horror had gone and all he felt now was a great tiredness and anger that this was the end of it. For this, that now was coming, he had very little curiosity. For years it had obsessed him; but now it meant nothing in itself. It was strange how easy being tired enough made it.

Now he would never write the things that he had saved to write until he knew enough to write them well. Well, he would not have to fail at trying to write them either. Maybe you could never write them, and that was why you put them off and delayed the starting. Well he would never know, now.

"I wish we'd never come," the woman said. She was looking at him holding the glass and biting his lip. "You never would have gotten anything like this in Paris. You always said you loved Paris. We could have stayed in Paris or gone anywhere. I'd have gone anywhere. I said I'd go anywhere you wanted. If you wanted to shoot we could have gone shooting in Hungary and been comfortable."

"Your bloody money," he said.

"That's not fair," she said. "It was always yours as much as mine. I left everything and I went wherever you wanted to go and I've done what you wanted to do. But I wish we'd never come here."

"You said you loved it."

"I did when you were all right. But now I hate it. I don't see why that had to happen to your leg. What have we done to have that happen to us?"

"I suppose what I did was to forget to put iodine on it when I first scratched it. Then I didn't pay any attention to it because I never infect. Then, later, when it got bad, it was probably using that weak carbolic solution when the other antiseptics ran out that paralyzed the minute blood vessels and started the gangrene." He looked at her, "What else?"

"I don't mean that."

"If we would have hired a good mechanic instead of a half baked kikuyu driver, he would have checked the oil and never burned out that bearing in the truck."

"I don't mean that."

"If you hadn't left your own people, your goddamned Old Westbury, Saratoga, Palm Beach people to take me on————"

"Why, I loved you. That's not fair. I love you now. I'll always love you. Don't you love me?"

"No," said the man. "I don't think so. I never have."

"Harry, what are you saying? You're out of your head."

"No. I haven't any head to go out of."

"Don't drink that," she said. "Darling, please don't drink that. We have to do everything we can."

"You do it," he said. "I'm tired."

Now in his mind he saw a railway station at Karagatch and he was standing with his pack and that was the headlight of the Simplon-Orient cutting the dark now and he was leaving Thrace then after the retreat. That was one of the things he had saved to write, with, in the morning at breakfast, looking out the window and seeing snow on the mountains in Bulgaria and Nansen's Secretary asking the old man if it were snow and the old man looking at it and saying, No, that's not snow. It's too early for snow. And the Secretary repeating to the other girls, No, you see. It's not snow and them all saying, It's not snow we were mistaken. But it was the snow all right and he sent them on into it when he evolved exchange of populations. And it was snow they tramped along in until they died that winter.

It was snow too that fell all Christmas week that year up in the Gauertal, that year they lived in the woodcutter's house with the big square porcelain stove that filled half the room, and they slept on mattresses filled with beech leaves, the time the deserter came with his feet bloody in the snow. He said the police were right behind him and they gave him woolen socks and held the gendarmes talking until the tracks had drifted over.

In Schrunz, on Christmas day, the snow was so bright it hurt your eyes when you looked out from the weinstube and saw every one coming home from church. That was where they walked up the sleigh-smoothed urine-yellowed road along the river with the steep pine hills, skis heavy on the shoulder, and where they ran that great run down the glacier above the Madlener-haus, the snow as smooth to see as cake frosting and as light as powder and he remembered the noiseless rush the speed made as you dropped down like a bird.

They were snow-bound a week in the Madlener-haus that time in the blizzard playing cards in the smoke by the lantern light and the stakes were higher all the time as Herr Lent lost more. Finally he lost it all. Everything, the skischule money and all the season's profit and then his capital. He could see him with his long nose, picking up the cards and then opening, "Sans Voir." There was always gambling then. When there was no snow you gambled and when there was too much you gambled. He thought of all the time in his life he had spent gambling.

But he had never written a line of that, nor of that cold, bright Christmas day with the mountains showing across the plain that Barker had flown across the lines to bomb the Austrian officers' leave train, machine-gunning them as they scattered and ran. He remembered Barker afterwards coming into the mess and starting to tell about it. And how quiet it got and then somebody saying, "You bloody murderous bastard."

Those were the same Austrians they killed then that he skied with later. No not the same. Hans, that he skied with all that year, had been in the Kaiser-Jägers and when they went hunting hares together up the little valley above the saw-mill they had talked of the fighting on Pasubio and of the attack on Perticara and Asalone and he had never written a word of that. Nor of Monte Corona, nor the Sette Communi, nor of Arsiero.

How many winters had he lived in the Vorarlberg and the Arlberg? It was four and then he remembered the man who had the fox to sell when they had walked into Bludenz, that time to buy presents, and the cherry-pit taste of good kirsch, the fast-slipping rush of running powder-snow on crust, singing "Hi! Ho! said Rolly!" as you ran down the last stretch to the steep drop, taking it straight, then running the orchard in three turns and out across the ditch and into the icy road behind the inn. Knocking your bindings loose, kicking the skis free and leaning them up against the wooden wall of the inn, the lamplight coming from the window, where inside, in the smoky, new-wine smelling warmth, they were playing the accordion.

"Where did we stay in Paris?" he asked the woman who was sitting by him in a canvas chair, now, in Africa.

"At the Crillon. You know that."

"Why do I know that?"

"That's where we always stayed."

"No. Not always."

"There and at the Pavillion Henri-Quatre in St. Germain. You said you loved it there."

"Love is a dunghill," said Harry. "And I'm the cock that gets on it to crow."

"If you have to go away," she said, "is it absolutely necessary to kill off everything you leave behind? I mean do you have to take away everything? Do you have to kill your horse, and your wife and burn your saddle and your armour?"

"Yes," he said. "Your damned money was my armour. My Swift and my Armour."

"Don't."

"All right. I'll stop that. I don't want to hurt you."

"It's a little bit late now."

"All right then. I'll go on hurting you. It's more amusing. The only thing I ever really liked to do with you I can't do now."

"No, that's not true. You liked to do many things and everything you wanted to do I did."

"Oh, for Christ sake stop bragging, will you?"

He looked at her and saw her crying.

"Listen," he said. "Do you think that it is fun to do this? I don't know why I'm doing it. It's trying to kill to keep yourself alive, I imagine. I was all right when we started talking. I didn't mean to start this, and now I'm crazy as a coot and being as cruel to you as I can be. Don't pay any attention, darling, to what I say. I love you, really. You know I love you. I've never loved any one else the way I love you."

He slipped into the familiar lie he made his bread and butter by.

"You're sweet to me."

"You bitch," he said. "You rich bitch. That's poetry. I'm full of poetry now. Rot and poetry. Rotten poetry."

"Stop it. Harry, why do you have to turn into a devil now?"

"I don't like to leave anything," the man said. "I don't like to leave things behind."

▰◟◝ ◞◜▰

It was evening now and he had been asleep. The sun was gone behind the hill and there was a shadow all across the plain and the small animals were feeding close to camp; quick dropping heads and switching tails, he watched them keeping well out away from the bush now. The birds no longer waited on the ground. They were all perched heavily in a tree. There were many more of them. His personal boy was sitting by the bed.

"Memsahib's gone to shoot," the boy said. "Does Bwana want?"

"Nothing."

She had gone to kill a piece of meat and, knowing how he liked to watch the game, she had gone well away so she would not disturb this little pocket of the plain that he could see. She was always thoughtful, he thought. On anything he knew about, or had read, or that she had ever heard.

It was not her fault that when he went to her he was already over. How could a woman know that you meant nothing that you said; that you spoke only from habit and to be comfortable? After he no longer meant what he said, his lies were more successful with women than when he had told them the truth.

It was not so much that he lied as that there was no truth to tell. He had had his life and it was over and then he went on living it again with different people and more money, with the best of the same places, and some new ones.

You kept from thinking and it was all marvellous. You were equipped with good insides so that you did not go to pieces that way, the way most of them had, and you made an attitude that you cared nothing for the work you used to do, now that you could no longer do it. But, in yourself, you said that you would write about these people; about the very rich; that you were really not of them but a spy in their country; that you would leave it and write of it and for once it would be written by some one who knew what he was writing of. But he would never do it, because each day of not writing, of comfort, of being that which he despised, dulled his ability and softened his will to work so that, finally, he did no work at all. The people he knew now were all much more comfortable when he did not work. Africa was where he had been happiest in the good time of his life, so he had come out here to start again. They had made this safari with the minimum of comfort. There was no hardship; but there was no luxury and he had thought that he could get back into training that way. That in some way he could work the fat off his soul the way a fighter went into the mountains to work and train in order to burn it out of his body.

She had liked it. She said she loved it. She loved anything that was exciting, that involved a change of scene, where there were new people and where things were pleasant. And he had felt the illusion of returning strength of will to work. Now if this was how it ended, and he knew it was, he must not turn like some snake biting itself because its back was broken. It wasn't this woman's fault. If it had not been she it would have been another. If he lived by a lie he should try to die by it. He heard a shot beyond the hill.

She shot very well this good, this rich bitch, this kindly caretaker and destroyer of his talent. Nonsense. He had destroyed his talent himself. Why should he blame this woman because she kept him well? He had destroyed his talent by not using it, by betrayals of himself and what he believed in, by drinking so much that he blunted the edge of his perceptions, by laziness, by sloth, and by snobbery, by pride and by prejudice, by hook and by crook. What was this? A catalogue of old books? What was his talent anyway? It was a talent all right but instead of using it, he had traded on it. It was never what he had done, but always what he could do. And he had chosen to make his living with something else instead of a pen or a pencil. It was strange, too, wasn't it, that when he fell in love with another woman, that woman should always have more money than the last one? But when he no longer was in love, when he was only lying, as to this woman, now, who had the most money of all, who had all the money there was, who had had a husband and children, who had taken lovers and been dissatisfied with them, and who loved him dearly as a writer, as a man, as a companion and as a proud possession; it was strange that when he did not love her at all and was lying, that he should be able to give her more for her money than when he had really loved.

We must all be cut out for what we do, he thought. However you make your living is where your talent lies. He had sold vitality, in one form or another, all his life and when your affections are not too involved you give much better value for the money. He had found that out but he would never write that, now, either. No, he would not write that, although it was well worth writing.

Now she came in sight, walking across the open toward the camp. She was wearing jodhpurs and carrying her rifle. The two boys had a Tommie slung and they were coming along behind her. She was still a good-looking woman, he thought, and she had a pleasant body. She had a great talent and appreciation for the bed, she was not pretty, but he liked her face, she read enormously, liked to ride and shoot and, certainly, she drank too much. Her husband had died when she was still a comparatively young woman and for a while she had devoted herself to her two just-grown children, who did not need her and were embarrassed at having her about, to her stable of horses, to books, and to bottles. She liked to read in the evening before dinner and she drank Scotch and soda while she read. By dinner she was fairly drunk and after a bottle of wine at dinner she was usually drunk enough to sleep.

That was before the lovers. After she had the lovers she did not drink so much because she did not have to be drunk to sleep. But the lovers bored her. She had been married to a man who had never bored her and these people bored her very much.

Then one of her two children was killed in a plane crash and after that was over she did not want the lovers, and drink being no anaesthetic she had to make another life. Suddenly, she had been acutely frightened of being alone. But she wanted some one that she respected with her.

It had begun very simply. She liked what he wrote and she had always envied the life he led. She thought he did exactly what he wanted to. The steps by which she had acquired him and the way in which she had finally fallen in love with him were all part of a regular progression in which she had built herself a new life and he had traded away what remained of his old life.

He had traded it for security, for comfort too, there was no denying that, and for what else? He did not know. She would have bought him anything he wanted. He knew that. She was a damned nice woman too. He would as soon be in bed with her as anyone; rather with her, because she was richer, because she was very pleasant and appreciative and because she never made scenes. And now this life that she had built again was coming to a term because he had not used iodine two weeks ago when a thorn had scratched his knee as they moved forward trying to photograph a herd of waterbuck standing, their heads up, peering while their nostrils searched the air, their ears spread wide to hear the first noise that would send them rushing into the bush. They had bolted, too, before he got the picture.

Here she came now.

He turned his head on the cot to look toward her. "Hello," he said.

"I shot a Tommy ram," she told him. "He'll make you good broth and I'll have them mash some potatoes with the Klim. How do you feel?"

"Much better."

"Isn't that lovely? You know I thought perhaps you would. You were sleeping when I left."

"I had a good sleep. Did you walk far?"

"No. Just around behind the hill. I made quite a good shot on the Tommy."

"You shoot marvellously, you know."

"I love it. I've loved Africa. Really. If *you're* all right it's the most fun that I've ever had. You don't know the fun it's been to shoot with you. I've loved the country."

"I love it too."

"Darling, you don't know how marvellous it is to see you feeling better. I couldn't stand it when you felt that way. You won't talk to me like that again, will you? Promise me?"

"No," he said. "I don't remember what I said."

"You don't have to destroy me. Do you? I'm only a middle-aged woman who loves you and wants to do what you want to do. I've been destroyed two or three times already. You wouldn't want to destroy me again, would you?"

"I'd like to destroy you a few times in bed," he said.

"Yes. That's the good destruction. That's the way we're made to be destroyed. The plane will be here tomorrow."

"How do you know?"

"I'm sure. It's bound to come. The boys have the wood all ready and the grass to make the smudge. I went down and looked at it again today. There's plenty of room to land and we have the smudges ready at both ends."

"What makes you think it will come tomorrow?"

"I'm sure it will. It's overdue now. Then, in town, they will fix up your leg and then we will have some good destruction. Not that dreadful talking kind."

"Should we have a drink? The sun is down."

"Do you think you should?"

"I'm having one."

"We'll have one together. *Molo, letti dui whiskey-soda!*" she called.

"You'd better put on your mosquito boots," he told her.

"I'll wait till I bathe . . ."

While it grew dark they drank and just before it was dark and there was no longer enough light to shoot, a hyena crossed the open on his way around the hill.

"That bastard crosses there every night," the man said. "Every night for two weeks."

"He's the one makes the noise at night. I don't mind it. They're a filthy animal though."

Drinking together, with no pain now except the discomfort of lying in the one position, the boys lighting a fire, its shadow jumping on the tents, he could feel the return of acquiescence in this life of pleasant surrender. She *was* very good to him. He had been cruel and unjust in the afternoon. She was a fine woman, marvellous really. And just then it occurred to him that he was going to die.

It came with a rush; not as as rush of water nor of wind; but of a sudden evil-smelling emptiness and the odd thing was that the hyena slipped lightly along the edge of it.

"What is it, Harry?" she asked him.

"Nothing," he said. "You had better move over to the other side. To windward."

"Did Molo change the dressing?"

"Yes. I'm just using the boric now."

"How do you feel?"

"A little wobbly."

"I'm going in to bathe," she said. "I'll be right out. I'll eat with you and then we'll put the cot in."

So, he said to himself, we did well to stop the quarrelling. He had never quarrelled much with this woman, while with the women that he loved he had quarrelled so much they had finally, always, with the corrosion of the quarrelling, killed what they had together. He had loved too much, demanded too much, and he wore it all out.

He thought about alone in Constantinople that time, having quarrelled in Paris before he had gone out. He had whored the whole time and then, when that was over, and he had failed to kill his loneliness, but only made it worse, he had written her, the first one, the one who left him, a letter telling her how he had never been able to kill it. . . . How when he thought he saw her outside the Regence *one time it made him go all faint and sick inside, and that he would follow a woman who looked like her in some way, along the Boulevard, afraid to see it was not she, afraid to lose the feeling it gave him. How every one he had slept with had only made him miss her more. How what she had done could never matter since he knew he could not cure himself of loving her. He wrote this letter at the Club, cold sober, and mailed it to New York asking her to write him at the office in Paris. That seemed safe. And that night missing her so much it made him feel hollow sick inside, he wandered up past Taxim's, picked a girl up and took her out to supper. He had gone to a place to dance with her afterward, she danced badly, and left her for a hot Armenian slut, that swung her belly against him so it almost scalded. He took her away from a British gunner subaltern after a row. The gunner asked him outside and they fought in the street on the cobbles in the dark. He'd hit him twice, hard, on the side of the jaw and when he didn't go down he knew he was in for a fight. The gunner hit him in the body, then beside his eye. He swung with his left again and landed and the gunner fell on him and grabbed his coat and tore the sleeve off and he clubbed him twice behind the ear and then smashed him with his right as he pushed him away. When the gunner went down his head hit first and he ran with the girl because they heard the M.P.'s coming. They got into a taxi and drove out to Rimmily Hissa along the Bosphorus, and around, and back in the cool night and went to bed and she felt as over-ripe as she looked but smooth, rose-petal, syrupy, smooth-bellied, big-breasted and needed no pillow under her buttocks, and he left her before she was awake looking blowsy enough in the first daylight and turned up at the Pera Palace with a black eye, carrying his coat because one sleeve was missing.*

That same night he left for Anatolia and he remembered, later on that trip, riding all day through fields of the poppies that they raised for opium and how strange it made you feel, finally, and all the distances seemed wrong, to where they had made the attack with the newly arrived Constantine officers, that did not know a god-damned thing, and the artillery had fired into the troops and the British observer had cried like a child.

That was the day he'd first seen dead men wearing white ballet skirts and upturned shoes with pompons on them. The Turks had come steadily and lumpily and he had seen the skirted men running and the officers shooting into them and running then themselves and he and the British observer had run too until his lungs ached and his mouth was full of the taste of pennies and they stopped behind some rocks and there were the Turks coming as lumpily as ever. Later he had seen the things that he could never think of and later still he had seen much worse. So when he got back to Paris that time he could not talk about it or stand to have it mentioned. And there in the café as he passed was that American poet with a pile of saucers in front of him and a stupid look on his potato face talking about the Dada movement with a Roumanian who said his name was Tristan Tzara, who always wore a monocle and had a headache, and, back at the apartment with his wife that now he loved again, the quarrel all over, the madness all over, glad to be home, the office sent his mail up to the flat. So then the letter in answer to the one he'd written came in on a platter one morning and when he saw the handwriting he went cold all over and tried to slip the letter underneath another. But his wife said, "Who is that letter from, dear?" and that was the end of the beginning of that.

He remembered the good times with them all, and the quarrels. They always picked the finest places to have the quarrels. And why had they always quarrelled when he was feeling best? He had never written any of that because, at first, he never wanted to hurt any one and then it seemed as though there was enough to write without it. But he had always thought that he would write it finally. There was so much to write. He had seen the world change; not just the events; although he had seen many of them and had watched the people, but he had seen the subtler change and he could remember how the people were at different times. He had been in it and he had watched it and it was his duty to write of it; but now he never would.

"How do you feel?" she said. She had come out from the tent now after her bath.

"All right."

"Could you eat now?" He saw Molo behind her with the folding table and the other boy with the dishes.

"I want to write," he said.

"You ought to take some broth to keep your strength up."

"I'm going to die tonight," he said. "I don't need my strength up."

"Don't be melodramatic, Harry, please," she said.

"Why don't you use your nose? I'm rotted half way up my thigh now. What the hell should I fool with broth for? Molo bring whiskey-soda."

"Please take the broth," she said gently.

"All right."

The broth was too hot. He had to hold it in the cup until it cooled enough to take it and then he just got it down without gagging.

"You're a fine woman," he said. "Don't pay any attention to me."

She looked at him with her well-known, well-loved face from *Spur* and *Town and Country*, only a little the worse for drink, only a little the worse for bed, but *Town and Country* never showed those good breasts and those useful thighs and those lightly small-of-back caressing hands, and as he looked and saw her well known pleasant smile, he felt death come again. This time there was no rush. It was a puff, as of a wind that makes a candle flicker and the flame go tall.

"They can bring me my net out later and hang it from the tree and build the fire up. I'm not going in the tent tonight. It's not worth moving. It's a clear night. There won't be any rain."

So this was how you died, in whispers that you did not hear. Well, there would be no more quarrelling. He could promise that. The one experience that he had never had he was not going to spoil now. He probably would. You spoiled everything. But perhaps he wouldn't.

"You can't take dictation, can you?"

"I never learned," she told him.

"That's all right."

There wasn't time, of course, although it seemed as though it telescoped so that you might put it all into one paragraph if you could get it right.

There was a log house, chinked white with mortar, on a hill above the lake. There was a bell on a pole by the door to call the people in to meals. Behind the house were fields and behind the fields was the timber. A line of lombardy poplars ran from the house to the dock. Other poplars ran along the point. A road went up to the hills along the edge of the timber and along that road he picked blackberries. Then that log house was burned down and all the guns that had been on deer foot racks above the open fire place were burned and afterwards their barrels, with the lead melted in the magazines, and the stocks burned away, lay out on the heap of ashes that were used to make lye for the big iron soap kettles, and you asked Grandfather if you could have them to play with, and he said, no. You see they were his guns still and he never bought any others. Nor did he hunt any more. The house was rebuilt in the same place out of lumber now and painted white and from its porch you saw the poplars and the lake beyond; but there were never any more guns. The barrels of the guns that had hung on the deer feet on the wall of the log house lay out there on the heap of ashes and no one ever touched them.

In the Black Forest, after the war, we rented a trout stream and there were two ways to walk to it. One was down the valley from Triberg and around the valley road in the shade of the trees that bordered the white road, and then up a side road that went up through the hills past many small farms, with the big Schwarzwald houses, until that road crossed the stream. That was where our fishing began.

The other way was to climb steeply up to the edge of the woods and then go across the top of the hills through the pine woods, and then out to the edge of a meadow and down across this meadow to the bridge. There were birches along the stream and it was not big, but narrow, clear and fast, with pools where it had cut under the roots of the birches. At the Hotel in Triberg the proprietor had a fine season. It was very pleasant and we were all great friends. The next year came the inflation and the money he had made the year before was not enough to buy supplies to open the hotel and he hanged himself.

You could dictate that, but you could not dictate the Place Contrescarpe where the flower sellers dyed their flowers in the street and the dye ran over the paving where the autobus started and the old men and the women, always drunk on wine and bad marc; and the children with their noses running in the cold; the smell of dirty sweat and poverty and drunkenness at the Café des Amateurs and the whores at the Bal Musette they lived above. The Concierge who entertained the trooper of the Garde Republicaine in her loge, his horse-hair-plumed helmet on a chair. The locataire across the hall whose husband was a bicycle racer and her joy that morning at the Cremerie when she had opened L'Auto and seen where he placed third in Paris-Tours, his first big race. She had blushed and laughed and then gone upstairs crying with the yellow sporting paper in her hand. The husband of the woman who ran the Bal Musette drove a taxi and when he, Harry, had to take an early plane the husband knocked upon the door to wake him and they each drank a glass of white wine at the zinc of the bar before they started. He knew his neighbors in that quarter then because they were all poor.

Around that Place *there were two kinds; the drunkards and the sportifs. The drunkards killed their poverty that way; the sportifs took it out in exercise. They were the descendants of the Communards and it was no struggle for them to know their politics. They knew who had shot their fathers, their relatives, their brothers, and their friends when the Versailles troops came in and took the town after the Commune and executed any one they could catch with calloused hands, or who wore a cap, or carried any other sign he was a working man. And in that poverty, and in that quarter across the street from a Boucherie Chevaline and a wine co-operative he had written the start of all he was to do. There never was another part of Paris that he loved like that, the sprawling trees, the old white plastered houses painted brown below, the long green of the autobus in that round square, the purple flower dye upon the paving, the sudden drop down the hill of the rue Cardinal Lemoine to the River, and the other way the narrow crowded world of the rue Mouffetard. The street that ran up toward the Pantheon and the other that he always took with the bicycle, the only asphalted street in all that quarter, smooth under the tires, with the high narrow houses and the cheap tall hotel where Paul Verlaine had died. There were only two rooms in the apartments where they lived and he had a room on the top floor of that hotel that cost him sixty francs a month where he did his writing, and from it he could see the roofs and chimney pots and all the hills of Paris.*

From the apartment you could only see the wood and coal man's place. He sold wine too, bad wine. The golden horse's head outside the Boucherie Chevaline where the carcasses hung yellow gold and red in the open window, and the green painted co-operative where they bought their wine; good wine and cheap. The rest was plaster walls and the windows of the neighbors. The neighbors who, at night, when some one lay drunk in the street, moaning and groaning in that typical French ivresse *that you were propaganded to believe did not exist, would open their windows and then the murmur of talk.*

"Where is the policeman? When you don't want him the bugger is always there. He's sleeping with some concierge. Get the Agent.*" Till some one threw a bucket of water from a window and the moaning stopped. "What's that? Water. Ah, that's intelligent." And the windows shutting. Marie, his femme de menage, protesting against the eight-hour day saying, "If a husband works until six he gets only a little drunk on the way home and does not waste too much. If he works only until five he is drunk every night and one has no money. It is the wife of the working man who suffers from this shortening of hours."*

"Wouldn't you like some more broth?" the woman asked him now.

"No, thank you very much. It is awfully good."

"Try just a little."

"I would like a whiskey-soda."

"It's not good for you."

"No. It's bad for me. Cole Porter wrote the words and the music. This knowledge that you're going mad for me."

"You know I like you to drink."

"Oh yes. Only it's bad for me."

When she goes, he thought. I'll have all I want. Not all I want but all there is. Ayee he was tired. Too tired. He was going to sleep a little while. He lay still and death was not there. It must have gone around another street. It went in pairs, on bicycles, and moved absolutely silently on the pavements.

No, he had never written about Paris. Not the Paris that he cared about. But what about the rest that he had never written?

What about the ranch and the silvered gray of the sage brush, the quick, clear water in the irrigation ditches, and the heavy green of the alfalfa. The trail went up into the hills and the cattle in the summer were shy as deer. The bawling and the steady noise and slow moving mass raising a dust as you brought them down in the fall. And behind the mountains, the clear sharpness of the peak in the evening light and, riding down along the trail in the moonlight, bright across the valley. Now he remembered coming down through the timber in the dark holding the horse's tail when you could not see and all the stories that he meant to write.

About the half-wit chore boy who was left at the ranch that time and told not to let any one get any hay, and that old bastard from the Forks who had beaten the boy when he had worked for him stopping to get some feed. The boy refusing and the old man saying he would beat him again. The boy got the rifle from the kitchen and shot him when he tried to come into the barn and when they came back to the ranch he'd been dead a week, frozen in the corral, and the dogs had eaten part of him. But what was left you packed on a sled wrapped in a blanket and roped on and you got the boy to help you haul it, and the two of you took it out over the road on skis, and sixty miles down to town to turn the boy over. He having no idea that he would be arrested. Thinking he had done his duty and that you were his friend and he would be rewarded. He'd helped to haul the old man in so everybody could know how bad the old man had been and how he'd tried to steal some feed that didn't belong to him, and when the sheriff put the handcuffs on the boy he couldn't believe it. Then he'd started to cry. That was one story he had saved to write. He knew at least twenty good stories from out there and he had never written one. Why?

"You tell them why," he said.

"Why what, dear?"

"Why nothing."

She didn't drink so much, now, since she had him. But if he lived he would never write about her, he knew that now. Nor about any of them. The rich were dull and they drank too much, or they played too much backgammon. They were dull and they were repetitious. He remembered poor Julian and his romantic awe of them and how he had started a story once that began, "The very rich are very different from you and me." And how some one had said to Julian, yes, they have more money. but that was not humorous to Julian. He thought they were a special glamourous race and when he found they weren't it wrecked him just as much as any other thing that wrecked him.

He had been contemptuous of those who wrecked. You did not have to like it because you understood it. He could beat anything, he thought, because no thing could hurt him if he did not care.

All right. Now he would not care for death. One thing he had always dreaded was the pain. He could stand pain as well as any man, until it went on too long, and wore him out, but here he had something that had hurt frightfully and just when he had felt it breaking him, the pain had stopped.

He remembered long ago when Williamson, the bombing officer, had been hit by a stick bomb some one in a German patrol had thrown as he was coming in through the wire that night and, screaming, had begged every one to kill him. He was a fat man, very brave, and a good officer, although addicted to fantastic shows. But that night he was caught in the wire, with a flare lighting him up and his bowels spilled out into the wire, so when they brought him in, alive, they had to cut him loose. Shoot me, Harry. For Christ sake shoot me. They had had an argument one time about our Lord never sending you anything you could not bear and some one's theory had been that meant that at a certain time the pain passed you out automatically. But he had always remembered Williamson, that night. Nothing passed out Williamson until he gave him all his morphine tablets that he had always saved to use himself and then they did not work right away.

Still this now, that he had, was very easy; and if it was no worse as it went on there was nothing to worry about. Except that he would rather be in better company.

He thought a little about the company that he would like to have.

No, he thought, when everything you do, you do too long, and do too late, you can't expect to find the people still there. The people all are gone. The party's over and you are with your hostess now.

I'm getting as bored with dying as with everything else, he thought.

"It's a bore," he said out loud.

"What is, my dear?"

"Anything you do too bloody long."

He looked at her face between him and the fire. She was leaning back in the chair and the firelight shone on her pleasantly lined face as he could see that she was sleepy. He heard the hyena make a noise just outside the range of the fire.

"I've been writing," he said. "But I got tired."

"Do you think you will be able to sleep?"

"Pretty sure. Why don't you turn in?"

"I like to sit here with you."

"Do you feel anything strange?" he asked her.

"No. Just a little sleepy."

"I do," he said.

He had just felt death come by again.

"You know the only thing I've never lost is curiosity," he said to her.

"You've never lost anything. You're the most complete man I've ever known."

"Christ," he said. "How little a woman knows. What is that? Your intuition?"

Because, just then, death had come and rested its head on the foot of the cot and he could smell its breath.

"Never believe any of that about a scythe and a skull," he told her. "It can be two bicycle policemen as easily, or be a bird. Or it can have a wide snout like a hyena."

It had moved up on him now, but it had no shape any more. It simply occupied space.

"Tell it to go away."

It did not go away but moved a little closer.

"You've got a hell of a breath," he told it. "You stinking bastard."

It moved up closer to him still and now he could not speak to it, and when it saw he could not speak it came a little closer, and now he tried to send it away without speaking, but it moved in on him so its weight was all upon his chest, and while it crouched there and he could not move, or speak, he heard the woman say, "Bwana is asleep now. Take the cot up very gently and carry it into the tent."

He could not speak to tell her to make it go away and it crouched now, heavier, so he could not breathe. And then, while they lifted the cot, suddenly it was all right and the weight went from his chest.

It was morning and had been morning for some time and he heard the plane. It showed very tiny and then made a wide circle and the boys ran out and lit the fires, using kerosene, and piled on grass so there were two big smudges at each end of the level place and the morning breeze blew them toward the camp and the plane circled twice more, low this time, and then glided down and levelled off and landed smoothly and, coming walking toward him, was old Compton in slacks, a tweed jacket and a brown felt hat.

"What's the matter, old cock?" Compton said.

"Bad leg," he told him. "Will you have some breakfast?"

"Thanks. I'll just have some tea. It's the Puss Moth you know. I won't be able to take the Memsahib. There's only room for one. Your lorry is on the way."

Helen had taken Compton aside and was speaking to him. Compton came back more cheery than ever.

"We'll get you right in," he said. "I'll be back for the Mem. Now I'm afraid I'll have to stop at Arusha to refuel. We'd better get going."

"What about the tea?"

"I don't really care about it you know."

The boys had picked up the cot and carried it around the green tents and down along the rock and out onto the plain and along past the smudges that were burning brightly now, the grass all consumed, and the wind fanning the fire, to the little plane. It was difficult getting him in, but once in he lay back in the leather seat, and the leg was stuck straight out to one side of the seat where Compton sat. Compton started the motor and got in. He waved to Helen and to the boys and, as the clatter moved into the old familiar roar, they swung around with Compie watching for wart-hog holes and roared, bumping, along the stretch between the fires and with the last bump rose and he saw them all standing below, waving, and the camp beside the hill, flattening now, and the plain spreading, clumps of trees, and the bush flattening, while the game trails ran now smoothly to the dry waterholes, and there was a new water that he had never known of. The zebra, small rounded backs now, and the wildebeeste, big-headed dots seeming to climb as they moved in long fingers across the plain, now scattering as the shadow came toward them, they were tiny now, and the movement had no gallop, and the plain as far as you could see, gray-yellow now and ahead old Compie's tweed back and the brown felt hat. Then they were over the first hills and the wildebeeste were trailing up them, and then they were over mountains with sudden depths of green-rising forest and the solid bamboo slopes, and then the heavy forest again, sculptured into the peaks and hollows until they crossed, and hills sloped down and then another plain, hot now, and purple brown, bumpy with heat and Compie looking back to see how he was riding. Then there were other mountains dark ahead.

And then instead of going on to Arusha they turned left, he evidently figured that they had the gas, looking down he saw a pink sifting cloud, moving over the ground, and in the air, like the first snow in a blizzard, that comes from nowhere, and he knew the locusts were coming up from the South. Then they began to climb and they were going to the East it seemed, and then it darkened and they were in a storm, the rain so thick it seemed like flying through a waterfall, and then they were out and Compie turned his head and grinned and pointed and there, ahead, all he could see, as wide as all the world, great, high, and unbelievably white in the sun, was the square top of Kilimanjaro. And then he knew that there was where he was going.

Just then the hyena stopped whimpering in the night and started to make a strange, human, almost crying sound. The woman heard it and stirred uneasily. She did not wake. In her dream she was at the house on Long Island and it was the night before her daughter's début. Somehow her father was there and he had been very rude. Then the noise the hyena made was so loud she woke and for a moment she did not know where she was and she was very afraid. Then she took the flashlight and shone it on the other cot that they had carried in after Harry had gone to sleep. She could see his bulk under the mosquito bar but somehow he had gotten his leg out and it hung down alongside the cot. The dressings had all come down and she could not look at it.

"Molo," she called, "Molo! Molo!"

Then she said, "Harry, Harry!" Then her voice rising, "Harry! Please, Oh Harry!"

There was no answer and she could not hear him breathing.

Outside the tent the hyena made the same strange noise that had awakened her. But she did not hear him for the beating of her heart.

QUESTIONS FOR DISCUSSION AND WRITING

1.   Important features of Hemingway's style are its spare understatement and its objective tone. Hemingway himself compared his style to an iceberg: "seven-eights of it under water for every part that shows." Analyze how Hemingway achieves this effect by examining the first few paragraphs of the story or another representative sampling.

2.   What is the relevance of the epigraph about the leopard carcass?

3.   Analyze the narrative voice. Notice that it is very tightly focused on Harry, but that it is divided into roman and italic passages. What is the distinction?

4.   We are well into the story before we learn that the man's name is Harry, and the story is almost over before we learn that the woman's name is Helen; for much of the story, they are called "the man" and "the woman." What is the effect of this handling of names?

5.   As Harry awaits death, he evaluates his life. What is his judgment of himself as a writer? As a man?

6.   How does Harry view women? What is his relationship with Helen like?

Jorge Luis Borges

Jorge Luis Borges (1899–1986) was one of the finest of the writers who created the Latin-American "Boom," the literary efflorescence that has placed Latin-American literature at the forefront of world literature in the past few decades. Born in Buenos Aires, Argentina, Borges spent the years between his fifteenth birthday and his twenty-second in Europe, where he became acquainted with avant-garde literary movements. Returning to Argentina in 1921, he lived for several years the life of a literary journalist and minor man of letters. A turning point came in 1937, when an accident left him with a severe head wound and possible brain damage. Borges began writing fiction to see if he could still develop a coherent narrative or argument. Over the next dozen or so years, he wrote most of the stories that were to make him famous, short narratives that weave together reality, fantasy, and philosophical puzzles and paradoxes and that he called simply "fictions." The first collection of these pieces, *The Garden of Forking Paths*, appeared in 1941; an expanded version, *Fictions*, followed in 1944. The main body of Borges' most characteristic work was completed with *The Aleph* (1949). Opposition to Juan Perón, the dictator who came to power in Argentina in 1946, cost Borges his job with the Buenos Aires library, but when Perón was overthrown in 1955, Borges was appointed director of the National Library of Argentina and, a year later, professor of English and North American Literature at the University of Buenos Aires. Although he lost his sight to a hereditary eye disease in the 1950s, he continued to write—mostly poetry—and to travel and lecture, especially in the United States, until his death in 1986.

THE GARDEN OF FORKING PATHS*

On page 22 of Liddell Hart's *History of World War I* you will read that an attack against the Serre-Montauban line by thirteen British divisions (supported by 1,400 artillery pieces) planned for the 24th of July, 1916, had to be postponed until the morning of the 29th. The torrential rains, Captain Liddell Hart comments, caused this delay, an insignificant one, to be sure.

The following statement, dictated, reread and signed by Dr. Yu Tsun, former professor of English at the *Hochschule* at Tsingtao, throws an unsuspected light over the whole affair. The first two pages of the document are missing.

" . . . and I hung up the receiver. Immediately afterwards, I recognized the voice that had answered in German. It was that of Captain Richard Madden. Madden's presence in Viktor Runeberg's apartment meant the end of our anxieties and—but this seemed, *or should have seemed*, very secondary to me—also the end of our lives. It meant that Runeberg had been arrested or murdered.[1] Before the sun set on that day, I would encounter the same fate. Madden was implacable. Or rather, he was obliged to be so. An Irishman at the service of England, a man accused of laxity and perhaps of treason, how could he fail to seize and be thankful for such a miraculous

*Translated by Donald A. Yates
[1] An hypothesis both hateful and odd. The Prussian spy Hans Rabener, alias Viktor Runeberg, attacked with drawn automatic the bearer of the warrant for his arrest, Captain Richard Madden. The latter, in self-defense, inflicted the wound which brought about Runeberg's death. (Note supplied by Borges's "editor.")

opportunity; the discovery, capture, maybe even the death of two agents of the German Reich? I went up to my room; absurdly I locked the door and threw myself on my back on the narrow iron cot. Through the window I saw the familiar roofs and the cloud-shaded six o'clock sun. It seemed incredible to me that that day without premonitions or symbols should be the one of my inexorable death. In spite of my dead father, in spite of having been a child in a symmetrical garden of Hai Feng, was I—now—going to die? Then I reflected that everything happens to a man precisely, precisely *now*. Centuries of centuries and only in the present do things happen; countless men in the air, on the face of the earth and the sea, and all that really is happening is happening to me . . . The almost intolerable recollection of Madden's horselike face banished these wanderings. In the midst of my hatred and terror (it means nothing to me now to speak of terror, now that I have mocked Richard Madden, now that my throat yearns for the noose) it occurred to me that that tumultuous and doubtless happy warrior did not suspect that I possessed the Secret. The name of the exact location of the new British artillery park on the River Ancre. A bird streaked across the gray sky and blindly I translated it into an airplane and that airplane into many (against the French sky) annihilating the artillery station with vertical bombs. If only my mouth, before a bullet shattered it, could cry out that secret name so it could be heard in Germany . . . My human voice was very weak. How might I make it carry to the ear of the Chief? To the ear of that sick and hateful man who knew nothing of Runeberg and me save that we were in Staffordshire and who was waiting in vain for our report in his arid office in Berlin, endlessly examining newspapers . . . I said out loud: *I must flee.* I sat up noiselessly, in a useless perfection of silence, as if Madden were already lying in wait for me. Something—perhaps the mere vain ostentation of proving my resources were nil—made me look through my pockets. I found what I knew I would find. The American watch, the nickel chain and the square coin, the key ring with the incriminating useless keys to Runeberg's apartment, the notebook, a letter which I resolved to destroy immediately (and which I did not destroy), a crown, two shillings and a few pence, the red and blue pencil, the handkerchief, the revolver with one bullet. Absurdly, I took it in my hand and weighed it in order to inspire courage within myself. Vaguely I thought that a pistol report can be heard at a great distance. In ten minutes my plan was perfected. The telephone book listed the name of the only person capable of transmitting the message; he lived in a suburb of Fenton, less than a half hour's train ride away.

I am a cowardly man. I say it now, now that I have carried to its end a plan whose perilous nature no one can deny. I know its execution was terrible. I didn't do it for Germany, no. I care nothing for a barbarous country which imposed upon me the abjection of being a spy. Besides, I know of a man from England—a modest man—who for me is no less great than Goethe. I talked with him for scarcely an hour, but during that hour he was Goethe . . . I did it because I sensed that the Chief somehow feared people of my race—for the innumerable ancestors who merge within me. I wanted to prove to him that a yellow man could save his armies. Besides, I had to flee from Captain Madden. His hands and his voice could call at my door at any moment. I dressed silently, bade farewell to myself in the mirror, went downstairs, scrutinized the peaceful street and went out. The station was not far from my home, but I judged it wise to take a cab. I argued that in this way I ran less risk of being recognized; the fact is that in the deserted street I felt myself visible and vulnerable, infinitely so. I remember that I told the cab driver to stop a short distance before the main entrance. I got out with voluntary, almost painful slowness; I was going to the village of Ashgrove but I bought a ticket for a more distant station. The train left within a very few minutes, at eight-fifty. I hurried; the next one would leave at nine-thirty. There was hardly a soul on the platform. I went through the coaches; I remember a few farmers, a woman dressed in mourning, a young boy who was reading with fervor the *Annals* of Tacitus, a wounded and happy soldier. The coaches jerked forward at last. A man whom I recognized ran in vain to the end of the platform. It was Captain Richard Madden. Shattered, trembling, I shrank into the far corner of the seat, away from the dreaded window.

From this broken state I passed into an almost abject felicity. I told myself that the duel had already begun and that I had won the first encounter by frustrating, even if for forty minutes, even if by a stroke of fate, the attack of my adversary. I argued that this slightest of victories foreshadowed a total victory. I argued (no less fallaciously) that my cowardly felicity proved that I was a man capable of carrying out the adventure successfully. From this weakness I took strength that did not abandon me. I foresee that man will resign himself each day to more atrocious undertakings; soon there will be no one but warriors and brigands; I give them this counsel: *The author of an atrocious undertaking ought to imagine that he has already accomplished it, ought to impose upon himself a future as irrevocable as the past.* Thus I proceeded as my eyes of a man already dead registered the elapsing of the day, which was perhaps the last, and the diffusion of the night. The train ran gently along, amid ash trees. It stopped, almost in the middle of the fields. No one announced the name of the station. "Ashgrove?" I asked a few lads on the platform. "Ashgrove," they replied. I got off.

A lamp enlightened the platform but the faces of the boys were in shadow. One questioned me, "Are you going to Dr. Stephen Albert's house?" Without waiting for my answer, another said, "The house is a long way from here, but you won't get lost if you take this road to the left and at every crossroads turn again to your left." I tossed them a coin (my last), descended a few stone steps and started down the solitary road. It went downhill slowly. It was of elemental earth; overhead the branches were tangled; the low, full moon seemed to accompany me.

For an instant, I thought that Richard Madden in some way had penetrated my desperate plan. Very quickly, I understood that that was impossible. The instructions to turn always to the left reminded me that such was the common procedure for discovering the central point of certain labyrinths. I have some understanding of labyrinths: not for nothing am I the great grandson of that Ts'ui Pên who was governor of Yunnan and who renounced worldly power in order to write a novel that might be even more populous than the *Hung Lu Meng* and to construct a labyrinth in which all men would become lost. Thirteen years he dedicated to the heterogeneous tasks, but the hand of a stranger murdered him—and his novel was incoherent and no one found the labyrinth. Beneath English trees I meditated on that lost maze: I imagined it inviolate and perfect at the secret crest of a mountain; I imagined it erased by rice fields or beneath the water; I imagined it infinite, no longer composed of octagonal kiosks and returning paths, but of rivers and provinces and kingdoms ... I thought of a labyrinth of labyrinths, of one sinuous spreading labyrinth that would encompass the past and the future and in some way involve the stars. Absorbed in these illusory images, I forgot my destiny of one pursued. I felt myself to be, for an unknown period of time, an abstract perceiver of the world. The vague, living countryside, the moon, the remains of the day worked on me, as well as the slope of the road which eliminated any possibility of weariness. The afternoon was intimate, infinite. The road descended and forked among the now confused meadows. A high-pitched, almost syllabic music approached and receded in the shifting of the wind, dimmed by leaves and distance. I thought that a man can be an enemy of other men, of the moments of other men, but not of a country: not of fireflies, words, gardens, streams of water, sunset. Thus I arrived before a tall, rusty gate. Between the iron bars I made out a poplar grove and a pavilion. I understood suddenly two things, the first trivial, the second almost unbelievable: the music came from the pavilion, and the music was Chinese. For precisely that reason I had openly accepted it without paying it any heed. I do not remember whether there was a bell or whether I knocked with my hand. The sparkling of the music continued.

From the rear of the house within a lantern approached: a lantern that the trees sometimes striped and sometimes eclipsed, a paper lantern that had the form of a drum and the color of the moon. A tall man bore it. I didn't see his face for the light blinded me. He opened the door and said slowly, in my own language: "I see that the pious Hsi P'êng persists in correcting my solitude. You no doubt wish to see the garden?"

I recognized the name of one of our consuls and I replied, disconcerted, "The garden?"

"The garden of forking paths."

Something stirred in my memory and I uttered with incomprehensible certainty, "The garden of my ancestor Ts'ui Pên."

"Your ancestor? Your illustrious ancestor? Come in."

The damp path zigzagged like those of my childhood. We came to a library of Eastern and Western books. I recognized bound in yellow silk several volumes of the Lost Encyclopedia, edited by the Third Emperor of the Luminous Dynasty but never printed. The record on the phonograph revolved next to a bronze phoenix. I also recall a *famille rose* vase and another, many centuries older, of that shade of blue which our craftsmen copied from the potters of Persia . . .

Stephen Albert observed me with a smile. He was, as I have said, very tall, sharp-featured, with gray eyes and a gray beard. He told me that he had been a missionary in Tientsin "before aspiring to become a Sinologist."

We sat down—I on a long, low divan, he with his back to the window and a tall circular clock. I calculated that my pursuer, Richard Madden, could not arrive for at least an hour. My irrevocable determination could wait.

"An astounding fate, that of Ts'ui Pên," Stephen Albert said. "Governor of his native province, learned in astronomy, in astrology, and in the tireless interpretation of the canonical books, chess player, famous poet and calligrapher—he abandoned all this in order to compose a book and a maze. He renounced the pleasures of both tyranny and justice, of his populous couch, of his banquets and even of erudition—all to close himself up for thirteen years in the Pavilion of the Limpid Solitude. When he died, his heirs found nothing save chaotic manuscripts. His family, as you may be aware, wished to condemn them to the fire; but his executor— a Taoist or Buddhist monk—insisted on their publication."

"We descendants of Ts'ui Pên," I replied, "continue to curse that monk. Their publication was senseless. The book is an indeterminate heap of contradictory drafts. I examined it once: in the third chapter the hero dies, in the fourth he is alive. As for the other undertaking of Ts'ui Pên, his labyrinth . . . "

"Here is Ts'ui Pên's labyrinth," he said, indicating a tall lacquered desk.

"An ivory labyrinth!" I exclaimed. "A minimum labyrinth."

"A labyrinth of symbols," he corrected. "An invisible labyrinth of time. To me, a barbarous Englishman, has been entrusted the revelation of this diaphanous mystery. After more than a hundred years, the details are irretrievable; but it is not hard to conjecture what happened. Ts'ui Pên must have said once: *I am withdrawing to write a book.* And another time: *I am withdrawing to construct a labyrinth.* Every one imagined two works; to no one did it occur that the book and the maze were one and the same thing. The Pavilion of the Limpid Solitude stood in the center of a garden that was perhaps intricate; that circumstance could have suggested to the heirs a physical labyrinth. Hs'ui Pên died; no one in the vast territories that were his came upon the labyrinth; the confusion of the novel suggested to me that *it* was the maze. Two circumstances gave me the correct solution of the problem. One: the curious legend that Ts'ui Pên had planned to create a labyrinth which would be strictly infinite. The other: a fragment of a letter I discovered."

Albert rose. He turned his back on me for a moment; he opened a drawer of the black and gold desk. He faced me and in his hands he held a sheet of paper that had once been crimson, but was now pink and tenuous and cross-sectioned. The fame of Ts'ui Pên as a calligrapher had been justly won. I read, uncomprehendingly and with fervor, these words written with a minute brush by a man of my blood: *I leave to the various futures (not to all) my garden of forking paths.* Wordlessly, I returned the sheet. Albert continued:

"Before unearthing this letter, I had questioned myself about the ways in which a book can be infinite. I could think of nothing other than a cyclic volume, a circular one. A book whose last page was identical with the first, a book which had the possibility of continuing indefinitely. I remembered too that night which is at the middle of the Thousand and One Nights when Scheherazade (through a magical oversight of the copyist) begins to relate word for word the story of the Thousand and One Nights, establishing the risk of coming once again to the night when she must repeat it, and thus on to infinity. I imagined as well a Platonic, hereditary work, transmitted from father to son, in which each new individual adds a chapter or corrects with pious care the pages of his elders. These conjectures diverted me; but none seemed to correspond, not even remotely, to the contradictory chapters of Ts'ui Pên. In the midst of this perplexity, I received from Oxford the manuscript you have examined. I lingered, naturally, on the sentence: *I leave to the various futures (not to all) my garden of forking paths.* Almost instantly, I understood: 'the garden of forking paths' was the chaotic novel; the phrase 'the various futures (not to all)' suggested to me the forking in time, not in space. A broad rereading of the work confirmed the theory. In all fictional works, each time a man is confronted with several alternatives, he chooses one and eliminates the others; in the fiction of Ts'ui Pên, he chooses—simultaneously—all of them. *He creates,* in this way, diverse futures, diverse times which themselves also proliferate and fork. Here, then, is the explanation of the novel's contradictions. Fang, let us say, has a secret; a stranger calls at his door; Fang resolves to kill him. Naturally, there are several possible outcomes: Fang can kill the intruder, the intruder can kill Fang, they both can escape, they both can die, and so forth. In the work of Ts'ui Pên, all possible outcomes occur; each one is the point of departure for other forkings. Sometimes, the paths of this labyrinth converge: for example, you arrive at this house, but in one of the possible pasts you are my enemy, in another, my friend. If you will resign yourself to my incurable pronunciation, we shall read a few pages."

His face, within the vivid circle of the lamplight, was unquestionably that of an old man, but with something unalterable about it, even immortal. He read with slow precision two versions of the same epic chapter. In the first, an army marches to battle across a lonely mountain; the horror of the rocks and shadows makes the men undervalue their lives and they gain an easy victory. In the second, the same army traverses a palace where a great festival is taking place; the resplendent battle seems to them a continuation of the celebration and they win the victory. I listened with proper veneration to these ancient narratives, perhaps less admirable in themselves than the fact that they had been created by my blood and were being restored to me by a man of a remote empire, in the course of a desperate adventure, on a Western isle. I remember the last words, repeated in each version like a secret commandment: *Thus fought the heroes, tranquil their admirable hearts, violent their swords, resigned to kill and to die.*

From that moment on, I felt about me and within my dark body an invisible, intangible swarming. Not the swarming of the divergent, parallel and finally coalescent armies, but a more inaccessible, more intimate agitation that they in some manner prefigured. Stephen Albert continued:

"I don't believe that your illustrious ancestor played idly with these variations. I don't consider it credible that he would sacrifice thirteen years to the infinite execution of a rhetorical experiment. In your country, the novel is a subsidiary form of literature; in Ts'ui Pên's time it was a despicable form. Ts'ui Pên was a brilliant novelist, but he was also a man of letters who doubtless did not consider himself a mere novelist. The testimony of his contemporaries proclaims—and his life fully confirms—his metaphysical and mystical interests. Philosophic controversy usurps a good part of the novel. I know that of all problems, none disturbed him so greatly nor worked upon him so much as the abysmal problem of time. Now then, the latter is the only problem that does not figure in the pages of the *Garden*. He does not even use the word that signifies *time*. How do you explain this voluntary omission?"

I proposed several solutions—all unsatisfactory. We discussed them. Finally, Stephen Albert said to me:

"In a riddle whose answer is chess, what is the only prohibited word?"

I thought a moment and replied, "The word *chess*."

"Precisely," said Albert. "*The Garden of Forking Paths* is an enormous riddle, or parable, whose theme is time; this recondite cause prohibits its mention. To omit a word always, to resort to inept metaphors and obvious periphrases, is perhaps the most emphatic way of stressing it. That is the tortuous method preferred, in each of the meanderings of his indefatigable novel, by the oblique Ts'ui Pên. I have compared hundreds of manuscripts, I have corrected the errors that the negligence of the copyists has introduced, I have guessed the plan of this chaos, I have re-established—I believe I have re-established—the primordial organization, I have translated the entire work: it is clear to me that not once does he employ the word 'time.' The explanation is obvious: *The Garden of Forking Paths* is an incomplete, but not false, image of the universe as Ts'ui Pên conceived it. In contrast to Newton and Schopenhauer, your ancestor did not believe in a uniform, absolute time. He believed in an infinite series of times, in a growing, dizzying net of divergent, convergent and parallel times. This network of times which approached one another, forked, broke off, or were unaware of one another for centuries, embraces *all* possibilities of time. We do not exist in the majority of these times; in some you exist, and not I; in others I, and not you; in others, both of us. In the present one, which a favorable fate has granted me, you have arrived at my house; in another, while crossing the garden, you found me dead; in still another, I utter these same words, but I am a mistake, a ghost."

"In every one," I pronounced, not without a tremble to my voice, "I am grateful to you and revere you for your re-creation of the garden of Ts'ui Pên."

"Not in all," he murmured with a smile. "Time forks perpetually toward innumerable futures. In one of them I am your enemy."

Once again I felt the swarming sensation of which I have spoken. It seemed to me that the humid garden that surrounded the house was infinitely saturated with invisible persons. Those persons were Albert and I, secret, busy and multiform in other dimensions of time. I raised my eyes and the tenuous nightmare dissolved. In the yellow and black garden there was only one man; but this man was as strong as a statue . . . this man was approaching along the path and he was Captain Richard Madden.

"The future already exists," I replied, "but I am your friend. Could I see the letter again?"

Albert rose. Standing tall, he opened the drawer of the tall desk; for the moment his back was to me. I had readied the revolver. I fired with extreme caution. Albert fell uncomplainingly, immediately. I swear his death was instantaneous—a lightning stroke.

The rest is unreal, insignificant. Madden broke in, arrested me. I have been condemned to the gallows. I have won out abominably; I have communicated to Berlin the secret name of the city they must attack. They bombed it yesterday; I read it in the same papers that offered to England the mystery of the learned Sinologist Stephen Albert who was murdered by a stranger, one Yu Tsun. The Chief had deciphered this mystery. He knew my problem was to indicate (through the uproar of the war) the city called Albert, and that I had found no other means to do so than to kill a man of that name. He does not know (no one can know) my innumerable contrition and weariness.

QUESTIONS FOR DISCUSSION AND WRITING

1. "The Garden of Forking Paths" is not only a frame story—one in which an "outer story" has embedded in it another story—it also is multiply framed, like a series of Chinese boxes. Furthermore, each of the threads of narrative, both framing and embedded, involves a text of some sort. Discuss the relation between the passage from Hart's *History of World War I*, the statement from Yu Tsun containing his account of how he transmitted the location of the British artillery base to Germany, and the story of how Yu Tsun's ancestor Ts'ui Pên wrote a novel and constructed a labyrinth, as explained by Stephen Albert.

2. Yu Tsun, on his way to Stephen Albert's house, reflects that, "The author of an atrocious undertaking ought to imagine that he has already accomplished it, ought to impose upon himself a future as irrevocable as the past." Does Yu Tsun, in some sense, do this himself?

3. One interpretation of "The Garden of Forking Paths" is that it is about the nature of fiction and that "The Garden of Forking Paths" (the story) is like *The Garden of Forking Paths* (Ts'ui Pên's labyrinth novel, which is embedded in the story). Discuss.

4. A complementary interpretation of the story might emphasize its use of fiction as a metaphor for human life and how it suggests that we organize our lives by constructing fictions that help us conceptualize human choice, time, and reality. Discuss.

Toshio Mori

Toshio Mori (1910–1980) was a pioneer of Japanese-American writing. He was born and spent his life in the San Francisco Bay area, except for the years of World War II, when he was interned, along with other Americans of Japanese descent, in a camp in Topaz Center, Utah. *Yokohama, California,* a collection of short stories set in the Bay area, was published in 1949. A second collection, *The Chauvinist and Other Stories,* and a novel, *Woman from Hiroshima,* were both published in 1979.

TOSHIO MORI

In the late afternoon he began wanting to go to the city. When the quitting time came he wanted very much to go to the city. All day the spell of bleakness and dullness witched him, and although the day was unusually warm and sunny he could not erase the spell. He wanted to do something, to do anything, to move, to get over the feeling that was disturbing him. He could think of nothing to do but go to the city, to crush and wipe out this ominous feeling of standing alone, walking alone, going alone, without a nod or a smile or caress or better, an understanding from someone.

Tonight Teruo boarded the bus, leaving behind what to him was sad and dark today, and looking forward, expectantly, hopefully, to the night and the city and the people to revive him, his spirit and the return of undivorced feeling toward the world, the people, the life. He was certain there was that quality in the city to reward him for his efforts. He would go to the friends, go to the girls' houses, go to the spots that would bring back the old days, and go to show if necessary, go everywhere, go to all the places and the people tonight to drown out his senseless strain and motion.

He sat, riding to the city, without a thought of the past which was this afternoon, deliberately forgetting, erasing the melancholia. Once he recalled the afternoon. Must you go tonight? his mother had said. Yes, I must go tonight, he had said. I must go no matter what else happens. And he meant it. Tonight he could not sit with the family and talk. Tonight he could not listen to the radio; he could not read. He could not, moreover, sit in silence like other nights, in constant wake of himself and the field he worked in the daytime. So he was doing right tonight. Something in the city would divert his attention or someone would see and understand the state he was in and would lend a hand. Everything would come out all right, he said to himself; everything must come out all right.

Teruo got off at Twelfth and Clay and walked down a block and turned up Eleventh Street. He headed straight for Tsuyuko's home without much thought. Then walking closer to the house that was gay and lively, he could see her sitting in the living room reading or listening to the short wave program from Japan or playing those sad melancholy songs on the Japanese records. He could see her running up to him when the doorbell rings and cry, Oh, hello! Teruo. How glad I am to see you!

He was confident she was home. And nearing her home he could see the bright lighted living room and knew she was home. She would always be home. That was her nature, he thought. So when she opened the door and squealed in delight he was certain now everything would turn out right.

"Oh, hello! Teruo," she said. "How delightful! Do come in!"

But that was not all. There were two young men in the room. He recognized one of them as Haruo Aratani and the other he did not know and Tsuyuko introduced him. They sat down and the conversation which was interrupted by his entrance was resumed. And between laughters and talk Tsuyuko asked him how he was getting along these days. He said he was just so-so.

The moment Teruo sat down he knew the place was not for him. There was the same gaiety and liveliness in the room, the same Tsuyuko of other nights, but it was not the same. As he sat in the midst of laughter and lively chatter he felt he was out of it all, alone, alien, orphaned. The contrast he was playing in the room, helplessly coming, shook him and the longer he remained in the room, the more he thought of this and the helplessness of himself. He sat forty minutes thinking, still hoping that something might happen, that some little bit of a thing or a gesture or a movement would change the makeup of the room to something that would resurrect him but it did not come. He sat ill, stifling, wanting to move, to talk, and that something did not happen and he did not move. Teruo left early, Tsuyuko saw him off at the door and told him to come again real soon. When he crossed the street to the other side he saw Tsuyuko through the window, returning to the living room that was gaiety and laughter and two young men.

He began to walk rapidly with no mind as to where he was going. For blocks he could think of nothing else. She was not at fault. She really was herself and the two young men were blameless. There was nothing that had irritated him, no incident, no envy or jealousy to be furious about. It made him all the more sad and deserted.

Just tonight, he thought. If we had been alone together, just tonight, it might have been different. She might understand, she might only have smiled and listened and said nothing and it might have done a world of good for him. Just to have her close to him tonight, to understand him as he understood his state of feeling, would have been sufficient. That was all he would ask for. She could go with the two young men anytime, anywhere, all the other times and that was all right. She could go as she pleased and that was right. But tonight, he thought, tonight was different.

After walking blocks of city blocks he remembered the home on Sixth Street. He could go and see Yuri. He was in town; this was the time to see her. He would talk to her. She was serious and read books and she might understand. In time, by talking and listening he might find the way to the outlet and forget the emptiness of self and dullness of time. She could understand; yes, she could.

He quickened his pace. Already it was nine o'clock. He must hasten to catch Yuri home. When he knocked on the door the mother came out. She said Yuri went out early and would not be home till late but wouldn't he come in and have tea. He declined; and having left the steps and the sidewalks of her block, he turned once more toward the city.

He could think of nothing else to do. He did not feel like going to a movie now. Through his head raced a number of names that were familiar. Names of his friends, names of his parents' intimates, and of special names, Bob, Tora, Kazumi, Sumio, Min, George. But the names did not come alive; he could think of nothing to do in the city, having now played his hunches and failed.

Reaching the town he went in Tabe Drug's soda fountain and sat and ordered a vanilla milkshake. Razzy, the soda jerker, remembered him and hailed. "How's the tricks?" he said. "Not so hot," Teruo said, "does the old gang still come in?" "Yes, you bet," Razzy said. "Tora, Sumio, Kazumi, Bob, Butch, Min, George."

"Have they come in recently?" Teruo said. "No, not for quite awhile," the soda jerker said. That was all.

While he was sipping his milkshake Sumio and his woman came in. Sumio came over and both slapped each other's back. "How's the old boy?" Sumio said. "Fine," said Teruo, "how are you?" "Great," said Sumio. They talked for a while about the old gang and the old days, and then Sumio went back to his table.

Five minutes later Teruo said goodbye and left.

He walked up Broadway toward the theatrical center thinking of going home now at nine forty-five. There was nothing to do but go home. All his efforts had failed, each effort making him more miserable and conscious of aloneness and sadness. He decided he might just as well go home and bury himself in the bed.

But approaching the theater, his eyes were attracted to the bright lights of its front, bright and cheery in illumination, suggesting hope and cheerfulness inside. He might as well, he thought, take a last fling for the night. So Teruo bought a ticket and went inside the Roosevelt Theater to see the vaudeville.

He remembered watching a comic with a little bit of an accordion and a big size accordion. With the little accordion he had a trick note that made a noise like a raspberry from a human mouth. Every once in while he would sound this note and the people laughed. He had a face like Harry Langdon or Lloyd Hamilton of the old silent pictures, looking pathetic and funny. He was trying to be funny and wasn't funny, and was funny for lack of it. Then Teruo remembered a lovely blonde singing into the microphone in her throaty voice, of being away from the Ozarks, of wanting to go back there, of seeing her pappy and the smell of chicken dinner, and of the Ozarks calling her back. It made him sad and her beautiful face and innocence made it all the more tragic and agonizing that she, with her beauty, should sing such sad songs. He could stand it no more. When the vaudeville was over he walked out of the theater missing the double features.

When Teruo reached home the house was dark. It was dead still as if no one were occupying the house but himself coming home and occupying the place. But he knew his parents were sleeping inside and his brothers were also sleeping.

He sat on the edge of the bed, making little noise, and began undressing. He was aware that the night was almost over, that tonight was almost through with him. But he knew he was not through with the state of his feeling. Instead, tonight increased the fervor of sadness and loneliness, and for a long while Teruo did not shut off his light.

He was still up at two in the morning. He could hear the breathing of his mother sleeping in the next room, and on the other side of the wall he could hear his brother snoring. He sat, aware that no one knew him as he knew himself. He knew even Mother and his brother Hajime could not see his state of feeling; that no one in this world would see, and if seeing would not see, unable to understand and share his state of feeling that was accumulating and had been accumulating since birth.

QUESTIONS FOR DISCUSSION AND WRITING

1. "Toshio Mori" is a third-person story about a young man named "Teruo," and yet it is given the author's name. What does this suggest about

its autobiographical content? About the nature of fiction? About the process of understanding ourselves by turning our lives into narrative?

2.   In the last line of the story, we are told of Teruo's "state of feeling that was accumulating and had been accumulating since birth." What is this state of feeling? Is it merely an adolescent sense of alienation and self-dramatization? Or does it seem to be something more? Does the story offer any clues?

3.   The critic Shirley Geok-lin Lim has written that Mori "seldom focuses on conflicts of dual identity but affirms instead the enfolding of Japanese identity in the American." Does this comment seem relevant to this story?

Tillie Olsen

Tillie Olsen (b. 1913) has had an unusual career. She was born in Omaha, Nebraska, into a working-class family that had fled persecution in czarist Russia. The coming of the 1929 depression forced her to drop out of high school. She worked as a factory laborer and then as a secretary and was active as a labor organizer. Although she published some fiction in the 1930s, the demands of work and child care left her little time to write until 1955, when her youngest child began school. Olsen won a creative-writing fellowship at Stanford University and published her first collection of short stories, *Tell Me a Riddle*, in 1961. It won an O. Henry Award for the best short story of the year for the title story. She has since published *Yonnondio* (1974), a novel begun when she was nineteen, and *Silences* (1978), a collection of essays.

I STAND HERE IRONING

I stand here ironing, and what you asked me moves tormented back and forth with the iron.

"I wish you would manage the time to come and talk with me about your daughter. I'm sure you can help me understand her. She's a youngster who needs help and whom I'm deeply interested in helping."

"Who needs help." . . . Even if I came, what good would it do? You think because I am her mother I have a key, or that in some way you could use me as a key? She has lived for nineteen years. There is all that life that has happened outside of me, beyond me.

And when is there time to remember, to sift, to weigh, to estimate, to total? I will start and there will be an interruption and I will have to gather it all together again. Or I will become engulfed with all I did or did not do, with what should have been and what cannot be helped.

She was a beautiful baby. The first and only one of our five that was beautiful at birth. You do not guess how new and uneasy her tenancy in her now-loveliness. You did not know her all those years she was thought homely, or see her poring over her baby pictures, making me tell her over and over how beautiful she had been—and would be, I would tell her—and was now, to the seeing eye. But the seeing eyes were few or nonexistent. Including mine.

I nursed her. They feel that's important nowadays. I nursed all the children, but with her, with all the fierce rigidity of first motherhood, I did like the books then said. Though her cries battered me to trembling and my breasts ached with swollenness, I waited till the clock decreed.

Why do I put that first? I do not even know if it matters, or if it explains anything.

She was a beautiful baby. She blew shining bubbles of sound. She loved motion, loved light, loved color and music and textures. She would lie on the floor in her blue overalls patting the surface so hard in ecstasy her hands and feet would blur. She was a miracle to me, but when she was eight months old I had to leave her daytimes with the woman downstairs to whom she was no miracle at all, for I worked or looked for work and for Emily's father, who "could no longer endure" (he wrote in his good-bye note) "sharing want with us."

I was nineteen. It was the pre-relief, pre-WPA world of the depression. I would start running as soon as I got off the streetcar, running up the stairs, the place smelling sour, and awake or asleep to startle awake, when she saw me she would break into a clogged weeping that could not be comforted, a weeping I can hear yet.

After a while I found a job hashing at night so I could be with her days, and it was better. But it came to where I had to bring her to his family and leave her.

It took a long time to raise the money for her fare back. Then she got chicken pox and I had to wait longer. When she finally came, I hardly knew her, walking quick and nervous like her father, looking like her father, thin, and dressed in a shoddy red that yellowed her skin and glared at the pockmarks. All the baby loveliness gone.

She was two. Old enough for nursery school they said, and I did not know then what I know now—the fatigue of the long day, and the lacerations of group life in the kinds of nurseries that are only parking places for children.

Except that it would have made no difference if I had known. It was the only place there was. It was the only way we could be together, the only way I could hold a job.

And even without knowing, I knew. I knew the teacher that was evil because all these years it has curdled into my memory, the little boy hunched in the corner, her rasp, "why aren't you outside, because Alvin hits you? that's no reason, go out, scaredy." I knew Emily hated it even if she did not clutch and implore "don't go Mommy" like the other children, mornings.

She always had a reason why we should stay home. Momma, you look sick. Momma, I feel sick. Momma, the teachers aren't there today, they're sick. Momma, we can't go, there was a fire there last night. Momma, it's a holiday today, no school, they told me.

But never a direct protest, never rebellion. I think of our others in their three-, four-year-oldness—the explosions, the tempers, the denunciations, the de-mands—and I feel suddenly ill. I put the iron down. What in me demanded that goodness in her? And what was the cost, the cost to her of such goodness?

The old man living in the back once said in his gentle way: "You should smile at Emily more when you look at her." What *was* in my face when I looked at her? I loved her. There were all the acts of love.

It was only with the others I remembered what he said, and it was the face of joy, and not of care or tightness or worry I turned to them—too late for Emily. She does not smile easily, let alone almost always as her brothers and sisters do. Her face is closed and sombre, but when she wants, how fluid. You must have seen it in her pantomimes, you spoke of her rare gift for comedy on the stage that rouses laughter out of the audience so dear they applaud and applaud and do not want to let her go.

Where does it come from, that comedy? There was none of it in her when she came back to me that second time, after I had had to send her away again. She had a new daddy now to learn to love, and I think perhaps it was a better time.

Except when we left her alone nights, telling ourselves she was old enough.

"Can't you go some other time, Mommy, like tomorrow?" she would ask. "Will it be just a little while you'll be gone? Do you promise?"

The time we came back, the front door open, the clock on the floor in the hall. She rigid awake. "It wasn't just a little while. I didn't cry. Three times I called you, just three times, and then I ran downstairs to open the door so you could come faster. The clock talked loud. I threw it away, it scared me what it talked."

She said the clock talked loud again that night I went to the hospital to have

Susan. She was delirious with the fever that comes before red measles, but she was fully conscious all the week I was gone and the week after we were home when she could not come near the new baby or me.

She did not get well. She stayed skeleton thin, not wanting to eat, and night after night she had nightmares. She would call for me, and I would rouse from exhaustion to sleepily call back: "You're all right, darling, go to sleep, it's just a dream," and if she still called, in a sterner voice, "now go to sleep, Emily, there's nothing to hurt you." Twice, only twice, when I had to get up for Susan anyhow, I went in to sit with her.

Now when it is too late (as if she would let me hold and comfort her like I do the others) I get up and go to her at once at her moan or restless stirring. "Are you awake, Emily? Can I get you something?" And the answer is always the same: "No, I'm all right, go back to sleep, Mother."

They persuaded me at the clinic to send her away to a convalescent home in the country where "she can have the kind of food and care you can't manage for her, and you'll be free to concentrate on the new baby." They still send children to that place. I see pictures on the society page of sleek young women planning affairs to raise money for it, or dancing at the affairs, or decorating Easter eggs or filling Christmas stockings for the children.

They never have a picture of the children so I do not know if the girls still wear those gigantic red bows and the ravaged looks on the every other Sunday when parents can come to visit "unless otherwise notified"—as we were notified the first six weeks.

Oh it is a handsome place, green lawns and tall trees and fluted flower beds. High up on the balconies of each cottage the children stand, the girls in their red bows and white dresses, the boys in white suits and giant red ties. The parents stand below shrieking up to be heard and the children shriek down to be heard, and between them the invisible wall: "Not to Be Contaminated by Parental Germs or Physical Affection."

There was a tiny girl who always stood hand in hand with Emily. Her parents never came. One visit she was gone. "They moved her to Rose Cottage," Emily shouted in explanation. "They don't like you to love anybody here."

She wrote once a week, a labored writing of a seven-year-old. "I am fine. How is the baby. If I write my leter nicly I well have a star. Love." There never was a star. We wrote every other day, letters she could never hold or keep but only hear read—once. "We simply do not have room for children to keep any personal possessions," they patiently explained when we pieced one Sunday's shrieking together to plead how much it would mean to Emily, who loved so to keep things, to be allowed to keep her letters and cards.

Each visit she looked frailer. "She isn't eating," they told us.

(They had runny eggs for breakfast or mush with lumps, Emily said later, I'd hold it in my mouth and not swallow. Nothing ever tasted good, just when they had chicken.)

It took us eight months to get her released home, and only the fact that she gained back so little of her seven lost pounds convinced the social worker.

I used to try to hold and love her after she came back, but her body would stay stiff, and after a while she'd push away. She ate little. Food sickened her, and I think much of life too. Oh she had physical lightness and brightness, twinkling by on skates, bouncing like a ball up and down up and down over the jump rope, skimming over the hill; but these were momentary.

She fretted about her appearance, thin and dark and foreign-looking at a time when every little girl was supposed to look or thought she should look a chubby blonde replica of Shirley Temple. The doorbell sometimes rang for her, but no one seemed to come and play in the house or be a best friend. Maybe because we moved so much.

There was a boy she loved painfully through two school semesters. Months later she told me how she had taken pennies from my purse to buy him candy. "Licorice was his favorite and I brought him some every day, but he still likes Jennifer better'n me. Why, Mommy?" The kind of question for which there is no answer.

School was a worry to her. She was not glib or quick in a world where glibness and quickness were easily confused with ability to learn. To her overworked and exasperated teachers she was an overconscientious "slow learner" who kept trying to catch up and was absent entirely too often.

I let her be absent, though sometimes the illness was imaginary. How different from my now-strictness about attendance with the others. I wasn't working. We had a new baby, I was home anyhow. Sometimes, after Susan grew old enough, I would keep her home from school, too, to have them all together.

Mostly Emily had asthma, and her breathing, harsh and labored, would fill the house with a curiously tranquil sound. I would bring the two old dresser mirrors and her boxes of collections to her bed. She would select beads and single earrings, bottle tops and shells, dried flowers and pebbles, old postcards and scraps, all sorts of oddments; then she and Susan would play Kingdom, setting up landscapes and furniture, peopling them with action.

Those were the only times of peaceful companionship between her and Susan. I have edged away from it, that poisonous feeling between them, that terrible balancing of hurts and needs I had to do between the two, and did so badly, those earlier years.

Oh there are conflicts between the others too, each one human, needing, demanding, hurting, taking—but only between Emily and Susan, no, Emily toward Susan that corroding resentment. It seems so obvious on the surface, yet it is not obvious. Susan, the second child, Susan, golden- and curly-haired and chubby, quick and articulate and assured, everything in appearance and manner Emily was not; Susan, not able to resist Emily's precious things, losing or sometimes clumsily breaking them; Susan telling jokes and riddles to company for applause while Emily sat silent (to say to me later: that was *my* riddle, Mother, I told it to Susan); Susan, who for all the five years' difference in age was just a year behind Emily in developing physically.

I am glad for that slow physical development that widened the difference between her and her contemporaries, though she suffered over it. She was too vulnerable for that terrible world of youthful competition, of preening and parading, of constant measuring of yourself against every other, of envy, "If I had that copper hair," "If I had that skin . . . " She tormented herself enough about not looking like the others, there was enough of the unsureness, the having to be conscious of words before you speak, the constant caring—what are they thinking of me? Without having it all magnified by the merciless physical drives.

Ronnie is calling. He is wet and I change him. It is rare there is such a cry now. That time of motherhood is almost behind me when the ear is not one's own but must always be racked and listening for the child cry, the child call. We sit for a while and I hold him, looking out over the city spread in charcoal with its soft aisles of light. "*Shoogily*," he breathes and curls closer. I carry him back to bed, asleep. *Shoogily*. A funny word, a family word, inherited from Emily, invented by her to say: *comfort*.

In this and other ways she leaves her seal, I say aloud. And startle at my saying it. What do I mean? What did I start to gather together, and try and make coherent? I was at the terrible, growing years. War years. I do not remember them well. I was working, there were four smaller ones now, there was not time for her. She had to help be a mother, and housekeeper, and shopper. She had to set her seal. Mornings of crisis and near hysteria trying to get lunches packed, hair combed, coats and shoes found, everyone to school or Child Care on time, the baby ready for transportation. And always the paper scribbled on by a smaller one, the book looked at by Susan then mislaid, the homework not done. Running out to that huge school where she was one, she was lost, she was a drop; suffering over the unpreparedness, stammering and unsure in her classes.

There was so little time left at night after the kids were bedded down. She would struggle over books, always eating (it was in those years she developed her enormous appetite that is legendary in our family) and I would be ironing, or preparing food for the next day, or writing V-mail to Bill, or tending the baby. Sometimes, to make me laugh, or out of her despair, she would imitate happenings or types at school.

I think I said once: "Why don't you do something like this in the school amateur show?" One morning she phoned me at work, hardly understandable through the weeping: "Mother, I did it. I won, I won; they gave me first prize; they clapped and clapped and wouldn't let me go."

Now suddenly she was Somebody, and as imprisoned in her difference as she had been in anonymity.

She began to be asked to perform at other high schools, even in colleges, then at city and statewide affairs. The first one we went to, I only recognized her that first moment when thin, shy, she almost drowned herself into the curtains. Then: Was this Emily? The control, the command, the convulsing and deadly clowning, the spell, then the roaring, stamping audience, unwilling to let this rare and precious laughter out of their lives.

Afterwards: You ought to do something about her with a gift like that—but without money or knowing how, what does one do? We have left it all to her, and the gift has as often eddied inside, clogged and clotted, as been used and growing.

She is coming. She runs up the stairs two at a time with her light graceful step, and I know she is happy tonight. Whatever it was that occasioned your call did not happen today.

"Aren't you ever going to finish ironing, Mother? Whistler painted his mother in a rocker. I'd have to paint mine standing over an ironing board." This is one of her communicative nights and she tells me everything and nothing as she fixes herself a plate of food out of the icebox.

She is so lovely. Why did you want me to come in at all? Why were you concerned? She will find her way.

She starts up the stairs to bed. "Don't get me up with the rest in the morning." "But I thought you were having midterms." "Oh, those," she comes back in, kisses me, and says quite lightly, "in a couple of years when we'll all be atom-dead they won't matter a bit."

She has said it before. She *believes* it. But because I have been dredging the past, and all that compounds a human being is so heavy and meaningful in me, I cannot endure it tonight.

I will never total it all. I will never come in to say: She was a child seldom smiled at. Her father left me before she was a year old. I had to work her first six years when there was work, or I sent her home and to his relatives. There were years she had care she hated. She was dark and thin and foreign-looking in a world where the prestige went to blondeness and curly hair and dimples, she was slow where glibness was prized. She was a child of anxious, not proud, love. We were poor and could not afford for her the soil of easy growth. I was a young mother, I was a distracted mother. There were other children pushing up, demanding. Her younger sister seemed all that she was not. There were years she did not want me to touch her. She kept too much in herself, her life was such she had to keep too much in herself. My wisdom came too late. She has much to her and probably little will come of it. She is a child of her age, of depression, of war, of fear.

Let her be. So all that is in her will not bloom—but in how many does it? There is still enough left to live by. Only help her to know—help make it so there is cause for her to know—that she is more than this dress on the ironing board, helpless before the iron.

QUESTIONS FOR DISCUSSION AND WRITING

1. "I Stand Here Ironing" has an unusual rhetorical structure. Look at the first sentence. Who is "I" and who is "you"? Are we to understand the story as literally spoken to the teacher? Or is the monologue an imaginary or hypothetical one? (Notice that "you" never interrupts or responds.) What is gained by such a rhetorical arrangement?

2. "I did not know then what I know now," the narrator says, and there is a sense that mistakes she made with Emily were not repeated with her younger children. Trace the difference in the story between youthful ignorance and later knowledge.

3. Some of the obstacles Emily faces are existential—in the nature of things—while others are caused by a flawed society. Can you distinguish between the two?

4. Emily develops a gift for comedy and wins recognition at school. Does the story give any indication of how she developed this gift? Consider the proposition that one of the themes of the story is the nature of art and that Emily's comedy is parallel to her mother's writing of this story.

Mary TallMountain

Mary TallMountain (b. 1918), of Athabaskan, Russian, and Scots-Irish descent, was born in the Alaskan bush but has lived for many years in San Francisco. Her books include *Nine Poems* (1979), *There Is No Word for Goodbye* (1981), *Green March Moons* (1987), and *The Light on the Tent Wall: A Bridging* (1990).

THE SINH OF NIGUUDZAGHA

Niguudzagha had been abroad since first light. He emerged silently from the stand of spruce and trudged along a small bridge of planks thrown down across the slough. The dark side of Graveyard Hill rose in front of him. Unhurriedly he climbed the long slanting path. His steps paused at intervals that he might rest and draw the sharp clean air deeply into his lungs. Strength flowed through his slender body and into the crevices of his brain. Here and there he stopped at a grave sunken beneath the grass, only its tilted wooden cross marking its presence. Names and images slipped through his mind, locking him so intensely into the past that it startled him when he found he had reached the crest of the Hill. The oldest gravehouses had fallen into scatters of boards and glass. Only the sturdiest remained. One of these stood at the point of the Hill, its corrugated iron walls leaning out to the river. At the roofpeak was nailed the large oval mirror of a bureau, the once ornate walnut frame buffeted and bleached white by storms. The glass was still intact. It flashed above the village like a watchful eye.

Wild rosebushes grew here, and the dry blossoms clung to bare stems. Niguudzagha stood motionless. With a stubby thumb he rubbed a rose into his palm and scattered its dust out on the wind. Parting the grasses, he came down upon the brow of the dome to the place where no graves were. He waited against the stillness of the Hill, his eyes lifted to the eastern rim of earth along which the mountains crouched like dark sleeping animals.

No-oy thrust his burning face out of the dark descent beyond the mountains.

A column of mist poured down the river, whitely muffling its broad curve. Far out in the Kaiyuh, little creeks swarmed in the meadows like coiled snakes. A moose stood haunch-deep in a lake, his immense antlered bulk a still, black speck. The waterways were filled with the distantly shrill commotion of feeding birds. A flurry of pale wings shaped itself roughly into a ladder, drifted south, and faded into enormous stretches of sky.

No-oy slipped higher with the imperceptible wheel of earth. His first blaze stuck across the mist and lighted Niguudzagha's thick white hair. Niguudzagha lowered himself stiffly into a bowl of tamped-down grass curtained by weeds that rattled sparse and faint in small gusts of wind. *No-oy* pressed heat through the heavy red plaid of his mackinaw and he held out his hands. His lips moved. Heat crept steadily into his flesh.

Dew lay on the bark and plants he had gathered and heaped loosely in the sack at his belt. The sack was worn and stained with juices from the plants. He had knotted it of string in squares to let the green creatures breathe. Gently he touched a leaf of dock, sensing through the paper-thin skin of his fingertips the rushing life under its hairy surface. He sniffed the sharp scent and murmured a few words. Leaning forward in the dry nest, he tucked the sack under the weeds. Then he lay back and let the earth clasp his narrow bones.

He was the last medicine man.

Closing his eyes, he summoned *sinh*. After a time, *sinh* floated down to him. His vision subtly altered. Against the screen of his eyelids he saw the people coming out of their cabins to the river, tiny shapes in barest motion upon the fastnesses of the land. Their voices floated up, no louder than the piping of insects. He sent *sinh* wandering through Nulato village, and the faces passed before him with their secrets. Niguudzagha was the oldest among the people. There was nothing he did not know about them. In this was power, but he demanded nothing of it. All he desired had been given. He felt regret only that a portion was now lost to them of the ancient and harmonious balance between the worlds in which they moved.

Andrew's face came before him. His clear questioning gaze fixed itself upon Niguudzagha's. Andrew, first son of Big Mike. His death had come in the time of leaves falling. He had gone out to set net for dog salmon. His canoe overturned. His faint shouts were heard from the shore, and then was heard only the voice of the river. When his friends reached the strong middle current, he was gone.

The people grieved because Niguudzagha could not perform the ceremonies for Andrew as in old times. The priests had warned them that to summon and speak with the *yeega'* of the dead in that manner was an evil thing. But there was a yet more serious matter. Andrew had gone into strange places and his wife and children could not lay him in the family plot. They were terrified. His spirit was surely lost. They implored Niguudzagha to find it. Having foreseen, he acquiesced. He performed the rite in the silence and secrecy of night beneath the cold dark river.

He imparted these matters to Andrew in reassuring soft mutters of Athabaskan. Andrew's face withdrew. Niguudzagha knew with a rush of certainty that he had gone safely to his right place. His *yeega'* roamed tranquil in the other world, much like this one except that there, it was the time of big snow. About him, speaking familiarly, the animals and birds attended him. He was set free of the other spirits who prowled fearsomely upon the earth. A shadow curtain had lifted from his senses, and he was one with the world above.

Creases of pleasure curved Niguudzagha's cheeks and he settled deep into the nest. His old clawlike hands clasped and loosened. He drifted slowly back to himself and was immediately seized by the warmth of *No-oy*. Looking up, he spoke into the great blazing eye: "Now it is made good."

Since his youth he had talked to *No-oy*. He was even then given over to the things of the earth. In the days of *esnaih*, when the band followed the call of animals and birds and of the fish of the river, he left the other children playing and wandered in lone places. As his years increased, he passed hours considering the ways of the earth and creatures. When he tried, his mind emptied of all but the great land breathing about him. A day came when he realized he had been lying on the ground engaged in speech with an alder tree.

At this Niguudzagha smiled, remembering that he had not feared that first messenger who would be one of his familiars. After his first speech with the alder, he ate and drank nothing for three days and kept silence as men did before the hunt. In the woods, fasting and faint, he sometimes fell down and lay unconscious. He awakened with a sense of having wandered timelessly in vast bright spaces beyond the world. He staggered when he stood. Incomprehensible words came from his lips. He began to fly out far above his mind, and crawling on his belly cried once to an unknown being: "Give me wisdom to counsel others!" When he emerged from the trance he did not know how he could have spoken so. It was the way elder persons talked.

Niguudzagha's mind flickered again to the people. Today they were in vital balance. Daily he assured himself of their well-being, for they were surrounded by the *yeega'* of unseen creatures. The mysteries, he thought, were beyond the small comprehension of any man. At certain seasons the spirits were honored in ceremonies by all the people gathered as one. He performed, alone with *sinh* and the lesser guides, other rites too potent for the telling. He never spoke of them, and never uttered the names of *yeega'*.

The people were loath to speak of these matters of the spirit world to the *Gisakk* priests. It was bad luck. *Yeega'* would be angered. But they confided, a little at a time and under subtle questioning. "Over us all is the Master of the world. Everything in the world is by him," they said. "He care about our game and fish. A man has to be careful. If he step on his catch or dirty it, it don't look right. It's like we don't care."

"One should never offend the giver of food, the avenger of waste?" one of the Fathers had asked Niguudzagha long ago.

Niguudzagha told him, "If we mistreat *yeega'*, then when the people are hard up, all this would come back and we would know we are being punished."

"You believe in God, then," the Father said.

With reluctance, Niguudzagha replied, "There is some Being who look down on us and see what we do. He is every place, but he has no name."

Now he scratched his head with a feeling of helplessness. He was sorry he had revealed this knowledge belonging to the people. But in a way, the Father seemed like another medicine man. Except for one thing. Niguudzagha had a persistent sense that he and the Father were not considered equals. Father wore a certain manner of authority. This went with the giving of orders, Niguudzagha thought. And only the Being of no name gave orders to the people until *Gisakk* came among them. As to himself, he knew he had always lived in the presence of the Being. This mysterious perception had been infused into him by the incessant dreams.

Gaagateeya', his grandfather, had understood. Grandfather was full of years and well accustomed to dreaming. One day he looked into the boy's face with eyes curtained by a white film. "Ah, Kuskaga!" he exclaimed.

That was Niguudzagha's name then, a name that meant harpoon for his parents had wished him to be keen and straight. The name had been worn by an ancestor deep in the past when the people lived by the sea. Kuskaga held himself utterly still for long periods, in the manner of the harpoon, waiting for that creature which he saw coming toward him in the watery, shifting shapes of the dreams.

The filmed eyes of Gaagateeya' wavered and Kuskaga thought they could see his face only as a blur. "You visit with the trees," Gaagateeya' said.

"Yes, my grandfather."

"You talk to trees?"

Kuskaga shuffled his feet restlessly. "They talk too," he said.

"Ahhh, my youngest son." Grandfather's white look glided out and fixed upon the gleam of *No-oy* dancing on the river. "You talk to any other?" The eyes shone purely, like dentalium shell.

"Many other." Kuskaga bent his head and studied the stones of the ground.

"Who?"

Hesitantly, "*Doyon . . . Nokinbaa . . . Gagaa . . . Dotson*".*

---

*Wolverine . . . Snowy Owl . . . King Salmon . . . Raven.

"Oho!" Grandfather said. "These you dream?"

"I don't know . . . " Kuskaga hesitated. "One time I talk to real *Dotson'* on a tree!"

"Oh, that fellow! What did he say?"

"He tell me I have to wait, that's all."

With a smile, Grandfather said, "You get scared and nervous, yah?"

"All the time," Kuskaga admitted.

Grandfather's eyes closed. After a while he said, "That's good." He pulled Kuskaga to his knee. "You have fourteen years now, isn't it? Always you wait for something and you wonder what is that thing. Now I tell you. You will be medicine man, I think."

Kuskaga's breath caught, and his mind circled among all he had seen and heard. At last he had received an answer to the endless puzzle of his mysterious actions. His chest tightened. "How can this be?"

"All these creatures are your helpers," Grandfather said. "They bring big message. First you will learn all about our people and the land we walk upon here. You will know animals and their *yeega'*. At a time when it is right, your *sinh* will come. When that happens, you will go far out of yourself. And you will be medicine man. But you will learn more. You will know the secret language of *sinh*. You will make *yeega'* songs and sing to game and fish. Then you will pass under the river."

At this Kuskaga shivered. He gasped, thinking: I dream too much. I have no strength. How can I do medicine man's work?

Grandfather smiled. His broad front teeth protruded, a wide space at each side like Beaver's. Kuskaga remembered with a shock that Grandfather was a medicine man of the old time. He had been named Gaagateeya' for Beaver, the builder. He passed under the river like Beaver.

Now Grandfather became animated. His voice came forth powerfully. "You will get strong and well, and you will lose fear. You will cure and counsel. All will come, if it is to be. It is a gift of the Being." His small bright face glowed toward his grandson.

Instantly Kuskaga knew Grandfather had heard his thought.

"I see you remember I make medicine before," Grandfather continued. "I just wait for you to get ready. I perceive much, youngest son."

Kuskaga stared at him. "Oh! You see with blind eyes?"

Gaagateeya' nodded. "Not just this place I see, but others. Where I may wish to be, I'm there." He raised his hand.

An exquisite pain flashed through Kuskaga's being. A breath of sudden wind stirred his hair. All about was a fluttering of wings and the raucous warning cries of *Dotson'*. A cloud drew across *No-oy's* face. Two feral eyes glowed in the darkened air, and Kuskaga hid his face behind his arm.

He felt himself return from an infinite distance.

"You see?" Grandfather said.

Kuskaga entered another condition. His dreams began to shift and change. Sometimes he took the shape of *Doyon*, and grunting, clawed the earth in rage. Once he went into the body of *Nokinbaa* and saw tiny scurrying moles and lemmings with such clarity that he felt an intense blood hunger.

He perceived ever more deeply into the meanings of his calling. Constantly he was accompanied by the cries of birds and the shuffling whirr of their wings. He prowled for miles back into the empty tundra, acquiring knowledge of the spirit of night and discerning the ways of its living things.

Gaageteeya' endlessly instructed his youngest son.

Kuskaga's face grew a solemnity that was transformed in rare moments by a great belly laugh that shook the length of his frame. He loomed skyward and his ebony eyes gazed down at Grandfather from his new height. The hollows between his ribs filled and he became lean and solid with muscle. The child's nervousness was replaced by a deepening serenity. He was nineteen when one day Gaagateeya' called him. Grandfather wore a look of pride that he quickly hid. His head came painfully erect between his crooked shoulders. "I call you youngest son no more," he said in the soft tones of Athabaskan.

Kuskaga squatted before him, his slim bronzed face intent. He fixed each detail of Grandfather's person solidly into his memory.

"Now I can teach you nothing."

"Ahhh," Kuskaga breathed.

"You must learn the rest of your part alone."

Kuskaga's *yeega'* was heavy. He stared at Grandfather's hands lying idle on his thighs, and he laid his own big hand over them. He felt the small knobs grown upon the ends of the fingers with a thrill of regret mingled with tenderness. Standing, he opened his *yeega'* to the powerful current that passed from Grandfather's *yeega'* into him. In silence he turned and strode away on the boardwalk. He felt the eyes of pearl gleaming behind him.

Only a few days later, in the early dusk of the month of freeze-up, Kuskaga sat on a log among dark spruce trees. Snow sifted lightly from their branches. The forest grew still, and the silence tensed all around. His nerves and muscles gathered and he quivered with anticipation.

There was a swift breath of wings upon his face.

And he passed profoundly into another place. He was almost dreaming, yet not wholly; it was more than dream: it was an endless thought in an absence of time, a slow flood carrying him to the center of existence. He flowed upon it, weightless.

The brown head appeared. An ivory disc of minute feathers lay flat around the immense yellow-moon eye with its fixed black pupil, staring past him. Now he glimpsed the beak, an ebony hook resting in the bronze breast overlaid with delicate creamy stripes blending into a body of dappled rust. Below, he saw the pale ruffled boots, and at last the merciless shining black talons, curled around a dead willow branch.

Suddenly feathers rippled and stood out. The talons shifted. The intricate tail feathers quivered. The brown head turned full to him. The ear tufts lifted high over the eyes, the eyes that dilated to unbearable intensity.

Great Horned Owl was asking a question.

Will you choose? came the words into Kuskaga's mind.

His larynx bobbed wildly in his throat. His fingers groped forward and dabbed at the exquisite feathers of the breast. Owl sidled away on the branch.

Tell Sinh. What do you want? Again the deep voice filled Kuskaga's mind. His mouth was full of dryness and he swallowed again. He was made dumb by the hammering of his heart.

Ho-hohoo ho ho -ho-hohoo ho ho. Often before, he had listened to the low call of Owl, but now his hearing had become painfully acute. The beak opened, and the hoots, pitched more loudly, hummed through him like the singing of a fine wire. Fierce yellow eyes flashed shut and open, and he saw their clean surfaces, flat as glass.

I call you Niguudzagha now. The voice was as sad as a mourning chant.

He perceived he had been in this place with Owl many times, grieving for the past, for the future of the people. With a flash of foreknowledge he envisioned all the smothered griefs of living. He endured upon his *yeega'* the weight of years falling with the force of a blow. It was too great. His tears fell, and he saw the wind spirit rising, the blowing snow.

Owl blinked rapidly. *Take my name, Niguudzagha.*

Ahhh. He had known these words by some means, unearthly it might be, in dreams or in another time. They were so familiar he had not recognized them for the words he had awaited all his life. There was an instant clamor or roaring, grunting and squawking from unseen presences all around. He shivered with the chill of their malice.

"Yes! It is my name. I claim it!"

As soon as he said the words, the din faded.

His head came up and he looked directly into the yellow eyes and he went closer, and closer, until he lay small and flat against Owl's enormous eye. He was plunged instantly into a vast and fiery brilliance. There came a rush more swift than wind. He entered the immense round darkness behind the eye of Owl.

He was naked in the place of no light, falling past the jagged walls of an abyss. Lightning streaked around him. Talons lifted him high and laid him belly down on the wings of Owl. They spiralled up toward a far splash of light. It grew larger and there appeared two towering dark cliffs whose feet stood in a river beside the colossal bones of ancient animals. The cliffs moved rumbling toward each other. Owl swooped through the narrowing gap, and it crashed shut. A bellow of fury echoed from the river as they emerged into a grove of alders.

Owl turned his head with a steady stare. There is the Woman, he muttered. She paced forward in a robe of feathers, gazing with a single eye of many flashing facets. In them was mirrored the dancing universe. Silently she offered him a basket glittering with gold and another, heaped with bitter bark. He grasped the basket of bark.

Smiling, the Woman thrust a harpoon straight through his heart, impaling him upon the back of Owl. The harpoon flew to his hand and he hurled it into the sky. Chanting in a new tongue, he flattened himself again upon Owl's mighty feathers, and everything fell away as they flew out over the cliffs of darkness.

His mind hummed: *Niguudzagha.* He was lying in a drift of snow. The dawn gaze of *No-oy* slanted through the spruces and found his eyes. He sat straight up. Sweat wadded his parka. "Medicine man." Now he uttered the words, savoring their sound. Bending his knees he stared meditatively at his boots. A set of deep scratches lay in the short dense reindeer hair of the calf of each boot.

And he remembered the flight.

He sat bemused. Gradually he was aware of an object lying beside him. Taking it up in delicate fingers, he blew away the dust of snow. It was only a small bundle. He held it, feeling for its *yeega'.* It was gentle, reassuring, and there was in it a true goodness. He opened the packet of pearly sealgut. It loosed familiar creatures' fur smells. Now that one was the fine curled feather of *Nikinbaa,* and here were two glossy feathers of *Dotson'.* These tufts were the stiff hairs of *Midziy,* the reindeer, plucked from his beard. And this was a piece of the white backbone of *Gaa!* Ahhh! This was the amulet of the creatures of his dreams!

"I am Niguudzagha," he shouted, jumping to his feet. He started to dance. He was surely going to burst right out of his body! Then he thought of Owl. There was the clear sense of his voice, coming again as it had in his dream. Or was it a dream?

This is your amulet. Great Horned Owl is your Sinh. You have taken his name. The splendid words rolled around him as a shower of snow fell on his hair and he saw the whipping shadows of rising wings.

*   *   *

Now Niguudzagha returned slowly from his reflections. His body lay flat and quiescent in the nest. His slitted eyes idly watched the play of *No-oy* who, halfway up the sky, flicked fingers of light through the clouds. The shadow of a reed fell across Niguudzagha's face. After these many years he had acquired a resemblance to Owl. It was chiefly in the fierce gaze of his black eyes. The dense white brows protruded like ear tufts, although they grew long and he had to cut them with his knife. His head with its full shock of hair was shaped like the round feathered skull of Owl. His bones were fine and almost as fragile as Owl's, and his loose garments had the layered appearance of plumage.

Unsteadily he got to his feet and swayed until his balance returned. He yawned gustily and stretched his arms to the sky like curved wings. He inched down the crooked trail that clung to the face of the Hill, hooking his powerful toes like talons.

He could have made the descent in the dark.

QUESTIONS FOR DISCUSSION AND WRITING

1. "The Sinh of Niguudzagha" is a memory story, in which the present action is only a frame for an extended memory. Summarize the present action and then outline the structure of the remembered action.

2. The story is in the third person, and yet it is so tightly focalized through Niguudzagha that we experience even his dreams and visions. Examine representative passages to see if there is any separation at all between the point of view of Niguudzagha and that of the narrator.

3. The story uses several Athabaskan words and yet only *Doyon, Nokinbaa, Gagaa,* and *Dotson'* are translated in a footnote. How do we learn what the other words mean: *no-oy, sinh, yeega', esnaih, Gisakk, Kuskaga, Gaagateeya', Niguudzagha, Midziy*? Is anything gained by having us puzzle out words like *sinh* and *Niguudzagha* from their context?

4. Part of the purpose of the story seems to be to get us to see the world from an Athabaskan point of view. How does TallMountain do this?

Wakako Yamauchi

Wakako Yamauchi (b. 1924), like her character Masako in "And the Soul Shall Dance," was born the daughter of an Issei (first-generation Japanese-American) farmer in the Imperial Valley of California; she now lives in Gardena, California. Her family was interned at the detention camp at Poston, Arizona, during World War II. Yamauchi is best known as a writer of short stories. "And the Soul Shall Dance" was first published in *Aiiieeeee! An Anthology of Asian American Writers* (1974). In 1977, Yamauchi adapted it into a play that was produced by the East/West Players of Los Angeles. It won both the Los Angeles Critics' Circle Award for the best new play of 1977 and a national award as the best new play in regional theater. A film version has been shown on public television, and the play is still frequently produced. The play version appears later in this volume. Among Yamauchi's other plays are *The Music Lessons, 12-1-A,* and *Memento.*

AND THE SOUL SHALL DANCE

It's all right to talk about it now. Most of the principals are dead, except, of course, me and my younger brother, and possibly Kiyoko Oka, who might be near forty-five now, because, yes, I'm sure of it, she was fourteen then. I was nine, and my brother about four, so he hardly counts at all. Kiyoko's mother is dead, my father is dead, my mother is dead, and her father could not have lasted all these years with his tremendous appetite for alcohol and pickled chilies—those little yellow ones, so hot they could make your mouth hurt; he'd eat them like peanuts and tears would surge from his bulging thyroid eyes in great waves and stream down the dark coarse terrain of his face.

My father farmed then in the desert basin resolutely named Imperial Valley, in the township called Westmoreland; twenty acres of tomatoes, ten of summer squash, or vice versa, and the Okas lived maybe a mile, mile and a half, across an alkaline road, a stretch of greasewood, tumbleweed and white sand, to the south of us. We didn't hobnob much with them, because you see, they were a childless couple and we were a family: father, mother, daughter, and son, and we went to the Buddhist church on Sundays where my mother taught Japanese, and the Okas kept pretty much to themselves. I don't mean they were unfriendly; Mr. Oka would sometimes walk over (he rarely drove) on rainy days, all dripping wet, short and squat under a soggy newspaper, pretending to need a plow-blade or a file, and he would spend the afternoon in our kitchen drinking sake and eating chilies with my father. As he got progressively drunker, his large mouth would draw down and with the stream of tears, he looked like a kindly weeping bullfrog.

Not only were they childless, impractical in an area where large families were looked upon as labor potentials, but there was a certain strangeness about them. I became aware of it the summer our bathhouse burned down, and my father didn't get right down to building another, and a Japanese without a bathhouse . . . well, Mr. Oka offered us the use of his. So every night that summer we drove to the Okas for our bath, and we came in frequent contact with Mrs. Oka, and this is where I found the strangeness.

Mrs. Oka was small and spare. Her clothes hung on her like loose skin and when she walked, the skirt about her legs gave her a sort of webbed look. She was pretty in spite of the boniness and the dull calico and the barren look; I know now she couldn't have been over thirty. Her eyes were large and a little vacant, although once I saw them fill with tears; the time I insisted we take the old Victrola over and we played our Japanese records for her. Some of the songs were sad, and I imagined the nostalgia she felt, but my mother said the tears were probably from yawning or from the smoke of her cigarettes. I thought my mother resented her for not being more hospitable; indeed, never a cup of tea appeared before us, and between them the conversation of women was totally absent: the rise and fall of gentle voices, the arched eyebrows, the croon of polite surprise. But more than this, Mrs. Oka was *different*.

Obviously she was shy, but some nights she disappeared altogether. She would see us drive into her yard and then lurch from sight. She was gone all evening. Where could she have hidden in that two-roomed house—where in that silent desert? Some nights she would wait out our visit with enormous forbearance, quietly pushing wisps of stray hair behind her ears and waving gnats away from her great moist eyes, and some nights she moved about with nervous agitation, her khaki canvas shoes slapping loudly as she walked. And sometimes there appeared to be welts and bruises on her usually smooth brown face, and she would sit solemnly, hands on lap, eyes large and intent on us. My mother hurried us home then: "Hurry Masako, no need to wash well; hurry."

You see, being so poky, I was always last to bathe. I think the Okas bathed after we left because my mother often reminded me to keep the water clean. The routine was to lather outside the tub (there were buckets and pans and a small wooden stool), rinse off the soil and soap, and then soak in the tub of hot hot water and contemplate. Rivulets of perspiration would run down the scalp.

When my mother pushed me like this, I dispensed with ritual, rushed a bar of soap around me and splashed about a pan of water. So hastily toweled, my wet skin trapped the clothes to me, impeding my already clumsy progress. Outside, my mother would be murmuring her many apologies and my father, I knew, would be carrying my brother whose feet were already sandy. We would hurry home.

I thought Mrs. Oka might be insane and I asked my mother about it, but she shook her head and smiled with her mouth drawn down and said that Mrs. Oka loved her sake. This was unusual, yes, but there were other unusual women we knew. Mrs. Nagai was bought by her husband from a geisha house; Mrs. Tani was a militant Christian Scientist; Mrs. Abe, the midwife, was occult. My mother's statement explained much: sometimes Mrs. Oka was drunk and sometimes not. Her taste for liquor and cigarettes was a step in the realm of men; unusual for a Japanese wife, but at that time, in that place, and to me, Mrs. Oka loved her sake in the way my father loved his, in the way of Mr. Oka, the way I loved my candy. That her psychology may have demanded this anesthetic, that she lived with something unendurable, did not occur to me. Nor did I perceive the violence of emotions that the purple welts indicated—or the masochism that permitted her to display these wounds to us.

In spite of her masculine habits, Mrs. Oka was never less than a woman. She was no lady in the area of social amenities; but the feminine in her was innate and never left her. Even in her disgrace, she was a small broken sparrow, slightly floppy, too slowly enunciating her few words, too carefully rolling her Bull Durham, cocking her small head and moistening the ocher tissue. Her aberration was a protest of the life assigned her; it was obstinate, but unobserved, alas, unheeded. "Strange" was the only concession we granted her.

Toward the end of summer, my mother said we couldn't continue bathing at the Okas'; when winter set in we'd all catch our death from the commuting and she'd always felt dreadful about our imposition on Mrs. Oka. So my father took the corrugated tin sheets he'd found on the highway and had been saving for some other use and built up our bathhouse again. Mr. Oka came to help.

While they raised the quivering tin walls, Mr. Oka began to talk. His voice was sharp and clear above the low thunder of the metal sheets.

He told my father he had been married in Japan previously to the present Mrs. Oka's older sister. He had a child by the marriage, Kiyoko, a girl. He had left the two to come to America intending to send for them soon, but shortly after his departure, his wife passed away from an obscure stomach ailment. At the time, the present Mrs. Oka was young and had foolishly become involved with a man of poor reputation. The family was anxious to part the lovers and conveniently arranged a marriage by proxy and sent him his dead wife's sister. Well that was all right, after all, they were kin, and it would be good for the child when she came to join them. But things didn't work out that way; year after year he postponed calling for his daughter, couldn't get the price of fare together, and the wife— ahhh, the wife, Mr. Oka's groan was lost in the rumble of his hammering.

He cleared his throat. The girl was now fourteen, he said, and begged to come to America to be with her own real family. Those relatives had forgotten the favor he'd done in accepting a slightly used bride, and now tormented his daughter for being forsaken. True, he'd not sent much money, but if they knew, if they only knew how it was here.

"Well," he sighed, "who could be blamed? It's only right she be with me anyway."

"That's right," my father said.

"Well, I sold the horse and some other things and managed to buy a third-class ticket on the Taiyo-Maru. Kiyoko will get here the first week of September." Mr. Oka glanced toward my father, but my father was peering into a bag of nails. "I'd be much obliged to you if your wife and little girl," he rolled his eyes toward me, "would take kindly to her. She'll be lonely."

Kiyoko-san came in September. I was surprised to see so very nearly a woman; short, robust, buxom: the female counterpart of her father; thyroid eyes and protruding teeth, straight black hair banded impudently into two bristly shucks, Cuban heels and white socks. Mr. Oka brought her proudly to us.

"Little Masako here," for the first time to my recollection, he touched me; he put his rough fat hand on the top of my head, "is very smart in school. She will help you with your school work, Kiyoko," he said.

I had so looked forward to Kiyoko-san's arrival. She would be my soul mate; in my mind I had conjured a girl of my own proportions: thin and tall, but with the refinement and beauty I didn't yet possess that would surely someday come to the fore. My disappointment was keen and apparent. Kiyoko-san stepped forward shyly, then retreated with a short bow and small giggle, her fingers pressed to her mouth.

My mother took her away. They talked for a long time—about Japan, about enrollment in American school, the clothes Kiyoko-san would need, and where to look for the best values. As I watched them, it occurred to me that I had been deceived: this was not a child, this was a woman. The smile pressed behind her fingers, the way of her nod, so brief, like my mother when father scolded her: the face was inscrutable, but something—maybe spirit—shrank visibly, like a piece of silk in water. I was disappointed; Kiyoko-san's soul was barricaded in her unenchanting appearance and the smile she fenced behind her fingers.

She started school from third grade, one below me, and as it turned out, she quickly passed me by. There wasn't much I could help her with except to drill her on pronunciation—the "L" and "R" sounds. Every morning walking to our rural school: land, leg, library, loan, lot; every afternoon returning home: run, rabbit, rim, rinse, roll. That was the extent of our communication; friendly but uninteresting.

One particularly cold November night—the wind outside was icy; I was sitting on my bed, my brother's and mine, oiling the cracks in my chapped hands by lamplight—someone rapped urgently at our door. It was Kiyoko-san; she was hysterical, she wore no wrap, her teeth were chattering, and except for the thin straw zori, her feet were bare. My mother led her to the kitchen, started a pot of tea, and gestured to my brother and me to retire. I lay very still but because of my brother's restless tossing and my father's snoring, was unable to hear much. I was aware, though, that drunken and savage brawling had brought Kiyoko-san to us. Presently they came to the bedroom. I feigned sleep. My mother gave Kiyoko-san a gown and pushed me over to make room for her. My mother spoke firmly: "Tomorrow you will return to them; you must not leave them again. They are your people." I could almost feel Kiyoko-san's short nod.

All night long I lay cramped and still, afraid to intrude into her hulking back. Two or three times her icy feet jabbed into mine and quickly retreated. In the morning I found my mother's gown neatly folded on the spare pillow. Kiyoko-san's place in bed was cold.

She never came to weep at our house again but I know she cried: her eyes were often swollen and red. She stopped much of her giggling and routinely pressed her fingers to her mouth. Our daily pronunciation drill petered off from lack of interest. She walked silently with her shoulders hunched, grasping her books with both arms, and when I spoke to her in my halting Japanese, she absently corrected my prepositions.

Spring comes early in the Valley; in February the skies are clear though the air is still cold. By March, winds are vigorous and warm and wild flowers dot the desert floor, cockleburs are green and not yet tenacious, the sand is crusty underfoot, everywhere there is the smell of things growing and the first tomatoes are showing green and bald.

As the weather changed, Kiyoko-san became noticeably more cheerful. Mr. Oka who hated so to drive could often be seen steering his dusty old Ford over the road that passes our house, and Kiyoko-san sitting in front would sometimes wave gaily to us. Mrs. Oka was never with them. I thought of these trips as the westernizing of Kiyoko-san: with a permanent wave, her straight black hair became tangles of tiny frantic curls; between her textbooks she carried copies of *Modern Screen* and *Photoplay*, her clothes were gay with print and piping, and she bought a pair of brown suede shoes with alligator trim. I can see her now picking her way gingerly over the deceptive white peaks of alkaline crust.

At first my mother watched their coming and going with vicarious pleasure. "Probably off to a picture show; the stores are all closed at this hour," she might say. Later her eyes would get distant and she would muse, "They've left her home again; Mrs. Oka is alone again, the poor woman."

Now when Kiyoko-san passed by or came in with me on her way home, my mother would ask about Mrs. Oka—how is she, how does she occupy herself these rainy days, or these windy or warm or cool days. Often the answers were polite: "Thank you, we are fine," but sometimes Kiyoko-san's upper lip would pull over her teeth, and her voice would become very soft and she would say, "Drink, always drinking, and fighting." At those times my mother would invariably say, "Endure, soon you will be marrying and going away."

Once a young truck driver delivered crates at the Oka farm and he dropped back to our place to tell my father that Mrs. Oka had lurched behind his truck while he was backing up, and very nearly let him kill her. Only the daughter pulling her away saved her, he said. Thoroughly unnerved, he stopped by to rest himself and talk about it. Never, never, he said in wide-eyed wonder, had he seen a drunken Japanese woman. My father nodded gravely, "Yes, it's unusual," he said and drummed his knee with his fingers.

Evenings were longer now, and when my mother's migraines drove me from the house in unbearable self-pity, I would take walks in the desert. One night with the warm wind against me, the dune primrose and yellow poppies closed and fluttering, the greasewood swaying in languid orbit, I lay on the white sand beneath a shrub and tried to disappear.

A voice sweet and clear cut through the half-dark of the evening:

> Red lips press against a glass
> Drink the purple wine
> > And the soul shall dance

Mrs. Oka appeared to be gathering flowers. Bending, plucking, standing, searching, she added to a small bouquet she clasped. She held them away; looked at them slyly, lids lowered, demure, then in a sudden and sinuous movement, she broke into a stately dance. She stopped, gathered more flowers, and breathed deeply into them. Tossing her head, she laughed—softly, beautifully, from her dark throat. The picture of her imagined grandeur was lost to me, but the delusion that transformed the bouquet of tattered petals and sandy leaves, and the aloneness of a desert twilight into a fantasy that brought such joy and abandon made me stir with discomfort. The sound broke Mrs. Oka's dance. Her eyes grew large and her neck tense—like a cat on the prowl. She spied me in the bushes. A peculiar chill ran through me. Then abruptly and with childlike delight, she scattered the flowers around her and walked away singing:

> Falling, falling, petals on a wind . . .

That was the last time I saw Mrs. Oka. She died before the spring harvest. It was pneumonia. I didn't attend the funeral, but my mother said it was sad. Mrs. Oka looked peaceful, and the minister expressed the irony of the long separation of Mother and Child and the short-lived reunion; hardly a year together, she said. We went to help Kiyoko-san address and stamp those black-bordered acknowledgements.

When harvest was over, Mr. Oka and Kiyoko-san moved out of the Valley. We never heard from them or saw them again and I suppose in a large city, Mr. Oka found some sort of work, perhaps as a janitor or a dishwasher and Kiyoko-san grew up and found someone to marry.

QUESTIONS FOR DISCUSSION AND WRITING

1. "And the Soul Shall Dance" is narrated by the mature Masako looking back on her childhood. What difference is there between her past perceptions of the Okas and her present understanding?

2. "And the Soul Shall Dance" is, in a sense, a mystery story, the mystery being what is wrong with Mrs. Oka. What are the successive understandings that Masako has of Mrs. Oka? How does her last encounter with Mrs. Oka alter her understanding?

3. Is "And the Soul Shall Dance" a story of immigration, of adaptation to a new country and a new culture? Discuss.

4. What is the connection between Kiyoko and Masako? Is Kiyoko in any sense a foil for Masako, acting out some of the conflicts that Masako feels? Discuss.

Rolando Hinojosa-Smith

Rolando Hinojosa-Smith (b. 1929) grew up in Mercedes, Texas, on the Mexican border, the son of a Mexican-American father, Manuel Guzman Hinojosa, and an Anglo mother, Carrie Effie Smith. He is generally regarded as the dean of Chicano/Chicana or Mexican-American writing. He writes in both Spanish and English, often translating his own work from one language to the other. His first novel, *Sketches of the Valley and Other Works* (1973), won the Quinto Sol Award for the best Mexican-American novel of the year. Other works include *Klail City* (1976), *Dear Rafe* (1981), *Rites and Witnesses* (1982), *Partners in Crime* (1985), and *Becky and Her Friends* (1990). Hinojosa-Smith, who holds a Ph.D. from the University of Illinois, is director of the Texas Center for Writers at the University of Texas–Austin.

ONE OF THOSE THINGS

Excerpt from *Klail City Enterprise-News* (March 15, 1970)

Klail City. (Special) Baldemar Cordero, 30, of 169 South Hidalgo Street, is in the city jail following a row in a bar in the city's Southside. Cordero is alleged to have fatally stabbed Arnesto Tamez, also 30, over the affections of one of the "hostesses" who works there. No bail had been set at press time.

One of Those Things*

There's no getting around it. I killed Ernesto Tamez at the *Aquí me quedo* bar. Now don't ask for details because I don't even know how it happened myself. But that Ernesto's done for. Laid him out. Cold.

Funny how things work out, huh? Just about yesterday at this time I was drinking with my brother-in-law, Beto Castañeda, the one who married my sister Marta, and we were following around and laughing about something I can't recall now when Tamez walks in cussing a blue streak. He lashed at me straight out and I let him get away with it; I just plain let him even though he and I didn't get along. Can you beat that?

You knew Tamez, didn't you? Once over at Félix Champion's place someone smashed a bottle over his head when Tamez broke that mirror, remember? Well, I haven't forgotten and that's why whenever I would see Tamez, I wouldn't exactly run away but I wasn't about to turn my back on him either.

Well, as I said, Beto and I were having some beers until, as usual, we'd run out of money or we'd get bagged, but without bothering anybody or cadging drinks or anything like that.

I've known Tamez and his whole clan from school, when they lived out in el Rebaje: Joaquín, the oldest, married Jovita de Anda. It's no secret she once had the morals of a henhouse chicken, but she seems to have straightened since she

---

* Editor's note: This tape recording made by Balde Cordero has been reproduced faithfully using conventional orthography; surely, what matters here may be the content, not the form. March 16, 1970. Klail City Workhouse.

married Joaquín. Emilio, the cripple, was left like that when he slipped and fell from a freight train at Chico Fernández' loading dock. Bertita married one of the Leal boys who turned out to be a hard worker. I think they moved to Muleshoe. They also say that's he's very rich and I hope so, because he worked hard and he deserves it. Bertita was no bargain, I'll say that; but she wasn't a bad woman. Ernesto was something else again. You know, I still can't figure it out how he got away with all his shit until I stabbed him at the *Aquí me quedo*. Oh, well . . .

There's no room for lying here. You know me, Hinojosa, just as you knew my parents. Beto and I started drinking at the *San Diego*, we then went to the *Diamond* and, still up to it, we went to the *Blue Bar* until the Reyna brothers came in. I sure don't have to tell you about them: even the pebbles on the street know that when they're wired on grass they grab a beer so that the cops will think they're drunk. Anyway, when the Reynas got there, Beto and I left so there wouldn't be any trouble. I'll tell you, ever since I beat the blue-eyed shit out of him at the *Diamond*, Anselmo Reyna treats me with great respect. But, seeing how they were wired and I mean they were baled and wired . . . Anyway, since we didn't want to start a ruckus, well, we just decided to go to the *Aquí me quedo*.

It's really odd, isn't it; if the Reynas hadn't shown up at the *Blue Bar*, nothing like this would've happened. Who am I kidding? When something is going to happen, it happens; why fight it. Ernesto had it coming and I just happened to be the one to give it to him. Just like that. Just like the queer bookkeeper at Torres' place, Luisito Monciváis, handing over merchandise. At times it scares me to think that I killed a human being. It's a mess, isn't it?

Look here, Hinojosa, . . . I remember the way of it all but not the when. You see, I can usually take a bunch of crap when I have to, but to be ridiculed like that, to be made to look like a fool? Add to it that I was half smashed, that Ernesto was a bastard, that he'd been bugging my ass for a long time now, and, to top it all off, he was just a plain no good ball busting phony son-of-a-bitch. Well, you know the rest; we went at it.

Beto told me later that the blood spurted all over his arm and face. Beto also said that I didn't bat an eye or anything. As for me, I can tell you I didn't hear anything: the screaming of the women, the rustle and bustle of the mob crowding over. Nothing.

I do remember going to the sidewalk and noticing a house full of people watching TV. Sitting there as innocent as I had been a mere five minutes before. I'm telling you, the idea of life and death is a frightening thing; to tell the truth, really, who knows anything about anything?

Have I told you that once, right in front of everybody, Ernesto snatched a woman from me at *El farol*? See what I mean? Another time he told a woman that I had the clap. Oh, I'm telling you that he pulled a lot of other shit but, you know, it was just one of those things; I didn't do anything about it. Maybe I should have put a stop to it then . . . but then again maybe not. Who's to say.

Well, last night he not only insulted me to my face, but he told me that I didn't have any balls or hair on my chest. Now you know no one says that to me unless I get along with him. I didn't say a thing, I just looked at him and the goddamn idiot probably thought I was afraid of him. He kept it up and then he brought one of the women who dances at the *Aquí me quedo* and right then and there he opens up again and brags that he has made me back down many times before. I think the woman was halfway scared and embarrassed but she was smart enough to shut the hell up all right. I sort of remember that my ears started buzzing as if instead of a hat I were wearing a hornet's nest. I could hear the buzzing, I could hear the dumb butt's grating voice, I could see the idiotic bitch grinning at me and then, suddenly, I heard a high-pitched piercing scream and saw Ernesto slithering out of the woman's arms.

I do remember that I took a deep breath and that I walked out of the place to the sidewalk where I could see the family sitting in the living room watching TV. Later on I realized that in my left hand I was still holding the pearl-handled knife that papá Albino had given me.

I went back into the bar and then walked out right back again. I didn't even try to run. What for? And, where would I go if everyone knew me? When I went back in I saw that they had poured water on the cement floor and swept the blood as if nothing had happened. They had taken Ernesto to the storage room where they keep the beer and the beef jerky they use for snacks. When don Manuel got there I handed him the knife myself. Later on I went with him in his car after he finished up in there. Then, to the tank, and here I am.

One of don Manuel's sons brought me some coffee early this morning and waited until I finished it. You know, I've tried to remember the exact moment when I buried my knife in that fool's chest and I can't. Absolutely blank. Too, it could be that I just don't want to remember ...

Beto left just as you came in; he's on his way over to the district attorney's office to make a statement. Who knows what's going to happen in the future, but right now I really feel bad about what I did last night ... That old saying about what's done is done is all talk. Believe me, it bothers me to think that I killed Ernesto Tamez. Sometimes I get to thinking that taking a man's life isn't worth the trouble.

What I did was wrong, I'll admit that, but sometimes I also think that if Ernesto were to insult me again, well, hell, I'd kill him again. The truth is, one never learns.

I won't tire you anymore. You can see I'm only repeating myself since this is the only thing on my mind. Thanks a lot for coming and I appreciate your bringing cigarettes. Perhaps some day I'll know, myself, why I killed him ... but who's to say, right? The man was going to die sometime and maybe I was destined to speed it up a little. See? There I go again.

Hey, before you leave: tell Mr. Royce I won't be at work tomorrow ... I'm sorry. Say, will you tell him that he owes me a week's pay, too ...

See you later, Hinojosa ... and thanks, huh?

Marta Tells Her Story*

... well, you know, when papá Albino died as a result of that accident up in Saginaw, Balde decided that we should stay there until the whole mess was straightened out. At first, the contractor who took us up from the Valley tried to cheat us out of our pay and Balde had to threaten him so that he would do something. With the little money we got, Balde hired a lawyer to sue Dailey Pickle. The lawyer was a young little guy but he sure made that pickle company pay us something called indemnity. When that business about dad was over, we paid off what we owed and we even had enough left for the Winter there while we were waiting to sign up with another contractor or could find work. (By this time, Beto was courting me but because I was in mourning, you understand, he couldn't come to see me.)

You've known Balde since he was little and, as dad used to say, what else is there

* Taped on March 17, 1970.

to say? Mom had been an invalid many years now and even with her pain and all, she kept making the trips with us. Anyway, there we were, several Mexican families in Saginaw, waiting for Winter with the intention of taking whatever work came along. The first one to get a job was Balde, as a port watchman; shortly afterward, he got Beto a job there too, as they became better friends and then, as you know, they became brothers-in-law when Beto and I were married.

At that time Balde was about 27 years old and had many opportunities to marry, but partly because of mom's illness and partly because his help was needed at home, he never did marry. When we returned to the Valley two years ago, he went on as before. Balde is a good man and a hard worker, and even when he would go out to drink, he avoided fights as much as he could in order not to neglect his obligations at home. (On many occasions he had to eat dirt, I know, but one can see that he was thinking of us and for that reason he tried to avoid the free-for-alls in the bars.) About the only thing I know about all of this is what Beto tells me, but then he seldom talks about his affairs. Once, by chance, I heard that Balde had given one of the Reynas a good beating but that was never mentioned at home.

It's very difficult to tell what I thought or what I said when that business of Neto Tamez happened. At first I couldn't picture it, you know, because I could not believe that my brother Balde could kill anyone. Don't think I'm saying this because Balde is a saint, but surely it must have been something terrible that Balde could not avoid. I will say that it had been very difficult for him to control himself and it may be that that night Ernesto just overdid it: Beto had told me that Neto Tamez had been insulting several times but since Beto rarely talks I can't always understand what he says. As for Balde, he would say nothing at all for the only thing he brought home from the streets was a smile. It's true that once in a while he looked serious, as if he were at a funeral or something, but I wasn't about to ask him anything. Well, as you can see, what with these two men, my housecleaning, the cooking and washing, and with mother in her condition, well, I hardly have time for gossip.

I'm not pretending to be innocent at all, it's just that I want you to know that much of what I know I heard from Beto, or from my friends who would come to visit or on the few occasions when Balde and Beto would discuss it. I am also telling you what I assumed, but I've already made it clear to you that one doesn't know everything; far from it. Everyone knows that Neto Tamez was always goading my brother Balde and that my brother would ignore him. I'm telling you that if Balde didn't let him have it before it was because he was thinking about us. That's the truth. The thing no one knows is why Neto acted the way he did toward my brother.

I'll tell you why: when we were in school Neto used to send me letters, he would follow me home and he would use the kids who were afraid of him as messengers. I never paid attention to him or encouraged him either. The girls told me that he wouldn't let other boys come near me as if he were my boss or something. This was years ago, and I never told Balde, but the first time I heard that Neto was making life miserable for Balde I knew, or thought I knew, why he was doing it. I don't know if Balde knew it or not but, as Beto says, anything is possible.

One time my friends told me that in one of those places like *La golondrina* and *El farolito*, Neto Tamez insulted Balde many times and in many different ways; either he would take his dancing partner from him, or he would say nasty things about Balde, or he would do some other low thing, but always with the same purpose: to make life miserable for him, don't you see? I'm not saying that Tamez went after him at all, but I am saying that he never passed up an opportunity to ridicule him until Balde would be forced to leave the place. Suffice it to say that living in the same town, practically in the same neighborhood, and taking so many insults took a great deal of patience. Balde did not show his anger at home and whether he came home drunk or sober he acted the same: he would kiss mom, he talked with us for a while and then he would light a cigarette and sit on the porch steps. Ha! compared to Balde, Beto, who doesn't talk much, is like a magpie?

That Tamez family is an odd bunch. When they lived in el Rebaje, it seems that that clan was always fighting with half the town. I remember when Joaquín, because of one of those things, had to marry Jovita de Anda, don Servando Tamez did not allow any of the de Andas to attend the wedding. They say that poor old don Marcial de Anda, a weak little bit of a man, cried like a baby. I remember seeing Emilio with his club foot strutting around the house like a policeman. It's a good thing doña Tula Tamez had died by that time. Poor woman would have been ashamed by it all. Possibly the only good thing to come out of that family was Bertita, who wanted to be Balde's girl. She finally married Ramiro Leal, the tortilla factory guy . . .

Well, anyway, yesterday, as soon as you left to go see Balde at the jail, don Manuel came by. He said he had come by to see mom but he really came to tell her not to worry about the bills. (Who would believe it! I've seen that man beat, pistol whip, kick and curse more than a hundred drunks and potheads only to take coffee to them in jail the next day. One thing's for sure, since don Manuel became a policeman, a woman can walk down the street alone and at night without being bothered.) As he was leaving, don Manuel told me we could get our groceries at Torres'.

Mom and I are broken hearted with Balde, but thank God I still have Beto. I hope the Tamez men don't come and bother him because then mom and I will really be ruined without a man in the house. Right now Beto is over at the District Attorney's office giving a statement.

Oh, Sr. Hinojosa, I don't know how this will all turn out; but whatever happens, it will be God's will.

ROMEO HINOJOSA
Attorney at Law

420 South Cerralvo   Tel. 843-1640

The following is a deposition, in English, made by Beto Castañeda, today, March 17, 1970, in the office of Mr. Robert A. Chapman, Assistant District Attorney for Belken County.

The aforementioned officer of the court gave me a copy of the statement as part of the testimony in the trial of *The State vs. Cordero,* set for August 23 of this year in the court of Judge Harrison Phelps who presides in the 139th District Court.

Romeo Hinojosa

Romeo Hinojosa

A DEPOSITION FREELY GIVEN

on this seventeenth day of March, 1970, by Mr. Gilberto Castañeda in room 218 of the Belken County Court House was duly taken, witnessed, and signed by Miss Helen Chacón, a legal interpreter and acting assistant deputy recorder for said County, as part of a criminal investigation assigned to Robert A. Chapman, assistant district attorney for the same County.

It is understood that Mr. Castañeda is acting solely as a deponent and is not a party to any civil or criminal investigation, proceeding, or violation which may be alluded to in this deposition.

"Well, my name is Gilberto Castañeda and I live at 169 South Hidalgo Street here in Klail. It is not my house; it belong to my mother-in-law, but I have live there since I marry Marta (Marta Cordero Castañeda, 28, 169 South Hidalgo Street, Klail City) about three years ago.

I am working at the Royce-Fedders tomato packing shed as a grader. My brother-in-law, Balde Cordero, work there too. He pack tomatoes and don't get pay for the hour, he get pay for what he pack and since I am a grader I make sure he get the same class tomato and that way he pack faster; he just get a tomato with the right hand and he wrap it with the left. He pack a lug of tomatoes so fast you don't see it and he does it fast because I am a good grader.

Balde is a good man. His father, don Albino, my father-in-law who die up in Saginaw, Michigan when Marta and I, you know, go together ... well, Balde is like don Albino, you understand? A good man. A right man. Me, I stay an orphan and when the Mejías take me when my father and my mother die in that train wreck—near Flora, don Albino tell the Mejías I must go to the school. I go to First Ward Elementary where Mr. Gold is principal. In First Ward I am a friend of Balde and there I meet Marta too. Later when I grow up I don't visit the house too much because of Marta, you know what I mean? Anyway, Balde is my friend and I have know him very well ... maybe more than nobody else. He's a good man.

Well, last night Balde and I took a few beers in some of the places near where we live. We drink a couple here and a couple there, you know, and we save the *Aquí me quedo* on South Missouri for last. It is there that I tell Balde a joke about the drunk guy who is going to his house and he hear the clock in the corner make two sounds. You know that one? Well, this drunk guy he hear the clock go bong-bong and he say that the clock is wrong for it give one o'clock two time. Well, Balde think that is funny ... Anyway, when I tell the joke in Spanish it's better. Well, there we are drinking a beer when Ernesto Tamez comes. Ernesto Tamez is like a woman, you know? Everytime he get in trouble he call his family to help him ... that is the way it is with him. Well, that night he bother Balde again. More than one time Balde has stop me when Tamez begin to insult. That Balde is a man of patience. This time Ernesto bring a *vieja* (woman) and Balde don't say nothing, nothing, nothing. What happen is that things get spooky, you know. Ernesto talking and burllándose de él (ridiculing him) and at the same time he have the poor woman by the arm. And then something happened. I don't know what happen, but *something* happen and fast.

I don't know. I really don't know. It all happen so fast——the knife, the blood squirt all over my face and arms, the woman try to get away, a loud really loud scream, not a *grito* (local Mexican yell) but more a woman screaming, you know what I mean? and then Ernesto fall on the cement.

Right there I look at Balde and his face is like a mask in asleep, you understand? No angry, no surprise, nothing. In his left hand he have the knife and he shake his head like he say "yes" and then he take a deep breath before he walk to the door. Look, it happen so fast no one move for a while. Then Balde come in and go out of the place and when don Manuel (constable for precinct No. 21) come in, Balde just hand over the knife. Lucas Barrón, you know, el Chorreao (a nickname), well, he wash the blood and sweep the floor before don Manuel get there. Don Manuel just shake his head and tell Balde to go to the car and wait. Don Manuel he walk to the back to see Ernesto and on the way out one of the women, I think it is *la güera Balín* (Amelia Cortez, 23, no known address, this city), try to make a joke but don Manuel he say "no estés chingando" (shut the hell up, or words to that effect) and after that don Manuel go about his own business. Me, I go to the door but all I see is Balde looking at a house across the street and he don't even know I come to say good-bye. Anyway, this morning a little boy of don Manuel say for me to come here and here I am."

Further deponent sayeth not.

Sworn to before me, this
    17th day of March, 1970

/s/ *Helen Chacón*   /s/ *Gilberto Castañeda*

    Helen Chacón   Gilberto Castañeda
    Acting Asst. Deputy Recorder
    Belken County

Excerpt from *The Klail City Enterprise-News* (August 24, 1970)

Klail City. (Special). Baldemar Cordero, 30, of 169 South Hidalgo Street, drew a 15 year sentence Harrison Phelps' 139th District Court, for the to the Huntsville State Prison in Judge murder of Ernesto Tamez last Spring. PICK UP.

Cordero is alleged to have fatally stabbed Ernesto Tanez, also 30, over the affections of one of the "hostesses" who works there. PICK UP.

No appeal had been made at press time.

QUESTIONS FOR DISCUSSION AND WRITING

1. "One of Those Things" is a documentary story—that is, it is told through a series of ostensibly authentic documents. Is there any point of view behind these varied documents? (Notice that the interviews with Balde Cordero and Marta Castañeda are addressed to "Hinojosa," and the deposition from Beto Castañeda, is preceded by a cover letter from "Romeo Hinojosa," a lawyer who seems to be defending Cordero in his murder trial.)

2. The documents contain a number of mistakes; for instance, Ernesto Tamez is referred to in the first newspaper story as "Arnesto Tamez," and the last newspaper story has some garbled passages. What is the function of these "mistakes"?

3. The title phrase is used by Balde Cordero in his interview; it seems to imply that the stabbing was a chance occurrence. Was it? The various documents build up a complex set of circumstances that led to the murder. What are they?

4. What sort of a society is depicted in "One of Those Things"? What sorts of codes and value systems do the characters live by?

Paule Marshall

Paule Marshall (b. 1929) was born on the island of Barbados in the Caribbean but grew up in Brooklyn. Her novels include *Brown Girl, Brownstones* (1959), *The Chosen Place, The Timeless People* (1969), *Praisesong for the Widow* (1984), and *Daughters* (1991). Short-story collections include *Soul Clap Hands and Sing,* (1961) and *Reena and Other Stories* (1984). Paule Marshall teaches writing at Virginia Commonwealth University in Richmond.

BARBADOS

Dawn, like the night which had preceded it, came from the sea. In a white mist tumbling like spume over the fishing boats leaving the island and the hunched, ghost shapes of the fishermen. In a white, wet wind breathing over the villages scattered amid the tall canes. The cabbage palms roused, their high headdresses solemnly saluting the wind, and along the white beach which ringed the island the casuarina trees began their moaning—a sound of women lamenting their dead within a cave.

The wind, smarting of the sea, threaded a wet skein through Mr. Watford's five hundred dwarf coconut trees and around his house at the edge of the grove. The house, Colonial American in design, seemed created by the mist—as if out of the dawn's formlessness had come, magically, the solid stone walls, the blind, broad windows and the portico of fat columns which embraced the main story. When the mist cleared, the house remained—pure, proud, a pristine white—disdaining the crude wooden houses in the village outside its high gate.

It was not the dawn settling around his house which awakened Mr. Watford, but the call of his Barbary doves from their hutch in the yard. And it was more the feel of that sound than the sound itself. His hands had retained, from the many times a day he held the doves, the feel of their throats swelling with that murmurous, mournful note. He lay abed now, his hands—as cracked and callused as a cane cutter's—filled with the sound, and against the white sheet which flowed out to the white walls he appeared profoundly alone, yet secure in loneliness, contained. His face was fleshless and severe, his black skin sucked deep into the hollow of his jaw, while under a high brow, which was like a bastion raised against the world, his eyes were indrawn and pure. It was as if during all his seventy years, Mr. Watford had permitted nothing to sight which could have affected him.

He stood up, and his body, muscular but stripped of flesh, appeared to be absolved from time, still young. Yet each clenched gesture of his arms, of his lean shank as he dressed in a faded shirt and work pants, each vigilant, snapping motion of his head betrayed tension. Ruthlessly he spurred his body to perform like a younger man's. Savagely he denied the accumulated fatigue of the years. Only sometimes when he paused in his grove of coconut trees during the day, his eyes tearing and the breath torn from his lungs, did it seem that if he could find a place hidden from the world and himself he would give way to exhaustion and weep from weariness.

Dressed, he strode through the house, his step tense, his rough hand touching the furniture from Grand Rapids which crowded each room. For some reason, Mr. Watford had never completed the house. Everywhere the walls were raw and unpainted, the furniture unarranged. In the drawing room with its coffered ceiling, he stood before his favorite piece, an old mantel clock which eked out the time. Reluctantly it whirred five and Mr. Watford nodded. His day had begun.

It was no different from all the days which made up the five years since his return to Barbados. Downstairs in the unfinished kitchen, he prepared his morning tea—tea with canned milk and fried bakes—and ate standing at the stove while lizards skittered over the unplastered walls. Then, belching and snuffling the way a child would, he put on a pith helmet, secured his pants legs with bicycle clasps and stepped into the yard. There he fed the doves, holding them so that their sound poured into his hands and laughing gently—but the laugh gave way to an irritable grunt as he saw the mongoose tracks under the hutch. He set the trap again.

The first heat had swept the island like a huge tidal wave when Mr. Watford, with that tense, headlong stride, entered the grove. He had planted the dwarf coconut trees because of their quick yield and because, with their stunted trunks, they always appeared young. Now as he worked, rearranging the complex of pipes which irrigated the land, stripping off the dead leaves, the trees were like cool, moving presences; the stiletto fronds wove a protective dome above him and slowly, as the day soared toward noon, his mind filled with the slivers of sunlight through the trees and the feel of earth in his hands, as it might have been filled with thoughts.

Except for a meal at noon, he remained in the grove until dusk surged up from the sea; then returning to the house, he bathed and dressed in a medical doctor's white uniform, turned on the lights in the parlor and opened the tall doors to the portico. Then the old women of the village on their way to church, the last hawkers caroling, "Fish, flying fish, a penny, my lady," the roistering saga-boys lugging their heavy steel drums to the crossroads where they would rehearse under the street lamps—all passing could glimpse Mr. Watford, stiff in his white uniform and with his head bent heavily over a Boston newspaper. The papers reached him weeks late but he read them anyway, giving a little savage chuckle at the thought that beyond his world that other world went its senseless way. As he read, the night sounds of the village welled into a joyous chorale against the sea's muffled cadence and the hollow, haunting music of the steel band. Soon the moths, lured in by the light, fought to die on the lamp, the beetles crashed drunkenly against the walls and the night—like a woman offering herself to him—became fragrant with the night-blooming cactus.

Even in America Mr. Watford had spent his evenings this way. Coming home from the hospital, where he worked in the boiler room, he would dress in his white uniform and read in the basement of the large rooming house he owned. He had lived closeted like this, detached, because America—despite the money and property he had slowly accumulated—had meant nothing to him. Each morning, walking to the hospital along the rutted Boston streets, through the smoky dawn light, he had known—although it had never been a thought—that his allegiance, his place, lay elsewhere. Neither had the few acquaintances he had made mattered. Nor the women he had occasionally kept as a younger man. After the first month their bodies would grow coarse to his hand and he would begin edging away. . . . So that he had felt no regret when, the year before his retirement, he resigned his job, liquidated his properties and, his fifty-year exile over, returned home.

The clock doled out eight and Mr. Watford folded the newspaper and brushed the burnt moths from the lamp base. His lips still shaped the last words he had read as he moved through the rooms, fastening the windows against the night air, which he had dreaded even as a boy. Something palpable but unseen was always, he believed, crouched in the night's dim recess, waiting to snare him. . . . Once in bed in his sealed room, Mr. Watford fell asleep quickly.

The next day was no different except that Mr. Goodman, the local shopkeeper, sent the boy for coconuts to sell at the racetrack and then came that evening to pay for them and to herald—although Mr. Watford did not know this—the coming of the girl.

That morning, taking his tea, Mr. Watford heard the careful tap of the mule's hoofs and looking out saw the wagon jolting through the dawn and the boy, still lax with sleep, swaying on the seat. He was perhaps eighteen and the muscles packed tightly beneath his lustrous black skin gave him a brooding strength. He came and stood outside the back door, his hands and lowered head performing the small, subtle rites of deference.

Mr. Watford's pleasure was full, for the gestures were those given only to a white man in his time. Yet the boy always nettled him. He sensed a natural arrogance like a pinpoint of light within his dark stare. The boy's stance exhumed a memory buried under the years. He remembered, staring at him, the time when he had worked as a yard boy for a white family, and had had to assume the same respectful pose while their flat, raw, Barbadian voices assailed him with orders. He remembered the muscles in his neck straining as he nodded deeply and a taste like alum on his tongue as he repeated the "Yes, please," as in a litany. But because of their whiteness and wealth, he had never dared hate them. Instead his rancor, like a boomerang, had rebounded, glancing past him to strike all the dark ones like himself, even his mother with her spindled arms and her stomach sagging with a child who was, invariably, dead at birth. He had been the only one of ten to live, the only one to escape. But he had never lost the sense of being pursued by the same dread presence which had claimed them. He had never lost the fear that if he lived too fully he would tire and death would quickly close the gap. His only defense had been a cautious life and work. He had been almost broken by work at the age of twenty when his parents died, leaving him enough money for the passage to America. Gladly had he fled the island. But nothing had mattered after his flight.

The boy's foot stirred the dust. He murmured, "Please, sir, Mr. Watford, Mr. Goodman at the shop send me to pick the coconut."

Mr. Watford's head snapped up. A caustic word flared, but died as he noticed a political button pinned to the boy's patched shirt with "Vote for the Barbados People's Party" printed boldly on it, and below that the motto of the party: "The Old Shall Pass." At this ludicrous touch (for what could this boy, with his splayed and shigoed feet and blunted mind, understand about politics?) he became suddenly nervous, angry. The button and its motto seemed, somehow, directed at him. He said roughly, "Well, come then. You can't pick any coconuts standing there looking foolish!"—and he led the way to the grove.

The coconuts, he knew, would sell well at the booths in the center of the track, where the poor were penned in like cattle. As the heat thickened and the betting grew desperate, they would clamor: "Man, how you selling the water coconuts?" and hacking off the tops they would pour rum into the water within the hollow centers, then tilt the coconuts to their heads so that the rum-sweetened water skimmed their tongues and trickled bright down their dark chins. Mr. Watford had stood among them at the track as a young man, as poor as they were, but proud. And he had always found something unutterably graceful and free in their gestures, something which had roused contradictory feelings in him: admiration, but just as strong, impatience at their easy ways, and shame. . . .

That night, as he sat in his white uniform reading, he heard Mr. Goodman's heavy step and went out and stood at the head of the stairs in a formal, proprietary pose. Mr. Goodman's face floated up into the light—the loose folds of flesh, the skin slick with sweat as if oiled, the eyes scribbled with veins and mottled, bold—as if each blemish there was a sin he proudly displayed or a scar which proved he had met life head-on. His body, unlike Mr. Watford's, was corpulent and, with the trousers caught up around his full crotch, openly concupiscent. He owned the one shop in the village which gave credit and a booth which sold coconuts at the race track, kept a wife and two outside women, drank a rum with each customer at his bar, regularly caned his fourteen children, who still followed him everywhere (even now they were waiting for him in the darkness beyond Mr. Watford's gate) and bet heavily at the races, and when he lost gave a loud hacking laugh which squeezed his body like a pain and left him gasping.

The laugh clutched him now as he flung his pendulous flesh into a chair and wheezed, "Watford, how? Man, I near lose house, shop, shirt and all at race today. I tell you, they got some horses from Trinidad in this meet that's making ours look like they running backwards. Be Jese, I wouldn't bet on a Bajan horse tomorrow if Christ heself was to give me the top. Those bitches might look good but they's nothing 'pon a track."

Mr. Watford, his back straight as the pillar he leaned against, his eyes unstained, his gaunt face planed by contempt, gave Mr. Goodman his cold, measured smile, thinking that the man would be dead soon, bloated with rice and rum—and somehow this made his own life more certain.

Sputtering with his amiable laughter, Mr. Goodman paid for the coconuts, but instead of leaving then as he usually did, he lingered, his eyes probing for a glimpse inside the house. Mr. Watford waited, his head snapping warily; then, impatient, he started toward the door and Mr. Goodman said, "I tell you, your coconut trees bearing fast enough even for dwarfs. You's lucky, man."

Ordinarily Mr. Watford would have waved both the man and his remark aside, but repelled more than usual tonight by Mr. Goodman's gross form and immodest laugh, he said—glad of the cold edge his slight American accent gave the words— "What luck got to do with it? I does care the trees properly and they bear, that's all. Luck! People, especially this bunch around here, it always looking to luck when the only answer is a little brains and plenty of hard work. . . ." Suddenly remembering the boy that morning and the political button, he added in loud disgust, "Look that half-foolish boy you does send here to pick the coconuts. Instead of him learning a trade and going to England where he might find work he's walking about with a political button. He and all in politics now! But that's the way with these down here. They'll do some of everything but work. They don't want work!" He gestured violently, almost dancing in anger. "They too busy spreeing."

The chair creaked as Mr. Goodman sketched a pained and gentle denial. "No, man," he said, "you wrong. Things is different to before. I mean to say, the young people nowadays is different to how we was. They not just sitting back and taking things no more. They not so frighten for the white people as we was. No, man. Now take that said same boy, for an example. I don't say he don't like a spree, but he's serious, you see him there. He's a member of this new Barbados People's Party. He wants to see his own color running the government. He wants to be able to make a living right here in Barbados instead of going to any cold England. And he's right!" Mr. Goodman paused at a vehement pitch, then shrugged heavily. "What the young people must do, nuh? They got to look at something . . ."

"Look to work!" And Mr. Watford thrust out a hand so that the horned knuckles caught the light.

"Yes, that's true—and it's up to we that got little something to give them work," Mr. Goodman said, and a sadness filtered among the dissipations in his eyes. "I mean to say we that got little something got to help out. In a manner of speaking, we's responsible . . ."

"Responsible!" The word circled Mr. Watford's head like a gnat and he wanted to reach up and haul it down, to squash it underfoot.

Mr. Goodman spread his hands; his breathing rumbled with a sigh. "Yes, in a manner of speaking. That's why, Watford man, you got to provide little work for some poor person down in here. Hire a servant at least! 'Cause I gon tell you something . . ." And he hitched forward his chair, his voice dropped to a wheeze. "People talking. Here you come back rich from big America and build a swell house and plant 'nough coconut trees and you still cleaning and cooking and thing like some woman. Man, it don't look good!" His face screwed in emphasis and he sat back. "Now, there's this girl, the daughter of a friend that just dead, and she need work bad enough. But I wouldn't like to see she working for these white people 'cause you know how those men will take advantage of she. And she'd make a good servant, man. Quiet and quick so, and nothing a-tall to feed and she can sleep anywhere about the place. And she don't have no boys always around her either. . . ." Still talking, Mr. Goodman eased from his chair and reached the stairs with surprising agility. "You need a servant," he whispered, leaning close to Mr. Watford as he passed. "It don't look good, man, people talking. I gon send she."

Mr. Watford was overcome by nausea. Not only from Mr. Goodman's smell—a stench of salt fish, rum and sweat—but from an outrage which was like a sediment in his stomach. For a long time he stood there almost kecking from disgust, until his clock struck eight, reminding him of the sanctuary within—and suddenly his cold laugh dismissed Mr. Goodman and his proposal. Hurrying in, he locked the doors and windows against the night air and, still laughing, he slept.

The next day, coming from the grove to prepare his noon meal, he saw her. She was standing in his driveway, her bare feet like strong dark roots amid the jagged stones, her face tilted toward the sun—and she might have been standing there always waiting for him. She seemed of the sun, of the earth. The folktale of creation might have been true with her: that along a riverbank a god had scooped up the earth—rich and black and warmed by the sun—and molded her poised head with its tufted braids and then with a whimsical touch crowned it with a sober brown felt hat which should have been worn by some stout English matron in a London suburb, had sculptured the passionless face and drawn a screen of gossamer across her eyes to hide the void behind. Beneath her bodice her small breasts were smooth at the crest. Below her waist, her hips branched wide, the place prepared for its load of life. But it was the bold and sensual strength of her legs which completely unstrung Mr. Watford. He wanted to grab a hoe and drive her off.

"What it 'tis you want?" he called sharply.

"Mr. Goodman send me."

"Send you for what?" His voice was shrill in the glare.

She moved. Holding a caved-in valise and a pair of white sandals, her head weaving slightly as though she bore a pail of water there or a tray of mangoes, she glided over the stones as if they were smooth ground. Her bland expression did not change, but her eyes, meeting his, held a vague trust. Pausing a few feet away, she curtsied deeply. "I's the new servant."

Only Mr. Watford's cold laugh saved him from anger. As always it raised him to a height where everything below appeared senseless and insignificant—especially his people, whom the girl embodied. From this height, he could even be charitable. And thinking suddenly of how she had waited in the brutal sun since morning without taking shelter under the nearby tamarind tree, he said, not unkindly, "Well, girl, go back and tell Mr. Goodman for me that I don't need no servant."

"I can't go back."

"How you mean can't?" His head gave its angry snap.

"I'll get lashes," she said simply. "My mother say I must work the day and then if you don't wish me, I can come back. But I's not to leave till night falling, if not I get lashes."

He was shaken by her dispassion. So much so that his head dropped from its disdaining angle and his hands twitched with helplessness. Despite anything he might say or do, her fear of the whipping would keep her there until nightfall, the valise and shoes in hand. He felt his day with its order and quiet rhythms threatened by her intrusion—and suddenly waving her off as if she were an evil visitation, he hurried into the kitchen to prepare his meal.

But he paused, confused, in front of the stove, knowing that he could not cook and leave her hungry at the door, nor could he cook and serve her as though he were the servant.

"Yes, please."

They said nothing more. She entered the room with a firm step and an air almost of familiarity, placed her valise and shoes in a corner and went directly to the larder. For a time Mr. Watford stood by, his muscles flexing with anger and his eyes bounding ahead of her every move, until, feeling foolish and frighteningly useless, he went out to feed his doves.

The meal was quickly done and as he ate he heard the dry slap of her feet behind him—a pleasant sound—and then silence. When he glanced back she was squatting in the doorway, the sunlight aslant the absurd hat and her face bent to a bowl she held in one palm. She ate slowly, thoughtfully, as if fixing the taste of each spoonful in her mind.

It was then that he decided to let her work the day and at nightfall to pay her a dollar and dismiss her. His decision held when he returned later from the grove and found tea awaiting him, and then through the supper she prepared. Afterward, dressed in his white uniform, he patiently waited out the day's end on the portico, his face setting into a grim mold. Then just as dusk etched the first dark line between the sea and sky, he took out a dollar and went downstairs.

She was not in the kitchen, but the table was set for his morning tea. Muttering at her persistence, he charged down the corridor, which ran the length of the basement, flinging open the doors to the damp, empty rooms on either side, and sending the lizards and the shadows long entrenched there scuttling to safety.

He found her in the small slanted room under the stoop, asleep on an old cot he kept there, her suitcase turned down beside the bed, and the shoes, dress and the ridiculous hat piled on top. A loose nightshift muted the outline of her body and hid her legs, so that she appeared suddenly defenseless, innocent, with a child's trust in her curled hand and in her deep breathing. Standing in the doorway, with his own breathing snarled and his eyes averted, Mr. Watford felt like an intruder. She had claimed the room. Quivering with frustration, he slowly turned away, vowing that in the morning he would shove the dollar at her and lead her like a cow out of his house. . . .

Dawn brought rain and a hot wind which set the leaves rattling and swiping at the air like distraught arms. Dressing in the dawn darkness, Mr. Watford again armed himself with the dollar and, with his shoulders at an uncompromising set, plunged downstairs. He descended into the warm smell of bakes and this smell, along with the thought that she had been up before him, made his hand knot with exasperation on the banister. The knot tightened as he saw her, dust swirling at her feet as she swept the corridor, her face bent solemn to the task. Shutting her out with a lifted hand, he shouted, "Don't bother sweeping. Here's a dollar. G'long back."

The broom paused and although she did not raise her head, he sensed her groping through the shadowy maze of her mind toward his voice. Behind the dollar which he waved in her face, her eyes slowly cleared. And, surprisingly, they held no fear. Only anticipation and a tenuous trust. It was as if she expected him to say something kind.

"G'long back!" His angry cry was a plea.

Like a small, starved flame, her trust and expectancy died and she said, almost with reproof, "The rain falling."

To confirm this, the wind set the rain stinging across the windows and he could say nothing, even though the words sputtered at his lips. It was useless. There was nothing inside her to comprehend that she was not wanted. His shoulders sagged under the weight of her ignorance, and with a futile gesture he swung away, the dollar hanging from his hand like a small sword gone limp.

She became as fixed and familiar a part of the house as the stones—and as silent. He paid her five dollar a week, gave her Mondays off and in the evenings, after a time, even allowed her to sit in the alcove off the parlor, while he read with his back to her, taking no more notice of her than he did the moths on the lamp.

But once, after many silent evenings together, he detected a sound apart from the night murmurs of the sea and village and the metallic tuning of the steel band, a low, almost inhuman cry of loneliness which chilled him. Frightened, he turned to find her leaning hesitantly toward him, her eyes dark with urgency, and her face tight with bewilderment and a growing anger. He started, not understanding, and her arm lifted to stay him. Eagerly she bent closer. But as she uttered the low cry again, as her fingers described her wish to talk, he jerked around, afraid that she would be foolish enough to speak and that once she did they would be brought close. He would be forced then to acknowledge something about her which he refused to grant; above all, he would be called upon to share a little of himself. Quickly he returned to his newspaper, rustling it to settle the air, and after a time he felt her slowly, bitterly, return to her silence. . . .

Like sand poured in a careful measure from the hand, the weeks flowed down to August and on the first Monday, August bank holiday, Mr. Watford awoke to the sound of the excursion buses leaving the village for the annual outing, their backfire pelleting the dawn calm and the ancient motors protesting the over-crowding. Lying there, listening, he saw with disturbing clarity his mother dressed for an excursion—the white headtie wound above her dark face and her head poised like a dancer's under the heavy outing basket of food. That set of her head had haunted his years, reappearing in the girl as she walked toward him the first day. Aching with the memory, yet annoyed with himself for remembering, he went downstairs.

The girl had already left for the excursion, and although it was her day off, he felt vaguely betrayed by her eagerness to leave him. Somehow it suggested ingratitude. It was as if his doves were suddenly to refuse him their song or his trees their fruit, despite the care he gave them. Some vital past which shaped the simple mosaic of his life seemed suddenly missing. An alien silence curled like coal gas throughout the house. To escape it he remained in the grove all day and, upon his return to the house, dressed with more care than usual, putting on a fresh, starched uniform, and solemnly brushing his hair until it lay in a smooth bush above his brow. Leaning close to the mirror, but avoiding his eyes, he cleaned the white rheum at their corners, and afterward pried loose the dirt under his nails.

Unable to read his papers, he went out on the portico to escape the unnatural silence in the house, and stood with his hands clenched on the balustrade and his taut body straining forward. After a long wait he heard the buses return and voices in gay shreds upon the wind. Slowly his hands relaxed, as did his shoulders under the white uniform; for the first time that day his breathing was regular. She would soon come.

But she did not come and dusk bloomed into night, with a fragrant heat and a full moon which made the leaves glint as though touched with frost. The steel band at the crossroads began the lilting songs of sadness and seduction, and suddenly—like shades roused by the night and the music—images of the girl flitted before Mr. Watford's eyes. He saw her lost amid the carousings in the village, despoiled; he imagined someone like Mr. Goodman clasping her lewdly or tumbling her in the canebrake. His hand rose, trembling, to rid the air of her; he tried to summon his cold laugh. But, somehow, he could not dismiss her as he had always done with everyone else. Instead, he wanted to punish and protect her, to find and lead her back to the house.

As he leaned there, trying not to give way to the desire to go and find her, his fist striking the balustrade to deny his longing, he saw them. The girl first, with the moonlight like a silver patina on her skin, then the boy whom Mr. Goodman sent for the coconuts, whose easy strength and the political button—"The Old Order Shall Pass"—had always mocked and challenged Mr. Watford. They were joined in a tender battle: the boy in a sport shirt riotous with color was reaching for the girl as he leaped and spun, weightless, to the music, while she fended him off with a gesture which was lovely in its promise of surrender. Her protests were little scattered bursts: "But, man, why don't you stop, nuh . . . ? But, you know, you getting on like a real-real idiot. . . ."

Each time she chided him he leaped higher and landed closer, until finally he eluded her arm and caught her by the waist. Boldly he pressed a leg between her tightly closed legs until they opened under his pressure. Their bodies cleaved into one whirling form and while he sang she laughed like a wanton, with her hat cocked over her ear. Dancing, the stones moiling underfoot, they claimed the night. More than the night. The steel band played for them alone. The trees were their frivolous companions, swaying as they swayed. The moon rode the sky because of them.

Mr. Watford, hidden by a dense shadow, felt the tendons which strung him together suddenly go limp; above all, an obscure belief which, like rare china, he had stored on a high shelf in his mind began to tilt. He sensed the familiar specter which hovered in the night reaching out to embrace him, just as the two in the yard were embracing. Utterly unstrung, incapable of either speech or action, he stumbled into the house, only to meet there an accusing silence from the clock, which had missed its eight o'clock winding, and his newspapers lying like ruined leaves over the floor.

He lay in bed in the white uniform, waiting for sleep to rescue him, his hands seeking the comforting sound of his doves. But sleep eluded him and instead of the doves, their throats tremulous with sound, his scarred hands filled with the shape of a woman he had once kept: her skin, which had been almost bruising in its softness; the buttocks and breasts spread under his hands to inspire both cruelty and tenderness. His hands closed to softly crush those forms, and the searing thrust of passion, which he had not felt for years, stabbed his dry groin. He imagined the two outside, their passion at a pitch by now, lying together behind the tamarind tree, or perhaps—and he sat up sharply—they had been bold enough to bring their lust into the house. Did he not smell their taint on the air? Restored suddenly, he rushed downstairs. As he reached the corridor, a thread of light beckoned him from her room and he dashed furiously toward it, rehearsing the angry words which would jar their bodies apart. He neared the door, glimpsed her through the small opening, and his step faltered; the words collapsed.

She was seated alone on the cot, tenderly holding the absurd felt hat in her lap, one leg tucked under her while the other trailed down. A white sandal, its strap broken, dangled from the foot and gently knocked the floor as she absently swung her leg. Her dress was twisted around her body—and pinned to the bodice, so that it gathered the cloth between her small breasts, was the political button the boy always wore. She was dreamily fingering it, her mouth shaped by a gentle, ironic smile and her eyes strangely acute and critical. What had transpired on the cot had not only, it seemed, twisted the dress around her, tumbled her hat and broken her sandal, but had also defined her and brought the blurred forms of life into focus for her. There was a woman's force in her aspect now, a tragic knowing and acceptance in her bent head, a hint about her of Cassandra watching the future wheel before her eyes.

Before those eyes which looked to another world, Mr. Watford's anger and strength failed him and he held to the wall for support. Unreasonably, he felt that he should assume some hushed and reverent pose, to bow as she had the day she had come. If he had known their names, he would have pleaded forgiveness for the sins he had committed against her and the others all his life, against himself. If he could have borne the thought, he would have confessed that it had been love, terrible in its demand, which he had always fled. And that love had been the reason for his return. If he had been honest, he would have whispered—his head bent and a hand shading his eyes—that unlike Mr. Goodman (whom he suddenly envied for his full life) and the boy with his political button (to whom he had lost the girl), he had not been willing to bear the weight of his own responsibility. . . . But all Mr. Watford could admit, clinging there to the wall, was, simply, that he wanted to live—and that the girl held life within her as surely as she held the hat in her hands. If he could prove himself better than the boy, he could win it. Only then, he dimly knew, would he shake off the pursuer which had given him no rest since birth. Hopefully, he staggered forward, his step cautious and contrite, his hands, quivering along the wall.

She did not see or hear him as he pushed the door wider. And for some time he stood there, his shoulders hunched in humility, his skin stripped away to reveal each flaw, his whole self offered in one outstretched hand. Still unaware of him, she swung her leg, and the dangling shoe struck a derisive note. Then, just as he had turned away that evening in the parlor when she had uttered her low call, she turned away now, refusing him.

Mr. Watford's body went slack and then stiffened ominously. He knew that he would have to wrest from her the strength needed to sustain him. Slamming the door, he cried, his voice cracked and strangled, "What you and him was doing in here? Tell me! I'll not have you bringing nastiness round here. Tell me!"

She did not start. Perhaps she had been aware of him all along and had expected his outburst. Or perhaps his demented eye and the desperation rising from him like a musk filled her with pity instead of fear. Whatever, her benign smile held and her eyes remained abstracted until his hand reached out to fling her back on the cot. Then, frowning, she stood up, wobbling a little on the broken shoe and holding the political button as if it was a new power which would steady and protect her. With a cruel flick of her arm she struck aside his hand and, in a voice as cruel, halted him. "But you best move and don't come holding on to me, you nasty, pissy old man. That's all you is, despite yuh big house and fancy furnitures and yuh newspapers from America. You ain't people, Mr. Watford, you ain't people!" And with a look and a lift of her head which made her condemnation final, she placed the hat atop her braids, and turning aside picked up the valise which had always lain, packed, beside the cot—as if even on the first day she had known that this night would come and had been prepared against it. . . .

Mr. Watford did not see her leave, for a pain squeezed his heart dry and the driven blood was a bright, blinding cataract over his eyes. But his inner eye was suddenly clear. For the first time it gazed mutely upon the waste and pretense which had spanned his years. Flung there against the door by the girls' small blow, his body slowly crumpled under the weariness he had long denied. He sensed that dark but unsubstantial figure which roamed the nights searching for him wind him in its chill embrace. He struggled against it, his hands clutching the air with the spastic eloquence of a drowning man. He moaned—and the anguished sound reached beyond the room to fill the house. It escaped to the yard and his doves swelled their throats, moaning with him.

QUESTIONS FOR DISCUSSION AND WRITING

1. "Barbados" is named for its setting. What does Barbados come to mean in the course of the story?

2. "Barbados" is a portrait of a fearful, life-denying man. How does Marshall account psychologically for Mr. Watford's temperament?

3. Does this story have a political dimension? Note Goodman's statement about what ought to be done for the local people and the boy's political button.

4. What happens at the end of the story? Does Watford die?

Hugo Martinez-Serros

Hugo Martinez-Serros (b. 1930) grew up in a poverty-stricken Mexican-American *barrio* (neighborhood) in south Chicago. A scholarship allowed him to attend the University of Chicago, where he received a B.A. in English in 1951. A Ph.D. from Northwestern University followed. He turned to writing fiction relatively late in life, publishing his first stories when he was fifty. His first collection of stories, set in his childhood neighborhood, is *The Last Laugh and Other Stories* (1988). Martinez-Serros is a professor of English at Lawrence University in Appleton, Wisconsin.

"LEARN! LEARN!"

José María Rivera always read important letters with a red pencil in his hand. They were letters written in *castellano*—he sometimes called it *cristiano*, his eyes rolling, his voice serious—by people who knew or should have known the language as well or better than he did, which is what made the letters important. He read first for spelling errors, rapidly, crossing out, adding, changing, circling, then he went back for a second reading to seize anything that had escaped his initial sweep. In repeated readings, finally, he concentrated on what the letters said.

There were few of these letters in the passing of a year. The two or three his brothers-in-law far off in Mexico wrote to his wife, letters that always provoked him to say in a louder than normal voice: *"Lástima de educación universitaria, no saben escribir."* A pity indeed, he never tired of thinking, they were educated at the university and just didn't know how to write. He said it as much to himself as to his wife, a perceptive woman who did not answer him. Years ago, before leaving Mexico, he had already developed the habit of saying things aloud to himself. And there were the other letters, rare strikes that came into his hands from friends who did not quite understand them, and from the friends of friends.

Chema—his friends called him that—had long ago stopped "editing" the *barrio semanarios*, weeklies. They had too many errors, the same ones over and over and they held no challenge for him. Besides, his anonymous letters to their editors had gone unheeded and he was not interested in writers who did not want to be redeemed. *"Cabrones, ojetes,* damned assholes," he had labeled them in the final letter, and as he wrote he shouted repeatedly to himself. *"¡Que se chinguen ésos!* Fuck them! *¡No tienen interés en aprender!* They're not interested in learning!"

The church bulletin of Our Lady of Guadalupe was another matter. The Riveras, whose destinies were in the hands of *don José*—his acquaintances called him that—were not church-going, but every Sunday *don* José sent one of his sons for the bulletin, warning him as he left, to be careful, *"Ten cuidado,"* and not to get lost in that den of corruption, *"No te vayas a perder en ese recinto de perversos."* Although the bulletin dealt exclusively with what Chema called *"cosas de beatas y maricones,* news for overly pious women and fairies"—births, marriages, deaths, baptisms, confirmations, first communions, fund-raising events, the activities of the Daughters of Our Most Holy Virgin of Guadalupe and of the Knights of the Virgin of Guadalupe—he acknowledged the excellence of its language, an excellence that was not without faults, however. The author of that bulletin was the *párroco*, Father Tortas, a Spaniard whom Chema called, "that overstuffed *gachupín,"* adding gleefully, *"Cuervo cargado de carnes y de cagada,* a crow bursting with flesh and shit."

314

José María mined every one of Father Tortas' bulletins, and every one yielded something, however small or imagined. But it was the nugget of indisputable error that filled him with intense pleasure and made him shout, *"Aprende de tu padre, sanguijuela,* learn from your master, parasite! This is your only creative act, it should be perfect! You have nothing else to do, *manos de señorita!* ¡Aprende! ¡Aprende! Learn! Learn! If I am the only one willing to kick your ass, so be it! Your voice is louder than it should be, you must answer for it!'' And José María taught the priest as well as he could, in anonymous letters that went out often but not regularly, for not all bulletins merited a complete letter. His sons, feeling themselves partners in this enterprise, delivered them to the church or the rectory, clandestinely, provocatively, under cover of the large crowds that moved in and out of the former or passed slowly by the latter.

There was no question of it, Father Tortas heeded portions of the anonymous letters and this made José María a better critic. Their conflict, the tip of the iceberg of their antagonisms, took place at the level of orthography, grammar, syntax, semantics. Sometimes José María applauded the priest's responses to particular challenges, for he would counter his unknown antagonist's thrusts with an ingenious verbal maze here, an extraordinarily subtle play on words there. At times the priest seemed to tweak his unknown critic by slipping into flagrant error. Chema begrudged the priest his mastery of the language and whispered to himself, *"Sí, dominas el castellano, pinche cura maricón,* you lousy fairy of a priest, you do know the language! You have this over my brothers-in-law, that wherever the hell they taught you, they taught you well, *manos de señorita."*

Juan Ginés Tortas' parishioners had never seen hands more beautiful than his. They had made José María think of the hands of figures in religious calendars. They were white, very white, the fingers slender and long and tapering into flat tips capped by manicured nails, a labyrinth of pale blue lines just under the skin. Hands surprisingly fleshless, firm and smooth. To his flock they seemed hands made for holding and displaying Christ, a living monstrance. Nearing fifty, Father Tortas was a big man with a bald pate. A sprinkle of white flakes fell from the hair that ringed his head, and his hands recurrently fluttered up to his shoulders to flick at the incessant snow. He dressed with an elegance that belied the notion that a priest's wardrobe is uniformly dull, and even his cassocks and robes were tailored to his personal desires. He had long ago assumed the practice, after Mass, of keeping his robes on and wearing them in his chambers. They intimidated parishioners he received there, giving him the distance he needed.

As seminarian and newly ordained priest, Juan Ginés, proud and serious by nature and gregarious by design, had been a competitor whose incentive was competition. He was a performer who excelled when he was surrounded by excellent performers. Drawn to material comfort, he had aspired to a position of prestige in some chancery, convinced that there he would find abundance and intellectual stimulation. But the young priest's impatience, buttressed by ambition and a knowledge of English, had driven him to the United States. He had imagined himself the Sepúlveda of the *mestizos* in Anglo-America, had envisioned himself in the American Hierarchy as the exegete of the Spanish-American text.

In the United States Juan Ginés saw the Canaan of his expectations crumble in the Babylon of his captivity in South Chicago. They had not told him as he would later tell himself—*"¡Me enviaron al culo de esta ciudad salchichera!"*—that South Chicago was the anus of sausage-making Chicago. He had come to a dead end when the world had seemed new to him, and for a time he had struggled to check his bitterness, winning small victories over his pride and ambition, but he could not vanquish them. He convinced himself that he had been intentionally misled, ultimately believing that they had exiled him unjustly. So it was that he made a sword of his disillusionment and a shield of what had been his expectations. His weight increased with his cynicism and his hair began to thin.

For more than twenty years Father Tortas had grieved the impatience that had led him to abandon Spain for the hope of rapid advancement in a city where, he discovered, it was reserved for priests with Irish surnames. Since then he had moved cautiously, slowly weighing alternatives on the scales of his distrust to arrive at decisions of consequence and inconsequence alike. He had pondered as long over the advisability of forming a parish baseball team as he had over the need for a second assistant. He scorned young people for their immaturity and lack of judgment, making them the target of diatribes delivered from the pulpit, subjecting them to inquisitional indignities in the intimacy of the confessional. And for more than twenty years he had indulged his pride with fantasies of what he could have been had he stayed in Spain: now a cardinal's secretary, now a bishop, now a cardinal. He became aloof, solitary, performed his duties with the aid of many, but drew nobody close to him and drew close to nobody, not even his assistant priests. Alone, he lived more in the world of what could have been than in the community where he ran out his time. What little affection he could summon he bestowed on his altar boys, who, uneasy in his presence, would not have passed their thirteenth year if he could have controlled their growth. Of his pastoral concerns in recent years only the composition of the church bulletin seemed to interest him. Not even his housekeeper really knew him.

On Saturday mornings Father Tortas sat at his desk and unhurriedly wrote the weekly bulletin on oversized sheets of lined paper. Working from a pad of notes, dates, symbols, he finished it in an hour, needing more time only if the bulletin was unusually long. But it never took more than two hours. His penmanship was clear, large and angular, marked by that stiffness characteristic of certain European hands. Typed by a volunteer whom the *párroco* had trained, the copy was taken to a local printer by noon and the finished product was delivered to the rectory before five. Chema's anonymous letters effected no obvious change in his routine. The priest gradually intensified his concentration, paid greater attention to expression, turned increasingly to figurative language, adopted a more sophisticated syntax and, except for rare instances, did not need additional time to produce the bulletin. Had he known this, José María, like those who measure others against themselves, would have been astounded by the facility and speed with which Father Tortas composed the document.

Like most of the men in the neighborhood, Chema worked in the steel mill. He was skilled at executing a variety of difficult and dangerous jobs that required strength, stamina and alertness. He did the jobs superbly, with an animal intelligence and grace that were incomparable among his fellow workers. He followed his nature in what he did, and what he did and how he did it were his only security in the mill since it was not unionized. But the work did not spend him; it failed to test his physical limits. It did not drain him of that need he felt to exhaust his energies. It failed to challenge his intelligence and he knew it always would.

Even the letters he wrote in English deserved at least one draft, and Chema composed them as well as he could. Inevitably he turned to one of his sons for help, a resource that pained them both since José María had to accept his son's judgment and the son had to suffer his father's detailed, time-consuming explanations.

"But you can't say that, that's Spanish, it's not said like that in English," his son explained to him in Spanish.

"Who says you can't? If you understand what you're doing you can do anything you want to with language.But you don't understand! *¡Lástima! ¡Aprende! ¡Aprende!*"

"I'm tellin' you, Pa, *no es inglés.*"

In some cases the son's advice was rejected. Having labored for an expression he thought poetic—"My determination to become a citizen is not different from the determination of the lion that, crippled, accepted Daniel's aid. My allegiance to the Daniel that is the United States could not be different from that of the lion to Daniel"—José María held fast to his creation over his son's protests, convinced that an adult would see what the youth had failed to appreciate. There was no antagonism between father and son, no rivalry, no dispute as to who knew English better. Both felt impatience: the father over his son's incomprehension of figurative language, the son over his father's insistence, which pulled ambivalently at the boy, who admired it even while it annoyed him. Together they hammered out a finished product and Chema then typed it, his fingers slowly pounding the keys of a winged, flightless Oliver. Chema was confident that the typewritten letter would impress its *gringo* reader.

But when José María wrote the most important letters, when he wrote letters in *castellano*—his own, his wife's—he prepared for the undertaking as carefully as Father Tortas might have readied everything for a Solemn High Mass. He spread newspaper over one end of the kitchen table to smooth its uneven surface, placed Bello's *Gramática de la lengua castellana* at his left elbow, a dictionary at his right, a half dozen sharp-pointed pencils and a block of unlined paper in front of him. His hands had worn through the covers of both books and he had skillfully rebuilt them. The dictionary was small, a desk copy often inadequate to his needs.

Imagining himself the addressee, José María gave himself selfishly to his letter, writing in intense pursuit of the perfection his mind projected just beyond his pencils. Always, after several days, he came close enough to that perfection to feel satisfied; on rare occasions he achieved it. Almost as a rule of thumb, the number of drafts his letters required equaled the number of pages per letter. His prose was solid, heavy at times, but he wielded it with ease and could make it leap and turn to his wishes. An isolated sentence might seem cumbrous, but it lost this quality in the configuration of a paragraph or passage. He shaped his prose as a blacksmith from Guanajuato fashioned wrought iron, heating it in the forge of his brain, hammering it over and over on the anvil of his judgment, plunging it finally into the cold water of acceptance, piece by piece, the overall design held in the eye of his intelligence. He read all finished letters to his wife:

Priest,

    I repeat what I have told you before: you have no imagination. Inasmuch as you refuse to think of your parishioners as human beings, as *hermanos* or *hijos,* insisting, rather, on seeing them as animals, *ovejas,* always *ovejas,* lend consistency, unity, to your vision by seeing yourself as a sheep dog rather than as a shepherd. At least give your parishioners a little variety. Call them fish, or doves, or better still, *burros.* You, of all people, must know how important, useful and docile *burros* are in the Hispanic world as well as in the bible. Read Vargas Vila, for you might learn from him how. . . .

On the second page of your bulletin, first paragraph of the section entitled BAPTISMS, you employ a passive construction incorrectly. I bring to your attention that in passive constructions with *se* it is the nature of the passive subject that determines the form the verb must take. . . .

The tools of Chema's mill work—hammers, pickaxes, pokers, shovels, drills, wrenches—had made his hands hard and his fingers were rooted in a ridge of calluses that spread to the base of his thick palms. His nails were dense, horny, a little longer than those of other men who did his kind of work. To shake his hand was to shake the hand of a man wearing a gauntlet. In that hand a pencil or pen seemed to grow small, almost disappearing in his fist, so that when he wrote, the script seemed to flow from a little tube he operated with the slight pressure of three fingers.

The writing was utterly controlled, swift, rhythmically winding and unwinding in fluid curves, the tall letters, all the same height, gracefully swayed from lower left to upper right, the crosses of the t's straight and slightly lengthened. It was elegant in its proportions, in the purity of its lines, in the inventiveness of its capital letters, in the almost-flourishes of occasional final letters that caught the eye with their air of effortless improvisation. The surprise of those who saw him write filled Chema with immense satisfaction, and he seized every opportunity to write that presented itself, even if it was only to sign his name. His Spanish letters were written in longhand. Nothing else would do.

He wrote with a Schaeffer fountain pen, white-dotted, medium point, in his judgment the finest writing instrument his money could buy. Several times a week he filled pages of a notebook with circles, ovals, straight and curved lines, all joined together and exactly alike. It gave him no pleasure to do these exercises. He performed them routinely, knowing that by doing them his hand would always be fully in control. On the subject of writing he spoke like a specialist:

"You hold the pen with little pressure, *apenitas,* about an inch and a half up from the point. The upper part rests in the cradle formed by the thumb and the index finger, *así.* And remember, this is the most important part, you write with the forearm, not with the wrist, *con el antebrazo.* The movement is from the elbow down, that way you never get tired: *¡Nunca!* And the test is in how loosely you hold the pen. Go ahead, pull it from between my fingers, you'll see how easy it is to do. You see *¡Aprende, aprende!*"

The Rivera children all wrote well. José María had seen to that. They regularly did exercises for him in notebooks, but none showed the signs of calligraphic precociousness he had shown when he was their age. And they spoke well enough, both languages, but especially Spanish. They spoke it better than their friends, which did not surprise José María, for he had convinced them that it was important to speak well. They had heard him dominate conversations with his friends, had heard the latter turn to their father to settle disputes about word meanings, had seen him reach for his dictionary to drive all doubt from the minds of his listeners.

As much as anything it was the dictionary test that impressed the Rivera children. José María did it not to show off but as a measure of himself in the presence of his children, as a way of showing them that they could learn as he had. He handed them his dictionary and they took turns opening it at random and reading him words that looked difficult. He would define them. He did it to show them that words belonged to anyone who wanted them, and they came to believe that success in life and the power of speech were closely linked, that one could not be important without knowing words.

The penmanship of the first anonymous letter had caught Father Tortas' attention. The letter's message had made him smile wryly. A man had written it, that much he could tell. But he knew that man was not one of his parishioners, for which one of them could write like that, express himself like that, have so little respect for him that he dared instruct him? *Hijo de puta,* he thought, what do you know, what do you know about me? Do you think that everyone can thrive in a sea of literacy? It had crushed him to learn that his parishioners were laborers, poor people of little education who had fled Mexico in search of something better. They defiled his language. He came to need those letters, anticipated them, counted on them to pique him, to make him think, to lift him from the drudgery of his daily life as did his weekly flights to the Loop, where he brushed elbows with his kind of people in elegant restaurants, theatres, museums. People who dressed like him, who shared his interests, who talked like him and ate like him. *Castrado,* he mused, if you had *cojones* you would show them to me, you would sign your name and show me your *mestizo* face. But you half-breeds have always been cowards. Only cowards live in the *culo* of Chicago and like it. I could find you out if I wanted, but I give your letters the importance they deserve—anonymity. You amuse me, *enano,* you faceless dwarf. Still, he wondered who his Momus might be.

As time passed, Father Tortas became convinced that his critic had to be one of the parish's heretics. Chema was his prime suspect, but without inquiry he could not learn enough about him to confirm his suspicions. In the end he abandoned all desire to ascertain who the offender was because it did not matter that he identify his anonymous correspondent. And he did not want to deter the man.

Once, several years before the priest brought out the bulletin, the two men had met. It was in the depths of *la crisis,* the Depression, and José María had been lucky to be working one and two days a week. His family was large, his children very young, and he needed additional work. They had learned to live without gas and electricity, but they could not do without food and clothing. There was always work to be done in the church and in the church's properties. Everybody knew this. Reluctantly, José María had gone to see the priest, driven to it by need and the hope of securing employment. He found Father Tortas in the sacristy.

"¿Señor cura?" José María said.

The priest turned to face a man in his thirties, lean and muscular, his Mexican physiognomy striking with its deepset eyes, prominent cheekbones and nose, a slight fleshiness around the mouth that drew attention away from the chin. He wore heavy work shoes, corduroy trousers, a denim shirt under a light jacket, and a wool cap pulled forward on his head. José María looked steadily into the other man's eyes.

"Aquí se me llama padre, around here people call me Father." The priest looked deliberately at the man's cap, as if telling him to remove it. Unruffled, José María understood but kept his hands at his sides. Then the priest asked, *"Eres una de mis ovejas?"* all the while thinking, whether you're mine or not you're a sheep.

"Soy hombre, I'm a man. *Vivo en este barrio,* I live in this neighborhood," he answered coldly, offended by the other's use of *tú.* Fucking priests, he thought, they're all alike.

"*¿Qué quieres?*" the priest asked, thinking, yes, you bastard, just what is it that you want?

Hijo de la chingada, Chema thought, *van dos veces,* that's twice you've done it now. Again, the answer was cold, "*No quiero nada,* I want nothing. I have come looking for work. I am a good painter, a fair plumber, a carpenter. I can repair anything that needs repairing. I am a good electrician too. Pay me what you like, *lo que quiera usted;* if you don't like my work, don't pay me anything. I need work."

"The men in this parish donate their skills to their *párroco.* Why should I hire you?"

"*Mire usted,* look," he said pointing to a wall of blistered paint above a large radiator. His "*Ahí arriba,*" accompanied by an upward thrust of the head, directed the priest's eyes to a badly cracked pane of glass just below the high ceiling. "You should hire me because my work stands up to time. Because I am not afraid of height."

Father Tortas sat down but did not offer the man a chair. He caught his right trouser leg just above the knee, pulled it up gently and crossed his legs. The black tailored material hung in a long smooth fold above a polished black dress shoe. "Do you have a family?"

"*Sí.*"

"Which is your church?"

"I do not have a church."

"*Lástima.* I do not hire heretics. If you want to work for me you must attend Mass here." Waving his hands back and forth between himself and José María he added, "Bring me your heretics. When I have made Catholics of all of you and you become sheep in my fold, I may hire you."

"I do better work than your Catholics."

Impatiently, the priest stood up, crossed the room, took his black Homburg from a rack and put it on. "*¿Cómo te llamas?*" he asked, as if knowing his name would give him some power over him.

"*Julio César,*" he answered with a smile. "*Y tú cura,*" he continued, "*seguramente te llamas Torquemada.*"

"I have no time for your insolence!" Tortas reached out to smooth a cassock that hung neatly on a hanger.

"Nor I for yours. I am leaving, please feel free to put on your dress." And he laughed, turned and left.

Father Tortas' experience with two of the Rivera boys was no better. On Sundays, after Mass, they posted themselves at the doors on his church to sell papers. He had shooed them away many times and once had managed to snatch their little *semanarios* tearing them to pieces and repulsing the boys as he might have driven money changers from his temple. But they kept coming back and he finally asked them in a threatening voice, "*¿Cómo se llama vuestro padre?*"

"*Don* José María Rivera," they answered fearlessly.

Furious, the priest shouted, "*¡Entre vosotros no hay don, como no sea don Mierda!* There isn't a *don* among you, unless it be *don* Shit!"

One of the boys answered him, saying, "*¡Para mierda, los curas!* If it's shit you have in mind, we should be talking about priests!" Chema laughed when the boys told him what had happened. Father Tortas kept distant from them after that.

When Chema's eldest son, at sixteen, found a part-time job at the Wilcox and Follet Book Company, it was the dictionaries that caught his attention. "They got dictionaries up the ass on the fourth floor!" he told his brothers. "Little ones, vest-pocket dictionaries, an' bigger'n bigger ones. The biggest are those big fat Websters with color-plates."

"Do they have 'em in Spanish?"

"Yeah. In all kinds of languages. In two languages too."

The plan took form slowly and when they had worked it out to the last detail they executed it, on a Saturday. On Sunday, when José María's youngest son brought him Father Tortas' bulletin, his other sons each brought him a dictionary, the first real gifts they had ever given him, gifts that Chema could not afford. (Three times in the air shaft, heart and hands had followed perfectly the trajectory of the falling books, three times had calculated precisely the moment at which to catch, three times had shuddered with the explosions, the grime-encrusted windows becoming banks of eyes as Chema's sons struggled to hide the books in a Boy Scout knapsack.) Chema's eyes bulged in disbelief as he fingered the three volumes: a thick, handsome *Sopena,* a *Velázquez* bilingual, and *Webster's* unabridged complete with color-plates.

Readying his table in the kitchen, his new *Sopena* as his right elbow, José María picked up the bulletin and began to read it aloud, a mocking edge in his voice:

> *Queridas ovejas,*
> I remind the Daughters of our Most Holy Virgin of Guadalupe and the Knights of the Virgin of Guadalupe. . . .

"*Ahora te chingas, cura,*" he exclaimed, "you're fucked now, priest, now you'll see who's who, *sabrás que soy tu padre, tu padre,* now you'll know once and for all who your master is! *¡Aprende! ¡Aprende!* Learn! Learn!"

And José María Rivera placed his hand on his new *Sopena.*

QUESTIONS FOR DISCUSSION AND WRITING

1. The protagonist of "Learn! Learn!" is Chema, the antagonist is Father Tortas, and the issue is their command of Spanish. Are they foils to each other? How? What does mastery of Spanish mean to each of them?

2. The scenic structure of "Learn! Learn!" is rather unusual in that the first two-thirds of the story is almost completely made up of habitual or typical action, and the only dramatic scenes appear in the last third of the story. How is the last third made more meaningful by the lengthy preparation in the first two-thirds?

3. "Learn! Learn!" is about two very different men trying to live in a place far from home. What strategies do Chema and Father Tortas, respectively, use to adapt to their environment?

Gerald Haslam

Gerald Haslam (b. 1937) grew up in Bakersfield, California, the son of an Anglo father and a Mexican-American mother. His books include *Okies: Selected Stories* (1973), *Masks: A Novel* (1976), *The Wages of Sin* (1980), *Hawk Flights: Visions of the West* (1983), *Snapshots: Glimpses of the Other California* (1985), *The Man Who Cultivated Fire* (1987), and *Voices of a Place* (1987). Gerald Haslam teaches at Sonoma State University in California.

HAWK'S FLIGHT: AN AMERICAN FABLE

Awake early, he had crept sleepily up the gully to relieve himself. He was not yet old enough to stand guard, and on mornings like this he was grateful to be sleeping inside beneath warm robes. There had been no one visible when he started up the gully, so he hadn't walked as far from home as usual. Still he walked too far. Savages leapt upon him before he could shout a warning and, in the instant before he was beaten unconscious, he realized fully it was the attack they had for so long dreaded.

He vaguely perceived that morning, yet through haze he heard shouts and screams from his village, frenzied yips of savages, pops and cracks of rifles. A child flashed up the gully past him with a mounted savage behind her. In a moment there was a scream, then the horseman rode back down the gully breathing hard. Painfully turning his head, he saw where the girl lay, her crushed head in a pool of blood, her tiny features stunned and askew.

Struggling to rise, he glimpsed, before collapsing, men trying to defend their families—his own father perhaps—and he caught the hot leer of one savage's eye. He knew he was done, that everyone was done, as he slipped back into the void.

How many hours or days or weeks they dragged him, leather thong round his neck, he could not say. He had stumbled and staggered barefoot over rocky ground for endless miles. When he fell, they jerked him until he was unconscious from choking, but always stopped to revive him just in time to deny him merciful death. Yet he was dead; he had died with his family back at the village. Only his body lived.

They dragged him finally into their compound where villagers beat and spat upon him. Children threw rocks at him, shouting in their incomprehensible tongue. He did not have to know their words to understand what they said. He was taken before their chief, a small, decorated man. There was a good deal of loud talk, again incomprehensible, then he was forced into a small wooden hut.

He needed water; he needed food; he needed rest. Lying painfully on a grass-covered corner of the hut, sleep came to him finally in the heat of the day. And he lived again in his dreams: Hawk flew wind away from the savages toward the hills where his people lay rotting; his mother and father and sisters and brothers waved to him as he flew beyond them toward Sacred Spring.

Before the Spring, he knelt and asked what his people had done that their homeland should be invaded by savages. But Sacred Spring did not answer. Are we to submit? he asked, incredulous. Are we to not fight back? The Spring gurgled, then belched forth red: blood flowed from wounded Earth. But I am only one, he said, and not even a warrior. Become a warrior, ordered Sacred Spring. I have no weapons, he said. Then it came to him: he was Hawk and he had the wind.

He awoke to find a cup of water and a metal plate with a few pieces of dried meat and hard bread on it. He wanted to bolt the food, but Hawk's battered face made chewing difficult, so he broke both meat and bread into tiny pieces which he softened in his mouth, then swallowed. Just as he finished his meal, he heard voices outside the hut, and gruff laughter. There was one small, low window in the dark hovel and suddenly a stream of urine sprayed through it. The laughter grew louder, some words were shouted, then the voices grew faint. Hawk peered out the window and saw three of the savage warriors striding away, their blue uniforms dark as death over the bright earth of the compound.

It was nearly night when several blue warriors threw open the door of his hut and pulled him out. Prodded to their chief again, Hawk felt strengthened from the food and able to breathe and draw life from the air. This time there were other human beings present, though they were of a rival clan. As the pale chief spoke, one of the human beings said to Hawk: "Now listen to this. I will tell you what their chief says." The man spoke poorly, but at least he could be understood. "The white chief says you and your clan have hurt many of his warriors. He says you are dangerous vermin. He says you must be an example. He says they will pull your neck with a rope until you are dead. He says their god will protect you." The human being who was not of his clan could not resist a comment of his own: "You and yours are lice," he added.

Hawk turned to face the other human being. "At least we have not become savages," he spat, and the other human being was ashamed and angry. He knew that Hawk, a boy not yet a warrior, had bested him. He said something to a savage in the strange tongue, and the blue warrior struck Hawk hard across the face. The other human being was even more ashamed when Hawk did not flinch.

Back in the wooden hovel, the boy again curled on the grass to sleep. His face hurt badly where the savage had struck him. He could neither open nor close his mouth. His head pulsed with pain each time his heart beat. He could not sleep and was sitting up when a very pale young savage visited him, accompanied by blue warriors. The savage held two pieces of wood tied together to represent the four sacred directions. The direction stick told Hawk that the savage was a shaman. So Hawk listened respectfully to words he could not understand while the pale shaman gestured and babbled. When the savage finally quieted, Hawk mumbled no, only that. The pale savage seemed to understand, and departed. He had been a weak shaman with no real power.

Hawk found himself feeling a strange kind of pity for these hopeless creatures who possessed no magic at all, no union with Earth or Sky, only the ability to hurt and kill. He could not even hate such creatures for they were beneath hate. They were sad and dangerous like a broken rattlesnake thrashing around wildly to kill whatever neared it because it could not save itself. They had great skill at destruction, but he could sense no life force in them.

Hawk flew wind again that night, flew high to the zenith where Old Man of the Ancients resided; Old Man was growing impatient with the savages. Hawk flew to the nadir and Earth Mother wept angrily over her torn land and dead children. It was a bad dream because the savages killed everything and everyone. And, in the instant before he awoke, the shattered, bleeding face of the little girl he had seen in the gully flooded him. It was a very bad dream, for he knew he must kill a savage.

They came for him early next morning, a mass of blue-shirted savages who bound his arms with leather straps, then led him around a building into a square where it seemed all the pale villagers were gathered around a wooden platform.

As he was thrust up the steps, he saw a rope—a rope for pulling his neck—draped over a crossbeam. Hawk was placed beneath the rope and the savages' chief stood at the front of the platform and spoke loudly to his people. At the same time, the wan shaman stood directly in front of Hawk, muttering tensely and senselessly into his face, holding his sticks in one hand. Another savage knelt behind Hawk and began to bind his legs. Hawk knew it was time, and he repeated to himself a warrior's song he had been learning as part of his training:

> Let us see, is this real,
> Let us see, is this real,
> This life I am living?
> You Powers who dwell everywhere,
> Let us see, is this real,
> This life I am living?

He leaned forward and bit the shaman's pallid white nose, at the same time kicking the man who sought to bind his legs. Then Hawk darted across the platform and kicked the startled chief behind a knee and the enemy leader crumpled directly in front of him. One more kick with all his leg behind it and Hawk felt the pale chief's head crumple. He had killed the savages' leader.

From all around him, blue savages fired their weapons, yet Hawk stood straight and tall, making no attempt to flee or dodge. Bullets smashed into his body, but they were too slow, for Hawk flew wind once more, high over the frantic scene and away, over plains and deserts, over brooding hills, over bleeding Sacred Spring. And Sacred Spring called to him as he soared: "Ho Warrior!"

QUESTIONS FOR DISCUSSION AND WRITING

1. Point of view is very important in this story. At what point does the reader realize that "he" is a Native American and that the "savages" are U.S. soldiers?

2. What Native American beliefs and moral codes does Hawk draw upon? Examine especially the dream scenes in which Hawk "flies wind" and the scene in which Hawk is condemned to hang, including the exchange with the Indian translator. You might compare Hawk's beliefs with those of Niguudzagha in "The Sinh of Niguudzagha," if you have read that story.

3. In what respect is this story "an American fable"?

Joyce Carol Oates

Joyce Carol Oates (b. 1938) grew up on a farm outside Lockport, New York, went to a high school near Buffalo, and earned a bachelor's degree at Syracuse University; she has drawn upon these upstate New York settings for some of her voluminous fiction. Since 1963, when she published her first collection of stories, *By the North Gate*, Oates has published more than twenty novels, fourteen collections of short stories, a number of books of poems, and several collections of essays. Her novels include *them* (1969), *Do with Me What You Will* (1973), *Son of the Morning* (1978), *Marya: A Life* (1986), *You Must Remember This* (1987), *American Appetites* (1988), *Because It Is Bitter, and Because It Is My Heart* (1990), *I Lock My Door Upon Myself* (1990), and *Black Water* (1992). "Where Are You Going, Where Have You Been?" appeared in the short-story collection *The Wheel of Love* (1970).

WHERE ARE YOU GOING, WHERE HAVE YOU BEEN?

For Bob Dylan

Her name was Connie. She was fifteen and she had a quick, nervous giggling habit of craning her neck to glance into mirrors or checking other people's faces to make sure her own was all right. Her mother, who noticed everything and knew everything and who hadn't much reason any longer to look at her own face, always scolded Connie about it. "Stop gawking at yourself. Who are you? You think you're so pretty?" she would say. Connie would raise her eyebrows at these familiar old complaints and look right through her mother, into a shadowy vision of herself as she was right at that moment: she knew she was pretty and that was everything. Her mother had been pretty once too, if you could believe those old snapshots in the album, but now her looks were gone and that was why she was always after Connie.

"Why don't you keep your room clean like your sister? How've you got your hair fixed—what the hell stinks? Hair spray? You don't see your sister using that junk."

Her sister June was twenty-four and still lived at home. She was a secretary in the high school Connie attended, and if that wasn't bad enough—with her in the same building—she was so plain and chunky and steady that Connie had to hear her praised all the time by her mother and her mother's sisters. June did this, June did that, she saved money and helped clean the house and cooked and Connie couldn't do a thing, her mind was all filled with trashy daydreams. Their father was away at work most of the time and when he came home he wanted supper and he read the newspaper at supper and after supper he went to bed. He didn't bother talking much to them, but around his bent head Connie's mother kept picking at her until Connie wished her mother was dead and she herself was dead and it was all over. "She makes me want to throw up sometimes," she complained to her friends. She had a high, breathless, amused voice that made everything she said sound a little forced, whether it was sincere or not.

There was one good thing: June went places with girl friends of hers, girls who were just as plain and steady as she, and so when Connie wanted to do that her mother had no objections. The father of Connie's best friend drove the girls the three miles to town and left them at a shopping plaza so they could walk through the stores or go to a movie, and when he came to pick them up again at eleven he never bothered to ask what they had done.

They must have been familiar sights, walking around the shopping plaza in their shorts and ballerina slippers that always scuffed the sidewalk, with charm bracelets jingling on their thin wrists; they would lean together to whisper and laugh secretly if someone passed who amused or interested them. Connie had long dark blond hair that drew anyone's eye to it, and she wore part of it pulled up on her head and puffed out and the rest of it she let fall down her back. She wore a pull-over jersey blouse that looked one way when she was at home and another way when she was away from home. Everything about her had two sides to it, one for home and one for anywhere that was not home: her walk, which could be childlike and bobbing, or languid enough to make anyone think she was hearing music in her head; her mouth, which was pale and smirking most of the time, but bright and pink on these evenings out; her laugh, which was cynical and drawling at home—"Ha, ha, very funny,"—but high-pitched and nervous anywhere else, like the jingling of the charms on her bracelet.

Sometimes they did go shopping or to a movie, but sometimes they went across the highway, ducking fast across the busy road, to a drive-in restaurant where older kids hung out. The restaurant was shaped like a big bottle, though squatter than a real bottle, and on its cap was a revolving figure of a grinning boy holding a hamburger aloft. One night in midsummer they ran across, breathless with daring, and right away someone leaned out a car window and invited them over, but it was just a boy from high school they didn't like. It made them feel good to be able to ignore him. They went up through the maze of parked and cruising cars to the bright-lit, fly-infested restaurant, their faces pleased and expectant as if they were entering a sacred building that loomed up out of the night to give them what haven and blessing they yearned for. They sat at the counter and crossed their legs at the ankles, their thin shoulders rigid with excitement, and listened to the music that made everything so good: the music was always in the background, like music at a church service, it was something to depend upon.

A boy named Eddie came in to talk with them. He sat backwards on his stool, turning himself jerkily around in semicircles and then stopping and turning back again, and after a while he asked Connie if she would like something to eat. She said she would and so she tapped her friend's arm on her way out—her friend pulled her face up into a brave, droll look—and Connie said she would meet her at eleven, across the way. "I just hate to leave her like that," Connie said earnestly, but the boy said that she wouldn't be alone for long. So they went out to his car, and on the way Connie couldn't help but let her eyes wander over the windshields and faces all around her; her face gleaming with a joy that had nothing to do with Eddie or even this place; it might have been the music. She drew her shoulders up and sucked in her breath with the pure pleasure of being alive, and just at that moment she happened to glance at a face a few feet from hers. It was a boy with shaggy black hair, in a convertible jalopy painted gold. He stared at her and then his lips widened into a grin. Connie slit her eyes at him and turned away, but she couldn't help glancing back and there he was, still watching her. He wagged a finger and laughed and said, "Gonna get you, baby," and Connie turned away again without Eddie noticing anything.

She spent three hours with him, at the restaurant where they ate hamburgers and drank Cokes in wax cups that were always sweating, and then down an alley a mile or so away, and when he left her off at five to eleven only the movie house was still open at the plaza. Her girl friend was there, talking with a boy. When

Connie came up, the two girls smiled at each other and Connie said, "How was the movie?" and the girl said "*You* should know." They rode off with the girl's father, sleepy and pleased, and Connie couldn't help but look back at the darkened shopping plaza with its big empty parking lot and its signs that were faded and ghostly now, and over at the drive-in restaurant where cars were still circling tirelessly. She couldn't hear the music at this distance.

Next morning June asked her how the movie was and Connie said, "So-so."

She and that girl and occasionally another girl went out several times a week, and the rest of the time Connie spent around the house—it was summer vacation—getting in her mother's way and thinking, dreaming about the boys she met. But all the boys fell back and dissolved into a single face that was not even a face but an idea, a feeling, mixed up with the urgent insistent pounding of the music and the humid night air of July. Connie's mother kept dragging her back to the daylight by finding things for her to do or saying suddenly, "What's this about the Pettinger girl?"

And Connie would say nervously, "Oh, her. That dope." She always drew thick clear lines between herself and such girls, and her mother was simple and kind enough to believe it. Her mother was so simple, Connie thought, that it was maybe cruel to fool her so much. Her mother went scuffling around the house in old bedroom slippers and complained over the telephone to one sister about the other, then the other called up and the two of them complained about the third one. If June's name was mentioned her mother's tone was approving, and if Connie's name was mentioned it was disapproving. This did not really mean she disliked Connie, and actually Connie thought that her mother preferred her to June just because she was prettier, but the two of them kept up a pretense of exasperation, a sense that they were tugging and struggling over something of little value to either of them. Sometimes, over coffee, they were almost friends, but something would come up—some vexation that was like a fly buzzing suddenly around their heads—and their faces were hard with contempt.

One Sunday Connie got up at eleven—none of them bothered with church—and washed her hair so that it could dry all day long in the sun. Her parents and sister were going to a barbecue at an aunt's house and Connie said no, she wasn't interested, rolling her eyes to let her mother know just what she thought of it. "Stay home alone then," her mother said sharply. Connie sat out back in a lawn chair and watched them drive away, her father quiet and bald, hunched around so that he could back the car out, her mother with a look that was still angry and not at all softened through the windshield, and in the back seat poor old June, all dressed up as if she didn't know what a barbecue was, with all the running yelling kids and the flies. Connie sat with her eyes closed in the sun, dreaming and dazed with the warmth about her as if this were a kind of love, the caresses of love, and her mind slipped over onto thoughts of the boy she had been with the night before and how nice he had been, how sweet it always was, not the way someone like June would suppose but sweet, gentle, the way it was in movies and promised in songs; and when she opened her eyes she hardly knew where she was, the back yard ran off into weeds and a fence-like line of trees and behind it the sky was perfectly blue and still. The asbestos "ranch house" that was now three years old startled her—it looked small. She shook her head as if to get awake.

It was too hot. She went inside the house and turned on the radio to drown out the quiet. She sat on the edge of her bed, barefoot, and listened for an hour and a half to a program called XYZ Sunday Jamboree, record after record of hard, fast, shrieking songs she sang along with, interspersed by exclamations from "Bobby

King": "An' look here, you girls at Napoleon's—Son and Charley want you to pay real close attention to this song coming up!"

And Connie paid close attention herself, bathed in a glow of slow-pulsed joy that seemed to rise mysteriously out of the music itself and lay languidly about the airless little room, breathed in and breathed out with each gentle rise and fall of her chest.

After a while she heard a car coming up the drive. She sat up once, startled, because it couldn't be her father so soon. The gravel kept crunching all the way in from the road—the driveway was long—and Connie ran to the window. It was a car she didn't know. It was an open jalopy, painted a bright gold that caught the sunlight opaquely. Her heart began to pound and her fingers snatched at her hair, checking it, and she whispered, "Christ. Christ," wondering how bad she looked. The car came to a stop at the side door and the horn sounded four short taps, as if this were a signal Connie knew.

She went into the kitchen and approached the door slowly, then hung out the screen door, her bare toes curling down off the step. There were two boys in the car and now she recognized the driver: he had shaggy, shabby black hair that looked crazy as a wig and he was grinning at her.

"I ain't late, am I?" he said.

"Who the hell do you think you are?" Connie said.

"Toldja I'd be out, didn't I?"

"I don't even know who you are."

She spoke sullenly, careful to show no interest or pleasure, and he spoke in a fast, bright monotone. Connie looked past him to the other boy, taking her time. He had fair brown hair, with a lock that fell onto his forehead. His sideburns gave him a fierce, embarrassed look, but so far he hadn't even bothered to glance at her. Both boys wore sunglasses. The driver's sunglasses were metallic and mirrored everything in miniature.

"You wanta come for a ride?" he said.

Connie smirked and let her hair fall loose over one shoulder.

"Don'tcha like my car? New paint job," he said. "Hey."

"What?"

"You're cute."

She pretended to fidget, chasing flies away from the door.

"Don'tcha believe me, or what?" he said.

"Look, I don't even know who you are," Connie said in disgust.

"Hey, Ellie's got a radio, see. Mine broke down." He lifted his friend's arm and showed her the little transistor radio the boy was holding, and now Connie began to hear the music. It was the same program that was playing inside the house.

"Bobby King?" she said.

"I listen to him all the time. I think he's great."

"He's kind of great," Connie said reluctantly.

"Listen, the guy's *great*. He knows where the action is."

Connie blushed a little, because the glasses made it impossible for her to see just what this boy was looking at. She couldn't decide if she liked him or if he was just a jerk, and so she dawdled in the doorway and wouldn't come down or go back inside. She said, "What's all that stuff painted on your car?"

"Can'tcha read it?" He opened the door very carefully, as if he were afraid it might fall off. He slid out just as carefully, planting his feet firmly on the ground, the tiny metallic world in his glasses slowing down like gelatine hardening, and in the midst of it Connie's bright green blouse. "This here is my name, to begin with," he said. ARNOLD FRIEND was written in tarlike black letters on the side, with a drawing of a round, grinning face that reminded Connie of a pumpkin, except it wore sunglasses. "I wanta introduce myself, I'm Arnold Friend and that's my real name and I'm gonna be your friend, honey, and inside the car's Ellie Oscar, he's kinda shy." Ellie brought his transistor radio up to his shoulder and balanced it there. "Now, these numbers are a secret code, honey," Arnold Friend explained. He read off the numbers 33, 19, 17 and raised his eyebrows at her to see what she thought of that, but she didn't think much of it. The left rear fender had been smashed and around it was written, on the gleaming gold background: DONE BY CRAZY WOMAN DRIVER. Connie had to laugh at that. Arnold Friend was pleased at her laughter and looked up at her. "Around the other side's a lot more—you wanta come and see them?"

"No."

"Why not?"

"Why should I?"

"Don'tcha wanta see what's on the car? Don'tcha wanta go for a ride?"

"I don't know."

"Why not?"

"I got things to do."

"Like what?"

"Things."

He laughed as if she had said something funny. He slapped his thighs. He was standing in a strange way, leaning back against the car as if he were balancing himself. He wasn't tall, only an inch or so taller than she would be if she came down to him. Connie liked the way he was dressed, which was the way all of them dressed: tight faded jeans stuffed into black, scuffed boots, a belt that pulled his waist in and showed how lean he was, and a white pull-over shirt that was a little soiled and showed the hard small muscles of his arms and shoulders. He looked as if he probably did hard work, lifting and carrying things. Even his neck looked muscular. And his face was a familiar face, somehow: the jaw and chin and cheeks slightly darkened because he hadn't shaved for a day or two, and the nose long and hawklike, sniffing as if she were a treat he was going to gobble up and it was all a joke.

"Connie, you ain't telling the truth. This is your day set aside for a ride with me and you know it," he said, still laughing. The way he straightened and recovered from his fit of laughing showed that it had been all fake.

"How do you know what my name is?" she said suspiciously.

"It's Connie."

"Maybe and maybe not."

"I know my Connie," he said, wagging his finger. Now she remembered him even better, back at the restaurant, and her cheeks warmed at the thought of how she had sucked in her breath just at the moment she passed him—how she must have looked to him. And he had remembered her. "Ellie and I come out here especially for you," he said. "Ellie can sit in the back. How about it?"

"Where?"

"Where what?"

"Where're we going?"

He looked at her. He took off the sunglasses and she saw how pale the skin around his eyes was, like holes that were not in shadow but instead in light. His eyes were like chips of broken glass that catch the light in an amiable way. He smiled. It was as if the idea of going for a ride somewhere, to someplace, was a new idea to him.

"Just for a ride, Connie sweetheart."

"I never said my name was Connie," she said.

"But I know what it is. I know your name and all about you, lots of things," Arnold Friend said. He had not moved yet but stood still leaning back against the side of his jalopy. "I took a special interest in you, such a pretty girl, and found out all about you—like I know your parents and sister are gone somewheres and I know where and how long they're going to be gone, and I know who you were with last night, and your best girl friend's name is Betty. Right?"

He spoke in a simple lilting voice, exactly as if he were reciting the words to a song. His smile assured her that everything was fine. In the car Ellie turned up the volume on his radio and did not bother to look around at them.

"Ellie can sit in the back seat," Arnold Friend said. He indicated his friend with a casual jerk of his chin, as if Ellie did not count and she should not bother with him.

"How'd you find out all that stuff?" Connie said.

"Listen: Betty Schultz and Tony Fitch and Jimmy Pettinger and Nancy Pettinger," he said in a chant. "Raymond Stanley and Bob Hutter—"

"Do you know all those kids?"

"I know everybody."

"Look, you're kidding. You're not from around here."

"Sure."

"But—how come we never saw you before?"

"Sure you saw me before," he said. He looked down at his boots, as if he were a little offended. "You just don't remember."

"I guess I'd remember you," Connie said.

"Yeah?" He looked up at this, beaming. He was pleased. He began to mark time with the music from Ellie's radio, tapping his fists lightly together. Connie looked away from his smile to the car, which was painted so bright it almost hurt her eyes to look at it. She looked at that name, ARNOLD FRIEND. And up at the front fender was an expression that was familiar—MAN THE FLYING SAUCERS. It was an expression kids had used the year before but didn't use this year. She looked at it for a while as if the words meant something to her that she did not yet know.

"What're you thinking about? Huh?" Arnold Friend demanded. "Not worried about your hair blowing around in the car, are you?"

"No."

"Think I maybe can't drive good?"

"How do I know?"

"You're a hard girl to handle. How come?" he said. "Don't you know I'm your friend? Didn't you see me put my sign in the air when you walked by?"

"What sign?"

"My sign." And he drew an X in the air, leaning out toward her. They were maybe ten feet apart. After his hand fell back to his side the X was still in the air, almost visible. Connie let the screen door close and stood perfectly still inside it, listening to the music from her radio and the boy's blend together. She stared at Arnold Friend. He stood there so stiffly relaxed, pretending to be relaxed, with one hand idly on the door handle as if he was keeping himself up that way and had no intention of ever moving again. She recognized most things about him, the tight jeans that showed his thighs and buttocks and the greasy leather boots and the tight shirt, and even that slippery friendly smile of his, that sleepy dreamy smile that all the boys used to get across ideas they didn't want to put into words. She recognized all this and also the singsong way he talked, slightly mocking, kidding, but serious and a little melancholy, and she recognized the way he tapped one fist against the other in homage to the perpetual music behind him. But all these things did not come together.

She said suddenly, "Hey, how old are you?"

His smile faded. She could see then that he wasn't a kid, he was much older—thirty, maybe more. At this knowledge her heart began to pound faster.

"That's a crazy thing to ask. Can'tcha see I'm your own age?"

"Like hell you are."

"Or maybe a couple of years older. I'm eighteen."

"Eighteen?" she said doubtfully.

He grinned to reassure her and lines appeared at the corners of his mouth. His teeth were big and white. He grinned so broadly his eyes became slits and she saw how thick the lashes were, thick and black as if painted with a black tarlike material. Then, abruptly, he seemed to become embarrassed and looked over his shoulder at Ellie. "*Him*, he's crazy," he said. "Ain't he a riot? He's a nut, a real character." Ellie was still listening to the music. His sunglasses told nothing about what he was thinking. He wore a bright orange shirt unbuttoned halfway to show his chest, which was a pale, bluish chest and not muscular like Arnold Friend's. His shirt collar was turned up all around and the very tips of the collar pointed out past his chin as if they were protecting him. He was pressing the transistor radio up against his ear and sat there in a kind of a daze, right in the sun.

"He's kinda strange," Connie said.

"Hey, she says you're kinda strange! Kinda strange!" Arnold Friend cried. He pounded on the car to get Ellie's attention. Ellie turned for the first time and Connie saw with shock that he wasn't a kid either—he had a fair, hairless face, cheeks reddened slightly as if the veins grew too close to the surface of his skin, the face of a forty-year-old baby. Connie felt a wave of dizziness rise in her at this sight and she stared at him as if waiting for something to change the shock of the moment, make it all right again. Ellie's lips kept shaping words, mumbling along with the words blasting in his ear.

"Maybe you two better go away," Connie said faintly.

"What? How come?" Arnold Friend cried. "We come out here to take you for a ride. It's Sunday." He had the voice of the man on the radio now. It was the same voice, Connie thought. "Don'tcha know it's Sunday all day? And honey, no matter who you were with last night, today you're with Arnold Friend and don't forget it! Maybe you better step out here," he said, and this last was in a different voice. It was a little flatter, as if the heat was finally getting to him.

"Hey."

"You two better leave."

"We ain't leaving until you come with us."

"Like hell I am—"

"Connie, don't fool around with me. I mean—I mean, don't fool *around*," he said shaking his head. He laughed incredulously. He placed his sunglasses on top of his head, carefully, as if he were indeed wearing a wig, and brought the stems down behind his ears. Connie stared at him, another wave of dizziness and fear rising in her so that for a moment he wasn't even in focus but was just a blur standing there against his gold car, and she had the idea that he had driven up the driveway all right but had come from nowhere before that and belonged nowhere and that everything about him and even about the music that was so familiar to her was only half real.

"If my father comes and sees you—"

"He ain't coming. He's at a barbecue."

"How do you know that?"

"Aunt Tillie's. Right now they're—uh—they're drinking. Sitting around," he said vaguely, squinting as if he were staring all the way to town and over to Aunt Tillie's back yard. Then the vision seemed to get clear and he nodded energetically. "Yeah. Sitting around. There's your sister in her blue dress, huh? And high heels, the poor sad bitch—nothing like you, sweetheart! And your mother's helping some fat woman with the corn, they're cleaning the corn—husking the corn—"

"What fat woman?" Connie cried.

"How do I know what fat woman, I don't know every goddamn fat woman in the world!" Arnold Friend laughed.

"Oh, that's Mrs. Hornsby. . . . Who invited her?" Connie said. She felt a little lightheaded. Her breath was coming quickly.

"She's too fat. I don't like them fat. I like them the way you are, honey," he said, smiling sleepily at her. They stared at each other for a while through the screen door. He said softly, "Now, what you're going to do is this: you're going to come out that door. You're going to sit up front with me and Ellie's going to sit in the back, the hell with Ellie, right? This isn't Ellie's date. You're my date. I'm your lover, honey."

"What? You're crazy—"

"Yes, I'm your lover. You don't know what that is but you will," he said. "I know that too. I know all about you. But look: it's real nice and you couldn't ask for nobody better than me, or more polite. I always keep my word. I'll tell you how it is, I'm always nice at first, the first time. I'll hold you so tight you won't think you have to try to get away or pretend anything because you'll know you can't. And I'll come inside you where it's all secret and you'll give in to me and you'll love me—"

"Shut up! You're crazy!" Connie said. She backed away from the door. She put her hands up against her ears as if she'd heard something terrible, something not meant for her. "People don't talk like that, you're crazy," she muttered. Her heart was almost too big now for her chest and its pumping made sweat break out all over her. She looked out to see Arnold Friend pause and then take a step toward the porch, lurching. He almost fell. But, like a clever drunken man, he managed to catch his balance. He wobbled in his high boots and grabbed hold of one of the porch posts.

"Honey?" he said. "You still listening?"

"Get the hell out of here!"

"Be nice, honey. Listen."

"I'm going to call the police—"

He wobbled again and out of the side of his mouth came a fast spat curse, an aside not meant for her to hear. But even this "Christ!" sounded forced. Then he began to smile again. She watched this smile come, awkward as if he were smiling from inside a mask. His whole face was a mask, she thought wildly, tanned down to his throat but then running out as if he had plastered make-up on his face but had forgotten about his throat.

"Honey—? Listen, here's how it is. I always tell the truth and I promise you this: I ain't coming in that house after you."

"You better not! I'm going to call the police if you—if you don't—"

"Honey," he said, talking right through her voice, "honey, I'm not coming in there but you are coming out here. You know why?"

She was panting. The kitchen looked like a place she had never seen before, some room she had run inside but that wasn't good enough, wasn't going to help her. The kitchen window had never had a curtain, after three years, and there were dishes in the sink for her to do—probably—and if you ran your hand across the table you'd feel something sticky there.

"You listening, honey?"

"—going to call the police—"

"Soon as you touch the phone I don't need to keep my promise and can come inside. You won't want that."

She rushed forward and tried to lock the door. Her fingers were shaking. "But why lock it," Arnold Friend said gently, talking right into her face. "It's just a screen door. It's just nothing." One of his boots was at a strange angle, as if his foot wasn't in it. It pointed out to the left, bent at the ankle. "I mean, anybody can break through a screen door and glass and wood and iron or anything else if he needs to, anybody at all, and specially Arnold Friend. If the place got lit up with a fire, honey, you'd come runnin' out into my arms, right into my arms an' safe at home—like you knew I was your lover and'd stopped fooling around. I don't mind a nice shy girl but I don't like no fooling around." Part of those words were spoken with a slight rhythmic lilt, and Connie somehow recognized them—the echo of a song from last year, about a girl rushing into her boy friend's arms and coming home again—

Connie stood barefoot on the linoleum floor, staring at him. "What do you want?" she whispered.

"I want you," he said.

"What?"

"Seen you that night and thought, that's the one, yes sir. I never needed to look anymore."

"But my father's coming back. He's coming to get me. I had to wash my hair first—" She spoke in a dry, rapid voice, hardly raising it for him to hear.

"No, your daddy is not coming and yes, you had to wash your hair and you washed it for me. It's nice and shining and all for me. I thank you, sweetheart," he said with a mock bow, but again he almost lost his balance. He had to bend and adjust his boots. Evidently his feet did not go all the way down; the boots must have been stuffed with something so that he would seem taller. Connie stared out at him and behind him at Ellie in the car, who seemed to be looking off toward Connie's right, into nothing. This Ellie said, pulling the words out of the air one after another as if he were just discovering them, "You want me to pull out the phone?"

"Shut your mouth and keep it shut," Arnold Friend said, his face red from bending over or maybe from embarrassment because Connie had seen his boots. "This ain't none of your business."

"What—what are you doing? What do you want?" Connie said. "If I call the police they'll get you, they'll arrest you—"

"Promise was not to come in unless you touch that phone, and I'll keep that promise," he said. He resumed his erect position and tried to force his shoulders back. He sounded like a hero in a movie, declaring something important. But he spoke too loudly and it was as if he were speaking to someone behind Connie. "I ain't made plans for coming in that house where I don't belong but just for you to come out to me, the way you should. Don't you know who I am?"

"You're crazy," she whispered. She backed away from the door but did not want to go into another part of the house, as if this would give him permission to come through the door. "What do you . . . you're crazy, you. . . ."

"Huh? What're you saying, honey?"

Her eyes darted everywhere in the kitchen. She could not remember what it was, this room.

"This is how it is, honey: you come out and we'll drive away, have a nice ride. But if you don't come out we're gonna wait till your people come home and then they're all going to get it."

"You want that telephone pulled out?" Ellie said. He held the radio away from his ear and grimaced, as if without the radio the air was too much for him.

"I toldja shut up, Ellie," Arnold Friend said, "you're deaf, get a hearing aid, right? Fix yourself up. This little girl's no trouble and's gonna be nice to me, so Ellie keep to yourself, this ain't your date—right? Don't hem in on me, don't hog, don't crush, don't bird dog, don't trail me," he said in a rapid, meaningless voice, as if he were running through all the expressions he'd learned but was no longer sure which of them was in style, then rushing on to new ones, making them up with his eyes closed. "Don't crawl under my fence, don't squeeze in my chipmunk hole, don't sniff my glue, suck my popsicle, keep your own greasy fingers on yourself!" He shaded his eyes and peered in at Connie, who was backed against the kitchen table. "Don't mind him, honey, he's just a creep. He's a dope. Right? I'm the boy for you and like I said, you come out here nice like a lady and give me your hand, and nobody else gets hurt, I mean, your nice old bald-headed daddy and your mummy and your sister in her high heels. Because listen: why bring them in this?"

"Leave me alone," Connie whispered.

"Hey, you know that old woman down the road, the one with the chickens and stuff—you know her?"

"She's dead!"

"Dead? What? You know her?" Arnold Friend said.

"She's dead—"

"Don't you like her?"

"She's dead—she's—she isn't here any more—"

"But don't you like her, I mean, you got something against her? Some grudge or something?" Then his voice dipped as if he were conscious of a rudeness. He touched the sunglasses perched up on top of his head as if to make sure they were still there. "Now, you be a good girl."

"What are you going to do?"

"Just two things, or maybe three," Arnold Friend said. "But I promise it won't last long and you'll like me the way you get to like people you're close to. You will. It's all over for you here, so come on out. You don't want your people in any trouble, do you?"

She turned and bumped against a chair or something, hurting her leg, but she ran into the back room and picked up the telephone. Something roared in her ear, a tiny roaring, and she was so sick with fear that she could do nothing but listen to it—the telephone was clammy and very heavy and her fingers groped down to the dial but were too weak to touch it. She began to scream into the phone, into the roaring. She cried out, she cried for her mother, she felt her breath start jerking back and forth in her lungs as if it were something Arnold Friend was stabbing her with again and again with no tenderness. A noisy sorrowful wailing rose all about her and she was locked inside it the way she was locked inside this house.

After a while she could hear again. She was sitting on the floor with her wet back against the wall.

Arnold Friend was saying from the door, "That's a good girl. Put the phone back."

She kicked the phone away from her.

"No, honey. Pick it up. Put it back right."

She picked it up and put it back. The dial tone stopped.

"That's a good girl. Now, you come outside."

She was hollow with what had been fear but what was now just an emptiness. All that screaming had blasted it out of her. She sat, one leg cramped under her, and deep inside her brain was something like a pinpoint of light that kept going and would not let her relax. She thought, I'm not going to see my mother again. She thought, I'm not going to sleep in my bed again. Her bright green blouse was all wet.

Arnold Friend said, in a gentle-loud voice that was like a stage voice, "The place where you came from ain't there any more, and where you had in mind to go is cancelled out. This place you are now—inside your daddy's house—is nothing but a cardboard box I can knock down any time. You know that and always did know it. You hear me?"

She thought, I have got to think. I have got to know what to do.

"We'll go out to a nice field, out in the country here where it smells so nice and it's sunny," Arnold Friend said. "I'll have my arms tight around you so you won't need to try to get away and I'll show you what love is like, what it does. The hell with this house! It looks solid all right," he said. He ran a fingernail down the screen and the noise did not make Connie shiver, as it would have the day before. "Now, put your hand on your heart, honey. Feel that? That feels solid too but we know better. Be nice to me, be sweet like you can because what else is there for a girl like you but to be sweet and pretty and give in?—and get away before her people come back?"

She felt her pounding heart. Her hand seemed to enclose it. She thought for the first time in her life that it was nothing that was hers, that belonged to her, but just a pounding, living thing inside this body that wasn't really hers either.

"You don't want them to get hurt," Arnold Friend went on. "Now, get up, honey. Get up all by yourself."

She stood.

"Now, turn this way. That's right. Come over here to me.—Ellie, put that away, didn't I tell you? You dope. You miserable creepy dope," Arnold Friend said. His words were not angry but only part of an incantation. The incantation was kindly. "Now, come out through the kitchen to me, honey, and let's see a smile, try it, you're a brave, sweet little girl and now they're eating corn and hot dogs cooked to bursting over an outdoor fire, and they don't know one thing about you and never did and honey, you're better than them because not a one of them would have done this for you."

Connie felt the linoleum under her feet; it was cool. She brushed her hair back out of her eyes. Arnold Friend let go of the post tentatively and opened his arms for her, his elbows pointing in toward each other and his wrists limp, to show that this was an embarrassed embrace and a little mocking, he didn't want to make her self-conscious.

She put out her hand against the screen. She watched herself push the door slowly open as if she were back safe somewhere in the other doorway, watching this body and this head of long hair moving out into the sunlight where Arnold Friend waited.

"My sweet little blue-eyed girl," he said in a half-sung sigh that had nothing to do with her brown eyes but was taken up just the same by the vast sunlit reaches of the land behind him and on all sides of him—so much land that Connie had never seen before and did not recognize except to know that she was going to it.

QUESTIONS FOR DISCUSSION AND WRITING

1. Analyze the narrative voice in this story. It follows Connie very closely. Is the point of view hers, or is there an ironic distance between the narrator and Connie?

2. Why does Connie go with Arnold Friend at the end, in spite of her fear of him?

3. The story is full of indirect references to fairy tales. Identify allusions to Sleeping Beauty, Cinderella, and The Three Little Pigs. Do any others occur to you?

4. Why do you think the story is dedicated to Bob Dylan?

Raymond Carver

Raymond Carver (1938–88) grew up in Clatskanie, a logging town in Oregon. He married at nineteen, just out of high school, and had two children. He attended Humboldt State College in California and did graduate work at the University of Iowa, all the while holding odd jobs to support his family. He taught writing for several years at Syracuse University. His first collection of stories, *Will You Please Be Quiet, Please,* was published in 1976 and was nominated for a National Book Award. Subsequent collections included *What We Talk About When We Talk About Love* (1981), *Cathedral* (1983), and *Where I'm Calling From* (1988). He died of lung cancer at the age of fifty.

WHAT WE TALK ABOUT WHEN WE TALK ABOUT LOVE

My friend Mel McGinnis was talking. Mel McGinnis is a cardiologist, and sometimes that gives him the right.

The four of us were sitting around his kitchen table drinking gin. Sunlight filled the kitchen from the big window behind the sink. There were Mel and me and his second wife, Teresa—Terri, we called her—and my wife, Laura. We lived in Albuquerque then. But we were all from somewhere else.

There was an ice bucket on the table. The gin and the tonic water kept going around, and we somehow got on the subject of love. Mel thought real love was nothing less than spiritual love. He said he'd spent five years in a seminary before quitting to go to medical school. He'd said he still looked back on those years in the seminary as the most important years in his life.

Terri said the man she lived with before she lived with Mel loved her so much he tried to kill her. Then Terri said, "He beat me up one night. He dragged me around the living room by my ankles. He kept saying, 'I love you, I love you, you bitch.' He went on dragging me around the living room. My head kept knocking on things." Terri looked around the table. "What do you do with love like that?"

She was a bone-thin woman with a pretty face, dark eyes, and brown hair that hung down her back. She liked necklaces made of turquoise, and long pendant earrings.

"My God, don't be silly. That's not love, and you know it," Mel said. "I don't know what you'd call it, but I sure know you wouldn't call it love."

"Say what you want to, but I know it was," Terri said. "It may sound crazy to you, but it's true just the same. People are different, Mel. Sure, sometimes he may have acted crazy. Okay. But he loved me. In his own way maybe, but he loved me. There was love there, Mel. Don't say there wasn't."

Mel let out his breath. He held his glass and turned to Laura and me. "The man threatened to kill me," Mel said. He finished his drink and reached for the gin bottle. "Terri's a romantic. Terri's of the kick-me-so-I'll-know-you-love-me school. Terri, hon, don't look that way." Mel reached across the table and touched Terri's cheek with his fingers. He grinned at her.

"Now he wants to make up," Terri said.

"Make up what?" Mel said. "What is there to make up? I know what I know. That's all."

"How'd we get started on this subject, anyway?" Terri said. She raised her glass and drank from it. "Mel always has love on his mind," she said. "Don't you, honey?" She smiled, and I thought that was the last of it.

337

"I just wouldn't call Ed's behavior love. That's all I'm saying, honey," Mel said. "What about you guys?" Mel said to Laura and me. "Does that sound like love to you?"

"I'm the wrong person to ask," I said. "I didn't even know the man. I've only heard his name mentioned in passing. I wouldn't know. You'd have to know the particulars. But I think what you're saying is that love is an absolute."

Mel said, "The kind of love I'm talking about is. The kind of love I'm talking about, you don't try to kill people."

Laura said, "I don't know anything about Ed, or anything about the situation. But who can judge anyone else's situation?"

I touched the back of Laura's hand. She gave me a quick smile. I picked up Laura's hand. It was warm, the nails polished, perfectly manicured. I encircled the broad wrist with my fingers, and I held her.

"When I left, he drank rat poison," Terri said. She clasped her arms with her hands. "They took him to the hospital in Santa Fe. That's where we lived then, about ten miles out. They saved his life. But his gums went crazy from it. I mean they pulled away from his teeth. After that, his teeth stood out like fangs. My God," Terri said. She waited a minute, then let go of her arms and picked up her glass.

"What people won't do!" Laura said.

"He's out of the action now," Mel said. "He's dead."

Mel handed me the saucer of limes. I took a section, squeezed it over my drink, and stirred the ice cubes with my finger.

"It gets worse," Terri said. "He shot himself in the mouth. But he bungled that too. Poor Ed," she said. Terri shook her head.

"Poor Ed nothing," Mel said. "He was dangerous."

Mel was forty-five years old. He was tall and rangy with curly soft hair. His face and arms were brown from the tennis he played. When he was sober, his gestures, all his movements, were precise, very careful.

"He did love me though, Mel. Grant me that," Terri said. "That's all I'm asking. He didn't love me the way you love me. I'm not saying that. But he loved me. You can grant me that, can't you?"

"What do you mean, he bungled it?" I said.

Laura leaned forward with her glass. She put her elbows on the table and held her glass in both hands. She glanced from Mel to Terri and waited with a look of bewilderment on her open face, as if amazed that such things happened to people you were friendly with.

"How'd he bungle it when he killed himself?" I said.

"I'll tell you what happened," Mel said. "He took this twenty-two pistol he'd bought to threaten Terri and me with. Oh, I'm serious, the man was always threatening. You should have seen the way we lived in those days. Like fugitives. I even bought a gun myself. Can you believe it? A guy like me? But I did. I bought one for self-defense and carried it in the glove compartment. Sometimes I'd have to leave the apartment in the middle of the night. To go to the hospital, you know? Terri and I weren't married then, and my first wife had the house and kids, the dog, everything, and Terri and I were living in this apartment here. Sometimes, as I say, I'd get a call in the middle of the night and have to go in to the hospital at two or three in the morning. It'd be dark out there in the parking lot, and I'd break into a sweat before I could even get to my car. I never knew if he was going to come up out of the shrubbery or from behind a car and start shooting. I mean, the man was crazy. He was capable of wiring a bomb, anything. He used to call my service at all hours and say he needed to talk to the doctor, and when I'd return the call, he'd say, 'Son of a bitch, your days are numbered.' Little things like that. It was scary, I'm telling you."

"I still feel sorry for him," Terri said.

"It sounds like a nightmare," Laura said. "But what exactly happened after he shot himself?"

Laura is a legal secretary. We'd met in a professional capacity. Before we knew it, it was a courtship. She's thirty-five, three years younger than I am. In addition to being in love, we like each other and enjoy one another's company. She's easy to be with.

"What happened?" Laura said.

Mel said, "He shot himself in the mouth in his room. Someone heard the shot and told the manager. They came in with a passkey, saw what had happened, and called an ambulance. I happened to be there when they brought him in, alive but past recall. The man lived for three days. His head swelled up to twice the size of a normal head. I'd never seen anything like it, and I hope I never do again. Terri wanted to go in and sit with him when she found out about it. We had a fight over it. I didn't think she should see him like that. I didn't think she should see him, and I still don't."

"Who won the fight?" Laura said.

"I was in the room with him when he died," Terri said. "He never came up out of it. But I sat with him. He didn't have anyone else."

"He was dangerous," Mel said. "If you call that love, you can have it."

"It was love," Terri said. "Sure, it's abnormal in most people's eyes. But he was willing to die for it. He did die for it."

"I sure as hell wouldn't call it love," Mel said. "I mean, no one knows what he did it for. I've seen a lot of suicides, and I couldn't say anyone ever knew what they did it for."

Mel put his hands behind his neck and tilted his chair back. "I'm not interested in that kind of love," he said. "If that's love, you can have it."

Terri said, "We were afraid. Mel even made a will out and wrote to his brother in California who used to be a Green Beret. Mel told him who to look for if something happened to him."

Terri drank from her glass. She said, "But Mel's right—we lived like fugitives. We were afraid. Mel was, weren't you, honey? I even called the police at one point, but they were no help. They said they couldn't do anything until Ed actually did something. Isn't that a laugh?" Terri said.

She poured the last of the gin into her glass and waggled the bottle. Mel got up from the table and went to the cupboard. He took down another bottle.

"Well, Nick and I know what love is," Laura said. "For us, I mean," Laura said. She bumped my knee with her knee. "You're supposed to say something now," Laura said, and turned her smile on me.

For an answer, I took Laura's hand and raised it to my lips. I made a big production out of kissing her hand. Everyone was amused.

"We're lucky," I said.

"You guys," Terri said. "Stop that now. You're making me sick. You're still on the honeymoon, for God's sake. You're still gaga, for crying out loud. Just wait. How long have you been together now? How long has it been? A year? Longer than a year?"

"Going on a year and a half," Laura said, flushed and smiling.

"Oh, now," Terri said. "Wait awhile."

She held her drink and gazed at Laura.

"I'm only kidding," Terri said.

Mel opened the gin and went around the table with the bottle.

"Here, you guys," he said. "Let's have a toast. I want to propose a toast. A toast to love. To true love," Mel said.

We touched glasses.

"To love," we said.

Outside in the backyard, one of the dogs began to bark. The leaves of the aspen that leaned past the window ticked against the glass. The afternoon sun was like a presence in this room, the spacious light of ease and generosity. We could have been anywhere, somewhere enchanted. We raised our glasses again and grinned at each other like children who had agreed on something forbidden.

"I'll tell you what real love is," Mel said. "I mean, I'll give you a good example. And then you can draw your own conclusions." He poured more gin into his glass. He added an ice cube and a sliver of lime. We waited and sipped our drinks. Laura and I touched knees again. I put a hand on her warm thigh and left it there.

"What do any of us really know about love?" Mel said. "It seems to me we're just beginners at love. We say we love each other and we do, I don't doubt it. I love Terri and Terri loves me, and you guys love each other too. You know the kind of love I'm talking about now. Physical love, that impulse that drives you to someone special, as well as love of the other person's being, his or her essence, as it were. Carnal love and, well, call it sentimental love, the day-to-day caring about the other person. But sometimes I have a hard time accounting for the fact that I must have loved my first wife too. But I did, I know I did. So I suppose I am like Terri in that regard. Terri and Ed." He thought about it and then he went on. "There was a time when I thought I loved my first wife more than life itself. But now I hate her guts. I do. How do you explain that? What happened to that love? What happened to it, is what I'd like to know. I wish someone could tell me. Then there's Ed. Okay, we're back to Ed. He loves Terri so much he tries to kill her and he winds up killing himself." Mel stopped talking and swallowed from his glass. "You guys have been together for eighteen months and you love each other. It shows all over you. You glow with it. But you both loved other people before you met each other. You've both been married before, just like us. And you probably loved other people before that too, even. Terri and I have been together five years, been married for four. And the terrible thing, the terrible thing is, but the good thing too, the saving grace, you might say, is that if something happened to one of us—excuse me for saying this—but if something happened to one of us tomorrow, I think the other one, the other person, would grieve for a while, you know, but then the surviving party would go out and love again, have someone else soon enough. All this, all of this love we're talking about, it would just be a memory. Maybe not even a memory. Am I wrong? Am I way off base? Because I want you to set me straight if you think I'm wrong. I want to know. I mean, I don't know anything, and I'm the first one to admit it."

"Mel, for God's sake," Terri said. She reached out and took hold of his wrist. "Are you getting drunk? Honey? Are you drunk?"

"Honey, I'm just talking," Mel said. "All right? I don't have to be drunk to say what I think. I mean, we're all just talking, right?" Mel said. He fixed his eyes on her.

"Sweetie, I'm not criticizing," Terri said.

She picked up her glass.

"I'm not on call today," Mel said. "Let me remind you of that. I am not on call," he said.

"Mel, we love you," Laura said.

Mel looked at Laura. He looked at her as if he could not place her, as if she was not the woman she was.

"Love you too, Laura," Mel said. "And you, Nick, love you too. You know something?" Mel said. "You guys are our pals," Mel said.

He picked up his glass.

Mel said, "I was going to tell you about something. I mean, I was going to prove a point. You see, this happened a few months ago, but it's still going on right now, and it ought to make us feel ashamed when we talk like we know what we're talking about when we talk about love."

"Come on now," Terri said. "Don't talk like you're drunk if you're not drunk."

"Just shut up for once in your life," Mel said very quietly. "Will you do me a favor and do that for a minute? So as I was saying, there's this old couple who had this car wreck out on the interstate. A kid hit them and they were all torn to shit and nobody was giving them much chance to pull through."

Terri looked at us and then back at Mel. She seemed anxious, or maybe that's too strong a word.

Mel was handing the bottle around the table.

"I was on call that night," Mel said. "It was May or maybe it was June. Terri and I had just sat down to dinner when the hospital called. There'd been this thing out on the interstate. Drunk kid, teenager, plowed his dad's pickup into this camper with this old couple in it. They were up in their mid-seventies, that couple. The kid—eighteen, nineteen, something—he was DOA. Taken the steering wheel through his sternum. The old couple, they were alive, you understand. I mean, just barely. But they had everything. Multiple fractures, internal injuries, hemorrhaging, contusions, lacerations, the works, and they each of them had themselves concussions. They were in a bad way, believe me. And, of course, their age was two strikes against them. I'd say she was worse off than he was. Ruptured spleen along with everything else. Both kneecaps broken. But they'd been wearing their seatbelts and, God knows, that's what saved them for the time being."

"Folks, this is an advertisement for the National Safety Council," Terri said. "This is your spokesman, Dr. Melvin R. McGinnis, talking." Terri laughed. "Mel," she said, "sometimes you're just too much. But I love you, hon," she said.

"Honey, I love you," Mel said.

He leaned across the table. Terri met him halfway. They kissed.

"Terri's right," Mel said as he settled himself again. "Get those seatbelts on. But seriously, they were in some shape, those oldsters. By the time I got down there, the kid was dead, as I said. He was off in a corner, laid out on a gurney. I took one look at the old couple and told the ER nurse to get me a neurologist and an orthopedic man and a couple of surgeons down there right away."

He drank from his glass. "I'll try to keep this short," he said. "So we took the two of them up to the OR and worked like fuck on them most of the night. They had these incredible reserves, those two. You see that once in a while. So we did everything that could be done, and toward morning we're giving them a fifty-fifty chance, maybe less than that for her. So here they are, still alive the next morning. So, okay, we move them into the ICU, which is where they both kept plugging away at it for two weeks, hitting it better and better on all the scopes. So we transfer them out to their own room."

Mel stopped talking. "Here," he said, "let's drink this cheapo gin the hell up. Then we're going to dinner, right? Terri and I know a new place. That's where we'll go, to this new place we know about. But we're not going until we finish up this cut-rate, lousy gin."

Terri said, "We haven't actually eaten there yet. But it looks good. From the outside, you know."

"I like food," Mel said. "If I had it to do all over again, I'd be a chef, you know? Right, Terri?" Mel said.

He laughed. He fingered the ice in his glass.

"Terri knows," he said. "Terri can tell you. But let me say this. If I could come back again in a different life, a different time and all, you know what? I'd like to come back as a knight. You were pretty safe wearing all that armor. It was all right being a knight until gunpowder and muskets and pistols came along."

"Mel would like to ride a horse and carry a lance," Terri said.

"Carry a woman's scarf with you everywhere," Laura said.

"Or just a woman," Mel said.

"Shame on you," Laura said.

Terri said, "Suppose you came back as a serf. The serfs didn't have it so good in those days," Terri said.

"The serfs never had it good," Mel said. "But I guess even the knights were vessels to someone. Isn't that the way it worked? But then everyone is always a vessel to someone. Isn't that right? Terri? But what I liked about knights, besides their ladies, was that they had that suit of armor, you know, and they couldn't get hurt very easy. No cars in those days, you know? No drunk teenagers to tear into your ass."

"Vassals," Terri said.

"What?" Mel said.

"Vassals," Terri said. "They were called vassals, not vessels."

"Vassals, vessels," Mel said, "what the fuck's the difference? you knew what I meant anyway. All right," Mel said. "So I'm not educated. I learned my stuff. I'm a heart surgeon, sure, but I'm just a mechanic. I go in and I fuck around and I fix things. Shit," Mel said.

"Modesty doesn't become you," Terri said.

"He's just a humble sawbones," I said. "But sometimes they suffocated in all that armor, Mel. They'd even have heart attacks if it got too hot and they were too tired and worn out. I read somewhere that they'd fall off their horses and not be able to get up because they were too tired to stand with all that armor on them. They got trampled by their own horses sometimes."

"That's terrible," Mel said. "That's a terrible thing, Nicky. I guess they'd just lay there and wait until somebody came along and made a shish kebab out of them."

"Some other vessel," Terri said.

"That's right," Mel said. "Some vassal would come along and spear the bastard in the name of love. Or whatever the fuck it was they fought over in those days."

"Same things we fight over these days," Terri said.

Laura said, "Nothing's changed."

The color was still high in Laura's cheeks. Her eyes were bright. She brought her glass to her lips.

Mel poured himself another drink. He looked at the label closely as if studying a long row of numbers. Then he slowly put the bottle down on the table and slowly reached for the tonic water.

"What about the old couple?" Laura said. "You didn't finish that story you started."

Laura was having a hard time lighting her cigarette. Her matches kept going out.

The sunshine inside the room was different now, changing, getting thinner. But the leaves outside the window were still shimmering, and I stared at the pattern they made on the panes and on the Formica counter. They weren't the same patterns, of course.

"What about the old couple?" I said.

"Older but wiser," Terri said.

Mel stared at her.

Terri said, "Go on with your story, hon. I was only kidding. Then what happened?"

"Terri, sometimes," Mel said.

"Please, Mel," Terri said. "Don't always be so serious, sweetie. Can't you take a joke?"

"Where's the joke?" Mel said.

He held his glass and gazed steadily at his wife.

"What happened?" Laura said.

Mel fastened his eyes on Laura. He said, "Laura, if I didn't have Terri and if I didn't love her so much, and if Nick wasn't my best friend, I'd fall in love with you. I'd carry you off, honey," he said.

"Tell your story," Terri said. "Then we'll go to that new place, okay?"

"Okay," Mel said. "Where was I?" he said. He stared at the table and then he began again.

"I dropped in to see each of them every day, sometimes twice a day if I was up doing other calls anyway. Casts and bandages, head to foot, the both of them. You know, you've seen it in the movies. That's just the way they looked, just like in the movies. Little eye-holes and nose-holes and mouth-holes. And she had to have her legs slung up on top of it. Well, the husband was very depressed for the longest while. Even after he found out that his wife was going to pull through, he was still very depressed. Not about the accident, though. I mean, the accident was one thing, but it wasn't everything. I'd get up to his mouth-hole, you know, and he'd say no, it wasn't the accident exactly but it was because he couldn't see her through his eye-holes. He said that was what was making him feel so bad. Can you imagine? I'm telling you, the man's heart was breaking because he couldn't turn his goddamn head and *see* his goddamn wife."

Mel looked around the table and shook his head at what he was going to say.

"I mean, it was killing the old fart just because he couldn't *look* at the fucking woman."

We all looked at Mel.

"Do you see what I'm saying?" he said.

Maybe we were a little drunk by then. I know it was hard keeping things in focus. The light was draining out of the room, going back through the window where it had come from. Yet nobody made a move to get up from the table to turn on the overhead light.

"Listen," Mel said. "Let's finish this fucking gin. There's about enough left here for one shooter all around. Then let's go eat. Let's go to the new place."

"He's depressed," Terri said. "Mel, why don't you take a pill?"

Mel shook his head. "I've taken everything there is."

"We all need a pill now and then," I said.

"Some people are born needing them," Terri said.

She was using her finger to rub at something on the table. Then she stopped rubbing.

"I think I want to call my kids," Mel said. "Is that all right with everybody? I'll call my kids," he said.

Terri said, "What if Marjorie answers the phone? You guys, you've heard us on the subject of Marjorie? Honey, you know you don't want to talk to Marjorie. It'll make you feel even worse."

"I don't want to talk to Marjorie," Mel said. "But I want to talk to my kids."

"There isn't a day goes by that Mel doesn't say he wishes she'd get married again. Or else die," Terri said. "For one thing," Terri said, "she's bankrupting us. Mel says it's just to spite him that she won't get married again. She has a boyfriend who lives with her and the kids, so Mel is supporting the boyfriend too."

"She's allergic to bees," Mel said. "If I'm not praying she'll get married again, I'm praying she'll get herself stung to death by a swarm of fucking bees."

"Shame on you," Laura said.

"Bzzzzzzz," Mel said, turning his fingers into bees and buzzing them at Terri's throat. Then he let his hands drop all the way to his sides.

"She's vicious," Mel said. "Sometimes I think I'll go up there dressed like a beekeeper. You know, that hat that's like a helmet with the plate that comes down over your face, the big gloves, and the padded coat? I'll knock on the door and let loose a hive of bees in the house. But first I'd make sure the kids were out, of course."

He crossed one leg over the other. It seemed to take him a lot of time to do it. Then he put both feet on the floor and leaned forward, elbows on the table, his chin cupped in his hands.

"Maybe I won't call the kids, after all. Maybe it isn't such a hot idea. Maybe we'll just go eat. How does that sound?"

"Sounds fine to me," I said. "Eat or not eat. Or keep drinking. I could head right on out into the sunset."

"What does that mean, honey?" Laura asked.

"It just means what I said," I said. "It means I could just keep going. That's all it means."

"I could eat something myself," Laura said. "I don't think I've ever been so hungry in my life. Is there something to nibble on?"

"I'll put out some cheese and crackers," Terri said.

But Terri just sat there. She did not get up to get anything.

Mel turned his glass over. He spilled it out on the table.

"Gin's gone," Mel said.

Terri said, "Now what?"

I could hear my heart beating. I could hear everyone's heart. I could hear the human noise we sat there making, not one of us moving, not even when the room went dark.

QUESTIONS FOR DISCUSSION AND WRITING

1. The only action in "What We Talk About When We Talk About Love" is four people's sitting around a table talking about love. Is this a plot? Does anything change from the beginning to the end?

2. What examples of love do the speakers cite, and what paradoxes and contradictions of love do they involve?

3. The first-person narration is in the voice of Nick. Does the point of view matter? Would the story be substantially different if it were told by any other of the four characters?

4. This story observes the classical unities of time, place, and action; it takes place at one time and in one place, and there is only one action—the conversation about love. How does this compression affect the story's impact?

5. The tone seems to change slightly in the last paragraph. What does it mean? Why has the room gone dark?

Toni Cade Bambara

Toni Cade Bambara (b. 1939) grew up in Harlem and was educated at Queens College and the City College of New York. After graduation, she did social work, as an investigator for the New York City Department of Welfare and as director of recreation in the Psychiatry Department of Metropolitan Hospital. Her first collection of short stories, the well-received *Gorilla, My Love,* appeared in 1972. It was followed by a second collection, *The Sea Birds Are Still Alive,* in 1977, and by a novel, *The Salt Eaters,* in 1980. Toni Cade Bambara lives in Philadelphia.

MEDLEY

I could tell the minute I got in the door and dropped my bag, I wasn't staying. Dishes piled sky-high in the sink looking like some circus act. Glasses all ghosty on the counter. Busted tea bags, curling cantaloupe rinds, white cartons from the Chinamen, green sacks from the deli, and that damn dog creeping up on me for me to wrassle his head or kick him in the ribs one. No, I definitely wasn't staying. Couldn't even figure why I'd come. But picked my way to the hallway anyway till the laundry-stuffed pillowcases stopped me. Larry's bass blocking the view to the bedroom.

"That you, Sweet Pea?"

"No, man, ain't me at all," I say, working my way back to the suitcase and shoving that damn dog out the way. "See ya round," I holler, the door slamming behind me, cutting off the words abrupt.

⚊⟋⟍⟋⟍⟍⚊

Quite naturally sitting cross-legged at the club, I embroider a little on the homecoming tale, what with an audience of two crazy women and a fresh bottle of Jack Daniels. Got so I could actually see shonuff toadstools growing in the sink. Cantaloupe seeds sprouting in the muck. A goddamn compost heap breeding near the stove, garbage gardens on the grill.

"Sweet Pea, you oughta hush, cause you can't possibly keep on lying so," Pot Limit's screaming, tears popping from her eyes. "Lawd hold my legs, cause this liar bout to kill me off."

"Never mind about Larry's housekeeping, girl," Sylvia's soothing me, sloshing perfectly good bourbon all over the table. "You can come and stay with me till your house comes through. It'll be like old times at Aunt Merriam's."

I ease back into the booth to wait for the next set. The drummer's fooling with the equipment, tapping the mikes, hoping he's watched, so I watch him. But feeling worried in my mind about Larry, cause I've been through days like that myself. Cold cream caked on my face from the day before, hair matted, bathrobe funky, not a clean pair of drawers to my name. Even the emergency ones, the draggy cotton numbers stuffed way in the back of the drawer under the scented paper gone. And no clean silverware in the box and the last of the paper cups gone too. Icebox empty cept for a rock of cheese and the lone water jug that ain't even half full that's how anyhow the thing's gone on. And not a clue as to the next step. But then Pot Limit'll come bamming on the door to say So-and-so's in town and can she have the card table for a game. Or Sylvia'll send a funny card inviting herself to dinner and even giving me the menu. Then I zoom through that house like a manic work brigade till me and the place ready for white-glove inspection. But what if somebody or other don't intervene for Larry, I'm thinking.

The drummer's messin round on the cymbals, head cocked to the side, rings sparkling. The other dudes are stepping out from behind the curtain. The piano man playing with the wah-wah doing splashy, breathy science fiction stuff. Sylvia checking me out to make sure I ain't too blue. Blue got hold to me, but I lean forward out of the shadows and babble something about how off the bourbon tastes these days. Hate worryin Sylvia, who is the kind of friend who bleeds at the eyes with your pain. I drain my glass and hum along with the opening riff of the guitar and I keep my eyes strictly off the bass player, whoever he is.

Larry Landers looked more like a bass player than ole Mingus himself. Got these long arms that drape down over the bass like they were grown special for that purpose. Fine, strong hands with long fingers and muscular knuckles, the dimples deep black at the joints. His calluses so other-colored and hard, looked like Larry had swiped his grandmother's tarnished thimbles to play with. He'd move in on that bass like he was going to hump it or something, slide up behind it as he lifted it from the rug, all slinky. He'd become one with the wood. Head dipped down sideways bobbing out the rhythm, feet tapping, legs jiggling, he'd look good. Thing about it, though, ole Larry couldn't play for shit. Couldn't never find the right placement for the notes. Never plucking with enough strength, despite the perfectly capable hands. Either you didn't hear him at all or what you heard was off. The man couldn't play for nuthin is what I'm saying. But Larry Landers was baad in the shower, though.

He'd soap me up and down with them great, fine hands, doing a deep bass walking in the back of his mouth. And I'd just have to sing, though I can't sing to save my life. But we'd have one hellafyin musical time in the shower, lemme tell you. "Green Dolphin Street" never sounded like nuthin till Larry bopped out them changes and actually made me sound good. On "My Funny Valentine" he'd do a whizzing sounding bow thing that made his throat vibrate real sexy and I'd cutesy up the introduction, which is, come to think of it, my favorite part. But the main number when the hot water started running out was "I Feel Like Making Love." That was usually the wind up of our repertoire cause you can imagine what that song can do to you in the shower and all.

Got so we spent a helluva lotta time in the shower. Just as well, cause didn't nobody call Larry for gigs. He a nice man, considerate, generous, baad in the shower, and good taste in music. But he just wasn't nobody's bass player. Knew all the stances, though, the postures, the facial expressions, had the choreography down. And right in the middle of supper he'd get some Ron Carter thing going in his head and hop up from the table to go get the bass. Haul that sucker right in the kitchen and do a number in dumb show, all the playing in his throat, the acting with his hands. But that ain't nuthin. I mean that can't get it. I can impersonate Betty Carter if it comes to that. The arms crooked just so, the fingers popping, the body working, the cap and all, the teeth, authentic. But I got sense enough to know I ain't nobody's singer. Actually, I am a mother, though I'm only just now getting it together. And too, I'm an A-1 manicurist.

Me and my cousin Sinbad come North working our show in cathouses at first. Set up a salon right smack in the middle of Miz Maybry's Saturday traffic. But that wasn't no kind of life to be bringing my daughter into. So I parked her at a boarding school till I could make some other kind of life. Wasn't no kind of life for Sinbad either, so we quit.

Our first shop was a three-chair affair on Austin. Had a student barber who could do anything—blow-outs, do's, corn rows, weird cuts, afros, press and curl, whatever you wanted. Plus he didn't gab you to death. And he always brought his sides and didn't blast em neither. He went on to New York and opened his own shop. Was a bootblack too then, an old dude named James Noughton, had a crooked back and worked at the post office at night, and knew everything about everything, read all the time.

"Whatcha want to know about Marcus Garvey, Sweet Pea?"

If it wasn't Garvey, it was the rackets or the trucking industry or the flora and fauna of Greenland or the planets or how the special effects in the disaster movies were done. One Saturday I asked him to tell me about the war, cause my nephew'd been drafted and it all seemed so wrong to me, our men over there in Nam fighting folks who fighting for the same things we are, to get that bloodsucker off our backs.

Well, what I say that for. Old dude gave us a deep knee bend, straight up eight-credit dissertation on World Wars I and II—the archduke getting offed, Africa cut up like so much cake, Churchill and his cigars, Gabriel Heatter on the radio, Hitler at the Olympics igging Owens, Red Cross doing Bloods dirty refusing donuts and bandages, A. Philip Randolph scaring the white folks to death, Mary McLeod Bethune at the White House, Liberty Bond drives, the Russian front, frostbite of the feet, the Jew stiffs, the gypsies no one mourned . . . the whole johnson. Talked straight through the day, Miz Mary's fish dinner growing cold on the radiator, his one and only customer walking off with one dull shoe. Fell out exhausted, his shoe rag limp in his lap, one arm draped over the left foot platform, the other clutching his heart. Took Sinbad and our cousin Pepper to get the old man home. I stayed with him all night with the ice pack and a fifth of Old Crow. He liked to die.

After while trade picked up and with a better class of folk too. Then me and Sinbad moved to North and Gaylord and called the shop Chez Sinbad. No more winos stumbling in or deadbeats wasting my time talking raunchy shit. The paperboy, the numbers man, the dudes with classier hot stuff coming in on Tuesday mornings only. We did up the place nice. Light globes from a New Orleans whorehouse, Sinbad likes to lie. Brown-and-black-and-silver-striped wallpaper. Lots of mirrors and hanging plants. Them old barber chairs spruced up and called antiques and damn if someone didn't buy one off us for eight hundred, cracked me up.

I cut my schedule down to ten hours in the shop so I could do private sessions with the gamblers and other business men and women who don't like sitting around the shop even though it's comfy, specially my part. Got me a cigar showcase with a marble top for serving coffee in clear glass mugs with heatproof handles too. My ten hours in the shop are spent leisurely. And my twenty hours out are making me a mint. Takes dust to be a mother, don't you know.

It was a perfect schedule once Larry Landers came into my life. He part-timed at a record shop and bartended at Topp's on the days and nights I worked at the shops. That gave us most of Monday and Wednesdays to listen to sides and hit the clubs. Gave me Fridays all to myself to study in the library and wade through them college bulletins and get to the museum and generally chart out a routine for when Debbie and me are a team. Sundays I always drive to Delaware to see her, and Larry detours to D.C. to see his sons. My bankbook started telling me I was soon going to be a full-time mama again and a college girl to boot, if I can ever talk myself into doing a school thing again, old as I am.

Life with Larry was cool. Not just cause he wouldn't hear about me going halves on the bills. But cause he was an easy man to be easy with. He liked talking softly and listening to music. And he liked having folks over for dinner and cards. Larry a real nice man and I liked him a lot. And I liked his friend Hector, who lived in the back of the apartment. Ole moon-face Hector went to school with Larry years ago and is some kind of kin. And they once failed in the funeral business together and I guess those stories of them times kinda keep them friends.

The time they had to put Larry's brother away is their best story, Hector's story really, since Larry got to play a little grief music round the edges. They decided to pass up a church service, since Bam was such a treacherous desperado wouldn't nobody want to preach over his body and wouldn't nobody come to hear no lies about the dearly departed untimely ripped or cut down or whatever. So Hector and Larry set up some kind of pop stand awning right at the gravesite, expecting close blood only. But seems the whole town turned out to make sure ole evil, hell-raising Bam was truly dead. Dudes straight from the barber chair, the striped ponchos blowing like wings, fuzz and foam on they face and all, lumbering up the hill to the hole taking bets and talking shit, relating how Ole Crazy Bam had shot up the town, shot up the jail, shot up the hospital pursuing some bootlegger who'd come up one keg short of the order. Women from all around come to demand the lid be lifted so they could check for themselves and be sure that Bam was stone cold. No matter how I tried I couldn't think of nobody bad enough to think on when they told the story of the man I'd never met.

Larry and Hector so bent over laughing bout the funeral, I couldn't hardly put the events in proper sequence. But I could surely picture some neighbor lady calling on Larry and Bam's mama reporting how the whole town had turned out for the burying. And the mama snatching up the first black thing she could find to wrap around herself and make an appearance. No use passing up a scene like that. And Larry prancing round the kitchen being his mama. And I'm too stunned to laugh, not at somebody's mama, and somebody's brother dead. But him and Hector laughing to beat the band and I can't help myself.

Thing about it, though, the funeral business stories are Hector's stories and he's not what you'd call a good storyteller. He never gives you the names, so you got all these he's and she's floating around. And he don't believe in giving details, so you got to scramble to paint your own pictures. Toward the end of that particular tale of Bam, all I could picture was the townspeople driving a stake through the dead man's heart, then hurling that coffin into the hole right quick. There was also something in that story about the civil rights workers wanting to make a case cause a white cop had cut Bam down. But looked like Hector didn't have a hold on that part of the story, so I just don't know.

Stories are not Hector's long suit. But he is an absolute artist on windows. Ole Moon-Face can wash some windows and make you cry about it too. Makes these smooth little turns out there on that little bitty sill just like he wasn't four stories up without a belt. I'd park myself at the breakfast counter and thread the new curtains on the rods while Hector mixed up the vinegar solution real cheflike. Wring out the rags just so, scrunch up the newspapers into soft wads that make you think of cat's paws. Hector was a cat himself out there on the sill, making these marvelous circles in the glass, rubbing the hardhead spots with a strip of steel wool he had pinned to his overalls.

Hector offered to do my car once. But I put a stop to that after that first time.

My windshield so clear and sparkling felt like I was in an accident and heading over the hood, no glass there. But it was a pleasure to have coffee and watch Hector. After while, though, Larry started hinting that the apartment wasn't big enough for four. I agreed, thinking he meant Earl had to go. Come to find Larry meant Hector, which was a real drag. I love to be around people who do whatever it is they do with style and care.

Larry's dog named Earl P. Jessup Bowers, if you can get ready for that. And I should mention straightaway that I do not like dogs one bit, which is why I was glad when Larry said somebody had to go. Cats are bad enough. Horses are a total drag. By the age of nine I was fed up with all that noble horse this and noble horse that. They got good PR, horses. But I really can't use em. Was a fire once when I was little and some dumb horse almost burnt my daddy up messin around, twisting, snorting, broncing, rearing up, doing everything but comin on out the barn like even the chickens had sense enough to do. I told my daddy to let that horse's ass burn. Horses be as dumb as cows. Cows just don't have good press agents is all.

I used to like cows when I was real little and needed to hug me something bigger than a goldfish. But don't let it rain, the dumbbells'll fall right in a ditch and you break a plow and shout yourself hoarse trying to get them fools to come up out the ditch. Chipmunks I don't mind when I'm at the breakfast counter with my tea and they're on their side of the glass doing Disney things in the yard. Blue jays are law-and-order birds, thoroughly despicable. And there's one prize fool in my Aunt Merriam's yard I will one day surely kill. He tries to "whip whip whip-poorwill" like the Indians do in the Fort This or That movies when they're signaling to each other closing in on George Montgomery but don't never get around to wiping that sucker out. But dogs are one of my favorite hatreds. All the time woofing, bolting down their food, slopping water on the newly waxed lino-leum, messin with you when you trying to read, chewin on the slippers.

Earl P. Jessup Bowers was an especial drag. But I could put up with Earl when Hector was around. Once Hector was gone and them windows got cloudy and gritty, I was through. Kicked that dog every chance I got. And after thinking what it meant, how the deal went down, place too small for four and it was Hector not Earl—I started moving up my calendar so I could get out of there. I ain't the kind of lady to press no ultimatum on no man. Like "Choose, me or the dog." That's unattractive. Kicking Hector out was too. An insult to me, once I got to thinking about it. Especially since I had carefully explained from jump street to Larry that I got one item on my agenda, making a home for me and my kid. So if anybody should've been given walking papers, should've been me.

~∿ ∕∕∕~

Anyway. One day Moody comes waltzing into Chez Sinbad's and tips his hat. He glances at his nails and glances at me. And I figure here is my house in a green corduroy suit. Pot Limit had just read my cards and the jack of diamonds kept coming up on my resource side. Sylvia and me put our heads together and figure it got to be some gambler or hustler who wants his nails done. What other jacks do I know to make my fortune? I'm so positive about Moody, I whip out a postcard from the drawer where I keep the emeries and write my daughter to start packing.

"How much you make a day, Miss Lady?"

"Thursdays are always good for fifty," I lie.

He hands me fifty and glances over at Sinbad, who nods that it's cool. "I'd like my nails done at four-thirty. My place."

"Got a customer at that time, Mr. Moody, and I like to stay reliable. How bout five-twenty?"

He smiles a slow smile and glances at Sinbad, who nods again, everything's cool. "Fine," he says. "And do you think you can manage a shave without cutting a person's throat?"

"Mr. Moody, I don't know you well enough to have just cause. And none of your friends have gotten to me yet with that particular proposition. Can't say what I'm prepared to do in the future, but for now I can surely shave you real careful-like."

Moody smiles again, then turns to Sinbad, who says it's cool and he'll give me the address. This look-nod dialogue burns my ass. That's like when you take a dude to lunch and pay the check and the waiter's standing there with *your* money in his paws asking *the dude* was everything all right and later for *you*. Shit. But I take down Moody's address and let the rest roll off me like so much steaming lava. I start packing up my little alligator case—buffer, batteries, clippers, emeries, massager, sifter, arrowroot and cornstarch, clear sealer, magnifying glass, and my own mixture of green and purple pigments.

"Five-twenty ain't five-twenty-one, is it, Miss Lady?"

"Not in my book," I say, swinging my appointment book around so he can see how full it is and how neatly the times are printed in. Course I always fill in phony names case some creep starts pressing me for a session.

For six Thursdays running and two Monday nights, I'm at Moody's bending over them nails with a miner's light strapped to my forehead, the magnifying glass in its stand, nicking just enough of the nails at the sides, tinting just enough with the color so he can mark them cards as he shuffles. Takes an hour to do it proper. Then I sift my talc concoction and brush his hands till they're smooth. Them cards move around so fast in his hands, he can actually tell me he's about to deal from the bottom in the next three moves and I miss it and I'm not new to this. I been a gambler's manicurist for more years than I care to mention. Ten times he'll cut and each time the same fifteen cards in the top cut and each time in exactly the same order. Incredible.

Now, I've known hands. My first husband, for instance. To see them hands work their show in the grandstands, at a circus, in a parade, the pari-mutuels—artistry in action. We met on the train. As a matter of fact, he was trying to burgle my bag. Some story to tell the grandchildren, hunh? I had to get him straight about robbing from folks. I don't play that. Ya gonna steal, hell, steal back some of them millions we got in escrow is my opinion. We spent three good years on the circuit. Then credit cards moved in. Then choke-and-grab muggers who killed the whole tradition. He was reduced to a mere shell of his former self, as they say, and took to putting them hands on me. I try not to think on when things went sour. Try not to think about them big slapping hands, only of them working hands. Moody's working hands were something like that, but even better. So I'm impressed and he's impressed. And he pays me fifty and tips me fifty and shuts up when I shave him and keeps his hands off my lovely person.

I'm so excited counting up my bread, moving up the calendar, making impulsive calls to Delaware and the two of us squealing over the wire like a coupla fools, that what Larry got to say about all these goings-on just rolls off my back like so much molten lead.

"Well, who be up there while he got his head in your lap and you squeezing his goddamn blackheads?"

"I don't squeeze his goddamn blackheads, Larry, on account of he don't have no goddamn blackheads. I give him a shave, a steam, and an egg-white face mask. And when I'm through, his face is as smooth as his hands."

"I'll bet," Larry says. That makes me mad cause I expect some kind of respect for my work, which is better than just good.

"And he doesn't have his head in my lap. He's got a whole barbershop set up on his solarium."

"His what?" Larry squinting at me, raising the wooden spoon he stirring the spaghetti with, and I raise the knife I'm chopping the onions with. Thing about it, though, he don't laugh. It's funny as hell to me, but Larry got no sense of humor sometimes, which is too bad cause he's a lotta fun when he's laughing and joking.

"It's not a bedroom. He's got this screened-in sun porch where he raises African violets and—"

"Please, Sweet Pea. Why don't you quit? You think I'm dumb?"

"I'm serious. I'm serious and I'm mad cause I ain't got no reason to lie to you whatever was going on, Larry." He turns back to the pot and I continue working on the sauce and I'm pissed off cause this is silly. "He sits in the barber chair and I shave him and give him a manicure."

"What else you be giving him? A man don't be paying a good-looking woman to come to his house and all and don't—"

"Larry, if you had the dough and felt like it, wouldn't you pay Pot Limit to come read your cards? And couldn't you keep your hands to yourself and she a good-looking woman? And couldn't you see yourself paying Sylvia to come and cook for you and no funny stuff, and she's one of the best-looking women in town?"

Larry cooled out fast. My next shot was to bring up the fact that he was insulting my work. Do I go around saying the women who pass up Bill the bartender and come to him are after his joint? No, cause I respect the fact that Larry Landers mixes the best piña coladas this side of Barbados. And he's flashy with the blender and the glasses and the whole show. He's good and I respect that. But he cooled out so fast I didn't have to bring it up. I don't believe in overkill, besides I like to keep some things in reserve. He cooled out so fast I realized he wasn't really jealous. He was just going through one of them obligatory male numbers, all symbolic, no depth.

Like the time this dude came into the shop to talk some trash and Sinbad got his ass on his shoulders, talking about the dude showed no respect for him cause for all he knew I could be Sinbad's woman. And me arguing that since that ain't the case, what's the deal? I mean why get hot over what if if what if ain't. Men are crazy. Now there is Sinbad, my blood cousin who grew up right in the same house like a brother damn near, putting me through simple-ass changes like that. Who's got time for grand opera and comic strips, I'm trying to make a life for me and my kid. But men are like that. Gorillas, if you know what I mean.

Like at Topp's sometimes. I'll drop in to have a drink with Larry when he's on the bar and then I leave. And maybe some dude'll take it in his head to walk me to the car. That's cool. I lay it out right quick that me and Larry are a we and then we take it from there, just two people gassing in the summer breeze and that's just fine. But don't let some other dude holler over something like "Hey, man, can you handle all that? Why don't you step aside, junior, and let a man . . ." and blah-de-da-de-dah. They can be the best of friends or total strangers just kidding around, but right away they two gorillas pounding on their chest, pounding on their chest and talking over my head, yelling over the tops of cars just like I'm not a person with some say-so in the matter. It's a man-to-man ritual that ain't got nothing to do with me. So I just get in my car and take off and leave them to get it on if they've a mind to. They got it.

But if one of the gorillas is a relative, or a friend of mine, or a nice kinda man I got in mind for one of my friends, I will stick around long enough to shout em down and point out that they are some ugly gorillas and are showing no respect for me and therefore owe me an apology. But if they don't fit into one of them categories, I figure it ain't my place to try to develop them so they can make the leap from gorilla to human. If their own mamas and daddies didn't care whether they turned out to be amoebas or catfish or whatever, it ain't my weight. I got my own weight. I'm a mother. So they got it.

Like I use to tell my daughter's daddy, the key to getting along and living with other folks is to keep clear whose weight is whose. His drinking, for instance, was not my weight. And him waking me up in the night for them long, rambling, ninety-proof monologues bout how the whole world's made up of victims, rescuers, and executioners and I'm the dirty bitch cause I ain't rescuing him fast enough to suit him. Then got so I was the executioner, to hear him tell it. I don't say nuthin cause my philosophy of life and death is this—I'll go when the wagon comes, but I ain't going out behind somebody's else's shit. I arranged my priorities long ago when I jumped into my woman stride. Some things I'll go off on. Some things I'll hold my silence and wait out. Some things I just bump off, cause the best solution to some problems is to just abandon them.

But I struggled with Mac, Debbie's daddy. Talked to his family, his church, AA, hid the bottles, threatened the liquor man, left a good job to pay nurse, mistress, kitten, buddy. But then he stopped calling me Dahlin and started calling me Mama. I don't play that. I'm my daughter's mama. So I split. Did my best to sweeten them last few months, but I'd been leaving for a long time.

The silliest thing about all of Larry's grumblings back then was Moody had no eyes for me and vice versa. I just like the money. And I like watching him mess around with the cards. He's exquisite, dazzling, stunning shuffling, cutting, marking, dealing from the bottom, the middle, the near top. I ain't never seen nothing like it, and I seen a whole lot. The thing that made me mad, though, and made me know Larry Landers wasn't ready to deal with no woman full grown was the way he kept bringing it up, always talking about what he figured was on Moody's mind, like what's on my mind don't count. So I finally did have to use up my reserves and point out to Larry that he was insulting my work and that I would never dream of accusing him of not being a good bartender, of just being another pretty face, like they say.

"You can't tell me he don't have eyes," he kept saying.

"What about my eyes? Don't my eyes count?" I gave it up after a coupla tries. All I know is, Moody wasn't even thinking about me. I was impressed with his work and needed the trade and vice versa.

One time, for instance, I was doing his hands on the solarium and thought I saw a glint of metal up under his jacket. I rearranged myself in the chair so I could work my elbow in there to see if he was carrying heat. I thought I was being cool about it.

"How bout keeping your tits on your side of the table, Miss Lady."

I would rather he think anything but that. I would rather he think I was clumsy in my work even. "Wasn't about tits, Moody. I was just trying to see if you had a holster on and was too lazy to ask."

"Would have expected you to. You a straight-up, direct kind of person." He opened his jacket away with the heel of his hand, being careful with his nails. I liked that.

"It's not about you," he said quietly, jerking his chin in the direction of the revolver. "Had to transport some money today and forgot to take it off. Sorry."

I gave myself two demerits. One for the tits, the other for setting up a situation where he wound up telling me something about his comings and goings. I'm too old to be making mistakes like that. So I apologized. Then gave myself two stars. He had a good opinion of me and my work. I did an extra-fine job on his hands that day.

Then the house happened. I had been reading the rental ads and For Sale columns for months and looking at some awful, tacky places. Then one Monday me and Sylvia lucked up on this cute little white-brick job up on a hill away from the street. Lots of light and enough room and not too much yard to kill me off. I paid money down and rushed them papers through. Got back to Larry's place all excited and found him with his mouth all poked out.

Half grumbling, half proposing, he hinted around that we all should live at his place like a family. Only he didn't quite lay it out plain in case of rejection. And I'll tell you something. I wouldn't want to be no man. Must be hard on the heart always having to get out there, setting yourself up to be possibly shot down, approaching the lady, calling, the invitation, the rap. I don't think I could handle it myself unless everybody was just straight up at all times from day one till the end. I didn't answer Larry's nonproposed proposal cause it didn't come clear to me till after dinner. So I just let my silence carry whatever meaning it will. Ain't nuthin too much changed from the first day he came to get me from my Aunt Merriam's place. My agenda is still to make a home for my girl. Marriage just ain't one of the things on my mind no more, not after two. Got no regrets or bad feelings about them husbands neither. Like the poem says, when you're handed a lemon, make lemonade, honey, make lemonade. That's Gwen Brooks' motto, that's mine too. You get a lemon, well, just make lemonade.

━━ ✦ ━━

"Going on the road next week," Moody announces one day through the steam towel. "Like you to travel with me, keep my hands in shape. Keep the women off my neck. Check the dudes at my back. Ain't asking you to carry heat or money or put yourself in no danger. But I could use your help." He pauses and I ease my buns into the chair, staring at the steam curling from the towel.

"Wicked schedule though—Mobile, Birmingham, Sarasota Springs, Jacksonville, then Puerto Rico and back. Can pay you two thousand and expenses. You're good, Miss Lady. You're good and you got good sense. And while I don't believe in nothing but my skill and chance, I gotta say you've brought me luck. You a lucky lady, Miss Lady."

He raises his hands and cracks his knuckles and it's like the talking towel has eyes as well cause damn if he ain't checking his cuticles.

"I'll call you later, Moody," I manage to say, mind reeling. With two thousand I can get my stuff out of storage, and buy Debbie a real nice bedroom set, pay tuition at the college too and start my three-credit-at-a-time grind.

Course I never dreamed the week would be so unnerving, exhausting, constantly on my feet, serving drinks, woofing sisters, trying to distract dudes, keeping track of fifty-leven umpteen goings on. Did have to carry the heat on three occasions and had to do a helluva lotta driving. Plus was most of the time holed up in the hotel room close to the phone. I had pictured myself lazying on the beach in Florida dreaming up cruises around the world with two matching steamer trunks with the drawers and hangers and stuff. I'd pictured traipsing through the casinos in Puerto

Rico ordering chicken salad and coffee liqueur and tipping the croupiers with blue chips. Shit no. Was work. And I sure as hell learned how Moody got his name. Got so we didn't even speak, but I kept those hands in shape and his face smooth and placid. And whether he won, lost, broke even, or got wiped out, I don't even know. He gave me my money and took off for New Orleans. That trip liked to kill me.

⬛〰 〰⬛

"You never did say nothing interesting about Moody," Pot Limit says insinuatingly, swinging her legs in from the aisle cause ain't nobody there to snatch so she might as well sit comfortable.

"Yeah, she thought she'd put us off the trail with a riproaring tale about Larry's housekeeping."

They slapping five and hunching each other and making a whole lotta noise, spilling Jack Daniels on my turquoise T-straps from Puerto Rico.

"Come on, fess up, Sweet Pea," they crooning. "Did you give him some?"

"Ahhh, yawl bitches are tiresome, you know that?"

"Naaw, naaw," say Sylvia, grabbing my arm. "You can tell us. We wantta know all about the trip, specially the nights." She winks at Pot Limit.

"Tell us about this Moody man and his wonderful hands one more time, cept we want to hear how the hands feeel on the flesh, honey." Pot Limit doing a bump and grind in the chair that almost makes me join in the fun, except I'm worried in my mind about Larry Landers.

Just then the piano player comes by and leans over Sylvia, blowing in her ear. And me and Pot Limit mimic the confectionary goings-on. And just as well, cause there's nothin to tell about Moody. It wasn't a movie after all. And in real life the good-looking gambler's got cards on his mind. Just like I got my child on my mind. Onliest thing to say about the trip is I'm five pounds lighter, not a shade darker, but two thousand closer toward my goal.

"Ease up," Sylvia says, interrupting the piano player to fuss over me. Then the drummer comes by and eases in on Pot Limit. And I ease back into the shadows of the booth to think Larry over.

I'm staring at the entrance half expecting Larry to come into Topp's, but it's not his night. Then too, the thing is ended if I'd only know it. Larry the kind of man you're either living with him or you're out. I for one would've liked us to continue, me and Debbie in our place, him and Earl at his. But he got so grumpy the time I said that, I sure wasn't gonna bring it up again. Got grumpy in the shower too, got so he didn't want to wash my back.

But that last night fore I left for Birmingham, we had us one crazy musical time in the shower. I kept trying to lure him into "Maiden Voyage," which I really can't do without back-up, cause I can't sing all them changes. After while he come out from behind his sulk and did a Jon Lucien combination on vocal and bass, alternating the sections, eight bars of singing words, eight bars of singing bass. It was baad. Then he insisted on doing "I Love You More Today Than Yesterday." And we like to break our arches, stomping out the beat against the shower mat.

The bathroom was all steamy and we had the curtains open so we could see the plants and watch the candles burning. I had bought us a big fat cake of sandalwood soap and it was matching them candles scent for scent. Must've been two o'clock in the morning and looked like the hot water would last forever and ever and ever. Larry finally let go of the love songs, which were making me feel kinda funny cause I thought it was understood that I was splitting, just like he'd always made it clear either I was there or nowhere.

Then we hit on a tune I don't even know the name of cept I like to scat and do my thing Larry calls Swahili wailing. He laid down the most intricate weaving, walking, bopping, strutting bottom to my singing I ever heard. It inspired me. Took that melody and went right on out that shower, them candles bout used up, the fatty soap long since abandoned in the dish, our bodies barely visible in the steamed-up mirrors walling his bathroom. Took that melody right on out the room and out of doors and somewhere out this world Larry changing instruments fast as I'm changing moods, colors. Took an alto solo and gave me a rest, worked an intro up on the piano playing the chords across my back, drove me all up into the high register while he weaved in and out around my head on a flute sounding like them chilly pipes of the Andes. And I was Yma Sumac for one minute there, up there breathing some rare air and losing my mind, I was so high on just sheer music. Music and water, the healthiest things in the world. And that hot water pounding like it was part of the group with a union card and all. And I could tell that if that bass could've fit in the tub, Larry would've dragged that bad boy in there and played the hell out of them soggy strings once and for all.

I dipped way down and reached way back for snatches of Jelly Roll Morton's "Deep Creek Blues" and Larry so painful, so stinging on the bass, could make you cry. Then I'm racing fast through Bessie and all the other Smith singers, Mildred Bailey, Billie and imitators, Betty Roche, Nat King Cole vintage 46, a little Joe Carroll, King Pleasure, some Babs. Found myself pulling lines out of songs I don't even like, but ransacked songs just for the meaningful lines or two cause I realized we were doing more than just making music together, and it had to be said just how things stood.

Then I was off again and lost Larry somewhere down there doing scales, sound like. And he went back to that first supporting line that had drove me up into the Andes. And he stayed there waiting for me to return and do some more Swahili wailing. But I was elsewhere and liked it out there and ignored the fact that he was aiming for a windup of "I Love You More Today Than Yesterday." I sang myself out till all I could ever have left in life was "Brown Baby" to sing to my little girl. Larry stayed on the ground with the same supporting line, and the hot water started getting funny and I knew my time was up. So I came crashing down, jarring the song out of shape, diving back into the melody line and somehow, not even knowing what song each other was doing, we finished up together just as the water turned cold.

QUESTIONS FOR DISCUSSION AND WRITING

1. What is the source of conflict in "Medley"? Who is the protagonist, who is the antagonist, and what issue divides them?

2. Perhaps the most striking thing about "Medley" is the voice of Sweet Pea, telling her story. What are some of the characteristics of Sweet Pea's mode of expression?

3. A recurring joke—and symbol—in the story is Sweet Pea and Larry's vocal duets in the shower. What do these duets reveal about their relationship?

4. One of Bambara's recurring projects in her fiction is to shatter stereotypes of black women. What stereotypes does the character of Sweet Pea shatter?

Maxine Hong Kingston

Maxine Hong Kingston was born in 1940 in Stockton, California. Her parents were Chinese immigrants who had had prestigious jobs in China but operated a laundry in the United States. Kingston was educated at the University of California, Berkeley, and became a public-school teacher, first in California and then in Hawaii. Her first book was *The Woman Warrior: Memoirs of a Girlhood Among Ghosts* (1976); it won a number of awards, including the National Book Critics Circle Award. *China Men* appeared in 1980; it dealt with her father and her male relatives as *The Woman Warrior* had dealt with her mother and her female relatives. A novel, *Tripmaster Monkey*, appeared in 1989.

NO NAME WOMAN

"You must not tell anyone," my mother said, "what I am about to tell you. In China your father had a sister who killed herself. She jumped into the family well. We say that your father has all brothers because it is as if she had never been born.

"In 1924 just a few days after our village celebrated seventeen hurry-up weddings—to make sure that every young man who went 'out on the road' would responsibly come home—your father and his brothers and your grandfather and his brothers and your aunt's new husband sailed for America, the Gold Mountain. It was your grandfather's last trip. Those lucky enough to get contracts waved good-bye from the decks. They fed and guarded the stowaways and helped them off in Cuba, New York, Bali, Hawaii. 'We'll meet in California next year,' they said. All of them sent money home.

"I remember looking at your aunt one day when she and I were dressing; I had not noticed before that she had such a protruding melon of a stomach. But I did not think, 'She's pregnant,' until she began to look like other pregnant women, her shirt pulling and the white tops of her black pants showing. She could not have been pregnant, you see, because her husband had been gone for years. No one said anything. We did not discuss it. In early summer she was ready to have the child, long after the time when it could have been possible.

"The village also had been counting. On the night the baby was to be born the villagers raided our house. Some were crying. Like a great saw, teeth strung with lights, files of people walked zigzag across our land, tearing the rice. Their lanterns doubled in the disturbing black water, which drained away through the broken bunds. As the villagers closed in, we could see that some of them, probably men and women we knew well, wore white masks. The people with long hair hung it over their faces. Women with short hair made it stand up on end. Some had tied white bands around their foreheads, arms, and legs.

"At first they threw mud and rocks at the house. Then they threw eggs and began slaughtering our stock. We could hear the animals scream their deaths— the roosters, the pigs, a last great roar from the ox. Familiar wild heads flared in our night windows; the villagers encircled us. Some of the faces stopped to peer at us, their eyes rushing like searchlights. The hands flattened against the panes, framed heads, and left red prints.

"The villagers broke in the front and the back doors at the same time, even though we had not locked the doors against them. Their knives dripped with the blood of our animals. They smeared blood on the doors and walls. One woman swung a chicken, whose throat she had slit, splattering blood in red arcs about her. We stood together in the middle of the house, in the family hall with the pictures and tables of ancestors around us, and looked straight ahead.

"At that time the house had only two wings. When the men came back, we would build two more to enclose our courtyard and a third one to begin a second courtyard. The villagers pushed through both wings, even your grandparents' rooms, to find your aunt's, which was also mine until the men returned. From this room a new wing for one of the younger families would grow. They ripped up her clothes and shoes and broke her combs, grinding them underfoot. They tore her work from the loom. They scattered the cooking fire and rolled the new weaving into it. We could hear them in the kitchen breaking our bowls and banging the pots. They overturned the great waist-high earthenware jugs; duck eggs, pickled fruits, vegetables burst out and mixed in acrid torrents. The old woman from the next field swept a broom through the air and loosed the spirits-of-the-broom over our heads. 'Pig.' 'Ghost.' 'Pig,' they sobbed and scolded while they ruined our house.

"When they left, they took sugar and oranges to bless themselves. They cut pieces from the dead animals. Some of them took bowls that were not broken and clothes that were not torn. Afterward we swept up the rice and sewed it back into sacks. But the smell from the spilled preserves lasted. Your aunt gave birth in the pigsty that night. The next morning when I went for the water, I found her and the baby plugging up the family well.

"Don't let your father know that I told you. He denies her. Now that you have started to menstruate, what happened to her could happen to you. Don't humiliate us. You wouldn't like to be forgotten as if you had never been born. The villagers are watchful."

Whenever she had warned us about life, my mother told stories that ran like this one, a story to grow up on. She tested our strength to establish realities. Those in the emigrant generations who could not reassert brute survival died young and far from home. Those of us in the first American generations have had to figure out how the invisible world the emigrants built around our childhoods fit in solid America.

The emigrants confused the gods by diverting their curses, misleading them with crooked streets and false names. They must try to confuse their offspring as well, who, I suppose, threaten them in similar ways—always trying to get things straight, always trying to name the unspeakable. The Chinese I know hide their names; sojourners take new names when their lives change and guard their real names with silence.

Chinese-Americans, when you try to understand what things in you are Chinese, how do you separate what is peculiar to childhood, to poverty, insanities, one family, your mother who marked your growing with stories, from what is Chinese? What is Chinese tradition and what is the movies?

If I want to learn what clothes my aunt wore, whether flashy or ordinary, I would have to begin, "Remember Father's drowned-in-the-well sister?" I cannot ask that. My mother has told me once and for all the useful parts. She will add nothing unless powered by Necessity, a riverbank that guides her life. She plants vegetable gardens rather than lawns; she carries the odd-shaped tomatoes home from the fields and eats food left for the gods.

Whenever we did frivolous things, we used up energy; we flew high kites. We children came up off the ground over the melting cones our parents brought home from work and the American movie on New Year's Day—*Oh, You Beautiful*

Doll with Betty Grable one year, and *She Wore a Yellow Ribbon* with John Wayne another year. After the one carnival ride each, we paid in guilt; our tired father counted his change on the dark walk home.

Adultery is extravagance. Could people who hatch their own chicks and eat the embryos and the heads for delicacies and boil the feet in vinegar for party food, leaving only the gravel, eating even the gizzard lining—could such people engender a prodigal aunt? To be a woman, to have a daughter in starvation time was a waste enough. My aunt could not have been the lone romantic who gave up everything for sex. Women in the old China did not choose. Some man had commanded her to lie with him and be his secret evil. I wonder whether he masked himself when he joined the raid on the family.

Perhaps she encountered him in the fields or on the mountain where the daughters-in-law collected fuel. Or perhaps he first noticed her in the marketplace. He was not a stranger because the village housed no strangers. She had to have dealings with him other than sex. Perhaps he worked an adjoining field, or he sold her the cloth for the dress she sewed and wore. His demand must have surprised, then terrified her. She obeyed him; she always did as she was told.

When the family found a young man in the next village to be her husband, she stood tractably beside the best rooster, his proxy, and promised before they met that she would be his forever. She was lucky that he was her age and she would be the first wife, an advantage secure now. The night she first saw him, he had sex with her. Then he left for America. She had almost forgotten what he looked like. When she tried to envision him, she only saw the black and white face in the group photograph the men had had taken before leaving.

The other man was not, after all, much different from her husband. They both gave orders: she followed. "If you tell your family, I'll beat you. I'll kill you. Be here again next week." No one talked sex, ever. And she might have separated the rapes from the rest of living if only she did not have to buy her oil from him or gather wood in the same forest. I want her fear to have lasted just as long as rape lasted so that the fear could have been contained. No drawn-out fear. But women at sex hazarded birth and hence lifetimes. The fear did not stop but permeated everywhere. She told the man, "I think I'm pregnant." He organized the raid against her.

On nights when my mother and father talked about their life back home, sometimes they mentioned an "outcast table" whose business they still seemed to be settling, their voices tight. In a commensal tradition, where food is precious, the powerful older people made wrongdoers eat alone. Instead of letting them start separate new lives like the Japanese, who could become samurais and geishas, the Chinese family, faces averted but eyes glowering sideways, hung on to the offenders and fed them leftovers. My aunt must have lived in the same house as my parents and eaten at an outcast table. My mother spoke about the raid as if she had seen it, when she and my aunt, a daughter-in-law to a different household, should not have been living together at all. Daughters-in-law lived with their husbands' parents, not their own; a synonym for marriage in Chinese is "taking a daughter-in-law." Her husband's parents could have sold her, mortgaged her, stoned her. But they had sent her back to her own mother and father, a mysterious act hinting at disgraces not told me. Perhaps they had thrown her out to deflect the avengers.

She was the only daughter; her four brothers went with her father, husband, and uncles "out on the road" and for some years became western men. When the goods were divided among the family, three of the brothers took land, and the youngest, my father, chose an education. After my grandparents gave their daughter away to her husband's family, they had dispensed all the adventure and all the property. They expected her alone to keep the traditional ways, which her brothers, now among the barbarians, could fumble without detection. The heavy, deep-rooted women were to maintain the past against the flood, safe for returning. But the rare urge west had fixed upon our family, and so my aunt crossed boundaries not delineated in space.

The work of preservation demands that the feelings playing about in one's guts not be turned into action. Just watch their passing like cherry blossoms. But perhaps my aunt, my forerunner, caught in a slow life, let dreams grow and fade and after some months or years went toward what persisted. Fear at the enormities of the forbidden kept her desires delicate, wire and bone. She looked at a man because she liked the way the hair was tucked behind his ears, or she liked the question-mark line of the long torso curving at the shoulder and straight at the hip. For warm eyes or a soft voice or a slow walk—that's all—a few hairs, a line, a brightness, a sound, a pace she gave up family. She offered us up for a charm that vanished with tiredness, a pigtail that didn't toss when the wind died. Why, the wrong lighting could erase the dearest thing about him.

It could very well have been, however, that my aunt did not take subtle enjoyment of her friend, but, a wild woman, kept rollicking company. Imagining her free with sex doesn't fit, though. I don't know any woman like that, or men either. Unless I see her life branching into mine, she gives me no ancestral help.

To sustain her being in love, she often worked at herself in the mirror, guessing at the colors and shapes that would interest him, changing them frequently in order to hit on the right combination. She wanted him to look back.

On a farm near the sea, a woman who tended her appearance reaped a reputation for eccentricity. All the married women blunt-cut their hair in flaps about their ears or pulled it back in tight buns. No nonsense. Neither style blew easily into heart-catching tangles. And at their weddings they displayed themselves in their long hair for the last time. "It brushed the backs of my knees," my mother tells us. "It was braided, and even so, it brushed the backs of my knees."

At the mirror my aunt combed individuality into her bob. A bun could have been contrived to escape the black streamers blowing in the wind or in quiet wisps about her face, but only the older women in our picture album wear buns. She brushed her hair back from her forehead, tucking the flaps behind her ears. She looped a piece of thread, knotted in a circle between her index fingers and thumbs, and ran the double strand across her forehead. When she closed her fingers as if she were making a pair of shadow geese bite, the string twisted together catching the little hairs. Then she pulled the thread away from her skin, ripping the hairs out neatly, her eyes watering from the needles of pain. Opening her fingers, she cleaned the thread, then rolled it along her hairline and the tops of her eyebrows. My mother did the same to me and my sisters and herself. I used to believe that the expression "caught by the short hairs" meant a captive held with a depilatory string. It especially hurt at the temples, but my mother said we were lucky we didn't have to have our feet bound when we were seven. Sisters used to sit on their beds and cry together, she said, as their mothers or their slaves removed the bandages for a few minutes each night and let the blood gush back into their veins. I hope that the man my aunt loved appreciated a smooth brow, that he wasn't just a tits-and-ass man.

Once my aunt found a freckle on her chin, at a spot that the almanac said predestined her for unhappiness. She dug it out with a hot needle and washed the wound with peroxide.

More attention to her looks than these pulling of hairs and pickings at spots would have caused gossip among the villagers. They owned work clothes and good clothes, and they wore good clothes for feasting the new seasons. But since a woman combing her hair hexes beginnings, my aunt rarely found an occasion to look her best. Women looked like great sea snails—the corded wood, babies, and laundry they carried were the whorls on their backs. The Chinese did not admire a bent back; goddesses and warriors stood straight. Still there must have been a marvelous freeing of beauty when a worker laid down her burden and stretched and arched.

Such commonplace loveliness, however, was not enough for my aunt. She dreamed of a lover for the fifteen days of New Year's, the time for families to exchange visits, money, and food. She plied her secret comb. And sure enough she cursed the year, the family, the village, and herself.

Even as her hair lured her imminent lover, many other men looked at her. Uncles, cousins, nephews, brothers would have looked, too, had they been home between journeys. Perhaps they had already been restraining their curiosity, and they left, fearful that their glances, like a field of nesting birds, might be startled and caught. Poverty hurt, and that was their first reason for leaving. But another, final reason for leaving the crowded house was the never-said.

She may have been unusually beloved, the precious only daughter, spoiled and mirror gazing because of the affection the family lavished on her. When her husband left, they welcomed the chance to take her back from the in-laws; she could live like the little daughter for just a while longer. There are stories that my grandfather was different from other people, "crazy ever since the little Jap bayoneted him in the head." He used to put his naked penis on the dinner table, laughing. And one day he brought home a baby girl, wrapped up inside his brown western-style greatcoat. He had traded one of his sons, probably my father, the youngest, for her. My grandmother made him trade back. When he finally got a daughter of his own, he doted on her. They must have all loved her, except perhaps my father, the only brother who never went back to China, having once been traded for a girl.

Brothers and sisters, newly men and women, had to efface their sexual color and present plain miens. Disturbing hair and eyes, a smile like no other threatened the ideal of five generations living under one roof. To focus blurs, people shouted face to face and yelled from room to room. The immigrants I know have loud voices, unmodulated to American tones even after years away from the village where they called their friendships out across the fields. I have not been able to stop my mother's screams in public libraries or over telephones. Walking erect (knees straight, toes pointed forward, not pigeon-toed, which is Chinese-feminine) and speaking in an inaudible voice, I have tried to turn myself American-feminine. Chinese communication was loud, public. Only sick people had to whisper. But at the dinner table, where the family members came nearest one another, no one could talk, not the outcasts nor any eaters. Every word that falls from the mouth is a coin lost. Silently they gave and accepted food with both hands. A preoccupied child who took his bowl with one hand got a sideways glare. A complete moment of total attention is due everyone alike. Children and lovers have no singularity here, but my aunt used a secret voice, a separate attentiveness.

She kept the man's name to herself throughout her labor and dying; she did not accuse him that he be punished with her. To save her inseminator's name she gave silent birth.

He may have been somebody in her own household, but intercourse with a man outside the family would have been no less abhorrent. All the village were kinsmen, and the titles shouted in loud country voices never let kinship be forgotten. Any man within visiting distance would have been neutralized as a lover—"brother," "younger brother," "older brother"—one hundred and fifteen relationship titles. Parents researched birth charts probably not so much to assure good fortune as to circumvent incest in a population that has but one hundred surnames. Everybody has eight million relatives. How useless then sexual mannerisms, how dangerous.

As it came from an atavism deeper than fear, I used to add "brother" silently to boys' names. It hexed the boys, who would or would not ask me to dance, and made them less scary and as familiar and deserving of benevolence as girls.

But, of course, I hexed myself also—no dates. I should have stood up, both arms waving, and shouted out across libraries, "Hey, you! Love me back." I had no idea, though, how to make attraction selective, how to control its direction and magnitude. If I made myself American-pretty so that the five or six Chinese boys in the class fell in love with me, everyone else—the Caucasian, Negro, and Japanese boys—would too. Sisterliness, dignified and honorable, made much more sense.

Attraction eludes control so stubbornly that whole societies designed to organize relationships among people cannot keep order, not even when they bind people to one another from childhood and raise them together. Among the very poor and the wealthy, brothers married their adopted sisters, like doves. Our family allowed some romance, paying adult brides' prices and providing dowries so that their sons and daughters could marry strangers. Marriage promises to turn strangers into friendly relatives—a nation of siblings.

In the village structure, spirits shimmered among the live creatures, balanced and held in equilibrium by time and land. But one human being flaring up into violence could open up a black hole, a maelstrom that pulled in the sky. The frightened villagers, who depended on one another to maintain the real, went to my aunt to show her a personal, physical representation of the break she had made in the "roundness." Misallying couples snapped off the future, which was to be embodied in true offspring. The villagers punished her for acting as if she could have a private life, secret and apart from them.

If my aunt betrayed the family at a time of large grain yields and peace, when many boys were born, and wings were being built on many houses, perhaps she might have escaped such severe punishment. But the men—hungry, greedy, tired of planting in dry soil, cuckolded—had had to leave the village in order to send food-money home. There were ghost plagues, bandit plagues, wars with the Japanese, floods. My Chinese brother and sister had died of an unknown sickness. Adultery, perhaps only a mistake during good times, became a crime when the village needed food.

The round moon cakes and round doorways, the round tables of graduated size that fit one roundness inside another, round windows and rice bowls—these talismen had lost their power to warn this family of the law: a family must be whole, faithfully keeping the descent line by having sons to feed the old and the dead, who in turn look after the family. The villagers came to show my aunt and her lover-in-hiding a broken house. The villagers were speeding up the circling of events because she was too shortsighted to see that her infidelity had already harmed the village, that waves of consequences would return unpredictably, sometimes in disguise, as now, to hurt her. This roundness had to be made coin-sized so that she would see its circumference: punish her at the birth of her baby. Awaken her to the inexorable. People who refused fatalism because they could invent small resources insisted on culpability. Deny accidents and wrest fault from the stars.

After the villagers left, their lanterns now scattering in various directions toward home, the family broke their silence and cursed her. "Aiaa, we're going to die. Death is coming. Death is coming. Look what you've done. You've killed us. Ghost! Dead ghost! Ghost! You've never been born." She ran out into the fields, far enough from the house so that she could no longer hear their voices, and pressed herself against the earth, her own land no more. When she felt the birth coming, she thought that she had been hurt. Her body seized together. "They've hurt me too much," she thought. "This is gall, and it will kill me." Her forehead and knees against the earth, her body convulsed and then released her onto her back. The black well of sky and stars went out and out and out forever; her body and her complexity seemed to disappear. She was one of the stars, a bright dot in the blackness, without home, without a companion, in eternal cold and silence. An agoraphobia rose in her, speeding higher and higher, bigger and bigger; she would not be able to contain it; there would be no end to fear.

Flayed, unprotected against space, she felt pain return, focusing her body. This pain chilled her—a cold, steady kind of surface pain. Inside, spasmodically, the other pain, the pain of the child, heated her. For hours she lay on the ground, alternately body and space. Sometimes a vision of normal comfort obliterated reality: she saw the family in the evening gambling at the dinner table, the young people massaging their elders' backs. She saw them congratulating one another, high joy on the mornings the rice shoots came up. When these pictures burst, the stars drew yet further apart. Black space opened.

She got to her feet to fight better and remembered that old-fashioned women gave birth in their pigsties to fool the jealous, pain-dealing gods, who do not snatch piglets. Before the next spasms could stop her, she ran to the pigsty, each step a rushing out into emptiness. She climbed over the fence and knelt in the dirt. It was good to have a fence enclosing her, a tribal person alone.

Laboring, this woman who had carried a child as a foreign growth that sickened her every day, expelled it at last. She reached down to touch the hot, wet, moving mass, surely smaller than anything human, and could feel that it was human after all—fingers, toes, nails, nose. She pulled it up on to her belly, and it lay curled there, butt in the air, feet precisely tucked one under the other. She opened her loose shirt and buttoned the child inside. After resting, it squirmed and thrashed and she pushed it up to her breast. It turned its head this way and that until it found her nipple. There, it made little snuffling noises. She clenched her teeth at its preciousness, lovely as a young calf, a piglet, a little dog.

She may have gone to the pigsty as a last act of responsibility: she would protect this child as she had protected its father. It would look after her soul, leaving supplies on her grave. But how would this tiny child without family find her grave when there would be no marker for her anywhere, neither in the earth nor the family hall? No one would give her a family hall name. She had taken the child with her into the wastes. At its birth the two of them had felt the same raw pain of separation, a wound that only the family pressing tight could close. A child with no descent line would not soften her life but only trail after her, ghostlike, begging her to give it purpose. At dawn the villagers on their way to the fields would stand around the fence and look.

Full of milk, the little ghost slept. When it awoke, she hardened her breasts against the milk that crying loosens. Toward morning she picked up the baby and walked to the well.

Carrying the baby to the well shows loving. Otherwise abandon it. Turn its face into the mud. Mothers who love their children take them along. It was probably a girl; there is some hope of forgiveness for boys.

"Don't tell anyone you had an aunt. Your father does not want to hear her name. She has never been born." I have believed that sex was unspeakable and words so strong and fathers so frail that "aunt" would do my father mysterious harm. I have thought that my family, having settled among immigrants who had also been their neighbors in the ancestral land, needed to clean their name, and a wrong word would incite the kinspeople even here. But there is more to this silence: they want me to participate in her punishment. And I have.

In the twenty years since I heard this story I have not asked for details nor said my aunt's name; I do not know it. People who can comfort the dead can also chase after them to hurt them further—a reverse ancestor worship. The real punishment was not the raid swiftly inflicted by the villagers, but the family's deliberately forgetting her. Her betrayal so maddened them, they saw to it that she would suffer forever, even after death. Always hungry, always needing, she would have to beg food from other ghosts, snatch and steal it from those whose living descendants give them gifts. She would have to fight the ghosts massed at crossroads for the buns a few thoughtful citizens leave to decoy her away from village and home so that the ancestral spirits could feast unharassed. At peace, they could act like gods, not ghosts, their descent lines providing them with paper suits and dresses, spirit money, paper houses, paper automobiles, chicken, meat, and rice into eternity—essences delivered up in smoke and flames, steam and incense rising from each rice bowl. In an attempt to make the Chinese care for people outside the family, Chairman Mao encourages us now to give our paper replicas to the spirits of outstanding soldiers and workers, no matter whose ancestors they may be. My aunt remains forever hungry. Goods are not distributed evenly among the dead.

My aunt haunts me—her ghost drawn to me because now, after fifty years of neglect, I alone devote pages of paper to her, though not origamied into houses and clothes. I do not think she always means me well. I am telling on her, and she was a spite suicide, drowning herself in the drinking water. The Chinese are always very frightened of the drowned one, whose weeping ghost, wet hair hanging and skin bloated, waits silently by the water to pull down a substitute.

QUESTIONS FOR DISCUSSION AND WRITING

1. "No Name Woman" begins: " 'You must not tell anyone,' my mother said, 'what I am about to tell you.' " How does this opening affect the way we read the story?

2. Analyze the structure of "No Name Woman." Does it have a plot in the ordinary sense? Notice that it begins with the mother's brief account of the aunt's suicide, then continues with an essayistic commentary on the themes of the aunt's story, and ends with a fuller, more imaginative retelling of the aunt's story. Is the "plot" the story of the aunt or Maxine Hong Kingston's confronting and coming to terms with this forbidden story?

3. "Chinese-Americans," Kingston writes, "when you try to understand what things in you are Chinese, how do you separate what is peculiar to childhood, to poverty, insanities, one family, your mother who marked your growing with stories, from what is Chinese? What is Chinese and what is the movies?" Could it be said that this passage articulates the action of "No Name Woman"? Is Kingston trying to define her ethnic identity as opposed to idiosyncratic family characteristics, to differentiate between "Chinese tradition" and "the movies"? Go through the story, identifying what Kingston seems to decide is "Chinese tradition."

Bharati Mukherjee

Bharati Mukherjee (b. 1940) was born and educated in Calcutta. She came to the United States in 1961 and studied at the University of Iowa Writer's Workshop, ultimately earning a Ph.D. Her first novel was *The Tiger's Daughter* (1971); her other novels are *Wife* (1975) and *Jasmine* (1989). She has published two short-story collections: *Darkness* (1985) and *The Middleman and Other Stories* (1988), the latter of which won the National Book Critics Circle Award. Mukherjee teaches creative writing at Columbia University and the City University of New York.

THE MANAGEMENT OF GRIEF

A woman I don't know is boiling tea the Indian way in my kitchen. There are a lot of women I don't know in my kitchen, whispering and moving tactfully. They open doors, rummage through the pantry, and try not to ask me where things are kept. They remind me of when my sons were small, on Mother's Day or when Vikram and I were tired, and they would make big, sloppy omelets. I would lie in bed pretending I didn't hear them.

Dr. Sharma, the treasurer of the Indo-Canada Society, pulls me into the hallway. He wants to know if I am worried about money. His wife, who has just come up from the basement with a tray of empty cups and glasses, scolds him, "Don't bother Mrs. Bhave with mundane details." She looks so monstrously pregnant her baby must be days overdue. I tell her she shouldn't be carrying heavy things. "Shaila," she says, smiling, "this is the fifth." Then she grabs a teenager by his shirttails. He slips his Walkman off his head. He has to be one of her four children; they have the same domed and dented foreheads. "What's the official word now?" she demands. The boy slips the headphones back on. "They're acting evasive, Ma. They're saying it could be an accident or a terrorist bomb."

All morning, the boys have been muttering, Sikh bomb, Sikh bomb. The men, not using the word, bow their heads in agreement. Mrs. Sharma touches her forehead at such a word. At least they've stopped talking about space debris and Russian lasers.

Two radios are going in the dining room. They are tuned to different stations. Someone must have brought the radios down from my boys' bedrooms. I haven't gone into their rooms since Kusum came running across the front lawn in her bathrobe. She looked so funny, I was laughing when I opened the door.

The big TV in the den is being whizzed through American networks and cable channels.

"Damn!" some man swears bitterly. "How can these preachers carry on like nothing's happened?" I want to tell him we're not that important. You look at the audience, and at the preacher in his blue robe with his beautiful white hair, the potted palm trees under a blue sky, and you know they care about nothing.

The phone rings and rings. Dr. Sharma's taken charge. "We're with her," he keeps saying, "Yes, yes, the doctor has given calming pills. Yes, yes, pills are having necessary effect." I wonder if pills alone explain this calm. Not peace, just a deadening quiet. I was always controlled, but never repressed. Sound can reach me, but my body is tensed, ready to scream. I hear their voices all around me. I hear my boys and Vikram cry, "Mommy, Shaila!" and their screams insulate me, like headphones.

The woman boiling water tells her story again and again. "I got the news first. My cousin from Halifax before six A.M., can you imagine? He'd gotten up for prayers and his son was studying for medical exams and he heard on a rock channel that something had happened to a plane. They said first it had disappeared from the radar, like a giant eraser just reached out. His father called me, so I said to him, what do you mean, 'something bad'? You mean a hijacking? And he said, *Behn,* there is no confirmation of anything yet, but check with your neighbors because a lot of them must be on that plane. So I called poor Kusum straight-away. I knew Kusum's husband and daughter were booked to go yesterday."

Kusum lives across the street from me. She and Satish had moved in less than a month ago. They said they needed a bigger place. All these people, the Sharmas and friends from Indo-Canada Society, had been there for the housewarming. Satish and Kusum made tandoori on their big gas grill and even the white neighbors piled their plates high with that luridly red, charred, juicy chicken. Their younger daughter had danced, and even our boys had broken away from the Stanley Cup telecast to put in a reluctant appearance. Everyone took pictures for their albums and for the community newspapers—another of our families had made it big in Toronto—and now I wonder how many of those happy faces are gone. "Why does God give us so much if all along He intends to take it away?" Kusum asks me.

I nod. We sit on carpeted stairs, holding hands like children. "I never once told him that I loved him," I say. I was too much the well-brought-up woman. I was so well brought up I never felt comfortable calling my husband by his first name.

"It's all right," Kusum says. "He knew. My husband knew. They felt it. Modern young girls have to say it because what they feel is fake."

Kusum's daughter Pam runs in with an overnight case. Pam's in her McDonald's uniform. "Mummy! You have to get dressed!" Panic makes her cranky. "A reporter's on his way here."

"Why?"

"You want to talk in your bathrobe?" She starts to brush her mother's long hair. She's the daughter who's always in trouble. She dates Canadian boys and hangs out in the mall, shopping for tight sweaters. The younger one, the goody-goody one according to Pam, the one with a voice so sweet that when she sang *bhajans* for Ethiopian relief even a frugal man like my husband wrote out a hundred-dollar check, *she* was on that plane. *She* was going to spend July and August with grandparents because Pam wouldn't go. Pam said she'd rather waitress at McDonald's. "If it's a choice between Bombay and Wonderland, I'm picking Wonderland," she'd said.

"Leave me alone," Kusum yells. "You know what I want to do? If I didn't have to look after you now, I'd hang myself."

Pam's young face goes blotchy with pain. "Thanks," she says, "don't let me stop you."

"Hush," pregnant Mrs. Sharma scolds Pam. "Leave your mother alone. Mr. Sharma will tackle the reporters and fill out the forms. He'll say what has to be said."

Pam stands her ground. "You think I don't know what Mummy's thinking? *Why her?* That's what. That's sick! Mummy wishes my little sister were alive and I were dead."

Kusum's hand in mine is trembly hot. We continue to sit on the stairs.

*   *   *

She calls before she arrives, wondering if there's anything I need. Her name is Judith Templeton and she's an appointee of the provincial government. "Multi-culturalism?" I ask, and she says "partially," but that her mandate is bigger. "I've been told you knew many of the people on the flight," she says. "Perhaps if you'd agree to help us reach the others . . . ?"

She gives me time at least to put on tea water and pick up the mess in the front room. I have a few *samosas* from Kusum's housewarming that I could fry up, but then I think, why prolong this visit?

Judith Templeton is much younger than she sounded. She wears a blue suit with a white blouse and a polka-dot tie. Her blond hair is cut short, her only jewelry is pearl-drop earrings. Her briefcase is new and expensive looking, a gleaming cordovan leather. She sits with it across her lap. When she looks out the front windows onto the street, her contact lenses seem to float in front of her light blue eyes.

"What sort of help do you want from me?" I ask. She has refused the tea, out of politeness, but I insist, along with some slightly stale biscuits.

"I have no experience," she admits. "That is, I have an M.S.W. and I've worked in liaison with accident victims, but I mean I have no experience with a tragedy of this scale—"

"Who could?" I ask.

"—and with the complications of culture, language, and customs. Someone mentioned that Mrs. Bhave is a pillar—because you've taken it more calmly."

At this, perhaps, I frown, for she reaches forward, almost to take my hand. "I hope you understand my meaning, Mrs. Bhave. There are hundreds of people in Metro directly affected, like you, and some of them speak no English. There are some widows who've never handled money or gone on a bus, and there are old parents who still haven't eaten or gone outside their bedrooms. Some houses and apartments have been looted. Some wives are still hysterical. Some husbands are in shock and profound depression. We want to help, but our hands are tied in so many ways. We have to distribute money to some people, and there are legal documents—these things can be done. We have interpreters, but we don't always have the human touch, or maybe the right human touch. We don't want to make mistakes, Mrs. Bhave, and that's why we'd like to ask you to help us."

"More mistakes, you mean," I say.

"Police matters are not in my hands," she answers.

"Nothing I can do will make any difference," I say. "We must all grieve in our own way."

"But you are coping very well. All the people said, Mrs. Bhave is the strongest person of all. Perhaps if the others could see you, talk with you, it would help them."

"By the standards of the people you call hysterical, I am behaving very oddly and badly, Miss Templeton." I want to say to her, *I wish I could scream, starve, walk into Lake Ontario, jump from a bridge.* "They would not see me as a model. I do not see myself as a model."

I am a freak. No one who has ever known me would think of me reacting this way. This terrible calm will not go away.

She asks me if she may call again, after I get back from a long trip that we all must make. "Of course," I say. "Feel free to call, anytime."

Four days later, I find Kusum squatting on a rock overlooking a bay in Ireland. It isn't a big rock, but it juts sharply out over water. This is as close as we'll ever get to them. June breezes balloon out her sari and unpin her knee-length hair. She has the bewildered look of a sea creature whom the tides have stranded.

It's been one hundred hours since Kusum came stumbling and screaming across my lawn. Waiting around the hospital, we've heard many stories. The police, the diplomats, they tell us things thinking that we're strong, that knowledge is helpful to the grieving, and maybe it is. Some, I know, prefer ignorance, or their own versions. The plane broke in two, they say. Unconsciousness was instantaneous. No one suffered. My boys must have just finished their breakfasts. They loved eating on planes, they loved the smallness of the plates, knives, and forks. Last year they saved the airline salt and pepper shakers. Half an hour more and they would have made it to Heathrow.

Kusum says that we can't escape our fate. She says that all those people—our husbands, my boys, her girl with the nightingale voice, all those Hindus, Christians, Sikhs, Muslims, Parsis, and the atheists on that plane—were fated to die together off this beautiful bay. She learned this from a swami in Toronto.

I have my Valium.

Six of us "relatives"—two widows and four widowers—chose to spend the day today by the waters instead of sitting in a hospital room and scanning photographs of the dead. That's what they call us now: relatives. I've looked through twenty-seven photos in two days. They're very kind to us, the Irish are very understanding. Sometimes understanding means freeing a tourist bus for this trip to the bay, so we can pretend to spy our loved ones through the glassiness of waves or in sun-speckled cloud shapes.

I could die here, too, and be content.

"What is that, out there?" She's standing and flapping her hands, and for a moment I see a head shape bobbing in the waves. She's standing in the water, I on the boulder. The tide is low, and a round, black, head-sized rock has just risen from the waves. She returns, her sari end dripping and ruined, and her face is a twisted remnant of hope, the way mine was a hundred hours ago, still laughing but inwardly knowing that nothing but the ultimate tragedy could bring two women together at six o'clock on a Sunday morning. I watch her face sag into blankness.

"That water felt warm, Shaila," she says at length.

"You can't," I say. "We have to wait for our turn to come."

I haven't eaten in four days, haven't brushed my teeth.

"I know," she says. "I tell myself I have no right to grieve. They are in a better place than we are. My swami says depression is a sign of our selfishness."

Maybe I'm selfish. Selfishly I break away from Kusum and run, sandals slapping against stones, to the water's edge. What if my boys aren't lying pinned under the debris? What if they aren't stuck a mile below that innocent blue chop? What if, given the strong currents . . .

Now I've ruined my sari, one of my best. Kusum has joined me, knee deep in water that feels to me like a swimming pool. I could settle in the water, and my husband would take my hand and the boys would slap water in my face just to see me scream.

"Do you remember what good swimmers my boys were, Kusum?"

"I saw the medals," she says.

One of the widowers, Dr. Ranganathan from Montreal, walks out to us, carrying his shoes in one hand. He's an electrical engineer. Someone at the hotel mentioned his work is famous around the world, something about the place where physics and electricity come together. He has lost a huge family, something indescribable. "With some luck," Dr. Ranganathan suggests to me, "a good swim-

mer could make it safely to some island. It is quite possible that there may be
many, many microscopic islets scattered around."

"You're not just saying that?" I tell Dr. Ranganathan about Vinod, my elder son.
Last year he took diving as well.

"It's a parent's duty to hope," he says. "It is foolish to rule out possibilities that
have not been tested. I myself have not surrendered hope."

Kusum is sobbing once again. "Dear lady," he says, laying his free hand on her
arm, and she calms down.

"Vinod is how old?" he asks me. He's very careful, as we all are. *Is*, not was.

"Fourteen. Yesterday he was fourteen. His father and uncle were going to take
him down to the Taj and give him a big birthday party. I couldn't go with them
because I couldn't get two weeks off from my stupid job in June." I process bills
for a travel agent. June is a big travel month.

Dr. Ranganathan whips the pockets of his suit jacket inside out. Squashed roses,
in darkening shades of pink, float on the water. He tore the roses off creepers in
somebody's garden. He didn't ask anyone if he could pluck the roses, but now
there's an article about it in the local papers. When you see an Indian person, it
says, please give them flowers.

"A strong youth of fourteen," he says, "can very likely pull to safety a younger
one."

My sons, though four years apart, were very close. Vinod wouldn't let Mithun
drown. *Electrical engineering*, I think, foolishly perhaps: this man knows important
secrets of the universe, things closed to me. Relief spins me lightheaded. No
wonder my boys' photographs haven't turned up in the gallery of photos of the
recovered dead. "Such pretty roses," I say.

"My wife loved pink roses. Every Friday I had to bring a bunch home. I used to
say, Why? After twenty-odd years of marriage you're still needing proof positive of
my love?" He has identified his wife and three of his children. Then others from
Montreal, the lucky ones, intact families with no survivors. He chuckles as he
wades back to shore. Then he swings around to ask me a question. "Mrs. Bhave,
you are wanting to throw in some roses for your loved ones? I have two big ones
left."

But I have other things to float: Vinod's pocket calculator; a half-painted model
B-52 for my Mithun. They'd want them on their island. And for my husband? For
him I let fall into the calm, glassy waters a poem I wrote in the hospital yesterday.
Finally he'll know my feelings for him.

"Don't tumble, the rocks are slippery," Dr. Ranganathan cautions. He holds
out a hand for me to grab.

Then it's time to get back on the bus, time to rush back to our waiting posts on
hospital benches.

Kusum is one of the lucky ones. The lucky ones flew here, identified in multipli-
cate their loved ones, then will fly to India with the bodies for proper ceremonies.
Satish is one of the few males who surfaced. The photos of faces we saw on the
walls in an office at Heathrow and here in the hospital are mostly of women.
Women have more body fat, a nun said to me matter-of-factly. They float better.

Today I was stopped by a young sailor on the street. He had loaded bodies, he'd
gone into the water when—he checks my face for signs of strength—when the
sharks were first spotted. I don't blush, and he breaks down. "It's all right," I say.
"Thank you." I heard about the sharks from Dr. Ranganathan. In his orderly

mind, science brings understanding, it holds no terror. It is the shark's duty. For every deer there is a hunter, for every fish a fisherman.

The Irish are not shy; they rush to me and give me hugs and some are crying. I cannot imagine reactions like that on the streets of Toronto. Just strangers, and I am touched. Some carry flowers with them and give them to any Indian they see.

After lunch, a policeman I have gotten to know quite well catches hold of me. He says he thinks he has a match for Vinod. I explain what a good swimmer Vinod is.

"You want me with you when you look at photos?" Dr. Ranganathan walks ahead of me into the picture gallery. In these matters, he is a scientist, and I am grateful. It is a new perspective. "They have performed miracles," he says. "We are indebted to them."

The first day or two the policemen showed us relatives only one picture at a time; now they're in a hurry, they're eager to lay out the possibilities, and even the probables.

The face on the photo is of a boy much like Vinod; the same intelligent eyes, the same thick brows dipping into a V. But this boy's features, even his cheeks, are puffier, wider, mushier.

"No." My gaze is pulled by other pictures. There are five other boys who look like Vinod.

The nun assigned to console me rubs the first picture with a fingertip. "When they've been in the water for a while, love, they look a little heavier." The bones under the skin are broken, they said on the first day—try to adjust your memories. It's important.

"It's not him. I'm his mother. I'd know."

"I know this one!" Dr. Ranganathan cries out, and suddenly, from the back of the gallery, "And this one!" I think he senses that I don't want to find my boys. "They are the Kutty brothers. They were also from Montreal." I don't mean to be crying. On the contrary, I am ecstatic. My suitcase in the hotel is packed heavy with dry clothes for my boys.

The policeman starts to cry. "I am so sorry, I am so sorry, ma'am. I really thought we had a match."

With the nun ahead of us and the policeman behind, we, the unlucky ones without their children's bodies, file out of the makeshift gallery.

From Ireland most of us go to India. Kusum and I take the same direct flight to Bombay, so I can help her clear customs quickly. But we have to argue with a man in uniform. He has large boils on his face. The boils swell and grow with sweat as we argue with him. He wants Kusum to wait in line and he refuses to take authority because his boss is on a tea break. But Kusum won't let her coffins out of sight, and I shan't desert her though I know that my parents, elderly and diabetic, must be waiting in a stuffy car in a scorching lot.

"You bastard!" I scream at the man with the popping boils. Other passengers press closer. "You think we're smuggling contraband in those coffins!"

Once upon a time we were well-brought-up women; we were dutiful wives who kept our heads veiled, our voices shy and sweet.

In India, I become, once again, an only child of rich, ailing parents. Old friends of the family come to pay their respects. Some are Sikh, and inwardly, involuntarily, I cringe. My parents are progressive people; they do not blame communities for a few individuals.

In Canada it is a different story now.

"Stay longer," my mother pleads. "Canada is a cold place. Why would you want to be by yourself?" I stay.

Three months pass. Then another.

"Vikram wouldn't have wanted you to give up things!" they protest. They call my husband by the name he was born with. In Toronto he'd changed to Vik so the men he worked with at his office would find his name as easy as Rod or Chris. "You know, the dead aren't cut off from us!"

My grandmother, the spoiled daughter of a rich zamindar, shaved her head with rusty razor blades when she was widowed at sixteen. My grandfather died of childhood diabetes when he was nineteen, and she saw herself as the harbinger of bad luck. My mother grew up without parents, raised indifferently by an uncle, while her true mother slept in a hut behind the main estate house and took her food with the servants. She grew up a rationalist. My parents abhor mindless mortification.

The zamindar's daughter kept stubborn faith in Vedic rituals; my parents rebelled. I am trapped between two modes of knowledge. At thirty-six, I am too old to start over and too young to give up. Like my husband's spirit, I flutter between worlds.

Courting aphasia, we travel. We travel with our phalanx of servants and poor relatives. To hill stations and to beach resorts. We play contract bridge in dusty gymkhana clubs. We ride stubby ponies up crumbly mountain trails. At tea dances, we let ourselves be twirled twice round the ballroom. We hit the holy spots we hadn't made time for before. In Varanasi, Kalighat, Rishikesh, Hardwar, astrologers and palmists seek me out and for a fee offer me cosmic consolations.

Already the widowers among us are being shown new bride candidates. They cannot resist the call of custom, the authority of their parents and older brothers. They must marry; it is the duty of a man to look after a wife. The new wives will be young widows with children, destitute but of good family. They will make loving wives, but the men will shun them. I've had calls from the men over crackling Indian telephone lines. "Save me," they say, these substantial, educated, successful men of forty. "My parents are arranging a marriage for me." In a month they will have buried one family and returned to Canada with a new bride and partial family.

I am comparatively lucky. No one here thinks of arranging a husband for an unlucky widow.

Then, on the third day of the sixth month into this odyssey, in an abandoned temple in a tiny Himalayan village, as I make my offering of flowers and sweetmeats to the god of a tribe of animists, my husband descends to me. He is squatting next to a scrawny sadhu in moth-eaten robes. Vikram wears the vanilla suit he wore the last time I hugged him. The sadhu tosses petals on a butter-fed flame, reciting Sanskrit mantras, and sweeps his face of flies. My husband takes my hand in his.

You're beautiful, he starts. Then, *What are you doing here?*

Shall I stay? I ask. He only smiles, but already the image is fading. *You must finish alone what we started together.* No seaweed wreathes his mouth. He speaks too fast, just as he used to when we were an envied family in our pink split-level. He is gone.

In the windowless altar room, smoky with joss sticks and clarified butter lamps, a sweaty hand gropes for my blouse. I do not shriek. The sadhu arranges his robe. The lamps hiss and sputter out.

When we come out of the temple, my mother says, "Did you feel something weird in there?"

My mother has no patience with ghosts, prophetic dreams, holy men, and cults. "No," I lie. "Nothing."

But she knows that she's lost me. She knows that in days I shall be leaving.

Kusum's put up her house for sale. She wants to live in an ashram in Hardwar. Moving to Hardwar was her swami's idea. Her swami runs two ashrams, the one in Hardwar and another here in Toronto.

"Don't run away," I tell her.

"I'm not running away," she says. "I'm pursuing inner peace. You think you or that Ranganathan fellow are better off?"

Pam's left for California. She wants to do some modeling, she says. She says when she comes into her share of the insurance money she'll open a yoga-cum-aerobics studio in Hollywood. She sends me postcards so naughty I daren't leave them on the coffee table. Her mother has withdrawn from her and the world.

The rest of us don't lose touch, that's the point. Talk is all we have, says Dr. Ranganathan, who has also resisted his relatives and returned to Montreal and to his job, alone. He says, Whom better to talk with than other relatives? We've been melted down and recast as a new tribe.

He calls me twice a week from Montreal. Every Wednesday night and every Saturday afternoon. He is changing jobs, going to Ottawa. But Ottawa is over a hundred miles away, and he is forced to drive two hundred and twenty miles a day from his home in Montreal. He can't bring himself to sell his house. The house is a temple, he says; the king-sized bed in the master bedroom is a shrine. He sleeps on a folding cot. A devotee.

There are still some hysterical relatives. Judith Templeton's list of those needing help and those who've "accepted" is in nearly perfect balance. Acceptance means you speak of your family in the past tense and you make active plans for moving ahead with your life. There are courses at Seneca and Ryerson we could be taking. Her gleaming leather briefcase is full of college catalogues and lists of cultural societies that need our help. She has done impressive work, I tell her.

"In the textbooks on grief management," she replies—I am her confidante, I realize, one of the few whose grief has not sprung bizarre obsessions—"there are stages to pass through: rejection, depression, acceptance, reconstruction." She has compiled a chart and finds that six months after the tragedy, none of us still rejects reality, but only a handful are reconstructing. "Depressed acceptance" is the plateau we've reached. Remarriage is a major step in reconstruction (though she's a little surprised, even shocked, over *how* quickly some of the men have taken on new families). Selling one's house and changing jobs and cities is healthy.

How to tell Judith Templeton that my family surrounds me, and that like creatures in epics, they've changed shapes? She sees me as calm and accepting but worries that I have no job, no career. My closest friends are worse off than I. I cannot tell her my days, even my nights, are thrilling.

She asks me to help with families she can't reach at all. An elderly couple in Agincourt whose sons were killed just weeks after they had brought their parents over from a village in Punjab. From their names, I know they are Sikh. Judith Templeton and a translator have visited them twice with offers of money for airfare to Ireland, with bank forms, power-of-attorney forms, but they have refused to sign, or to leave their tiny apartment. Their sons' money is frozen in the bank. Their sons' investment apartments have been trashed by tenants, the furnishings sold off. The parents fear that anything they sign or any money they receive will end the company's or the country's obligations to them. They fear they are selling their sons for two airline tickets to a place they've never seen.

The high-rise apartment is a tower of Indians and West Indians, with a sprinkling of Orientals. The nearest bus-stop kiosk is lined with women in saris. Boys practice cricket in the parking lot. Inside the building, even I wince a bit from the ferocity of onion fumes, the distinctive and immediate Indianness of frying ghee, but Judith Templeton maintains a steady flow of information. These poor old people are in imminent danger of losing their place and all their services.

I say to her, "They are Sikh. They will not open up to a Hindu woman." And what I want to add is, as much as I try not to, I stiffen now at the sight of beards and turbans. I remember a time when we all trusted each other in this new country, it was only the new country we worried about.

The two rooms are dark and stuffy. The lights are off, and an oil lamp sputters on the coffee table. The bent old lady has let us in, and her husband is wrapping a white turban over his oiled, hip-length hair. She immediately goes to the kitchen, and I hear the most familiar sound of an Indian home, tap water hitting and filling a teapot.

They have not paid their utility bills, out of fear and inability to write a check. The telephone is gone; electricity and gas and water are soon to follow. They have told Judith their sons will provide. They are good boys, and they have always earned and looked after their parents.

We converse a bit in Hindi. They do not ask about the crash and I wonder if I should bring it up. If they think I am here merely as a translator, then they may feel insulted. There are thousands of Punjabi speakers, Sikhs, in Toronto to do a better job. And so I say to the old lady, "I too have lost my sons, and my husband, in the crash."

Her eyes immediately fill with tears. The man mutters a few words which sound like a blessing. "God provides and God takes away," he says.

I want to say, But only men destroy and give back nothing. "My boys and my husband are not coming back," I say. "We have to understand that."

Now the old woman responds. "But who is to say? Man alone does not decide these things." To this her husband adds his agreement.

Judith asks about the bank papers, the release forms. With a stroke of the pen, they will have a provincial trustee to pay their bills, invest their money, send them a monthly pension.

"Do you know this woman?" I ask them.

The man raises his hand from the table, turns it over, and seems to regard each finger separately before he answers. "This young lady is always coming here, we make tea for her, and she leaves papers for us to sign." His eyes scan a pile of papers in the corner of the room. "Soon we will be out of tea, then will she go away?"

The old lady adds, "I have asked my neighbors and no one else gets *angrezi* visitors. What have we done?"

"It's her job," I try to explain. "The government is worried. Soon you will have no place to stay, no lights, no gas, no water."

"Government will get its money. Tell her not to worry, we are honorable people."

I try to explain the government wishes to give money, not take. He raises his hand. "Let them take," he says. "We are accustomed to that. That is no problem."

"We are strong people," says his wife. "Tell her that."

"Who needs all this machinery?" demands the husband. "It is unhealthy, the bright lights, the cold air on a hot day, the cold food, the four gas rings. God will provide, not government."

"When our boys return," the mother says.

Her husband sucks his teeth. "Enough talk," he says.

Judith breaks in. "Have you convinced them?" The snaps on her cordovan briefcase go off like firecrackers in that quiet apartment. She lays the sheaf of legal papers on the coffee table. "If they can't write their names, an X will do—I've told them that."

Now the old lady has shuffled to the kitchen and soon emerges with a pot of tea and two cups. "I think my bladder will go first on a job like this," Judith says to me, smiling. "If only there was some way of reaching them. Please thank her for the tea. Tell her she's very kind."

I nod in Judith's direction and tell them in Hindi, "She thanks you for the tea. She thinks you are being very hospitable but she doesn't have the slightest idea what it means."

I want to say, Humor her. I want to say, My boys and my husband are with me too, more than ever. I look in the old man's eyes and I can read his stubborn, peasant message: *I have protected this woman as best I can. She is the only person I have left. Give to me or take from me what you will, but I will not sign for it. I will not pretend that I accept.*

In the car, Judith says, "You see what I'm up against? I'm sure they're lovely people, but their stubbornness and ignorance are driving me crazy. They think signing a paper is signing their sons' death warrants, don't they?"

I am looking out the window. I want to say, *In our culture, it is a parent's duty to hope.*

"Now Shaila, this next woman is a real mess. She cries day and night, and she refuses all medical help. We may have to—"

"Let me out at the subway," I say.

"I beg your pardon?" I can feel those blue eyes staring at me.

It would not be like her to disobey. She merely disapproves, and slows at a corner to let me out. Her voice is plaintive. "Is there anything I said? Anything I did?"

I could answer her suddenly in a dozen ways, but I choose not to. "Shaila? Let's talk about it," I hear, then slam the door.

A wife and mother begins her new life in a new country, and that life is cut short. Yet her husband tells her, Complete what we have started. We, who stayed out of politics and came halfway around the world to avoid religious and political feuding, have been the first in the New World to die from it. I no longer know what we started, nor how to complete it. I write letters to the editors of local papers and to members of Parliament. Now at least they admit it was a bomb. One MP answers back, with sympathy, but with a challenge. You want to make a difference? Work on a campaign. Work on mine. Politicize the Indian voter.

My husband's old lawyer helps me set up a trust. Vikram was a saver and a careful investor. He had saved the boys' boarding school and college fees. I sell the pink house at four times what we paid for it and take a small apartment downtown. I am looking for a charity to support.

We are deep in the Toronto winter, gray skies, icy pavements. I stay indoors, watching television. I have tried to assess my situation, how best to live my life, to complete what we began so many years ago. Kusum has written me from Hardwar that her life is now serene. She has seen Satish and has heard her daughter sing again. Kusum was on a pilgrimage, passing through a village, when she heard a young girl's voice, singing one of her daughter's favorite *bhajans*. She followed the music through the squalor of a Himalayan village, to a hut where a young girl, an exact replica of her daughter, was fanning coals under the kitchen fire. When she appeared, the girl cried out, "Ma!" and ran away. What did I think of that?

I think I can only envy her.

Pam didn't make it to California, but writes me from Vancouver. She works in a department store, giving makeup hints to Indian and Oriental girls. Dr. Ranganathan has given up his commute, given up his house and job, and accepted an academic position in Texas, where no one knows his story and he has vowed not to tell it. He calls me now once a week.

I wait, I listen and I pray, but Vikram has not returned to me. The voices and the shapes and the nights filled with visions ended abruptly several weeks ago.

I take it as a sign.

One rare, beautiful, sunny day last week, returning from a small errand on Yonge Street, I was walking through the park from the subway to my apartment. I live equidistant from the Ontario Houses of Parliament and the University of Toronto. The day was not cold, but something in the bare trees caught my attention. I looked up from the gravel, into the branches and the clear blue sky beyond. I thought I heard the rustling of larger forms, and I waited a moment for voices. Nothing.

"What?" I asked.

Then as I stood in the park looking north to Queen's Park and west to the university, I heard the voices of my family one last time. *Your time has come,* they said. *Go, be brave.*

I do not know where this voyage I have begun will end. I do not know which direction I will take. I dropped the package on a park bench and started walking.

QUESTIONS FOR DISCUSSION AND WRITING

1. Shaila Bhave, the narrator of "The Management of Grief," tells her story in the present tense. What is the effect of this use of the historical present?

2. How do the characters in the story manage their grief?

3. Shaila tells about her grandmother, who "kept stubborn faith in Vedic rituals," and her mother, who rebelled and "grew up a rationalist." Shaila

says of herself that she is "trapped between two modes of knowledge." What are the two modes for Shaila? Explore the theme of "fluttering between two worlds" in the story.

4. The plane crash is based upon an actual terrorist bombing. You might be interested in looking up newspaper accounts of the incident. Or, perhaps even better, you might construct an account of the Sikh–Hindu rivalry and the bombing on the basis of internal evidence in the story.

Simon J. Ortiz

Simon J. Ortiz (b. 1941) is a member of the Acoma Pueblo tribe. He was born in Albuquerque, New Mexico, and studied at Fort Lewis College, the University of New Mexico, and the University of Iowa. He has taught at a number of colleges and universities, including San Diego State University; Navajo Community College in Tsaile, New Mexico; the University of New Mexico; and Lewis and Clark College. Known primarily as a poet, he has published a number of collections of poems, including *Naked in the Wind* (1971), *Going for the Rain* (1976), *A Good Journey* (1977), and *From Sand Hill: Rising in This Heart Which Is Our America* (1981). But he is also an accomplished writer of fiction; his stories are collected in *Fightin': New and Collected Stories* (1983).

KAISER AND THE WAR

Kaiser got out of the state pen when I was in the fourth grade. I don't know why people called him Kaiser. Some called him Hitler too, since he was Kaiser, but I don't think he cared at all what they called him. He was probably just glad to get out of the state pen.

Kaiser got into the state pen because he didn't go into the army. That's what my father said anyway, and because he was a crazy nut, according to some people, which was probably why he didn't want to go into the army in the first place, which was what my father said also.

The army wanted him anyway, or maybe they didn't know he was crazy or supposed to be. They came for him out at home on the reservation, and he said he wasn't going to go because he didn't speak good English. Kaiser didn't go to school more than just the first or second grade. He said what he said in Indian and his sister said it in English for him. The army men, somebody from the county draft board, said they'd teach him English, don't worry about it, and how to read and write and give him clothes and money when he got out of the army so that he could start regular as any American. Just like anybody else, and they threw in stuff about how it would be good for our tribe and the people of the U.S.A.

Well, Kaiser, who didn't understand that much English anyway, listened quietly to his sister telling him what the army draft-board men were saying. He didn't ask any questions, just once in a while said, "Yes," like he'd been taught to say in the first grade. Maybe some of the interpretation was lost the way his sister was doing it, or maybe he went nuts like some people said he did once in a while because the next thing he did was to bust out the door and start running for Black Mesa.

The draft-board men didn't say anything at first, and then they got pretty mad. Kaiser's sister cried because she didn't want Kaiser to go into the army, but she didn't want him running out just like that either. She had gone to the Indian school in Albuquerque, and she had learned that stuff about patriotism, duty, honor—even if you were said to be crazy.

At about that time, their grandfather, Faustin, cussed in Indian at the draft-board men. Nobody had noticed when he came into the house, but there he was, fierce-looking as hell as usual, although he wasn't fierce at all. Then he got mad at his granddaughter and the men, asked what they were doing in his house, making the women cry and not even sitting down like friendly people did. Old Faustin and the army confronted each other. The army men were confused and

378

getting more and more nervous. The old man told the girl to go out of the room, and he'd talk to the army himself, although he didn't speak a word of English except "goddammey," which didn't sound too much like English but he threw it in once in a while anyway.

Those army men tried to get the girl to come back, but the old man wouldn't let her. He told her to get to grinding corn or something useful. They tried sign language, and when Faustin figured out what they were waving their hands around for, he laughed out loud. He wouldn't even take the cigarettes offered him, so the army men didn't say anything more. The last thing they did, though, was give the old man a paper, but they didn't explain what it was for. They probably hoped it would get read somehow.

Well, after they left, the paper did get read by the girl, and she told Faustin what it was about. The law was going to come and take Kaiser to jail because he wouldn't go into the army by himself. Grandfather Faustin sat down and talked quietly to himself for a while and then he got up to look for Kaiser.

Kaiser was on his way home by then, and his grandfather told him what was going to happen. They sat down by the side of the road and started to make plans. Kaiser would go hide up on Black Mesa and maybe go all the way to Brushy Mountain if the law really came to poking around seriously. Faustin would take him food and tell him the news once in a while.

Everybody in the village knew what was going on pretty soon. Some approved, and some didn't. Some thought it was pretty funny. My father, who couldn't go in the army even if he wanted to because there were too many of us kids, laughed about it for days. The people who approved of it and thought it funny were the ones who knew Kaiser was crazy and that the army must be even crazier. The ones who disapproved were mostly those who were scared of him. A lot of them were the parents or brother of girls who they must have suspected of liking Kaiser. Kaiser was pretty good-looking and funny in the way he talked for a crazy guy. And he was a hard worker. He worked every day out in the fields or up at the sheep camp for his parents while they were alive and for his sister and nephew and grandfather. These people, who were scared of him and said he should have gone into the army perhaps it'll do him good, didn't want him messing around their daughters or sisters, which they said he did from time to time. Mostly these people were scared he would do *something*, and there was one too many nuts around in the village anyway, they said.

My old man didn't care though. He was buddies with Kaiser. When there was a corn dance up at the community hall they would have a whole lot of fun singing and laughing and joking, and once in a while when someone brought around a bottle or two they would really get going and the officers of the tribe would have to warn them to behave themselves.

Kaiser was O.K. though. He came around home a lot. His own kinsfolks didn't care for him too much because he was crazy, and they didn't go out of their way to invite him to eat or spend the night when he dropped by their homes and it happened to get dark before he left. My mother didn't mind him around. When she served him something to eat, she didn't act like he was nuts, or supposed to be; she just served him and fussed over him like he was a kid, which Kaiser acted like a lot of the time. I guess she didn't figure a guy who acted like a kid was crazy.

Right after we finished eating, if it happened to be supper, my own grandfather, who was a medicine man, would talk to him and to all of us kids who were usually paying only half attention. He would tell us advice, about how the world was, how each person, everything, was important. And then he would tell us stories about the olden times. Legends mostly, about the *katzina,* Spider Woman, where our *hano,* people came from. Some of the stories were funny, some sad, and some pretty boring. Kaiser would sit there, not saying anything except *"Eheh,"* which is what you're supposed to say once in a while to show that you're listening to the olden times.

After half of us kids were asleep, Grandfather would quit talking, only Kaiser wouldn't want him to quit and he'd ask for more, but Grandfather wouldn't tell any more. What Kaiser would do was start telling himself about the olden times. He'd lie on the floor in the dark, or sometimes up on the roof which was where he'd sleep in the summer, talking. And sometimes he'd sing, which is also part of the old times. I would drift off to sleep just listening to him.

Well, he didn't come around home after he went up on Black Mesa. He just went up there and stayed there. The law, which was the County Sheriff, an officer, and the Indian Agent from the Indian Affairs office in Albuquerque, came out to get him, but nobody would tell them where he was. The law had a general idea where he was, but that didn't get them very far because they didn't know the country around Black Mesa. It's rougher than hell up there, just a couple of sheep camps in a lot of country.

The Indian Agent had written a letter to the officers of the tribe that they would come up for Kaiser on a certain day. There were a lot of people waiting for them when they drove up to the community meeting hall. The County Sheriff had a bulging belly and he had a six-shooter strapped to his hip. When the men standing outside the community hall saw him step out of the government car, they made jokes. Just like the Lone Ranger, someone said. The law didn't know what they were laughing about, and they said, Hello, and paid no attention to what they couldn't understand.

Faustin was among them. But he was silent and he smoked a roll-your-own. The Agent stopped before him, and Faustin took a slow drag on his roll-your-own but didn't look at the man.

"Faustin, my old friend," the Agent said. "How are you?"

The old man didn't say anything. He let the tobacco smoke out slowly and looked straight ahead. Someone in the crowd told Faustin what the Agent had said, but the old man didn't say anything at all.

The law thought he was praying or that he was a wise man contemplating his answer, the way he was so solemn-like, so they didn't press him. What Faustin was doing was ignoring the law. He didn't want them to talk with him. He turned to a man at his side.

"Tell this man I do not want to talk. I can't understand what they're saying in American anyway. And I don't want anyone to tell me what they say. I'm not interested." He looked at the government then, and he dismissed their presence with his indignation.

"The old man isn't gonna talk to you." someone said.

The Agent and Sheriff Big Belly glared at the man. "Who's in charge around here?" the Sheriff said.

The Indians laughed. They joked by calling each other big belly. The Governor of the tribe and two chiefs came soon. They greeted the law, and then they went into the meeting hall to confer about Kaiser.

"Well, have you brought Kaiser?" the Indian Agent asked, although he saw that they hadn't and knew that they wouldn't.

"No," the Governor said. And someone translated for him. "He will not come."

"Well, why don't you bring him? If he doesn't want to come, why don't you bring him? A bunch of you can bring him," the Agent said. He was becoming irritated.

The Governor, chiefs, and men talked to each other. One old man held the floor a while, until others got tired of him telling about the old times and how it was and how the Americans had said a certain thing and did another and so forth. Someone said, "We can bring him. Kaiser should come by himself anyway. Let's go get him." He was a man who didn't like Kaiser. He looked around carefully when he got through speaking and sat down.

"Tell the Americans that is not the way," one of the chiefs said. "If our son wants to meet these men he will come." And the law was answered with the translation.

"I'll be a son-of-a-bitch," the Sheriff said, and the Indians laughed quietly. He glared at them and they stopped. "Let's go get him ourselves," he continued.

The man who had been interpreting said, "He is crazy."

"Who's crazy?" the Sheriff yelled, like he was refuting an accusation. "I think you're all crazy."

"Kaiser, I think he is crazy," the interpreter said like he was ashamed of saying so. He stepped back, embarrassed.

Faustin then came to the front. Although he said he didn't want to talk with the law, he shouted. "Go get Kaiser yourself. If he's crazy, I hope he kills you. Go get him."

"O.K.," the Agent said when the interpreter finished. "We'll go get him ourselves. Where is he?" The Agent knew no one would tell him, but he asked it anyway.

With that, the Indians assumed the business that the law came to do was over, and that the law had resolved what it came to do in the first place. The Indians began to leave.

"Wait," the Agent said. "We need someone to go with us. He's up on Black Mesa, but we need someone to show us where."

The men kept on leaving. "We'll pay you. The government will pay you to go with us. You're deputized," the Agent said. "Stop them, Sheriff," he said to the County Sheriff, and the Sheriff yelled, "Stop, come back here," and put a hand to his six-shooter. When he yelled, some of the Indians looked at him to laugh. He sure looked funny and talked funny. But some of them came back. "All right, you're deputies, you'll get paid," the Sheriff said. Some of them knew what that meant, others weren't too sure. Some of them decided they'd come along for the fun of it.

The law and the Indians piled into the government car and a pickup truck which belonged to one of the deputies who was assured that he would get paid more than the others.

Black Mesa is fifteen miles back on the reservation. There are dirt roads up to it, but they weren't very good; nobody uses them except sheepherders and hunters in the fall. Kaiser knew what he was doing when he went up there, and he probably saw them when they were coming. But it wouldn't have made any difference, because when the law and the deputies came up to the foot of the mesa they still weren't getting anywhere. The deputies, who were still Indians, wouldn't tell or didn't really know where Kaiser was at the moment. So they sat for a couple of hours at the foot of the mesa, debating what should be done. The law tried to get the deputies to talk. The Sheriff was boiling mad at this time, getting madder too, and he was for *persuading* one of the deputies into telling where Kaiser was exactly. But he reasoned the deputy wouldn't talk, being that he was Indian too, and so he shut up for a while. He had figured out why the Indians laughed so frequently even though it was not as loud as before they were deputized.

Finally, they decided to walk up Black Mesa. It's rough going, and when they didn't know which was the best way to go up they found it was even rougher. The real law dropped back one by one to rest on a rock or under a piñon tree until only the deputies were left. They watched the officer from the Indian Affairs office sitting on a fallen log some yards back. He was the last one to keep up so far, and he was unlacing his shoes. The deputies waited patiently for him to start again and for the others to catch up.

"It's sure hot," one of the deputies said.

"Yes, maybe it'll rain soon," another said.

"No, it rained for the last time last month. Maybe next year."

"Snow then," another said.

They watched the Sheriff and the Indian Agent walking toward them half a mile back. One of them limped.

"Maybe the Americans need a rest," someone said. "We walked a long ways."

"Yes, they might be tired," another said. "I'll go tell that one that we're going to stop to rest," he said, and walked back to the law sitting on the log. "We gonna stop to rest," he told the law. The law didn't say anything as he massaged his feet. And the deputy walked away to join the others.

They didn't find Kaiser that day or the next day. The deputies said they could walk all over the mesa without finding him for all eternity, but they wouldn't find him. They didn't mind walking, they said. As long as they got paid for their time. Their crops were already in, and they'd just hire someone to haul winter wood for them now that they had the money. But they refused to talk. The ones who wanted to tell where Kaiser was, if they knew, didn't say so out loud, but they didn't tell anyway so it didn't make any difference. They were too persuaded by the newly found prosperity of employment.

The Sheriff, exhausted by the middle of the second day of walking the mesa, began to sound like he was for going back to Albuquerque. Maybe Kaiser'd come in by himself; he didn't see any sense in looking for some Indian anyway just to get him into the army. Besides, he'd heard the Indian was crazy. When the Sheriff had first learned the Indian's name was Kaiser he couldn't believe it, but he was assured that wasn't his real name, just something he was called because he was crazy. But the Sheriff didn't feel any better or less tired, and he was getting jumpy about the crazy part.

At the end of the second day, the law decided to leave. Maybe we'll come back, they said. We'll have to talk this over with the Indian Affairs officials. Maybe it'll be all right if that Indian doesn't have to be in the army after all. And they left. The Sheriff, his six-shooter off his hip now, was pretty tired out, and he didn't say anything.

The officials for the Indian Affairs didn't give up though. They sent back some more men. The County Sheriff decided it wasn't worth it; besides, he had a whole county to take care of. And the Indians were deputized again. More of them volunteered this time; some had to be turned away. They had figured out how to work it; they wouldn't have to tell, if they knew, where Kaiser was. All they would have to do was walk and say from time to time, "Maybe he's over there by that canyon. Used to be there was some good hiding places back when the Apache and Navajo were raising hell." And some would go over there and some in the other direction, investigating good hiding places. But after camping around Black Mesa for a week this time, the Indian Affairs gave up. They went by Faustin's house the day they left for Albuquerque and left a message: the government would wait, and when Kaiser least expected it, they would get him and he would have to go to jail.

Kaiser decided to volunteer for the army. He had decided to after he had watched the law and the deputies walk all over the mesa. Grandfather Faustin had come to visit him up at one of the sheep camps, and the old man gave him all the news at home, and then he told Kaiser the message the government had left.

"O.K.," Kaiser said. And he was silent for a while and nodded his head slowly like his grandfather did. "I'll join the army."

"No," his grandfather said. "I don't want you to. I will not allow you."

"Grandfather, I do not have to mind you. If you were my grandfather or uncle on my mother's side, I would listen to you and probably obey you, but you are not, and so I will not obey you."

"You are really crazy then," Grandfather Faustin said. "If that's what you want to do, go ahead." He was angry and he was sad, and he got up and put his hand on his grandson's shoulder and blessed him in the people's way. After that the old man left. It was in the evening when he left the sheep camp, and he walked a long time away from Black Mesa before he started to sing.

The next day, Kaiser showed up at home. He ate with us, and after we ate we sat in the living room with my grandfather.

"So you've decided to go into the Americans' army," my grandfather said. None of us kids, nor even my parents, had known he was going, but my grandfather had known all along. He probably knew as soon as Kaiser had walked into the house. Maybe even before that.

My grandfather blessed him then, just like Faustin had done, and he talked to him of how a man should behave and what he should expect. Just general things, and Grandfather turned sternly toward us kids, who were playing around as usual. My father and mother talked with him too, and when they were through, my grandfather put corn meal in Kaiser's hand for him to pray with. Our parents told us kids to tell Kaiser goodbye and good luck, and after we did he left.

The next thing we heard was that Kaiser was in the state pen.

Later on, some people went to visit him up at the state pen. He was O.K. and getting fat, they said, and he was getting on O.K. with everybody, the warden told them. And when someone had asked Kaiser if he was O.K., he said he was fine and he guessed he would be American pretty soon, being that he was around them so much. The people left Kaiser some home-baked bread and dried meats and came home after being assured by the warden that he'd get out pretty soon, maybe right after the war. Kaiser was a model inmate. When the visitors got home to the reservation, they went and told Faustin his grandson was O.K., getting fat and happy as any American. Old Faustin didn't have anything to say about that.

Well, the war was over after a while. Faustin died sometime near the end of it. Nobody had heard him mention Kaiser at all. Kaiser's sister and nephew were the only ones left at their home. Sometimes someone would ask about Kaiser, and his sister or nephew would say, "Oh, he's fine. He'll be home pretty soon. Right after the war." But after the war was over, they just said he was fine.

My father and a couple of other guys went down to the Indian Affairs office to see what they could find out about Kaiser. They were told that Kaiser was going to stay in the pen longer now because he had tried to kill somebody. Well, he just went crazy one day, and he made a mistake, so he'll just have to stay in for a couple more years or so, the Indian Affairs said. That was the first anybody heard of Kaiser trying to kill somebody, and some people said why the hell didn't they put him in the army for that like they wanted to in the first place. So Kaiser remained in the pen long after the war was over, and most of the guys who had gone into the army from the tribe had come home. When he was due to get out, the Indian Affairs sent a letter to the Governor, and several men from the village went to get him.

My father said Kaiser was quiet all the way home on the bus. Some of the guys tried to joke with him, but he just wouldn't laugh or say anything. When they got off the bus at the highway and began to walk home, the guys broke into song, but that didn't bring Kaiser around. He kept walking quiet and reserved in his gray suit. Someone joked that Kaiser probably owned the only suit in the whole tribe.

"You lucky so-and-so. You look like a rich man," the joker said. The others looked at him sharply and he quit joking, but Kaiser didn't say anything.

When they reached his home, his sister and nephew were very happy to see him. They cried and laughed at the same time, but Kaiser didn't do anything except sit at the kitchen table and look around. My father and the other guys gave him advice and welcomed him home again and left.

After that, Kaiser always wore his gray suit. Every time you saw him he was wearing it. Out in the fields or at the plaza watching the *katzina,* he wore the suit. He didn't talk much any more, my father said, and he didn't come around home any more either. The suit was getting all beat-up looking, but he just kept on wearing it so that some people began to say that he was showing off.

"That Kaiser," they said, "he's always wearing his suit, just like he was an American or something. Who does he think he is anyway?" And they'd snicker, looking at Kaiser with a sort of envy. Even when the suit was torn and soiled so that it hardly looked anything like a suit, Kaiser wore it. And some people said, "When he dies, Kaiser is going to be wearing his suit." And they said that like they wished they had gotten a suit like Kaiser's.

Well, Kaiser died, but without his gray suit. He died up at one of his distant relative's sheep camps one winter. When someone asked about the suit, they were told by Kaiser's sister that it was rolled up in some newspaper at their home. She said that Kaiser had told her, before he went up to the sheep camp, that she was to send it to the government. But, she said, she couldn't figure out what he meant, whether Kaiser had meant the law or somebody, maybe the state pen or the Indian Affairs.

The person who asked about the suit wondered about Kaiser's instructions. He couldn't figure out why Kaiser wanted to send a beat-up suit back. And then he figured, Well, maybe that's the way it was when you either went into the state pen or the army and became an American.

QUESTIONS FOR DISCUSSION AND WRITING

1. The narrator of "Kaiser and the War" is not a major participant in the action but an anonymous observer and member of the tribe. How does this affect the narrative? What point of view does the narrator represent?

2. What do we know of Kaiser's motives, as they come to us through the narrator? Why, for example, does he decide to volunteer for the army?

3. "Kaiser and the War" starts off as a comedy and ends on a much darker note. Identify both comic and tragic elements.

4. "Kaiser and the War" is about the confrontation of two cultures. How do the Native Americans and the whites fail to understand each other?

Leslie Marmon Silko

Leslie Marmon Silko (b. 1948) comes from a family part Mexican, part Laguna Pueblo, part Anglo. She became well known as the author of *Ceremony* (1977), a novel about how a distraught veteran of World War II finds peace by rediscovering the ceremonies of his Native American heritage. Her other books include *Laguna Woman: Poems* (1974); *Storyteller* (1981), a collection of short stories and poems; and *Almanac of the Dead* (1991), a novel. She lives on a ranch outside Tucson, Arizona.

YELLOW WOMAN

My thigh clung to his with dampness, and I watched the sun rising up through the tamaracks and willows. The small brown water birds came to the river and hopped across the mud, leaving brown scratches in the alkali-white crust. They bathed in the river silently. I could hear the water, almost at our feet where the narrow fast channel bubbled and washed green ragged moss and fern leaves. I looked at him beside me, rolled in the red blanket on the white river sand. I cleaned the sand out of the cracks between my toes, squinting because the sun was above the willow trees. I looked at him for the last time, sleeping on the white river sand.

I felt hungry and followed the river south the way we had come the afternoon before, following our footprints that were already blurred by lizard tracks and bug trails. The horses were still lying down, and the black one whinnied when he saw me but he did not get up—maybe it was because the corral was made out of thick cedar branches and the horses had not yet felt the sun like I had. I tried to look beyond the pale red mesas to the pueblo. I knew it was there, even if I could not see it, on the sandrock hill above the river, the same river that moved past me now and had reflected the moon last night.

The horse felt warm underneath me. He shook his head and pawed the sand. The bay whinnied and leaned against the gate trying to follow, and I remembered him asleep in the red blanket beside the river. I slid off the horse and tied him close to the other horse, I walked north with the river again, and the white sand broke loose in footprints over footprints.

"Wake up."

He moved in the blanket and turned his face to me with his eyes still closed. I knelt down to touch him.

"I'm leaving."

He smiled now, eyes still closed. "You are coming with me, remember?" He sat up now with his bare dark chest and belly in the sun.

"Where?"

"To my place."

"And will I come back?"

He pulled his pants on. I walked away from him, feeling him behind me and smelling the willows.

"Yellow Woman," he said.

I turned to face him. "Who are you?" I asked.

He laughed and knelt on the low, sandy bank, washing his face in the river. "Last night you guessed my name, and you knew why I had come."

I stared past him at the shallow moving water and tried to remember the night, but I could only see the moon in the water and remember his warmth around me.

"But I only said that you were him and that I was Yellow Woman—I'm not really her—I have my own name and I come from the pueblo on the other side of the mesa. Your name is Silva and you are a stranger I met by the river yesterday afternoon."

He laughed softly. "What happened yesterday has nothing to do with what you will do today, Yellow Woman."

"I know—that's what I'm saying—the old stories about the ka'tsina [kachina] spirit and Yellow Woman can't mean us."

My old grandpa liked to tell those stories best. There is one about Badger and Coyote who went hunting and were gone all day, and when the sun was going down they found a house. There was a girl living there alone, and she had light hair and eyes and she told them that they could sleep with her. Coyote wanted to be with her all night so he sent Badger into a prairie-dog hole, telling him he thought he saw something in it. As soon as Badger crawled in, Coyote blocked up the entrance with rocks and hurried back to Yellow Woman.

"Come here," he said gently.

He touched my neck and I moved close to him to feel his breathing and to hear his heart. I was wondering if Yellow Woman had known who she was—if she knew that she would become part of the stories. Maybe she'd had another name that her husband and relatives called her so that only the ka'tsina from the north and the storytellers would know her as Yellow Woman. But I didn't go on; I felt him all around me, pushing me down into the white river sand.

Yellow Woman went away with the spirit from the north and lived with him and his relatives. She was gone for a long time, but then one day she came back and she brought twin boys.

"Do you know the story?"

"What story?" He smiled and pulled me close to him as he said this. I was afraid lying there on the red blanket. All I could know was the way he felt, warm, damp, his body beside me. This is the way it happens in the stories, I was thinking, with no thought beyond the moment she meets the ka'tsina spirit and they go.

"I don't have to go. What they tell in stories was real only then, back in time immemorial, like they say."

He stood up and pointed at my clothes tangled in the blanket. "Let's go," he said.

I walked beside him, breathing hard because he walked fast, his hand around my wrist. I had stopped trying to pull away from him, because his hand felt cool and the sun was high, drying the river bed into alkali. I will see someone, eventually I will see someone, and then I will be certain that he is only a man—some man from nearby—and I will be sure that I am not Yellow Woman. Because she is from out of time past and I live now and I've been to school and there are highways and pickup trucks that Yellow Woman never saw.

It was an easy ride north on horseback. I watched the change from the cottonwood trees along the river to the junipers that brushed past us in the foothills, and finally there were only piñons, and when I looked up at the rim of the mountain plateau I could see pine trees growing on the edge. Once I stopped to look down, but the pale sandstone had disappeared and the river was gone and the dark lava hills were all around. He touched my hand, not speaking, but always singing softly a mountain song and looking into my eyes.

I felt hungry and wondered what they were doing at home now—my mother, my grandmother, my husband, and the baby. Cooking breakfast, saying, "Where did she go?—maybe kidnapped." And Al going to the tribal police with the details: "She went walking along the river."

The house was made with black lava rock and red mud. It was high above the spreading miles of arroyos and long mesas. I smelled a mountain smell of pitch and buck brush. I stood there beside the black horse, looking down on the small, dim country we had passed, and I shivered.

"Yellow Woman, come inside where it's warm."

He lit a fire in the stove. It was an old stove with a round belly and an enamel coffeepot on top. There was only the stove, some faded Navajo blankets, and a bedroll and cardboard box. The floor was made of smooth adobe plaster, and there was one small window facing east. He pointed at the box.

"There's some potatoes and the frying pan." He sat on the floor with his arms around his knees pulling them close to his chest and he watched me fry the potatoes. I didn't mind him watching me because he was always watching me—he had been watching me since I came upon him sitting on the river bank trimming leaves from a willow twig with his knife. We ate from the pan and he wiped the grease from his fingers on his Levi's.

"Have you brought women here before?" He smiled and kept chewing, so I said. "Do you always use the same tricks?"

"What tricks?" He looked at me like he didn't understand.

"The story about being a ka'tsina from the mountains. The story about Yellow Woman."

Silva was silent; his face was calm.

"I don't believe it. Those stories couldn't happen now," I said.

He shook his head and said softly, "But someday they will talk about us, and they will say, 'Those two lived long ago when things like that happened.' "

He stood up and went out. I ate the rest of the potatoes and thought about things—about the noise the stove was making and the sound of the mountain wind outside. I remembered yesterday and the day before, and then I went outside.

I walked past the corral to the edge where the narrow trail cut through the black rim rock. I was standing in the sky with nothing around me but the wind that came down from the blue mountain peak behind me. I could see faint mountain images in the distance miles across the vast spread of mesas and valleys and plains. I wondered who was over there to feel the mountain wind on those sheer blue edges—who walks on the pine needles in those blue mountains.

"Can you see the pueblo?" Silva was standing behind me.

I shook my head. "We're too far away."

"From here I can see the world." He stepped out on the edge. "The Navajo reservation begins over there." He pointed to the east. "The Pueblo boundaries are over here." He looked below us to the south, where the narrow trail seemed to come from. "The Texans have their ranches over there, starting with that valley, the Concho Valley. The Mexicans run some cattle over there too."

"Do you ever work for them?"

"I steal from them," Silva answered. The sun was dropping behind us and the shadows were filling the land below. I turned away from the edge that dropped forever into the valleys below.

"I'm cold," I said, "I'm going inside." I started wondering about this man who could speak the Pueblo language so well but who lived on a mountain and rustled cattle. I decided that this man Silva must be Navajo, because Pueblo men didn't do things like that.

"You must be a Navajo."

Silva shook his head gently. "Little Yellow Woman," he said, "you never give up, do you? I have told you who I am. The Navajo people know me, too." He knelt down and unrolled the bedroll and spread the extra blankets out on a piece of canvas. The sun was down, and the only light in the house came from outside—the dim orange light from sundown.

I stood there and waited for him to crawl under the blankets.

"What are you waiting for?" he said, and I lay down beside him. He undressed me slowly like the night before beside the river—kissing my face gently and running his hands up and down my belly and legs. He took off my pants and then he laughed.

"Why are you laughing?"

"You are breathing so hard."

I pulled away from him and turned my back on him.

He pulled me around and pinned me down with his arms and chest. "You don't understand, do you, little Yellow Woman? You will do what I want."

And again he was all around me with his skin slippery against mine, and I was afraid because I understood that his strength could hurt me. I lay underneath him and I knew that he could destroy me. But later, while he slept beside me, I touched his face and I had a feeling—the kind of feeling for him that overcame me that morning along the river. I kissed him on the forehead and he reached out for me.

When I woke up in the morning he was gone. It gave me a strange feeling because for a long time I sat there on the blankets and looked around the little house for some object of his—some proof that he had been there or maybe that he was coming back. Only the blankets and the cardboard box remained. The .30-30 that had been leaning in the corner was gone, and so was the knife I had used the night before. He was gone, and I had my chance to go now. But first I had to eat, because I knew it would be a long walk home.

I found some dried apricots in the cardboard box, and I sat down on a rock at the edge of the plateau rim. There was no wind and the sun warmed me. I was surrounded by silence. I drowsed with apricots in my mouth, and I didn't believe that there were highways or railroads or cattle to steal.

When I woke up, I stared down at my feet in the black mountain dirt. Little black ants were swarming over the pine needles around my foot. They must have smelled the apricots. I thought about my family far below me. They would be wondering about me, because this had never happened to me before. The tribal police would file a report. But if old Grandpa weren't dead he would tell them what happened—he would laugh and say, "Stolen by a ka'tsina, a mountain spirit. She'll come home—they usually do." There are enough of them to handle things. My mother and grandmother will raise the baby like they raised me. Al will find someone else, and they will go on like before, except that there will be a story about the day I disappeared while I was walking along the river. Silva had come for me; he said he had. I did not decide to go. I just went. Moonflowers blossom in the sand hills before dawn, just as I followed him. That's what I was thinking as I wandered along the trail through the pine trees.

It was noon when I got back. When I saw the stone house I remembered that I had meant to go home. But that didn't seem important any more, maybe because

there were little blue flowers growing in the meadow behind the stone house and
the gray squirrels were playing in the pines next to the house. The horses were
standing in the corral, and there was a beef carcass hanging on the shady side of
a big pine in front of the house. Flies buzzed around the clotted blood that hung
from the carcass. Silva was washing his hands in a bucket full of water. He must
have heard me coming because he spoke to me without turning to face me.

"I've been waiting for you."

"I went walking in the big pine trees."

I looked into the bucket full of bloody water with brown-and-white animal hairs
floating in it. Silva stood there letting his hand drip, examining me intently.

"Are you coming with me?"

"Where?" I asked him.

"To sell the meat in Marquez."

"If you're sure it's O.K."

"I wouldn't ask you if it wasn't," he answered.

He sloshed the water around in the bucket before he dumped it out and set the
bucket upside down near the door. I followed him to the corral and watched him
saddle the horses. Even beside the horses he looked tall, and I asked him again if
he wasn't Navajo. He didn't say anything; he just shook his head and kept cinch-
ing up the saddle.

"But Navajos are tall."

"Get on the horse," he said, "and let's go."

The last thing he did before we started down the steep trail was to grab the
.30-30 from the corner. He slid the rifle into the scabbard that hung from his
saddle.

"Do they ever try to catch you?" I asked.

"They don't know who I am."

"Then why did you bring the rifle?"

"Because we are going to Marquez where the Mexicans live."

The trail leveled out on a narrow ridge that was steep on both sides like an animal
spine. On one side I could see where the trail went around the rocky gray hills and
disappeared into the southeast where the pale sandrock mesas stood in the distance near my home. On the other side was a trail that went west, and as I looked
far into the distance I thought I saw the little town. But Silva said no, that I was
looking in the wrong place, that I just thought I saw houses. After that I quit
looking off into the distance; it was hot and the wildflowers were closing up their
deep-yellow petals. Only the waxy cactus flowers bloomed in the bright sun, and
I saw every color that a cactus blossom can be; the white ones and the red ones
were still buds, but the purple and the yellow were blossoms, open full and the
most beautiful of all.

Silva saw him before I did. The white man was riding a big gray horse, coming
up the trail towards us. He was traveling fast and the gray horse's feet sent rocks
falling off the trail into the dry tumbleweeds. Silva motioned for me to stop and
we watched the white man. He didn't see us right away, but finally his horse
whinnied at our horses and he stopped. He looked at us briefly before he lapped
the gray horse across the three hundred yards that separated us. He stopped his
horse in front of Silva, and his young fat face was shadowed by the brim of his hat.
He didn't look mad, but his small, pale eyes moved from the blood-soaked gunny
sacks hanging from my saddle to Silva's face and then back to my face.

"Where did you get the fresh meat?" the white man asked.

"I've been hunting," Silva said, and when he shifted his weight in the saddle the leather creaked.

"The hell you have, Indian. You've been rustling cattle. We've been looking for the thief for a long time."

The rancher was fat, and sweat began to soak through his white cowboy shirt and the wet cloth stuck to the thick rolls of belly fat. He almost seemed to be panting from the exertion of talking, and he smelled rancid, maybe because Silva scared him.

Silva turned to me and smiled. "Go back up the mountain, Yellow Woman."

The white man got angry when he heard Silva speak in a language he couldn't understand. "Don't try anything, Indian. Just keep riding to Marquez. We'll call the state police from there."

The rancher must have been unarmed because he was very frightened and if he had a gun he would have pulled it out then. I turned my horse around and the rancher yelled, "Stop!" I looked at Silva for an instant and there was something ancient and dark—something I could feel in my stomach—in his eyes, and when I glanced at his hand I saw his finger on the trigger of the .30-30 that was still in the saddle scabbard. I slapped my horse across the flank and the sacks of raw meat swung against my knees as the horse leaped up the trail. It was hard to keep my balance, and once I thought I felt the saddle slipping backward; it was because of this that I could not look back.

I didn't stop until I reached the ridge where the trail forked. The horse was breathing deep gasps and there was a dark film of sweat on its neck. I looked down in the direction I had come from, but I couldn't see the place. I waited. The wind came up and pushed warm air past me. I looked up at the sky, pale blue and full of thin clouds and fading vapor trails left by jets.

I think four shots were fired—I remember hearing four hollow explosions that reminded me of deer hunting. There could have been more shots after that, but I couldn't have heard them because my horse was running again and the loose rocks were making too much noise as they scattered around his feet.

Horses have a hard time running downhill, but I went that way instead of uphill to the mountain because I thought it was safer. I felt better with the horse running southeast past the round gray hills that were covered with cedar trees and black lava rock. When I got to the plain in the distance I could see the dark green patches of tamaracks that grew along the river; and beyond the river I could see the beginning of the pale sandrock mesas. I stopped the horse and looked back to see if anyone was coming; then I got off the horse and turned the horse around, wondering if it would go back to its corral under the pines on the mountain. It looked back at me for a moment and then plucked a mouthful of green tumbleweeds before it trotted back up the trail with its ears pointed forward, carrying its head daintily to one side to avoid stepping on the dragging reins. When the horse disappeared over the last hill, the gunny sacks full of meat were still swinging and bouncing.

I walked toward the river on a wood-hauler's road that I knew would eventually lead to the paved road. I was thinking about waiting beside the road for someone to drive by, but by the time I got to the pavement I had decided it wasn't very far to walk if I followed the river back the way Silva and I had come.

The river water tasted good, and I sat in the shade under a cluster of silvery willows. I thought about Silva, and I felt sad at leaving him; still, there was something strange about him, and I tried to figure it out all the way back home.

I came back to the place on the river bank where he had been sitting the first time I saw him. The green willow leaves that he had trimmed from the branch were still lying there, wilted in the sand. I saw the leaves and I wanted to go back to him—to kiss him and to touch him—but the mountains were too far away now. And I told myself, because I believe it, he will come back sometime and be waiting again by the river.

I followed the path up from the river into the village. The sun was getting low, and I could smell supper cooking when I got to the screen door of my house. I could hear their voices inside—my mother was telling my grandmother how to fix the Jell-O and my husband, Al, was playing with the baby. I decided to tell them that some Navajo had kidnaped me, but I was sorry that old Grandpa wasn't alive to hear my story because it was the Yellow Woman stories he liked to tell best.

QUESTIONS FOR DISCUSSION AND WRITING

1. How would you characterize the narrator-protagonist of "Yellow Woman"? Do her motivations and reactions seem realistic?

2. "Yellow Woman" stories, as the story indicates, were variations on the theme of "Yellow Woman" being abducted by an evil spirit called a *ka'tsina* or *kachina*. What is the relation between this story and a traditional Yellow Woman story? Is Silva teasing or is he really a *kachina*? List the details suggesting that he is supernatural. Then list the details suggesting that he is an ordinary man.

3. What happens at the end of the story? Does Silva kill the rancher? Note that the speaker expects Silva to return. What is gained by leaving the ending indefinite?

Kim Chi-wŏn

Kim Chi-wŏn (b. 1943) is the daughter of Ch'oe Chŏng-hŭi, one of the most famous women writers in modern Korea. Kim Chi-wŏn immigrated to the United States in the 1970s. Much of her fiction deals with the challenges facing Korean immigrant women in New York City, where she lives.

A CERTAIN BEGINNING*

Yun-ja floated on the blue swells, her face toward the dazzling sun. At first the water had chilled her, but now it felt agreeable, almost responding to her touch. Ripples slapped about her ears, and a breeze brushed the wet tip of her nose. Sailboats eased out of the corner of her eye and into the distance. She heard the drone of powerboats, the laughter of children, and the babble of English, Spanish, and other tongues blending indistinguishably like faraway sounds in a dream. Her only reaction to all this was an occasional blink. She felt drugged by the sun.

Yun-ja straightened herself in the water and looked for Chŏng-il. There he was, sitting under the beach umbrella with his head tilted back, drinking something. From her distant vantage point, twenty-seven-year-old Chŏng-il looked as small as a Boy Scout. He reminded her of a houseboy she had seen in a photo of some American soldiers during the Korean War.

"Life begins all over after today," Yun-ja thought. She had read in a woman's magazine that it was natural for a woman who was alone after a divorce, even a long-awaited one, to be lonely, to feel she had failed, because in any society a happy marriage is considered a sign of a successful life. And so a divorced woman ought to make radical changes in her life-style. The magazine article had suggested getting out of the daily routine—sleeping as late as you want, eating what you want, throwing a party in the middle of the week, getting involved in new activities. "My case is a bit different, but like the writer says, I've got to start over again. But how? How is my life going to be different?" Yun-ja hadn't the slightest idea how to start a completely new life. Even if she were to begin sleeping all day and staying up all night, what difference would it make if she hadn't changed inwardly? Without a real change the days ahead would be boring and just blend together, she thought. Day would drift into night; she would find herself hardly able to sleep and another empty day would dawn. And how tasteless the food eaten alone; how unbearable to hear only the sound of her own chewing. These thoughts hadn't occurred to her before. "He won't be coming anymore starting tomorrow," she thought. The approaching days began to look meaningless.

Several days earlier, Chŏng-il had brought some soybean sprouts and tofu to Yun-ja's apartment and had begun making soybean-paste soup. Yun-ja was sitting on the old sofa, knitting.

"Mrs. Lee, how about a trip to the beach to celebrate our 'marriage'? A honeymoon, you know?"

Yun-ja laughed. She and Chŏng-il found nothing as funny as the word *marriage*. Chŏng-il also laughed, to show that his joke was innocent.

* *Translated by Bruce and Ju-Chan Fulton.*

"Marriage" to Chŏng-il meant the permanent resident card he was obtaining. He and Yun-ja were already formally married, but it was the day he was to receive the green card he had been waiting for that Chŏng-il called his "wedding day."

Chŏng-il had paid Yun-ja fifteen hundred dollars to marry him so that he could apply for permanent residency in the U.S. Until his marriage he had been pursued by the American immigration authorities for working without the proper visa.

"Americans talk about things like inflation, but they're still a superpower. Don't they have anything better to do than track down foreign students?" Chŏng-il had said the day he met Yun-ja. His eyes had been moist with tears.

Now, almost two months later, Chŏng-il had his permanent resident card and Yun-ja the fifteen hundred dollars. And today their relationship would come to an end.

Chŏng-il ambled down the beach toward the water, his smooth bronze skin gleaming in the sun. He shouted to Yun-ja and smiled, but she couldn't make out the words. Perhaps he was challenging her to a race, or asking how the water was.

Yun-ja had been delighted when Ki-yŏng's mother, who had been working with her at a clothing factory in Chinatown, sounded her out about a contract marriage with Chŏng-il. "He came here on a student visa," the woman had explained. "My husband tells me his older brother makes a decent living in Seoul. . . . The boy's been told to leave the country, so his bags are packed and he's about to move to a different state. . . . It's been only seven months since he came to America. . . . Just his luck—other Korean students work here without getting caught. . . ."

"Why not?" Yun-ja had thought. If only she could get out of that sunless, roach-infested Manhattan basement apartment that she had been sharing with a young Chinese woman. And her lower back had become stiff as a board from too many hours of piecework at the sewing machine. All day long she was engulfed by Chinese speaking in strange tones and sewing machines whirring at full tilt. Yun-ja had trod the pedals of her sewing machine in the dusty air of the factory, the pieces of cloth she handled feeling unbearably heavy. Yes, life in America had not been easy for Yun-ja, and so she decided to give herself a vacation. With the fifteen hundred dollars from a contract marriage she could get a sunny room where she could open the window and look out on the street.

And now her wish had come true. She had gotten a studio apartment on the West Side, twenty minutes by foot from the end of a subway line, and received Chŏng-il as a "customer," as Ki-yŏng's mother had put it.

After quitting her job Yun-ja stayed in bed in the morning, listening to the traffic on the street below. In the evening, Chŏng-il would return from his temporary accounting job. Yun-ja would greet him like a boardinghouse mistress, and they would share the meal she had prepared. Her day was divided between the time before he arrived and the time after.

Thankful for his meals, Chŏng-il would sometimes go grocery shopping and occasionally he would do the cooking, not wishing to feel obligated to Yun-ja.

Chŏng-il swam near. "Going to stay in forever?" he joked. His lips had turned blue.

"Anything left to drink?" she asked.

"There's some Coke, and I got some water just now."

Chŏng-il had bought everything for this outing—Korean-style grilled beef, some Korean delicacies, even paper napkins.

"Mrs. Lee, this is a good place for clams—big ones too. A couple of them will fill you up—or so they say. Let's go dig a few. Then we can go home, steam them up, and have them with rice. A simple meal, just right for a couple of tired bodies. What do you think?"

Instead of answering, Yun-ja watched Chŏng-il's head bobbing like a watermelon. "So he's thinking about dropping by my place. . . . Will he leave at eleventhirty again, on our last day? Well, he has to go there anyway to pick up his things." While eating lunch, she had mentally rehearsed some possible farewells at her apartment: "I guess you'll be busy with school again pretty soon," or "Are you moving into a dorm?"

Yun-ja was worried about giving Chŏng-il the impression that she was making a play for him. At times she had wanted to hand Chŏng-il a fresh towel or some lotion when he returned sopping wet from the shower down the hall, but she would end up simply ignoring him.

Yun-ja thought about the past two months. Each night after dinner at her apartment Chŏng-il would remain at the table and read a book or newspaper. At eleven-thirty he would leave to spend the night with a friend who lived two blocks away. Chŏng-il had been told by his lawyer that a person ordered out of the country who then got married and applied for a permanent resident card could expect to be investigated by the Immigration and Naturalization Service. And so he and Yun-ja had tried to look like a married couple. This meant that Chŏng-il had to be seen with Yun-ja. He would stay as late as he could at her apartment, and he kept a pair of pajamas, some old shoes, and other belongings there.

Tick, tick, tick. . . . Yun-ja would sit knitting or listening to a record, while Chŏng-il read a book or wrote a letter. Pretending to be absorbed in whatever they were doing, both would keep stealing glances at their watches. . . . Tick, tick, tick. . . .

At eleven-thirty Chŏng-il would strap on his watch and get up. Jingling his keys, he would mumble "Good night" or "I'm going." Yun-ja would remain where she was and pretend to be preoccupied until his lanky, boyish figure had disappeared out the door.

It hadn't always been that way. During the first few days after their marriage they would exchange news of Korea or talk about life in America—U.S. immigration policy, the high prices, the unemployment, or whatever. And when Chŏng-il left, Yun-ja would see him to the door. The silent evenings had begun the night she had suggested they live together. That night Chŏng-il had brought some beer and they had sung some children's ditties, popular tunes, and other songs they both knew. The people in the next apartment had pounded on the wall in protest. Chŏng-il and Yun-ja had lowered their voices, but only temporarily. It was while Chŏng-il was bringing tears of laughter to Yun-ja, as he sang and clowned around, that she had broached the subject: Why did Chŏng-il want to leave right at eleventhirty every night only to sleep at a friend's apartment where he wasn't really welcome? He could just as easily curl up in a corner of her apartment at night and the two of them could live together like a big sister and her little brother—now wouldn't that be great? Immediately Chŏng-il's face had hardened and Yun-ja had realized her blunder. That was the last time Chŏng-il had brought beer to the apartment. The lengthy conversations had stopped and Chŏng-il no longer entertained Yun-ja with songs.

Yun-ja had begun to feel resentful as Chŏng-il rose and left like clockwork each night. "Afraid I'm going to bite, you little stinker!" she would think, pouting at the sound of the key turning in the door. "It's a tug-of-war. You want to keep on my good side, so you sneak looks at me to see how I'm feeling. You're scared I might call off the marriage. It's true, isn't it—if I said I didn't want to go through with it, what would you do? Where would you find another unmarried woman with a green card? Would you run off to another state? Fat chance!"

The evening following her ill-advised proposal to live together, Yun-ja had left her apartment around the time Chŏng-il was to arrive. She didn't want him to think she was sitting around the apartment waiting for him. She walked to a nearby playground that she had never visited before and watched a couple of Asian children playing with some other children. She wondered if being gone when Chŏng-il arrived would make things even more awkward between them. She wanted to return and tell him that her suggestion the previous evening had had no hidden meaning. Yun-ja had no desire to become emotionally involved with Chŏng-il. This was not so much because of their thirteen-year age difference (though Yun-ja still wasn't used to the idea that she was forty), but because Yun-ja had no illusions about marriage.

The man Yun-ja had married upon graduating from college had done well in business, and around the time of their divorce seven years later he had become a wealthy man, with a car and the finest house in Seoul's Hwagok neighborhood.

"Let's get a divorce; you can have the house," he had said one day.

Yun-ja was terribly shocked.

"But why? . . . Is there another woman?"

"No, it's not that. I just don't think I'm cut out for marriage."

In desperation Yun-ja had suggested a trial separation. But her husband had insisted on the divorce, and one day he left, taking only a toiletry kit and some clothes. Yun-ja had wept for days afterward. She was convinced that another woman had come on the scene, and sometimes she secretly kept an eye on her husband's office on T'oegye Avenue to try to confirm this.

"Was there really no other woman?" she asked herself at the playground. "Did he want the divorce because he was tired of living with me?" Their only baby had been placed in an incubator at birth, but the sickly child had died. Being a first-time mother had overwhelmed Yun-ja. "Maybe he just got sick and tired of everything. Or maybe he just wanted to stop living with me and go somewhere far away—that's how I felt toward him when he stayed out late." She had heard recently that he had remarried.

"Are you Korean?"

Yun-ja looked up to see a withered old Korean woman whose hair was drawn into a bun the size of a walnut. Yun-ja was delighted to see another Korean, though she couldn't help feeling conspicuous because of the older woman's traditional Korean clothing, which was made of fine nylon gauze.

Before Yun-ja could answer, the woman plopped herself down and drew a crimson pack of cigarettes from the pocket of her bloomers.

"Care for one, miss?"

"No, thank you."

The old woman lit a cigarette and began talking as if she were ripe for a quarrel: "Ah me, this city isn't fit for people to live in. It's a place for animals, that's what. In Korea I had a nice warm room with a laminated floor, but here no one takes their shoes off and the floors are all messy."

"Can't you go back to Korea?"

"Are you kidding? Those darn sons of mine won't let me. I have to babysit their kids all day long. Whenever I see a plane I start crying—I tell you! To think that I flew over here on one of those damned things!"

The old woman's eyes were inflamed, as if she cried every day, and now fresh tears gathered. Yun-ja looked up and watched the plane they had spotted. It had taken off from the nearby airport and seemed to float just above them as it climbed into the sky. Its crimson and emerald green landing lights winked.

"I don't miss my hometown the way this grandmother does. And I don't feel like crying at the sight of that plane," thought Yun-ja. Her homeland was the source of her shame. She had had to get away from it—there was no other way.

It was around seven when Yun-ja returned from the playground.

Chŏng-il opened the door. "Did you go somewhere?" he asked politely, like a schoolboy addressing his teacher.

Yun-ja was relieved to have been spoken to first.

"I was talking with an elderly Korean woman."

"The one who goes around in Korean clothes? Was she telling you how bad it is here in America?"

"You know her?"

"Oh, she's notorious—latches on to every Korean she sees."

This ordinary beginning to the evening would eventually yield to a silent stand-off, taut like the rope in a tug-of-war.

Chŏng-il's joking reference to "marriage" the evening he had offered to take Yun-ja to the beach had come easily because his immigration papers had finally been processed. All he had to do was see his lawyer and sign them, and he would get his permanent resident card.

Though it was six o'clock, it was still bright as midday. It was a muggy August evening, and the small fan in the wall next to the window stuttered, as if it were panting in the heat of Yun-ja's top-floor apartment.

Realizing that Chŏng-il was only joking, Yun-ja stopped knitting. She got up and put a record on. The reedy sound of a man's mellow voice unwound from the cheap stereo:

Now that we're about to part
Take my hand once again. . . .

Yun-ja abruptly turned off the stereo. "Listening to songs makes me feel even hotter," she said.

Several days later, after Chŏng-il had obtained his permanent resident card, he borrowed a car and took Yun-ja to the beach, as promised. Yun-ja had thought it a kind of token of his gratitude, like the flowers or wine you give to the doctor who delivered your baby, or a memento you give to your teacher at graduation.

They stayed late at the beach to avoid the Friday afternoon rush hour. As the day turned to evening, the breeze became chilly and the two of them stayed out of the water, sitting together on the cool sand. Whether it was because they were outside or because this was their last day together, Yun-ja somehow felt that the tug-of-war between them had eased. But the parting words a couple might have said to each other were missing: "Give me a call or drop me a line and let me know how things are going." Chŏng-il did most of the talking, and Yun-ja found his small talk refreshing. He told her about getting measles at age nine, practicing martial arts in college, and going around Seoul in the dog days of summer just to get a driver's license so he could work while going to school in America. And he talked about a book he'd read, entitled *Papillon*.

"If you have Papillon's will, the sky's the limit on what you can do in America.

You've heard Koreans when they get together here. They're always talking about the Chinese. The first-generation Chinese saved a few pennies doing unskilled labor when the subways were built. The second generation opened up small laundries or noodle stands. Buying houses and educating the kids didn't happen until the third generation. Whenever I hear that, I realize that Koreans want to do everything in a hurry—I'm the same way. They sound like they want to accomplish in a couple of years what it took the Chinese three generations to do.... When I left Korea I told my friends and my big brother not to feel bad if I didn't write, because I might not be able to afford the postage. My brother bought me an expensive fountain pen and told me that if I went hungry in the States I should sell it and buy myself a meal. And then my older sister had a gold ring made for me. I put the damned thing on my finger, got myself decked out in a suit for the plane ride, and then on the way over I was so excited I couldn't eat a thing—not a thing. The stewardess was probably saying to herself, 'Here's a guy who's never been on a plane before.' That damned ring—I must have looked like a jerk!''

Yun-ja related a few details about the elderly Korean woman she had met in the park. (Why did her thoughts return so often to this grandmother?) Then she told Chŏng-il a little about herself, realizing he had probably already learned through Ki-yŏng's mother that she was just another divorcée with no one to turn to.

The cool wind picked up as the sunlight faded, and they put their clothes on over their swimsuits. Chŏng-il's shirt was inside out, and Yun-ja could read the brand name on the neck tag.

"Your shirt's inside out."

Chŏng-il roughly pulled the shirt off and put it on right side out. Her steady gaze seemed to annoy him.

The beach was deserted except for a few small groups and some young couples lying on the sand nearby, exchanging affections. Hundreds of sea gulls began to gather. The birds frightened Yun-ja. Their wings looked ragged; their sharp, ceaselessly moving eyes seemed treacherous. Yun-ja felt as if their pointed beaks were about to bore into her eyes, maybe even her heart. She folded the towel she had been sitting on and stood up.

"Let's get going."

More gulls had alighted on the nearly empty parking lot, which stretched out as big as a football field.

"Want to get a closer look?" Chŏng-il asked as he started the car.

"They'll fly away."

"Not if we go slow. God, there must be thousands of them."

The car glided in a slow circle around the sea gulls. Just as Chŏng-il had said, the birds stayed where they were. Yun-ja watched them through the window, her fear now gone.

They pulled out onto the highway and the beach grew distant. A grand sunset flared up in the dark blue sky. The outline of distant hills and trees swung behind the car and gradually disappeared. Yun-ja noticed that Chŏng-il had turned on the headlights.

"You must be beat," Chŏng-il said. "Why don't you lean back and make yourself comfortable."

Perhaps because he was silent for a time, Yun-ja somehow felt his firm, quiet manner in the smooth, steady motion of the car. She wondered what to do when they arrived at her apartment. Invite him in? Arrange to meet him somewhere the following day to give him his things? But the second idea would involve seeing him again.... The tide hadn't been low, so they hadn't been able to dig clams.... "I'll

bet I've looked like a nobody to him, a woman who's hungry for love and money."
Yun-ja recalled something Chŏng-il had once told her: "After I get my degree
here, write a couple of books, and make a name for myself, I'd like to go back to
Korea. Right now there are too many Ph.D.'s over there. I know I wouldn't find
a job if I went back with just a degree."

"And for the rest of your life," Yun-ja now thought, "I'll be a cheap object for
you to gossip about. You'll say, 'I was helpless when they told me to leave the
country—so I bought myself a wife who was practically old enough to be my
mother. What a pain in the neck—especially when she came up with the idea of
living together.' And at some point in the future when you propose to your
sweetheart, maybe you'll blabber something like 'I have a confession to make—
I've been married before. . . .'"

Chŏng-il drove on silently. His hand on the steering wheel was fine and delicate—a student's hand. Yun-ja felt like yanking that hand, biting it, anything to
make him see things her way, to make him always speak respectfully of her in the
future.

Chŏng-il felt Yun-ja's gaze and stole a glance at her. The small face that had
been angled toward his was now looking straight ahead. "She's no beauty—maybe
it's that thin body of her that makes her look kind of shriveled up—but sometimes
she's really pretty. Especially when it's hot. Then that honey-colored skin of hers
gets a nice shine to it and her eyelashes look even darker." But Chŏng-il had
rarely felt comfortable enough to examine Yun-ja's face.

"Mrs. Lee, did you ever have any children?"

"One—it died."

Chŏng-il lit a cigarette. Her toneless voice rang in his ears. "She doesn't seem
to have any feelings. No expression, no interest in others, it even sounds as if her
baby's death means nothing to her. True—time has a way of easing the pain. I
don't show any emotion either when I tell people that my father died when I was
young and my mother passed away when I was in college. Probably it's the same
with her. But her own baby? How can she said 'It died' just like that?"

He had known from the beginning, through Ki-yŏng's mother, that Yun-ja was
a single woman with no money. It had never occurred to him when he paid
Ki-yŏng's mother the first installment of the fifteen hundred dollars that a woman
with such a common name as Yun-ja might have special qualities. What had he
expected her to be like, this woman who was to become his wife in name only?
Well, a woman who had led a hard life, but who would vaguely resemble Ki-yŏng's
mother—short permed hair, a calf-length sack dress, white sandals—a woman in
her forties who didn't look completely at ease in Western-style clothing. But the
woman Ki-yŏng's father had taken him to meet at the bus stop was thin and petite
with short, straight hair and a sleeveless dress. Her eyelids had a deep double fold,
and her skin had a dusky sheen that reminded Chŏng-il of Southeast Asian women.
She was holding a pair of sunglasses, and a large handbag hung from her long,
slender arm.

As they walked the short distance to Ki-yŏng's mother's for dinner that first
night, Chŏng-il had felt pity for this woman who didn't even come up to his
shoulders. He had also felt guilty and ill at ease. But Yun-ja had spoken nonchalantly: "So you're a student? Well, I just found an apartment yesterday. I'll be
moving in three days from now. We can go over a little later and I'll show you
around. It's really small—kitchen, bathroom, living room, and bedroom all in
one." To Chŏng-il this breezy woman of forty or so acted like an eighteen-year-old

girl. "This woman's marrying me for money." He felt regretful, as if he were buying an aging prostitute.

"Why don't you two forget about the business part of it and get married for real?" Ki-yŏng's mother had said at dinner. And when she sang a playful rendition of the wedding march, Chŏng-il had felt like crawling under the table. Yun-ja had merely laughed.

The traffic between the beach and the city was heavy, occasionally coming to a standstill. Among the procession of vehicles Yun-ja and Chŏng-il noticed cars towing boats, cars carrying bicycles, cars with tents and shovels strapped to their roof racks.

As Chŏng-il drove by shops that had closed for the day, he thought of all the time he had spent on the phone with his older brother in Korea, of all the hard-earned money he had managed to scrounge from him (did his sister-in-law know about that?)—all because of this permanent resident card. And now he couldn't even afford tuition for next semester. These thoughts depressed him. But then he bucked up: Now that he had his green card (his chest swelled at the idea), there was no reason he couldn't work. "I'll take next semester off, put my nose to the grindstone, and by the following semester I'll have my tuition." And now that he was a permanent resident, his tuition would be cut in half. He made some mental calculations: How much could he save by cutting his rent and food to the bone? "But you can't cut down on the food too much," Chŏng-il reminded himself. There were students who had ended up sick and run-down, who couldn't study or do other things as a result. "This woman Yun-ja really has it easy—doesn't have to study. All she has to do is eat and sleep, day after day." Chŏng-il felt it was disgraceful that a young, intelligent Korean such as himself was living unproductively in America, as if he had no responsibilities to his family or country. "Why am I busting my butt to be here? Is the education really that wonderful?" In English class back in Korea he had vaguely dreamed of studying in America. Or rather he had liked the idea of hearing people say he had studied there. More shameful than this was the impulse he had to stay on in America. "What about the other people from abroad who live in the States—do they feel guilty about their feelings for their country, too?" He had read diatribes about America's corrupt material civilization. But he couldn't figure out what was so corrupt about it, and that bothered him. He wanted to see just what a young Korean man could accomplish in the world, and he wanted to experience the anger of frustration rather than the calm of complacency. He wanted knowledge, and recognition from others. But this woman Yun-ja didn't even seem to realize she was Korean.

The car pulled up on a street of six-story apartment buildings whose bricks were fading. Children were running and bicycling on the cement sidewalk; elderly couples strolled hand in hand, taking in the evening. Chŏng-il got out, unpacked the cooler and the towels, and loaded them on his shoulder. He and Yun-ja had the elevator to themselves. Yun-ja felt anxious and lonely, as if she had entered an unfamiliar neighborhood at dusk. She braced herself against the side of the elevator as it accelerated and slowed. When she was young it seemed the world belonged to her, but as time went on these "belongings" had disappeared; now she felt as if she had nothing. When it came time to part from someone, her heart ached as if she were separating from a lover. "Am I so dependent on people that I drove my husband away? Nobody wants to be burdened with me, so they all leave—even my baby. . . . I wonder if that old woman at the playground went back to Korea. Maybe she's still smoking American cigarettes and bending the ear of every Korean she sees here. Maybe I'll end up like her when I'm old. Already my body feels like a dead weight because of my neuralgia—God forbid that I latch on to just anybody and start telling a sob story."

Yun-ja unlocked the door to the apartment and turned on the light.

Today the small, perfectly square room looked cozy and intimate to them. They smelled the familiar odors, which had been intensified by the summer heat.

But Chŏng-il felt awkward when he saw that Yun-ja had packed his trunk and set it on the sofa. If only he could unpack it and return the belongings to their places.

"You must feel pretty sticky—why don't you take a shower?" Yun-ja said.

Chŏng-il returned from washing his salt-encrusted body to find Yun-ja cleaning the sand from the doorway. She had changed to a familiar, well-worn yellow dress. The cooler had been emptied and cleaned, the towels put away. Yun-ja had shampooed, and comb marks were still visible in her wet hair. Chŏng-il tried to think of something to say, gave up, and tiptoed to the sofa to sit down. "She's already washed her hair, changed, and started sweeping up," he thought. As Yun-ja bustled about, she looked to Chŏng-il as if she had just blossomed.

"Shouldn't I offer him some dinner?" Yun-ja thought as she swept up the sand. "He went to the trouble of borrowing a car and taking me out—the least I can do is give him a nice meal. And where would he eat if he left now? He'd probably fill up on junk food. . . . But if I offer to feed him, he might think I had something in mind. And when I've paid people for something, they never offered me dinner, did they?"

"How about some music?" Chŏng-il mumbled. He got up, walked stiffly to the stereo, and placed the needle on the record that happened to be on the turntable. The rhythm of a Flamenco guitar filled the room. Although Chŏng-il didn't pay much attention to the music Yun-ja played, it seemed that this was a new record. "Why have I been afraid of this woman? You'd think she was a witch or something."

"If that woman sinks her hooks into you, you've had it." Chŏng-il had heard this from his roommate, Ki-yŏng's father, and goodness knows how many others. "Nothing happened again today?" the roommate would joke when Chŏng-il returned in the evening from Yun-ja's apartment. "When it comes to you-know-what, nothing beats a middle-aged woman. I hope you're offering good service in return for those tasty meals you're getting."

The shrill voices of the children and the noise of airplanes and traffic were drowned out by the guitar music. The odor of something rotten outside wafted in with the heat of the summer night.

Chŏng-il began to feel ashamed. Here he was about to run out on this woman he'd used in return for a measly sum of money—a woman whose life he had touched. He had visited this room for almost two months, and now he wished he could spend that time over again. "Why didn't I try to make it more enjoyable?" he asked himself. He and Yun-ja had rarely listened to music, and when they had gone strolling in the nearby park after dinner he had felt uneasy, knowing that they did this only so that others would see the two of them together.

Yun-ja finished sweeping the sand up and sat down at the round dinner table. "If you're hungry, why don't you help yourself to some leftovers from yesterday's dinner? There's some lettuce and soybean paste and a little rice too."

Yun-ja's hair had dried, and a couple of strands of it drooped over her forehead. She looked pretty to Chŏng-il.

"And some marinated peppers," she continued.

Chŏng-il's body stiffened. This offer of dinner was a signal that it was time for him to leave. He rose and fumbled for something appropriate to say about the past two months. The blood rushed to his head and his face burned. Finally he blurted out, "What would you say if I . . . proposed to you?" Then he flung open the door as if he were being chased out. In his haste to leave he sent one of Yun-ja's sandals flying from the doorway toward the gas range. The door slammed shut behind him.

Yun-ja sprang up from the table. "What did he say?" Her body prickled, as if she were yielding to a long-suppressed urge to urinate. "I don't believe in marriage," she told herself. "Not after what I went through." She rushed to the door and looked through the peephole into the hall. She saw Chŏng-il jab futilely at the elevator button and then run toward the stairway.

"The boy proposed to me—I should be thankful," Yun-ja thought. Like water reviving a dying tree, hot blood began to buzz through her sleepy veins. This long-forgotten sensation of warmth made her think that maybe their relationship had been pointing in this direction all along. "It was fun prettying myself up the day I met him. And before that, didn't I expect some good times with him even though we weren't really married?"

Yun-ja turned and looked around the room. There was Chŏng-il's trunk on the sofa. "But he'd end up leaving me too." Suddenly she felt very vulnerable. Everything about her, starting with her age and the divorce, and then all the little imperfections—the wrinkles around the eyes, the occasional drooling in her sleep—reared up in her mind. "But I'm not going to let my shortcomings get me down," she reassured herself. "It's time to make a stand."

QUESTIONS FOR DISCUSSION AND WRITING

1. "A Certain Beginning" takes place on the final day of Yun-ja and Chŏng-il's "marriage," and the rest of the story is told in memories and flashbacks. Analyze these inset scenes and the way they relate to the present action.

2. The first part of the story is focalized through Yun-ja exclusively, but halfway through the story we suddenly shift to Chŏng-il's point of view, and thereafter the points of view alternate. Where does this happen, and what is its effect?

3. At one point in the story, Yun-ja thinks of the old Korean woman in the park and thinks: "Why did her thoughts return so often to this grandmother?" Can you answer the question?

4. Explore differences in the story: between American and Korean, between men and women, between young and old, and between the elements of whatever other oppositions you see.

5. What does the title mean? Does it refer to the ending of the story? Is there a prospect of a future for Yun-ja and Chŏng-il?

Stuart Dybek

Stuart Dybek (b. 1942) grew up in the Pilsen neighborhood of south Chicago. His book of poems, *Brass Knuckles,* was published in 1979. It was followed by two collections of short stories, *Childhood and Other Neighborhoods* (1980) and *The Coast of Chicago* (1990).

CHOPIN IN WINTER

The winter Dzia-Dzia came to live with us in Mrs. Kubiac's building on Eighteenth Street was the winter that Mrs. Kubiac's daughter, Marcy, came home pregnant from college in New York. Marcy had gone there on a music scholarship, the first person in Mrs. Kubiac's family to go to high school, let alone college.

Since she had come home I had seen her only once. I was playing on the landing before our door, and as she came up the stairs we both nodded hi. She didn't look pregnant. She was thin, dressed in a black coat, its silvery fur collar pulled up around her face, her long blonde hair tucked into the collar. I could see the snowflakes on the fur turning to beads of water under the hall light bulb. Her face was pale and her eyes the same startled blue as Mrs. Kubiac's.

She passed me almost without noticing and continued up the next flight of stairs, then paused and, leaning over the banister, asked, "Are you the same little boy I used to hear crying at night?"

Her voice was gentle, yet kidding.

"I don't know," I said.

"If your name is Michael and if your bedroom window is on the fourth floor right below mine, then you are," she said. "When you were little sometimes I'd hear you crying your heart out at night. I guess I heard what your mother couldn't. The sound traveled up."

"I really woke you up?"

"Don't worry about that. I'm a very light sleeper. Snow falling wakes me up. I used to wish I could help you as long as we were both up together in the middle of the night with everyone else snoring."

"I don't remember crying," I said.

"Most people don't once they're happy again. It looks like you're happy enough now. Stay that way, kiddo." She smiled. It was a lovely smile. Her eyes seemed surprised by it. "Too-da-loo." She waved her fingers.

"Too-da-loo." I waved after her. A minute after she was gone I began to miss her.

Our landlady, Mrs. Kubiac, would come downstairs for tea in the afternoons and cry while telling my mother about Marcy. Marcy, Mrs. Kubiac said, wouldn't tell her who the child's father was. She wouldn't tell the priest. She wouldn't go to church. She wouldn't go anywhere. Even the doctor had to come to the house, and the only doctor that Marcy would allow was Dr. Shtulek, her childhood doctor.

"I tell her, 'Marcy, darling, you have to do something,'" Mrs. Kubiac said. "What about all the sacrifices, the practice, the lessons, teachers, awards? Look at rich people—they don't let anything interfere with what they want.'"

Mrs. Kubiac told my mother these things in strictest confidence, her voice at

402

first a secretive whisper, but growing louder as she recited her litany of troubles. The louder she talked the more broken her English became, as if her worry and suffering were straining the language past its limits. Finally, her feelings overpowered her; she began to weep and lapsed into Bohemian, which I couldn't understand.

I would sit out of sight beneath the dining-room table, my plastic cowboys galloping through a forest of chair legs, while I listened to Mrs. Kubiac talk about Marcy. I wanted to hear everything about her, and the more I heard the more precious the smile she had given me on the stairs became. It was like a secret bond between us. Once I became convinced of that, listening to Mrs. Kubiac seemed like spying. I was Marcy's friend and conspirator. She had spoken to me as if I was someone apart from the world she was shunning. Whatever her reasons for the way she was acting, whatever her secrets, I was on her side. In daydreams I proved my loyalty over and over.

At night we could hear her playing the piano—a muffled rumbling of scales that sounded vaguely familiar. Perhaps I actually remembered hearing Marcy practicing years earlier, before she had gone on to New York. The notes resonated through the kitchen ceiling while I wiped the supper dishes and Dzia-Dzia sat soaking his feet. Dzia-Dzia soaked his feet every night in a bucket of steaming water into which he dropped a tablet that fizzed, immediately turning the water bright pink. Between the steaming water and pink dye, his feet and legs, up to the knees where his trousers were rolled, looked permanently scalded.

Dzia-Dzia's feet seemed to be turning into hooves. His heels and soles were swollen nearly shapeless and cased in scaly calluses. Nails, yellow as a horse's teeth, grew gnarled from knobbed toes. Dzia-Dzia's feet had been frozen when as a young man he walked most of the way from Krakow to Gdansk in the dead of winter escaping service in the Prussian army. And later he had frozen them again mining for gold in Alaska. Most of what I knew of Dzia-Dzia's past had mainly to do with the history of his feet.

Sometimes my uncles would say something about him. It sounded as if he had spent his whole life on the move—selling dogs to the Igorot in the Philippines after the Spanish-American War; mining coal in Johnstown, Pennsylvania; working barges on the Great Lakes; riding the rails out West. No one in the family wanted much to do with him. He had deserted them so often, my uncle Roman said, that it was worse than growing up without a father.

My grandma had referred to him as *Pan Djabel,* "Mr. Devil," though the way she said it sounded as if he amused her. He called her a *gorel,* a hillbilly, and claimed that he came from a wealthy, educated family that had been stripped of their land by the Prussians.

"Landowners, all right!" Uncle Roman once said to my mother. "Besides acting like a bastard, according to Ma, he actually *was* one in the literal sense."

"Romey, shhh, what good's bitter?" my mother said.

"Who's bitter, Ev? It's just that he couldn't even show up to bury her. I'll never forgive that."

Dzia-Dzia hadn't been at Grandma's funeral. He had disappeared again, and no one had known where to find him. For years Dzia-Dzia would simply vanish without telling anyone, then suddenly show up out of nowhere to hang around for a while, ragged and smelling of liquor, wearing his two suits one over the other, only to disappear yet again.

"Want to find him? Go ask the bums on skid row," Uncle Roman would say.

My uncles said he lived in boxcars, basements, and abandoned buildings. And when, from the window of a bus, I'd see old men standing around trash fires behind billboards, I'd wonder if he was among them.

Now that he was very old and failing he sat in our kitchen, his feet aching and numb as if he had been out walking down Eighteenth Street barefoot in the snow.

It was my aunts and uncles who talked about Dzia-Dzia "failing." The word always made me nervous. I was failing, too—failing spelling, English, history, geography, almost everything except arithmetic, and that only because it used numbers instead of letters. Mainly, I was failing penmanship. The nuns complained that my writing was totally illegible, that I spelled like a DP, and threatened that if I didn't improve they might have to hold me back.

Mother kept my failures confidential. It was Dzia-Dzia's they discussed during Sunday visits in voices pitched just below the level of an old man's hearing. Dzia-Dzia stared fiercely but didn't deny what they were saying about him. He hadn't spoken since he had reappeared, and no one knew whether his muteness was caused by senility or stubbornness, or if he'd gone deaf. His ears had been frozen as well as his feet. Wiry white tufts of hair that matched his horned eyebrows sprouted from his ears. I wondered if he would hear better if they were trimmed.

Though Dzia-Dzia and I spent the evenings alone together in the kitchen, he didn't talk any more than he did on Sundays. Mother stayed in the parlor, immersed in her correspondence courses in bookkeeping. The piano rumbled above us through the ceiling. I could feel it more than hear it, especially the bass notes. Sometimes a chord would be struck that made the silverware clash in the drawer and the glasses hum.

Marcy had looked very thin climbing the stairs, delicate, incapable of such force. But her piano was massive and powerful-looking. I remembered going upstairs once with my mother to visit Mrs. Kubiac. Marcy was away at school then. The piano stood unused—top lowered, lid down over the keys—dominating the apartment. In the afternoon light it gleamed deeply, as if its dark wood were a kind of glass. Its pedals were polished bronze and looked to me more like pedals I imagined motormen stamping to operate streetcars.

"Isn't it beautiful, Michael?" my mother asked.

I nodded hard, hoping that Mrs. Kubiac would offer to let me play it, but she didn't.

"How did it get up here?" I asked. It seemed impossible that it could fit through a doorway.

"Wasn't easy," Mrs. Kubiac said, surprised. "Gave Mr. Kubiac a rupture. It come all the way on the boat from Europe. Some old German, a great musician, brang it over to give concerts, then got sick and left it. Went back to Germany. God knows what happened to him—I think he was a Jew. They auctioned it off to pay his hotel bill. That's life, huh? Otherwise who could afford it? We're not rich people."

"It must have been very expensive anyway," my mother said.

"Only cost me a marriage," Mrs. Kubiac said, then laughed, but it was forced. "That's life too, huh?" she asked. "Maybe a woman's better off without a husband?" And then, for just an instant, I saw her glance at my mother, then look away. It was a glance I had come to recognize from people when they caught themselves saying something that might remind my mother or me that my father had been killed in the war.

*   *   *

The silverware would clash and the glasses hum. I could feel it in my teeth and bones as the deep notes rumbled through the ceiling and walls like distant thunder. It wasn't like listening to music, yet more and more often I would notice Dzia-Dzia close his eyes, a look of concentration pinching his face as his body swayed slightly. I wondered what he was hearing. Mother had said once that he'd played the fiddle when she was a little girl, but the only music I'd even seen him show any interest in before was the "Frankie Yankovitch Polka Hour," which he turned up loud and listened to with his ear almost pressed to the radio. Whatever Marcy was playing, it didn't sound like Frankie Yankovitch.

Then one evening, after weeks of silence between us, punctuated only by grunts, Dzia-Dzia said, "That's boogie-woogie music."

"What, Dzia-Dzia?" I asked, startled.

"Music the boogies play."

"You mean from upstairs? That's Marcy."

"She's in love with a colored man."

"What are you telling him, Pa?" Mother demanded. She had just happened to enter the kitchen while Dzia-Dzia was speaking.

"About boogie-woogie." Dzia-Dzia's legs jiggled in the bucket so that the pink water sloshed over onto the linoleum.

"We don't need that kind of talk in the house."

"What talk, Evusha?"

"He doesn't have to hear that prejudice in the house," Mom said. "He'll pick up enough on the street."

"I just told him boogie-woogie."

"I think you better soak your feet in the parlor by the heater," Mom said. "We can spread newspaper."

Dzia-Dzia sat, squinting as if he didn't hear.

"You heard me, Pa. I said soak your feet in the parlor," Mom repeated on the verge of shouting.

"What, Evusha?"

"I'll yell as loud as I have to, Pa."

"Boogie-woogie, boogie-woogie, boogie-woogie," the old man muttered as he left the kitchen, slopping barefoot across the linoleum.

"Go soak your head while you're at it," Mom muttered behind him, too quietly for him to hear.

Mom had always insisted on polite language in the house. Someone who failed to say "please" or "thank you" was as offensive to her ears as someone who cursed. "The word is 'yes,' not 'yeah,' " she would correct. Or "If you want 'hey,' go to a stable." She considered "ain't" a form of laziness, like not picking up your dirty socks.

Even when they got a little drunk at the family parties that took place at our flat on Sundays, my uncles tried not to swear—and they had all been in the army and the marines. Nor were they allowed to refer to the Germans as Krauts, or the Japanese as Nips. As far as Mom was concerned, of all the misuses of language, racial slurs were the most ignorant, and so the most foul.

My uncles didn't discuss the war much anyway, though whenever they got together there was a certain feeling in the room as if beneath the loud talk and joking they shared a deeper, sadder mood. Mom had replaced the photo of my father in his uniform with an earlier photo of him sitting on the running board of the car they'd owned before the war. He was grinning and petting the neighbor's Scottie. That one and their wedding picture were the only photos that Mom kept out. She knew I didn't remember my father, and she seldom talked about him. But there were a few times when she would read aloud parts of his letters. There was one passage in particular that she read at least once a year. It had been written while he was under bombardment, shortly before he was killed.

> When it continues like this without letup you learn what it is to really hate. You begin to hate them as a people and want to punish them all—civilians, women, children, old people—it makes no difference, they're all the same, none of them innocent, and for a while your hate and anger keep you from going crazy with fear. But if you let yourself hate and believe in hate, then no matter what else happens, you've lost. Eve, I love our life together and want to come home to you and Michael, as much as I can, the same man who left.

I wanted to hear more but didn't ask. Perhaps because everyone seemed to be trying to forget. Perhaps because I was afraid. When the tears would start in Mom's eyes I caught myself wanting to glance away as Mrs. Kubiac had.

There was something more besides Mom's usual standards for the kind of language allowed in the house that caused her to lose her temper and kick Dzia-Dzia out of his spot in the kitchen. She had become even more sensitive, especially where Dzia-Dzia was concerned, because of what had happened with Shirley Popel's mother.

Shirley's mother had died recently. Mom and Shirley had been best friends since grade school, and after the funeral, Shirley came back to our house and poured out the story.

Her mother had broken a hip falling off a curb while sweeping the sidewalk in front of her house. She was a constantly smiling woman without any teeth who, everyone said, looked like a peasant. After forty years in America she could barely speak English, and even in the hospital refused to remove her babushka.

Everyone called her Babushka, Babush for short, which meant "granny," even the nuns at the hospital. On top of her broken hip, Babush caught pneumonia, and one night Shirley got a call from the doctor saying Babush had taken a sudden turn for the worse. Shirley rushed right over, taking her thirteen-year-old son, Rudy. Rudy was Babushka's favorite, and Shirley hoped that seeing him would instill the will to live in her mother. It was Saturday night and Rudy was dressed to play at his first dance. He wanted to be a musician and was wearing clothes he had bought with money saved from his paper route. He'd bought them at Smoky Joe's on Maxwell Street—blue suede loafers, electric-blue socks, a lemon-yellow one-button roll-lapel suit with padded shoulders and pegged trousers, and a parrot-green satin shirt. Shirley thought he looked cute.

When they got to the hospital they found Babush connected to tubes and breathing oxygen.

"Ma," Shirley said, "Rudy's here."

Babush raised her head, took one look at Rudy, and smacked her gray tongue. "Rudish," Babush said, "you dress like nigger." Then suddenly her eyes rolled; she fell back, gasped, and died.

"And those were her last words to any of us, Ev," Shirley wept, "words we'll carry the rest of our lives, but especially poor little Rudy—*you dress like nigger.*"

For weeks after Shirley's visit, no matter who called, Mom would tell them Shirley's story over the phone.

"Those aren't the kind of famous last words we're going to hear in this family if I can help it," she promised more than once, as if it were a real possibility. "Of course," she'd sometimes add, "Shirley always has let Rudy get away with too much. I don't see anything cute about a boy going to visit his grandmother at the hospital dressed like a hood."

Any last words Dzia-Dzia had he kept to himself. His silence, however, had already been broken. Perhaps in his own mind that was a defeat that carried him from failing to totally failed. He returned to the kitchen like a ghost haunting his old chair, one that appeared when I sat alone working on penmanship.

No one else seemed to notice a change, but it was clear from the way he no longer soaked his feet. He still kept up the pretense of sitting there with them in the bucket. The bucket went with him the way ghosts drag chains. But he no longer went through the ritual of boiling water: boiling it until the kettle screeched for mercy, pounding so the linoleum puddled and steam clouded around him, and finally dropping in the tablet that fizzed furiously pink, releasing a faintly metallic smell like a broken thermometer.

Without his bucket steaming, the fogged windows cleared. Mrs. Kubiac's building towered a story higher than any other on the block. From our fourth-story window I could look out at an even level with the roofs and see the snow gathering on them before it reached the street.

I sat at one end of the kitchen table copying down the words that would be on the spelling test the next day. Dzia-Dzia sat at the other, mumbling incessantly, as if finally free to talk about the jumble of the past he'd never mentioned—wars, revolutions, strikes, journeys to strange places, all run together, and music, especially Chopin. "Chopin," he'd whisper hoarsely, pointing to the ceiling with the reverence of nuns pointing to heaven. Then he'd close his eyes and his nostrils would widen as if he were inhaling the fragrance of sound.

It sounded no different to me, the same muffled thumping and rumbling we'd been hearing ever since Marcy had returned home. I could hear the intensity in the crescendos that made the silverware clash, but it never occurred to me to care what she was playing. What mattered was that I could hear her play each night, could feel her playing just a floor above, almost as if she were in our apartment. She seemed that close.

"Each night Chopin—it's all she thinks about, isn't it?"

I shrugged.

"You don't know?" Dzia-Dzia whispered, as if I were lying and he was humoring me.

"How should I know?"

"And I suppose how should you know the 'Grande Valse brillante' when you hear it either? How should you know Chopin was twenty-one when he composed it?—about the same age as the girl upstairs. He composed it in Vienna, before he went to Paris. Don't they teach you that in school? What are you studying?"

"Spelling."

"Can you spell *dummkopf*?"

The waves of the keyboard would pulse through the warm kitchen and I would become immersed in my spelling words, and after that in penmanship. I was in remedial penmanship. Nightly penmanship was like undergoing physical therapy. While I concentrated on the proper slant of my letters my left hand smeared graphite across the loose-leaf paper.

Dzia-Dzia, now that he was talking, no longer seemed content to sit and listen in silence. He would continually interrupt.

"Hey, Lefty, stop writing with your nose. Listen how she plays."

"Don't shake the table, Dzia-Dzia."

"You know this one? No? 'Valse brillante.'"

"I thought that was the other one."

"What other one? The E-flat? That's 'Grande Valse brillante.' This one's A-flat. Then there's another A-flat—Opus 42—called 'Grande Valse.' Understand?"

He rambled on like that about A- and E-flat and sharps and opuses and I went back to compressing my capital *M*'s. My homework was to write five hundred of them. I was failing penmanship yet again, my left hand, as usual, taking the blame it didn't deserve. The problem with *M* wasn't my hand. It was that I had never been convinced that the letters could all be the same widths. When I wrote, *M* automatically came out twice as broad as *N, H*, double the width of *I*.

"This was Paderewski's favorite waltz. She plays it like an angel."

I nodded, staring in despair at my homework. I had made the mistake of interconnecting the *M*'s into long strands. They hummed in my head, drowning out the music, and I wondered if I had been humming aloud. "Who's Paderewski?" I asked, thinking it might be one of Dzia-Dzia's old friends, maybe from Alaska.

"Do you know who's George Washington, who's Joe DiMaggio, who's Walt Disney?"

"Sure."

"I thought so. Paderewski was like them, except he played Chopin. Understand? See, deep down inside, Lefty, you know more than you think."

Instead of going into the parlor to read comics or play with my cowboys while Mom pored over her correspondence courses, I began spending more time at the kitchen table, lingering over my homework as an excuse. My spelling began to improve, then took a turn toward perfection; the slant of my handwriting reversed toward the right; I began to hear melodies in what had sounded like muffled scales.

Each night Dzia-Dzia would tell me more about Chopin, describing the preludes or ballades or mazurkas, so that even if I hadn't heard them I could imagine them, especially Dzia-Dzia's favorites, the nocturnes, shimmering like black pools.

"She's playing her way through the waltzes," Dzia-Dzia told me, speaking as usual in his low, raspy voice as if we were having a confidential discussion. "She's young but already knows Chopin's secret—a waltz can tell more about the soul than a hymn."

By my bedtime the kitchen table would be shaking so much that it was impossible to practice penmanship any longer. Across from me, Dzia-Dzia, his hair, eyebrows, and ear tufts wild and white, swayed in his chair, with his eyes squeezed closed and a look of rapture on his face as his fingers pummeled the tabletop. He played the entire width of the table, his body leaning and twisting as his fingers swept the keyboard, left hand pounding at those chords that jangled silverware, while his right raced through runs across tacky oilcloth. His feet pumped the empty bucket. If I watched him, then closed my eyes, it sounded as if two pianos were playing.

One night Dzia-Dzia and Marcy played so that I expected at any moment the table would break and the ceiling collapse. The bulbs began to flicker in the overhead fixture, then went out. The entire flat went dark.

"Are the lights out in there, too?" Mom yelled from the parlor. "Don't worry, it must be a fuse."

The kitchen windows glowed with the light of snow. I looked out. All the buildings down Eighteenth Street were dark and the streetlights were out. Spraying wings of snow, a snow-removal machine, its yellow lights revolving, disappeared down Eighteenth like the last blinks of electricity. There wasn't any traffic. The block looked deserted, as if the entire city was deserted. Snow was filling the emptiness, big flakes floating steadily and softly between the darkened buildings, coating the fire escapes, while on the roofs a blizzard swirled up into the clouds.

Marcy and Dzia-Dzia never stopped playing.

"Michael, come in here by the heater, or if you're going to stay in there put the burners on," Mom called.

I lit the burners on the stove. They hovered in the dark like blue crowns of flame, flickering Dzia-Dzia's shadow across the walls. His head pitched, his arms flew up as he struck the notes. The walls and windowpanes shook with gusts of wind and music. I imagined plaster dust wafting down, coating the kitchen, a fine network of cracks spreading through the dishes.

"Michael?" Mother called.

"I'm sharpening my pencil." I stood by the sharpener grinding it as hard as I could, then sat back down and went on writing. The table rocked under my point, but the letters formed perfectly. I spelled new words, words I'd never heard before, yet as soon as I wrote them their meanings were clear, as if they were in another language, one in which words were understood by their sounds, like music. After the lights came back on I couldn't remember what they meant and threw them away.

Dzia-Dzia slumped back in his chair. He was flushed and mopped his forehead with a paper napkin.

"So, you liked that one," he said. "Which one was it?" he asked. He always asked me that, and little by little I had begun recognizing their melodies.

"The polonaise," I guessed. "In A-flat major."

"Ahhh," he shook his head in disappointment. "You think everything with a little spirit is the polonaise."

"The 'Revolutionary' étude!"

"It was a waltz," Dzia-Dzia said.

"How could that be a waltz?"

"A posthumous waltz. You know what 'posthumous' means?"

"What?"

"It means music from after a person's dead. The kind of waltz that has to carry back from the other side. Chopin wrote it to a young woman he loved. He kept his feelings for her secret but never forgot her. Sooner or later feelings come bursting out. The dead are as sentimental as anyone else. You know what happened when Chopin died?"

"No."

"They rang the bells all over Europe. It was winter. The Prussians heard them. They jumped on their horses. They had cavalry then, no tanks, just horses. They rode until they came to the house where Chopin lay on a bed next to a grand piano. His arms were crossed over his chest, and there was plaster drying on his hands and face. The Prussians rode right up the stairs and barged into the room, slashing with their sabers, their horses stamping and kicking up their front hooves. They hacked the piano and stabbed the music, then wadded up the music into the piano, spilled on kerosene from the lamps, and set it on fire. Then they rolled Chopin's piano to the window—it was those French windows, the kind that open out and there's a tiny balcony. The piano wouldn't fit, so they rammed it through, taking out part of the wall. It crashed three stories into the street, and when it hit it made a sound that shook the city. The piano lay there smoking, and the Prussians galloped over it and left. Later, some of Chopin's friends snuck back and removed his heart and sent it in a little jeweled box to be buried in Warsaw.''

Dzia-Dzia stopped and listened. Marcy had begun to play again very faintly. If he had asked me to guess what she was playing I would have said a prelude, the one called "The Raindrop."

I heard the preludes on Saturday nights, sunk up to my ears in bathwater. The music traveled from upstairs through the plumbing, and resonated as clearly underwater as if I had been wearing earphones.

There were other places I discovered where Marcy's playing carried. Polonaises sometimes reverberated down an old trash chute that had been papered over in the dining room. Even in the parlor, provided no one else was listening to the radio or flipping pages of a newspaper, it was possible to hear the faintest hint of mazurkas around the sealed wall where the stovepipe from the space heater disappeared into what had once been a fireplace. And when I went out to play on the landing, bundled up as if I was going out to climb on the drifts piled along Eighteenth Street, I could hear the piano echoing down the hallways. I began to creep higher up the stairs to the top floor, until finally I was listening at Mrs. Kubiac's door, ready to jump away if it should suddenly open, hoping I would be able to think of some excuse for being there, and at the same time almost wishing they would catch me.

I didn't mention climbing the stairs in the hallway, nor any of the other places I'd discovered, to Dzia-Dzia. He never seemed interested in anyplace other than the kitchen table. It was as if he were attached to the chair, rooted in his bucket.

"Going so early? Where you rushing off to?'' he'd ask at the end of each evening, no matter how late, when I'd put my pencil down and begun buckling my books into my satchel.

I'd leave him sitting there, with his feet in his empty bucket, and his fingers, tufted with the same white hair as his ears, still tracing arpeggios across the tabletop, though Marcy had already stopped playing. I didn't tell him how from my room, a few times lately after everyone was asleep, I could hear her playing as clearly as if I were sitting at her feet.

Marcy played less and less, especially in the evenings after supper, which had been her regular time.

Dzia-Dzia continued to shake the table nightly, eyes closed, hair flying, fingers thumping, but the thump of his fingers against the oilcloth was the only sound other than his breathing—rhythmic and labored as if he were having a dream or climbing a flight of stairs.

I didn't notice at first, but Dzia-Dzia's solos were the start of his return to silence.

"What's she playing, Lefty?'' he demanded more insistently than ever, as if still testing whether I knew.

Usually now, I did. But after a while I realized he was no longer testing me. He was asking because the sounds were becoming increasingly muddled to him. He seemed able to feel the pulse of the music but could no longer distinguish the melodies. By asking me, he hoped perhaps that if he knew what Marcy was playing he would hear it clearly himself.

Then he began to ask what she was playing when she wasn't playing at all.

I would make up answers. "The polonaise . . . in A-flat major.''

"The polonaise! You always say that. Listen harder. Are you sure it's not a waltz?"

"You're right, Dzia-Dzia. It's the 'Grande Valse'. "

"The 'Grande Valse' . . . which one is that?"

"A-flat, Opus 42. Paderewski's favorite, remember? Chopin wrote it when he was twenty-one, in Vienna."

"In Vienna?" Dzia-Dzia asked, then pounded the table with his fist. "Don't tell me numbers and letters! A-flat, Z-sharp, Opus o, Opus, 1,000! Who cares? You make it sound like a bingo game instead of Chopin."

I was never sure if he couldn't hear because he couldn't remember, or couldn't remember because he couldn't hear. His hearing itself seemed sharp enough.

"Stop scratching with that pencil all the time, Lefty, and I wouldn't have to ask you what she's playing," he'd complain.

"You'd hear better, Dzia-Dzia, if you'd take the kettle off the stove."

He was slipping back into his ritual of boiling water. The kettle screeched like a siren. The windows fogged. Roofs and weather vanished behind a slick of steam. Vapor ringed the overhead light bulbs. The vaguely metallic smell of the fizzing pink tablets hung at the end of every breath.

Marcy played hardly at all by then. What little she played was muffled, far off as if filtering through the same fog. Sometimes, staring at the steamed windows, I imagined Eighteenth Street looked that way, with rings of vapor around the streetlights and headlights, clouds billowing from exhaust pipes and manhole covers, breaths hanging, snow swirling like white smoke.

Each night water hissed from the kettle's spout as from a blown valve, rumbling as it filled the bucket, brimming until it slopped over onto the warped linoleum. Dzia-Dzia sat, bony calves half submerged, trousers rolled to his knees. He was wearing two suits again, one over the other, always a sure sign he was getting ready to travel, to disappear without saying good-bye. The fingers of his left hand drummed unconsciously along the tabletop as his feet soaked. Steam curled up the arteries of his scalded legs, hovered over his lap, smoldered up the buttons of his two vests, traced his mustache and white tufts of hair until it enveloped him. He sat in a cloud, eyes glazed, fading.

⚊⚊⚊⚊⚊

I began to go to bed early. I would leave my homework unfinished, kiss Mother good night, and go to my room.

My room was small, hardly space for more than the bed and bureau. Not so small, though, that Dzia-Dzia couldn't have fit. Perhaps, had I told him that Marcy played almost every night now after everyone was sleeping, he wouldn't have gone back to filling the kitchen with steam. I felt guilty, but it was too late, and I shut the door quickly before steam could enter and fog my window.

It was a single window. I could touch it from the foot of the bed. It opened onto a recessed, three-sided air shaft and faced the roof of the building next door. Years ago a kid my age named Freddy had lived next door and we still called it Freddy's roof.

Marcy's window was above mine. The music traveled down as clearly as Marcy said my crying had traveled up. When I closed my eyes I could imagine sitting on the Oriental carpet beside her huge piano. The air shaft actually amplified the music just as it had once amplified the arguments between Mr. and Mrs. Kubiac, especially the shouting on those nights after Mr. Kubiac had moved out, when he would return drunk and try to move back in. They'd argued mostly in Bohemian, but when Mr. Kubiac started beating her, Mrs. Kubiac would yell out in English, "Help me, police, somebody, he's killing me!" After a while the police would usually come and haul Mr. Kubiac away. I think sometimes Mom called them. One night Mr. Kubiac tried to fight off the police, and they gave him a terrible beating. "You're killing him in front of my eyes!" Mrs. Kubiac began to scream. Mr. Kubiac broke away and, with the police chasing him, ran down the hallways pounding on doors, pleading for people to open up. He pounded on our door. Nobody in the building let him in. That was their last argument.

The room was always cold. I'd slip, still wearing my clothes, under the goose-feather–stuffed *piersyna* to change into my pajamas. It would have been warmer with the door open even a crack, but I kept it closed because of the steam. A steamed bedroom window reminded me too much of the winter I'd had pneumonia. It was one of the earliest things I could remember: the gurgling hiss of the vaporizer and smell of benzoin while I lay sunk in my pillows watching steam condense to frost on the pane until daylight blurred. I could remember trying to scratch through the frost with the key to a windup mouse so that I could see how much snow had fallen, and Mother catching me. She was furious that I had climbed out from under the warmth of my covers and asked me if I wanted to get well or to get sicker and die. Later, when I asked Dr. Shtulek if I was dying, he put his stethoscope to my nose and listened. "Not yet." He smiled. Dr. Shtulek visited often to check my breathing. His stethoscope was cold like all the instruments in his bag, but I liked him, especially for unplugging the vaporizer. "We don't need this anymore," he confided. Night seemed very still without its steady exhaling. The jingle of snow chains and the scraping of shovels carried from Eighteenth Street. Maybe that was when I first heard Marcy practicing scales. By then I had grown used to napping during the day and lying awake at night. I began to tunnel under my *piersyna* to the window and scrape at the layered frost. I scraped for nights, always afraid I would get sick again for disobeying. Finally, I was able to see the snow on Freddy's roof. Something had changed while I'd been sick—they had put a wind hood on the tall chimney that sometimes blew smoke into our flat. In the dark it looked as if someone was standing on the roof in an old-fashioned helmet. I imagined it was a German soldier. I'd heard Freddy's landlord was German. The soldier stood at attention, but his head slowly turned back and forth and hooted with each gust of wind. Snow drove sideways across the roof, and he stood banked by drifts, smoking a cigar. Sparks flew from its tip. When he turned completely around to stare in my direction with his faceless face, I'd duck and tunnel back under my *piersyna* to my pillows and pretend to sleep. I believed a person asleep would be shown more mercy than a person awake. I'd lie still, afraid he was marching across the roof to peer in at me through the holes I'd scraped. It was a night like that when I heard Mother crying. She was walking from room to room crying like I'd never heard anyone cry before. I must have called out because she came into my room and tucked the covers around me. "Everything will be all right," she whispered; "go back to sleep." She sat on my bed, toward the foot where she could look out the window, crying softly until her shoulders began to shake. I lay pretending to sleep. She cried like that for nights after my father was killed. It was my mother, not I, whom Marcy had heard.

It was only after Marcy began playing late at night that I remembered my mother crying. In my room, with the door shut against the steam, it seemed she was playing for me alone. I would wake already listening and gradually realize that the music had been going on while I slept, and that I had been shaping my dreams to it. She played only nocturnes those last weeks of winter. Sometimes they seemed to carry over the roofs, but mostly she played so softly that only the air shaft made it possible to hear. I would sit huddled in my covers beside the window listening, looking out at the white dunes on Freddy's roof. The soldier was long gone, his helmet rusted off. Smoke blew unhooded; black flakes with sparking edges wafted out like burning snow. Soot and music and white gusts off the crests buffeted the pane. Even when the icicles began to leak and the streets to turn to brown rivers of slush, the blizzard in the air shaft continued.

Marcy disappeared during the first break in the weather. She left a note that read: "Ma, don't worry."

"That's all," Mrs. Kubiac said, unfolding it for my mother to see. "Not even 'love,' not even her name signed. The whole time I kept telling her 'do something,' she sits playing the piano, and now she does something, when it's too late, unless she goes to some butcher. Ev, what should I do?"

My mother helped Mrs. Kubiac call the hospitals. Each day they called the morgue. After a week, Mrs. Kubiac called the police, and when they couldn't find Marcy, any more than they had been able to find Dzia-Dzia, Mrs. Kubiac began to call people in New York—teachers, old roommates, landlords. She used our phone. "Take it off the rent," she said. Finally, Mrs. Kubiac went to New York herself to search.

When she came back from New York she seemed changed, as if she'd grown too tired to be frantic. Her hair was a different shade of gray so that now you'd never know it had once been blonde. There was a stoop to her shoulders as she descended the stairs on the way to novenas. She no longer came downstairs for tea and long talks. She spent much of her time in church, indistinguishable among the other women from the old country, regulars at the morning requiem mass, wearing babushkas and dressed in black like a sodality of widows, droning endless mournful litanies before the side altar of the Black Virgin of Czesto-chowa.

By the time a letter from Marcy finally came, explaining that the entire time she had been living on the South Side in a Negro neighborhood near the university, and that she had a son whom she'd named Tatum Kubiac—"Tatum" after a famous jazz pianist—it seemed to make little difference. Mrs. Kubiac visited once but didn't go back. People had already learned to glance away from her when certain subjects were mentioned—daughters, grandchildren, music. She had learned to glance away from herself. After she visited Marcy she tried to sell the piano, but the movers couldn't figure how to get it downstairs, nor how anyone had ever managed to move it in.

It took time for the music to fade. I kept catching wisps of it in the air shaft, behind walls and ceilings, under bathwater. Echoes traveled the pipes and wall-papered chutes, the bricked-up flues and dark hallways. Mrs. Kubiac's building seemed riddled with its secret passageways. And, when the music finally disap-peared, its channels remained, conveying silence. Not an ordinary silence of absence and emptiness, but a pure silence beyond daydream and memory, as intense as the music it replaced, which, like music, had the power to change whoever listened. It hushed the close-quartered racket of the old building. It had always been there behind the creaks and drafts and slamming doors, behind the staticky radios, and the flushings and footsteps and crackling fat, behind the wails

of vacuums and kettles and babies, and the voices with their scraps of conversation
and arguments and laughter floating out of flats where people locked themselves
in with all that was private. Even after I no longer missed her, I could still hear the
silence left behind.

QUESTIONS FOR DISCUSSION AND WRITING

1. "Chopin in Winter" seems to have two plot lines: the story of Marcy and
the story of Dzia-Dzia. How are they related?

2. "Chopin in Winter" has a first-person narrator: a mature man looking
back on childhood experiences. To what extent does he express his boyhood
perspective on the material, and to what extent does he bring an adult
understanding?

3. What does the story of Shirley Popel's mother's last words have to do with
the rest of the story?

4. What does the title mean?

Ann Beattie

Ann Beattie (b. 1947), who began publishing her fiction in the 1970s, is often grouped with Raymond Carver and a few other writers of their generation as a "minimalist," a writer who deals with ordinary, even banal characters and trivial, seemingly meaningless events in a flat, understated style. She grew up in a suburb of Washington, D.C., and was educated at American University and the University of Connecticut. After publishing some stories in *The New Yorker,* she published her first collection of short stories, *Distortions,* and her first novel, *Chilly Scenes of Winter,* both in 1976. Later novels include *Falling in Place* (1980), *Love Always* (1985), and *Picturing Will* (1990). Later story collections include *Scenes and Surprises* (1979), *Jacklighting* (1981), *The Burning House* (1982), and *Where You'll Find Me* (1986).

WEEKEND

On Saturday morning Lenore is up before the others. She carries her baby into the living room and puts him in George's favorite chair, which tilts because its back legs are missing, and covers him with a blanket. Then she lights a fire in the fireplace, putting fresh logs on a few embers that are still glowing from the night before. She sits down on the floor beside the chair and checks the baby, who has already gone back to sleep—a good thing, because there are guests in the house. George, the man she lives with, is very hospitable and impetuous; he extends invitations whenever old friends call, urging them to come spend the weekend. Most of the callers are his former students—he used to be an English professor—and when they come it seems to make things much worse. It makes *him* much worse, because he falls into smoking too much and drinking and not eating, and then his ulcer bothers him. When the guests leave, when the weekend is over, she has to cook bland food: applesauce, oatmeal, puddings. And his drinking does not taper off easily anymore; in the past he would stop cold when the guests left, but lately he only tapers down from Scotch to wine, and drinks wine well into the week—a lot of wine, perhaps a whole bottle with his meal—until his stomach is much worse. He is hard to live with. Once when a former student, a woman named Ruth, visited them—a lover, she suspected—she overheard George talking to her in his study, where he had taken her to see a photograph of their house before he began repairing it. George had told Ruth that she, Lenore, stayed with him because she was simple. It hurt her badly, made her actually dizzy with surprise and shame, and since then, no matter who the guests are, she never feels quite at ease on the weekends. In the past she enjoyed some of the things she and George did with their guests, but since overhearing what he said to Ruth she feels that all their visitors have been secretly told the same thing about her. To her, though, George is usually kind. But she is sure that is the reason he has not married her, and when he recently remarked on their daughter's intelligence (she is five years old, a girl named Maria) she found that she could no longer respond with simple pride; now she feels spite as well, feels that Maria exists as proof of her own good genes. She has begun to expect perfection of the child. She knows this is wrong, and she has tried hard not to communicate her anxiety to Maria, who is already, as her kindergarten teacher says, "untypical."

At first Lenore loved George because he was untypical, although after she had moved in with him and lived with him for a while she began to see that he was not

415

exceptional but a variation on a type. She is proud of observing that, and she harbors the discovery—her silent response to his low opinion of her. She does not know why he found her attractive—in the beginning he did—because she does not resemble the pretty, articulate young women he likes to invite, with their lovers or girl friends, to their house for the weekend. None of these young women have husbands; when they bring a man with them at all they bring a lover, and they seem happy not to be married. Lenore, too, is happy to be single—not out of conviction that marriage is wrong but because she knows that it would be wrong to be married to George if he thinks she is simple. She thought at first to confront him with what she had overheard, to demand an explanation. But he can weasel out of any corner. At best, she can mildly fluster him, and later he will only blame it on Scotch. Of course she might ask why he has all these women come to visit, why he devotes so little time to her or the children. To that he would say that it was the quality of the time they spent together that mattered, not the quantity. He has already said that, in fact, without being asked. He says things over and over so that she will accept them as truths. And eventually she does. She does not like to think long and hard, and when there is an answer—even his answer—it is usually easier to accept it and go on with things. She goes on with what she has always done: tending the house and the children and George, when he needs her. She likes to bake and she collects art postcards. She is proud of their house, which was bought cheaply and improved by George when he was still interested in that kind of work, and she is happy to have visitors come there, even if she does not admire them or even like them.

Except for teaching a night course in photography at a junior college once a week, George has not worked since he left the university two years ago, after he was denied tenure. She cannot really tell if he is unhappy working so little, because he keeps busy in other ways. He listens to classical music in the morning, slowly sipping herbal teas, and on fair afternoons he lies outdoors in the sun, no matter how cold the day. He takes photographs, and walks alone in the woods. He does errands for her if they need to be done. Sometimes at night he goes to the library or goes to visit friends; he tells her that these people often ask her to come too, but he says she would not like them. This is true—she would not like them. Recently he has done some late-night cooking. He has always kept a journal, and he is a great letter writer. An aunt left him most of her estate, ten thousand dollars, and said in her will that he was the only one who really cared, who took the time, again and again, to write. He had not seen his aunt for five years before she died, but he wrote regularly. Sometimes Lenore finds notes that he has left for her. Once, on the refrigerator, there was a long note suggesting clever Christmas presents for her family that he had thought of while she was out. Last week he scotch-taped a slip of paper to a casserole dish that contained leftover veal stew, saying: "This was delicious." He does not compliment her verbally, but he likes to let her know that he is pleased.

A few nights ago—the same night they got a call from Julie and Sarah, saying they were coming for a visit—she told him that she wished he would talk more, that he would confide in her.

"Confide what?" he said.

"You always take that attitude," she said. "You pretend that you have no thoughts. Why does there have to be so much silence?"

"I'm not a professor anymore," he said. "I don't have to spend every minute *thinking.*"

But he loves to talk to the young women. He will talk to them on the phone for as much as an hour; he walks with them through the woods for most of the day when they visit. The lovers the young women bring with them always seem to fall behind; they give up and return to the house to sit and talk to her, or to help with the preparation of the meal, or to play with the children. The young woman and George come back refreshed, ready for another round of conversation at dinner.

A few weeks ago one of the young men said to her, "Why do you let it go on?" They had been talking lightly before that—about the weather, the children—and then, in the kitchen, where he was sitting shelling peas, he put his head on the table and said, barely audibly, "Why do you let it go on?" He did not raise his head, and she stared at him, thinking that she must have imagined his speaking. She was surprised—surprised to have heard it, and surprised that he had said nothing after that, which made her doubt that he had spoken.

"Why do I let what go on?" she said.

There was a long silence. "Whatever this sick game is, I don't want to get involved in it," he said at last. "It was none of my business to ask. I understand that you don't want to talk about it."

"But it's really cold out there," she said. "What could happen when it's freezing out?"

He shook his head, the way George did, to indicate that she was beyond understanding. But she wasn't stupid, and she knew what might be going on. She had said the right thing, had been on the right track, but she had to say what she felt, which was that nothing very serious could be happening at that moment because they were walking in the woods. There wasn't even a barn on the property. She knew perfectly well that they were talking.

When George and the young woman had come back, he fixed hot apple juice, into which he trickled rum. Lenore was pleasant, because she was sure of what had not happened; the young man was not, because he did not think as she did. Still at the kitchen table, he ran his thumb across a pea pod as though it were a knife.

This weekend Sarah and Julie are visiting. They came on Friday evening. Sarah was one of George's students—the one who led the fight to have him rehired. She does not look like a troublemaker; she is pale and pretty, with freckles on her cheeks. She talks too much about the past, and this upsets him, disrupts the peace he has made with himself. She tells him that they fired him because he was "in touch" with everything, that they were afraid of him because he was so in touch. The more she tells him the more he remembers, and then it is necessary for Sarah to say the same things again and again; once she reminds him, he seems to need reassurance—needs to have her voice, to hear her bitterness against the members of the tenure committee. By evening they will both be drunk. Sarah will seem both agitating and consoling, Lenore and Julie and the children will be upstairs, in bed. Lenore suspects that she will not be the only one awake listening to them. She thinks that in spite of Julie's glazed look she is really very attentive. The night before, when they were all sitting around the fireplace talking, Sarah made a gesture and almost upset her wineglass, but Julie reached for it and stopped it from toppling over. George and Sarah were talking so energetically that they did not notice. Lenore's eyes met Julie's as Julie's hand shot out. Lenore feels that she is like Julie: Julie's face doesn't betray emotion, even when she is interested, even when she cares deeply. Being the same kind of person, Lenore can recognize this.

Before Sarah and Julie arrived Friday evening, Lenore asked George if Sarah was his lover.

"Don't be ridiculous," he said. "You think every student is my lover? Is Julie my lover?"

She said, "That wasn't what I said."

"Well, if you're going to be preposterous, go ahead and say that," he said. "If you think about it long enough, it would make a lot of sense, wouldn't it?"

He would not answer her question about Sarah. He kept throwing Julie's name into it. Some other woman might then think that he was protesting too strongly— that Julie really was his lover. She thought no such thing. She also stopped suspecting Sarah, because he wanted that, and it was her habit to oblige him.

He is twenty-one years older than Lenore. On his last birthday he was fifty-five. His daughter from his first marriage (his *only* marriage; she keeps reminding herself that they are not married, because it often seems that they might as well be) sent him an Irish country hat. The present made him irritable. He kept putting it on and putting it down hard on his head. "She wants to make me a laughable old man," he said. "She wants me to put this on and go around like a fool." He wore the hat all morning, complaining about it, frightening the children. Eventually, to calm him, she said, "She intended *nothing.*" She said it with finality, her tone so insistent that he listened to her. But having lost his reason for bitterness, he said, "Just because you don't think doesn't mean others don't think." Is he getting old? She does not want to think of him getting old. In spite of his ulcer, his body is hard. He is tall and handsome, with a thick mustache and a thin black goatee, and there is very little gray in his kinky black hair. He dresses in tight-fitting blue jeans and black turtleneck sweaters in the winter, and old white shirts with the sleeves rolled up in the summer. He pretends not to care about his looks, but he does. He shaves carefully, scraping slowly down each side of his goatee. He orders his soft leather shoes from a store in California. After taking one of his long walks—even if he does it twice a day—he invariably takes a shower. He always looks refreshed, and very rarely admits any insecurity. A few times, at night in bed, he has asked, "Am I still the man of your dreams?" And when she says yes he always laughs, turning it into a joke, as if he didn't care. She knows he does. He pretends to have no feeling for clothing, but actually he cares so strongly about his turtlenecks and shirts (a few are Italian silk) and shoes that he will have no others. She has noticed that the young women who visit are always vain. When Sarah arrived, she was wearing a beautiful silk scarf, pale as conch shells.

Sitting on the floor on Saturday morning, Lenore watches the fire she has just lit. The baby, tucked in George's chair, smiles in his sleep, and Lenore thinks what a good companion he would be if only he were an adult. She gets up and goes into the kitchen and tears open a package of yeast and dissolves it, with sugar and salt, in hot water, slushing her fingers through it and shivering because it is so cold in the kitchen. She will bake bread for dinner—there is always a big meal in the early evening when they have guests. But what will she do for the rest of the day? George told the girls the night before that on Saturday they would walk in the woods, but she does not really enjoy hiking, and George will be irritated because of the discussion the night before, and she does not want to aggravate him. "You are unwilling to challenge anyone," her brother wrote her in a letter that came a few days ago. He has written her for years—all the years she has been with George— asking when she is going to end the relationship. She rarely writes back because she knows her answers sound too simple. She has a comfortable house. She cooks. She keeps busy and she loves her two children. "It seems unkind to say *but*," her brother writes, "but . . ." It is true; she likes simple things. Her brother, who is a lawyer in Cambridge, cannot understand that.

Lenore rubs her hand down the side of her face and says good morning to Julie and Sarah, who have come downstairs. Sarah does not want orange juice; she already looks refreshed and ready for the day. Lenore pours a glass for Julie. George calls from the hallway, "Ready to roll?" Lenore is surprised that he wants to leave so early. She goes into the living room. George is wearing a denim jacket, his hands in the pockets.

"Morning," he says to Lenore. "You're not up for a hike, are you?"

Lenore looks at him, but does not answer. As she stands there, Sarah walks around her and joins George in the hallway and he holds the door open for her. "Let's walk to the store and get Hershey bars to give us energy for a long hike," George says to Sarah. They are gone. Lenore finds Julie still in the kitchen, waiting for the water to boil. Julie says that she had a bad night and she is happy not to be going with George and Sarah. Lenore fixes tea for them. Maria sits next to her on the sofa, sipping orange juice. The baby likes company, but Maria is a very private child; she would rather that she and her mother were always alone. She has given up being possessive about her father. Now she gets out a cardboard box and takes out her mother's collection of postcards, which she arranges on the floor in careful groups. Whenever she looks up, Julie smiles nervously at her; Maria does not smile, and Lenore doesn't prod her. Lenore goes into the kitchen to punch down the bread, and Maria follows. Maria has recently gotten over chicken pox, and there is a small new scar in the center of her forehead. Instead of looking at Maria's blue eyes, Lenore lately has found herself focusing on the imperfection.

As Lenore is stretching the loaves onto the cornmeal-covered baking sheet, she hears the rain start. It hits hard on the garage roof.

After a few minutes Julie comes into the kitchen. "They're caught in this downpour," Julie says. "If Sarah had left the car keys, I could go get them."

"Take my car and pick them up," Lenore says, pointing with her elbow to the keys hanging on a nail near the door.

"But I don't know where the store is."

"You must have passed it driving to our house last night. Just go out of the driveway and turn right. It's along the main road."

Julie gets her purple sweater and takes the car keys. "I'll be right back," she says.

Lenore can sense that she is glad to escape from the house, that she is happy the rain began.

In the living room Lenore turns the pages of a magazine, and Maria mutters a refrain of "Blue, blue, dark blue, green blue," noticing the color every time it appears. Lenore sips her tea. She puts a Michael Hurley record on George's stereo. Michael Hurley is good rainy-day music. George has hundreds of records. His students used to love to paw through them. Cleverly, he has never made any attempt to keep up with what is currently popular. Everything is jazz or eclectic: Michael Hurley, Keith Jarrett, Ry Cooder.

Julie comes back. "I couldn't find them," she says. She looks as if she expects to be punished.

Lenore is surprised. She is about to say something like "You certainly didn't look very hard, did you?" but she catches Julie's eye. She looks young and afraid, and perhaps even a little crazy.

"Well, we tried," Lenore says.

Julie stands in front of the fire, with her back to Lenore. Lenore knows she is thinking that she is dense—that she does not recognize the implications.

"They might have walked through the woods instead of along the road," Lenore says. "That's possible."

"But they would have gone out to the road to thumb when the rain began, wouldn't they?"

Perhaps she misunderstood what Julie was thinking. Perhaps it has never occurred to Julie until now what might be going on.

"Maybe they got lost," Julie says. "Maybe something happened to them."

"Nothing happened to them," Lenore says. Julie turns around and Lenore catches the small point of light in her eye again. "Maybe they took shelter under a tree," she says. "Maybe they're screwing. How should I know?"

It is not a word Lenore often uses. She usually tries not to think about that at all, but she can sense that Julie is very upset.

"Really?" Julie says. "Don't you care, Mrs. Anderson?"

Lenore is amused. There's a switch. All the students call her husband George and her Lenore; now one of them wants to think there's a real adult here to explain all this to her.

"What am I going to do?" Lenore says. She shrugs.

Julie does not answer.

"Would you like me to pour you tea?" Lenore asks.

"Yes," Julie says. "Please."

George and Sarah return in the middle of the afternoon. George says that they decided to go on a spree to the big city—it is really a small town he is talking about, but calling it the big city gives him an opportunity to speak ironically. They sat in a restaurant bar, waiting for the rain to stop, George says, and then they thumbed a ride home. "But I'm completely sober," George says, turning for the first time to Sarah. "What about you?" He is all smiles. Sarah lets him down. She looks embarrassed. Her eyes meet Lenore's quickly, and jump to Julie. The two girls stare at each other, and Lenore, left with only George to look at, looks at the fire and then gets up to pile on another log.

Gradually it becomes clear that they are trapped together by the rain. Maria undresses her paper doll and deliberately rips a feather off its hat. Then she takes the pieces to Lenore, almost in tears. The baby cries, and Lenore takes him off the sofa, where he has been sleeping under his yellow blanket, and props him in the space between her legs as she leans back on her elbows to watch the fire. It's her fire, and she has the excuse of presiding over it.

"How's my boy?" George says. The baby looks, and looks away.

It gets dark early, because of the rain. At four-thirty George uncorks a bottle of Beaujolais and brings it into the living room, with four glasses pressed against his chest with his free arm. Julie rises nervously to extract the glasses, thanking him too profusely for the wine. She gives a glass to Sarah without looking at her.

They sit in a semicircle in front of the fire and drink the wine. Julie leafs through magazines—*New Times, National Geographic*—and Sarah holds a small white dish painted with gray-green leaves that she has taken from the coffee table; the dish contains a few shells and some acorn caps, a polished stone or two, and Sarah lets these objects run through her fingers. There are several such dishes in the house, assembled by George. He and Lenore gathered the shells long ago, the first time they went away together, at a beach in North Carolina. But the acorn caps, the shiny turquoise and amethyst stones—those are there, she knows, because George likes the effect they have on visitors; it is an expected unconventionality, really. He has also acquired a few small framed pictures, which he points out to guests who are more important than worshipful students—tiny oil paintings of fruit, prints with small details from the unicorn tapestries. He pretends to like small, elegant things. Actually, when they visit museums in New York he goes first to El Grecos and big Mark Rothko canvases. She could never get him to admit that what he said or did was sometimes false. Once, long ago, when he asked if he was still the man of her dreams, she said, "We don't get along well anymore." "Don't talk about it," he said—no denial, no protest. At best, she could say things and get away with them; she could never get him to continue such a conversation.

At the dinner table, lit with white candles burning in empty wine bottles, they eat off his grandmother's small flowery plates. Lenore looks out a window and sees, very faintly in the dark, their huge oak tree. The rain has stopped. A few stars have come out, and there are glints on the wet branches. The oak tree grows very close to the window. George loved it when her brother once suggested that some of the bushes and trees should be pruned away from the house so it would not always be so dark inside; it gave him a chance to rave about the beauty of nature, to say that he would never tamper with it. "It's like a tomb in here all day," her brother had said. Since moving here, George has learned the names of almost all the things that are growing on the land: he can point out abelia bushes, spirea, laurels. He subscribes to *National Geographic* (although she rarely sees him looking at it). He is at last in touch, he says, being in the country puts him in touch. He is saying it now to Sarah, who has put down her ivory-handled fork to listen to him. He gets up to change the record. Side two of the Telemann record begins softly.

Sarah is still very much on guard with Lenore; she makes polite conversation with her quickly when George is out of the room. "You people are so wonderful," she says. "I wish my parents could be like you."

"George would be pleased to hear that," Lenore says, lifting a small piece of pasta to her lips.

When George is seated again, Sarah, anxious to please, tells him, "If only my father could be like you."

"Your father," George says. "I won't have that analogy." He says it pleasantly, but barely disguises his dismay at the comparison.

"I mean, he cares about nothing but business," the girl stumbles on.

The music, in contrast, grows lovelier.

Lenore goes into the kitchen to get the salad and hears George say, "I simply won't let you girls leave. Nobody leaves on a Saturday."

There are polite protests, there are compliments to Lenore on the meal—there is too much talk. Lenore has trouble caring about what's going on. The food is warm and delicious. She pours more wine and lets them talk.

"Godard, yes, I know . . . panning that row of honking cars *so* slowly, that long line of cars stretching on and on."

She has picked up the end of George's conversation. His arm slowly waves out over the table, indicating the line of motionless cars in the movie.

"That's a lovely plant," Julie says to Lenore.

"It's Peruvian ivy," Lenore says. She smiles. She is supposed to smile. She will not offer to hack shoots off her plant for these girls.

Sarah asks for a Dylan record when the Telemann finishes playing. White wax drips onto the wood table. George waits for it to solidify slightly, then scrapes up the little circles and with thumb and index finger flicks them gently toward Sarah. He explains (although she asked for no particular Dylan record) that he has only Dylan before he went electric. And "Planet Waves"—"because it's so romantic. That's silly of me, but true." Sarah smiles at him. Julie smiles at Lenore. Julie is being polite, taking her cues from Sarah, really not understanding what's going on. Lenore does not smile back. She has done enough to put them at ease. She is tired now, brought down by the music, a full stomach, and again the sounds of rain outside. For dessert there is homemade vanilla ice cream, made by George, with small black vanilla-bean flecks in it. He is still drinking wine, though; another bottle has been opened. He sips wine and then taps his spoon on his ice cream, looking at Sarah. Sarah smiles, letting them all see the smile, then sucks the ice cream off her spoon. Julie is missing more and more of what's going on. Lenore watches as Julie strokes her hand absently on her napkin. She is wearing a thin silver choker and—Lenore notices for the first time—a thin silver ring on the third finger of her right hand.

"It's just terrible about Anna," George says, finishing his wine, his ice cream melting, looking at no one in particular, although Sarah was the one who brought up Anna the night before, when they had been in the house only a short time— Anna dead, hit by a car, hardly an accident at all. Anna was also a student of his. The driver of the car was drunk, but for some reason charges were not pressed. (Sarah and George have talked about this before, but Lenore blocks it out. What can she do about it? She met Anna once: a beautiful girl, with tiny, childlike hands, her hair thin and curly—wary, as beautiful people are wary.) Now the driver has been flipping out, Julie says, and calling Anna's parents, wanting to talk to them to find out why it has happened.

The baby begins to cry. Lenore goes upstairs, pulls up more covers, talks to him for a minute. He settles for this. She goes downstairs. The wine must have affected her more than she realizes; otherwise, why is she counting the number of steps?

In the candlelit dining room, Julie sits alone at the table. The girl has been left alone again; George and Sarah took the umbrellas, decided to go for a walk in the rain.

◄◄◄ ►►►

It is eight o'clock. Since helping Lenore load the dishes into the dishwasher, when she said what a beautiful house Lenore had, Julie has said very little. Lenore is tired, and does not want to make conversation. They sit in the living room and drink wine.

"Sarah is my best friend," Julie says. She seems apologetic about it. "I was so out of it when I came back to college. I was in Italy, with my husband, and suddenly I was back in the States. I couldn't make friends. But Sarah wasn't like the other people. She cared enough to be nice to me."

"How long have you been friends?"

"For two years. She's really the best friend I've ever had. We understand things—we don't always have to talk about them."

"Like her relationship with George," Lenore says.

Too direct. Too unexpected. Julie has no answer.

"You act as if you're to blame," Lenore says.

"I feel strange because you're such a nice lady."

A nice lady! What an odd way to speak. Has she been reading Henry James? Lenore has never known what to think of herself, but she certainly thinks of herself as being more complicated than a "lady."

"Why do you look that way?" Julie asks. "You *are* nice. I think you've been very nice to us. You've given up your whole weekend."

"I always give up my weekends. Weekends are the only time we socialize, really. In a way, it's good to have something to do."

"But to have it turn out like this . . ." Julie says. "I think I feel so strange because when my own marriage broke up I didn't even suspect. I mean, I couldn't act the way you do, anyway, but I—"

"For all I know, nothing's going on," Lenore says. "For all I know, your friend is flattering herself, and George is trying to make me jealous." She puts two more logs on the fire. When these are gone, she will either have to walk to the woodshed or give up and go to bed. "Is there something . . . *major* going on?" she asks.

Julie is sitting on the rug, by the fire, twirling her hair with her finger. "I didn't know it when I came out here," she says. "Sarah's put me in a very awkward position."

"But do you know how far it has gone?" Lenore asks, genuinely curious now.

"No," Julie says.

No way to know if she's telling the truth. Would Julie speak the truth to a lady? Probably not.

"Anyway," Lenore says with a shrug, "I don't want to think about it all the time."

"I'd never have the courage to live with a man and not marry," Julie says. "I mean, I wish I had, that we hadn't gotten married, but I just don't have that kind of . . . I'm not secure enough."

"You have to live somewhere," Lenore says.

Julie is looking at her as if she does not believe that she is sincere. Am I? Lenore wonders. She has lived with George for six years, and sometimes she thinks she has caught his way of playing games, along with his colds, his bad moods.

"I'll show you something," Lenore says. She gets up, and Julie follows. Lenore puts on the light in George's study, and they walk through it to a bathroom he has converted to a darkroom. Under a table, in a box behind another box, there is a stack of pictures. Lenore takes them out and hands them to Julie. They are pictures that Lenore found in his darkroom last summer; they were left out by mistake, no doubt, and she found them when she went in with some contact prints he had left in their bedroom. They are high-contrast photographs of George's face. In all of them he looks very serious and very sad; in some of them his eyes seem to be narrowed in pain. In one, his mouth is open. It is an excellent photograph of a man in agony, a man about to scream.

"What are they?" Julie whispers.

"Pictures he took of himself," Lenore says. She shrugs. "So I stay," she says.

Julie nods. Lenore nods, taking the pictures back. Lenore has not thought until this minute that this may be why she stays. In fact, it is not the only reason. It is just a very demonstrable, impressive reason. When she first saw the pictures, her own face had become as distorted as George's. She had simply not known what to do. She had been frightened and ashamed. Finally she put them in an empty box, and put the box behind another box. She did not even want him to see the horrible pictures again. She does not know if he has ever found them, pushed back against the wall in that other box. As George says, there can be too much communication between people.

Later, Sarah and George come back to the house. It is still raining. It turns out that they took a bottle of brandy with them, and they are both drenched and drunk. He holds Sarah's finger with one of his. Sarah, seeing Lenore, lets his finger go. But then he turns—they have not even said hello yet—and grabs her up, spins her around, stumbling into the living room, and says, "I am in love."

Julie and Lenore watch them in silence.

"See no evil," George says, gesturing with the empty brandy bottle to Julie.

"Hear no evil," George says, pointing to Lenore. He hugs Sarah closer. "I speak no evil. I speak the truth. I am in love!"

Sarah squirms away from him, runs from the room and up the stairs in the dark.

George looks blankly after her, then sinks to the floor and smiles. He is going to pass it off as a joke. Julie looks at him in horror, and from upstairs Sarah can be heard sobbing. Her crying awakens the baby.

"Excuse me," Lenore says. She climbs the stairs and goes into her son's room, and picks him up. She talks gently to him, soothing him with lies. He is too sleepy to be alarmed for long. In a few minutes he is asleep again, and she puts him back in his crib. In the next room Sarah is crying more quietly now. Her crying is so awful that Lenore almost joins in, but instead she pats her son. She stands in the dark by the crib and then at last goes out and down the hallway to her bedroom. She takes off her clothes and gets into the cold bed. She concentrates on breathing normally. With the door closed and Sarah's door closed, she can hardly hear her. Someone taps lightly on her door.

"Mrs. Anderson," Julie whispers. "Is this your room?"

"Yes," Lenore says. She does not ask her in.

"We're going to leave. I'm going to get Sarah and leave. I didn't want to just walk out without saying anything."

Lenore just cannot think how to respond. It was really very kind of Julie to say something. She is very close to tears, so she says nothing.

"Okay," Julie says, to reassure herself. "Good night. We're going."

There is no more crying. Footsteps. Miraculously, the baby does not wake up again, and Maria has slept through all of it. She has always slept well. Lenore herself sleeps worse and worse, and she knows that George walks much of the night, most nights. She hasn't said anything about it. If he thinks she's simple, what good would her simple wisdom do him?

The oak tree scrapes against the window in the wind and rain. Here on the second floor, under the roof, the tinny tapping is very loud. If Sarah and Julie say anything to George before they leave, she doesn't hear them. She hears the car start, then die out. It starts again—she is praying for the car to go—and after conking out once more it rolls slowly away, crunching gravel. The bed is no warmer; she shivers. She tries hard to fall asleep. The effort keeps her awake. She squints her eyes in concentration instead of closing them. The only sound in the house is the electric clock, humming by her bed. It is not even midnight.

She gets up, and without turning on the light, walks downstairs. George is still in the living room. The fire is nothing but ashes and glowing bits of wood. It is as cold there as it was in the bed.

"That damn bitch," George says. "I should have known she was a stupid little girl."

"You went too far," Lenore says. "I'm the only one you can go too far with."

"Damn it," he says, and pokes the fire. A few sparks shoot up. "Damn it," he repeats under his breath.

His sweater is still wet. His shoes are muddy and ruined. Sitting on the floor by the fire, his hair matted down on his head, he looks ugly, older, unfamiliar.

She thinks of another time, when it was warm. They were walking on the beach together, shortly after they met, gathering shells. Little waves were rolling in. The sun went behind the clouds and there was a momentary illusion that the clouds were still and the sun was racing ahead of them. "Catch me," he said, breaking away from her. They had been talking quietly, gathering shells. She was so surprised at him for breaking away that she ran with all her energy and did catch him, putting her hand out and taking hold of the band of his swimming trunks as he veered into the water. If she hadn't stopped him, would he really have run far out into the water, until she couldn't follow anymore? He turned on her, just as abruptly as he had run away, and grabbed her and hugged her hard, lifted her high. She had clung to him, held him close. He had tried the same thing when he came back from the walk with Sarah, and it hadn't worked.

"I wouldn't care if their car went off the road," he says bitterly.

"Don't say that," she says.

They sit in silence, listening to the rain. She slides over closer to him, puts her hand on his shoulder and leans her head there, as if he could protect her from the awful things he has wished into being.

QUESTIONS FOR DISCUSSION AND WRITING

1. Analyze the narrator's voice in this story. The story is largely told from Lenore's point of view. Is the narrator's attitude identical to Lenore's, or is there some ironic distance?

2. How would you characterize George and Lenore's relationship? Is Lenore purely a victim of a self-centered and callous man?

3. What is the effect of telling the entire story in the present tense?

4. We are told that "At first Lenore loved George because he was untypical, although after she had moved in with him and lived with him for a while she began to see that he was not exceptional but a variation on a type." What is the "type"?

5. In the last sentence of the story, Lenore sits close to George "as if he could protect her from the awful things he has wished into being." What are the "awful things," and in what sense has George "wished" them "into being"?

Linda Hogan

Linda Hogan (b. 1947) is a Chickasaw who was born in Colorado and educated at the University of Colorado. She has published several books of poems, including *Eclipse* (1983), *Seeing Through the Sun* (1985), and *Savings* (1988). Her novel *Mean Spirit* appeared in 1990.

AUNT MOON'S YOUNG MAN

That autumn when the young man came to town, there was a deep blue sky. On their way to the fair, the wagons creaked into town. One buckboard, driven by cloudy white horses, carried a grunting pig inside its wooden slats. Another had cages of chickens. In the heat, the chickens did not flap their wings. They sounded tired and old, and their shoulders drooped like old men.

There was tension in the air. Those people who still believed in omens would turn to go home, I thought, white chicken feathers caught on the wire cages they brought, reminding us all that the cotton was poor that year and that very little of it would line the big trailers outside the gins.

A storm was brewing over the plains, and beneath its clouds a few people from the city drove dusty black motorcars through town, angling around the statue of General Pickens on Main Street. They refrained from honking at the wagons and the white, pink-eyed horses. The cars contained no animal life, just neatly folded stacks of quilts, jellies, and tomato relish, large yellow gourds, and pumpkins that looked like the round faces of children through half-closed windows.

"The biting flies aren't swarming today," my mother said. She had her hair done up in rollers. It was almost dry. She was leaning against the window frame, looking at the ink-blue trees outside. I could see Bess Evening's house through the glass, appearing to sit like a small, hand-built model upon my mother's shoulder. My mother was a dreamer, standing at the window with her green dress curved over her hip.

Her dress was hemmed slightly shorter on one side than on the other. I decided not to mention it. The way she leaned, with her abdomen tilted out, was her natural way of standing. She still had good legs, despite the spidery blue veins she said came from carrying the weight of us kids inside her for nine months each. She also blamed us for her few gray hairs.

She mumbled something about "the silence before the storm" as I joined her at the window.

She must have been looking at the young man for a long time, pretending to watch the sky. He was standing by the bushes and the cockscombs. There was a flour sack on the ground beside him. I thought at first it might be filled with something he brought for the fair, but the way his hat sat on it and a pair of black boots stood beside it, I could tell it held his clothing, and that he was passing through Pickens on his way to or from some city.

"It's mighty quiet for the first day of fair," my mother said. She sounded far away. Her eyes were on the young stranger. She unrolled a curler and checked a strand of hair.

We talked about the weather and the sky, but we both watched the young man. In the deep blue of sky his white shirt stood out like a light. The low hills were fire-gold and leaden.

One of my mother's hands was limp against her thigh. The other moved down from the rollers and touched the green cloth at her chest, playing with a flaw in the fabric.

"Maybe it was the tornado," I said about the stillness in the air. The tornado had passed through a few days ago, touching down here and there. It exploded my cousin's house trailer, but it left his motorcycle standing beside it, untouched. "Tornadoes have no sense of value," my mother had said. "They are always taking away the saints and leaving behind the devils."

The young man stood in that semi-slumped, half-straight manner of fullblood Indians. Our blood was mixed like Heinz 57, and I always thought of purebloods as better than us. While my mother eyed his plain moccasins, she patted her rolled hair as if to put it in order. I was counting the small brown flowers in the blistered wallpaper, the way I counted ceiling tiles in the new school, and counted each step when I walked.

I pictured Aunt Moon inside her house up on my mother's shoulder. I imagined her dark face above the yellow oilcloth, her hands reflecting the yellow as they separated dried plants. She would rise slowly, as I'd seen her do, take a good long time to brush out her hair, and braid it once again. She would pet her dog, Mister, with long slow strokes while she prepared herself for the fair.

My mother moved aside, leaving the house suspended in the middle of the window, where it rested on a mound of land. My mother followed my gaze. She always wanted to know what I was thinking or doing. "I wonder," she said, "why in tarnation Bess's father built that house up there. It gets all the heat and wind."

I stuck up for Aunt Moon. "She can see everything from there, the whole town and everything."

"Sure, and everything can see her. A wonder she doesn't have ghosts."

I wondered what she meant by that, everything seeing Aunt Moon. I guessed by her lazy voice that she meant nothing. There was no cutting edge to her words.

"And don't call her Aunt Moon." My mother was reading my mind again, one of her many tricks. "I know what you're thinking," she would say when I thought I looked expressionless. "You are thinking about finding Mrs. Mark's ring and holding it for a reward."

I would look horrified and tell her that she wasn't even lukewarm, but the truth was that I'd been thinking exactly those thoughts. I resented my mother for guessing my innermost secrets. She was like God, everywhere at once knowing everything. I tried to concentrate on something innocent. I thought about pickles. I was safe; she didn't say a word about dills or sweets.

Bess, Aunt Moon, wasn't really my aunt. She was a woman who lived alone and had befriended me. I liked Aunt Moon and the way she moved, slowly, taking up as much space as she wanted and doing it with ease. She had wide lips and straight eyelashes.

Aunt Moon dried medicine herbs in the manner of her parents. She knew about plants, both the helpful ones and the ones that were poisonous in all but the smallest of doses. And she knew how to cut wood and how to read the planets. She told me why I was stubborn. It had to do with my being born in May. I believed her because my father was born a few days after me, and he was stubborn as all get out, even compared to me.

Aunt Moon was special. She had life in her. The rest of the women in town were cold in the eye and fretted over their husbands. I didn't want to be like them. They condemned the men for drinking and gambling, but even after the loudest quarrels, ones we'd overhear, they never failed to cook for their men. They'd cook platters of lard-fried chicken, bowls of mashed potatoes, and pitchers of creamy flour gravy.

Bess called those meals "sure death by murder."

Our town was full of large and nervous women with red spots on their thin-skinned necks, and we had single women who lived with brothers and sisters or took care of an elderly parent. Bess had comments on all of these: "They have eaten their anger and grown large," she would say. And there were the sullen ones who took care of men broken by the war, women who were hurt by the men's stories of death and glory but never told them to get on with living, like I would have done.

Bessie's own brother, J.D., had gone to the war and returned with softened, weepy eyes. He lived at the veterans hospital and he did office work there on his good days. I met him once and knew by the sweetness of his eyes that he had never killed anyone, but something about him reminded me of the lonely old shacks out on cotton farming land. His eyes were broken windows.

"Where do you think that young man is headed?" my mother asked.

Something in her voice was wistful and lonely. I looked at her face, looked out the window at the dark man, and looked back at my mother again. I had never thought about her from inside the skin. She was the mind reader in the family, but suddenly I knew how she did it. The inner workings of the mind were clear in her face, like words in a book. I could even feel her thoughts in the pit of my stomach. I was feeling embarrassed at what my mother was thinking when the stranger crossed the street. In front of him an open truck full of prisoners passed by. They wore large white shirts and pants, like immigrants from Mexico. I began to count the flowers in the wallpaper again, and the truckful of prisoners passed by, and when it was gone, the young man had also vanished into thin air.

Besides the young man, another thing I remember about the fair that year was the man in the bathroom. On the first day of the fair, the prisoners were bending over like great white sails, their black and brown hands stuffing trash in canvas bags. Around them the children washed and brushed their cows and raked fresh straw about their pigs. My friend Elaine and I escaped the dust-laden air and went into the women's public toilets, where we shared a stolen cigarette. We heard someone open the door, and we fanned the smoke. Elaine stood on the toilet seat so her sisters wouldn't recognize her shoes. Then it was silent, so we opened the stall and stepped out. At first the round dark man, standing by the door, looked like a woman, but then I noticed the day's growth of beard at his jawline. He wore a blue work shirt and a little straw hat. He leaned against the wall, his hand moving inside his pants. I grabbed Elaine, who was putting lipstick on her cheeks like rouge, and pulled her outside the door, the tube of red lipstick still in her hand.

Outside, we nearly collapsed by a trash can, laughing. "Did you see that? It was a man! In the women's bathroom." She smacked me on the back.

We knew nothing of men's hands inside their pants, so we began to follow him like store detectives, but as we rounded a corner behind his shadow, I saw Aunt Moon walking away from the pigeon cages. She was moving slowly with her cane, through the path's sawdust, feathers and sand.

"Aunt Moon, there was a man in the bathroom," I said, and then remembered the chickens I wanted to tell her about. Elaine ran off. I didn't know if she was still following the man or not, but I'd lost interest when I saw Aunt Moon.

"Did you see those chickens that lay the green eggs?" I asked Aunt Moon.

She wagged her head no, so I grabbed her free elbow and guided her past the pigeons with curly feathers and the turkeys with red wattles, right up to the chickens.

"They came all the way from South America. They sell for five dollars, can you imagine?" Five dollars was a lot for chickens when we were still recovering from the Great Depression, men were still talking about what they'd done with the CCC, and children still got summer complaint and had to be carried around crippled for months.

She peered into the cage. The eggs were smooth and resting in the straw. "I'll be" was all she said.

I studied her face for a clue as to why she was quiet, thinking she was mad or something. I wanted to read her thoughts as easily as I'd read my mother's. In the strange light of the sky, her eyes slanted a bit more than usual. I watched her carefully. I looked at the downward curve of her nose and saw the young man reflected in her eyes. I turned around.

On the other side of the cage that held the chickens from Araucania was the man my mother had watched. Bess pretended to be looking at the little Jersey cattle in the distance, but I could tell she was seeing that man. He had a calm look on his face and his dark chest was smooth as oil where his shirt was opened. His eyes were large and black. They were fixed on Bess like he was a hypnotist or something magnetic that tried to pull Bess Evening toward it, even though her body stepped back. She did step back, I remember that, but even so, everything in her went forward, right up to him.

I didn't know if it was just me or if his presence charged the air, but suddenly the oxygen was gone. It was like the fire at the Fisher Hardware when all the air was drawn into the flame. Even the chickens clucked softly, as if suffocating, and the cattle were more silent in the straw. The pulse in everything changed.

I don't know what would have happened if the rooster hadn't crowed just then, but he did, and everything returned to normal. The rooster strutted and we turned to watch him.

Bessie started walking away and I went with her. We walked past the men and boys who were shooting craps in a cleared circle. One of them rubbed the dice between his hands as we were leaving, his eyes closed, his body's tight muscles willing a winning throw. He called me Lady Luck as we walked by. He said, "There goes Lady Luck," and he tossed the dice.

At dinner that evening we could hear the dance band tuning up in the make-shift beer garden, playing a few practice songs to the empty tables with their red cloths. They played "The Tennessee Waltz." For a while, my mother sang along with it. She had brushed her hair one hundred strokes and now she was talking and regretting talking all at the same time. "He was such a handsome man," she said. My father wiped his face with a handkerchief and rested his elbows on the table. He chewed and looked at nothing in particular. "For the longest time he stood there by the juniper bushes."

My father drank some coffee and picked up the newspaper. Mother cleared the table, one dish at a time and not in stacks like usual. "His clothes were neat. He must not have come from very far away." She moved the salt shaker from the end of the table to the center, then back again.

"I'll wash," I volunteered.

Mother said, "Bless you," and touched herself absently near the waist, as if to remove an apron. "I'll go get ready for the dance," she said.

My father turned a page of the paper.

The truth was, my mother was already fixed up for the dance. Her hair looked soft and beautiful. She had slipped into her new dress early in the day, "to break it in," she said. She wore nylons and she was barefoot and likely to get a runner. I would have warned her, but it seemed out of place, my warning. Her face was softer than usual, her lips painted to look full, and her eyebrows were much darker than usual.

"Do you reckon that young man came here for the rodeo?" She hollered in from the living room, where she powdered her nose. Normally she made up in front of the bathroom mirror, but the cabinet had been slammed and broken mysteriously one night during an argument so we had all taken to grooming ourselves in the small framed mirror in the living room.

I could not put my finger on it, but all the women at the dance that night were looking at the young man. It wasn't exactly that he was handsome. There was something else. He was alive in his whole body while the other men walked with great effort and stiffness, even those who did little work and were still young. Their male bodies had no language of their own in the way that his did. The women themselves seemed confused and lonely in the presence of the young man, and they were ridiculous in their behavior, laughing too loud, blushing like schoolgirls, or casting him a flirting eye. Even the older women were brighter than usual. Mrs. Tubby, whose face was usually as grim as the statue of General Pickens, the Cherokee hater, played with her necklace until her neck had red lines from the chain. Mrs. Tens twisted a strand of her hair over and over. Her sister tripped over a chair because she'd forgotten to watch where she was going.

The men, sneaking drinks from bottles in paper bags, did not notice any of the fuss.

Maybe it was his hands. His hands were strong and dark.

I stayed late, even after wives pulled their husbands away from their ball game talk and insisted they dance.

My mother and father were dancing. My mother smiled up into my father's face as he turned her this way and that. Her uneven skirt swirled a little around her legs. She had a run in her nylons, as I predicted. My father, who was called Peso by the townspeople, wore his old clothes. He had his usual look about him, and I noticed that faraway, unfocused gaze on the other men too. They were either distant or they were present but rowdy, embarrassing the women around them with the loud talk of male things: work and hunting, fights, this or that pretty girl. Occasionally they told a joke, like, "Did you hear the one about the traveling salesman?"

The dancers whirled around the floor, some tapping their feet, some shuffling, the women in new dresses and dark hair all curled up like in movie magazines, the men with new leather boots and crew cuts. My dad's rear stuck out in back, the way he danced. His hand clutched my mother's waist.

That night, Bessie arrived late. She was wearing a white dress with a full gathered skirt. The print was faded and I could just make out the little blue stars on the cloth. She carried a yellow shawl over her arm. Her long hair was braided as usual in the manner of the older Chickasaw women, like a wreath on her head. She was different from the others with her bright shawls. Sometimes she wore a heavy shell necklace or a collection of bracelets on her arm. They jangled when she talked with me, waving her hands to make a point. Like the time she told me that the soul is a small woman inside the eye who leaves at night to wander new places.

No one had ever known her to dance before, but that night the young man and Aunt Moon danced together among the artificial geraniums and plastic carnations. They held each other gently like two breakable vases. They didn't look at each other or smile the way the other dancers did; that's how I knew they liked each other. His large dark hand was on the small of her back. Her hand rested tenderly on his shoulder. The other dancers moved away from them and there was empty space all around them.

My father went out into the dark to smoke and to play a hand or two of poker. My mother went to sit with some of the other women, all of them pulling their damp hair away from their necks and letting it fall back again, or furtively putting on lipstick, fanning themselves, and sipping their beers.

"He puts me in the mind of a man I once knew," said Mrs. Tubby.

"Look at them," said Mrs. Tens. "Don't you think he's young enough to be her son?"

With my elbows on my knees and my chin in my hands, I watched Aunt Moon step and square when my mother loomed up like a shadow over the bleachers where I sat.

"Young lady," she said in a scolding voice. "You were supposed to go home and put the children to bed."

I looked from her stern face to my sister Susan, who was like a chubby angel sleeping beside me. Peso Junior had run off to the gambling game, where he was pushing another little boy around. My mother followed my gaze and looked at Junior. She put her hands on her hips and said, "Boys!"

My sister Roberta, who was twelve, had stayed close to the women all night, listening to their talk about the fullblood who had come to town for a rodeo or something and who danced so far away from Bessie that they didn't look friendly at all except for the fact that the music had stopped and they were still waltzing.

Margaret Tubby won the prize money that year for the biggest pumpkin. It was 220.4 centimeters in circumference and weighed 190 pounds and had to be carried on a stretcher by the volunteer firemen. Mrs. Tubby was the town's chief social justice. She sat most days on the bench outside the grocery store. Sitting there like a full-chested hawk on a fence, she held court. She had watched Bess Evening for years with her sharp gold eyes. "This is the year I saw it coming," she told my mother, as if she'd just been dying for Bess to go wrong. It showed up in the way Bess walked, she said, that the woman was coming to a no good end just like the rest of her family had done.

"When do you think she had time to grow that pumpkin?" Mother asked as we escaped Margaret Tubby's court on our way to the store. I knew what she meant, that Mrs. Tubby did more time with gossip than with her garden.

Margaret was even more pious than usual at that time of year when the green tent revival followed on the heels of the fair, when the pink-faced men in white shirts arrived and, really, every single one of them was a preacher. Still, Margaret Tubby kept her prize money to herself and didn't give a tithe to any church.

With Bess Evening carrying on with a stranger young enough to be her son, Mrs. Tubby succeeded in turning the church women against her once and for all. When Bessie walked down the busy street, one of the oldest dances of women took place, for women in those days turned against each other easily, never thinking they might have other enemies. When Bess appeared, the women stepped away. They vanished from the very face of earth that was named Comanche Street. They disappeared into the Oklahoma redstone shops like swallows swooping into their small clay nests. The women would look at the new bolts of red cloth in Terwilligers with feigned interest, although they would never have worn red, even to a dog fight. They'd purchase another box of face powder in the five and dime, or drink cherry phosphates at the pharmacy without so much as tasting the flavor.

But Bessie was unruffled. She walked on in the empty mirage of heat, the sound of her cane blending in with horse hooves and the rhythmic pumping of oil wells out east.

At the store, my mother bought corn meal, molasses, and milk. I bought penny candy for my younger sisters and for Peso Junior with the money I earned by helping Aunt Moon with her remedies. When we passed Margaret Tubby on the way out, my mother nodded at her, but said to me, "That pumpkin grew fat on gossip. I'll bet she fed it with nothing but all-night rumors." I thought about the twenty-five-dollar prize money and decided to grow pumpkins next year.

My mother said, "Now don't you get any ideas about growing pumpkins, young lady. We don't have room enough. They'd crowd out the cucumbers and tomatoes."

My mother and father won a prize that year, too. For dancing. They won a horse lamp for the living room. "We didn't even know it was a contest," my mother said, free from the sin of competition. Her face was rosy with pleasure and pride. She had the life snapping out of her like hot grease, though sometimes I saw that life turn to a slow and restless longing, like when she daydreamed out the window where the young man had stood that day.

Passing Margaret's post and giving up on growing a two-hundred-pound pumpkin, I remembered all the things good Indian women were not supposed to do. We were not supposed to look into the faces of men. Or laugh too loud. We were not supposed to learn too much from books because that kind of knowledge was a burden to the soul. Not only that, it always took us away from our loved ones. I was jealous of the white girls who laughed as loud as they wanted and never had rules. Also, my mother wanted me to go to college no matter what anyone else said or thought. She said I was too smart to stay home and live a life like hers, even if the other people thought book learning would ruin my life.

Aunt Moon with her second sight and heavy breasts managed to break all the rules. She threw back her head and laughed out loud, showing off the worn edges of her teeth. She didn't go to church. She did a man's work, cared for animals, and chopped her own wood. The gossiping women said it was a wonder Bessie Evening was healthy at all and didn't have female problems—meaning with her body, I figured.

The small woman inside her eye was full and lonely at the same time.

Bess made tonics, remedies, and cures. The church women, even those who gossiped, slipped over to buy Bessie's potions at night and in secret. They'd never admit they swallowed the "snake medicine," as they called it. They'd say to Bess, "What have you got to put the life back in a man? My sister has that trouble, you know." Or they'd say, "I have a friend who needs a cure for the sadness." They bought remedies for fever and coughing fits, for sore muscles and for sleepless nights.

Aunt Moon had learned the cures from her parents, who were said to have visited their own sins upon their children, both of whom were born out of wedlock from the love of an old Chickasaw man and a young woman from one of those tribes up north. Maybe a Navajo or something, the people thought.

But Aunt Moon had numerous talents and I respected them. She could pull cotton, pull watermelons, and pull babies with equal grace. She even delivered those scrub cattle, bred with Holsteins too big for them, caesarean. In addition to that, she told me the ways of the world and not just about the zodiac or fortune cards. "The United States is in love with death," she would say. "They sleep with it better than with lovers. They celebrate it on holidays, the Fourth of July, even in spring when they praise the loss of a good man's body."

She would tend her garden while I'd ask questions. What do you think about heaven? I wanted to know. She'd look up and then get back to pulling the weeds. "You and I both would just grump around up there with all those righteous people. Women like us weren't meant to live on golden streets. We're Indians," she'd say as she cleared out the space around a bean plant. "We're like these beans. We grew up from mud." And then she'd tell me how the people emerged right along with the crawdads from the muddy female swamps of the land. "And what is gold anyway? Just something else that comes from mud. Look at the conquistadors." She pulled a squash by accident. "And look at the sad women of this town, old already and all because of gold." She poked a hole in the ground and replanted the roots of the squash. "Their men make money, but not love. They give the women gold rings, gold-rimmed glasses, gold teeth, but their skin dries up for lack of love. Their hearts are little withered raisins." I was embarrassed by the mention of making love, but I listened to her words.

This is how I came to call Bessie Evening by the name of Aunt Moon: She'd been teaching me that animals and all life should be greeted properly as our kinfolk. "Good day, Uncle," I learned to say to the longhorn as I passed by on the road. "Good morning, cousins. Is there something you need?" I'd say to the sparrows. And one night when the moon was passing over Bessie's house, I said, "Hello, Aunt Moon. I see you are full of silver again tonight." It was so much like Bess Evening, I began to think, that I named her after the moon. She was sometimes full and happy, sometimes small and weak. I began saying it right to her ears: "Auntie Moon, do you need some help today?"

She seemed both older and younger than thirty-nine to me. For one thing, she walked with a cane. She had developed some secret ailment after her young daughter died. My mother said she needed the cane because she had no mortal human to hold her up in life, like the rest of us did.

But the other thing was that she was full of mystery and she laughed right out loud, like a Gypsy, my mother said, pointing out Bessie's blue-painted walls, bright clothes and necklaces, and all the things she kept hanging from her ceiling. She decorated outside her house, too, with bits of blue glass hanging from the trees, and little polished quartz crystals that reflected rainbows across the dry hills.

Aunt Moon had solid feet, a light step, and a face that clouded over with emotion and despair one moment and brightened up like light the next. She'd beam and say to me, "Sassafras will turn your hair red," and throw back her head to laugh, knowing full well that I would rinse my dull hair with sassafras that very night, ruining my mother's pans.

I sat in Aunt Moon's kitchen while she brewed herbals in white enamel pans on the woodstove. The insides of the pans were black from sassafras and burdock and other plants she picked. The kitchen smelled rich and earthy. Some days it was hard to breathe from the combination of woodstove heat and pollen from the plants, but she kept at it and her medicine for cramps was popular with the women in town.

Aunt Moon made me proud of my womanhood, giving me bags of herbs and an old eagle feather that had been doctored by her father back when people used to pray instead of going to church. "The body divines everything," she told me, and sometimes when I was with her, I knew the older Indian world was still here and

I'd feel it in my skin and hear the night sounds speak to me, hear the voice of water tell stories about people who lived here before, and the deep songs came out from the hills.

One day I found Aunt Moon sitting at her table in front of a plate of untouched toast and wild plum jam. She was weeping. I was young and didn't know what to say, but she told me more than I could ever understand. "Ever since my daughter died," she told me, "my body aches to touch her. All the mourning has gone into my bones." Her long hair was loose that day and it fell down her back like a waterfall, almost to the floor.

After that I had excuses on the days I saw her hair loose. "I'm putting up new wallpaper today," I'd say, or "I have to help Mom can peaches," which was the truth.

"Sure," she said, and I saw the tinge of sorrow around her eyes even though she smiled and nodded at me.

Canning the peaches, I asked my mother what it was that happened to Aunt Moon's daughter.

"First of all," my mother set me straight, "her name is Bess, not Aunt Moon." Then she'd tell the story of Willow Evening. "That pretty child was the light of that woman's eye," my mother said. "It was all so fast. She was playing one minute and the next she was gone. She was hanging on to that wooden planter and pulled it right down onto her little chest."

My mother touched her chest. "I saw Bessie lift it like it weighed less than a pound—did I already tell you that part?"

All I had seen that day was Aunt Moon holding Willow's thin body. The little girl's face was already gone to ashes and Aunt Moon blew gently on her daughter's skin, even though she was dead, as if she could breathe the life back into her one more time. She blew on her skin the way I later knew that women blow sweat from lovers' faces, cooling them. But I knew nothing of any kind of passion then.

The planter remained on the dry grassy mound of Aunt Moon's yard, and even though she had lifted it, no one else, not even my father, could move it. It was still full of earth and dead geraniums, like a monument to the child.

"That girl was all she had," my mother said through the steam of boiling water. "Hand me the ladle, will you?"

The peaches were suspended in sweet juice in their clear jars. I thought of our lives—so short, the skin so soft around us that we could be gone any second from our living—thought I saw Willow's golden brown face suspended behind glass in one of the jars.

The men first noticed the stranger, Isaac, when he cleaned them out in the poker game that night at the fair. My father, who had been drinking, handed over the money he'd saved for the new bathroom mirror and took a drunken swing at the young man, missing him by a foot and falling on his bad knee. Mr. Tubby told his wife he lost all he'd saved for the barber shop business, even though everyone in town knew he drank it up long before the week of the fair. Mr. Tens lost his Mexican silver ring. It showed up later on Aunt Moon's hand.

Losing to one another was one thing. Losing to Isaac Cade meant the dark young man was a card sharp and an outlaw. Even the women who had watched the stranger all that night were sure he was full of demons.

The next time I saw Aunt Moon, it was the fallow season of autumn, but she seemed new and fresh as spring. Her skin had new light. Gathering plants, she smiled at me. Her cane moved aside the long dry grasses to reveal what grew underneath. Mullein was still growing, and holly.

I sat at the table while Aunt Moon ground yellow ochre in a mortar. Isaac came in from fixing the roof. He touched her arm so softly I wasn't sure she felt it. I had never seen a man touch a woman that way.

He said hello to me and he said, "You know those fairgrounds? That's where the three tribes used to hold sings." He drummed on the table, looking at me, and sang one of the songs. I said I recognized it, a song I sometimes dreamed I heard from the hill.

A red handprint appeared on his face, like one of those birthmarks that only show up in the heat or under the strain of work or feeling.

"How'd you know about the fairgrounds?" I asked him.

"My father was from here." He sat still, as if thinking himself into another time. He stared out the window at the distances that were in between the blue curtains.

I went back to Aunt Moon's the next day. Isaac wasn't there, so Aunt Moon and I tied sage in bundles with twine. I asked her about love.

"It comes up from the ground just like corn," she said. She pulled a knot tighter with her teeth.

Later, when I left, I was still thinking about love. Outside where Bess had been planting, black beetles were digging themselves under the turned soil, and red ants had grown wings and were starting to fly.

When I returned home, my mother was sitting outside the house on a chair. She pointed at Bess Evening's house. "With the man there," she said, "I think it best you don't go over to Bessie's house anymore."

I started to protest, but she interrupted. "There are no ands, ifs, or buts about it."

I knew it was my father who made the decision. My mother had probably argued my point and lost to him again, and lost some of her life as well. She was slowed down to a slumberous pace. Later that night as I stood by my window looking toward Aunt Moon's house, I heard my mother say, "God damn them all and this whole damned town."

"There now," my father said. "There now."

"She's as dark and stained as those old black pans she uses," Margaret Tubby said about Bess Evening one day. She had come to pick up a cake from Mother for the church bake sale. I was angered by her words. I gave her one of those "looks could kill" faces, but I said nothing. We all looked out the window at Aunt Moon. She was standing near Isaac, looking at a tree. It leapt into my mind suddenly, like lightning, that Mrs. Tubby knew about the blackened pans. That would mean she had bought cures from Aunt Moon. I was smug about this discovery.

Across the way, Aunt Moon stood with her hand outstretched, palm up. It was filled with roots or leaves. She was probably teaching Isaac about the remedies. I knew Isaac would teach her things also, older things, like squirrel sickness and porcupine disease that I'd heard about from grandparents.

Listening to Mrs. Tubby, I began to understand why, right after the fair, Aunt Moon had told me I would have to fight hard to keep my life in this town. Mrs. Tubby said, "Living out of wedlock! Just like her parents." She went on, "History repeats itself."

I wanted to tell Mrs. Tubby a thing or two myself. "History, my eye," I wanted to say. "You're just jealous about the young man." But Margaret Tubby was still angry that her husband had lost his money to the stranger, and also because she probably still felt bad about playing with her necklace like a young girl that night at the fair. My mother said nothing, just covered the big caramel cake and handed it over to Mrs. Tubby. My mother looked like she was tired of fools and that included me. She looked like the woman inside her eye had just wandered off.

I began to see the women in Pickens as ghosts. I'd see them in the library looking at the stereopticons, and in the ice cream parlor. The more full Aunt Moon grew, the more drawn and pinched they became.

The church women echoed Margaret. "She's as stained as her pans," they'd say, and they began buying their medicines at the pharmacy. It didn't matter that their coughs returned and that their children developed more fevers. It didn't matter that some of them could not get pregnant when they wanted to or that Mrs. Tens grew thin and pale and bent. They wouldn't dream of lowering themselves to buy Bessie's medicines.

My mother ran hot water into the tub and emptied one of her packages of bubble powder in it. "Take a bath," she told me. "It will steady your nerves."

I was still crying, standing at the window, looking out at Aunt Moon's house through the rain.

The heavy air had been broken by an electrical storm earlier that day. In a sudden crash, the leaves flew off their trees, the sky exploded with lightning, and thunder rumbled the earth. People went to their doors to watch. It scared me. The clouds turned green and it began to hail and clatter.

That was when Aunt Moon's old dog, Mister, ran off, went running like crazy through the town. Some of the older men saw him on the street. They thought he was hurt and dying because of the way he ran and twitched. He butted right into a tree and the men thought maybe he had rabies or something. They meant to put him out of his pain. One of them took aim with a gun and shot him, and when the storm died down and the streets misted over, everything returned to heavy stillness and old Mister was lying on the edge of the Smiths' lawn. I picked him up and carried his heavy body up to Aunt Moon's porch. I covered him with sage, like she would have done.

Bess and Isaac had gone over to Alexander that day to sell remedies. They missed the rain, and when they returned, they were happy about bringing home bags of beans, ground corn, and flour.

I guess it was my mother who told Aunt Moon about her dog.

That evening I heard her wailing. I could hear her from my window and I looked out and saw her with her hair all down around her shoulders like a black shawl. Isaac smoothed back her hair and held her. I guessed that all the mourning was back in her bones again, even for her little girl, Willow.

That night my mother sat by my bed. "Sometimes the world is a sad place," she said and kissed my hot forehead. I began to cry again.

"Well, she still has the burro," my mother said, neglecting to mention Isaac.

I began to worry about the burro and to look after it. I went over to Aunt Moon's against my mother's wishes, and took carrots and sugar to the gray burro. I scratched his big ears.

By this time, most of the younger and healthier men had signed up to go to Korea and fight for their country. Most of the residents of Pickens were mixed-blood Indians and they were even more patriotic than white men. I guess they wanted to prove that they were good Americans. My father left and we saw him off at the depot. I admit I missed him saying to me, "The trouble with you is you think too much." Old Peso, always telling people what their problems were. Margaret Tubby's lazy son had enlisted because, as his mother had said, "It would make a man of him," and when he was killed in action, the townspeople resented Isaac, Bess Evening's young man, even more since he did not have his heart set on fighting the war.

Aunt Moon was pregnant the next year when the fair came around again, and she was just beginning to show. Margaret Tubby had remarked that Bess was visiting all those family sins on another poor child.

This time I was older. I fixed Mrs. Tubby in my eyes and I said, "Miss Tubby, you are just like history, always repeating yourself."

She pulled her head back into her neck like a turtle. My mother said, "Hush, Sis. Get inside the house." She put her hands on her hips. "I'll deal with you later." She almost added, "Just wait till your father gets home."

Later, I felt bad, talking that way to Margaret Tubby so soon after she lost her son.

Shortly after the fair, we heard that the young man inside Aunt Moon's eye was gone. A week passed and he didn't return. I watched her house from the window and I knew, if anyone stood behind me, the little house was resting up on my shoulder.

Mother took a nap and I grabbed the biscuits off the table and snuck out.

"I didn't hear you come in," Aunt Moon said to me.

"I didn't knock," I told her. "My mom just fell asleep. I thought it'd wake her up."

Aunt Moon's hair was down. Her hands were on her lap. A breeze came in the window. She must not have been sleeping and her eyes looked tired. I gave her the biscuits I had taken off the table. I lied and told her my mother had sent them over. We ate one.

Shortly after Isaac was gone, Bess Evening again became the focus of the town's women. Mrs. Tubby said, "Bessie would give you the shirt off her back. She never deserved a no good man who would treat her like dirt and then run off." Mrs. Tubby went over to Bess Evening's and bought enough cramp remedy from the pregnant woman to last her and her daughters for the next two years.

Mrs. Tens lost her pallor. She went to Bessie's with a basket of jellies and fruits, hoping in secret that Bess would return Mr. Tens's Mexican silver ring now that the young man was gone.

The women were going to stick by her; you could see it in their squared shoulders. They no longer hid their purchases of herbs. They forgot how they'd looked at Isaac's black eyes and lively body with longing that night of the dance. If they'd had dowsing rods, the split willow branches would have flown up to the sky, so much had they twisted around the truth of things and even their own natures. Isaac was the worst of men. Their husbands, who were absent, were saints who loved them. Every morning when my mother said her prayers and forgot she'd damned the town and everybody in it, I heard her ask for peace for Bessie Evening, but she never joined in with the other women who seemed happy over Bessie's tragedy.

Isaac was doubly condemned in his absence. Mrs. Tubby said, "What kind of fool goes off to leave a woman who knows about tea leaves and cures for diseases of the body and the mind alike? I'll tell you what kind, a card shark, that's what."

Someone corrected her. "Card *sharp*, dearie, not *shark*."

Who goes off and leaves a woman whose trees are hung with charming stones, relics, and broken glass, a woman who hangs sage and herbs to dry on her walls and whose front porch is full of fresh-cut wood? Those women, how they wanted to comfort her, but Bess Evening would only go to the door, leave them standing outside on the steps, and hand their herbs to them through the screen.

My cousins from Denver came for the fair. I was going to leave with them and get a job in the city for a year or so, then go on to school. My mother insisted she could handle the little ones alone now that they were bigger, and that I ought to go. It was best I made some money and learned what I could, she said.

"Are you sure?" I asked while my mother washed her hair in the kitchen sink.

"I'm sure as the night's going to fall." She sounded light-hearted, but her hands stopped moving and rested on her head until the soap lather began to disappear. "Besides, your dad will probably be home any day now."

I said, "Okay then, I'll go. I'll write you all the time." I was all full of emotion, but I didn't cry.

"Don't make promises you can't keep," my mother said, wrapping a towel around her head.

I went to the dance that night with my cousins, and out in the trees I let Jim Tens kiss me and promised him that I would be back. "I'll wait for you," he said. "And keep away from those city boys."

I meant it when I said, "I will."

He walked me home, holding my hand. My cousins were still at the dance. Mom would complain about their late city hours. Once she even told us that city people eat supper as late as eight o'clock P.M. We didn't believe her.

After Jim kissed me at the door, I watched him walk down the street. I was surprised that I didn't feel sad.

I decided to go to see Aunt Moon one last time. I was leaving at six in the morning and was already packed and I had taken one of each herb sample I'd learned from Aunt Moon, just in case I ever needed them.

I scratched the burro's gray face at the lot and walked up toward the house. The window was gold and filled with lamplight. I heard an owl hooting in the distance and stopped to listen.

I glanced in the window and stopped in my tracks. The young man, Isaac, was there. He was speaking close to Bessie's face. He put his finger under her chin and lifted her face up to his. He was looking at her with soft eyes and I could tell there were many men and women living inside their eyes that moment. He held her cane across the back of her hips. With it, he pulled her close to him and held her tight, his hands on the cane pressing her body against his. And he kissed her. Her hair was down around her back and shoulders and she put her arms around his neck. I turned to go. I felt dishonest and guilty for looking in at them. I began to run.

I ran into the bathroom and bent over the sink to wash my face. I wiped Jim Tens's cold kiss from my lips. I glanced up to look at myself in the mirror, but my face was nothing, just shelves of medicine bottles and aspirin. I had forgotten the mirror was broken.

From the bathroom door I heard my mother saying her prayers, fervently, and louder than usual. She said, "Bless Sis's Aunt Moon and bless Isaac, who got arrested for trading illegal medicine for corn, and forgive him for escaping from jail."

She said this so loud, I thought she was talking to me. Maybe she was. Now how did she read my mind again? It made me smile, and I guessed I was reading hers.

All the next morning, driving through the deep blue sky, I thought how all the women had gold teeth and hearts like withered raisins. I hoped Jim Tens would marry one of the Tubby girls. I didn't know if I'd ever go home or not. I had Aunt Moon's herbs in my bag, and the eagle feather wrapped safe in a scarf. And I had a small, beautiful woman in my eye.

QUESTIONS FOR DISCUSSION AND WRITING

1. "Aunt Moon's Young Man" is a female-maturation narrative. What experiences does the young narrator undergo, and how does Aunt Moon serve as a role model?

2. When does "Aunt Moon's Young Man" take place? What indications of the time are given in the story? How does the time affect the action?

3. The narrator at one point says that Aunt Moon told her that "the soul is a small woman inside the eye who leaves at night to wander new places." Trace this image through the story and describe its significance.

4. Several sets of value systems clash in "Aunt Moon's Young Man." Discuss the value systems of the town, of the narrator's parents, of Margaret Tubby, and of Aunt Moon.

Amy Tan

Amy Tan (b. 1952) grew up in Oakland, California, the daughter of parents who had immigrated from China just two-and-a-half years before she was born. She visited China for the first time in 1987 and returned to write her first book, the enormously successful *Joy Luck Club* (1989). A second novel, *The Kitchen God's Wife* (1991), was equally successful. Amy Tan lives in San Francisco.

TWO KINDS

My mother believed you could be anything you wanted to be in America. You could open a restaurant. You could work for the government and get good retirement. You could buy a house with almost no money down. You could become rich. You could become instantly famous.

"Of course you can be prodigy, too," my mother told me when I was nine. "You can be best anything. What does Auntie Lindo know? Her daughter, she is only best tricky."

America was where all my mother's hopes lay. She had come here in 1949 after losing everything in China: her mother and father, her family home, her first husband, and two daughters, twin baby girls. But she never looked back with regret. There were so many ways for things to get better.

We didn't immediately pick the right kind of prodigy. At first my mother thought I would be a Chinese Shirley Temple. We'd watch Shirley's old movies on TV as though they were training films. My mother would poke my arm and say, "*Ni kan*"—You watch. And I would see Shirley tapping her feet, or singing a sailor song, or pursing her lips into a very round O while saying, "Oh my goodness."

"*Ni kan,*" said my mother as Shirley's eyes flooded with tears. "You already know how. Don't need talent for crying!"

Soon after my mother got this idea about Shirley Temple, she took me to a beauty training school in the Mission district and put me in the hands of a student who could barely hold the scissors without shaking. Instead of getting big fat curls, I emerged with an uneven mass of crinkly black fuzz. My mother dragged me off to the bathroom and tried to wet down my hair.

"You look like Negro Chinese," she lamented, as if I had done this on purpose.

The instructor of the beauty training school had to lop off those soggy clumps to make my hair even again. "Peter Pan is very popular these days," the instructor assured my mother. I now had hair the length of a boy's, with straight-across bangs that hung at a slant two inches above my eyebrows. I liked the haircut and it made me actually look forward to my future fame.

In fact, in the beginning, I was just as excited as my mother, maybe even more so. I pictured this prodigy part of me as many different images, trying each one on for size. I was a dainty ballerina girl standing by the curtains, waiting to hear the right music that would send me floating on my tiptoes. I was like the Christ Child lifted out of the straw manger, crying with holy indignity. I was Cinderella stepping from her pumpkin carriage with sparkly cartoon music filling the air.

In all of my imaginings, I was filled with a sense that I would soon become *perfect*.

440

My mother and father would adore me. I would be beyond reproach. I would never feel the need to sulk for anything.

But sometimes the prodigy in me became impatient. "If you don't hurry up and get me out of here, I'm disappearing for good," it warned. "And then you'll always be nothing."

Every night after dinner, my mother and I would sit at the Formica kitchen table. She would present new tests, taking her examples from stories of amazing children she had read in *Ripley's Believe It or Not,* or *Good Housekeeping, Reader's Digest,* and a dozen other magazines she kept in a pile in our bathroom. My mother got these magazines from people whose houses she cleaned. And since she cleaned many houses each week, we had a great assortment. She would look through them all, searching for stories about remarkable children.

The first night she brought out a story about a three-year-old boy who knew the capitals of all the states and even most of the European countries. A teacher was quoted as saying the little boy could also pronounce the names of the foreign cities correctly.

"What's the capital of Finland?" my mother asked me, looking at the magazine story.

All I knew was the capital of California, because Sacramento was the name of the street we lived on in Chinatown. "Nairobi!" I guessed, saying the most foreign word I could think of. She checked to see if that was possibly one way to pronounce "Helsinki" before showing me the answer.

The tests got harder—multiplying numbers in my head, finding the queen of hearts in a deck of cards, trying to stand on my head without using my hands, predicting the daily temperatures in Los Angeles, New York, and London.

One night I had to look at a page from the Bible for three minutes and then report everything I could remember. "Now Jehoshaphat had riches and honor in abundance and . . . that's all I remember, Ma," I said.

And after seeing my mother's disappointed face once again, something inside of me began to die. I hated the tests, the raised hopes and failed expectations. Before going to bed that night, I looked in the mirror above the bathroom sink and when I saw only my face staring back—and that it would always be this ordinary face—I began to cry. Such a sad, ugly girl! I made high-pitched noises like a crazed animal, trying to scratch out the face in the mirror.

And then I saw what seemed to be the prodigy side of me—because I had never seen that face before. I looked at my reflection, blinking so I could see more clearly. The girl staring back at me was angry, powerful. This girl and I were the same. I had new thoughts, willful thoughts, or rather thoughts filled with lots of won'ts. I won't let her change me, I promised myself. I won't be what I'm not.

So now on nights when my mother presented her tests, I performed listlessly, my head propped on one arm. I pretended to be bored. And I was. I got so bored I started counting the bellows of the foghorns out on the bay while my mother drilled me in other areas. The sound was comforting and reminded me of the cow jumping over the moon. And the next day, I played a game with myself, seeing if my mother would give up on me before eight bellows. After a while I usually counted only one, maybe two bellows at most. At last she was beginning to give up hope.

Two or three months had gone by without any mention of my being a prodigy again. And then one day my mother was watching "The Ed Sullivan Show" on TV.

The TV was old and the sound kept shorting out. Every time my mother got halfway up from the sofa to adjust the set, the sound would go back on and Ed would be talking. As soon as she sat down, Ed would go silent again. She got up, the TV broke into loud piano music. She sat down. Silence. Up and down, back and forth, quiet and loud. It was like a stiff embraceless dance between her and the TV set. Finally she stood by the set with her hand on the sound dial.

She seemed entranced by the music, a little frenzied piano piece with this mesmerizing quality, sort of quick passages and then teasing lilting ones before it returned to the quick playful parts.

"*Ni kan,*" my mother said, calling me over with hurried hand gestures. "Look here."

I could see why my mother was fascinated by the music. It was being pounded out by a little Chinese girl, about nine years old, with a Peter Pan haircut. The girl had the sauciness of a Shirley Temple. She was proudly modest like a proper Chinese child. And she also did this fancy sweep of a curtsy, so that the fluffy skirt of her white dress cascaded slowly to the floor like the petals of a large carnation.

In spite of these warning signs, I wasn't worried. Our family had no piano and we couldn't afford to buy one, let alone reams of sheet music and piano lessons. So I could be generous in my comments when my mother bad-mouthed the little girl on TV.

"Play note right, but doesn't sound good! No singing sound," complained my mother.

"What are you picking on her for?" I said carelessly. "She's pretty good. Maybe she's not the best, but she's trying hard." I knew almost immediately I would be sorry I said that.

"Just like you," she said. "Not the best. Because you not trying." She gave a little huff as she let go of the sound dial and sat down on the sofa.

The little Chinese girl sat down also to play an encore of "Anitra's Dance" by Grieg. I remember the song, because later on I had to learn how to play it.

Three days after watching "The Ed Sullivan Show," my mother told me what my schedule would be for piano lessons and piano practice. She had talked to Mr. Chong, who lived on the first floor of our apartment building. Mr. Chong was a retired piano teacher and my mother had traded housecleaning services for weekly lessons and a piano for me to practice on every day, two hours a day, from four until six.

When my mother told me this, I felt as though I had been sent to hell. I whined and then kicked my foot a little when I couldn't stand it anymore.

"Why don't you like me the way I am? I'm *not* a genius! I can't play the piano. And even if I could, I wouldn't go on TV if you paid me a million dollars!" I cried.

My mother slapped me. "Who ask you be genius?" she shouted. "Only ask you be your best. For you sake. You think I want you be genius? Hnnh? What for! Who ask you!"

"So ungrateful," I heard her mutter in Chinese. "If she had as much talent as she has temper, she would be famous now."

Mr. Chong, whom I secretly nicknamed Old Chong, was very strange, always tapping fingers to the silent music of an invisible orchestra. He looked ancient in my eyes. He had lost most of the hair on top of his head and he wore thick glasses and had eyes that always looked tired and sleepy. But he must have been younger than I thought, since he lived with his mother and was not yet married.

I met Old Lady Chong once and that was enough. She had this peculiar smell like a baby that had done something in its pants. And her fingers felt like a dead person's, like an old peach I once found in the back of the refrigerator; the skin just slid off the meat when I picked it up.

I soon found out why Old Chong had retired from teaching piano. He was deaf. "Like Beethoven!" he shouted to me. "We're both listening only in our head!" And he would start to conduct his frantic silent sonatas.

Our lessons went like this. He would open the book and point to different things, explaining their purpose: "Key! Treble! Bass! No sharps or flats! So this is C major! Listen now and play after me!"

And then he would play the C scale a few times, a simple chord, and then, as if inspired by an old, unreachable itch, he gradually added more notes and running trills and a pounding bass until the music was really something quite grand.

I would play after him, the simple scale, the simple chord, and then I just played some nonsense that sounded like a cat running up and down on top of garbage cans. Old Chong smiled and applauded and then said, "Very good! But now you must learn to keep time!"

So that's how I discovered that Old Chong's eyes were too slow to keep up with the wrong notes I was playing. He went through the motions in half-time. To help me keep rhythm, he stood behind me, pushing down on my right shoulder for every beat. He balanced pennies on top of my wrists so I would keep them still as I slowly played scales and arpeggios. He had me curve my hand around an apple and keep that shape when playing chords. He marched stiffly to show me how to make each finger dance up and down, staccato like an obedient little soldier.

He taught me all these things, and that was how I also learned I could be lazy and get away with mistakes, lots of mistakes. If I hit the wrong notes because I hadn't practiced enough, I never corrected myself. I just kept playing in rhythm. And Old Chong kept conducting his own private reverie.

So maybe I never really gave myself a fair chance. I did pick up the basics pretty quickly, and I might have become a good pianist at that young age. But I was so determined not to try, not to be anybody different that I learned to play only the most earsplitting preludes, the most discordant hymns.

Over the next year, I practiced like this, dutifully in my own way. And then one day I heard my mother and her friend Lindo Jong both talking in a loud bragging tone of voice so others could hear. It was after church, and I was leaning against the brick wall wearing a dress with stiff white petticoats. Auntie Lindo's daughter, Waverly, who was about my age, was standing farther down the wall about five feet away. We had grown up together and shared all the closeness of two sisters squabbling over crayons and dolls. In other words, for the most part, we hated each other. I thought she was snotty. Waverly Jong had gained a certain amount of fame as "Chinatown's Littlest Chinese Chess Champion."

"She bring home too many trophy," lamented Auntie Lindo that Sunday. "All day she play chess. All day I have no time do nothing but dust off her winnings." She threw a scolding look at Waverly, who pretended not to see her.

"You lucky you don't have this problem," said Auntie Lindo with a sigh to my mother.

And my mother squared her shoulders and bragged: "Our problem worser than yours. If we ask Jing-mei wash dish, she hear nothing but music. It's like you can't stop this natural talent."

And right then, I was determined to put a stop to her foolish pride.

*   *   *

A few weeks later, Old Chong and my mother conspired to have me play in a talent show which would be held in the church hall. By then, my parents had saved up enough to buy me a secondhand piano, a black Wurlitzer spinet with a scarred bench. It was the showpiece of our living room.

For the talent show, I was to play a piece called "Pleading Child" from Schumann's *Scenes from Childhood*. It was a simple, moody piece that sounded more difficult than it was. I was supposed to memorize the whole thing, playing the repeat parts twice to make the piece sound longer. But I dawdled over it, playing a few bars and then cheating, looking up to see what notes followed. I never really listened to what I was playing. I daydreamed about being somewhere else, about being someone else.

The part I liked to practice best was the fancy curtsy: right foot out, touch the rose on the carpet with a pointed foot, sweep to the side, left leg bends, look up and smile.

My parents invited all the couples from the Joy Luck Club to witness my debut. Auntie Lindo and Uncle Tin were there. Waverly and her two older brothers had also come. The first two rows were filled with children both younger and older than I was. The littlest ones got to go first. They recited simple nursery rhymes, squawked out tunes on miniature violins, twirled Hula Hoops, pranced in pink ballet tutus, and when they bowed or curtsied, the audience would sigh in unison, "Awww," and then clap enthusiastically.

When my turn came, I was very confident. I remember my childish excitement. It was as if I knew, without a doubt, that the prodigy side of me really did exist. I had no fear whatsoever, no nervousness. I remember thinking to myself, This is it! This is it! I looked out over the audience, at my mother's blank face, my father's yawn, Auntie Lindo's stiff-lipped smile, Waverly's sulky expression. I had on a white dress layered with sheets of lace, and a pink bow in my Peter Pan haircut. As I sat down I envisioned people jumping to their feet and Ed Sullivan rushing up to introduce me to everyone on TV.

And I started to play. It was so beautiful. I was so caught up in how lovely I looked that at first I didn't worry how I would sound. So it was a surprise to me when I hit the first wrong note and I realized something didn't sound quite right. And then I hit another and another followed that. A chill started at the top of my head and began to trickle down. Yet I couldn't stop playing, as though my hands were bewitched. I kept thinking my fingers would adjust themselves back, like a train switching to the right track. I played this strange jumble through two repeats, the sour notes staying with me all the way to the end.

When I stood up, I discovered my legs were shaking. Maybe I had just been nervous and the audience, like Old Chong, had seen me go through the right motions and had not heard anything wrong at all. I swept my right foot out, went down on my knee, looked up and smiled. The room was quiet, except for Old Chong, who was beaming and shouting, "Bravo! Bravo! Well done!" But then I saw my mother's face, her stricken face. The audience clapped weakly, and as I walked back to my chair, with my whole face quivering as I tried not to cry, I heard a little boy whisper loudly to his mother, "That was awful," and the mother whispered back, "Well, she certainly tried."

And now I realized how many people were in the audience, the whole world it seemed. I was aware of eyes burning into my back. I felt the shame of my mother and father as they sat stiffly throughout the rest of the show.

We could have escaped during intermission. Pride and some strange sense of honor must have anchored my parents to their chairs. And so we watched it all: the eighteen-year-old boy with a fake mustache who did a magic show and juggled flaming hoops while riding a unicycle. The breasted girl with white makeup who sang from *Madame Butterfly*, and got honorable mention. And the eleven-year-old boy who won first prize playing a tricky violin song that sounded like a busy bee.

After the show, the Hsus, the Jongs, and the St. Clairs from the Joy Luck Club came up to my mother and father.

"Lots of talented kids," Auntie Lindo said vaguely, smiling broadly.

"That was somethin' else," said my father, and I wondered if he was referring to me in a humorous way, or whether he even remembered what I had done.

Waverly looked at me and shrugged her shoulders. "You aren't a genius like me," she said matter-of-factly. And if I hadn't felt so bad, I would have pulled her braids and punched her stomach.

But my mother's expression was what devastated me: a quiet, blank look that said she had lost everything. I felt the same way, and it seemed as if everybody were now coming up, like gawkers at the scene of an accident, to see what parts were actually missing. When we got on the bus to go home, my father was humming the busy-bee tune and my mother was silent. I kept thinking she wanted to wait until we got home before shouting at me. But when my father unlocked the door to our apartment, my mother walked in and then went to the back, into the bedroom. No accusations. No blame. And in a way, I felt disappointed. I had been waiting for her to start shouting, so I could shout back and cry and blame her for all my misery.

I assumed my talent-show fiasco meant I never had to play the piano again. But two days later, after school, my mother came out of the kitchen and saw me watching TV.

"Four clock," she reminded me as if it were any other day. I was stunned, as though she were asking me to go through the talent-show torture again. I wedged myself more tightly in front of the TV.

"Turn off TV," she called from the kitchen five minutes later.

I didn't budge. And then I decided. I didn't have to do what my mother said anymore. I wasn't her slave. This wasn't China. I had listened to her before and look what happened. She was the stupid one.

She came out of the kitchen and stood in the arched entryway of the living room. "Four clock," she said once again, louder.

"I'm not going to play anymore," I said nonchalantly. "Why should I? I'm not a genius."

She walked over and stood in front of the TV. I saw her chest was heaving up and down in an angry way.

"No!" I said, and I now felt stronger, as if my true self had finally emerged. So this was what had been inside me all along.

"No! I won't!" I screamed.

She yanked me by the arm, pulled me off the floor, snapped off the TV. She was frighteningly strong, half pulling, half carrying me toward the piano as I kicked the throw rugs under my feet. She lifted me up and onto the hard bench. I was sobbing by now, looking at her bitterly. Her chest was heaving even more and her mouth was open, smiling crazily as if she were pleased I was crying.

"You want me to be someone that I'm not!" I sobbed. "I'll never be the kind of daughter you want me to be!"

"Only two kinds of daughters," she shouted in Chinese. "Those who are obedient and those who follow their own mind! Only one kind of daughter can live in this house. Obedient daughter!''

"Then I wish I wasn't your daughter. I wish you weren't my mother,'' I shouted. As I said these things I got scared. I felt like worms and toads and slimy things were crawling out of my chest, but it also felt good, as if this awful side of me had surfaced, at last.

"Too late change this,'' said my mother shrilly.

And I could sense her anger rising to its breaking point. I wanted to see it spill over. And that's when I remembered the babies she had lost in China, the ones we never talked about. "Then I wish I'd never been born!'' I shouted. "I wish I were dead! Like them.''

It was as if I had said the magic words. Alakazam!—and her face went blank, her mouth closed, her arms went slack, and she backed out of the room, stunned, as if she were blowing away like a small brown leaf, thin, brittle, lifeless.

It was not the only disappointment my mother felt in me. In the years that followed, I failed her so many times, each time asserting my own will, my right to fall short of expectations. I didn't get straight A's. I didn't become class president. I didn't get into Stanford. I dropped out of college.

For unlike my mother, I did not believe I could be anything I wanted to be. I could only be me.

And for all those years, we never talked about the disaster at the recital or my terrible accusations afterward at the piano bench. All that remained unchecked, like a betrayal that was now unspeakable. So I never found a way to ask her why she had hoped for something so large that failure was inevitable.

And even worse, I never asked her what frightened me the most: Why had she given up hope?

For after our struggle at the piano, she never mentioned my playing again. The lessons stopped. The lid to the piano was closed, shutting out the dust, my misery, and her dreams.

So she surprised me. A few years ago, she offered to give me the piano, for my thirtieth birthday. I had not played in all those years. I saw the offer as a sign of forgiveness, a tremendous burden removed.

"Are you sure?'' I asked shyly. "I mean, won't you and Dad miss it?''

"No, this your piano,'' she said firmly. "Always your piano. You only one can play.''

"Well, I probably can't play anymore,'' I said. "It's been years.''

"You pick up fast,'' said my mother, as if she knew this was certain. "You have natural talent. You could been genius if you want to.''

"No, I couldn't.''

"You just not trying,'' said my mother. And she was neither angry nor sad. She said it as if to announce a fact that could never be disproved. "Take it,'' she said.

But I didn't at first. It was enough that she had offered it to me. And after that, every time I saw it in my parents' living room, standing in front of the bay windows, it made me feel proud, as if it were a shiny trophy I had won back.

Last week I sent a tuner over to my parents' apartment and had the piano reconditioned, for purely sentimental reasons. My mother had died a few months before and I had been getting things in order for my father, a little bit at a time. I put the jewelry in special silk pouches. The sweaters she had knitted in yellow, pink, bright orange—all the colors I hated—I put those in moth-proof boxes. I found some old Chinese silk dresses, the kind with little slits up the sides. I rubbed the old silk against my skin, then wrapped them in tissue and decided to take them home with me.

After I had the piano tuned, I opened the lid and touched the keys. It sounded even richer than I remembered. Really, it was a very good piano. Inside the bench were the same exercise notes with handwritten scales, the same secondhand music books with their covers held together with yellow tape.

I opened up the Schumann book to the dark little piece I had played at the recital. It was on the left-hand side of the page, "Pleading Child." It looked more difficult than I remembered. I played a few bars, surprised at how easily the notes came back to me.

And for the first time, or so it seemed, I noticed the piece on the right-hand side. It was called "Perfectly Contented." I tried to play this one as well. It had a lighter melody but the same flowing rhythm and turned out to be quite easy. "Pleading Child" was shorter but slower; "Perfectly Contented" was longer but faster. And after I played them both a few times, I realized they were two halves of the same song.

QUESTIONS FOR DISCUSSION AND WRITING

1. What is the nature of the conflict between the narrator and her mother? Is it just over whether the girl will be a "prodigy" or not? Or does this overt conflict express deeper differences?

2. Despite the girl's insistence that she is ordinary and like everyone else, one side of her is attracted to what she calls "the prodigy side of me." Trace this ambivalence through the story.

3. "Two Kinds" can be read as a story of assimilation, of finding a place in a new country. Trace this process through both the mother's and the daughter's actions.

4. At the end of the story, the daughter, now grown, plays both "Pleading Child" and its companion piece, "Perfectly Contented," and realizes that "they were two halves of the same song." How does this final episode form a suitable conclusion to the story?

Louise Erdrich

Louise Erdrich, born in 1954 of German-American and Chippewa parents, grew up in North Dakota as part of the Turtle Mountain Band of Chippewa. She was educated at Dartmouth College and Johns Hopkins University. Her first book was *Jacklight* (1979), a collection of poetry. Her first novel was *Love Medicine* (1984). It was followed by *The Beet Queen* (1986), *Tracks* (1988), and *The Crown of Columbus* (1991), the last written in collaboration with Michael Dorris, her husband and a fine novelist himself. Erdrich and Dorris live in New Hampshire.

AMERICAN HORSE

The woman sleeping on the cot in the woodshed was Albertine American Horse. The name was left over from her mother's short marriage. The boy was the son of the man she had loved and let go. Buddy was on the cot too, sitting on the edge because he'd been awake three hours watching out for his mother and besides, she took up the whole cot. Her feet hung over the edge, limp and brown as two trout. Her long arms reached out and slapped at things she saw in her dreams.

Buddy had been knocked awake out of hiding in a washing machine while herds of policemen with dogs searched through a large building with many tiny rooms. When the arm came down, Buddy screamed because it had a blue cuff and sharp silver buttons. "Tss," his mother mumbled, half awake, "wasn't nothing." But Buddy sat up after her breathing went deep again, and he watched.

There was something coming and he knew it.

It was coming from very far off but he had a picture of it in his mind. It was a large thing made of metal with many barbed hooks, points, and drag chains on it, something like a giant potato peeler that rolled out of the sky, scraping clouds down with it and jabbing or crushing everything that lay in its path on the ground.

Buddy watched his mother. If he woke her up, she would know what to do about the thing, but he thought he'd wait until he saw it for sure before he shook her. She was pretty, sleeping, and he liked knowing he could look at her as long and close up as he wanted. He took a strand of her hair and held it in his hands as if it was the rein to a delicate beast. She was strong enough and could pull him along like the horse their name was.

Buddy had his mother's and his grandmother's name because his father had been a big mistake.

"They're all mistakes, even your father. But *you* are the best thing that ever happened to me."

That was what she said when he asked.

Even Kadie, the boyfriend crippled from being in a car wreck, was not as good a thing that had happened to his mother as Buddy was. "He was a medium-sized mistake," she said. "He's hurt and I shouldn't even say that, but it's the truth." At the moment, Buddy knew that being the best thing in his mother's life, he was also the reason they were hiding from the cops.

He wanted to touch the satin roses sewed on her pink tee shirt, but he knew he shouldn't do that even in her sleep. If she woke up and found him touching the roses, she would say, "Quit that, Buddy." Sometimes she told him to stop hugging her like a gorilla. She never said that in the mean voice she used when he oppressed her, but when she said that he loosened up anyway.

There were times he felt like hugging her so hard and in such a special way that she would say to him, "Let's get married." There were also times he closed his eyes and wished that she would die, only a few times, but still it haunted him that his wish might come true. He and Uncle Lawrence would be left alone. Buddy wasn't worried, though, about his mother getting married to somebody else. She had said to her friend, Madonna, "All men suck," when she thought Buddy wasn't listening. He had made an uncertain sound, and when they heard him they took him in their arms.

"Except for you, Buddy," his mother said. "All except for you and maybe Uncle Lawrence, although he's pushing it."

"The cops suck the worst, though," Buddy whispered to his mother's sleeping face, "because they're after us." He felt tired again, slumped down, and put his legs beneath the blanket. He closed his eyes and got the feeling that the cot was lifting up beneath him, that it was arching its canvas back and then traveling, traveling very fast and in the wrong direction for when he looked up he saw the three of them were advancing to meet the great metal thing with hooks and barbs and all sorts of sharp equipment to catch their bodies and draw their blood. He heard its insides as it rushed toward them, purring softly like a powerful motor and then they were right in its shadow. He pulled the reins as hard as he could and the beast reared, lifting him. His mother clapped her hand across his mouth.

"Okay," she said. "Lay low. They're outside and they're gonna hunt."

She touched his shoulder and Buddy leaned over with her to look through a crack in the boards.

They were out there all right, Albertine saw them. Two officers and that social worker woman. Vicki Koob. There had been no whistle, no dream, no voice to warn her that they were coming. There was only the crunching sound of cinders in the yard, the engine purring, the dust sifting off their car in a fine light brownish cloud and settling around them.

The three people came to a halt in their husk of metal—the car emblazoned with the North Dakota State Highway Patrol emblem which is the glowing profile of the Sioux policeman, Red Tomahawk, the one who killed Sitting Bull. Albertine gave Buddy the blanket and told him that he might have to wrap it around him and hide underneath the cot.

"We're gonna wait and see what they do." She took him in her lap and hunched her arms around him. "Don't you worry," she whispered against his ear. "Lawrence knows how to fool them."

Buddy didn't want to look at the car and the people. He felt his mother's heart beating beneath his ear so fast it seemed to push the satin roses in and out. He put his face to them carefully and breathed the deep, soft powdery woman smell of her. That smell was also in her little face cream bottles, in her brushes, and around the washbowl after she used it. The satin felt so unbearably smooth against his cheek that he had to press closer. She didn't push him away, like he expected, but hugged him still tighter until he felt as close as he had ever been to back inside her again where she said he came from. Within the smells of her things, her soft skin, and the satin of her roses, he closed his eyes then, and took his breaths softly and quickly with her heart.

They were out there, but they didn't dare get out of the car yet because of Lawrence's big, ragged dogs. Three of these dogs had loped up the dirt driveway with the car. They were rangy, alert, and bounced up and down on their cushioned paws like wolves. They didn't waste their energy barking, but positioned themselves quietly, one at either car door and the third in front of the bellied-out screen door to Uncle Lawrence's house. It was six in the morning but the wind was up already, blowing dust, ruffling their short moth-eaten coats. The big brown one on Vicki Koob's side had unusual black and white markings, stripes almost, like a hyena and he grinned at her, tongue out and teeth showing.

"Shoo!" Miss Koob opened her door with a quick jerk.

The brown dog sidestepped the door and jumped before her, tiptoeing. Its dirty white muzzle curled and its eyes crossed suddenly as if it was zeroing its cross-hair sights in on the exact place it would bite her. She ducked back and slammed the door.

"It's mean," she told Officer Brackett. He was printing out some type of form. The other officer, Harmony, a slow man, had not yet reacted to the car's halt. He had been sitting quietly in the back seat, but now he rolled down his window and with no change in expression unsnapped his holster and drew his pistol out and pointed it at the dog on his side. The dog smacked down on its belly, wiggled under the car and was out and around the back of the house before Harmony drew his gun back. The other dogs vanished with him. From wherever they had disappeared to they began to yap and howl, and the door to the low shoebox-style house fell open.

"Heya, what's going on?"

Uncle Lawrence put his head out the door and opened wide the one eye he had in working order. The eye bulged impossibly wider in outrage when he saw the police car. But the eyes of the two officers and Miss Vicki Koob were wide open too because they had never seen Uncle Lawrence in his sleeping get up or, indeed, witnessed anything like it. For his ribs, which were cracked from a bad fall and still mending, Uncle Lawrence wore a thick white corset laced up the front with a striped sneakers' lace. His glass eye and his set of dentures were still out for the night so his face puckered here and there, around its absences and scars, like a damaged but fierce little cake. Although he had a few gray streaks now, Uncle Lawrence's hair was still thick, and because he wore a special contraption of elastic straps around his head every night, two oiled waves always crested on either side of his middle part. All of this would have been sufficient to astonish, even without the most striking part of his outfit—the smoking jacket. It was made of black satin and hung open around his corset, dragging a tassled belt. Gold thread dragons struggled up the lapels and blasted their furry red breath around his neck. As Lawrence walked down the steps, he put his arms up in surrender and the gold tassels in the inner seams of his sleeves dropped into view.

"My heavens, what a sight." Vicki Koob was impressed.

"A character," apologized Officer Harmony.

As a tribal police officer who could be counted on to help out the State Patrol, Harmony thought he always had to explain about Indians or get twice as tough to show he did not favor them. He was slow-moving and shy but two jumps ahead of other people all the same, and now, as he watched Uncle Lawrence's splendid approach, he gazed speculatively at the torn and bulging pocket of the smoking jacket. Harmony had been inside Uncle Lawrence's house before and knew that above his draped orange-crate shelf of war medals a blue-black German luger was hung carefully in a net of flat-headed nails and fishing line. Thinking of this deadly exhibition, he got out of the car and shambled toward Lawrence with a dreamy little smile of welcome on his face. But when he searched Lawrence, he found that the bulging pocket held only the lonesome-looking dentures from Lawrence's empty jaw. They were still dripping denture polish.

"I had been cleaning them when you arrived," Uncle Lawrence explained with acid dignity.

He took the toothbrush from his other pocket and aimed it like a rifle.

"Quit that, you old idiot." Harmony tossed the toothbrush away. "For once you ain't done nothing. We came for your nephew."

Lawrence looked at Harmony with a faint air of puzzlement.

"Ma Frere, listen," threatened Harmony amiably, "those two white people in the car came to get him for the welfare. They got papers on your nephew that give them the right to take him."

"Papers?" Uncle Lawrence puffed out his deeply pitted cheeks. "Let me see them papers."

The two of them walked over to Vicki's side of the car and she pulled a copy of the court order from her purse. Lawrence put his teeth back in and adjusted them with busy workings of his jaw.

"Just a minute," he reached into his breast pocket as he bent close to Miss Vicki Koob. "I can't read these without I have in my eye."

He took the eye from his breast pocket delicately, and as he popped it into his face the social worker's mouth fell open in a consternated O.

"What is this," she cried in a little voice.

Uncle Lawrence looked at her mildly. The white glass of the eye was cold as lard. The black iris was strangely charged and menacing.

"He's nuts," Brackett huffed along the side of Vicki's neck. "Never mind him."

Vicki's hair had sweated down her nape in tiny corkscrews and some of the hairs were so long and dangly now that they disappeared into the zippered back of her dress. Brackett noticed this as he spoke into her ear. His face grew red and the backs of his hands prickled. He slid under the steering wheel and got out of the car. He walked around the hood to stand with Leo Harmony.

"We could take you in too," said Brackett roughly. Lawrence eyed the officers in what was taken as defiance. "If you don't cooperate, we'll get out the handcuffs," they warned.

One of Lawrence's arms was stiff and would not move until he'd rubbed it with witch hazel in the morning. His older arm worked fine though, and he stuck it out in front of Brackett.

"Get them handcuffs," he urged them. "Put me in a welfare home."

Brackett snapped one side of the handcuffs on Lawrence's good arm and the other to the handle of the police car.

"That's to hold you," he said. "We're wasting our time. Harmony, you search that little shed over by the tall grass and Miss Koob and myself will search the house."

"My rights is violated!" Lawrence shrieked suddenly. They ignored him. He tugged at the handcuff and thought of the good heavy file he kept in his tool box and the German luger oiled and ready but never loaded, because of Buddy, over his shelf. He should have used it on these bad ones, even Harmony in his big-time white man job. He wouldn't last long in that job anyway before somebody gave him what for.

"It's a damn scheme," said Uncle Lawrence, rattling his chains against the car. He looked over at the shed and thought maybe Albertine and Buddy had sneaked away before the car pulled into the yard. But he sagged, seeing Albertine move like a shadow within the boards. "Oh, it's all a damn scheme," he muttered again.

"I want to find that boy and salvage him," Vicki Koob explained to Officer Brackett as they walked into the house. "Look at his family life—the old man crazy as a bedbug, the mother intoxicated somewhere."

Brackett nodded, energetic, eager. He was a short hopeful redhead who failed consistently to win the hearts of women. Vicki Koob intrigued him. Now, as he watched, she pulled a tiny pen out of an ornamental clip on her blouse. It was attached to a retractable line that would suck the pen back, like a child eating one strand of spaghetti. Something about the pen on its line excited Brackett to the point of discomfort. His hand shook as he opened the screendoor and stepped in, beckoning Miss Koob to follow.

They could see the house was empty at first glance. It was only one rectangular room with whitewashed walls and a little gas stove in the middle. They had already come through the cooking lean-to with the other stove and washstand and rusty old refrigerator. That refrigerator had nothing in it but some wrinkled potatoes and a package of turkey necks, Vicki Koob noted in her perfect-bound notebook. The beds along the walls of the big room were covered with quilts that Albertine's mother, Sophie, had made from bits of old wool coats and pants that the Sisters sold in bundles at the mission. There was no one hiding beneath the beds. No one was under the little aluminum dinette table covered with a green oilcloth, or the soft brown wood chairs tucked up to it. One wall of the big room was filled with neatly stacked crates of things—old tools and springs and small half-dismantled appliances. Five or six television sets were stacked against the wall. Their control panels spewed colored wires and at least one was cracked all the way across. Only the topmost set, with coathanger antenna angled sensitively to catch the bounding signals around Little Shell, looked like it could possibly work.

Not one thing escaped Vicki Koob's trained and cataloguing gaze. She made note of the cupboard that held only commodity flour and coffee. The unsanitary tin oil drum beneath the kitchen window, full of empty surplus pork cans and beer bottles, caught her eye as did Uncle Lawrence's physical and mental deteriorations. She quickly described these "benchmarks of alcoholic dependency within the extended family of Woodrow (Buddy) American Horse" as she walked around the room with the little notebook open, pushed against her belly to steady it. Although Vicki had been there before, Albertine's presence had always made it difficult for her to take notes.

"Twice the maximum allowable space between door and threshold," she wrote now. "Probably no insulation. Two three-inch cracks in walls inadequately sealed with white-washed mud." She made a mental note but could see no point in describing Lawrence's stuffed reclining chair that only reclined, the shadeless lamp with its plastic orchid in the bubble glass base, or the three-dimensional picture of Jesus that Lawrence had once demonstrated to her. When plugged in, lights rolled behind the water the Lord stood on so that he seemed to be strolling although he never actually went forward, of course, but only pushed the glowing waves behind him forever like a poor tame rat in a treadmill.

Brackett cleared his throat with a nervous rasp and touched Vicki's shoulder. "What are you writing?"

She moved away and continued to scribble as if thoroughly absorbed in her work. "Officer Brackett displays an undue amount of interest in my person," she wrote. "Perhaps?"

He snatched playfully at the book, but she hugged it to her chest and moved off smiling. More curls had fallen, wetted to the base of her neck. Looking out the window, she sighed long and loud.

"All night on brush rollers for this. What a joke."

Brackett shoved his hands in his pockets. His mouth opened slightly, then shut with a small throttled cluck.

When Albertine saw Harmony ambling across the yard with his big brown thumbs in his belt, his placid smile, and his tiny black eyes moving back and forth, she put Buddy under the cot. Harmony stopped at the shed and stood quietly. He spread his arms to show her he hadn't drawn his big police gun.

"Ma Cousin," he said in the Michif dialect that people used if they were relatives or sometimes if they needed gas or a couple of dollars, "why don't you come out here and stop this foolishness?"

"I ain't your cousin," Albertine said. Anger boiled up in her suddenly. "I ain't related to no pigs."

She bit her lip and watched him through the cracks, circling, a big tan punching dummy with his boots full of sand so he never stayed down once he fell. He was empty inside, all stale air. But he knew how to get to her so much better than a white cop could. And now he was circling because he wasn't sure she didn't have a weapon, maybe a knife or the German luger that was the only thing that her father, Albert American Horse, had left his wife and daughter besides his name. Harmony knew that Albertine was a tall strong woman who took two big men to subdue when she didn't want to go in the drunk tank. She had hard hips, broad shoulders, and stood tall like her Sioux father, the American Horse who was killed threshing in Belle Prairie.

"I feel bad to have to do this," Harmony said to Albertine. "But for godsakes, let's nobody get hurt. Come on out with the boy, why don't you? I know you got him in there."

Albertine did not give herself away this time. She let him wonder. Slowly and quietly she pulled her belt through its loops and wrapped it around and around her hand until only the big oval buckle with turquoise chunks shaped into a butterfly stuck out over her knuckles. Harmony was talking but she wasn't listening to what he said. She was listening to the pitch of his voice, the tone of it that would tighten or tremble at a certain moment when he decided to rush the shed. He kept talking slowly and reasonably, flexing the dialect from time to time, even mentioning her father.

"He was a damn good man. I don't care what they say, Albertine, I knew him."

Albertine looked at the stone butterfly that spread its wings across her fist. The wings looked light and cool, not heavy. It almost looked like it was ready to fly. Harmony wanted to get to Albertine through her father but she would not think about American Horse. She concentrated on the sky blue stone.

Yet the shape of the stone, the color, betrayed her.

She saw her father suddenly, bending at the grille of their old gray car. She was small then. The memory came from so long ago it seemed like a dream—narrowly focused, snapshot-clear. He was bending by the grille in the sun. It was hot summer. Wings of sweat, dark blue, spread across the back of his work shirt. He always wore soft blue shirts, the color of shade cloudier than this stone. His stiff hair had grown out of its short haircut and flopped over his forehead. When he stood up and turned away from the car, Albertine saw that he had a butterfly.

"It's dead," he told her. "Broke its wings and died on the grille."

She must have been five, maybe six, wearing one of the boy's tee shirts Mama bleached in Hilex-water. American Horse took the butterfly, a black and yellow one, and rubbed it on Albertine's collarbone and chest and arms until the color and the powder of it were blended into her skin.

"For grace," he said.

And Albertine had felt a strange lightening in her arms, in her chest, when he did this and said, "For grace." The way he said it, grace meant everything the butterfly was. The sharp delicate wings. The way it floated over grass. The way its wings seemed to breathe fanning in the sun. The wisdom of the way it blended into flowers or changed into a leaf. In herself she felt the same kind of possibilities and closed her eyes almost in shock or pain, she felt so light and powerful at that moment.

Then her father had caught her and thrown her high into the air. She could not remember landing in his arms or landing at all. She only remembered the sun filling her eyes and the world tipping crazily behind her, out of sight.

"He was a damn good man," Harmony said again.

Albertine heard his starched uniform gathering before his boots hit the ground. Once, twice, three times. It took him four solid jumps to get right where she wanted him. She kicked the plank door open when he reached for the handle and the corner caught him on the jaw. He faltered, and Albertine hit him flat on the chin with the butterfly. She hit him so hard the shock of it went up her arm like a string pulled taut. Her fist opened, numb, and she let the belt unloop before she closed her hand on the tip end of it and sent the stone butterfly swooping out in a wide circle around her as if it was on the end of a leash. Harmony reeled backward as she walked toward him swinging the belt. She expected him to fall but he just stumbled. And then he took the gun from his hip.

Albertine let the belt go limp. She and Harmony stood within feet of each other, breathing. Each heard the human sound of air going in and out of the other person's lungs. Each read the face of the other as if deciphering letters carved into softly eroding veins of stone. Albertine saw the pattern of tiny arteries that age, drink, and hard living had blown to the surface of the man's face. She saw the spoked wheels of his iris and the arteries like tangled threads that sewed him up. She saw the living net of springs and tissue that held him together, and trapped him. She saw the random, intimate plan of his person.

She took a quick shallow breath and her face went strange and tight. She saw the black veins in the wings of the butterfly, roads burnt into a map, and then she was located somewhere in the net of veins and sinew that was the tragic complexity of the world so she did not see Officer Brackett and Vicki Koob rushing toward her, but felt them instead like flies caught in the same web, rocking it.

"Albertine!" Vicki Koob had stopped in the grass. Her voice was shrill and tight. "It's better this way, Albertine. We're going to help you."

Albertine straightened, threw her shoulders back. Her father's hand was on her chest and shoulders lightening her wonderfully. Then on wings of her father's hands, on dead butterfly wings, Albertine lifted into the air and flew toward the others. The light powerful feeling swept her up the way she had floated higher, seeing the grass below. It was her father throwing her up into the air and out of danger. Her arms opened for bullets but no bullets came. Harmony did not shoot. Instead, he raised his fist and brought it down hard on her head.

Albertine did not fall immediately, but stood in his arms a moment. Perhaps she gazed still farther back behind the covering of his face. Perhaps she was completely stunned and did not think as she sagged and fell. Her face rolled forward and hair covered her features, so it was impossible for Harmony to see with just what particular expression she gazed into the head-splitting wheel of light, or blackness, that overcame her.

Harmony turned the vehicle onto the gravel road that led back to town. He had convinced the other two that Albertine was more trouble than she was worth, and so they left her behind, and Lawrence too. He stood swearing in his cinder driveway as the car rolled out of sight. Buddy sat between the social worker and Officer Brackett. Vicki tried to hold Buddy fast and keep her arm down at the same time, for the words she'd screamed at Albertine had broken the seal of antiperspirant beneath her arms. She was sweating now as though she'd stored an ocean up inside of her. Sweat rolled down her back in a shallow river and pooled at her waist and between her breasts. A thin sheen of water came out on her forearms, her face. Vicki gave an irritated moan but Brackett seemed not to take notice, or take offense at least. Air-conditioned breezes were sweeping over the seat anyway, and very soon they would be comfortable. She smiled at Brackett over Buddy's head. The man grinned back. Buddy stirred. Vicki remembered the emergency chocolate bar she kept in her purse, fished it out, and offered it to Buddy. He did not react, so she closed his fingers over the package and peeled the paper off one end.

The car accelerated. Buddy felt the road and wheels pummeling each other and the rush of the heavy motor purring in high gear. Buddy knew that what he'd seen in his mind that morning, the thing coming out of the sky with barbs and chains, had hooked him. Somehow he was caught and held in the sour tin smell of the pale woman's armpit. Somehow he was pinned between their pounds of breathless flesh. He looked at the chocolate in his hand. He was squeezing the bar so hard that a thin brown trickle had melted down his arm. Automatically he put the bar in his mouth.

As he bit down he saw his mother very clearly, just as she had been when she carried him from the shed. She was stretched flat on the ground, on her stomach, and her arms were curled around her head as if in sleep. One leg was drawn up and it looked for all the world like she was running full tilt into the ground, as though she had been trying to pass into the earth, to bury herself, but at the last moment something had stopped her.

There was no blood on Albertine, but Buddy tasted blood now at the sight of her, for he bit down hard and cut his own lip. He ate the chocolate, every bit of it, tasting his mother's blood. And when he had the chocolate down inside him and all licked off his hands, he opened his mouth to say thank you to the woman, as his mother had taught him. But instead of a thank you coming out he was astonished to hear a great rattling scream, and then another, rip out of him like pieces of his own body and whirl onto the sharp things all around him.

QUESTIONS FOR DISCUSSION AND WRITING

1. Point of view is used very complexly and interestingly in "American Horse." Trace the successive points of view and comment on their effect.

2. One of the story's contrasts between the Native American characters and the white characters is in the way the sexes interact and see one another.

Trace references to this subject through the story. What other contrasts do you see between the Indian world and the white world?

3. What happens when Harmony overcomes Albertine? What distracts her and makes her vulnerable to his attack? What is fantasy and what is reality in her perceptions of the attack? (Compare with the fantasy in "Hawk's Flight: An American Fable.")

4. Trace the generational theme in the story, from Albert American Horse to his daughter Albertine to her son Buddy. What is passed along in this sequence?

Julia Alvarez

Julia Alvarez was born in the Dominican Republic and moved to the United States with her family when she was ten years old. She has taught writing in schools in Kentucky, California, Vermont, Washington, D.C., and Illinois. She now teaches at Middlebury College in Vermont. Her first book was a collection of poetry, *Homecoming* (1986). *How the Garcia Girls Lost Their Accents,* a collection of linked short stories, from which "Daughter of Invention" is taken, appeared in 1991.

DAUGHTER OF INVENTION

For a period after they arrived in this country, Laura García tried to invent something. Her ideas always came after the sightseeing visits she took with her daughters to department stores to see the wonders of this new country. On his free Sundays, Carlos carted the girls off to the Statue of Liberty or the Brooklyn Bridge or Rockefeller Center, but as far as Laura was concerned, these were men's wonders. Down in housewares were the true treasures women were after.

Laura and her daughters would take the escalator, marveling at the moving staircase, she teasing them that this might be the ladder Jacob saw with angels moving up and down to heaven. The moment they lingered by a display, a perky saleslady approached, no doubt thinking a young mother with four girls in tow fit the perfect profile for the new refrigerator with automatic defrost or the heavy duty washing machine with the prewash soak cycle. Laura paid close attention during the demonstrations, asking intelligent questions, but at the last minute saying she would talk it over with her husband. On the drive home, try as they might, her daughters could not engage their mother in conversation, for inspired by what she had just seen, Laura had begun inventing.

She never put anything actual on paper until she had settled her house down at night. On his side of the bed her husband would be conked out for an hour already, his Spanish newspapers draped over his chest, his glasses propped up on his bedside table, looking out eerily at the darkened room like a disembodied bodyguard. In her lighted corner, pillows propped behind her, Laura sat up inventing. On her lap lay one of those innumerable pads of paper her husband brought home from his office, compliments of some pharmaceutical company, advertising tranquilizers or antibiotics or skin cream. She would be working on a sketch of something familiar but drawn at such close range so she could attach a special nozzle or handier handle, the thing looked peculiar. Her daughters would giggle over the odd doodles they found in kitchen drawers or on the back shelf of the downstairs toilet. Once Yoyo was sure her mother had drawn a picture of a man's you-know-what; she showed her sisters her find, and with coy, posed faces they inquired of their mother what she was up to. *Ay,* that was one of her failures, she explained to them, a child's double-compartment drinking glass with an outsized, built-in straw.

Her daughters would seek her out at night when she seemed to have a moment to talk to them: they were having trouble at school or they wanted her to persuade their father to give them permission to go into the city or to a shopping mall or a movie—in broad daylight, Mami! Laura would wave them out of her room. "The problem with you girls . . . ." The problem boiled down to the fact that they wanted to become Americans and their father—and their mother, too, at first—would have none of it.

"You girls are going to drive me crazy!" she threatened, if they kept nagging. "When I end up in Bellevue, you'll be safely sorry!"

She spoke in English when she argued with them. And her English was a mishmash of mixed-up idioms and sayings that showed she was "green behind the ears," as she called it.

If her husband insisted she speak in Spanish to the girls so they wouldn't forget their native tongue, she'd snap, "When in Rome, do unto the Romans."

Yoyo, the Big Mouth, had become the spokesman for her sisters, and she stood her ground in that bedroom. "We're not going to that school anymore, Mami!"

"You have to." Her eyes would widen with worry. "In this country, it is against the law not to go to school. You want us to get thrown out?"

"You want us to get killed? Those kids were throwing stones today!"

"Sticks and stones don't break bones," she chanted. Yoyo could tell, though, by the look on her face, it was as if one of those stones the kids had aimed at her daughters had hit her. But she always pretended they were at fault. "What did you do to provoke them? It takes two to tangle, you know."

"Thanks, thanks a lot, Mom!" Yoyo stormed out of that room and into her own. Her daughters never called her *Mom* except when they wanted her to feel how much she had failed them in this country. She was a good enough Mami, fussing and scolding and giving advice, but a terrible girlfriend parent, a real failure of a Mom.

Back she went to her pencil and pad, scribbling and tsking and tearing off sheets, finally giving up, and taking up her *New York Times*. Some nights, though, if she got a good idea, she rushed into Yoyo's room, a flushed look on her face, her tablet of paper in her hand, a cursory knock on the door she'd just thrown open. "Do I have something to show you, Cuquita!"

This was Yoyo's time to herself, after she finished her homework, while her sisters were still downstairs watching TV in the basement. Hunched over her small desk, the overhead light turned off, her desk lamp poignantly lighting only her paper, the rest of the room in warm, soft, uncreated darkness, she wrote her secret poems in her new language.

"You're going to ruin your eyes!" Laura began, snapping on the overly bright overhead light, scaring off whatever shy passion Yoyo, with the blue thread of her writing, had just begun coaxing out of a labyrinth of feelings.

"Oh, Mami!" Yoyo cried out, her eyes blinking up at her mother. "I'm writing."

"*Ay*, Cuquita." That was her communal pet name for whoever was in her favor. "Cuquita, when I make a million, I'll buy you your very own typewriter." (Yoyo had been nagging her mother for one just like the one her father had bought to do his order forms at home.) "Gravy on the turkey" was what she called it when someone was buttering her up. She buttered and poured. "I'll hire you your very own typist."

Down she plopped on the bed and held out her pad. "Take a guess, Cuquita?" Yoyo studied the rough sketch a moment. Soap sprayed from the nozzle head of a shower when you turned the knob a certain way? Instant coffee with creamer already mixed in? Time-released water capsules for your potted plants when you were away? A keychain with a timer that would go off when your parking meter was about to expire? (The ticking would help you find your keys easily if you mislaid them.) The famous one, famous only in hindsight, was the stick person dragging a square by a rope—a suitcase with wheels? "Oh, of course," Yoyo said, humoring her. "What every household needs: a shower like a car wash, keys ticking like a bomb, luggage on a leash!" By now, it had become something of a family joke, their Thomas Edison Mami, their Benjamin Franklin Mom.

Her face fell. "Come on now! Use your head." One more wrong guess, and she'd show Yoyo, pointing with her pencil to the different highlights of this incredible new wonder. "Remember that time we took the car to Bear Mountain, and we re-ah-lized that we had forgotten to pack an opener with our pick-a-nick?" (Her daughters kept correcting her, but she insisted this was how it should be said.) "When we were ready to eat we didn't have any way to open the refreshments cans?" (This before fliptop lids, which she claimed had crossed her mind.) "You know what this is now?" Yoyo shook her head. "Is a car bumper, but see this part is a removable can opener. So simple and yet so necessary, eh?"

"Yeah, Mami. You should patent it." Yoyo shrugged as her mother tore off the scratch paper and folded it, carefully, corner to corner, as if she were going to save it. But then, she tossed it in the wastebasket on her way out of the room and gave a little laugh like a disclaimer. "It's half of one or two dozen of another."

None of her daughters were very encouraging. They resented her spending time on those dumb inventions. Here they were trying to fit in America among Americans; they needed help figuring out who they were, why the Irish kids whose grandparents had been micks were calling them spics. Why had they come to this country in the first place? Important, crucial, final things, and here was their own mother, who didn't have a second to help them puzzle any of this out, inventing gadgets to make life easier for the American Moms.

Sometimes Yoyo challenged her. "Why, Mami? Why do it? You're never going to make money. The Americans have already thought of everything, you know that."

"Maybe not. Maybe, just maybe, there's something they've missed that's important. With patience and calm, even a burro can climb a palm." This last was one of her many Dominican sayings she had imported into her scrambled English.

"But what's the point?" Yoyo persisted.

"Point, point, does everything need a point? Why do you write poems?"

Yoyo had to admit it was her mother who had the point there. Still, in the hierarchy of things, a poem seemed much more important than a potty that played music when a toilet-training toddler went in its bowl.

They talked about it among themselves, the four girls, as they often did now about the many puzzling things in this new country.

"Better she reinvents the wheel than be on our cases all the time," the oldest, Carla, observed. In the close quarters of an American nuclear family, their mother's prodigious energy was becoming a real drain on their self-determination. Let her have a project. What harm could she do, and besides, she needed that acknowledgement. It had come to her automatically in the old country from being a de la Torre. "García de la Torre," Laura would enunciate carefully, giving her maiden as well as married name when they first arrived. But the blank smiles had never heard of her name. She would show them. She would prove to these Americans what a smart woman could do with a pencil and pad.

She had a near miss once. Every night, she liked to read *The New York Times* in bed before turning off her light, to see what the Americans were up to. One night, she let out a yelp to wake up her husband beside her. He sat bolt upright, reaching for his glasses which in his haste, he knocked across the room. "*¿Qué pasa? ¿Qué pasa?*" What is wrong? There was terror in his voice, the same fear she'd heard in the Dominican Republic before they left. They had been watched there; he was followed. They could not talk, of course, though they had whispered to each other in fear at night in the dark bed. Now in America, he was safe, a success even; his Centro de Medicina in the Bronx was thronged with the sick and the homesick yearning to go home again. But in dreams, he went back to those awful days and long nights, and his wife's screams confirmed his secret fear: they had not gotten away after all; the SIM had come for them at last.

"*Ay*, Cuco! Remember how I showed you that suitcase with little wheels so we should not have to carry those heavy bags when we traveled? Someone stole my idea and made a million!" She shook the paper in his face. "See, see! This man was no *bobo!* He didn't put all his pokers on a back burner. I kept telling you, one of these days my ship would pass me by in the night!" She wagged her finger at her husband and daughters, laughing all the while, one of those eerie laughs crazy people in movies laugh. The four girls had congregated in her room. They eyed their mother and each other. Perhaps they were all thinking the same thing, wouldn't it be weird and sad if Mami did end up in Bellevue?

"*¡Ya, ya!*" She waved them out of her room at last. "There is no use trying to drink spilt milk, that's for sure."

It was the suitcase rollers that stopped Laura's hand; she had weathervaned a minor brainstorm. And yet, this plagiarist had gotten all the credit, and the money. What use was it trying to compete with the Americans: they would always have the head start. It was their country, after all. Best stick close to home. She cast her sights about—her daughters ducked—and found her husband's office in need. Several days a week, dressed professionally in a white smock with a little name tag pinned on the lapel, a shopping bag full of cleaning materials and rags, she rode with her husband in his car to the Bronx. On the way, she organized the glove compartment or took off the address stickers from the magazines for the waiting room because she had read somewhere how by means of these stickers drug addict patients found out where doctors lived and burglarized their homes looking for syringes. At night, she did the books, filling in columns with how much money they had made that day. Who had time to be inventing silly things!

She did take up her pencil and pad one last time. But it was to help one of her daughters out. In ninth grade, Yoyo was chosen by her English teacher, Sister Mary Joseph, to deliver the Teacher's Day address at the school assembly. Back in the Dominican Republic growing up, Yoyo had been a terrible student. No one could ever get her to sit down to a book. But in New York, she needed to settle somewhere, and since the natives were unfriendly, and the country inhospitable, she took root in the language. By high school, the nuns were reading her stories and compositions out loud in English class.

But the spectre of delivering a speech brown-nosing the teachers jammed her imagination. At first she didn't want to and then she couldn't seem to write that speech. She should have thought of it as "a great honor," as her father called it. But she was mortified. She still had a slight accent, and she did not like to speak in public, subjecting herself to her classmates' ridicule. It also took no great figuring to see that to deliver a eulogy for a convent full of crazy, old, overweight nuns was no way to endear herself to her peers.

But she didn't know how to get out of it. Night after night, she sat at her desk, hoping to polish off some quick, noncommittal little speech. But she couldn't get anything down.

The weekend before the assembly Monday morning Yoyo went into a panic. Her mother would just have to call in tomorrow and say Yoyo was in the hospital, in a coma.

Laura tried to calm her down. "Just remember how Mister Lincoln couldn't think of anything to say at the Gettysburg, but then, bang! *Four score and once upon a time ago,*" she began reciting. "Something is going to come if you just relax. You'll see, like the Americans say, *Necessity is the daughter of invention.* I'll help you."

That weekend, her mother turned all her energy towards helping Yoyo write her speech. "Please, Mami, just leave me alone, please," Yoyo pleaded with her. But Yoyo would get rid of the goose only to have to contend with the gander. Her father kept poking his head in the door just to see if Yoyo had "fulfilled your obligations," a phrase he had used when the girls were younger and he'd check to see whether they had gone to the bathroom before a car trip. Several times that weekend around the supper table, he recited his own high school valedictorian speech. He gave Yoyo pointers on delivery, notes on the great orators and their tricks. (Humbleness and praise and falling silent with great emotion were his favorites.)

Laura sat across the table, the only one who seemed to be listening to him. Yoyo and her sisters were forgetting a lot of their Spanish, and their father's formal, florid diction was hard to understand. But Laura smiled softly to herself, and turned the lazy Susan at the center of the table around and around as if it were the prime mover, the first gear of her attention.

That Sunday evening, Yoyo was reading some poetry to get herself inspired: Whitman's poems in an old book with an engraved cover her father had picked up in a thrift shop next to his office. *I celebrate myself and sing myself. . . . He most honors my style who learns under it to destroy the teacher.* The poet's words shocked and thrilled her. She had gotten used to the nuns, a literature of appropriate sentiments, poems with a message, expurgated texts. But here was a flesh and blood man, belching and laughing and sweating in poems. *Who touches this book touches a man.*

That night, at last, she started to write, recklessly, three, five pages, looking up once only to see her father passing by the hall on tiptoe. When Yoyo was done, she read over her words, and her eyes filled. She finally sounded like herself in English!

As soon as she had finished that first draft, she called her mother to her room. Laura listened attentively while Yoyo read the speech out loud, and in the end, her eyes were glistening too. Her face was soft and warm and proud. "*Ay,* Yoyo, you are going to be the one to bring our name to the headlights in this country! That is a beautiful, beautiful speech I want for your father to hear it before he goes to sleep. Then I will type it for you, all right?"

Down the hall they went, mother and daughter, faces flushed with accomplishment. Into the master bedroom where Carlos was propped up on his pillows, still awake, reading the Dominican papers, already days old. Now that the dictatorship had been toppled, he had become interested in his country's fate again. The interim government was going to hold the first free elections in thirty years. History was in the making, freedom and hope were in the air again! There was still some question in his mind whether or not he might move his family back. But Laura had gotten used to the life here. She did not want to go back to the old country where, de la Torre or not, she was only a wife and a mother (and a failed one at that, since she had never provided the required son). Better an independent nobody than a high-class houseslave. She did not come straight out and disagree with her husband's plans. Instead, she fussed with him about reading the papers in bed, soiling their sheets with those poorly printed, foreign tabloids. "*The*

Times is not that bad!'' she'd claim if her husband tried to humor her by saying they shared the same dirty habit.

The minute Carlos saw his wife and daughter filing in, he put his paper down, and his face brightened as if at long last his wife had delivered the son, and that was the news she was bringing him. His teeth were already grinning from the glass of water next to his bedside lamp, so he lisped when he said, "Eh-speech, eh-speech!"

"It is so beautiful, Cuco," Laura coached him, turning the sound on his TV off. She sat down at the foot of the bed. Yoyo stood before both of them, blocking their view of the soldiers in helicopters landing amid silenced gun reports and explosions. A few weeks ago it had been the shores of the Dominican Republic. Now it was the jungles of Southeast Asia they were saving. Her mother gave her the nod to begin reading.

Yoyo didn't need much encouragement. She put her nose to the fire, as her mother would have said, and read from start to finish without looking up. When she concluded, she was a little embarrassed at the pride she took in her own words. She pretended to quibble with a phrase or two, then looked questioningly to her mother. Laura's face was radiant. Yoyo turned to share her pride with her father.

The expression on his face shocked both mother and daughter. Carlos's tooth-less mouth had collapsed into a dark zero. His eyes bored into Yoyo, then shifted to Laura. In barely audible Spanish, as if secret microphones or informers were all about, he whispered to his wife, "You will permit her to read *that*?"

Laura's eyebrows shot up, her mouth fell open. In the old country, any whisper of a challenge to authority could bring the secret police in their black V.W.'s. But this was America. People could say what they thought. "What is wrong with her speech?" Laura questioned him.

"What ees wrrrong with her eh-speech?" Carlos wagged his head at her. His anger was always more frightening in his broken English. As if he had mutilated the language in his fury—and now there was nothing to stand between them and his raw, dumb anger. "What is wrong? I will tell you what is wrong. It show no gratitude. It is boastful. *I celebrate myself? The best student learns to destroy the teacher?*" He mocked Yoyo's plagiarized words. "That is insubordinate. It is improper. It is disrespecting of her teachers—" In his anger he had forgotten his fear of lurking spies: each wrong he voiced was a decibel higher than the last outrage. Finally, he shouted at Yoyo, "As your father, I forbid you to make that eh-speech!"

Laura leapt to her feet, a sign that *she* was about to deliver her own speech. She was a small woman, and she spoke all her pronouncements standing up, either for more projection or as a carry-over from her girlhood in convent schools where one asked for, and literally, took the floor in order to speak. She stood by Yoyo's side, shoulder to shoulder. They looked down at Carlos. "That is no tone of voice—" She began.

But now, Carlos was truly furious. It was bad enough that his daughter was rebelling, but here was his own wife joining forces with her. Soon he would be surrounded by a houseful of independent American women. He too leapt from the bed, throwing off his covers. The Spanish newspapers flew across the room. He snatched the speech out of Yoyo's hands, held it before the girl's wide eyes, a vengeful, mad look in his own, and then once, twice, three, four, countless times, he tore the speech into shreds.

"Are you crazy?" Laura lunged at him. "Have you gone mad? That is her speech for tomorrow you have torn up!"

"Have *you* gone mad?" He shook her away. "You were going to let her read that . . . that insult to her teachers?"

"Insult to her teachers!" Laura's face had crumpled up like a piece of paper. On it was written a love note to her husband, an unhappy, haunted man. "This is America, Papi, America! You are not in a savage country anymore!"

Meanwhile, Yoyo was on her knees, weeping wildly, collecting all the little pieces of her speech, hoping that she could put it back together before the assembly tomorrow morning. But not even a sibyl could have made sense of those tiny scraps of paper. All hope was lost. "He broke it, he broke it," Yoyo moaned as she picked up a handful of pieces.

Probably, if she had thought a moment about it, she would not have done what she did next. She would have realized her father had lost brothers and friends to the dictator Trujillo. For the rest of his life, he would be haunted by blood in the streets and late night disappearances. Even after all these years, he cringed if a black Volkswagen passed him on the street. He feared anyone in uniform: the meter maid giving out parking tickets, a museum guard approaching to tell him not to get too close to his favorite Goya.

On her knees, Yoyo thought of the worst thing she could say to her father. She gathered a handful of scraps, stood up, and hurled them in his face. In a low, ugly whisper, she pronounced Trujillo's hated nickname: "Chapita! You're just another Chapita!"

It took Yoyo's father only a moment to register the loathsome nickname before he came after her. Down the halls they raced, but Yoyo was quicker than he and made it into her room just in time to lock the door as her father threw his weight against it. He called down curses on her head, ordered her on his authority as her father to open that door! He throttled that doorknob, but all to no avail. Her mother's love of gadgets saved Yoyo's hide that night. Laura had hired a locksmith to install good locks on all the bedroom doors after the house had been broken into once while they were away. Now if burglars broke in again, and the family were at home, there would be a second round of locks for the thieves to contend with.

"Lolo," she said, trying to calm him down. "Don't you ruin my new locks."

Finally he did calm down, his anger spent. Yoyo heard their footsteps retreating down the hall. Their door clicked shut. Then, muffled voices, her mother's rising in anger, in persuasion, her father's deeper murmurs of explanation and self-defense. The house fell silent a moment, before Yoyo heard, far off, the gun blasts and explosions, the serious, self-important voices of newscasters reporting their TV war.

A little while later, there was a quiet knock at Yoyo's door, followed by a tentative attempt at the door knob. "Cuquita?" her mother whispered. "Open up, Cuquita."

"Go away," Yoyo wailed, but they both knew she was glad her mother was there, and needed only a moment's protest to save face.

Together they concocted a speech: two brief pages of stale compliments and the polite commonplaces on teachers, a speech wrought by necessity and without much invention by mother and daughter late into the night on one of the pads of paper Laura had once used for her own inventions. After it was drafted, Laura typed it up while Yoyo stood by, correcting her mother's misnomers and missayings.

Yoyo came home the next day with the success story of the assembly. The nuns had been flattered, the audience had stood up and given "our devoted teachers a standing ovation," what Laura had suggested they do at the end of the speech.

She clapped her hands together as Yoyo recreated the moment. "I stole that from your father's speech, remember? Remember how he put that in at the end?" She quoted him in Spanish, then translated for Yoyo into English.

That night, Yoyo watched him from the upstairs hall window, where she'd retreated the minute she heard his car pull up in front of the house. Slowly, her father came up the driveway, a grim expression on his face as he grappled with a large, heavy cardboard box. At the front door, he set the package down carefully and patted all his pockets for his house keys. (If only he'd had Laura's ticking key chain!) Yoyo heard the snapping open of locks downstairs. She listened as he struggled to maneuver the box through the narrow doorway. He called her name several times, but she did not answer him.

"My daughter, your father, he love you very much," he explained from the bottom of the stairs. "He just want to protect you." Finally, her mother came up and pleaded with Yoyo to go down and reconcile with him. "Your father did not mean to harm. You must pardon him. Always it is better to let bygones be forgotten, no?"

Downstairs, Yoyo found her father setting up a brand new electric typewriter on the kitchen table. It was even better than her mother's. He had outdone himself with all the extra features: a plastic carrying case with Yoyo's initials decaled below the handle, a brace to lift the paper upright while she typed, an erase cartridge, an automatic margin tab, a plastic hood like a toaster cover to keep the dust away. Not even her mother could have invented such a machine!

But Laura's inventing days were over just as Yoyo's were starting up with her school-wide success. Rather than the rolling suitcase everyone else in the family remembers, Yoyo thinks of the speech her mother wrote as her last invention. It was as if, after that, her mother had passed on to Yoyo her pencil and pad and said, "Okay, Cuquita, here's the buck. You give it a shot."

QUESTIONS FOR DISCUSSION AND WRITING

1. Analyze the point of view of this story. Who is the main character? How does a sentence like the following contribute to our understanding of the point of view: "Probably, if she had thought a moment about it, she would not have done what she did next"?

2. Whomever we regard as the main character, Laura, Carlos, and Yoyo are all important in the story, and each of the three undergoes difficulties in adjusting to life in the United States. Trace the experiences of each in this process.

3. The theme of language is important in the story. Trace this theme through Laura's malapropisms, Yoyo's writing and her school speech, the model of Whitman, and Carlos's first tearing up Yoyo's speech and then giving her a typewriter.

Don Belton

Don Belton, a native of Philadelphia, has been a reporter for *Newsweek* and currently teaches writing at the University of Michigan. His first novel, *Almost Midnight*, was published in 1986.

MY SOUL IS A WITNESS

Come on up . . . my castle's rockin'
—Blues

The night exhales a treasury of stars. You are in the blacked-out backseat of a limousine floating along Upper East Side Manhattan. There is a crowd of reporters with a camera crew outside your building. You fan out your hair and draw it into a knot at your neck. You wrap your face and head in a tulle black veil. Then you put on the dark glasses. The car stops at the canopied entrance to the building. You are a shimmery blur as you are swept into the glass-and-marble lobby and sent floating up in the special elevator. All the while, your teeth flash inside the veil.

You drank too much vodka on the *Concorde*.

The living room is a jack-in-the-box. Statuary, paintings, plates, and mirrors jump out at you. You come and sit on the sofa, stepping from satiny shoes. You lay back your head, closing your eyes. It feels good to relax. You feel the muscles around your eyes relax. Your perfect teeth unclench. In another room a telephone rings, and then you hear the whir of paper passing automatically through a fax machine. You stand and pace the living room and then the entire apartment.

You have not slept here for years. It is hard to believe: when you bought the apartment a decade ago, you imagined yourself, in its peaceable library, reading books in the shine of the lighted fireplace. You dreamed of Sunday mornings in the desert-vast bedroom, spreading the sheets of *The New York Times* across the bed, sipping coffee drawn from a machine, listening to the jazz albums you collected in your early twenties. You said you craved a life filled with books, your own cooking, and other people's music. You believed there might be a man in time whose qualities would enhance your own, who would admire your secret face—who would stay.

But now the apartment houses a six-person staff managing your career in the United States. It still amazes you how easily your home has become a headquarters. How easily you ceased to be the "I" you fought so hard to achieve and began manifesting as "we." The apartment is a prop, a part of the machinery that throws your outsize image at the world.

Here you meet with reporters when your albums are released. Business meetings are conducted in the dining room among gilt mirrors and Venetian glassware. Bodyguards double as waiters. Journalists sip champagne in an atmosphere of chintz and Ming-dynasty horses. You have a private suite of rooms with a king-sized bed, remote-control television sets and stereo systems; there is a mirrored dressing room crammed with unfamiliar clothes. Computerized telephones, bedside, by the couch, desk, and in the bathroom, blink relentlessly. The bathroom offers bone-handled toothbrushes, horn combs, exotic toothpastes and headache cures. The bathtub has a whirlpool and a twenty-four-karat gold grab bar. Lying in the deep tub, in an aura of flowers, you push the loofah sponge from your thighs.

You feel sick and longing.

At exactly seven-thirty, abandoning spilled boxes, belts, powder, and shoes, you emerge from your rooms wearing a short black tasseled dress. Makeup sparkles on your face like blossom dust.

The cook has arrived and filled the apartment with the smells of grilled salmon and beef Peregourdine. In the living room you pour yourself a glass of wine. Fresh flowers have started arriving in profusion, massive bouquets of lilies, camellias, and roses, forty to a bunch.

You pause between worlds, discarnate somehow, unmanifest, waiting for your transformation. You haven't fully arrived. You still feel the motion of the plane. It seems you are always on a plane these days. You break a Valium in half and wash it down with wine.

More than twenty years ago your name exploded into celebrity. Twenty years ago you were still the lead singer of the Jewelettes, four gawky Cinderellas singing with ghetto wistfulness and spurious sighs. Soon you looked more like sepia-toned debutantes than ghetto girls, as coolly mannered as Snow White princesses from Shaker Heights or Grosse Pointe. The Jewelettes: Frances Deal, Marie LaBerth, Lucinda Blood, and Beryl Hopkins.

You think, Where are those other girls? Gone like the fur coats, glamour wigs, dream houses, and big Cadillac convertibles bought on fast new money. Those other girls were like sparks from the flash paper used to herald the acts in the old rhythm and soul revues.

But you still fascinate, riding success like a smooth glissando. You are the fire that burns up everything in your way. You surpass everything and everybody. You surpass your music, as much a model as a singer, as much a face as a sound. The sound is a soul/pop seduction with a built-in cry. In the 1960s it was the sound of a woman crying for freedom that transfixed the world. Later it became the sound of a woman crying for a vision. Your devouring voice still stalks the world looking for a home.

A test pressing of your new album arrived by messenger while you were in the bath. You put the disc on the turntable. Soon the rumbling music vibrates you to your bone. You listen to the jungling mix of horns, drumbeats, and guitars. Then you hear your own voice soaring over the top, stretching out the rhythm, snaking and twisting the time.

You look out your high windows at a panorama of New York City. You light a cigarette. You feel a chill at the small of your back and gradually become present. You are here.

New York has changed since you were last in this room. A new feeling has entered the city. This knowledge reaches you beneath the blaring music, and a muscle around your left eye twitches. You read the change in the mute suspended panorama. The city has a different look, new people. You sense trip wires have been laid for you by your enemies.

The living room with its wraparound windows facing all of New York and the world becomes your stage. You consider the drama of your public life—your magazine covers, industry awards, record-breaking sales, your marriages and re-marriages and the lovers who turn into soul-murderers in the dark.

And now this new album and a seventeen-city concert tour, product endorsements, hotel rooms, private jets, parties. Oblivion.

You are always scheming to steal back the limelight and steal it back again and again. Your prayer is: *Let me not be forsaken until I have shown strength to this generation and power to every one that is to come.* And your prayer is: *Bring me up again from the depths of the earth.*

You remove the record from the turntable. You hate the whole sound of the new album. The entire album has the sound of mockery with something ugly howling in the mix.

When the production contracts were drawn up for the album, you told the record producer, "Give me a hit. That's all."

You weren't joking.

You record music you no longer love. Your music no longer expresses your spirit. You've become a simulator. You rehearse every whisper and moan you deliver with letter-perfection. Your early music was structured around voices. You *had* to sing in those days because all you had was the sound your soul made in your body to reach an audience. You couldn't hide behind arrangements, haute couture costumes, and special effects. It would have cost your life to stand on the stage of the Apollo or the Uptown trying to sing something you didn't understand. Those black audiences would have torn you apart.

You came out on those stages, scratching up the floor with your two-dollar high heels, trying to dance in a too-tight gown made from a Simplicity pattern. They weren't studying your smile or the bend of your bright auburn wig. They were waiting. You were naked to them. They were close enough to look right into your eyes, and they were willing to carry you, but you had to show them your heart. You would have wrenched it from the center of your breasts if need be to work up a feeling. They were shriving for your soul while you were up there. You messed up your face with the depth of pain and love pouring through you. You kept up your ragged shuffling and chanting until you were fused with a power that rocks the ceaselessly coming waves of the ocean. Until the tears streamed down your face and your hands gave benedictions of release and blood pardon.

You wish you could cry those tears again. Perhaps they would wash away the years that have pushed you further and further from your audience and from your song. Now you play the big money venues. Most of your audience watches you perform on the giant video monitors set up around the arena or through binoculars or as a diffused light at the center of a dark stadium.

You have become a radiant source of light.

As for your records, your voice now comes clothed in jarring hooks and computer-programmed crashes to penetrate even the mind centered on the ghoulish flame of a drug pipe.

Your voice strains under the burden of cigarettes and isolation. Your voice is blocked up with your own anger and wonderment. You are at a loss to express what you have lived and seen in a pop song. Still your records sell as if imbued with a diabolical charm.

Something stings your hand. The cigarette has burned away to the space between your fingers. You fling it from you as if it were a wasp. It is a moment before you realize it is only a burning cigarette end and retrieve it from the carpet.

Kneeling on the floor for the cigarette, you feel a stealing stroke of nausea, then exhaustion. You hit your arm against the coffee table and, moaning, fall back on your side. Your hair sweeps your face, flipping back. You stretch out on your back, holding your stomach, then your head. You feel hot. You feel as though your head were about to blow apart. Your prayer is: *I can't die here. Not now. Not here alone without anyone who loves me and knows me. Don't let me die before I reach my safe harbor.* Your eyes roll back, watching the ceiling. The ceiling looks so remote—a mute blazing-white world above your head.

You tell yourself to breathe. You try to concentrate on your breath. You breathe soundly and resolutely, listening to the air enter and leave through your mouth until you become all breath, all air. Fire and brimstone fall from the walls and ceiling. The fire catches first in your brain. Next your skin catches. You cry and sweat. Your head throbs, breaking into burning cinders. You are so hot you cannot stand it. Your clothes catch fire from your skin.

Your body burns and rolls on the floor.

You keep on breathing. Through the time on the floor your soul keeps on breathing and watching.

You remember yourself, as the fire disappears. You are supreme, self-existent, single and self-producing.

No one has pierced your mystery.

Next the waters of your spirit begin to break. You walk down a terraced mountain to greet the waves. You are the sea-witch, the mirror of heaven.

The wind refreshes you, anoints your shoulders, neck and face. The wind brings fragrances of Africa and the Caribbean, Newark, Haiti, New Orleans—everywhere your people rush in the move of life with their smells and voices. Even the voice of their laughter and the smell of their fear. Smells of their fiery food and the fucking-dance of their regeneration. The wind is filled with their voices whispering together. Their whispers are like kisses imprinting your whole body with information. Telling you a vocabulary of feelings.

When the waters break, they leap the boundaries of the sea. They overtake the shore. And with them break the glamorous waters of your pain. The waters toss you like a reeling ship. You rock and reel. You toss. You go down. You drown in emerald water. There are emeralds and rare rubies in the sea's foam. The emeralds are your blood pride and the rubies your blood guiltiness. You fall to the sea's floor.

The impact of the fall stuns your mind and knocks the breath out of your soul. You are hours on the watery floor, unconscious, angels and demons fighting to bear you away.

Suddenly breath returns to your body with the whir of electricity returning to a whole city after a power failure.

You simply rise.

QUESTIONS FOR DISCUSSION AND WRITING

1. Who is the speaker in this story? Are the "I" and the "you" two sides of a single self? Or is the "I" strictly a separate consciousness?

2. What aesthetic is advanced by the story? The narrator contrasts the pure art of the singer's early days with the corruption and commercialization of her present. What criteria are being used?

3. What literally happens at the end of the story? Does the singer die? Can we be sure? Whether she dies or not, what sort of inner experience does she go through?

4. The story has an epigraph from a blues song. How is it relevant? Is there a suggestion that the story itself is structured musically, like a blues? What analogies exist between the story and a song?

Becky Birtha

Becky Birtha has published two collections of short stories: *For Nights Like This One: Stories of Loving Women* (1983) and *Lovers' Choice* (1987). She is also the author of *The Forbidden Poems* (1991). She lives in Philadelphia.

JOHNNIERUTH

Summertime. Nighttime. Talk about steam heat. This whole city get like the bathroom when somebody in there taking a shower with the door shut. Nights like that, can't nobody sleep. Everybody be outside, sitting on they steps or else dragging half they furniture out on the sidewalk—kitchen chairs, card tables—even bringing TVs outside.

Womenfolks, mostly. All the grown women around my way look just the same. They all big—stout. They got big bosoms and big hips and fat legs, and they always wearing runover house shoes and them shapeless, flowered numbers with the buttons down the front. 'Cept on Sunday. Sunday morning they all turn into glamour girls, in them big hats and long gloves, with they skinny high heels and they skinny selves in them tight girdles—wouldn't nobody ever know what they look like the rest of the time.

When I was a little kid, I didn't wanna grow up, 'cause I never wanted to look like them ladies. I heard Miz Jenkins down the street one time say she don't mind being fat 'cause that way her husband don't get so jealous. She say it's more than one way to keep a man. Me, I don't have me no intentions of keeping no man. I never understood why they was in so much demand anyway, when it seem like all a woman can depend on 'em for is making sure she keep on having babies.

We got enough children in my neighborhood. In the summertime even the little kids allowed to stay up till eleven or twelve o'clock at night—playing in the street and hollering and carrying on—don't never seem to get tired. Don't nobody care, long as they don't fight.

Me—I don't hang around no front steps no more. Hot nights like that, I get out my ten-speed and I be gone.

That's what I like to do more than anything else in the whole world. Feel that wind in my face keeping me cool as an air conditioner, shooting along like a snowball. My bike light as a kite. I can really get up some speed.

All the guys around my way got ten-speed bikes. Some of the girls got 'em, too, but they don't ride 'em at night. They pedal around during the day, but at nighttime they just hang around out front, watching babies and running they mouth. I didn't get my Peugeot to be no conversation piece.

My mama don't like me to ride at night. I tried to point out to her that she ain't never said nothing to my brothers, and Vincent a year younger than me. (And Langston two years older, in case "old" is the problem.) She say, "That's different, Johnnieruth. You're a girl." Now I wanna know how is anybody gonna know that. I'm skinny as a knifeblade turned sideways, and all I ever wear is blue jeans and a Wrangler jacket. But if I bring that up, she liable to get started in on how come I can't be more of a young lady, and fourteen is old enough to start taking more pride in my appearance, and she gonna be ashamed to admit I'm her daughter.

I just tell her that my bike be moving so fast can't nobody hardly see me, and couldn't catch me if they did. Mama complain to her friends how I'm wild and she

469

can't do nothing with me. She know I'm gonna do what I want no matter what she say. But she know I ain't getting in no trouble, neither.

Like some of the boys I know stole they bikes, but I didn't do nothing like that. I'd been saving my money ever since I can remember, every time I could get a nickel or a dime outa anybody.

When I was a little kid, it was hard to get money. Seem like the only time they ever give you any was on Sunday morning, and then you had to put it in the offering. I used to hate to do that. In fact, I used to hate everything about Sunday morning. I had to wear all them ruffly dresses—that shiny slippery stuff in the wintertime that got to make a noise every time you move your ass a inch on them hard old benches. And that scratchy starchy stuff in the summertime with all them scratchy crinolines. Had to carry a pocketbook and wear them shiny shoes. And the church we went to was all the way over on Summit Avenue, so the whole damn neighborhood could get a good look. At least all the other kids'd be dressed the same way. The boys think they slick 'cause they get to wear pants, but they still got to wear a white shirt and a tie; and them dumb hats they wear can't hide them baldheaded haircuts, 'cause they got to take the hats off in church.

There was one Sunday when I musta been around eight. I remember it was before my sister Corletta was born, 'cause right around then was when I put my foot down about that whole sanctimonious routine. Anyway, I was dragging my feet along Twenty-fifth Street in back of Mama and Vincent and them, when I spied this lady. I only seen her that one time, but I still remember just how she look. She don't look like nobody I ever seen before. I *know* she don't live around here. She real skinny. But she ain't no real young woman, neither, She could be old as my mama. She ain't nobody's mama—I'm sure. And she ain't wearing Sunday clothes. She got on blue jeans and a man's blue working shirt, with the tail hanging out. She got patches on her blue jeans, and she still got her chin stuck out like she some kinda African royalty. She ain't carrying no shiny pocketbook. It don't look like she care if she got any money or not, or who know it, if she don't. She ain't wearing no house shoes, or stockings or high heels neither.

Mama always speak to everybody, but when she pass by this lady she make like she ain't even seen her. But I get me a real good look, and the lady stare right back at me. She got a funny look on her face, almost like she think she know me from someplace. After she pass on by, I had to turn around to get another look, even though Mama say that ain't polite. And you know what? She was turning around, too, looking back at me. And she give me a great big smile.

I didn't know too much in them days, but that's when I first got to thinking about how it's got to be different ways to be, from the way people be around my way. It's got to be places where it don't matter to nobody if you all dressed up on Sunday morning or you aint. That's how come I started saving money. So, when I got enough, I could go away to someplace like that.

Afterwhile I begun to see there wasn't no point in waiting around for handouts, and I started thinking of ways to earn my own money. I used to be running errands all the time—mailing letters for old Grandma Whittaker and picking up cigarettes and newspapers up the corner for everybody. After I got bigger, I started washing cars in the summer, and shoveling people sidewalk in the wintertime. Now I got me a newspaper route. Ain't never been no girl around here with no paper route, but I guess everybody got it figured out by now that I aint' gonna be like nobody else.

The reason I got me my Peugeot was so I could start to explore. I figured I better start looking around right now, so when I'm grown, I'll know exactly where I wanna go. So I ride around every chance I get.

Last summer I used to ride with the boys a lot. Sometimes eight to ten of us'd just go cruising around the streets together. All of a sudden my mama decide she don't want me to do that no more. She say I'm too old to be spending so much time with boys. (That's what they tell you half the time, and the other half the time they worried 'cause you ain't interested in spending more time with boys. Don't make much sense.) She want me to have some girl friends, but I never seem to fit in with none of the things the girls doing. I used to think I fit in more with the boys.

But I seen how Mama might be right, for once. I didn't like the way the boys was starting to talk about girls sometimes. Talking about what some girl be like from the neck on down, and talking all up underneath somebody clothes and all. Even though I wasn't really friends with none of the girls, I still didn't like it. So now I mostly just ride around by myself. And Mama don't like that neither—you just can't please her.

This boy that live around the corner on North Street, Kenny Henderson, started asking me one time if I don't ever be lonely, 'cause he always see me by myself. He say don't I ever think I'd like to have me somebody special to go places with and stuff. Like I'd pick him if I did! Made me wanna laugh in his face. I do be lonely, a lotta times, but I don't tell nobody. And I ain't met nobody yet that I'd really rather be with than be by myself. But I will someday. When I find that special place where everybody different, I'm gonna find somebody there I can be friends with. And it ain't gonna be no dumb boy.

I found me one place already that I like to go to a whole lot. It ain't even really that far away—by bike—but it's on the other side of the Avenue. So I don't tell Mama and them I go there, 'cause they like to think I'm right around the neighborhood someplace. But this neighborhood too dull for me. All the houses look just the same—no porches, no yards, no trees—not even no parks around here. Every block look so much like every other block it hurt your eyes to look at afterwhile. So I ride across Summit Avenue and go down that big steep hill there, and then make a sharp right at the bottom and cross the bridge over the train tracks. Then I head on out the boulevard—that's the nicest part, with all them big trees making a tunnel over the top, and lightning bugs shining in the bushes. At the end of the boulevard you get to this place call the Plaza.

It's something like a little park—the sidewalks is all bricks and they got flowers planted all over the place. The same kind my mama grow in that painted-up tire she got out front masquerading like a garden decoration—only seem like they smell sweeter here. It's a big high fountain right in the middle, and all the streetlights is the real old-fashion kind. That Plaza is about the prettiest place I ever been.

Sometimes something going on there. Like a orchestra playing music or some man or lady singing. One time they had a show with some girls doing some kinda foreign dances. They look like they were around my age. They all had on these fancy costumes, with different color ribbons all down they back. I wouldn't wear nothing like that, but it looked real pretty when they was dancing.

I got me a special bench in one corner where I like to sit, 'cause I can see just about everything, but wouldn't nobody know I was there. I like to sit still and think, and I like to watch people. A lotta people be coming there at night—to look at the shows and stuff, or just to hang out and cool off. All different kinda people.

This one night when I was sitting over in that corner where I always be at, there was this lady standing right near my bench. She mostly had her back turned to me and she didn't know I was there, but I could see her real good. She had on this shiny purple shirt and about a million silver bracelets. I kinda liked the way she look. Sorta exotic, like she maybe come from California or one of the islands. I mean she had class—standing there posing with her arms folded. She walk away a little bit. Then turn around and walk back again. Like she waiting for somebody.

Then I spotted this dude coming over. I spied him all the way 'cross the Plaza. Looking real fine. Got on a three-piece suit. One of them little caps sitting on a angle. Look like leather. He coming straight over to this lady I'm watching and then she seen him, too, and she start to smile, but she don't move till he got right up next to her. And then I'm gonna look away, 'cause I can't stand to watch nobody hugging and kissing on each other, but all of a sudden I see it ain't no dude at all. It's another lady.

Now I can't stop looking. They smiling at each other like they ain't seen one another in ten years. Then the one in the purple shirt look around real quick— but she don't look just behind her—and sorta pull the other one right back into the corner where I'm sitting at, and then they put they arms around each other and kiss—for a whole long time. Now I really know I oughta turn away, but I can't. And I know they gonna see me when they finally open they eyes. And they do.

They both kinda gasp and back up, like I'm the monster that just rose up outta the deep. And then I guess they can see I'm only a girl, and they look at one another—and start to laugh! Then they just turn around and start to walk away like it wasn't nothing at all. But right before they gone, they both look around again, and see I still ain't got my eye muscles and my jaw muscles working right again yet. And the one lady wink at me. And the other one say, "Catch you later."

I can't stop staring at they backs, all the way across the Plaza. And then, all of a sudden, I feel like I got to be doing something, got to be moving.

I wheel on outta the Plaza and I'm just concentrating on getting up my speed. 'Cause I can't figure out what to think. Them two women kissing and then, when they get caught, just laughing about it. And here I'm laughing, too, for no reason at all. I'm sailing down the boulevard laughing like a lunatic, and then I'm singing at the top of my lungs. And climbing that big old hill up to Summit Avenue is just as easy as being on a escalator.

QUESTIONS FOR DISCUSSION AND WRITING

1. "Johnnieruth" is a maturation story, a story about some aspect of a young person's growing up. What sort of development is Johnnieruth going through at the time of the story, and how does the experience described in the story help advance her growth?

2. "Johnnieruth" is a first-person story, told in the voice of fourteen-year-old Johnnieruth. Are there any points in the story where the reader is likely to understand the situation better than Johnnieruth?

3. What does the sight of the lesbians kissing mean to Johnnieruth? Is it just a glimpse of a more exotic world than her mother's world, or is there a suggestion that the lesbians are acting out sexual feelings that Johnnieruth has?

4. "Johnnieruth" is full of references to gender, to what is perceived as "masculine" and "feminine." Trace this subject through the story.

Michelle Cliff

Michelle Cliff was born in Jamaica in 1946. She was educated at Wagner College in New York and at the Warburg Institute of the University of London. Her first book was a collection of poetry, *Claiming an Identity They Taught Me to Despise* (1980). *Abeng* (1984) is a novel set in Jamaica about a friendship between the light-skinned Claire Savage and the darker-skinned Zoe. Claire's story is continued in *No Telephone to Heaven* (1987). Cliff has also published *The Land of Look Behind* (1985), a collection of poems and prose, from which "If I Could Write This in Fire, I Would Write This in Fire" is taken. Michelle Cliff lives in Santa Cruz, California.

IF I COULD WRITE THIS IN FIRE, I WOULD WRITE THIS IN FIRE

I

We were standing under the waterfall at the top of Orange River. Our chests were just beginning to mound—slight hills on either side. In the center of each were our nipples, which were losing their sideways look and rounding into perceptible buttons of dark flesh. Too fast it seemed. We touched each other, then, quickly and almost simultaneously, raised our arms to examine the hairs growing underneath. Another sign. Mine was wispy and light-brown. My friend Zoe had dark hair curled up tight. In each little patch the riverwater caught the sun so we glistened.

The waterfall had come about when my uncles dammed up the river to bring power to the sugar mill. Usually, when I say "sugar mill" to anyone not familiar with the Jamaican countryside or for that matter my family, I can tell their minds cast an image of tall smokestacks, enormous copper cauldrons, a man in a broad-brimmed hat with a whip, and several dozens of slaves—that is, if they have any idea of how large sugar mills once operated. It's a grandiose expression—like plantation, verandah, out-building. (Try substituting farm, porch, outside toilet.) To some people it even sounds romantic.

Our sugar mill was little more than a round-roofed shed, which contained a wheel and woodfire. We paid an old man to run it, tend the fire, and then either bartered or gave the sugar away, after my grandmother had taken what she needed. Our canefield was about two acres of flat land next to the river. My grandmother had six acres in all—one donkey, a mule, two cows, some chickens, a few pigs, and stray dogs and cats who had taken up residence in the yard.

Her house had four rooms, no electricity, no running water. The kitchen was a shed in the back with a small pot-bellied stove. Across from the stove was a mahogany counter, which had a white enamel basin set into it. The only light source was a window, a small space covered partly by a wooden shutter. We washed our faces and hands in enamel bowls with cold water carried in kerosene tins from the river and poured from enamel pitchers. Our chamber pots were enamel also, and in the morning we carefully placed them on the steps at the side of the house where my grandmother collected them and disposed of their contents. The out-house was about thirty yards from the back door—a "closet" as we called it—infested with lizards capable of changing color. When the door was shut it was totally dark, and the lizards made their presence known by the noise of their scurrying through the torn newspaper, or the soft shudder when they dropped from the walls. I remember most clearly the stench of the toilet, which seemed to hang in the air in that climate.

But because every little piece of reality exists in relation to another little piece, our situation was not that simple. It was to our yard that people came with news first. It was in my grandmother's parlor that the Disciples of Christ held their meetings.

Zoe lived with her mother and sister on borrowed ground in a place called Breezy Hill. She and I saw each other almost every day on our school vacations over a period of three years. Each morning early—as I sat on the cement porch with my coffee cut with condensed milk—she appeared: in her straw hat, school tunic faded from blue to gray, white blouse, sneakers hanging around her neck. We had coffee together, and a piece of hard-dough bread with butter and cheese, waited a bit and headed for the river. At first we were shy with each other. We did not start from the same place.

There was land. My grandparents' farm. And there was color.

(My family was called *red*. A term which signified a degree of whiteness. "We's just a flock of red people," a cousin of mine said once.) In the hierarchy of shades I was considered among the lightest. The countrywomen who visited my grand-mother commented on my "tall" hair—meaning long. Wavy, not curly.

I had spent the years from three to ten in New York and spoke—at first—like an American. I wore American clothes: shorts, slacks, bathing suit. Because of my American past I was looked upon as the creator of games. Cowboys and Indians. Cops and Robbers. Peter Pan.

(While the primary colonial identification for Jamaicans was English, American colonialism was a strong force in my childhood—and of course continues today. We were sent American movies and American music. American aluminum com-panies had already discovered bauxite on the island and were shipping the ore to their mainland. United Fruit bought our bananas. White Americans came to Montego Bay, Ocho Rios, and Kingston for their vacations and their cruise ships docked in Port Antonio and other places. In some ways America was seen as a better place than England by many Jamaicans. The farm laborers sent to work in American agribusiness came home with dollars and gifts and new clothes; there were few who mentioned American racism. Many of the middle class who emi-grated to Brooklyn or Staten Island or Manhattan were able to pass into the white American world—saving their blackness for other Jamaicans or for trips home; in some cases, forgetting it altogether. Those middle-class Jamaicans who could not pass for white managed differently—not unlike the Bajans in Paule Marshall's *Brown Girl, Brownstones*—saving, working, investing, buying property. Completely separate in most cases from Black Americans.)

*   *   *

I was someone who had experience with the place that sent us triple features of B-grade westerns and gangster movies. And I had tall hair and light skin. And I was the granddaughter of my grandmother. So I had power. I was the cowboy, Zoe was my sidekick, the boys we knew were Indians. I was the detective, Zoe was my "girl," the boys were the robbers. I was Peter Pan, Zoe was Wendy Darling, the boys were the lost boys. And the terrain around the river—jungled and dark green—was Tombstone, or Chicago, or Never-Never Land.

This place and my friendship with Zoe never touched my life in Kingston. We did not correspond with each other when I left my grandmother's home.

I never visited Zoe's home the entire time I knew her. It was a given; never suggested, never raised.

Zoe went to a state school held in a country church in Red Hills. It had been my mother's school. I went to a private all-girls school where I was taught by white Englishwomen and pale Jamaicans. In her school the students were caned as punishment. In mine the harshest punishment I remember was being sent to sit under the *lignum vitae* to "commune with nature." Some of the girls were out-and-out white (English and American), the rest of us were colored—only a few were dark. Our uniforms were blood-red gabardine, heavy and hot. Classes were held in buildings meant to recreate England: damp with stone floors, facing onto a cloister, or quad as they called it. We began each day with the headmistress leading us in English hymns. The entire school stood for an hour in the zinc-roofed gymnasium.

Occasionally a girl fainted, or threw up. Once, a girl had a grand mal seizure. To any such disturbance the response was always "keep singing." While she flailed on the stone floor, I wondered what the mistresses would do. We sang "Faith of Our Fathers," and watched our classmate as her eyes rolled back in her head. I thought of people swallowing their tongues. This student was dark—here on a scholarship—and the only woman who came forward to help her was the gamesmistress, the only dark teacher. She kneeled beside the girl and slid the white web belt from her tennis shorts, clamping it between the girl's teeth. When the seizure was over, she carried the girl to a tumbling mat in a corner of the gym and covered her so she wouldn't get chilled.

Were the other women unable to touch this girl because of her darkness? I think that now. Her darkness and her scholarship. She lived on Windward Road with her grandmother; her mother was a maid. But darkness is usually enough for women like those to hold back. Then, we usually excused that kind of behavior by saying they were "ladies." (We were constantly being told we should be ladies also. One teacher went so far as to tell us many people thought Jamaicans lived in trees and we had to show these people they were mistaken.) In short, we felt insufficient to judge the behavior of these women. The English ones (who had the corner on power in the school) had come all this way to teach us. Shouldn't we treat them as the missionaries they were certain they were? The creole Jamaicans had a different role: they were passing on to those of us who were light-skinned the creole heritage of collaboration, assimilation, loyalty to our betters. We were expected to be willing subjects in this outpost of civilization.

*   *   *

The girl left school that day and never returned.

After prayers we filed into our classrooms. After classes we had games: tennis, field hockey, rounders (what the English call baseball), netball (what the English call basketball). For games we were divided into "houses"—groups named for Joan of Arc, Edith Cavell, Florence Nightingale, Jane Austen. Four white heroines. Two martyrs. One saint. Two nurses. (None of us knew then that there were Black women with Nightingale at Scutari.) One novelist. Three involved in whitemen's wars. Two dead in whitemen's wars. *Pride and Prejudice.*

Those of us in Cavell wore red badges and recited her last words before a firing squad in W. W. I: "Patriotism is not enough. I must have no hatred or bitterness toward anyone."

Sorry to say I grew up to have exactly that.

Looking back: To try and see when the background changed places with the foreground. To try and locate the vanishing point: where the lines of perspective converge and disappear. Lines of color and class. Lines of history and social context. Lines of denial and rejection. When did *we* (the light-skinned middle-class Jamaicans) take over for *them* as oppressors? I need to see when and how this happened. When what should have been reality was overtaken by what was surely unreality. When the house nigger became master.

"What's the matter with you? You think you're white or something?"
"Child, what you want to know 'bout Garvey for? The man was nothing but a damn fool."
"They not our kind of people."

Why did we wear wide-brimmed hats and try to get into Oxford? Why did we not return?

Great Expectations: a novel about origins and denial, about the futility and tragedy of that denial, about attempting assimilation. We learned this novel from a light-skinned Jamaican woman—she concentrated on what she called the "love affair" between Pip and Estella.

Looking back: Through the last page of *Sula.* "And the loss pressed down on her chest and came up into her throat. 'We was girls together,' she said as though explaining something." It was Zoe, and Zoe alone, I thought of. She snapped into my mind and I remembered no one else. Through the greens and blues of the riverbank. The flame of red hibiscus in front of my grandmother's house. The cracked grave of a former landowner. The fruit of the ackee which poisons those who don't know how to prepare it.

"What is to become of us?"
We borrowed a baby from a woman and used her as our dolly. Dressed and undressed her. Dipped her in the riverwater. Fed her with the milk her mother had left with us: and giggled because we knew where the milk had come from.

A letter: "I am desperate. I need to get away. I beg you one fifty-dollar."

*   *   *

I send the money because this is what she asks for. I visit her on a trip back home. Her front teeth are gone. Her husband beats her and she suffers blackouts. I sit on her chair. She is given birth control pills which aggravate her "condition." We boil up sorrel and ginger. She is being taught by Peace Corps volunteers to embroider linen mats with little lambs on them and gives me one as a keepsake. We cool off the sorrel with a block of ice brought from the shop nearby. The shopkeeper immediately recognizes me as my grandmother's granddaughter and refuses to sell me cigarettes. (I am twenty-seven.) We sit in the doorway of her house, pushing back the colored plastic strands which form a curtain, and talk about Babylon and Dred. About Manley and what he's doing for Jamaica. About how hard it is. We walk along the railway tracks—no longer used—to Crooked River and the post office. Her little daughter walks beside us and we recite a poem for her: "Mornin' buddy/Me no buddy fe wunna/Who den, den I saw?" and on and on.

I can come and go. And I leave. To complete my education in London.

II

Their goddam kings and their goddam queens. Grandmotherly Victoria spreading herself thin across the globe. Elizabeth II on our t.v. screens. We stop what we are doing. We quiet down. We pay our respects.

1981: In Massachusetts I get up at 5 A.M. to watch the royal wedding. I tell myself maybe the IRA will intervene. It's got to be better than starving themselves to death. Better to be a kamikaze in St. Paul's Cathedral than a hostage in Ulster. And last week Black and white people smashed storefronts all over the United Kingdom. But I really don't believe we'll see royal blood on t.v. I watch because they once ruled us. In the back of the cathedral a Maori woman sings an aria from Handel, and I notice that she is surrounded by the colored subjects.

To those of us in the commonwealth the royal family was the perfect symbol of hegemony. To those of us who were dark in the dark nations, the prime minister, the parliament barely existed. We believed in royalty—we were convinced in this belief. Maybe it played on some ancestral memories of West Africa—where other kings and queens had been. Altars and castles and magic.

The faces of our new rulers were everywhere in my childhood. Calendars, newsreels, magazines. Their presences were often among us. Attending test matches between the West Indians and South Africans. They were our landlords. Not always absentee. And no matter what Black leader we might elect—were we to choose independence—we would be losing something almost holy in our impudence.

WE ARE HERE BECAUSE YOU WERE THERE
BLACK PEOPLE AGAINST STATE BRUTALITY
BLACK WOMEN WILL NOT BE INTIMIDATED
WELCOME TO BRITAIN ... WELCOME TO SECOND-CLASS
CITIZENSHIP
(slogans of the Black movement in Britain)

*   *   *

Indian women cleaning the toilets in Heathrow airport. This is the first thing I notice. Dark women in saris trudging buckets back and forth as other dark women in saris—some covered by loosefitting winter coats—form a line to have their passports stamped.

The triangle trade: molasses/rum/slaves. Robinson Crusoe was on a slave-trading journey. Robert Browning was a mulatto. Holding pens. Jamaica was a seasoning station. Split tongues. Sliced ears. Whipped bodies. The constant pretense of civility against rape. Still. Iron collars. Tinplate masks. The latter a precaution: to stop the slaves from eating the sugar cane.

A pregnant woman is to be whipped—they dig a hole to accommodate her belly and place her face down on the ground. Many of us became light-skinned very fast. Traced ourselves through bastard lines to reach the duke of Devonshire. The earl of Cornwall. The lord of this and the lord of that. Our mothers' rapes were the thing unspoken.

You say: But Britain freed her slaves in 1833. Yes.

Tea plantations in India and Ceylon. Mines in Africa. The Cape-to-Cairo Railroad. Rhodes scholars. Suez Crisis. The whiteman's bloody burden. Boer War. Bantustans. Sitting in a theatre in London in the seventies. A play called *West of Suez*. A lousy play about British colonials. The finale comes when several well-known white actors are machine-gunned by several lesser-known Black actors. (As Nina Simone says: "This is a show tune but the show hasn't been written for it yet.)

The red empire of geography classes. "The sun never sets on the British empire and you can't trust it in the dark." Or with the dark peoples. "Because of the Industrial Revolution European countries went in search of markets and raw materials." Another geography (or was it a history) lesson.

Their bloody kings and their bloody queens. Their bloody peers. Their bloody generals. Admirals. Explorers. Livingstone. Hillary. Kitchener. All the bwanas. And all their beaters, porters, sherpas. Who found the source of the Nile. Victoria Falls. The tops of mountains. Their so-called discoveries reek of untruth. How many dark people died so they could misname the physical features in their blasted gazetteer. A statistic we shall never know. Dr. Livingstone, I presume you are here to rape our land and enslave our people.

There are statues of these dead white men all over London.

An interesting fact: The swearword "bloody" is a contraction of "by my lady"—a reference to the Virgin Mary. They do tend to use their ladies. Name ages for them. Places for them. Use them as screens, inspirations, symbols. And many of the ladies comply. While the national martyr Edith Cavell was being executed by the Germans in 1915 in Belgium (called "poor little Belgium" by the allies in the war), the Belgians were engaged in the exploitation of the land and peoples of the Congo.

*   *   *

And will we ever know how many dark peoples were "imported" to fight in whitemen's wars. Probably not. Just as we will never know how many hearts were cut from African people so that the Christian doctor might be a success—i.e., extend a whiteman's life. Our Sister Killjoy observes this from her black-eyed squint.

Dr. Schweitzer—humanitarian, authority on Bach, winner of the Nobel Peace Prize—on the people of Africa: "The Negro is a child, and with children nothing can be done without the use of authority. We must, therefore, so arrange the circumstances of our daily life that my authority can find expression. With regard to Negroes, then, I have coined the formula: 'I am your brother, it is true, but your elder brother.'" (*On the Edge of the Primeval Forest*, 1961)

They like to pretend we didn't fight back. We did: with obeah, poison, revolution. It simply was not enough.

"Colonies . . . these places where 'niggers' are cheap and the earth is rich." (W.E.B. DuBois, "The Souls of White Folk")

A cousin is visiting me from Cal Tech where he is getting a degree in engineering. I am learning about the Italian Renaissance. My cousin is recognizably Black and speaks with an accent. I am not and I do not—unless I am back home, where the "twang" comes upon me. We sit for some time in a bar in his hotel and are not served. A light-skinned Jamaican comes over to our table. He is an older man—a professor at the University of London. "Don't bother with it, you hear. They don't serve us in this bar." A run-of-the-mill incident for all recognizably Black people in this city. But for me it is not.

Henry's eyes fill up, but he refuses to believe our informant. "No, man, the girl is just busy." (The girl is a fifty-year-old white woman, who may just be following orders. But I do not mention this. I have chosen sides.) All I can manage to say is, "Jesus Christ, I hate the fucking English." Henry looks at me. (In the family I am known as the "lady cousin." It has to do with how I look. And the fact that I am twenty-seven and unmarried—and for all they know, unattached. They do not know that I am really the lesbian cousin.) Our informant says—gently, but with a distinct tone of disappointment—"My dear, is that what you're studying at the university?"

You see—the whole business is very complicated.

Henry and I leave without drinks and go to meet some of his white colleagues at a restaurant I know near Covent Garden Opera House. The restaurant caters to theatre types and so I hope there won't be a repeat of the bar scene—at least they know how to pretend. Besides, I tell myself, the owners are Italian *and* gay; they *must* be halfway decent. Henry and his colleagues work for an American company which is paying their way through Cal Tech. They mine bauxite from the hills in the middle of the island and send it to the United States. A turnaround occurs at dinner: Henry joins the whitemen in a sustained mockery of the waiters: their accents and the way they walk. He whispers to me: "Why you want to bring us to a battyman's den, lady?" (*Battyman* = *faggot* in Jamaican.) I keep quiet.

* * *

We put the whitemen in a taxi and Henry walks me to the underground station. He asks me to sleep with him. (It wouldn't be incest. His mother was a maid in the house of an uncle and Henry has not seen her since his birth. He was taken into the family. She was let go.) I say that I can't. I plead exams. I can't say that I don't want to. Because I remember what happened in the bar. But I can't say that I'm a lesbian either—even though I want to believe his alliance with the whitemen at dinner was forced: not really him. He doesn't buy my excuse. "Come on, lady, let's do it. What's the matter, you 'fraid?" I pretend I am back home and start patois to show him somehow I am not afraid, not English, not white. I tell him he's a married man and he tells me he's a ram goat. I take the train to where I am staying and try to forget the whole thing. But I don't. I remember our different skins and our different experiences within them. And I have a hard time realizing that I am angry with Henry. That to him—no use in pretending—a queer is a queer.

1981: I hear on the radio that Bob Marley is dead and I drive over the Mohawk Trail listening to a program of his music and I cry and cry and cry. Someone says: "It wasn't the ganja that killed him, it was poverty and working in a steel foundry when he was young."

I flash back to my childhood and a young man who worked for an aunt I lived with once. He taught me to smoke ganja behind the house. And to peel an orange with the tip of a machete without cutting through the skin—"Love" it was called: a necklace of orange rind the result. I think about him because I heard he had become a Rastaman. And then I think about Rastas.

We are sitting on the porch of an uncle's house in Kingston—the family and I—and a Rastaman comes to the gate. We have guns but they are locked behind a false closet. We have dogs but they are tied up. We are Jamaicans and know that Rastas mean no harm. We let him in and he sits on the side of the porch and shows us his brooms and brushes. We buy some to take back to New York. "Peace, missis."

There were many Rastas in my childhood. Walking the roadside with their goods. Sitting outside their shacks in the mountains. The outsides painted bright— sometimes with words. Gathering at Palisadoes Airport to greet the Conquering Lion of Judah. They were considered figures of fun by most middle-class Jamaicans. Harmless—like Marcus Garvey.

Later: white American hippies trying to create the effect of dred in their straight white hair. The ganja joint held between their straight white teeth. "Man, the grass is good." Hanging out by the Sheraton pool. Light-skinned Jamaicans also dred-locked, also assuming the ganja. Both groups moving to the music but not the words. Harmless. "Peace, brother."

III

My grandmother: "Let us thank God for a fruitful peace."
My grandfather: "Let us rescue the perishing world."

This evening on the road in western Massachusetts there are pockets of fog. Then clear spaces. Across from a pond a dog staggers in front of my headlights. I look closer and see that his mouth is foaming. He stumbles to the side of the road—I go to call the police.

I drive back to the house, radio playing "difficult" piano pieces. And I think about how I need to say all this. This is who I am. I am not what you allow me to be. Whatever you decide me to be. In a bookstore in London I show the woman at the counter my book and she stares at me for a minute, then says: "You're a Jamaican." "Yes." "You're not at all like our Jamaicans."

Encountering the void is nothing more nor less than understanding invisibility. Of being fogbound.

Then: It was never a question of passing. It was a question of hiding. Behind Black and white perceptions of who we were—who they thought we were. Tropics. Plantations. Calypso. Cricket. We were the people with the musical voices and the coronation mugs on our parlor tables. I would be whatever figure these foreign imaginations cared for me to be. It would be so simple to let others fill in for me. So easy to startle them with a flash of anger when their visions got out of hand—but never to sustain the anger for myself.
It could become a life lived within myself. A life cut off. I know who I am but you will never know who I am. I may in fact lose touch with who I am.

I hid from my real sources. But my real sources were also hidden from me.

Now: It is not a question of relinquishing privilege. It is a question of grasping more of myself. I have found that in the real sources are concealed my survival. My speech. My voice. To be colonized is to be rendered insensitive. To have those parts necessary to sustain life numbed. And this is in some cases—in my case—perceived as privilege. The test of a colonized person is to walk through a shantytown in Kingston and not bat an eye. This I cannot do. Because part of me lives there—and as I grasp more of this part I realize what needs to be done with the rest of my life.

Sometimes I used to think we were like the Marranos—the Sephardic Jews forced to pretend they were Christians. The name was given to them by the Christians, and meant "pigs." But once out of Spain and Portugal, they became Jews openly again. Some settled in Jamaica. They knew who the enemy was and acted for their own survival. But they remained Jews always.

We also knew who the enemy was—I remember jokes about the English. Saying they stank, saying they were stingy, that they drank too much and couldn't hold their liquor, that they had bad teeth, were dirty and dishonest, were limey bastards, and horse-faced bitches. We said the men only wanted to sleep with Jamaican women. And that the women made pigs of themselves with Jamaican men.

But of course this was seen by us—the light-skinned middle class—with a double vision. We learned to cherish that part of us that was them—and to deny the part that was not. Believing in some cases that the latter part had ceased to exist.

*   *   *

None of this is as simple as it may sound. We were colorists and we aspired to oppressor status. (Of course, almost any aspiration instilled by western civilization is to oppressor status: success, for example.) Color was the symbol of our potential: color taking in hair "quality," skin tone, freckles, nose-width, eyes. We did not see that color symbolism was a method of keeping us apart: in the society, in the family, between friends. Those of us who were light-skinned, straight-haired, etc., were given to believe that we could actually attain whiteness—or at least those qualities of the colonizer which made him superior. We were convinced of white supremacy. If we failed, we were not really responsible for our failures: we had all the advantages—but it was that one persistent drop of blood, that single rogue gene that made us unable to conceptualize abstract ideas, made us love darkness rather than despise it, which was to be blamed for our failure. Our dark part had taken over; an inherited imbalance in which the doom of the creole was sealed.

I am trying to write this as clearly as possible, but as I write I realize that what I say may sound fabulous, or even mythic. It is. It is insane.

Under this system of colorism—the system which prevailed in my childhood in Jamaica, and which has carried over to the present—rarely will dark and light people co-mingle. Rarely will they achieve between themselves an intimacy informed with identity. (I should say here that I am using the categories light and dark both literally and symbolically. There are dark Jamaicans who have achieved lightness and the "advantages" which go with it by their successful pursuit of oppressor status.)

Under this system light and dark people will meet in those ways in which the light-skinned person imitates the oppressor. But imitation goes only so far; the light-skinned person becomes an oppressor in fact. He/she will have a dark chauffeur, a dark nanny, a dark maid, and a dark gardener. These employees will be paid badly. Because of the slave past, because of their dark skin, the servants of the middle class have been used according to the traditions of the slavocracy. They are not seen as workers for their own sake, but for the sake of the family who has employed them. It was not until Michael Manley became prime minister that a minimum wage for houseworkers was enacted—and the indignation of the middle class was profound.

During Manley's leadership the middle class began to abandon the island in droves. Toronto. Miami. New York. Leaving their houses and businesses behind and sewing cash into the tops of suitcases. Today—with a new regime—they are returning; "Come back to the way things used to be" the tourist advertisement on American t.v. says. "Make it Jamaica again. Make it your own."

But let me return to the situation of houseservants as I remember it: They will be paid badly, but they will be "given" room and board. However, the key to the larder will be kept by the mistress in her dresser drawer. They will spend Christmas with the family of their employers and be given a length of English wool for trousers or a few yards of cotton for dresses. They will see their children on their days off; their extended family will care for the children the rest of the time. When the employers visit their relations in the country, the servants may be asked along—oftentimes the servants of the middle class come from the same part of the countryside their employers have come from. But they will be expected to work while they are there. Back in town, there are parts of the house they are allowed to move freely around; other parts they are not allowed to enter. When the family watches the t.v. the servant is allowed to watch also, but only while standing in a doorway. The servant may have a radio in his/her room, also a dresser and a cot. Perhaps a mirror. There will usually be one ceiling light. And one small square louvered window.

A true story: One middle-class Jamaican woman ordered a Persian rug from Harrod's in London. The day it arrived so did her new maid. She was going downtown to have her hair touched up, and told the maid to vacuum the rug. She told the maid she would find the vacuum cleaner in the same shed as the power mower. And when she returned she found that the fine nap of her new rug had been removed.

The reaction of the mistress was to tell her friends that the "girl" was backward. She did not fire her until she found that the maid had scrubbed the teflon from her new set of pots, saying she thought they were coated with "nastiness."

The houseworker/mistress relationship in which one Black woman is the oppressor of another Black woman is a cornerstone of the experience of many Jamaican women.

I remember another true story: In a middle-class family's home one Christmas, a relation was visiting from New York. This woman had brought gifts for everybody, including the house-maid. The maid had been released from a mental institution recently, where they had "treated" her for depression. This visiting light-skinned woman had brought the dark woman a bright red rayon blouse and presented it to her in the garden one afternoon, while the family was having tea. The maid thanked her softly, and the other woman moved toward her as if to embrace her. Then she stopped, her face suddenly covered with tears, and ran into the house, saying, "My God, I can't, I can't."

We are women who come from a place almost incredible in its beauty. It is a beauty which can mask a great deal and which has been used in that way. But that the beauty is there is a fact. I remember what I thought the freedom of my childhood, in which the fruitful place was something I took for granted. Just as I took for granted Zoe's appearance every morning on my school vacations—in the sense that I knew she would be there. That she would always be the one to visit me. The perishing world of my grandfather's graces at the table, if I ever seriously thought about it, was somewhere else.

Our souls were affected by the beauty of Jamaica, as much as they were affected by our fears of darkness.

There is no ending to this piece of writing. There is no way to end it. As I read back over it, I see that we/they/I may become confused in the mind of the reader; but these pronouns have always co-existed in my mind. The Rastas talk of the "I and I"—a pronoun in which they combine themselves with Jah. Jah is a contraction of Jahweh and Jehova, but to me always sounds like the beginning of Jamaica. I and Jamaica is who I am. No matter how far I travel—how deep the ambivalence

I feel about ever returning. And Jamaica is a place in which we/they/I connect
and disconnect—change place.

QUESTIONS FOR DISCUSSION AND WRITING

1.   "If I Could Write This in Fire, I Would Write This in Fire" follows Cliff's
experiences very closely and has been described as an "autobiographical
essay." Nevertheless it has claim to be regarded as autobiographical fiction
because of the many fictional devices it employs. Identify some of these.

2.   The story is quite allusive. Go through the story and identify difficult
references—to "ganja," for example, or to "Rastamen" or to "Michael Manley." Look up these allusions. What effect does dropping unexplained Jamaican terms into the text have?

3.   It could be argued that the theme of the story is the formation of the
speaker's identify. Trace this process through the story.

4.   In the episode with her cousin Henry in London, the speaker hides the
fact that she is "the lesbian cousin." How is homosexuality related to the
other issues in the story?

5.   Near the end of the story, Cliff writes that "we/they/I may become
confused in the mind of the reader." What confusions are there in her use
of these pronouns?

6.   Rather than conventional paragraphs, "If I Could Write This in Fire, I
Would Write This in Fire" is structured in short sections with white spaces
between them. What is the effect of this typographical arrangement?

Steven Corbin

Steven Corbin teaches at the University of California at Los Angeles. His first novel, *No Easy Place to Be* (1989), is set in Harlem during the Harlem Renaissance of the 1920s.

UPWARD BOUND

The summer between sophomore and junior years in high school, I had the opportunity to attend college. Upward Bound was a year-round, government-funded program designed for academically gifted inner-city students to whet their taste for college life. The locale was Upper Montclair, New Jersey. The school Montclair State College.

Out of my element, I wasn't certain how I felt about being away from home for six weeks. Accustomed to a raucous, crime-ridden, poverty-ravaged neighborhood, I wasn't used to the open space of green campus, the rolling hills, the serenity. Arriving at the campus, I wanted to turn around and go home.

Stone Hall, the boys' dormitory, was located—or isolated, as it were—at the northern end of campus. One was forced to tour the entire campus en route to breakfast at Freeman Hall. My room—luckily I didn't have a roommate—was all of one hundred square feet. There was hardly space to bend over. But it was mine. All mine. Compared to the cramped bedroom I shared with two brothers at home, this was the Taj Mahal.

Though only the first day, it seemed, by the chatter and laughter ringing through the halls, that everyone knew one another. A familiar alienation; I never fit in. As a child, some of my playmates wondered why I'd abruptly desert them in a game of stickball and run home to draw pictures and write poetry. Male members of my family considered me weird for not sharing their enthusiasm for professional contact sports. They didn't understand why crashing helmets on the thirty-two-yard line and pulverizing left hooks to the jaw in a boxing ring were, to me, insufferable. And, as I was fifteen-and-a-half years old—going on sixteen in four months—my peers were beginning to speculate about why I was seemingly not into pussy. Why I never talked about it. Hell, I'd never even had any.

Walking down the dormitory's corridor, which seemed to go on forever, I surreptitiously glanced into several rooms where students were getting acquainted through loud, animated discussions, laughter, swearing, water balloon and pillow fights. I felt fortunate about rooming alone. Unless I could choose my roommate, I was in no mood for surprises. Be just my luck to be paired with a star quarterback who plastered *Playboy* centerfolds along his wall and who, in the middle of the night, might ask me to make myself scarce so that he could ravish the coed he'd managed to slip into the dormitory against the counselors' knowledge.

Put simply, I didn't know if I could endure the next six weeks.

Evening. A cool breeze calmed the campus, the towering pine trees whispering to each other, bowing, curtsying, swaying as if in a mating dance, sunlight peeking through the leaves in quick snatches. The sun slowly set, tinges of burnt orange dramatically reflecting off the skyscrapers of New York's skyline on the far eastern horizon.

Dr. Greene, the program director, was winding up a tedious welcoming speech

485

in the dining hall, and made special mention of the students attending for the first time. As my eyes panned the room, studying the brown, black, yellow faces I knew would never become my friends, I wondered just what the hell I was doing there. So far, what I liked best about being tucked miles away from home was the cafeteria. All you could eat. The perpetually ravenous, skinny teenager that I was, my insatiable appetite was often unfulfilled at home. My mother, a factory worker, struggled to feed and clothe three growing sons, and though we'd eat three meals a day, I never got as much as my appetite demanded. Dr. Greene told us why we, the academically promising black and Puerto Rican and some Asian students, had been chosen, driving his point home by paternally placing his hands upon the shoulders of Angel Rodriguez, who'd be attending Harvard in the fall.

Bored, my mind wandered to my home in Jersey City. I could see my brothers, both poor eaters, sweating it out in the hot and sticky, roach-infested kitchen, languidly devouring their food, distractedly twisting their hair, cheeks puffed out like hamsters storing seed. In my family I was the best eater—which meant I'd eat anything. Garbage mouth, they called me. My younger brothers were finicky, which drove my mother crazy. She professed two basic philosophies about food. A child of the Depression, she abhorred the waste of food. Secondly, she never refused a hungry person a meal. In our home we were never sent to bed without dinner as a punishment, regardless of what we'd done. "Because," she was known to say, as her mother had before her, "people gotta eat, and food ends up as shit, anyhow."

Before classes began that week, students were cramming in as much partying as possible. The dance season kicked off in Chapin Hill, the girls' dormitory, where they played mostly 45s and Shing-a-linged and grinded the night away. I felt suspended inside a bubble of isolation, so distanced from it all, balancing myself on the periphery, though I could reach out and touch any one of them. From outside on the veranda, I could smell marijuana seeping through the open windows, carried by the pine-sweetened breeze, and I hoped for an invitation to take a hit.

Surprisingly, the blacks and Latins seemed to mingle, which was uncharacteristic of the territorial neighborhoods we hailed from. The music even fluctuated from the smooth, sweet soul of The Temptations and the raw, sweaty funk of James Brown, to the brassy, timbal-punctuated salsa rhythms of Ray Barretto and Willi Colon. The Puerto Ricans—the PRs, we called them—were jazzed about teaching blacks their style of dancing; mambo, cha-cha, and merengue; they were no more enthusiastic than the blacks who were eager to learn.

I couldn't get into it.

I could dance all right. I could even do the mambo and cha-cha. But I'd been spoiled by having spent my weekends in Greenwich Village with members of my track team. We frequented gay bars where we were never carded. So, sitting there in Chapin Hall on the campus of Montclair State, listening to the slow, uptempo, and salsa music, it wasn't as if I didn't want to dance. I refused to dance with girls. In all of my two years in high school, I'd never been forced to before. I wasn't about to start now. I knew myself. Knew what I wanted. And it didn't come in a skirt and panty hose. Nearly all the good-looking guys on the dance floor grabbed at anything with breasts while I, sitting forlorn and unapproachable, squeezed into a dark corner, fantasized that they'd grab for me instead.

This simply isn't working out, I kept thinking.

And just as the party was over, and we headed back to our separate dormitories in compliance with the eleven o'clock curfew, and I was feeling sorry for myself for being cast into yet another social circumstance where I didn't fit, walking back alone to Stone Hall while, seemingly, everyone had someone, a friend, a room-mate, a lover to talk to, the warm night air ignited with mosquitoes, lightning bugs, crickets whirring, the breezy fragrance of pine, it happened suddenly, as if a cone of celestial light had been thrown upon the darkness.

I saw *him*.

The boys' showers were crowded.

With my towel, I had to wait in line for an available stall. I was uncomfortable standing in the buff before a group of males. Changing clothes in my high school locker room for Phys. Ed., I'd protect and guard myself as if something immea-surably valuable existed beneath my towel. Conversely, watching other boys soap their lean bodies became a pastime, a ritual I would come to live for every morn-ing for the next six weeks. Sight-seeing, I called it.

I stepped into the shower. Adjusting the hot water, I took the bar of soap, turned, glanced over my shoulder, and nearly gasped out loud. There *he* was. In the op-posite stall, *he*—I thought I heard someone call him Lorenzo—caught sight of me dropping the soap, nearly tripping over myself to retrieve it. I tried to calm my shaky hands, to slide the soap across my body and work up a lather as I'd done a thousand times before. Whenever I could, I tried to steal glimpses of him without appearing obvious. That's all I needed. For my secret to be unleashed among a bunch of hormone-exploding, homophobic, perhaps fag-bashing teenage boys I didn't know. I thought that he caught me staring several times. My eyes met his, then dropped when I thought he wasn't looking. He must've noticed me checking him out. Suddenly he turned away. My view had been reduced to his backside and the hefty calves of his hairy legs. He, too, had dropped his soap. I used the opportunity to exchange a smile with him. He didn't return it. And if I wasn't mistaken, he flashed me a dirty look. The "What the hell're you staring at? You faggot!" look. For the remainder of the shower, I kept to myself. But I had to look at him once more. When I turned, he was gone. In his place stood an obese buy who sang out loud while he bathed. Unflinchingly, he stared at my nakedness. He swung around to adjust the water. When he turned back, I, too, was gone.

During my classes I daydreamed about my family back home. How my brothers were faring in my absence. The brother closest to me in age had begun an experimentation of sorts in our drug-infested community. He'd made the quan-tum leap from diet pills to heroin. By age fifteen he was shooting up, or main-lining, as the phrase went. It concerned me gravely. Though we'd always been close and acted as utmost confidants for each other—I was closer to no one than my brother—I had felt compelled to tell my mother of his doings, but my loyalties to him wouldn't allow me to part my lips. He'd assured me that he had it under control. But then so did many others who were no longer around to tell about it. The crowd I ran with was nothing to write home to my mother about, either—especially the boys from my high school track team who accompanied me to Greenwich Village gay bars on weekends—but the crowd my brother hung with was another story. I even thought myself "better" than my brother because I "snorted" heroin occasionally, while he was doing heroin as junkies did it. Telling my mother—or my father, who didn't live with us—might break the sinewy chain of our male bond. And consequently he could turn around and tell my parents that I slept with guys.

As a child, I was in touch with my sexuality at an age when most boys didn't know how to write their name. Though I couldn't divulge or exercise it, except through bonding games of Truth and Dare with the neighborhood boys, I never experienced shame or remorse over it. Later, as a teenager, I even thought myself superior to straight boys. They were not as bright or creatively talented as I was. They didn't know themselves as I knew myself. They were not as discerning as I. I was privy to two worlds; they, one. They knew virtually nothing about sensitivity—maybe individually, but not as a group. They couldn't open up and reveal themselves as I could. They couldn't make love. Oh, they could fuck. But they couldn't really love their women. I knew. My female friends and my mother and her sisters chronically complained about it.

That wasn't true of gay boys. We could go for hours without climaxing, caressing and cuddling with endless foreplay. Masters & Johnson even wrote a *Newsweek* cover story about it, detailing their sex study findings, substantiating it with statistics and laboratory observations.

My baby brother was still young enough that I didn't feel cause to worry. Not yet. In a few years that would sweep by as swiftly as this six-week college stint, there was no telling what he'd be subjected to. Coming of age in our community, there was little chance that he wouldn't dip and dab in hardcore drugs. In our neighborhood it was recreation. While suburban middle-class kids went away to summer camps and vacations along the Jersey shore, we turned to deserted parking lots, rooftops, and abandoned buildings to experiment furtively with chemicals capable of wiping us out in a single afternoon.

"Your dime," my smart-aleck brother said, answering the phone.

"It's me, bucket head."

"Yo!" my brother said. His voice was hoarse, scratchy. Heroin coated.

"What's happening?"

I pictured him with a needle in his arm, slumped in a corner on the bathroom floor, his dilated pupils flickering to the back of his head, while Ma cooked dinner in the kitchen next door, assuming he was taking a leak.

"You're what's happening, man," my brother said, "How's college?"

"It's okay. Where's Ma?"

"She ain't here. She'll be back later."

"How's everything at home?"

"Same ol' shit, man."

"Why's your voice so raspy?"

"It ain't—"

"Are you? . . . You know."

"What?"

"You know."

"Yeah, I'm high, if that's what you mean. I only do it once in a while."

I sighed heavily into the mouthpiece. "I don't know," I said, defeated.

"Know what?" His joviality turned defensive.

"Well, I was just thinking that . . . well, what if Mommy or Daddy found out—"

"You mean, what if you *told* them, right?"

"Well, sometimes Ma asks me about the crowd you run around with—"

"Yeah, and she asks me how come you never go out with girls, but do I tell on you?"

"But what I do won't kill me."

"Oh, yes, it will. If I tell Ma or Daddy, it will."

Watching a grainy, black-and-white Malcolm X documentary in class, my mouth gaped at the rare opportunity this afforded. Everything I'd ever seen or heard about Malcolm X had been through the bigoted American press, which continually berated and lambasted him. But Professor Maddox—a black man who jokingly made it clear that he was no relation whatsoever to Lester of Alabama—heralded the slain leader's immense contributions to the black community, especially in the way of fostering black pride. Because of Malcolm, he said, we'd ceased being "colored" *and* "Negro" and for once took unadulterated pride in being exactly what we were: black. I found this fascinating. It might've been the moment I realized that I would be getting a special, even alternative education in this Upward Bound program.

At any given moment in the dormitory all I ever heard about was pussy. Pussy this. Pussy that. And yet, when the opportunities availed themselves, these pussy-crazed juveniles engaged in antics beyond my comprehension. One day there had even been a fistfight between two roommates. Apparently, one fellow admitted a bunch of the guys into the room in the middle of the night while his roommate slept. Several of the boys took turns prodding his open lips with their erections or sticking them against his teeth. When he woke up, I could hear the noise from my second-floor room, though the incident happened upstairs and down the hall.

My optimism shattered when it became common knowledge on campus that *he*—Lorenzo Gonzales, a Cuban—relentlessly chased a cute black girl from his high school who made no bones about the fact that she had another "real" boyfriend back home. While she went steady with Shorty, her beau in Jersey City, Lorenzo was a hobby she could indulge during her spare time. I thought her stupid, even cruel. How, I wondered, could she pass up this sexy Latin hunk of toned flesh with the mink-brown eyes and thick eyebrows? He adored her and didn't care who knew it. I admired his tenacity. It was rumored that reports of his liaison with Maxie had gotten back to Shorty and inevitably there'd be a showdown. I hoped as much. That's what he'd get for messing around with someone who didn't want him half as badly as I.

As much as we attended classes, studied, and composed term papers, there were just as many recreational outlets. It took little or no excuse to throw a party, even if it was only playing records in the Rec Room. Not unlike in the streets and schools we'd left behind for six weeks, drugs flowed and passed hands with similar frequency and visibility. Despite our status as so-called academically gifted students, many of us couldn't shake inner-city habits like marijuana, amphetamines, barbiturates, cocaine, and heroin. Removed from the world, we weren't allowed to leave the campus unless chaperoned by one of the counselors. Similarly, we were prohibited from harboring anyone else on campus or in our dormitories, aside from Visitation Day. Neither of which stopped us from periodically sneaking off campus to buy drugs in nearby New York City. Curfew was taken seriously. Campus legend boasted that someone had been fifteen minutes late getting back to his dormitory. The counselors called his parents and announced that they'd be delivering him back to Jersey City within the hour. Like clockwork, one-two-three, he was gone.

*   *   *

As my warped sense of humor disseminated among my peers, I began to relish a popularity I hadn't anticipated. People were a lot friendlier than I'd given them credit for. Usually it was effortless to befriend girls. Easier to get along with, there was less to prove with them, which allowed me to be myself. With the guys, I'd feel pressured to discuss the Yankees, the Knicks, the Mets, the Jets. And of course, pussy.

There were two other guys like me. They liked boys, too, I could tell. Over the weeks we became friends. But we never let on about ourselves among each other. Like a secret code, we always talked around it. They, like me, never pursued the girls or even discussed them. We talked about everything *but* sports and pussy. I wanted to invite them to hang out with my friends and me at Stonewall or the Bon Soir in the Village when the six weeks were through. Yet I felt as if I'd be violating the tacit code we perpetuated. So I said nothing.

There were times, especially on Friday and Saturday nights, when I'd sit atop a hill near Stone Hall overlooking the rolling hills, the green pastures, and the New Jersey Turnpike. Beyond that, New York shone like the Emerald City in *The Wizard of Oz*. No matter what fun I was having with the Upward Bound students, it never equaled the antics I was missing with my friends in the Village. Given the hour, I knew precisely where they were and what they were doing. At eight o'clock or so, they were arriving at the PATH Ninth Street train station, crossing the street, passing by Trude Heller's. They'd walk to Nathan's on the corner of Eighth Street and Sixth Avenue, then continue up the street to Bon Soir. Friday and Saturday nights my crowd openly cruised, even harassed good-looking guys and gave "street shows" for the busloads of tourists who flashed their cameras like paparazzi. By two o'clock in the morning they'd be hitting Nathan's for a bite. Then they'd end up at the Pitts Street pool for a swim and whatever, or Stonewall in the Village, or Bosco's in Harlem, or another after-hours spot somewhere between Brooklyn and the Bronx.

I joined the newspaper staff as a reporter. Our campus rag was called *Up*. The stores were average, the graphics mediocre. The outstanding newspaper feature was the art work. Sketched by some incredibly talented artist, it put everything else to shame. When I looked closer to examine the signature, I read the initials L.G. Could it be? I thought. Upon further inquiry, I was told that Lorenzo Gonzales had long ago established quite a reputation as an artist. He did much of the impressive work in his high school yearbook. There was nothing or no one he couldn't draw. I believed that and appreciated his talent, since sketching was one of the first artistic outlets I had exhibited as a child.

I never again saw him during my favorite part of the morning, watching wet flesh. He was either leaving when I arrived, vice versa, or I saw him nowhere near the showers at all.

Dr. Greene, his assistants, and counselors took us on field trips. We were exposed to cultural and artistic events relevant to us as blacks, Latins, and Asians. During the six weeks, we visited New York several times to see Broadway plays, such as *Purlie Victorious* and *Two Gentlemen of Verona*. We toured the Metropolitan and Guggenheim museums. Saw R&B and salsa concerts at Madison Square Garden, recitals and operas at the Met. They took us to Boston to see James Earl Jones play *Othello*. In Philadelphia, my one and only time there, we saw the cracked Liberty Bell on the Fourth of July. We frequented the movies and shopping malls, where we spent our weekly stipend. And once, they took us, by bus, to Washington, D.C., for the weekend where we did all the usual tours of the virgin white buildings that housed our government. Except it wasn't that new to me. When I was a child, my parents visited Virginia annually to see my father's family. We passed through D.C., to and from, and took rolls of slides on the steps of the Capitol or the Lincoln Memorial.

"Who do you think is the most athletic?" I asked my closeted friends one night, sitting in the dormitory, passing around a joint, whistling through clenched teeth.

"What?"

"You heard me."

"Franklin," one said.

"Elijah," the other said.

"What about Lorenzo?" I said.

"Oh, yeah!"

"I forgot about Lorenzo!"

Their emphatic responses to Lorenzo struck a chord. I decided to explore it.

"And . . ." I said, slowly and deliberately, sucking in a lungful of marijuana, "don't you think he's the cutest, too?"

Eyes dropped to the floor. The room turned suddenly quiet. I had gone too far.

"Well?" I went further.

"What do you mean, cute?" one said.

"C'mon. Cute is cute," I said. "Okay . . . I'll say it first. I think . . . he's the cutest boy on campus."

Eyes lifted slowly from the floor.

"Well . . ." one said, his eyes moving around the room, eyes moist, cloudy, and glossed by Panamanian Red, "if you think he's cute . . . then . . . I think so, too."

"Me . . . too," the other said. We burst into a round of forced laughter.

"And how about Maxie Bryant?" I said. "See how she treats him? Don't they make a terrible couple?"

"He's a fool for her. I don't understand it," one said.

"Bitch," the other said.

"This conversation will stay in this room, won't it?" one said.

I liked thinking of Lorenzo as my proverbial "first love," though he'd never said one word to me. Except I'd been involved in an affair earlier that year. Ramon Diaz—my track teammates teased me about my proclivities for Latin men—was actually my first love. He was twenty-one, I fifteen, though I lied and said I was sixteen. A Brooklyn Puerto Rican, he lived near Jay Street Boro Hall with his lover. I didn't find out about the lover until emotionally it was too late. Anyway, he was a dog. I was willing to do "anything" for him. He knew it, and used me accordingly.

I was awakened one night by loud whispering outside my door. Whoever it was—I didn't recognize the voice—stood outside the corridor telling someone that a faggot lived in this particular room. I was convinced that it was meant for me to hear. As the voices subsided and I turned over to get back to sleep, I heard something roll under my door. Quickly I jumped up, turned on the light, and noticed a blue-and-white firecracker, its fuse fizzling. A dud, it never went off.

A couple of hours later that same night, I heard rooms being broken into by the dorm director and counselors. They were ransacking the rooms in search of illicit drugs. Some students were quick enough to flush whatever they had down the toilet. Those not so lucky were apprehended, and told to start packing. I had a few joints and a two-dollar glassine bag or two of heroin—a deuce, we called it. Why they never bothered to raid me, I don't know. Nor did I bother to flush any of my drugs.

As the six weeks inched to a close, I discovered a thing or two. Without a doubt, I would attend college after graduation. Additionally, I'd developed a desire to go away to school which, before the Montclair experience, had never occurred to me.

The annual banquet was approaching—Upward Bound's version of a prom. The students got dressed up, had corsages, made dates, and attended the dinner where we would receive awards, say good-bye to each other, and party the last night away.

I anguished over whom to ask. This brand of protocol worked against my grain. Finally, after much contemplation and process of elimination, I asked a girl who'd be an easy, sure bet.

When I asked, Patrice replied affirmatively before I could finish the question.

I speculated about my father's pride in my accomplishments. After the first four weeks at Montclair State, I'd been chosen as one of the exemplary students to be written about in a newspaper article in our home town. Everyone read the *Jersey Journal,* and I felt that Daddy had seen the article and my photograph. It might've been the first time in years that he had seen me, in a photograph or otherwise. He lived all of seven blocks away from my mother, brothers, and me. But the divorce between him and my mother had been so bitter that for some twisted reason he took it out on his children as well. None of us ever understood his despicable behavior. Before the breakup he'd been a caring father, as good as any.

Despite his comparatively well-to-do economic status, his frequent fishing trips to Costa Rica, or the fact that he hit the numbers for several thousand dollars several times a year, he never gave us a penny. Adding insult to injury, he was characteristically delinquent with his child support payments. Frequently my mother was forced to confront him in a court of law for a measly forty dollars a week. "Ain't that a damn shame," my mother and her sisters would say, my aunts shaking their heads and sucking their tongues in unison. While he traipsed about town in silks, mohair, monogrammed jackets, and designer shirts, his three boys wore the same pants to school every day, their shoes had holes in the soles—especially mine—and we hardly got anything new unless it was Christmas or Easter. Even then, nothing was guaranteed.

My father had groomed me academically. Throughout grade school he encouraged my straight-A report cards and convinced me that I would be attending college. *College.* That word frightened me. I thought yeah, I'm smart all right—the word they used in those days in lieu of bright or gifted—but I didn't think I had what it took to survive a college education. This was highly unusual. My father entertained middle-class values amid a low-economic neighborhood. I know of no other fathers on the block, or mothers, who insisted that their children were to attend college.

Now that I was performing the deeds my father expected of me, it seemed to hardly matter to him. Not once did he ever call to congratulate me or tell me to keep up the good work. Although he never pressured me to be a lawyer or a doctor or any other kind of professional, he had always let me know that he expected something important from me. Now he didn't seem to give a rat's hair what I did academically.

*   *   *

I was awakened by light taps on my window. Frightened, I glanced up at the window above my bed. I rubbed my eyes, blinked them repeatedly, but I couldn't believe them.

Lorenzo, a look of desperation distorting his face, was asking me to let him in. I had no idea what he wanted. Or what he was doing on the ledge outside my window in the middle of the night. I might've fantasized the situation along the lines of some Romeo and Romeo romance. But his facial expression said something entirely different. I hurried and opened my window so that he could crawl in.

At first he said nothing, panting, out of breath. He motioned me to "Shh!" with his forefinger pressed against his lips. When he caught his breath, he told me that he'd been out past curfew. He'd gone to New York to buy drugs, and he promised to slip me a free bag for my troubles. Groggily, I accepted the reward for my deed.

"Thanks a lot, man," he said. "What's your name again?"

I knew that he knew my name. He also knew I had the hots for him. He was playing it safe.

"You know my name," I replied.

"Well, thanks a lot."

"Anytime."

"Well," he said, clearing his throat, his discomfort apparent as he searched for the next thing to say. "So, man, who you taking to the banquet tomorrow night?"

"Patrice Jackson. . . . You?" It was weird, knowing the answer before asking the question.

"Maxie," he said, anxiously jiggling the change in his pocket.

"Of course."

"Hey, man, I didn't know you and Patrice had a thing."

"Maybe that's because we don't."

"Oh. . . . Well, anyway, she's cute."

"Yeah, I guess."

"It's late," he said, looking at his watch, as if he hadn't known that before waking me up. He slapped his forehead with the palm of his hand. "I really should be going—"

"Are you and Maxie going steady?"

"Why?"

"Just asking," I said, now embarrassed by my prying—embarrassment stemming from the suspicion in his inflection. "I think you two make a nice couple."

"Well, man," he said, removing his shoes, tiptoeing across the floor, opening the door, turning to shake my hand. He looked both ways before stepping into the corridor, and whispered, "Thanks a lot for helping me out tonight. If there's anything I can do for you, man, let me know."

After he left, I clicked off the light and climbed back into bed.

In the darkness, against the whirring of crickets, the buzzing of mosquitoes, my back sticking to the humid, muggy, sweat-soaked sheets, I masturbated. Fourth time that day. All of them over him.

At the banquet I watched Lorenzo more than my own date. Admittedly, he and Maxie made an attractive couple. As speeches were read and awards handed out to the high achievers, I worried about having to kiss Patrice at the end of the night. Contemplating it there at our table, I realized that I'd never kissed a girl. Would she expect me to kiss her? Would she kiss me back?

My contributions to the campus newspaper were cited by Dr. Greene and Professor Maddox. I was asked to stand, which I did. The entire room broke into a thunderous applause, which startled me. I hadn't known I was so well-liked. In the distance I could see Lorenzo clapping loudest and whistling with his pinkies stuck in the corners of his mouth. As soon as he had finished clapping and whistling, he placed his arm around Maxie's bare shoulder, and I sensed a quickly passing wave of jealousy.

Toward the end of the night Lorenzo approached me, slapped me five, and reiterated how grateful he was to me for letting him in my window. Apparently, two other people had refused, afraid they'd be expelled along with him if caught. "Too bad we didn't have the chance to know each other better," he said.

Too bad, indeed, I thought.

All I could think of was having to kiss Patrice. Should it be a peck? On the cheek or the lips? Is she expecting tongue? Or more? I knew she expected something by the way she kept looking at me, and the manner and tone she employed when she spoke. I'd never heard it before. She was acting as if we were going together. She hadn't had a boyfriend all summer. Perhaps she needed an escort to make a statement. All week long, her roommate and girlfriends had teased me about her wherever I saw them—in class, the cafeteria, the bookstore. Sounded as if she'd told them we'd been engaged.

I'd known Patrice over the past six weeks as a fellow student and acquaintance. Like other students, she was as significant to me as the mosquito buzzing in my ear the night before.

Yet just this side of a week, her innocuous expectations had vexed me. I resented her for it. But I soothed myself with my only option. Control. Take charge, I told myself. She's the girl, and she expects you to be in control. She'd accept whatever I gave her. Even if it was a handshake.

When I walked her back to Chapin Hall, we stood on the wide veranda gazing nervously into each other's eyes. She obviously wanted me to kiss her. I was fumbling, and flirted with the idea of pecking her on the cheek before fleeing into the pitch darkness. After tonight I never have to see her again, I reminded myself.

I wrapped my arms around her, pulled her to me, and planted the kiss upon her lips for which I assumed she'd been waiting all night.

It was easier than I'd thought.

I just imagined it was Lorenzo.

QUESTIONS FOR DISCUSSION AND WRITING

1. Near the beginning of "Upward Bound," the narrator contrasts his home, "raucous, crime-ridden, poverty-ravaged," with "the open space of green campus, the rolling hills, the serenity" and says, "I wanted to turn around and go home," thus comically establishing the two worlds of the story: the home in the ghetto and the temporary retreat of Montclair State College. How do the two balance each other? Relate the narrator's attitudes toward his father, mother, and brother to his attitudes toward his fellow students in the Upward Bound program.

2. Describe the narrator's sense of his own identity. How does he describe

himself? What does he value most about himself? How does he contrast himself with most other people?

3. Does the story have a single central action? In some ways, it seems a rather rambling account of the summer. Is there a coherent progression underlying the seemingly random narrative?

4. Is the narrator really "upward bound"?

Michael Martone

Michael Martone (b. 1955) grew up in Fort Wayne, Indiana, and was educated at Butler University, Indiana University, and Johns Hopkins University. His first book was a collection of poems: *At a Loss* (1977). It was followed by a short-story collection, *Alive and Dead in Indiana* (1984); a collection of prose poems, *Return to Powers* (1985); and another collection of stories, *Safety Patrol* (1988). *Alive and Dead in Indiana* was reissued in revised form as *Fort Wayne Is Seventh on Hitler's List* (1990). Michael Martone teaches at Iowa State University.

FORT WAYNE IS SEVENTH ON HITLER'S LIST

This is a city of poets. Every Wednesday, when the sirens go off, a poet will tell you that, after thirty years, Fort Wayne is still seventh on Hitler's bombing list. And you half expect to hear the planes, a pitch lower than the sirens, their names as recognizable as those of automobiles. Heinkels lumber out of the east, coast up Taylor Street, or follow the Pennsy from one GE plant to another. Stukas dive on the wire-and-die works, starting their run at the International Harvester bell tower, left standing on purpose, and finish by strafing the Tokheim yards. Junkers wheel, and Messerschmitts circle. All the time there would be sirens.

Grandfather keeps his scrapbooks upstairs in the window seat of the empty bedroom. When he dies, they are to be mine, and I am to give them to the Air Force Museum at Wright-Patterson Air Force Base. Grandfather started keeping these scrapbooks when he felt the time was right for war. He felt the war coming. In the years before the war, the scrapbooks that he kept were pieces of the world he found— a field outside of Peking where old people go to die, a man being buried alive, all the All-American football teams of those years, the bar of soap Dillinger used at the Crown Point jail, a man cut into three parts by a train, a Somalian warrior with no clothes on. These things made sense to Grandfather.

A real poet knows how to bomb his own city.

In the window seat where Grandfather keeps his finished scrapbooks, there is also his collection of missals, all the handouts from Wendell Willkie's campaign, and everything Father Coughlin ever wrote. The scrapbooks have interesting covers. There is one with a mallard duck on the wing worked into the leather. One is made of wood and has an oak leaf carved into it. Most, though, have only company names or *Season's Greetings*.

I have never been able to read all the scrapbooks. They are in no order, and nothing in them is. Every page is dated with the newspaper itself. He went straight through the book. One day I can read about the Battle of Britain, the next day VE day, the next the Soviet Pact. I have never gotten to the bottom of the window seat. Once I found Hitler's list.

There are cottonwoods along the rivers. In the spring, a poet will look up at the undefended sky and announce, "At any moment we could be destroyed."

* * *

When I was little, I would practice making bomb noises, the whistling sound of a bomb falling. I would take a deep breath, form my lips, begin. I could make it sound as if the bomb were falling away from me, or on me, by modulating the volume, adjusting its fade or rise. I preferred the perspective of the plane, starting with the loud high note. A second or two of silence as the bomb is out of earshot. Then the tiny puff of air reaching me from the ground.

This is why old men smoke at night in the middle of parks. They do it to attract bombers.

Mother remembers certain things about the war. She remembers making dolls out of hollyhocks, taping butcher paper on the windows, and not being able to look at the newspaper until Grandfather had cut out the things he wanted. Once, in the A&P, she lost her underwear while waiting in line to buy milk. There was no rubber to hold up the underwear. She tells me this story every time I think I have troubles. Mother danced in the USO shows for the troops from Baer Field and Casad. Once she shared the stage with Bob Hope.

The whole city watches as the skywriter finishes the word.

SURRENDER

Before going through the scrapbooks, I would sit on the window seat as if to hold the lid on. I would look out over the front lawn, across Poinsette to Hamilton Park. Through the pine trees and the blooming cherries, I could see the playground and the circling tether ball, the pavilion, the war memorial, the courts. I wasn't old enough to change the world.

At a high-school bake sale, the frosted gingerbread men remind a teacher of her students drilling on the football field during the war. They wore letter jackets with shiny white sleeves, or bright sweaters with stripes and decorations. They carried brooms at trail arms in the sunset.

How does evil get into the world?

Witches. Or children crying, "Catch me, if you can."

I watch Mother feed a baby. "Nnnnaaawwwhh," she goes, "here it comes in for a landing." She conducts the spoon on a yawing course, approaching. "Open the hangar door," she orders.

Mother looks at me as the baby sucks the spoon. "Remember?" she says.

"I remember," I say.

She sends out the second wave of creamed cereal.

In the fall, the new Chevrolets arrive, and Hafner sets up his old searchlight. It is surplus from the war, painted silver now. The diesel motor rotates the light. The light itself comes from a flame magnified and reflected into a beam. People come across the street to look. They look at the new cars lined up.

From Hafner's lot, you can look across the St. Joe River, south, to where three other beams sweep back and forth in the night. Those are coming from Allen County Motors, Jim Kelley Buick, and DeHaven Chevrolet. From the west is the lone light of Means Cadillac tracing a tight circle and toppling over into a broad arc, catching for an instant the tip of the bank building downtown and righting itself like a top. To the north is another battery of lights playing off one another, intersecting, some moving faster than others. Toward you and away. Bench's AMC, Northway Plymouth, Ayres' Pontiac. The illusion of depth in the night. The general vicinity of each source.

What are they looking for?

Something new is in the world.

There was a Looney Tunes cartoon Engineer John showed almost every day on his TV show. It was made during the war. Hitler, upset with the way the war is going, flies a mission himself, only to have the plane dismantled over Russia by "Gremlins from the Kremlin."

I would look through the scrapbooks to see how it really happened.

There has been a plane circling all day. There appears to be a streak of smoke coming from its tail. But I'm sure it's some kind of banner too high to read.

In the scrapbook with the wood cover, there is a picture of Gypsy Rose Lee selling war bonds.

This is the only picture in all of Grandfather's scrapbooks where he's made a note. It says: *I bet the Lord is pleased.*

During the war, the top hemisphere of the streetlight globes were painted with a black opaque glaze. They stayed that way after the war. No one seems to mind. Parts of dead insects show in the lower half of the globe. There's more and more of them in there summer after summer.

Grandfather read meters for his living. During the war, he was made block warden because everyone remembered the way he'd kept calm during *The War of the Worlds.* They also figured that he knew a little bit about electricity.

The city practiced blackouts all the time because they'd heard that Fort Wayne was seventh on the list. One night everyone stumbled into Hamilton Park for a demonstration. A man from the Civil Defense wanted to emphasize the importance of absolute dark, lights really out. Grandfather said that the man lit a match when the rest of the city was all dark. He said that you could see the whole park and the faces of everyone in the park. They were all looking at the match. He said you could see the houses. He said you could read the street sign. *Poinsette.*

The man blew out the match with one breath. The people went home in the dark.

Were they wishing they could do something about the stars?

They kept German prisoners in camps near the Nickel Plate yards. People would go out to the camps and look at the prisoners. Everyone felt very safe, even the women. Many of the prisoners had worked on streets downtown, or in the neighborhoods, and were friendly with the people.

Some of these prisoners stayed in town after the war. Some sent for their families. You ask them, they'll tell you—Fort Wayne is a good place to live.

In one of Grandfather's scrapbooks, there is a series of pictures taken from the nose of a B-17. The first picture is of the bombs falling away from the plane. In the background are the city streets already burning. In the second picture, the nose of another bomber is working its way into the frame and under the bombs, smaller now by seconds. The third picture shows the plane in the path of the falling bombs. One has already taken away the stabilizer without exploding. The perspective is really terrifying. The fourth picture shows the plane skidding into its tailspin. All this time the bombs are falling. And the fifth picture is the plane falling with the bombs.

Grandfather has arranged these pictures to be read down the page. One after the other.

Casad is a GSO depot built during the war just outside of town. I go there sometimes to watch them dust the fields nearby, the fertile strip near the bend in the Maumee. High school kids race by on the township roads on their way to Ohio to drink. I don't know if they even use Casad for anything now.

Casad was built to be confusing from the air. All you can see, even from across the road, are mounds of different-colored stones. Some of the piles are real, others are only camouflaged roofs. If you look closely at some of them, you can see a small ventilation pipe or maybe some type of window. The important things are underground. There are stories that date from the war of one-ton chunks of rubber in storage. They feared the damage that would be caused if they dropped any during transportation. Tin, copper, nickel, tungsten, and mercury were all supposed to have been stored there. From the road, quarry piles and sandpiper tents hump out of sight through the cornfield to the river.

It must all look pretty harmless from the sky.

The high school kids will stop on the way back. Late at night, they will sit on the hoods of their cars guessing which of the shadows are real. They are waiting to sober up and weave home.

Mother remembers his Prospero at the Civic Theatre. He lived here years ago. The only time I saw Robert Lansing act was on the TV show where he played the wing commander and flew B-17s. All I remember now are the shots in the cramped cockpit with the flights of bombers in the background. Most of the action took place on that tiny set, two seats and the man in the turret, aft, always moving as the actors talked or rocked from the flack or were riddled by "bandits" or feathered the number three engine.

Robert Lansing visited our high school and talked about acting. He said there was a method that allowed him to use his past experiences in new situations. He said he was afraid to fly. He told us this standing in the middle of the gym floor, targeted in the cross hairs of the time-line.

In the stores downtown, there were bowls of lemon drops and cherry drops next to the cash registers. The merchants have broken into some of the supplies of the bomb shelters in the basements of their stores. They found that the water had soured years ago in the tins. The candy is sweet even though it is over twenty years old. They say the candy and water have been replaced in the bomb shelters. "No sense letting anything go to waste," they say. Every time you buy something, the person running the register will say, "Have some candy." And then they will mention where the candy comes from.

The small drums the candy came in are being used as wastebaskets. They are painted drab. Sometimes, the stenciled CANDY has been crossed out. The Civil

Defense emblem can still be seen—the pyramid in the circle, pointing up to the sky.

Grandfather saw Bob Hope in the coffee shop of the Hotel Anthony. He showed him the clipping he had been carrying around for years, the one about Mother dancing in Bob Hope's show. Grandfather said that he wished Bob Hope could be home for Christmas but was grateful that someone did what Bob Hope did.

In the fall, the wind turns the trees to silent puffs of smoke.

Grandfather wants to know why I want to be a poet. He shows me a clipping of Eldon Lapp, who goes to our church. There is a picture of Eldon in his flight jacket and soft hat. During the war, Eldon was shot down over Germany. Before his capture, he lived for months in the Black Forest. He survived that long with the aid of another flyer who had been trained as a Boy Scout and had been in Germany during a world jamboree. This flyer knew all the tricks—how to fish with a line and makeshift hook, how to conceal a trail, how to secure a camp, how to read signs. Eldon swore then that if he got out of this alive he would dedicate his life to scouting.

"That's vocation," Grandfather says to me.

The Kiwanis Club sponsors airplane rides all summer. Taking off from Baer Field, the tour flies over most of the city. I saw the Wayne Knitting Mill's tall smokestack, *Wayne* built right into the bricks. I flew by the elevators, followed Main Street downtown and circled the courthouse. Then over the Old Fort, looking defenseless, and the filtration plant with the ponds. I followed the Maumee from the three rivers downstream, sweeping by the old Studebaker plant, Zollner Piston, all the wire-and-die works, Magnavox. Then banking up the bypass, north, over the shopping centers and malls and their parking lots, over Eckrich and the campus, to my house.

I could see my house. I knew it even from the air. There were people in the front yard I did not know, looking up, shielding their eyes, waving.

Grandfather, all you can see are the contrails. The plodding lines of the bombers and the lyric corkscrews of their escort. It is how this city chooses to die. Daylight raids, everyone is watching. This is the American Way. To see it coming. The bombs are inverted exclamations at the beginning of their sentence.

I can hear the planes looking for the city each night. I keep my eyes closed as they fly over the house. Their engines pulse like the sirens. It is a patient sound. And I wait too.

I want for them to drop the flares, or for a few of them to come in lower. We did not ask for this. They fly by overhead. You can hear them, but you cannot see them. They are showing no lights. Low clouds. No stars.

They go on, on some heading to the west. But they will be back later. Then, further east, there will come the panting sound, almost comic, as they drop the bombs randomly, hoping to hit something, and then, empty, go back to where they came from.

Tarsk and Hartup have been taking aerial photographs for years. All the merchants and the schools, each new mayor, every public place has one of their pictures. Sometimes the picture is of one building and at other times of whole blocks. There are calendars, too, that everyone gets from Lincoln Life. In Mike's Car Wash people will try to find their house in the picture that hangs in the lobby while their car is being dried. Every day Tarsk and Hartup fly over the city taking pictures—but no matter what picture you look at, someone will always point out what is missing, or what has since disappeared.

QUESTIONS FOR DISCUSSION AND WRITING

1. "Fort Wayne Is Seventh on Hitler's List" begins, "This is a city of poets." What does Martone mean? Trace the idea of poetry through the story.

2. The story does not have a plot in the ordinary sense. Is there any structure or progression?

3. "Fort Wayne Is Seventh on Hitler's List," like Michelle Cliff's "If I Could Write This in Fire, I Would Write This in Fire," is organized in short passages separated by white spaces. Compare the use and effect of these separate little sections in the two pieces.

4. Who is the narrator of "Fort Wayne Is Seventh on Hitler's List"? What is the *tone* of the narration?

A FICTION
CASEBOOK

🙙 🙚

One of the pleasures of reading fiction is discussing it with others. You have done this in class and perhaps outside of class as well. An extension of this sharing of responses is reading published criticism of fiction, responding to it, and incorporating insights from the criticism into your own study. Of course, this is best done after you have studied the work thoroughly yourself; it is easy to be influenced too much by published work, if only because it *looks* so authoritative in print.

This casebook on fiction (there will be others on poetry and drama) provides you with the basic materials for practicing using secondary material (criticism and other writing about literature) in your own study and writing. First comes a very famous story, Charlotte Perkins Gilman's "The Yellow Wallpaper" (1892). It might be best to read this carefully and work out your own interpretation before you go on to read the interpretations of others. Then come a series of documents about "The Yellow Wallpaper." First is an essay Gilman herself wrote twenty-one years after publishing the story: "Why I Wrote 'The Yellow Wallpaper.'" Then comes a fairly comprehensive overview of the story: Elaine R. Hedges's "Afterword to 'The Yellow Wallpaper.'" And finally comes an exchange of ideas on "The Yellow Wallpaper" that was first published in *Tulsa Studies in Women's Literature.* The exchange opens with Paula Treichler's essay "Escaping the Sentence: Diagnosis and Discourse in 'The Yellow Wallpaper.'" Karen Ford and Carol Thomas Neely reply to Treichler's essay in two shorter essays. And finally Treichler responds to Ford's and Neely's criticisms in an essay called "The Wall Behind the Yellow Wallpaper." The whole thing adds up to a lively debate over the meaning of a complex and interesting story. Read Gilman's and Hedges's essays and the Treichler-Ford-Neely exchange carefully after you have worked out your own interpretation of "The Yellow Wallpaper." Then turn to the following essay: "Writing from Sources: Fiction."

Charlotte Perkins Gilman

Charlotte Perkins Gilman (1860–1935) was born in Hartford, Connecticut. Her father, a member of the Beecher family that produced the minister Henry Ward Beecher and Harriet Beecher Stowe, who wrote *Uncle Tom's Cabin*, deserted the family shortly after Charlotte's birth. She married an artist named Charles Stetson when she was twenty-four and quickly had a daughter. Bouts of severe depression drove her to S. Weir Mitchell, the most famous neurologist of the day, who prescribed the "rest cure" described in "The Yellow Wallpaper." She recovered only after she had resumed a normal life. Gilman was divorced in 1892 and embarked on a career as a feminist writer and lecturer. She married her cousin George Houghton Gilman in 1900. Her sociological writing included *Women and Economics* (1898), *Concerning Children* (1900), *The Home* (1904), *Man-Made World* (1911), and *His Religion and Hers* (1923). Her fiction, most of which was didactic, included the novels *Moving the Mountain* (1911), *Herland* (1915), and *With Her in Ourland* (1916). Her autobiography, *The Living of Charlotte Perkins Gilman*, appeared in 1933. Diagnosed with advanced breast cancer, Gilman killed herself in 1935.

THE YELLOW WALLPAPER

It is very seldom that mere ordinary people like John and myself secure ancestral halls for the summer.

A colonial mansion, a hereditary estate, I would say a haunted house, and reach the height of romantic felicity—but that would be asking too much of fate!

Still I will proudly declare that there is something queer about it.

Else, why should it be let so cheaply? And why have stood so long untenanted?

John laughs at me, of course, but one expects that in marriage.

John is practical in the extreme. He has no patience with faith, an intense horror of superstition, and he scoffs openly at any talk of things not to be felt and seen and put down in figures.

John is a physician, and *perhaps*—(I would not say it to a living soul, of course, but this is dead paper and a great relief to my mind—) *perhaps* that is one reason I do not get well faster.

You see he does not believe I am sick!

And what can one do?

If a physician of high standing, and one's own husband, assures friends and relatives that there is really nothing the matter with one but temporary nervous depression—a slight hysterical tendency—what is one to do?

My brother is also a physician, and also of high standing, and he says the same thing.

So I take phosphates or phosphites—whichever it is, and tonics, and journeys, and air, and exercise, and am absolutely forbidden to "work" until I am well again.

Personally, I disagree with their ideas.

Personally, I believe that congenial work, with excitement and change, would do me good.

But what is one to do?

I did write for a while in spite of them; but it *does* exhaust me a good deal—having to be so sly about it, or else meet with heavy opposition.

I sometimes fancy that in my condition if I had less opposition and more society and stimulus—but John says the very worst thing I can do is to think about my condition, and I confess it always makes me feel bad.

So I will let it alone and talk about the house.

The most beautiful place! It is quite alone, standing well back from the road, quite three miles from the village. It makes me think of English places that you read about, for there are hedges and walls and gates that lock, and lots of separate little houses for the gardeners and people.

There is a *delicious* garden! I never saw such a garden—large and shady, full of box-bordered paths, and lined with long grape-covered arbors with seats under them.

There were greenhouses, too, but they are all broken now.

There was some legal trouble, I believe, something about the heirs and co-heirs; anyhow, the place has been empty for years.

That spoils my ghostliness, I am afraid, but I don't care—there is something strange about the house—I can feel it.

I even said so to John one moonlight evening, but he said what I felt was a *draught*, and shut the window.

I get unreasonably angry with John sometimes. I'm sure I never used to be so sensitive. I think it is due to this nervous condition.

But John says if I feel so, I shall neglect proper self-control; so I take pains to control myself—before him, at least, and that makes me very tired.

I don't like our room a bit. I wanted one downstairs that opened on the piazza and had roses all over the window, and such pretty old-fashioned chintz hangings! but John would not hear of it.

He said there was only one window and not room for two beds, and no near room for him if he took another.

He is very careful and loving, and hardly lets me stir without special direction.

I have a schedule prescription for each hour in the day; he takes all care from me, and so I feel basely ungrateful not to value it more.

He said we came here solely on my account, that I was to have perfect rest and all the air I could get. "Your exercise depends on your strength, my dear," said he, "and your food somewhat on your appetite; but air you can absorb all the time." So we took the nursery at the top of the house.

It is a big, airy room, the whole floor nearly, with windows that look all ways, and air and sunshine galore. It was nursery first and then playroom and gymnasium, I should judge; for the windows are barred for little children, and there are rings and things in the walls.

The paint and paper look as if a boys' school had used it. It is stripped off—the paper—in great patches all around the head of my bed, about as far as I can reach, and in a great place on the other side of the room low down. I never saw a worse paper in my life.

One of those sprawling flamboyant patterns committing every artistic sin.

It is dull enough to confuse the eye in following, pronounced enough to constantly irritate and provoke study, and when you follow the lame uncertain curves for a little distance they suddenly commit suicide—plunge off at outrageous angles, destroy themselves in unheard of contradictions.

The color is repellent, almost revolting; a smouldering unclean yellow, strangely faded by the slow-turning sunlight.

It is a dull yet lurid orange in some places, a sickly sulphur tint in others.

No wonder the children hated it! I should hate it myself if I had to live in this room long.

There comes John, and I must put this away,—he hates to have me write a word.

We have been here two weeks, and I haven't felt like writing before, since that first day.

I am sitting by the window now, up in this atrocious nursery, and there is nothing to hinder my writing as much as I please, save lack of strength.

John is away all day, and even some nights when his cases are serious.

I am glad my case is not serious!

But these nervous troubles are dreadfully depressing.

John does not know how much I really suffer. He knows there is no *reason* to suffer, and that satisfies him.

Of course it is only nervousness. It does weigh on me so not to do my duty in any way!

I meant to be such a help to John, such a real rest and comfort, and here I am a comparative burden already!

Nobody would believe what an effort it is to do what little I am able,—to dress and entertain, and order things.

It is fortunate Mary is so good with the baby. Such a dear baby!

And yet I *cannot* be with him, it makes me so nervous.

I suppose John never was nervous in his life. He laughs at me so about this wallpaper!

At first he meant to repaper the room, but afterwards he said that I was letting it get the better of me, and that nothing was worse for a nervous patient than to give way to such fancies.

He said that after the wallpaper was changed it would be the heavy bedstead, and then the barred windows, and then that gate at the head of the stairs, and so on.

"You know the place is doing you good," he said, "and really, dear, I don't care to renovate the house just for a three months' rental."

"Then do let us go downstairs," I said, "there are such pretty rooms there."

Then he took me in his arms and called me, a blessed little goose, and said he would go down cellar, if I wished, and have it whitewashed into the bargain.

But he is right enough about the beds and windows and things.

It is an airy and comfortable room as any one need wish, and, of course, I would not be so silly as to make him uncomfortable just for a whim.

I'm really getting quite fond of the big room, all but that horrid paper.

Out of one window I can see the garden, those mysterious deep-shaded arbors, the riotous old-fashioned flowers, and bushes and gnarly trees.

Out of another I get a lovely view of the bay and a little private wharf belonging to the estate. There is a beautiful shaded lane that runs down there from the house. I always fancy I see people walking in these numerous paths and arbors, but John has cautioned me not to give way to fancy in the least. He says that with my imaginative power and habit of story-making, a nervous weakness like mine is sure to lead to all manner of excited fancies, and that I ought to use my will and good sense to check the tendency. So I try.

I think sometimes that if I were only well enough to write a little it would relieve the press of ideas and rest me.

But I find I get pretty tired when I try.

It is so discouraging not to have any advice and companionship about my work.

When I get really well, John says we will ask Cousin Henry and Julia down for a long visit; but he says he would as soon put fireworks in my pillow-case as to let me have those stimulating people about now.

I wish I could get well faster.

But I must not think about that. This paper looks to me as if it *knew* what a vicious influence it had!

There is a recurrent spot where the pattern lolls like a broken neck and two bulbous eyes stare at you upside down.

I get positively angry with the impertinence of it and the everlastingness. Up and down and sideways they crawl, and those absurd, unblinking eyes are everywhere. There is one place where two breadths didn't match, and the eyes go all up and down the line, one a little higher than the other.

I never saw so much expression in an inanimate thing before, and we all know how much expression they have! I used to lie awake as a child and get more entertainment and terror out of blank walls and plain furniture than most children could find in a toy-store.

I remember what a kindly wink the knobs of our big, old bureau used to have, and there was one chair that always seemed like a strong friend.

I used to feel that if any of the other things looked too fierce I could always hop into that chair and be safe.

The furniture in this room is no worse than inharmonious, however, for we had to bring it all from downstairs. I suppose when this was used as a playroom they had to take the nursery things out, and no wonder! I never saw such ravages as the children have made here.

The wallpaper, as I said before, is torn off in spots, and it sticketh closer than a brother—they must have had perseverance as well as hatred.

Then the floor is scratched and gouged and splintered, the plaster itself is dug out here and there, and this great heavy bed which is all we found in the room, looks as if it had been through the wars.

But I don't mind it a bit—only the paper.

There comes John's sister. Such a dear girl as she is, and so careful of me! I must not let her find me writing.

She is a perfect and enthusiastic housekeeper, and hopes for no better profession. I verily believe she thinks it is the writing which made me sick!

But I can write when she is out, and see her a long way off from these windows.

There is one that commands the road, a lovely shaded winding road, and one that just looks over the country. A lovely country, too, full of great elms and velvet meadows.

This wallpaper has a kind of subpattern in a different shade, a particularly irritating one, for you can only see it in certain lights, and not clearly then.

But in the places where it isn't faded and where the sun is just so—I can see a strange, provoking, formless sort of figure, that seems to skulk about behind that silly and conspicuous front design.

There's sister on the stairs!

Well, the Fourth of July is over! The people are all gone and I am tired out. John thought it might do me good to see a little company, so we just had mother and Nellie and the children down for a week.

Of course I didn't do a thing. Jennie sees to everything now.

But it tired me all the same.

John says if I don't pick up faster he shall send me to Weir Mitchell in the fall.

But I don't want to go there at all. I had a friend who was in his hands once, and she says he is just like John and my brother, only more so!

Besides, it is such an undertaking to go so far.

I don't feel as if it was worth while to turn my hand over for anything, and I'm getting dreadfully fretful and querulous.

I cry at nothing, and cry most of the time.

Of course I don't when John is here, or anybody else, but when I am alone.

And I am alone a good deal just now. John is kept in town very often by serious cases, and Jennie is good and lets me alone when I want her to.

So I walk a little in the garden or down that lovely lane, sit on the porch under the roses, and lie down up here a good deal.

I'm getting really fond of the room in spite of the wallpaper. Perhaps *because* of the wallpaper.

It dwells in my mind so!

I lie here on this great immovable bed—it is nailed down, I believe—and follow that pattern about by the hour. It is as good as gymnastics, I assure you. I start, we'll say, at the bottom, down in the corner over there where it has not been touched, and I determine for the thousandth time that I *will* follow that pointless pattern to some sort of a conclusion.

I know a little of the principle of design, and I know this thing was not arranged on any laws of radiation, or alternation, or repetition, or symmetry, or anything else that I ever heard of.

It is repeated, of course, by the breadths, but not otherwise.

Looked at in one way each breadth stands alone, the bloated curves and flourishes—a kind of "debased Romanesque" with *delirium tremens* go waddling up and down in isolated columns of fatuity.

But, on the other hand, they connect diagonally, and the sprawling outlines run off in great slanting waves of optic horror, like a lot of wallowing seaweeds in full chase.

The whole thing goes horizontally, too, at least it seems so, and I exhaust myself in trying to distinguish the order of its going in that direction.

They have used a horizontal breadth for a frieze, and that adds wonderfully to the confusion.

There is one end of the room where it is almost intact, and there, when the crosslights fade and the low sun shines directly upon it, I can almost fancy radiation after all,—the interminable grotesque seems to form around a common centre and rush off in headlong plunges of equal distraction.

It makes me tired to follow it. I will take a nap I guess.

I don't know why I should write this.

I don't want to.

I don't feel able.

And I know John would think it absurd. But I *must* say what I feel and think in some way—it is such a relief!

But the effort is getting to be greater than the relief.

Half the time now I am awfully lazy, and lie down ever so much.

John says I mustn't lose my strength, and has me take cod liver oil and lots of tonics and things, to say nothing of ale and wine and rare meat.

Dear John! He loves me very dearly, and hates to have me sick. I tried to have a real earnest reasonable talk with him the other day, and tell him how I wish he would let me go and make a visit to Cousin Henry and Julia.

But he said I wasn't able to go, nor able to stand it after I got there; and I did not make out a very good case for myself, for I was crying before I had finished.

It is getting to be a great effort for me to think straight. Just this nervous weakness I suppose.

And dear John gathered me up in his arms, and just carried me upstairs and laid me on the bed, and sat by me and read to me till it tired my head.

He said I was his darling and his comfort and all he had, and that I must take care of myself for his sake, and keep well.

He says no one but myself can help me out of it, that I must use my will and self-control and not let any silly fancies run away with me.

There's one comfort, the baby is well and happy, and does not have to occupy this nursery with the horrid wallpaper.

If we had not used it, that blessed child would have! What a fortunate escape! Why, I wouldn't have a child of mine, an impressionable little thing, live in such a room for worlds.

I never thought of it before, but it is lucky that John kept me here after all, I can stand it so much easier than a baby, you see.

Of course I never mention it to them any more—I am too wise,—but I keep watch of it all the same.

There are things in that paper that nobody knows but me, or ever will.

Behind that outside pattern the dim shapes get clearer every day.

It is always the same shape, only very numerous.

And it is like a woman stooping down and creeping about behind that pattern. I don't like it a bit. I wonder—I begin to think—I wish John would take me away from here!

It is so hard to talk with John about my case, because he is so wise, and because he loves me so.

But I tried it last night.

It was moonlight. The moon shines in all around just as the sun does.

I hate to see it sometimes, it creeps so slowly, and always comes in by one window or another.

John was asleep and I hated to waken him, so I kept still and watched the moonlight on that undulating wallpaper till I felt creepy.

The faint figure behind seemed to shake the pattern, just as if she wanted to get out.

I got up softly and went to feel and see if the paper *did* move, and when I came back John was awake.

"What is it, little girl?" he said. "Don't go walking about like that—you'll get cold."

I thought it was a good time to talk, so I told him that I really was not gaining here, and that I wished he would take me away.

"Why, darling!" said he, "our lease will be up in three weeks, and I can't see how to leave before.

"The repairs are not done at home, and I cannot possibly leave town just now. Of course if you were in any danger, I could and would, but you really are better, dear, whether you can see it or not. I am a doctor, dear, and I know. You are gaining flesh and color, your appetite is better, I feel really much easier about you."

"I don't weigh a bit more," said I, "nor as much; and my appetite may be better in the evening when you are here, but it is worse in the morning when you are away!"

"Bless her little heart!" said he with a big hug, "she shall be as sick as she pleases! But now let's improve the shining hours by going to sleep, and talk about it in the morning!"

"And you won't go away?" I asked gloomily.

"Why, how can I, dear? It is only three weeks more and then we will take a nice little trip of a few days while Jennie is getting the house ready. Really dear you are better!"

"Better in body perhaps—" I began, and stopped short, for he sat up straight and looked at me with such a stern, reproachful look that I could not say another word.

"My darling," said he, "I beg of you, for my sake and for our child's sake, as well as for your own, that you will never for one instant let that idea enter your mind! There is nothing so dangerous, so fascinating, to a temperament like yours. It is a false and foolish fancy. Can you not trust me as a physician when I tell you so?"

So of course I said no more on that score, and we went to sleep before long. He thought I was asleep first, but I wasn't, and lay there for hours trying to decide whether that front pattern and the back pattern really did move together or separately.

On a pattern like this, by daylight, there is a lack of sequence, a defiance of law, that is a constant irritant to a normal mind.

The color is hideous enough, and unreliable enough, and infuriating enough, but the pattern is torturing.

You think you have mastered it, but just as you get well underway in following, it turns a back-somersault and there you are. It slaps you in the face, knocks you down, and tramples upon you. It is like a bad dream.

The outside pattern is a florid arabesque, reminding one of a fungus. If you can imagine a toadstool in joints, an interminable string of toadstools, budding and sprouting in endless convolutions—why, that is something like it.

That is, sometimes!

There is one marked peculiarity about this paper, a thing nobody seems to notice but myself, and that is that it changes as the light changes.

When the sun shoots in through the east window—I always watch for that first long, straight ray—it changes so quickly that I never can quite believe it.

That is why I watch it always.

By moonlight—the moon shines in all night when there is a moon—I wouldn't know it was the same paper.

At night in any kind of light, in twilight, candlelight, lamplight, and worst of all by moonlight, it becomes bars! The outside pattern I mean, and the woman behind it is as plain as can be.

I didn't realize for a long time what the thing was that showed behind, that dim sub-pattern, but now I am quite sure it is a woman.

By daylight she is subdued, quiet. I fancy it is the pattern that keeps her so still. It is so puzzling. It keeps me quiet by the hour.

I lie down ever so much now. John says it is good for me, and to sleep all I can.

Indeed he started the habit by making me lie down for an hour after each meal.

It is a very bad habit I am convinced, for you see I don't sleep.

And that cultivates deceit, for I don't tell them I'm awake—O no!

The fact is I am getting a little afraid of John.

He seems very queer sometimes, and even Jennie has an inexplicable look.

It strikes me occasionally, just as a scientific hypothesis,—that perhaps it is the paper!

I have watched John when he did not know I was looking, and come into the room suddenly on the most innocent excuses, and I've caught him several times *looking at the paper!* And Jennie too. I caught Jennie with her hand on it once.

She didn't know I was in the room, and when I asked her in a quiet, a very quiet voice, with the most restrained manner possible, what she was doing with the paper—she turned around as if she had been caught stealing, and looked quite angry—asked me why I should frighten her so!

Then she said that the paper stained everything it touched, that she had found yellow smooches on all my clothes and John's, and she wished we would be more careful!

Did not that sound innocent? But I know she was studying that pattern, and I am determined that nobody shall find it out but myself!

Life is very much more exciting now than it used to be. You see I have something more to expect, to look forward to, to watch. I really do eat better, and am more quiet than I was.

John is so pleased to see me improve! He laughed a little the other day, and said I seemed to be flourishing in spite of my wallpaper.

I turned it off with a laugh. I had no intention of telling him it was *because* of the wallpaper—he would make fun of me. He might even want to take me away.

I don't want to leave now until I have found it out. There is a week more, and I think that will be enough.

I'm feeling ever so much better! I don't sleep much at night, for it is so interesting to watch developments; but I sleep a good deal in the daytime.

In the daytime it is tiresome and perplexing.

There are always new shoots on the fungus, and new shades of yellow all over it. I cannot keep count of them, though I have tried conscientiously.

It is the strangest yellow, that wallpaper! It makes me think of all the yellow things I ever saw—not beautiful ones like buttercups, but old foul, bad yellow things.

But there is something else about that paper—the smell! I noticed it the moment we came into the room, but with so much air and sun it was not bad. Now we have had a week of fog and rain, and whether the windows are open or not, the smell is here.

It creeps all over the house.

I find it hovering in the dining-room, skulking in the parlor, hiding in the hall, lying in wait for me on the stairs.

It gets into my hair.

Even when I go to ride, if I turn my head suddenly and surprise it—there is that smell!

Such a peculiar odor, too! I have spent hours in trying to analyze it, to find what it smelled like.

It is not bad—at first, and very gentle, but quite the subtlest, most enduring odor I ever met.

In this damp weather it is awful, I wake up in the night and find it hanging over me.

It used to disturb me at first. I thought seriously of burning the house—to reach the smell.

But now I am used to it. The only thing I can think of that it is like is the *color* of the paper! A yellow smell.

There is a very funny mark on this wall, low down, near the mopboard. A streak that runs round the room. It goes behind every piece of furniture, except the bed, a long, straight, even *smooch,* as if it had been rubbed over and over.

I wonder how it was done and who did it, and what they did it for. Round and round and round—round and round and round!—it makes me dizzy!

I really have discovered something at last.

Through watching so much at night, when it changes so, I have finally found out.

The front pattern *does* move—and no wonder! The woman behind shakes it!

Sometimes I think there are a great many women behind, and sometimes only one, and she crawls around fast, and her crawling shakes it all over.

Then in the very bright spots she keeps still, and in the very shady spots she just takes hold of the bars and shakes them hard.

And she is all the time trying to climb through. But nobody could climb through that pattern—it strangles so; I think that is why it has so many heads.

They get through, and then the pattern strangles them off and turns them upside down, and makes their eyes white!

If those heads were covered or taken off it would not be half so bad.

I think that woman gets out in the daytime!

And I'll tell you why—privately—I've seen her!

I can see her out of every one of my windows!

It is the same woman, I know, for she is always creeping, and most women do not creep by daylight.

I see her in that long shaded lane, creeping up and down. I see her in those dark grape arbors, creeping all around the garden.

I see her on the long road under the trees, creeping along, and when a carriage comes she hides under the blackberry vines.

I don't blame her a bit. It must be very humiliating to be caught creeping by daylight!

I always lock the door when I creep by daylight. I can't do it at night, for I know John would suspect something at once.

And John is so queer now, that I don't want to irritate him. I wish he would take another room! Besides, I don't want anybody to get that woman out at night but myself.

I often wonder if I could see her out of all the windows at once.

But, turn as fast as I can, I can only see out of one at one time.

And though I always see her, she *may* be able to creep faster than I can turn!

I have watched her sometimes away off in the open country, creeping as fast as a cloud shadow in a high wind.

If only that top pattern could be gotten off from the under one! I mean to try it, little by little.

I have found out another funny thing, but I shan't tell it this time! It does not do to trust people too much.

There are only two more days to get this paper off, and I believe John is beginning to notice. I don't like the look in his eyes.

And I heard him ask Jennie a lot of professional questions about me. She had a very good report to give.

She said I slept a good deal in the daytime.

John knows I don't sleep very well at night, for all I'm so quiet!

He asked me all sorts of questions, too, and pretended to be very loving and kind.

As if I couldn't see through him!

Still, I don't wonder he acts so, sleeping under this paper for three months.

It only interests me, but I feel sure John and Jennie are secretly affected by it.

Hurrah! This is the last day, but it is enough. John is to stay in town over night, and won't be out until this evening.

Jennie wanted to sleep with me—the sly thing! but I told her I should undoubtedly rest better for a night all alone.

That was clever, for really I wasn't alone a bit! As soon as it was moonlight and that poor thing began to crawl and shake the pattern, I got up and ran to help her.

I pulled and she shook, I shook and she pulled, and before morning we had peeled off yards of that paper.

A strip about as high as my head and half around the room.

And then when the sun came and that awful pattern began to laugh at me, I declared I would finish it to-day!

We go away to-morrow, and they are moving all my furniture down again to leave things as they were before.

Jennie looked at the wall in amazement, but I told her merrily that I did it out of pure spite at the vicious thing.

She laughed and said she wouldn't mind doing it herself, but I must not get tired.

How she betrayed herself that time!

But I am here, and no person touches this paper but me,—not *alive!*

She tried to get me out of the room—it was too patent! But I said it was so quiet and empty and clean now that I believed I would lie down again and sleep all I could; and not to wake me even for dinner—I would call when I woke.

So now she is gone, and the servants are gone, and the things are gone, and there is nothing left but that great bedstead nailed down, with the canvas mattress we found on it.

We shall sleep downstairs to-night, and take the boat home to-morrow.

I quite enjoy the room, now it is bare again.

How those children did tear about here!

This bedstead is fairly gnawed!

But I must get to work.

I have locked the door and thrown the key down into the front path.

I don't want to go out, and I don't want to have anybody come in, till John comes.

I want to astonish him.

I've got a rope up here that even Jennie did not find. If that woman does get out, and tries to get away, I can tie her!

But I forgot I could not reach far without anything to stand on!

This bed will *not* move!

I tried to lift and push it until I was lame, and then I got so angry I bit off a little piece at one corner—but it hurt my teeth.

Then I peeled off all the paper I could reach standing on the floor. It sticks horribly and the pattern just enjoys it! All those strangled heads and bulbous eyes and waddling fungus growths just shriek with derision!

I am getting angry enough to do something desperate. To jump out of the window would be admirable exercise, but the bars are too strong even to try.

Besides I wouldn't do it. Of course not. I know well enough that a step like that is improper and might be misconstrued.

I don't like to *look* out of the windows even—there are so many of those creeping women, and they creep so fast.

I wonder if they all come out of that wallpaper as I did?

But I am securely fastened now by my well-hidden rope—you don't get *me* out in the road there!

I suppose I shall have to get back behind the pattern when it comes night, and that is hard!

It is so pleasant to be out in this great room and creep around as I please!

I don't want to go outside. I won't, even if Jennie asks me to.

For outside you have to creep on the ground, and everything is green instead of yellow.

But here I can creep smoothly on the floor, and my shoulder just fits in that long smooch around the wall, so I cannot lose my way.

Why there's John at the door!

It is no use, young man, you can't open it!

How he does call and pound!

Now he's crying for an axe.

It would be a shame to break down that beautiful door!

"John dear!" said I in the gentlest voice, "the key is down by the front steps, under a plaintain leaf!"

That silenced him for a few moments.

Then he said—very quietly indeed, "Open the door, my darling!"

"I can't," said I. "The key is down by the front door under a plaintain leaf!"

And then I said it again, several times, very gently and slowly, and said it so often that he had to go and see, and he got it of course, and came in. He stopped short by the door.

"What is the matter?" he cried. "For God's sake, what are you doing!"

I kept on creeping just the same, but I looked at him over my shoulder.

"I've got out at last," said I, "in spite of you and Jane. And I've pulled off most of the paper, so you can't put me back!"

Now why should that man have fainted? But he did, and right across my path by the wall, so that I had to creep over him every time!

WHY I WROTE "THE YELLOW WALLPAPER"*

By Charlotte Perkins Gilman

Many and many a reader has asked that. When the story first came out, in the *New England Magazine* about 1891, a Boston physician made protest in *The Transcript.* Such a story ought not to be written, he said; it was enough to drive anyone mad to read it.

Another physician, in Kansas I think, wrote to say that it was the best description of incipient insanity he had ever seen, and—begging my pardon—had I been there?

Now the story of the story is this:

For many years I suffered from a severe and continuous nervous breakdown

* Originally published in *The Forerunner*, October 1913.

tending to melancholia—and beyond. During about the third year of this trouble I went, in devout faith and some faint stir of hope, to a noted specialist in nervous diseases, the best known in the country. This wise man put me to bed and applied the rest cure, to which a still-good physique responded so promptly that he concluded there was nothing much the matter with me, and sent me home with solemn advice to "live as domestic a life as far as possible," to "have but two hours' intellectual life a day," and "never to touch pen, brush, or pencil again" as long as I lived. This was in 1887.

I went home and obeyed those directions for some three months, and came so near the borderline of utter mental ruin that I could see over.

Then, using the remnants of intelligence that remained, and helped by a wise friend, I cast the noted specialist's advice to the winds and went to work again—work, the normal life of every human being; work, in which is joy and growth and service, without which one is a pauper and a parasite—ultimately recovering some measure of power.

Being naturally moved to rejoicing by this narrow escape, I wrote "The Yellow Wallpaper," with its embellishments and additions, to carry out the ideal (I never had hallucinations or objections to my mural decorations) and sent a copy to the physician who so nearly drove me mad. He never acknowledged it.

The little book is valued by alienists and as a good specimen of one kind of literature. It has, to my knowledge, saved one woman from a similar fate—so terrifying her family that they let her out into normal activity and she recovered.

But the best result is this. Many years later I was told that the great specialist had admitted to friends of his that he had altered his treatment of neurasthenia since reading "The Yellow Wallpaper."

It was not intended to drive people crazy, but to save people from being driven crazy, and it worked.

AFTERWORD TO "THE YELLOW WALLPAPER"*

By Elaine R. Hedges

"The Yellow Wallpaper" is a small literary masterpiece. For almost fifty years it has been overlooked, as has its author, one of the most commanding feminists of her time. Now, with the new growth of the feminist movement, Charlotte Perkins Gilman is being rediscovered, and "The Yellow Wallpaper" should share in that rediscovery. The story of a woman's mental breakdown, narrated with superb psychological and dramatic precision, it is, as William Dean Howells said of it in 1920, a story to "freeze our . . . blood."[1]

The story was wrenched out of Gilman's own life, and is unique in the canon of her works. Although she wrote other fiction—short stories and novels—and much poetry as well, none of it ever achieved the power and directness, the imaginative authenticity of this piece. Polemical intent often made her fiction dry and clumsily didactic; and the extraordinary pressures of publishing deadlines under which she

---

* First published in *The Yellow Wallpaper* by Charlotte Perkins Gilman. Old Westbury, N.Y.: Feminist Press, 1973.
[1] William Dean Howells, ed., *The Great Modern American Stories* (New York: Boni and Liveright, 1920), p. vii.

worked made careful composition almost impossible. (During one seven-year period she edited and published her own magazine, *The Forerunner,* writing almost all of the material for it—a sum total, she estimated, of twenty-one thousand words per month or the equivalent of twenty-eight books.)

Charlotte Perkins Gilman was an active feminist and primarily a nonfiction writer: the author of *Women and Economics,* a witty, bitingly satirical analysis of the situation of women in her society, which was used as a college text in the 1920s and translated into seven languages; and the author of many other nonfiction works dealing with the socioeconomic status of women. She was also an indefatigable and inspiring lecturer. Her work during the last decade of the nineteenth century and the first two of the twentieth has led one recent historian to say that she was "the leading intellectual in the women's movement in the United States" in her time.[2]

That interest in her has recently revived is satisfying, and only just. In the past few years several masters theses and doctoral dissertations have been written about her, and *Women and Economics* was reissued in 1966. The recent acquisition of her personal papers by the Schlesinger Library of Radcliffe College is bound to lead to further research and publication. Even "The Yellow Wallpaper" has resurfaced in several anthologies. However, tucked away among many other selections and frequently with only brief biographical information about its author, the story will not necessarily find in these anthologies the wide audience it deserves.[3]

Yet it does deserve the widest possible audience. For aside from the light it throws on the personal despairs, and the artistic triumph over them, of one of America's foremost feminists, the story is one of the rare pieces of literature we have by a nineteenth-century woman which directly confronts the sexual politics of the male-female, husband-wife relationship. In its time (and presumably still today, given its appearance in the anthology *Psychopathology and Literature*), the story was read essentially as a Poe-esque tale of chilling horror—and as a story of mental aberration. It is both of these. But it is more. It is a feminist document, dealing with sexual politics at a time when few writers felt free to do so, at least so candidly. Three years after Gilman published her story, Kate Chopin published *The Awakening,* a novel so frank in its treatment of the middle-class wife and her prescribed submissive role that it lost its author both reputation and income. It is symptomatic of their times that both Gilman's story and Chopin's novel end with the self-destruction of their heroines.

It wasn't easy for Charlotte Perkins Gilman to get her story published. She sent it first to William Dean Howells, and he, responding to at least some of its power and authenticity, recommended it to Horace Scudder, editor of *The Atlantic Monthly,* then the most prestigious magazine in the United States. Scudder rejected the story, according to Gilman's account in her autobiography, with a curt note:

---

[2] Carl Degler, ed., *Women and Economics* (reprint ed., New York: Harper and Row, 1966), p. xiii.

[3] Leslie Y. Rabkin, ed., *Psychopathology and Literature* (San Francisco: Chandler Publications, 1966); Elaine Gottlieb Hemley and Jack Matthews, eds., *The Writer's Signature: Idea in Story and Essay* (Glenview, Ill.: Scott, Foresman, Co., 1972); Gail Parker, ed., *The Oven Birds: American Women on Womanhood, 1820–1920* (Garden City, N.Y.: Anchor Books, 1972). The last of these anthologies is the only one that puts "The Yellow Wallpaper" into the context of the struggle of American women for self-, social, and political expression. However, Dr. Parker's treatment of Gilman in her introduction is negative and sometimes factually shaky. Nor does she discuss the story itself in any detail.

Dear Madam,

Mr. Howells has handed me this story. I could not forgive myself if I made others as miserable as I have made myself!

Sincerely yours,[4]
H.E. Scudder

In the 1890s editors, and especially Scudder, still officially adhered to a canon of "moral uplift" in literature, and Gilman's story, with its heroine reduced at the end to the level of a groveling animal, scarcely fitted the prescribed formula. One wonders, however, whether hints of the story's attack on social mores—specifically on the ideal of the submissive wife—came through to Scudder and unsettled him?

The story was finally published, in May 1892, in *The New England Magazine*, where it was greeted with strong but mixed feelings. Gilman was warned that such stories were "perilous stuff," which should not be printed because of the threat they posed to the relatives of such "deranged" persons as the heroine.[5] The implications of such warnings—that women should "stay in their place," that nothing could or should be done except maintain silence or conceal problems—are fairly clear. Those who praised the story, for the accuracy of its portrayal and its delicacy of touch, did so on the grounds that Gilman had captured in literature, from a medical point of view, the most "detailed account of incipient insanity."[6] Howells' admiration for the story, when he reprinted it in 1920 in the *Great Modern American Stories*, limited itself to the story's "chilling" quality. Again, however, no one seems to have made the connection between the insanity and the sex, or sexual role, of the victim, no one explored the story's implications for male-female relationships in the nineteenth century.

To appreciate fully these relationships, and hence the meaning of Gilman's story, requires biographical background. Born in 1860 in Connecticut, Charlotte Perkins grew up in Rhode Island and her childhood and youth were hard. Her mother bore three children in three years; one child died; after the birth of the third the father abandoned the family. Charlotte said of her mother that her life was "one of the most painfully thwarted I have ever known." Her mother had been idolized as a young girl, had had many suitors, and was then left with two children after a few brief years of marriage. Did the conflicting patterns imposed on women at that time (and still today)—"belle of the ball" versus housewife and producer of children—contribute to, or indeed even account for, the destruction of her marriage? Gilman suggests that the father may have left the family because the mother had been told that if she were to have another child she might die.[7] In any event, the effect of the broken marriage on Charlotte was painful. According to Gilman's autobiography, her mother sacrificed both her own and her daughter's need for love, out of an understandably desperate yet inevitably self-destructive need for protection against further betrayal; the mother seems literally to have refused as much as a light physical caress. It was her way of initiating Charlotte into the sufferings that life would hold for a woman.

---

[4] Charlotte Perkins Gilman, *The Living of Charlotte Perkins Gilman. An Autobiography* (New York: D. Appleton-Century Co., 1935), p. 119.
[5] Ibid., p. 120. It is interesting to note that the writer of this letter, a doctor, ascribed the heroine's problem to "an *heredity* of mental derangement." (My italics.)
[6] Ibid., p. 120.
[7] Ibid., p. 5. "Whether the doctor's dictum was the reason [for the father's abandoning the family] or merely a reason I do not know," Gilman writes in her autobiography.

Growing up without tenderness Charlotte grew up also, perhaps as a result of the treatment she received, determined to develop her willpower and refusing to be defeated. Her own description of herself at sixteen is of a person who had "My mother's profound religious tendency and implacable sense of duty; my father's intellectual appetite; a will power, well developed, from both; a passion of my own for scientific knowledge, for real laws of life; an insatiable demand for perfection in everything. . . ."[8] These traits would characterize her, and her work, throughout her life.

That, at seventeen, she could write, "Am going to try hard this winter to see if I cannot enjoy myself like other people" is both painful indication of the deprivations of her childhood and tribute to the strengths she wrested from those deprivations.[9] She had inherited the New England Puritan tradition of duty and responsibility: what she described as the development of "noble character."[10] (She was related to the famous Beecher family; Harriet Beecher Stowe was her great-aunt.) On the whole her Puritan heritage served her well; but it had its painful effects, as would be seen in her first marriage.

By the time she was in her late teens Charlotte Perkins had begun seriously to ponder "the injustices under which women suffered."[11] Although not in close touch with the suffrage movement (with which indeed she never in her later career directly associated herself, finding its objectives too limited for her own more radical views on the need for social change), she was becoming increasingly aware of such current developments as the entrance of some young women into colleges—and the ridicule they received—of the growing numbers of young women in the working population, of a few books being written that critically examined the institution of marriage, and of the somewhat more open discussion of matters of sexuality and chastity. She began to write poems—one in defense of prostitutes—and to pursue her own independent thinking. Her commitment was to change a world which she saw as unhappy and confused: she would use logic, argument, and demonstration; she would write and she would lecture.

Meanwhile she had met Charles Stetson, a Providence, Rhode Island, artist. She was drawn to him by his artistic ability, his ideals, and his loneliness—so much like her own. The story of their courtship, as she recounts it in her autobiography, is evidence of the effects on her of the life of self-denial she had led. There was, she says, "no natural response of inclination or desire, no question of, 'Do I love him?' only, 'Is it right?' " Only after reluctance and refusal, and at a time when he had met with "a keen personal disappointment," did she agree to marry him.[12] Actually, her motives in marrying and her expectations of marriage are, until further evidence is available, difficult to sort out. Although her autobiography stresses her sense of duty and pity there seems also to be evidence, from some early notebooks and journals at the Schlesinger Library, that love and companionship were also involved. But what is clear is that Charlotte Perkins knew she was facing the crucial question so many nineteenth-century women had to face: marriage or a career. A woman *"should* be able to have marriage and motherhood, and do her work in the world also," she argued.[13] Yet she was not convinced by her own argument—what

---

[8] Ibid., p. 44.
[9] Ibid.
[10] Ibid., p. 45.
[11] Ibid., p. 61.
[12] Ibid., pp. 82, 83.
[13] Ibid., p. 83 (My italics.)

models did she have? And her fears that marriage and motherhood might incapacitate her for her "work in the world" would prove to be true, for her as for most women in our society.

Although she claims to have been happy with her husband, who was "tender" and "devoted," and helped with the housework, and toward whom she felt "the natural force of sex-attraction," she soon began to experience periods of depression: ". . . something was going wrong from the first." As she describes it, "A sort of gray fog drifted across my mind, a cloud that grew and darkened." Increasingly she felt weak, sleepless, unable to work. A year after the marriage she gave birth to a daughter and within a month of the birth she became, again in her own words, "a mental wreck." "There was a constant dragging weariness. . . . Absolute incapacity. Absolute misery."[14]

It would seem that Charlotte Perkins Stetson felt trapped by the role assigned the wife within the conventional nineteenth century marriage. If marriage meant children and too many children meant incapability for other work; if she saw her father's abandonment and her mother's coldness as the result of this sexual-marital bind; if she saw herself as victimized by marriage, the woman playing the passive role—then she was simply seeing clearly.

It was out of this set of marital circumstances, but beyond that out of her larger social awareness of the situation of women in her century, that "The Yellow Wallpaper" emerged five years later. Witness to the personal and social anguish of its author, the story is also an indictment of the incompetent medical advice she received. Charlotte Perkins Stetson was sent to the most preeminent "nerve specialist" of her time, Dr. S. Weir Mitchell of Philadelphia, and it was his patronizing treatment of her that seems ultimately to have provoked her to write her story. Dr. Mitchell could not fit Mrs. Stetson into either of his two categories of victims of what was then called "nervous prostration": businessmen exhausted from too much work or society women exhausted from too much play. His prescription for her health was that she devote herself to domestic work and to her child, confine herself to, at most, two hours of intellectual work a day, and "never touch pen, brush or pencil as long as you live."[15]

After a month in Dr. Mitchell's sanitarium Charlotte Stetson returned home. She reports that she almost lost her mind. Like the heroine in her story, she would often "crawl into remote closets and under beds—to hide from the grinding pressure of that profound distress."[16]

In 1887, after four years of marriage, Charlotte Perkins Stetson and her husband agreed to a separation and a divorce. It was an obvious necessity. When away from him—she had made a trip to California shortly after the onset of her illness—she felt healthy and recovered. When she returned to her family she began again to experience depression and fatigue.

For the rest of her life Charlotte Perkins would suffer from the effects of this nervous breakdown. Her autobiography reveals her as a woman of iron will, but also as one who was constantly troubled by periods of severe fatigue and lethargy, against which she fought constantly. Her formidable output of writing, traveling, and lecturing, in the years after her first marriage, would seem to have been wrested from a slim budget of energy, but energy so carefully hoarded and di-

---

[14] Ibid., pp. 83, 87–8, 89, 91.
[15] Ibid., p. 96.
[16] Ibid.

rected that it sustained her through over thirty years as a leading feminist writer and lecturer.

In 1890 Charlotte Perkins Stetson moved to California, where, struggling for economic survival as a woman alone, she began lecturing on the status of women. The years between 1890 and 1894 were, she recalls, the hardest of her life. She was fighting against public opinion, against outright hostility, as she gave her lectures on socialism and freedom for women. She taught school, kept a boarding house, edited newspapers, all the time writing and speaking. She accepted her husband's new marriage to her best friend, to whom she relinquished her child, and this action led to even greater public hostility, of course, against which she had to fight. In the midst of this most difficult period of her life she produced "The Yellow Wallpaper."

The story is narrated with clinical precision and aesthetic tact. The curt, chopped sentences, the brevity of the paragraphs, which often consist of only one or two sentences, convey the taut, distraught mental state of the narrator. The style creates a controlled tension: everything is low key and understated. The stance of the narrator is all, and it is a very complex stance indeed, since she is ultimately mad and yet, throughout her descent into madness, in many ways more sensible than the people who surround and cripple her. As she tells her story the reader has confidence in the reasonableness of her arguments and explanations.

The narrator is a woman who has been taken to the country by her husband in an effort to cure her of some undefined illness—a kind of nervous fatigue. Although her husband, a doctor, is presented as kindly and well meaning, it is soon apparent that his treatment of his wife, guided as it is by nineteenth-century attitudes toward women, is an important source of her affliction and a perhaps inadvertent but nonetheless vicious abettor of it. Here is a woman who, as she tries to explain to anyone who will listen, wants very much to *work*. Specifically, she wants to write (and the story she is narrating is her desperate and secret attempt both to engage in work that is meaningful to her and to retain her sanity). But the medical advice she receives, from her doctor/husband, from her brother, also a doctor, and from S. Weir Mitchell, explicitly referred to in the story, is that she do nothing. The prescribed cure is total rest and total emptiness of mind. While she craves intellectual stimulation and activity, and at one point poignantly expresses her wish for "advice and companionship" (one can read today respect and equality) in her work, what she receives is the standard treatment meted out to women in a patriarchal society. Thus her husband sees her as a "blessed little goose."[17] She is his "little girl" and she must take care of herself for his sake. Her role is to be "a rest and comfort to him." That he often laughs at her is, she notes forlornly and almost casually at one point, only what one expects in marriage.

Despite her pleas he will not take her away from this house in the country which she hates. What he does, in fact, is choose for her a room in the house that was formerly a nursery. It is a room with barred windows originally intended to prevent small children from falling out. It is the room with the fateful yellow wallpaper. The narrator herself had preferred a room downstairs; but this is 1890 and, to use Virginia Woolf's phrase, there is no choice for this wife of "a room of one's own."

Without such choice, however, the woman has been emotionally and intellec-

---

[17] "The Yellow Wall-Paper," *The New England Magazine,* May 1892, p. 649.

tually violated. In fact, her husband instills guilt in her. They have come to the country, he says "solely on [her] account." Yet this means that he must be away all day, and many nights, dealing with his patients.

The result in the woman is subterfuge. With her husband she cannot be her true self but must pose; and this, as she says, "makes me very tired." Finally, the fatigue and the subterfuge are unbearable. Increasingly she concentrates her attention on the wallpaper in her room—a paper of a sickly yellow that both disgusts and fascinates her. Gilman works out the symbolism of the wallpaper beautifully, without ostentation. For, despite all the elaborate descriptive detail devoted to it, the wallpaper remains mysteriously, hauntingly undefined and only vaguely visuable. But such, of course, is the situation of this wife, who identifies herself with the paper. The paper symbolizes her situation as seen by the men who control her and hence her situation as seen by herself. How can she define herself?

The wallpaper consists of "lame uncertain curves" that suddenly "commit suicide—destroy themselves in unheard-of contradictions." There are pointless patterns in the paper, which the narrator nevertheless determines to pursue to some conclusion. Fighting for her identity, for some sense of independent self, she observes the wallpaper and notes that just as she is about to find some pattern and meaning in it, it "slaps you in the face, knocks you down, and tramples upon you."

Inevitably, therefore, the narrator, imprisoned within the room, thinks she discerns the figure of a woman behind the paper. The paper is barred—that is part of what pattern it has, and the woman is trapped behind the bars, trying to get free. Ultimately, in the narrator's distraught state, there are a great many women behind the patterned bars, all trying to get free.

Given the morbid social situation that by now the wallpaper has come to symbolize, it is no wonder that the narrator begins to see it as staining everything it touches. The sickly yellow color runs off, she imagines, on her husband's clothes as well as on her own.

But this woman, whom we have come to know so intimately in the course of her narrative, and to admire for her heroic efforts to retain her sanity despite all opposition, never does get free. Her insights, and her desperate attempts to define and thus cure herself by tracing the bewildering pattern of the wallpaper and deciphering its meaning, are poor weapons against the male certainty of her husband, whose attitude toward her is that "bless her little heart" he will *allow* her to be "as sick as she pleases."

It is no surprise to find, therefore, that at the end of the story the narrator both does and does not identify with the creeping women who surround her in her hallucinations. The women creep out of the wallpaper, they creep through the arbors and lanes and along the roads outside the house. Women must creep. The narrator knows this. She has fought as best she could against creeping. In her perceptivity and in her resistance lie her heroism (her heroineism). But at the end of the story, on her last day in the house, as she peels off yards and yards of wallpaper and creeps around the floor, she has been defeated. She is totally mad.

But in her mad-sane way she has seen the situation of women for what it is. She has wanted to strangle the woman behind the paper—tie her with a rope. For that woman, the tragic product of her society, is of course the narrator's self. By rejecting that woman she might free the other, imprisoned woman within herself. But the only available rejection is suicidal, and hence she descends into madness. Madness is her only freedom, as, crawling around the room, she screams at her husband that she has finally "got out"—outside the wallpaper—and can't be put back.[18]

Earlier in the story the heroine gnawed with her teeth at the nailed-down bed in her room: excruciating proof of her sense of imprisonment. Woman as prisoner; woman as child or cripple; woman, even, as a fungus growth, when at one point in her narrative the heroine describes the women whom she envisions behind the wallpaper as "strangled heads and bulbous eyes and waddling fungus growths." These images permeate Gilman's story. If they are the images men had of women, and hence that women had of themselves, it is not surprising that madness and suicide bulk large in the work of late nineteenth-century women writers. "Much madness is divinest sense . . . Much sense the starkest madness," Emily Dickinson had written some decades earlier; and she had chosen spinsterhood as one way of rejecting society's "requirements" regarding woman's role as wife. One thinks, too, of Edith Wharton's *The House of Mirth,* with its heroine, Lily Bart, "manacled" by the bracelets she wears. Raised as a decorative item, with no skills or training, Lily must find a husband, if she is to have any economic security. Her bracelets, intended to entice young bachelors, are really her chains. Lily struggles against her fate, trying to retain her independence and her moral integrity. In the end, however, she commits suicide.

Such suicides as that of Lily, or of Kate Chopin's heroine mentioned earlier, as well as the madness that descends upon the heroine in "The Yellow Wallpaper," are all deliberate dramatic indictments, by women writers, of the crippling social pressures imposed on women in the nineteenth century and the sufferings they thereby endured: women who could not attend college although their brothers could; women expected to devote themselves, their lives, to aging and ailing parents; women treated as toys or as children and experiencing who is to say how much loss of self-confidence as a result. It is to this entire class of defeated, or even destroyed women, to this large body of wasted, or semi-wasted talent, that "The Yellow Wallpaper" is addressed.

The heroine in "The Yellow Wallpaper" is destroyed. She has fought her best against husband, brother, doctor, and even against women friends (her husband's sister, for example, is "a perfect and enthusiastic housekeeper, and hopes for no better profession"). She has tried, in defiance of all the social and medical codes of her time, to retain her sanity and her individuality. But the odds are against her and she fails.

Charlotte Perkins Stetson Gilman did not fail. She had been blighted, damaged, like the heroine in her story, by society's attitudes toward women. But having written the story she transcended the heroine's fate—although at what inner cost we shall never know. She went on to carve out a famous career as a feminist lecturer and writer. From the 1890s until about 1920 she was in demand as a speaker both in the United States and abroad, and her books were read on both continents. The books, especially *Women and Economics,* attacked the social and economic system that enslaved and humiliated women. About this enslavement

[18] At this point, at the end of her story, Gilman has the narrator say to her husband, "I've got out at last, . . . in spite of you and Jane." There has been no previous reference to a "Jane" in the story, and so one must speculate as to the reference. It could conceivably be a printer's error, since there are both a Julia and a Jennie in the story (Jennie is the housekeeper and functions as a guardian/imprisoner for the heroine, and Julia is an ineffectual female relative). On the other hand, it could be that Gilman is referring here to the narrator herself, to the narrator's sense that she had gotten free of both her husband and her "Jane" self: free, that is, of herself as defined by marriage and society.

and humiliation she was adamant, as some of her more striking metaphors show:
That women are kept, like horses:

> The labor of women in the house, certainly, enables men to produce more
> wealth than they otherwise could; and in this way women are economic factors
> in society. But so are horses. The labor of horses enables men to produce more
> wealth than they otherwise could. The horse is an economic factor in society.
> But the horse is not economically independent, nor is the woman.[19]

That women are used like cows:

> The wild cow is a female. She has healthy calves, and milk enough for them.
> And that is all the femininity she needs. Otherwise than that she is bovine
> rather than feminine. She is a light, strong, swift, sinewy creature, able to run,
> jump and fight, if necessary. We, for economic uses, have artificially developed
> the cow's capacity for producing milk. She has become a walking milk-
> machine, bred and tended to that express end, her value measured in quarts.[20]

Women's ineffectual domestic status was the target of some of Gilman's strongest attacks. As she said elsewhere in *Women and Economics,* the same world exists
for women as for men,

> the same human energies and human desires and ambitions within. But all
> that she may wish to have, all that she may wish to do, must come through a
> single channel and a single choice. Wealth, power, social distinction, fame—
> not only these, but home and happiness, reputation, ease and pleasure, her
> bread and butter,—all, must come to her through a small gold ring.[21]

The damaging effects on women of being manacled to that small gold ring she
explored in detail. Women are bred for marriage, yet they cannot actively pursue
it but must sit passively and wait to be chosen. The result is strain and hypocrisy,
and an overemphasis on sex or "femininity." "For, in her position of economic
dependence in the sex-relation, sex-distinction is with her not only a means of
attracting a mate, as with all creatures, but a means of getting her livelihood, as is
the case with no other creature under heaven."[22]

Gilman was not opposed to the home nor to domestic work. She believed
indeed that the home tended to produce such qualities, necessary for the development of the human race, as kindness and caring. But her evolutionary approach to social change enabled her to see that the institution of the home had
not developed consonant to the development of other institutions in society.
Women, and children, were imprisoned within individual homes, where the
women had no recognized economic independence and the children often suffocated, "noticed, studied, commented on, and incessantly interfered with. . . .
How can they grow up without injury?"[23] For, she argued, in the home as presently established there can be neither freedom nor equality. Rather, there is

---

[19] *Women and Economics,* p. 13.

[20] Ibid., pp. 43–44.

[21] Ibid. p. 71.

[22] Ibid., p. 38.

[23] *The Home: Its Work and Influence* (New York: Charlton Co., 1910), pp. 40–41.

"ownership": a dominant father, a more or less subservient mother, and an utterly dependent child. Injustice, rather than justice, was the result.

In her attack on the nuclear family Gilman thus anticipated many current complaints. Or, one should rather say, that more than half a century after she began her campaign against women's subservient status we are still struggling with the problems she diagnosed and described.

Her suggested solutions included community kitchens, whereby the work of cooking would be more efficiently and sociably performed, leaving those women free for other occupations who were not adept at this particular skill but meanwhile making that skill economically respectable; and childcare centers—even if only play space on walled-in roofs of city apartment buildings—to release the child and the mother from the tyranny of the individual family.

Work must be respected: this was one of Gilman's basic tenets, but women must be admitted into the human work world on equal terms with men. The domestic work they do must be respected, and they must be free to do other kinds of work as well. Gilman believed in continuing human progress (she wrote a utopian novel, *Moving the Mountain,* in which women had achieved true equality with men), and she saw the situation of women in the nineteenth century as thwarting this progress as well as thwarting their own development. For some human beings to be classified as horses, or cows, or sexual objects, was to impoverish not only themselves but human society as a whole.

She herself refused to be so thwarted. In 1900 she married her cousin, George Houston Gilman, and she continued to work until the day when she chose her own death. Suffering from breast cancer, she chose not to be a burden to others. She took chloroform and died. It was her final willed choice.

ESCAPING THE SENTENCE: DIAGNOSIS AND DISCOURSE IN "THE YELLOW WALLPAPER"*

By Paula A. Treichler

Almost immediately in Charlotte Perkins Gilman's story "The Yellow Wallpaper," the female narrator tells us she is "sick." Her husband, "a physician of high standing," has diagnosed her as having a "temporary nervous depression—a slight hysterical tendency."[1] Yet her journal—in whose words the story unfolds—records her own resistance to this diagnosis and, tentatively, her suspicion that the medical treatment it dictates—treatment that confines her to a room in an isolated country estate—will not cure her. She suggests that the diagnosis itself, by undermining her own conviction that her "condition" is serious and real, may indeed be one reason why she does not get well.

A medical diagnosis is a verbal formula representing a constellation of physical symptoms and observable behaviors. Once formulated, it dictates a series of therapeutic actions. In "The Yellow Wallpaper," the diagnosis of hysteria or depression, conventional "women's diseases" of the nineteenth century, sets in motion a therapeutic regimen which involves language in several ways. The nar-

* Originally published in *Tulsa Studies in Women's Literature* 3 (1984): 61–77.
[1] Charlotte Perkins Gilman, *The Yellow Wallpaper* (Old Westbury, New York: The Feminist Press, 1973), p. 13. Subsequent references are cited parenthetically in the text.

rator is forbidden to engage in normal social conversation; her physical isolation is in part designed to remove her from the possibility of over-stimulating intellectual discussion. She is further encouraged to exercise "self-control" and avoid expressing negative thoughts and fears about her illness; she is also urged to keep her fancies and superstitions in check. Above all, she is forbidden to "work"—to write. Learning to monitor her own speech, she develops an artificial feminine self who reinforces the terms of her husband's expert diagnosis: this self attempts to speak reasonably and in "a very quiet voice," refrains from crying in his presence, and hides the fact that she is keeping a journal. This male-identified self disguises the true underground narrative: a confrontation with language.

Because she does not feel free to speak truthfully "to a living soul," she confides her thoughts to a journal—"dead paper"—instead. The only safe language is dead language. But even the journal is not altogether safe. The opening passages are fragmented as the narrator retreats from topic after topic (the first journal entry consists of 39 separate paragraphs). The three points at which her language becomes more discursive carry more weight by contrast. These passages seem at first to involve seemingly unobjectionable, safe topics: the house, her room, and the room's yellow wallpaper. Indeed, the very first mention of the wallpaper expresses conventional hyperbole: "I never saw worse paper in my life." But the language at once grows unexpected and intense:

> One of those sprawling flamboyant patterns committing every artistic sin.
> It is dull enough to confuse the eye in following, pronounced enough to constantly irritate and provoke study, and when you follow the lame uncertain curves for a little distance they suddenly commit suicide—plunge off at outrageous angles, destroy themselves in unheard of contradictions (13).

Disguised as an acceptable feminine topic (interest in decor), the yellow wallpaper comes to occupy the narrator's entire reality. Finally, she rips it from the walls to reveal its real meaning. Unveiled, the yellow wallpaper is a metaphor for women's discourse. From a conventional perspective, it first seems strange, flamboyant, confusing, outrageous: the very act of women's writing produces discourse which embodies "unheard of contradictions." Once freed, it expresses what is elsewhere kept hidden and embodies patterns that the patriarchal order ignores, suppresses, fears as grotesque, or fails to perceive at all. Like all good metaphors, the yellow wallpaper is variously interpreted by readers to represent (among other things) the "pattern" which underlies sexual inequality, the external manifestation of neurasthenia, the narrator's unconscious, the narrator's situation within patriarchy.[2] But an emphasis on discourse—writing, the act of speaking, lan-

---

[2] Umberto Eco describes a "good metaphor" as one which, like a good joke, offers a shortcut through the labyrinth of limitless semiosis. "Metaphor, Dictionary, and Encyclopedia," *New Literary History,* 15 (Winter 1984), 255–71. Though there is relatively little criticism on "The Yellow Wallpaper" to date, the wallpaper seems to be a fruitful metaphor for discussions of madness, women's relationship to medicine, sexual inequality, marriage, economic dependence, and sexuality. An introduction to these issues is provided by Elaine R. Hedges in her "Afterword," *The Yellow Wallpaper,* pp. 37–63 (pp. 514–523 in this anthology). Hedges also cites a number of nineteenth-century responses to the story. A useful though condescending discussion of the story in the light of Gilman's own life is Mary A. Hill, "Charlotte Perkins Gilman: A Feminist's Struggle with Womanhood," *Massachusetts Review,* 21 (Fall 1980), 503–26. A Bachelardian critical reading is Mary Beth Pringle, " 'La Poetique De L'Espace' in Charlotte Perkins Gilman's 'The Yellow Wallpaper,' " *The French-American Review,* 3 (Winter 1978/ Spring 1979), 15–22. See also Loralee MacPike, "Environment as Psychopathological Symbolism in 'The Yellow Wallpaper,' " *American Literary Realism 1870–1910,* 8 (Summer 1975), 286–88, and Beate Schopp-Schilling, " 'The Yellow Wallpaper': A Rediscovered 'Realistic' Story," *American Literary Realism 1870–1910,* 8 (Summer 1975), 284–86.

guage—draws us to the central issue in this particular story: the narrator's alienation from work, writing, and intellectual life. Thus the story is inevitably
concerned with the complicated and charged relationship between women and
language: analysis then illuminates particular points of conflict between patriarchal language and women's discourse. This conflict in turn raises a number of
questions relevant for both literary and feminist scholarship: In what senses can
language be said to be oppressive to women? How do feminist linguistic innovations seek to escape this oppression? What is the relationship of innovation to
material conditions? And what does it mean, theoretically, to escape the sentence
that the structure of patriarchal language imposes?

i. The Yellow Wallpaper

The narrator of "The Yellow Wallpaper" has come with her husband to an isolated country estate for the summer. The house, a "colonial mansion," has been
untenanted for years through some problem with inheritance. It is "the most
beautiful place!" The grounds contain "hedges and walls and gates that lock, and
lots of separate little houses for the gardeners and people" (11). Despite this
palatial potential to accommodate many people, the estate is virtually deserted
with nothing growing in its greenhouses. The narrator perceives "something
queer about it" and believes it may be haunted.

She is discouraged in this and other fancies by her sensible physician-husband
who credits only what is observable, scientific, or demonstrable through facts and
figures. He has scientifically diagnosed his wife's condition as merely "a temporary nervous depression"; her brother, also a noted physician, concurs in this
opinion. Hence husband and wife have come as physician and patient to this
solitary summer mansion in quest of cure. The narrator reports her medical
regimen to her journal, together with her own view of the problem:

> So I take phosphates or phosphites—whichever it is, and tonics, and jour-
> neys, and air, and exercise, and am absolutely forbidden to "work" until I am
> well again.
> Personally, I disagree with their ideas.
> Personally, I believe that congenial work, with excitement and change,
> would do me good.
> But what is one to do?(10).

Her room at the top of the house seems once to have been a nursery or a playroom with bars on the windows and "rings and things on the walls." The room
contains not much more than a mammoth metal bed. The ugly yellow wallpaper has
been stripped off in patches—perhaps by the children who formerly inhabited the
room. In this "atrocious nursery" the narrator increasingly spends her time. Her
husband is often away on medical cases, her baby makes her nervous, and no other
company is permitted her. Disturbed by the wallpaper, she asks for another room
or for different paper; her husband urges her not to give way to her "fancies."
Further, he claims that any change would lead to more change: "after the wallpaper was changed it would be the heavy bedstead, and then the barred windows,
and then that gate at the head of the stairs, and so on"(14). So no changes are
made, and the narrator is left alone with her "imaginative power and habit of story-
making" (15). In this stimulus-deprived environment, the "pattern" of the wallpaper becomes increasingly compelling: the narrator gradually becomes intimate
with its "principle of design" and unconventional connections. The figure of a

woman begins to take shape behind the superficial pattern of the paper. The more the wallpaper comes alive, the less inclined is the narrator to write in her journal—"dead paper." Now with three weeks left of the summer and her relationship with the wallpaper more and more intense, she asks once more to be allowed to leave. Her husband refuses: "I cannot possibly leave town just now. Of course if you were in any danger, I could and would, but you really are better, dear, whether you can see it or not. I am a doctor, dear, and I know" (23). She expresses the fear that she is not getting well. "Bless her little heart!" he responds, "She shall be as sick as she pleases" (24). When she hesitantly voices the belief that she may be losing her mind, he reproaches her so vehemently that she says no more. Instead, in the final weeks of the summer, she gives herself up to the wallpaper. "Life is very much more exciting now than it used to be," she tells her journal. "You see I have something more to expect, to look forward to, to watch. I really do eat better, and am more quiet than I was" (27). She reports that her husband judges her "to be flourishing in spite of my wall-paper."

She begins to strip off the wallpaper at every opportunity in order to free the woman she perceives is trapped inside. She becomes increasingly aware of this woman and other female figures creeping behind the surface pattern of the wallpaper: there is a hint that the room's previous female occupant has left behind the marks of her struggle for freedom. Paranoid by now, the narrator attempts to disguise her obsession with the wallpaper. On the last day, she locks herself in the room and succeeds in stripping off most of the remaining paper. When her husband comes home and finally unlocks the door, he is horrified to find her creeping along the walls of the room. "I've got out at last," she tells him triumphantly, "And I've pulled off most of the paper, so you can't put me back" (36). Her husband faints, and she is obliged to step over him each time she circles the room.

"The Yellow Wallpaper" was read by nineteenth-century readers as a harrowing case study of neurasthenia. Even recent readings have treated the narrator's madness as a function of her individual psychological situation. A feminist reading emphasizes the social and economic conditions which drive the narrator—and potentially all women—to madness. In these readings, the yellow wallpaper represents (1) the narrator's own mind, (2) the narrator's unconscious, (3) the "pattern" of social and economic dependence which reduces women to domestic slavery. The woman in the wallpaper represents (1) the narrator herself, gone mad, (2) the narrator's unconscious, (3) all women. While these interpretations are plausible and fruitful, I interpret the wallpaper to be women's writing or women's discourse, and the woman in the wallpaper to be the representation of women that becomes possible only after women obtain the right to speak. In this reading, the yellow wallpaper stands for a new vision of women—one which is constructed differently from the representation of women in patriarchal language. The story is thus in part about the clash between two modes of discourse: one powerful, "ancestral," and dominant; the other new, "impertinent," and visionary. The story's outcome makes a statement about the relationship of a visionary feminist project to material reality.

ii. Diagnosis and Discourse

It is significant that the narrator of "The Yellow Wallpaper" is keeping a journal, confiding to "dead paper" the unorthodox thoughts and perceptions she is reluctant to tell to a "living soul." Challenging and subverting the expert prescription that forbids her to write, the journal evokes a sense of urgency and danger. "There comes John," she tells us at the end of her first entry, "and I must put this away—he hates to have me write a word" (13). We, her readers, are thus from the beginning her confidantes, implicated in forbidden discourse.

Contributing to our suspense and sense of urgency is the ambiguity of the narrator's "condition," whose etiology is left unstated in the story. For her physician-husband, it is a medical condition of unknown origin to be medically managed. Certain imagery (the "ghostliness" of the estate, the "trouble" with the heirs) suggests hereditary disease. Other evidence points toward psychological causes (e.g., postpartum depression, failure to adjust to marriage and mother-hood). A feminist analysis moves beyond such localized causes to implicate the economic and social conditions which, under patriarchy, make women domestic slaves. In any case, the fact that the origin of the narrator's condition is never made explicit intensifies the role of diagnosis in putting a name to her "condi-tion."

Symptoms are crucial for the diagnostic process. The narrator reports, among other things, exhaustion, crying, nervousness, synesthesia, anger, paranoia, and hallucination. "Temporary nervous depression" (coupled with a "slight hysteri-cal tendency") is the medical term that serves to diagnose or define these symp-toms. Once pronounced, and reinforced by the second opinion of the narrator's brother, this diagnosis not only names reality but also has considerable power over what that reality is now to be: it dictates the narrator's removal to the "ancestral halls" where the story is set and generates a medical therapeutic regimen that includes physical isolation, "phosphates or phosphites," air, and rest. Above all, it forbids her to "work." The quotation marks, registering her husband's per-spective, discredit the equation of writing with true work. The diagnostic language of the physician is coupled with the paternalistic language of the husband to create a formidable array of controls over her behavior.

I use "diagnosis," then, as a metaphor for the voice of medicine or science that speaks to define women's condition. Diagnosis is powerful and public; represent-ing institutional authority, it dictates that money, resources, and space are to be expended as consequences in the "real world." It is a male voice that privileges the rational, the practical, and the observable. It is the voice of male logic and male judgment which dismisses superstition and refuses to see the house as haunted or the narrator's condition as serious. It imposes controls on the female narrator and dictates how she is to perceive and talk about the world. It is en-forced by the "ancestral halls" themselves: the rules are followed even when the physician-husband is absent. In fact, the opening imagery—"ancestral halls," "a colonial mansion," "a haunted house"—legitimizes the diagnostic process by placing it firmly within an institutional frame: medicine, marriage, patriarchy. All function in the story to define and prescribe.

In contrast, the narrator in her nursery room speaks privately to her journal. At first she expresses her views hesitantly, "personally." Her language includes a number of stereotypical features of "women's language": not only are its topics limited, it is marked formally by exclamation marks, italics, intensifiers, and rep-etition of the impotent refrain, "What is one to do?"[3] The journal entries at this

---

[3] "Women's language" is discussed in Robin Lakoff, *Language and Woman's Place* (New York: Harper and Row, 1975); Casey Miller and Kate Swift, *Words and Women* (New York: Anchor/Doubleday, 1976); Barrie Thorne, Cheris Kramarae, and Nancy Henley, eds., "Introduction," *Language, Gender and Society* (Rowley, Mass.: Newbury House, 1983); Cheris Kramarae, *Women and Men Speaking* (Rowley, Mass.: Newbury House, 1981); Sally McConnell-Ginet, Ruth Borker, and Nelly Furman, eds., *Women and Language in Literature and Society* (New York: Praeger, 1980); Mary Ritchie Key, *Male/Female Language* (Metuchen, New Jersey: Scarecrow Press, 1975); and Paula A. Treichler, "Verbal Subversions in Dorothy Parker: 'Trapped like a Trap in a Trap,' " *Language and Style*, 13 (Fall 1980), 46–61.

early stage are very tentative and clearly shaped under the stern eye of male judgment. Oblique references only hint at an alternative reality. The narrator writes, for example, that the wallpaper has been "'torn off'" and "'stripped away,'" yet she does not say by whom. Her qualms about her medical diagnosis and treatment remain unspoken except in her journal, which functions only as a private respite, a temporary relief. "Dead paper," it is not truly subversive.

Nevertheless, the narrator's language almost from the first does serve to call into question both the diagnosis of her condition and the rules established to treat it. As readers, therefore, we are not permitted wholehearted confidence in the medical assessment of the problem. It is not that we doubt the existence of her "condition," for it obviously causes genuine suffering; but we come to doubt that the diagnosis names the real problem—the narrator seems to place her own inverted commas around the words "temporary nervous depression" and "slight hysterical tendency"—and perceive that whatever its nature it is exacerbated by the rules established for its cure.

For this reason, we are alert to the possibility of an alternative vision. The yellow wallpaper provides it. Representing a different reality, it is "living paper," aggressively alive: "You think you have mastered it, but just as you get well underway in following, it turns a back-somersault and there you are. It slaps you in the face, knocks you down, and tramples upon you. It is like a bad dream" (25). The narrator's husband refuses to replace the wallpaper, "whitewash" the room, or let her change rooms altogether on the grounds that other changes will then be demanded. The wallpaper is to remain: acknowledgment of its reality is the first step toward freedom. Confronting it at first through male eyes, the narrator is repelled and speculates that the children who inhabited the room before her attacked it for its ugliness. There is thus considerable resistance to the wallpaper and an implied rejection of what it represents, even by young children.

But the wallpaper exerts its power and, at the same time, the narrator's journal entries falter; "I don't know why I should write this" (21), she says, about halfway through the story. She makes a final effort to be allowed to leave the room; when this fails, she becomes increasingly absorbed by the wallpaper and by the figure of a woman that exists behind its confusing surface pattern. This figure grows clearer to her, to the point where she can join her behind the paper and literally act within it. At this point, her language becomes bolder: she completes the predicates that were earlier left passively hanging. Describing joint action with the woman in the wallpaper, she tells us that the room has come to be damaged at the hands of women: "I pulled and she shook, I shook and she pulled, and before morning we had peeled off yards of that paper" (32); "I am getting angry enough to do something desperate" (34). From an increasingly distinctive perspective, she sees an alternative reality beneath the repellent surface pattern in which the figures of women are emerging. Her original perception is confirmed: the patriarchal house is indeed "haunted" by figures of women. The room is revealed as a prison inhabited by its former inmates, whose struggles have nearly destroyed it. Absorbed almost physically by "living paper"—writing—she strives to liberate the women trapped within the ancestral halls, women with whom she increasingly identifies. Once begun, liberation and identification are irreversible: "I've got out at last . . ." cries the narrator, "And I've pulled off most of the paper, so you can't put me back!" (36).

This ending of "The Yellow Wallpaper" is ambiguous and complex. Because the narrator's final proclamation is both triumphant and horrifying, madness in the story is both positive and negative. On the one hand, it testifies to an alternative reality and challenges patriarchy head on. The fact that her unflappable husband faints when he finds her establishes the dramatic power of her new freedom. Defying the judgment that she suffers from a "temporary nervous depression," she has followed her own logic, her own perceptions, her own projects to this final scene in which madness is seen as a kind of transcendent sanity. This engagement with the yellow wallpaper constitutes a form of the "work" which has been forbidden—women's writing. As she steps over the patriarchal body, she leaves the authoritative voice of diagnosis in shambles at her feet. Forsaking "women's language" forever, her new mode of speaking—an unlawful language—escapes "'the sentence" imposed by patriarchy.

On the other hand, there are consequences to be paid for this escape. As the ending of the narrative, her madness will no doubt commit her to more intense medical treatment, perhaps to the dreaded Weir Mitchell of whom her husband has spoken. The surrender of patriarchy is only temporary: her husband has merely fainted, after all, not died, and will no doubt move swiftly and severely to deal with her. Her individual escape is temporary and compromised.

But there is yet another sense in which "The Yellow Wallpaper" enacts a clash between diagnosis and women's discourse. Asked once whether the story was based on fact, Gilman replied "I had been as far as one could go and get back."[4] Gilman based the story on her own experience of depression and treatment. For her first visit to the noted neurologist S. Weir Mitchell, she prepared a detailed case history of her own illness, constructed in part from her journal entries. Mitchell was not impressed: he "only thought it proved conceit" (*The Living,* 95). He wanted obedience from patients, not information. "Wise women," he wrote elsewhere, "choose their doctors and trust them. The wisest ask the fewest questions."[5] Gilman reproduced in her journal Mitchell's prescription for her:

> Live as domestic a life as possible. Have your child with you all the time. (Be it remarked that if I did but dress the baby it left me shaking and crying—certainly far from a healthy companionship for her to say nothing of the effect on me.) Lie down an hour after every meal. Have but two hours intellectual life a day. And never touch pen, brush or pencil as long as you live (*The Living,* 96).

Gilman spent several months trying to follow Mitchell's prescription, a period of intense suffering for her:

> I could not read nor write nor paint nor sew nor talk nor listen to talking, nor anything. I lay on that lounge and wept all day. The tears ran down into my ears on either side. I went to bed crying, woke in the night crying, sat on the edge of the bed in the morning and cried—from sheer continuous pain (*The Living,* 121).

At last, in a "moment of clear vision," Gilman realized that for her the traditional domestic role was at least in part the cause of her distress. She left her husband and with her baby went to California to be a writer and a feminist activist. Three years later she wrote "The Yellow Wallpaper." After the story was published, she

[4] Charlotte Perkins Gilman, *The Living of Charlotte Perkins Gilman: An Autobiography* (New York: Appleton-Century, 1935), p. 121. Subsequent references are cited parenthetically in the text.
[5] S. Weir Mitchell, *Doctor and Patient* (Philadelphia: Lippincott, 1888), p. 48.

sent a copy to Mitchell. If it in any way influenced his treatment of women in the future, she wrote, "I have not lived in vain" (*The Living*, 121).

There are several points to note here with respect to women's discourse. Gilman's use of her own journal to create a fictional journal which in turn becomes a published short story problematizes and calls our attention to the journal form. The terms "depression" and "hysteria" signal a non-textual as well as a textual conundrum: contemporary readers could (and some did) read the story as a realistic account of madness; for feminist readers (then and now) who bring to the text some comprehension of medical attitudes toward women in the nineteenth century, such a non-ironic reading is not possible. Lest we miss Gilman's point, her use of a real proper name in her story, Weir Mitchell's, draws explicit attention to the world outside the text.[6]

Thus "The Yellow Wallpaper" is not merely a fictional challenge to the patriarchal diagnosis of women's condition. It is also a public critique of a real medical treatment. Publication of the story added power and status to Gilman's words and transformed the journal form from a private to a public setting. Her published challenge to diagnosis has now been read by thousands of readers. By living to tell the tale, the woman who writes escapes the sentence that condemns her to silence.

iii. Escaping the Sentence

To call "The Yellow Wallpaper" a struggle between diagnosis and discourse is to characterize the story in terms of language. More precisely, it is to contrast the signification procedures of patriarchal medicine with discursive disruptions that call those procedures into question. A major problem in "The Yellow Wallpaper" involves the relationship of the linguistic sign to the signified, of language to "reality." Diagnosis, highlighted from the beginning by the implicit inverted commas around diagnostic phrases ("a slight hysterical tendency"), stands in the middle of an equation which translates a phenomenological perception of the human body into a finite set of signs called "symptoms"—fever, exhaustion, nervousness, pallor, and so on—which are in turn assembled to produce a "diagnosis"; this sign generates treatment, a set of prescriptions that impinge once more upon the "'real" human body. Part of the power of diagnosis as a scientific

---

[6] A feminist understanding of medical treatment of women in the nineteenth century is, however, by no means uncomplicated. An analysis frequently quoted is that by Barbara Ehrenreich and Deirdre English, *For Her Own Good: 150 Years of the Experts' Advice to Women* (Garden City, New York: Anchor/Doubleday, 1979). Their analysis should be supplemented by Regina Morantz, "The Lady and her Physician," in *Clio's Consciousness Raised: New Perspectives on the History of Women*, eds. Mary S. Hartman and Lois Banner (New York: Harper Colophon, 1974), pp. 38–53; as well as by Ludi Jordanova, "Conceptualizing Power Over Women," *Radical Science Journal*, 12 (1982), 124–28. Attention to the progressive aspects of Weir Mitchell's treatment of women is given by Morantz and by Suzanne Poirier, "The Weir Mitchell Rest Cure: Four Women who 'Took Charge,'" paper presented at the conference Women's Health: Taking Care and Taking Charge, Morgantown, West Virginia, 1982 (Author's affiliation: Humanistic Studies Program, Health Sciences Center, University of Illinois at Chicago). See also Barbara Sicherman, "The Uses of Diagnosis: Doctors, Patients, and Neurasthenia," *Journal of the History of Medicine and Allied Sciences*, 32 (January 1977), 33–54; Carroll Smith-Rosenberg and Charles Rosenberg, "The Female Animal: Medical and Biological Views of Woman and Her Role in Nineteenth-Century America," rpt. in *Concepts of Health and Disease: Interdisciplinary Perspectives*, eds. Arthur Caplan, H. Tristram Engelhardt, Jr., and James J. McCartney (Reading, Mass.: Addison-Wesley, 1981), pp. 281–303; and Ann Douglas Wood, "'The Fashionable Diseases': Women's Complaints and Their Treatment in Nineteenth-Century America," in *Clio's Consciousness Raised: New Perspectives on the History of Women*, pp. 1–22.

process depends upon a notion of language as transparent, as *not* the issue. Rather the issue is the precision, efficiency, and plausibility with which a correct diagnostic sign is generated by a particular state of affairs that is assumed to exist in reality. In turn, the diagnostic sign is not complete until its clinical implications have been elaborated as a set of concrete therapeutic practices designed not merely to refer to but actually to change the original physical reality. Chary with its diagnostic categories (as specialized lexicons go), medicine's rich and intricate descriptive vocabulary testifies to the history of its mission: to translate the realities of the human body into human language and back again. As such, it is a perfect example of language which "reflects" reality and simultaneously "produces" it.[7]

Why is this interesting? And why is this process important in "The Yellow Wallpaper"? Medical diagnosis stands as a prime example of an authorized linguistic process (distilled, respected, high-paying) whose representational claims are strongly supported by social, cultural, and economic practices. Even more than most forms of male discourse, the diagnostic process is multiply-sanctioned.[8] "The Yellow Wallpaper" challenges both the particular "sentence" passed on the narrator and the elaborate sentencing process whose presumed representational power can sentence women to isolation, deprivation, and alienation from their own sentencing possibilities. The right to author or originate sentences is at the heart of the story and what the yellow wallpaper represents: a figure for women's discourse, it seeks to escape the sentence passed by medicine and patriarchy. Before looking more closely at what the story suggests about the nature of women's discourse, we need to place somewhat more precisely this notion of "the sentence."

Diagnosis is a "sentence" in that it is simultaneously a linguistic entity; a declaration or judgment, and a plan for action in the real world whose clinical consequences may spell dullness, drama, or doom for the diagnosed. Diagnosis may be, then, not merely a sentence but a death sentence. This doubling of the word "sentence" is not mere playfulness. "I sat down and began to speak," wrote Anna Kavan in *Asylum Piece*, describing the beginning of a woman's mental breakdown, "driving my sluggish tongue to frame words that seemed useless even before they were uttered." This physically exhausting process of producing sentences is generalized: "Sometimes I think that some secret court must have tried and condemned me, unheard, to this heavy sentence."[9] The word "sentence" is both sign and signified, word and act, declaration and discursive consequence. Its duality emphasizes the difficulty of an analysis which privileges purely semiotic relationships on the one hand or the representational nature of language on the other. In "The Yellow Wallpaper," the diagnosis of hysteria may be a sham: it may be socially constituted or merely individually expedient quite apart from even a conventional representational relationship. But it dictates a rearrangement of

---

[7] The notion that diagnosis is socially constituted through doctor-patient interaction is discussed by Marianne A. Paget, "On the Work of Talk: Studies in Misunderstanding," in *The Social Organization of Doctor-Patient Communication*, eds. Sue Fisher and Alexandra Dundas Todd (Washington, D.C.: Center for Applied Linguistics, 1983), pp. 55–74. See also Barbara Sicherman, "The Uses of Diagnosis."

[8] Discussions of the multiple sanctions for medicine and science include Shelley Day, "Is Obstetric Technology Depressing?" *Radical Science Journal*, 12 (1982), 17–45; Donna J. Haraway, "In the Beginning was the Word: The Genesis of Biological Theory," *Signs*, 6 (Spring 1981), 469–81; Bruno Latour and Steve Woolgar, *Laboratory Life: Social Construction of Scientific Facts* (Beverly Hills: Sage, 1979); Evan Stark, "What is Medicine?" *Radical Science Journal*, 12 (1982), 46–89; and P. Wright and A. Treacher, eds., *The Problem of Medical Knowledge* (Edinburgh: Edinburgh University Press, 1982).

[9] Anna Kavan, *Asylum Piece* (1940; rpt. New York: Michael Kesend, 1981), pp. 63, 65.

material reality nevertheless. The sentence may be unjust, inaccurate, or irrelevant, but the sentence is served anyway.[10]

The sentence is of particular importance in modern linguistics, where it has dominated inquiry for twenty-five years and for more than seventy years has been the upper cut-off point for the study of language: consideration of word sequences and meaning beyond the sentence has been typically dismissed as too untidy and speculative for linguistic science. The word "sentence" also emphasizes the technical concentration, initiated by structuralism but powerfully developed by transformational grammar, on syntax (formal grammatical structure at the sentence level). The formulaic sentence S→NP+VP which initiates the familiar tree diagram of linguistic analysis could well be said to exemplify the tyranny of syntax over the study of semantics (meaning) and pragmatics (usage). As a result, as Sally McConnell-Ginet has argued, linguistics has often failed to address those aspects of language with which women have been most concerned: on the one hand, the semantic or non-linguistic conditions underlying given grammatical structures, and on the other, the contextual circumstances in which linguistic structures are actually used.[11] One can generalize and say that signs alone are of less interest to women than are the processes of signification which link signs to semantic and pragmatic aspects of speaking. To "escape the sentence" is to move beyond the boundaries of formal syntax.

But is it to move beyond language? In writing about language over the last fifteen years, most feminist scholars in the United States have argued that language creates as well as reflects reality and hence that feminist linguistic innovation helps foster more enlightened social conditions for women. A more conservative position holds that language merely reflects social reality and that linguistic reform is hollow unless accompanied by changes in attitudes and socio-economic conditions that also favor women's equality. Though different, particularly in their support for innovation, both positions more or less embody a view that there is a non-linguistic reality to which language is related in sys-

---

[10] Reviewing medical evidence in "The Yellow Wallpaper," Suzanne Poirier suggests that a diagnosis of "neurasthenia" would have been more precise but that in any case, given the narrator's symptoms, the treatment was inappropriate and probably harmful. " 'The Yellow Wallpaper' as Medical Case History," paper presented to the Faculty Seminar in Medicine and Society, University of Illinois College of Medicine at Urbana-Champaign, April 13, 1983. On the more general point, two recent contrasting analyses are offered by Umberto Eco, "Metaphor, Dictionary, Encyclopedia," who poses a world of language resonant with purely semiotic, intertextual relationships, and John Haiman, "Dictionaries and Encyclopedias," *Lingua*, 50 (1980), 329–57, who argues for the total interrelatedness of linguistic and cultural knowledge.

[11] Sally McConnell-Ginet, "Linguistics and the Feminist Challenge," in *Women and Language in Literature and Society*, pp. 3–25. The linguistic formula S→NP+VP means that Sentence is rewritten as (consists of) Noun Phrase + Verb Phrase. Sentences are "generated" as tree diagrams that move downward from the abstract entity S to individual components of actual sentences. It could be said that linguistics misses the forest for the trees. But the fact that the study of women and language *has* concentrated on meaning and usage does not mean that syntax might not be relevant for feminist analysis. Potentially fruitful areas might include analysis of passive versus active voice (for example, see my "The Construction of Ambiguity in *The Awakening*: A Linguistic Analysis," in *Women and Language in Literature and Society*, pp. 239–57), of nominalization (a linguistic process particularly characteristic of male bureaucracies and technologies), of cases (showing underlying agency and other relationships), of negation and interrogation (two grammatical processes implicated by "women's language," Note 3), and of the relationship between deep and surface structure. Julia Penelope Stanley has addressed a number of these areas; see, for example, "Passive Motivation," *Foundations of Language*, 13 (1975), 25–39. Pronominalization, of course, has been a focus for feminist analysis for some time.

tematic ways.[12] Recent European writing challenges the transparency of such a division, arguing that at some level reality is inescapably linguistic. The account of female development within this framework emphasizes the point at which the female child comes into language (and becomes a being now called female); because she is female, she is from the first alienated from the processes of symbolic representation. Within this symbolic order, a phallocentric order, she is frozen, confined, curtailed, limited, and represented as "lack," as "other." To make a long story short, there is as yet no escaping the sentence of male-determining discourse.[13]

According to this account, "the sentence," for women, is inescapably bound up with the symbolic order. Within language, says Luce Irigaray for example, women's fate is a "death sentence."[14] Irigaray's linguistic innovations attempt to disrupt this "law of the father" and exemplify the possibilities for a female language which "has nothing to do with the syntax which we have used for centuries, namely, that constructed according to the following organization: subject, predicate, or, subject, verb, object."[15] Whatever the realities of that particular claim, at the moment there are persuasive theoretical, professional, and political reasons for feminists to pay attention to what I will now more officially call discourse, which encompasses linguistic and formalistic considerations, yet goes beyond strict formalism to include both semantics and pragmatics. It is thus concerned not merely with speech, but with the conditions of speaking. With this notion of "sentencing," I have tried to suggest a process of language production in which an individual word, speech, or text is linked to the conditions under which it was (and could have been) produced as well as to those under which it is (and could be) read and interpreted. Thus the examination of diagnosis and discourse in a text is at once a study of a set of representational practices, of mechanisms for control and opportunities for resistance, and of communicational possibilities in fiction and elsewhere.[16]

In "The Yellow Wallpaper" we see consequences of the "'death sentence." Woman is represented as childlike and dysfunctional. Her complaints are wholly circular, merely confirming the already-spoken patriarchal diagnosis. She is constituted and defined within the patriarchal order of language and destined, like Athena in Irigaray's analysis, to repeat her father's discourse "without much

---

[12] See, for example, Maija Blaubergs, "An Analysis of Classic Arguments Against Changing Sexist Language," in *The Voices and Words of Women and Men*, ed. Cheris Kramarae (Oxford: Pergamon Press, 1980), pp. 135–47; Francine Frank, "Women's Language in America: Myth and Reality," in *Women's Language and Style*, eds. Douglas Butturff and Edmund L. Epstein (Akron, Ohio: L&S Books, 1978), pp. 47–61; Mary Daly, *Gyn/Ecology* (Boston: Beacon, 1978); and Wendy Martyna, "The Psychology of the Generic Masculine," in *Women and Language in Literature and Society*, pp. 69–78. A general source is Barrie Thorne, Cheris Kramarae, and Nancy Henley, eds., *Language, Gender and Society* (Rowley, Mass.: Newbury House, 1983).

[13] See, for example, Juliet Mitchell and Jacqueline Rose, eds., *Feminine Sexuality: Jacques Lacan and the école freudienne* (New York: W. W. Norton, 1982), pp. 1–57.

[14] Luce Irigaray, "Veiled Lips," trans. Sara Speidel, *Mississippi Review*, 33 (Winter/Spring 1983), 99. See also Luce Irigaray, "Women's Exile: Interview with Luce Irigaray," trans. Couze Venn, *Ideology and Consciousness*, 1 (1977), 62–76; and Cary Nelson, "Envoys of Otherness: Difference and Continuity in Feminist Criticism," in *For Alma Mater: Theory and Practice in Feminist Scholarship*, eds. Paula A. Treichler, Cheris Kramarae, and Beth Stafford (Urbana: University of Illinois Press, 1985).

[15] Luce Irigaray, "Women's Exile," 64.

[16] See the discussion of discourse in Meaghan Morris, "A-Mazing Grace: Notes on Mary Daly's Poetics," *Intervention*, 16 (1982), 70–92.

understanding."[17] "Personally," she says, and "I sometimes fancy"; this is acceptable language in the ancestral halls. Her attempts to engage in different, serious
language—self-authored—are given up; to write in the absence of patriarchal
sanction requires "having to be so sly about it, or else meet with heavy opposition" (10) and is too exhausting. Thus the narrator speaks the law of the father
in the form of a "women's language" which is prescribed by patriarchy and exacts
its sentence upon her: not to author sentences of her own.

The yellow wallpaper challenges this sentence. In contrast to the orderly, evac-
uated patriarchal estate, the female lineage that the wallpaper represents is thick
with life, expression, and suffering. Masquerading as a symptom of "madness,"
language animates what had been merely an irritating and distracting pattern:

> This paper looks to me as if it *knew* what a vicious influence it had!
> There is a recurrent spot where the pattern lolls like a broken neck and two
> bulbous eyes stare at you upside down.
> I get positively angry with the impertinence of it and the everlastingness. Up
> and down and sideways they crawl, and those absurd, unblinking eyes are
> everywhere (16).

The silly and grotesque surface pattern reflects women's conventional representation; one juxtaposition identifies "that silly and conspicuous front design" with
"sister on the stairs!" (18). In the middle section of the story, where the narrator
attempts to convey her belief that she is seriously ill, the husband-physician is
quoted verbatim (23–25), enabling us to see the operation of male judgment at
first hand. He notes an improvement in her symptoms: "You are gaining flesh and
color, your appetite is better, I feel really much easier about you." The narrator
disputes these statements: "I don't weigh a bit more, nor as much; and my appetite may be better in the evening when you are here, but it is worse in the
morning when you are away!" His response not only pre-empts further talk of
facts, it reinforces the certainty of his original diagnosis and confirms his view of
her illness as non-serious: " 'Bless her little heart!' said he with a big hug, 'she
shall be as sick as she pleases!' " (24).

His failure to let her leave the estate initiates a new relationship to the wallpaper. She begins to see women in the pattern. Until now, we as readers have
acquiesced in the fiction that the protagonist is keeping a journal, a fiction initially supported by journal-like textual references. This now becomes difficult to
sustain: how can the narrator keep a journal when, as she tells us, she is sleeping,
creeping, or watching the wallpaper the whole time? In her growing paranoia,
would she confide in a journal she could not lock up? How did the journal get into
our hands? Because we are nevertheless reading this "journal," we are forced to
experience a contradiction: the narrative is unfolding in an impossible form. This
embeds our experience of the story in self-conscious attention to its construction.

---

[17] Luce Irigaray, "Veiled Lips," 99–101. According to Irigaray's account, Apollo, "the always-already-
speaking," drives away the chorus of women (the Furies) who want revenge for Clytemnestra's murder. His words convey his repulsion for the chaotic, non-hierarchical female voice: "Heave in torment,
black froth erupting from your lungs"; "Never touch my halls, you have no right"; "Out you flock
without a herdsman—out!" Calling for the forgetting of bloodshed, Athena, embodying the father's
voice and the father's law, pronounces the patriarchal sentence on the matriarchal chorus: the women
will withdraw to a subterranean cavern where they will be permitted to establish a cult, perform
religious rites and sacrifices, and remain "loyal and propitious to the land." They are removed from
positions of influence, their words destined to have only subterranean meaning.

A new tone enters as she reports that she defies orders to take naps by not actually sleeping: "And that cultivates deceit, for I don't tell them I'm awake—O no!" (26). This crowing tone announces a decisive break from the patriarchal order. She mocks her husband's diagnosis by diagnosing for herself why he "seems very queer sometimes": "It strikes me occasionally, just as a scientific hypothesis,—that perhaps it is the paper!" (26–27).

The wallpaper never becomes attractive. It remains indeterminate, complex, unresolved, disturbing; it continues to embody, like the form of the story we are reading, "unheard of contradictions." By now the narrator is fully engrossed by it and determined to find out its meaning. During the day—by "normal" standards—it remains "tiresome and perplexing" (28). But at night she sees a woman, or many women, shaking the pattern and trying to climb through it. Women "get through," she perceives, "and then the pattern strangles them off and turns them upside down, and makes their eyes white!" (30). The death sentence imposed by patriarchy is violent and relentless. No one escapes.

The story is now at its final turning point: "I have found out another funny thing," reports the narrator, "but I shan't tell it this time! It does not do to trust people too much" (31). This is a break with patriarchy—and a break with us. What she has discovered, which she does not state, is that she and the woman behind the paper are the same. This is communicated syntactically by contrasting sentences: "This bedstead is fairly gnawed!" she tells us, and then: "I bit off a little piece [of the bedstead] at one corner" (34). "If that woman does get out, and tries to get away, I can tie her!" and "But I am securely fastened now by my well-hidden rope" (34–35). The final passages are filled with crowing, "impertinent" language: "Hurrah!" "The sly thing!" "No person touches this paper but me,—not *alive!*" (32–33). Locked in the room, she addresses her husband in a dramatically different way: "It is no use, young man, you can't open it!"

She does not make this declaration aloud. In fact, she appears to have difficulty even making herself understood and must repeat several times the instructions to her husband for finding the key to the room. At first we think she may be too mad to speak proper English. But then we realize that he simply is unable to accept a statement of fact from her, his little goose, until she has "said it so often that he had to go and see" (36). Her final triumph is her public proclamation, "I've got out at last . . . you can't put me back!" (36).

There is a dramatic shift here both in *what* is said and in *who* is speaking. Not only has a new "impertinent" self emerged, but this final voice is collective, representing the narrator, the woman behind the wallpaper, and women elsewhere and everywhere. The final vision itself is one of physical enslavement, not liberation: the woman, bound by a rope, circles the room like an animal in a yoke. Yet that this vision has come to exist and to be expressed changes the terms of the representational process. That the husband-physician must at last listen to a woman speaking—no matter what she says—significantly changes conditions for speaking. Though patriarchy may be only temporarily unconscious, its ancestral halls will never be precisely the same again.

We can return now to the questions raised at the outset. Language in "The Yellow Wallpaper" is oppressive to women in the particular form of a medical diagnosis, a set of linguistic signs whose representational claims are authorized by society and whose power to control women's fate, whether or not those claims are valid, is real. Representation has real, material consequences. In contrast, women's power to originate signs is monitored; and, once produced, no legitimating social apparatus is available to give those signs substance in the real world.

Linguistic innovation, then, has a dual fate. The narrator in "The Yellow Wallpaper" initially speaks a language authorized by patriarchy, with genuine language ("work") forbidden her. But as the wallpaper comes alive she devises a different, "impertinent" language which defies patriarchal control and confounds the predictions of male judgment (diagnosis). The fact that she becomes a creative and involved language user, producing sentences which break established rules, *in and of itself* changes the terms in which women are represented in language and extends the conditions under which women will speak.

Yet language is intimately connected to material reality, despite the fact that no direct correspondence exists. The word is theory to the deed: but the deed's existence will depend upon a complicated set of material conditions. The narrator of "The Yellow Wallpaper" is not free at the end of the story because she has temporarily escaped her sentence: though she has "got out at last," her triumph is to have sharpened and articulated the nature of women's condition; she remains physically bound by a rope and locked in a room. The conditions she has diagnosed must change before she and other women will be free. Thus women's control of language is left metaphorical and evocative: the story only hints at possibilities for change. Woman is both passive and active, subject and object, sane and mad. Contradictions remain, for they are inherent in women's current "condition."

Thus to "escape the sentence" involves both linguistic innovation and change in material conditions: both change in what is said and change in the conditions of speaking. The escape of individual women may constitute a kind of linguistic self-help which has intrinsic value as a contribution to language but which functions socially and politically to isolate deviance rather than to introduce change. Representation is not without consequences. Thus the study of women and language must involve the study of discourse, which encompasses both form and function as well as the representational uncertainty their relationship entails. As a metaphor, the yellow wallpaper is never fully resolved: it can be described, but its meaning cannot be fixed. It remains trivial and dramatic, vivid and dowdy, compelling and repulsive: these multiple meanings run throughout the story in contrast to the one certain meaning of patriarchal diagnosis. If diagnosis is the middle of an equation that freezes material flux in a certain sign, the wallpaper is a disruptive center that chaotically fragments any attempt to fix on it a single meaning. It offers a lesson in language, whose sentence is perhaps not always destined to escape us.

"THE YELLOW WALLPAPER" AND WOMEN'S DISCOURSE*

By Karen Ford

Paula Treichler's essay "Escaping the Sentence: Diagnosis and Discourse in 'The Yellow Wallpaper' " offers one of the first close and thorough readings of a short story which has long been of interest to feminists but which is also read and employed by psychologists, historians, sociologists, and literary critics. Although the story has had many readers, remarkably little has been written about it. Treichler's essay provides at once a close reading and a challenging thesis around

* Originally published in *Tulsa Studies in Women's Literature* 4 (1985): 309–14.

which discussion can begin. Each time I have taught "The Yellow Wallpaper," students insist that it describes the progression of one person's neurosis, for instance that it is the tale of one woman's mental breakdown caused specifically by postpartum depression. Yet, many details, like the narrator's lack of a name, argue against her individuality, and similarly, the primer-like names of the husband and sister-in-law—John and Mary—suggest they are merely representatives for Husbands and In-laws. In fact, the most individual name in the story—Weir Mitchell—points away from the narrator and toward the effects of his very specific treatment on people like her. Moreover, as Treichler has shown, "a feminist reading emphasizes the social and economic conditions which drive the narrator—and potentially all women—to madness" (64). In addition to liberating "The Yellow Wallpaper" from overly idiosyncratic readings, Treichler's essay raises two important issues for readers of Gilman's story and for feminist critics in particular: first, through her discussion of diagnosis, she works toward a definition of "patriarchal discourse"; and, second, through her close reading of the story, she problematizes the image of the wallpaper, thereby calling into question the notion of women's discourse.

There can be no doubt that the narrator dwells in the middle of Patriarchy. She is living in "ancestral halls" (9), has just given birth to a boy, is surrounded by men—her husband, her brother, and somewhere in the background, Weir Mitchell—and even the female or females in the house appear to be cardboard figures cut out by the patriarchy—first Mary, the virgin mother who "is so good with the baby" (14) and later Jennie (a word which means a female donkey or beast of burden) who "is a perfect and enthusiastic housekeeper, and hopes for no better profession" (17–18). Whatever language emerges from this setting can safely be considered "male." Further, John is identified in relation to the patriarchy first and in relation to his wife only afterwards: he is "a physician of high standing and one's own husband" (10). In "The Yellow Wallpaper" the physician is the quintessential man, and his talk, therefore, is the epitome of male discourse. Thus Treichler's definitions of the physician's talk—of diagnosis—clarify the nature of this discourse. It is "powerful and public; representing institutional authority, it dictates . . . it privileges the rational, the practical, and the observable"(65), and even more important, it "translate[s] the realities of the human body into human language and back again. As such, it is a perfect example of language which 'reflects' reality and simultaneously 'produces' it" (69).

As recent discussions of women's language and women's relation to language have shown, "women's discourse" is difficult, and perhaps even impossible, to define. Treichler's analysis of the wallpaper at first acknowledges this by summarizing a variety of interpretations of the meaning of the paper. However, when Treichler offers an alternative reading of the image, she reduces the plurality, fixing the significance of the wallpaper too rigidly. She says:

> While these interpretations are plausible and fruitful, I interpret the wallpaper to be women's writing or women's discourse, and the women in the wallpaper to be the representation of women that becomes possible only after women obtain their right to speak. In this reading, the yellow wallpaper stands for a new vision of women—one which is constructed differently from the representation of women in patriarchal language. (64)

Although I resist the apparent determinacy of this interpretation, considering the wallpaper as discourse clearly generates important results. Treichler is able to uncover a line of female kinship that challenges the male ancestry. Also, the narrator's crucial shift in tone to impertinence is foregrounded as Treichler establishes the causal link between the wallpaper and the narrator's revolt. And even within this reading, Treichler recognizes that "the story only hints at possibilities for change" (74), that "as metaphor, the yellow wallpaper is never fully resolved . . . its meaning cannot be fixed" (75). Nevertheless, her analysis raises several questions. First, if the wallpaper stands for a new vision of women, why is the narrator tearing it down? Next, how can it be a "representation of women that becomes possible only after women obtain their right to speak," if it grows more vivid as the narrator becomes less verbal? Moreover, if the narrator comes into her own through the wallpaper, then why does she become more and more a victim of male diagnosis as she becomes further engaged with the wallpaper—that is, although she does free the woman inside the paper, she is tied up, locked in a room, creeping on all fours like the child John has accused her of being, and moving in a circle that sketches the futility of her liberation through madness. Despite these reservations, I am interested in the notion that the wallpaper represents women's discourse to the extent that the wallpaper is impossible to define.

In fact, the narrator herself answers some of these questions when she attempts to describe the paper: it "commit[s] every artistic sin": "It is dull enough to confuse the eye in following, pronounced enough to constantly irritate and provoke study, and when you follow the lame uncertain curves for a little distance they suddenly commit suicide—plunge off at outrageous angles, destroy themselves in unheard of contradictions" (13). As she describes it, the wallpaper does seem to resemble all-too-familiar assessments of women's language—first, it "sins" against established forms; it is dull, confusing, irritating, yet nevertheless provoking. Further, the narrator clearly comes to embody the wallpaper's aesthetic when she begins creeping as though she, like its designs, is lame. The most crucial element of her description, however, is the "unheard of contradictions." This, I think, is a key to understanding male and female discourse in the story.

"The Yellow Wallpaper" is replete with contradictions. The conjunction of contradiction—"but"—occurs 56 times in this short space and there are numerous instances of other words—and, so, only, besides—employed to mean "but." Every time the narrator speaks, she is interrupted and contradicted until she begins to interrupt and contradict herself. On the opening page she attempts to gain verbal leverage by vigorously beginning sentences that express her opinions with the word "personally."

Personally, I disagree with their ideas.

Personally, I believe that congenial work . . . would do me good. (10)

as though to give emphasis and substance to points she knows will be lost on her husband. And, indeed, to him the word "personally," coming from her, signifies that the ideas to follow can be ignored as mere opinion. As Treichler has shown, the narrator has her own plan for recovery including visits with friends and, most important, a return to her writing. But John contradicts these possibilities. The wallpaper, in fact, sometimes appears like male discourse in its capacity to contradict and immobilize the women who are trapped within it. In this view, the narrator releases herself (and other women) from the paper by tearing it down. *Her* contradictions, however, are "unheard." She can only counter John's dictums literally by refusing to speak, or, metaphorically, by revealing the blankness behind the wallpaper. As Treichler notes, the narrator becomes less verbal as she moves further into the world of the wallpaper. Tearing down the paper, then, is not the construction of women's discourse; rather, it signals a retreat from discourse precisely because language is male-controlled. The idea of contradiction captures this relationship between male and female discourse in "The Yellow Wallpaper." Far more significant than what they say is the fact that John's talk persists while hers falters.

In *New French Feminisms* Xavière Gauthier notes that traditional work in women's language offers two points of view that Gauthier describes as "flip sides of the same prejudiced coin" (162), because they both describe women's writing in relation to men's. First is the notion that if men write one way—straightforwardly, rationally—then women write in the opposite way—intuitively, sensitively. The second idea is that women are just slow learners who will write like men when they catch up.

As an alternative to these views, Gauthier and others suggest another possibility, pointing to "blank pages, gaps, borders, spaces and silence, holes in discourse . . . the aspect of feminine writing which is the most difficult to verbalize because it becomes compromised, rationalized, masculinized as it explains itself. . . . If the reader feels a bit disoriented in this new space, one which is obscure and silent, it proves perhaps, that it is women's space" (164). If the narrator in "The Yellow Wallpaper" in any sense discovers women's discourse, it exists in the blankness behind the wallpaper. She certainly associates that blankness with freedom: "I've pulled off most of the paper, so you can't put me back!" (36). But is this freedom of expression, and if so, at what cost does she achieve it?

There is much evidence in women's writing—both in fiction and in theory—of this retreat to what Gauthier calls "this new space," and to what Gilman describes as the blank spaces behind the wallpaper. In fact, "The Yellow Wallpaper" narrator participates in a long tradition in women's writing of retreat to such a state. In the location of such a place outside language and outside male influence and in the tendency for women to find other women there, this new space can be symbolically connected to the pre-Oedipal (in Freud's terms) or the Imaginary (in Lacan's). Marianne Hirsch compares this state to the pre-Oedipal phase outlined in psychoanalytic writing:

> Attachment to this phase is characterized by fusion, fluidity, mutuality, continuity and lack of differentiation, as well as by the heroines' refusal of a heterosexual social reality that violates their psychological needs, a reality defined by images of fragmentation, separation, discontinuity, alienation, and self-denial. Faced with the break between psychological needs and social imperatives, literary convention finds only one possible resolution: the heroine's death. (27)

I would add to death the heroine's madness, especially since most of the deaths in this tradition are preceded by madness. Hirsch looks beyond the self-destructiveness of these endings and sees, like "The Yellow Wallpaper" narrator, some cause for elation:

> if we look at what adulthood and maturity mean for the female protagonists of these texts, at the confinement, discontinuity, and stifling isolation that define marriage and motherhood, they do not present positive options. . . . I submit that the heroines' allegiance to childhood, pre-Oedipal desire, spiritual with-

drawal, and ultimately death is not neurotic but a realistic and paradoxically fulfilling reaction to an impossible contradiction (27–28).

Hirsch's reading redeems the lives and deaths of many heroines, both literary and actual—notably, Bertha Mason in *Jane Eyre* who dwells in madness and plunges to her death; Edna Pontellier in *The Awakening*, Rachel Vinrace in *The Voyage Out*, and Maggie Tulliver in *The Mill on the Floss* who drown; Lily Bart in *The House of Mirth*, Madame Bovary, and the wife and mother in "A Sorrowful Woman" who die by drugs; or Joan Ogden in *The Unlit Lamp* who simply gives up the ghost. These are only a few of the characters whose lives might seem less bitterly wasted under such a reading. But however dignified and victorious these resolutions into madness and death may seem in relation to the compromised life of marriage and motherhood, they are not ultimately acceptable. As the holes, blanks, gaps, and borders (that Gauthier proposes are the sites of women's language) are no substitute for words on the center of the page; lethargy, depravity, and suicide are not alternatives to a fulfilling life.

Fortunately, recent developments in the tradition of women's writing make it no longer necessary to celebrate silences. In the last ten years or so—but not exclusively, since there have always been women writing whose visions were positive—the endings of women's stories are turning the tables on a patriarchy that imposes sentences of madness and death as the only alternatives to marriage, motherhood, and conformity. Thus in Zora Neale Hurston's *Their Eyes Were Watching God*, the *hero* is bitten by a rabid dog and goes mad, and the *heroine* has to shoot him to save herself. In Alice Walker's "Really, Doesn't Crime Pay?" the narrator tries to behead her frustrating husband with a chain saw (he is saved in the nick of time when the noise awakens him). In Joanna Russ's *On Strike Against God*, two women are practicing target shooting at the end of the book when a

> respectably dressed Professorial type appeared in the gap in the front hedge ... saying, amused—as if it were any of his business!—"What are you girls doing?" Jean had swung the gun around, quite coldly. And pulled back the safety catch. "Get out!" He turned pale and backing away, vanished behind the hedge. (97)

More recently, in *The Color Purple*, Walker envisions a new phase of the tradition when her heroine can transcend oppression *and* anger through writing, working, and loving women. And finally, in *Sources*, a long poem published two years ago, Adrienne Rich associates women's new possibilities specifically with their ability to use language:

> When
> I speak of an end to suffering I don't mean anesthesia.
> I mean knowing the world, and my place in it, not in
> order to stare with bitterness or detachment, but as a
> powerful and womanly series of choices: and here I
> write the words, in their fullness:
> powerful; womanly. (35)

Clearly, these endings are more possible in a world where women can work, write, refuse marriage, love more freely, own guns, and operate buzz saws. The connection Treichler discovers in "The Yellow Wallpaper" between women's discourse and self-discovery is applicable to contemporary developments in women's literature where women—writers and characters—are proving that language can be both powerful and womanly.

WORKS CITED

Gauthier, Xavière. "Is There Such a Thing As Women's Writing?" In *New French Feminisms: An Anthology*. Ed. Elaine Marks and Isabelle de Courtivron. New York: Schocken Books, 1981. 161–64.
Gilman, Charlotte Perkins. *The Yellow Wallpaper*. Old Westbury, NY: The Feminist Press, 1973.
Hirsch, Marianne, "Spiritual *Bildung*: The Beautiful Soul as Paradigm." In *The Voyage In*. Ed. Elizabeth Abel, Marianne Hirsch, and Elizabeth Langland. Hanover: University Press of New England, 1983, 23–48.
Rich, Adrienne. *Sources*. Woodside, CA: The Heyeck Press, 1983.
Russ, Joanna. *On Strike Against God*. Trumansburg, NY: The Crossing Press, Out & Out Books, 1980.
Treichler, Paula. "Escaping the Sentence: Diagnosis and Discourse in 'The Yellow Wallpaper.'" *Tulsa Studies in Women's Literature* 3 (1984): 61–77.

ALTERNATIVE WOMEN'S DISCOURSE*

By Carol Thomas Neely

While I disagree with Paula Treichler's interpretation of the yellow wallpaper, I agree with her—as do most feminist critics, scholars, writers—that patriarchal discourse is oppressive to women, and that women must analyze its oppressiveness, exploit its practices for their own ends, disrupt and displace it (though they cannot, I think, replace it) with women's discourses. Her paper illuminates these issues. I also agree with her clear explication of a controversial point—that the differences between men's and women's language are not primarily or most interestingly at the level of style—of syntax, semantics, semiotics—but at the level of context—of crucial differences in the ways the two discourses are produced, are received, become efficacious. While Treichler's metaphor of "diagnosis" and her pun on "sentence" aptly point to this crucial feature of discourse, I think they embody some of the difficulties which have plagued all attempts to theorize or practice such a discourse. When women's language is reduced to the level of style alone, attempts to isolate or prescribe stylistic features which are or should be peculiar to women's discourse fail either because some men have used these features too in the service of politics oppressive to women or because the prescriptions do not serve the purposes of all women language users. On the other hand, attempts to contextualize language tend to embed it so deeply in institutional contexts that discussion shifts from language to discourse to wider social issues so that problems peculiar to language usage get lost. Diagnosis, for example, is both a linguistic and a social issue. While changing speech practices in diagnostic situations can have some impact on institutionalized medicine, broader changes in the institution would be required to sustain these practices. Discussions of women's language are often either too particular and stylistic to be of broad practical use (as with the French feminists' call for an *écriture féminine*) or too intertwined with critiques of patriarchal institutions to be of much theoretical use (as in the discourse of midwifery).

In what follows, inspired by Treichler's collocation of women/diagnosis/discourse, I will examine some of the difficulties in the attempt to escape the patri-

* Originally published in *Tulsa Studies in Women's Literature* 4 (1985): 315–21.

archal sentence and author new sentences. First I will analyze why such an escape is not achieved by the narrator of "The Yellow Wallpaper"; second I will explore Virginia Woolf's prescriptions for female discourse; and third, I will survey some recent variations on her strategies.

The yellow wallpaper in Charlotte Perkins Gilman's story is, I think, more appropriately and usefully defined as a representation of patriarchal discourse (as perceived by women who look at it close up for too long) than of women's discourse: I read the story's ending not as any kind of a victory for the narrator but as her defeat. She confirms the diagnosis of her husband the doctor by complying with it and therefore depriving herself of discourse altogether. As part of the ancestral home, the yellow wallpaper is emblematic of the aging and restrictive institutions of patriarchy. It is ancient, reminding the narrator of "old, foul, bad yellow things" (14). It is contradictory at every level—it is "dull" yet "flamboyant" (5), changes but is always the same, has a pattern which cannot be followed to a logical conclusion. Tenacious and oppressive, it is hard to get off the walls. It has bars which trap the narrator's imprisoned doubles; it "strangles" them (15) and it "keeps [the narrator] quiet by the hour" (13). "You think you have mastered it, but just as you get well underway, it turns a back somersault and tramples upon you. It is like a bad dream" (12). In all of these ways it is a visual representation of and symbolic accomplice to the husband's discourse and diagnosis, which is likewise repetitive, inescapable, and contradictory. She is, he tells her, sick and not sick, weak but required to be strong; she must not give in to "fancies" (7) but is offered no alternatives to them; she is supposed to change herself but is not allowed to change anything else—not the wallpaper, the room, the house, the marriage.

As she grows "fond" of her room (9), the wallpaper elicits from her voluntary compliance with her husband's prescriptions (which at first she had questioned). He opposes her writing, and when the wallpaper makes her "tired" (10) she ceases, as Treichler notes, even the surreptitious journal-keeping. He refuses to let her see friends, and she herself eventually refuses all communication with her sister-in-law and fellow prisoner who shares her interest in and dislike of the wallpaper (and who is, it seems, identified more with the woman who is trying to get out of the wallpaper than with the paper itself [see also 8, 13, 14]). Eventually the narrator reconstitutes for herself in extremity the conditions of her oppression: confinement, infantilization, trivialization, banishment from discourse, madness. She locks herself in her room, giving only her husband the power to release her (when she tells him where the key is), gnaws at the bedstead, ropes herself to the walls and "creeps" (18–19) round and round them. Although at the end she has dismantled patriarchal discourse in wonderfully literal ways—the wallpaper is torn down and her husband has fainted—she has confirmed and not escaped its diagnosis because she has no alternate discourse and no context out of which to create one—no work, no women friends to provide "advice and companionship" (7), no contact with her body or with the adult sexuality represented by the chained-down bed which her husband has retreated from and the child downstairs which she has retreated from. In short the narrator attains none of the conditions for discourse identified by later writers and seized by Gilman herself—who ran from her "cure" to friends, who wrote journals, stories, and theoretical work, who supported herself, and who used this story to express her own experience of breakdown—to indict Weir Mitchell and force change in his practices, and to warn women against him. Interestingly, in Gilman's later, more didactic fiction, an older woman doctor is sometimes the hero who brings about the happy—and feminist—resolution (see also "Mr. Pebbles' Heart" and *The Crux* in Gilman).

In 1897, ten years after Gilman escaped her prescribed treatment, Virginia Woolf, at 15, experienced "symptoms" associated with a breakdown two years earlier following her mother's death; her doctor prescribed a modified version of the Weir Mitchell treatment which forbade school, regular studies, and excitement ("no reading, no writing," Trombley, 77), and required at least four hours outdoors every day. This treatment had the effect of cutting Woolf off from formal education and friendship with peers while confining her in the care of her powerful father and her stepsister, Stella Duckworth; her time outdoors was usually spent gardening or running errands for the rest of the family (DeSalvo, 79–83). The diary which she started in this year records her feelings of anger and despair at this regimen, often expressed through a persona, a "Miss Jan."[1] This crucial diary began for Woolf forty-three years of prodigious writing—diaries, letters, essays, reviews, lectures, stories, novels. In 1941, she again experienced symptoms of breakdown, dreaded another imposition of the rest cure, and found that writing had failed her, that, according to a journal entry, "the writing 'I' has vanished. No audience. No echo. Thats [sic] part of one's death" (Dinnage, 4). She committed suicide, leaving behind a thrice-revised suicide note.

Woolf serves as an exemplary model of women's writing and, in *A Room of One's Own*, she explicitly creates a new form of discourse to subvert the patriarchal lecture format whose incitements to pomposity, vanity, and authoritarianism she hated. This work she called "talks to girls" (*Letters*, 4:102); it is, as Jane Marcus suggested in a talk on *A Room of One's Own*, a "trialogue" between women writers, women students, and women readers from which men are excluded (Marcus' talk, on *A Room of One's Own* as a narrative of lesbian seduction, occurred at the National Women's Studies Association annual meeting in June 1983). Within this congenial "trialogue" format, Woolf explores the nature of oppressive male discourse and the conditions necessary to create alternate women's discourse. The writing on women by men which the narrator finds in the British Museum has precisely the characteristics of the yellow wallpaper; it is contradictory, interminable, angry, and powerful—and it makes no sense to the women reading it. When Woolf declares men's sentences inappropriate for women's use, her metaphor points to three aspects of the inadequacy of male discourse—its style, its forms, its content. These limitations are even clearer, I think, in Woolf's original formulation of the problem in her essay "Women and Fiction": "It is a sentence made by men; it is too loose [syntactically], too heavy [with the weight of formal conventions], too pompous [with its freight of male values and male power] for women's use" (48). Women writing must "knock into shape"(*Room*, 80) the sentences, the genres, the values of men.

In order to create this alternate discourse, however, women must first achieve the conditions of writing which Woolf outlines in *A Room of One's Own*, "Women and Fiction,"and "Professions for Women." They must have 500 pounds and a room of their own—that is, financial, social, and psychological independence. They must have a tradition of women's writing to place themselves within, must be

---

[1] I am indebted for this information to a talk by Louise DeSalvo on Woolf's 1897 diary (which she and Mitchell Leaska are editing along with other early diaries) delivered at a Woolf session at the 1983 Annual Meeting of the National Women's Studies Association in Columbus, Ohio. My view of Woolf at fifteen owes a great deal to this talk as well as to DeSalvo's article, "1897: Woolf at Fifteen." My view of *A Room of One's Own* in the discussion below is indebted to Jane Marcus' talk at the same session.

able to, as Woolf says, "think back through our mothers" (*Room,* 79). They must have an audience of women to write for, one which is symbolically present in the fictionalized lecture format of *A Room of One's Own*. Women writers must kill the "Angel in the House," the representation in male discourse of ideal womanhood, "immensely sympathetic . . . immensely charming . . . utterly unselfish" ("Professions," 59). The creeping phantom women in "The Yellow Wallpaper" seem to me a kind of grotesque counter-representation of this Angel—a vision of her as she appears to women who are unable either to be her or to kill her; as Woolf says of this specter: "she was always creeping back when I thought I had dispatched her" ("Professions," 60). More difficult still, the woman writing female discourse must represent in it the aspects of herself that the Angel stereotype has repressed—must "tell the truth about my experiences as a body," as Woolf put it ("Professions," 62). This was a problem Woolf did not feel that she or other women writers had yet solved. Her ideal of the great artist as androgynous is, I think, a way of evading the problem altogether. Contemporary feminists have also flirted with the idea of androgyny, but most have not found it theoretically or practically viable. But all other aspects of Woolf's critique of patriarchy and her strategies for creating an alternate discourse have been advocated, extended, or achieved by her female predecessors. In particular, academic women have appropriated the lecture format as Woolf did and have made it into a crucial form of women's discourse—the place where one can acquire the conditions for speech which the narrator of "The Yellow Wallpaper" lacked: a space for self-expression, audiences who listen, "companionship and advice," contact with a suppressed tradition.

I now want to look at four enormously varied subsequent attempts to create alternate women's discourse; the first two are more textual, the last two more material.[2] The first, H.D.'s *Tribute to Freud,* is a kind of counter case history, a visionary translation of H.D.'s analysis by Freud, which revises and completes it. Although an idiosyncratic case of female discourse, it is of special interest because psychoanalysis is one of the most powerful forms of contemporary diagnosis; H.D.'s response to her analysis prefigures more recent and more theoretical debates and interactions between psychoanalysis and feminism. "The Professor is not always right," (18, 96) H.D. reiterates in her *Tribute*. She analyzes Freud, includes in her account childhood material which she has neglected/refused to tell him, and displaces without denying his interpretations. At the center of her account is her revision of Freud's "translation" (44) of her "writing on the wall" at Corfu. The Professor reads the experience as a "hallucination," a "Dangerous symptom" (41, 46), which he interprets as revealing "desire for union with her mother" (44). Her lengthy description, in contrast, represents the writing as a prophetic, visionary confirmation of her vocation as a poet. The vision and the interpretation culminate in the image of Niké, Victory, winged and ascending (55–56). This symbol she opposes to Freud's representation of women, his "favorite statue, a little Athena/Niké who, although she has lost her spear, is, Freud

---

[2] Since my topic here is written discourse, I do not include the results of recent studies of men's and women's conversation in heterosexual groups which have identified a variety of gender differences in conversation. The most significant and interesting of these have to do not with content or style but with the control exerted over the conditions of conversation. In mixed conversations between social equals, men control when conversation starts and stops, which topics get discussed, and for how long. They interrupt women more often than women interrupt them and they interrupt them sooner. For these and other differences see, for example, the essays in Thorne.

announces, "perfect" (69).[3] H.D.'s written and rewritten accounts of her analysis, first in journals and letters, then in *Tribute,* and again later in "Advent" allowed her to participate in her analysis on equal terms with Sigmund, the professor, master, father, explorer, and "blameless physician" (101) whom she revered and whose name she interpreted to mean "victorious mouth or voice or utterance" (88). This active participation as well as Freud's brilliant and sensitive treatment of her were perhaps the reasons for the practical success of the treatment—it did, apparently, remove her writer's block and depression and generate a long creative period (although there were later breakdowns).

A second strategy for creating women's discourse, the French feminists' call for a female language, *l'écriture féminine,* also emerges from and defines itself in relation to psychoanalytic theory and practice. Like H.D.'s *Tribute,* it too speaks—at a metaphorical level—to Woolf's problem of "telling the truth about my experiences as a body." Certain French feminists urge women to create a uniquely female style compounded of and celebrating the female body, female desire, the unconscious, heterogeneity. This source is to be reflected in the textual features of the writing—structure, syntax, sentence length, imagery. While the project is a tantalizing one and the writing advocating it has a special power, *l'écriture féminine* has been widely and rightly criticized for its murky attempts at self-definition, its reification of conservative, dualistic, gender stereotypes, and its failure to pay attention to the material conditions for discourse.[4] It seems to me to sentence women to a perpetual "Otherness" and to prescribe for them a style which may be even more circumscribed and less useful than that which patriarchy allows.

In contrast to French feminists, American feminists have concentrated less on writing the body and more on finding language which will enable them to reappropriate their own bodies, to analyze and express their own sexuality and sexual practices. They have advocated a communal discourse such as is the goal of one of the earliest and most popular American feminist texts, *Our Bodies, Ourselves.* From such apparently unproblematic beginnings have followed years of dialogue and conflict; the latest stage of this discourse is represented by a collection of position papers, "The Female Sexuality Debates," in *Signs,* Autumn 1984. In these passionate, painful debates, feminist theory, women's sexual practice, and women's discourse are complexly, confusingly, and perhaps dangerously intertwined. The debate is about what theory of sexuality, which sexual practices, and what representations of them are good for women. Some of the issues are whether heterosexuality is identical to rape, whether lesbian practices, lesbian identification, a lesbian continuum is essential to feminist theory/practice, whether pornography is an appropriate discourse for the representation of female sexuality, whether sexual practices such as incest, sadomasochism, adult/child sexuality are to be condemned, tolerated, advocated. The debates thus center on what practices and/or discourses of sexuality are appropriate to women. They imply the inextricability of language and sexuality, questioning whether *any* sexual practices or discourses are free from the dominant discourse in which "bodies, skills, and

---

[3] My exploration of H.D.'s relation to Freud is indebted to a talk by Adalaide Morris on Freud and H.D. at a special session, "Encounters with Freud," at the 1983 Annual Meeting of the Modern Language Association of America, New York City.

[4] Two of the best known documents of *l'écriture féminine* are Luce Irigaray, "When Our Lips Speak Together," and Hélène Cixous, "The Laugh of the Medusa," in *New French Feminisms.* See also other essays on women's style in this volume. For some criticisms, see "Variations on Common Themes," 212–30 in *New French Feminisms* and essays by Ann Jones and Hélène Wenzel in *Feminist Studies.*

pleasures are . . . linguistically sexuated and scientized" and "center on mastery and monolithic identity" (125). The number of positions taken even within this fairly moderate gathering suggests that women do not yet agree and probably will never agree on what it means to "tell the truth about my experience as a body" or on whether this is possible; their opportunities for expressing a variety of such truths are, however, far greater than Woolf's were.

The last example of an alternative discourse, the least textual and most material, is the midwifery model of pregnancy and childbirth, a radically different diagnosis with radically different implications for "treatment" (the word, in fact, is not even appropriate) from those prescribed by the dominant medical model. The two are contrasted in Barbara Katz Rothman's *Giving Birth: Alternatives in Childbirth* (originally titled, *In Labor, Women and Power in the Birthplace*). In the medical paradigm, pregnancy is defined as a doctor-managed "disease" with "symptoms." It is either "high" or "low" risk; the mother is passive machinery, the child a parasite who belongs to the father and to the doctor who "delivers" it (36–40, 131–38). This model encourages medical intervention at all stages of the process from anti-miscarriage drugs to anti-nausea drugs to drug-induced labor and doctor's rupture of the membranes and use of forceps—practices which benefit the medical establishment more than the mother and baby. According to the alternate midwifery discourse, pregnancy is a normal process, not a disease, one which the mother and child experience together and which mother and midwife facilitate together by communicating as equals. Rather than using medical intervention to force anomalous labors into the stages defined in obstetrics texts, midwives, for example, abandon or redefine these stages based on their experiences with laboring mothers (264–70). This is a potentially powerful and radical alternative discourse, one by women, for women, about women, and based on women's experiences and their articulation of these experiences. It calls into question the language, accuracy, psychological effects, and medical efficacy of the dominant discourse; it provides an alternative to it which is both linguistic and practical—midwifery-assisted home births. But obviously both the practical consequences and the theoretical implications of this discourse are limited.

In spite, then, of these varied alternatives, the notion of women's discourse remains elusive. As conceived it is too narrowly textual or too widely contextual, too idiosyncratic or too amorphous, too prescriptive or too undecidable. Most discouragingly, women's discourse remains so intertwined with the patriarchal discourse it tries to displace that it is difficult to be sure such a female-centered discourse is really there. Hence Paula Treichler's interpretation of the yellow wallpaper and mine are not, perhaps, as antithetical as they might at first appear to be. Women's writing is still a part of the dominant patriarchal discourse; hence the wallpaper can represent both women's writing and patriarchy's absorption of it. Tearing the wallpaper down can be seen then as partially a victory, partially a defeat. In spite of such defeats and in spite of the difficulties in defining women's discourse, the struggle with its contradictions is an important and necessary weapon in the struggle against the contradictory and confining representations of women in patriarchal discourse.

WORKS CITED

H.D. *Tribute to Freud*, 1956; rpt. Boston: David R. Godine, 1974

DeSalvo, Louise. "1897: Virginia Woolf at Fifteen." In *Virginia Woolf: A Feminist Slant*. Ed. Jane Marcus. Lincoln: University of Nebraska Press, 1983:78–108.

Dinnage, Rosemary. "The Last Act." Rev. of *The Diary of Virginia Woolf, Vol. 5 (1936–1941)*, ed. Anne Olivier Bell. *The New York Review of Books*. 8 Nov. 1984: 3–4.

"The Feminist Sexuality Debates." *Signs* 10, 1 (Autumn, 1984): 106–35.

Gilman, Charlotte Perkins. *The Charlotte Perkins Gilman Reader*. Ed. Ann J. Lane. New York: Pantheon, 1980.

Jones, Ann Rosalind. "Writing the Body: Toward an Understanding of L'Ecriture Féminine." *Feminist Studies* 7, 2 (Summer, 1981):247–63.

Marks, Elaine and Isabelle de Courtivron, ed. *New French Feminisms*. Amherst: University of Massachusetts Press, 1980.

Our Bodies, Ourselves. By The Boston Women's Health Collective. New York: Simon and Schuster, 1971.

Rothman, Barbara Katz. *Giving Birth: Alternatives in Childbirth*. New York: Penguin, 1984.

Thorne, Barrie, Cheris Kramerae and Nancy Henley, ed. *Language, Gender, and Society*. Rowley, MA: Newbury House, 1983.

Trombley, Stephen. *'All that Summer She Was Mad': Virginia Woolf and Her Doctors*. London: Junction Books, 1981.

Wenzel, Hélène Vivienne. "The Text as Body/Politics: An Appreciation of Monique Wittig's Writings in Context." *Feminist Studies* 7, 2 (Summer, 1981):264–87.

Woolf, Virginia. *A Room of One's Own*. New York: Harcourt Brace Jovanovich, 1957.

——— *Letters, Vol. 4*. ed. Nigel Nicolson with Joanne Trautmann. London: Hogarth Press, 1978.

——— "Professions for Women" and "Women and Fiction" in Woolf, *Women and Writing*. Ed. Michelle Barrett. New York: Harcourt Brace Jovanovich, 1979.

THE WALL BEHIND THE YELLOW WALLPAPER: RESPONSE TO CAROL NEELY AND KAREN FORD*

By Paula Treichler

I thank Carol Neely and Karen Ford for taking the time to respond to my essay on "The Yellow Wallpaper." It is a real pleasure to have intelligent and thoughtful readings of one's work, whether or not the authors "agree" with it. I found their comments particularly useful in thinking through more clearly some general issues about language and feminist literary analysis. I will talk about three of these issues here: (1) problematic aspects of the term "women's discourse"; (2) problems with the notion of an "alternative discourse"; and (3) the difficulty of interpreting the metaphor of the yellow wallpaper.

The term "women's discourse" has various meanings in current feminist writing which include (a) a specific discursive tradition or set of practices, such as *l'écriture féminine,* (b) literary or scholarly texts written by women, (c) literary or scholarly texts written by feminists, (d) "women's language" in the sense of a cluster of empirically-specifiable stylistic, interactional, lexical, or semantic characteristics ascribed to women's talk in naturalistic settings, (e) language use by women within such traditionally female cultural domains as the consciousness-raising group, the nursing profession, or the home birth setting, (f) an envisioned or visionary women's language which exists apart from the structures and entailments attributed to "man-made language"; and (g) any example of talk or writing by any woman under any circumstances.

Obviously, there can be real problems in theorizing or practicing "women's discourse" when the term itself is so slippery, referring now to the hypothesis that certain specific linguistic features (such as tag questions) are gender-marked, now to the incontrovertible fact that female human beings do produce utterances and texts, and now to a visionary language which can exist only "outside of" patriarchal discourse. This points to the importance of situating discussions fairly pre-

* Originally published in *Tulsa Studies in Women's Literature* 4 (1985): 323–30.

cisely, as I tried to do in my essay by talking about women's discourse in the context of medical diagnosis, a highly institutionalized form of "patriarchal discourse." Ford's discussion of female literary narratives and Neely's of midwifery and childbirth discourse (which I'll say more about below) are similarly and usefully situated.

Of course the term *discourse* in much contemporary scholarship is also defined rather loosely. It is not interchangeable with *language,* a term that signifies an abstract structured system (and in linguistics the product rather than the raw material of analysis). *Discourse* implies language in process—that is, spoken and written communicative practices embedded within the materiality of the speech stream or the written text. In linguistics, the term refers to linguistic productions larger than the sentence, entailing the analysis of any given utterance or sentence in terms of its immediate discursive context. Discourse also implies a movement back and forth, a body of ongoing linguistic interaction between engaged participants situated in time and space—language, that is, inseparable from its social contexts. The title of my essay, "Escaping the Sentence," argued for the study of language as discourse. "Women's discourse" is not a merely descriptive term but rather is concerned with the entire process (even "the apparatus") through which gendered utterances are produced. What are the rights, privileges, and prohibitions operating on male and female speakers in authoring utterances? Under what conditions is "gender" in discourse created and maintained? How are gender prescriptions disrupted, evaded, or redefined? With what interpretations and consequences? In the same sense, the term "patriarchal discourse" involves, loosely speaking, the production of language that works to articulate, codify, and maintain various forms of authority, power, and control.

To assume a formal dichotomy, then, between "patriarchal discourse" and "women's discourse" is false, just as it is false to assume that "language" is patriarchal and therefore that "women's discourse" must be something other than "language." It seems inaccurate even to say that there is a dominant "mainstream" patriarchal discourse and a subordinate women's discourse which exists as a kind of undercurrent. On the contrary, there are within a given culture or civilization multiple discourses which have evolved in multiple contexts: each has its own life, its own imperatives, its own contestations, and its own strategies for engendering speakers, subjects, and listeners. Though perhaps the notion has value for specific literary or psychoanalytic arguments, it does not make much sense to me linguistically to say that women have developed "outside language." But I think we can say that certain linguistic practices and discursive traditions may evolve outside the policed territory of specific discourses—areas that are "blank" as far as those discourses are concerned. We might think of language as a vast geographical terrain which different people and groups inhabit and "work over" in many different ways—cohabiting a given territory perhaps, perhaps struggling over it, sometimes evolving diverse practices for cultivating the same type of terrain, sometimes attending to new areas that have lain fallow. Discourse, then, might be seen as a specialized and institutionalized set of practices for inhabiting and cultivating a given piece of terrain—and enabling us to have access to that terrain at all. Language is thus inhabited by both "patriarchy" and "women," as well as many other inhabitants with their various voices and discourse practices. "Dominance" or "subordination" is not something that comes with the territory (language) but is rather established through interaction with a complex of other factors such as local politics and mapmaking practices.

Despite problems with this somewhat simple-minded analogy, it illuminates my argument here that women's discourse is never truly "alternative" but rather inhabits the same terrain as the "patriarchal discourse" it challenges. Current discourses on childbirth, to use one of Carol Neely's examples, clarify this notion of a contested terrain. The women's health movement/midwifery model does indeed offer, as Neely states, a "potentially powerful and radical alternative discourse" in contrast to that of organized medicine. But the ways in which the medical and the midwifery models of childbirth are now intertwined in the U.S. constitute a compelling social and linguistic drama with significant social, economic, and ideological consequences. The two discourses do not stand apart from each other as two separate alternatives. Though the women's health movement capitalizes on the idea of "natural" childbirth, for example, there has been considerable discussion of how that term is to be used (see Rothman, 161, and Oakley, 12–17 and 236–49); moreover, anthropological studies of birth (such as those by Margaret Mead and Niles Newton, and by Brigitte Jordan) argue that no models of birth are "natural"—all are culturally constructed. The term "natural" nevertheless functions strategically to reappropriate for women a definition taken away from them in fairly concrete ways by the medical profession. A 1920 landmark paper by the influential obstetrician and gynecologist Joseph B. DeLee, for example, introduced a definition of the birth process as pathological and abnormal: we do not call it "normal," he argued to his colleagues, when a baby's head is crushed in a door and it dies of cerebral hemorrhage; yet "when a baby's head is crushed against a tight pelvic floor and a hemorrhage in the brain kills it, we call this normal, at least we say that the function is natural, not pathogenic" (40). DeLee was arguing specifically for the routine use of forceps in delivery but his work more broadly legitimated a medical definition of childbirth as abnormal, providing a theoretical grounding for a high degree of medical intervention as well as a lexicon elaborating upon the notion of the pregnant woman as a patient (see Jordan, 35) and of childbirth as a pathological event. (Both Jordan and Oakley offer theoretical discussions of this definition process and its implications).

Challenges to this definition have come from many directions over the past two decades. The feminist writer Gena Corea, for example, charged that the language of obstetrics textbooks characterizes the pregnant woman's body as hostile territory and the medical staff as a kind of SWAT team, poised at all times for swift and aggressive intervention. Challenges have also come from consumers, the women's health movement, the home birth movement, and organized midwifery (groups that sometimes overlap), and more recently from insurance organizations and from state and federal agencies. As these challenges gain strength and legitimacy and the struggle grows over the meaning of the term *childbirth,* ideological and economic issues are invoked and articulated with increasing intensity. The ideological issues raised in the voluminous literature include, on the one hand, the medical profession's responsibility to provide mother and baby with "safe" medical care, the importance of medical expertise and authority, the right to earn money in a free market economy, and the intrinsic value of technological progress, and, on the other hand, the importance of egalitarian decision-making in health care, a woman's right to control her own body, and the importance of free choice in a democracy. Economic issues include the high cost of medical and hospital care, the deregulation of the health care system, changing patterns of reimbursement from insuring agencies and other third party payers, the declining birth rate, and the "oversupply" of physicians and other health care professionals. The bottom line is competition on the part of physicians to maintain their "market share" of low-risk births, organized movements among midwives in many states toward professional legitimation and institutionalization, and in general an atmosphere in which definitional pluralism and professional coexistence are increasingly difficult. Indeed, the childbirth issue served as the focal case study in the Federal Trade Commission's 1979 determination that many practices of organized medicine constituted restraint of trade (the case study, conducted and reported by Lewin and Associates, Inc. is summarized in Lubic as well). In state after state, consumers, health care professionals, researchers, policy-makers, and others are asking whether and how to regulate the "childbirth revolution" through training, certification, licensure, and legalization. Obstetricians and family practitioners suppress their differences in order to present a unified position opposing non-medical births; nurse-midwives hold back from endorsing lay midwifery to protect their own still tenuous legitimacy. In short, the discourse on childbirth, these days, emerges from a patchwork of theoretical arguments, case studies, legal battles, proposed and enacted legislation, lobbying campaigns, public dramas, alliances and schisms between and within various constituencies, and the findings of a highly disputatious research literature.

Thus women's discourse on childbirth is not entirely "by women, for women, about women and based on women's experiences and the articulation of those experiences." It is not autonomous but rather generated out of resistance and implicated in ongoing day-to-day struggles for survival and legitimacy. So it may also function variously to engage and maintain the loyalties of its constituencies, undermine the power of the medical establishment, argue its case to the public and the press, dramatize the risks and dangers of medical intervention and hospital birth, and highlight its own safety and cost-effectiveness.

In the same way, "The Yellow Wallpaper" does not present two clear alternative discourses but rather shows in graphic and claustrophobic detail how the same terrain—language—may be differently inhabited. It is a story about language as it is embodied in a very specific type of "patriarchal discourse": the medical diagnosis and its representation of women. This was, and is, a highly policed terrain in which attempts at counter-discourse are discouraged or forbidden (see the accounts by Paget, Burgess, or Scully and Bart). In the same space, the narrator attempts to produce a counter-diagnosis. My argument is that this is a very difficult thing to do, requiring her to work around the edges of a highly circumscribed and policed discourse which restricts the conditions under which she can speak at all. Karen Ford's analysis of the "unheard of contradictions" in the narrator's language—the recurrent anomalies in the even flow of conventional speech—supports this. It would be too optimistic to say that the narrator deliberately evolves an alternative discourse. Yet in the final scene, she does not in fact act in conformity to the patriarchal diagnosis that her sickness is temporary, superficial, and essentially "normal" but instead to her own: that she (woman/women) is genuinely sick and her condition serious. If diagnosis is constructed through discourse, then her different discourse forces a new diagnosis. That she overthrows her early conformity to male-prescribed language is a significant triumph.

The yellow wallpaper embodies this complex cacophony of discourses that come to exist within the terrain the narrator inhabits. As I said in my essay, ultimately the wallpaper "is a disruptive center that chaotically fragments any attempt to fix on it a single meaning." This does not mean that it can mean anything but that meaning itself, in the narrator's struggle to arrive through language at a different understanding of her "condition," is not ultimately fixed.

As I've tried to indicate in my sketch of current discourses on childbirth, to talk about "women's discourse" is to point to a set of conditions for speaking and hearing, and to sites where new strategies and contestations may originate; it is not a fixed, formal entity. I would therefore back away from Ford's conclusion that "language is male-controlled" and remain with the more specific charge that the discourse of medical diagnosis is a prime example of patriarchal discourse. It was perhaps too global an extension on my part to make diagnosis do duty for all forms of "patriarchal discourse," though discussions like Oakley's and Paget's do suggest characteristics shared among different discourses that have been oppressive in their representations of women.

Ford and Neely argue in their different ways that the conditions of speaking have changed, offering more women now those conditions that Woolf suggested would further self-expression: space, audiences who listen, "companionship and advice," and contact with a suppressed tradition. But the contemporary developments in literature by women noted by Ford far surpass women's visible impact on medical texts. Despite the struggles for meaning over the past two decades and the complex mingling of discourses around childbirth that I have sketched above, one has seen little sign of this turbulence in major medical textbooks, which seem astonishingly insulated from widespread social upheaval. There is perhaps some evidence that this is changing: the index to the 1976 edition of the textbook *Williams' Obstetrics* (Pritchard and MacDonald) includes the entry:

CHAUVINISM, MALE, variable amounts, 1–923.

In the 1980 edition, the entry reads:

CHAUVINISM, MALE, voluminous amounts, 1–1102.

The entry is absent from the 1985 edition; rather one finds a number of points in the text itself where feminist concerns are implicitly addressed. To claim a relationship between the index entries and more central textual changes is not possible without concrete evidence. One can claim, however, that the kind of individual changes that, alone, may constitute what I called in my essay "linguistic self-help" are now, in 1985, beginning to be reinforced and sustained by what Neely refers to as "broader changes in the institution" of medicine. In obstetrics practice, I noted a number of these above. Broad economic changes still need to be repeatedly negotiated in local instances. But as hospitals decorate birthing rooms with yards of chintz, encourage obstetricians to involve the whole family in the "birth experience," and create brochures outlining how "natural" it is to deliver a baby in the hospital, can broader changes in medical textbooks and other forms of medical discourse be far behind?

My point is, however, that this is a discourse in which a single index entry still constitutes at the moment a significant feminist subversion. And it is in the context of this discourse that I place the heroic linguistic resistances of the narrator of "The Yellow Wallpaper," who is, as Neely writes, "supposed to change herself but is not allowed to change anything else."

Whose discourse does the yellow wallpaper represent? Discourse is not a covering, like a jacket that fits one sex or the other, or a surface that can be removed or destroyed. The wallpaper is not an artificial covering over reality, a mere surface that can be stripped away; rather it is an aggressive materiality, full of contradictions and impossibilities. When the wallpaper appears finally to be wrestled away from the wall, the narrator is not outside language or beyond language: she never does arrive at such a space, for language is all we know. The most we can do is to situate ourselves within the terrain, inhabit and work it differently. This may suggest new ways of seeing. Indeed the narrator moves "through" the patterns that come with the room to a different view: behind the wallpaper is the wall itself. This is a new representation of women's condition.

Like Carol Neely, I'm not sure that our readings are ultimately incompatible, for we are talking about the narrator's engagement with language. But we do diverge in terms of what we find interesting and compelling about this text. For me it is the dual sentencing of the female narrator, achieved through diagnosis, to a gendered existence both in discourse and in her physical isolation. The confounding throughout of the literary and the "real," the symbolic and the material, gives the narrative some of its impossible and contradictory qualities: Gilman fuses an imaginary fantasy with a social commentary on real (indeed experienced) conditions, she uses a medical case history (another form of "patriarchal discourse") to attack medical practice, and she enfolds us within a world of contradictions and impossibilities whose revelations, nevertheless, will perhaps help us and others escape. Literary analysis works toward resolution and closure, and I found both Karen Ford's and Carol Neely's interpretations of the yellow wallpaper metaphor logical and persuasive. But discourse in "The Yellow Wallpaper" remains an open and contested terrain. We don't know exactly whose discourse is whose, or what it means, or how it will all come out in the end.

In escaping the sentence, the narrator overturns the physician's patriarchal diagnosis but doesn't escape the consequences that this reversal will impose: behind the yellow wallpaper is the wall. In this representation, women are not free. Furthermore, women are still constructed linguistic entities. It is not possible to escape language, only to use it differently, to different ends. To say that the narrator achieves a counter-diagnosis is not to say that she has achieved victory in any total sense. She will not escape, but her words have revealed the wall that confines her. So have Gilman's, an escapee whose account of her experience enlists us, as readers, to continue to work toward changing the nature of medical discourse and the consequences of medical encounters for women.

WORKS CITED

Burgess, Ann Wolbert. "Physician Sexual Misconduct and Patients' Responses." *American Journal of Psychiatry* 138, no. 10, October 1981, 1335–42.

Corea, Gena. *The Hidden Malpractice: How American Medicine Treats Women as Patients and Professionals.* New York: William Morrow, 1977.

DeLee, Joseph B. "The Prophylactic Forceps Operation." *American Journal of Obstetrics and Gynecology,* January, 1920, 34–44.

Jordan, Brigitte. *Birth in Four Cultures.* Montreal: Eden Press, 1983.

Lewin and Associates, Inc. "Competition Among Health Practitioners: The Influence of the Medical Profession on the Health Manpower Market. Volume II: The Childbearing Center Case Study." Washington, D.C.: Federal Trade Commission, 1981.

Lubic, Ruth Watson. "Alternative Maternity Care: Resistance and Change." In *Childbirth: Alternatives to Medical Control,* ed. Shelly Romalis. Austin: University of Texas Press, 1981, 217–49.

Mead, Margaret and Niles Newton. "Cultural Patterning of Perinatal Behavior." In *Childbearing: Its Social and Psychological Aspects,* ed. Stephen A. Richardson and Alan Guttmacher. Baltimore: Williams and Wilkins, 1967, 142–244.

Oakley, Ann. *The Captured Womb: A History of the Medical Care of Pregnant Women.* Oxford: Basil Blackwell, 1984.

Paget, Marianne A. "On the Work of Talk: Studies in Misunderstandings." In *The Social Organization of Doctor-Patient Communication,* ed. Sue Fisher and Alexandra Dundas Todd. Washington, D.C.: Center for Applied Linguistics, 1983, 55–74.

Pritchard, Jack A. and Paul C. MacDonald. *Williams' Obstetrics.* New York: Appleton-Century-Crofts, 1976, 1980, and 1985.

Rothman, Barbara Katz. "Awake and Aware, or False Consciousness: The Cooption of Childbirth Reform in America." In *Childbirth: Alternatives to Medical Control,* ed. Shelly Romalis. Austin: University of Texas Press, 1981, 150–80.

Scully, Diana and Pauline Bart. "A Funny Thing Happened on the Way to the Orifice: Women in Gynecology Textbooks." *American Journal of Sociology* 78, 1973, 1045–50.

Writing from Sources:
Fiction

ॐ

If writing a critical paper about a literary work is like a little monologue or lecture, writing a paper that draws upon others' interpretations is a little like a conversation. It is not exactly like a conversation, because the writer's voice is still the dominant one, but at least alternative views are taken into account.

These alternative views can be used in various ways. One familiar pattern is to construct an essay as a reply to an interpretation you disagree with. Karen Ford's and Carol Thomas Neely's essays on "The Yellow Wallpaper" are of this kind. Paula Treichler's essay argues that the wallpaper symbolizes "women's writing" or "a new vision of women." Karen Ford points out several objections to this reading ("If the wallpaper stands for a new vision of women, why is the narrator tearing it down?"); nevertheless, she picks up Treichler's argument and pushes it somewhat further. Carol Thomas Neely, in contrast, disagrees with Treichler and develops an alternative interpretation: "The yellow wallpaper . . . is more appropriately and usefully defined as a representation of patriarchal discourse (as perceived by women who look at it close up for too long) than of women's discourse: I read the story's ending not as any kind of victory for the narrator but as her defeat." Another possible way to use a published interpretation is to agree with it and then develop it further than the author did. This is what Ford does, even with an interpretation she can accept only provisionally. The important thing is not whether you agree or disagree with the source you cite but that you define your relationship to it clearly and that you subordinate the source to your own argument.

TO QUOTE OR NOT TO QUOTE. Suppose, then, that you have worked out an interpretation of a piece of fiction and have defined your position in relation to one or more previous, published interpretations, either in agreement or disagreement. In presenting these previous interpretations, how do you decide whether to paraphrase or to quote directly? The rule of thumb here is to quote only when you would gain by quoting something which you would miss by paraphrasing. Such gains might occur if the passage in question were distinctive in expression in an important way or if the point you were making required consideration of the precise wording. Otherwise, paraphrase and summary are usually clearer and more economical. Look at Karen Ford's opening paragraph, for example. Most of the paragraph is devoted to summing up and describing Treichler's essay, and yet she quotes Treichler only once, in the passage beginning "a feminist reading emphasizes. . . ." In the rest of the paragraph, Ford summarizes Treichler in her own words; here she apparently felt that Treichler's exact choice of words was important.

The same rule of thumb applies to the primary source, the piece of fiction being analyzed and interpreted, except that the precise wording is likely to be more important and hence cited more often. Look at Ford's second paragraph, for example. Here she is describing the patriarchal world of "The Yellow Wallpaper," making the point that "Whatever language emerges from this setting can safely be considered 'male.'" Nuances of language, then, are important, and so Ford weaves four important phrases from the story into her own sentences. At the end of the paragraph, she returns to Treichler and incorporates into her own text two quotations from Treichler's essay on the subject of patriarchal language. Notice, though, that Ford retains control of the paragraph; her quotations both from the Gilman story and from Treichler's essay are so short and so well integrated into the paragraph that they never threaten to take over the development of the paragraph.

FOOTNOTES VERSUS WORKS CITED. Notice that the essays on "The Yellow Wallpaper" follow two methods of documentation or citation of sources. Treichler's original essay uses footnotes to give sources. Notice that she not only footnotes quoted material but also uses the footnotes to give additional bibliographical information, discuss subordinate points, and generally supplement the main text. Her footnotes can also be used as a model of form. References to a book look like this:

> Charlotte Perkins Gilman, *The Yellow Wallpaper* (Old Westbury, N.Y.: The Feminist Press, 1973), p. 13.

An article in a periodical is cited this way:

> Umberto Eco, "Metaphor, Dictionary, and Encyclopedia," *New Literary History*, 15 (Winter 1984), 255–71.

An example of a citation of an essay in an edited book appears in footnote 6:

> Regina Morantz, "The Lady and Her Physician," in *Clio's Consciousness Raised: New Perspectives on the History of Women*, eds. Mary S. Hartman and Lois Banner (New York: Harper Colophon, 1974), pp. 38–53.

Footnote 6 also offers a model for a citation of an unpublished paper:

> Suzanne Poirier, "The Weir Mitchell Rest Cure: Four Women Who 'Took Charge,'" paper presented at the conference Women's Health: Taking Care and Taking Charge, Morgantown, West Virginia, 1982.

Footnote 9 contains an example of a citation of a reprinted book:

>   Anna Kavan, *Asylum Piece* (1940; rpt. New York: Michael Kesend, 1981), pp. 63, 65.

Notice that the original date of publication is given first, then the publication information on the edition actually used. Here, as in all the examples, you should follow the exact form, including punctuation, so that your footnotes are completely consistent, both with themselves and with standard practice.

Footnotes of the sort that Treichler provides are obviously very useful in providing supplementary material, including bibliographical references, without clogging the main text. But there is another system, used by Ford and Neely and by Treichler herself in her second essay. This is the "Works Cited" method. In this method, the author alludes to the writer of another work in the text and gives the page number in parentheses. The full reference is given in a list called "Works Cited." For example, when Ford cites a critic named Xavière Gauthier, she writes:

>   In *New French Feminisms* Xavière Gauthier notes that traditional work in women's language offers two points of view that Gauthier describes as "flip sides of the same prejudiced coin" (162), because they both describe women's writing in relation to men's.

Then, in the "Works Cited" list, the reference appears:

>   Gauthier, Xavière. "Is There Such a Thing As Women's Writing?" in *New French Feminisms: An Anthology*. Ed. Elaine Marks and Isabelle de Courtivron. New York: Schocken Books, 1981, 161–64.

Notice that the form for citations is slightly different for footnotes and for "Works Cited."

Notice also that Carol Thomas Neely uses both footnotes *and* a "Works Cited" list in her essay. Her footnotes, though, are not bibliographical, as the footnotes in Treichler's first essay are; they give supplementary discussion of the ideas in the text, and if a work is referred to, it is identified briefly, as it would be if it were in the main text, and cited fully in the "Works Cited" list.

Writing from sources about literature takes a little practice. Rather than referring to one text, you are referring to several, and you must take care to keep your references clear. Taking other readings into account can enrich your own writing immensely—if it is done well. The key is probably being sure that you have a well-worked-out interpretation of your own and that you keep the secondary works you cite subordinate to your own argument, contributing to it but not taking it over.

II

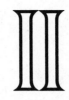

POETRY

Reading Poetry Critically

𝄢 𝄐 𝄑

When we began the study of fiction, we observed that the term *fiction* itself is full of ambiguities and complexities. The term *poetry* is at least as ambiguous and complex. What is poetry? Etymology doesn't help as much with poetry as it does with fiction. As we saw, *fiction* comes from the Latin *fictus,* "formed," a fact that emphasizes the artful shapeliness of fiction rather than its falsity. *Poetry* comes from the Greek *poiein,* "to create." Poets are creators, and poetry is what they create. The etymology suggests the high prestige of poetry but not its nature.

Most attempts to define poetry include several features, in various combinations. One is *form:* Poetry is language arranged according to a formal system (broken into lines of similar length, with a regular rhythm, employing rhyme in a fixed pattern, etc.). Another is *content:* Poetry deals with intense, vivid, personal experience in such a way as to partially recreate that experience in the reader. A third has to do with the *language* of poetry: Poetic language is unusual language, to the extent that the emphasis shifts from what is said to how it is said.

There are two things wrong with these definitions: They don't apply to everything that we call poetry, and they do apply to a great many things that we do not call poetry. Free verse, for example, does not follow a regular metrical scheme, and a poem such as Pope's *Essay on Criticism* deals with factual material rather than with "intense, vivid, personal experience." On the other hand, literary prose often deals with intense personal experience in unusual and beautiful language, and a verse like "Thirty days hath September" is not ordinarily thought of as poetry even though it uses a regular verse form.

Perhaps the only definition of poetry possible (though it is a very circular one) is that it is "anything that people agree to call poetry." The history of poetry is too long and varied to be contained in a single definition, and what an Elizabethan sonnet, an eighteenth-century satire, an Emily Dickinson poem, and a Navaho chant have in common is probably less interesting than the ways in which they differ. That is why books that print medieval lyrics next to modern American poems are a little unsettling. Poetry is much more interesting if it is contextualized, read in the light of its own time and place. Often the best question we can ask is not "What is poetry?" but "How did this culture seem to define poetry, and what work did it seem to do in the culture?"

Reading poetry is not fundamentally different from reading fiction, and much of what we learned about fiction applies also to poetry, especially in regard to point of view, metaphor, and theme. But some elements of poetry are distinctive. In the following pages, we will consider, first, *dramatic situation,* the implied speaker, audience, and circumstances of a poetic text. Then we will go on to consider *form and structure,* learning how to identify common verse forms and how to describe uncommon or unique forms. From there, we will go on to *diction,* the language of poetry; to *metaphor;* and to *theme.* After we have looked at each of these elements of poetry, we will pull them all together in a general reading of a single poem, Amy Clampitt's "Stacking the Straw."

Our study of the interpretation of poetry, then, will be like our study of the interpretation of fiction in at least one respect: It will move back and forth between analysis and synthesis, between separate consideration of the "elements" of poetry and, overall, global interpretations. As with fiction, the first, intuitive understanding will be important as a guide to further analysis. Going systematically through the "elements of poetry" will ensure that we don't miss some important feature. And finally, discriminating between *reading, interpretation,* and *criticism* will help us understand our own relationship to the poetic text. The last thing we will do is consider some of the special problems that *writing about poetry* presents.

Let us begin by reading Donne's "The Sun Rising," Coleridge's "Frost at Midnight," and Joy Harjo's "Your Phone Call at Eight A.M." in preparation for a consideration of dramatic situation.

John Donne

John Donne (1572–1631) spent his life at or near the English court, and his poetry is essentially coterie poetry—difficult, witty poetry to be read by a small group of like-minded friends. Yet it is something more, for it continues to find delighted readers now, almost four hundred years after it was written. After a youth spent in traveling and voluminous reading, Donne became, at the age of twenty-six, private secretary to a powerful court official named Sir Thomas Egerton. He lost this position, however, and was even imprisoned briefly when he secretly married Lady Egerton's sixteen-year-old niece, Ann More. The next few years were difficult for Donne. When he was forty-three, at the urging of King James, Donne entered the Anglican ministry. He eventually became Dean of St. Paul's Cathedral and was known as one of the greatest preachers in England. Donne's poetry and that of his followers was labeled by later critics as "Metaphysical," by which is meant poetry built around "conceits" (elaborate metaphors) and that combines unexpected language and content. His early poetry (of which "A Valediction: Forbidding Mourning" is an example) was primarily love poetry, his later poetry mainly religious poetry; both, however, used many of the same techniques.

THE SUN RISING

> Busy old fool, unruly sun,
> Why dost thou thus,

Through windows and through curtains call on us?
Must to thy motions lovers' seasons run?
    Saucy pedantic wretch, go chide 5
    Late school boys and sour prentices,
    Go tell court huntsmen that the King will ride,
    Call country ants to harvest offices;[1]
Love, all alike, no season knows nor clime,
Nor hours, days, months, which are the rags of time. 10

    Thy beams, so reverend and strong
    Why shouldst thou think?
I could eclipse and cloud them with a wink,
But that I would not lose her sight so long;
    If her eyes have not blinded thine, 15
    Look, and tomorrow late, tell me,
    Whether both th' Indias of spice and mine[2]
Be where thou leftst them, or lie here with me.
Ask for those kings whom thou saw'st yesterday,
And thou shalt hear, All here in one bed lay. 20

    She is all states, and all princes, I,
    Nothing else is.
Princes do but play us; compared to this,
All honor's mimic, all wealth alchemy.[3]
    Thou, sun, art half as happy as we, 25
    In that the world's contracted thus;
    Thine age asks ease, and since thy duties be
    To warm the world, that's done in warming us.
Shine here to us, and thou art everywhere;
This bed thy center is,[4] these walls, thy sphere. 30

Samuel Taylor Coleridge

In the poetic partnership that William Wordsworth and Samuel Taylor Coleridge (1772–1834) formed, Wordsworth was to write poems on "ordinary life," whereas Coleridge was to direct his efforts at "persons and characters supernatural, or at least romantic." It is only one of many contrasts the two used to describe their close, complementary relationship and that others have continued to use. After an erratic performance at Cambridge, which included an enlistment in the army under the name of Silas Tomkyn Comberbacke and an ill-fated project with the poet Robert Southey to establish a utopian community in Pennsylvania, Coleridge settled down with his wife, Sara, whom he had married as part of the Pennsylvania project, on an annuity provided him by the Wedgwood family, manufacturers of fine dishes. He met Wordsworth in 1795 and became a close friend and collaborator. Literary work, though, was slowed by opium, which had first been prescribed for rheumatism and to which, by 1802, he was hopelessly addicted. In his later years, he was cared for by a sympathetic physician named James Gillman and

---

[1] Harvest jobs.   [2] East India was the source of spices, the West Indies the source of gold.
[3] That is, fraudulent.   [4] The center of the sun's orbit.

managed to produce several books of poetry; *Biographia Literaria,* his book of criticism and literary theory; and several other prose works.

FROST AT MIDNIGHT

The frost performs its secret ministry,
Unhelped by any wind. The owlet's cry
Came loud—and hark, again! loud as before.
The inmates of my cottage, all at rest,
Have left me to that solitude, which suits   5
Abtruser musings: save that at my side
My cradled infant slumbers peacefully.
'Tis calm indeed! so calm, that it disturbs
And vexes meditation with its strange
And extreme silentness. Sea, hill, and wood,   10
This populous village! Sea, and hill, and wood,
With all the numberless goings-on of life,
Inaudible as dreams! the thin blue flame
Lies on my low-burnt fire, and quivers not;
Only that film, which fluttered on the grate,   15
Still flutters there, the sole unquiet thing.[1]
Methinks, its motion in this hush of nature
Gives it dim sympathies with me who live,
Making it a companionable form,
Whose puny flaps and freaks the idling Spirit   20
By its own moods interprets, everywhere
Echo or mirror seeking of itself,
And makes a toy of Thought.
                                        But O! how oft,
How oft, at school, with most believing mind,   25
Presageful, have I gazed upon the bars,
To watch that fluttering *stranger!* and as oft
With unclosed lids, already had I dreamt
Of my sweet birth-place, and the old church-tower,
Whose bells, the poor man's only music, rang   30
From morn to evening, all the hot Fair-day,
So sweetly, that they stirred and haunted me
With a wild pleasure, falling on mine ear
Most like articulate sounds of things to come!
So gazed I, till the soothing things, I dreamt,   35
Lulled me to sleep, and sleep prolonged my dreams!
And so I brooded all the following morn,
Awed by the stern preceptor's face, mine eye
Fixed with mock study on my swimming book:
Save if the door half opened, and I snatched   40
A hasty glance, and still my heart leaped up,

---

[1] "In all parts of the kingdom these films are called *strangers* and supposed to portend the arrival of some absent friend" (Coleridge's note). The "film" is a piece of soot fluttering on the grate.

For still I hoped to see the *stranger's* face,
Townsman, or aunt, or sister more beloved
My playmate when we both were clothed alike![2]

Dear Babe, that sleepest cradled by my side,   45
Whose gentle breathings, heard in this deep calm,
Fill up the interspersèd vacancies
And momentary pauses of the thought!
My babe so beautiful! it thrills my heart
With tender gladness, thus to look at thee,   50
And think that thou shalt learn far other lore,
And in far other scenes! For I was reared
In the great city, pent 'mid cloisters dim,
And saw nought lovely but the sky and stars.
But *thou*, my babe! shalt wander like a breeze   55
By lakes and sandy shores, beneath the crags
Of ancient mountain, and beneath the clouds,
Which image in their bulk both lakes and shores
And mountain crags: so shalt thou see and hear
The lovely shapes and sounds intelligible   60
Of that eternal language, which thy God
Utters, who from eternity doth teach
Himself in all, and all things in himself.
Great universal Teacher! he shall mold
Thy spirit, and by giving make it ask.   65

Therefore all seasons shall be sweet to thee,
Whether the summer clothe the general earth
With greenness, or the redbreast sit and sing
Betwixt the tufts of snow on the bare branch
Of mossy apple-tree, while the nigh thatch   70
Smokes in the sun-thaw; whether the eavedrops fall
Heard only in the trances of the blast,
Or if the secret ministry of frost
Shall hang them up in silent icicles,
Quietly shining to the quiet Moon.   75

Joy Harjo

Joy Harjo (b. 1951) is of the Creek (Muscogee) tribe of Native Americans. She was born in Tulsa, Oklahoma, and earned a B.A. at the University of New Mexico and an M.F.A. from the Iowa Writers Workshop. She currently teaches at the University of Arizona. A recurring theme in Harjo's work is the search for unity within the fragmentation of modern life, a search that often involves seeking to recover a harmony in traditional Native American ways. Her collections of poetry include *What Moon Drove Me to This?* (1979), *She Had Some Horses* (1983), and *In Mad Love and War* (1990). *Secrets from the Center of the World,* a collaboration with

---

[2] That is, when he and his sister both wore baby clothes, not differentiated by sex.

the photographer Stephen Strom, was published in 1989. Harjo is also a film-maker and plays tenor saxophone in big bands.

YOUR PHONE CALL AT EIGHT A.M.

Your phone call at eight A.M. could
have been a deadly rope.
All the colors of your voice
were sifted out. The barest part flew
through the wires. Then tight-roped   5
into the comfort of my own home,
where I surrounded myself with smoke
of piñon, with cedar and sage.
Protected the most dangerous places,
for more than survival, I always   10
mean. But what you wanted, this morning
you said, was a few words
and not my heart. What you wanted . . .
But the skeleton of your voice
clicked barely perceptible,   15
didn't you hear it?
And what you said you wanted
was easy enough, a few books
some pages, anything, to cancel
what your heart ever saw in me that you didn't.   20
But you forgot to say that part.
Didn't even recognize it when it
came winging out of you—
the skeleton's meat and blood,
all that you didn't want to remember   25
when you called at eight a.m. . . . .
But that's all right because
this poem isn't for you
but for me
after all   30

DRAMATIC SITUATION

There is no fixed order in which to consider the elements of a poem. But it usually works well to begin with a general, overall survey of the poem and to wait for smaller features until later. Analyzing the *dramatic situation* is usually a good first move. To identify the dramatic situation is to consider the poem as if it were a miniature play or a single speech in a play. The elements of the dramatic situation are the speaker, the person addressed, and the context. From the context, it is an easy step to summarizing what the speaker says. Such a summary is sometimes called the *paraphrasable prose content*. The term acknowledges that the full content of a good poem can never be captured in a paraphrase, but it is useful, nevertheless, to arrive at a common understanding of what the sentences of the poem say, *as sentences,* not necessarily as lines of verse.

Take a look at Donne's "The Sun Rising," for instance. The first line tells us immediately who is being addressed: "Busy old fool, unruly sun." Somebody is talking to the sun, but who? We have to wait a few lines to gradually pick up the identity of the speaker and the situation. The third line refers to "us," suggesting that the speaker is not alone; and the fourth says that lovers should not be governed by the risings and settings of the sun, suggesting that the speaker is a lover. By the end of the second stanza, if not before, all is clear: The speaker is a man who is in bed with his lover. Of course, the poem raises questions about who is *really* being addressed. After all, to talk to the sun is to ensure not being heard, and as the poem goes on, we realize that the real intended auditor is the loved one, to whom the poem is an elaborate compliment. And because we are reading the poem, the ultimate intended audience may be ourselves. But much of the fun of the poem is the pretense that the poem is spoken by a man in bed with a woman and that he is pretending to scold the sun for coming up too soon.

(How do we identify the genders involved? Notice that the loved one is referred to with feminine pronouns: *her* and *she.* But what about the male speaker? The only direct evidence that the speaker is male is the fact that he calls himself "all princes" [line 21]. Otherwise, the speaker theoretically could be imagined as female, and the liaison a homosexual one. The point here is not to argue for such an improbable reading but to suggest that nothing should be taken for granted in analyzing dramatic situations.)

As for the paraphrasable prose content, notice that it is structured by progressively greater exaggeration. The speaker begins by telling the sun that lovers are not governed by its movements (stanza 1). He then says that he could eclipse the sun just by closing his eyes, but that he doesn't want to lose the time for gazing at his love. He goes on to ask the sun (if it has not been blinded by the brilliance of the loved one's eyes) if the Orient and the West Indies and all the kings of the world are still where they were or if they are now all in the lovers' bed (stanza 2). This last statement sets up the climactic exaggerations of stanza 3. The loved one is "all states," and the lover is "all princes." The entire world is contracted to the bedroom and the bed, and the sun (which after all is very old) can warm the world just by warming the lovers.

This paraphrase misses a lot of what makes the poem funny and meaningful— the variations on the motif of time, for instance, and the half-joking, half-serious triumph of the private over the public. But it is a rough map of the poem and can serve as the basis of more detailed study later.

If the speaker in "The Sun Rising" seems to be talking past his ostensible audience, the sun, to his loved one and past the loved one to readers of his poem, Coleridge's "Frost at Midnight" presents equal, if very different, complexities. The first stanza of this poem is devoted to little else than describing the dramatic situation: The speaker sits in a cottage, the other inhabitants of which are asleep. He sits before an open fire, and at his side is his sleeping infant. It is a calm, frosty night outside. The implied audience of the first two verse paragraphs is left vague and unspecified. With stanza 3 the speaker turns to the sleeping child and addresses him for the rest of the poem. Because the child is asleep, he can hardly be called an audience in the ordinary sense. The discourse of "Frost at Midnight" is highly problematical, though problematical in so conventionalized a way that we hardly notice its artificiality. We can read the poem as an interior monologue. (It would be rather grotesque to imagine the speaker soliloquizing aloud to the sleeping house.) But the poem has none of the fragmentation, associational structure, and incoherence of a real interior monologue. The dramatic situation is merely an occasion to set up a conventionalized dramatic monologue, rather like Hamlet's soliloquies, that we can take as unspoken thoughts if we like.

Much of the content of the poem is an exploration of the meaning of the dramatic situation. In the first stanza, Coleridge (as we may agree to call the speaker) describes the setting and situation and compares the fluttering "stranger" of soot in the fire with his own restless spirit, forever seeking echoes of itself in nature. The second stanza is a memory of childhood, which he spent lost in dreams, reveries, and presentiments of things to come. In the third stanza, he turns to the child and declares that he will be reared in the country, which will give him a better relationship with the world than the speaker, who was reared in the city, has. The poem ends with a half-hope, half-prayer that "all seasons shall be sweet" to the child, whether summer, which clothes "the general earth / With greenness," or winter, when "the secret ministry of frost" hangs eavedrops up in silent icicles. As with "The Sun Rising," a prose paraphrase of "Frost at Midnight" omits most of what makes the poem interesting. But it can serve as the basis for more subtle and detailed study of the poem.

Joy Harjo's "Your Phone Call at Eight A.M." rings yet another set of variations on the conventions and ambiguities of a dramatic situation. The speaker seems to be a woman addressing her lover about an upsetting early-morning telephone call. Is the lover present? Has he returned to the speaker? Has the speaker gone to meet him? Is the poem part of a later telephone call? Part of a letter? All these questions are left unresolved until the last four lines of the poem:

> But that's all right because
> this poem isn't for you
> but for me
> after all

These last lines force us to abruptly revise our understanding of the poem. What we took to be a speech addressed to the lover either directly or through the medium of a telephone call or letter we are now told is "a poem" that is not for the lover but for the speaker.

The telephone call has been upsetting. The speaker offers a series of metaphors for it: a deadly rope—a hangman's rope or a lariat, a filter that "sifted out" the colors of the lover's voice, which was left a clicking skeleton. The speaker has sensed a retreat from intimacy in the lover's voice; he wants something "to cancel / what your heart ever saw in me that you didn't."

Is "Your Phone Call at Eight A.M." about love or about poetry? Or is it about both? Those last four lines, after the earlier part of the poem that seemed to be a rather emotional speech by a woman unsure of her lover, turn the poem into something altogether different—not a rebuke of the lover but an attempt to deal with a painful experience by articulating it in language. The poem is not for the lover but for the speaker "after all."

(Genders are even more problematic here than in "The Sun Rising." Notice that all the pronouns are ungendered [*you, me,* etc.]. We have read the speaker as female and the person addressed as male. But the speaker could be male and the person addressed could be female, or the two could be the same sex, either male or female. The temptation to read the "I" as female comes from the fact that the poem is by a female poet. But poets can and do adopt *personae* completely unlike themselves. The only reason for interpreting the poem as being from woman to man is that Harjo does not *seem* to be writing here from an invented perspective. However, she may be.)

The dramatic situations of some poems are very concrete and specific; those of others are vague and indeterminate. But working out the dramatic situation and the paraphrasable prose content of any poem can lead us into close analysis not only of the premises of the poem but also into nuances of voice, tone, and implication. It's often a good starting point.

Read the following poems carefully: Shakespeare's "Shall I Compare Thee to a Summer's Day?", Whitman's "When I Heard the Learn'd Astronomer," Galway Kinnell's "First Song," and Sonia Sanchez's "A Song." They will serve as the basis for a discussion of *form* and *structure*.

William Shakespeare

William Shakespeare (1564–1616) is best known for his plays. But if he had written nothing but his nondramatic verse, he would still hold a high place in English literature. He wrote several poems on classical or mythological themes, notably *Venus and Adonis* (1593), *The Rape of Lucrece* (1594), and *The Phoenix and the Turtle* (1601). His sonnets, apparently written for private circulation rather than for publication, were published without his authorization in 1609. And the plays contain many songs that contribute in a variety of ways to the development of plot, character, or theme.

SONNET 18: SHALL I COMPARE THEE TO A SUMMER'S DAY?

> Shall I compare thee to a summer's day?
> Thou art more lovely and more temperate:
> Rough winds do shake the darling buds of May,
> And summer's lease hath all too short a date:
> Sometime too hot the eye of heaven shines,   5
> And often is his gold complexion dimmed;
> And every fair from fair sometimes declines,
> By chance or nature's changing course untrimmed;
> But thy eternal summer shall not fade,
> Nor lose possession of that fair thou ow'st;   10
> Nor shall death brag thou wander'st in his shade,
> When in eternal lines to time thou grow'st:
> So long as men can breathe, or eyes can see,
> So long lives this, and this gives life to thee.

Walt Whitman

"The United States themselves are essentially the greatest poem," Walt Whitman (1819–92) wrote in the preface to the first edition of *Leaves of Grass,* and he devoted his life to finding the words and forms for this poem. Whitman grew up in New York, first on Long Island and then in Brooklyn. He left school when he was eleven and was eventually apprenticed to a printer. Printing led to journalism, and between the ages of nineteen and thirty-one Whitman was caught up in the daily pressures of newspaper work. In about 1850, he underwent something of a transformation. He began to wear workman's clothes, grew a full beard, and began to think of himself as a potential bard and prophet of an ideal America. The first edition of *Leaves of Grass*, privately published by Whitman himself, appeared in 1855. The rest of Whitman's life was devoted primarily to producing further editions of *Leaves of Grass*, each with added poems and revisions and rearrangements of earlier ones. Whitman suffered a stroke in 1873 and moved in with his brother's family in Camden, New Jersey. He lived there until his death in 1892, the center of a cult of worldwide admirers and followers.

WHEN I HEARD THE LEARN'D ASTRONOMER

When I heard the learn'd astronomer,
When the proofs, the figures, were ranged in columns before me,
When I was shown the charts and diagrams, to add, divide, and measure
    them,
When I sitting heard the astronomer where he lectured with much applause
    in the lecture-room,
How soon unaccountable I became tired and sick,   5
Till rising and gliding out I wander'd off by myself,
In the mystical moist night-air, and from time to time,
Look'd up in perfect silence at the stars.

Galway Kinnell

Galway Kinnell (b. 1927) was born in Providence, Rhode Island, and educated at Princeton University and the University of Rochester. His first book of poems appeared in 1960: *What a Kingdom It Was*. Since then, he has published about twenty books of poetry. In 1983, his *Selected Poems* won both the Pulitzer Prize and the American Book Award. Kinnell describes his progress as a poet in terms of openness. As he has developed, he has given up the often intricate, traditional rhyme schemes of his early poetry in favor of simpler diction and form. Like many of his fellow modern poets—Marianne Moore and Ted Hughes, for example—he has written extensively about animals, finding in the identification with an animal a passage between the world of nature and that of human beings.

FIRST SONG

Then it was dusk in Illinois, the small boy
After an afternoon of carting dung
Hung on the rail fence, a sapped thing
Weary to crying. Dark was growing tall
And he began to hear the pond frogs all   5
Calling on his ear with what seemed their joy.

Soon their sound was pleasant for a boy
Listening in the smoky dusk and the nightfall
Of Illinois, and from the fields two small
Boys came bearing cornstalk violins   10
And they rubbed the cornstalk bows with resins
And the three sat there scraping of their joy.

It was now fine music the frogs and the boys
Did in the towering Illinois twilight make
And into dark in spite of a shoulder's ache   15
A boy's hunched body loved out of a stalk
The first song of his happiness, and the song woke
His heart to the darkness and into the sadness of joy.

Sonia Sanchez

Sonia Sanchez (b. 1934), born in Birmingham, Alabama, moved with her family
to Harlem when she was nine. She was graduated from Hunter College in 1955.
An African-American, she joined the Nation of Islam in 1972 and advocates
black militancy in response to white violence. She is a playwright as well as a
poet; her plays include *The Bronx Is Next* (1970), *Sister Son/ji* (1971), and *I'm
Black When I'm Singing, I'm Blue When I Ain't* (1982). Poetry collections include
Homecoming (1969), *We a BaddDDD People* (1970), *A Blues Book for Blue Black
Magical Women* (1974), *I've Been a Woman: New and Selected Poems* (1979), and
Under a Soprano Sky (1987). Sanchez is a professor of English at Temple Uni-
versity in Philadelphia.

A SONG

take my virginity
and convert it to maternity
wait around a century or two
and see what i'll do.

take my body give it yo' brand   5
stitch my breasts on the fatherland
wait around a decade or two
and see just what i'll do.

place my dreams on any back stair
tune my eyes for yo' nightmare   10
wait around a century or two
and see what i'll finally do.

suck my breath until i stutter
listen to the sounds i utter
wait around a decade or two   15
and see just what i'll do.

take my daughter one sunday morn
drape her in dresses to be torn
wait around a century or two
and see what i'll finally do.   20

bury me early all dressed in white
find yourself a brand new wife
wait around a decade or two
and see what she'll finally do.
and see what she'll finally do.   25

FORM AND STRUCTURE

Working out the *dramatic situation* of a poem is a good way of getting an overview
of a poem. So is analysis of *form* and *structure*. These terms are similar in meaning
in most contexts. But with poetry, we use the word *form* to refer to the metrical
arrangement of a poem, and the word *structure* to refer to the arrangement of
thought.

Form

Many students resist analyzing the form of a poem, finding such analysis dull and
mechanical. You don't have to know music theory, they say, to appreciate a song;
why should you have to do a metrical analysis of a poem in order to appreciate it?
They have a point; no amount of metrical analysis will help us understand what a
poem says, much less evaluate that meaning. And yet in literature and especially
in poetry, how a thing is said is at least as important as the thing that is said, and
it is difficult to see how a person could appreciate the way a poem makes its
statement without understanding the formal rules the poem has followed.

An analysis of a poem's form involves identifying four things:

1. the dominant rhythm of the poem,
2. the length of the lines,
3. the number of lines in a stanza, and
4. the rhyme scheme of a stanza.

To identify the dominant rhythm of a poem, identify the kind of *metrical foot* that
predominates. There are four important kinds of foot: iamb, trochee, anapest,
and dactyl. The *iamb* (or *iambic foot*) is the most common rhythm in English. (It
is easy, for example, to identify iambic rhythms in everyday conversation or in
such utilitarian writing as that found in newspaper stories.) An iamb is an unstressed syllable followed by a stressed one: ˘ ´. Here is a line, for example, from
Wordsworth's *The Prelude:*

Fair séed / time hád / my soúl, / and Í / grĕw úp.

There may be other rhythms in the poem, but the iambic rhythm predominates.
Here are the first two lines of Browning's "The Bishop Orders His Tomb at St.
Praxed's Church":

> Vanity / saith / the preach- / er, / vanity!
>
> Draw round / my bed: / is An- / selm keep- /ing back?

The word "vanity" in the first line (twice) is obviously not iambic but a triple rhythm (a *dactyl*, we shall see later). But the poem quickly settles into the predominantly iambic rhythm of the second line.

A *trochee* (or *trochaic foot*) is the opposite of an iamb. It is a stressed syllable followed by an unstressed one: ´ ˘. Here, for example, are the first lines from Blake's "Song of Innocence":

> Piping / down the / valleys / wild
>
> Piping / songs of / pleasant / glee
>
> On a / cloud I / saw a / child
>
> And he / laughing / said to / me.

The iamb and the trochee are duple rhythms, like 2/4 and 4/4 in music. The principal triple rhythms in poetry are anapestic and dactyllic. An *anapest* (or *anapestic foot*) has two unstressed syllables followed by a stressed one.

> 'Twas the night / before Christ- / mas and all / through the house . . .

The anapestic rhythms of "A Visit from St. Nicholas" have a singsong, rather comical effect. In Byron's "The Destruction of Sennacherib," the rhythms imitate horses' hooves:

> The Assyr- / ian came down / like the wolf / on the fold,
>
> And his co- / horts were gleam- / ing in pur- / ple and gold.

The *dactyl* (*dactylic foot*) consists of a stressed syllable followed by two unstressed ones, basically the same rhythm as 3/4 time in music, as in Tennyson's "The Charge of the Light Brigade":

> Half a league, / half a league,
>
> Half a league / onward,
>
> All in the / valley of / Death
>
> Rode the six / hundred.

There are other kinds of rhythm as well. A *spondee* has two stressed syllables (´ ´). A *pyrric* has two unstressed syllables (˘ ˘). An *amphibrach* has the rhythm of unstressed, stressed, unstressed (˘ ´ ˘); an *amphimacer* has the opposite one of stressed, unstressed, stressed (´ ˘ ´). But the ability to recognize iambs, trochees, anapests, and dactyls will allow you to analyze the basic rhythm of almost any poem.

In addition to the basic rhythm of a poem—the predominant kind of foot—we need to note the number of feet in each line. Here are the terms for the common line lengths:

monometer	one foot
dimeter	two feet
trimeter	three feet
tetrameter	four feet
pentameter	five feet
hexameter	six feet
heptameter	seven feet
octameter	eight feet

And finally, in order to describe a verse form, we need to give the number of lines in a stanza and the rhyme scheme.

One final caution: Scanning poetry (identifying its rhythms) is not an exact science. Different readers may place the stress differently; there are many levels of stress, not just stressed and unstressed; and different readers may put more stresses and therefore feet into a given line than other readers do. The purpose of scansion is not to arrive at perfect agreement but to recognize basic patterns and thus to be able to recognize when the basic pattern is being broken. To say that a poem is in iambic pentameter is not to say that every foot is an iamb and that every line has five feet. It is merely to say that the basic pattern—the point of departure, if you will—is iambic pentameter and that variations are variations from that pattern.

To see how all this works, let us take a look at Shakespeare's Sonnet 18: "Shall I Compare Thee to a Summer's Day?" Let us mark the stresses and the division into feet in the first couple of lines of the poem:

Shall Í / compáre / thee tŏ / a súm- / mer's dáy?

Thóu art / more lóve- / lў and / more témp- / ĕrate

Even this much analysis shows that most of the feet are iambs and that the lines have five feet. In other words, the lines are in iambic pentameter. There are several other kinds of feet (*substitutions*), but the basic pattern is iambic pentameter.

Next we should see how many lines are in this one-stanza poem, and we find that there are fourteen. We check the rhyme scheme and find the following: ababcdcdefefgg. We can now describe the poem as "fourteen lines of iambic pentameter, rhymed ababcdcdefefgg." We should recognize this as an English or Shakespearean sonnet (perhaps not a big surprise if we are analyzing something called "Sonnet 18" by Shakespeare!). Sometimes we will discover that the verse form of the poem we are studying conforms to a standard model, and sometimes we will find that the verse form was apparently invented for this one poem or perhaps has been used before but has no name. Either piece of information is good to know. (A guide to common English verse forms follows this essay.)

For a very different example, take a look at Whitman's "When I Heard the Learn'd Astronomer." This poem may be marked for stresses:

When I heard the learn'd astronomer,

When the proofs, the figures, were ranged in columns before me ...

There is some preponderance of iambs here, but no more than one would expect in even a prose passage. Similarly, there seems to be no regular line length. Line 1 seems to have three stresses and therefore three feet; line 2 seems to have five. Line 3 seems to have eight. There is no end-rhyme. All these observations tell us that "When I Heard the Learn'd Astronomer" is in *free verse*, verse that does not use traditional meter and rhyme.

Does the fact that a poem is in free verse mean that there is nothing more to be said about its form? Not at all. Look again at "When I Heard the Learn'd Astronomer." Is there *any* pattern in the lines? Notice that the first four lines are the most varied in length and seem wordy and prosaic, especially the third and fourth lines. The last four lines, by contrast, are comparatively regular. Each has five feet, and the last line is a perfectly regular iambic pentameter line:

Look'd up / in per- / fect si- / lence at / the stars.

"When I Heard the Learn'd Astronomer," short as it is, has two settings—the lecture-room and the out-of-doors—and the change in line length corresponds exactly to the change of setting. Is it too fanciful to say that the long, irregular first four lines suggest the noise, pedantry, and wordiness of the lecture-room and that the comparative brevity and regularity of the last four lines suggest the silence and serenity of the natural order?

Sonnet 18 uses a familiar form in a traditional way, whereas "When I Heard the Learn'd Astronomer" abandons traditional form for free verse. For a very different example, look at Galway Kinnell's "First Song."

Then it was / dusk in / Ill-i- / nois, the / small boy
After an / after- / noon of / carting / dung
Hung on the / rail / fence, / a sapped / thing
Weary to / crying. / Dark was / growing / tall
And he be- / gan to / hear the / pond frogs / all
Calling / on his ear / with what / seemed their / joy.

What pattern can we find here? There are many substitutions, but the basic pattern seems to be trochaic, and there seem to be five feet in each line. (This pattern would be confirmed and would be even clearer if we scanned the other two stanzas as well.) Each stanza, then, consists of six lines of trochaic pentameter. The rhyme scheme seems to be abbcca. (In the first stanza, *dung* and *thing* are not exact rhymes, but a look at the second and third lines of the other stanzas confirms that they are meant as rhymes and are, in fact, half-rhymes.

"First Song," then, consists of three six-line stanzas of trochaic pentameter, rhymed abbcca. A glance at the "Guide to Verse Forms" (following this section) shows that this is not an established form with a name and a history. Nevertheless, it is made up of familiar elements. Each stanza is basically three couplets, with the second and third couplets placed between the two lines of the first couplet, in a kind of nested structure. The regularity of line length and the frequency of rhyme make this poem perhaps seem more regular than it is, and the use of an ad hoc form and the frequent liberties taken with it give the poem, conversely, a modern tone.

Finally, for yet another very different example of form, look at Sonia Sanchez's "A Song." The title and the look of the quatrains on the page prepare us to read this poem as a simple song lyric, perhaps in ballad stanza. But if we look closely at the form, we find that it is not ballad stanza at all but a very free handling of the quatrain. In the first place, the rhyme scheme is not abab or abcb but is rather aabb. (In the last, five-line stanza, the fifth line is a repetition of line four, like a tag or coda on a song.) The lines are not alternating tetrameter and trimeter, as we would expect in ballad stanza, but are rather three lines of tetrameter followed by a line of trimeter. The rhythm is quite free:

táke / mý vĭr- / gínĭ- / tý

aňd cónvért / iť tŏ / matérn- / ĭtý

waǐt ă- / roúnd ă / céntŭrý / oř two

aňd séе / what I'ĺl / dó.

The basic rhythm is trochaic, but it is varied so much that it is almost unrecognizable, and the poem has something of the naturalness and irregularity of conversation rather than the singsong regularity we associate with ballads. We might call "A Song" an "art-ballad," a poem that builds on the tradition of the ballad quatrain but varies it so much that it could never be mistaken for a folk-song.

The four very different examples of Shakespeare's Sonnet 18, Whitman's "When I Heard the Learn'd Astronomer," Kinnell's "First Song," and Sanchez's "A Song" identify the stages in the process of describing a poem's form:

1. identification of basic rhythm, line length, number of lines in a stanza, and rhyme scheme;
2. determination whether the form is a standard, traditional one or not; and
3. description of the appropriateness of the form to the content of the poem.

Structure

Consideration of the content of poems brings us to another way of looking at the overall organization of a poem: analysis of its *structure*. Whereas *form* refers to the arrangement of the actual words and sentences of a poem on the page, *structure* refers to the arrangement of thought. How is the content structured? Does it ask a question at the beginning and go on to answer it? Does it describe a scene and then interpret its meaning? Does it make a generalization and then provide an example (or three or four examples)? Does it tell a story?

Let us review the four poems the form of which we have just analyzed and analyze their structures as well. In Shakespeare's Sonnet 18, the poet announces what he is going to do in the first line—"Shall I compare thee to a summer's day?"—and then goes on to do it. But there are a number of little surprises and unexpected turns along the way. The first point that Shakespeare makes in his comparison is that "Thou art more lovely and more temperate," and the rest of the first eight lines (the *octave*) are devoted to the defects of summer's days: It is sometimes windy, summer doesn't last long, sometimes it's too hot or too cloudy.

Nature, in general, is too changeable. But then Shakespeare makes a surprising statement (at the beginning of the last six lines or *sestet,* where we would expect a shift or turn in the thought): "But thy eternal summer shall not fade." Here is a paradox. Human beings are mortal, and we usually contrast our temporality with the timelessness of nature. But here the speaker is saying that the loved one is less subject to change than nature is. The rest of the sestet is devoted to unraveling this paradox. The loved one is immortal and unchanging because she has been written about in this poem:

> So long as men can breathe, or eyes can see,
> So long lives this [this poem], and this gives life to thee.

The poem is a sophisticated joke: What seems at first an elaborate compliment to a lady turns out to be by the end a piece of self-congratulation by the poet. The subject is not love, as we think at first, but art and our ability to escape time by fleeing from nature into art.

A structural analysis comes very close to being a summary or paraphrase of the poem, and indeed it may make use of summary and paraphrase. But at its best, a structural analysis should not just sum up the content of a poem but describe the way the content is laid out: the order of ideas and the reasons for that order.

We have already touched on one structural feature of Whitman's "When I Heard the Learn'd Astronomer," its division into an indoor scene and an outdoor scene. But before we observe this, we have to realize that, short as it is, "When I Heard the Learn'd Astronomer" is a narrative poem; it tells a little story about the speaker, who went to an astronomy lecture, became "tired and sick," and went outside and "look'd up in perfect silence at the stars." "When I Heard the Learn'd Astronomer" is a little fable or parable about the relation between human achievement and nature, and notice that the implied conclusion is almost the opposite of Shakespeare's in Sonnet 18. Shakespeare suggests (with whatever degree of seriousness) that nature is changeable and unreliable, whereas human art can convey immortality. Human art makes Whitman "tired and sick," and he can be restored only by direct contact with the silent perfection of nature. The conflict of art and nature is dramatized on the tiny stage of the poem, with four rambling, wordy lines devoted to art and four taut, economical lines devoted to nature.

Galway Kinnell's "First Song" is another narrative, though here not a first-person account of a recent event, as "When I Heard the Learn'd Astronomer" seems to be, but a third-person account of childhood experience told from an adult perspective. (We may suspect that the story is autobiographical, despite the third-person distance from "the small boy.") Like Whitman's slight anecdote, Kinnell's story about a farm boy is short on action but rich in suggestion.

The three stanzas structure the action in three parts. In the first stanza, the boy is exhausted after a day of hauling manure. By the third stanza, the boy, who was "a sapped thing / Weary to crying" in the first stanza, has become happy; his music on the cornstalk violin is "the first song of his happiness." Stanza 2 is transitional between the sorrow of stanza 1 and the joy of stanza 3. The boy listens to the pond frogs croaking "with what seemed their joy," and two boys arrive carrying cornstalk violins.

What is the meaning of the boy's experience? The anecdote upon which "First Song" is based is an initiation narrative, a story of how a young person is introduced to some aspect of adult experience, in this case the power of art. The boy's song is the "first song of his happiness," and it woke "His heart to the darkness and into the sadness of joy." The song of the cornstalk violins is a special kind of art, especially close to nature. The boy hears two kinds of music, the croaking of the frogs expressing "what seemed their joy" and the music of the cornstalk violins. They are the music of nature and the music of art, and the two blend in the "towering Illinois twilight."

It may not be pushing things too far to note that "First Song" takes up again the topic of nature and art treated in Sonnet 18 and "When I Heard the Learn'd Astronomer." If Shakespeare sees art as superior to nature, offering the hope of a kind of immortality, and if Whitman sees human achievements as dwarfed by the grandeur of nature, then Kinnell seems to see art as best when it is in harmony with nature, when the materials of art are humble, like cornstalks, and when the song of the boys blends with the song of the frogs.

The structure of Sanchez's "A Song" is obviously very different, being not a story but a chant or incantation. The six stanzas follow a single pattern: two lines in imperative voice that tell a man to do something to the speaker ("take my virginity," "take my body give it yo' brand," etc.), then a variation on

> wait around a century or two
> and see what i'll do.

These variations follow a pattern. The stanzas alternate between "wait around a century or two" and "wait around a decade or two" for the third line, and "and see just what i'll do" and "and see what i'll finally do" for the fourth line. The last stanza, dealing with the "brand new wife," ends with the variation "and see what she'll finally do." Except for the last variation, it is hard to see that these changes have significant thematic implications; they seem to be variations for the sake of variation, to avoid mechanical repetition.

The progression of the stanzas is another matter. The violence done to woman by man seems to escalate as the poem progresses, from childbearing ("take my virginity / and convert it to maternity") to appropriation of female children ("take my daughter one sunday morn / drape her in dresses to be torn") and what amounts to murder ("bury me early all dressed in white / find yourself a brand new wife"). This last stanza, with its switch from "see what i'll finally do" to "see what she'll finally do," enlarges the subject of the poem from a sense of personal grievance to one of feminist solidarity. If justice is not done in this generation, it will be done in the future.

We have considered form and structure separately, and they must initially be analyzed that way. But ideally they should finally merge, complementing and reinforcing each other. Thus the two four-line units of "When I Heard the Learn'd Astronomer" harmonize with the contrasts between indoors and outdoors, human knowledge and nature, and talk about the stars and the stars themselves upon which the poem is built. Similarly, the three stanzas of "First Song" match the three stages in the boy's experience, from exhaustion to the awakening of the senses to "the first song of his happiness" in stanza 3. And the six quatrains of "A Song" offer an opportunity to express the escalating list of grievances upon which Sanchez structures her poem.

We have touched on *diction*, the word choice poets make, in the course of analyzing other elements. But for more extended study of diction, read the following poems: Tennyson's "The Lady of Shalott," Blake's "The Sick Rose," Michael Blumenthal's "Advice to My Students: How to Write a Poem," and Stephen Shu Ning Liu's "At the King's Funeral."

A GUIDE TO VERSE FORMS

The most common verse forms are arranged here by the number of lines in a stanza, from one to fourteen. Other features of the form are given, along with an example.

One line

The idea of a one-line stanza is rather peculiar. But this is a convenient place to describe *blank verse,* which does not have stanzas. Blank verse is unrhymed iambic pentameter. It has irregular verse paragraphs rather than stanzas. It is the principal verse form of Shakespeare's plays and has been used in many of the long, serious poems in English and American literature, including Milton's *Paradise Lost,* Wordsworth's *Prelude,* Tennyson's *Idylls of the King,* and many of Robert Frost's poems, including "The Death of the Hired Man."

> Of man's first disobedience, and the fruit
> Of that forbidden tree whose mortal taste
> Brought death into the world, and all our woe,
> With loss of Eden, til one greater Man
> Restore us, and regain the blissful seat,
> Sing, Heavenly Muse. . . .
>
> from John Milton, *Paradise Lost*

Two lines

A two-line stanza is called a *couplet.* A distinctive form of couplet is the *heroic couplet,* which is defined as a couplet of iambic pentameter, closed and end-stopped. A couplet is closed if it expresses a complete thought and ends with a terminal mark of punctuation, such as a period or semicolon. It is end-stopped if the first line ends in a pause, not running over into the second line. It was Pope's principal verse form and is strongly identified with English neoclassical verse, though it has been used in other periods.

> What dire offense from amorous causes springs,
> What mighty contests rise from trivial things,
> I sing—This verse to Caryll, Muse! is due:
> This, even Belinda may vouchsafe to view:
> Slight is the subject, but not so the praise,
> If she inspire, and he approve my lays.
>
> from Alexander Pope, *The Rape of the Lock*

The *tetrameter couplet* has also been widely used in English, usually, though not always, for satiric or comic verse.

> The farmer's goose, who in the stubble,
> Has fed without restraint or trouble,
> Grown fat with corn and sitting still,
> Can scarce get o'er the barn door sill;
>
> from Jonathan Swift, "The Progress of Poetry"

Three lines

Three-line stanzas are rare in English. The only widely used one is *terza rima,* the Italian stanza used by Dante for the *Divine Comedy.* Terza rima has three-line stanzas linked by the following rhyming pattern: aba bcb cdc, ded, and so on.

> O wild West Wind, thou breath of Autumn's being,
> Thou, from whose unseen presence the leaves dead
> Are driven, like ghosts from an enchanter fleeing,
>
> Yellow, and black, and pale, and hectic red,
> Pestilence-stricken multitudes: O Thou,
> Who chariotest to their dark wintry bed
>
> The winged seeds, where they lie cold and low,
> Each like a corpse within its grave, until
> Thine azure sister of the Spring shall blow
>
> Her clarion o'er the dreaming earth, and fill
> (Driving sweet buds like flocks to feed in air)
> With living hues and odours plain and hill:
>
> Wild Spirit, which art moving everywhere;
> Destroyer and Preserver; hear, O hear!
>
> from Percy Bysshe Shelley, "Ode to the West Wind"

Four lines

Four-line stanzas are called *quatrains.* There is a wide variety of types, depending on the length of line and the rhyme pattern. In *ballad stanza,* lines 1 and 3 are tetrameter, and lines 2 and 4 are trimeter; the rhyme scheme is either abab or abcb.

> There lived a wife at Usher's Well,
>   And a wealthy wife was she;
> She had three stout and stalwart sons,
>   And sent them o'er the sea.
>
> from "The Wife at Usher's Well"

Heroic quatrains use all iambic pentameter lines and rhyme abab:

> The curfew tolls the knell of parting day,
>   The lowing herd wind slowly o'er the lea,
> The plowman homeward plods his weary way,
>   And leaves the world to darkness and to me.
>
> from Thomas Gray, "Elegy Written in a Country Churchyard"

Seven lines

Rhyme royal is so called because King James I of Scotland used it in "The Kingis Quair." It consists of seven lines of iambic pentameter rhymed ababbcc. It can be thought of as a quatrain followed by two couplets, with line 4 serving as both the last line of the quatrain and the first line of the first couplet.

> They flee from me, that sometime did me seek,
> With naked foot stalking in my chamber.
> I have seen them, gentle, tame, and meek,
> That now are wild, and do not remember
> That sometime they put themselves in danger
> To take bread at my hand; and now they range,
> Busily seeking with a continual change.
>
> from Thomas Wyatt, "They Flee from Me"

Eight lines

Ottava rima is an eight-line stanza, as its Italian name indicates. Its lines are all iambic pentameter, and the rhyme scheme is abababcc. It was introduced into English, like terza rima and the sonnet, by Thomas Wyatt in the early sixteenth century; but its most famous use is by Byron in *Don Juan*. Byron turned the form to comic purposes by using strained rhymes and using the final couplet for a witty twist. But it can also be used for serious purposes, as it was by Yeats in "Sailing to Byzantium" and "Among School Children."

> I walk through the long schoolroom questioning;
> A kind old nun in a white hood replies;
> The children learn to cipher and to sing,
> To study reading-books and history,
> To cut and sew, be neat in everything
> In the best modern way—the children's eyes
> In momentary wonder stare upon
> A sixty–year–old smiling public man.
>
> from William Butler Yeats, "Among School Children"

Nine Lines

Spenserian stanza was invented by Edmund Spenser for *The Faerie Queene*. It consists of nine lines, of which the first eight are iambic pentameter and the last is iambic hexameter (an *alexandrine*). The rhyme scheme is ababbcbcc.

> St. Agnes' Eve—Ah, bitter chill it was!
> The owl, for all his feathers, was a-cold;
> The hare limped trembling through the frozen grass,
> And silent was the flock in woolly fold;
> Numb were the Beadsman's fingers, while he told
> His rosary, and while his frosted breath,
> Like pious incense from a censer old,
> Seemed taking flight for heaven, without a death,
> Past the sweet Virgin's picture, while his prayer he saith.
>
> from John Keats, "The Eve of Saint Agnes"

Fourteen lines

Probably the most widely used verse form in English is the sonnet: fourteen lines of iambic pentameter, linked by a fixed rhyme scheme. Introduced into English from Italian by Thomas Wyatt in the early sixteenth century, it has been used by most of the major English poets. There are two kinds of sonnets (with many

individual variants). The Italian or Petrarchan sonnet is rhymed abbaabba cde-
cde. (Francesco Petrarch [1304–74] was a famous Italian sonneteer.) Notice that
the Italian sonnet breaks naturally into an eight-line *octave* and a six-line *sestet*. It
therefore lends itself to a structure of statement and counterstatement.

> I met a traveler from an antique land
> Who said: Two vast and trunkless legs of stone
> Stand in the desert . . . Near them, on the sand,
> Half sunk, a shattered visage lies, whose frown,
> And wrinkled lip, and sneer of cold command,
> Tell that its sculptor well those passions read
> Which yet survive, stamped on these lifeless things,
> The hand that mocked them, and the heart that fed:
> And on the pedestal these words appear;
> "My name is Ozymandias, king of kings:
> Look on my works, ye Mighty, and despair!"
> Nothing beside remains. Round the decay
> Of that colossal wreck, boundless and bare
> The lone and level sands stretch far away.

Percy Bysshe Shelley, "Ozymandias"

The English or Shakespearean sonnet is arranged as three quatrains and a couplet: abab cdcd efef gg. Although the English sonnet can be divided into an octave
(containing two quatrains) and a sestet (containing a quatrain and a couplet), a
stronger break follows the twelfth line, with the capping couplet offering an
opportunity for an epigrammatic conclusion, a sudden reversal, or a similar climactic effect.

> Since there's no help, come let us kiss and part;
> Nay, I have done, you get no more of me,
> And I am glad, yea glad with all my heart
> That thus so cleanly I myself can free;
> Shake hands forever, cancel all our vows,
> And when we meet at any time again,
> Be it not seen in either of our brows
> That we one jot of former love retain.
> Now at the last gasp of love's latest breath,
> When, his pulse failing, passion speechless lies,
> When faith is kneeling by his bed of death,
> And innocence is closing up his eyes.
>   Now if thou wouldst, when all have given him over,
>   From death to life thou mightst him yet recover.

Michael Drayton, Sonnet 61

The most common variant of the English sonnet is the Spenserian sonnet, in
which the quatrains are linked by common rhymes: abab bcbc cdcd ee.

Composite forms

There are several other standard verse forms, including some very complicated
ones such as the *villanelle* and the *sestina*. But more important for our present purposes is to recognize that a great many poems are written in ad hoc forms, invented

just for that one poem. Such forms, though, are usually composite, in that they consist of some combination of couplets, quatrains, or other familiar forms. Look at the first poem in this section, for example, Donne's "The Sun Rising."

> Busy old fool, unruly sun,
> Why dost thou thus,
> Through windows and through curtains call on us?
> Must to thy motions lovers' seasons run?
> Saucy pedantic wretch, go chide
> Late school boys and sour prentices,
> Go tell court huntsmen that the King will ride,
> Call country ants to harvest offices;
> Love, all alike, no season knows nor clime,
> Nor hours, days, months, which are the rags of time.

This stanza can be described as made up of two quatrains and a couplet: abba cdcd ee. This structure is somewhat concealed, however, by the variations in line length. The number of feet in each line is this: 4255 4444 55. This combination of short and long lines is one of the major devices Donne uses to give his poem its informal, conversational tone despite the regularity of its metrical form.

Irregular forms

There is no law that poets have to be perfectly regular and consistent in their use of verse forms. A significant amount of poetry in English uses traditional rhythms and rhymes but uses them irregularly. Here is the beginning of John Milton's "Lycidas," for example:

> Yet once more, O ye laurels and once more
> Ye myrtles brown with ivy never sere,
> I come to pluck your berries harsh and crude,
> And with forced fingers rude,
> Shatter your leaves before the mellowing year.

The rhymes here go abccb. This does not set up a pattern that is repeated in the poem. Line 1, like a number of other lines in the poem, is left unrhymed, and all that we can say of the lines that are rhymed is that the rhyme is likely to occur within the next few lines. Line length is also irregular. The basic pattern is iambic pentameter. But line 4 is two feet short, and through the rest of the poem occasional lines are trimeter or tetrameter rather than pentameter. Such freedom and irregularity are associated in English poetry with *odes*, poems written in celebration of someone or something, as "Lycidas" is an elegiac ode, written as a memorial to Edward King.

Free verse

Free verse is verse that does not use traditional meter or rhyme. It is especially associated with modern poetry, although there are examples in the earlier history of poetry, for example, in the poems of the eighteenth-century Christopher Smart. To say that free verse does not use traditional meter or rhyme is not to say that it is formless. It merely uses different formal devices. Here is the first section from Walt Whitman's *Song of Myself*, for example:

I celebrate myself, and sing myself,
And what I assume you shall assume,
For every atom belonging to me as good belongs to you.

I loaf and invite my soul,
I lean and loaf at my ease observing a spear of summer
    grass.

My tongue, every atom of my blood, formed from this
    soil, this air,
Born here of parents born here from parents the same,
    and their parents the same,
I, now thirty-seven years old in perfect health begin,
Hoping to cease not till death.

Creeds and schools in abeyance,
Retiring back a while sufficed at what they are, but
    never forgotten.
I harbor for good or bad, I permit to speak at every
    hazard,
Nature without check with original energy.

This certainly does not look or sound like traditional poetry, but no one would mistake it for prose, even if it were not broken into lines typographically. The basic unit here is the line, and the principles of organization are balance, parallelism, and repetition. The first three lines, for example, balance contrasting phrases: "I celebrate myself / and sing myself," "what I assume / you shall assume," and "every atom belonging to me as good / belongs to you." Complete lines as well as half-lines are balanced against one another as in the two lines of the second verse paragraph. And the paragraphs themselves are linked by parallels and echoes; look, for example, at the distribution of clauses that begin with "I" through the four paragraphs. Describing the form of free verse is more difficult than recognizing a conventional verse form, but it is just as important a part of understanding and interpretation.

Alfred, Lord Tennyson

Alfred, Lord Tennyson (1809–92), the most popular of the English Victorian poets in his own day, was something of a self-made man. Born into a chaotic family of twelve children of an alcoholic clergyman in Lincolnshire, he had to leave Cambridge University without a degree because of family problems, financial and otherwise. While there, however, he formed the resolution to become a poet and developed a close friendship with a fellow student, Arthur Hallam, who became engaged to Tennyson's sister. Volumes of verse appeared in 1830, 1832, and 1842. He came into his maturity, however, with *In Memoriam* (1850), a long poem in commemoration of Hallam, who had died suddenly in 1833. The year 1850 was also marked by his appointment as poet laureate of England (succeeding Wordsworth), and his long-postponed marriage to Emily Sellwood. Tennyson's life after 1850 was that of a Victorian institution. His poetry brought him a good income, and each successive publication found a wide readership.

THE LADY OF SHALOTT

Part I

On either side the river lie
Long fields of barley and of rye,
That clothe the wold[1] and meet the sky;
And through the field the road runs by
    To many-towered Camelot,[2]   5
And up and down the people go,
Gazing where the lilies blow[3]
Round an island there below,
    The island of Shalott.

Willows whiten, aspens quiver,   10
Little breezes dusk and shiver
Through the wave that runs forever
By the island in the river
    Flowing down to Camelot.
Four gray walls, and four gray towers,   15
Overlook a space of flowers,
And the silent isle imbowers
    The Lady of Shalott.

By the margin, willow-veiled,
Slide the heavy barges trailed   20
By slow horses; and unhailed
The shallop[4] flitteth silken-sailed
    Skimming down to Camelot;
But who hath seen her wave her hand?
Or at the casement seen her stand?   25
Or is she known in all the land,
    The Lady of Shalott?

Only reapers, reaping early
In among the bearded barley,
Hear a song that echoes cheerly   30
From the river winding clearly,
    Down to towered Camelot;
And by the moon the reaper weary,
Piling sheaves in uplands airy,
Listening whispers " 'Tis the fairy   35
    Lady of Shalott."

Part II

There she weaves by night and day
A magic web with colors gay.

---

[1] A moor or bare plain.   [2] Legendary palace of King Arthur.
[3] Bloom.   [4] A small boat.

She has heard a whisper say,
A curse is on her if she stay   40
    To look down to Camelot.
She knows not what the curse may be,
And so she weaveth steadily,
And little other care hath she,
    The Lady of Shalott.   45

And moving through a mirror clear[5]
That hangs before her all the year,
Shadows of the world appear.
There she sees the highway near
    Winding down to Camelot;   50
There the river eddy whirls,
And there the surly village churls,
And the red cloaks of market girls,
    Pass onward from Shalott.

Sometimes a troop of damsels glad,   55
An abbot on an ambling pad,[6]
Sometimes a curly shepherd lad,
Or long-haired page in crimson clad,
    Goes by to towered Camelot;
And sometimes through the mirror blue   60
The knights come riding two and two:
She hath no loyal knight and true,
    The Lady of Shalott.

But in her web she still delights
To weave the mirror's magic sights,   65
For often through the silent nights
A funeral, with plumes and lights
    And music, went to Camelot;
Or when the moon was overhead,
Came two young lovers lately wed: 70
"I am half sick of shadows," said
    The Lady of Shalott.

Part III

A bowshot from her bower eaves,
He rode between the barley sheaves,
The sun came dazzling through the leaves,   75
And flamed upon the brazen greaves[7]
    Of bold Sir Lancelot.
A red-cross knight[8] forever kneeled

---

[5] Weavers used mirrors, placed behind the loom, to watch the other side of their work.
[6] An easy-gaited saddle horse.
[7] Leg pieces of armor.
[8] The knight of holiness in Edmund Spenser's *Faerie Queene* (1590).

To a lady in his shield,
That sparkled on the yellow field,
    Beside remote Shalott.   80

The gemmy bridle glittered free,
Like to some branch of stars we see
Hung in the golden Galaxy.
The bridle bells rang merrily   85
    As he rode down to Camelot;
And from his blazoned baldric[9] slung
A mighty silver bugle hung,
And as he rode his armor rung,
    Beside remote Shalott.   90

All in the blue unclouded weather
Thick-jeweled shone the saddle leather,
The helmet and the helmet feather,
Burned like one burning flame together,
    As he rode down to Camelot;   95
As often through the purple night,
Below the starry clusters bright,
Some bearded meteor, trailing light,
    Moves over still Shalott.

His broad clear brow in sunlight glowed;   100
On burnished hooves his war horse trode;
From underneath his helmet flowed
His coal-black curls as on he rode,
    As he rode down to Camelot.
From the bank and from the river,   105
He flashed into the crystal mirror,
"Tirra lirra," by the river
    Sang Sir Lancelot.

She left the web, she left the loom,
She made three paces through the room,
She saw the water lily bloom,   110
She saw the helmet and the plume,
    She looked down to Camelot.
Out flew the web and floated wide;
The mirror cracked from side to side;   115
"The curse is come upon me," cried
    The Lady of Shalott.

Part IV

In the stormy east wind straining,
The pale yellow woods were waning,

---

[9] A belt, usually ornamented, worn diagonally across the chest to support a sword or bugle.

The broad stream in his banks complaining,   120
Heavily the low sky raining
   Over towered Camelot;
Down she came and found a boat
Beneath a willow left afloat,
And round about the prow she wrote,   125
   The Lady of Shalott.

And down the river's dim expanse
Like some bold seër in a trance,
Seeing all his own mischance—
With a glassy countenance   130
   Did she look to Camelot.
And at the closing of the day
She loosed the chain, and down she lay;
The broad stream bore her far away,
   The Lady of Shalott.   135

Lying, robed in snowy white,
That loosely flew to left and right—
The leaves upon her falling light—
Through the noises of the night
   She floated down to Camelot;   140
And as the boat-head wound along
The willowy hills and fields among,
They heard her singing her last song,
   The Lady of Shalott.

Heard a carol, mournful, holy,   145
Chanted loudly, chanted lowly,
Till her blood was frozen slowly,
And her eyes were darkened wholly,
   Turned to towered Camelot.
For ere she reached upon the tide   150
The first house by the waterside,
Singing in her song she died,
   The Lady of Shalott.

Under tower and balcony,
By garden wall and gallery,   155
A gleaming shape she floated by,
Dead-pale between the houses high,
   Silent into Camelot.
Out upon the wharfs they came,
Knight and burgher, lord and dame,   160
And round the prow they read her name,
   The Lady of Shalott.

Who is this? and what is here?
And in the lighted palace near

Died the sound of royal cheer;
And they crossed themselves for fear,
　　All the knights at Camelot:
But Lancelot mused a little space;
He said, "She has a lovely face;
God in his mercy lend her grace,
　　The Lady of Shalott."

Gerard Manley Hopkins

Gerard Manley Hopkins (1844–89) was in some ways a poet born out of his time. He wrote in the nineteenth century; he found his audience in the twentieth. Hopkins was born into the Church of England. At Oxford University, he fell under the influence of the Oxford Movement, which was reviving ritual and dogma within the church; he eventually converted to Catholicism and joined, in 1868, the Society of Jesus. After ordination and service in a number of parishes, he was sent to Dublin in 1884 as Professor of Classics at University College, Dublin. Hopkins had written poetry before he became a priest but had given it up. After several years, he began writing again, though not for publication; he did not believe his church superiors would approve. His poetry was published long after his death by his friend Robert Bridges. Hopkins's poetry is full of innovations we might call modern: a loose system of meter Hopkins called "sprung rhythm," a strange, sometimes extravagant diction that coins words, revives archaic ones, and mixes "high" and "low" words, and a use of incongruity that recalls the Metaphysicals.

FELIX RANDAL

Felix Randal the farrier,[1] O is he dead then? my duty all ended,
Who have watched his mould of man, big-boned and hardy-handsome
Pining, pining, till time when reason rambled in it and some
Fatal four disorders, fleshed there, all contended?

Sickness broke him. Impatient, he cursed at first, but mended
Being anointed and all; though a heavenlier heart began some
Months earlier, since I had our sweet reprieve and ransom
Tendered to him.[2] Ah well, God rest him all road ever[3] he offended!

This seeing the sick endears them to us, us too it endears.
My tongue had taught thee comfort, touch had quenched thy tears,
Thy tears that touched my heart, child, Felix, poor Felix Randal;

How far from then forethought of, all thy more boisterous years,
When thou at the random[4] grim forge, powerful amidst peers,
Didst fettle[5] for the great grey drayhorse his bright and battering
　　sandal!

5

10

[1] Blacksmith.　　[2] Heard his confession and given him absolution.
[3] In whatever way.　　[4] Built of irregularly shaped stones.　　[5] Prepare.

Michael Blumenthal

Michael Blumenthal (b. 1949) was raised in Manhattan, the son of Jewish refugees from Hitler's Germany who spoke only German in their home. He earned a degree in philosophy from the State University of New York at Binghamton and then took a law degree at Cornell. Since giving up the practice of law to practice poetry, he has worked as a teacher, speechwriter, editor, and arts administrator, and he now teaches at Harvard. His poetry is notable for its comic-ironic tone. His collections include *Days We Would Rather Know* (1984), *Laps* (1984), *Against Romance* (1987), and *The Wages of Goodness* (1992).

ADVICE TO MY STUDENTS: HOW TO WRITE A POEM

Forget, now, for a moment
that you were the blond boy
whose father jumped off the bridge
when you were only eleven. Forget
that you are the brokenhearted,   5
the cuckolded, the windswept lover
alone beneath the dangling pines.
Forget that you are the girl
of the godless cry, that no one
took you into his arms   10
during the cold night, that you have cried
from the fathomless depths
like a blue whale, and the world
has called back to you only its oracles
of relinquishment and moonlight.   15
Forget, now, my young friends,
everything you can never forget,
and hear, in the untamed wind,
in the perorations of the ravishing air,
the words for your life: *omelette,*   20
divestiture, Prokofiev, stars.
Forget, even as you gaze up at them,
the astral bodies and the heavenly bodies,
forget, even, your own ravenous body
and call out, into the beckoning light,   25
the names of everything you have
never known: flesh and blood, stone
and interlude, marmalade and owl—
those first syllables of your new world:
your clear and forgotten life.   30

Stephen Shu Ning Liu

Stephen Shu Ning Liu (b. 1930) was born in Fu-Ling, China. He briefly studied at Nanking University, taught Chinese in Taiwan for one year, and emigrated to America in 1952. He earned a doctorate at the University of North Dakota and now teaches at Clark County Community College in Las Vegas. He has published poems in more than 200 magazines, and in 1982 he collected them, translated them into Chinese, and published them in a bilingual format as *Dream Journeys to China* (Beijing: New World Press, 1982).

AT THE KING'S FUNERAL

More than 80,000 mourners anguish
and faint in the hot sun.
"Don't say he was fat," cried one of his
female fans. "They made him look fat
in the coffin. Please don't say he was fat."   5

The King of Rock 'n' Roll collapsed
in his 18-room mansion. He was 42, over
200 pounds, motionless, inflexible.
Flags dipped through much of the South;
tears stained a million people's cheeks.   10

"My life's over," sobbed a 17-year-old girl
from Michigan. She clutched an armful of purple
flowers from the ground. "I couldn't take anything
yellow or pink," she resolved. "Purple flowers
are sad like myself."   15

Only the cicadas cry in joy over the demise
of their rival. Consistently, they will sing
loud at the Forest Hill Cemetery,
and they will rock 'n' roll the streets
with the return of summer, in Memphis, Tennessee.   20

DICTION

Diction, or word choice, is arguably more important in poetry than in other genres. Or perhaps we should say that it is important in a different way. Language is certainly important in fiction and drama, but fiction has narrative and characters to hold our attention as well, and drama has both these and stage action and spectacle, too. Poetry *can* have narrative and characters; but to a greater extent than in fiction and drama, these exist in poetry only through words. It is possible to think of a good novelist who is clumsy with words (Theodore Dreiser, for instance) or a good playwright (Eugene O'Neill). But it is hard to imagine a good poet who is not adept with words. So in order to understand poetry, we need to pay close attention to the ways poets use language.

There are two dimensions to this subject. One is the kind of vocabulary a poet draws upon for a poem or perhaps for all of his or her poetry. The history of poetry in English has been a history of the establishment of various kinds of "poetic diction," each of which has been overthrown by subsequent generations. Shakespeare's Petrarchan contemporaries fell into a kind of formulaic diction that Shakespeare parodied in "My Mistress' Eyes Are Nothing Like the Sun" and that Donne reformed by using all sorts of "unpoetic" technical and scientific terms in his own poetry. In the eighteenth century, Pope's lesser contemporaries wrote in a cramped, genteel, and euphemistic vocabulary that became increasingly formulaic until Wordsworth, at the dawn of the nineteenth century, called for a poetic diction that would be "a selection of the real language of men." Romanticism began with a revitalization of the language of poetry; it ended, early in the following century, with a poetic diction as narrow and mechanical as that of the neoclassicists had been. The early modern poets worked a revolution in language as radical as the early romantics had, and the twentieth century has, for the most part, maintained a somewhat broader and more inclusive language of poetry than previous ages have, although individual poets have cultivated their own personal vocabularies.

Describing where an individual poem or poet stands in relation to these various "poetic dictions" has a distinctly subjective element to it (although we should always be prepared to give examples to support our judgments). We might find a particular poem's diction to be "earthy," "colloquial," and "simple," or, on the other hand, "abstract," "self-consciously literary," and "complex." We might note the presence of "technical" words or "archaic" diction.

The other dimension of the study of poetic diction is the analysis of particular word choices in a poem: precise denotations and connotations of a word, its novelty or unexpectedness, and its actual sound within the context. Think of the first stanza of Robert Herrick's brief "Upon Julia's Clothes," for example:

> Whenas in silks my Julia goes,
> Then, then, methinks how sweetly flows
> That liquefaction of her clothes.

The effect of these lines is almost completely dependent upon the surprising choice of the word "liquefaction." Why does it seem so right? We don't ordinarily think of a woman's clothes as turning to liquid, and of course they do so here only metaphorically. Julia's clothes "flow," as water does, and presumably the swishing sound of her silks is like the rushing of water. But the sound of the word "liquefaction" is like the rushing of water, too. The pleasure we take in the rightness of the word "liquefaction" is not an intellectual pleasure—it is more nearly a sensuous pleasure—but it is a poetic one nevertheless.

The four poems we have just read—by Tennyson, Hopkins, Michael Blumenthal, and Stephen Shu Ning Liu—employ very different kinds of diction. Comparing them will suggest something of the range of possible poetic languages.

Tennyson's "The Lady of Shalott" is, most literally, a brief, courtly Arthurian narrative, a romantic story about a maiden on an island who is under a curse that says she will die if she looks directly at Arthur's palace at Camelot. Tempted by the sight of Sir Lancelot, she does look at Camelot and dies, as she floats in a boat past Camelot. The story is very tantalizing, and we may speculate about its meaning. Is it about the necessary withdrawal of the Tennysonian artist from life? The lady of

Shalott is a kind of artist, weaving into her magic web the sights she sees reflected in her mirror. Is Tennyson saying that if an artist leaves the world of art for involvement in the real world, he or she dies as an artist? The story seems to have a sexual dimension, too. When the lady sees two newlyweds, she says that she is "half sick of shadows," and it is after all a handsome man (with a history of illicit sexuality) who tempts the lady out of her isolation.

Whatever conclusions we come to about theme, Tennyson obviously invokes a dreamy, chivalric, fairy-tale world in "The Lady of Shalott." Part of this effect is the work of metrics. Tennyson uses a nine-line stanza with only three rhymes: aaaa b ccc b. The b rhyme is the same in all stanzas—"Camelot"/"Shalott"—except in stanza 9, where "Lancelot" takes the place of "Camelot," and stanza 12, where it takes the place of "Shalott." The effect of such multiple rhymes is almost hypnotic; we are lulled by the repetitions of rhymes and refrains almost as the lady of Shalott is lulled.

Diction contributes to the creation of this world, too. The language is slightly archaic. A field is a "wold," and we get such verb forms as "flitteth" and "weaveth." Boats in this world are "shallops," girls are "damsels," and boys are "lads." Archaism is less important, though, than a kind of filtering of the language that results in a very special fairy-tale diction. What this diction is can be clarified by noting what it is not, what sorts of words would definitely be outside the verbal world of "The Lady of Shalott." Could we say that the lady of Shalott "blew her nose," that she "belched," that she "scratched her head"? Could we say that she was "sexually excited" by the sight of Lancelot? Could we refer to the "class conflict" between those anonymous reapers and the knights at Camelot? Could we refer to the "hegemony" the court exercises over the neighborhood? Obviously, the answer to all these questions is "no." The language of realism would not work in the dream-world of "The Lady of Shalott." Realistic references to the physical body or to physical functions, to believable motivations, or to political matters all would break the spell of the poem, which depends upon a special vocabulary that evokes the long ago and the far away.

The language of "The Lady of Shalott" slips along smoothly and sweetly, weaving a kind of narcotic spell. The language of Gerard Manley Hopkins' "Felix Randal" is just the opposite: awkward, knotty, obscure, continually calling attention to itself. Hopkins often seems to be hunting for obscure words that fit his purposes and holding them up for us to taste and savor. Why call Felix Randal a "farrier," rather than a blacksmith? "Farrier" is a perfectly good piece of British English from the Latin for "iron": *ferrum*. But even in the 1880s, when Hopkins wrote the poem, it was slightly quaint and was rapidly being replaced by "blacksmith." No matter. Hopkins seems to have used it *because* it was unfamiliar and would slow us down, maybe even make us look it up (and probably also because it alliterates with "Felix Randal" and because the "iron" in the word anticipates the "bright and battering sandal" of the last line).

Diction is not the only thing in this poem that is "counter, original, spare, strange" (as Hopkins said in another poem, "Pied Beauty"). What about the rhythm of the lines? Would anyone notice at first that this is a sonnet? And what of the syntax? What about the clause "till time when reason rambled in it and some / Fatal four disorders, fleshed there, all contended"?

The tortured diction of the poem matches these other deformations. We might look at the juxtaposition of the theological ("our sweet reprieve and ransom") with the provincially colloquial ("all road ever he offended"). But let us look instead at the astonishing last line:

Didst fettle for the great grey drayhorse his bright
and battering sandal!

Rhythm is important here. Those extra stressed syllables—"great grey drayhorse,"
"bright and battering sandal"—are undoubtedly meant to imitate Felix Randal's
hammer on the anvil. But the choice of words is important, too. What is the effect
of using "fettle" instead of the more common "prepare"? And what about calling
a horseshoe a "bright and battering sandal"? Hopkins is engaged in a process of
"estrangement" here, a "making strange" of his subject. His simple, working-
class parishioner becomes a heroic, almost mythic figure as Hopkins uses strange,
unexpected terms to represent him, a figure suggesting the infinite variety, the
"pied beauty," of life as opposed to the gray anonymity of death.

Michael Blumenthal's "Advice to My Students: How to Write a Poem" is a poem
about the language of poetry. In encouraging his students to hear "the words of
your life," Blumenthal is giving advice very much in the spirit of Hopkins, who
found in "farrier" and "fettle" words for Felix Randal's life. Superficially, Blumenthal's advice seems to counsel a rather impersonal kind of poetry. His students are to forget their own personal woes and find the words for their lives:
"omelette / divestiture, Prokofiev, stars." And yet perhaps Blumenthal may be encouraging his students to write a more profoundly personal kind of poetry. His advice
is full of paradoxes: His students are to forget "everything you can never forget,"
and they are to call out "the names of everything you have / never known."
Poetry, perhaps, is to be found not in a recital of autobiographical woes but in the
particularities of words, not only *"omelette / divestiture, Prokofiev, stars"* but also
"flesh and blood, stone / and interlude, marmalade and owl," the "first syllables
of your new world." In a final paradox, words will lead the apprentice poets to
"your clear and forgotten life," a life deeper than that implied by the woes of
confessional poetry.

Stephen Shu Ning Liu's "At the King's Funeral," brief as it is, plays several
kinds of diction off against one another. The naïve language of Elvis Presley's
mourners is juxtaposed to the more sober language of the main speaker: "Don't
say he was fat. . . . They made him look fat / in the coffin. Please don't say he was
fat." But the speaker himself shifts dictions in the course of the poem. He begins
in a detached, reportorial style full of exact numbers: 80,000 mourners, an 18-
room mansion, 42 years old, over 200 pounds. But in the last stanza the diction
shifts from the neutral, journalistic style of the first part to a more subjective,
evocative style:

Only the cicadas cry in joy over the demise
of their rival. Consistently, they will sing
loud at the Forest Hill Cemetery,
and they will rock 'n' roll the streets
with the return of summer, in Memphis, Tennessee.

In this last stanza (or paragraph, in this prose poem), Elvis Presley becomes a
force of nature, rival of the cicadas, who "cry in joy" over his death and who will
"rock 'n' roll" the Memphis streets when summer returns. There is much that is
absurd about the cult of Elvis Presley, and the first three stanzas take note of the
absurdity. But in the last stanza, Presley is treated with dignity and even something
like awe, and much of this effect turns around the startling word choice in having
the cicadas "rock 'n' roll" the streets of Memphis.

Poems do not just "use" language; they *are* language, and close attention to them as language is always rewarding.

We have unavoidably touched several times already on the metaphoric dimension in poetry—in our consideration of the cornstalk violins in "First Song," for example, or the lady and the tower in "The Lady of Shalott." Prepare for a fuller treatment of metaphor by reading Shakespeare's Sonnet 130: "My Mistress' Eyes Are Nothing Like the Sun," Blake's "The Sick Rose," Ana Castillo's "Women Are Not Roses," and Diana Chang's "On Being in the Midwest."

Matthew Arnold

Matthew Arnold (1822–88) was one of the most important literary and social critics of Victorian England, as well as an accomplished poet. His father was headmaster of Rugby School, where Arnold spent his childhood. After an indifferent career at Oxford, Arnold became at the age of twenty-five an inspector of schools, a post he held for thirty-five years. He had already published a volume of poetry; others followed, and in 1857 he was appointed Professor of Poetry at Oxford University, a largely honorary part-time position. By the time he was thirty-eight, his career as a poet was virtually finished; in his later years he wrote mostly criticism, including two volumes of *Essays in Criticism* (1865 and 1888), *Culture and Anarchy* (1869), and *Literature and Dogma* (1873). In both his poetry and prose, in various ways, Arnold's major theme was how to live a decent life in a modern, industrialized society.

DOVER BEACH

The sea is calm tonight.
The tide is full, the moon lies fair
Upon the straits;—on the French coast the light
Gleams and is gone; the cliffs of England stand,
Glimmering and vast, out in the tranquil bay. 5
Come to the window, sweet is the night-air!
Only, from the long line of spray
Where the sea meets the moon-blanched land,
Listen! you hear the grating roar
Of pebbles which the waves draw back, and fling, 10
At their return, up the high strand,
Begin, and cease, and then again begin,
With tremulous cadence slow, and bring
The eternal note of sadness in.

Sophocles[1] long ago 15
Heard it on the Aegean, and it brought
Into his mind the turbid ebb and flow
Of human misery; we

[1] Greek tragic playwright (c. 496–c. 406 B.C.). Arnold is probably thinking of lines 583ff. of Sophocles' *Antigone*, where the chorus compares the vengeance of the gods to waves breaking unceasingly on the shore.

Find also in the sound a thought,
Hearing it by this distant northern sea.   20

The Sea of Faith
Was once, too, at the full, and round earth's shore
Lay like the folds of a bright girdle furled.
But now I only hear
Its melancholy, long, withdrawing roar,   25
Retreating, to the breath
Of the night-wind, down the vast edges drear
And naked shingles of the world.

Ah, love, let us be true
To one another! for the world, which seems   30
To lie before us like a land of dreams,
So various, so beautiful, so new,
Hath really neither joy, nor love, nor light,
Nor certitude, nor peace, nor help for pain;
And we are here as on a darkling plain   35
Swept with confused alarms of struggle and flight,
Where ignorant armies clash by night.

William Shakespeare

William Shakespeare (1564–1616) is best known for his plays. But if he had
written nothing but his nondramatic verse, he would still hold a high place in
English literature. He wrote several poems on classical or mythological themes,
notably *Venus and Adonis* (1593), *The Rape of Lucrece* (1594), and *The Phoenix and
the Turtle* (1601). His sonnets, apparently written for private circulation rather
than for publication, were published without his authorization in 1609. And the
plays contain many songs that contribute in a variety of ways to the development
of plot, character, or theme.

SONNET 130: MY MISTRESS' EYES ARE NOTHING
LIKE THE SUN

My mistress' eyes are nothing like the sun;
Coral is far more red than her lips' red;
If snow be white, why then her breasts are dun;
If hairs be wires, black wires grow on her head.
I have seen roses damasked,[1] red and white,   5
But no such roses see I in her cheeks;
And in some perfumes is there more delight
Than in the breath that from my mistress reeks.
I love to hear her speak, yet well I know

---

[1] Variegated in color.

That music hath a far more pleasing sound;   10
I grant I never saw a goddess go;
My mistress, when she walks, treads on the ground.
And yet, by heaven, I think my love as rare
As any she belied with false compare.

William Blake

One of the most unusual, interesting, and profound of the English poets is William
Blake (1757–1827). Born in London, he had no formal education except at art
school and in a seven-year apprenticeship, from age fourteen to twenty-one, to an
engraver. Blake married Catherine Boucher when he was twenty-four; she was
illiterate, but Blake taught her to read and she assisted him with engraving and
printing. He had already begun to practice the art that he was to pursue for the
rest of his life: making engravings that incorporated both a poetic text and a
pictorial illustration or decoration around it. To read a Blake poem without its
original engraving reproduced as well is to miss at least half of his mixed-media
form. The subject of Blake's poetry is primarily a myth of human history, beginning with *The Four Zoas* (c.1795–1803) and continuing through *Milton* (c.1800–
1810) and *Jerusalem* (c.1804–20). But he also wrote a series of short but powerful
poems, in *Songs of Innocence and of Experience* (1794). Of the poems reprinted in
this book, "The Lamb" is from the *Songs of Innocence,* and "The Tyger" and
"London" are from the *Songs of Experience.*

THE SICK ROSE

O Rose, thou art sick!
The invisible worm
That flies in the night,
In the howling storm,

Has found out thy bed   5
Of crimson joy,
And his dark secret love
Does thy life destroy.

Ana Castillo

Ana Castillo (b. 1953), of Aztec heritage, was born and grew up in Chicago. In her
poems and fiction, Castillo explores sexual politics. Her volumes of poetry include
Otro Canto [*Another Song*] (1977), *The Invitation* (1979), *Women Are Not Roses*
(1984), and *My Father Was a Toltec* (1988). She has also written two novels: *The
Mixquiahuala Letters* (1986) and *Sapognoia* (1988).

WOMEN ARE NOT ROSES

Women have no
beginning
only continual
flows.

Though rivers flow   5
women are not
rivers.

Women are not
roses
they are not oceans   10
or stars.

i would like to tell
her this but
i think she
already knows.   15

Diana Chang

Diana Chang was born (in 1934) in New York but grew up in China with her
mother, who was Eurasian. She returned to the United States as an adult. Best
known as a novelist, she has published six novels. (Her short story "The Oriental
Contingent" appears in the fiction section of this book.) Her volumes of poetry
include *The Horizon Is Definitely Speaking* (1982) and *What Matisse Is After* (1984).
A painter as well as a writer, Chang teaches creative writing at Barnard College.

ON BEING IN THE MIDWEST

Don't you feel it's like being in the midst of a long novel?
Have I ever known anything about beginnings and endings?

Or is what I feel like marriage
with precariousness receding in a rear-view mirror?

Where was it I once steadied myself for sudden dawnings   5
and the earth could collapse like a cape?

I try out my thoughts in order to understand:
If I go far in any direction
would I find I have remained?
There must be ways to leave oneself behind   10

This is experience where light is broad
and daybreak and dusk support one like land

I remember how the edge takes the body away
and burning water puts out the sun

and seas begin to travel   15
in silver shaken out,
stars scattering,
shores moved by hungry weather

Here, parole has been revoked
and this, with me in its tidelessness,   20

has come down with an even breathing of massed secrets

METAPHOR AND METONYMY

Rhetoricians, ever since classical times, have identified and labeled literally dozens of figures of speech that can be used in poetry. Many of them can safely be ignored, but a few are especially useful. Two of the most useful are *metaphor* and *metonymy*. Both of these (and most other rhetorical devices) can be used in prose as well as in poetry, and what was said about metaphors in fiction applies also to poetry.

Metaphor involves a comparison. It transfers a term from the object it ordinarily designates to another object that it designates only by implicit comparison. When we use a phrase like "the roses in her cheeks," we are transferring the term "roses" from its ordinary context (gardens) to one it can designate only by comparison (a woman's face). This comparison is very simple: Roses and the woman's cheeks are both red or pink. But the comparison may suggest other common features: beauty, fragrance, naturalness. The phrase "the red food coloring in her cheeks" would not work, even though both the food coloring and the cheeks are red. Successful metaphors are complex and work on all levels of meaning.

Metaphor establishes a connection between two things based on similarity; *metonymy* establishes a connection based on contiguity or association. The saying "the pen is mightier than the sword" means something like, "writing, and its ability to influence people's opinions, is more powerful than military force." Here the pen stands for writing and the sword for military force not because they are similar but because they are associated with (contiguous to) the respective activities. Specifically, they are instruments by which those activities are carried out. One form that metonymy can take is *synecdoche*, the rhetorical figure in which the part stands for the whole or vice versa, or, to put it another way, a less inclusive term is used for a more inclusive one or vice versa. If we say, "All hands on deck," we are using a less inclusive term (hands) for a more inclusive one (sailors). If we refer to a police officer as "the law," on the other hand, we are using a more inclusive term (the law) for a less inclusive one (a police officer). If I refer to my car as "a bucket of bolts," I am using a metaphor. I am suggesting that my car and a bucket of bolts have something in common (both produce a metallic clatter, maybe). If on the other hand I refer to it as my "wheels," I am using a metonym that is also a synecdoche. Wheels are not *like* my car; they are *a part of* my car. I am letting the part (the wheels) represent the whole (the car).

The term *metonym* can also accurately be used to refer to separate details in a description. Because no verbal description can ever be exhaustive, the details that a writer chooses "stand for," in a sense, the thing being described and are thus metonymic.

To illustrate these points, let us look at Matthew Arnold's "Dover Beach." A quick survey of the poem will clarify the dramatic situation. A man and a woman are in a room, possibly in a hotel, overlooking the beach at Dover, in England, on the English Channel. It is a moonlit night. The man is speaking. He first describes the scene from the window and then gives his associations with it. The sound of the surf on the beach reminds him of human misery, and the ebbing of the tide reminds him of the decline of faith. At the end of the poem, he tells the woman that they should be true to one another, because the world is too chaotic to offer anything else to rely on. "Dover Beach," then, is one of many nineteenth-century poems (Coleridge's "Frost at Midnight" is another) in which the poet describes a natural scene and then interprets its meaning.

The first verse paragraph of "Dover Beach" is devoted to setting the scene, and Arnold selects five or six details to represent the scene: The sea is calm; the tide is full; the moon is fair; a light from the coast of France across the Channel gleams a moment and disappears; the famous white cliffs of Dover are in view, "glimmering and vast." And finally and most important, he hears the rhythmic roar of waves striking the shore. So far we have had a series of metonymic details and no metaphors as yet, although we are getting close to metaphor in the last line, where the narrator hears in the sound of the waves "the eternal note of sadness."

In the next two paragraphs, Arnold converts some of his metonymic details to metaphors. First, he observes that Sophocles also associated the sound of waves striking the shore with "the turbid ebb and flow / Of human misery." Then, in the third paragraph, he explicitly establishes his metaphors. The sea is like the Sea of Faith, which once was full but is now on the ebb. (The simile of the "bright girdle" may be rather obscure. Arnold seems to mean that the sea at high tide lies tight around the shore like a close-fitting garment, but at low tide the fit is looser.) The roar of the waves is the melancholy sound of faith receding "down the vast edges drear / And naked shingles of the world."

The last paragraph, in which the speaker makes his appeal for personal loyalty in the absence of any larger meanings, is built around two more similes. (A simile is an explicit comparison, whereas a metaphor is an implicit one; a simile uses "like," "as," or another comparison word.) The world appears to them, young and in love, to be like "a land of dreams"—various, beautiful, and new. But the world is really like a "darkling plain / Swept with confused alarms of struggle and flight, / Where ignorant armies clash by night."

"Dover Beach" is quite appropriately named. The beach is not merely the setting of the poem but its subject. It is first described and then interpreted in two ways, first as it appears to be ("a land of dreams") and then as it really is ("a darkling plain").

Why does discriminating between metonyms and metaphors matter? Studying these figures of speech gives us a glimpse into the way the mind constructs meaning. Metonymy is associated with realism, with the perception of external reality. Metaphor engages the human ability to make connections, to grasp similarities between disparate things. Thus in "Dover Beach," we see Arnold engaging in the process of making meaning by beginning with metonyms—separate details of the scene before him—and moving on to convert those metonyms into metaphors, the night scene of the opening lines, for example, becoming the "darkling plain" of the last lines.

Shakespeare's Sonnet 130: "My Mistress' Eyes Are Nothing Like the Sun," Blake's "The Sick Rose," and Ana Castillo's "Women Are Not Roses" offer an opportunity to compare three different metaphoric treatments of roses. "My Mistress' Eyes Are Nothing Like the Sun" is a comic critique of metaphor, specifically the stale, formulaic, exaggerated metaphor of the Petrarchan tradition of love poetry. One need not have read a great deal of this sort of Elizabethan poetry to get the joke; the poems Shakespeare is parodying are ones that claim that the mistress' eyes *are* like the sun, her lips are redder than coral, her breasts are whiter than snow, and her cheeks contain roses. Shakespeare's poem proceeds by refusing to metaphorize; his mistress' eyes are "nothing like the sun," her lips are not nearly as red as coral, her breasts are "dun" compared to snow, etc.

The immediate object of Shakespeare's satire is hackneyed Petrarchan poetry. But more generally it is the power of metaphor to deceive rather than illuminate. "False compare," by which a woman is represented as having eyes like the sun, movements like a goddess, and a voice sweeter than music, loses the real woman in a fog of exaggerations. Shakespeare's mistress is better loved by not being subjected to this sort of absurd idealization. The poem has a feminist dimension as well. Putting a woman on a pedestal is an ambiguous compliment at best; it is sometimes (maybe always) a way of avoiding dealing with the real woman, the one as rare, Shakespeare says, "As any she belied with false compare."

William Blake's "The Sick Rose" is at the opposite pole from the hackneyed poems Shakespeare satirized in "My Mistress' Eyes." If their use of a rose metaphorically was facile, over-obvious, and fundamentally false, Blake's use of it is far from facile or obvious. As a matter of fact, it is so oblique and puzzling as to resist interpretation at all. How is the rose sick? It appears to be from the worm, but what is a worm that is invisible and "flies in the night, / In the howling storm"? What could a rose's "bed / Of crimson joy" be? And how could the worm's "dark secret love" destroy the rose's life?

Blake seems to have written a poem that lacks surface coherence. If we abandon the search for literal meaning and move to the metaphorical meaning we may do better. The rose is a traditional metaphor for youth, beauty, and female sexuality. (Look at the medieval poem *The Romance of the Rose*, for example.) The worm traditionally stands for death, corruption, and male sexuality. The poem, on this level, seems to be about the destructive potential of sexual passion (perhaps even about venereal disease). In this reading, the rose does not have the "bed / Of crimson joy"; it *is* that bed, and the "howling storm" in which the worm flies is perhaps the storm of passion. For whatever reason, the beauty of the rose is destined to attract the force that will destroy its life. The difficulty of fitting all this together in a surface narrative about a rose and a worm is not necessarily a failing in the poem. The mystery of the literal meaning and the evocativeness of the metaphor make this a haunting, troubling poem.

Ana Castillo's "Women Are Not Roses" is built around the cultural connection of roses with women that Shakespeare ridiculed in "My Mistress' Eyes Are Nothing Like the Sun" and that Blake used for the dreamlike imagery of "The Sick Rose." The poem is so spare and economical that the dramatic situation is left indefinite. Who is the speaker? Is it a man or a woman? Who is the "she" of the last stanza? The poem begins with a proposition: "Women have no / beginning / only continual / flows." The statement is a version of a cliché that might be called the *la donna mobile* ("woman is changeable") stereotype: Women have fluid, constantly changing, boundaryless personalities. The middle two stanzas counter this initial statement with a repudiation of feminine stereotypes: Women are not rivers, roses, oceans, or stars. The last stanza shifts from the declarative propositions of the first three stanzas to a more grounded dramatic statement: "I would like to tell / her this but / i think she / already knows." Again, who is the "she"? Is she a woman who made the initial statement? Is she "woman," an individualized figure embodying all women?

As in the otherwise very different "The Sick Rose," the surface meaning of "Women Are Not Roses" is left vague and open, and the poem is perhaps more effective for that reason. "Women Are Not Roses" is a little drama of sexual stereotypes minimally framed by an implicit dramatic situation.

Finally, Diana Chang's "On Being in the Midwest" is a good example of a poem devoted to the statement and exploration of a single metaphor. The midwestern landscape becomes a metaphor for a state of mind, or, more than that, a way of being in the world. And this landscape is never directly described; the poem is all metaphor and no metonymy. Within her global metaphor, Chang uses smaller-scale metaphors and similes. Being in the Midwest is like being "in the midst of a long novel," far from "beginnings and endings." Within her evocation of the midwestern landscape are references to life near the coasts:

> Where was it I once steadied myself for sudden dawnings
> and the earth could collapse like a cape?

And

> I remember how the edge takes the body away
> and burning water puts out the sun
>
> and seas begin to travel
> in silver shaken out,
> stars scattering,
> shores moved by hungry weather.

Chang seems ambivalent about the midwest. The plains and prairies seem stable and supportive:

> This is experience where light is broad
> and daybreak and dusk support one like land.

On the other hand, "There must be ways to leave oneself behind," something that is hard to do where one can travel for a long time without encountering any change.

Chang writes, "I try out my thoughts in order to understand," and that might stand as a summary of the way poets use metaphor and metonymy. In the work of the best poets, figures of speech are not merely ornamental. They are epistemological, ways of exploring experience and its meaning. By offering ways to "try out one's thoughts in order to understand," they are not just "poetic devices" but come close to the heart of poetry itself as a way of knowing.

Finally, we should consider *theme* in poetry. As preparation for this, read Nelly Wong's "Not from the Food" and Frank Bidart's "Happy Birthday."

Nelly Wong

Nelly Wong was born (in 1934) and raised in Oakland, California. She works as an administrative assistant at San Francisco State University and is active in the clerical workers' union, AFSCME 3218, the Freedom Socialist Party, and Radical Women (a socialist feminist organization). Her books include *Dreams in Harrison Railroad Park* (1977) and *The Death of the Long Steam Lady* (1986). She has been featured, along with Mitsuye Yamada, in a documentary film: *Mitsuye and Nelly: Asian American Poets,* produced by Allie Light and Irving Saraf.

NOT FROM THE FOOD

Once I organized a dinner
for office friends
and I was proud when I ordered
barbecued spareribs, eggroll appetizers
bird's nest soup   5
empress chicken with asparagus
peking duck and thousand-layer buns
lobster cantonese
mushrooms, grass, black, button
yang chow fried rice   10
sweet and sour rock cod
oolong tea
fortune cookies
and almond delight
and I was prouder still   15
when I invited my guests
to tour dark alleys
the sing-song waves of faces
peeping from second-story windows
pointing to ducks, squabs,   20
thousand-year-old eggs
me on the perimeter
of Chinatown
with my office friends
gulping wine, holding my nose,   25
masked, playing oriental,
inscrutable, wise.
Now standing
before a brass spittoon
I recall that time   30
and I want to puke
not from the food, my friend,
not from the food

Frank Bidart

Frank Bidart was born in Bakersfield, California in 1939 and went to the University of California at Riverside. He went to graduate school at Harvard, where he studied with Robert Lowell. He has remained in the East, where he is now a professor of English at Wellesley College. The word "cinematic" often is used in connection with Bidart's poetry; his poems, which often represent extreme states of mind, are built up from vividly imagined scenes and images often abruptly juxtaposed, as in cinematic montage. His books include *Golden State* (1973), *The Book of the Body* (1977), *The Sacrifice* (1983), and *In the Western Night: Collected Poems, 1965–1990* (1990).

HAPPY BIRTHDAY

Thirty-three, goodbye—
the awe I feel

is not that you won't come again, or why—

or even that after
a time, we think of those who are dead   5

with a sweetness that cannot be explained—

but that I've read the trading-cards:
RALPH TEMPLE CYCLIST CHAMPION TRICK RIDER

WILLIE HARRADON CYCLIST
THE YOUTHFUL PHENOMENON   10

F. F. IVES CYCLIST
100 MILES 6 H. 25 MIN. 30 SEC.

—as the fragile metal of their
wheels stopped turning, as they

took on wives, children, accomplishments, all those   15
predilections which also insisted on ending,

they could not tell themselves from what they had done.

Terrible to dress in the clothes
of a period that must end.

They didn't plan it that way—   20
they didn't plan it that way.

THEME

In a sense we have been considering theme in our discussions of all the poems thus far. It is hard to imagine discussing dramatic situation, structure, or diction, for example, without having some sort of conception of what the poem means. But it might be well to consider theme directly and separately, as we did with fiction, however artificial that isolation may be. Theme means the same thing in reference to poetry that it does in reference to fiction: "the central idea of a literary work stated as a generalization about human experience." And we usually arrive at a statement of theme the same way with poetry that we do with fiction, by moving back and forth between the general and the particular. We first articulate a tentative version of the theme after one or two readings and then successively modify it as we work out the specific details of the poem. The suggestion made in the section "Writing About Fiction" that when considering the elements of fiction we should implicitly add "and theme" to each ("plot and theme," "character and theme," etc.) applies also to poetry. Even such a matter as verse form has thematic implications and can best be considered in terms of meaning.

Sometimes a poem contains a thematic passage that can be taken as the starting point, at least, for a statement of theme. The very title of Ana Castillo's "Women Are Not Roses" comes close to being a thematic statement. We might want to recast it in more general terms—"The reality of women is different from the stereotyped images by which they are portrayed"—but the basic idea is the same. In "Dover Beach," Arnold is quite explicit about the thematic content of his poem:

> . . . the world, which seems
> To lie before us like a land of dreams,
> So various, so beautiful, so new,
> Hath really neither joy, nor love, nor light,
> Nor certitude, nor peace, nor help for pain;
> And we are here as on a darkling plain
> Swept with confused alarms of struggle and flight,
> Where ignorant armies clash by night.

We might want to recast this, along the lines of "The modern world has lost all sense of purpose and meaning." But the thematic statement merely summarizes the original lines, gaining in economy what it sacrifices in beauty.

Other poems may lack any sort of explicit thematic statement, and we may have to produce our own generalizations about the implied meaning. What is the theme of Joy Harjo's "Your Phone Call at Eight A.M."? The poem is a dramatic monologue in the form of a telephone call to a lover after an earlier cold, wounding phone call. It ends, you remember, with these lines:

> But that's all right because
> this poem isn't for you
> but for me
> after all[.]

We might experiment with a thematic statement for "Your Phone Call at Eight A.M." along these lines: "Poetry is a rich, nuanced, many-layered mode of discourse that can protect one against the sort of sterile and skeletal discourse sometimes used as an offensive or defensive weapon." Many other statements would work as well for a theme of this poem, and any, including this one, would have to be progressively refined as we studied the poem.

Let us look at thematic issues in the two poems we did not discuss earlier: Nelly Wong's "Not from the Food" and Frank Bidart's "Happy Birthday." "Not from the Food" is a narrative poem in which the narrator, who is Chinese-American, remembers an occasion on which she organized a Chinese dinner and a tour of Chinatown for her Anglo office friends. Structurally, we can see the poem as divided into two very unequal parts, which correspond to the two sentences in the poem, the first made up of the first twenty-seven lines, the second made up of the last six lines. This division also corresponds to the temporal structure of the poem. Lines 1–30 describe the incident in the past; lines 28–33 describe the speaker's present attitude toward the incident. This brief final return to the present from the memory of the dinner is marked by an abrupt change of tone; after the romantic and colorful catalogue of Chinese dishes in the earlier part of the poem, the speaker says in the last part of the poem that the memory of the dinner makes her "want to puke." Why so negative an attitude toward the memory? The key is in lines 25–27, when the narrator remembers herself,

> gulping wine, holding my nose,
> masked, playing oriental,
> inscrutable, wise.

Can we make a tentative statement of theme from these observations? How about this: "It is a shameful thing to curry favor by presenting one's own ethnic group as exotic and quaint"? Assuming that this is at least an initial approximation of the poem's theme, would "Not from the Food" be a better poem if Wong had made it explicit, as Arnold, say, did in "Dover Beach"? The answer, obviously, is "no." The main strength of "Not from the Food" is not the truth or falsity of its theme but the way Wong has developed that theme in language. The tension in the poem is as much between two dictions, two kinds of writing, as it is between two attitudes toward ethnicity, and one is presented in terms of the other. In the first part of the poem the long catalogue of Chinese dishes is lush and poetic in itself:

> barbecued spareribs, eggroll appetizers
> bird's nest soup
> empress chicken with asparagus
> peking duck and thousand-layer buns. . . .

Although Wong disapproves of this exoticizing now, she can recreate the charm of the Chinatown culture and the pleasure she took in showing it to her friends. The abrupt, ugly "I want to puke" is effective because we have been lulled into the same sort of romanticizing Wong did in the past. Recognition of the theme Wong is working with is only the beginning of an adequate interpretation of the poem.

Frank Bidart's "Happy Birthday" is, if anything, more oblique than "Not from the Food" in its development of its theme. A good first step may be to analyze the grammatical structure of the poem. As "Not from the Food" was made up of two sentences, "Happy Birthday" is made up of three sentences, although if it were punctuated differently, with periods for some of the dashes, it would contain five or six independent clauses. The poem seems to have been written on or soon after the speaker's thirty-fourth birthday; it opens with his bidding the age of thirty-three goodbye. He then tries to define the "awe" he feels. It is not because of the mystery of the linear structure of time, which means that the past never returns, or because of the "sweetness" of our memories of the dead, but because of the feelings aroused by trading cards of great bicycle racers. The speaker sees the racers frozen in time at the height of their achievements but imagines also their later lives when they took on "wives, children, accomplishments," until they lost their identities in their accomplishments, victims of time. Even the clothes we wear are a reminder of temporality: "Terrible to dress in the clothes / of a period that must end." In the last lines, he highlights human beings' helplessness against time: "They didn't plan it that way— / they didn't plan it that way."

"Happy Birthday" deals with one of the oldest subjects in the history of poetry: the tragedy of human beings' subjection to time and its ravages. Bidart makes it fresh by grounding the poem in concrete realities—the trading cards, for instance—and by capturing the associational thought processes of a young man just coming to terms with his inevitable decline and death.

There is no formula for working out what we call the theme or ideational content of a poem. We may look within the poem itself for thematic statements or for passages that can be restated as themes. We can examine a poem's division into sentences and trace the sequences of ideas independently of line division. We can intuitively construct a statement of theme and then replace it or revise it as we study the separate parts of the poem. The articulation of theme, so long as it concerns itself not just with *what* is said but *how* it is said as well, is close to being synonymous with reading and interpreting poetry.

With poetry as with fiction, interpretation is not complete with just analysis. After things have been taken apart, they must be put back together again in a balanced, holistic reading. We will do this with Amy Clampitt's "Stacking the Straw."

Amy Clampitt

Amy Clampitt was born (in 1920) and reared in rural Iowa. After graduation from Grinnell College, she moved to New York, where she worked as a librarian for the National Audubon Society and as a freelance researcher and editor. Although she had been writing poetry and fiction for years, she did not begin publishing until 1978, when she was fifty-eight years old. Her first book, *The Kingfisher,* appeared in 1983. It was followed by *What the Light Was Like* (1985) and *Archaic Figure* (1987). Clampitt has a distinctive poetic voice, using a rich syntax and vocabulary to deal with subjects less often drawn from her New York years than from her Iowa ones.

STACKING THE STRAW

In those days the oatfields'
fenced-in vats of running platinum,
the yellower alloy of wheat and barley,
whose end, however gorgeous all that trammeled
rippling in the wind, came down   5
to toaster-fodder, cereal
as a commodity, were a rebuke
to permanence—to bronze or any metal
less utilitarian than the barbed braids
that marked off a farmer's property,   10
or the stoked dinosaur of a steam engine
that made its rounds from farm to farm,
after the grain was cut and bundled,

and powered the machine that did the
    threshing.   15

Strawstacks' beveled loaves, a shape
that's now extinct, in those days were
the nearest thing the region had
to monumental sculpture. While hayracks
and wagons came and went, delivering bundles,   20
carting the winnowed ore off to the granary,

a lone man with a pitchfork stood aloft
beside the hot mouth of the blower,
building about himself, forkful
by delicately maneuvered forkful,   25
a kind of mountain, the golden
stuff of mulch, bedding for animals.
I always thought of him with awe—
a craftsman whose evolving altitude
gave him the aura of a hero. He'd come down   30
from the summit of the season's effort
black with the baser residues of that
discarded gold. Saint Thomas of Aquino[1]
also came down from the summit
of a lifetime's effort, and declared   35
that everything he'd ever done was straw.

---

[1] Saint Thomas Aquinas (1225–74) wrote the *Summa Theologica,* which synthesized Aristotelian philosophy and Christian belief, thus creating the official Catholic philosophy.

From Reading to
Interpretation and
Criticism

Ͽ Ϩ Ϩ

So far in our study of poetry we have taken things apart by breaking poetry down into its "elements"—dramatic situation, form, structure, diction, metaphor and metonymy, and theme. But finally we have to put things back together and arrive at a balanced general interpretation of the poem. Or, to adopt the terms we used with fiction, we should arrive at a general reading, interpretation, and criticism of the poem. These registers of reading apply to poetry as much as they do to fiction. As with fiction, at the *reading* stage, we ask ourselves, "What does the poem say?" This involves analysis of the dramatic situation, analysis of sentence structure and production of a prose paraphrase of the poem, identification of form and structure, analysis of diction, and rhetorical analysis, including identification of metaphors and metonyms. With the identification of theme, we move into the *interpretation* stage, in which we ask ourselves not "What does the poem say?" but "What does the poem mean?" As with fiction, reading and interpretation will not be separated as neatly as in our description but will involve moving back and forth between analysis of detail and articulation of theme, between the particular and the general, each being constantly adjusted in the light of the other. And again, as with fiction, we should identify ourselves as closely as we can with the viewpoint and themes of the poem, so we feel we are reading and interpreting the poem as nearly as possible in the way the poet would want us to read and interpret it.

Criticism is different. As with fiction, in moving into the stage of criticism, we try to see the individual work that we have read and interpreted in a larger context. No longer do we try to "move out of ourselves" to identify ourselves as closely as possible with the point of view of a work; now we try to place the poem's themes and values in relation to our own themes and values and within a larger historical perspective.

Let us illustrate this process by examining Amy Clampitt's fine poem "Stacking the Straw." The first three words of this poem help us immediately to identify the *dramatic situation.* "In those days" suggests that the speaker is an older person

607

looking back on the past, when things were done differently. The audience and the situation are generalized—the audience is just "the reader," and there is no specific setting—but the voice of the poem is mature and reflective.

As to *form,* the poem is in free verse:

> Ĭn thŏse / dáys, / thĕ oát- / fíelds'
>
> fenćed-ĭn / váts ŏf / rúnning / plătĭ- / nŭm,
>
> thĕ yél- / lŏwĕr / állŏy̆ / ŏf whéat / ănd bárlĕy,
>
> whŏse énd, / hŏwĕv̆- / er gór- / geŏus áll / thăt trámmellĕd
>
> rĭpplĭng / ĭn thĕ wĭnd, / căme dówn
>
> to toást- / er fód- / er, cér- / eăl
>
> ăs ă cŏmmód- / ĭty̆. . . .

This is free verse without the great variations in line length of a Whitman. Even the look of the poem on the page shows that the lines are of similar length, mostly with between three and five accents per line. The effect of this comparative regularity is to make the verse sound somewhat like irregular blank verse.

The *structure* of the poem is that of a generalized memory. What is described is not any particular action in any particular year but rather habitual, recurring action, of the sort repeated year after year. The first twenty lines of the poem describe the practice of threshing; the last fifteen concentrate on a single figure, the man who stacked the straw as it came out the blower of the threshing machine. In the last four lines, Saint Thomas of Aquino (or Aquinas) is unexpectedly brought in because he declared at the end of his life that "everything he's ever done was straw."

It is difficult in this poem to separate structure from *figuration* or from the use of *metaphor* and *metonymy,* because a chain of metaphors does much to structure the poem. These are metaphors of precious metals and, more generally, of esteemed and long-lasting cultural products. Thus in the opening lines, oats are called "running platinum," and wheat and barley are called "the yellower alloy." But the grain, as commodity, is expendable and thus a "rebuke" to any metal less utilitarian than barbed wire and the steam engine that drove the thresher. The strawstack and the stacker are similarly described in heroic, archaic terms. The strawstacks were the "nearest thing the region had / to monumental sculpture," while the stacker, who rose higher and higher as the strawstack grew, had "the aura of a hero." The straw itself is gold, "the golden / stuff of mulch," "discarded gold." The *diction* of the poem reinforces this idealizing tendency. The subject may be homespun but the language is not; the grain is "winnowed ore," and the stacker builds "about himself, forkful / by delicately maneuvered forkful, a kind of mountain, the golden / stuff of mulch, bedding for animals."

How are we to interpret this poem? The poem is built around a contrast between the humble and the heroic, and Clampitt seems to want us to see the humble in heroic terms. The oats, wheat, and barley are platinum and gold; the stacker has the "aura of a hero" as he builds a golden mountain. It is tempting to see this opposition as a contrast between nature and culture, the natural and the artificial. But of course gold and platinum are as "natural" as wheat is, and grain, domesticated and cultivated by farmers, is itself not wholly natural. But what is important is not what these materials "really" are but how they are perceived, and Amy Clampitt wants to complicate our perception of the relative worth of precious metals and monumental sculpture as opposed to grain and strawstacks. She suggests, to make a thematic statement much more blunt and heavy-handed than her ironically elegant poem, that farming has a heroic quality and that grain, though a perishable commodity, should be treasured along with silver and gold.

If we try to contextualize this theme, we are moving from *interpretation* to *criticism*. "Stacking the Straw" belongs to a genre of poetry celebrating rural life that goes back to the Greek poet Hesiod's *Works and Days* (eighth century B.C.) and the Roman poet Virgil's *Georgics* (30 B.C.). In our own country and century, the poetry of farming has been cultivated most successfully by Robert Frost. Rural poetry does not have a single stance toward the country. The most common themes in rural poetry have been frank idealization ("God made the country, man made the town"), a realistic view of the rigors of rural life, and the use of the country as a microcosm, where the conflicts of life can be examined in a comparatively simple context. The last of these perhaps roughly describes Frost's poetic practice and perhaps Amy Clampitt's as well. Rural poetry of this sort is most likely to be written by a city person who looks back on rural life, as Clampitt does, from far away in time and space and brings to her subject an urbane irony and psychic distance.

Writing About Poetry

𝄞 𝄢 𝄢

The points made in the earlier section "Writing About Fiction" apply also to poetry. The best way of studying poetry is to write about it, to produce a text upon the text. We all generate such texts mentally as we read; it could be argued that poetry is not just the words on the page but also the interaction between the printed page and the mental poem that each reader creates in response. The most useful kind of writing about poetry is not just an exercise but an effort to articulate that mental poem, clarifying and enriching one's response to the poem.

The skills needed to write a critical essay on poetry are for the most part those needed to write about fiction or any other topic: the ability to frame a strong thesis, to develop it logically and with concrete evidence, to organize well-developed paragraphs, to construct good sentences, and to employ a precise and adequate vocabulary. But poetry offers its own special challenges. The most obvious one is that the interpretation of poetry usually turns upon subtle and precise matters of expression and that therefore anyone writing about it cannot be content with general references but must quote extensively. The ability to quote gracefully, to move easily back and forth between the poet's language and one's own commentary, is a skill that must be developed. The best way to develop it is probably to read some criticism by someone whose work you admire and see how he or she handles quotations.

There are several stages in the planning and writing of a good paper about poetry. Suppose that you are asked to write about the following poem.

IT IS A BEAUTEOUS EVENING

by William Wordsworth

It is a beauteous evening, calm and free,
The holy time is quiet as a Nun

610

> Breathless with adoration; the broad sun
> Is sinking down in its tranquility;
> The gentleness of heaven broods o'er the Sea;
> Listen! the mighty Being is awake,
> And doth with his eternal motion make
> A sound like thunder—everlastingly.
> Dear Child! dear Girl! that walkest with me here,
> If thou appear untouched by solemn thought,
> Thy nature is not therefore less divine:
> Thou liest in Abraham's bosom all the year,
> And worship'st at the Temple's inner shrine,
> God being with thee when we know it not.

PREWRITING. The first step in preparing to write about a poem is to gather material, which in this case means making a set of close observations about the poem that can later be worked into an interpretation. The list of "elements" of poetry that we have been using will be of help here. Marching through it systematically will ensure that no major aspect of the poem is overlooked.

1. *Dramatic situation.* It is evening by the sea, and an older person, probably a man, is speaking to a younger person, a girl. (If we want to look outside the poem for identification, we find that the speaker is Wordsworth, at the age of thirty-two, and the girl is Caroline, his natural daughter whose mother was a Frenchwoman, Annette Vallon. Caroline was ten years old in 1802, when the poem was written.)

2. *Form and structure.* The poem is fourteen lines of iambic pentameter rhymed ABBACDDCEFGEGF and is thus an Italian sonnet. (The variation in the rhyme scheme of the sestet is common and does not make the sonnet irregular.) As usual, there is a break or a turn in thought between the octave and the sestet. The octave describes the scene before the speaker, in terms that emphasize nature's holiness. In the sestet, the speaker turns to the girl (whose presence we are not aware of earlier) and tells her that if she seems less moved by the sight, her nature is not less divine. As a child, she is always closer to nature than older people are.

3. *Diction.* The language of the poem is dignified, serious, and even religious. The poem uses a number of archaic, "poetic" forms: *thou, thy, dost, walkest,* and so on.

4. *Figuration; use of metaphor and metonymy.* Wordsworth, in describing the natural scene, selects several metonymic details: the quietness of the scene, the sinking sun, the "gentleness" of the sky over the sea, and the noise of the waves. Most of these details are presented through metaphors drawn from religion or the contemplative life. The time is "holy" and "quiet as a Nun / Breathless with adoration," the sun sinks down in its "tranquility," the "gentleness of heaven broods o'er the Sea," and the sea itself is associated with God: It is a "mighty Being" who "doth with his eternal motion make / A sound like thunder—everlastingly." In the second part of the poem, the girl is said to be "divine," and her closeness to nature is presented in religious terms, as lying "in Abraham's bosom" (see Luke 16:22) and worshipping at "the Temple's inner shrine."

5. *Theme.* "It Is a Beauteous Evening" expresses both Wordsworth's reverence for nature and his view of childhood. The poem presents a paradox in that the Wordsworthian speaker responds deeply and emotionally to the natural scene. The little girl who is his companion seems indifferent to the scene; yet Wordsworth praises her for being closer to nature than he is, because she is a child.

PLANNING AND WRITING A FIRST DRAFT. By the time you have finished the prewriting study of the poem, a number of possible topics will probably have occurred to you. Perhaps you are interested in the sonnet and would like to write on "Wordsworth's Use of the Sonnet Form in 'It Is a Beauteous Evening.' " Maybe what you observed about Wordsworth's figures of speech struck you, and you would like to write about "Metaphor and Metonymy in 'It Is a Beauteous Evening.' " You may have noticed the peculiarity in the poem that the nonhuman aspects of nature are all personified (the evening, the sun, the sea), whereas the only human besides the speaker is presented as outside life in some way ("in Abraham's bosom" or "at the Temple's inner shrine"). This would produce a paper on "Human and Nonhuman in 'It Is a Beauteous Evening.' "

Whatever you find most interesting and promising for a paper, you should experiment with developing it into a thesis sentence. Remember that a thesis sentence should bite off neither too much nor too little. If the thesis sentence is too broad and sweeping, you may find it impossible to develop convincingly. If it is too narrow and timid, it may strike the reader as tedious and obvious. Suppose that you have noticed the way things are gendered in "It Is a Beauteous Evening"; the evening is feminine ("a Nun") but the sea is masculine (a "mighty Being" with *his* eternal motion), while the sun appears to be neuter (*its*). In the sestet, a speaker who is apparently masculine addresses a feminine listener, who nevertheless "liest in Abraham's bosom." Is there material for a paper here? To find out, we would have to turn our observations into a thesis sentence that doesn't just report the observations but draws some conclusion from them. "Wordsworth assigns genders to everything in 'It Is a Beauteous Evening' " does not suggest any interpretation of the observation; it is too narrow for a thesis sentence. "Wordsworth views nature as essentially feminine" is too broad; you cannot generalize about Wordsworth's thinking on the basis of one sonnet. (Also, it doesn't fit the facts; one aspect of nature at least, the sea, is masculine in the poem.) "In 'It Is a Beauteous Evening,' Wordsworth describes our relationship to nature in gendered terms" might work better; it suggests an interpretation of the poem that is narrow enough to be supported by the evidence and broad enough to be interesting.

Once you have at least a working thesis, you need to plan the organization of your essay. How are you going to present your thesis? How are you going to structure your development? Would it be better to work your way through the poem sequentially or to adopt a topical organization? At this point, it might be well to jot down an outline, as simple as three key words in order or as complicated as a sentence outline, with subtopics spelled out in complete sentences.

Once the essay is thoroughly planned, it is time to do a first draft. There are various ways of writing first drafts. Some people like to write very quickly, or even talk their paper into a tape recorder, to be transcribed later, so as to capture the clarity we often bring to oral explanations. Others like to think on paper or at a typewriter or computer keyboard, revising as they go along, so the draft takes longer but is more polished when it is finished.

REVISING AND WRITING THE FINAL DRAFT. Once the first draft is written, you need some distance and objectivity. The best way to get this is to let time elapse. If you have allowed yourself adequate time, you can let the paper sit at least overnight. When you return to it, it will be much easier to spot shaky logic, weak support for your points, inadequately developed paragraphs, and awkwardly constructed sentences. Another good way to get a fresh look, whether you have let time pass or not, is to read the paper aloud, either to somebody else or to yourself. Lots of things that look good on the page reveal their awkwardness when read aloud. Once you have done your revisions, you are ready to prepare the finished paper. This is the point at which to double check all quotations (it is very easy to copy lines of poetry inaccurately!), check doubtful spellings, and in general make the paper impeccable mechanically.

Poems for Further Reading

ॐ ॐ

Anonymous

"Barbara Allan" and "Sir Patrick Spens" are English popular ballads, anonymous narrative songs the origins of which are unknown and which have been preserved by being passed down orally. They may have originated as early as the Middle Ages, but few were written down before the eighteenth century. Many of them are surprisingly effective as poetry, often telling a tragic tale in a spare, economical, objective style with little moralizing. Most of the ballads exist in multiple forms, reflecting the number of "informants" from whose singing or recitation they were transcribed. "Barbara Allan" and "Sir Patrick Spens" are given here in a Scottish or northern dialect, reflecting where these versions were collected. Many of the English popular ballads appear in American versions as well, having been brought to America by immigrants and undergoing a separate development in the New World.

BARBARA ALLAN

It was in and about the Martinmas[1] time,
    When the green leaves were a-fallin',
That Sir John Graeme in the West Country
    Fell in love with Barbara Allan.

He sent his man down through the town   5
    To the place where she was dwellin':

[1] The Feast of St. Martin falls on November 11.

614

"O haste and come to my master dear,
  Gin[2] ye be Barbara Allan."

O slowly, slowly rase[3] she up,
  To the place where he was lyin',   10
And when she drew the curtain by:
  "Young man, I think you're dyin'."

"O it's I'm sick, and very, very sick,
  And 'tis a' for Barbara Allan."
"O the better for me ye sal[4] never be,   15
  Though your heart's blood were a-spillin'.

"O dinna ye mind,[5] young man," said she,
  "When ye the cups were fillin',
That ye made the healths gae[6] round and round,
  And slighted Barbara Allan?"   20

He turned his face unto the wall,
  And death with him was dealin':
"Adieu, adieu, my dear friends all,
  And be kind to Barbara Allan."

And slowly, slowly, rase she up,   25
  And slowly, slowly left him;
And sighing said she could not stay,
  Since death of life had reft[7] him.

She had not gane[8] a mile but twa,[9]
  When she heard the dead-bell knellin',   30
And every jow[10] that the dead-bell ga'ed[11]
  It cried, "Woe to Barbara Allan!"

"O mother, mother, make my bed,
  O make it soft and narrow:
Since my love died for me today,   35
  I'll die for him tomorrow."

SIR PATRICK SPENS

The king sits in Dumferline town,
  Drinking the blude-reid[1] wine:
"O whar will I get a guid sailor
  To sail this ship of mine?"

---

[2] If.   [3] Rose.
[4] Shall.   [5] Don't you remember.   [6] Go.   [7] Deprived.
[8] Gone.   [9] But a mile or two.   [10] Stroke.   [11] Gave.
[1] Blood-red.

Up and spak an eldern[2] knicht, 5
 Sat at the king's richt knee:
"Sir Patrick Spens is the best sailor
 That sails upon the sea."

The king has written a braid[3] letter
 And signed it wi' his hand, 10
And sent it to Sir Patrick Spens,
 Was walking on the sand.

The first line that Sir Patrick read,
 A loud lauch[4] lauched he;
The next line that Sir Patrick read, 15
 The tear blinded his ee.[5]

"O wha[6] is this has done this deed,
 This ill deed done to me,
To send me out this time o' the year,
 To sail upon the sea? 20

"Make haste, make haste, my mirry men all,
 Our guid ship sails the morn."
"O say na sae,[7] my master dear,
 For I fear a deadly storm.

"Late late yestre'en I saw the new moon 25
 Wi' the auld[8] moon in her arm,
And I fear, I fear, my dear master,
 That we will come to harm."

O our Scots nobles were richt laith[9]
 To weet[10] their cork-heeled shoon,[11] 30
But lang owre[12] a' the play were played
 Their hats they swam aboon.[13]

O lang, lang may their ladies sit,
 Wi' their fans into their hand,
Or e'er they see Sir Patrick Spens 35
 Come sailing to the land.

O lang, lang may the ladies stand,
 Wi' their gold kembs[14] in their hair,
Waiting for their ain[15] dear lords,
 For they'll see thame na mair.[16] 40

Half o'er,[17] half o'er to Aberdour
 It's fifty fadom[18] deep,

---

[2] Elderly. [3] Broad. [4] Laugh. [5] Eye. [6] Who. [7] O say not so.
[8] Old. [9] Loath. [10] Wet. [11] Shoes. [12] Ere. [13] Above.
[14] Combs. [15] Own. [16] More. [17] Halfway over. [18] Fathoms.

And there lies guid Sir Patrick Spens,
Wi' the Scots lords at his feet.

Edmund Spenser

Edmund Spenser (1552–99), generally regarded as the greatest nondramatic
poet of the English Renaissance, was born in London, was educated at Cambridge,
and spent most of his life in the service of powerful men, including Dr. John
Young, Bishop of Rochester; the Earl of Leicester, Queen Elizabeth's favorite
courtier; and Lord Grey of Wilton, Lord Deputy of Ireland. His major works
include the pastoral poem *The Shepheardes Calender;* a sequel named *Colin Clouts
Come Home Againe;* a sonnet cycle, *Amoretti;* two marriage poems, *Epithalamion* and
Prothalamion; and his masterpiece, the romantic epic *The Faerie Queene.* (Spenser's
poems are always published in original-spelling versions, since his spellings were
already archaic in his own day and were employed self-consciously.)

SONNET 37

What guyle is this, that those her golden tresses,
She doth attyre under a net of gold:
And with sly[1] skill so cunningly them dresses,
That which is gold or heare, may scarse be told?
Is it that mens frayle eyes, which gaze too bold,   5
She may entangle in that golden snare:
And being caught may craftily enfold,
Theyr weaker harts, which are not wel aware?
Take heed therefore, myne eyes, how ye doe stare
Henceforth too rashly on that guilefull net,   10
In which if ever ye entrappéd are,
Out of her bands ye by no meanes shall get.
Fondnesse[2] it were for any being free,
To covet fetters, though they golden bee.

SONNET 75

One day I wrote her name upon the strand,
But came the waves and washéd it away:
Agayne I wrote it with a second hand,
But came the tyde, and made my paynes his pray.
"Vayne man," sayd she, "that doest in vaine assay,   5
A mortall thing so to immortalize,
For I my selve shall lyke to this decay,
And eek[1] my name bee wypéd out lykewize."
"Not so," quod[2] I, "let baser things devize
To dy in dust, but you shall live by fame: 10

[1] Clever.   [2] Foolishness.
[1] Also.   [2] Quoth.

My verse your vertues rare shall eternize,
And in the hevens wryte your glorious name.
Where whenas death shall all the world subdew,
Our love shall live, and later life renew."

Christopher Marlowe

Christopher Marlowe (1564–93) was born in Canterbury and educated at Cambridge University. While still at Cambridge, he began to write plays and probably became a spy for Queen Elizabeth's government. His plays include the two-part *Tamburlaine*, about a world conqueror; the tragedies *The Jew of Malta* and *Dr. Faustus;* and a history play, *Edward II.* In addition, he wrote a sizable amount of lyric and narrative poetry and a number of translations from Latin. He was killed in a tavern brawl at the age of twenty-nine.

THE PASSIONATE SHEPHERD TO HIS LOVE

Come live with me and be my love,
And we will all the pleasures prove[1]
That valleys, groves, hills, and fields,
Woods, or steepy mountain yields.

And we will sit upon the rocks,   5
Seeing the shepherds feed their flocks,
By shallow rivers to whose falls
Melodious birds sing madrigals.

And I will make thee beds of roses
And a thousand fragrant posies,   10
A cap of flowers, and a kirtle
Embroidered all with leaves of myrtle;

A gown made of the finest wool
Which from our pretty lambs we pull;
Fair lined slippers for the cold,   15
With buckles of the purest gold;

A belt of straw and ivy buds,
With coral clasps and amber studs:
And if these pleasures may thee move,
Come live with me, and be my love.   20

The shepherds' swains shall dance and sing
For thy delight each May morning:
If these delights thy mind may move,
Then live with me and be my love.

[1] Test, experience.

William Shakespeare

William Shakespeare (1564–1616) is best known for his plays. But if he had written nothing but his nondramatic verse, he would still hold a high place in English literature. He wrote several poems on classical or mythological themes, notably *Venus and Adonis* (1593), *The Rape of Lucrece* (1594), and *The Phoenix and the Turtle* (1601). His sonnets, apparently written for private circulation rather than for publication, were published without his authorization in 1609. And the plays contain many songs, which contribute in a variety of ways to the development of plot, character, or theme.

IT WAS A LOVER AND HIS LASS

FROM *As You Like It*

It was a lover and his lass,
    With a hey, and a ho, and a hey nonino,
That o'er the green corn field did pass
    In springtime, the only pretty ring time,
When birds do sing, hey ding a ding, ding: 5
Sweet lovers love the spring.

Between the acres of the rye,
    With a hey, and a ho, and a hey nonino,
These pretty country folks would lie,
    In springtime, etc.   10

This carol they began that hour,
    With a hey, and a ho, and a hey nonino,
How that a life was but a flower
    In springtime, etc.

And therefore take the present time,   15
    With a hey, and a ho, and a hey nonino;
For love is crownéd with the prime
    In springtime, etc.

OH MISTRESS MINE

FROM *Twelfth Night*

Oh mistress mine! where are you roaming?
Oh! stay and hear; your true love's coming,
    That can sing both high and low.
Trip no further, pretty sweeting;
Journeys end in lovers meeting,   5
    Every wise man's son doth know.

What is love? 'tis not hereafter;
Present mirth hath present laughter;
  What's to come is still unsure:
In delay there lies no plenty;   10
Then come kiss me, sweet and twenty,
  Youth's a stuff will not endure.

FEAR NO MORE THE HEAT O' THE SUN

FROM *Cymbeline*

Fear no more the heat o' the sun,
  Nor the furious winter's rages;
Thou thy worldly task hast done,
  Home art gone, and ta'en thy wages:
Golden lads and girls all must,   5
As chimney-sweepers, come to dust.

Fear no more the frown o' the great;
  Thou art past the tyrant's stroke;
Care no more to clothe and eat;
  To thee the reed is as the oak: 10
The scepter, learning, physic, must
All follow this, and come to dust.

Fear no more the lightning flash,
  Nor the all-dreaded thunder stone;[1]
Fear not slander, censure rash;   15
  Thou hast finished joy and moan:
All lovers young, all lovers must
Consign to thee, and come to dust.

No exorciser harm thee!
Nor no witchcraft charm thee!   20
Ghost unlaid forbear thee!
Nothing ill come near thee!
Quiet consummation have;
And renowned be thy grave!

SONNET 55

Not marble, nor the gilded monuments
Of princes, shall outlive this powerful rhyme;
But you shall shine more bright in these contents
Than unswept stone, besmeared with sluttish time.
When wasteful war shall statues overturn,   5
And broils root out the work of masonry,

---

[1] Thunder was thought to be caused by the crashing of "aerial stones" (meteorites).

Nor Mars his sword nor war's quick fire shall burn
The living record of your memory.
'Gainst death and all-oblivious enmity
Shall you pace forth; your praise shall still find room   10
Even in the eyes of all posterity
That wear this world out to the ending doom.
So, till the judgment that yourself arise,
You live in this, and dwell in lovers' eyes.

SONNET 116

Let me not to the marriage of true minds
Admit impediments. Love is not love
Which alters when it alteration finds,
Or bends with the remover to remove:
Oh, no! it is an ever-fixéd mark,   5
That looks on tempests and is never shaken;
It is the star to every wandering bark.
Whose worth's unknown, although his height be taken.
Love's not Time's fool, though rosy lips and cheeks
Within his bending sickle's compass come;   10
Love alters not with his brief hours and weeks,
But bears it out even to the edge of doom.
If this be error and upon me proved,
I never writ, nor no man ever loved.

Ben Jonson

Shakespeare's great contemporary Ben Jonson (1572–1637) was indebted, far
more than Shakespeare was, to the Latin classics. In his youth he worked as a
bricklayer and served in the army. But while still in his twenties, he began working
as an actor and playwright in the London theater. Although he wrote classical
tragedies such as *Sejanus* (1603), he excelled in satiric comedies such as *Every Man
in His Humor* (1598), *Volpone* (1606), and *The Alchemist* (1610). Later, Jonson
came to specialize in masques—elaborately staged allegorical spectacles performed at court and culminating in a compliment to the king or queen—and was
named poet laureate in 1616. In his later years, he was the literary dictator of
London and gathered around himself a number of younger poets such as Robert
Herrick, Thomas Carew, and Sir John Suckling, who called themselves the "Sons
of Ben." These poets carried the Jonsonian tradition into the "Cavalier" school
of seventeenth-century poetry.

ON MY FIRST DAUGHTER[1]

Here lies, to each her parents' ruth,[2]
Mary, the daughter of their youth;

---

[1] Nothing is known of this daughter except the information given in the poem itself.
[2] Grief.

Yet all heaven's gifts being heaven's due,
It makes the father less to rue.
At six months' end she parted hence   5
With safety of her innocence;
Whose soul heaven's queen, whose name she bears,
In comfort of her mother's tears,
Hath placed amongst her virgin-train:
Where, while that severed doth remain,   10
This grave partakes the fleshly birth;
Which cover lightly, gentle earth!

ON MY FIRST SON[1]

Farewell, thou child of my right hand,[2] and joy;
My sin was too much hope of thee, loved boy:
Seven years thou wert lent to me, and I thee pay,
Exacted by thy fate, on the just day.
O could I lose all father[3] now! for why   5
Will man lament the state he should envy,
To have so soon 'scaped world's and flesh's rage,
And, if no other misery, yet age?
Rest in soft peace, and asked, say, "Here doth lie
Ben Jonson his best piece of poetry."   10
For whose sake henceforth all his vows be such
As what he loves may never like too much.

SONG: TO CELIA[1]

Drink to me only with thine eyes,
And I will pledge with mine;
Or leave a kiss but in the cup,
And I'll not look for wine.
The thirst that from the soul doth rise,   5
Doth ask a drink divine:
But might I of Jove's nectar sup,
I would not change for thine.

I sent thee late a rosy wreath,
Not so much honoring thee,   10
As giving it a hope, that there
It could not withered be.
But thou thereon did'st only breathe,
And sent'st it back to me;

---

[1] Jonson's son Benjamin was born in 1596 and died on his seventh birthday.
[2] *Benjamin* means "child of my right hand" in Hebrew, implying dexterity and good fortune.
[3] Thoughts of being a father.
[1] This famous song, despite its grace in English, was adapted from five passages in the *Epistles* of Philostratus, a Greek writer of the third century A.D.

Since when it grows and smells, I swear, 15
Not of itself, but thee.

John Donne

John Donne (1572–1631) spent his life at or near the English court, and his poetry is essentially coterie poetry—difficult, witty poetry to be read by a small group of like-minded friends. Yet it is something more, for it continues to find delighted readers now, almost four hundred years after it was written. After a youth spent in traveling and voluminous reading, Donne became, at the age of twenty-six, private secretary to a powerful court official named Sir Thomas Egerton. He lost this position, however, and was even imprisoned briefly when he secretly married Lady Egerton's sixteen-year-old niece, Ann More. The next few years were difficult for Donne. When he was forty-three, at the urging of King James, Donne entered the Anglican ministry. He eventually became Dean of St. Paul's Cathedral and was known as one of the greatest preachers in England. Donne's poetry and that of his followers was labeled by later critics as "Metaphysical," by which is meant poetry built around "conceits" (elaborate metaphors) and that combines unexpected language and content. His early poetry (of which "A Valediction: Forbidding Mourning" is an example) was primarily love poetry, his later poetry mainly religious poetry; both, however, used many of the same techniques.

A VALEDICTION: FORBIDDING MOURNING[1]

As virtuous men pass mildly away,
    And whisper to their souls to go,
Whilst some of their sad friends do say
    The breath goes now, and some say, No;

So let us melt, and make no noise, 5
    No tear-floods, nor sigh-tempests move,
'Twere profanation of our joys
    To tell the laity our love.

Moving of th' earth brings harms and fears,
    Men reckon what it did and meant; 10
But trepidation of the spheres,
    Though greater far, is innocent.[2]

Dull sublunary[3] lovers' love
    (Whose soul is sense) cannot admit
Absence, because it doth remove 15
    Those things which elemented[4] it.

---

[1] A valediction is a farewell. Donne addressed the poem to his wife when he left for a trip to the continent in 1612.
[2] That is, earthquakes are regarded as bad omens, but irregular movement of the celestial spheres (in the geocentric Ptolemaic system) is not regarded as dangerous.
[3] "Beneath the moon," that is, ordinary, subject to change.   [4] Composed.

But we by a love so much refined
   That our selves know not what it is,
Inter-assuréd of the mind,
   Care less, eyes, lips, and hands to miss.   20

Our two souls therefore, which are one,
   Though I must go, endure not yet
A breach, but an expansion,
   Like gold to airy thinness beat.

If they be two, they are two so   25
   As stiff twin compasses are two;
Thy soul, the fixed foot, makes no show
   To move, but doth, if th' other do.

And though it in the center sit,
   Yet when the other far doth roam,   30
It leans and harkens after it,
   And grows erect, as that comes home.

Such wilt thou be to me, who must
   Like th' other foot, obliquely run;
Thy firmness makes my circle just,   35
   And makes me end where I begun.[5]

Robert Herrick

Robert Herrick (1591–1674) came from a family of goldsmiths; an analogy is often drawn between goldsmithing and Herrick's own rich and ornamental art. Herrick was educated at Cambridge University and entered the Anglican ministry when he was thirty-two. A friend and disciple of Ben Jonson, Herrick found it hard to tear himself away from London, but in 1629, when he was thirty-nine, he accepted a church in faraway Devonshire. He continued to write poetry and in 1648 had it published in a single volume containing both secular and religious poems. The secular poems were called *Hesperides*, and the religious ones *Noble Numbers;* there were about 1,200 poems in all. Herrick's poems were largely ignored until the nineteenth century, when they were revived and he came to be regarded as one of the great seventeenth-century poets.

DELIGHT IN DISORDER

A sweet disorder in the dress
Kindles in clothes a wantonness.
A lawn[1] about the shoulders thrown
Into a fine distractión;
An erring lace, which here and there   5
Enthralls the crimson stomacher;[2]

---

[5] The circle symbolizes perfection.
[1] Thin scarf.   [2] The lower part of a bodice.

A cuff neglectful, and thereby
Ribbons to flow confusedly;
A winning wave, deserving note,
In the tempestuous petticoat;   10
A careless shoestring, in whose tie
I see a wild civility;
Do more bewitch me than when art
Is too precise in every part.

UPON JULIA'S CLOTHES

Whenas in silks my Julia goes,
Then, then, methinks, how sweetly flows
That liquefaction of her clothes.

Next, when I cast mine eyes, and see
That brave[1] vibration, each way free,   5
O, how that glittering taketh me!

CORINNA'S GOING A-MAYING

Get up! get up for shame! the blooming morn
Upon her wings presents the god unshorn.[1]
   See how Aurora throws her fair
   Fresh-quilted colors through the air:[2]
   Get up, sweet slug-a-bed, and see   5
   The dew bespangling herb and tree.
Each flower has wept and bowed toward the east
Above an hour since, yet you not dressed;
   Nay, not so much as out of bed?
   When all the birds have matins said,   10
   And sung their thankful hymns, 'tis sin,
   Nay, profanation to keep in,
Whenas a thousand virgins on this day
Spring, sooner than the lark, to fetch in May.[3]

Rise, and put on your foliage, and be seen   15
To come forth, like the springtime, fresh and green,
   And sweet as Flora.[4] Take no care
   For jewels for your gown or hair;
   Fear not; the leaves will strew
   Gems in abundance upon you;   20
Besides, the childhood of the day has kept,

[1] Splendid.
[1] Apollo, the sun god. His hair is the rays of the sun and so is never cut.
[2] Aurora is the goddess of the dawn. She is throwing back her covers after the night's sleep.
[3] Blossoms to trim the house on May Day (May 1).
[4] Flora was the Roman goddess of flowers and vegetation.

Against you come, some orient[5] pearls unwept;
   Come and receive them while the light
   Hangs on the dew-locks of the night,
   And Titan[6] on the eastern hill   25
   Retires himself, or else stands still
Till you come forth. Wash, dress, be brief in praying:
Few beads[7] are best when once we go a-Maying.

Come, my Corinna, come; and, coming, mark
How each field turns a street,[8] each street a park   30
   Made green and trimmed with trees; see how
   Devotion gives each house a bough
   Or branch: each porch, each door ere this,
   An ark, a tabernacle is,[9]
Made up of whitethorn neatly interwove,   35
As if here were those cooler shades of love.
   Can such delights be in the street
   And open fields, and we not see 't?
   Come, we'll abroad; and let's obey
   The proclamation made for May,   40
And sin no more, as we have done, by staying;
But, my Corinna, come, let's go a-Maying.

There's not a budding boy or girl this day
But is got up and gone to bring in May;
   A deal of youth, ere this, is come   45
   Back, and with whitethorn laden home.
   Some have dispatched their cakes and cream
   Before that we have left to dream;
And some have wept, and wooed, and plighted troth,
And chose their priest, ere we can cast off sloth.   50
   Many a green-gown[10] has been given,
   Many a kiss, both odd and even;[11]
Many a glance, too, has been sent
From out the eye, love's firmament;
Many a jest told of the keys betraying   55
This night, and locks picked; yet we're not a-Maying.

Come, let us go while we are in our prime,
And take the harmless folly of the time.
   We shall grow old apace, and die
   Before we know our liberty.   60
   Our life is short, and our days run
   As fast away as does the sun;
And, as a vapor or a drop of rain
Once lost, can ne'er be found again;

---

[5] Eastern, oriental.   [6] The sun.   [7] Prayerbeads.   [8] Turns into a street.
[9] The Hebrew Ark of the Covenant. Herrick is playfully presenting Maying as a religion of nature.
[10] Gown made green by rolling in the grass.
[11] In kissing games, kisses are awarded in odd or even numbers.

So when or you or I are made 65
A fable, song, or fleeting shade,
All love, all liking, all delight
Lies drowned with us in endless night.
Then while time serves, and we are but decaying,
Come, my Corinna, come, let's go a-Maying. 70

George Herbert

George Herbert (1593–1633) seemed destined for political prominence when, after his graduation from Cambridge, he was named Public Orator at the university. The Orator's job was to speak for the university (in Latin) on public occasions; the post was often a stepping stone to political advancement. Herbert instead entered the Anglican ministry, accepting a church at Bemerton, in Salisbury. Here he distinguished himself for piety and conscientiousness. His service lasted only three years before he died of tuberculosis at the age of forty. He left behind a manuscript of poems that was printed after his death with the title *The Temple*. Herbert is a Metaphysical poet and shares with Donne a fondness for the ingenious conceit. But his devotional poetry has a quietness and serenity that Donne's lacks.

THE COLLAR

I struck the board[1] and cried, "No more;
        I will abroad!
What? shall I ever sigh and pine?
My lines and life are free, free as the road,
Loose as the wind, as large as store. 5
        Shall I be still in suit?[2]
Have I no harvest but a thorn
To let me blood, and not restore
What I have lost with cordial[3] fruit?
        Sure there was wine 10
Before my sighs did dry it; there was corn
    Before my tears did drown it.
Is the year only lost to me?
    Have I no bays[4] to crown it,
No flowers, no garlands gay? all blasted? 15
        All wasted?
Not so, my heart; but there is fruit,
        And thou hast hands.
Recover all thy sigh-blown age
On double pleasures: leave thy cold dispute 20

[1] Table.   [2] Still in attendance on someone.   [3] Stimulating, heartwarming.
[4] Laurel of glory, especially poetic glory.

Of what is fit and not. Forsake thy cage,
    Thy rope of sands,[5]
Which petty thoughts have made, and made to thee
    Good cable, to enforce and draw,

        And be thy law,   25
While thou didst wink[6] and wouldst not see.
        Away! take heed;
        I will abroad.
Call in thy death's-head[7] there; tie up thy fears.
        He that forbears   30
    To suit and serve his need,
        Deserves his load."
But as I raved and grew more fierce and wild
    At every word,
Methought I heard one calling, *Child!*   35
    And I replied, *My Lord.*

THE PULLEY

When God at first made man,
Having a glass of blessings standing by,
    "Let us," said he, "pour on him all we can.
Let the world's riches, which dispersèd lie,
    Contract into a span."   5

So strength first made a way;
Then beauty flowed, then wisdom, honor, pleasure.
    When almost all was out, God made a stay,
Perceiving that, alone of all his treasure,
    Rest in the bottom lay.[1]   10

"For if I should," said he,
"Bestow this jewel also on my creature,
    He would adore my gifts instead of me,
And rest in Nature, not the God of Nature;
    So both should losers be.   15

"Yet let him keep the rest,
But keep them with repining restlessness.
    Let him be rich and weary, that at least,
If goodness lead him not, yet weariness
    May toss him to my breast."   20

[5] Imaginary, ineffective limitations on behavior.
[6] Shut one's eyes to.   [7] A skull, a Christian reminder of mortality.
[1] *Rest* means both "repose" and "the remainder" here. The working of the two against each other is the "pulley" of the title.

John Milton

John Milton (1608–74) was born into a middle-class family in London. While still a child, he was recognized as something of a prodigy, especially in learning language. Formal instruction at Cambridge was followed by further intensive independent study. After two years' travel on the continent, he returned to England to witness the English Revolution, which overthrew and executed the king and placed Oliver Cromwell at the head of the state. Milton enthusiastically supported the Revolution and became Latin Secretary to Cromwell's Council of State. He lost his eyesight in 1652, probably through years of strain. When the monarchy was restored in 1660, Milton was at first in some danger, but he managed to escape with a fine. *Paradise Lost,* Milton's biblical epic written to "justify the ways of God to man," appeared in 1667. *Paradise Regained,* a poem about Christ's temptation in the wilderness, and *Samson Agonistes,* a tragic poem, followed. "Lycidas" was written when Milton was in his late twenties to commemorate the death by drowning of a college classmate, Edward King. It is in the form of a pastoral elegy: that is, it is developed as the song of a shepherd mourning the loss of a friend.

LYCIDAS

In this monody[1] the author bewails a learned friend, unfortunately drowned in his passage from Chester on the Irish Seas, 1637. And by occasion foretells the ruin of our corrupted clergy, then in their height.

>   Yet once more, O ye laurels, and once more
> Ye myrtles brown, with ivy never sere,[2]
> I come to pluck your berries harsh and crude,[3]
> And with forced fingers rude,
> Shatter your leaves before the mellowing year.   5
> Bitter constraint, and sad occasion dear,
> Compels me to disturb your season due;
> For Lycidas is dead, dead ere his prime,
> Young Lycidas, and hath not left his peer.
> Who would not sing for Lycidas? He knew   10
> Himself to sing, and build the lofty rhyme.
> He must not float upon his watery bier
> Unwept, and welter to the parching wind,
> Without the meed of some melodious tear.
>   Begin then, sisters of the sacred well[4]   15
> That from beneath the seat of Jove doth spring,
> Begin, and somewhat loudly sweep the string.
> Hence with denial vain, and coy excuse;
> So may some gentle Muse
> With lucky words favor my destined urn,   20

---

[1] In Greek drama, a "monody" was a portion of a chorus sung by a single voice.
[2] Laurels, myrtles, and ivy are all evergreens associated with poetic inspiration.
[3] Unripe.
[4] The nine muses were said to live near the sacred "well" or spring on Mt. Helicon.

And as he passes turn,
And bid fair peace be to my sable shroud.
For we were nursed upon the selfsame hill,
Fed the same flock, by fountain, shade, and rill.
    Together both, ere the high lawns[5] appeared   25
Under the opening eyelids of the morn,
We drove afield, and both together heard
What time the grayfly winds her sultry horn,
Battening our flocks with the fresh dews of night,
Oft till the star that rose at evening bright   30
Toward Heaven's descent had sloped his westering wheel.
Meanwhile the rural ditties were not mute,
Tempered to th' oaten flute,[6]
Rough satyrs danced, and fauns with cloven heel
From the glad sound would not be absent long,   35
And old Damoetas[7] loved to hear our song.
    But O the heavy change, now thou art gone,
Now thou art gone, and never must return!
Thee, shepherd, thee the woods and desert caves,
With wild thyme and the gadding[8] vine o'ergrown,   40
And all their echoes mourn.
The willows and the hazel copses green
Shall now no more be seen,
Fanning their joyous leaves to thy soft lays.
As killing as the canker to the rose,   45
Or taint-worm to the weanling herds that graze,
Or frost to flowers that their gay wardrobe wear,
When first the white thorn blows;[9]
Such, Lycidas, thy loss to shepherd's ear.
    Where were ye, nymphs, when the remorseless deep   50
Closed o'er the head of our loved Lycidas?
For neither were ye playing on the steep,
Where your old Bards, the famous Druids[10] lie,
Nor on the shaggy top of Mona high,
Nor yet where Deva spreads her wizard stream: 55
Ay me! I fondly dream—
Had ye been there—for what could that have done?
What could the Muse[11] herself that Orpheus bore,
The Muse herself, for her inchanting[12] son
Whom universal Nature did lament,   60
When by the rout that made the hideous roar,
His gory visage down the stream was sent,

---

[5] Upland pastures.   [6] Shepherds' panpipes.
[7] A stock pastoral name. "Damoetas" was probably a tutor King and Milton shared at Cambridge.
[8] Straggling.   [9] Blossoms.
[10] The druids were priests of Celtic Britain. The "steep" is the mountain Kerig-y-Druidion in Wales, where druids were reputed to be buried. "Mona" is the island of Anglesey, and "Deva" is the river Dee. Kerig-y-Druidion, Anglesey, and the river Dee are all in the west, near where King was drowned.
[11] The mother of Orpheus was Calliope, the muse of epic poetry.
[12] The obsolete verb form of "incantation." It implies both "chanting" and "enchanting."

Down the swift Hebrus to the Lesbian shore?[13]
   Alas! What boots[14] it with incessant care
To tend the homely slighted shepherd's trade, 65
And strictly meditate the thankless Muse?[15]
Were it not better done as others use,
To sport with Amaryllis in the shade,
Or with the tangles of Neaera's hair?[16]
Fame is the spur that the clear spirit doth raise 70
(That last infirmity of noble mind)
To scorn delights, and live laborious days;
But the fair guerdon[17] when we hope to find,
And think to burst out into sudden blaze,
Comes the blind Fury[18] with th' abhorréd shears, 75
And slits the thin spun life. "But not the praise,"
Phoebus[19] replied, and touched my trembling ears;
"Fame is no plant that grows on mortal soil,
Nor in the glistering foil[20]
Set off to th' world, nor in broad rumor lies, 80
But lives and spreads aloft by those pure eyes,
And perfect witness of all-judging Jove;
As he pronounces lastly on each deed,
Of so much fame in Heaven expect thy meed."
   O fountain Arethuse,[21] and thou honored flood, 85
Smooth-sliding Mincius, crowned with vocal reeds,
That strain I heard was of a higher mood.
But now my oat[22] proceeds,
And listens to the herald of the sea[23]
That came in Neptune's plea. 90
He asked the waves, and asked the felon winds,
"What hard mishap hath doomed this gentle swain?"
And questioned every gust of rugged wings
That blows from off each beakéd promontory;
They knew not of his story, 95
And sage Hippotades[24] their answer brings,
That not a blast was from his dungeon strayed,
The air was calm, and on the level brine,

---

[13] A mob (or "rout") of crazed Thracian women tore Orpheus to pieces and threw his head into the river Hebrus. It floated, singing all the way, down the river and out in the Aegean Sea to the island of Lesbos.
[14] Profits.   [15] Study to write poetry.
[16] *Amaryllis* and *Neaera* are stock pastoral names for pretty nymphs.
[17] Reward.
[18] Atropos, one of the three Fates, carried scissors to cut the thread of human life. Milton makes her a Fury to emphasize her horribleness.
[19] Phoebus Apollo, god of poetry. Touching the ears of one's listeners was, in Roman times, a request that they remember what is said.
[20] Shiny, thin metal, used as a background for jewels to make them look more sparkling.
[21] Arethusa was a fountain in Sicily, Mincius a river in Lombardy. Both are stock placenames in pastoral poetry.
[22] Pipe; song.
[23] The herald is Triton, sent by Neptune to plead his master's innocence in Lycidas' death.
[24] Another name for Aeolus, god of the winds.

Sleek Panope[25] with all her sisters played.
It was that fatal and perfidious bark   100
Built in th' eclipse,[26] and rigged with curses dark,
That sunk so low that sacred head of thine.
    Next Camus,[27] reverend sire, went footing slow,
His mantle hairy, and his bonnet sedge,
Inwrought with figures dim, and on the edge   105
Like that sanguine flower inscribed with woe.[28]
"Ah! who hath reft," quoth he, "my dearest pledge?"
Last came and last did go
The pilot of the Galilean lake,[29]
Two massy keys he bore of metals twain   110
(The golden opes, the iron shuts amain[30]).
He shook his mitered locks,[31] and stern bespake:
"How well could I have spared for thee, young swain,
Enow[32] of such as for their bellies' sake,
Creep and intrude, and climb into the fold!   115
Of other care they little reckoning make,
Than how to scramble at the shearers' feast,
And shove away the worthy bidden guest.
Blind mouths![33] That scarce themselves know how to hold
A sheep-hook,[34] or have learned aught else the least   120
That to the faithful herdsman's art belongs!
What recks it them?[35] What need they? They are sped;
And when they list,[36] their lean and flashy songs
Grate on their scrannel[37] pipes of wretched straw.
The hungry sheep look up, and are not fed,   125
But swoln with wind, and the rank mist they draw,
Rot inwardly, and foul contagion spread,
Besides what the grim wolf with privy paw[38]
Daily devours apace, and nothing said.
But that two-handed engine at the door[39]   130
Stands ready to smite once, and smite no more."
    Return, Alpheus,[40] the dread voice is past,
That shrunk thy streams; return, Sicilian muse,
And call the vales, and bid them hither cast
Their bells and flowerets of a thousand hues.   135
Ye valleys low where the mild whispers use,[41]

---

[25] Chief sea nymph.   [26] Eclipses were thought to portend unlucky times.
[27] Personification of the river Cam and, hence, of Cambridge University, through whose grounds it runs.
[28] The hyacinth, named for a youth accidentally killed by Apollo. Its petals supposedly have "AI," "AI," the Greek sound of mourning, on them.
[29] St. Peter, who carries keys that lock and unlock the gates of Heaven.
[30] Permanently.
[31] St. Peter, as the first bishop of the Christian church, wears a bishop's miter.
[32] Enough.   [33]They have no vision, only appetites.
[34] A bishop's staff is shaped like a shepherd's crook.   [35] "What do they care?"
[36] Want to; choose.   [37] Harsh.   [38] Roman Catholicism.
[39] The nature of the "two-handed engine" has never been satisfactorily explained.
[40] Alpheus was a river-god who wooed the nymph Arethusa, for whom the fountain was named. (See line 85.)
[41] Are used, or accustomed, to being heard.

Of shades and wanton winds, and gushing brooks,
On whose fresh lap the swart star[42] sparely looks,
Throw hither all your quaint enameled eyes,
That on the green turf suck the honeyed showers,   140
And purple all the ground with vernal flowers.
Bring the rathe[43]primrose that forsaken dies.
The tufted crow-toe, and pale jessamine,
The white pink, and the pansy freaked[44] with jet,
The glowing violet,   145
The musk-rose, and the well attired woodbine.
With cowslips wan that hang the pensive head,
And every flower that sad embroidery wears:
Bid amaranthus[45] all his beauty shed,
And daffadillies fill their cups with tears,   150
To strew the laureate hearse[46] where Lycid lies.
For so to interpose a little ease,
Let our frail thoughts dally with false surmise.[47]
Ay me! Whilst thee the shores and sounding seas
Wash far away, where'er thy bones are hurled,   155
Whether beyond the stormy Hebrides,[48]
Where thou perhaps under the whelming tide
Visit'st the bottom of the monstrous world;
Or whether thou, to our moist vows denied,
Sleep'st by the fable of Bellerus old,[49]   160
Where the great vision of the guarded mount
Looks toward Namancos and Bayona's hold;[50]
Look homeward angel now, and melt with ruth:[51]
And, O ye dolphins,[52] waft the hapless youth.
    Weep no more, woeful shepherds, weep no more,   165
For Lycidas your sorrow is not dead,
Sunk though he be beneath the watery floor,
So sinks the day-star[53] in the ocean bed,
And yet anon repairs his drooping head,
And tricks[54] his beams, and with new-spangled ore,   170
Flames in the forehead of the morning sky:
So Lycidas sunk low, but mounted high,
Through the dear might of him that walked the waves,
Where other groves, and other streams along,
With nectar pure his oozy locks he laves,   175
And hears the unexpressive nuptial song,[55]
In the blest kingdoms meek of joy and love.
There entertain him all the saints above,

---

[42] Sirius, the Dog Star, which appears during the hot days of late summer.
[43] Early.   [44] Flecked.   [45] An imaginary flower that never fades.
[46] Bier decorated with laurels.
[47] The "false surmise" is the thought that the body of Lycidas has been recovered and can be buried.
[48] Islands off the west coast of Scotland.
[49] Bellerus was a fabled giant supposed to be buried on Land's End in Cornwall.
[50] The "guarded mount" is St. Michael's Mount in Cornwall. Milton imagines St. Michael looking across the sea to Namancos and Bayona, in northern Spain.
[51] Pity.
[52] Dolphins carried the poet Arion safely to shore after a wreck because they loved his verses.
[53] The sun.   [54] Dresses.   [55] Inexpressible wedding song. See Revelation, chapter 19.

In solemn troops and sweet societies
That sing, and singing in their glory move,   180
And wipe the tears forever from his eyes.
Now, Lycidas, the shepherds weep no more;
Henceforth thou art the genius[56] of the shore,
In thy large recompense, and shalt be good
To all that wander in that perilous flood.   185
    Thus sang the uncouth swain[57] to th' oaks and rills,
While the still morn went out with sandals gray;
He touched the tender stops of various quills,[58]
With eager thought warbling his Doric[59] lay.
And now the sun had stretched out all the hills,   190
And now was dropped into the western bay;
At last he rose, and twitched his mantle blue:
Tomorrow to fresh woods, and pastures new.

WHEN I CONSIDER HOW MY LIGHT IS SPENT

When I consider how my light is spent
   Ere half my days, in this dark world and wide,
   And that one talent which is death to hide,
   Lodged with me useless, though my soul more bent
To serve therewith my Maker, and present   5
   My true account, lest he returning chide;
   "Doth God exact day-labor, light denied?"
   I fondly ask; but Patience to prevent
That murmur, soon replies, "God doth not need
   Either man's work or his own gifts; who best   10
   Bear his mild yoke, they serve him best. His state
Is kingly. Thousands at his bidding speed
   And post o'er land and ocean without rest:
   They also serve who only stand and wait."

Andrew Marvell

Andrew Marvell (1621–78) attended Cambridge University and was for some
years tutor to the daughter of Sir Thomas Fairfax, general of the Parliamentary
forces in the English Civil War. In 1657, he became the assistant of John Milton,
the Latin Secretary for the Commonwealth; after the Restoration, he seemed to
have been responsible for saving Milton from imprisonment and possible execution. From 1659 until his death in 1678, Marvell was a Member of Parliament,
representing Hull. He published nothing of his poetry during his lifetime except
a few satires. The main body of his work was published after his death, and Marvell

[56] Presiding spirit.
[57] Unschooled shepherd. (It was a convention of pastoral poetry that the poet be represented as an
ignorant shepherd.)
[58] The pipes of his panpipe.   [59] Simple and rustic.

has become recognized as one of the most accomplished of the seventeenth-century English poets.

THE GARDEN

How vainly men themselves amaze[1]
To win the palm, the oak, or bays,[2]
And their incessant labors see
Crowned from some single herb, or tree,
Whose short and narrow-vergéd shade   5
Does prudently their toils upbraid;
While all flowers and all trees do close[3]
To weave the garlands of repose!

Fair Quiet, have I found thee here,
And Innocence, thy sister dear?   10
Mistaken long, I sought you then
In busy companies of men.
Your sacred plants, if here below,
Only among the plants will grow;
Society is all but rude   15
To this delicious solitude.

No white nor red was ever seen
So amorous as this lovely green.
Fond lovers, cruel as their flame,
Cut in these trees their mistress' name: 20
Little, alas, they know or heed
How far these beauties hers exceed!
Fair trees, wheresoe'er your barks I wound,
No name shall but your own be found.[4]

When we have run our passion's heat,   25
Love hither makes his best retreat.
The gods, that mortal beauty chase,
Still in a tree did end their race:
Apollo haunted Daphne so,
Only that she might laurel grow;   30
And Pan did after Syrinx speed,
Not as a nymph, but for a reed.[5]

What wondrous life is this I lead!
Ripe apples drop about my head;

---

[1] Bewilder.
[2] Crowns for athletics (palm), civic merit (oak), and poetry (bay, or laurel).   [3] Join.
[4] Marvell whimsically proposes to carve in the bark of trees not the name of a loved one but tree names, such as "oak" or "maple."
[5] Ovid, in the *Metamorphoses*, tells how Apollo pursued Daphne until she turned into a laurel and how Pan pursued Syrinx until she turned into a reed, from which he made panpipes.

The luscious clusters of the vine   35
Upon my mouth do crush their wine;
The nectarine and curious[6] peach
Into my hands themselves do reach;
Stumbling on melons, as I pass,
Insnared with flowers, I fall on grass.   40

Meanwhile the mind, from pleasure less,[7]
Withdraws into its happiness;
The mind, that ocean where each kind
Does straight its own resemblance find;[8]
Yet it creates, transcending these,   45
Far other worlds and other seas,
Annihilating all that's made
To a green thought in a green shade.[9]

Here at the fountain's sliding foot,
Or at some fruit tree's mossy root,   50
Casting the body's vest[10] aside,
My soul into the boughs does glide:
There, like a bird, it sits and sings,
Then whets[11] and combs its silver wings,
And, till prepared for longer flight,   55
Waves in its plumes the various light.[12]

Such was that happy garden-state,
While man there walked without a mate:
After a place so pure and sweet,
What other help could yet be meet!   60
But 'twas beyond a mortal's share
To wander solitary there:
Two paradises 'twere in one
To live in paradise alone.

How well the skillful gardener drew   65
Of flowers and herbs this dial[13] new,
Where, from above, the milder sun
Does through a fragrant zodiac run;
And as it works, th' industrious bee
Computes its time as well as we!   70
How could such sweet and wholesome hours
Be reckoned but with herbs and flowers?

[6] Exquisite.   [7] Compressed and drawn in upon itself to enjoy pleasure.
[8] The ocean was thought to contain a counterpart of every animal on dry land. The mind is like an ocean, then, because it contains a mental image of everything in the outside world.
[9] Green (contemplation) should be contrasted with the red (passion) and white (innocence) of line 17.
[10] Vestment or clothing. The body itself is being represented as clothing for the soul.
[11] Preens.
[12] Varied or many-colored light of this world, as opposed to the pure white light of eternity.
[13] A sundial made of flowers.

BERMUDAS

Where the remote Bermudas ride,
In th' ocean's bosom unespied,
From a small boat that rowed along,
The listening winds received this song:

"What should we do but sing His praise,   5
That led us through the watery maze
Unto an isle so long unknown,
And yet far kinder than our own?
Where He the huge sea monsters wracks,[1]
That lift the deep upon their backs;   10
He lands us on a grassy stage,
Safe from the storms, and prelate's rage.[2]
He gave us this eternal spring
Which here enamels everything,
And sends the fowls to us in care,   15
On daily visits through the air;
He hangs in shades the orange bright,
Like golden lamps in a green night,
And does in the pomegranates close
Jewels more rich than Ormus[3] shows;   20
He makes the figs our mouths to meet,
And throws the melons at our feet;
But apples[4] plants of such a price,
No tree could ever bear them twice;
With cedars, chosen by His hand,   25
From Lebanon, He stores the land;
And makes the hollow seas, that roar,
Proclaim the ambergris[5] on shore;
He cast (of which we rather boast)
The Gospel's pearl upon our coast,   30
And in these rocks for us did frame
A temple, where to sound His name.
O! let our voice His praise exalt,
Till it arrive at heaven's vault,
Which, thence (perhaps) rebounding, may   35
Echo beyond the Mexique Bay."[6]

Thus sung they in the English boat,
An holy and a cheerful note;
And all the way, to guide their chime,
With falling oars they kept the time.   40

---

[1] Wrecks; destroys.   [2] The rage of bishops.
[3] Variant of Ormuz or Hormuz; jewel trading center in Persia (present-day Iran).
[4] Pineapples.
[5] A waxy substance formed in the intestines of sperm whales and often found floating in the ocean or washed ashore. It is used as a fixative in the manufacture of perfumes.
[6] Gulf of Mexico.

TO HIS COY MISTRESS

   Had we but world enough, and time,
This coyness, lady, were no crime.
We would sit down, and think which way
To walk, and pass our long love's day.
Thou by the Indian Ganges' side   5
Shouldst rubies find; I by the tide
Of Humber would complain.[1] I would
Love you ten years before the flood,
And you should, if you please, refuse
Till the conversion of the Jews.[2]   10
My vegetable love should grow
Vaster than empires and more slow;
An hundred years should go to praise
Thine eyes, and on thy forehead gaze;
Two hundred to adore each breast,   15
But thirty thousand to the rest;
An age at least to every part,
And the last age should show your heart.
For, lady, you deserve this state,[3]
Nor would I love at lower rate.   20
   But at my back I always hear
Time's wingéd chariot hurrying near;
And yonder all before us lie
Deserts of vast eternity.
Thy beauty shall no more be found,   25
Nor, in thy marble vault, shall sound
My echoing song; then worms shall try
That long-preserved virginity,
And your quaint honor turn to dust,
And into ashes all my lust: 30
The grave's a fine and private place,
But none, I think, do there embrace.
   Now therefore, while the youthful hue
Sits on thy skin like morning dew,
And while thy willing soul transpires   35
At every pore with instant fires,[4]
Now let us sport us while we may,
And now, like amorous birds of prey,
Rather at once our time devour
Than languish in his slow-chapped[5] power.   40
Let us roll all our strength and all

[1] The Humber river (which flows through Marvell's home town of Hull) is a comically dull stream to compare to the famous Ganges river of India.
[2] Folk belief was that the Jews would be converted to Christianity just before the Last Judgment.
[3] Dignity.
[4] *Transpires:* breathes forth. *Instant fires:* immediate passions.
[5] Slow-jawed. (Time is represented as slowly chewing up the world.)

Our sweetness up into one ball,
And tear our pleasures with rough strife
Through the iron gates of life:
Thus, though we cannot make our sun   45
Stand still, yet we will make him run.

Katherine Philips

Katherine Philips (1631–64) grew up in London in a wealthy merchant family.
She received a good education and was married at the age of sixteen to a prosperous man in his fifties, a staunch supporter of Cromwell and the Revolution.
Philips was a prolific poet and translator and was the center of a literary circle that
included Abraham Cowley and Henry Vaughan. Her collected poems were published in a pirated edition in the year of her death.

AGAINST LOVE

Hence, Cupid! with your cheating toys,
Your real Griefs, and painted Joys,
Your Pleasure which itself destroys.
Lovers like men in fevers burn and rave,
And only what will injure them do crave.   5
Men's weakness makes Love so severe,
They give him power by their fear,
And make the shackles which they wear.
    Who to another does his heart submit;
    Makes his own Idol, and then worships it.   10
Him whose heart is all his own,
Peace and liberty does crown;
He apprehends no killing frown.
    He feels no raptures which are joys diseas'd,
    And is not much transported, but still pleas'd.   15

Aphra Behn

Very little is known about the life of Aphra Behn (1640–89), dramatist, novelist,
poet, and apparently the first Englishwoman to earn a living with her writing. She
may have spent some time as a child in Surinam (Dutch Guiana), the setting of
her novel *Oroonoko* (1688). Back in England, she married a London merchant
named Behn when she was eighteen; he died eight years later. Next she seems to
have been employed by Charles II on secret service in the Netherlands. If so, she
was not well rewarded; by 1667, she was back in London, in debt, and eventually
in debtors' prison. On her release, she turned to writing as a source of income.
Her first play, *The Forc'd Marriage,* was produced in 1671. Sixteen others followed,
including her dramatic masterpiece *The Rover* (1677 and 1681). In addition, she
wrote twelve histories and novels, as well as poetry and translations.

SONG: A THOUSAND MARTYRS I HAVE MADE

A thousand martyrs I have made,
   All sacrific'd to my desire;
A thousand beauties have betray'd,
   That languish in resistless fire.
The untam'd heart to hand I brought,   5
And fixed the wild and wandering thought.

I never vow'd nor sigh'd in vain
   But both, tho' false, were well receiv'd.
The fair are pleas'd to give us pain,
   And what they wish is soon believ'd.   10
And tho' I talk'd of wounds and smart,
Love's pleasures only touched my heart.

Alone the glory and the spoil
   I always laughing bore away;
The triumphs, without pain or toil,   15
   Without the hell, the heav'n of joy.
And while I thus at random rove
Despis'd the fools that whine for love.

LOVE ARMED

Love[1] in Fantastic Triumph sat,
Whilst Bleeding Hearts around him flowed,
For whom Fresh pains he did Create,
And strange Tyrannic power he showed;
From thy Bright Eyes he took his fire,   5
Which round about, in sport he hurled;
But 'twas from mine he took desire,
Enough to undo the Amorous World.

From me he took his sighs and tears,
From thee his Pride and Cruelty;   10
From me his Languishments and Fears,
And every Killing Dart from thee;
Thus thou and I, the God[1] have armed.
And set him up a Deity;
But my poor Heart alone is harmed,   15
Whilst thine the Victor is, and free.

---

[1] Personified as a god: Cupid.

Anne Bradstreet

Anne Bradstreet (c. 1612–72) was the author of the first published book of poetry written by a resident of America. Her father, Thomas Dudley, was a devout Puritan who managed the estate of the Puritan Earl of Lincoln. She was married at sixteen to Simon Bradstreet, a young graduate of Cambridge and an associate of her father. Two years later, both the Dudley and the Bradstreet families sailed with Governor John Winthrop and the Massachusetts Bay emigrants for the New World. Simon Bradstreet was a leader in the Massachusetts Bay Company and eventually became Governor of the Colony. Anne Bradstreet, who had written poems for her father when she was growing up, continued to write in the New World. Without telling her, a brother-in-law, John Woodbridge, took a manuscript collection of her poems to London and had it printed there, under the title *The Tenth Muse,* in 1650. Many of Bradstreet's poems are religious or meditative, but a fair number of them are secular and domestic.

THE AUTHOR TO HER BOOK[1]

Thou ill-formed offspring of my feeble brain,
Who after birth didst by my side remain,
Till snatched from thence by friends, less wise than true,
Who thee abroad, exposed to public view,
Made thee in rags, halting to th' press to trudge,   5
Where errors were not lessened (all may judge).
At thy return my blushing was not small,
My rambling brat (in print) should mother call,
I cast thee by as one unfit for light,
Thy visage was so irksome in my sight;   10
Yet being mine own, at length affection would
Thy blemishes amend, if so I could:
I washed thy face, but more defects I saw,
And rubbing off a spot still made a flaw.
I stretched thy joints to make thee even feet,[2]   15
Yet still thou run'st more hobbling than is meet;
In better dress to trim thee was my mind,
But nought save homespun cloth i' th' house I find.
In this array 'mongst vulgars[3] may'st thou roam.
In critic's hands beware thou dost not come,   20
And take thy way where yet thou art not known;
If for thy father asked, say thou hadst none;
And for thy mother, she alas is poor,
Which caused her thus to send thee out of door.

---

[1] Bradstreet wrote this poem for the second edition of *The Tenth Muse,* which was published in 1678.
[2] Bradstreet is punning on *feet,* meaning both parts of the body and metrical units.
[3] Common people.

TO MY DEAR AND LOVING HUSBAND

If ever two were one, then surely we.
If ever man were loved by wife, then thee;
If ever wife was happy in a man,
Compare with me, ye women, if you can.
I prize thy love more than whole mines of gold   5
Or all the riches that the East doth hold.
My love is such that rivers cannot quench,
Nor ought but love from thee, give recompense.
Thy love is such I can no way repay,
The heavens reward thee manifold, I pray.   10
Then while we live, in love let's so persevere
That when we live no more, we may live ever.

Edward Taylor

Edward Taylor (c. 1642–1729) was an American Puritan minister whose poetry
was not generally known until the 1930s, when his poetic manuscripts were discovered in the Yale University library. He has since become recognized as an
American Metaphysical poet comparable to John Donne, if not as accomplished.
Taylor was born in Leicestershire, England, and emigrated to America when he
was twenty-six years old in order to avoid signing an oath of loyalty to the Church
of England. He attended Harvard for three years, where he prepared for the
ministry. He was asked to take a church in Westfield, Massachusetts, then on the
western frontier. He agreed and spent the rest of his life in Westfield, ministering
to his congregation and, as we know now, writing poetry.

UPON A WASP CHILLED WITH COLD

The bear that breathes the northern blast[1]
Did numb, torpedo-like,[2] a wasp
Whose stiffened limbs encramped, lay bathing
In Sol's[3] warm breath and shine as saving,
Which with her hands she chafes and stands   5
Rubbing her legs, shanks, thighs, and hands.
Her petty toes, and fingers' ends
Nipped with this breath, she out extends
Unto the sun, in great desire
To warm her digits at that fire.   10
Doth hold her temples in this state
Where pulse doth beat, and head doth ache.
Doth turn, and stretch her body small,

---

[1] The constellation in the north, Ursa Major or the Great Bear.
[2] A torpedo is a fish like an electric eel that delivers an electrical shock.
[3] The sun's.

Doth comb her velvet capital.[4]
As if her little brain pan were   15
A volume of choice precepts clear.
As if her satin jacket hot
Contained apothecary's shop[5]
Of nature's receipts, that prevails
To remedy all her sad ails,   20
As if her velvet helmet high
Did turret[6] rationality.
She fans her wing up to the wind
As if her pettycoat were lined,
With reason's fleece, and hoists sails   25
And humming flies in thankful gales
Unto her dun curled[7] palace hall
Her warm thanks offering for all.

    Lord, clear my misted sight that I
May hance view Thy divinity,   30
Some sparks whereof thou up dost hasp[8]
Within this little downy wasp
In whose small corporation[9] we
A school and a schoolmaster see,
Where we may learn, and easily find   35
A nimble spirit bravely mind
Her work in every limb: and lace
It up neat with a vital grace,
Acting each part though ne'er so small
Here of this fustian[10] animal.   40
Till I enravished climb into
The Godhead on this ladder do,
Where all my pipes inspired upraise
An heavenly music furred[11] with praise.

HUSWIFERY[1]

Make me, O Lord, Thy spinning wheel complete.[2]
    Thy Holy Word my distaff make for me.
Make mine affections Thy swift flyers neat
    And make my soul Thy holy spool to be.

---

[4] Head.   [5] Drugstore. "Receipts" are recipes or prescriptions.
[6] Contain.   [7] Dark curved.   [8] Enclose.   [9] Body.
[10] Fustian was coarse cloth; metaphorically it also referred to melodramatic acting.
[11] Decorated, as with fur.
[1] Huswifery: housekeeping, here used to mean weaving.
[2] Taylor's development of the conceit of the poet as God's spinning wheel involves some technical terms in weaving. The "distaff" is a staff around which is wound the unspun wool. "Flyers" control the spinning of the thread. The "spool" twists the thread, and the "reel" takes up the finished thread. "Quills" are bobbins, and "fulling mills" are used to clean the newly woven cloth with fuller's earth.

My conversation make to Thy reel   5
And reel the yarn thereon spun of Thy wheel.

Make me Thy loom then, knit therein this twine:
And make Thy Holy Spirit, Lord, wind quills:
Then weave the web Thyself. The yarn is fine.
Thine ordinances make my fulling mills.   10
Then dye the same in heavenly colors choice,
All pinked with varnished flowers of paradise.[3]

Then clothe therewith mine understanding, will,
Affections, judgment, conscience, memory,
My words, and actions, that their shine may fill   15
My ways with glory and Thee glorify.
Then mine appeal shall display before Ye
That I am clothed in holy robes for glory.

Anne Finch

Anne Finch (1661–1722) was born into a noble English family and married into
an even nobler one, becoming thereby countess of Winchelsea. She moved in
artistic circles, was a friend of both Jonathan Swift and Alexander Pope, and was
a prolific and accomplished poet herself. Her work was largely forgotten until
recent feminist critics' revival of earlier female poets.

TRAIL ALL YOUR PIKES

Trail all your pikes, dispirit[1] every drum,
March in a slow procession from afar,
Ye silent, ye dejected, men of war.
Be still the hautboys,[2] and the flute be dumb!
Display no more, in vain, the lofty banner;   5
For see where on the bier before ye lies
The pale, the fall'n, the untimely sacrifice
To your mistaken shrine, to your false idol Honour.

TO THE NIGHTINGALE

Exert thy voice, sweet harbinger[1] of spring!
    This moment is thy time to sing,
    This moment I attend to praise,
And set my numbers to thy lays.[2]
    Free as thine shall be my song   5

---

[3] "Pinked": decorated. "Varnished": shiny.
[1] Muffle; take away their capacity to inspire.   [2] Oboes.
[1] Herald.   [2] Songs.

As thy music, short or long.
Poets, wild as thee, were born,
  Pleasing best when unconfined,
  When to please is least designed,
Soothing but their cares to rest;   10
  Cares do still their thoughts molest,
  And still the unhappy poet's breast,
Like thine, when best he sings, is placed against a thorn.[3]

  She begins. Let all be still!
    Muse, thy promise now fulfil!   15
  Sweet, oh sweet! still sweeter yet!
  Can thy words such accents fit,
  Canst thou syllables refine,
  Melt a sense that shall retain
  Still some spirit of the brain,   20
  Till with sounds like these it join?
    'Twill not be! then change thy note,
    Let division shake thy throat.[4]
  Hark! division now she tries,
  Yet as far as the Muse outflies.   25
    Cease then, prithee, cease thy tune!
    Trifler, wilt thou sing till June?
  Till thy business all lies waste,
  And the time of building's past?
    Thus we poets that have speech,   30
  Unlike what thy forests teach,
    If a fluent vein be shown
    That's transcendent to our own,
  Criticize, reform, or preach,
  Or censure what we cannot reach.   35

Alexander Pope

Alexander Pope (1688–1744) is the exemplary poet of the neoclassic period in England. His genius is for polish, wit, and social commentary rather than for personal emotion and self-revelation, a genius that found perfect expression in the heroic couplet he used in most of his poems. He had to make his own way in the literary circles of his time. As a Catholic, he could not attend a university or receive patronage. He was further handicapped by ill health; tuberculosis of the spine when he was a child left him partially disabled. Pope's first successes, written when he was in his early twenties, were the versified critical work *An Essay on Criticism* (1711) and the mock-epic *Rape of the Lock* (1712). Translations of Homer's epics and an edition of Shakespeare's plays gave him financial security. In his later years he turned to topical satire, often casting his poems in the form of

---

[3] Legend has it that the nightingale sometimes commits suicide by placing his breast against a thorn and singing as he dies.
[4] "Division" is a seventeenth-century musical term meaning ornamentation of a melody line in singing.

imitations of the satires of Horace, thus implying a parallel between his own London and Horace's Rome. "Epistle II. To a Lady. Of the Characters of Women" is one of four "epistles" or "moral essays" Pope wrote. The first is on the characters of men; the third and fourth are on the use of riches. Pope's view of women in "Epistle II" expresses the misogyny of his age. Its charm is in the vividness of its satire of feminine types and the grace of the closing compliment to Martha Blount, Pope's close friend and the lady to whom the poem is addressed. Most of the stock Latin names conceal actual women of Pope's and Blount's acquaintance, but they will not be identified in the notes.

EPISTLE II. TO A LADY

Of The Characters Of Women

Nothing so true as what you once let fall,
"Most women have no characters at all."
Matter too soft a lasting mark to bear,
And best distinguished by black, brown, or fair.
How many pictures[1] of one nymph we view,   5
All how unlike each other, all how true!
Arcadia's countess, here, in ermined pride,
Is, there, Pastora by a fountain side.
Here Fannia, leering on her own good man,
And there, a naked Leda with a swan.[2]   10
Let then the fair one beautifully cry,
In Magdalen's loose hair and lifted eye,
Or dressed in smiles of sweet Cecilia shine,[3]
With simpering angels, palms, and harps divine;
Whether the charmer sinner it, or saint it,   15
If folly grow romantic,[4] I must paint it.
Come then, the colors and the ground[5] prepare!
Dip in the rainbow, trick her off in air;
Choose a firm cloud, before it fall, and in it
Catch, ere she change, the Cynthia[6] of this minute.   20
Rufa, whose eye quick-glancing o'er the park,
Attracts each light gay meteor of a spark,
Agrees as ill with Rufa studying Locke,[7]
As Sappho's diamonds with her dirty smock,
Or Sappho at her toilet's greasy task,   25
With Sappho fragrant at an evening masque:
So morning insects that in muck begun,
Shine, buzz, and flyblow in the setting sun.

---

[1] Pope organizes the poem around a stroll through an imaginary picture gallery. Eighteenth-century ladies often had themselves painted in mythological costumes and settings.
[2] Zeus took the shape of a swan in order to seduce the mortal Leda.
[3] These lines describe stock poses in which St. Mary Magdalen and St. Cecilia, patron saint of music, were painted.
[4] Fanciful.   [5] First coats of paint on a canvas before the figures were sketched in.
[6] Goddess of the moon, hence changeable.
[7] John Locke, English philosopher and author of *An Essay Concerning Human Understanding* (1690).

How soft is Silia! fearful to offend,
The frail one's advocate, the weak one's friend: 30
To her, Calista proved her conduct nice,
And good Simplicius asks of her advice.
Sudden, she storms! she raves! You tip the wink,
But spare your censure; Silia does not drink.
All eyes may see from what the change arose,   35
All eyes may see—a pimple on her nose.
    Papillia, wedded to her amorous spark,[8]
Sighs for the shades—"How charming is a park!"
A park is purchased, but the fair he sees
All bathed in tears—"Oh, odious, odious trees!"   40
    Ladies, like variegated tulips, show;
'Tis to their changes half their charms we owe;
Fine by defect, and delicately weak,
Their happy spots the nice admirer take,
'T'was thus Calypso once each heart alarmed,   45
Awed without virtue, without beauty charmed;
Her tongue bewitched as oddly as her eyes,
Less wit than mimic, more a wit than wise;
Strange graces still, and stranger flights she had,
Was just not ugly, and was just not mad;   50
Yet ne'er so sure our passion to create,
As when she touched the brink of all we hate.
    Narcissa's nature, tolerably mild,
To make a wash,[9] would hardly stew a child;
Has even been proved to grant a lover's prayer,   55
And paid a tradesman once to make him stare,
Gave alms at Easter, in a Christian trim,
And made a widow happy, for a whim.
Why then declare good nature is her scorn,
When 'tis by that alone she can be borne?   60
Why pique all mortals, yet affect a name?
A fool to pleasure, yet a slave to fame:
Now deep in Taylor and the *Book of Martyrs,*[10]
Now drinking citron[11] with his Grace and Chartres.
Now conscience chills her, and now passion burns;   65
And atheism and religion take their turns;
A very heathen in the carnal part,
Yet still a sad, good Christian at her heart.
    See Sin in state, majestically drunk;
Proud as a peeress, prouder as a punk;[12]   70
Chaste to her husband, frank to all beside,
A teeming mistress, but a barren bride.

---

[8] A young dandy; a lover.   [9] Cosmetic lotion.

[10] Jeremy Taylor, a seventeenth-century cleric, wrote *Holy Living and Holy Dying.* John Foxe's *Acts and Monuments* (often called *Book of Martyrs*) was an account of the Protestants who lost their lives under Mary Queen of Scots; it was common in Protestant households in the eighteenth century.

[11] Brandy flavored with "citron": lemon or orange peel. "His Grace" (the Duke of Wharton) and Francis Chartres were well-known libertines.

[12] Prostitute.

What then? let blood and body bear the fault,
Her head's untouched, that noble seat of thought:
Such this day's doctrine—in another fit   75
She sins with poets through pure love of wit.
What has not fired her bosom or her brain?
Caesar and Tallboy,[13] Charles and Charlemagne.
As Helluo,[14] late dictator of the feast,
The nose of hautgout,[15] and the tip of taste,   80
Criticked your wine, and analyzed your meat,
Yet on plain pudding deigned at home to eat;
So Philomedé, lecturing all mankind
On the soft passion, and the taste refined,
The address, the delicacy—stoops at once,   85
And makes her hearty meal upon a dunce.

    Flavia's a wit, has too much sense to pray;
To toast our wants and wishes, is her way;
Nor asks of God, but her stars, to give
The mighty blessing, "while we live, to live."   90
Then all for death, that opiate of the soul!
Lucretia's dagger, Rosamonda's bowl.[16]
Say, what can cause such impotence of mind?
A spark too fickle, or a spouse too kind.
Wise wretch! with pleasures too refined to please,   95
With too much spirit to be e'er at ease,
With too much quickness ever to be taught,
With too much thinking to have common thought:
You purchase pain with all that joy can give,
And die of nothing but a rage to live.   100

    Turn then from wits; and look on Simo's mate,
No ass so meek, no ass so obstinate.
Or her, that owns her faults, but never mends,
Because she's honest, and the best of friends:
Or her, whose life the Church and scandal share,   105
Forever in a passion, or a prayer:
Or her, who laughs at hell, but (like her Grace)
Cries, "Ah! how charming, if there's no such place!"
Or who in sweet vicissitude appears
Of mirth and opium, ratafie[17] and tears,   110
The daily anodyne, and nightly draught,
To kill those foes to fair ones, time and thought.
Woman and fool are two hard things to hit,
For true no-meaning puzzles more than wit.

    But what are these to great Atossa's mind?   115
Scarce once herself, by turns all womankind!
Who, with herself, or others, from her birth

---

[13] A crude character in Richard Brome's play *The Jovial Crew* (1641).
[14] Glutton (Latin).
[15] Anything with a strong scent, such as slightly rancid meat.
[16] Tarquin raped Lucretia, who then killed herself. (See, for example, Shakespeare's *Rape of Lucrece*.)
Rosamunda was the mistress of Henry II; Queen Eleanor forced her to drink poison.
[17] An alcoholic drink flavored with apricot pits.

Finds all her life one warfare upon earth:
Shines in exposing knaves, and painting fools,
Yet is whate'er she hates and ridicules.   120
No thought advances, but her eddy brain
Whisks it about, and down it goes again.
Full sixty years the world has been her trade,
The wisest fool much time has ever made.
From loveless youth to unrespected age,   125
No passion gratified except her rage.
So much the fury still outran the wit,
The pleasure missed her, and the scandal hit.
Who breaks with her, provokes revenge from hell,
But he's a bolder man who dares be well:[18]   130
Her every turn with violence pursued,
Nor more a storm her hate than gratitude:
To that each passion turns, or soon or late;
Love, if it makes her yield, must make her hate:
Superiors? death! and equals? what a curse!   135
But an inferior not dependent? worse.
Offend her, and she knows not to forgive;
Oblige her, and she'll hate you while you live:
But die, and she'll adore you—Then the bust
And temple rise—then fall again to dust.   140
Last night, her lord was all that's good and great;
A knave this morning, and his will a cheat.
Strange! by the means defeated of the ends,
By spirit robbed of power, by warmth of friends,
By wealth of followers! without one distress   145
Sick of herself through very selfishness!
Atossa, cursed with every granted prayer,
Childless with all her children, wants an heir.
To heirs unknown descends the unguarded store,
Or wanders, Heaven-directed, to the poor.   150
  Pictures like these, dear Madam, to design,
Asks no firm hand, and no unerring line;
Some wandering touches, some reflected light,
Some flying stroke alone can hit 'em right:
For how should equal colors do the knack?[19]   155
Chameleons who can paint in white and black?
  "Yet Chloe sure was formed without a spot—"
Nature in her then erred not, but forgot.
"With every pleasing, every prudent part,
Say, what can Chloe want?"—She wants a heart.   160
She speaks, behaves, and acts just as she ought;
But never, never, reached one generous thought.
Virtue she finds too painful an endeavor,
Content to dwell in decencies forever.
So very reasonable, so unmoved,   165
As never yet to love, or to be loved.

[18] Be in her favor.   [19] Do the trick.

She, while her lover pants upon her breast,
Can mark the figures on an Indian chest;
And when she sees her friend in deep despair,
Observes how much a chintz exceeds mohair.   170
Forbid it Heaven, a favor or a debt
She e'er should cancel—but she may forget.
Safe is your secret still in Chloe's ear;
But none of Chloe's shall you ever hear.
Of all her dears she never slandered one,   175
But cares not if a thousand are undone.
Would Chloe know if you're alive or dead?
She bids her footman put it in her head.
Chloe is prudent—Would you too be wise?
Then never break your heart when Chloe dies.   180
    One certain portrait may (I grant) be seen,
Which heaven has varnished out, and made a *Queen*.[20]
The same forever! and described by all
With Truth and Goodness, as with crown and ball.
Poets heap virtues, painters gems at will,   185
And show their zeal, and hide their want of skill.
'Tis well—but, artists! who can paint or write,
To draw the naked is your true delight.
That robe of quality so struts and swells,
None see what parts of Nature it conceals: 190
The exactest traits of body or of mind,
We owe to models of an humble kind
If Queensberry[21] to strip there's no compelling,
'Tis from a handmaid we must take a Helen.
From peer to bishop 'tis no easy thing   195
To draw the man who loves his God, or king:
Alas! I copy (or my draft would fail)
From honest Mah'met or plain Parson Hale.[22]
    But grant, in public men sometimes are shown,
A woman's seen in private life alone: 200
Our bolder talents in full light displayed;
Your virtues open fairest in the shade.
Bred to disguise, in public 'tis you hide;
There, none distinguish 'twixt your shame or pride,
Weakness or delicacy; all so nice,   205
That each may seem a virtue, or a vice.
    In men, we various ruling passions find;
In women, two almost divide the kind;
Those, only fixed, they first or last obey,
The love of pleasure, and the love of sway.[23]   210
    That, Nature gives; and where the lesson taught
Is but to please, can pleasure seem a fault?

[20] Queen Caroline.   [21] The Duchess of Queensberry was a famous beauty.
[22] George I had a Turkish servant named Mahomet. Dr. Stephen Hales, an Anglican clergyman, was a friend of Pope.
[23] Power.

Experience, this; by man's oppression cursed,
They seek the second not to lose the first.
    Men, some to business, some to pleasure take   215
But every woman is at heart a rake;
Men, some to quiet, some to public strife;
But every lady would be queen for life.
    Yet mark the fate of a whole sex of queens!
Power all their end, but beauty all the means: 220
In youth they conquer, with so wild a rage,
As leaves them scarce a subject in their age:
For foreign glory, foreign joy, they roam;
No thought of peace or happiness at home.
But wisdom's triumph is well-timed retreat,   225
As hard a science to the fair as great!
Beauties, like tyrants, old and friendless grown,
Yet hate repose, and dread to be alone,
Worn out in public, weary every eye,
Nor leave one sigh behind them when they die.   230
    Pleasures the sex, as children birds, pursue,
Still out of reach, yet never out of view,
Sure, if they catch, to spoil the toy at most,
To covet flying, and regret when lost:
As last, to follies youth could scarce defend,   235
It grows their age's prudence to pretend;
Ashamed to own they gave delight before,
Reduced to feign it, when they give no more;
As hags hold sabbaths,[24] less for joy than spite,
So these their merry, miserable night;   240
Still round and round the ghosts of beauty glide,
And haunt the places where their honor died.
    See how the world its veterans rewards!
A youth of frolics, an old age of cards;
Fair to no purpose, artful to no end,   245
Young without lovers, old without a friend;
A fop their passion, but their prize a sot;
Alive, ridiculous, and dead, forgot!
    Ah friend! to dazzle let the vain design;
To raise the thought, and touch the heart be thine!   250
That charm shall grow, while what fatigues the Ring[25]
Flaunts and goes down, an unregarded thing:
So when the sun's broad beam has tired the sight,
All mild ascends the moon's more sober light,
Serene in virgin modesty she shines,   255
And unobserved the glaring orb declines.
    Oh! blest with temper, whose unclouded ray
Can make tomorrow cheerful as today;
She, who can love a sister's charms, or hear
Sighs for a daughter with unwounded ear;   260

---

[24] Black masses held by witches ("hags").
[25] A fashionable drive in London's Hyde Park.

She, who ne'er answers till a husband cools,
Or, if she rules him, never shows she rules;
Charms by accepting, by submitting sways,
Yet has her humor most, when she obeys;
Let fops or fortune fly which way they will;   265
Disdains all loss of tickets or Codille;[26]
Spleen, vapors, or smallpox, above them all,
And mistress of herself, though China[27] fall.
   And yet, believe me, good as well as ill,
Woman's at best a contradiction still.   270
Heaven, when it strives to polish all it can
Its last best work, but forms a softer man;
Picks from each sex, to make the favorite blest,
Your love of pleasure, our desire of rest:
Blends, in exception to all general rules,   275
Your taste of follies, with our scorn of fools:
Reserve with frankness, art with truth allied,
Courage with softness, modesty with pride;
Fixed principles, with fancy ever new;
Shakes all together, and produces—you.   280
   Be this a woman's fame: with this unblest,
Toasts live a scorn, and queens may die a jest.
This Phoebus promised (I forget the year)
When those blue eyes first opened on the sphere;
Ascendant Phoebus watched that hour with care,   285
Averted half your parents' simple prayer;
And gave you beauty, but denied the pelf
That buys your sex a tyrant o'er itself.
The generous god, who wit and gold refines,
And ripens spirits as he ripens mines,[28]   290
Kept dross for duchesses, the world shall know it,
To you gave sense, good humor, and a poet.

Thomas Gray

"Elegy Written in a Country Churchyard" has for more than two centuries been
one of a handful of poems written in English best known to the general reader,
both as a whole and as a source of memorable phrases ("the short and simple
annals of the poor," "the paths of glory lead but to the grave"). Its author,
Thomas Gray (1716–71), was a quiet, retiring professor of history at Cambridge
University. Educated at Cambridge, he returned there to teach after extensive
travel on the continent. A literary scholar as well as a historian, he studied the then
little-known fields of medieval poetry and Norse and Welsh folklore. These interests, along with his love of wild, picturesque scenery and the respect for humble
life shown in the "Elegy," anticipate some of the qualities later to be known as
Romantic.

[26] The tickets are lottery tickets. "Codille" is the loss of a hand at the card game of ombre.
[27] Both the country and crockery.
[28] The sun ("Phoebus") was thought to ripen precious metals in the ground.

ELEGY WRITTEN IN A COUNTRY CHURCHYARD

The curfew tolls the knell of parting day,
  The lowing herd wind slowly o'er the lea,
The plowman homeward plods his weary way,
  And leaves the world to darkness and to me.

Now fades the glimmering landscape on the sight,   5
  And all the air a solemn stillness holds,
Save where the beetle wheels his droning flight,
  And drowsy tinklings lull the distant folds;

Save that from yonder ivy-mantled tower
  The moping owl does to the moon complain   10
Of such, as wandering near her secret bower,
  Molest her ancient solitary reign.

Beneath those rugged elms, that yew tree's shade,
  Where heaves the turf in many a moldering heap,
Each in his narrow cell forever laid,   15
  The rude[1] forefathers of the hamlet sleep.

The breezy call of incense-breathing Morn,
  The swallow twittering from the straw-built shed,
The cock's shrill clarion, or the echoing horn,[2]
  No more shall rouse them from their lowly bed.   20

For them no more the blazing hearth shall burn,
  Or busy housewife ply her evening care;
No children run to lisp their sire's return,
  Or climb his knees the envied kiss to share.

Oft did the harvest to their sickle yield,   25
  Their furrow oft the stubborn glebe[3] has broke;
How jocund did they drive their team afield!
  How bowed the woods beneath their sturdy stroke!

Let not Ambition mock their useful toil,
  Their homely joys, and destiny obscure;   30
Nor Grandeur hear with a disdainful smile
  The short and simple annals of the poor.

The boast of heraldry,[4] the pomp of power,
  And all that beauty, all that wealth e'er gave,
Awaits alike the inevitable hour.   35
  The paths of glory lead but to the grave.

Nor you, ye proud, impute to these the fault,
  If Memory o'er their tomb no trophies[5] raise,

---

[1] Humble; unsophisticated.   [2] The hunter's horn.   [3] Ground; soil.   [4] Aristocracy.
[5] Carved figures representing a dead person's accomplishments.

Where through the long-drawn aisle and fretted[6] vault
  The pealing anthem swells the note of praise. 40

Can storied urn or animated bust[7]
  Back to its mansion call the fleeting breath?
Can Honor's voice provoke[8] the silent dust,
  Or Flattery soothe the dull cold ear of Death?

Perhaps in this neglected spot is laid 45
  Some heart once pregnant with celestial fire;
Hands that the rod of empire might have swayed,
  Or waked to ecstasy the living lyre.

But Knowledge to their eyes her ample page
  Rich with the spoils of time did ne'er unroll; 50
Chill Penury repressed their noble rage,
  And froze the genial current of the soul.

Full many a gem of purest ray serene,
  The dark unfathomed caves of ocean bear:
Full many a flower is born to blush unseen, 55
  And waste its sweetness on the desert air.

Some village Hampden,[9] that with dauntless breast
  The little tyrant of his fields withstood;
Some mute inglorious Milton here may rest,
  Some Cromwell guiltless of his country's blood. 60

The applause of listening senates to command,
  The threats of pain and ruin to despise,
To scatter plenty o'er a smiling land,
  And read their history in a nation's eyes.

Their lot forbade: nor circumscribed alone 65
  Their growing virtues, but their crimes confined;
Forbade to wade through slaughter to a throne,
  And shut the gates of mercy on mankind,

The struggling pangs of conscious truth to hide,
  To quench the blushes of ingenuous shame, 70
Or heap the shrine of Luxury and Pride
  With incense kindled at the Muse's flame.

Far from the madding crowd's ignoble strife,
  Their sober wishes never learned to stray;
Along the cool sequestered vale of life 75
  They kept the noiseless tenor of their way.

---

[6] Ornamented with repeated and symmetrical figures, often in relief.
[7] *Storied urn:* inscribed funeral urn. *Animated:* lifelike.   [8] Call forth.
[9] John Hampton (1594–1643) was a military hero in the Parliamentary army in the English Civil War.

Yet even these bones from insult to protect
　　Some frail memorial still erected nigh,
With uncouth rhymes and shapeless sculpture decked,
　　Implores the passing tribute of a sigh.　　　　　　　　80

Their name, their years, spelt by the unlettered Muse,
　　The place of fame and elegy supply:
And many a holy text around she strews,
　　That teach the rustic moralist to die.

For who to dumb Forgetfulness a prey,　　　　　　　　85
　　This pleasing anxious being e'er resigned,
Left the warm precincts of the cheerful day,
　　Nor cast one longing lingering look behind?

On some fond breast the parting soul relies,
　　Some pious drops the closing eye requires;　　　　　90
Even from the tomb the voice of Nature cries,
　　Even in our ashes live their wonted fires.

For thee, who mindful of the unhonored dead
　　Dost in these lines their artless tale relate;
If chance, by lonely contemplation led,　　　　　　　95
　　Some kindred spirit shall inquire thy fate,

Haply some hoary-headed swain may say,
　　"Oft have we seen him at the peep of dawn
Brushing with hasty steps the dews away
　　To meet the sun upon the upland lawn.　　　　　　100

"There at the foot of yonder nodding beech
　　That wreathes its old fantastic roots so high,
His listless length at noontide would he stretch,
　　And pore upon the brook that babbles by.

"Hard by yon wood, now smiling as in scorn,　　　　　105
　　Muttering his wayward fancies he would rove,
Now drooping, woeful wan, like one forlorn,
　　Or crazed with care, or crossed in hopeless love.

"One morn I missed him on the customed hill,
　　Along the heath and near his favorite tree;　　　　110
Another came; nor yet beside the rill,
　　Nor up the lawn, nor at the wood was he;

"The next with dirges due in sad array
　　Slow through the churchway path we saw him borne.
Approach and read (for thou canst read) the lay,　　　115
　　Graved on the stone beneath yon aged thorn."

The Epitaph

Here rests his head upon the lap of Earth
A youth to Fortune and to Fame unknown.
Fair Science[10] *frowned not on his humble birth,*
And Melancholy marked him for her own.

Large was his bounty, and his soul sincere,   5
Heaven did a recompense as largely send:
He gave to Misery all he had, a tear,
He gained from Heaven ('twas all he wished) a friend.

No farther seek his merits to disclose,
Or draw his frailties from their dread abode   10
(There they alike in trembling hope repose),
The bosom of his Father and his God.

Phillis Wheatley

Phillis Wheatley (c. 1753–84) was the first published black poet in America. Born in Africa, probably in northwest Africa in the area of present-day Senegal and Gambia, she was brought to Boston and sold when she was about seven years old. She was bought by a prosperous and generous tailor, John Wheatley, probably as a companion for his wife, Susannah. The Wheatleys seem to have recognized her intelligence very early and taught her to read and write. In 1773, John Wheatley took her to London and arranged for the publication of a collection of her poems: *Poems on Various Subjects, Religious and Moral.* Wheatley was freed when the Wheatleys died, and she married a free black named John Peters. She spent several years in great poverty and died in 1784, at the age of about thirty. Wheatley's favorite poets were Milton, Pope, and Gray, and her own verse is influenced rather too heavily by them. Nevertheless, her work is noteworthy because it preceded by nearly a century any other significant black writing in America.

ON BEING BROUGHT FROM AFRICA TO AMERICA

'Twas mercy brought me from my pagan land,
Taught my benighted soul to understand
That there's a God, that there's a Savior too:
Once I redemption neither sought nor knew.
Some view our sable[1] race with scornful eye.   5
"Their color is a diabolic dye."
Remember, Christians, Negroes, black as Cain,[2]
May be refined, and join the angelic train.

[10] Learning.
[1] Black.
[2] God set a mark upon Cain for killing his brother Abel. The color of blacks has sometimes been called the mark of Cain.

TO S.M.,[1] A YOUNG AFRICAN PAINTER, ON SEEING HIS WORKS

To show the laboring bosom's deep intent,
And thought in living characters to paint,
When first thy pencil did those beauties give,
And breathing figures learnt from thee to live,
How did those prospects give my soul delight, 5
A new creation rushing on my sight?
Still, wondrous youth! each noble path pursue,
On deathless glories fix thine ardent view:
Still may the painter's and the poet's fire
To aid thy pencil, and thy verse conspire! 10
And may the charms of each seraphic[2] theme
Conduct thy footsteps to immortal fame!
High to the blissful wonders of the skies
Elate thy soul, and raise thy wishful eyes.
Thrice happy, when exalted to survey 15
That splendid city, crowned with endless day,
Whose twice six gates[3] on radiant hinges ring:
Celestial Salem[4] blooms in endless spring.

Calm and serene thy moments glide along,
And may the muse inspire each future song! 20
Still, with the sweets of contemplation blest,
May peace with balmy wings your soul invest!
But when these shades of time are chased away,
And darkness ends in everlasting day,
On what seraphic pinions shall we move, 25
And view the landscape in the realms above?
There shall thy tongue in heavenly murmurs flow,
And there my muse with heavenly transport glow:
No more to tell of Damon's[5] tender sighs,
Or rising radiance of Aurora's[6] eyes, 30
For nobler themes demand a nobler strain,
And purer language on the ethereal plain.
Cease, gentle muse! the solemn gloom of night
Now seals the fair creation from my sight.

Charlotte Smith

Charlotte Smith (1749–1806), though principally known as a novelist, was also an able, if rather conventional, poet. She was in her thirties when, married and with ten children, she found herself the sole support of her family, her husband being

---

[1] Scipio Moorhead, servant of a Boston minister named John Moorhead.
[2] Angelic.
[3] Heaven is said to have twelve gates (the same number of the tribes of Israel).
[4] Jerusalem.
[5] Damon and Pythias were legendary friends in classical mythology.
[6] Personification of the dawn.

imprisoned for debt. A collection of poems, *Elegiac Sonnets* (1784), was reasonably successful, but Smith turned to fiction as a more popular and thus more lucrative form. Her gothic novel *Emmeline* (1788) was very successful, her dozen or so later ones less so, because of their occasionally didactic tone.

VERSES INTENDED TO HAVE BEEN PREFIXED TO THE NOVEL OF *EMMELINE*, BUT THEN SUPPRESSED.

O'erwhelm'd with sorrow, and sustaining long
"The proud man's contumely, th'oppressor's wrong,"[1]
Languid despondency, and vain regret,
Must my exhausted spirit struggle yet?
Yes!—Robb'd myself of all that fortune gave,   5
Even of all hope—but shelter in the grave,
Still shall the plaintive lyre essay its powers
To dress the cave of Care with Fancy's flowers,
Maternal Love the fiend Despair withstand,
Still animate the heart and guide the hand,   10
—May you, dear objects of my anxious care,
Escape the evils I was born to bear!
Round *my* devoted head while tempests roll,
Yet there, where I have treasured up my soul,
May the soft rays of dawning hope impart   15
Reviving Patience to my fainting heart;—
And when its sharp solicitudes shall cease,
May I be conscious in the realms of peace
That every tear which swells my children's eyes,
From sorrows past, not present ills arise.   20
Then, with some friend who loves to share your pain,
For 'tis my boast that *some* such friends remain,
By filial grief, and fond remembrance prest,
You'll seek the spot where all my sorrows rest;
Recall my hapless days in sad review,   25
The long calamities I bore for you,
And—with an happier fate—resolve to prove
How well you merited your mother's love.

THE DEAD BEGGAR, AN ELEGY ADDRESSED TO A LADY, WHO WAS AFFECTED AT SEEING THE FUNERAL OF A NAMELESS PAUPER, BURIED AT THE EXPENCE OF THE PARISH, IN THE CHURCH-YARD AT BRIGHTHELMSTONE, IN NOVEMBER 1792.

Swells then thy feeling heart, and streams thine eye
O'er the deserted being, poor and old,

---

[1] See *Hamlet*, III.1.71. Smith reverses the line, which reads in Shakespeare, "Th' oppressor's wrong, the proud man's contumely."

Whom cold, reluctant, Parish Charity
   Consigns to mingle with his kindred mould?

Mourn'st thou, that *here* the time-worn sufferer ends   5
   Those evil days still threatening woes to come;
Here, where the friendless feel no want of friends,
   Where even the houseless wanderer finds an home?

What tho' no kindred crowd in sable forth,
   And sigh, or seem to sigh, around his bier;   10
Tho' o'er his coffin with the humid earth
   No children drop the unavailing tear?

Rather rejoice that *here* his sorrows cease,
   Whom sickness, age, and poverty oppress'd;
Where Death, the Leveller, restores to peace   15
   The wretch who living knew not where to rest.

Rejoice, that tho' an outcast spurn'd by fate,
   Thro' penury's rugged path his race he ran;
In earth's cold bosom, equall'd with the great,
   Death vindicates the insulted rights of Man.   20

Rejoice, that tho' severe his earthly doom,
   And rude, and sown with thorns the way he trod,
Now, (where unfeeling Fortune cannot come)
   He rests upon the mercies of his God.

William Blake

One of the most unusual, interesting, and profound of the English poets is William
Blake (1757–1827). Born in London, he had no formal education except at art
school and in a seven-year apprenticeship, from age fourteen to twenty-one, to an
engraver. Blake married Catherine Boucher when he was twenty-four; she was
illiterate, but Blake taught her to read and she assisted him with engraving and
printing. He had already begun to practice the art that he was to pursue for the
rest of his life: making engravings that incorporated both a poetic text and a
pictorial illustration or decoration around it. To read a Blake poem without its
original engraving reproduced as well is to miss at least half of his mixed-media
form. The subject of Blake's poetry is primarily a myth of human history, beginning with *The Four Zoas* (c. 1795–1803) and continuing through *Milton* (c. 1800–
1810) and *Jerusalem* (c. 1804–1820). But he also wrote a series of short but
powerful poems, in *Songs of Innocence and of Experience* (1794). Of the poems
reprinted in this book, "The Lamb" is from the *Songs of Innocence* and "The
Tyger" and "London" are from the *Songs of Experience*.

THE LAMB

Little Lamb, who made thee?
Dost thou know who made thee?
Gave thee life & bid thee feed,
By the stream & o'er the mead;
Gave thee clothing of delight,   5
Softest clothing wooly bright;
Gave thee such a tender voice,
Making all the vales rejoice!
  Little Lamb who made thee?
  Dost thou know who made thee?   10

Little Lamb I'll tell thee,
Little Lamb I'll tell thee!
He is called by thy name,
For he calls himself a Lamb:
He is meek & he is mild,   15
He became a little child:
I a child & thou a lamb,
We are called by his name.
  Little Lamb God bless thee.
  Little Lamb God bless thee.   20

THE TYGER

Tyger! Tyger! burning bright
In the forests of the night,
What immortal hand or eye
Could frame thy fearful symmetry?

In what distant deeps or skies   5
Burnt the fire of thine eyes?
On what wings dare he aspire?
What the hand, dare seize the fire?

And what shoulder, & what art,
Could twist the sinews of thy heart?   10
And when thy heart began to beat,
What dread hand? & what dread feet?

What the hammer? what the chain?
In what furnace was thy brain?
What the anvil? What dread grasp   15
Dare its deadly terrors clasp?

When the stars threw down their spears,
And water'd heaven with their tears,
Did he smile his work to see?
Did he who made the Lamb make thee?   20

Tyger! Tyger! burning bright
In the forests of the night,
What immortal hand or eye
Dare frame thy fearful symmetry?

LONDON

I wander thro' each charter'd street,
Near where the charter'd Thames does flow,
And mark in every face I meet
Marks of weakness, marks of woe.

In every cry of every man,   5
In every Infant's cry of fear,
In every voice, in every ban,
The mind-forg'd manacles I hear.

How the Chimney-sweeper's cry
Every blackning Church appalls;   10
And the hapless Soldier's sigh
Runs in blood down Palace walls.

But most thro' midnight streets I hear
How the youthful Harlot's curse
Blasts the new-born Infant's tear,   15
And blights with plagues the Marriage hearse.

William Wordsworth

William Wordsworth (1770–1850) was born in the Lake District, in northwest England. His mother died when he was eight, his father when William was thirteen. Despite an inheritance that was tied up in litigation, he was able to enter Cambridge University when he was seventeen. Travel in France followed college; he met a woman there named Annette Vallon with whom he had a daughter. Money difficulties and the French Revolution kept them apart. Back in England, Wordsworth settled in a cottage in Dorsetshire with his sister Dorothy and began a long and fruitful friendship with Samuel Taylor Coleridge. In 1798, they published a collaborative book, *Lyrical Ballads,* which along with a preface Wordsworth added to the second edition in 1800 became the key document in English literary Romanticism. In 1799, Wordsworth and Dorothy moved back to the Lake District. Most of Wordsworth's best poetry had been written by 1807; although he lived until 1850, most of his later poetry represents a noticeable falling off. Wordsworth's most characteristic poetry is that not only of nature but of nature as perceived in childhood and remembered in maturity. All three of the poems included here represent variations on that theme.

LINES COMPOSED A FEW MILES
ABOVE TINTERN ABBEY

Five years have passed; five summers, with the length
Of five long winters! and again I hear
These waters, rolling from their mountain-springs
With a soft inland murmur. Once again
Do I behold these steep and lofty cliffs,   5
That on a wild secluded scene impress
Thoughts of more deep seclusion; and connect
The landscape with the quiet of the sky.
The day is come when I again repose
Here, under this dark sycamore, and view   10
These plots of cottage ground, these orchard tufts,
Which at this season, with their unripe fruits,
Are clad in one green hue, and lose themselves
'Mid groves and copses. Once again I see
These hedgerows, hardly hedgerows, little lines   15
Of sportive wood run wild; these pastoral farms,
Green to the very door; and wreaths of smoke
Sent up, in silence, from among the trees!
With some uncertain notice, as might seem
Of vagrant dwellers in the houseless woods,   20
Or of some Hermit's cave, where by his fire
The Hermit sits alone.

                    These beauteous forms,
Through a long absence, have not been to me
As is a landscape to a blind man's eye;   25
But oft, in lonely rooms, and 'mid the din
Of towns and cities, I have owed to them,
In hours of weariness, sensations sweet,
Felt in the blood, and felt along the heart;
And passing even into my purer mind,   30
With tranquil restoration—feelings too
Of unremembered pleasure; such, perhaps,
As have no slight or trivial influence
On that best portion of a good man's life,
His little, nameless, unremembered, acts   35
Of kindness and of love. Nor less, I trust,
To them I may have owed another gift,
Of aspect more sublime; that blessed mood,
In which the burthen of the mystery,
In which the heavy and the weary weight   40
Of all this unintelligible world,
Is lightened—that serene and blessed mood,
In which the affections gently lead us on—
Until, the breath of this corporeal frame
And even the motion of our human blood   45
Almost suspended, we are laid asleep
In body, and become a living soul;

While with an eye made quiet by the power
Of harmony, and the deep power of joy,
We see into the life of things. 50

      If this
Be but a vain belief, yet, oh! how oft—
In darkness and amid the many shapes
Of joyless daylight; when the fretful stir
Unprofitable, and the fever of the world, 55
Have hung upon the beatings of my heart—
How oft, in spirit, have I turned to thee,
O sylvan Wye! thou wanderer through the woods,
How often has my spirit turned to thee!

  And now, with gleams of half-extinguished thought, 60
With many recognitions dim and faint,
And somewhat of a sad perplexity,
The picture of the mind revives again;
While here I stand, not only with the sense
Of present pleasure, but with pleasing thoughts 65
That in this moment there is life and food
For future years. And so I dare to hope,
Though changed, no doubt, from what I was when first
I came among these hills; when like a roe
I bounded o'er the mountains, by the sides 70
Of the deep rivers, and the lonely streams,
Wherever nature led—more like a man
Flying from something that he dreads than one
Who sought the thing he loved. For nature then
(The coarser pleasures of my boyish days, 75
And their glad animal movements all gone by)
To me was all in all.—I cannot paint
What then I was. The sounding cataract
Haunted me like a passion; the tall rock,
The mountain, and the deep and gloomy wood, 80
Their colors and their forms, were then to me
An appetite; a feeling and a love,
That had no need of a remote charm,
By thought supplied, nor any interest
Unborrowed from the eye.—That time is past, 85
And all its aching joys are now no more,
And all its dizzy raptures. Not for this
Faint I, nor mourn nor murmur; other gifts
Have followed; for such loss, I would believe,
Abundant recompense. For I have learned 90
To look on nature, not as in the hour
Of thoughtless youth; but hearing oftentimes
The still, sad music of humanity,
Nor harsh nor grating, though of ample power
To chasten and subdue. And I have felt 95
A presence that disturbs me with the joy
Of elevated thoughts; a sense sublime

Of something far more deeply interfused,
Whose dwelling is the light of setting suns,
And the round ocean and the living air,   100
And the blue sky, and in the mind of man:
A motion and a spirit, that impels
All thinking things, all objects of all thought,
And rolls through all things. Therefore am I still
A lover of the meadows and the woods,   105
And mountains; and of all that we behold
From this green earth; of all the mighty world
Of eye, and ear—both what they half create,
And what perceive; well pleased to recognize
In nature and the language of the sense   110
The anchor of my purest thoughts, the nurse,
The guide, the guardian of my heart, and soul
Of all my moral being.

               Nor perchance,
If I were not thus taught, should I the more   115
Suffer my genial spirits[1] to decay:
For thou art with me here upon the banks
Of this fair river; thou my dearest Friend,[2]
My dear, dear Friend; and in thy voice I catch
The language of my former heart, and read   120
My former pleasures in the shooting lights
Of thy wild eyes. Oh! yet a little while
May I behold in thee what I was once,
My dear, dear Sister! and this prayer I make,
Knowing that Nature never did betray   125
The heart that loved her; 'tis her privilege,
Through all the years of this our life, to lead
From joy to joy: for she can so inform
The mind that is within us, so impress
With quietness and beauty, and so feed   130
With lofty thoughts, that neither evil tongues,
Rash judgments, nor the sneers of selfish men,
Nor greetings where no kindness is, nor all
The dreary intercourse of daily life,
Shall e'er prevail against us, or disturb   135
Our cheerful faith, that all which we behold
Is full of blessings. Therefore let the moon
Shine on thee in thy solitary walk;
And let the misty mountain winds be free
To blow against thee: and, in after years,   140
When these wild ecstasies shall be matured
Into a sober pleasure; when thy mind
Shall be a mansion for all lovely forms,
Thy memory be as a dwelling place
For all sweet sounds and harmonies; oh! then,   145

---

[1] Creative powers. ("Genial," here, is the adjective form of "genius.")
[2] His sister Dorothy.

If solitude, or fear, or pain, or grief
Should be thy portion, with what healing thoughts
Of tender joy wilt thou remember me,
And these my exhortations! Nor, perchance—
If I should be where I no more can hear   150
Thy voice, nor catch from thy wild eyes these gleams
Of past existence—wilt thou then forget
That on the banks of this delightful stream
We stood together; and that I, so long
A worshiper of Nature, hither came   155
Unwearied in that service; rather say
With warmer love—oh! with far deeper zeal
Of holier love. Nor wilt thou then forget,
That after many wanderings, many years
Of absence, these steep woods and lofty cliffs,   160
And this green pastoral landscape, were to me
More dear, both for themselves and for thy sake!

MY HEART LEAPS UP WHEN I BEHOLD

My heart leaps up when I behold
A rainbow in the sky:
So was it when my life began;
So is it now I am a man;
So be it when I shall grow old,   5
    Or let me die!
The Child is father of the Man;
And I could wish my days to be
Bound each to each by natural piety.

THE WORLD IS TOO MUCH WITH US

The world is too much with us; late and soon
Getting and spending, we lay waste our powers:
Little we see in Nature that is ours;
We have given our hearts away, a sordid boon!
The sea that bares her bosom to the moon;   5
The winds that will be howling at all hours,
And are up-gathered now like sleeping flowers;
For this, for everything, we are out of tune;
It moves us not.—Great God! I'd rather be
A pagan suckled in a creed outworn;   10
So might I, standing on this pleasant lea,
Have glimpses that would make me less forlorn;
Have sight of Proteus[1] rising from the sea;
Or hear old Triton blow his wreathèd horn.

---

[1] A sea-god, as is Triton.

Samuel Taylor Coleridge

In the poetic partnership that William Wordsworth and Samuel Taylor Coleridge (1772–1834) formed, Wordsworth was to write poems on "ordinary life," whereas Coleridge was to direct his efforts at "persons and characters supernatural, or at least romantic." It is only one of many contrasts the two used to describe their close, complementary relationship and that others have continued to use. After an erratic performance at Cambridge, which included an enlistment in the army under the name of Silas Tomkyn Comberbacke and an ill-fated project with the poet Robert Southey to establish a utopian community in Pennsylvania, Coleridge settled down with his wife, Sara, whom he had married as part of the Pennsylvania project, on an annuity provided him by the Wedgwood family, manufacturers of fine dishes. He met Wordsworth in 1795 and became a close friend and collaborator. Literary work, though, was slowed by opium, which had first been prescribed for rheumatism and to which, by 1802, he was hopelessly addicted. In his later years, he was cared for by a sympathetic physician named James Gillman and managed to produce several books of poetry; *Biographia Literaria,* his book of criticism and literary theory; and several other prose works.

KUBLA KHAN[1]

In Xanadu did Kubla Khan
A stately pleasure-dome decree:
Where Alph, the sacred river, ran
Through caverns measureless to man
   Down to a sunless sea.   5
So twice five miles of fertile ground
With walls and towers were girdled round:
And here were gardens bright with sinuous rills,
Where blossomed many an incense-bearing tree,
And here were forests ancient as the hills,   10
Enfolding sunny spots of greenery.

But oh! that deep romantic chasm which slanted
Down the green hill athwart a cedarn cover!
A savage place! as holy and enchanted
As e'er beneath a waning moon was haunted   15
By woman wailing for her demon-lover!

---

[1] "Kubla Khan" originated, by Coleridge's own account, as an opium dream. In a note on a manuscript of "Kubla Khan," Coleridge wrote: "This fragment with a good deal more, not recoverable, composed, in a sort of reverie brought on by two grains of opium, taken to check a dysentery, at a farmhouse between Porlock and Linton, a quarter of a mile from Culbone Church, in the fall of the year, 1797." Coleridge had fallen asleep while reading this sentence from Samuel Purchas's *Purchas his Pilgrimage,* a fanciful seventeenth-century travel book: "In Xamdu did Cublai Can build a stately Palace, encompassing sixteen miles of plaine ground with a wall, wherein are fertile Meddowes, pleasant springs, delightful Streames, and all sorts of beasts of chase and game, and in the middest thereof a sumptuous house of pleasure, which may be removed from place to place." Waking with the poem complete in his mind, Coleridge began to write it down but was interrupted by a "person from Porlock." When the visitor left, Coleridge found that the dream-poem had vanished from his mind.

And from this chasm, with ceaseless turmoil seething,
As if this earth in fast thick pants were breathing,
A mighty fountain momently was forced,
Amid whose swift half-intermitted burst   20
Huge fragments vaulted like rebounding hail,
Or chaffy grain beneath the thresher's flail:
And 'mid these dancing rocks at once and ever
It flung up momently the sacred river.
Five miles meandering with a mazy motion   25
Through wood and dale the sacred river ran,
Then reached the caverns measureless to man,
And sank in tumult to a lifeless ocean:
And 'mid this tumult Kubla heard from far
Ancestral voices prophesying war!   30
    The shadow of the dome of pleasure
    Floated midway on the waves;
    Where was heard the mingled measure
    From the fountain and the caves.
It was a miracle of rare device,   35
A sunny pleasure-dome with caves of ice!

    A damsel with a dulcimer
    In a vision once I saw:
    It was an Abyssinian maid,
    And on her dulcimer she played,   40
    Singing of Mount Abora.
Could I revive within me
Her symphony and song,
To such a deep delight 'twould win me,
That with music loud and long,   45
I would build that dome in air,
That sunny dome! those caves of ice!
And all who heard should see them there,
And all should cry, Beware! Beware!
His flashing eyes, his floating hair!   50
Weave a circle round him thrice,
And close your eyes with holy dread,
For he on honey-dew hath fed,
And drunk the milk of Paradise.

Percy Bysshe Shelley

No writer better speaks for the revolutionary strain in English romantic poetry than Percy Bysshe Shelley (1792–1822). Born into an aristocratic family in Sussex, Shelley seemed destined to take his place in the social establishment. Instead, he was expelled from Oxford for writing an atheistic pamphlet; eloped with a young woman, Harriet Westbrook, who was being persecuted, Shelley was convinced, by her father; became a disciple of the radical William Godwin; fell in love with Godwin's daughter, Mary Wollstonecraft Godwin; and fled with her to France. In the midst of all this activity, he found time to write, publishing his first major poem, *Queen Mab,* in 1813. When Harriet killed herself, Shelley married Mary and moved with her to Italy, never to return to England. Shelley's masterpiece, the epic *Prometheus Unbound,* his tragedy *The Cenci,* "Ode to the West Wind," and many of his finest lyrics were all written in 1819, when he was twenty-seven. In 1822, Shelley and his friend Edward Williams were drowned when a storm upset their boat on the Gulf of Spezia.

ODE TO THE WEST WIND

I

O wild West Wind, thou breath of Autumn's being,
Thou, from whose unseen presence the leaves dead
Are driven, like ghosts from an enchanter fleeing,

Yellow, and black, and pale, and hectic red,
Pestilence-stricken multitudes: O thou,   5
Who chariotest to their dark wintry bed

The wingéd seeds, where they lie cold and low,
Each like a corpse within its grave, until
Thine azure sister of the Spring shall blow

Her clarion o'er the dreaming earth, and fill   10
(Driving sweet buds like flocks to feed in air)
With living hues and odors plain and hill:

Wild Spirit, which art moving everywhere;
Destroyer and preserver; hear, oh hear!

II

Thou on whose stream, mid the steep sky's commotion,   15
Loose clouds like earth's decaying leaves are shed,
Shook from the tangled boughs of Heaven and Ocean,

Angels of rain and lightning: there are spread
On the blue surface of thine aëry surge,
Like the bright hair uplifted from the head   20

Of some fierce Maenad,[1] even from the dim verge
Of the horizon to the zenith's height,
The locks of the approaching storm. Thou dirge

Of the dying year, to which this closing night
Will be the dome of a vast sepulcher,   25
Vaulted with all thy congregated might

[1] Crazed female worshipper of Dionysus.

Of vapors, from whose solid atmosphere
Black rain, and fire, and hail will burst: oh, hear!

III

Thou who didst waken from his summer dreams
The blue Mediterranean, where he lay,   30
Lulled by the coil of his crystálline streams,

Beside a pumice isle in Baiae's bay,[2]
And saw in sleep old palaces and towers
Quivering within the wave's intenser day,

All overgrown with azure moss and flowers   35
So sweet, the sense faints picturing them! Thou
For whose path the Atlantic's level powers

Cleave themselves into chasms, while far below
The sea-blooms and the oozy woods which wear
The sapless foliage of the ocean, know   40

Thy voice, and suddenly grown gray with fear,
And tremble and despoil themselves: oh, hear!

IV

If I were a dead leaf thou mightest bear;
If I were a swift cloud to fly with thee;
A wave to pant beneath thy power, and share   45

The impulse of thy strength, only less free
Than thou, O uncontrollable! If even
I were as in my boyhood, and could be

The comrade of thy wanderings over Heaven,
As then, when to outstrip thy skiey speed   50
Scarce seemed a vision; I would ne'er have striven

As thus with thee in prayer in my sore need.
O, lift me as a wave, a leaf, a cloud!
I fall upon the thorns of life! I bleed!

A heavy weight of hours has chained and bowed   55
One too like thee: tameless, and swift, and proud.

V

Make me thy lyre, even as the forest is:
What if my leaves are falling like its own!
The tumult of thy mighty harmonies

---

[2] "Baiae's bay," west of Naples, has islands of volcanic rock ("pumice") and was the site of the villas of Roman emperors ("old palaces and towers").

Will take from both a deep, autumnal tone,   60
Sweet though in sadness. Be thou, Spirit fierce,
My spirit! Be thou me, impetuous one!

Drive my dead thoughts over the universe
Like withered leaves to quicken a new birth!
And, by the incantation of this verse,   65

Scatter, as from an unextinguished hearth
Ashes and sparks, my words among mankind!
Be through my lips to unawakened earth

The trumpet of a prophecy! O, Wind,
If Winter comes, can Spring be far behind?   70

William Cullen Bryant

William Cullen Bryant (1794–1878) was born and grew up in Massachusetts. Family finances prevented his going to Yale as he had hoped to do; instead, he studied for and passed the bar examination. Meanwhile he had begun to write poetry. The publication of his "Thanatopsis" (the title means "meditation on death") in 1817 gave him something of a reputation. He published a short collection of his *Poems* in 1821. In 1825, Bryant moved to New York to become an editor of the *New-York Review and Atheneum Magazine.* The magazine failed, but Bryant moved to the *Evening Post,* where he stayed for the rest of his life, eventually as part owner and editor-in-chief. He continued to write, periodically issuing successive versions of his *Collected Poems* and writing a series of travel books. In his seventies, he translated the *Iliad* and the *Odyssey.* Bryant's reputation was very high in his own day. From our perspective, he perhaps seems less an accomplished artist than a genteel voice expressing the concerns of his moment in American history.

TO A WATERFOWL

Whither, 'midst falling dew,
While glow the heavens with the last steps of day,
Far, through their rosy depths, dost thou pursue
    Thy solitary way?

Vainly the fowler's eye   5
Might mark thy distant flight, to do thee wrong,
As, darkly seen against the crimson sky,
    Thy figure floats along.

Seek'st thou the plashy[1] brink
Of weedy lake, or marge of river wide,   10
Or where the rocking billows rise and sink
    On the chaféd ocean side?

[1] Marshy. (A "plash" is a pool.)

There is a Power, whose care
Teaches thy way along that pathless coast,
The desert and illimitable air,   15
    Lone wandering, but not lost,

All day thy wings have fanned,
At that far height, the cold thin atmosphere;
Yet stoop not, weary, to the welcome land,
    Though the dark night is near.   20

And soon that toil shall end,
Soon shalt thou find a summer home, and rest,
And scream among thy fellows; reeds shall bend,
    Soon, o'er thy sheltered nest.

Thou'rt gone, the abyss of heaven   25
Hath swallowed up thy form, yet, on my heart
Deeply hath sunk the lesson thou hast given,
    And shall not soon depart.

He, who, from zone to zone,
Guides through the boundless sky thy certain flight,   30
In the long way that I must trace alone,
    Will lead my steps aright.

THE PRAIRIES[1]

These are the Gardens of the Desert, these
The unshorn fields, boundless and beautiful,
And fresh as the young earth, ere man had sinned—[2]
The prairies. I behold them for the first,
And my heart swells, while the dilated sight   5
Takes in the encircling vastness. Lo! they stretch
In airy undulations, far away,
As if the ocean, in his gentlest swell,
Stood still, with all his rounded billows fixed,
And motionless for ever.—Motionless?—   10
No—they are all unchained again. The clouds
Sweep over with their shadows, and beneath
The surface rolls and fluctuates to the eye;
Dark hollows seem to glide along and chase
The sunny ridges. Breezes of the South!   15
Who toss the golden and the flame-like flowers,
And pass the prairie-hawk that, poised on high,
Flaps his broad wings, yet moves not—ye have played
Among the palms of Mexico and vines

---

[1] Bryant wrote this poem after visiting his brothers on the Illinois frontier in 1832.
[2] Bryant later replaced this reference to the Garden of Eden with this line: "For which the speech of England has no name—." (The word "prairie" is adopted from the French.)

Of Texas, and have crisped the limpid brooks   20
That from the fountains of Sonora[3] glide
Into the calm Pacific—have ye fanned
A nobler or a lovelier scene than this?
Man hath no part in all this glorious work:
The hand that built the firmament hath heaved   25
And smoothed these verdant swells, and sown their slopes
With herbage, planted them with island groves,
And hedged them round with forests. Fitting floor
For this magnificent temple of the sky—
With flowers whose glory and whose multitude   30
Rival the constellations! The great heavens
Seem to stoop down upon the scene in love,—
A nearer vault, and of a tenderer blue,
Than that which bends above the eastern hills.

    As o'er the verdant waste I guide my steed,   35
Among the high rank grass that sweeps his sides,
The hollow beating of his footstep seems
A sacrilegious sound. I think of those
Upon whose rest he tramples. Are they here—
The dead of other days!—and did the dust   40
Of these fair solitudes once stir with life
And burn with passion? Let the mighty mounds[4]
That overlook the rivers, or that rise
In the dim forest crowded with old oaks,
Answer. A race, that long has passed away,   45
Built them;—a disciplined and populous race
Heaped, with long toil, the earth, while yet the Greek
Was hewing the Pentelicus[5] to forms
Of symmetry, and rearing on its rock
The glittering Parthenon. These ample fields   50
Nourished their harvests, here their herds were fed,
When haply by their stalls the bison lowed,
And bowed his maned shoulder to the yoke.
All day this desert murmured with their toils,
Till twilight blushed and lovers walked, and wooed   55
In a forgotten language, and old tunes,
From instruments of unremembered form,
Gave the soft winds a voice. The red man came—
The roaming hunter tribes, warlike and fierce,
And the mound-builders vanished from the earth.   60
The solitude of centuries untold
Has settled where they dwelt. The prairie wolf
Hunts in their meadows, and his fresh dug den
Yawns by my path. The gopher mines the ground

---

[3] A river in northwest Mexico.
[4] Indian burial mounds. Bryant follows the belief, common at the time, that they were built by a race earlier than the Indians.
[5] Greek mountain that produced the finest grade of white building marble.

Where stood their swarming cities. All is gone— 65
All—save the piles of earth that hold their bones—
The platforms where they worshipped unknown gods—
The barriers which they builded from the soil
To keep the foe at bay—till o'er the walls
The wild beleaguerers broke, and, one by one, 70
The strong holds of the plain were forced, and heaped
With corpses. The brown vultures of the wood
Flocked to those vast uncovered sepulchres,
And sat, unscared and silent, at their feast.
Haply some solitary fugitive, 75
Lurking in marsh and forest, till the sense
Of desolation and of fear became
Bitterer than death, yielded himself to die.
Man's better nature triumphed. Kindly words
Welcomed and soothed him; the rude conquerors 80
Seated the captive with their chiefs. He chose
A bride among their maidens. And at length
Seemed to forget,—yet ne'er forgot,—the wife
Of his first love, and her sweet little ones
Butchered, amid their shrieks, with all his race. 85
  Thus change the forms of being. Thus arise
Races of living things, glorious in strength,
And perish, as the quickening breath of God
Fills them, or is withdrawn. The red man too—
Has left the blooming wilds he ranged so long, 90
And, nearer to the Rocky Mountains, sought
A wider hunting ground. The beaver builds
No longer by these streams, but far away,
On waters whose blue surface ne'er gave back
The white man's face—among Missouri's springs, 95
And pools whose issues swell the Oregan,[6]
He rears his little Venice.[7] In these plains
The bison feeds no more. Twice twenty leagues
Beyond remotest smoke of hunter's camp,
Roams the majestic brute, in herds that shake 100
The earth with thundering steps—yet here I meet
His ancient footprints stamped beside the pool.
  Still this great solitude is quick with life.
Myriads of insects, gaudy as the flowers
They flutter over, gentle quadrupeds, 105
And birds, that scarce have learned the fear of man
Are here, and sliding reptiles of the ground,
Startlingly beautiful. The graceful deer
Bounds to the wood at my approach. The bee,
A more adventurous colonist than man, 110
With whom he came across the eastern deep,
Fills the savannas with his murmurings,

[6] Columbia River.
[7] That is, a city built in the water.

And hides his sweets, as in the golden age,
Within the hollow oak. I listen long
To his domestic hum, and I think I hear   115
The sound of that advancing multitude
Which soon shall fill these deserts. From the ground
Comes up the laugh of children, the soft voice
Of maidens, and the sweet and solemn hymn
Of Sabbath worshippers. The low of herds   120
Blends with the rustling of the heavy grain
Over the dark-brown furrows. All at once.
A fresher wind sweeps by, and breaks my dream,
And I am in the wilderness alone.

John Keats

The poetry of John Keats (1795–1821)—concrete and sensuous, full of the love
of life, masterly in its command of language—is remarkable. Even more remarkable is that it was written by one who was dead at twenty-six; further, the bulk of
it was written in nine months, between January and September 1819. Keats was
born in London. His father, who ran a livery stable, died when Keats was eight; his
mother, when he was fourteen. His guardian arranged an apprenticeship for
Keats with an apothecary. Keats qualified as an apothecary himself, but he almost
immediately abandoned medicine for poetry, which he had started writing when
he was eighteen. His most ambitious early work is *Endymion* (1817), a lush allegory
of the poet's quest for ideal beauty. In 1818, Keats watched his younger brother
Tom die of tuberculosis, began to develop symptoms of the disease himself, and
fell deeply in love with a pretty eighteen-year-old girl named Fanny Brawne. The
year 1819 saw Keats write his greatest poems: *The Eve of St. Agnes, La Belle Dame sans
Merci,* the six great odes, *Lamia,* and a number of other poems. A year and a half
after this burst of creative energy, he was dead.

ON FIRST LOOKING INTO CHAPMAN'S HOMER[1]

Much have I traveled in the realms of gold,
And many goodly states and kingdoms seen:
Round many western islands have I been
Which bards in fealty to Apollo[2] hold.
Oft of one wide expanse had I been told   5
That deep-browed Homer ruled as his demesne;[3]
Yet did I never breathe its pure serene
Till I heard Chapman speak out loud and bold:
Then felt I like some watcher of the skies
When a new planet swims into his ken;   10

---

[1] The Elizabethan poet George Chapman translated the *Iliad* and the *Odyssey.* Charles Cowden Clarke,
Keats's teacher and friend, introduced him to the translations.
[2] Greek god of poetry.
[3] Realm.

Or like stout Cortez[4] when with eagle eyes
He stared at the Pacific—and all his men
Looked at each other with a wild surmise—
Silent, upon a peak in Darien.

ODE ON A GRECIAN URN

I

Thou still unravished bride of quietness,
    Thou foster-child of silence and slow time,
Sylvan historian, who canst thus express
    A flowery tale more sweetly than our rhyme:
What leaf-fringed legend haunts about thy shape   5
    Of deities or mortals, or of both,
        In Tempe or the dales of Arcady?[1]
What men or gods are these? What maidens loth?
    What mad pursuit? What struggle to escape?
        What pipes and timbrels? What wild ecstasy?   10

II

Heard melodies are sweet, but those unheard
    Are sweeter; therefore, ye soft pipes, play on;
Not to the sensual ear, but, more endeared,
    Pipe to the spirit ditties of no tone:
Fair youth, beneath the trees, thou canst not leave   15
    Thy song, nor ever can those trees be bare;
        Bold Lover, never, never canst thou kiss,
Though winning near the goal—yet, do not grieve;
    She cannot fade, though thou hast not thy bliss,
        Forever wilt thou love, and she be fair!   20

III

Ah, happy, happy boughs! that cannot shed
    Your leaves, nor ever bid the spring adieu;
And, happy melodist, unweariéd,
    Forever piping songs for ever new;
More happy love! more happy, happy love!   25
    Forever warm and still to be enjoyed,
        Forever panting, and forever young;
All breathing human passion far above,
    That leaves a heart high-sorrowful and cloyed,
        A burning forehead, and a parching tongue.   30

---

[4] It was Balboa, not Cortez, who first saw the Pacific Ocean from Darien, a mountain in Panama.
[1] *Tempe:* a beautiful valley in Greece that has come to stand for rural beauty. *Arcady:* a Greek state identified with the pastoral ideal.

IV

Who are these coming to the sacrifice?
    To what green altar, O mysterious priest,
Lead'st thou that heifer lowing at the skies,
    And all her silken flanks with garlands dressed?
What little town by river or sea shore,   35
    Or mountain-built with peaceful citadel,
        Is emptied of this folk, this pious morn?
And, little town, thy streets for evermore
    Will silent be; and not a soul to tell
        Why thou art desolate, can e'er return.   40

V

O Attic[2] shape! Fair attitude! with brede[3]
    Of marble men and maidens overwrought,
With forest branches and the trodden weed;
    Thou, silent form, dost tease us out of thought
As doth eternity: Cold Pastoral!   45
    When old age shall this generation waste,
        Thou shalt remain, in midst of other woe
Than ours, a friend to man, to whom thou say'st,
    "Beauty is truth, truth beauty,"—that is all
        Ye know on earth, and all ye need to know.   50

ODE TO A NIGHTINGALE

I

My heart aches, and a drowsy numbness pains
    My sense, as though of hemlock[1] I had drunk,
Or emptied some dull opiate to the drains
    One minute past, and Lethe-wards[2] had sunk:
'Tis not through envy of thy happy lot,   5
    But being too happy in thine happiness,—
        That thou, light-wingéd Dryad[3] of the trees,
            In some melodious plot
Of beechen green, and shadows numberless,
    Singest of summer in full-throated ease.   10

II

O, for a draft of vintage! that hath been
    Cooled a long age in the deep-delvéd earth,

---

[2] Greek.
[3] An interwoven pattern.
[1] A poisonous herb.
[2] Toward Lethe, the river of forgetfulness in the Greek underworld.
[3] Wood nymph.

Tasting of Flora[4] and the country green,
  Dance, and Provençal[5] song, and sunburnt mirth!
O for a beaker full of the warm South,   15
  Full of the true, the blushful Hippocrene,[6]
    With beaded bubbles winking at the brim,
      And purple-stainéd mouth;
    That I might drink, and leave the world unseen,
      And with thee fade away into the forest dim: 20

III

Fade far away, dissolve, and quite forget
  What thou among the leaves hast never known,
The weariness, the fever, and the fret
  Here, where men sit and hear each other groan;
Where palsy shakes a few, sad, last gray hairs,   25
  Where youth grows pale, and specter-thin, and dies;
    Where but to think is to be full of sorrow
      And leaden-eyed despairs,
    Where Beauty cannot keep her lustrous eyes,
      Or new Love pine at them beyond to-morrow.   30

IV

Away! away! for I will fly to thee,
  Not charioted by Bacchus and his pards,[7]
But on the viewless wings of Poesy,
  Though the dull brain perplexes and retards:
Already with thee! tender is the night,   35
  And haply the Queen-Moon is on her throne,
    Clustered around by all her starry Fays;[8]
      But here there is no light,
    Save what from heaven is with the breezes blown
      Through verdurous glooms and winding mossy ways. 40

V

I cannot see what flowers are at my feet,
  Nor what soft incense hangs upon the boughs,
But, in embalméd darkness, guess each sweet
  Wherewith the seasonable month endows
The grass, the thicket, and the fruit-tree wild;   45
  White hawthorn, and the pastoral eglantine;
    Fast fading violets covered up in leaves;
      And mid-May's eldest child,
    The coming musk-rose, full of dewy wine,
      The murmurous haunt of flies on summer eves.   50

---

[4] Flowers, after the Roman goddess of flowers.
[5] Of Provence, the region in southern France renowned for its troubadours.
[6] Wine; figuratively, water from the fountain of the Muses on Mt. Helicon.
[7] Bacchus, the god of wine, was often depicted in a chariot drawn by leopards ("pards").
[8] Fairies.

VI

Darkling I listen; and, for many a time
  I have been half in love with easeful Death.
Called him soft names in many a muséd[9] rhyme,
    To take into the air my quiet breath;   55
Now more than ever seems it rich to die,
  To cease upon the midnight with no pain,
      While thou art pouring forth thy soul abroad
        In such an ecstasy!
  Still wouldst thou sing, and I have ears in vain—   60
    To thy high requiem become a sod.

VII

Thou wast not born for death, immortal Bird!
  No hungry generations tread thee down;
The voice I hear this passing night was heard   65
  In ancient days by emperor and clown:[10]
Perhaps the self-same song that found a path   65
  Through the sad heart of Ruth,[11] when, sick for home,
    She stood in tears amid the alien corn;
      The same that oft-times hath
Charmed magic casements, opening on the foam
  Of perilous seas, in faery lands forlorn.   70

VIII

Forlorn! the very word is like a bell
  To toll me back from thee to my sole self!
Adieu! the fancy cannot cheat so well
  As she is famed to do, deceiving elf.
Adieu! adieu! thy plaintive anthem fades   75
  Past the near meadows, over the still stream,
    Up the hill-side; and now 'tis buried deep
      In the next valley-glades:
Was it a vision, or a waking dream?
  Fled is that music:—Do I wake or sleep?   80

Emily Brontë

Emily Brontë (1818–48) is best known for her passionate, romantic novel *Wuthering Heights*. But she also wrote a number of haunting, if eccentric, poems. These poems were part of a long, serial narrative that she wrote as a child with her sisters, Charlotte and Anne, about an imaginary kingdom named Gondal. The poems, which were first published in 1846, were dramatic speeches spoken by various lovers in the Gondal narrative and express versions of love similar to the intense, transcendent passion of Catherine Earnshaw and Heathcliff in *Wuthering Heights*.

---

[9] Thought-out; meditated.
[10] Rustic.
[11] The young widow in the Biblical Book of Ruth.

REMEMBRANCE

Cold in the earth—and the deep snow piled above thee,
Far, far removed, cold in the dreary grave!
Have I forgot, my only Love, to love thee,
Severed at last by Time's all-severing wave?

Now, when alone, do my thoughts no longer hover 5
Over the mountains, on that northern shore,
Resting their wings where heath and fern leaves cover
Thy noble heart forever, ever more?

Cold in the earth—and fifteen wild Decembers,
From those brown hills, have melted into spring; 10
Faithful, indeed, is the spirit that remembers
After such years of change and suffering!

Sweet Love of youth, forgive, if I forget thee,
While the world's tide is bearing me along;
Other desires and other hopes beset me, 15
Hopes which obscure, but cannot do thee wrong!

No later light has lightened up my heaven,
No second morn has ever shone for me;
All my life's bliss from thy dear life was given,
All my life's bliss is in the grave with thee. 20

But, when the days of golden dreams had perished,
And even Despair was powerless to destroy,
Then did I learn how existence could be cherished,
Strengthened, and fed without the aid of joy.

Then did I check the tears of useless passion— 25
Weaned my young soul from yearning after thine;
Sternly denied its burning wish to hasten
Down to that tomb already more than mine.

And, even yet, I dare not let it languish,
Dare not indulge in memory's rapturous pain; 30
Once drinking deep of that divinest anguish,
How could I seek the empty world again?

NO COWARD SOUL IS MINE

No coward soul is mine,
No trembler in the world's storm-troubled sphere!
I see Heaven's glories shine,
And Faith shines equal, arming me from Fear.

O God within my breast,   5
Almighty ever-present Deity!
Life, that in me hast rest
As I, undying Life, have power in thee!

Vain are the thousand creeds
That move men's hearts, unutterably vain;   10
Worthless as withered weeds,
Or idlest froth, amid the boundless main

To waken doubt in one
Holding so fast by thy infinity,
So surely anchored on   15
The steadfast rock of Immortality.

With wide-embracing love
Thy spirit animates eternal years,
Pervades and broods above,
Changes, sustains, dissolves, creates and rears.   20

Though earth and moon were gone,
And suns and universes ceased to be,
And thou were left alone,
Every Existence would exist in thee.

There is not room for Death,   25
Nor atom that his might could render void
Since thou art Being and Breath,
And what thou art may never be destroyed.

Elizabeth Barrett Browning

Elizabeth Barrett Browning (1806–61) was educated in the home of her wealthy
and solicitous father. She apparently suffered a spinal injury at the age of thirteen
that left her a semi-invalid. She nevertheless earned a considerable reputation as
a poet, with a translation of Aeschylus' *Prometheus Bound* (1833), *The Seraphim, and
Other Poems* (1838), and *Poems* (1844). When she was forty, she married the as yet
comparatively unknown poet Robert Browning and moved to Italy with him.
Sonnets from the Portuguese is a sequence of forty-four sonnets dedicated to Robert
Browning. The title was probably meant to disguise the sonnets' personal origin.
Because Robert's nickname for Elizabeth was "the Portuguese" (because of her
dark complexion and because she had written a poem, "Catrina to Camoëns," in
the voice of a Portuguese girl loved by the sixteenth-century poet Camoëns),
Sonnets from the Portuguese, as a title, was something of an in-joke as well.

FROM SONNETS FROM THE PORTUGUESE

21

Say over again, and yet once over again,
That thou dost love me. Though the word repeated

Should seem "a cuckoo song," as thou dost treat it,
Remember, never to the hill or plain,
Valley and wood, without her cuckoo strain   5
Comes the fresh Spring in all her green completed.
Belovéd, I, amid the darkness greeted
By a doubtful spirit voice, in that doubt's pain
Cry, "Speak once more—thou lovest!" Who can fear
Too many stars, though each in heaven shall roll,   10
Too many flowers, though each shall crown the year?
Say thou dost love me, love me, love me—toll
The silver iterance!—only minding, Dear,
To love me also in silence with thy soul.

43

How do I love thee! Let me count the ways.
I love thee to the depth and breadth and height
My soul can reach, when feeling out of sight
For the ends of Being and ideal Grace.
I love thee to the level of every day's   5
Most quiet need, by sun and candlelight.
I love thee freely, as men strive for Right;
I love thee purely, as they turn from Praise.
I love thee with the passion put to use
In my old griefs, and with my childhood's faith.   10
I love thee with a love I seemed to lose
With my lost saints—I love thee with the breath,
Smiles, tears, of all my life!—and, if God choose,
I shall but love thee better after death.

Alfred, Lord Tennyson

Alfred, Lord Tennyson (1809–92), the most popular of the English Victorian
poets in his own day, was something of a self-made man. Born into a chaotic
family of twelve children of an alcoholic clergyman in Lincolnshire, he had to
leave Cambridge University without a degree because of family problems, financial and otherwise. While there, however, he formed the resolution to become
a poet and developed a close friendship with a fellow student, Arthur Hallam,
who became engaged to Tennyson's sister. Volumes of verse appeared in 1830,
1832, and 1842. He came into his maturity, however, with *In Memoriam* (1850),
a long poem in commemoration of Hallam, who had died suddenly in 1833.
The year 1850 was also marked by his appointment as poet laureate of England
(succeeding Wordsworth) and his long-postponed marriage to Emily Sellwood.
Tennyson's life after 1850 was that of a Victorian institution. His poetry brought
him a good income, and each successive publication found a wide readership.
"Ulysses," published in the 1842 *Poems*, is a comparatively early poem. In it,
Tennyson builds upon a suggestion by Dante that long after the events in the
Odyssey ended, the aged Ulysses set out on another voyage of exploration in the
west.

ULYSSES

It little profits that an idle king,
By this still hearth, among these barren crags,
Matched with an aged wife, I mete and dole
Unequal laws[1] unto a savage race,
That hoard, and sleep, and feed, and know not me.   5

I cannot rest from travel; I will drink
Life to the lees. All times I have enjoyed
Greatly, have suffered greatly, both with those
That loved me, and alone; on shore, and when
Through scudding drifts[2] the rainy Hyades   10
Vexed the dim sea. I am become a name;
For always roaming with a hungry heart
Much have I seen and known—cities of men
And manners, climates, councils, governments,
Myself not least, but honored of them all—   15
And drunk delight of battle with my peers,
Far on the ringing plains of windy Troy.
I am a part of all that I have met;
Yet all experience is an arch wherethrough
Gleams that untraveled world whose margin fades   20
Forever and forever when I move.
How dull it is to pause, to make an end,
To rust unburnished, not to shine in use!
As though to breathe were life! Life piled on life
Were all too little, and of one to me   25
Little remains; but every hour is saved
From that eternal silence, something more,
A bringer of new things; and vile it were
For some three suns to store and hoard myself,
And this gray spirit yearning in desire   30
To follow knowledge like a sinking star,
Beyond the utmost bound of human thought.

This is my son, mine own Telemachus,
To whom I leave the scepter and the isle—
Well-loved of me, discerning to fulfill   35
This labor, by slow prudence to make mild
A rugged people, and through soft degrees
Subdue them to the useful and the good.
Most blameless is he, centered in the sphere
Of common duties, decent not to fail   40
In office of tenderness, and pay
Meet adoration to my household gods,
When I am gone. He works his work, I mine.

---

[1] "Unequal" because some are rewarded, others punished.
[2] Driving showers. The Hyades are a group of stars thought to signal rain.

There lies the port; the vessel puffs her sail;
There gloom the dark, broad seas. My mariners, 45
Souls that have toiled, and wrought, and thought with me—
That ever with a frolic welcome took
The thunder and the sunshine, and opposed
Free hearts, free foreheads—you and I are old;
Old age hath yet his honor and his toil. 50
Death closes all; but something ere the end,
Some work of noble note, may yet be done,
Not unbecoming men that strove with Gods.
The lights begin to twinkle from the rocks;
The long day wanes; the slow moon climbs; the deep 55
Moans round with many voices. Come, my friends,
'Tis not too late to seek a newer world.
Push off, and sitting well in order smite
The sounding furrows; for my purpose holds
To sail beyond the sunset, and the baths 60
Of all the western stars,[3] until I die.
It may be that the gulfs will wash us down;
It may be we shall touch the Happy Isles,[4]
And see the great Achilles, whom we knew.
Though much is taken, much abides; and though 65
We are not now that strength which in old days
Moved earth and heaven, that which we are, we are—
One equal temper of heroic hearts,
Made weak by time and fate, but strong in will
To strive, to seek, to find, and not to yield. 70

Robert Browning

Robert Browning (1812–89) was born in London. He attended a boarding school near his home and was briefly a student at the University of London, but he was largely self-educated through a program of intensive reading. He published his first poem, *Pauline,* when he was twenty-one, but, fearing the excessive self-revelation of poetry, he turned to playwriting, encouraged by the leading actor-manager W. C. Macready. After a series of failures, he returned to poetry, publishing *Dramatic Lyrics,* a collection of dramatic monologues, in 1842. A turning point came when he met Elizabeth Barrett in 1845. The two eloped and moved to Italy, where they lived happily until Elizabeth's death in 1861, after which Browning returned to England to live. His collection of poems *Men and Women* appeared in 1855; other volumes followed, including the book-length narrative poem *The Ring and the Book* (1868). By the time of his death in 1889, he rivaled Tennyson in popularity. Browning's most notable achievement is the development of the dramatic monologue, a poem entirely spoken by a dramatic character like an extended speech in a play. Many have found a distinctly modern quality in the multiple ironies that are set up by Browning's use of the form.

[3] In Greek cosmology, the flat Earth was surrounded by the outer ocean into which the stars descended.
[4] Elysium, where the Greek heroes went after death.

MY LAST DUCHESS[1]

Ferrara

That's my last Duchess painted on the wall,
Looking as if she were alive. I call
That piece a wonder, now: Frà Pandolf's hands
Worked busily a day, and there she stands.
Will't please you sit and look at her? I said   5
"Frà Pandolf" by design, for never read
Strangers like you that pictured countenance,
The depth and passion of its earnest glance,
But to myself they turned (since none puts by
The curtain I have drawn for you, but I)   10
And seemed as they would ask me, if they durst,
How such a glance came there; so, not the first
Are you to turn and ask thus. Sir, 'twas not
Her husband's presence only, called that spot
Of joy into the Duchess' cheek: perhaps   15
Frà Pandolf chanced to say "Her mantle laps
Over my lady's wrist too much," or "Paint
Must never hope to reproduce the faint
Half-flush that dies along her throat": such stuff
Was courtesy, she thought, and cause enough   20
For calling up that spot of joy. She had
A heart—how shall I say?—too soon made glad,
Too easily impressed; she liked what'er
She looked on, and her looks went everywhere.
Sir, 'twas all one! My favor at her breast,   25
The dropping of the daylight in the West,
The bough of cherries some officious fool
Broke in the orchard for her, the white mule
She rode with round the terrace—all and each
Would draw from her alike the approving speech,   30
Or blush, at least. She thanked men—good! but thanked
Somehow—I know not how—as if she ranked
My gift of a nine-hundred-years-old name
With anybody's gift. Who'd stoop to blame
This sort of trifling? Even had you skill   35
In speech—(which I have not)—to make your will
Quite clear to such an one, and say, "Just this
Or that in you disgusts me; here you miss,
Or there exceed the mark"—and if she let
Herself be lessoned so, nor plainly set   40
Her wits to yours, forsooth, and made excuse
—E'en then would be some stooping; and I choose
Never to stoop. Oh sir, she smiled, no doubt,

---

[1] "My Last Duchess" was inspired by a historical character, Alfonso II, a sixteenth-century Duke of Ferrara in Italy. His youthful wife, Lucrezia, died after three years of marriage, and the Duke negotiated to marry a niece of the Count of Tyrol.

Whene'er I passed her; but who passed without
Much the same smile? This grew; I gave commands;   45
Then all smiles stopped together. There she stands
As if alive. Will't please you rise? We'll meet
The company below, then. I repeat.
The Count your master's known munificence
Is ample warrant that no just pretense   50
Of mine for dowry will be disallowed;
Though his fair daughter's self, as I avowed
At starting, is my object. Nay, we'll go
Together down, sir. Notice Neptune, though,
Taming a sea horse, thought a rarity,   55
Which Claus of Innsbruck cast in bronze for me!

FRA LIPPO LIPPI[1]

I am poor brother Lippo, by your leave!
You need not clap your torches to my face.
Zooks,[2] what's to blame? you think you see a monk!
What, 'tis past midnight, and you go the rounds,
And here you catch me at an alley's end   5
Where sportive ladies leave their doors ajar?
The Carmine's[3] my cloister: hunt it up,
Do—harry out, if you must show your zeal,
Whatever rat, there, haps on his wrong hole,
And nip each softling of a wee white mouse,   10
Weke, weke, that's crept to keep him company!
Aha, you know your betters! Then, you'll take
Your hand away that's fiddling on my throat,
And please to know me likewise. Who am I?
Why, one, sir, who is lodging with a friend   15
Three streets off—he's a certain . . . how d'ye call?
Master—a . . . Cosimo of the Medici,[4]
I' the house that caps the corner. Boh! you were best!
Remember and tell me, the day you're hanged,
How you affected such a gullet's gripe![5]   20
But you,[6] sir, it concerns you that your knaves
Pick up a manner nor discredit you:
Zooks, are we pilchards,[7] that they sweep the streets
And count fair prize what comes into their net?
He's Judas to a tittle, that man is![8]   25
Just such a face! Why, sir, you make amends.

[1] Lippo Lippi was an actual fifteenth-century painter. Browning derived his information about him from Giorgio Vasari's *Lives of the Painters.*
[2] A short form of "Gadzooks," a mild oath.
[3] Santa Maria del Carmine, the cloister of Carmelite friars to which Lippi belonged.
[4] Member of a powerful Florentine family and Lippi's patron.
[5] "How you dared to grip my throat!"   [6] The officer in charge of the night watchmen.
[7] Little fish.   [8] "He [one of the watchmen] could be a model for Judas, to the last detail."

Lord, I'm not angry! Bid your hangdogs go
Drink out this quarter-florin to the health
Of the munificent House that harbors me
(And many more beside, lads! more beside!)   30
And all's come square again. I'd like his face—
His, elbowing on his comrade in the door
With the pike and lantern—for the slave that holds
John Baptist's head a-dangle by the hair
With one hand ("Look you, now," as who should say)   35
And his weapon in the other, yet unwiped!
It's not your chance to have a bit of chalk,
A wood-coal or the like? or you should see!
Yes, I'm the painter, since you style me so.
What, brother Lippo's doings, up and down,   40
You know them and they take you? like enough!
I saw the proper twinkle in your eye—
'Tell you, I liked your looks at very first.
Let's sit and set things straight now, hip to haunch.
Here's spring come, and the nights one makes up bands   45
To roam the town and sing out carnival,[9]
And I've been three weeks shut within my mew,[10]
A-painting for the great man, saints and saints
And saints again. I could not paint all night—
Ouf! I leaned out of window for fresh air.   50
There came a hurry of feet and little feet,
A sweep of lute-strings, laughs, and whifts of song—
Flower o' the broom,
Take away love, and our earth is a tomb!
Flower o' the quince,   55
I let Lisa go, and what good in life since?
Flower o' the thyme—and so on. Round they went.
Scarce had they turned the corner when a titter
Like the skipping of rabbits by moonlight—three slim shapes,
And a face that looked up . . . zooks, sir, flesh and blood,   60
That's all I'm made of! Into shreds it went,
Curtain and counterpane and coverlet,
All the bed-furniture—a dozen knots,
There was a ladder! Down I let myself,
Hands and feet, scrambling somehow, and so dropped,   65
And after them. I came up with the fun
Hard by Saint Laurence,[11] hail fellow, well met—
Flower o' the rose,
If I've been merry, what matter who knows?
And so as I was stealing back again   70
To get to bed and have a bit of sleep
Ere I rise up tomorrow and go work
On Jerome knocking at his poor old breast

---

[9] Festivities preceding Lent; Mardi Gras.   [10] Enclosure.   [11] A church in Florence.

With his great round stone to subdue the flesh,[12]
You snap me of the sudden, Ah, I see!   75
Though your eye twinkles still, you shake your head—
Mine's shaved—a monk, you say—the sting's in that!
If Master Cosimo announced himself,
Mum's the word naturally; but a monk!
Come, what am I a beast for? tell us, now!   80
I was a baby when my mother died
And father died and left me in the street.
I starved there, God knows how, a year or two
On fig skins, melon parings, rinds and shucks,
Refuse and rubbish. One fine frosty day,   85
My stomach being empty as your hat,
The wind doubled me up and down I went.
Old Aunt Lapaccia trussed me with one hand
(Its fellow was a stinger as I knew),
And so along the wall, over the bridge,   90
By the straight cut to the convent. Six words there,
While I stood munching my first bread that month:
"So, boy, you're minded," quoth the good fat father
Wiping his mouth, 'twas refection time[13]—
"To quit this very miserable world?   95
Will you renounce" . . . "the mouthful of bread?" thought I;
By no means! Brief, they made a monk of me;
I did renounce the world, its pride and greed,
Palace, farm, villa, shop, and banking house,
Trash, such as these poor devils of Medici   100
Have given their hearts to—all at eight years old.
Well, sir, I found in time, you may be sure,
'Twas not for nothing—the good bellyful,
The warm serge and the rope that goes all round,
And day-long blessed idleness beside!   105
"Let's see what the urchin's fit for"—that came next.
Not overmuch their way, I must confess.
Such a to-do! They tried me with books:
Lord, they'd have taught me Latin in pure waste!
Flower o' the clove,   110
All the Latin I construe is "amo," I love!
But, mind you, when a boy starves in the streets
Eight years together, as my fortune was,
Watching folk's faces to know who will fling
The bit of half-stripped grape bunch he desires,   115
And who will curse or kick him for his pains—
Which gentleman processional and fine,
Holding a candle to the Sacrament,
Will wink and let him lift a plate and catch
The droppings of the wax to sell again,   120

---

[12] St. Jerome was notable for his self-punishing asceticism.   [13] Mealtime.

Or holla for the Eight[14] and have him whipped—
How say I?—nay, which dog bites, which lets drop
His bone from the heap of offal in the street—
Why, soul and sense of him grow sharp alike,
He learns the look of things, and none the less   125
For admonition from the hunger-pinch.
I had a store of such remarks, be sure,
Which, after I found leisure, turned to use.
I drew men's faces on my copybooks,
Scrawled them within the antiphonary's marge,[15]   130
Joined legs and arms to the long music-notes,
Found eyes and nose and chin for A's and B's,
And made a string of pictures of the world
Betwixt the ins and outs of verb and noun,
On the wall, the bench, the door. The monks looked black.   135
"Nay," quoth the Prior,[16] "turn him out, d' ye say?
In no wise. Lose a crow and catch a lark.
What if at last we get our man of parts,
We Carmelites, like those Camaldolese
And Preaching Friars,[17] to do our church up fine   140
And put the front on it that ought to be!"
And hereupon he bade me daub away.
Thank you! my head being crammed, the walls a blank,
Never was such prompt disemburdening.
First, every sort of monk, the black and white,   145
I drew them, fat and lean: then, folk at church,
From good old gossips waiting to confess
Their cribs of barrel droppings, candle ends—
To the breathless fellow at the altar-foot,
Fresh from his murder, safe and sitting there   150
With the little children round him in a row
Of admiration, half for his beard and half
For that white anger of his victim's son
Shaking a fist at him with one fierce arm,
Signing himself with the other because of Christ   155
(Whose sad face on the cross sees only this
After the passion[18] of a thousand years)
Till some poor girl, her apron o'er her head
(Which the intense eyes looked through), came at eve
On tiptoe, said a word, dropped in a loaf,   160
Her pair of earrings and a bunch of flowers
(The brute took growling), prayed, and so was gone.
I painted all, then cried " 'Tis ask and have;
Choose, for more's ready!"—laid the ladder flat,
And showed my covered bit of cloister wall.   165
The monks closed in a circle and praised loud
Till checked, taught what to see and not to see,

---

[14] Magistrates of Florence.   [15] Margins of the songbook.
[16] Head of the convent.   [17] *Camaldolese:* Benedictine monks. *Preaching Friars:* Dominican monks.
[18] Suffering.

Being simple bodies—"That's the very man!
Look at the boy who stoops to pat the dog!
That woman's like the Prior's niece who comes   170
To care about his asthma: it's the life!"
But there my triumph's straw-fire flared and funked;[19]
Their betters took their turn to see and say:
The Prior and the learned pulled a face
And stopped all that in no time. "How? what's here?   175
Quite from the mark of painting, bless us all!
Faces, arms, legs and bodies like the true
As much as pea and pea! it's devil's game!
Your business is not to catch men with show,
With homage to the perishable clay,   180
But lift them over, ignore it all,
Make them forget there's such a thing as flesh.
Your business is to paint the souls of men—
Man's soul, and it's a fire, smoke . . . no, it's not . . .
It's vapor done up like a newborn babe—   185
(In that shape when you die it leaves your mouth)
It's . . . well, what matters talking, it's the soul!
Give us no more of body than shows soul!
Here's Giotto,[20] with his Saint a-praising God,
That sets us praising—why not stop with him?   190
Why put all thoughts of praise out of our head
With wonder at lines, colors, and what not?
Paint the soul, never mind the legs and arms!
Rub all out, try at it a second time.
Oh, that white smallish female with the breasts,   195
She's just my niece . . . Herodias,[21] I would say—
Who went and danced and got men's heads cut off!
Have it all out!" Now, is this sense, I ask?
A fine way to paint soul, by painting body
So ill, the eye can't stop there, must go further   200
And can't fare worse! Thus, yellow does for white
When what you put for yellow's simply black,
And any sort of meaning looks intense
When all beside itself means and looks naught.
Why can't a painter lift each foot in turn,   205
Left foot and right foot, go a double step,
Make his flesh liker and his soul more like,
Both in their order? Take the prettiest face,
The Prior's niece . . . patron-saint—is it so pretty
You can't discover if it means hope, fear,   210
Sorrow or joy? won't beauty go with these?
Suppose I've made her eyes all right and blue,
Can't I take breath and try to add life's flash,

---

[19] Went up in smoke.
[20] Giotto (1276–1337) was a great Florentine painter who painted in the stylized medieval manner rather than in Lippi's more realistic style.
[21] Salome, whose dance ended in the beheading of John the Baptist. See Matthew 14:1–2.

And then add soul and heighten them threefold?
Or say there's beauty with no soul at all—   215
(I never saw it—put the case the same—)
If you get simple beauty and naught else,
You get about the best thing God invents:
That's somewhat: and you'll find the soul you have missed,
Within yourself, when you return him thanks.   220
"Rub all out!" Well, well, there's my life, in short,
And so the thing has gone on ever since.
I'm grown a man no doubt, I've broken bounds:
You should not take a fellow eight years old
And make him swear to never kiss the girls.   225
I'm my own master, paint now as I please—
Having a friend, you see, in the Corner-house![22]
Lord, it's fast holding by the rings in front—
Those great rings serve more purposes than just
To plant a flag in, or tie up a horse!   230
And yet the old schooling sticks, the old grave eyes
Are peeping o'er my shoulders as I work,
The heads shake still—"It's art's decline, my son!
You're not of the true painters, great and old;
Brother Angelico's the man, you'll find;   235
Brother Lorenzo stands his single peer:[23]
Fag on at flesh, you'll never make the third!"
Flower o' the pine,
You keep you mistr . . . manners, and I'll stick to mine!
I'm not the third, then: bless us, they must know!   240
Don't you think they're the likeliest to know,
They with their Latin? So, I swallow my rage,
Clench my teeth, suck my lips in tight, and paint
To please them—sometimes do and sometimes don't;
For, doing most, there's pretty sure to come   245
A turn, some warm eve finds me at my saints—
A laugh, a cry, the business of the world—
(*Flower o' the peach,*
Death for us all, and his own life for each!)
And my whole soul revolves, the cup runs over,   250
The world and life's too big to pass for a dream,
And I do these wild things in sheer despite,
And play the fooleries you catch me at,
In pure rage! The old mill-horse, out at grass
After hard years, throws up his stiff heels so,   255
Although the miller does not preach to him
The only good of grass is to make chaff.[24]
What would men have? Do they like grass or no—
May they or mayn't they? all I want's the thing
Settled forever one way. As it is,   260

[22] The palace of the Medici.
[23] Fra Angelico (1387–1455) and Lorenzo Monaco (1370–1425).   [24] Straw.

You tell too many lies and hurt yourself:
You don't like what you only like too much,
You do like what, if given you at your word,
You find abundantly detestable.
For me, I think I speak as I was taught;   265
I always see the garden and God there
A-making man's wife: and, my lesson learned,
The value and significance of flesh,
I can't unlearn ten minutes afterwards.

You understand me: I'm a beast, I know.   270
But see, now—why, I see as certainly
As that the morning star's about to shine,
What will hap some day. We've a youngster here
Comes to our convent, studies what I do,
Slouches and stares and lets no atom drop: 275
His name is Guidi[25]—he'll not mind the monks—
They call him Hulking Tom, he lets them talk—
He picks my practice up—he'll paint apace,
I hope so—though I never live so long,
I know what's sure to follow. You be judge!   280
You speak no Latin more than I, belike;
However, you're my man, you've seen the world
—The beauty and the wonder and the power,
The shapes of things, their colors, lights and shades,
Changes, surprises—and God made it all!   285
—For what? Do you feel thankful, aye or no,
For this fair town's face, yonder river's line,
The mountain round it and the sky above,
Much more the figures of man, woman, child,
These are the frame to? What's it all about?   290
To be passed over, despised? or dwelt upon,
Wondered at? oh, this last of course!—you say.
But why not do as well as say—paint these
Just as they are, careless what comes of it?
God's works—paint any one, and count it crime   295
To let a truth slip. Don't object, "His works
Are here already; nature is complete:
Suppose you reproduce her—(which you can't)
There's no advantage! You must beat her, then."
For, don't you mark? we're made so that we love   300
First when we see them painted, things we have passed
Perhaps a hundred times nor cared to see;
And so they are better, painted—better to us,
Which is the same thing. Art was given for that;
God uses us to help each other so,   305

[25] Guidi or Masaccio (1401–28) was a contemporary of Lippi's, though he may have been Lippi's teacher rather than his student. His paintings survive in the chapel of Santa Maria del Carmine, Lippi's church.

Lending our minds out. Have you noticed, now,
Your cullion's[26] hanging face? A bit of chalk,
And trust me but you should, though! How much more,
If I drew higher things with the same truth!
That were to take the Prior's pulpit-place,   310
Interpret God to all of you! Oh, oh,
It makes me mad to see what men shall do
And we in our graves! This world's no blot for us,
Nor blank; it means intensely, and means good:
To find its meaning is my meat and drink.   315
"Aye, but you don't so instigate to prayer!"
Strikes in the Prior: "when your meaning's plain
It does not say to folk—remember matins,
Or, mind you fast next Friday!" Why, for this
What need of art at all? A skull and bones,   320
Two bits of stick nailed crosswise, or, what's best,
A bell to chime the hour with, does as well.
I painted a Saint Laurence[27] six months since
At Prato, splashed the fresco in fine style:
"How looks my painting, now the scaffold's down?"   325
I ask a brother: "Hugely," he returns—
"Already not one phiz of your three slaves
Who turn the Deacon off his toasted side,
But it's scratched and prodded to our heart's content,
The pious people have so eased their own   330
With coming to say prayers there in a rage:
We get on fast to see the bricks beneath.
Expect another job this time next year,
For pity and religion grow i' the crowd—
Your painting serves its purpose!" Hang the fools!   335

—That is—you'll not mistake an idle word
Spoke in a huff by a poor monk, God wot,
Tasting the air this spicy night which turns
The unaccustomed head like Chianti wine!
Oh, the church knows! don't misreport me, now!   340
It's natural a poor monk out of bounds
Should have his apt word to excuse himself:
And hearken how I plot to make amends.
I have bethought me: I shall paint a piece
... There's for you! Give me six months, then go, see   345
Something in Sant' Ambrogios![28] Bless the nuns!
They want a cast o' my office.[29] I shall paint
God in the midst, Madonna and her babe,
Ringed by a bowery flowery angel brood,

---

[26] Rascal's.
[27] Saint Laurence was martyred by burning. *Prato:* town near Florence. *Fresco:* technique of painting
quickly on wet plaster.
[28] Another church in Florence.   [29] Sample of my work.

Lilies and vestments and white faces, sweet 350
As puff on puff of grated orris-root[30]
When ladies crowd to Church at midsummer.
And then i' the front, of course a saint or two—
Saint John, because he saves the Florentines,
Saint Ambrose, who puts down in black and white 355
The convent's friends and gives them a long day,
And Job, I must have him there past mistake,
The man of Uz (and Us without the z,
Painters who need his patience). Well, all these
Secured at their devotion, up shall come 360
Out of a corner when you least expect,
As one by a dark stair into a great light,
Music and talking, who but Lippo! I—
Mazed, motionless and moonstruck—I'm the man!
Back I shrink—what is this I see and hear? 365
I, caught up with my monk's things by mistake,
My old serge gown and rope that goes all round,
I, in this presence, this pure company!
Where's a hole, where's a corner for escape?
Then steps a sweet angelic slip of a thing 370
Forward, puts out a soft palm—"Not so fast!"
—Addresses the celestial presence, "nay—
He made you and devised you, after all,
Though he's none of you! Could Saint John there draw—
His camel-hair[31] make up a painting-brush? 375
We come to bother Lippo for all that,
Iste perfecit opus!"[32] So, all smile—
I shuffle sideways with my blushing face
Under the cover of a hundred wings
Thrown like a spread of kirtles when you're gay 380
And play hot cockles,[33] all the doors being shut,
Till, wholly unexpected, in there pops
The hothead husband! Thus I scuttle off
To some safe bench behind, not letting go
The palm of her, the little lily thing 385
That spoke the good word for me in the nick,
Like the Prior's niece . . . Saint Lucy, I would say.
And so all's saved for me, and for the church
A pretty picture gained. Go, six months hence!
Your hand, sir, and good-by: no lights, no lights! 390
The street's hushed, and I know my own way back,
Don't fear me! There's the gray beginning. Zooks!

[30] Cosmetic powder made from the sweet-smelling roots of the orris flower. The picture Lippi is describing is the *Coronation of the Virgin*, a painting that Browning actually saw in Florence.
[31] St. John was said to dress in camel-hair. See Mark 1:16.
[32] "This man made the work." These words are actually painted in *The Coronation of the Virgin*, next to a figure representing Fra Lippo Lippi.
[33] *Kirtles:* skirts. *Hot cockles:* a game that involves wearing a blindfold.

Walt Whitman

"The United States themselves are essentially the greatest poem," Walt Whitman (1819–92) wrote in the preface to the first edition of *Leaves of Grass,* and he devoted his life to finding the words and forms for this poem. Whitman grew up in New York, first on Long Island and then in Brooklyn. He left school when he was eleven and was eventually apprenticed to a printer. Printing led to journalism, and between the ages of nineteen and thirty-one Whitman was caught up in the daily pressures of newspaper work. In about 1850, he underwent something of a transformation. He began to wear workman's clothes, grew a full beard, and began to think of himself as a potential bard and prophet of an ideal America. The first edition of *Leaves of Grass,* privately published by Whitman himself, appeared in 1855. The rest of Whitman's life was devoted primarily to producing further editions of *Leaves of Grass,* each with added poems and revisions and rearrangements of earlier ones. Whitman suffered a stroke in 1873 and moved in with his brother's family in Camden, New Jersey. He lived there until his death in 1892, the center of a cult of worldwide admirers and followers.

CAVALRY CROSSING A FORD

A line in long array where they wind betwixt green islands,
They take a serpentine course, their arms flash in the sun—hark to the musical
    clank,
Behold the silvery river, in it the splashing horses loitering stop to drink,
Behold the brown-faced men, each group, each person, a picture, the negligent
    rest on the saddles,
Some emerge on the opposite bank, others are just entering the ford—   5
    while,
Scarlet and blue and snowy white,
The guidon flags flutter gayly in the wind.

TO A LOCOMOTIVE IN WINTER

Thee for my recitative,
Thee in the driving storm even as now, the snow, the winter-day declining,
Thee in thy panoply,[1] thy measur'd dual throbbing and thy beat convulsive,
Thy black cylindric body, golden brass and silvery steel,
Thy ponderous side-bars, parallel and connecting rods, gyrating, shuttling at
    thy sides,   5
Thy metrical, now swelling pant and roar, now tapering in the distance,
Thy great protruding head-light fix'd in front,
Thy long, pale, floating vapor-pennants, tinged with delicate purple,
Thy dense and murky clouds out-belching from thy smoke-stack,
Thy knitted frame, thy springs and valves, the tremulous twinkle of thy
    wheels,   10

[1] Suit of armor.

Thy train of cars behind, obedient, merrily following,
Through gale or calm, now swift, now slack, yet steadily careering;
Type of the modern—emblem of motion and power—pulse of the
    continent,
For once come serve the Muse and merge in verse, even as here I see thee,
With storm and buffeting gusts of wind and falling snow,   15
By day thy warning ringing bell to sound its notes,
By night thy silent signal lamp to swing.

Fierce-throated beauty!
Roll through my chant with all thy lawless music, thy swinging lamps at
    night,
Thy madly-whistled laughter, echoing, rumbling like an earthquake, rousing
    all,   20
Law of thyself complete, thine own track firmly holding,
(No sweetness debonair of tearful harp or glib piano thine,)
Thy trills of shrieks by rocks and hills return'd,
Launch'd o'er the prairies wide, across the lakes,
To the free skies unpent and glad and strong.   25

Christina Rossetti

Christina Rossetti (1830–94) is often thought of, accurately if inadequately, as
the poet who, along with her brother Dante Gabriel Rossetti, best translated into
poetry the aesthetic principles of the Pre-Raphaelite painters. Twelve years
younger than Dante Gabriel, she remained single and spent much of her life
caring for an elderly father, who died in 1854, and mother, who died in 1886. She
was deeply religious and wrote many devotional poems. *Goblin Market and Other
Poems* (1862) was the first collection of Pre-Raphaelite poetry to find a large
readership. The Pre-Raphaelite Brotherhood was a group of painters—John Ever-
ett Millais, William Holman Hunt, and Dante Gabriel Rossetti were the most
prominent—who shared certain artistic goals. They wanted to reform English
painting by repudiating the reigning academic style in favor of the manner of
medieval painting ("pre-Raphael"), which they defined as using simple forms
and pure colors. The simple style of "Goblin Market" and its lush, colorful
descriptions are equivalents of painterly values. Its lyricism and its haunting, tantalizing themes are more a matter of Rossetti's talent than of Pre-Raphaelite
principles.

GOBLIN MARKET

Morning and evening
Maids heard the goblins cry:
"Come buy our orchard fruits,
Come buy, come buy:
Apples and quinces,   5
Lemons and oranges,
Plump unpecked cherries,

Melons and raspberries,
Bloom-down-cheeked peaches,
Swart-headed mulberries,   10
Wild free-born cranberries,
Crabapples, dewberries,
Pineapples, blackberries,
Apricots, strawberries;—
All ripe together   15
In summer weather,—
Morns that pass by,
Fair eyes that fly;
Come buy, come buy:
Our grapes fresh from the vine,   20
Pomegranates full and fine,
Dates and sharp bullaces,
Rare pears and greengages,
Damsons[1] and bilberries,
Taste them and try: 25
Currants and gooseberries,
Bright-fire-like barberries,
Figs to fill your mouth,
Citrons from the South,
Sweet to tongue and sound to eye;   30
Come buy, come buy."
Evening by evening
Among the brookside rushes,
Laura bowed her head to hear,
Lizzie veiled her blushes: 35
Crouching close together
In the cooling weather,
With clasping arms and cautioning lips,
With tingling cheeks and finger tips.
"Lie close," Laura said,   40
Pricking up her golden head:
"We must not look at goblin men,
We must not buy their fruits:
Who knows upon what soil they fed
Their hungry thirsty roots?"   45
"Come buy," call the goblins
Hobbling down the glen.
"Oh," cried Lizzie, "Laura, Laura,
You should not peep at goblin men."
Lizzie covered up her eyes,   50
Covered close lest they should look;
Laura reared her glossy head,
And whispered like the restless brook:
'Look, Lizzie, look, Lizzie,
Down the glen tramp little men.   55
One hauls a basket,

---

[1] Bullaces, greengages, and damsons are kinds of plums.

One bears a plate,
One lugs a golden dish
Of many pounds' weight.
How fair the vine must grow   60
Whose grapes are so luscious;
How warm the wind must blow
Through those fruit bushes."
"No," said Lizzie: "No, no, no;
Their offers should not charm us,   65
Their evil gifts would harm us."
She thrust a dimpled finger
In each ear, shut eyes and ran:
Curious Laura chose to linger
Wondering at each merchant man.   70
One had a cat's face,
One whisked a tail,
One tramped at a rat's pace,
One crawled like a snail,
One like a wombat[2] prowled obtuse and furry, 75
One like a ratel[3] tumbled hurry skurry.
She heard a voice like voice of doves
Cooing all together:
They sounded kind and full of loves
In the pleasant weather.   80

Laura stretched her gleaming neck
Like a rush-imbedded swan,
Like a lily from the beck,[4]
Like a moonlit poplar branch,
Like a vessel at the launch   85
When its last restraint is gone.

Backwards up the mossy glen
Turned and trooped the goblin men,
With their shrill repeated cry,
"Come buy, come buy."   90
When they reached where Laura was
They stood stock still upon the moss,
Leering at each other,
Brother with queer brother;
Signaling each other,   95
Brother with sly brother.
One set his basket down,
One reared his plate;
One began to weave a crown
Of tendrils, leaves, and rough nuts brown   100
(Men sell not such in any town):

[2] A kind of Australian marsupial that resembles a small bear.
[3] Honey badger.
[4] Brook.

One heaved the golden weight
Of dish and fruit to offer her:
"Come buy, come buy," was still their cry.
Laura stared but did not stir,   105
Longed but had no money.
The whisk-tailed merchant bade her taste
In tones as smooth as honey.
The cat-faced purr'd,
The rat-paced spoke a word   110
Of welcome, and the snail-paced even was heard;
One parrot-voiced and jolly
Cried "Pretty Goblin" still for "Pretty Polly";
One whistled like a bird.

But sweet-tooth Laura spoke in haste: 115
"Good Folk, I have no coin;
To take were to purloin:
I have no copper in my purse,
I have no silver either,
And all my gold is on the furze   120
That shakes in windy weather
Above the rusty heather."
"You have much gold upon your head,"
They answered all together:
"Buy from us with a golden curl."   125
She clipped a precious golden lock,
She dropped a tear more rare than pearl,
Then sucked their fruit globes fair or red.
Sweeter than honey from the rock,
Stronger than man-rejoicing wine,   130
Clearer than water flowed that juice;
She never tasted such before,
How should it cloy with length of use?
She sucked and sucked and sucked the more
Fruits which that unknown orchard bore;   135
She sucked until her lips were sore;
Then flung the emptied rinds away
But gathered up one kernel stone,
And knew not was it night or day
As she turned home alone.   140

Lizzie met her at the gate
Full of wise upbraidings:
"Dear, you should not stay so late,
Twilight is not good for maidens;
Should not loiter in the glen   145
In the haunts of goblin men.
Do you not remember Jeanie,
How she met them in the moonlight,
Took their gifts both choice and many,
Ate their fruits and wore their flowers   150

Plucked from bowers
Where summer ripens at all hours?
But ever in the noonlight
She pined and pined away;
Sought them by night and day,   155
Found them no more, but dwindled and grew gray;
Then fell with the first snow,
While to this day no grass will grow
Where she lies low:
I planted daisies there a year ago   160
That never blow.⁵
You should not loiter so."
"Nay, hush," said Laura:
"Nay, hush, my sister:
I ate and ate my fill,   165
Yet my mouth waters still:
Tomorrow night I will
Buy more"; and kissed her.
"Have done with sorrow;
I'll bring you plums tomorrow   170
Fresh on their mother twigs,
Cherries worth getting;
You cannot think what figs
My teeth have met in,
What melons icy-cold   175
Piled on a dish of gold
Too huge for me to hold,
What peaches with a velvet nap,
Pellucid grapes without one seed:
Odorous indeed must be the mead   180
Whereon they grow, and pure the wave they drink
With lilies at the brink,
And sugar-sweet their sap."

Golden head by golden head,
Like two pigeons in one nest   185
Folded in each other's wings,
They lay down in their curtained bed:
Like two blossoms on one stem,
Like two flakes of new-fallen snow,
Like two wands of ivory   190
Tipped with gold for awful⁶ kings.
Moon and stars gazed in at them,
Wind sang to them lullaby,
Lumbering owls forebore to fly,
Not a bat flapped to and fro   195
Round their nest:
Cheek to cheek and breast to breast
Locked together in one nest.

⁵ Blossom.   ⁶ Awe-inspiring.

Early in the morning
When the first cock crowed his warning, 200
Neat like bees, as sweet and busy,
Laura rose with Lizzie:
Fetched in honey, milked the cows,
Aired and set to rights the house,
Kneaded cakes of whitest wheat, 205
Cakes for dainty mouths to eat,
Next churned butter, whipped up cream,
Fed their poultry, sat and sewed;
Talked as modest maidens should:
Lizzie with an open heart, 210
Laura in an absent dream,
One content, one sick in part;
One warbling for the mere bright day's delight,
One longing for the night.

At length slow evening came: 215
They went with pitchers to the reedy brook;
Lizzie most placid in her look,
Laura most like a leaping flame,
They drew the gurgling water from its deep.
Lizzie plucked purple and rich golden flags, 220
Then turning homeward said: "The sunset flushes
Those furthest loftiest crags;
Come, Laura, not another maiden lags.
No willful squirrel wags,
The beasts and birds are fast asleep." 225
But Laura loitered still among the rushes.
And said the bank was steep.

And said the hour was early still,
The dew not fallen, the wind not chill;
Listening ever, but not catching 230
The customary cry,
"Come buy, come buy,"
With its iterated jingle
Of sugar-baited words:
Not for all her watching 235
Once discerning even one goblin
Racing, whisking, tumbling, hobbling—
Let alone the herds
That used to tramp along the glen,
In groups or single, 240
Of brisk fruit-merchant men.
Till Lizzie urged, "O Laura, come;
I hear the fruit-call, but I dare not look:
You should not loiter longer at this brook:
Come with me home. 245
The stars rise, the moon bends her arc,
Each glow-worm winks her spark,
Let us get home before the night grows dark:

For clouds may gather
Though this is summer weather, 250
Put out the lights and drench us through:
Then if we lost our way what should we do?"
Laura turned cold as stone
To find her sister heard that cry alone,
That goblin cry, 255
"Come buy our fruits, come buy."
Must she then buy no more such dainty fruit?
Must she no more such succous[7] pasture find,
Gone deaf and blind?
Her tree of life dropped from the root: 260
She said not one word in her heart's sore ache:
But peering through the dimness, nought discerning,
Trudged home, her pitcher dripping all the way;
So crept to bed, and lay
Silent till Lizzie slept; 265
Then sat up in a passionate yearning.
And gnashed her teeth for balked desire, and wept
As if her heart would break.

Day after day, night after night,
Laura kept watch in vain 270
In sullen silence of exceeding pain.
She never caught again the goblin cry,
"Come buy, come buy";—
She never spied the goblin men
Hawking their fruits along the glen: 275
But when the noon waxed bright
Her hair grew thin and gray;
She dwindled, as the fair full moon doth turn
To swift decay and burn
Her fire away. 280

One day remembering her kernelstone
She set it by a wall that faced the south;
Dewed it with tears, hoped for a root,
Watched for a waxing shoot,
But there came none. 285
It never saw the sun,
It never felt the trickling moisture run:
While with sunk eyes and faded mouth
She dreamed of melons, as a traveler sees
False waves in desert drouth 290
With shade of leaf-crowned trees,
And burns the thirstier in the sandful breeze.

She no more swept the house,
Tended the fowls or cows,
Fetched honey, kneaded cakes of wheat, 295

[7] Juicy; succulent.

Brought water from the brook:
But sat down listless in the chimneynook
And would not eat.
Tender Lizzie could not bear
To watch her sister's cankerous care,   300
Yet not to share.
She night and morning
Caught the goblins' cry:
"Come buy our orchard fruits,
Come buy, come buy":—   305
Beside the brook, along the glen,
She heard the tramp of goblin men,
The voice and stir
Poor Laura could not hear;
Longed to buy fruit to comfort her,   310
But feared to pay too dear.
She thought of Jeanie in her grave,
Who should have been a bride;
But who for joys brides hope to have
Fell sick and died   315
In her gay prime,
In earliest winter time,
With the first glazing rime,
With the snow-fall of crisp winter time.

Till Laura dwindling   320
Seemed knocking at Death's door.
Then Lizzie weighed no more
Better and worse;
But put a silver penny in her purse,
Kissed Laura, crossed the heath with clumps of furze   325
At twilight, halted by the brook:
And for the first time in her life
Began to listen and look.

Laughed every goblin
When they spied her peeping: 330
Came towards her hobbling,
Flying, running, leaping,
Puffing and blowing,
Chuckling, clapping, crowing,
Cluckling and gobbling,   335
Mopping and mowing,[8]
Full of airs and graces,
Pulling wry faces,
Demure grimaces,
Cat-like and rat-like,   340
Ratel- and wombat-like,
Snail-paced in a hurry,

---

[8] Moping and making faces.

Parrot-voiced and whistler,
Helter skelter, hurry skurry,
Chattering like magpies, 345
Fluttering like pigeons,
Gliding like fishes,—
Hugged her and kissed her:
Squeezed her and caressed her:
Stretched up their dishes, 350
Panniers, and plates:
"Look at our apples
Russet and dun,
Bob at our cherries,
Bite at our peaches, 355
Citrons and dates,
Grapes for the asking,
Pears red with basking
Out in the sun,
Plums on their twigs; 360
Pluck them and suck them,—
Pomegranates, figs."

"Good folk," said Lizzie,
Mindful of Jeanie:
"Give me much and many": 365
Held out her apron,
Tossed them her penny.
"Nay, take a seat with us,
Honor and eat with us,"
They answered grinning: 370
"Our feast is but beginning.
Night yet is early,
Warm and dew-pearly,
Wakeful and starry:
Such fruits as these 375
No man can carry;
Half their bloom would fly,
Half their dew would dry,
Half their flavor would pass by.
Sit down and feast with us, 380
Be welcome guest with us,
Cheer you and rest with us."—
"Thank you," said Lizzie: "But one waits
At home alone for me:
So without further parleying, 385
If you will not sell me any
Of your fruits though much and many,
Give me back my silver penny
I tossed you for a fee."—
They began to scratch their pates, 390
No longer wagging, purring,
But visibly demurring,

Grunting and snarling.
One called her proud,
Cross-grained, uncivil;   395
Their tones waxed loud,
Their looks were evil.
Lashing their tails
They trod and hustled her,
Elbowed and jostled her,   400
Clawed with their nails,
Barking, mewing, hissing, mocking,
Tore her gown and soiled her stocking,
Twitched her hair out by the roots,
Stamped upon her tender feet,   405
Held her hands and squeezed their fruits
Against her mouth to make her eat.

White and golden Lizzie stood,
Like a lily in a flood,—
Like a rock of blue-veined stone   410
Lashed by tides obstreperously,—
Like a beacon left alone
In a hoary roaring sea,
Sending up a golden fire,—
Like a fruit-crowned orange-tree   415
White with blossoms honey-sweet
Sore beset by wasp and bee,—
Like a royal virgin town
Topped with gilded dome and spire
Close beleaguered by a fleet   420
Mad to tug her standard down.

One may lead a horse to water,
Twenty cannot make him drink.
Though the goblins cuffed and caught her,
Coaxed and fought her,   425
Bullied and besought her,
Scratched her, pinched her black as ink,
Kicked and knocked her,
Mauled and mocked her,
Lizzie uttered not a word;   430
Would not open lip from lip
Lest they should cram a mouthful in:
But laughed in heart to feel the drip
Of juice that syruped all her face,
And lodged in dimples of her chin,   435
And streaked her neck which quaked like curd.
At last the evil people,
Worn out by her resistance,
Flung back her penny, kicked their fruit
Along whichever road they took   440
Not leaving root or stone or shoot;

Some writhed into the ground,
Some dived into the brook
With ring and ripple,
Some scudded on the gale without a sound,   445
Some vanished in the distance.

In a smart, ache, tingle,
Lizzie went her way;
Knew not was it night or day;
Sprang up the bank, tore through the furze,   450
Threaded copse and dingle,⁹
And heard her penny jingle
Bouncing in her purse,—
Its bounce was music to her ear.
She ran and ran   455
As if she feared some goblin man
Dogged her with gibe or curse
Or something worse:
But not one goblin skurried after,
Nor was she pricked by fear;   460
The kind heart made her windy-paced
That urged her home quite out of breath with haste
And inward laughter.

She cried, "Laura," up the garden,
"Did you miss me?   465
Come and kiss me.
Never mind my bruises,
Hug me, kiss me, suck my juices
Squeezed from goblin fruits for you,
Goblin pulp and goblin dew.   470
Eat me, drink me, love me;
Laura, make much of me;
For your sake I have braved the glen
And had to do with goblin merchant men."

Laura started from her chair,   475
Flung her arms up in the air,
Clutched her hair:
"Lizzie, Lizzie, have you tasted
For my sake the fruit forbidden?
Must your light like mine be hidden,   480
Your young life like mine be wasted,
Undone in mine undoing,
And ruined in my ruin,
Thirsty, cankered, goblin-ridden?"—
She clung about her sister,   485
Kissed and kissed and kissed her:
Tears once again

⁹ Thicket and wooded valley.

Refreshed her shrunken eyes,
Dropping like rain
After long sultry drouth;   490
Shaking with anguish, fear, and pain,
She kissed and kissed her with a hungry mouth.

Her lips began to scorch,
That juice was wormwood to her tongue,
She loathed the feast: 495
Writhing as one possessed she leaped and sung,
Rent all her robe, and wrung
Her hands in lamentable haste,
And beat her breast,
Her locks streamed like the torch   500
Borne by a racer at full speed,
Or like the mane of horses in their flight,
Or like an eagle when she stems[10] the light
Straight toward the sun,
Or like a caged thing freed,   505
Or like a flying flag when armies run.

Swift fire spread through her veins, knocked at her heart,
Met the fire smoldering there
And overbore its lesser flame;
She gorged on bitterness without a name: 510
Ah fool, to choose such part
Of soul-consuming care!
Sense failed in the mortal strife:
Like the watch-tower of a town
Which an earthquake shatters down,   515
Like a lightning-stricken mast,
Like a wind-uprooted tree
Spun about,
Like a foam-topped waterspout
Cast down headlong in the sea,   520
She fell at last;
Pleasure past and anguish past,
Is it death or is it life?

Life out of death.
That night long Lizzie watched by her,   525
Counted her pulse's flagging stir,
Felt for her breath,
Held water to her lips, and cooled her face
With tears and fanning leaves.
But when the first birds chirped about their eaves,   530
And early reapers plodded to the place
Of golden sheaves,

[10] Makes headway against.

And dew-wet grass
Bowed in the morning winds so brisk to pass,
And new buds with new day   535
Opened of cup-like lilies on the stream,
Laura awoke as from a dream,
Laughed in the innocent old way,
Hugged Lizzie but not twice or thrice;
Her gleaming locks showed not one thread of gray,   540
Her breath was sweet as May,
And light danced in her eyes.

Days, weeks, months, years
Afterwards, when both were wives
With children of their own;   545
Their mother-hearts beset with fears,
Their lives bounded up in tender lives;
Laura would call the little ones
And tell them of her early prime,
Those pleasant days long gone   550
Of not-returning time:
Would talk about the haunted glen,
The wicked quaint fruit-merchant men,
The fruits like honey to the throat
But poison in the blood   555
(Men sell not such in any town):
Would tell them how her sister stood
In deadly peril to do her good,
And win the fiery antidote:
Then joining hands to little hands   560
Would bid them cling together,—
"For there is no friend like a sister
In calm or stormy weather;
To cheer one on the tedious way,
To fetch one if one goes astray,   565
To lift one if one totters down,
To strengthen whilst one stands."

Emily Dickinson

Emily Dickinson (1830–86) was born in Amherst, Massachusetts, in the house in which she was to live her entire life. She was fairly gregarious when she was young; as she aged, she became increasingly reclusive. She dressed always in white, kept always to her house, and communicated with strangers only through a half-open door that hid her from sight. In her 56 years, she wrote nearly 1,800 poems, of which only 7 were published during her lifetime. The others, discovered after her death, were finally definitively published in 1955. She is now regarded, with Whitman, as the greatest of nineteenth-century American poets. Read first as the eccentric, ethereal "belle of Amherst," she is now increasingly read as a sophisticated critic of her culture.

249: WILD NIGHTS—WILD NIGHTS!

Wild Nights—Wild Nights!
Were I with thee
Wild Nights should be
Our luxury!

Futile—the Winds—   5
To a Heart in port—
Done with the Compass—
Done with the Chart!

Rowing in Eden—
Ah, the Sea!   10
Might I but moor—Tonight—
In Thee!

754: MY LIFE HAD STOOD—A LOADED GUN

My Life had stood—a Loaded Gun—
In Corners—till a Day
The Owner passed—identified—
And carried Me away—

And now We roam in Sovereign Woods   5
And now We hunt the Doe—
And every time I speak for Him—
The Mountains straight reply—

And do I smile, such cordial light
Upon the Valley glow—   10
It is as a Vesuvian[1] face
Had let its pleasure through—

And when at Night—Our good Day done—
I guard My Master's Head—
'Tis better than the Eider-Duck's   15
Deep Pillow—to have shared—

To foe of His—I'm deadly foe—
None stir the second time—
On whom I lay a Yellow Eye—
Or an emphatic Thumb—   20

Though I than He—may longer live
He longer must—than I—
For I have but the power to kill,
Without—the power to die—

[1] A face capable of erupting, like Mt. Vesuvius, the volcano overlooking the Bay of Naples in Italy.

1755: TO MAKE A PRAIRIE IT TAKES A CLOVER AND ONE BEE

To make a prairie it takes a clover and one bee,
One clover, and a bee,
And revery.
The revery alone will do,
If bees are few.   5

Lewis Carroll

Charles Lutwidge Dodgson (1832–98), under his own name, published a number of treatises on mathematics; he was a lecturer in mathematics at Oxford as well as a deacon in the Church of England. As Lewis Carroll, he published two master-pieces of Victorian nonsense: *Alice in Wonderland* (1865) and *Through the Looking-Glass* (1871). "Jabberwocky" is one of the many songs scattered through the two books, this one from *Through the Looking-Glass.* Later in the book, Humpty Dumpty explains the odd words. Using the example of "slithy," which contains both "lithe" and "slimy," he says the words are "portmanteau" words. (One word is inside another, as something might be inside a portmanteau, or suitcase.) James Joyce used much the same method for the coinages in his experimental novel *Finnegans Wake,* although he did not read *Through the Looking-Glass* until after he had written a substantial part of *Finnegans Wake.*

JABBERWOCKY

'Twas brillig, and the slithy toves
　　Did gyre and gimble in the wabe;
All mimsy were the borogoves,
　　And the mome raths outgrabe.[1]

"Beware the Jabberwock, my son!   5
　　The jaws that bite, the claws that catch!
Beware the Jubjub bird, and shun
　　The frumious Bandersnatch!"

He took his vorpal sword in hand:
　　Long time the manxome foe he sought—   10
So rested he by the Tumtum tree,
　　And stood awhile in thought.

[1] When Humpty Dumpty, later in *Through the Looking-Glass,* "explains" the poem, he gives these definitions of the words in the first stanza: *Brillig:* "four o'clock in the afternoon—the time you begin *broiling* things for dinner"; *slithy:* "lithe and slimy"; *toves:* "something like badgers—they're something like lizards—and they're something like corkscrews"; *gyre:* "to go round and round like a gyroscope"; *gimble:* "to make holes like a gimlet"; *wabe:* "the grass plot around a sundial . . . because it goes a long way before it, and a long way behind it . . . and a long way beyond it on each side"; *mimsy:* "flimsy and miserable"; *borogoves:* "a thin shabby-looking bird with its feathers sticking out all round—something like a mop"; *mome:* "short for 'from home' "; *rath:* "a sort of green pig"; *outgrabe:* "outgribing is something between bellowing and whispering, with a kind of sneeze in the middle."

And as in uffish thought he stood,
   The Jabberwock, with eyes of flame,
Came whiffling through the tulgey wood,   15
   And burbled as it came!

One, two! One, two! And through and through
   The vorpal blade went snicker-snack!
He left it dead, and with its head
   He went galumphing back.   20

"And hast thou slain the Jabberwock?
   Come to my arms, my beamish boy!
O frabjous day! Callooh! Callay!"
   He chortled in his joy.

'Twas brillig, and the slithy toves   25
   Did gyre and gimble in the wabe;
All mimsy were the borogoves,
   And the mome raths outgrabe.

Thomas Hardy

The career of Thomas Hardy (1840–1928) breaks sharply into two parts. From 1872 until 1896, he published a series of novels that placed him in the first rank of nineteenth-century English novelists. Then, frustrated and angered by the hostile reception of *Jude the Obscure,* he resolved to turn exclusively to poetry and, from 1898 until his death, produced a body of work that gave him an honored place in modern poetry. Hardy grew up near Dorchester in southwest England, the area that was the fictional "Wessex" of his novels. He was apprenticed to an architect when he was fifteen; after six years he went to London to work as an architect. Instead, he began to write novels, beginning with *Desperate Remedies* (1871) and ending with *Jude the Obscure* (1896). Hardy was preoccupied in both his fiction and his poetry with the natural and the inner forces that control human destiny, with such forces as environment and coincidence as well as human passions and desires. The novels are tragic; the term is not too strong for many of his lyric poems, brief as they are.

DRUMMER HODGE[1]

1

They throw in Drummer Hodge, to rest
   Uncoffined—just as found:
His landmark is a kopje-crest[2]
   That breaks the veldt around;

[1] Hodge was a British soldier killed in the Boer War in South Africa (1899–1902).
[2] A small hill. (The word is South African Dutch, or Afrikaans.)

And foreign constellations west[3]
 Each night above his mound.

2

Young Hodge the Drummer never knew—
 Fresh from his Wessex home—
The meaning of the broad Karoo,[4]
 The Bush, the dusty loam,
And why uprose to nightly view
 Strange stars amid the gloam.[5]

3

Yet portion of that unknown plain
 Will Hodge forever be;
His homely Northern breast and brain
 Grow to some Southern tree,
And strange-eyed constellations reign
 His stars eternally.

THE DARKLING[1] THRUSH

I leant upon a coppice gate[2]
 When Frost was specter-gray,
And Winter's dregs made desolate
 The weakening eye of day.
The tangled bine-stems[3] scored the sky
 Like strings of broken lyres,
And all mankind that haunted nigh
 Had sought their household fires.

The land's sharp features seemed to be
 The Century's corpse[4] outleant,
His crypt the cloudy canopy,
 The wind his death-lament.
The ancient pulse of germ and birth
 Was shrunken hard and dry,
And every spirit upon earth
 Seemed fervorless as I.

At once a voice arose among
 The bleak twigs overhead
In a fullhearted evensong

---

[3] Set. Because South Africa is in the southern hemisphere, different constellations are visible from those seen in England.
[4] Plain. The "Bush" is any uncleared land. [5] Twilight. [1] In the dark.
[2] Gate leading to a grove of trees. [3] Bare branches of shrubs.
[4] The corpse of the nineteenth century. Hardy wrote this poem on New Year's Eve, 1899.

Of joy illimited;   20
An aged thrush, frail, gaunt, and small,
  In blast-beruffled plume,
Had chosen thus to fling his soul
  Upon the growing gloom.

So little cause for carolings   25
  Of such ecstatic sound
Was written on terrestrial things
  Afar or nigh around,
That I could think there trembled through
  His happy good-night air   30
Some blessed Hope, whereof he knew
  And I was unaware.

CHANNEL FIRING[1]

That night your great guns, unawares,
Shook all our coffins as we lay,
And broke the chancel window-squares,
We thought it was the Judgment Day

And sat upright. While drearisome   5
Arose the howl of wakened hounds:
The mouse let fall the altar-crumb,
The worms drew back into the mounds,

The glebe cow[2] drooled. Till God called, "No;
It's gunnery practice out at sea   10
Just as before you went below;
The world is as it used to be:

"All nations striving strong to make
Red war yet redder. Mad as hatters
They do no more for Christés[3] sake   15
Than you who are helpless in such matters.

"That this is not the judgment hour
For some of them's a blessed thing,
For if it were they'd have to scour
Hell's floor for so much threatening. . . .   20

"Ha, ha. It will be warmer when
I blow the trumpet (if indeed
I ever do; for you are men,
And rest eternal sorely need)."

---

[1] This poem was written in April 1914. The channel firing is gunnery practice in the English Channel. World War I broke out four months later (August 4, 1914).
[2] Cow in a small field (a "glebe").
[3] The archaic spelling and pronunciation heighten the ballad quality of the poem.

So down we lay again. "I wonder,   25
Will the world ever saner be,"
Said one, "than when He sent us under
In our indifferent century!"

And many a skeleton shook his head.
"Instead of preaching forty year,"   30
My neighbor Parson Thirdly said,
"I wish I had stuck to pipes and beer."

Again the guns disturbed the hour,
Roaring their readiness to avenge,
As far inland as Stourton Tower,   35
And Camelot, and starlit Stonehenge.[4]

Gerard Manley Hopkins

Gerard Manley Hopkins (1844–89) was in some ways a poet born out of his time.
He wrote in the nineteenth century; he found his audience in the twentieth. Hopkins was born into the Church of England. At Oxford University, he fell under the influence of the Oxford Movement, which was reviving ritual and dogma within the church; he eventually converted to Catholicism and joined, in 1868, the Society of Jesus. After ordination and service in a number of parishes, he was sent to Dublin in 1884 as Professor of Classics at University College, Dublin. Hopkins had written poetry before he became a priest but had given it up. After several years, he began writing again, though not for publication; he did not believe his church superiors would approve. His poetry was published long after his death by his friend Robert Bridges. Hopkins's poetry is full of innovations we might call modern: a loose system of meter Hopkins called "sprung rhythm," a strange, sometimes extravagant diction that coins words, revives archaic ones, and mixes "high" and "low" words, and a use of incongruity that recalls the Metaphysicals.

GOD'S GRANDEUR

The world is charged with the grandeur of God.
   It will flame out, like shining from shook foil;[1]
   It gathers to a greatness, like the ooze of oil
Crushed.[2] Why do men then now not reck his rod?
Generations have trod, have trod, have trod;   5
   And all is seared with trade; bleared, smeared with toil;
   And wears man's smudge and shares man's smell: the soil
Is bare now, nor can foot feel, being shod.

And for all this, nature is never spent;
   There lives the dearest freshness deep down things;   10

---

[4] The placenames, all in "Wessex," combine historic periods. There is a village named "Stour Head," which Hardy calls "Stour Tower" or "Stourton" in his fiction. Camelot was the legendary seat of King Arthur's court. Stonehenge is the prehistoric stone circle on Salisbury Plain.
[1] Thin metal as in "tinfoil," though Hopkins said he had gold foil in mind.
[2] As olive oil is crushed from olives.

And though the last lights off the black West went
  Oh, morning, at the brown brink eastward, springs—
Because the Holy Ghost over the bent
  World broods with warm breast and with ah! bright wings.

SPRING AND FALL

To a Young Child

Márgarét, áre you gríeving
Over Goldengrove unleaving?
Leáves, like the things of man, you
With your fresh thoughts care for, can you?
Áh! ás the heart grows older   5
It will come to such sights colder
By and by, nor spare a sigh
Though worlds of wanwood leafmeal[1] lie;
And yet you *will* weep and know why.
Now no matter, child, the name: 10
Sórrow's spríngs áre the same.
Nor mouth had, no nor mind, expressed
What heart heard of, ghost guessed:[2]
It ís the blight man was born for,
It is Margaret you mourn for.   15

William Butler Yeats

William Butler Yeats (1865–1939) is often called the greatest poet writing in
English in the twentieth century. That he did so from outside England is not
unprecedented; the twentieth century has seen the flourishing of several English-
language literatures other than England's. Yeats was born in Dublin. He briefly
attended art school but soon left to devote himself to poetry. His earliest poems
were dreamy, Pre-Raphaelite affairs; as he matured, his poetry became more
complex, perhaps in response to both the contradictions of historical events and
the model of literary modernists. He lived through cataclysmic change in his
homeland: the growing cultural nationalism of the Irish Literary Revival, the 1916
Rising, the Civil War of 1921–22, and the founding of an independent state.
Underlying the surface conflicts of his poetry is a deeper conflict between what he
sometimes called "power" and "knowledge," which took many forms, including
political commitment versus aestheticism, involvement in the world versus escap-
ism, and simplicity versus complexity.

[1] *Wanwood* seems to mean "dark wood" (O.E. *wann:* "dark," "livid"). *Leafmeal* seems to mean
"having fallen one by one," on the analogy of *piecemeal.*
[2] "What the physical being heard of, the spirit guessed" [i.e., human mortality].

THE STOLEN CHILD

Where dips the rocky highland
Of Sleuth Wood[1] in the lake,
There lies a leafy island
Where flapping herons wake
The drowsy water rats; 5
There we've hid our faery vats,
Full of berries
And of reddest stolen cherries.
Come away, O human child!
To the waters and the wild 10
With a faery, hand in hand,
For the world's more full of weeping than you can understand.

Where the wave of moonlight glosses
The dim gray sands with light,
Far off by furthest Rosses 15
We foot it all the night,
Weaving olden dances
Mingling hands and mingling glances
Till the moon has taken flight;
To and fro we leap 20
And chase the frothy bubbles,
While the world is full of troubles
And is anxious in its sleep.
Come away, O human child!
To the waters and the wild 25
With a faery, hand in hand,
For the world's more full of weeping than you can understand.

Where the wandering water gushes
From the hills above Glen-Car,
In pools among the rushes 30
That scarce could bathe a star,
We seek for slumbering trout
And whispering in their ears
Give them unquiet dreams;
Leaning softly out 35
From ferns that drop their tears
Over the young streams.
Come away, O human child!
To the waters and the wild
With a faery, hand in hand, 40
For the world's more full of weeping than you can understand.

Away with us he's going,
The solemn-eyed:

[1] All the places mentioned are in the neighborhood of Sligo, in western Ireland, where Yeats spent time as a child with his maternal grandparents.

He'll hear no more the lowing
Of the calves on the warm hillside   45
Or the kettle on the hob
Sing peace into his breast,
Or see the brown mice bob
Round and round the oatmeal chest.
For he comes, the human child,   50
To the waters and the wild
With a faery, hand in hand,
From a world more full of weeping than he can understand.

THE LAKE ISLE OF INNISFREE[1]

I will arise and go now, and go to Innisfree,
And a small cabin build there, of clay and wattles[2] made:
Nine bean-rows will I have there, a hive for the honeybee,
And live alone in the bee-loud glade.

And I shall have some peace there, for peace comes dropping slow,   5
Dropping from the veils of the morning to where the cricket sings;
There midnight's all a glimmer, and noon a purple glow,
And evening full of the linnet's wings.

I will arise and go now, for always night and day
I hear lake water lapping with low sounds by the shore;   10
While I stand on the roadway, or on the pavements gray,
I hear it in the deep heart's core.

EASTER 1916[1]

I have met them at close of day
Coming with vivid faces
From counter or desk among gray
Eighteenth-century houses.
I have passed with a nod of the head   5
Or polite meaningless words,
Or have lingered awhile and said
Polite meaningless words,
And thought before I had done
Of a mocking tale or a gibe   10
To please a companion
Around the fire at the club,

[1] Innisfree (in-ish-free) is an island in Lough Gill, County Sligo, near Yeats' grandparents' home. Some of the details of the poem are drawn from Henry David Thoreau's *Walden*.
[2] Stakes, interwoven with branches.
[1] The Easter Rising took place on Easter Monday, 1916. A small group of rebels tried to seize power from the British. They occupied the General Post Office in Dublin and proclaimed a free state. The rebellion collapsed, and the leaders were executed. It had a strong effect on public opinion, however.

Being certain that they and I
But lived where motley is worn:
All changed, changed utterly:
A terrible beauty is born.   15

That woman's days were spent
In ignorant good will,
Her nights in argument
Until her voice grew shrill.
What voice more sweet than hers   20
When, young and beautiful,
She rode to harriers?[2]
This man had kept a school
And rode our wingéd horse;[3]   25
This other his helper and friend
Was coming into his force;
He might have won fame in the end,
So sensitive his nature seemed,
So daring and sweet his thought.   30
This other man I had dreamed
A drunken, vainglorious lout.[4]
He had done most bitter wrong
To some who are near my heart,
Yet I number him in the song;   35
He, too, has resigned his part
In the casual comedy;
He, too, has been changed in his turn,
Transformed utterly:
A terrible beauty is born.   40

Hearts with one purpose alone
Through summer and winter seem
Enchanted to a stone
To trouble the living stream.
The horse that comes from the road,   45
The rider, the birds that range
From cloud to tumbling cloud,
Minute by minute they change;
A shadow of cloud on the stream
Changes minute by minute;   50
A horse-hoof slides on the brim,
And a horse plashes within it;
The long-legged moorhens dive,
And hens to moorcocks call;
Minute by minute they live: 55
The stone's in the midst of all.

---

[2] Constance Gore-Booth (afterward Countess Markiewicz), whom Yeats had known in Sligo.
[3] Patrick Pearse, a schoolteacher and poet. His "helper and friend" is Thomas MacDonagh.
[4] Major John MacBride, who had offended Yeats by marrying Maud Gonne, with whom Yeats was in love. The marriage took place in 1903; the couple separated after two years.

Too long a sacrifice
Can make a stone of the heart.
O when may it suffice?
That is Heaven's part, our part   60
To murmur name upon name,
As a mother names her child
When sleep at last has come
On limbs that had run wild.
What is it but nightfall?   65
No, no, not night but death;
Was it needless death after all?
For England may keep faith
For all that is done and said.
We know their dream; enough   70
To know they dreamed and are dead;
And what if excess of love
Bewildered them till they died?
I write it out in a verse—
MacDonagh and MacBride   75
And Connolly[5] and Pearse
Now and in time to be,
Wherever green is worn,
Are changed, changed utterly:
A terrible beauty is born.   80

LEDA AND THE SWAN[1]

A sudden blow: the great wings beating still
Above the staggering girl, her thighs caressed
By the dark webs, her nape caught in his bill,
He holds her helpless breast upon his breast.

How can those terrified vague fingers push   5
The feathered glory from her loosening thighs?
And how can body, laid in that white rush,
But feel the strange heart beating where it lies?

A shudder in the loins engenders there
The broken wall, the burning roof and tower[2]   10
And Agamemnon dead.
                              Being so caught up,
So mastered by the brute blood of the air,

[5] James Connelly, the leader, with Pearse, of the Rising. All the rebels named, except Constance
Gore-Booth, were executed by firing squad.
[1] In Greek mythology, Zeus took the form of a swan in order to seduce the mortal Leda.
[2] According to the myth, the coupling of Zeus and Leda produced twin girls: Helen of Troy and
Clytemnestra, wife of the Greek general Agamemnon. Helen was the cause of the Trojan War and the
destruction of Troy (the "broken wall, the burning roof and tower") and Clytemnestra was responsible for "Agamemnon dead."

Did she put on his knowledge with his power
Before the indifferent beak could let her drop?

Robert Frost

For about fifty years, from 1914 until his death, Robert Frost (1874–1963) personified poetry to many Americans. Gentle, rural, homespun, he seemed to embody the poet as American cracker-barrel philosopher. But careful readers recognized that beneath the folksy manner, Frost's vision of the world was tough, modern, and even pessimistic at times. Frost was born in California. When he was eleven, his father died and the family moved to Massachusetts. When Frost was graduated from high school, he married his co-valedictorian, had four children, and drifted through a number of jobs for twenty years. In 1912, he took his family to England, where he published his first book of poetry, *A Boy's Will* (1913). After a second book, *North of Boston* (1914), Frost came back to America, bought a farm in New Hampshire, and settled in for a long life of writing poetry and carrying on an active schedule of readings and lectures. Through his many volumes, Frost maintained a consistent approach. He used traditional verse forms (very skillfully); he built up a poetic voice as a gentle, thoughtful New Englander; and he took as his subject New England rural life, with its characters, its daily rhythms, and its relationship to nature.

MENDING WALL

Something there is that doesn't love a wall,
That sends the frozen-ground-swell under it,
And spills the upper boulders in the sun;
And makes gaps even two can pass abreast.
The work of hunters is another thing: 5
I have come after them and made repair
Where they have left not one stone on a stone,
But they would have the rabbit out of hiding,
To please the yelping dogs. The gaps I mean,
No one has seen them made or heard them made,   10
But at spring mending-time we find them there.
I let my neighbor know beyond the hill;
And on a day we meet to walk the line
And set the wall between us once again.
We keep the wall between us as we go.   15
To each the boulders that have fallen to each.
And some are loaves and some so nearly balls
We have to use a spell to make them balance:
'Stay where you are until our backs are turned!'
We wear our fingers rough with handling them.   20
Oh, just another kind of outdoor game,
One on a side. It comes to little more:
There where it is we do not need the wall:
He is all pine and I am apple orchard.

My apple trees will never get across   25
And eat the cones under his pines, I tell him.
He only says, 'Good fences make good neighbors.'
Spring is the mischief in me, and I wonder
If I could put a notion in his head:
'*Why* do they make good neighbors: Isn't it   30
Where there are cows? But here there are no cows.
Before I built a wall I'd ask to know
What I was walling in or walling out,
And to whom I was like to give offense.
Something there is that doesn't love a wall,   35
That wants it down.' I could say 'Elves' to him,
But it's not elves exactly, and I'd rather
He said it for himself. I see him there
Bringing a stone grasped firmly by the top
In each hand, like an old-stone savage armed.   40
He moves in darkness as it seems to me,
Not of woods only and the shade of trees.
He will not go behind his father's saying,
And he likes having thought of it so well
He says again, 'Good fences make good neighbors.'   45

THE ROAD NOT TAKEN

Two roads diverged in a yellow wood,
And sorry I could not travel both
And be one traveler, long I stood
And looked down one as far as I could
To where it bent in the undergrowth;   5

Then took the other, as just as fair,
And having perhaps the better claim,
Because it was grassy and wanted wear;
Though as for that the passing there
Had worn them really about the same,   10

And both that morning equally lay
In leaves no step had trodden black.
Oh, I kept the first for another day!
Yet knowing how way leads on to way,
I doubted if I should ever come back.   15

I shall be telling this with a sigh
Somewhere ages and ages hence:
Two roads diverged in a wood, and I—
I took the one less traveled by,
And that has made all the difference.   20

Wallace Stevens

"The poem of the act of the mind" was how Wallace Stevens (1879–1955) defined modern poetry in "Of Modern Poetry"; the phrase does nicely for Stevens' own poetry. Stevens was preoccupied with perception, with the interplay between the mind and the outside world (as Wordsworth and his fellow Romantics were before him); all his poems are "poems of the act of the mind." Stevens grew up in Reading, Pennsylvania. He attended Harvard but dropped out after three years and went to law school. Decided upon a literary career but unwilling to rely upon poetry for a living, he took a job with the Hartford Accident and Indemnity Company, headquartered in Hartford, Connecticut. He continued to work for the insurance company from 1916 until his death in 1955. His first collection of poems, *Harmonium,* appeared in 1923; many collections followed. A book of lectures and criticism, *The Necessary Angel,* was published in 1951, and Stevens' *Collected Poems* appeared in 1954.

THE SNOW MAN

One must have a mind of winter
To regard the frost and the boughs
Of the pine-trees crusted with snow;

And have been cold a long time
To behold the junipers shagged with ice,   5
The spruces rough in the distant glitter

Of the January sun; and not to think
Of any misery in the sound of the wind,
In the sound of a few leaves,

Which is the sound of the land   10
Full of the same wind
That is blowing in the same bare place

For the listener, who listens in the snow,
And, nothing himself, beholds
Nothing that is not there and the nothing that is.   15

OF MODERN POETRY

The poem of the mind in the act of finding
What will suffice. It has not always had
To find: the scene was set; it repeated what
Was in the script.
              Then the theatre was changed   5
To something else. Its past was a souvenir.

It has to be living, to learn the speech of the place.
It has to face the men of the time and to meet
The women of the time. It has to think about war
And it has to find what will suffice. It has   10
To construct a new stage. It has to be on that stage
And, like an insatiable actor, slowly and
With meditation, speak words that in the ear,
In the delicatest ear of the mind, repeat,
Exactly, that which it wants to hear, at the sound   15
Of which, an invisible audience listens,
Not to the play, but to itself, expressed
In an emotion as of two people, as of two
Emotions becoming one. The actor is
A metaphysician in the dark, twanging   20
An instrument, twanging a wiry string that gives
Sounds passing through sudden rightnesses, wholly
Containing the mind, below which it cannot descend,
Beyond which it has no will to rise.
                                        It must   25
Be the finding of a satisfaction, and may
Be of a man skating, a woman dancing, a woman
Combing. The poem of the act of the mind.

William Carlos Williams

William Carlos Williams (1883–1963), like his close contemporary Wallace
Stevens, was an American modernist who stayed at home, spiritually as well as
physically, unlike those other American modernists T. S. Eliot and Ezra Pound.
Eliot and Pound lived in Europe and saw their poetry as international. Even more
than Stevens, Williams saw his work as being "in the American grain" (to quote
the title of one of his books of essays), closely linked to the physical fact of the
American landscape. Williams was born in Rutherford, New Jersey. He earned an
M.D. at the University of Pennsylvania, interned in New York City, did postdoc-
toral work in Germany, and practiced pediatric medicine in Rutherford for almost
forty years, until 1951, when the first of a series of strokes forced retirement upon
him. His first major book was *Spring and All* (1923). Most of his poetry was short,
but at the end of his life he published the epic *Paterson,* which takes Paterson, New
Jersey, to be exemplary in some ways of American history and American life.

SPRING AND ALL

By the road to the contagious hospital[1]
under the surge of the blue
mottled clouds driven from the
northeast—a cold wind. Beyond, the

---

[1] Hospital for contagious diseases.

waste of broad, muddy fields
brown with dried weeds, standing and fallen   5

patches of standing water
the scattering of tall trees

All along the road the reddish
purplish, forked, upstanding, twiggy   10
stuff of bushes and small trees
with dead, brown leaves under them
leafless vines—

Lifeless in appearance, sluggish
dazed spring approaches—   15

They enter the new world naked,
cold, uncertain of all
save that they enter. All about them
the cold, familiar wind—

Now the grass, tomorrow   20
the stiff curl of wildcarrot leaf
One by one objects are defined—
It quickens:[2] clarity, outline of leaf

But now the stark dignity of
entrance—Still, the profound change   25
has come upon them: rooted, they
grip down and begin to awaken

BURNING THE CHRISTMAS GREENS

Their time past, pulled down
cracked and flung to the fire
—go up in a roar

All recognition lost, burnt clean
clean in the flame, the green   5
dispersed, a living red,
flame red, red blood wakes
on the ash—

and ebbs to a steady burning
the rekindled bed become   10
a landscape of flame

[2] Comes to life.

At the winter's midnight
we went to the trees, the coarse
holly, the balsam and
the hemlock for their green   15

At the thick of the dark
the moment of the cold's
deepest plunge we brought branches
cut from the green trees

to fill our need, and over   20
doorways, about paper Christmas
bells covered with tinfoil
and fastened by red ribbons

we stuck the green prongs
in the windows hung   25
woven wreaths and above pictures
the living green. On the

mantle we built a green forest
and among those hemlock
sprays put a herd of small   30
white deer as if they

were walking there. All this!
and it seemed gentle and good
to us. Their time past,
relief! The room bare. We   35

stuffed the dead grate
with them upon the half burnt out
log's smoldering eye, opening
red and closing under them

and we stood there looking down.   40
Green is a solace
a promise of peace, a fort
against the cold (though we

did not say so) a challenge
above the snow's   45
hard shell. Green (we might
have said) that, where

small birds hide and dodge
and lift their plaintive
rallying cries, blocks for them   50
and knocks down

the unseeing bullets of
the storm. Green spruce boughs
pulled down by a weight of
snow—Transformed!   55

Violence leaped and appeared.
Recreant! roared to life
as the flame rose through and
our eyes recoiled from it.

In the jagged flames green   60
to red, instant and alive. Green!
those sure abutments . . . Gone!
lost to mind

and quick in the contracting
tunnel of the grate   65
appeared a world! Black
mountains, black and red—as

yet uncolored—and ash white,
an infant landscape of shimmering
ash and flame and we, in   70
that instant, lost,

breathless to be witnesses,
as if we stood
ourselves refreshed among
the shining fauna of that fire.   75

H. D. (Hilda Doolittle)

Hilda Doolittle (1886–1961), who wrote under the pen name H. D., was known
during her lifetime as perhaps the quintessential Imagist poet. The term was Ezra
Pound's; Imagists were to abandon regular rhythm and rhyme as well as discursive, explanatory passages and rely instead upon the power of vivid images. H. D.
was an Imagist, it was true, but we have come to recognize that she was much more
than that. She grew up in Bethlehem, Pennsylvania. When her father, an astronomer, took a job as director of the observatory at the University of Pennsylvania,
Hilda met Ezra Pound, then an undergraduate. After two years at Bryn Mawr, she
moved to London, where Pound continued to advise her and suggested the name
H. D. She also met and married the English poet Richard Aldington. When the
marriage broke up after Aldington returned from World War I, H. D. became the
lover and the lifelong friend of Winifred Ellerman, a wealthy Englishwoman who
wrote under the name Bryher. In addition to short Imagist poems, H. D. wrote
fiction and autobiography, most notably perhaps *Tribute to Freud* (1956), an account of her psychoanalysis with Sigmund Freud. Her long poem *Helen in Egypt*
was published in 1961.

SEA ROSE

Rose, harsh rose,
marred and with stint of petals,
meagre flower, thin,
sparse of leaf,

more precious   5
than a wet rose,
single on a stem—
you are caught in the drift.

Stunted, with small leaf,
you are flung on the sand,   10
you are lifted
in the crisp sand
that drives in the wind.

Can the spice-rose
drip such acrid fragrance   15
hardened in a leaf?

HELEN[1]

All Greece hates
the still eyes in the white face,
the lustre as of olives
where she stands,
and the white hands.   5

All Greece reviles
the wan face when she smiles,
hating it deeper still
when it grows wan and white,
remembering past enchantments   10
and past ills.

Greece sees unmoved,
God's daughter, born of love,
the beauty of cool feet
and slenderest knees,   15
could love indeed the maid,
only if she were laid,
white ash amid funereal cypresses.

[1] Helen of Troy, whose elopement with Paris was the cause of the Trojan War.

Marianne Moore

Marianne Moore (1887–1972) grew up in Pennsylvania and was graduated from Bryn Mawr College with a degree in biology and histology. (She often used scientific and technical language in her poetry.) After graduating in 1909, traveling in Europe, and teaching for four years at the United States Indian School in Carlisle, Pennsylvania, she lived with her mother in Brooklyn until the mother's death in 1947. She became editor of *The Dial,* an influential literary magazine, in 1925. The poet H. D. and her friend Winifred Ellerman (Bryher) arranged without her knowledge to have Moore's first book of poems published in England: *Poems* (1921). It was followed by many other volumes, and a *Complete Poems* was published in 1967. Moore was a witty and ingenious poet, best known for her complex verse forms. But her poetry is full of ideas as well, about the nature of poetry (and the poetry of nature, especially animals) and about human value systems.

POETRY

I, too, dislike it: there are things that are important beyond
    all this fiddle.
  Reading it, however, with a perfect contempt for it, one
    discovers in
  it after all, a place for the genuine. 5
    Hands that can grasp, eyes
    that can dilate, hair that can rise
      if it must, these things are important not because a

high-sounding interpretation can be put upon them but because
    they are 10
  useful. When they become so derivative as to become
    unintelligible,
  the same thing may be said for all of us, that we
    do not admire what
    we cannot understand: the bat 15
      holding on upside down or in quest of something to

eat, elephants pushing, a wild horse taking a roll, a tireless wolf
    under
  a tree, the immovable critic twitching his skin like a horse that
    feels a flea, the base- 20
  ball fan, the statistician—
    nor is it valid
      to discriminate against 'business documents and

school-books';[1] all these phenomena are important. One must

---

[1] "Diary of Tolstoy (Dutton) p. 84. 'Where the boundary between prose and poetry lies, I shall never be able to understand. The question is raised in manuals of style, yet the answer to it lies beyond me.

make a distinction   25
however: when dragged into prominence by half poets, the
    result is not poetry,
nor till the poets among us can be
    'literalists of
    the imagination'[2]—above   30
        insolence and triviality and can present

for inspection, 'imaginary gardens with real toads in them', shall
    we have
it. In the meantime, if you demand on the one hand,
the raw material of poetry in   35
    all its rawness and
    that which is on the other hand
        genuine, you are interested in poetry.

NEVERTHELESS

you've seen a strawberry
        that's had a struggle; yet
        was, where the fragments met,

a hedgehog or a star-
        fish for the multitude   5
        of seeds. What better food

than apple seeds—the fruit
        within the fruit—locked in
        like counter-curved twin

hazelnuts? Frost that kills   10
        the little rubber-plant-
        leaves of *kok-saghyz*[1] -stalks, can't

harm the roots; they still grow
        in frozen ground. Once where
        there was a prickly-pear-   15

leaf clinging to barbed wire,
        a root shot down to grow
        in earth two feet below;

Poetry is verse; prose is not verse. Or else poetry is everything with the exception of business documents and school books' " (Moore's note).

[2] "Yeats' *Ideas of Good and Evil* (A. H. Bullen), p. 182. 'The limitation of his view was from the very
intensity of his vision; he was a too literal realist of imagination, as others are of nature; and because
he believed that the figures seen by the mind's eye, when exalted by inspiration, were "external
existences," symbols of divine essences, he hated every grace of style that might obscure their linea-
ments' " (Moore's note).

[1] Russian dandelion.

as carrots form mandrakes[2]
 or ram's-horn root some-
  times. Victory won't come   20

to me unless I go
 to it; a grape tendril
  ties a knot in knots till

knotted thirty times—so   25
 the bound twig that's undergone and over-gone, can't stir.

The weak overcomes its
 menace, the strong over-
  comes itself. What is there   30

like fortitude! What sap
 went through that little thread
  to make the cherry red!

T. S. Eliot

T. S. Eliot (1888–1965) was an overpowering influence on English and American poets during the first two-thirds of the twentieth century, and, though his stock has fallen considerably—the critic Harold Bloom has disparagingly called Eliot and Ezra Pound "The Cowley and Cleveland of this age"—his impact on several generations of poets must still be reckoned with. Eliot was born in St. Louis into a wealthy family. After attending Harvard, he settled in England, supporting himself first by teaching, then by working in a bank, and finally by working in publishing. "The Love Song of J. Alfred Prufrock" and "Preludes" (both 1915) attracted some attention, but "The Waste Land" (1922) caused a sensation, seeming to capture the sense of futility and meaninglessness of the postwar period. Eliot himself was far from finding the world meaningless, growing steadily more conservative in his literary tastes, his politics and his religion. *Four Quartets* (1935–43) expressed religious belief as strongly as "The Waste Land" had seemed to express the opposite. In his later years, Eliot turned to playwriting, in a series of verse dramas that developed religious themes in the mode of drawing-room comedy.

THE LOVE SONG OF J. ALFRED PRUFROCK

S'io credessi che mia resposta fosse
a persona che mai tornasse al mondo,
questa fiamma staria senza più scosse.
Ma per ciò che giammai di questo fondo
non tornò vivo alcun, s'i'odo il vero,
senza terma d'infamia ti respondo.[1]

---

[2] Mandrakes have a divided root said to resemble two legs.
[1] These words are spoken in the *Divine Comedy* to Dante by the spirit of Guido da Montefeltro, speaking from a flickering flame in the eighth circle of Hell. (See next page for English translation.)

Let us go then, you and I,
When the evening is spread out against the sky
Like a patient etherised upon a table;
Let us go, through certain half-deserted streets,
The muttering retreats   5
Of restless nights in one-night cheap hotels
And sawdust restaurants with oyster-shells:
Streets that follow like a tedious argument
Of insidious intent
To lead you to an overwhelming question . . .   10
Oh, do not ask, 'What is it?'
Let us go and make our visit.

In the room the women come and go
Talking of Michelangelo.

The yellow fog that rubs its back upon the window-panes,   15
The yellow smoke that rubs its muzzle on the window-panes,
Licked its tongue into the corners of the evening,
Lingered upon the pools that stand in drains,
Let fall upon its back the soot that falls from chimneys,
Slipped by the terrace, made a sudden leap,   20
And seeing that it was a soft October night,
Curled once about the house, and fell asleep.

And indeed there will be time
For the yellow smoke that slides along the street
Rubbing its back upon the window-panes;   25
There will be time, there will be time
To prepare a face to meet the faces that you meet;
There will be time to murder and create,
And time for all the works and days[2] of hands
That lift and drop a question on your plate;   30
Time for you and time for me,
And time yet for a hundred indecisions,
And for a hundred visions and revisions,
Before the taking of a toast and tea.

In the room the women come and go   35
Talking of Michelangelo.

If I believed that my reply were to anyone
who would ever return to the world,
this flame would remain quiet,
but since no one from this ditch
has ever returned alive, if I hear the truth,
I will answer without fear or infamy.
　　　　　Dante, *Inferno* XXVII.61–66,
　　　　　trans. H. R. Huse.

[2] An allusion to the *Works and Days* of the eighth-century Greek poet Hesiod. The allusion is ironic, since the *Works and Days* deals with the real labor of peasants rather than with the idle chatter of this scene.

And indeed there will be time
To wonder, 'Do I dare?' and, 'Do I dare?'
Time to turn back and descend the stair,
With a bald spot in the middle of my hair— 40
(They will say: 'How his hair is growing thin!)
My morning coat, my collar mounting firmly to the chin,
My necktie rich and modest, but asserted by a simple pin—
(They will say: 'But how his arms and legs are thin!')
Do I dare 45
Disturb the universe?
In a minute there is time
For decisions and revisions which a minute will reverse.

For I have known them all already, known them all—
Have known the evenings, mornings, afternoons, 50
I have measured out my life with coffee spoons;
I know the voices dying with a dying fall
Beneath the music from a farther room.
    So how should I presume?

And I have known the eyes already, known them all— 55
The eyes that fix you in a formulated phrase,
And when I am formulated, sprawling on a pin,
When I am pinned and wriggling on the wall,
Then how should I begin
To spit out all the butt-ends of my days and ways? 60
    And how should I presume?

And I have known the arms already, known them all—
Arms that are braceleted and white and bare
(But in the lamplight, downed with light brown hair!)?
Is it perfume from a dress 65
That makes me so digress?
Arms that lie along a table, or wrap about a shawl.
    And should I then presume?
    And how should I begin?

        .   .   .   .   .   .

Shall I say, I have gone at dusk through narrow streets 70
And watched the smoke that rises from the pipes
Of lonely men in shirt-sleeves, leaning out of windows? . . .

I should have been a pair of ragged claws
Scuttling across the floors of silent seas.

        .   .   .   .   .   .

And the afternoon, the evening, sleeps so peacefully! 75
Smoothed by long fingers,
Asleep . . . tired . . . or it malingers,
Stretched on the floor, here beside you and me.
Should I, after tea and cakes and ices,
Have the strength to force the moment to its crisis? 80
But though I have wept and fasted, wept and prayed,

Though I have seen my head (grown slightly bald) brought in upon a
    platter,[3]
I am no prophet—and here's no great matter;
I have seen the moment of my greatness flicker,
And I have seen the eternal Footman hold my coat, and snicker,   85
And in short, I was afraid.

And would it have been worth it, after all,
After the cups, the marmalade, the tea,
Among the porcelain, among some talk of you and me,
Would it have been worth while,   90
To have bitten off the matter with a smile,
To have squeezed the universe into a ball
To roll it towards some overwhelming question,
To say: 'I am Lazarus,[4] come from the dead,
Come back to tell you all, I shall tell you all'—   95
If one, settling a pillow by her head,
    Should say: 'That is not what I meant at all.
    That is not it, at all.'

And would it have been worth it, after all,
Would it have been worth while,
After the sunsets and the dooryards and the sprinkled streets,   100
After the novels, after the teacups, after the skirts that trail along the floor—
And this, and so much more?—
It is impossible to say just what I mean!
But as if a magic lantern threw the nerves in patterns on a screen:
Would it have been worth while   105
If one, settling a pillow or throwing off a shawl,
And turning toward the window, should say:
    'That is not it at all,
    That is not what I meant, at all.'

     110
No! I am not Prince Hamlet, nor was meant to be;
Am an attendant lord, one that will do
To swell a progress,[5] start a scene or two,
Advise the prince; no doubt, an easy tool,
Deferential, glad to be of use,   115
Politic, cautious, and meticulous;
Full of high sentence,[6] but a bit obtuse;
At times, indeed, almost ridiculous—
Almost, at times, the Fool.

I grow old . . . I grow old . . .   120
I shall wear the bottoms of my trousers rolled.

---

[3] John the Baptist was beheaded and his head brought in upon a platter at the request of Salome. See
Matthew 14:1–12.
[4] Lazarus was raised from the dead by Jesus. See John 11:1–44.
[5] A ceremonial procession, often represented in Elizabethan plays.
[6] Sententiously expressed opinions.

Shall I part my hair behind? Do I dare to eat a peach?
I shall wear white flannel trousers, and walk upon the beach.
I have heard the mermaids singing, each to each.

I do not think that they will sing to me.   125

I have seen them riding seaward on the waves
Combing the white hair of the waves blown black
When the wind blows the water white and back.

We have lingered in the chambers of the sea
By sea-girls wreathed with seaweed red and brown   130
Till human voices wake us, and we drown.

Edna St. Vincent Millay

Edna St. Vincent Millay (1892–1950) grew up in Maine, one of three daughters reared by a single mother. She was graduated from Vassar College in 1917 and moved to Greenwich Village, where she acted and wrote articles and plays as well as poetry. In 1923, she married the widower of the well-known feminist Inez Mulholland. She was quite prolific, publishing a volume every year or so for a quarter-century. She won the Pulitzer Prize in 1923. Her literary reputation waned for a time, probably because of her conservative, traditional style, but her work has begun to attract readers and critics again.

LOVE IS NOT ALL: IT IS NOT MEAT NOR DRINK

Love is not all: it is not meat nor drink
Nor slumber nor a roof against the rain;
Nor yet a floating spar to men that sink
And rise and sink and rise and sink again;
Love can not fill the thickened lung with breath,   5
Nor clean the blood, nor set the fractured bone;
Yet many a man is making friends with death
Even as I speak, for lack of love alone.
It well may be that in a difficult hour,
Pinned down by pain and moaning for release,   10
Or nagged by want past resolution's power,
I might be driven to sell your love for peace,
Or trade the memory of this night for food.
It well may be. I do not think I would.

ON THOUGHT IN HARNESS

My falcon to my wrist
Returns
From no high air.

I sent her toward the sun that burns
Above the mist;   5
But she has not been there.

Her talons are not cold; her beak
Is closed upon no wonder;
Her head stinks of its hood, her feathers reek
Of me, that quake at the thunder.   10

Degraded bird, I give you back your eyes forever, ascend now
    whither you are tossed;
Forsake this wrist, forsake this rhyme;
Soar, eat ether, see what has never been seen; depart, be lost,
But climb.

Langston Hughes

Langston Hughes (1902–67) was one of the most able and successful African-
American writers of the first half of the twentieth century. Born in Joplin, Missouri, Hughes spent much of his childhood in Cleveland, where he was graduated
from high school. After a year at Columbia University, Hughes held a series of
menial jobs for several years, continuing, however, to write and publish poetry. He
gravitated to Harlem, where he became one of the leading figures in the Harlem
Renaissance, that flowering of African-American art in the 1920s. His first book of
poetry, *The Weary Blues*, appeared in 1926. By 1930, Hughes was not only a
well-known writer but also an acknowledged leader of African-American writing.
He published collections of African-American writing and his own poetry, fiction,
plays and screenplays, and a series of comic sketches about a character named
Jesse B. Semple, a sort of black Will Rogers; Hughes collected the Semple sketches
into four volumes. Hughes, unlike many of his fellow African-American writers,
delighted in black speech and culture and delighted in recreating it in his writing.

THE NEGRO SPEAKS OF RIVERS

I've known rivers:
I've known rivers ancient as the world and older than the flow of
    human blood in human veins.

My soul has grown deep like the rivers.

I bathed in the Euphrates when dawns were young.   5
I built my hut near the Congo and it lulled me to sleep.
I looked upon the Nile and raised the pyramids above it.
I heard the singing of the Mississippi when Abe Lincoln
    went down to New Orleans, and I've seen its muddy
    bosom turn all golden in the sunset.   10

I've known rivers:
Ancient, dusky rivers.

My soul has grown deep like the rivers.

FREEDOM TRAIN

I read in the papers about the
    Freedom Train.
I heard on the radio about the
    Freedom Train.
I seen folks talkin' about the   5
    Freedom Train.
Lord, I been a-waitin' for the
    Freedom Train!

Down South in Dixie only train I see's
Got a Jim Crow car set aside for me.   10
I hope there ain't no Jim Crow on the Freedom Train,
No back door entrance to the Freedom Train,
No signs FOR COLORED on the Freedom Train,
No WHITE FOLKS ONLY on the Freedom Train.

      I'm gonna check up on this   15
        Freedom Train.

Who's the engineer on the Freedom Train?
Can a coal black man drive the Freedom Train?
Or am I still a porter on the Freedom Train?
Is there ballot boxes on the Freedom Train?   20
When it stops in Mississippi will it be made plain
Everybody's got a right to board the Freedom Train?

      Somebody tell me about this
        Freedom Train!

The Birmingham station's marked COLORED and WHITE.   25
The white folks go left, the colored go right—
They even got a segregated lane.
Is that the way to get aboard the Freedom Train?

      I got to know about this
        Freedom Train!   30

If my children ask me, *Daddy, please explain*
Why there's Jim Crow stations for the Freedom Train?
What shall I tell my children? . . . *You* tell me—
'Cause freedom ain't freedom when a man ain't free.

      But maybe they explains it on the   35
        Freedom Train.

When my grandmother in Atlanta, 83 and black,
Gets in line to see the Freedom,
Will some white man yell, *Get back!*
A Negro's got no business on the Freedom Track!   40

>Mister, I thought it were the
>   Freedom Train!

Her grandson's name was Jimmy. He died at Anzio.
He died for real. It warn't no show.
The freedom that they carryin' on this Freedom Train,   45
Is it for real—or just a show again?

>Jimmy wants to know about the
>   Freedom Train.

Will *his* Freedom Train come zoomin' down the track
Gleamin' in the sunlight for white and black?   50
Not stoppin' at no stations marked COLORED nor WHITE,
Just stoppin' in the fields in the broad daylight,
Stoppin' in the country in the wide-open air
Where there never was no Jim Crow signs nowhere,
No Welcomin' Committees, nor Politicians of note,   55
No Mayors and such for which colored can't vote,
And nary a sign of a color line—
For the Freedom Train will be yours and mine!

Then maybe from their graves in Anzio
The G.I.'s who fought will say, *We wanted it so!*   60
Black men and white will say, *Ain't it fine?*
At home they got a train that's yours and mine!

>Then I'll shout, *Glory for the*
>   *Freedom Train!*
>I'll holler, *Blow your whistle,*   65
>   *Freedom Train!*
>*Thank God-A-Mighty! Here's the*
>   *Freedom Train!*
>*Get on board our Freedom Train!*

Gwendolyn Brooks

Gwendolyn Brooks was born (in 1917) in Topeka, Kansas, and grew up in Chicago, where she has continued to live. Her poetry collection *A Street in Bronzeville* (1945) first brought her name before the public; it was something of an African-American *Spoon River Anthology* in its evocation of the characters in a black community. In 1950, she became the first African-American to win the Pulitzer Prize, for her collection *Annie Allen* (1949). In the 1960s Brooks's work changed its character somewhat, as she wrote more simply and drew more upon African-American forms. The Poet Laureate of Illinois, Brooks uses her position and standing to help other African-American writers, especially young ones.

WE REAL COOL

The Pool Players. Seven at the Golden Shovel.

We real cool. We
Left school. We

Lurk late. We
Strike straight. We

Sing sin. We   5
Thin gin. We

Jazz June. We
Die soon.

A BRONZEVILLE MOTHER LOITERS IN MISSISSIPPI.
MEANWHILE, A MISSISSIPPI MOTHER BURNS BACON

From the first it had been like a
Ballad. It had the beat inevitable. It had the blood.
A wildness cut up, and tied in little bunches,
Like the four-line stanzas of the ballads she had never quite
Understood—the ballads they had set her to, in school.   5

Herself: the milk-white maid, the "maid mild"
Of the ballad. Pursued
By the Dark Villain. Rescued by the Fine Prince.
The Happiness-Ever-After.
That was worth anything.   10
It was good to be a "maid mild."
That made the breath go fast.

Her bacon burned. She
Hastened to hide it in the step-on can, and
Drew more strips from the meat case. The eggs and sour-
    milk biscuits   15
Did well. She set out a jar
Of her new quince preserve.

. . . But there was a something about the matter of the
    Dark Villain.
He should have been older, perhaps.
The hacking down of a villain was more fun to think about   20
When his menace possessed undisputed breadth, undisputed
    height,
And a harsh kind of vice.
And best of all, when his history was cluttered
With the bones of many eaten knights and princesses.

The fun was disturbed, then all but nullified   25
When the Dark Villain was a blackish child
Of fourteen, with eyes still too young to be dirty,
And a mouth too young to have lost every reminder
Of its infant softness.

That boy must have been surprised! For   30
These were grown-ups. Grown-ups were supposed to be
    wise.
And the Fine Prince—and that other—so tall, so broad,
    so
Grown! Perhaps the boy had never guessed
That the trouble with grown-ups was that under the
    magnificent shell of adulthood, just under,
Waited the baby full of tantrums.   35
It occurred to her that there may have been something
Ridiculous in the picture of the Fine Prince
Rushing (rich with the breadth and height and
Mature solidness whose lack, in the Dark Villain, was
    impressing her,
Confronting her more and more as this first day after the
    trial   40
And acquittal wore on) rushing
With his heavy companion to hack down (unhorsed)
That little foe.
So much had happened, she could not remember now what
    that foe had done
Against her, or if anything had been done.   45
The one thing in the world that she did know and knew
With terrifying clarity was that her composition
Had disintegrated. That, although the pattern prevailed,
The breaks were everywhere. That she could think
Of no thread capable of the necessary   50
Sew-work.

She made the babies sit in their places at the table.
Then, before calling Him, she hurried
To the mirror with her comb and lipstick. It was necessary
To be more beautiful than ever.   55
The beautiful wife.
For sometimes she fancied he looked at her as though
Measuring her. As if he considered, Had she been worth It?
Had *she* been worth the blood, the cramped cries, the little
    stuttering bravado,
The gradual dulling of those Negro eyes,   60
The sudden, overwhelming *little-boyness* in that barn?
Whatever she might feel or half-feel, the lipstick necessity
    was something apart. He must never conclude
That she had not been worth It.

He sat down, the Fine Prince, and
Began buttering a biscuit. He looked at his hands.   65

He twisted in his chair, he scratched his nose.
He glanced again, almost secretly, at his hands.
More papers were in from the North, he mumbled. More
    meddling headlines.
With their pepper-words, "bestiality," and "barbarism,"
    and
"Shocking."   70
The half-sneers he had mastered for the trial worked
    across
His sweet and pretty face.

What he'd like to do, he explained, was kill them all.
The time lost. The unwanted fame.
Still, it had been fun to show those intruders   75
A thing or two. To show that snappy-eyed mother,
That sassy, Northern, brown-black————

Nothing could stop Mississippi.
He knew that. Big Fella
Knew that.   80
And, what was so good, Mississippi knew that.
Nothing and nothing could stop Mississippi.
They could send in their petitions, and scar
Their newspapers with bleeding headlines. Their governors
Could appeal to Washington. . . .   85

"What I want," the older baby said, "is 'lasses on my
    jam."
Whereupon the younger baby
Picked up the molasses pitcher and threw
The molasses in his brother's face. Instantly
The Fine Prince leaned across the table and slapped   90
The small and smiling criminal.

She did not speak. When the Hand
Came down and away, and she could look at her child,
At her baby-child,
She could think only of blood.   95
Surely her baby's cheek
Had disappeared, and in its place, surely,
Hung a heaviness, a lengthening red, a red that had no end.
She shook her head. It was not true, of course.
It was not true at all. The   100
Child's face was as always, the
Color of the paste in her paste-jar.
She left the table, to the tune of the children's lamenta-
    tions, which were shriller
Than ever. She
Looked out of a window. She said not a word. *That*   105
Was one of the new Somethings—
The fear,
Tying her as with iron.

Suddenly she felt his hands upon her. He had followed her
To the window. The children were whimpering now.   110
Such bits of tots. And she, their mother,
Could not protect them. She looked at her shoulders, still
Gripped in the claim of his hands. She tried, but could not
  resist the idea
That a red ooze was seeping, spreading darkly, thickly,
  slowly,
Over her white shoulders, her own shoulders,   115
And over all of Earth and Mars.

He whispered something to her, did the Fine Prince, something
About love, something about love and night and intention.

She heard no hoof-beat of the horse and saw no flash of
  the shining steel.

He pulled her face around to meet   120
His, and there it was, close close,
For the first time in all those days and nights.
His mouth, wet and red,
So very, very, very red,
Closed over hers.   125

Then a sickness heaved within her. The courtroom Coca-
  Cola,
The courtroom beer and hate and sweat and drone,
Pushed like a wall against her. She wanted to bear it.
But his mouth would not go away and neither would the
Decapitated exclamation points in that Other Woman's
  eyes.   130

She did not scream.
She stood there.
But a hatred for him burst into glorious flower,
And its perfume enclasped them—big,
Bigger than all magnolias.   135

The last bleak news of the ballad.
The rest of the rugged music.
The last quatrain.

Mary TallMountain

Mary TallMountain (b. 1918) is an Athabaskan Indian and is also part Russian and Scots-Irish. Born in Alaska, she lives now in San Francisco but returns frequently to Alaska to teach and conduct workshops among the native people. She did not begin writing until 1970. Since then, she has published *Nine Poems* (1979) and *There Is No Word for Goodbye* (1981), which won a Pushcart Prize.

THE LAST WOLF

the last wolf hurried toward me
through the ruined city
and I heard his baying echoes
down the steep smashed warrens
of Montgomery Street and past   5
the few ruby-crowned highrises
left standing
their lighted elevators useless

passing the flickering red and green
of traffic signals   10
baying his way eastward
in the mystery of his wild loping gait
closer the sounds in the deadly night
through clutter and rubble of quiet blocks

I heard his voice ascending the hill   15
and at last his low whine as he came
floor by empty floor to the room
where I sat
in my narrow bed looking west, waiting
I heard him snuffle at the door and   20
I watched
he trotted across the floor

he laid his long gray muzzle
on the spare white spread
and his eyes burned yellow   25
his small dotted eyebrows quivered

Yes, I said.
I know what they have done.

THE IVORY DOG FOR MY SISTER

oh sister
how those Nulato sled dogs howl
at sunset it

haunted me a lifetime
by river's edge they mourn   5
passing the hours
of summer

all day
they lie chained
bury their noses under   10

fluffy Malemute tail plumes
grey-blue eyes watch the People
getting ready the nets and
fishwheels

under strong skulls they   15
remember winter
the rushing freedom how they
leap and bark and when the
harness tangles
how the whip whistles down to nudge   20
their furry backs

Clem says fifty years ago he
and a half wolf husky named Moose
worked the team how
icy the air   25
how white
the flowing breaths
of men and dogs

the ivory dog
from Nulato a piece of my life   30
I thought he could tell you
about the moving of time and
what it is to wait
he's done it so long now
sister   35
the ivory dog is true

Now watching you in lamplight,
I see scarlet berries
Ripened,
Your sunburned fingers plucking them.   40
With hesitant words,
With silence,
From inmost space
I call you
Out of the clay.   45

It is time at last,
This dawn.
Stir. Wake. Rise.
Glide gentle between my bones,
Grasp my heart. Now   50
Walk beside me. Feel
How these winds move, the way
These mornings breathe.
Let me see you new
In this light.   55

You—
Wrapped in brown,
Myself repeated
Out of dark and different time.

Amy Clampitt

Amy Clampitt was born (in 1920) and reared in rural Iowa. After graduation from
Grinnell College, she moved to New York, where she worked as a librarian for the
National Audubon Society and as a freelance researcher and editor. Although she
had been writing poetry and fiction for years, she did not begin publishing until
1978, when she was fifty-eight years old. Her first book, *The Kingfisher*, appeared in
1983. It was followed by *What the Light Was Like* (1985) and *Archaic Figure* (1987).
Clampitt has a distinctive poetic voice, using a rich syntax and vocabulary to deal
with subjects less often drawn from her New York years than from her Iowa ones.

IOLA, KANSAS

Riding all night, the bus half empty, toward the interior,
among refineries, trellised and turreted illusory cities,
the crass, the indispensable wastefulness of oil rigs
offshore, the homunculi swigging at the gut of a continent:

the trailers, the semis, the vans, the bumper stickers,   5
slogans in day-glo invoking the name of Jesus, who knows
what it means: the air waves, the brand name, the backyard
Barbie-doll barbecue, graffiti in video, the burblings,

the dirges: *heart like a rock, I said Kathy I'm lost,*
the scheme is a mess, we've left Oklahoma, its cattle,   10
sere groves of pecan trees interspersing the horizonless
belch and glare, the alluvium of the auto junkyards,

we're in Kansas now, we've turned off the freeway,
we're meandering, as again night falls, among farmsteads,
the little towns with the name of a girl on the watertower,   15
the bandstand in the park at the center, the churches

alight from within, perpendicular banalities of glass
candy-streaked purple-green-yellow (who is this Jesus?),
the strangeness of all there is, whatever it is, growing
stranger, we've come to a rest stop, the name of the girl   20

on the watertower is Iola: no video, no vending machines,
but Wonder Bread sandwiches, a pie: "It's boysenberry,
I just baked it today," the woman behind the counter
believably says, the innards a purply glue, and I eat it

with something akin to reverence: free refills from   25
the Silex on the hot plate, then back to our seats,
the loud suction of air brakes like a thing alive, and
the voices, the sleeping assembly raised, as by an agency

out of the mystery of the interior, to a community—
and through some duct in the rock I feel my heart go out,   30
out here in the middle of nowhere (the scheme is a mess)
to the waste, to the not knowing who or why, and am happy.

Mitsuye Yamada

Mitsuye Yamada was born (in 1923) in Kyushu, Japan, but her family emigrated
to America and she grew up in Seattle, Washington. When World War II broke
out, her family, along with other Japanese-Americans, was sent to an internment
camp in Idaho. Her collection of poems *Camp Notes and Other Poems* (1976) deals
with this experience and was partially written while she was in the camp. A second
collection, *Desert Run: Poems and Stories,* was published in 1989. She now lives in
California, where she teaches at Cypress College.

THE CLUB

He beat me with the hem of a kimono
worn by a Japanese woman
this prized
painted
wooden statue   5
carved to perfection
in Japan or maybe Hong Kong.

She was usually on display
in our living room atop his bookshelf
among his other overseas treasures   10
I was never to touch.
She posed there most of the day
her head tilted
her chin resting lightly
on the white pointed fingertips   15
of her right hand
her black hair
piled high on her head
her long slim neck bared
to her shoulders.   20
An invisible hand
under the full sleeve
clasped her kimono
close to her body

its hem flared 25
gracefully around her feet.

That hem
made fluted red marks
on these freckled arms
my shoulders 30
my back.
That head
inside his fist
made camel
bumps 35
on his knuckles.
I prayed for her
that her pencil thin neck
would not snap
or his rage would be unendurable. 40
She held fast for me
didn't even chip or crack.

One day, we were talking
as we often did the morning after.
Well, my sloe-eyed beauty, I said 45
have you served him enough?
I dared to pick her up with one hand
I held her gently by the flowing robe
around her slender legs.
She felt lighter than I had imagined. 50
I stroked her cold thighs
with the tips of my fingers
and felt a slight tremor.

I carried her into the kitchen and wrapped her
in two sheets of paper towels 55
We're leaving
I whispered
you and I
together.

I placed her 60
between my clothes in my packed suitcase.
That is how we left him
forever.

Mari Evans

Mari Evans was born (in 1923) in Toledo, Ohio, and attended the University of Toledo. She has taught at Indiana University, Purdue, Northwestern, Cornell, Washington University in St. Louis, and the State University of New York–Albany.

She has published three books of poetry—*Where Is All the Music?* (1968), *I Am a Black Woman* (1970), and *Night Star* (1980)—as well as two plays and two children's books. She is also the editor of *Black Women Writers 1950–80: A Critical Evaluation* (1984).

I AM A BLACK WOMAN

I am a black woman
the music of my song
some sweet arpeggio of tears
is written in a minor key
and I   5
can be heard humming in the night
Can be heard
          humming
in the night

I saw my mate leap screaming to the sea   10
and I/with these hands/cupped the lifebreath
from my issue in the canebrake
I lost Nat's swinging body in a rain of tears[1]
and heard my son scream all the way from Anzio[2]
for Peace he never knew. . . . I   15
learned Da Nang and Pork Chop Hill[3]
in anguish
Now my nostrils know the gas
and these trigger tire/d fingers
seek the softness in my warrior's beard   20

I
am a black woman
tall as a cypress
strong
beyond all definition still   25
defying place
and time
and circumstance
    assailed
        impervious   30
          indestructible
Look
    on me and be
renewed

[1] Nat Turner (1800–31) led an abortive slave rebellion and was hanged. The first two memories, of the mate leaping into the sea and of having a child in the canebrake, are apparently generalized vignettes of slave life.
[2] Town in central Italy and scene of a major World War II battle.
[3] Scenes of bloody engagements in Vietnam and Korea, respectively.

early in the mornin

early in the mornin
j w brown
whippin' his woman
knockin' her around
said "answer my question   5
if you please"
(how she goin' to answer
on her knees
groanin' 'Buddy, Buddy!
wake up and go   10
get L C and Mar'gret—he's
hurtin' me so . .')

Buddy went flyin
down the stairs in
brown pants over his   15
underwear but
L C and Margaret wouldn't stir
said: "Buddy we sympathize
with her . . . but from what you say
far as we can see   20
if she'd answer his question
he'd let her be"

she never did answer
(far as we could hear)
but the sight of that child   25
in his underwear his
head bent down
shoes untied and all
comin' back alone
down the empty Mall   30
was sad.
More than I could bear.
Makes you wonder if
anybody cares
anywhere   35

Galway Kinnell

Galway Kinnell was born (in 1927) in Providence, Rhode Island, and educated at
Princeton University and the University of Rochester. His first book of poems
appeared in 1960: *What a Kingdom It Was*. Since then, he has published about
twenty books of poetry. In 1983, his *Selected Poems* won both the Pulitzer Prize and
the American Book Award. Kinnell describes his progress as a poet in terms of
openness. As he has developed, he has given up the often intricate, traditional
rhyme schemes of his early poetry in favor of simpler diction and form. Like many

of his fellow modern poets—Marianne Moore and Ted Hughes, for example—he
has written extensively about animals, finding in the identification with an animal
a passage between the world of nature and that of human beings.

THE PORCUPINE

1

Fatted
on herbs, swollen on crabapples,
puffed up on bast and phloem,[1] ballooned
on willow flowers, poplar catkins, first
leafs of aspen and larch,   5
the porcupine
drags and bounces his last meal through ice,
mud, roses and goldenrod, into the stubbly high fields.

2

In character
he resembles us in seven ways: 10
he puts his mark on outhouses,
he alchemizes by moonlight,
he shits on the run,
he uses his tail for climbing,
he chuckles softly to himself when scared,   15
he's overcrowded if there's more than one of him per five
     acres,
his eyes have their own inner redness.

3

Digger of
goings across floors, of hesitations
at thresholds, of   20
handprints of dread
at doorpost or window jamb, he would
gouge the world
empty of us, hack and crater
it   25
until it is nothing, if that
could rid it of all our sweat and pathos.
Adorer of axe
handles aflow with grain, of arms
of Morris chairs, of hand   30
crafted objects

---

[1] Technical names for parts of plants. *Bast* is the woody outer layer of the stems of such plants as flax
and hemp. *Phloem* is the food-conducting tissue of vascular plants.

steeped in the juice of fingertips,
of surfaces wetted down
with fist grease and elbow oil,
of clothespins that have   35
grabbed our body-rags by underarm and crotch . . .

Unimpressed—bored—
by the whirl of the stars, by *these*
he's astonished, ultra-
Rilkean angel![2]   40

for whom the true
portion of the sweetness of earth
is one of those bottom-heavy, glittering, saccadic[3]
bits
of salt water that splash down   45
the haunted ravines of a human face.

4

A farmer shot a porcupine three times
as it dozed on a tree limb. On
the way down it tore open its belly
on a broken   50
branch, hooked its gut,
and went on falling. On the ground
it sprang to its feet, and
paying out gut heaved
and spartled through a hundred feet of goldenrod   55
before
the abrupt emptiness.

5

The Avesta[4]
puts porcupine killers
into hell for nine generations, sentencing them   60
to gnaw out
each other's hearts for the
salts of desire.

I roll
this way and that in the great bed, under   65
the quilt
that mimics this country of broken farms and woods,
the fatty sheath of the man

[2] Rainer Maria Rilke (1875–1926), in his *Duino Elegies*, constructed a hierarchical cosmology from animals to angels.
[3] Having to do with a rapid, intermittent eye movement.
[4] Sacred writing of the ancient Persians.

melting off,
the self-stabbing coil   70
of bristles reversing, blossoming outward—
a red-eyed, hard-toothed, arrow-stuck urchin
tossing up mattress feathers,
pricking the
woman beside me until she cries.   75

6

In my time I have
crouched, quills erected,
Saint
Sebastian[5] of the
scared heart, and been   80
beat dead with a locust club
on the bare snout.
And fallen from high places
I have fled, have
jogged   85
over fields of goldenrod,
terrified, seeking home,
and among flowers
I have come to myself empty, the rope
strung out behind me   90
in the fall sun
suddenly glorified with all my blood.

7

And tonight I think I prowl broken
skulled or vacant as a
sucked egg in the wintry meadow, softly chuckling, blank   95
template of myself, dragging
a starved belly through the lichflowered acres,
where
burdock looses the ark of its seed
and thistle holds up its lost bloom   100
and rosebushes in the wind scrape their dead limbs
for the forced-fire
of roses.

Peter Blue Cloud

Peter Blue Cloud is an Akwesasne Mohawk, born (in 1927) in Quebec and now living in northern California. A former structural ironworker, he has published several volumes of poetry, including *Coyote and Friends* (1976), *Turtle, Bear, and Wolf* (1976), *Back Then Tomorrow* (1978), *White Corn Sister* (1979), and *Elderberry Flute Song* (1982).

[5]St. Sebastian was martyred by being shot full of arrows.

STONE MOUNTAIN FACE

Charlie bends to feed the stove
dry oak, and the fire throws
a glow of red in early morning,
I take the pot of coffee and pour
our cups full, and the dog   5
thumps her tail upon the floor

her nose twitching in sleep
and from the odor of deerhide
soaking in a bucket, I roll
a smoke and we listen to   10
the steady beat of rain against
the roof and dripping to ground

"yes, I was thinking of the drum
we are trying to make
and trying to dream its shape   15
and sound, but the images weren't
clear at all, and the rain was
drumming all night, so I came
over to ask if you'd heard its
shape and sound yet,"   20
                    Charlie
asked this, sipping coffee and
the firebox door was still open
and our shadows were quivering
giants across the floor and wall   25
and the sharp odor of ripe hide
stung the room, and I hesitated,

awhile, remembering a strange dream
mixed with the outdoor thru window
earlier visions of the night, of   30
lightning upright walking the
sagebrush land, electric-charged
walkers become outlines
of bright colored dancing, dancing
acrid puffs of power of feet   35
to ground, dancing a frenzy
across sand dunes to the west
toward the first low hills
of Storm Mountain, where clouds
of dark waters are born   40

and reflect themselves in the lake
of a tamarack village up there
in the midst of fir and cedar
where bear and deer wander, "no,
I heard no shape or sound but   45
saw a thing, a wondrous, though

frightening thing, I can't remember
just what it might be, a thought
of my own imagining, or something
I'm to know about later, maybe,''   50
and Charlie looked at the hide
soaking, floating, staring

                                        and

beckoned me with a hand,
I leaned toward the bucket   55
and looked, and then stared,
a shiver sort of at my neck
as I saw the twisted face the
folds of hide portrayed, and
"yes, I think that's what it   60

wants to be, and I guess we
have to do it.'' and right then
began a frantic pace to do
a thing we didn't know just
what or why, but knew only   65
that it was ours to do, and

                                        don't

thank me hastily, the oak tree
whispered, as I cut slim branches,
and basket willow, too, hoped   70
I knew what it was all about, and
sapling maple thongs peeled
slippery singing, questioned my
fingers nervous haste, as rain
now slowed to drizzle waiting,   75
and four hands in a harmony
of expectation began to fashion
a hoop and frame, peeling and
bending and lashing fast with
swift, sure fingers.   80

then hands again in counter motion
twisting the deerhide to dryness,
the acrid odor dilating nostrils
and racing pulses, forcibly,
as does the blood smells of   85
fresh killed creatures.

and in a silence of concentration
we lashed the hide to frame
with a coiling lace of maple,
and cut, and inserted fingers   90
pulling, tearing, forcing
the shape of a face known,
uneven and crude, mouth
curled and open over hide teeth,
close to fire, the face was leaned,   95

then we pried open paint cans
and dipped with fingers, and
the face was given a lightning
flash of white, and streaking
dots of blue, and orange lips,   100
brown earth eye circles and
black night hollow cheeks,

Now long and flowing strands of maple
were tied to frame and knotted
then hide which was head   105
of the face we had fashioned.
and we looked at it only once,
finished and drying further
close to stove's heat,
        then   110
we drove to the leveling-off
place of Storm Mountain, close
to tamarack village, beneath an old
fir, there we stood the face, against
the mound of roots and tilted stone,   115
    and sat beneath a neighbor cedar,
to join the forming storm above
our heads, and maybe walked
about on stabbing lightning legs,
and the black and writhing clouds   120
were our stomachs in the mind
of storm thinking, as branches
    whipped in storm dance,
and saplings like grass in earth dance,
heads low to ground, backs arched,   125
in willing pain,
                    the drumming
of rainfingers to shivering branches,
the howling slapping wind,
                            and   130
    the after calm,
    and two old men
                    bent with age
slowly
    making their way   135
    down Storm Mountain.

Maya Angelou

Perhaps the best known of the many accomplishments of Maya Angelou (b. 1928)
is her ongoing, multivolume autobiography, beginning with *I Know Why the Caged
Bird Sings* (1970) and continuing through four more volumes. She was born in St.
Louis but with her brother Bailey went to Stamps, Arkansas, to live with their
grandmother when their parents divorced. This is recounted in *I Know Why the
Caged Bird Sings*. She later studied music and dance and toured Europe and North

Africa in *Porgie and Bess*. Angelou has taken an active part in public life, carrying on a heavy schedule of lecturing and serving as Northern Coordinator for the Southern Christian Leadership Conference. She is also a member of the advisory board of the Women's Prison Association and of the board of trustees of the American Film Institute and has held many other posts. She has published several volumes of poetry, including *Just Give Me a Cool Drink of Water 'fore I Diiie* (1971), *Oh Pray My Wings Are Gonna Fit Me Well* (1975), and *Shaker, Why Don't You Sing?* (1983).

A GOOD WOMAN FEELING BAD

The blues may be the life you've led
Or midnight hours in
An empty bed. But persecuting
Blues I've known
Could stalk   5
Like tigers, break like bone,

Pend like rope in
A gallows tree,
Make me curse
My pedigree,   10

Bitterness thick on
A rankling tongue,
A psalm to love that's
Left unsung,

Rivers heading north   15
But ending South,
Funeral music
In a going-home mouth.

All riddles are blues,
And all blues are sad,   20
And I'm only mentioning
Some blues I've had.

A GEORGIA SONG

We swallow the odors of Southern cities,
Fat back boiled to submission,
Tender evening poignancies of
Magnolia and the great green
Smell of fresh sweat.   5
In Southern fields,
The sound of distant
Feet running, or dancing,

And the liquid notes of
Sorrow songs,   10
Waltzes, screams and
French quadrilles float over
The loam of Georgia.

Sing me to sleep, Savannah.

Clocks run down in Tara's halls and dusty   15
Flags droop their unbearable
Sadness.

Remember our days, Susannah

Oh, the blood-red clay,
Wet still with ancient   20
Wrongs, and Abenaa
Singing her Creole airs to
Macon.
We long, dazed, for winter evenings
And a whitened moon,   25
And the snap of controllable fires.

Cry for our souls, Augusta.

We need a wind to strike
Sharply, as the thought of love
Betrayed can stop the heart.   30
An absence of tactile
Romance, no lips offering
Succulence, nor eyes
Rolling, disconnected from
A Sambo face.   35

Dare us new dreams, Columbus.

A cool new moon, a
Winter's night, calm blood,
Sluggish, moving only
Out of habit, we need   40
Peace.

Oh Atlanta, oh deep, and
Once lost city,

Chant for us a new song. A song
Of Southern peace.   45

Maurice Kenny

Maurice Kenny is an Akwesasne Mohawk and was born (in 1929) and reared in upstate New York. His first collection of poetry was *Dead Letters Sent* (1959). He has now published ten volumes of poetry, including *The Mama Poems* (1984), for which he won the American Book Award, *Is Summer This Bear* (1985), *Rain and Other Fictions* (1985), *Greyhounding This America* (1986), and *Between Two Rivers: Selected Poems* (1987).

NORTH

In Memory of My Father

sun rises over mountain lakes
fox breakfasts in the berry patch
mice tug grains into the burrow
grass has a way of growing

north by the old trail   5
north by the Susquehanna
north by the Freeway
north by the Alleghany or Mohawk
airlines that sweep you into north country,
deerland, Thousand Islands;   10
north by semis that scoop up the north
and wrap its aluminum soil about
your Thanksgiving turkey
and freeze your pudding in the refrigerator

north by any path would be north   15
north . . . by north star, northern
northern country of villages and cowpens
cheese factories and crab apples, trout
diseased elms and sick roots
fenced meadows slit by snowmobiles   20
sky cracked by television wires,
and hunters blizzard to cabins
by dead deer . . . the last kept
them abandoned in the north snow
from home in Staten Island   25

north of strawberry fields, milkweed
north of maples running sap to boil
north, north country, northern New York
where corn grew to the table and squash
and bean covered the valleys   30
north of strawberry fields, north of sumac
north of smoke, north of tomorrow, today
of yesterday that was and is and will be

for strawberries grow forever
and wolves will cross the frozen river   35
under the flight of geese

sun humps over hills and horses
muskrats in the stream
swimming to shore with a mouthful of mud
the bee sipping honey   40
minnows in the creek

grass has a way of growing
north, north along the old trail

guard the eastern gate

LAND

1976

Torn, tattered, yet rugged
in the quick incline of bouldered hills
crab appled, cragged, lightning-struck birch, cedar;
wilderness muzzled; forests . . . kitchen tables and bedposts
of foreign centuries; meadows cowed   5
beyond redemption, endurance, violated
by emigres' feet, and vineyards alien
to indigenous squash and berry,
fragile lupine and iris of the pond;
while wounded willows bend in the snow   10
blown north by the west wind

1820

spring lifts under drifts, saplings
hold to the breeze, larks sing, strawberries
crawl from under snow, woodchucks run
stone walls of new cemeteries and orchards;   15
apples blossom, thistle bloom

(Madame de Feriet's ghost prowls the miraged bridge
spanning Black River and her mansion lanterns
glow in the clear darkness of the French dream,
hazeled in the richness of her opulence   20

the lands she would hold out to tenants for rent
have neither clearings nor plows;
the disillusionment loried her trunks to France,
her mansion to ashes, her bridge to dust in 1871,
her savings to pittance, her dream to agony   25

Madame de Feriet gave her French aristocratic manner
to a signpost at the edge of the country road,
tangled now by yellow roses and purple vetch)

1976

April lifts from under the drifts of grey
snow piled by plows ruthless in their industrial   30
might to free roads and make passage
for trucks and automobiles to hurry to the grave
with dead horses in the far pasture
that no longer sustains the hunger of bleating lambs

virgin spring lifts, its muddy face scarred   35
and mapped with trails of progress, its smoke
rising in pine, maple, flowering aspen,
chicory weed and clods, manure of waste, whey,
abandoned farm houses and barns shaking in the wind . . .
blind old men caught without canes in the storm;   40
spring bloody in its virginity, its flow corrupted,
raped in zoned courts of law that struck quarried hills . . .
a great god's lance thrust in the quickness of electric sun

rage of spring rivers, swollen with anger . . .
cold voice growling through the night . . . swirling,   45
swallowing the soft shoulders of shoreline;
the rage of the aged shackled to history
and the crumbling bones of its frame, fisted against
the night, shaking the cane against the dark, the bats
fluttering in the balmy summer eve, fireflies creeping   50
through the young green grass of the long fresh meadows

1812

the north, the north aches in the bones, the land,
in the elms' limbs gently singing in that August
breeze, bereft of holiday and festival, ghost and voice . . .
tunneled by gophers; ticks and fleas stuck to an old dog's back   55

(General Brown marched his men to Sacketts Harbor,
struck the British in the red belly
and went home to lift a pint to his deeds
and captured acres, to ville a town, erect a fence)

1976

the gooseberry is diseased, and the elm,   60
stone walls broken, sky cracked, pheasants
and young muskrats sterilized, and fields

mulleins are my arms

mulleins are my arms
and chicory
the sinew of my flesh;
May strawberries
are the blood of my legs   5
and the sun of summer;
maples are my head
and the sugar the sap of my tongue
that runs in the warm wind;
crocus are my eyes;   10
turtle the feet of my winter

seasons are a rumble of
herded old cows
coming to barn from pastures
before snow covers corn,   15
and the mare jumps the fence
crazy from glittering stones

marvelous is the miracle of spring
and, also, the weight of winter;
the plum which ripens,   20
drops seeds into pockets of earth
vacated by gophers;
the rabbits that sleep,
and the bear

incredible is the force of April,   25
and the lust of January;
in the summer of the second year
mulleins grow another branch,

chicory spreads to another field

Stephen Shu Ning Liu

Stephen Shu Ning Liu was born in 1930 in Fu-Ling, China. He briefly studied at Nanking University, taught Chinese in Taiwan for one year, and emigrated to America in 1952. He earned a doctorate at the University of North Dakota and now teaches at Clark County Community College in Las Vegas. He has published poems in more than two hundred magazines; in 1982 he collected them, translated them into Chinese, and published them in a bilingual format as *Dream Journeys to China* (New World Press, Beijing, China, 1982). His poem "At the King's Funeral" appears earlier in this section on page 589.

NIGHT SAILING

A night in Las Vegas, jazz-mad,
the smoke-riding wind suffers insomnia,
fanning my sampan, I know not how,
through the furry gorges on Yangtze:

a mountain pass yellows in October: 5
beyond the clearing of an orange grove
her cottage sits glimmering in the sun.
What is she doing in the house,
embroidering a fan, recalling
sparrow-awakening fields, silk-green,   10
where dragonflies glided in pairs?
And what promises under a cloud, how long ago?

I float into the half-illumined trees,
as if into the sea, against the wind
that capsizes my boat and hurls me far away   15
from her door, in night Las Vegas, jazz-mad.

HOME THOUGHTS

I've seen July the Fourth in the Chicago sky,
I've seen New Year's Eve at Times Square, yet I
like better the first star burning above our
dark oakwoods, in one of those frog-mad evenings.

I've heard cataracts at Jasper Park,   5
I've heard thunder surfs along the Monterey Bay,
yet my mind turns to a mountain stream prattling
through the summer, like a loquacious village wench.

I've drained exotic gin inside a palace,
I've tasted confections from a queen's plate,   10
yet all I've missed is a sip from a bowl of
sweetened lotus roots, lake-water-cool.

I've traveled through the sun's fiery arch,
I've watched ivory gulches on the moon, yet I would
give ten heavens away for one-acre grass of home   15
and a stone sleep, in one of those frog-mad evenings.

THE WILD HORSE STAR

A palmist entreats me, in blurred Brooklyn:
in a minute, I'm overwhelmed by the cries
of Old Yang, the iron-mouth fortuneteller

in that village of weeping willows;
even on a raining day,   5
wearing their saucer-shaped bamboo hats,
country folks stood outside Yang's door,
outnumbering the meadow mushrooms.

"With all your treasures," Old Yang said
to my mother, shaking his white-sedged beard,   10
"you can't make your son stay in this land,
for the Wild Horse Star winks at him."
And in the silk rain of the early spring,
that foreboding voice haunted us:
"Beware the Wild Horse Star, beware!"   15
Mother gave him a silver dollar, and as we
walked home that morning, what did she say
while some catkins fell from the willow tree?

Rosario Morales

Rosario Morales (b. 1930) was born and reared in New York City. She was studying at Hunter College when she and her husband decided to move to Puerto Rico
to protest the Korean War. They remained there for five years, farming part of an
abandoned coffee plantation. Her work has been published in a number of anthologies, and she has co-authored a book with her daughter Aurora: *Getting Home
Alive* (1986).

MY REVOLUTION

My revolution is not starched and ironed
  (Stand over the ironing board, wield the hot iron)
It is not ass-girdled and breast-bound
  (Wiggle and worm into it every morning, wiggle and worm out
    of it every night)   5
My revolution is not white-gloved and white-suited
  (Soak it and scrub it and bleach it . . . and wear it?
    Only with care!)
It's not thick-soled and heavy high-booted
  (Lift the left foot. Down. Now lift the other.)   10

My revolution is comfortable
  hard-wearing
    long-standing
      versatile!
I can wear it in the fields   15
I can wear it to go dancing
    do the dishes
    do the laundry
    see the movie
    do the marching   20

My revolution is not cut from a pattern, *I* designed it.

It's homemade and hand-crafted
It's got seams to let out
   and hems to let down
      tucks to take in   25
         darts to take out.

My revolution is comfortable
   hard-wearing
      long-lasting
         versatile!   30

My revolution fits
So well
Sometimes
I don't know I'm wearing it.

So, when your revolution doesn't fit   35
   ain't your size
   chokes
   binds
   climbs up your crotch
   bites into your breasts   40
   or rubs your heels raw

  Give it back!
  Turn it in!
  Ask for a refund!
     and make yourself another   45
      make one of your very own.

OLD

Una[1]

My mother at thirty was as luminous as a Puerto Rican dawn over
the cream sand beaches curving in and out and around the island.
She was like the moist fruit of the mango, like the fronds of the royal
palm in the wind. And I knew thirty was what I was going to be
when I lost the skeleton I wore, when I grew old, grew beautiful and   5
free.

Dos

Skin
practicing to be old—

[1] "One." The sections of the poems are numbered in Spanish (*Una, Dos, Tres,* etc.).

lining up,
squaring off: 10
tracings
etchings
bas relief.

Look!
Over the blue   15
creek beds of my veins,
how the wrinkling
ripples sparkle
in the sun.

Tres

Que clase de vieja[2] will I be when I knew none, grew up in New York   20
City when El Barrio[3] was young like me and grandmothers grew in
Puerto Rico, when grandmothers were kept fresh in boxes of pictures under the bed and became flesh only the summer I was going
to be ten. We took a long sickening boat ride of a week to the magical landscape of Naranjito and on its one street I became "¡Mira!   25
la hija de Lola, la de Mercedes."[4] Abuela[5] Mercedes was just like
her photograph: large, cotton-wrapped, her breasts squared off onto her
middle, hammocks of face dripping onto her chin, cushions of
her melting into the brown floorboards. She smelled like maduros frying. And while the music from the jukebox across the street flies about   30
her shoulders, crashes into the hibiscus bush, the guayaba, and as she
stands imperturbable, solid, only her flesh giving way, I am comforted
and afraid.

I cannot turn to my other grandmother. Abuela Rosario sat small,
sat thin, sat straight and hard in a hard chair, knobbed hands on   35
a knobbed stick. She beat one girl and ten boys into adulthood,
and my father beat me, and I beat my babies and bit my hands and
looked for knobs.

Cuatro

Crow's wings not feet—pinions
anchored to my eyes.   40
They spread in flight only

---

[2] "What kind of old woman."   [3] "Neighborhood" (the Puerto Rican section of New York).
[4] "Look! The daughter of Lola, of Mercedes."   [5] "Grandmother."

when I smile.
I smile.

Cinco

She warned me as she added sugar to the roasting coffee beans to
blacken the brew, "Don't go out into the damp air, the cool night,   45
after a day tostando café[6] in an open pan over a hot fire, porque te
va' a pa'mar."[7] She said, "¡Cuidao, o te va' a pa'mar!"[8] And she meant
that the moment I hit the evening chill my warm skin would shrivel
and wrinkle and ruck, a surrealer Rip Van Winkle. Only a moment
would go by and I'd be old, old, older than old doña Cornelia her-   50
self, who always carefully wrapped a towel around her head and shoulders like a shawl before she left her burnt-sugar brown kitchen and
stepped out beneath the banana leaves hiding the stars.

Seis

Maga was Jane's mother, my best friend's mother, was Alabama-born,
high-born, white as her hair, and even after twenty years in Puerto   55
Rico couldn't speak Spanish, and her a communist like her red-haired
daughter, like her Puerto Rican son-in-law, like me.

I wanted to be like her when I grew old, I wanted the freedom to
say what I liked, when I liked, to whom I liked. I wanted to pour
Lapsang Souchong out of a china teapot into the endless afternoon   55
and tell others what to do and how to do it. I wanted what I thought it
felt like, sitting tall and high-handed, hair cut short and crisp,
straight spine keeping the cops from stepping through the door to
take her son-in-law César away, lean slacks bending, lean hands reaching to grasp the garden weeds and smack the roots free of soil, grasp-   60
ing, too, at her daughter's home, her son, her time and when Jane
died, she reached for mine.

I couldn't give you that! But oh, Maga, will I sit as you sat, lone-
handed, sipping tepid tea into the night?

Siete

Stop!   65
I don't want my scalp

---

[6] "Roasting coffee."   [7] "Because you will freeze."   [8] "Careful! Or you're going to freeze."

shining through a few thin hairs.
Don't want my neck skin to hang—
    neglected cobweb—in the corner of my chin.

Stop! at ruckling ruches of skin   70
    at soft sags,
        bags of tongue tickling breast and belly.
    at my carved face.

No further.
Stop.   75

Ocho

no quiero morir[9]

Gary Snyder

The poetry of Gary Snyder (b. 1930) combines Zen Buddhism with left-wing politics, Native American lore, and ecology in search of an inner, spiritual order. Born in San Francisco and raised in Portland, Oregon, Snyder earned a B.A. in anthropology at Reed College and did further study at Indiana University and Berkeley. He has traveled widely in Japan and India and has spent three extended periods studying Buddhism in Japanese monasteries. He has published more than twenty-five volumes of poetry and won the Pulitzer Prize in 1975.

RIPRAP[1]

Lay down these words
Before your mind like rocks.
        placed solid, by hands
In choice of place, set
Before the body of the mind   5
        in space and time:
Solidity of bark, leaf, or wall
        riprap of things:
Cobble of milky way,
        straying planets,   10
These poems, people,
        lost ponies with
Dragging saddles—

[9] "I don't want to die."
[1] Riprap is an assemblage of broken stone laid down as a foundation in water or soft ground.

and rocky sure-foot trails.
The worlds like an endless   15
    four-dimensional
Game of *Go*.
        ants and pebbles
In the thin loam, each rock a word
        a creek-washed stone   20
Granite: ingrained
        with torment of fire and weight
Crystal and sediment linked hot
        all change, in thoughts,
As well as things.   25

AXE HANDLES

One afternoon the last week in April
Showing Kai how to throw a hatchet
One-half turn and it sticks in a stump.
He recalls the hatchet-head
Without a handle, in the shop   5
And go gets it, and wants it for his own.
A broken-off axe handle behind the door
Is long enough for a hatchet,
We cut it to length and take it
With the hatchet head   10
And working hatchet, to the wood block.
There I begin to shape the old handle
With the hatchet, and the phrase
First learned from Ezra Pound
Rings in my ears!   15
"When making an axe handle
        the pattern is not far off."
And I say this to Kai
"Look: We'll shape the handle
By checking the handle   20
Of the axe we cut with—"
And he sees. And I hear it again:
It's in Lu Ji's *Wên Fu*, fourth century
A.D. "Essay on Literature"—in the
Preface: "In making the handle   25
Of an axe
By cutting wood with an axe
The model is indeed near at hand."
My teacher Shih-hsiang Chen
Translated that and taught it years ago   30
And I see: Pound was an axe,
Chen was an axe, I am an axe
And my son a handle, soon
To be shaping again, model
And tool, craft of culture,   35
How we go on.

Carter Revard

Carter Revard (Osage, b. 1931) grew up in the country outside Pawhuska, Oklahoma, with six brothers and sisters. He went to the University of Tulsa on a scholarship from a radio program named Whiz Kids, studied at Oxford on a Rhodes scholarship, and then earned a doctorate in English at Yale. He is now professor of English at Washington University in St. Louis, where he teaches Chaucer and historical linguistics. Revard's poetry is collected in *Ponca War Dancers* (1980). His poetry is quite varied, but he seems to have found his poetic voice in the speech of his native Oklahoma.

SUPPORT YOUR LOCAL POLICE DOG

The night before my Uncle Carter got shot
Trying to hijack a load of bootleg whiskey,
He dressed fit to kill, put on his lilac hairoil,
And leaned down to the mirror in our living room
To comb the hair back over his bald spot, humming   5
'Corinne, Corinne, where have you been so long?'
I don't know if 'Corinne' tipped the other bunch off,
But I hope he put it to her before they killed him.
I bet if there was any he was getting his.
—Jesus, I never saw him standing still   10
Or lying down, till they led me past his coffin.
He should have been a lord in Boswell's time,
Though he'd most likely been laid up with gout
Before he was forty, had that kind of drive.
More drive than brains though. Hell, man out on parole   15
For robbing a bank, and his hip not very long healed
Where the cop in ambush shot him trying to surrender,
Had no more sense than go after those bottled-in-bonders
From Kansas City. You KNOW they'd be in cahoots
With all the local crooks and laws. We couldn't   20
See why he'd let himself get talked into trying.
My Uncle Dwain said it was a put-up job,
Carter knew too much, the gang had him bumped off.

Well, the last time I was home for a visit,
Leaving behind these earnest city people   25
Who keep DISCOVERING crime and poverty
Like tin cans tied to their suburbs' purebred tails
Till they run frothing, yapping for law and order,
I thought of the big police dog Carter brought home
His last time there and kenneled by the chickenhouse: 30

Nobody was going to steal OUR stock, by God.
(Later the damn dog got to killing turkeys
On a neighbor's place; we had to let it be shot.)
—The gilt mirror he'd gazed at his bald spot in
Had been demoted, now hung dim in the bathroom.   35

I patted my Old Spice lather on and shaved
As suavely as he had combed, and smelled as good.
He never lived to grow white whiskers like mine;
I knew the smartest crooks don't ever need guns,
And I would never walk out into the night   40
To get myself shot down, the way he did.
I've got more brains. But while he lived, I admit,
He was my favorite uncle; guts, charm, and drive.
He would have made a perfect suburban mayor—
Or maybe, manager for some liquor chain.   45

DRIVING IN OKLAHOMA

On humming rubber along this white concrete
    lighthearted between the gravities
of source and destination like a man
        halfway to the moon
    in this bubble of tuneless whistling   5
at seventy miles an hour from the windvents,
        over prairie swells rising
    and falling, over the quick offramp
    that drops to its underpass and the truck
        thundering beneath as I cross   10
with the country music twanging out my windows,
        I'm grooving down this highway feeling
technology is freedom's other name when
        —a meadowlark
    comes sailing across my windshield   15
        with breast shining yellow
    and five notes pierce
        the windroar like a flash
        of nectar on mind
gone as the country music swells up and   20
        drops me wheeling down
    my notch of cement-bottomed sky
    between home and away
                                and wanting
to move again through country that a bird   25
    has defined wholly with song
        and maybe next time see how
    he flies so easy, when he sings.

Thomas C. Dent

Thomas C. Dent was born (in 1932) and grew up in New Orleans. He was
educated at Morehouse College and Goddard College and has worked in journalism and public relations. He was one of the founders of the Umbra writers'
workshop in New York; of *Callaloo*, an important periodical of black writing; and

of the Congo Square Writers Union of New Orleans. Collections of his poems
include *Magnolia Street* (1976, rpt. 1987) and *Blue Lights and River Songs* (1982).
He has also written a number of plays.

POEM FOR WILLIE MAYS[1]

<pre>
to catch a fly ball
is pluckin cherries from
                              a tree
easy lazy fluid function
                              motion   5
disconbomulating a
thousand stark stone
skyscrapers
is
Willie Ricks makin a   10
                              fool
of the Mississippi state
                              highway patrol
pretendin to be
                              a good nigger   15
is
the sun comin up &
      goin down
                              every day
to form a dark-hued people   20
who understand
                              the red of sun-ray
                              the blue of night-hue
is
the Viet Cong launching   25
a surprise raid
in the Mekon Delta[2]
is
sho-be-do-be-do
laughing at   30
oooh-la-la
without oooh-la-la knowing it be
laughed at
is
Monk[3] ripping off terse messages   35
is caressed Miles[4] whispers
is
</pre>

---

[1] Famous baseball player with the New York (later San Francisco) Giants (1951–72). He hit 660 home
runs, the third highest total on record.
[2] Delta of the Mekon (or Mekong) River near Ho Chi Minh City (Saigon), scene of heavy fighting in
the Vietnam War.
[3] Thelonious Monk (1917–82), famous black jazz pianist.
[4] Miles Davis (1926–1990), famous black jazz trumpeter.

a whole stadium
of dancing minds eyes.

Willie Mays catching a fly ball   40
is rhythm
on a honeymoon
with space

SECRET MESSAGES

(For Danny Barker)

rain
rain drenches the city[1]
as we move past
stuffed black mammies
chained to Royal St. praline shops   5
check it out

past Bourbon St. beer cans
shadowed moorish cottages
ships slipping down the riversnake past
images of the bullet-riddled bodies of   10
Mark Essex & Bras Coupe
buried in the beckoning of the blk
shoeshine boy
when it rains it pours
check it out   15

past blk tap-dancers of the shit-eating grin
the nickle & dime shake-a-leg
shades of weaving flambeau[2] carriers
of the dripping oil & the grease-head
"we *are* mardi gras" one said   20
check it out

past that to where you play yr banjo
"it's plantation time agin" you say to us
& we laugh . . .
outside a blk cabdriver helps crippled   25
Sweet Emma into the front seat
she done boogied the piano another night
for maybe the 250th year
she laughs loudly to herself as tourists
watch   30
there is an Ashanti[3] saying
when one hears something but does not understand, they say:
            "like singing to the white man"
check it out

---

[1] New Orleans, as the street names indicate.   [2] Torch.   [3] Major ethnic group in Ghana.

tripping past raindrops with the ancient slick-haired   35
Jelly Roll piano player[4]
to listen to some "modern musicians"
at Lu & Charlie's
& the old piano player saying
"they can play a little bit can't they"   40
teasing our god of fallen masks
check it out . . .

& maybe someday when nobody is
checking it out
the drummers will come to life in   45
St. Louis No. 1 at midnight
beating out the secret messages
& all the masks will drop.
jest like we said they would.
secret messages   50
secret messages of the gods.

rain
rain drenches the city
as we move past grinning stuffed black mammies
the god of fallen masks offstage   55
waiting, waiting . . .

Etheridge Knight

Etheridge Knight was born (in 1931) in Corinth, Mississippi, and was largely
self-educated. *Poems from Prison* (1968), Knight's first book, as the title indicates,
was published while Knight was serving a prison sentence. *Black Voices from Prison*
(1971) was published soon after he was released. Further collections include *Belly
Song and Other Poems* (1975) and *Born of a Woman* (1980). The University of
Pittsburgh Press has published his collected poems, *The Essential Etheridge Knight*
(1986). In 1985 he was given the Shelley Memorial Award by the Poetry Society
of America.

THE IDEA OF ANCESTRY

1

Taped to the wall of my cell are 47 pictures: 47 black
faces: my father, mother, grandmothers (1 dead), grandfathers (both dead), brothers, sisters, uncles, aunts,
cousins (1st & 2nd), nieces, and nephews. They stare
across the space at me sprawling on my bunk. I know   5
their dark eyes, they know mine. I know their style,

---

[4] Pianist in the style of Jelly Roll Morton (1885–1941).

they know mine. I am all of them, they are all of me;
they are farmers, I am a thief, I am me, they are thee.

I have at one time or another been in love with my mother,
1 grandmother, 2 sisters, 2 aunts (1 went to the asylum),   10
and 5 cousins. I am now in love with a 7 yr old niece
(she sends me letters written in large block print, and
her picture is the only one that smiles at me).

I have the same name as 1 grandfather, 3 cousins, 3 nephews,
and 1 uncle. The uncle disappeared when he was 15, just took   15
off and caught a freight (they say). He's discussed each year
when the family has a reunion, he causes uneasiness in
the clan, he is an empty space. My father's mother, who is 93
and who keeps the Family Bible with everybody's birth dates
(and death dates) in it, always mentions him. There is no   20
place in her Bible for "whereabouts unknown."

                                    2

Each fall the graves of my grandfathers call me, the brown
hills and red gullies of mississippi send out their electric
messages, galvanizing my genes. Last yr / like a salmon quitting
the cold ocean-leaping and bucking up his birthstream / I   25
hitchhiked my way from L.A. with 16 caps[1] in my pocket and a
monkey on my back. And I almost kicked it with the kinfolks.
I walked barefooted in my grandmother's backyard / I smelled the
    old
land and the woods / I sipped cornwhiskey from fruit jars with the
    men /
I flirted with the women / I had a ball till the caps ran out   30
and my habit came down. That night I looked at my grandmother
and split / my guts were screaming for junk / but I was almost
contented / I had almost caught up with me.
(The next day in Memphis I cracked a croaker's crib for a fix).

This yr there is a gray stone wall damming my stream, and when   35
the falling leaves stir my genes, I pace my cell or flop on my bunk
and stare at 47 black faces across the space. I am all of them,
they are all of me, I am me, they are thee, and I have no children
to float in the space between.

---

[1] E.g., of heroin.

FOR LANGSTON HUGHES

Gone   Gone
Another weaver of black dreams has gone
we sat in June Bug's pad with the shades drawn
and the air thick with holy smoke, and we heard
the Lady[1] sing Langston before we knew his name.   5
and when Black Bodies stopped swinging[2] June
Bug, TG and I went out and swung on some white cats.
now I don't think the Mythmaker meant for us to do *that*
but we didn't know what else to do.

Gone   Gone   10
Another weaver of black dreams has gone

Audre Lorde

Audre Lorde (1934–92) was born in New York of parents from Grenada. She was educated at the University of Mexico, Hunter College, and Columbia University, with degrees in library science, and worked for several years as a librarian. Her first book was *The First Cities* (1968); it was followed by *Cables to Rage* (1970), *From a Land Where Other People Live* (1973), *New York Head Shop and Museum* (1975), *The Black Unicorn* (1978), *Chosen Poems: Old and New* (1982), and *Our Dead Behind Us* (1986). She also published an autobiographical novel (or "biomythography," as she called it): *Zami: A New Spelling of My Name* (1982). Lorde's early poetry was quiet and introspective. It grew steadily more emphatic and political, as she turned to themes of feminism, racial justice, and lesbianism. For the last seven years of her life, she lived on the island of St. Croix in the Virgin Islands, where she was known by an African name, "Gamba Adisa," a name that reflects her interest in pan-African issues.

STATIONS

Some women love
to wait
for life   for a ring
in the June light   for a touch
of the sun to heal them   for another   5
woman's voice   to make them whole
to untie their hands
put words in their mouths
form to their passages   sound
to their screams   for some other sleeper   10
to remember   their future   their past.

---

[1] Billie Holiday (1915–59), black jazz singer whose nickname was "Lady Day."
[2] Billie Holiday is singing "Strange Fruit," a song by Lewis Allen about lynching.

Some women wait for their right
train   in the wrong station
in the alleys of morning
for the noon to holler   15
the night come down.

Some women wait for love
to rise up
the child of their promise
to gather from earth   20
what they do not plant
to claim pain for labor
to become
the tip of an arrow   to aim
at the heart of now   25
but it never stays.

Some women wait for visions
that do not return
where they were not welcome
naked   30
for invitations to places
they always wanted
to visit
to be repeated.

Some women wait for themselves   35
around the next corner
and call the empty spot peace
but the opposite of living
is only not living
and the stars do not care.   40

Some women wait for something
to change   and nothing
does change
so they change
themselves.   45

CALL

Holy ghost woman
stolen out of your name
Rainbow Serpent
whose faces have been forgotten
Mother   loosen my tongue or adorn me   5
with a lighter burden
Aido Hwedo is coming.[1]

[1] "*Aido Hwedo:* The Rainbow Serpent; also a representation of all ancient divinities who must be
worshipped but whose names and faces have been lost in time" (Lorde's note).

On worn kitchen stools and tables
we are piecing our weapons together
scraps of different histories
do not let us shatter   10
any altar
she who scrubs the capitol toilets, listening
is your sister's youngest daughter
gnarled Harriet's anointed
you have not been without honor   15
even the young guerrilla has chosen
yells as she fires into the thicket
Aido Hwedo is coming.

I have written your names on my cheekbone   20
dreamed your eyes   flesh my epiphany
most ancient goddesses   hear me
enter
I have not forgotten your worship
nor my sisters
nor the sons of my daughters   25
my children watch for your print
in their labors
and they say Aido Hwedo is coming.

I am a Black woman   turning
mouthing your name as a password   30
through seductions   self-slaughter
and I believe in the holy ghost
mother
in your flames beyond our vision
blown light through the fingers of women   35
enduring   warring
sometimes outside your name
we do not choose all our rituals
Thandi Modise   winged girl of Soweto   40
brought fire back home in the snout of a mortar
and passes the word from her prison cell   whispering
Aido Hwedo is coming.

Rainbow Serpent who must not go
unspoken   45
I have offered up the safety of separations
sung the spirals of power
and what fills the spaces
before power unfolds or flounders
in desirable nonessentials   50
I am a Black woman   stripped down
and praying
my whole life has been an altar
worth its ending
and I say Aido Hwedo is coming.   55

I may be a weed in the garden
of women I have loved
who are still
trapped in their season
but even they shriek   60
as they rip burning gold from their skins
Aido Hwedo is coming.

We are learning by heart
what has never been taught
you are my given   fire-tongued   65
Oya Seboulisa Mawu Afrekete[2]
and now we are mourning our sisters
lost to the false hush of sorrow
to hardness and hatchets and childbirth
and we are shouting   70
Rosa Parks and Fannie Lou Hamer
Assata Shakur and Yaa Asantewa
my mother and Winnie Mandela[3] are singing
in my throat
the holy ghosts' linguist   75
one iron silence broken
Aido Hwedo is calling
calling
your daughters are named
and conceiving   80
Mother   loosen my tongue
or adorn me
with a lighter burden
Aido Hwedo is coming.

Aido Hwedo is coming.   85

Aido Hwedo is coming.

N. Scott Momaday

N. Scott Momaday (Kiowa) was born (in 1934) in Lawton, Oklahoma, and grew up
in New Mexico. He did his undergraduate work at the University of New Mexico
and his graduate work at Stanford University, where he received a Ph.D. In 1968,
he published his first novel, *House Made of Dawn,* which won the Pulitzer Prize. It
was followed the next year by *The Way to Rainy Mountain,* a mingling of Kiowa myth,
history, and autobiography. Since then, he has published another novel, *The Ancient*

---

[2] Names of African goddesses.
[3] Various strong women. Rosa Parks began the Montgomery bus strike when she refused to give up her
bus seat to a white man (Dec. 1, 1955). Fannie Lou Hamer (1918–77) was one of the founders of the
Student Non-Violent Coordinating Committee, 1961. Assata Shakur (b. 1947) was a member of the
Black Panther Party who was convicted in 1977 on flimsy evidence of killing a New Jersey state
policeman. Two years later, she escaped from prison and fled to Cuba, where she now lives. Winnie
Mandela (b. 1934) is a South African political activist.

Child (1989); two collections of poetry, *Angle of Geese and Other Poems* (1974) and *The Gourd Dancer: Poems* (1976); and an autobiography, *The Names: A Memoir* (1976). Momaday is Regent's Professor of English at the University of Arizona.

PLAINVIEW: 1

There in the hollow of the hills I see,
Eleven magpies stand away from me.

Low light upon the rim; a wind informs
This distance with a gathering of storms

And drifts in silver crescents on the grass,   5
Configurations that appear, and pass.

There falls a final shadow on the glare,
A stillness on the dark, erratic air.

I do not hear the longer wind that lows
Among the magpies. Silence disclose,   10

Until no rhythms of unrest remain,
Eleven magpies standing in the plain.

They are illusion—wind and rain revolve—
And they recede in darkness, and dissolve.

PLAINVIEW: 2

I saw an old Indian
At Saddle Mountain
He drank and dreamed of drinking
And a blue-black horse

Remember my horse running   5
    Remember my horse
Remember my horse running
    Remember my horse

Remember my horse wheeling
    Remember my horse   10
Remember my horse wheeling
    Remember my horse

Remember my horse blowing
    Remember my horse
Remember my horse blowing   15
    Remember my horse

Remember my horse standing
  Remember my horse
Remember my horse standing
  Remember my horse   20

Remember my horse hurting
  Remember my horse
Remember my horse hurting
  Remember my horse

Remember my horse falling   25
  Remember my horse
Remember my horse falling
  Remember my horse

Remember my horse dying
  Remember my horse   30
Remember my horse dying
  Remember my horse

A horse is one thing
An Indian another
An old horse is old   35
An old Indian is sad

I saw an old Indian
At Saddle Mountain
He drank and dreamed of drinking
And a blue-black horse   40

Remember my horse running
  Remember my horse
Remember my horse wheeling
  Remember my horse
Remember my horse blowing   45
  Remember my horse
Remember my horse standing
  Remember my horse
Remember my horse hurting
  Remember my horse   50
Remember my horse falling
  Remember my horse
Remember my horse dying
  Remember my horse
Remember my blue-black horse   55
Remember my blue-black horse
  Remember my horse
  Remember my horse
Remember
Remember   60

PLAINVIEW: 3

The sun appearing: a pendant
of clear cutbeads, flashing;
a drift of pollen and glitter
lapping, and overlapping night;
a prairie fire.   5

PLAINVIEW: 4[1]

Johnny cake and venison and sassafras tea,
Johnny cake and venison and sassafras tea.

Just there another house, Poor Buffalo's house.
The paint is gone from the wood, and the people are
gone from the house. Once upon a time I saw the people   5
there, in the windows and the yard. An old woman
lived there, one of whose girlhood I have often dreamed.
She was Milly Durgan of Texas, and a Kiowa captive.

Aye, Milly Durgan, you've gone now to be
Away in the country and captivity;   10
Aye, Milly Durgan, you've gone from your home
Away to the prairie forever to roam.

The warm wind lies about the house in March,
and there is a music in it, as I have heard, an
American song.   15

And it's ladies to the center
and it's gents around the row,
And we'll rally round the canebrake
and shoot the buffalo.

Sonia Sanchez

Sonia Sanchez was born (in 1934) in Birmingham, Alabama, but moved with her family to Harlem when she was nine. She graduated from Hunter College in 1955. An African-American, she joined the Nation of Islam in 1972 and advocates black militancy in response to white violence. She is a playwright as well as a poet; her plays include *The Bronx Is Next* (1970), *Sister Son/ji* (1971), and *I'm Black When I'm Singing, I'm Blue When I Ain't* (1982). Poetry collections include *Homecoming* (1969), *We a BaddDDD People* (1970), *A Blues Book for Blue Black Magical Women* (1974), *I've Been a Woman: New and Selected Poems* (1979), and *Under a Soprano Sky* (1987). Sanchez is Professor of English at Temple University.

---

[1] "The lines in italics are from two American folk songs, 'The Texian Boys' and 'Shoot the Buffalo' " (Momaday's note).

POEM NO. 10

you keep saying you were always there
waiting for me to see you.
                              you said that once
on the wings of a pale green butterfly
you rode across san francisco's hills   5
and touched my hair as i caressed
a child called militancy
you keep saying you were always there

holding my small hand
                  as i walked   10
unbending indiana streets i could not see around
and you grew a black mountain
of curves and i turned
and became soft again
you keep saying you were always there   15

repeating my name softly
                  as i slept in
slow pittsburgh blues and you made me
sweat nite dreams that danced
and danced until the morning   20
rained yo/red delirium

you keep saying you were always there
you keep saying you were always there
            will you stay love
                  now that i am here?   25

BLUES

i love a twenty yr old weekends
dig him way down until he's glad.
yeh. i love a twenty yr old weekends
dig him way down until he's glad
you see what my wanting you has   5
done gone and made me badddddd.

watched for you each evening
stood right outside my do
said i watched for you each evening
stood right outside my do   10
but you never came in and
i couldn't stand still no mo

what do you do when you need
a man so much it hurt?

i say where do you go when you   15
need a man so much it hurt?
you make it down to the corner
and start digging in the dirt.

yeh. i love a twenty yr old weekends
dig him way down until he's dry   20
yeh. i love a twenty yr old weekends
dig him way down until he's dry
you see what my needing you
has done gone and made me try.

you see what my needing you   25
has done gone and made me try.

Mark Strand

Mark Strand was born (in 1934) in Canada but moved to the United States with his parents when he was a child. He earned a B.F.A. at Yale and an M.A. at the University of Iowa. His first book of poetry was *Sleeping with One Eye Open* (1964). It was followed by *Reasons for Moving* (1968), *Darker: Poems* (1970), *The Story of Our Lives* (1973), *The Sergeantville Notebook* (1973), *Elegy for My Father* (1973), and *The Late Hour* (1978). Strand's *Selected Poems* appeared in 1980. Strand's poetry is often compared to Wallace Stevens's, because of its abstraction and its concern with perception.

KEEPING THINGS WHOLE

In a field
I am the absence
of field.
This is
always the case.   5
Wherever I am
I am what is missing.

When I walk
I part the air
and always   10
the air moves in
to fill the spaces
where my body's been.
We all have reasons
for moving.   15
I move
to keep things whole.

WHERE ARE THE WATERS OF CHILDHOOD?

See where the windows are boarded up,
where the gray siding shines in the sun and salt air
and the asphalt shingles on the roof have peeled or fallen off,
where tiers of oxeye daisies float on a sea of grass?
That's the place to begin.   5

Enter the kingdom of rot,
smell the damp plaster, step over the shattered glass,
the pockets of dust, the rags, the soiled remains of a mattress,
look at the rusted stove and sink, at the rectangular stain
on the wall where Winslow Homer's *Gulf Stream* hung.   10
Go to the room where your father and mother
would let themselves go in the drift and pitch of love,
and hear, if you can, the creak of their bed,
then go to the place where you hid.

Go to your room, to all the rooms whose cold, damp air you   15
      breathed,
to all the unwanted places where summer, fall, winter, spring,
seem the same unwanted season, where the trees you knew
      have died
and other trees have risen. Visit that other place
you barely recall, that other house half hidden.

See the two dogs burst into sight, When you leave,   20
they will cease, snuffed out in the glare of an earlier light.
Visit the neighbors down the block; he waters his lawn,
she sits on her porch, but not for long.
When you look again they are gone.

Keep going back, back to the field, flat and sealed in mist.   25
On the other side, a man and a woman are waiting;
they have come back, your mother before she was gray,
your father before he was white.

Now look at the North West Arm, how it glows a deep
      cerulean blue.
See the light on the grass, the one leaf burning, the cloud   30
that flares. You're almost there, in a moment your parents
will disappear, leaving you under the light of a vanished star,
under the dark of a star newly born. Now is the time.

Now you invent the boat of your flesh and set it upon the
      waters
and drift in the gradual swell, in the laboring salt.   35
Now you look down. The waters of childhood are there.

Nelly Wong

Nelly Wong was born (in 1934) and raised in Oakland, California. She works as an administrative assistant at San Francisco State University and is active in the clerical workers' union, AFSCME 3218, the Freedom Socialist Party, and Radical Women (a socialist feminist organization). Her books include *Dreams in Harrison Railroad Park* (1977) and *The Death of the Long Steam Lady* (1986). She has been featured, along with Mitsuye Yamada, in a documentary film: *Mitsuye and Nelly: Asian American Poets,* produced by Allie Light and Irving Saraf. Her poem "Not From the Food" appears earlier in this section on page 601.

DREAMS IN HARRISON RAILROAD PARK

We sit on a green bench in Harrison Railroad Park.
As we rest, I notice my mother's thighs
thin as my wrists.
I want to hug her
but I am afraid.   5

A bearded man comes by, asks for a cigarette.
We shake our heads, hold out our empty hands.
He shuffles away and picks up
a half-smoked stub.
His eyes light up.   10
Enclosed by the sun he dreams
temporarily.

Across the street an old woman hobbles by.
My mother tells me: She is unhappy here.
She thinks she would be happier   15
back home.
But she has forgotten.

My mother's neighbor dreams
of warm nights in Shanghai,
of goldfish swimming in a courtyard pond,   20
of having a young maid
anoint her tiny bound feet.

And my mother dreams
of wearing dresses that hang in her closet,
of swallowing soup without pain,   25
of coloring eggs
for an unborn grandson.

I turn and touch my mother's eyes.
They are wet
and I dream   30
and I dream
of embroidering
new skin.

Amiri Baraka

Amiri Baraka was born (in 1934) LeRoi Jones in Newark, N.J. He went to Howard University in Washington, D.C., served in the Air Force, and then earned an M.A. in German literature at Columbia University. In the late fifties and early sixties, Jones (as he was then called) founded a magazine named *Yugen* and the Totem Press in New York, publishing the work of such writers as Charles Olson, Robert Duncan, Gary Snyder, and Frank O'Hara. He also founded the Black Arts Repertory Theatre in Harlem, for which he wrote such powerful plays as *Dutchman* (1964) and *Experimental Death Unit No. 1* (1965). In 1966 he changed his name to Amiri Baraka and moved to the slums of Newark, N.J. Here he founded Spirit House, a community center committed to social and political action. Baraka has been enormously prolific, publishing over seventy-five books. Key poetry publications are *Preface to a Twenty-Volume Suicide Note* (1961), *Black Magic: Poetry 1961–1967* (1969), and *Selected Poetry* (1979). Also published in 1979 was *Selected Plays and Prose*.

LOOK FOR YOU YESTERDAY,
HERE YOU COME TODAY

Part of my charm:
        envious blues feeling
        separation of church & state
        grim calls from drunk debutantes

Morning never aids me in my quest.   5
I have to trim my beard in solitude.
I try to hum lines from "The Poet In New York."[1]

People saw metal all around the house on Saturdays. The Phone
                                    rings.

terrible poems come in the mail. Descriptions of celibate parties   10
                      torn trousers: Great Poets dying
                      with their strophes on. & me
                      incapable of a simple straightforward
                      anger.

It's so diffuse   15
being alive. Suddenly one is aware
        that nobody really gives a damn.
        My wife is pregnant with *her* child.
        "It means nothing to me," sez Strindberg.[2]

An avalanche of words   20
could cheer me up. Words from Great Sages.
        Was James Karolis a great sage??
        Why did I let Ora Matthews beat him up
        in the bathroom? Haven't I learned my lesson.

[1] Poem by the Spanish poet Federico Garcia Lorca (1898–1936).
[2] August Strindberg (1849–1912), great Swedish playwright and a famous misogynist.

I would take up painting
if I cd think of a way to do it
better than Leonardo. Than Bosch.
Than Hogarth. Than Kline.[3]

Frank walked off the stage, singing
"My silence is as important as Jack's incessant yatter."

I am a mean hungry sorehead
Do I have the capacity for grace??

To arise one smoking spring
& find one's youth has taken off
for greener parts.

A sudden blankness in the day
as if there were no afternoon.
& all my piddling joys retreated
to their own dopey mythic worlds.

The hours of the atmosphere
grind their teeth like hags.

              (When will world war two be over?)

I stood up on a mailbox
waving my yellow tee-shirt
watching the gray tanks
stream up Central Ave.

            All these thots
            are Flowers of Evil[4]
            cold & lifeless
            as subway rails

the sun like a huge cobblestone
flaking its brown slow rays
primititi

      once, twice. My life
      seems over & done with.
      Each morning I rise
      like a sleep walker
      & rot a little more.

All the lovely things I've known have disappeared.
I have all my pubic hair & am lonely.
There is probably no such place as Battle Creek, Michigan!

---

[3] Famous artists: Leonardo da Vinci (1452–1519), Hieronymus Bosch (c. 1450–1516), William Hogarth (1697–1764), and Franz Kline (1910–62).
[4] Name of a famous collection of poems by Charles Baudelaire (1821–67).

Tom Mix[5] dead in a Boston Nightclub
before I realized what happened.

People laugh when I tell them about Dickie Dare!

What is one to do in an alien planet   65
where the people breathe New Ports?
Where is my space helmet, I sent for it
3 lives ago ... when there were box tops.

What has happened to box tops??

O, God ... I must have a belt that glows green   70
in the dark. Where is my Captain Midnight decoder??
I can't understand what Superman is saying!

THERE *MUST* BE A LONE RANGER!!!

* * * *

but this also   75
is part of my charm.
A maudlin nostalgia
that comes on
like terrible thoughts about death.

How dumb to be sentimental about anything   80
To call it love
& cry pathetically
into the long black handkerchief
of the years.

"Look for you yesterday
Here you come today   85
Your mouth wide open
But what you got to say?"

—part of my charm

old envious   blues feeling
ticking like   a big cobblestone clock.   90

I hear the reel running out ...
the spectators are impatient for popcorn:
It was only a selected short subject

F. Scott Charon[6]
will soon be glad-handing me   95
like a legionnaire

[5] Cowboy movie star of the 1920s.
[6] Baraka combines F. Scott Fitzgerald (1896–1940), American novelist, with Charon, boatman over
the Styx who rowed the newly dead to Hades in Greek mythology.

My silver bullets all gone
My black mask trampled in the dust

& Tonto way off in the hills
moaning like Bessie Smith.[7]

100

DAS KAPITAL

Strangling women in the suburban bush
they bodies laid around rotting while martinis are drunk
the commuters looking for their new yorkers feel a draft
& can get even drunker watching the teevee later on the Ford
replay. There will be streams of them coming, getting off   5
near where the girls got killed. Two of them strangled by
the maniac.
There are maniacs hidden everywhere cant you see? By the dozens
and double dozens, maniacs by the carload (tho they *are*
a minority). But they terrorize us uniformly, all over the place   10
we look at the walls of our houses, the garbage cans parked full
strewn around our defaulting cities, and we cd get scared. A rat
eases past us on his way to a banquet, can you hear the cheers raised
through the walls, full of rat humor. Blasts of fire, some woman's son will
   stumble
and die with a pool of blood around his head. But it wont be the maniac.
   These old houses
crumble, the unemployed stumble by us straining, ashy fingered, harassed.   15
   The air is cold
winter heaps above us consolidating itself in degrees. We need a aspirin or
   something, and
pull our jackets close. The baldhead man on the television set goes on in a
   wooden way
his unappetizing ignorance can not be stood, or understood. The people
   turn the channel
looking for Good Times and get a negro with a pulldown hat. Flashes of
   maniac shadows before   20
bed, before you pull down the shade you can see the leaves being blown
   down the street
too dark now to see the writing on them, the dates, and amounts we owe.
   The streets too
will soon be empty, after the church goers go on home having been saved
   again from the
Maniac . . . except a closeup of the chief mystic's face rolling down to his
   hands will send
shivers through you, looking for traces of the maniacs life. Even there
   among the mythophrenics.   25

What can you do? It's time finally to go to bed. The shadows close around
   and the room is still

---

[7] Great blues singer (1894?–1937).

Most of us know there's a maniac loose. Our lives a jumble of frustrations
    and unfilled
capacities. The dead girls, the rats noise, the flashing somber lights, the
    dead voice on
television, was that blood and hair beneath the preacher's fingernails? A
    few other clues

we mull them over as we go to sleep, the skeletons of dollarbills, traces of
    dead used up   30
labor, lead away from the death scene until we remember a quiet fit that
    everywhere
is the death scene. Tomorrow you got to hit it sighs through us like the
    wind, we got to
hit it, like an old song at radio city, working for the yanqui dollarrrrr, when
    we were
children, and then we used to think it was not the wind, but the maniac
    scratching against
our windows. Who is the maniac, and why everywhere at the same time . . .   35

Diana Chang

Diana Chang was born (in 1934) in New York but grew up in China with her
mother, who was Eurasian. She returned to the United States as an adult. Best
known as a novelist, she has published six novels. (Her short story "The Oriental
Contingent" appears in the fiction section of this book.) Her volumes of poetry
include *The Horizon is Definitely Speaking* (1982) and *What Matisse Is After* (1984).
A painter as well as a writer, Chang teaches creative writing at Barnard College.

ON THE FLY

You reconnoiter. Following, I swat and sulk.
You're in my hair.

Go, go!
You lay causeways through the air,
return to touch my wrist,   5

rise on your smile.

Now where are you?
I search bare lanes,
hold out honey.

We while away the night.   10
My knee, my cheek
exist because of you.
You bank through my arms.
As though in love, I career after you.

Again, I tear you out of my hair.   15
Wings akimbo, you bite hard.
This—my live-in—is a falling out.

At last I know to throw open windows.
Either you will or won't
. . . stay.   20

The cup we shared is filled with moonlight.
As at an amphitheater
when the music was new,
I sat like you rubbing your hands—
so much to relish together.   25

Is the silence now saying
you were staking only air?

You took up no room, really,
now high, then there.

Largeness now   30
has me residing

unkissed
unsettled

no longer flying

and nowhere   35

Joy Kogawa

Joy Kogawa was born (in 1935) in Vancouver, British Columbia. Canada, like the
United States, interned citizens of Japanese ancestry during the Second World
War. Kogawa's family was sent first to a camp in central British Columbia, then to
one in Alberta. She was educated at the University of Alberta, the Toronto Con-
servatory of Music, and the University of Saskatchewan; she now lives in Toronto.
Her novel *Obasan* (1981), about Canada's internment of Japanese citizens, won
both the Books in Canada First Novel Award and the Canadian Authors Association Book of the Year Award. A children's version of *Obasan* is entitled *Naomi's
Road* (1986).

ANCESTORS' GRAVES IN KURAKAWA

Down down across the open sea to Shikoku
To story book island of mist and mystery
By train and bus through remote mountain villages
Following my father's boyhood backwards

Retracing the mountain path he crossed on rice husk slippers   5
With his dreams of countries beyond seas beyond seas
His dreams still intact, his flight perpetual
Back down the steep red mountain path
To the high hillside grave of my ancestors
Grey and green ferns hang down   10
Edging my faint beginnings with shades
Maintaining muteness in a wordless flickering
The hiddenness stretches beyond my reach
Strange dew drops through cedar incense
And I greet the dead who smile through trees   15
Accepting the pebbles that melt through my eyes.

WOODTICK

The spring day the teen on his bike slanted his caucasian eyes
At my eight year old beautiful daughter
And taunted gibberish
I was eight years old and the Japs were
Enemies of Canada and the big white boys   5
And their golden haired sisters who
Lived in the ghost town of Slocan
Were walking together, crowding me
Off the path of the mountain, me running
Into the forest to escape   10
Into the pine brown and green lush dark
And getting lost and fearing woodticks
Which burrowed into your scalp beneath
Thick black hair follicles and could only be
Dug out by a doctor with hot needles—   15
Fearing sudden slips caused by melting snow
And steep ravines and the thick silence of
Steaming woods and cobwebs, so listening
For the guiding sound of their laughter
To lead me back to the path and   20
Following from a safe distance unseen
Till near the foot of the mountain
Then running past faster than their laughter
Home, vowing never to go again to the mountain
Alone—and Deidre whispers to walk faster   25
Though I tell her there are no
Woodticks in Saskatoon.

SNAKES

Suddenly in the woods a
Green and yellow snake as if he
Slithered down my back

A moving rope of wind slinking an instant
Barber shop sign round my spine   5
And as I clambered out of the woods—
Suddenly on the path a presence
Of children, one fearful whispering
"Chinese" and the other
Moving swiftly past—   10

Jay Wright

Jay Wright was born (in 1935) in Albuquerque, New Mexico, and graduated from
the University of California at Berkeley. He currently lives in New Hampshire. His
first book of poetry was *Death as History* (1967). It was followed by *The Homecoming
Singer* (1971), *Soothsayers and Omens* (1976), *Dimensions of History* (1976), *The
Double Invention of Komo* (1980), and *Elaine's Book* (1988). *Selected Poems* was published in 1987 by the Princeton University Press. Wright is a complex poet. He
describes his work as an effort "to uncover the weave." For him, the "weave" of
black culture includes strands from anthropology and symbolism, gospel and jazz,
African religion, and Native American cosmology, as well as white Western culture.

THE HOMECOMING SINGER

The plane tilts in to Nashville,
coming over the green lights
like a toy train skipping past
the signals on a track.
The city is livid with lights,   5
as if the weight of all the people
shooting down her arteries
had inflamed them.
It's Friday night,
and people are home for the homecomings.   10
As I come into the terminal,
a young black man, in a vested gray suit,
paces in the florid Tennessee air,
breaks into a run like a halfback
in open field, going past the delirious faces,   15
past the poster of Molly Bee,
in her shiny chaps, her hips tilted forward
where the guns would be, her legs set,
as if she would run, as if she were
a cheerleader who doffs her guns   20
on Saturday afternoon and careens
down the sidelines after some broken field runner,
who carries it in, for now,
for all the state of Tennessee
with its nut smelling trees,   25

its stolid little stone walls
set out under thick blankets of leaves,
its crisp lights dangling on the porches
of homes that top the graveled driveways,
where people who cannot yodel or yell   30
putter in the grave October afternoons,
waiting for Saturday night and the lights
that spatter on Molly Bee's silver chaps.
I don't want to think of them,
or even of the broken field runner in the terminal,   35
still looking for his girl, his pocket
full of dates and parties, as I come
into this Friday night of homecomings
and hobble over the highway in a taxi
that has its radio tuned to country music.   40
I come up to the campus,
with a large wreath jutting up
under the elegant dormitories,
where one girl sits looking down at the shrieking cars,
as the lights go out, one by one, around her   45
and the laughter drifts off, rising, rising,
as if it would take flight away
from the livid arteries of Nashville.
Now, in sleep, I leave my brass-headed bed,
and see her enter with tall singers,   50
they in African shirts, she in a robe.
She sits, among them, as a golden lance
catches her, suddenly chubby, with soft lips
and unhurried eyes, quite still in the movement
around her, waiting, as the other voices fade,   55
as the movement stops, and starts to sing,
her voice moving up from its tart entrance
until it swings as freely
as an ecstatic dancer's foot,
rises and plays among the windows   60
as it would with angels and falls,
almost visible, to return to her,
and leave her shaking with the tears
I'm ashamed to release, and leave her
twisting there on that stool with my shame   65
for the livid arteries, the flat Saturdays,
the inhuman homecomings of Nashville.
I kneel before her. She strokes my hair,
as softly as she would a cat's head
and goes on singing, her voice shifting   70
and bringing up the Carolina calls,
the waterboy, the railroad cutter, the jailed,
the condemned, all that had been forgotten
on this night of homecomings, all
that had been misplaced in those livid arteries.   75
She finishes, and leaves,

her shy head tilted and wrinkled,
in the green-tinged lights of the still campus.
I close my eyes and listen,
as she goes out to sing this city home.　　　　　　　80

THE INVENTION
OF A GARDEN

I'm looking out of the window,
from the second floor,
into a half-eaten patio,
where the bugs dance deliriously
and the flowers sniff at bits of life.　　　　　5
I touch my burned-out throat,
with an ache to thrust
my fingers to the bone,
run them through the wet
underpinnings of my skin,　　　　　10
in the thick blood, around
the craggèd vertebrae.
I have dreamed of armored insects,
taking flight through my stomach wall,
the fissured skin refusing to close,　　　　　15
or bleed, but gaping
like the gory lips of an oyster,
stout and inviting, clefts of flesh
rising like the taut membrane of a drum,
threatening to explode and spill　　　　　20
the pent-up desires I hide.
Two or three birds
invent a garden,
he said,
and I have made a bath　　　　　25
to warm the intrepid robins
that glitter where the sun
deserts the stones.
They come, and splash, matter-of-factly,
in the coral water, sand-driven　　　　　30
and lonely as sandpipers
at the crest of a wave.
Could I believe in the loneliness
of beaches, where sand crabs
duck camouflaged in holes,　　　　　35
and devitalized shrubs and shells
come up to capture the shore?
More, than in this garrisoned room,
where this pencil scratches
in the ruled-off lines,　　　　　40
making the only sound

that will contain the taut,
unopened drum that beats the dance
for bugs and garden-creating birds.

June Jordan

June Jordan was born (in 1936) in New York to parents who were Jamaican
immigrants. She was educated at Barnard College and has taught at a number of
colleges and universities, including Connecticut College, The City College of New
York, Sarah Lawrence College, Yale University, and the State University of New
York at Stony Brook. Currently, she is Professor of Afro-American Studies and
Women's Studies at the University of California, Berkeley. Jordan is a prolific
writer, having written plays and children's books as well as poetry. Her collections
of poetry include *Some Changes* (1971), *New Days: Poems of Exile and Return* (1974),
Things That I Do in the Dark: Selected Poetry (1977; rev. 1981), *Living Room: New
Poems 1980–84* (1985), and *Naming Our Destiny: New and Selected Poems* (1989).

POEM FOR GRANVILLE IVANHOE JORDAN
November 4, 1890–December 21, 1974

Dedicated to Stephen Henderson

I

At the top of your tie
the dressy maroon number
with one/small
gravy stain
remaining   5

the knot is now too narrow for your neck

a ridiculous a dustfree/shiny box confines
your arms and legs
accustomed to a boxer's hunch a wrestler's hauling
energies at partial rest   10

3 or 4 A.M. a thousand nights
who stubbornly retrieved your own
into
illumination
              bright beyond blindfiling of   15
              a million letters at the Post Office which
              never forwarded even one
              of a hundred
              fantasies
              your kitchenkept plans   20
keeping you awake

West Indian in kitchen exile
alone between the days
and studying the National Geographic Magazines
white explorations and   25
excitement
in the places you were forced to leave

                              no shoes
                              no teeth

but oxlike shoulders   30
and hazel eyes that watered
slightly
from the reading you did teach yourself to do

West Indian in kitchen exile
omnivorous consumer of thick   35
kitchen table catalogs
of seeds for sale
for red
bright flowers

seeds   40

slick and colorful
on the quick
lush pages
advertising pear and
apple trees   45
or peaches
in first bloom

                    who saved for money orders
                    for the flowers
                    for the trees   50
                    who used a spade
                    and shovel
                    heavily and well
                    to plant the Brooklyn backyard
                    innocent of all   55
                    the succulent
                    the gorgeous schemes
                    you held between your fingers
                    like a simple
                    piece of paper   60

Jesus, Daddy
what did you expect

an orange grove
a eucalyptus

roses
from the cities that despised the sweet calypso
of your trust?   65

II

Who stole the mustache from your face?
It's gone.
Who took it away?   70
Why did you stop there

> *on your knees*

at eighty four

> *a man*

down on your knees   75

> *in inconceivable but willing*
> *prayer/your life*
> *God's baby in gray hair*

What pushed you from your own two feet?

> *my father*   80

III

To this you have come

> *a calm a concrete pit*

contains your corpse
above the spumespent ending of the surf
against the mountain trees and fertile pitch   85
of steeply clinging dirt

> *"Sleep on Beloved*
> *Take Thy Rest"*

the minister
eyes bare beneath the island light   90
intones a feeling mumbo jumbo

> *"ashes to ashes*
> *dust to dust"*

the village men
wrists strained to lumped up veins and cartilage   95
(from carrying the casket)
do not pray
they do not sing

"A-bide with me,
fast falls the eventide"   100

It's afternoon
It's hot
It's lit by sun that cannot be undone

by death

CAMEO NO. I

Abraham Lincoln shit he never walked nowhere to read
a book tell all about it all about
the violation the continuous the fuck my face
the dark and evil dark is evil no good dark
the evil and continuous   5
the light the white the literature he read was
lying blood to leech the life away

believe the Abraham the Lincoln log the literature
the books he read the book he wrote down put
down   10
put you on the rawhide prairie
emancipated proclaiming
Illinois the noise
the boombang bothering my life
the crapcrashchaos print the words   15
the sprightly syllable destruction
nobody black black nobody black nobody
black
nobody

man   20

he no Abraham no kind
a president a power walk the miles and read the piles of
pages pale to murder real

                    no wonder he was so depressed

that character   25
cost me almost
my whole
future   times

CAMEO NO. II

The name of this poem is

George Washington
somebody want me to think he bad

he bad

George Washington the father of this country   5
the most the first the holy-poly ghost
the father of this country
took my mother

anyway you want to take that

George the father hypocrite   10
his life some other bit
than freedom down to every man

George Washington he think he big
he trade my father for a pig

his ordinary   15
extraordinary human
slaves 300 people Black
and bleeding life beholden to the Presidential
owner underneath the powder of his wicked wig
he think he big   20

he pull a blackman from his pocket
put a pig inside the other one
George Washington

the father of this country
stocked   25
by declarations at the auction block

Prez Washington he say
"give me niggers
let me pay

by check"   30
(Check the father of this country
what he say:)

"I always pay for niggers
let them stay
like vermin   35
at Mount Vernon"

impeccable in battle
ManKill Number One
the revolutionary head
aristocratic raider at the vulnerable   40
slavegirl bed

Americanus Rex
Secretus Blanco-Bronco-Night-Time-Sex

the father of this country
leading privileges of rape and run   45

George Washington

somebody tell me how he bad he big

I know how he
the great great great great
great great proto-   50

typical

Lucille Clifton

Lucille Clifton was born (in 1936) in Depew, New York, and was educated at Howard University in Washington and Fredonia State Teachers College in New York. She worked for the New York State Division of Employment and for the United States Office of Education before turning to full-time teaching and writing. Clifton is now Professor of English at the University of California, Santa Cruz. She has written twenty-one children's books as well as poetry. Major poetry collections include *Good Times: Poems* (1969), *Good News About the Earth* (1972), *An Ordinary Woman* (1974), *Two-Headed Woman* (1980), and *Next: New Poems* (1987). She also has written an autobiography: *Generations: A Memoir* (1976).

SOME JESUS

adam and eve

the names
of the things
bloom in my mouth

my body opens
into brothers   5

▪
cain

the land of nod
is a desert
on my head   i
plant tears
every morning   10
my brother
don't rise up

▪
moses

i walk on bones
snakes twisting

in my hand   15
locusts breaking my mouth
an old man
leaving slavery
home is burning in me
like a bush   20
God got his eye on

■

solomon

i bless the black
skin of the woman
and the black
night turning around her   25
like a star's bed
and the black
sound of delilah
across his prayers
for they have made me   30
wise

■

job

job easy
is the pride
of God

job hard   35
the pride
of job

i come to rags
like a good baby
to breakfast   40

■

daniel

i have learned
some few things
like when a man
walk manly
he don't stumble   45
even in the lion's den

■

jonah

what i remember
is green

in the trees
and the leaves   50
and the smell of mango
and yams
and if i had a drum
i would send to the brothers
—Be care full of the ocean—   55

■

john

somebody coming in blackness
like a star
and the world be a great bush
on his head
and his eyes be fire   60
in the city
and his mouth be true as time

he be calling the people brother
even in the prison
even in the jail   65

i'm just only a baptist preacher
somebody bigger than me coming
in blackness like a star

■

mary

this kiss
as soft as cotton   70

over my breasts
all shiny bright

something is in this night
oh Lord have mercy on me

i feel a garden   75
in my mouth

between my legs
i see a tree

■

joseph

something about this boy
has spelled my tongue   80

so even when my fingers tremble
on mary
my mouth cries only
Jesus   Jesus   Jesus

■

the calling of the disciples

some Jesus   85
has come on me

i throw down my nets
into water he walks

i loose the fish
he feeds to cities   90

and everybody calls me
an old name

as i follow out
laughing like God's fool
behind this Jesus   95

■

the raising of lazarus

the dead shall rise again
whoever say
dust must be dust
don't see the trees
smell rain   100
remember africa
everything that goes
can come
stand up
even the dead shall rise   105

■

palm sunday

so here come i
home again
and the people glad
giving thanks
glorying in the brother   110
laying turnips
for the mule to walk on

waving beets
and collards in the air

■

good friday

i rise up above my self   115
like a fish flying

men will be gods
if they want it

■

easter sunday

while i was in the middle of the night
I saw red stars and black stars   120
pushed out of the sky by white ones
and i knew as sure as jungle
is the father of the world
i must slide down like a great dipper of stars
and lift men up   125

■

spring song

the green of Jesus
is breaking the ground
and the sweet
smell of delicious Jesus
is opening the house and   130
the dance of Jesus music
has hold of the air and
the world is turning
in the body of Jesus and
the future is possible   135

■

Larry Neal

Larry Neal (1937–81) was born in Atlanta, Georgia, and reared in Philadelphia.
He was educated at Lincoln University and the University of Pennsylvania. An
associate of Amiri Baraka, he collaborated with him in editing an important
anthology of the Black Arts Movement, *Black Fire* (1968). Neal's poetry collections
are *Black Boogaloo* (1969) and *Hoodoo Hollerin' Bebop Ghosts* (1975).

MALCOLM X—AN AUTOBIOGRAPHY[1]

I am the Seventh Son of the son
who was also the seventh.
I have drunk deep of the waters of my ancestors,
have traveled the soul's journey toward cosmic harmony—
the Seventh Son.   5

Have walked slick avenues
and seen grown men, fall, to die in a blue doom
of death and ancestral agony;
have seen old men glide, shadowless, feet barely
touching the pavements.   10

I sprang out of the Midwestern plains
the bleak Michigan landscape, the black blues of Kansas
City, these kiss-me-nights;
out of the bleak Michigan landscape wearing the slave name
Malcolm Little.   15

Saw a brief vision in Lansing when I was seven, and in
my momma's womb heard the beast cry death;
a landscape on which white robed figures ride, and my
Garvey father[2] silhouetted against the night-fire
gun in hand,   20
form outlined against a panorama of violence.

Out of the Midwestern bleakness, I sprang, pushed eastward,
past shack on country nigger shack, across the wilderness
of North America.
I hustler. I pimp. I unfulfilled black man   25
bursting with destiny.
New York City Slim called me Big Red,
and there was no escape, close nights of the smell of death.
Pimp. Hustler. The day fills these rooms.
I'm talking about New York, Harlem.   30
Talking about the neon madness.
Talking about ghetto eyes and nights
Talking about death protruding across the room
Talking about Small's Paradise.
Talking about cigarette butts, and rooms smelly with white   35
sex-flesh, and dank sheets, and being on the run.
Talking about cocaine illusions.
Talking about stealing and selling.

---

[1] The poem follows closely the *Autobiography of Malcolm X*, as told to Alex Haley (1964).
[2] Malcolm's father was a follower of Marcus Garvey (1887–1940), founder of the Universal Negro Improvement Society and leader of a "back to Africa" movement.

Talking about these New York cops who smell
of blood and money.   40
I am Big Red, tiger, vicious, Big Red, bad nigger, will kill.

But there is rhythm here
Its own special substance:
I hear Billie[3] sing, no Good Man, and dig Prez,[4] wearing
the Zoot suit of life, the Porkpie hat tilted at the   45
correct angle; through the Harlem smoke of beer and
whiskey, I understand the mystery of the Signifying
Monkey;
in a blue haze of inspiration
I reach for the totality of being.   50
I am at the center of a swirl of events.
War and death.
Rhythm.
Hot women.
I think life a commodity bargained   55
for across the bar in Small's.

I perceive the echoes of Bird[5]
and there is a gnawing the maw
of my emotions.

And then there is jail.   60
America is the world's greatest jailer,
and we are all in jails
holy spirits contained like magnificent
birds of wonder.
I now understand my father urged on by the ghost of Garvey,   65
and see a small brown man standing in a corner.[6]
The cell. Cold. Dank.
The light around him vibrates.
(Am I crazy?)
But to understand is to submit to a more perfect will,   70
a more perfect order.
To understand is to surrender the imperfect self
for a more perfect self.

Allah formed man, I follow
and shake within the very depth of my most interesting being;   75
and I bear witness to the Message of Allah
and I bear witness; all praise is due Allah.

---

[3] Billie Holiday (1915–59), black jazz singer.
[4] Lester Young (1909–59), great black tenor saxophonist. Billie Holiday gave him the nickname "President," later shortened to "Prez."
[5] A vision of Elijah Muhammad (1897–1975), founder of the Black Muslims.

LADY'S DAYS[1]

More song. birds follow the sun.
rain comes . . .
we drive South, me and Billie
rain.

Was it D.C.; or the hick towns   5
of square yokels come to hear the Lady sing?

Rain. these nights on the road, the car, these
towns lingering blue in her voice.

South where birds go.
I remember them faces   10
the soft and the hard
faces scarred, wailing
for the song and the moan
digging the gardenia thing[2]
she was into . . .   15
                    Lady's days

Digging the song as it turned soft
in her mouth
digging as the mouth turned softly
in the song . . .   20
They dug you, yeah
heavy smoke moaning
room shifting under red spotlights
And then there was the Philly bust.
Hey now lover, you said, don't worry . . .   25
some towns are like that . . . But the music
is somewhere else . . .

Those were copasetic times, eh Mama?
Down the hall, morning rises bright
and weird in Lester's horn.[3]   30
We watch the sun scat over the river
and then our bodies merge into his song.
                    Lady's days

Now rain
on the road again, rain.   35
Herbie is driving
you sleep, pressed against my chest . . .
I can still hear Prez's[4] solo

---

[1] The nickname of Billie Holiday, the great jazz singer, was "Lady Day."
[2] Billie Holiday's trademark was a gardenia, worn over her ear.
[3] Lester Young, tenor saxophonist.   [4] Lester Young's nickname was "Prez."

from last night's gig . . .
the light dreams   40
the warm woman in my arms
and her mellow voice hovering over us . . .
My woman
Billie beautiful
My woman, Lady Day   45
child of the God of Song . . .
heavy smell of alcohol and moan
spotlights for the Lady
raining gardenias and blues.

Faces. the pain rides them   50
more pain
their pain
ghosts ride them
your voice rides them
shifting under red spotlights . . .   55
smoke.

One night between sets, I asked you what it meant.
the pain raining
and the moans of scars and gardenias.
I had just finished running some scales   60
in quiet sixteenths when I asked you:
Is that the way it is Billie baby?
I recall you humming a line from
one of my solos
and then you laughed, that real pretty laugh.   65
Slow power of the blues, you said.
you said, you said that it had to go
down that way; honey, ain't gotta be no
reason for towns, faces, moans . . .

Ishmael Reed

Ishmael Reed (b. 1938) is better known as a novelist than a poet, but he has
published several volumes of poetry that have some of the same qualities—energy,
humor, and outrageousness—as such novels as *Yellow Back Radio Broke-Down*. Reed
was born in Chattanooga, Tennessee, and educated at the University of Buffalo.
He has been active in publishing and promoting ethnic literature, as cofounder of
the Yardbird Press, the Before Columbus Foundation, and Ishmael Reed and Al
Young's Quilt. His collections of poetry include *Catechism of d neoamerican hoodoo
church* (1970), *Conjure: Selected Poems 1963–1970* (1972), *Chattanooga* (1978), *A
Secretary to the Spirits* (1978), and *New and Collected Poems* (1988).

I AM A COWBOY IN THE BOAT OF RA

*'The devil must be forced to reveal any such physical evil
(potions, charms, fetishes, etc.) still outside the body
and these must be burned.'*
> Rituale Romanum, *published 1947, endorsed by the
> coat-of-arms and introductory letter from
> Francis cardinal Spellman*

I am a cowboy in the boat of Ra,[1]
sidewinders in the saloons of fools
bit my forehead   like   O
the untrustworthiness of Egyptologists
who do not know their trips. Who was that   5
dog-faced man?[2] they asked, the day I rode
from town.

School marms with halitosis cannot see
the Nefertiti[3] fake chipped on the run by slick
germans, the hawk behind Sonny Rollins' head[4] or   10
the ritual beard of his axe;[5] a longhorn winding
its bells thru the Field of Reeds.

I am a cowboy in the boat of Ra. I bedded
down with Isis,[6] Lady of the Boogaloo, dove
down deep in her horny, stuck up her Wells-Far-ago   15
in daring midday getaway. 'Start grabbing the
blue,' I said from top of my double crown.

I am a cowboy in the boat of Ra. Ezzard Charles[7]
of the Chisholm Trail. Took up the bass but they
blew off my thumb. Alchemist in ringmanship but a   20
sucker for the right cross.

I am a cowboy in the boat of Ra. Vamoosed from
the temple i bide my time. The price on the wanted
poster was a-going down, outlaw alias copped my stance
and moody greenhorns were making me dance;   25
     while my mouth's
shooting iron got its chambers jammed.

I am a cowboy in the boat of Ra. Boning-up in
the ol West i bide my time. You should see
me pick off these tin cans whippersnappers. I   30
write the motown long plays for the comeback of

---

[1] Sun-god; the creator and father of all things in ancient Egyptian religion.
[2] Anubis, Egyptian god of the dead, had the head of a dog.
[3] Queen of Egypt (c. 1372–1350 B.C.). There is a famous limestone bust of Nefertiti in the Berlin
Museum; Reed is suggesting that it is a fake.
[4] Great jazz tenor saxophone player of the 1950s.   [5] Musical instrument.
[6] A nature goddess and the chief goddess of ancient Egypt.
[7] Heavyweight boxing champion of the world, 1949–51.

Osiris.[8] Make them up when stars stare at sleeping
steer out here near the campfire. Women arrive
on the backs of goats and throw themselves on
my Bowie.[9]   35

I am a cowboy in the boat of Ra. Lord of the lash,
the Loup Garou[10] Kid. Half breed son of Pisces and
Aquarius. I hold the souls of men in my pot. I do
the dirty boogie with scorpions. I make the bulls
keep still and was the first swinger to grape the taste.   40

I am a cowboy in his boat. Pope Joan[11] of the
Ptah Ra. C/mere a minute willya doll?
Be a good girl and
bring me my Buffalo horn of black powder
bring me my headdress of black feathers   45
bring me my bones of Ju-Ju[12] snake
go get my eyelids of red paint.
Hand me my shadow

I'm going into town after Set[13]

I am a cowboy in the boat of Ra   50

look out Set   here i come Set
to get Set   to sunset Set
to unseat Set   to Set down Set

                        usurper of the Royal couch
                        —imposter RAdio of Moses' bush[14]   55
                        party pooper O hater of dance
                        vampire outlaw of the milky way

WHY I OFTEN ALLUDE TO OSIRIS

ikhnaton[1] looked like
prophet jones, who brick
by brick broke up a

---

[8] God of the underworld in ancient Egyptian religion. Both the brother and the husband of Isis, he symbolized the creative forces of nature.
[9] A large hunting knife, named after the Texas hero Jim Bowie.
[10] "Werewolf" (French). In voodoo, a berserk priest.
[11] Mythical female pope, supposed to have lived in the ninth century A.D. *Ptah Ra:* Chief god of the ancient Egyptian city of Memphis.
[12] In voodoo, a fetish or charm.
[13] Brother and enemy of Osiris.
[14] Moses heard the voice of God in a burning bush commanding him to lead the Hebrews out of Egypt (see Exodus 3:2).
[1] Egyptian king (c. 1372–54 B.C.). He abandoned the ancient polytheism of Egypt and taught the worship of one god, the sun.

french chateau & set it
down in detroit. he was   5
'elongated' like prophet
jones & had a hairdresser's
taste.
ikhnaton moved cities for
his mother-in-law &   10
each finger of his hands
bore rings.

ikhnaton brought re
ligious fascism to egypt.

where once man animals   15
plants & stars freely
roamed thru each other's
rooms, ikhnaton came up
with the door.

(a lot of people in new york   20
go for him—museum curators
politicians & tragic mulattoes)

i'll take osiris any
time.
prefiguring JB he   25
funky chickened into
ethiopia & everybody had
a good time. osiris in
vented the popcorn, the
slow drag & the lindy hop.[2]   30

he'd rather dance than rule.

BEWARE: DO NOT READ THIS POEM

tonite, *thriller* was
abt an ol woman, so vain she
surrounded her self w/
   many mirrors

It got so bad that finally she   5
locked herself indoors & her
whole life became the
   mirrors

one day the villagers broke
into her house, but she was too   10

---

[2] The funky chicken, the slow drag, and the lindy hop are all dances of the 1950s.

swift for them. she disappeared
    into a mirror
each tenant who bought the house
after that, lost a loved one to
    the ol woman in the mirror:
    first a little girl
    then a young woman
    then the young woman/s husband   15

the hunger of this poem is legendary
it has taken in many victims   20
back off from this poem
it has drawn in yr feet
back off from this poem
it has drawn in yr legs
back off from this poem   25
it is a greedy mirror
you are into this poem. from
    the waist down
nobody can hear you can they?
this poem has had you up to here   30
    belch
this poem aint got no manners
you cant call out frm this poem
relax now & go w/this poem
move & roll on to this poem   35

    do not resist this poem
    this poem has yr eyes
    this poem has his head
    this poem has his arms
    this poem has his fingers   40
    this poem has his fingertips

this poem is the reader & the
    reader this poem

statistic: the us bureau of missing persons reports
    that in 1968 over 100,000 people disappeared   45
    leaving no solid clues
        nor trace   only
a space   in the lives of their friends

Charles Simic

Charles Simic was born (in 1938) in Yugoslavia and emigrated to the United States with his family when he was a boy. He went to the University of Chicago and New York University. Currently, he is Professor of English at the University of New Hampshire. Simic writes poems that combine a surface simplicity with an unsettling, mysterious, or surrealist content, sometimes linked to political distrust.

His books include *Dismantling the Silence* (1971), *Return to a Place Lit by a Glass of Milk* (1974), *Charon's Cosmology* (1977), *Classic Ballroom Dances* (1980), *Austerities* (1982), *Selected Poems* (1985), *Unending Blues* (1986), and *The World Doesn't End* (1989). Simic was awarded a MacArthur "genius" grant in 1984 and won the Pulitzer Prize in 1990.

SUMMER MORNING

I love to stay in bed
All morning,
Covers thrown off, naked,
Eyes closed, listening.

Outside they are opening   5
Their primers
In the little school
Of the corn field.

There's a smell of damp hay,
Of horses, laziness,   10
Summer sky and eternal life.

I know all the dark places
Where the sun hasn't reached yet,
Where the last cricket
Has just hushed; anthills   15
Where it sounds like it's raining;
Slumbering spiders spinning wedding dresses.

I pass over the farmhouses
Where the little mouths open to suck,
Barnyards where a man, naked to the waist,   20
Washes his face and shoulders with a hose,
Where the dishes begin to rattle in the kitchen.

The good tree with its voice
Of a mountain stream
Knows my steps.   25
It, too, hushes.

I stop and listen:
Somewhere close by
A stone cracks a knuckle,
Another rolls over in its sleep.   30

I hear a butterfly stirring
Inside a caterpillar,
I hear the dust talking
Of last night's storm.

Further ahead, someone   35
Even more silent
Passes over the grass
Without bending it.

And all of a sudden!
In the midst of that quiet,   40
It seems possible
To live simply on this earth.

MY SHOES

Shoes, secret face of my inner life:
Two gaping toothless mouths,
Two partly decomposed animal skins
Smelling of mice-nests.

My brother and sister who died at birth   5
Continuing their existence in you,
Guiding my life
Toward their incomprehensible innocence.

What use are books to me
When in you it is possible to read   10
The Gospel of my life on earth
And still beyond, of things to come?

I want to proclaim the religion
I have devised for your perfect humility
And the strange church I am building   15
With you as the altar.

Ascetic and maternal, you endure:
Kin to oxen, to Saints, to condemned men,
With your mute patience, forming
The only true likeness of myself.   20

Michael Van Walleghen

Michael Van Walleghen (b. 1938) did his undergraduate work at Wayne State
University and then earned an M.F.A. from the Iowa Writers Workshop. He now
teaches at the University of Illinois. His books include *The Wichita Poems* (1975);
More Trouble with the Obvious (1980), which won the Lamont Prize; *Blue Tango*
(1989); and the forthcoming *Tall Birds Stalking*.

MORE TROUBLE WITH THE
OBVIOUS

A baby bird has fallen from its tree and lies feebly peeping dead center of the
bright circle under our streetlight. What is there to do but bring it in? We
dutifully prepare a shoebox, then mix up the baby food and hamburger of an
old routine we know by heart, the ritual we've learned as children—but the
truth is, in all the years since childhood, neither my wife nor I can remember   5
having saved a single bird. We won't save this one either, trembling weakly
now on the kitchen table, refusing to do so much as open its beak for our
ridiculous food.

It lives with us two days, then dies suddenly in my hand—of "heart attack" my
neighbor says. "Young birds like that almost always die of heart attack." He   10
says this pounding nails in his porch and I believe him. In fact, I feel stupid
for having mentioned it at all. A heart attack. Of course. The best thing would
have been not to touch it. Perhaps it would have found a place to hide; and
then, in the morning, its mother might have flown down to feed it. In any
case, it's dead now and buried in the garden. The same garden, by the way,   15
from which my neighbor's cat wrestled a live snake once into the hubbub of
our barbecue.

But then I seem to have always had trouble with the obvious. Once, when a
friend died, and after my parents had told me he had died, I came around the
next morning anyway to call him out for school. His mother came to the door   20
weeping and told me Orville couldn't go to school that day. I felt as if I had
been walking in my sleep. I knew my parents hadn't lied, and I certainly knew
what death meant; but somehow, until that moment, I must have thought it
was just a dream I'd had. At school, another friend said he thought Orville
died from eating donuts every night for supper. I had no trouble at all be-   25
lieving that. By then, donuts made about as much sense as anything.

A baby bird has fallen from its tree . . . someone you love perhaps is dying in
another city. There must be something we can do. I remember one Sunday
Orville and I got down on our knees in an alley and asked the Blessed Mother
for a kite. When we found a rolled-up kite in the next ashcan with the rubber   30
bands still on it, we *knew* it was a miracle. And we were glad, of course; but
neither one of us, I think, was overwhelmed. We just believed in miracles and
thought they happened all the time. We thought the birds we found needed
milk and bread. We thought when they got big they would be our friends, do
us wonderful favors, and keep us company forever.   35

THE HONEYMOON
OF THE MUSE

You're right. There's nothing
much to see out here but corn

and soybeans. Wake me up
when we get to Denver. Yawning

this, the tired muse gives up 5
but Illinois goes on forever

with detours through Homer,
Sadorus, Villa Grove . . .

towns nestled at the foot
of nothing—and therefore 10

precarious somehow, fitfully
alpine, as if the sky itself

might suddenly collapse
and wipe them out entirely.

Are we there yet? Where's 15
the meadow, the hillside,

the shepherd with his flute?
Let's stop and ask directions.

Poor kid. She thinks Denver
is a kind of honeymoon resort 20

located high on the slopes
of Mount Parnassus. She thinks

I'm rich and the airplane roar
of my broken muffler means simply

that my car can also fly. Why 25
not? She can believe anything.

So here we are slowing down
for Villa Grove . . . two scarce blocks

of houses, body shops and shattered
Chinese elms. No Denver certainly 30

but rare enough, a jewel really,
set high in the rugged mountains

of central Illinois. "Look . . ."
I whisper, kissing her perfect ear,

"there's a liquor store that's open 35
and a vacancy at the Villa Pines!"

Paula Gunn Allen

Paula Gunn Allen (b. 1939) describes herself as being of Laguna/Sioux/Lebanese/Jewish heritage. Her family spoke five languages when she was growing up in New Mexico. She has a Ph.D. from the University of New Mexico and currently is professor of Native American studies at the University of California, Berkeley. She is the author of *Skin and Bones: Poems 1979–87* (1988) and six other books of poetry; a novel, *The Woman Who Owned the Shadows* (1983); and a book of essays, *The Sacred Hoop: Recovering the Feminine in American Indian Tradition* (1986). She has also edited *Studies in American Indian Literature* (1983) and *Spider Woman's Granddaughters: Traditional Tales and Contemporary Writing by Native American Women* (1989).

POWWOW 79, DURANGO

haven't been to one in almost three years
there's six drums and 200 dancers a few
booths piled with jewelry and powwow stuff
some pottery and oven bread
everyone gathers   5
stands for the grand entry
two flag songs
and the opening prayer by some guy
works for the BIA
who asks our father   10
to bless our cars
to heal our hearts
to let the music here tonight
make us better, cool
hurts and unease   15
in his son's name, amen.
my daughter arrives, stoned,
brown face ashy from the weed,
there's no toilet paper
in the ladies room she accuses me   20
there's never any toilet paper
in the *ladies* room at a powwow she glares
changes
calms
its like being home after a long time   25
are you gonna dance I ask
here's my shawl
not dressed right she says
the new beaded ties I bought her swing
from her long dark braids   30
why not you have dark blue on I say
look.
we step inside the gym
eyes sweep the rubber floor

jackets, jeans, down-filled vests,   35
sweatshirts all dark blue.
have to look close to pick out
occasional brown or red on older folks
the dark brown faces rising on the bleachers
the dark hair on almost every head   40
ever see so many Indians
you're dressed right
we look at the bleachers
quiet like shadows
the people sit watching the floor below   45
where dancers circle the beating drums
exploding color in the light.

LOS ANGELES, 1980

The death culture swarms
over the land bringing
honeysuckle eucalyptus palm
ivy brick and unfinished wood
torn from forests to satisfy organic   5
craving. The death society walks
hypnotized by its silent knowledge
nor does it hear the drum quiet
to the core.
The trees know.   10
Look.
They are dying.
The small birds who walk heedless
of the people swarming around them
know: they peck at sesame seeds trucked   15
from factories far away and crumbs
dropped from Rainbow buns. They
do not fly at human approach. They
act as if we are not there.

The dying generation does not know.   20
Boys offer me papers that shriek
of impending death: *Klan and Nazis Unite!*
the headlines proclaim. I must be aware, be
ware. The rally forming on the steps
beyond the plaza swirls with belief   25
that protest can change something, a
transformation needed, longed for,
that does not ever seem to come.
"It's getting worse," the young beard
assures me. His hair, teeth, skin   30
gleam with assured elegance.
"I know," I reply.

The dying generation moves purposefully:
well-dressed in Jantzen and Wrangler,
Gucchi and Adidas, clothes, bodies,   35
smiles gleaming, cool in the practiced
superiority of well-cut, natural fiber
clothes and vitamin-drenched consciousness,
they live their truth. They cannot count
the cost. But their silent hearts beat   40
slow with knowledge their bodies share
with the birds.

On my way to this New Jerusalem
on a smog-shrouded hill, I passed
fine stores filled with hidden omen,   45
dedicated to health and cleanliness,
luxury and the One True Path.
I could see they were there to save
my life. One brick-front shop's
bronze-tasteful sign announced: 50
Weight and Smoking Control Center.
In its smoky glass I saw
my own reflection:
short, fat, a black cigarette
in my hand, my self-cut hair   55
greying, my worn clothes mocking
the expensive, seductive sign.
I could see how I am
neither healthy nor wealthy.
But I am wise   60
enough to know
that death comes in pretty packages too,
and all around me
the dying air agreed.

The death people do not know   65
what they create, or how they hide
from the consequences of their dreams.
Wanting the good they slide
into an unforgiving destiny.
Alfalfa sprout, sesame seed,   70
no meat, no cigarettes: what will change
the inexorable dying we are facing?

No rally, no headline, no designer jean
can do more than hasten it.
We are related, after all.   75
the beautiful
wealthy
sun children and I.
We wander together into a smoky tomorrow,
seeing the clouds of darkness gather   80

on the surrounding hills.
shroud the sea, cover and oppose our
brightest dreams.
The dying grows silent
around us   85
and we walk
still believing it need not be.

Frank Bidart

Frank Bidart was born (in 1939) in Bakersfield, California, and went to the University of California at Riverside. He went to graduate school at Harvard, where he studied with Robert Lowell. He has remained in the East and is now Professor of English at Wellesley College. The word "cinematic" often is used in connection with Bidart's poetry; his poems, which often represent extreme states of mind, are built up from vividly imagined scenes and images often abruptly juxtaposed, as in cinematic montage. His books include *Golden State* (1973), *The Book of the Body* (1977), *The Sacrifice* (1983), and *In the Western Night: Collected Poems, 1965–1990* (1991). His poem "Happy Birthday" appears earlier in this section on page 602.

ANOTHER LIFE

Peut-être n'es-tu pas suffisamment mort.
C'est ici la limite de notre domaine. De-
vant toi coule un fleuve.[1]

                                        Valéry.

"—In a dream I never *exactly* dreamed,
but that is, somehow, the quintessence
of what I *might* have dreamed,
                         Kennedy is in Paris

again; it's '61; once again   5
some new national life seems possible,
though desperately, I try to remain unduped,
even cynical . . .
             He's standing in an open car,

brilliantly lit, bright orange   10
next to a grey de Gaulle, and they stand
not far from me, slowly moving up the Champs-Elysées . . .

---

[1] "Perhaps you are not sufficiently dead. Here is the limit of our domain. Before you flows a river." The quotation is from the prose dialogue *Eupalinos, or The Architect* by the French poet Paul Valéry (1871–1945). The speaker is Socrates, addressing Phaedrus, and the setting is the underworld. The river referred to is the river of Time.

Bareheaded in the rain, he gives a short
choppy wave, smiling like a sun god.

—I stand and   15
look, suddenly at peace; once again mindlessly
moved,
            as they bear up the fields of Elysium

the possibility of Atlantic peace,

reconciliation between all that power, energy,   20
optimism,—
            and an older wisdom, without
illusions, without force, the austere source
of nihilism, corrupted only by its dream of Glory . . .

But no—; as I   25
watch, the style is

                        not quite right—;

                        Kennedy is *too* orange . . .

And de Gaulle, white, dead
white, ghost white, not even grey . . .   30

                                    As my heart
began to grieve for my own awkwardness and
ignorance, which would never be
soothed by the informing energies
                        of whatever   35
wisdom saves,—

            I saw a young man, almost
my twin, who had written
                        'MONSTER'
in awkward lettering with a crayon across   40
the front of his sweat shirt.
                        He was gnawing on his arm,

in rage and anger gouging up
pieces of flesh—; but as I moved to stop him, somehow
help him,   45
            suddenly he looked up,

and began, as I had, to look at Kennedy and de Gaulle:

and then abruptly, almost as if I were seeing him
through a camera lens, his figure
split in two,—   50
            or doubled,—

and all the fury
                    drained from his stunned, exhausted face . . .

But only for a moment. Soon his eyes turned down
to the word on his chest. The two figures   55
again became one,

and with fresh energy he attacked the mutilated arm . . .

—Fascinated, I watched as this
pattern, this cycle,
                    repeated several times.   60

Then he reached out and touched me.

—Repelled,
        I pulled back . . . But he became
frantic, demanding that I become
the body he split into: 65
                    'It's harder
to manage *each* time! Please,
give me your energy;—*help me!*'

                    —I said it was impossible,
there was *no part* of us the same: 70
we were just watching a parade together:
(and then, as he reached for my face)
                    leave me *alone!*

He smirked, and said
I was never alone.   75

                    I told him to go to hell.

He said that this was hell.

                    —I said it was impossible,
there was *no part* of us the same:
we were just watching a parade together: 80
                              when I saw

Grief, avenging Care, pale
Disease, Insanity, Age, and Fear,
                    —all the raging desolations

which I had come to learn were my patrimony;   85
the true progeny of my parents' marriage;
the gifts hidden within the mirror;

—standing guard at the gate of this place,
triumphant,
                    striking poses   90
                              eloquent of the disasters they embodied . . .

—I took several steps to the right, and saw
Kennedy was paper-thin,
                    as was de Gaulle;
mere cardboard figures   95
whose possible real existence
lay buried beneath a million tumbling newspaper photographs ...

—I turned, and turned, but now all that was left
was an enormous
                    fresco;—on each side, the unreadable   100
                                fresco of my life ..."

Judy Grahn

Judy Grahn was born (in 1940) in Chicago and lived there until she was nine,
when her parents moved to New Mexico. She graduated from San Francisco State
University and has continued to live and work in the Bay area. She writes for, as
well as about, "common" women and is committed to developing an accessible
feminist and lesbian working-class aesthetic. Her poetry up to 1977 has been
collected in a volume named *The Work of a Common Woman* (1978). Other books
include *The Queen of Wands* (1982), and *Another Mother Tongue: Gay Words, Gay
Worlds* (1984).

THE COMMON WOMAN

I. Helen, at 9 am, at noon, at 5:15

Her ambition is to be more shiny
and metallic, black and purple as
a thief at midday; trying to make it
in a male form, she's become as
stiff as possible.   5
Wearing trim suits and spike heels,
she says "bust" instead of breast;
somewhere underneath she
misses love and trust, but she feels
that spite and malice are the   10
prices of success. She doesn't realize
yet, that she's missed success, also,
so her smile is sometimes still
genuine. After a while she'll be a real
killer, bitter and more wily, better at   15
pitting the men against each other
and getting the other women fired.
She constantly conspires.
Her grief expresses itself in fits of fury
over details, details take the place of meaning,   20
money takes the place of life.
She believes that people are lice

who eat her, so she bites first; her
thirst increases year by year and by the time
the sheen has disappeared from her black hair,   25
and tension makes her features unmistakably
ugly, she'll go mad. No one in particular
will care. As anyone who's had her for a boss
will know
the common woman is as common   30
as the common crow.

II. Ella, in a square apron, along Highway 80

She's a copperheaded waitress,
tired and sharp-worded, she hides
her bad brown tooth behind a wicked
smile, and flicks her ass   35
out of habit, to fend off the pass
that passes for affection.
She keeps her mind the way men
keep a knife—keen to strip the game
down to her size. She has a thin spine,   40
swallows her eggs cold, and tells lies.
She slaps a wet rag at the truck drivers
if they should complain. She understands
the necessity for pain, turns away
the smaller tips, out of pride, and   45
keeps a flask under the counter. Once,
she shot a lover who misused her child.
Before she got out of jail, the courts had pounced
and given the child away. Like some isolated lake,
her flat blue eyes take care of their own stark   50
bottoms. Her hands are nervous, curled, ready
to scrape.
The common woman is as common
as a rattlesnake.

III. Nadine, resting on her neighbor's stoop

She holds things together, collects bail,   55
makes the landlord patch the largest holes.
At the Sunday social she would spike
every drink, and offer you half of what she knows,
which is plenty. She pokes at the ruins of the city
like an armored tank; but she thinks   60
of herself as a ripsaw cutting through
knots in wood. Her sentences come out
like thick pine shanks
and her big hands fill the air like smoke.
She's a mud-chinked cabin in the slums,   65
sitting on the doorstep counting
rats and raising 15 children,

half of them her own. The neighborhood
would burn itself out without her;
one of these days she'll strike the spark herself.   70
She's made of grease
and metal, with a hard head
that makes the men around her seem frail.
The common woman is as common as
a nail.   75

IV. *Carol, in the park, chewing on straws*

She has taken a woman lover
whatever shall we do
she has taken a woman lover
how lucky it wasnt you
And all the day through she smiles and lies   80
and grits her teeth and pretends to be shy,
or weak, or busy. Then she goes home
and pounds her own nails, makes her own
bets, and fixes her own car, with her friend.
She goes as far   85
as women can go without protection
from men.
On weekends, she dreams of becoming a tree;
a tree that dreams it is ground up
and sent to the paper factory, where it   90
lies helpless in sheets, until it dreams
of becoming a paper airplane, and rises
on its own current; where it turns into a
bird, a great coasting bird that dreams of becoming
more free, even, than that—a feather, finally, or   95
a piece of air with lightning in it.
        she has taken a woman lover
        whatever can we say
She walks around all day
quietly, but underneath it   100
she's electric;
angry energy inside a passive form.
The common woman is as common
as a thunderstorm.

V. *Detroit Annie, hitchhiking*

Her words pour out as if her throat were a broken   105
artery and her mind were cut-glass, carelessly handled.
You imagine her in a huge velvet hat with great
dangling black feathers,
but she shaves her head instead
and goes for three-day midnight walks.   110
Sometimes she goes down to the dock and dances
off the end of it, simply to prove her belief

that people who cannot walk on water
are phonies, or dead.
When she is cruel, she is very, very   115
cool and when she is kind she is lavish.
Fishermen think perhaps she's a fish, but they're all
fools. She figured out that the only way
to keep from being frozen was to
stay in motion, and long ago converted   120
most of her flesh into liquid. Now when she
smells danger, she spills herself all over,
like gasoline, and lights it.
She leaves the taste of salt and iron
under your tongue, but you dont mind.   125
The common woman is as common
as the reddest wine.

VI. *Margaret, seen through a picture window*

After she finished her first abortion
she stood for hours and watched it spinning in the
toilet, like a pale stool.   .   130
Some distortion of the rubber
doctors with their simple tubes and
complicated prices,
still makes her feel guilty.
White and yeasty.   135
All her broken bubbles push her down
into a shifting tide, where her own face
floats above her like the whole globe.
She lets her life go off and on
in a slow strobe.   140
At her last job she was fired for making
strikes, and talking out of turn;
now she stays home, a little blue around the edges.
Counting calories and staring at the empty
magazine pages, she hates her shape   145
and calls herself overweight.
Her husband calls her a big baboon.
Lusting for changes, she laughs through her
teeth, and wanders from room to room.
The common woman is as solemn as a monkey   150
or a new moon.

VII. *Vera, from my childhood*

Solemnly swearing, to swear as an oath to you
who have somehow gotten to be a pale old woman;
swearing, as if an oath could be wrapped around
your shoulders   155
like a new coat:
For your 28 dollars a week and the bastard boss

you never let yourself hate;
and the work, all the work you did at home
where you never got paid;   160
For your mouth that got thinner and thinner
until it disappeared as if you had choked on it,
watching the hard liquor break your fine husband down
into a dead joke.
For the strange mole, like a third eye   165
right in the middle of your forehead;
for your religion which insisted that people
are beautiful golden birds and must be preserved;
for your persistent nerve
and plain white talk—   170
the common woman is as common
as good bread
as common as when you couldnt go on
but did.
For all the world we didnt know we held in common   175
all along
the common woman is as common as the best of bread
and will rise
and will become strong—I swear it to you
I swear it to you on my own head   180
I swear it to you on my common
woman's
head

Miguel Algarin

Miguel Algarin was born (in 1941) in Santurce, Puerto Rico. In the fifties he and
his family moved to New York, first to Spanish Harlem and then to Queens. He
received a B.A. from the University of Wisconsin, an M.A. from Pennsylvania State
University, and a Ph.D. from Rutgers University where he currently serves on the
faculty of the English and Caribbean Studies departments. Algarin was one of the
first to identify the group known as "Nuyoricans," Puerto Ricans more at home
in New York than in Puerto Rico. He is a leader in the Nuyorican arts community,
having founded the Nuyorican Poets' Cafe, a gathering place for Nuyorican writers. He himself has written poetry, plays, and translations. His books of poetry
include *Mongo Affair* (1978), *On Call* (1980), *Body Bee Calling from the 21st Century*
(1982), and *The Time Is Now/Ya es tiempo* (1984).

"ALWAYS THROW THE FIRST PUNCH"

My uncle always insisted,
"strike the first punch,
put your enemy on the run,"
I always threw the first punch,

I remember   5
"attack, attack, attack,
put the hurting
on his limbs,"
I remember,
I remember   10
the night my uncle
got angry because I said
his wife thought his nuts
were christmas walnuts
and that she cracked them   15
every day of the year,
his left arm twitched,
I leapt at him
and struck first.

TAOS PUEBLO INDIANS: 700 STRONG ACCORDING TO BOBBY'S LAST CENSUS

It costs $1.50 for my van to enter
Taos Pueblo Indian land,
adobe huts, brown tanned Indian red skin
reminding me of brown Nuyorican people,
young Taos Pueblo Indians   5
ride the back of a pick up truck
with no memories of mustangs
controlled by their naked calves and thighs,
rocky, unpaved roads, red brown dirt,
a stream bridged by wide trunk planks,   10
young warriors unloading thick trunks
for the village drum makers to work,
tourists bringing the greens,
Indian women fry flour and bake bread,
older men attend curio shops,   15
the center of the village is a parking lot
into which America's mobile homes
pour in with their air conditioned cabins, color
T.V., fully equipped kitchens, bathrooms
with flushing toilets and showers,   20
A.M. & F.M. quadrophonic stereo sound,
cameras, geiger counters, tents,
hiking boots, fishing gear and mobile telephones,
"restricted" signs are posted round the parking lot
making the final stage for the zoo   25
where the natives approach selling
American Jewelry made in Phoenix
by a foster American Indian from Brooklyn
who runs a missionary profit making turquoise jewelry shop

"Ma, is this clean water?   30
do the Indians drink out of this water?
is it all right for me to drink it?"
the young white substitute teacher's daughter
wants to drink some Indian water,
young village school children recognize her,   35
and in her presence the children snap
quick attentive looks that melt into
"boy am I glad I'm not in school"
gestures as we pass,
but past, past this living room zoo,   40
out there on that ridge,
over there, over that ridge,
on the other side of that mountain,
is that Indian land too?
are there leaders and governments over that ridge?   45
does Indian law exist there?
who would the Pueblo Indian send
to a formal state meeting
with the heads of street government,
who would we plan war with?   50
can we transport arms earmarked for ghetto
warriors, can we construct our street
government constitutions on your land?
when orthodox Jews from Crown Heights
receive arms from Israel in their territorial struggle   55
with local Brooklyn Blacks,
can we raise your flag
in the Lower East Side
as a sign of our mutual treaty of protection?
"hey you you're not supposed to walk in our water,"   60
"stay back we're busy making bread,"
these were besides your "restricted zones"
the most authoritative words
spoken by your native tongue,
the girl's worry about her drinking water   65
made Raúl remove his Brazilian made shoes
from the Pueblo Indian drinking cup,
the old woman's bread warning
froze me dead on the spot
"go buy something in the shop,   70
you understand me, go buy something,"
I didn't buy I just strolled on by the curio shops
till I came across Bobby the police officer,
taught at Santa Fe, though he could've gone on to Albuquerque,
Taos Pueblo Indians   75
sending their officers of the law to be trained
in neighboring but foreign cities like in New Mexico
proves that Taos Pueblo Indians
ignore that a soldier belongs to his trainer
that his discipline, his habitual muscle response   80

belongs to his drill sergeant master:
"our laws are the same as up in town"
too bad Bobby! they could be your laws,
it's your land!
then flashing past as I leave Taos Bobby speeds   85
towards the reservation in a 1978 GMC van with two red flashers
on top bringing Red Cross survival rations to the Taos Pueblo Indians
respectfully frying bread for tourists
behind their sovereign borders.

Geary Hobson

Geary Hobson, Cherokee, Quapaw, and Chickasaw, was born in 1941 in Chicot
County, Arkansas. He edited a standard collection of Native American writing, *The
Remembered Earth* (1979). His own latest book of poetry is *Deer Hunting and Other
Poems* (1988). He teaches in the English department of the University of Okla-
homa.

DEER HUNTING

1

"God dammit, Al. Are you gonna help me
cut up this deer, or
are you gonna stand there all day
drinking deer and yakking?"
    Knives flash in savage motion   5
flesh from hide quickly severs
as the two men rip the pelt tail downwards
from the head. The hide but not
the head is kept. Guts spew forth
in a riot of heat and berries and shit,   10
as is quickly kicked into the trash hole.
    Hooves are whacked off,
and thrown also to the waste hole—
a rotted hollow stump.
But the antler rack is saved,   15
sawed from the crown with a hand-saw,
trophy of the hunt,
like gold teeth carried home
from the wars
in small cigar boxes.   20
    Men stand around in little groups,
bragging how the deer fell to their rifles
and throw their empties into the stump-hole.
    Al walks to the stump, unzips his pants.
"Hell, Bob, you're so fucking slow,   25
I could skin ten deer while you're doing one

and I'll show you up just as soon
as I take a piss."
   The hounds,
tired from the slaughter,   30
watch the men. They whine
for flesh denied them
and turn to pans filled with Purina.

2

"Now, watch me, ungilisi, grandson,
as I prepare this deer   35
which the Great Spirit has given to us
for meat."
   The old man hangs the carcass
feet-first from the pecan tree
with gentleness   40
like the handling of spider-webbing
for curing purposes.
   Slow cuts around the hooves,
quick slices of the knives as
the grandfather and father   45
part the hide from the meat.
The young boy—now a man—
stands shy and proud,
his initiating kill before him,
like a prayer unexpected,   50
his face still smeared
with the deer's blood of blessing.
   The hide is taken softly,
the head and antlers brought easily with it,
in a downward pull by the two men.   55
   Guts in a tumbling rush
fall into the bucket
to be cooked with the hooves
into a strength stew
for the hunting dogs   60
brothers who did their part in the chase.
   The three men share the raw liver,
eating it to become
part of the deer.
   The older man cuts   65
a small square of muscle
from the deer's dead flank,
and tosses it solemnly into the bushes
behind him, giving back part of the deer's swiftness
to the place from which it came.   70
   Softly, thankfully, the old man
breathes to the woods,
and turns and smiles at his grandson,
now become a man.

CENTRAL HIGHLANDS, VIET NAM, 1968

1

An eagle glides above the plain
where mice scurry in a vortex
of smoke and blood.
Wings dip, soar downward
in a clash   5
of fire
and upheaval
of earth and bone.

2

You will die, Dull Knife,
and your people,
and your vanquisher's descendants   10
will weep over their father's deeds.

3

In the mountains of Viet Nam
the Meo people, too,
will pass
from this world in napalm flashes   15
and burnt-out hillsides
and all that will be left
to give
will be
the helpless tears   20
of history future.

4

The eagle flies blindly
into the smoke of his past.

Simon J. Ortiz

Simon J. Ortiz (b. 1941) is from Acoma Pueblo in New Mexico. He has a master's
degree from the University of Iowa and has taught at a number of colleges and
universities. He writes both fiction and poetry, and his story "Kaiser and the War"
appears in the fiction section of this anthology. His collection of poems *Going for
the Rain* (1976) is based on a journey he made across the United States looking
for Indians and the way they live. Other poetry collections include *A Good Journey*
(1977) and *From Sand Creek* (1981).

TWO WOMEN

She is a Navajo woman sitting at her loom.
The sun is not far up, but she has already prepared
her husband's and sons' breakfasts,
and they have eaten and left.
Today, her husband will pull the weeds   5
from among the pumpkin, squash, and cornplants
in their small field at the mouth of Redwater Wash.
The two sons have driven their sheep and goats
to the Hill With White Stones. And she is left
in the calm of her work at the loom.   10

Quickly, Grandmother,
the Spider spins,
quick flips and turns,
the colors.

O the colors, Grandmother,   15
I saw in the two-days-ago rainbow.

O Grandmother Spider, the sun is shining
through your loom.

She works gently, her skirt flared out,
in the sun of this morning's Summer.   20

Desbah is grinding corn into meal.
The kernels of the corn are blue
with a small scattering of whites;
they are hard and she can hear them
crack sharply under the handstone   25
she is using. She reaches into a sack
for the corn and puts them on the stone.
Her father, Silversmith, brought it
one evening to her. He had it tied
on his horse with some rope,   30
and it was wrapped in some canvas cloth.
As she stops momentarily grinding,
she can hear him again say, "This stone
for the grinding of corn is for my child.
The man who gets her will be pleased,   35
but he will not like to carry this heavy thing
around," and he had laughed with his love
and hopes for her. Silversmith had gone
on ahead many years ago, and she never did
have a man get her.   40

She can hear the blue and white kernels
crack sharply on the heavy stone.

MANY FARMS NOTES

taken on a Many Farms,
Arizona trip, Spring 1973

1

Hawk circles
on wind roads
only he knows
how to follow
to the center.

2

Hawk's bright eyes
read trees, stones,
points in horizon,
movements, how wind
and shadows play
tricks, and sudden
rabbit flurry
which reminds him
of his empty stomach.

3

A Tuba City girl asks me
if I ever write from paintings.
I tell her that I write
with visions in my head.

4

I'm walking out of Gallup.
He calls, "Hey, my fren,
where you going too fas'?"
"Many Farms."
"Good lucks."
I smile for his good thoughts.

5

A wind vision:
if you look into the Chinle Valley,
you will see the Woman's cover,
a tapestry her Old Mother worked
for 10 million years or so.

6

On the way south to the junction,   30
I looked to the northeast
and couldn't decide whether that point
in the distance beyond the Defiance uplift
was Sonsela Butte or Fluted Rock.

7

The L.A. Kid was a city child   35
and a Navajo rodeo queen,
who said she'd seen me on the road
coming out of Window Rock,
said her friend had said,
"I think that was him;   40
we just passed him up,"
and felt so bad,
said she was born in L.A.
but wasn't really a city girl
and visited her homeland   45
every Summer, and said
her mother was from Lukachukai.

8

Bear occurs several times, of course:

The day before I went to Many Farms,
received a card from Snyder,   50
said he'd "spent a day watching grizzly bear"
grizzling at the San Diego Zoo.

Navajo girl had a painting of Bear.
He was facing east and looking up.
A line was drawn through him,   55
from chest to tail, rainbow muted colors,
and I said, "That line seems to be both
the horizon and the groundline where you start."

She told me about what the people say.
Don't ever whistle at night where bears are,   60
because female bears do that
when there are courting bears around.
Remember that: don't whistle
in the dark, horny Bear night.

That Navajo girl asked me   65
what I thought about polygamy.
I told her I thought it was a good idea
but not for keeps, and we laughed.
I wonder how many wives Bear has?

9

For Monday night supper, we had   70
mutton ribs, round steak,
good Isleta bread, tortillas,
broccoli, green chili, potatoes,
gravy, coffee, and apple pie.
The mutton was tough and Francis said,   75
"You gotta be tough
to live on this land."

10

After I got out of the back
of a red pickup truck,
I walked for about a mile   80
and met three goats, two sheep and a lamb
by the side of the road.
I was wearing a bright red wool cap
pulled over my ears,
and I suppose they thought I was maybe weird   85
because they were all ears and eyes.
I said, "Yaahteh, my friends.
I'm from Acoma, just passing through."
The goat with the bell jingled it
in greeting a couple of times.   90
I could almost hear the elder sheep
telling the younger, "You don't see
many Acoma poets passing through here."

11

"What would you say that the main theme
of your poetry is?"   95
"To put it as simply as possible,
I say it this way: to recognize
the relationships I share with everything."
I would like to know well the path
from just east of Black Mountain   100
to the gray outcropping of Roof Butte
without having to worry
about the shortest way possible.

12

I worried about two women discussing how
to get rid of a Forming Child   105
without too much trouble, whether
it would be in the hospital in Gallup
or in Ganado.
Please forgive my worry and my concern.

13

"Are you going to Gallup, shima?"   110
"Yes."
"One dollar and fifty cents, please."

Rayna Green

Rayna Green (b. 1942) is a Cherokee from Oklahoma. She holds a Ph.D. in folklore and works at the Smithsonian Institution in Washington, where she heads a program in Native American scientific and technical development. Her poems have appeared in a number of magazines and anthologies. She currently is working on a detective novel named *Give-Away*, whose protagonist is a female Indian detective named Ramona Sixkiller.

WHEN I CUT MY HAIR

when I cut my hair
at thirty-five
Grandma said she'd forgive me
for cutting it
without her permission   5

but I cried out everytime
I touched my head

years from then
and Grandma dead
it came back to me last night when   10
you said you wanted it all

your rich body grounding me safe
the touch of your hair
took me out
I saw pigeon feathers   15
red wool
and fur

and it wrapped me
with the startled past
so sudden   20
your hair falling all around us

I touched center
and forgave myself

COOSAPONAKEESA (MARY MATHEWS MUSGROVE BOSOMSWORTH), LEADER OF THE CREEKS, 1700–1783

for Joy Harjo

what kind of lovers could they have been
these colonists

good enough to marry them everyone
or was it something else that made her take them on

all woman   5
part swamp rat
half horse
she rode through Georgia
It was hers and the Creeks'
and Oglethorpe wanted it all   10

But she rolled with him too
and kept them at bay
for too long
'til they said
she'd sold out for the goods   15

the money and velvet was what she loved
sure enough
but Ossabaw and Sapelo and Savannah more
so she fought them with sex and war
and anything that worked   20
until they rolled over her

The Creeks say Mary came back as Sherman
just to see what they'd taken away
burned to the ground
and returned to her once more   25

The Creek girls in Oklahoma
laugh like Mary now
wild and good
they'll fight you for it
and make you want everything all over again   30

no deals this time though
it's all
or nothing

Marilyn Hacker

Marilyn Hacker was born in 1942 in New York City and educated at New York University and the Art Students League. She has taught writing at several univer-

sities and divides her time between New York and Paris, where she spends part of
each year with her daughter. Hacker's first book, *Presentation Piece* (1974) won
both the Lamont Prize and the National Book Award. Her poetic voice is a
distinctive one; one critic has characterized her tone as "rakish." It is witty, ironic,
and self-mocking. *Presentation Piece* was followed by *Separations* (1976), *Taking
Notice* (1980), and *Assumptions* (1985). *Love, Death, and the Changing of the Seasons*
(1986) is a novel in sonnets that tells the story of a passionate lesbian relationship
from beginning to end. *The Hang-Glider's Daughter: New and Selected Poems* and
Going Back to the River both appeared in 1990.

FEELING AND FORM

for Sandy Moore and for Susanne K. Langer

Dear San: Everybody doesn't write poetry.
A lot of people doodle profiles, write
something they think approximates poetry
because nobody taught them to read poetry.
Rhyming or trailing gerunds, clumps of words   5
straggle a page, unjustified—poetry?
It's not like talking, so it must be poetry.
Before they learn to write, all children draw
pictures grown-ups teach them how not to draw.
Anyone learns/unlearns the craft of poetry   10
too. The fourth grader who gets a neat like-
ness of Mom in crayon's not unlike

the woman who sent you her Tone Poem, who'd like
her admiration praised. That isn't poetry,
unless she did the work that makes it like   15
this, any, work, in outrage, love, or lik-
ing an apple's October texture. Write
about anything—I wish I could. It's like
the still-lives you love: you don't have to like
apples to like Cezanne. I do like words,   20
which is why I make things out of words
and listen to their hints, resounding like
skipping-stones radiating circles, drawing context from text, the way I've watched you draw

a pepper shaker on a table, draw   25
it again, once more, until it isn't like
anything but your idea of a drawing, like an idea of movement, drawing its shape from sequence. You write poetry.
I was a clever child who liked to draw,   30
and did it well, but when I watch you draw,
you rubber-face like I do when I write:
chewed lip, cat-tongue, smiles, scowls that go with right

choices, perplexed, deliberate, withdrawn
in worked play, conscious of the spaces words
or lines make as you make them, without words   35

for instant exegesis. Molding words
around a shape's analogous to drawing these coffee-cups in settings words
describe, but whose significance leaves words   40
unsaid, because it's drawn, because it's like
not my blue mug, but inked lines. Chosen words
—I couldn't write *your white mug*—collect words
they're meant, or drawn to, make mental space poetry
extends beyond the page. If you thought poetry   45
were merely nicely ordered private words
for two eyes only, why would you say, "Write
me a letter, dammit!" This is a letter, right?

Wrong. Form intimates fiction. I could write
me as a mathematician, weave in words   50
implying *you* a man, sixteen, a right-
handed abstract expressionist. I'd write
untruths, from which some other *you* could draw
odd inferences. Though I don't, I write
you, and you're the Donor on the right-   55
hand panel, kneeling in sable kirtle. Like-
ly I'm the lady left of you, who'd like
to peer into your missal, where the writing (legible Gothic) lauds in Latin poetry
the Lady at the center. Call her poetry,   60

virtual space, or Bona Dea. Poetry
dovetails contradictions. If I write
a private *you* a public discourse, words
tempered and stroked will draw you where you draw
these lines, and yours, convergent, made, unlike;   65

that likelihood draws words I write to poetry.

CONTE

(Cinderella, sometime after the affair of the glass/fur slipper)

First of all, I'm bored. It's not
what you'd think. Every day, meetings
I can't attend. I sit and sit and stick
my fingers with petit-point needles. Ladies
ignore me, or tell me all their petty secrets   5
(petty because *they* can't attend meetings)
about this man or that. Even his mistress
—*you* would have assumed he had a mistress—

gritted her teeth and had me come to lunch
and whined about the way she was mistreated.   10
And I suppose she's right, she was mistreated.
The plumbing is appalling, but I won't
go into that. He is forever brooding
on lost choices he might have made; before
three days had passed, I'd heard, midnight to dawn,   15
about the solitary life he craved.
Why not throw it all up, live on the coast
and fish, no, no, impossible with wives!
Why *not* throw it all up, live on the coast,
or cut my hair, teach (what?) little girls   20
and live at home with you? I schooled myself
for this, despised *you* for going to meetings,
reading instead of scrubbing, getting fat
(scorn of someone who burns off bread and puddings).
I made enduring tedium my virtue.   25
I'll have to keep my virtue. I could envy
you, but I'm sick of envy. Please allow
me now, at least, to call you sisters. Yours, C.

Haki Madhubuti

Haki Madhubuti (b. 1942; originally known as Don L. Lee) was prominent in the
flowering of black culture in Chicago in the 1960s. He was a founding member of
OBAC (Organization of Black American Culture), and has remained in Chicago,
operating the Third World Press and the Institute of Positive Education. Madhubuti was born in Little Rock, Arkansas, and was educated at Roosevelt University
and the University of Illinois, Chicago. He earned an M.F.A. at the University of
Iowa. Madhubuti's volumes of poetry include *Think Black* (1968), *Black Pride*
(1968), *Don't Cry, Scream* (1969), *We Walk the Way of the New World* (1970), and
Earthquakes and Survival Missions: Poetry and Essays of Black Renewal (1984).

THE SECRETS OF THE VICTORS

(the only fair fight is the one that is won)
Anglo-Saxon Proverb

forever define the enemy as less than garbage,
his women as whores & gutter scum,
their children as thieves & beggars,
the men as rapists, child molesters & cannibals,
their civilization as savage and   5
beautifully primitive.

as you confiscate the pagans' land, riches & women
curse them to your god for not being productive,
for not inventing barbwire and DDT,

perpetually portray the **natives**   10
as innocent & simple minded while eagerly
preparing to convert them to **your way.**

dispatch your merchants with
tins & sweets, rot gut & cheap wines.
dispatch your priest armed with   15
words of fear, conditional love and
fairy tales about strangers dying for you.
dispatch your military
to protect your new labor pool.

if there is resistance   20
or any show of defiance
act swiftly & ugly & memorably
when you kill a man
leave debilitating fear in the hearts of his
father, brothers, uncles, friends & unborn sons.   25
if doubt exist as to your determination
wipe the earth with his
women, girl children & all that's sacred;
drunken them in bodacious horror.
upon quiet, summon the ministers to   30
bless the guilty as you publicly
break their necks.
after their memories fade intensify the teaching.

instruct your holy men
to curse violence   while   35
proclaiming the Land Safe
introducing
the thousand year Reign of the Victors
as your Scholars
re-write the history.   40

SAFISHA

1

our joining into one proceeded like
sand through a needle's eye.
slow, bursting for enlargement & uncertainty.
a smoothing of passion and ideas
into spirited permanence and love.   5

there are decades of caring in you,
children loving that makes the father
in me active and responsible.
you forecasted the decline of marble shooting

& yo yo tricks, knowing too that hopscotch   10
& double dutch could retard early minds if
not balanced with challenges and language.

you are what brothers talk about
when serious & committed to loving life.
when examples are used to capture dreams   15
you are that woman.
for me you are summer at midlife,
daring spirit and middlenoon love
and the reason i return.

                                   2

dark women are music   20
some complicated well worked
rhythms
others   simple melodies.
you are like soft piano
black keys dancing between   25
& not becoming the white.
you bring dance & vision into our lives.
it is good & good
to be your
man.   30

LADY DAY[1]

hearing from you are smiles in winter
you   as you are
you warm and illuminating spaces
bring
blooming fruit in iceage times   5
with heated heated voices

believe me when i say
men will listen to you
most
will try to please you   10

there will be sun & thunder & mudslides
in your life
you will satisfy your days with work & laughter
and sunday songs.
your nights like most nights will   15
conjure up memories of easier seasons
happier suntimes and coming years

[1] Nickname of Billie Holiday (1915–59), great jazz singer. Madhubuti, however, seems not to be thinking so much of Billie Holiday specifically as of the connotations of her nickname.

earthcolors and rainbows will enter your heart
when least expected
often
in small enduring ways   like this
lovesong.

20

Louise Glück

Louise Glück was born (in 1943) in New York City and studied at Sarah Lawrence College and Columbia University. She has taught at Williams College in Massachusetts since 1983. Her volumes of poetry include *Firstborn* (1968), *The House on Marshland* (1975), *The Garden* (1976), *Teh* (1976), *Descending Figure* (1980), *The Triumph of Achilles* (1985), and *Ararat* (1990). Much of Glück's poetry is personal and domestic, but is so spare and lacking in circumstantial detail that it seems mythic.

FOR MY MOTHER

It was better when we were
together in one body.
Thirty years. Screened
through the green glass
of your eye, moonlight   5
filtered into my bones
as we lay
in the big bed, in the dark,
waiting for my father.
Thirty years. He closed   10
your eyelids with
two kisses. And then spring
came and withdrew from me
the absolute
knowledge of the unborn,   15
leaving the brick stoop
where you stand, shading
your eyes, but it is
night, the moon
is stationed in the beech tree,   20
round and white among
the small tin markers of the stars:
Thirty years. A marsh
grows up around the house.
Schools of spores circulate   25
behind the shades, drift through
gauze flutterings of vegetation.

POEM

In the early evening, as now, a man is bending
over his writing table.
Slowly he lifts his head; a woman
appears, carrying roses.
Her face floats to the surface of the mirror,   5
marked with the green spokes of rose stems.

It is a form
of suffering: then always the transparent page
raised to the window until its veins emerge
as words finally filled with ink.   10

And I am meant to understand
what binds them together
or to the gray house held firmly in place by dusk

because I must enter their lives:
it is spring, the pear tree   15
filming with weak, white blossoms.

THE SCHOOL CHILDREN

The children go forward with their little satchels.
And all morning the mothers have labored
to gather the late apples, red and gold,
like words of another language.

And on the other shore   5
are those who wait behind great desks
to receive these offerings.

How orderly they are—the nails
on which the children hang
their overcoats of blue or yellow wool.   10

And the teachers shall instruct them in silence
and the mothers shall scour the orchards for a way out,
drawing to themselves the gray limbs of the fruit trees
bearing so little ammunition.

Susan Griffin

Susan Griffin (b. 1943) lives and teaches privately in Berkeley, California. She has
won an Emmy Award for her play *Voices*. Her books of poetry include *Like the Iris
of an Eye* (1976) and *Unremembered Country* (1987).

GRANDMOTHER

After so long
she died.
Eighty years old,
they said,
"She had a long life;   5
she didn't suffer
when she went."
That's not the point.
But what is?
We should have all got   10
together
after all of these years,
strung out all over
the state, but she
would not have   15
a funeral and was
burned. She was
my Grandmother,
held me on her lap
when I was young.   20
I wept on her
breast and combed her
white hair, and
loved her for the way
her arms knew   25
my pain. She taught me
to read, and brush my
teeth, iron my clothes,
scramble eggs,
spread jam on bread,   30
clean up crumbs from
all the tables, grind
meat, stifle laughs,
grit my teeth, say the
right thing,   35
shake hands, watch to see
if my slip was hanging, to
put my hair in a french roll
wear mascara and
use a lip brush,   40
file my nails, bathe in
oil. She saved little things for me.
Her things, she'd say,
"My things, let me show
you my things; don't   45
let a stranger
who doesn't know
their value, touch

my things." The crystal
polar bears, the   50
rose plates,
the chair we could never
sit in. I don't want them.
I want
my Grandmother   55
so we might
do what we
should have done
in life,
sit down together   60
drunk or tired and
worn down or crazy with
ecstasy, so we might
sit down together
and sing out our grief.   65

GRANDFATHER

He leaned forward
the emphysema like silver
in his lungs,
"Those niggers,"
he coughed and   5
confided in me,
"they're all savages."
Dear Grandpa
of the carnation flower garden
and polished Dodge,   10
I remember you
fingering your nitrate ties,
pulling cigarettes from
leather cases, you
whispered about   15
"those niggers,"
and stood behind the
swinging door
as women brought you
plates of roast beef   20
and shined the kitchen floor.
He's in the cemetery
now, this old man
who liked to wink at me
and slip me shots of bourbon   25
behind my Grandma's back.
He played the mandolin and
told us stories—his
mind was full of
crime. The seven little   30

indians, the lady
in the lake. His argot
came from selling cars,
so much
was traded in, and now   35
there are more highways to
travel nowhere by. But
nothing
works against death; the savages
in his heart are coming home,   40
and they are his children
more savage than ever he dreamed

Lance Henson

Lance Henson (b. 1944) is a Cheyenne who grew up in Oklahoma and Texas. He did his undergraduate work at Oklahoma College of Liberal Arts, Chickasha, and received an M.A. in creative writing from the University of Tulsa. Henson's poetry is based upon traditional Cheyenne beliefs augmented by the teachings of Carl Jung. He believes that Native American culture offers images that can lead American culture from "the fetters of adolescence into the dark mysterious world of manhood." Henson has published a number of books of poetry, including *Selected Poems, 1970–1983* (1984).

warrior nation trilogy

1

from the mountains we come
lifting our voices for the beautiful
road you have given

we are the buffalo people
we dwell in the light of our father sun   5
in the shadow of our mother earth

we are the beautiful people
we roam the great plains without fear
in our days the land has taught us oneness
we alone breathe with the rivers   10
we alone hear the song of the stones

2

oh ghost that follows me
find in me strength to know the wisdom
of this life

take me to the mountain of my grandfather   15
i have heard him all night
singing among the summer leaves

3

great spirit (maheo)

make me whole
i have come this day with my spirit   20
i am not afraid
for i have seen in vision
the white buffalo
grazing the frozen field
which grows near the full circle   25
of this
world

five poems for coyote from cheyenne country

1

he is rust
      in moonlight

2

when the roadman paused
      we heard our brothers voice

3

in snow   5
   one track

4

eight without ears
hang upside down from fence posts
near hammon oklahoma

5

the moonlight splashes   10
in their
eyes

at the ramada inn

an aquarium of popcorn
bursts from visions of miss emilys
picture
just inside lawton at one fifteen
in the morning   5
it bourbon and seven
the tables are a shiny tin
whisper
the juke box occasionally skips
four miles distant   10
on a windy cemetery hill
a stone eagle that marks geronimos
grave
rises into the night
if i had to name this hour   15
i would hold it up to the light
and ask to be
something more

Pedro Pietri

Pedro Pietri (b. 1944) is a New York Puerto Rican poet. A playwright as well as a poet, he has had his plays produced in New York, California, and Puerto Rico, some in productions directed by Jose Ferrer and Joseph Papp. His collections of poetry include *Puerto Rican Obituary* (1973), *Lost in the Museum of Natural History* (1981), and *Traffic Violations* (1983).

INTERMISSION FROM MONDAY

have to leave the city
because sidewalks are sidewalks
parking meters are parking meters
and heavy traffic is very heavy
I know I will miss myself very much   5
every single second I am not around
but if I don't get out of town
blank walls might become blank walls
and that I cannot tolerate at all

have to leave the city   10
before my breakfast gets suspicious
and calls an ambulance to take me away
applauding a battle that was lost
because it made society safe for anxiety
O my lunch will be extremely lonely   15

and get cold and have to be discarded
when I am not around to stare at it
in the presence of gigantic noise makers

have to leave the city
when what you see is what you see   20
and what you don't see you don't see
and the imagination is classified
as excess luggage at the airport
where picture frames are picture frames
and the lines get longer and longer   25
for first class tickets on a bookshelf
where a poet has become a poet
to everyone except himself

INTERMISSION FROM FRIDAY

You don't remember what you did
Last night
You were too sober to walk
A straight line
Something about the way you don't   5
Comb your hair lately
Intimidates your dead english teacher
Who keeps coming
Back to life to make sure you don't
Get a raise or promotion   10

The invisible shades of your window
Keep coming down
And going all the way up unassisted
You want to laugh
As loud as possible but you know   15
What will happen
To all the nursery rhymes you learned
If you confess
That the sandwich you just ordered
Tried to take a bite   20
At you when your back was turned

Eternal balloon venders remind you
Mental illness isn't
A joke to make you rich and famous
You salute them   25
Doubting and fearing their presence.
You want to be left
Alone—but should the phone not ring
For a few weeks
You will lose your mind wondering   30
What you did wrong?

The neon eyes of discarded crucifix
You keep hidden
Around your exposed naked neck
Misdirects you
To the commotion trumpets and drums
And dynamite makes
In a parade to commemorate amnesia

Again you want to laugh outloudly
But to be on
The safe side of your insanity
You stand upsidedown
On your head and announce that you
Are not crazy yet!
Your last request is a prophylactic
Your last words are
If I have sin please congratulate me

THE NIGHT IS OUT OF SIGHT

In a dream I wasn't having yet
My father was expelled
From heaven and hell for walking
Through a few thousand walls
Under the influence of alcohol

Assured me everything was real
And unreal enough to frighten
Those who are dead serious about
What they are going to laugh at
The next time they get uptight

We sat down on bar stools to talk
About our magnificent mother
Whose hair has become a bouquet
Of flowers that are endless
In the smile of sad expressions

We got very drunk staying sober
And when daylight was finally over
We came to the sane conclusion
All conversations end with hello
& all greetings begin with farewell

He congratulated me for refusing
To remove my hat & stop dressing
In black regardless of the weather
Or the occasion—there is nothing
Anyone alive can do right or wrong

He said before deciding the time
Had come to discontinue talking
& continue walking through walls
To be discovered by other days &
Nights that make metaphor possible   30

So we departed to poetry forever
& ever to never again listen
To the ringing of alarm clocks
Reminding us nothing ever happens
If we must keep track of time   35

Sherley Anne Williams

Sherley Anne Williams (b. 1944) grew up in Bakersfield, California, and was educated at California State University at Fresno, Howard University, and Brown University. She has taught at Federal City College, California State University at Fresno, and California State University at San Diego, where she has been head of the English department. Her books include *The Peacock Poems* (1975), *Some One Sweet Angel Chile* (1982), and a novel, *Dessa Rose* (1986).

I WANT ARETHA[1] TO SET
THIS TO MUSIC:

I surprise girlhood
in your face; I know
my own, have been a
prisoner of my own
dark skin and fleshy   5
lips, walked that same high
butty strut despite
all this; rejected
the mask my mother
wore so stolidly   10
through womanhood and
wear it now myself.

I see the mask, sense
the girl and the woman
you became, wonder   15
if mask and woman
are one, if pain is
the sum of all your
knowing, victim the
only game you learned.   20

Old and in pain and
bearing up bearing up

---

[1] Aretha Franklin (b. 1942), famous American soul singer.

and hurt and age These
are the signs of our
womanhood but I'll
make book Bessie[2] did
more than just endure.

■

hear it?

                    hear it?

Oh I'm lonesome now   30
    but I won't be lonesome long
Say I'm lonely now
    but I don't need to be lonesome long
You know it take a man wid some style and passion
    to make a single woman sing these lonely songs   35

    one-sided bed Blues

Never had a man to talk to me
    to say the things he say
Never had a man talk like this, honey,
    say the things you say.   40
Man talk so strong
    till I can't tell Night from Day.

His voice be low words come slow
    and he be movin all the while
His voice be low words come slow   45
    and he be movin, Lawd! all the while.
I'm his radio and he sho
    know how to tune my dial.

My bed one-sided from me
    sleepin alone all the time   50
My bed *wop*-sided from me
    sleepin alone so much of the time
And the fact that it empty
    show how this man is messin wid my mind.

■

    what's out there knockin   55
    Is what the world
    don't get enough of

■

[2] Bessie Smith (1898?—1937), American blues singer.

you were never miss brown to me

I

We were not raised to look in
a grown person's mouth when they
spoke or to say ma'am or sir—
only the last was sometimes
thought fast even rude but daddy   5
dismissed this: it was yea and
nay in the Bible and this
was a New Day. He liked even
less honorary forms—Uncle,
Aunt, Big Mamma—mamma to   10
who? he would ask. Grown
people were Mr. and Miss
admitting one child in many
to the privilege of their
given names. We were raised to   15
make "Miss Daisy" an emblem
of kinship and love; you
were never Miss Brown to me.

II

I call you Miss in tribute
to the women of that time,   20
the mothers of friends, the friends
of my mother, mamma
herself, women of mystery
and wonder who traveled some
to get to that Project. In the   25
places of their childhoods, the
troubles they had getting grown,
the tales of men they told among
themselves as we sat unnoted
at their feet we saw some image   30
of a past and future self.
The world had loved them even
less than their men but this did
not keep them from scheming on
its favor. It was this that   35
made them grown and drew from our
unmannerly mouths "Miss"
before their first names.

I call
you Daisy and acknowledge   40
my place in this line: I am
the women of my childhood

just as I was the women of
my youth, one with these women
of silence who lived on the   45
cusp of their time and knew it;
who taught what it is to be grown.

Miguel Piñero

Miguel Piñero (1946–88) is perhaps best known as the playwright who wrote *Short Eyes* (1974). Piñero was born in Puerto Rico and emigrated to the United States when he was a child. He began writing *Short Eyes,* a play about prison life, when he was serving a term in Ossining Correctional Facility ("Sing Sing"). Originally produced by a company of convicts and ex-convicts, eventually it was produced by Joseph Papp at the New York Public Theatre. It won the Obie award for Best Off-Broadway Play of 1973–74 and has been produced all over the world. Piñero wrote a number of other plays and was also an accomplished poet. His poems first appeared in *Nuyorican Poetry* (1975), which he edited with Miguel Algarin and which presented for the first time the poetry of a new group of New York Puerto Rican writers. A collection of his poetry, *La Bodega Sold Dreams,* was published in 1980. Piñero died at the age of forty-two.

LA BODEGA[1] SOLD DREAMS

dreamt i was a poet
&
writin' silver sailin' songs
words
strong & powerful crashin' thru   5
walls of steel & concrete
erected in minds weak
&
those asleep
replacin' a hobby of paper candy   10
wrappin', collectin'
potent to pregnate sterile young
thoughts

i dreamt i was this poeta
words glitterin' brite & bold   15
strikin' a new rush for gold
in las bodegas
where our poets' words & songs
are sung
but   20
sunlite stealin' thru venetian
blinds

---

[1] "The grocery store" (Spanish.)

eyes hatin', workin' of time
clock
sweatin'   25
&
swearin'
&
slavin'
for the final dime   30
runnin' a maze
a token ride
perspiration insultin' poets
pride
words stoppin' on red   35
goin' on green
poets' dreams
endin' in a factoría as one
in a million
unseen   40

buyin' bodega sold dreams . . .

A LOWER EAST SIDE POEM

Just once before I die
I want to climb up on a
tenement sky
to dream my lungs out till
I cry   5
then scatter my ashes thru
the Lower East Side.

So let me sing my song tonight
let me feel out of sight
and let all eyes be dry   10
when they scatter my ashes thru
the Lower East Side.

From Houston to 14th Street
from Second Avenue to the mighty D
here the hustlers & suckers meet   15
the faggots & freaks will all get
high
on the ashes that have been scattered
thru the Lower East Side.

There's no other place for me to be   20
there's no other place that I can see
there's no other town around that
brings you up or keeps you down

no food little heat sweeps by
fancy cars & pimps' bars & juke saloons   25
& greasy spoons make my spirits fly
with my ashes scattered thru the
Lower East Side . . .

A thief, a junkie I've been
committed every known sin   30
Jews and Gentiles . . . Bums and Men
of style . . . run away child
police shooting wild . . .
mother's futile wails . . . pushers
making sales . . . dope wheelers   35
& cocaine dealers . . . smoking pot
streets are hot & feed off those who bleed to death . . .

all that's true
all that's true
all that is true   40
but this ain't no lie
when I ask that my ashes be scattered thru
the Lower East Side.

So here I am, look at me
I stand proud as you can see   45
pleased to be from the Lower East
a street fighting man
a problem of this land
I am the Philosopher of the Criminal Mind
a dweller of prison time   50
a cancer of Rockefeller's[1] ghettocide
this concrete tomb is my home
to belong to survive you gotta be strong
you can't be shy less without request
someone will scatter your ashes thru   55
the Lower East Side.

I don't wanna be buried in Puerto Rico
I don't wanna rest in long island cemetery
I wanna be near the stabbing shooting
gambling fighting & unnatural dying   60
& new birth crying
so please when I die . . .
don't take me far away
keep me near by
take my ashes and scatter them thru out   65
the Lower East Side . . .

---

[1] Nelson Rockefeller, Governor of New York, 1966–73.

Linda Hogan

Linda Hogan (b. 1947) is a Chickasaw writer from Gene Autry, Oklahoma. She is a successful fiction writer as well as a poet; her story "Aunt Moon's Young Man" appears in the fiction section of this book. She was educated at the University of Colorado and now teaches at the University of Minnesota. Her poetry collections include *Eclipse* (1983), *Seeing Through the Sun* (1985), and *Savings* (1988). A novel, *Mean Spirit*, was published in 1990.

LEAVING

Good-bye, divisions of people:
    those hickory-chopping,
    the hump hunters,
    skunk people
    dung people   5
    people who live under trees
    who live in broken houses
    and parts of houses.
    Their house worn out people
    are the meanest of all.   10

My house-cut-off people, I'm saying good-bye
to that person behind me.
She's the one
who tried to please her father,
the one an uncle loved for her dark hair.   15

White coyote behind me
light up your eyes, your white shadows,
your white round mouth
in its cage of black trees, a moon
running from branch to branch.   20
Moon that lives in the water,
snapping turtle that crawled out
at me.

Good-bye shooting horse
    above a dead man's grave.   25
Let that blessed rain.
where fish descended from the sky
                  evaporate.

Silver lures, minnows
in that river who is the moon   30
living in a broken house,
who is the coyote
dwelling among the blackjack broken off
people, the turtle

who lives in its round white shell,
   I can tell you good-bye.   35

Good-bye to the carved bone beads
I found by the river. They can grow back
their flesh,
   their small beating hearts,   40
   air in the bones
   and gray wings they fly
   away from me.

Good-bye to the milky way
   who lives in his old worn out place,   45
   dog white
   his trail.

All my people are weeping
when I step out of my old skin
like a locust singing good-bye,   50
feet still clinging
to the black walnut tree.
They say I've burned all my brown sticks
for telling time
and still it passes away.   55

SONG FOR MY NAME

Before sunrise
think of brushing out an old woman's
dark braids.
Think of your hands,
fingertips on the soft hair.   5

If you have this name,
your grandfather's dark hands
lead horses toward the wagon
and a cloud of dust follows,
ghost of silence.   10

That name is full of women
with black hair
and men with eyes like night.
It means no money
tomorrow.   15

Such a name my mother loves
while she works gently
in the small house.
She is a white dove
and in her own land   20

the mornings are pale,
birds sing into the white curtains
and show off their soft breasts.

If you have a name like this,
there's never enough water.   25
There is too much heat.
When lightning strikes, rain
refuses to follow.
It's my name,
that of a woman living   30
between the white moon
and the red sun, waiting to leave.
It's the name that goes with me
back to earth
no one else can touch.   35

R. T. Smith

R. T. Smith (b. 1947) is a Lumbee/Tuscarora Indian, born in Washington, D.C., and educated at the University of North Carolina–Charlotte and Appalachian State University. He is currently Alumni Writer-in-Residence at Auburn University in Alabama. His ten books of poetry include *Waking Under Snow* (1975), *Good Water* (1979), *Rural Route* (1981), and *Banish Misfortune* (1988).

GOYATHLAY[1]

Athabascan for "yawner," a boy's
habit before he learned the secret
language of the raiders, before
the elders knew he was a far seer.
He ran after the jackrabbit   5
and killed sidewinders with stones.
He prayed in the hogan or rode
his father's horse to bring
more corn to the tiswin makers.
He shot his arrows at rain crows.   10
On the mesa he spoke to storm clouds,
and the women loved him. His voice
was hard as chert.[2] It was darker.
A Chiricahua, he followed Cochise
across the border and earned   15
fame for stealing. The Mexicans
who had coined "Apache" from Zuñi

---

[1] As Smith explains, the real name of Geronimo (c. 1829–1909), leader of the Chiricahua Apache
Indians. The poem recounts the main events in his public life.
[2] A hard siliceous rock.

words for "enemy," called him
"Geronimo." "Jerome," a saint's
name that intrigued him. A war   20
leader, stoic, often wounded, he
saw the new reservation abolished
and took to the mountains,
drinking rain, gnawing on belt
leather. We know the story: 25
he was invisible, a nightmare,
a treacherous demon with genius
for guerilla moves, the perfect
desert creature, a Gila monster
adored by his warriors: Naiche,   30
Perico, Mangus and Fun. Chatto
he thought was the brown servant
of Chi-den, the Great Evil. He
strove to honor Ussen, the Greater
Good Spirit. He spoke Spanish.   35
He shot cattle and rose from sage,
from caliche³ and mist, from nowhere,
a myth with a Winchester, a wraith,
an icon of absolute scorn.
Hummingbirds on the ridge swarmed   40
to the flash of his red bandanna.
Untrackable, he eluded even Tom
Horn and painted his face purple
with the yellow sunstripe. Then
he surrendered, calling it wisdom,   45
calling it medicine and fatigue.
After the Skeleton Canyon Treaty
he was sent east on the Southern
Pacific. In San Antone the crowd
wished to lynch him. He sold his   50
buttons for souvenirs. By candles
he sewed on more. At Fort Pickens
he and his kin suffered from miasma,
the Florida climate. He smoked
cigars and stared at tourists.   55
A debutante fainted. He learned to
weave baskets, to till the soil.
He advised his children and wives
to obey their captors in silence.
He rarely slept and stared at stars.   60
He scrawled autographs and met
the young Walter Reed.⁴ He spoke
to the ocean and walked alone,
homesick for the White Mountains.

³ Hard desert soil.
⁴ U.S. Army surgeon who headed a commission to investigate a yellow-fever outbreak in Cuba. The commission demonstrated that the fever was transmitted by mosquitos.

More magician than council chief,   65
he remembered General Miles as
a man with a sneer. His torso
was strange with scars, an eye cut,
half shut forever. Lead lodged
in his tendons. He limped. In '94   70
they shipped him out west again,
to Fort Sill, after his wife Ga-ah
died of Bright's.[5] He played cards
and wore an officer's blue tunic
over his long shirt. For a quarter   75
he would print his name on bows
he carved. He loved tortillas
and would not eat hog. He taught
the prisoners to boil the salt
from their water. Always he was   80
a chanter, though his son Chappo
was the best dancer. In Oklahoma
he joined the Dutch Reformed and
took another wife. He gambled
and saw Christ as divine. Goyathlay   85
still saw the wide spirit world
but could no longer cure the Ghost
Sickness. In Roosevelt's first
inaugural gala, he waved at
his old enemies. In Saint Louis   90
he was a World's Fair attraction,
a man who had murdered and run
wild in the shadows, a bewildering
eater of cactus and roots. He
watched the sunrise to recall   95
the "heshke," the killer craze,
with sadness and ached for piñon
and ocotillo[6] shade. He worked
in the garden and wove the willow.
His family and clan loved him. He   100
drove to market and made the laws.
At eighty, still pious, still fierce,
he fell from a wagon, drunk on
his craft sales. He died alone,
an exile who yearned for canyons   105
and rock sheer, spoor and a circle
of elders, magpies rising against
red dawn. He could hear dust
blowing and ponies at great distance.
He gave his name to our acts   110
of airborne abandon.[7] He mourned

---

[5] Bright's disease, a chronic inflammation of the kidneys.
[6] Desert trees. Piñon is a pine-like tree, ocotilla a cactus-like one.
[7] Airborne troops traditionally yell "Geronimo!" when they parachute out of an airplane.

the wilderness as it vanished.
He wept only in his cold cell.
He killed with no venom and kept
vigils. Named for a saint, he swept 115
away with the wind but visits us
still. He yawned and chased arrows,
a boy who ran with the antelope,
a man who hid behind the moon,
who almost saved a renegade nation, 120
a man who fasted in the rain.

Sandra Maria Esteves

Sandra Maria Esteves (b. 1948) grew up in the Bronx, New York. She has been
active in the Nuyorican movement, both as a poet and as an activist and organizer.
She has also been active in the theater, as writer and as producer-director with the
African Caribbean Poetry Theater. Her books include *Yerba Buena: dibujos y poemas*
(1980), *Tropical Rains: A Bilingual Downpour* (1984), and *Bluestown Mockingbird
Mamba* (1990).

FOR FIDEL CASTRO

Cubano
I was but a child when you marched
a hundred thousand miles
in a war/spectacle media event rating higher
than Cleopatra, The Ten Commandments, and The Robe 5

But those who were sleeping awoke
when you arrived
warrior son of your country
new breed, pure soul, hombre
vowed to the flame truth 10

After blood was a birth
a new child to be nourished to health
ripped from an old bag of shells
hanging free from the sky

The growing is slow 15
the wound still bleeds
and the ocean stands in endless vigil

Twenty years later
this womantree has
thickly rooted in cement 20
mass profusions and
infinite rebellions

Here, from this land
  where chrome fades into plastic and famished spirit
I read the shells you have cast into the river   25
analyze the signs with the sea
and extend my palms to you as strength.

SOME PEOPLE ARE ABOUT JAM

Dedicated to Rich Bartee, the D-train Poetsinger

Whether they are drunk or sober
  rich or poor they jam everywhere
with everyone, and it doesn't matter when
        day or night there is always time for jamming
              from three a.m. to six in the afternoon   5
in any room of the house or any streetcorner
they jam in supermarkets funerals department stores
        rooftops, wherever they find people they jam
thru rain or sun, sleet or snow they will jam if they can
  (and even when they are not jamming   10
              they are thinking of new ways to jam
        and new people to jam with)
but one thing is certain
              they cannot be stopped from jamming
        even if you took their money and threw them in jail   15
they'd jam
        because jamming is what they are about

              I once knew someone who tried to jam on the subway
the police arrested him for disorderly conduct
        saying that jamming wasn't allowed   20
  he tried to convince them that jamming was really good therapy
        they didn't agree
  so they jammed him up good in the only way they knew how

Now he doesn't jam because he is dead
        but some say he's still jamming in the ether   25
  or in the air or wherever it is where his spirit remains
some say they have even seen him jamming
        somewhere between their dreams and the moon
a few wanted to bottle his jams and sell them wholesale
        but it had already been done with other people's jams   30
and the jamming market was low
  so in order to create a new market they printed pictures of him
  jamming on tee shirts with the letters J-A-M
              written over his head
        which they hoped to sell to his many friends   35
most of whom were women because they appreciated his jams
    much more than men, although there are some men
        who have jammed with him

and they will tell you
that he was about jam   40
it was all he ever did
and it didn't matter if he was drunk or sober
he jammed all the time

In fact, he believed so much in the power of jam
that he dedicated his life to it   45
spent all his time with it
tried to convince people to incorporate jam
into their vocabularies
and refused to do anything that did not include jam

People would ask him, "Why do you jam so much?"   50
and he would tell them
that without jam life wasn't worth living
that jam was the most necessary ingredient
to the existence of man on this planet
(and to the existence of women too   55
because jam was not the exclusive property of men)
it belonged to everyone
especially children
and he was always taking jam lessons from them
he learned that jamming wasn't limited   60
to size shape sex or race
that one could jam alone.

With one person

Or with one thousand people

And that's just what he did, he jammed   65
and jammed, and jammed
hoping that people would follow his example.

Albert Goldbarth

Albert Goldbarth was born in 1948 in Chicago and educated at the University of
Illinois–Chicago and at the University of Iowa, where he received an M.F.A. He has
taught at the University of Texas since 1977. Goldbarth's parents were religious
Jews, and Jewishness often forms part of the subject matter of his poetry, which
tends to be witty, voluble, and even baroque. He has published over a dozen chap-
books of poetry; *Original Light: New and Selected Poems 1973–1983* appeared in 1983.

BEFORE

The class was History, that's
what I wanted—the bridge
the bent Yid ragman took reluctantly

between steamship and sweatshop, or
older than that: the landbridge   5
something almost a horse was
grazing its way to Alaska
across on something almost hooves,
or older: something almost a leg
that was the grayveined print of a leg   10
in a web, before a bridge could be anything
more than a body's own
furthest extension. I was
seventeen. It was sunny. I'd come
from History, and before that   15
from a lineage of ragpickers,
songpluckers, kettlemenders, renderers
of humpfat for the candles, masters of
disputation over a nuance of scripture,
debtors, diddlers, elegiasts and jewelers   20
—history too, though the textbook
didn't say it. The page said Presidents
and paper. I wanted something from
before paper—wasps,
the fluted home of their making.   25
I wanted the first bone
of my bones. I wanted the word
before the alphabet, the word like a suckstone
working up spit. And then I stopped,
near Washtenaw and Ainslie, on the bridge   30
above the sewerage ditch, and sun
as if meeting a challenge made the stars
of a constellation-story burn
that urban rut's otherwise lustreless
flow. It was the sign of The Cart,   35
and there too, in the story, sun
bedazzled dull surfaces: all those heaps
of garment-district scraps he peddled,
a few abused tin pots, and who knows
how or why but some wholeskinned Spanish onions,   40
wool socks, and a single tired rose. I
still remember this: his humming something
tuneless, as if from before the idea of song
took full root in American soil—but
like the rose, though it drooped, though maybe   45
the worm ate in it, his song was handsome,
a lady would accept it and understand. And
this: my face was reflected, wavery
but ascertainably wide-eyed, on his pots.
Or in the sewerage currents—and then the   50
stars shifted, light was
sun again, and I was something almost
a man, on its way home,
humming its wanting. I was a boy

with a book. And this was long before 55
I'd learn to have words for what I wanted,
but what I wanted was something
like a bottle with a notepage in it,
thrown to sea—the clarity of glass,
but from before glass; and the urgency 60
of that written note, before writing.
—Maybe the water itself,
the message its salt.

A HISTORY OF CIVILIZATION

In the dating bar, the potted ferns lean down
conspiratorially, little spore-studded
elopement ladders. The two top buttons
of every silk blouse have already half-undone all
introduction. Slices of smile, slices of sweet brie, 5
dark and its many white wedges. In back

of the bar, the last one-family grocer's is necklaced
over and over: strings of leeks, greek olives, sardines.
The scoops stand at attention in the millet barrel,
the cordovan sheen of the coffee barrel, the kidney beans. 10
And a woman whose pride is a clean linen apron polishes
a register as intricate as a Sicilian shrine. In back

of the grocery, dozing and waking in fitful starts
by the guttering hearth, a ring of somber-gabardined grandpas
plays dominoes. Their stubble picks up the flicker like filaments 15
still waiting for the bulb or the phone to be invented. Even their
coughs, their phlegms, are in an older language. They move the simple
pieces of matching numbers. In back

of the back room, in the unlit lengths of storage, it's
that season: a cat eyes a cat. The sacks and baskets 20
are sprayed with the sign of a cat's having eyed a cat, and
everything to do with rut and estrus comes down to a few
sure moves. The dust motes drift, the continents.
In the fern bar a hand tries a knee, as if unplanned.

Wendy Rose

Wendy Rose (b. 1948) a Hopi/Miwok Indian, is an anthropologist as well as an
artist and poet. She teaches at the University of California at Berkeley and edits
the *American Indian Quarterly*, one of the major journals of Native American culture. Her books of poetry include *Lost Copper* (1980), *What Happened When the Hopi
Hit New York* (1982), and *The Halfbreed Chronicles* (1985).

TRUGANINNY

"Truganinny, the last of the Tasmanians, had seen the stuffed and mounted body of her husband and it was her dying wish that she be buried in the outback or at sea for she did not wish her body to be subjected to the same indignities. Upon her death she was nevertheless stuffed and mounted and put on display for over eighty years."

Paul Coe, Australian Aborigine activist, 1972

You will need
to come closer
for little is left
of this tongue
and what I am saying   5
is important.

I am
the last one.

I whose nipples
wept white mist   10
and saw so many
dead daughters
their mouths empty and round
their breathing stopped
their eyes gone gray.   15

Take my hand
black into black
as yellow clay
is a slow melt
to grass gold   20
of earth

and I am melting
back to the Dream.

Do not leave
for I would speak,   25
I would sing
another song.

Your song.

They will take me.
Already they come;   30
even as I breathe
they are waiting for me
to finish my dying.

We old ones
take such   35
a long time.

Please
take my body
to the source of night,
to the great black desert   40
where Dreaming was born.
Put me under
the bulk of a mountain
or in the distant sea,
put me where   45
they will not
find me.

KITTY

(That first night I slept next to a Gypsy and she looked at my hands and said I would survive. I knew then I would live because she had said so . . . next morning she was cold, dead you know . . .)
—*paraphrased from the narrative of Kitty Felix Hart, as she escorted her son, a Canadian doctor, around Auschwitz in 1978. When she was freed from the death camp, she fled to England and became a medical technician. Parenthetical statements are paraphrased from her narrative.*

I am still preparing
this tomboy hair
split like cake
beribboned
hands jittery   5
from the razor
and emptied
of girlhood
so fast

       (Mengele stood there. I had to strip   10
       completely and then I had to run. I had typhus,
       could hardly stand and was out of my head
       but if you couldn't run,
       you would be selected)

I came to know   15
the bones of my hands
gripping hunger
like a mandolin
and I would someday
paint the scars   20
red, renew it all
and show my children
the rails we rode
some of us dying
and some of us   25
praying, falling
from the cattle cars
like straw.

We approached
crowded into a single smell   30
and on the horizon
as the train began to slow
the flicker and rise
of fire, a glow

       (You got quite accustomed to bodies   35
       just heaped up. I carried them from
       the infectious hut; that was my job.
       Like this now: just one, two, three
       and throw them down. I had to load
       my friends on. That finished me,   40
       that really finished me. My mother
       stopped me from going on
       the electric fence ...)

Don't let the bones
be cast away   45
but keep them
like heirlooms;
lock them up
and guard them,
your grandfather,   50
his sons, everyone.
Forget if they grew deformed,
if they came to coat
the blue of test tubes,
if they resided   55
for a time
in the lab. Remember
machine guns,
wire fences
surrounded by knives,   60
mines buried beyond
and buried beyond that
where you stand now
in canyons of clay
burned faceless   65
my naked people.

       Ask the plains
       of barley stubble,
       the mud marked
       by Nazi boots,   70
              the small strong flowers
                 she has
                 survived

       Ask the smoking
       Polish sky,   75
       the flat lack

<pre>
of mountains,
        the fat spotted brown cattle
              she has
              survived   80

Ask the birches
tingling black
in brittle smoke,
the words wept
in English,   85
remembered
in Polish,
tears that wipe
the ovens clean
            and run the river to purity   90
              she has
              survived
              she has
              survived
</pre>

Leslie Marmon Silko

Leslie Marmon Silko (b. 1948) has identified her mixed heritage—Laguna, Mexican, white—as a fundamental element in her art: "I suppose at the core of my writing is the attempt to identify what it is to be a half-breed or mixed blooded person; what it is like to grow up neither white nor fully traditional Indian." Silko was born in Albuquerque, New Mexico, and grew up on the Laguna Pueblo reservation. She was educated at the University of New Mexico and is now Professor of English at the University of Arizona. The line between poetry and prose is not fixed in Silko's work. Her fiction sometimes incorporates passages of poetry, and her poetry emphasizes narrative rather than ornate language. Her first book was a collection of poems, *Laguna Woman* (1974), but it was her next work, *Ceremony* (1977), a novel, that made her name well known. *Storyteller* (1981) mixes poems and short stories. Her most recent book is *Almanac of the Dead* (1991). (Silko's story "Yellow Woman" appears in the fiction section of this book.)

PRAYER TO THE PACIFIC

<pre>
I traveled to the ocean
            distant
                  from my southwest land of sandrock
                  to the moving blue water
            Big as the myth of origin.   5

Pale
pale water in the yellow-white light of
                        sun   floating west
                              to China
                        where ocean herself was born.   10
Clouds that blow across the sand are wet.
</pre>

Squat in the wet sand and speak to the Ocean:
       I return to you   turquoise   the red coral you sent us,
              sister spirit of Earth.
Four round stones in my pocket   I carry back the ocean   15
          to suck and to taste.

Thirty thousand years ago
          Indians came riding across the ocean
          carried by giant sea turtles.
Waves were high that day   20
       great sea turtles waded   slowly out
            from the gray sundown sea.
Grandfather Turtle rolled in the sand   four times
         and disappeared
            swimming into the sun.   25

And so   from that time
      immemorial,
          as the old people say,
rain clouds drift from the west
          gift from the ocean.   30

Green leaves in the wind
Wet earth on my feet
      swallowing raindrops
          clear from China.

DEER DANCE/FOR YOUR RETURN

for Denny

If this
will hasten your return
then I will hold myself above you all night
blowing softly
down-feathered clouds   5
that drift above the spruce
and hide your eyes
as you are born back
to the mountain.

Years ago   10
through the yellow oak leaves
antlers polished like stones
in the canyon stream-crossing
      Morning turned in the sky
      when I saw you   15
      and I wanted the gift
      you carry on moon-color shoulders
      so big

                    the size of you
                    holds the long winter.   20

You have to come home with me before
a long way down the mountain
The people welcome you.

I took
the best red blanket for you   25
the turquoise   the silver rings
were very old
                something familiar for you
                blue corn meal saved special.

While others are sleeping   30
I tie feathers on antlers
whisper close to you
                we have missed you
                I have longed for you.

Losses are certain   35
in the pattern of this dance
Over the terrain a hunter travels
blind curves in the trail
seize the breath
until it leaps away   40
loose again
to run the hills.
                Go quickly.

How beautiful
this last time
I touch you   45
                to believe
                and hasten the return
                of lava-slope hills and
                your next-year heart   50
Mine still beats
in the tall grass
where you stopped.
                Go quickly.

Year by year   55
after the first snowfall
I will walk these hills and
        pray you will come again
I will go with a heart full for you
        to wait your return.   60

The neck pulse slacks,
then smoothes.
It has been a long time

Sundown forms change
Faces are unfamiliar   65
    As the last warmth goes
    from under my hand
    Hooves scatter rocks
    down the hillside
    and I turn to you   70
The run
for the length of the mountain
is only beginning.

Victor Hernandez Cruz

The poet and novelist Ishmael Reed has told of doing a poetry reading at Benjamin Franklin High School in 1966 and telling the audience that one of the best American poets was a student there: "When I mentioned [Victor Hernandez Cruz's] name, the students and teachers gasped. Victor Cruz, who has since that time gained a reputation as an international bilingual poet, was failing Spanish." Hernandez Cruz was born (in 1949) in Puerto Rico and moved with his family to Spanish Harlem when he was five. His first book of poems, *Papo Got His Gun,* was published when he was only seventeen. His poetry is influenced by the music of the Caribbean: "My family life was full of music, guitars and conga drums, maracas and songs. My mother sang songs. Even when it was five below zero in New York she sang warm tropical ballads." His work has made him the best known of the New York Puerto Rican poets. Later poetry collections include *Snaps* (1969), *Mainland* (1973), *Tropicalization* (1976), *By-Lingual Wholes* (1982), and *Rhythm, Content & Flavor* (1989).

today is a day of great joy

when they stop poems
in the mail   & clap
their hands & dance to
them
when women become pregnant   5
by the side of poems
the strongest sounds   making
the river go along

it is a great day

as poems fall down to   10
movie crowds   in restaurants
in bars

when poems start to
knock down walls   to
choke politicians   15

when poems scream &
begin to break the air

that is the time of
true poets   that is
the time of greatness   20

a true poet   aiming
poems & watching things
fall to the ground

it is a great day.

going uptown to visit miriam

on the train
old ladies playing football
going for empty seats

very funny persons

the train riders   5
                    are silly people
                    i am a train rider

but no one knows where i am
going to take this train

to take this train   10
to take this train

the ladies   read popular
paperbacks   because they
are popular   they get off
at 42 to change for the   15
westside line   or off
59 for the department store

the train pulls in & out
the white walls   dark-
ness   white walls   dark-   20
ness

ladies looking up   i
wonder where they going
the dentist   pick up
husband pick up wife   25
pick up kids
pick up ?grass?
to library   to museum
to laundromat   to school

but no one knows where i am   30
going to take this train

to take this train

to visit miriam
to visit miriam

& to kiss her   35
on the cheek
& hope i don't
see sonia on the
street

But no one knows where i'm taking   40
this train
         taking this train
         to visit miriam.

POEM

Your head it waves outside
You are as deep and heavy as the ocean
Night and day
Cabo Rojo[1]   the stars
Day and night   5
Arecibo   music in green
It rains   Rain washes coconuts
The mangos they fall off the trees
In midnights   You hear them falling
Sunshine   sol   10
Your eyes they become one with the light
It is early   Early Early Early
And the rooster is early
Like a natural alarm
The music of the morning   15

Your head is full of the ocean and
The mystery of the sea shells
It moves like the waves

Moving outside the rhythms of life
Dawn birth deep in the mountains   20
Your eyes   they move
In and out of the woods
They look for spirits

---

[1] The places mentioned in this poem are all in Puerto Rico.

Here is where our mothers are from
From this land sitting   25
All pregnant with sweetness
And trees that want to be the wind

Walking through the little space
The trees make
You want to laugh   30
In this lonely night there is music
And you do
And you don't stop
And the music is right behind you

Coquí   Coquí   Coquí   Coquí   35

Here is where the journey started
And you laugh as tall as palm trees
And you taste as good as pasteles[2]
You dance toward the silver of the stars
Everything moves with you   40
Like a tropical train.

Shawn Wong

Shawn Wong was born (in 1949) in Oakland, California, and grew up in Berkeley,
California. He was educated at San Francisco State University and the University
of California, Berkeley. He is presently a professor in the American Ethnic Studies
department at the University of Washington. Wong was one of the coeditors of a
landmark collection of Asian-American writing, *Aiiieeeee! An Anthology of Asian
American Writers* (1974) and its sequel *The Big Aiiieeeee! An Anthology of Chinese
American and Japanese American Writing* (1991). Wong has published a great deal
of poetry in magazines and has published a novel: *Homebase* (1979).

LOVE AMONG FRIENDS

In trust you showed me a photograph
of a ragged girl with long black hair
cradling a wounded baby.
She pretends to whisper rhymes to her sister
saying all the time, "Renew these bones."   5
Calmly, you tell me that there are places
where children
have learned to lie down like tigers
and watch for the fire,
the blue fire.   10

[2] Pastries.

Then you asked me to understand your spirit
because of love among friends.
To carry the wounded children,
to cradle their blue arms in mine.
Spring passes by in a moment of dreams   15
and we too have learned to sleep like tigers
to watch for the fire that is precious
blue and ceaselessly blue.

Being a mother you said
that you would pay for everything   20
not in guilt, but by commitment.
You must dream at night of your own
children lost in a world of red clouds.

This is not tragedy, do not concern yourself
with the children's fear,   25
they have seen nothing else, never sleep
long enough for dreams.
There are places like the Plain of Jars[1] to dream about,
and there are cold, restless places to sleep in.

ELEGY FOR A GREENHOUSE

For Arthur Okamura

Okamura's greenhouse fell down today
his colored cows were munching on a field
of moonlit nasturtiums
and used the nails of the roof for toothpicks.
The moonlight strikes the cows   5
coloring them black
and moon.
Their sides glow like walking atlases
the moon white countries
lost in their black hide oceans.   10
The seesaw of greenhouse windows in the wind
and the crash is a voice saying,
"Japanese artists make bad gardeners!"
They let their gardens grow
out of sight   15
pruning and nurturing the roots.

Michael Blumenthal

Michael Blumenthal (b. 1949) was raised in Manhattan, the son of Jewish refugees from Hitler's Germany, who spoke only German in the home. He earned a
degree in philosophy from the State University of New York at Binghamton and

---

[1] Plateau in Laos where several hundred ancient carved funerary urns have been discovered.

then took a law degree at Cornell. Since giving up the practice of law to write poetry, he has worked as a teacher, speech writer, editor, and arts administrator, and now teaches at Harvard. His poetry is notable for its comic-ironic tone. His collections include *Sympathetic Magic* (1980), *Days We Would Rather Know* (1984), and *Laps* (1984). His poem, "Advice to My Students: How to Write a Poem," appears earlier in this book in the introduction to poetry.

AGAINST ROMANCE

The two lovers tangled in the thicket
of their terrible passion do not yet know
one another, but they are delighted,
nonetheless, to be here, on this spring day,
among the periwinkles and crocuses,   5
because it is part of their beautiful image
of what love is, because they have been
to the cinema and can imagine, now,
a Mozart concerto or a Chopin nocturne
playing in the background, they can imagine   10
they are like the lovers in Bonnard's *Terrace*,[1]
but supine beneath the horse chestnuts
and magnolias, and that it is all part
of love's wild and ancient choreography
that has brought them here, something   15
as orderly and fated as sunrise, as simple
as the planets, and that now they will stroll happily
ever after into the sweet movie of their lives,
the light always at a perfect angle to the camera,
the beasts always trumpeted out from the brush   20
at the perfect moment, the obstacles
reshaping themselves like a boy's hand
placed under a blanket to amuse a kitten.
For months, maybe for years, they go on like this—
munching jackfruit in some beautiful tropic,   25
stalking the wild mushrooms of some pristine forest,
until they become the myth of themselves
they have been so long making,
the stars of their own enterprise,
and when life turns its dimmed lights up   30
once again and the theater empties,
they find the stranger love always delivers up
to the desperate, they see, at last, the reel
never shown at the theater—the one where
no music plays in the background, no blossom   35
rides the stem of the plucked flower,
and no face looks back at the smitten lover
but his own—hungry as it ever was, hungry
to reach back into the darkness, now, for real.

[1] A painting by the French painter Pierre Bonnard (1867–1947).

Carolyn Forché

In one sense, all poetry is "political poetry"; it implies or assumes a way of life that depends on political considerations, whether acknowledged or not. But Carolyn Forché (b. 1950) has practiced political poetry in a narrower and more explicit sense. The result is both powerful poetry and a powerful political statement. Forché was born in Detroit and earned a B.A. in, significantly, the two fields of international relations and creative writing. She went on to an M.F.A. in writing at Bowling Green University in Ohio. Her first book, *Gathering the Tribes* (1976) won the coveted Yale Series of Younger Poets Award. After some temporary teaching jobs, she worked for two years, 1978–80, in El Salvador as a writer and human rights activist. She dealt with this experience in *The Country Between Us* (1981), a collection of poems that was chosen as the Lamont Selection of the Academy of American Poets. Forché's work as reporter and poet raises the question of what the United States' involvement should be in El Salvadoran politics and, more generally, the dilemma of the committed individual confronting the horrors of twentieth-century history.

RETURN

For Josephine Crum

Upon my return to America, Josephine:
the iced drinks and paper umbrellas, clean
toilets and Los Angeles palm trees moving
like lean women, I was afraid more than
I had been, even of motels so much so   5
that for months every tire blow-out
was final, every strange car near the house
kept watch and I strained even to remember
things impossible to forget. You took
my stories apart for hours, sitting   10
on your sofa with your legs under you
and fifty years in your face.
              So you know
now, you said, what kind of money
is involved and that *campesinos*[1] knife   15
one another and you know you should
not trust anyone and so you find a few
people you will trust. You know the mix
of machetes with whiskey, the slip of the tongue
that costs hundreds of deaths.   20
You've seen the pits where men and women
are kept the few days it takes without
food and water. You've heard the cocktail
conversation on which their release depends.
So you've come to understand why   25

---

[1] Peasants; farm workers.

men and women of good will read
torture reports with fascination.
Such things as water pumps
and co-op farms are of little importance
and take years.   30
It is not Che Guevara, this struggle.
Camillo Torres is dead. Victor Jara
was rounded up with the others, and José
Martí is a landing strip for planes
from Miami to Cuba.[2] Go try on   35
Americans your long, dull story
of corruption, but better to give
them what they want: Lil Milagro Ramirez,
who after years of commitment did not
know what year it was, how she walked   40
with help and was forced to shit in public.
Tell them about the razor, the live wire,
dry ice and concrete, grey rats and above all
who fucked her, how many times and when.
Tell them about retaliation: José lying   45
on the flat bed truck, waving his stumps
in your face, his hands cut off by his
captors and thrown to the many acres
of cotton, lost, still, and holding
the last few lumps of leeched earth.   50
Tell them of José in his last few hours
and later how, many months later,
a labor leader was cut to pieces and buried.
Tell them how his friends found
the soldiers and made them dig him up   55
and ask forgiveness of the corpse, once
it was assembled again on the ground
like a man. As for the cars, of course
they watch you and for this don't flatter
yourself. We are all watched. We are   60
all assembled.

       Josephine, I tell you
I have not rested, not since I drove
those streets with a gun in my lap,
not since all manner of speaking has   65
failed and the remnant of my life
continues onward. I go mad, for example,
in the Safeway, at the many heads
of lettuce, papayas and sugar, pineapples
and coffee, especially the coffee.   70

---

[2] Latin American patriots and revolutionaries. Ché Guevara (1928–67) was a Cuban revolutionary who helped Castro in his rise to power. Camillo Torres was a Colombian reformist priest killed in action with revolutionary guerrillas in 1967. José Martí (1853–95) founded the Cuban Revolutionary Party. He died at the beginning of the final Cuban insurrection against Spain.

And when I speak with American men,
there is some absence of recognition:
their constant Scotch and fine white
hands, many hours of business, penises
hardened by motor inns and a faint   75
resemblance to their wives. I cannot
keep going. I remember the American
attaché in that country: his tanks
of fish, his clicking pen, his rapt
devotion to reports. His wife wrote   80
his reports. She said as much as she
gathered him each day from the embassy
compound, that she was tired of covering
up, sick of his drinking and the loss
of his last promotion. She was a woman   85
who flew her own plane, stalling out
after four martinis to taxi on an empty
field in the *campo*[3] and to those men
and women announce she was there to help.
She flew where she pleased in that country   90
with her drunken kindness, while Marines
in white gloves were assigned to protect
her husband. It was difficult work, what
with the suspicion on the rise in smaller
countries that gringos die like other men.   95
I cannot, Josephine, talk to them.

And so, you say, you've learned a little
about starvation: a child like a supper scrap
filling with worms, many children strung
together, as if they were cut from paper   100
and all in a delicate chain. And that people
who rescue physicists, lawyers and poets
lie in their beds at night with reports
of mice introduced into women, of men
whose testicles are crushed like eggs.   105
That they cup their own parts
with their bedsheets and move themselves
slowly, imagining bracelets affixing
their wrists to a wall where the naked
are pinned, where the naked are tied open   110
and left to the hands of those who erase
what they touch. We are all erased
by them, and no longer resemble decent
men. We no longer have the hearts,
the strength, the lives of women.   115
Your problem is not your life as it is
in America, not that your hands, as you

[3] Countryside.

tell me, are tied to do something. It is
that you were born to an island of greed
and grace where you have this sense   120
of yourself as apart from others. It is
not your right to feel powerless. Better
people than you were powerless.
You have not returned to your country,
but to a life you never left.   125

Ray A. Young Bear

Ray A. Young Bear (b. 1950) has been a lifelong resident of the Mesquakie (Red
Earth) Tribal Settlement in central Iowa. Since 1984 he has been performing
with his own drum and dance troupe, presenting authentic Mesquakie music and
dancing. His volumes of poetry include *Winter of the Salamander* (1980), *The Invisible Musician* (1990), and *Black Eagle Child: The Facepaint Narratives* (1991).

THE REASON WHY I AM AFRAID EVEN THOUGH
I AM A FISHERMAN

Who is there
to witness the ice
as it gradually forms itself
from the cold rock-hard banks
to the middle of the river?   5
Is the wind chill a factor?
Does the water at some point
negotiate and agree to stop
moving and become frozen?
When you do not know the answers   10
to these immediately you are afraid,
and to even think in this inquisitive
manner is contrary to the precept
that life is in everything.
Me, I am not a man;   15
I respect the river
for not knowing its secret,
for answers have nothing
to do with cause and occurrence.
It doesn't matter how early   20
I wake to see the sun shine
through the ice-fishing hole;
only the ice along
with my foolishness
decides when   25
to break.

THE LANGUAGE OF WEATHER

The summer rain isn't here yet,
but I hear and see the approaching
shadow of its initial messenger:
Thunder.
The earth's bright horizon   5
sends a final sunbeam directly
toward me, skimming across the tops
of clouds and hilly woodland.
All in one moment, in spite
of my austerity, everything   10
is aligned: part-land, part-cloud,
part-sky, part-sun and part-self.
I am the only one to witness
this renascence.
Before darkness replaces the light   15
in my eyes, I meditate briefly
on the absence of religious
importunity; no acknowledgement
whatsoever for the Factors
which make my existence possible.   20
My parents, who are hurrying
to overturn the reddish-brown dirt
around the potato plants, begin to talk
above the rumbling din.
"Their mouths are opening.   25
See that everyone in the household
releases part of ourselves
to our Grandfathers."
While raindrops begin to cool
my face and arms, lightning   30
breaks a faraway cottonwood
in half; small clouds of red
garden dust are kicked into
the frantic air by grasshoppers
in retreat.   35
I think of the time I stood
on this same spot years ago,
but it was under moonlight,
and I was watching this beautiful
electrical force dance above   40
another valley.
In the daylight distance,
a stray spirit whose guise
is a Whirlwind, spins and attempts
to communicate from its ethereal   45
loneliness.

Michael Madonick

Michael Madonick was born (in 1950) and raised in the Bronx, New York. He was educated at Rollins College and the University of Oregon and has won the Academy of American Poets Prize and the New Jersey Council on the Arts Distinguished Artist Award. Currently, he is teaching at the University of Illinois.

LETTER TO MY EX-WIFE WHO IS HAVING LUNCH WITH HAROLD BLOOM TOMORROW

Dear Marianna, Our lives are full of accident and I know
that is no way to start a letter, particularly if you choose
to share it, if I may be so bold as to be familiar, with
Harold. This morning, when I saw the red Rufous Hummingbird whine
in its display flight through the rhododendrons that line   5
the gate to the convent of Discalced Carmelite Nuns near the top
of Greenhill Road, I was of course reminded of our telephone
conversation about "Variations On a Summer Day," specifically the line,
"Damariscotta da da doo." But leave that to another note. The stars,
now, as stars are out West, are larger than the keen eyes of the weak-   10
fish that thrived once near the shores of New Haven. I have been
much interested in night, its demarcations, the land's
end poem that comes as seldom to my shore as Kansas'; and
the moon, the green moon that Stevens hardly speaks of
directly, which is large in the circle of things. Not that I care much   15
to talk of anxieties or almonds but lately, in talking
with you of your troubles, I am as impotent as a Jew without a sense
of judgement. Here, where the trees still remember how to grow
and salmon show themselves whole in the river, not dressed like Diane
Von Furstenburg on a Wedgewood platter at the Yale   20
Alumni Luncheon, I must admit to some
jealousies. I think I could love Harold,
myself, were it not for bad dreams and all that deconstruction
and angst spread like chopped-liver at a rabbi's funeral. But I did
not start this letter to raise such subjects as Flaubert's   25
umbrellas, the six D.A.R. women, tight-lipped and stealing
glances at the newly professed Benedictine running
in cut-offs through the rain, or my cousin, Milton
Finkel, whose name is still an embarrassment. I don't know why
I started this, at night, I would tell you if I knew, when I could be walking   30
under the pale green water
tower that rises, as a matter
of fact and not significance, like
so many other things. Sex
was always a problem for us. I could never concentrate well,   35
and for that I am sorry. But who's to say
that in its own way life wasn't better
without sweating and puddles on the sheets. If
Harold lays a hand on you
I'll kill him. Love, Ramon.   40

WHITE DEER

Dog. Unicorn. Deer. I find you on the way
Up my driveway, glaring at my car, as the target

Glares at the arrow. But the car stares back,
Losing its headlights' steel light in the powder

Of your powdered coat. And I think, at first,   5
You are a neighbor's dog, but then, believe

You leapt the fence of that medieval tapestry
And landed in the cloister of my woods. Dog.

Unicorn. How hard you stare this metal down,
As if it were some awkward armor you outran   10

A thousand years before. Too soon I see the rest,
Your family in dark suit behind you, standing

Like stone near the salt block, and I conjugate
again. Dog. Unicorn. Deer. And all

That Mystery once allowed succumbs to fact.   15

Jorie Graham

Jorie Graham (b. 1951) had a cosmopolitan childhood. The daughter of a journalist and a sculptor, she spent her childhood in Italy, studied at the Sorbonne,
took a degree in film studies from New York University, and then earned an
M.F.A. from the Iowa Writers Workshop where she now teaches. Graham is a
nature poet, though in a sense closer to Wallace Stevens than to William Wordsworth. She sees the world as being like a text for her to read, with equal attentiveness to text and reader. Her collections include *Hybrids of Plants and Ghosts*
(1980), *Erosion* (1983), and *The End of Beauty* (1987).

MIND

The slow overture of rain,
each drop breaking
without breaking into
the next, describes
the unrelenting, syncopated   5
mind. Not unlike
the hummingbirds
imagining their wings
to be their heart, and swallows
believing the horizon   10
to be a line they lift

and drop. What is it
they cast for? The poplars,
advancing or retreating,
lose their stature   15
equally, and yet stand firm,
making arrangements
in order to become
imaginary. The city
draws the mind in streets,   20
and streets compel it
from their intersections
where a little
belongs to no one. It is
what is driven through   25
all stationary portions
of the world, gravity's
stake in things. The leaves,
pressed against the dank
window of November   30
soil, remain unwelcome
till transformed, parts
of a puzzle unsolvable
till the edges give a bit
and soften. See how   35
then the picture becomes clear,
the mind entering the ground
more easily in pieces,
and all the richer for it.

MY GARDEN, MY DAYLIGHT

My neighbor brings me bottom fish—
    tomcod, rockcod—
a fist of ocean. He comes out
    from the appletrees between us
holding his gift like a tight   5
    spool of thread.

Once a week he brings me fresh-catch,
    boned and skinned
and rolled up like a tongue. I freeze them,
    speechless, angelic   10
instruments. I have a choir of them.
    Alive, they feed

driving their bodies through the mud,
    mud through their flesh.
See how white they become. High above,   15
    the water thins
to blue, then air, then less . . .
    These aren't as sweet

as those that shine up there,
    quick schools   20
forever trying to slur over, become water.
    But these belong to us
who cannot fall out of this world
    but only deeper

into it, driving it into the white   25
    of our eyes. Muddy
daylight, we utter it, we drown in it.
    You can stay dry
if you can step between the raindrops
    mother's mother   30

said. She's words now you can't hear.
    I try to wind my way
between what's here: chalk, lily, milk
    titanium, snow—
as far as I can say   35
    these appleblossoms house

five shades of white, and yet
    I know there's more.
Between my held breath and its small hot
    death, a garden,   40
Whiteness, grows. Its icy fruit
    seems true,

it glows. *For free* he says
    so that I can't refuse.

Joy Harjo

Joy Harjo (b. 1951) is of the Creek (Muscogee) tribe of Native Americans. She was born in Tulsa, Oklahoma, and earned a B.A. from the University of New Mexico and an M.F.A. from the Iowa Writers Workshop. She currently teaches at the University of Arizona. A recurring theme in Harjo's work is the search for unity within the fragmentation of modern life, a search that often involves seeking to recover a harmony in traditional Indian ways. Her collections of poetry include *What Moon Drove Me to This?* (1979), *She Had Some Horses* (1983), and *In Mad Love and War* (1990). *Secrets from the Center of the World*, a collaboration with the photographer Stephen Strom, was published in 1989. Harjo is also a filmmaker and plays tenor saxophone in big bands. Her poem, "Your Phone Call at Eight A.M.," appears earlier in this book in the introduction to poetry.

REMEMBER

Remember the sky that you were born under,
know each of the star's stories.
Remember the moon, know who she is. I met her

in a bar once in Iowa City.
Remember the sun's birth at dawn, that is the   5
strongest point of time. Remember sundown
and the giving away to night.
Remember your birth, how your mother struggled
to give you form and breath. You are evidence of
her life, and her mother's, and hers.   10
Remember your father, his hands cradling
your mother's flesh, and maybe her heart, too
and maybe not.
He is your life, also.
Remember the earth whose skin you are.   15
Red earth yellow earth white earth brown earth
black earth we are earth.
Remember the plants, trees, animal life who all have their
tribes, their families, their histories, too. Talk to them,
listen to them. They are alive poems.   20
Remember the wind. Remember her voice. She knows the
origin of this universe. I heard her singing Kiowa war
dance songs at the corner of Fourth and Central once.
Remember that you are all people and that all people
are you.   25
Remember that you are this universe and that this
universe is you.
Remember that all is in motion, is growing, is you.
Remember that language comes from this.
Remember the dance that language is, that life is.   30
Remember
to remember.

SHE HAD SOME HORSES

She had some horses.

She had horses who were bodies of sand.
She had horses who were maps drawn of blood.
She had horses who were skins of ocean water.
She had horses who were the blue air of sky.   5
She had horses who were fur and teeth.
She had horses who were clay and would break.
She had horses who were splintered red cliff.

She had some horses.

She had horses with long, pointed breasts.   10
She had horses with full, brown thighs.
She had horses who laughed too much.
She had horses who threw rocks at glass houses.
She had horses who licked razor blades.

She had some horses.   15

She had horses who danced in their mothers' arms.
She had horses who thought they were the sun, and their
bodies shone and burned like stars.
She had horses who waltzed nightly on the moon.
She had horses who were much too shy, and kept quiet   20
in stalls of their own making.

She had some horses.

She had horses who liked Creek stomp dance songs.
She had horses who cried in their beer.
She had horses who spit at male queens who made   25
them afraid of themselves.
She had horses who said they weren't afraid.
She had horses who lied.
She had horses who told the truth, who were stripped bare
of their tongues.   30

She had some horses.

She had horses who called themselves, "horse."
She had horses who called themselves, "spirit," and kept
their voices secret and to themselves.
She had horses who had no names.   35
She had horses who had books of names.

She had some horses.

She had horses who whispered in the dark, who were afraid to speak.
She had horses who screamed out of fear of the silence, who
carried knives to protect themselves from ghosts.   40
She had horses who waited for destruction.
She had horses who waited for resurrection.

She had some horses.

She had horses who got down on their knees for any savior.
She had horses who thought their high price had saved them.   45
She had horses who tried to save her, who climbed in her
bed at night and prayed as they raped her.

She had some horses.

She had some horses she loved.
She had some horses she hated.   50
These were the same horses.

Garrett Kaoru Hongo

Garrett Kaoru Hongo was born (in 1951) in Hawaii of Japanese-American parents. He grew up in California and studied at Pomona College, the University of Michigan, and the University of California–Irvine, where he earned an M.F.A. in writing. Hongo was founding director of a Seattle theater group named the Asian Exclusion Act. He collaborated with Alan Lau and Lawson Inada on a book of poetry called *The Buddha Bandits Down Highway 99* (1978). His own books of poetry include *Yellow Light* (1982) and *The River of Heaven* (1988).

ANCESTRAL GRAVES, KAHUKU[1]

for Edward Hirsch

Driving off Kam Highway along the North Shore,
    past the sugar mill,
Rusting and silent, a haunt for crows
    and the quick mongoose,
Cattle egrets and papaya trees in the wet fields   5
    wheeling on their muddy gears;

We turn left, *makai* towards the sea,
    and by the old *"76,"*
Its orange globe a target for wind
    and the rust, and the bleeding light;   10
Down a chuckholed gravel road
    between state-built retirement homes
And the old village of miscellaneous shotguns
    overgrown with vines, yellow *hau* flowers,
And the lavish hearts and green embroidery of bougainvillaea   15
    stitching through their rotting screens.

At the golf course, built by Castle & Cooke
    by subscription, 60 some years ago,
We swing past Hole No. 7 and its dying grass
    worn by generations of the poor   20
And losing out to the traps and dunes
    pushing in from the sea.

It's a dirt road, finally,
    two troughs of packed earth
And a strip of bermuda all the way   25
    to the sandy point
Where, opposite the homely sentinels
    of three stripped and abandoned cars
Giving in to the rain and its brittle decay,
    a wire fence   30

[1] Kahuku Point is on the north side of the island of Oahu, Hawaii.

Opens to the hard scrabble of a shallow beach
    and the collapsing stones
And the rotting stakes,
    o-kaimyō for the dead,
Of this plantation-tough   35
    cemetery-by-the-sea.

We get out, and I guide you,
    as an aunt did once for me,
Over the drying tufts and patchy carpeting
    of temple moss   40
Yellowing in the saline earth,
    pointing out,
As few have in any recent time,
    my family graves
And the mayonnaise jars empty of flowers,   45
    the broken saucers
Where rice cakes and mandarins were stacked,
    the weather-smoothed
Shards of unglazed pots for sand and incense
    and their chowders of ash.   50

The wind slaps through our clothes
    and kicks a sand-cloud
Up to our eyes, and I remember
    to tell you
how the *tsunami* in '46 took out   55
    over half the gravesites,
Tore through two generations,
    most of our dead
Gone in one night, bones and tombstones
    up and down the beach,   60
Those left, half-in, half-out of the broken cliff
    harrowed by the sea.

I remember to say that the land,
    what's left of it,
Still belongs to the growers,   65
    the same as built the golf course,
Who own, even in death,
    those they did in life,
And that the sea came then
    through a vicious tenderness   70
Like the Buddha's, reaching
    from his lotus-seat
And ushering all the lost and incapable
    from this heaven to its source.

I read a few names—   75
    this one's the priest,
His fancy stone scripted with ideograms
    carved almost plain by the wind now,

And this one, Yaeko, my grandfather's sister
    who bedded down one night 80
In the canefields and with a Scotsman
    and was beaten to death
For the crime—
    a hoe handle they say—
Struck by her own father, 85
    mythic and unabsolved.

Our shame is not her love,
    whether idyll or rape
Behind the green shrouds and whispering tassels
    of sugar cane, 90
Not is it the poor gruel of their daily lives
    or the infrequent
Pantomime of worship they engaged in
    odd Saturdays;
It is its effacement, the rough calligraphy 95
    on rotting wood
Worn smooth and illegible,
    the past
Like a name whispered in a shallow grave
    just above tideline 100
That speaks to us in a quiet woe
    without forgiveness
As we move off, back toward our car,
    the grim and constant
Muttering from the sea 105
    a cool sutra in our ears.

THE CADENCE OF SILK

When I lived in Seattle, I loved watching
the Sonics play basketball; something
about that array of trained and energetic
bodies set in motion to attack a more
sluggish, less physically intelligent opponent 5
appealed to me, taught me about cadence
and play, the offguard breaking free
before the rebound, "releasing," as is said
in the parlance of the game, getting to
the center's downcourt pass and streaking 10
to the basket for a scoopshot layup
off the glass, all in rhythm, all in
perfect declensions of action, smooth
and strenuous as Gorgiasian rhetoric.[1]
I was hooked on the undulant ballet 15
of the pattern offense, on the set play

---

[1] Gorgias (c.483–c.375), Greek rhetorician and philosopher.

back-door under the basket, and, at times,
even on the auctioneer's pace and elocution
of the play-by-play man. Now I watch
the Lakers, having returned to Los Angeles   20
some years ago, love them even more than
the Seattle team, long since broken up and aging.
The Lakers are incomparable, numerous
options for any situation, their players
the league's quickest, most intelligent,   25
and, it is my opinion, frankly, the most *cool.*
Few bruisers, they are sleek as arctic seals,
especially the small forward
as he dodges through the key, away from
the ball, rubbing off his man on the screen,   30
setting for his shot. Then, slick as spit,
comes the ball from the point guard,
and my man goes up, cradling the ball
in his right hand like a waiter balancing
a tray piled with champagne in stemmed glasses,   35
cocking his arm and bringing the ball
back behind his ear, pumping, letting fly then
as he jumps, popcorn-like, in the corner,
while the ball, launched, slung dextrously
with a slight backspin, slashes through   40
the basket's silk net with a small,
sonorous splash of completion.

Brigit Pegeen Kelly

Brigit Pegeen Kelly was born (in 1951) in Palo Alto, California, and grew up in
Bloomington, Indiana. She was educated at Indiana University and the University
of Oregon. Kelly has worked as a nurse, an actress, and a counselor and is currently teaching at the University of Illinois. She won the Yale Series of Younger
Poets Prize in 1987 and is the author of *To the Place of Trumpets* (1988).

IMAGINING THEIR OWN HYMNS

What fools they are to believe the angels
in this window are in ecstasy. They
do not smile. Their eyes are rolled back in annoyance
not in bliss, as my mother's eyes roll back
when she finds us in the dirt with the cider—   5
flies and juice blackening our faces and hands.
When the sun comes up behind the angels
then even in their dun robes they are beautiful,
with their girlish hair and their mean lit faces,
but they do not love the light. As I   10
do not love it when I am made clean

for the ladies who bring my family money.
They stroke my face and smooth my hair. So sweet,
they say, so good, but I am not sweet or good.
I would take one of the possums we kill   15
in the dump by the woods where the rats slide
like dark boats into the dark stream and leave it
on the heavy woman's porch just to think
of her on her knees scrubbing and scrubbing
at a stain that will never come out.   20
And these angels that the women turn to
are not good either. They are sick of Jesus,
who never stops dying, hanging there white
and large, his shadow blue as pitch, and blue
the bruise on his chest, with spread petals,   25
like the hydrangea blooms I tear from
Mrs. Macht's bush and smash on the sidewalk.
One night they will get out of here. One night
when the weather is turning cold and a few
candles burn, they will leave St. Blase standing   30
under his canopy of glass lettuce
and together, as in a wedding march,
their pockets full of money from the boxes
for the sick poor, they will walk down the aisle,
imagining their own hymns, past the pews   35
and the water fonts in which small things float,
down the streets of our narrow town, while
the bells ring and the birds fly up in the fields
beyond—and they will never come back.

YOUNG WIFE'S LAMENT

The mule that lived on the road
where I was married
would bray to wake the morning,
but could not wake me.
How many summers I slept   5
lost in my hair. How many
mules on how many hills singing.
Back of a deep ravine
he lived, above a small river
on a beaten patch of land.   10
I walked up in the day and walked down,
having been given nothing
else to do. The road grew no longer,
I grew no wiser, my husband
was away selling things to people who buy.   15
He went up the road, too, but
the road was full of doors for him,
the road was his belt and,
one notch at a time, he loosened it

on his way. I would sit   20
on the hill of stones and look down
on the trees, on the lake
far away with its boats and those
who ride in boats
and I could not pray. Some of us   25
have mule minds,
are foolish as sails whipping
in the wind, senseless
as sheets rolling through the fields,
some of us are not given   30
even a wheel of the tinker's cart
upon which to pray.
When I came back I pumped water
in the yard under the trees
by the fence where the cows came up,   35
but water is not wisdom
and change is not made by wishes.
Else I would have ridden something,
even a mule, over
those hills and away.   40

Judith Ortiz Cofer

Judith Ortiz Cofer (b. 1952) was born in Hormigueros, Puerto Rico. Her father
was in the army and was frequently reassigned, and so the family lived in a variety
of places while she was growing up. She graduated from high school in Augusta,
Georgia, attended Augusta College, and earned an M.A. at Florida Atlantic University. Cofer also studied at Oxford University on an English Speaking Union of
America scholarship. She is the author of two collections of poetry, *Peregrina*
(1985) and *Terms of Survival* (1989), and has also published a novel, *The Line of
the Sun* (1989).

THE IDEA OF ISLANDS

The place where I was born,
that mote in a cartographer's eye,
interests you?
Today Atlanta is like a port city
enveloped in mist. The temperature   5
is plunging with the abandon
of a woman rushing to a rendezvous.
Since you ask, things were simpler
on the island. Food and shelter
were never the problem. Most days,   10
a hat and a watchful eye were all
one needed for protection, the climate being
rarely inclement. Fruit could be plucked

from trees languishing under the weight
of their own fecundity. The thick sea
spewed out fish that crawled into the pots
of women whose main occupation was to dress
each other's manes with scarlet hibiscus,
which as you may know, blooms
without restraint in the tropics.
I was always the ambitious one, overdressed
by my neighbors' standards, and unwilling
to eat mangoes three times a day.
In truth, I confess to spending my youth
guarding the fire by the beach, waiting
to be rescued from the futile round
of paradisial life.
How do I like the big city?
City lights are just as bright
as the stars that enticed me then;
the traffic ebbs and rises like the tides
and in a crowd,
everyone is an island.

THEY NEVER GROW OLD

I am speaking of that hollow-eyed race
of bone-embraced tubercular women and men,
the last of whom I caught a glimpse of
in the final days of my childhood.

Every family had one
hidden away in a sanitarium—
a word whispered when certain names
came up in conversation. And when I asked
my mother what it meant, she said,
a very clean place.

Once, I saw one; a rare
appearance by a distant cousin
our family tried to keep invisible.
From a neighbor's house across the road,
I looked upon the visitor in a white dress
that seemed to hang upon her skeletal frame
like a starched garment on a wire hanger.
She held a handkerchief to her mouth
the entire time. The circle of polite relatives
sat back in the chairs around her.
The coffee cup at her side would later
be discarded, the chair she floated on—she seemed
to have no volume or weight—would be scrubbed
with something so strong, it made one cry; the whole house
sanitized and disinfected after her brief stay.

Though these sad, thin cousins were rarely seen
in our living rooms, they were a presence in the attics
and closets where we kept all our unwanted kin.

And they too had their heroes and myths.

As a girl I heard the story of two young people,   30
put away to die and forgotten,
who met in the cool, pine-scented corridors
of their hospital prison, and fell in love.
Desperate to be together, they escaped
into the night. It was a young woman   35
who found them under an embankment bridge,
a damp place where a creek one could step over ran.
Lying in each others' arms, their bodies marbleized
with fever and morning dew. They were a frieze
in a Roman catacomb: Eros and Psyche in repose.   40

Moved by their plight, the girl brought them food
and a blanket. But dying creatures are easy to track,
and they were soon found by townspeople scandalized
that the ill should want to make love. A priest
was called in before a doctor. I surmise   45
that they died in separate beds.
                          Back then, I was convinced
the story of the dying lovers clinging to each other
in the dark cave, was the most romantic thing I would ever hear,
the spot on their lungs that killed them, I imagined   50
as a privileged place on the body's ordinary geography.

I too wanted to live in *a very clean place,*
where fragile as a pale pink rosebud I would sit
among my many satin pillows and wait for the man with whom
I would never grow old, to rescue me from a dull life.   55
Death and love once again confused
by one too young to see the difference.

Rita Dove

Rita Dove was born (in 1952) in Akron, Ohio. She graduated from Miami University of Ohio, earned an M.A. at the Iowa Writers Workshop, and was a Fulbright Fellow at the University of Tübingen, Germany. She is now a professor of English at the University of Virginia. Her books of poetry include *The Yellow House on the Corner* (1980), *Museum* (1983), *Thomas and Beulah* (1986), and *Grace Notes* (1989). *Thomas and Beulah,* a book-length narrative poem that uses episodes from the lives of Dove's grandparents to tell the story of black families of their generation, won the 1987 Pulitzer Prize. *Fifth Sunday,* a collection of short stories, was published in 1985, and *Through the Ivory Gate,* a novel, was published in 1992.

GEOMETRY

I prove a theorem and the house expands:
the windows jerk free to hover near the ceiling,
the ceiling floats away with a sigh.

As the walls clear themselves of everything
but transparency, the scent of carnations   5
leaves with them. I am out in the open

and above the windows have hinged into butterflies,
sunlight glinting where they've intersected.
They are going to some point true and unproven.

PARSLEY[1]

1. The Cane Fields[2]

There is a parrot imitating spring
in the palace, its feathers parsley green.
Out of the swamp the cane appears

to haunt us, and we cut it down. El General
searches for a word; he is all the world   5
there is. Like a parrot imitating spring,

we lie down screaming as rain punches through
and we come up green. We cannot speak an R—
out of the swamp, the cane appears

and then the mountain we call in whispers *Katalina*.[3]   10
The children gnaw their teeth to arrowheads.
There is a parrot imitating spring.

El General has found his word: *perejil.*
Who says it, lives. He laughs, teeth shining
out of the swamp. The cane appears   15

in our dreams, lashed by wind and streaming.
And we lie down. For every drop of blood
there is a parrot imitating spring.
Out of the swamp the cane appears.

---

[1] "On October 2, 1957, Rafael Trujillo (1891–1961), dictator of the Dominican Republic, ordered 20,000 blacks killed because they could not pronounce the letter 'r' in *perejil*, the Spanish word for parsley" (Dove's note).

[2] That is, sugar cane.

[3] Katarina (since the speaker "cannot speak an R").

2. *The Palace*

The word the general's chosen is parsley.   20
It is fall, when thoughts turn
to love and death; the general thinks
of his mother, how she died in the fall
and he planted her walking cane at the grave
and it flowered, each spring stolidly forming   25
four-star blossoms. The general

pulls on his boots, he stomps to
her room in the palace, the one without
curtains, the one with a parrot
in a brass ring. As he paces he wonders   30
Who can I kill today. And for a moment
the little knot of screams
is still. The parrot, who has traveled

all the way from Australia in an ivory
cage, is, coy as a widow, practising   35
spring. Ever since the morning
his mother collapsed in the kitchen
while baking skull-shaped candies
for the Day of the Dead,[4] the general
has hated sweets. He orders pastries   40
brought up for the bird; they arrive

dusted with sugar on a bed of lace.
The knot in his throat starts to twitch;
he sees his boots the first day in battle
splashed with mud and urine   45
as a soldier falls at his feet amazed—
how stupid he looked!—at the sound
of artillery. *I never thought it would sing*
the soldier said, and died. Now

the general sees the fields of sugar   50
cane, lashed by rain and streaming.
He sees his mother's smile, the teeth
gnawed to arrowheads. He hears
the Haitians sing without R's
as they swing the great machetes: 55
Katalina, they sing, *Katalina*.

mi madle, mi amol en muelte.[5] God knows
his mother was no stupid woman; she
could roll an R like a queen. Even
a parrot can roll an R! In the bare room   60

---

[4] The Roman Catholic festival of Corpus Christi.
[5] That is, *mi madre, mi amor en muerte*, "my mother, my love in death."

the bright feathers arch in a parody
of greenery, as the last pale crumbs
disappear under the blackened tongue. Someone

calls out his name in a voice
so like his mother's, a startled tear   65
splashes the tip of his right boot.
My mother, my love in death.
The general remembers the tiny green sprigs
men of his village wore in their capes
to honor the birth of a son. He will   70
order many, this time, to be killed

for a single, beautiful word.

Alberto Alvaro Rios

Alberto Alvaro Rios was born (in 1952) and grew up in Nogales, Arizona, on the border between Mexico and the United States; his father was Mexican, his mother English. Both a poet and a fiction writer, he has published the poetry collection *Whispering to Fool the Wind* (1982) and the short story collection *The Iguana Killer: Twelve Stories of the Heart* (1984), as well as *Five Indiscretions* (1985) and *Teodora Luna's Two Kisses* (1990). (His story "Johnny Ray" appears in the fiction section of this book.) Rios teaches at the University of Arizona, Tempe.

MI ABUELO[1]

Where my grandfather is in the ground
where you can hear the future
like an Indian with his ear at the tracks.
A pipe leads down to him so that sometimes
he whispers what will happen to a man   5
in town or how he will meet the best
dressed woman tomorrow and how the best
man at her wedding will chew the ground
next to her. Mi abuelo is the man
who speaks through all the mouths in my house.   10
An echo of me hitting the pipe sometimes
to stop him from saying *my hair is a*
sieve is the only other sound. It is a phrase
that among all others is the best,
he says, and *my hair is a sieve* is sometimes   15
repeated for hours out of the ground
when I let him, which is not often.
An abuelo should be much more than a man
like you! He stops then, and speaks: *I am a man*

[1] "My grandfather." (Spanish).

who has served ants with the attitude   20
of a waiter, who has made each smile as only
an ant who is fat can, and they liked me best,
but there is nothing left. Yet I know he ground
green coffee beans as a child, and sometimes
he will talk about his wife, and sometimes   25
about when he was deaf and a man
cured him by mail and he heard groundhogs
talking, or about how he walked with a cane
he chewed on when he got hungry.
At best, mi abuelo is a liar.   30
I see an old picture of him at nani's[2] with an
off-white yellow center mustache and sometimes
that's all I know for sure. He talks best
about these hills, *slowest waves,* and where this man
is going, and I'm convinced his hair is a sieve,   35
that his fever is cooled now underground.
Mi abuelo is an ordinary man.
I look down the pipe, sometimes, and see a
ripple-topped stream in its best suit, in the ground.

NANI

Sitting at her table, she serves
the sopa de arroz[1] to me
instinctively, and I watch her,
the absolute *mamá,* and eat words
I might have had to say more   5
out of embarrassment. To speak,
now-foreign words I used to speak,
too, dribble down her mouth as she serves
me albondigas.[2] No more
than a third are easy to me.   10
By the stove she does something with words
and looks at me only with her
back. I am full. I tell her
I taste the mint, and watch her speak
smiles at the stove. All my words   15
make her smile. Nani never serves
herself, she only watches me
with her skin, her hair. I ask for more.

I watch the *mamá* warming more
tortillas for me. I watch her   20
fingers in the flame for me.
Near her mouth, I see a wrinkle speak
of a man whose body serves

---

[2] Grandmama's.   [1] "Rice soup."   [2] "Meatballs."

the ants like she serves me, then more words
from more wrinkles about children, words 25
about this and that, flowing more
easily from these other mouths. Each serves
as a tremendous string around her,
holding her together. They speak
nani was this and that to me 30
and I wonder just how much of me
will die with her, what were the words
I could have been, was. Her insides speak
through a hundred wrinkles, now, more
than she can bear, steel around her, 35
shouting, then, What is this thing she serves?

She asks me if I want more.
I own no words to stop her.
Even before I speak, she serves.

Gary Soto

Gary Soto (b. 1952) has taken as his poetic subject the lives of Mexican-American farm workers; one critic has called him "an existentialist Cesar Chavez." He was born in Fresno, California, and was educated at California State University, Fresno, and at the University of California, Irvine. He now teaches at San Diego State University. His books include *The Elements of San Joaquin* (1977), *The Tale of Sunlight* (1978), *Father Is a Pillow Tied to a Broom* (1980), *Where Sparrows Work Hard* (1981), and *Black Hair* (1985).

BLACK HAIR

At eight I was brilliant with my body.
In July, that ring of heat
We all jump through, I sat in the bleachers
Of Romain Playground, in the lengthening
Shade that rose from our dirty feet. 5
The game before us was more than baseball.
It was a figure—Hector Moreno
Quick and hard with turned muscles,
His crouch the one I assumed before an altar
Of worn baseball cards, in my room. 10

I came here because I was Mexican, a stick
Of brown light in love with those
Who could do it—the triple and hard slide,
The gloves eating balls into double plays.
What could I do with 50 pounds, my shyness, 15
My black torch of hair, about to go out?
Father was dead, his face no longer

Hanging over the table or our sleep,
And mother was the terror of mouths
Twisting hurt by butter knives.   20

In the bleachers I was brilliant with my body,
Waving players in and stomping my feet,
Growing sweaty in the presence of white shirts.
I chewed sunflower seeds. I drank water
And bit my arm through the late innings.   25
When Hector lined balls into deep
Center, in my mind I rounded the bases
With him, my face flared, my hair lifting
Beautifully, because we were coming home
To the arms of brown people.   30

ODE TO THE YARD SALE

A toaster,
A plate
Of pennies,
A plastic rose
Staring up   5
To the sky.
It's Saturday
And two friends,
Merchants of
The salvageable heart,   10
Are throwing
Things onto
The front lawn—
A couch,
A beanbag,   15
A table to clip
Poodles on,
Drawers of
Potato mashers,
Spoons, knives   20
That signaled
To the moon
For help.
Rent is due.
It's somewhere   25
On this lawn,
Somewhere among
The shirts we've
Looked good in,
Taken off before   30
We snuggled up
To breasts
That almost made

Us gods.
It'll be a good   35
Day, because
There's much
To sell,
And the pitcher
Of water   40
Blue in the shade,
Clear in the
Light, with
The much-handled
Scotch the color   45
Of leaves
Falling at our
Shoes, will
Get us through
The afternoon   50
Rush of old
Ladies, young women
On their way
To becoming nurses,
Bachelors of   55
The twice-dipped
Tea bag. It's
An eager day:
Wind in the trees,
Laughter of   60
Children behind
Fences. Surely
People will arrive
With handbags
And wallets,   65
To open up coffee
Pots and look
In, weigh pans
In each hand,
And prop hats   70
On their heads
And ask, "How do
I look?" (foolish
To most,
Beautiful to us).   75
And so they
Come, poking
At the clothes,
Lifting salt
And pepper shakers   80
For their tiny music,
Thumbing through
Old magazines
For someone

They know,   85
As we sit with
Our drinks
And grow sad
That the ashtray
Has been sold,   90
A lamp, a pillow,
The fry pans
That were action
Packed when
We cooked,   95
Those things
We threw so much
Love on, day
After day,
Sure they would   100
Mean something
When it came
To this.

Jimmy Santiago Baca

Jimmy Santiago Baca (b. 1952) wrote the poems in his first collection, *Immigrants in Our Own Land* (1979), while he was in prison. He now lives on a small farm outside Albuquerque, New Mexico. Other collections include *Poems Taken from My Yard* (1986) and *Martin & Meditations on the South Valley* (1987).

ANCESTOR

It was a time when they were afraid of him.
My father, a bare man, a gypsy, a horse
with broken knees no one would shoot.
Then again, he was like the orange tree,
and young women plucked from him sweet fruit.   5
To meet him, you must be in the right place,
even his sons and daughter, we wondered
where was papa now and what was he doing.
He held the mystique of travelers
that pass your backyard and disappear into the trees. 10
Then, when you follow, you find nothing,
not a stir, not a twig displaced from its bough.
And then he would appear one night.
Half covered in shadows and half in light,
his voice quiet, absorbing our unspoken thoughts.   15
When his hands lay on the table at breakfast,
they were hands that had not fixed our crumbling home,
hands that had not taken us into them
and the fingers did not gently rub along our lips.

They were hands of a gypsy that filled our home
with love and safety, for a moment;
with all the shambles of boards and empty stomachs,
they filled us because of the love in them.
Beyond the ordinary love, beyond the coordinated life,
beyond the sponging of broken hearts,
came the untimely word, the fallen smile, the quiet tear,
that made us grow up quick and romantic.
Papa gave us something: when we paused from work,
my sister fourteen years old working the cotton fields,
my brother and I running like deer,
we would pause, because we had a papa no one could catch,
who spoke when he spoke and bragged and drank,
he bragged about us: he did not say we were smart,
nor did he say we were strong and were going to be rich someday.
He said we were good. He held us up to the world for it to see,
three children that were good, who understood love in a quiet way,
who owned nothing but calloused hands and true freedom,
and that is how he made us: he offered us to the wind,
to the mountains, to the skies of autumn and spring.
He said, "Here are my children! Care for them!"
And he left again, going somewhere like a child
with a warrior's heart, nothing could stop him.
My grandmother would look at him for a long time,
and then she would say nothing.
She chose to remain silent, praying each night,
guiding down like a root in the heart of earth,
clutching sunlight and rains to her ancient breast.
And I am the blossom of many nights.
A threefold blossom: my sister is as she is,
my brother is as he is, and I am as I am.
Through sacred ceremony of living, daily living,
arose three distinct hopes, three loves,
out of the long felt nights and days of yesterday.

IMMIGRANTS IN OUR OWN LAND

We are born with dreams in our hearts,
looking for better days ahead.
At the gates we are given new papers,
our old clothes are taken
and we are given overalls like mechanics wear.
We are given shots and doctors ask questions.
Then we gather in another room
where counselors orient us to the new land
we will now live in. We take tests.
Some of us were craftsmen in the old world,
good with our hands and proud of our work.
Others were good with their heads.
They used common sense like scholars

use glasses and books to reach the world.
But most of us didn't finish high school.   15

The old men who have lived here stare at us,
from deep disturbed eyes, sulking, retreated.
We pass them as they stand around idle,
leaning on shovels and rakes or against walls.
Our expectations are high: in the old world,   20
they talked about rehabilitation,
about being able to finish school,
and learning an extra good trade.
But right away we are sent to work as dishwashers,
to work in fields for three cents an hour.   25
The administration says this is temporary
So we go about our business, blacks with blacks,
poor whites with poor whites,
chicanos and indians by themselves.
The administration says this is right,   30
no mixing of cultures, let them stay apart,
like in the old neighborhoods we came from.

We came here to get away from false promises,
from dictators in our neighborhoods,
who wore blue suits and broke our doors down   35
when they wanted, arrested us when they felt like,
swinging clubs and shooting guns as they pleased.
But it's no different here. It's all concentrated.
The doctors don't care, our bodies decay,
our minds deteriorate, we learn nothing of value.   40
Our lives don't get better, we go down quick.

My cell is crisscrossed with laundry lines,
my T-shirts, boxer shorts, socks and pants are drying.
Just like it used to be in my neighborhood:
from all the tenements laundry hung window to window.   45
Across the way Joey is sticking his hands
through the bars to hand Felipé a cigarette,
men are hollering back and forth cell to cell,
saying their sinks don't work,
or somebody downstairs hollers angrily   50
about a toilet overflowing,
or that the heaters don't work.

I ask Coyote next door to shoot me over
a little more soap to finish my laundry.
I look down and see new immigrants coming in,   55
mattresses rolled up and on their shoulders,
new haircuts and brogan boots,
looking around, each with a dream in their heart,
thinking they'll get a chance to change their lives.

But in the end, some will just sit around 60
talking about how good the old world was.
Some of the younger ones will become gangsters.
Some will die and others will go on living
without a soul, a future, or a reason to live.
Some will make it out of here with hate in their eyes, 65
but so very few make it out of here as human
as they came in, they leave wondering what good they are now
as they look at their hands so long away from their tools,
as they look at themselves, so long gone from their families,
so long gone from life itself, so many things have changed. 70

Ana Castillo

Ana Castillo, who is of Aztec heritage, was born (in 1953) and grew up in Chicago. In her poems and fiction, Castillo explores sexual politics. Her volumes of poetry include *Otro Canto* [Another Song] (1977), *The Invitation* (1979), *Women Are Not Roses* (1984), and *My Father Was a Toltec* (1988). She has also written two novels: *The Mixquiahuala Letters* (1986) and *Sapognoia* (1988).

NAPA, CALIFORNIA

Dedicado al Sr. Chávez, sept '75[1]

We pick
   the bittersweet grapes
   at harvest
   one
     by 5
       one
with leather worn hands
       as they pick
       at our dignity
       and wipe our pride 10
       away
       like the sweat we wipe
       from our sun-beaten brows
       at midday
In fields 15
   so vast
   that our youth seems
   to pass before us
   and we have grown

[1] "Dedicated to Señor Chavez, Sept. '75." César Chavez organized the wine-grape pickers in California, first organizing the National Farm Workers Association and then the United Farm Workers, which became a member union of the AFL-CIO in 1972.

20

very
    very
        old
            by dusk . . .
                (buenos pues, ¿qué vamos a hacer, Ambrosio?
                ¡bueno pues, seguirle, compadre, seguirle!

25

                ¡Ay, Mama!
                Sí pues, ¿qué vamos a hacer, compadre?
                ¡Seguirle, Ambrosio, seguirle!) [2]
We pick
    with a desire
    that only survival

30

    inspires
While the end
    of each day only brings
    a tired night

35

    that waits for the sun
    and the land
    that in turn waits
    for us . . .

A COUNTER-REVOLUTIONARY PROPOSITION

Let's forget
that Everything matters
for a while: beneath
the covers
we'll block out the   5
afternoon sun, icycled
windows; a pile of bills
instead of Christmas cards;
Christian and Jews, land
reform news, another old   10
lady beat to death in a cold
water flat; a friend who needs
a fix, big time dealer taking
a sip from a coconut out
in the Bahamas; Mamá and menopause;   15
another leak in the basement:

Let's forget
all this
for just a while and make
a little love . . .   20
and make a little love,
instead.

---

[2] "Well then, what are we going to do, Ambrosio? Well then, follow him, my friend! Ah Mama! Well then, what are we going to do, my friend? Follow him, Ambrosio, follow him!"

Lorna Dee Cervantes

Lorna Dee Cervantes was born (in 1954) into a working-class Mexican family in San Francisco and grew up in San Jose. She was educated at San Jose City College and San Jose State University. Cervantes has been active in Chicano/Chicana community affairs as a member of the Chicana Theatre Group and as an organizer for the Centro Cultural de la Gente (People's Cultural Center). She also founded the Mango Press, a small press that publishes a literary magazine and books of poetry. Her own poetry was published in *Emplumada* (1981).

UNCLE'S FIRST RABBIT

He was a good boy
making his way through
the Santa Barbara pines,
sighting the blast of fluff
as he leveled the rifle,   5
and the terrible singing began.
He was ten years old,
hunting his grandpa's supper.
He had dreamed of running,
shouldering the rifle to town,   10
selling it, and taking the next
train out.
        Fifty years
have passed and he still hears
that rabbit "just like a baby."   15
He remembers how the rabbit
stopped keening under the butt
of his rifle, how he brought
it home with tears streaming
down his blood soaked jacket.   20
"That bastard. That bastard."
He cried all night and the week
after, remembering that voice
like his dead baby sister's,
remembering his father's drunken   25
kicking that had pushed her
into birth. She had a voice
like that, growing faint
at its end; his mother rocking,
softly, keening. He dreamed   30
of running, running
the bastard out of his life.
He would forget them, run down
the hill, leave his mother's
silent waters, and the sounds   35
of beating night after night.
        When war came,

he took the man's vow. He was
finally leaving and taking
the bastard's last bloodline   40
with him. At war's end, he could
still hear her, her soft
body stiffening under water
like a shark's. The color
of the water, darkening, soaking,   45
as he clung to what was left
of a ship's gun. Ten long hours
off the coast of Okinawa, he sang
so he wouldn't hear them.
He pounded their voices out   50
of his head, and awakened
to find himself slugging the bloodied
face of his wife.
    Fifty years
have passed and he has not run   55
the way he dreamed. The Paradise
pines shadow the bleak hills
to his home. His hunting hounds,
dead now. His father, long dead.
His wife, dying, hacking in the bed   60
she has not let him enter for the last
thirty years. He stands looking,
he mouths the words, "Die you bitch,
I'll live to watch you die." He turns,
entering their moss-soft livingroom.   65
He watches out the picture window
and remembers running: how he'll
take the new pickup to town, sell it,
and get the next train out.

VISIONS OF MEXICO WHILE AT A WRITING SYMPOSIUM
IN PORT TOWNSEND, WASHINGTON

México

When I'm that far south, the old words
molt off my skin, the feathers
of all my nervousness.
My own words somersault naturally as my name,
joyous among all those meadows: Michoacán,   5
Vera Cruz, Tenochtitlán, Oaxaca . . .
Pueblos green on the low hills
where men slap handballs below acres of maíz.[1]
I watch and understand.

---

[1] Corn.

My frail body has never packed mud 10
or gathered in the full weight of the harvest.
Alone with the women in the adobe, I watch men,
their taut faces holding in all their youth.
This far south we are governed by the law
of the next whole meal. We work 15
and watch seabirds elbow their wings
in migratory ways, those mispronouncing gulls
coming south
to refuge or gameland.

I don't want to pretend I know more 20
and can speak all the names. I can't.
My sense of this land can only ripple through my veins
like the chant of an epic corrido.[2]
I come from a long line of eloquent illiterates
whose history reveals what words don't say. 25
Our anger is our way of speaking,
the gesture is an utterance more pure than word.
We are not animals
but our senses are keen and our reflexes,
accurate punctuation. 30
All the knifings in a single night, low-voiced
scufflings, sirens, gunnings . . .
We hear them
and the poet within us bays.

Washington

I don't belong this far north. 35
The uncomfortable birds gawk at me.
They hem and haw from their borders in the sky.
I heard them say: México is a stumbling comedy.
A loose-legged Cantinflas woman
acting with Pancho Villa drunkenness.[3] 40
Last night at the tavern
this was all confirmed
in a painting of a woman: her glowing
silk skin, a halo
extending from her golden coiffure 45
while around her, dark-skinned men with Jap slant eyes
were drooling in a caricature of machismo.
Below it, at the bar, two Chicanas
hung at their beers. They had painted black
birds that dipped beneath their eyelids. 50
They were still as foam while the men

[2] Street ballad.
[3] *Cantinflas:* popular Mexican comic film actor (1911–93). *Pancho Villa:* Mexican bandit and revolutionary (c. 1877–1923).

fiddled with their asses, absently;
the bubbles of their teased hair snapped
open in the forced wind of the beating fan.
there are songs in my head I could sing you   55
songs that could drone away
all the Mariachi bands you thought you ever heard
songs that could tell you what I know
or have learned from my people
but for that   I need words   60
simple black nymphs between white sheets of paper
obedient words   obligatory words   words I steal
in the dark when no one can hear me

as pain sends seabirds south from the cold
I come north   65
to gather my feathers
for quills

Aurora Levins Morales

Aurora Levins Morales was born (in 1954) in Puerto Rico. Her mother was a New
York Puerto Rican, her father a Jewish-American. Her parents moved back to the
United States when she was a small child, and she grew up in various cities where
her father's work as a college professor took them: Rochester, New York; Ann
Arbor, Michigan; New York City; and Chicago. Her poetry and fiction have been
published in a number of periodicals and collections, and in 1986 she co-authored
a book, *Getting Home Alive,* with her mother, Rosario Morales. (Rosario Morales's
contribution to this volume is represented elsewhere in this book.)

SUGAR POEM

Poetry
is something refined
in your vocabulary,
taking its place at the table
in a silver bowl: essence   5
of culture.

I come from the earth
where the cane was grown.
I know
the knobbed rooting,   10
green spears, heights of
caña[1]

---

[1] Sugar cane.

against the sky,
purple plumed.
I know the backache   15
of the machetero.[2]
the arc of steel
cutting, cutting,
the rhythm of harvest
leaving acres of sharp spikes   20
that wound the feet—
and the sweet smoke
of the llamarada:[3]
rings of red fire burning
dark sugar into the wind.   25

My poems grow from the ground.
I know what they are made of:
heavy, raw and green.

Sugar,
you say, is sweet.   30
One teaspoon in a cup of coffee . . .
life's not so bad.

Caña, I reply,
yields many things:
molasses   35
for the horses,
rum for the tiredness
of the machetero,
industrial
alcohol to cleanse,   40
distill, to burn
as fuel.

I don't write my poems
for anybody's sweet tooth.

My poems are acetylene torches   45
welding steel.
My poems are flamethrowers
cutting paths through the world.
My poems are bamboo spears
opening the air.   50
They come from the earth,
common and brown.

[2] Field worker; one who uses the *machete* or cane knife.
[3] Blaze; bonfire.

CLASS POEM

This is my poem in celebration of my middle class privilege
This is my poem to say out loud
I'm glad I had food, and shelter, and shoes,
glad I had books and travel, glad there was air and light
and room for poetry.   5

This poem is for Tita, my best friend
who played in the dirt with me
and married at eighteen (which was late) and who was a scientist
but instead she bore six children   and four of them died
Who wanted to know the exact location of color   10
in the hibiscus petal, and patiently peeled away the thinnest,
most translucent layers to find it
and who works in a douche bag factory in Maricao.

This poem is for the hunger of my mother
discovering books at thirteen in the New York Public Library   15
who taught me to read when I was five
and when we lived on a coffee farm
subscribed to a mail-order library,
who read the Blackwell's catalogue
like a menu of delights   20
and when we moved from Puerto Rico to the States
we packed 100 boxes of books and 40 of everything else.

This poem is for my father's immigrant Jewish family.
For my great-grandfather Abe Sackman
who worked in Bridgeport making nurse's uniforms   25
and came home only on weekends, for years, and who painted
on bits of old wooden crates, with housepaint,
birds and flowers for his great-grandchildren
and scenes of his old-country childhood.

This poem celebrates my father the scientist   30
who left the microscope within reach,
with whom I discovered the pomegranate eye of the fruitfly,
and yes, the exact location of color in a leaf.

This poem celebrates my brother the artist
who began to draw when he was two,   35
and so my parents bought him reams of paper
and when he used them up, bought him more,
and today it's a silkscreen workshop
and posters that travel around the world,
and I'm glad for him   and for Pop with his housepaints   40
and Tita staining the cement with crushed flowers
searching for color
and my mother shutting out the cries of her first-born

ten minutes at a time
to sketch the roofs and elevated tracks   45
in red-brown pastels.

This is for Norma
who died of parasites in her stomach when she was four
I remember because her mother wailed her name
screaming and sobbing   50
one whole afternoon in the road in front of our school
and for Angélica
who caught on fire while stealing kerosene for her family
and died in pain
because the hospital she was finally taken to   55
knew she was poor
and would not give her the oxygen she needed to live
but wrapped her in greased sheets
so that she suffocated.

This is a poem against the wrapped sheets,   60
against guilt.

This is a poem to say:
my choosing to suffer gives nothing
to Tita and Norma and Angélica
and that not to use the tongue, the self-confidence, the training   65
my privilege bought me
is to die again for people who are already dead
and who wanted to live.

And in case anyone here confuses the paraphernalia
with the thing itself   70
let me add that I lived with rats and termites
no carpet   no stereo   no TV
that the bath came in buckets and was heated on the stove
that I read by kerosene lamp and had Sears mail-order clothes
and that that has nothing to do   75
with the fact of my privilege.

Understand, I know exactly what I got: protection and choice
and I am through apologizing.
I am going to strip apology from my voice
my posture   80
my apartment
my clothing
my dreams
because the voice that says the only true puertorican
is a dead or dying puertorican   85
is the enemy's voice—
the voice that says
"How can you let yourself shine when Tita, when millions
are daily suffocating in those greased sheets . . ."

I refuse to join them there.   90
I will not suffocate.
I will not hold back.
Yes, I had books and food and shelter and medicine
and I intend to survive.

Cathy Song

Cathy Song was born in 1955 in Hawaii of Chinese-American parents. She was educated at the University of Hawaii, Wellesley College, and Boston University. Her book *Picture Bride* won the Yale Younger Poets Award for 1982. She has also published *Frameless Windows, Squares of Light* (1988).

LOST SISTER

1

In China,
even the peasants
named their first daughters
Jade—
the stone that in the far fields   5
could moisten the dry season,
could make men move mountains
for the healing green of the inner hills
glistening like slices of winter melon.

And the daughters were grateful: 10
they never left home.
To move freely was a luxury
stolen from them at birth.
Instead, they gathered patience,
learning to walk in shoes   15
the size of teacups,
without breaking—
the arc of their movements
as dormant as the rooted willow,
as redundant as the farmyard hens.   20
But they traveled far
in surviving,
learning to stretch the family rice,
to quiet the demons,
the noisy stomachs.   25

2

There is a sister
across the ocean,

who relinquished her name,
diluting jade green
with the blue of the Pacific.   30
Rising with a tide of locusts,
she swarmed with others
to inundate another shore.
In America,
there are many roads   35
and women can stride along with men.

But in another wilderness,
the possibilities,
the loneliness,
can strangulate like jungle vines.   40
The meager provisions and sentiments
of once belonging—
fermented roots, Mah-Jongg tiles and firecrackers—
set but a flimsy household
in a forest of nightless cities.   45
A giant snake rattles above,
spewing black clouds into your kitchen.
Dough-faced landlords
slip in and out of your keyholes,
making claims you don't understand,   50
tapping into your communication systems
of laundry lines and restaurant chains.

You find you need China:
your one fragile identification,
a jade link   55
handcuffed to your wrist.

You remember your mother
who walked for centuries,
footless—
and like her,   60
you have left no footprints,
but only because
there is an ocean in between,
the unremitting space of your rebellion.

THE SEAMSTRESS

1

I work best in a difficult light,
proud of these intelligent hands
like blind fingertips pressing upon
the fine, irresistible seams.

This is my world; my work: 5
to occupy a lean-to of a room
with a tin roof that slants
so on one side, an entire
wall without windows.

My spine bent over the Singer   10
has over the years conformed
into the silhouette of a coat hanger.
If I move about, it is with the slow
descent of the spider,
attached to an invisible thread,   15
I let myself down off the chair.

It is my hands that take
their miraculous flight, flying
from the cloth they guide toward
the continuous drone of the needle.   20
Hands moist and white like lilies.
The white gloved hands of the magician.

I turn bolts of cloth into wedding dresses
like chiffon cakes in the summer.
The frayed mothers arrive with their daughters.   25
I pin them in the afternoon fittings,
drape the veil about their soft faces
as if it were mosquito netting.

2

Moving among the orchids this morning,
I see the straw hat and slippered feet   30
of my ninety-two-year-old father.
I am the second of his four unmarried daughters.

He leaves a trail of water
behind him, dragging the hose
through the grass, around the hedges.   35
The heavy-whiskered jackfruit are ripening.
He will pick them with a muslin sack
wired to the end of a fishing pole.

His attachment to the world
is in the daily application of a skill.   40
It is the cultivating of orchids,
the most highly evolved species of flowers.
For me, it is the deft turning
of a sleeve, a pleat, or a collar.

He carries a spray of the smallest   45
variety past the screen door, each orchid
delicately and elaborately unfurled

like the ornate headpieces
my mother would make from threads
of black silk when as a girl   50
she was a dollmaker's apprentice in Japan.

With her we lived in a world of miniatures.
The world got swallowed up
into the smallest square of concentration.
My sisters and I became nearsighted,   55
squinting in the hot, still room,
relying on our agile fingers
to duplicate with scraps of silk
a shrunken world. Ornamented dolls
no more than twelve inches high   60
holding musical instruments.
Looking up to meet the room
swirling as if in a cloud of insects,
there were times when we fell
to the floor from exhaustion   65
and the sudden readjustment of vision;
our legs still tucked, as we were taught, beneath us.

3

The dolls are encased in glass boxes
displayed like shrines around the room.
The last one was made twenty years ago   70
just before my mother died.
Haruko, my third sister, keeps them dusted,
plucking at the occasional termites
that squeeze through the glass corners
to gorge their amber bodies on the brocaded silk.   75

My eyes sting today again
as though one of my sisters
nearby were peeling onions.
We each keep to our discreet part of the house,
crossing polite paths to murmur over meals.   80

It seems I have always lived
in this irregular room, rarely needing
to see beyond the straight seams that fit neatly,
the snaps that fasten securely in my mind.
The world for me is the piece of cloth   85
I have at the moment beneath my hands.
I am not surprised
by how little the world changes.
My father carrying the green hose
across the grass, a ribbon of water   90
trickling down his shoulder,
staining the left pocket

of his gray, loose-fitting shirt.
The wedding dresses each white, dusty summer.
Someone very quiet once lived here.   95

Diane Burns

Diane Burns (b. 1957) is a Native American, of the Chemehuevi tribe on her
father's side, of the Anishinabe (Chippawa) on her mother's. She was educated at
the Institute of American Indian Arts in Santa Fe, New Mexico, and is a painter
and illustrator as well as a poet. She belongs to the Poets' Overland Expeditionary
Troupe, which performs poetry in theatrical settings, and she has read her work
all over the country. Her poems are collected in *Riding the One-Eyed Ford* (1981).

GADOSHKIBOS

Gadoshkibos
the warrior
He would sign no treaties
"Foolish" he called them
The whites are crazy   5
The whites are crazy
they sang around the fires at night
when the Anishinabe knew the trappers were gone.

Gadoshkibos
great grandfather   10
died in ecstacy
Nakota arrow in his throat, cries
The whites are crazy
Why fight among each other when we know?
The real enemy rushes us like buffaloes into a trap.   15

Gadoshkibos
son of the same
lays at night with his wives.
They ran, hid, but now
they stay put year round.   20
The whites are crazy.
The children starve on commodity food
and he wonders where the Anishinabe warriors have gone.

Gadoshkibos'
wife, the second,   25
struggles with her garden
ground is good with blood
spilled there and she knows
the whites are crazy
and she handles her hoe like a rifle.   30
Her sisters in the nations watch the children and know they must wait.

Gadoshkibos
the latest one
reads sociology
at Pomona State   35
and studies just why
the whites are crazy.
Summertimes he goes back to the blanket
and he wanders the woods and wonders where the warriors have gone.

BIG FUN

I don't care if you're married I still love you
I don't care if you're married
After the party's over
I will take you home in my One-Eyed Ford
Way yah hi yo, Way yah hi yo!   5

   Modene!
   the roller derby queen!
   She's Anishinabe,
     that means Human Being!
That's H for hungry!   10
and B for frijoles!
     frybread!
     Tortillas!
     Watermelon!
     Pomona!   15
Take a sip of this
and a drag of that!
At the rancheria fiesta
It's tit for tat!
Low riders and Levis   20
go fist in glove!
Give it a little pat
a push or a shove
Move it or lose it!
Take straight or bruise it!   25
Everyone
has her fun
when the sun
is all done
We're all one   30
make a run
hide your gun
Hey!
I'm no nun!
'49 in the hills above[1]   35
     Ventura
Them Okies gotta drum

---

[1] A '49 celebration is a dance or party held after a more formal powwow or tribal celebration is over.

I'm from Oklahoma
I got no one to call my own
if you will be my honey   40
I will be your sugar pie, way hi yah,
Way yah hey way yah hi yah!

We're gonna sing all night
bring your blanket
or   45
be that way then!

Dwight Okita

Dwight Okita was born (in 1958) and grew up in Chicago. His Japanese-American parents were sent to relocation camps during World War II. His father was released to fight with other Japanese-Americans in a special army unit, the 442nd Battalion. Okita was educated at the University of Illinois, Chicago, and is active in the Chicago theater and performance community.

IN RESPONSE TO EXECUTIVE ORDER 9066:
ALL AMERICANS OF JAPANESE DESCENT
MUST REPORT TO RELOCATION CENTERS

Dear Sirs:
Of course I'll come. I've packed my galoshes
and three packets of tomato seeds. Janet calls them
"love apples." My father says where we're going
they won't grow.   5

I am a fourteen-year-old girl with bad spelling
and a messy room. If it helps any, I will tell you
I have always felt funny using chopsticks
and my favorite food is hot dogs.
My best friend is a white girl named Denise—   10
we look at boys together. She sat in front of me
all through grade school because of our names:
O'Connor, Ozawa. I know the back of Denise's head very well.
I tell her she's going bald. She tells me I copy on tests.
We're best friends.   15

I saw Denise today in Geography class.
She was sitting on the other side of the room.
"You're trying to start a war," she said, "giving secrets away
to the Enemy, Why can't you keep your big mouth shut?"
I didn't know what to say.   20
I gave her a packet of tomato seeds
and asked her to plant them for me, told her
when the first tomato ripens
to miss me.

CROSSING WITH THE LIGHT

All these nights, all these traffic lights.
And love, that busy street.

And scientists would stand in white coats and talk
amongst themselves about the Doppler Effect:
how love takes longer to arrive than to depart,   5
a car approaching in the oncoming lane, what happens
when source and observer are drawing closer together.

And poets would see love in the parking of a car,
love in the rear-view mirror, love in the slowing
of tires between yellow lines.   10
"Stay with me in this parking lot," the driver
would say. "All my life, I have held this space
for someone like you."

Meanwhile back at the curb,
we were waiting.   15

I wanted to stand here and watch
the city run out of things to say
and the cars out of gas
till everything was stopped—
and you would be the first thing to move.   20

But nights like these, you can look both ways
and still not see it coming. Nights like these
you want to walk away from headlights.

Meanwhile back at the curb . . .
we were crossing. Shoes lifting   25
over pavement, steady as rain
"Red Rover, Red Rover, let . . ."
That someone would be waiting on the other side—
not waiting to cross, not waiting for signs
waiting only for you this time.   30

Something in your stride asks,
"This one? This time? Is *this* it?"
And a voice that comes from the street,
from the cracks in the sidewalk,
from the curb you stand on and all the curbs   35
you've ever stood on and waited at—
a voice that says,
"Yes. This one. This time. This is the place."

Janice Mirikitani

Janice Mirikitani is a third-generation Japanese-American. She is program director of San Francisco's Glide Foundation, a multicultural community center. Marikitani has edited three anthologies, and her own books include *Shedding Silence* (1976) and *Awake in the River* (1978).

JADE

The woman insisted
my name must be Jade.
Your name's not Jade?
Well, it should be.
It suits you, jewel of the orient.

I knew a young hooker
called Jade.
She had red dyed hair
and yellow teeth
bucked around a perpetual candy bar.   5
They called her Jade
because she was Clyde's
jewel of the orient.
Her real name was Sumiko ...
Hardy or Johnson or Smith.   10
She was from Concord.
Boring, she said,
and kept running away
from home. Her father
would come looking for her,   15
beat her again,
drag her home
while her mother
babbled and bawled in Japanese.
Concord was boring.   20
Jade kept running away,
Clyde's jewel of the orient.
He took care of her well,
and she couldn't wait
to see him, her hunger   25
like locusts in drought,
to put the cold needle to her vein,
blood blossoming in the
dropper like bougainvillea
pushing the heroin through,   30
her eyes exploding with green lights,
the cold encasing
each corpuscle,
rushing through
heart to the spine,   35

a freeze settling in each
vertebrae until
she's as cold as stone,
metabolism at zero degrees,
speech center numbed   40
and life as still as icicles.
Pain, boredom, loneliness
like a frosty pillow
where she lays her nodding
head.   45
    I wanted to tell
    the woman who kept
    insisting my name was Jade
about Jade.
who od'd. Her jaundiced body   50
found on her cold floor
mattress,
roaches crawling in her ears,
her dead eyes, glassy
as jewels.   55

BREAKING TRADITION

For my daughter

My daughter denies she is like me,
her secretive eyes avoid mine.
    She reveals the hatreds of womanhood
    already veiled behind music and smoke and telephones.
I want to tell her about the empty room   5
    of myself.
    This room we lock ourselves in
    where whispers live like fungus,
    giggles about small breasts and cellulite,
    where we confine ourselves to jealousies,   10
    bedridden by menstruation.
    This waiting room where we feel our hands
    are useless, dead speechless clamps
    that need hospitals and forceps and kitchens
    and plugs and ironing boards to make them useful.   15
I deny I am like my mother. I remember why:
    She kept her room neat with silence,
    defiance smothered in requirements to be otonashii,[1]
    passion and loudness wrapped in an obi,[2]
    her steps confined to ceremony,   20
    the weight of her sacrifice she carried like

---

[1] Gentle, self-effacing (Japanese).
[2] Wide sash, part of traditional Japanese feminine dress.

a foetus. Guilt passed on in our bones.
I want to break tradition—unlock this room
    where women dress in the dark.
    Discover the lies my mother told me.   25
    The lies that we are small and powerless
    that our possibilities must be compressed
    to the size of pearls, displayed only as
    passive chokers, charms around our neck.
Break Tradition.   30
    I want to tell my daughter of this room
    of myself
    filled with tears of shakuhachi,[3]
    the light in my hands,
    poems about madness,   35
    the music of yellow guitars,
    sounds shaken from barbed wire and
    goodbyes and miracles of survival.

My daughter denies she is like me
    her secretive eyes are walls of smoke   40
    and music and telephones.
    her pouting ruby lips, her skirts
    swaying to salsa, Madonna and the Stones.
    her thighs displayed in carnivals of color.
    I do not know the contents of her room.   45
She mirrors my aging.

She is breaking tradition.

Donna Kate Rushin

Donna Kate Rushin is a poet and teacher who lives in Boston. She has also worked
in theater and radio. Her work has been published in journals and in the anthology *This Bridge Called My Back*.

THE BRIDGE POEM

I've had enough
I'm sick of seeing and touching
Both sides of things
Sick of being the damn bridge for everybody

Nobody   5
Can talk to anybody
Without me
Right?

---

[3] Japanese straight flute.

I explain my mother to my father my father to my little sister
My little sister to my brother my brother to the white feminists   10
The white feminists to the Black church folks the Black church folks
To the ex-hippies the ex-hippies to the Black separatists the
Black separatists to the artists the artists to my friends' parents . . .

Then
I've got to explain myself   15
To everybody

I do more translating
Than the Gawdamn U.N.

Forget it
I'm sick of it   20

I'm sick of filling in your gaps

Sick of being your insurance against
The isolation of your self-imposed limitations
Sick of being the crazy at your holiday dinners
Sick of being the odd one at your Sunday Brunches   25
Sick of being the sole Black friend to 34 individual white people

Find another connection to the rest of the world
Find something else to make you legitimate
Find some other way to be political and hip

I will not be the bridge to your womanhood   30
Your manhood
Your human-ness

I'm sick of reminding you not to
Close off too tight for too long

I'm sick of mediating with your worst self   35
On behalf of your better selves

I am sick
Of having to remind you
To breathe
Before you suffocate   40
Your own fool self

Forget it
Stretch or drown
Evolve or die

The bridge I must be   45
Is the bridge to my own power
I must translate

My own fears
Mediate
My own weaknesses   50

I must be the bridge to nowhere
But my true self
And then
I will be useful

THE BLACK BACK-UPS

This is dedicated to Merry Clayton, Cissy Houston, Vonetta Washington, Dawn, Carrietta McClellen, Rosie Farmer, Marsha Jenkins and Carolyn Williams. This is for all the Black women who sang back-up for Elvis Presley, John Denver, James Taylor, Lou Reed, Etc. Etc. Etc.

    I said Hey Babe   5
    Take a Walk on the Wild Side
    I said Hey Babe
    Take a Walk on the Wild Side

    And the colored girls say

    Do dodo do do dodododo   10
    Do dodo do do dodododo
    Do dodo do do dodododo ooooo

This is for my Great Grandmother Esther, my Grandmother Addie, my Grand-mother called Sister, my Great Aunt Rachel, my Aunt Hilda, my Aunt Tine, my Aunt Breda, my Aunt Gladys, my Aunt Helen, my Aunt Ellie, my Cousin   15
Barbara, my Cousin Dottie and my Great Great Aunt Vene

This is dedicated to all of the Black women riding on buses and subways Back and forth to the Main Line, Haddonfield, N.J., Cherry Hill and Chevy Chase. This is for the women who spend their summers in Rockport, Newport, Cape Cod and Camden, Maine. This is for the women who open bundles of dirty   20
laundry sent home from ivy-covered campuses

    And the colored girls say

    Do dodo do do dodododo
    Do dodo do do dodododo
    Do dodo do do dodododo ooooo   25

    Jane Fox   Jane Fox
    Calling Jane Fox
    Where are you Jane?

    My Great Aunt Rachel worked for the Foxes
    Ever since I can remember   30
    There was The Boy

Whose name I never knew
And there was The Girl
Whose name was Jane

My Aunt Rachel brought Jane's dresses for me to wear 35
Perfectly Good Clothes
And I should've been glad to get them
Perfectly Good Clothes
No matter they didn't fit quite right
Perfectly Good Clothes Jane 40
Brought home in a brown paper bag with an air of
Accomplishment and excitement
Perfectly Good Clothes
Which I hated

It's not that I have anything *personal* against *you* Jane 45

It's just that I felt guilty
For hating those clothes

I mean
Can you get to the irony of it Jane?

And the colored girls say 50

Do dodo do do dodododo
Do dodo do do dodododo
Do dodo do do dodododo ooooo

At school
In Ohio
I swear to Gawd 55
There was always somebody
Telling me that the only person
In their whole house
Who listened and understood them
Despite the money and the lessons 60
Was the housekeeper
And I knew it was true
But what was I supposed to say?

I know it's true 65
I watch them getting off the train
And moving slowly toward the Country Squire
With their uniform in their shopping bag
And the closer they get to the car
The more the two little kids jump and laugh 70
And even the dog is about to
Turn inside out
Because they just can't wait until she gets there
Edna Edna   Wonderful Edna
(But Aunt Edna to me, or Gram, or Miz Johnson, or Sister 75
Johnson on Sundays)

And the colored girls say

Do dodo do do dodododo
Do dodo do do dodododo
Do dodo do do dodododo ooooo   80

This is for Hattie McDaniels, Butterfly McQueen, Ethel Waters
Saphire
Saphronia
Ruby Begonia
Aunt Jemima   85
Aunt Jemima on the Pancake Box
Aunt Jemima on the Pancake Box?

AuntJemimaonthepancakebox?
auntjemimaonthepancakebox?
Ainchamamaonthepancakebox?   90
Ain't chure Mama on the pancake box?

Mama Mama
Get offa that damn box
And come home to me

And my Mama leaps offa that box   95
She swoops down in her nurse's cape
Which she wears on Sunday
And on Wednesday night prayer meeting
And she wipes my forehead
And she fans my face for me   100
And she makes me a cup o' tea
And it don't do a thing for my real pain
Except she is my Mama
Mama Mommy Mommy Mammy Mammy
Mam-mee Mam-mee   105
I'd Walk a mill-yon miles
For one o' your smiles

This is for the Black Back-ups
This is for my mama and your mama
My grandma and your grandma   110
This is for the thousand thousand Black Back-Ups

And the colored girls say

Do dodo   do do   dodododo
Do do   do   do   do
        Do   do   115
                             do
Do
                    do

Roberta Hill Whiteman

Roberta Hill Whiteman is a member of the Oneida tribe of Wisconsin. She grew up around Green Bay and was educated at the University of Wisconsin and the University of Montana. She now teaches at the University of Wisconsin–Eau Claire. Her poems are collected in *Star Quilt* (1984).

THE LONG PARENTHESIS

For my students at the Wisconsin
State Reformatory, Fall 1977

I didn't want to walk through remote control doors,
the bars, peeling paint, a fifties beige. I didn't hope to save you,
just to teach dashes, colons, the verb you need
for better days outside. My card: "Education."
The Lieutenant warned: "You smile, it's rape   5
and all your fault. I've filed each armed and dangerous.
Never shut the door." The scar across his left eye
burned brighter than his shirt.

I've been here before. My father wore his heart out on you cons,
Twenty-nine years of math, gum on the ass of his second suit,   10
he served his time. Imprisoned by an ache, he couldn't return,
kept seeing the spoon pierce his student's throat,
the death rattle fill the hall, blood dry on his palm.
The library door was open; the guards were hours away.
He kept saying one of you had drowned.   15
This mold for a society could make the seas decay.

You live the long parenthesis; each of you a man
who listens to the water drip, sees dust hang in each tier,
whose dash and strut and rebel glare,
ah, rebel that I am, had made you seed for anarchy   20
or harbingers of war. I'm glad I found you
flesh, sweat, excuses. For weeks your number dropped:
one went home, collared the next day on another warrant,
one anxious in his learning found morning in the hole.

Seven of you were left: three races in one room, four billboards   25
peppered with holes, six windows faced concrete.
What records can they keep of inappropriate looks?
At first you thought, "a woman.'" I memorized restraint.
When others peered inside, I began to shut the door.
Our classroom needed thunder, a forest lit with moths, the smell   30
of blooming sweet flag and faces clean of such arrogant despair.
I see you, each writing his escape:

one locked up more inside than bars will ever do;
one sharpened foreign rhetoric like an unforgiving blade;
one puffed up for flight, a comic-loving sparrow;   35
one craved a mean piano and almost didn't pass;
one smiled at me for weeks and must have worked in secret;
one walked in like a leopard, practiced in his moves;
one, with sleight of hand, planned to reraise himself.
I dragged those early lessons like a red ant does her sand.   40

Pile one wall there, a peephole here, so each can see the other,
human and alive. My passion's equally vain.
We're out of place in this tyranny of routine,
the suave American Dream where one of every six
guards the thick or dead. Scraping all at once like winter weeds,   45
we hassled with a future that strongarmed us back to now.
We con ourselves: just one chance to snatch a generous pitfall.
Your eyes need time to heal, and healing's hard in there.

We live by more than breath. Behind the all pervading air,
creation quickened seed, flower, fruit and pith. Love's always   50
changing form. A self that stays divided finds an early grave
or mirrors still more misery in parentheses again. Draw miracles
from yourself. Stumbling in the dark, I'm too vulnerable for answers,
but that delicious morning when you're free, I hope good deeds
take shape behind you, like scarves drawn from a magic hat   55
one after the other shimmer boldly in the wind.

STAR QUILT

These are notes to lightning in my bedroom.
A star forged from linen thread and patches.
Purple, yellow, red like diamond suckers, children

of the star gleam on sweaty nights. The quilt unfolds
against sheets, moving, warm clouds of Chinook.   5
It covers my cuts, my red birch clusters under pine.

Under it your mouth begins a legend,
and wide as the plain, I hope Wisconsin marshes
promise your caress. The candle locks

us in forest smells, your cheek tattered   10
by shadow. Sweetened by wings, my mothlike heart
flies nightly among geraniums.

We know of land that looks lonely,
but isn't, of beef with hides of velveteen,
of sorrow, an eddy in blood.   15

Star quilt, sewn from dawn light by fingers
of flint, take away those touches
meant for noisier skins,

anoint us with grass and twilight air,
so we may embrace, two bitter roots   20
pushing back into the dust.

A POETRY CASEBOOK

🙖 🙖

It is very rewarding to study a number of poems by the same poet. The entire body of a poet's work has some of the same characteristics as a single poem: a central theme or set of themes, recurring images and metaphors, a beginning, middle, and end. We cannot include the entire body of any poet's work in this book, of course, but in this section you will have an opportunity to study a range of poems by a single poet and to read some published criticism of his work. The poet is Michael S. Harper, one of the most accomplished of contemporary African-American poets, and we are including eight of his poems.

Also included are a 1981 essay by Harper himself on his work and three critical essays on Harper's work. John F. Callahan's "The Testifying Voice in Michael Harper's *Images of Kin*," although formally an essay-review of Harper's 1977 selected poems, *Images of Kin*, goes beyond that purpose to offer a broad survey of some of Harper's principal themes and techniques. Father Joseph A. Brown's 1986 essay, "Their Long Scars Touch Ours: A Reflection on the Poetry of Michael Harper," also offers broad generalizations about Harper's career (finding Harper's main subject to be *"Death* in all its manifestations"); it also offers close readings of several of the Harper poems included here. The fourth essay, "Black Poetry and Black Music; History and Tradition: Michael Harper and John Coltrane," by the German critic Günter H. Lenz, is only one section of a much longer essay. It takes up a single important aspect of Harper's poetry, his use of jazz as inspiration, subject, and metaphor, and especially the influence upon him of the great tenor saxophonist John Coltrane.

This casebook will provide you with the opportunity to read several poems by the same poet, compare the poems, identify recurring concerns and formal techniques, and generally get a feel for his work. And it will also provide you with some examples of professional criticism of poetry and give you a chance to enter the critical dialogue concerning the work of a gifted and rewarding poet.

Michael S. Harper

Michael S. Harper was born (in 1938) and grew up in Brooklyn. He remembers that, "My parents weren't rich, but they had a good record collection," and early on he formed an enthusiasm for the great jazz musicians of his youth, who have provided him with much of the inspiration for his poetry. When he was thirteen, he and his parents moved to Los Angeles where he attended high school and what is now California State University. He went on to earn an M.F.A. at the Iowa Writers Workshop. After teaching in Portland, Oregon; Hayward, California; and Urbana, Illinois, Harper became a professor of English and director of the writing program at Brown University, where he still teaches. His books include *Dear John, Dear Coltrane* (1970), *History Is Your Own Heartbeat* (1971), *Photographs: Negatives: History as Apple Tree* (1972), *Song: I Want a Witness* (1972), *Debridement* (1973), *Nightmare Begins Responsibility* (1974), *Images of Kin: New and Selected Poems* (1977), and *Healing Song for the Inner Ear* (1984).

DEAR JOHN, DEAR COLTRANE[1]

a love supreme, a love supreme
a love supreme, a love supreme

Sex fingers toes
in the marketplace
near your father's church
in Hamlet, North Carolina—[2]   5
witness to this love
in this calm fallow
of these minds,
there is no substitute for pain: 10
genitals gone or going,
seed burned out,
you tuck the roots in the earth,
turn back, and move
by river through the swamps,   15
singing: *a love supreme, a love supreme;*
what does it all mean?

Loss, so great each black
woman expects your failure
in mute change, the seed gone.   20
You plod up into the electric city—
your song now crystal and
the blues. You pick up the horn
with some will and blow
into the freezing night: 25
a love supreme, a love supreme—

Dawn comes and you cook
up the thick sin 'tween

---

[1] John Coltrane (1926–67) was the leading jazz saxophonist of his generation. "A Love Supreme" (recorded 1965) is one of his compositions.
[2] Place of Coltrane's birth.

impotence and death, fuel
the tenor sax cannibal   30
heart, genitals and sweat
that makes you clean—
a love supreme, a love supreme—

Why you so black?
cause I am   35
why you so funky?
cause I am
why you so black?
cause I am
why you so sweet?   40
cause I am
why you so black?
cause I am
a love supreme, a love supreme:

So sick   45
you couldn't play *Naima*,³
so flat we ached
for song you'd concealed
with your own blood,
your diseased liver gave   50
out its purity,
the inflated heart
pumps out, the tenor kiss,
tenor love:
a love supreme, a love supreme—   55
a love supreme, a love supreme—

AMERICAN HISTORY

Those four black girls blown up
in that Alabama church¹
remind me of five hundred
middle passage blacks,²
in a net, under water   5
in Charleston harbor
so *redcoats*³ wouldn't find them.
Can't find what you can't see
can you?

---

³ Another of Coltrane's compositions (recorded 1966).
¹ In 1963 opponents of civil rights exploded a bomb in a black church in Birmingham, Alabama,
killing four little girls.
² The Middle Passage was the middle part of the slaveships' route from Africa to America; that is, the
crossing of the Atlantic Ocean.
³ British soldiers.

REUBEN, REUBEN[1]

I reach from pain
to music great enough
to bring me back,
swollenhead, madness,
lovefruit, a pickle of hate   5
so sour my mouth twicked
up and would not sing;
there's nothing in the beat
to hold it in
melody and turn human skin;   10
a brown berry gone
to rot just two days on the branch;
we've lost a son
the music, *jazz*, comes in.

HERE WHERE COLTRANE IS

Soul and race
are private dominions,
memories and modal
songs, a tenor blossoming,
which would paint suffering   5
a clear color but is not in
this Victorian house
without oil in zero degree
weather and a forty-mile-an-hour wind;
it is all a well-knit family: 10
a love supreme.
Oak leaves pile up on walkway
and steps, catholic as apples
in a special mist of clear white
children who love my children.   15
I play "Alabama"[1]
on a warped record player
skipping the scratches
on your faces over the fibrous
conical hairs of plastic   20
under the wooden floors.

Dreaming on a train from New York
to Philly, you hand out six
notes which become an anthem
to our memories of you: 25

[1] Reuben Masai Harper, one of two of Harper's sons who died in infancy.
[1] Composition by John Coltrane. Coltrane began writing "Alabama" on a train between New York and Philadelphia (see lines 22–27).

oak, birch, maple,
apple, cocoa, rubber.
For this reason Martin is dead;
for this reason Malcolm is dead;
for this reason Coltrane is dead;[2]   30
in the eyes of my first son are the browns
of these men and their music.

HIGH MODES: VISION AS RITUAL: CONFIRMATION

Black Man Go Back To The Old Country
Black Man Go Back To The Old Country
Black Man Go Back To The Old Country
Black Man Go Back To The Old Country

And you went back home for the images,   5
the brushwork packing the mud
into the human form; and the ritual:
Black Man Go Back To The Old Country.

We danced, the chocolate trees and samba
leaves wetting the paintbrush, and babies   10
came in whispering of one, oneness,
otherness, forming each man in his music,
one to one: and we touched, *contact-high,*
high modes,[1] *contact-high,* and the images,
contact-high, man to man, came back.   15
Black Man Go Back To The Old Country.

The grooves turned in a human face,
Lady Day,[2] blue and green, modally,
and we touched, *contact-high,* high modes:
Black Man Go Back To The Old Country.   20

Bird was a mode from the old country;[3]
Bud Powell bowed in modality, blow Bud;
Louis Armstrong touched the old country,
and brought it back, around corners;
Miles is a mode; Coltrane is, power,   25
Black Man Go Back To The Old Country

---

[2] Martin Luther King (1929–68); Malcolm X (1925–65); John Coltrane (1926–67).
[1] Harper has written of the term *modality* (*mode, modal*): "My poems are *modal.* By modality I mean the creation of an environment so intense by its life and force as to revivify and regenerate, spiritually, man and community; modality assumes contact, touch, between human beings, one to one, and an environment of spirit that revitalizes man, individually and culturally."
[2] Nickname of American jazz singer Billie Holiday (1915–59).
[3] The jazz musicians named in these lines are Charlie "Bird" Parker (alto saxophone), Bud Powell (piano), Louis Armstrong (trumpet), Miles Davis (trumpet), and John Coltrane (tenor and soprano saxophones).

Black Man Go Back To The Old Country
Black Man Go Back To The Old Country

And we go back to the well: Africa,
the first mode, and man, modally,   30
touched the land of the continent,
modality: we are one; a man is another
man's face, modality, in continuum,
from man, to man, *contact-high,* to man,
contact-high, to man, high modes, oneness,   35
contact-high, man to man, *contact-high:*

Black Man Go Back To The Old Country
Black Man Go Back To The Old Country
Black Man Go Back To The Old Country
Black Man Go Back To The Old Country   40

CONTINUOUS VISIT

Your canoe stops
near a sunflower patch
where your daughters
swim in two weedy ditches
off our shaky docks,   5
cast frogs, hooked through
their mouths,
bass not yet biting.

Moose pie, creamed
beans and Jell-O   10
opt new appetites,
your girls beach
sandpiled in towels;
under forty oaks
you read chronicles   15
from typed peach paper,
last year's spirits
pitched in its threshing,
blood from the suture
of my family.   20

This suture is race
as it is blood,
long as the frozen
lake building messages
on typewritten paper,   25
faces of my ancestors,
warm in winter only
as their long scars touch ours.

NIGHTMARE BEGINS RESPONSIBILITY[1]

I place these numbed wrists to the pane
watching white uniforms whisk over
him[2] in the tube-kept
prison
fear what they will do in experiment   5
watch my gloved stickshifting gasolined hands
breathe *boxcar-information-please* infirmary tubes
distrusting white-pink mending paperthin
silkened end hairs, distrusting tubes
shrunk in his *trunk-skincapped*   10
shaven head, in thighs
distrusting-white-hands-picking-baboon-light
on this son who will not make his second night
of this wardstrewn intensive airpocket
where his father's asthmatic   15
hymns of *night-train*, train done gone
his mother can only know that he has flown
up into essential calm unseen corridor
going boxscarred home, *mamaborn, sweetsonchild*
gonedowntown into *researchtestingwarehousebatteryacid* 20
mama-son-done-gone/me telling her 'nother
train tonight, no music, no breathstroked
heartbeat in my infinite distrust of them:

and of my distrusting self
white-doctor-who-breathed-for-him-all-night   25
say it for two sons gone,
say nightmare, say it loud
panebreaking heartmadness:
nightmare begins responsibility.

ALICE[1]

'The word made stone, the stone word'
'A RITE is an action the very form of which is the result of a Divine
Revelation.'

I

You stand waist-high in snakes
beating the weeds for the gravebed

---

[1] An allusion to the American poet Delmore Schwartz's *In Dreams Begin Responsibilities* (1938). Schwartz took the title from the epigraph to William Butler Yeats's volume *Responsibilities* (1914): "In dreams begins responsibility." Yeats attributes the line to an "Old Play."
[2] One of the two sons Harper and his wife lost in infancy.
[1] The black American novelist Alice Walker (b. 1944). This poem is based on an incident in which Harper and Walker searched for the grave of the writer Zora Neale Hurston. Walker has given her own version of this incident in an essay "In Search of Zora Neale Hurston," *Ms* (1974), reprinted in *In Search of Our Mothers' Gardens* (1983).

a quarter mile from the nearest
relative, an open field in Florida: lost,
looking for Zora, and when she speaks   5
from her sunken chamber to call
you to her side, she calls
you her distant cousin, her sister
come to mark her burial place
with bright black stone.   10
She has known you would do this—
her crooked stick, her straight lick—
and the lie you would have to tell
to find her, and that you lied
to her relatives in a conjure-riddle   15
of the words you have uttered,
calling her to communion.

A black rock of ages you have placed
where there was no marker,
and though the snakes abound   20
in this preserve from ancestral space,
you have paid your homage
in traditional line, the face open:
your face in the woman-light of surrender
toughened in what you were.   25

II

Floods of truth flow from your limbs
of these pages in a vision swollen
in experience and pain:
that child you stepped into blossom
of a man's skull beaten into smile   30
of submission, you gathering horse nectar
for offering over a baby's crusted gasp,
for centuries of motherhood and atonement
for which you write, and the rite written.

And for this I say your name: Alice,   35
my grandmother's name, your name,
conjured in snake-infested field
where Zora Neale welcomed you home,
and where I speak from now
on higher ground of her risen   40
black marker where you have written
your name in hers, and in mine.

A NARRATIVE OF THE LIFE AND TIMES OF
JOHN COLTRANE: PLAYED BY HIMSELF

Hamlet, North Carolina

I don't remember train whistles,
or corroding trestles of ice
seeping from the hangband,
vaulting northward in shining triplets,
but the feel of the reed on my tongue   5
haunts me even now, my incisors
pulled so the pain wouldn't lurk
on "Cousin Mary";

in High Point I stared
at the bus which took us to band   10
practice on Memorial Day;
I could hardly make out, in the mud,
placemarks, separations of skin
sketched in plates above the rear bumper.

Mama asked, "what's the difference   15
'tween North and South Carolina,"
a capella notes of our church choir
doping me into arpeggios,
into *sheets of sound* labeling me
into dissonance.   20

I never liked the photo taken with
Bird, Miles without sunglasses,[1]
me in profile almost out of exposure;
these were my images of movement;
when I hear the sacred songs,   25
auras of my mother at the stove,
I play the blues:

what good does it do to complain:
one night I was playing with Bostic,[2]
blacking out, coming alive only to melodies   30
where I could play my parts:
And then, on a train to Philly,
I sang "Naima" locking the door
without exit no matter what song
I sang; with remonstrations on the ceiling   35
of that same room I practiced in
on my back when too tired to stand,
I broke loose from crystalline habits
I thought would bring me that sound.

---

[1] "Bird" is Charlie Parker, "Miles," Miles Davis. Coltrane played for some years with the Miles Davis quintet.
[2] Earl Bostic (1913–65), alto saxophonist and bandleader.

MY POETIC TECHNIQUE AND THE HUMANIZATION OF THE AMERICAN AUDIENCE*

by Michael S. Harper

The geographical division of the country into political districts and regions with complementary agricultural and economic systems underlies much of Afro-American poetic symbolism. That the star points north is not important because of some abstract, or mystical or religious conception, but because it brought into conjunction Biblical references, concrete social conditions and the human will to survive—including the fact that if you got safely across certain socio-geographical boundaries you were in freedom. Writers have made much of the North Star but they forget that a hell of a lot of slaves were running away to the West, 'going to the nation, going to the territory,' because as Mark Twain knew, that too was an area of Negro freedom. When people get to telling stories based on their cooperate experience, quite naturally such patterns turn up. Because as significant scenes in which human will is asserted, they help organize and focus narrative. They become more poetic the further we are removed from the actual experience, and their symbolic force is extended through repetition.[1]

I was fortunate enough to be born at home, delivered by my grandfather, and so there was much lore attached to my birth, much signifying. My parents weren't rich, but they had a good record collection, and they prohibited me from playing any of their 78's, which was a guarantee that I'd investigate in my own time, always when they were out of the house. After dusting the records, and making sure the needle was in place, the records in the appropriate order, every item in place, I'd forget not to hum the songs I'd heard, and would get caught with a smile. I also had the habit of riding the subway trains on what we called off-days, days when we took off from school, all the Jewish holidays in particular. I'd been riding the subways since I was five, but my parents didn't know it, and it took them three years to catch me. On that fateful day I was illegally riding after school, and passed my father as he went to work. I knew he'd seen me, though he never let on, and I decided to get on the next train and continue riding. At the next express I got off, intending to turn around and go back home to the inevitable whipping when I heard a tapping on a window of another train—it was my grandmother. She waved faintly with a hint of a smile. Music and trains! Coltrane. One learns most by getting caught doing the things you love; it leaves an impression.

I knew Bessie Smith and Billie Holiday from birth, and I was a horn man: President Lester Young; Coleman Superhawk Hawkins; Big Bad Ben Webster; Charles Chan Parker, alias the Bird; John William Coltrane, alias the Trane. There's a story that Trane was searching for a particular tone on his horn. He had what we thought was a perfect embouchure, but his teeth hurt constantly, so he searched for a soft reed which would ease the pain. After searching for a year, each session killing his chops, he gave it up completely. There was no easy way to get that sound—play through the pain to a *love supreme*.

* Originally published in *Black American Literature and Humanism*, ed. R. Baxter Miller. (Lexington: University Press of Kentucky, 1981).
[1] Michael S. Harper and Robert B. Stepto, "Study and Experience: An Interview with Ralph Ellison," *Massachusetts Review* 18 (Autumn 1977): 435.

I wrote, secretly, in high school, buried in the back of some English class for fear I'd be asked to stand and recite a memorized poem of Donne, Shakespeare, or John Keats. Luckily I tore up all these efforts, switched to prose and short dramatic forms until I was almost through college. I was working on the postal facing table, the middle-class equivalent to the pool hall. Almost everybody in sight had advanced degrees. It was there I learned about Tolstoi and *So What* Dostoevski, as one of my partners used to call the Russian underground man. My partner had discovered Miles Davis. When I went to the Writers Workshop at the University of Iowa, I was the only blood in either fiction or poetry, and I was enrolled in both. Several teachers asked me was I going to be another James Baldwin—one of the faculty members was so obsessed with Baldwin he knew I'd known Mr. Baldwin—I had read Baldwin's novels and essays, but hadn't met Baldwin personally. I began to specialize in retorts to affronts. You met Isaac Singer? You been hunting with Hemingway? But this kind of humor didn't go over very well. All the writers in the workshop at the time were victims of the New Criticism, the poets writing in rhyme and meter, the fiction writers reading James and Forster.

I hung out with the football players during the era of Iowa's great dynasty. The best lineman on the team, Al Hinton, would creep over to my garage apartment behind one of the few Black families in Iowa City, and ask me if I knew anyone who could teach him to draw. We were dancing to "Gypsy Woman" and playing tonk. I used to stay in the library until closing time, 2 a.m., to avoid the cold. My first and only poem on the worksheet in the poetry class was a poem dedicated to Miles Davis, "Alone," which I've since cut to three lines. It was my bible. How would it be to solo with that great tradition of the big bands honking you on? Could one do it in a poem? I'd taken my survey courses, studied my Donne and Shakespeare, got hot at the Moor of Venice, hotter at Prospero (me mad Caliban) and gone on to American literature without Frederick Douglass, Du Bois, Johnson, or Toomer. Richard Wright I remember most clearly because he was talked about in Brooklyn when I was a kid. I read all his books in one weekend because none of his books had ever been taken out of the school library. I took offense at O'Neill's Brutus Jones (as I'd despised Vachel Lindsay's "Congo" poem), and T. S. Eliot's remarks on the ending of "All God's Chillun Got Wings" (neither play large enough for the torso of Paul Robeson), and searched for the cadence of street talk in the inner ear of the great musicians, the great blues singers.

This brings me to church. My mother was Episcopal; my father Catholic; I was a Baptist because of the great singing. Every Sunday I had to *hit the meter* (put money in the collection box), hit the holy water, and take the subway to 52nd Street to catch Bird play. One morning, just after 9 a.m., Bird came out a side door, his sax in a triply reinforced Macy's shopping bag: "Boy, how come you not in church?" he asked, but I was quick, told him I'd been and took up his horn case, the handles raggedly stringed. He took us, three or four kids all under ten, to the subway station; changed a quarter, gave us each a nickel, told us not to sneak on the train going home, and disappeared uptown.

I have images of musicians at their best and when they were down and out; their playing never faltered—the other musicians wouldn't tolerate anything less than a journeyman job, a little extra inspiration. My people were good storytellers. Some of my personal kin walked north and west during the Civil War from North Carolina, South Carolina, and Virginia, and one ancestor came from Chatham—Ontario, Canada. I was surprised to find their images in books, not Stowe's *Uncle Tom's Cabin*, the play version differing greatly from the text of the novel, but Douglass' 1845 narrative written by himself. Douglass' rhetoric, the notion of having each slave carry on his person an articulate pass, is my ticket to freedom.

I have gotten letters from "friends" praising my knowledge of history, but I learned a little terminology from a zoology teacher in Los Angeles who had us count somites in his worms. He told me I shouldn't study because I'd never get into medical school; I should pick up a broom and forget the microscope. He, of course, was being scrutinized for future reference. A new critic once wrote, "nigger your breed ain't metaphysical," and of course we're not. The poet, Sterling Brown, whose record I heard in the library in San Francisco fifteen years ago ("the strong men, keep a-comin' on / the strong men, git stronger") coined an infamous retort—"cracker your breed ain't exegetical."

I wrote about my "Grandfather" because he was a hero in the highest sense, though he waited tables in white clothes. He taught me to study Sugar Ray's left-hook technique, to step inside someone's sense of time, of theatre, of the stage and arena, and to floor show to one's own tune. Ellison called it *antagonistic cooperation;* Wright called it the switchblade of the movie-screen. Language and rhetoric is essential power. Why else were the slaves prohibited from reading, from learning to pen their own sagas? All great art is finally testamental, and its technical brilliance never shadows the content of the song. Deliver the melody, make sure the harmony's correct, play as long as you like, but play sweet, and don't forget the ladies.

A final note on the blues is that they always say *yes* to life; meet life's terms but never accept them: "been down so long that down don't worry me / road so rocky, won't be rocky long." Johnny Hodges must have said this to Duke on tour: "you run them verbs (the key of G), I'll drive the thought (the rabbit on his own rainbow)."

I'll make a coda on the American audience, which is vast potentially. "I wish you'd buy more books," said Huck to Tom—meanwhile Jim was bringing his family to freedom. The landscape of the poem is the contour of the face reading the Declaration of Independence. How many White Jeffersons are there in this country, anyway? When I interviewed for my present duty at Brown University, all that slave trade money came back to haunt me once again, a man yelled out from the genteel back of the room that I was an impostor borrowing from musicians. Couldn't I do something about my accent? People were embarrassed for him. He was quickly ushered out, and the East Side returned to normal, good old Providence with its old money and the mafia flair. I remembered that Douglass had been run out of Providence to New Bedford after an abolitionist meeting, and it's rumored that John Brown (the fanatical one) came all the way from Oberlin, Ohio, to meet the best gunsmith in town, a Black infantryman from the Black Regiment of Rhode Island.

"Straight, no Chaser," said the musician. He must have meant the street corner and the library. With some lies thrown in, this has been a riff in honor of my ancestors and a little stretching of the truth to make the point. Here is one more lie to make the audience sweet. When I was in South Africa in 1977 on an American Specialist Program, all by myself, I landed at Jan Smuts airport in Johannesburg at about 2:30 a.m. I was carrying Sterling Brown's *Southern Road* and Robert Hayden's *Angle of Ascent* and some of my own books, one with Coltrane's image on the cover. I was first addressed in Afrikaans, but not being colored, I answered in American, "I'm from Brooklyn . . . you ever heard of Jackie Robinson?" It took me awhile to get through customs. I was staying at the Holiday Inn right at the airport so all I had to do was wait for the little van picking up customers. I stood there for a few minutes, a few Whites not far away. When the driver, a Black South African, approached I got ready to board. I was first in line. Telling me to wait, the driver held up his hand to me, boarded all the White passengers, and drove off. I stood there taking names so to speak. When the driver returned, he apologized for not taking me in the van with the other passengers. He wanted to know where I came from and then he asked—"What language do you speak when the White people aren't around?" I said, "English," and he said, "No, no." What language did I speak when the White people weren't around? The second time he asked I changed my response to "American." "Brother," he inquired, "when Blacks are among themselves, don't they speak *jazz?*" I nodded, *right on,* brother. Send more Afro-Americans from the states; bring your record collections. The battle of the big bands begins.

THE TESTIFYING VOICE IN MICHAEL HARPER'S
*IMAGES OF KIN**

by John F. Callahan

For Michael Harper the mission of poetry is bound up with eloquence and the magic of the spoken word, the oral tradition. Harper is a poet whose vision of personal and national experience is worked out in the Afro-American grain—that tradition of pain and rejuvenation expressed in the sorrow songs, the blues, and folktales, the whole range of Afro-American oral tradition, a tradition, it is important to remember, which also touches formal American/Afro-American rhetorical patterns, from Abraham Lincoln and Frederick Douglass in the nineteenth century to Martin Luther King in the nineteen-fifties and -sixties. Harper is alert to the possibilities of rhetoric and the complexities of that ancient and American rhetoric tradition whose purpose was to challenge, vex, please, persuade, and, at last, illuminate the audience. He is a poet not of paradox but of the paradoxical, of simplicity in the midst of complexities, affirmation in the midst of tragedy—but affirmations so aware of the incongruities of eloquence that his voice intensifies the sense of tragedy and devastation.

Make no mistake about Harper's allegiance to a single complex, diverse tradition. Much as he recognizes and heeds points of departure between American and Afro-American cultural patterns, Harper is a major American poet for the same reasons and in the same work that he is a major Afro-American poet. His stance is deliberately chosen, and defiant toward any who try to subordinate either the American or Afro-American aspect of his tradition, experience, or language. Harper's purpose, like Du Bois's at the turn of this century, is to turn the notion (and fact) of double-consciousness, of racial and cultural polarity, into a strength, an energy, a source of wholeness. Like Du Bois, Harper wishes nothing to be lost in the passage to a "better and truer self."

At forty, Harper has written a dozen or more extraordinary poems, poems long-lived and stunningly original, poems that transform his stance as an American/Afro-American poet into a reality with the power of illumination. *Images of Kin* (Urbana: Univ. of Illinois Press, 1977) is a collection of Harper's best and most representative work. Beginning with *Healing Songs,* a selection of recent, previously uncollected poems, and "Uplift From a Dark Tower," Harper's impor-

* Originally published in *Black American Literature Forum* 13 (Fall, 1979).

tant poem stalking Booker T. Washington's connection with the Trask family and its Yaddo estate, *Images of Kin* reverses chronological lines and travels back through Harper's prolific earlier volumes: *Nightmare Begins Responsibility* (1975); *Debridement* (1973); *Song: I Want a Witness* (1972); *History Is Your Own Heartbeat* (1971); and *Dear John, Dear Coltrane* (1970).

Arranging and organizing one's poems can be a difficult and perplexing task, particularly this early when the writer's trajectory may not yet be clear. In the case of *Images of Kin* Harper seems to have been governed by an urge to see, feel, and make known the past in the present moment—understandably, given his emphasis on healing and transformation. Nevertheless, in my view the cutting edge of the current work is somewhat dulled by its being presented first. In the sense that Yeats called poetry a quarrel with ourselves it may be that some of the current poems need the dramatic declaration and details of the early work, particularly *Dear John, Dear Coltrane* and *History Is Your Own Heartbeat*. Not that Harper's early poetry is always simple and direct. It is not, and neither is the later work inaccessible or uncompelling, but I think that even the best of the current poems ("Tongue-Tied in Black and White," "Bristol: Bicentenary Remembrances of Trade," and "Smoke," for instance) are richer for the contexts worked out and made familiar in earlier poems. The moments of controlled eloquence in the current poems might have a greater impact if the collection were arranged chronologically. Another related quarrel I have with *Images of Kin* is with the decision to include large selections from the three long poems comprising *Debridement*. As an admirer of the title poem's experiments with vernacular, documentary, and bureaucratic idioms, I regret that the book is out of print, but excerpting it as Harper has done in *Images of Kin* does the poem less than justice. This is even truer of the excerpts reprinted here from the long poems on John Brown and Richard Wright. For me the *Debridement* selections overload the collection, blur its focus; the editors at Illinois should have seen this and, recognizing the merits of *Debridement,* reissued it separately from *Images of Kin*.

There is, too, the matter of language. Occasionally, in the recent poems, "Healing Song" for example, I sense a blurring of idiom as if Harper were slipping out of the grooves of a naturally-crafted, improvisatory style into an over-elaborated, overloaded imagery:

> Ragboned Bob Hayden, shingled in slime,
> reaches for his cereus ladder of midnight flight,
> his seismographic heartbeats
> sphinctered in rhiney polygraphs of light;
> Dee-troit born and half-blind
> in diction of arena and paradise,
> his ambient nightmare-dreams streak his tongue. . . .

From an arresting beginning—"Ragboned Bob Hayden"—the stanza's imagery becomes so carefully wrought as to be overwrought or even careless in the sense that complications do duty for complexity. Yet tucked away in the passage are two finely-tuned lines evoking Hayden's outer and inner landscape, his gifts, afflictions and compensations: "Dee-troit born and half-blind/in diction of arena and paradise." The beat thins into a ballad rhythm and melody subtly expressive of the blending of Afro-American and American culture and idiom. The voice modulates to a frequency at which the spoken word reverberates out from words written on the page.

Again, I am reminded of an aphorism of Du Bois: "The problem of the twentieth century," he wrote in 1900, "is the problem of the color-line. . . ." To a large extent the problem of poetry is the problem of voice, and for Harper, because of his consciously-honed identity and stance as an American/Afro-American poet, the problem of voice becomes a matter of voice-line. Certainly, the fact and metaphor of lines persistently mark Harper's work. Lines connect and demarcate; they suggest the points of contact and points of departure between American and Afro-American tradition; between the official word, usually written, and the oral tradition, its anecdotes and improvisatory, embellishing forms shaping what Ralph Ellison has called the "unofficial stream" of American history. Harper is interested in lines of ancestry and kinship, ties made visible by blood and heredity, and those other ties manifest but less visible, ties formed by the shared experience of American life.

Going back to voice, I regard Harper's reputation secure because of the continuing impact, the originality and importance, of what I call his performance poems, in most cases poems written by 1970. In these stunning poems from *Dear John, Dear Coltrane* and *History Is Your Own Heartbeat* he worked out the problem of voice. He found a formal way to shape the idioms and strands of his experience and tradition into a voice capable of expressing many styles, many frequencies, many lines of speech and experience. And performance here is no less complex a word than voice. I mean to suggest the fluidities and possibilities Ralph Ellison had in mind when he said that "in improvised jazz performance and creation can consist of a single complex act." Performance is a metaphor for the poet's role as well as a way of writing poetry. For Harper the Afro-American performance metaphor brings the poet and his poems to the testing ground of the world; sometimes the locale of a poem is the arena in the sense of a combat zone in which the poet, like the jazz musician of the '20s, '30s, '40s, and '50s, contends for a place in the culture.

It is no accident or coincidence that Harper's performance poems tend to focus on musicians or, as with "Ode to Tenochtitlan" or "Biafra Blues," on historical action that compels a merging of musical with poetic techniques. Nor is it surprising that Harper desires to make the bond between himself and his reader/listener akin to that between the Afro-American musician and his audience. Harper develops this relationship knowing thoroughly the tradition, doubtless recalling the lines spoken in Sterling Brown's "Ma Rainey" before and after she has done her stuff:

> I talked to a fellow, an' the fellow say,
> "She jes' catch hold of us, somekindaway."

And then, after the performance:

> Dere wasn't much more de fellow say:
> She jes' gits hold of us dataway.

Performance is transformational, rejuvenating—this is made clear in Brown's poems by the shift into folk idiom and the merging of the narrator and his folk character into almost a single presence, or, in any case, a common voice.

In a departure from Sterling Brown's idiomatic performance poems and in the subtle manner of the jazz musicians he writes about, Harper puts himself—the active voice of his consciousness—somewhere near the center of his performance poems. The form is testamental and the intent transformational in the manner of the blues. The forms of address vary and are often interchangeable among I, you, and me; yet, no matter what the apparent subject matter, the modality of tradition which Harper seeks is always achieved *somehow* by the force of his presence, his personality—above all, his voice. All this centrality of consciousness is consistent with Harper's notion of modality. It is, he says, "always about relationships," "always about energy." In the case of Harper's best poetry, performance is the form through which the energies of private and public life are joined, as he writes of Tommy Smith and John Carlos in "Ode to Tenochtitlan," joined in

> a style so resilient
> and chromatic the pure
> needs of their bodies
> bulge through metric
> distances in their
> special rhythms.

This unity between public and private experience seems a necessity in Harper's imagination despite, even because of, the realities of danger and struggle; and every time the reliable test is the test of style.

There is too a paradox, a reversal, which follows upon the extended meaning of performance in Harper's work. Often his poems about private life and intimate experience ("Deathwatch" and "Mission") assume a public rhetoric, a style and frame of reference close to oratory, while poems about public figures and histor- ical reality are imbued with a passionate intensity and purity of intention that are next door to intimacy ("Dear John, Dear Coltrane" and " 'Bird Lives': Charles Parker"). It may be that as a poet of performance in these early poems Harper wrote of love as combat and combat as love in another variation on the theme of American/Afro-American literature and experience; i.e., that for men, whether they contend with women and family or with the forces of society and nature, love and intimacy follow from contention; that is, from shared participation in combat or, more complexly, from struggle.

From the Declaration of Independence forward there has been confusion in American life between love and politics, and in Afro-American experience the pursuit of happiness has been a right necessarily tested out in both the public and private domains. Certainly, many of Harper's family poems convey the sense that there is no such thing as a home-court advantage and that in America one's private environment may be the unfriendliest arena of all.

Contrariwise, the closest Harper comes to a state of peace and rest may be in the final stanza of "History as Apple Tree," a poem whose participants are Harper and the ghosts of historical figures and whose action is a solitary ritual that illuminates the past uniquely in Harper's consciousness:

> As black man I steal away
> in the night to the apple tree,
> place my arm in the rich grave,
> black sachem on a family plot,
> take up a chuck of apple root,
> let it become my skeleton,
> become my own myth:
> my arm the historical branch,
> my name the bruised fruit,
> black human photograph: apple tree.

The image gradually appears and develops like a *still* photograph; phosphorescent in their suggestion of quiet thought on the poet's part, the lines perhaps compel silence from those responsive to his vision.

Leaving aside further speculation about the nature of performance, let me characterize the diverse human frequencies articulated in these Harper poems. In the best poems false ties are sundered, true connections made, as the music of contact plays over the full range of human feeling and perception.

"Dear John, Dear Coltrane": antiphonally, playfully:

> why you so funky?
> cause I am
> why you so black?
> cause I am
> why you so sweet?
> cause I am

"Love Medley: Patrice Cuchulain": a voice wonderful and full of wonder coming home to what Yeats called the "deep heart's core":

> what is birth but death
> with complexity: blood, veins,
> machinery and love: our names.

"This Is My Son's Song: *'Ungie, Hi Ungie'* ": tenderly with the sudden power of illumination:

> the glow in his eyes
> is for himself, will and love:an ex-
> clamation of your name:
> *"Ungie, hi Ungie"*: you are saved.

" 'Bird Lives': Charles Parker": a climactic fury of love and protection both too late and too soon:

> In the first wave, the musicians,
> out there, alone, in the first wave;
> everywhere you went Massey Hall,
> Sweden, New Rochelle, *Birdland*
> nameless bird, Blue Note, Carnegie,
> tuxedo junction, out of nowhere,
> *confirmation, confirmation, confirmation:*
> *Bird Lives! Bird Lives!* and you do;
> Dead—

I, you, he, they: these pronouns tend toward we, and the effect is that along with Harper we pass in and out of other lives to glimpses—images and illuminations—of the life we share.

After *History Is Your Own Heartbeat* Harper shifts away from the kind of ritual poem of performance which had demanded that he become his material, specifically that he become the articulate horns of Coltrane and Parker in order to illuminate their lives in his poetic voice. There had been, even in the ritualized refrain of a poem like "High Modes"—*"Black Man Go Back To The Old Coun-*

try"—an unmistakable participation by Harper in his exhortations. With *Song: I Want a Witness*, a decade is over, and after 1970 Harper appears to distance himself from his material. The involvement remains; it is the identification that has passed away. What Harper has done is to express detachment in rhetorical terms as a reflex of voice. The effect is sometimes a tour de force. No one better evokes the aftereffects and changing racial sensibilities of the '70s than Harper in the title poem from this volume and, indeed, his detached tone is both a warning to his people and a way of testifying that he himself intends to keep his guard up higher in coming days:

> This scene is about power,
> terror, producing
> love and pain and pathology;
> in an army of white dust,
> blacks here to *testify*
> and *testify* and *testify*,
> and *redeem*, and *redeem*,
> in black smoke coming,
> as they wave their arms
> as they wave their tongues.

There is a tautness here, a controlled anger, and certainly a clarity that beneath the illusions and rhetoric of the '60s racial attitudes have not changed utterly—or even very much—in America. Like the early poem "Black Spring," "Song: I Want a Witness" is a parable. In "Black Spring" Harper went to biology for a metaphor; here the political and military situation described stands also for the social and cultural situation, and the victims' response evokes the sacrificial role blacks are expected to perform in the purification of America, even as they are destroyed. In any case the poem seems to be *about* the expectation of performance, performance unfree and stereotyped, and not to *embody* performance in the manner of the earlier work.

I have mentioned how in the *Photographs/Negatives* section of *Song: I Want a Witness* Harper goes against the grain of performance to explore, usually in silence at night, alone, recesses of self left somewhat unattended in earlier volumes. Many of the best poems in the 1975 volume *Nightmare Begins Responsibility* are poems about the struggle and craft of the Afro-American heroic tradition. The heroism in question is often understated, its drama the drama of anecdotes told and retold. Its participants are relatives, athletes, writers, the wives of these figures—those who helped shape Harper and the character of his style. Without exception these poems require an act of kinship whose authenticity is tested in the grooves of the poet's voice. In the poems for literary ancestors, Harper tests his skill at linking folk speech with contemporary Afro-American idiom and both with a vernacular common to all American speech. In "Br'er Sterling and the Rocker," a variation on and mixture of both folk poetry and the sonnet, Harper explores the compatibilities between standard American vernacular and what he has called "needful black idiom":

> Listen Br'er Sterling
> steel-drivin' man, folk-said, folk-sayin',
> that chair's a blues-harnessed star
> turnin' on its earthy axis. . . .

This language is colloquial, its spoken quality mostly one with the common American tongue with some phrases and certainly its rhythm and energy owing to Afro-American idiom. At the same time phrases like "blues-harnessed star" and "earthy axis," while not esoteric or obscure, somewhat derive their texture from the witty, metaphysical habits of modern poetry, often a poetry of the solitary muse. The phrases place a formulaic, written overlay on the spoken word. It is hard to imagine someone improvising them, as it is to imagine Harper not improvising, in blues tradition, the last two lines:

> Miss Daisy, latch on that star's arc,
> hold on sweet mama; Br'er Sterling's rocker glows.

Here, and elsewhere in his best work, Harper aspires to an idiom in which the written word participates in the illusion that what has been written is truly spoken, made up before our witnessing eyes. So we hear "the tongue/gone pure," as Harper has written of Sterling Brown's folk poetry; we sense the realization of tradition in the present moment and feel the spirit of the word move us in rejuvenation.

"Grandfather," "Blackjack," "Buck," "Roland," "Gains"—there is an extraordinary quality to these poems of kinship and tradition, an intense energy that fuses rhetoric and references with immediate experience. Using that "diction of arena and paradise" he attributes to Robert Hayden, Harper rewires the frayed lines connecting individual personality and Afro-American traditions of struggle, survival, and stoical sacrifice which have kept the tradition alive.

In the current poems there is the same story to be rediscovered, reconstructed, and told. "Bristol: Bicentenary Remembrances of Trade" is the most compelling and important. Harper visits libraries, great houses and museums, leafs through handbooks, notes the presence of black Jamaicans still as far (or farther) outside the pale of British life as in Edmund Burke's time. All this is history, but how does it cohere? What does it illuminate? Writing of his train ride, his transportation to London on the return trip from England in 1976, Harper intuits from his travel rhythms and the headlines something of the lingering meaning of the middle passage:

> The train to Paddington
> is quick, hot-shades cover the windows
> from a setting sun; newspapers gleam
> in smeared headlines of Soweto, my black
> baggage hangs on the rack above my head
> as I rock to waystation in London
> and the transport home to old shores
> in Rhode Island.

Repeated here and in a poem like "Uplift From a Dark Tower" are acts of investigation, new discoveries of the keys to kinship and tradition. "And there are keys," Harper has insisted and continues to insist. One key is articulation of the spoken and the written word. And this is the prospect for the long haul of Harper's poetry—further variations of that musical and historical consciousness found in those voices which his voice has hinted at throughout *Images of Kin*.

THEIR LONG SCARS TOUCH OURS: A REFLECTION ON THE POETRY OF MICHAEL HARPER*

by Joseph A. Brown, SJ

In the manner of those musical artists he most admires, Michael Harper devotes his poetic energy to acts of reverence for the giants of his cultural tradition and to attempts to establish his own extensions of their roles as witnesses of human possibilities. His poetry symbolizes a clear variation on a classic theme of Afro-American culture: double-consciousness, and, in the words of one of Harper's collaborators-in-interpretation Robert Stepto, the peering through the veil by the "articulate kinsman."

Through the convention of *dedications,* many poets tell their audiences where they are "coming from." Poems as responses to previous works, poems as homages, elegies and appreciations are all part of the poetic self-enfranchisement in the Olympian Club. Michael Harper participates in this time-honored self-authenticating process, seemingly devoting most of his output to the sharing of "images" of his kin. But it is in the *how* of Harper's commitment to dedications that his own vocation of poet is brought into the center spotlight. It is important to see Harper's longstanding meditation on the life and art of John Coltrane as a reflection on how Harper views himself as an Afro-American artist.

The understanding of Afro-American art must begin with the music and with the musicians. The cultural critics (beginning with Du Bois) and the artists themselves attest to this. Not only can the art-form itself be traced backwards—jazz from blues from spirituals from traditional African musical styles—but the motives and impulses and intentions of music-making can be traced through history. The tracing of the line through history marks one of the primary concerns of "modern" Afro-American art and culture, starting with the time known as the Negro Renaissance. In his discussion of scholarship on the "borrowings" of Afro-American music, John Lovell makes a claim for artistic intention that needs to be studied:

> ... the basic issue is in how the borrowing is made. The key factor in this basic issue is the original purpose of the creator. If he begins with a creative design to express, depict, criticize or exalt his own life, he is entitled, as Shakespeare did, to use any available realistic or legendary material.[1]

Lovell's remarks are applicable to the music Charlie Parker created when he borrowed "Embraceable You," to the result of Coltrane's borrowing of "My Favorite Things," and to the changes Harper works on Delmore Schwartz when *In Dreams Begin Responsibilities* becomes *Nightmare Begins Responsibility*. It is not really "borrowing"; it is using available material as an introduction to virtuosity. As such the act of performance, be it musical or literary, carries with it political and social overtones that are often overlooked.

From the days when Phillis Wheatley had to prove to skeptical audiences that not only could she read and write, but that she could compose verses "on demand," Afro-American poets have been challenged, dismissed or accepted on the

---

* Originally published in *Callaloo* 9:1 (Winter 1986).
[1] John Lovell, Jr., *Black Song: The Forge and the Flame* (New York: Macmillan, 1972), p. 14.

basis of their control of traditional (European and Euro-American) techniques. The usual result was that the Afro-American artist was found never quite as "good" as the inspiration. It would be altogether logical for Afro-American poets—from Paul Laurence Dunbar to Countee Cullen and Langston Hughes, to Melvin Tolson and Gwendolyn Brooks—to throw away their pens and run into the night screaming, "Anxiety of Influence! Anxiety of Influence!" when judged in comparison to James Whitcomb Riley, Walt Whitman, John Keats, Edna Millay, Edwin Arlington Robinson, T. S. Eliot or the others in the host of names used to "prove" that no matter how hard they tried, these children of Africa could never manage to match or surpass their European or Euro-American brothers and sisters.

But that act of frustration and rage seldom occurred, at least not with any terminal finality. Dunbar could feel his "traditional" verse never got an adequate reading, Cullen could resist being lectured to stick with "Negro" themes and Brooks could be re-born into the dispensation of 1960s militance, but—with the exception of Amiri Baraka—none of the contemporary Afro-American poets still being read have tried to erase their self-connection with their early poetic role models. In fact, it may be argued that this identification with previous poets will ensure an audience for these Afro-American poets for years to come. Let the argument commence with Michael Harper as our guide.

In *Nightmare Begins Responsibility*, Harper presents, as an introduction, a set of aphorisms entitled, "Kin." The sentences are set forth as a basic chord structure of the songs he will perform throughout the book. As such, they are useful to the reader, enabling one to keep in mind just what themes are important to the writer, and they are useful in determining whether the writer fulfills his self-imposed intentions. Several of these aphorisms are especially pertinent as descriptions of the vocation of the *Poet* as Harper sees himself:

> These are my first values: Understanding, Conscience, and Ability.

> Transformation is the spice of life transformed.

> Man must add to nature. Effort is that which is added.
> The aim of effort is to make it.

> Meet life's terms but never accept them.

> "Straight, No Chaser" said the musician.[2]

As a human being, Harper believes that "life's terms" must be met; and as a poet, Harper argues that the existing techniques and traditions of poetry must be confronted. It is enough to master the forms, because in mastery the artist demonstrates power. But something must be added to nature, to the "available realistic or legendary material." The world in which Michael Harper lives is not significantly different from the world of Paul Laurence Dunbar or John Coltrane. That world is the real and legendary *America*, a world where the souls of black folk are continually threatened with dreams which turn into nightmares. For Harper, technique is natural, the easy part of poetry. What he wrestles with in his poetry is what he sets out for himself in his declaration of intentions: understanding and conscience. Harper's methodology derives from the music of his maturity. If the

---

[2] Michael Harper, *Nightmare Begins Responsibility* (Urbana: University of Illinois Press, 1975), p. 3.

dream becomes a nightmare, if the legend is a lie, say so; confront the wall head-on, swallow the fire straight, with no soothing "chaser":

> Human beings are capable of all kinds of possibility, combination, and diversity. But if one has a vision of history as myth as lie, one has a closed, reductive view of things. Of course the fantasy of white supremist America with its closed myths has always been a fantasy of a white country. Out of that kind of fantasy came genocide, Indian massacres, fugitive slave laws, manifest destiny, open-door policies, Vietnam, Detroit, East Saint Louis, Watts, the Mexican War, Chicago and the Democratic Convention of 1968.[3]

Harper considers the nightmare and finds it suffocating; the walls of reality close in. The alternative to this closed, reductive view of things is, obviously, an open-ended breaking through of "what seems to be," thereby giving precedence to the *effort* involved in taking life straight. In describing his concept of effort, Harper invokes the presence and example of John Coltrane:

> One of the things that is important about Coltrane's music is the energy and passion with which he approached his instrument and music. Such energy was perhaps akin to the nature of oppression generally and the kind of energy it takes to break oppressive conditions, oppressive musical structures, and oppressive societal structures.[4]

Harper finds relevance in the performer, as much as in the performance. This is true of his comments on Coltrane and it is equally true of all his poetic subjects. Therefore, it makes sense to search through Harper's poems for examples of how he reflects upon his own growing awareness of the poet-as-performer. In the interview just quoted, Harper says, "It's my responsibility to articulate." He dwells upon this point in his poetry by centering on the moment when words fail him, at the moment when his experiences seem most constricting. *Death* in all its manifestations is the subject matter of Michael Harper's poetic career. How he has fought a way for himself out of the tomb, the temptation to eternally reside in nightmares; how he wills himself to construct a ladder of saints as a way of remembering those who instruct him in open-ended, "modal" living; how, finally, he offers his performance as a sign of hope and encouragement to his readers— all of these place Michael Harper where he wants to be: the child of the great performing blues artists.

When Harper invokes the names of his chosen ancestral poets, it is their physical power that he celebrates, their effort to endure that he takes comfort in. On Dunbar:

> Minstrel and mask:
> a landscape of speech and body
> burned in verbal space,
> the match cinder unstandard:[5]

The point of view expressed in this excerpt of Harper's commemoration of Dunbar is common to the other poems Harper dedicates to fellow writers. He is their

---

[3] John O'Brien, *Interviews with Black Writers* (New York: Liveright, 1973), p. 98.
[4] O'Brien.
[5] *Nightmare*, p. 80.

audience, listening and watching, not reading. He values them because they attempt to connect with the past, with family, with cultural traditions. He applauds these writers' attempts to leave words as signposts for others. Harper collected a set of poems-to-writers in a section of *Nightmare,* entitled, "Sterling Letters." In the first poem, Sterling Brown is identified with Br'er Rabbit (surely an active, performing hero if there ever was one in the Afro-American tradition). Brown, about to launch himself into space, is described as rocking, talking—doubletalking—and "steel-drivin'." Ernest Gaines is presented as nighttime storyteller to a believing, though critical audience (the listening poet). Sterling Brown is also described teaching and giving poetry readings. In other places in *Images of Kin,* John Berryman is remembered reading and lecturing, eventually leaping into the Mississippi to his death (p. 9); Robert Hayden is cast in the role of his own mythic character, Icarus (p. 14); and Galway Kinnell is valued as reader, searcher for history and is blended into one of his own images, that of a "kite being drawn off into the Hebrides" (p. 18). In the poems dedicated to Richard Wright ("The Meaning of Protest," "Heartblow: Messages," and "Afterword: A Film"), Harper gives homage to the fiction writer by casting him as a character in his own works. Placed as these poems are, directly after Harper's sequence on John Brown, it is hard not to sense that Wright's *persona,* as prophet of the nightmare haunting white America, makes him an apt companion to Brown, Tubman and the other names Harper records in his tributes to those who believed that "The price of repression is greater than the cost of liberty."[6]

It is in the last poem of *Nightmare,* "Alice," that Harper describes himself best, while focusing on another writer. From the inscription on, Harper makes his case for the writer as child of the tradition, upholder of ritual, possessor of history, and prophet of the people. His sense of history, summed up in the title *History Is Your Own Heartbeat,* is found in this poem as an assumption. The poetic act challenges, undoes, time itself. As was the case with his poem on Dunbar, here also Harper makes those who are dead become present by the invocation of the name. In a most classic sense, the act of writing bestows immortality. For Harper, the poet must be actively engaged in searching out the worthy saints, chanting their name; must carve the "testimony in stone," and guide the reader to these complex signs for instruction and confirmation. The poem begins with the dramatic pose:

> You stand waist-high in snakes
> beating the weeds for the gravebed
> a quarter mile from the nearest
> relative, an open field in Florida: lost,
> looking for Zora . . .

Harper establishes more than a dramatic picture of Alice Walker. He uses her own words, her own recreation of the event and interprets it in the light of his own perennial concerns. In the process, he manages to brush against a few of the snakes waiting to bite all contemporary artists. To be modern is to be lost in a world that is hostile. The ache derived from an existential awareness of one's condition is often the conclusion of modern literature. The journey to such an awareness is just as often the subject of this literature. For Harper and *his* subject, it is the beginning. Life's terms are met, but are not accepted in the sense that death shall have dominion.

[6] Michael Harper, *Images of Kin* (Urbana: University of Illinois Press, 1977), pp. 71–97.

> ... and when she speaks
> from her sunken chamber to call
> you to her side, she calls
> you her distant cousin, her sister
> come to mark her burial place
> with bright black stone.

Zora Neale Hurston's own work in traditional religious practices of Afro-Americans, in Haiti especially but elsewhere in the south, is utilized here. The snakes are complex presences, both threatening and familiar. In her own telling of the story, Walker calls out to Zora, asking for help in finding the grave. When Walker and her companions discover what is probably the "sunken chamber," Walker thanks one of the women for staying by her side during the search and adds, "Zora thanks you too."[7] Although it is narrated as a moment of nervous release, the remark tends to highlight the fact that Zora was called, the gravesite was located; that Walker is "close" to Hurston.

What is a submerged implication in Walker's essay becomes a focal point in Harper's poem. In order to bring harmony to the scene, the ancestor, in the best African tradition, manipulates the present. What is subtle in Walker becomes certainty in Harper. The poem not only restates the basic scene of the essay; the spirit of Hurston is brought into focus by using her own words, her quotation of folklore. If it *is* Hurston who is managing this moment, she does so by being linked to the power of the tradition and by making that tradition effect the result. Walker says she was at her most hopeless when she called out "Zora!" Harper says she was lost. Both would agree that Hurston was also lost. To bring all into harmony each actor—including the poet who has placed himself at the scene and made himself privy to the intentions of Hurston's ghost—must fulfill a rite handed down by the community. Hurston went searching for her past and was given the words of a proverb: Her crooked stick, her straight lick. Walker went looking for her own past, her literary ancestor, and must become possessed by the spirit of her whom she sought. Walker must stand among snakes, must employ "lies" and conjure-riddles, much in the way Hurston had to dissemble in order to perform her anthropological researches. The poet also acts out a part, similar to that performed by the two women. He "conjures" them both to appear before the reader. He retrieves a possibly lost moment and makes of the poem a monument to the effort expended in restoring the dead to life. What he says of Walker, could be said of him:

> A black rock of ages you have placed
> where there was no marker,
> and though the snakes abound
> in this preserve from ancestral space,
> you have paid your homage
> in traditional line, the face open:

Harper wants the reader to say this of him.

It has been his responsibility, also, to stand lost and to call up the dead, for comfort and for direction. He ends this homage to Alice and Zora by connecting the specific act of restoration to his own work, his spot among the snakes. In his

---

[7] Alice Walker, *In Search of Our Mothers' Gardens* (New York: Harcourt Brace Jovanovich, 1983), p. 105.

closing comments, Harper uses the visionary, prophetic language clearly and directly:

> And for this I say your name: Alice,
> my grandmother's name, your name,
> conjured in snake-infested field
> where Zora Neale welcomed you home,
> and where I speak from now
> on higher ground of her risen
> black marker where you have written
> your name in hers, and in mine.[8]

By writing/uttering the word, by manipulating the realities normally permissible to poetry, Harper has brought into existence a community of courageous nurturing women. His grandmother is described as a woman who "reigned" in her kitchen, who was in some sense gifted with second-sight, who was, for her children, a rock in a weary and threatening land.[9] He says he stands on "higher ground." He has achieved that height by being lifted up, transported, by the ritual (rite) he has initiated. Vision comes from ecstacy; the ecstatic state induced by chanting the names of the ancestral spirits leads to possession.

What is common to many religions becomes, for Michael Harper, a method and a motive for writing poetry. While all would know that Zora Neale Hurston is worth the black stone marker—her place in literature attests to that—Alice Braxton Johnson achieves equal stature through the effort of her grandson. Alice Walker is worth honoring for what she has done for Zora. The justification for this honor, as it is presented in this poem, is that Walker has done what Harper has done for his "mother." He and Walker are merged into the same passion and energy because they have restored the "traditional line." By linking the famous with the obscure, Harper acts out the role of both poet and prophet. The act of connection is the act of metaphor. It is the poet who welds the elements together for the revelation that occurs. It is the prophetic vision that allows him to see into history and bend the crooked into the straight, to redeem that which had been lost. When Alice Walker found what she hoped was the grave of Zora Hurston, she became healed by that act of courage and that act of faith. "It must be so because I need it to be so." Harper gives his blessing to that act by erasing all doubt and ambivalence in his version of the story. It *was* so. By offering himself and Walker as examples, he presents the reader with their lives and their writings and markers to go and do likewise. In the best sense of the tradition of call-and-response, this poem demands more than an act of contemplation from the reader. A display of poetic craft is blended with a call to participate in the ritual.

Sound—*noise*—is the act of defiance performed by the poet in the face of death. *Silence,* in the poetry of Michael Harper, is the most frequent representation of ultimate brokenness. It is this reliance on sound that Michael Harper studies and learns from the musicians he values. He must do with words on a page what they learned to do with their voices, their instrumental extensions of themselves, in front of audiences. In this regard, it is worth noting that live performances are most remembered and most often poetically recreated; recorded song is seldom mentioned in reference to his musicians. Life is song, for Harper. The air is living,

---

[8] *Nightmare,* p. 96.
[9] *Nightmare,* p. 73.

full of sounds, whisperings, resonances, promises. When silence fills the air, when no words can be found to articulate the deepest feelings of the poet, he nevertheless presents himself and his struggle for words to his audience. Much like the classic blues of Bessie Smith or Billie Holiday, Harper's poems undercut and comment upon themselves. The words here proclaim that no words are possible. The angle of the head, the posture of the singer, the rhythm of the song itself, the ironic and ambivalent inflections of the lyrics—are all part of a blues performance at its best.

So, too, with the Harper poems that are most evocative of that musical tradition. The poet gives us the dramatic incident, explains his utter frustration, shows us the effort to face the problem, straight/no chaser, and in the process of talking himself through the problem he performs his solution. This performing tradition has an echo of ordination: one chosen from among the people to offer sacrifice on their behalf. The blues performer is "set apart" in order to represent the best possible reaction—that reaction that the audience most values—and applies the standard of the audience to the specific issue before them all. No moment or matter is too private to be exorcised in a healing song. One of Harper's most famous poems proves this point, incorporating all of the themes and postures so far discussed:

REUBEN, REUBEN

I reach from pain
to music great enough
to bring me back
swollenhead, madness,
lovefruit, a pickle of hate
so sour my mouth twicked
up and would not sing;
there's nothing in the beat
to hold it in
melody and turn human skin;
a brown berry gone
to rot just two days on the branch;
we've lost a son,
the music, jazz, comes in.[10]

Although not named such, this poem is a song (though the title is allusive enough to be a clue). The circularity of movement in the first two lines positions the poet, once again, in a visionary space. He is an intersecting point, through whom the pain, nightmare of death and the healing music pass. The word choices, the short, clipped lines, the keening quality of all the "in" and "ing" rhymes—all participate in echoing the nasal quality of a Holiday performance or the high-register assault of Coltrane on the soprano sax. Holiday's classic "Strange Fruit" provides a ladder through the song, from *lovefruit* and *madness*, to *rot* and *branch*. Let me sing about how I cannot sing; for unless I sing about it, I will be forever lost in hate.

Though *humility* has, in recent years, become suspect as a virtue when applied to Afro-American life, it is a quality of Michael Harper's poetry. The virtue of humility should be viewed with suspicion when it is imposed on a person, or urged

[10] Michael Harper, *Dear John, Dear Coltrane* (Pittsburgh: University of Pittsburgh Press, 1970), p. 64.

as a way of life. As a self-chosen virtue, it can become a way of maintaining sanity. The root meaning of the word comes from *Humus,* meaning *of the earth.* The old song, "Live Humble," could be an admonition to live with one's feet upon the ground, as much as a demand to keep one's face pressed to the ground. It is, at best, this virtue of humility, a method of maintaining one's balance, by relying always on the truth of one's situation. The admonition to take life straight, with no chaser, connects here, also. In the title poem of *Dear John, Dear Coltrane,* Harper uses his clinical precision to list the truth of Coltrane's genius. In the midst of this truth-telling, the dead-end distraction of drugs is mentioned, the destructiveness of racism is spelled out, the doubts inherent in forging new ground are confronted. The listing moves from the most humble to the most sublime. The list itself is seamless, connective. To be humble is to live the truth, the whole truth:

> Why you so black?
> cause I am
> why you so funky?
> cause I am
> why you so black?
> cause I am
> why you so sweet?
> cause I am
> why you so black?
> cause I am
> a love supreme, a love supreme:[11]

In this chorus, the repetition equates the few descriptions, finally blending them all into the last statement. The circularity is present once again. The movement is both up—to the supreme—and down—to the funky.

From 1970 to 1984, Harper had meditated deeply on the life of Coltrane, bringing each new version of investigation before the audience. Like all good singers of the tradition, Harper never sings the same person the same way twice. He also never loses the theme no matter how many years pass between the sessions. "Dear John, Dear Coltrane" was written/spoken to the man. Much has gone into the understanding of the poet, so that in his most recent collection there is "A Narrative of the Life and Times of John Coltrane: Played by Himself." The final stanzas of each poem are worth comparing:

> So sick
> you couldn't play *Naima,*
> so flat we ached
> for song you'd concealed
> with your own blood,
> your diseased liver gave
> out its purity,
> the inflated heart
> pumps out, the tenor kiss,
> tenor love:
> *a love supreme, a love supreme—*
> *a love supreme, a love supreme—*

Judgment and accusation, however muted, are presented in these words. The poet is in the audience, never fully able to understand what takes place within the artist,

---

[11] *Dear John,* p. 74.

even though the medical report can be read. There is not enough truth in this assessment to bring words of comfort. The final quotation is an anchor for the faith of the listener/observer. Something more is being demanded, even as excuses are being made for its absence. Both the musician and the listening poet are aware of what has been lost, even while what is being performed is all that can be given.

By becoming the scribe of the musician from the inside, the artist/audience frame is erased by the poet. Intentions and resolutions are presented from within. Therefore, the same historical performance is read differently:

> what good does it do to complain:
> one night I was playing with Bostic,
> blacking out, coming alive only to melodies
> where I could play my parts:
> And then, on a train to Philly,
> I sang "Naima" locking the door
> without exit no matter what song
> I sang; with remonstrations on the ceiling
> of that same room I practiced in
> on my back when too tired to stand,
> I broke loose from crystalline habits
> I thought would bring me that sound.[12]

Zora returned from the dead to call "Alice" and possess her. In his humility, the poet opens himself to the same confrontation. Coltrane speaks to him, answers the veiled complaint of the earlier poem. Where the listener dwelt on death, the artist celebrated his breaking through a wall of death. The same song has been seen from different places within the same man—the poet. The artist—both Coltrane and Harper, merged here—sees his own judgments written on the ceiling in the darkness and he uses his art to subdue and transform the nightmare into song. The musician becomes his song. The physical positioning of the artist in the last stanza—on his back, practicing—leads to his being identified with the sound he sends upward, pumping out "a love supreme" as a "tenor kiss/tenor love." He broke loose. And he returns to tell his story to and through the poet.

The medical condition of John Coltrane represents one other aspect of Michael Harper's consistent practice in writing. Disease, sickness, diminishment are all preludes to death. Harper has become a pathologist, searching for the wounds, the death, of his people within them and within him so that the healing power of his poetry can have its effect. Reuben's name is recorded, his dying is noted over and over. Parents, grandparents, relatives, friends, people known only through stories, are met and learned in that moment when silence overtakes them. Harper becomes their sound, so that no matter how feeble the breaths, how unattended their passing, they are not forever lost. In this servant's role, Harper employs, as could be expected, the mystical apparatus to become one of his subjects. He speaks for the community, in all senses of the term. This process is best summed up in the title, *Song: I Want a Witness*. The truth of Harper's career is that—much like the hero of Hawthorne's short story, "The Great Stone Face"—he becomes that which he seeks. The summing-up title for all of Harper's work could be, *Song: I AM MY WITNESS*. In one of the poems in *Song*, Harper outlines the journey

---

[12] Michael Harper, *Healing Song for the Inner Ear* (Urbana: University of Illinois Press, 1985), p. 92.

taken in his career. He also shares the essence of his own special place within the circle of witnessing saints: "Continuous Visit."

The poem begins with the dramatic stage, nature; once again the scene is filled with ambivalent details—sunflower patches and weedy ditches. Invisible—therefore, uncatchable—bass are linked with "cast frogs, hooked through / their mouths." Live, stable oak trees provide a backdrop for the reading of chronicles typed on "peach paper," implying the death of trees for the furtherance of culture. Two families are contrasted; the daughters of the person addressed as "you" in the poem and the family of the poet. The poet and his family belong in the space, but the "you" is an intruder, bringing along death and destruction. This is brought to the fore of the discussion:

> you read chronicles
> from typed peach paper,
> last year's spirits
> pitched in its threshing,
> blood from the suture
> of my family.
> This suture is race
> as it is blood,
> long as the frozen
> lake building messages
> on typewritten paper,
> faces of my ancestors,
> warm in winter only
> as their long scars touch ours.[13]

Whatever knowledge the poet possesses comes to him in vision. His position in the poem is hidden; what reads like an assumption is given weight and force by the utter difference between the two opponents. The silent intruder brings things into the space, things which have been transformed out of the elements of nature. The intruder is weak, employing technology to effect what the poet accomplishes merely with his desire to know. Because of the intrusional attributes of the "other," no one can assume that this moment is the "continuous visit" spoken of in the title of the poem. Rather, the poet belongs to this place; it is where he comes to visit with nature and his ancestors. The presence of the intruder heightens the poet's awareness of his own (the poet's) natural right to be where he is, to be doing what he is doing. The family, the blood, and the environment write messages upon the poet, instructing him in the ways of history. The presence of the intruder breaks the flow of the communication. Disruption forces the poet to repair his own condition. Effort must be expended in order to bring the world back into ecological balance. The poet must perform an operation: he must suture the wound caused by the possessor of technology—who is, here and throughout the poetry of Harper, America, the Bringer of Genocide, of War, of Riot. The intruder brings winter into the world of the poet. Calling on his ancestors, the poet warms his blood, and heals the wound within himself. It is his attitude that weaves the continuous seam that is the suture. It is his person that is the suture within the poem. With his world momentarily broken into, the poet refuses to allow distraction to grow into obsession. He distances himself from the intruder by dwelling upon the presence of those who claim the space with a better

---

[13] Michael Harper, *Song: I Want a Witness* (Pittsburgh: University of Pittsburgh Press, 1972), p. 16.

title. Later on in the book, Harper begins his cycle on History, Heartbeats, Night-mares and Photographs:

> Nightmare begins responsibility.

> The Indian is the root of an apple tree;
> history, symbol, presence: these voices
> are not lost on us, or them.[14]

Given the language and the drama of "Continuous Visit," it would be reasonable to speculate that the ancestors of the long scars, who live in the trees, fish, frozen lakes and in the memory of the speaker are here at the root: the Indians of North America. Harper, once open to the voices of his ancestors, allows himself to become a child of all who have been scarred by the long winter of America. Because they come to him, call to him, use him for their prophet, their voices are not lost on us.

He performs a needed role, both as a representative voice and as a symbol of the healing act. The song he sings gives witness to the creative act: the poet binds that which has been wounded, says words of power over the hurt and bleeding heart and invites those who read him to dig deeply—to the root where life still speaks.

FROM BLACK POETRY AND BLACK MUSIC; HISTORY AND TRADITION: MICHAEL HARPER AND JOHN COLTRANE*

by Günter H. Lenz

In 1970, Michael Harper wrote about his first book of poetry, *Dear John, Dear Coltrane* (1970):

> John Coltrane was the epitome of a new style, his music and being the vision of liberation of the sensibility expressed through the man and his art, the tenor and soprano saxophones the vehicles for the larger man, a force so overwhelming as to be revolutionary to perception and sensibility themselves. My vision has been slow in coming to the surface. What concerns me is the articulation of *consciousness,* the ability to deal with contingencies and create a new liberating vision which frees rather than imprisons.
>
> Some of the themes of my poems are: History and the development of an historical consciousness which frees us from the past; *modes* of perception, the relationship between ideal, real, and material modes of individual perception; myths, distinctions between truth and lie, the one the patterning of particular experiences into universals, the other the incapacity to accept facts as partic-ular because of the demands of a system (one of which is the closed system of white supremacy, one dimensional, cyclic, repetitious in design and in error); personality, the deepening of historical consciousness to facilitate an awaken-ing, psychic and real.

[14] *Witness,* p. 43.
* Originally published in *History and Tradition in Afro-American Literature,* ed. Günter H. Lenz. (Frank-furt: Campus, 1984).

My poems are *modal*. By modality I mean the creation of an environment so intense by its life and force as to revivify and regenerate, spiritually, man and community; modality assumes contact, touch, between human beings, one to one, and an environment of spirit that revitalizes man, individually and culturally. Man is the original *mode;* what he does is modal—the musicians, Bud, Bird, Trane, Lady, Bessie, Pres, Fats, Mingus, Elvin, Max, McCoy, Miles, were and are modal; man's being, his sensibility in action, contact, with another human being, is modality. The blues singer says 'I' but the audience assumes 'We'; out of such energy comes community and freedom. A Love Supreme.[1]

Harper's statement is a condensation of the world view and poetics which he had worked out during the 1960s and which he would further elaborate during the following decade. It clearly reveals the key role the new black music of John Coltrane and others had played in his development as a black poet. Two years later, Harper confirmed this, when he said in an interview: "I felt my influences were more musical than poetic. This doesn't mean that I haven't read a great deal of poetry, I have. But I think in terms of music I've been most heavily influenced by Charlie Parker, Miles Davis, Bessie Smith, Billie Holiday, John Coltrane, and Thelonius Monk."[2] It was, most of all, John Coltrane's playing that communicated to him a new "total liberation of the sensibility." "I loved John Coltrane and I loved his music. I loved the kind of intensity he brought to his playing and I love his commitment." (O'Brien, p. 97) Coltrane showed him what *modality* as a non-Western concept of life, understanding, and creation means, the power of the "both/and" instead of the Cartesian "either/or," the "unity in diversity," the "continuum" of black culture as space (comprising all black nations), and as time (history/tradition), and kinship. Coltrane's music helped him to articulate his "vision" of "history and the development of an historical consciousness" for black Americans, and it expressed to him the "energy and passion" it takes "to break oppressive conditions, oppressive musical strictures, and oppressive societal situations." (O'Brien, p. 98) Harper understood the "urgency of his playing" as a "cry" for "community" which the "fragmentation that this society produces" had destroyed.[3] He had read and taught black poets, but he knew that in order to find his own voice as a poet, he had to ground his own work in a viable community and tradition he could not find among those poets. "I think the most important thing having to do with thematic influence is the need I have to connect my work with a tradition which I came out of and which I understood. And that tradition was the black musical tradition." (O'Brien, p. 99)

From the beginning, Michael Harper wrote poems about black musicians, about Miles Davis, Charlie Parker, Bud Powell, McCoy Tyner, Paul Chambers, Wes Montgomery, Elvin Jones, but also Bessie Smith, Mahalia Jackson, Billie Holiday, and James Brown. The poems affirm the basic unity of all kinds of black music, yet they are not so much about "the music," but about the personalities of the musicians, the meaning of their playing or singing as a communication of experiential reality and of triumphs over oppression and suffering. The poems Harper has written about John Coltrane over the years create and reveal in their statements (as well

---

[1] Michael Harper, in *Natural Process: An Anthology of New Black Poetry* (New York: Hill and Wang, 1970), pp. 42–43. [The original footnotes have been renumbered for this excerpted version.]

[2] Michael Harper in John O'Brien, ed., *Interviews with Black Writers* (New York: Liveright, 1973), p. 97 (hereafter referred to as O'Brien).

[3] Abraham Chapman, "An Interview with Michael S. Harper," *Arts in Society* 11 (1975), p. 470 (hereafter referred to as Chapman).

as in their images, metaphors, rhythmical motifs which recur again and again and are confirmed or transformed) complex interrelationships among the poems, among the past, the present, and the future, among the various realms and planes of being and experience. If the sequence of Coltrane poems expresses continuity, inclusiveness, complexity, it, at the same time, is deeply concerned with, and affected by, change.

The first poem in *Dear John, Dear Coltrane*, "Brother John," dedicated to the painter John O. Stewart as well as to John Coltrane, is a rhythmic chant to the black man, an incantation of Bird, Miles, and Trane, an affirmation of the blackness and the being ("I'm a black man; I am") of *all* black people.[4] "Dirge for Trane," written after Coltrane's death, introduces a poetic motif, "Gone, gone, gone, gone, gone—," that will come up again and again in Harper's poetry, "another brother gone." It testifies to the death toll black Americans have had to pay in American history, in political life and especially among musicians, a commemoration of their suffering and victimization. But at the same time it is used in the poems to evoke an awareness of the continuity, or the strength of tradition, of ancestors who continue to be a living presence in the black community.

Harper's title poem "Dear John, Dear Coltrane" (pp. 74–75), written before Coltrane's death, is a supreme expression of Coltrane's impact and message and of Harper's efforts as a poet to transform the quality of Coltrane's *personality and music*, of his album *A Love Supreme*, into black poetry. It begins and ends with Harper chanting (in his performance of the poem with cellist Ron DeVaughn) "a love supreme" in the same way Coltrane does on his record.[5] The phrase recurs several times to mark rapid switches of focus and of the tone of the poet's voice, from the personal and biographical to the culture in general, from the present to the violence and brutality in black history, from narrative to a juxtaposition of images, from testimony to "prophecy," from Coltrane's "song now crystal and / the blues" to an "antiphonal, call response / retort stanza" that "simulates the black church, and gives the answer of renewal to any question raised— '*cause i am.*'"[6] Coltrane is celebrated as a master, as a force of purification, redemption, and love. By creating out of suffering he affirms the black experience and black manhood and urgently longs for a "we," for black community.

> Dawn comes and you cook
> up the thick sin 'tween
> impotence and death, fuel
> the tenor sax cannibal
> heart, genitals and sweat
> that makes you clean—
> *a love supreme, a love supreme—*
>
> *Why you so black?*
> *cause I am*

---

[4] Michael Harper, *Dear John, Dear Coltrane* (Pittsburgh: University of Pittsburgh Press, 1970), pp. 3–4. Harper's books will hereafter be quoted in the text as follows: *Dear John, Dear Coltrane: DJ; History Is Your Own Heartbeat* (Urbana: University of Illinois Press, 1971): *HH; Song: I Want a Witness* (Pittsburgh: University of Pittsburgh Press, 1972): *S; Debridement* (Garden City, N.Y.: Doubleday, 1973): *D; Nightmare Begins Responsibility* (Urbana: University of Illinois Press, 1975): *NBR.*

[5] Michael Harper, poetry reading with Ron DeVaughn, cello, *Black Box 9* (Washington, D.C.: The New Classroom, 1976).

[6] Liner notes to the double-LP *John Coltrane, 1957–1958* (Bellaphon/prestige BLST 6513), hereafter referred to as "liner notes."

Why you so funky?
cause I am
Why you so black?
cause I am
why you so sweet?
cause I am
why you so black?
cause I am
a love supreme, a love supreme:

So sick
you couldn't play Naima,
so flat we ached
for song you'd concealed
with your own blood,
your diseased liver gave
out its purity,
the inflated heart
pumps out, the tenor kiss,
tenor love:
a love supreme, a love supreme—
a love supreme, a love supreme—   (*DJ*, p. 74)

"Dear John, Dear Coltrane" is not so much a poem *about* black music, but condenses in its images and rhythms, in its poetical "testamental process" (liner notes) the various dimensions of black music as the central force of the black experience which Harper develops more extensively in other poems in his first book. "Reuben, Reuben," a very private poem on the death of his infant son, "a brown berry gone," talks about the redemptive power of black music: "we've lost a son, / the music, *jazz*, comes in" (p. 64). "Dead-Day: Malcolm, Feb. 21" is about Malcolm's death in 1969, about "our love for you," and takes up as the final line "Another brother gone" (p. 82). "Ode to Tenochtitlan" (pp. 85–86) brings together the black power salute to Tommy Smith and John Carlos at the Olympic Games in Mexico City in 1968 and John Coltrane's death, "ANOTHER BROTHER GONE—", "as a twin black spirit, / brother's come on home." And the final poem in the volume, "Biafra Blues" (pp. 87–88), uses the continuous repetition of the same motif as a comment on the brutality and insanity of the Biafra War:

There is no famine
there is no genocide
only a community
in revolt, only
the refinement of oil
slicks, only a black
smell, sunken, aglow:
another brother gone
another brother gone
. . . . (*DJ*, p. 88)

Harper's second book of poetry *History Is Your Own Heartbeat* (1971) is about kinship, history, and "a modal myth in language": "It involves the titans of black music and its history. . . . It assumes . . . that there is an African continuum . . . , an unbroken continuity of beliefs and concepts of the black people who have an unbroken African residual in their lives and are essentially connected to Africa. This concept involves a world-view which has always been antithetical to America, with its concepts of manifest destiny, slavery, westward expansion, and so on." (O'Brien, pp. 102–103) The poems attempt to reveal and communicate this alternative mode not by offering a new "definition" of history as something "out there," as an anonymous force, but by looking for "history" in the "heartbeats" of kin, in one's own family and ancestors as well as in the extended network and institutions of past and present, "locating oneself in time and space and land-scape," in the rituals of black culture, especially the blues (Chapman, p. 469). "There is a relationship between the single beating heart and all hearts beating. And there's a relationship between a single historical story and the stories which are modulated on their own heartbeats." (O'Brien, p. 105) It is this "history" Harper claims, and this "landscape" he explores, in *History Is Your Own Heartbeat*.

The first part of the book, "Ruth's Blues," "a kind of introduction into the blues using contemporary modes of speech and metaphor" and "psychic and literal in its anatomy of a midwestern family" (O'Brien, pp. 100–101), discovers the continuity and strength of kinship and ancestry in the life experience of a specific *individual,* Harper's mother-in-law. The poems read the inscriptions of history in the human body and are all located in one particular *American* land-scape. The poems of the second part, "History As Personality," establish the network of *individuals,* private and cultural, contemporary and historical, to whom the poet owes his own *spiritual, artistic,* and *cultural* growth and "vision" (p. 51). At the same time, they set out to define the aesthetic status of the poems by associating them with a wide spectrum of cultural forms and media, poems as "blues" (pp. 37, 46, 62), "music" (pp. 38, 42, 71), "photographs" (p. 43), "folksong" (pp. 48, 66), "ritual" (p. 50), "dance" (p. 52), "song in America" (p. 53), "parables in stone" (p. 64), "newsletter" (p. 68), "dream" (p. 72), "culture as science as language as cannibal" (p. 75).

The poem "Here Where Coltrane Is" (*HH,* pp. 32–33) at the end of Part One serves as a "bridge" to Part Two. The title confirms the *place* ("Here") and the continual *presence* ("Is") John Coltrane and his music have in Harper's *own life* and in the culture. The poem is about living in a place in Portland, Oregon, "in this Victorian house," in a particular season in the year ("Oak leaves pile up on walkway / and steps"), "in zero degree / weather and forty-mile an hour wind," and it is about the poet's listening to Coltrane's music, a particular record, "I play 'Alabama' / on a warped record player." But these *private* memories are living parts of the "eternality of music, color, race, and culture" (O'Brien, p. 101), as are the modal songs, *uniting* the poet and his kin and Coltrane into a "well-knit family":

> Soul and race
> are private dominions,
> memories and modal
> songs, a tenor blossoming,
>
> . . . .
> it is all a well-knit family:
> *a love supreme.*   (*HH,* p. 32)[7]

---

[7] The importance of "kinship" in Harper's poetry is discussed in Robert B. Stepto's "Michael S. Harper, Poet as Kinsman: The Family Sequences," *Massachusetts Review,* 17 (1976), pp. 477–502.

In recreating his own "emotional landscape" and the natural environment at the time, the poet "reconciles" the historical and the mythical, "black tradition in the family and natural history" (Coltrane's "six notes" and "oak, birch, maple / apple, cocoa, rubber"). If this, to Michael Harper, is the message, or the revelation, of the poem, it is his *poetic strategy* that makes the *poem as a whole* a "testimony" of the "images of process," of black music as modal "aesthetic vision." The poem is a "recontextualization" of a complex "experience" "in poetic terms" (Chapman, p. 466). It is, in fact, a palimpsest of several trans-formations of "real life" experience into communication and art that reflect upon one another and establish a living tradition in black culture (art) and the sequence of generations. The poet, *"here* where Coltrane *is,"* listens to "Alabama" and evokes the private, natural, and cultural context of the experience *in poetic terms,* in his sounds and images. He re-writes *his own poem* "American History" from *Dear John, Dear Coltrane* where he had related the death of "those four girls blown up / in that Alabama church" (p. 62) to the death of five hundred "middle passage blacks" in Charleston during slavery, by revisioning the historical event through his response to Coltrane's recording of "Alabama" which itself was a *musical* expression and communication of an experience Coltrane had on a train from New York to Philadelphia.[8] Coltrane's experience of reading the *speech* Martin Luther King had composed was, in its turn, a reenactment of King's rhetorical transformation of reports he had heard of the bombing of the church in Birmingham, Alabama (Chapman, p. 466). Where King in his eulogy "translated" the meaning of that historical moment into a particular prose rhythm of the tradition of the black sermon, Coltrane took his rhythm and his contemporary idiom of the blues tradition and composed the melody of "Alabama" and recorded it with his group. Harper tries to find the poetic equivalent to the rhythm and melody of "Alabama" by drawing on the continuum of the Afro-American culture, religious and secular, and he *transforms* and *transcends* the energy and the message of King's sermon and Coltrane's music in "Alabama" (that virtually ends in the "simulation of a human cry" indicating both the limits and the origin of music) into the revelation of poetry.

This experimental and aesthetic interaction among the various levels and perspectives of the poem explains why, to Michael Harper, the poet, there is no contradiction, no mutual exclusiveness, between the black church, revolutionary politics, and black music. And it confirms to him the continuity of the black cultural and communal tradition that has to be claimed for and by his son, by future generations.[9]

> For this reason Martin is dead;
> for this reason Malcolm is dead;
> for this reason Coltrane is dead;
> in the eyes of my first son are the browns
> of these men and their music.   (*HH,* p. 33)

Autobiography, family, family history, landscape, language, church, jazz, art, politics, history, and myth are revealed as belonging to one continuum of the Afro-American experience, a continuum, however, that by no means should be mistaken as simply assuring harmony and happiness but has always been charac-

[8] Cf. Amiri Baraka's poem "AM/TRAK," *Selected Poetry* (New York: Morrow, 1979), pp. 332–37.
[9] Cf. Stepto, "Michael S. Harper," p. 487.

terized, in American history, by suffering, violence, oppression, and resistance.

The third part of *History Is Your Own Heartbeat,* "High Modes," is "a ritual poem in nine parts," a testimonial to the living and human power of black speech and black music that explores "what is happening" (see epigraph, p. 77), the tensions and the potential of Afro-American history.[10] It is dedicated to a friend of Harper's, a black painter, and works out in images and sounds what the Afro-American "modal myth in language" as an alternative to the Western rationalistic world-view and language of system and either/or means in America:

> This grid, ideal,
> intersecting squares,
> system, thought,
> western wall,
> migrating phoenix,
> death to all.
> ("Apollo Vision: The Nature of the Grid," *HH,* p. 91)

As black people cannot live in this "Greek-oriented, finally schizophrenic vision of the rationalist mode" that is characterized by the *absence* of everything vital ("no ritual; no dance; / no song; no spirit; / no man; no mode; / . . . ," *HH,* p. 90), they must uncover its "imperialistic" effects and demythologize the American myths of "manifest destiny, slavery, westward expansion." They must remember that "History for us [Americans] begins / with murder and enslavement / not with discovery," as Harper quotes from W. C. Williams' *In the American Grain* in "Zeus Muse: History as Culture" (*HH,* pp. 86–87; O'Brien, pp. 102, 106). The first poem in this section, " 'Bird Lives'; Charles Parker in St. Louis" (*HH,* pp. 70–80) is a dirge for "another brother gone" and recalls the suffering, the self-destruction of his life ("What is the meaning of music? / what is the meaning of war? / What is the meaning of oppression?"). But the poem also reminds us of his achievement by his "blowing" and "screaming" the "implayable" to transform his "pain," "blues and racism" into "confirmation" (a title of one of his recordings), into a forceful legacy to his community.

The last poem of "High Modes" (and of the book) is a final summing up of Harper's philosophy in a complex pattern of poetical motifs, images, and rhythms: "High Modes: Vision as Ritual: Confirmation" (*HH,* pp. 94–95). The recurring motifs, "another brother gone" and "a love supreme," have been transformed into "Black Man Go Back To The Old Country" that opens and closes the poem, marks its structure, gives direction to the process of black culture, conjures the images of the past, and confirms the continuing presence and power of the ancestral rituals and myths, of the "contract," "man to man." In the "brush-work" of the painter, in his images and "human form[s]" the traditional community rituals came alive again so that "we" could take part and "dance," "oneness, / otherness, forming each man in his music, / one to one: and we touched, *contact-high,* / high modes, *contact-high,* and the images, / *contact-high,* man to man, came back." That in the paintings the "music" of "oneness" and "high modes" can be seen, or revealed, is the achievement of black musicians. Billie Holiday, Louis Armstrong, Miles Davis were and are "modes from the old

---

[10] Interpreting Harper's poetic use of "ritual" and "myth," I have found Victor Turner's analysis in terms of process and drama most helpful. See *Drama, Fields, and Metaphors: Symbolic Action in Human Society* (Ithaca, N.Y.: Cornell University Press, 1974) and *The Ritual Process: Structure and Anti-Structure* (Ithaca, N.Y.: Cornell University Press, 1969).

country," who "brought it back" from "Africa, / the first mode," "going back to one's origins, trying to excavate what one comes out of, both in literal and cosmological terms, so as to try to recontextualize and put together a clearer picture of one's responsibilities in terms of the continuum and artistic traditional heritage" (Chapman, p. 470). The testimonial quality of black music finds its fulfillment in "Coltrane is, power," the last words in this part of the poem before it returns to its refrain *Black Man Go Back To The Old Country.* "As Harper elaborates in his liner notes to a Coltrane album: "Coltrane's music is the recognition and embodiment of life-force; his music is testamental in modal forms of expression that unfold in their many modal aspects. His music testifies to life; one is witness to the spirit of life; and one is rejuvenated and renewed in a living experience, the music that provides images strong enough to give back that power that renews . . . *Coltrane is thus power beyond definition."*

> And we go back to the well: Africa,
> the first mode, and man, modally,
> touched the land of the continent,
> modality: we are one; a man is another
> man's face, modality, in continuum,
> from man, to man, *contact-high,* to man,
> *contact-high,* to man, high modes, oneness,
> *contact-high,* man to man, *contact-high:*
> *Black Man Go Back To The Old Country*
> *Black Man Go Back To The Old Country*
> *Black Man Go Back To The Old Country*
> *Black Man Go Back To The Old Country*   (*HH,* p. 95)

In this final part of the poem, Harper evokes African spirituality, Nommo, the "magical power of the word" (Janheinz Jahn), and he celebrates the "energizing" power of Coltrane's music that has made his own work as a poet possible "both in terms of historical-aesthetic vision, and in terms of technique." Music and poetry being "complementary," the poet must "carry that particular tradition, and [Coltrane's] placement in it, into the human fabric, the fabric of humane relations, to make his music part of a living reality, seen and unseen" (Chapman, pp. 468–469). Coltrane's *music* provides *images* of process strong enough to energize the poet, as black music is "a continuous process of fluidity in the passage of creation, human creation, contingent human experience, ancestral reality, black history, aesthetic vision" (liner notes). That means, Coltrane in his playing most profoundly incorporates and communicates the meaning of the *Afro-American tradition.* "Coltrane is a groove in the black tradition, the history and culture of black people; he constantly reused his roots in a testamental way, in the spirit of the blues. The blues was Trane's vocabulary; and the blues is always a secular testament to life that is optimistic in its profundity. His music is therefore aggressive, for it grows out of a living experience; and his music is the total environment of the jam session, the jazz set as the expression of the interaction of forces, his present and past modalities" (liner notes). By having "plugged into the tradition" of the blues mode as well as of the spirituals, gospel songs, sermons, and religious rituals of the black church, Coltrane "continues" and "reclaims" the African continuum, black culture as fundamentally permeated by a non-Western philosophy of life and history. Yet *continuation* is not enough. Actually, as the mode of music, and of poetry, is process, reclaiming and continuing the traditions means *transformation* and *transcendence.* Coltrane "reused" the blues, "recreated" it, carried "the tradition into a dimension of expression, into an area of possibility never taken before, for extension and overextension is a device of our aesthetic vision" (Chapman, p. 470).

This process of *transcendence and recreation* has important implications. Transcendence always is recreation, a renewal at (and of) the sources of the black cultural tradition that "reveals its own truth on its own terms." In their development, black music and black poetry will always have to go back to the oral tradition, to its origin in the human cry, in human speech, in the rhythm of life: "Creation is recreating traditions, black musical traditions recreated out of human speech, the attuned human ear, the pulsing, rhythmic heart" (liner notes). At the same time, this creation is not a return to the past in the sense of celebrating one's "roots," but a critical reappropriation and testing of the legacy of the past, or its symbols and rituals. This means, for *black Americans,* the discovery that the key role of *music* in their cultural tradition is not simply an outflowing of the African spiritual continuum, but the result of particular *historical* events and developments on American soil: music was *"the only explicit device open to [Black people] while they were enslaved"* (Chapman, p. 469, Harper's emphasis). Therefore there is "a tremendous amount of history, metaphor, cultural information, and detail, in the music of Black Americans," in its sounds as well as in its verbal forms.

It is out of this historical experience and awareness that the singing and playing of the black musician has always aimed at collective expression, has always spoken for the black community (and its problems), as his music is the "total environment of the jam session." "The blues singer sings 'I,' but the assumption by the listening community is 'we;' for the musician speaks for us all" (liner notes). As Coltrane's music expresses the Afro-American tradition as one of survival and resistance to oppression and as his playing grows out of the living experience of Black America today, his music necessarily will be "aggressive": "I suspect that one of the reasons why [Coltrane's life] expired had something to do with the kind of fragmentation that this society produces, particularly among Black people, and *that the kind of community he was crying for, that urgency of which his playing was a symbol,* was not about to come at this time" (Chapman, p. 470, my emphasis). In *re-creating* and *transcending* the Afro-American cultural traditions in music, the mode of Coltrane's music reveals itself as inherently *political,* and his playing is experienced as a "cry of my people" (Archie Shepp) for their African American past, for their kin, for fundamental revolutionary *change* (Amiri Baraka), for the creation of a "new humanism" (Harper).

Writing from Sources: Poetry

ʒℛ ℛℭ

The section "Writing from Sources: Fiction" emphasized the mechanics of writing from sources: when to quote, how to write a footnote, how to construct a "Works Cited" list. These points apply also to writing about poetry from sources, and you should use the earlier section for reference. In this section, we will consider the more general question of how to read secondary material for prospective use in your own writing.

We have reprinted four pieces here. The first is a charming anecdotal piece by Harper himself about his early days and the influences that shaped him as a poet. Then there are three critical essays on Harper's poetry: a review-essay by John F. Callahan on Harper's *Images of Kin: New and Selected Poems* (1977); a general overview of Harper's work by Joseph A. Brown, called "'Their Long Scars Touch Ours: A Reflection on the Poetry of Michael Harper"; and an essay called "Black Poetry and Black Music; History and Tradition: Michael Harper and John Coltrane," by Günter H. Lenz, on Harper's use of the jazz saxophonist John Coltrane as both subject and inspiration.

As we would expect, the three critical essays contain both general and specific material, broad generalizations about Harper's work, and analyses of specific poems offered in support of the generalizations. One way to use their ideas is to look for different interpretations of the same poems, state the disagreements, and then try to judge among them. Both Brown and Lenz, for example, have fairly detailed analyses of "Dear John, Dear Coltrane." One could summarize their opinions and then offer one's own. The trouble with this is that Brown and Lenz say similar things about the poem. They did not write their essays in opposition to one another, and to read their work as representing contesting views is to strain things a bit.

A more useful way to use these critics' work in one's own writing might be to look for the large generalizations and quote or summarize them as springboards into one's own interpretations. Let us take another look at the essays, identify their central points, and imagine how we might use them in our own work.

Harper's own little autobiographical sketch is unpretentious; Harper himself describes it as "a riff in honor of my ancestors and a little stretching of the truth to make the point." The imagery is neat. A "riff" is a melodic phrase in jazz, and Harper often presents himself as a jazz musician taking a solo; he often raises, too, the issue of truthfulness in poetry. In spite of its informality, the sketch has a lot to tell us about the forces that shaped Harper as a poet: the jazz records in his parents' collection, his reaction to literature surveys with no black writers, the black church, his reading of history. "Straight, no chaser," Harper says, quoting the title of a well-known jazz piece. The phrase recurs throughout his work, usually meaning something like, "Give me the truth straight, without softening it with illusions," and in this essay Harper tells us the ways he has found toward the truth.

John F. Callahan's major point is suggested in his title: "The Testifying Voice in Michael Harper's *Images of Kin*." To "testify" in the black church is to stand up and speak to the congregation of one's experience of God, and for Callahan, Harper's best poems are "performance poems," poems like "Dear John, Dear Coltrane" or "Reuben, Reuben," in which Harper metaphorically stands and testifies or, to change the metaphor, stands and takes a solo, *a la* John Coltrane. To write these poems, Harper "worked out the problem of voice. He found a formal way to shape the idioms and strands of his experience and tradition into a voice capable of expressing many styles, many frequencies, many lines of speech and experience." Callahan's portrait of Harper as testifier or jazzman is largely metaphorical, and not everyone would agree on the poems in which Harper's characteristic "voice" is heard and those in which it is not. But when Callahan points out the difference, in a poem named "Br'er Sterling and the Rocker," between "literary" lines like

> that chair's a blues-harnessed star
> turnin' on its earthy axis

and lines that sound as if they had been improvised in a blues song, like

> Miss Daisy, latch on that star's arc,
> hold on sweet mama; Br'er Sterling's rocker glows,

we can see his point, agree with it or not.

Joseph A. Brown's essay has many points of similarity to Callahan's; like Callahan, he emphasizes Harper's role of the poet-as-performer. But Brown's treatment of Harper's metaphoric performance emphasizes its function of comforting and providing hope in the face of death. Harper's poems are full of death and suffering. On the public level, "American History" is a matter of four little girls blown up in a Birmingham church and five hundred slaves in a net dragged down to drown in Charleston Harbor. On the personal level, it is his son dying in "Reuben, Reuben" and "Nightmare Begins Responsibility." His poetry is full of dirges, for John Coltrane, Zora Neale Hurston, Malcolm X, Martin Luther King. For Brown,

> *Death* in all its manifestations is the subject matter of Michael Harper's poetic career. How he fought a way for himself out of the tomb, the temptation to eternally reside in nightmares; how he wills himself to construct a ladder of saints as a way of remembering those who instructed him in open-ended, "modal" living; how, finally, he offers his

performance as a sign of hope and encouragement to his readers—all of these place Michael Harper where he wants to be: the child of the great performing blues artists.

Brown supports his view of Harper's work with close analyses of several poems. How he does this is well worth careful study.

If Brown's view of Harper's work shares common ground with Callahan's, Günter H. Lenz's essay, "Black Poetry and Black Music; History and Tradition: Michael Harper and John Coltrane," has many points of agreement with both of them. But in analyzing the many poems Harper has written about John Coltrane over the years, his emphasis is not so much on Harper as a metaphoric performer as on the themes and metaphors that Harper has developed in these poems:

> The poems Harper has written about John Coltrane over the years create and reveal in their statements (as well as in their images, metaphors, rhythmical motifs which occur again and again and are confirmed or transformed), complex interrelationships among the poems, among the past, the present, and the future, among the various realms and planes of being and experience.

Lenz is very inclusive in his definition of what constitutes a poem about John Coltrane, and in his readings of a variety of Harper poems he demonstrates the way Harper tries to emulate the healing, unifying power that he finds in Coltrane's music.

Callahan, Brown, and Lenz are themselves "writing from sources," and the ways they handle quotations and documentation provide good models for us. Beginners in writing from sources often make two common errors which might be called *No It's Not* and *Me Too*. Writers guilty of *No It's Not* quote only to disagree and to use the rejected quotation as a springboard for their own views. There are times when quoting something in order to disagree with it is perfectly appropriate, when you believe that a dominant or widely held opinion is wrong, for example. But to let your own work turn into a string of corrections of other people's work is not productive.

The other error, *Me Too*, is the exact opposite: quoting only passages that you agree with and using the quotations to support a position otherwise unsupported. A more formal name for this error is "arguing from authority," and it makes for a poor argument. If you want to make the point that Michael Harper draws an analogy between jazz and poetry, and in order to develop the point you quote Critic A, who says that Michael Harper draws an analogy between jazz and poetry, and then you go on to quote Critics B and C, who say ditto, you have said the same thing four times but have not developed your argument. Three examples of Harper's equation of jazz and poetry would be much more convincing than three authorities saying the same thing.

Finally, let us take a look at how our writers use secondary material. Harper, who is writing an autobiographical sketch, and Callahan, who is writing a review, use no footnotes. But Brown and Lenz draw on other critics' work frequently and document their borrowings extensively. Both treat the writers they quote from as neither inferior and in need of correction nor superior and capable of validating their points by mere assertion, but as equal participants in a critical conversation. Look at Brown's first quotation, for example. He quotes the critic John Lovell on the subject of "borrowings" in Afro-American music. Lovell thinks borrowing is all right if it serves the borrower's purpose to "express, depict, criticize, or exalt his own life." In the first place, Brown quotes enough so that we can follow

Lovell's reasoning; we are not asked to accept his views merely on the basis of his supposed authority. In the second place, Brown follows the quotation by neither *No It's Not* nor *Me Too* but with some examples of Lovell's point. The quoted person is a stimulus to thought, not a substitute for it. Harper himself is the person Brown quotes most frequently, and he does it economically, so that each quotation, whether from Harper's poetry or his prose, makes exactly the point it is intended to make, not just some generally applicable one. And notice that Brown follows up every quotation with a summary or commentary on it; the quotation is not left to speak for itself.

The most elaborate use of sources and documentation is in Lenz's essay. Notice that he begins with a lengthy quotation from Harper, which he follows with a longer passage of his own in which he interprets what Harper has to say. In this paragraph, too, notice how skillfully Lenz uses short quoted phrases from Harper within his own sentences, so as to get the flavor of Harper's language without quoting great blocks of his work.

Notice, too, Lenz's use of parenthetical attribution for texts that he is going to quote frequently. For example, when discussing John O'Brien's *Interviews with Black Writers,* he gives it a footnote the first time he quotes it (footnote 2), says in the footnote "(hereafter referred to as O'Brien)," and then identifies it within parentheses in the main text after that. Footnote 4 arranges not only parenthetical attribution for Harper's poems but also abbreviations for his volumes of poetry, to be even more economical. If Lenz did not use these devices, he would have three times as many footnotes, and the reader would probably find it wearisome flipping back to the notes so often.

Some of Lenz's footnotes and parenthetical attributions give the sources of quotations, but a number of them do not. Footnote 5, for example, cites a tape recording of Harper reading "Dear John, Dear Coltrane" in order to substantiate Lenz's statement that he chants "a love supreme" like Coltrane. Footnote 8 cites another poet's treatment of Coltrane's composing "Alabama," to compare with Harper's. Footnote 10 cites an anthropologist not quoted in the text but on whom Lenz has drawn for his concepts of "ritual" and "myth" in Harper's work.

Both Brown's and Lenz's essays repay close study of how they make quoted material seem to be voices in an interesting conversation rather than stiff, pedantic conventions, surely our goal in writing from sources.

III

DRAMA

Reading Drama Critically

ℑℛ ℛℒ

Reading literature, no matter what the genre, requires a number of skills: the ability to read carefully, to imagine people and events, and to think about the meaning of experience. But certain skills seem more crucial to certain genres. Reading fiction, for example, seems to require an ability to empathize and even identify with people sometimes very different from oneself. Reading poems requires a good ear for language, the sound of words, and the nuances of meaning.

Reading drama requires a number of skills, but the most important one is perhaps the skill to visualize concrete stage pictures when reading a play. Drama, unlike fiction or poetry, employs not one medium but two: the printed page and the theater. Attempts have been made in the past to privilege one medium over the other. Romantic literary critics held, for example, that Shakespeare was better read than performed; no actual production could be as good as the one in the reader's imagination. Certain theater people, on the other hand, deny that plays are literature at all. They do not even like the word *plays* and instead use the word *scripts*, regarding the printed text as only a guide to stage performance. Either view ignores the fact that plays are both read *and* performed. Drama is both a literary art, like fiction and poetry, and a performance art, like music and dance; dramatic texts are both plays and scripts.

The double nature of plays means that the best skill one can have in reading them is the ability to imagine productions of them. A pencil, one of the best aids to reading, can be used for underlining, marginal comments, and general notes. When you read plays, it can also be used to make rough sketches of settings, floor plans, and the stage picture at important moments. Some good readers of plays actually move toy figures or chess pieces around a floor plan in order to visualize spatial relationships.

The point is not just to figure out the "right" stage pictures—any play can be well staged in a number of ways—nor is it just to keep two actors from occupying the same space at the same time. The point of thoughtful visualization and concretization is to see how various meanings might be created on the stage. The key question is "why?" Why should the actors be arranged on the stage in a certain way at a certain time? What range of options has the playwright given us? And of course the disposition of the actors on the stage is not the only consideration. How should a certain line be spoken? Should two actors look at each other at a certain time? Who is listening to whom? Who is looking at whom? And, in both cases, why?

This kind of concrete, visual analysis of plays is not just desirable, it is absolutely necessary if you are to understand drama. Part of the nature of drama is that it be left somewhat open to interpretation by the director or, in our case, the reader. The good reader of drama has to see what is left out that would ordinarily be supplied in fiction and use his or her imagination to flesh out the text.

And visualizing, important as it is, is not the only tool we have for analyzing drama. The language of drama is meant to be spoken and heard, and reading scenes aloud is important. Verbalizing is as important as visualizing. Many of the literary elements we studied in fiction and poetry—plot, character, theme, figurative elements—appear also in drama, often in slightly different ways. In studying fiction and poetry, we used several texts to illustrate each element. The length of most plays makes this impossible. So we will use one play, Alice Childress's long one-act play *Wine in the Wilderness*, as our demonstration text. Read it carefully and then read the following sections, which will use *Wine in the Wilderness* to introduce the most important elements of drama, to discuss reading, interpretation, and criticism as they apply to the study of drama, and to discuss some special issues in writing about drama.

Alice Childress

Alice Childress (b. 1920), in a career in the theater that spans more than fifty years, has become one of the most successful African-American playwrights in the history of the American theater, though she remains largely unknown to the general public. Born in Charleston, South Carolina, she was educated, first, in the schools of Harlem, New York; she later studied in the Radcliffe Institute for Independent Study, from which she graduated in 1968. At twenty-one she became a member of the company of the American Negro Theater in New York and remained with them for twelve years. Her first play, *Florence,* was produced in New York in 1949, and her play *Trouble in Mind* won an Obie award in 1956. Other major plays are *Gold Through the Trees* (1952), *Wedding Band* (1966), *Wine in the Wilderness* (1969), *Sea Island Song* (1977), and *Moms: A Praise Play for a Black Comedienne* (1987). Her most frequently produced play is perhaps *Wedding Band,* the story of an interracial romance; it starred Eartha Kitt in the New York production. *Trouble in Mind* is a play about the theater, in which black actors must decide whether to participate in a play about lynching that the white director regards as daring and liberal, but that the actors see as dated and demeaning. In 1977 her children's book *A Hero Ain't Nothin' But a Sandwich* (1973) was made into a film for which Childress wrote the screenplay.

WINE IN THE WILDERNESS

CHARACTERS

BILL JAMESON, *An artist aged thirty-three*
OLDTIMER, *An old roustabout character in his sixties*
SONNY-MAN, *A writer aged twenty-seven*

CYNTHIA, *A social worker aged twenty-five. She is Sonny-Man's wife*
TOMMY, *A woman factory worker aged thirty*

SCENE: *A one room apartment in a Harlem Tenement. It used to be a three room apartment but the tenant has broken out walls and is half finished with a redecorating job. The place is now only partly reminiscent of its past tawdry days, plaster broken away and lathing exposed right next to a new brick-faced portion of wall. The kitchen is not a part of the room. There is a three-quarter bed covered with an African throw, a screen is placed at the foot of the bed to insure privacy when needed. The room is obviously black dominated, pieces of sculpture, wall hangings, paintings. An artist's easel is standing with a drapery thrown across it so the empty canvas beneath it is hidden. Two other canvases the same size are next to it, they too are covered and conceal paintings. The place is in a beautiful, rather artistic state of disorder. The room also reflects an interest in other darker peoples of the world. . . . A Chinese incense-burner Buddha, an American Indian feathered war helmet, a Mexican serape, a Japanese fan, a West Indian travel poster. There is a kitchen table, chairs, floor cushions, a couple of box crates, books, bookcases, plenty of artist's materials. There is a small raised platform for model posing. On the platform is a backless chair.*

The tail end of a riot is going on out in the street. Noise and screaming can be heard in the distance, . . . running feet, voices shouting over loudspeakers.

OFFSTAGE VOICES Offa the street! Into your homes! Clear the street! (*The whine of a bullet is heard*) Cover that roof! It's from the roof! (BILL *is seated on the floor with his back to the wall, drawing on a large sketch pad with a charcoal pencil. He is very absorbed in his task but flinches as he hears the bullet sound, ducks and shields his head with upraised hand, . . . then resumes sketching. The telephone rings, he reaches for phone with caution, pulls it toward him by the cord in order to avoid going near window or standing up)*

BILL   Hello? Yeah, my phone is on. How the hell I'm gonna be talkin' to you if it's not on? *(Sound of glass breaking in the distance)* I could lose my damn life answerin' the phone. Sonny-Man, what the hell you callin' me up for! I thought you and Cynthia might be downstairs dead. I banged on the floor and hollered down the air-shaft, no answer. No stuff! Thought yall was dead. I'm sittin' here drawin' a picture in your memory. In a bar! Yall sittin' in a bar? See there, you done blew the picture that's in your memory . . . No kiddin', they wouldn't let you in the block? Man, they can't keep you outta your own house. Found? You found who? Model? What model? Yeah, yeah, thanks, . . . but I like to find my own models. No! Don't bring nobody up here in the middle of a riot . . . Hey, Sonny-Man! Hey!

(Sound of yelling and rushing footsteps in the hall)

WOMAN'S VOICE *(Offstage)*   Dammit, Bernice! The riot is over! What you hidin' in the hall for? I'm in the house, your father's in the house, . . . and you out here hidin' in the hall!
GIRL'S VOICE *(Offstage)*   The house might burn down!
BILL   Sonny-Man, I can't hear you!
WOMAN'S VOICE *(Offstage)*   If it do burn down, what the hell you gon' do, run off and leave us to burn up by ourself? The riot is over. The police say it's over! Get back in the house!

(Sound of running feet and a knock on the door)

BILL   They say it's over. Man, they oughta let you on your own block, in your own house . . . Yeah, we still standing', this seventy year old house got guts. Thank you, yeah, thanks but I like to pick my own models. You drunk? Can't you hear when I say not to . . . Okay, all right, bring her . . . *(Frantic knocking at the door)* I gotta go. Yeah, yeah, bring her. I gotta go . . . *(Hangs up phone and opens the door for* OLDTIMER. *The old man is carrying a haul of loot . . . two or three bottles of liquor, a ham, a salami and a suit with price tags attached)* What's this! Oh, no, no, no, Oldtimer, not here. . . . *(Faint sound of a police whistle)* The police after you? What you bring that stuff in here for?
OLDTIMER *(Runs past* BILL *to C. as he looks for a place to hide the loot)*   No, no, they not really after me but . . . I was in the basement so I could stash this stuff, . . . but a fella told me they pokin' round down there . . . in the back yard pokin' round . . . the police doin' a lotta pokin' round.
BILL   If the cops are searchin' why you wanna dump your troubles on me?
OLDTIMER   I don't wanta go to jail. I'm too old to go to jail. What we gonna do?
BILL   We can throw it the hell outta the window. Didn't you think of just throwin' it away and not worry 'bout jail?
OLDTIMER   I can't do it. It's like . . . I'm Oldtimer but my hands and arms is somebody else that I don't know-a-tall. *(BILL *pulls stuff out of* OLDTIMER'S *arms and places loot on the kitchen table.* OLDTIMER'S *arms fall to his sides)* Thank you, son.

BILL   Stealin' ain't worth a bullet through your brain, is it? You wanna get shot down and drown in your own blood, . . . for what? A suit, a bottle of whiskey? Gonna throw your life away for a damn ham?

OLDTIMER   But I ain' really stole nothin', Bill, cause I ain' no thief. Them others, . . . they smash the windows, they run in the stores and grab and all. Me, I pick up what they left scatter in the street. Things they drop . . . things they trample underfoot. What's in the street ain' like stealin'. This is leavin's. What I'm gon' do if the police come?

BILL   *(Starts to gather the things in the tablecloth that is on the table)*   I'll throw it out the air-shaft window.

OLDTIMER   *(Places himself squarely in front of the air-shaft window)*   I be damn. Uh-uh, can't let you do it, Billy-Boy. *(Grabs the liquor and holds on)*

BILL   *(Wraps the suit, the ham and the salami in the tablecloth and ties the ends together in a knot)*   Just for now, then you can go down and get it later.

OLDTIMER   *(Getting belligerent)*   I say I ain't gon' let you do it.

BILL   Sonny-Man calls this "The people's revolution." A revolution should not be looting and stealing. Revolutions are for liberation. *(Oldtimer won't budge from before the window)* Okay, man, you win, it's all yours. *(Walks away from OLDTIMER and prepares his easel for sketching)*

OLDTIMER   Don't be mad with me, Billy-Boy, I couldn' help myself.

BILL   *(At peace with the old man)*   No hard feelin's.

OLDTIMER   *(As he uncorks bottle)*   I don't blame you for bein' fed up with us, . . . fella like you oughta be fed up with your people sometime. Hey, Billy, let's you and me have a little taste together.

BILL   Yeah, why not.

OLDTIMER   *(At table pouring drinks)*   You mustn't be too hard on me. You see, you talented, you got somethin' on the ball, you gonna make it on past these white folk, . . . but not me, Billy-boy, it's too late in the day for that. Time, time, time, . . . time done put me down. Father Time is a bad white cat. Whatcha been paintin' and drawin' lately? You can paint me again if you wanta, . . . no charge. Paint me 'cause that might be the only way I get to stay in the world after I'm dead and gone. Somebody'll look up at your paintin' and say, . . . "Who's that?" And you say, . . . "That's Oldtimer." *(BILL joins OLDTIMER at table and takes one of the drinks)* Well here's lookin' at you and goin' down me. *(Gulps drink down)*

BILL   *(Raising his glass)*   Your health, oldtimer.

OLDTIMER   My day we didn't have all this grants and scholarship like now. Whatcha been doin!?

BILL   I'm working on the third part of a triptych.

OLDTIMER   A what tick?

BILL   A triptych.

OLDTIMER   Hot-damn, that call for another drink. Here's to the trip-tick. Down the hatch. What is one-a-those?

BILL   It's three paintings that make one work . . . three paintings that make one subject.

OLDTIMER   Goes together like a new outfit . . . hat, shoes and suit.

BILL   Right. The title of my triptych is . . . "Wine In The Wilderness" . . . Three canvases on black womanhood . . .

OLDTIMER   *(Eyes light up)*   Are they naked pitchers?

BILL   *(Crosses to paintings)*   No, all fully clothed.

OLDTIMER   *(Wishing it was a naked picture)*   Man, ain' nothin' dirty 'bout naked pitchers. That's art. What you call artistic.

BILL   Right, right, right, but these are with clothes. That can be artistic too. *(Uncovers one of the canvases and reveals paintings of a charming little girl in Sunday dress and hair ribbon)* I call her . . . "Black girlhood."

OLDTIMER   Awwwww, that's innocence! Don't know what it's all about. Ain't that the little child that live right down the street? Yeah. That call for another drink.

BILL   Slow down, Oldtimer, wait till you see this. *(Covers the painting of the little girl, then uncovers another canvas and reveals a beautiful woman, deep mahogany complexion, she is cold but utter perfection, draped in startling colors of African material, very "Vogue" looking. She wears a golden head-dress sparkling with brilliants and sequins applied over the paint)* There she is . . . "Wine In The Wilderness" . . . Mother Africa, regal, black womanhood in her noblest form.

OLDTIMER   Hot damn. I'd die for her, no stuff, . . . oh, man. "Wine In The Wilderness."

BILL   Once, a long time ago, a poet named Omar told us what a paradise life could be if a man had a loaf of bread, a jug of wine and . . . a woman singing to him in the wilderness. She is the woman, she is the bread, she is the wine, she is the singing. This Abyssinian maiden is paradise, . . . perfect black womanhood.

OLDTIMER   *(Pours for* BILL *and himself)*   To our Abyssinian maiden.

BILL   She's the Sudan, the Congo River, the Egyptian Pyramids . . . Her thighs are African Mahogany . . . she speaks and her words pour forth sparkling clear as the waters . . . Victoria Falls.

OLDTIMER   Ow! Victoria Falls! She got a pretty name.

BILL   *(Covers her up again)*   Victoria Falls is a waterfall not her name. Now, here's the one that calls for a drink. *(Snatches cover from the empty canvas)*

OLDTIMER   *(Stunned by the empty canvas)*   Your . . . your pitcher is gone.

BILL   Not gone, . . . she's not painted yet. This will be the third part of the triptych. This is the unfinished third of "Wine In The Wilderness." She's gonna be the kinda chick that is grass roots, . . . no, not grass roots, . . . I mean she's underneath the grass roots. The lost woman, . . . what the society has made out of our women. She's as far from my African queen as a woman can get and still be female, she's as close to the bottom as you can get without crackin' up . . . she's ignorant, unfeminine, coarse, rude . . . vulgar . . . a poor, dumb chick that's had her behind kicked until it's numb . . . and the sad part is . . . she ain't together, you know, . . . there's no hope for her.

OLDTIMER   Oh, man, you talkin' 'bout my first wife.

BILL   A chick that ain' fit for nothin' but to . . . to . . . just pass her by.

OLDTIMER   Yeah, later for her. When you see her, cross over to the other side of the street.

BILL   If you had to sum her up in one word it would be nothin'!

OLDTIMER   *(Roars with laughter)*   That call for a double!

BILL   *(Beginning to slightly feel the drinks. He covers the canvas again)*   Yeah, that's a double! The kinda woman that grates on your damn nerves. And Sonny-Man just called to say he found her runnin' round in the middle-a this riot, Sonny-Man say she's the real thing from underneath them grass roots. A back-country chick right outta the wilds of Mississippi, . . . but she ain' never been near there. Born in Harlem, raised right here in Harlem, . . . but back country. Got the picture?

OLDTIMER   *(Full of laughter)*   When . . . when . . . when she get here let's us stomp her to death.

BILL   Not till after I paint her. Gonna put her right here on this canvas. *(Pats the canvas, walks in a strut around the table)* When she gets put down on canvas, . . . then triptych will be finished.

OLDTIMER *(Joins him in the strut)* Trip-tick will be finish . . . trip-tick will be finish . . .

BILL Then "Wine In The Wilderness" will go up against the wall to improve the view of some post office . . . or some library . . . or maybe a bank . . . and I'll win a prize . . . and the queen, my black queen will look down from the wall so the messed up chicks in the neighborhood can see what a woman oughta be . . . and the innocent child on one side of her and the messed up chick on the other side of her . . . MY STATEMENT.

OLDTIMER *(Turning the strut into a dance)* Wine in the wilderness . . . up against the wall . . . wine in the wilderness . . . up against the wall . . .

WOMAN FROM UPSTAIRS APT. *(Offstage)* What's the matter! The house on fire?

BILL *(Calls upstairs through the air-shaft window)* No, baby! We down here paintin' pictures!

(Sound of police siren in distance)

WOMAN FROM UPSTAIRS APT. *(Offstage)* So much-a damn noise! Cut out the noise! *(To her husband, hysterically)* Percy! Percy! You hear a police siren! Percy! That a fire engine?!

BILL Another messed up chick. *(Gets a rope and ties it to* OLDTIMER's *bundle)* Got an idea. We'll tie the rope to the bundle, . . . then . . . *(Lowers bundle out of window)* lower the bundle outta the window . . . and tie it to this nail here behind the curtain. Now! Nobody can find it except you and me . . . Cops come, there's no loot. *(Ties rope to nail under curtain)*

OLDTIMER Yeah, yeah, loot long gone 'til I want it. *(Makes sure window knot is secure)* It'll be swingin' in the breeze free and easy. *(There is knocking on the door)*

SONNY-MAN Open up! Open up! Sonny-Man and company.

BILL *(Putting finishing touches on securing knot to nail)* Wait, wait, hold on. . . .

SONNY-MAN And-a here we come!

(Pushes the door open. Enters room with his wife CYNTHIA *and* TOMMY. SONNY-MAN *is in high spirits. He is in his late twenties, his wife* CYNTHIA *is a bit younger. She wears her hair in a natural style, her clothing is tweedy and in good, quiet taste.* SONNY-MAN *is wearing slacks and a dashiki over a shirt.* TOMMY *is dressed in a mis-matched skirt and a sweater, wearing a wig that is not comical, but is wiggy looking. She has the habit of smoothing it every once in a while, patting to make sure it's in place. She wears sneakers and bobby sox, carries a brown paper sack)*

CYNTHIA You didn't think it was locked, did you?

BILL Door not locked? *(Looking over* TOMMY)

TOMMY You oughta run him outta town, pushin' open people's door.

BILL Come right on in.

SONNY-MAN *(Standing behind* TOMMY *and pointing down at her to draw* BILL's *attention)* Yes, sireeeeee.

CYNTHIA Bill, meet a friend-a ours . . . This is Miss Tommy Fields. Tommy, meet a friend-a ours . . . this is Bill, Jameson . . . Bill, Tommy.

BILL Tommy, if I may call you that . . .

TOMMY *(Likes him very much)* Help yourself, Bill. It's a pleasure. Bill Jameson, well, all right.

BILL   The pleasure is all mine. Another friend-a ours, Oldtimer.

TOMMY   *(With respect and warmth)*   How are you, Mr. Timer?

BILL   *(Laughs along with others,* OLDTIMER *included)*   What you call him, baby?

TOMMY   Mr. Timer, . . . ain't that what you say?   *(They all laugh expansively)*

BILL   No, sugar pie, that's not his name, . . . we just say . . . "Oldtimer," that's what everybody call him. . . .

OLDTIMER   Yeah, they all call me that . . . everybody say that . . . OLDTIMER.

TOMMY   That's cute, . . . but what's your name?

BILL   His name *is* . . . er . . . er . . . What *is* your name?

SONNY-MAN   Dog-bite, what's your name, man?

(There is a significant moment of self-consciousness as CYNTHIA, SONNY *and* BILL *realize they don't know* OLDTIMER*'s name)*

OLDTIMER   Well, it's . . . Edmond L. Matthews.

TOMMY   Edmond *L.* Matthews. What's the L for?

OLDTIMER   Lorenzo, . . . Edmond Lorenzo Matthews.

BILL AND SONNY-MAN   Edmond Lorenzo Matthews.

TOMMY   Please to meetcha, Mr. Matthews.

OLDTIMER   Nobody call me that in a long, long time.

TOMMY   I'll call you Oldtimer like the rest but I like to know who I'm meetin'. (OLDTIMER *gives her a chair)* There you go. He's a gentleman too. Bet you can tell my feet hurt. I got one corn, . . . and that one is enough. Oh, it'll ask you for somethin'.

(General laughter. BILL *indicates to* SONNY-MAN *that* TOMMY *seems right.* CYNTHIA *and* OLDTIMER *take seats near* TOMMY*)*

BILL   You rest yourself, baby, er . . . er . . . Tommy. You did say Tommy.

TOMMY   I cut it to Tommy . . . Tommy-Marie, I use both of 'em sometime.

BILL   How 'bout some refreshment?

SONNY-MAN   Yeah, how 'bout that.   *(Pouring drinks)*

TOMMY   Don't yall carry me too fast, now.

BILL   *(Indicating liquor bottles)*   I got what you see and also some wine . . . couple-a cans-a beer.

TOMMY   I'll take the wine.

BILL   Yeah, I knew it.

TOMMY   Don't wanta start nothin' I can't keep up.

*(*OLDTIMER *slaps his thigh with pleasure)*

BILL   That's all right, baby, you just a wine-o.

TOMMY   You the one that's got the wine, not me.

BILL   I use this for cookin'.

TOMMY   You like to get loaded while you cook?

*(*OLDTIMER *is having a ball)*

BILL   *(As he pours wine for* TOMMY*)*   Oh, baby, you too much.

OLDTIMER   *(Admiring* TOMMY*)*   Oh, Lord, I wish, I wish, I wish I was young again.

TOMMY   *(Flirtatiously)*   Lively as you are, . . . I don't know what we'd do with you if you got any younger.

OLDTIMER   Oh, hush now!

SONNY-MAN *(Whispering to* BILL *and pouring drinks)* Didn't I tell you! Know what I'm talking' about. You dig? All the elements, man.

TOMMY *(Worried about what the whispering means)* Let's get somethin' straight. I didn't come bustin' in on the party, . . . I was asked. If you married and any wives or girl-friends round here . . . I'm innocent. Don't wanta get shot at or jumped on. Cause I wasn't doin' a thing but mindin' my business! . . . *(Saying the last in loud tones to be heard in other rooms)*

OLDTIMER Jus' us here, that's all.

BILL I'm single, baby. Nobody wants a poor artist.

CYNTHIA Oh, honey, we wouldn't walk you into a jealous wife or girl friend.

TOMMY You paint all-a these pitchers?

*(*BILL *and* SONNY-MAN *hand out drinks)*

BILL Just about. Your health, baby, to you.

TOMMY *(Lifts her wine glass)* All right, and I got one for you. . . . Like my grampaw used-ta say, . . . Here's to the men's collars and the women's skirts, . . . may they never meet. *(General laughter)*

OLDTIMER But they ain't got far to go before they do.

TOMMY *(Suddenly remembers her troubles)* Niggers, niggers . . . niggers . . . I'm sick-a niggers, ain't you? A nigger will mess up everytime . . . Lemmie tell you what the niggers done . . .

BILL Tommy, baby, we don't use that word around here. We can talk about each other a little better than that.

CYNTHIA Oh, she doesn't mean it.

TOMMY What must I say?

BILL Try Afro-Americans.

TOMMY Well, . . . the Afro-Americans burnt down my house.

OLDTIMER Oh, no they didn't!

TOMMY Oh, yes they did . . . it's almost burn down. Then the firemen nailed up my door . . . the door to my room, nailed up shut tight with all I got in the world.

OLDTIMER Shame, what a shame.

TOMMY A *damn* shame. My clothes . . . Everything gone. This riot blew my life. All I got is gone like it never was.

OLDTIMER I know it.

TOMMY My transistor radio . . . that's gone.

CYNTHIA Ah, gee.

TOMMY The transistor . . . and a brand new pair-a shoes I never had on one time . . . *(Raises her right hand)* If I never move, that's the truth . . . new shoes gone.

OLDTIMER Child, when hard luck fall it just keep fallin'.

TOMMY And in my top dresser drawer I got a my-on-ase jar with forty-one dollars in it. The fireman would not let me in to get it . . . And it was a Afro-American fireman, don't-cha know.

OLDTIMER And you ain't got no place to stay. *(*BILL *is studying her for portrait possibilities)*

TOMMY *(Rises and walks around room)* That's a lie. I always got some place to go. I don't wanta boast but I ain't never been no place that I can't go back the second time. Woman I use to work for say . . . "Tommy, any time, any time you want a sleep-in place you come right here to me." . . . And that's Park Avenue, my own private bath and T.V. set . . . But I don't want that . . . so I make it on out here to the dress factory. I got friends . . . not a lot of 'em . . . but a few *good* ones. I call my friend—girl and her mother . . . they say . . . "Tommy, you come here, bring yourself over here." So Tommy got a roof with no sweat. (*Looks at torn walls*) Looks like the Afro-Americans got to you too. Breakin' up, breakin' down, . . . that's all they know.

BILL   No, Tommy, . . . I'm re-decorating the place . . .

TOMMY   You mean you did this yourself?

CYNTHIA   It's gonna be wild . . . brick-face walls . . . wall to wall carpet.

SONNY-MAN   She was breakin' up everybody in the bar . . . had us all laughin' . . . crackin' us up. In the middle of a riot . . . she's gassin' everybody!

TOMMY   No need to cry, it's sad enough. They hollerin' whitey, whitey . . . but who they burn out? Me.

BILL   The brothers and sisters are tired, weary of the endless get-no-where struggle.

TOMMY   I'm standin' there in the bar . . . tellin' it like it is . . . next thing I know they talkin' about bringin' me to meet you. But you know what I say? Can't nobody pick nobody for nobody else. It don't work. And I'm standin' there in a mis-match skirt and top and these sneaker-shoes. I just went to put my dresses in the cleaner . . . Oh, Lord, wonder if they burn down the cleaner. Well, no matter, when I got back it was all over . . . They went in the grocery store, rip out the shelves, pull out all the groceries . . . the hams . . . the . . . the . . . the can goods . . . everything . . . and then set fire . . . Now who you think live over the grocery? Me, that's who. I don't even go to the store lookin' this way . . . but this would be the time, when . . . folks got a fella they want me to meet.

BILL   (*Suddenly self-conscious*) Tommy, they thought . . . they thought I'd like to paint you . . . that's why they asked you over.

TOMMY   (*Pleased by the thought but she can't understand it*) Paint me? For what? If he was gonna paint somebody seems to me it'd be one of the pretty girls they show in the beer ads. They even got colored on television now, . . . brushin' their teeth and smokin' cigarettes, . . . some of the prettiest girls in the world. He could get them, . . . couldn't you?

BILL   Sonny-Man and Cynthia were right. I want to paint you.

TOMMY   (*Suspiciously*) Naked, with no clothes on?

BILL   No, baby, dressed just as you are now.

OLDTIMER   Wearin' clothes is also art.

TOMMY   In the cleaner I got a white dress with a orlon sweater to match it, maybe I can get it out tomorrow and pose in that.

(CYNTHIA, OLDTIMER *and* SONNY-MAN *are eager for her to agree*)

BILL   No, I will paint you today, Tommy, just as you are, holding your brown paper bag.

TOMMY   Mmmmmm, me holdin' the damn bag, I don' know 'bout that.

BILL   Look at it this way, tonight has been a tragedy.

TOMMY   Sure in hell has.

BILL   And so I must paint you tonight, . . . Tommy in her moment of tragedy.

TOMMY   I'm tired.

BILL   Damn, baby, all you have to do is sit there and rest.

TOMMY   I'm hungry.

SONNY-MAN   While you're posin' Cynthia can run down to our house and fix you some eggs.

CYNTHIA   (*Gives her husband a weary look*) Oh, Sonny, that's such a lovely idea.

SONNY-MAN   Thank you, darlin', I'm in there, . . . on the beam.

TOMMY *(Ill at ease about posing)* I don't want no eggs. I'm goin' to find some Chinee food.

BILL I'll go. If you promise to stay here and let me paint you, . . . I'll get you anything you want.

TOMMY *(Brightening up)* Anything I want. Now, how he sound? All right, you comin' on mighty strong there. "Anything you want." When last you heard somebody say that? . . . I'm warnin' you, now, . . . I'm free, single and disengage, . . . so you better watch yourself.

BILL *(Keeping her away from ideas of romance)* Now this is the way the program will go down. First I'll feed you, then I'll paint you.

TOMMY Okay, I'm game, I'm a good sport. First off, I want me some Chinee food.

CYNTHIA Order up, Tommy, the treat's on him.

TOMMY How come it is you never been married? All these girls runnin' round Harlem lookin' for husbands. *(To CYNTHIA)* I don't blame 'em, 'cause I'm lookin' for somebody myself.

BILL I've been married, married and divorced, she divorced me, Tommy, so maybe I'm not much of a catch.

TOMMY Look at it this-a-way. Some folks got bad taste. That woman had bad taste. *(All laugh except BILL who pours another drink)* Watch it, Bill, you gonna rust the linin' of your stomach. Ain't this a shame? The riot done wipe me out and I'm sittin' here havin' me a ball. Sittin' here ballin'! *(As BILL refills her glass)* Hold it, that's enough. Likker ain' my problem.

OLDTIMER I'm havin' me a good time.

TOMMY Know what I say 'bout divorce. *(Slaps her hands together in a final gesture)* Anybody don' wantcha, . . . later, let em go. That's bad taste for you.

BILL Tommy, I don't wanta ever get married again. It's me and my work. I'm not gettin' serious about anybody. . . .

TOMMY He's spellin' at me, now. Nigger, . . . I mean Afro-American . . . I ain' ask you nothin'. You hinkty, I'm hinkty too. I'm independent as a hog on ice, . . . and a hog on ice is dead, cold, well-preserved . . . and don't need a mother-grabbin' thing. *(All laugh heartily except BILL and CYNTHIA)* I know models get paid. I ain't no square but this is a special night and so this one'll be on the house. Show you my heart's in the right place.

BILL I'll be glad to pay you, baby.

TOMMY You don't really like me, do you? That's all right, sometime it happen that way. You can't pick for *nobody*. Friends get to matchin' up friends and they mess up everytime. Cynthia and Sonny-Man done messed up.

BILL I like you just fine and I'm glad and grateful that you came.

TOMMY Good enough. *(Extends her hand. They slap hands together)* You 'n me friends?

BILL Friends baby, friends. *(Putting rock record on)*

TOMMY *(Trying out the model stand)* Okay, Dad! Let's see 'bout this *anything I want* jive. Want me a bucket-a Egg Foo Yong, and you get you a shrimp-fry rice, we split that and each have some-a both. Make him give you the soy sauce, the hot mustard and the duck sauce too.

BILL Anything else, baby?

TOMMY Since you ask, yes. If your money hold out, get me a double order egg roll. And a half order of the sweet and sour spare ribs.

BILL *(To OLDTIMER and SONNY-MAN)* Come on, come on. I need some strong men to help me bring back your order, baby.

TOMMY *(Going into her dance . . . simply standing and going through some boo-ga-loo motions)* Better go get it 'fore I think up some more to go 'long with it. *(The men laugh and vanish out of the door. Steps heard descending stairs)* Turn that off. *(CYNTHIA turns off record player)* How could I forget your name, good as you been to me this day. Thank you, Cynthia, thank you. I *like* him. Oh, I *like* him. But I don't wanta push him too fast. Oh, I got to play these cards right.

CYNTHIA *(A bit uncomfortable)* Oh, Honey, . . . Tommy, you don't want a poor artist.

TOMMY Tommy's not lookin' for a meal ticket. I been doin' for myself all my life. It takes two to make it in this high-price world. A black man see a hard way to go. The both of you gotta pull together. That way you accomplish.

CYNTHIA I'm a social worker . . . and I see so many broken homes. Some of these men! Tommy, don't be in a rush about the marriage thing.

TOMMY Keep it to yourself, . . . but I was thirty my last birthday and haven't even been married. I coulda been. Oh, yes, indeed, coulda been. But I don't want any and everybody. What I want with a no-good piece-a nothin'? I'll never forget what the Reverend Martin Luther King said . . . "I have a dream." I like him sayin' it 'cause truer words have never been spoke. *(Straightening the room)* I have a dream, too. Mine is to find a man who'll treat me just half-way decent . . . just to meet me half-way is all I ask, to smile, be kind to me. Somebody in my corner. Not to wake up by myself in the mornin' and face this world all alone.

CYNTHIA About Bill, it's best not to ever count on anything, anything at all, Tommy.

TOMMY *(This remark bothers her for a split second but she shakes it off)* Of course, Cynthia, that's one of the foremost rules of life. Don't count on *nothin'!*

CYNTHIA Right, don't be too quick to put your trust in these men.

TOMMY You put your trust in one and got yourself a husband.

CYNTHIA Well, yes, but what I mean is . . . Oh, you know. A man is a man and Bill is also an artist and his work comes before all else and there are other factors . . .

TOMMY *(Sits facing CYNTHIA)* What's wrong with me?

CYNTHIA I don't know what you mean.

TOMMY Yes you do. You tryin' to tell me I'm aimin' too high by lookin' at Bill.

CYNTHIA Oh, no my dear.

TOMMY Out there in the street, in the bar, you and your husband were so sure that he'd *like* me and want to paint my picture.

CYNTHIA But he does want to paint you, he's very eager to . . .

TOMMY But why? Somethin' don't fit right.

CYNTHIA *(Feeling sorry for TOMMY)* If you don't want to do it, just leave and that'll be that.

TOMMY Walk out while he's buyin' me what I ask for, spendin' his money on me? That'd be too dirty. *(Looks at books. Takes one from shelf)* Books, books, books everywhere. "Afro-American History." I like that. What's wrong with me, Cynthia? Tell me, I won't get mad with you, I swear. If there's somethin' wrong that I can change, I'm ready to do it. Eighth grade, that's all I had of school. You a social worker, I know that mean college. I come from poor people. *(Examining the book in her hand)* Talkin' 'bout poverty this and poverty that and studyin' it. When you in it you don't be studyin' 'bout it. Cynthia, I remember my mother tyin' up her stockin's with strips-a rag 'cause she didn't have no garters. When I get home from school she'd say, . . . "Nothin' much here to eat." Nothin' much might be grits, or bread and coffee. I got sick-a all that, got me a job. Later for school.

CYNTHIA   The Matriarchal Society.

TOMMY   What's that?

CYNTHIA   A Matriarchal Society is one in which the women rule . . . the women have the power . . . the women head the house.

TOMMY   We didn't have nothin' to rule over, not a pot nor a window. And my papa picked hisself up and run off with some finger-poppin' woman and we never hear another word 'til ten, twelve years later when a undertaker call up and ask if Mama wanta come claim his body. And don'cha know, mama went on over and claim it. A woman need a man to claim, even if it's a dead one. What's wrong with me? Be honest.

CYNTHIA   You're a fine person . . .

TOMMY   Go on, I can take it.

CYNTHIA   You're too brash. You're too used to looking out for yourself. It makes us lose our femininity . . . It makes us hard . . . it makes us seem very hard. We do for ourselves too much.

TOMMY   If I don't, who's gonna do for me?

CYNTHIA   You have to let the black man have his manhood again. You have to give it back, Tommy.

TOMMY   I didn't take it from him, how I'm gonna give it back? What else is the matter with me? You had school, I didn't. I respect that.

CYNTHIA   Yes, I've had it, the degree and the whole bit. For a time I thought I was about to move into another world, the so-called "integrated" world, a place where knowledge and knowhow could set you free and open all the doors, but that's a lie. I turned away from that idea. The first thing I did was give up dating white fellas.

TOMMY   I never had none to give up. I'm not soundin' on you. White folks, nothin' happens when I look at 'em. I don't hate 'em, don't love 'em, . . . just nothin' shakes a-tall. The dullest people in the world. The way they talk . . . "Oh, hooty, hooty, hoo" . . . break it down for me to A, B, C's. That Bill . . . I like him, with his black, uppity, high-handed ways. What do you do to get a man you want? A social worker oughta tell you things like that.

CYNTHIA   Don't chase him . . . at least don't let it look that way. Let him pursue you.

TOMMY   What if he won't? Men don't chase me much, not the kind I like.

CYNTHIA   *(Rattles off instructions glibly)* Let him do the talking. Learn to listen. Stay in the background a little. Ask his opinion . . . "What do *you* think, Bill?"

TOMMY   Mmmmm, "Oh, hooty, hooty, hoo."

CYNTHIA   But why count on him? There are lots of other nice guys.

TOMMY   You don't think he'd go for me, do you?

CYNTHIA   *(Trying to be diplomatic)* Perhaps you're not really his type.

TOMMY   Maybe not, but he's mine. I'm so lonesome . . . I'm *lonesome* . . . I want somebody to love. Somebody to say . . . "That's all right," when the World treats me mean.

CYNTHIA   Tommy, I think you're too good for Bill.

TOMMY   I don't wanta hear that. The last man that told me I was too good for him . . . was tryin' to get away. He's good enough for me. *(Straightening room)*

CYNTHIA   Leave the room alone. What we need is a little more sex appeal and a little less washing, cooking and ironing. (TOMMY *puts down the room straightening*) One more thing, . . . do you have to wear that wig?

TOMMY   *(A little sensitive)* I like how your hair looks. But some of the naturals I don't like. Can see all the lint caught up in the hair like it hasn't been combed since know not when. You a Muslim?

CYNTHIA   No.

TOMMY   I'm just sick-a hair, hair, hair. Do it this way, don' do it, leave it natural, straighten it, process, no process. I get sick-a hair and talkin' 'bout it and foolin' with it. That's why I wear the wig.

CYNTHIA   I'm sure your own must be just as nice or nicer than that.

TOMMY   It oughta be. I only paid nineteen ninety five for this.

CYNTHIA   You ought to go back to usin' your own.

TOMMY   *(Tensely)*   I'll be givin' that some thought.

CYNTHIA   You're pretty nice people just as you are. Soften up, Tommy. You might surprise yourself.

TOMMY   I'm listenin'.

CYNTHIA   Expect more. Learn to let men open doors for you . . .

TOMMY   What if I'm standin' there and they don't open it?

CYNTHIA   *(Trying to level with her)*   You're a fine person. He wants to paint you, that's all. He's doing a kind of mural thing and we thought he would enjoy painting you. I'd hate to see you expecting more out of the situation than what's there.

TOMMY   Forget it, sweetie-pie, don' nothin' happen that's not suppose to.

(Sound of laughter in the hall. BILL, OLDTIMER *and* SONNY-MAN *enter)*

BILL   No Chinese restaurant left, baby! It's wiped out. Gone with the revolution.

SONNY-MAN   *(To* CYNTHIA*)*   Baby, let's move, split the scene, get on with it, time for home.

BILL   The revolution is here. Whatta you do with her? You paint her!

SONNY-MAN   You write her . . . you write the revolution. I'm gonna write the revolution into a novel nine hundred pages long.

BILL   Dance it! Sing! "Down in the cornfield Hear dat mournful sound . . . *(*SONNY-MAN *and* OLDTIMER *harmonize)* Dear old Massa am-a sleepin' A-sleepin' in the cold, cold ground." Now for "Wine In The Wilderness!" Trip-tych will be finished.

CYNTHIA   *(In* BILL's *face)*   "Wine In The Wilderness," huh? Exploitation!

SONNY-MAN   Upstairs, all out, come on, Oldtimer. Folks can't create in a crowd. Cynthia, move it, baby.

OLDTIMER   *(Starting toward the window)*   My things! I got a package.

SONNY-MAN   *(Heads him off)*   Up and out. You don't have to go home, but you have to get outta here. Happy paintin', yall. *(One backward look and they are all gone)*

BILL   Whatta night, whatta night, whatta night, baby. It will be painted, written, sung and discussed for generations.

TOMMY   *(Notices nothing that looks like Chinese food. He is carrying a small bag and a container)*   Where's the Foo Yong?

BILL   They blew the restaurant, baby. All I could get was a couple-a franks and a orange drink from the stand.

TOMMY   *(Tensely)*   You brought me a frank-footer? That's what you think-a me, a frank-footer?

BILL   Nothin' to do with what I think. Place is closed.

TOMMY   *(Quietly surly)*   This is the damn City-a New York, any hour on the clock they sellin' the chicken in the basket, barbecue ribs, pizza pie, hot pastrami samitches; and you brought me a frank-footer?

BILL   Baby, don't break bad over somethin' to eat. The smart set, the jet set, the beautiful people, kings and queens eat frankfurters.

TOMMY If a queen sent you out to buy her a bucket-a Foo Yong, you wouldn't come back with no lonely-ass frank-footer.

BILL Kill me 'bout it, baby! Go 'head and shoot me six times. That's the trouble with our women, yall always got your mind on food.

TOMMY Is that our trouble? *(Laughs)* Maybe you right. Only two things to do. Either eat the frankfooter or walk on outta here. You got any mustard?

BILL *(Gets mustard from the refrigerator)* Let's face it, our folks are not together. The brothers and sisters have busted up Harlem, . . . no plan, no nothin'. There's your black revolution, heads whipped, hospital full and we still in the same old bag.

TOMMY *(Seated at the kitchen table)* Maybe what everybody need is somebody like you, who know how things oughta go, to get on out there and start some action.

BILL You still mad about the frankfurter?

TOMMY No. I keep seein' pitchers of what was in my room and how it all must be spoiled now. *(Sips the orange drink)* A orange never been near this. Well, it's cold. *(Looking at an incense burner)* What's that?

BILL An incense burner, was given to me by the Chinese guy, Richard Lee. I'm sorry they blew his restaurant.

TOMMY Does it help you to catch the number?

BILL No, baby, I just burn incense sometime.

TOMMY For what?

BILL Just 'cause I feel like it. Baby, ain't you used to nothin'?

TOMMY Ain't used to burnin' incent for nothin'.

BILL *(Laughs)* Burnin' what?

TOMMY That stuff.

BILL What did you call it?

TOMMY Incent.

BILL It's not incent, baby. It's incense.

TOMMY Like the sense you got in your head. In-sense. Thank you. You're a very correctable person, aint you?

BILL Let's put you on canvas.

TOMMY *(Stubbornly)* I have to eat first.

BILL That's another thing 'bout black women, they wanta eat 'fore they do anything else. Tommy, . . . Tommy, . . . I bet your name is Thomasina. You look like a Thomasina.

TOMMY You could sit there and guess til your eyes pop out and you never would guess my first name. You might could guess the middle name but not the first one.

BILL Tell it to me.

TOMMY My name is Tomorrow.

BILL How's that?

TOMMY Tomorrow, . . . like yesterday and *tomorrow*, and the middle name is just plain Marie. That's what my father name me, Tomorrow Marie. My mother say he thought it had a pretty sound.

BILL Crazy! I never met a girl named Tomorrow.

TOMMY They got to callin' me Tommy for short, so I stick with that. Tomorrow Marie, . . . Sound like a promise that can never happen.

BILL *(Straightens chair on stand. He is very eager to start painting)* That's what Shakespeare said, . . . "Tomorrow and tomorrow and tomorrow." Tomorrow, you will be on this canvas.

TOMMY *(Still uneasy about being painted)* What's the hurry? Rome wasn't built in a day, . . . that's another saying.

BILL   If I finish in time, I'll enter you in an exhibition.

TOMMY   *(Loses interest in the food. Examines the room. Looks at portraits on the wall)*   He looks like somebody I know or maybe saw before.

BILL   That's Frederick Douglass. A man who used to be a slave. He escaped and spent his life trying to make us all free. He was a great man.

TOMMY   Thank you, Mr. Douglass. Who's the light colored man? *(Indicates a frame next to the Douglass)*

BILL   He's white. That's John Brown. They killed him for tryin' to shoot the country outta the slavery bag. He dug us, you know. Old John said, "Hell no, slavery must go."

TOMMY   I heard all about him. Some folks say he was crazy.

BILL   If he had been shootin' at *us* they wouldn't have called him a nut.

TOMMY   School wasn't a great part-a my life.

BILL   If it was you wouldn't-a found out too much 'bout black history cause the books full-a nothin' but whitey, . . . all except the white ones who dug us, . . . they not there either. Tell me, . . . who was Elijah Lovejoy?

TOMMY   Elijah Lovejoy, . . . Mmmmmmm. I don't know. Have to do with the Bible?

BILL   No, that's another white fella, . . . Elijah had a printin' press and the main thing he printed was "Slavery got to go." Well the man moved in on him, smashed his press time after time . . . but he kept puttin' it back together and doin' his thing. So, one final day, they came in a mob and burned him to death.

TOMMY   *(Blows her nose with sympathy as she fights tears)*   That's dirty.

BILL   *(As TOMMY glances at titles in book cases)*   Who was Monroe Trotter?

TOMMY   Was he white?

BILL   No, soul brother. Spent his years tryin' to make it all right. Who was Harriet Tubman?

TOMMY   I heard-a her. But don't put me through no test, Billy. *(Moving around studying pictures and books)* This room is full-a things I don't know nothin' about. How'll I get to know?

BILL   Read, go to the library, book stores, ask somebody.

TOMMY   Okay, I'm askin'. Teach me things.

BILL   Aw, baby, why torment yourself? Trouble with our women, . . . they all wanta be great brains. Leave somethin' for a man to do.

TOMMY   *(Eager to impress him)*   What you think-a Martin Luther King?

BILL   A great guy. But it's too late in the day for the singin' and prayin' now.

TOMMY   What about Malcolm X.?

BILL   Great cat . . . but there again . . . Where's the program?

TOMMY   What about Adam Powell? I voted for him. That's one thing 'bout me. I vote. Maybe if everybody vote for the right people . . .

BILL   The ballot box. It would take me all my life to straighten you on that hype.

TOMMY   I got the time.

BILL   You gonna wind up with a king size headache. The Matriarchy gotta go. Yall throw them suppers together, keep your husband happy, raise the kids.

TOMMY   I don't have a husband. Course, that could be fixed. *(Leaving the unspoken proposal hanging in the air)*

BILL   You know the greatest thing you could do for your people? Sit up there and let me put you down on canvas.

TOMMY   Bein' married and havin' a family might be good for your people as a race, but I was thinkin' 'bout myself a little.

BILL   Forget yourself sometime, sugar. On that canvas you'll be givin' and givin' and givin' . . . That's where you can do your thing best. What you stallin' for?

TOMMY *(Returns to table and sits in chair)* I . . . I don't want to pose in this outfit.

BILL *(Patience is wearing thin)* Why, baby, why?

TOMMY I don't feel proud-a myself in this.

BILL Art, baby, we talkin' art. Whatcha want . . . Ribbons? Lace? False eyelashes?

TOMMY No, just my white dress with the orlon sweater, . . . or anything but this what I'm wearin'. You oughta see me in that dress with my pink linen shoes. Oh, hell, the shoes are gone. I forgot 'bout the fire . . .

BILL Oh, stop fightin' me! Another thing . . . our women don't know a damn thing 'bout bein' feminine. *Give in* sometime. It won't kill you. You tellin' me how to paint? Maybe you oughta hang out your shingle and give art lessons! You too damn opinionated. You gonna pose or you not gonna pose? Say somethin'!

TOMMY You makin' me nervous! Hollerin' at me. My mama never holler at me. Hollerin'.

BILL I'll soon be too tired to pick up the brush, baby.

TOMMY *(Eye catches picture of white woman on the wall)* That's a white woman! Bet you never hollered at her and I bet she's your girlfriend . . . too, and when she posed for her pitcher I bet yall was laughin' . . . and you didn't buy her no frankfooter!

BILL *(Feels a bit smug about his male prowess)* Awww, come on, cut that out, baby. That's a little blonde, blue-eyed chick who used to pose for me. That ain't where it's at. This is a new day, the deal is goin' down different. This is the black moment, doll. Black, black, black is bee-yoo-tee-full. Got it? *Black is beautiful.*

TOMMY Then how come it is that I don't *feel* beautiful when you *talk* to me?!!

BILL That's your hang-up, not mine. You supposed to stretch forth your wings like Ethiopia, shake off them chains that been holdin' you down. Langston Hughes said let 'em see how beautiful you are. But you determined not to ever be beautiful. Okay, that's what makes you Tommy.

TOMMY Do you *have* a girl friend? And who is she?

BILL *(Now enjoying himself to the utmost)* Naw, naw, naw, doll. I *know* people, but none-a this "tie-you-up-and-I-own-you" jive. I ain't mistreatin' nobody and there's enough-a me to go around. That's another thing with our women, . . . they wanta *latch* on. Learn to play it by ear, roll with the punches, cut down on some-a this "got-you-to-the-grave" kinda relationship. Was today all right? Good, be glad, . . . take what's at hand because tomorrow never comes, it's always today. *(She begins to cry)* Awwww, I didn't mean it that way . . . I forgot your name. *(He brushes her tears away)* You act like I belong to you. You're jealous of a picture?

TOMMY That's how women are, always studyin' each other and wonderin' how they look up 'gainst the next person.

BILL *(A bit smug)* That's human nature. Whatcha call healthy competition.

TOMMY You think she's pretty?

BILL She was, perhaps still is. Long, silky hair. She could sit on her hair.

TOMMY *(With bitter arrogance)* Doesn't *everybody*?

BILL You got a head like a rock and gonna have the last word if it kills you. Baby, I bet you could knock out Muhammad Ali in the first round, then rare back and scream like Tarzan . . . "Now, I am the greatest!" *(He is very close to her and is amazed to feel a great sense of physical attraction)* What we arguin' bout? *(Looks her over as he looks away. He suddenly wants to put the conversation on a more intimate level. His eye is on the bed)* Maybe tomorrow would be a better time for paintin'. Wanna freshen up, take a bath, baby? Water's nice n' hot.

TOMMY *(Knows the sound and turns to check on the look. Notices him watching the bed. Starts weeping)* No, I don't! Nigger!

BILL   Was that nice? What the hell, let's paint the picture. Or are you gonna hold that back too?

TOMMY I'm posin'. Shall I take off the wig?

BILL   No, it's a part of your image, ain't it? You must have a reason for wearin' it.

(TOMMY snatches up her orange drink and sits in the model's chair)

TOMMY *(With defiance)* Yes, I wear it cause you and those like you go for long, silky hair, and this is the only way I can have some without burnin' my mother-grabbin' brains out. Got it? *(She accidentally knocks over container of orange drink into her lap)* Hell, I can't wear this. I'm soaked through. I'm not gonna catch no double pneumonia sittin' up here wringin' wet while you paint and holler at me.

BILL   Bitch!

TOMMY You must be talkin' bout your mama!

BILL   Shut up! Aw, shut-up! *(Phone rings. He finds an African throw-cloth and hands it to her)* Put this on. Relax, don't go way mad, and all the rest-a that jazz. Change, will you? I apologize. I'm sorry. *(He picks up phone)* Hello, survivor of a riot speaking. Who's calling? *(TOMMY retires behind the screen with the throw. During the conversation she undresses and wraps the throw around her. We see TOMMY and BILL, but they can't see each other)* Sure, told you not to worry. I'll be ready for the exhibit. If you don't dig it, don't show it. Not time for you to see it yet. Yeah, yeah, next week. You just make sure your exhibition room is big enough to hold the crowds that's gonna congregate to see this fine chick I got here. *(This perks* TOMMY's *ears up)* You ought see her. The finest black woman in the world . . . No, . . . the finest *any* woman in the world . . . This gorgeous satin chick is . . . is . . . black velvet moonlight . . . an ebony queen of the universe . . . (TOMMY *can hardly believe her ears)* One look at her and you go back to Spice Islands . . . She's Mother Africa. . . . You flip, double flip. She has come through everything that has been put on her . . . *(He unveils the gorgeous woman he has painted . . . "Wine In the Wilderness."* TOMMY *believes he is talking about her)* Regal . . . grand . . . magnificent, fantastic. . . . You would vote her the woman you'd most like to meet on a desert island, or around the corner from anywhere. She's here with me now . . . and I don't know if I want to show her to you or anybody else . . . I'm beginnin' to have this deep attachment . . . She sparkles, man, Harriet Tubman, Queen of the Nile . . . sweetheart, wife, mother, sister, friend. . . . The night . . . a black diamond . . . A dark, beautiful dream . . . A cloud with a silvery lining . . . Her wrath is a storm over the Bahamas. "Wine In The Wilderness" . . . The memory of Africa . . . The *now* of things . . . but best of all and most important . . . She's tomorrow . . . she's my tomorrow . . . (TOMMY *is dressed in the African wrap. She is suddenly awakened to the feeling of being loved and admired. She removes the wig and fluffs her hair. Her hair under the wig must not be an accurate, well-cut Afro . . . but should be rather attractive natural hair. She studies herself in a mirror. We see her taller, more relaxed and sure of herself. Perhaps braided hair will go well with Afro robe)* Aw, man, later. You don't believe in nothin'! *(He covers "Wine In The Wilderness." Is now in a glowing mood)* Baby, whenever you ready. *(She emerges from behind the screen. Dressed in the wrap, sans wig. He is astounded)* Baby, what. . . ? Where . . . where's the wig?

TOMMY I don't think I want to wear it, Bill.

BILL   That is very becoming . . . the drape thing.

TOMMY Thank you.

BILL I don't know what to say.

TOMMY It's time to paint. *(Steps up on the model stand and sits in the chair. She is now a queen, relaxed and smiling her appreciation for his past speech to the art dealer. Her feet are bare)*

BILL *(Mystified by the change in her. Tries to do a charcoal sketch)* It is quite late.

TOMMY Makes me no difference if it's all right with you.

BILL *(Wants to create the other image)* Could you put the wig back on?

TOMMY You don't really like wigs, do you?

BILL Well, no.

TOMMY Then let's have things the way you like.

BILL *(Has no answer for this. He makes a haphazard line or two as he tries to remember the other image)* Tell me something about yourself, . . . anything.

TOMMY *(Now on sure ground)* I was born in Baltimore, Maryland and raised here in Harlem. My favorite flower is "Four O'clocks," that's a bush flower. My wearin' flower, corsage flower, is pink roses. My mama raised me, mostly by herself, God rest the dead. Mama belonged to "The Eastern Star." Her father was a "Mason." If a man in the family is a "Mason" any woman related to him can be an "Eastern Star." My grandfather was a member of "The Prince Hall Lodge." I had a uncle who was an "Elk," . . . a member of "The Improved Benevolent Protective Order of Elks of the World": "The Henry Lincoln Johnson Lodge." You know, the white "Elks" are called "The Benevolent Protective Order of Elks" but the black "Elks" are called "The *Improved* Benevolent Protective Order of Elks of *the World*." That's because the black "Elks" got the copyright first but the white "Elks" took us to court about it to keep us from usin' the name. Over fifteen hundred black folk went to jail for wearin' the "Elk" emblem on their coat lapel. Years ago, . . . that's what you call history.

BILL I didn't know about that.

TOMMY Oh, it's understandable. Only way I heard 'bout John Brown was because the black "Elks" bought his farmhouse where he trained his men to attack the government.

BILL The black "Elks" bought the John Brown Farm? What did they do with it?

TOMMY They built a outdoor theater and put a perpetual light in his memory, . . . and they buildin' cottages there, one named for each state in the union and . . .

BILL How do you know about it?

TOMMY Well, our "Elks" helped my cousin go through school with a scholarship. She won a speaking contest and wrote a composition titled "Onward and Upward, O, My Race." That's how she won the scholarship. Coreen knows all that Elk history.

BILL *(Seeing her with new eyes)* Tell me some more about you, Tomorrow Marie. I bet you go to church.

TOMMY Not much as I used to. Early in life I pledged myself in the A.M.E. Zion Church.

BILL *(Studying her face, seeing her for the first time)* A.M.E.

TOMMY A.M.E. That's African Methodist Episcopal. We split off from the white Methodist Episcopal and started our own in the year Seventeen hundred and ninety six. We built our first buildin' in the year 1800. How 'bout that?

BILL That right?

TOMMY Oh, I'm just showin' off. I taught Sunday School for two years and you had to know the history of A.M.E. Zion . . . or else you couldn't teach. My great, great grandparents was slaves.

BILL   Guess everybody's was.

TOMMY   Mine was slaves in a place called Sweetwater Springs, Virginia. We tried to look it up one time but somebody at Church told us that Sweetwater Springs had become a part of Norfolk . . . so we didn't carry it any further . . . As it would be a expense to have a lawyer trace your people.

BILL   *(Throws charcoal pencil across room)*   No good! It won't work! I can't work anymore.

TOMMY   Take a rest. Tell me about you.

BILL   *(Sits on bed)*   Everybody in my family worked for the Post Office. They bought a home in Jamaica, Long Island. Everybody on that block bought an aluminum screen door with a duck on it, . . . or was it a swan? I guess that makes my favorite flower crab grass and hedges. I have a lot of bad dreams. *(TOMMY massages his temples and the back of his neck)* A dream like suffocating, dying of suffocation. The worst kinda dream. People are standing in a weird looking art gallery, they're looking and laughing at everything I've ever done. My work begins to fade off the canvas, right before my eyes. Everything I've ever done is laughed away.

TOMMY   Don't be so hard on yourself. If I was smart as you I'd wake up singin' every mornin'. *(There is the sound of thunder. He kisses her)* When it thunders that's the angels in heaven playin' with their hoops, rollin' their hoops and bicycle wheels in the rain. My Mama told me that.

BILL   I'm glad you're here. Black *is* beautiful, you're beautiful, A.M.E. Zion, Elks, pink roses, bush flower, . . . blooming out of the slavery of Sweetwater Springs, Virginia.

TOMMY   I'm gonna take a bath and let the riot and the hell of living go down the drain with the bath water.

BILL   Tommy, Tommy, Tomorrow Marie, let's save each other, let's be kind and good to each other while it rains and the angels roll those hoops and bicycle wheels. *(They embrace. The sound of rain)*

(Music in as lights come down. As lights fade down to darkness, music comes in louder. There is a flash of lightning. We see TOMMY *and* BILL *in each other's arms. It is very dark. Music up louder, then softer and down to very soft. Music is mixed with the sound of rain beating against the window. Music slowly fades as gray light of dawn shows at window. Lights go up gradually. The bed is rumpled and empty.* BILL *is in the bathroom.* TOMMY *is at the stove turning off the coffee pot. She sets table with cups and saucers, spoons.* TOMMY *'s hair is natural, she wears another throw [African design] draped around her. She sings and hums a snatch of a joyous spiritual)*

TOMMY   "Great day, Great day, the world's on fire, Great day . . ." *(Calling out to* BILL *who is in bath)* Honey, I found the coffee, and it's ready. Nothin' here to go with it but a cucumber and a Uneeda biscuit.

BILL   *(Offstage. Joyous yell from offstage)*   Tomorrow and tomorrow and tomorrow! Good mornin', Tomorrow!

TOMMY   *(More to herself than to* BILL*)*   "Tomorrow and tomorrow." That's Shakespeare. *(Calls to* BILL*)* You say that was Shakespeare?

BILL   *(Offstage)*   Right, baby, right!

TOMMY   I bet Shakespeare was black! You know how we love poetry. That's what give him away. I bet he was passin'. *(Laughs)*

BILL   *(Offstage)*   Just you wait, one hundred years from now all the honkys gonna claim our poets just like they stole our blues. They gonna try to steal Paul Laurence Dunbar and LeRoi and Margaret Walker.

TOMMY *(To herself)* God moves in a mysterious way, even in the middle of a riot. *(A knock on the door)* Great day, great day the world's on fire ... *(Opens the door. OLDTIMER enters. He is soaking wet. He does not recognize her right away)*

OLDTIMER 'Scuse me, I must be in the wrong place.

TOMMY *(Patting her hair)* This is me. Come on in, Edmond Lorenzo Matthews. I took off my hair-piece. This is me.

OLDTIMER *(Very distracted and worried)* Well, howdy-do and good mornin'. *(He has had a hard night of drinking and sleeplessness)* Where Billy-boy? It pourin' down some rain out there. *(Makes his way to the window)*

TOMMY What's the matter?

OLDTIMER *(Raises the window and starts pulling in the cord, the cord is weightless and he realizes there is nothing on the end of it)* No, no, it can't be. Where is it? It's gone! *(Looks out the window)*

TOMMY You gonna catch your death. You wringin' wet.

OLDTIMER Yall take my things in? It was a bag-a loot. A suit and some odds and ends. It was my loot. Yall took it in?

TOMMY No. *(Realizes his desperation. She calls to BILL through the closed bathroom door)* Did you take in any loot that was outside the window?

BILL *(Offstage)* No.

TOMMY He said "no."

OLDTIMER *(Yells out window)* Thieves, ... dirty thieves ... lotta good it'll do you ...

TOMMY *(Leads him to a chair, dries his head with a towel)* Get outta the wet things. You smell just like a whiskey still. Why don't you take care of yourself. *(Dries off his hands)*

OLDTIMER Drinkin' with the boys. Likker was everywhere all night long.

TOMMY You got to be better than this.

OLDTIMER Everything I ever put my hand and mind to do, it turn out wrong, ... Nothin' but mistakes ... When you don' know, you don' know. I don' know nothin'. I'm ignorant.

TOMMY Hush that talk ... You know lotsa things, everybody does. *(Helps him remove wet coat)*

OLDTIMER Thanks. How's the trip-tick?

TOMMY The what?

OLDTIMER *Trip-tick.* That's a paintin'.

TOMMY See there, you know more about art than I do. What's a trip-tick? Have some coffee and explain me a trip-tick.

OLDTIMER *(Proud of his knowledge)* Well, I tell you, ... a trip-tick is a paintin' that's in three parts ... but they all belong together to be looked at all at once. Now ... this is the first one ... a little innocent girl ... *(Unveils picture)*

TOMMY She's sweet.

OLDTIMER And this is "Wine In The Wilderness" ... The Queen of the Universe ... the finest chick in the world.

TOMMY *(Tommy is thoughtful as he unveils the second picture)* That's not me.

OLDTIMER No, you gonna be this here last one. The worst gal in town. A messed-up chick that—that—*(He unveils the third canvas and is face to face with the almost blank canvas, then realizes what he has said. He turns to see the stricken look on TOMMY's face)*

TOMMY The messed-up chick, *that's* why they brought me here, ain't it? That's why he wanted to paint me! Say it!

OLDTIMER No, I'm lyin', I didn't mean it. It's the society that messed her up. Awwwwww, Tommy, don't look that-a-way. It's art, ... it's only art ... He couldn't mean you, . . . it's art . . . *(The door opens.* CYNTHIA *and* SONNY-MAN *enter)*

SONNY-MAN   Anybody want a ride down . . . down . . . down . . . downtown? What's wrong? Excuse me . . . *(Starts back out)*

TOMMY   *(Blocking the exit to* CYNTHIA *and* SONNY-MAN *)* No, come on in. Stay with it . . . "Brother" . . . "Sister." Tell 'em what a trip-tick is, Oldtimer.

CYNTHIA *(Very ashamed)*   Oh, no.

TOMMY   You don't have to tell 'em. They already know. The messed-up chick! How come you didn't pose for that, my sister? The messed-up chick lost her home last night, . . . burnt out with no place to go. You and Sonny-Man gave me comfort, you cheered me up and took me in, . . . *took me in!*

CYNTHIA   Tommy, we didn't know you, we didn't mean . . .

TOMMY   It's all right! I was lost but now I'm found! Yeah, the blind can see! *(She dashes behind the screen and puts on her clothing, sweater, skirt etc.)*

OLDTIMER *(Goes to bathroom door)*   Billy, come out!

SONNY-MAN   Billy, step out here, please! *(*BILL *enters shirtless, wearing dungarees)* Oldtimer let it out 'bout the trip-tych.

BILL   The rest of you move on.

TOMMY *(Looking out from behind screen)*   No, don't go a step. You brought me here, see me out!

BILL   Tommy, let me explain it to you.

TOMMY *(Coming out from behind screen)*   I gotta check out my apartment, and my clothes and money. Cynthia, . . . I can't wait for anybody to open the door or look out for me and all that kinda crap you talk. A bunch-a liars!

BILL   Oldtimer, why you . . .

TOMMY   Leave him the hell alone. He ain' said nothin' that ain' so!

SONNY-MAN   Explain to the sister that some mistakes have been made.

BILL   Mistakes have been made, baby. The mistakes were yesterday, this is to-day . . .

TOMMY   Yeah, and I'm Tomorrow, remember? Trouble is I was Tommin' to you, to all of you, . . . "Oh, maybe they gon' like me." . . . I was your fool, thinkin' writers and painters know moren' me, that maybe a little bit of you would rub off on me.

CYNTHIA   We are wrong. I knew it yesterday. Tommy, I told you not to expect anything out of this . . . this arrangement.

BILL   This is a relationship, not an arrangement.

SONNY-MAN   Cynthia, I tell you all the time, keep outta other people's business. What the hell you got to do with who's gonna get what outta what? You and Oldtimer, yakkin' and yakkin'. *(To* OLDTIMER*)* Man, you mouth gonna kill you.

BILL   It's me and Tommy. Clear the room.

TOMMY   Better not. I'll kill him! The "black people" this and the "Afro-American" . . . that . . . You ain' got no use for none-a us. Oldtimer, you their fool too. 'Til I got here they didn't even know your damn name. There's something inside-a me that says I ain' suppose to let *nobody* play me cheap. Don't care how much they know! *(She sweeps some of the books to the floor)*

BILL   Don't you have any forgiveness in you? Would I be beggin' you if I didn't care? Can't you be generous enough . . .

TOMMY   Nigger, I been too damn generous with you, already. All-a these people know I wasn't down here all night posin' for no pitcher, nigger!

BILL   Cut that out, Tommy, and you not going anywhere!

TOMMY   You wanna bet? Nigger!

BILL   Okay, you called it, baby, I did act like a low, degraded person . . .

TOMMY *(Combing out her wig with her fingers while holding it)*   Didn't call you no low, degraded person. Nigger! *(To* CYNTHIA *who is handing her a comb)* "Do you have to wear a wig?" Yes! To soften the blow when yall go up side-a my head with a baseball bat. *(Going back to taunting* BILL *and ignoring* CYNTHIA'*s comb)* Nigger!

BILL   That's enough-a that. You right and you're wrong too.

TOMMY   Ain't a-one-a us you like that's alive and walkin' by you on the street . . . you don't like flesh and blood niggers.

BILL   Call me that, baby, but don't call yourself. That what you think of yourself?

TOMMY   If a black somebody is in a history book, or printed on a pitcher, or drawed on a paintin', . . . or if they're a statue, . . . dead, and outta the way, and can't talk back, then you dig 'em and full-a so much-a damn admiration and talk 'bout *"our"* history. But when you run into us livin' and breathin' ones, with the life's blood still pumpin' through us, . . . then you comin' on 'bout how we ain' never together. You hate us, that's what! *You hate black me!*

BILL *(Stung to the heart, confused and saddened by the half truth which applies to himself)* I never hated you, I never will, no matter what you or any of the rest of you do to *make* me hate you. I won't! Hell, woman, why do you say that! Why would I hate you?

TOMMY   Maybe I look too much like the mother that give birth to you. Like the Ma and Pa that worked in the post office to buy you a house and a screen door with a damn duck on it. And you so ungrateful you didn't even like it.

BILL   No, I didn't, baby. I don't like screen doors with ducks on 'em.

TOMMY   You didn't like who was livin' behind them screen doors. Phoney Nigger!

BILL   That's all! Damnit! don't go there no more!

TOMMY   Hit me, so I can tear this place down and scream bloody murder.

BILL *(Somewhere between laughter and tears)*   Looka here, baby, I'm willin' to say I'm wrong, even in fronta the room fulla people . . .

TOMMY *(Through clenched teeth)*   Nigger.

SONNY-MAN   The sister is upset.

TOMMY   And you stop callin' me "the" sister, . . . if you feelin' so brotherly why don't you say *"my"* sister? Ain't no we-ness in your talk. "The" Afro-American, "the" black man, there's no we-ness in you. Who do you think *you* are?

SONNY-MAN   I was talkin' in general er . . . *my* sister, 'bout the masses.

TOMMY   There he go again. "The" masses. Tryin' to make out like we pitiful and you got it made. You the masses your damn self and don't even know it. *(Another angry look at* BILL*)* Nigger.

BILL *(Pulls dictionary from shelf)*   Let's get this ignorant "nigger" talk squared away. You can stand some education.

TOMMY   You *treat* me like a nigger, that's what. I'd rather be called one than treated that way.

BILL *(Questions* TOMMY*)*   What is a nigger? *(Talks as he is trying to find word)* A nigger is a low, degraded person, *any* low degraded person. I learned that from my teacher in the fifth grade.

TOMMY   Fifth grade is a liar! Don't pull that dictionary crap on me.

BILL *(Pointing to the book)*   Webster's New World Dictionary of The American Language, College Edition.

TOMMY   I don't need to find out what no college white folks say nigger is.

BILL   I'm tellin' you it's a low, degraded person. Listen. *(Reads from the book)* Nigger, N-i-g-g-e-r, . . . A Negro . . . A member of any dark-skinned people . . . Damn. *(Amazed by dictionary description)*

SONNY-MAN   Brother Malcolm *said* that's what they meant, ... nigger is a Negro, Negro is a nigger.

BILL *(Slowly finishing his reading)*   A vulgar, offensive term of hostility and contempt. Well, so much for the fifth grade teacher.

SONNY-MAN   No, they do not call low, degraded white folks niggers. Come to think of it, did you ever hear whitey call Hitler a nigger? Now if some whitey digs us, ... the others might call him a nigger-*lover,* but they don't call him no nigger.

OLDTIMER   No, they don't.

TOMMY *(Near tears)*   When they say "nigger," just dry-long-so, they mean educated you and uneducated me. They hate you and call you "nigger," I called you "nigger" but I love you. *(There is dead silence in the room for a split second)*

SONNY-MAN *(Trying to establish peace)*   There you go. There you go.

CYNTHIA *(Cautioning* SONNY-MAN*)*   Now is not the time to talk, darlin'.

BILL   You love me? Tommy, that's the greatest compliment you could ...

TOMMY *(Sorry she said it)*   You must be runnin' a fever, nigger, I ain' said nothin' 'bout lovin' you.

BILL *(In a great mood)*   You did, yes, you did.

TOMMY   Well, you didn't say it to me.

BILL   Oh, Tommy, ...

TOMMY *(Cuts him off abruptly)*   And don't you dare say it now. I'm tellin' you, ... it ain't to be said now. *(Checks through her paper bag to see if she has everything. Starts to put on the wig, changes her mind, holds it to end of scene. Turns to the others in the room)* Oldtimer, ... my brothers and my sister.

OLDTIMER   I wish I was a thousand miles away, I'm so sorry. *(He sits at the foot of the model stand)*

TOMMY   I don't stay mad, it's here today and gone tomorrow. I'm sorry your feelin's got hurt, ... but when I'm hurt I turn and hurt back. Somewhere, in the middle of last night, I thought the old me was gone, ... lost forever, and gladly. But today was flippin' time, so back I flipped. Now it's "turn the other cheek" time. If I can go through life other-cheekin' the white folk, ... guess yall can be other-cheeked too. But I'm goin' back to the nitty-gritty crowd, where the talk is we-ness and us-ness. I hate to do it but I have to thank you 'cause I'm walkin' out with much more than I brought in. *(Goes over and looks at the queen in the "Wine In The Wilderness" painting)* Tomorrow-Marie had such a lovely yesterday. *(*BILL *takes her hand, she gently removes it from his grasp)* Bill, I don't have to wait for anybody's by-your-leave to be a "Wine In The Wilderness" woman. I can be it if I wanta, ... and I *am.* I am. I am. I'm not the one you made up and painted, the very pretty lady who can't talk back, ... but I'm "Wine In The Wilderness" ... alive and kickin', me ... Tomorrow-Marie, cussin' and fightin' and lookin' out for my damn self 'cause ain' nobody else 'round to do it, dontcha know. And, Cynthia, if my hair is straight, or if it's natural, or if I wear a wig, or take it off, ... that's all right; because wigs ... shoes ... hats ... bags ... and even this ... *(She picks up the African throw she wore a few moments before ... fingers it)* They're just what you call ... access ... *(Fishing for the word)* ... like what you wear with your Easter outfit ...

CYNTHIA   Accessories.

TOMMY   Thank you, my sister. Accessories. Somethin' you add on or take off. The real thing is takin' place on the inside ... that's where the action is. That's "Wine In The Wilderness," ... a woman that's a real one and a good one. And yall just better believe I'm it. *(She proceeds to the door)*

BILL Tommy. *(She turns. He takes the beautiful queen, "Wine In The Wilderness" from the easel)* She's not it at all, Tommy. This chick on the canvas, . . . nothin' but accessories, a dream I drummed up outta the junk room of my mind. *(Places the "queen" to one side)* You are and . . . *(Points to* OLDTIMER*)* . . . Edmund Lorenzo Matthews . . . the real beautiful people, . . . Cynthia . . .

CYNTHIA *(Bewildered and unbelieving)* Who? Me?

BILL Yeah, honey, you and Sonny-Man, don't know how beautiful you are. *(Indicates the other side of model stand)* Sit there.

SONNY-MAN *(Places cushions on the floor at the foot of the model stand)* Just sit here and be my beautiful self. *(To* CYNTHIA*)* Turn on, baby, we gonna get our picture took.

*(*CYNTHIA *smiles)*

BILL Now there's Oldtimer, the guy who was here before there were scholarships and grants and stuff like that, the guy they kept outta the schools, the man the factories wouldn't hire, the union wouldn't let him join . . .

SONNY-MAN Yeah, yeah, rap to me. Where you goin' with it, man? Rap on.

BILL I'm makin' a triptych.

SONNY-MAN Make it, man.

BILL *(Indicating* CYNTHIA *and* SONNY-MAN*)* On the other side, Young Man and Woman, workin' together to do our thing.

TOMMY *(Quietly)* I'm goin' now.

BILL But you belong up there in the center, "Wine In The Wilderness" . . . that's who you are. *(Moves the canvas of "the little girl" and places a sketch pad on the easel)* The nightmare, about all that I've done disappearing before my eyes. It was a good nightmare. I was painting in the dark, all head and no heart. I couldn't see until you came, baby. *(To* CYNTHIA, SONNY-MAN *and* OLDTIMER*)* Look at Tomorrow. She came through the biggest riot of all, . . . somethin' called "Slavery," and she's even comin' through the "now" scene, . . . folks laughin' at her, even her own folks laughin' at her. And look *how* . . . with her head high up like she's poppin' her fingers at the world. *(Takes up charcoal pencil and tears old page off sketch pad so he can make a fresh drawing)* Aw, let me put it down, Tommy. "Wine In The Wilderness," you gotta let me put it down so all the little boys and girls can look up and see you on the wall. And you know what they're gonna say? "Hey, don't she look like somebody we know?" *(*TOMMY *slowly returns and takes her seat on the stand.* TOMMY *is holding the wig in her lap. Her hands are very graceful looking against the texture of the wig)* And they'll be right, you're somebody they know . . . *(He is sketching hastily. There is a sound of thunder and the patter of rain)* Yeah, roll them hoops and bicycle wheels.

(Music in low. Music up higher as Bill continues to sketch)

CURTAIN

Wine in the Wilderness and the Elements of Drama

꒱ ꒰ ꒱

As far as we know, the first piece of criticism of drama was Aristotle's *Poetics*, written in the fourth century B.C. Extraordinarily, this essay, written over 2300 years ago, continues to influence the way we analyze drama, even though the drama most of us know is very different from the Greek tragedies and comedies Aristotle knew. The very idea of dividing drama up into its "elements" for analysis is Aristotle's; we continue to do this not only for drama but for fiction and poetry as well. Aristotle identified six elements of drama: plot, character, diction, thought, spectacle, and song. We can modernize this list a bit so that it fits kinds of drama other than Greek tragedy, and come up with these elements: subgenre, staging and stage metaphors, plot, character, language, and theme. Let us talk through these elements, drawing upon *Wine in the Wilderness* for illustration.

SUBGENRE. Subgenres traditionally have been more important in drama than in fiction and poetry. There is no equivalent in those other genres to the pervasiveness with which plays, from the beginning to very near the present, have been categorized as either tragedies or comedies. The definitions of both are classic problems in dramatic criticism. But tragedy has generally been defined as the story of a protagonist engaged in a morally significant struggle that ends in defeat or death, while comedy, through laughter, celebrates life and fertility. There are, of course, fiction subgenres (the maturation novel, the artist-novel), and poetic ones (the elegy, the ode), but audiences have never expected all novels and all poetry to fit into some subgenre in the way they have expected all (or nearly all) drama to do. (There have been other dramatic subgenres, too, such as history plays and romances, but these are insignificant compared to the power of the tragic and comic models.)

Some of the earlier plays in this anthology illustrate the subgenres of tragedy and comedy very well. *Medea* is clearly a tragedy; *Tartuffe* and *The Importance of Being Earnest* are clearly comedies. *The Tempest* is a little different; it is a dramatic romance. It is only in the last century that the majority of plays have not been either clearly comic or clearly tragic. Some playwrights, especially popular, commercial ones, still practice more or less straight comedy—Neil Simon, for instance (though many of his later plays have a more complex tone); tragedy has been a harder subgenre to cast in modern terms. Most serious plays since the last part of the nineteenth century have been neither comic nor tragic but a mixture of the two. Ibsen, Strindberg, and Chekhov, Pirandello, Brecht, and Beckett all wrote plays with both comic and tragic elements. There is no general agreement about what to call plays like this; "tragicomedy," "mixed genres," "realistic drama," have all been tried, but it is hard to find a single term that suits the wide range of subject matter and technique of the modern theater.

How would you describe the subgenre to which *Wine in the Wilderness* belongs? Obviously neither tragedy nor comedy, it belongs to a type with which we are all familiar: plays that are generally realistic in style, but which exercise a certain amount of artistic license to shape the material to make certain points. The term *expressive realism* has been used for plays of this sort, and it is a useful one; it could be applied to most serious modern plays for the stage, for film, and for television. Bill Jameson's studio, the people who come into it, and what they do there are reasonably convincing, but we would never mistake them for a "slice of life." This is not "Candid Camera" but an artistically constructed representation of life arranged to develop certain themes. Labels—whether "tragedy" and "comedy" or "expressive realism"—are not important. What is important is to recognize that in a play like *Wine in the Wilderness* it is never enough that the action be convincingly realistic; it is made more orderly, more patterned than life usually is, in order to make an artistic statement.

STAGING AND STAGE METAPHORS. "Staging" means the world that opens up to us when the curtain or the lights go up on a play. It consists of the setting but also the context of the setting, whatever is outside the walls of the setting. It also includes the kinds of things that go on onstage, not the detailed minutiae of stage movement but the kinds of stage pictures we are presented with.

When we are considering the staging of a play, we are dealing with *theatricalized* space. We theatricalize space, or people, or actions when we set them off for observation within a theatrical framework. Nothing on stage is merely itself. By being placed on stage, it becomes part of a field of meaning and invites interpretation. When we walk into a room in real life, we may or may not be justified in asking ourselves, "What does this room mean?" We are always justified in asking this question when we look at what's on stage (or on a movie or television screen, for that matter).

The staging of *Wine in the Wilderness* is very suggestive. Bill Jameson's studio-apartment in Harlem is described in detail:

> It used to be a three room apartment but the tenant has broken out walls and is half finished with a redecorating job. The place is now only partially reminiscent of its past tawdry days, plaster broken away and lathing exposed right next to a new brick-faced portion of wall.

Why is the apartment being remodeled? And why does the play take place when the job is only "half finished"? Notice that the play is about change and flux, about the building of a new African-American identity, especially in regard to gender issues. It would probably be overstating the case to call the room a "symbol" of cultural change—the mode is realistic rather than symbolic—but the half-remodeled room suggests meanings, tones, ideas, and moods in a way that a "real" room would not necessarily do.

If the set of *Wine in the Wilderness* says, "change," it also says two other things: "blackness" and "art." That same first stage direction says:

> The room is obviously *black* dominated, pieces of sculpture, wall hangings, paintings. . . . The room also reflects an interest in other darker peoples of the world . . . A Chinese incense-burner Buddha, an American Indian feathered war helmet, a Mexican serape, a Japanese fan, a West Indian travel poster.

Other details of the room tell us that it is an artist's studio as well as an apartment: an easel with an empty canvas on it, other canvases, the small raised platform for model posing, and even the general effect of being in "a beautiful, rather artistic state of disorder."

All these carefully worked out details could be regarded as being in the service of characterization; Bill is an artist who is in the midst of an unfinished project of exploring black identity through his art. But the room-as-sign transcends the individual character and becomes an arena where themes of blackness, gender, and art are going to be hammered out in the course of the play.

Staging, though, is not just a matter of setting, in the narrow sense of the word; it also involves the larger world that the play suggests. Outside Bill Jameson's studio lies Harlem, and Harlem is rioting. The first thing we hear is offstage voices from the street—"Offa the street! Into your homes! Clear the street!" and the first thing we see is Bill sitting on the floor, sketching, and flinching at each gunshot. This is a strong image with which to begin the play, and it suggests the crisis in racial affairs that the play is going to deal with in more abstract, theoretical terms. (It is interesting that the riot is never explained. The date of the play would suggest that it is part of the civil disturbances that followed the assassination of Martin Luther King, Jr., but the play never confirms that. Perhaps the suggestive power of the background riot is greater by never being tied down to particular events.)

Another kind of contextualization leads us not into the riots offstage in *Wine in the Wilderness* but to the play's *self-referentiality*, to the way it calls attention to itself as a play. This self-referentiality takes the common form of having the play contain as its subject a work of art. Notice that we have two works of art called "Wine in the Wilderness," not only Bill Jameson's unfinished triptych but the play in which it appears, and Alice Childress does not make the mistakes Bill makes. Her "wine in the wilderness" is not the dream African princess of Bill's painting, but the real woman Tommy, whom Bill eventually comes to recognize as the best image of black womanhood. And when, at the end of the play, Bill recognizes that all the other characters are instances of black identity and begins to paint them, we realize that this is what Alice Childress has been doing all through the play. *Wine in the Wilderness*, in other words, is a *metaplay*, a play about art, a play that takes its own status as a work of art as a metaphor for its subject.

If we take *Wine in the Wilderness*'s self-referentiality as a central metaphor, then obviously we are using "metaphor" in a slightly unusual sense. We think of metaphors as figures of speech, verbal, rhetorical flourishes. And yet the metaphor "Understanding black identity is like writing a play" is never articulated in the play, merely implied. It is, in other words, a nonverbal, theatrical metaphor, of the kind we should be on the lookout for in our further reading of drama.

What is true of a stage setting in the style of expressive realism—that it is a field of heightened meaning—is true also of other styles, even those of completely different theaters. The huge, bare, all-purpose amphitheaters where Greek tragedies were staged and the bare scaffolding that constituted the setting for Renaissance plays were equally meaningful and appropriate theatricalized spaces for the dramas staged there.

PLOT. Of his six elements of drama, Aristotle rather surprisingly declared that the most important is plot. We tend to think of character development and revelation as the most important goal of literature, including drama, and to think of plot, in serious literature, only as a way of revealing character. But for Aristotle plot was "the first principle, and, as it were, the soul of a tragedy." It is perhaps less important to retrace Aristotle's reasoning in reaching this conclusion about Greek tragedy than to consider the nature of plot in drama in general and to compare it to plot in fiction. Dramatic plots and fictional plots are really very similar, and most of what was said earlier in the book about plots in fiction holds true also for plots in drama: 1) they consist of a series of scenes and thus have a *scenic structure;* 2) these scenes are a selective way of telling an implied *story;* 3) plots generally follow the course of a *conflict* between value systems usually represented in some way by a *protagonist* and an *antagonist,* a course that moves from *exposition,* through *development* or *rising action* to *climax* and *denouement* or *falling action;* and 4) plots follow certain *ordering principles,* such as parallelism and symmetry, which give them unity and coherence.

The most obvious difference between plots in fiction and plots in drama is perhaps the different balance in them between what Aristotle called *mimesis* and *diagesis. Mimesis* and *diagesis* can be roughly defined as "action" and "commentary." In *mimetic* passages, the characters do something; in *diagetic* passages, either they or the narrator comment on, interpret, or explain the actions. We are less patient with diagesis in drama than in fiction, and we generally feel that unless a play translates its material into significant action it is insufficiently "dramatized." Fiction, on the other hand, with its often intrusive narrative voice, can tolerate less action and more diagetic commentary.

Wine in the Wilderness has a beautifully constructed plot. Look at the scenic structure, for instance. (The play is not divided into "scenes," in the strict sense, but we can take a scene to be a sequence among a certain grouping of characters.) The play has eight scenes:

1. Bill alone, sketching and talking on the telephone.
2. Bill and Oldtimer.
3. Bill, Oldtimer, Sonny-Man, Cynthia, and Tommy.
4. Cynthia and Tommy.
5. Bill, Oldtimer, Sonny-Man, Cynthia, and Tommy.
6. Bill and Tommy. (This scene contains the fade-out and fade-in representing the night passing.)
7. Tommy and Oldtimer.
8. Bill, Oldtimer, Sonny-Man, Cynthia, and Tommy.

Notice, from this outline, that this play, which turns around a painted triptych, is itself structured like a triptych. The central panel is the long central scene between Bill and Tommy, the first panel is what leads up to that scene, and the third panel is what follows it. There is nothing mechanical about this three-part structure—the characters' comings and goings are handled very naturally—but there is something very satisfying formally about the stage gradually emptying to leave Bill and Tommy alone and then, after the central scene, gradually filling up again. Notice, too, that the play opens with Bill alone on stage, sketching, and ends with him sketching, but this time with all the other characters posing in tableau for him. So the play, like Bill's paintings, is "framed" by these sketching scenes.

If we look at the plot structure of *Wine in the Wilderness* in terms of the development and resolution of a conflict, we find a structure that supplements and complements the tripartite structure. Obviously, Bill is the protagonist and his project is to use Tommy to complete his allegorical triptych of black womanhood, to consist of a painting of a little girl called "Black Girlhood," another of a fantasized African princess called "Wine in the Wilderness," and a third, as yet unpainted, of what Bill calls the "lost woman," the sort of woman, "ignorant, unfeminine, coarse, rude, vulgar," that represents what society has made of actual African-American women.

Tommy, earthy, tough, shrewd, and loving, unwittingly plays the antagonist to Bill's project—unwittingly because of course Bill does not tell her what he wants her to model and through a misunderstanding Tommy thinks she is to be the "Wine in the Wilderness" figure. The climactic confrontation comes when Old-timer clumsily reveals to Tommy that Bill used her to model not Wine in the Wilderness but "the worst gal in town." The confrontation results, though, not just in the triumph of Tommy and the defeat of Bill, but in the conversion of Bill to a wiser view of black womanhood. The conversion is from idealism to realism. The fantasy African princess that was "Wine in the Wilderness" is rejected: "This chick on the canvas, . . . nothin' but accessories, a dream I drummed up outta the junk room of my mind." The real Wine in the Wilderness is not only Tommy but Oldtimer, Sonny-Man, and Cynthia as well, all of whom take their places on the modelling stand at the end of the play.

CHARACTER. As in fiction, in drama there comes a point where plot and character practically merge, since the major way we come to know characters is to observe their actions, while their actions can hardly be understood except in terms of their personalities and motivations.

With dramatic characters, as with fictional ones, there is a double movement toward individuality and away from it toward representativeness. We like to have strong, sharply individualized characters and at the same time we like to feel that they "stand for" something larger than themselves. Or, as we put it in regard to fictional characters, we want to understand characters as individual, idiosyncratic people and at the same time see how they are parts of systems.

Interestingly enough, the tension between the generalizing tendency and the particularizing tendency in the way we understand people is a strong theme in *Wine in the Wilderness*. Bill, at the beginning of the play, generalizes and idealizes people, specifically women, to the point of stereotyping. "Wine in the Wilderness" in his painting is "cold but utter perfection, draped in startling colors of African material, very 'Vogue' looking," "Mother Africa, regal, black womanhood in her noblest form." By the end of the play, he has had this illusion shattered and realizes not only that the funny, tough, individualistic Tommy is the real "Wine in the Wilderness," but that his other friends are also representative figures in the panorama of black identity. Cynthia and Sonny-Man are "Young Man and Woman, workin' together to do our thing," while even the comic, drunken, thieving Oldtimer is a kind of personification of Black History:

> the guy who was here before there were scholarships and grants and stuff like that, the guy they kept outta the schools, the man the factories wouldn't hire, the union wouldn't let him join. . . .

We may regret that the lively, earthy characters of the play vanish at the end into these cold, allegorical figures; Tommy is a much more interesting character than "Wine in the Wilderness" is. But do they vanish? The ending may be a piece of comic irony. Bill says he has come to terms with reality, but he seems to be up to his own tricks, turning Tommy into Wine in the Wilderness and Sonny-Man and Cynthia into Young Man and Woman. The characters all belong to a system—they are all aspects of black identity—but paradoxically they can be part of an abstract system only so long as they preserve their individuality as well. (Of course, Tommy's double nature is suggested by her two names, the realistic "Tommy" and the metaphoric "Tomorrow.")

LANGUAGE. Aristotle said that a good tragedy should use language "embellished with every kind of artistic ornament." He was thinking, though, of Greek tragedies written in a highly artificial verse, which made no attempt to capture the rhythms of colloquial speech and which was punctuated periodically by choric odes which were chanted by a chorus and which were even more stylized than the formal dialogue.

The plays in this anthology use a wide variety of dramatic languages, from the formal verse of the English translation of *Medea* to the blank verse and prose of *The Tempest,* the comically rhymed couplets of Richard Wilbur's translation of Molière's *Tartuffe,* and the stylized banter of Wilde's *The Importance of Being Earnest.* But what of the modern, realistic, prose plays like *Wine in the Wilderness*? Is there any equivalent in them for Aristotle's "language embellished with every kind of artistic ornament"?

Even within *Wine in the Wilderness,* there is a considerable range of uses of language. Childress has the dramatist's knack of giving her characters different voices. Consider a passage like this one, for example:

OLDTIMER . . . Whatcha been doin!?
BILL I'm working on the third part of a triptych.
OLDTIMER A what tick?
BILL A triptych.
OLDTIMER Hot-damn, that call for another drink. Here's to the trip-tick. Down the hatch. What is one-a-those?
BILL It's three paintings that make one work . . . three paintings that make one subject.

Childress gets low comedy here out of the contrast between Bill's rather precise speech and Oldtimer's black street speech. The contrast in ways of talking is not always just a comic device, though. Look closely at Tommy's language, for instance. She is often very funny, but it is because she uses language wittily. We laugh with her rather than at her, as we tend to do with Oldtimer. The contrast between Bill's manner of speaking and hers reinforces the thematic conflict of the play.

Other dimensions of language are important in plays, too. Silence—the absence of language—is an important dramatic device, and studying the way the playwright uses pauses and silent action is often illuminating. Speed and tempo are important, too; actors and directors are careful to pace scenes carefully, varying the tempo as appropriate, and readers should be attentive to these considerations as well.

THEME. After a certain point in the analysis of a play (or a story or poem), the notion of literary "elements" becomes quite forced. To think of plot as an "element" seems to suggest that it can be put in or taken out of a play at will. But if you take out the plot of, say, *Wine in the Wilderness,* is anything left? Can the element of character be separated from that of plot? If you remove the plot and there is nothing for the characters to do, can it be said that there are any characters left? Obviously, the idea of a literary work being made up of separate "elements" is a critical fiction that must eventually be abandoned in favor of a more integrated reading.

If there is something odd about thinking of plot and character as elements, the same is even more true of theme, which we have defined as "the central idea of a literary work stated as a generalization about human experience." A central theme states the implications of every part of a literary work; if it is an "element" of a work, it is an element that sums up the implications of every other element. These complexities do not mean that the concept of theme is invalid, but merely that we must not fall into what we might call the cookbook fallacy of literary study, the notion that the elements of literature are like cooking ingredients and that literary works are the product of combining some plot, character, and diction, mixing well, and perhaps adding a dash of theme at the end.

Keeping these qualifications in mind, can we nevertheless experiment with some thematic statements for *Wine in the Wilderness?* In the course of analyzing various elements in the play, we have identified a number of topics the play touches on, including change, art, and ethnic identity. One other topic we have not yet touched on is gender. Is it significant that it is black womanhood that is problematic for Bill Jameson and not black manhood? Or, to put it another way, could the genders be inverted in this play without other major changes? Could Bill Jameson be a woman artist painting a triptych about black manhood and could Tommy be a man she seduces? The answer obviously is "no"; the play deals with specific issues that apply to black women and not to black men. Notice how sexist Bill Jameson's original conception of "Wine in the Wilderness" is. His plan for the second and third panels is an example of the stereotypes of Virgin and Whore which feminists have found deeply embedded in our culture. Bill either idealizes women ("Mother Africa, regal, black womanhood in her noblest form") or degrades them ("as far from my African queen as a woman can get and still be female"). What he cannot do, until he meets Tommy, is interact with a real, complex woman without putting her either on a pedestal or in the mud.

What is *Wine in the Wilderness* about? We might state the theme as "The real 'wine in the wilderness' is the black woman as she is, not as men imagine her to be." Or we might say, "Defining ethnic identity is like painting a picture or writing a play." Or we might try, "In a time of rapid change, African-Americans need to find a proud sense of their identity." Certainly none of these thematic statements is wrong; all express ideas found in the play. But they all seem either too broad or too narrow to capture the real content of the play. "A sense of ethnic identity should be based on reality, not on false idealizations," might come closer to capturing the theme of the play on the same level of generalization as the play itself.

From Reading to
Interpretation and
Criticism

༄༅ ༄༅

As with fiction and poetry, we have taken an "elements of literature" approach to drama, tracing the neo-Aristotelian elements of subgenre, staging and stage metaphors, plot, character, language, and theme through *Wine in the Wilderness*. With fiction and poetry, we suggested placing this analytical, part-by-part approach within a larger critical method based on a progression through three "registers" of reading. The same suggestion holds for drama. In the first stage, simply *reading,* we answer as fully as possible the question, "What does the play say?" This stage corresponds fairly closely to our analysis of the first five "elements of drama": subgenre, staging and stage metaphors, plot, character, and language.

At this point, we do not concern ourselves too much with large themes; instead, we try to describe the play as precisely as possible. We ask ourselves such questions as, "Does this play belong to a recognizable subgenre, such as tragedy, comedy, or metaplay?" "What is the dramatic world that the play creates through its staging: its sets, the implied world outside the sets, its people, its stage pictures?" "How is the plot structured?" "What is the central conflict?" "How is the conflict brought to a climax, and how is it resolved?" "What are the characters like and what sort of a system do they form?" "On what issues are they compared and contrasted?" "What sorts of stage languages are employed?"

With *interpretation,* we move from "What does the play say?" to "What does the play mean?" This corresponds closely to our consideration of the theme or themes of *Wine in the Wilderness,* our formulation of some of the ideas in the play, and our attempt to distinguish between central, organizing themes and secondary ones.

In the registers of both reading and interpretation, we try to stay as close as possible to the playwright's vision, as we understand it. We try to read empathetically, setting aside our own beliefs and ideas and trying to identify as closely as possible with the playwright's. When we move into the register of *criticism,* however, we try to place the play within a larger contextual framework than the playwright did. Here we ask ourselves not "What does the play say?" or "What

1013

does the play mean?" but "What is the larger historical and cultural context within which this play should be placed?"

There is no single, fixed context for a literary work, of course, and we cannot pretend to identify the "correct" background against which to read a novel or poem or play. So any "critical" remarks we might make will have to be, as usual, tentative and suggestive rather than authoritative and definitive. But we might consider placing the play against the broad background of the modern debate over the relation of art and revolution, and against the somewhat narrower one of the cultural history of African Americans in the 1960s.

One of the striking things about the action of the play is that it takes place in the middle of a riot. Bullets are whizzing past the apartment when the play begins, and Bill Jameson is sitting on the floor, sketching, well away from the windows and flinching every time he hears a gunshot. There is fear among the neighbors that the house is going to be burned down. This seems an odd beginning for a play that is going to turn around the issue of what sort of images should appear in a three-panel painting about black womanhood. Childress could easily have left out the riot; no plot point depends on it. By putting it in and furthermore featuring it so prominently at the beginning of the play, she seems to imply some relationship between racial rioting and artistic images of black womanhood.

There has been such a relationship in romantic and postromantic thought ever since Percy Bysshe Shelley wrote that poets are "the unacknowledged legislators of the world." Shelley seems to have meant (and he has been taken to have meant) that important social change begins with changes in the areas that poets deal with: ideas, emotions, the imagination. In other words, we cannot bring about social changes until we can first imagine them. Bill Jameson's spiritual ancestors include not only Shelley but also Matthew Arnold and those modern poets, painters, and composers who have believed that fundamental change first must be a change in the way we think. His descendants include Winton Marsalis, Spike Lee, and other contemporary artists who are attempting to represent black culture truthfully.

There is also a much more immediate cultural context for *Wine in the Wilderness:* the black culture movements of the 1960s. The civil rights movement that eventually outlawed segregation was accompanied by such movements as the Black Arts Movement, which sought to build racial pride through the pursuit of a "black aesthetic" and the encouragement of black achievement in the arts. (A "black aesthetic" is the belief that black culture should find its own artistic forms rather than employing ones rooted in white culture.) Significant figures in these movements were Amiri Baraka (Leroi Jones), Haki Madhubuti (Don L. Lee), and Gwendolyn Brooks, among others. (See their introductions in the poetry section of this book.) The gender theme of *Wine in the Wilderness* anticipates later criticism of the black cultural movements of the sixties as being too male-oriented. Childress's celebration of the real black woman (as opposed to sentimental idealizations) in the figure of Tommy anticipates later celebrations by such playwrights as Ntozake Shange and such novelists as Alice Walker and Toni Morrison.

There are a number of other "contexts" within which *Wine in the Wilderness* might be placed. One might be theatrical. What theater first produced the play? Were the theater's other offerings that season written by white playwrights or by black ones? In other words, was this play first presented within a framework of black drama, white drama, or racially mixed drama? What sorts of audiences attended the first production? Subsequent productions? Does the play seem to be written for a black audience, a white audience, or a mixed audience? Or the context might be aesthetic. What is the relation of *Wine in the Wilderness* to a black aesthetic? Is Childress using a white, Western theatrical form for a black subject, or is there something innovative in the play's form?

Obviously, none of these critical questions could be answered solely on the basis of a reading of *Wine in the Wilderness*. All would require some research and collateral reading. A simple starting point might simply be to ask, "What was happening in the United States in 1969?" Thumbing through news magazines from 1969, not only for public movements such as the Vietnam protest movement but also for information about gender roles, popular music, and other such cultural phenomena, can help bring a play like *Wine in the Wilderness* into sharper focus. And this is the purpose of the reading register we call *criticism:* to return the literary work, which may have been read in isolation, back to its cultural contexts, whether historical, philosophical, political, or aesthetic.

Writing About Drama

ℨℛ ℛℨ

For the most part, writing about drama is like writing about fiction or poetry or anything else. It requires careful, thoughtful work at all three stages of writing: prewriting, writing, and revision. The main difference between writing about fiction or poetry and writing about drama is the challenge of reading and interpreting plays *as drama*. It is possible to study a play as if it were just a rather eccentrically printed short story all in dialogue. But to do so is to ignore the play's distinctive qualities and to limit yourself unnecessarily in what you can say. Let us think through the process of writing an essay on *Wine in the Wilderness*, laying particular stress on the play as drama.

PREWRITING. In writing a critical essay on literature, the more time and thought that go into the prewriting stage, the easier the rest of the process is going to be and the better the final result is likely to be. In earlier sections on writing about fiction and poetry, it was suggested that the best prewriting tool was a pencil—for marginal annotations, for notes, and for outlines of all sorts, from associational "web" outlines to final plans for the paper's organization. All this is also true of getting ready to write a paper on drama. But in addition, the prewriting stage in writing about drama should include detailed consideration of the play in performance. This involves imagining what the play would look like on the stage, at least at key moments. Pencil sketches of the floor plan and the stage picture at important points might be enough to help you visualize the play (especially if you have had some stage experience). A simple model of the stage, with a floor plan drawn on a large sheet of paper and with chess pieces representing the characters, might be a help in thinking out the staging.

Look at the first stage direction in *Wine in the Wilderness*, which describes the set. It seems remarkably detailed. But notice how much freedom Childress has given the director and designer. We are told that there are shouts and gunshots in the street and that Bill stays away from the windows. But where are the windows? Is it a corner apartment, with windows in the back wall and one side wall? Are all the windows in the back wall, as if there were other apartments on each side? A little later, an "airshaft window" is mentioned; where is it? Where is the door to the apartment? The door to the kitchen? To the bathroom? What time of day is it? Again, we are not told, but it seems likely that it is nighttime. Rioting and looting are more likely to take place under cover of night, and Sonny-Man and Cynthia call from a bar. If it is night and dark outside the windows, are there flashes of light or reflections of flames from the burning buildings? How is the apartment itself lighted?

In the middle of the play the lights go down briefly to indicate the passing of the night, and while they are down we see lightning outside the windows. When the lights come up again, it is the "gray light of dawn." Is this passage from darkness into light, from night into dawn, symbolic at all? If it is not as written, would it be justifiable to try to make it significant in production?

The key elements in the room are the bed, with a screen at its foot for privacy, and the raised platform on which the model is to pose. Again, we are not told where these should be placed in the room. Where would you place them? A minimum consideration is that they not be in the way, but ideally they should be placed in such a way as to make possible significant arrangements of the actors. Should the platform be upstage (away from the audience) with a special light on it, so that when people are on it they look as if they were already a picture? Should the easel be placed so the audience can see what Bill is sketching? Why or why not?

The point of all these questions (and many, many more) is not to provide material directly for your paper; a paper about where the bed is placed in *Wine in the Wilderness* would be tedious. The point is to help you think concretely about the play as a text for performance. Once you pin yourself down on whether it's dark outside or not, you can decide whether you want to write a paper on "The Significance of Light in *Wine in the Wilderness*." Once you decide where the bed with its concealing screen and the platform go, you might see the possibility of a paper on "Looking and Being Looked at in *Wine in the Wilderness*." Both these topics (and many more) grow out of a full awareness of the performance dimensions of a play text.

Working out performance possibilities of a play will probably involve reading it at least three times, once quickly to get the overall plot and characters, another time more slowly to visualize performance and working out specifically the playwright's instructions, even when they are vague, and once more fairly quickly with your own staging in mind to check whether it works or not or needs any improvement. Deciding on a topic and working it up to the point of beginning writing might take two or three more readings, as you refine the topic, develop it into a thesis sentence, and gather details to support your argument.

Of course performance possibilities are not the only source of ideas for papers; thinking them out helps you get a feel for the play. But you may decide to write about one of the elements of drama as it appears in *Wine in the Wilderness* ("Setting as Metaphor in *Wine in the Wilderness*," "Black English and the Language of *Wine in the Wilderness*," "Painting as Metaphor in *Wine in the Wilderness*") or about some aspects of the play's cultural context ("*Wine in the Wilderness* and the Black Aesthetic," "Gender Roles in *Wine in the Wilderness*") or about a key scene ("The Scene Between Bill and Tommy in *Wine in the Wilderness*," "The Last Scene in *Wine in the Wilderness*"). Generating good paper topics is not easy, but there are methodical ways of turning them up. If you can think of several possibilities and can select the one that seems most promising, you have a much better chance of producing a successful paper.

WRITING. If you do your prewriting thoroughly, writing the first draft of the paper should go fairly quickly. People differ greatly in the fluency and speed with which they write. Some people can dash off a first draft as quickly as they can get the words on paper, while others work much more slowly, considering several versions of each sentence before selecting one as the best. But relatively speaking, if you find writing the first draft unusually slow and difficult, you might take that as a sign of some flaw in the plan. If it is hard to articulate and explain the thesis, it may be because the thesis itself is vague and needs sharpening up. If the transitions are difficult between one section and the next, it may be because they're out of logical sequence. If the sections of the first draft are seriously out of balance, with one section much longer or much shorter than presumably parallel sections, you should reconsider whether the points are really parallel.

One sort of problem may be presented by the length of the average play. A full-length play is considerably longer than either a lyric poem or a short story, and you may find it difficult to decide how to represent it in your paper. (Writing about a novel, of course, presents an even greater challenge.) You may feel that one or two scenes are all that you can deal with in a short paper and yet feel that that is not enough to represent the whole play. The key to this is probably to avoid overweighting your paper with either large generalizations about the entire play or specific references to particular scenes, and instead move back and forth between the two kinds of material. Include some generalizations about the play as a whole and then support them with close analysis of selected scenes. (Except in special circumstances, the assumption in most literature classes is that you are writing for an audience that has read the work you are writing about and therefore you need not summarize it.)

Writing a first draft is a way of testing your ideas and your plan for presenting them. You should not expect the first draft to be the final one. If it exposes the strengths and weaknesses of your argument and gives you a text to develop, it has done its work.

REVISION. The main challenge in revision is not making changes but deciding what changes to make. Once we have sweated out a first draft, most of us are so close to the subject that we have trouble thinking of alternatives to the choices we have made. We need to recover our objectivity. There are several ways to do this. One is simply letting time pass. Even if you only put the first draft away overnight, the time will move you away from the text enough so that you can see alternatives you were not able to see when you just finished the draft. Another way to get a fresh point of view is to include a fresh person in the process. Get a friend to read the paper and react to it. Or, better yet, read the paper aloud to a friend. Often the presence of a real audience instead of a hypothetical one will reveal passages that are poorly explained. Even if the friend doesn't offer any criticism, seeing the paper through his or her eyes often gives us the needed distance. (Hint: if a friend is not available, read the paper to your cat. Anything to escape the solitude of your own skull.)

Revisions usually go quickly once you have decided what changes to make. Sometimes revision requires that you return to the play for more evidence to support your points or to look for contrary evidence that might make you revise your points. But usually revision involves sharpening the presentation of an argument, not altering its basic content. The last step in revision, of course, is making the final draft, the one you are going to submit, mechanically impeccable, with the accuracy of all quotations checked, the spelling of all doubtful words confirmed, and the form of the paper absolutely perfect. A clean, accurate manuscript sends a message to the reader that, since you are careful in small things, you can be trusted on the big issues as well.

Euripides and the Greek Theater

Drama, more than poetry or fiction, is dependent upon social institutions; people are not going to write plays unless there is a theater to perform them. A suitable theater to encourage great writing has existed only three times in Western history: in the Greece of the fifth century B.C.; in Western Europe in the Renaissance, from about 1575 to 1700; and from the late nineteenth century to the present.

Euripides was the third of the three great tragedians of Periclean Athens. The lives of Aeschylus, Sophocles, and Euripides overlapped. Aeschylus was born in about 525 B.C.; both Sophocles and Euripides died in 406 B.C. So the lives of the great playwrights covered only a little over a hundred years, and they were active in the theater for a shorter time.

The Greek theater underwent rapid development during the comparatively brief time it flourished. It had originated in Greek religion. Dionysus, god of wine, fertility, and the irrational, was worshipped through chanted choral poems called *dithyrambs,* performed on circular stone platforms used to thresh grain in villages throughout Greece. Dithyramb became drama when the celebrants gradually stopped singing *about* Dionysus and began to impersonate him. (The first to do so was said to have been named Thespis; hence the name "thespians" for actors.)

By the time Aeschylus began writing, in about the third decade of the fifth century, fully developed plays, not all on the subject of Dionysus, were being written and produced in specially built theaters during seasonal festivals. Greek theaters preserved some of the features of their humble origins as village threshing platforms. Their central acting area was the *orchestra,* a round stone platform built at the bottom of a hillside that could form a natural amphitheater. Behind the orchestra was a building, called the *scene building,* which not only provided a background to the action but also provided doors for entrances and exists, dressing rooms, and storerooms for costumes and props. (See diagram.)

Greek plays were performed by a handful of actors and a chorus. Aristotle, who provides much of the information we have about the Greek theater, said that the chorus numbered fifty in Aeschylus's time, but that Sophocles reduced it to twelve and Euripides raised it again to fifteen. The earliest plays (of which none survives) apparently used only one actor and the chorus. By Aeschylus's time, two actors were used, and Sophocles introduced a third actor (which Aeschylus, too, used in his later plays). Of course, this does not mean that there could be only two or three characters. Each actor played several parts. It does mean, though, that no more than three characters could ever be on stage at the same time (unless one was a nonspeaking role).

Some Greek theaters were enormous; the Theater of Dionysus in Athens seated about 25,000 people; so productions of Greek tragedies were more like spectacular outdoor pageants than intimate modern plays. Actors wore elaborate masks, carved to communicate at a distance what sort of character they were playing. Performances were accompanied by instrumental music, and the chorus danced as well as chanted during the choral sections of the plays.

The structure of the Greek theater is closely related to the vision of life held by the Greek playwrights. Most Greek plays take place "before the palace" because of the difficulty in altering the appearance of the orchestra and the scene building. And so Greek plays deal overwhelmingly with public life. There are no real love scenes in Greek tragedies and few private, domestic scenes, but there are many public ceremonies and rituals—audiences with kings, official homecomings,

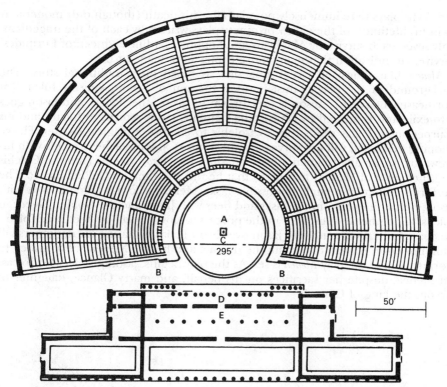

Plan of the Theater of Dionysus at Athens. A. Orchestra B. Chorus Entrance C. Altar to Dionysus D. Skene.

royal proclamations, and the like. Often, individual passion and family strife are in the background of the tragic plots, but they remain in the background, off-stage. Greek tragedy takes place on the boundary between public and private life, where sometimes private guilt impinges upon public responsibility. It is life lived "before the palace."

The three great tragedians differed not just in their theatrical technique but in their views of life. Aeschylus was known to his contemporaries as the "poet of violence" because of his fondness for spectacular stage effects: Prometheus nailed to his rock, the Furies pursuing Orestes (which according to contemporary accounts made pregnant women in the audience miscarry). There was a strain of the epic in Aeschylus. His best plays are sweeping culture-histories (the *Oresteia*, the *Persians, Prometheus Bound*).

Aeschylus was interested in entire societies and their relation to the gods. Sophocles was a humanist more interested in the individual than in the group and more interested in the relationships among human beings than in their dealings with the gods. Aeschylus's vision is most fully expressed in the titanic trilogy the *Oresteia;* Sophocles' in his Theban plays, which were not written as a trilogy but were linked in subject and theme: *Oedipus the King, Oedipus at Colonus,* and *Antigone.*

Euripides (c. 480–406 B.C.), born forty-five years after Aeschylus and sixteen years after Sophocles, speaks with a voice different from either of theirs—ironic, skeptical, and disillusioned—a voice that many have found prophetically "modern.'' His plays were immensely popular after his death (though only moderately so in his lifetime); of the eighty or ninety plays written by each of the tragedians, only seven each survive by Aeschylus and Sophocles, while eighteen of Euripides' survive, an indication that many more copies were made of his.

Medea, like almost all Greek tragedies, is based on a traditional story. The background of the play is this: Jason is the son of Aeson, king of Iolcus (in northeastern Greece). Aeson is overthrown by his brother Pelias, and Jason goes into exile and is tutored by Chiron the Centaur. Jason returns to Iolcus, and his usurper-uncle Pelias sends him to Colchis to capture a magical Golden Fleece (hoping that Jason will not survive the adventure). Jason reaches Colchis with his crew, the Argonauts (named after their ship, the *Argo*). Aeetes (King of Colchis and the father of Medea) tells Jason that he will give him the Golden Fleece if he performs certain seemingly impossible tasks. Medea, who has fallen in love with Jason, helps him perform the tasks and flees with Jason and the Golden Fleece to Iolcus, killing her own brother in the process to slow pursuit by Aeetes. In Iolcus, Medea uses her magic to help Jason overthrow Pelias by having his daughters kill him. But Jason is unable to claim the throne, and he and Medea are banished to Corinth, where the play *Medea* is set. As the play begins, Jason has decided to cast off Medea, despite her sacrifices on his behalf, and marry Glauce, daughter of Creon, the king of Corinth.

MEDEA*

CHARACTERS

NURSE
TUTOR *to Medea's sons*
MEDEA
CHORUS *of Corinthian women*
CREON, *king of Corinth*

JASON
AEGEUS, *king of Athens*
MESSENGER
MEDEA'S TWO CHILDREN

SCENE: *Before* JASON'S *house in Corinth*

NURSE: If only they had never gone! If the Argo's hull
  Never had winged out through the grey-blue jaws of rock[1]
  And on towards Colchis! If that pine on Pelion's[2] slopes
  Had never felt the axe, and fallen, to put oars
  Into those heroes' hands, who went at Pelias' bidding
  To fetch the golden fleece! Then neither would Medea,
  My mistress, ever have set sail for the walled town
  Of Iolcus, mad with love for Jason; nor would she,
  When Pelias' daughters, at her instance, killed their father,
  Have come with Jason and her children to live here   10
  In Corinth; where, coming as an exile, she has earned
  The citizens' welcome; while to Jason she is all
  Obedience—and in marriage that's the saving thing,
  When a wife obediently accepts her husband's will.

  But now her world has turned to enmity, and wounds her
  Where her affection's deepest. Jason has betrayed
  His own sons, and my mistress, for a royal bed,
  For alliance with the king of Corinth. He has married
  Glauce, Creon's daughter. Poor Medea! Scorned and shamed,
  She raves, invoking every vow and solemn pledge   20
  That Jason made her, and calls the gods as witnesses
  What thanks she has received for her fidelity.
  She will not eat; she lies collapsed in agony,
  Dissolving the long hours in tears. Since first she heard
  Of Jason's wickedness, she has not raised her eyes,
  Or moved her cheek from the hard ground; and when her friends
  Reason with her, she might be a rock or wave of the sea,
  For all she hears—unless, maybe, she turns away
  Her lovely head, speaks to herself alone, and wails
  Aloud for her dear father, her own land and home,   30
  Which she betrayed and left, to come here with this man
  Who now spurns and insults her. Poor Medea! Now
  She learns through pain what blessings they enjoy who are not

---

* *Translated by Philip Vellacott.*
[1] The Symplegades, two mythical rocks at the strait of Bosporus, said to crush ships that sailed between them.
[2] A mountain in Thessaly.

Uprooted from their native land. She hates her sons:
To see them is no pleasure to her. I am afraid
Some dreadful purpose is forming in her mind. She is
A frightening woman; no one who makes an enemy
Of her will carry off an easy victory.

Here come the boys, back from their running. They've no thought
Of this cruel blow that's fallen on their mother. Well,   40
They're young; young heads and painful thoughts don't go together.

Enter the TUTOR *with* MEDEA'S TWO SONS.

TUTOR: Old nurse and servant of my mistress's house, tell me,
  What are you doing, standing out here by the door,
  All alone, talking to yourself, harping on trouble?
  Eh? What does Medea say to being left alone?
NURSE: Old friend, tutor of Jason's sons, an honest slave
  Suffers in her own heart the blow that strikes her mistress.
  It was too much, I couldn't bear it; I had to come
  Out here and tell my mistress's wrongs to earth and heaven.
TUTOR: Poor woman! Has she not stopped crying yet?   50
NURSE: Stopped crying?
  I envy you. Her grief's just born—not yet half-grown.
TUTOR: Poor fool—though she's my mistress and I shouldn't say it—
  She had better save her tears. She has not heard the worst.
NURSE: The worst? What now? Don't keep it from me. What has happened?
TUTOR: Why, nothing's happened. I'm sorry I said anything.
NURSE: Look—we're both slaves together: don't keep me in the dark.
  Is it so great a secret? I can hold my tongue.
TUTOR: I'd gone along to the benches where the old men play
  At dice, next to the holy fountain of Peirene;   60
  They thought I was not listening; and I heard one say
  That Creon king of Corinth means to send these boys
  Away from here—to banish them, and their mother too.
  Whether the story's true I don't know. I hope not.
NURSE: But surely Jason won't stand by and see his sons
  Banished, even if he has a quarrel with their mother?
TUTOR: Old love is ousted by new love. Jason's no friend
  To this house.
NURSE: Then we're lost, if we must add new trouble
  To old, before we're rid of what we had already.   70
TUTOR: But listen: it's no time to tell Medea this.
  Keep quiet, say nothing about it.
NURSE: Children, do you hear
  What sort of father Jason is to you? My curse
  On—No! No curse; he is my master. All the same,
  He is guilty: he has betrayed those near and dear to him.
TUTOR: What man's not guilty? It's taken you a long time to learn
  That everybody loves himself more than his neighbour.
  These boys are nothing to their father: he's in love.
NURSE: Run into the house, boys. Everything will be all right.   80

[*The* CHILDREN *move away a little.*]

You do your best to keep them by themselves, as long
As she's in this dark mood; don't let them go to her.
I've watched her watching them, her eye like a wild bull's.
There's something that she means to do; and I know this:
She'll not relax her rage till it has found its victim.
God grant she strike her enemies and not her friends!

MEDEA'*s voice is heard from inside the house.*

MEDEA: Oh, oh! What misery, what wretchedness!
  What shall I do? If only I were dead!
NURSE: There! You can hear; it is your mother
  Racking her heart, racking her anger.   90
  Quick, now, children, hurry indoors;
  And don't go within sight of her,
  Or anywhere near her; keep a safe distance.
  Her mood is cruel, her nature dangerous,
  Her will fierce and intractable.
  Come on, now, in with you both at once.

[*The* CHILDREN *go in, and the* TUTOR *follows.*]

The dark cloud of her lamentations
Is just beginning. Soon, I know,
It will burst aflame as her anger rises.
Deep in passion and unrelenting,   100
What will she do now, stung with insult?
MEDEA [*indoors*]: Do I not suffer? Am I not wronged? Should I not weep?
  Children, your mother is hated, and you are cursed:
  Death take you, with your father, and perish his whole house!
NURSE: Oh, the pity of it! Poor Medea!
  Your children—why, what have *they* to do
  With their father's wickedness? Why hate *them*?
  I am sick with fear for you, children, terror
  Of what may happen. The mind of a queen
  Is a thing to fear. A queen is used   110
  To giving commands, not obeying them;
  And her rage once roused is hard to appease.

To have learnt to live on the common level
Is better. No grand life for me,
Just peace and quiet as I grow old.
The middle way, neither great nor mean,
Is best by far, in name and practice.
To be rich and powerful brings no blessing;
Only more utterly
Is the prosperous house destroyed, when the gods are angry.   120

Enter the CHORUS *of Corinthian women.*

CHORUS:
> I heard her voice, I heard
> That unhappy woman from Colchis
> Still crying, not calm yet.
> Old Nurse, tell us about her.
> As I stood by the door I heard her
> Crying inside the palace.
> And my own heart suffers too
> When Jason's house is suffering;
> For that is where my loyalty lies.

NURSE: Jason's house? It no longer exists; all that is finished.   130
> Jason is a prisoner in a princess's bed;
> And Medea is in her room
> Melting her life away in tears;
> No word from any friend can give her comfort.

MEDEA [*still from indoors*]:
> Come, flame of the sky,
> Pierce through my head!
> What do I gain from living any longer?
> Oh, how I hate living! I want
> To end my life, leave it behind, and die.   140

CHORUS:
> O Zeus, and Earth, and Light,
> Do you hear the chanted prayer
> Of a wife in her anguish?

[*turning to the door and addressing* MEDEA]

> What madness is this? The bed you long for—
> Is it what others shrink from?
> Is it death you demand?
> Do not pray that prayer, Medea!
> If your husband is won to a new love—
> The thing is common; why let it anger you?
> Zeus will plead your cause.   150
> Check this passionate grief over your husband
> Which wastes you away.

MEDEA: Mighty Themis! Dread Artemis![3]
> Do you see how I am used—
> In spite of those great oaths I bound him with—
> By my accursed husband?—
> Oh, may I see Jason and his bride
> Ground to pieces in their shattered palace
> For the wrong they have dared to do to me, unprovoked!
> O my father, my city, you I deserted;   160
> My brother I shamefully murdered!

NURSE: Do you hear what my mistress is saying,
> Clamouring to Themis, hearer of prayer,
> And to Zeus, who is named guardian of men's oaths?

---

[3] Themis: goddess of justice. Artemis: virgin goddess and protectress of women and children.

It is no trifling matter
That can end a rage like hers.
CHORUS: I wish she would come out here and let us see her
  And talk to her; if she would listen
  Perhaps she would drop this fierce resentful spirit,
  This passionate indignation.   170
  As a friend I am anxious to do whatever I can.
  Go, nurse, persuade her to come out to us.
  Tell her we are all on her side.
  Hurry, before she does harm—to those in there;
  This passion of hers is an irresistible flood.
NURSE: I will. I fear I shall not persuade her;
  Still I am glad to do my best.
  Yet as soon as any of us servants
  Goes near to her, or tries to speak,
  She glares at us like a mad bull   180
  Or a lioness guarding her cubs.

[*The* NURSE *goes to the door, where she turns.*]

The men of old times had little sense;
If you called them fools you wouldn't be far wrong.
They invented songs, and all the sweetness of music,
To perform at feasts, banquets, and celebrations;
But no one thought of using
Songs and stringed instruments
To banish the bitterness and pain of life.
Sorrow is the real cause
Of deaths and disasters and families destroyed.   190
If music could cure sorrow it would be precious;
But after a good dinner why sing songs?
When people have fed full they're happy already.

The NURSE *goes in.*

CHORUS:
  I heard her sobbing and wailing,
  Shouting shrill, pitiful accusations
  Against her husband who has betrayed her.
  She invokes Themis, daughter of Zeus,
  Who witnessed those promises which drew her
  Across from Asia to Hellas, setting sail at night,
  Threading the salt strait,   200
  Key and barrier to the Pontic Sea.[4]

MEDEA *comes out. She is not shaken with weeping, but cool and self-possessed.*

MEDEA: Women of Corinth, I would not have you censure me,
  So I have come. Many, I know, are proud at heart,
  Indoors or out; but others are ill spoken of

---

[4] The Black Sea.

As supercilious, just because their ways are quiet.
There is no justice in the world's censorious eyes.
They will not wait to learn a man's true character;
Though no wrong has been done them, one look—and they hate.
Of course a stranger must conform; even a Greek
Should not annoy his fellows by crass stubbornness. 210
I accept my place; but this blow that has fallen on me
Was not to be expected. It has crushed my heart.
Life has no pleasure left, dear friends. I want to die.
Jason was my whole life; he knows that well. Now he
Has proved himself the most contemptible of men.

Surely, of all creatures that have life and will, we women
Are the most wretched. When, for an extravagant sum,
We have bought a husband,[5] we must then accept him as
Possessor of our body. This is to aggravate
Wrong with worse wrong. Then the great question: will the man 220
We get be bad or good? For women, divorce is not
Respectable; to repel the man, not possible.

Still more, a foreign woman, coming among new laws,
New customs, needs the skill of magic, to find out
What her home could not teach her, how to treat the man
Whose bed she shares. And if in this exacting toil
We are successful, and our husband does not struggle
Under the marriage yoke, our life is enviable.
Otherwise, death is better. If a man grows tired
Of the company at home, he can go out, and find 230
A cure for tediousness. We wives are forced to look
To one man only. And, they tell us, we at home
Live free from danger, they go out to battle: fools!
I'd rather stand three times in the front line than bear
One child.
      But the same arguments do not apply
To you and me. You have this city, your father's home,
The enjoyment of your life, and your friends' company.
I am alone; I have no city; now my husband
Insults me. I was taken as plunder from a land 240
At the earth's edge. I have no mother, brother, nor any
Of my own blood to turn to in this extremity.

So, I make one request. If I can find a way
To work revenge on Jason for his wrongs to me,
Say nothing. A woman's weak and timid in most matters;
The noise of war, the look of steel, makes her a coward.
But touch her right in marriage, and there's no bloodier spirit.
CHORUS: I'll do as you ask. To punish Jason will be just.
I do not wonder that you take such wrongs to heart.

[CREON *approaches*.]

---

[5] Medea is referring to the custom of dowries.

But look, Medea; I see Creon, King of Corinth; 250
He must have come to tell you of some new decision.
CREON: You there, Medea, scowling rage against your husband!
I order you out of Corinth; take your sons and go
Into exile. Waste no time; I'm here to see this order
Enforced. And I'm not going back into my palace
Until I've put you safe outside my boundaries.
MEDEA: Oh! this is the cruel end of my accursed life!
My enemies have spread full sail; no welcoming shore
Waits to receive and save me. Ill-treated as I am,
Creon, I ask: for what offence do you banish me? 260
CREON: I fear you. Why wrap up the truth? I fear that you
May do my daughter some irreparable harm.
A number of things contribute to my anxiety.
You're a clever woman, skilled in many evil arts;
You're barred from Jason's bed, and that enrages you.
I learn too from reports, that you have uttered threats
Of revenge on Jason and his bride and his bride's father.
I'll act first, then, in self-defence. I'd rather make you
My enemy now, than weaken, and later pay with tears.
MEDEA: My reputation, yet again! Many times, Creon, 270
It has been my curse and ruin. A man of any shrewdness
Should never have his children taught to use their brains
More than their fellows. What do you gain by being clever?
You neglect your own affairs; and all your fellow citizens
Hate you. Those who are fools will call you ignorant
And useless, when you offer them unfamiliar knowledge.
As for those thought intelligent, if people rank
You above *them*, that is a thing they will not stand.
I know this from experience: because I am clever,
They are jealous; while the rest dislike me. After all, 280
I am not so clever as all that.
               So you, Creon,
Are afraid—of what? Some harm that I might do to you?
Don't let *me* alarm you, Creon. I'm in no position—
A woman—to wrong a king. You have done me no wrong.
You've given your daughter to the man you chose. I hate
My husband—true; but you had every right to do
As you have done. So now I bear no grudge against
Your happiness: marry your daughter to him, and good luck
To you both. But let me live in Corinth. I will bear 290
My wrongs in silence, yielding to superior strength.
CREON: Your words are gentle; but my blood runs cold to think
What plots you may be nursing deep within your heart.
In fact, I trust you so much less now than before.
A woman of hot temper—and a man the same—
Is a less dangerous enemy than one quiet and clever.
So out you go, and quickly; no more arguing.
I've made my mind up; you're my enemy. No craft
Of yours will find a way of staying in my city.
MEDEA: I kneel to you, I beseech you by the young bride, your child. 300
CREON: You're wasting words; you'll never make me change my mind.

MEDEA: I beg you! Will you cast off pity, and banish me?
CREON: I will: I have more love for my family than for you.
MEDEA: My home, my country! How my thoughts turn to you now!
CREON: I love my country too—next only to my daughter.
MEDEA: Oh, what an evil power love has in people's lives!
CREON: That would depend on circumstances, I imagine.
MEDEA: Great Zeus, remember who caused all this suffering!
CREON: Go, you poor wretch, take all my troubles with you! Go!
MEDEA: I know what trouble is; I have no need of more.   310
CREON: In a moment you'll be thrown out neck and crop. Here, men!
MEDEA: No, no, not that! But, Creon, I have one thing to ask.
CREON: You seem inclined, Medea, to give me trouble still.
MEDEA: I'll go. [*She still clings to him.*] It was not *that* I begged.
CREON: Then why resist?
     Why will you not get out?
MEDEA: This one day let me stay,
     To settle some plan for my exile, make provision
     For my two sons, since their own father is not concerned
     To help them. Show some pity: you are a father too,   320
     You should feel kindly towards them. For myself, exile
     Is nothing. I weep for them; their fate is very hard.
CREON: I'm no tyrant by nature. My soft heart has often
     Betrayed me; and I know it's foolish of me now;
     Yet none the less, Medea, you shall have what you ask.
     But take this warning: if tomorrow's holy sun
     Finds you or them inside my boundaries, you die.
     That is my solemn word. Now stay here, if you must,
     This one day. You can hardly in one day accomplish
     What I am afraid of.   330

Exit CREON.

CHORUS:
     Medea, poor Medea!
     Your grief touches our hearts.
     A wanderer, where can you turn?
     To what welcoming house?
     To what protecting land?
     How wild with dread and danger
     Is the sea where the gods have set your course!

MEDEA: A bad predicament all round—yes, true enough;
     But don't imagine things will end as they are now.
     Trials are yet to come for this new-wedded pair;   340
     Nor shall those nearest to them get off easily.

     Do you think I would ever have fawned so on this man,
     Except to gain my purpose, carry out my schemes?
     Not one touch, not one word: yet he—oh, what a fool!
     By banishing me at once he could have thwarted me
     Utterly; instead, he allows me to remain one day.
     Today three of my enemies I shall strike dead:

Father and daughter; and *my* husband.
I have in mind so many paths of death for them,
I don't know which to choose. Should I set fire to the house,   350
And burn the bridal chamber? Or creep up to their bed
And drive a sharp knife through their guts? There is one fear:
If I am caught entering the house, or in the act,
I die, and the last laugh goes to my enemies.
The best is the direct way, which most suits my bent:
To kill by poison.
So—say they are dead: what city will receive me then?
What friend will guarantee my safety, offer land
And home as sanctuary? None. I'll wait a little.
If some strong tower of help appears, I'll carry out   360
This murder cunningly and quietly. But if Fate
Banishes me without resource, I will myself
Take sword in hand, harden my heart to the uttermost,
And kill them both, even if I am to die for it.

For, by Queen Hecate,[6] whom above all divinities
I venerate, my chosen accomplice, to whose presence
My central hearth is dedicated, no one of them
Shall hurt me and not suffer for it! Let me work:
In bitterness and pain they shall repent this marriage,
Repent their houses joined, repent my banishment.   370

Come! Lay your plan, Medea; scheme with all your skill.
On to the deadly moment that shall test your nerve!
You see now where you stand. Your father was a king,
His father was the Sun-god:[7] you must not invite
Laughter from Jason and his new allies, the tribe
Of Sisyphus.[8] You know what you must do. Besides—

[*She turns to the* CHORUS.]

We were born women—useless for honest purposes,
But in all kinds of evil skilled practitioners.
CHORUS: Streams of the sacred rivers flow uphill;
    Tradition, order, all things are reversed: 380
        Deceit is *men*'s device now,
        Men's oaths are gods' dishonour.
    Legend will now reverse our reputation;
    A time comes when the female sex is honoured;
        That old discordant slander
        Shall no more hold us subject.
    Male poets of past ages, with their ballads
    Of faithless women, shall go out of fashion;
        For Phoebus,[9] Prince of Music,
        Never bestowed the lyric inspiration   390

---

[6] Goddess of witchcraft.
[7] Medea's father, King Aeetes, was the son of the sun-god Helios.
[8] A legendary early king of Corinth.
[9] Apollo, god of music and poetry.

Through female understanding—
Or we'd find themes for poems,
We'd counter with our epics against man.
Oh, Time is old; and in his store of tales
    Men figure no less famous
    Or infamous than women.

So you, Medea, wild with love,
Set sail from your father's house,
Threading the Rocky Jaws of the eastern sea;
And here, living in a strange country,   400
Your marriage lost, your bed solitary,
You are driven beyond the borders,
An exile with no redress.
The grace of sworn oaths is gone;
Honour remains no more
In the wide Greek world, but is flown to the sky.
Where can you turn for shelter?
Your father's door is closed against you;
Another is now mistress of your husband's bed;
A new queen rules in your house.   410

Enter JASON

JASON: I have often noticed—this is not the first occasion—
    What fatal results follow from ungoverned rage.
    You could have stayed in Corinth, still lived in this house,
    If you had quietly accepted the decisions
    Of those in power. Instead, you talked like a fool; and now
    You are banished. Well, your angry words don't upset *me*;
    Go on as long as you like reciting Jason's crimes.
    But after your abuse of the King and the princess
    Think yourself lucky to be let off with banishment.
    I have tried all the time to calm them down; but you   420
    Would not give up your ridiculous tirades against
    The royal family. So, you're banished. However, I
    Will not desert a friend. I have carefully considered
    Your problem, and come now, in spite of everything,
    To see that you and the children are not sent away
    With an empty purse, or unprovided. Exile brings
    With it a train of difficulties. You no doubt
    Hate me: but I could never bear ill-will to you.
MEDEA: You filthy coward!—if I knew any worse name
    For such unmanliness I'd use it—so, you've come!   430
    You, my worst enemy, come to me! Oh, it's not courage,
    This looking friends in the face after betraying them.
    It is not even audacity; it's a disease,
    The worst a man can have, pure shamelessness. However,
    It is as well you came; to say what I have to say
    Will ease my heart; to hear it said will make you wince.

I will begin at the beginning. When you were sent

To master the fire-breathing bulls, yoke them, and sow
The deadly furrow, then I saved your life; and that
Every Greek who sailed with you in the Argo knows.   440
The serpent that kept watch over the Golden Fleece,
Coiled round it fold on fold, unsleeping—it was I
Who killed it, and so lit the torch of your success.[10]
I willingly deceived my father; left my home;
With you I came to Iolcus by Mount Pelion,
Showing much love and little wisdom. There I put
King Pelias to the most horrible of deaths[11]
By his own daughters' hands, and ruined his whole house.
And in return for this you have the wickedness
To turn me out, to get yourself another wife,   450
Even after I had borne you sons! If you had still
Been childless I could have pardoned you for hankering
After this new marriage. But respect for oaths has gone
To the wind. Do you, I wonder, think that the old gods
No longer rule? Or that new laws are now in force?
You must know you are guilty of perjury to me.

My poor right hand, which you so often clasped! My knees
Which you then clung to! How we are besmirched and mocked
By this man's broken vows, and all our hopes deceived!

Come, I'll ask your advice as if you were a friend.   460
Not that I hope for any help from you; but still,
I'll ask you, and expose your infamy. Where now
Can I turn? Back to my country and my father's house,
Which I betrayed to come with you? Or to Iolcus,
To Pelias's wretched daughters? What a welcome they
Would offer me, who killed their father! Thus it stands:
My friends at home now hate me; and in helping you
I have earned the enmity of those I had no right
To hurt. For my reward, you have made me the envy
Of Hellene women everywhere! A marvellous   470
Husband I have, and faithful too, in the name of pity;
When I'm banished, thrown out of the country without a friend,
Alone with my forlorn waifs. Yes, a shining shame
It will be to you, the new-made bridegroom, that your own sons,
And I who saved your life, are begging beside the road!

O Zeus! Why have you given us clear signs to tell
True gold from counterfeit; but when we need to know
Bad *men* from good, the flesh bears no revealing mark?
CHORUS: The fiercest anger of all, the most incurable,
Is that which rages in the place of dearest love.   480
JASON: I have to show myself a clever speaker, it seems.
This hurricane of recrimination and abuse
Calls for good seamanship: I'll furl all but an inch
Of sail, and ride it out. To begin with, since you build

[10] Medea lists the tasks she helped Jason to accomplish to win the Golden Fleece.
[11] Medea told Pelias' daughter that they could restore his youth by boiling him in a cauldron.

To such a height your services to me, I hold
That credit for my successful voyage was solely due
To Aphrodite,[12] no one else divine or human.
I admit, you have intelligence; but, to recount
How helpless passion drove you then to save my life
Would be invidious; and I will not stress the point.   490
Your services, so far as they went, were well enough;
But in return for saving me you got far more
Than you gave. Allow me, in the first place, to point out
That you left a barbarous land to become a resident
Of Hellas;[13] here you have known justice; you have lived
In a society where force yields place to law.
Moreover, here your gifts are widely recognized,
You are famous; if you still lived at the ends of the earth
Your name would never be spoken. Personally, unless
Life brings me fame, I long neither for hoards of golds,   500
Nor for a voice sweeter than Orpheus![14]—Well, *you* began
The argument about my voyage; and that's my answer.

As for your scurrilous taunts against my marriage with
The royal family, I shall show you that my action
Was wise, not swayed by passion, and directed towards
Your interests and my children's.—No, keep quiet! When I
Came here from Iolcus as a stateless exile, dogged
And thwarted by misfortunes—why, what luckier chance
Could I have met, than marriage with the King's daughter?
It was not, as you resentfully assume, that I   510
Found your attractions wearisome, and was smitten with
Desire for a new wife; nor did I specially want
To raise a numerous family—the sons we have
Are enough, I'm satisfied; but I want to ensure
First—and the most important—that we should live well
And not be poor; I know how a poor man is shunned
By all his friends. Next, that I could bring up my sons
In a manner worthy of my descent; have other sons,
Perhaps, as brothers to your children; give them all
An equal place, and so build up a closely-knit   520
And prosperous family. *You* need no more children, do you?
While *I* thought it worth while to ensure advantages
For those I have, by means of those I hope to have.

Was such a plan, then, wicked? Even you would approve
If you could govern your sex-jealousy. But you women
Have reached a state where, if all's well with your sex-life,
You've everything you wish for; but when *that* goes wrong,
At once all that is best and noblest turns to gall.
If only children could be got some other way,

[12] Goddess of love.
[13] Greece.
[14] A legendary harpist who sang so sweetly he could enchant nature. He was one of the Argonauts.

Without the female sex! If women didn't exist, 530
Human life would be rid of all its miseries.
CHORUS: Jason, you have set your case forth very plausibly.
But to my mind—though you may be surprised at this—
You are acting wrongly in thus abandoning your wife.
MEDEA: No doubt I differ from many people in many ways.
To me, a wicked man who is also eloquent
Seems the most guilty of them all. He'll cut your throat
As bold as brass, because he knows he can dress up murder
In handsome words. He's not so clever after all.
You dare outface me now with glib high-mindedness! 540
One word will throw you: if you were honest, you ought first
To have won me over, not got married behind my back.
JASON: No doubt, if I had mentioned it, you would have proved
Most helpful. Why, even now you will not bring yourself
To calm this raging temper.
MEDEA: That was not the point;
But you're an ageing man, and an Asiatic wife
Was no longer respectable.
JASON: Understand this:
It's not for the sake of any woman that I have made 550
This royal marriage, but, as I've already said,
To ensure your future, and to give my children brothers
Of royal blood, and build security for us all.
MEDEA: I loathe your prosperous future; I'll have none of it,
Nor none of your security—it galls my heart.
JASON: You know—you'll change your mind and be more sensible.
You'll soon stop thinking good is bad, and striking these
Pathetic poses when in fact you're fortunate.
MEDEA: Go on, insult me: you have a roof over your head.
I am alone, an exile. 560
JASON: It was your own choice.
Blame no one but yourself.
MEDEA: *My* choice? What did I do?
Did I make you my wife and then abandon you?
JASON: You called down wicked curses on the King and his house.
MEDEA: I did. On your house too Fate sends me as a curse.
JASON: I'll not pursue this further. If there's anything else
I can provide to meet the children's needs or yours,
Tell me; I'll gladly give whatever you want, or send
Letters of introduction, if you like, to friends 570
Who will help you.—Listen: to refuse such help is mad.
You've everything to gain if you give up this rage.
MEDEA: Nothing would induce me to have dealings with your friends,
Nor to take any gift of yours; so offer none.
A lying traitor's gifts carry no luck.
JASON: Very well.
I call the gods to witness that I have done my best
To help you and the children. You make no response
To kindness; friendly overtures you obstinately
Reject. So much the worse for you. 580

MEDEA: Go! You have spent
  Too long out here. You are consumed with craving for
  Your newly-won bride. Go, enjoy her!

[*Exit* JASON.]

                                        It may be—
  And God uphold my words—that this your marriage-day
  Will end with marriage lost, loathing and horror left.
CHORUS:
        Visitations of love that come
        Raging and violent on a man
        Bring him neither good repute nor goodness.
        But if Aphrodite descends in gentleness   590
        No other goddess brings such delight.
        Never, Queen Aphrodite,
        Loose against me from your golden bow,
        Dipped in sweetness of desire,
        Your inescapable arrow!

        Let Innocence, the gods' loveliest gift,
        Choose me for her own;
        Never may the dread Cyprian[15]
        Craze my heart to leave old love for new,
        Sending to assault me   600
        Angry disputes and feuds unending;
        But let her judge shrewdly the loves of women
        And respect the bed where no war rages.

        O my country, my home!
        May the gods save me from becoming
        A stateless refugee
        Dragging out an intolerable life
        In desperate helplessness!
        That is the most pitiful of all griefs;
        Death is better. Should such a day come to me   610
        I pray for death first.
        Of all pains and hardships none is worse
        Than to be deprived of your native land.
        This is no mere reflection derived from hearsay;
        It is something we have seen.
        You, Medea, have suffered the most shattering of blows;
        Yet neither the city of Corinth
        Nor any friend has taken pity on you.
        May dishonour and ruin fall on the man
        Who, having unlocked the secrets   620
        Of a friend's frank heart, can then disown him!
        He shall be no friend of mine.

Enter AEGEUS.[16]

---

[15] Aphrodite, goddess of love. She first appeared in Cyprus.
[16] Father of Theseus, the great mythic ruler of Athens.

AEGEUS: All happiness to you, Medea! Between old friends
  There is no better greeting.
MEDEA: All happiness to you,
  Aegeus, son of Pandion the wise! Where have you come from?
AEGEUS: From Delphi, from the ancient oracle of Apollo.
MEDEA: The centre of the earth,[17] the home of prophecy:
  Why did you go?
AEGEUS: To ask for children; that my seed   630
  May become fertile.
MEDEA: Why, have you lived so many years
  Childless?
AEGEUS: Childless I am; so some fate has ordained.
MEDEA: You have a wife, or not?
AEGEUS: I am married.
MEDEA: And what answer
  Did Phoebus give you about children?
AEGEUS: His answer was
  Too subtle for me or any human interpreter.   640
MEDEA: Is it lawful for me to hear it?
AEGEUS: Certainly; a brain
  Like yours is what is needed.
MEDEA: Tell me, since you may.
AEGEUS: He commanded me 'not to unstop the wineskin's neck'—
MEDEA: Yes—until when?
AEGEUS: Until I came safe home again.
MEDEA: I see. And for what purpose have you sailed to Corinth?
AEGEUS: You know the King of Troezen, Pittheus, son of Pelops?
MEDEA: Yes, a most pious man.   650
AEGEUS: I want to ask his advice
  About this oracle.
MEDEA: He is an expert in such matters.
AEGEUS: Yes, and my closest friend. We went to the wars together.
MEDEA: I hope you will get all you long for, and be happy.
AEGEUS: But you are looking pale and wasted: what is the matter?
MEDEA: Aegeus, my husband's the most evil man alive.
AEGEUS: Why, what's this? Tell me all about your unhappiness.
MEDEA: Jason has betrayed me, though I never did him wrong.
AEGEUS: What has he done? Explain exactly.   660
MEDEA: He has taken
  Another wife, and made her mistress of *my* house.
AEGEUS: But such a thing is shameful! He has never dared—
MEDEA: It is so. Once he loved me; now I am disowned.
AEGEUS: Was he tired of you? Or did he fall in love elsewhere?
MEDEA: Oh, passionately. He's not a man his friends can trust.
AEGEUS: Well, if—as you say—he's a bad lot, let him go.
MEDEA: It's royalty and power he's fallen in love with.
AEGEUS: What?
  Go on. Who's the girl's father?   670
MEDEA: Creon, King of Corinth.

---

[17] The Navelstone, believed to be the center of the earth, was located at Delphi.

AEGEUS: I see. Then you have every reason to be upset.

MEDEA: It is the end of everything! What's more, I'm banished.

AEGEUS: Worse still—extraordinary! Why, who has banished you?

MEDEA: Creon has banished me from Corinth.

AEGEUS: And does Jason
  Accept this? How disgraceful!

MEDEA: Oh, no! He protests.
  But he's resolved to bear it bravely.—Aegeus, see,
  I touch your beard as a suppliant, embrace your knees,   680
  Imploring you to have pity on my wretchedness.
  Have pity! I am an exile; let me not be friendless.
  Receive me in Athens;[18] give me a welcome in your house.
  So may the gods grant you fertility, and bring
  Your life to a happy close. You have not realized
  What good luck chance has brought you. I know certain drugs
  Whose power will put an end to your sterility.
  I promise you shall beget children.

AEGEUS: I am anxious,
  For many reasons, to help you in this way, Medea;   690
  First, for the gods' sake, then this hope you've given me
  Of children—for I've quite despaired of my own powers.
  This then is what I'll do: once you can get to Athens
  I'll keep my promise and protect you all I can.
  But I must make this clear first: I do not intend
  To take you with me away from Corinth. If you come
  Yourself to Athens, you shall have sanctuary there;
  I will not give you up to anyone. But first
  Get clear of Corinth without help; the Corinthians too
  Are friends of mine, and I don't wish to give offence.   700

MEDEA: So be it. Now confirm your promise with an oath,
  And all is well between us.

AEGEUS: Why? Do you not trust me?
  What troubles you?

MEDEA: I trust you; but I have enemies—
  Not only Creon, but the house of Pelias.
  Once you are bound by oaths you will not give me up
  If they should try to take me out of your territory.
  But if your promise is verbal, and not sworn to the gods,
  Perhaps you will make friends with them, and agree to do   710
  What they demand. I've no power on my side, while they
  Have wealth and all the resources of a royal house.

AEGEUS: Your forethought is remarkable; but since you wish it
  I've no objection. In fact, the taking of an oath
  Safeguards me; since I can confront your enemies
  With a clear excuse; while *you* have full security.
  So name your gods.

MEDEA: Swear by the Earth under your feet,
  By the Sun, my father's father, and the whole race of gods.

---

[18] Athens was legendary for its hospitality to strangers.

AEGEUS: Tell me what I shall swear to do or not to do.   720
MEDEA: Never yourself to expel me from your territory;
  And, if my enemies want to take me away, never
  Willingly, while you live, to give me up to them.
AEGEUS: I swear by Earth, and by the burning light of the Sun,
  And all the gods, to keep the words you have just spoken.
MEDEA: I am satisfied. And if you break your oath, what then?
AEGEUS: Then may the gods do to me as to all guilty men.
MEDEA: Go now, and joy be with you. Everything is well.
  I'll reach your city as quickly as I can, when I
  Have carried out my purpose and achieved my wish.   730

AEGEUS *clasps her hand and hurries off.*

CHORUS: May Hermes, protector of travellers, bring you
  Safe to your home, Aegeus; may you accomplish
  All that you so earnestly desire;
  For your noble heart wins our goodwill.
MEDEA: O Zeus! O Justice, daughter of Zeus! O glorious Sun!
  Now I am on the road to victory; now there's hope!
  I shall see my enemies punished as they deserve.
  Just where my plot was weakest, at that very point
  Help has appeared in this man Aegeus; he is a haven
  Where I shall find safe mooring, once I reach the walls   740
  Of the city of Athens. Now I'll tell you all my plans:
  They'll not make pleasant hearing.

[MEDEA'S NURSE *has entered; she listens in silence.*]

                              First I'll send a slave
  To Jason, asking him to come to me; and then
  I'll give him soft talk; tell him he has acted well,
  Tell him I think this royal marriage which he has bought
  With my betrayal is for the best and wisely planned.
  But I shall beg that my children be allowed to stay.
  Not that I would think of leaving sons of mine behind
  On enemy soil for those who hate me to insult;   750
  But in my plot to kill the princess they must help.
  I'll send them to the palace bearing gifts, a dress
  Of soft weave and a coronet of beaten gold.
  If she takes and puts on this finery, both she
  And all who touch her will expire in agony;
  With such a deadly poison I'll anoint my gifts.

  However, enough of that. What makes me cry with pain
  Is the next thing I have to do. I will kill my sons.
  No one shall take my children from me. When I have made
  Jason's whole house a shambles,[19] I will leave Corinth   760
  A murderess, flying from my darling children's blood.

___
[19] A slaughterhouse.

Yes, I can endure guilt, however horrible;
The laughter of my enemies I will not endure.

Now let things take their course. What use is life to me?
I have no land, no home, no refuge from despair.
My folly was committed long ago, when I
Was ready to desert my father's house, won over
By eloquence from a Greek, whom with God's help I now
Will punish. He shall never see alive again
The sons he had from me. From his new bride he never   770
Shall breed a son; she by my poison, wretched girl,
Must die a hideous death. Let no one think of me
As humble or weak or passive; let them understand
I am of a different kind: dangerous to my enemies,
Loyal to my friends. To such a life glory belongs.
CHORUS: Since you have told us everything, and since I want
  To be your friend, and also to uphold the laws
  Of human life—I tell you, you must not do this!
MEDEA: No other thing is possible. You have excuse
  For speaking so: you have not been treated as I have.   780
CHORUS: But—to kill your own children! Can you steel your heart?
MEDEA: This is the way to deal Jason the deepest wound.
CHORUS: This way will bring you too the deepest misery.
MEDEA: Let be. Until it is done words are unnecessary.
  Nurse! You are the one I use for messages of trust.
  Go and bring Jason here. As you're a loyal servant,
  And a woman, breathe no word about my purposes.

Exit NURSE.

CHORUS: The people of Athens, sons of Erechtheus,
    have enjoyed their prosperity
  Since ancient times. Children of blessed gods,   790
  They grew from holy soil unscorched by invasion.
  Among the glories of knowledge their souls are pastured;
  They walk always with grace under the sparkling sky.
  There long ago, they say, was born golden-haired Harmony,
  Created by the nine virgin Muses[20] of Pieria.

  They say that Aphrodite dips her cup
  In the clear stream of the lovely Cephisus;[21]
  It is she who breathes over the land the breath
  Of gentle honey-laden winds; her flowing locks
  She crowns with a diadem of sweet-scented roses,   800
  And sends the Loves to be enthroned beside Knowledge,
  And with her to create excellence in every art.

  Then how will such a city,
  Watered by sacred rivers,

[20] Goddesses of the arts, worshipped at the Pierian spring, Mount Olympus.
[21] River near Athens.

A country giving protection to its friends—
How will Athens welcome
You, the child-killer
Whose presence is pollution?
Contemplate the blow struck at a child,
Weigh the blood you take upon you.   810
Medea, by your knees,
By every pledge or appeal we beseech you,
Do not slaughter your children!

Where will you find hardness of purpose?
How will you build resolution in hand or heart
To face horror without flinching?
When the moment comes, and you look at them—
The moment for you to assume the role of murderess—
How will you do it?
When your sons kneel to you for pity,   820
Will you stain your fingers with their blood?
Your heart will melt; you will know you cannot.

Enter JASON *from the palace. Two maids come from the house to attend* MEDEA.

JASON: You sent for me: I have come. Although you hate me, I
    Am ready to listen. You have some new request; what is it?
MEDEA: Jason, I ask you to forgive the things I said.
    You must bear with my violent temper; you and I
    Share many memories of love. I have been taking
    Myself to task. 'You are a fool.' I've told myself,
    'You're mad, when people try to plan things for the best,
    To be resentful, and pick quarrels with the King   830
    And with your husband; what he's doing will help us all.
    His wife is royal; her sons will be my sons' brothers.
    Why not throw off your anger? What is the matter, since
    The gods are making kind provision? After all
    I have two children still to care for; and I know
    We came as exiles, and our friends are few enough.'
    When I considered this, I saw my foolishness;
    I saw how useless anger was. So now I welcome
    What you have done; I think you are wise to gain for us
    This new alliance, and the folly was all mine.   840
    I should have helped you in your plans, made it my pleasure
    To get ready your marriage-bed, attend your bride.
    But we women—I won't say we are bad by nature,
    But we are what we are. You, Jason, should not copy
    Our bad example, or match yourself with us, showing
    Folly for folly. I give in; I was wrong just now,
    I admit. But I have thought more wisely of it since.
    Children, children! Are you indoors? Come out here.

[*The* CHILDREN *come out. Their* TUTOR *follows.*]

Children,

Greet your father, as I do, and put your arms round him.　　850
Forget our quarrel, and love him as your mother does.
We have made friends; we are not angry any more.
There, children; take his hand.

[*She turns away in a sudden flood of weeping.*]

　　　　　　　　　　　Forgive me; I recalled
What pain the future hides from us.

[*After embracing* JASON *the* CHILDREN *go back to* MEDEA.]

　　　　　　　　　　Oh children! Will you
All your lives long, stretch out your hands to me like this?
Oh, my tormented heart is full of tears and terrors.
After so long, I have ended my quarrel with your father;
And now, see! I have drenched this young face with my tears.　　860
CHORUS: I too feel fresh tears fill my eyes. May the course of evil
　Be checked now, go no further!
JASON:　　　　　　　　　I am pleased, Medea,
That you have changed your mind; though indeed I do not blame
Your first resentment. Only naturally a woman
Is angry when her husband marries a second wife.
You have had wiser thoughts; and though it has taken time,
You have recognized the right decision. This is the act
Of a sensible woman. As for you, my boys, your father
Has taken careful thought, and, with the help of the gods,　　870
Ensured a good life for you. Why, in time, I'm sure,
You with your brothers will be leading men in Corinth.
Only grow big and strong. Your father, and those gods
Who are his friends, have all the rest under control.
I want to see you, when you're strong, full-grown young men,
Tread down my enemies.

[*Again* MEDEA *breaks down and weeps.*]

　　　　　　　　What's this? Why these floods of tears?
Why are you pale? Did you not like what I was saying?
Why do you turn away?
MEDEA:　　　　　　It is nothing. I was thinking　　880
About these children.
JASON:　　　　　I'll provide for them. Cheer up.
MEDEA: I will. It is not that I mean to doubt your word.
　But women—are women; tears come naturally to us.
JASON: Why do you grieve so over the children?
MEDEA:　　　　　　　　　　　I'm their mother.
When you just now prayed for them to live long, I wondered
Whether it would be so; and grief came over me.
But I've said only part of what I had to say;
Here is the other thing. Since Creon has resolved　　890
To send me out of Corinth, I fully recognize
That for me too this course is best. If I lived here
I should become a trouble both to you and him.
People believe I bear a grudge against you all.

So I must go. But the boys—I would like *them* to be
Brought up in your care. Beg Creon to let them stay.
JASON: I don't know if I can persuade him; but I'll try.
MEDEA: Then—get your wife to ask her father to let them stay.
JASON: Why, certainly; I'm pretty sure she'll win him over.
MEDEA: She will, if she's like other women. But I too   900
Can help in this. I'll send a present to your wife—
The loveliest things to be found anywhere on earth.
The boys shall take them.—One of you maids, go quickly, bring
The dress and golden coronet.—They will multiply
Her happiness many times, when she can call her own
A royal, noble husband, and these treasures, which
My father's father the Sun bequeathed to his descendants.

[*A slave has brought a casket, which* MEDEA *now hands to her sons.*]

Boys, hold these gifts. Now carry them to the happy bride,
The princess royal; give them into her own hands.
Go! She will find them all that such a gift should be.   910
JASON: But why deprive yourself of such things, foolish woman?
Do you think a royal palace is in want of dresses?
Or gold, do you suppose? Keep them, don't give them away.
If my wife values me at all she will yield to *me*
More than to costly presents, I am sure of that.
MEDEA: Don't stop me. Gifts, they say, persuade even the gods;
With mortals, gold outweighs a thousand arguments.
The day is hers; from now on *her* prosperity
Will rise to new heights. She is royal and young. To buy
My sons from exile I would give life, not just gold.   920
Come, children, go both of you into this rich palace;
Kneel down and beg your father's new wife, and my mistress,
That you may not be banished. And above all, see
That she receives my present into her own hands.
Go quickly; be successful, and bring good news back,
That what your mother longs for has been granted you.

Exit JASON *followed by the* CHILDREN *and the* TUTOR.

CHORUS:
    Now I have no more hope,
    No more hope that the children can live;
    They are walking to murder at this moment.
    The bride will receive the golden coronet,   930
    Receive her merciless destroyer;
    With her own hands she will carefully fit
    The adornment of death round her golden hair.

    She cannot resist such loveliness, such heavenly gleaming;
    She will enfold herself
    In the dress and the wreath of wrought gold,
    Preparing her bridal beauty
    To enter a new home—among the dead.
    So fatal is the snare she will fall into,

So inevitable the death that awaits her;   940
From its cruelty there is no escape.

And you, unhappy Jason, ill-starred in marriage,
You, son-in-law of kings:
Little you know that the favour you ask
Will seal your sons' destruction
And fasten on your wife a hideous fate.
O wretched Jason!
So sure of destiny, and so ignorant!

Your sorrow next I weep for, pitiable mother;
You, for jealousy of your marriage-bed,   950
Will slaughter your children;
Since, disregarding right and loyalty,
Your husband has abandoned you
And lives with another wife.

The TUTOR *returns from the palace with the two* CHILDREN.

TUTOR: Mistress! These two boys are reprieved from banishment.
  The princess took your gifts from them with her own hand,
  And was delighted. They have no enemies in the palace.

[MEDEA *is silent.*]

  Well, bless my soul!
  Isn't that good news? Why do you stand there thunderstruck?
MEDEA [*to herself*]: How cruel, how cruel!   960
TUTOR: That's out of tune with the news I brought.
MEDEA: How cruel life is!
TUTOR: Have I, without knowing it,
  Told something dreadful, then? I thought my news was good.
MEDEA: Your news is what it is. I am not blaming you.
TUTOR: Then why stand staring at the ground, with streaming eyes?
MEDEA: Strong reason forces me to weep, old friend. The gods,
  And my own evil-hearted plots, have led to this.
TUTOR: Take heart, mistress; in time your sons will bring you home.
MEDEA: Before then, I have others to send home.—Oh, gods!   970
  She weeps.
TUTOR: You're not the only mother parted from her sons.
  We are all mortal; you must not bear grief so hard.
MEDEA: Yes, friend. I'll follow your advice. Now go indoors
  And get things ready for them, as on other days.

[*Exit* TUTOR. *The* CHILDREN *come to* MEDEA.]

  O children, children! You have a city, and a home;
  And when we have parted, there you both will stay for ever,
  You motherless, I miserable. And I must go
  To exile in another land, before I have had

My joy of you, before I have seen you growing up, 980
Becoming prosperous. I shall never see your brides,
Adorn your bridal beds, and hold the torches high.
My misery is my own heart, which will not relent.
All was for nothing, then—these years of rearing you,
My care, my aching weariness, and the wild pains
When you were born. Oh, yes, I once built many hopes
On you; imagined, pitifully, that you would care
For my old age, and would yourselves wrap my dead body
For burial. How people would envy me my sons!
That sweet, sad thought has faded now. Parted from you, 990
My life will be all pain and anguish. You will not
Look at your mother any more with these dear eyes.
You will have moved into a different sphere of life.

Dear sons, why are you staring at me so? You smile
At me—your last smile: why?

[*She weeps. The* CHILDREN *go from her a little, and she turns to the* CHORUS.]

Oh, what am I to do?
Women, my courage is all gone. Their young, bright faces—
I can't do it. I'll think no more of it. I'll take them
Away from Corinth. Why should I hurt *them,* to make
Their father suffer, when I shall suffer twice as much 1000
Myself? I won't do it. I won't think of it again.

What is the matter with me? Are my enemies
To laugh at me? Am I to let them off scot free?
I must steel myself to it. What a coward I am,
Even tempting my own resolution with soft talk.
Boys, go indoors.

[*The* CHILDREN *go to the door, but stay there watching her.*]

If there is any here who finds it
Not lawful to be present at my sacrifice,
Let him see to it. My hand shall not weaken.

Oh, my heart, don't, don't do it! Oh, miserable heart, 1010
Let them be! Spare your children! We'll all live together
Safely in Athens; and they will make you happy. . . . No!
No! No! By all the fiends of hate in hell's depths, no!
I'll not leave sons of mine to be the victims of
My enemies' rage. In any case there is no escape,
The thing's done now. Yes, now—the golden coronet
Is on her head, the royal bride is in her dress,
Dying, I know it. So, since I have a sad road
To travel, and send these boys on a still sadder road,
I'll speak to them. Come, children; give me your hand, dear son; 1020
Yours too. Now we must say goodbye. Oh, darling hand,

And darling mouth; your noble, childlike face and body!
Dear sons, my blessing on you both—but there, not here!
All blessing here your father has destroyed. How sweet
To hold you! And children's skin is soft, and their breath pure.
Go! Go away! I can't look at you any longer;
My pain is more than I can bear.

[*The* CHILDREN *go indoors.*]

                                                  I understand
The horror of what I am going to do; but anger,
The spring of all life's horror, masters my resolve.   1030

MEDEA *goes to stand looking towards the palace.*

CHORUS:
       I have often engaged in arguments,
       And become more subtle, and perhaps more heated,
       Than is suitable for women;
       Though in fact women too have intelligence,
       Which forms part of our nature and instructs us—
       Not all of us, I admit; but a certain few
       You might perhaps find, in a large number of women—
       A few not incapable of reflection;

       And this is my opinion: those men or women
       Who never had children of their own at all   1040
       Enjoy the advantage in good fortune
       Over those who are parents. Childless people
       Have no means of knowing whether children are
       A blessing or a burden; but being without them
       They live exempt from many troubles.

       While those who have growing up in their homes
       The sweet gift of children I see always
       Burdened and worn with incessant worry,
       First, how to rear them in health and safety,
       And bequeath them, in time, enough to live on;   1050
       And then this further anxiety:
       They can never know whether all their toil
       Is spent for worthy or worthless children.

       And beyond the common ills that attend
       All human life there is one still worse:
       Suppose at last they are pretty well off,
       Their children have grown up, and, what's more,
       Are kind and honest: then what happens?
       A throw of chance—and there goes Death
       Bearing off your child into the unknown.   1060

       Then why should mortals thank the gods,
       Who add to their load, already grievous,

This one more grief, for their children's sake,
Most grievous of all?
MEDEA: Friends, I have long been waiting for a message from the palace.
  What is to happen next? I see a slave of Jason's
  Coming, gasping for breath. He must bring fearful news.

Enter a MESSENGER.

MESSENGER: Medea! Get away, escape! Oh, what a thing to do!
  What an unholy, horrible thing! Take ship, or chariot,
  Any means you can, but escape!   1070
MEDEA: Why should I escape?
MESSENGER: She's dead—the princess, and her father Creon too,
  They're both dead, by your poisons.
MEDEA: Your news is excellent.
  I count you from today my friend and benefactor.
MESSENGER: What? Are you sane, or raving mad? When you've committed
  This hideous crime against the royal house, you're glad
  At hearing of it? Do you not tremble at such things?
MEDEA: I could make suitable reply to that, my friend.
  But take your time now; tell me, how did they die? You'll give   1080
  Me double pleasure if their death was horrible.
MESSENGER: When your two little boys came hand in hand, and entered
  The palace with their father, where the wedding was,
  We servants were delighted. We had all felt sorry
  To hear how you'd been treated; and now the word went round
  From one to another, that you and Jason had made it up.
  So we were glad to see the boys; one kissed their hand,
  Another their fair hair. Myself, I was so pleased,
  I followed with them to the princess's room. Our mistress—
  The one we now call mistress in your place—before   1090
  She saw your pair of boys coming, had eyes only
  For Jason; but seeing them she dropped her eyes, and turned
  Her lovely cheek away, upset that they should come
  Into her room. Your husband then began to soothe
  Her sulkiness, her girlish temper. 'You must not,'
  He said, 'be unfriendly to our friends. Turn your head round,
  And give up feeling angry. Those your husband loves
  You must love too. Now take these gifts,' he said, 'and ask
  Your father to revoke their exile for my sake.'
  So, when she saw those lovely things, she was won over,   1100
  And agreed to all that Jason asked. At once, before
  He and your sons were well out of the house, she took
  The embroidered gown and put it round her. Then she placed
  Over her curls the golden coronet, and began
  To arrange her hair in a bright mirror, smiling at
  Her lifeless form reflected there. Then she stood up,
  And to and fro stepped daintily about the room
  On white bare feet, and many times she would twist back
  To see how the dress fell in clear folds to the heel.

  Then suddenly we saw a frightening thing. She changed   1110
  Colour; she staggered sideways, shook in every limb.

She was just able to collapse on to a chair,
Or she would have fallen flat. Then one of her attendants,
An old woman, thinking that perhaps the anger of Pan[22]
Or some other god had struck her, chanted the cry of worship.
But then she saw, oozing from the girl's lips, white froth;
The pupils of her eyes were twisted out of sight;
The blood was drained from all her skin. The old woman knew
Her mistake, and changed her chant to a despairing howl.
One maid ran off quickly to fetch the King, another   1120
To look for Jason and tell him what was happening
To his young bride; the whole palace was filled with a clatter
Of people running here and there.
                                        All this took place
In a few moments, perhaps while a fast runner might run
A hundred yards; and she lay speechless, with eyes closed.
Then she came to, poor girl, and gave a frightful scream,
As two torments made war on her together: first
The golden coronet round her head discharged a stream
Of unnatural devouring fire: while the fine dress   1130
Your children gave her—poor miserable girl!—the stuff
Was eating her clear flesh. She leapt up from her chair,
On fire, and ran, shaking her head and her long hair
This way and that, trying to shake off the coronet.
The ring of gold was fitted close and would not move;
The more she shook her head the fiercer the flame burned.
At last, exhausted by agony, she fell to the ground;
Save to her father, she was unrecognizable.
Her eyes, her face, were one grotesque disfigurement;
Down from her head dripped blood mingled with flame; her flesh,   1140
Attacked by the invisible fangs of poison, melted
From the bare bone, like gum-drops from a pine-tree's bark—
A ghastly sight. Not one among us dared to touch
Her body. What we'd seen was lesson enough for us.

But suddenly her father came into the room.
He did not understand, poor man, what kind of death
Had struck his child. He threw himself down at her side,
And sobbed aloud, and kissed her, and took her in his arms,
And cried, 'Poor darling child, what god destroyed your life
So cruelly? Who robs me of my only child,   1150
Old as I am, and near my grave? Oh, let me die   —
With you, my daughter!' Soon he ceased his tears and cries,
And tried to lift his aged body upright; and then,
As ivy sticks to laurel-branches, so he stuck
Fast to the dress. A ghastly wrestling then began;
He struggled to raise up his knee, she tugged him down.
If he used force, he tore the old flesh off his bones.
At length the King gave up his pitiful attempts;
Weakened with pain, he yielded, and gasped out his life.
Now, joined in death, daughter and father—such a sight   1160

[22] The nature-god Pan was said to be able to inflict fits of terror (the origin of the word "panic").

As tears were made for—they lie there.
To you, Medea,
I have no more to say. You will yourself know best
How to evade reprisal. As for human life,
It is a shadow, as I have long believed. And this
I say without hesitation: those whom most would call
Intelligent, the propounders of wise theories—
Their folly is of all men's the most culpable.
Happiness is a thing no man possesses. Fortune
May come now to one man, now to another, as
Prosperity increases; happiness never.

Exit MESSENGER.

CHORUS: Today we see the will of Heaven, blow after blow,
  Bring down on Jason justice and calamity.
MEDEA: Friends, now my course is clear: as quickly as possible
  To kill the children and then fly from Corinth; not
  Delay and so consign them to another hand
  To murder with a better will. For they must die,
  In any case; and since they must, then I who gave
  Them birth will kill them. Arm yourself, my heart: the thing
  That you must do is fearful, yet inevitable.
  Why wait, then? My accursed hand, come, take the sword;
  Take it, and forward to your frontier of despair.
  No cowardice, no tender memories; forget
  That you once loved them, that of your body they were born.
  For one short day forget your children; afterwards
  Weep: though you kill them, they were your beloved sons.
  Life has been cruel to me.

MEDEA *goes into the house.*

CHORUS: Earth, awake! Bright arrows of the Sun,
  Look! Look down on the accursed woman
  Before she lifts up a murderous hand
  To pollute it with her children's blood!
  For they are of your own golden race;
  And for mortals to spill blood that grew
  In the veins of gods is a fearful thing.
  Heaven-born brightness, hold her, stop her,
  Purge the palace of her, this pitiable
  Bloody-handed fiend of vengeance!

  All your care for them lost! Your love
  For the babes you bore, all wasted, wasted!
  Why did you come from the blue Symplegades
  That hold the gate of the barbarous sea?
  Why must this rage devour your heart
  To spend itself in slaughter of children?
  Where kindred blood pollutes the ground
  A curse hangs over human lives;
  And murder measures the doom that falls

1170

1180

1190

1200

By Heaven's law on the guilty house.
A child's scream is heard from inside the house.
CHORUS: Do you hear? The children are calling for help.
  O cursed, miserable woman!
CHILDREN'S VOICES: Help, help! Mother, let me go! Mother, don't kill us!   1210
CHORUS: Shall we go in?
  I am sure we ought to save the children's lives.
CHILDREN'S VOICES: Help, help, for the gods' sake! She is killing us!
  We can't escape from her sword!
CHORUS: O miserable mother, to destroy your own increase,
  Murder the babes of your body!
  Stone and iron you are, as you resolved to be.

  There was but one in time past,
  One woman that I have heard of,
  Raised hand against her own children.   1220
  It was Ino,[23] sent out of her mind by a god,
  When Hera, the wife of Zeus,
  Drove her from her home to wander over the world.
  In her misery she plunged into the sea
  Being defiled by the murder of her children;
  From the steep cliff's edge she stretched out her foot,
  And so ended,
  Joined in death with her two sons.

  What can be strange or terrible after this?
  O bed of women, full of passion and pain,   1230
  What wickedness, what sorrow you have caused on the earth!

Enter JASON, *running and breathless.*

JASON: You women standing round the door there! Is Medea
  Still in the house?—vile murderess!—or has she gone
  And escaped? I swear she must either hide in the deep earth
  Or soar on wings into the sky's abyss, to escape
  My vengeance for the royal house.—She has killed the King
  And the princess! Does she expect to go unpunished?

  Well, I am less concerned with her than with the children.
  Those who have suffered at her hands will make her suffer;
  I've come to save my sons, before Creon's family   1240
  Murder them in revenge for this unspeakable
  Crime of their mother's.
CHORUS: Jason, you have yet to learn
  How great your trouble is; or you would not have spoken so.
JASON: What trouble? Is Medea trying to kill me too?
CHORUS: Your sons are dead. Their mother has killed both your sons.
JASON: What? Killed my sons? That word kills me.
CHORUS: They are both dead.

---

[23] Hera, Zeus' consort, drove Ino to madness and suicide because she helped rear Dionysus, son of
Zeus and Semele.

JASON: Where are they? Did she kill them out here, or indoors?
CHORUS: Open that door, and see them lying in their blood.   1250
JASON: Slaves, there! Unbar the doors! Open, and let me see
  Two horrors: my dead sons, and the woman I will kill.

JASON *batters at the doors.* MEDEA *appears above the roof, sitting in a chariot*
  drawn by dragons, with the bodies of the two children beside her.

MEDEA: Jason! Why are you battering at these doors, seeking
  The dead children and me who killed them? Stop! Be quiet.
  If you have any business with me, say what you wish.
  Touch us you cannot, in this chariot which the Sun
  Has sent to save us from the hands of enemies.
JASON: You abomination! Of all women most detested
  By every god, by me, by the whole human race!
  You could endure—a mother!—to lift sword against   1260
  Your own little ones; to leave me childless, my life wrecked.
  After such murder do you outface both Sun and Earth—
  Guilty of gross pollution? May the gods blast your life!
  I am sane now; but I was mad before, when I
  Brought you from your palace in a land of savages
  Into a Greek home—you, a living curse, already
  A traitor both to your father and your native land.
  The vengeance due for your sins the gods have cast on me.
  You had already murdered your brother at his own hearth
  When first you stepped on board my lovely Argo's hull.   1270
  That was your beginning. Then you became my wife, and bore
  My children; now, out of mere sexual jealousy,
  You murder them! In all Hellas there is not one woman
  Who could have done it; yet in preference to them
  I married you, chose hatred and murder for my wife—
  No woman, but a tiger; a Tuscan Scylla[24]—but more savage.
  Ah, what's the use? If I cursed you all day, no remorse
  Would touch you, for your heart's proof against feeling. Go!
  Out of my sight, polluted fiend, child-murderer!
  Leave me to mourn over my destiny: I have lost   1280
  My young bride; I have lost the two sons I begot
  And brought up; I shall never see them alive again.
MEDEA: I would if necessary have answered at full length
  Everything you have said; but Zeus the father of all
  Knows well what service I once rendered you, and how
  You have repaid me. You were mistaken if you thought
  You could dishonour my bed and live a pleasant life
  And laugh at me. The princess was wrong too, and so
  Was Creon, when he took you for his son-in-law
  And thought he could exile me with impunity.   1290
  So now, am I a tiger, Scylla?—Hurl at me
  What names you please! I've reached your heart; and that is right.
JASON: You suffer too; my loss is yours no less.
MEDEA: It is true;

[24] A monster who, with Charybdis, attacked ships sailing through the strait of Messina.

But my pain's a fair price, to take away your smile.

JASON: O children, what a wicked mother Fate gave you!

MEDEA: O sons, your father's treachery cost you your lives.

JASON: It was not my hand that killed my sons.

MEDEA: No, not your hand;
    But your insult to me, and your new-wedded wife.   1300

JASON: You thought *that* reason enough to murder them, that I
    No longer slept with you?

MEDEA: And is that injury
    A slight one, do you imagine, to a woman?

JASON: Yes,
    To a modest woman; but to you—the whole world lost.

MEDEA: I can stab too: your sons are dead!

JASON: Dead? No! They live—
    To haunt your life with vengeance.

MEDEA: Who began this feud?   1310
    The gods know.

JASON: Yes—they know the vileness of your heart.

MEDEA: Loathe on! Your bitter voice—how I abhor the sound!

JASON: As I loathe yours. Let us make terms and part at once.

MEDEA: Most willingly. What terms? What do you bid me do?

JASON: Give me my sons for burial and mourning rites.

MEDEA: Oh, no! I will myself convey them to the temple
    Of Hera[25] Acraea; there in the holy precinct I
    Will bury them with my own hand, to ensure that none
    Of my enemies shall violate or insult their graves.   1320
    And I will ordain an annual feast and sacrifice
    To be solemnized for ever by the people of Corinth,
    To expiate this impious murder. I myself
    Will go to Athens, city of Erechtheus,[26] to make my home
    With Aegeus son of Pandion. You, as you deserve,
    Shall die an unheroic death, your head shattered
    By a timber from the Argo's hull.[27] Thus wretchedly
    Your fate shall end the story of your love for me.

JASON: The curse of children's blood be on you!
    Avenging Justice blast your being!   1330

MEDEA: What god will hear your imprecation,
    Oath-breaker, guest-deceiver, liar?

JASON: Unclean, abhorrent child-destroyer!

MEDEA: Go home: your wife waits to be buried.

JASON: I go—a father once; now childless.

MEDEA: You grieve too soon. Old age is coming.

JASON: Children, how dear you were!

MEDEA: To their mother; not to you.

JASON: Dear—and you murdered them?

MEDEA: Yes, Jason, to break your heart.   1340

JASON: I long to fold them in my arms;
    To kiss their lips would comfort me.

---

[25] Hera was said to protect wives and marriage.

[26] Legendary king of Athens.

[27] Jason died in Corinth in a freak accident when a timber from his old ship the Argo fell on his head.

MEDEA: *Now* you have loving words, now kisses for them:
  Then you disowned them, sent them into exile.
JASON: For God's sake, let me touch their gentle flesh.
MEDEA: You shall not. It is waste of breath to ask.
JASON:

    Zeus, do you hear how I am mocked
    Rejected, by this savage beast
    Polluted with her children's blood?

    But now, as time and strength permit,   1350
    I will lament this grievous day,
    And call the gods to witness, how
    You killed my sons, and now refuse
    To let me touch or bury them.
    Would God I had not bred them,
    Or ever lived to see
    Them dead, you their destroyer!

During this speech the chariot has moved out of sight.
CHORUS: Many are the Fates which Zeus in Olympus dispenses;
  Many matters the gods bring to surprising ends.
  The things we thought would happen do not happen;
  The unexpected God makes possible;   1360
  And such is the conclusion of this story.[28]

QUESTIONS FOR DISCUSSION AND WRITING

1. In one of his more infuriating speeches (ll. 474–525), Jason tells Medea that she is a "barbarian" and is fortunate to be a resident in Hellas. Jason, of course, ignores the fact that in Colchis, it was he who was the "barbarian" and Medea helped him. In many ways this play is about "outsiders" (or, if you like, the Other). Identify the various kinds of outsiders in the play and trace out the ironic contradictions in their treatment.

2. Lines 1–38 constitute one of Euripides' "non-dramatic" prologues (one addressed directly to the audience). What functions does this prologue serve, besides giving background information? How is the Nurse characterized? What issues of moral judgment are raised?

3. Why does Euripides have the chorus made up of Corinthian women? What point of view do they represent throughout the play?

4. In lines 370–71, Medea tells the chorus:

        We were born women—useless for honest purposes,
        But in all kinds of evil skilled practitioners.

Medea frequently casts her quarrel with Jason as a quarrel between men and women. Trace everything that she has to say about the genders and identify ironies.

---

[28] The chorus's last speech is formulaic and was used by Euripides for a number of plays.

5.   In line 447–48, Medea, speaking to Jason, identifies herself as one who upholds the laws of the "old gods" and asks Jason if he believes that "new laws" are now in force. What does she mean, and what values does she associate with the "old gods" and the "new gods"?

6.   It has been suggested that Euripides' central subject is the irrational. Certainly it is an important theme in *Medea*. Jason insists that he is doing the rational thing and that Medea is behaving irrationally. Trace this contrast through the play, identifying ironies and contradictions where appropriate.

7.   *Dramatic irony* is the term we use for a situation in which the characters and the audience have different degrees of knowledge of the situation. In lines 912–16, the tutor announces joyfully that the princess has accepted Medea's gifts and is puzzled by the reception he gets. Analyze the dramatic irony in this scene.

8.   The climactic actions of *Medea*, the killing of Glauce and Creon and the killing of Medea's sons, take place offstage, in accordance with ordinary Greek dramatic practice. Analyze how these actions are presented to the audience.

9.   What beliefs about the world does *Medea* seem to imply? What role do the gods play in human affairs? What strengths and weaknesses do humans have? What virtues are most important, what vices most to be avoided? What is the relationship of the rational and the irrational in human life?

Shakespeare and the Early Modern Theatre

William Shakespeare (1564–1616) is generally agreed to be not only the greatest playwright but the greatest writer in history, not only in the English-speaking world but internationally. This status is not an unmixed blessing; it has attracted around Shakespeare a web of idealization, myth, and misunderstanding that periodically must be cleared away if we are to understand the real nature of his accomplishment.

Shakespeare was born in Stratford-upon-Avon, the son of a Stratford businessman, and was educated at the Stratford grammar school. When he was eighteen he married Anne Hathaway; they had three children. Little else is known of his early life until he appeared in London as a playwright in 1592. In 1594, when he was thirty, he became a member, as both actor and playwright, of a theater company called the Lord Chamberlain's Men. (They were later known as the King's Men after Queen Elizabeth died and was succeeded by James I.) It was for this company that he wrote his thirty-six or so plays. In 1599 he became part-owner of the Globe Theater; later he also acquired a share in the Blackfriars Theater. He retired to Stratford in 1613, when he was forty-nine, and died three years later.

Shakespeare's career came at the peak of a long period of theatrical development. The classical theater of Greece and Rome had been forgotten throughout the early Middle Ages. The theater was reinvented through the ceremonies of the Christian Church, thus rooting it in religion as the Greek theater had been. Starting with brief dramatized sections of the mass, medieval church drama developed religious allegories and dramatizations of biblical stories that were presented on the church grounds at special festivals. This drama inspired a secular equivalent consisting of simple farces and allegories. By the end of the sixteenth century, theater companies were thriving in England, the rediscovery of classical drama offered a model for structuring dramatic texts, and there was a lively, broadly based audience for native drama.

The theater that Shakespeare wrote for was very different from the gigantic amphitheaters of ancient Greece. Touring companies at first set up their stages in the inner courtyards of inns, and these became the models when theaters were purpose-built. These theaters were two- or three-storied buildings with open courtyards in the center. (See drawing.) The windows and balconies opening onto the courtyard provided the most expensive seats. The courtyard itself provided standing room at the lowest prices. On one side of the courtyard was erected a scaffold stage, which thrust into the courtyard. This stage was covered with a wooden roof to keep off rain and sunshine. At the back of the stage was a curtained alcove, with doors on each side for entrances and exits. The deck of the roof provided a second acting area called the "above." On a third level, another chamber provided space for musicians and makers of such sound effects as rolling cannon balls for thunder. The only sets were stage pieces such as thrones, which could be quickly moved on and off. There was no provision for artificial lighting; performances took place in daylight hours.

This seemingly primitive theater was actually quite a flexible and sophisticated theater space, offering a wide variety of acting areas. It, like the Greek theater, can be read as a manifestation of a governing idea of its age: the unbounded human imagination. As the Greek theater, with its round stone platform in front of a scene building, had lent itself to stories about people in their social roles, "before

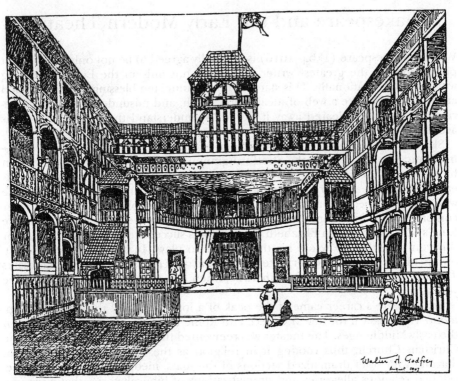

A modern reconstruction of an Elizabethan theater

the palace," so the Shakespearean theater offered a space that, by the exercise of the imagination, could transform itself instantly into any place. Shakespeare wrote about this feature of his theater in the Prologue to *Henry V*, where he laments that his theater, "this wooden O," cannot contain the setting of his story, "the vasty fields of France." The irony, of course, is that in the play that follows, the theater does contain those French fields, perhaps better than anything could until the invention of motion pictures.

The structure of Shakespearean drama follows the possibilities of his theater, as the structure of Greek drama followed the possibilities of the Greek theater. Plays can be described loosely as having closed or open structures. Plays with closed structures have few characters and few scenes, take place in continuous or nearly continuous time and in one place or a few places, and have single, highly unified plots. Greek drama is a good example; so is the modern realistic play.

Plays with open structures are the opposite: they have many characters and many scenes, cover a wide range of times and places, and often have more than one plot. The "epic" plays of Bertolt Brecht are an example; so generally are films. And so are Shakespeare's plays, which tend to have large casts and many separate scenes, take place in a variety of locations and often over a period of weeks or months, and have at least two plot-lines.

The physical theater Shakespeare wrote for did not make this approach to playwriting necessary, but made it possible. If a large company of actors is economically viable, and if there are no sets to be changed, there is no reason not to write large-scale, inclusive plays that range widely over time and space and incorporate a wide range of experience. Shakespeare's bare stage was microcosmic, and it is perhaps no accident that his theater was named the Globe. (The fact that the space beneath the stage, reached by a trapdoor, was called "hell" and the roof over the stage was painted with stars and called "the heavens" encouraged the same thought.)

The basic unit of a Shakespeare play is the scene. The modern practice of numbering scenes and identifying their setting is rather misleading, since the only thing that marks off a Shakespearean scene in authentic, bare-stage performance is the clearing of the stage. When all the actors on stage go off, we know a scene is ending, and when another group of actors comes on, we know another is beginning. Sometimes the place is identified (a ship at sea, before Prospero's cell); often the scene takes place in an unidentified, indeterminate place (another part of the island).

There can be fifty or more of these scenes; *The Tempest*, with nine scenes, has one of the most closed forms among Shakespeare's plays. However many there are, they are related by a great many links, usually based on contrast. A large-scale scene is followed by a small one, a main-plot scene is followed by a subplot scene, a comic scene is followed by a serious one, and so on. Or a public scene (a coronation, a royal audience) can be followed by a private scene (a love scene or a scene between mother and child), for the Greek emphasis upon public life has given way to a Shakespearean balancing of public and private life. The effect is of a complex world built up of bits and pieces, an imaginative world so comprehensive that many have compared it to the real one.

THE TEMPEST

NAMES OF THE ACTORS

ALONSO, *King of Naples*
SEBASTIAN, *his brother*
PROSPERO, *the right Duke of Milan*
ANTONIO, *his brother, the usurping Duke*
  of Milan
FERDINAND, *son to the King of Naples*
GONZALO, *an honest old counselor*
ADRIAN AND FRANCISCO, *lords*
CALIBAN, *a savage and deformed slave*
TRINCULO, *a jester*
STEPHANO, *a drunken butler*
MASTER *of a ship*

BOATSWAIN
MARINERS

MIRANDA, *daughter to Prospero*
ARIEL, *an airy spirit*
IRIS,
CERES,
JUNO,   } [*spirits*]
NYMPHS,
REAPERS,

[*Other Spirits serving* PROSPERO]

THE SCENE: [*A ship at sea; afterwards*] *an uninhabited island.*

ACT I

Scene I. [A ship at sea.]

A tempestuous noise of thunder and lightning heard.
Enter a SHIPMASTER *and a* BOATSWAIN.

MAST. Boatswain![1]
BOATS. Here, master. What cheer?[2]
MAST. Good, speak to the mariners; fall to't yarely,[3] or we run ourselves
  aground! Bestir, bestir!   *Exit.*

Enter MARINERS.

BOATS. Heigh, my hearts! Cheerly, cheerly, my hearts! Yare, yare! Take
  in the topsail! Tend[4] to the master's whistle! Blow till thou burst thy
  wind, if room enough![5]

Enter ALONSO, SEBASTIAN, ANTONIO, FERDINAND, GONZALO, *and others.*

ALON. Good boatswain, have care. Where's the master? Play the[6] men.
BOATS. I pray now, keep below.
ANT. Where is the master, bos'n?   10
BOATS. Do you not hear him? You mar our labor. Keep your cabins: you
  do assist the storm!
GON. Nay, good, be patient.

---

[1] **master,** captain. [Notes to *The Tempest* are by Oscar James Campbell.]
[2] **what cheer?** How do we fare?   [3] **yarely,** promptly.   [4] **tend,** attend.
[5] **if room,** if there is open sea.   [6] **play the,** play the part of.

BOATS. When the sea is. Hence! What cares these roarers[7] for the name of king? To cabin! Silence! Trouble us not!

GON. Good, yet remember whom thou hast aboard.

BOATS. None that I more love than myself. You are a counselor: if you can command these elements to silence and work the peace of the present,[8] we will not hand[9] a rope more; use your authority. If you cannot, give thanks you have lived so long, and make yourself ready in your cabin for the mischance of the hour, if it so hap.—Cheerly, good hearts!—Out of our way, I say. *Exit.*

GON. I have great comfort from this fellow. Methinks he hath no drowning mark upon him; his complexion is perfect gallows![10] Stand fast, good Fate, to his hanging! Make the rope of his destiny our cable, for our own doth little advantage. If he be not born to be hanged, our case is miserable. *Exeunt.*

Re-enter BOATSWAIN.

BOATS. Down with the topmast! Yare! Lower, lower! Bring her to try with main course![11] (*A cry within.*) A plague upon this howling! They are louder than the weather or our office.[12]

Enter SEBASTIAN, ANTONIO, *and* GONZALO.

Yet again? What do you here? Shall we give o'er[13] and drown? Have you a mind to sink?

SEB. A pox o'[14] your throat, you bawling, blasphemous, incharitable dog!

BOATS. Work you then.

ANT. Hang, cur, hang, you whoreson, insolent noisemaker! We are less afraid to be drowned than thou art.

GON. I'll warrant him for[15] drowning, though the ship were no stronger than a nutshell and as leaky as an unstanched wench.

BOATS. Lay her ahold, ahold![16] Set her two courses![17] Off to sea again! Lay her off![18]

Enter MARINERS, *wet.*

MARINERS. All lost! To prayers, to prayers! All lost!

[*Exeunt.*]

BOATS. What, must our mouths be cold?[19]

GON. The King and Prince at prayers! Let's assist them, For our case is as theirs.

SEB. I am out of patience.

ANT. We are merely[20] cheated of our lives by drunkards.

---

[7] **roarers,** i.e., the winds and waves.   [8] **work . . . present,** i.e., calm the present storm.
[9] **hand,** handle.
[10] **his . . . gallows,** an allusion to the proverb, "He who is born to be hanged, will never be drowned"; **complexion,** face.   [11] **Bring . . . main course,** bring her close to the wind under mainsail.
[12] **our office,** the noise of our orders.   [13] **give o'er,** give up.   [14] **A pox o',** a plague on.
[15] **warrant him,** guarantee him; **for,** against.   [16] **ahold,** close to the wind.
[17] **two courses,** two sails, i.e., foresail and mainsail.   [18] **off,** i.e., away from shore.
[19] **What . . . cold,** the boatswain here takes to drink.   [20] **merely,** completely.

This wide-chopped[21] rascal—would thou mightst lie drowning
The washing of ten tides![22]

GON.   He'll be hanged yet,   50
  Though every drop of water swear against it
  And gape at wid'st to glut[23] him.

A confused noise within: "Mercy on us—
  We split, we split!—Farewell, my wife and children!—
  Farewell, brother!—We split, we split, we split!"

                                                      [*Exit* BOATSWAIN.]

ANT. Let's all sink with the King.
SEB.   Let's take leave of him.
                                    Exeunt [ANTONIO *and* SEBASTIAN].
GON. Now would I give a thousand furlongs of sea for an acre of barren
  ground—long heath, brown furze,[24] anything. The wills above be
  done, but I would fain die a dry death.   60

                                                                      Exit.

Scene II. [The island. Before Prospero's cell.]

Enter PROSPERO *and* MIRANDA.

MIR. If by your art, my dearest father, you have
  Put the wild waters in this roar, allay[1] them.
  The sky, it seems, would pour down stinking pitch
  But that the sea, mounting to the welkin's[2] cheek,
  Dashes the fire out. O, I have suffered
  With those that I saw suffer! a brave[3] vessel
  (Who had no doubt some noble creature in her)
  Dashed all to pieces! O, the cry did knock
  Against my very heart! Poor souls, they perished!
  Had I been any god of power, I would   10
  Have sunk the sea within the earth or ere
  It should the good ship so have swallowed and
  The fraughting souls within her.
PROS.   Be collected.[4]
  No more amazement.[5] Tell your piteous heart
  There's no harm done.
MIR.   O, woe the day!
PROS.   No harm.
  I have done nothing but in care of thee,
  Of thee my dear one, thee my daughter, who   20
  Art ignorant of what thou art, naught knowing

---

[21] **wide-chopped,** wide-mouthed and so "insolent."
[22] **ten tides,** the punishment for a pirate was to be hanged on the shore and left till three tides flowed
over him.   [23] **glut,** swallow.
[24] **long heath, brown furze,** the phrase means "no matter how worthless"; **heath,** heather; **furze,**
evergreen shrub.

[1] **allay,** calm.   [2] **welkin's,** sky's.   [3] **brave,** gallant.
[4] **fraughting,** forming her cargo; **collected,** calm.   [5] **amazement,** alarm.

Of whence I am; nor that I am more better
Than Prospero, master of a full[6] poor cell,
And thy no greater father.
MIR.   More to know
Did never meddle[7] with my thoughts.
PROS.   'Tis time
I should inform thee farther. Lend thy hand
And pluck my magic garment from me. So,

                              [*Takes off his magic robe.*]

Lie there, my art. Wipe thou thine eyes; have comfort.   30
The direful spectacle of the wrack, which touched
The very virtue[8] of compassion in thee,
I have with such provision[9] in mine art
So safely ordered[10] that there is no soul—
No, not so much perdition[11] as an hair
Betid[12] to any creature in the vessel
Which thou heardst cry, which thou sawst sink. Sit down;
For thou must now know farther.
MIR.   You have often
Begun to tell me what I am, but stopped   40
And left me to a bootless inquisition,[13]
Concluding, "Stay! Not yet."
PROS.   The hour's now come;
The very minute bids thee ope thine ear.
Obey, and be attentive. Canst thou remember
A time before we came unto this cell?
I do not think thou canst, for then thou wast not
Out[14] three years old.
MIR.   Certainly, sir, I can.
PROS. By what? By any other house or person?   50
Of anything the image tell me that
Hath kept with thy remembrance.
MIR.   'Tis far off,
And rather like a dream than an assurance
That my remembrance warrants.[15] Had I not
Four or five women once that tended me?
PROS. Thou hadst, and more, Miranda. But how is it
That this lives in thy mind? What seest thou else
In the dark backward[16] and abysm of time?
If thou rememb'rest aught ere thou camest here,   60
How thou camest here thou mayst.
MIR.   But that I do not.
PROS. Twelve year since, Miranda, twelve year since,
Thy father was the Duke of Milan and
A prince of power.

---

[6] **full,** thoroughly.   [7] **meddle,** mingle.
[8] **very virtue,** essential nature.   [9] **provision,** foresight.
[10] **ordered,** managed.   [11] **perdition,** loss.
[12] **Betid,** happened.   [13] **bootless inquisition,** profitless inquiry.   [14] **Out,** fully.
[15] **remembrance warrants,** memory guarantees.   [16] **dark backward,** dim past.

Mir.   Sir, are not you my father?

Pros. Thy mother was a piece[17] of virtue, and
  She said thou wast my daughter; and thy father
  Was Duke of Milan; and his only heir
  A princess—no worse issued.[18]   70

Mir.   O the heavens!
  What foul play had we that we came from thence?
  Or blessed was't we did?

Pros.   Both, both, my girl!
  By foul play, as thou sayst, were we heaved thence,
  But blessedly holp hither.

Mir.   O, my heart bleeds
  To think o' the teen that I have turned you to,[19]
  Which is from[20] my remembrance! Please you, farther.

Pros. My brother, and thy uncle, called Antonio—   80
  I pray thee mark me—that a brother should
  Be so perfidious!—he whom next thyself
  Of all the world I loved, and to him put[21]
  The manage of my state, as at that time
  Through all the seignories[22] it was the first,
  And Prospero the prime[23] duke, being so reputed
  In dignity, and for the liberal arts[24]
  Without a parallel; those being all my study,
  The government I cast upon my brother
  And to my state[25] grew stranger, being transported   90
  And rapt in secret[26] studies—thy false uncle—
  Dost thou attend me?

Mir.   Sir, most heedfully,

Pros. Being once perfected[27] how to grant suits,
  How to deny them, who t' advance, and who
  To trash for overtopping,[28] new-created
  The creatures that were mine, I say, or changed 'em,
  Or else new-formed 'em; having both the key[29]
  Of officer and office, set all hearts i' the state[30]
  To what tune pleased his ear, that[31] now he was   100
  The ivy which had hid my princely trunk
  And sucked my verdure out on 't.[32] Thou attendst not!

Mir. O, good sir, I do.

Pros.   I pray thee mark me.
  I thus neglecting worldly ends, all dedicated
  To closeness,[33] and the bettering of my mind

---

[17] **piece,** masterpiece.   [18] **no worse issued,** descended from no lower stock.
[19] **teen . . . to,** sorrow I have forced you to recall.   [20] **from,** out of.   [21] **put,** entrusted.
[22] **signories,** dukedoms.   [23] **prime,** first in importance.
[24] **liberal arts,** learning.   [25] **state,** duties of government.
[26] **secret,** occult, i.e., magic.   [27] **Being . . . perfected,** having learned perfectly.
[28] **trash for over-topping,** to clip to keep from growing too high, i.e., to restrain from becoming too
ambitious; **new created,** made over (so that they were no longer loyal to me).
[29] **key,** the tuning key.   [30] **state,** government.
[31] **that,** so that.   [32] **on 't,** of it.   [33] **closeness,** privacy.

With that which, but by being so retired,[34]
O'erprized all popular rate,[35] in my false brother
Awakened an evil nature, and my trust,
Like a good parent, did beget of him
A falsehood in its contrary[36] as great   110
As my trust was, which had indeed no limit,
A confidence sans bound. He being thus lorded,[37]
Not only with what my revenue yielded
But what my power[38] might else exact, like one
Who having unto truth, by telling of it,[39]
Made such a sinner of his memory
To credit his own lie,[40] he did believe
He was indeed the Duke, out o' the substitution[41]
And executing the outward face[42] of royalty   120
With all prerogative. Hence his ambition growing—
Dost thou hear?
MIR.   Your tale, sir, would cure deafness.
PROS. To have no screen between this part he played
And him he played it for, he needs will be
Absolute Milan.[43] Me (poor man) my library
Was dukedom large enough! Of temporal[44] royalties
He thinks me now incapable; confederates[45]
(So dry[46] he was for sway) with the King of Naples
To give him annual tribute, do him homage,   130
Subject his coronet to his crown, and bend
The dukedom yet unbowed (alas, poor Milan!)
To most ignoble stooping.
MIR.   O the heavens!
PROS. Mark his condition, and the event;[47] then tell me
If this might be a brother.
MIR.   I should sin
To think but nobly of my grandmother.
Good wombs have borne bad sons.
PROS.   Now the condition.   140
This King of Naples, being an enemy
To me inveterate, hearkens my brother's suit;
Which was, that he, in lieu o' the premises,[48]
Of homage and I know not how much tribute,

---

[34] **but . . . retired,** but for the fact that it kept me out of touch with the duties of my office.
[35] **o'erprized . . . rate,** (would have) surpassed in value all popular estimate.
[36] **falsehood,** treachery; **contrary,** opposite kind.
[37] **lorded,** made lord (i.e., supreme ruler) of the state.
[38] **power,** i.e., tyrannical power.   [39] **it,** i.e., his lie.
[40] **Who . . . lie,** who by telling a lie often has so corrupted his memory as to mistake his lie for the truth.
[41] **out . . . substitution,** by reason of acting as my substitute.
[42] **executing . . . face,** performing the obvious duties.   [43] **Absolute Milan,** actual Duke of Milan.
[44] **temporal,** i.e., as contrasted with "spiritual"; **royalties,** royal prerogatives.
[45] **confederates,** conspires.   [46] **dry,** thirsty.
[47] **condition,** the terms of his agreement; **event,** result.
[48] **in . . . premises,** in return for the stipulations.

Should presently[49] extirpate me and mine
Out of the dukedom and confer fair Milan,
With all the honors, on my brother. Whereon,[50]
A treacherous army levied, one midnight
Fated to the purpose, did Antonio open
The gates of Milan; and, i' the dead of darkness,　　　　150
The ministers[51] for the purpose hurried thence
Me and thy crying self.

MIR.　　　　　　　　　Alack, for pity!
I, not rememb'ring how I cried out then,
Will cry it o'er again. It is a hint[52]
That wrings mine eyes to't.

PROS.　　　　　　　　　Hear a little further,
And then I'll bring thee to the present business
Which now's upon's; without the which this story
Were most impertinent.[53]　　　　　　　　　　　　160

MIR.　　　　　　　　　Wherefore did they not
That hour destroy us?

PROS.　　　　　　　　　Well demanded, wench.[54]
My tale provokes that question. Dear, they durst not,
So dear the love my people bore me; nor set[55]
A mark so bloody on the business; but
With colors fairer[56] painted their foul ends.
In few,[57] they hurried us aboard a bark,
Bore us some leagues to sea; where they prepared
A rotten carcass of a butt, not rigged,　　　　　　　170
Nor tackle, sail, nor mast; the very rats
Instinctively have quit it. There they hoist us,
To cry to the sea, that roared to us; to sigh
To the winds, whose pity, sighing back again,
Did us but loving wrong.

MIR.　　　　　　　　　Alack, what trouble
Was I then to you!

PROS.　　　　　　　　　O, a cherubin
Thou wast that did preserve me! Thou didst smile,
Infused with a fortitude from heaven,　　　　　　　　180
When I have decked[58] the sea with drops full salt,
Under my burden groaned; which raised in me
An undergoing stomach,[59] to bear up
Against what should ensue.

MIR.　　　　　　　　　How came we ashore?

PROS. By providence divine.
Some food we had, and some fresh water, that
A noble Neapolitan, Gonzalo,
Out of his charity, who being then appointed

---

[49] **presently,** at once.　　[50] **whereon,** i.e., in carrying out this agreement.
[51] **ministers,** agents.　　[52] **hint,** occasion.
[53] **impertinent,** irrelevant.　　[54] **wench,** here used affectionately.
[55] **set,** i.e., dare set.　　[56] **colors,** i.e., pretexts; **fairer,** more specious.
[57] **few,** short.　　[58] **decked,** covered.　　[59] **undergoing stomach,** courage to endure.

Master of this design, did give us, with   190
Rich garments, linens, stuffs, and necessaries
Which since have steaded much. So, of his gentleness,[60]
Knowing I loved my books, he furnished me
From mine own library with volumes that
I prize above my dukedom.

Mir.   Would I might
But ever see that man!

Pros.   Now I arise.
Sit still, and hear the last of our sea-sorrow.
Here in this island we arrived; and here   200
Have I, thy schoolmaster, made thee more profit
Than other princess can, that have more time
For vainer hours, and tutors not so careful.

Mir. Heavens thank you for't! And now I pray you, sir,—
For still 'tis beating in my mind,—your reason
For raising this sea-storm?

Pros.   Know thus far forth.
By accident most strange, bountiful Fortune
(Now my dear lady[61]) hath mine enemies
Brought to this shore; and by my prescience   210
I find my zenith[62] doth depend upon
A most auspicious star, whose influence
If now I court not, but omit,[63] my fortunes
Will ever after droop. Here cease more questions.
Thou art inclined to sleep. 'Tis a good dullness,[64]
And give it way. I know thou canst not choose.

                                    [Miranda *sleeps.*]
Come away,[65] servant, come! I am ready now.
Approach, my Ariel. Come!

Enter Ariel.

Ariel. All hail, great master! Grave sir, hail! I come
To answer thy best pleasure; be't to fly,   220
To swim, to dive into the fire, to ride
On the curled clouds. To thy strong bidding task[66]
Ariel and all his quality.[67]

Pros.   Hast thou, spirit,
Performed to point[68] the tempest that I bade thee?

Ariel. To every article.
I boarded the King's ship. Now on the beak,[69]
Now in the waist, the deck, in every cabin,
I flamed amazement.[70] Sometime I'ld divide
And burn in many places; on the topmast,   230

---

[60] **steaded,** helped; **gentleness,** nobility of nature.   [61] **dear lady,** kind patroness.
[62] **my zenith,** rising to the top of my fortune.   [63] **omit,** ignore.
[64] **dullness,** drowsiness.   [65] **away,** hither.   [66] **task,** put to the test.
[67] **quality,** skill.   [68] **to point,** to the most exact detail.   [69] **beak,** prow.
[70] **flamed amazement,** caused terror by becoming flame (i.e., he became St. Elmo's fire).

The yards, and bowsprit would I flame distinctly,[71]
Then meet and join. Jove's lightnings, the precursors
O' the dreadful thunderclaps, more momentary[72]
And sight-outrunning were not. The fire and cracks[73]
Of sulphurous roaring the most mighty Neptune
Seem to besiege and make his bold waves tremble;
Yea, his dread trident shake.

PROS.   My brave[74] spirit!
Who was so firm, so constant, that this coil[75]
Would not infect his reason?   240

ARIEL.   Not a soul
But felt a fever of the mad[76] and played
Some tricks of desperation. All but mariners
Plunged in the foaming brine and quit the vessel,
Then all afire with me. The King's son Ferdinand,
With hair up-staring[77] (then like reeds, not hair),
Was the first man that leapt; cried "Hell is empty,
And all the devils are here!"

PROS.   Why, that's my spirit!
But was not this nigh shore?   250

ARIEL.   Close by, my master.

PROS. But are they, Ariel, safe?

ARIEL.   Not a hair perished.
On their sustaining[78] garments not a blemish,
But fresher than before; and as thou badest me,
In troops I have dispersed them 'bout the isle.
The King's son have I landed by himself,
Whom I left cooling of the air with sighs
In an odd angle[79] of the isle, and sitting,
His arms in this sad knot.[80]   260

PROS.   Of the King's ship
The mariners say how thou hast disposed,
And all the rest o' the fleet.

ARIEL.   Safely in harbor
Is the King's ship; in the deep nook where once
Thou calledst me up at midnight to fetch dew
From the still-vexed Bermoothes,[81] there she's hid;
The mariners all under hatches stowed,
Who, with a charm joined to their suff'red labor,
I have left asleep; and for[82] the rest o' the fleet,   270
Which I dispersed, they all have met again,
And are upon the Mediterranean float[83]
Bound sadly home for Naples,
Supposing that they saw the King's ship wracked
And his great person perish.

---

[71] **distinctly,** in several places at once.   [72] **momentary,** instantaneous.
[73] **cracks,** sharp, loud noises.   [74] **brave,** fine.
[75] **coil,** turmoil.   [76] **fever . . . mad,** such fever as madmen feel.
[77] **up-staring,** standing on end.   [78] **sustaining,** holding them up.
[79] **odd angle,** out-of-the-way spot.   [80] **this sad knot,** folded sadly, in this way.
[81] **still-vexed Bermoothes,** ever storm-beaten Bermuda.   [82] **for,** as for.   [83] **float,** sea.

PROS.   Ariel, thy charge
  Exactly is performed; but there's more work.
  What is the time o' the day?
ARIEL.   Past the mid season.
PROS. At least two glasses.[84] The time 'twixt six and now   280
  Must by us both be spent most preciously.[85]
ARIEL. Is there more toil? Since thou dost give me pains,[86]
  Let me remember thee what thou hast promised,
  Which is not yet performed me.
PROS.   How now? moody?
  What is't thou canst demand?
ARIEL.   My liberty.
PROS. Before the time be out? No more!
ARIEL.   I prithee,
  Remember I have done thee worthy service,   290
  Told thee no lies, made no mistakings, served
  Without or grudge or grumblings. Thou didst promise
  To bate[87] me a full year.
PROS.   Dost thou forget
  From what a torment I did free thee?
ARIEL.   No.
PROS. Thou dost; and thinkst it much to tread the ooze
  Of the salt deep,
  To run upon the sharp wind of the North,
  To do me business in the veins o' the earth   300
  When it is baked with frost.
ARIEL.   I do not, sir.
PROS. Thou liest, malignant thing! Hast thou forgot
  The foul witch Sycorax, who with age and envy[88]
  Was grown into a hoop? Hast thou forgot her?
ARIEL. No, sir.
PROS.   Thou hast. Where was she born?
  Speak! Tell me!
ARIEL. Sir, in Argier.[89]
PROS.   O, was she so? I must   310
  Once in a month recount what thou hast been,
  Which thou forgetst. This damned witch Sycorax,
  For mischiefs manifold, and sorceries terrible
  To enter human hearing, from Argier
  Thou knowst was banished. For one thing[90] she did
  They would not take her life. Is not this true?
ARIEL. Ay, sir.
PROS. This blue-eyed[91] hag was hither brought with child
  And here was left by the sailors. Thou, my slave,
  As thou reportst thyself, wast then her servant;   320
  And, for thou wast a spirit too delicate

---

[84] **glasses,** hourglasses, hours.   [85] **preciously,** i.e., as though each moment were precious.
[86] **pains,** hard tasks.   [87] **bate me,** reduce my term of service by.
[88] **envy,** malice.   [89] **Argier,** Algiers.
[90] **for one thing,** because of one good deed.   [91] **blue-eyed,** with dark circles under her eyes.

To act her earthy and abhorred commands,
Refusing her grand hests,[92] she did confine thee,
By help of her more potent ministers,[93]
And in her most unmitigable rage,
Into a cloven pine; within which rift
Imprisoned thou didst painfully remain
A dozen years; within which space she died
And left thee there; where thou didst vent thy groans
As fast as mill wheels strike.[94] Then was this island   330
(Save for the son that she did litter here,
A freckled whelp, hag-born[95]) not honored with
A human shape.   \

ARIEL.   Yes, Caliban, her son.

PROS. Dull thing, I say so! he, that Caliban
Whom now I keep in service. Thou best knowst
What torment I did find thee in. Thy groans
Did make wolves howl and penetrate the breasts
Of ever-angry bears. It was a torment
To lay upon the damned, which Sycorax   340
Could not again undo. It was mine art,
When I arrived and heard thee, that made gape
The pine, and let thee out.

ARIEL.   I thank thee, master.

PROS. If thou more murmurst, I will rend an oak
And peg thee in his knotty entrails till
Thou hast howled away twelve winters.

ARIEL.   Pardon, master.
I will be correspondent[96] to command
And do my spriting gently.[97]   350

PROS.   Do so; and after two days
I will discharge thee.

ARIEL.   That's my noble master!
What shall I do? Say what! What shall I do?

PROS. Go make thyself like a nymph o' the sea. Be subject
To no sight but thine and mine; invisible
To every eyeball else. Go take this shape
And hither come in't. Go! Hence with diligence!

                                               Exit [ARIEL].

Awake, dear heart, awake! Thou hast slept well.
Awake!   360

MIR.   The strangeness of your story put
Heaviness[98] in me.

PROS.   Shake it off. Come on.
We'll visit Caliban, my slave, who never
Yields us kind answer.

MIR.   'Tis a villain, sir,

---

[92] **grand hests,** important commands.   [93] **ministers,** agents.
[94] **As ... strike,** as fast as the clacks of water mills.   [95] **hag-born,** born of a witch.
[96] **correspondent,** submissive.   [97] **gently,** quietly, i.e., without complaint.
[98] **Heaviness,** drowsiness.

I do not love to look on.

PROS.   But as 'tis,
We cannot miss[99] him. He does make our fire,
Fetch in our wood, and serves in offices[100]
That profit us. What, ho! slave! Caliban!
Thou earth, thou! Speak!   370

CAL. (*Within*)   There's wood enough within.

PROS. Come forth, I say! There's other business for thee.
Come, thou tortoise! When?[101]

Enter ARIEL *like a water nymph.*

Fine apparition! My quaint[102] Ariel,
Hark in thine ear.

ARIEL.   My lord, it shall be done.   *Exit.*

PROS. Thou poisonous slave, got by the Devil himself
Upon thy wicked dam, come forth!   380

Enter CALIBAN

CAL. As wicked dew as e'er my mother brushed
With raven's feather from unwholesome fen
Drop on you both! A southwest[103] blow on ye
And blister you all o'er!

PROS. For this, be sure, tonight thou shalt have cramps,
Side-stitches that shall pen thy breath up; urchins[104]
Shall, for that vast[105] of night that they may work,
All exercise[106] on thee; thou shalt be pinched
As thick as honeycomb, each pinch more stinging
Than bees that made 'em.   390

CAL.   I must eat my dinner.
This island's mine by Sycorax my mother,
Which thou takest from me. When thou camest first,
Thou strokedst me and made much of me; wouldst give me
Water with berries in't; and teach me how
To name the bigger light, and how the less,
That burn by day, and night; and then I loved thee
And showed thee all the qualities[107] o' the isle,
The fresh springs, brine-pits, barren place and fertile.
Cursed be I that did so! All the charms   400
Of Sycorax—toads, beetles, bats light on you!
For I am all the subjects that you have,
Which[108] first was mine own king; and here you sty me
In this hard rock, whiles you do keep from me
The rest o' the island.

[99] **miss,** do without.   [100] **offices,** duties.
[101] **When?** an exclamation of impatience.   [102] **quaint,** ingenious.
[103] **southwest,** southwest wind in England was supposed to bring infection with its fog.
[104] **urchins,** imps in the shape of hedgehogs.   [105] **vast,** abyss.
[106] **exercise,** practice.   [107] **qualities,** properties.   [108] **Which,** who.

PROS.   Thou most lying slave,
  Whom stripes may move, not kindness! I have used thee
  (Filth as thou art) with humane care, and lodged thee
  In mine own cell till thou didst seek to violate
  The honor of my child.   410
CAL. O ho, O ho! Would't had been done!
  Thou didst prevent me; I had peopled else
  This isle with Calibans.
MIR.   Abhorred slave,
  Which any print of goodness wilt not take,
  Being capable of all ill! I pitied thee,
  Took pains to make thee speak, taught thee each hour
  One thing or other. When thou didst not, savage,
  Know thine own meaning, but wouldst gabble like
  A thing most brutish, I endowed thy purposes   420
  With words that made them known. But thy vile race,
  Though thou didst learn, had that in't which good natures
  Could not abide to be with. Therefore wast thou
  Deservedly confined into this rock, who hadst
  Deserved more than a prison.
CAL. You taught me language, and my profit on't
  Is, I know how to curse. The red plague rid you[109]
  For learning me your language!
PROS.   Hag-seed,[110] hence!
  Fetch us in fuel; and be quick, thou'rt best,[111]   430
  To answer other business. Shrugst thou, malice?[112]
  If thou neglectst or dost unwillingly
  What I command, I'll rack thee with old[113] cramps,
  Fill all thy bones with aches, make thee roar
  That beasts shall tremble at thy din.
CAL.   No, pray thee.
  [*Aside*] I must obey. His art is of such pow'r
  It would control my dam's god, Setebos,[114]
  And make a vassal of him.
PROS.   So, slave; hence!   440

                                           Exit CALIBAN.

Enter FERDINAND; *and* ARIEL, *invisible, playing and singing.*

                          ARIEL'*s song.*

                  Come unto these yellow sands,
                      And then take hands.
                  Curtsied when you have and kissed,

---

[109] **red plague rid you,** i.e., the bubonic plague destroy you.
[110] **Hag-seed,** son of a witch.   [111] **thou'rt best,** it would be best for you.
[112] **answer,** attend to; **malice,** malignant creature.
[113] **old,** a lot of.   [114] **Setebos,** a god or devil thought to be worshiped by American savages.

The wild waves whist,[115]
Foot it featly[116] here and there;
And, sweet sprites, the burden bear.
Hark, hark!

BURDEN[117] *dispersedly.*[118] Bow, wow!
   The watchdogs bark.
BURDEN *dispersedly.* Bow, wow!
ARIEL.   Hark, hark! I hear   450
      The strain of strutting chanticleer
      Cry, cock-a-diddle-dowe.

FER. Where should this music be? I' the air, or the earth?
   It sounds no more; and sure it waits upon
   Some god o' the island. Sitting on a bank,
   Weeping again the King my father's wrack,
   This music crept by me upon the waters,
   Allaying both their fury and my passion
   With its sweet air. Thence I have followed it,   460
   Or it hath drawn me rather; but 'tis gone.
   No, it begins again.

ARIEL's *song.*

      Full fathom five thy father lies;
         Of his bones are coral made;
      Those are pearls that were his eyes;
         Nothing of him that doth fade
      But doth suffer a sea-change
      Into something rich and strange.
      Sea nymphs hourly ring his knell:

BURDEN. Ding-dong.   470

      Hark! now I hear them—Ding-dong bell.

FER. The ditty does remember[119] my drowned father.
   This is no mortal business, nor no sound
   That the earth owes.[120] I hear it now above me.
PROS. The fringed curtains of thine eye advance[121]
   And say what thou seest yond.
MIR.   What is't? a spirit?
   Lord, how it looks about! Believe me, sir,
   It carries a brave[122] form. But 'tis a spirit.
PROS. No, wench. It eats, and sleeps, and hath such senses   480

---

[115] **whist,** being hushed.   [116] **featly,** gracefully.
[117] **burden,** refrain.   [118] **dispersedly,** coming from different directions.
[119] **ditty,** words to the song; **remember,** commemorate.
[120] **owes,** possesses.   [121] **advance,** lift up.
[122] **brave,** handsome, gallant.

As we have, such. This gallant which thou seest
Was in the wrack; and, but he's something stained[123]
With grief (that's beauty's canker[124]), thou mightst call him
A goodly[125] person. He hath lost his fellows
And strays about to find 'em.

MIR.   I might call him
A thing divine, for nothing natural
I ever saw so noble.

PROS. [*Aside*]   It goes on, I see,   490
As my soul prompts it. Spirit, fine spirit! I'll free thee
Within two days for this.

FER.   Most sure, the goddess
On whom these airs attend![126] Vouchsafe my pray'r
May know if you remain[127] upon this island,
And that you will some good instruction give
How I may bear me here. My prime[128] request,
Which I do last pronounce, is (O you wonder!)
If you be maid or no?[129]

MIR.   No wonder, sir,
But certainly a maid.   500

FER.   My language? Heavens!
I am the best of them that speak this speech,
Were I but where 'tis spoken.

PROS.   How? the best?
What wert thou if the King of Naples heard thee?

FER. A single[130] thing, as I am now, that wonders
To hear thee speak of Naples.[131] He does hear me;
And that he does I weep. Myself am Naples,
Who with mine eyes, never since at ebb, beheld
The King, my father, wracked.   510

MIR.   Alack, for mercy!

FER. Yes, faith, and all his lords, the Duke of Milan
And his brave son being twain.

PROS. [*Aside*]   The Duke of Milan
And his more braver daughter could control[132] thee,
If now 'twere fit to do't. At the first sight
They have changed eyes.[133] Delicate Ariel,
I'll set thee free for this!—A word, good sir.
I fear you have done yourself some wrong.[134] A word!

MIR. Why speaks my father so ungently? This   520
Is the third man that e'er I saw; the first
That e'er I sighed for. Pity move my father
To be inclined my way!

---

[123] **something,** somewhat; **stained,** spoiled.
[124] **canker,** canker-worm or caterpillar that eats the rosebuds.
[125] **goodly,** handsome.   [126] **attend,** accompany.
[127] **May know,** may gain the knowledge from you; **remain,** dwell.
[128] **prime,** first.   [129] **or no,** i.e., or a goddess.
[130] **single,** solitary and so "helpless."   [131] **Naples,** king of Naples.
[132] **control,** confute.   [133] **changed eyes,** i.e., have eyes for each other only.
[134] **done . . . wrong,** have not been true to your better nature.

Fer.   O, if a virgin,
And your affection not gone forth, I'll make you
The Queen of Naples.
Pros.   Soft,[135] sir! one word more.
[*Aside*] They are both in either's pow'rs. But this swift business
I must uneasy make, lest too light[136] winning
Make the prize light.[137]—One word more! I charge thee   530
That thou attend me. Thou dost here usurp
The name thou owest[138] not, and hast put thyself
Upon this island as a spy, to win it
From me, the lord on't.
Fer.   No, as I am a man!
Mir. There's nothing ill can dwell in such a temple.
If the ill spirit have so fair a house,
Good things will strive to dwell with't.[139]
Pros.   Follow me.—
Speak not you for him; he's a traitor.—Come!   540
I'll manacle thy neck and feet together;
Sea water shalt thou drink; thy food shall be
The fresh brook mussels, withered roots, and husks
Wherein the acorn cradled. Follow.
Fer.   No.
I will resist such entertainment[140] till
Mine enemy has more power.

                    He draws, and is charmed from moving.
Mir.   O dear father,
Make not too rash a trial of him, for
He's gentle, and not fearful.[141]   550
Pros.   What, I say,
My foot[142] my tutor?—Put thy sword up, traitor!
Who makest a show but darest not strike, thy conscience
Is so possessed with guilt. Come, from thy ward![143]
For I can here disarm thee with this stick[144]
And make thy weapon drop.
Mir.   Beseech you,[145] father!
Pros. Hence! Hang not on my garments.
Mir.   Sir, have pity.
I'll be his surety.   560
Pros.   Silence! One word more
Shall make me chide thee, if not hate thee. What,
An advocate for an impostor? Hush!
Thou thinkst there is no more such shapes as he,
Having seen but him and Caliban. Foolish wench!

---

[135] **Soft,** wait a minute.   [136] **uneasy,** difficult; **light,** easy.
[137] **light,** lightly valued.   [138] **owest,** ownest.
[139] **strive . . . 't,** strive to occupy the same house (in order to drive out the evil spirit).
[140] **entertainment,** treatment.   [141] **gentle,** well-born; **not fearful,** no coward.
[142] **foot,** an inferior part of the body, i.e., Miranda.
[143] **Come . . . ward,** abandon your posture of defense.   [144] **stick,** his magic wand.
[145] **Beseech you,** i.e., I beseech you.

To[146] the most of men this is a Caliban,
And they to him are angels.

MIR.   My affections
Are then most humble. I have no ambition
To see a goodlier[147] man.   570

PROS.   Come on, obey!
Thy nerves[148] are in their infancy again
And have no vigor in them.

FER.   So they are.
My spirits,[149] as in a dream, are all bound up.
My father's loss, the weakness which I feel,
The wrack of all my friends, nor this man's threats
To whom I am subdued, are but light to me,
Might I but through my prison once a day
Behold this maid. All corners else o' the earth   580
Let liberty make use of;[150] space enough
Have I in such a prison.

PROS. [*Aside*]   It works.   [*To* FERDINAND]
Come on.—
Thou hast done well, fine Ariel! [*To* FERDINAND] Follow me.—
[*To* ARIEL] Hark what thou else shalt do me.

MIR.   Be of comfort.
My father's of a better nature, sir,
Than he appears by speech. This is unwonted
Which now came from him.   590

PROS.   Thou shalt be as free
As mountain winds; but then exactly do
All points of my command.

ARIEL.   To the syllable.

PROS. Come, follow.—Speak not for him.

                                                            Exeunt.

ACT II

Scene I. [Another part of the island.]

Enter ALONSO, SEBASTIAN, ANTONIO, GONZALO, ADRIAN, FRANCISCO, *and others.*

GON. Beseech you, sir, be merry. You have cause
  (So have we all) of joy; for our escape
  Is much beyond our loss. Our hint of[1] woe
  Is common. Every day some sailor's wife,
  The master of some merchant, and the merchant,[2]
  Have just our theme of woe; but for[3] the miracle,
  I mean our preservation, few in millions

---

[146] **To,** in comparison with.   [147] **goodlier,** handsomer.
[148] **nerves,** sinews.   [149] **spirits,** energies.
[150] **All . . . use of,** let those who are free have all the rest of the world.

[1] **hint of,** occasion for.
[2] **merchant,** merchantman; **merchant,** i.e., the owner.   [3] **for,** as for.

Can speak like us. Then wisely, good sir, weigh
Our sorrow with our comfort.
ALON.   Prithee peace.   10
SEB. He receives comfort like cold porridge.
ANT. The visitor[4] will not give him o'er so.[5]
SEB. Look, he's winding up the watch of his wit; by-and-by it will strike.
GON. Sir—
SEB. One. Tell.[6]
GON. When every grief is entertained[7] that's offered,
    Comes to the entertainer—
SEB. A dollar.[8]
GON. Dolor comes to him, indeed. You have spoken truer than you
    purposed.   20
SEB. You have taken it wiselier[9] than I meant you should.
GON. Therefore, my lord—
ANT. Fie, what a spendthrift is he of his tongue!
ALON. I prithee spare.[10]
GON. Well, I have done. But yet—
SEB. He will be talking.
ANT. Which, of he or Adrian, for a good wager, first begins to crow?
SEB. The old cock.[11]
ANT. The cock'rel.[12]
SEB. Done! The wager?   30
ANT. A laughter.[13]
SEB. A match!
ADR. Though this island seem to be desert—
ANT. Ha, ha, ha!
SEB. So, you're paid.[14]
ADR. Uninhabitable and almost inaccessible—
SEB. Yet—
ADR. Yet—
ANT. He could not miss't.
ADR. It must needs be of subtle, tender, and delicate temperance.[15]   40
ANT. Temperance[16] was a delicate wench.
SEB. Ay, and a subtle, as he most learnedly delivered.[17]
ADR. The air breathes upon us here most sweetly.
SEB. As if it had lungs, and rotten ones.
ANT. Or as 'twere perfumed by a fen.
GON. Here is everything advantageous to life.
ANT. True; save means to live.
SEB. Of that there's none, or little.
GON. How lush and lusty the grass looks! how green!
ANT. The ground indeed is tawny.   50

---

[4] **visitor,** spiritual counsellor.   [5] **give . . . so,** give him up with so little preaching.
[6] **tell,** count.   [7] **entertained,** accepted (without resistance).
[8] **dollar,** pun on "dolor," meaning grief.   [9] **taken it wiselier,** understood my remark more subtly.
[10] **spare,** i.e., your words.   [11] **The old cock,** Gonzalo.   [12] **The cock'rel,** Adrian.
[13] **laughter,** i.e., the winner has a laugh on the loser; **laughter,** also means a nest of eggs.
[14] **you're paid,** i.e., you've had your laugh.   [15] **temperance,** temperature.
[16] **Temperance,** a character in a morality play or in Chapman's *May Day* (1611).
[17] **delivered,** reported.

SEB. With an eye[18] of green in't.

ANT. He misses not much.

SEB. No; he doth but mistake the truth totally.

GON. But the rarity of it[19] is—which is indeed almost beyond credit—

SEB. As many vouched rarities[20] are.

GON. That our garments, being, as they were, drenched in the sea, hold,
  notwithstanding, their freshness and gloss, being rather new-dyed
  than stained with salt water.

ANT. If but one of his pockets could speak,[21] would it not say he lies?

SEB. Ay, or very falsely pocket up[22] his report.   60

GON. Methinks our garments are now as fresh as when we put them on
  first in Afric, at the marriage of the King's fair daughter Claribel to the
  King of Tunis.

SEB. 'Twas a sweet marriage, and we prosper well in our return.

ADR. Tunis was never graced before with such a paragon to their queen.

GON. Not since widow Dido's time.

ANT. Widow? A pox o' that![23] How came that "widow" in? Widow Dido!

SEB. What if he had said "widower Aeneas" too? Good lord, how you
  take it!

ADR. "Widow Dido," said you? You make me study of that. She was of   70
  Carthage, not of Tunis.

GON. This Tunis, sir, was Carthage.

ADR. Carthage?

GON. I assure you, Carthage.

ANT. His word is more than the miraculous harp.[24]

SEB. He hath raised the wall, and houses too.[25]

ANT. What impossible matter will he make easy next?

SEB. I think he will carry this island home in his pocket and give it his
  son for an apple.

ANT. And, sowing the kernels of it in the sea, bring forth more islands.   80

GON. Ay!

ANT. Why, in good time![26]

GON. Sir, we were talking that our garments seem now as fresh as when
  we were at Tunis at the marriage of your daughter, who is now Queen.

ANT. And the rarest that e'er came there.

SEB. Bate,[27] I beseech you, widow Dido.

ANT. O, widow Dido? Ay, widow Dido!

GON. Is not, sir, my doublet as fresh as the first day I wore it? I mean, in
  a sort.

ANT. That "sort" was well fished for.[28]   90

GON. When I wore it at your daughter's marriage.

ALON. You cram these words into mine ears against

---

[18] **eye,** touch.   [19] **rarity of it,** strange thing about it.
[20] **vouched rarities,** strange tales vouched for by their narrators.
[21] **pockets . . . speak,** and say they were wet.
[22] **pocket up,** accept without examining.   [23] **of that,** about that.
[24] **miraculous harp,** Amphion is said to have made the walls of Thebes rise by playing on his harp.
[25] **the . . . too,** i.e., of Carthage (by identifying it with Tunis).
[26] **in good time,** that's a good idea.   [27] **bate,** subtract, except.
[28] **That . . . for,** the word "sort" was a lucky catch.

The stomach of my sense.[29] Would I had never
Married my daughter there! for, coming thence,
My son is lost; and, in my rate,[30] she too,
Who is so far from Italy removed
I ne'er again shall see her. O thou mine heir
Of Naples and of Milan, what strange fish
Hath made his meal on thee?

FRAN.   Sir, he may live.   100
I saw him beat the surges under him
And ride upon their backs. He trod the water,
Whose enmity he flung aside, and breasted
The surge most swol'n that met him. His bold head
'Bove the contentious waves he kept, and oared
Himself with his good arms in lusty stroke
To the shore, that o'er his wave-worn basis[31] bowed,
As[32] stooping to relieve him. I not doubt
He came alive to land.

ALON.   No, no, he's gone.   110

SEB. Sir, you may thank yourself for this great loss,
    That would not bless our Europe with your daughter,
    But rather lose her to an African,
    Where she, at least, is banished from your eye
    Who[33] hath cause to wet the grief on't.

ALON.   Prithee peace.

SEB. You were kneeled to and importuned otherwise[34]
    By all of us; and the fair soul herself
    Weighed,[35] between loathness and obedience, at
    Which end o' the beam should[36] bow. We have lost your son,   120
    I fear, forever. Milan and Naples have
    Mo[37] widows in them of this business' making
    Than we bring men to comfort them.
    The fault's your own.

ALON.   So is the dear'st[38] o' the loss.

GON. My Lord Sebastian,
    The truth you speak doth lack some gentleness,
    And time[39] to speak it in. You rub the sore
    When you should bring the plaster.

SEB.   Very well.   130

ANT. And most chirurgeonly.[40]

GON. It is foul weather in us all, good sir,
    When you are cloudy.

SEB.   Foul weather?

ANT.   Very foul.

---

[29] **stomach . . . sense,** inclination of my feelings.   [30] **rate,** estimation.
[31] **his,** its; **basis,** base.   [32] **As,** as if.   [33] **Who,** i.e., the eye.
[34] **importuned otherwise,** begged him to do otherwise, i.e., not to marry his daughter to the King of Tunis.
[35] **Weighed,** balanced.
[36] **beam,** the bar at the ends of which the two balances hung; **should,** i.e., she should.
[37] **Mo,** more.   [38] **dear'st,** worst.   [39] **time,** fitting time.   [40] **chirurgeonly,** like a surgeon.

GON. Had I plantation of[41] this isle, my lord—

ANT. He'd sow't with nettle seed.

SEB.   Or docks, or mallows.

GON. And were the king on't, what would I do?

SEB. 'Scape being drunk, for want of wine.   140

GON. I' the commonwealth I would by contraries[42]
   Execute all things; for no kind of traffic
   Would I admit; no name of magistrate;
   Letters[43] should not be known; riches, poverty,
   And use of service,[44] none; contract, succession,
   Bourn, bound of land, tilth,[45] vineyard, none;
   No use of metal, corn, or wine, or oil;
   No occupation; all men idle, all;
   And women too, but innocent and pure;
   No sovereignty.   150

SEB.   Yet he would be king on't.

ANT. The latter end of his commonwealth forgets the beginning.

GON. All things in common nature should produce
   Without sweat or endeavor. Treason, felony,
   Sword, pike, knife, gun, or need of any engine[46]
   Would I not have; but nature should bring forth,
   Of it own kind, all foison,[47] all abundance,
   To feed my innocent people.

SEB. No marrying 'mong his subjects?

ANT. None, man! All idle[48]—whores and knaves.   160

GON. I would with such perfection govern, sir,
   T'excel[49] the golden age.

SEB.   Save his Majesty!

ANT. Long live Gonzalo!

GON.   And—do you mark me, sir?

ALON. Prithee no more. Thou dost talk nothing to me.

GON. I do well believe your Highness; and did it to minister occasion[50]
   to these gentlemen, who are of such sensible[51] and nimble lungs that
   they always use to laugh at nothing.

ANT. 'Twas you we laughed at.   170

GON. Who in this kind of merry fooling am nothing to you. So you may
   continue, and laugh at nothing still.

ANT. What a blow was there given!

SEB. An it had not fall'n flatlong.[52]

GON. You are gentlemen of brave metal.[53] You would lift the moon out
   of her sphere if she would continue in it five weeks without changing.

Enter ARIEL [*invisible*], *playing solemn music.*

---

[41] **plantation of,** the charter to colonize.
[42] **by contraries,** by methods the direct opposite of the usual ones.
[43] **Letters,** learning.   [44] **service,** ceremony.
[45] **Bourn,** boundary; **tilth,** tillage.   [46] **engine,** military machines.
[47] **it,** its; **foison,** plenty.   [48] **idle,** worthless.
[49] **T'excel,** as to excel.   [50] **minister occasion,** furnish opportunity (for laughter).
[51] **sensible,** sensitive.   [52] **An,** if; **flatlong,** with the flat of the sword.
[53] **brave metal,** fine spirit.

SEB. We would so, and then go a-batfowling.[54]
ANT. Nay, good my lord, be not angry.
GON. No, I warrant you. I will not adventure[55] my discretion so weakly.
    Will you laugh me asleep, for I am very heavy?[56]   180
ANT. Go sleep, and hear us.[57]
                [*All sleep except* ALONSO, SEBASTIAN, *and* ANTONIO.]
ALON. What, all so soon asleep? I wish mine eyes
    Would, with themselves, shut up my thoughts. I find
    They are inclined to do so.
SEB.   Please you, sir
    Do not omit the heavy offer[58] of it.
    It seldom visits sorrow; when it doth,
    It is a comforter.
ANT.   We two, my lord,
    Will guard your person while you take your rest,   190
    And watch your safety.
ALON.   Thank you. Wondrous heavy.
                     [ALONSO *sleeps. Exit* ARIEL.]
SEB. What a strange drowsiness possesses them!
ANT. It is the quality o' the climate.
SEB.   Why
    Doth it not then our eyelids sink? I find not
    Myself disposed to sleep.
ANT.   Nor I. My spirits are nimble.[59]
    They fell together all, as by consent.[60]
    They dropped as by a thunderstroke. What might,   200
    Worthy Sebastian—O, what might?—No more!
    And yet methinks I see it in thy face,
    What thou shouldst be. The occasion speaks thee,[61] and
    My strong imagination sees a crown
    Dropping upon thy head.
SEB.   What? Art thou waking?
ANT. Do you not hear me speak?
SEB.   I do; and surely
    It is a sleepy language, and thou speakst
    Out of thy sleep. What is it thou didst say?   210
    This is a strange repose, to be asleep
    With eyes wide open; standing, speaking, moving—
    And yet so fast asleep.
ANT.   Noble Sebastian,
    Thou letst thy fortune sleep—die, rather; winkst[62]
    Whiles thou are waking.[63]
SEB.   Thou dost snore distinctly;
    There's meaning in thy snores.

---

[54] **a-batfowling,** hunting birds at night with a light and a stick with which to beat the bushes.
[55] **adventure,** risk.   [56] **heavy,** drowsy.
[57] **hear us,** i.e., let our laughter put you to sleep.
[58] **omit,** fail to accept; **heavy offer,** the invitation which your drowsiness extends.
[59] **nimble,** alert.   [60] **consent,** agreement.
[61] **speaks thee,** proclaims thee [king].   [62] **winkst,** Do you close your eyes [to this chance]?
[63] **waking,** awake.

ANT. I am more serious than my custom. You
    Must be so too, if heed me;[64] which to do   220
    Trebles thee o'er.
SEB.   Well, I am standing water.[65]
ANT. I'll teach you how to flow.
SEB.   Do so. To ebb
    Hereditary sloth instructs me.
ANT.   O,
    If you but knew how you the purpose[66] cherish
    Whiles thus you mock it! how, in stripping[67] it,
    You more invest it! Ebbing men[68] indeed
    (Most often) do so near the bottom run   230
    By[69] their own fear or sloth.
SEB.   Prithee say on.
    The setting[70] of thine eye and cheek proclaim
    A matter[71] from thee; and a birth, indeed,
    Which throes thee much to yield.[72]
ANT.   Thus, sir:
    Although this lord of weak remembrance,[73] this
    Who shall be of as little memory
    When he is earthed,[74] hath here almost persuaded
    (For he's a spirit of persuasion, only   240
    Professes[75] to persuade) the King his son's alive,
    'Tis as impossible that he's undrowned
    As he that sleeps here swims.
SEB.   I have no hope[76]
    That he's undrowned.
ANT.   O, out of that no hope
    What great hope have you! No hope that way is
    Another way so high a hope that even
    Ambition cannot pierce a wink beyond,[77]
    But doubts discovery there.[78] Will you grant with me   250
    That Ferdinand is drowned?
SEB.   He's gone.
ANT.   Then tell me,
    Who's the next heir of Naples?
SEB.   Claribel.
ANT. She that is Queen of Tunis; she that dwells
    Ten leagues beyond man's life; she that from Naples
    Can have no note,[79] unless the sun were post—
    The man i' the moon's too slow—till newborn chins

---

[64] **if heed me,** if you pay attention to me.
[65] **Trebles ... o'er,** makes you three times as great; **standing water,** i.e., when the tide neither ebbs nor flows.
[66] **purpose,** i.e., to be king.   [67] **stripping,** i.e., of pretense.
[68] **invest it,** clothe it with reality; **Ebbing men,** men who are stranded when their fortune ebbs.
[69] **By,** because of.   [70] **setting,** fixed expression.
[71] **matter,** i.e., of importance.   [72] **throes,** pains; **yield,** utter.   [73] **remembrance,** memory.
[74] **earthed,** buried, i.e., the memory of him after he is dead will be as short as his own.
[75] **only Professes,** his sole profession is.   [76] **hope,** expectation.
[77] **wink,** the least bit; **beyond,** i.e., hope of the crown.
[78] **But ... there,** but must doubt the truth of what it sees there.   [79] **note,** information.

Be rough and razorable; she that from whom[80]　　　　　　　　　260
We all were sea-swallowed, though some cast[81] again,
And, by that destiny, to perform an act
Whereof what's past is prologue, what to come,
In yours and my discharge.[82]
SEB.　　　　　　　　　　　　What stuff is this? How say you?
'Tis true my brother's daughter's Queen of Tunis;
So is she heir of Naples; 'twixt which regions
There is some space.
ANT.　　　　　　　　A space whose ev'ry cubit
Seems to cry out "How shall that Claribel　　　　　　　　270
Measure us back to Naples? Keep[83] in Tunis,
And let Sebastian wake!" Say this were death
That now hath seized them, why, they were[84] no worse
Than now they are. There be that[85] can rule Naples
As well as he that sleeps; lords that can prate
As amply and unnecessarily
As this Gonzalo. I myself could make
A chough of as deep chat. O, that you bore[86]
The mind that I do! What a sleep were this
For your advancement! Do you understand me?　　　　　　280
SEB. Methinks I do.
ANT.　　　　　　　　And how does your content[87]
Tender[88] your own good fortune?
SEB.　　　　　　　　　　　　I remember
You did supplant your brother Prospero.
ANT.　　　　　　　　　　　　　　True.
And look how well my garments sit upon me,
Much feater[89] than before! My brother's servants
Were then my fellows; now they are my men.
SEB. But, for[90] your conscience—　　　　　　　　　290
ANT. Ay, sir! Where lies that? If 'twere a kibe,[91]
'Twould put me to[92] my slipper; but I feel not
This deity in my bosom. Twenty consciences
That stand 'twixt me and Milan, candied be they
And melt, ere they molest![93] Here lies your brother,
No better than the earth he lies upon
If he were that which now he's like—that's dead;
Whom I with this obedient steel (three inches of it)
Can lay to bed forever; whiles you, doing thus,

---

[80] **from whom,** returning from whom.　　　[81] **cast,** (1) vomited up, (2) cast for a role in a play.
[82] **discharge,** performance, i.e., yours and mine to perform.
[83] **Measure us back,** find her way back to us; **Keep,** stay.
[84] **them,** i.e., all the sleepers; **were,** would be.　　　[85] **that,** those who.
[86] **chough . . . chat,** a crow talk as deep stuff; **bore,** had.
[87] **content,** pleasure.
[88] **Tender,** regard; i.e., With how much pleasure do you regard?
[89] **feater,** more becomingly.　　　[90] **for,** as to.
[91] **kibe,** sore heel.　　　[92] **put me to,** force me to wear.
[93] **Twenty . . . molest,** let the twenty consciences that stand between me and the duchy of Milan be frozen stiff and then melt like candy rather than disturb me.

To the perpetual wink[94] for aye might put   300
This ancient morsel,[95] this Sir Prudence, who
Should not upbraid our course. For[96] all the rest,
They'll take suggestion[97] as a cat laps milk;
They'll tell the clock to any business[98] that
We say befits the hour.
SEB.   Thy case, dear friend,
Shall be my precedent. As thou gotst Milan,
I'll come by Naples. Draw thy sword. One stroke
Shall free thee from the tribute which thou payest,
And I the King shall love thee.   310
ANT.   Draw together;
And when I rear my hand, do you the like,
To fall it[99] on Gonzalo.   [*They draw.*]
SEB.   O, but one word!

                                                    [*They converse apart.*]

Enter ARIEL, [*invisible*], *with music and song.*

ARIEL. My master through his art foresees the danger
That you, his friend,[100] are in, and sends me forth
(For else his project dies[101]) to keep them living.
                              Sings in GONZALO's *ear.*

          While you here do snoring lie,
          Open-eyed conspiracy
                    His time doth take.   320
          If of life you keep a care,
          Shake off slumber and beware.
                    Awake, awake!

ANT. Then let us both be sudden.
GON. [*Wakes*] Now good angels preserve the King!
ALON. [*Wakes*] Why, how now? Ho, awake! Why are you drawn?[102]
   Wherefore this ghastly looking?
GON.   What's the matter?
SEB. Whiles we stood here securing your respose,
   Even now, we heard a hollow burst of bellowing   330
   Like bulls, or rather lions. Did't not wake you?
   It struck mine ear most terribly.
ALON.   I heard nothing.
ANT. O, 'twas a din to fright a monster's ear,
   To make an earthquake! Sure it was the roar
   Of a whole herd of lions.
ALON.   Heard you this, Gonzalo?

---

[94] **perpetual wink,** everlasting sleep.   [95] **morsel,** piece of a man.
[96] **For,** as for.   [97] **take suggestion,** act on our suggestion.
[98] **tell . . . business,** count the strokes and say when it is the proper time for.
[99] **fall it,** let it fall.   [100] **his friend,** Gonzalo.
[101] **project dies,** plan miscarries.   [102] **Why . . . drawn?** Why have you drawn your swords?

GON. Upon mine honor, sir, I heard a humming,[103]
   And that a strange one too, which did awake me.
   I shaked you, sir, and cried. As mine eyes opened,   340
   I saw their weapons drawn. There was a noise;
   That's verily.[104] 'Tis best we stand upon our guard,
   Or that we quit this place. Let's draw our weapons.
ALON. Lead off this ground, and let's make further search
   For my poor son.
GON.   Heavens keep him from these beasts!
   For he is sure i' the island.
ALON.   Lead away.
ARIEL. Prospero my lord shall know what I have done.
   So, King, go safely on to seek thy son.   350

                                  Exeunt.

Scene II. [Another part of the island.]

Enter CALIBAN *with a burden of wood. A noise of thunder heard.*

CAL. All the infections that the sun sucks up
   From bogs, fens, flats, on Prosper fall and make him
   By inchmeal[1] a disease! His spirits hear me,
   And yet I needs must curse. But they'll nor pinch,
   Fright me with urchins-shows,[2] pitch me i' the mire,
   Nor lead me, like a firebrand,[3] in the dark
   Out of my way, unless he bid 'em; but
   For every trifle are they set upon me;
   Sometime like apes that mow[4] and chatter at me,
   And after bite me; then like hedgehogs which   10
   Lie tumbling in my barefoot way and mount
   Their pricks at my footfall; sometime am I
   All wound with adders, who with cloven tongues
   Do hiss me into madness.

Enter TRINCULO.

                Lo, now, lo!
   Here comes a spirit of his, and to torment me
   For bringing wood in slowly. I'll fall flat;
   Perchance he will not mind[5] me.   *[Lies down.]*
TRIN. Here's neither bush nor shrub to bear off[6] any weather at all, and
   another storm brewing. I hear it sing i' the wind. Yond same black   20
   cloud, yond huge one, looks like a foul bombard[7] that would shed his
   liquor. If it should thunder as it did before, I know not where to hide

---

[103] **humming,** i.e., Ariel's song.   [104] **verily,** the truth.

[1] **By inchmeal,** inch by inch.   [2] **urchin-shows,** apparition of goblins.
[3] **firebrand,** will-o'-the wisp.   [4] **mow,** make faces.
[5] **mind,** notice.   [6] **bear off,** keep off.
[7] **bombard,** a wine jug made of black leather, so called because of its fancied resemblance to a cannon.

my head. Yond same cloud cannot choose but fall[8] by pailfuls. What
have we here? a man or a fish? dead or alive? A fish: he smells like a
fish; a very ancient and fishlike smell; a kind of, not of the newest,
poor John.[9] A strange fish! Were I in England now, as once I was, and
had but this fish painted, not a holiday fool there but would give a
piece of silver. There would this monster make a man. Any strange
beast there makes a man.[10] When they will not give a doit[11] to relieve
a lame beggar, they will lay out ten to see a dead Indian. Legged like   30
a man! and his fins like arms! Warm, o' my troth! I do now let loose
my opinion, hold it no longer: this is no fish, but an islander, that hath
lately suffered by a thunderbolt. [*Thunder.*] Alas, the storm is come
again! My best way is to creep under his gaberdine.[12] There is no
other shelter hereabout. Misery acquaints a man with strange bedfel-
lows. I will here shroud[13] till the dregs of the storm be past.

                                                            [*Creeps under* CALIBAN's *garment.*]

Enter STEPHANO, *singing;* [*a bottle in his hand*].

STE.   I shall no more to sea, to sea;
                                        Here shall I die ashore.

This is a very scurvy[14] tune to sing at a man's funeral.
Well, here's my comfort.   *Drinks.*   40

        The master, the swabber, the boatswain, and I,
            The gunner, and his mate,
        Loved Mall, Meg, and Marian, and Margery,
            But none of us cared for Kate.
            For she had a tongue with a tang,
            Would cry to a sailor "Go hang!"
        She loved not the savor of tar nor of pitch;
        Yet a tailor might scratch her where'er she did
            itch.
            Then to sea, boys, and let her go hang!   50

This is a scurvy tune too; but here's my comfort.

                                                                        Drinks.

CAL. Do not torment me! O!
STE. What's the matter? Have we devils here? Do you put tricks upon's
    with savages and men of Inde,[15] ha? I have not 'scaped drowning to be
    afeard now of your four legs;[16] for it hath been said, "As proper[17] a
    man as ever went on four legs cannot make him give ground"; and it
    shall be said so again, while Stephano breathes at nostrils.
CAL. The spirit torments me. O!
STE. This is some monster of the isle, with four legs, who hath got, as I

---

[8] **cannot . . . fall,** cannot help falling.   [9] **poor John,** salted hake (a kind of codfish).
[10] **makes a man,** makes a man's fortune.   [11] **doit,** the smallest coin—half a farthing.
[12] **gaberdine,** a long cloak.   [13] **shroud,** cover myself.
[14] **scurvy,** mean, "lousy."   [15] **Inde,** the Indies (East or West).
[16] **your four legs,** any four-legged creature.   [17] **proper,** handsome.

take it, an ague. Where the devil should he learn our language? I will   60
give him some relief, if it be but for that. If I can recover[18] him, and
keep him tame, and get to Naples with him, he's a present for any
emperor that ever trod on neat's leather.[19]

CAL. Do not torment me prithee! I'll bring my wood home faster.

STE. He's in his fit[20] now and does not talk after the wisest.[21] He shall
taste of my bottle. If he have never drunk wine afore, it will go near to
remove his fit. If I can recover him and keep him tame, I will not take
too much for him;[22] he shall pay for him that hath him, and that
soundly.

CAL. Thou dost me yet but little hurt. Thou wilt anon; I know it by thy   70
trembling.[23] Now Prosper works upon thee.

STE. Come on your ways.[24] Open your mouth. Here is that which will
give language to you, cat.[25] Open your mouth. This will shake your
shaking, I can tell you, and that soundly. [*Gives* CALIBAN *drink.*] You
cannot tell who's your friend. Open your chaps[26] again.

TRIN. I should know that voice. It should be—but he is drowned; and
these are devils. O, defend[27] me!

STE. Four legs and two voices—a most delicate monster! His forward
voice now is to speak well of his friend; his backward voice is to utter
foul speeches and to detract.[28] If all the wine in my bottle will recover   80
him, I will help his ague. Come! [*Gives drink.*] Amen! I will pour some
in thy other mouth.

TRIN. Stephano!

STE. Doth thy other mouth call me? Mercy, mercy! This is a devil, and no
monster. I will leave him; I have no long spoon.[29]

TRIN. Stephano! If thou beest Stephano, touch me and speak to me; for
I am Trinculo—be not afeard—thy good friend Trinculo.

STE. If thou beest Trinculo, come forth. I'll pull thee by the lesser legs.
If any be Trinculo's legs, these are they. [*Pulls him out.*] Thou art very
Trinculo indeed! How camest thou to be the siege of this moon-   90
calf?[30] Can he vent Trinculos?

TRIN. I took him to be killed with a thunderstroke. But art thou not
drowned, Stephano? I hope now thou art not drowned. Is the storm
overblown? I hid me under the dead mooncalf's gaberdine for fear of
the storm. And art thou living, Stephano? O Stephano, two Neapoli-
tans 'scaped?

STE. Prithee do not turn me about. My stomach is not constant.[31]

CAL. [*Aside*] These be fine things, an if they be not sprites. That's a
brave[32] god and bears celestial liquor. I will kneel to him.

STE. How didst thou 'scape? How camest thou hither? Swear by this   100

---

[18] **recover,** cure.   [19] **neat's leather,** a shoe made out of cowhide.
[20] **fit,** fit of fever.   [21] **after the wisest,** in the most intelligent way.
[22] **I will . . . for him,** i.e., no price will be too high for him.
[23] **trembling,** a sign of being possessed of a devil.
[24] **Come . . . ways,** an expression of encouragement.
[25] **cat,** an allusion to the proverb, "Good liquor will make a cat speak."
[26] **chaps,** jaws.   [27] **defend,** God defend.   [28] **detract,** slander.
[29] **long spoon,** an allusion to the proverb, "He that sups with the Devil has need of a long spoon."
[30] **siege,** excrement; **moon-calf,** monster, congenital idiot.
[31] **constant,** settled.   [32] **brave,** fine.

bottle how thou camest hither. I escaped upon a butt of sack which
the sailors heaved o'erboard, by this bottle, which I made of the bark
of a tree with mine own hands since I was cast ashore.

CAL. I'll swear upon that bottle to be thy true subject, for the liquor is
not earthly.

STE. Here! Swear then how thou escapedst.

TRIN. Swum ashore, man, like a duck. I can swim like a duck, I'll be
sworn.

STE. Here, kiss the book.[33] [*Gives him drink.*] Though thou canst swim
like a duck, thou art made like a goose.   110

TRIN. O Stephano, hast any more of this?

STE. The whole butt, man. My cellar is in a rock by the seaside, where my
wine is hid. How now, mooncalf? How does thine ague?

CAL. Hast thou not dropped from heaven?

STE. Out o' the moon, I do assure thee. I was the Man i' the Moon when
time was.[34]

CAL. I have seen thee in her, and I do adore thee. My mistress showed
me thee, and thy dog, and thy bush.[35]

STE. Come, swear to that; kiss the book. I will furnish it anon with new
contents. Swear.   [CALIBAN *drinks.*]   120

TRIN. By this good light, this is a very shallow monster! I afeard of him?
A very weak monster! The Man i' the Moon? A most poor credulous
monster! Well drawn,[36] monster, in good sooth.

CAL. I'll show thee every fertile inch o' the island; and I will kiss thy foot.
I prithee be my god.

TRIN. By this light, a most perfidious and drunken monster! When's
god's asleep he'll rob his bottle.

CAL. I'll kiss thy foot. I'll swear myself thy subject.

STE. Come on then. Down, and swear!   130

TRIN. I shall laugh myself to death at this puppy-headed monster. A most
scurvy monster! I could find in my heart to beat him—

STE. Come, kiss.

TRIN. But that the poor monster's in drink. An abominable monster!

CAL. I'll show thee the best springs; I'll pluck thee berries;
I'll fish for thee, and get thee wood enough.
A plague upon the tyrant that I serve!
I'll bear him no more sticks, but follow thee,
Thou wondrous man.

TRIN. A most ridiculous monster, to make a wonder of a poor drunkard!   140

CAL. I prithee let me bring thee where crabs[37] grow;
And I with my long nails will dig thee pignuts,
Show thee a jay's nest, and instruct thee how
To snare the nimble marmoset;[38] I'll bring thee

---

[33] **kiss the book,** he gives him the bottle instead of the Bible on which to take an oath.

[34] **when time was,** once upon a time.

[35] **thy dog and thy bush,** there was a folk tradition that a peasant was banished to the moon for
gathering brush on Sunday. His dog went along, as did the last bush he had cut.

[36] **Well drawn,** i.e., that was a good swig; **drawn,** swigged.   [37] **crabs,** crab-apples.

[38] **marmoset,** a small monkey.

To clust'ring filberts, and sometimes I'll get thee
Young scamels[39] from the rock. Wilt thou go with me?
STE. I prithee now lead the way without any more talking. Trinculo, the
King and all our company else being drowned, we will inherit[40] here.
Here, bear my bottle. Fellow Trinculo, we'll fill him by-and-by[41] again.

CALIBAN *sings drunkenly.*

CAL. Farewell, monster; farewell, farewell!   150
TRIN. A howling monster! a drunken monster!

CAL.   No more dams I'll make for fish,
                        Nor fetch in firing
                        At requiring,
                   Nor scrape trencher,[42] nor wash dish.
                        'Ban, 'Ban, Ca—Caliban
                   Has a new master. Get a new man.

Freedom, highday! highday, freedom! freedom, highday, freedom!
STE. O brave monster! lead the way.

Exeunt.

ACT III

Scene I. [Before PROSPERO's cell.]

Enter FERDINAND, *bearing a log.*

FER. There be some sports are painful, and their labor[1]
   Delight in them sets off;[2] some kinds of baseness
   Are nobly undergone, and most poor[3] matters
   Point to rich ends. This my mean task
   Would be as heavy to me as odious, but
   The mistress which I serve quickens what's dead
   And makes my labors pleasures. O, she is
   Ten times more gentle than her father's crabbed;
   And he's composed of harshness! I must remove
   Some thousands of these logs and pile them up,   10
   Upon a sore injunction.[4] My sweet mistress
   Weeps when she sees me work, and says such baseness[5]
   Had never like executor. I forget;[6]
   But these sweet thoughts do even refresh my labors.
   Most busy least when I do it.[7]

Enter MIRANDA; *and* PROSPERO [*behind, unseen*].

---

[39] **scamels,** probably sea gulls.   [40] **inherit,** take possession.
[41] **by-and-by,** right away.   [42] **trencher,** wooden plate.

[1] **labor,** fatigue.   [2] **sets off,** cancels.
[3] **Are,** which are; **most poor,** the poorest.
[4] **sore injunction,** an order under severe penalties.   [5] **baseness,** menial toil.
[6] **I forget,** i.e., to work (in thinking about my sweet mistress).
[7] **least,** i.e., when I seem least busy; **do it,** i.e., forget it (my work and merely think of her).

MIR.   Alas, now pray you
Work not so hard! I would the lightning had
Burnst up those logs that you are enjoined to pile!
Pray set it down and rest you. When this burns,
'Twill weep[8] for having wearied you. My father   20
Is hard at study; pray now rest yourself;
He's safe for these three hours.
FER.   O most dear mistress,
The sun will set before I shall discharge
What I must strive to do.
MIR.   If you'll sit down,
I'll bear your logs the while. Pray give me that.
I'll carry it to the pile.
FER.   No, precious creature.
I had rather crack my sinews, break my back,   30
Than you should such dishonor undergo
While I sit lazy by.
MIR.   It would become me
As well as it does you; and I should do it
With much more ease; for my good will is to it,
And yours it is against.
PROS. [*Aside*]   Poor worm, thou art infected!
This visitation[9] shows it.
MIR.   You look wearily.
FER. No, noble mistress. 'Tis fresh morning with me   40
When you are by at night. I do beseech you,
Chiefly that I might set it in my prayers,
What is your name?
MIR.   Miranda. O my father,
I have broke your hest to say so!
FER.   Admired[10] Miranda!
Indeed the top of admiration, worth
What's dearest[11] to the world! Full many a lady
I have eyed with best regard,[12] and many a time
The harmony of their tongues hath into bondage   50
Brought my too diligent ear; for several virtues[13]
Have I liked several women; never any
With so full soul but some defect in her
Did quarrel with the noblest grace she owed,[14]
And put it to the foil;[15] but you, O you,
So perfect and so peerless, are created
Of every creature's best!
MIR.   I do not know
One of my sex; no woman's face remember,
Save, from my glass, mine own; nor have I seen   60
More that I may call men than you, good friend,

---

[8] **weep,** i.e., exude sap.   [9] **visitation,** visit (upon Ferdinand).
[10] **hest,** command; **Admired,** admirable.   [11] **What's dearest,** whatever is most valuable.
[12] **regard,** gaze.   [13] **several virtues,** particular excellencies.
[14] **owed,** owned.   [15] **put . . . foil,** made it ineffective.

And my dear father. How features are abroad[16]
I am skill-less[17] of; but, by my modesty
(The jewel in my dower), I would not wish
Any companion in the world but you;
Nor can imagination form a shape,
Besides yourself, to like of.[18] But I prattle
Something too wildly, and my father's precepts
I therein do forget.
FER.   I am, in my condition,[19]   70
A prince, Miranda; I do think, a king
(I would not so!), and would no more endure
This wooden slavery than to suffer
The flesh fly blow[20] my mouth. Hear my soul speak!
The very instant that I saw you, did
My heart fly to your service, there resides,
To make me slave to it; and for your sake
Am I this patient log-man.
MIR.   Do you love me?
FER. O heaven, O earth, bear witness to this sound,   80
And crown what I profess with kind event[21]
If I speak true! if hollowly, invert[22]
What best is boded me to mischief![23] I,
Beyond all limit of what else[24] i' the world,
Do love, prize, honor you.
MIR.   I am a fool
To weep at what I am glad of.
PROS. [*Aside*]   Fair[25] encounter
Of two most rare affections![26] Heavens rain grace
On that which breeds between 'em!   90
FER.   Wherefore weep you?
MIR. At mine unworthiness, that dare not offer
What I desire to give, and much less take
What I shall die to want.[27] But this is trifling;
And all the more it seeks to hide itself,
The bigger bulk it shows. Hence, bashful cunning!
And prompt me plain and holy innocence!
I am your wife, if you will marry me;
If not, I'll die your maid. To be your fellow[28]
You may deny me; but I'll be your servant,   100
Whether you will or no.
FER.   My mistress,[29] dearest!
And I thus humble ever.
MIR.   My husband then?
FER. Ay, with a heart as willing

---

[16] **how . . . abroad,** what beauty is like out in the world.   [17] **skill-less,** ignorant.
[18] **like of,** be pleased with.   [19] **condition,** rank.
[20] **blow,** deposit eggs on.   [21] **event,** outcome.   [22] **hollowly,** insincerely; **invert,** convert.
[23] **boded,** destined (by Fate); **mischief,** ill fortune.
[24] **limit,** bounds; **what else,** everything else, whatever it may be.   [25] **Fair,** fortunate.
[26] **affections,** dispositions.   [27] **want,** be without.
[28] **maid,** maid-servant; **fellow,** wife.   [29] **mistress,** lady-love.

As bondage e'er of freedom. Here's my hand.
MIR. And mine, with my heart in't; and now farewell
  Till half an hour hence.
FER.   A thousand thousand!

            Exeunt [FERDINAND *and* MIRANDA *severally*].

PROS. So glad of this as they I cannot be,   110
  Who are surprised withal;[30] but my rejoicing
  At nothing can be more. I'll to my book;
  For yet ere suppertime must I perform
  Much business appertaining.[31]

                                                            Exit.

Scene II. [Another part of the island.]

Enter CALIBAN, STEPHANO, *and* TRINCULO.

STE. Tell not me![1] When the butt is out, we will drink water; not a drop
  before. Therefore bear[2] up and board 'em! Servant monster, drink to
  me.

TRIN. Servant monster? The folly of this island![3] They say there's but five
  upon this isle. We are three of them. If the other two be brained like
  us, the state totters.

STE. Drink, servant monster, when I bid thee. Thy eyes are almost set[4] in
  thy head.

TRIN. Where should they be set else? He were a brave monster indeed
  if they were set in his tail.   10

STE. My man-monster hath drowned his tongue in sack. For my part, the
  sea cannot drown me. I swam, ere I could recover[5] the shore, five-
  and-thirty leagues off and on, by this light. Thou shalt be my lieutenant, monster, or my standard.[6]

TRIN. Your lieutenant, if you list; he's no standard.

STE. We'll not run, Monsieur Monster.

TRIN. Nor go[7] neither; but you'll lie like dogs, and yet say nothing
  neither.

STE. Mooncalf, speak once in thy life, if thou beest a good mooncalf.

CAL. How does thy honor? Let me lick thy shoe. I'll not serve him; he is   20
  not valiant.

TRIN. Thou liest, most ignorant monster! I am in case to justle[8] a constable. Why, thou deboshed[9] fish thou, was there ever man a coward
  that hath drunk so much sack as I today? Wilt thou tell a monstrous
  lie, being but half a fish and half a monster?

CAL. Lo, how he mocks me! Wilt thou let him, my lord?

TRIN. "Lord" quoth he? That a monster should be such a natural![10]

CAL. Lo, lo, again! Bite him to death I prithee.

STE. Trinculo, keep a good tongue in your head. If you prove a muti-

---

[30] **withal,** at it.   [31] **appertaining,** i.e., to the marriage.
[1] **Tell me not,** don't talk to me (about drinking more slowly).   [2] **bear,** sail.
[3] **The . . . island,** what a place for fools this island must be!   [4] **set,** fixed (in a drunken stare).
[5] **recover,** reach.   [6] **standard,** standard-bearer.
[7] **go,** walk.   [8] **in case,** in a condition; **justle,** wrestle with.
[9] **deboshed,** debauched.   [10] **natural,** idiot.

neer—the next tree! The poor monster's my subject, and he shall not   30
suffer indignity.

CAL. I thank my noble lord. Wilt thou be pleased to hearken once again
to the suit I made to thee?

STE. Marry, will I. Kneel and repeat it; I will stand, and so shall Trinculo.

Enter ARIEL, *invisible.*

CAL. As I told thee before, I am subject to a tyrant,[11]
    A sorcerer, that by his cunning hath
    Cheated me of the island.

ARIEL. Thou liest.

CAL.   Thou liest, thou jesting monkey thou!
    I would my valiant master would destroy thee.   40
    I do not lie.

STE. Trinculo, if you trouble him any more in's tale, by this hand, I will
supplant some of your teeth.

TRIN. Why, I said nothing.

STE. Mum, then, and no more.—Proceed.

CAL. I say by sorcery he got this isle;
    From me he got it. If thy greatness will
    Revenge it on him—for I know thou darest,
    But this thing dare not—

STE. That's most certain.   50

CAL. Thou shalt be lord of it, and I'll serve thee.

STE. How now shall this be compassed?[12]
    Canst thou bring me to the party?

CAL. Yea, yea, my lord! I'll yield him thee asleep,
    Where thou mayst knock a nail into his head.

ARIEL. Thou liest, thou canst not.

CAL. What a pied ninny's this! Thou scurvy patch![13]
    I do beseech thy greatness give him blows
    And take his bottle from him. When that's gone,
    He shall drink naught but brine, for I'll not show him
    Where the quick freshes[14] are.   60

STE. Trinculo, run into no further danger. Interrupt the monster one
word further and, by this hand, I'll turn my mercy out o' doors and
make a stockfish[15] of thee.

TRIN. Why, what did I? I did nothing. I'll go farther off.

STE. Didst thou not say he lied?

ARIEL. Thou liest.

STE. Do I so? Take thou that! [*Strikes* TRINCULO.]
    As you like this, give me the lie another time.

TRIN. I did not give thee the lie. Out o' your wits, and hearing too? A pox   70
o' your bottle! This can sack and drinking do. A murrain[16] on your

---

[11] **tyrant,** usurper.   [12] **compassed,** brought to pass.

[13] **pied,** parti-colored, i.e., clad in a jester's motley; **patch,** fool.

[14] **quick freshes,** springs of running fresh water.

[15] **stockfish,** cod, because it was beaten to make it soft enough for cooking.

[16] **murrain,** a pestilence attacking cattle.

monster, and the Devil take your fingers!

CAL. Ha, ha, ha!

STE. Now forward with your tale.—Prithee stand further off.

CAL. Beat him enough. After a little time
I'll beat him too.

STE.   Stand farther.—Come, proceed.

CAL. Why, as I told thee, 'tis a custom with him
I' the afternoon to sleep. There thou mayst brain him,
Having first seized his books, or with a log   80
Batter his skull, or paunch[17] him with a stake,
Or cut his weasand[18] with thy knife. Remember
First to possess his books; for without them
He's but a sot,[19] as I am, nor hath not
One spirit to command. They all do hate him
As rootedly as I. Burn but his books.
He has brave utensils[20] (for so he calls them)
Which, when he has a house, he'll deck withal.
And that most deeply to consider is
The beauty of his daughter. He himself   90
Calls her a nonpareil.[21] I never saw a woman
But only Sycorax my dam and she;
But she as far surpasseth Sycorax
As great'st does least.

STE.   Is it so brave a lass?

CAL. Ay, lord. She will become thy bed, I warrant,
And bring thee forth brave brood.

STE. Monster, I will kill this man. His daughter and I will be king and
queen, save our Graces! and Trinculo and thyself shall be viceroys.
Dost thou like the plot, Trinculo?   100

TRIN. Excellent.

STE. Give me thy hand. I am sorry I beat thee; but while thou livest, keep
a good tongue in thy head.

CAL. Within this half hour will he be asleep.
Wilt thou destroy him then?

STE.   Ay, on mine honor.

ARIEL. This will I tell my master.

CAL. Thou makest me merry; I am full of pleasure.
Let us be jocund. Will you troll the catch[22]
You taught me but whilere?[23]   110

STE. At thy request, monster, I will do reason, any reason.[24] Come on,
Trinculo, let us sing.   *Sings.*

Flout 'em and scout 'em[25]
And scout 'em and flout 'em!
Thought is free.

---

[17] **paunch,** disembowel.   [18] **weasand,** windpipe.
[19] **sot,** simpleton.   [20] **brave utensils,** fine ornaments.
[21] **nonpareil,** paragon.
[22] **troll the catch,** sing the round (for three voices).   [23] **but whilere,** only a little while ago.
[24] **any reason,** anything reasonable.
[25] **Flout,** mock; **scout,** jeer at.

CAL. That's not the tune.

ARIEL *plays the tune on a tabor*[26] *and pipe.*

STE. What is this same?

TRIN. This is the tune of our catch, played by the picture of Nobody.[27]

STE. If thou beest a man, show thyself in thy likeness. If thou beest a
    devil, take 't as thou list.   120

TRIN. O, forgive me my sins!

STE. He that dies pays all debts.[28] I defy thee.
    Mercy upon us!

CAL. Art thou afeard?

STE. No, monster, not I.

CAL. Be not afeard. The isle is full of noises,[29]
    Sounds, and sweet airs that give delight and hurt not.
    Sometimes a thousand twangling[30] instruments
    Will hum about mine ears; and sometime voices
    That,[31] if I then had waked after long sleep,   130
    Will make me sleep again; and then, in dreaming,
    The clouds methought would open and show riches
    Ready to drop upon me, that, when I waked,
    I cried to dream again.

STE. This will prove a brave[32] kingdom to me, where I shall have my
    music for nothing.

CAL. When Prospero is destroyed.

STE. That shall be by-and-by. I remember the story.[33]

TRIN. The sound is going away. Let's follow it, and after do our work.

STE. Lead, monster; we'll follow. I would I could see this taborer! He   140
    lays it on.

TRIN. Wilt come? I'll follow Stephano.

Exeunt.

Scene III. [Another part of the island.]

Enter ALONSO, SEBASTIAN, ANTONIO, GONZALO, ADRIAN, FRANCISCO, *etc.*

GON. By'r Lakin,[1] I can go no further, sir!
    My old bones ache. Here's a maze trod indeed
    Through forthrights and meanders. By your patience,[2]
    I needs must rest me.

ALON.   Old lord, I cannot blame thee,
    Who am myself attached[3] with weariness
    To the dulling of my spirits.[4] Sit down and rest.
    Even here I will put off my hope, and keep it

---

[26] **tabor,** a small drum.

[27] **picture of Nobody,** refers to a picture on the title page of a play *No-body and Some-body* (1606). The
figure is all head, neck, arms, legs, and particularly nose, and so has no body.

[28] **He . . . debts,** i.e., you cannot collect debts from a dead man.

[29] **noises,** musical sounds.   [30] **twangling,** loud.   [31] **that,** so that.

[32] **brave,** fine.   [33] **by-and-by,** at once; **the story,** i.e., what you have said.

[1] **By'r Lakin,** by our Lady, the Blessed Virgin.

[2] **forthrights and meanders,** straight paths and winding paths; **By . . . patience,** if you will be patient
enough to allow me.

[3] **attached,** seized.   [4] **spirits,** vital spirits, vitality.

No longer for my flatterer. He is drowned
Whom thus we stray to find; and the sea mocks   10
Our frustrate search on land. Well, let him go.
ANT. [*Aside to* SEBASTIAN] I am right glad that he's so out of hope.
Do not for one repulse forego the purpose
That you resolved t' effect.
SEB. [*Aside to* ANTONIO] The next advantage[5]
Will we take throughly.
ANT. [*Aside to* SEBASTIAN] Let it be tonight;
For, now they are oppressed with travel, they
Will not nor cannot use such vigilance
As when they are fresh.   20
SEB. [*Aside to* ANTONIO] I say tonight. No more.

Solemn and strange music; and PROSPERO *on the top* (*invisible*).

ALON. What harmony is this? My good friends, hark!
GON. Marvelous sweet music!

*Enter several strange Shapes, bringing in a banquet;[6] and dance about it with
gentle actions of salutations; and, inviting the King, etc., to eat, they depart.*

ALON. Give us kind keepers,[7] heavens! What were these?
SEB. A living drollery.[8] Now I will believe
That there are unicorns; that in Arabia
There is one tree, the phoenix' throne, one phoenix
At this hour reigning there.
ANT.   I'll believe both;
And what does else want credit,[9] come to me,   30
And I'll be sworn 'tis true. Travelers ne'er did lie,
Though fools at home condemn 'em.
GON.   If in Naples
I should report this now, would they believe me?
If I should say, I saw such islanders
(For certes these are people of the island),
Who, though they are of monstrous shape, yet, note,
Their manners are more gentle, kind, than of
Our human generation you shall find
Many—nay, almost any.   40
PROS. [*Aside*]   Honest[10] lord,
Thou hast said well; for some of you there present
Are worse than devils.
ALON.   I cannot too much muse[11]
Such shapes, such gesture,[12] and such sound, expressing
(Although they want the use of tongue) a kind
Of excellent dumb discourse.

[5] **advantage,** advantageous opportunity.
[6] **banquet,** light refreshments, usually sweets, fruit, and wine.
[7] **keepers,** guardian angels.   [8] **drollery,** puppet show.
[9] **does . . . credit,** is incredible.   [10] **Honest,** honorable.
[11] **muse,** wonder at.   [12] **gesture,** demeanor.

PROS. [*Aside*]   Praise in departing.[13]
FRAN. They vanished strangely.
SEB.   No matter, since   50
  They have left their viands behind; for we have stomachs.[14]
  Will't please you taste of what is here?
ALON.   Not I.
GON. Faith, sir, you need not fear. When we were boys,
  Who would believe that there were mountaineers
  Dewlapped[15] like bulls, whose throats had hanging at 'em
  Wallets of flesh? or that there were such men
  Whose heads stood in their breasts? which now we find
  Each putter-out of five for one[16] will bring us
  Good warrant of.   60
ALON.   I will stand to,[17] and feed;
  Although my last, no matter, since I feel
  The best[18] is past. Brother, my lord the Duke,
  Stand to, and do as we.

Thunder and lightning. Enter ARIEL, *like a harpy; claps his wings upon the
table; and with a quaint device*[19] *the banquet vanishes.*

ARIEL. You are three men of sin, whom destiny—
  That hath to instrument[20] this lower world
  And what is in't—the never-surfeited sea
  Hath caused to belch up you, and on this island,
  Where man doth not inhabit—you 'mongst men
  Being most unfit to live. I have made you mad;   70
  And even with suchlike valor[21] men hang and drown
  Their proper[22] selves.
                    [ALONSO, SEBASTIAN, *etc., draw their swords.*]
                    You fools! I and my fellows
  Are ministers of Fate. The elements,
  Of whom your swords are tempered, may as well
  Wound the loud winds, or with bemocked-at stabs
  Kill the still-closing waters, as diminish
  One dowle[23] that's in my plume. My fellow ministers
  Are like[24] invulnerable. If you could hurt,
  Your swords are now too massy[25] for your strengths   80
  And will not be uplifted. But remember
  (For that's my business to you) that you three
  From Milan did supplant good Prospero;
  Exposed unto the sea, which hath requit[26] it,
  Him and his innocent child; for which foul deed
  The powers, delaying (not forgetting), have

---

[13] **Praise in departing,** the proverb was "Praise at the parting."   [14] **stomachs,** appetites.
[15] **Dewlapped,** i.e., having a fold of skin or goiter under the neck.
[16] **Each . . . one,** each traveler who insures his safe return home at a premium of 1 to 5, or 20 percent.
[17] **stand to,** take the risk.   [18] **best,** i.e., the best part of life.
[19] **harpy,** foul creature, half bird, half woman; **quaint device,** ingenious stage machine.
[20] **to instrument,** as its instrument.   [21] **suchlike valor,** i.e., the courage of madness.
[22] **proper,** own.   [23] **dowle,** a tiny downy feather.
[24] **like,** likewise.   [25] **massy,** heavy.   [26] **requit,** requited it (i.e., the crime).

Incensed the seas and shores, yea, all the creatures,[27]
Against your peace. Thee of thy son, Alonso,
They have bereft; and do pronounce by me
Ling'ring perdition[28] (worse than any death   90
Can be at once) shall step by step attend
You and your ways; whose wraths to guard you from,
Which here, in this most desolate isle, else falls
Upon your heads, is nothing but heart's sorrow
And a clear[29] life ensuing.

He vanishes in thunder; then, to soft music, enter the Shapes again, and dance,
with mocks and mows,[30] and carrying out the table.

PROS. [*Aside*] Bravely the figure of this harpy hast thou
    Performed, my Ariel; a grace it had, devouring.[31]
    Of my instruction hast thou nothing bated[32]
    In what thou hadst to say. So, with good life[33]
    And observation strange, my meaner ministers[34]   100
    Their several kinds[35] have done. My high charms work,
    And these, mine enemies, are all knit up
    In their distractions.[36] They now are in my pow'r;
    And in these fits I leave them, while I visit
    Young Ferdinand, whom they suppose is drowned,
    And his and mine loved darling.   [*Exit above.*]
GON. I' the name of something holy, sir, why stand you
    In this strange stare?
ALON.   O, it is monstrous, monstrous!
    Methought the billows spoke and told me of it;   110
    The winds did sing it to me; and the thunder,
    That deep and dreadful organ pipe, pronounced
    The name of Prosper. It did bass my trespass.[37]
    Therefore my son i' the ooze is bedded; and
    I'll seek him deeper than e'er plummet sounded
    And with him there lie mudded.   *Exit.*
SEB.   But one fiend at a time,
    I'll fight their legions o'er![38]
ANT.   I'll be thy second.
                          Exeunt [SEBASTIAN *and* ANTONIO].
GON. All three of them are desperate. Their great guilt,   120
    Like poison given to work a great time after,
    Now 'gins to bite the spirits. I do beseech you,
    That are of suppler joints, follow them swiftly

[27] **Incensed,** aroused; **all the creatures,** all creation.
[28] **perdition,** destruction.   [29] **clear,** guiltless.
[30] **mocks and mows,** mocking gestures and grimaces.
[31] **devouring,** i.e., even while you were devouring the banquet.
[32] **bated,** left undone.   [33] **with good life,** in a lifelike manner.
[34] **observation strange,** careful attention (to my commands); **meaner ministers,** inferior [to Ariel] agents.
[35] **several kinds,** particular tasks.   [36] **In ... distractions,** each in his special form of madness.
[37] **did ... trespass,** publish my trespass in a bass voice.   [38] **o'er,** one after another.

And hinder them from what this ecstasy[39]
May now provoke them to.

ADR.   Follow, I pray you.

Exeunt omnes.

ACT IV

Scene I. [Before Prospero's cell.]

Enter PROSPERO, FERDINAND, *and* MIRANDA.

PROS. If I have too austerely punished you,
    Your compensation makes amends; for I
    Have given you here a third[1] of mine own life,
    Or[2] that for which I live; who once again
    I tender to thy hand. All thy vexations
    Were but my trials of thy love, and thou
    Hast strangely[3] stood the test. Here, afore heaven,
    I ratify this my rich gift. O Ferdinand,
    Do not smile at me that I boast her off,[4]
    For thou shalt find she will outstrip all praise   10
    And make it halt[5] behind her.

FER.   I do believe it
    Against an oracle.[6]

PROS. Then, as my gift, and thine own acquisition
    Worthily purchased,[7] take my daughter. But
    If thou dost break her virgin-knot before
    All sanctimonious[8] ceremonies may
    With full and holy rite be minist'red,
    No sweet aspersion[9] shall the heavens let fall
    To make this contract grow; but barren hate,   20
    Sour-eyed disdain, and discord shall bestrew
    The union of your bed with weeds so loathly
    That you shall hate it both. Therefore take heed,
    As Hymen's lamp shall light you![10]

FER.   As I hope
    For quiet days, fair issue, and long life,
    With such love as 'tis now, the murkiest den,
    The most opportune place, the strong'st suggestion[11]
    Our worser genius[12] can, shall never melt
    Mine honor into lust, to[13] take away   30

---

[39] **ecstasy,** frenzy.   [1] **third,** Miranda; the other thirds are himself and his kingdom.
[2] **Or,** in other words.   [3] **strangely,** unusually well.
[4] **boast her off,** exhibit her virtues by boasting.   [5] **halt,** limp.
[6] **Against an oracle,** i.e., even though an oracle should declare the opposite to be true.
[7] **purchased,** won.   [8] **sanctimonious,** sacred.
[9] **aspersion,** sprinkling (of dew as holy water).
[10] **Hymen's,** Hymen was the Greek and Roman god of marriage; **light you,** i.e., that the marriage torch
    not burn smokily, for that was a bad omen.
[11] **suggestion,** temptation.   [12] **worser genius,** evil attendant spirit.
[13] **to,** so as to.

The edge of that day's celebration
When I shall think or[14] Phoebus' steeds are foundered
Or Night kept chained below.
PROS.   Fairly spoke.
  Sit then and talk with her; she is thine own.
  What, Ariel! my industrious servant, Ariel!

Enter ARIEL.

ARIEL. What would my potent master? Here I am.
PROS. Thou and thy meaner fellows your last service
  Did worthily perform; and I must use you
  In such another trick. Go bring the rabble,[15]   40
  O'er whom I give thee pow'r, here to this place.
  Incite them to quick motion; for I must
  Bestow upon the eyes of this young couple
  Some vanity of mine art.[16] It is my promise,
  And they expect it from me.
ARIEL.   Presently?[17]
PROS. Ay, with a twink.[18]
ARIEL. Before you can say "Come" and "Go,"
  And breathe twice and cry, "So, so,"
  Each one, tripping on his toe,   50
  Will be here with mop and mow.[19]
  Do you love me master? No?
PROS. Dearly, my delicate Ariel. Do not approach
  Till thou dost hear me call.
ARIEL.   Well! I conceive.[20]   *Exit.*
PROS. Look thou be true. Do not give dalliance[21]
  Too much the rein. The strongest oaths are straw
  To the fire i' the blood. Be more abstemious,
  Or else good night your vow!
FER.   I warrant you, sir.   60
  The white cold virgin snow upon my heart
  Abates the ardor of my liver.[22]
PROS.   Well.
  Now come, my Ariel! Bring a corollary[23]
  Rather than want a spirit. Appear, and pertly![24]
  No tongue! All eyes! Be silent.   *Soft music.*

Enter IRIS.

IRIS. Ceres, most bounteous lady, thy rich leas[25]

---

[14] **or,** either.   [15] **rabble,** i.e., the lesser spirits.
[16] **vanity,** slight example; **art,** magic.   [17] **Presently,** immediately.
[18] **twink,** twinkle (of an eye).   [19] **mop and mow,** grin and grimace.
[20] **conceive,** understand (what you want).   [21] **dalliance,** fondling.
[22] **liver,** the supposed seat of the passions.   [23] **corollary,** surplus (of spirits).
[24] **pertly,** quickly.   [25] **leas,** fields.

Of wheat, rye, barley, vetches,[26] oats, and pease;
Thy turfy mountains, where live nibbling sheep,
And flat meads thatched with stover,[27] them to keep; ₇₀
Thy banks with pioned and twilled brims,[28]
Which spongy April at thy hest[29] betrims
To make cold nymphs chaste crowns; and thy broom groves,[30]
Whose shadow the dismissed[31] bachelor loves,
Being lasslorn; thy pole-clipt[32] vineyard;
And thy sea-marge, sterile and rocky-hard,
Where thou thyself dost air[33]—the queen o' the sky,
Whose wat'ry arch[34] and messenger am I,
Bids thee leave these,[35] and with her sovereign Grace,

JUNO descends.

Here on this grass-plot, in this very place, ₈₀
To come and sport. Her peacocks fly amain;[36]
Approach, rich Ceres, her to entertain.

Enter CERES.

CERES. Hail, many-colored messenger, that ne'er
Dost disobey the wife of Jupiter,
Who, with thy saffron wings, upon my flow'rs
Diffusest honey drops, refreshing show'rs,
And with each end of thy blue bow dost crown
My bosky acres and my unshrubbed down,[37]
Rich scarf to my proud earth—why hath thy queen
Summoned me hither to this short-grassed green? ₉₀
IRIS. A contract of true love to celebrate
And some donation freely to estate[38]
On the blest lovers.
CERES.   Tell me, heavenly bow,
If Venus or her son, as thou dost know,
Do now attend the queen. Since they did plot
The means that dusky Dis[39] my daughter got,
Her and her blind boy's scandaled[40] company
I have forsworn.
IRIS.   Of her society
Be not afraid. I met her Deity ₁₀₀
Cutting the clouds towards Paphos,[41] and her son

---

[26] **vetches,** grass for fodder.   [27] **stover,** another sort of fodder grass.
[28] **pioned . . . brims,** furrowed and ridged edges.   [29] **hest,** command.
[30] **cold,** passionless; **broom groves,** thickets of broom.
[31] **dismissed,** rejected.   [32] **pole-clipt,** with vines clinging to poles.
[33] **air,** take the air.   [34] **wat'ry arch,** rainbow.
[35] **these,** i.e., the places just enumerated.   [36] **amain,** swiftly.
[37] **bosky,** covered with shrubs and bushes; **down,** open upland.
[38] **donation,** i.e., that expressed in the song of blessing; **estate,** bestow.
[39] **means,** scheme by which; **Dis,** Pluto, who carried Proserpine, Ceres' daughter, off to make her Queen of the Lower World.
[40] **scandaled,** scandalous.   [41] **Paphos,** a town in Cyprus, sacred to Venus.

Dove-drawn with her. Here thought they to have done
Some wanton charm upon this man and maid,
Whose vows are, that no bed-right shall be paid
Till Hymen's torch be lighted; but in vain.
Mars's hot minion[42] is returned again;
Her waspish-headed[43] son has broke his arrows,
Swears he will shoot no more, but play with sparrows
And be a boy right out.   110

[*Enter* JUNO.]

CERES.   Highest queen of state,[44]
  Great Juno, comes; I know her by her gait.
JUNO. How does my bounteous sister? Go with me
  To bless this twain, that they may prosperous be
  And honored in their issue.

They sing.

JUNO.   Honor, riches, marriage blessing,
               Long continuance, and increasing,
               Hourly joys be still[45] upon you!
               Juno sings her blessings on you.

CERES.   Earth's increase, foison plenty,[46]   120
               Barns and garners never empty,
               Vines with clust'ring bunches growing,
               Plants with goodly burden bowing;
               Spring come to you at the farthest
               In the very end of harvest!
               Scarcity and want shall shun you,
               Ceres' blessing so is on you.

FER. This is a most majestic vision, and
  Harmonious charmingly. May I be bold
  To think these spirits?   130
PROS.   Spirits, which by mine art
  I have from their confines called to enact
  My present fancies.
FER.   Let me live here ever!
  So rare a wond'red father and a wise
  Makes this place Paradise.
               JUNO *and* CERES *whisper, and send* IRIS *on employment.*
PROS.   Sweet now, silence!
  Juno and Ceres whisper seriously.

---

[42] **hot minion,** lustful darling (Venus).   [43] **waspish-headed,** irritable.
[44] **right out,** outright; **state,** majesty.   [45] **still,** always.
[46] **foison plenty,** plentiful harvest.

There's something else to do. Hush and be mute,
Or else our spell is marred. 140
IRIS. You nymphs, called Naiads, of the wind'ring brooks,
With your sedged crowns[47] and ever-harmless looks,
Leave your crisp[48] channels, and on this green land
Answer your summons. Juno does command.
Come, temperate[49] nymphs, and help to celebrate
A contract of true love. Be not too late.

Enter certain NYMPHS.

You sunburned sicklemen, of August weary,
Come hither from the furrow and be merry.
Make holiday. Your rye-straw hats put on,
And these fresh nymphs encounter[50] every one 150
In country footing.[51]

Enter certain REAPERS, *properly habited. They join with the* NYMPHS *in a graceful dance; towards the end whereof* PROSPERO *starts suddenly and speaks; after which, to a strange, hollow, and confused noise, they heavily vanish.*[52]

PROS. [*Aside*] I had forgot that foul conspiracy
Of the beast Caliban and his confederates
Against my life. The minute of their plot
Is almost come.— [*To the* SPIRITS] Well done! Avoid![53] No more!
FER. This is strange. Your father's in some passion
That works him strongly.
MIR.   Never till this day
Saw I him touched with anger so distempered.[54]
PROS. You do look, my son, in a moved sort, 160
As if you were dismayed. Be cheerful, sir.
Our revels now are ended. These our actors,
As I foretold you, were all spirits and
Are melted into air, into thin air;
And, like the baseless fabric[55] of this vision,
The cloud-capped towers, the gorgeous palaces,
The solemn temples, the great globe itself,
Yea, all which it inherit, shall dissolve,
And, like this insubstantial pageant faded,
Leave not a rack[56] behind. We are such stuff 170
As dreams are made on, and our little life
Is rounded[57] with a sleep. Sir, I am vexed.

---

[47] **sedged crowns,** garlands of sedge (sweet-flag).   [48] **crisp,** curled, rippling.
[49] **temperate,** chaste.   [50] **fresh,** young and pretty; **encounter,** join (as partners).
[51] **footing,** dances.   [52] **heavily vanish,** vanish slowly and reluctantly.
[53] **Avoid,** begone.   [54] **distempered,** violent.
[55] **baseless fabric,** structure lacking a foundation.   [56] **rack,** vestige.
[57] **rounded,** surrounded.

Bear with my weakness. My old brain is troubled.
Be not disturbed with my infirmity.
If you be pleased, retire into my cell
And there repose. A turn or two I'll walk
To still my beating[58] mind.

FER. ⎱
MIR. ⎰ We wish your peace.   *Exeunt.*

Enter ARIEL.

PROS. Come with a thought![59] I thank thee, Ariel. Come.
ARIEL. Thy thoughts I cleave to.[60] What's thy pleasure?   180
PROS. Spirit, we must prepare to meet with Caliban.
ARIEL. Ay, my commander. When I presented[61] Ceres,
    I thought to have told thee of it, but I feared
    Lest I might anger thee.
PROS. Say again, where didst thou leave these varlets?[62]
ARIEL. I told you, sir, they were redhot with drinking;
    So full of valor that they smote the air
    For breathing in their faces, beat the ground
    For kissing of their feet; yet always bending[63]
    Towards their project.[64] Then I beat my tabor;   190
    At which like unbacked[65] colts they pricked their ears,
    Advanced[66] their eyelids, lifted up their noses
    As they smelt music. So I charmed their ears
    That calf-like they my lowing followed through
    Toothed briers, sharp furzes, pricking goss,[67] and thorns,
    Which ent'red their frail shins. At last I left them
    I' the filthy mantled[68] pool beyond your cell,
    There dancing up to the chins, that the foul lake
    O'erstunk their feet.
PROS.   This was well done, my bird.   200
    Thy shape invisible retain thou still.
    The trumpery[69] in my house, go bring it hither
    For stale[70] to catch these thieves.
ARIEL.   I go, I go.   *Exit.*
PROS. A devil, a born devil, on whose nature
    Nurture[71] can never stick! on whom my pains,
    Humanely taken, all, all lost, quite lost!
    And as with age his body uglier grows,
    So his mind cankers.[72] I will plague them all,
    Even to roaring.   210

---

[58] **beating,** excited.   [59] **with a thought,** on the instant.
[60] **Thy . . . to,** I am at hand whenever you think of me.   [61] **presented,** acted the part of.
[62] **varlets,** scoundrels.   [63] **bending,** directing their course.
[64] **project,** i.e., the murder of Prospero.   [65] **unbacked,** unbroken.
[66] **Advanced,** lifted.   [67] **goss,** gorse (spiny evergreen shrub).
[68] **filthy mantled,** covered with scum.   [69] **trumpery,** showy stuff.
[70] **stale,** decoy.   [71] **Nurture,** education.
[72] **cankers,** corrodes.

Enter ARIEL, *loaden with glistering*[73] *apparel, etc.*

                     Come, hang them on this line.[74]
[PROSPERO *and* ARIEL *remain, invisible.*]

Enter CALIBAN, STEPHANO, *and* TRINCULO, *all wet.*

CAL. Pray you tread softly, that the blind mole may not
    Hear a foot fall. We now are near his cell.
STE. Monster, your fairy, which you say is a harmless fairy, has done little
    better than played the Jack[75] with us.
TRIN. Monster, I do smell all horse-piss, at which my nose is in great
    indignation.
STE. So is mine. Do you hear, monster? If I should take a displeasure
    against you, look you—
TRIN. Thou wert but a lost monster.   220
CAL. Good my lord, give me thy favor still.
    Be patient, for the prize I'll bring thee to
    Shall hoodwink[76] this mischance. Therefore speak softly.
    All's hushed as midnight yet.
TRIN. Ay, but to lose our bottles in the pool—
STE. There is not only disgrace and dishonor in that, monster, but an
    infinite loss.
TRIN. That's more to me than my wetting. Yet this is your harmless fairy,
    monster.
STE. I will fetch off[77] my bottle, though I be o'er ears for my labor.   230
CAL. Prithee, my king, be quiet. Seest thou here?
    This is the mouth o' the cell. No noise, and enter.
    Do that good[78] mischief which may make this island
    Thine own forever, and I, thy Caliban,
    For aye thy foot-licker.
STE. Give me thy hand. I do begin to have bloody thoughts.
TRIN. O King Stephano! O peer![79] O worthy Stephano, look what a
    wardrobe here is for thee!
CAL. Let it alone, thou fool! It is but trash.
TRIN. O ho, monster! we know what belongs to a frippery.[80] O King   240
    Stephano!
STE. Put off that gown, Trinculo. By this hand, I'll have that gown!
TRIN. Thy Grace[81] shall have it.
CAL. The dropsy drown this fool! What do you mean
    To dote thus on such luggage? Let 't alone,[82]
    And do the murder first. If he awake,

---

[73] **glistering,** glittering.   [74] **line,** linden tree.   [75] **Jack,** knave.
[76] **hoodwink,** blind yourself to.   [77] **fetch off,** rescue.   [78] **good,** profitable (to us).
[79] **O . . . peer,** Trinculo refers to an old ballad the first lines of which were,
                  King Stephen was a worthy peer,
                  His breeches cost him but a crown.
[80] **frippery,** a second-hand clothing shop.   [81] **Thy Grace,** your Majesty.
[82] **Let 't alone,** let it alone.

From toe to crown he'll fill our skins with pinches,
Make us strange stuff.[83]

STE. Be you quiet, monster. Mistress line, is not this my jerkin?[84]
[*Takes it down.*] Now is the jerkin under the line.[85] Now, jerkin, you   250
are like to lose your hair[86] and prove a bald jerkin.

TRIN. Do, do! We steal by line and level,[87] an't like your Grace.[88]

STE. I thank thee for that jest. Here's a garment for't. Wit shall not go
unrewarded while I am king of this country. "Steal by line and level"
is an excellent pass of pate.[89] There's another garment for't.

TRIN. Monster, come put some lime[90] upon your fingers, and away with
the rest!

CAL. I will have none on't. We shall lose our time
And all be turned to barnacles,[91] or to apes
With foreheads villainous low.   260

STE. Monster, lay-to your fingers. Help to bear this away where my
hogshead of wine is, or I'll turn you out of my kingdom. Go to, carry
this.

TRIN. And this.

STE. Ay, and this.

A noise of hunters heard. Enter divers SPIRITS *in shape of dogs and hounds,
hunting them about,* PROSPERO *and* ARIEL *setting them on.*

PROS. Hey, Mountain, hey!

ARIEL. Silver! there it goes, Silver!

PROS. Fury, Fury! There, Tyrant, there! Hark, hark![92]
[CALIBAN, STEPHANO, *and* TRINCULO *are driven out.*]
Go, charge my goblins that they grind their joints
With dry convulsions,[93] shorten up their sinews   270
With aged cramps, and more pinch-spotted make them
Than pard or cat o' mountain.[94]

ARIEL.   Hark, they roar.

PROS. Let them be hunted soundly. At this hour
Lie at my mercy all mine enemies.
Shortly shall all my labors end, and thou
Shalt have the air at freedom. For a little
Follow, and do me service.   *Exeunt.*

---

[83] **Make . . . stuff,** transform us into some strange substance.   [84] **jerkin,** short jacket.

[85] **under the line,** a pun on "line" meaning (1) linden, (2) equator.

[86] **lose your hair,** i.e., as a result of a tropical fever.

[87] **Do, do,** keep on, you are doing fine; **line,** plumb line; **level,** carpenter's level.

[88] **an't . . . Grace,** if your majesty approve (the pun).

[89] **pass of pate,** sally of wit.   [90] **lime,** bird-lime.

[91] **barnacles,** geese, that were strangely thought to develop from barnacles.

[92] **hark,** equivalent to "sic 'em."

[93] **dry convulsions,** cramps which come when the joints seem to be dry from age.

[94] **pard,** leopard; **cat o' mountain,** catamount or mountain lion.

ACT V

Scene I. [Before the cell of Prospero.]

Enter PROSPERO *in his magic robes, and* ARIEL.

PROS. Now does my project gather to a head.
  My charms crack not,[1] my spirits obey, and Time
  Goes upright with his carriage.[2] How's the day?
ARIEL. On the sixth hour, at which time, my lord,
  You said our work should cease.
PROS.   I did say so
  When first I raised the tempest. Say, my spirit,
  How fares the King and 's followers?
ARIEL.   Confined together
  In the same fashion as you gave in charge,   10
  Just as you left them—all prisoners, sir,
  In the line grove which weather-fends[3] your cell.
  They cannot budge till your release. The King,
  His brother, and yours abide all three distracted,
  And the remainder mourning over them,
  Brimful of sorrow and dismay; but chiefly
  Him that you termed, sir, the good old Lord Gonzalo.
  His tears run down his beard like winter's drops
  From eaves of reeds.[4] Your charm so strongly works 'em,
  That if you now beheld them, your affections[5]   20
  Would become tender.
PROS.   Dost thou think so, spirit?
ARIEL. Mine would, sir, were I human.
PROS.   And mine shall.
  Hast thou, which art but air, a touch, a feeling
  Of their afflictions, and shall not myself,
  One of their kind, that relish all[6] as sharply
  Passion[7] as they, be kindlier moved than thou art?
  Though with their high wrongs I am struck to the quick,
  Yet with my nobler[8] reason 'gainst my fury   30
  Do I take part. The rarer action is
  In virtue than in vengeance.[9] They being penitent,
  The sole drift[10] of my purpose doth extend
  Not a frown further. Go, release them, Ariel.
  My charms I'll break, their senses I'll restore,
  And they shall be themselves.

---

[1] **crack not,** show no flaw.
[2] **Goes upright,** i.e., does not stoop, his burden is so light; **carriage,** burden.
[3] **line,** linden; **weather-fends,** protects from wind and rain.
[4] **reeds,** thatched roofs.   [5] **affections,** feelings.
[6] **relish all,** feel quite.   [7] **Passion,** suffer.
[8] **nobler,** i.e., than fury.
[9] **the . . . vengeance,** it is a finer action to be controlled by reason than to take vengeance.
[10] **drift,** intention.

ARIEL.   I'll fetch them, sir.   *Exit.*
PROS. [*Makes a magic circle with his staff*] Ye elves of hills, brooks, stand-
      ing[11] lakes, and groves,
  And ye that on the sands with printless[12] foot   40
  Do chase the ebbing Neptune,[13] and do fly him
  When he comes back; you demipuppets[14] that
  By moonshine do the green sour ringlets[15] make,
  Whereof the ewe not bites; and you, whose pastime
  Is to make midnight[16] mushrumps, that rejoice
  To hear the solemn curfew;[17] by whose aid
  (Weak masters though ye be) I have bedimmed
  The noontide sun, called forth the mutinous[18] winds,
  And 'twixt the green sea and the azured vault[19]
  Set roaring war; to the dread rattling thunder   50
  Have I given fire[20] and rifted Jove's stout oak
  With his own bolt; the strong-based promontory
  Have I made shake and by the spurs[21] plucked up
  The pine and cedar; graves at my command
  Have waked their sleepers, oped, and let 'em forth
  By my so potent art. But this rough magic
  I here abjure; and when I have required
  Some heavenly music (which even now I do)
  To work mine end upon their senses that[22]
  This airy charm is for, I'll break my staff,[23]   60
  Bury it certain fathoms in the earth,
  And deeper than did ever plummet sound
  I'll drown my book.[24]   *Solemn music.*

Here enters ARIEL *before; then* ALONSO, *with a frantic gesture,*[25] *attended by*
GONZALO; SEBASTIAN *and* ANTONIO *in like manner, attended by* ADRIAN
and FRANCISCO. *They all enter the circle which* PROSPERO *had made, and there
stand charmed; which* PROSPERO *observing, speaks.*

  A solemn air, and the best comforter
  To an unsettled fancy, cure thy brains,
  Now useless, boiled within thy skull! There stand,
  For you are spell-stopped.[26]
  Holy Gonzalo, honorable man,
  Mine eyes, ev'n sociable to the show[27] of thine,

---

[11] **standing,** tideless.   [12] **printless,** leaving no footprint.
[13] **ebbing Neptune,** the outgoing tide.
[14] **demipuppets,** half as big as figures of a puppet show.
[15] **green . . . ringlets,** circles of dark green grass, supposed to be made by fairies dancing in a ring.
[16] **midnight,** produced by fairy art at midnight.
[17] **curfew,** because after it has sounded at 9 P.M. fairy creatures may wander where they wish.
[18] **mutinous,** turbulent.   [19] **azured vault,** the blue sky.
[20] **given fire,** set off.   [21] **spurs,** roots.   [22] **that,** whom.
[23] **staff,** magic wand.   [24] **book,** i.e., one containing magic formulas for controlling spirits.
[25] **gesture,** mien.   [26] **spell-stopped,** rendered motionless by the spell.
[27] **sociable,** sympathetic; **show,** appearance.

Fall fellowly drops.[28] The charm dissolves apace;   70
And as the morning steals upon the night,
Melting the darkness, so their rising senses
Begin to chase the ignorant fumes[29] that mantle
Their clearer reason. O good Gonzalo,
My true preserver, and a loyal sir[30]
To him thou followst! I will pay thy graces
Home[31] both in word and deed. Most cruelly
Didst thou, Alonso, use me and my daughter.
Thy brother was a furtherer in the act.
Thou art pinched for't now, Sebastian. Flesh and blood,   80
You, brother mine, that entertained[32] ambition,
Expelled remorse and nature; who, with Sebastian
(Whose inward pinches therefore are most strong),
Would here have killed your king, I do forgive thee,
Unnatural though thou art. Their understanding
Begins to swell, and the approaching tide
Will shortly fill the reasonable shore,[33]
That now lies foul and muddy. Not one of them
That yet looks on me or would know me. Ariel,
Fetch me the hat and rapier in my cell.   90
I will discase[34] me, and myself present
As I was sometime Milan.[35] Quickly, spirit!
Thou shalt ere long be free.

[*Exit* ARIEL *and returns immediately.*]

ARIEL *sings and helps to attire him.*

> Where the bee sucks, there suck I;
> In a cowslip's bell I lie;
> There I couch when owls do cry.
> On the bat's back I do fly
> After summer merrily.
> Merrily, merrily shall I live now
> Under the blossom that hangs on the bough.   100

PROS. Why, that's my dainty Ariel![36] I shall miss thee,
But yet thou shalt have freedom. So, so, so.
To the King's ship, invisible as thou art!
There shalt thou find the mariners asleep
Under the hatches. The master and the boatswain

---

[28] **Fall . . . drops,** shed sympathetic tears.
[29] **ignorant fumes,** fumes which rose and covered the brain, thus causing unconsciousness.
[30] **sir,** gentleman.   [31] **pay . . . Home,** fully repay your favors.
[32] **entertained,** welcomed.   [33] **reasonable shore,** shore of reason.
[34] **discase me,** remove my magician's robe.
[35] **sometime Milan,** formerly Duke of Milan.
[36] **that's . . . Ariel,** referring to Ariel's deftness in helping him to change his clothes.

Being awake, enforce them to this place,
And presently,[37] I prithee.
ARIEL. I drink the air before me, and return
   Or ere your pulse twice beat.   *Exit.*
GON. All torment, trouble, wonder, and amazement   110
   Inhabits here. Some heavenly power guide us
   Out of this fearful country!
PROS.   Behold, sir King,
   The wronged Duke of Milan, Prospero.
   For more assurance that a living prince
   Does now speak to thee, I embrace thy body,
   And to thee and thy company I bid
   A hearty welcome.
ALON.   Whe'r thou beest he or no,
   Or some enchanted trifle to abuse[38] me,   120
   As late I have been, I not know. Thy pulse
   Beats, as of flesh and blood; and, since I saw thee,
   The affliction of my mind amends, with which,
   I fear, a madness held me. This must crave
   (An if this be at all) a most strange story.
   Thy dukedom I resign and do entreat
   Thou pardon me my wrongs.[39] But how should Prospero
   Be living and be here?
PROS.   First, noble friend,
   Let me embrace thine age,[40] whose honor cannot   130
   Be measured or confined.
GON.   Whether this be
   Or be not, I'll not swear.
PROS.   You do yet taste[41]
   Some subtleties[42] o' the isle, that will not let you
   Believe things certain.[43] Welcome, my friends all.
   [*Aside to* SEBASTIAN *and* ANTONIO] But you, my brace of lords, were I
      so minded,
   I here could pluck[44] his Highness' frown upon you,
   And justify you[45] traitors. At this time   140
   I will tell no tales.
SEB. [*Aside*]   The Devil speaks in him.
PROS.   No.
   For you, most wicked sir, whom to call brother
   Would even infect my mouth, I do forgive
   Thy rankest fault—all of them; and require
   My dukedom of thee, which perforce I know
   Thou must restore.
ALON.   If thou beest Prospero,

---

[37] **presently,** at once.   [38] **trifle,** apparition caused by enchantment; **abuse,** deceive.
[39] **my wrongs,** wrongs I have done you.
[40] **age,** i.e., aged body.   [41] **taste,** are under the influence of.
[42] **subtleties,** illusions.   [43] **things certain,** the reality of things.
[44] **pluck,** bring down.   [45] **justify you,** prove you to be.

Give us particulars of thy preservation;   150
How thou hast met us here, who three hours since
Were wracked upon this shore; where I have lost
(How sharp the point of this remembrance is!)
My dear son Ferdinand.

PROS.   I am woe[46] for't, sir.

ALON. Irreparable is the loss, and patience
Says it is past her cure.

PROS.   I rather think
You have not sought her help, of whose soft grace[47]
For the like loss I have her sovereign aid   160
And rest[48] myself content.

ALON.   You the like loss?

PROS. As great to me as late;[49] and, supportable
To make the dear[50] loss, have I means much weaker
Than you may call to comfort you; for I
Have lost my daughter.

ALON.   A daughter?
O heavens, that they were living both in Naples,
The King and Queen there! That[51] they were, I wish
Myself were muddled in that oozy bed   170
Where my son lies. When did you lose your daughter?

PROS. In this last tempest. I perceive these lords
At this encounter do so much admire[52]
That they devour[53] their reason, and scarce think
Their eyes do offices of truth,[54] their words
Are natural breath. But, howsoev'r[55] you have
Been justled from your senses, know for certain
That I am Prospero, and that very duke
Which was thrust forth of Milan, who most strangely
Upon this shore, where you were wracked, was landed   180
To be the lord on't. No more yet of this;
For 'tis a chronicle of day by day,
Not a relation for a breakfast, nor
Befitting this first meeting. Welcome, sir.
This cell's my court. Here have I few attendants,
And subjects none abroad.[56] Pray you look in.
My dukedom since you have given me again,
I will requite[57] you with as good a thing,
At least bring forth a wonder to content[58] ye
As much as me my dukedom.   190

     Here PROSPERO *discovers*[59] FERDINAND *and* MIRANDA *playing at chess.*

---

[46] **woe,** worry.   [47] **soft grace,** comforting favor.   [48] **rest,** remain.
[49] **as late,** and as recently happened.
[50] **dear,** deeply felt.   [51] **that,** provided that.   [52] **admire,** wonder.
[53] **devour,** swallow, destroy.
[54] **do offices of truth,** perform their functions properly.
[55] **howsoev'r,** however much.   [56] **abroad,** i.e., elsewhere on the island.
[57] **requite,** pay back.   [58] **wonder,** marvel; **content,** please.
[59] **discovers,** reveals (by drawing the curtain of the inner stage).

MIR. Sweet lord, you play me false.

FER.   No, my dearest love,
   I would not for the world.

MIR. Yes, for a score[60] of kingdoms you should wrangle,
   And I would call it fair play.[61]

ALON.   If this prove
   A vision of the island, one dear son
   Shall I twice lose.

SEB.   A most high miracle!

FER. Though the seas threaten, they are merciful.   200
   I have cursed them without cause.   *[Kneels.]*

ALON.   Now all the blessings
   Of a glad father compass thee about!
   Arise, and say how thou camest here.

MIR.   O, wonder!
   How many goodly[62] creatures are there here!
   How beauteous mankind is! O brave[63] new world
   That has such people in't!

PROS.   'Tis new to thee.

ALON. What is this maid with whom thou wast at play?   210
   Your eld'st[64] acquaintance cannot be three hours.
   Is she the goddess that hath severed us
   And brought us thus together?

FER.   Sir, she is mortal;
   But by immortal providence she's mine.
   I chose her when I could not ask my father
   For his advice, nor thought I had one. She
   Is daughter to this famous Duke of Milan,
   Of whom so often I have heard renown
   But never saw before; of whom I have   220
   Received a second life; and second father
   This lady makes him to me.

ALON.   I am hers.[65]
   But, O, how oddly will it sound that I
   Must ask my child forgiveness!

PROS.   There, sir, stop.
   Let us not burden our remembrance with
   A heaviness[66] that's gone.

GON.   I have inly wept,
   Or should have spoke ere this. Look down, you gods,   230
   And on this couple drop a blessed crown!
   For it is you that have chalked forth[67] the way
   Which brought us hither.

ALON.   I say amen, Gonzalo.

---

[60] **score,** (1) wager, (2) twenty.
[61] **you . . . fair play,** I should allow you to argue that you had played fair.
[62] **goodly,** comely.   [63] **brave,** splendid.
[64] **eld'st,** longest possible.
[65] **hers,** her father's, i.e., I accept her as a daughter.
[66] **heaviness,** grief.   [67] **chalked forth,** marked out.

Gon. Was Milan thrust from Milan that his issue
   Should become kings of Naples? O, rejoice
   Beyond a common joy, and set it down
   With gold on lasting pillars: In one voyage
   Did Claribel her husband find at Tunis,
   And Ferdinand her brother found a wife   240
   Where he himself was lost; Prospero his dukedom
   In a poor isle; and all of us ourselves
   When no man was his own.[68]
Alon. [*To* Ferdinand *and* Miranda] Give me your hands.
   Let grief and sorrow still embrace his heart
   That doth not wish you joy.
Gon.   Be it so! Amen!

Enter Ariel, *with the* Master *and* Boatswain *amazedly*[69] *following.*

   O, look, sir; look, sir! Here is more of us!
   I prophesied, if a gallows were on land,
   This fellow could not drown. Now, blasphemy,[70]   250
   That swearst grace o'erboard,[71] not an oath on shore?
   Hast thou no mouth by land? What is the news?
Boats. The best news is that we have safely[72] found
   Our king and company; the next, our ship,
   Which, but three glasses[73] since, we gave out split,
   Is tight and yare[74] and bravely rigged as when
   We first put out to sea.
Ariel. [*Aside to* Prospero] Sir, all this service
   Have I done since I went.
Pros. [*Aside to* Ariel] My tricksy[75] spirit!   260
Alon. These are not natural events; they strengthen
   From strange to stranger. Say, how came you hither?
Boats. If I did think, sir, I were well awake,
   I'ld strive to tell you. We were dead of sleep[76]
   And (how we know not) all clapped under hatches,
   Where, but even now, with strange and several[77] noises
   Of roaring, shrieking, howling, jingling chains,
   And mo[78] diversity of sounds, all horrible,
   We were awaked; straightway at liberty;[79]
   Where we, in all her trim, freshly beheld[80]   270
   Our royal, good and gallant ship, our master[81]

---

[68] **When . . . own,** when no man was in his right wits (because of the enchantment).
[69] **amazedly,** distractedly.   [70] **blasphemy,** blasphemous fellow.
[71] **swearst . . . o'erboard,** drives God's protection away from the ship by swearing.
[72] **safely,** safe and sound.   [73] **glasses,** hours.
[74] **yare,** ready, seaworthy.   [75] **tricksy,** roguish.
[76] **of sleep,** asleep.   [77] **several,** particular.   [78] **mo,** more.
[79] **at liberty,** released from our confinement (under the hatches).
[80] **trim,** rigging; **freshly,** as good as new.   [81] **master,** captain.

Cap'ring to eye her. On a trice,[82] so please you,
Even in a dream, were we divided from them
And were brought moping[83] hither.

ARIEL. [*Aside to* PROSPERO]   Was't well done?

PROS. [*Aside to* ARIEL] Bravely, my diligence.[84]
   Thou shalt be free.

ALON. This is as strange a maze[85] as e'er men trod,
   And there is in this business more than nature
   Was ever conduct of. Some oracle[86]   280
   Must rectify[87] our knowledge.

PROS.   Sir, my liege,
   Do not infest your mind with beating on[88]
   The strangeness of this business. At picked[89] leisure,
   Which shall be shortly, single I'll resolve you[90]
   (Which to you shall seem probable[91]) of every
   These happened accidents;[92] till when, be cheerful
   And think of each thing well. [*Aside to* ARIEL] Come hither, spirit.
   Set Caliban and his companions free.
   Untie the spell. [*Exit* ARIEL.]How fares my gracious sir?[93]   290
   There are yet missing of your company
   Some few odd lads that you remember not.

Enter ARIEL, *driving in* CALIBAN, STEPHANO, *and* TRINCULO, *in their stol'n
apparel.*

STE. Every man shift for all the rest, and let no man take care for himself;
   for all is but fortune. Coragio, bully[94] monster, coragio!

TRIN. If these be true spies which I wear in my head, here's a goodly
   sight.

CAL. O Setebos, these be brave spirits indeed!
   How fine[95] my master is! I am afraid
   He will chastise me.

SEB.   Ha, ha!   300
   What things are these, my Lord Antonio?
   Will money buy 'em?

ANT.   Very like. One of them
   Is a plain fish and no doubt marketable.

---

[82] **capering,** i.e., dancing for joy; **on a trice,** in an instant.
[83] **moping,** bewildered.
[84] **Bravely,** splendidly; **diligence,** diligent fellow.
[85] **maze,** confusion.
[86] **conduct,** guide; **oracle,** i.e., message from Heaven.
[87] **rectify,** proclaim correct.
[88] **infest,** harass; **beating on,** dwelling upon.
[89] **picked,** chosen.
[90] **single,** i.e., when I am alone with you; **resolve you,** clear up your doubts.
[91] **Which,** i.e., my explanation; **probable,** reasonable.
[92] **every . . . accidents,** all the events that have happened.
[93] **gracious sir,** Alonzo.   [94] **bully,** fine.
[95] **fine,** splendidly dressed.

PROS. Mark but the badges[96] of these men, my lords,
  Then say if they be true.[97] This misshapen knave,
  His mother was a witch, and one so strong
  That could control the moon, make flows and ebbs,
  And deal in her command without her power.[98]   310
  These three have robbed me, and this demidevil
  (For he's a bastard one) had plotted with them
  To take my life. Two of these fellows you
  Must know and own;[99] this thing of darkness I
  Acknowledge mine.
CAL.   I shall be pinched to death.
ALON. Is not this Stephano, my drunken butler?
SEB. He is drunk now. Where had he wine?
ALON. And Trinculo is reeling ripe.[100] Where should they
  Find this grand liquor that hath gilded[101] 'em?   320
  How camest thou in this pickle?[102]
TRIN. I have been in such a pickle, since I saw you last, that I fear me will
  never out of my bones. I shall not fear fly-blowing.[103]
SEB. Why, how now, Stephano?
STE. O, touch me not! I am not Stephano, but a cramp.
PROS. You'ld be king o' the isle, sirrah?
STE. I should have been a sore one then.
ALON. This is as strange a thing as e'er I looked on.
PROS. He is as disproportioned in his manners
  As in his shape. Go, sirrah, to my cell;   330
  Take with you your companions. As you look
  To have my pardon, trim it handsomely.
CAL. Ay, that I will! and I'll be wise hereafter,
  And seek for grace.[104] What a thrice-double ass
  Was I to take this drunkard for a god
  And worship this dull fool!
PROS.   Go to! Away!
ALON. Hence, and bestow your luggage where you found it.
SEB. Or stole it rather.

[*Exeunt* CALIBAN, STEPHANO, *and* TRINCULO.]

PROS. Sir, I invite your Highness and your train   340
  To my poor cell, where you shall take your rest
  For this one night; which, part of it, I'll waste[105]
  With such discourse as, I not doubt, shall make it

---

[96] **badges,** emblems worn on the arms of retainers to show to what family they belonged. The stolen garments are the badges of these men.
[97] **true,** honest.
[98] **deal . . . power,** act in the area of her (the moon's) authority with power greater than hers.
[99] **own,** i.e., admit to be your servants.
[100] **reeling ripe,** ripe for reeling, so drunk he can't walk straight.
[101] **gilded,** flushed, intoxicated.
[102] **in this pickle,** to be pickled in this way.
[103] **fly-blowing,** i.e., because pickled meat is never fly-blown.
[104] **grace,** forgiveness.   [105] **waste,** spend.

Go quick away—the story of my life,
And the particular accidents[106] gone by
Since I came to this isle; and in the morn
I'll bring you to your ship, and so to Naples,
Where I have hope to see the nuptial
Of these our dear-beloved solemnized;
And thence retire me to my Milan, where   350
Every third thought shall be my grave.
ALON.   I long
To hear the story of your life, which must
Take the ear strangely.
PROS.   I'll deliver all;[107]
And promise you calm seas, auspicious gales,
And sail[108] so expeditious that shall catch
Your royal fleet far off.—My Ariel, chick,
That is thy charge. Then to the elements
Be free, and fare thou well.—Please you draw near.[109]   360

Exeunt omnes.

EPILOGUE

Spoken by PROSPERO

Now my charms are all o'erthrown,
And what strength I have's mine own,
Which is most faint. Now 'tis true
I must be here confined by you,
Or sent to Naples. Let me not,
Since I have my dukedom got
And pardoned the deceiver, dwell
In this bare island by your spell;
But release me from my bands[1]
With the help of your good hands.[2]   10
Gentle breath[3] of yours my sails
Must fill, or else my project fails,
Which was to please. Now I want[4]
Spirits to enforce, art to enchant;
And my ending is despair
Unless I be relieved by prayer,[5]
Which pierces so that it assaults
Mercy itself and frees all faults.[6]

---

[106] **accidents,** events.
[107] **Take,** charm; **deliver all,** tell everything.   [108] **sail,** trip.
[109] **draw near,** i.e., enter my cave.

[1] **bands,** bonds.   [2] **hands,** i.e., applause.   [3] **Gentle breath,** favorable comment.
[4] **want,** lack.
[5] **prayer,** i.e., the one he is now making to the audience.
[6] **Mercy,** God's mercy; **frees,** gains forgiveness for.

As you from crimes[7] would pardoned be,
Let your indulgence[8] set me free.   20

Exit.

QUESTIONS FOR DISCUSSION AND WRITING

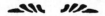

1.   *The Tempest* is unique among Shakespeare's plays for having a central symbol as its title. Most of his plays are named for their main character (*Hamlet*) or characters (*Romeo and Juliet*), with a phrase describing the play (*The Comedy of Errors*), or with a vaguely appropriate thematic tag (*All's Well That Ends Well*). What is the function of the tempest other than bringing the royal party under Prospero's control? As a natural symbol of disorder, is it echoed by other instances of disorder brought to order?

2.   There are three groups of characters in the play whose activities amount to three separate plots. There is the Prospero group (Prospero, Miranda, Ariel, Caliban, and Ferdinand). Then there is the court group (Alonso, Sebastian, Antonio, Gonzalo, Adrian, and Francisco) and the commoner group (Trinculo, Stephano, and, later, Caliban). Are there parallels among these groups?

3.   *The Tempest* has been read as a *metaplay,* a play about plays, with Prospero as the master playwright-director and the others as unwitting actors in the drama of restoration and reconciliation he has set up. Trace the implications of this interpretation through the play.

4.   In Prospero's account of his overthrow (I.ii), does he take any responsibility himself? What are the implications of his story?

5.   Compare Ariel and Caliban as "good servant" and "bad servant." How do they differ in their history and behavior?

6.   Part of the action of *The Tempest* is the struggle to act neither more nor less than human but exactly human. Trace this theme throughout the play.

7.   Prospero recurringly has been identified with Shakespeare, and his renunciation of his magical powers (V.i.40–64) has been called "Shakespeare's farewell to his art" (*The Tempest* is his last play, apart from a collaboration). Is there any more than sentimentality to this notion? Does magic equal poetry throughout the play?

8.   Another famous speech that has been read autobiographically is Prospero's "Our revels now are ended" (IV.i.167–78). How is this speech related to the rest of the play?

9.   Prospero's government of the island and his subjugation of Ariel and Caliban have been read as an enactment of the process of English colonization, which was proceeding rapidly when the play was written. Is this a viable interpretation?

---

[7] **crimes,** sins.
[8] **indulgence,** lack of censure.

10. The relationship between Prospero and Miranda is a crucial one. How would you characterize it? How is it related to the themes of the play?

11. Like all Shakespeare's plays, *The Tempest* deals with both public, political issues and private, personal and familial ones. Can you identify some public issues and some private ones and show how they are related?

Molière and the Neoclassical Theater

From our perspective, over three centuries later, the theaters of Shakespeare and Jean-Baptiste Poquelin, whose stage name was Molière (1622–73), were products of the same historical movement, the Renaissance culmination of a long tradition of medieval theater. The theaters of Shakespeare and Molière were very different, however, despite their proximity in time and geography and their similar ancestries.

Molière was born into a prosperous middle-class family in Paris; his father was an upholsterer who counted the king among his customers. Molière was being prepared for a career in law when, at the age of twenty-one, he announced that he was going to become an actor. Part of the attraction of the theater was the beautiful and gifted Madeleine Béjart. With Béjart, her brother Joseph, and her sister Genevieve, Molière founded a troupe called *L'Illustre Théâtre*. After two years of failure in Paris, the Illustrious Theater started a tour of the provinces that lasted for twelve years. During this time, Molière became a brilliant comic actor and a playwright as well.

Returning to Paris, *L'Illustre Théâtre* won the patronage of, first, the king's brother and eventually Louis XIV himself, who conferred on Molière's company the title of "Troupe of the King" and had it entertain at Versailles and other locations of the court, as well as in the magnificent Palais-Royal theater in Paris. The company performed Molière's *School for Wives* (1662), *Tartuffe* (1664), *The Miser* (1668), *The Doctor in Spite of Himself* (1666), *The Misanthrope* (1666), *The Would-Be Gentleman* (1671), *The Imaginary Invalid* (1673), and many other works. *Tartuffe* caused a scandal on its first performances and Louis XIV ordered the production suspended. Molière revised it three years later, hoping to remove some of the objections to it, but again it was forbidden. On February 17, 1673, Molière was performing the role of the hypochondriac Argan in his last play, *The Imaginary Invalid,* when he collapsed, hemorrhaging from the lungs from advanced tuberculosis; he died later that night.

The theaters for which Molière wrote differed considerably from Shakespeare's Globe. The earliest seventeenth-century French theaters were converted from unused indoor tennis courts, survivals of a short-lived vogue for tennis. These and later theaters were long, narrow rooms with a raised stage at one end, an ornate proscenium arch, and a front curtain, much like a modern stage. The stage, unlike Shakespeare's, represented a particular place throughout, depicted in scenery drawn in perspective and made of wood and canvas. This scenery remained in place throughout the play; because of both the difficulty of shifting scenery and the influence of the idea of "unity of place" (the limitation of a play to one location), no attempt was made to change the set in the course of the action.

The neoclassic theater, like the Greek and Shakespearean theaters, shaped and limited the dramatic worlds that could be created in it. Not for Molière is the open space before palaces where kings meet their subjects, as in Greek drama, or the bare scaffolding upon which Shakespeare could erect settings of the imagination. The rooms in bourgeois houses, like the one in Orgon's house where *Tartuffe* takes place, do not suggest struggles between men and gods or the comprehensive visions of Shakespeare. What they do suggest is Molière's dramatic territory, the cramped, obsessive, and comic complications of middle-class social life and the monsters it engenders.

By Molière's day, especially in France, critics had turned against the "irregularities" of Shakespeare's complex dramaturgy and had formulated "rules" that were thought to codify classical practice. These rules dealt with verisimilitude, distinct genres, decorum, stage morality, and the unities of time, place, and action. Verisimilitude, or faithfulness to life, demanded the elimination of the supernatural and the avoidance of such conventions as soliloquies. It also demanded that the playwright present not eccentric individuals but "representative" and "universal" characters and actions. Tragedy and comedy were to be kept distinct from each other; there were to be no serious scenes in comedy or comic scenes in tragedy as there were in Shakespeare. "Decorum," or fittingness, meant that characters were to behave in accordance with their age group, rank, profession, and gender. There were to be no cowardly soldiers or manly women. (Of course, decorum meant that characters behaved in accordance with the age's clichés.) Neoclassic artistic morality demanded that the good be rewarded and the bad punished, in other words, that "poetic justice" be observed. And finally, in a misunderstanding of Aristotle's *Poetics* and of the practice of the Greek and Roman playwrights, the "unities" were to be observed. The "unity of place" meant that a play could be set in only one place; the "unity of time" meant that it could deal with a period only as long as the time of representation, or, alternatively, with a period of twenty-four hours or less; and the "unity of action" meant that it could have only one plot (no subplots, Shakespearean-style).

These tenets of the neoclassic theater are generally followed by Molière in his comedies, though he was far from being a slave to them. More relevant than the rules of the critics was the popular folk comedy of the French countryside, with its stock characters, its slapstick action, and its preoccupation with sexual intrigue. Molière revived this comedy and used it to deal with contemporary fashions and customs. The result was the "character comedy" for which he is lastingly known.

TARTUFFE*

CHARACTERS

MME PERNELLE, *Orgon's mother*
ORGON, *Elmire's husband*
ELMIRE, *Orgon's wife*
DAMIS, *Orgon's son, Elmire's stepson*
MARIANE, *Orgon's daughter, Elmire's*
    stepdaughter, in love with Valère
VALÈRE, *in love with Mariane*

CLÉANTE, *Orgon's brother-in-law*
TARTUFFE, *a hypocrite*
DORINE, *Mariane's lady's-maid*
M. LOYAL, *a bailiff*
A POLICE OFFICER
FLIPOTE, *Mme Pernelle's maid*

The scene throughout: ORGON's *house in Paris*

ACT I

Scene 1

MADAME PERNELLE and FLIPOTE, her maid
        ELMIRE   DORINE   CLÉANTE
        MARIANE   DAMIS

MADAME PERNELLE: Come, come, Flipote; it's time I left this place.
ELMIRE: I can't keep up, you walk at such a pace.
MADAME PERNELLE: Don't trouble, child; no need to show me out.
    It's not your manners I'm concerned about.
ELMIRE: We merely pay you the respect we owe.
    But, Mother, why this hurry? Must you go?
MADAME PERNELLE: I must. This house appalls me. No one in it
    Will pay attention for a single minute.
    Children, I take my leave much vexed in spirit.
    I offer good advice, but you won't hear it.   10
    You all break in and chatter on and on.
    It's like a madhouse with the keeper gone.
DORINE: If . . .
MADAME PERNELLE: Girl, you talk too much, and I'm afraid
    You're far too saucy for a lady's-maid.
    You push in everywhere and have your say.
DAMIS: But . . .
MADAME PERNELLE: You, boy, grow more foolish every day.
    To think my grandson should be such a dunce!
    I've said a hundred times, if I've said it once,   20
    That if you keep the course on which you've started,
    You'll leave your worthy father broken-hearted.
MARIANE: I think . . .
MADAME PERNELLE: And you, his sister, seem so pure,

---

* *Translated by Richard Wilbur.*

So shy, so innocent, and so demure.
But you know what they say about still waters.
I pity parents with secretive daughters.
ELMIRE: Now, Mother . . .
MADAME PERNELLE: And as for you, child, let me add   30
That your behavior is extremely bad,
And a poor example for these children, too.
Their dear, dead mother did far better than you.
You're much too free with money, and I'm distressed
To see you so elaborately dressed.
When it's one's husband that one aims to please,
One has no need of costly fripperies.
CLÉANTE: Oh, Madame, really . . .
MADAME PERNELLE: You are her brother, Sir,
And I respect and love you; yet if I were   40
My son, this lady's good and pious spouse,
I wouldn't make you welcome in my house.
You're full of worldly counsels which, I fear,
Aren't suitable for decent folk to hear.
I've spoken bluntly, Sir; but it behooves us
Not to mince words when righteous fervor moves us.
DAMIS: Your man Tartuffe is full of holy speeches . . .
MADAME PERNELLE: And practises precisely what he preaches.
He's a fine man, and should be listened to.
I will not hear him mocked by fools like you.
DAMIS: Good God! Do you expect me to submit   50
To the tyranny of that carping hypocrite?
Must we forgo all joys and satisfactions
Because that bigot censures all our actions?
DORINE: To hear him talk—and he talks all the time—
There's nothing one can do that's not a crime.
He rails at everything, your dear Tartuffe.
MADAME PERNELLE: Whatever he reproves deserves reproof.
He's out to save your souls, and all of you
Must love him, as my son would have you do.
DAMIS: Ah no, Grandmother, I could never take   60
To such a rascal, even for my father's sake.
That's how I feel, and I shall not dissemble.
His every action makes me seethe and tremble
With helpless anger, and I have no doubt
That he and I will shortly have it out.
DORINE: Surely it is a shame and a disgrace
To see this man usurp the master's place—
To see this beggar who, when first he came,
Had not a shoe or shoestring to his name
So far forget himself that he behaves   70
As if the house were his, and we his slaves.
MADAME PERNELLE: Well, mark my words, your souls would fare far better
If you obeyed his precepts to the letter.
DORINE: You see him as a saint. I'm far less awed;
In fact, I see right through him. He's a fraud.

MADAME PERNELLE: Nonsense!
DORINE: His man Laurent's the same, or worse;
  I'd not trust either with a penny purse.
MADAME PERNELLE: I can't say what his servant's morals may be;
  His own great goodness I can guarantee.   80
  You all regard him with distaste and fear
  Because he tells you what you're loath to hear,
  Condemns your sins, points out your moral flaws,
  And humbly strives to further Heaven's cause.
DORINE: If sin is all that bothers him, why is it
  He's so upset when folk drop in to visit?
  Is Heaven so outraged by a social call
  That he must prophesy against us all?
  I'll tell you what I think: if you ask me,
  He's jealous of my mistress' company.   90
MADAME PERNELLE: Rubbish! (*To* ELMIRE.) He's not alone, child, in
    complaining
  Of all your promiscuous entertaining.
  Why, the whole neighborhood's upset, I know,
  By all these carriages that come and go,
  With crowds of guests parading in and out
  And noisy servants loitering about.
  In all of this, I'm sure there's nothing vicious;
  But why give people cause to be suspicious?
CLÉANTE: They need no cause; they'll talk in any case.   100
  Madam, this world would be a joyless place
  If, fearing what malicious tongues might say,
  We locked our doors and turned our friends away.
  And even if one did so dreary a thing,
  D'you think those tongues would cease their chattering?
  One can't fight slander; it's a losing battle;
  Let us instead ignore their tittle-tattle.
  Let's strive to live by conscience' clear decrees,
  And let the gossips gossip as they please.
DORINE: If there is talk against us, I know the source: 110
  It's Daphne and her little husband, of course.
  Those who have greatest cause for guilt and shame
  Are quickest to besmirch a neighbor's name.
  When there's a chance for libel, they never miss it;
  When something can be made to seem illicit
  They're off at once to spread the joyous news,
  Adding to fact what fantasies they choose.
  By talking up their neighbor's indiscretions
  They seek to camouflage their own transgressions,
  Hoping that others' innocent affairs   120
  Will lend a hue of innocence to theirs,
  Or that their own black guilt will come to seem
  Part of a general shady color-scheme.
MADAME PERNELLE: All that is quite irrelevant. I doubt
  That anyone's more virtuous and devout
  Than dear Orante; and I'm informed that she

Condemns your mode of life most vehemently.
DORINE: Oh, yes, she's strict, devout, and has no taint
  Of worldliness; in short, she seems a saint.
  But it was time which taught her that disguise;   130
  She's thus because she can't be otherwise.
  So long as her attractions could enthrall,
  She flounced and flirted and enjoyed it all,
  But now that they're no longer what they were
  She quits a world which fast is quitting her,
  And wears a veil of virtue to conceal
  Her bankrupt beauty and her lost appeal.
  That's what becomes of old coquettes today:
  Distressed when all their lovers fall away,
  They see no recourse but to play the prude,   140
  And so confer a style on solitude.
  Thereafter, they're severe with everyone,
  Condemning all our actions, pardoning none,
  And claiming to be pure, austere, and zealous
  When, if the truth were known, they're merely jealous,
  And cannot bear to see another know
  The pleasures time has forced them to forgo.
MADAME PERNELLE (*initially to* ELMIRE): That sort of talk is what you like
    to hear;
  Therefore you'd have us all keep still, my dear,   150
  While Madam rattles on the livelong day.
  Nevertheless, I mean to have my say.
  I tell you that you're blest to have Tartuffe
  Dwelling, as my son's guest, beneath this roof;
  That Heaven has sent him to forestall its wrath
  By leading you, once more, to the true path;
  That all he reprehends is reprehensible,
  And that you'd better heed him, and be sensible.
  These visits, balls, and parties in which you revel
  Are nothing but inventions of the Devil.   160
  One never hears a word that's edifying:
  Nothing but chaff and foolishness and lying,
  As well as vicious gossip in which one's neighbor
  Is cut to bits with epee, foil, and saber.
  People of sense are driven half-insane
  At such affairs, where noise and folly reign
  And reputations perish thick and fast.
  As a wise preacher said on Sunday last,
  Parties are Towers of Babylon, because
  The guests all babble on with never a pause;   170
  And then he told a story which, I think . . .
  (*To* CLÉANTE.) I heard that laugh, Sir, and I saw that wink!
  Go find your silly friends and laugh some more!
  Enough; I'm going; don't show me to the door.
  I leave this household much dismayed and vexed;
  I cannot say when I shall see you next.
  (*Slapping* FLIPOTE.) Wake up, don't stand there gaping into space!

I'll slap some sense into that stupid face.
Move, move, you slut.

Scene 2

Cléante
Dorine

Cléante: I think I'll stay behind;
  I want no further pieces of her mind.
  How that old lady . . .
Dorine: Oh, what wouldn't she say
  If she could hear you speak of her that way!
  She'd thank you for the *lady*, but I'm sure
  She'd find the *old* a little premature.
Cléante: My, what a scene she made, and what a din!
  And how this man Tartuffe has taken her in!
Dorine: Yes, but her son is even worse deceived;   10
  His folly must be seen to be believed.
  In the late troubles, he played an able part
  And served his king with wise and loyal heart,
  But he's quite lost his senses since he fell
  Beneath Tartuffe's infatuating spell.
  He calls him brother, and loves him as his life,
  Preferring him to mother, child, or wife.
  In him and him alone will he confide;
  He's made him his confessor and his guide;
  He pets and pampers him with love more tender   20
  Than any pretty mistress could engender,
  Gives him the place of honor when they dine,
  Delights to see him gorging like a swine,
  Stuffs him with dainties till his guts distend,
  And when he belches, cries "God bless you, friend!"
  In short, he's mad; he worships him; he dotes;
  His deeds he marvels at, his words he quotes,
  Thinking each act a miracle, each word
  Oracular as those that Moses heard.
  Tartuffe, much pleased to find so easy a victim,   30
  Has in a hundred ways beguiled and tricked him,
  Milked him of money, and with his permission
  Established here a sort of Inquisition.
  Even Laurent, his lackey, dares to give
  Us arrogant advice on how to live;
  He sermonizes us in thundering tones
  And confiscates our ribbons and colognes.
  Last week he tore a kerchief into pieces
  Because he found it pressed in a *Life of Jesus:*
  He said it was a sin to juxtapose   40
  Unholy vanities and holy prose.

Scene 3

ELMIRE   DAMIS   DORINE
MARIANE   CLÉANTE

ELMIRE: (*to* CLÉANTE): You did well not to follow; she stood in the door
  And said *verbatim* all she'd said before.
  I saw my husband coming. I think I'd best
  Go upstairs now, and take a little rest.
CLÉANTE: I'll wait and greet him here; then I must go.
  I've really only time to say hello.
DAMIS: Sound him about my sister's wedding, please.
  I think Tartuffe's against it, and that he's
  Been urging Father to withdraw his blessing.
  As you well know, I'd find that most distressing.   10
  Unless my sister and Valère can marry,
  My hopes to wed *his* sister will miscarry,
  And I'm determined . . .
DORINE: He's coming.

Scene 4

ORGON
CLÉANTE
DORINE

ORGON: Ah, Brother, good-day.
CLÉANTE: Well, welcome back. I'm sorry I can't stay.
  How was the country? Blooming, I trust, and green?
ORGON: Excuse me, Brother; just one moment.
  (*To* DORINE.)   Dorine . . .
  (*To* CLÉANTE.) To put my mind at rest, I always learn
  The household news the moment I return.
  (*To* DORINE.) Has all been well, these two days I've been gone?
  How are the family? What's been going on?
DORINE: Your wife, two days ago, had a bad fever,   10
  And a fierce headache which refused to leave her.
ORGON: Ah. And Tartuffe?
DORINE: Tartuffe? Why, he's round and red,
  Bursting with health, and excellently fed.
ORGON: Poor fellow!
DORINE: That night, the mistress was unable
  To take a single bite at the dinner-table.
  Her headache-pains, she said, were simply hellish.
ORGON: Ah. And Tartuffe?
DORINE: He ate his meal with relish,   20
  And zealously devoured in her presence
  A leg of mutton and a brace of pheasants.
ORGON: Poor fellow!
DORINE: Well, the pains continued strong,
  And so she tossed and tossed the whole night long,

Now icy-cold, now burning like a flame.
We sat beside her bed till morning came.
ORGON: Ah. And Tartuffe?
DORINE: Why, having eaten, he rose
    And sought his room, already in a doze,   30
    Got into his warm bed, and snored away
    In perfect peace until the break of day.
ORGON: Poor fellow!
DORINE: After much ado, we talked her
    Into dispatching someone for the doctor.
    He bled her, and the fever quickly fell.
ORGON: Ah. And Tartuffe?
DORINE: He bore it very well.
    To keep his cheerfulness at any cost,
    And make up for the blood *Madame* had lost,   40
    He drank, at lunch, four beakers full of port.
ORGON: Poor fellow!
DORINE: Both are doing well, in short.
    I'll go and tell *Madame* that you've expressed
    Keen sympathy and anxious interest.

Scene 5

ORGON
CLÉANTE

CLÉANTE: That girl was laughing in your face, and though
    I've no wish to offend you, even so
    I'm bound to say that she had some excuse.
    How can you possibly be such a goose?
    Are you so dazed by this man's hocus-pocus
    That all the world, save him, is out of focus?
    You've given him clothing, shelter, food, and care;
    Why must you also . . .
ORGON: Brother, stop right there.
    You do not know the man of whom you speak.   10
CLÉANTE: I grant you that. But my judgment's not so weak
    That I can't tell, by his effect on others . . .
ORGON: Ah, when you meet him, you two will be like brothers!
    There's been no loftier soul since time began.
    He is a man who . . . a man who . . . an excellent man.
    To keep his precepts is to be reborn,
    And view this dunghill of a world with scorn.
    Yes, thanks to him I'm a changed man indeed.
    Under his tutelage my soul's been freed
    From earthly loves, and every human tie: 20
    My mother, children, brother, and wife could die,
    And I'd not feel a single moment's pain.
CLÉANTE: That's a fine sentiment, Brother; most humane.
ORGON: Oh, had you seen Tartuffe as I first knew him,
    Your heart, like mine, would have surrendered to him.
    He used to come into our church each day

And humbly kneel nearby, and start to pray.
He'd draw the eyes of everybody there
By the deep fervor of his heartfelt prayer;
He'd sigh and weep, and sometimes with a sound   30
Of rapture he would bend and kiss the ground;
And when I rose to go, he'd run before
To offer me holy-water at the door.
His serving-man, no less devout than he,
Informed me of his master's poverty;
I gave him gifts, but in his humbleness
He'd beg me every time to give him less.
"Oh, that's too much," he'd cry, "too much by twice!
I don't deserve it. The half, Sir, would suffice."
And when I wouldn't take it back, he'd share   40
Half of it with the poor, right then and there.
At length, Heaven prompted me to take him in
To dwell with us, and free our souls from sin.
He guides our lives, and to protect my honor
Stays by my wife, and keeps an eye upon her;
He tells me whom she sees, and all she does,
And seems more jealous than I ever was!
And how austere he is! Why, he can detect
A mortal sin where you would least suspect;
In smallest trifles, he's extremely strict.   50
Last week, his conscience was severely pricked
Because, while praying, he had caught a flea
And killed it, so he felt, too wrathfully.
CLÉANTE: Good God, man! Have you lost your common sense—
        Or is this all some joke at my expense?
        How can you stand there and in all sobriety . . .
ORGON: Brother, your language savors of impiety.
        Too much free-thinking's made your faith unsteady,
        And as I've warned you many times already,
        'Twill get you into trouble before you're through. 60
CLÉANTE: So I've been told before by dupes like you:
        Being blind, you'd have all others blind as well;
        The clear-eyed man you call an infidel,
        And he who sees through humbug and pretense
        Is charged, by you, with want of reverence.
        Spare me your warnings, Brother; I have no fear
        Of speaking out, for you and Heaven to hear,
        Against affected zeal and pious knavery.
        There's true and false in piety, as in bravery,
        And just as those whose courage shines the most   70
        In battle, are the least inclined to boast,
        So those whose hearts are truly pure and lowly
        Don't make a flashy show of being holy.
        There's a vast difference, so it seems to me,
        Between true piety and hypocrisy:
        How do you fail to see it, may I ask?
        Is not a face quite different from a mask?

Cannot sincerity and cunning art,
Reality and semblance, be told apart?
Are scarecrows just like men, and do you hold   80
That a false coin is just as good as gold?
Ah, Brother, man's a strangely fashioned creature
Who seldom is content to follow Nature,
But recklessly pursues his inclination
Beyond the narrow bounds of moderation,
And often, by transgressing Reason's laws,
Perverts a lofty aim or noble cause.
A passing observation, but it applies.
ORGON: I see, dear Brother, that you're profoundly wise;
You harbor all the insight of the age.   90
You are our one clear mind, our only sage,
The era's oracle, its Cato too,
And all mankind are fools compared to you.
CLÉANTE: Brother, I don't pretend to be a sage,
Nor have I all the wisdom of the age.
There's just one insight I would dare to claim:
I know that true and false are not the same;
And just as there is nothing I more revere
Than a soul whose faith is steadfast and sincere,
Nothing that I more cherish and admire   100
Than honest zeal and true religious fire,
So there is nothing that I find more base
Than specious piety's dishonest face—
Than these bold mountebanks, these histrios
Whose impious mummeries and hollow shows
Exploit our love of Heaven, and make a jest
Of all that men think holiest and best;
These calculating souls who offer prayers
Not to their Maker, but as public wares,
And seek to buy respect and reputation   110
With lifted eyes and sighs of exaltation;
These charlatans, I say, whose pilgrim souls
Proceed, by way of Heaven, toward earthly goals,
Who weep and pray and swindle and extort,
Who preach the monkish life, but haunt the court,
Who make their zeal the partner of their vice—
Such men are vengeful, sly, and cold as ice,
And when there is an enemy to defame
They cloak their spite in fair religion's name,
Their private spleen and malice being made   120
To seem a high and virtuous crusade,
Until, to mankind's reverent applause,
They crucify their foe in Heaven's cause.
Such knaves are all too common; yet, for the wise,
True piety isn't hard to recognize,
And, happily, these present times provide us
With bright examples to instruct and guide us.
Consider Ariston and Périandre;

Look at Oronte, Alcidamas, Clitandre;
Their virtue is acknowledged; who could doubt it?   130
But you won't hear them beat the drum about it.
They're never ostentatious, never vain,
And their religion's moderate and humane;
It's not their way to criticize and chide:
They think censoriousness a mark of pride,
And therefore, letting others preach and rave,
They show, by deeds, how Christians should behave.
They think no evil of their fellow man,
But judge of him as kindly as they can.
They don't intrigue and wangle and conspire;   140
To lead a good life is their one desire;
The sinner wakes no rancorous hate in them;
It is the sin alone which they condemn;
Nor do they try to show a fiercer zeal
For Heaven's cause than Heaven itself could feel.
These men I honor, these men I advocate
As models for us all to emulate.
Your man is not their sort at all, I fear:
And, while your praise of him is quite sincere,
I think that you've been dreadfully deluded.   150
ORGON: Now then, dear Brother, is your speech concluded?
CLÉANTE: Why, yes.
ORGON: Your servant, Sir. (*He turns to go.*)
CLÉANTE: No, Brother; wait.
  There's one more matter. You agreed of late
  That young Valère might have your daughter's hand.
ORGON: I did.
CLÉANTE: And set the date, I understand.
ORGON: Quite so.
CLÉANTE: You've now postponed it; is that true?   160
ORGON: No doubt.
CLÉANTE: The match no longer pleases you?
ORGON: Who knows?
CLÉANTE: D'you mean to go back on your word?
ORGON: I won't say that.
CLÉANTE: Has anything occurred
  Which might entitle you to break your pledge?
ORGON: Perhaps.
CLÉANTE: Why must you hem, and haw, and hedge?
  The boy asked me to sound you in this affair . . .   170
ORGON: It's been a pleasure.
CLÉANTE: But what shall I tell Valère?
ORGON: Whatever you like.
CLÉANTE: But what have you decided?
  What are your plans?
ORGON: I plan, Sir, to be guided
  By Heaven's will.
CLÉANTE: Come, Brother, don't talk rot.
  You've given Valère your word; will you keep it, or not?

ORGON: Good day.

CLÉANTE: This looks like poor Valère's undoing;
  I'll go and warn him that there's trouble brewing.

ACT II

Scene 1

ORGON
MARIANE

ORGON: Mariane.

MARIANE: Yes, Father?

ORGON: A word with you; come here.

MARIANE: What are you looking for?

ORGON (*peering into a small closet*): Eavesdroppers, dear.
  I'm making sure we shan't be overheard.
  Someone in there could catch our every word.
  Ah, good, we're safe. Now, Mariane, my child,
  You're a sweet girl who's tractable and mild,
  Whom I hold dear, and think most highly of.

MARIANE: I'm deeply grateful, Father, for your love.

ORGON: That's well said, Daughter; and you can repay me
  If, in all things, you'll cheerfully obey me.

MARIANE: To please you, Sir, is what delights me best.

ORGON: Good, good. Now, what d'you think of Tartuffe, our guest?

MARIANE: I, Sir?

ORGON: Yes. Weigh your answer; think it through.

MARIANE: Oh, dear. I'll say whatever you wish me to.

ORGON: That's wisely said, my Daughter. Say of him, then,
  That he's the very worthiest of men,
  And that you're fond of him, and would rejoice
  In being his wife, if that should be my choice.
  Well?

MARIANE: What?

ORGON: What's that?

MARIANE: I . . .

ORGON: Well?

MARIANE: Forgive me, pray.

ORGON: Did you not hear me?

MARIANE: Of *whom*, Sir, must I say
  That I am fond of him, and would rejoice
  In being his wife, if that should be your choice?

ORGON: Why, of Tartuffe.

MARIANE: But, Father, that's false, you know.
  Why would you have me say what isn't so?

ORGON: Because I am resolved it shall be true.
  That it's my wish should be enough for you.

MARIANE: You can't mean, Father . . .

ORGON: Yes, Tartuffe shall be

Allied by marriage to this family,   40
And he's to be your husband, is that clear?
It's a father's privilege . . .

Scene 2

DORINE
ORGON
MARIANE

ORGON (*to* DORINE):   What are you doing in here?
   Is curiosity so fierce a passion
   With you, that you must eavesdrop in this fashion?
DORINE: There's lately been a rumor going about—
   Based on some hunch or chance remark, no doubt—
   That you mean Mariane to wed Tartuffe.
   I've laughed it off, of course, as just a spoof.
ORGON: You find it so incredible?
DORINE: Yes, I do.
   I won't accept that story, even from you.   10
ORGON: Well, you'll believe it when the thing is done.
DORINE: Yes, yes, of course. Go on and have your fun.
ORGON: I've never been more serious in my life.
DORINE: Ha!
ORGON: Daughter, I mean it; you're to be his wife.
DORINE: No, don't believe your father; it's all a hoax.
ORGON: See here, young woman . . .
DORINE: Come, Sir, no more jokes;
   You can't fool us.
ORGON: How dare you talk that way?   20
DORINE: All right, then; we believe you, sad to say.
   But how a man like you, who looks so wise
   And wears a moustache of such splendid size,
   Can be so foolish as to . . .
ORGON: Silence, please!
   My girl, you take too many liberties.
   I'm master here, as you must not forget.
DORINE: Do let's discuss this calmly; don't be upset.
   You can't be serious, Sir, about this plan.
   What should that bigot want with Mariane?   30
   Praying and fasting ought to keep him busy.
   And then, in terms of wealth and rank, what is he?
   Why should a man of property like you
   Pick out a beggar son-in-law?
ORGON: That will do.
   Speak of his poverty with reverence.
   His is a pure and saintly indigence
   Which far transcends all worldly pride and pelf.
   He lost his fortune, as he says himself,
   Because he cared for Heaven alone, and so   40
   Was careless of his interests here below.

I mean to get him out of his present straits
And help him to recover his estates—
Which, in his part of the world, have no small fame.
Poor though he is, he's a gentleman just the same.
DORINE: Yes, so he tells us; and, Sir, it seems to me
  Such pride goes very ill with piety.
  A man whose spirit spurns this dungy earth
  Ought not to brag of lands and noble birth;
  Such worldly arrogance will hardly square   50
  With meek devotion and the life of prayer.
  ... But this approach, I see, has drawn a blank;
  Let's speak, then, of his person, not his rank.
  Doesn't it seem to you a trifle grim
  To give a girl like her to a man like him?
  When two are so ill-suited, can't you see
  What the sad consequence is bound to be?
  A young girl's virtue is imperilled, Sir,
  When such a marriage is imposed on her;
  For if one's bridegroom isn't to one's taste,   60
  It's hardly an inducement to be chaste,
  And many a man with horns upon his brow
  Has made his wife the thing that she is now.
  It's hard to be a faithful wife, in short,
  To certain husbands of a certain sort,
  And he who gives his daughter to a man she hates
  Must answer for her sins at Heaven's gates.
  Think, Sir, before you play so risky a role.
ORGON: This servant-girl presumes to save my soul!
DORINE: You would do well to ponder what I've said.   70
ORGON: Daughter, we'll disregard this dunderhead.
  Just trust your father's judgment. Oh, I'm aware
  That I once promised you to young Valère;
  But now I hear he gambles, which greatly shocks me;
  What's more, I've doubts about his orthodoxy.
  His visits to church, I note, are very few.
DORINE: Would you have him go at the same hours as you,
  And kneel nearby, to be sure of being seen?
ORGON: I can dispense with such remarks, Dorine.
  (*To* MARIANE.) Tartuffe, however, is sure of Heaven's blessing,   80
  And that's the only treasure worth possessing.
  This match will bring you joys beyond all measure;
  Your cup will overflow with every pleasure;
  You two will interchange your faithful loves
  Like two sweet cherubs, or two turtle-doves.
  No harsh word shall be heard, no frown be seen,
  And he shall make you happy as a queen.
DORINE: And she'll make him a cuckold, just wait and see.
ORGON: What language!
DORINE: Oh, he's a man of destiny;   90
  He's *made* for horns, and what the stars demand
  Your daughter's virtue surely can't withstand.

ORGON: Don't interrupt me further. Why can't you learn
   That certain things are none of your concern?
DORINE: It's for your own sake that I interfere.

(*She repeatedly interrupts* ORGON *just as he is turning to speak to his daughter:*)

ORGON: Most kind of you. Now, hold your tongue, d'you hear?
DORINE: If I didn't love you . . .
ORGON: Spare me your affection.
DORINE: I love you, Sir, in spite of your objection.
ORGON: Blast!   100
DORINE: I can't bear, Sir, for your honor's sake,
   To let you make this ludicrous mistake.
ORGON: You mean to go on talking?
DORINE: If I didn't protest
   This sinful marriage, my conscience couldn't rest.
ORGON: If you don't hold your tongue, you little shrew . . .
DORINE: What, lost your temper? A pious man like you?
ORGON: Yes! Yes! You talk and talk. I'm maddened by it.
   Once and for all, I tell you to be quiet.
DORINE: Well, I'll be quiet. But I'll be thinking hard.   110
ORGON: Think all you like, but you had better guard
   That saucy tongue of yours, or I'll . . .
   (*Turning back to* MARIANE.)   Now, child,
   I've weighed this matter fully.
DORINE (*aside*):   It drives me wild
   That I can't speak.

(ORGON *turns his head, and she is silent.*)

ORGON: Tartuffe is no young dandy,
   But, still, his person . . .
DORINE (*aside*):   Is as sweet as candy.
ORGON: Is such that, even if you shouldn't care   120
   For his other merits . . .

(*He turns and stands facing* DORINE, *arms crossed.*)

DORINE (*aside*):   They'll make a lovely pair.
   If I were she, no man would marry me
   Against my inclination, and go scot-free.
   He'd learn, before the wedding-day was over,
   How readily a wife can find a lover.
ORGON (*to* DORINE): It seems you treat my orders as a joke.
DORINE: Why, what's the matter? 'Twas not to you I spoke.
ORGON: What *were* you doing?
DORINE: Talking to myself, that's all.   130
ORGON: Ah! (*Aside.*) One more bit of impudence and gall,
   And I shall give her a good slap in the face.

(*He puts himself in position to slap her;* DORINE, *whenever he glances at her, stands immobile and silent:*)

> Daughter, you shall accept, and with good grace,
> The husband I've selected . . . Your wedding-day . . .
> (*To* DORINE.) Why don't you talk to yourself?

DORINE: I've nothing to say.

ORGON: Come, just one word.

DORINE: No thank you, Sir. I pass.

ORGON: Come, speak; I'm waiting.

DORINE: I'd not be such an ass.   140

ORGON (*turning to* MARIANE): In short, dear Daughter, I mean to be
>   obeyed,
> And you must bow to the sound choice I've made.

DORINE (*moving away*): I'd not wed such a monster, even in jest.

(ORGON *attempts to slap her, but misses.*)

ORGON: Daughter, that maid of yours is a thorough pest;
> She makes me sinfully annoyed and nettled.
> I can't speak further; my nerves are too unsettled.
> She's so upset me by her insolent talk,
> I'll calm myself by going for a walk.

Scene 3   150

DORINE
MARIANE

DORINE (*returning*): Well, have you lost your tongue, girl? Must I play
> Your part, and say the lines you ought to say?
> Faced with a fate so hideous and absurd,
> Can you not utter one dissenting word?

MARIANE: What good would it do? A father's power is great.

DORINE: Resist him now, or it will be too late.

MARIANE: But . . .

DORINE: Tell him one cannot love at a father's whim;
> That you shall marry for yourself, not him;
> That since it's you who are to be the bride,   10
> It's you, not he, who must be satisfied;
> And that if his Tartuffe is so sublime,
> He's free to marry him at any time.

MARIANE: I've bowed so long to Father's strict control,
> I couldn't oppose him now, to save my soul.

DORINE: Come, come, Mariane. Do listen to reason, won't you?
> Valère has asked for your hand. Do you love him, or don't you?

MARIANE: Oh, how unjust of you! What can you mean
> By asking such a question, dear Dorine?
> You know the depth of my affection for him;   20
> I've told you a hundred times how I adore him.

DORINE: I don't believe in everything I hear;
  Who knows if your professions were sincere?
MARIANE: They were, Dorine, and you do me wrong to doubt it;
  Heaven knows that I've been all too frank about it.
DORINE: You love him, then?
MARIANE: Oh, more than I can express.
DORINE: And he, I take it, cares for you no less?
MARIANE: I think so.
DORINE: And you both, with equal fire,   30
  Burn to be married?
MARIANE: That is our one desire.
DORINE: What of Tartuffe, then? What of your father's plan?
MARIANE: I'll kill myself, if I'm forced to wed that man.
DORINE: I hadn't thought of that recourse. How splendid!
  Just die, and all your troubles will be ended!
  A fine solution. Oh, it maddens me
  To hear you talk in that self-pitying key.
MARIANE: Dorine, how harsh you are! It's most unfair.
  You have no sympathy for my despair.   40
DORINE: I've none at all for people who talk drivel
  And, faced with difficulties, whine and snivel.
MARIANE: No doubt I'm timid, but it would be wrong . . .
DORINE: True love requires a heart that's firm and strong.
MARIANE: I'm strong in my affection for Valère,
  But coping with my father is his affair.
DORINE: But if your father's brain has grown so cracked
  Over his dear Tartuffe that he can retract
  His blessing, though your wedding-day was named,
  It's surely not Valère who's to be blamed.   50
MARIANE: If I defied my father, as you suggest,
  Would it not seem unmaidenly, at best?
  Shall I defend my love at the expense
  Of brazenness and disobedience?
  Shall I parade my heart's desires, and flaunt . . .
DORINE: No, I ask nothing of you. Clearly you want
  To be Madame Tartuffe, and I feel bound
  Not to oppose a wish so very sound.
  What right have I to criticize the match?
  Indeed, my dear, the man's a brilliant catch.   60
  Monsieur Tartuffe! Now, there's a man of weight!
  Yes, yes, Monsieur Tartuffe, I'm bound to state,
  Is quite a person; that's not to be denied;
  'Twill be no little thing to be his bride.
  The world already rings with his renown;
  He's a great noble—in his native town;
  His ears are red, he has a pink complexion,
  And all in all, he'll suit you to perfection.
MARIANE: Dear God!
DORINE: Oh, how triumphant you will feel   70
  At having caught a husband so ideal!
MARIANE: Oh, do stop teasing, and use your cleverness

To get me out of this appalling mess.
Advise me, and I'll do whatever you say.
DORINE: Ah no, a dutiful daughter must obey
Her father, even if he weds her to an ape.
You've a bright future; why struggle to escape?
Tartuffe will take you back where his family lives,
To a small town aswarm with relatives—
Uncles and cousins whom you'll be charmed to meet. 80
You'll be received at once by the elite,
Calling upon the bailiff's wife, no less—
Even, perhaps, upon the mayoress,
Who'll sit you down in the *best* kitchen chair.
Then, once a year, you'll dance at the village fair
To the drone of bagpipes—two of them, in fact—
And see a puppet-show, or an animal act.
Your husband . . .
MARIANE: Oh, you turn my blood to ice!
Stop torturing me, and give me your advice. 90
DORINE (*threatening to go*): Your servant, Madam.
MARIANE: Dorine, I beg of you . . .
DORINE: No, you deserve it; this marriage must go through.
MARIANE: Dorine!
DORINE: No.
MARIANE: Not Tartuffe! You know I think him . . .
DORINE: Tartuffe's your cup of tea, and you shall drink him.
MARIANE: I've always told you everything, and relied . . .
DORINE: No. You deserve to be tartuffified.
MARIANE: Well, since you mock me and refuse to care,
I'll henceforth seek my solace in despair: 100
Despair shall be my counsellor and friend,
And help me bring my sorrows to an end.

(*She starts to leave.*)

DORINE: There now, come back; my anger has subsided.
You do deserve some pity, I've decided.
MARIANE: Dorine, if Father makes me undergo
This dreadful martyrdom, I'll die, I know.
DORINE: Don't fret; it won't be difficult to discover
Some plan of action . . . But here's Valère, your lover.

Scene 4

VALÈRE
MARIANE
DORINE

VALÈRE: Madame, I've just received some wondrous news
Regarding which I'd like to hear your views.
MARIANE: What news?
VALÈRE: You're marrying Tartuffe.

MARIANE: I find
  That Father does have such a match in mind.
VALÈRE: Your father, Madame . . .
MARIANE: . . . has just this minute said
  That it's Tartuffe he wishes me to wed.
VALÈRE: Can he be serious?   10
MARIANE: Oh, indeed he can;
  He's clearly set his heart upon the plan.
VALÈRE: And what position do you propose to take, Madam?
MARIANE: Why—I don't know.
VALÈRE: For heaven's sake—
  You don't know?
MARIANE: No.
VALÈRE: Well, well!
MARIANE: Advise me, do.
VALÈRE: Marry the man. That's my advice to you.   20
MARIANE: That's your advice?
VALÈRE: Yes.
MARIANE: Truly?
VALÈRE: Oh, absolutely.
  You couldn't choose more wisely, more astutely.
MARIANE: Thanks for this counsel; I'll follow it, of course.
VALÈRE: Do, do; I'm sure 'twill cost you no remorse.
MARIANE: To give it didn't cause your heart to break.
VALÈRE: I gave it, Madam, only for your sake.
MARIANE: And it's for your sake that I take it, Sir.   30
DORINE (*withdrawing to the rear of the stage*): Let's see which fool will prove
    the stubborner.
VALÈRE: So! I am nothing to you, and it was flat
    Deception when you . . .
MARIANE: Please, enough of that.
  You've told me plainly that I should agree
  To wed the man my father's chosen for me,
  And since you've designed to counsel me so wisely,
  I promise, Sir, to do as you advise me.
VALÈRE: Ah, no, 'twas not by me that you were swayed.   40
  No, your decision was already made;
  Though now, to save appearances, you protest
  That you're betraying me at my behest.
MARIANE: Just as you say.
VALÈRE: Quite so. And I now see
  That you were never truly in love with me.
MARIANE: Alas, you're free to think so if you choose.
VALÈRE: I choose to think so, and here's a bit of news:
  You've spurned my hand, but I know where to turn
  For kinder treatment, as you shall quickly learn.   50
MARIANE: I'm sure you do. Your noble qualities
  Inspire affection . . .
VALÈRE: Forget my qualities, please.
  They don't inspire you overmuch, I find.
  But there's another lady I have in mind

Whose sweet and generous nature will not scorn
To compensate me for the loss I've borne.
MARIANE: I'm no great loss, and I'm sure that you'll transfer
    Your heart quite painlessly from me to her.
VALÈRE: I'll do my best to take it in my stride.   60
    The pain I feel at being cast aside
    Time and forgetfulness may put an end to.
    Or if I can't forget, I shall pretend to.
    No self-respecting person is expected
    To go on loving once he's been rejected.
MARIANE: Now, that's a fine, high-minded sentiment.
VALÈRE: One to which any sane man would assent.
    Would you prefer it if I pined away
    In hopeless passion till my dying day?
    Am I to yield you to a rival's arms   70
    And not console myself with other charms?
MARIANE: Go then: console yourself; don't hesitate.
    I wish you to; indeed, I cannot wait.
VALÈRE: You wish me to?
MARIANE: Yes.
VALÈRE: That's the final straw.
    Madam, farewell. Your wish shall be my law.

(*He starts to leave, and then returns: this repeatedly:*)

MARIANE: Splendid.
VALÈRE (*coming back again*):
                 This breach, remember, is of your making;   80
    It's you who've driven me to the step I'm taking.
MARIANE: Of course.
VALÈRE (*coming back again*):
                 Remember, too, that I am merely
    Following your example.
MARIANE: I see that clearly.
VALÈRE: Enough. I'll go and do your bidding, then.
MARIANE: Good.
VALÈRE (*coming back again*):
                 You shall never see my face again.   90
MARIANE: Excellent.
VALÈRE (*walking to the door, then turning about*):
                 Yes?
MARIANE: What?
VALÈRE: What's that? What did you say?
MARIANE: Nothing. You're dreaming.
VALÈRE: Ah. Well, I'm on my way.
    Farewell, *Madame.*

(*He moves slowly away.*)

MARIANE: Farewell.
DORINE (*to* MARIANE):   If you ask me,   100

Both of you are as mad as mad can be.
Do stop this nonsense, now. I've only let you
Squabble so long to see where it would get you.
Whoa there, Monsieur Valère!

(*She goes and seizes* VALÈRE *by the arm; he makes a great show of resistance.*)

VALÈRE: What's this, Dorine?
DORINE: Come here.
VALÈRE: No, no, my heart's too full of spleen.
  Don't hold me back; her wish must be obeyed.
DORINE: Stop!
VALÈRE: It's too late now; my decision's made.   110
DORINE: Oh, pooh!
MARIANE (*aside*):   He hates the sight of me, that's plain.
  I'll go, and so deliver him from pain.
DORINE (*leaving* VALÈRE, *running after* MARIANE):
  And now *you* run away! Come back.
MARIANE: No, no.
  Nothing you say will keep me here. Let go!
VALÈRE (*aside*): She cannot bear my presence, I perceive.
  To spare her further torment, I shall leave.
DORINE (*leaving* MARIANE, *running after* VALÈRE): Again! You'll not es-   120
  cape, Sir; don't you try it.
  Come here, you two. Stop fussing, and be quiet.

(*She takes* VALÈRE *by the hand, then* MARIANE, *and draws them together.*)

VALÈRE (*to* DORINE): What do you want of me?
MARIANE (*To* DORINE):   What is the point of this?
DORINE: We're going to have a little armistice.
  (*To* VALÈRE.) Now weren't you silly to get so overheated?
VALÈRE: Didn't you see how badly I was treated?
DORINE (*to* MARIANE): Aren't you a simpleton, to have lost your head?
MARIANE: Didn't you hear the hateful things he said?
DORINE (*to* VALÈRE): You're both great fools. Her sole desire, Valère,   130
  Is to be yours in marriage. To that I'll swear.
  (*To* MARIANE.) He loves you only, and he wants no wife
  But you, Mariane. On that I'll stake my life.
MARIANE (*to* VALÈRE): Then why you advised me so, I cannot see.
VALÈRE (*to* MARIANE): On such a question, why ask advice of *me?*
DORINE: Oh, you're impossible. Give me your hands, you two.
  (*To* VALÈRE.)   Yours first.
VALÈRE (*giving* DORINE *his hand*): But why?
DORINE (*to* MARIANE):   And now a hand from you.
MARIANE (*also giving* DORINE *her hand*):   140
  What are you doing?
DORINE: There: a perfect fit.
  You suit each other better than you'll admit.

(VALÈRE *and* MARIANE *hold hands for some time without looking at each other.*)

VALÈRE (*turning toward* MARIANE): Ah, come, don't be so haughty. Give
   a man
  A look of kindness, won't you, Mariane?

(MARIANE *turns toward* VALÈRE *and smiles.*)

DORINE: I tell you, lovers are completely mad!
VALÈRE (*to* MARIANE): Now come, confess that you were very bad
  To hurt my feelings as you did just now.
  I have a just complaint, you must allow.　　　　　　　　　　150
MARIANE: *You* must allow that you were most unpleasant . . .
DORINE: Let's table that discussion for the present;
  Your father has a plan which must be stopped.
MARIANE: Advise us, then; what means must we adopt?
DORINE: We'll use all manner of means, and all at once.
  (*To* MARIANE.) Your father's addled; he's acting like a dunce.
  Therefore you'd better humor the old fossil.
  Pretend to yield to him, be sweet and docile,
  And then postpone, as often as necessary,
  The day on which you have agreed to marry.　　　　　　　　160
  You'll thus gain time, and time will turn the trick.
  Sometimes, for instance, you'll be taken sick,
  And that will seem good reason for delay;
  Or some bad omen will make you change the day—
  You'll dream of muddy water, or you'll pass
  A dead man's hearse, or break a looking-glass.
  If all else fails, no man can marry you
  Unless you take his ring and say "I do."
  But now, let's separate. If they should find
  Us talking here, our plot might be divined.　　　　　　　　170
  (*To* VALÈRE.) Go to your friends, and tell them what's occurred,
  And have them urge her father to keep his word.
  Meanwhile, we'll stir her brother into action,
  And get Elmire, as well, to join our faction.
  Good-bye.
VALÈRE (*to* MARIANE):
        Though each of us will do his best,
  It's your true heart on which my hopes shall rest.
MARIANE (*to* VALÈRE): Regardless of what Father may decide,
  None but Valère shall claim me as his bride.　　　　　　　180
VALÈRE: Oh, how those words content me! Come what will . . .
DORINE: Oh, lovers, lovers! Their tongues are never still.
  Be off, now.
VALÈRE (*turning to go, then turning back*):
        One last word . . .
DORINE:　　　　　　　　　　　　　　No time to chat:
  You leave by this door; and *you* leave by that.

(DORINE *pushes them, by the shoulders, toward opposing doors.*)

ACT III

Scene 1

DAMIS
DORINE

DAMIS: May lightning strike me even as I speak,
  May all men call me cowardly and weak,
  If any fear or scruple holds me back
  From settling things, at once, with that great quack!
DORINE: Now, don't give way to violent emotion.
  Your father's merely talked about this notion,
  And words and deeds are far from being one.
  Much that is talked about is left undone.
DAMIS: No, I must stop that scoundrel's machinations;
  I'll go and tell him off; I'm out of patience.   10
DORINE: Do calm down and be practical. I had rather
  My mistress dealt with him—and with your father.
  She has some influence with Tartuffe, I've noted.
  He hangs upon her words, seems most devoted,
  And may, indeed, be smitten by her charm.
  Pray Heaven it's true! 'Twould do our cause no harm.
  She sent for him, just now, to sound him out
  On this affair you're so incensed about;
  She'll find out where he stands, and tell him, too,
  What dreadful strife and trouble will ensue   20
  If he lends countenance to your father's plan.
  I couldn't get in to see him, but his man
  Says that he's almost finished with his prayers.
  Go, now. I'll catch him when he comes downstairs.
DAMIS: I want to hear this conference, and I will.
DORINE: No, they must be alone.
DAMIS: Oh, I'll keep still.
DORINE: Not you. I know your temper. You'd start a brawl,
  And shout and stamp your foot and spoil it all.
  Go on.   30
DAMIS: I won't; I have a perfect right...
DORINE: Lord, you're a nuisance! He's coming; get out of sight.

(DAMIS *conceals himself in a closet at the rear of the stage.*)

Scene 2

TARTUFFE
DORINE

TARTUFFE (*observing* DORINE, *and calling to his manservant offstage*):
  Hang up my hair-shirt, put my scourge in place,
  And pray, Laurent, for Heaven's perpetual grace.

I'm going to the prison now, to share
My last few coins with the poor wretches there.
DORINE (*aside*): Dear God, what affectation! What a fake!
TARTUFFE: You wished to see me?
DORINE: Yes . . .
TARTUFFE (*taking a handkerchief from his pocket*):
                                 For mercy's sake,   10
Please take this handkerchief, before you speak.
DORINE: What?
TARTUFFE: Cover that bosom, girl. The flesh is weak,
And unclean thoughts are difficult to control.
Such sights as that can undermine the soul.
DORINE: Your soul, it seems, has very poor defenses,
And flesh makes quite an impact on your senses.
It's strange that you're so easily excited;
My own desires are not so soon ignited,
And if I saw you naked as a beast,   20
Not all your hide would tempt me in the least.
TARTUFFE: Girl, speak more modestly; unless you do,
I shall be forced to take my leave of you.
DORINE: Oh, no, it's I who must be on my way;
I've just one little message to convey.
Madame is coming down, and begs you, Sir,
To wait and have a word or two with her.
TARTUFFE: Gladly.
DORINE (*aside*):   *That* had a softening effect!
I think my guess about him was correct.
TARTUFFE: Will she be long?   30
DORINE: No: that's her step I hear.
Ah, here she is, and I shall disappear.

Scene 3

ELMIRE
TARTUFFE

TARTUFFE: May Heaven, whose infinite goodness we adore,
Preserve your body and soul forevermore,
And bless your days, and answer thus the plea
Of one who is its humblest votary.
ELMIRE: I thank you for that pious wish. But please,
Do take a chair and let's be more at ease.

(*They sit down.*)

TARTUFFE: I trust that you are once more well and strong?
ELMIRE: Oh, yes: the fever didn't last for long.
TARTUFFE: My prayers are too unworthy, I am sure,
To have gained from Heaven this most gracious cure;   10
But lately, Madam, my every supplication
Has had for object your recuperation.

ELMIRE: You shouldn't have troubled so. I don't deserve it.
TARTUFFE: Your health is priceless, Madam, and to preserve it
   I'd gladly give my own, in all sincerity.
ELMIRE: Sir, you outdo us all in Christian charity.
   You've been most kind. I count myself your debtor.
TARTUFFE: 'Twas nothing, Madam. I long to serve you better.
ELMIRE: There's a private matter I'm anxious to discuss.
   I'm glad there's no one here to hinder us.   20
TARTUFFE: I too am glad; it floods my heart with bliss
   To find myself alone with you like this.
   For just this chance I've prayed with all my power—
   But prayed in vain, until this happy hour.
ELMIRE: This won't take long, Sir, and I hope you'll be
   Entirely frank and unconstrained with me.
TARTUFFE: Indeed, there's nothing I had rather do
   Than bare my inmost heart and soul to you.
   First, let me say that what remarks I've made
   About the constant visits you are paid   30
   Were prompted not by any mean emotion,
   But rather by a pure and deep devotion,
   A fervent zeal . . .
ELMIRE: No need for explanation.
   Your sole concern, I'm sure, was my salvation.
TARTUFFE (*taking* ELMIRE*'s hand and pressing her fingertips*): Quite so;
   and such great fervor do I feel . . .
ELMIRE: Ooh! Please! You're pinching!
TARTUFFE: 'Twas from excess of zeal.
   I never meant to cause you pain, I swear.   40
   I'd rather . . .

(*He places his hand on* ELMIRE*'s knee.*)

ELMIRE: What can your hand be doing there?
TARTUFFE: Feeling your gown; what soft, fine-woven stuff!
ELMIRE: Please, I'm extremely ticklish. That's enough.

(*She draws her chair away;* TARTUFFE *pulls his after her.*)

TARTUFFE (*fondling the lace collar of her gown*): My, my, what lovely
   lacework on your dress!
   The workmanship's miraculous, no less.
   I've not seen anything to equal it.
ELMIRE: Yes, quite. But let's talk business for a bit.
   They say my husband means to break his word   50
   And give his daughter to you, Sir. Had you heard?
TARTUFFE: He did once mention it. But I confess
   I dream of quite a different happiness.
   It's elsewhere, Madam, that my eyes discern
   The promise of that bliss for which I yearn.
ELMIRE: I see: you care for nothing here below.
TARTUFFE: Ah, well—my heart's not made of stone, you know.

ELMIRE: All your desires mount heavenward, I'm sure,
  In scorn of all that's earthly and impure.
TARTUFFE: A love of heavenly beauty does not preclude 60
  A proper love for earthly pulchritude;
  Our senses are quite rightly captivated
  By perfect works our Maker has created.
  Some glory clings to all that Heaven has made;
  In you, all Heaven's marvels are displayed.
  On that fair face, such beauties have been lavished,
  The eyes are dazzled and the heart is ravished;
  How could I look on you, O flawless creature,
  And not adore the Author of all Nature,
  Feeling a love both passionate and pure 70
  For you, his triumph of self-portraiture?
  At first, I trembled lest that love should be
  A subtle snare that Hell had laid for me;
  I vowed to flee the sight of you, eschewing
  A rapture that might prove my soul's undoing;
  But soon, fair being, I became aware
  That my deep passion could be made to square
  With rectitude, and with my bounden duty.
  I thereupon surrendered to your beauty.
  It is, I know, presumptuous on my part 80
  To bring you this poor offering of my heart,
  And it is not my merit, Heaven knows,
  But your compassion on which my hopes repose.
  You are my peace, my solace, my salvation;
  On you depends my bliss—or desolation;
  I bide your judgment and, as you think best,
  I shall be either miserable or blest.
ELMIRE: Your declaration is most gallant, Sir,
  But don't you think it's out of character?
  You'd have done better to restrain your passion 90
  And think before you spoke in such a fashion.
  It ill becomes a pious man like you . . .
TARTUFFE: I may be pious, but I'm human too:
  With your celestial charms before his eyes,
  A man has not the power to be wise.
  I know such words sound strangely, coming from me,
  But I'm no angel, nor was meant to be,
  And if you blame my passion, you must needs
  Reproach as well the charms on which it feeds.
  Your loveliness I had no sooner seen 100
  Than you became my soul's unrivalled queen;
  Before your seraph glance, divinely sweet,
  My heart's defenses crumbled in defeat,
  And nothing fasting, prayer, or tears might do
  Could stay my spirit from adoring you.
  My eyes, my sighs have told you in the past
  What now my lips make bold to say at last,
  And if, in your great goodness, you will deign

To look upon your slave, and ease his pain,—
If, in compassion for my soul's distress,   110
You'll stoop to comfort my unworthiness,
I'll raise to you, in thanks for that sweet manna,
An endless hymn, an infinite hosanna.
With me, of course, there need be no anxiety,
No fear of scandal or of notoriety.
These young court gallants, whom all the ladies fancy,
Are vain in speech, in action rash and chancy;
When they succeed in love, the world soon knows it;
No favor's granted them but they disclose it
And by the looseness of their tongues profane   120
The very altar where their hearts have lain.
Men of my sort, however, love discreetly,
And one may trust our reticence completely.
My keen concern for my good name insures
The absolute security of yours;
In short, I offer you, my dear Elmire,
Love without scandal, pleasure without fear.
ELMIRE: I've heard your well-turned speeches to the end,
And what you urge I clearly apprehend.
Aren't you afraid that I may take a notion   130
To tell my husband of your warm devotion,
And that, supposing he were duly told,
His feelings toward you might grow rather cold?
TARTUFFE: I know, dear lady, that your exceeding charity
Will lead your heart to pardon my temerity;
That you'll excuse my violent affection
As human weakness, human imperfection;
And that—O fairest!—you will bear in mind
That I'm but flesh and blood, and am not blind.
ELMIRE: Some women might do otherwise, perhaps,   140
But I shall be discreet about your lapse;
I'll tell my husband nothing of what's occurred
If, in return, you'll give your solemn word
To advocate as forcefully as you can
The marriage of Valère and Mariane,
Renouncing all desire to dispossess
Another of his rightful happiness,
And . . .

Scene 4

DAMIS
ELMIRE
TARTUFFE

DAMIS (*emerging from the closet where he has been hiding*):
    No! We'll not hush up this vile affair;
    I heard it all inside that closet there,
    Where Heaven, in order to confound the pride

Of this great rascal, prompted me to hide.
Ah, now I have my long-awaited chance
To punish his deceit and arrogance,
And give my father clear and shocking proof
Of the black character of his dear Tartuffe.
ELMIRE: Ah no, Damis; I'll be content if he   10
  Will study to deserve my leniency.
  I've promised silence—don't make me break my word;
  To make a scandal would be too absurd.
  Good wives laugh off such trifles, and forget them;
  Why should they tell their husbands, and upset them?
DAMIS: You have your reasons for taking such a course,
  And I have reasons, too, of equal force.
  To spare him now would be insanely wrong.
  I've swallowed my just wrath for far too long
  And watched this insolent bigot bringing strife   20
  And bitterness into our family life.
  Too long he's meddled in my father's affairs,
  Thwarting my marriage-hopes, and poor Valère's.
  It's high time that my father was undeceived,
  And now I've proof that can't be disbelieved—
  Proof that was furnished me by Heaven above.
  It's too good not to take advantage of.
  This is my chance, and I deserve to lose it
  If, for one moment, I hesitate to use it.
ELMIRE: Damis . . .   30
DAMIS: No, I must do what I think right.
  Madam, my heart is bursting with delight,
  And, say whatever you will, I'll not consent
  To lose the sweet revenge on which I'm bent.
  I'll settle matters without more ado;
  And here, most opportunely, is my cue.

Scene 5

ORGON   TARTUFFE
DAMIS   ELMIRE

DAMIS: Father, I'm glad you've joined us. Let us advise you
  Of some fresh news which doubtless will surprise you.
  You've just now been repaid with interest
  For all your loving-kindness to our guest.
  He's proved his warm and grateful feelings toward you;
  It's with a pair of horns he would reward you.
  Yes, I surprised him with your wife, and heard
  His whole adulterous offer, every word.
  She, with her all too gentle disposition,
  Would not have told you of his proposition;   10
  But I shall not make terms with brazen lechery,
  And feel that not to tell you would be treachery.

ELMIRE: And I hold that one's husband's peace of mind
   Should not be spoilt by tattle of this kind.
   One's honor doesn't require it: to be proficient
   In keeping men at bay is quite sufficient.
   These are my sentiments, and I wish, Damis,
   That you had heeded me and held your peace.

Scene 6

ORGON
DAMIS
TARTUFFE

ORGON: Can it be true, this dreadful thing I hear?
TARTUFFE: Yes, Brother, I'm a wicked man, I fear:
   A wretched sinner, all depraved and twisted,
   The greatest villain that has ever existed.
   My life's one heap of crimes, which grows each minute;
   There's naught but foulness and corruption in it;
   And I perceive that Heaven, outraged by me,
   Has chosen this occasion to mortify me.
   Charge me with any deed you wish to name;
   I'll not defend myself, but take the blame.   10
   Believe what you are told, and drive Tartuffe
   Like some base criminal from beneath your roof;
   Yes, drive me hence, and with a parting curse:
   I shan't protest, for I deserve far worse.
ORGON (*to* DAMIS): Ah, you deceitful boy, how dare you try
   To stain his purity with so foul a lie?
DAMIS: What! Are you taken in by such a bluff?
   Did you not hear . . . ?
ORGON: Enough, you rogue, enough!
TARTUFFE: Ah, Brother, let him speak: you're being unjust.   20
   Believe his story; the boy deserves your trust.
   Why, after all, should you have faith in me?
   How can you know what I might do, or be?
   Is it on my good actions that you base
   Your favor? Do you trust my pious face?
   Ah, no, don't be deceived by hollow shows;
   I'm far, alas, from being what men suppose;
   Though the world takes me for a man of worth,
   I'm truly the most worthless man on earth.
   (*To* DAMIS.) Yes, my dear son, speak out now: call me the chief   30
   Of sinners, a wretch, a murderer, a thief;
   Load me with all the names men most abhor;
   I'll not complain; I've earned them all, and more;
   I'll kneel here while you pour them on my head
   As a just punishment for the life I've led.
ORGON (*to* TARTUFFE): This is too much, dear Brother.
   (*To* DAMIS.)
                                 Have you no heart?

DAMIS: Are you so hoodwinked by this rascal's art . . . ?

ORGON: Be still, you monster. 40

    (*To* TARTUFFE.) Brother, I pray you, rise.

    (*To* DAMIS.) Villain!

DAMIS: But . . .

ORGON: Silence!

DAMIS: Can't you realize . . . ?

ORGON: Just one word more, and I'll tear you limb from limb.

TARTUFFE: In God's name, Brother, don't be harsh with him.

    I'd rather far be tortured at the stake

    Than see him bear one scratch for my poor sake.

ORGON (*to* DAMIS): Ingrate! 50

TARTUFFE: If I must beg you, on bended knee,

    To pardon him . . .

ORGON (*falling to his knees, addressing* TARTUFFE):

                  Such goodness cannot be!

    (*To* DAMIS.) Now, *there's* true charity!

DAMIS: What, you . . . ?

ORGON: Villain, be still!

    I know your motives; I know you wish him ill:

    Yes, all of you—wife, children, servants, all—

    Conspire against him and desire his fall, 60

    Employing every shameful trick you can

    To alienate me from this saintly man.

    Ah, but the more you seek to drive him away,

    The more I'll do to keep him. Without delay,

    I'll spite this household and confound its pride

    By giving him my daughter as his bride.

DAMIS: You're going to force her to accept his hand?

ORGON: Yes, and this very night, d'you understand?

    I shall defy you all, and make it clear

    That I'm the one who gives the orders here. 70

    Come, wretch, kneel down and clasp his blessed feet,

    And ask his pardon for your black deceit.

DAMIS: I ask that swindler's pardon? Why, I'd rather . . .

ORGON: So! You insult him, and defy your father!

    A stick! A stick! (*To* TARTUFFE.) No, no—release me, do.

    (*To* DAMIS.) Out of my house this minute! Be off with you,

    And never dare set foot in it again.

DAMIS: Well, I shall go, but . . .

ORGON: Well, go quickly, then.

    I disinherit you; an empty purse 80

    Is all you'll get from me—except my curse!

Scene 7

ORGON
TARTUFFE

ORGON: How he blasphemed your goodness! What a son!

TARTUFFE: Forgive him, Lord, as I've already done.

(*To* ORGON.) You can't know how it hurts when someone tries
　To blacken me in my dear Brother's eyes.
ORGON: Ahh!
TARTUFFE:　　The mere thought of such ingratitude
　Plunges my soul into so dark a mood . . .
　Such horror grips my heart . . . I gasp for breath,
　And cannot speak, and feel myself near death.
ORGON: (*He runs, in tears, to the door through which he has just driven*　　　10
　　his son.) You blackguard! Why did I spare you? Why did I not
　Break you in little pieces on the spot?
　Compose yourself, and don't be hurt, dear friend.
TARTUFFE: These scenes, these dreadful quarrels, have got to end.
　I've much upset your household, and I perceive
　That the best thing will be for me to leave.
ORGON: What are you saying!
TARTUFFE:　　　　　　　　　They're all against me here;
　They'd have you think me false and insincere.
ORGON: Ah, what of that? Have I ceased believing in you?　　　　　　20
TARTUFFE: Their adverse talk will certainly continue,
　And charges which you now repudiate
　You may find credible at a later date.
ORGON: No, Brother, never.
TARTUFFE:　　　　　　　　Brother, a wife can sway
　Her husband's mind in many a subtle way.
ORGON: No, no.
TARTUFFE:　　To leave at once is the solution;
　Thus only can I end their persecution.
ORGON: No, no, I'll not allow it; you shall remain.　　　　　　　　30
TARTUFFE: Ah, well; 'twill mean much martyrdom and pain,
　But if you wish it . . .
ORGON:　　　　　Ah!
TARTUFFE:　　　　　　　Enough; so be it.
　But one thing must be settled, as I see it.
　For your dear honor, and for our friendship's sake,
　There's one precaution I feel bound to take.
　I shall avoid your wife, and keep away . . .
ORGON: No, you shall not, whatever they may say.
　It pleases me to vex them, and for spite　　　　　　　　　　　40
　I'd have them see you with her day and night.
　What's more, I'm going to drive them to despair
　By making you my only son and heir;
　This very day, I'll give to you alone
　Clear deed and title to everything I own.
　A dear, good friend and son-in-law-to-be
　Is more than wife, or child, or kin to me.
　Will you accept my offer, dearest son?
TARTUFFE: In all things, let the will of Heaven be done.
ORGON: Poor fellow! Come, we'll go draw up the deed.　　　　　　50
　Then let them burst with disappointed greed!

ACT IV

Scene 1

CLÉANTE
TARTUFFE

CLÉANTE: Yes, all the town's discussing it, and truly,
    Their comments do not flatter you unduly.
    I'm glad we've met, Sir, and I'll give my view
    Of this sad matter in a word or two.
    As for who's guilty, that I shan't discuss;
    Let's say it was Damis who caused the fuss;
    Assuming, then, that you have been ill-used
    By young Damis, and groundlessly accused,
    Ought not a Christian to forgive, and ought
    He not to stifle every vengeful thought?   10
    Should you stand by and watch a father make
    His only son an exile for your sake?
    Again I tell you frankly, be advised:
    The whole town, high and low, is scandalized;
    This quarrel must be mended, and my advice is
    Not to push matters to a further crisis.
    No, sacrifice your wrath to God above,
    And help Damis regain his father's love.
TARTUFFE: Alas, for my part I should take great joy
    In doing so. I've nothing against the boy.   20
    I pardon all, I harbor no resentment;
    To serve him would afford me much contentment.
    But Heaven's interest will not have it so:
    If he comes back, then I shall have to go.
    After his conduct—so extreme, so vicious—
    Our further intercourse would look suspicious.
    God knows what people would think! Why, they'd describe
    My goodness to him as a sort of bribe;
    They'd say that out of guilt I made pretense
    Of loving-kindness and benevolence—   30
    That, fearing my accuser's tongue, I strove
    To buy his silence with a show of love.
CLÉANTE: Your reasoning is badly warped and stretched,
    And these excuses, Sir, are most far-fetched.
    Why put yourself in charge of Heaven's cause?
    Does Heaven need our help to enforce its laws?
    Leave vengeance to the Lord, Sir; while we live,
    Our duty's not to punish, but forgive;
    And what the Lord commands, we should obey
    Without regard to what the world may say.   40
    What! Shall the fear of being misunderstood
    Prevent our doing what is right and good?
    No, no; let's simply do what Heaven ordains,
    And let no other thoughts perplex our brains.

TARTUFFE: Again, Sir, let me say that I've forgiven
  Damis, and thus obeyed the laws of Heaven;
  But I am not commanded by the Bible
  To live with one who smears my name with libel.
CLÉANTE: Were you commanded, Sir, to indulge the whim
  Of poor Orgon, and to encourage him   50
  In suddenly transferring to your name
  A large estate to which you have no claim?
TARTUFFE: 'Twould never occur to those who know me best
  To think I acted from self-interest.
  The treasures of this world I quite despise;
  Their specious glitter does not charm my eyes;
  And if I have resigned myself to taking
  The gift which my dear Brother insists on making,
  I do so only, as he well understands,
  Lest so much wealth fall into wicked hands,   60
  Lest those to whom it might descend in time
  Turn it to purposes of sin and crime,
  And not, as I shall do, make use of it
  For Heaven's glory and mankind's benefit.
CLÉANTE: Forget these trumped-up fears. Your argument
  Is one the rightful heir might well resent;
  It *is* a moral burden to inherit
  Such wealth, but give Damis a chance to bear it.
  And would it not be worse to be accused
  Of swindling, than to see that wealth misused?   70
  I'm shocked that you allowed Orgon to broach
  This matter, and that you feel no self-reproach;
  Does true religion teach that lawful heirs
  May freely be deprived of what is theirs?
  And if the Lord has told you in your heart
  That you and young Damis must dwell apart,
  Would it not be the decent thing to beat
  A generous and honorable retreat,
  Rather than let the son of the house be sent,
  For your convenience, into banishment?   80
  Sir, if you wish to prove the honesty
  Of your intentions . . .
TARTUFFE: Sir, it is half-past three.
  I've certain pious duties to attend to,
  And hope my prompt departure won't offend you.
CLÉANTE (*alone*): Damn.

Scene 2

ELMIRE   CLÉANTE
MARIANE   DORINE

DORINE: Stay, Sir, and help Mariane, for Heaven's sake!
  She's suffering so, I fear her heart will break.

Her father's plan to marry her off tonight
Has put the poor child in a desperate plight.
I hear him coming. Let's stand together, now,
And see if we can't change his mind, somehow,
About this match we all deplore and fear.

Scene 3

ORGON   MARIANE   DORINE
ELMIRE   CLÉANTE

ORGON: Hah! Glad to find you all assembled here.
  (*To* MARIANE.) This contract, child, contains your happiness,
  And what it says I think your heart can guess.
MARIANE (*falling to her knees*): Sir, by that Heaven which sees me here
    distressed,
  And by whatever else can move your breast,
  Do not employ a father's power, I pray you,
  To crush my heart and force it to obey you,
  Nor by your harsh commands oppress me so
  That I'll begrudge the duty which I owe—   10
  And do not so embitter and enslave me
  That I shall hate the very life you gave me.
  If my sweet hopes must perish, if you refuse
  To give me to the one I've dared to choose,
  Spare me at least—I beg you, I implore—
  The pain of wedding one whom I abhor;
  And do not, by a heartless use of force,
  Drive me to contemplate some desperate course.
ORGON (*feeling himself touched by her*): Be firm, my soul. No human
    weakness, now.   20
MARIANE: I don't resent your love for him. Allow
  Your heart free rein, Sir; give him your property,
  And if that's not enough, take mine from me;
  He's welcome to my money; take it, do,
  But don't, I pray, include my person too.
  Spare me, I beg you; and let me end the tale
  Of my sad days behind a convent veil.
ORGON: A convent! Hah! When crossed in their amours,
  All lovesick girls have the same thought as yours.
  Get up! The more you loathe the man, and dread him,   30
  The more ennobling it will be to wed him.
  Marry Tartuffe, and mortify your flesh!
  Enough; don't start that whimpering afresh.
DORINE: But why . . . ?
ORGON: Be still, there. Speak when you're spoken to.
  Not one more bit of impudence out of you.
CLÉANTE: If I may offer a word of counsel here . . .
ORGON: Brother, in counseling you have no peer;
  All your advice is forceful, sound, and clever;

I don't propose to follow it, however.   40
ELMIRE (*to* ORGON): I am amazed, and don't know what to say;
   Your blindness simply takes my breath away.
   You are indeed bewitched, to take no warning
   From our account of what occurred this morning.
ORGON: Madam, I know a few plain facts, and one
   Is that you're partial to my rascal son;
   Hence, when he sought to make Tartuffe the victim
   Of a base lie, you dared not contradict him.
   Ah, but you underplayed your part, my pet;
   You should have looked more angry, more upset.   50
ELMIRE: When men make overtures, must we reply
   With righteous anger and a battle-cry?
   Must we turn back their amorous advances
   With sharp reproaches and with fiery glances?
   Myself, I find such offers merely amusing,
   And make no scenes and fusses in refusing;
   My taste is for good-natured rectitude,
   And I dislike the savage sort of prude
   Who guards her virtue with her teeth and claws,
   And tears men's eyes out for the slightest cause: 60
   The Lord preserve me from such honor as that,
   Which bites and scratches like an alley-cat!
   I've found that a polite and cool rebuff
   Discourages a lover quite enough.
ORGON: I know the facts, and I shall not be shaken.
ELMIRE: I marvel at your power to be mistaken.
   Would it, I wonder, carry weight with you
   If I could *show* you that our tale was true?
ORGON: Show me?
ELMIRE: Yes.   70
ORGON: Rot.
ELMIRE: Come, what if I found a way
   To make you see the facts as plain as day?
ORGON: Nonsense.
ELMIRE: Do answer me; don't be absurd.
   I'm not now asking you to trust our word.
   Suppose that from some hiding-place in here
   You learned the whole sad truth by eye and ear—
   What would you say of your good friend, after that?
ORGON: Why, I'd say . . . nothing, by Jehoshaphat!   80
   It can't be true.
ELMIRE: You've been too long deceived,
   And I'm quite tired of being disbelieved.
   Come now: let's put my statements to the test,
   And you shall see the truth made manifest.
ORGON: I'll take that challenge. Now do your uttermost.
   We'll see how you make good your empty boast.
ELMIRE (*to* DORINE): Send him to me.
DORINE: He's crafty; it may be hard
   To catch the cunning scoundrel off his guard.   90

ELMIRE: No, amorous men are gullible. Their conceit
  So blinds them that they're never hard to cheat.
  Have him come down (*To* CLÉANTE *&* MARIANE.) Please leave us, for
    a bit.

Scene 4

ELMIRE
ORGON

ELMIRE: Pull up this table, and get under it.
ORGON: What?
ELMIRE: It's essential that you be well-hidden.
ORGON: Why there?
ELMIRE: Oh, Heavens! Just do as you are bidden.
  I have my plans; we'll soon see how they fare.
  Under the table, now; and once you're there,
  Take care that you are neither seen nor heard.
ORGON: Well, I'll indulge you, since I gave my word
  To see you through this infantile charade.   10
ELMIRE: Once it is over, you'll be glad we played.
  (*To her husband, who is now under the table.*) I'm going to act quite
    strangely, now, and you
  Must not be shocked at anything I do.
  Whatever I may say, you must excuse
  As part of that deceit I'm forced to use.
  I shall employ sweet speeches in the task
  Of making that impostor drop his mask;
  I'll give encouragement to his bold desires,
  And furnish fuel to his amorous fires.   20
  Since it's for your sake, and for his destruction,
  That I shall seem to yield to his seduction,
  I'll gladly stop whenever you decide
  That all your doubts are fully satisfied.
  I'll count on you, as soon as you have seen
  What sort of man he is, to intervene,
  And not expose me to his odious lust
  One moment longer than you feel you must.
  Remember: you're to save me from my plight
  Whenever . . . He's coming! Hush! Keep out of sight!   30

Scene 5

TARTUFFE
ELMIRE
ORGON

TARTUFFE: You wish to have a word with me, I'm told.
ELMIRE: Yes. I've a little secret to unfold.
  Before I speak, however, it would be wise
  To close that door, and look about for spies.

(TARTUFFE *goes to the door, closes it, and returns.*)

The very last thing that must happen now
Is a repetition of this morning's row.
I've never been so badly caught off guard.
Oh, how I feared for you! You saw how hard
I tried to make that troublesome Damis
Control his dreadful temper, and hold his peace. 10
In my confusion, I didn't have the sense
Simply to contradict his evidence;
But as it happened, that was for the best,
And all has worked out in our interest.
This storm has only bettered your position;
My husband doesn't have the least suspicion,
And now, in mockery of those who do,
He bids me be continually with you.
And that is why, quite fearless of reproof,
I now can be alone with my Tartuffe, 20
And why my heart—perhaps too quick to yield—
Feels free to let its passion be revealed.
TARTUFFE: Madam, your words confuse me. Not long ago,
You spoke in quite a different style, you know.
ELMIRE: Ah, Sir, if that refusal made you smart,
It's little that you know of woman's heart,
Or what that heart is trying to convey
When it resists in such a feeble way!
Always, at first, our modesty prevents
The frank avowal of tender sentiments; 30
However high the passion which inflames us,
Still, to confess its power somehow shames us.
Thus we reluct, at first, yet in a tone
Which tells you that our heart is overthrown,
That what our lips deny, our pulse confesses,
And that, in time, all noes will turn to yesses.
I fear my words are all too frank and free,
And a poor proof of woman's modesty;
But since I'm started, tell me, if you will—
Would I have tried to make Damis be still, 40
Would I have listened, calm and unoffended,
Until your lengthy offer of love was ended,
And been so very mild in my reaction,
Had your sweet words not given me satisfaction?
And when I tried to force you to undo
The marriage-plans my husband has in view,
What did my urgent pleading signify
If not that I admired you, and that I
Deplored the thought that someone else might own
Part of a heart I wished for mine alone? 50
TARTUFFE: Madam, no happiness is so complete
As when, from lips we love, come words so sweet;
Their nectar floods my every sense, and drains
In honeyed rivulets through all my veins.

To please you is my joy, my only goal;
Your love is the restorer of my soul;
And yet I must beg leave, now, to confess
Some lingering doubts as to my happiness.
Might this not be a trick? Might not the catch
Be that you wish me to break off the match
With Mariane, and so have feigned to love me?
I shan't quite trust your fond opinion of me
Until the feelings you've expressed so sweetly
Are demonstrated somewhat more concretely,
And you have shown, by certain kind concessions,
That I may put my faith in your professions.

ELMIRE (*She coughs, to warn her husband.*) Why be in such a hurry?
   Must my heart
Exhaust its bounty at the very start?
To make that sweet admission cost me dear,
But you'll not be content, it would appear,
Unless my store of favors is disbursed
To the last farthing, and at the very first.

TARTUFFE: The less we merit, the less we dare to hope,
And with our doubts, mere words can never cope.
We trust no promised bliss till we receive it;
Not till a joy is ours can we believe it.
I, who so little merit your esteem,
Can't credit this fulfillment of my dream,
And shan't believe it, Madam, until I savor
Some palpable assurance of your favor.

ELMIRE: My, how tyrannical your love can be,
And how it flusters and perplexes me!
How furiously you take one's heart in hand,
And make your every wish a fierce command!
Come, must you hound and harry me to death?
Will you not give me time to catch my breath?
Can it be right to press me with such force,
Give me no quarter, show me no remorse,
And take advantage, by your stern insistence,
Of the fond feelings which weaken my resistance?

TARTUFFE: Well, if you look with favor upon my love,
Why, then, begrudge me some clear proof thereof?

ELMIRE: But how can I consent without offense
To Heaven, toward which you feel such reverence?

TARTUFFE: If Heaven is all that holds you back, don't worry.
I can remove that hindrance in a hurry.
Nothing of that sort need obstruct our path.

ELMIRE: Must one not be afraid of Heaven's wrath?

TARTUFFE: Madam, forget such fears, and be my pupil,
And I shall teach you how to conquer scruple.
Some joys, it's true, are wrong in Heaven's eyes;
Yet Heaven is not averse to compromise;
There is a science, lately formulated,
Whereby one's conscience may be liberated,
And any wrongful act you care to mention

May be redeemed by purity of intention.
I'll teach you, Madam, the secrets of that science;
Meanwhile, just place on me your full reliance.
Assuage my keen desires, and feel no dread: 110
The sin, if any, shall be on my head.

(ELMIRE *coughs, this time more loudly.*)

You've a bad cough.
ELMIRE: Yes, yes. It's bad indeed.
TARTUFFE (*producing a little paper bag*): A bit of licorice may be what you
     need.
ELMIRE: No, I've a stubborn cold, it seems. I'm sure it
     Will take much more than licorice to cure it.
TARTUFFE: How aggravating.
ELMIRE: Oh, more than I can say.
TARTUFFE: If you're still troubled, think of things this way: 120
     No one shall know our joys, save us alone,
     And there's no evil till the act is known;
     It's scandal, Madam, which makes it an offense,
     And it's no sin to sin in confidence.
ELMIRE (*having coughed once more*): Well, clearly I must do as you require,
     And yield to your importunate desire.
     It is apparent, now, that nothing less
     Will satisfy you, and so I acquiesce.
     To go so far is much against my will;
     I'm vexed that it should come to this; but still,   130
     Since you are so determined on it, since you
     Will not allow mere language to convince you,
     And since you ask for concrete evidence, I
     See nothing for it, now, but to comply.
     If this is sinful, if I'm wrong to do it,
     So much the worse for him who drove me to it.
     The fault can surely not be charged to me.
TARTUFFE: Madam, the fault is mine, if fault there be,
     And . . .
ELMIRE: Open the door a little, and peek out;   140
     I wouldn't want my husband poking about.
TARTUFFE: Why worry about the man? Each day he grows
     More gullible; one can lead him by the nose.
     To find us here would fill him with delight,
     And if he saw the worst, he'd doubt his sight.
ELMIRE: Nevertheless, do step out for a minute
     Into the hall, and see that no one's in it.

Scene 6

ORGON
ELMIRE

ORGON (*coming out from under the table*): That man's a perfect monster,
     I must admit!
     I'm simply stunned. I can't get over it.

ELMIRE: What, coming out so soon? How premature!
  Get back in hiding, and wait until you're sure.
  Stay till the end, and be convinced completely;
  We mustn't stop till things are proved concretely.
ORGON: Hell never harbored anything so vicious!
ELMIRE: Tut, don't be hasty. Try to be judicious.
  Wait, and be certain that there's no mistake.   10
  No jumping to conclusions, for Heaven's sake!

(*She places* ORGON *behind her, as* TARTUFFE *re-enters.*)

Scene 7

TARTUFFE
ELMIRE
ORGON

TARTUFFE (*not seeing* ORGON): Madam, all things have worked out to
    perfection;
  I've given the neighboring rooms a full inspection;
  No one's about; and now I may at last . . .
ORGON (*intercepting him*): Hold on, my passionate fellow, not so fast!
  I should advise a little more restraint.
  Well, so you thought you'd fool me, my dear saint!
  How soon you wearied of the saintly life—
  Wedding my daughter, and coveting my wife!
  I've long suspected you, and had a feeling   10
  That soon I'd catch you at your double-dealing.
  Just now, you've given me evidence galore;
  It's quite enough; I have no wish for more.
ELMIRE (*To* TARTUFFE): I'm sorry to have treated you so slyly,
  But circumstances forced me to be wily.
TARTUFFE: Brother, you can't think . . .
ORGON: No more talk from you;
  Just leave this household, without more ado.
TARTUFFE: What I intended . . .
ORGON: That seems fairly clear.   20
  Spare me your falsehoods and get out of here.
TARTUFFE: No, I'm the master, and you're the one to go!
  This house belongs to me, I'll have you know,
  And I shall show you that you can't hurt *me*
  By this contemptible conspiracy,
  That those who cross me know not what they do,
  And that I've means to expose and punish you,
  Avenge offended Heaven, and make you grieve
  That ever you dared order me to leave.

Scene 8

ELMIRE
ORGON

ELMIRE: What was the point of all that angry chatter?
ORGON: Dear God, I'm worried. This is no laughing matter.

ELMIRE: How so?
ORGON: I fear I understood his drift.
  I'm much disturbed about that deed of gift.
ELMIRE: You gave him . . . ?
ORGON: Yes, it's all been drawn and signed.
  But one thing more is weighing on my mind.
ELMIRE: What's that?
ORGON: I'll tell you; but first let's see if there's   10
  A certain strong-box in his room upstairs.

ACT V

Scene 1

ORGON
CLÉANTE

CLÉANTE: Where are you going so fast?
ORGON: God knows!
CLÉANTE: Then wait;
  Let's have a conference, and deliberate
  On how this situation's to be met.
ORGON: That strong-box has me utterly upset;
  This is the worst of many, many shocks.
CLÉANTE: Is there some fearful mystery in that box?
ORGON: My poor friend Argas brought that box to me
  With his own hands, in utmost secrecy;   10
  'Twas on the very morning of his flight.
  It's full of papers which, if they came to light,
  Would ruin him—or such is my impression.
CLÉANTE: Then why did you let it out of your possession?
ORGON: Those papers vexed my conscience, and it seemed best
  To ask the counsel of my pious guest.
  The cunning scoundrel got me to agree
  To leave the strong-box in his custody,
  So that, in case of an investigation,
  I could employ a slight equivocation   20
  And swear I didn't have it, and thereby,
  At no expense to conscience, tell a lie.
CLÉANTE: It looks to me as if you're out on a limb.
  Trusting him with that box, and offering him
  That deed of gift, were actions of a kind
  Which scarcely indicate a prudent mind.
  With two such weapons, he has the upper hand,
  And since you're vulnerable, as matters stand,
  You erred once more in bringing him to bay.
  You should have acted in some subtler way.   30
ORGON: Just think of it: behind that fervent face,
  A heart so wicked, and a soul so base!
  I took him in, a hungry beggar, and then . . .

Enough, by God! I'm through with pious men:
Henceforth I'll hate the whole false brotherhood,
And persecute them worse than Satan could.
CLÉANTE: Ah, there you go—extravagant as ever!
Why can you not be rational? You never
Manage to take the middle course, it seems,
But jump, instead, between absurd extremes.   40
You've recognized your recent grave mistake
In falling victim to a pious fake;
Now, to correct that error, must you embrace
An even greater error in its place,
And judge our worthy neighbors as a whole
By what you've learned of one corrupted soul?
Come, just because one rascal made you swallow
A show of zeal which turned out to be hollow,
Shall you conclude that all men are deceivers,
And that, today, there are no true believers?   50
Let atheists make that foolish inference;
Learn to distinguish virtue from pretense,
Be cautious in bestowing admiration,
And cultivate a sober moderation.
Don't humor fraud, but also don't asperse
True piety; the latter fault is worse,
And it is best to err, if err one must,
As you have done, upon the side of trust.

Scene 2

DAMIS
ORGON
CLÉANTE

DAMIS: Father, I hear that scoundrel's uttered threats
Against you; that he pridefully forgets
How, in his need, he was befriended by you,
And means to use your gifts to crucify you.
ORGON: It's true, my boy. I'm too distressed for tears.
DAMIS: Leave it to me, Sir; let me trim his ears.
Faced with such insolence, we must not waver.
I shall rejoice in doing you the favor
Of cutting short his life, and your distress.
CLÉANTE: What a display of young hotheadedness!   10
Do learn to moderate your fits of rage.
In this just kingdom, this enlightened age,
One does not settle things by violence.

Scene 3

MADAME PERNELLE   DORINE · ORGON
MARIANE   DAMIS   CLÉANTE
ELMIRE

MADAME PERNELLE: I hear strange tales of very strange events.
ORGON: Yes, strange events which these two eyes beheld.
   The man's ingratitude is unparalleled.
   I save a wretched pauper from starvation,
   House him, and treat him like a blood relation,
   Shower him every day with my largesse,
   Give him my daughter, and all that I possess;
   And meanwhile the unconscionable knave
   Tries to induce my wife to misbehave;
   And not content with such extreme rascality,   10
   Now threatens me with my own liberality,
   And aims, by taking base advantage of
   The gifts I gave him out of Christian love,
   To drive me from my house, a ruined man,
   And make me end a pauper, as he began.
DORINE: Poor fellow!
MADAME PERNELLE: No, my son, I'll never bring
   Myself to think him guilty of such a thing.
ORGON: How's that?
MADAME PERNELLE: The righteous always were maligned.   20
ORGON: Speak clearly, Mother. Say what's on your mind.
MADAME PERNELLE: I mean that I can smell a rat, my dear.
   You know how everybody hates him, here.
ORGON: That has no bearing on the case at all.
MADAME PERNELLE: I told you a hundred times, when you were small,
   That virtue in this world is hated ever;
   Malicious men may die, but malice never.
ORGON: No doubt that's true, but how does it apply?
MADAME PERNELLE: They've turned you against him by a clever lie.
ORGON: I've told you, I was there and saw it done.   30
MADAME PERNELLE: Ah, slanderers will stop at nothing, Son.
ORGON: Mother, I'll lose my temper . . . For the last time,
   I tell you I was witness to the crime.
MADAME PERNELLE: The tongues of spite are busy night and noon,
   And to their venom no man is immune.
ORGON: You're talking nonsense. Can't you realize
   I saw it; saw it; saw it with my eyes?
   Saw, do you understand me? Must I shout it
   Into your ears before you'll cease to doubt it?
MADAME PERNELLE: Appearances can deceive, my son. Dear me,   40
   We cannot always judge by what we see.
ORGON: Drat! Drat!
MADAME PERNELLE: One often interprets things awry;
   Good can seem evil to a suspicious eye.

ORGON: Was I to see his pawing at Elmire
  As an act of charity?
MADAME PERNELLE: Till his guilt is clear,
  A man deserves the benefit of the doubt.
  You should have waited, to see how things turned out.
ORGON: Great God in Heaven, what more proof did I need?   50
  Was I to sit there, watching, until he'd . . .
  You drive me to the brink of impropriety.
MADAME PERNELLE: No, no, a man of such surpassing piety
  Could not do such a thing. You cannot shake me.
  I don't believe it, and you shall not make me.
ORGON: You vex me so that, if you weren't my mother,
  I'd say to you . . . some dreadful thing or other.
DORINE: It's your turn now, Sir, not to be listened to;
  You'd not trust us, and now she won't trust you.
CLÉANTE: My friends, we're wasting time which should be spent   60
  In facing up to our predicament.
  I fear that scoundrel's threats weren't made in sport.
DAMIS: Do you think he'd have the nerve to go to court?
ELMIRE: I'm sure he won't: they'd find it all too crude
  A case of swindling and ingratitude.
CLÉANTE: Don't be too sure. He won't be at a loss
  To give his claims a high and righteous gloss;
  And clever rogues with far less valid cause
  Have trapped their victims in a web of laws.
  I say again that to antagonize   70
  A man so strongly armed was most unwise.
ORGON: I know it; but the man's appalling cheek
  Outraged me so, I couldn't control my pique.
CLÉANTE: I wish to Heaven that we could devise
  Some truce between you, or some compromise.
ELMIRE: If I had known what cards he held, I'd not
  Have roused his anger by my little plot.
ORGON (*to* DORINE, *as* M. LOYAL *enters*): What is that fellow looking for?
    Who is he?
  Go talk to him—and tell him that I'm busy.   80

Scene 4

MONSIEUR LOYAL	DAMIS	ELMIRE
MADAME PERNELLE	MARIANE	CLÉANTE
ORGON	DORINE	

MONSIEUR LOYAL: Good day, dear sister. Kindly let me see
  Your master.
DORINE: He's involved with company,
  And cannot be disturbed just now, I fear.
MONSIEUR LOYAL: I hate to intrude; but what has brought me here
  Will not disturb your master, in any event.
  Indeed, my news will make him most content.

DORINE: Your name?

MONSIEUR LOYAL: Just say that I bring greetings from
    Monsieur Tartuffe, on whose behalf I've come.   10

DORINE (*to* ORGON): Sir, he's a very gracious man, and bears
    A message from Tartuffe, which, he declares,
    Will make you most content.

CLÉANTE: Upon my word,
    I think this man had best be seen, and heard.

ORGON: Perhaps he has some settlement to suggest.
    How shall I treat him? What manner would be best?

CLÉANTE: Control your anger, and if he should mention
    Some fair adjustment, give him your full attention.

MONSIEUR LOYAL: Good health to you, good Sir. May Heaven confound   20
    Your enemies, and may your joys abound.

ORGON (*aside, to* CLÉANTE): A gentle salutation: it confirms
    My guess that he is here to offer terms.

MONSIEUR LOYAL: I've always held your family most dear;
    I served your father, Sir, for many a year.

ORGON: Sir, I must ask your pardon; to my shame,
    I cannot now recall your face or name.

MONSIEUR LOYAL: Loyal's my name; I come from Normandy,
    And I'm a bailiff, in all modesty.
    For forty years, praise God, it's been my boast   30
    To serve with honor in that vital post,
    And I am here, Sir, if you will permit
    The liberty, to serve you with this writ . . .

ORGON: To—*what?*

MONSIEUR LOYAL: Now, please, Sir, let us have no friction:
    It's nothing but an order of eviction.
    You are to move your goods and family out
    And make way for new occupants, without
    Deferment or delay, and give the keys . . .

ORGON: I? Leave this house?   40

MONSIEUR LOYAL: Why yes, Sir, if you please.
    This house, Sir, from the cellar to the roof,
    Belongs now to the good Monsieur Tartuffe,
    And he is lord and master of your estate
    By virtue of a deed of present date,
    Drawn in due form, with clearest legal phrasing . . .

DAMIS: Your insolence is utterly amazing!

MONSIEUR LOYAL: Young man, my business here is not with you,
    But with your wise and temperate father, who,
    Like every worthy citizen, stands in awe   50
    Of justice, and would never obstruct the law.

ORGON: But . . .

MONSIEUR LOYAL: Not for a million, Sir, would you rebel
    Against authority; I know that well.
    You'll not make trouble, Sir, or interfere
    With the execution of my duties here.

DAMIS: Someone may execute a smart tattoo
    On that black jacket of yours, before you're through.

MONSIEUR LOYAL: Sir, bid your son be silent. I'd much regret
  Having to mention such a nasty threat   60
  Of violence, in writing my report.
DORINE (*aside*): This man Loyal's a most disloyal sort!
MONSIEUR LOYAL: I love all men of upright character,
  And when I agreed to serve these papers, Sir,
  It was your feelings that I had in mind.
  I couldn't bear to see the case assigned
  To someone else, who might esteem you less
  And so subject you to unpleasantness.
ORGON: What's more unpleasant than telling a man to leave
  His house and home?   70
MONSIEUR LOYAL: You'd like a short reprieve?
  If you desire it, Sir, I shall not press you,
  But wait until tomorrow to dispossess you.
  Splendid. I'll come and spend the night here, then,
  Most quietly, with half a score of men.
  For form's sake, you might bring me, just before
  You go to bed, the keys to the front door.
  My men, I promise, will be on their best
  Behavior, and will not disturb your rest.
  But bright and early, Sir, you must be quick   80
  And move out all your furniture, every stick:
  The men I've chosen are both young and strong,
  And with their help it shouldn't take you long.
  In short, I'll make things pleasant and convenient,
  And since I'm being so extremely lenient,
  Please show me, Sir, a like consideration,
  And give me your entire cooperation.
ORGON (*aside*): I may be all but bankrupt, but I vow
  I'd give a hundred louis, here and now,
  Just for the pleasure of landing one good clout   90
  Right on the end of that complacent snout.
CLÉANTE: Careful; don't make things worse.
DAMIS: My bootsole itches
  To give that beggar a good kick in the breeches.
DORINE: Monsieur Loyal, I'd love to hear the whack
  Of a stout stick across your fine broad back.
MONSIEUR LOYAL: Take care: a woman too may go to jail if
  She uses threatening language to a bailiff.
CLÉANTE: Enough, enough, Sir. This must not go on.
  Give me that paper, please, and then begone.   100
MONSIEUR LOYAL: Well, *au revoir*. God give you all good cheer!
ORGON: May God confound you, and him who sent you here!

Scene 5

ORGON   ELMIRE   DORINE
CLÉANTE   MADAME PERNELLE   DAMIS
MARIANE

ORGON: Now, Mother, was I right or not? This writ
  Should change your notion of Tartuffe a bit.
  Do you perceive his villainy at last?
MADAME PERNELLE: I'm thunderstruck. I'm utterly aghast.
DORINE: Oh, come, be fair. You mustn't take offense
  At this new proof of his benevolence.
  He's acting out of selfless love, I know.
  Material things enslave the soul, and so
  He kindly has arranged your liberation
  From all that might endanger your salvation.   10
ORGON: Will you not ever hold your tongue, you dunce?
CLÉANTE: Come, you must take some action, and at once.
ELMIRE: Go tell the world of the low trick he's tried.
  The deed of gift is surely nullified
  By such behavior, and public rage will not
  Permit the wretch to carry out his plot.

Scene 6

VALÈRE   ELMIRE   DAMIS
ORGON   MARIANE   DORINE
CLÉANTE   MADAME PERNELLE

VALÈRE: Sir, though I hate to bring you more bad news,
  Such is the danger that I cannot choose.
  A friend who is extremely close to me
  And knows my interest in your family
  Has, for my sake, presumed to violate
  The secrecy that's due to things of state,
  And sends me word that you are in a plight
  From which your one salvation lies in flight.
  That scoundrel who's imposed upon you so
  Denounced you to the King an hour ago   10
  And, as supporting evidence, displayed
  The strong-box of a certain renegade
  Whose secret papers, so he testified,
  You had disloyally agreed to hide.
  I don't know just what charges may be pressed,
  But there's a warrant out for your arrest;
  Tartuffe has been instructed, furthermore,
  To guide the arresting officer to your door.

CLÉANTE: He's clearly done this to facilitate
His seizure of your house and your estate. 20
ORGON: That man, I must say, is a vicious beast!
VALÈRE: Quick, Sir; you mustn't tarry in the least.
My carriage is outside, to take you hence;
This thousand louis should cover all expense.
Let's lose no time, or you shall be undone;
The sole defense, in this case, is to run.
I shall go with you all the way, and place you
In a safe refuge to which they'll never trace you.
ORGON: Alas, dear boy, I wish that I could show you
My gratitude for everything I owe you. 30
But now is not the time; I pray the Lord
That I may live to give you your reward.
Farewell, my dears; be careful . . .
CLÉANTE: Brother, hurry.
We shall take care of things; you needn't worry.

Scene 7

THE OFFICER	ELMIRE	DORINE
TARTUFFE	MARIANE	CLÉANTE
VALÈRE	MADAME PERNELLE	DAMIS
ORGON		

TARTUFFE: Gently, Sir, gently; stay right where you are.
No need for haste; your lodging isn't far.
You're off to prison, by order of the Prince.
ORGON: This is the crowning blow, you wretch; and since
It means my total ruin and defeat,
Your villainy is now at last complete.
TARTUFFE: You needn't try to provoke me; it's no use.
Those who serve Heaven must expect abuse.
CLÉANTE: You are indeed most patient, sweet, and blameless.
DORINE: How he exploits the name of Heaven! It's shameless. 10
TARTUFFE: Your taunts and mockeries are all for naught;
To do my duty is my only thought.
MARIANE: Your love of duty is most meritorious,
And what you've done is little short of glorious.
TARTUFFE: All deeds are glorious, Madam, which obey
The sovereign prince who sent me here today.
ORGON: I rescued you when you were destitute;
Have you forgotten that, you thankless brute?
TARTUFFE: No, no, well I remember everything;
But my first duty is to serve my King. 20
That obligation is so paramount
That other claims, beside it, do not count;
And for it I would sacrifice my wife,
My family, my friend, or my own life.
ELMIRE: Hypocrite!

DORINE: All that we most revere, he uses
 To cloak his plots and camouflage his ruses.
CLÉANTE: If it is true that you are animated
 By pure and loyal zeal, as you have stated,
 Why was this zeal not roused until you'd sought   30
 To make Orgon a cuckold, and been caught?
 Why weren't you moved to give your evidence
 Until your outraged host had driven you hence?
 I shan't say that the gift of all his treasure
 Ought to have damped your zeal in any measure;
 But if he is a traitor, as you declare,
 How could you condescend to be his heir?
TARTUFFE (*to the* OFFICER): Sir, spare me all this clamor; it's growing shrill.
 Please carry out your orders, if you will.
OFFICER: Yes, I've delayed too long, Sir. Thank you kindly.   40
 You're just the proper person to remind me.
 Come, you are off to join the other boarders
 In the King's prison, according to his orders.
TARTUFFE: Who? I, Sir?
OFFICER: Yes.
TARTUFFE: To prison? This can't be true!
OFFICER: I owe an explanation, but not to you.
 (*To* ORGON.) Sir, all is well; rest easy, and be grateful.
 We serve a Prince to whom all sham is hateful,
 A Prince who sees into our inmost hearts,   50
 And can't be fooled by any trickster's arts.
 His royal soul, though generous and human,
 Views all things with discernment and acumen;
 His sovereign reason is not lightly swayed,
 And all his judgments are discreetly weighed.
 He honors righteous men of every kind,
 And yet his zeal for virtue is not blind,
 Nor does his love of piety numb his wits
 And make him tolerant of hypocrites.
 'Twas hardly likely that this man could cozen   60
 A King who's foiled such liars by the dozen.
 With one keen glance, the King perceived the whole
 Perverseness and corruption of his soul,
 And thus high Heaven's justice was displayed:
 Betraying you, the rogue stood self-betrayed.
 The King soon recognized Tartuffe as one
 Notorious by another name, who'd done
 So many vicious crimes that one could fill
 Ten volumes with them, and be writing still.
 But to be brief: our sovereign was appalled   70
 By this man's treachery toward you, which he called
 The last, worst villainy of a vile career,
 And bade me follow the impostor here
 To see how gross his impudence could be,
 And force him to restore your property.
 Your private papers, by the King's command,

I hereby seize and give into your hand.
The King, by royal order, invalidates
The deed which gave this rascal your estates,
And pardons, furthermore, your grave offense   80
In harboring an exile's documents.
By these decrees, our Prince rewards you for
Your loyal deeds in the late civil war,
And shows how heartfelt is his satisfaction
In recompensing any worthy action,
How much he prizes merit, and how he makes
More of men's virtues than of their mistakes.
DORINE: Heaven be praised!
MADAME PERNELLE: I breathe again, at last.
ELMIRE: We're safe.
MARIANE: I can't believe the danger's past.   90
ORGON (*to* TARTUFFE): Well, traitor, now you see ...
CLÉANTE: Ah, Brother, please,
Let's not descend to such indignities.
Leave the poor wretch to his unhappy fate,
And don't say anything to aggravate
His present woes; but rather hope that he
Will soon embrace an honest piety,
And mend his ways, and by a true repentance
Move our just King to moderate his sentence.   100
Meanwhile, go kneel before your sovereign's throne
And thank him for the mercies he has shown.
ORGON: Well said: let's go at once and, gladly kneeling,
Express the gratitude which all are feeling.
Then, when that first great duty has been done,
We'll turn with pleasure to a second one,
And give Valère, whose love has proven so true,
The wedded happiness which is his due.

QUESTIONS FOR DISCUSSION AND WRITING

1.   Most of Molière's comedies, including *Tartuffe*, follow the New Comedy
pattern of a struggle between the forces of youth and the forces of age; youth
is embodied in a young couple who want to marry and age in the form of
parents and older people who try to block their marriage. Trace this pattern
through *Tartuffe*. Identify the forces on each side.

2.   Who is the protagonist of *Tartuffe?* One is tempted, of course, to say that
the title character (the most memorable character) is the protagonist. But
does Orgon have claim to being considered the protagonist? Perhaps the
question revolves around what the theme of the play is. Is it hypocrisy or the
naiveté that makes one vulnerable to being taken in by hypocrisy? How do
these alternatives alter our reading of the play?

3.   Molière's plays are structured around a series of comic "turns." That is, each scene tends to be organized around a comic device, often quite broad. Take sample scenes of *Tartuffe* and analyze their comic devices. (Act I, scene 1, and Act I, scene 4, are good scenes to start with.)

4.   Molière often has a "touchstone" character in his plays, one who expresses the standard of common sense from which the comic obsessives depart. Cléante plays this role in *Tartuffe,* and he expresses his philosophy in Act I, scene 5. Trace his argument and consider it as the thematic center of the play.

5.   Dorine and Elmire are also characters with good sense. Identify scenes in which they express the corrective to the excesses of the other characters. Do class and gender affect these positions?

6.   A central theme of *Tartuffe* is the difficulty of discerning what is real behind unreliable appearances, a theme articulated by Cléante: "Is not a face quite different from a mask? / Cannot sincerity and cunning art, / Reality and semblance, be told apart?" (I.5.76–78). Orgon, of course, cannot tell what Tartuffe is really like. But do the other characters have any trouble with this problem? (Look at scene II.4, for example, between Valère and Mariane.)

7.   Tartuffe is, of course, the main deceiver in the play. But is he ever deceived himself? Examine specifically Act III, scene 3, in which Tartuffe tries to seduce Elmire.

8.   Orgon and his family are saved from Tartuffe only by a *deus ex machina* in the form of the King's pardon brought by the Officer in the last scene. What does this ending imply about the power of good to overcome evil? How is the King characterized, and how does his characterization relate to the themes of the play?

Oscar Wilde and the Nineteenth-Century Theater

Oscar Wilde (1854–1900) was born in Dublin, the son of a father who was a well-known surgeon and a mother who was a writer. He distinguished himself as a student of classics at Trinity College, Dublin, and then won a fellowship to Oxford, where he came under the influence of the aesthetic theories of John Ruskin and Walter Pater. After graduation, Wilde settled in London where he established himself as a flamboyant spokesman for aestheticism, the credo of "art for art's sake," which he found not only in French literature but also in a line of English poets and critics going back through Ruskin and Pater to John Keats.

Wilde published work in a variety of forms. His literary and cultural criticism included *The Decay of Lying* (1889) and *The Soul of Man Under Socialism* (1891). His novel *The Picture of Dorian Gray* (1891), about a man whose vices leave him physically young and attractive while his hidden portrait becomes a horrible image of his degeneration, created a sensation. He also published several volumes of poetry. His greatest successes, though, were a series of witty, epigrammatic comedies which were produced between 1892 and 1895; these included *Lady Windermere's Fan, A Woman of No Importance, An Ideal Husband,* and, most notably, *The Importance of Being Earnest* (1895).

Wilde's success crumbled into disaster in 1895 when he was arrested for homosexuality (then a serious crime), convicted, and sentenced to two years imprisonment with hard labor. Since 1891 Wilde, who was married with two sons, had carried on an affair with a young aristocrat, Lord Alfred Douglas. Wilde's conviction led to his bankruptcy and divorce. When he was released from prison, he settled in France, where he lived under an assumed name, sick and dependent on his friends for support. He died three years later, at the age of forty-six.

It is paradoxical to present *The Importance of Being Earnest* as representative of the nineteenth-century theater, because the most notable feature of the play is the thoroughness with which it demolishes with laughter the established pieties of Victorian culture. The comic paradox of the title is that the theme of the play is the importance of *not* being earnest. Wilde's subtitle for the play was "A Trivial Comedy for Serious People"; what "serious people" would take away from this trivial comedy was a skepticism about some of the most cherished aspects of Victorian society: marriage, property, morality, class relationships, and death. The play operates by arousing laughter through distortions of scale. The Victorian preoccupation with right behavior is seen in a new light when wrong behavior is defined as eating too many cucumber sandwiches. And the importance of good breeding is somewhat undercut when one is the offspring of a handbag.

Despite the comic subversiveness of its theme, *The Importance of Being Earnest* gives a clear and accurate sense of the sort of theater of which it is both a parody and an example. The stylized permanent setting of Molière's stage has become the peep-hole stage of the modern proscenium theater. Settings can be realistic and flexible: There is an elaborate separate setting for each of the acts of *The Importance of Being Earnest*. Lighting, first with gas and then with electricity, can achieve complex illusionary effects, and stage properties can be real. An imaginary "fourth wall" separates the stage from the audience, which gazes through this invisible wall at a world seemingly as real as its own. Such a theater constantly raises questions of reality and illusion. We are asked to observe people who look and act very much like ourselves, but who speak in a series of hilarious one-liners, whose lives follow stereotyped plot patterns, and whose values seem to invert the beliefs most people hold. As a result, we are constantly being faced with the problem of deciding what in this secondary world is "true" (like our lives) and "false" (not like them).

The twentieth-century theater has not stayed locked in the dramaturgy of *The Importance of Being Earnest*. It has used a diversity of stages: thrust, arena, outdoor, indoor, large, small. But in many ways the picture-frame, illusionistic stage of the Victorians has been the point from which the many stages of twentieth-century theater have departed.

THE IMPORTANCE OF BEING EARNEST

THE PERSONS OF THE PLAY

JOHN WORTHING, J.P.
ALGERNON MONCRIEFF
REV. CANON CHASUBLE, D.D.
MERRIMAN, *butler*
LANE, *manservant*

LADY BRACKNELL
HON.[1] GWENDOLEN FAIRFAX
CECILY CARDEW
MISS PRISM, *governess*

THE SCENES OF THE PLAY

ACT I   *Algernon Moncrieff's Flat in Half-Moon Street, W.*
ACT II   *The Garden at the Manor House, Woolton.*
ACT III *Drawing-Room at the Manor House, Woolton.*

FIRST ACT

SCENE. *Morning-room in* ALGERNON's *flat in Half-Moon Street.[2] The room is luxuriously and artistically furnished. The sound of a piano is heard in the adjoining room.*

*(*LANE *is arranging afternoon tea on the table, and after the music has ceased,* ALGERNON *enters.)*

ALGERNON   Did you hear what I was playing, Lane?
LANE   I didn't think it polite to listen, sir.
ALGERNON   I'm sorry for that, for your sake. I don't play accurately—anyone can play accurately—but I play with wonderful expression. As far as the piano is concerned, sentiment is my forte. I keep science for life.
LANE   Yes, sir.
ALGERNON   And, speaking of the science of life, have you got the cucumber sandwiches cut for Lady Bracknell?
LANE   Yes, sir. *(Hands them on a salver.)*
ALGERNON   *(Inspects them, takes two, and sits down on the sofa.)* Oh! . . . by the way, Lane, I see from your book[3] that on Thursday night, when Lord Shoreham and Mr. Worthing were dining with me, eight bottles of champagne are entered as having been consumed.
LANE   Yes, sir; eight bottles and a pint.
ALGERNON   Why is it that at a bachelor's establishment the servants invariably drink the champagne? I ask merely for information.
LANE   I attribute it to the superior quality of the wine, sir. I have often observed that in married households the champagne is rarely of a first-rate brand.
ALGERNON   Good Heavens! Is marriage so demoralizing as that?
LANE   I believe it *is* a very pleasant state, sir. I have had very little experience of it myself up to the present. I have only been married once. That was in consequence of a misunderstanding between myself and a young person.
ALGERNON   *(Languidly.)* I don't know that I am much interested in your family life, Lane.

---

[1] Honorable. The title indicates that she is the daughter of a viscount or a baron.
[2] A fashionable street in the West End of London.   [3] Record book of wines.

LANE   No, sir; it is not a very interesting subject. I never think of it myself.

ALGERNON   Very natural, I am sure. That will do, Lane, thank you.

LANE   Thank you, sir.   (LANE *goes out.*)

ALGERNON   Lane's views on marriage seem somewhat lax. Really, if the lower orders don't set us a good example, what on earth is the use of them? They seem, as a class, to have absolutely no sense of moral responsibility.

(Enter LANE.*)*

LANE   Mr. Ernest Worthing.

(Enter JACK.*)*   (LANE *goes out.*)

ALGERNON   How are you, my dear Ernest? What brings you up to town?

JACK   Oh, pleasure, pleasure! What else should bring one anywhere? Eating as usual, I see, Algy!

ALGERNON   *(Stiffly.)* I believe it is customary in good society to take some slight refreshment at five o'clock. Where have you been since last Thursday?

JACK   *(Sitting down on the sofa.)* In the country.

ALGERNON   What on earth do you do there?

JACK   *(Pulling off his gloves.)* When one is in town one amuses oneself. When one is in the country one amuses other people. It is excessively boring.

ALGERNON   And who are the people you amuse?

JACK   *(Airily.)* Oh, neighbours, neighbours.

ALGERNON   Got nice neighbours in your part of Shropshire?

JACK   Perfectly horrid! Never speak to one of them.

ALGERNON   How immensely you must amuse them! *(Goes over and takes sandwich.)* By the way, Shropshire is your county, is it not?

JACK   Eh? Shropshire? Yes, of course. Hallo! Why all these cups? Why cucumber sandwiches? Why such reckless extravagance in one so young? Who is coming to tea?

ALGERNON   Oh! merely Aunt Augusta and Gwendolen.

JACK   How perfectly delightful!

ALGERNON   Yes, that is all very well; but I am afraid Aunt Augusta won't quite approve of your being here.

JACK   May I ask why?

ALGERNON   My dear fellow, the way you flirt with Gwendolen is perfectly disgraceful. It is almost as bad as the way Gwendolen flirts with you.

JACK   I am in love with Gwendolen. I have come up to town expressly to propose to her.

ALGERNON   I thought you had come up for pleasure? . . . I call that business.

JACK   How utterly unromantic you are!

ALGERNON   I really don't see anything romantic in proposing. It is very romantic to be in love. But there is nothing romantic about a definite proposal. Why, one may be accepted. One usually is, I believe. Then the excitement is all over. The very essence of romance is uncertainty. If ever I get married, I'll certainly try to forget the fact.

JACK   I have no doubt about that, dear Algy. The Divorce Court was specially invented for people whose memories are so curiously constituted.

ALGERNON   Oh! there is no use speculating on that subject. Divorces are made in Heaven—(JACK *puts out his hand to take a sandwich.* ALGERNON *at once interferes.*)

Please don't touch the cucumber sandwiches. They are ordered specially for Aunt Augusta. *(Takes one and eats it.)*

JACK   Well, you have been eating them all the time.

ALGERNON   That is quite a different matter. She is my aunt. *(Takes plate from below.)* Have some bread and butter. The bread and butter is for Gwendolen. Gwendolen is devoted to bread and butter.

JACK   *(Advancing to table and helping himself.)* And very good bread and butter it is too.

ALGERNON   Well, my dear fellow, you need not eat as if you were going to eat it all. You behave as if you were married to her already. You are not married to her already, and I don't think you ever will be.

JACK   Why on earth do you say that?

ALGERNON   Well, in the first place girls never marry the men they flirt with. Girls don't think it right.

JACK   Oh, that is nonsense!

ALGERNON   It isn't. It is a great truth. It accounts for the extraordinary number of bachelors that one sees all over the place. In the second place, I don't give my consent.

JACK   Your consent!

ALGERNON   My dear fellow, Gwendolen is my first cousin. And before I allow you to marry her, you will have to clear up the whole question of Cecily. *(Rings bell.)*

JACK   Cecily! What on earth do you mean? What do you mean, Algy, by Cecily? I don't know anyone of the name of Cecily.

(Enter LANE.)

ALGERNON   Bring me that cigarette case Mr. Worthing left in the smoking-room the last time he dined here.

LANE   Yes, sir.   *(LANE goes out.)*

JACK   Do you mean to say you have had my cigarette case all this time? I wish to goodness you had let me know. I have been writing frantic letters to Scotland Yard[4] about it. I was very nearly offering a large reward.

ALGERNON   Well, I wish you would offer one. I happen to be more than usually hard up.

JACK   There is no good offering a large reward now that the thing is found.

(Enter LANE with the cigarette case on a salver. ALGERNON takes it at once. LANE goes out.)

ALGERNON   I think that is rather mean of you, Ernest, I must say. *(Opens case and examines it.)* However, it makes no matter, for, now that I look at the inscription inside, I find that the thing isn't yours after all.

JACK   Of course it's mine. *(Moving to him.)* You have seen me with it a hundred times, and you have no right whatsoever to read what is written inside. It is a very ungentlemanly thing to read a private cigarette case.

ALGERNON   Oh! it is absurd to have a hard-and-fast rule about what one should read and what one shouldn't. More than half of modern culture depends on what one shouldn't read.

JACK   I am quite aware of the fact, and I don't propose to discuss modern culture.

---

[4] Police headquarters in London.

It isn't the sort of thing one should talk of in private. I simply want my cigarette case back.

ALGERNON   Yes; but this isn't your cigarette case. This cigarette case is a present from someone of the name of Cecily, and you said you didn't know anyone of that name.

JACK   Well, if you want to know, Cecily happens to be my aunt.

ALGERNON   Your aunt!

JACK   Yes. Charming old lady she is, too. Lives at Tunbridge Wells.[5] Just give it back to me, Algy.

ALGERNON   *(Retreating to back of sofa.)* But why does she call herself Cecily if she is your aunt and lives at Tunbridge Wells? *(Reading.)* "From little Cecily with her fondest love."

JACK   *(Moving to sofa and kneeling upon it.)* My dear fellow, what on earth is there in that? Some aunts are tall, some aunts are not tall. That is a matter that surely an aunt may be allowed to decide for herself. You seem to think that every aunt should be exactly like your aunt! That is absurd! For Heaven's sake give me back my cigarette case. *(Follows* ALGERNON *round the room.)*

ALGERNON   Yes. But why does your aunt call you her uncle. "From little Cecily, with her fondest love to her dear Uncle Jack." There is no objection, I admit, to an aunt being a small aunt, but why an aunt, no matter what her size may be, should call her own nephew her uncle, I can't quite make out. Besides, your name isn't Jack at all; it is Ernest.

JACK   It isn't Ernest; it's Jack.

ALGERNON   You have always told me it was Ernest. I have introduced you to everyone as Ernest. You answer to the name of Ernest. You look as if your name was Ernest. You are the most earnest looking person I ever saw in my life. It is perfectly absurd your saying that your name isn't Ernest. It's on your cards. Here is one of them. *(Taking it from case.)* "Mr. Ernest Worthing, B. 4, The Albany."[6] I'll keep this as a proof that your name is Ernest if ever you attempt to deny it to me, or to Gwendolen, or to anyone else. *(Puts the card in his pocket.)*

JACK   Well, my name is Ernest in town and Jack in the country, and the cigarette case was given to me in the country.

ALGERNON   Yes, but that does not account for the fact that your small Aunt Cecily, who lives at Tunbridge Wells, calls you her dear uncle. Come, old boy, you had much better have the thing out at once.

JACK   My dear Algy, you talk exactly as if you were a dentist. It is very vulgar to talk like a dentist when one isn't a dentist. It produces a false impression.

ALGERNON   Well, that is exactly what dentists always do. Now, go on! Tell me the whole thing. I may mention that I have always suspected you of being a confirmed and secret Bunburyist; and I am quite sure of it now.

JACK   Bunburyist? What on earth do you mean by a Bunburyist?

ALGERNON   I'll reveal to you the meaning of that incomparable expression as soon as you are kind enough to inform me why you are Ernest in town and Jack in the country.

JACK   Well, produce my cigarette case first.

ALGERNON   Here it is. *(Hands cigarette case.)* Now produce your explanation, and pray make it improbable. *(Sits on sofa.)*

JACK   My dear fellow, there is nothing improbable about my explanation at all. In

[5] A fashionable resort town in southern England.
[6] An elegant apartment building near Piccadilly Circus.

fact it's perfectly ordinary. Old Mr. Thomas Cardew, who adopted me when I was a little boy, made me in his will guardian to his granddaughter, Miss Cecily Cardew. Cecily, who addresses me as her uncle from motives of respect that you could not possibly appreciate, lives at my place in the country under the charge of her admirable governess, Miss Prism.

ALGERNON   Where is that place in the country, by the way?

JACK   That is nothing to you, dear boy. You are not going to be invited. . . . I may tell you candidly that the place is not in Shropshire.

ALGERNON   I suspected that, my dear fellow! I have Bunburyed all over Shropshire on two separate occasions. Now, go on. Why are you Ernest in town and Jack in the country?

JACK   My dear Algy, I don't know whether you will be able to understand my real motives. You are hardly serious enough. When one is placed in the position of guardian, one has to adopt a very high moral tone on all subjects. It's one's duty to do so. And as a high moral tone can hardly be said to conduce very much to either one's health or one's happiness, in order to get up to town I have always pretended to have a younger brother of the name of Ernest, who lives in the Albany, and gets into the most dreadful scrapes. That, my dear Algy, is the whole truth pure and simple.

ALGERNON   The truth is rarely pure and never simple. Modern life would be very tedious if it were either, and modern literature a complete impossibility!

JACK   That wouldn't be at all a bad thing.

ALGERNON   Literary criticism is not your forte, my dear fellow. Don't try it. You should leave that to people who haven't been at a University. They do it so well in the daily papers. What you really are is a Bunburyist. I was quite right in saying you were a Bunburyist. You are one of the most advanced Bunburyists I know.

JACK   What on earth do you mean?

ALGERNON   You have invented a very useful young brother called Ernest, in order that you may be able to come up to town as often as you like. I have invented an invaluable permanent invalid called Bunbury, in order that I may be able to go down into the country whenever I choose. Bunbury is perfectly invaluable. If it wasn't for Bunbury's extraordinary bad health, for instance, I wouldn't be able to dine with you at Willis's tonight, for I have been really engaged[7] to Aunt Augusta for more than a week.

JACK   I haven't asked you to dine with me anywhere tonight.

ALGERNON   I know. You are absurdly careless about sending out invitations. It is very foolish of you. Nothing annoys people so much as not receiving invitations.

JACK   You had much better dine with your Aunt Augusta.

ALGERNON   I haven't the smallest intention of doing anything of the kind. To begin with, I dined there on Monday, and once a week is quite enough to dine with one's own relations. In the second place, whenever I do dine there I am always treated as a member of the family, and sent down with[8] either no woman at all, or two. In the third place, I know perfectly well whom she will place me next to, tonight. She will place me next Mary Farquhar, who always flirts with her own husband across the dinner-table. That is not very pleasant. Indeed, it is not even decent . . . and that sort of thing is enormously on the increase. The amount of women in London who flirt with their own husbands is perfectly scandalous. It looks so bad. It is simply washing one's clean linen in public.

---

[7] Committed to attend her party.   [8] Escort as a dinner partner.

Besides, now that I know you to be a confirmed Bunburyist, I naturally want to talk to you about Bunburying. I want to tell you the rules.

JACK   I am not a Bunburyist at all. If Gwendolen accepts me, I am going to kill my brother, indeed I think I'll kill him in any case. Cecily is a little too much interested in him. It is rather a bore. So I am going to get rid of Ernest. And I strongly advise you to do the same with Mr. . . . with your invalid friend who has the absurd name.

ALGERNON   Nothing will induce me to part with Bunbury, and if you ever get married, which seems to me extremely problematic, you will be very glad to know Bunbury. A man who marries without knowing Bunbury has a very tedious time of it.

JACK   That is nonsense. If I marry a charming girl like Gwendolen, and she is the only girl I ever saw in my life that I would marry, I certainly won't want to know Bunbury.

ALGERNON   Then your wife will. You don't seem to realize, that in married life three is company and two is none.

JACK   (*Sententiously.*) That, my dear young friend, is the theory that the corrupt French Drama has been propounding for the last fifty years.

ALGERNON   Yes; and that the happy English home has proved in half the time.

JACK   For heaven's sake, don't try to be cynical. It's perfectly easy to be cynical.

ALGERNON   My dear fellow, it isn't easy to be anything nowadays. There's such a lot of beastly competition about. (*The sound of an electric bell is heard.*) Ah! that must be Aunt Augusta. Only relatives, or creditors, ever ring in that Wagnerian[9] manner. Now, if I get her out of the way for ten minutes, so that you can have an opportunity for proposing to Gwendolen, may I dine with you tonight at Willis's?

JACK   I suppose so, if you want to.

ALGERNON   Yes, but you must be serious about it. I hate people who are not serious about meals. It is so shallow of them.

(*Enter* LANE.)

LANE   Lady Bracknell and Miss Fairfax.

(ALGERNON *goes forward to meet them. Enter* LADY BRACKNELL *and* GWENDOLEN.)

LADY BRACKNELL   Good afternoon, dear Algernon, I hope you are behaving very well.

ALGERNON   I'm feeling very well, Aunt Augusta.

LADY BRACKNELL   That's not quite the same thing. In fact the two things rarely go together. (*Sees* JACK *and bows to him with icy coldness.*)

ALGERNON   (*To* GWENDOLEN.) Dear me, you are smart![10]

GWENDOLEN   I am always smart! Aren't I, Mr. Worthing?

JACK   You're quite perfect, Miss Fairfax.

GWENDOLEN   Oh! I hope I am not that. It would leave no room for developments, and I intend to develop in many directions. (GWENDOLEN *and* JACK *sit down together in the corner.*)

LADY BRACKNELL   I'm sorry if we are a little late, Algernon, but I was obliged to call on dear Lady Harbury. I hadn't been there since her poor husband's death.

---

[9] Loud. Wagner's epic operas were the source of many Victorian jokes.
[10] Elegant or fashionable.

I never saw a woman so altered; she looks quite twenty years younger. And now I'll have a cup of tea, and one of those nice cucumber sandwiches you promised me.

ALGERNON   Certainly, Aunt Augusta. (*Goes over to tea-table.*)

LADY BRACKNELL   Won't you come and sit here, Gwendolen?

GWENDOLEN   Thanks, Mamma, I'm quite comfortable where I am.

ALGERNON   (*Picking up empty plate in horror.*) Good heavens! Lane! Why are there no cucumber sandwiches? I ordered them specially.

LANE   (*Gravely.*) There were no cucumbers in the market this morning, sir. I went down twice.

ALGERNON   No cucumbers!

LANE   No, sir. Not even for ready money.

ALGERNON   That will do, Lane, thank you.

LANE   Thank you, sir.

ALGERNON   I am greatly distressed, Aunt Augusta, about there being no cucumbers, not even for ready money.

LADY BRACKNELL   It really makes no matter, Algernon. I had some crumpets[11] with Lady Harbury, who seems to me to be living entirely for pleasure now.

ALGERNON   I hear her hair has turned quite gold from grief.

LADY BRACKNELL   It certainly has changed its colour. From what cause I, of course, cannot say. (ALGERNON *crosses and hands tea.*) Thank you. I've quite a treat for you tonight, Algernon. I am going to send you down with Mary Farquhar. She is such a nice woman, and so attentive to her husband. It's delightful to watch them.

ALGERNON   I am afraid, Aunt Augusta, I shall have to give up the pleasure of dining with you tonight after all.

LADY BRACKNELL   (*Frowning.*) I hope not, Algernon. It would put my table completely out. Your uncle would have to dine upstairs. Fortunately he is accustomed to that.

ALGERNON   It is a great bore, and, I need hardly say, a terrible disappointment to me, but the fact is I have just had a telegram to say that my poor friend Bunbury is very ill again. (*Exchanges glances with* JACK.) They seem to think I should be with him.

LADY BRACKNELL   It is very strange. This Mr. Bunbury seems to suffer from curiously bad health.

ALGERNON   Yes; poor Bunbury is a dreadful invalid.

LADY BRACKNELL   Well, I must say, Algernon, that I think it is high time that Mr. Bunbury made up his mind whether he was going to live or to die. This shilly-shallying with the question is absurd. Nor do I in any way approve of the modern sympathy with invalids. I consider it morbid. Illness of any kind is hardly a thing to be encouraged in others. Health is the primary duty of life. I am always telling that to your poor uncle, but he never seems to take much notice . . . as far as any improvement in his ailments goes. I should be obliged if you would ask Mr. Bunbury, from me, to be kind enough not to have a relapse on Saturday, for I rely on you to arrange my music for me. It is my last reception, and one wants something that will encourage conversation, particularly at the end of the season[12] when everyone has practically said whatever they had to say, which, in most cases, was probably not much.

ALGERNON   I'll speak to Bunbury, Aunt Augusta, if he is still conscious, and I think I can promise you he'll be all right by Saturday. Of course the music is a

---

[11] A kind of muffin.   [12] The London social season, from May through July.

great difficulty. You see, if one plays good music, people don't listen, and if one plays bad music, people don't talk. But I'll run over the programme I've drawn out, if you will kindly come into the next room for a moment.

LADY BRACKNELL Thank you, Algernon. It is very thoughtful of you. *(Rising, and following* ALGERNON.*)* I'm sure the programme will be delightful, after a few expurgations. French songs I cannot possibly allow. People always seem to think that they are improper, and either look shocked, which is vulgar, or laugh, which is worse. But German sounds a thoroughly respectable language, and indeed, I believe is so. Gwendolen, you will accompany me.

GWENDOLEN Certainly, Mamma.

*(*LADY BRACKNELL *and* ALGERNON *go into the music-room,* GWENDOLEN *remains behind.)*

JACK Charming day it has been, Miss Fairfax.

GWENDOLEN Pray don't talk to me about the weather, Mr. Worthing. Whenever people talk to me about the weather, I always feel quite certain that they mean something else. And that makes me so nervous.

JACK I do mean something else.

GWENDOLEN I thought so. In fact, I am never wrong.

JACK And I would like to be allowed to take advantage of Lady Bracknell's temporary absence . . .

GWENDOLEN I would certainly advise you to do so. Mamma has a way of coming back suddenly into a room that I have often had to speak to her about.

JACK *(Nervously.)* Miss Fairfax, ever since I met you I have admired you more than any girl . . . I have ever met since . . . I met you.

GWENDOLEN Yes, I am quite aware of the fact. And I often wish that in public, at any rate, you had been more demonstrative. For me you have always had an irresistible fascination. Even before I met you I was far from indifferent to you. *(*JACK *looks at her in amazement.)* We live, as I hope you know, Mr. Worthing, in an age of ideals. The fact is constantly mentioned in the more expensive monthly magazines, and has reached the provincial pulpits I am told: and my ideal has always been to love someone of the name of Ernest. There is something in that name that inspires absolute confidence. The moment Algernon first mentioned to me that he had a friend called Ernest, I knew I was destined to love you.

JACK You really love me, Gwendolen?

GWENDOLEN Passionately!

JACK Darling! You don't know how happy you've made me.

GWENDOLEN My own Ernest!

JACK But you don't really mean to say that you couldn't love me if my name wasn't Ernest?

GWENDOLEN But your name is Ernest.

JACK Yes, I know it is. But supposing it was something else? Do you mean to say you couldn't love me then?

GWENDOLEN *(Glibly.)* Ah! that is clearly a metaphysical speculation, and like most metaphysical speculations has very little reference at all to the actual facts of real life, as we know them.

JACK Personally, darling, to speak quite candidly, I don't much care about the name of Ernest . . . I don't think the name suits me at all.

GWENDOLEN It suits you perfectly. It is a divine name. It has a music of its own. It produces vibrations.

JACK   Well, really, Gwendolen, I must say that I think there are lots of other much nicer names. I think Jack, for instance, a charming name.

GWENDOLEN   Jack? . . . No, there is very little music in the name Jack, if any at all, indeed. It does not thrill. It produces absolutely no vibrations. . . . I have known several Jacks, and they all, without exception, were more than usually plain. Besides, Jack is a notorious domesticity for John! And I pity any woman who is married to a man called John. She would probably never be allowed to know the entrancing pleasure of a single moment's solitude. The only really safe name is Ernest.

JACK   Gwendolen, I must get christened at once—I mean we must get married at once. There is no time to be lost.

GWENDOLEN   Married, Mr. Worthing?

JACK   (*Astounded.*) Well . . . surely. You know that I love you, and you led me to believe, Miss Fairfax, that you were not absolutely indifferent to me.

GWENDOLEN   I adore you. But you haven't proposed to me yet. Nothing has been said at all about marriage. The subject has not even been touched on.

JACK   Well . . . may I propose to you now?

GWENDOLEN   I think it would be an admirable opportunity. And to spare you any possible disappointment, Mr. Worthing, I think it only fair to tell you quite frankly beforehand that I am fully determined to accept you.

JACK   Gwendolen!

GWENDOLEN   Yes, Mr. Worthing, what have you got to say to me?

JACK   You know what I have got to say to you.

GWENDOLEN   Yes, but you don't say it.

JACK   Gwendolen, will you marry me? (*Goes on his knees.*)

GWENDOLEN   Of course I will, darling. How long you have been about it! I am afraid you have had very little experience in how to propose.

JACK   My own one, I have never loved anyone in the world but you.

GWENDOLEN   Yes, but men often propose for practice. I know my brother Gerald does. All my girl-friends tell me so. What wonderfully blue eyes you have, Ernest! They are quite, quite blue. I hope you will always look at me just like that, especially when there are other people present.

(*Enter* LADY BRACKNELL.)

LADY BRACKNELL   Mr. Worthing! Rise, sir, from this semi-recumbent posture. It is most indecorous.

GWENDOLEN   Mamma! (*He tries to rise; she restrains him.*) I must beg you to re-tire. This is no place for you. Besides, Mr. Worthing has not quite finished yet.

LADY BRACKNELL   Finished what, may I ask?

GWENDOLEN   I am engaged to Mr. Worthing, Mamma. (*They rise together.*)

LADY BRACKNELL   Pardon me, you are not engaged to anyone. When you do become engaged to someone, I, or your father, should his health permit him, will inform you of the fact. An engagement should come on a young girl as a surprise, pleasant or unpleasant, as the case may be. It is hardly a matter that she could be allowed to arrange for herself. . . . And now I have a few questions to put to you, Mr. Worthing. While I am making these inquiries, you, Gwendolen, will wait for me below in the carriage.

GWENDOLEN   (*Reproachfully.*) Mamma!

LADY BRACKNELL   In the carriage, Gwendolen! (GWENDOLEN *goes to the door. She and* JACK *blow kisses to each other behind* LADY BRACKNELL*'s back.* LADY BRACKNELL *looks vaguely about as if she could not understand what the noise was. Finally turns around.)* Gwendolen, the carriage!

GWENDOLEN   Yes, Mamma. *(Goes out, looking back at* JACK.*)*

LADY BRACKNELL   *(Sitting down.)* You can take a seat, Mr. Worthing.

(Looks in her pocket for note-book and pencil.)

JACK   Thank you, Lady Bracknell, I prefer standing.

LADY BRACKNELL   *(Pencil and note-book in hand.)* I feel bound to tell you that you are not down on my list of eligible young men, although I have the same list as the dear Duchess of Bolton has. We work together, in fact. However, I am quite ready to enter your name, should your answers be what a really affectionate mother requires. Do you smoke?

JACK   Well, yes, I must admit I smoke.

LADY BRACKNELL   I am glad to hear it. A man should always have an occupation of some kind. There are far too many idle men in London as it is. How old are you?

JACK   Twenty-nine.

LADY BRACKNELL   A very good age to be married at. I have always been of opinion that a man who desires to get married should know either everything or nothing. Which do you know?

JACK   *(After some hesitation.)* I know nothing, Lady Bracknell.

LADY BRACKNELL   I am pleased to hear it. I do not approve of anything that tampers with natural ignorance. Ignorance is like a delicate exotic fruit; touch it and the bloom is gone. The whole theory of modern education is radically unsound. Fortunately in England, at any rate, education produces no effect whatsoever. If it did, it would prove a serious danger to the upper classes, and probably lead to acts of violence in Grosvenor Square.[13] What is your income?

JACK   Between seven and eight thousand a year.

LADY BRACKNELL   *(Makes a note in her book.)* In land, or in *investments?*

JACK   In investments, chiefly.

LADY BRACKNELL   That is satisfactory. What between the duties expected of one during one's lifetime, and the duties exacted from one after one's death,[14] land has ceased to be either a profit or a pleasure. It gives one position, and prevents one from keeping it up. That's all that can be said about land.

JACK   I have a country house with some land, of course, attached to it, about fifteen hundred acres, I believe; but I don't depend on that for my real income. In fact, as far as I can make out, the poachers are the only people who make anything out of it.

LADY BRACKNELL   A country house! How many bedrooms? Well, that point can be cleared up afterwards. You have a town house, I hope? A girl with a simple, unspoiled nature, like Gwendolen, could hardly be expected to reside in the country.

JACK   Well, I own a house in Belgrave Square,[15] but it is let by the year to Lady Bloxham. Of course, I can get it back whenever I like, at six months' notice.

LADY BRACKNELL   Lady Bloxham? I don't know her.

JACK   Oh, she goes about very little. She is a lady considerably advanced in years.

---

[13] Fashionable area in the West End of London.
[14] The pun refers to "death duties" (inheritance taxes).
[15] Another fashionable West End address.

LADY BRACKNELL   Ah, nowadays that is no guarantee of respectability of character. What number in Belgrave Square?

JACK   149.

LADY BRACKNELL   *(Shaking her head.)* The unfashionable side. I thought there was something. However, that could easily be altered.

JACK   Do you mean the fashion, or the side?

LADY BRACKNELL   *(Sternly.)* Both, if necessary, I presume. What are your politics?

JACK   Well, I am afraid I really have none. I am a Liberal Unionist.[16]

LADY BRACKNELL   Oh, they count as Tories. They dine with us. Or come in the evening, at any rate. Now to minor matters. Are your parents living?

JACK   I have lost both my parents.

LADY BRACKNELL   Both? . . . That seems like carelessness. Who was your father? He was evidently a man of some wealth. Was he born in what the Radical papers call the purple of commerce, or did he rise from the ranks of aristocracy?

JACK   I am afraid I really don't know. The fact is, Lady Bracknell, I said I had lost my parents. It would be nearer the truth to say that my parents seem to have lost me. . . . I don't actually know who I am by birth. I was . . . well, I was found.

LADY BRACKNELL   Found!

JACK   The late Mr. Thomas Cardew, an old gentleman of a very charitable and kindly disposition, found me, and gave me the name of Worthing, because he happened to have a first-class ticket for Worthing in his pocket at the time. Worthing is a place in Sussex. It is a seaside resort.

LADY BRACKNELL   Where did the charitable gentleman who had a first-class ticket for this seaside resort find you?

JACK   *(Gravely.)* In a handbag.

LADY BRACKNELL   A handbag?

JACK   *(Very seriously.)* Yes, Lady Bracknell, I was in a handbag—a somewhat large, black leather handbag with handles to it—an ordinary handbag, in fact.

LADY BRACKNELL   In what locality did this Mr. James, or Thomas, Cardew come across this ordinary handbag?

JACK   In the cloakroom at Victoria Station. It was given to him in mistake for his own.

LADY BRACKNELL   The cloakroom at Victoria Station?

JACK   Yes. The Brighton line.

LADY BRACKNELL   The line is immaterial. Mr. Worthing, I confess I feel somewhat bewildered by what you have just told me. To be born, or at any rate, bred in a handbag, whether it had handles or not, seems to me to display a contempt for the ordinary decencies of family life that remind one of the worst excesses of the French Revolution. And I presume you know what that unfortunate movement led to? As for the particular locality in which the handbag was found, a cloakroom at a railway station might serve to conceal a social indiscretion— has probably, indeed, been used for that purpose before now—but it could hardly be regarded as an assured basis for a recognized position in good society.

JACK   May I ask you then what you would advise me to do? I need hardly say I would do anything in the world to ensure Gwendolen's happiness.

LADY BRACKNELL   I would strongly advise you, Mr. Worthing, to try and acquire some relations as soon as possible, and to make a definite effort to produce at any rate one parent, of either sex, before the season is quite over.

---

[16] A group of members of the Liberal Party who in 1886 formed an alliance with the Conservatives to oppose Home Rule for Ireland.

JACK   Well, I don't see how I could possibly manage to do that. I can produce the handbag at any moment. It is in my dressing-room at home. I really think that should satisfy you, Lady Bracknell.

LADY BRACKNELL   Me, sir! What has it to do with me? You can hardly imagine that I and Lord Bracknell would dream of allowing our only daughter—a girl brought up with the utmost care—to marry into a cloakroom, and form an alliance with a parcel? Good morning, Mr. Worthing!

(LADY BRACKNELL sweeps out in majestic indignation.)

JACK   Good morning! *(ALGERNON, from the other room, strikes up the Wedding March. JACK looks perfectly furious, and goes to the door.)* For goodness' sake don't play that ghastly tune, Algy! How idiotic you are!

(The music stops, and ALGERNON enters cheerily.)

ALGERNON   Didn't it go off all right, old boy? You don't mean to say Gwendolen refused you? I know it is a way she has. She is always refusing people. I think it is most ill-natured of her.

JACK   Oh, Gwendolen is as right as a trivet.[17] As far as she is concerned, we are engaged. Her mother is perfectly unbearable. Never met such a gorgon[18] . . . I don't really know what a gorgon is like, but I am quite sure that Lady Bracknell is one. In any case, she is a monster, without being a myth, which is rather unfair . . . I beg your pardon, Algy, I suppose I shouldn't talk about your own aunt in that way before you.

ALGERNON   My dear boy, I love hearing my relations abused. It is the only thing that makes me put up with them at all. Relations are simply a tedious pack of people who haven't got the remotest knowledge of how to live, nor the smallest instinct about when to die.

JACK   Oh, that is nonsense!

ALGERNON   It isn't!

JACK   Well, I won't argue about the matter. You always want to argue about things.

ALGERNON   That is exactly what things were originally made for.

JACK   Upon my word, if I thought that, I'd shoot myself. . . . *(A pause.)* You don't think there is any chance of Gwendolen becoming like her mother in about a hundred and fifty years, do you, Algy?

ALGERNON   All women become like their mothers. That is their tragedy. No man does. That's his.

JACK   Is that clever?

ALGERNON   It is perfectly phrased! and quite as true as any observation in civilized life should be.

JACK   I am sick to death of cleverness. Everybody is clever nowadays. You can't go anywhere without meeting clever people. The thing has become an absolute public nuisance. I wish to goodness we had a few fools left.

ALGERNON   We have.

JACK   I should extremely like to meet them. What do they talk about?

ALGERNON   The fools! Oh! about the clever people, of course.

---

[17] A three-legged stand. The expression means "steady, reliable."
[18] Repulsively ugly or terrifying woman, from mythical women (like Medusa) with snakes for hair, and eyes that turned anyone who looked at them to stone.

JACK   What fools!

ALGERNON   By the way, did you tell Gwendolen the truth about your being Ernest in town, and Jack in the country?

JACK   *(In a very patronizing manner.)* My dear fellow, the truth isn't quite the sort of thing one tells to a nice sweet refined girl. What extraordinary ideas you have about the way to behave to a woman!

ALGERNON   The only way to behave to a woman is to make love to her, if she is pretty, and to someone else if she is plain.

JACK   Oh, that is nonsense.

ALGERNON   What about your brother? What about the profligate Ernest?

JACK   Oh, before the end of the week I shall have got rid of him. I'll say he died in Paris of apoplexy. Lots of people die of apoplexy, quite suddenly, don't they?

ALGERNON   Yes, but it's hereditary, my dear fellow. It's a sort of thing that runs in families. You had much better say a severe chill.

JACK   You are sure a severe chill isn't hereditary, or anything of that kind?

ALGERNON   Of course it isn't!

JACK   Very well, then. My poor brother Ernest is carried off suddenly in Paris, by a severe chill. That gets rid of him.

ALGERNON   But I thought you said that . . . Miss Cardew was a little too much interested in your poor brother Ernest? Won't she feel his loss a good deal?

JACK   Oh, that is all right. Cecily is not a silly romantic girl, I am glad to say. She has got a capital appetite, goes long walks, and pays no attention at all to her lessons.

ALGERNON   I would rather like to see Cecily.

JACK   I will take very good care you never do. She is excessively pretty, and she is only just eighteen.

ALGERNON   Have you told Gwendolen yet that you have an excessively pretty ward who is only just eighteen?

JACK   Oh! one doesn't blurt these things out to people. Cecily and Gwendolen are perfectly certain to be extremely great friends. I'll bet you anything you like that half an hour after they have met, they will be calling each other sister.

ALGERNON   Women only do that when they have called each other a lot of other things first. Now, my dear boy, if we want to get a good table at Willis's, we really must go and dress. Do you know it is nearly seven?

JACK   *(Irritably.)* Oh! It always is nearly seven.

ALGERNON   Well, I'm hungry.

JACK   I never knew you when you weren't. . . .

ALGERNON   What shall we do after dinner? Go to the theatre?

JACK   Oh no! I loathe listening.

ALGERNON   Well, let us go to the club?

JACK   Oh, no! I hate talking.

ALGERNON   Well, we might trot round to the Empire[19] at ten?

JACK   Oh no! I can't bear looking at things. It is so silly.

ALGERNON   Well, what shall we do?

JACK   Nothing!

ALGERNON   It is awfully hard work doing nothing. However, I don't mind hard work where there is no definite object of any kind.

(Enter LANE.*)*

---

[19] A music hall in Leicester Square.

LANE   Miss Fairfax.

(Enter GWENDOLEN. LANE *goes out.)*

ALGERNON   Gwendolen, upon my word!

GWENDOLEN   Algy, kindly turn your back. I have something very particular to say to Mr. Worthing.

ALGERNON   Really, Gwendolen, I don't think I can allow this at all.

GWENDOLEN   Algy, you always adopt a strictly immoral attitude towards life. You are not quite old enough to do that. *(*ALGERNON *retires to the fireplace.)*

JACK   My own darling!

GWENDOLEN   Ernest, we may never be married. From the expression on Mamma's face I fear we never shall. Few parents nowadays pay any regard to what their children say to them. The old-fashioned respect for the young is fast dying out. Whatever influence I ever had over Mamma, I lost at the age of three. But although she may prevent us from becoming man and wife, and I may marry someone else, and marry often, nothing that she can possibly do can alter my eternal devotion to you.

JACK   Dear Gwendolen!

GWENDOLEN   The story of your romantic origin, as related to me by Mamma, with unpleasing comments, has naturally stirred the deeper fibres of my nature. Your Christian name has an irresistible fascination. The simplicity of your character makes you exquisitely incomprehensible to me. Your town address at the Albany I have. What is your address in the country?

JACK   The Manor House, Woolton, Hertfordshire.

*(*ALGERNON, *who has been carefully listening, smiles to himself, and writes the address on his shirt-cuff. Then picks up the Railway Guide.)*

GWENDOLEN   There is a good postal service, I suppose? It may be necessary to do something desperate. That of course will require serious consideration. I will communicate with you daily.

JACK   My own one!

GWENDOLEN   How long do you remain in town?

JACK   Till Monday.

GWENDOLEN   Good! Algy, you may turn round now.

ALGERNON   Thanks, I've turned round already.

GWENDOLEN   You may also ring the bell.

JACK   You will let me see you to your carriage, my own darling?

GWENDOLEN   Certainly.

JACK   *(To* LANE, *who now enters.)* I will see Miss Fairfax out.

LANE   Yes, sir. (JACK *and* GWENDOLEN *go off.)*

*(*LANE *presents several letters on a salver to* ALGERNON. *It is to be surmised that they are bills, as* ALGERNON *after looking at the envelopes, tears them up.)*

ALGERNON   A glass of sherry, Lane.

LANE   Yes, sir.

ALGERNON   Tomorrow, Lane, I'm going Bunburying.

LANE   Yes, sir.

ALGERNON   I shall probably not be back till Monday. You can put up my dress clothes, my smoking jacket, and all the Bunbury suits. . . .

LANE   Yes, sir. *(Handing sherry.)*
ALGERNON   I hope tomorrow will be a fine day, Lane.
LANE   It never is, sir.
ALGERNON   Lane, you're a perfect pessimist.
LANE   I do my best to give satisfaction, sir.

(Enter JACK. LANE *goes off.)*

JACK   There's a sensible, intellectual girl! The only girl I ever cared for in my life. *(*ALGERNON *is laughing immoderately.)* What on earth are you so amused at?
ALGERNON   Oh, I'm a little anxious about poor Bunbury, that is all.
JACK   If you don't take care, your friend Bunbury will get you into a serious scrape some day.
ALGERNON   I love scrapes. They are the only things that are never serious.
JACK   Oh, that's nonsense, Algy. You never talk anything but nonsense.
ALGERNON   Nobody ever does.

*(*JACK *looks indignantly at him, and leaves the room.* ALGERNON *lights a cigarette, reads his shirt-cuff, and smiles.)*

Act-Drop.[20]

SECOND ACT

SCENE. *Garden at the Manor House. A flight of grey stone steps leads up to the house. The garden, an old-fashioned one, full of roses. Time of year, July. Basket chairs, and a table covered with books, are set under a large yew tree.*
   *(*MISS PRISM[21] *discovered seated at the table.* CECILY *is at the back watering flowers.)*

MISS PRISM   *(Calling.)* Cecily, Cecily! Surely such a utilitarian occupation as the watering of flowers is rather Moulton's duty than yours? Especially at a moment when intellectual pleasures await you. Your German grammar is on the table. Pray open it at page fifteen. We will repeat yesterday's lesson.
CECILY   *(Coming over very slowly.)* But I don't like German. It isn't at all a becoming language. I know perfectly well that I look quite plain after my German lesson.
MISS PRISM   Child, you know how anxious your guardian is that you should improve yourself in every way. He laid particular stress on your German, as he was leaving for town yesterday. Indeed, he always lays stress on your German when he is leaving for town.
CECILY   Dear Uncle Jack is so very serious! Sometimes he is so serious that I think he cannot be quite well.
MISS PRISM   *(Drawing herself up.)* Your guardian enjoys the best of health, and his gravity of demeanour is especially to be commended in one so comparatively young as he is. I know no one who has a higher sense of duty and responsibility.

---

[20] A front curtain used between acts.
[21] Miss Prism's name has been related to the phrase "prunes and prisms." The phrase occurs in Charles Dickens's *Little Dorrit* (chapter 41), where a teacher of young ladies has her pupils say "prunes and prisms" over and over to give "a pretty form to the lips."

CECILY   I suppose that is why he often looks a little bored when we three are together.

MISS PRISM   Cecily! I am surprised at you. Mr. Worthing has many troubles in his life. Idle merriment and triviality would be out of place in his conversation. You must remember his constant anxiety about that unfortunate young man his brother.

CECILY   I wish Uncle Jack would allow that unfortunate young man, his brother, to come down here sometimes. We might have a good influence over him, Miss Prism. I am sure you certainly would. You know German, and Geology, and things of that kind influence a man very much. (CECILY *begins to write in her diary.*)

MISS PRISM   *(Shaking her head.)* I do not think that even I could produce any effect on a character that according to his own brother's admission is irretrievably weak and vacillating. Indeed I am not sure that I would desire to reclaim him. I am not in favour of this modern mania for turning bad people into good people at a moment's notice. As a man sows so let him reap. You must put away your diary, Cecily. I really don't see why you should keep a diary at all.

CECILY   I keep a diary in order to enter the wonderful secrets of my life. If I didn't write them down I should probably forget all about them.

MISS PRISM   Memory, my dear Cecily, is the diary that we all carry about with us.

CECILY   Yes, but it usually chronicles the things that have never happened, and couldn't possibly have happened. I believe that memory is responsible for nearly all the three-volume novels that Mudie sends us.[22]

MISS PRISM   Do not speak slightingly of the three-volume novel, Cecily. I wrote one myself in earlier days.

CECILY   Did you really, Miss Prism? How wonderfully clever you are! I hope it did not end happily? I don't like novels that end happily. They depress me so much.

MISS PRISM   The good ended happily, and the bad unhappily. That is what fiction means.

CECILY   I suppose so. But it seems very unfair. And was your novel ever published?

MISS PRISM   Alas! no. The manuscript unfortunately was abandoned. I use the word in the sense of lost or mislaid. To your work, child, these speculations are profitless.

CECILY   *(Smiling.)* But I see dear Dr. Chasuble coming up through the garden.

MISS PRISM   *(Rising and advancing.)* Dr. Chasuble! This is indeed a pleasure.

(Enter CANON CHASUBLE.*)*

CHASUBLE   And how are we this morning? Miss Prism, you are, I trust, well?

CECILY   Miss Prism has just been complaining of a slight headache. I think it would do her so much good to have a short stroll with you in the Park, Dr. Chasuble.

MISS PRISM   Cecily, I have not mentioned anything about a headache.

CECILY   No, dear Miss Prism, I know that, but I felt instinctively that you had a headache. Indeed I was thinking about that, and not about my German lesson, when the Rector came in.

CHASUBLE   I hope, Cecily, you are not inattentive.

---

[22] Mudie's Circulating Library was a commercial library that rented out copies of three-volume Victorian novels.

CECILY   Oh, I am afraid I am.

CHASUBLE   That is strange. Were I fortunate enough to be Miss Prism's pupil, I would hang upon her lips. (MISS PRISM *glares.*) I spoke metaphorically.—My metaphor was drawn from bees. Ahem! Mr. Worthing, I suppose, has not returned from town yet?

MISS PRISM   We do not expect him till Monday afternoon.

CHASUBLE   Ah yes, he usually likes to spend his Sunday in London. He is not one of those whose sole aim is enjoyment, as, by all accounts, that unfortunate young man his brother seems to be. But I must not disturb Egeria[23] and her pupil any longer.

MISS PRISM   Egeria? My name is Lætitia, Doctor.

CHASUBLE   (*Bowing.*) A classical allusion merely, drawn from the pagan authors. I shall see you both no doubt at Evensong?[24]

MISS PRISM   I think, dear Doctor, I will have a stroll with you. I find I have a headache after all, and a walk might do it good.

CHASUBLE   With pleasure, Miss Prism, with pleasure. We might go as far as the schools and back.

MISS PRISM   That would be delightful. Cecily, you will read your Political Economy in my absence. The chapter on the Fall of the Rupee you may omit. It is somewhat too sensational. Even these metallic problems have their melodramatic side.

(*Goes down the garden with* DR. CHASUBLE.)

CECILY   (*Picks up books and throws them back on table.*) Horrid Political Economy! Horrid Geography! Horrid, horrid German!

(*Enter* MERRIMAN *with a card on a salver.*)

MERRIMAN   Mr. Ernest Worthing has just driven over from the station. He has brought his luggage with him.

CECILY   (*Takes the card and reads it.*) "Mr. Ernest Worthing, B.4 The Albany, W." Uncle Jack's brother! Did you tell him Mr. Worthing was in town?

MERRIMAN   Yes, Miss. He seemed very much disappointed. I mentioned that you and Miss Prism were in the garden. He said he was anxious to speak to you privately for a moment.

CECILY   Ask Mr. Ernest Worthing to come here. I suppose you had better talk to the housekeeper about a room for him.

MERRIMAN   Yes, Miss.   (MERRIMAN *goes off.*)

CECILY   I have never met any really wicked person before. I feel rather frightened. I am so afraid he will look just like everyone else.

(*Enter* ALGERNON, *very gay and debonair.*)

He does!

ALGERNON   (*Raising his hat.*) You are my little cousin Cecily, I'm sure.

CECILY   You are under some strange mistake. I am not little. In fact, I believe I am more than usually tall for my age. (ALGERNON *is rather taken aback.*) But I am

---

[23] Classical name for a female teacher of young women.   [24] Evening church services.

your cousin Cecily. You, I see from your card, are Uncle Jack's brother, my cousin Ernest, my wicked cousin Ernest.

ALGERNON   Oh! I am not really wicked at all, cousin Cecily. You mustn't think that I am wicked.

CECILY   If you are not, then you have certainly been deceiving us all in a very inexcusable manner. I hope you have not been leading a double life, pretending to be wicked and being really good all the time. That would be hypocrisy.

ALGERNON   *(Looks at her in amazement.)* Oh! Of course I have been rather reckless.

CECILY   I am glad to hear it.

ALGERNON   In fact, now you mention the subject, I have been very bad in my own small way.

CECILY   I don't think you should be so proud of that, though I am sure it must have been very pleasant.

ALGERNON   It is much pleasanter being here with you.

CECILY   I can't understand how you are here at all. Uncle Jack won't be back till Monday afternoon.

ALGERNON   That is a great disappointment. I am obliged to go up by the first train on Monday morning. I have a business appointment that I am anxious . . . to miss.

CECILY   Couldn't you miss it anywhere but in London?

ALGERNON   No; the appointment is in London.

CECILY   Well, I know, of course, how important it is not to keep a business engagement, if one wants to retain any sense of the beauty of life, but still I think you had better wait till Uncle Jack arrives. I know he wants to speak to you about your emigrating.

ALGERNON   About my what?

CECILY   Your emigrating. He has gone up to buy your outfit.

ALGERNON   I certainly wouldn't let Jack buy my outfit. He has no taste in neckties at all.

CECILY   I don't think you will require neckties. Uncle Jack is sending you to Australia.[25]

ALGERNON   Australia? I'd sooner die.

CECILY   Well, he said at dinner on Wednesday night, that you would have to choose between this world, the next world, and Australia.

ALGERNON   Oh, well! The accounts I have received of Australia and the next world are not particularly encouraging. This world is good enough for me, cousin Cecily.

CECILY   Yes, but are you good enough for it?

ALGERNON   I'm afraid I'm not that. That is why I want you to reform me. You might make that your mission, if you don't mind, cousin Cecily.

CECILY   I'm afraid I've no time, this afternoon.

ALGERNON   Well, would you mind my reforming myself this afternoon?

CECILY   It is rather quixotic of you. But I think you should try.

ALGERNON   I will. I feel better already.

CECILY   You are looking a little worse.

ALGERNON   That is because I am hungry.

CECILY   How thoughtless of me. I should have remembered that when one is

---

[25] Originally a penal colony, Australia by 1895 was a favorite place to send unpromising family members to get them out of the way.

going to lead an entirely new life, one requires regular and wholesome meals. Won't you come in?

ALGERNON   Thank you. Might I have a button-hole first?[26] I never have any appetite unless I have a button-hole first.

CECILY   A Maréchal Niel?[27] *(Picks up scissors.)*

ALGERNON   No, I'd sooner have a pink rose.

CECILY   Why? *(Cuts a flower.)*

ALGERNON   Because you are like a pink rose, cousin Cecily.

CECILY   I don't think it can be right for you to talk to me like that. Miss Prism never says such things to me.

ALGERNON   Then Miss Prism is a short-sighted old lady. (CECILY *puts the rose in his button-hole.)* You are the prettiest girl I ever saw.

CECILY   Miss Prism says that all good looks are a snare.

ALGERNON   They are a snare that every sensible man would like to be caught in.

CECILY   Oh! I don't think I would care to catch a sensible man. I shouldn't know what to talk to him about.

(They pass into the house, MISS PRISM *and* DR. CHASUBLE *return.)*

MISS PRISM   You are too much alone, dear Dr. Chasuble. You should get married. A misanthrope I can understand—a womanthrope, never!

CHASUBLE   *(With a scholar's shudder.)* Believe me, I do not deserve so neologistic a phrase. The precept as well as the practice of the Primitive Church was distinctly against matrimony.

MISS PRISM   *(Sententiously.)* That is obviously the reason why the Primitive Church has not lasted up to the present day. And you do not seem to realize, dear Doctor, that by persistently remaining single, a man converts himself into a permanent public temptation. Men should be more careful; this very celibacy leads weaker vessels astray.

CHASUBLE   But is a man not equally attractive when married?

MISS PRISM   No married man is ever attractive except to his wife.

CHASUBLE   And often, I've been told, not even to her.

MISS PRISM   That depends on the intellectual sympathies of the woman. Maturity can always be depended on. Ripeness can be trusted. Young women are green. (DR. CHASUBLE *starts.)* I spoke horticulturally. My metaphor was drawn from fruits. But where is Cecily?

CHASUBLE   Perhaps she followed us to the schools.

(Enter JACK *slowly from the back of the garden. He is dressed in the deepest mourning, with crape hatband and black gloves.)*

MISS PRISM   Mr. Worthing!

CHASUBLE   Mr. Worthing?

MISS PRISM   This is indeed a surprise. We did not look for you till Monday afternoon.

JACK   *(Shakes* MISS PRISM*'s hand in a tragic manner.)* I have returned sooner than I expected. Dr. Chasuble, I hope you are well?

---

[26] A flower for a man's lapel.   [27] A variety of yellow rose.

CHASUBLE   Dear Mr. Worthing, I trust this garb of woe does not betoken some terrible calamity?

JACK   My brother.

MISS PRISM   More shameful debts and extravagance?

CHASUBLE   Still leading his life of pleasure?

JACK   *(Shaking his head.)* Dead!

CHASUBLE   Your brother Ernest dead?

JACK   Quite dead.

MISS PRISM   What a lesson for him! I trust he will profit by it.

CHASUBLE   Mr. Worthing, I offer you my sincere condolence. You have at least the consolation of knowing that you were always the most generous and forgiving of brothers.

JACK   Poor Ernest! He had many faults, but it is a sad, sad blow.

CHASUBLE   Very sad indeed. Were you with him at the end?

JACK   No. He died abroad; in Paris, in fact. I had a telegram last night from the manager of the Grand Hotel.

CHASUBLE   Was the cause of death mentioned?

JACK   A severe chill, it seems.

MISS PRISM   As a man sows, so shall he reap.[28]

CHASUBLE   *(Raising his hand.)* Charity, dear Miss Prism, charity! None of us are perfect. I myself am peculiarly susceptible to draughts. Will the interment take place here?

JACK   No. He seemed to have expressed a desire to be buried in Paris.

CHASUBLE   In Paris! *(Shakes his head.)* I fear that hardly points to any very serious state of mind at the last. You would no doubt wish me to make some slight allusion to this tragic domestic affliction next Sunday. (JACK *presses his hand convulsively.)* My sermon on the meaning of the manna in the wilderness can be adapted to almost any occasion, joyful, or, as in the present case, distressing. *(All sigh.)* I have preached it at harvest celebrations, christenings, confirmations, on days of humiliation and festal days. The last time I delivered it was in the Cathedral, as a charity sermon on behalf of the Society for the Prevention of Discontent among the Upper Orders. The Bishop, who was present, was much struck by some of the analogies I drew.

JACK   Ah! that reminds me, you mentioned christenings, I think, Dr. Chasuble? I suppose you know how to christen all right? (DR. CHASUBLE *looks astounded.)* I mean, of course, you are continually christening, aren't you?

MISS PRISM   It is, I regret to say, one of the Rector's most constant duties in this parish. I have often spoken to the poorer classes on the subject. But they don't seem to know what thrift is.

CHASUBLE   But is there any particular infant in whom you are interested, Mr. Worthing? Your brother was, I believe unmarried, was he not?

JACK   Oh, yes.

MISS PRISM   *(Bitterly.)* People who live entirely for pleasure usually are.

JACK   But it is not for any child, dear Doctor. I am very fond of children. No! the fact is, I would like to be christened myself, this afternoon, if you have nothing better to do.

CHASUBLE   But surely, Mr. Worthing, you have been christened already?

JACK   I don't remember anything about it.

CHASUBLE   But have you any grave doubts on the subject?

---

[28] See Galatians VI.7.

JACK   I certainly intend to have. Of course I don't know if the thing would bother you in any way, or if you think I am a little too old now.

CHASUBLE   Not at all. The sprinkling, and, indeed, the immersion of adults is a perfectly canonical practice.

JACK   Immersion!

CHASUBLE   You need have no apprehensions. Sprinkling is all that is necessary, or indeed I think advisable. Our weather is so changeable. At what hour would you wish the ceremony performed?

JACK   Oh, I might trot round about five if that would suit you.

CHASUBLE   Perfectly, perfectly! In fact I have two similar ceremonies to perform at that time. A case of twins that occurred recently in one of the outlying cottages on your own estate. Poor Jenkins the carter, a most hardworking man.

JACK   Oh! I don't see much fun in being christened along with other babies. It would be childish. Would half-past five do?

CHASUBLE   Admirably! Admirably! *(Takes out watch.)* And now, dear Mr. Worthing, I will not intrude any longer into a house of sorrow. I would merely beg you not to be too much bowed down by grief. What seems to us bitter trials are often blessings in disguise.

MISS PRISM   This seems to me a blessing of an extremely obvious kind.

(Enter CECILY *from the house.)*

CECILY   Uncle Jack! Oh, I am pleased to see you back. But what horrid clothes you have got on! Do go and change them.

MISS PRISM   Cecily!

CHASUBLE   My child! my child! *(*CECILY *goes towards* JACK; *he kisses her brow in a melancholy manner.)*

CECILY   What is the matter, Uncle Jack? Do look happy! You look as if you had a toothache, and I have got such a surprise for you. Who do you think is in the dining-room? Your brother!

JACK   Who?

CECILY   Your brother Ernest. He arrived about half an hour ago.

JACK   What nonsense! I haven't got a brother!

CECILY   Oh, don't say that. However badly he may have behaved to you in the past he is still your brother. You couldn't be so heartless as to disown him. I'll tell him to come out. And you will shake hands with him, won't you, Uncle Jack? *(Runs back into the house.)*

CHASUBLE   These are very joyful tidings.

MISS PRISM   After we had all been resigned to his loss, his sudden return seems to me peculiarly distressing.

JACK   My brother is in the dining-room? I don't know what it all means. I think it is perfectly absurd.

(Enter ALGERNON *and* CECILY *hand in hand. They come slowly up to* JACK.*)*

JACK   Good heavens! *(Motions* ALGERNON *away.)*

ALGERNON   Brother John, I have come down from town to tell you that I am very sorry for all the trouble I have given you, and that I intend to lead a better life in the future. *(*JACK *glares at him and does not take his hand.)*

CECILY   Uncle Jack, you are not going to refuse your own brother's hand?

JACK   Nothing will induce me to take his hand. I think his coming down here disgraceful. He knows perfectly well why.

CECILY   Uncle Jack, do be nice. There is some good in everyone. Ernest has just been telling me about his poor invalid friend Mr. Bunbury whom he goes to visit so often. And surely there must be much good in one who is kind to an invalid, and leaves the pleasures of London to sit by a bed of pain.

JACK   Oh! he has been talking about Bunbury, has he?

CECILY   Yes, he has told me all about poor Mr. Bunbury, and his terrible state of health.

JACK   Bunbury! Well, I won't have him talk to you about Bunbury or about anything else. It is enough to drive one perfectly frantic.

ALGERNON   Of course I admit that the faults were all on my side. But I must say that I think that Brother John's coldness to me is peculiarly painful. I expected a more enthusiastic welcome, especially considering it is the first time I have come here.

CECILY   Uncle Jack, if you don't shake hands with Ernest, I will never forgive you.

JACK   Never forgive me?

CECILY   Never, never, never!

JACK   Well, this is the last time I shall ever do it.

(Shakes hands with ALGERNON *and glares.)*

CHASUBLE   It's pleasant, is it not, to see so perfect a reconciliation? I think we might leave the two brothers together.

MISS PRISM   Cecily, you will come with us.

CECILY   Certainly, Miss Prism. My little task of reconciliation is over.

CHASUBLE   You have done a beautiful action today, dear child.

MISS PRISM   We must not be premature in our judgments.

CECILY   I feel very happy. *(They all go off.)*

JACK   You young scoundrel, Algy, you must get out of this place as soon as possible. I don't allow any Bunburying here.

(Enter MERRIMAN.*)*

MERRIMAN   I have put Mr. Ernest's things in the room next to yours, sir. I suppose that is all right?

JACK   What?

MERRIMAN   Mr. Ernest's luggage, sir. I have unpacked it and put it in the room next to your own.

JACK   His luggage?

MERRIMAN   Yes, sir. Three portmanteaus,[29] a dressing-case, two hat boxes, and a large luncheon-basket.

ALGERNON   I am afraid I can't stay more than a week this time.

JACK   Merriman, order the dog-cart[30] at once. Mr. Ernest has been suddenly called back to town.

MERRIMAN   Yes, sir. *(Goes back into the house.)*

ALGERNON   What a fearful liar you are, Jack. I have not been called back to town at all.

JACK   Yes, you have.

---

[29] Large leather suitcases.
[30] A small two-wheel cart drawn by a horse and carrying two people seated back-to-back.

ALGERNON I haven't heard anyone call me.

JACK Your duty as a gentleman calls you back.

ALGERNON My duty as a gentleman has never interfered with my pleasures in the smallest degree.

JACK I can quite understand that.

ALGERNON Well, Cecily is a darling.

JACK You are not to talk of Miss Cardew like that. I don't like it.

ALGERNON Well, I don't like your clothes. You look perfectly ridiculous in them. Why on earth don't you go up and change? It is perfectly childish to be in deep mourning for a man who is actually staying for a whole week with you in your house as a guest. I call it grotesque.

JACK You are certainly not staying with me for a whole week as a guest or anything else. You have got to leave . . . by the four-five train.

ALGERNON I certainly won't leave you so long as you are in mourning. It would be most unfriendly. If I were in mourning you would stay with me, I suppose. I should think it very unkind if you didn't.

JACK Well, will you go if I change my clothes?

ALGERNON Yes, if you are not too long. I never saw anybody take so long to dress, and with such little result.

JACK Well, at any rate, that is better than being always overdressed as you are.

ALGERNON If I am occasionally a little overdressed, I make up for it by being always immensely overeducated.

JACK Your vanity is ridiculous, your conduct an outrage, and your presence in my garden utterly absurd. However, you have got to catch the four-five, and I hope you will have a pleasant journey back to town. This Bunburying, as you call it, has not been a great success for you.   (*Goes into the house.*)

ALGERNON I think it has been a great success. I'm in love with Cecily, and that is everything.

(*Enter* CECILY *at the back of the garden. She picks up the can and begins to water the flowers.*)

But I must see her before I go, and make arrangements for another Bunbury. Ah, there she is.

CECILY Oh, I merely came back to water the roses. I thought you were with Uncle Jack.

ALGERNON He's gone to order the dog-cart for me.

CECILY Oh, is he going to take you for a nice drive?

ALGERNON He's going to send me away.

CECILY Then have we got to part?

ALGERNON I am afraid so. It's very painful parting.

CECILY It is always painful to part from people whom one has known for a very brief space of time. The absence of old friends one can endure with equanimity. But even a momentary separation from anyone to whom one has just been introduced is almost unbearable.

ALGERNON Thank you.

(*Enter* MERRIMAN.)

MERRIMAN The dog-cart is at the door, sir. (ALGERNON *looks appealingly at* CECILY.)

CECILY It can wait, Merriman . . . for . . . five minutes.

MERRIMAN   Yes, Miss.   *(Exit* MERRIMAN.*)*

ALGERNON   I hope, Cecily, I shall not offend you if I state quite frankly and openly that you seem to me to be in every way the visible personification of absolute perfection.

CECILY   I think your frankness does you great credit, Ernest. If you will allow me I will copy your remarks into my diary. *(Goes over to table and begins writing in diary.)*

ALGERNON   Do you really keep a diary? I'd give anything to look at it. May I?

CECILY   Oh no. *(Puts her hand over it.)* You see, it is simply a very young girl's record of her own thoughts and impressions, and consequently meant for publication. When it appears in volume form I hope you will order a copy. But pray, Ernest, don't stop. I delight in taking down from dictation. I have reached "absolute perfection." You can go on. I am quite ready for more.

ALGERNON   *(Somewhat taken aback.)* Ahem! Ahem!

CECILY   Oh, don't cough, Ernest. When one is dictating one should speak fluently and not cough. Besides, I don't know how to spell a cough.

(Writes as ALGERNON *speaks.)*

ALGERNON   *(Speaking very rapidly.)* Cecily, ever since I first looked upon your wonderful and incomparable beauty, I have dared to love you wildly, passionately, devotedly, hopelessly.

CECILY   I don't think that you should tell me that you love me wildly, passionately, devotedly, hopelessly. Hopelessly doesn't seem to make much sense, does it?

ALGERNON   Cecily!

(Enter MERRIMAN.*)*

MERRIMAN   The dog-cart is waiting, sir.

ALGERNON   Tell it to come round next week, at the same hour.

MERRIMAN   *(Looks at* CECILY, *who makes no sign.)* Yes, sir.   *(*MERRIMAN *retires.)*

CECILY   Uncle Jack would be very much annoyed if he knew you were staying on till next week, at the same hour.

ALGERNON   Oh, I don't care about Jack. I don't care for anybody in the whole world but you. I love you, Cecily. You will marry me, won't you?

CECILY   You silly boy! Of course. Why, we have been engaged for the last three months.

ALGERNON   For the last three months?

CECILY   Yes, it will be exactly three months on Thursday.

ALGERNON   But how did we become engaged?

CECILY   Well, ever since dear Uncle Jack first confessed to us that he had a younger brother who was very wicked and bad, you of course have formed the chief topic of conversation between myself and Miss Prism. And of course a man who is much talked about is always very attractive. One feels there must be something in him after all. I daresay it was foolish of me, but I fell in love with you, Ernest.

ALGERNON   Darling! And when was the engagement actually settled?

CECILY   On the 14th of February last. Worn out by your entire ignorance of my existence, I determined to end the matter one way or the other, and after a long struggle with myself I accepted you under this dear old tree here. The next day

I bought this little ring in your name, and this is the little bangle with the true lovers' knot I promised you always to wear.

ALGERNON   Did I give you this? It's very pretty, isn't it?

CECILY   Yes, you've wonderfully good taste, Ernest. It's the excuse I've always given for your leading such a bad life. And this is the box in which I keep all your dear letters. *(Kneels at table, opens box, and produces letters tied up with blue ribbon.)*

ALGERNON   My letters! But my own sweet Cecily, I have never written you any letters.

CECILY   You need hardly remind me of that, Ernest. I remember only too well that I was forced to write your letters for you. I always wrote three times a week, and sometimes oftener.

ALGERNON   Oh, do let me read them, Cecily?

CECILY   Oh, I couldn't possibly. They would make you far too conceited. *(Replaces box.)* The three you wrote me after I had broken off the engagement are so beautiful, and so badly spelled, that even now I can hardly read them without crying a little.

ALGERNON   But was our engagement ever broken off?

CECILY   Of course it was. On the 22nd of March. You can see the entry if you like. *(Shows diary.)* "Today I broke off my engagement with Ernest. I feel it is better to do so. The weather still continues charming."

ALGERNON   But why on earth did you break it off? What had I done? I had done nothing at all. Cecily, I am very much hurt indeed to hear you broke it off. Particularly when the weather was so charming.

CECILY   It would hardly have been a really serious engagement if it hadn't been broken off at least once. But I forgave you before the week was out.

ALGERNON   *(Crossing to her, and kneeling.)* What a perfect angel you are, Cecily.

CECILY   You dear romantic boy. *(He kisses her, she puts her fingers through his hair.)* I hope your hair curls naturally, does it?

ALGERNON   Yes, darling, with a little help from others.

CECILY   I am so glad.

ALGERNON   You'll never break off our engagement again, Cecily?

CECILY   I don't think I could break it off now that I have actually met you. Besides, of course, there is the question of your name.

ALGERNON   Yes, of course. *(Nervously.)*

CECILY   You must not laugh at me, darling, but it had always been a girlish dream of mine to love someone whose name was Ernest. *(ALGERNON rises, CECILY also.)* There is something in that name that seems to inspire absolute confidence. I pity any poor married woman whose husband is not called Ernest.

ALGERNON   But, my dear child, do you mean to say you could not love me if I had some other name?

CECILY   But what name?

ALGERNON   Oh, any name you like—Algernon—for instance. . . .

CECILY   But I don't like the name of Algernon.

ALGERNON   Well, my own dear, sweet, loving little darling, I really can't see why you should object to the name of Algernon. It is not at all a bad name. In fact, it is rather an aristocratic name. Half of the chaps who get into Bankruptcy Court are called Algernon. But seriously, Cecily . . . *(Moving to her.)* . . . if my name was Algy, couldn't you love me?

CECILY   *(Rising.)* I might respect you, Ernest, I might admire your character, but I fear that I should not be able to give you my undivided attention.

ALGERNON   Ahem! Cecily! *(Picking up hat.)* Your Rector here is, I suppose, thoroughly experienced in the practice of all the rites and ceremonials of the Church?

CECILY   Oh, yes, Dr. Chasuble is a most learned man. He has never written a single book, so you can imagine how much he knows.

ALGERNON   I must see him at once on a most important christening—I mean on most important business.

CECILY   Oh!

ALGERNON   I shan't be away more than half an hour.

CECILY   Considering that we have been engaged since February the 14th, and that I only met you today for the first time, I think it is rather hard that you should leave me for so long a period as half an hour. Couldn't you make it twenty minutes?

ALGERNON   I'll be back in no time.

(Kisses her and rushes down the garden.)

CECILY   What an impetuous boy he is! I like his hair so much. I must enter his proposal in my diary.

(Enter MERRIMAN.)

MERRIMAN   A Miss Fairfax has just called to see Mr. Worthing. On very important business Miss Fairfax states.

CECILY   Isn't Mr. Worthing in his library?

MERRIMAN   Mr. Worthing went over in the direction of the Rectory some time ago.

CECILY   Pray ask the lady to come out here; Mr. Worthing is sure to be back soon. And you can bring tea.

MERRIMAN   Yes, miss.   *(Goes out.)*

CECILY   Miss Fairfax! I suppose one of the many good elderly women who are associated with Uncle Jack in some of his philanthropic work in London. I don't quite like women who are interested in philanthropic work. I think it is so forward of them.

(Enter MERRIMAN.)

MERRIMAN   Miss Fairfax.

(Enter GWENDOLEN.)   *(Exit MERRIMAN.)*

CECILY   *(Advancing to meet her.)* Pray let me introduce myself to you. My name is Cecily Cardew.

GWENDOLEN   Cecily Cardew? *(Moving to her and shaking hands.)* What a very sweet name! Something tells me that we are going to be great friends. I like you already more than I can say. My first impressions of people are never wrong.

CECILY   How nice of you to like me so much after we have known each other such a comparatively short time. Pray sit down.

GWENDOLEN   *(Still standing up.)* I may call you Cecily, may I not?

CECILY   With pleasure!

GWENDOLEN   And you will always call me Gwendolen, won't you?

CECILY   If you wish.

GWENDOLEN   Then that is all quite settled, is it not?

CECILY   I hope so. (*A pause. They both sit down together.*)

GWENDOLEN   Perhaps this might be a favourable opportunity for my mentioning who I am. My father is Lord Bracknell. You have never heard of Papa, I suppose?

CECILY   I don't think so.

GWENDOLEN   Outside the family circle, Papa, I am glad to say, is entirely unknown. I think that is quite as it should be. The home seems to me to be the proper sphere for the man. And certainly once a man begins to neglect his domestic duties he becomes painfully effeminate, does he not? And I don't like that. It makes men so very attractive. Cecily, Mamma, whose views on education are remarkably strict, has brought me up to be extremely short-sighted; it is part of her system; so do you mind my looking at you through my glasses?

CECILY   Oh! not at all, Gwendolen. I am very fond of being looked at.

GWENDOLEN   (*After examining* CECILY *carefully through a lorgnette.*) You are here on a short visit I suppose.

CECILY   Oh no! I live here.

GWENDOLEN   (*Severely.*) Really? Your mother, no doubt, or some female relative of advanced years, resides here also?

CECILY   Oh no! I have no mother, nor, in fact, any relations.

GWENDOLEN   Indeed?

CECILY   My dear guardian, with the assistance of Miss Prism, has the arduous task of looking after me.

GWENDOLEN   Your guardian?

CECILY   Yes, I am Mr. Worthing's ward.

GWENDOLEN   Oh! It is strange he never mentioned to me that he had a ward. How secretive of him! He grows more interesting hourly. I am not sure, however, that the news inspires me with feelings of unmixed delight. (*Rising and going to her.*) I am very fond of you, Cecily; I have liked you ever since I met you! But I am bound to state that now that I know that you are Mr. Worthing's ward, I cannot help expressing a wish you were—well just a little older than you seem to be—and not quite so very alluring in appearance. In fact, if I may speak candidly—

CECILY   Pray do! I think that whenever one has anything unpleasant to say, one should always be quite candid.

GWENDOLEN   Well, to speak with perfect candour, Cecily, I wish that you were fully forty-two, and more than usually plain for your age. Ernest has a strong upright nature. He is the very soul of truth and honour. Disloyalty would be as impossible to him as deception. But even men of the noblest possible moral character are extremely susceptible to the influence of the physical charms of others. Modern, no less than ancient history, supplies us with many most painful examples of what I refer to. If it were not so, indeed, history would be quite unreadable.

CECILY   I beg your pardon, Gwendolen, did you say Ernest?

GWENDOLEN   Yes.

CECILY   Oh, but it is not Mr. Ernest Worthing who is my guardian. It is his brother—his elder brother.

GWENDOLEN   (*Sitting down again.*) Ernest never mentioned to me that he had a brother.

CECILY   I am sorry to say they have not been on good terms for a long time.

GWENDOLEN   Ah! that accounts for it. And now that I think of it I have never heard any man mention his brother. The subject seems distasteful to most men. Cecily, you have lifted a load from my mind. I was growing almost anxious. It would have been terrible if any cloud had come across a friendship like ours, would it not? Or course you are quite, quite sure that it is not Mr. Ernest Worthing who is your guardian?

CECILY   Quite sure. *(A pause.)* In fact, I am going to be his.

GWENDOLEN   *(Enquiringly.)* I beg your pardon?

CECILY   *(Rather shy and confidingly.)* Dearest Gwendolen, there is no reason why I should make a secret of it to you. Our little county newspaper is sure to chronicle the fact next week. Mr. Ernest Worthing and I are engaged to be married.

GWENDOLEN   *(Quite politely, rising.)* My darling Cecily, I think there must be some slight error. Mr. Ernest Worthing is engaged to me. The announcement will appear in the *Morning Post* on Saturday at the latest.

CECILY   *(Very politely, rising.)* I am afraid you must be under some misconception. Ernest proposed to me exactly ten minutes ago. *(Shows diary.)*

GWENDOLEN   *(Examines diary through her lorgnette carefully.)* It is certainly very curious, for he asked me to be his wife yesterday afternoon at 5:30. If you would care to verify the incident, pray do so. *(Produces diary of her own.)* I never travel without my diary. One should always have something sensational to read in the train. I am so sorry, dear Cecily, if it is any disappointment to you, but I am afraid *I* have the prior claim.

CECILY   It would distress me more than I can tell you, dear Gwendolen, if it caused you any mental or physical anguish, but I feel bound to point out that since Ernest proposed to you he clearly has changed his mind.

GWENDOLEN   *(Meditatively.)* If the poor fellow has been entrapped into any foolish promise I shall consider it my duty to rescue him at once, and with a firm hand.

CECILY   *(Thoughtfully and sadly.)* Whatever unfortunate entanglement my dear boy may have got into, I will never reproach him with it after we are married.

GWENDOLEN   Do you allude to me, Miss Cardew, as an entanglement? You are presumptuous. On an occasion of this kind it becomes more than a moral duty to speak one's mind. It becomes a pleasure.

CECILY   Do you suggest, Miss Fairfax, that I entrapped Ernest into an engagement? How dare you? This is no time for wearing the shallow mask of manners. When I see a spade I call it a spade.

GWENDOLEN   *(Satirically.)* I am glad to say that I have never seen a spade. It is obvious that our social spheres have been widely different.

(Enter MERRIMAN, *followed by the footman. He carries a salver, table cloth, and plate stand.* CECILY *is about to retort. The presence of the servants exercises a restraining influence, under which both girls chafe.)*

MERRIMAN   Shall I lay tea here as usual, Miss?

CECILY   *(Sternly, in a calm voice.)* Yes, as usual. *(*MERRIMAN *begins to clear table and lay cloth. A long pause.* CECILY *and* GWENDOLEN *glare at each other.)*

GWENDOLEN   Are there many interesting walks in the vicinity, Miss Cardew?

CECILY   Oh! yes! a great many. From the top of one of the hills quite close one can see five counties.

GWENDOLEN   Five counties! I don't think I should like that. I hate crowds.

CECILY   *(Sweetly.)* I suppose that is why you live in town? *(GWENDOLEN bites her lip, and beats her foot nervously with her parasol.)*

GWENDOLEN   *(Looking round.)* Quite a well-kept garden this is, Miss Cardew.

CECILY   So glad you like it, Miss Fairfax.

GWENDOLEN   I had no idea there were any flowers in the country.

CECILY   Oh, flowers are as common here, Miss Fairfax, as people are in London.

GWENDOLEN   Personally I cannot understand how anybody manages to exist in the country, if anybody who is anybody does. The country always bores me to death.

CECILY   Ah! This is what the newspapers call agricultural depression, is it not? I believe the aristocracy are suffering very much from it just at present. It is almost an epidemic amongst them, I have been told. May I offer you some tea, Miss Fairfax?

GWENDOLEN   *(With elaborate politeness.)* Thank you. *(Aside.)* Detestable girl! But I require tea!

CECILY   *(Sweetly.)* Sugar?

GWENDOLEN   *(Superciliously.)* No, thank you. Sugar is not fashionable any more. *(CECILY looks angrily at her, takes up the tongs and puts four lumps of sugar into the cup.)*

CECILY   *(Severely.)* Cake or bread and butter?

GWENDOLEN   *(In a bored manner.)* Bread and butter, please. Cake is rarely seen at the best houses nowadays.

CECILY   *(Cuts a very large slice of cake, and puts it on the tray.)* Hand that to Miss Fairfax.

(MERRIMAN does so, and goes out with footman. GWENDOLEN drinks the tea and makes a grimace. Puts down cup at once, reaches out her hand to the bread and butter, looks at it, and finds it is cake. Rises in indignation.)

GWENDOLEN   You have filled my tea with lumps of sugar, and though I asked most distinctly for bread and butter, you have given me cake. I am known for the gentleness of my disposition, and the extraordinary sweetness of my nature, but I warn you, Miss Cardew, you may go too far.

CECILY   *(Rising.)* To save my poor, innocent, trusting boy from the machinations of any other girl there are no lengths to which I would not go.

GWENDOLEN   From the moment I saw you I distrusted you. I felt that you were false and deceitful. I am never deceived in such matters. My first impressions of people are invariably right.

CECILY   It seems to me, Miss Fairfax, that I am trespassing on your valuable time. No doubt you have many other calls of a similar character to make in the neighbourhood.

(Enter JACK.)

GWENDOLEN   *(Catching sight of him.)* Ernest! My own Ernest!

JACK   Gwendolen! Darling! *(Offers to kiss her.)*

GWENDOLEN   *(Drawing back.)* A moment! May I ask if you are engaged to be married to this young lady? *(Points to CECILY.)*

JACK   *(Laughing.)* To dear little Cecily! Of course not! What could have put such an idea into your pretty little head?

GWENDOLEN   Thank you. You may! *(Offers her cheek.)*

CECILY   *(Very sweetly.)* I knew there must be some misunderstanding, Miss Fairfax. The gentleman whose arm is at present round your waist is my dear guardian, Mr. John Worthing.

GWENDOLEN   I beg your pardon?

CECILY   This is Uncle Jack.

GWENDOLEN   *(Receding.)* Jack! Oh!

(Enter ALGERNON. *)*

CECILY   Here is Ernest.

ALGERNON   *(Goes straight over to* CECILY *without noticing anyone else.)* My own love! *(Offers to kiss her.)*

CECILY   *(Drawing back.)* A moment, Ernest! May I ask you—are you engaged to be married to this young lady?

ALGERNON   *(Looking round.)* To what young lady? Good heavens! Gwendolen!

CECILY   Yes! to good heavens, Gwendolen, I mean to Gwendolen.

ALGERNON   *(Laughing.)* Of course not! What could have put such an idea into your pretty little head?

CECILY   Thank you. *(Presenting her cheek to be kissed.)* You may. (ALGERNON *kisses her.)*

GWENDOLEN   I felt there was some slight error, Miss Cardew. The gentleman who is now embracing you is my cousin, Mr. Algernon Moncrieff.

CECILY   *(Breaking away from* ALGERNON.*)* Algernon Moncrieff! Oh! *(The two girls move towards each other and put their arms round each other's waists as if for protection.)*

CECILY   Are you called Algernon?

ALGERNON   I cannot deny it.

CECILY   Oh!

GWENDOLEN   Is your name really John?

JACK   *(Standing rather proudly.)* I could deny it if I liked. I could deny anything if I liked. But my name certainly is John. It has been John for years.

CECILY   *(To* GWENDOLEN.*)* A gross deception has been practised on both of us.

GWENDOLEN   My poor wounded Cecily!

CECILY   My sweet wronged Gwendolen!

GWENDOLEN   *(Slowly and seriously.)* You will call me sister, will you not? *(They embrace.* JACK *and* ALGERNON *groan and walk up and down.)*

CECILY   *(Rather brightly.)* There is just one question I would like to be allowed to ask my guardian.

GWENDOLEN   An admirable idea! Mr. Worthing, there is just one question I would like to be permitted to put to you. Where is your brother Ernest? We are both engaged to be married to your brother Ernest, so it is a matter of some importance to us to know where your brother Ernest is at present.

JACK   *(Slowly and hesitatingly.)* Gwendolen—Cecily—it is very painful for me to be forced to speak the truth. It is the first time in my life that I have ever been reduced to such a painful position, and I am really quite inexperienced at doing anything of the kind. However I will tell you quite frankly that I have no brother Ernest. I have no brother at all. I never had a brother in my life, and I certainly have not the smallest intention of ever having one in the future.

CECILY   *(Surprised.)* No brother at all?

JACK   *(Cheerily.)* None!

GWENDOLEN   *(Severely.)* Had you never a brother of any kind?

JACK *(Pleasantly.)* Never. Not even of any kind.

GWENDOLEN I am afraid it is quite clear, Cecily, that neither of us is engaged to be married to anyone.

CECILY It is not a very pleasant position for a young girl suddenly to find herself in. Is it?

GWENDOLEN Let us go into the house. They will hardly venture to come after us there.

CECILY No, men are so cowardly, aren't they?

(They retire into the house with scornful looks.)

JACK This ghastly state of things is what you call Bunburying, I suppose?

ALGERNON Yes, and a perfectly wonderful Bunbury it is. The most wonderful Bunbury I have ever had in my life.

JACK Well, you've no right whatsoever to Bunbury here.

ALGERNON That is absurd. One has a right to Bunbury anywhere one chooses. Every serious Bunburyist knows that.

JACK Serious Bunburyist! Good heavens!

ALGERNON Well, one must be serious about something, if one wants to have any amusement in life. I happen to be serious about Bunburying. What on earth you are serious about I haven't got the remotest idea. About everything, I should fancy. You have such an absolutely trivial nature.

JACK Well, the only small satisfaction I have in the whole of this wretched business is that your friend Bunbury is quite exploded. You won't be able to run down to the country quite so often as you used to do, dear Algy. And a very good thing too.

ALGERNON Your brother is a little off colour, isn't he, dear Jack? You won't be able to disappear to London quite so frequently as your wicked custom was. And not a bad thing either.

JACK As for your conduct towards Miss Cardew, I must say that your taking in a sweet, simple, innocent girl like that is quite inexcusable. To say nothing of the fact that she is my ward.

ALGERNON I can see no possible defence at all for your deceiving a brilliant, clever, thoroughly experienced young lady like Miss Fairfax. To say nothing of the fact that she is my cousin.

JACK I wanted to be engaged to Gwendolen, that is all. I love her.

ALGERNON Well, I simply wanted to be engaged to Cecily. I adore her.

JACK There is certainly no chance of your marrying Miss Cardew.

ALGERNON I don't think there is much likelihood, Jack, of you and Miss Fairfax being united.

JACK Well, that is no business of yours.

ALGERNON If it was my business, I wouldn't talk about it. *(Begins to eat muffins.)* It is very vulgar to talk about one's business. Only people like stockbrokers do that, and then merely at dinner parties.

JACK How you can sit there, calmly eating muffins when we are in this horrible trouble, I can't make out. You seem to me to be perfectly heartless.

ALGERNON Well, I can't eat muffins in an agitated manner. The butter would probably get on my cuffs. One should always eat muffins quite calmly. It is the only way to eat them.

JACK I say it's perfectly heartless your eating muffins at all, under the circumstances.

ALGERNON   When I am in trouble, eating is the only thing that consoles me. Indeed, when I am in really great trouble, as anyone who knows me intimately will tell you, I refuse everything except food and drink. At the present moment I am eating muffins because I am unhappy. Besides, I am particularly fond of muffins. *(Rising.)*

JACK   *(Rising.)* Well, that is no reason why you should eat them all in that greedy way. *(Takes muffins from* ALGERNON.*)*

ALGERNON   *(Offering tea-cake.)* I wish you would have tea-cake instead. I don't like tea-cake.

JACK   Good heavens! I suppose a man may eat his own muffins in his own garden.

ALGERNON   But you have just said it was perfectly heartless to eat muffins.

JACK   I said it was perfectly heartless of you, under the circumstances. That is a very different thing.

ALGERNON   That may be. But the muffins are the same. *(He seizes the muffin-dish from* JACK.*)*

JACK   Algy, I wish to goodness you would go.

ALGERNON   You can't possibly ask me to go without having some dinner. It's absurd. I never go without my dinner. No one ever does, except vegetarians and people like that. Besides I have just made arrangements with Dr. Chasuble to be christened at a quarter to six under the name of Ernest.

JACK   My dear fellow, the sooner you give up that nonsense the better. I made arrangements this morning with Dr. Chasuble to be christened myself at 5:30, and I naturally will take the name of Ernest. Gwendolen would wish it. We can't both be christened Ernest. It's absurd. Besides, I have a perfect right to be christened if I like. There is no evidence at all that I ever have been christened by anybody. I should think it extremely probable I never was, and so does Dr. Chasuble. It is entirely different in your case. You have been christened already.

ALGERNON   Yes, but I have not been christened for years.

JACK   Yes, but you have been christened. That is the important thing.

ALGERNON   Quite so. So I know my constitution can stand it. If you are not quite sure about your ever having been christened, I must say I think it rather dangerous your venturing on it now. It might make you very unwell. You can hardly have forgotten that someone very closely connected with you was very nearly carried off this week in Paris by a severe chill.

JACK   Yes, but you said yourself that a severe chill was not hereditary.

ALGERNON   It usen't to be, I know—but I daresay it is now. Science is always making wonderful improvements in things.

JACK   *(Picking up the muffin-dish.)* Oh, that is nonsense; you are always talking nonsense.

ALGERNON   Jack, you are at the muffins again! I wish you wouldn't. There are only two left. *(Takes them.)* I told you I was particularly fond of muffins.

JACK   But I hate tea-cake.

ALGERNON   Why on earth then do you allow tea-cake to be served up for your guests? What ideas you have of hospitality!

JACK   Algernon! I have already told you to go. I don't want you here. Why don't you go!

ALGERNON   I haven't quite finished my tea yet! and there is still one muffin left.

*(*JACK *groans, and sinks into a chair,* ALGERNON *still continues eating.)*

Act-Drop.

THIRD ACT

SCENE. *Morning-room at the Manor House.* GWENDOLEN *and* CECILY *are at the window, looking out into the garden.*

GWENDOLEN   The fact that they did not follow us at once into the house, as anyone else would have done, seems to me to show that they have some sense of shame left.

CECILY   They have been eating muffins. That looks like repentance.

GWENDOLEN   *(After a pause.)* They don't seem to notice us at all. Couldn't you cough?

CECILY   But I haven't got a cough.

GWENDOLEN   They're looking at us. What effrontery!

CECILY   They're approaching. That's very forward of them.

GWENDOLEN   Let us preserve a dignified silence.

CECILY   Certainly. It's the only thing to do now.

(Enter JACK *followed by* ALGERNON. *They whistle some dreadful popular air from a British opera.)*

GWENDOLEN   This dignified silence seems to produce an unpleasant effect.

CECILY   A most distasteful one.

GWENDOLEN   But we will not be the first to speak.

CECILY   Certainly not.

GWENDOLEN   Mr. Worthing, I have something very particular to ask you. Much depends on your reply.

CECILY   Gwendolen, your common sense is invaluable. Mr. Moncrieff, kindly answer me the following question. Why did you pretend to be my guardian's brother?

ALGERNON   In order that I might have an opportunity of meeting you.

CECILY   *(To* GWENDOLEN.*)* That certainly seems a satisfactory explanation, does it not?

GWENDOLEN   Yes, dear, if you can believe him.

CECILY   I don't. But that does not affect the wonderful beauty of his answer.

GWENDOLEN   True. In matters of grave importance, style, not sincerity is the vital thing. Mr. Worthing, what explanation can you offer to me for pretending to have a brother? Was it in order that you might have an opportunity of coming up to town to see me as often as possible?

JACK   Can you doubt it, Miss Fairfax?

GWENDOLEN   I have the gravest doubts upon the subject. But I intend to crush them. This is not the moment for German scepticism.[31] *(Moving to* CECILY.*)* Their explanations appear to be quite satisfactory, especially Mr. Worthing's. That seems to me to have the stamp of truth upon it.

CECILY   I am more than content with what Mr. Moncrieff said. His voice alone inspires one with absolute credulity.

GWENDOLEN   Then you think we should forgive them?

CECILY   Yes. I mean no.

---

[31] Nineteenth-century German biblical scholars had the reputation of being rigorously skeptical.

GWENDOLEN   True! I had forgotten. There are principles at stake that one can-
not surrender. Which of us should tell them? The task is not a pleasant one.
CECILY   Could we not both speak at the same time?
GWENDOLEN   An excellent idea! I nearly always speak at the same time as other
people. Will you take the time from me?
CECILY   Certainly. (GWENDOLEN *beats time with uplifted finger.*)
GWENDOLEN AND CECILY   (*Speaking together.*) Your Christian names are still an
insuperable barrier. That is all!
JACK AND ALGERNON   (*Speaking together.*) Our Christian names! Is that all? But we
are going to be christened this afternoon.
GWENDOLEN   (*To* JACK.) For my sake you are prepared to do this terrible thing?
JACK   I am.
CECILY   (*To* ALGERNON.) To please me you are ready to face this fearful ordeal?
ALGERNON   I am!
GWENDOLEN   How absurd to talk of the equality of the sexes! Where questions of
self-sacrifice are concerned, men are infinitely beyond us.
JACK   We are. (*Clasps hands with* ALGERNON.)
CECILY   They have moments of physical courage of which we women know ab-
solutely nothing.
GWENDOLEN   (*To* JACK.) Darling!
ALGERNON   (*To* CECILY.) Darling. (*They fall into each other's arms.*)

(*Enter* MERRIMAN. *When he enters he coughs loudly seeing the situation.*)

MERRIMAN   Ahem! Ahem! Lady Bracknell!!
JACK   Good heavens!

(*Enter* LADY BRACKNELL. *The couples separate in alarm. Exit* MERRIMAN.)

LADY BRACKNELL   Gwendolen! What does this mean?
GWENDOLEN   Merely that I am engaged to be married to Mr. Worthing, Mamma.
LADY BRACKNELL   Come here. Sit down. Sit down immediately. Hesitation of any
kind is a sign of mental decay in the young, of physical weakness in the old.
(*Turns to* JACK.) Apprised, sir, of my daughter's sudden flight by her trusty
maid, whose confidence I purchased by means of a small coin, I followed her
at once by a luggage train. Her unhappy father is, I am glad to say, under the
impression that she is attending a more than usually lengthy lecture by the University Extension Scheme on the influence of a permanent income on thought.
I do not propose to undeceive him. Indeed I have never undeceived him on
any question. I would consider it wrong. But of course, you will clearly understand that all communication between yourself and my daughter must cease immediately from this moment. On this point, as indeed on all points, I am firm.
JACK   I am engaged to be married to Gwendolen, Lady Bracknell!
LADY BRACKNELL   You are nothing of the kind, sir. And now, as regards Alger-
non! . . . Algernon!
ALGERNON   Yes, Aunt Augusta.
LADY BRACKNELL   May I ask if it is in this house that your invalid friend Mr.
Bunbury resides?
ALGERNON   (*Stammering.*) Oh! No! Bunbury doesn't live here. Bunbury is some-
where else at present. In fact, Bunbury is dead.

LADY BRACKNELL Dead! When did Mr. Bunbury die? His death must have been extremely sudden.

ALGERNON *(Airily.)* Oh! I killed Bunbury this afternoon. I mean poor Bunbury died this afternoon.

LADY BRACKNELL What did he die of?

ALGERNON Bunbury? Oh, he was quite exploded.

LADY BRACKNELL Exploded! Was he the victim of a revolutionary outrage? I was not aware that Mr. Bunbury was interested in social legislation. If so, he is well punished for his morbidity.

ALGERNON My dear Aunt Augusta, I mean he was found out! The doctors found out that Bunbury could not live, that is what I mean—so Bunbury died.

LADY BRACKNELL He seems to have had great confidence in the opinion of his physicians. I am glad, however, that he made up his mind at the last to some definite course of action, and acted under proper medical advice. And now that we have finally got rid of this Mr. Bunbury, may I ask, Mr. Worthing, who is that young person whose hand my nephew Algernon is now holding in what seems to me a peculiarly unnecessary manner?

JACK That lady is Miss Cecily Cardew, my ward. *(LADY BRACKNELL bows coldly to CECILY.)*

ALGERNON I am engaged to be married to Cecily, Aunt Augusta.

LADY BRACKNELL I beg your pardon?

CECILY Mr. Moncrieff and I are engaged to be married, Lady Bracknell.

LADY BRACKNELL *(With a shiver, crossing to the sofa and sitting down.)* I do not know whether there is anything peculiarly exciting in the air of this particular part of Hertfordshire, but the number of engagements that go on seems to me considerably above the proper average that statistics have laid down for our guidance. I think some preliminary enquiry on my part would not be out of place. Mr. Worthing, is Miss Cardew at all connected with any of the larger railway stations in London? I merely desire information. Until yesterday I had no idea that there were any families or persons whose origin was a Terminus. *(JACK looks perfectly furious, but restrains himself.)*

JACK *(In a clear, cold voice.)* Miss Cardew is the granddaughter of the late Mr. Thomas Cardew of 149, Belgrave Square, S.W.; Gervase Park, Dorking, Surrey; and the Sporran, Fifeshire, N.B.[32]

LADY BRACKNELL That sounds not unsatisfactory. Three addresses always inspire confidence, even in tradesmen. But what proof have I of their authenticity?

JACK I have carefully preserved the Court Guides of the period. They are open to your inspection, Lady Bracknell.

LADY BRACKNELL *(Grimly.)* I have known strange errors in that publication.

JACK Miss Cardew's family solicitors are Messrs. Markby, Markby, and Markby.

LADY BRACKNELL Markby, Markby, and Markby? A firm of the very highest position in their profession. Indeed I am told that one of the Mr. Markbys is occasionally to be seen at dinner parties. So far I am satisfied.

JACK *(Very irritably.)* How extremely kind of you, Lady Bracknell! I have also in my possession, you will be pleased to hear, certificates of Miss Cardew's birth, baptism, whooping cough, registration, vaccination, confirmation, and the measles; both the German and the English variety.

LADY BRACKNELL Ah! A life crowded with incident, I see; though perhaps some-

---

[32] North Britain (Scotland).

what too exciting for a young girl. I am not myself in favour of premature experiences. *(Rises, looks at her watch.)* Gwendolen! the time approaches for our departure. We have not a moment to lose. As a matter of form, Mr. Worthing, I had better ask you if Miss Cardew has any little fortune?

JACK   Oh! about a hundred and thirty thousand pounds in the Funds.[33] That is all. Good-bye, Lady Bracknell. So pleased to have seen you.

LADY BRACKNELL   *(Sitting down again.)* A moment, Mr. Worthing. A hundred and thirty thousand pounds! And in the Funds! Miss Cardew seems to me a most attractive young lady, now that I look at her. Few girls of the present day have any really solid qualities, any of the qualities that last, and improve with time. We live, I regret to say, in an age of surfaces. *(To* CECILY.*)* Come over here, dear. *(*CECILY *goes across.)* Pretty child! your dress is sadly simple, and your hair seems almost as nature might have left it. But we can soon alter all that. A thoroughly experienced French maid produces a really marvelous result in a very brief space of time. I remember recommending one to young Lady Lancing, and after three months her own husband did not know her.

JACK   *(Aside.)* And after six months nobody knew her.

LADY BRACKNELL   *(Glares at* JACK *for a few moments. Then bends, with a practised smile, to* CECILY.*)* Kindly turn round, sweet child. *(*CECILY *turns completely round.)* No, the side view is what I want. *(*CECILY *presents her profile.)* Yes, quite as I expected. There are distinct social possibilities in your profile. The two weak points in our age are its want of principle and its want of profile. The chin a little higher, dear. Style largely depends on the way the chin is worn. They are worn very high, just at present. Algernon!

ALGERNON   Yes, Aunt Augusta!

LADY BRACKNELL   There are distinct social possibilities in Miss Cardew's profile.

ALGERNON   Cecily is the sweetest, dearest, prettiest girl in the whole world. And I don't care twopence about social possibilities.

LADY BRACKNELL   Never speak disrespectfully of Society, Algernon. Only people who can't get into it do that. *(To* CECILY.*)* Dear child, of course you know that Algernon has nothing but his debts to depend upon. But I do not approve of mercenary marriages. When I married Lord Bracknell I had no fortune of any kind. But I never dreamed for a moment of allowing that to stand in my way. Well, I suppose I must give my consent.

ALGERNON   Thank you, Aunt Augusta.

LADY BRACKNELL   Cecily, you may kiss me!

CECILY   *(Kisses her.)* Thank you, Lady Bracknell.

LADY BRACKNELL   You may also address me as Aunt Augusta for the future.

CECILY   Thank you, Aunt Augusta.

LADY BRACKNELL   The marriage, I think, had better take place quite soon.

ALGERNON   Thank you, Aunt Augusta.

CECILY   Thank you, Aunt Augusta.

LADY BRACKNELL   To speak frankly, I am not in favour of long engagements. They give people the opportunity of finding out each other's character before marriage, which I think is never advisable.

JACK   I beg your pardon for interrupting you, Lady Bracknell, but this engagement is quite out of the question. I am Miss Cardew's guardian, and she cannot marry without my consent until she comes of age. That consent I absolutely decline to give.

---

[33] Government bonds.

LADY BRACKNELL   Upon what grounds may I ask? Algernon is an extremely, I may almost say an ostentatiously, eligible young man. He has nothing, but he looks everything. What more can one desire?

JACK   It pains me very much to have to speak frankly to you, Lady Bracknell, about your nephew, but the fact is that I do not approve at all of his moral character. I suspect him of being untruthful. *(ALGERNON and CECILY look at him in indignant amazement.)*

LADY BRACKNELL   Untruthful! My nephew Algernon? Impossible! He is an Oxonian.

JACK   I fear there can be no possible doubt about the matter. This afternoon, during my temporary absence in London on an important question of romance, he obtained admission to my house by means of the false pretence of being my brother. Under an assumed name he drank, I've just been informed by my butler, an entire pint bottle of my Perrier-Jouet, Brut, '89; a wine I was specially reserving for myself. Continuing his disgraceful deception, he succeeded in the course of the afternoon in alienating the affections of my only ward. He subsequently stayed to tea, and devoured every single muffin. And what makes his conduct all the more heartless is, that he was perfectly well aware from the first that I have no brother, that I never had a brother, and that I don't intend to have a brother, not even of any kind! I distinctly told him so myself yesterday afternoon.

LADY BRACKNELL   Ahem! Mr. Worthing, after careful consideration I have decided entirely to overlook my nephew's conduct to you.

JACK   That is very generous of you, Lady Bracknell. My own decision, however, is unalterable. I decline to give my consent.

LADY BRACKNELL   *(To CECILY.)* Come here, sweet child. *(CECILY goes over.)* How old are you, dear?

CECILY   Well, I am really only eighteen, but I always admit to twenty when I go to evening parties.

LADY BRACKNELL   You are perfectly right in making some slight alteration. Indeed, no woman should ever be quite accurate about her age. It looks so calculating . . . . *(In a meditative manner.)* Eighteen, but admitting to twenty at evening parties. Well, it will not be very long before you are of age and free from the restraints of tutelage. So I don't think your guardian's consent is, after all, a matter of any importance.

JACK   Pray excuse me, Lady Bracknell, for interrupting you again, but it is only fair to tell you that according to the terms of her grandfather's will Miss Cardew does not come legally of age till she is thirty-five.

LADY BRACKNELL   That does not seem to me to be a grave objection. Thirty-five is a very attractive age. London society is full of women of the very highest birth who have, of their own free choice, remained thirty-five for years. Lady Dumbleton is an instance in point. To my own knowledge she has been thirty-five ever since she arrived at the age of forty, which was many years ago now. I see no reason why our dear Cecily should not be even still more attractive at the age you mention than she is at present. There will be a large accumulation of property.

CECILY   Algy, could you wait for me till I was thirty-five?

ALGERNON   Of course I could, Cecily. You know I could.

CECILY   Yes, I felt it instinctively, but I couldn't wait all that time. I hate waiting even five minutes for anybody. It always makes me rather cross. I am not punctual myself, I know, but I do like punctuality in others, and waiting, even to be married, is quite out of the question.

ALGERNON   Then what is to be done, Cecily?

CECILY   I don't know, Mr. Moncrieff.

LADY BRACKNELL   My dear Mr. Worthing, as Miss Cardew states positively that she cannot wait till she is thirty-five—a remark which I am bound to say seems to me to show a somewhat impatient nature—I would beg of you to reconsider your decision.

JACK   But my dear Lady Bracknell, the matter is entirely in your own hands. The moment you consent to my marriage to Gwendolen, I will most gladly allow your nephew to form an alliance with my ward.

LADY BRACKNELL   *(Rising and drawing herself up.)* You must be quite aware that what you propose is out of the question.

JACK   Then a passionate celibacy is all that any of us can look forward to.

LADY BRACKNELL   That is not the destiny I propose for Gwendolen. Algernon, of course, can choose for himself. *(Pulls out her watch.)* Come, dear; *(*GWENDOLEN *rises)* we have already missed five, if not six, trains. To miss any more might expose us to comment on the platform.

(Enter DR. CHASUBLE. *)*

CHASUBLE   Everything is quite ready for the christenings.

LADY BRACKNELL   The christenings, sir! Is not that somewhat premature?

CHASUBLE   *(Looking rather puzzled, and pointing to* JACK *and* ALGERNON. *)* Both these gentlemen have expressed a desire for immediate baptism.

LADY BRACKNELL   At their age? The idea is grotesque and irreligious! Algernon, I forbid you to be baptized. I will not hear of such excesses. Lord Bracknell would be highly displeased if he learned that that was the way in which you wasted your time and money.

CHASUBLE   Am I to understand then that there are to be no christenings at all this afternoon?

JACK   I don't think that, as things are now, it would be of much practical value to either of us, Dr. Chasuble.

CHASUBLE   I am grieved to hear such sentiments from you, Mr. Worthing. They savour of the heretical views of the Anabaptists,[34] views that I have completely refuted in four of my unpublished sermons. However, as your present mood seems to be one peculiarly secular, I will return to the church at once. Indeed, I have just been informed by the pew-opener that for the last hour and a half Miss Prism has been waiting for me in the vestry.

LADY BRACKNELL   *(Starting.)* Miss Prism! Did I hear you mention a Miss Prism?

CHASUBLE   Yes, Lady Bracknell. I am on my way to join her.

LADY BRACKNELL   Pray allow me to detain you for a moment. This matter may prove to be one of vital importance to Lord Bracknell and myself. Is this Miss Prism a female of repellant aspect, remotely connected with education?

CHASUBLE   *(Somewhat indignantly.)* She is the most cultivated of ladies, and the very picture of respectability.

LADY BRACKNELL   It is obviously the same person. May I ask what position she holds in your household?

CHASUBLE   *(Severely.)* I am a celibate, madam.

JACK   *(Interposing.)* Miss Prism, Lady Bracknell, has been for the last three years Miss Cardew's esteemed governess and valued companion.

---

[34] A seventeenth-century Protestant sect whose views on baptism were regarded as heretical by the Church of England.

LADY BRACKNELL   In spite of what I hear of her, I must see her at once. Let her be sent for.

CHASUBLE   *(Looking off.)* She approaches; she is nigh.

(Enter MISS PRISM *hurriedly.)*

MISS PRISM   I was told you expected me in the vestry, dear Canon. I have been waiting for you there for an hour and three quarters. *(Catches sight of* LADY BRACKNELL *who has fixed her with a stony glare.* MISS PRISM *grows pale and quails. She looks anxiously round as if desirous to escape.)*

LADY BRACKNELL   *(In a severe, judicial voice.)* Prism! *(*MISS PRISM *bows her head in shame.)* Come here, Prism! *(*MISS PRISM *approaches in a humble manner.)* Prism! Where is that baby? *(General consternation. The* CANON *starts back in horror.* AL-GERNON *and* JACK *pretend to be anxious to shield* CECILY *and* GWENDOLEN *from hearing the details of a terrible public scandal.)* Twenty-eight years ago, Prism, you left Lord Bracknell's house, Number 104, Upper Grosvenor Street, in charge of a perambulator that contained a baby, of the male sex. You never returned. A few weeks later, through the elaborate investigations of the Metropolitan police, the perambulator was discovered at midnight, standing by itself in a remote corner of Bayswater. It contained the manuscript of a three-volume novel of more than usually revolting sentimentality. *(*MISS PRISM *starts in involuntary indignation.)* But the baby was not there! *(Everyone looks at* MISS PRISM.*)* Prism! Where is that baby? *(A pause.)*

MISS PRISM   Lady Bracknell, I admit with shame that I do not know. I only wish I did. The plain facts of the case are these. On the morning of the day you mention, a day that is for ever branded on my memory, I prepared as usual to take the baby out in its perambulator. I had also with me a somewhat old, but capacious handbag, in which I had intended to place the manuscript of a work of fiction that I had written during my few unoccupied hours. In a moment of mental abstraction, for which I never can forgive myself, I deposited the manu-script in the bassinette, and placed the baby in the handbag.

JACK   *(Who has been listening attentively.)* But where did you deposit the handbag?

MISS PRISM   Do not ask me, Mr. Worthing.

JACK   Miss Prism, this is a matter of no small importance to me. I insist on knowing where you deposited the handbag that contained that infant.

MISS PRISM   I left it in the cloakroom of one of the larger railway stations in London.

JACK   What railway station?

MISS PRISM   *(Quite crushed.)* Victoria. The Brighton line. *(Sinks into a chair.)*

JACK   I must retire to my room for a moment. Gwendolen, wait here for me.

GWENDOLEN   If you are not too long, I will wait here for you all my life.

(Exit JACK *in great excitement.)*

CHASUBLE   What do you think this means, Lady Bracknell?

LADY BRACKNELL   I dare not even suspect, Dr. Chasuble. I need hardly tell you that in families of high position strange coincidences are not supposed to occur. They are hardly considered the thing.

(Noises heard overhead as if someone was throwing trunks about. Everyone looks up.)

CECILY   Uncle Jack seems strangely agitated.

CHASUBLE   Your guardian has a very emotional nature.

LADY BRACKNELL   This noise is extremely unpleasant. It sounds as if he was having an argument. I dislike arguments of any kind. They are always vulgar, and often convincing.

CHASUBLE   *(Looking up.)* It has stopped now. *(The noise is redoubled.)*

LADY BRACKNELL   I wish he would arrive at some conclusion.

GWENDOLEN   This suspense is terrible. I hope it will last.

(Enter JACK *with a handbag of black leather in his hand.)*

JACK   *(Rushing over to* MISS PRISM.*)* Is this the handbag, Miss Prism? Examine it carefully before you speak. The happiness of more than one life depends on your answer.

MISS PRISM   *(Calmly.)* It seems to be mine. Yes, here is the injury it received through the upsetting of a Gower Street omnibus in younger and happier days. Here is the stain on the lining caused by the explosion of a temperance beverage, an incident that occurred at Leamington. And here, on the lock, are my initials. I had forgotten that in an extravagant mood I had had them placed there. The bag is undoubtedly mine. I am delighted to have it so unexpectedly restored to me. It has been a great inconvenience being without it all these years.

JACK   *(In a pathetic voice.)* Miss Prism, more is restored to you than this handbag. I was the baby you placed in it.

MISS PRISM   *(Amazed.)* You?

JACK   *(Embracing her.)* Yes . . . mother!

MISS PRISM   *(Recoiling in indignant astonishment.)* Mr. Worthing! I am unmarried!

JACK   Unmarried! I do not deny that is a serious blow. But after all, who has the right to cast a stone against one who has suffered? Cannot repentance wipe out an act of folly? Why should there be one law for men, and another for women? Mother, I forgive you. *(Tries to embrace her again.)*

MISS PRISM   *(Still more indignant.)* Mr. Worthing, there is some error. *(Pointing to* LADY BRACKNELL.*)* There is the lady who can tell you who you really are.

JACK   *(After a pause.)* Lady Bracknell, I hate to seem inquisitive, but would you kindly inform me who I am?

LADY BRACKNELL   I am afraid that the news I have to give you will not altogether please you. You are the son of my poor sister, Mrs. Moncrieff, and consequently Algernon's elder brother.

JACK   Algy's elder brother! Then I have a brother after all. I knew I had a brother! I always said I had a brother! Cecily—how could you have ever doubted that I had a brother? *(Seizes hold of* ALGERNON.*)* Dr. Chasuble, my unfortunate brother. Miss Prism, my unfortunate brother. Gwendolen, my unfortunate brother. Algy, you young scoundrel, you will have to treat me with more respect in the future. You have never behaved to me like a brother in all your life.

ALGERNON   Well, not till today, old boy, I admit. I did my best, however, though I was out of practice. *(Shakes hands.)*

GWENDOLEN   *(To* JACK.*)* My own! But what own are you? What is your Christian name, now that you have become someone else?

JACK   Good heavens! . . . I had quite forgotten that point. Your decision on the subject of my name is irrevocable, I suppose?

GWENDOLEN   I never change, except in my affections.

CECILY   What a noble nature you have, Gwendolen!

JACK   Then the question had better be cleared up at once. Aunt Augusta, a moment. At the time when Miss Prism left me in the handbag, had I been christened already?

LADY BRACKNELL   Every luxury that money could buy, including christening, had been lavished on you by your fond and doting parents.

JACK   Then I was christened! That is settled. Now, what name was I given? Let me know the worst.

LADY BRACKNELL   Being the eldest son you were naturally christened after your father.

JACK   *(Irritably.)* Yes, but what was my father's Christian name?

LADY BRACKNELL   *(Meditatively.)* I cannot at the present moment recall what the General's Christian name was. But I have no doubt he had one. He was eccentric, I admit. But only in later years. And that was the result of the Indian climate, and marriage, and indigestion, and other things of that kind.

JACK   Algy! Can't you recollect what our father's Christian name was?

ALGERNON   My dear boy, we were never even on speaking terms. He died before I was a year old.

JACK   His name would appear in the Army Lists of the period, I suppose, Aunt Augusta?

LADY BRACKNELL   The General was essentially a man of peace, except in his domestic life. But I have no doubt his name would appear in any military directory.

JACK   The Army Lists of the last forty years are here. These delightful records should have been my constant study. *(Rushes to bookcase and tears the books out.)* M. Generals . . . Mallam, Maxbohm, Magley, what ghastly names they have— Markby, Migsby, Mobbs, Moncrieff! Lieutenant 1840, Captain, Lieutenant-Colonel, Colonel, General 1869, Christian names, Ernest John. *(Puts book very quietly down and speaks quite calmly.)* I always told you, Gwendolen, my name was Ernest, didn't I? Well, it is Ernest after all. I mean it naturally is Ernest.

LADY BRACKNELL   Yes, I remember now that the General was called Ernest. I knew I had some particular reason for disliking the name.

GWENDOLEN   Ernest! My own Ernest! I felt from the first that you could have no other name!

JACK   Gwendolen, it is a terrible thing for a man to find out suddenly that all his life he has been speaking nothing but the truth. Can you forgive me?

GWENDOLEN   I can. For I feel that you are sure to change.

JACK   My own one!

CHASUBLE   *(To* MISS PRISM.*)* Lætitia! *(Embraces her.)*

MISS PRISM   *(Enthusiastically.)* Frederick! At last!

ALGERNON   Cecily! *(Embraces her.)* At last!

JACK   Gwendolen! *(Embraces her.)* At last!

LADY BRACKNELL   My nephew, you seem to be displaying signs of triviality.

JACK   On the contrary, Aunt Augusta, I've now realized for the first time in my life the vital Importance of Being Earnest.

CURTAIN.

QUESTIONS FOR DISCUSSION AND WRITING

1. Act I of *The Importance of Being Earnest* takes place in London; Acts II and III take place in the country. What meanings does the country have in the play? (Shakespeare often has his characters withdraw from the city or court to a "green world," where they are transformed; the island serves this function in *The Tempest*. Is Hertfordshire a "green world" in this sense?)

2. *The Importance of Being Earnest,* like *Tartuffe,* employs the New Comedy plot: a young couple (in this case two young couples) want to marry, are blocked by social forces embodied in older people, but overcome the opposition and marry. What are the blocking forces embodied in Prism, Chasuble, and Bracknell, and how are they overcome?

3. Part of the fun of *The Importance of Being Earnest* is the duplication of so many things, especially the lovers. Jack and Algernon are similar but amusingly different as well, as are Gwendolyn and Cecily. Explain. Consider also Lane and Merriman, Miss Prism and Canon Chasuble, and Lord and Lady Bracknell.

4. There are many sources of laughter in *The Importance of Being Earnest,* including comedy of character, comedy of situation, and verbal comedy. First, what is comic about the characters in the play?

5. Second, what is comic about the situations in the play?

6. Third, what is comic about the language in the play? The most obvious example is the epigrams. How do they work? Look at this example, from early in Act I: "Really, if the lower orders don't set us a good example, what on earth is the use of them?" This quip works on the Wildean principle of topsy-turvydom: a Victorian cliché is stood on its head. Look at some other examples and see what other comic devices Wilde uses.

7. What aspects of society become the subjects of comedy in *The Importance of Being Earnest?* The epigram quoted in question 6 turns a commonplace about class upside down. What other topics are the subject of laughter?

The Modern Theater

༄༅ ༄༅

Luis Valdez

Luis Valdez (b. 1940) was born into a family of migrant farm workers in Delano, California. He attended San Jose State College (now University) on a scholarship. After graduation he became an organizer for the United Farm Workers, founded by Cesar Chavez to organize the largely Mexican migrant farm workers in California to help them achieve decent pay and working conditions. In 1965, he founded the Teatro Campesino (Farm Workers' Theater). The goals of the *teatro* were to educate and inspire farm workers and to encourage them to join the union. The theater's first productions were short, propaganda plays called *actos*. Valdez had worked with the San Francisco Mime Troupe, and he adopted some features of its style, including farcical exaggeration, stereotyped characters, masks, improvisation, and direct social commentary. The *actos* were performed by unemployed farm workers in such spaces as streets, union halls, or the back of trucks next to vineyards. Valdez has called the *actos* "collaborative work"; the actors helped develop the dialogue by improvising during rehearsal.

The Teatro Campesino did not confine itself long to the subject of the organization of farm workers but turned to more general themes of Chicano identity. (The term *Chicano*, which means "Mexican-American," was first used pejoratively, but was adopted as a term of pride by Mexican-American activists in the 1960s.) *Los Vendidos* (*The Sellouts*), for example, explores farcically various Chicano stereotypes and satirizes those who give up their identity for the sake of being accepted by a racist white society. In longer, more complex plays, such as *Dark Root of a Scream* (1971) and *La gran carpa de los rasquachis* (*The Great Tent of the Underdogs,* 1973), Valdez combines contemporary social issues with traditional Mexican myth and allegory. *Zoot Suit* (1978) was a hit play in Los Angeles and became the first Chicano play to be produced on Broadway. It was made into a film in 1982. In 1987 Valdez wrote and directed the successful Hollywood film *La Bamba*, the story of the Chicano pop singer Richie Valens.

LOS VENDIDOS[1]

CHARACTERS

HONEST SANCHO
SECRETARY
FARM WORKER
JOHNNY
REVOLUCIONARIO
MEXICAN-AMERICAN

[*Scene:* HONEST SANCHO'S *Used Mexican Lot and Mexican Curio Shop. Three models are on display in* HONEST SANCHO'S *shop: to the right, there is a* REVOLUCIONARIO, *complete with sombrero, carrilleras, and carabina 30-30.*[2] *At center, on the floor, there is the* FARM WORKER, *under a broad straw sombrero. At stage left is the Pachuco, filero*[3] *in hand.*]
    HONEST SANCHO *is moving among his models, dusting them off and preparing for another day of business.*]

SANCHO: Bueno, bueno, mis monos, vamos a ver a quien vendemos ahora, ¿no?[4]
    [*To audience.*] ¡Quihubo! I'm Honest Sancho and this is my shop. Antes fuí contratista pero ahora logré tener mi negocito.[5] All I need now is a customer. [*A bell rings offstage.*] Ay, a customer!
SECRETARY   [*Entering*]: Good morning, I'm Miss Jiménez from—
SANCHO: ¡Ah, una chicana! Welcome, welcome Señorita Jiménez.
SECRETARY   [*Anglo pronunciation*]: JIM-enez.
SANCHO: ¿Qué?
SECRETARY: My name is Miss JIM-enez. Don't you speak English? What's wrong with you?
SANCHO: Oh, nothing, Señorita JIM-enez. I'm here to help you.
SECRETARY: That's better. As I was starting to say, I'm a secretary from Governor Reagan's office,[6] and we're looking for a Mexican type for the administration.
SANCHO: Well, you come to the right place, lady. This is Honest Sancho's Used Mexican lot, and we got all types here. Any particular type you want?
SECRETARY: Yes, we were looking for somebody suave—
SANCHO: Suave.
SECRETARY: Debonair.
SANCHO: De buen aire.
SECRETARY: Dark.
SANCHO: Prieto.
SECRETARY: But of course not too dark.
SANCHO: No muy prieto.
SECRETARY: Perhaps, beige.

---

[1] "The Sellouts."
[2] *Revolucionario,* "Revolutionary," *carrilleras,* "cartridge belts"; *carabina 30-30,* "30-30 carbine."
[3] *Pachuco,* "urban tough guy"; *filero,* "blade."
[4] "Well, well, my darlings, let's see who we can sell now, O.K.?"
[5] "I used to be a contractor, but now I've succeeded in having my own little business."
[6] Ronald Reagan was governor of California from 1967 to 1975.

SANCHO: Beige, just the tone. Así como cafecito con leche, ¿no?[7]

SECRETARY: One more thing. He must be hard-working.

SANCHO: That could only be one model. Stop right over here to the center of the shop, lady. [*They cross to the farm worker.*] This is our standard farm worker model. As you can see, in the words of our beloved Senator George Murphy, he is "built close to the ground." Also take special notice of his four-ply Goodyear huaraches, made from the rain tire. This wide-brimmed sombrero is an extra added feature—keeps off the sun, rain, and dust.

SECRETARY: Yes, it does look durable.

SANCHO: And our farm worker model is friendly. Muy amable.[8] Watch. [*Snaps his fingers.*]

FARM WORKER: [*Lifts up head*]: Buenos días, señorita. [*His head drops.*]

SECRETARY: My, he's friendly.

SANCHO: Didn't I tell you? Loves his patrones! But his most attractive feature is that he's hard working. Let me show you. [*Snaps fingers.* FARM WORKER *stands.*]

FARM WORKER: ¡El jale![9] [*He begins to work.*]

SANCHO: As you can see, he is cutting grapes.

SECRETARY: Oh, I wouldn't know.

SANCHO: He also picks cotton. [*Snap.* FARM WORKER *begins to pick cotton.*]

SECRETARY: Versatile isn't he?

SANCHO: He also picks melons. [*Snap.* FARM WORKER *picks melons.*] That's his slow speed for late in the season. Here's his fast speed. [*Snap.* FARM WORKER *picks faster.*]

SECRETARY: ¡Chihuahua! . . . I mean, goodness, he sure is a hard worker.

SANCHO: [*Pulls the* FARM WORKER *to his feet*]: And that isn't the half of it. Do you see these little holes on his arms that appear to be pores? During those hot sluggish days in the field, when the vines or the branches get so entangled, it's almost impossible to move; these holes emit a certain grease that allow our model to slip and slide right through the crop with no trouble at all.

SECRETARY: Wonderful. But is he economical?

SANCHO: Economical? Señorita, you are looking at the Volkswagen of Mexicans. Pennies a day is all it takes. One plate of beans and tortillas will keep him going all day. That, and chile. Plenty of chile. Chile jalapenos, chile verde, chile colorado. But, of course, if you do give him chile [*Snap.* FARM WORKER *turns left face. Snap.* FARM WORKER *bends over.*] then you have to change his oil filter once a week.

SECRETARY: What about storage?

SANCHO: No problem. You know these new farm labor camps our Honorable Governor Reagan has built out by Parlier or Raisin City? They were designed with our model in mind. Five, six, seven, even ten in one of those shacks will give you no trouble at all. You can also put him in old barns, old cars, river banks. You can even leave him out in the field overnight with no worry!

SECRETARY: Remarkable.

SANCHO: And here's an added feature: Every year at the end of the season, this model goes back to Mexico and doesn't return, automatically, until next Spring.

SECRETARY: How about that. But tell me: does he speak English?

SANCHO: Another outstanding feature is that last year this model was programmed to go out on STRIKE! [*Snap.*]

---

[7] "Like coffee with milk, no?"   [8] "Very friendly."   [9] "The job!"

FARM WORKER: ¡HUELGA! ¡HUELGA! Hermanos, sálganse de esos files.[10]
[*Snap. He stops.*]
SECRETARY: No! Oh no, we can't strike in the State Capitol.
SANCHO: Well, he also scabs. [*Snap.*]
FARM WORKER: Me vendo barato, ¿y qué?[11] [*Snap.*]
SECRETARY: That's much better, but you didn't answer my question. Does he
speak English?
SANCHO: Bueno . . . no, pero[12] he has other—
SECRETARY: No.
SANCHO: Other features.
SECRETARY: NO! He just won't do!
SANCHO: Okay, okay pues. We have other models.
SECRETARY: I hope so. What we need is something a little more sophisticated.
SANCHO: Sophisti—¿qué?
SECRETARY: An urban model.
SANCHO: Ah, from the city! Step right back. Over here in this corner of the shop
is exactly what you are looking for. Introducing our new 1969 JOHNNY PA-
CHUCO model! This is our fast-back model. Streamlined. Built for speed,
low-riding, city life. Take a look at some of these features. Mag shoes, dual
exhausts, green chartreuse paint-job, dark-tint windshield, a little poof on top.
Let me just turn him on. [*Snap.* JOHNNY *walks to stage center with a pachuco
bounce.*]
SECRETARY: What was that?
SANCHO: That, señorita, was the Chicano shuffle.
SECRETARY: Okay, what does he do?
SANCHO: Anything and everything necessary for city life. For instance, survival:
He knife fights. [*Snap.* JOHNNY *pulls out switch blade and swings at* SECRETARY.]
[SECRETARY *screams.*]
SANCHO: He dances. [*Snap.*]
JOHNNY: [*Singing*]: "Angel Baby, my Angel Baby . . ." [*Snap.*]
SANCHO: And here's a feature no city model can be without. He gets arrested,
but not without resisting, of course. [*Snap.*]
JOHNNY: ¡En la madre, la placa![13] I didn't do it! I didn't do it! [JOHNNY *turns and
stands up against an imaginary wall, legs spread out, arms behind his back.*]
SECRETARY: Oh no, we can't have arrests! We must maintain law and order.
SANCHO: But he's bilingual!
SECRETARY: Bilingual?
SANCHO: Simón que yes.[14] He speaks English! Johnny, give us some English.
[*Snap.*]
JOHNNY [*Comes downstage*]: Fuck-you!
SECRETARY: [*Gasps*]: Oh! I've never been so insulted in my whole life!
SANCHO: Well, he learned it in your school.
SECRETARY: I don't care where he learned it.
SANCHO: But he's economical!
SECRETARY: Economical?
SANCHO: Nickels and dimes. You can keep Johnny running on hamburgers,
Taco Bell tacos, Lucky Lager beer, Thunderbird wine, yesca—
SECRETARY: Yesca?

---

[10] "Strike! Strike! Brothers, leave those rows."   [11] "I come cheap. So what?"
[12] "Well . . . no, but"   [13] "Geez, the cops!"   [14] "Yeah, sure."

SANCHO: Mota.
SECRETARY: Mota?
SANCHO: Leños[15] . . . Marijuana. [*Snap;* JOHNNY *inhales on an imaginary joint.*]
SECRETARY: That's against the law!
JOHNNY [*Big smile, holding his breath*]: Yeah.
SANCHO: He also sniffs glue. [*Snap.* JOHNNY *inhales glue, big smile.*]
JOHNNY: That's too much man, ése.[16]
SECRETARY: No, Mr. Sancho, I don't think this—
SANCHO: Wait a minute, he has other qualities I know you'll love. For example, an inferiority complex. [*Snap.*]
JOHNNY [*To* SANCHO]: You think you're better than me, huh ése? [*Swings switch blade.*]
SANCHO: He can also be beaten and he bruises, cut him and he bleeds; kick him and he—[*He beats, bruises and kicks* PACHUCO.] would you like to try it?
SECRETARY: Oh, I couldn't.
SANCHO: Be my guest. He's a great scapegoat.
SECRETARY: No, really.
SANCHO: Please.
SECRETARY Well, all right. Just once [*She kicks* PACHUCO.] Oh, he's so soft.
SANCHO: Wasn't that good? Try again.
SECRETARY [*Kicks* PACHUCO]: Oh, he's so wonderful! [*She kicks him again.*]
SANCHO: Okay, that's enough, lady. You ruin the merchandise. Yes, our Johnny Pachuco model can give you many hours of pleasure. Why, the L.A.P.D. just bought twenty of these to train their rookie cops on. And talk about maintenance. Señorita, you are looking at an entirely self-supporting machine. You're never going to find our Johnny Pachuco model on the relief rolls. No, sir, this model knows how to liberate.
SECRETARY: Liberate?
SANCHO: He steals. [*Snap.* JOHNNY *rushes the* SECRETARY *and steals her purse.*]
JOHNNY: ¡Dame esa bolsa, vieja![17] [*He grabs the purse and runs. Snap by* SANCHO. *He stops.*]

[SECRETARY *runs after* JOHNNY *and grabs purse away from him, kicking him as she goes.*]

SECRETARY: No, no, no! We can't have any *more* thieves in the State Administration. Put him back.
SANCHO: Okay, we still got other models. Come on, Johnny, we'll sell you to some old lady. [SANCHO *takes* JOHNNY *back to his place.*]
SECRETARY: Mr. Sancho, I don't think you quite understand what we need. What we need is something that will attract the women voters. Something more traditional, more romantic.
SANCHO: Ah, a lover. [*He smiles meaningfully.*] Step right over here, señorita. Introducing our standard Revolucionario and/or Early California Bandit type. As you can see he is well-built, sturdy, durable. This is the International Harvester of Mexicans.
SECRETARY: What does he do?
SANCHO: You name it, he does it. He rides horses, stays in the mountains, crosses deserts, plains, rivers, leads revolutions, follows revolutions, kills, can be killed, serves as a martyr, hero, movie star—did I say movie star? Did you ever see *Viva*

---

[15] "Joints."   [16] "fellow."   [17] "Gimme that bag, old lady!"

Zapata? Viva Villa? Villa Rides? Pancho Villa Returns? Pancho Villa Goes Back? Pancho Villa Meets Abbott and Costello —

SECRETARY: I've never seen any of those.

SANCHO: Well, he was in all of them. Listen to this. [*Snap.*]

REVOLUCIONARIO   [*Scream*]: ¡VIVA VILLAAAAA!

SECRETARY: That's awfully loud.

SANCHO: He has a volume control. [*He adjusts volume. Snap.*]

REVOLUCIONARIO   [*Mousey voice*]: ¡Viva Villa!

SECRETARY: That's better.

SANCHO: And even if you didn't see him in the movies, perhaps you saw him on TV. He makes commercials. [*Snap.*]

REVOLUCIONARIO: Is there a Frito Bandito in your house?

SECRETARY: Oh yes, I've seen that one!

SANCHO: Another feature about this one he is that he is economical. He runs on raw horsemeat and tequila!

SECRETARY: Isn't that rather savage?

SANCHO: Al contrario,[18] it makes him a lover. [*Snap.*]

REVOLUCIONARIO   [*To* SECRETARY]: ¡Ay, mamasota, cochota, ven pa'ca![19] [*He grabs* SECRETARY *and folds her back—Latin-Lover style.*]

SANCHO   [*Snap.* REVOLUCIONARIO *goes back upright.*]: Now wasn't that nice?

SECRETARY: Well, it was rather nice.

SANCHO: And finally, there is one outstanding feature about this model I KNOW the ladies are going to love: He's a GENUINE antique! He was made in Mexico in 1910!

SECRETARY: Made in Mexico?

SANCHO: That's right. Once in Tijuana, twice in Guadalajara, three times in Cuernavaca.

SECRETARY: Mr. Sancho, I thought he was an American product.

SANCHO: No, but—

SECRETARY: No, I'm sorry. We can't buy anything but American-made products. He just won't do.

SANCHO: But he's an antique!

SECRETARY: I don't care. You still don't understand what we need. It's true we need Mexican models such as these, but it's more important that he be *American.*

SANCHO: American?

SECRETARY: That's right, and judging from what you've shown me, I don't think you have what we want. Well, my lunch hour's almost over; I better—

SANCHO: Wait a minute! Mexican but American?

SECRETARY: That's correct.

SANCHO: Mexican but ... [*A sudden flash.*] AMERICAN! Yeah, I think we've got exactly what you want. He just came in today! Give me a minute. [*He exits. Talks from backstage.*] Here he is in the shop. Let me just get some papers off. There. Introducing our new 1970 Mexican-American! Ta-ra-ra-ra-ra-ra-RA-RAAA!

[*Sancho brings out the* MEXICAN-AMERICAN *model, a clean-shaven middle-class type in a business suit, with glasses.*]

SECRETARY   [*Impressed*]: Where have you been hiding this one?

SANCHO: He just came in this morning. Ain't he a beauty? Feast your eyes on

[18] "On the contrary."   [19] "Hey, big mama, get over here!"

him! Sturdy U.S. STEEL frame, streamlined, modern. As a matter of fact, he is built exactly like our Anglo models except that he comes in a variety of darker shades: naugahyde, leather, or leatherette.

SECRETARY: Naugahyde.

SANCHO: Well, we'll just write that down. Yes, señorita, this model represents the apex of American engineering! He is bilingual, college educated, ambitious! Say the word "acculturate" and he accelerates. He is intelligent, well-mannered, clean—did I say clean? [*Snap.* MEXICAN-AMERICAN *raises his arm.*] Smell.

SECRETARY [*Smells*]: Old Sobaco, my favorite.

SANCHO [*Snap.* MEXICAN-AMERICAN *turns toward Sancho*]: Eric! [*To* SECRETARY.] We call him Eric García. [*To* ERIC.] I want you to meet Miss JIM-enez, Eric.

MEXICAN-AMERICAN: Miss JIM-enez, I am delighted to make your acquaintance. [*He kisses her hand.*]

SECRETARY: Oh, my, how charming!

SANCHO: Did you feel the suction? He has seven especially engineered suction cups right behind his lips. He's a charmer all right!

SECRETARY: How about boards? Does he function on boards?

SANCHO: You name them, he is on them. Parole boards, draft boards, school boards, taco quality control boards, surf boards, two-by-fours.

SECRETARY: Does he function in politics?

SANCHO: Señorita, you are looking at a political MACHINE. Have you ever heard of the OEO, EOC, COD, WAR ON POVERTY? That's our model! Not only that, he makes political speeches.

SECRETARY: May I hear one?

SANCHO: With pleasure. [*Snap.*] Eric, give us a speech.

MEXICAN-AMERICAN: Mr. Congressman, Mr. Chairman, members of the board, honored guests, ladies and gentlemen. [SANCHO *and* SECRETARY *applaud.*] Please, please. I come before you as a Mexican-American to tell you about the problems of the Mexican. The problems of the Mexican stem from one thing and one thing alone: He's stupid. He's uneducated. He needs to stay in school. He needs to be ambitious, forward-looking, harder-working. He needs to think American, American, American, AMERICAN, AMERICAN, AMERICAN. GOD BLESS AMERICA! GOD BLESS AMERICA! GOD BLESS AMERICA!! [*He goes out of control.*]

[SANCHO *snaps frantically and the* MEXICAN-AMERICAN *finally slumps forward, bending at the waist.*]

SECRETARY: Oh my, he's patriotic too!

SANCHO: Si, señorita, he loves his country. Let me just make a little adjustment here. [*Stands* MEXICAN-AMERICAN *up.*]

SECRETARY: What about upkeep? Is he economical?

SANCHO: Well, no, I won't lie to you. The Mexican-American costs a little bit more, but you get what you pay for. He's worth every extra cent. You can keep him running on dry Martinis, Langendorf bread.

SECRETARY: Apple pie?

SANCHO: Only Mom's. Of course, he's also programmed to eat Mexican food on ceremonial functions, but I must warn you: an overdose of beans will plug up his exhaust.

SECRETARY: Fine! There's just one more question: HOW MUCH DO YOU WANT FOR HIM?

SANCHO: Well, I tell you what I'm gonna do. Today and today only, because

you've been so sweet, I'm gonna let you steal this model from me! I'm gonna
let you drive him off the lot for the simple price of—let's see taxes and license
included—$15,000.

SECRETARY: Fifteen thousand DOLLARS? For a MEXICAN!

SANCHO: Mexican? What are you talking, lady? This is a Mexican-AMERICAN!
We had to melt down two pachucos, a farm worker and three gabachos[20] to
make this model! You want quality, but you gotta pay for it! This is no cheap
run-about. He's got class!

SECRETARY: Okay, I'll take him.

SANCHO: You will?

SECRETARY: Here's your money.

SANCHO: You mind if I count it?

SECRETARY: Go right ahead.

SANCHO: Well, you'll get your pink slip in the mail. Oh, do you want me to wrap
him up for you? We have a box in the back.

SECRETARY: No, thank you. The Governor is having a luncheon this afternoon,
and we need a brown face in the crowd. How do I drive him?

SANCHO: Just snap your fingers. He'll do anything you want.

[SECRETARY *snaps.* MEXICAN-AMERICAN *steps forward.*]

MEXICAN-AMERICAN: RAZA QUERIDA, ¡VAMOS LEVANTANDO ARMAS PARA
LIBERARNOS DE ESTOS DESGRACIADOS GABACHOS QUE NOS EXPLO-
TAN! VAMOS.[21]

SECRETARY: What did he say?

SANCHO: Something about lifting arms, killing white people, etc.

SECRETARY: But he's not supposed to say that!

SANCHO: Look, lady, don't blame me for bugs from the factory. He's your
Mexican-American; you bought him, now drive him off the lot!

SECRETARY: But he's broken!

SANCHO: Try snapping another finger.

[SECRETARY *snaps.* MEXICAN-AMERICAN *comes to life again.*]

MEXICAN-AMERICAN: ¡ESTA GRAN HUMANIDAD HA DICHO BASTA! Y SE
HA PUESTO EN MARCHA! ¡BASTA! ¡BASTA! ¡VIVA LA RAZA! ¡VIVA LA
CAUSA! ¡VIVA LA HUELGA! ¡VIVAN LOS BROWN BERETS! ¡VIVAN LOS
ESTUDIANTES![22] ¡CHICANO POWER!

[The MEXICAN-AMERICAN *turns toward the* SECRETARY, *who gasps and backs up. He
keeps turning toward the* PACHUCO, FARM WORKER, *and* REVOLUCIONARIO, *snapping
his fingers and turning each of them on, one by one.*]

PACHUCO [*Snap. To* SECRETARY]: I'm going to get you, baby! ¡Viva La Raza!

FARM WORKER [*Snap. To* SECRETARY]: ¡Viva la huelga! ¡Viva la Huelga! ¡VIVA LA
HUELGA!

---

[20] "Whites."

[21] "Beloved countrymen, let us take up arms to liberate ourselves from those damned whites who
exploit us! Let's go!"

[22] "This great mass of humanity has said enough! And it has begun to march! Enough! Enough!
Long live La Raza [the Chicanos]! Long live the cause! Long live the strike! Long live the Brown
Berets! Long live the students!

REVOLUCIONARIO [*Snap. To* SECRETARY]: ¡Viva la revolución! ¡VIVA LA REVOLU-CION!

[*The three models join together and advance toward the* SECRETARY *who backs up and runs out of the shop screaming.* SANCHO *is at the other end of the shop holding his money in his hand. All freeze. After a few seconds of silence, the* PACHUCO *moves and stretches, shaking his arms and loosening up. The* FARM WORKER *and* REVOLUCIONARIO *do the same.* SANCHO *stays where he is, frozen to his spot.*]

JOHNNY: Man, that was a long one, ése.[23] [*Others agree with him.*]

FARM WORKER: How did we do?

JOHNNY: Perty good, look all that lana,[24] man! [*He goes over to* SANCHO *and removes the money from his hand.* SANCHO *stays where he is.*]

REVOLUCIONARIO: En la madre, look at all the money.

JOHNNY: We keep this up, we're going to be rich.

FARM WORKER: They think we're machines.

REVOLUCIONARIO: Burros.

JOHNNY: Puppets.

MEXICAN-AMERICAN: The only thing I don't like is—how come I always got to play the goddamn Mexican-American?

JOHNNY: That's what you get for finishing high school.

FARM WORKER: How about our wages, ése?

JOHNNY: Here it comes right now. $3,000 for you, $3,000 for you, $3,000 for you, and $3,000 for me. The rest we put back into the business.

MEXICAN-AMERICAN: Too much, man. Heh, where you vatos[25] going tonight?

FARM WORKER: I'm going over to Concha's. There's a party.

JOHNNY: Wait a minute, vatos. What about our salesman? I think he needs an oil job.

REVOLUCIONARIO: Leave him to me.

[*The* PACHUCO, FARM WORKER, *and* MEXICAN-AMERICAN *exit, talking loudly about their plans for the night. The* REVOLUCIONARIO *goes over to* SANCHO, *removes his derby hat and cigar, lifts him up and throws him over his shoulder.* SANCHO *hangs loose, lifeless.*]

REVOLUCIONARIO [*To audience*]: He's the best model we got! ¡Ajua![26] [*Exit.*]
[*End.*]

QUESTIONS FOR DISCUSSION AND WRITING

1. The idea of selling stereotyped Mexicans at "Honest Sancho's Used Mexican Lot" sounds like a gag for a comedy sketch on, say, *Saturday Night Live*. But it works very well as the central metaphor for a fairly detailed satire on stereotyping. Stereotyping treats people as things, for example, so these people literally are things. What other features of stereotyping are represented here?

2. Notice that the Secretary is not an obvious racist but is interested in buying a Mexican for a superficially praiseworthy purpose: so Mexicans will

---

[23] "man." [24] "money." [25] "guys." [26] "Wow!"

be represented in the governor's administration. What is being satirized here?

3.   After presenting three stereotypes—the Farm Worker, the Pachuco, and the Revolucionario—Honest Sancho brings out the climactic stereotype, the Mexican-American. What is the satiric point here?

4.   At the end of the play, the models seem to become human, while Sancho seems to become a model ("the best model we got"). In a 1973 television production, made by Valdez himself, he used another ending; a scientist replaces people of Mexican descent with Mexican-American models. These models will become Chicanos, with their own values, rather than assimilated Mexican-Americans. In another production, the men decide to use the $15,000 to build a community center. What do you think of these various endings?

5.   In his introduction to the published texts of the *actos*, Valdez writes that the Theatro Campesino formulated the following purposes for the *actos:*

> Actos: Inspire the audience to social action. Illuminate specific points about social
>   problems. Satirize the opposition. Show or hint at a solution. Express what
>   people are feeling.

Does *Los Vendidos* seem to carry out these purposes? How? All of them equally? Some more than others?

6.   Is it appropriate to judge a play like *Los Vendidos* by the same criteria as, say, *The Tempest*? What are appropriate criteria for evaluating *Los Vendidos*?

Wakako Yamauchi

Wakako Yamauchi (b. 1924) grew up in the Imperial Valley of California. Like Masako in *And the Soul Shall Dance,* she was the daughter of truck farmers. In 1942 she and her family were confined with other Japanese-Americans at an internment camp in Poston, Arizona. Best known as a short-story writer, Yamauchi based the play on a short story she had written in 1974. (It is reprinted in the fiction section of this anthology.) She developed the short story into a play in 1977, when it was produced by the East/West Players in Los Angeles. It won the Los Angeles Critics' Circle Award for the best new play of 1977 and the American Theater Critics Association Award for the best play of 1977 not produced in New York. It has been produced frequently since and has had a television production. Yamauchi's other plays include *The Music Lessons,* about a widow and her daughter, both of whom fall in love with a farm laborer, and *12-1-A,* about a Japanese-American family incarcerated in a World War II detention camp.

AND THE SOUL SHALL DANCE

CHARACTERS

MURATA, *40, Issei*[1] *farmer.*
HANA, *Issei wife of Murata.*
MASAKO, *11, Nisei*[2] *daughter of the Muratas.*
OKA, *45, Issei farmer.*
EMIKO, *30, wife of Oka.*
KIYOKO, *14, Oka's daughter.*

PLACE AND TIME.   *The action of the play takes place on and between two small farms in Southern California's Imperial Valley in the early 1930s.*

ACT I

Scene 1

Summer 1935, afternoon. Interior of the Murata house. The set is spare. There is a kitchen table, four chairs, a bed, and on the wall, a calendar indicating the year and month: June, 1935. There is a doorway leading to the other room. Props are: a bottle of sake, two cups, a dish of chiles, a phonograph, and two towels hanging on pegs on the wall. A wide wooden bench sits outside.

The bathhouse has just burned to the ground due to the carelessness of MASAKO, *Nisei daughter, 11. Off stage there are sounds of* MURATA, *40, Issei farmer, putting out the fire.*

Inside the house HANA MURATA, *Issei wife, in a drab house dress, confronts* MASAKO (*wearing summer dress of the era*). MASAKO *is sullen and somewhat defiant.* HANA *breaks the silence.*

HANA: How could you be so careless, Masako? You know you should be extra careful with fire. How often have I told you? Now the whole bathhouse is gone. I told you time and again, when you stoke a fire, you should see that everything is swept into the fireplace.

[MURATA *enters. He's dressed in old work clothes. He suffers from heat and exhaustion.*]

MURATA: [*Coughing.*] Shack went up like a match box . . . This kind of weather dries everything . . . just takes a spark to make a bonfire out of dry timber.
HANA: Did you save any of it?
MURATA: No. Couldn't . . .
HANA: [*To* MASAKO.] How many times have I told you . . .

[MASAKO *moves nervously.*]

MURATA: No use crying about it now. *Shikata ga nai.* It's gone now. No more bathhouse. That's all there is to it.
HANA: But you've got to tell her. Otherwise she'll make the same mistake. You'll be building a bathhouse every year.

---

[1] First-generation Japanese-American.   [2] Second-generation Japanese-American.

[MURATA *removes his shirt and wipes off his face. He throws his shirt on a chair and sits at the table.*]

MURATA: *Baka!* Ridiculous!

MASAKO: I didn't do it on purpose.

[*She goes to the bed, opens a book.* HANA *follows her.*]

HANA: I know that but you know what this means? It means we bathe in a bucket ... inside the house. Carry water in from the pond, heat it on the stove ... We'll use more kerosene.

MURATA: Tub's still there. And the fireplace. We can still build a fire under the tub.

HANA: [*Shocked.*] But no walls! Everyone in the country can see us!

MURATA: Wait 'til dark then. Wait 'til dark.

HANA: We'll be using a lantern. They'll still see us.

MURATA: Angh! Who? Who'll see us? You think everyone in the country waits to watch us take a bath? Hunh? You know how stupid you sound? Ridiculous!

HANA: [*Defensively.*] It'll be inconvenient.

[HANA *is saved by a rap on the door.* OKA, *Issei neighbor, 45, enters. He is short and stout, dressed in faded work clothes.*]

OKA: Hello! Hello! Oi! What's going on here? Hey! Was there some kind of fire?

[HANA *rushes to the door to let* OKA *in. He stamps the dust from his shoes and enters.*]

HANA: Oka-san![3] You just wouldn't believe ... We had a terrible thing happen.

OKA: Yeah. Saw the smoke from down the road. Thought it was your house. Came rushing over. Is the fire out?

[MURATA *half rises and sits back again. He's exhausted.*]

MURATA: [*Gesturing.*] Oi, oi. Come in ... sit down. No big problem. It was just our bathhouse.

OKA: Just the *furoba*, eh?

MURATA: Just the bath.

HANA. Our Masako was careless and the *furoba* caught fire. There's nothing left of it but the tub.

[MASAKO *looks up from her book, pained. She makes a very small sound.*]

OKA: Long as the tub's there, no problem. I'll help you with it. [*He starts to roll up his sleeves.* MURATA *looks at him.*]

MURATA: What ... now? Now?

OKA: Long as I'm here.

HANA: Oh, Papa. Aren't we lucky to have such friends?

MURATA: [*To* HANA.] Hell, we can't work on it now. The ashes are still hot. I

---

[3] The suffix *-san* indicates respect or courtesy, like the English *Mr., Mrs.,* or *Ms.* The suffixes *-chan* and *-kun* (as in *Masako-chan* and *Nagata-kun*) are affectionate or diminutive.

just now put the damned fire out. Let me rest a while. [*To* OKA.] Oi, how about a little *sake*? [*Gesturing to* HANA.] Make *sake* for Oka-san. [OKA *sits at the table.* HANA *goes to prepare the sake. She heats it, gets out the cups and pours it for the men.*] I'm tired . . . I am *tired.*

HANA: Oka-san has so generously offered his help . . .

[OKA *is uncomfortable. He looks around and sees* MASAKO *sitting on the bed.*]

OKA: Hello, there, Masako-chan. You studying?

MASAKO: No, it's summer vacation.

MURATA: [*Sucking in his breath.*] Kids nowadays . . . no manners . . .

HANA: She's sulking because I had to scold her.

[MASAKO *makes a small moan.*]

MURATA: Drink, Oka-san.

OKA: [*Swallowing.*] Ahhh, that's good.

MURATA: Eh, you not working today?

OKA: No . . . no . . . I took the afternoon off today. I was driving over to Nagatas' when I saw this big black cloud of smoke coming from your yard.

HANA: It went up so fast . . .

MURATA: What's up at Nagatas'? [*To* HANA]. Get the chiles out. Oka-san loves chiles.

[HANA *opens a jar of chiles and puts them on a plate. She serves the men and gets her mending basket and walks to* MASAKO. MASAKO *makes room for her on the bed.*]

OKA: [*Helping himself.*] Ah, chiles. [MURATA *looks at* OKA, *the question unanswered.*] Well, I want to see him about my horse. I'm thinking of selling my horse.

MURATA: Sell your horse!

OKA: [*He scratches his head.*] The fact is, I need some money. Nagata-san's the only one around made money this year, and I'm thinking he might want another horse.

MURATA: Yeah, he made a little this year. And he's talking big . . . big! Says he's leasing twenty more acres this fall.

OKA: Twenty acres?

MURATA: Yeah. He might want another horse.

OKA: Twenty acres, eh?

MURATA: That's what he says. But you know his old woman makes all the decisions. [OKA *scratches his head.*]

HANA: They're doing all right.

MURATA: Henh. Nagata-kun's so hen-pecked, it's pathetic. Peko-peko. [*He makes motions of a hen pecking.*]

OKA: [*Feeling the strain.*] I better get over there.

MURATA: Why the hell you selling your horse?

OKA: I need cash.

MURATA: Oh, yeah. I could use some too. Seems like everyone's getting out of the depression but the poor farmers. Nothing changes for us. We go on and on planting our tomatoes and summer squash and eating them . . . Well, at least it's healthy.

HANA: Papa, do you have lumber?

MURATA: Lumber? For what?

HANA: The bath.

MURATA: [*Impatiently.*] Don't worry about that. We need more *sake* now.

[HANA *rises to serve him.*]

OKA: You sure Nagata-kun's working twenty more acres?

MURATA: Last I heard. What the hell; if you need a few bucks, I can loan you . . .

OKA: A few hundred. I need a few hundred dollars.

MURATA: Oh, a few hundred. But what the hell you going to do without a horse? Out here a man's horse is as important as his wife.

OKA: [*Seriously.*] I don't think Nagata will buy my wife. [*The men laugh, but* HANA *doesn't find it so funny.* MURATA *glances at her. She fills the cups again.* OKA *makes a half-hearted gesture to stop her.* MASAKO *watches the pantomime carefully.* OKA *swallows his drink in one gulp.*] I better get moving.

MURATA: What's the big hurry?

OKA: Like to get the horse business done.

MURATA: Ehhhh . . . relax. Do it tomorrow. He's not going to die, is he?

OKA: [*Laughing.*] Hey he's a good horse. I want to get it settled today. If Nagata-kun won't buy, I got to find someone else. You think maybe Kawaguchi . . . ?

MURATA: Not Kawaguchi . . . Maybe Yamamoto.

HANA: What is all the money for, Oka-san? Does Emiko-san need an operation?

OKA: Nothing like that . . .

HANA: Sounds very mysterious.

OKA: No mystery, Mrs. No mystery. No sale, no money, no story.

MURATA: [*Laughing.*] That's a good one. "No sale, no money, no . . ." Eh, Mama. [*He points to the empty cups.* HANA *fills the cups and goes back to* MASAKO.]

HANA: [*Muttering.*] I see we won't be getting any work done today. [*To* MASAKO]. Are you reading again? Maybe we'd still have a bath if you . . .

MASAKO: I didn't do it on purpose.

MURATA: [*Loudly.*] I sure hope you know what you're doing. Oka-kun. What'd you do without a horse?

OKA: I was hoping you'd lend me yours now and then . . . [*He looks at* HANA.] I'll pay for some of the feed.

MURATA: [*Emphatically waving his hand.*] Sure! Sure!

OKA: The fact is, I need that money. I got a daughter in Japan and I just got to send for her this year.

[HANA *comes to life. She puts down her mending and sits at the table.*]

HANA: A daughter? You have a daughter in Japan? Why, I didn't know you had children. Emiko-san and you . . . I thought you were childless.

OKA: [*Scratching his head.*] We are. I was married before.

MURATA: You son-of-a-gun!

HANA: Is that so? How old is your daughter?

OKA: Kiyoko must be . . . fifteen now. Yeah, fifteen.

HANA: Fifteen! Oh, that *would* be too old for Emiko-san's child. Is Kiyoko-san living with relatives in Japan?

OKA: [*Reluctantly.*] Yeah, with grandparents. With Shizue's parents. Well, the fact is, Shizue, that's my first wife, and Emiko were sisters. They come from a family with no sons. I was a boy when I went to work for the family . . . as an apprentice . . . they're blacksmiths. Later I married Shizue and took on the family name—you know, *yoshi*—because they had no sons.[4] My real name is Sakakihara.

MURATA: Sakakihara! That's a great name!

HANA: A magnificent name!

OKA: No one knows me by that here.

MURATA: Should have kept that . . . Sakakihara.

OKA: [*Muttering.*] I don't even know myself by that name.

HANA: And Shizue-san passed away and you married Emiko-San?

OKA: Oh, yeah. Shizue and I lived with the family for a while and we had the baby . . . that's, you know, Kiyoko . . . [*The liquor has affected him and he's become less inhibited.*] Well, while I was serving apprentice with the family, they always looked down their noses at me. After I married, it got worse . . . That old man . . . Angh! He was terrible! Always pushing me around, making me look bad in front of my wife and kid. That old man was mean . . . ugly!

MURATA: Yeah. I heard about that apprentice work—*detchi-boko* . . . Heard it was damned humiliating.

OKA: That's the God's truth!

MURATA: Never had to do it myself. I came to America instead. They say *detchi-boko* is bloody hard work.

OKA: The work's all right. I'm not afraid of work. It's the humiliation! I hated them! Pushing me around like I was still a boy . . . Me, a grown man! And married to their daughter! [MURATA *groans in sympathy.*] Well, Shizue and I talked it over and we decided the best thing was to get away. We thought if I came to America and made some money . . . you know, send her money until we had enough, I'd go back and we'd leave the family . . . you know, move to another province . . . start a small business, maybe in the city, a noodle shop or something.

MURATA: That's everyone's dream. Make money, go home and live like a king.

OKA: I worked like a dog. Sent every penny to Shizue. And then she died. She died on me!

[HANA *and* MURATA *observe a moment of silence in respect for* OKA*'s anguish.*]

HANA: And you married Emiko-san.

OKA: I didn't marry her. They married her to me! Right after Shizue died.

HANA: But Oka-san, you were lucky . . .

OKA: Before the body was cold! No respect! By proxy. The old man wrote me they were arranging a marriage by proxy for me and Emiko. They said she'd grown to be a beautiful woman and would serve me well.

HANA: Emiko-san *is* a beautiful woman.

OKA: And they sent her to me. Took care of everything! Immigration, fare, everything.

HANA: But she's your sister-in-law—Kiyoko's aunt. It's good to keep the family together.

OKA: That's what I thought. But hear this: Emiko was the favored one. Shizue was not so pretty, not so smart. They were grooming Emiko for a rich man—his name was Yamoto—lived in a grand house in the village. They sent her to

---

[4] "Yoshi is a procedure wherein a man is married into a family that has no sons and is obliged to carry the wife's family name and continue the lineage." [Yamauchi's note]

schools; you know, the culture thing: tea ceremony, you know, all that. They didn't even like me, and suddenly they married her to me.

MURATA: Yeah. You don't need all that formal training to make it over here. Just a strong back.

HANA: And a strong will.

OKA: It was all arranged. I couldn't do anything about it.

HANA: It'll be all right. With Kiyoko coming ...

OKA: [*Dubiously.*] I hope so ... I never knew human beings could be so cruel. You know how they mistreated my daughter? You know after Emiko came over, things got from bad to worse and I *never* had enough money to send to Kiyoko.

MURATA: They don't know what it's like here. They think money's picked off the ground here.

OKA: And they treated Kiyoko so bad. They told her I forgot about her. They told her I didn't care—they said I abandoned her. Well, she knew better. She wrote to me all the time and I always told her I'd send for her ... soon as I got the money. [*He shakes his head.*] I just got to do something this year.

HANA: She'll be happier here. She'll know her father cares.

OKA: Kids tormented her for not having parents.

MURATA: Kids are cruel.

HANA: Masako will help her. She'll help her get started at school. She'll make friends ... she'll be all right.

OKA: I hope so. She'll need friends. [*He considers he might be making a mistake after all.*] What could I say to her? Stay there? It's not what you think over here? I can't help her? I just have to do this thing. I just have to do this one thing for her.

MURATA: Sure ...

HANA: Don't worry. It'll work out fine.

[MURATA *gestures to* HANA. *She fills the cup.*]

MURATA: You talk about selling your horse, I thought you were pulling out.

OKA: I wish I could. But there's nothing else I can do.

MURATA: Without money, yeah ...

OKA: You can go into some kind of business with money, but a man like me ... no education ... there's no kind of job I can do. I'd starve in the city.

MURATA: Dishwashing, maybe. Janitor ...

OKA: At least here we can eat. Carrots, maybe, but we can eat.

MURATA: All the carrots we been eating 'bout to turn me into a rabbit.

[*They laugh.* HANA *starts to pour more wine for* OKA *but he stops her.*]

OKA: I better not drink any more. Got to drive to Nagata-san's yet. [*He rises and walks over to* MASAKO.] You study hard, don't you? You'll teach Kiyoko English, eh? When she gets here ...

HANA: Oh, yes. She will.

MURATA: Kiyoko-san could probably teach her a thing or two.

OKA: She won't know about American ways ...

MASAKO: I'll help her.

HANA: Don't worry, Oka-san. She'll have a good friend in our Masako. [*They move toward the door.*]

OKA: Well, thanks for the *sake.* I guess I talk too much when I drink. [*He scratches*

his head and laughs.] Oh. I'm sorry about the fire. By the way, come to my house
for your bath . . . until you build yours again.

HANA: [*Hesitantly.*] Oh, uh . . . thank you. I don't know if . . .

MURATA: Good! Good! Thanks a lot. I need a good hot bath tonight.

OKA: Tonight, then.

MURATA: We'll be there.

HANA: [*Bowing.*] Thank you very much. *Sayonara.*

OKA: [*Nodding.*] See you tonight.

[OKA *leaves.* HANA *faces her husband as soon as the door closes.*]

HANA: Papa. I don't know about going over there.

MURATA: [*Surprised.*] Why?

HANA: Well, Emiko-san . . .

MURATA: [*Irritated.*] What's the matter with you? We need a bath and Oka's
invited us over.

HANA: [*To* MASAKO.] Help me clear the table. [MASAKO *reluctantly leaves her book
and begins to clear the table.*] Papa, you know we've been neighbors already three,
four years and Emiko-san's never been very hospitable.

MURATA: She's shy, that's all.

HANA: Not just shy . . . she's strange. I feel like she's pushing me off . . . she
makes me feel like—I don't know—like I'm prying or something.

MURATA: Maybe you are.

HANA: And never put out a cup of tea . . . If she had all the training in the graces
. . . why, a cup of tea . . .

MURATA: So if you want tea, ask for it.

HANA: I can't do that, Papa. She's strange . . . I don't know . . . [*To* MASAKO.]
When we go there, be very careful not to say anything wrong.

MASAKO: I never say anything anyway.

HANA: [*Thoughtfully.*] Would you believe the story Oka-san just told? Why, I
never knew . . .

MURATA: There're lot of things you don't know. Just because a man don't . . .
talk about them, don't mean he don't feel . . . don't think about . . .

HANA: [*Looking around.*] We'll have to take something . . . There's nothing to
take . . . Papa, maybe you can dig up some carrots.

MURATA: God, Mama, be sensible. They got carrots. Everybody's got carrots.

HANA: Something . . . maybe I should make something.

MURATA: Hell, they're not expecting anything.

HANA: It's not good manners to go empty-handed.

MURATA: We'll take the *sake.*

[HANA *grimaces.* MASAKO *sees the record player.*]

MASAKO: I know, Mama. We can take the Victrola! We can play records for Mrs.
Oka. Then nobody has to talk.

[MURATA *laughs.*]

Fade out.

Scene 2

That evening. We see the exterior wall of the Okas' weathered house. There is a workable screen door and a large screened window. Outside there is a wide wooden bench that can accommodate three or four people. There is one separate chair and a lantern stands against the house.

The last rays of the sun light the area in a soft golden glow. This light grows gray as the scene progresses and it is quite dark at the end of the scene.

Through the screened window, EMIKO OKA, *Issei woman, 30, can be seen walking erratically back and forth. She wears a drab cotton dress but her grace and femininity come through. Her hair is bunned back in the style of Issei women of the era.*

OKA *sits cross-legged on the bench. He wears a Japanese summer robe* (yukata) *and fans himself with a round Japanese fan.*

The Muratas enter. MURATA *carries towels and a bottle of* sake. HANA *carries the Victrola, and* MASAKO *a package containing their* yukatas.

OKA: [*Standing to receive the Muratas.*] Oh, you've come. Welcome!
MURATA: Yah ... Good of you to ask us.
HANA: [*Bowing.*] Yes, thank you very much. [*To* MASAKO.] Say "hello," Masako.
MASAKO: Hello.
HANA: And "thank you."
MASAKO: Thank you.

[OKA *makes motion of protest.* EMIKO *stops her pacing and watches from the window.*]

HANA: [*Glancing briefly at the window.*] And how is Emiko-san this evening?
OKA: [*Turning toward the house.*] Emi! Emiko!
HANA: That's all right. Don't call her out. She must be busy.
OKA: [*Half rising.*] Emiko!

[EMIKO *comes to the door.* HANA *starts a deep bow toward the door.*]

MURATA: *Konbanwa!* (*"Good evening!"*)
HANA: *Konbanwa,* Emiko-san. I feel so bad about this intrusion. Your husband has told you, our bathhouse was destroyed by fire and he graciously invited us to come use yours.

[EMIKO *shakes her head.*]

OKA: I didn't have a chance to ...

[HANA *recovers and nudges* MASAKO.]

HANA: Say hello to Mrs. Oka.
MASAKO: Hello, Mrs. Oka.

[HANA *lowers the Victrola on the bench.*]

OKA: What's this? You brought a phonograph?
MASAKO: It's a Victrola.

HANA: [*Laughing indulgently.*] Yes. Masako wanted to bring this over and play
   some records.
MURATA: [*Extending the wine.*] Brought a little *sake* too.
OKA: [*Taking the bottle*] Ah, now that I like. Emiko, bring out the cups.

[*He waves at his wife, but she doesn't move. He starts to ask again, but decides to get them
himself. He enters the house and returns with two cups. EMIKO seats herself on the single
chair. The Muratas unload their paraphernalia; OKA pours the wine, the men drink, HANA
chatters and sorts the records, MASAKO stands by, helping her.*]

HANA: Yes, our Masako loves to play records. I like records too . . . and Papa,
   he . . .
MURATA: [*Watching* EMIKO.] They take me back home. The only way I can get
   there . . . in my mind.
HANA: Do you like music, Emiko-san? [EMIKO *looks vague but smiles faintly.*] Oka-
   san, you like them, don't you?
OKA: Yeah. But I don't have a player. No chance to hear them.
MURATA: I had to get this for them. They wouldn't leave me alone until I got it.
   Well . . . a phonograph . . . what the hell, they got to have *some* fun.
HANA: We don't have to play them, if you'd rather not . . .
OKA: Play. Play them.
HANA;   I thought we could listen to them and relax. [*She extends some records to*
   EMIKO.] Would you like to look through these, Emiko-san? [EMIKO *doesn't re-
   spond. She pulls out a sack of Bull Durham and starts to roll a cigarette.* HANA *pushes*
   MASAKO *to her.*] Take these to her. [MASAKO *moves toward* EMIKO *with the records.*
   MASAKO *stands watching her as she lights her cigarette.*] Some of these are very old.
   You might know them, Emiko-san. [*She sees* MASAKO *watching* EMIKO.] Masako,
   bring those over here. [*She laughs uncomfortably.*] You might like this one, Emiko-
   san. . . [*She starts the player.*] Do you know it?

[*The record whines out* "Kago No Tori."[5] EMIKO *listens with her head cocked. She smokes
her cigarette. She becomes wrapped in nostalgia and memories of the past.* MASAKO *watches
her carefully.*]

MASAKO: [*Whispering.*] Mama, she's crying.

[*Startled,* HANA *and* MURATA *look toward* EMIKO.]

HANA: [*Pinching* MASAKO.] Shhh. The smoke is in her eyes.
MURATA: Did you bring the record I like, Mama?

[EMIKO *rises abruptly and enters the house.*]

MASAKO: There were tears, Mama.
HANA: From yawning. Masako. [*Regretfully, to* OKA.] I'm afraid we've offended
   her.
OKA: [*Unaware.*] Hunh? Aw . . . no . . . pay no attention . . . no offense . . .

---

[5] "The Caged Bird." The lyrics appear at the end of the play.

[MASAKO *looks toward the window.* EMIKO *stands forlornly and slowly drifts into a dance.*]

HANA: I'm very sorry. Children, you know ... they'll say anything, anything that's on their minds.

[MURATA *notices* MASAKO *watching* EMIKO *through the window and tries to divert her attention.*]

MURATA: The needles. Masako, where're the needles?
MASAKO: [*Still watching.*] I forgot them.

[HANA *sees what's going on.* OKA *is unaware.*]

HANA: Masako, go take your bath now. Masako ...

[MASAKO *reluctantly picks up her towel and leaves.*]

OKA: Yeah, yeah ... take your bath.
MURATA: [*Sees* EMIKO *still dancing.*] Change the record, Mama.
OKA: [*Still unaware.*] That's kind of sad.
MURATA: No use to get sick over a record. We're supposed to enjoy.

[HANA *stops the record.* EMIKO *disappears from the window.* HANA *selects a lively* ondo— *"Tokyo Ondo."*]

HANA: We'll find something more fun. [*The three begin to tap to the music.*] Can't you just see the festival? The dancers, the bright *kimonos*, the paper lanterns bobbing in the wind, the fireflies ... How nostalgic ... Oh, how nostalgic ...

[*From the side of the house* EMIKO *appears. Her hair is down, she wears an old straw hat. She dances in front of the Muratas. They're startled. After the first shock, they watch with frozen smiles. They try to join* EMIKO*'s mood but something is missing.* OKA *is grieved. He finally stands as though he's had enough.* EMIKO, *now close to the door, ducks into the house.*]

HANA: That was pretty ... very nice ...

[OKA *settles down and grunts.* MURATA *clears his throat and* MASAKO *returns from her bath.*]

MURATA: You're done already? [*He's glad to see her.*]
MASAKO: I wasn't very dirty. The water was too hot.
MURATA: Good! Just the way I like it.
HANA: Not dirty?
MURATA: [*Picking up his towel.*] Come on, Mama ... scrub my back.
HANA: [*Laughing embarrassedly.*] Oh, oh ... well ... [*She stops the player.*] Masako, now don't forget ... crank the machine and change the needle now and then.
MASAKO: I didn't bring them.
HANA: Oh. Oh ... all right. I'll be back soon ... don't forget ... crank.

[*She leaves with her husband.* OKA *and* MASAKO *are alone.* OKA *is awkward and falsely hearty.*]

OKA: So! So you don't like hot baths, eh?

MASAKO: Not too hot.

OKA: [*Laughing.*] I thought you like it real hot. Hot enough to burn the house down. That's a little joke. [MASAKO *busies herself with the records to conceal her annoyance.*] I hear you're real good in school. Always top of the class.

MASAKO: It's a small class. Only two of us.

OKA: When Kiyoko comes, you'll help her in school, yeah? You'll take care of her . . . a favor for me, eh?

MASAKO: Okay.

OKA: You'll be her friend, eh?

MASAKO: Okay.

OKA: That's good. That's good. You'll like her. She's a nice girl too. [OKA *stands, yawns, and stretches.*] I'll go for a little walk now.

[*He touches his crotch to indicate his purpose.* MASAKO *turns her attention to the records and selects one, "The Soul Shall Dance,"*[6] *and begins to sway to the music. The song draws* EMIKO *from the house. She looks out the window, sees* MASAKO *is alone and begins to slip into a dance.*]

EMIKO: Do you like that song, Masa-chan? [MASAKO *is startled and draws back. She remembers her mother's warning. She doesn't know what to do. She nods.*] That's one of my favorite songs. I remember in Japan I used to sing it so often . . . my favorite song . . . [*She sings along with the record.*]

> Akai kuchibiru
> Kappu ni yosete
> Aoi sake nomya
> Kokoro ga odoru . . .

Do you know what that means, Masa-Chan?

MASAKO: I think so . . . The soul will dance?

EMIKO: Yes, yes, that's right.

> The soul shall dance. Red lips against a glass
> Drink the green . . .

MASAKO: Wine?

EMIKO: [*Nodding*] Drink the green wine.

MASAKO: Green? I thought wine is purple.

EMIKO: [*Nodding.*] Wine is purple . . . but this is a green liqueur. [EMIKO *holds up one of the china cups as though it were crystal, and looks at it as though the light were shining through it and she sees the green liquid.*] It's good . . . it warms your heart.

MASAKO: And the soul dances.

EMIKO: Yes.

MASAKO: What does it taste like? The green wine . . .

EMIKO: Oh, it's like . . . it's like . . .

---

[6] See the full lyric at the end of the play.

[*The second verse starts. "Kurai yoru yume, Setsunasa yo, Aoi sake nomya, Yume mo odoru . . ."*]

MASAKO: In the dark night . . .
EMIKO: Dreams are unbearable . . . insufferable . . . [*She turns sad.*]
MASAKO: Drink the . . .
EMIKO: [*Nodding.*] Drink the green wine . . .
MASAKO: And the dreams will dance.
EMIKO: [*Softly.*] I'll be going back one day . . .
MASAKO: To where?
EMIKO: My home . . . Japan . . . my real home. I'm planning to go back.
MASAKO: By yourself?
EMIKO: [*Nodding.*] Oh, yes. It's a secret. You can keep a secret?
MASAKO: Unhn. I have lots of secrets . . . all my own . . . [*The music stops.* EMIKO *sees* OKA *approaching and disappears into the house.* MASAKO *attends to the record and does not know* EMIKO *is gone.*] Secrets I never tell anyone.
OKA: Secrets? What kind of secrets? What did she say?
MASAKO: Oh, Nothing.
OKA: What did you talk about?
MASAKO: Nothing . . . Mrs. Oka was talking about the song. She was telling me what it meant . . . about the soul.
OKA: [*Scoffing.*] Heh! What does she know about soul? [*Calming down.*] Ehhh . . . some people don't have them . . . souls.
MASAKO: [*Timidly.*] I thought . . . I think everyone has a soul. I read in a book . . .
OKA: [*Laughing.*] Maybe . . . maybe you're right. I'm not an educated man, you know . . . I don't know too much about books. When Kiyoko comes you can talk to her about it. Kiyoko is very . . . [*From inside the house, we hear* EMIKO *begin to sing loudly at the name* KIYOKO *as though trying to drown it out.* OKA *stops talking. Then resumes.*] Kiyoko is very smart. You'll have a good time with her. She'll learn your language fast. How old did you say you are?
MASAKO: Almost twelve.

[*By this time* OKA *and* MASAKO *are shouting, trying to be heard above* EMIKO's *singing.*]

OKA: Kiyoko is fifteen . . . Kiyoko . . . [OKA *is exasperated. He rushes into the house seething.* MASAKO *hears* OKA's *muffled rage. "Behave yourself" and "kitchigai" come through.* MASAKO *slinks to the window and looks in.* OKA *slaps* EMIKO *around.* MASAKO *reacts to the violence.* OKA *comes out.* MASAKO *returns to the bench in time. He pulls his fingers through his hair and sits next to* MASAKO. *She very slightly draws away.*] Want me to light a lantern?
MASAKO: [*Shaken.*] No . . . ye- . . . okay . . .
OKA: We'll get a little light here . . .

[*He lights the lantern as the Muratas return from their bath. They are in good spirits.*]

MURATA: Ahhhh . . . Nothing like a good hot bath.
HANA: So refreshing . . .
MURATA: A bath should be taken hot and slow. Don't know how Masako gets through so fast.
HANA: She probably doesn't get in the tub.
MASAKO: I do. [*Everyone laughs.*] Well I do.

[EMIKO *comes out. She has a large purple welt on her face. She sits on the separate chair, hands folded, quietly watching the Muratas. They look at her with alarm.* OKA *engages himself with his fan.*]

HANA: Oh! Emiko-san . . . what . . . ah-ah . . . whaa . . . [*She draws a deep breath.*] What a nice bath we had . . . such a lovely bath. We do appreciate your hos . . . pitality. Thank you so much.

EMIKO: Lovely evening, isn't it?

HANA: Very lovely. Very. Ah, a little warm, but nice . . . Did you get a chance to hear the records? [*Turning to* MASAKO.] Did you play the records for Mrs. Oka?

MASAKO: Ye- . . . no . . . The needle was . . .

EMIKO: Yes, she did. We played the records together.

MURATA: Oh, you played the songs together?

EMIKO: Yes . . . yes . . .

MURATA: That's nice . . . Masako can understand pretty good, eh?

EMIKO: She understand everything . . . everything I say.

MURATA: [*Withdrawing.*] Oh, yeah? Eh, Mama, we ought to be going . . . [*He closes the player.*] Hate to bathe and run but . . .

HANA: Yes, yes. Tomorrow is a busy day. Come, Masako.

EMIKO: Please . . . stay a little longer.

MURATA: Eh, well, we got to be going.

HANA: Why, thank you, but . . .

EMIKO: It's still quite early.

OKA: [*Indicating he's ready to say goodbye.*] Enjoyed the music. And the *sake.*

EMIKO: The records are very nice. Makes me remember Japan. I sang those songs . . . those very songs . . . Did you know I used to sing?

HANA: [*Politely.*] Why, no . . . no. I didn't know that. You must have a very lovely voice.

EMIKO: Yes.

HANA: No, I didn't know that. That's very nice.

EMIKO: Yes, I sang. My parents were very strict . . . they didn't like it. They said it was frivolous. Imagine?

HANA: Yes, I can imagine. Things were like that . . . in those days singing was not considered proper for nice . . . I mean, only for women in the profess- . . .

MURATA: We better get home, Mama.

HANA: Yes, yes. What a shame you couldn't continue with it.

EMIKO: In the city I did do some classics: the dance, and the *koto,* and the flower, and, of course, the tea . . . [*She makes the proper gesture for the different disciplines.*] All those. Even some singing . . . classics, of course.

HANA: [*Politely.*] Of course.

EMIKO: All of it is so disciplined . . . so disciplined. I was almost a *natori.*[7]

HANA: Oh! How nice.

EMIKO: But everything changed.

HANA: Oh!

EMIKO: I was sent here to America. [*She glares at* OKA.]

HANA: Oh, too bad . . . I mean, too bad about your *natori.*

MURATA: [*Loudly to* OKA.] So did you see Nagata today?

OKA: Oh, yeah. Yeah.

MURATA: What did he say? Is he interested?

---

[7] Certified performer.

OKA: Yeah. Yeah. He's interested.
MURATA: He likes the horse, eh?
OKA: Ah ... yeah.
MURATA: I knew he'd like him. I'd buy him myself if I had the money.
OKA: Well, I have to take him over tomorrow. He'll decide then.
MURATA: He'll buy ... he'll buy. You'd better go straight over to the ticket office
   and get that ticket. Before you—ha-ha—spend the money.
OKA: Ha-ha. Yeah.
HANA: It'll be so nice when Kiyoko-san comes to join you. I know you're looking
   forward to it.
EMIKO: [*Confused.*] Oh ... oh ...
HANA: Masako is so happy. It'll be good for her too.
EMIKO: I had more freedom in the city ... I lived with an aunt and she let me
   ... She wasn't so strict.

[MURATA *and* MASAKO *have their gear together and stand ready to leave.*]

MURATA: Good luck on the horse tomorrow.
OKA: Yeah, thanks.
HANA: [*Bowing.*] Many, many thanks.
OKA: [*Nodding toward the* sake.] Thanks for the *sake.*
HANA: [*Bowing again.*] Goodnight, Emiko-san. We'll see you again soon. We'll
   bring the records too.
EMIKO: [*Softly.*] Those songs ... those very songs ...
MURATA: Let's go, Mama.

[*The Muratas pull away. Light follows them and grows dark on the Okas. The Muratas
begin walking home.*]

HANA: That was uncomfortable.
MASAKO: What's the matter with ...
HANA: Shhhh!
MURATA: I guess Oka has his problems.
MASAKO: Is she really *kitchigai?*
HANA;   Of course not. She's not crazy. Don't say that word, Masako.
MASAKO: I heard Mr. Oka call her that.
HANA: He called her that?
MASAKO: I ... I think so.
HANA: You heard wrong. Masako. Emiko-san isn't crazy. She just likes her drinks.
   She had too much to drink tonight.
MASAKO: Oh.
HANA: She can't adjust to this life. She can't get over the good times she had in
   Japan. Well, it's not easy ... but one has to know when to bend ... like the
   bamboo. When the winds blow, bamboo bends. You bend or crack. Remember
   that, Masako.
MURATA: [*Laughing wryly.*] Bend, eh? Remember that, Mama.
HANA: [*Softly.*] You don't know ... it isn't ever easy.
MASAKO: Do you want to go back to Japan, Mama?
HANA: Everyone does.
MASAKO: Do you, Papa?
MURATA: I'll have to make some money first.

MASAKO: I don't. Not me. Not Kiyoko . . .

HANA: After Kiyoko-san comes, Emiko will have company and things will
straighten out. She has nothing to live on but her memories. She doesn't have
any friends. At least I have my friends at church . . . at least I have that. She must
get awful lonely.

MASAKO: I know that. She tried to make friends with me.

HANA: She did? What did she say?

MASAKO: Well, sort of . . .

HANA: What did she say?

MASAKO: She didn't say anything. I just felt it. Maybe you should be her friend,
Mama.

MURATA: Poor woman. We could have stayed longer.

HANA: But you wanted to leave. I tried to be friendly. You saw that. It's not easy
to talk to Emiko. She either closes up, you can't pry a word from her, or else she
goes on and on. . . all that . . . that . . . about the *koto* and tea and the flower . . .
I mean, what am I supposed to say? She's so unpredictable. And the drinking . . .

MURATA: All right, all right, Mama.

MASAKO: Did you see her black eye?

HANA: [*Calming down.*] She probably hurt herself. She wasn't very steady.

MASAKO: Oh, no. Mr. Oka hit her.

HANA: I don't think so.

MASAKO: He hit her. I saw him.

HANA: You saw that? Papa, do you hear that. She saw them. That does it. We're
not going there again.

MURATA: Aww . . . Oka wouldn't do that. Not in front of a kid.

MASAKO: Well, they didn't do it in front of me. They were in the house.

MURATA: You see . . .

HANA: That's all right. You just have to fix the bathhouse. Either that or we're
going to bathe at home . . . in a bucket. We're not going . . . we'll bathe at home.
[MURATA *mutters to himself.*] What?

MURATA: I said all right, it's the bucket then. I'll get to it when I can.

[HANA *passes* MURATA *and walks ahead.*]

Fade out.

Scene 3

Same evening. Lights crossfade to the exterior of the Oka house. The Muratas have just left.
EMIKO *sits on the bench. Her back is to* OKA. OKA, *still standing, looks at her contemp-*
tuously as she takes the bottle and one of the cups to pour herself a drink.

OKA: Nothing more disgusting than a drunk woman. [EMIKO *ignores him.*] You
make a fool of yourself. *Washi baka ni shite!* You make a fool of me! [EMIKO
doesn't move.]

EMIKO: One can only make a fool of one's self.

OKA: You learn that in the fancy schools, eh? [EMIKO *examines the pattern of her*
cup.] Eh? Eh? Answer me! [EMIKO *ignores.*] I'm talking to you. Answer me!
[*Menacing.*] You don't get away with that. You think you're so fine . . . [EMIKO
looks off into the horizon. OKA *turns her roughly around.*] When I talk, you listen!
[EMIKO *turns away again.* OKA *pulls the cup from her hand.*] Goddamnit! What'd

you think my friends think of you? What kind of ass they think I am? [*He grabs her shoulders.*]

EMIKO: Don't touch me . . . don't touch me.

OKA: Who the hell you think you are? "Don't touch me, don't touch me." Who the hell! High and mighty, eh? Too good for me, eh? Don't put on the act for me . . . I know who you are.

EMIKO: Tell me who I am, Mister Smart Peasant.

OKA: Shut your fool mouth, goddamnit! Sure! I'll tell you. I know all about you . . . Shizue told me. The whole village knows.

EMIKO: Shizue!

OKA: Yeah! Shizue. Embarrassed the hell out of her, your own sister.

EMIKO: Embarrassed? I have nothing to be ashamed of. I don't know what you're talking about.

OKA: [*Derisively.*] You don't know what I'm talking about. I know. The whole village knows. They're all laughing at you. At me! Stupid Oka got stuck with a second-hand woman. I didn't say anything because . . .

EMIKO: I'm not second-hand!

OKA: Who you trying to fool? I know. Knew long time ago . . . Shizue wrote me all about your affairs in Tokyo. The men you were mess- . . .

EMIKO: Affairs? Men?

OKA: That man you were messing with . . . I knew all along. I didn't say anything because you . . . I . . .

EMIKO: I'm not ashamed of it.

OKA: You're not ashamed! What the hell! Your father thought he was pulling a fast one on me . . . thought I didn't know nothing . . . thought I was some kind of dumb ass . . . I didn't say nothing because Shizue's dead . . . Shizue's dead. I was willing to give you a chance.

EMIKO: [*Laughing.*] A chance?

OKA: Yeah! A chance! Laugh! Give a *joro* another chance. Sure, I'm stupid . . . dumb.

EMIKO: I'm not a whore. I'm true . . . He knows I'm true.

OKA: True! Ha!

EMIKO: You think I'm untrue just because I let . . . let you . . . There's only one man for me.

OKA: Let me [*Obscene gesture.*] you? I can do what I want with you. Your father palmed you off on me—like a dog or cat—an animal . . . couldn't do nothing with you. Even that rich dumb Yamoto wouldn't have you. Your father—greedy father—so proud . . . making big plans for you . . . for himself. Ha! The whole village laughing at him. . . [EMIKO *hangs her head.*] Shizue told me. And she was working like a dog . . . trying to keep your goddamn father happy . . . doing my work and yours.

EMIKO: My work?

OKA: Yeah, your work too! She killed herself working! She killed herself . . . [*He has tender memories of his dull, uncomplaining wife.*] Up in the morning getting the fires started, working the bellows, cleaning the furnace, cooking, and late at night working with the sewing . . . tending the baby . . . [*He mutters.*] The goddamn family killed her. And you . . . you out there in Tokyo with the fancy clothes, doing the [*He sneers.*] dance, the tea, the flower, the *koto*, and the . . . [*Obscene gesture.*]

EMIKO: [*Hurting.*] Achhhh . . .

OKA: Did you have fun? Did you have fun on your sister's blood? [EMIKO *doesn't answer.*] Did you? He must have been a son-of-bitch . . . What would make that goddamn greedy old man send his prize mare to a plow horse like me? What kind of bum was he that your father . . .

EMIKO: He's not a bum . . . he's not a bum.

OKA: Was he Korean? Was he *Etta?* That's the only thing I could figure.

EMIKO: I'm true to him. Only him.

OKA: True? You think he's true to you? You think he waits for you? Remembers you? *Aho!* Think he cares?

EMIKO: [*Nodding quietly.*] He does.

OKA: And waits ten years? *Baka!* Go back to Japan and see. You'll find out. Go back to Japan. *Kaire!*

EMIKO: In time.

OKA: In time? How about now?

EMIKO: I can't now.

OKA: Ha! Now! Go now! Who needs you? Who needs you? You think a man waits ten years for a woman? You think you're some kind of . . . of . . . diamond . . . treasure . . . he's going to wait his life for you? Go to him. He's probably married with ten kids. Go to him. Get out! Goddamn *joro* . . . Go! Go!

[OKA *sweeps* EMIKO *off the bench.*]

EMIKO: [*Hurting.*] Ahhhh! I . . . I don't have the money. Give me money to . . .

OKA: If I had money I would give it to you ten years ago. You think I been eating this *kuso* for ten years because I like it?

EMIKO: You're selling the horse . . . Give me the . . .

OKA: [*Scoffing.*] That's for Kiyoko. I owe you nothing.

EMIKO: Ten years, you owe me.

OKA: Ten years of what? Misery? You gave me nothing. I give you nothing. You want to go, pack your bag and start walking. Try cross the desert. When you get dry and hungry, think about me.

EMIKO: I'd die out there.

OKA: Die! You think I didn't die here?

EMIKO: I didn't do anything to you.

OKA: No, no you didn't. All I wanted was a little comfort and . . . you . . . no, you didn't. No. So you die. We all die. Shizue died. If she was here, she wouldn't treat me like this . . . [*He thinks of his poor dead wife.*] Ah, I should have brought her with me. She'd be alive now. We'd be poor but happy . . . like . . . like Murata and his wife . . . and the kid . . .

EMIKO: I wish she were alive too. I'm not to blame for her dying. I didn't know . . . I was away. I loved her. I didn't want her to die . . . I . . .

OKA: [*Softening.*] I know that. I'm not blaming you for that . . . And it's not my fault what happened to you either . . . [EMIKO *is silent and* OKA *mistakes that for a change in attitude. He is encouraged.*] You understand that, eh? I didn't ask for you. It's not my fault you're here in this desert . . . with . . . with me . . . [EMIKO *weeps.* OKA *reaches out.*]. I know I'm too old for you. It's hard for me too . . . but this is the way it is. I just ask you be kinder . . . understand it wasn't my fault. Try make it easier for me . . . for yourself too.

[OKA *touches her and she shrinks from his touch.*]

EMIKO: Ach!

OKA: [*Humiliated again.*] Goddamn it! I didn't ask for you! *Aho!* If you was smart

you'd done as your father said . . . cut out that *saru shibai* with the *Etta* . . .
married the rich Yamoto. Then you'd still be in Japan. Not here to make my life
so miserable. [EMIKO *is silent.*] And you can have your *Etta* . . . and anyone else
you want. Take them all on . . . [OKA *is worn out. It's hopeless.*] God, why do we
do this all the time? Fighting, fighting all the time. There must be a better way
to live . . . there must be another way.

[OKA *waits for a response, gives up, and enters the house.* EMIKO *watches him leave and
pours herself another drink. The storm has passed, the alcohol takes over. She turns to the
door* OKA *disappeared into.*]

EMIKO: Because I must keep the dream alive . . . the dream is all I live for. I am
only in exile now. Because if I give in, all I've lived before . . . will mean nothing
. . . will be for nothing . . . Because if I let you make me believe this is all there
is to my life, the dream would die . . . I would die . . . [*She pours another drink and
feels warm and good.*]

Fade out.

ACT II

Scene 1

Mid-September, afternoon. Muratas' kitchen. The calendar reads September. MASAKO *is at
the kitchen table with several books. She thumbs through a Japanese magazine.* HANA *is with
her sewing.*

MASAKO: Do they always wear kimonos in Japan, Mama?
HANA: Most of the time.
MASAKO: I wonder if Kiyoko will be wearing a kimono like this?
HANA: [*Peering into* MASAKO's *magazine.*] They don't dress like that . . . not for
every day.
MASAKO: I wonder what she's like.
HANA: Probably a lot like you. What do you think she's like?
MASAKO: She's probably taller.
HANA: Mr. Oka isn't tall.
MASAKO: And pretty . . .
HANA: [*Laughing.*] Mr. Oka . . . Well, I don't suppose she'll look like her father.
MASAKO: Mrs. Oka is pretty.
HANA: She isn't Kiyoko-san's real mother, remember.
MASAKO: Oh. That's right.
HANA: But they are related. Well, we'll soon see.
MASAKO: I thought she was coming in September. It's already September.
HANA: Papa said Oka-san went to San Pedro a few days ago. He should be back
soon with Kiyoko-san.
MASAKO: Didn't Mrs. Oka go too?
HANA: [*Glancing toward the Oka house.*] I don't think so. I see lights in their house
at night.
MASAKO: Will they bring Kiyoko over to see us?
HANA: Of course. First thing, probably. You'll be very nice to her, won't you?

[MASAKO *leaves the table and finds another book.*]

MASAKO: Sure. I'm glad I'm going to have a friend. I hope she likes me.

HANA: She'll like you. Japanese girls are very polite, you know.

MASAKO: We have to be or our Mamas get mad at us.

HANA: Then I should be getting mad at you more often.

MASAKO: It's often enough already. Mama. [*She opens a hardback book.*] Look at this, Mama . . . I'm going to show her this book.

HANA: She won't be able to read at first.

MASAKO: I love this story. Mama, this is about people like us—settlers—it's about the prairie. We live in a prairie, don't we?

HANA: Prairie? Does that mean desert?

MASAKO: I think so.

HANA: [*Nodding and looking bleak.*] We live in a prairie.

MASAKO: It's about the hardships and the floods and droughts and how they have nothing but each other.

HANA: [*Nodding.*] We have nothing but each other. But these people—they're white people.

MASAKO: [*Nodding.*] Sure, Mama. They come from the east. Just like you and Papa came from Japan.

HANA: We come from the far far east. That's different. White people are different from us.

MASAKO: I know that.

HANA: White people among white people . . . that's different from Japanese among white people. You know what I'm saying?

MASAKO: I know that. How come they don't write books about us . . . about Japanese people?

HANA: Because we're nobodies here.

MASAKO: If I didn't read these, there'd be nothing for me . . .

HANA: Some of the things you read, you're never going to know.

MASAKO: I can dream, though.

HANA: [*Sighing.*] Sometimes the dreaming makes the living harder. Better to keep your head out of the clouds.

MASAKO: That's not much fun.

HANA: You'll have fun when Kiyoko-san comes. You can study together, you can sew, and sometimes you can try some of those fancy American recipes.

MASAKO: Mama, you have to have chocolate and cream and things like that.

HANA: We'll get them.

[*We hear the putt-putt of* OKA*'s old car.* MASAKO *and* HANA *pause and listen.* MASAKO *runs to the window.*]

MASAKO: I think it's them!

HANA: The Okas?

MASAKO: It's them! It's them!

[HANA *stands and looks out. She removes her apron and puts away her sewing.*]

HANA: Two of them. Emiko-san isn't with them. Let's go outside.

[OKA *and* KIYOKO, *14, enter.* OKA *is wearing his going-out clothes: a sweater, white shirt, dark pants, but no tie.* KIYOKO *walks behind him. She is short, chunky, broadchested and very self-conscious. Her hair is straight and banded into two shucks. She wears a conserv-*]

ative cotton dress, white socks and two-inch heels. OKA *is proud. He struts in, his chest puffed out.*]

OKA: Hello, hello ... We're here. We made it! [*He pushes* KIYOKO *forward.*] This is my daughter, Kiyoko. [*To* KIYOKO.] Murata-san ... remember I was talking about? My friends ...

KIYOKO: [*Barely audible, bowing deeply.*] *Hajime mashite yoroshiku onegai shimasu* ...

HANA: [*Also bowing formally.*] I hope your journey was pleasant.

OKA: [*While the women are still bowing, he pushes* KIYOKO *toward* MASAKO.] This is Masako-chan; I told you about her ...

[MASAKO *is shocked at* KIYOKO*'s appearance. The girl she expected is already a woman. She stands with her mouth agape and withdraws noticeably.* HANA *rushes in to fill the awkwardness.*]

HANA: Say hello, Masako. My goodness, where are your manners? [*She laughs apologetically.*] In this country they don't make much to-do about manners. [*She stands back to examine* KIYOKO.] My, my, I didn't picture you so grown up. My, my ... Tell me, how was your trip?

OKA: [*Proudly.*] We just drove in from Los Angeles just this morning. We spent the night in San Pedro and the next two days we spent in Los Angeles ... you know, Japanese town.

HANA: How nice!

OKA: Kiyoko was so excited. Twisting her head this way and that—couldn't see enough with her big eyes. [*He imitates her fondly.*] She's from the country, you know ... just a big country girl. Got all excited about the Chinese dinner—we had a Chinese dinner. She never ate it before.

[KIYOKO *covers her mouth and giggles.*]

HANA: Chinese dinner!

OKA: Oh, yeah. Duck, pakkai, chow mein, seaweed soup ... the works!

HANA: A feast!

OKA: Oh, yeah. Like a holiday. Two holidays. Two holidays in one.

HANA: [*Pushes* MASAKO *forward.*]. Two holidays in one! Kiyoko-san, our Masako has been looking forward to meeting you.

KIYOKO: [*Bowing again.*] *Hajime mashite* ...

HANA: She's been thinking of all sorts of things she can do with you: sewing, cooking ...

MASAKO: Oh, Mama.

[KIYOKO *covers her mouth and giggles.*]

HANA: It's true, Kiyoko-san. She's been looking forward to having a best friend.

[KIYOKO *giggles again and* MASAKO *pulls away.*]

OKA: Kiyoko, you shouldn't be so shy. The Muratas are my good friends and you should feel free with them. Ask anything, say anything ... right?

HANA: Of course, of course. [*She is slightly annoyed with* MASAKO.] Masako, go in and start the tea. [MASAKO *enters the house.*] I'll call Papa. He's in the yard. Papa!

Oka-san is here! [*To* KIYOKO] Now tell me, how was your trip? Did you get seasick?

KIYOKO: [*Bowing and nodding.*] *Eh* (''yes''). A little . . .

OKA: Tell her. Tell her how sick you got.

[KIYOKO *covers her mouth and giggles.*]

HANA: Oh, I know, I know, I was too. That was a long time ago. I'm sure things are improved now. Tell me about Japan . . . what is it like now? They say it's so changed . . . modern . . .

OKA: Kiyoko comes from the country . . . backwoods. Nothing changes much there from century to century.

HANA: Ah! That's true. That's why I love Japan. And you wanted to leave. It's unbelievable. To come here!

OKA: She always dreamed about it.

HANA: Well, it's not really that bad.

OKA: No, it's not that bad. Depends on what you make of it.

HANA: That's right. What you make of it. I was just telling Masako today . . .

[MURATA *enters. He rubs his hands to take off the soil and comes in grinning. He shakes* OKA*'s hand.*]

MURATA: Oi, oi . . .

OKA: Yah . . . I'm back. This is my daughter.

MURATA: No! She's beautiful!

OKA: Finally made it. Finally got her here.

MURATA: [*To* KIYOKO.] Your father hasn't stopped talking about you all summer.

HANA: And Masako too.

KIYOKO: [*Bowing.*] *Hajime mashite* . . .

MURATA: [*Acknowledging with a short bow.*] Yah. How'd you like the trip?

OKA: I was just telling your wife—had a good time in Los Angeles. Had a couple of great dinners, took in the cinema—Japanese pictures, bought her some American clothes.

HANA: Oh, you bought that in Los Angeles.

MURATA: Got a good price for your horse, eh? Lots of money, eh?

OKA: Nagata's a shrewd bargainer. Heh. It don't take much money to make her happy. She's a country girl.

MURATA: That's all right. Country's all right. Country girl's the best.

OKA: Had trouble on the way back.

MURATA: Yeah?

OKA: Fan belt broke.

MURATA: That'll happen.

OKA: Lucky I was near a gasoline station. We were in the mountains. Waited in a restaurant while it was getting fixed.

HANA: Oh, that was good.

OKA: Guess they don't see Japanese much. Stare? Terrible! Took them a long time to wait on us. Dumb waitress practically threw the food at us. Kiyoko felt bad.

HANA: Ahh! That's too bad . . . too bad. That's why I always pack a lunch when we take trips.

MURATA: They'll spoil the day for you ... those barbarians!

OKA: Terrible food too. Kiyoko couldn't swallow the dry bread and bologna.

HANA: That's the food they eat!

MURATA: Let's go in ... have a little wine. Mama, we got wine? This is a celebration.

HANA: I think so ... a little ... [*They enter the house talking.* MASAKO *has made the tea, and* HANA *begins to serve the wine.*] How is your mother? Was she happy to see you?

KIYOKO: Oh, she ... yes ...

HANA: I just know she was surprised to see you so grown up. Of course, you remember her from Japan, don't you?

KIYOKO: [*Nodding.*] *Eh* ("yes"). I can barely remember. I was very young ...

HANA: Of course. But you do, don't you?

KIYOKO: She was gone most of the time ... at school in Tokyo. She was very pretty, I remember that.

HANA: She's still very pretty.

KIYOKO: *Eh.* She was always laughing. She was much younger then.

HANA: Oh now, it hasn't been that long ago.

[MASAKO *leaves the room to go outside. The following dialogue continues muted as light goes dim in the house and focuses on* MASAKO. EMIKO *enters, is drawn to the* MURATA *window and listens.*]

OKA: We stayed at an inn on East First Street. *Shizuokaya.* Whole inn filled with Shizuoka people ... talking the old dialect. Thought I was in Japan again.

MURATA: That right?

OKA: Felt good. Like I was in Japan again.

HANA: [*To* KIYOKO.] Did you enjoy Los Angeles?

KIYOKO: [*Nodding.*] *Eh.*

OKA: That's as close as I'll get to Japan.

MURATA: *Mattakuna!* That's for sure.

[*Outside* MASAKO *becomes aware of* EMIKO.]

MASAKO: Why don't you go in?

EMIKO: Oh. Oh. Why don't you?

MASAKO: They're all grown-ups in there. I'm not grown up.

EMIKO: [*Softly.*] All grown-ups ... Maybe I'm not either. [*Her mood changes.*] Masa-chan, do you have a boy friend?

MASAKO: I don't like boys. They don't like me.

EMIKO: Oh, that will change. You will change. I was like that too.

MASAKO: Besides, there're none around here ... Japanese boys ... There are some at school, but they don't like girls.

HANA: [*Calling from the kitchen.*] Masako ...

[MASAKO *doesn't answer.*]

EMIKO: Your mother is calling you.

MASAKO: [*Answering her mother.*] *Nani?* ("What?")

HANA: [*From the kitchen.*] Come inside now.

EMIKO: You'll have a boy friend one day.

MASAKO: Not me.

EMIKO: You'll fall in love one day. Someone will make the inside of you light up, and you'll know you're in love. [*She relives her own experience.*] Your life will change . . . grow beautiful. It's good, Masa-chan. And this feeling you'll remember the rest of your life . . . will come back to you . . . haunt you . . . keep you alive . . . five, ten years . . . no matter what happens . . . keep you alive.

HANA: [*From the kitchen.*] Masako . . . come inside now.

[MASAKO *turns aside to answer and* EMIKO *slips away.*]

MASAKO: What, Mama?

[HANA *comes out.*]

HANA: Come inside. Don't be so unsociable. Kiyoko wants to talk to you.

MASAKO: [*Watching* EMIKO *leave.*] She doesn't want to talk to me. You're only saying that.

HANA: What's the matter with you? Don't you want to make friends with her?

MASAKO: She's not my friend. She's your friend.

HANA: Don't be so silly. She's only fourteen.

MASAKO: Fifteen. They said fifteen. She's your friend. She's an old lady.

HANA: Don't say that.

MASAKO: I don't like her.

HANA: Shhh! Don't say that.

MASAKO: She doesn't like me either.

HANA: Ma-chan. Remember your promise to Mr. Oka? You're going to take her to school, teach her the language, teach her the ways of Americans.

MASAKO: She can do it herself. You did.

HANA: That's not nice, Ma-chan.

MASAKO: I don't like the way she laughs.

[*She imitates* KIYOKO *holding her hand to her mouth and giggling and bowing.*]

HANA: Oh, how awful! Stop that. That's the way the girls do in Japan. Maybe she doesn't like your ways either. That's only a difference in manners. What you're doing now is considered very bad manners. [*She changes tone.*] Ma-chan. . . just wait—when she learns to read and speak, you'll have so much to say to each other. Come on, be a good girl and come inside.

MASAKO: It's just old people in there, Mama. I don't want to go in.

[HANA *calls* KIYOKO *away from the table and speaks confidentially to her.*]

HANA: Kiyoko-san, please come here a minute. Maybe it's better for you to talk to Masako alone. [KIYOKO *leaves the table and walks to* HANA *outside.*] Masako has a lot of things to tell you about . . . what to expect in school and things . . .

MURATA: [*Calling from the table.*] Mama, put out something . . . chiles . . . for Oka-san.

[HANA *leaves the two girls and enters the house.* KIYOKO *and* MASAKO *stand awkwardly,* KIYOKO *glancing shyly at* MASAKO.]

MASAKO: Do you like it here?
KIYOKO: [*Nodding.*] *Eh.*

[*There's an uncomfortable pause.*]

MASAKO: School will be starting next week . . .
KIYOKO: [*Nodding.*] *Eh.*
MASAKO: Do you want to walk to school with me?
KIYOKO: [*Nodding.*] Ah.

[MASAKO *rolls her eyes and tries again.*]

MASAKO: I leave at 7:30.
KIYOKO: Ah.

[*There's a long pause.* MASAKO *finally gives up and moves off stage.*]

MASAKO: I have to do something.

[KIYOKO *watches her leave and uncertainly moves back to the house.* HANA *looks up at* KIYOKO *coming in alone, sighs, and quietly pulls out a chair for her.*]

Fade out.

Scene 2

November night. Interior of the Murata house. Lamps are lit. The family is at the kitchen table. HANA *sews,* MASAKO *does her homework,* MURATA *reads the paper. They're dressed in warm robes and having tea. Outside thunder rolls in the distance and lightning flashes.*

HANA: It'll be *ohigan* ("an autumn festival") soon.
MURATA: Something to look forward to.
HANA: We will need sweet rice for *omochi* ("rice cakes").
MURATA: I'll order it next time I go to town.
HANA: [*To* MASAKO.] How is school? Getting a little harder?
MASAKO: Not that much. Sometimes the arithmetic is hard.
HANA: How is Kiyoko-san doing? Is she getting along all right?
MASAKO: She's good in arithmetic. She skipped a grade already.
HANA: Already? That's good news. Only November and she skipped a grade! At this rate she'll be through before you.
MASAKO: Well, she's older.
MURATA: Sure, she's older, Mama.
HANA: Has she made any friends?
MASAKO: No. She follows me around all day. She understands okay, but she doesn't talk. She talks like, you know . . . she says "ranchi" for lunch and "ranchi" for ranch too, and like that. Kids laugh and copy behind her back. It's hard to understand her.
HANA: You understand her, don't you?
MASAKO: I'm used to it. [MURATA *smiles secretly.*]
HANA: You should tell the kids not to laugh; after all, she's trying. Maybe you

should help her practice those words . . . show her what's she's doing wrong.

MASAKO: I already do. Our teacher told me to do that.

MURATA: [*Looking up from his paper.*] You ought to help her all you can.

HANA: And remember when you started school and you couldn't speak English either.

MASAKO: I help her.

[MURATA *rises and goes to the window. The night is cold. Lightning flashes and the wind whistles.*]

MURATA: Looks like a storm coming up. Hope we don't have a freeze.

HANA: If it freezes, we'll have another bad year. Maybe we ought to start the smudge pots.

MURATA: [*Listening.*] It's starting to rain. Nothing to do now but pray.

HANA: If praying is the answer, we'd be in Japan now . . . rich.

MURATA: [*Wryly.*] We're not dead yet. We still have a chance. [HANA *glares at this small joke.*] Guess I'll turn in.

HANA: Go to bed . . . go to bed. I'll sit up and worry.

MURATA: If worrying was the answer, we'd be around the world twice and in Japan. Come on, Mama. Let's go to bed. It's too cold tonight to be mad. [*There's an urgent knock on the door. The family react to it.*] Dareh da! ("Who is it!") [MURATA *goes to the door and pauses.*] Who is it!

KIYOKO: [*Weakly.*] It's me . . . help me . . .

[MURATA *opens the door and* KIYOKO *enters. She's dressed in a kimono with a shawl thrown over. Her legs are bare except for a pair of straw zori. Her hair is stringy from the rain and she trembles from the cold.*]

MURATA: My God! Kiyoko-san! What's the matter?

HANA: Kiyoko-san! What is it?

MURATA: What happened?

KIYOKO: [*Gasping.*] They're fighting . . . they're fighting.

MURATA: Ah . . . don't worry . . . those things happen. No cause to worry. Mama, make tea for her. Sit down and catch your breath. I'll take you home when you're ready.

HANA: Papa, I'll take care of it.

MURATA: Let me know when you're ready to go home.

HANA: It must be freezing out there. Try to get warm. Try to calm yourself.

MURATA: Kiyoko-san . . . don't worry.

[HANA *waves* MASAKO *and* MURATA *off.* MURATA *leaves.* MASAKO *goes to her bed in the kitchen.*]

HANA: Papa, I'll take care of it.

KIYOKO: [*Looking at* MURATA's *retreating form.*] I came to ask your help.

HANA: You ran down here without a lantern? You could have fallen and hurt yourself.

KIYOKO: I don't care . . . I don't care.

HANA: You don't know, Kiyoko-san. It's treacherous out there . . . snakes, spiders . . .

KIYOKO: I must go back . . . I . . . I . . . you . . . please come with me.

HANA: First, first, we must get you warm . . . Drink your tea.

KIYOKO: But they might kill each other. They're fighting like animals. Help me stop them!

[HANA *goes to the stove to warm a pot of soup.*]

HANA: I cannot interfere in a family quarrel.

KIYOKO: It's not a quarrel . . . it's a . . .

HANA: That's all it is. A family squabble. You'll see. Tomorrow . . .

[KIYOKO *rises and puts her hand on* HANA's *arm.*]

KIYOKO: Not just a squabble . . . please! [*She starts toward the door but* HANA *restrains her.*]

HANA: Now listen. Listen to me, Kiyoko-san. I've known your father and mother a little while now. I suspect it's been like this for years. Every family has some kind of trouble.

KIYOKO: Not like this . . . not like this.

HANA: Some have it better—some worse. When you get married, you'll understand. Don't worry. Nothing will happen. [*She takes a towel from the wall and dries* KIYOKO's *hair.*] You're chilled to the bone. You'll catch your death.

KIYOKO: I don't care . . . I want to die.

HANA: Don't be silly. It's not that bad.

KIYOKO: They started drinking early in the afternoon. They make some kind of brew and hide it somewhere in the desert.

HANA: It's illegal to make it. That's why they hide it. That home brew is poison to the body . . . and the mind too.

KIYOKO: It makes them crazy. They drink it all the time and quarrel constantly. I was in the other room studying. I try so hard to keep up with school.

HANA: We were talking about you just this evening. Masako says you're doing so well . . . you skipped a grade?

KIYOKO: It's hard . . . hard . . . I'm too old for the class and the children . . . [*She remembers all her problems and starts to cry again.*]

HANA: It's always hard in a new country.

KIYOKO: They were bickering and quarreling all afternoon. Then something happened. All of a sudden I saw them on the floor . . . hitting and . . . and . . . He was hitting her in the stomach, the face . . . I tried to stop them, but they were so . . . drunk.

HANA: There, there . . . It's probably all over now.

KIYOKO: Why does it happen like this? Nothing is right. Everywhere I go . . . Masa-chan is so lucky. I wish my life was like hers. I can hardly remember my real mother.

HANA: Emiko-san is almost a real mother to you. She's blood kin.

KIYOKO: She hates me. She never speaks to me. She's so cold. I want to love her but she won't let me. She hates me.

HANA: I don't think that's true, Kiyoko-san.

KIYOKO: I know it's true.

HANA: No. I don't think you have anything to do with it. It's this place. She hates it. This place is so lonely and alien.

KIYOKO: Then why didn't she go back? Why did they stay here?

HANA: You don't know. It's not so simple. Sometimes I think . . .

KIYOKO: Then why don't they make the best of it here? Like you?

HANA: That isn't easy either. Believe me. [*She goes to the stove to stir the soup.*] Sometimes ... sometimes the longing for homeland fills me with despair. Will I never return again? Will I never see my mother, my father, my sisters again? But what can one do? There are responsibilities here ... children ... [*She draws a sharp breath.*] And another day passes ... another month ... another year. Eventually everything passes. [*She takes the soup to* KIYOKO.] Did you have supper tonight?

KIYOKO: [*Bowing gratefully.*] Ah. When my ... my aunt gets like this, she doesn't cook. No one eats. I don't get hungry anymore.

HANA: Cook for yourself. It's important to keep your health.

KIYOKO: I left Japan for a better life here ...

HANA: It isn't easy for you, is it? But you must remember your filial duty.

KIYOKO: It's so hard.

HANA: But you can make the best of it here, Kiyoko-san. And take care of yourself. You owe that to yourself. Eat. Keep well. It'll be better, you'll see. And sometimes it'll seem worse. But you'll survive. We do, you know ... we do ... [*She looks around.*] It's getting late.

KIYOKO: [*Apprehensively.*] I don't want to go back.

HANA: You can sleep with Masako tonight. Tomorrow you'll go back. And you'll remember what I told you. [*She puts her arms around* KIYOKO, *who is overcome with self-pity and begins to weep quietly.*] Life is never easy, Kiyoko-san. Endure. Endure. Soon you'll be marrying and going away. Things will not always be this way. And you'll look back on this ... this night and you'll ...

[*There is a rap on the door.* HANA *exchanges glances with* KIYOKO *and goes to answer it. She opens it a crack.* OKA *has come looking for* KIYOKO. *He's dressed in an overcoat and holds a wet newspaper over his head.*]

OKA: Ah! I'm sorry to bother you so late at night ... the fact is ...

HANA: Oka-san ...

OKA: [*Jovially.*] Good evening, good evening ... [*He sees* KIYOKO.] Ah ... there you are ... Did you have a nice visit?

HANA: [*Irritated.*] Yes, she's here.

OKA: [*Still cheerful.*] Thought she might be. Ready to come home now?

HANA: She came in the rain.

OKA: [*Ignoring* HANA*'s tone.*] That's foolish of you, Kiyoko. You might catch cold.

HANA: She was frightened by your quarreling. She came for help.

OKA: [*Laughing with embarrassment.*] Oh! Kiyoko, that's nothing to worry about. It's just we had some disagreement ...

HANA: That's what I told her, but she was frightened all the same.

OKA: Children are ...

HANA: Not children, Oka-san. Kiyoko. Kiyoko was terrified. I think that was a terrible thing to do to her.

OKA: [*Rubbing his head.*] Oh, I ... I ...

HANA: If you had seen her a few minutes ago ... hysterical ... shaking ... crying ... wet and cold to the bone ... out of her mind with worry.

OKA: [*Rubbing his head.*] Oh ... I ... don't know what she was so worried about.

HANA: You. You and Emiko fighting like you were going to kill each other.

OKA: [*There's nothing more to hide. He lowers his head in penitence.*] Aaaaachhhhhhh ...

HANA: I know I shouldn't tell you this, but there's one or two things I have to say: You sent for Kiyoko-san and now she's here. You said yourself she had a bad time in Japan, and now she's having a worse time. It isn't easy for her in a strange new country; the least you can do is try to keep her from worrying . . . especially about yourselves. I think it's terrible what you're doing to her . . . terrible!

OKA: [*Bowing in deep humility.*] I am ashamed . . .

HANA: I think she deserves better. I think you should think about that.

OKA: [*Still in his bow.*] I thank you for this reminder. It will never happen again. I promise.

HANA: I don't need that promise. Make it to Kiyoko-san.

OKA: [*To* KIYOKO.] Come with Papa now. He did a bad thing. He'll be a good Papa from now. He won't worry his little girl again. All right? All right? [*They move to the door.*]

KIYOKO: Thank you so much. [*She takes* MURATA's *robe and tries to return it.*]

OKA: Madam. I thank you again.

HANA: [*To* KIYOKO.] That's all right. You can bring it back tomorrow. [*Aside to* KIYOKO.] Remember . . . remember what we talked about. [*Loudly.*] Goodnight, Oka-san.

[*They leave.* HANA *goes to* MASAKO, *who lies on the bed. She covers her.* MURATA *appears from the bedroom. He's heard it all. He and* HANA *exchange a glance and together they retire to their room.*]

Fade out.

Scene 3

The next morning. The Murata house and yard. HANA *and* MURATA *have already left the house to examine the rain damage in the fields.* MASAKO *prepares to go to school. She puts on a coat and picks up her books and lunch bag. Meanwhile,* KIYOKO *slips quietly into the yard. She wears a coat and carries* MURATA's *robe and sets it on the outside bench.* MASAKO *walks out and is surprised to see* KIYOKO.

MASAKO: Hi. I thought you'd be . . . sick today.

KIYOKO: Oh. I woke up late.

MASAKO: [*Scrutinizing* KIYOKO's *face.*] Your eyes are red.

KIYOKO: [*Averting her eyes.*] Oh. I . . . got . . . sand in it. Yes.

MASAKO: Do you want to use eye drops? We have eye drops in the house.

MIYOKO: Oh . . . no. That's all right.

MASAKO: That's what you call bloodshot.

KIYOKO: Oh.

MASAKO: My father gets it a lot. When he drinks too much.

KIYOKO: Oh . . .

[MASAKO *notices* KIYOKO *doesn't have her lunch.*]

MASAKO: Where's your lunch bag?

KIYOKO: I . . . forgot it.

MASAKO: Did you make your lunch today?

KIYOKO: Yes. Yes, I did. But I forgot it.

MASAKO: Do you want to go back and get it?

KIYOKO: No, that's all right. [*They are silent for a while.*] We'll be late.

MASAKO: Do you want to practice your words?

KIYOKO: [*Thoughtfully.*] Oh . . .

MASAKO: Say, "My."

KIYOKO: My?

MASAKO: Eyes . . .

KIYOKO: Eyes.

MASAKO: Are . . .

KIYOKO: Are.

MASAKO: Red.

KIYOKO: Red.

MASAKO: Your eyes are red. [KIYOKO *doesn't repeat it.*] I . . . [KIYOKO *doesn't cooperate.*] Say, "I."

KIYOKO: I.

MASAKO: Got . . .

KIYOKO: Got.

MASAKO: Sand . . . [KIYOKO *balks.*] Say, "I."

KIYOKO: [*Sighing.*] I.

MASAKO: Reft . . .

KIYOKO: Reft.

MASAKO: My . . .

KIYOKO: My.

MASAKO: Runch . . .

KIYOKO: Run . . . Lunch. [*She stops.*] Masako-san, you are mean. You are hurting me.

MASAKO: It's a joke! I was just trying to make you laugh!

KIYOKO: I cannot laugh today.

MASAKO: Sure you can. You can laugh. Laugh! Like this! [*She makes a hearty laugh.*]

KIYOKO: I cannot laugh when you make fun of me.

MASAKO: Okay, I'm sorry. We'll practice some other words then, okay? [KIYOKO *doesn't answer.*] Say, "Okay."

KIYOKO: [*Reluctantly.*] Okay . . .

MASAKO: Okay, then . . . um . . . um . . . [*She still teases and talks rapidly.*] Say . . . um . . . "She sells sea shells on the sea shore." [KIYOKO *turns away indignantly.*] Aw, come on, Kiyoko! It's just a joke. Laugh!

KIYOKO: [*Imitating sarcastically.*] Ha-ha-ha! Now you say, *"Kono kyaku wa yoku kaki ku kyaku da!"*

MASAKO: Sure! I can say it! Kono kyaku waki ku kyoku kaku . . .

KIYOKO: That's not right.

MASAKO: Koki kuki kya . . .

KIYOKO: No.

MASAKO: Okay, then. You say, "Sea sells she shells . . . shu . . . sss . . ."

[*They both laugh,* KIYOKO *with her hands over her mouth.*]

MASAKO: [*Taking* KIYOKO's *hands from her mouth.*] Not like that! Like this! [*She gives a big belly laugh.*]

KIYOKO: Like this? [*She imitates* MASAKO.]

MASAKO: Yeah, that's right! You're not mad anymore?

KIYOKO: I'm not mad anymore.

MASAKO: Okay. You can share my lunch today because we're . . .

KIYOKO: "Flends?"

[MASAKO *looks at* KIYOKO, *they giggle and move on.* HANA *and* MURATA *come in from assessing the storm's damage. They are dressed warmly.* HANA *is depressed.* MURATA *tries hard to be cheerful.*]

MURATA: It's not so bad, Mama.

HANA: Half the ranch is flooded . . . at least half.

MURATA: No-no. A quarter, maybe. It's sunny today . . . it'll dry.

HANA: The seedlings will rot.

MURATA: No, no. It'll dry. It's all right—better than I expected.

HANA: If we have another bad year, no one will lend us money for the next crop.

MURATA: Don't worry. If it doesn't drain by tomorrow, I'll replant the worst places. We still have some seed left. Yeah, I'll replant . . .

HANA: More work.

MURATA: Don't worry, Mama. It'll be all right.

HANA: [*Quietly.*] Papa, where will it end? Will we always be like this—always at the mercy of the weather—prices—always at the mercy of the Gods?

MURATA: [*Patting* HANA's *back.*] Things will change. Wait and see. We'll be back in Japan by . . . in two years . . . guarantee . . . Maybe sooner.

HANA: [*Dubiously.*] Two years . . .

MURATA: [*Finds the robe on the bench.*] Ah, look, Mama. Kiyoko-san brought back my robe.

HANA: [*Sighing.*] Kiyoko-san . . . poor Kiyoko-san . . . and Emiko-san.

MURATA: Ah, Mama. We're lucky. We're lucky, Mama.

[HANA *smiles sadly at* MURATA.]

Fade out.

Scene 4

The following spring, afternoon. Exterior of the Oka house. OKA *is dressed to go out. He wears a sweater, long-sleeved white shirt, dark pants, no tie. He puts his foot on the bench to wipe off his shoe with the palm of his hand. He straightens his sleeve, removes a bit of lint and runs his fingers through his hair. He hums under his breath.* KIYOKO *comes from the house. Her hair is frizzled with a permanent wave, she wears a gaudy new dress and a pair of new shoes. She carries a movie magazine*—Photoplay *or* Modern Screen.

OKA: [*Appreciatively.*] Pretty. Pretty.

KIYOKO: [*Turning for him.*] It's not too *hadeh?*[8] I feel strange in colors.

OKA: Oh no. Young girls should wear bright colors. There's time enough to wear gray when you get old. Old lady colors. [KIYOKO *giggles.*] Sure you want to go to the picture show? It's such a nice day . . . shame to waste in a dark hall.

KIYOKO: Where else can we go?

OKA: We can go to the Muratas.

---

[8] Gaudy.

KIYOKO: All dressed up?

OKA: Or Nagatas. I'll show him what I got for my horse.

KIYOKO: [*Laughing.*] Oh, I love the pictures.

OKA: We don't have many nice spring days like this. Here the season is short. Summer comes in like a dragon . . . right behind . . . breathing fire . . . like a dragon. You don't know the summers here. They'll scare you. [*He tousles KI-YOKO's hair and pulls a lock of it. It springs back. He shakes his head in wonder.*] Goddamn. Curly hair. Never thought curly hair could make you so happy.

KIYOKO: [*Giggling.*] All the American girls have curly hair.

OKA: Your friend Masako like it?

KIYOKO: [*Nodding.*] She says her mother will never let her get a permanent wave.

OKA: She said that, eh? Bet she's wanting one.

KIYOKO: I don't know about that.

OKA: Bet she's wanting some of your pretty dresses too.

KIYOKO: Her mother makes all her clothes.

OKA: Buying is just as good. Buying is better. No trouble that way.

KIYOKO: Masako's not so interested in clothes. She loves the pictures, but her mother won't let her go. Some day, can we take Masako with us?

OKA: If her mother lets her come. Her mother's got a mind of her own . . . a stiff back.

KIYOKO: But she's nice.

OKA: [*Dubiously.*] Oh, yeah. Can't be perfect, I guess. Kiyoko, after the harvest I'll have money and I'll buy you the prettiest dress in town. I'm going to be lucky this year. I feel it.

KIYOKO: You're already too good to me . . . dresses, shoes, permanent wave . . . movies . . .

OKA: That's nothing. After the harvest, just wait . . .

KIYOKO: Magazines . . . You do enough. I'm happy already.

OKA: You make me happy too, Kiyoko. You make me feel good . . . like a man again . . . [*That statement bothers him.*] One day you're going to make a young man happy. [KIYOKO *giggles.*] Someday we going to move from here.

KIYOKO: But we have good friends here, Papa.

OKA: Next year our lease will be up and we got to move.

KIYOKO: The ranch is not ours?

OKA: No. In America, Japanese cannot own land. We lease and move every two, three years. Next year we going to go someplace where there's young fellows. There's none good enough for you here. [*He watches* KIYOKO *giggle.*] Yeah. You going to make a good wife. Already a good cook. I like your cooking.

KIYOKO: [*A little embarrassed.*] Shall we go now?

OKA: Yeah. Put the magazine away.

KIYOKO: I want to take it with me.

OKA: Take it with you?

KIYOKO: Last time, after we came back, I found all my magazines torn in half.

OKA: [*Looking toward the house.*] Torn?

KIYOKO: This is the only one I have left.

OKA: [*Not wanting to deal with it.*] All right. All right.

[*The two prepare to leave when the door opens.* EMIKO *stands there, her hair is unkempt and she looks wild. She holds an empty can in one hand, the lid in the other.*]

EMIKO: Where is it?

[OKA *tries to make a hasty departure.*]

KIYOKO: Where is what?

[OKA *pushes* KIYOKO *ahead of him, still trying to make a getaway.*]

EMIKO: Where is it? Where is it? What did you do with it? [EMIKO *moves toward* OKA. *He can't ignore her and he stops.*]

OKA: [*With false unconcern to* KIYOKO.] Why don't you walk on ahead to the Muratas?

KIYOKO: We're not going to the pictures?

OKA: We'll go. First you walk to the Muratas. Show them your new dress. I'll meet you there.

[KIYOKO *picks up a small package and exits.* OKA *sighs and shakes his head.*]

EMIKO: [*Shaking the can.*] Where is it? What did you do with it?

OKA: [*Feigning surprise.*] With what?

EMIKO: You know what. You stole it. You stole my money.

OKA. *Your* money?

EMIKO: I've been saving that money.

OKA: Yeah? Well, where'd you get it? Where'd you get it, eh? You stole it from me! Dollar by dollar . . . You stole it from me! Out of my pocket!

EMIKO: I saved it!

OKA: From my pocket!

EMIKO: It's mine! I saved for a long time . . . Some of it I brought from Japan.

OKA: *Bakayuna!*[9] What'd you bring from Japan? Nothing but some useless kimonos. [OKA *starts to leave but* EMIKO *hangs on to him.*]

EMIKO: Give back my money! Thief!

OKA: [*Swings around and balls his fists but doesn't strike.*] Goddamn! Get off me!

EMIKO: [*Now pleading.*] Please give it back . . . please . . . please . . . [*She starts to stroke him.* OKA *pulls her hands away and pushes her from him.*] Oni!

OKA: [*Seething.*] Oni? What does that make you? *Oni baba?* Yeah, that's what you are . . . a devil!

EMIKO: It's mine! Give it back . . .

OKA: The hell! You think you can live off me and steal my money too? How stupid you think I am?

EMIKO: [*Tearfully.*] But I've paid . . . I've paid . . .

OKA: With what?

EMIKO: You know I've paid.

OKA: [*Scoffing.*] You call that paying?

EMIKO: What did you do with it?'

OKA: I don't have it.

EMIKO: It's gone? It's gone?

OKA: Yeah! It's gone. I spent it. The hell! Every last cent.

EMIKO: The new clothes . . . the curls . . . restaurants . . . pictures . . . shoes . . . My money . . . my going-home money . . .

OKA: You through?

EMIKO: What will I do? What will . . .

[9] Stupid woman.

OKA: I don't care what you do. Walk. Use your feet. Swim to Japan. I don't care.
I give you no more than you gave me. Now I don't want anything. I don't care
what you do. [*He walks away.*]

[EMIKO *still holds the empty can. Off stage we hear* OKA's *car door slam and the sound of
his old car starting off. Accustomed to crying alone, she doesn't utter a sound. Her shoulders
begin to shake, her dry soundless sobs turn to a silent laugh. She wipes the dust gently from
the can as though comforting a friend. Her movements become sensuous, her hands move on
to her own body, around her throat, over her breasts, to her hips, caressing, soothing,
reminding her of her lover's hands.*]

Fade out.

Scene 5

Same day, late afternoon. Exterior of the Murata house. The light is soft. HANA *is sweeping
the yard;* MASAKO *hangs a glass wind chime on the exposed wall.*

HANA: [*Directing* MASAKO.] There . . . there. That's a good place.
MASAKO: Here?
HANA: [*Nodding.*] It must catch the slightest breeze. [*Sighing and listening.*] It
brings back so much . . . That's the reason I never hung one before. I guess it
doesn't matter much any more . . .
MASAKO: I thought you liked to think about Japan.
HANA: [*Laughing sadly.*] I didn't want to hear the sound so often . . . get too used
to it. Sometimes you hear something too often, after a while you don't hear it
anymore . . . I didn't want that to happen. The same thing happens to feelings
too, I guess. After a while you don't feel any more. You're too young to understand that yet.
MASAKO: I understand, Mama.
HANA: Wasn't it nice of Kiyoko-san to give us the *furin?*
MASAKO: I love it. I don't know anything about Japan, but it makes me feel
something too.
HANA: Maybe someday when you're grown up, gone away, you'll hear it and
remember yourself as this little girl . . . remember this old house, the ranch, and
. . . your old mama . . .
MASAKO: That's kind of scary.

[EMIKO *enters unsteadily. She carries a bundle wrapped in a colorful scarf "furoshiki." In
the package are two beautiful kimonos.*]

HANA: Emiko-san! What a pleasant surprise! Please sit down. We were just hanging the *furin.* It was so sweet of Kiyoko-san to give it to Masako. She loves it.

[EMIKO *looks mildly interested. She acts as normal as she can throughout the scene, but at
times drops her facade, revealing her desperation.*]

EMIKO: Thank you. [*She sets her bundle on the bench but keeps her hand on it.*]
HANA: Your family was here earlier. [EMIKO *smiles vaguely.*] On their way to the
pictures, I think. [*To* MASAKO.] Make tea for us, Ma-chan.
EMIKO: Please don't . . .
HANA: Kiyoko-san was looking so nice—her hair all curly . . . Of course, in our
day, straight black hair was desirable. Of course, times change.

EMIKO: Yes.

HANA: But she did look fine. My, my, a colorful new dress, new shoes, a permanent wave—looked like a regular American girl. Did you choose her dress?

EMIKO: No . . . I didn't go.

HANA: You know, I didn't think so. Very pretty, though. I liked it very much. Of
course, I sew all Masako's clothes. It saves money. It'll be nice for you to make
things for Kiyoko-san too. She'd be so pleased. I know she'd be pleased . . .
[*While* HANA *talks,* EMIKO *plucks nervously at her package. She waits for* HANA *to stop
talking.*] Emiko-san, is everything all right?

EMIKO: [*Smiling nervously.*] Yes.

HANA: Masako, please go make tea for us. See if there aren't any more of those
crackers left. Or did you finish them? [*To* EMIKO.] We can't keep anything in
this house. She eats everything as soon as Papa brings it home. You'd never
know it, she's so skinny. We never have anything left for company.

MASAKO: We hardly ever have company anyway.

[HANA *gives her daughter a strong look, and* MASAKO *goes into the house.* EMIKO *is lost
in her own thoughts. She strokes her package.*]

HANA: Is there something you . . . I can help you with? [*Very gently.*] Emiko-san?

EMIKO: [*Suddenly frightened.*] Oh no. I was thinking . . . Now that . . . now that . . .
Masa-chan is growing up . . . older . . .

HANA: [*Relieved.*] Oh, yes. She's growing fast.

EMIKO: I was thinking . . . [*She stops, puts the package on her lap and is lost again.*]

HANA: Yes, she is growing. Time goes on fast. I think she'll be taller than me
soon. [*She laughs weakly, stops and looks puzzled.*]

EMIKO: Yes.

[EMIKO*'s depression pervades the atmosphere.* HANA *is affected by it. The two women sit in
silence. A small breeze moves the wind chimes. At the moment light grows dim on the two
lonely figures.* MASAKO *comes from the house with a tray of tea. The light returns to normal
again.*]

HANA: [*Gently.*] You're a good girl.

[MASAKO *looks first to* EMIKO *then to her mother. She sets the tray on the bench and stands
near* EMIKO, *who seems to notice her for the first time.*]

EMIKO: How are you?

[HANA *pours the tea and serves her.*]

HANA: Emiko-san, is there something I can do for you?

EMIKO: There's . . . I was . . . I . . . Masa-chan will be a young lady soon . . .

HANA: Oh, well, now I don't know about "lady."

EMIKO: Maybe she would like a nice . . . nice . . . [*She unwraps her package.*] . . . I
have kimonos . . . I wore in Japan for dancing . . . maybe she can . . . if you like,
I mean. They'll be nice on her . . . she's so slim . . .

[EMIKO *shakes out a robe.* HANA *and* MASAKO *are impressed.*]

HANA: Ohhhh! Beautiful!

MASAKO: Oh, Mama! Pretty! [HANA *and* MASAKO *finger the material.*] Gold
threads, Mama.

HANA: Brocade!

EMIKO: Maybe Masa-chan would like them. I mean for her school programs . . .
Japanese school . . .

HANA: Oh, no! Too good for country. People will be envious of us . . . wonder
where we got them.

EMIKO: I mean for festivals . . . *Obon, Hana Matsuri* . . .

HANA: Oh, but you have Kiyoko-san now. You should give them to her. Has she
seen them?

EMIKO: Oh . . . no . . .

HANA: She'll love them. You should give them to her . . . not our Masako.

EMIKO: I thought . . . I mean I was thinking of . . . if you could give me a little . . .
if you could pay . . . manage to give me something for . . .

HANA: But these gowns, Emiko-san—they're worth hundreds.

EMIKO: I know, but I'm not asking for that. Whatever you can give . . . only as
much as you can give.

MASAKO: Mama?

HANA: Masako, Papa doesn't have that kind of money.

EMIKO: Anything you can give . . . anything . . .

MASAKO: Ask Papa.

HANA: There's no use asking. I know he can't afford it.

EMIKO: [*Looking at* MASAKO.] A little at a time.

MASAKO: Mama?

HANA: [*Finally.*] No, Masako. This is a luxury. [HANA *folds the gowns and puts them
away.* MASAKO *is disappointed.* EMIKO *is devastated.* HANA *sees this and tries to find
some way to help.*] Emiko-San, I hope you understand . . . [EMIKO *is silent trying to
gather her resources.*] I know you can sell them and get the full price somewhere.
Let's see . . . a family with a lot of growing daughters . . . someone who did well
last year . . . Nagatas have no girls . . . Umedas have girls but no money . . . Well,
let's see . . . Maybe not here in this country town. Ah . . . You can take them to
the city, Los Angeles, and sell them to a store . . . or Terminal Island . . . lots of
wealthy fishermen there. Yes, that would be the place. Why, it's no problem,
Emiko-san. Have your husband take them there. I know you'll get your money.
He'll find a buyer. I know he will.

EMIKO: Yes.

[EMIKO *finishes folding and ties the scarf. She sits quietly.*]

HANA: Please have your tea. I'm sorry. . . I really would like to take them for
Masako but it just isn't possible. You understand, don't you? [EMIKO *nods.*]
Please don't feel so . . . so bad. It's not really a matter of life or death, is it?
Emiko-san?

[EMIKO *nods again.* HANA *sips her tea.*]

MASAKO: Mama? If you could ask Papa . . .

HANA: Oh, the tea is cold. Masako could you heat the kettle?

EMIKO: No more. I must be going. [*She picks up her package and rises slowly.*]

HANA: [*Looking helpless.*] So soon? Emiko-san, please stay. [EMIKO *starts to go.*]
Masako will walk with you. [*She pushes* MASAKO *forward.*]

EMIKO: It's not far.
HANA: Emiko-san? You'll be all right?
EMIKO: Yes . . . yes . . . yes . . .
HANA: [*Calling as* EMIKO *exits.*] I'm sorry, Emiko-san.
EMIKO: Yes . . .

[MASAKO *and* HANA *watch as* EMIKO *leaves. The light grows dim as though a cloud passed over.* EMIKO *exits.* HANA *strokes* MASAKO*'s hair.*]

HANA: Your hair is so black and straight . . . nice . . .

[*They stand close. The wind chimes tinkle; light grows dim. Light returns to normal.* MURATA *enters. He sees this tableau of mother and child and is puzzled.*]

MURATA: What's going on here?

[*The two women part.*]

HANA: Oh . . . nothing . . . nothing . . .
MASAKO: Mrs. Oka was here. She had two kimo- . . .
HANA: [*Putting her hand on* MASAKO*'s shoulder.*] It was nothing . . .
MURATA: Eh? What'd she want?
HANA: Later, Papa. Right now, I'd better fix supper.
MURATA: [*Looking at the sky.*] Strange how the sun comes and goes. Maybe I didn't need to irrigate—looks like rain. [*He remembers and is exasperated.*] Ach! I forgot to shut the water.
MASAKO: I'll do it, Papa.
HANA: Masako, that gate's too heavy for you.
MURATA: She can handle it. Take out the pin and let the gate fall all the way down. All the way. And put the pin back. Don't forget to put the pin back.
HANA: And be careful. Don't fall in the canal.

[MASAKO *leaves.*]

MURATA: What's the matter with that girl?
HANA: Nothing. Why?
MURATA: Usually have to beg her to do . . .
HANA: She's growing up.
MURATA: Must be that time of the month.
HANA: Oh, Papa, she's too young for that yet.
MURATA: [*Genially as they enter the house.*] Got to start some time. Looks like I'll be out-numbered soon. I'm out-numbered already.

[HANA *glances at him and quietly sets about preparations for supper.* MURATA *removes his shirt and sits at the table with a paper. Light fades slowly.*]

Fade out.

Scene 6

Same evening. Exterior, desert. There is at least one shrub. MASAKO *appears, walking slowly. From a distance we hear* EMIKO *singing the song "And the Soul Shall Dance."*

MASAKO *looks around, sees the shrub and crouches under it.* EMIKO *appears. She's dressed in her beautiful kimono tied loosely at her waist. She carries a branch of sage. Her hair is loose.*

EMIKO: *Akai kuchibiru / Kappu ni yosete / Aoi sake nomya / Kokoro ga odoru . . . Kurai yoru no yume / Setsu nasa yo . . .*

[*She breaks into a dance, laughs mysteriously, turns round and round, acting out a fantasy.* MASAKO *stirs uncomfortably,* EMIKO *senses a presence. She stops, drops her branch and walks off stage singing as she goes.*]

EMIKO: *Aoi sake nomya / Yume mo odoru . . .*

[MASAKO *watches as* EMIKO *leaves. She rises slowly and picks up the branch* EMIKO *has left. She looks at the branch, moves forward a step and looks off to the point where* EMIKO *disappeared. Light slowly fades until only the image of* MASAKO*'s face remains etched in the mind.*]

Fade out.

KOKORO GA ODORU*

Akai Kuchibiru
Kappu ni yosete
Aoi sake nomya
Kokoro ga odoru

Kurai yoru no yume
Setsu nasa yo
Aoi sake nomya
Yume mo odoru

Asa no munashisa
Yume wo chirasu
Sora to kokoro wa
Sake shidai

Futari wakare no
Samishisa yo
Hitori sake nomya
Kokoro ga odoru

* *Lyric by Wakako Yamauchi*

AND THE SOUL SHALL DANCE*

Red lips
Press against a glass
Drink the green wine
And the soul shall dance

Dark night dreams
Are unbearable
Drink the green wine
And the dreams will dance

Morning's reality
Scatter the dreams
Sky and soul
Depend on the wine

The loneliness of
The two apart
Drink the wine alone
And the soul shall dance

KAGO NO TORI**

Aitasa, mita sa ni
Kowa sa wo wasure
Kurai yomichi wo
Tada hitori

**Popular Song*

THE CAGED BIRD**

(She)
   In the desire to meet her
   And the wish to see her
   He forgets his fear and
   Walks the dark streets alone.

(He)

Aini kita no ni	Though I've come to tryst
Naze dete awanu?	Why do you not come out?
Boku no yobu koye	My voice calling you—
Wasure taka?	Have you forgotten it?

(She)

Anata no yobu koye	Your voice calling me
Wasure ma senu ga	I have not forgotten, but
Deru ni derareru	To leave, to be able to leave—
Kago no tori	No choice for the caged bird.

QUESTIONS FOR DISCUSSION AND WRITING

1. *And the Soul Shall Dance* offers an unusual opportunity to compare a fictional treatment of a story with a dramatic treatment. Reread the short story of the same title upon which this play is based. How did Yamauchi develop a very brief short story into a full-length play? What scenes are in the play that are not in the short story? What scenes are in the short story that are not in the play? What is lost by not having the narrative voice of the adult Masako looking back on this incident of her childhood? What, if anything, is gained? Compare the handling of particular scenes in the short story and the play. Notice that sometimes an incident narrated in a sentence or two in the story takes up a lengthy scene in the play.

2. *And the Soul Shall Dance* opens with Masako just having accidentally burned down the bathhouse. Is this an appropriate beginning aside from the fact that it makes it more natural for the Muratas to visit the Okas more often? Is the fire symbolic in any way?

3. Masako is the only character in the play who is a *Nisei* (second-generation Japanese-American). She has never seen Japan and must rely on the account of others for her notions of the land of her ancestors. How is Japan represented to Masako in the memories of her family and the Okas?

4. *And the Soul Shall Dance* is organized by binary oppositions. There are two families and so two houses, two married couples, two daughters, two countries (one present, the other remembered). What is the meaning of these oppositions?

5. In some ways, Emiko is the central character in the play. Is she presented on the whole sympathetically or unsympathetically? Do the other characters differ in their response to her? Is she characterized in the same way in the story and play?

6. There is an emphasis in *And the Soul Shall Dance* on watching. Masako, especially, is recurringly in the position of glimpsing a troubling tableau, culminating in the final scene, where she, hidden behind a bush, watches Emiko sing and dance. What are the effect and meaning of these scenes?

7. A major theme of *And the Soul Shall Dance* is assimilation or, more precisely, the difficulty of moving from one culture to another, preserving some things and discarding others. What difficulties do the various characters have in coming to be at home in America? What does the play seem to say in general about the topic?

Marsha Norman

Marsha Norman (b. 1947) grew up in Louisville, Kentucky. After completing a B.A. degree in philosophy at Agnes Scott College in Decatur, Georgia, she returned to Louisville to do graduate work at the University of Louisville and to work with emotionally disturbed children at Kentucky Central State Hospital. Louisville is the home of the Actors Theater, a regional theater that has had remarkable success in attracting and encouraging new playwrights. In 1976 its director, Jon Jory, asked Norman to write a play about the issue of busing to achieve racial balance in Louisville schools. Norman agreed, but before she finished, the play had turned into *Getting Out,* the story of a disturbed girl with whom Norman had worked at the hospital and who subsequently had been convicted of murder. Actors Theater produced the play in 1977; a New York production followed the next year.

Getting Out established the pattern for Norman's subsequent plays: a deeply troubled central character, usually a woman, engages in struggles that raise difficult philosophical and moral problems. This was the pattern followed, in a very different way, by *'night Mother,* a two-character play about a deeply unhappy woman with a failed marriage and a delinquent son. This woman tries to explain her decision to commit suicide to her incredulous and horrified mother; the suicide ends the play.

'night Mother won the 1983 Pulitzer Prize for Drama. *Traveler in the Dark* (1984), which had productions in Cambridge, Massachusetts, and Los Angeles, was less well received. The story of a struggle between a rationalistic doctor and his minister-father for control of the doctor's son, the play struck reviewers as too schematic in its structure and too murky in its theme. It had an obvious relevance to Norman's development as a playwright, however. Norman has written a number of other plays, including *Third and Oak: The Laundromat and the Pool Hall* (1978), *The Holdup* (1983), and *The Secret Garden* (1991).

GETTING OUT

CHARACTERS

ARLENE, *a thin, drawn woman in her
late twenties who has just served an
eight-year prison term for murder.*
ARLIE, *Arlene at various times earlier in
her life.*
BENNIE, *an Alabama prison guard in his
fifties.*
GUARD *(Evans).*
GUARD *(Caldwell).*
DOCTOR, *a psychiatrist in a juvenile
institution.*

MOTHER, *Arlene's mother.*
SCHOOL PRINCIPAL, *female.*
RONNIE, *a teenager in a juvenile
institution.*
CARL, *Arlene's former pimp and partner
in various crimes, in his late twenties.*
WARDEN, *superintendent of Pine Ridge
Correctional Institute for Women.*
RUBY, *Arlene's upstairs neighbor, a cook
in a diner, also an ex-con, in her late
thirties.*

PLAYWRIGHT'S NOTES

Arlie is the violent kid Arlene was until her last stretch in prison. Arlie may walk
through the apartment quite freely, but no one there will acknowledge her presence. Most of her scenes take place in the prison areas.

Arlie, in a sense, is Arlene's memory of herself, called up by fears, needs and
even simple word cues. The memory haunts, attacks and warns. But mainly, the
memory will not go away.

Arlie's life should be as vivid as Arlene's, if not as continuous. There must be
hints in both physical type and gesture that Arlie and Arlene are the same person,
though seen at different times in her life. They both speak with a country twang,
but Arlene is suspicious and guarded, withdrawal is always a possibility. Arlie is
unpredictable and incorrigible. The change seen in Arlie during the second act
represents a movement toward the adult Arlene, but the transition should never
be complete. Only in the final scene are they enjoyably aware of each other.

The life in the prison "surround" needs to convince without distracting. The
guards do not belong to any specific institution, but rather to all the places where
Arlene has done time.

PROLOGUE

*Beginning five minutes before the houselights come down, the following announcements are
broadcast over the loudspeaker. A woman's voice is preferred, a droning tone is essential.*

LOUDSPEAKER VOICE: Kitchen workers, all kitchen workers report immediately
to the kitchen. Kitchen workers to the kitchen. The library will not be open
today. Those scheduled for book checkout should remain in morning work
assignments. Kitchen workers to the kitchen. No library hours today. Library
hours resume tomorrow as usual. All kitchen workers to the kitchen.

Frances Mills, you have a visitor at the front gate. All residents and staff, all
residents and staff. . . . Do not, repeat, do not, walk on the front lawn today or
use the picnic tables on the front lawn during your break during lunch or
dinner.

Your attention please. The exercise class for Dorm A residents has been cancelled. Mrs. Fischer should be back at work in another month. She thanks you for your cards and wants all her girls to know she had an eight-pound baby girl.

Doris Creech, see Mrs. Adams at the library before lunch. Frances Mills, you have a visitor at the front gate. The Women's Associates' picnic for the beauty school class has been postponed until Friday. As picnic lunches have already been prepared, any beauty school member who so wishes, may pick up a picnic lunch and eat it at her assigned lunch table during the regular lunch period.

Frances Mills, you have a visitor at the front gate. Doris Creech to see Mrs. Adams at the library before lunch. I'm sorry, that's Frankie Hill, you have a visitor at the front gate. Repeat, Frankie Hill, not Francis Mills, you have a visitor at the front gate.

ACT ONE

The play is set in a dingy one-room apartment in a rundown section of downtown Louisville, Kentucky. There is a twin bed and one chair. There is a sink, an apartment-size combination stove and refrigerator, and a counter with cabinets above. Dirty curtains conceal the bars on the outside of the single window. There is one closet and a door to the bathroom. The door to the apartment opens into a hall.

A catwalk stretches above the apartment and a prison cell, stage right, connects to it by stairways. An area downstage and another stage left complete the enclosure of the apartment by playing areas for the past. The apartment must seem imprisoned.

Following the prologue, lights fade to black and the warden's voice is heard on tape.

WARDEN'S VOICE: The Alabama State Parole Board hereby grants parole to Holsclaw, Arlene, subject having served eight years at Pine Ridge Correctional Institute for the second-degree murder of a cab driver in conjunction with a filling station robbery involving attempted kidnapping of attendant. Crime occurred during escape from Lakewood State Prison where subject Holsclaw was serving three years for forgery and prostitution. Extensive juvenile records from the state of Kentucky appended hereto.

As the warden continues, light comes up on ARLENE, *walking around the cell, waiting to be picked up for the ride home.* ARLIE *is visible, but just barely, down center.*

WARDEN'S VOICE: Subject now considered completely rehabilitated is returned to Kentucky under interstate parole agreement in consideration of family residence and appropriate support personnel in the area. Subject will remain under the supervision of Kentucky parole officers for a period of five years. Prospects for successful integration into community rated good. Psychological evaluation, institutional history and health records attached in Appendix C, this document.

BENNIE'S VOICE: Arlie!

ARLENE *leaves the cell as light comes up on* ARLIE, *seated down center. She tells this story rather simply. She enjoys it, but its horror is not lost on her. She may be doing some semiabsorbing activity such as painting her toenails.*

ARLIE: So, there was this little kid, see, this creepy little fucker next door. Had glasses an somethin' wrong with his foot. I don't know, seven, maybe. Anyhow, ever time his daddy went fishin', he'd bring this kid back some frogs. They built this little fence around 'em in the backyard like they was pets or somethin'. An we'd try to go over an see 'em but he'd start screamin' to his mother to come out an git rid of us. Real snotty like. So we got sick of him bein' such a goody-goody an one night me an June snuck over there an put all his dumb ol' frogs in this sack. You never heared such a fuss. (*Makes croaking sounds*) Slimy bastards, frogs. We was plannin' to let 'em go all over the place, but when they started jumpin' an all, we just figured they was askin' for it. So, we taken 'em out front to the porch an we throwed 'em, one at a time, into the street. (*Laughs*) Some of 'em hit cars goin' by but most of 'em jus' got squashed, you know, runned over? It was great, seein' how far we could throw 'em, over back of our backs an under our legs an God, it was really fun watchin' 'em fly through the air then *splat* (*Claps hands*) all over somebody's car window or somethin'. Then the next day, we was waitin' and this little kid comes out in his backyard lookin' for his stupid frogs and he don't see any an he gets so crazy, cryin' and everything. So me an June goes over an tells him we seen this big mess out in the street, an he goes out an sees all them frogs' legs and bodies an shit all over and everwhere, an, man, it was so funny. We 'bout killed ourselves laughin'. Then his mother come out and she wouldn't let him go out an pick up all the pieces, so he jus' had to stand there watchin' all the cars go by smush his little babies right into the street. I's gonna run out an git him a frog's head, but June yellin' at me "Arlie, git over here fore some car slips on them frog guts an crashes into you." (*Pause*) I never had so much fun in one day in my whole life.

ARLIE *remains seated as* ARLENE *enters the apartment. It is late evening. Two sets of footsteps are heard coming up the stairs.* ARLENE *opens the door and walks into the room. She stands still, surveying the littered apartment.* BENNIE *is heard dragging a heavy trunk up the stairs.* BENNIE *is wearing his guard uniform. He is a heavy man, but obviously used to physical work.*

BENNIE   (*From outside*): ARLIE?
ARLENE: Arlene.
BENNIE: Arlene? (*Bringing the trunk just inside the door*)
ARLENE: Leave it. I'll git it later.
BENNIE: Oh, now, let me bring it in for you. You ain't as strong as you was.
ARLENE: I ain't as mean as I was. I'm strong as ever. You go on now. (*Beginning to walk around the room*)
ARLIE   (*Irritated, as though someone is calling her*): Lay off! (*Gets up and walks past* BENNIE)
BENNIE   (*Scoots the trunk into the room a little further*): Go on where, Arlie?
ARLENE: I don't know where. How'd I know where you'd be goin'?
BENNIE: I can't go till I know you're gonna do all right.
ARLENE: Look, I'm gonna do all right. I done all right before Pine Ridge, an I done all right at Pine Ridge. An I'm gonna do all right here.
BENNIE: But you don't know nobody. I mean, nobody nice.
ARLENE: Lay off.
BENNIE: Nobody to take care of you.
ARLENE   (*Picking up old newspapers and other trash from the floor*): I kin take care of myself. I been doin' it long enough.
BENNIE: Sure you have, an you landed yourself in prison doin' it, Arlie girl.
ARLENE   (*Wheels around*): Arlie girl landed herself in prison. Arlene is out, okay?
BENNIE: Hey, now, I know we said we wasn't gonna say nuthin' about that, but

I been lookin' after you for a long time. I been watchin' you eat your dinner for
eight years now. I got used to it, you know?

ARLENE: Well, you kin jus' git unused to it.

BENNIE: Then why'd you ask me to drive you all the way up here?

ARLENE: I didn't, now. That was all your big ideal.

BENNIE: And what were you gonna do? Ride the bus, pick up some soldier, git
yourself in another mess of trouble?

ARLIE struts back into the apartment, speaking as if to a soldier in a bar.

ARLIE: Okay, who's gonna buy me a beer?

ARLENE: You oughta go by Fort Knox on your way home.

ARLIE: Fuckin' soldiers, don't care where they get theirself drunk.

ARLENE: You'd like it.

ARLIE: Well, Arlie girl, take your pick.

ARLENE: They got tanks right out on the grass to look at.

ARLIE (*Now appears to lean on a bar rail*): You git that haircut today, honey?

BENNIE: I just didn't want you given your twenty dollars the warden gave you to
the first pusher you come across.

ARLIE laughs.

ARLENE: That's what you think I been waitin' for?

A guard appears and motions for ARLIE to follow him.

ARLIE: Yeah! I heard ya.

The guard takes ARLIE to the cell and slams the door.

BENNIE: But God almighty, I hate to think what you'd done to the first ol' bugger
tried to make you in that bus station. You got grit, Arlie girl. I gotta credit you
for that.

ARLIE (*From the cell, as she dumps a plate of food on the floor*): Officer!

BENNIE: The screamin' you'd do. Wake the dead.

ARLENE: Uh-huh.

BENNIE (*Proudly*): An there ain't nobody can beat you for throwin' plates.

ARLIE: Are you gonna clean up this shit or do I have to sit here and look at it till
I vomit?

A guard comes in to clean it up.

BENNIE: Listen, ever prison in Alabama's usin' plastic forks now on account of
what you done.

ARLENE: You can quit talkin' just anytime now.

ARLIE: Some life you got, fatso. Bringin' me my dinner then wipin' it off the
walls. (*Laughs*)

BENNIE: Some of them officers was pretty leery of you. Even the chaplain.

ARLENE: No he wasn't either.

BENNIE: Not me, though. You was just wild, that's all.

ARLENE: Animals is wild, not people. That's what he said.

ARLIE (*Mocking*): Good behavior, good behavior. Shit.

BENNIE: Now what could that four-eyes chaplain know about wild? (ARLENE *looks up sharply*) Okay. Not wild, then . . .

ARLIE: I kin git outta here anytime I want. (*Leaves the cell*)

BENNIE: But you got grit, Arlie.

ARLENE: I have said for you to call me Arlene.

BENNIE: Okay okay.

ARLENE: Huh?

BENNIE: Don't git riled. You want me to call you Arlene, then Arlene it is. Yes ma'am. Now, (*Slapping the trunk*) where do you want this? (*No response*) Arlene, I said, where do you want this trunk?

ARLENE: I don't care. (BENNIE *starts to put it at the foot of the bed*) No! (*Then calmer*) I seen it there too long. (BENNIE *is irritated*) Maybe over here. (*Points to a spot near the window*) I could put a cloth on it and sit an look out the . . . (*She pulls the curtains apart, sees the bars on the window*) What's these bars doin' here?

BENNIE (*Stops moving the trunk*): I think they're to keep out burglars, you know. (*Sits on the trunk*)

ARLENE: Yeah, I know.

ARLIE *appears at the catwalk, as if stopped during a break-in.*

ARLIE: We ain't breakin' in, cop, we're just admirin' this beautiful window.

ARLENE: I don't want them there. Pull them out.

BENNIE: You can't go tearin' up the place, Arlene. Landlord wouldn't like it.

ARLIE (*To the unseen policeman*): Maybe I got a brick in my hand and maybe I don't.

BENNIE: Not one bit.

ARLIE: An I'm standin' on this garbage can because I like to, all right?

ARLENE (*Walking back toward* BENNIE): I ain't gonna let no landlord tell me what to do.

BENNIE: The landlord owns the building. You gotta do what he says or he'll throw you out right on your pretty little behind. (*Gives her a familiar pat*)

ARLENE (*Slaps his hand away*): You watch your mouth. I won't have no dirty talk.

ARLIE: Just shut the fuck up, cop! Go bust a wino or somethin'. (*Returns to the cell*)

ARLENE (*Points down right*): Here, put the trunk over here.

BENNIE (*Carrying the trunk over to the spot she has picked*): What you got in here, anyhow? Rocks? Rocks from the rock pile?

ARLENE: That ain't funny.

BENNIE: Oh sweetie, I didn't mean nuthin' by that.

ARLENE: And I ain't your sweetie.

BENNIE: We really did have us a rock pile, you know, at the old men's prison, yes we did. And those boys, time they did nine or ten years carryin' rocks around, they was pret-ty mean, I'm here to tell you. And strong? God.

ARLENE: Well, what did you expect? (*Beginning to unpack the trunk*)

BENNIE: You're tellin' me. It was dumb, I kept tellin' the warden that. They coulda killed us all, easy, anytime, that outfit. Except, we did have the guns.

ARLENE: Uh-huh.

BENNIE: One old bastard sailed a throwin' rock at me one day, woulda took my eye out if I hadn't turned around just then. Still got the scar, see? (*Reaches up to the back of his head*)

ARLENE: You shoot him?

BENNIE: Nope. Somebody else did. I forget who. Hey! (*Walking over to the window*) These bars won't be so bad. Maybe you could get you some plants so's you don't even see them. Yeah, plants'd do it up just fine. Just fine.

ARLENE (*Pulls a cheaply framed picture of Jesus out of the trunk*): Chaplain give me this.

BENNIE: He got it for free, I bet.

ARLENE: Now, look here. The chaplain was good to me, so you can shut up about him.

BENNIE (*Backing down*): Fine. Fine.

ARLENE: Here. (*Handing him the picture*) You might as well be useful fore you go.

BENNIE: Where you want it?

ARLENE: Don't matter.

BENNIE: Course it matters. Wouldn't want me puttin' it inside the closet, would you? You gotta make decisions now, Arlene. Gotta decide things.

ARLENE: I don't care.

BENNIE (*Insisting*): Arlene.

ARLENE (*Pointing to a prominent position on the apartment wall, center*): There.

BENNIE: Yeah. Good place. See it first thing when you get up.

ARLENE *lights a cigarette, as* ARLIE *retrieves a hidden lighter from the toilet in the cell.*

ARLIE: There's ways . . . gettin' outta bars . . . (*Lights a fire in the cell, catching her blouse on fire too*)

BENNIE (*As* ARLIE *is lighting the fire*): This ol' nail's pretty loose. I'll find something better to hang it with . . . somewhere or other . . .

ARLIE *screams and the doctor runs toward her, getting the attention of a guard who has been goofing off on the catwalk.*

ARLIE: Let me outta here! There's a fuckin' fire in here!

The doctor arrives at the cell, pats his pockets as if looking for the keys.

ARLIE: Officer!

DOCTOR: Guard!

Guard begins his run to the cell.

ARLIE: It's burnin' me!

DOCTOR: Hurry!

GUARD (EVANS): I'm comin'! I'm comin'!

DOCTOR: What the hell were you—

GUARD (EVANS) (*Fumbling for the right key*): Come on, come on.

DOCTOR (*Urgent*): For Chrissake!

The guard gets the door open, they rush in. The doctor, wrestling ARLIE *to the ground, opens his bag.*

DOCTOR: Lay still, dammit.

ARLIE *collapses. The doctor gives an injection.*

DOCTOR: (*Grabbing his hand*): Ow!

GUARD (EVANS)   (*Lifting* ARLIE *up to the bed*): Get bit, Doc?

DOCTOR: You going to let her burn this place down before you start payin' attention up there?

GUARD (EVANS)   (*Walks to the toilet, feels under the rim*): Uh-huh.

BENNIE: There, that what you had in mind?

ARLENE: Yeah, thanks.

GUARD (EVANS):   She musta had them matches hid right here.

BENNIE   (*Staring at the picture he's hung*): How you think he kept his beard trimmed all nice?

ARLENE   (*Preoccupied with unloading the trunk*): Who?

BENNIE   (*Pointing to the picture*): Jesus.

DOCTOR: I'll have to report you for this, Evans.

ARLENE: I don't know.

DOCTOR: That injection should hold her. I'll check back later. (*Leaves*)

GUARD (EVANS)   (*Walking over to the bed*): Report me, my ass. We got cells don't have potties, Holsclaw. (*Begins to search her and the bed, handling her very roughly*) So where is it now? Got it up your pookie, I bet. Oh, that'd be good. Doc comin' back an me with my fingers up your . . . roll over . . . don't weigh hardly nuthin', do you, dollie?

BENNIE: Never seen him without a moustache either.

ARLENE: Huh?

BENNIE: The picture.

GUARD (EVANS):   Aw now . . . (*Finding the lighter under the mattress*) That wasn't hard at all. Don't you know 'bout hide an seek, Arlie, girl? Gonna hide somethin', hide it where it's fun to find it. (*Standing up, going to the door*) Crazy fuckin' someday-we-ain't-gonna-come-save-you bitch!

Guard slams cell door and leaves.

BENNIE: Well, Arlie girl, that ol' trunk's 'bout as empty as my belly.

ARLENE: You have been talkin' 'bout your belly ever since we left this mornin'.

BENNIE: You hungry? Them hotdogs we had give out around Nashville.

ARLENE: No. Not really.

BENNIE: You gotta eat, Arlene.

ARLENE: Says who?

BENNIE   (*Laughs*): How 'bout I pick us up some chicken, give you time to clean yourself up. We'll have a nice little dinner, just the two of us.

ARLENE: I git sick if I eat this late. Besides, I'm tired.

BENNIE: You'll feel better soon's you git somethin' on your stomach. Like I always said, "Can't plow less'n you feed the mule."

ARLENE: I ain't never heard you say that.

BENNIE: There's lots you don't know about me, Arlene. You been seein' me ever day, but you ain't been payin' attention. You'll get to like me now we're out.

ARLENE: You . . . was always out.

BENNIE: Yes sir, I'm gonna like bein' retired. I kin tell already. An I can take care of you, like I been, only now—

ARLENE: You tol' me you was jus' takin' a vacation.

BENNIE: I was gonna tell you.

ARLENE: You had some time off an nothin' to do . . .

BENNIE: Figured you knew already.

ARLENE: You said you ain't never seen Kentucky like you always wanted to. Now you tell me you done quit at the prison?

BENNIE: They wouldn't let me drive you up here if I was still on the payroll, you know. Rules, against the rules. Coulda got me in big trouble doin' that.

ARLENE: You ain't goin' back to Pine Ridge?

BENNIE: Nope.

ARLENE: An you drove me all the way up here plannin' to stay here?

BENNIE: I was thinkin' on it.

ARLENE: Well what are you gonna do?

BENNIE (*Not positive, just a possibility*): Hardware.

ARLENE: Sell guns?

BENNIE (*Laughs*): Nails. Always wanted to. Some little store with bins and barrels full of nails and screws. Count 'em out. Put 'em in little sacks.

ARLENE: I don't need nobody hangin' around remindin' me where I been.

BENNIE: We had us a good time drivin' up here, didn't we? You throwin' that tomato outta the car . . . hit that no litterin' sign square in the middle. (*Grabs her arm as if to feel the muscle*) Good arm you got.

ARLENE (*Pulling away sharply*): Don't you go grabbin' me.

BENNIE: Listen, you take off them clothes and have yourself a nice hot bath. (*Heading for the bathroom*) See, I'll start the water. And me, I'll go get us some chicken. (*Coming out of the bathroom*) You like slaw or potato salad?

ARLENE: Don't matter.

BENNIE (*Asking her to decide*): Arlene . . .

ARLENE: Slaw.

BENNIE: One big bucket of slaw comin' right up. An extra rolls. You have a nice bath, now, you hear? I'll take my time so's you don't have to hurry fixin' yourself up.

ARLENE: I ain't gonna do no fixin'.

BENNIE (*A knowing smile*): I know how you gals are when you get in the tub. You got any bubbles?

ARLENE: What?

BENNIE: Bubbles. You know, stuff to make bubbles with. Bubble bath.

ARLENE: I thought you was goin'.

BENNIE: Right. Right. Goin' right now.

BENNIE *leaves, locking the door behind him. He has left his hat on the bed.* ARLENE *checks the stove and refrigerator.*

GUARD (CALDWELL) (*Opening the cell door, carrying a plastic dinner carton*): Got your grub, girlie.

ARLIE: Get out!

GUARD (CALDWELL): Can't. Doc says you gotta take the sun today.

ARLIE: You take it! I ain't hungry.

The guard and ARLIE *begin to walk to the downstage table area.*

GUARD (CALDWELL): You gotta eat, Arlie.

ARLIE: Says who?

GUARD (CALDWELL): Says me. Says the warden. Says the Department of Corrections. Brung you two rolls.

ARLIE: And you know what you can do with your—

GUARD (CALDWELL):   Stuff 'em in your bra, why don't you?

ARLIE: Ain't you got somebody to go beat up somewhere?

GUARD (CALDWELL):   Gotta see you get fattened up.

ARLIE: What do you care?

ARLENE goes into the bathroom.

GUARD (CALDWELL):   Oh, we care all right. (*Setting the food down on the table*) Got us a two-way mirror in the shower room. (*She looks up, hostile*) And you don't know which one it is, do you? (*He forces her onto the seat*) Yes ma'am. Eat. (*Pointing to the food*) We sure do care if you go gittin' too skinny. (*Walks away but continues to watch her*) Yes ma'am. We care a hog-lickin' lot.

ARLIE   (*Throws the whole carton at him*): Sons-a-bitches!

Mother's knock is heard on the apartment door.

MOTHER'S VOICE: Arlie? Arlie girl you in there?

ARLENE walks out of the bathroom. She stands still, looking at the door. ARLIE hears the knock at the same time and slips into the apartment and over to the bed, putting the pillow between her legs and holding the yellow teddy bear ARLENE has unpacked. The knocking gets louder.

MOTHER'S VOICE: Arlie?

ARLIE   (*Pulling herself up weakly on one elbow, speaking with the voice of a very young child*): Mama? Mama?

ARLENE walks slowly toward the door.

MOTHER'S VOICE   (*Now pulling the door knob from the outside, angry that the door is locked*): Arlie? I know you're in there.

ARLIE: I can't git up, Mama. (*Hands between her legs*) My legs is hurt.

MOTHER'S VOICE: What's takin' you so long?

ARLENE   (*Smoothing out her dress*): Yeah, I'm comin'. (*Puts BENNIE's hat out of sight under the bed*) Hold on.

MOTHER'S VOICE: I brung you some stuff but I ain't gonna stay here all night.

ARLENE opens the door and stands back. MOTHER looks strong but badly worn. She is wearing her cab driver's uniform and is carrying a plastic laundry basket stuffed with cleaning fluids, towels, bug spray, etc.

ARLENE: I didn't know if you'd come.

MOTHER: Ain't I always?

ARLENE: How are you?

ARLENE moves as if to hug her. MOTHER stands still, ARLENE backs off.

MOTHER: 'Bout the same. (*Walking into the room*)

ARLENE: I'm glad to see you.

MOTHER   (*Not looking at ARLENE*): You look tired.

ARLENE: It was a long drive.

MOTHER (*Putting the laundry basket on the trunk*): Didn't fatten you up none, I see. (*Walks around the room, looking the place over*) You always was too skinny. (ARLENE *straightens her clothes again*) Shoulda beat you like your daddy did. Make you eat.

ARLIE: Nobody done this to me, Mama. (*Protesting, in pain*) No! No!

MOTHER: He weren't a mean man, though, your daddy.

ARLIE: Was . . . (*Quickly*) my bike. My bike hurt me. The seat bumped me.

MOTHER: You remember that black chewing gum he got you when you was sick?

ARLENE: I remember he beat up on you.

MOTHER: Yeah, (*Proudly*) and he was real sorry a coupla times. (*Looking in the closet*) Filthy dirty. Hey! (*Slamming the closet door.* ARLENE *jumps at the noise*) I brung you all kinda stuff. Just like Candy not leavin' you nuthin'. (*Walking back to the basket*) Some kids I got.

ARLIE (*Curling up into a ball*): No, Mama, don't touch it. It'll git well. It git well before.

ARLENE: Where is Candy?

MOTHER: You got her place so what do you care? I got her outta my house so whatta I care? This'll be a good place for you.

ARLENE (*Going to the window*): Wish there was a yard, here.

MOTHER (*Beginning to empty the basket*): Nice things, see? Bet you ain't had no colored towels where you been.

ARLENE: No.

MOTHER (*Putting some things away in cabinets*): No place like home. Got that up on the kitchen wall now.

ARLIE: I don't want no tea, Mama.

ARLENE: Yeah?

MOTHER (*Repeating* ARLENE'*s answers*): No . . . yeah? . . . You forgit how to talk? I ain't gonna be here all that long. Least you can talk to me while I'm here.

ARLENE: You ever git that swing you wanted?

MOTHER: Dish towels, an see here? June sent along this teapot. You drink tea, Arlie?

ARLENE: No.

MOTHER: June's havin' another baby. Don't know when to quit, that girl. Course, I ain't one to talk. (*Starting to pick up trash on the floor*)

ARLENE: Have you seen Joey?

ARLIE: I'm tellin' you the truth.

MOTHER: An Ray . . .

ARLIE (*Pleading*): Daddy didn't do nuthin' to me.

MOTHER: Ray ain't had a day of luck in his life.

ARLIE: Ask him. He saw me fall on my bike.

MOTHER: Least bein' locked up now, he'll keep off June till the baby gits here.

ARLENE: Have you seen Joey?

MOTHER: Your daddy ain't doin' too good right now. Man's been dyin' for ten years, to hear him tell it. You'd think he'd git tired of it an jus' go ahead . . . pass on.

ARLENE (*Wanting an answer*): Mother . . .

MOTHER: Yeah, I seen 'im. 'Bout two years ago. Got your stringy hair.

ARLENE: You got a picture?

MOTHER: You was right to give him up. Foster homes is good for some kids.

ARLIE: Where's my Joey-bear? Yellow Joey-bear? Mama?

ARLENE: How'd you see him?

MOTHER: I was down at Detention Center pickin' up Pete. (*Beginning her serious cleaning now*)

ARLENE (*Less than interested*): How is he?

MOTHER: I could be workin' at the Detention Center I been there so much. All I gotta do's have somethin' big goin' on an I git a call to come after one of you. Can't jus' have kids, no, gotta be pickin' 'em up all over town.

ARLENE: You was just tellin' me—

MOTHER: Pete is taller, that's all.

ARLENE: You was just tellin' me how you saw Joey.

MOTHER: I'm comin' back in the cab an I see him waitin' for the bus.

ARLENE: What'd he say?

MOTHER: Oh, I didn't stop. (ARLENE *looks up quickly, hurt and angry*) If the kid don't even know you, Arlie, he sure ain't gonna know who I am.

ARLENE: How come he couldn't stay at Shirley's?

MOTHER: 'Cause Shirley never was crazy about washin' more diapers. She's the only smart kid I got. Anyway, social worker only put him there till she could find him a foster home.

ARLENE: But I coulda seen him.

MOTHER: Thatta been trouble, him bein' in the family. Kid wouldn't have known who to listen to, Shirley or you.

ARLENE: But I'm his mother.

MOTHER: See, now you don't have to be worryin' about him. No kids, no worryin'.

ARLENE: He just had his birthday, you know.

ARLIE: Don't let Daddy come in here, Mama. Just you an me. Mama?

ARLENE: When I git workin', I'll git a nice rug for this place. He could come live here with me.

MOTHER: Fat chance.

ARLENE: I done my time.

MOTHER: You never really got attached to him anyway.

ARLENE: How do you know that?

MOTHER: Now don't you go gettin' het up. I'm telling you . . .

ARLENE: But . . .

MOTHER: Kids need rules to go by an he'll get 'em over there.

ARLIE (*Screaming*): No Daddy! I didn't tell her nuthin'. I didn't! I didn't! (*Gets up from the bed, terrified*)

MOTHER: Here, help me with these sheets. (*Hands ARLENE the sheets from the laundry basket*) Even got you a spread. Kinda goes with them curtains. (ARLENE *is silent*) You ain't thanked me, Arlie girl.

ARLENE (*Going to the other side of the bed*): They don't call me Arlie no more. It's Arlene now.

ARLENE *and* MOTHER *make up the bed.* ARLIE *jumps up, looks around and goes over to* MOTHER's *purse. She looks through it hurriedly and pulls out the wallet. She takes some money and runs down left, where she is caught by a school principal.*

PRINCIPAL: Arlie? You're in an awfully big hurry for such a little girl. (*Brushes at* ARLIE's *hair*) That is you under all that hair, isn't it? (ARLIE *resists this gesture*) Now, you can watch where you're going.

ARLIE: Gotta git home.

PRINCIPAL: But school isn't over for another three hours. And there's peanut butter and chili today.

ARLIE: Ain't hungry. (*Struggling free*)

The principal now sees ARLIE*'s hands clenched behind her back.*

PRINCIPAL: What do you have in your hands, Arlie?

ARLIE: Nuthin'.

PRINCIPAL: Let me see your hands, Arlie. Open up your hands.

ARLIE *brings her hands around in front, opening them, showing crumpled dollars.*

ARLIE: It's my money. I earned it.

PRINCIPAL (*Taking the money*): And how did we earn this money?

ARLIE: Doin' things.

PRINCIPAL: What kind of things?

ARLIE: For my daddy.

PRINCIPAL: Well, we'll see about that. You'll have to come with me.

ARLIE *resists as the principal pulls her.*

ARLIE: No.

PRINCIPAL: Your mother was right after all. She said put you in a special school. (*Quickly*) No, what she said was put you away somewhere and I said, no, she's too young, well I was wrong. I have four hundred other children to take care of here and what have I been doing? Breaking up your fights, talking to your truant officer and washing your writing off the bathroom wall. Well, I've had enough. You've made your choice. You *want* out of regular school and you're going to *get* out of regular school.

ARLIE (*Becoming more violent*): You can't make me go nowhere, bitch!

PRINCIPAL (*Backing off in cold anger*): I'm not making you go. You've earned it. You've worked hard for this, well, they're used to your type over there. They'll know exactly what to do with you. (*She stalks off, leaving* ARLIE *alone*)

MOTHER (*Smoothing out the spread*): Spread ain't new, but it don't look so bad. Think we got it right after we got you. No, I remember now. I was pregnant with you an been real sick the whole time.

ARLENE *lights a cigarette,* MOTHER *takes one,* ARLENE *retrieves the pack quickly.*

MOTHER: Your daddy brung me home this big bowl of chili an some jelly doughnuts. Some fare from the airport give him a big tip. Anyway, I'd been eatin' peanut brittle all day, only thing that tasted any good. Then in he come with this chili an no sooner'n I got in bed I thrown up all over everwhere. Lucky I didn't throw you up, Arlie girl. Anyhow, that's how come us to get a new spread. This one here. (*Sits on the bed*)

ARLENE: You drivin' the cab any?

MOTHER: Any? Your daddy ain't drove it at all a long time now. Six years, seven maybe.

ARLENE: You meet anybody nice?

MOTHER: Not anymore. Mostly drivin' old ladies to get their shoes. Guess it got around the nursin' homes I was reliable. (*Sounds funny to her*) You remember that time I took you drivin' with me that night after you been in a fight an that soldier bought us a beer? Shitty place, hole in the wall?

ARLENE: You made me wait in the car.

MOTHER   (*Standing up*): Think I'd take a child of mine into a dump like that?

ARLENE: You went in.

MOTHER: Weren't no harm in it. (*Walking over for the bug spray*) I didn't always look so bad, you know.

ARLENE: You was pretty.

MOTHER   (*Beginning to spray the floor*): You could look better'n you do. Do somethin' with your hair. I always thought if you'd looked better you wouldn't have got in so much trouble.

ARLENE   (*Pleased and curious*): Joey got my hair?

MOTHER: And skinny.

ARLENE: I took some beauty school at Pine Ridge.

MOTHER: Yeah, a beautician?

ARLENE: I don't guess so.

MOTHER: Said you was gonna work.

ARLENE: They got a law here. Ex-cons can't get no license.

MOTHER: Shoulda stayed in Alabama, then. Worked there.

ARLENE: They got a law there, too.

MOTHER: Then why'd they give you the trainin'?

ARLENE: I don't know.

MOTHER: Maybe they thought it'd straighten you out.

ARLENE: Yeah.

MOTHER: But you are gonna work, right?

ARLENE: Yeah. Cookin' maybe. Somethin' that pays good.

MOTHER: You? Cook? (*Laughs*)

ARLENE: I could learn it.

MOTHER: Your daddy ain't never forgive you for that bologna sandwich. (AR-LENE *laughs a little, finally enjoying a memory*) Oh, I wish I'd seen you spreadin' that Colgate on that bread. He'd have smelled that toothpaste if he hadn't been so sloshed. Little snotty-nosed kid tryin' to kill her daddy with a bologna sandwich. An him bein' so pleased when you brung it to him . . . (*Laughing*)

ARLENE: He beat me good.

MOTHER: Well, now, Arlie, you gotta admit you had it comin' to you. (*Wiping tears from laughing*)

ARLENE: I guess.

MOTHER: You got a broom?

ARLENE: No.

MOTHER: Well, I got one in the cab I brung just in case. I can't leave it here, but I'll sweep up fore I go. (*Walking toward the door*) You jus' rest till I git back. Won't find no work lookin' the way you do.

MOTHER *leaves.* ARLENE *finds some lipstick and a mirror in her purse, makes an attempt to look better while* MOTHER *is gone.*

ARLIE   (*Jumps up, as if talking to another kid*): She is not skinny!

ARLENE   (*Looking at herself in the mirror*): I guess I could . . .

ARLIE: And she don't have to git them stinking permanents. Her hair just comes outta her head curly.

ARLENE: Some lipstick.

ARLIE (*Serious*): She drives the cab to buy us stuff, 'cause we don't take no charity from nobody, 'cause we got money 'cause she earned it.

ARLENE (*Closing the mirror, dejected, afraid* MOTHER *might be right*): But you're too skinny and you got stringy hair. (*Sitting on the floor*)

ARLIE (*More angry*): She drives at night 'cause people needs rides at night. People goin' to see their friends that are sick, or people's cars broken down an they gotta get to work at the ... nobody calls my mama a whore!

MOTHER (*Coming back in with the broom*): If I'd known you were gonna sweep up with your butt, I wouldn't have got this broom. Get up! (*Sweeps at* ARLENE *to get her to move*)

ARLIE: You're gonna take that back or I'm gonna rip out all your ugly hair and stuff it down your ugly throat.

ARLENE (*Tugging at her own hair*): You still cut hair?

MOTHER (*Noticing some spot on the floor*): Gonna take a razor blade to get out this paint.

ARLENE: Nail polish.

ARLIE: Wanna know what I know about your mama? She's dyin'. Somethin's eatin' up her insides piece by piece, only she don't want you to know it.

MOTHER (*Continuing to sweep*): So, you're callin' yourself Arlene, now?

ARLENE: Yes.

MOTHER: Don't want your girlie name no more?

ARLENE: Somethin' like that.

MOTHER: They call you Arlene in prison?

ARLENE: Not at first when I was bein' hateful. Just my number then.

MOTHER: You always been hateful.

ARLENE: There was this chaplain, he called me Arlene from the first day he come to talk to me. Here, let me help you. (*She reaches for the broom*)

MOTHER: I'll do it.

ARLENE: You kin rest.

MOTHER: Since when? (ARLENE *backs off*) I ain't hateful, how come I got so many hateful kids? (*Sweeping harder now*) Poor dumb-as-hell Pat, stealin' them wigs, Candy screwin' since day one, Pete cuttin' up ol' Mac down at the grocery, June sellin' dope like it was Girl Scout cookies, and you ... thank God I can't remember it all.

ARLENE (*A very serious request*): Maybe I could come out on Sunday for ... you still make that pot roast?

MOTHER (*Now sweeping over by the picture of Jesus*): That your picture?

ARLENE: That chaplain give it to me.

MOTHER: The one give you your "new name."

ARLENE: Yes.

MOTHER: It's crooked. (*Doesn't straighten it*)

ARLENE: I liked those potatoes with no skins. An that ketchup squirter we had, jus' like in a real restaurant.

MOTHER: People that run them institutions now, they jus' don't know how to teach kids right. Let 'em run around an get in more trouble. They should get you up at the crack of dawn an set you to scrubbin' the floor. That's what kids need. Trainin'. Hard work.

ARLENE (*A clear request*): I'll probably git my Sundays off.

MOTHER: Sunday ... is my day to clean house now.

ARLENE gets the message, finally walks over to straighten the picture. MOTHER now feels a little bad about this rejection, stops sweeping for a moment.

MOTHER: I woulda wrote you but I didn't have nuthin' to say. An no money to send, so what's the use?

ARLENE: I made out.

MOTHER: They pay you for workin'?

ARLENE: 'Bout three dollars a month.

MOTHER: How'd you make it on three dollars a month? (*Answers her own question*) You do some favors?

ARLENE   (*Sitting down in the chair under the picture, a somewhat smug look*): You jus' can't make it by yourself.

MOTHER   (*Pauses, suspicious, then contemptuous*): You play, Arlie?

ARLENE: You don't know nuthin' about that.

MOTHER: I hear things. Girls callin' each other "mommy" an bringin' things back from the canteen for their "husbands." Makes me sick. You get family, Arlie, what you want with that playin'? Don't want nobody like that in my house.

ARLENE: You don't know what you're talkin' about.

MOTHER: I still got two kids at home. Don't want no bad example. (*Not finishing the sweeping. Has all the dirt in one place, but doesn't get it up off the floor yet*)

ARLENE: I could tell them some things.

MOTHER   (*Vicious*): Like about that cab driver.

ARLENE: Look, that was a long time ago. I wanna work, now, make somethin' of myself. I learned to knit. People'll buy nice sweaters. Make some extra money.

MOTHER: We sure could use it.

ARLENE: An then if I have money, maybe they'd let me take Joey to the fair, buy him hotdogs an talk to him. Make sure he ain't foolin' around.

MOTHER: What makes you think he'd listen to you? Alice, across the street? Her sister took care her kids while she was at Lexington. You think they pay any attention to her now? Ashamed, that's what. One of 'em told me his mother done died. Gone to see a friend and died there.

ARLENE: Be different with me and Joey.

MOTHER: He don't even know who you are, Arlie.

ARLENE   (*Wearily*): Arlene.

MOTHER: You forgot already what you was like as a kid. At Waverly, tellin' them lies about that campin' trip we took, sayin' your daddy made you watch while he an me . . . you know. I'd have killed you then if them social workers hadn't been watchin'.

ARLENE: Yeah.

MOTHER: Didn't want them thinkin' I weren't fit. Well, what do they know? Each time you'd get out of one of them places, you'd be actin' worse than ever. Go right back to that junkie, pimp, Carl, sellin' the stuff he steals, savin' his ass from the police. He follow you home this time, too?

ARLENE: He's got four more years at Bricktown.

MOTHER: Glad to hear it. Here . . . (*Handing her a bucket*) Water.

ARLENE fills up the bucket and MOTHER washes several dirty spots on the walls, floor and furniture. ARLENE knows better than to try to help. The doctor walks downstage to find ARLIE for their counseling session.

DOCTOR: So you refuse to go to camp?

ARLIE: Now why'd I want to go to your fuckin' camp? Camp's for babies. You can go shit in the woods if you want to, but I ain't goin'.

DOCTOR: Oh, you're goin'.

ARLIE: Wanna bet?

MOTHER: Arlie, I'm waitin'. (*For the water*)

ARLIE: 'Sides, I'm waitin'.

DOCTOR: Waiting for what?

ARLIE: For Carl to come git me.

DOCTOR: And who is Carl?

ARLIE: Jus' some guy. We're goin' to Alabama.

DOCTOR: You don't go till we say you can go.

ARLIE: Carl's got a car.

DOCTOR: Does he have a driver's license to go with it?

ARLIE (*Enraged, impatient*): I'm goin' now.

ARLIE *stalks away, then backs up toward the doctor again. He has information she wants.*

DOCTOR: Hey!

ARLENE: June picked out a name for the baby?

MOTHER: Clara . . . or Clarence. Got it from this fancy shampoo she bought.

ARLIE: I don't feel good. I'm pregnant, you know.

DOCTOR: The test was negative.

ARLIE: Well, I should know, shouldn't I?

DOCTOR: No. You want to be pregnant, is that it?

ARLIE: I wouldn't mind. Kids need somebody to bring 'em up right.

DOCTOR: Raising children is a big responsibility, you know.

ARLIE: Yeah, I know it. I ain't dumb. Everybody always thinks I'm so dumb.

DOCTOR: You could learn if you wanted to. That's what the teachers are here for.

ARLIE: Shit.

DOCTOR: Or so they say.

ARLIE: All they teach us is about geography. Why'd I need to know about Africa. Jungles and shit.

DOCTOR: They want you to know about other parts of the world.

ARLIE: Well, I ain't going there so whatta I care?

DOCTOR: What's this about Cindy?

ARLIE (*Hostile*): She told Mr. Dawson some lies about me.

DOCTOR: I bet.

ARLIE: She said I fuck my daddy for money.

DOCTOR: And what did you do when she said that?

ARLIE: What do you think I did? I beat the shit out of her.

DOCTOR: And that's a good way to work out your problem?

ARLIE (*Proudly*): She ain't done it since.

DOCTOR: She's been in traction, since.

ARLIE: So, whatta I care? She say it again, I'll do it again. Bitch!

ARLENE (*Looking down at the dirt* MOTHER *is gathering on the floor*): I ain't got a can. Just leave it.

MOTHER: And have you sweep it under the bed after I go? (*Wraps the dirt in a piece of newspaper and puts it in her laundry basket*)

DOCTOR (*Looking at his clipboard*): You're on unit cleanup this week.

ARLIE: I done it last week!

DOCTOR: Then you should remember what to do. The session is over. (*Getting up, walking away*) And stand up straight! And take off that hat!

DOCTOR *and* ARLIE *go offstage as* MOTHER *finds* BENNIE*'s hat.*

MOTHER: This your hat?
ARLENE: No.
MOTHER: Guess Candy left it here.
ARLENE: Candy didn't leave nuthin'.
MOTHER: Then whose is it? (ARLENE *doesn't answer*) Do you know whose hat this
    is? (ARLENE *knows she made a mistake*) I'm askin' you a question and I want an
    answer. (ARLENE *turns her back*) Whose hat is this? You tell me right now, whose
    hat is this?
ARLENE: It's Bennie's.
MOTHER: And who's Bennie?
ARLENE: Guy drove me home from Pine Ridge. A guard.
MOTHER   (*Upset*): I knew it. You been screwin' a goddamn guard. (*Throws the hat
    on the bed*)
ARLENE: He jus' drove me up here, that's all.
MOTHER: Sure.
ARLENE: I git sick on the bus.
MOTHER: You expect me to believe that?
ARLENE: I'm tellin' you, he jus'—
MOTHER: No man alive gonna drive a girl five hundred miles for nuthin'.
ARLENE: He ain't never seen Kentucky.
MOTHER: It ain't Kentucky he wants to see.
ARLENE: He ain't gettin' nuthin' from me.
MOTHER: That's what you think.
ARLENE: He done some nice things for me at Pine Ridge. Gum, funny stories.
MOTHER: He'd be tellin' stories all right, tellin' his buddies where to find you.
ARLENE: He's gettin' us some dinner right now.
MOTHER: And how're you gonna pay him? Huh? Tell me that.
ARLENE: I ain't like that no more.
MOTHER: Oh you ain't. I'm your mother. I know what you'll do.
ARLENE: I tell you I ain't.
MOTHER: I knew it. Well, when you got another bastard in you, don't come
    cryin' to me, 'cause I done told you.
ARLENE: Don't worry.
MOTHER: An I'm gettin' myself outta here fore your boyfriend comes back.
ARLENE   (*Increasing anger*): He ain't my boyfriend.
MOTHER: I been a lotta things, but I ain't dumb, Arlene. ("ARLENE" *is mocking.*)
ARLENE: I didn't say you was. (*Beginning to know how this is going to turn out*)
MOTHER: Oh no? You lied to me!
ARLENE: How?
MOTHER: You took my spread without even sayin' thank you. You're hintin' at
    comin' to my house for pot roast just like nuthin' ever happened, an all the
    time you're hidin' a goddamn guard under your bed. (*Furious*) Uh-huh.
ARLENE   (*Quietly*): Mama?
MOTHER   (*Cold, fierce*): What?
ARLENE: What kind of meat makes a pot roast?
MOTHER: A roast makes a pot roast. Buy a roast. Shoulder, chuck . . .
ARLENE: Are you comin' back?
MOTHER: You ain't got no need for me.
ARLENE: I gotta ask you to come see me?

MOTHER: I come tonight, didn't I, an nobody asked me?

ARLENE: Just forgit it.

MOTHER   (*Getting her things together*): An if I hadn't told them about this apartment, you wouldn't be out at all, how 'bout that!

ARLENE: Forgit it!

MOTHER: Don't you go talkin' to me that way. You remember who I am. I'm the one took you back after all you done all them years. I brung you that teapot. I scrubbed your place. You remember that when you talk to me.

ARLENE: Sure.

MOTHER: Uh-huh. (*Now goes to the bed, rips off the spread and stuffs it in her basket*) I know I shouldn't have come. You ain't changed a bit.

ARLENE: Same hateful brat, right?

MOTHER   (*Arms full, heading for the door*): Same hateful brat. Right.

ARLENE   (*Rushing toward her*): Mama . . .

MOTHER: Don't you touch me.

MOTHER *leaves.* ARLENE *stares out the door, stunned and hurt. Finally, she slams the door and turns back into the room.*

ARLENE: No! Don't you touch Mama, Arlie.

RONNIE, *a fellow juvenile offender, runs across the catwalk, waving a necklace and being chased by* ARLIE.

RONNIE: Arlie got a boyfriend, Arlie got a boyfriend. (*Throws the necklace downstage*) Whoo!

ARLIE   (*Chasing him*): Ronnie, you ugly mother, I'll smash your fuckin'—

ARLENE   (*Getting more angry*): You might steal all—

RONNIE   (*Running down the stairs*): Arlie got a boyfriend . . .

ARLIE: Gimme that necklace or I'll—

ARLENE: —or eat all Mama's precious pot roast.

RONNIE   (*As they wrestle downstage*): You'll tell the doctor on me? And get your private room back? (*Laughing*)

ARLENE   (*Cold and hostile*): No, don't touch Mama, Arlie. 'Cause you might slit Mama's throat. (*Goes into the bathroom*)

ARLIE: You wanna swallow all them dirty teeth?

RONNIE: Tell me who give it to you.

ARLIE: No, you tell me where it's at.

RONNIE *breaks away, pushing* ARLIE *in the opposite direction, and runs for the necklace.*

RONNIE: It's right here. (*Drops it down his pants*) Come an git it.

ARLIE: Oh now, that was really ignorant, you stupid pig.

RONNIE   (*Backing away, daring her*): Jus' reach right in. First come, first served.

ARLIE: Now, how you gonna pee after I throw your weenie over the fence?

RONNIE: You ain't gonna do that, girl. You gonna fall in love.

ARLIE *turns vicious, pins* RONNIE *down, attacking. This is no longer play. He screams. The doctor appears on the catwalk.*

DOCTOR: Arlie! (*Heads down the stairs to stop this*)

CARL's Voice   (*From outside the apartment door*): Arlie!
DOCTOR: Arlie!
ARLIE: Stupid, ugly—
RONNIE: Help!

ARLIE *runs away and hides down left.*

DOCTOR: That's three more weeks of isolation, Arlie. (*Bending down to* RONNIE)
    You all right? Can you walk?
RONNIE   (*Looking back to* ARLIE *as he gets up in great pain*): She was tryin' to kill me.
DOCTOR: Yeah. Easy now. You should've known, Ronnie.
ARLIE   (*Yelling at* RONNIE): You'll get yours, crybaby.
CARL's VOICE: Arlie . . .
ARLIE: Yeah, I'm comin'!
CARL's VOICE: Bad-lookin' dude says move your ass an open up this here door,
    girl.

ARLENE *does not come out of the bathroom.* CARL *twists the door knob violently, then kicks
in the door and walks in.* CARL *is thin and cheaply dressed.* CARL's *walk and manner are
imitative of black pimps, but he can't quite carry it off.*

CARL: Where you at, mama?
ARLENE: Carl?
CARL: Who else? You 'spectin' Leroy Brown?
ARLENE: I'm takin' a bath!
CARL   (*Walking toward the bathroom*): I like my ladies clean. Matter of professional
    pride.
ARLENE: Don't come in here.
CARL   (*Mocking her tone*): Don't come in here. I seen it all before, girl.
ARLENE: I'm gittin' out. Sit down or somethin'.
CARL   (*Talking loud enough for her to hear him through the door*): Ain't got the time.
    (*Opens her purse, then searches the trunk*) Jus' come by to tell you it's tomorrow. We
    be takin' our feet to the New York street. (*As though she will be pleased*) No more
    fuckin' around with these jiveass southern turkeys. We're goin' to the big city,
    baby. Get you some red shades and some red shorts an' the johns be linin' up
    fore we hit town. Four tricks a night. How's that sound? No use wearin' out that
    cute ass you got. Way I hear it, only way to git busted up there's be stupid, an
    I ain't lived this long bein' stupid.
ARLENE   (*Coming out of the bathroom wearing a towel*): That's exactly how you lived
    your whole life—bein' stupid.
CARL: Arlie . . . (*Moving in on her*) be sweet, sugar.
ARLENE: Still got your curls.
CARL   (*Trying to bug her*): You're looking okay yourself.
ARLENE: Oh, Carl. (*Noticing the damage to the door, breaking away from any closeness
    he might try to force*)
CARL   (*Amused*): Bent up your door, some.
ARLENE: How come you're out?
CARL: Sweetheart, you done broke out once, been nabbed and sent to Pine
    Ridge and got yourself paroled since I been in. I got a right to a little free time
    too, ain't that right?
ARLENE: You escape?

CARL: Am I standin' here or am I standin' here? They been fuckin' with you, I can tell.

ARLENE: They gonna catch you.

CARL (*Going to the window*): Not where we're going. Not a chance.

ARLENE: Where you goin' they won't git you?

CARL: Remember that green hat you picked out for me down in Birmingham? Well, I ain't ever wore it yet, but I kin wear it in New York 'cause New York's where you wear whatever you feel like. One guy tol' me he saw this dude wearin' a whole ring of feathers round' his leg, right here (*Grabs his leg above the knee*) an he weren't in no circus nor no Indian neither.

ARLENE: I ain't seen you since Birmingham. How come you think I wanna see you now?

ARLIE *appears suddenly, confronts* CARL.

ARLIE (*Pointing as if there is a trick waiting*): Carl, I ain't goin' with that dude, he's weird.

CARL: 'Cause we gotta go collect the johns' money, that's "how come."

ARLIE: I don't need you pimpin' for me.

ARLENE (*Very strong*): I'm gonna work.

CARL: Work?

ARLENE: Yeah.

CARL: What's this "work"?

ARLIE: You always sendin' me to them ol' droolers . . .

CARL: You kin do two things, girl—

ARLIE: They slobberin' all over me . . .

CARL: Breakin' out an hookin'.

ARLIE: They tyin' me to the bed!

ARLENE: I mean real work.

ARLIE (*Now screaming, gets further away from him*): I could git killed working for you. Some sicko, some crazy drunk . . .

ARLIE *goes offstage. A guard puts her in the cell sometime before* BENNIE*'s entrance.*

CARL: You forget, we seen it all on TV in the day room, you bustin' outta Lakewood like that. Fakin' that palsy fit, then beatin' the guard half to death with his own key ring. Whoo-ee! Then that spree you went on . . . stoppin' at that fillin' station for some cash, then kidnappin' the old dude pumpin' the gas.

ARLENE: Yeah.

CARL: Then that cab driver comes outta the bathroom an tries to mess with you and you shoots him with his own piece. (*Fires an imaginary pistol*) That there's nice work, mama. (*Going over to her, putting his arms around her*)

ARLENE: That gun . . . it went off, Carl.

CARL (*Getting more determined with his affection*): That's what guns do, doll. They go off.

BENNIE'S VOICE (*From outside*): Arlene? Arlene?

CARL: Arlene? (*Jumping up*) Well, la-de-da.

BENNIE *opens the door, carrying the chicken dinners. He is confused, seeing* ARLENE *wearing a towel and talking to* CARL.

ARLENE: Bennie, this here's Carl.

CARL: You're interruptin', Jack. Me an Arlie got business.

BENNIE: She's callin' herself Arlene.

CARL: I call my ladies what I feel like, chicken man, an you call yourself "gone."

BENNIE: I don't take orders from you.

CARL: Well, you been takin' orders from somebody, or did you git that outfit at the army surplus store?

ARLENE: Bennie brung me home from Pine Ridge.

CARL   (*Walking toward him*): Oh, it's a guard now, is it? That chicken break out or what? (*Grabs the chicken*)

BENNIE: I don't know what you're doin' here, but—

CARL: What you gonna do about it, huh? Lock me up in the toilet? You an who else, Batman?

BENNIE   (*Taking the chicken back, walking calmly to the counter*): Watch your mouth, punk.

CARL   (*Kicks a chair toward* BENNIE): Punk!

ARLENE   (*Trying to stop this*): I'm hungry.

BENNIE: You heard her, she's hungry.

CARL   (*Vicious*): Shut up! (*Mocking*) Ossifer.

BENNIE: Arlene, tell this guy if he knows what's good for him . . .

CARL   (*Walking to the counter where* BENNIE *has left the chicken*): Why don't you write me a parkin' ticket? (*Shoves the chicken on the floor*) Don't fuck with me, dad. It ain't healthy.

BENNIE *pauses. A real standoff. Finally,* BENNIE *bends down and picks up the chicken.*

BENNIE: You ain't worth dirtyin' my hands.

CARL *walks by him, laughing.*

CARL: Hey, Arlie. I got some dude to see. (*For* BENNIE*'s benefit as he struts to the door*) What I need with another beat-up guard? All that blood, jus' ugly up my threads. (*Very sarcastic*) Bye y'all.

ARLENE: Bye, Carl.

CARL *turns back quickly at the door, stopping* BENNIE, *who was following him.*

CARL: You really oughta shine them shoes, man. (*Vindictive laugh, slams the door in* BENNIE*'s face*)

BENNIE   (*Relieved, trying to change the atmosphere*): Well, how 'bout if we eat? You'll catch your death dressed like that.

ARLENE: Turn around then.

ARLENE *gets a shabby housecoat from the closet. She puts it on over her towel, buttons it up, then pulls the towel out from under it. This has the look of a prison ritual.*

BENNIE   (*As she is dressing*): Your parole officer's gonna tell you to keep away from guys like that . . . for your own good, you know. Those types, just like the suckers on my tomatoes back home. Take everything right outta you. Gotta pull 'em off, Arlie, uh, Arlene.

ARLENE: Now, I'm decent now.

BENNIE: You hear what I said?

ARLENE (*Going to the bathroom for her hairbrush*): I told him that. That's exactly what I did tell him.

BENNIE: Who was that anyhow? (*Sits down on the bed, opens up the chicken*)

ARLENE (*From the bathroom*): Long time ago, me an Carl took a trip together.

BENNIE: When you was a kid, you mean?

ARLENE: I was at this place for kids.

BENNIE: And Carl was there?

ARLENE: No, he picked me up an we went to Alabama. There was this wreck an all. I ended up at Lakewood for forgery. It was him that done it. Got me pregnant too.

BENNIE: That was Joey's father?

ARLENE: Yeah, but he don't know that. (*Sits down*)

BENNIE: Just as well. Guy like that, don't know what they'd do.

ARLENE: Mother was here while ago. Says she's seen Joey. (*Taking a napkin from* BENNIE)

BENNIE: Wish I had a kid. Life ain't, well, complete, without no kids to play ball with an take fishin'. Dorrie, though, she had them backaches an that neuralgia, day I married her to the day she died. Good woman though. No drinkin', no card playin', real sweet voice . . . what was that song she used to sing? . . . Oh, yeah . . .

ARLENE: She says Joey's a real good-lookin' kid.

BENNIE: Well, his mom ain't bad.

ARLENE: At Lakewood, they tried to git me to have an abortion.

BENNIE: They was just thinkin' of you, Arlene.

ARLENE (*Matter-of-fact, no self-pity*): I told 'em I'd kill myself if they done that. I would have too.

BENNIE: But they took him away after he was born.

ARLENE: Yeah. (BENNIE *waits, knowing she is about to say more*) An I guess I went crazy after that. Thought if I could jus' git out an find him . . .

BENNIE: I don't remember any of that on the TV.

ARLENE: No.

BENNIE: Just remember you smilin' at the cameras, yellin' how you tol' that cab driver not to touch you.

ARLENE: I never seen his cab. (*Forces herself to eat*)

ARLIE (*In the cell, holding a pillow and singing*): Rock-a-bye baby, in the tree top, when the wind blows, the cradle will . . . (*Not remembering*) cradle will . . . (*Now talking*) What you gonna be when you grow up, pretty boy baby? You gonna be a doctor? You gonna give people medicine an take out they . . . no, don't be no doctor . . . be . . . be a preacher . . . sayin' Our Father who is in heaven . . . heaven, that's where people go when they dies, when doctors can't save 'em or somebody kills 'em fore they even git a chance to . . . no, don't be no preacher neither . . . be . . . go to school an learn good (*Tone begins to change*) so you kin . . . make everbody else feel so stupid all the time. Best thing you to be is stay a baby 'cause nobody beats up on babies or puts them . . . (*Much more quiet*) that ain't true, baby. People is mean to babies, so you stay right here with me so nobody kin git you an make you cry an they lay one finger on you (*Hostile*) an I'll beat the screamin' shit right out of 'em. They even blow on you an I'll kill 'em.

BENNIE *and* ARLENE *have finished their dinner.* BENNIE *puts one carton of slaw in the refrigerator, then picks up all the paper, making a garbage bag out of one of the sacks.*

BENNIE: Ain't got a can, I guess. Jus' use this ol' sack for now.
ARLENE: I ain't never emptyin' another garbage can.
BENNIE: Yeah, I reckon you know how by now. (*Yawns*) You 'bout ready for bed?
ARLENE   (*Stands up*): I s'pose.
BENNIE   (*Stretches*): Little tired myself.
ARLENE   (*Dusting the crumbs off the bed*): Thanks for the chicken.
BENNIE: You're right welcome. You look beat. How 'bout I rub your back. (*Grabs her shoulders*)
ARLENE   (*Pulling away*): No. (*Walking to the sink*) You go on now.
BENNIE: Oh come on. (*Wiping his hands on his pants*) I ain't all that tired.
ARLENE: *I'm* tired.
BENNIE: Well, see then, a back rub is just what the doctor ordered.
ARLENE: No. I don't . . . (*Pulling away*)

BENNIE *grabs her shoulders and turns her around, sits her down hard on the trunk, starts rubbing her back and neck.*

BENNIE: Muscles git real tightlike, right in here.
ARLENE: You hurtin' me.
BENNIE: Has to hurt a little or it won't do no good.
ARLENE   (*Jumps, he has hurt her*): Oh, stop it! (*She slips away from him and out into the room. She is frightened*)
BENNIE   (*Smiling, coming after her, toward the bed*): Be lot nicer if you was layin' down. Wouldn't hurt as much.
ARLENE: Now, I ain't gonna start yellin'. I'm jus' tellin' you to go.
BENNIE   (*Straightens up as though he's going to cooperate*): Okay then. I'll jus' git my hat.

He reaches for the hat, then turns quickly, grabs her and throws her down on the bed. He starts rubbing again.

BENNIE: Now, you just relax. Don't you go bein' scared of me.
ARLENE: You ain't gettin' nuthin' from me.
BENNIE: I don't want nuthin', honey. Jus' tryin' to help you sleep.
ARLENE   (*Struggling*): Don't you call me honey.

BENNIE *stops rubbing, but keeps one hand on her back. He rubs her hair with his free hand.*

BENNIE: See? Don't that feel better?
ARLENE: Let me up.
BENNIE: Why, I ain't holdin' you down.
ARLENE: Then let me up.
BENNIE   (*Takes hands off*): Okay. Git up.

ARLENE *turns over slowly, begins to lift herself up on her elbows.* BENNIE *puts one hand on her leg.*

ARLENE: Move your hand. (*She gets up, moves across the room*)

BENNIE: I'd be happy to stay here with you tonight. Make sure you'll be all right. You ain't spent a night by yourself for a long time.

ARLENE: I remember how.

BENNIE: Well how you gonna git up? You got a alarm?

ARLENE: It ain't all that hard.

BENNIE (*Puts one hand in his pocket, leers a little*): Oh yeah it is. (*Walks toward her again*) Gimme a kiss. Then I'll go.

ARLENE (*Edging along the counter, seeing she's trapped*): You stay away from me.

BENNIE *reaches for her, clamping her hands behind her, pressing up against her.*

BENNIE: Now what's it going to hurt you to give me a little ol' kiss?

ARLENE (*Struggling*): Git out! I said git out!

BENNIE: You don't want me to go. You're jus' beginning to git interested. Your ol' girlie temper's flarin' up. I like that in a woman.

ARLENE: Yeah, you'd love it if I'd swat you one. (*Getting away from him*)

BENNIE: I been hit by you before. I kin take anything you got.

ARLENE: I could mess you up good.

BENNIE: Now, Arlie. You ain't had a man in a long time. And the ones you had been no-count.

ARLENE: Git out!

She slaps him. He returns the slap.

BENNIE (*Moving in*): Ain't natural goin' without it too long. Young thing like you. Git all shriveled up.

ARLENE: All right, you sunuvabitch, you asked for it!

She goes into a violent rage, hitting and kicking him. BENNIE *overpowers her capably, prison-guard style.*

BENNIE (*Amused*): Little outta practice, ain't you?

ARLENE (*Screaming*): I'll kill you, you creep!

The struggle continues, BENNIE *pinning her arms under his legs as he kneels over her on the bed.* ARLENE *is terrified and in pain.*

BENNIE: You will? You'll kill ol' Bennie . . . kill ol' Bennie like you done that cab driver?

A cruel reminder he employs to stun and mock her. ARLENE *looks as though she has been hit.* BENNIE, *still fired up, unzips his pants.*

ARLENE (*Passive, cold and bitter*): This how you got your Dorrie, rapin'?

BENNIE (*Unbuttoning his shirt*): That what you think this is, rape?

ARLENE: I oughta know.

BENNIE: Uh-huh.

ARLENE: First they unzip their pants.

BENNIE *pulls his shirttail out.*

ARLENE: Sometimes they take off their shirt.
BENNIE: They do huh?
ARLENE: But mostly, they just pull it out and stick it in.

BENNIE *stops, finally hearing what she has been saying. He straightens up, obviously shocked. He puts his arms back in his shirt.*

BENNIE: Don't you call me no rapist. (*Pause, then insistent*) No, I ain't no rapist,
    Arlie. (*Gets up, begins to tuck his shirt back in and zip up his pants*)
ARLENE: And I ain't Arlie.

ARLENE *remains on the bed as he continues dressing.*

BENNIE: No, I guess you ain't.
ARLENE   (*Quietly and painfully*): Arlie coulda killed you.
                                    END OF ACT ONE

PROLOGUE

These announcements are heard during the last five minutes of the intermission.

LOUDSPEAKER VOICE: Garden workers will, repeat, will, report for work this af-
    ternoon. Bring a hat and raincoat and wear boots. All raincoats will be checked
    at the front gate at the end of work period and returned to you after supper.
        Your attention please. A checkerboard was not returned to the recreation
    area after dinner last night. Anyone with information regarding the black and
    red checkerboard missing from the recreation area will please contact Mrs.
    Duvall after lunch. No checkerboards or checkers will be distributed until this
    board is returned.
        Betty Rickey and Mary Alice Wolf report to the laundry. Doris Creech and
    Arlie Holsclaw report immediately to the superintendent's office. The movie
    this evening will be *Dirty Harry* starring Clint Eastwood. Doris Creech and Arlie
    Holsclaw report to the superintendent's office immediately.
        The bus from St. Mary's this Sunday will arrive at 1:00 P.M. as usual. Those
    residents expecting visitors on that bus will gather on the front steps promptly
    at 1:20 and proceed with the duty officer to the visiting area after it has been
    confirmed that you have a visitor on the bus.
        Attention all residents. Attention all residents. (*Pause*) Mrs. Helen Carson has
    taught needlework classes here at Pine Ridge for thirty years. She will be retiring
    at the end of this month and moving to Florida where her husband has bought
    a trailer park. The resident council and the superintendent's staff has decided
    on a suitable retirement present. We want every resident to participate in this
    project—which is—a quilt, made from scraps of material collected from the
    residents and sewn together by residents and staff alike. The procedure will be
    as follows. A quilting room has been set up in an empty storage area just off the
    infirmary. Scraps of fabric will be collected as officers do evening count. Those
    residents who would enjoy cutting up old uniforms and bedding no longer in
    use should sign up for this detail with your dorm officer. If you would like to

sign your name or send Mrs. Carson some special message on your square of fabric, the officers will have tubes of embroidery paint for that purpose. The backing for the quilt has been donated by the Women's Associates as well as the refreshments for the retirement party to be held after lunch on the thirtieth. Thank you very much for your attention and participation in this worthwhile tribute to someone we are all very fond of here. You may resume work at this time. Doris Creech and Arlie Holsclaw report to the superintendent's office immediately.

ACT TWO

Lights fade. When they come up, it is the next morning. ARLENE *is asleep on the bed.* ARLIE *is locked in a maximum-security cell. We do not see the officer to whom she speaks.*

ARLIE: No, I don't have to shut up, neither. You already got me in seg-re-ga-tion, what else you gonna do? I got all day to sleep, while everybody else is out bustin' ass in the laundry. (*Laughs*) Hey! I know . . . you ain't gotta go do no dorm count, I'll just tell you an you jus' sit. Huh? You 'preciate that? Ease them corns you been moanin' about . . . yeah . . . okay. Write this down. (*Pride, mixed with alternating contempt and amusement*) Startin' down by the john on the back side, we got Mary Alice. Sleeps with her pillow stuffed in her mouth. Says her mom says it'd keep her from grindin' down her teeth or somethin'. She be suckin' that pillow like she gettin' paid for it. (*Laughs*) Next, it's Betty the Frog. Got her legs all opened out like some fuckin' . . . (*Makes croaking noises*) Then it's Doris eatin' pork rinds. Thinks somebody gonna grab 'em outta her mouth if she eats 'em during the day. Doris ain't dumb. She fat, but she ain't dumb. Hey! You notice how many girls is fat here? Then it be Rhonda, snorin', Marvene, wheezin', and Suzanne, coughin'. Then Clara an Ellie be still whisperin'. Family shit, who's gettin' outta line, which girls is gittin' a new work 'signment, an who kin git extra desserts an for how much. Them's the two really run this place. My bed right next to Ellie, for sure it's got some of her shit hid in it by now. Crackers or some crap gonna leak out all over my sheets. Last time I found a fuckin' grilled cheese in my pillow. Even had two of them little warty pickles. Christ! Okay. Linda and Lucille. They be real quiet, but they ain't sleepin'. Prayin', that's them. Linda be sayin' them Hell Marys till you kin just about scream. An Lucille, she tol' me once she didn't believe in no God, jus' some stupid spirits whooshin' aroun' everwhere makin' people do stuff. Weird. Now, I'm goin' back down the other side, there's . . . (*Screams*) I'd like to see you try it! I been listenin' at you for the last three hours. Your husband's gettin' laid off an your lettuce is gettin' eat by rabbits. Crap City. *You* shut up! Whadda I care if I wake everybody up? I want the nurse . . . I'm gittin' sick in here . . . an there's bugs in here!

The light comes up in the apartment. Faint morning traffic sounds are heard. ARLENE *does not wake up. The warden walks across the catwalk. A guard catches up with him near* ARLIE*'s cell.* BENNIE *is stationed at the far end of the walk.*

LOUDSPEAKER VOICE: Dorm A may now eat lunch.
GUARD (EVANS): Warden, I thought 456 . . . (*Nodding in* ARLIE*'s direction*) was leavin' here.

WARDEN: Is there some problem?

GUARD (EVANS):   Oh, we can take care of her all right. We're just tired of takin' her shit, if you'll pardon the expression.

ARLIE: You ain't seen nuthin' yet, you mother.

WARDEN: Washington will decide on her transfer. Till then, you do your job.

GUARD (EVANS):   She don't belong here. Rest of—

LOUDSPEAKER VOICE: Betty Rickey and Mary Alice Wolf report to the laundry.

GUARD (EVANS):   Most of these girls are mostly nice people, go along with things. She needs a cage.

ARLIE   (*Vicious*): I need a knife.

WARDEN   (*Very curt*): Had it occurred to you that we could send the rest of them home and just keep her? (*Walks away*)

LOUDSPEAKER VOICE: Dorm A may now eat lunch. A Dorm to lunch.

GUARD (EVANS)   (*Turning around, muttering to himself*): Oh, that's a swell idea. Let everybody out except bitches like Holsclaw. (*She makes an obscene gesture at him, he turns back toward the catwalk*) Smartass warden, thinks he's runnin' a hotel.

BENNIE: Give you some trouble, did she?

GUARD (EVANS):   I can wait.

BENNIE: For what?

GUARD (EVANS):   For the day she tries gettin' out an I'm here by myself. I'll show that screechin' slut a thing or two.

BENNIE: That ain't the way, Evans.

GUARD (EVANS):   The hell it ain't. Beat the livin'—

BENNIE: Outta a little thing like her? Gotta do her like all the rest. You got your shorts washed by givin' Betty Rickey Milky Ways. You git your chairs fixed givin' Frankie Hill extra time in the shower with Lucille Smith. An you git ol' Arlie girl to behave herself with a stick of gum. Gotta have her brand, though.

GUARD (EVANS):   You screwin' that wildcat?

BENNIE   (*Starts walk to* ARLIE*'s cell*): Watch. (ARLIE *is silent as he approaches, but is watching intently*) Now, (*To nobody in particular*) where was that piece of Juicy Fruit I had in this pocket. Gotta be here somewhere. (*Takes a piece of gum out of his pocket and drops it within* ARLIE*'s reach*) Well, (*Feigning disappointment*) I guess I already chewed it. (ARLIE *reaches for the gum and gets it*) Oh, (*Looking down at her now*) how's it goin', kid?

ARLIE *says nothing more, but unwraps the gum and chews it.* BENNIE *leaves the cell area, motioning to the other guard as if to say, "See, that's how it's done." A loud siren goes by in the street below the apartment.* ARLENE *bolts up out of bed, then turns back to it quickly, making it up in a frenzied, ritual manner. As she tucks the spread up under the pillow, the siren stops and so does she. For the first time, now, she realizes where she is and the inappropriateness of the habit she has just played out. A jackhammer noise gets louder. She walks over to the window and looks out. There is a wolf-whistle from a worker below. She shuts the window in a fury. She looks around the room as if trying to remember what she is doing there. She looks at her watch, now aware that it is late and that she has slept in her clothes.*

ARLENE: People don't sleep in their clothes, Arlene. An people git up fore noon.

ARLENE *makes a still-disoriented attempt to pull herself together—changing shoes, combing her hair, washing her face—as prison life continues on the catwalk. The warden walks toward* ARLIE, *stopping some distance from her but talking directly to her, as he checks files of papers.*

WARDEN: Good afternoon, Arlie.

ARLIE: Fuck you. (WARDEN *walks away*) Wait! I wanna talk to you.

WARDEN: I'm listening.

ARLIE: When am I gittin' outta here?

WARDEN: That's up to you.

ARLIE: The hell it is.

WARDEN: When you can show that you can be with the other girls, you can get out.

ARLIE: How'm I supposed to prove that bein' in here?

WARDEN: And then you can have mail again and visitors.

ARLIE: You're just fuckin' with me. You ain't ever gonna let me out. I been in this ad-just-ment room four months, I think.

WARDEN: Arlie, you see the other girls in the dorm walking around, free to do whatever they want? If we felt the way you seem to think we do, everyone would be in lockup. When you get out of segregation, you can go to the records office and have your time explained to you.

ARLIE: It won't make no sense.

WARDEN: They'll go through it all very slowly . . . when you're eligible for parole, how many days of good time you have, how many industrial days you've earned, what constitutes meritorious good time . . . and how many days you're set back for your write-ups and all your time in segregation.

ARLIE: I don't even remember what I done to git this lockup.

WARDEN: Well, I do. And if you ever do it again, or anything like it again, you'll be right back in lockup where you will stay until you forget *how* to do it.

ARLIE: What was it?

WARDEN: You just remember what I said.

ARLENE: Now then . . . (*Sounds as if she has something in mind to do. Looks as though she doesn't*)

ARLIE: What was it?

WARDEN: Oh, and Arlie, the prison chaplain will be coming by to visit you today.

ARLIE: I don't want to see no chaplain!

WARDEN: Did I ask you if you wanted to see the chaplain? No, I did not. I said, the chaplain will be coming by to visit you today. (*To an unseen guard*) Mrs. Roberts, why hasn't this light bulb been replaced?

ARLIE   (*Screaming*): Get out of my hall!

The warden walks away. ARLENE *walks to the refrigerator and opens it. She picks out the carton of slaw* BENNIE *put there last night. She walks away from the door, then turns around, remembering to close it. She looks at the slaw, as a guard comes up to* ARLIE's *cell with a plate.*

ARLENE: I ain't never eatin' no more scrambled eggs.

GUARD (CALDWELL):   Chow time, cutie pie.

ARLIE: These eggs ain't scrambled, they's throwed up! And I want a fork!

ARLENE *realizes she has no fork, then fishes one out of the garbage sack from last night. She returns to the bed, takes a bite of slaw and gets her wallet out of her purse. She lays the bills out on the bed one at a time.*

ARLENE: That's for coffee ... and that's for milk and bread ... an that's cookies
    ... an cheese and crackers ... and shampoo an soap ... and bacon an
    livercheese. No, pickle loaf ... an ketchup and some onions ... an peanut
    butter an jelly ... and shoe polish. Well, ain't no need gettin' everything all at
    once. Coffee, milk, ketchup, cookies, cheese, onions, jelly. Coffee, milk ... oh,
    shampoo ...

There is a banging on the door.

RUBY'S VOICE   (*Yelling*): Candy, I gotta have my five dollars back.
ARLENE   (*Quickly stuffing her money back in her wallet*): Candy ain't here!
RUBY'S VOICE: It's Ruby, upstairs. She's got five dollars I loaned her ... Arlie?
    That Arlie? Candy told me her sister be ...

ARLENE *opens the door hesitantly.*

RUBY: It is Arlie, right?
ARLENE: It's Arlene. (*Does not extend her hand*)
RUBY: See, I got these shoes in layaway ... (*Puts her hand back in her pocket*) she
    said you been ... you just got ... you seen my money?
ARLENE: No.
RUBY: I don't get 'em out today they go back on the shelf.
ARLENE   (*Doesn't understand*): They sell your shoes?
RUBY: Yeah. Welcome back.
ARLENE: Thank you.
RUBY: She coulda put it in my mailbox.

RUBY *starts to leave.* ARLENE *is closing the door when* RUBY *turns around.*

RUBY: Uh ... listen ... if you need a phone, I got one most of the time.
ARLENE: I do have to make this call.
RUBY: Ain't got a book though ... well, I got one but it's holdin' up my bed.
    (*Laughs*)
ARLENE: I got the number.
RUBY: Well, then ...
ARLENE: Would you ... wanna come in?
RUBY: You sure I'm not interruptin' anything?
ARLENE: I'm s'posed to call my parole officer.
RUBY: Good girl. Most of them can't talk but you call 'em anyway. (ARLENE *does
    not laugh*) Candy go back to that creep?
ARLENE: I guess.
RUBY: I's afraid of that. (*Looking around*) Maybe an envelope with my name on
    it? Really cleaned out the place, didn't she?
ARLENE: Yeah. Took everything.

They laugh a little.

RUBY: Didn't have much. Didn't do nuthin' here 'cept ... sleep.
ARLENE: Least the rent's paid till the end of the month. I'll be workin' by then.
RUBY: You ain't seen Candy in a while.
ARLENE: No. Think she was in the seventh grade when—

RUBY: She's growed up now, you know.

ARLENE: Yeah. I was thinkin' she might come by.

RUBY: Honey, she won't be comin' by. He keeps all his . . . (*Starting over*) his place is pretty far from here. But . . . (*Stops, trying to decide what to say*)

ARLENE: But what?

RUBY: But she had a lot of friends, you know. *They* might be comin' by.

ARLENE: Men, you mean.

RUBY: Yeah. (*Quietly, waiting for* ARLENE's *reaction*)

ARLENE (*Realizing the truth*): Mother said he was her boyfriend.

RUBY: I shouldn't have said nuthin'. I jus' didn't want you to be surprised if some john showed up, his tongue hangin' out an all. (*Sits down on the bed*)

ARLENE: It's okay. I shoulda known anyway. (*Now suddenly angry*) No, it ain't okay. Guys got their dirty fingernails all over her. Some pimp's out buyin' green pants while she. . . . Goddamn her.

RUBY: Hey now, that ain't your problem. (*Moves toward her,* ARLENE *backs away*)

ARLIE (*Pointing*): You stick your hand in here again Doris an I'll bite it off.

RUBY: She'll figure it out soon enough.

ARLIE (*Pointing to another person*): An you, you ain't my mama, so you can cut the mama crap.

ARLENE: I wasn't gonna cuss no more.

RUBY: Nuthin' in the parole rules says you can't get pissed. My first day outta Gilbertsville I done the damn craziest . . . (ARLENE *looks around, surprised to hear she had done time*) Oh yeah, a long time ago, but . . . hell, I heaved a whole gallon of milk right out the window my first day.

ARLENE (*Somewhat cheered*): It hit anybody?

RUBY: It bounced! Made me feel a helluva lot better. I said, "Ruby, if a gallon of milk can bounce back, so kin you."

ARLENE: That's really what you thought?

RUBY: Well, not exactly. I had to keep sayin' it for 'bout a year fore I finally believed it. I's moppin' this lady's floor once an she come in an heard me sayin' "gallon a milk, gallon a milk," fired me. She did. Thought I was too crazy to mop her floors.

RUBY *laughs, but is still bitter.* ARLENE *wasn't listening.* RUBY *wants to change the subject now.*

RUBY: Hey! You have a good trip? Candy said you was in Arkansas.

ARLENE: Alabama. It was okay. This guard, well he used to be a guard, he just quit. He ain't never seen Kentucky, so he drove me. (*Watching for* RUBY's *response*)

RUBY: Pine Ridge?

ARLENE: Yeah.

RUBY: It's coed now, ain't it?

ARLENE: Yeah. That's dumb, you know. They put you with men so's they can git you if you're seen with 'em.

RUBY: S'posed to be more natural, I guess.

ARLENE: I guess.

RUBY: Well, I say it sucks. Still a prison. No matter how many pictures they stick up on the walls or how many dirty movies they show, you still gotta be counted five times a day. (*Now beginning to worry about* ARLENE's *silence*) You don't seem like Candy said.

ARLENE: She tell you I was a killer?

RUBY: More like the meanest bitch that ever walked. I seen lots worse than you.

ARLENE: I been lots worse.

RUBY: Got to you, didn't it?

ARLENE *doesn't respond, but* RUBY *knows she's right.*

RUBY: Well, you jus' gotta git over it. Bein' out, you gotta—

ARLENE: Don't you start in on me.

RUBY   (*Realizing her tone*): Right, sorry.

ARLENE: It's okay.

RUBY: Ex-cons is the worst. I'm sorry.

ARLENE: It's okay.

RUBY: Done that about a year ago. New waitress we had. Gave my little goin'-
straight speech, "No booze, no men, no buyin' on credit," shit like that, she
quit that very night. Stole my fuckin' raincoat on her way out. Some speech,
huh? (*Laughs, no longer resenting this theft*)

ARLENE: You a waitress?

RUBY: I am the Queen of Grease. Make the finest french fries you ever did see.

ARLENE: You make a lot of money?

RUBY: I sure know how to. But I ain't about to go back inside for doin' it.
Cookin' out's better'n eatin' in, I say.

ARLENE: You think up all these things you say?

RUBY: Know what I hate? Makin' salads—cuttin' up all that stuff 'n floppin' it in
a bowl. Some day . . . some day . . . I'm gonna hear "tossed salad" an I'm gonna
do jus' that. Toss out a tomato, toss out a head of lettuce, toss out a big ol'
carrot. (*Miming the throwing and enjoying herself immensely*)

ARLENE   (*Laughing*): Be funny seein' all that stuff flyin' outta the kitchen.

RUBY: Hey Arlene! (*Gives her a friendly pat*) You had your lunch yet?

ARLENE   (*Pulling away immediately*): I ain't hungry.

RUBY   (*Carefully*): I got raisin toast.

ARLENE: No. (*Goes over to the sink, twists knobs as if to stop a leak*)

ARLIE: Whaddaya mean, what did she do to me? You got eyes or is they broke?
You only seein' what you feel like seein'. I git ready to protect myself from a
bunch of weirdos an then you look.

ARLENE: Sink's stopped up. (*Begins to work on it*)

ARLIE: You ain't seein' when they's leavin' packs of cigarettes on my bed an then
thinking I owe 'em or somethin'.

RUBY: Stopped up, huh? (*Squashing a bug on the floor*)

ARLIE: You ain't lookin' when them kitchen workers lets up their mommies in
line nights they know they only baked half enough brownies.

RUBY: Let me try.

ARLIE: You ain't seein' all the letters comin' in an goin' out with visitors. I'll tell
you somethin'. One of them workmen buries dope for Betty Rickey in little
plastic bottles under them sticker bushes at the water tower. You see that? No,
you only seein' me. Well, you don't see shit.

RUBY   (*A quiet attempt*): Gotta git you some Drano if you're gonna stay here.

ARLIE: I'll tell you what she done. Doris brung me some rollers from the beauty-
school class. Three fuckin' pink rollers. Them plastic ones with the little holes.
I didn't ask her. She jus' done it.

RUBY: Let me give her a try.

ARLENE: I can fix my own sink.

ARLIE: I's stupid. I's thinkin' maybe she were different from all them others. Then that night everbody disappears from the john and she's wantin' to brush my hair. Sure, brush my hair. How'd I know she was gonna crack her head open on the sink. I jus' barely even touched her.

RUBY   (*Walking to the bed now, digging through her purse*): Want a Chiclet?

ARLIE: You ain't asked what she was gonna do to me. Huh? When you gonna ask that? You don't give a shit about that 'cause Doris such a good girl.

ARLENE   (*Giving up*): Don't work.

RUBY: We got a dishwasher quittin' this week if you're interested.

ARLENE: I need somethin' that pays good.

RUBY: You type?

ARLENE: No.

RUBY: Do any clerk work?

ARLENE: No.

RUBY: Any keypunch?

ARLENE: No.

RUBY: Well, then I hate to tell you, but all us old-timers already got all the good cookin' and cleanin' jobs. (*Smashes another bug, goes to the cabinet to look for the bug spray*) She even took the can of Raid! Just as well, empty anyway. (ARLENE *doesn't respond*) She hit the bugs with it. (*Still no response*) Now, there's that phone call you are talkin' about.

ARLENE: Yeah.

RUBY   (*Walking toward the door*): An I'll git you that number for the dishwashin' job, just in case. (ARLENE *backs off*) How 'bout cards? You play any cards? Course you do. I get sick of beatin' myself all the time at solitaire. Damn borin' bein' so good at it.

ARLENE   (*Goes for her purse*): Maybe I'll jus' walk to the corner an make my call from there.

RUBY: It's always broke.

ARLENE: What?

RUBY: The phone . . . at the corner. Only it ain't at the corner. It's inside the A & P.

ARLENE: Maybe it'll be fixed.

RUBY: Look, I ain't gonna force you to play cards with me. It's time for my programs anyway.

ARLENE: I gotta git some pickle loaf an . . . things.

RUBY: Suit yourself. I'll be there if you change your mind.

ARLENE: I have some things I gotta do here first.

RUBY   (*Trying to leave on a friendly basis*): Look, I'll charge you a dime if it'll make you feel better.

ARLENE   (*Takes her seriously*): Okay.

RUBY   (*Laughs, then realizes* ARLENE *is serious*): Mine's the one with the little picture of Johnny Cash on the door.

RUBY *leaves. Singing to the tune of* "*I'll Toe the Line*," BENNIE *walks across the catwalk carrying a tray with cups and a pitcher of water.* ARLENE *walks toward the closet. She is delaying going to the store, but is determined to go. She checks little things in the room, remembers to get a scarf, changes shoes, checks her wallet. Finally, as she is walking out, she stops and looks at the picture of Jesus, then moves closer, having noticed a dirty spot. She goes back into the bathroom for a tissue, wets it in her mouth, then dabs at the offending spot. She puts the tissue in her purse, then leaves the room when noted.*

BENNIE: I keep my pants up with a piece of twine. I keep my eyes wide open all the time. Da da da da-da da da da da da. If you'll be mine, please pull the twine.

ARLIE: You can't sing for shit.

BENNIE   (*Starts down the stairs toward* ARLIE*'s cell*): You know what elephants got between their toes?

ARLIE: I don't care.

BENNIE: Slow natives. (*Laughs*)

ARLIE: That ain't funny.

GUARD (EVANS)   (*As* BENNIE *opens* ARLIE*'s door*): Hey, Davis.

BENNIE: Conversation is rehabilitatin', Evans. Want some water?

ARLIE: Okay.

BENNIE: How about some Kool-Aid to go in it? (*Gives her a glass of water*)

ARLIE: When does the chaplain come?

BENNIE: Want some gum?

ARLIE: Is it today?

BENNIE: Kool-Aid's gone up, you know. Fifteen cents and tax. You get out, you'll learn all about that.

ARLIE: Does the chaplain come today?

BENNIE   (*Going back up the catwalk*): Income tax, sales tax, property tax, gas and electric, water, rent—

ARLIE: Hey!

BENNIE: Yeah, he's comin', so don't mess up.

ARLIE: I ain't.

BENNIE: What's he tell you anyway, get you so starry-eyed?

ARLIE: He jus' talks to me.

BENNIE: I talk to you.

ARLIE: Where's Frankie Hill?

BENNIE: Gone.

ARLIE: Out?

BENNIE: Pretty soon.

ARLIE: When.

BENNIE: Miss her don't you? Ain't got nobody to bullshit with. Stories you gals tell . . . whoo-ee!

ARLIE: Get to cut that grass now, Frankie, honey.

BENNIE: Huh?

ARLIE: Stupidest thing she said. (*Gently*) Said first thing she was gonna do when she got out—

ARLENE *leaves the apartment.*

BENNIE: Get laid.

ARLIE: Shut up. First thing was gonna be going to the garage. Said it always smelled like car grease an turpur . . . somethin'.

BENNIE: Turpentine.

ARLIE: Yeah, an gasoline, wet. An she'll bend down an squirt oil in the lawn-mower, red can with a long pointy spout. Then cut the grass in the backyard, up an back, up an back. They got this grass catcher on it. Says she likes scoopin' up that cut grass an spreadin' it out under the trees. Says it makes her real hungry for some lunch. (*A quiet curiosity about all this*)

BENNIE: I got a power mower, myself.

ARLIE: They done somethin' to her. Took out her nerves or somethin'. She . . .

BENNIE: She jus' got better, that's all.

ARLIE: Hah. Know what else? They give her a fork to eat with last week. A fork. A fuckin' fork. Now how long's it been since I had a fork to eat with?

BENNIE (*Getting ready to leave the cell*): Wish I could help you with that, honey.

ARLIE (*Loud*): Don't call me honey.

BENNIE (*Locks the door behind him*): That's my girl.

ARLIE: I ain't your girl.

BENNIE (*On his way back up the stairs*): Screechin' wildcat.

ARLIE (*Very quiet*): What time is it?

ARLENE *walks back into the apartment. She is out of breath and has some trouble getting the door open. She is carrying a big sack of groceries. As she sets the bag on the counter, it breaks open, spilling cans and packages all over the floor. She just stands and looks at the mess. She takes off her scarf and sets down her purse, still looking at the spilled groceries. Finally, she bends down and picks up the package of pickle loaf. She starts to put it on the counter, then turns suddenly and throws it at the door. She stares at it as it falls.*

ARLENE: Bounce? (*In disgust*) Shit.

ARLENE *sinks to the floor. She tears open the package of pickle loaf and eats a piece of it. She is still angry, but is completely unable to do anything about her anger.*

ARLIE: Who's out there? Is anybody out there? (*Reading*) Depart from evil and do good. (*Yelling*) Now, you pay attention out there 'cause this is right out of the Lord's mouth. (*Reading*) And dwell, that means live, dwell for-ever-more. (*Speaking*) That's like for longer than I've been in here or longer than . . . this Bible the chaplain give me's got my name right in the front of it. Hey! Somebody's s'posed to be out there watchin' me. Wanna hear some more? (*Reading*) For the Lord for . . . (*The word is forsaketh*) I can't read in here, you turn on my light, you hear me? Or let me out and I'll go read it in the TV room. Please let me out. I won't scream or nuthin'? I'll just go right to sleep, okay? Somebody! I'll go right to sleep. Okay? You won't even know I'm there. Hey! Goddammit, somebody let me out of here, I can't stand it in here anymore. Somebody! (*Her spirit finally broken*)

ARLENE (*She draws her knees up, wraps her arms around them and rests her head on her arms*): Jus' gotta git a job an make some money an everything will be all right. You hear me, Arlene? You git yourself up an go find a job. (*Continues to sit*) An you kin start by cleanin' up this mess you made 'cause food don't belong on the floor.

ARLENE *still doesn't get up.* CARL *appears in the doorway of the apartment. When he sees* ARLENE *on the floor, he goes into a fit of vicious, sadistic laughter.*

CARL: What's happenin', mama? You havin' lunch with the bugs?

ARLENE (*Quietly*): Fuck off.

CARL (*Threatening*): What'd you say?

ARLENE (*Reconsidering*): Go away.

CARL: You watch your mouth or I'll close it up for you.

ARLENE *stands up now.* CARL *goes to the window and looks out, as if checking for someone.*

ARLENE: They after you, ain't they?

CARL *sniffs, scratches at his arm. He finds a plastic bag near the bed, stuffed with brightly colored knitted things. He pulls out baby sweaters, booties and caps.*

CARL: What the fuck is this?
ARLENE: You leave them be.
CARL: You got a baby hid here somewhere? I found its little shoes. (*Laughs, dangling them in front of him*)
ARLENE   (*Chasing him*): Them's mine.
CARL: Aw sugar, I ain't botherin' nuthin'. Just lookin'. (*Pulls more out of the sack, dropping one or two booties on the floor, kicking them away*)
ARLENE   (*Picking up what he's dropped*): I ain't tellin' you again. Give me them.
CARL   (*Turns around quickly, walking away with a few of the sweaters*): How much these go for?
ARLENE: I don't know yet.
CARL: I'll jus' take care of 'em for you—a few coin for the trip. You *are* gonna have to pay your share, you know.
ARLENE: You give me them. I ain't goin' with you. (*She walks toward him*)
CARL: You ain't?

Mocking, ARLENE *walks up close to him now, taking the bag in her hands. He knocks her away and onto the bed.*

CARL: Straighten up, girlie. (*Now kneels over her*) You done forgot how to behave yourself. (*Moves as if to threaten her, but kisses her on the forehead, then moves out into the room*)
ARLENE   (*Sitting up*): I worked hard on them things. They's nice, too, for babies and little kids.
CARL: I bet you fooled them officers good, doin' this shit. (*Throws the bag in the sink*)
ARLENE: I weren't—
CARL: I kin see that scene. They sayin' . . . (*Puts on a high southern voice*) "I'd jus' love one a them nice yella sweaters."
ARLENE: They liked them.
CARL: Those turkeys, sure they did. Where else you gonna git your free sweaters an free washin' an free step-right-up-git-your-convict-special-shoe-shine. No, don't give me no money, officer. I's jus' doin' this 'cause I likes you.
ARLENE: They give 'em for Christmas presents.
CARL   (*Checks the window again, then peers into the grocery sack*): What you got sweet, mama? (*Pulls out a box of cookies and begins to eat them*)
ARLIE: I'm sweepin', Doris, 'cause it's like a pigpen in here. So you might like it, but I don't, so if you got some mops, I'll take one of them too.
ARLENE: You caught another habit, didn't you?
CARL: You turned into a narc or what?
ARLENE: You scratchin' an sniffin' like crazy.
CARL: I see a man eatin' cookies an that's what you see too.

ARLENE: An you was laughin' at me sittin' on the floor! You got cops lookin' for you an you ain't scored yet this morning. You better get yourself back to prison where you can git all you need.

CARL: Since when Carl couldn't find it if he really wanted it?

ARLENE: An I bought them cookies for me.

CARL: An I wouldn't come no closer if I's you.

ARLENE (*Stops, then walks to the door*): Then take the cookies an git out.

CARL (*Imitating* BENNIE): Oh, please, Miss Arlene, come go with Carl to the big city. We'll jus' have us the best time.

ARLENE: I'm gonna stay here an git a job an save up money so's I kin git Joey. (*Opening the door*) Now, I ain't s'posed to see no ex-cons.

CARL (*Big laugh*): You don't know nobody else. Huh, Arlie? Who you know ain't a con-vict?

ARLENE: I'll meet 'em.

CARL: And what if they don't wanna meet you? You ain't exactly a nice girl, you know. An you gotta be jivin' about that job shit. (*Throws the sack of cookies on the floor*)

ARLENE (*Retrieving the cookies*): I kin work.

CARL: Doin' what?

ARLENE: I don't know. Cookin', cleanin', somethin' that pays good.

CARL: You got your choice, honey. You can do cookin' an cleanin' *or* you can do somethin' that pays good. You ain't gonna git rich working on your knees. You come with me an you'll have money. You stay here, you won't have shit.

ARLENE: Ruby works an she does okay.

CARL: You got any Kool-Aid? (*Looking in the cabinets, moving* ARLENE *out of his way*) Ruby who?

ARLENE: Upstairs. She cooks. Works nights an has all day to do jus' what she wants.

CARL: And what, exactly, do she do? See flicks take rides in cabs to pick up see-through shoes?

ARLENE: She watches TV, plays cards, you know.

CARL: Yeah, I know. Sounds just like the day room in the fuckin' joint.

ARLENE: She likes it.

CARL (*Exasperated*): All right. Say you stay here an *finally* find yourself some job. (*Grabs the picture of Jesus off the wall*) This your boyfriend?

ARLENE: The chaplain give it to me.

CARL: Say it's dishwashin', okay? (ARLENE *doesn't answer*) Okay?

ARLENE: Okay. (*Takes the picture, hangs it back up*)

CARL: An you git maybe seventy-five a week. Seventy-five for standin' over a sink full of greasy gray water, fishin' out blobs of bread an lettuce. People puttin' pieces of chewed-up meat in their napkins and you gotta pick it out. Eight hours a day, six days a week, to make seventy-five lousy pictures of Big Daddy George. Now, how long it'll take you to make seventy-five workin' for me?

ARLENE: A night.

She sits on the bed, CARL *pacing in front of her.*

CARL: Less than a night. Two hours maybe. Now, it's the same fuckin' seventy-five bills. You can either work all week for it or make it in two hours. You work two hours a night for me an how much you got in a week? (ARLENE *looks puzzled by the multiplication required. He sits down beside her, even more disgusted*) Two seventy-five's is a hundred and fifty. Three hundred-and-fifties is four hundred and fifty. You stay here you git seventy-five a week. You come with me an you git four hundred and fifty a week. Now, four hundred and fifty, Arlie, is *more* than seventy-five. You stay here you gotta work eight hours a day and your hands git wrinkled and your feet swell up. (*Suddenly distracted*) There was this guy at Bricktown had webby toes like a duck. (*Back now*) You come home with me you work two hours a night an you kin sleep all mornin' an spend the day buyin' eyelashes and tryin' out perfume. Come home, have some guy openin' the door for you sayin', "Good evenin', Miss Holsclaw, nice night now ain't it?" (*Puts his arm around her*)

ARLENE: It's Joey I'm thinkin' about.

CARL: If you was a kid, would you want your mom to git so dragged out washin' dishes she don't have no time for you an no money to spend on you? You come with me, you kin send him big orange bears an Sting-Ray bikes with his name wrote on the fenders. He'll like that. Holsclaw. (*Amused*) Kinda sounds like coleslaw, don't it? Joey be tellin' all his friends 'bout his mom livin' up in New York City an bein' so rich an sendin' him stuff all the time.

ARLENE: I want to be with him.

CARL   (*Now stretches out on the bed, his head in her lap*): So, fly him up to see you. Take him on that boat they got goes roun' the island. Take him up to the Empire State Building, let him play King Kong. (*Rubs her hair, unstudied tenderness*) He be talkin' 'bout that trip his whole life.

ARLENE   (*Smoothing his hair*): I don't want to go back to prison, Carl.

CARL   (*Jumps up, moves toward the refrigerator*): There any chocolate milk? (*Distracted again*) You know they got this motel down in Mexico named after me? Carlsbad Cabins. (*Proudly*) Who said anything about goin' back to prison? (*Slams the refrigerator door, really hostile*) What do you think I'm gonna be doin'? Keepin' you out, that's what!

ARLENE   (*Stands up*): Like last time? Like you gettin' drunk? Like you lookin' for kid junkies to beat up?

CARL: God, ain't it hot in this dump. You gonna come or not? You wanna wash dishes, I could give a shit. (*Yelling*) But you comin' with me, you say it right now, lady! (*Grabs her by the arm*) Huh?

There is a knock on the door.

RUBY'S VOICE: Arlene?

CARL   (*Yelling*): She ain't here!

RUBY'S VOICE   (*Alarmed*): Arlene! You all right?

ARLENE: That's Ruby I was tellin' you about.

CARL   (*Catches ARLENE's arm again, very rough*): We ain't through!

RUBY   (*Opening the door*): Hey! (*Seeing the rough treatment*) Goin' to the store. (*Very firm*) Thought maybe you forgot somethin'.

CARL   (*Turns ARLENE loose*): You this cook I been hearin' about?

RUBY: I cook. So what?

CARL: Buys you nice shoes, don't it, cookin'? Why don't you hock your watch an have somethin' done to your hair? If you got a watch.

RUBY: Why don't you drop by the coffee shop. I'll spit in your eggs.

CARL: They let you bring home the half-eat chili dogs?

RUBY: You . . . you got half-eat chili dogs for brains. (*To* ARLENE) I'll stop by later. (*Contemptuous look for* CARL)

ARLENE: No. Stay.

CARL *gets the message. He goes over to the sink to get a drink of water out of the faucet, then looks down at his watch.*

CARL: Piece of shit. (*Thumps it with his finger*) Shoulda took the dude's hat, Jack. Guy preachin' about the end of the world ain't gonna own a watch that works.

ARLENE (*Walks over to the sink, bends over* CARL): You don't need me. I'm gittin' too old for it, anyway.

CARL: I don't discuss my business with strangers in the room. (*Heads for the door*)

ARLENE: When you leavin'?

CARL: Six. You wanna come, meet me at this bar. (*Gives her a brightly colored matchbook*) I'm havin' my wheels delivered.

ARLENE: You stealin' a car?

CARL: Take a cab. (*Gives her a dollar*) You don't come . . . well, I already laid it out for you. I ain't never lied to you, have I girl?

ARLENE: No.

CARL: Then you be there. That's all the words I got. (*Makes an unconscious move toward her*) I don't beg nobody. (*Backs off*) Be there.

He turns abruptly and leaves. ARLENE *watches him go, folding up the money in the matchbook. The door remains open.*

ARLIE (*Reading, or trying to, from a small Testament*): For the Lord forsaketh not his saints, but the seed of the wicked shall be cut off.

RUBY *walks over to the counter, starts to pick up some of the groceries lying on the floor, then stops.*

RUBY: I 'magine you'll want to be puttin' these up yourself. (ARLENE *continues to stare out the door*) He do this?

ARLENE: No.

RUBY: Can't trust these sacks. I seen bag boys punchin' holes in 'em at the store.

ARLENE: Can't trust anybody. (*Finally turning around*)

RUBY: Well, you don't want to trust him, that's for sure.

ARLENE: We spent a lot of time together, me an Carl.

RUBY: He live here?

ARLENE: No, he jus' broke outta Bricktown near where I was. I got word there sayin' he'd meet me. I didn't believe it then, but he don't lie, Carl don't.

RUBY: You thinkin' of goin' with him?

ARLENE: They'll catch him. I told him but he don't listen.

RUBY: Funny ain't it, the number a men come without ears.

ARLENE: How much that dishwashin' job pay?

RUBY: I don't know. Maybe seventy-five.

ARLENE: That's what he said.

RUBY: He tell you you was gonna wear out your hands and knees grubbin' for nuthin', git old an be broke an never have a nice dress to wear? (*Sitting down*)

ARLENE: Yeah.

RUBY: He tell you nobody's gonna wanna be with you 'cause you done time?

ARLENE: Yeah.

RUBY: He tell you your kid gonna be ashamed of you an nobody's gonna believe you if you tell 'em you changed?

ARLENE: Yeah.

RUBY: Then he was right. (*Pauses*) But when you make your two nickels, you can keep both of 'em.

ARLENE   (*Shattered by these words*): Well, I can't do that.

RUBY: Can't do what?

ARLENE: Live like that. Be like bein' dead.

RUBY: You kin always call in sick . . . stay home, send out for pizza an watch your Johnny Carson on TV . . . or git a bus way out Preston Street an go bowlin'.

ARLENE   (*Anger building*): What am I gonna do? I can't git no work that will pay good 'cause I can't do nuthin'. It'll be years fore I have a nice rug for this place. I'll never even have some ol' Ford to drive around, I'll never take Joey to no fair. I won't be invited home for pot roast and I'll have to wear this fuckin' dress for the rest of my life. What kind of life is that?

RUBY: It's outside.

ARLENE: Outside? Honey I'll either be *inside* this apartment or *inside* some kitchen sweatin' over the sink. Outside's where you get to do what you want, not where you gotta do some shit job jus' so's you can eat worse than you did in prison. That ain't why I quit bein' so hateful, so I could come back and rot in some slum.

RUBY   (*Word "slum" hits hard*): Well, you can wash dishes to pay the rent on your "slum," or you can spread your legs for any shit that's got the ten dollars.

ARLENE   (*Not hostile*): I don't need you agitatin' me.

RUBY: An I don't live in no slum.

ARLENE   (*Sensing* RUBY*'s hurt*): Well, I'm sorry . . . it's just . . . I thought . . . (*Increasingly upset*)

RUBY   (*Finishing her sentence*): . . . it was gonna be different. Well, it ain't. And the sooner you believe it, the better off you'll be.

A guard enters ARLIE*'s cell.*

ARLIE: Where's the chaplain? I got somethin' to tell him.

ARLENE: They said I's . . .

GUARD (CALDWELL):   He ain't comin'.

ARLENE: . . . he tol' me if . . . I thought once Arlie . . .

ARLIE: It's Tuesday. He comes to see me on Tuesday.

GUARD (CALDWELL):   Chaplain's been transferred, dollie. Gone. Bye-bye. You know.

ARLENE: He said the meek, meek, them that's quiet and good . . . the meek . . . as soon as Arlie . . .

RUBY: What, Arlene? Who said what?

ARLIE: He's not comin' back?

ARLENE: At Pine Ridge there was . . .

ARLIE: He woulda told me if he couldn't come back.

ARLENE: I was . . .

GUARD (CALDWELL):   He left this for you.

ARLENE: I was . . .

GUARD (CALDWELL):   Picture of Jesus, looks like.

ARLENE: . . . this chaplain . . .

RUBY   (*Trying to call her back from this hysteria*): Arlene . . .

ARLIE   (*Hysterical*): I need to talk to him.

ARLENE: This chaplain . . .

ARLIE: You tell him to come back and see me.

ARLENE: I was in lockup . . .

ARLIE (*A final, anguished plea*): I want the chaplain!

ARLENE: I don't know . . . years . . .

RUBY: And . . .

ARLENE: This chaplain said I had . . . said Arlie was my hateful self and she was hurtin' me and God would find some way to take her away . . . and it was God's will so I could be the meek . . . the meek, them that's quiet and good an git whatever they want . . . I forgit that word . . . they git the earth.

RUBY: Inherit.

ARLENE: Yeah. And that's why I done it.

RUBY: Done what?

ARLENE: What I done. 'Cause the chaplain he said . . . I'd sit up nights waitin' for him to come talk to me.

RUBY: Arlene, what did you do? What are you talkin' about?

ARLENE: They tol' me . . . after I's out an it was all over . . . they said after the chaplain got transferred . . . I didn't know why he didn't come no more till after . . . they said it was three whole nights at first, me screamin' to God to come git Arlie an kill her. They give me this medicine an thought I's better then . . . that night it happened, the officer was in the dorm doin' count . . . an they didn't hear nuthin' but they come back out where I was an I'm standin' there tellin' 'em to come see, real quiet I'm tellin' 'em, but there's all this blood all over my shirt an I got this fork I'm holdin' real tight in my hand . . . (*Clenches one hand now, the other hand fumbling with the front of her dress as if she's going to show Ruby*) this fork, they said Doris stole it from the kitchen an give it to me so I'd kill myself and shut up botherin' her . . . an there's all these holes all over me where I been stabbin' myself an I'm sayin' Arlie is dead for what she done to me, Arlie is dead an it's God's will . . . I didn't scream it, I was jus' sayin' it over and over . . . Arlie is dead, Arlie is dead . . . they couldn't git that fork outta my hand till . . . I woke up in the infirmary an they said I almost died. They said they's glad I didn't. (*Smiling*) They said did I feel better now an they was real nice, bringing me chocolate puddin' . . .

RUBY: I'm sorry, Arlene.

RUBY *reaches out for her, but* ARLENE *pulls away sharply.*

ARLENE: I'd be eatin' or jus' lookin' at the ceiling an git a tear in my eye, but it'd jus' dry up, you know, it didn't run out or nuthin'. An then pretty soon, I's well, an officers was sayin' they's seein' such a change in me an givin' me yarn to knit sweaters an how'd I like to have a new skirt to wear an sometimes lettin' me chew gum. They said things ain't never been as clean as when I's doin' the housekeepin' at the dorm. (*So proud*) An then I got in the honor cottage an nobody was foolin' with me no more or nuthin'. An I didn't git mad like before or nuthin'. I jus' done my work an knit . . . an I don't think about it, what happened, 'cept . . . (*Now losing control*) People here keep callin' me Arlie an . . . (*Has trouble saying* "ARLIE") I didn't mean to do it, what I done . . .

RUBY: Oh, honey . . .

ARLENE: I did . . . (*This is very difficult*) I mean, Arlie was a pretty mean kid, but I did . . . (*Very quickly*) I didn't know what I . . .

ARLENE *breaks down completely, screaming, crying, falling over into* RUBY*'s lap.*

ARLENE   (*Grieving for this lost self*): Arlie!

RUBY *rubs her back, her hair, waiting for the calm she knows will come.*

RUBY   (*Finally, but very quietly*): You can still ... (*Stops to think of how to say it*) ...
you can still love people that's gone.

RUBY *continues to hold her tenderly, rocking as with a baby. A terrible crash is heard on the
steps outside the apartment.*

BENNIE'S VOICE: Well, chicken-pluckin', hog-kickin' shit!
RUBY: Don't you move now, it's just somebody out in the hall.
ARLENE: That's—
RUBY: It's okay Arlene. Everything's gonna be just fine. Nice and quiet now.
ARLENE: That's Bennie that guard I told you about.
RUBY: I'll get it. You stay still now. (*She walks to the door and looks out into the hall,
hands on hips*) Why you dumpin' them flowers on the stairs like that? Won't git
no sun at all! (*Turns back to* ARLENE) Arlene, there's a man plantin' a garden out
in the hall. You think we should call the police or get him a waterin' can?

BENNIE *appears in the doorway, carrying a box of dead-looking plants.*

BENNIE: I didn't try to fall, you know.
RUBY   (*Blocking the door*): Well, when you git ready to *try*, I wanna watch!
ARLENE: I thought you's gone.
RUBY   (*To* BENNIE): You got a visitin' pass?
BENNIE   (*Coming into the room*): Arlie ... (*Quickly*) Arlene. I brung you some
plants. You know, plants for your window. Like we talked about, so's you don't
see them bars.
RUBY   (*Picking up one of the plants*): They sure is scraggly-lookin' things. Next
time, git plastic.
BENNIE: I'm sorry I dropped 'em, Arlene. We kin get 'em back together an
they'll do real good. (*Setting them down on the trunk*) These ones don't take the
sun. I asked just to make sure. Arlene?
RUBY: You up for seein' this petunia killer?
ARLENE: It's okay. Bennie, this is Ruby, upstairs.
BENNIE   (*Bringing one flower over to show* ARLENE, *stuffing it back into its pot*): See?
It ain't dead.
RUBY: Poor little plant. It comes from a broken home.
BENNIE   (*Walks over to the window, getting the box and holding it up*): That's gonna
look real pretty. Cheerful-like.
RUBY: Arlene ain't gettin' the picture yet. (*Walking to the window and holding her
plant up too, posing*) Now.

ARLENE *looks, but is not amused.*

BENNIE   (*Putting the plants back down*): I jus' thought, after what I done last night
... I jus' wanted to do somethin' nice.
ARLENE   (*Calmer now*): They is nice. Thanks.
RUBY: Arlene says you're a guard.
BENNIE: I was. I quit. Retired.

ARLENE: Bennie's goin' back to Alabama.

BENNIE: Well, I ain't leavin' right away. There's this guy at the motel says the bass is hittin' pretty good right now. Thought I might fish some first.

ARLENE: Then he's goin' back.

BENNIE (*To* RUBY *as he washes his hands*): I'm real fond of this little girl. I ain't goin' till I'm sure she's gonna do okay. Thought I might help some.

RUBY: Arlene's had about all the help she can stand.

BENNIE: I got a car, Arlene. An money. An ... (*Reaching into his pocket*) I brung you some gum.

ARLENE: That's real nice, too. An I 'preciate what you done, bringin' me here an all, but ...

BENNIE: Well, look. Least you can take my number at the motel an give me a ring if you need somethin'. (*Holds out a piece of paper*) Here, I wrote it down for you. (ARLENE *takes the paper*) Oh, an somethin' else, these towel things ... (*Reaching into his pocket, pulling out a package of towelettes*) they was in the chicken last night. I thought I might be needin' 'em, but they give us new towels every day at that motel.

ARLENE: Okay then. I got your number.

BENNIE (*Backing up toward the door*): Right. Right. Any ol' thing, now. Jus' any ol' thing. You even run outta gum an you call.

RUBY: Careful goin' down.

ARLENE: Bye Bennie.

BENNIE: Right. The number now. Don't lose it. You know, in case you need somethin'.

ARLENE: No.

BENNIE *leaves,* ARLENE *gets up and picks up the matchbook* CARL *gave her and holds it with* BENNIE*'s piece of paper.* RUBY *watches a moment, sees* ARLENE *trying to make this decision, knows that what she says now is very important.*

RUBY: We had this waitress put her phone number in matchbooks, give 'em to guys left her nice tips. Anyway, one night this little ol' guy calls her and comes over and says he works at this museum an he don't have any money but he's got this hat belonged to Queen Victoria. An she felt real sorry for him so she screwed him for this little ol' lacy hat. Then she takes the hat back the next day to the museum thinkin' she'll git a reward or somethin' an you know what they done? (*Pause*) Give her a free membership. Tellin' her thanks so much an we're so grateful an wouldn't she like to see this mummy they got downstairs ... an all the time jus' stallin' ... waiting 'cause they called the police.

ARLENE: You do any time for that?

RUBY (*Admitting the story was about her*): County jail.

ARLENE (*Quietly, looking at the matchbook*): County jail. (*She tears up the matchbook and drops it in the sack of trash*) You got any Old Maids?

RUBY: Huh?

ARLENE: You know.

RUBY (*Surprised and pleased*): Cards?

ARLENE (*Laughs a little*): It's the only one I know.

RUBY: Old Maid, huh? (*Not her favorite game*)

ARLENE: I gotta put my food up first.

RUBY: 'Bout an hour?

ARLENE: I'll come up.

RUBY: Great. (*Stops by the plants on her way to the door, smiles*) These plants is real
ugly.

RUBY *exits.* ARLENE *watches her, then turns back to the groceries still on the floor. Slowly,
but with great determination, she picks up the items one at a time and puts them away in
the cabinet above the counter.* ARLIE *appears on the catwalk. There is one light on each of
them.*

ARLIE: Hey! You 'member that time we was playin' policeman an June locked me
up in Mama's closet an then took off swimmin'? An I stood around with them
dresses itchin' my ears an crashin' into that door tryin' to git outta there? It was
dark in there. So, finally, (*Very proud*) I went around an peed in all Mama's
shoes. But then she come home an tried to git in the closet only June taken the
key so she said, "Who's in there?" an I said, "It's me!" and she said, "What you
doin' in there?" an I started gigglin' an she started pullin' on the door an
yellin', "Arlie, what you doin' in there?" (*Big laugh*)

ARLENE *has begun to smile during the story. Now they speak together, both standing as
Mama did, one hand on her hip.*

ARLIE AND ARLENE: Arlie, what you doin' in there?
ARLENE   (*Still smiling and remembering, stage dark except for one light on her face*): Aw
shoot.

Light dims on ARLENE*'s fond smile as* ARLIE *laughs once more.*

END OF PLAY

QUESTIONS FOR DISCUSSION AND WRITING

1.   What does the title mean? The immediate meaning is, of course, getting
out of prison, but does Arlene need to "get out" of anything else?

2.   The central theatrical device of *Getting Out* is the simultaneous presence
on the stage of past and present: Arlene and Arlie; the apartment and the
prison. What are the implications of this splitting? Is Arlie Arlene's memories? Does Arlene have two selves? Notice Arlene's account, near the end of
the play, of what the chaplain told her before she left prison.

3.   Often in the play, there are parallels and links between what Arlie is
doing in the past and what Arlene is doing in the present. Pick out selected
scenes and trace these links.

4.   The prison and the apartment seem to represent opposites for Arlene,
and yet they sometimes appear to be the same. The apartment has bars on the
windows, and Arlene, late in the play, tells Ruby that having the apartment
and dishwashing job is not being "outside" at all: "Honey I'll either be *inside*
this apartment or *inside* some kitchen sweatin' over the sink. Outside's where
you get to do what you want, not where you gotta do some shit job jus' so's

you can eat worse than you did in prison." Trace this parallel between prison and the life open to Arlene outside. How does the idea of "imprisonment" transcend its literal meaning and become a metaphor in the play?

5. What is wrong with Arlene psychologically? What reasons are given for her temperament?

6. *Getting Out* has a "happy ending" in that Arlene seems to have decided to get a job, live within the law, and eventually get her son back. What influences lead her to conquer "Arlie" and reform her life? Do you find the reform credible?

7. In the Prologues to the two acts, a "loudspeaker voice" makes prison announcements, although the primary setting is the apartment. What is the status of this voice, and how does it function in the play?

8. The play begins and ends with stories narrated by Arlie/Arlene. Arlie's first lines in Act I are the story of how she and a friend killed a neighbor boy's pet frogs, and Act II ends with the story of how June locked her in their mother's closet. Why are these stories appropriate, and how do they function in the play?

9. What is Bennie's function in the play? Is he in some ways a foil to Arlene? Is he confronting similar problems in his own life?

Sam Shepard

"I'm pulled," Sam Shepard (b. 1943) has written, "toward images that shine in the middle of junk. Like cracked headlights shining on a deer's eyes. I've been influenced by Jackson Pollock, Little Richard, Cajun fiddles, and the Southwest." "Images that shine in the middle of junk" is a fine description of his plays, which are superficially realistic but really organized around a series of striking, dream-like images surrounded by and sometimes even made up of the junk of our culture: rock music, brand names, cowboy films, and science fiction.

Shepard was born in Fort Sheridan, Illinois, but grew up in Southern California, where the pop culture of cars, drugs, and rock music was to shape his later writing. After briefly attending a junior college and holding a number of menial jobs—including hot-walking horses at Santa Anita race track, herding and shearing sheep, and picking oranges—Shepard headed for New York, where he worked as a waiter, played drums with a band called the Holy Modal Rounders, and wrote brief, surrealistic plays for off-off-Broadway theaters. His first full-length play, *La Turista*, was produced in 1967. By the end of the sixties, Shepard had written almost twenty plays and had begun to receive recognition for his work: a Yale University fellowship and a Rockefeller grant in 1967 and a Guggenheim grant in 1968.

In 1971, Shepard moved to England, where he continued his prolific output, which included one of his best plays, *Tooth of Crime* (1972), which layers a *High Noon*-style shootout with the trappings of rock stars, science fiction, astrology, and gangster movies, all in a futuristic, invented slang. Returning to the United States in 1974, Shepard settled in California, where he worked with the Magic Theater of San Francisco, which did the premier productions of most of his plays. In the late seventies, Shepard turned to writing a series of plays that were longer and more realistic than his early work, though still dominated by dream images. These include his "family trilogy," which consists of *Curse of the Starving Class* (1976), *Buried Child* (1978), and *True West* (1980). *Buried Child* won the 1979 Pulitzer Prize for drama. His plays also include *Fool for Love* (1983) and *A Lie of the Mind* (1985). In 1978, Shepard's career took another turn. He appeared as an actor in Terence Malick's film *Days of Heaven;* since then he has become a major movie star, with principal roles in *Resurrection* (1981), *Raggedy Man* (1981), *Frances* (1982), *The Right Stuff* (1983), *Country* (1984), the film version of *Fool for Love* (1985), and *Crimes of the Heart* (1987).

Sam Shepard dominated the American theater of the 1970s and '80s as Eugene O'Neill did the theater of the 1920s and '30s and Arthur Miller and Tennessee Williams did the theater of the 1950s and '60s. Like the work of those earlier playwrights, Shepard's plays capture the myths and cultural symbols of American life in a sometimes troubling but always powerful way.

TRUE WEST

CHARACTERS

AUSTIN: *early thirties, light blue sports shirt, light tan cardigan sweater, clean blue jeans, white tennis shoes*

LEE: *his older brother, early forties, filthy white t-shirt, tattered brown overcoat covered with dust, dark blue baggy suit pants from the Salvation Army, pink suede belt, pointed black forties dress shoes scuffed up, holes in the soles, no socks, no hat, long pronounced sideburns, "Gene Vincent" hairdo, two days' growth of beard, bad teeth.*

SAUL KIMMER: *late forties, Hollywood producer, pink and white flower print sports shirt, white sports coat with matching polyester slacks, black and white loafers.*

MOM: *early sixties, mother of the brothers, small woman, conservative white skirt and matching jacket, red shoulder bag, two pieces of matching red luggage.*

True West was first performed at the Magic Theatre in San Francisco on July 10, 1980. The director was Robert Woodruff, and the cast was as follows:

AUSTIN *Peter Coyote*
LEE *Jim Haynie*
SAUL KIMMER *Tom Dahlgreen*
MOM *Carol McElheney*

SCENE: *All nine scenes take place on the same set; a kitchen and adjoining alcove of an older home in a Southern California suburb, about 40 miles east of Los Angeles. The kitchen takes up most of the playing area to stage left. The kitchen consists of a sink, upstage center, surrounded by counter space, a wall telephone, cupboards, and a small window just above it bordered by neat yellow curtains. Stage left of sink is a stove. Stage right, a refrigerator. The alcove adjoins the kitchen to stage right. There is no wall division or door to the alcove. It is open and easily accessible from the kitchen and defined only by the objects in it: a small round glass breakfast table mounted on white iron legs, two matching white iron chairs set across from each other. The two exterior walls of the alcove which prescribe a corner in the upstage right are composed of many small windows, beginning from a solid wall about three feet high and extending to the ceiling. The windows look out to bushes and citrus trees. The alcove is filled with all sorts of house plants in various pots, mostly Boston ferns hanging in planters at different levels. The floor of the alcove is composed of green synthetic grass.*

All entrances and exits are made stage left from the kitchen. There is no door. The actors simply go off and come onto the playing area.

NOTE ON SET AND COSTUME: *The set should be constructed realistically with no attempt to distort its dimensions, shapes, objects, or colors. No objects should be introduced which might draw special attention to themselves other than the props demanded by the script. If a stylistic "concept" is grafted onto the set design it will only serve to confuse the evolution of the characters' situation, which is the most important focus of the play.*

Likewise, the costumes should be exactly representative of who the characters are and not added onto for the sake of making a point to the audience.

NOTE ON SOUND: *The coyote of Southern California has a distinct yapping, dog-like bark, similar to a hyena. This yapping grows more intense and maniacal as the pack grows in numbers, which is usually the case when they lure and kill pets from suburban yards. The sense of growing frenzy in the pack should be felt in the background, particularly in Scenes 7 and 8. In any case, these coyotes never make the long, mournful, solitary howl of the Hollywood stereotype.*

The sound of crickets can speak for itself.

These sounds should also be treated realistically even though they sometimes grow in volume and numbers.

ACT ONE

Scene 1

Night. Sound of crickets in dark. Candlelight appears in alcove, illuminating AUSTIN, *seated at glass table hunched over a writing notebook, pen in hand, cigarette burning in ashtray, cup of coffee, typewriter on table, stacks of paper, candle burning on table.*

Soft moonlight fills kitchen illuminating LEE, *beer in hand, six-pack on counter behind him. He's leaning against the sink, mildly drunk; takes a slug of beer.*

LEE: So, Mom took off for Alaska, huh?

AUSTIN: Yeah.

LEE: Sorta' left you in charge.

AUSTIN: Well, she knew I was coming down here so she offered me the place.

LEE: You keepin' the plants watered?

AUSTIN: Yeah.

LEE: Keepin' the sink clean? She don't like even a single tea leaf in the sink ya' know.

AUSTIN: (*trying to concentrate on writing*)   Yeah, I know.

(*pause*)

LEE: She gonna' be up there a long time?

AUSTIN: I don't know.

LEE: Kinda' nice for you, huh? Whole place to yourself.

AUSTIN: Yeah, it's great.

LEE: Ya' got crickets anyway. Tons a' crickets out there. (*looks around kitchen*) Ya' got groceries? Coffee?

AUSTIN: (*Looking up from writing*) What?

LEE: You got coffee?

AUSTIN: Yeah.

LEE: At's good. (*short pause*) Real coffee? From the bean?

AUSTIN: Yeah. You want some?

LEE: Naw. I brought some uh—(*motions to beer*)

AUSTIN: Help yourself to whatever's—(*motions to refrigerator*)

LEE: I will. Don't worry about me. I'm not the one to worry about. I mean I can uh—(*pause*) You always work by candlelight?

AUSTIN: No—uh—Not always.

LEE: Just sometimes?

AUSTIN: (*puts pen down, rubs his eyes*) Yeah. Sometimes it's soothing.

LEE: Isn't that what the old guys did?

AUSTIN: What old guys?

LEE: The forefathers. You know.

AUSTIN: Forefathers?

LEE: Isn't that what they did? Candlelight burning into the night? Cabins in the wilderness.

AUSTIN: (*rubs hand through his hair*)   I suppose.

LEE: I'm not botherin' you am I? I mean I don't wanna break into yer uh— concentration or nothin'.

AUSTIN: No, it's all right.

LEE: That's good. I mean I realize that yer line a' work demands a lota' concentration.

AUSTIN: It's okay.

LEE: You probably think that I'm not fully able to comprehend somethin' like that, huh?

AUSTIN: Like what?

LEE: That stuff yer doin'. That art. You know. Whatever you call it.

AUSTIN: It's just a little research.

LEE: You may not know it but I did a little art myself once.

AUSTIN: You did?

LEE: Yeah! I did some a' that. I fooled around with it. No future in it.

AUSTIN: What'd you do?

LEE: Never mind what I did! Just never mind about that. (*pause*) It was ahead of its time.

(*pause*)

AUSTIN: So, you went out to see the old man, huh?

LEE: Yeah, I seen him.

AUSTIN: How's he doing?

LEE: Same. He's doin' just about the same.

AUSTIN: I was down there too, you know.

LEE: What d'ya want, an award? You want some kinda' medal? You were down there. He told me all about you.

AUSTIN: What'd he say?

LEE: He told me. Don't worry.

(*pause*)

AUSTIN: Well—

LEE: You don't have to say nothin'.

AUSTIN: I wasn't.

LEE: Yeah, you were gonna' make somethin' up. Somethin' brilliant.

(*pause*)

AUSTIN: You going to be down here very long, Lee?

LEE: Might be. Depends on a few things.

AUSTIN: You got some friends down here?

LEE: (*laughs*)   I know a few people. Yeah.

AUSTIN: Well, you can stay here as long as I'm here.

LEE: I don't need your permission do I?

AUSTIN: No.

LEE: I mean she's my mother too, right?

AUSTIN: Right.

LEE: She might've just as easily asked me to take care of her place as you.
AUSTIN: That's right.
LEE: I mean I know how to water plants.

(*long pause*)

AUSTIN: So you don't know how long you'll be staying then?
LEE: Depends mostly on houses, ya' know.
AUSTIN: Houses?
LEE: Yeah. Houses. Electric devices. Stuff like that. I gotta' make a little tour first.

(*short pause*)

AUSTIN: Lee, why don't you just try another neighborhood, all right?
LEE: (*laughs*)   What'sa' matter with this neighborhood? This is a great neighborhood. Lush. Good class a' people. Not many dogs.
AUSTIN: Well, our uh—Our mother just happens to live here. That's all.
LEE: Nobody's gonna' know. All they know is somethin's missing. That's all. She'll never even hear about it. Nobody's gonna' know.
AUSTIN: You're going to get picked up if you start walking around here at night.
LEE: Me? I'm gonna' git picked up? What about you? You stick out like a sore thumb. Look at you. You think yer regular lookin'?
AUSTIN: I've got too much to deal with here to be worrying about—
LEE: Yer not gonna' have to worry about me! I've been doin' all right without you. I haven't been anywhere near you for five years! Now isn't that true?
AUSTIN: Yeah.
LEE: So you don't have to worry about me. I'm a free agent.
AUSTIN: All right.
LEE: Now all I wanna' do is borrow yer car.
AUSTIN: No!
LEE: Just fer a day. One day.
AUSTIN: No!
LEE: I won't take it outside a twenty mile radius. I promise ya'. You can check the speedometer.
AUSTIN: You're not borrowing my car! That's all there is to it.

(*pause*)

LEE: Then I'll just take the damn thing.
AUSTIN: Lee, look—I don't want any trouble, all right?
LEE: That's a dumb line. That is a dumb fuckin' line. You git paid fer dreamin' up a line like that?
AUSTIN: Look, I can give you some money if you need money.

(LEE *suddenly lunges at* AUSTIN, *grabs him violently by the shirt and shakes him with tremendous power*)

LEE: Don't you say that to me! Don't you ever say that to me! (*just as suddenly he turns him loose, pushes him away and backs off*) You may be able to git away with that with the old man. Git him tanked up for a week! Buy him off with yer Hollywood blood money, but not me! I can git my own money my own way. Big money!

AUSTIN: I was just making an offer.
LEE: Yeah, well keep it to yourself!

(*long pause*)

   Those are the most monotonous fuckin' crickets I ever heard in my life.
AUSTIN: I kinda' like the sound.
LEE: Yeah. Supposed to be able to tell the temperature by the number a' pulses. You believe that?
AUSTIN: The temperature?
LEE: Yeah. The air. How hot it is.
AUSTIN: How do you do that?
LEE: I don't know. Some woman told me that. She was a botanist. So I believed her.
AUSTIN: Where'd you meet her?
LEE: What?
AUSTIN: The woman botanist?
LEE: I met her on the desert. I been spendin' a lota' time on the desert.
AUSTIN: What were you doing out there?
LEE: (*pause, stares in space*)   I forgit. Had me a pit bull there for a while but I lost him.
AUSTIN: Pit bull?
LEE: Fightin' dog. Damn I made some good money off that little dog. Real good money.

(*pause*)

AUSTIN: You could come up north with me, you know.
LEE: What's up there?
AUSTIN: My family.
LEE: Oh, that's right, you got the wife and kiddies now don't ya'. The house, the car, the whole slam. That's right.
AUSTIN: You could spend a couple days. See how you like it. I've got an extra room.
LEE: Too cold up there.

(*pause*)

AUSTIN: You want to sleep for a while?
LEE: (*pause, stares at* AUSTIN)   I don't sleep.

(*lights to black*)

Scene 2

Morning. AUSTIN *is watering plants with a vaporizer,* LEE *sits at glass table in alcove drinking beer.*

LEE: I never realized the old lady was so security-minded.
AUSTIN: How do you mean?
LEE: Made a little tour this morning. She's got locks on everything. Locks and double-locks and chain locks and—What's she got that's so valuable?

AUSTIN: Antiques I guess. I don't know.

LEE: Antiques? Brought everything with her from the old place, huh. Just the same crap we always had around. Plates and spoons.

AUSTIN: I guess they have personal value to her.

LEE: Personal value. Yeah. Just a lota' junk. Most of it's phony anyway. Idaho decals. Now who in the hell wants to eat offa' plate with the state of Idaho starin' ya' in the face. Every time ya' take a bite ya' get to see a little bit more.

AUSTIN: Well it must mean something to her or she wouldn't save it.

LEE: Yeah, well personally I don't wanna' be invaded by Idaho when I'm eatin'. When I'm eatin' I'm home. Ya' know what I'm sayin'? I'm not driftin', I'm home. I don't need my thoughts swept off to Idaho. I don't need that!

(*pause*)

AUSTIN: Did you go out last night?

LEE: Why?

AUSTIN: I thought I heard you go out.

LEE: Yeah, I went out. What about it?

AUSTIN: Just wondered.

LEE: Damn coyotes kept me awake.

AUSTIN: Oh yeah, I heard them. They must've killed somebody's dog or something.

LEE: Yappin' their fool heads off. They don't yap like that on the desert. They howl. These are city coyotes here.

AUSTIN: Well, you don't sleep anyway do you?

(*pause,* LEE *stares at him*)

LEE: You're pretty smart aren't ya?

AUSTIN: How do you mean?

LEE: I mean you never had any more on the ball than I did. But here you are gettin' invited into prominent people's houses. Sittin' around talkin' like you know somethin'.

AUSTIN: They're not so prominent.

LEE: They're a helluva' lot more prominent than the houses I get invited into.

AUSTIN: Well you invite yourself.

LEE: That's right. I do. In fact I probably got a wider range a' choices than you do, come to think of it.

AUSTIN: I wouldn't doubt it.

LEE: In fact I been inside some pretty classy places in my time. And I never even went to an Ivy League school either.

AUSTIN: You want some breakfast or something?

LEE: Breakfast?

AUSTIN: Yeah. Don't you eat breakfast?

LEE: Look, don't worry about me pal. I can take care a' myself. You just go ahead as though I wasn't even here, all right?

(AUSTIN *goes into kitchen, makes coffee*)

AUSTIN: Where'd you walk to last night?

(*pause*)

LEE: I went up in the foothills there. Up in the San Gabriels. Heat was drivin' me crazy.

AUSTIN: Well, wasn't it hot out on the desert?

LEE: Different kinda' heat. Out there it's clean. Cools off at night. There's a nice little breeze.

AUSTIN: Where were you, the Mojave?

LEE: Yeah. The Mojave. That's right.

AUSTIN: I haven't been out there in years.

LEE: Out past Needles there.

AUSTIN: Oh yeah.

LEE: Up here it's different. This country's real different.

AUSTIN: Well, it's been built up.

LEE: Built up? Wiped out is more like it. I don't even hardly recognize it.

AUSTIN: Yeah. Foothills are the same though, aren't they?

LEE: Pretty much. It's funny goin' up in there. The smells and everything. Used to catch snakes up there, remember?

AUSTIN: You caught snakes.

LEE: Yeah. And you'd pretend you were Geronimo or some damn thing. You used to go right out to lunch.

AUSTIN: I enjoyed my imagination.

LEE: That what you call it? Looks like yer still enjoyin' it.

AUSTIN: So you just wandered around up there, huh?

LEE: Yeah. With a purpose.

AUSTIN: See any houses?

(*pause*)

LEE: Couple. Couple a' real nice ones. One of 'em didn't even have a dog. Walked right up and stuck my head in the window. Not a peep. Just a sweet kinda' suburban silence.

AUSTIN: What kind of a place was it?

LEE: Like a paradise. Kinda' place that sorta' kills ya' inside. Warm yellow lights. Mexican tile all around. Copper pots hangin' over the stove. Ya' know like they got in the magazines. Blonde people movin' in and outa' the rooms, talkin' to each other. (*pause*) Kinda' place you wish you sorta' grew up in, ya' know.

AUSTIN: That's the kind of place you wish you'd grown up in?

LEE: Yeah, why not?

AUSTIN: I thought you hated that kind of stuff.

LEE: Yeah, well you never knew too much about me did ya'?

(*pause*)

AUSTIN: Why'd you go out to the desert in the first place?

LEE: I was on my way to see the old man.

AUSTIN: You mean you just passed through there?

LEE: Yeah. That's right. Three months of passin' through.

AUSTIN: Three months.

LEE: Somethin' like that. Maybe more. Why?

AUSTIN: You lived on the Mojave for three months?

LEE: Yeah. What'sa' matter with that?

AUSTIN: By yourself?

LEE: Mostly. Had a couple a' visitors. Had that dog for a while.

AUSTIN: Didn't you miss people?

LEE: (*laughs*) People?

AUSTIN: Yeah. I mean I go crazy if I have to spend three nights in a motel by myself.

LEE: Yer not in a motel now.

AUSTIN: No, I know. But sometimes I have to stay in motels.

LEE: Well, they got people in motels don't they?

AUSTIN: Strangers.

LEE: Yer friendly aren't ya'? Aren't you the friendly type?

(*pause*)

AUSTIN: I'm going to have somebody coming by here later, Lee.

LEE: Ah! Lady friend?

AUSTIN: No, a producer.

LEE: Aha! What's he produce?

AUSTIN: Film. Movies. You know.

LEE: Oh, movies. Motion pictures! A big wig huh?

AUSTIN: Yeah.

LEE: What's he comin' by here for?

AUSTIN: We have to talk about a project.

LEE: Whadya' mean, "a project"? What's "a project"?

AUSTIN: A script.

LEE: Oh. That's what yer doin' with all these papers?

AUSTIN: Yeah.

LEE: Well, what's the project about?

AUSTIN: We're uh—it's a period piece.

LEE: What's "a period piece"?

AUSTIN: Look, it doesn't matter. The main thing is we need to discuss this alone. I mean—

LEE: Oh, I get it. You want me outa' the picture.

AUSTIN: Not exactly. I just need to be alone with him for a couple of hours. So we can talk.

LEE: Yer afraid I'll embarrass ya' huh?

AUSTIN: I'm not afraid you'll embarrass me!

LEE: Well, I tell ya' what— Why don't you just gimme the keys to yer car and I'll be back here around six o'clock or so. That give ya' enough time?

AUSTIN: I'm not loaning you my car, Lee.

LEE: You want me to just git lost huh? Take a hike? Is that it? Pound the pavement for a few hours while you bullshit yer way into a million bucks.

AUSTIN: Look, it's going to be hard enough for me to face this character on my own without—

LEE: You don't know this guy?

AUSTIN: No I don't know— He's a producer. I mean I've been meeting with him for months but you never get to know a producer.

LEE: Yer tryin' to hustle him? Is that it?

AUSTIN: I'm not trying to hustle him! I'm trying to work out a deal! It's not easy.

LEE: What kinda' deal?

AUSTIN: Convince him it's a worthwhile story.

LEE: He's not convinced? How come he's comin' over here if he's not convinced? I'll convince him for ya'.

AUSTIN: You don't understand the way things work down here.
LEE: How do things work down here?

(*pause*)

AUSTIN: Look, if I loan you my car will you have it back here by six?
LEE: On the button. With a full tank a' gas.
AUSTIN: (*digging in his pocket for keys*) Forget about the gas.
LEE: Hey, these days gas is gold, old buddy.

(AUSTIN *hands the keys to* LEE)

You remember that car I used to loan you?
AUSTIN: Yeah.
LEE: Forty Ford. Flathead.
AUSTIN: Yeah.
LEE: Sucker hauled ass didn't it?
AUSTIN: Lee, it's not that I don't want to loan you my car—
LEE: You are loanin' me yer car.

(LEE *gives* AUSTIN *a pat on the shoulder, pause*)

AUSTIN: I know. I just wish—
LEE: What? You wish what?
AUSTIN: I don't know. I wish I wasn't—I wish I didn't have to be doing business down here. I'd like to just spend some time with you.
LEE: I thought it was "Art" you were doin'.

(LEE *moves across kitchen toward exit, tosses keys in his hand*)

AUSTIN: Try to get it back here by six, okay?
LEE: No sweat. Hey, ya' know, if that uh—story of yours doesn't go over with the guy—tell him I got a couple a' "projects" he might be interested in. Real commercial. Full a' suspense. True-to-life stuff.

(LEE *exits,* AUSTIN *stares after* LEE *then turns, goes to papers at table, leafs through pages, lights fade to black*)

Scene 3

Afternoon. Alcove, SAUL KIMMER *and* AUSTIN *seated across from each other at table.*

SAUL: Well, to tell you the truth, Austin, I have never felt so confident about a project in quite a long time.
AUSTIN: Well, that's good to hear, Saul.
SAUL: I am absolutely convinced we can get this thing off the ground. I mean we'll have to make a sale to television and that means getting a major star. Somebody bankable. But I think we can do it. I really do.
AUSTIN: Don't you think we need a first draft before we approach a star?
SAUL: No, no, not at all. I don't think it's necessary. Maybe a brief synopsis. I don't want you to touch the typewriter until we have some seed money.
AUSTIN: That's fine with me.

SAUL: I mean it's a great story. Just the story alone. You've really managed to
    capture something this time.
AUSTIN: I'm glad you like it, Saul.

(LEE *enters abruptly into kitchen carrying a stolen television set, short pause*)

LEE: Aw shit, I'm sorry about that. I am really sorry, Austin.
AUSTIN: (*standing*) That's all right.
LEE: (*moving toward them*) I mean I thought it was way past six already. You said
    to have it back here by six.
AUSTIN: We were just finishing up. (*to* SAUL) This is my, uh—brother, Lee.
SAUL: (*standing*) Oh, I'm very happy to meet you.

(LEE *sets T.V. on sink counter, shakes hands with* SAUL)

LEE: I can't tell ya' how happy I am to meet you, sir.
SAUL: Saul Kimmer.
LEE: Mr. Kipper.
SAUL: Kimmer.
AUSTIN: Lee's been living out on the desert and he just uh—
SAUL: Oh, that's terrific! (*to* LEE) Palm Springs?
LEE: Yeah. Yeah, right. Right around in that area. Near uh—Bob Hope Drive
    there.
SAUL: Oh I love it out there. I just love it. The air is wonderful.
LEE: Yeah. Sure is. Healthy.
SAUL: And the golf. I don't know if you play golf, but the golf is just about the
    best.
LEE: I play a lota' golf.
SAUL: Is that right?
LEE: Yeah. In fact I was hoping I'd run into somebody out here who played a
    little golf. I've been lookin' for a partner.
SAUL: Well, I uh—
AUSTIN: Lee's just down for a visit while our mother's in Alaska.
SAUL: Oh, your mother's in Alaska?
AUSTIN: Yes. She went up there on a little vacation. This is her place.
SAUL: I see. Well isn't that something. Alaska.
LEE: What kinda' handicap do ya' have, Mr. Kimmer?
SAUL: Oh I'm just a Sunday duffer really. You know.
LEE: That's good 'cause I haven't swung a club in months.
SAUL: Well we ought to get together sometime and have a little game. Austin, do
    you play?

(SAUL *mimes a Johnny Carson golf swing for Austin*)

AUSTIN: No, I don't uh—I've watched it on T.V.
LEE: (*to* SAUL) How 'bout tomorrow morning? Bright and early. We could get
    out there and put in eighteen holes before breakfast.
SAUL: Well, I've got uh—I have several appointments—
LEE: No, I mean real early. Crack a'dawn. While the dew's still thick on the
    fairway.
SAUL: Sounds really great.

LEE: Austin could be our caddie.

SAUL: Now that's an idea. (*laughs*)

AUSTIN: I don't know the first thing about golf.

LEE: There's nothin' to it. Isn't that right, Saul? He'd pick it up in fifteen minutes.

SAUL: Sure. Doesn't take long. 'Course you have to play for years to find your true form. (*chuckles*)

LEE: (*to* AUSTIN)   We'll give ya' a quick run-down on the club faces. The irons, the woods. Show ya' a couple pointers on the basic swing. Might even let ya' hit the ball a couple times. Whadya' think, Saul?

SAUL: Why not. I think it'd be great. I haven't had any exercise in weeks.

LEE: 'At's the spirit! We'll have a little orange juice right afterwards.

(*pause*)

SAUL: Orange juice?

LEE: Yeah! Vitamin C! Nothin' like a shot a' orange juice after a round a' golf. Hot shower. Snappin' towels at each other's privates. Real sense a' fraternity.

SAUL: (*smiles at* AUSTIN)   Well, you make it sound very inviting, I must say. It really does sound great.

LEE: Then's it's a date.

SAUL: Well, I'll call the country club and see if I can arrange something.

LEE: Great! Boy, I sure am sorry that I bustled in on ya' all in the middle of yer meeting.

SAUL: Oh that's quite all right. We were just about finished anyway.

LEE: I can wait out in the other room if you want.

SAUL: No really—

LEE: Just got Austin's color T.V. back from the shop. I can watch a little amateur boxing now.

(LEE *and* AUSTIN *exchange looks*)

SAUL: Oh—Yes.

LEE: You don't fool around in television, do you, Saul?

SAUL: Uh—I have in the past. Produced some T.V. specials. Network stuff. But it's mainly features now.

LEE: That's where the big money is, huh?

SAUL: Yes. That's right.

AUSTIN: Why don't I call you tomorrow, Saul, and we'll get together. We can have lunch or something.

SAUL: That'd be terrific.

LEE: Right after the golf.

(*pause*)

SAUL: What?

LEE: You can have lunch right after the golf.

SAUL: Oh, right.

LEE: Austin was tellin' me that yer interested in stories.

SAUL: Well, we develop certain projects that we feel have commercial potential.

LEE: What kinda' stuff do ya' go in for?

SAUL: Oh, the usual. You know. Good love interest. Lots of action. (*chuckles at* AUSTIN)

LEE: Westerns?

SAUL: Sometimes.

AUSTIN: I'll give you a ring, Saul.

(AUSTIN *tries to move* SAUL *across the kitchen but* LEE *blocks their way*)

LEE: I got a Western that'd knock yer lights out.

SAUL: Oh really?

LEE: Yeah. Contemporary Western. Based on a true story. 'Course I'm not a writer like my brother here. I'm not a man of the pen.

SAUL: Well—

LEE: I mean I can tell ya' a story off the tongue but I can't put it down on paper. That don't make any difference though does it?

SAUL: No, not really.

LEE: I mean plenty a' guys have stories don't they? True-life stories. Musta' been a lota' movies made from real life.

SAUL: Yes. I suppose so.

LEE: I haven't seen a good Western since "Lonely Are the Brave." You remember that movie?

SAUL: No, I'm afraid I—

LEE: Kirk Douglas. Helluva' movie. You remember that movie, Austin?

AUSTIN: Yes.

LEE: (*to* SAUL) The man dies for the love of a horse.

SAUL: Is that right.

LEE: Yeah. Ya' hear the horse screamin' at the end of it. Rain's comin' down. Horse is screamin'. Then there's a shot. BLAM! Just a single shot like that. Then nothin' but the sound of rain. And Kirk Douglas is ridin' in the ambulance. Ridin' away from the scene of the accident. And when he hears that shot he knows that his horse has died. He knows. And you see his eyes. And his eyes die. Right inside his face. And then his eyes close. And you know that he's died too. You know that Kirk Douglas has died from the death of his horse.

SAUL: (*eyes* AUSTIN *nervously*) Well, it sounds like a great movie. I'm sorry I missed it.

LEE: Yeah, you shouldn't a' missed that one.

SAUL: I'll have to try to catch it some time. Arrange a screening or something. Well, Austin, I'll have to hit the freeway before rush hour.

AUSTIN: (*ushers him toward exit*) It's good seeing you, Saul.

(AUSTIN *and* SAUL *shake hands*)

LEE: So ya' think there's room for a real Western these days? A true-to-life Western?

SAUL: Well, I don't see why not. Why don't you uh—tell the story to Austin and have him write a little outline.

LEE: You'd take a look at it then?

SAUL: Yes. Sure. I'll give it a read-through. Always eager for new material. (*smiles at* AUSTIN)

LEE: That's great! You'd really read it then huh?

SAUL: It would just be my opinion of course.

LEE: That's all I want. Just an opinion. I happen to think it has a lota' possibilities.

SAUL: Well, it was great meeting you and I'll—

(SAUL *and* LEE *shake*)

LEE: I'll call you tomorrow about the golf.

SAUL: Oh. Yes, right.

LEE: Austin's got your number, right?

SAUL: Yes.

LEE: So long, Saul. (*gives* SAUL *a pat on the back*)

(SAUL *exits,* AUSTIN *turns to* LEE, *looks at T.V. then back to* LEE)

AUSTIN: Give me the keys.

(AUSTIN *extends his hand toward* LEE, LEE *doesn't move, just stares at* AUSTIN, *smiles, lights to black*)

Scene 4

Night. Coyotes in distance, fade, sound of typewriter in dark, crickets, candlelight in alcove, dim light in kitchen, lights reveal AUSTIN *at glass table typing,* LEE *sits across from him, foot on table, drinking beer and whiskey, the T.V. is still on sink counter,* AUSTIN *types for a while, then stops.*

LEE: All right, now read it back to me.

AUSTIN: I'm not reading it back to you, Lee. You can read it when we're finished. I can't spend all night on this.

LEE: You got better things to do?

AUSTIN: Let's just go ahead. Now what happens when he leaves Texas?

LEE: Is he ready to leave Texas yet? I didn't know we were that far along. He's not ready to leave Texas.

AUSTIN: He's right at the border.

LEE: (*sitting up*)   No, see, this is one a' the critical parts. Right here. (*taps paper with beer can*) We can't rush through this. He's not right at the border. He's a good fifty miles from the border. A lot can happen in fifty miles.

AUSTIN: It's only an outline. We're not writing an entire script now.

LEE: Well ya' can't leave things out even if it is an outline. It's one a' the most important parts. Ya' can't go leavin' it out.

AUSTIN: Okay, okay. Let's just—get it done.

LEE: All right. Now. He's in the truck and he's got his horse trailer and his horse.

AUSTIN: We've already established that.

LEE: And he sees this other guy comin' up behind him in another truck. And that truck is pullin' a gooseneck.

AUSTIN: What's a gooseneck?

LEE: Cattle trailer. You know the kind with a gooseneck, goes right down in the bed a' the pick-up.

AUSTIN: Oh. All right. (*types*)

LEE: It's important.

AUSTIN: Okay. I got it.

LEE: All these details are important.

(AUSTIN *types as they talk*)

AUSTIN: I've got it.

LEE: And this other guy's got his horse all saddled up in the back a' the goose-neck.

AUSTIN: Right.

LEE: So both these guys have got their horses right along with 'em, see.

AUSTIN: I understand.

LEE: Then this first guy suddenly realizes two things.

AUSTIN: The guy in front?

LEE: Right. The guy in front realizes two things almost at the same time. Simultaneous.

AUSTIN: What were the two things?

LEE: Number one, he realizes that the guy behind him is the husband of the woman he's been—

(LEE *makes gesture of screwing by pumping his arm*)

AUSTIN: (*sees* LEE's *gesture*)   Oh. Yeah.

LEE: And number two, he realizes he's in the middle of tornado country.

AUSTIN: What's "tornado country"?

LEE: Panhandle.

AUSTIN: Panhandle?

LEE: Sweetwater. Around in that area. Nothin'. Nowhere. And number three—

AUSTIN: I thought there was only two.

LEE: There's three. There's a third unforeseen realization.

AUSTIN: And what's that?

LEE: That he's runnin' outa' gas.

AUSTIN: (*stops typing*)   Come on, Lee.

(AUSTIN *gets up, moves to kitchen, gets a glass of water*)

LEE: Whadya' mean, "come on"? That's what it is. Write it down! He's runnin' outa' gas.

AUSTIN: It's too—

LEE: What? It's too what? It's too real! That's what ya' mean isn't it? It's too much like real life!

AUSTIN: It's not like real life! It's not enough like real life. Things don't happen like that.

LEE: What! Men don't fuck other men's women?

AUSTIN: Yes. But they don't end up chasing each other across the Panhandle. Through "tornado country."

LEE: They do in this movie!

AUSTIN: And they don't have horses conveniently along with them when they run out of gas! And they don't run out of gas either!

LEE: These guys run outa' gas! This is my story and one a' these guys runs outa' gas!

AUSTIN: It's just a dumb excuse to get them into a chase scene. It's contrived.

LEE: It is a chase scene! It's already a chase scene. They been chasin' each other fer days.

AUSTIN: So now they're supposed to abandon their trucks, climb on their horses and chase each other into the mountains?

LEE: (*standing suddenly*) There aren't any mountains in the Panhandle! It's flat!

(LEE *turns violently toward windows in alcove and throws beer can at them*)

LEE: Goddamn these crickets! (*yells at crickets*) Shut up out there! (*pause, turns back toward table*) This place is like a fuckin' rest home here. How're you supposed to think!

AUSTIN: You wanna' take a break?

LEE: No, I don't wanna' take a break! I wanna' get this done! This is my last chance to get this done.

AUSTIN: (*moves back into alcove*) All right. Take it easy.

LEE: I'm gonna' be leavin' this area. I don't have time to mess around here.

AUSTIN: Where are you going?

LEE: Never mind where I'm goin'! That's got nothin' to do with you. I just gotta' get this done. I'm not like you. Hangin' around bein' a parasite offa' other fools. I gotta' do this thing and get out.

(*pause*)

AUSTIN: A parasite? Me?

LEE: Yeah, you!

AUSTIN: After you break into people's houses and take their televisions?

LEE: They don't need their televisions! I'm doin' them a service.

AUSTIN: Give me back my keys, Lee.

LEE: Not until you write this thing! You're gonna' write this outline thing for me or that car's gonna' wind up in Arizona with a different paint job.

AUSTIN: You think you can force me to write this? I was doing you a favor.

LEE: Git off yer high horse will ya'! Favor! Big favor. Handin' down favors from the mountain top.

AUSTIN: Let's just write it, okay? Let's sit down and not get upset and see if we can just get through this.

(AUSTIN *sits at typewriter*)

(*pause*)

LEE: Yer not gonna' even show it to him, are ya'?

AUSTIN? What?

LEE: This outline. You got no intention of showin' it to him. Yer just doin' this 'cause yer afraid a' me.

AUSTIN: You can show it to him yourself.

LEE: I will, boy! I'm gonna' read it to him on the golf course.

AUSTIN: And I'm not afraid of you either.

LEE: Then how come yer doin' it?

AUSTIN: (*pause*) So I can get my keys back.

(*pause as* LEE *takes keys out of his pocket slowly and throws them on table, long pause,* AUSTIN *stares at keys*)

LEE: There. Now you got yer keys back.

(AUSTIN *looks up at* LEE *but doesn't take keys*)

LEE: Go ahead. There's yer keys.

(AUSTIN *slowly takes keys off table and puts them back in his own pocket*)

Now what're you gonna' do? Kick me out?

AUSTIN: I'm not going to kick you out, Lee.
LEE: You couldn't kick me out, boy.
AUSTIN: I know.
LEE: So you can't even consider that one. (*pause*) You could call the police. That'd be the obvious thing.
AUSTIN: You're my brother.
LEE: That don't mean a thing. You go down to the L.A. Police Department there and ask them what kinda' people kill each other the most. What do you think they'd say?
AUSTIN: Who said anything about killing?
LEE: Family people. Brothers. Brothers-in-law. Cousins. Real American-type people. They kill each other in the heat mostly. In the smog-alerts. In the brush fire season. Right about this time a' year.
AUSTIN: This isn't the same.
LEE: Oh no? What makes it different?
AUSTIN: We're not insane. We're not driven to acts of violence like that. Not over a dumb movie script. Now sit down.

(*long pause,* LEE *considers which way to go with it*)

LEE: Maybe not. (*he sits back down at table across from* AUSTIN) Maybe you're right. Maybe we're too intelligent, huh? (*pause*) We got our heads on our shoulders. One of us has even got a Ivy League diploma. Now that means somethin' don't it? Doesn't that mean somethin'?
AUSTIN: Look, I'll write this thing for you, Lee. I don't mind writing it. I just don't want to get all worked up about it. It's not worth it. Now, come on. Let's just get through it, okay?
LEE: Nah. I think there's easier money. Lotsa' places I could pick up thousands. Maybe millions. I don't need this shit. I could go up to Sacramento Valley and steal me a diesel. Ten thousand a week dismantling one a' those suckers. Ten thousand a week!

(LEE *opens another beer, puts his foot back up on table*)

AUSTIN: No, really, look, I'll write it out for you. I think it's a great idea.
LEE: Nah, you got yer own work to do. I don't wanna' interfere with yer life.
AUSTIN: I mean it'd be really fantastic if you could sell this. Turn it into a movie. I mean it.

(*pause*)

LEE: Ya' think so huh?

AUSTIN: Absolutely. You could really turn your life around, you know. Change things.

LEE: I could get me a house maybe.

AUSTIN: Sure you could get a house. You could get a whole ranch if you wanted to.

LEE: (*laughs*) A ranch? I could get a ranch?

AUSTIN: 'Course you could. You know what a screenplay sells for these days?

LEE: No. What's it sell for?

AUSTIN: A lot. A whole lot of money.

LEE: Thousands?

AUSTIN: Yeah. Thousands.

LEE: Millions?

AUSTIN: Well—

LEE: We could get the old man outa' hock then.

AUSTIN: Maybe.

LEE: Maybe? Whadya' mean, maybe?

AUSTIN: I mean it might take more than money.

LEE: You were just tellin' me it'd change my whole life around. Why wouldn't it change his?

AUSTIN: He's different.

LEE: Oh, he's of a different ilk huh?

AUSTIN: He's not gonna' change. Let's leave the old man out of it.

LEE: That's right. He's not gonna' change but I will. I'll just turn myself right inside out. I could be just like you then, huh? Sittin' around dreamin' stuff up. Gettin' paid to dream. Ridin' back and forth on the freeway just dreamin' my fool head off.

AUSTIN: It's not all that easy.

LEE: It's not, huh?

AUSTIN: No. There's a lot of work involved.

LEE: What's the toughest part? Deciding whether to jog or play tennis?

(*long pause*)

AUSTIN: Well, look. You can stay here—do whatever you want to. Borrow the car. Come in and out. Doesn't matter to me. It's not my house. I'll help you write this thing or—not. Just let me know what you want. You tell me.

LEE: Oh. So now suddenly you're at my service. Is that it?

AUSTIN: What do you want to do, Lee?

(*long pause,* LEE *stares at him then turns and dreams at windows*)

LEE: I tell ya' what I'd do if I still had that dog. Ya' wanna' know what I'd do?

AUSTIN: What?

LEE: Head out to Ventura. Cook up a little match. God that little dog could bear down. Lota' money in dog fightin'. Big money.

(*pause*)

AUSTIN: Why don't we try to see this through, Lee. Just for the hell of it. Maybe you've really got something here. What do you think?

(*pause,* LEE *considers*)

LEE: Maybe so. No harm in tryin' I guess. You think it's such a hot idea. Besides,
I always wondered what'd be like to be you.
AUSTIN: You did?
LEE: Yeah, sure. I used to picture you walkin' around some campus with yer arms
fulla' books. Blondes chasin' after ya'.
AUSTIN: Blondes? That's funny.
LEE: What's funny about it?
AUSTIN: Because I always used to picture you somewhere.
LEE: Where'd you picture me?
AUSTIN: Oh, I don't know. Different places. Adventures. You were always on
some adventure.
LEE: Yeah.
AUSTIN: And I used to say to myself, "Lee's got the right idea. He's out there in
the world and here I am. What am I doing?"
LEE: Well you were settin' yourself up for somethin'.
AUSTIN: I guess.
LEE: We better get started on this thing then.
AUSTIN: Okay.

(AUSTIN *sits up at typewriter, puts new paper in*)

LEE: Oh. Can I get the keys back before I forget?

(AUSTIN *hesitates*)

You said I could borrow the car if I wanted, right? Isn't that what you said?
AUSTIN: Yeah. Right.

(AUSTIN *takes keys out of his pocket, sets them on table,* LEE *takes keys slowly, plays with
them in his hand*)

LEE: I could get a ranch, huh?
AUSTIN: Yeah. We have to write it first though.
LEE: Okay. Let's write it.

(*lights start dimming slowly to end of scene as* AUSTIN *types,* LEE *speaks*)

So they take off after each other straight into an endless black prairie. The sun
is just comin' down and they can feel the night on their backs. What they don't
know is that each one of 'em is afraid, see. Each one separately thinks that he's
the only one that's afraid. And they keep ridin' like that straight into the night.
Not knowing. And the one who's chasin' doesn't know where the other one is
taking him. And the one who's being chased doesn't know where he's going.

(*lights to black, typing stops in the dark, crickets fade*)

ACT TWO

Scene 5

Morning. LEE *at the table in alcove with a set of golf clubs in a fancy leather bag.* AUSTIN *at sink washing a few dishes.*

AUSTIN: He really liked it, huh?

LEE: He wouldn't a' gave me these clubs if he didn't like it.

AUSTIN: He gave you the clubs?

LEE: Yeah. I told ya' he gave me the clubs. The bag too.

AUSTIN: I thought he just loaned them to you.

LEE: He said it was part a' the advance. A little gift like. Gesture of his good faith.

AUSTIN: He's giving you an advance?

LEE: Now what's so amazing about that? I told ya' it was a good story. You even said it was a good story.

AUSTIN: Well that is really incredible, Lee. You know how many guys spend their whole lives down here trying to break into this business? Just trying to get in the door?

LEE: (*pulling clubs out of bag, testing them*)   I got no idea. How many?

(*pause*)

AUSTIN: How much of an advance is he giving you?

LEE: Plenty. We were talkin' big money out there. Ninth hole is where I sealed the deal.

AUSTIN: He made a firm commitment?

LEE: Absolutely.

AUSTIN: Well, I know Saul and he doesn't fool around when he says he likes something.

LEE: I thought you said you didn't know him.

AUSTIN: Well, I'm familiar with his tastes.

LEE: I let him get two up on me goin' into the back nine. He was sure he had me cold. You shoulda' seen his face when I pulled out the old pitching wedge and plopped it pin-high, two feet from the cup. He 'bout shit his pants. "Where'd a guy like you ever learn how to play golf like that?", he says.

(LEE *laughs,* AUSTIN *stares at him*)

AUSTIN: 'Course there's no contract yet. Nothing's final until it's on paper.

LEE: It's final, all right. There's no way he's gonna' back out of it now. We gambled for it.

AUSTIN: Saul gambled?

LEE: Yeah, sure. I mean he liked the outline already so he wasn't risking that much. I just guaranteed it with my short game.

(*pause*)

AUSTIN: Well, we should celebrate or something. I think Mom left a bottle of champagne in the refrigerator. We should have a little toast.

(AUSTIN *gets glasses from cupboard, goes to refrigerator, pulls out bottle of champagne*)

LEE: You shouldn't oughta' take her champagne, Austin. She's gonna' miss that.
AUSTIN: Oh, she's not going to mind. She'd be glad we put it to good use. I'll get her another bottle. Besides, it's perfect for the occasion.

(*pause*)

LEE: Yer gonna' get a nice fee fer writin' the script a' course. Straight fee.

(AUSTIN *stops, stares at* LEE, *puts glasses and bottles on table, pause*)

AUSTIN: I'm writing the script?
LEE: That's what he said. Said we couldn't hire a better screenwriter in the whole town.
AUSTIN: But I'm already working on a script. I've got my own project. I don't have time to write two scripts.
LEE: No, he said he was gonna' drop that other one.

(*pause*)

AUSTIN: What? You mean mine? He's going to drop mine and do yours instead?
LEE: (*smiles*)   Now look, Austin, it's jest beginner's luck ya' know. I mean I sank a fifty foot putt for this deal. No hard feelings.

(AUSTIN *goes to phone on wall, grabs it, starts dialing*)

He's not gonna' be in, Austin. Told me he wouldn't be in 'till late this afternoon.
AUSTIN: (*stays on phone, dialing, listens*)   I can't believe this. I just can't believe it. Are you sure he said that? Why would he drop mine?
LEE: That's what he told me.
AUSTIN: He can't do that without telling me first. Without talking to me at least. He wouldn't just make a decision like that without talking to me!
LEE: Well I was kinda' surprised myself. But he was real enthusiastic about my story.

(AUSTIN *hangs up phone violently, paces*)

AUSTIN: What'd he say! Tell me everything he said!
LEE: I been tellin' ya'! He said he liked the story a whole lot. It was the first authentic Western to come along in a decade.
AUSTIN: He liked that story! Your story?
LEE: Yeah! What's so surprisin' about that?
AUSTIN: It's stupid! It's the dumbest story I ever heard in my life.
LEE: Hey, hold on! That's my story yer talkin' about!
AUSTIN: It's a bullshit story! It's idiotic. Two lamebrains chasing each other across Texas! Are you kidding? Who do you think's going to go see a film like that?
LEE: It's not a film! It's a movie. There's a big difference. That's somethin' Saul told me.

AUSTIN: Oh he did, huh?

LEE: Yeah, he said, "In this business we make movies, American movies. Leave the films to the French."

AUSTIN: So you got real intimate with old Saul huh? He started pouring forth his vast knowledge of cinema.

LEE: I think he liked me a lot, to tell ya' the truth. I think he felt I was somebody he could confide in.

AUSTIN: What'd you do, beat him up or something?

LEE: (*stands fast*) Hey, I've about had it with the insults, buddy! You think yer the only one in the brain department here? Yer the only one that can sit around and cook things up? There's other people got ideas too, ya' know!

AUSTIN: You must've done something. Threatened him or something. Now what'd you do, Lee?

LEE: I convinced him!

(LEE *makes sudden menacing lunge toward* AUSTIN, *wielding golf club above his head, stops himself, frozen moment, long pause,* LEE *lowers club*)

AUSTIN: Oh, Jesus. You didn't hurt him, did you?

(*long silence,* LEE *sits back down at table*)

Lee! Did you hurt him?

LEE: I didn't do nothin' to him! He liked my story. Pure and simple. He said it was the best story he's come across in a long, long time.

AUSTIN: That's what he told me about my story! That's the same thing he said to me.

LEE: Well, he musta' been lyin'. He musta' been lyin' to one of us anyway.

AUSTIN: You can't come into this town and start pushing people around. They're gonna' put you away!

LEE: I never pushed anybody around! I beat him fair and square. (*pause*) They can't touch me anyway. They can't put a finger on me. I'm gone. I can come in through the window and go out though the door. They never knew what hit 'em. You, yer stuck. Yer the one that's stuck. Not me. So don't be warnin' me what to do in this town.

(*pause,* AUSTIN *crosses to table, sits at typewriter, rests*)

AUSTIN: Lee, come on, level with me, will you? It doesn't make any sense that suddenly he'd throw my idea out the window. I've been talking to him for months. I've got too much at stake. Everything's riding on this project.

LEE: What's yer idea?

AUSTIN: It's just a simple love story.

LEE: What kinda' love story?

AUSTIN: (*stands, crosses into kitchen*) I'm not telling you!

LEE: Ha! 'Fraid I'll steal it huh? Competition's gettin' kinda' close to home isn't it?

AUSTIN: Where did Saul say he was going?

LEE: He was gonna' take my story to a couple studios.

AUSTIN: That's *my* outline you know! I wrote that outline! You've got no right to be peddling it around.

LEE: You weren't ready to take credit for it last night.
AUSTIN: Give me my keys!
LEE: What?
AUSTIN: The keys! I want my keys back!
LEE: Where you goin?
AUSTIN: Just give me my keys! I gotta' take a drive. I gotta' get out of here for a
   while.
LEE: Where you gonna' go, Austin?
AUSTIN: (*pause*)   I might just drive out to the desert for a while. I gotta' think.
LEE: You can think here just as good. This is the perfect setup for thinkin'. We
   got some writin' to do here, boy. Now let's just have us a little toast. Relax. We're
   partners now.

(LEE *pops the cork on the champagne bottle, pours two drinks as the lights fade to black*)

Scene 6

Afternoon. LEE *and* SAUL *in kitchen,* AUSTIN *in alcove.*

LEE: Now you tell him. You tell him, Mr. Kipper.
SAUL: Kimmer.
LEE: Kimmer. You tell him what you told me. He don't believe me.
AUSTIN: I don't want to hear it.
SAUL: It's really not a big issue, Austin. I was simply amazed by your brother's
   story and—
AUSTIN: Amazed? You lost a bet! You gambled with my material!
SAUL: That's really beside the point, Austin. I'm ready to go all the way with your
   brother's story. I think it has a great deal of merit.
AUSTIN: I don't want to hear about it, okay? Go tell it to the executives! Tell it
   to somebody who's going to turn it into a package deal or something. A T.V.
   series. Don't tell it to me.
SAUL: But I want to continue with your project too, Austin. It's not as though we
   can't do both. We're big enough for that aren't we?
AUSTIN: "We"? *I* can't do both! I don't know about "we."
LEE: (*to* SAUL)   See, what'd I tell ya'. He's totally unsympathetic.
SAUL: Austin, there's no point in our going to another screenwriter for this. It
   just doesn't make sense. You're brothers. You know each other. There's a
   familiarity with the material that just wouldn't be possible otherwise.
AUSTIN: There's no familiarity with the material! None! I don't know what "tornado country" is. I don't know what a "gooseneck" is. And I don't want to
   know! (*pointing to* LEE) He's a hustler! He's a bigger hustler than you are! If you
   can't see that, then—
LEE: (*to* AUSTIN)   Hey, now hold on. I didn't have to bring this bone back to you,
   boy. I persuaded Saul here that you were the right man for the job. You don't
   have to go throwin' up favors in my face.
AUSTIN: Favors! I'm the one who wrote the fuckin' outline! You can't even spell.
SAUL: (*to* AUSTIN)   Your brother told me about the situation with your father.

(*pause*)

AUSTIN: What? (*looks at* LEE)

SAUL: That's right. Now we have a clear-cut deal here, Austin. We have big studio money standing behind this thing. Just on the basis of your outline.

AUSTIN: (*to* SAUL) What'd he tell you about my father?

SAUL: Well—that he's destitute. He needs money.

LEE: That's right. He does.

(AUSTIN *shakes his head, stares at them both*)

AUSTIN: (*to* LEE) And this little assignment is supposed to go toward the old man? A charity project? Is that what this is? Did you cook this up on the ninth green too?

SAUL: It's a big slice, Austin.

AUSTIN: (*to* LEE) I gave him money! I already gave him money. You know that. He drank it all up!

LEE: This is a different deal here.

SAUL: We can set up a trust for your father. A large sum of money. It can be doled out to him in parcels so he can't misuse it.

AUSTIN: Yeah, and who's doing the doling?

SAUL: Your brother volunteered.

(AUSTIN *laughs*)

LEE: That's right. I'll make sure he uses it for groceries.

AUSTIN: (*to* SAUL) I'm not doing this script! I'm not writing this crap for you or anybody else. You can't blackmail me into it. You can't threaten me into it. There's no way I'm doing it. So just give it up. Both of you.

(*long pause*)

SAUL: Well, that's it then. I mean this is an easy three hundred grand. Just for a first draft. It's incredible, Austin. We've got three different studios all trying to cut each other's throat to get this material. In one morning. That's how hot it is.

AUSTIN: Yeah, well, you can afford to give me a percentage on the outline then. And you better get the genius here an agent before he gets burned.

LEE: Saul's gonna' be my agent. Isn't that right, Saul?

SAUL: That's right. (*to* AUSTIN) Your brother has really got something, Austin. I've been around too long not to recognize it. Raw talent.

AUSTIN: He's got a lota' balls is what he's got. He's taking you right down the river.

SAUL: Three hundred thousand, Austin. Just for a first draft. Now you've never been offered that kind of money before.

AUSTIN: I'm not writing it.

(*pause*)

SAUL: I see. Well—

LEE: We'll just go to another writer then. Right, Saul? Just hire us somebody with some enthusiasm. Somebody who can recognize the value of a good story.

SAUL: I'm sorry about this, Austin.

AUSTIN: Yeah.

SAUL: I mean I was hoping we could continue both things but now I don't see how it's possible.

AUSTIN: So you're dropping my idea altogether. Is that it? Just trade horses midstream? After all these months of meetings.

SAUL: I wish there was another way.

AUSTIN: I've got everything riding on this, Saul. You know that. It's my only shot. If this falls through—

SAUL: I have to go with what my instincts tell me—

AUSTIN: Your instincts!

SAUL: My gut reaction.

AUSTIN: You lost! That's your gut reaction. You lost a gamble. Now you're trying to tell me you like his story? How could you possibly fall for that story? It's as phony as Hopalong Cassidy. What do you see in it? I'm curious.

SAUL: It has the ring of truth, Austin.

AUSTIN: (*laughs*)   Truth?

LEE: It is true.

SAUL: Something about the real West.

AUSTIN: Why? Because it's got horses? Because it's got grown men acting like little boys?

SAUL: Something about the land. Your brother is speaking from experience.

AUSTIN: So am I!

SAUL: But nobody's interested in love these days, Austin. Let's face it.

LEE: That's right.

AUSTIN: (*to* SAUL)   He's been camped out on the desert for three months. Talking to cactus. What's he know about what people wanna' see on the screen! I drive on the freeway every day. I swallow the smog. I watch the news in color. I shop in the Safeway. I'm the one who's in touch! Not him!

SAUL: I have to go now, Austin.

(SAUL *starts to leave*)

AUSTIN: There's no such thing as the West anymore! It's a dead issue! It's dried up, Saul, and so are you.

(SAUL *stops and turns to* AUSTIN)

SAUL: Maybe you're right. But I have to take the gamble, don't I?

AUSTIN: You're a fool to do this, Saul.

SAUL: I've always gone on my hunches. Always. And I've never been wrong. (*to* LEE) I'll talk to you tomorrow, Lee.

LEE: All right, Mr. Kimmer.

SAUL: Maybe we could have some lunch.

LEE: Fine with me. (*smiles at* AUSTIN)

SAUL: I'll give you a ring.

(SAUL *exits, lights to black as brothers look at each other from a distance*)

Scene 7

Night. Coyotes, crickets, sound of typewriter in dark, candlelight up on LEE *at typewriter struggling to type with one finger system,* AUSTIN *sits sprawled out on kitchen floor with whiskey bottle, drunk.*

AUSTIN: (*singing, from floor*)

> Red sails in the sunset
> Way out on the blue
> Please carry my loved one
> Home safely to me
>
> Red sails in the sunset—

LEE: (*slams fist on table*)   Hey! Knock it off will ya'! I'm tryin' to concentrate here.
AUSTIN: (*laughs*)   You're tryin' to concentrate?
LEE: Yeah. That's right.
AUSTIN: Now you're tryin' to concentrate.
LEE: Between you, the coyotes and the crickets a thought don't have much of a chance.
AUSTIN: "Between me, the coyotes and the crickets." What a great title.
LEE: I don't need a title! I need a thought.
AUSTIN: (*laughs*)   A thought! Here's a thought for ya'—
LEE: I'm not askin' fer yer thoughts! I got my own. I can do this thing on my own.
AUSTIN: You're going to write an entire script on your own?
LEE: That's right.

(*pause*)

AUSTIN: Here's a thought. Saul Kimmer—
LEE: Shut up will ya'!
AUSTIN: He thinks we're the same person.
LEE: Don't get cute.
AUSTIN: He does! He's lost his mind. Poor old Saul. (*giggles*) Thinks we're one and the same.
LEE: Why don't you ease up on that champagne.
AUSTIN: (*holding up bottle*)   This isn't champagne any more. We went through the champagne a long time ago. This is serious stuff. The days of champagne are long gone.
LEE: Well, go outside and drink it.
AUSTIN: I'm enjoying your company, Lee. For the first time since your arrival I am finally enjoying your company. And now you want me to go outside and drink alone?
LEE: That's right.

(LEE *reads through paper in typewriter, makes an erasure*)

AUSTIN: You think you'll make more progress if you're alone? You might drive yourself crazy.
LEE: I could have this thing done in a night if I had a little silence.
AUSTIN: Well you'd still have the crickets to contend with. The coyotes. The

sounds of the police helicopters prowling above the neighborhood. Slashing their searchlights down through the streets. Hunting for the likes of you.

LEE: I'm a screenwriter now! I'm legitimate.

AUSTIN: (*laughing*) A screenwriter!

LEE: That's right. I'm on salary. That's more'n I can say for you. I got an advance coming.

AUSTIN: This is true. This is very true. An advance. (*pause*) Well, maybe I oughta' go out and try my hand at your trade. Since you're doing so good at mine.

LEE: Ha!

(LEE *attempts to type some more but gets the ribbon tangled up, starts trying to re-thread it as they continue talking*)

AUSTIN: Well why not? You don't think I've got what it takes to sneak into people's houses and steal their T.V.s?

LEE: You couldn't steal a toaster without losin' yer lunch.

(AUSTIN *stands with a struggle, supports himself by the sink*)

AUSTIN: You don't think I could sneak into somebody's house and steal a toaster?

LEE: Go take a shower or somethin' will ya!

(LEE *gets more tangled up with the typewriter ribbon, pulling it out of the machine as though it was fishing line*)

AUSTIN: You really don't think I could steal a crumby toaster? How much you wanna' bet I can't steal a toaster! How much? Go ahead! You're a gambler aren't you? Tell me how much yer willing to put on the line. Some part of your big advance? Oh, you haven't got that yet, have you? I forgot.

LEE: All right: I'll bet you your car that you can't steal a toaster without gettin' busted.

AUSTIN: You already got my car!

LEE: Okay, your house then.

AUSTIN: What're you gonna' give me? I'm not talkin' about my house and my car, I'm talkin' about what are you gonna' give me. You don't have nothin' to give me.

LEE: I'll give you—shared screen credit. How 'bout that? I'll have it put in the contract that this was written by the both of us.

AUSTIN: I don't want my name on that piece of shit! I want something of value. You got anything of value? You got any tidbits from the desert? Any rattlesnake bones? I'm not a greedy man. Any little personal treasure will suffice.

LEE: I'm gonna' just kick yer ass out in a minute.

AUSTIN: Oh, so now you're gonna' kick me out! Now I'm the intruder. I'm the one who's invading your precious privacy.

LEE: I'm trying to do some screenwriting here!

(LEE *stands, picks up typewriter, slams it down hard on table, pause, silence except for crickets*)

AUSTIN: Well, you got everything you need. You got plenty a' coffee? Groceries.

You got a car. A contract. (*pause*) Might need a new typewriter ribbon but other than that you're pretty well fixed. I'll just leave ya' alone for a while.

(AUSTIN *tries to steady himself to leave,* LEE *makes a move toward him*)

LEE: Where are you goin'?
AUSTIN: Don't worry about me. I'm not the one to worry about.

(AUSTIN *weaves toward exit, stops*)

LEE: What're you gonna' do? Just go wander out into the night?
AUSTIN: I'm gonna' make a little tour.
LEE: Why don't ya' just go to bed for Christ's sake. Yer makin' me sick.
AUSTIN: I can take care a' myself. Don't worry about me.

(AUSTIN *weaves badly in another attempt to exit, he crashes to the floor,* LEE *goes to him but remains standing*)

LEE: You want me to call your wife for ya' or something?
AUSTIN: (*from floor*) My wife?
LEE: Yeah. I mean maybe she can help ya' out. Talk to ya' or somethin'.
AUSTIN: (*struggles to stand again*) She's five hundred miles away. North. North of here. Up in the North country where things are calm. I don't need any help. I'm gonna' go outside and I'm gonna' steal a toaster. I'm gonna' steal some other stuff too. I might even commit bigger crimes. Bigger than you ever dreamed of. Crimes beyond the imagination!

(AUSTIN *manages to get himself vertical, tries to head for exit again*)

LEE: Just hang on a minute, Austin.
AUSTIN: Why? What for? You don't need my help, right? You got a handle on the project. Besides, I'm lookin' forward to the smell of the night. The bushes. Orange blossoms. Dust in the driveways. Rain bird sprinklers. Lights in people's houses. You're right about the lights, Lee. Everybody else is livin' the life. Indoors. Safe. This is a paradise down here. You know that? We're livin' in a paradise. We've forgotten about that.
LEE: You sound just like the old man now.
AUSTIN: Yeah, well, we all sound alike when we're sloshed. We just sorta' echo each other.
LEE: Maybe if we could work on this together we could bring him back out here. Get him settled down some place.

(AUSTIN *turns violently toward* LEE, *takes a swing at him, misses and crashes to the floor again,* LEE *stays standing*)

AUSTIN: I don't want him out here! I've had it with him! I went all the way out there! I went out of my way. I gave him money and all he did was play Al Jolson records and spit at me! I gave him money!

(*pause*)

LEE: Just help me a little with the characters, all right? You know how to do it, Austin.

AUSTIN: (*on the floor, laughs*) The characters!

LEE: Yeah. You know. The way they talk and stuff. I can hear it in my head but I can't get it down on paper.

AUSTIN: What characters?

LEE: The guys. The guys in the story.

AUSTIN: Those aren't characters.

LEE: Whatever you call 'em then. I need to write somethin' out.

AUSTIN: Those are illusions of characters.

LEE: I don't give a damn what ya' call 'em! You know what I'm talkin' about!

AUSTIN: Those are fantasies of a long lost boyhood.

LEE: I gotta' write somethin' out on paper!!

(*pause*)

AUSTIN: What for? Saul's gonna' get you a fancy screenwriter isn't he?

LEE: I wanna' do it myself!

AUSTIN: Then do it! Yer on your own now, old buddy. You bulldogged yer way into contention. Now you gotta' carry it through.

LEE: I will but I need some advice. Just a couple a' things. Come on, Austin. Just help me get 'em talkin' right. It won't take much.

AUSTIN: Oh, now you're having a little doubt huh? What happened? The pressure's on, boy. This is it. You gotta' come up with it now. You don't come up with a winner on your first time out they just cut your head off. They don't give you a second chance ya' know.

LEE: I got a good story! I know it's a good story. I just need a little help is all.

AUSTIN: Not from me. Not from yer little old brother. I'm retired.

LEE: You could save this thing for me, Austin. I'd give ya' half the money. I would. I only need half anyway. With this kinda' money I could be a long time down the road. I'd never bother ya' again. I promise. You'd never even see me again.

AUSTIN: (*still on floor*) You'd disappear?

LEE: I would for sure.

AUSTIN: Where would you disappear to?

LEE: That don't matter. I got plenty a' places.

AUSTIN: Nobody can disappear. The old man tried that. Look where it got him. He lost his teeth.

LEE: He never had any money.

AUSTIN: I don't mean that. I mean his teeth! His real teeth. First he lost his real teeth, then he lost his false teeth. You never knew that did ya'? He never confided in you.

LEE: Nah, I never knew that.

AUSTIN: You wanna' drink?

(AUSTIN *offers bottle to* LEE, LEE *takes it, sits down on kitchen floor with* AUSTIN, *they share the bottle*)

Yeah, he lost his real teeth one at a time. Woke up every morning with another tooth lying on the mattress. Finally, he decides he's gotta' get 'em all pulled out but he doesn't have any money. Middle of Arizona with no money and no insurance and every morning another tooth is lying on the mattress. (*takes a drink*) So what does he do?

LEE: I dunno'. I never knew about that.

AUSTIN: He begs the government. G.I. Bill or some damn thing. Some pension plan he remembers in the back of his head. And they send him out the money.

LEE: They did?

(*they keep trading the bottle between them, taking drinks*)

AUSTIN: Yeah. They send him the money but it's not enough money. Costs a lot to have yer teeth yanked. They charge by the individual tooth, ya' know. I mean one tooth isn't equal to another tooth. Some are more expensive. Like the big ones in the back—

LEE: So what happened?

AUSTIN: So he locates a Mexican dentist in Juarez who'll do the whole thing for a song. And he takes off hitchhiking to the border.

LEE: Hitchhiking?

AUSTIN: Yeah. So how long you think it takes him to get to the border? A man his age.

LEE: I dunno.

AUSTIN: Eight days it takes him. Eight days in the rain and the sun and every day he's droppin' teeth on the blacktop and nobody'll pick him up 'cause his mouth's full a' blood.

(*pause, they drink*)

So finally he stumbles into the dentist. Dentist takes all his money and all his teeth. And there he is, in Mexico, with his gums sewed up and his pockets empty.

(*long silence, AUSTIN drinks*)

LEE: That's it?

AUSTIN: Then I go out to see him, see. I go out there and I take him out for a nice Chinese dinner. But he doesn't eat. All he wants to do is drink Martinis outa' plastic cups. And he takes his teeth out and lays 'em on the table 'cause he can't stand the feel of 'em. And we ask the waitress for one a' those doggie bags to take the chop suey home in. So he drops his teeth in the doggie bag along with the chop suey. And then we go out to hit all the bars up and down the highway. Says he wants to introduce me to all his buddies. And in one a' those bars, in one a' those bars up and down the highway, he left that doggie bag with his teeth laying in the chop suey.

LEE: You never found it?

AUSTIN: We went back but we never did find it. (*pause*) Now that's a true story. True to life.

(*they drink as lights fade to black*)

Scene 8

Very early morning, between night and day. No crickets, coyotes yapping feverishly in distance before light comes up, a small fire blazes up in the dark from alcove area, sound of

LEE *smashing typewriter with a golf club, lights coming up,* LEE *seen smashing typewriter methodically then dropping pages of his script into a burning bowl set on the floor of alcove, flames leap up,* AUSTIN *has a whole bunch of stolen toasters lined up on the sink counter along with* LEE'S *stolen T.V., the toasters are of a wide variety of models, mostly chrome,* AUSTIN *goes up and down the line of toasters, breathing on them and polishing them with a dish towel, both men are drunk, empty whiskey bottles and beer cans litter floor of kitchen, they share a half empty bottle on one of the chairs in the alcove,* LEE *keeps periodically taking deliberate ax-chops at the typewriter using a nine-iron as* AUSTIN *speaks, all of their mother's house plants are dead and drooping.*

AUSTIN: (*polishing toasters*)   There's gonna' be a general lack of toast in the neighborhood this morning. Many, many unhappy, bewildered breakfast faces. I guess it's best not to even think of the victims. Not to even entertain it. Is that the right psychology?

LEE: (*pauses*)   What?

AUSTIN: Is that the correct criminal psychology? Not to think of the victims?

LEE: What victims?

(LEE *takes another swipe at the typewriter with nine-iron, adds pages to the fire*)

AUSTIN: The victims of crime. Of breaking and entering. I mean is it a prerequisite for a criminal not to have a conscience?

LEE: Ask a criminal.

(*pause,* LEE *stares at* AUSTIN)

What're you gonna' do with all those toasters? That's the dumbest thing I ever saw in my life.

AUSTIN: I've got hundreds of dollars worth of household appliances here. You may not realize that.

LEE: Yeah, and how many hundreds of dollars did you walk right past?

AUSTIN: It was toasters you challenged me to. Only toasters. I ignored every other temptation.

LEE: I never challenged you! That's no challenge. Anybody can steal a toaster.

(LEE *smashes typewriter again*)

AUSTIN: You don't have to take it out on my typewriter ya' know. It's not the machine's fault that you can't write. It's a sin to do that to a good machine.

LEE: A sin?

AUSTIN: When you consider all the writers who never even had a machine. Who would have given an eyeball for a good typewriter. Any typewriter.

(LEE *smashes typewriter again*)

AUSTIN: (*polishing toasters*)   All the ones who wrote on matchbook covers. Paper bags. Toilet paper. Who had their writing destroyed by their jailers. Who persisted beyond all odds. Those writers would find it hard to understand your actions.

(LEE *comes down on typewriter with one final crushing blow of the nine-iron then collapses in one of the chairs, takes a drink from bottle, pause*)

AUSTIN: (*after pause*) Not to mention demolishing a perfectly good golf club. What about all the struggling golfers? What about Lee Trevino? What do you think he would've said when he was batting balls around with broomsticks at the age of nine. Impoverished.

(*pause*)

LEE: What time is it anyway?
AUSTIN: No idea. Time stands still when you're havin' fun.
LEE: Is it too late to call a woman? You know any women?
AUSTIN: I'm a married man.
LEE: I mean a local woman.

(AUSTIN *looks out at light through window above sink*)

AUSTIN: It's either too late or too early. You're the nature enthusiast. Can't you tell the time by the light in the sky? Orient yourself around the North Star or something?
LEE: I can't tell anything.
AUSTIN: Maybe you need a little breakfast. Some toast! How 'bout some toast?

(AUSTIN *goes to cupboard, pulls out loaf of bread and starts dropping slices into every toaster,* LEE *stays sitting, drinks, watches* AUSTIN)

LEE: I don't need toast. I need a woman.
AUSTIN: A woman isn't the answer. Never was.
LEE: I'm not talkin' about permanent. I'm talkin' about temporary.
AUSTIN: (*putting toast in toasters*) We'll just test the merits of these little demons. See which brands have a tendency to burn. See which one can produce a perfectly golden piece of fluffy toast.
LEE: How much gas you got in yer car?
AUSTIN: I haven't driven my car for days now. So I haven't had an opportunity to look at the gas gauge.
LEE: Take a guess. You think there's enough to get me to Bakersfield?
AUSTIN: Bakersfield? What's in Bakersfield?
LEE: Just never mind what's in Bakersfield! You think there's enough goddamn gas in the car!
AUSTIN: Sure.
LEE: Sure. You could care less, right. Let me run outa' gas on the Grapevine. You could give a shit.
AUSTIN: I'd say there was enough gas to get you just about anywhere, Lee. With your determination and guts.
LEE: What the hell time is it anyway?

(LEE *pulls out his wallet, starts going through dozens of small pieces of paper with phone numbers written on them, drops some on the floor, drops others in the fire*)

AUSTIN: Very early. This is the time of morning when the coyotes kill people's cocker spaniels. Did you hear them? That's what they were doing out there. Luring innocent pets away from their homes.
LEE: (*searching through his papers*) What's the area code for Bakersfield? You know?

AUSTIN: You could always call the operator.

LEE: I can't stand that voice they give ya'.

AUSTIN: What voice?

LEE: That voice that warns you that if you'd only tried harder to find the number in the phone book you wouldn't have to be calling the operator to begin with.

(LEE *gets up, holding a slip of paper from his wallet, stumbles toward phone on wall, yanks receiver, starts dialing*)

AUSTIN: Well I don't understand why you'd want to talk to anybody else anyway. I mean you can talk to me. I'm your brother.

LEE: (*dialing*)   I wanna' talk to a woman. I haven't heard a woman's voice in a long time.

AUSTIN: Not since the botanist?

LEE: What?

AUSTIN: Nothing. (*starts singing as he tends toast*)

> Red sails in the sunset
> Way out on the blue
> Please carry my loved one
> Home safely to me

LEE: Hey, knock it off will ya'! This is long distance here.

AUSTIN: Bakersfield?

LEE: Yeah, Bakersfield. It's Kern County.

AUSTIN: Well, what county are *we* in?

LEE: You better get yourself a 7-Up, boy.

AUSTIN: One county's as good as another.

(AUSTIN *hums "Red Sails" softly as* LEE *talks on phone*)

LEE: (*to phone*)   Yeah, operator look—first off I wanna' know the area code for Bakersfield. Right. Bakersfield! Okay. Good. Now I wanna' know if you can help me track somebody down. (*pause*) No, no I mean a phone number. Just a phone number. Okay. (*holds a piece of paper up and reads it*) Okay, the name is Melly Ferguson. Melly. (*pause*) I dunno'. Melly. Maybe. Yeah. Maybe Melanie. Yeah. Melanie Ferguson. Okay. (*pause*) What? I can't hear ya' so good. Sounds like yer under the ocean. (*pause*) You got ten Melanie Fergusons? How could that be? Ten Melanie Fergusons in Bakersfield? Well gimme all of 'em then. (*pause*) What d'ya' mean? Gimme all ten Melanie Fergusons! That's right. Just a second. (*to* AUSTIN) Gimme a pen.

AUSTIN: I don't have a pen.

LEE: Gimme a pencil then!

AUSTIN: I don't have a pencil.

LEE: (*to phone*)   Just a second, operator. (*to* AUSTIN) Yer a writer and ya' don't have a pen or a pencil!

AUSTIN: I'm not a writer. You're a writer.

LEE: I'm on the phone here! Get me a pen or a pencil.

AUSTIN: I gotta' watch the toast.

LEE: (*to phone*)   Hang on a second, operator.

(LEE *lets the phone drop then starts pulling all the drawers in the kitchen out on the floor and dumping the contents, searching for a pencil,* AUSTIN *watches him casually*)

LEE: (*crashing through drawers, throwing contents around kitchen*)   This is the last time I try to live with people, boy! I can't believe it. Here I am! Here I am again in a desperate situation! This would never happen out on the desert. I would never be in this kinda' situation out on the desert. Isn't there a pen or a pencil in this house! Who lives in this house anyway!

AUSTIN: Our mother.

LEE: How come she don't have a pen or a pencil! She's a social person isn't she? Doesn't she have to make shopping lists? She's gotta' have a pencil. (*finds a pencil*) Aaha! (*he rushes back to phone, picks up receiver*) All right operator. Operator? Hey! Operator! Goddammit!

(LEE *rips the phone off the wall, and throws it down, goes back to chair and falls into it, drinks, long pause*)

AUSTIN: She hung up?

LEE: Yeah, she hung up. I knew she was gonna' hang up. I could hear it in her voice.

(LEE *starts going through his slips of paper again*)

AUSTIN: Well, you're probably better off staying here with me anyway. I'll take care of you.

LEE: I don't need takin' care of! Not by you anyway.

AUSTIN: Toast is almost ready.

(Austin *starts buttering all the toast as it pops up*)

LEE: I don't want any toast.

(*long pause*)

AUSTIN: You gotta' eat something. Can't just drink. How long have we been drinking, anyway?

LEE: (*looking through slips of paper*)   Maybe it was Fresno. What's the area code for Fresno? How could I have lost that number! She was beautiful.

(*pause*)

AUSTIN: Why don't you just forget about that, Lee. Forget about the woman.

LEE: She had green eyes. You know what green eyes do to me?

AUSTIN: I know but you're not gonna' get it on with her now anyway. It's dawn already. She's in Bakersfield for Christ's sake.

(*long pause,* LEE *considers the situation*)

LEE: Yeah. (*looks at windows*) It's dawn?

AUSTIN: Let's just have some toast and—

LEE: What is this bullshit with the toast anyway! You make it sound like salvation

or something. I don't want any goddamn toast! How many times I gotta' tell ya'!
(LEE *gets up, crosses upstage to windows in alcove, looks out,* AUSTIN *butters toast*)
AUSTIN: Well it is like salvation sort of. I mean the smell. I love the smell of toast.
   And the sun's coming up. It makes me feel like anything's possible. Ya' know?
LEE: (*back to* AUSTIN, *facing windows upstage*)   So go to church why don't ya'.
AUSTIN: Like a beginning. I love beginnings.
LEE: Oh yeah. I've always been kinda' partial to endings myself.
AUSTIN: What if I come with you, Lee?
LEE: (*pause as* LEE *turns toward* AUSTIN)   What?
AUSTIN: What if I come with you out to the desert?
LEE: Are you kiddin'?
AUSTIN: No. I'd just like to see what it's like.
LEE: You wouldn't last a day out there, pal.
AUSTIN: That's what you said about the toasters. You said I couldn't steal a
   toaster, either.
LEE: A toaster's got nothin' to do with the desert.
AUSTIN: I could make it, Lee. I'm not that helpless. I can cook.
LEE: Cook?
AUSTIN: I can.
LEE: So what! You can cook. Toast.
AUSTIN: I can make fires. I know how to get fresh water from condensation.

(AUSTIN *stacks buttered toast up in a tall stack on plate*)

(LEE *slams table*)

LEE: It's not somethin' you learn out of a Boy Scout handbook!
AUSTIN: Well how do you learn it then! How're you supposed to learn it!

(*pause*)

LEE: Ya' just learn it, that's all. Ya' learn it 'cause ya' have to learn it. You don't
   have to learn it.
AUSTIN: You could teach me.
LEE: (*stands*)   What're you, crazy or somethin'? You went to college. Here, you
   are down here, rollin' in bucks. Floatin' up and down in elevators. And you
   wanna' learn how to live on the desert!
AUSTIN: I do, Lee. I really do. There's nothin' down here for me. There never
   was. When we were kids here it was different. There was a life here then. But
   now—I keep comin' down here thinkin' it's the fifties or somethin'. I keep
   finding myself getting off the freeway at familiar landmarks that turn out to be
   unfamiliar. On the way to appointments. Wandering down streets I thought I
   recognized that turn out to be replicas of streets I remember. Streets I misre-
   member. Streets I can't tell if I lived on or saw in a postcard. Fields that don't
   even exist anymore.
LEE: There's no point cryin' about that now.
AUSTIN: There's nothin' real down here, Lee! Least of all me!
LEE: Well I can't save you from that!
AUSTIN: You can let me come with you.
LEE: No dice, pal.
AUSTIN: You could let me come with you, Lee!

LEE: Hey, do you actually think I chose to live out in the middle a' nowhere? Do ya'? Ya' think it's some kinda' philosophical decision I took or somethin'? I'm livin' out there 'cause I can't make it here! And yer bitchin' to me about all yer success!

AUSTIN: I'd cash it all in in a second. That's the truth.

LEE: (*pause, shakes his head*) I can't believe this.

AUSTIN: Let me go with you.

LEE: Stop sayin' that will ya'! Yer worse than a dog.

(AUSTIN *offers out the plate of neatly stacked toast to* LEE)

AUSTIN: You want some toast?

(LEE *suddenly explodes and knocks the plate out of* AUSTIN's *hand, toast goes flying, long frozen moment where it appears* LEE *might go all the way this time when* AUSTIN *breaks it by slowly lowering himself to his knees and begins gathering the scattered toast from the floor and stacking it back on the plate,* LEE *begins to circle* AUSTIN *in a slow, predatory way, crushing pieces of toast in his wake, no words for a while,* AUSTIN *keeps gathering toast, even the crushed pieces*)

LEE: Tell ya' what I'll do, little brother. I might just consider makin' you a deal. Little trade. (AUSTIN *continues gathering toast as* LEE *circles him through this*) You write me up this screenplay thing just like I tell ya'. I mean you can use all yer usual tricks and stuff. Yer fancy language. Yer artistic hocus pocus. But ya' gotta' write everything like I say. Every move. Every time they run outa' gas, they run outa' gas. Every time they wanna' jump on a horse, they do just that. If they wanna' stay in Texas, by God they'll stay in Texas! (*Keeps circling*) And you finish the whole thing up for me. Top to bottom. And you put my name on it. And I own all the rights. And every dime goes in my pocket. You do all that and I'll sure enough take ya' with me to the desert. (LEE *stops, pause, looks down at* AUSTIN) How's that sound?

(*pause as* AUSTIN *stands slowly holding plate of demolished toast, their faces are very close, pause*)

AUSTIN: It's a deal.

(LEE *stares straight into* AUSTIN's *eyes, then he slowly takes a piece of toast off the plate, raises it to his mouth and takes a huge crushing bite never taking his eyes off* AUSTIN's, *as* LEE *crunches into the toast the lights black out*)

Scene 9

Mid-day. No sound, blazing heat, the stage is ravaged; bottles, toasters, smashed type-writer, ripped out telephone, etc. All the debris from previous scene is now starkly visible in intense yellow light, the effect should be like a desert junkyard at high noon, the cool-ness of the preceding scenes is totally obliterated. AUSTIN *is seated at table in alcove, shirt open, pouring with sweat, hunched over a writing notebook, scribbling notes desperately with a ballpoint pen.* LEE *with no shirt, beer in hand, sweat pouring down his chest, is walking a slow circle around the table, picking his way through the objects, sometimes kicking them aside.*

LEE: (*as he walks*)   All right, read it back to me. Read it back to me!

AUSTIN: (*scribbling at top speed*)   Just a second.

LEE: Come on, come on! Just read what ya' got.

AUSTIN: I can't keep up! It's not the same as if I had a typewriter.

LEE: Just read what we got so far. Forget about the rest.

AUSTIN: All right. Let's see—okay—(*wipes sweat from his face, reads as* LEE *circles*) Luke says uh—

LEE: Luke?

AUSTIN: Yeah.

LEE: His name's Luke? All right, all right—we can change the names later. What's he say? Come on, come on.

AUSTIN: He says uh—(*reading*) "I told ya' you were a fool to follow me in here. I know this prairie like the back a' my hand."

LEE: No, no, no! That's not what I said. I never said that.

AUSTIN: That's what I wrote.

LEE: It's not what I said. I never said "like the back a' my hand." That's stupid. That's one a' those—whadya' call it? Whadya' call that?

AUSTIN: What?

LEE: Whadya' call it when somethin's been said a thousand times before. Whadya' call that?

AUSTIN: Um—a cliché?

LEE: Yeah. That's right. Cliché. That's what that is. A cliché. "The back a' my hand." That's stupid.

AUSTIN: That's what you said.

LEE: I never said that! And even if I did, that's where yer supposed to come in. That's where yer supposed to change it to somethin' better.

AUSTIN: Well how am I supposed to do that and write down what you say at the same time?

LEE: Ya' just do, that's all! You hear a stupid line you change it. That's yer job.

AUSTIN: All right. (*makes more notes*)

LEE: What're you changin' it to?

AUSTIN: I'm not changing it. I'm just trying to catch up.

LEE: Well change it! We gotta' change that, we can't leave that in there like that. ". . . the back a' my hand." That's dumb.

AUSTIN: (*stops writing, sits back*)   All right.

LEE: (*pacing*)   So what'll we change it to?

AUSTIN: Um—How 'bout—"I'm on intimate terms with this prairie."

LEE: (*to himself considering line as he walks*)   "I'm on intimate terms with this prairie." Intimate terms, intimate terms. Intimate—that means like uh—sexual right?

AUSTIN: Well—yeah—or—

LEE: He's on sexual terms with the prairie? How dya' figure that?

AUSTIN: Well it doesn't necessarily have to mean sexual.

LEE: What's it mean then?

AUSTIN: It means uh—close—personal—

LEE: All right. How's it sound? Put it into the uh—the line there. Read it back. Let's see how it sounds. (*to himself*) "Intimate terms."

AUSTIN: (*scribbles in notebook*)   Okay. It'd go something like this: (*reads*) "I told ya' you were a fool to follow me in here. I'm on intimate terms with this prairie."

LEE: That's good. I like that. That's real good.

AUSTIN: You do?

LEE: Yeah. Don't you?

AUSTIN: Sure.

LEE: Sounds original now. "Intimate terms." That's good. Okay. Now we're cookin'! That has a real ring to it.

(AUSTIN *makes more notes,* LEE *walks around, pours beer on his arms and rubs it over chest feeling good about the new progress, as he does his* MOM *enters unobtrusively down left with her luggage, she stops and stares at the scene still holding luggage as the two men continue, unaware of her presence,* AUSTIN *absorbed in his writing,* LEE *cooling himself off with beer*)

LEE: (*continues*)   "He's on intimate terms with this prairie." Sounds real mysterious and kinda' threatening at the same time.

AUSTIN: (*writing rapidly*)   Good.

LEE: Now—(LEE *turns and suddenly sees* MOM, *he stares at her for a while, she stares back,* AUSTIN *keeps writing feverishly, not noticing,* LEE *walks slowly over to* MOM *and takes a closer look, long pause*)

LEE: Mom?

(AUSTIN *looks up suddenly from his writing, sees* MOM, *stands quickly, long pause,* MOM *surveys the damage*)

AUSTIN: Mom. What're you doing back?

MOM: I'm back.

LEE: Here, lemme take those for ya.

(LEE *sets beer on counter, then takes both her bags but doesn't know where to set them down in the sea of junk so he just keeps holding them*)

AUSTIN: I wasn't expecting you back so soon. I thought uh—How was Alaska?

MOM: Fine.

LEE: See any igloos?

MOM: No. Just glaciers.

AUSTIN: Cold huh?

MOM: What?

AUSTIN: It must've been cold up there?

MOM: Not really.

LEE: Musta' been colder than this here. I mean we're havin' a real scorcher here.

MOM: Oh? (*she looks at damage*)

LEE: Yeah. Must be in the hundreds.

AUSTIN: You wanna' take your coat off, Mom?

MOM: No. (*pause, she surveys space*) What happened in here?

AUSTIN: Oh um—Me and Lee were just sort of celebrating and uh—

MOM: Celebrating?

AUSTIN: Yeah. Uh—Lee sold a screenplay. A story, I mean.

MOM: Lee did?

AUSTIN: Yeah.

MOM: Not you?

AUSTIN: No. Him.

MOM: (*to* LEE)   You sold a screenplay?

LEE: Yeah. That's right. We're just sorta' finishing it up right now. That's what we're doing here.

AUSTIN: Me and Lee are going out to the desert to live.

MOM: You and Lee?

AUSTIN: Yeah. I'm taking off with Lee.

MOM: (*she looks back and forth at each of them, pause*) You gonna go live with your father?

AUSTIN: No. We're going to a different desert, Mom.

MOM: I see. Well, you'll probably wind up on the same desert sooner or later. What're all those toasters doing here?

AUSTIN: Well—we had kind of a contest.

MOM: Contest?

LEE: Yeah.

AUSTIN: Lee won.

MOM: Did you win a lot of money, Lee?

LEE: Well not yet. It's comin' in any day now.

MOM: (*to* LEE) What happened to your shirt?

LEE: Oh. I was sweatin' like a pig and I took it off.

(AUSTIN *grabs* LEE's *shirt off the table and tosses it to him*, LEE *sets down suitcases and puts his shirt on*)

MOM: Well, it's one hell of a mess in here, isn't it?

AUSTIN: Yeah, I'll clean it up for you, Mom. I just didn't know you were coming back so soon.

MOM: I didn't either.

AUSTIN: What happened?

MOM: Nothing. I just started missing all my plants.

(*she notices dead plants*)

AUSTIN: Oh.

MOM: Oh, they're all dead aren't they. (*she crosses toward them, examines them closely*) You didn't get a chance to water I guess.

AUSTIN: I was doing it and then Lee came and—

LEE: Yeah I just distracted him a whole lot here, Mom. It's not his fault.

(*pause, as* MOM *stares at plants*)

MOM: Oh well, one less thing to take care of I guess. (*turns toward brothers*) Oh, that reminds me—You boys will probably never guess who's in town. Try and guess.

(*long pause, brothers stare at her*)

AUSTIN: Whadya' mean, Mom?

MOM: Take a guess. Somebody very important has come to town. I read it, coming down on the Greyhound.

LEE: Somebody very important?

MOM: See if you can guess. You'll never guess.

AUSTIN: Mom—we're trying to uh—(*points to writing pad*)

MOM: Picasso. (*pause*) Picasso's in town. Isn't that incredible? Right now.

(*pause*)

AUSTIN: Picasso's dead, Mom.

MOM: No, he's not dead. He's visiting the museum. I read it on the bus. We have to go down there and see him.

AUSTIN: Mom—

MOM: This is the chance of a lifetime. Can you imagine? We could all go down and meet him. All three of us.

LEE: Uh— I don't think I'm really up fer meetin' anybody right now. I'm uh— What's his name?

MOM: Picasso! Picasso! You've never heard of Picasso? Austin, you've heard of Picasso.

AUSTIN: Mom, we're not going to have time.

MOM: It won't take long. We'll just hop in the car and go down there. An opportunity like this doesn't come along every day.

AUSTIN: We're gonna be leavin' here, Mom!

(*pause*)

MOM: Oh.

LEE: Yeah.

(*pause*)

MOM: You're both leaving?

LEE: (*looks at* AUSTIN) Well we were thinkin' about that before but now I—

AUSTIN: No, we are! We're both leaving. We've got it all planned.

MOM: (*to* AUSTIN) Well you can't leave. You have a family.

AUSTIN: I'm leaving. I'm getting out of here.

LEE: (*to* MOM) I don't really think Austin's cut out for the desert do you?

MOM: No. He's not.

AUSTIN: I'm going with you, Lee!

MOM: He's too thin.

LEE: Yeah, he'd just burn up out there.

AUSTIN: (*to* LEE) We just gotta' finish this screenplay and then we're gonna' take off. That's the plan. That's what you said. Come on, let's get back to work, Lee.

LEE: I can't work under these conditions here. It's too hot.

AUSTIN: Then we'll do it on the desert.

LEE: Don't be tellin' me what we're gonna do!

MOM: Don't shout in the house.

LEE: We're just gonna' have to postpone the whole deal.

AUSTIN: I can't postpone it! It's gone past postponing! I'm doing everything you said. I'm writing down exactly what you tell me.

LEE: Yeah, but you were right all along see. It is a dumb story. "Two lamebrains chasin' each other across Texas." That's what you said, right?

AUSTIN: I never said that.

(LEE *sneers in* AUSTIN'*s face then turns to* MOM)

LEE: I'm gonna' just borrow some a' your antiques, Mom. You don't mind do ya'? Just a few plates and things. Silverware.

(LEE *starts going through all the cupboards in kitchen pulling out plates and stacking them on counter as* MOM *and* AUSTIN *watch*)

MOM: You don't have any utensils on the desert?
LEE: Nah, I'm fresh out.
AUSTIN: (*to* LEE) What're you doing?
MOM: Well some of those are very old. Bone China.
LEE: I'm tired of eatin' outa' my bare hands, ya' know. It's not civilized.
AUSTIN: (*to* LEE) What're you doing? We made a deal!
MOM: Couldn't you borrow the plastic ones instead? I have plenty of plastic ones.
LEE: (*as he stacks plates*) It's not the same. Plastic's not the same at all. What I need is somethin' authentic. Somethin' to keep me in touch. It's easy to get outa' touch out there. Don't worry, I'll get em' back to ya'.

(AUSTIN *rushes up to* LEE, *grabs him by shoulders*)

AUSTIN: You can't just drop the whole thing, Lee!

(LEE *turns, pushes* AUSTIN *in the chest knocking him backwards into the alcove,* MOM *watches numbly,* LEE *returns to collecting the plates, silverware, etc.*)

MOM: You boys shouldn't fight in the house. Go outside and fight.
LEE: I'm not fightin'. I'm leavin'.
MOM: There's been enough damage done already.
LEE: (*his back to* AUSTIN *and* MOM, *stacking dishes on counter*) I'm clearin' outa' here once and for all. All this town does is drive a man insane. Look what it's done to Austin there. I'm not lettin' that happen to me. Sell myself down the river. No sir. I'd rather be a hundred miles from nowhere than let that happen to me.

(*during this* AUSTIN *has picked up the ripped-out phone from the floor and wrapped the cord tightly around both his hands, he lunges at* LEE *whose back is still to him, wraps the cord around* LEE'*s neck, plants a foot in* LEE'*s back and pulls back on the cord, tightening it,* LEE *chokes desperately, can't speak and can't reach* AUSTIN *with his arms,* AUSTIN *keeps applying pressure on* LEE'*s back with his foot, bending him into the sink,* MOM *watches*)

AUSTIN: (*tightening cord*) You're not goin' anywhere! You're not takin' anything with you. You're not takin' my car! You're not takin' the dishes! You're not takin' anything! You're stayin' right here!
MOM: You'll have to stop fighting in the house. There's plenty of room outside to fight. You've got the whole outdoors to fight in.

(LEE *tries to tear himself away, he crashes across the stage like an enraged bull dragging* AUSTIN *with him, he snorts and bellows but* AUSTIN *hangs on and manages to keep clear of* Lee'*s attempts to grab him, they crash into the table, to the floor,* LEE *is face down thrashing wildly and choking,* AUSTIN *pulls cord tighter, stands with one foot planted on* LEE'*s back and the cord stretched taut*)

Austin: (*holding cord*)   Gimme back my keys, Lee! Take the keys out! Take 'em out!

(Lee *desperately tries to dig in his pockets, searching for the car keys,* Mom *moves closer*)

Mom: (*calmly to* Austin)   You're not killing him, are you?
Austin: I don't know. I don't know if I'm killing him. I'm stopping him. That's all. I'm just stopping him.

(Lee *thrashes but* Austin *is relentless*)

Mom: You oughta' let him breathe a little.
Austin: Throw the keys out, Lee!

(Lee *finally gets keys out and throws them on floor but out of* Austin's *reach,* Austin *keeps pressure on cord, pulling* Lee's *neck back,* Lee *gets one hand to the cord but can't relieve the pressure*)

Reach me those keys would ya', Mom.

Mom: (*not moving*)   Why are you doing this to him?
Austin: Reach me the keys!
Mom: Not until you stop choking him.
Austin: I can't stop choking him! He'll kill me if I stop choking him!
Mom: He won't kill you. He's your brother.
Austin: Just get me the keys would ya'!

(*pause.* Mom *picks keys up off floor, hands them to* Austin)

Austin: (*to* Mom)   Thanks.
Mom: Will you let him go now?
Austin: I don't know. He's not gonna' let me get outa' here.
Mom: Well you can't kill him.
Austin: I can kill him! I can easily kill him. Right now. Right here. All I gotta' do is just tighten up. See? (*he tightens cord,* Lee *thrashes wildly,* Austin *releases pressure a little, maintaining control*) Ya' see that?
Mom: That's a savage thing to do.
Austin: Yeah, well, don't tell me I can't kill him because I can. I can just twist. I can just keep twisting. (Austin *twists the cord tighter,* Lee *weakens, his breathing changes to a short rasp*)
Mom: Austin!

(Austin *relieves pressure,* Lee *breathes easier but* Austin *keeps him under control*)

Austin: (*eyes on* Lee, *holding cord*)   I'm goin' to the desert. There's nothing stopping me. I'm going by myself to the desert.

(Mom *moving toward her luggage*)

Mom: Well, I'm going to go check into a motel. I can't stand this anymore.
Austin: Don't go yet!

(Mom *pauses*)

MOM: I can't stay here. This is worse than being homeless.
AUSTIN: I'll get everything fixed up for you, Mom. I promise. Just stay for a
  while.
MOM: (*picking up luggage*) You're going to the desert.
AUSTIN: Just wait!

(LEE *thrashes,* AUSTIN *subdues him,* MOM *watches holding luggage, pause*)

MOM: It was the worst feeling being up there. In Alaska. Staring out a window.
  I never felt so desperate before. That's why when I saw that article on Picasso I
  thought—
AUSTIN: Stay here, Mom. This is where you live.

(*she looks around the stage*)

MOM: I don't recognize it at all.

(*she exits with luggage,* AUSTIN *makes a move toward her but* LEE *starts to struggle and*
AUSTIN *subdues him again with cord, pause*)

AUSTIN: (*holding cord*) Lee? I'll make ya' a deal. You let me get outa' here. Just
  let me get to my car. All right, Lee? Gimme a little headstart and I'll turn you
  loose. Just gimme a little headstart. All right?

(LEE *makes no response,* AUSTIN *slowly releases tension on cord, still nothing from* LEE)

AUSTIN: Lee?

(LEE *is motionless,* AUSTIN *very slowly begins to stand, still keeping a tenuous hold on the
cord and his eyes riveted to* LEE *for any sign of movement,* AUSTIN *slowly drops the cord and
stands, he stares down at* LEE *who appears to be dead*)

AUSTIN: (*whispers*) Lee?

(*pause.* AUSTIN *considers, looks toward exit, back to* LEE, *then makes a small movement as
if to leave. Instantly* LEE *is on his feet and moves toward exit, blocking* AUSTIN'S *escape.
They square off to each other, keeping a distance between them. pause, a single coyote heard
in distance, lights fade softly into moonlight, the figures of the brothers now appear to be
caught in a vast desert-like landscape, they are very still but watchful for the next move, lights
go slowly to black as the after-image of the brothers pulses in the dark, coyote fades*)

QUESTIONS FOR DISCUSSION AND WRITING

  1. What does the title of *True West* mean? What is the "true west"? You
might consider also the "untrue west," the mythology of the west which the
play explores.

2. In scene 7, Austin says that Saul Kimmer thinks that Austin and Lee are "the same person." In what sense might this be true?

3. *True West* is full of stories within stories. One is Lee's absurd idea for a screenplay. (See especially scene 4.) What is the relationship between this story and the plot of *True West?*

4. Another such story within a story is that of the boys' father and his teeth, of which Austin says (scene 7) that it's "a true story—true to life," perhaps the true west. What is a true story, in Austin's terms, and what makes it true?

5. Sound effects are important in the play. Trace the use of crickets and coyotes. What do they seem to stand for?

6. The desert takes on a considerable symbolic significance in the play. Trace references to it. What does it seem to mean? Consider it in the context of the other locations mentioned in the play: the Los Angeles suburbs, Hollywood, Alaska. Do the places have symbolic dimensions?

7. The entrance of the mother at the end of the play comes as a shock. How does the scene contribute to the play? What is the function of her absurd belief that Picasso is in town? How does her entry into the play suggest that we consider the play as about family relationships?

8. *True West* is a play about art and the artistic process. What does it have to say on the subject?

9. Lee is a professional thief, and in the course of the play Austin tries his hand at theft as well. What does stealing seem to stand for in the value system of the play?

10. *True West* is quite a violent play, from Lee's assault on the typewriter with the golf club to the brothers' struggle at the end of the play. What is the function of the violence?

August Wilson

August Wilson (b. 1945) found fame in 1984, when *Ma Rainey's Black Bottom* opened in New York. But this "instant" success was preceded by over fifteen years' work in the theater and was followed by a series of other plays that made Wilson one of the most prolific, ambitious, and skilled of contemporary American dramatists.

Wilson grew up in Pittsburgh. When he was twenty-three he founded Black Horizons, an activist black theater company; he has also been affiliated with Playwrights Center in Minneapolis and New Playwrights of New York. He had productions of his early plays in St. Paul, Minnesota; Pittsburgh; and New York. His career was galvanized when in 1981 Lloyd Richards, dean of the Yale School of Drama and director of the Yale Repertory Theater, read *Ma Rainey's Black Bottom.* Richards first staged the play at Yale and then directed the 1984 Broadway production. He has remained closely affiliated with Wilson, has helped in the development of his plays, and has directed the first productions of all of them since *Ma Rainey*.

Wilson is engaged in writing a series of ten plays, one for each decade of the twentieth century, about black life in America. By 1993, five of the plays had been completed: *Joe Turner's Come and Gone* (1986), set in 1911; *Ma Rainey's Black Bottom* (1984), set in 1927; *The Piano Lesson* (1987), set in 1936; *Fences* (1985), set in 1957; and *Two Trains Running* (1989), set in 1969.

Wilson has said that music is at least as important a source of his plays as historical research is. And of none of his plays is this more true than *Ma Rainey's Black Bottom.* With the starting point an actual recording session in Chicago in 1927 (the recordings from which have been reissued), Wilson imaginatively creates in the microcosm of the studio the patterns of power, control, and cultural appropriation that have shaped black experience in America.

MA RAINEY'S BLACK BOTTOM

They tore the railroad down
so the Sunshine Special can't run
I'm going away baby
build me a railroad of my own
                    —Blind Lemon Jefferson

CHARACTERS

STURDYVANT	LEVEE
IRVIN	MA RAINEY
CUTLER	POLICEMAN
TOLEDO	DUSSIE MAE
SLOW DRAG	SYLVESTER

THE SETTING

There are two playing areas: what is called the "band room," and the recording studio. The band room is at stage left and is in the basement of the building. It is entered through a door up left. There are benches and chairs scattered about, a piano, a row of lockers, and miscellaneous paraphernalia stacked in a corner and long since forgotten. A mirror hangs on a wall with various posters.

The studio is upstairs at stage right, and resembles a recording studio of the late 1920's. The entrance is from a hall on the right wall. A small control booth is at the rear and its access is gained by means of a spiral staircase. Against one wall there is a line of chairs, and a horn through which the control room communicates with the performers. A door in the rear wall allows access to the band room.

THE PLAY

It is early March in Chicago, 1927. There is a bit of a chill in the air. Winter has broken but the wind coming off the lake does not carry the promise of spring. The people of the city are bundled and brisk in their defense against such misfortunes as the weather, and the business of the city proceeds largely undisturbed.

Chicago in 1927 is a rough city, a bruising city, a city of millionaires and derelicts, gangsters and rough-house dandies, whores and Irish grandmothers who move through its streets fingering long black rosaries. Somewhere a man is wrestling with the taste of a woman in his cheek. Somewhere a dog is barking. Somewhere the moon has fallen through a window and broken into thirty pieces of silver.

It is one o'clock in the afternoon. Secretaries are returning from their lunch, the noon Mass at St. Anthony's is over, and the priest is mumbling over his vestments while the altar boys practice their Latin. The procession of cattle cars through the stockyards continues unabated. The busboys in Mac's Place are cleaning away the last of the corned beef and cabbage, and on the city's Southside, sleepy-eyed negroes move lazily toward their small cold water flats and rented rooms to await the onslaught of night, which will find them crowded in the bars and juke joints both dazed and dazzling in their rapport with life. It is with these negroes that our concern lies most heavily: their values, their attitudes, and particularly their music.

It is hard to define this music. Suffice it to say that it is music that breathes and touches. That connects. That is in itself a way of being, separate and distinct from any other. This music is called blues. Whether this music came from Alabama or Mississippi or other parts of the South doesn't matter anymore. The men and women who make this music have learned it from the narrow crooked streets of East St. Louis, or the streets of the city's Southside, and the Alabama or Mississippi roots have been strangled by the northern manners and customs of free men of definite and sincere worth, men for whom this music often lies at the forefront of their conscience and concerns. Thus they are laid open to be consumed by it; its warmth and redress, its braggadocio and roughly poignant comments, its vision and prayer, which would instruct and allow them to reconnect, to reassemble and gird up for the next battle in which they would be both victim and the ten thousand slain.

ACT ONE

The lights come up in the studio, IRVIN *enters, carrying a microphone. He is a tall, fleshy man who prides himself on his knowledge of blacks and his ability to deal with them. He hooks up the microphone, blows into it, taps it, etc. He crosses over to the piano, opens it, and fingers a few keys.* STURDYVANT *is visible in the control booth. Preoccupied with money, he is insensitive to black performers and prefers to deal with them at arm's length. He puts on a pair of earphones.*

STURDYVANT: (*Over speaker.*) Irv . . . let's crack that mike, huh? Let's do a check on it.

IRVIN: (*Crosses to mike, speaks into it.*)   Testing . . . one . . . two . . . three . . . (*There is a loud feedback.* STURDYVANT *fiddles with the dials.*) Testing . . . one . . . two . . . three . . . testing. How's that, Mel?

(STURDYVANT *doesn't respond.*)

Testing . . . one . . . two . . .

STURDYVANT: (*Taking off earphones.*) Okay . . . that checks. We got a good reading.

(*Pause.*)

You got that list, Irv?

IRVIN: Yeah . . . yeah, I got it. Don't worry about nothing.

STURDYVANT: Listen, Irv . . . you keep her in line, okay? I'm holding you responsible for her . . . If she starts any of her . . .

IRVIN: Mel, what's with the goddamn horn? you wanna talk to me . . . okay! I can't talk to you over the goddamn horn . . . Christ!

STURDYVANT: I'm not putting up with any shenanigans. You hear, Irv?

(IRVIN *crosses over to the piano and mindlessly runs his fingers over the keys.*)

I'm just not gonna stand for it. I want you to keep her in line. Irv?

(STURDYVANT *enters from the control booth.*)

Listen, Irv . . . you're her manager . . . she's your responsibility . . .

IRVIN: Okay, okay, Mel . . . let me handle it.

STURDYVANT: She's your responsibility. I'm not putting up with any Royal Highness . . . Queen of the Blues bullshit!

IRVIN: Mother of the Blues, Mel. Mother of the Blues.

STURDYVANT: I don't care what she calls herself. I'm not putting up with it. I just
    want to get her in here . . . record those songs on that list . . . and get her out.
    Just like clockwork, huh?

IRVIN: Like clockwork, Mel. You just stay out of the way and let me handle it.

STURDYVANT: Yeah . . . yeah . . . you handled it last time. Remember? She
    marches in here like she owns the damn place . . . doesn't like the songs we
    picked out . . . and says her throat is sore . . . doesn't want to do more than one
    take . . .

IRVIN: Okay . . . okay . . . I was here! I know all about it.

STURDYVANT: Complains about the building being cold . . . and then . . . trips
    over the mike wire and threatens to sue me. That's taking care of it?

IRVIN: I've got it all worked out this time. I talked with her last night. Her throat
    is fine . . . We went over the songs together . . . I got everything straight, Mel.

STURDYVANT: Irv, that horn player . . . the one who gave me those songs . . . is he
    gonna be here today? Good. I want to hear more of that sound. Times are
    changing. This is a tricky business now. We've got to jazz it up . . . put in
    something different. You know, something wild . . . with a lot of rhythm.

(*Pause.*)

You know what we put out last time, Irv? We put out garbage last time. It was
garbage. I don't even know why I bother with this anymore.

IRVIN: You did all right last time, Mel. Not as good as you did before, but you did
    all right.

STURDYVANT: You know how many records we sold in New York? You wanna see
    the sheet? And you know what's in New York, Irv? Harlem. Harlem's in New
    York, Irv.

IRVIN: Okay, so they didn't sell in New York. But look at Memphis . . . Birming-
    ham . . . Atlanta. Christ, you made a bundle.

STURDYVANT: It's not the money, Irv. You know I couldn't sleep last night? This
    business is bad for my nerves. My wife is after me to slow down and take a
    vacation. Two more years and I'm gonna get out . . . get into something re-
    spectable. Textiles. That's a respectable business. You know what you could do
    with a shipload of textiles from Ireland?

(*A buzzer is heard offstage.*)

IRVIN: Why don't you go upstairs and let me handle it, Mel?

STURDYVANT: Remember . . . you're responsible for her.

(STURDYVANT *exits to the control booth.* IRVIN *crosses to get the door.* CUTLER, SLOW
DRAG, *and* TOLEDO *enter.* CUTLER *is in his mid-fifties, as are most of the others. He plays
guitar and trombone and is the leader of the group, possibly because he is the most sensible.
His playing is solid and almost totally unembellished. His understanding of his music is
limited to the chord he is playing at the time he is playing it. He has all the qualities of a
loner except the introspection.* SLOW DRAG, *the bass player, is perhaps the one most bored
by life. He resembles* CUTLER, *but lacks* CUTLER'*s energy. He is deceptively intelligent,
though, as his name implies, he appears to be slow. He is a rather large man with a wicked
smile. Innate African rhythms underlie everything he plays, and he plays with an ease that
is at times startling.* TOLEDO *is the piano player. In control of his instrument, he understands and recognizes that its limitations are an extension of himself. He is the only one in*

the group who can read. He is self-taught but misunderstands and misapplies his knowledge, though he is quick to penetrate to the core of a situation and his insights are thought-provoking. All of the men are dressed in a style of clothing befitting the members of a successful band of the era.)

IRVIN: How you boys doing, Cutler? Come on in.

(*Pause.*)

Where's Ma? Is she with you?

CUTLER: I don't know, Mr. Irvin. She told us to be here at one o'clock. That's all I know.

IRVIN:'   Where's . . . huh . . . the horn player? Is he coming with Ma?

CUTLER: Levee's supposed to be here same as we is. I reckon he'll be here in a minute. I can't rightly say.

IRVIN: Well, come on . . . I'll show you to the band room, let you get set up and rehearsed. You boys hungry? I'll call over to the deli and get some sandwiches. Get you fed and ready to make some music. Cutler . . . here's the list of songs we're gonna record.

STURDYVANT: (*Over speaker.*) Irvin, what's happening? Where's Ma?

IRVIN: Everything under control, Mel. I got it under control.

STURDYVANT: Where's Ma? How come she isn't with the band?

IRVIN: She'll be here in a minute, Mel. Let me get these fellows down to the band room, huh?

(*They exit the studio. The lights go down in the studio and up on the band room.* IRVIN *opens the door and allows them to pass as they enter.*)

You boys go ahead and rehearse. I'll let you know when Ma comes.

(IRVIN *exits.* CUTLER *hands* TOLEDO *the list of songs.*)

CUTLER: What we got here, Toledo?

TOLEDO: (*Reading.*) We got . . . "Prove It on Me" . . . "Hear Me Talking to You" . . . "Ma Rainey's Black Bottom" . . . and "Moonshine Blues."

CUTLER: Where Mr. Irvin go? Them ain't the songs Ma told me.

SLOW DRAG: I wouldn't worry about it if I were you, Cutler. They'll get it straightened out. Ma will get it straightened out.

CUTLER: I just don't want no trouble about these songs, that's all. Ma ain't told me them songs. She told me something else.

SLOW DRAG: What she tell you?

CUTLER: This "Moonshine Blues" wasn't in it. That's one of Bessie's songs.

TOLEDO: Slow Drag's right . . . I wouldn't worry about it. Let them straighten it up.

CUTLER: Levee know what time he supposed to be here?

SLOW DRAG: Levee gone out to spend your four dollars. He left the hotel this morning talking about he was gonna go buy some shoes. Say it's the first time he ever beat you shooting craps.

CUTLER: Do he know what time he supposed to be here? That's what I wanna know. I ain't thinking about no four dollars.

SLOW DRAG: Levee sure was thinking about it. That four dollars liked to burn a hole in his pocket.

CUTLER: Well, he's supposed to be here at one o'clock. That's what time Ma said. That nigger get out in the streets with that four dollars and ain't no telling when he's liable to show. You ought to have seen him at the club last night, Toledo. Trying to talk to some gal Ma had with her.

TOLEDO: You ain't got to tell me. I know how Levee do.

(*Buzzer is heard offstage.*)

SLOW DRAG: Levee tried to talk to that gal and got his feelings hurt. She didn't want no part of him. She told Levee he'd have to turn his money green before he could talk with her.

CUTLER: She out for what she can get. Anybody could see that.

SLOW DRAG: That's why Levee run out to buy some shoes. He's looking to make an impression on that gal.

CUTLER: What the hell she gonna do with his shoes? She can't do nothing with the nigger's shoes.

(SLOW DRAG *takes out a pint bottle and drinks.*)

TOLEDO: Let me hit that, Slow Drag.

SLOW DRAG: (*Handing him the bottle.*) This some of that good Chicago bourbon!

(*The door opens and* LEVEE *enters, carrying a shoe box. In his early thirties,* LEVEE *is younger than the other men. His flamboyance is sometimes subtle and sneaks up on you. His temper is rakish and bright. He lacks fuel for himself and is somewhat of a buffoon. But it is an intelligent buffoonery, clearly calculated to shift control of the situation to where he can grasp it. He plays trumpet. His voice is strident and totally dependent on his manipulation of breath. He plays wrong notes frequently. He often gets his skill and talent confused with each other.*)

CUTLER: Levee ... where Mr. Irvin go?

LEVEE: Hell, I don't know. I ain't none of his keeper.

SLOW DRAG: What you got there, Levee?

LEVEE: Look here, Cutler ... I got me some shoes!

(LEVEE *takes the shoes out of the box and starts to put them on.*)

TOLEDO: How much you pay for something like that, Levee?

LEVEE: Eleven dollars. Four dollars of it belong to Cutler.

SLOW DRAG: Levee say if it wasn't for Cutler ... he wouldn't have no new shoes.

CUTLER: I ain't thinking about Levee or his shoes. Come on ... let's get ready to rehearse.

SLOW DRAG: I'm with you on that score, Cutler. I wanna get out of here. I don't want to be around here all night. When it comes time to go up there and record them songs ... I just wanna go up there and do it. Last time it took us all day and half the night.

TOLEDO: Ain't but four songs on the list. Last time we recorded six songs.

SLOW DRAG: It felt like it was sixteen!

LEVEE: (*Finishes with his shoes.*)   Yeah! Now I'm ready! I can play some good music now! (*He goes to put up his old shoes and looks around the room.*) Damn! They done changed things around. Don't never leave well enough alone.

TOLEDO: Everything changing all the time. Even the air you breathing change. You got monoxide, hydrogen . . . changing all the time. Skin changing . . . different molecules and everything.

LEVEE: Nigger, what is you talking about? I'm talking about the room. I ain't talking about no skin and air. I'm talking about something I can see! Last time the band room was upstairs. This time it's downstairs. Next time it be over there. I'm talking about what I can see. I ain't talking about no molecules or nothing.

TOLEDO: Hell, I know what you talking about. I just said everything changin.' I know what you talking about, but you don't know what I'm talking about.

LEVEE: That door! Nigger, you see that door? That's what I'm talking about. That door wasn't there before.

CUTLER: Levee, you wouldn't know your right from your left. This is where they used to keep the recording horns and things . . . and damn if that door wasn't there. How in hell else you gonna get in here? Now, if you talking about they done switched rooms, you right. But don't go telling me that damn door wasn't there!

SLOW DRAG: Damn the door and let's get set up. I wanna get out of here.

LEVEE: Toledo started all that about the door. I'm just saying that things change.

TOLEDO: What the hell you think I was saying? Things change. The air and everything. Now you gonna say you was saying it. You gonna fit two propositions on the same track . . . run them into each other, and because they crash, you gonna say it's the same train.

LEVEE: Now this nigger talking about trains! We done went from the air to the skin to the door . . . and now trains. Toledo, I'd just like to be inside your head for five minutes. Jest to see how you think. You done got more shit piled up and mixed up in there than the devil got sinners. You been reading too many goddamn books.

TOLEDO: What you care about how much I read? I'm gonna ignore you 'cause you ignorant.

(LEVEE *takes off his coat and hangs it in the locker.*)

SLOW DRAG: Come on, let's rehearse the music.

LEVEE: You ain't gotta rehearse that . . . ain't nothing but old jug-band music. They need one of them jug bands for this.

SLOW DRAG: Don't make no difference. Long as we get paid.

LEVEE: That ain't what I'm talking about, nigger. I'm talking about art!

SLOW DRAG: What's drawing got to do with it?

LEVEE: Where you get this nigger from, Cutler? He sound like one of them Alabama niggers.

CUTLER: Slow Drag's all right. It's you talking all that weird shit about art. Just play the piece, nigger. You wanna be one of them . . . what you call . . . virtuoso or something, you in the wrong place. You ain't no Buddy Bolden or King Oliver . . . you just an old trumpet player come a dime a dozen. Talking about art.

LEVEE: What is you? I don't see your name in lights.

CUTLER: I just play the piece. Whatever they want. I don't go talking about art and criticizing other people's music.

LEVEE: I ain't like you, Cutler. I got talent! Me and this horn . . . we's tight. If my daddy knowed I was gonna turn out like this, he would've named me Gabriel. I'm gonna get me a band and make me some records. I done give Mr. Sturdyvant some of my songs I wrote and he say he's gonna let me record them when I get my band together.

(*Takes some papers out of his pocket.*)

I just gotta finish the last part of this song. And Mr. Sturdyvant want me to write another part to this song.

SLOW DRAG: How you learn to write music, Levee?

LEVEE: I just picked it up . . . like you pick up anything. Miss Eula used to play the piano . . . she learned me a lot. I knows how to play *real* music . . . not this old jug-band shit. I got style!

TOLEDO: Everybody got style. Style ain't nothing but keeping the same idea from beginning to end. Everybody got it.

LEVEE: But everybody can't play like I do. Everybody can't have their own band.

CUTLER: Well, until you get your own band where you can play what you want, you just play the piece and stop complaining. I told you when you came on here, this ain't none of them hot bands. This is an accompaniment band. You play Ma's music when you here.

LEVEE: I got sense enough to know that. Hell, I can look at you all and see what kind of band it is. I can look at Toledo and see what kind of band it is.

TOLEDO: Toledo ain't said nothing to you now. Don't let Toledo get started. You can't even spell music, much less play it.

LEVEE: What you talking about? I can spell music. I got a dollar say I can spell it! Put your dollar up. Where your dollar?

(TOLEDO *waves him away.*)

Now come on. Put your dollar up. Talking about I can't spell music.

(LEVEE *peels a dollar off his roll and slams it down on the bench beside* TOLEDO.)

TOLEDO: All right, I'm gonna show you. Cutler. Slow Drag. You hear this? The nigger betting me a dollar he can spell music. I don't want no shit now!

(TOLEDO *lays a dollar down beside* LEVEE's.)

All right. Go ahead. Spell it.

LEVEE: It's a bet then. Talking about I can't spell music.

TOLEDO: Go ahead, then. Spell it. Music. Spell it.

LEVEE: I can spell it, nigger! M-U-S-I-K. There!

(*He reaches for the money.*)

TOLEDO: Naw! Naw! Leave that money alone! You ain't spelled it.

LEVEE: What you mean I ain't spelled it? I said M-U-S-I-K!

TOLEDO: That ain't how you spell it! That ain't how you spell it! It's M-U-S-I-C,
C, nigger. Not K! C! M-U-S-I-C!
LEVEE: What you mean, C? Who say it's C?
TOLEDO: Cutler. Slow Drag. Tell this fool.

(*They look at each other and then away.*)

Well, I'll be a monkey's uncle!

(TOLEDO *picks up the money and hands* LEVEE *his dollar back.*)

Here's your dollar back, Levee. I done won it, you understand. I done won the
dollar. But if don't nobody know but me, how am I gonna prove it to you?
LEVEE: You just mad 'cause I spelled it.
TOLEDO: Spelled what! M-U-S-I-K don't spell nothing. I just wish there was some
way I could show you the right and wrong of it. How you gonna know something
if the other fellow don't know if you're right or not? Now I can't even be sure
that I'm spelling it right.
LEVEE: That's what I'm talking about. You don't know it. Talking about C. You
ought to give me that dollar I won from you.
TOLEDO: All right. All right. I'm gonna show you how ridiculous you sound. You
know the Lord's Prayer?
LEVEE: Why? You wanna bet a dollar on that?
TOLEDO: Just answer the question. Do you know the Lord's Prayer or don't you?
LEVEE: Yeah, I know it. What of it?
TOLEDO: Cutler?
CUTLER: What you Cutlering me for? I ain't got nothing to do with it.
TOLEDO: I just want to show the man how ridiculous he is.
CUTLER: Both of you all sound like damn fools. Arguing about something silly.
Yeah, I know the Lord's Prayer. My daddy was a deacon in the church. Come
asking me if I know the Lord's Prayer. Yeah, I know it.
TOLEDO: Slow Drag?
SLOW DRAG: Yeah.
TOLEDO: All right. Now I'm gonna tell you a story to show just how ridiculous he
sounds. There was these two fellows, see. So, the one of them go up to this
church and commence to taking up the church learning. The other fellow see
him out on the road and he say, "I done heard you taking up the church
learning," say, "Is you learning anything up there?" The other one say, "Yeah,
I done take up the church learning and I's learning all kinds of things about the
Bible and what it say and all. Why you be asking?" The other one say, "Well, do
you know the Lord's Prayer?" And he say, "Why, sure I know the Lord's Prayer,
I'm taking up learning at the church ain't I? I know the Lord's Prayer backwards
and forwards." And the other fellow says, "I bet you five dollars you don't know
the Lord's Prayer, 'cause I don't think you knows it. I think you be going up the
church 'cause the Widow Jenkins be going up there and you just wanna be
sitting in the same room with her when she cross them big, fine pretty legs she
got." And the other one say, "Well, I'm gonna prove you wrong and I'm gonna
bet you that five dollars." So he say, "Well, go on and say it then." So he
commenced to saying the Lord's Prayer. He say, "Now I lay me down to sleep,
I pray the Lord my soul to keep." The other one say, "Here's your five dollars.
I didn't think you knew it."

(*They all laugh.*)

Now, that's just how ridiculous Levee sound. Only 'cause I knowed how to spell music, I still got my dollar.

LEVEE: That don't prove nothing. What's that supposed to prove?

(TOLEDO *takes a newspaper out of his back pocket and begins to read.*)

TOLEDO: I'm through with it.

SLOW DRAG: Is you all gonna rehearse this music or ain't you?

(CUTLER *takes out some papers and starts to roll a reefer.*)

LEVEE: How many times you done played them songs? What you gotta rehearse for?

SLOW DRAG: This a recording session. I wanna get it right the first time and get on out of here.

CUTLER: Slow Drag's right. Let's go on and rehearse and get it over with.

LEVEE: You all go and rehearse, then. I got to finish this song for Mr. Sturdyvant.

CUTLER: Come on, Levee . . . I don't want no shit now. You rehearse like everybody else. You in the band like everybody else. Mr. Sturdyvant just gonna have to wait. You got to do that on your own time. This is the band's time.

LEVEE: Well, what is you doing? You sitting there rolling a reefer talking about let's rehearse. Toledo reading a newspaper. Hell, I'm ready if you wanna rehearse. I just say there ain't no point in it. Ma ain't here. What's the point in it?

CUTLER: Nigger, why you gotta complain all the time?

TOLEDO: Levee would complain if a gal ain't laid across his bed just right.

CUTLER: That's what I know. That's why I try to tell him just play the music and forget about it. It ain't no big thing.

TOLEDO: Levee ain't got an eye for that. He wants to tie on to some abstract component and sit down on the elemental.

LEVEE: This is get-on-Levee time, huh? Levee ain't said nothing except this some old jug-band music.

TOLEDO: Under the right circumstances you'd play anything. If you know music, then you play it. Straight on or off to the side. Ain't nothing abstract about it.

LEVEE: Toledo, you sound like you got a mouth full of marbles. You the only cracker-talking nigger I know.

TOLEDO: You ought to have learned yourself to read . . . then you'd understand the basic understanding of everything.

SLOW DRAG: Both of you all gonna drive me crazy with that philosophy bullshit. Cutler, give me a reefer.

CUTLER: Ain't you got some reefer? Where's your reefer? Why you all the time asking me?

SLOW DRAG: Cutler, how long I done known you? How long we been together? Twenty-two years. We been doing this together for twenty-two years. All up and down the back roads, the side roads, the front roads . . . We done played the juke joints, the whorehouses, the barn dances, and city sit-downs . . . I done lied for you and lied with you . . . We done laughed together, fought together, slept in the same bed together, done sucked on the same titty . . . and now you don't wanna give me no reefer.

CUTLER: You see this nigger trying to talk me out of my reefer, Toledo? Running

all that about how long he done knowed me and how we done sucked on the
same titty. Nigger, you *still* ain't getting none of my reefer!

TOLEDO: That's African.

SLOW DRAG: What? What you talking about? What's African?

LEVEE: I know he ain't talking about me. You don't see me running around in
no jungle with no bone between my nose.

TOLEDO: Levee, you worse than ignorant. You ignorant without a premise.

(*Pauses.*)

Now, what I was saying is what Slow Drag was doing is African. That's what you
call an African conceptualization. That's when you name the gods or call on the
ancestors to achieve whatever your desires are.

SLOW DRAG: Nigger, I ain't no African! I ain't doing no African nothing!

TOLEDO: Naming all those things you and Cutler done together is like trying to
solicit some reefer based on a bond of kinship. That's African. An ancestral
retention. Only you forgot the name of the gods.

SLOW DRAG: I ain't forgot nothing. I was telling the nigger how cheap he is.
Don't come talking that African nonsense to me.

TOLEDO: You just like Levee. No eye for taking an abstract and fixing it to a
specific. There's so much that goes on around you and you can't even see it.

CUTLER: Wait a minute . . . wait a minute. Toledo, now when this nigger . . .
when an African do all them things you say and name all the gods and whatnot
. . . then what happens?

TOLEDO: Depends on if the gods is sympathetic with his cause for which he is
calling them with the right names. Then his success comes with the right
proportion of his naming. That's the way that go.

CUTLER: (*Taking out a reefer.*)   Here, Slow Drag. Here's a reefer. You done talked
yourself up on that one.

SLOW DRAG: Thank you. You ought to have done that in the first place and saved
me all the aggravation.

CUTLER: What I wants to know is . . . what's the same titty we done sucked on.
That's what I want to know.

SLOW DRAG: Oh, I just threw that in there to make it sound good.

(*They all laugh.*)

CUTLER: Nigger, you ain't right.

SLOW DRAG: I knows it.

CUTLER: Well, come on . . . let's get it rehearsed. Time's wasting.

(*The musicians pick up their instruments.*)

Let's do it, "Ma Rainey's Black Bottom." One . . . two . . .
You know what to do.

(*They begin to play.* LEVEE *is playing something different. He stops.*)

LEVEE: Naw! Naw! We ain't doing it that way.

(TOLEDO *stops playing, then* SLOW DRAG.)

We doing my version. It say so right there on that piece of paper you got. Ask Toledo. That's what Mr. Irvin told me . . . say it's on the list he gave you.

CUTLER: Let me worry about what's on the list and what ain't on the list. How you gonna tell me what's on the list?

LEVEE: 'Cause I know what Mr. Irvin told me! Ask Toledo!

CUTLER: Let me worry about what's on the list. You just play the song I say.

LEVEE: What kind of sense it make to rehearse the wrong version of the song? That's what I wanna know. Why you wanna rehearse that version?

SLOW DRAG: You supposed to rehearse what you gonna play. That's the way they taught me. Now, *whatever* version we gonna play . . . let's go on and rehearse it.

LEVEE: That's what I'm trying to tell the man.

CUTLER: You trying to tell me what we is and ain't gonna play. And that ain't none of your business. Your business is to play what I say.

LEVEE: Oh, I see now. You done got jealous 'cause Mr. Irvin using my version. You done got jealous 'cause I proved I know something about music.

CUTLER: What the hell . . . nigger, you talk like a fool! What the hell I got to be jealous of you about? The day I get jealous of you I may as well lay down and die.

TOLEDO: Levee started all that 'cause he too lazy to rehearse.

(*To* LEVEE.)

You ought to just go on and play the song . . . What difference does it make?

LEVEE: Where's the paper? Look at the paper! Get the paper and look at it! See what it say. Gonna tell me I'm too lazy to rehearse.

CUTLER: We ain't talking about the paper. We talking about you understanding where you fit in when you around here. You just play what I say.

LEVEE: Look . . . I don't care what you play! All right? It don't matter to me. Mr. Irvin gonna straighten it up! I don't care what you play.

CUTLER: Thank you.

(*Pauses.*)

Let's play this "Hear Me Talking to You" till we find out what's happening with the "Black Bottom." Slow Drag, you sing Ma's part.

(*Pauses.*)

"Hear Me Talking to You." Let's do it. One . . . Two . . .
You know what to do.

(*They play.*)

SLOW DRAG: (*Singing*)

> Rambling man makes no change in me
> I'm gonna ramble back to my used-to-be
> Ah, you hear me talking to you
> I don't bite my tongue

You wants to be my man
You got to fetch it with you when you come.

Eve and Adam in the garden taking a chance
Adam didn't take time to get his pants
Ah, you hear me talking to you
I don't bite my tongue
You wants to be my man
You got to fetch it with you when you come.

Our old cat swallowed a ball of yarn
When the kittens were born they had sweaters on
Ah, you hear me talking to you
I don't bite my tongue
You wants to be my man
You got to fetch it with you when you come.

(IRVIN *enters. The musicians stop playing.*)

IRVIN: Any of you boys know what's keeping Ma?
CUTLER: Can't say, Mr. Irvin. She'll be along directly, I reckon. I talked to her this morning, she says she'll be here in time to rehearse.
IRVIN: Well, you boys go ahead.

(*He starts to exit.*)

CUTLER: Mr. Irvin, about these songs . . . Levee say . . .
IRVIN: Whatever's on the list, Cutler. You got that list I gave you?
CUTLER: Yessir, I got it right here.
IRVIN: Whatever's on there. Whatever that says.
CUTLER: I'm asking about this "Black Bottom" piece . . . Levee say . . .
IRVIN: Oh, it's on the list. "Ma Rainey's Black Bottom" on the list.
CUTLER: I know it's on the list. I wanna know what version. We got two versions of that song.
IRVIN: Oh. Levee's arrangement. We're using Levee's arrangement.
CUTLER: Okay. I got that straight. Now, this "Moonshine Blues" . . .
IRVIN: We'll work it out with Ma, Cutler. Just rehearse whatever's on the list and use Levee's arrangement on that "Black Bottom" piece.

(*He exits.*)

LEVEE: See, I told you! It don't mean nothing when I say it. You got to wait for Mr. Irvin to say it. Well, I told you the way it is.
CUTLER: Levee, the sooner you understand it ain't what you say, or what Mr. Irvin says . . . it's what Ma say that counts.
SLOW DRAG: Don't nobody say when it come to Ma. She's gonna do what she wants to do. Ma says what happens with her.
LEVEE: Hell, the man's the one putting out the record! He's gonna put out what he wanna put out!
SLOW DRAG: He's gonna put out what Ma want him to put out.

LEVEE: You heard what the man told you . . . "Ma Rainey's Black Bottom,"
Levee's arrangement. There you go! That's what he told you.

SLOW DRAG: What you gonna do, Cutler?

CUTLER: Ma ain't told me what version. Let's go on and play it Levee's way.

TOLEDO: See, now . . . I'll tell you something. As long as the colored man look to
white folks to put the crown on what he say . . . as long as he looks to white folks
for approval . . . then he ain't never gonna find out who he is and what he's
about. He's just gonna be about what white folks want him to be about. That's
one sure thing.

LEVEE: I'm just trying to show Cutler where he's wrong.

CUTLER: Cutler don't need you to show him nothing.

SLOW DRAG: (*Irritated.*)   Come on, let's get this shit rehearsed! You all can bicker
afterward!

CUTLER: Levee's confused about who the boss is. He don't know Ma's the boss.

LEVEE: Ma's the boss on the road! We at a recording session. Mr. Sturdyvant and
Mr. Irvin say what's gonna be here! We's in Chicago, we ain't in Memphis! I
don't know why you all wanna pick me about it, shit! I'm with Slow Drag . . .
Let's go on and get it rehearsed.

CUTLER: All right. All right. I know how to solve this. "Ma Rainey's Black Bottom." Levee's version. Let's do it. Come on.

TOLEDO: How that first part go again, Levee?

LEVEE: It go like this.

(*He plays.*)

That's to get the people's attention to the song. That's when you and Slow Drag
come in with the rhythm part. Me and Cutler play on the breaks.

(*Becoming animated.*)

Now we gonna dance it . . . but we ain't gonna countrify it. This ain't no barn
dance. We gonna play it like . . .

CUTLER: The man ask you how the first part go. He don't wanna hear all that.
Just tell him how the piece go.

TOLEDO: I got it. I got it. Let's go. I know how to do it.

CUTLER: "Ma Rainey's Black Bottom." One . . . two . . . You know what to do.

(*They begin to play.* LEVEE *stops.*)

LEVEE: You all got to keep up now. You playing in the wrong time. Ma come in
over the top. She got to find her own way in.

CUTLER: Nigger, will you let us play this song? When you get your band . . . then
you tell them that nonsense. We know how to play the piece. I was playing music
before you was born. Gonna tell me how to play . . . All right. Let's try it again.

SLOW DRAG: Cutler, wait till I fix this. This string started to unravel.

(*Playfully.*)

And you know I want to play Levee's music right.

LEVEE: If you was any kind of musician, you'd take care of your instrument. Keep it in tip-top order. If you was any kind of musician, I'd let you be in my band.

SLOW DRAG: Shhheeeeet!

(*He crosses to get his string and steps on* LEVEE'*s shoes.*)

LEVEE: Damn, Slow Drag! Watch them big-ass shoes you got.

SLOW DRAG: Boy, ain't nobody done nothing to you.

LEVEE: You done stepped on my shoes.

SLOW DRAG: Move them the hell out the way, then. You was in my way . . . I wasn't in your way.

(CUTLER *lights up another reefer.* SLOW DRAG *rummages around in his belongings for a string.* LEVEE *takes out a rag and begins to shine his shoes.*)

You can shine these when you get done, Levee.

CUTLER: If I had them shoes Levee got, I could buy me a whole suit of clothes.

LEVEE: What kind of difference it make what kind of shoes I got? Ain't nothing wrong with having nice shoes. I ain't said nothing about your shoes. Why you wanna talk about me and my Florsheims?

CUTLER: Any man who takes a whole week's pay and puts it on some shoes—you understand what I mean, what you walk around on the ground with—is a fool! And I don't mind telling you.

LEVEE: (*Irritated.*)   What difference it make to you, Cutler?

SLOW DRAG: The man ain't said nothing about your shoes. Ain't nothing wrong with having nice shoes. Look at Toledo.

TOLEDO: What about Toledo?

SLOW DRAG: I said ain't nothing wrong with having nice shoes.

LEVEE: Nigger got them clodhoppers! Old brogans! He ain't nothing but a sharecropper.

TOLEDO: You can make all the fun you want. It don't mean nothing. I'm satisfied with them and that's what counts.

LEVEE: Nigger, why don't you get some decent shoes? Got nerve to put on a suit and tie with them farming boots.

CUTLER: What you just tell me? It don't make no difference about the man's shoes. That's what you told me.

LEVEE: Aw, hell, I don't care what the nigger wear. I'll be honest with you. I don't care if he went barefoot.

(SLOW DRAG *has put his string on the bass and is tuning it.*)

Play something for me, Slow Drag.

(SLOW DRAG *plays.*)

A man got to have some shoes to dance like this! You can't dance like this with them clodhoppers Toledo got.

(LEVEE *sings.*)

> Hello Central give me Doctor Jazz.
> He's got just what I need I'll say he has   635

> When the world goes wrong and I have got the blues
> He's the man who makes me get on my dancing shoes.

TOLEDO: That's the trouble with colored folks ... always wanna have a good time. Good times done got more niggers killed than God got ways to count. What the hell having a good time mean? That's what I wanna know.

LEVEE: Hell, nigger ... it don't need explaining. Ain't you never had no good time before?

TOLEDO: The more niggers get killed having a good time, the more good times niggers wanna have.

(SLOW DRAG *stops playing.*)

There's more to life than having a good time. If there ain't, then this is a piss-poor life we're having ... if that's all there is to be got out of it.

SLOW DRAG: Toledo, just 'cause you like to read them books and study and whatnot ... that's your good time. People get other things they likes to do to have a good time. Ain't no need you picking them about it.

CUTLER: Niggers have been having a good time before you was born, and they gonna keep having a good time after you gone.

TOLEDO: Yeah, but what else they gonna do? Ain't nobody talking about making the lot of the colored man better for him here in America.

LEVEE: Now you gonna be Booker T. Washington.

TOLEDO: Everybody worried about having a good time. Ain't nobody thinking about what kind of world they gonna leave their youngens. "Just give me the good time, that's all I want." It just makes me sick.

SLOW DRAG: Well, the colored man's gonna be all right. He got through slavery, and he'll get through whatever else the white man put on him. I ain't worried about that. Good times is what makes life worth living. Now, you take the white man ... The white man don't know how to have a good time. That's why he's troubled all the time. He don't know how to have a good time. He don't know how to laugh at life.

LEVEE: That's what the problem is with Toledo ... reading all them books and things. He done got to the point where he forgot how to laugh and have a good time. Just like the white man.

TOLEDO: I know how to have a good time as well as the next man. I said, there's got to be more to life than having a good time. I said the colored man ought to be doing more than just trying to have a good time all the time.

LEVEE: Well, what is you doing, nigger? Talking all them highfalutin ideas about making a better world for the colored man. What is you doing to make it better? You playing the music and looking for your next piece of pussy same as we is. What is you doing? That's what I wanna know. Tell him, Cutler.

CUTLER: You all leave Cutler out of this. Cutler ain't got nothing to do with it.

TOLEDO: Levee, you just about the most ignorant nigger I know. Sometimes I wonder why I ever bother to try and talk with you.

LEVEE: Well, what is you doing? Talking that shit to me about I'm ignorant! What is you doing? You just a whole lot of mouth. A great big windbag. Thinking you smarter than everybody else. What is you doing, huh?

TOLEDO: It ain't just me, fool! It's everybody! What you think ... I'm gonna solve the colored man's problems by myself? I said, we. You understand that? We. That's every living colored man in the world got to do his share. Got to do his part. I ain't talking about what I'm gonna do . . . or what you or Cutler or Slow Drag or anybody else. I'm talking about all of us together. What all of us is gonna do. That's what I'm talking about, nigger!

LEVEE: Well, why didn't you say that, then?

CUTLER: Toledo, I don't know why you waste your time on this fool!

TOLEDO: That's what I'm trying to figure out.

LEVEE: Now there go Cutler with his shit. Calling me a fool. You wasn't even in the conversation. Now you gonna take sides and call me a fool.

CUTLER: Hell, I was listening to the man. I got sense enough to know what he was saying. I could tell it straight back to you.

LEVEE: Well, you go on with it. But I'll tell you this . . . I ain't gonna be too many more of your fools. I'll tell you that. Now you put that in your pipe and smoke it.

CUTLER: Boy, ain't nobody studying you. Telling me what to put in my pipe. Who's you to tell me what to do?

LEVEE: All right, I ain't nobody. Don't pay me no mind. I ain't nobody.

TOLEDO: Levee, you ain't nothing but the devil.

LEVEE: There you go! That's who I am. I'm the devil. I ain't nothing but the devil.

CUTLER: I can see that. That's something you know about. You know all about the devil.

LEVEE: I ain't saying what I know. I know plenty. What you know about the devil? Telling me what I know. What you know?

SLOW DRAG: I know a man sold his soul to the devil.

LEVEE: There you go! That's the only thing I ask about the devil . . . to see him coming so I can sell him this one I got. 'Cause if there's a god up there, he done went to sleep.

SLOW DRAG: Sold his soul to the devil himself. Name of Eliza Cotter. Lived in Tuscaloosa County, Alabama. The devil came by and he done upped and sold him his soul.

CUTLER: How you know the man done sold his soul to the devil, nigger? You talking that old-woman foolishness.

SLOW DRAG: Everybody know. It wasn't no secret. He went around working for the devil and everybody knowed it. Carried him a bag . . . one of them carpet-bags. Folks say he carried the devil's papers and whatnot where he put your fingerprint on the paper with blood.

LEVEE: Where he at now? That's what I want to know. He can put my whole handprint if he want to!

CUTLER: That's the damndest thing I ever heard! Folks kill me with that talk.

TOLEDO: Oh, that's real enough, all right. Some folks go arm in arm with the devil, shoulder to shoulder, and talk to him all the time. That's real, ain't nothing wrong in believing that.

SLOW DRAG: That's what I'm saying. Eliza Cotter is one of them. All right. The man living up in an old shack on Ben Foster's place, shoeing mules and horses, making them charms and things in secret. He done hooked up with the devil, showed up one day all fancied out with just the finest clothes you ever seen on a colored man . . . dressed just like one of them crackers . . . and carrying this bag with them papers and things. All right. Had a pocketful of money, just living the life of a rich man. Ain't done no more work or nothing. Just had him a string of women he run around with and throw his money away on. Bought him a big fine house . . . Well, it wasn't all that big, but it did have one of them white picket fences around it. Used to hire a man once a week just to paint that fence. Messed around there and one of the fellows of them gals he was messing with got fixed on him wrong and Eliza killed him. And he laughed about it. Sheriff come and arrest him, and then let him go. And he went around in that town laughing about killing this fellow. Trial come up, and the judge cut him loose. He must have been in converse with the devil too ... 'cause he cut him loose and give him a bottle of whiskey! Folks ask what done happened to make him change, and he'd tell them straight out he done sold his soul to the devil and ask them if they wanted to sell theirs 'cause he could arrange it for them. Preacher see him coming, used to cross on the other side of the road. He'd just stand there and laugh at the preacher and call him a fool to his face.

CUTLER: Well, whatever happened to this fellow? What come of him? A man who, as you say, done sold his soul to the devil is bound to come to a bad end.

TOLEDO: I don't know about that. The devil's strong. The devil ain't no push-over.

SLOW DRAG: Oh, the devil had him under his wing, all right. Took good care of him. He ain't wanted for nothing.

CUTLER: What happened to him? That's what I want to know.

SLOW DRAG: Last I heard, he headed north with that bag of his, handing out hundred-dollar bills on the spot to whoever wanted to sign on with the devil. That's what I hear tell of him.

CUTLER: That's a bunch of fool talk. I don't know how you fix your mouth to tell that story. I don't believe that.

SLOW DRAG: I ain't asking you to believe it. I'm just telling you the facts of it.

LEVEE: I sure wish I knew where he went. He wouldn't have to convince me long. Hell, I'd even help him sign people up.

CUTLER: Nigger, God's gonna strike you down with that blasphemy you talking.

LEVEE: Oh, shit! God don't mean nothing to me. Let him strike me! Here I am, standing right here. What you talking about he's gonna strike me? Here I am! Let him strike me! I ain't scared of him. Talking that stuff to me.

CUTLER: All right. You gonna be sorry. You gonna fix yourself to have bad luck. Ain't nothing gonna work for you. (*Buzzer sounds offstage.*)

LEVEE: Bad luck? What I care about some bad luck? You talking simple. I ain't knowed nothing but bad luck all my life. Couldn't get no worse. What the hell I care about some bad luck? Hell, I eat it everyday for breakfast! You dumber than I thought you was ... talking about bad luck.

CUTLER: All right, nigger, you'll see! Can't tell a fool nothing. You'll see!

IRVIN: (IRVIN *enters the studio, checks his watch, and calls down the stairs.*) Cutler ... you boys' sandwiches are up here ... Cutler?

CUTLER: Yessir, Mr. Irvin ... be right there.

TOLEDO: I'll walk up there and get them.

(TOLEDO *exits. The lights go down in the band room and up in the studio.* IRVIN *paces back and forth in an agitated manner.* STURDYVANT *enters.*)

STURDYVANT: Irv, what's happening? Is she here yet? Was that her?

IRVIN: It's the sandwiches, Mel. I told you ... I'll let you know when she comes, huh?

STURDYVANT: What's keeping her? Do you know what time it is? Have you looked
   at the clock? You told me she'd be here. You told me you'd take care of it.

IRVIN: Mel, for chrissakes! What do you want from me? What do you want me to
   do?

STURDYVANT: Look what time it is, Irv. You told me she'd be here.

IRVIN: She'll be here, okay? I don't know what's keeping her. You know they're
   always late, Mel.

STURDYVANT: You should have went by the hotel and made sure she was on time.
   You should have taken care of this. That's what you told me, huh? "I'll take care
   of it."

IRVIN: Okay! Okay! I didn't go to the hotel! What do you want me to do? She'll
   be here, okay? The band's here . . . she'll be here.

STURDYVANT: Okay, Irv. I'll take your word. But if she doesn't come . . . if she
   doesn't come . . .

(STURDYVANT *exits to the control booth as* TOLEDO *enters.*)

TOLEDO: Mr. Irvin . . . I come up to get the sandwiches.

IRVIN: Say . . . uh . . . look . . . one o'clock, right? She said one o'clock.

TOLEDO: That's what time she told us. Say be here at one o'clock.

IRVIN: Do you know what's keeping her? Do you know why she ain't here?

TOLEDO: I can't say, Mr. Irvin. Told us one o'clock.

(*The buzzer sounds,* IRVIN *goes to the door. There is a flurry of commotion as* MA RAINEY
enters, followed closely by the POLICEMAN, DUSSIE MAE, *and* SYLVESTER. MA RAINEY *is
a short, heavy woman. She is dressed in a full-length fur coat with matching hat, an
emerald-green dress, and several strands of pearls of varying lengths. Her hair is secured by
a headband that matches her dress. Her manner is simple and direct, and she carries herself
in a royal fashion.* DUSSIE MAE *is a young, darkskinned woman whose greatest asset is the
sensual energy which seems to flow from her. She is dressed in a fur jacket and a tight-fitting
canary-yellow dress.* SYLVESTER *is an Arkansas country boy, the size of a fullback. He wears
a new suit and coat, in which he is obviously uncomfortable. Most of the time, he stutters
when he speaks.*)

MA RAINEY: Irvin . . . you better tell this man who I am! You better get him
   straight!

IRVIN: Ma, do you know what time it is? Do you have any idea? We've been
   waiting . . .

DUSSIE MAE: (*To* SYLVESTER.)   If you was watching where you was going . . .

SYLVESTER: I was watching . . . What you mean?

IRVIN: (*Notices* POLICEMAN.)   What's going on here? Officer, what's the matter?

MA RAINEY: Tell the man who he's messing with!

POLICEMAN: Do you know this lady?

MA RAINEY: Just tell the man who I am! That's all you gotta do.

POLICEMAN: Lady, will you let me talk, huh?

MA RAINEY: Tell the man who I am!

IRVIN: Wait a minute . . . wait a minute! Let me handle it. Ma, will you let me
   handle it?

MA RAINEY: Tell him who he's messing with!

IRVIN: Okay! Okay! Give me a chance! Officer, this is one of our recording artists
   . . . Ma Rainey.

MA RAINEY: Madame Rainey! Get it straight! Madame Rainey! Talking about taking me to jail!

IRVIN: Look, Ma . . . give me a chance, okay? Here . . . sit down. I'll take care of it. Officer, what's the problem?

DUSSIE MAE: (*to* SYLVESTER.) It's all your fault.

SYLVESTER: I ain't done nothing . . . Ask Ma.

POLICEMAN: Well . . . when I walked up on the incident . . .

DUSSIE MAE: Sylvester wrecked Ma's car.

SYLVESTER: I d-d-did not! The m-m-man ran into me!

POLICEMAN: (*To* IRVIN.) Look, buddy. . . if you want it in a nutshell, we got her charged with assault and battery.

MA RAINEY: Assault and what for what!

DUSSIE MAE: See . . . we was trying to get a cab . . . and so Ma . . .

MA RAINEY: Wait a minute! I'll tell you if you wanna know what happened. (*She points to* SYLVESTER.) Now, that's Sylvester. That's my nephew. He was driving my car . . .

POLICEMAN: Lady, we don't know whose car he was driving.

MA RAINEY: That's my car!

DUSSIE MAE *and* SYLVESTER: That's Ma's car!

MA RAINEY: What you mean you don't know whose car it is? I bought and paid for that car.

POLICEMAN: That's what you say, lady . . . We still gotta check.

(*To* IRVIN.)

They hit a car on Market Street. The guy said the kid ran a stoplight.

SYLVESTER: What you mean? The man c-c-come around the corner and hit m-m-me!

POLICEMAN: While I was calling a paddy wagon to haul them to the station, they try to hop into a parked cab. The cabbie said he was waiting on a fare . . .

MA RAINEY: The man was just sitting there. Wasn't waiting for nobody. I don't know why he wanna tell that lie.

POLICEMAN: Look, lady . . . will you let me tell the story?

MA RAINEY: Go ahead and tell it then. But tell it right!

POLICEMAN: Like I say . . . she tries to get in this cab. The cabbie's waiting on a fare. She starts creating a disturbance. The cabbie gets out to try and explain the situation to her . . . and she knocks him down.

DUSSIE MAE: She ain't hit him! He just fell!

SYLVESTER: He just s-s-s-slipped!

POLICEMAN: He claims she knocked him down. We got her charged with assault and battery.

MA RAINEY: If that don't beat all to hell. I ain't touched the man! The man was trying to reach around me to keep his car door closed. I opened the door and it hit him and he fell down. I ain't touched the man!

IRVIN: Okay. Okay . . . I got it straight now, Ma. You didn't touch him. All right? Officer, can I see you for a minute?

DUSSIE MAE: Ma was just trying to open the door.

SYLVESTER: He j-j-just got in t-t-the way!

MA RAINEY: Said he wasn't gonna haul no colored folks . . . if you want to know the truth of it.

IRVIN: Okay, Ma . . . I got it straight now. Officer?

(IRVIN *pulls the* POLICEMAN *off to the side.*)

MA RAINEY: (*Noticing* TOLEDO.)   Toledo, Cutler and everybody here?
TOLEDO: Yeah, they down in the band room. What happened to your car?
STURDYVANT: (*Entering.*)   Irv, what's the problem? What's going on? Officer . . .
IRVIN: Mel, let me take care of it. I can handle it.
STURDYVANT: What's happening? What the hell's going on?
IRVIN: Let me handle it, Mel, huh?

(STURDYVANT *crosses over to* MA RAINEY.)

STURDYVANT: What's going on, Ma. What'd you do?
MA RAINEY: Sturdyvant, get on away from me! That's the last thing I need . . . to
go through some of your shit!
IRVIN: Mel, I'll take care of it. I'll explain it all to you. Let me handle it, huh?

(STURDYVANT *reluctantly returns to the control booth.*)

POLICEMAN: Look, buddy, like I say . . . we got her charged with assault and
battery . . . and the kid with threatening the cabbie.
SYLVESTER: I ain't done n-n-nothing!
MA RAINEY: You leave the boy out of it. He ain't done nothing. What's he
supposed to have done?
POLICEMAN: He threatened the cabbie, lady! You just can't go around threaten-
ing people.
SYLVESTER: I ain't done nothing to him! He's the one talking about he g-g-
gonna get a b-b-baseball bat on me! I just told him what I'd do with it. But I ain't
done nothing 'cause he didn't get the b-b-bat!
IRVIN: (*Pulling the* POLICEMAN *aside.*)   Officer . . . look here . . .
POLICEMAN: We was on our way down to the precinct . . . but I figured I'd do you
a favor and bring her by here. I mean, if she's as important as she says she is . . .
IRVIN: (*Slides a bill from his pocket.*)   Look, Officer . . . I'm Madame Rainey's manager . . . It's good to meet you.

(*He shakes the* POLICEMAN*'s hand and passes him the bill.*)

As soon as we're finished with the recording session, I'll personally stop by the
precinct house and straighten up this misunderstanding.
POLICEMAN: Well . . . I guess that's all right. As long as someone is responsible
for them.

(*He pockets the bill and winks at* IRVIN.)

No need to come down . . . I'll take care of it myself. Of course, we wouldn't
want nothing like this to happen again.
IRVIN: Don't worry, Officer . . . I'll take care of everything. Thanks for your help.

(IRVIN *escorts the* POLICEMAN *to the door and returns. He crosses over to* MA RAINEY.)

Here, Ma . . . let me take your coat.

(*To* SYLVESTER.)

I don't believe I know you.
MA RAINEY: That's my nephew, Sylvester.
IRVIN: I'm very pleased to meet you. Here . . . you can give me your coat.
MA RAINEY: That there is Dussie Mae.
IRVIN: Hello . . .

(DUSSIE MAE *hands* IRVIN *her coat.*)

Listen, Ma, just sit there and relax. The boys are in the band room rehearsing. You just sit and relax a minute.
MA RAINEY: I ain't for no sitting. I ain't never heard of such. Talking about taking me to jail. Irvin, call down there and see about my car.
IRVIN: Okay, Ma . . . I'll take care of it. You just relax.

(IRVIN *exits with the coats.*)

MA RAINEY: Why you all keep it so cold in here? Sturdyvant try and pinch every penny he can. You all wanna make some records, you better put some heat on in here or give me back my coat.
IRVIN: (*Entering.*) We got the heat turned up, Ma. It's warming up. It'll be warm in a minute.
DUSSIE MAE: (*Whispering to* MA RAINEY.) Where's the bathroom?
MA RAINEY: It's in the back. Down the hall next to Sturdyvant's office. Come on, I'll show you where it is. Irvin, call down there and see about my car. I want my car fixed today.
IRVIN: I'll take care of everything, Ma.

(*He notices* TOLEDO.)

Say . . . uh . . . uh . . .
TOLEDO: Toledo.
IRVIN: Yeah . . . Toledo. I got the sandwiches, you can take down to the rest of the boys. We'll be ready to go in a minute. Give you boys a chance to eat and then we'll be ready to go.

(IRVIN *and* TOLEDO *exit. The lights go down in the studio and come up in the band room.*)

LEVEE: Slow Drag, you ever been to New Orleans?
SLOW DRAG: What's in New Orleans that I want?
LEVEE: How you call yourself a musician and ain't never been to New Orleans.
SLOW DRAG: You ever been to Fat Back, Arkansas?

(*Pauses.*)

All right, then. Ain't never been nothing in New Orleans that I couldn't get in Fat Back.
LEVEE: That's why you backwards. You just an old country boy talking about Fat Back, Arkansas, and New Orleans in the same breath.

CUTLER: I been to New Orleans. What about it?

LEVEE: You ever been to Lula White's?

CUTLER: Lula White's? I ain't never heard of it.

LEVEE: Man, they got some gals in there just won't wait! I seen a man get killed
   in there once. Got drunk and grabbed one of the gals wrong . . . I don't know
   what the matter of it was. But he grabbed her and she stuck a knife in him all
   the way up to the hilt. He ain't even fell. He just stood there and choked on his
   own blood. I was just asking Slow Drag 'cause I was gonna take him to Lula
   White's when we get down to New Orleans and show him a good time. Introduce him to one of them gals I know down there.

CUTLER: Slow Drag don't need you to find him no pussy. He can take care of his
   own self. Fact is . . . you better watch your gal when Slow Drag's around. They
   don't call him Slow Drag for nothing.

(*He laughs.*)

Tell him how you got your name, Slow Drag.

SLOW DRAG: I ain't thinking about Levee.

CUTLER: Slow Drag break a woman's back when he dance. They had this contest
   one time in this little town called Bolingbroke about a hundred miles outside
   of Macon. We was playing for this dance and they was giving twenty dollars to
   the best slow draggers. Slow Drag looked over the competition, got down off the
   bandstand, grabbed hold of one of them gals, and stuck to her like a fly to jelly.
   Like wood to glue. Man had that gal whooping and hollering so . . . everybody
   stopped to watch. This fellow come in . . . this gal's fellow . . . and pulled a knife
   a foot long on Slow Drag. 'Member that, Slow Drag?

SLOW DRAG: Boy that mama was hot! The front of her dress was wet as a dishrag!

LEVEE: So what happened? What the man do?

CUTLER: Slow Drag ain't missed a stroke. The gal, she just look at her man with
   that sweet dizzy look in her eye. She ain't about to stop! Folks was clearing out,
   ducking and hiding under tables, figuring there's gonna be a fight. Slow Drag
   just looked over the gal's shoulder at the man and said, "Mister, if you'd quit
   hollering and wait a minute . . . you'll see I'm doing you a favor. I'm helping this
   gal win ten dollars so she can buy you a gold watch." The man just stood there
   and looked at him, all the while stroking that knife. Told Slow Drag, say, "All
   right, then, nigger. You just better make damn sure you win." That's when folks
   started calling him Slow Drag. The women got to hanging around him so bad
   after that, them fellows in that town ran us out of there.

(TOLEDO *enters, carrying a small cardboard box with the sandwiches.*)

LEVEE: Yeah . . . well, them gals in Lula White's will put a harness on his ass.

TOLEDO: Ma's up there. Some kind of commotion with the police.

CUTLER: Police? What the police up there for?

TOLEDO: I couldn't get it straight. Something about her car. They gone now . . .
   she's all right. Mr. Irvin sent some sandwiches.

(LEVEE *springs across the room.*)

LEVEE: Yeah, all right. What we got here?

(*He takes two sandwiches out of the box.*)

TOLEDO: What you doing grabbing two? There ain't but five in there . . . How you figure you get two?

LEVEE: 'Cause I grabbed them first. There's enough for everybody . . . What you talking about? It ain't like I'm taking food out of nobody's mouth.

CUTLER: That's all right. He can have mine too. I don't want none.

(LEVEE *starts toward the box to get anther sandwich.*)

TOLEDO: Nigger, you better get out of here. Slow Drag, you want this?

SLOW DRAG: Naw, you can have it.

TOLEDO: With Levee around, you don't have to worry about no leftovers. I can see that.

LEVEE: What's the matter with you? Ain't you eating two sandwiches? Then why you wanna talk about me? Talking about there won't be no leftovers with Levee around. Look at your own self before you look at me.

TOLEDO: That's what you is. That's what we all is. A leftover from history. You see now, I'll show you.

LEVEE: Aw, shit . . . I done got the nigger started now.

TOLEDO: Now, I'm gonna show you how this goes . . . where you just a leftover from history. Everybody come from different places in Africa, right? Come from different tribes and things. Soonawhile they began to make one big stew. You had the carrots, the peas, and potatoes and whatnot over here. And over there you had the meat, the nuts, the okra, corn . . . and then you mix it up and let it cook right through to get the flavors flowing together . . . then you got one thing. You got a stew.

Now you take and eat the stew. You take and make your history with that stew. All right. Now it's over. Your history's over and you done ate the stew. But you look around and you see some carrots over here, some potatoes over there. That stew's still there. You done made your history and it's still there. You can't eat it all. So what you got? You got some leftovers. That's what it is. You got leftovers and you can't do nothing with it. You already making you another history . . . cooking you another meal, and you don't need them leftovers no more. What to do?

See, we's the leftovers. The colored man is the leftovers. Now, what's the colored man gonna do with himself? That's what we waiting to find out. But first we gotta know we the leftovers. Now, who knows that? You find me a nigger that knows that and I'll turn any whichaway you want me to. I'll bend over for you. You ain't gonna find that. And that's what the problem is. The problem ain't with the white man. The white man knows you just a leftover. 'Cause he the one who done the eating and he know what he done ate. But we don't know that we been took and made history out of. Done went and filled the white man's belly and now he's full and tired and wants you to get out the way and let him be by himself. Now, I know what I'm talking about. And if you wanna find out, you just ask Mr. Irvin what he had for supper yesterday. And if he's an honest white man . . . which is asking for a whole heap of a lot . . . he'll tell you he done ate your black ass and if you please I'm full up with you . . . so go on and get off the plate and let me eat something else.

SLOW DRAG: What that mean? What's eating got to do with how the white man treat you? He don't treat you no different according to what he ate.

TOLEDO: I ain't said it had nothing to do with how he treat you.

CUTLER: The man's trying to tell you something, fool!

SLOW DRAG: What he trying to tell me? Ain't you here? Why you say he was trying to tell *me* something? Wasn't he trying to tell you too?

LEVEE: He was trying all right. He was trying a whole heap. I'll say that for him. But trying ain't worth a damn. I got lost right there trying to figure out who puts nuts in their stew.

SLOW DRAG: I knowed that before. My grandpappy used to put nuts in his stew. He and my grandmama both. That ain't nothing new.

TOLEDO: They put nuts in their stew all over Africa. But the stew they eat, and the stew your grandpappy made, and all the stew that you and me eat, and the stew Mr. Irvin eats . . . ain't in no way the same stew. That's the way that go. I'm through with it. That's the last you know me to ever try and explain something to you.

CUTLER: (*After a pause.*)   Well, time's getting along . . . Come on, let's finish rehearsing.

LEVEE: (*Stretching out on a bench.*)   I don't feel like rehearsing. I ain't nothing but a leftover. You go and rehearse with Toledo . . . He's gonna teach you how to make a stew.

SLOW DRAG: Cutler, what you gonna do? I don't want to be around here all day.

LEVEE: I know my part. You all go on and rehearse your part. You all need some rehearsal.

CUTLER: Come on, Levee, get up off your ass and rehearse the songs.

LEVEE: I already know them songs . . . What I wanna rehearse them for?

SLOW DRAG: You in the band, ain't you? You supposed to rehearse when the band rehearse.

TOLEDO: Levee think he the king of the barnyard. He thinks he's the only rooster know how to crow.

LEVEE: All right! All right! Come on, I'm gonna show you I know them songs. Come on, let's rehearse. I bet you the first one mess be Toledo. Come on . . . I wanna see if he know how to crow.

CUTLER: "Ma Rainey's Black Bottom," Levee's version. Let's do it.

(*They begin to rehearse. The lights go down in the band room and up in the studio.* MA RAINEY *sits and takes off her shoe, rubs her feet.* DUSSIE MAE *wanders about looking at the studio.* SYLVESTER *is over by the piano.*)

MA RAINEY: (*Singing to herself.*)

> Oh, Lord, these dogs of mine
> They sure do worry me all the time
> The reason why I don't know
> Lord, I beg to be excused
> I can't wear me no sharp-toed shoes.
> I went for a walk.
> I stopped to talk
> Oh, how my corns did bark.

DUSSIE MAE: It feels kinda spooky in here. I ain't never been in no recording studio before. Where's the band at?

MA RAINEY: They off somewhere rehearsing. I don't know where Irvin went to.

All this hurry up and he goes off back there with Sturdyvant. I know he better come on 'cause Ma ain't gonna be waiting. Come here . . . let me see that dress.

(DUSSIE MAE *crosses over.* MA RAINEY *tugs at the dress around the waist, appraising the fit.*)

That dress looks nice. I'm gonna take you tomorrow and get you some more things before I take you down to Memphis. They got clothes up here you can't get in Memphis. I want you to look nice for me. If you gonna travel with the show you got to look nice.

DUSSIE MAE: I need me some more shoes. These hurt my feet.

MA RAINEY: You get you some shoes that fit your feet. Don't you be messing around with no shoes that pinch your feet. Ma know something about bad feet. Hand me my slippers out my bag over yonder.

(DUSSIE MAE *brings the slippers.*)

DUSSIE MAE: I just want to get a pair of them yellow ones. About a half-size bigger.

MA RAINEY: We'll get you whatever you need. Sylvester, too . . . I'm gonna get him some more clothes. Sylvester, tuck your clothes in. Straighten them up and look nice. Look like a gentleman.

DUSSIE MAE: Look at Sylvester with that hat on.

MA RAINEY: Sylvester, take your hat off inside. Act like your mama taught you something. I know she taught you better than that.

(SYLVESTER *bangs on the piano.*)

Come on over here and leave that piano alone.

SYLVESTER: I ain't d-d-doing nothing to the p-p-piano. I'm just l-l-looking at it.

MA RAINEY: Well. Come on over here and sit down. As soon as Mr. Irvin comes back, I'll have him take you down and introduce you to the band.

(SYLVESTER *comes over.*)

He's gonna take you down there and introduce you in a minute . . . have Cutler show you how your part go. And when you get your money, you gonna send some of it home to your mama. Let her know you doing all right. Make her feel good to know you doing all right in the world.

(DUSSIE MAE *wanders about the studio and opens the door leading to the band room. The strains of* LEVEE'S *version of "Ma Rainey's Black Bottom" can be heard.* IRVIN *enters.*)

IRVIN: Ma, I called down to the garage and checked on your car. It's just a scratch. They'll have it ready for you this afternoon. They're gonna send it over with one of their fellows.

MA RAINEY: They better have my car fixed right too. I ain't going for that. Brand-new car . . . they better fix it like new.

IRVIN: It was just a scratch on the fender, Ma . . . They'll take care of it . . . don't worry . . . they'll have it like new.

MA RAINEY: Irvin, what is that I hear? What is that the band's rehearsing? I know they ain't rehearsing Levee's "Black Bottom." I know I ain't hearing that?

IRVIN: Ma, listen . . . that's what I wanted to talk to you about. Levee's version of that song . . . it's got a nice arrangement . . . a nice horn intro . . . It really picks it up . . .

MA RAINEY: I ain't studying Levee nothing. I know what he done to that song and I don't like to sing it that way. I'm doing it the old way. That's why I brought my nephew to do the voice intro.

IRVIN: Ma, that's what the people want now. They want something they can dance to. Times are changing. Levee's arrangement gives the people what they want. It gets them excited . . . makes them forget about their troubles.

MA RAINEY: I don't care what you say, Irvin. Levee ain't messing up my song. If he got what the people want, let him take it somewhere else. I'm singing Ma Rainey's song. I ain't singing Levee's song. Now that's all there is to it. Carry my nephew on down there and introduce him to the band. I promised my sister I'd look out for him and he's gonna do the voice intro on the song my way.

IRVIN: Ma, we just figured that . . .

MA RAINEY: Who's this "we"? What you mean "we"? I ain't studying Levee nothing. Come talking this "we" stuff. Who's "we"?

IRVIN: Me and Sturdyvant. We decided that it would . . .

MA RAINEY: You decided huh? I'm just a bump on the log. I'm gonna go which ever way the river drift. Is that it? You and Sturdyvant decided.

IRVIN: Ma, it was just that we thought it would be better.

MA RAINEY: I ain't got good sense. I don't know nothing about music. I don't know what's a good song and what ain't. You know more about my fans than I do.

IRVIN: It's not that, Ma. It would just be easier to do. It's more what the people want.

MA RAINEY: I'm gonna tell you something, Irvin . . . and you go on up there and tell Sturdyvant. What you all say don't count with me. You understand? Ma listens to her heart. Ma listens to the voice inside her. That's what counts with Ma. Now, you carry my nephew on down there . . . tell Cutler he's gonna do the voice intro on that "Black Bottom" song and that Levee ain't messing up my song with none of his music shit. Now, if that don't set right with you and Sturdyvant . . . then I can carry my black bottom on back down South to my tour, 'cause I don't like it up here no ways.

IRVIN: Okay, Ma . . . I don't care. I just thought . . .

MA RAINEY: Damn what you thought! What you look like telling me how to sing my song? This Levee and Sturdyvant nonsense . . . I ain't going for it! Sylvester, go on down there and introduce yourself. I'm through playing with Irvin.

SYLVESTER: Which way you go? Where they at?

MA RAINEY: Here . . . I'll carry you down there myself.

DUSSIE MAE: Can I go? I wanna see the band.

MA RAINEY: You stay your behind up here. Ain't no cause in you being down there. Come on, Sylvester.

IRVIN: Okay, Ma. Have it your way. We'll be ready to go in fifteen minutes.

MA RAINEY: We'll be ready to go when Madame says we're ready. That's the way it goes around here.

(MA RAINEY *and* SYLVESTER *exit. The lights go down in the studio and up in the band room.* MA RAINEY *enters with* SYLVESTER.)

Cutler, this here is my nephew Sylvester. He's gonna do that voice intro on the "Black Bottom" song using the old version.

LEVEE: What you talking about? Mr. Irvin say he's using my version. What you talking about?

MA RAINEY: Levee, I ain't studying you or Mr. Irvin. Cutler, get him straightened out on how to do his part. I ain't thinking about Levee. These folks done messed with the wrong person this day. Sylvester, Cutler gonna teach you your part. You go ahead and get it straight. Don't worry about what nobody else say.

(MA RAINEY *exits.*)

CUTLER: Well, come on in, boy. I'm Cutler. You got Slow Drag . . . Levee . . . and that's Toledo over there. Sylvester, huh?

SYLVESTER: Sylvester Brown.

LEVEE: I done wrote a version of that song what picks it up and sets it down in the people's lap! Now she come talking this! You don't need that old circus bullshit! I know what I'm talking about. You gonna mess up the song, Cutler, and you know it.

CUTLER: I ain't gonna mess up nothing. Ma say . . .

LEVEE: I don't care what Ma say! I'm talking about what the intro gonna do to the song. The people's in the North ain't gonna buy all that tent-show nonsense. They wanna hear some music!

CUTLER: Nigger, I done told you time and again . . . you just in the band. You plays the piece . . . whatever they want! Ma says what to play! Not you! You ain't here to be doing no creating, Your job is to play whatever Ma says!

LEVEE: I might not play nothing! I might quit!

CUTLER: Nigger, don't nobody care if you quit. Whose heart you gonna break?

TOLEDO: Levee ain't gonna quit. He got to make some money to keep him in shoe polish.

LEVEE: I done told you all . . . you all don't know me. You don't know what I'll do.

CUTLER: I don't think nobody too much give a damn! Sylvester, here's the way your part go. The band plays the intro . . . I'll tell you where to come in. The band plays the intro and then you say, "All right, boys, you done seen the rest . . . Now I'm gonna show you the best. Ma Rainey's gonna show you her black bottom." You got that?

(SYLVESTER *nods.*)

Let me hear you say it one time.

SYLVESTER: "All right, boys, you done s-s-seen the rest n-n-now I'm gonna show you the best. M-m-m-m-m-m-ma Rainey's gonna s-s-show you her black b-b-bottom."

LEVEE: What kind of . . . All right, Cutler! Let me see you fix that! You straighten that out! You hear that shit, Slow Drag? How in the hell the boy gonna do the part and he can't even talk!

SYLVESTER: W-w-w-who's you to tell me what to do, nigger! This ain't your band! Ma tell me to d-d-d-do it and I'm gonna do it. You can go to hell, n-n-n-igger!

LEVEE: B-b-b-boy, ain't nobody studying you. You go on and fix that one, Cutler. You fix that one and I'll . . . I'll shine your shoes for you. You go on and fix that one!

TOLEDO: You say you Ma's nephew, huh?

SYLVESTER: Yeah. So w-w-what that mean?

TOLEDO: Oh, I ain't meant nothing . . . I was just asking.

SLOW DRAG: Well, come on and let's rehearse so the boy can get it right.

LEVEE: I ain't rehearsing nothing! You just wait till I get my band. I'm gonna record that song and show you how it supposed to go!

CUTLER: We can do it without Levee. Let him sit on over there. Sylvester, you remember your part?

SYLVESTER: I remember it pretty g-g-g-good.

CUTLER: Well, come on, let's do it, then.

(*The band begins to play.* LEVEE *sits and pouts.* STURDYVANT *enters the band room.*)

STURDYVANT: Good . . . you boys are rehearsing, I see.

LEVEE: (*Jumping up.*)   Yessir! We rehearsing. We know them songs real good.

STURDYVANT: Good! Say, Levee, did you finish that song?

LEVEE: Yessir, Mr. Sturdyvant. I got it right here. I wrote that other part just like you say. It go like:

> You can shake it, you can break it
> You can dance at any hall
> You can slide across the floor
> You'll never have to stall
> My jelly, my roll,
> Sweet Mama, don't you let it fall.

Then I put that part in there for the people to dance, like you say, for them to forget about their troubles.

STURDYVANT: Good! Good! I'll just take this. I wanna see you about your songs as soon as I get the chance.

LEVEE: Yessir! As soon as you get the chance, Mr. Sturdyvant.

(STURDYVANT *exits.*)

CUTLER: You hear Levee? You hear this nigger? "Yessuh, we's rehearsing, boss."

SLOW DRAG: I heard him. Seen him too. Shuffling them feet.

TOLEDO: Aw, Levee can't help it none. He's like all of us. Spooked up with the white men.

LEVEE: I'm spooked up with him, all right. You let one of them crackers fix on me wrong. I'll show you how spooked up I am with him.

TOLEDO: That's the trouble of it. You wouldn't know if he was fixed on you wrong or not. You so spooked up by him you ain't had the time to study him.

LEVEE: I studies the white man. I got him studied good. The first time one fixes on me wrong, I'm gonna let him know just how much I studied. Come telling me I'm spooked up with the white man. You let one of them mess with me, I'll show you how spooked up I am.

CUTLER: You talking out your hat. The man come in here, call you a boy, tell you to get off your ass and rehearse, and you ain't had nothing to say to him, except "Yessir!"

LEVEE: I can say "yesssir" to whoever I please. What you got to do with it? I know how to handle white folks. I been handling them for thirty-two years, and now

you gonna tell me how to do it. Just 'cause I say "yessir" don't mean I'm
spooked up with him. I know what I'm doing. Let me handle him my way.

CUTLER: Well, go on and handle it, then.

LEVEE: Toledo, you always messing with somebody! Always agitating somebody
with that old philosophy bullshit you be talking. You stay out of my way about
what I do and say. I'm my own person. Just let me alone.

TOLEDO: You right, Levee. I apologize. It ain't none of my business that you
spooked up by the white man.

LEVEE: All right! See! That's the shit I'm talking about. You all back up and leave
Levee alone.

SLOW DRAG: Aw, Levee, we was all just having fun. Toledo ain't said nothing
about you he ain't said about me. You just taking it all wrong.

TOLEDO: I ain't meant nothing by it, Levee.

(*Pauses.*)

Cutler, you ready to rehearse?

LEVEE: Levee got to be Levee! And he don't need nobody messing with him
about the white man—cause you don't know nothing about me. You don't know
Levee. You don't know nothing about what kind of blood I got! What kind of
heart I got beating here!

(*He pounds his chest.*)

I was eight years old when I watched a gang of white mens come into my daddy's
house and have to do with my mama any way they wanted.

(*Pauses.*)

We was living in Jefferson County, about eighty miles outside of Natchez. My
daddy's name was Memphis . . . Memphis Lee Green . . . had him near fifty acres
of good farming land. I'm talking about good land! Grow anything you want!
He done gone off of shares and bought this land from Mr. Hallie's widow
woman after he done passed on. Folks called him an uppity nigger 'cause he
done saved and borrowed to where he could buy this land and be independent.

(*Pauses.*)

It was coming on planting time and my daddy went into Natchez to get him
some seed and fertilizer. Called me, say, "Levee, you the man of the house now.
Take care of your mama while I'm gone." I wasn't but a little boy, eight years
old.

(*Pauses.*)

My mama was frying up some chicken when them mens come in that house.
Must have been eight or nine of them. She standing there frying that chicken
and them mens come and took hold of her just like you take hold of a mule and
make him do what you want.

(*Pauses.*)

There was my mama with a gang of white mens. She tried to fight them off, but I could see where it wasn't gonna do her any good, I didn't know what they were doing to her . . . but I figured whatever it was they may as well do to me too. My daddy had a knife that he kept around there for hunting and working and whatnot. I know where he kept it and I went and got it.

I'm gonna show you how spooked up I was by the white man. I tried my damnedest to cut one of them's throat! I hit him on the shoulder with it. He reached back and grabbed hold of that knife and whacked me across the chest with it.

(LEVEE *raises his shirt to show a long, ugly scar.*)

That's what made them stop. They was scared I was gonna bleed to death. My mama wrapped a sheet around me and carried me two miles down to the Furlow place and they drove me up to Doc Albans. He was waiting on a calf to be born, and say he ain't had time to see me. They carried me up to Miss Etta, the midwife, and she fixed me up.

My daddy came back and acted like he done accepted the facts of what happened. But he got the names of them mens from mama. He found out who they was and then we announced we was moving out of that county. Said good-bye to everybody . . . all the neighbors. My daddy went and smiled in the face of one of them crackers who had been with my mama. Smiled in his face and sold him our land. We moved over with relations in Caldwell. He got us settled in and then he took off one day. I ain't never seen him since. He sneaked back, hiding up in the woods, laying to get them eight or nine men.

(*Pauses.*)

He got four of them before they got him. They tracked him down in the woods. Caught up with him and hung him and set him afire.

(*Pauses.*)

My daddy wasn't spooked up by the white man. Nosir! And that taught me how to handle them. I seen my daddy go up and grin in this cracker's face . . . smile in his face and sell him his land. All the while he's planning how he's gonna get him and what he's gonna do to him. That taught me how to handle them. So you all just back up and leave Levee alone about the white man. I can smile and say yessir to whoever I please. I got time coming to me. You all just leave Levee alone about the white man.

(*There is a long pause.* SLOW DRAG *begins playing on the bass and sings.*)

SLOW DRAG: (*Singing.*)

> If I had my way
> If I had my way
> If I had my way
> I would tear this old building down.

ACT TWO

(The lights come up in the studio. The musicians are setting up their instruments. Ma Rainey walks about shoeless, singing softly to herself. Levee stands near Dussie Mae, who hikes up her dress and crosses her leg. Cutler speaks to Irvin off to the side.)

CUTLER: Mr. Irvin, I don't know what you gonna do. I ain't got nothing to do with it, but the boy can't do the part. He stutters. He can't get it right. He stutters right through it every time.

IRVIN: Christ! Okay. We'll ... Shit! We'll just do it like we planned. We'll do Levee's version. I'll handle it, Cutler. Come on, let's go. I'll think of something.

(He exits to the control booth.)

MA RAINEY: *(Calling Cutler over.)* Levee's got his eyes in the wrong place. You better school him, Cutler.

CUTLER: Come on, Levee ... let's get ready to play! Get your mind on your work!

IRVIN: *(Over speaker.)* Okay, boys, we're gonna do "Moonshine Blues" first. "Moonshine Blues," Ma.

MA RAINEY: I ain't doing no "Moonshine" nothing. I'm doing the "Black Bottom" first. Come on, Sylvester.

(To Irvin.)

Where's Sylvester's mike? You need a mike for Sylvester. Irvin ... get him a mike.

IRVIN: Uh ... Ma, the boys say he can't do it. We'll have to do Levee's version.

MA RAINEY: What you mean he can't do it? Who say he can't do it? What boys say he can't do it?

IRVIN: The band, Ma ... the boys in the band.

MA RAINEY: What band? The band work for me! I say what goes! Cutler, what's he talking about? Levee, this some of your shit?

IRVIN: He stutters, Ma. They say he stutters.

MA RAINEY: I don't care if he do. I promised the boy he could do the part ... and he's gonna do it! That's all there is to it. He don't stutter all the time. Get a microphone down here for him.

IRVIN: Ma, we don't have time. We can't ...

MA RAINEY: If you wanna make a record, you gonna find time. I ain't playing with you, Irvin. I can walk out of here and go back to my tour. I got plenty fans. I don't need to go through all of this. Just go and get the boy a microphone.

(Irvin and Sturdyvant consult in the booth, Irvin exits.)

STURDYVANT: All right, Ma ... we'll get him a microphone. But if he messes up ... He's only getting one chance ... The cost ...

MA RAINEY: Damn the cost. You always talking about the cost. I make more money for this outfit than anybody else you got put together. If he messes up he'll just do it till he gets it right. Levee, I know you had something to do with this. You better watch yourself.

LEVEE: It was Cutler!

SYLVESTER: It was you! You the only one m-m-mad about it.

LEVEE: The boy stutter. He can't do the part. Everybody see that. I don't know why you want the boy to do the part no ways.

MA RAINEY: Well, can or can't . . . he gonna do it! You ain't got nothing to do with it!

LEVEE: I don't care what you do! He can sing the whole goddamned song for all I care!

MA RAINEY: Well, all right. Thank you.

(IRVIN *enters with a microphone and hooks it up. He exits to the control booth.*)

MA RAINEY: Come on, Sylvester. You just stand here and hold your hands like I told you. Just remember the words and say them . . . That's all there is to it. Don't worry about messing up. If you mess up, we'll do it again. Now, let me hear you say it. Play for him, Cutler.

CUTLER: One . . . two . . . you know what to do.

(*The band begins to play and* SYLVESTER *curls his fingers and clasps his hands together in front of his chest, pulling in opposite directions as he says his lines.*)

SYLVESTER: "All right, boys, you d-d-d-done s-s-s-seen the best . . .

(LEVEE *stops playing.*)

Now I'm g-g-g-gonna show you the rest . . . Ma R-r-rainey's gonna show you her b-b-b-black b-b-b-bottom." (*The rest of the bands stops playing.*)

MA RAINEY: That's all right. That's real good. You take your time, you'll get it right.

STURDYVANT: (*Over speaker.*) Listen, Ma . . . now, when you come in, don't wait so long to come in. Don't take so long on the intro, huh?

MA RAINEY: Sturdyvant, don't you go trying to tell me how to sing. You just take care of that up there and let me take care of this down here. Where's my Coke?

IRVIN: Okay, Ma. We're all set up to go up here. "Ma Rainey's Black Bottom," boys.

MA RAINEY: Where's my Coke? I need a Coke. You ain't got no Coke down here? Where's my Coke?

IRVIN: What's the matter, Ma? What's . . .

MA RAINEY: Where's my Coke? I need a Coca-Cola.

IRVIN: Uh . . . Ma, look, I forgot the Coke, huh? Let's do it without it, huh? Just this one song. What say, boys?

MA RAINEY: Damn what the band say! You know I don't sing nothing without my Coca-Cola!

STURDYVANT: We don't have any, Ma. There's no Coca-Cola here. We're all set up and we'll just go ahead and . . .

MA RAINEY: You supposed to have Coca-Cola. Irvin knew that. I ain't singing nothing without my Coca-Cola!

(*She walks away from the mike, singing to herself.* STURDYVANT *enters from the control booth.*)

STURDYVANT: Now, just a minute here, Ma. You come in an hour late ... we're way behind schedule as it is ... the band is set up and ready to go ... I'm burning my lights ... I've turned up the heat ... We're ready to make a record and what? You decide you want a Coca-Cola?

MA RAINEY: Sturdyvant, get out of my face.

(IRVIN *enters*.)

Irvin ... I told you to keep him away from me.

IRVIN: Mel, I'll handle it.

STURDYVANT: I'm tired of her nonsense, Irv. I'm not gonna put up with this!

IRVIN: Let me handle it, Mel. I know how to handle her.

(IRVIN *to* MA RAINEY.)

Look, Ma ... I'll call down to the deli and get you a Coke. But let's get started, huh? Sylvester's standing there ready to go ... the band's set up ... let's do this one song, huh?

MA RAINEY: If you too cheap to buy me a Coke, I'll buy my own. Slow Drag! Sylvester, go with Slow Drag and get me a Coca-Cola.

(SLOW DRAG *comes over*.)

Slow Drag, walk down to that store on the corner and get me three bottles of Coca-Cola. Get out my face, Irvin. You all just wait until I get my Coke. It ain't gonna kill you.

IRVIN: Okay, Ma. Get your Coke, for chrissakes! Get your Coke!

(IRVIN *and* STURDYVANT *exit into the hallway followed by* SLOW DRAG *and* SYLVESTER. TOLEDO, CUTLER *and* LEVEE *head for the band room*.)

MA RAINEY: Cutler, come here a minute. I want to talk to you.

(CUTLER *crosses over somewhat reluctantly*.)

What's all this about "the boys in the band say"? I tells you what to do. I says what the matter is with the band. I say who can and can't do what.

CUTLER: We just say 'cause the boy stutter ...

MA RAINEY: I know he stutters. Don't you think I know he stutters? This is what's gonna help him.

CUTLER: Well, how can he do the part if he stutters? You want him to stutter through it? We just thought it be easier to go on and let Levee do it like we planned.

MA RAINEY: I don't care if he stutters or not! He's doing the part and I don't wanna hear any more of this shit about what the band says. And I want you to find somebody to replace Levee when we get to Memphis. Levee ain't nothing but trouble.

CUTLER: Levee's all right. He plays good music when he puts his mind to it. He know how to write music too.

MA RAINEY: I don't care what he know. He ain't nothing but bad news. Find somebody else. I know it was his idea about who to say who can do what.

(DUSSIE MAE *wanders over to where they are sitting.*)

Dussie Mae, go sit your behind down somewhere and quit flaunting yourself
around.

DUSSIE MAE: I ain't doing nothing.

MA RAINEY: Well, just go on somewhere and stay out of the way.

CUTLER: I been meaning to ask you, Ma . . . about these songs. This "Moonshine
Blues" . . . that's one of them songs Bessie Smith sang, I believes.

MA RAINEY: Bessie what? Ain't nobody thinking about Bessie. I taught Bessie.
She ain't doing nothing but imitating me. What I care about Bessie? I don't care
if she sell a million records. She got her people and I got mine. I don't care what
nobody else do. Ma was the *first* and don't you forget it!

CUTLER: Ain't nobody said nothing about that. I just said that's the same song
she sang.

MA RAINEY: I been doing this a long time. Ever since I was a little girl. I don't
care what nobody else do. That's what gets me so mad with Irvin. White folks try
to be put out with you all the time. Too cheap to buy me a Coca-Cola. I lets them
know it, though. Ma don't stand for no shit. Wanna take my voice and trap it in
them fancy boxes with all them buttons and dials . . . and then too cheap to buy
me a Coca-Cola. And it don't cost but a nickel a bottle.

CUTLER: I knows what you mean about that.

MA RAINEY: They don't care nothing about me. All they want is my voice. Well,
I done learned that, and they gonna treat me like I want to be treated no matter
how much it hurt them. They back there now calling me all kinds of names . . .
calling me everything but a child of god. But they can't do nothing else. They
ain't got what they wanted yet. As soon as they get my voice down on them
recording machines, then it's just like if I'd be some whore and they roll over
and put their pants on. Ain't got no use for me then. I know what I'm talking
about. You watch. Irvin right there with the rest of them. He don't care nothing
about me either. He's been my manager for six years, always talking about
sticking together, and the only time he had me in his house was to sing for some
of his friends.

CUTLER: I know how they do.

MA RAINEY: If you colored and can make them some money, then you all right
with them. Otherwise, you just a dog in the alley. I done made this company
more money from my records than all the other recording artists they got put
together. And they wanna balk about how much this session is costing them.

CUTLER: I don't see where it's costing them all what they say.

MA RAINEY: It ain't! I don't pay that kind of talk no mind.

(*The lights go down on the studio and come up on the band room.* TOLEDO *sits reading a
newspaper.* LEVEE *sings and hums his song.*)

LEVEE: (*singing.*)

> You can shake it, you can break it
> You can dance at any hall
> You can slide across the floor
> You'll never have to stall
> My jelly, my roll,
> Sweet Mama, don't you let it fall.

Wait till Sturdyvant hear me play that! I'm talking about some real music. Toledo! I'm talking about *real* music!

(*The door opens and* DUSSIE MAE *enters.*)

Hey, mama! Come on in.

DUSSIE MAE: Oh, hi! I just wanted to see what it looks like down here.

LEVEE: Well, come on in . . . I don't bite.

DUSSIE MAE: I didn't know you could really write music. I thought you was just jiving me at the club last night.

LEVEE: Naw, baby . . . I knows how to write music. I done give Mr. Sturdyvant some of my songs and he says he's gonna let me record them. Ask Toledo. I'm gonna have my own band! Toledo, ain't I give Mr. Sturdyvant some of my songs I wrote?

TOLEDO: Don't get Toledo mixed up in nothing.

(*He exits.*)

DUSSIE MAE: You gonna get your own band sure enough?

LEVEE: That's right! Levee Green and his Footstompers.

DUSSIE MAE: That's real nice.

LEVEE: That's what I was trying to tell you last night. A man what's gonna get his own band need to have a woman like you.

DUSSIE MAE: A woman like me wants somebody to bring it and put it in my hand. I don't need nobody wanna get something for nothing and leave me standing in my door.

LEVEE: That ain't Levee's style, sugar. I got more style than that. I knows how to treat a woman. Buy her presents and things . . . treat her like she wants to be treated.

DUSSIE MAE: That's what they all say . . . till it come time to be buying the presents.

LEVEE: When we get down to Memphis, I'm gonna show you what I'm talking about. I'm gonna take you out and show you a good time. Show you Levee knows how to treat a woman.

DUSSIE MAE: When you getting your own band?

LEVEE: (*Moves closer to slip his arm around her.*)   Soon as Mr. Sturdyvant say. I done got my fellows already picked out. Getting me some good fellows know how to play real sweet music.

DUSSIE MAE: (*Moves away.*)   Go on now, I don't go for all that pawing and stuff. When you get your own band, maybe we can see about this stuff you talking.

LEVEE: (*Moving toward her.*)   I just wanna show you I know what the women like. They don't call me Sweet Lemonade for nothing.

(LEVEE *takes her in his arms and attempts to kiss her.*)

DUSSIE MAE: Stop it now. Somebody's gonna come in here.

LEVEE: Naw they ain't. Look here, sugar . . . what I wanna know is . . . can I introduce my red rooster to your brown hen?

DUSSIE MAE: You get your band, then we'll see if that rooster know how to crow.

(*He grinds up against her and feels her buttocks.*)

LEVEE: Now I know why my grandpappy sat on the back porch with his straight razor when grandma hung out the wash.

DUSSIE MAE: Nigger, you crazy!

LEVEE: I bet you sound like the midnight train from Alabama when it crosses the Mason-Dixon line.

DUSSIE MAE: How's you get so crazy?

LEVEE: It's women like you . . . drives me that way.

(*He moves to kiss her as the lights go down in the band room and up in the studio.* MA RAINEY *sits with* CUTLER *and* TOLEDO.)

MA RAINEY: It sure done got quiet in here. I never could stand no silence. I always got to have some music going on in my head somewhere. It keeps things balanced. Music will do that. It fills things up. The more music you got in the world, the fuller it is.

CUTLER: I can agree with that. I got to have my music too.

MA RAINEY: White folks don't understand about the blues. They hear it come out, but they don't know how it got there. They don't understand that's life's way of talking. You don't sing to feel better. You sing 'cause that's a way of understanding life.

CUTLER: That's right. You get that understanding and you done got a grip on life to where you can hold your head up and go on to see what else life got to offer.

MA RAINEY: The blues help you get out of bed in the morning. You get up knowing you ain't alone. There's something else in the world. Something's been added by that song. This be an empty world without the blues. I take that emptiness and try to fill it up with something.

TOLEDO: You fill it up with something the people can't be without, Ma. That's why they call you the Mother of the Blues. You fill up that emptiness in a way ain't nobody ever thought of doing before. And now they can't be without it.

MA RAINEY: I ain't started the blues way of singing. The blues always been here.

CUTLER: In the church sometimes you find that way of singing. They got blues in the church.

MA RAINEY: They say I started it . . . but I didn't. I just helped it out. Filled up that empty space a little bit. That's all. But if they wanna call me the Mother of the Blues, that's all right with me. It don't hurt none.

(SLOW DRAG *and* SYLVESTER *enter with the Cokes.*)

It sure took you long enough. That store ain't but on the corner.

SLOW DRAG: That one was closed. We had to find another one.

MA RAINEY: Sylvester, go and find Mr. Irvin and tell him we ready to go.

(SYLVESTER *exits. The lights in the band room come up while the lights in the studio stay one.* LEVEE *and* DUSSIE MAE *are kissing.* SLOW DRAG *enters. They break their embrace.* DUSSIE MAE *straightens up her clothes.*)

SLOW DRAG: Cold out. I just wanted to warm up with a little sip.

(*He goes to his locker, takes out his bottle and drinks.*)

Ma got her Coke, Levee. We about ready to start.

(SLOW DRAG *exits.* LEVEE *attempts to kiss* DUSSIE MAE *again.*)

DUSSIE MAE: No ... Come on! I got to go. You gonna get me in trouble.

(*She pulls away and exits up the stairs.* LEVEE *watches after her.*)

LEVEE: Good God! Happy birthday to the lady with the cakes!

(*The lights go down in the band room and come up in the studio.* MA RAINEY *drinks her Coke.* LEVEE *enters from the band room. The musicians take their places.* SYLVESTER *stands by his mike.* IRVIN *and* STURDYVANT *look on from the control booth.*)

IRVIN: We're all set up here, Ma. We're all set to go. You ready down there?
MA RAINEY: Sylvester, you just remember your part and say it. That's all there is
   to it. (*To* IRVIN.) Yeah, we ready.
IRVIN: Okay, boys. "Ma Rainey's Black Bottom." Take one.
CUTLER: One ... two ... You know what to do.

(*The band plays.*)

SYLVESTER: All right, boys, you d-d-d-done s-s-seen the rest. . . .
IRVIN: Hold it!

(*The band stops.* STURDYVANT *changes the recording disk and nods to* IRVIN.)

   Okay. Take two.
CUTLER: One ... two ... You know what to do.

(*The band plays.*)

SYLVESTER: All right, boys, you done seen the rest ... now I'm gonna show you
   the best. Ma Rainey's g-g-g-gonna s-s-show you her b-b-black bottom.
IRVIN: Hold it! Hold it!

(*The band stops.* STURDYVANT *changes the recording disk.*)

   Okay. Take Three. Ma, let's do it without the intro, huh? No voice intro ... you
   just come in singing.
MA RAINEY: Irvin, I done told you ... the boy's gonna do the part. He don't
   stutter all the time. Just give him a chance. Sylvester, hold your hands like I told
   you and just relax. Just relax and concentrate.
IRVIN: All right. Take three.
CUTLER: One ... two ... You know what to do.

(*The band plays.*)

SYLVESTER: All right, boys, you done seen the rest ... now I'm gonna show you
   the best. Ma Rainey's gonna show you her black bottom.
MA RAINEY: (*Singing.*)

Way down south in Alabamy
I got a friend they call dancing Sammy
Who's crazy about all the latest dances
Black Bottom stomping, two babies prancing
The other night at a swell affair
As soon as the boys found out that I was there
They said, come on, Ma, let's go to the cabaret.
When I got there, you ought to hear them say,
I want to see the dance you call the black bottom
I want to learn that dance
I want to see the dance you call your big black bottom
It'll put you in a trance.
All the boys in the neighborhood
They say your black bottom is really good
Come on and show me your black bottom
I want to learn that dance
I want to see the dance you call the black bottom
I want to learn that dance
Come on and show the dance you call your big black bottom
It puts you in a trance.
Early last morning about the break of day
Grandpa told my grandma, I heard him say,
Get up and show your old man your black bottom
I want to learn that dance

(*Instrumental break.*)

          I done showed you all my black bottom
          You ought to learn that dance.

IRVIN: Okay, that's good, Ma. That sounded great! Good job, boys!

MA RAINEY: (*To* SYLVESTER.)   See! I told you. I knew you could do it. You just have to put your mind to it. Didn't he do good, Cutler? Sound real good. I told him he could do it.

CUTLER: He sure did. He did better than I thought he was gonna do.

IRVIN: (*Entering to remove* SYLVESTER's *mike.*)   Okay boys ... Ma ... let's do "Moonshine Blues" next, huh? "Moonshine Blues," boys.

STURDYVANT: (*Over speaker.*)   Irv! Something's wrong down there. We don't have it right.

IRVIN: What? What's the matter, Mel ...

STURDYVANT: We don't have it right. Something happened. We don't have the godddamn song recorded!

IRVIN: What's the matter? Mel, what happened? You sure you don't have nothing?

STURDYVANT: Check that mike, huh, Irv. It's the kid's mike. Something's wrong with the mike. We've got everything all screwed up here.

IRVIN: Christ almighty! Ma, we got to do it again. We don't have it. We didn't record the song.

MA RAINEY: What you mean you didn't record it? What was you and Sturdyvant doing up there?

IRVIN: (*Following the mike wire.*)   Here ... Levee must have kicked the plug out.

LEVEE: I ain't done nothing: I ain't kicked nothing!

SLOW DRAG: If Levee had his mind on what he's doing . . .

MA RAINEY: Levee, if it ain't one thing, it's another. You better straighten your-self up!

LEVEE: Hell . . . it ain't my fault. I ain't done nothing!

STURDYVANT: What's the matter with that mike, Irv? What's the problem?

IRVIN: It's the cord, Mel. The cord's all chewed up. We need another cord.

MA RAINEY: This is the most disorganized . . . Irvin, I'm going home! Come on. Come on, Dussie.

(MA RAINEY *walks past* STURDYVANT *as he enters from the control booth. She exits offstage to get her coat.*)

STURDYVANT: (*To* IRVIN.)   Where's she going?

IRVIN: She said she's going home.

STURDYVANT: Irvin, you get her! If she walks out of here . . .

(MA RAINEY *enters carrying her and* DUSSIE MAE*'s coats.*)

MA RAINEY: Come on, Sylvester.

IRVIN: (*Helping her with her coat.*)   Ma . . . Ma . . . listen. Fifteen minutes! All I ask is fifteen minutes!

MA RAINEY: Come on, Sylvester, get your coat.

STURDYVANT: Ma, if you walk out of this studio . . .

IRVIN: Fifteen minutes, Ma!

STURDYVANT: You'll be through . . . washed up! If you walk out on me . . .

IRVIN: Mel, for chrissakes, shut up and let me handle it!

(*He goes after* MA RAINEY, *who has started for the door.*) Ma, listen. These records are gonna be hits! They're gonna sell like crazy! Hell, even Sylvester will be a star. Fifteen minutes. That's all I'm asking! Fifteen minutes.

MA RAINEY: (*Crosses to a chair and sits with her coat on.*) Fifteen minutes! You hear me, Irvin? Fifteen minutes . . . and then I'm gonna take my black bottom on back down to Georgia. Fifteen minutes. Then Madame Rainey is leaving!

IRVIN: (*Kisses her.*)   All right, Ma . . . fifteen minutes. I promise.

(*To the band.*)

You boys go ahead and take a break. Fifteen minutes and we'll be ready to go.

CUTLER: Slow Drag, you got any of that bourbon left?

SLOW DRAG: Yeah, there's some down there.

CUTLER: I could use a little nip.

(CUTLER *and* SLOW DRAG *exit to the band room, followed by* LEVEE *and* TOLEDO. *The lights go down in the studio and up in the band room.*)

SLOW DRAG: Don't make me no difference if she leave or not. I was kinda hoping she would leave.

CUTLER: I'm like Mr. Irvin . . . After all this time we done put in here, it's best to go ahead and get something out of it.

TOLEDO: Ma gonna do what she wanna do, that's for sure. If I was Mr. Irvin, I'd best go on and get them cords and things hooked up right. And I wouldn't take no longer than fifteen minutes doing it.

CUTLER: If Levee had his mind on his work, we wouldn't be in this fix. We'd be up there finishing up. Now we got to go back and see if that boy get that part right. Ain't no telling if he ever get that right again in his life.

LEVEE: Hey, Levee ain't done nothing!

SLOW DRAG: Levee up there got one eye on the gal and the other on his trumpet.

CUTLER: Nigger, don't you know that's Ma's gal?

LEVEE: I don't care whose gal it is. I ain't done nothing to her. I just talk to her like I talk to anybody else.

CUTLER: Well, that being Ma's gal, and that being that boy's gal, is one and two different things. The boy is liable to kill you . . . but you' ass gonna be out there scraping the concrete looking for a job if you messing with Ma's gal.

LEVEE: How am I messing with her? I ain't done nothing to the gal. I just asked her her name. Now, if you telling me I can't do that, then Ma will just have to go to hell.

CUTLER: All I can do is warn you.

SLOW DRAG: Let him hang himself, Cutler. Let him string his neck out.

LEVEE: I ain't done nothing to the gal! You all talk like I done went and done something to her. Leave me go with my business.

CUTLER: I'm through with it. Try and talk to a fool . . .

TOLEDO: Some mens got it worse than others . . . this foolishness I'm talking about. Some mens is excited to be fools. That excitement is something else. I know about it. I done experienced it. It makes you feel good to be a fool. But it don't last long. It's over in a minute. Then you got to tend with the consequences. You got to tend with what comes after. That's when you wish you had learned something about it.

LEVEE: That's the best sense you made all day. Talking about being a fool. That's the only sensible thing you said today. Admitting you was a fool.

TOLEDO: I admits it, all right. Ain't nothing wrong with it. I done been a little bit of everything.

LEVEE: Now you're talking. You's as big a fool as they make.

TOLEDO: Gonna be a bit more things before I'm finished with it. Gonna be foolish again. But I ain't never been the same fool twice. I might be a different kind of fool, but I ain't gonna be the same fool twice. That's where we part ways.

SLOW DRAG: Toledo, you done been a fool about a woman?

TOLEDO: Sure. Sure I have. Same as everybody.

SLOW DRAG: Hell, I ain't never seen you mess with no woman. I thought them books was your woman.

TOLEDO: Sure I messed with them. Done messed with a whole heap of them. And gonna mess with some more. But I ain't gonna be no fool about them. What you think? I done come in the world full-grown, with my head in a book? I done been young. Married. Got kids. I done been around and I done loved women to where you shake in your shoes just at the sight of them. Feel it all up and down your spine.

SLOW DRAG: I didn't know you was married.

TOLEDO: Sure. Legally. I been married legally. Got the papers and all. I done been through life. Made my marks. Followed some signs on the road. Ignored some others. I done been all through it. I touched and been touched by it. But I ain't never been the same fool twice. That's what I can say.

LEVEE: But you been a fool. That's what counts. Talking about I'm a fool for asking the gal her name and here you is one yourself.

TOLEDO: Now, I married a woman. A good woman. To this day I can't say she wasn't a good woman. I can't say nothing bad about her. I married that woman with all the good graces and intentions of being hooked up and bound to her for the rest of my life. I was looking for her to put me in my grave. But, you see . . . it ain't all the time what you' intentions and wishes are. She went out and joined the church. All right. There ain't nothing wrong with that. A good Christian woman going to church and wanna do right by her God. There ain't nothing wrong with that. But she got up there, got to seeing them good Christian mens and wondering why I ain't like that. Soon she figure she got a heathen on her hands. She figured she couldn't live like that. The church was more important than I was. So she left. Packed up one day and moved out. To this day I ain't never said another word to her. Come home one day and my house was empty! And I sat down and figured out that I was a fool not to see that she needed something that I wasn't giving her. Else she wouldn't have been up there at the church in the first place. I ain't blaming her. I just said it wasn't gonna happen to me again. So, yeah, Toledo been a fool about a woman. That's part of making life.

CUTLER: Well, yeah, I been a fool too. Everybody done been a fool once or twice. But, you see, Toledo, what you call a fool and what I call a fool is two different things. I can't see where you was being a fool for that. You ain't done nothing foolish. You can't help what happened, and I wouldn't call you a fool for it. A fool is responsible for what happens to him. A fool cause it to happen. Like Levee . . . if he keeps messing with Ma's gal and his feet be out there scraping the ground. That's a fool.

LEVEE: Ain't nothing gonna happen to Levee. Levee ain't gonna let nothing happen to him. Now, I'm gonna say it again. I asked the gal her name. That's all I done. And if that's being a fool, then you looking at the biggest fool in the world . . . 'cause I sure as hell asked her.

SLOW DRAG: You just better not let Ma see you ask her. That's what the man's trying to tell you.

LEVEE: I don't need nobody to tell me nothing.

CUTLER: Well, Toledo, all I gots to say is that from the looks of it . . . from your story . . . I don't think life did you fair.

TOLEDO: Oh, life is fair. It's just in the taking what it gives you.

LEVEE: Life ain't shit. You can put it in a paper bag and carry it around with you. It ain't got no balls. Now, death . . . death got some style! Death will kick your ass and make you wish you never been born! That's how bad death is! But you can rule over life. Life ain't nothing.

TOLEDO: Cutler, how's your brother doing?

CUTLER: Who, Nevada? Oh, he's doing all right. Staying in St. Louis. Got a bunch of kids, last I heard.

TOLEDO: Me and him was all right with each other. Done a lot of farming together down in Plattsville.

CUTLER: Yeah, I know you all was tight. He in St. Louis now. Running an elevator, last I hear about it.

SLOW DRAG: That's better than stepping in muleshit.

TOLEDO: Oh, I don't know now. I liked farming. Get out there in the sun . . .

smell that dirt. Be out there by yourself . . . nice and peaceful. Yeah, farming was all right by me. Sometimes I think I'd like to get me a little old place . . . but I done got too old to be following behind one of them balky mules now.

LEVEE: Nigger talking about life is fair. And ain't got a pot to piss in.

TOLEDO: See, now, I'm gonna tell you something. A nigger gonna be dissatisfied no matter what. Give a nigger some bread and butter . . . and he'll cry 'cause he ain't got no jelly. Give him some jelly, and he'll cry 'cause he ain't got no knife to put it on with. If there's one thing I done learned in this life, it's that you can't satisfy a nigger no matter what you do. A nigger's gonna make his own dissatisfaction.

LEVEE: Niggers got a right to be dissatisfied. Is you gonna be satisfied with a bone somebody done throwed you when you see them eating the whole hog?

TOLEDO: You lucky they let you be an entertainer. They ain't got to accept your way of entertaining. You lucky and don't even know it. You's entertaining and the rest of the people is hauling wood. That's the only kind of job for the colored man.

SLOW DRAG: Ain't nothing wrong with hauling wood. I done hauled plenty wood. My daddy used to haul wood. Ain't nothing wrong with that. That's honest work.

LEVEE: That ain't what I'm talking about. I ain't talking about hauling no wood. I'm talking about being satisfied with a bone somebody done throwed you. That's what's the matter with you all. You satisfied sitting in one place. You got to move on down the road from where you sitting . . . and all the time you got to keep an eye out for that devil who's looking to buy up souls. And hope you get lucky and find him!

CUTLER: I done told you about that blasphemy. Talking about selling your soul to the devil.

TOLEDO: We done the same thing, Cutler. There ain't no difference. We done sold Africa for the price of tomatoes. We done sold ourselves to the white man in order to be like him. Look at the way you dressed . . . That ain't African. That's white man. We trying to be just like him. We done sold who we are in order to become someone else. We's imitation white men.

CUTLER: What else we gonna be, living over here?

LEVEE: I'm Levee. Just me. I ain't no imitation nothing!

SLOW DRAG: You can't change who you are by how you dress. That's what I got to say.

TOLEDO: It ain't all how you dress. It's how you act, how you see the world. It's how you follow life.

LEVEE: It don't matter what you talking about. I ain't no imitation white man. And I don't want to be no white man. As soon as I get my band together and make them records like Mr. Sturdyvant done told me I can make, I'm gonna be like Ma and tell the white man just what he can do. Ma tell Mr. Irvin she gonna leave . . . and Mr. Irvin get down on his knees and beg her to stay! That's the way I gonna be! Make the white man respect me!

CUTLER: The white man don't care nothing about Ma. The colored folks made Ma a star. White folks don't care nothing about who she is . . . what kind of music she make.

SLOW DRAG: That's the truth about that. You let her go down to one of them white-folks hotels and see how big she is.

CUTLER: Hell, she ain't got to do that. She can't even get a cab up here in the North. I'm gonna tell you something. Reverend Gates . . . you know Reverend

Gates? . . . Slow Drag know who I'm talking about. Reverend Gates . . . now I'm gonna show you how this go where the white man don't care a thing about who you is. Reverend Gates was coming from Tallahassee to Atlanta, going to see his sister, who was sick at that time with the consumption. The train come up through Thomasville, then past Moultrie, and stopped in this little town called Sigsbee . . .

LEVEE: You can stop telling that right there! That train don't stop in Sigsbee. I know what train you talking about. That train got four stops before it reach Macon to go on to Atlanta. One in Thomasville, one in Moultrie, one in Cordele . . . and it stop in Centerville.

CUTLER: Nigger, I know what I'm talking about. You gonna tell me where the train stop?

LEVEE: Hell, yeah, if you talking about it stop in Sigsbee. I'm gonna tell you the truth.

CUTLER: I'm talking about *this* train! I don't know what train you been riding. I'm talking about *this* train!

LEVEE: Ain't but one train. Ain't but one train come out of Tallahassee heading north to Atlanta, and it don't stop at Sigsbee. Tell him, Toledo . . . that train don't stop at Sigsbee. The only train that stops at Sigsbee is the Yazoo Delta, and you have to transfer at Moultrie to get it!

CUTLER: Well, hell, maybe that what he done! I don't know. I'm just telling you the man got off the train at Sigsbee . . .

LEVEE: All right . . . you telling it. Tell it your way. Just make up anything.

SLOW DRAG: Levee, leave the man alone and let him finish.

CUTLER: I ain't paying Levee no never mind.

LEVEE: Go and tell it your way.

CUTLER: Anyway . . . Reverend Gates got of this train in Sigsbee. The train done stopped there and he figured he'd get off and check the schedule to be sure he arrive in time for somebody to pick him up. All right. While he's there checking the schedule, it come upon him that he had to go to the bathroom. Now, they ain't had no colored rest rooms at the station. The only colored rest room is an outhouse they got sitting way back two hundred yards or so from the station. All right. He in the outhouse and the train go off and leave him there. He don't know nothing about this town. Ain't never been there before—in fact, ain't never even heard of it before.

LEVEE: I heard of it! I know just where it's at . . . and he ain't got off no train coming out of Tallahassee in Sigsbee!

CUTLER: The man standing there, trying to figure out what he's gonna do . . . where this train done left him in this strange town. It started getting dark. He see where the sun's getting low in the sky and he's trying to figure out what he's gonna do, when he noticed a couple of white fellows standing across the street from this station. Just standing there, watching him. And then two or three more come up and joined the other ones. He look around, ain't seen no colored folks nowhere. He didn't know what was getting in these here fellows' minds, so he commence to walking. He ain't knowed where he was going. He just walking down the railroad tracks when he hear them call him. "Hey, nigger!" See, just like that. "Hey, nigger!" He kept on walking. They called him some more and he just keep walking. Just going down the tracks. And then he heard a gunshot where somebody done fired a gun in the air. He stopped then, you know.

TOLEDO: You don't even have to tell me no more. I know the facts of it. I done heard the same story a hundred times. It happened to me too. Same thing.

CUTLER: Naw, I'm gonna show you how the white folks don't care nothing about who or what you is. They crowded around him. These gang of mens made a circle around him. Now, he's standing there, you understand ... got his cross around his neck like them preachers wear. Had his little Bible with him what he carry all the time. So they crowd on around him and one of them ask who he is. He told them he was Reverend Gates and that he was going to see his sister who was sick and the train left without him. And they said, "Yeah, nigger ... but can you dance?" He looked at them and commenced to dancing. One of them reached up and tore his cross off his neck. Said he was committing a heresy by dancing with a cross and Bible. Took his Bible and tore it up and had him dancing till they got tired of watching him.

SLOW DRAG: White folks ain't never had no respect for the colored minister.

CUTLER: That's the only way he got out of there alive ... was to dance. Ain't even had no respect for a man of God! Wanna make him into a clown. Reverend Gates sat right in my house and told me that story from his own mouth. So ... the white folks don't care nothing about Ma Rainey. She's just another nigger who they can use to make some money.

LEVEE: What I wants to know is ... if he's a man of God, then where the hell was God when all of this was going on? Why wasn't God looking out for him? Why didn't God strike down them crackers with some of this lightning you talk about to me?

CUTLER: Levee, you gonna burn in hell.

LEVEE: What I care about burning in hell? You talk like a fool ... burning in hell. Why didn't God strike some of them crackers down? Tell me that! That's the question! Don't come telling me this burning-in-hell shit! He a man of God ... why didn't God strike some of them crackers down? I'll tell you why! I'll tell you the truth! It's sitting out there as plain as day! 'Cause he a white man's God. That's why! God ain't never listened to no nigger's prayers. God take a nigger's prayers and throw them in the garbage. God don't pay niggers no mind. In fact ... God hate niggers! Hate them with all the fury in his heart. Jesus don't love you, nigger! Jesus hate your black ass! Come talking that shit to me. Talking about burning in hell! God can kiss my ass.

(CUTLER *can stand no more. He jumps up and punches* LEVEE *in the mouth. The force of the blow knocks* LEVEE *down and* CUTLER *jumps on him.*)

CUTLER: You worthless ... That's my God! That's my God! That's my God! You wanna blaspheme my God!

(TOLEDO *and* SLOW DRAG *grab* CUTLER *and try to pull him off* LEVEE.)

SLOW DRAG: Come on, Cutler ... let it go! It don't mean nothing!

(CUTLER *has* LEVEE *down on the floor and pounds on him with a fury.*)

CUTLER: Wanna blaspheme my God! You worthless ... talking about my God!

(TOLEDO *and* SLOW DRAG *succeeded in pulling* CUTLER *off* LEVEE, *who is bleeding at the nose and mouth.*)

LEVEE: Naw, let him go! Let him go!

(*He pulls out a knife.*)

That's your God, huh? That's your God, huh? Is that right? Your God, huh? All right. I'm gonna give your God a chance. I'm gonna give your God a chance. I'm gonna give him a chance to save your black ass.

(LEVEE *circles* CUTLER *with the knife.* CUTLER *picks up a chair to protect himself.*)

TOLEDO: Come on, Levee . . . put the knife up!
LEVEE: Stay out of this, Toledo!
TOLEDO: That ain't no way to solve nothing.

(LEVEE *alternately swipes at* CUTLER *during the following.*)

LEVEE: I'm calling Cutler's God! I'm talking to Cutler's God! You hear me? Cutler's God! I'm calling Cutler's God. Come on and save this nigger! Strike me down before I cut his throat!
SLOW DRAG: Watch him, Cutler! Put that knife up, Levee!
LEVEE: (*To* CUTLER.) I'm calling your God! I'm gonna give him a chance to save you! I'm calling your God! We gonna find out whose God he is!
CUTLER: You gonna burn in hell, nigger!
LEVEE: Cutler's God! Come on and save this nigger! Come on and save him like you did my mama! Save him like you did my mama! I heard her when she called you! I heard her when she said, "Lord, have mercy! Jesus, help me! Please, God, have mercy on me, Lord Jesus, help me!" And did you turn your back? Did you turn your back, motherfucker? Did you turn your back?

(LEVEE *becomes so caught up in his dialogue with God that he forgets about* CUTLER *and begins to stab upward in the air, trying to reach God.*)

Come on! Come on and turn your back on me! Turn your back on me! Come on! Where is you? Come on and turn your back on me! Turn your back on me, motherfucker! I'll cut your heart out! Come on, turn your back on me! Come on! What's the matter? Where is you? Come on and turn your back on me! Come on, what you scared of? Turn your back on me! Come on! Coward, motherfucker!

(LEVEE *folds his knife and stands triumphantly.*)

Your God ain't shit, Cutler.

(*The lights fade to black.*)

MA RAINEY: (*Singing.*)

> Ah, you hear me talking to you
> I don't bite my tongue
> You wants to be my man
> You got to fetch it with you when you come.

(*Lights come up in the studio. The last bars of the last song of the session are dying out.*)

IRVIN: (*Over speaker.*)   Good! Wonderful! We have that, boys. Good session. That's
  great, Ma. We've got ourselves some winners.

TOLEDO: Well, I'm glad that's over.

MA RAINEY: Slow Drag, where you learn to play that bass at? You had it singing!
  I heard you! Had that bass jumping all over the place.

SLOW DRAG: I was following Toledo. Nigger got them long fingers striding all
  over the piano. I was trying to keep up with him.

TOLEDO: That's what you supposed to do, ain't it? Play the music. Ain't nothing
  abstract about it.

MA RAINEY: Cutler, you hear Slow Drag on that bass? He make it do what he
  want it to do! Spank it just like you spank a baby.

CUTLER: Don't be telling him that. Nigger's head get so big his hat won't fit him.

SLOW DRAG: If Cutler tune that guitar up, we would really have something.

CUTLER: You wouldn't know what a tuned-up guitar sounded like if you heard
  one.

TOLEDO: Cutler was talking. I heard him moaning. He was all up in it.

MA RAINEY: Levee . . . what is that you doing? Why you playing all them notes?
  You play ten notes for every one you supposed to play. It don't call for that.

LEVEE: You supposed to improvise on the theme. That's what I was doing.

MA RAINEY: You supposed to play the song the way I sing it. The way everybody
  else play it. You ain't supposed to go off by yourself and play what you want.

LEVEE: I was playing the song. I was playing it the way I felt it.

MA RAINEY: I couldn't keep up with what was going on. I'm trying to sing the
  song and you up there messing up my ear. That's what you was doing. Call
  yourself playing music.

LEVEE: Hey . . . I know what I'm doing. I know what I'm doing, all right. I know
  how to play music. You all back up and leave me alone about my music.

CUTLER: I done told you . . . it ain't about *your* music. It's about *Ma's* music.

MA RAINEY: That's all right, Cutler. I done told you what to do.

LEVEE: I don't care what you do. You supposed to improvise on the theme. Not
  play note for note the same thing over and over again.

MA RAINEY: You just better watch yourself. You hear me?

LEVEE: What I care what you or Cutler do? Come telling me to watch myself.
  What's that supposed to mean?

MA RAINEY: All right . . . you gonna find out what it means.

LEVEE: Go ahead and fire me. I don't care. I'm gonna get my own band anyway.

MA RAINEY: You keep messing with me.

LEVEE: Ain't nobody studying you. You ain't gonna do nothing to me. Ain't
  nobody gonna do nothing to Levee.

MA RAINEY: All right, nigger . . . you fired!

LEVEE: You think I care about being fired? I don't care nothing about that. You
  doing me a favor.

MA RAINEY: Cutler, Levee's out! He don't play in my band no more.

LEVEE: I'm fired . . . Good! Best thing that ever happened to me. I don't need
  this shit!

(LEVEE *exits to the band room.* IRVIN *enters from the control booth.*)

MA RAINEY: Cutler, I'll see you back at the hotel.

IRVIN: Okay, boys . . . you can pack up. I'll get your money for you.

CUTLER: That's cash money, Mr. Irvin. I don't want no check.

IRVIN: I'll see what I can do. I can't promise you nothing.

CUTLER: As long as it ain't no check. I ain't got no use for a check.

IRVIN: I'll see what I can do, Cutler.

(CUTLER, TOLEDO, *and* SLOW DRAG *exit to the band room.*)

Oh, Ma, listen . . . I talked to Sturdyvant, and he said . . . Now, I tried to talk him out of it . . . He said the best he can do is to take twenty-five dollars of your money and give it to Sylvester.

MA RAINEY: Take what and do what? If I wanted the boy to have twenty-five dollars of my money, I'd give it to him. He supposed to get his own money. He supposed to get paid like everybody else.

IRVIN: Ma, I talked to him . . . He said . . .

MA RAINEY: Go talk to him again! Tell him if he don't pay that boy, he'll never make another record of mine again. Tell him that. You supposed to be my manager. All this talk about sticking together. Start sticking! Go on up there and get that boy his money!

IRVIN: Okay, Ma . . . I'll talk to him again. I'll see what I can do.

MA RAINEY: Ain't no see about it! You bring that boy's money back here!

(IRVIN *exits. The lights stay on in the studio and come up in the band room. The men have their instruments packed and sit waiting for* IRVIN *to come and pay them.* SLOW DRAG *has a pack of cards.*)

SLOW DRAG: Come on, Levee, let me show you a card trick.

LEVEE: I don't want to see no card trick. What you wanna show me for? Why you wanna bother me with that?

SLOW DRAG: I was just trying to be nice.

LEVEE: I don't need you to be nice to me. What I need you to be nice to me for? I ain't gonna be nice to you. I ain't even gonna let you be in my band no more.

SLOW DRAG: Toledo, let me show you a card trick.

CUTLER: I just hope Mr. Irvin don't bring no check down here. What the hell I'm gonna do with a check?

SLOW DRAG: All right now . . . pick a card. Any card . . . go on . . . take any of them. I'm gonna show you something.

TOLEDO: I agrees with you, Cutler. I don't want no check either.

CUTLER: It don't make no sense to give a nigger a check.

SLOW DRAG: Okay, now. Remember your card. Remember which one you got. Now . . . you put it back in the deck. Anywhere you want. I'm gonna show you something.

(TOLEDO *puts the card in the deck.*)

You remember your card? All right. Now I'm gonna shuffle the deck. Now . . . I'm gonna show you what card you picked. Don't say nothing now. I'm gonna tell you what card you picked.

CUTLER: Slow Drag, that trick is as old as my mama.

SLOW DRAG: Naw, naw . . . wait a minute! I'm gonna show him his card . . . There it go! The six of diamonds. Ain't that your card? Ain't that it?

TOLEDO: Yeah, that's it . . . the six of diamonds.

SLOW DRAG: Told you! Told you I'd show him what it was!

(*The lights fade in the band room and come up full on the studio.* STURDYVANT *enters with* IRVIN.)

STURDYVANT: Ma, is there something wrong? Is there a problem?

MA RAINEY: Sturdyvant, I want you to pay that boy his money.

STURDYVANT: Sure, Ma. I got it right here. Two hundred for you and twenty-five for the kid, right?

(STURDYVANT *hands the money to* IRVIN, *who hands it to* MA RAINEY *and* SYLVESTER.)

Irvin misunderstood me. It was all a mistake. Irv made a mistake.

MA RAINEY: A mistake, huh?

IRVIN: Sure, Ma. I made a mistake. He's paid, right? I straightened it out.

MA RAINEY: The only mistake was when you found out I hadn't signed the release forms. That was the mistake. Come on, Sylvester.

(*She starts to exit.*)

STURDYVANT: Hey, Ma . . . come on, sign the forms, huh?

IRVIN: Ma . . . come on now.

MA RAINEY: Get your coat, Sylvester. Irvin, where's my car?

IRVIN: It's right out front, Ma. Here . . . I got the keys right here. Come on, sign the forms, huh?

MA RAINEY: Irvin, give me my car keys!

IRVIN: Sure, Ma . . . just sign the forms, huh?

(*He gives her the keys, expecting a trade-off.*)

MA RAINEY: Send them to my address and I'll get around to them.

IRVIN: Come on, Ma . . . I took care of everything, right? I straightened everything out.

MA RAINEY: Give me the pen, Irvin.

(*She signs the forms.*)

You tell Sturdyvant . . . one more mistake like that and I can make my records someplace else.

(*She turns to exit.*)

Sylvester, straighten up your clothes. Come on Dussie Mae. (*She exits, followed by* DUSSIE MAE *and* SYLVESTER. *The lights go down in the studio and come up on the band room.*)

CUTLER: I know what's keeping him so long. He up there writing our checks. You watch. I ain't gonna stand for it. He ain't gonna bring me no check down here. If he do, he's gonna take it right back upstairs and get some cash.

TOLEDO: Don't get yourself all worked up about it. Wait and see. Think positive.

CUTLER: I am thinking positive. He positively gonna give me some cash. Man give me a check last time . . . you remember . . . we went all over Chicago trying to get it cashed. See a nigger with a check, the first thing they think is he done stole it someplace.

LEVEE: I ain't had no trouble cashing mine.

CUTLER: I don't visit no whorehouses.

LEVEE: You don't know about my business. So don't start nothing. I'm tired of you as it is. I ain't but two seconds off your ass no way.

TOLEDO: Don't you all start nothing now.

CUTLER: What the hell I care what you tired of. I wasn't even talking to you. I was talking to this man right here.

(IRVIN *and* STURDYVANT *enter.*)

IRVIN: Okay, boys. Mr. Sturdyvant has your pay.

CUTLER: As long as it's cash money, Mr. Sturdyvant. 'Cause I have too much trouble trying to cash a check.

STURDYVANT: Oh, yes . . . I'm aware of that. Mr. Irvin told me you boys prefer cash, and that's what I have for you.

(*He starts handing out the money.*)

That was a good session you boys put in . . . That's twenty-five for you. Yessir, you boys really know your business and we are going to . . . Twenty-five for you . . . We are going to get you back in here real soon . . . twenty-five . . . and have another session so you can make some more money . . . and twenty-five for you. Okay, thank you, boys. You can get your things together and Mr. Irvin will make sure you find your way out.

IRVIN: I'll be out front when you get your things together, Cutler.

(IRVIN *exits.* STURDYVANT *starts to follow.*)

LEVEE: Mr. Sturdyvant, sir. About them songs I give you? . . .

STURDYVANT: Oh, yes, . . . uh . . . Levee. About them songs you gave me. I've thought about it and I just don't think the people will buy them. They're not the type of songs we're looking for.

LEVEE: Mr. Sturdyvant, sir . . . I done got my band picked out and they's real good fellows. They knows how to play real good. I know if the peoples hear the music, they'll buy it.

STURDYVANT: Well, Levee, I'll be fair with you . . . but they're just not the right songs.

LEVEE: Mr. Sturdyvant, you got to understand about that music. That music is what the people is looking for. They's tired of jug-band music. They wants something that excites them. Something with some fire to it.

STURDYVANT: Okay, Levee. I'll tell you what I'll do. I'll give you five dollars apiece for them. Now that's the best I can do.

LEVEE: I don't want no five dollars, Mr. Sturdyvant. I wants to record them songs, like you say.

STURDYVANT: Well, Levee, like I say . . . they just aren't the kind of songs we're looking for.

LEVEE: Mr. Sturdyvant, you asked me to write them songs. Now, why didn't you tell me that before when I first gave them to you? You told me you was gonna let me record them. What's the difference between then and now?

STURDYVANT: Well, look . . . I'll pay you for your trouble . . .

LEVEE: What's the difference, Mr. Sturdyvant? That's what I wanna know.

STURDYVANT: I had my fellows play your songs, and when I heard them, they just didn't sound like the kind of songs I'm looking for right now.

LEVEE: You got to hear *me* play them. Mr. Sturdyvant! You ain't heard *me* play them. That's what's gonna make them sound right.

STURDYVANT: Well, Levee, I don't doubt that really. It's just that . . . well, I don't think they'd sell like Ma's records. But I'll take them off your hands for you.

LEVEE: The people's tired of jug-band music, Mr. Sturdyvant. They wants something that's gonna excite them! They wants something with some fire! I don't know what fellows you had playing them songs . . . but if I could play them! I'd set them down in the people's lap! Now you told me I could record them songs!

STURDYVANT: Well, there's nothing I can do about that. Like I say, it's five dollars apiece. That's what I'll give you. I'm doing you a favor. Now, if you write any more, I'll help you out and take them off your hands. The price is five dollars apiece. Just like now.

(*He attempts to hand* LEVEE *the money, finally shoves it in* LEVEE*'s coat pocket and is gone in a flash.* LEVEE *follows him to the door and it slams in his face. He takes the money from his pocket, balls it up and throws it on the floor. The other musicians silently gather up their belongings.* TOLEDO *walks past* LEVEE *and steps on his shoe.*)

LEVEE: Hey! Watch it . . . Shit, Toledo! You stepped on my shoe!

TOLEDO: Excuse me there, Levee.

LEVEE: Look at that! Look at that! Nigger, you stepped on my shoe. What you do that for?

TOLEDO: I said I'm sorry.

LEVEE: Nigger gonna step on my goddamn shoe! You done fucked up my shoe! Look at that! Look at what you done to my shoe, nigger! I ain't stepped on your shoe! What you wanna step on my shoe for?

CUTLER: The man said he's sorry.

LEVEE: Sorry! How the hell he gonna be sorry after he gone ruint my shoe? Come talking about sorry!

(*Turns his attention back to* TOLEDO.)

Nigger, you stepped on my shoe! You know that?

(LEVEE *snatches his shoe off his foot and holds it up for* TOLEDO *to see.*)

See what you done done?

TOLEDO: What you want me to do about it? It's done now. I said excuse me.

LEVEE: Wanna go and fuck up my shoe like that. I ain't done nothing to your shoe. Look at this!

(TOLEDO *turns and continues to gather up his things.* LEVEE *spins him around by his shoulder.*)

LEVEE: Naw . . . Naw . . . look what you done!

(*He shoves the shoe in* TOLEDO*'s face.*)

Look at that! That's my shoe! Look at that! You did it! You did it! You fucked up my shoe! You stepped on my shoe with them raggedy-ass clodhoppers!

TOLEDO: Nigger, ain't nobody studying you and your shoe! I said excuse me. If you can't accept that, then the hell with it. What you want me to do?

(LEVEE *is in a near rage, breathing hard. He is trying to get a grip on himself, as even he senses, or perhaps only he senses, he is about to lose control. He looks around, uncertain of what to do.* TOLEDO *has gone back to packing, as have* CUTLER *and* SLOW DRAG. *They purposefully avoid looking at* LEVEE *in hopes he'll calm down if he doesn't have an audience. All the weight in the world suddenly falls on* LEVEE *and he rushes at* TOLEDO *with his knife in his hand.*)

LEVEE: Nigger, you stepped on my shoe!

(*He plunges the knife into* TOLEDO*'s back up to the hilt.* TOLEDO *lets out a sound of surprise and agony.* CUTLER *and* SLOW DRAG *freeze.* TOLEDO *falls backward with* LEVEE, *his hand still on the knife, holding him up.* LEVEE *is suddenly faced with the realization of what he has done. He shoves* TOLEDO *forward and takes a step back.* TOLEDO *slumps to the floor.*)

He . . . he stepped on my shoe. He did. Honest, Cutler, he stepped on my shoe. What he do that for? Toledo, what you do that for? Cutler, help me. He stepped on my shoe, Cutler. (*He turns his attention to* TOLEDO). Toledo! Toledo, get up.

(*He crosses to* TOLEDO *and tries to pick him up.*)

It's okay, Toledo. Come on . . . I'll help you. Come on, stand up now. Levee'll help you.

(TOLEDO *is limp and heavy and awkward. He slumps back to the floor.* LEVEE *gets mad at him.*)

Don't look at me like that! Toledo! Nigger, don't look at me like that! I'm warning you, nigger! Close your eyes! Don't you look at me like that! (*He turns to* CUTLER)

Tell him to close his eyes. Cutler. Tell him don't look at me like that.

CUTLER: Slow Drag, get Mr. Irvin down here.

(*The sound of a trumpet is heard,* LEVEE*'s trumpet, a muted trumpet struggling for the highest possibilities and blowing pain and warning.*)

(*Blackout.*)

QUESTIONS FOR DISCUSSION AND WRITING

1. Describe the set of *Ma Rainey's Black Bottom* or, even better, make a sketch of it. What sorts of ironies and relationships does it suggest? What sorts of stage effects does it make possible? How does it suggest a metaphor?

2. The dialogue of the five band members tends not to be straightforward and purposeful but spiraling and rambling. We often have to see the point of some topic of discussion through a process of association rather than strict logic. Discuss the "meaning" (in this sense) of the following passages: the bet over the spelling of "music," the Lord's Prayer joke, Toledo's discussion of "Africanness," the story of the man who sold his soul to the devil, Toledo's speech about leftovers, Levee's long speech about his childhood, Ma Rainey's description of the blues, Toledo's account of his marriage, and the story of Reverend Gates and its aftermath.

3. Several of the original reviewers found the ending forced and unconvincing. Do you agree? What events lead to the stabbing? What relevance does it have to the issues of the play?

4. Certain topics recur in the musicians' conversations: music, male/female relations, religion, and race. Trace each throughout the play. How do the musicians disagree? How does each topic show the effects of white racism?

5. A basic conflict in *Ma Rainey* (as in Wilson's cycle-in-progress as a whole) is that between those who accept and celebrate their African roots and those who try to deny them. How does this conflict appear in *Ma Rainey*?

6. The song "Ma Rainey's Black Bottom" refers to a white hit song and dance from 1926, "Black Bottom." What stance does Ma Rainey's song take toward this song? Does it parody it? With all its stereotypes and *double entendres*, is it humiliating for Ma Rainey to sing it?

A DRAMA CASEBOOK

ℰℛ   ℛℰ

The third of our casebooks, the one on drama, is devoted to David Henry Hwang's *M. Butterfly,* which won a Tony Award in 1988 as the best play of the year, and which deals with issues of the meeting of different cultures that have recurred frequently in this anthology. First read *M. Butterfly.* It is followed by four commentaries on the play: Hwang's own "Afterword" to the published version of the play, a review of the first production by Frank Rich of the *New York Times,* a feminist essay on the play, and a brief attack on it in the introduction to a collection of Asian-American writing. After you have read the plays and the commentaries, read the essay "Writing from Sources: Drama," which will supply a few suggestions for using the secondary material in the casebook.

David Henry Hwang

David Henry Hwang (b. 1957) is one of the most eloquent writers who have dramatized the situation of, immediately, the Chinese-American and, more generally, the "hyphenated American," whatever the country of origin. Hwang was born in Los Angeles of Chinese-American immigrants. He was educated at Stanford University and the Yale School of Drama. His first play, *FOB*, was produced while he was still an undergraduate; the title means "fresh off the boat," and the play concerns the relations between recent immigrants and ABCs (American Born Chinese). Hwang's next two plays reworked conventions of the Chinese opera (*The Dance and the Railroad*) and television situation comedy (*Family Devotions*). The first three plays, along with *The House of Sleeping Beauties,* a play based on Japanese materials, were published in 1983 as *Broken Promises: Four Plays.*

By the mid-eighties, Hwang had won critical acclaim and a number of prizes, including an Obie award in 1981, but none of his plays had been very successful commercially. This changed in 1988, when *M. Butterfly* opened in New York. The play won a Tony Award as the best play of 1988 and has had many productions around the world. The bizarre story of a French diplomat who carried on a lengthy affair with a Chinese actress without ever realizing that she was a man, the play seems to have been taken as a tragicomic fable about how we imagine, more than actually know, people different from ourselves.

M. BUTTERFLY

PLAYWRIGHT'S NOTES

A former French diplomat and a Chinese opera singer have been sentenced to six years in jail for spying for China after a two-day trial that traced a story of clandestine love and mistaken sexual identity. . . . Mr. Bouriscot was accused of passing information to China after he fell in love with Mr. Shi, whom he believed for twenty years to be a woman.

—*The New York Times*, May 11, 1986

This play was suggested by international newspaper accounts of a recent espionage trial. For purposes of dramatization, names have been changed, characters created, and incidents devised or altered, and this play does not purport to be a factual record of real events or real people.

> "I could escape this feeling
> With my China girl . . ."

—David Bowie & Iggy Pop

CHARACTERS

KUROGO
RENE GALLIMARD
SONG LILING
MARC/MAN #2/ CONSUL SHARPLESS
RENEE/WOMAN AT PARTY/GIRL IN
    MAGAZINE

COMRADE CHIN/SUZUKI/SHU FANG
HELGA
M. TOULON/MAN #1/JUDGE

SETTING
The action of the play takes place in a Paris prison in the present, and in recall, during the decade 1960 to 1970 in Beijing, and from 1966 to the present in Paris.

ACT ONE

Scene 1

M. GALLIMARD'*s prison cell. Paris. Present.*
Lights fade up to reveal RENE GALLIMARD, *65, in a prison cell. He wears a comfortable bathrobe, and looks old and tired. The sparsely furnished cell contains a wooden crate upon which sits a hot plate with a kettle, and a portable tape recorder.* GALLIMARD *sits on the crate staring at the recorder, a sad smile on his face.*
Upstage SONG, *who appears as a beautiful woman in traditional Chinese garb, dances a traditional piece from the Peking Opera, surrounded by the percussive clatter of Chinese music.*
Then, slowly, lights and sound cross-fade; the Chinese opera music dissolves into a Western opera, the "Love Duet" from Puccini's Madame Butterfly. SONG *continues dancing, now to the Western accompaniment. Though her movements are the same, the difference in music now gives them a balletic quality.*

GALLIMARD *rises, and turns upstage towards the figure of* SONG, *who dances without acknowledging him.*

GALLIMARD: Butterfly, Butterfly . . .

He forces himself to turn away, as the image of SONG *fades out, and talks to us.*

GALLIMARD: The limits of my cell are as such: four-and-a-half meters by five.
There's one window against the far wall; a door, very strong, to protect me from autograph hounds. I'm responsible for the tape recorder, the hot plate, and this charming coffee table.

When I want to eat, I'm marched off to the dining room—hot, steaming slop appears on my plate. When I want to sleep, the light bulb turns itself off—the work of fairies. It's an enchanted space I occupy. The French—we know how to run a prison.

But, to be honest, I'm not treated like an ordinary prisoner. Why? Because I'm a celebrity. You see, I make people laugh.

I never dreamed this day would arrive. I've never been considered witty or clever. In fact, as a young boy, in an informal poll among my grammar school classmates, I was voted "least likely to be invited to a party." It's a title I managed to hold onto for many years. Despite some stiff competition.

But now, how the tables turn! Look at me: the life of every social function in Paris. Paris? Why be modest? My fame has spread to Amsterdam, London, New York. Listen to them! In the world's smartest parlors. I'm the one who lifts their spirits!

With a flourish, GALLIMARD *directs our attention to another part of the stage.*

Scene 2

A party. Present.
Lights go up on a chic-looking parlor, where a well-dressed trio, two men and one woman, make conversation. GALLIMARD *also remains lit; he observes them from his cell.*

WOMAN: And what of Gallimard?
MAN 1:   Gallimard?
MAN 2:   Gallimard!
GALLIMARD (*To us*):   You see? They're all determined to say my name, as if it were some new dance.
WOMAN: He still claims not to believe the truth.
MAN 1:   What? Still? Even since the trial?
WOMAN: Yes. Isn't it mad?
MAN 2 (*Laughing*):   He says . . . it was dark . . . and she was very modest!

The trio break into laughter.

MAN 1:   So—what? He never touched her with his hands?
MAN 2:   Perhaps he did, and simply misidentified the equipment. A compelling case for sex education in the schools.
WOMAN: To protect the National Security—the Church can't argue with that.
MAN 1:   That's impossible! How could he not know?
MAN 2:   Simple ignorance.

MAN 1: For twenty years?

MAN 2: Time flies when you're being stupid.

WOMAN: Well, I thought the French were ladies' men.

MAN 2: It seems Monsieur Gallimard was overly anxious to live up to his national reputation.

WOMAN: Well, he's not very good-looking.

MAN 1: No, he's not.

MAN 2: Certainly not.

WOMAN: Actually, I feel sorry for him

MAN 2: A toast! To Monsieur Gallimard!

WOMAN: Yes! To Gallimard!

MAN 1: To Gallimard!

MAN 2: Vive la différence!

They toast, laughing. Lights down on them.

Scene 3

M. GALLIMARD *'s cell.*

GALLIMARD: (*Smiling*): You see? They toast me. I've become patron saint of the socially inept. Can they really be so foolish? Men like that—they should be scratching at my door, begging to learn my secrets! For I, Rene Gallimard, you see, I have known, and been loved by . . . the Perfect Woman.

Alone in this cell, I sit night after night, watching our story play through my head, always searching for a new ending, one which redeems my honor, where she returns at last to my arms. And I imagine you—my ideal audience—who come to understand and even, perhaps just a little, to envy me.

He turns on his tape recorder. Over the house speakers, we hear the opening phrases of Madame Butterfly.

GALLIMARD: In order for you to understand what I did and why, I must introduce you to my favorite opera: *Madame Butterfly*. By Giacomo Puccini. First produced at La Scala, Milan, 1904, it is now beloved throughout the Western world.

As GALLIMARD *describes the opera, the tape segues in and out to sections he may be describing.*

GALLIMARD: And why not? Its heroine, Cio-Cio-San, also known as Butterfly, is a feminine ideal, beautiful and brave. And its hero, the man for whom she gives up everything, is—(*He pulls out a naval officer's cap from under his crate, pops it on his head, and struts about*)—not very good-looking, not too bright, and pretty much a wimp: Benjamin Franklin Pinkerton of the U.S. Navy. As the curtain rises, he's just closed on two great bargains: one on a house, the other on a woman—call it a package deal.

. Pinkerton purchased the rights to Butterfly for one hundred yen—in modern currency, equivalent to about . . . sixty-six cents. So, he's feeling pretty pleased with himself as Sharpless, the American consul, arrives to witness the marriage.

MARC, *wearing an official cap to designate* SHARPLESS, *enters and plays the character.*

SHARPLESS/MARC: Pinkerton!

PINKERTON/GALLIMARD: Sharpless! How's it hangin'? It's a great day, just great. Between my house, my wife, and the rickshaw ride in from town, I've saved nineteen cents just this morning.

SHARPLESS: Wonderful. I can see the inscription on your tombstone already: "I saved a dollar, here I lie." (*He looks around*) Nice house.

PINKERTON: It's artistic. Artistic, don't you think? Like the way the shoji screens slide open to reveal the wet bar and disco mirror ball? Classy, huh? Great for impressing the chicks.

SHARPLESS: "Chicks"? Pinkerton, you're going to be a married man!

PINKERTON: Well, sort of.

SHARPLESS: What do you mean?

PINKERTON: This country—Sharpless, it is okay. You got all these geisha girls running around—

SHARPLESS: I know! I live here!

PINKERTON: Then, you know the marriage laws, right? I split for one month, it's annulled!

SHARPLESS: Leave it to you to read the fine print. Who's the lucky girl?

PINKERTON: Cio-Cio-San. Her friends call her Butterfly. Sharpless, she eats out of my hand!

SHARPLESS: She's probably very hungry.

PINKERTON: Not like American girls. It's true what they say about Oriental girls. They want to be treated bad!

SHARPLESS: Oh, please!

PINKERTON: It's true!

SHARPLESS: Are you serious about this girl?

PINKERTON: I'm marrying her, aren't I?

SHARPLESS: Yes—with generous trade-in terms.

PINKERTON: When I leave, she'll know what it's like to have loved a real man. And I'll even buy her a few nylons.

SHARPLESS: You aren't planning to take her with you?

PINKERTON: Huh? Where?

SHARPLESS: Home!

PINKERTON: You mean, America? Are you crazy? Can you see her trying to buy rice in St. Louis?

SHARPLESS: So, you're not serious.

Pause.

PINKERTON/GALLIMARD (*As* PINKERTON): Consul, I am a sailor in port. (*As* GALLIMARD) They then proceed to sing the famous duet, "The Whole World Over."

The duet plays on the speakers. GALLIMARD, *as* PINKERTON, *lipsyncs his lines from the opera.*

GALLIMARD: To give a rough translation: "The whole world over, the Yankee travels, casting his anchor wherever he wants. Life's not worth living unless he can win the hearts of the fairest maidens, then hotfoot it off the premises ASAP." (*He turns towards* MARC) In the preceding scene, I played Pinkerton, the womanizing cad, and my friend Marc from school . . . (MARC *bows grandly for our benefit*) played Sharpless, the sensitive soul of reason. In life, however, our positions were usually—no, always—reversed.

Scene 4

Ecole Nationale, Aix-en-Provence. 1947.

GALLIMARD: No, Marc, I think I'd rather stay home.

MARC: Are you crazy?! We are going to Dad's condo in Marseille! You know what happened last time?

GALLIMARD: Of course I do.

MARC: Of course you don't! You never know. . . . They stripped, Rene!

GALLIMARD: Who stripped?

MARC: The girls!

GALLIMARD: Girls? Who said anything about girls?

MARC: Rene, we're a buncha university guys goin' up to the woods. What are we gonna do—talk philosophy?

GALLIMARD: What girls? Where do you get them?

MARC: Who cares? The point is, they come. On trucks. Packed in like sardines. The back flips open, babes hop out, we're ready to roll.

GALLIMARD: You mean, they just—?

MARC: Before you know it, every last one of them—they're stripped and splashing around my pool. There's no moon out, they can't see what's going on, their boobs are flapping, right? You close your eyes, reach out—it's grab bag, get it? Doesn't matter whose ass is between whose legs, whose teeth are sinking into who. You're just in there, going at it, eyes closed, on and on for as long as you can stand. (*Pause*) Some fun, huh?

GALLIMARD: What happens in the morning?

MARC: In the morning, you're ready to talk some philosophy. (*Beat*) So how 'bout it?

GALLIMARD: Marc, I can't . . . I'm afraid they'll say no—the girls. So I never ask.

MARC: You don't have to ask! That's the beauty—don't you see? They don't have to say yes. It's perfect for a guy like you, really.

GALLIMARD: You go ahead . . . I may come later.

MARC: Hey, Rene—it doesn't matter that you're clumsy and got zits—they're not looking!

GALLIMARD: Thank you very much.

MARC: Wimp.

MARC *walks over to the other side of the stage, and starts waving and smiling at women in the audience.*

GALLIMARD (*To us*): We now return to my version of *Madame Butterfly* and the events leading to my recent conviction for treason.

GALLIMARD *notices* MARC *making lewd gestures.*

GALLIMARD: Marc, what are you doing?

MARC: Huh? (*Sotto voce*) Rene, there're a lotta great babes out there. They're probably lookin' at me and thinking, "What a dangerous guy."

GALLIMARD: Yes—how could they help but be impressed by your cool sophistication?

GALLIMARD *pops the Sharpless cap on* MARC's *head, and points him offstage.* MARC *exits, leering.*

Scene 5

M. GALLIMARD's *cell.*

GALLIMARD: Next, Butterfly makes her entrance. We learn her age—fifteen . . . but very mature for her years.

Lights come up on the area where we saw SONG *dancing at the top of the play. She appears there again, now dressed as Madame Butterfly, moving to the "Love Duet."* GALLIMARD *turns upstage slightly to watch, transfixed.*

GALLIMARD: But as she glides past him, beautiful, laughing softly behind her fan, don't we who are men sigh with hope? We, who are not handsome, nor brave, nor powerful, yet somehow believe, like Pinkerton, that we deserve a Butterfly. She arrives with all her possessions in the folds of her sleeves, lays them all out, for her man to do with as he pleases. Even her life itself—she bows her head as she whispers that she's not even worth the hundred yen he paid for her. He's already given too much, when we know he's really had to give nothing at all.

Music and lights on SONG *out.* GALLIMARD *sits at his crate.*

GALLIMARD: In real life, women who put their total worth at less than sixty-six cents are quite hard to find. The closest we come is in the pages of these magazines. (*He reaches into his crate, pulls out a stack of girlie magazines, and begins flipping through them*) Quite a necessity in prison. For three or four dollars, you get seven or eight women.

I first discovered these magazines at my uncle's house. One day, as a boy of twelve. The first time I saw them in his closet . . . all lined up—my body shook. Not with lust—no, with power. Here were women—a shelfful—who would do exactly as I wanted.

The "Love Duet" creeps in over the speakers. Special comes up, revealing, not SONG *this time, but a pinup girl in a sexy negligee, her back to us.* GALLIMARD *turns upstage and looks at her.*

GIRL: I know you're watching me.
GALLIMARD: My throat . . . it's dry.
GIRL: I leave my blinds open every night before I go to bed.
GALLIMARD: I can't move.
GIRL: I leave my blinds open and the lights on.
GALLIMARD: I'm shaking. My skin is hot, but my penis is soft. Why?
GIRL: I stand in front of the window.
GALLIMARD: What is she going to do?
GIRL: I toss my hair, and I let my lips part . . . barely.
GALLIMARD: I shouldn't be seeing this. It's so dirty. I'm so bad.
GIRL: Then, slowly, I lift off my nightdress.
GALLIMARD: Oh, god. I can't believe it. I can't—
GIRL: I toss it to the ground.
GALLIMARD: Now, she's going to walk away. She's going to—
GIRL: I stand there, in the light, displaying myself.

GALLIMARD: No. She's—why is she naked?

GIRL: To you.

GALLIMARD: In front of a window? This is wrong. No—

GIRL: Without shame.

GALLIMARD: No, she must . . . like it.

GIRL: I like it.

GALLIMARD: She . . . she wants me to see.

GIRL: I want you to see.

GALLIMARD: I can't believe it! She's getting excited!

GIRL: I can't see you. You can do whatever you want.

GALLIMARD: I can't do a thing. Why?

GIRL: What would you like me to do . . . next?

Lights go down on her. Music off. Silence, as GALLIMARD *puts away his magazines. Then he resumes talking to us.*

GALLIMARD: Act Two begins with Butterfly staring at the ocean. Pinkerton's been called back to the U.S., and he's given his wife a detailed schedule of his plans. In the column marked "return date," he's written "when the robins nest." This failed to ignite her suspicions. Now, three years have passed without a peep from him. Which brings a response from her faithful servant, Suzuki.

COMRADE CHIN *enters, playing* SUZUKI.

SUZUKI: Girl, he's a loser. What'd he ever give you? Nineteen cents and those ugly Day-Glo stockings? Look, it's finished! Kaput! Done! And you should be glad! I mean, the guy was a woofer! He tried before, you know—before he met you, he went down to geisha central and plunked down his spare change in front of the usual candidates—everyone else gagged! These are hungry prostitutes, and they were not interested, get the picture? Now, stop slathering when an American ship sails in, and let's make some bucks—I mean, yen! We are broke!

Now, what about Yamadori? Hey, hey—don't look away—the man is a prince—figuratively, and, what's even better, literally. He's rich, he's handsome, he says he'll die if you don't marry him—and he's even willing to overlook the little fact that you've been deflowered all over the place by a foreign devil. What do you mean, "But he's Japanese?" You're Japanese! You think you've been touched by the whitey god? He was a sailor with dirty hands!

SUZUKI *stalks offstage.*

GALLIMARD: She's also visited by Consul Sharpless, sent by Pinkerton on a minor errand.

MARC *enters, as* SHARPLESS.

SHARPLESS: I hate this job.

GALLIMARD: This Pinkerton—he doesn't show up personally to tell his wife he's abandoning her. No, he sends a government diplomat . . . at taxpayer's expense.

SHARPLESS: Butterfly? Butterfly? I have some bad—I'm going to be ill. Butterfly, I came to tell you—

GALLIMARD: Butterfly says she knows he'll return and if he doesn't she'll kill herself rather than go back to her own people. (*Beat*) This causes a lull in the conversation.

SHARPLESS: Let's put it this way . . .

GALLIMARD: Butterfly runs into the next room, and returns holding—

Sound cue: a baby crying. SHARPLESS, *"seeing" this, backs away.*

SHARPLESS: Well, good. Happy to see things going so well. I suppose I'll be going now. Ta ta. Ciao. (*He turns away. Sound cue out*) I hate this job. (*He exits*)

GALLIMARD: At that moment, Butterfly spots in the harbor an American ship— the *Abramo Lincoln!*

Music cue: "The Flower Duet." SONG, *still dressed as* BUTTERFLY, *changes into a wedding kimono, moving to the music.*

GALLIMARD: This is the moment that redeems her years of waiting. With Suzuki's help, they cover the room with flowers—

CHIN, *as* SUZUKI, *trudges onstage and drops a lone flower without much enthusiasm.*

GALLIMARD: —and she changes into her wedding dress to prepare for Pinkerton's arrival.

SUZUKI *helps* BUTTERFLY *change.* HELGA *enters, and helps* GALLIMARD *change into a tuxedo.*

GALLIMARD: I married a woman older than myself—Helga.

HELGA: My father was ambassador to Australia. I grew up among criminals and kangaroos.

GALLIMARD: Hearing that brought me to the altar—

HELGA *exits*

GALLIMARD: —where I took a vow renouncing love. No fantasy woman would ever want me, so, yes, I would settle for a quick leap up the career ladder. Passion, I banish, and in its place—practicality!

   But my vows had long since lost their charm by the time we arrived in China. The sad truth is that all men want a beautiful woman, and the uglier the man, the greater the want.

SUZUKI *makes final adjustments of* BUTTERFLY's *costume, as does* GALLIMARD *of his tuxedo.*

GALLIMARD: I married late, at age thirty-one. I was faithful to my marriage for eight years. Until the day when, as a junior-level diplomat in puritanical Peking, in a parlor at the German ambassador's house, during the "Reign of a Hundred Flowers," I first saw her . . . singing the death scene from *Madame Butterfly*.

SUZUKI *runs offstage.*

Scene 6

German ambassador's house. Beijing. 1960.
The upstage special area now becomes a stage. Several chairs face upstage, representing

*seating for some twenty guests in the parlor. A few "diplomats"—*RENEE, MARC, TOU-
LON *—in formal dress enter and take seats.*

GALLIMARD *also sits down, but turns towards us and continues to talk. Orchestral
accompaniment on the tape is now replaced by a simple piano.* SONG *picks up the death scene
from the point where* BUTTERFLY *uncovers the hara-kiri knife.*

GALLIMARD: The ending is pitiful. Pinkerton, in an act of great courage, stays
  home and sends his American wife to pick up Butterfly's child. The truth, long
  deferred, has come up to her door.

SONG, *playing* BUTTERFLY, *sings the lines from the opera in her own voice—which, though
not classical, should be decent.*

SONG: "Con onor muore / chi non puo serbar / vita con onore."
GALLIMARD (*Simultaneously*):   "Death with honor / Is better than life / Life with
  dishonor."

The stage is illuminated; we are now completely within an elegant diplomat's residence.
SONG *proceeds to play out an abbreviated death scene. Everyone in the room applauds.*
SONG, *shyly, takes her bows. Others in the room rush to congratulate her.* GALLIMARD
remains with us.

GALLIMARD: They say in opera the voice is everything. That's probably why I'd
  never before enjoyed opera. Here . . . here was a Butterfly with little or no
  voice—but she had the grace, the delicacy . . . I believed this girl. I believed her
  suffering. I wanted to take her in my arms—so delicate, even I could protect
  her, take her home, pamper her until she smiled.

Over the course of the preceding speech, SONG *has broken from the upstage crowd and moved
directly upstage of* GALLIMARD.

SONG: Excuse me. Monsieur . . . ?

GALLIMARD *turns upstage, shocked.*

GALLIMARD: Oh! Gallimard. Mademoiselle . . . ? A beautiful . . .
SONG: Song Liling.
GALLIMARD: A beautiful performance.
SONG: Oh, please.
GALLIMARD: I usually—
SONG: You make me blush. I'm no opera singer at all.
GALLIMARD: I usually don't like *Butterfly.*
SONG: I can't blame you in the least.
GALLIMARD: I mean, the story—
SONG: Ridiculous.
GALLIMARD: I like the story, but . . . what?
SONG: Oh, you like it?
GALLIMARD: I . . . what I mean is, I've always seen it played by huge women in so
  much bad makeup.
SONG: Bad makeup is not unique to the West.
GALLIMARD: But, who can believe them?
SONG: And you believe me?

GALLIMARD: Absolutely. You were utterly convincing. It's the first time—

SONG: Convincing? As a Japanese woman? The Japanese used hundreds of our
people for medical experiments during the war, you know. But I gather such an
irony is lost on you.

GALLIMARD: No! I was about to say, it's the first time I've seen the beauty of the
story.

SONG: Really?

GALLIMARD: Of her death. It's a . . . a pure sacrifice. He's unworthy, but what
can she do? She loves him . . . so much. It's a very beautiful story.

SONG: Well, yes, to a Westerner.

GALLIMARD: Excuse me?

SONG: It's one of your favorite fantasies, isn't it? The submissive Oriental woman
and the cruel white man.

GALLIMARD: Well, I didn't quite mean . . .

SONG: Consider it this way: what would you say if a blonde homecoming queen
fell in love with a short Japanese businessman? He treats her cruelly, then goes
home for three years, during which time she prays to his picture and turns down
marriage from a young Kennedy. Then, when she learns he has remarried, she
kills herself. Now, I believe you would consider this girl to be a deranged idiot,
correct? But because it's an Oriental who kills herself for a Westerner—ah!—
you find it beautiful.

Silence.

GALLIMARD: Yes . . . well . . . I see your point . . .

SONG: I will never do Butterfly again, Monsieur Gallimard. If you wish to see
some real theatre, come to the Peking Opera sometime. Expand your mind.

SONG *walks offstage.*

GALLIMARD (*To us*):   So much for protecting her in my big Western arms.

Scene 7

M. GALLIMARD's *apartment. Beijing. 1960.*
GALLIMARD *changes from his tux into a casual suit.* HELGA *enters.*

GALLIMARD: The Chinese are an incredibly arrogant people.

HELGA: They warned us about that in Paris, remember?

GALLIMARD: Even Parisians consider them arrogant. That's a switch.

HELGA: What is it that Madame Su says? "We are a very old civilization." I never
know if she's talking about her country or herself.

GALLIMARD: I walk around here, all I hear every day, everywhere is how *old* this
culture is. The fact that "old" may be synonymous with "senile" doesn't occur
to them.

HELGA: You're not going to change them. "East is east, west is west, and . . ."
whatever that guy said.

GALLIMARD: It's just that—silly. I met . . . at Ambassador Koening's tonight—you
should've been there.

HELGA: Koening? Oh god. no. Did he enchant you all again with the history of
Bavaria?

GALLIMARD: No. I met, I suppose, the Chinese equivalent of a diva. She's a
singer in the Chinese opera.

HELGA: They have an opera, too? Do they sing in Chinese? Or maybe—in Italian?

GALLIMARD: Tonight, she did sing in Italian.

HELGA: How'd she manage that?

GALLIMARD: She must've been educated in the West before the Revolution. Her French is very good also. Anyway, she sang the death scene from *Madame Butterfly.*

HELGA: *Madame Butterfly!* Then I should have come. (*She begins humming, floating around the room as if dragging long kimono sleeves*) Did she have a nice costume? I think it's a classic piece of music.

GALLIMARD: That's what *I* thought, too. Don't let her hear you say that.

HELGA: What's wrong?

GALLIMARD: Evidently the Chinese hate it.

HELGA: She hated it, but she performed it anyway? Is she perverse?

GALLIMARD: They hate it because the white man gets the girl. Sour grapes if you ask me.

HELGA: Politics again? Why can't they just hear it as a piece of beautiful music? So, what's in their opera?

GALLIMARD: I don't know. But, whatever it is, I'm sure it must be *old.*

Helga exits.

Scene 8

Chinese opera house and the streets of Beijing. 1960.
  The sound of gongs clanging fills the stage.

GALLIMARD: My wife's innocent question kept ringing in my ears. I asked around, but no one knew anything about the Chinese opera. It took four weeks, but my curiosity overcame my cowardice. This Chinese diva—this unwilling Butterfly—what did she do to make her so proud?

  The room was hot, and full of smoke. Wrinkled faces, old women, teeth missing—a man with a growth on his neck, like a human toad. All smiling, pipes falling from their mouths, cracking nuts between their teeth, a live chicken pecking at my foot—all looking, screaming, gawking . . . at her.

The upstage area is suddenly hit with a harsh white light. It has become the stage for the Chinese opera performance. Two dancers enter, along with SONG. GALLIMARD *stands apart, watching.* SONG *glides gracefully amidst the two dancers. Drums suddenly slam to a halt.* SONG *strikes a pose, looking straight at* GALLIMARD. *Dancers exit. Light change. Pause, then* SONG *walks right off the stage and straight up to* GALLIMARD.

SONG: Yes. You. White man. I'm looking straight at you.

GALLIMARD: Me?

SONG: You see any other white men? It was too easy to spot you. How often does a man in my audience come in a tie?

SONG starts to remove her costume. Underneath, she wears simple baggy clothes. They are now backstage. The show is over.

SONG: So, you are an adventurous imperialist?

GALLIMARD: I . . . thought it would further my education.

SONG: It took you four weeks. Why?

GALLIMARD: I've been busy.

SONG: Well, education has always been undervalued in the West, hasn't it?

GALLIMARD (*Laughing*):   I don't think it's true.

SONG: No, you wouldn't. You're a Westerner. How can you objectively judge your own values?

GALLIMARD: I think it's possible to achieve some distance.

SONG: Do you? (*Pause*) It stinks in here. Let's go.

GALLIMARD: These are the smells of your loyal fans.

SONG: I love them for being my fans, I hate the smell they leave behind. I too can distance myself from my people. (*She looks around, then whispers in his ear*) "Art for the masses" is a shitty excuse to keep artists poor. (*She pops a cigarette in her mouth*) Be a gentleman, will you? And light my cigarette.

GALLIMARD *fumbles for a match.*

GALLIMARD: I don't . . . smoke.

SONG   (*Lighting her own*): Your loss. Had you lit my cigarette, I might have blown a puff of smoke right between your eyes. Come.

They start to walk about the stage. It is a summer night on the Beijing streets. Sounds of the city play on the house speakers.

SONG: How I wish there were even a tiny cafe to sit in. With cappuccinos, and men in tuxedos and bad expatriate jazz.

GALLIMARD: If my history serves me correctly, you weren't even allowed into the clubs in Shanghai before the Revolution.

SONG: Your history serves you poorly, Monsieur Gallimard. True, there were signs reading "No dogs and Chinamen." But a woman, especially a delicate Oriental woman—we always go where we please. Could you imagine it otherwise? Clubs in China filled with pasty, big-thighed white women, while thousands of slender lotus blossoms wait just outside the door? Never. The clubs would be empty. (*Beat*) We have always held a certain fascination for you Caucasian men, have we not?

GALLIMARD: But . . . that fascination is imperialist, or so you tell me.

SONG: Do you believe everything I tell you? Yes. It is always imperialist. But sometimes . . . sometimes, it is also mutual. Oh—this is my flat.

GALLIMARD: I didn't even—

SONG: Thank you. Come another time and we will further expand your mind.

SONG *exits.* GALLIMARD *continues roaming the streets as he speaks to us.*

GALLIMARD: What was that? What did she mean, "Sometimes . . . it is mutual?" Women do not flirt with me. And I normally can't talk to them. But tonight, I held up my end of the conversation.

Scene 9

GALLIMARD*'s bedroom. Beijing. 1960.*
   HELGA *enters.*

HELGA: You didn't tell me you'd be home late.

GALLIMARD: I didn't intend to. Something came up.

HELGA: Oh? Like what?

GALLIMARD: I went to the . . . to the Dutch ambassador's home.

HELGA: Again?

GALLIMARD: There was a reception for a visiting scholar. He's writing a six-volume treatise on the Chinese revolution. We all gathered that meant he'd have to live here long enough to actually write six volumes, and we all expressed our deepest sympathies.

HELGA: Well, I had a good night too. I went with the ladies to a martial arts demonstration. Some of those men—when they break those thick boards—(*She mimes fanning herself*) whoo-whoo!

HELGA *exits. Lights dim.*

GALLIMARD: I lied to my wife. Why? I've never had any reason to lie before. But what reason did I have tonight? I didn't do anything wrong. That night, I had a dream. Other people, I've been told, have dreams where angels appear. Or dragons, or Sophia Loren in a towel. In my dream, Marc from school appeared.

MARC *enters, in a nightshirt and cap.*

MARC: Rene! You met a girl!

GALLIMARD *and* MARC *stumble down the Beijing streets. Night sounds over the speakers.*

GALLIMARD: It's not that amazing, thank you.

MARC: No! It's so monumental, I heard about it halfway around the world in my sleep!

GALLIMARD: I've met girls before, you know.

MARC: Name one. I've come across time and space to congratulate you. (*He hands* GALLIMARD *a bottle of wine*)

GALLIMARD: Marc, this is expensive.

MARC: On those rare occasions when you become a formless spirit, why not steal the best?

MARC *pops open the bottle, begins to share it with* GALLIMARD.

GALLIMARD: You embarrass me. She . . . there's no reason to think she likes me.

MARC: "Sometimes, it is mutual"?

GALLIMARD: Oh.

MARC: "Mutual"? "Mutual"? What does that mean?

GALLIMARD: You heard!

MARC: It means the money is in the bank, you only have to write the check!

GALLIMARD: I am a married man!

MARC: And an excellent one too. I cheated after . . . six months. Then again and again, until now—three hundred girls in twelve years.

GALLIMARD: I don't think we should hold that up as a model.

MARC: Of course not! My life—it is disgusting! Phooey! Phooey! But, you—you are the model husband.

GALLIMARD: Anyway, it's impossible. I'm a foreigner.

MARC: Ah, yes. She cannot love you, it is taboo, but something deep inside her heart . . . she cannot help herself . . . she must surrender to you. It is her destiny.

GALLIMARD: How do you imagine all this?

MARC: The same way you do. It's an old story. It's in our blood. They fear us,

Rene. Their women fear us. And their men—their men hate us. And, you know something? They are all correct.

They spot a light in a window.

MARC: There! There, Rene!
GALLIMARD: It's her window.
MARC: Late at night—it burns. The light—it burns for you.
GALLIMARD: I won't look. It's not respectful.
MARC: We don't have to be respectful. We're foreign devils.

Enter SONG, *in a sheer robe. The "One Fine Day" aria creeps in over the speakers. With her back to us,* SONG *mimes attending to her toilette. Her robe comes loose, revealing her white shoulders.*

MARC: All your life you've waited for a beautiful girl who would lay down for you. All your life you've smiled like a saint when it's happened to every other man you know. And you see them in magazines and you see them in movies. And you wonder, what's wrong with me? Will anyone beautiful ever want me? As the years pass, your hair thins and you struggle to hold onto even your hopes. Stop struggling, Rene. The wait is over. (*He exits*)
GALLIMARD: Marc? Marc?

At that moment, SONG, *her back still towards us, drops her robe. A second of her naked back, then a sound cue: a phone ringing, very loud. Blackout, followed in the next beat by a special up on the bedroom area, where a phone now sits.* GALLIMARD *stumbles across the stage and picks up the phone. Sound cue out. Over the course of his conversation, area lights fill in the vicinity of his bed. It is the following morning.*

GALLIMARD: Yes? Hello?
SONG (*Offstage*): Is it very early?
GALLIMARD: Why, yes.
SONG (*Offstage*):   How early?
GALLIMARD: It's . . . it's 5:30. Why are you—?
SONG (*Offstage*):   But it's light outside. Already.
GALLIMARD: It is. The sun must be in confusion today.

Over the course of SONG*'s next speech, her upstage special comes up again. She sits in a chair, legs crossed, in a robe, telephone to her ear.*

SONG: I waited until I saw the sun. That was as much discipline as I could manage for one night. Do you forgive me?
GALLIMARD: Of course . . . for what?
SONG: Then I'll ask you quickly. Are you really interested in the opera?
GALLIMARD: Why, yes. Yes I am.
SONG: Then come again next Thursday. I am playing *The Drunken Beauty*. May I count on you?
GALLIMARD: Yes. You may.
SONG: Perfect. Well, I must be getting to bed. I'm exhausted. It's been a very long night for me.

SONG *hangs up; special on her goes off.* GALLIMARD *begins to dress for work.*

Scene 10

SONG LILING's *apartment. Beijing. 1960.*

GALLIMARD: I returned to the opera that next week, and the week after that . . . she keeps our meetings so short—perhaps fifteen, twenty minutes at most. So I am left each week with a thirst which is intensified. In this way, fifteen weeks have gone by. I am starting to doubt the words of my friend Marc. But no, not really. In my heart, I know she has . . . an interest in me. I suspect this is her way. She is outwardly bold and outspoken, yet her heart is shy and afraid. It is the Oriental in her at war with her Western education.

SONG (*Offstage*): I will be out in an instant. Ask the servant for anything you want.

GALLIMARD: Tonight, I have finally been invited to enter her apartment. Though the idea is almost beyond belief, I believe she is afraid of me.

GALLIMARD *looks around the room. He picks up a picture in a frame, studies it. Without his noticing,* SONG *enters, dressed elegantly in a black gown from the twenties. She stands in the doorway looking like Anna May Wong.*

SONG: That is my father.

GALLIMARD (*Surprised*): Mademoiselle Song!

She glides up to him, snatches away the picture.

SONG: It is very good that he did not live to see the Revolution. They would, no doubt, have made him kneel on broken glass. Not that he didn't deserve such a punishment. But he is my father. I would've hated to see it happen.

GALLIMARD: I'm very honored that you've allowed me to visit your home.

SONG *curtsys.*

SONG: Thank you. Oh! Haven't you been poured any tea?

GALLIMARD: I'm really not—

SONG (*To her offstage servant*): Shu-Fang! Cha! Kwai-lah! (*To* GALLIMARD) I'm sorry. You want everything to be perfect—

GALLIMARD: Please.

SONG: —and before the evening even begins—

GALLIMARD: I'm really not thirsty.

SONG: —it's ruined.

GALLIMARD (*Sharply*): Mademoiselle Song!

SONG *sits down.*

SONG: I'm sorry.

GALLIMARD: What are you apologizing for now?

Pause; SONG *starts to giggle.*

SONG: I don't know!

GALLIMARD *laughs.*

GALLIMARD: Exactly my point.

SONG: Oh, I am silly. Lightheaded. I promise not to apologize for anything else
   tonight, do you hear me?
GALLIMARD: That's a good girl.

SHU-FANG, *a servant girl, comes out with a tea tray and starts to pour.*

SONG (*To* SHU-FANG):   No! I'll pour myself for the gentleman!

SHU-FANG, *staring at* GALLIMARD, *exits.*

SONG: No, I . . . I don't even know why I invited you up.
GALLIMARD: Well, I'm glad you did.

SONG *looks around the room.*

SONG: There is an element of danger to your presence.
GALLIMARD: Oh?
SONG: You must know.
GALLIMARD: It doesn't concern me. We both know why I'm here.
SONG: It doesn't concern me either. No . . . well perhaps . . .
GALLIMARD: What?
SONG: Perhaps I am slightly afraid of scandal.
GALLIMARD: What are we doing?
SONG: I'm entertaining you. In my parlor.
GALLIMARD: In France, that would hardly—
SONG: France. France is a country living in the modern era. Perhaps even ahead
   of it. China is a nation whose soul is firmly rooted two thousand years in the
   past. What I do, even pouring the tea for you now . . . it has . . . implications.
   The walls and windows say so. Even my own heart, strapped inside this Western
   dress . . . even it says things—things I don't care to hear.

SONG *hands* GALLIMARD *a cup of tea.* GALLIMARD *puts his hand over both the teacup
and* SONG*'s hand.*

GALLIMARD: This is a beautiful dress.
SONG: Don't.
GALLIMARD: What?
SONG: I don't even know if it looks right on me.
GALLIMARD: Believe me—
SONG: You are from France. You see so many beautiful women.
GALLIMARD: France? Since when are the European women—?
SONG: Oh! What am I trying to do, anyway!

SONG *runs to the door, composes herself, then turns towards* GALLIMARD.

SONG: Monsieur Gallimard, perhaps you should go.
GALLIMARD: But . . . why?
SONG: There's something wrong about this.
GALLIMARD: I don't see what.
SONG: I feel . . . I am not myself.
GALLIMARD: No. You're nervous.

SONG: Please. Hard as I try to be modern, to speak like a man, to hold a Western woman's strong face up to my own . . . in the end, I fail. A small, frightened heart beats too quickly and gives me away. Monsieur Gallimard, I'm a Chinese girl. I've never . . . never invited a man up to my flat before. The forwardness of my actions makes my skin burn.

GALLIMARD: What are you afraid of? Certainly not me, I hope.

SONG: I'm a modest girl.

GALLIMARD: I know. And very beautiful. (*He touches her hair*)

SONG: Please—go now. The next time you see me, I shall again be myself.

GALLIMARD: I like you the way you are right now.

SONG: You are a cad.

GALLIMARD: What do you expect? I'm a foreign devil.

GALLIMARD *walks downstage.* SONG *exits.*

GALLIMARD (*To us*): Did you hear the way she talked about Western women? Much differently than the first night. She does—she feels inferior to them—and to me.

Scene 11

The French embassy. Beijing. 1960.
GALLIMARD *moves towards a desk.*

GALLIMARD: I determined to try an experiment. In *Madame Butterfly,* Cio-Cio-San fears that the Western man who catches a butterfly will pierce its heart with a needle, then leave it to perish. I began to wonder: had I, too, caught a butterfly who would writhe on a needle?

MARC *enters, dressed as a bureaucrat, holding a stack of papers. As* GALLIMARD *speaks,* MARC *hands papers to him. He peruses, then signs, stamps or rejects them.*

GALLIMARD: Over the next five weeks, I worked like a dynamo. I stopped going to the opera, I didn't phone or write her. I knew this little flower was waiting for me to call, and, as I wickedly refused to do so, I felt for the first time that rush of power—the absolute power of a man.

MARC *continues acting as the bureaucrat, but he now speaks as himself.*

MARC: Rene! It's me!

GALLIMARD: Marc—I hear your voice everywhere now. Even in the midst of work.

MARC: That's because I'm watching you—all the time.

GALLIMARD: You were always the most popular guy in school.

MARC: Well, there's no guarantee of failure in life like happiness in high school. Somehow I knew I'd end up in the suburbs working for Renault and you'd be in the Orient picking exotic women off the trees. And they say there's no justice.

GALLIMARD: That's why you were my friend?

MARC: I gave you a little of my life, so that now you can give me some of yours. (*Pause*) Remember Isabelle?

GALLIMARD: Of course I remember! She was my first experience.

MARC: We all wanted to ball her. But she only wanted me.

GALLIMARD: I had her.

MARC: Right. You balled her.

GALLIMARD: You were the only one who ever believed me.

MARC: Well, there's a good reason for that. (*Beat*) C'mon. You must've guessed.

GALLIMARD: You told me to wait in the bushes by the cafeteria that night. The next thing I knew, she was on me. Dress up in the air.

MARC: She never wore underwear.

GALLIMARD: My arms were pinned to the dirt.

MARC: She loved the superior position. A girl ahead of her time.

GALLIMARD: I looked up, and there was this woman . . . bouncing up and down on my loins.

MARC: Screaming, right?

GALLIMARD: Screaming, and breaking off the branches all around me, and pounding my butt up and down into the dirt.

MARC: Huffing and puffing like a locomotive.

GALLIMARD: And in the middle of all this, the leaves were getting into my mouth, my legs were losing circulation, I thought, "God. So this is *it*?"

MARC: You thought that?

GALLIMARD: Well, I was worried about my legs falling off.

MARC: You didn't have a good time?

GALLIMARD: No, that's not what I—I had a great time!

MARC: You're sure?

GALLIMARD: Yeah. Really.

MARC: 'Cuz I wanted you to have a good time.

GALLIMARD: I did.

Pause.

MARC: Shit. (*Pause*) When all is said and done, she was kind of a lousy lay, wasn't she? I mean, there was a lot of energy there, but you never knew what she was doing with it. Like when she yelled "I'm coming!"—hell, it was so loud, you wanted to go "Look, it's not that big a deal."

GALLIMARD: I got scared. I thought she meant someone was actually coming. (*Pause*) But, Marc?

MARC: What?

GALLIMARD: Thanks.

MARC: Oh, don't mention it.

GALLIMARD: It was my first experience.

MARC: Yeah. You got her.

GALLIMARD: I got her.

MARC: Wait! Look at that letter again!

GALLIMARD *picks up one of the papers he's been stamping, and rereads it.*

GALLIMARD (*To us*): After six weeks, they began to arrive. The letters.

Upstage special on SONG, *as Madame Butterfly. The scene is underscored by the "Love Duet."*

SONG: Did we fight? I do not know. Is the opera no longer of interest to you? Please come—my audiences miss the white devil in their midst.

GALLIMARD *looks up from the letter, towards us.*

GALLIMARD (*To us*): A concession, but much too dignified. (*Beat; he discards the letter*) I skipped the opera again that week to complete a position paper on trade.

The bureaucrat hands him another letter.

SONG: Six weeks have passed since last we met. Is this your practice—to leave friends in the lurch? Sometimes I hate you, sometimes I hate myself, but always I miss you.

GALLIMARD (*To us*): Better, but I don't like the way she calls me "friend." When a woman calls a man her "friend," she's calling him a eunuch or a homosexual. (*Beat; he discards the letter*) I was absent from the opera for the seventh week, feeling a sudden urge to clean out my files.

Bureaucrat hands him another letter.

SONG: Your rudeness is beyond belief. I don't deserve this cruelty. Don't bother to call. I'll have you turned away at the door.

GALLIMARD (*To us*): I didn't. (*He discards the letter; bureaucrat hands him another*) And then finally, the letter that concluded my experiment.

SONG: I am out of words. I can hide behind dignity no longer. What do you want? I have already given you my shame.

GALLIMARD *gives the letter back to* MARC, *slowly. Special on* SONG *fades out.*

GALLIMARD (*To us*): Reading it, I became suddenly ashamed. Yes, my experiment had been a success. She was turning on my needle. But the victory seemed hollow.

MARC: Hollow?! Are you crazy?

GALLIMARD: Nothing, Marc. Please go away.

MARC (*Exiting, with papers*): Haven't I taught you anything?

GALLIMARD: "I have already given you my shame." I had to attend a reception that evening. On the way, I felt sick. If there is a God, surely he would punish me now. I had finally gained power over a beautiful woman, only to abuse it cruelly. There must be justice in the world. I had the strange feeling that the ax would fall this very evening.

Scene 12

AMBASSADOR TOULON's *residence. Beijing. 1960.*
Sound cue: party noises. Light change. We are now in a spacious residence. TOULON, *the French ambassador, enters and taps* GALLIMARD *on the shoulder.*

TOULON: Gallimard? Can I have a word? Over here.

GALLIMARD (*To us*): Manuel Toulon. French ambassador to China. He likes to think of us all as his children. Rather like God.

TOULON: Look, Gallimard, there's not much to say. I've liked you. From the day you walked in. You were no leader, but you were tidy and efficient.

GALLIMARD: Thank you, sir.

TOULON: Don't jump the gun. Okay, our needs in China are changing. It's embarrassing that we lost Indochina. Someone just wasn't on the ball there. I don't mean you personally, of course.

GALLIMARD: Thank you, sir.

TOULON: We're going to be doing a lot more information-gathering in the future. The nature of our work here is changing. Some people are just going to have to go. It's nothing personal.

GALLIMARD: Oh.

TOULON: Want to know a secret? Vice-Consul LeBon is being transferred.

GALLIMARD (*To us*): My immediate superior!

TOULON: And most of his department.

GALLIMARD (*To us*): Just as I feared! God has seen my evil heart—

TOULON: But not you.

GALLIMARD (*To us*): —and he's taking her away just as . . . (*To* TOULON) Excuse me, sir?

TOULON: Scare you? I think I did. Cheer up, Gallimard. I want you to replace LeBon as vice-consul.

GALLIMARD: You—? Yes, well, thank you, sir.

TOULON: Anytime.

GALLIMARD: I . . . accept with great humility.

TOULON: Humility won't be part of the job. You're going to coordinate the revamped intelligence division. Want to know a secret? A year ago, you would've been out. But the past few months, I don't know how it happened, you've become this new aggressive confident . . . thing. And they also tell me you get along with the Chinese. So I think you're a lucky man, Gallimard. Congratulations.

They shake hands. TOULON *exits. Party noises out.* GALLIMARD *stumbles across a darkened stage.*

GALLIMARD: Vice-consul? Impossible! As I stumbled out of the party, I saw it written across the sky: There is no God. Or, no—say that there is a God. But that God . . . understands. Of course! God who creates Eve to serve Adam, who blesses Solomon with his harem but ties Jezebel to a burning bed—that God is a man. And he understands! At age thirty-nine, I was suddenly initiated into the way of the world.

Scene 13

SONG LILING's *apartment. Beijing. 1960.*
SONG *enters, in a sheer dressing gown.*

SONG: Are you crazy?

GALLIMARD: Mademoiselle Song—

SONG: To come here—at this hour? After . . . after eight weeks?

GALLIMARD: It's the most amazing—

SONG: You bang on my door? Scare my servants, scandalize the neighbors?

GALLIMARD: I've been promoted. To vice-consul.

Pause.

SONG: And what is that supposed to mean to me?

GALLIMARD: Are you my Butterfly?

SONG: What are you saying?

GALLIMARD: I've come tonight for an answer: are you my Butterfly?

SONG: Don't you know already?

GALLIMARD: I want you to say it.

SONG: I don't want to say it.

GALLIMARD: So, that is your answer?

SONG: You know how I feel about—

GALLIMARD: I do remember one thing.

SONG: What?

GALLIMARD: In the letter I received today.

SONG: Don't.

GALLIMARD: "I have already given you my shame."

SONG: It's enough that I even wrote it.

GALLIMARD: Well, then—

SONG: I shouldn't have it splashed across my face.

GALLIMARD: —if that's all true—

SONG: Stop!

GALLIMARD: Then what is one more short answer?

SONG: I don't want to!

GALLIMARD: Are you my Butterfly? (*Silence; he crosses the room and begins to touch her hair*) I want from you honesty. There should be nothing false between us. No false pride.

Pause.

SONG: Yes, I am. I am your Butterfly.

GALLIMARD: Then let me be honest with you. It is because of you that I was promoted tonight. You have changed my life forever. My little Butterfly, there should be no more secrets: I love you.

He starts to kiss her roughly. She resists slightly.

SONG: No . . . no . . . gently . . . please, I've never . . .

GALLIMARD: No?

SONG: I've tried to appear experienced, but . . . the truth is . . . no.

GALLIMARD: Are you cold?

SONG: Yes. Cold.

GALLIMARD: Then we will go very, very slowly.

He starts to caress her; her gown begins to open.

SONG: No . . . let me . . . keep my clothes . . .

GALLIMARD: But . . .

SONG: Please . . . it all frightens me. I'm a modest Chinese girl.

GALLIMARD: My poor little treasure.

SONG: I am your treasure. Though inexperienced, I am not . . . ignorant. They teach us things, our mothers, about pleasing a man.

GALLIMARD: Yes?

SONG: I'll do my best to make you happy. Turn off the lights.

GALLIMARD *gets up and heads for a lamp.* SONG, *propped up on one elbow, tosses her hair back and smiles.*

SONG: Monsieur Gallimard?
GALLIMARD: Yes, Butterfly?
SONG: "Vieni, vieni!"
GALLIMARD: "Come, darling."
SONG: "Ah! Dolce notte!"
GALLIMARD: "Beautiful night."
SONG: "Tutto estatico d'amor ride il ciel!'
GALLIMARD: "All ecstatic with love, the heavens are filled with laughter."

He turns off the lamp. Blackout.

ACT TWO

Scene 1

M. GALLIMARD*'s cell. Paris. Present.*
  Lights up on GALLIMARD. *He sits in his cell, reading from a leaflet.*

GALLIMARD: This, from a contemporary critic's commentary on *Madame Butter-fly:* "Pinkerton suffers from . . . being an obnoxious bounder whom every man in the audience itches to kick." Bully for us men in the audience! Then, in the same note: "Butterfly is the most irresistibly appealing of Puccini's 'Little Women.' Watching the succession of her humiliations is like watching a child under torture." (*He tosses the pamphlet over his shoulder*) I suggest that, while we men may all want to kick Pinkerton, very few of us would pass up the oppor-tunity to *be* Pinkerton.

GALLIMARD *moves out of his cell.*

Scene 2

GALLIMARD *and* BUTTERFLY*'s flat. Beijing. 1960.*
  We are in a simple but well-decorated parlor. GALLIMARD *moves to sit on a sofa, while* SONG, *dressed in a chong sam, enters and curls up at his feet.*

GALLIMARD (*To us*):   We secured a flat on the outskirts of Peking. Butterfly, as I was calling her now, decorated our "home" with Western furniture and Chi-nese antiques. And there, on a few stolen afternoons or evenings each week, Butterfly commenced her education.
SONG: The Chinese men—they keep us down.
GALLIMARD: Even in the "New Society"?
SONG: In the "New Society," we are all kept ignorant equally. That's one of the exciting things about loving a Western man. I know you are not threatened by a woman's education.
GALLIMARD: I'm no saint, Butterfly.
SONG: But you come from a progressive society.
GALLIMARD: We're not always reminding each other how "old" we are, if that's what you mean.
SONG: Exactly. We Chinese—once, I suppose, it is true, we ruled the world. But

so what? How much more exciting to be part of the society ruling the world today. Tell me—what's happening in Vietnam?

GALLIMARD: Oh, Butterfly—you want me to bring my work home?

SONG: I want to know what you know. To be impressed by my man. It's not the particulars so much as the fact that you're making decisions which change the shape of the world.

GALLIMARD: Not the world. At best, a small corner.

TOULON *enters, and sits at a desk upstage.*

Scene 3

French embassy. Beijing. 1961.

GALLIMARD *moves downstage, to* TOULON*'s desk.* SONG *remains upstage, watching.*

TOULON: And a more troublesome corner is hard to imagine.

GALLIMARD: So, the Americans plan to begin bombing?

TOULON: This is very secret, Gallimard: yes. The Americans don't have an embassy here. They're asking us to be their eyes and ears. Say Jack Kennedy signed an order to bomb North Vietnam, Laos. How would the Chinese react?

GALLIMARD: I think the Chinese will squawk—

TOULON: Uh-huh.

GALLIMARD: —but, in their hearts, they don't even like Ho Chi Minh.

Pause.

TOULON: What a bunch of jerks. Vietnam was *our* colony. Not only didn't the Americans help us fight to keep them, but now, seven years later, they've come back to grab the territory for themselves. It's very irritating.

GALLIMARD: With all due respect, sir, why should the Americans have won our war for us back in '54 if we didn't have the will to win it ourselves?

TOULON: You're kidding, aren't you?

Pause.

GALLIMARD: The Orientals simply want to be associated with whoever shows the most strength and power. You live with the Chinese, sir. Do you think they like Communism?

TOULON: I live in China. Not with the Chinese.

GALLIMARD: Well, I—

TOULON: *You* live with the Chinese.

GALLIMARD: Excuse me?

TOULON: I can't keep a secret.

GALLIMARD: What are you saying?

TOULON: Only that I'm not immune to gossip. So, you're keeping a native mistress. Don't answer. It's none of my business. (*Pause*) I'm sure she must be gorgeous.

GALLIMARD: Well . . .

TOULON: I'm impressed. You have the stamina to go out into the streets and hunt one down. Some of us have to be content with the wives of the expatriate community.

GALLIMARD: I do feel . . . fortunate.

TOULON: So, Gallimard, you've got the inside knowledge—what *do* the Chinese
   think?
GALLIMARD: Deep down, they miss the old days. You know, cappuccinos, men in
   tuxedos—
TOULON: So what do we tell the Americans about Vietnam?
GALLIMARD: Tell them there's a natural affinity between the West and the Ori-
   ent.
TOULON: And that you speak from experience?
GALLIMARD: The Orientals are people too. They want the good things we can
   give them. If the Americans demonstrate the will to win, the Vietnamese will
   welcome them into a mutually beneficial union.
TOULON: I don't see how the Vietnamese can stand up to American firepower.
GALLIMARD: Orientals will always submit to a greater force.
TOULON: I'll note your opinions in my report. The Americans always love to hear
   how "welcome" they'll be. (*He starts to exit*)
GALLIMARD: Sir?
TOULON: Mmmm?
GALLIMARD: This . . . rumor you've heard.
TOULON: Uh-huh?
GALLIMARD: How . . . widespread do you think it is?
TOULON: It's only widespread within this embassy. Where nobody talks because
   everybody is guilty. We were worried about you, Gallimard. We thought you
   were the only one here without a secret. Now you go and find a lotus blossom
   . . . and top us all. (*He exits*)
GALLIMARD (*To us*):   Toulon knows! And he approves! I was learning the bene-
   fits of being a man. We form our own clubs, sit behind thick doors, smoke—and
   celebrate the fact that we're still boys. (*He starts to move downstage, towards Song*)
   So, over the—

Suddenly COMRADE CHIN *enters.* GALLIMARD *backs away.*

GALLIMARD (*To* SONG):   No! Why does she have to come in?
SONG: Rene, be sensible. How can they understand the story without her? Now,
   don't embarrass yourself.

GALLIMARD *moves down center.*

GALLIMARD (*To us*):   Now, you will see why my story is so amusing to so many
   people. Why they snicker at parties in disbelief. Please—try to understand it
   from my point of view. We are all prisoners of our time and place. (*He exits*)

Scene 4

GALLIMARD *and* BUTTERFLY's *flat. Beijing. 1961.*

SONG (*To us*):   1961. The flat Monsieur Gallimard rented for us. An evening
   after he has gone.
CHIN: Okay, see if you can find out when the Americans plan to start bombing
   Vietnam. If you can find out what cities, even better.
SONG: I'll do my best, but I don't want to arouse his suspicions.
CHIN: Yeah, sure, of course. So, what else?

SONG: The Americans will increase troops in Vietnam to 170,000 soldiers with 120,000 militia and 11,000 American advisors.

CHIN (*Writing*): Wait, wait. 120,000 militia and—

SONG: —11,000 American—

CHIN: —American advisors. (*Beat*) How do you remember so much?

SONG: I'm an actor.

CHIN: Yeah. (*Beat*) Is that how come you dress like that?

SONG: Like what, Miss Chin?

CHIN: Like that dress! You're wearing a dress. And every time I come here, you're wearing a dress. Is that because you're an actor? Or what?

SONG: It's a . . . disguise, Miss Chin.

CHIN: Actors, I think they're all weirdos. My mother tells me actors are like gamblers or prostitutes or—

SONG: It helps me in my assignment.

Pause.

CHIN: You're not gathering information in any way that violates Communist Party principles, are you?

SONG: Why would I do that?

CHIN: Just checking. Remember: when working for the Great Proletarian State, you represent our Chairman Mao in every position you take.

SONG: I'll try to imagine the Chairman taking my positions.

CHIN: We all think of him this way. Good-bye, comrade. (*She starts to exit*) Comrade?

SONG: Yes?

CHIN: Don't forget: there is no homosexuality in China!

SONG: Yes, I've heard.

CHIN: Just checking. (*She exits*)

SONG (*To us*): What passes for a woman in modern China.

GALLIMARD *sticks his head out from the wings.*

GALLIMARD: Is she gone?

SONG: Yes, Rene. Please continue in your own fashion.

Scene 5

Beijing. 1961–63.

GALLIMARD *moves to the couch where* SONG *still sits. He lies down in her lap, and she strokes his forehead.*

GALLIMARD (*To us*): And so, over the years 1961, '62, '63, we settled into our routine, Butterfly and I. She would always have prepared a light snack and then, ever so delicately, and only if I agreed, she would start to pleasure me. With her hands, her mouth . . . too many ways to explain, and too sad, given my present situation. But mostly we would talk. About my life. Perhaps there is nothing more rare than to find a woman who passionately listens.

SONG *remains upstage, listening, as* HELGA *enters and plays a scene downstage with* GALLIMARD.

HELGA: Rene, I visited Dr. Bolleart this morning.

GALLIMARD: Why? Are you ill?

HELGA: No, no. You see, I wanted to ask him ... that question we've been discussing.

GALLIMARD: And I told you, it's only a matter of time. Why did you bring a doctor into this? We just have to keep trying—like a crapshoot, actually.

HELGA: I went, I'm sorry. But listen: he says there's nothing wrong with me.

GALLIMARD: You see? Now, will you stop—?

HELGA: Rene, he says he'd like you to go in and take some tests.

GALLIMARD: Why? So he can find there's nothing wrong with both of us?

HELGA: Rene, I don't ask for much. One trip! One visit! And then, whatever you want to do about it—you decide.

GALLIMARD: You're assuming he'll find something defective!

HELGA: No! Of course not! Whatever he finds—if he finds nothing, we decide what to do about nothing! But go!

GALLIMARD: If he finds nothing, we keep trying. Just like we do now.

HELGA: But at least we'll know! (*Pause*) I'm sorry. (*She starts to exit*)

GALLIMARD: Do you really want me to see Dr. Bolleart?

HELGA: Only if you want a child, Rene. We have to face the fact that time is running out. Only if you want a child. (*She exits*)

GALLIMARD (*To Song*):   I'm a modern man, Butterfly. And yet, I don't want to go. It's the same old voodoo. I feel like God himself is laughing at me if I can't produce a child.

SONG: You men of the West—you're obsessed by your odd desire for equality. Your wife can't give you a child, and *you're* going to the doctor?

GALLIMARD: Well, you see, she's already gone.

SONG: And because this incompetent can't find the defect, you now have to subject yourself to him? It's unnatural.

GALLIMARD: Well, what is the "natural" solution?

SONG: In Imperial China, when a man found that one wife was inadequate, he turned to another—to give him his son.

GALLIMARD: What do you—? I can't ... marry you, yet.

SONG: Please. I'm not asking you to be my husband. But I am already your wife.

GALLIMARD: Do you want to ... have my child?

SONG: I thought you'd never ask.

GALLIMARD: But, your career ... your—

SONG: Phooey on my career! That's your Western mind, twisting itself into strange shapes again. Of course I love my career. But what would I love most of all? To feel something inside me—day and night—something I know is yours. (*Pause*) Promise me ... you won't go to this doctor. Who is this Western quack to set himself as judge over the man I love? I know who is a man, and who is not. (*She exits*)

GALLIMARD (*To us*):   Dr. Bolleart? Of course I didn't go. What man would?

Scene 6

Beijing. 1963.
Party noises over the house speakers. RENEE *enters, wearing a revealing gown.*

GALLIMARD: 1963. A party at the Austrian embassy. None of us could remember the Austrian ambassador's name, which seemed somehow appropriate. (*To* RENEE) So, I tell the Americans, Diem must go. The U.S. wants to be respected by the Vietnamese, and yet they're propping up this nobody seminarian as her president. A man whose claim to fame is his sister-in-law imposing fanatic "moral order" campaigns? Oriental women—when they're good, they're very good, but when they're bad, they're Christians.

RENEE: Yeah.

GALLIMARD: And what do you do?

RENEE: I'm a student. My father exports a lot of useless stuff to the Third World.

GALLIMARD: How useless?

RENEE: You know. Squirt guns, confectioner's sugar, hula hoops . . .

GALLIMARD: I'm sure they appreciate the sugar.

RENEE: I'm here for two years to study Chinese.

GALLIMARD: Two years?

RENEE: That's what everybody says.

GALLIMARD: When did you arrive?

RENEE: Three weeks ago.

GALLIMARD: And?

RENEE: I like it. It's primitive, but . . . well, this is the place to learn Chinese, so here I am.

GALLIMARD: Why Chinese?

RENEE: I think it'll be important someday.

GALLIMARD: You do?

RENEE: Don't ask me when, but . . . that's what I think.

GALLIMARD: Well, I agree with you. One hundred percent. That's very farsighted.

RENEE: Yeah, Well of course, my father thinks I'm a complete weirdo.

GALLIMARD: He'll thank you someday.

RENEE: Like when the Chinese start buying hula hoops?

GALLIMARD: There're a billion bellies out there.

RENEE: And if they end up taking over the world—well, then I'll be lucky to know Chinese too, right?

Pause.

GALLIMARD: At this point, I don't see how the Chinese can possibly take—

RENEE: You know what I *don't* like about China?

GALLIMARD: Excuse me? No—what?

RENEE: Nothing to do at night.

GALLIMARD: You come to parties at embassies like everyone else.

RENEE: Yeah, but they get out at ten. And then what?

GALLIMARD: I'm afraid the Chinese idea of a dance hall is a dirt floor and a man with a flute.

RENEE: Are you married?

GALLIMARD: Yes. Why?

RENEE: You wanna . . . fool around?

Pause.

GALLIMARD: Sure.

RENEE: I'll wait for you outside. What's your name?

GALLIMARD: Gallimard. Rene.

RENEE: Weird. I'm Renee too. (*She exits*)

GALLIMARD (*To us*):   And so, I embarked on my first extraextramarital affair. Renee was picture perfect. With a body like those girls in the magazines. If I put a tissue paper over my eyes, I wouldn't have been able to tell the difference. And it was exciting to be with someone who wasn't afraid to be seen completely naked. But is it possible for a woman to be *too* uninhibited, *too* willing, so as to seem almost too . . . masculine?

Chuck Berry blares from the house speakers, then comes down in volume as RENEE *enters, toweling her hair.*

RENEE: You have a nice weenie.
GALLIMARD: What?
RENEE: Penis. You have a nice penis.
GALLIMARD: Oh. Well, thank you. That's very . . .
RENEE: What—can't take a compliment?
GALLIMARD: No, it's very . . . reassuring.
RENEE: But most girls don't come out and say it, huh?
GALLIMARD: And also . . . what did you call it?
RENEE: Oh. Most girls don't call it a "weenie," huh?
GALLIMARD: It sounds very—
RENEE: Small, I know.
GALLIMARD: I was going to say, "young."
RENEE: Yeah. Young, small, same thing. Most guys are pretty, uh, sensitive about that. Like, you know, I had a boyfriend back home in Denmark. I got mad at him once and called him a little weeniehead. He got so mad! He said at least I should call him a great big weeniehead.
GALLIMARD: I suppose I just say "penis."
RENEE: Yeah. That's pretty clinical. There's "cock," but that sounds like a chicken. And "prick" is painful, and "dick" is like you're talking about some-one who's not in the room.
GALLIMARD: Yes. It's a . . . bigger problem than I imagined.
RENEE: I—I think maybe it's because I really don't know what to do with them—that's why I call them "weenies."
GALLIMARD: Well, you did quite well with . . . mine.
RENEE: Thanks, but I mean, really *do* with them. Like, okay, have you ever looked at one? I mean, really?
GALLIMARD: No, I suppose when it's part of you, you sort of take it for granted.
RENEE: I guess. But, like, it just hangs there. This little . . . flap of flesh. And there's so much fuss that we make about it. Like, I think the reason we fight wars is because we wear clothes. Because no one knows—between the men, I mean—who has the bigger . . . weenie. So, if I'm a guy with a small one, I'm going to build a really big building or take over a really big piece of land or write a really long book so the other men don't know, right? But, see, it never really works, that's the problem. I mean, you conquer the country, or whatever, but you're still wearing clothes, so there's no way to prove absolutely whose is bigger or smaller. And that's what we call a civilized society. The whole world run by a bunch of men with pricks the size of pins. (*She exits*)
GALLIMARD (*To us*):   This was simply not acceptable.

A high-pitched chime rings through the air. SONG, *dressed as Butterfly, appears in the upstage special. She is obviously distressed. Her body swoons as she attempts to clip the stems of flowers she's arranging in a vase.*

GALLIMARD: But I kept up our affair, wildly, for several months. Why? I believe because of Butterfly. She knew the secret I was trying to hide. But, unlike a Western woman, she didn't confront me, threaten, even pout. I remembered the words of Puccini's *Butterfly:*

SONG: "Noi siamo gente avvezza / alle piccole cose / umili e silenziose."

GALLIMARD: "I come from a people / Who are accustomed to little / Humble and silent." I saw Pinkerton and Butterfly, and what she would say if he were unfaithful . . . nothing. She would cry, alone, into those wildly soft sleeves, once full of possessions, now empty to collect her tears. It was her tears and her silence that excited me, every time I visited Renee.

TOULON (*Offstage*): Gallimard!

TOULON enters. GALLIMARD turns towards him. During the next section, SONG, up center, begins to dance with the flowers. It is a drunken dance, where she breaks small pieces off the stems.

TOULON: They're killing him.

GALLIMARD: Who? I'm sorry? What?

TOULON: Bother you to come over at this late hour?

GALLIMARD: No . . . of course not.

TOULON: Not after you hear my secret. Champagne?

GALLIMARD: Um . . . thank you.

TOULON: You're surprised. There's something that you've wanted, Gallimard. No, not a promotion. Next time. Something in the world. You're not aware of this, but there's an informal gossip circle among intelligence agents. And some of ours heard from some of the Americans—

GALLIMARD: Yes?

TOULON: That the U.S. will allow the Vietnamese generals to stage a coup . . . and assassinate President Diem.

The chime rings again. TOULON freezes. GALLIMARD turns upstage and looks at BUT-TERFLY, who slowly and deliberately clips a flower off its stem. GALLIMARD turns back towards TOULON.

GALLIMARD: I think . . . that's a very wise move!

TOULON unfreezes.

TOULON: It's what you've been advocating. A toast?

GALLIMARD: Sure. I consider this a vindication.

TOULON: Not exactly. "To the test. Let's hope you pass."

They drink. The chime rings again. TOULON freezes. GALLIMARD turns upstage, and SONG clips another flower.

GALLIMARD (*To TOULON*): The test?

TOULON (*Unfreezing*): It's a test of everything you've been saying. I personally think the generals probably will stop the Communists. And you'll be a hero. But if anything goes wrong, then your opinions won't be worth a pig's ear. I'm sure that won't happen. But sometimes it's easier when they don't listen to you.

GALLIMARD: They're your opinions too, aren't they?

TOULON: Personally, yes.

GALLIMARD: So we agree.

TOULON: But my opinions aren't on that report. Yours are. Cheers.

TOULON *turns away from* GALLIMARD *and raises his glass. At that instant* SONG *picks up the vase and hurls it to the ground. It shatters.* SONG *sinks down amidst the shards of the vase, in a calm, childlike trance. She sings softly, as if reciting a child's nursery rhyme.*

SONG (*Repeat as necessary*):   "The whole world over, the white man travels, setting anchor, wherever he likes. Life's not worth living, unless he finds, the finest maidens, of every land . . ."

GALLIMARD *turns downstage towards us.* SONG *continues singing.*

GALLIMARD: I shook as I left his house. That coward! That worm! To put the burden for his decisions on my shoulders!
  I started for Renee's. But no, that was all I needed. A schoolgirl who would question the role of the penis in modern society. What I wanted was revenge. A vessel to contain my humiliation. Though I hadn't seen her in several weeks, I headed for Butterfly's.

GALLIMARD *enters* SONG's *apartment.*

SONG: Oh! Rene . . . I was dreaming!
GALLIMARD: You've been drinking?
SONG: If I can't sleep, then yes, I drink. But then, it gives me these dreams which—Rene, it's been almost three weeks since you visited me last.
GALLIMARD: I know. There's been a lot going on in the world.
SONG: Fortunately I am drunk. So I can speak freely. It's not the world, it's you and me. And an old problem. Even the softest skin becomes like leather to a man who's touched it too often. I confess I don't know how to stop it. I don't know how to become another woman.
GALLIMARD: I have a request.
SONG: Is this a solution? Or are you ready to give up the flat?
GALLIMARD: It may be a solution. But I'm sure you won't like it.
SONG: Oh well, that's very important. "Like it?" Do you think I "like" lying here alone, waiting, always waiting for your return? Please—don't worry about what I may not "like."
GALLIMARD: I want to see you . . . naked.

Silence.

SONG: I thought you understood my modesty. So you want me to—what—strip? Like a big cowboy girl? Shiny pasties on my breasts? Shall I fling my kimono over my head and yell "ya-hoo" in the process? I thought you respected my shame!
GALLIMARD: I believe you gave me your shame many years ago.
SONG: Yes—and it is just like a white devil to use it against me. I can't believe it. I thought myself so repulsed by the passive Oriental and the cruel white man. Now I see—we are always most revolted by the things hidden within us.
GALLIMARD: I just mean—
SONG: Yes?
GALLIMARD: —that it will remove the only barrier left between us.
SONG: No, Rene. Don't couch your request in sweet words. Be yourself—a cad—

and know that my love is enough, that I submit—submit to the worst that you can give me. (*Pause*) Well, come. Strip me. Whatever happens, know that you have willed it. Our love, in your hands. I'm helpless before my man.

GALLIMARD *starts to cross the room.*

GALLIMARD: Did I not undress her because I knew, somewhere deep down, what I would find? Perhaps. Happiness is so rare that our mind can turn somersaults to protect it.

At the time, I only knew that I was seeing Pinkerton stalking towards his Butterfly, ready to reward her love with his lecherous hands. The image sickened me, pulled me to my knees, so I was crawling towards her like a worm. By the time I reached her, Pinkerton . . . had vanished from my heart. To be replaced by something new, something unnatural, that flew in the face of all I'd learned in the world—something very close to love.

He grabs her around the waist; she strokes his hair.

GALLIMARD: Butterfly, forgive me.
SONG: Rene . . .
GALLIMARD: For everything. From the start.
SONG: I'm . . .
GALLIMARD: I want to—
SONG: I'm pregnant. (*Beat*) I'm pregnant. (*Beat*) I'm pregnant.

(*Beat.*)

GALLIMARD: I want to marry you!

Scene 7
GALLIMARD *and* BUTTERFLY*'s flat. Beijing. 1963.*
Downstage, SONG *paces as* COMRADE CHIN *reads from her notepad. Upstage,* GALLI-MARD *is still kneeling. He remains on his knees throughout the scene, watching it.*

SONG: I need a baby.
CHIN (*From pad*): He's been spotted going to a dorm.
SONG: I need a baby.
CHIN: At the Foreign Language Institute.
SONG: I need a baby.
CHIN: The room of a Danish girl . . . What do you mean, you need a baby?!
SONG: Tell Comrade Kang—last night, the entire mission, it could've ended.
CHIN: What do you mean?
SONG: Tell Kang—he told me to strip.
CHIN: *Strip?!*
SONG: Write!
CHIN: I tell you, I don't understand nothing about this case anymore. Nothing.
SONG: He told me to strip, and I took a chance. Oh, we Chinese, we know how to gamble.
CHIN (*Writing*): " . . . told him to strip."
SONG: My palms were wet, I had to make a split-second decision.
CHIN: Hey! Can you slow down?!

Pause.

SONG: You write faster, I'm the artist here. Suddenly, it hit me—"All he wants is
for her to submit. Once a woman submits, a man is always ready to become
'generous.' "

CHIN: You're just gonna end up with rough notes.

SONG: And it worked! He gave in! Now, if I can just present him with a baby. A
Chinese baby with blond hair—he'll be mine for life!

CHIN: Kang will never agree! The trading of babies has to be a counterrevolutionary act!

SONG: Sometimes, a counterrevolutionary act is necessary to counter a counter-
revolutionary act.

Pause.

CHIN: Wait.

SONG: I need one . . . in seven months. Make sure it's a boy.

CHIN: This doesn't sound like something the Chairman would do. Maybe you'd
better talk to Comrade Kang yourself.

SONG: Good. I will.

CHIN *gets up to leave.*

SONG: Miss Chin? Why, in the Peking Opera, are women's roles played by men?

CHIN: I don't know. Maybe, a reactionary remnant of male—

SONG: No. (*Beat*) Because only a man knows how a woman is supposed to act.

CHIN *exits. Song turns upstage, towards* GALLIMARD.

GALLIMARD (*Calling after* CHIN): Good riddance! (*To* SONG) I could forget all
that betrayal in an instant, you know. If you'd just come back and become
Butterfly again.

SONG: Fat chance. You're here in prison, rotting in a cell. And I'm on a plane,
winging my way back to China. Your President pardoned me of our treason, you
know.

GALLIMARD: Yes, I read about that.

SONG: Must make you feel . . . lower than shit.

GALLIMARD: But don't you, even a little bit, wish you were here with me?

SONG: I'm an artist, Rene. You were my greatest . . . acting challenge. (*She laughs*)
It doesn't matter how rotten I answer, does it? You still adore me. That's why I
love you, Rene. (*She points to us*) So—you were telling your audience about the
night I announced I was pregnant.

GALLIMARD *puts his arms around* SONG's *waist. He and* SONG *are in the positions they
were in at the end of Scene 6.*

Scene 8

Same.

GALLIMARD: I'll divorce my wife. We'll live together here, and then later in
France.

SONG: I feel so . . . ashamed.

GALLIMARD: Why?

SONG: I had begun to lose faith. And now, you shame me with your generosity.

GALLIMARD: Generosity? No, I'm proposing for very selfish reasons.

SONG: Your apologies only make me feel more ashamed. My outburst a moment ago!

GALLIMARD: Your outburst? What about my request?!

SONG: You've been very patient dealing with my . . . eccentricities. A Western man, used to women freer with their bodies—

GALLIMARD: It was sick! Don't make excuses for me.

SONG: I have to. You don't seem willing to make them for yourself.

Pause.

GALLIMARD: You're crazy.

SONG: I'm happy. Which often looks like crazy.

GALLIMARD: Then make me crazy. Marry me.

Pause.

SONG: No.

GALLIMARD: What?

SONG: Do I sound silly, a slave, if I say I'm not worthy?

GALLIMARD: Yes. In fact you do. No one has loved me like you.

SONG: Thank you. And no one ever will. I'll see to that.

GALLIMARD: So what is the problem?

SONG: Rene, we Chinese are realists. We understand rice, gold, and guns. You are a diplomat. Your career is skyrocketing. Now, what would happen if you divorced your wife to marry a Communist Chinese actress?

GALLIMARD: That's not being realistic. That's defeating yourself before you begin.

SONG: We must conserve our strength for the battles we can win.

GALLIMARD: That sounds like a fortune cookie!

SONG: Where do you think fortune cookies come from?

GALLIMARD: I don't care.

SONG: You do. So do I. And we should. That is why I say I'm not worthy. I'm worthy to love and even to be loved by you. But I am not worthy to end the career of one of the West's most promising diplomats.

GALLIMARD: It's not that great a career! I made it sound like more than it is!

SONG: Modesty will get you nowhere. Flatter yourself, and you flatter me. I'm flattered to decline your offer. (*She exits*)

GALLIMARD (*To us*): Butterfly and I argued all night. And, in the end, I left, knowing I would never be her husband. She went away for several months—to the countryside, like a small animal. Until the night I received her call.

A baby's cry from offstage. SONG *enters, carrying a child.*

SONG: He looks like you.

GALLIMARD: Oh! (*Beat; he approaches the baby*) Well, babies are never very attractive at birth.

SONG: Stop!

GALLIMARD: I'm sure he'll grow more beautiful with age. More like his mother.

SONG: "Chi vide mai / a bimbo del Giappon . . . "

GALLIMARD: "What baby, I wonder, was ever born in Japan"—or China, for that matter—

SONG: " . . . occhi azzurrini?"

GALLIMARD: "With azure eyes"—they're actually sort of brown, wouldn't you say?

SONG: "E il labbro."

GALLIMARD: "And such lips!" (*He kisses* SONG) And such lips.

SONG: "E i ricciolini d'oro schietto?"

GALLIMARD: "And such a head of golden"—if slightly patchy—"curls?"

SONG: I'm going to call him "Peepee."

GALLIMARD: Darling, could you repeat that because I'm sure a rickshaw just flew by overhead.

SONG: You heard me.

GALLIMARD: "Song Peepee"? May I suggest Michael, or Stephan, or Adolph?

SONG: You may, but I won't listen.

GALLIMARD: You can't be serious. Can you imagine the time this child will have in school?

SONG: In the West, yes.

GALLIMARD: It's worse than naming him Ping Pong or Long Dong or—

SONG: But he's never going to live in the West, is he?

Pause.

GALLIMARD: That wasn't my choice.

SONG: It is mine. And this is my promise to you: I will raise him, he will be our child, but he will never burden you outside of China.

GALLIMARD: Why do you make these promises? I want to be burdened! I want a scandal to cover the papers!

SONG (*To us*):   Prophetic.

GALLIMARD: I'm serious.

SONG: So am I. His name is as I registered it. And he will never live in the West.

SONG *exits with the child.*

GALLIMARD (*To us*):   It is possible that her stubbornness only made me want her more. That drawing back at the moment of my capitulation was the most brilliant strategy she could have chosen. It is possible. But it is also possible that by this point she could have said, could have done . . . anything, and I would have adored her still.

Scene 9

Beijing. 1966.

A driving rhythm of Chinese percussion fills the stage.

GALLIMARD: And then, China began to change. Mao became very old, and his cult became very strong. And, like many old men, he entered his second childhood. So he handed over the reins of state to those with minds like his own. And children ruled the Middle Kingdom with complete caprice. The doctrine of the Cultural Revolution implied continuous anarchy. Contact between Chinese and foreigners became impossible. Our flat was confiscated. Her fame and my money now counted against us.

Two dancers in Mao suits and red-starred caps enter, and begin crudely mimicking revolutionary violence, in an agitprop fashion.

GALLIMARD: And somehow the American war went wrong too. Four hundred thousand dollars were being spent for every Viet Cong killed; so General Westmoreland's remark that the Oriental does not value life the way Americans do was oddly accurate. Why weren't the Vietnamese people giving in? Why were they content instead to die and die and die again?

TOULON *enters.*

TOULON: Congratulations, Gallimard.
GALLIMARD: Excuse me, sir?
TOULON: Not a promotion. That was last time. You're going home.
GALLIMARD: What?
TOULON: Don't say I didn't warn you.
GALLIMARD: I'm being transferred . . . because I was wrong about the American war?
TOULON: Of course not. We don't care about the Americans. We care about your mind. The quality of your analysis. In general, everything you've predicted here in the Orient . . . just hasn't happened,
GALLIMARD: I think that's premature.
TOULON: Don't force me to be blunt. Okay, you said China was ready to open to Western trade. The only thing they're trading out there are Western heads. And, yes, you said the Americans would succeed in Indochina. You were kidding, right?
GALLIMARD: I think the end is in sight.
TOULON: Don't be pathetic. And don't take this personally. You were wrong. It's not your fault.
GALLIMARD: But I'm going home.
TOULON: Right. Could I have the number of your mistress? (*Beat*) Joke! Joke! Eat a croissant for me.

TOULON *exits.* SONG, *wearing a Mao suit, is dragged in from the wings as part of the upstage dance. They "beat" her, then lampoon the acrobatics of the Chinese opera, as she is made to kneel onstage.*

GALLIMARD (*Simultaneously*): I don't care to recall how Butterfly and I said our hurried farewell. Perhaps it was better to end our affair before it killed her.

GALLIMARD *exits.* COMRADE CHIN *walks across the stage with a banner reading: "The Actor Renounces His Decadent Profession!" She reaches the kneeling* SONG. *Percussion stops with a thud. Dancers strike poses.*

CHIN: Actor-oppressor, for years you have lived above the common people and looked down on their labor. While the farmer ate millet—
SONG: I ate pastries from France and sweetmeats from silver trays.
CHIN: And how did you come to live in such an exalted position?

Song: I was a plaything for the imperialists!
Chin: What did you do?
Song: I shamed China by allowing myself to be corrupted by a foreigner . . .
Chin: What does this mean? The People demand a full confession!
Song: I engaged in the lowest perversions with China's enemies!
Chin: What perversions? Be more clear!
Song: I let him put it up my ass!

Dancers look over, disgusted.

Chin: Aaaa-ya! How can you use such sickening language?!
Song: My language . . . is only as foul as the crimes I committed . . .
Chin: Yeah. That's better. So—what do you want to do now?
Song: I want to serve the people.

Percussion starts up, with Chinese strings.

Chin: What?
Song: I want to serve the people!

Dancers regain their revolutionary smiles, and begin a dance of victory.

Chin: What?!
Song: I want to serve the people!!

Dancers unveil a banner: "The Actor Is Rehabilitated!" Song *remains kneeling before* Chin, *as the dancers bounce around them, then exit. Music out.*

Scene 10

A commune. Hunan Province. 1970.

Chin: How you planning to do that?
Song: I've already worked four years in the fields of Hunan, Comrade Chin.
Chin: So? Farmers work all their lives. Let me see your hands.

Song *holds them out for her inspection.*

Chin: Goddamn! Still so smooth! How long does it take to turn you actors into
        good anythings? Hunh. You've just spent too many years in luxury to be any
        good to the Revolution.
Song: I served the Revolution.
Chin: Serve the Revolution? Bullshit! You wore dresses! Don't tell me—I was
        there. I saw you! You and your white vice-consul! Stuck up there in your flat,
        living off the People's Treasury! Yeah, I knew what was going on! You two
        . . . homos! Homos! Homos! (*Pause; she composes herself*) Ah! Well . . . you will
        serve the people, all right. But not with the Revolution's money. This time, you
        use your own money.
Song: I have no money.
Chin: Shut up! And you won't stink up China anymore with your pervert stuff.
        You'll pollute the place where pollution begins—the West.
Song: What do you mean?

CHIN: Shut up! You're going to France. Without a cent in your pocket. You find your consul's house, you make him pay your expenses—

SONG: No.

CHIN: And you give us weekly reports! Useful information!

SONG: That's crazy. It's been four years.

CHIN: Either that, or back to rehabilitation center!

SONG: Comrade Chin, he's not going to support me! Not in France! He's a white man! I was just his plaything—

CHIN: Oh yuck! Again with the sickening language? Where's my stick?

SONG: You don't understand the mind of a man.

Pause.

CHIN: Oh no? No I don't? Then how come I'm married, huh? How come I got a man? Five, six years ago, you always tell me those kind of things, I felt very bad. But not now! Because what does the Chairman say? He tells us *I'm* now the smart one, you're now the nincompoop! *You're* the blockhead, the harebrain, the nitwit! You think you're so smart? You understand "The Mind of a Man"? Good! Then *you* go to France and be a pervert for Chairman Mao!

CHIN *and* SONG *exit in opposite directions.*

Scene 11

Paris. 1968-70.
GALLIMARD *enters.*

GALLIMARD: And what was waiting for me back in Paris? Well, better Chinese food than I'd eaten in China. Friends and relatives. A little accounting, regular schedule, keeping track of traffic violations in the suburbs. . . . And the indignity of students shouting the slogans of Chairman Mao at me—in French.

HELGA: Rene? Rene? (*She enters, soaking wet*) I've had a . . . a problem. (*She sneezes*)

GALLIMARD: You're wet.

HELGA: Yes, I . . . coming back from the grocer's. A group of students, waving red flags, they—

GALLIMARD *fetches a towel.*

HELGA: —they ran by, I was caught up along with them. Before I knew what was happening—

GALLIMARD *gives her the towel.*

HELGA: Thank you. The police started firing water cannons at us. I tried to shout, to tell them I was the wife of a diplomat, but—you know how it is . . . (*Pause*) Needless to say, I lost the groceries. Rene, what's happening to France?

GALLIMARD: What's—? Well, nothing, really.

HELGA: Nothing?! The storefronts are in flames, there's glass in the streets, buildings are toppling—and I'm wet!

GALLIMARD: Nothing! . . . that I care to think about.

HELGA: And is that why you stay in this room?

GALLIMARD: Yes, in fact.

HELGA: With the incense burning? You know something? I hate incense. It smells so sickly sweet.

GALLIMARD: Well, I hate the French. Who just smell—period!

HELGA: And the Chinese were better?

GALLIMARD: Please—don't start.

HELGA: When we left, this exact same thing, the riots—

GALLIMARD: No, no . . .

HELGA: Students screaming slogans, smashing down doors—

GALLIMARD: Helga—

HELGA: It was all going on in China, too. Don't you remember?!

GALLIMARD: Helga! Please! (*Pause*) You have never understood China, have you? You walk in here with these ridiculous ideas, that the West is falling apart, that China was spitting in our faces. You come in, dripping of the streets, and you leave water all over my floor. (*He grabs* HELGA's *towel, begins mopping up the floor*)

HELGA: But it's the truth!

GALLIMARD: Helga, I want a divorce.

Pause; GALLIMARD *continues, mopping the floor.*

HELGA: I take it back. China is . . . beautiful. Incense, I like incense.

GALLIMARD: I've had a mistress.

HELGA: So?

GALLIMARD: For eight years.

HELGA: I knew you would. I knew you would the day I married you. And now what? You want to marry her?

GALLIMARD: I can't. She's in China.

HELGA: I see. You want to leave. For someone who's not here, is that right?

GALLIMARD: That's right.

HELGA: You can't live with her, but still you don't want to live with me.

GALLIMARD: That's right.

Pause.

HELGA: Shit. How terrible that I can figure that out. (*Pause*) I never thought I'd say it. But, in China, I was happy. I knew, in my own way, I knew that you were not everything you pretended to be. But the pretense—going on your arm to the embassy ball, visiting your office and the guards saying, "Good morning, good morning, Madame Gallimard"—the pretense . . . was very good indeed. (*Pause*) I hope everyone is mean to you for the rest of your life. (*She exits*)

GALLIMARD (*To us*): Prophetic.

MARC *enters with two drinks.*

GALLIMARD (*To* MARC): In China, I was different from all other men.

MARC: Sure. You were white. Here's your drink.

GALLIMARD: I felt . . . touched.

MARC: In the head? Rene, I don't want to hear about the Oriental love goddess.

Okay? One night—can we just drink and throw up without a lot of conversation?

GALLIMARD: You still don't believe me, do you?

MARC: Sure I do. She was the most beautiful, et cetera, et cetera, blasé blasé.

Pause.

GALLIMARD: My life in the West has been such a disappointment.

MARC: Life in the West is like that. You'll get used to it. Look, you're driving me away. I'm leaving. Happy, now? (*He exits, then returns*) Look, I have a date tomorrow night. You wanna come? I can fix you up with—

GALLIMARD: Of course. I would love to come.

Pause.

MARC: Uh—on second thought, no. You'd better get ahold of yourself first.

He exits; GALLIMARD *nurses his drink.*

GALLIMARD (*To us*): This is the ultimate cruelty, isn't it? That I can talk and talk and to anyone listening, it's only air—too rich a diet to be swallowed by a mundane world. Why can't anyone understand? That in China, I once loved, and was loved by, very simply, the Perfect Woman.

SONG *enters, dressed as Butterfly in wedding dress.*

GALLIMARD (*To* SONG): Not again. My imagination is hell. Am I asleep this time? Or did I drink too much?

SONG: Rene?

GALLIMARD: God, it's too painful! That you speak?

SONG: What are you talking about? Rene—touch me.

GALLIMARD: Why?

SONG: I'm real. Take my hand.

GALLIMARD: Why? So you can disappear again and leave me clutching at the air? For the entertainment of my neighbors who—?

SONG *touches* GALLIMARD.

SONG: Rene?

GALLIMARD *takes* SONG*'s hand. Silence.*

GALLIMARD: Butterfly? I never doubted you'd return.

SONG: You hadn't . . . forgotten—?

GALLIMARD: Yes, actually, I've forgotten everything. My mind, you see—there wasn't enough room in this hard head—not for the world *and* for you. No, there was only room for one. (*Beat*) Come, look. See? Your bed has been waiting, with the Klimt poster you like, and—see? The xiang lu [incense burner] you gave me?

SONG: I . . . I don't know what to say.

GALLIMARD: There's nothing to say. Not at the end of a long trip. Can I make you some tea?

SONG: But where's your wife?

GALLIMARD: She's by my side. She's by my side at last.

GALLIMARD reaches to embrace SONG. SONG sidesteps, dodging him.

GALLIMARD: Why?!

SONG (*To us*): So I did return to Rene in Paris. Where I found—

GALLIMARD: Why do you run away? Can't we show them how we embraced that evening?

SONG: Please. I'm talking.

GALLIMARD: You have to do what I say! I'm conjuring you up in *my* mind!

SONG: Rene, I've never done what you've said. Why should it be any different in your mind? Now split—the story moves on, and I must change.

GALLIMARD: I welcomed you into my home! I didn't have to, you know! I could've left you penniless on the streets of Paris! But I took you in!

SONG: Thank you.

GALLIMARD: So . . . please . . . don't change.

SONG: You know I have to. You know I will. And anyway, what difference does it make? No matter what your eyes tell you, you can't ignore the truth. You already know too much.

GALLIMARD exits. SONG turns to us.

SONG: The change I'm going to make requires about five minutes. So I thought you might want to take this opportunity to stretch your legs, enjoy a drink, or listen to the musicians. I'll be here, when you return, right where you left me.

SONG goes to a mirror in front of which is a wash basin of water. She starts to remove her makeup as stagelights go to half and houselights come up.

ACT THREE

Scene 1

A courthouse in Paris. 1986.

As he promised, SONG has completed the bulk of his transformation, onstage by the time the houselights go down and the stagelights come up full. He removes his wig and kimono, leaving them on the floor. Underneath, he wears a well-cut suit.

SONG: So I'd done my job better than I had a right to expect. Well, give him some credit, too. He's right—I was in a fix when I arrived in Paris. I walked from the airport into town, then I located, by blind groping, the Chinatown district. Let me make one thing clear: whatever else may be said about the Chinese, they are stingy! I slept in doorways three days until I could find a tailor who would make me this kimono on credit. As it turns out, maybe I didn't even need it. Maybe he would've been happy to see me in a simple shift and mascara. But . . . better safe than sorry.

That was 1970, when I arrived in Paris. For the next fifteen years, yes, I lived a very comfy life. Some relief, believe me, after four years on a fucking commune in Nowheresville, China. Rene supported the boy and me, and I did some demonstrations around the country as part of my "cultural exchange" cover. And then there was the spying.

Song *moves upstage, to a chair.* Toulon *enters as a judge, wearing the appropriate wig and robes. He sits near* Song. *It's 1986, and* Song *is testifying in a courtroom.*

Song: Not much at first. Rene had lost all his high-level contacts. Comrade Chin wasn't very interested in parking-ticket statistics. But finally, at my urging, Rene got a job as a courier, handling sensitive documents. He'd photograph them for me, and I'd pass them on to the Chinese embassy.

Judge: Did he understand the extent of his activity?

Song: He didn't ask. He knew that I needed those documents, and that was enough.

Judge: But he must've known he was passing classified information.

Song: I can't say.

Judge: He never asked what you were going to do with them?

Song: Nope.

Pause.

Judge: There is one thing that the court—indeed, that all of France—would like to know.

Song: Fire away.

Judge: Did Monsieur Gallimard know you were a man?

Song: Well, he never saw me completely naked. Ever.

Judge: But surely, he must've . . . how can I put this?

Song: Put it however you like. I'm not shy. He must've felt around?

Judge: Mmmmm.

Song: Not really. I did all the work. He just laid back. Of course we did enjoy more . . . complete union, and I suppose he *might* have wondered why I was always on my stomach, but . . . But what you're thinking is, "Of course a wrist must've brushed . . . a hand hit . . . over twenty years!" Yeah. Well, Your Honor, it was my job to make him think I was a woman. And chew on this: it wasn't all that hard. See, my mother was a prostitute along the Bundt before the Revolution. And, uh, I think it's fair to say she learned a few things about Western men. So I borrowed her knowledge. In service to my country.

Judge: Would you care to enlighten the court with this secret knowledge? I'm sure we're all very curious.

Song: I'm sure you are. (*Pause*) Okay, Rule One is: Men always believe what they want to hear. So a girl can tell the most obnoxious lies and the guys will believe them every time—"This is my first time"—"That's the biggest I've ever seen"—or *both*, which, if you really think about it, is not possible in a single lifetime. You've maybe heard those phrases a few times in your own life, yes, Your Honor?

Judge: It's not my life, Monsieur Song, which is on trial today.

Song: Okay, okay, just trying to lighten up the proceedings. Tough room.

Judge: Go on.

Song: Rule Two: As soon as a Western man comes into contact with the East— he's already confused. The West has sort of an international rape mentality towards the East. Do you know rape mentality?

Judge: Give us your definition, please.

SONG: Basically, "Her mouth says no, but her eyes say yes."

The West thinks of itself as masculine—big guns, big industry, big money—so the East is feminine—weak, delicate, poor . . . but good at art, and full of inscrutable wisdom—the feminine mystique.

Her mouth says no, but her eyes say yes. The West believes the East, deep down, *wants* to be dominated—because a woman can't think for herself.

JUDGE: What does this have to do with my question?

SONG: You expect Oriental countries to submit to your guns, and you expect Oriental women to be submissive to your men. That's why you say they make the best wives.

JUDGE: But why would that make it possible for you to fool Monsieur Gallimard? Please—get to the point.

SONG: One, because when he finally met his fantasy woman, he wanted more than anything to believe that she was, in fact, a woman. And second, I am an Oriental. And being an Oriental, I could never be completely a man.

Pause.

JUDGE: Your armchair political theory is tenuous, Monsieur Song.

SONG: You think so? That's why you'll lose in all your dealings with the East.

JUDGE: Just answer my question: did he know you were a man?

Pause.

SONG: You know, Your Honor, I never asked.

Scene 2

Same.

Music from the "Death Scene" from Butterfly *blares over the house speakers. It is the loudest thing we've heard in this play.*

GALLIMARD *enters, crawling towards* SONG's *wig and kimono.*

GALLIMARD: Butterfly? Butterfly?

SONG *remains a man, in the witness box, delivering a testimony we do not hear.*

GALLIMARD (*To us*): In my moment of greatest shame, here, in this courtroom—with that . . . person up there, telling the world. . . . What strikes me especially is how shallow he is, how glib and obsequious . . . completely . . . without substance! The type that prowls around discos with a gold medallion stinking of garlic. So little like my Butterfly.

Yet even in this moment my mind remains agile, flipflopping like a man on a trampoline. Even now, my picture dissolves, and I see that . . . witness . . . talking to me.

SONG *suddenly stands straight up in his witness box, and looks at* GALLIMARD.

SONG: Yes. You. White man.

SONG *steps out of the witness box, and moves downstage towards* GALLIMARD. *Light change.*

GALLIMARD (*To* SONG): Who? Me?

SONG: Do you see any other white men?

GALLIMARD: Yes. There're white men all around. This is a French courtroom.

SONG: So you are an adventurous imperialist. Tell me, why did it take you so long? To come back to this place?

GALLIMARD: What place?

SONG: This theatre in China. Where we met many years ago.

GALLIMARD (*To us*): And once again, against my will, I am transported.

Chinese opera music comes up on the speakers. SONG *begins to do opera moves, as he did the night they met.*

SONG: Do you remember? The night you gave your heart?

GALLIMARD: It was a long time ago.

SONG: Not long enough. A night that turned your world upside down.

GALLIMARD: Perhaps.

SONG: Oh, be honest with me. What's another bit of flattery when you've already given me twenty years' worth? It's a wonder my head hasn't swollen to the size of China.

GALLIMARD: Who's to say it hasn't?

SONG: Who's to say? And what's the shame? In pride? You think I could've pulled this off if I wasn't already full of pride when we met? No, not just pride. Arrogance. It takes arrogance, really—to believe you can will, with your eyes and your lips, the destiny of another. (*He dances*) C'mon. Admit it. You still want me. Even in slacks and a button-down collar.

GALLIMARD: I don't see what the point of—

SONG: You don't? Well maybe, Rene, just maybe—I want you.

GALLIMARD: You do?

SONG: Then again, maybe I'm just playing with you. How can you tell? (*Reprising his feminine character, he sidles up to* GALLIMARD) "How I wish there were even a small cafe to sit in. With men in tuxedos, and cappuccinos, and bad expatriate jazz." Now you want to kiss me, don't you?

GALLIMARD (*Pulling away*): What makes you—?

SONG: —so sure? See? I take the words from your mouth. Then I wait for you to come and retrieve them. (*He reclines on the floor*)

GALLIMARD: Why?! Why do you treat me so cruelly?

SONG: Perhaps I *was* treating you cruelly. But now—I'm being nice. Come here, my little one.

GALLIMARD: I'm not your little one!

SONG: My mistake. It's I who am *your* little one, right?

GALLIMARD: Yes, I—

SONG: So come get your little one. If you like. I may even let you strip me.

GALLIMARD: I mean, you were! Before . . . but not like this!

SONG: I was? Then perhaps I still am. If you look hard enough. (*He starts to remove his clothes*)

GALLIMARD: What—what are you doing?

SONG: Helping you to see through my act.

GALLIMARD: Stop that! I don't want to! I don't—

SONG: Oh, but you asked me to strip, remember?

GALLIMARD: What? That was years ago! And I took it back!

SONG: No. You postponed it. Postponed the inevitable. Today, the inevitable has come calling.

From the speakers, cacophony: BUTTERFLY *mixed in with Chinese gongs.*

GALLIMARD: No! Stop! I don't want to see!

SONG: Then look away.

GALLIMARD: You're only in my mind! All this is in my mind! I order you! To stop!

SONG: To what? To strip? That's just what I'm—

GALLIMARD: No! Stop! I want you—!

SONG: You want me?

GALLIMARD: To stop!

SONG: You know something, Rene? Your mouth says no, but your eyes say yes. Turn them away. I dare you.

GALLIMARD: I don't have to! Every night, you say you're going to strip, but then I beg you and you stop!

SONG: I guess tonight is different.

GALLIMARD: Why? Why should that be?

SONG: Maybe I've become frustrated. Maybe I'm saying "Look at me, you fool!" Or maybe I'm just feeling . . . sexy. (*He is down to his briefs*)

GALLIMARD: Please. This is unnecessary. I know what you are.

SONG: Do you? What am I?

GALLIMARD: A—a man.

SONG: You don't really believe that.

GALLIMARD: Yes I do! I knew all the time somewhere that my happiness was temporary, my love a deception. But my mind kept the knowledge at bay. To make the wait bearable.

SONG: Monsieur Gallimard—the wait is over.

SONG *drops his briefs. He is naked. Sound cue out. Slowly, we and* SONG *come to the realization that what we had thought to be* GALLIMARD's *sobbing is actually his laughter.*

GALLIMARD: Oh god! What an idiot! Of course!

SONG: Rene—what?

GALLIMARD: Look at you! You're a man! (*He bursts into laughter again*)

SONG: I fail to see what's so funny!

GALLIMARD: "You fail to see—!" I mean, you never did have much of a sense of humor, did you? I just think it's ridiculously funny that I've wasted so much time on just a man!

SONG: Wait, I'm not "just a man."

GALLIMARD: No? Isn't that what you've been trying to convince me of?

SONG: Yes, but what I mean—

GALLIMARD: And now, I finally believe you, and you tell me it's not true? I think you must have some kind of identity problem.

SONG: Will you listen to me?

GALLIMARD: Why?! I've been listening to you for twenty years. Don't I deserve a vacation?

SONG: I'm not just any man!

GALLIMARD: Then, what exactly are you?

SONG: Rene, how can you ask—? Okay, what about this?

He picks up Butterfly's robes, starts to dance around. No music.

GALLIMARD: Yes, that's very nice. I have to admit.

SONG *holds out his arm to* GALLIMARD.

SONG: It's the same skin you've worshiped for years. Touch it.
GALLIMARD: Yes, it does feel the same.
SONG: Now—close your eyes.

SONG *covers* GALLIMARD*'s eyes with one hand. With the other,* SONG *draws* GALLIMARD*'s hand up to his face.* GALLIMARD, *like a blind man, lets his hands run over* SONG*'s face.*

GALLIMARD: This skin, I remember. The curve of her face, the softness of her cheek, her hair against the back of my hand . . .
SONG: I'm your Butterfly. Under the robes, beneath everything, it was always me. Now, open your eyes and admit it—you adore me. (*He removes his hand from* GALLIMARD*'s eyes*)
GALLIMARD: You, who knew every inch of my desires—how could you, of all people, have made such a mistake?
SONG: What?
GALLIMARD: You showed me your true self. When all I loved was the lie. A perfect lie, which you let fall to the ground—and now, it's old and soiled.
SONG: So—you never really loved me? Only when I was playing a part?
GALLIMARD: I'm a man who loved a woman created by a man. Everything else—simply falls short.

Pause.

SONG: What am I supposed to do now?
GALLIMARD: You were a fine spy, Monsieur Song, with an even finer accomplice. But now I believe you should go. Get out of my life!
SONG: Go where? Rene, you can't live without me. Not after twenty years.
GALLIMARD: I certainly can't live with you—not after twenty years of betrayal.
SONG: Don't be so stubborn! Where will you go?
GALLIMARD: I have a date . . . with my Butterfly.
SONG: So, throw away your pride. And come . . .
GALLIMARD: Get away from me! Tonight, I've finally learned to tell fantasy from reality. And, knowing the difference, I choose fantasy.
SONG: *I'm* your fantasy!
GALLIMARD: You? You're as real as hamburger. Now get out! I have a date with my Butterfly and I don't want your body polluting the room! (*He tosses* SONG*'s suit at him*) Look at these—you dress like a pimp.
SONG: Hey! These are Armani slacks and—! (*He puts on his briefs and slacks*) Let's just say . . . I'm disappointed in you, Rene. In the crush of your adoration, I thought you'd become something more. More like . . . a woman.
     But no. Men. You're like the rest of them. It's all in the way we dress, and make up our faces, and bat our eyelashes. You really have so little imagination!
GALLIMARD: You, Monsieur Song? Accuse me of too little imagination? You, if anyone, should know—I am pure imagination. And in imagination I will remain. Now get out!

GALLIMARD *bodily removes* SONG *from the stage, taking his kimono.*

SONG: Rene! I'll never put on those robes again! You'll be sorry!

GALLIMARD (*To* SONG):   I'm already sorry! (*Looking at the kimono in his hands*) Exactly as sorry . . . as a Butterfly.

Scene 3
M. GALLIMARD*'s prison cell. Paris. Present.*

GALLIMARD: I've played out the events of my life night after night, always searching for a new ending to my story, one where I leave this cell and return forever to my Butterfly's arms.

　　Tonight I realize my search is over. That I've looked all along in the wrong place. And now, to you, I will prove that my love was not in vain—by returning to the world of fantasy where I first met her.

He picks up the kimono; dancers enter.

GALLIMARD: There is a vision of the Orient that I have. Of slender women in chong sams and kimonos who die for the love of unworthy foreign devils. Who are born and raised to be the perfect women. Who take whatever punishment we give them, and bounce back, strengthened by love, unconditionally. It is a vision that has become my life.

Dancers bring the wash basin to him and help him make up his face.

GALLIMARD: In public, I have continued to deny that Song Liling is a man. This brings me headlines, and is a source of great embarrassment to my French colleagues, who can now be sent into a coughing fit by the mere mention of Chinese food. But alone, in my cell, I have long since faced the truth.

　　And the truth demands a sacrifice. For mistakes made over the course of a lifetime. My mistakes were simple and absolute—the man I loved was a cad, a bounder. He deserved nothing but a kick in the behind, and instead I gave him . . . all my love.

　　Yes—love. Why not admit it all? That was my undoing, wasn't it? Love warped my judgment, blinded my eyes, rearranged the very lines on my face . . . until I could look in the mirror and see nothing but . . . a woman.

Dancers help him put on the Butterfly wig.

GALLIMARD: I have a vision. Of the Orient. That, deep within its almond eyes, there are still women. Women willing to sacrifice themselves for the love of a man. Even a man whose love is completely without worth.

Dancers assist GALLIMARD *in donning the kimono. They hand him a knife.*

GALLIMARD: Death with honor is better than life . . . life with dishonor. (*He sets himself center stage, in a seppuku position*) The love of a Butterfly can withstand many things—unfaithfulness, loss, even abandonment. But how can it face the one sin that implies all others? The devastating knowledge that, underneath it all, the object of her love was nothing more, nothing less than . . . a man. (*He sets the tip of the knife against his body*) It is 19– –. And I have found her at last. In a prison on the outskirts of Paris. My name is Rene Gallimard—also known as Madame Butterfly.

GALLIMARD *turns upstage and plunges the knife into his body, as music from the "Love Duet" blares over the speakers. He collapses into the arms of the dancers, who lay him reverently on the floor. The image holds for several beats. Then a tight special up on* SONG, *who stands as a man, staring at the dead* GALLIMARD. *He smokes a cigarette; the smoke filters up through the lights. Two words leave his lips.*

SONG: Butterfly? Butterfly?

Smoke rises as lights fade slowly to black.

END OF PLAY

QUESTIONS FOR DISCUSSION AND WRITING

1. What does the stage look like in *M. Butterfly,* and what does it represent? Notice that the initial description of the setting says that, apart from the prison, the play takes place "in recall," and in Act II, scene 11, Gallimard says, "You have to do what I say! I'm conjuring you up in *my* mind!"

2. At the beginning of Act I, scene 2, Gallimard says that he has "known, and been loved by . . . the Perfect Woman!" What does he mean, and in what sense might he be right?

3. Puccini's opera *Madame Butterfly* is very important in *M. Butterfly*. What are its functions, and how does it contribute to the play?

4. Gallimard, and some of the other characters, break the "fourth wall" convention by addressing the audience directly and even interacting with it, as when Marc flirts with the women in the audience in Act I, scene 4. How do these acknowledgments that the stage is a stage affect the way we react to the play?

5. In Act I, scene 5, Gallimard says that he was "not handsome, nor brave, nor powerful," and he conjures up the image of a pinup girl from a sex magazine. What does this scene have to do with the major themes of the play?

6. When Gallimard and Song first meet (Act I, scene 6), they discuss the plot of *Madame Butterfly* and Song tells Gallimard, "It's one of your favorite fantasies, isn't it? The submissive Oriental woman and the cruel white man." Is Song right, judging from Gallimard's later behavior?

7. Through Act I, scenes 8–13, Song seduces Gallimard in such a way that she can keep her secret. How does she do this?

8. In Act II, scene 3, Gallimard gives Toulon some political advice about Vietnam. And as Toulon tells him later, he is almost comically wrong in everything he says. Given that Gallimard (and other Westerners) see the

Orient as feminine and the West as masculine, how have gender issues distorted his political thinking?

9. Compare Song and Renee, Gallimard's partner in his "extraextramarital" affair. Notice that in Act II, scene 6, when Gallimard wants
comforting after Toulon makes him responsible for the embassy's advice, he
goes to "Butterfly" instead of Renee:

> I started for Renee's. But no, that was all I needed. A schoolgirl who
> would question the role of the penis in modern society. What I wanted
> was revenge. A vessel to contain my humiliation. Though I hadn't seen
> her in several weeks, I headed for Butterfly's.

Does Butterfly "question the role of the penis in modern society"?

10. In Act II, scene 7, Song tells Chin that women's roles are played by men
in the Peking Opera, because "only a man knows how a woman is supposed
to act." What does she mean?

11. In the final scene between Song and Gallimard (Act III, scene 2), Song
tries to get Gallimard to admit that he is still attracted to his "Butterfly," even
though she is a man. What is the point of this scene? that there is a strain of
homosexuality in Gallimard? or that his dream "Butterfly" cannot be embodied in this man?

12. Just before he kills himself in the last scene, Gallimard dresses and
makes up as Butterfly and says "My name is Rene Gallimard—also known as
Madame Butterfly." What is the point of this final switch of identities?

AFTERWORD*

by David Henry Hwang

It all started in May of 1986, over casual dinner conversation. A friend asked, had I heard about the French diplomat who'd fallen in love with a Chinese actress, who subsequently turned out to be not only a spy, but a man? I later found a two-paragraph story in *The New York Times*. The diplomat, Bernard Bouriscot, attempting to account for the fact that he had never seen his "girlfriend" naked, was quoted as saying, "I thought she was very modest. I thought it was a Chinese custom."

Now, I am aware that this is *not* a Chinese custom, that Asian women are no more shy with their lovers than are women of the West. I am also aware, however, that Bouriscot's assumption was consistent with a certain stereotyped view of Asians as bowing, blushing flowers. I therefore concluded that the diplomat must have fallen in love, not with a person, but with a fantasy stereotype. I also inferred that, to the extent the Chinese spy encouraged these misperceptions, he must have played up to and exploited this image of the Oriental woman as demure and submissive. (In general, by the way, we prefer the term "Asian" to "Oriental," in the same way "Black" is superior to "Negro." I use the term "Oriental" specifically to denote an exotic or imperialistic view of the East.)

I suspected there was a play here. I purposely refrained from further research, for I was not interested in writing docudrama. Frankly, I didn't want the "truth" to interfere with my own speculations. I told Stuart Ostrow, a producer with whom I'd worked before, that I envisioned the story as a musical. I remember going so far as to speculate that it could be some "great *Madame Butterfly*–like tragedy." Stuart was very intrigued, and encouraged me with some early funding.

Before I can begin writing, I must "break the back of the story," and find some angle which compels me to set pen to paper. I was driving down Santa Monica Boulevard one afternoon, and asked myself, "What did Bouriscot think he was getting in this Chinese actress?" The answer came to me clearly: "He probably thought he had found Madame Butterfly."

The idea of doing a deconstructivist *Madame Butterfly* immediately appealed to me. This, despite the fact that I didn't even know the plot of the opera! I knew Butterfly only as a cultural stereotype; speaking of an Asian woman, we would sometimes say, "She's pulling a Butterfly," which meant playing the submissive Oriental number. Yet, I felt convinced that the libretto would include yet another lotus blossom pining away for a cruel Caucasian man, and dying for her love. Such a story has become too much of a cliché not to be included in the archetypal East-West romance that started it all. Sure enough, when I purchased the record, I discovered it contained a wealth of sexist and racist clichés, reaffirming my faith in Western culture.

Very soon after, I came up with the basic "arc" of my play: the Frenchman fantasizes that he is Pinkerton and his lover is Butterfly. By the end of the piece, he realizes that it is he who has been Butterfly, in that the Frenchman has been duped by love; the Chinese spy, who exploited that love, is therefore the real Pinkerton. I wrote a proposal to Stuart Ostrow, who found it very exciting. (On

---

* This essay by Hwang originally appeared in the Penguin edition of *M. Butterfly* (1989).

the night of the Tony Awards, Stuart produced my original two-page treatment, and we were gratified to see that it was, indeed, the play I eventually wrote.)

I wrote a play, rather than a musical, because, having "broken the back" of the story, I wanted to start immediately and not be hampered by the lengthy process of collaboration. I would like to think, however, that the play has retained many of its musical roots. So *Monsieur Butterfly* was completed in six weeks between September and mid-October, 1986. My wife, Ophelia, thought *Monsieur Butterfly* too obvious a title, and suggested I abbreviate it in the French fashion. Hence, *M. Butterfly,* far more mysterious and ambiguous, was the result.

I sent the play to Stuart Ostrow as a courtesy, assuming he would not be interested in producing what had become a straight play. Instead, he flew out to Los Angeles immediately for script conferences. Coming from a background in the not-for-profit theater, I suggested that we develop the work at a regional institution. Stuart, nothing if not bold, argued for bringing it directly to Broadway.

It was also Stuart who suggested John Dexter to direct. I had known Dexter's work only by its formidable reputation. Stuart sent the script to John, who called back the next day, saying it was the best play he'd read in twenty years. Naturally, this predisposed me to like him a great deal. We met in December in New York. Not long after, we persuaded Eiko Ishioka to design our sets and costumes. I had admired her work from afar ever since, as a college student, I had seen her poster for *Apocalypse Now* in Japan. By January, 1987, Stuart had optioned *M. Butterfly,* Dexter was signed to direct, and the normally sloth-like pace of commercial theater had been given a considerable prod.

On January 4, 1988, we commenced rehearsals. I was very pleased that John Lithgow had agreed to play the French diplomat, whom I named Rene Gallimard. Throughout his tenure with us, Lithgow was every inch the center of our company, intelligent and professional, passionate and generous. B. D. Wong was forced to endure a five-month audition period before we selected him to play Song Liling. Watching B. D.'s growth was one of the joys of the rehearsal process, as he constantly attained higher levels of performance. It became clear that we had been fortunate enough to put together a company with not only great talent, but also wonderful camaraderie.

As for Dexter, I have never worked with a director more respectful of text and bold in the uses of theatricality. On the first day of rehearsal, the actors were given movement and speech drills. Then Dexter asked that everyone not required at rehearsal leave the room. A week later, we returned for an amazingly thorough run-through. It was not until that day that I first heard my play read, a note I direct at many regional theaters who "develop" a script to death.

We opened in Washington, D.C., at the National Theatre, where *West Side Story* and *Amadeus* had premiered. On the morning after opening night, most of the reviews were glowing, except for *The Washington Post.* Throughout our run in Washington, Stuart never pressured us to make the play more "commercial" in reaction to that review. We all simply concluded that the gentleman was possibly insecure about his own sexual orientation and therefore found the play threatening. And we continued our work.

Once we opened in New York, the play found a life of its own. I suppose the most gratifying thing for me is that we had never compromised to be more "Broadway"; we simply did the work we thought best. That our endeavor should be rewarded to the degree it has is one of those all-too-rare instances when one's own perception and that of the world are in agreement.

Many people have subsequently asked me about the "ideas" behind the play.

From our first preview in Washington, I have been pleased that people leaving the theater were talking not only about the sexual, but also the political, issues raised by the work.

From my point of view, the "impossible" story of a Frenchman duped by a Chinese man masquerading as a woman always seemed perfectly explicable; given the degree of misunderstanding between men and women and also between East and West, it seemed inevitable that a mistake of this magnitude would one day take place.

Gay friends have told me of a derogatory term used in their community: "Rice Queen"—a gay Caucasian man primarily attracted to Asians. In these relationships, the Asian virtually always plays the role of the "woman"; the Rice Queen, culturally and sexually, is the "man." This pattern of relationships had become so codified that, until recently, it was considered unnatural for gay Asians to date one another. Such men would be taunted with a phrase which implied they were lesbians.

Similarly, heterosexual Asians have long been aware of "Yellow Fever"—Caucasian men with a fetish for exotic Oriental women. I have often heard it said that "Oriental women make the best wives." (Rarely is this heard from the mouths of Asian men, incidentally.) This mythology is exploited by the Oriental mail-order bride trade which has flourished over the past decade. American men can now send away for catalogues of "obedient, domesticated" Asian women looking for husbands. Anyone who believes such stereotypes are a thing of the past need look no further than Manhattan cable television, which advertises call girls from "the exotic east, where men are king; obedient girls, trained in the art of pleasure."

In these appeals, we see issues of racism and sexism intersect. The catalogues and TV spots appeal to a strain in men which desires to reject Western women for what they have become—independent, assertive, self-possessed—in favor of a more reactionary model—the pre-feminist, domesticated geisha girl.

That the Oriental woman is penultimately feminine does not of course imply that she is always "good." For every Madonna there is a whore; for every lotus blossom there is also a dragon lady. In popular culture, "good" Asian women are those who serve the White protagonist in his battle against her own people, often sleeping with him in the process. Stallone's *Rambo II*, Cimino's *Year of the Dragon*, Clavell's *Shogun*, Van Lustbader's *The Ninja* are all familiar examples.

Now our considerations of race and sex intersect the issue of imperialism. For this formula—good natives serve Whites, bad natives rebel—is consistent with the mentality of colonialism. Because they are submissive and obedient, good natives of both sexes necessarily take on "feminine" characteristics in a colonialist world. Gunga Din's unfailing devotion to his British master, for instance, is not so far removed from Butterfly's slavish faith in Pinkerton.

It is reasonable to assume that influences and attitudes so pervasively displayed in popular culture might also influence our policymakers as they consider the world. The neo-Colonialist notion that good elements of a native society, like a good woman, desire submission to the masculine West speaks precisely to the heart of our foreign policy blunders in Asia and elsewhere.

For instance, Frances Fitzgerald wrote in *Fire in the Lake*, "The idea that the United States could not master the problems of a country as small and underdeveloped as Vietnam did not occur to Johnson as a possibility." Here, as in so many other cases, by dehumanizing the enemy, we dehumanize ourselves. We become the Rice Queens of *realpolitik*.

M. Butterfly has sometimes been regarded as an anti-American play, a diatribe against the stereotyping of the East by the West, of women by men. Quite to the contrary, I consider it a plea to all sides to cut through our respective layers of cultural and sexual misperception, to deal with one another truthfully for our mutual good, from the common and equal ground we share as human beings.

For the myths of the East, the myths of the West, the myths of men, and the myths of women—these have so saturated our consciousness that truthful contact between nations and lovers can only be the result of heroic effort. Those who prefer to bypass the work involved will remain in a world of surfaces, misperceptions running rampant. This is, to me, the convenient world in which the French diplomat and the Chinese spy lived. This is why, after twenty years, he had learned nothing at all about his lover, not even the truth of his sex.

D.H.H.

New York City
September, 1988

REVIEW OF *M. BUTTERFLY**

by Frank Rich

It didn't require genius for David Henry Hwang to see that there were the makings of a compelling play in the 1986 newspaper story that prompted him to write *M. Butterfly*. Here was the incredible true-life tale of a career French foreign service officer brought to ruin—conviction for espionage—by a bizarre 20-year affair with a Beijing Opera diva. Not only had the French diplomat failed to recognize that his lover was a spy; he'd also failed to figure out that "she" was a he in drag. "It was dark, and she was very modest," says Gallimard (John Lithgow), Mr. Hwang's fictionalized protagonist, by half-joking way of explanation. When we meet him in the prison cell where he reviews his life, Gallimard has become, according to own understatement, "the patron saint of the socially inept."

But if this story is a corker, what is it about, exactly? That's where Mr. Hwang's imagination, one of the most striking to emerge in the American theater in this decade, comes in, and his answer has nothing to do with journalism. This playwright, the author of *The Dance and the Railroad* and *Family Devotions*, does not tease us with obvious questions such as is she or isn't she?, or does he know or doesn't he? Mr. Hwang isn't overly concerned with how the opera singer, named Song Liling (B. D. Wong), pulled his hocus-pocus in the boudoir, and he refuses to explain away Gallimard by making him a closeted, self-denying homosexual. An inversion of Puccini's *Madama Butterfly*, *M. Butterfly* is also the inverse of most American plays. Instead of reducing the world to an easily digested cluster of sexual or familial relationships, Mr. Hwang cracks open a liaison to reveal a sweeping, universal meditation on two of the most heated conflicts—men versus women, East versus West—of this or any other time.

As a piece of playwriting that manages to encompass phenomena as diverse as the origins of the Vietnam War and the socio-economic code embedded in Gior-

---

* *New York Times*, Mar. 21, 1988.

gio Armani fashions, *M. Butterfly* is so singular that one hates to report that a visitor to the Eugene O'Neill Theater must overcome a number of obstacles to savor it. Because of some crucial and avoidable lapses—a winning yet emotionally bland performance from Mr. Lithgow and inept acting in some supporting roles—the experience of seeing the play isn't nearly as exciting as thinking about it after the curtain has gone down. The production only rises to full power in its final act, when the evening's triumphant performance, Mr. Wong's mesmerizing account of the transvestite diva, hits its own tragic high notes. Until then, one must settle for being grateful that a play of this ambition has made it to Broadway, and that the director, John Dexter, has realized as much of Mr. Hwang's far-ranging theatricality as he has.

As usual, Mr. Hwang demands a lot from directors, actors and theatergoers. A 30-year-old Chinese-American writer from Los Angeles, he has always blended Oriental and Western theater in his work, and *M. Butterfly* does so on an epic scale beyond his previous plays, let alone such similarly minded Western hybrids as *Pacific Overtures* or *Nixon in China*. While ostensibly constructed as a series of Peter Shafferesque flashbacks narrated by Gallimard from prison, the play is as intricate as an infinity of Chinese boxes. Even as we follow the narrative of the lovers' affair, it is being refracted through both overt and disguised burlesque deconstructions of *Madama Butterfly*. As Puccini's music collides throughout with a percussive Eastern score by Lucia Hwong, so Western storytelling and sassy humor intermingle with flourishes of martial-arts ritual, Chinese opera (Cultural Revolution Maoist agitprop included) and Kabuki. Now and then, the entire mix is turned inside out, Genet and Pirandello style, to remind us that fantasy isn't always distinguishable from reality and that actors are not to be confused with their roles.

The play's form—whether the clashing and blending of Western and Eastern cultures or of male and female characters—is wedded to its content. It's Mr. Hwang's starting-off point that a cultural icon like *Madama Butterfly* bequeaths the sexist and racist roles that burden Western men: Gallimard believes he can become "a real man" only if he can exercise power over a beautiful and submissive woman, which is why he's so ripe to be duped by Song Liling's impersonation of a shrinking butterfly. Mr. Hwang broadens his message by making Gallimard an architect of the Western foreign policy in Vietnam. The diplomat disastrously reasons that a manly display of American might can bring the Viet Cong to submission as easily as he or Puccini's Pinkerton can overpower a Madama Butterfly.

Lest that ideological leap seem too didactic, the playwright shuffles the deck still more, suggesting that the roles played by Gallimard and Song Liling run so deep that they cross the boundaries of nations, cultures, revolutions and sexual orientations. That Gallimard was fated to love "a woman created by a man" proves to be figuratively as well as literally true: we see that the male culture that inspired his "perfect woman" is so entrenched that the attitudes of *Madama Butterfly* survive in his cherished present-day porno magazines. Nor is the third world, in Mr. Hwang's view, immune from adopting the roles it condemns in foreign devils. We're sarcastically told that men continue to play women in Chinese opera because "only a man knows how a woman is supposed to act." When Song Liling reassumes his male "true self," he still must play a submissive Butterfly to Gallimard—whatever his or Gallimard's actual sexual persuasions—unless he chooses to play the role of aggressor to a Butterfly of his own.

Mr. Hwang's play is not without its repetitions and its overly explicit bouts of thesis mongering. When the playwright stops trusting his own instinct for the mysterious, the staging often helps out. Using Eiko Ishioka's towering, blood-red Oriental variant on the abstract sets Mr. Dexter has employed in *Equus* and the Metropolitan Opera *Dialogues of the Carmelites*, the director stirs together Mr. Hwang's dramatic modes and settings until one floats to a purely theatrical imaginative space suspended in time and place. That same disorienting quality can be found in Mr. Wong's Song Liling—a performance that, like John Lone's in the early Hwang plays, finds even more surprises in the straddling of cultures than in the blurring of genders.

But Mr. Dexter's erratic handling of actors, also apparent in his Broadway *Glass Menagerie* revival, inflicts a serious toll. John Getz and Rose Gregorio, as Gallimard's oldest pal and wife, are wildly off-key, wrecking the intended high-style comedy of the all-Western scenes. Mr. Lithgow, onstage virtually throughout, projects intelligence and wit, and his unflagging energy drives and helps unify the evening. Yet this engaging, ironic Gallimard never seems completely consumed by passion, whether the eroticism of imperialism or of the flesh, and the performance seems to deepen more in pitch than despair from beginning to end. Though *M. Butterfly* presents us with a visionary work that bridges the history and culture of two worlds, the production stops crushingly short of finding the gripping human drama that merges Mr. Hwang's story with his brilliant play of ideas.

DAVID HWANG'S *M. BUTTERFLY:* PERPETUATING THE MISOGYNIST MYTH*

by Gabrielle Cody

An an Asian I identify with Song (Butterfly). As a man I identify with Gallimard. That willful self-delusion is something I know I've experienced as a man; I've been good at self-delusion when I've wanted to be. The really sexist things Gallimard says are things that I know on some level work in my own soul and color my relationships with women. Pleasure in giving pain to a woman is not that far removed I think, from a lot of male experiences.

D. H. Hwang, New York Times, *March, 1988.*

David Henry Hwang's *M. Butterfly* will continue to intoxicate audiences with the paper-thin Orient of toy parasols in exotic cocktails. His effortless brand of liberalism has the wry smoothness of the businessman's final pitch at Happy Hour. But Hwang has a diplomatic passport of sorts which allows him to travel from one thought to another about cultural or sexual politics without any real thinking to declare. His aim is to discuss imperialism in the context of sexism from a Man-Of-The-Eighties point of view and draw some subversive conclusions. To compare the Orient to a woman and to link imperialism to machismo or to suggest that the West has plundered her virgin soils and culture are not new ideas. The correspondence between sexual and cultural violation, between rape and Coca-Cola diplomacy, has long been established. In America, Vietnam comes to mind, and not coincidentally, since American involvement there was the result of earlier

*Originally published in *Theater* 20:2 (Spring 1989):24–27.

French incursion in Indochina, which isn't all that far from the diplomatic milieu in which Hwang's play is set.

M. Butterfly, as its title suggests, is the reworking of a tale from a Belasco play which Puccini saw in London at the turn-of-the-century and used as the basis for his opera at La Scala, in Milan in 1904. Puccini's Pinkerton, a United States Navy officer, is leasing a house in Nagasaki and preparing to marry Cio-Cio San, a fifteen-year-old Geisha girl, with the convenient provision that each contract can be cancelled on a month's notice. Pinkerton makes it perfectly clear to his friend Sharpless, the American consul and his best man, that he only intends to maintain his vows to Butterfly until he finds the American girl of his dreams. By the second act, Cio-Cio San has borne him a child, appropriately named Trouble; Pinkerton has long since left Nagasaki, perhaps never to return. But Butterfly is certain he will be back, as promised, in the spring, when the robins nest. When she's told they've already nested three times over, she remains impervious. Soon however, she spots a ship in the distance, the *Abraham Lincoln* carrying her beloved back to her. But the next morning it is Pinkerton's wife Kate, not he, who appears in order to retrieve his son and take him back to America. When Cio-Cio San realizes who Kate is, and what she has come for, she places an American flag and a doll in her child's arms, blindfolds him and stabs herself. The curtain falls as the remorseful Pinkerton arrives, screaming her name, only to find her on the floor, dying.

Besides the opera, *M. Butterfly* is also based on a 1986 newspaper article which told the bizarre story of a French diplomat arrested on charges of spying for the Chinese government with the help of his Chinese mistress. Stationed in China in the 1960s, he had met and fallen in love with a Peking opera diva who allegedly bore him a child. During his trial, however, the actress was revealed to be a man, a fact the diplomat denied knowing anything about. The actress was later expelled from France and the diplomat sentenced to six years in a Paris jail.

We first encounter René Gallimard in his prison cell, a small figure against the enormous cherry red and jet black walls that represent Peking, his past. As though caught in the design of a giant morsel of laquered sashimi, Gallimard paces about nervously trying to retrieve the pieces of his story. But already he is transfixed by the memory of Puccini's score and the appearance of an opera singer, who, in the first of a series of flashbacks, performs Butterfly's death aria for Western diplomats. Her apparent delight with his shy request to see her again moves him to exclaim: "I had finally gained power over a beautiful woman!" An unsurprising aside, since earlier on he discloses his sexual fear of women, wishing he were more like his colleagues whom Hwang endows with stereotypically French libidos. Gallimard envies their insatiable sexual appetites, the patriotic zest with which they maintain their colonial prerogative. "Their women fear us and their men hate us," says his friend Marc with pride as he urges the shy diplomat to pursue Song Liling. Gallimard's questionable virility leads him to believe in his rights as an underdog of French machismo, a kind of second-class Romeo in search of a romantic exploit: "We who are not handsome, not brave, nor powerful, yet somehow believe, like Pinkerton, that we deserve a Butterfly." But despite the pleasure of his new conquest he ponders the nature of power and worries that he might be piercing his Butterfly's heart, again, like Pinkerton: "Had I caught a butterfly that could ride on a needle?" he asks wearily.

Gallimard's memories of his idyllic courtship are regularly interrupted by Parisian commentary on the shocking revelations of 1986:

WOMAN: He still claims not to believe the truth.
MAN: What? Still? Even since the trial?
WOMAN: Yes. Isn't it mad?
MAN: (Laughing) He says . . . it was dark and she was very modest!

It is a clever technique on Hwang's part to have characters within the play pose the how-did-they-do-it and what-did-they-do questions for the audience. These after all, constitute the tantalizing lining of the play's dramaturgical kimono and they help to make Gallimard's ambiguous sexuality a safe dramatic icon:

MAN 1: So—what? He never touched her with his hands?
MAN 2: Perhaps he did, and simply misidentified the equipment. A compelling case for sex education in the schools.
GALLIMARD: You see, they toast me. I've become the patron saint of the socially inept . . . they should be scratching at my door, begging to learn my secrets! for I, René Gallimard, you see, I have known, and been loved by . . . the Perfect Woman.

But Hwang never fully challenges his protagonist's motive for falling in love with a woman, or a man, beyond Gallimard's childish Western fascination with the Orient. Instead, he relies on an endless series of attempts to trivialize the Frenchman's sexual power over Butterfly and impotence with his wife. Hwang makes René's flippant naiveté the play's central ideology rather than its target. Exchanges between Gallimard and his wife are symptomatic of Hwang's attraction to caricature over characterization:

GALLIMARD: I married a woman older than myself—Helga.
HELGA: My father was ambassador to Australia. I grew up among criminals and kangaroos.
GALLIMARD: Hearing that brought me to the altar—.

Absent from Hwang's tiresome repartée is any clear denunciation of what it parodies: there are no exchanges here, only punch lines offered as substitutes for thinking. Consequently, his dialogue has the effect of narrowing the play's discourse to such an extent that another work emerges, a kind of perverse cancellation of thought, a frenzied cover-up of the very questions the play supposedly exists to answer.

Another example of obfuscation is B. D. Wong's interpretation of Song Liling. Under the direction of John Dexter, Wong adopts the tradition of Onnagata—the Oriental principle which stipulates that only a man can act the part of a woman because only he can idealize her, whereas a woman can only be her—and violates its main purpose. Onnagata players often already trained in Kabuki for years, study the Geishas and infuse their work with great attention to realistic detail. Their aim is to portray the beauty and delicacy of a woman with the utmost precision. But Wong deliberately plays Butterfly as a man-playing-at-being-a-woman, self-consciously endowing her with Gallimard's fantasy of how an Oriental woman should behave—the equivalent in the West, of third-rate transvestism. Thus Butterfly's grotesque idealized femaleness dismisses the Onnagata intention altogether and destroys the premise Hwang had established earlier: that Gallimard is enamored of female Oriental passivity. There is no woman here to fall in love with because her impersonation exists in a marginal relationship to its male portrayer and as such has no reality. Her presence, in short, is not female, a fact Gallimard later confesses he had suspected but not challenged: "Did I not undress her because I knew, somewhere deep down, what I would find? Perhaps. Happiness is so rare that our mind can turn somersaults to protect it."

Not only does Hwang take the female gender out of Butterfly by over-feminizing her, he takes the Orient out of her by over-Orientalizing her. Picture a tall, mannered silhouette, desperately submitting to the stylized discomfort of high heels, eye-lashes combatting the weight of too much mascara, fingers flirtatiously taunting the air with exaggerated femininity. This is the creature who, when Gallimard, in a brief moment of lucidity asks to see her naked, will respond with studied Oriental coyness: "What do you want? I have already given you my shame." Butterfly's culture is now implicated in her inauthenticity and exploited to maintain the male actor's female identity.

Yet Hwang also cleverly invests Song Liling with the politically correct tirades of the play; in response to Gallimard's mesmerized reaction to her performance as Butterfly she says: "It's one of your favorite fantasies, isn't it? The submissive Oriental woman and the cruel white man?" or "Why in the Peking Opera are women's roles played by men? Because only a man knows how a woman is supposed to act," hoping to raise the Frenchman's consciousness and at the same time absolving Hwang from transcending the elementary level of the play's concerns.

But Song Liling has been spying for her government. In tender moments she has been extracting from her lover the secrets foreign policies are so often shaped by. And when the Cultural Revolution arrives, their menage is broken up and Gallimard returns to Paris. ("So what was waiting for me in Paris? Well, better Chinese food than I had ever had in China.") His return is the pivotal point of the play, when Madame Butterfly the woman, becomes M. Butterfly the man. The build-up to this lengthy, on-stage transformation, during which Wong removes all material evidence of femininity, is meant to be the dramatic climax of the play, its ultimate coup de théâtre. Yet, the combination of circus-like drum rolls and the arrogant simplicity with which this cosmetic crossing-over from one gender to another occurs, renders it painfully devoid of meaning. We applaud the dexterous expertise of the actor rather than the significance of his transformation. The "removal" of woman and the "putting on" of man have a strange violence to them, perhaps because there is no woman to remove at all, only the vestiges of what too often adds up to womanhood in the male imagination: Make-up, false eyelashes, earrings, high heels and submissive behavior.

When M. Butterfly turns to the audience, his hair is slicked back and his face now reveals a boyish masculinity. He throws off his kimono with the emphatic precision of a bullfighter's last thrust, killing the woman he never was, and adjusts to the comfort of a smart Armani suit. Then, with years of resentment towards Gallimard for his Western romanticization of the Orient, Butterfly arrives in Paris where he challenges his lover's confused sexuality; "Admit it. You still want me even in slacks and a button-down collar" he says. But the Frenchman, having only loved the illusion of a woman, replies with typical Western guilt: "You showed me your true self. When all I wanted was the lie." Gallimard, (to Frank Rich's great sigh of relief: "Hwang refuses to explain away Gallimard by making him a closeted, self-denying homosexual") denies the possibility of having loved a man, known it and liked it all along: "I am a man who loved a woman created by a man. Everything else simply falls short." Instead, out of shame, he becomes Butterfly's informant in exchange for his silence and is soon imprisoned on charges of espionage.

Gallimard, rejected by society, humiliated by Butterfly's accusations, no longer

Un Homme in the eyes of the world, engages in the reverse cosmetic cross-over that Butterfly had performed moments earlier. He metaphorically castrates himself by taking the failed man "off" and putting the idealized woman "on." Soon he is dressed in Madama Butterfly's kimono, his face painted in the Geisha tradition, literally transformed into the image of the operatic heroine whose amorous suffering for a Westerner made her beautiful to him:

> . . . Love. Why not admit it all? That was my undoing, wasn't it? Love warped my judgment, blinded my eyes, rearranged the very lines on my face . . . until I could look in the mirror and see nothing but . . . a woman.

And as he puts on Madama Butterfly's wig, Gallimard becomes the woman of his dreams: a victim of his own anesthetization of pain.

The real play underneath *M. Butterfly*'s seductive theatricality has very little to do with exposing sexism or cultural imperialism. Hwang's fascination with the facile reversal of gender is his greatest self-indictment; rather than examine the cultural and political circumstances that determine gendered behavior and make it easier to believe in than to challenge, he concludes that male and female cannot be reconciled in one person. The larger consequence of this notion is that male and female cannot be reconciled in society without one having power over the other. Gallimard becomes a "woman" out of failure and shame. Butterfly remains a "man" out of anger and revenge. Hwang's rejection of human complexity in his characters leads one to wonder why he chose this story. What does its theatrical elaboration conceal? Was Gallimard's self-inflicted punishment the only sexual morality available to him? Finally, why does the most lyrically compelling moment of the play express Gallimard's most reactionary sentiments?

> There is a vision of the Orient that I have. Of slender women in chong sams and kimonos who die for the love of unworthy foreign devils. Who are born and raised to be the perfect woman . . . I have a vision. Of the Orient. That deep within its almond eyes, there are still women. Women willing to sacrifice themselves for the love of a man. Even a man whose love is completely without warmth.

Hwang gives us no alternative but to leave with the image of a dying woman on a floor, and the beauty of sacrifice in our minds.

FROM THE INTRODUCTION TO *THE BIG AIIIEEEEE!**

by Jeffery Paul Chan, Frank Chin, Lawson Fusao Inada, and Shawn Wong

The American-born, exclusively English-speaking Asian Americans were dominated by the Christian vision of China as a country without a history and a philosophy without substance. The social Darwinist philosophers and fictioners of

*New York: Meridian Books, 1991.

the turn of the century taught history we now accept as both fact and stereotype, feeling there is no other history to know.

We begin another year angry! Another decade, and another Chinese American ventriloquizing the same old white Christian fantasy of little Chinese victims of "the original sin of being born to a brutish, sadomasochistic culture of cruelty and victimization" fleeing to America in search of freedom from everything Chinese and seeking white acceptance, and of being victimized by stupid white racists and then being reborn in acculturation and honorary whiteness. Every Chinese American book ever published in the United States of America by a major publisher has been a Christian autobiography or autobiographical novel. Yung Wing's *My Life in China and America* (1909: Henry Holt); Leong Gor Yun's *Chinatown Inside Out* (1936: Barrows Mussey); Pardee Lowe's *Father and Glorious Descendent* (1943: Little, Brown); Jade Snow Wong's *Fifth Chinese Daughter* (1950: Little, Brown); Virginia Lee's *The House That Tai-Ming Built* (1963: Macmillan); Chuang Hua's *Crossing* (1968: Dial Press); Betty Lee Sung's autobiographical expressionist pseudo-sociological *Mountain of Gold* (1972: Macmillan); Maxine Hong Kingston's *The Woman Warrior* (1976: Alfred A. Knopf), *China Men* (1980: Knopf), and *Tripmaster Monkey* (1989: Knopf); and Amy Tan's *The Joy Luck Club* (1989: G. P. Putnam) all tell the story that Will Irwin, the Christian social Darwinist practitioner of white racist love, wanted told in *Pictures of Old Chinatown* (1908) about how the "Chinese transformed themselves from our race adversaries to our dear subject people. . . ." The China and Chinese America portrayed in these works are the products of white racist imagination, not fact, not Chinese culture, and not Chinese or Chinese American literature.

If the woman warrior Fa Mulan; Monkey, of the childhood classic *Journey to the West*; China's language, culture, and history; the heroes, ducks, and swans of the Chinese fairy tale are all fake, as depicted in the Christian works, then what is real? No one questions the fact that, before the 1960s, the majority of Chinese Americans were non-Christian bachelor Chinamen. Only four works by Chinese American authors do not suck off the white Christian fantasy of the Chinese as a Shangri-La people. Two were novels published by major publishing houses— Diana Chang's *Frontiers of Love* (1956: Random House) and Louis Chu's *Eat a Bowl of Tea* (1961: Lyle Stuart). Shawn Wong's novel, *Homebase* (1979: I. Reed Books), and Frank Chin's collection of short stories, *The Chinaman Pacific & Frisco R.R. Co.* (1988: Coffee House Press), were published by small presses. However, these works alone do not prove the Christian works to be either fake or white racist. To do that, we have to turn to the history of the Asian Chinese and Japanese in white Christianity and in Western historiography, philosophy, social science, and literature.

For the truth of the Chinese culture and history that has been carried and developed into Chinese American institutions by the first Chinese Americans, we have to confront the real Fa Mulan, the real Monkey, the real Chinese first-person pronoun, the real Chinese words for "woman" and "slave" as they exist in the culture and texts of Chinese childhood literature, the ethics that the fairy tales and heroic traditions teach, and the sensibility that they express.

The Christian social Darwinist bias of twentieth-century white American culture combined with the Christian mission, the racist acts of Congress, and the statutes and city ordinances to emphasize the fake Chinese American dream over the Chinese American reality, the belief over the fact, and the fake over the real, until the stereotype has completely displaced history in the white sensibility. It is an article of white liberal American faith today that Chinese men, at their best, are effeminate closet queens like Charlie Chan and, at their worst, are homosexual menaces like Fu Manchu. No wonder David Henry Hwang's derivative *M. Butterfly* won the Tony for best new play of 1988. The good Chinese man, at his best, is the fulfillment of white male homosexual fantasy, literally kissing white ass. Now Hwang and the stereotype are inextricably one.

Writing from Sources: Drama

༄ ༅ ༆

The commentary in the Casebook on Fiction emphasized the *form* of writing from sources: the ways quotations can be worked into your writing and conventional forms for footnotes, "works cited" lists, and bibliographies. The Casebook on Poetry concentrated on the more general questions of how to read secondary material for prospective use in your own writing and the range of rhetorical uses to which your reading can be put.

These topics obviously are still relevant to writing about drama from sources, and you should refer to them while you are working with *M. Butterfly* and the four secondary sources we have reprinted here. But here we will concentrate on a different topic: dealing with violently disagreeing judgments and interpretations of a work. The various critics we read on "The Yellow Wallpaper" had minor disagreements, primarily on matters of emphasis, but all seemed to like the story and to think that it was well worth close attention. The same thing was true of John F. Callahan, Joseph A. Brown, and Günter H. Lenz, who wrote on Michael S. Harper's poems; the critics clearly admired Harper as a poet and directed their efforts toward illuminating the poems rather than calling their value into doubt.

The same thing cannot be said of the four commentaries on *M. Butterfly* included here. David Henry Hwang's own "Afterword" to the play obviously treats it as a success as a work of art and one substantial enough to bear interpretation and clarification. Frank Rich's review of the New York production, predictably, is more qualified in its assessment of the play than Hwang is himself. He admires the play's ambition, but comments that the audience "must overcome a number of obstacles to savor it." Some of these obstacles are in the play itself; others are in the production.

The pieces by Gabrielle Cody and by Jeffery Paul Chan, et al., are an altogether different matter. Cody not only dislikes the play, she seems to be angered by it. In her opening sentence, she calls the world of the play "the paper-thin Orient of toy parasols in exotic cocktails." She goes on to say that "Hwang has a diplomatic passport of sorts which allows him to travel from one thought to another about cultural or sexual politics without any real thinking to declare." Chan, Chin, Inada, and Wong are even more negative, if briefer. The play's meaning, they say, is that the "good Chinese man, at his best, is the fulfillment of white male homosexual fantasy, literally kissing white ass. Now Hwang and the stereotype are inextricably one."

There are several conclusions to be drawn from such wildly disparate interpretations of the play. One is a healthy skepticism about any one interpretation. Too often inexperienced writers are unrealistically reverent toward their sources. "If it's published, it must be right," is the attitude. But all four of these comments cannot be right. Things that Hwang apparently thought were successful about the production, Frank Rich found weak. And the two negative pieces, Cody's and Chan, et al.'s, attack the play not only for different reasons but for incompatible and even contradictory ones.

And what does "right" mean, in this context? The word is meaningless in reference to taste or value judgments. If one person says, "I like this play" or, what amounts to much the same thing, "This is a good play," while another one says, "I dislike this play," or "This is a bad play," can one be said to be wrong and the other right? In reference to likes and dislikes, there is little we can say except, everyone to his or her own taste.

The other point our *M. Butterfly* interpretations suggest is the necessity of contextualizing. These four pieces were written in very different circumstances, and their striking disagreements are perhaps less surprising when those differences are taken into account.

Hwang's "Afterword" is not intended as an evaluation of the play. The playwright is obviously not an objective judge of his own work, and Hwang's only reference to whether the play is a success or not is humorous and self-deprecating; when the director John Dexter read the play, he said it was the best play he had read in twenty years, a fact, Hwang writes, that "predisposed me to like him a great deal." Rather than evaluation, Hwang wants to describe the play's origin in a newspaper story's description of a real event, the reason he chose to add *Madame Butterfly* to the newspaper facts, and the course of the play through rehearsals up to its first performance. He also summarizes some of the ideas he consciously sought to develop in the play, notably the questioning of the stereotype that Orientals, and especially Oriental women, want to be dominated. This stereotype has political as well as sexual implications: "This formula—good natives serve Whites, bad natives rebel—is consistent with the mentality of colonialism."

The role of a theater reviewer is quite specific. To "explain" the meaning of a play is not so important as to tell the readers whether they should go to see it or not. Reviewers may do some skillful interpretation along the way, as Frank Rich does in this review, but their job is primarily to supply consumer information, of the same order as restaurant reviews, movie reviews, and television reviews. For this reason, almost every aspect of a dramatic production—the text of the play, the acting, the direction, the designs, even the comfort of the theater—is evaluated, in order to reach the conclusion, explicit or implicit, "Go see this play," or "Don't go see this play." For this reason, students of dramatic literature need to be very careful in using reviews (which are often the fullest source of commentary on a play); they need to separate out description, interpretation, and evaluation. Rich finds John Lithgow's performance as Gallimard "winning yet emotionally bland." Obviously this is a judgment on Rich's part, and others might disagree; whether they do or not, the comment seems to apply to Lithgow rather than to anything inherent in the role of Gallimard. Or does it? Rich says that "this engaging, ironic Gallimard never seems completely consumed by passion, whether the eroticism of imperialism or of the flesh." Since we have had the opportunity to read the play, as Rich probably had not, perhaps we should ask ourselves whether the coolness is in the role rather than in the acting. We might also ask ourselves if the timid Gallimard *should* ever be "completely controlled by passion." This sort of translation from the rhetorical stance of the reviewer to that of the dramatic critic is necessary if we are to use theater reviews as sources.

Gabrielle Cody's essay "David Hwang's *M. Butterfly*: Perpetuating the Misogynist Myth" has a third context. The essay appeared in *Theater*, a journal published by the Yale School of Drama, which is devoted to plays on the Yale Repertory Theater's schedule. Essays in this journal tend not to refer to previous interpretations, with footnotes and bibliography, but rather to advance an original argument. Cody obviously is a feminist critic, though the question of what sort of feminist critic she is is harder to answer. If we look in the essay for the "misogynist myth" referred to in the title, we may have some difficulty locating it, since Cody assumes that everyone has the same understanding of the misogynist myth that she does. But perhaps it is to be found near the end of the essay where Cody writes:

> Hwang's fascination with the facile reversal of gender is his greatest self-indictment; rather than examine the cultural and political circumstances that determine gendered behavior and make it easier to believe in than to challenge, he concludes that male and female cannot be reconciled in one person. The larger consequence of this notion is that male and female cannot be reconciled in society without one having control over the other.

Is the "misogynist myth," then, the idea that male and female cannot be reconciled either in the individual or in society? If so, we might conclude that Cody's feminist criticism requires that a work include wholesome images of characters in whom male and female qualities are combined in one person.

Also, on the basis of the examples of Song and Gallimard, can we conclude that "male and female cannot be reconciled in one person"? This play, with its sardonic tone and its deeply flawed characters, seems an inappropriate place to look for such universal implications. Cody seems to have little ear for irony. She takes Gallimard's speech beginning "There is a vision of the Orient that I have," and rightly says that it is "reactionary" but wrongly implies that it expresses Hwang's own sentiments because it is "lyrically compelling." By acting out the logical implications of his entanglement in the plot of *Madame Butterfly*, Gallimard is demonstrating for us the "wealth of sexist and racist cliches" that Hwang found in the opera, not asserting their truth, whether Cody finds them "lyrically compelling" or not.

Other readers may interpret Cody's essay differently and perhaps more favorably. The point is that secondary material should be given this sort of skeptical scrutiny and should not be taken at face value. And even an argument that is flawed as a whole can offer interesting points for consideration in our own work. Cody, after all, is dealing with a central aspect of the play: its treatment of the politics of gender. Questions that she raises may prompt us to somewhat different answers.

Finally, the passage by Chan, Chin, Inada, and Wong is an even briefer and more dismissive attack on the play than Cody's. Again, contextualization is in order. This passage appears in the Introduction to *The Big Aiiieeeee! An Anthology of Chinese American and Japanese American Literature* (New York: Meridian, 1991). *The Big Aiiieeeee!* is a revision and expansion of *Aiiieeeee! An Anthology of Asian American Writers,* originally published in 1974. The title is explained in the preface to *Aiiieeeee!* by saying that the anthology collects the work of Asian-Americans, "who got their China and Japan from the radio, off the silver screen, from television, out of comic books, from the pushers of white American culture that pictured the yellow man as something that when wounded, sad, or angry, or swearing, or wondering whined, shouted, or screamed 'aiiieeeee!' " Both versions of the book, then, were devoted to opposing American pop-culture stereotypes of Asians. These stereotypes of Asians, the editors argue, follow, for the Chinese, the white Christian missionary fantasy of "little Chinese victims of 'the original sin of being born to a brutish, sadomasochistic culture of cruelty and victimization' fleeing to America in search of freedom from everything Chinese and seeking white acceptance, and of being victimized by stupid white racists and then being reborn in acculturation and honorary whiteness." They find some of the most honored of Asian-American books, including Maxine Hong Kingston's *The Woman Warrior* and Amy Tan's *The Joy Luck Club,* to be versions of this racist myth.

M. Butterfly is a version of it, too, according to Chan, et al. Song, according to the editors, is "the fulfillment of white male homosexual fantasy." This reading of the play would be hard to support. Far from "kissing white ass," as the editors describe him, Song, in control through the entire affair, manages Gallimard's delusion and ends the play coolly in control, while the Western Gallimard, caught in the destructive Orientalist fantasies of *Madame Butterfly,* follows her in death.

Chan, et al.'s reading of *M. Butterfly* makes better sense in the context of a general critique of American literary representations of Asians. Their brief comment may be inaccurate and unfair, but it does bring out a dimension of the play otherwise neglected, the representation in the play of the East, not as woman, but as passive homosexual. And like Cody's essay, it raises a question that can be answered in ways other than the one in which the critic answers it. Cody's essay places the play in the context of feminism and feminist literary theory; it asks the question, "What feminist implications does *M. Butterfly* have?" Chan, et al.'s selection places it in the context of Orientalism, of Western representation of the East, and asks the questions, "What is the relation of *M. Butterfly* to the tradition of Asian-Americans writing about Asians? How does the play shatter or perpetuate stereotypes of Asians?"

We need not accept the details, or even the broad outlines, of a critical argument in order to make good use of it in our own writing. Sometimes asking the right question is as valuable as giving the right answer.

Glossary

Accent In poetry, a rhythmically significant emphasis given to a particular syllable. Stress.

Allegory In literature, a narrative in which each character, object, and event is symbolic of an idea or a moral or religious principle.

Alliteration The occurrence in a phrase, or especially in a passage of poetry, of a series of words with the same initial sound, as, for example, in "When to the sessions of sweet silent thought" (Shakespeare, Sonnet 30).

Allusion An indirect reference in a literary work to a person, place, event, or other text.

Anapest A metrical foot made up of two short syllables followed by a long one: ⏑ ⏑ ′.

Antagonist In a fictional or dramatic narrative, the character who opposes the main character or protagonist.

Assonance Repetition in a passage, especially a line of poetry, of the same vowel sound (without similar consonants, as in rhyme): *golden, grove; mad, cat.*

Ballad stanza A four-line stanza often used in both folk ballads and art ballads, in which the second and fourth lines rhyme; the first and third lines have four metrical feet and the second and fourth have three.

Bildungsroman "Development novel" (German). A novel (or by extension any narrative) that deals with the process of growing up.

Blank verse Unrhymed iambic pentameter.

Carpe diem "Seize the day" (Latin). The common poetic theme of making the most of life before death comes.

Caesura A pause in a line of verse caused by sense or natural speech rhythms rather than by metrical considerations.

CHARACTER A person in a literary work or the combination of qualities that makes a literary personage a distinctive individual. Writers usually make their characters credible through verisimilitude (likeness to reality), but literary characters differ in some obvious ways from real people. They tend to be simpler and more understandable, and to appear in the company of other characters whose qualities complement their own (**foil** characters).

CLIMAX In narrative structure, the point of greatest intensity, usually the point at which the conflicting forces upon which the narrative is built confront each other most directly and decisively.

CLOSED COUPLET A couplet that is grammatically complete within itself (practically speaking, one that ends with a period or a semicolon).

CLOSED DRAMATIC STRUCTURE Term used for the structure of plays that have few characters and few scenes; that take place in continuous or nearly continuous time and in one place or only a few places; and that have single, highly unified plots; plays that, in other words, observe the "unities." Greek plays and modern realistic plays both ordinarily employ closed structures.

COMEDY The term comedy has been extended in reference from stage comedy to apply to any humorous literary work. Interpretations of comedy have ranged from the satiric (comedy as a chastener of folly) to the vitalistic (comedy as a celebration of life and fecundity), with many stages between.

CONNOTATION A secondary or suggested meaning in addition to the primary one. See also **denotation.**

CONSONANCE Repetition of terminal consonants, as in, for example, *train* and *tone.* See also **assonance.**

COUPLET A unit of verse made up of two rhyming lines in the same meter.

CRITICISM "Criticism" of literature can mean many things, from a simple, explanatory gloss of a literary text to a complex examination of the relationship of a literary text to some system of psychology, a political position, or a philosophy of language. In this book, the term "criticism" is used as the critic Robert Scholes uses it, to refer to a stage of literary study, following "reading" and "interpretation," in which the text is placed in a broad context historically, culturally, and philosophically.

DACTYL A metrical foot consisting of an accented syllable followed by two unaccented ones: ´ ˘ ˘.

DENOTATION The primary or explicit meaning, as opposed to any "connotation," or suggested meaning. The terms "denotation" and "connotation" apply primarily to words, although they may be applied in an extended sense to any unit of meaning in a text, to a character or a situation, for example. See also **connotation.**

DÉNOUEMENT The outcome or resolution of a plot. The term is originally a French word meaning "unravelling." The metaphor is that of a plot being like the tying of a knot that is then untied or unravelled at the end. See also **plot.**

DEUS EX MACHINA "God from a machine," originally a god brought in by a crane to resolve the action of a Greek play; by extension, any artificial or improbable character or other device brought in at the end of a **story** to resolve a situation or untangle a **plot.**

DIAGESIS   A passage in a literary work where the author, either in his or her own voice or in that of one of the characters, interrupts the action to comment on, interpret, or explain it. Diagesis is usually contrasted to mimesis. See **mimesis.**

DIALOGUE   The spoken portions of a play, or a conversational passage in a piece of poetry or fiction.

DICTION   The choice and use of words in a literary work. Significant features of the diction of a work might be its level of formality, its geographical associations (use of regional idioms, for example), and its use of technical or specialized vocabularies (use of botanical terms, for example).

DIMETER   A verse line consisting of two metrical feet.

DOUBLE PLOT   A plot with two distinct sequences of events, often involving different characters. Shakespeare frequently balanced a main plot with a contrasting subplot.

DRAMATIC IRONY   The dramatic effect produced by leading an audience to see an incongruity between a situation on stage and what is said about it, while the characters remain unaware of the incongruity.

DRAMATIC SITUATION   In the analysis of poetry, the speaker, the person addressed, and the context of the address.

DYNAMIC CHARACTER   A character who changes in the course of a literary work, as opposed to a **static character,** who does not change.

ELEGY   Poem composed as a lament for one who is dead.

END-STOPPED LINE   A line of poetry which comes to a grammatical conclusion at its end.

ENGLISH SONNET   A sonnet with the rhyme scheme ABABCDCDEFEFGG, that contains, in other words, three quatrains and a concluding couplet. Also called a Shakespearean sonnet.

EPIC   A long narrative poem that celebrates the deeds of a legendary or traditional hero.

FALLING ACTION   The final action in a plot, in which loose ends are tied up and some indication is given of future prospects. See **dénouement.**

FICTION   The genre of literature to which novels and short stories belong, as distinct from poetry and drama. Etymologically and historically, the emphasis in the term is on its artistic form rather than on its falsity.

FIGURE OF SPEECH   An expression that uses words in a nonliteral and intensive way in order to produce a vivid and illuminating effect. The most important figures of speech are metaphor and metonymy. See **metaphor** and **metonymy**.

FOCALIZATION   The process by which the action of a narrative is presented from the perspective of one of the characters. To say that a story is **focalized** through a certain character is not exactly the same as saying that the story is told from that character's **point of view,** since the use of a point of view requires that the text be in the voice of the character in question, while focalization does not.

FOIL CHARACTER   A secondary character whose qualities and actions contrast with those of the main character and thus illuminate them.

FOOT A metrical unit ordinarily consisting of one stressed syllable and one or more unstressed syllables.

FORM In literary study, form usually refers to the literary type to which a work belongs (sonnet, maturation-novel, one-act play) rather than to the work's organization of ideas, which is usually referred to as **structure.**

FRAME STORY A story that gives the circumstances for the telling of a story. The narrative that gives the circumstances is called the **frame,** while the story that is told is the **embedded story.**

FREE VERSE Verse that does not follow conventional patterns of meter, stanzas, and rhyme.

HALF-STRESS Rhythmic stress on a syllable that is stronger than on an unstressed syllable but that falls short of full stress. Also called "secondary stress."

HEROIC COUPLET A couplet made up of iambic pentameter lines that are closed (grammatically complete at the end of the couplet) and end-stopped (with each line ending at a grammatical pause).

IAMB A metrical foot consisting of an unstressed syllable followed by a stressed one: ⌣′.

IAMBIC PENTAMETER Poetry consisting of lines of five iambic feet each.

IMAGE Vivid evocation of sensory experience. Descriptions that evoke the appearance of things are *visual images*. Such senses as taste and smell may also be drawn upon. Images usually come in groups in literature, making up "chains" of related images.

INTERPRETATION The question of what constitutes an adequate interpretation of a literary work is much debated; the answer depends on the school of **criticism** to which one adheres. This book follows the critic Robert Scholes by defining interpretation as the process of answering the question, "What does the work mean?" or, "What is the theme of the work?" Interpretation is distinct from criticism, which should follow interpretation and which asks the question, "What are the contexts for the meaning of the work?"

IRONY Incongruity between what is expected and what actually happens in a work of literature. **Verbal irony** turns around a sharp contrast between apparent and intended meanings, which are often diametrical opposites. **Irony of circumstance** involves not language so much as situations which contrast with expectations. See also **dramatic irony.**

ITALIAN SONNET A sonnet that rhymes ABBAABBACDECDE. (There may be some variation in the *sestet* or last six lines.) The principal break is between the *octave* (first eight lines) and the *sestet* rather than between the first twelve lines and the final couplet, as in an English sonnet. The Italian sonnet is also called the Petrarchan sonnet. See also **sonnet.**

LIMITED-OMNISCIENT NARRATOR A narrator whose knowledge is limited to what he or she sees and hears directly.

METAPHOR A figure of speech that turns around an implicit comparison. In a metaphor, a term is detached from something to which it applies in reality and is attached instead to something to which it applies only by comparison or analogy. In the phrase "the morning of life," for example, "morning" is taken from "day," to which it ordinarily applies, and is applied by analogy to "life." A **dramatic metaphor** or **stage metaphor** is not necessarily verbal but is established by a play's physical features. In Samuel Beckett's *Waiting for Godot,* for example, the metaphor "Life is waiting by the side of the road for someone who never comes" is never explicitly stated but is implicit in the setting and action.

METAPLAY   A play whose subject is wholly or partially drama itself. Such a play usually uses the elements of drama as metaphors for life. Shakespeare's *Hamlet,* for example, exploits many parallels between the theater and life, including the ambiguous meaning of "acting."

METER   The rhythmic pattern of poetry, defined in terms of the number and kind of metrical units, or feet, in a typical line.

METONYMY   A figure of speech in which an attribute or commonly associated feature is used to represent something. One kind of metonymy is **synecdoche,** in which the attribute is actually part of the thing represented. For example, in "All hands on deck!" "hands" is used to mean "sailors." Synecdoche may also use a more inclusive term for an less inclusive one: "the law" for a policeman, for example.

MIMESIS   The imitation of life in literature. Mimesis is usually identified with action in a story or play, while diagesis is associated with talk or explanation. See **diagesis.**

NARRATOR   The person who tells the story in a work of fiction. The narrator may be an individualized character in the work or an implied speaker who is not specifically individualized. See also **omniscient narrator, limited-omniscient narrator, reliable narrator,** and **unreliable narrator.**

OCTAVE   The first eight lines of a sonnet.

ODE   A lengthy lyric poem in praise of a person or thing; thus, a poem written in an exalted and often rather free style.

OMNISCIENT NARRATOR   A narrator who knows everything about a story, including the characters' unspoken thoughts and feelings.

OPEN DRAMATIC STRUCTURE   Term used for the structure of plays that have many characters and many scenes, that take place across an extended time and in a number of places, and that have more than one plot line. Shakespeare's plays and modern films both often employ open structures.

ORCHESTRA   The round stone platform that formed the main acting area in the Greek theater.

OTTAVA RIMA   A verse form with a stanza of eight iambic pentameter lines rhymed ABABABCC.

PARAPHRASE   A recasting of a literary work, especially a poem, in one's own words, for the purpose of simplification or clarification.

PENTAMETER   A line of verse containing five metrical feet.

PERSONA   An author's self-presentation in a literary work. The persona may be very unlike the author (as when an author has adopted a persona of the opposite sex) or very like the author. Even when the author and the persona seem exactly the same, the term "persona" reminds us that the self-presentation is artificial and self-constructed, not directly "real." (*Persona* means "mask" in Latin.)

PERSONIFICATION   A rhetorical device whereby inanimate objects or abstract ideas are represented as having human qualities, as in "Famine stalked the land."

PETRARCHAN SONNET   See **sonnet; Italian sonnet.**

PLOT   The series of events that constitute the action of a narrative. The stages of a plot are usually analyzed as (1) *exposition* (presentation of the initial situation and the revelation of a conflict), (2) *complication* or *rising action* (the development of the conflict), (3) *climax* (the point at which the conflict is most direct and at the end of which the conflict is resolved), and (4) *dénouement* or *falling action* (the winding up or "untying" of the action, creating an anticipation of conditions after the plot ends).

POETIC DICTION   A pejorative term, referring to a clichéd sort of stale "poetic" language such as the artificial language of second-rate neoclassic poetry or the sentimental clichés of late Victorian verse.

POINT OF VIEW   The narrative perspective of a story, including both the teller of the story and the time when it is taking place. Point of view is not exactly the same as narrative voice, since a story may be told from a particular point of view even though the narrative voice doing the telling may be an anonymous third-person omniscient one.

PROTAGONIST   The main character in a story or play.

QUATRAIN   Four-line stanza.

READING   In this book, the first stage of literary study, in which the principal question is, "What does the work say?" Reading should be followed by **interpretation** ("What does the work mean?"), then by **criticism** ("What is the context for the work's meaning?").

REALISM   The literary style that aims at verisimilitude, or faithfulness, to the appearance of life. **Expressive realism** adds to verisimilitude the arrangement of detail for expressive purposes.

RELIABLE NARRATOR   A narrator who is objective and whose version of events we are meant to trust.

RHYME ROYAL   A verse form that uses a stanza of seven lines of iambic pentameter rhymed ABABBCC.

RISING ACTION   The portion of a **plot** that follows the *exposition* and precedes the *climax,* where the principal conflict is developed.

RUN-ON LINE   A line of poetry that does not end with a grammatical conclusion but continues grammatically into the next line. The opposite of **end-stopped line.**

SCENE   A unit of a play with a fixed setting and continuous action; by extension, a passage in a narrative with the same features. Analyzing the **scenic structure** of a short story or novel is often a useful step in understanding the structure of the work.

SCENE BUILDING   The *skene* or building that formed the backdrop to the action in the Greek theater.

SELF-REFERENTIALITY   The phenomenon by which a literary work calls attention to its own status as a literary work. A play-within-a-play, for example, is usually a self-referential device, since it reminds us that the play within which it appears is also an invented work.

SESTET   The last six lines of a sonnet, often presenting a turn in the content, a contrast to the **octave** or first eight lines.

SETTING   The location or locations of the action of a literary work. Literary settings are seldom merely realistic or utilitarian; they almost always have some metaphoric dimension. See **metaphor.**

SHAKESPEAREAN SONNET.   See **sonnet; English sonnet.**

SHORT STORY   Short stories are notoriously hard to define, since they differ so much in length, form, and content. However, their brevity (usually fifty pages or less) determines some of their common features: concentration on a single character and on a single scene, organization around a single effect, and observation of the unities of time, place, and action.

SIMILE   A figure of speech in which two things are compared, using a term such as "like" or "as": "He is as strong as an ox."

SONNET   A single-stanza poem consisting of fourteen lines of rhymed iambic pentameter. See also **English sonnet** and **Italian sonnet.**

SPENSERIAN STANZA   A verse form which uses a stanza of nine lines, of which the first eight are iambic pentameter and the ninth is iambic hexameter (an alexandrine). The rhyme scheme is ABABBCBCC.

STANZA   Division of a poem, identified by a common pattern of meter, rhyme, and number of lines.

STATIC CHARACTER   One who does not change in the course of the work in which he or she appears. See also **dynamic character.**

STORY   In literary criticism, "story" means the chronological series of incidents that form the raw material of a narrative. From the materials of the story, a plot is formed through a process of selection, reshaping, and emphasis.

STREAM OF CONSCIOUSNESS   Technique of fiction by which a character's thoughts and feelings are given as a continuous stream rather than as discrete units.

STRESS   Metrically significant emphasis given to a syllable or word in a line of poetry.

STRUCTURE   The arrangement of materials within a literary work. If a poem asks a question and then goes on to answer it, or makes a generalization and gives three examples, or arranges three scenes into a short narrative, these features constitute the poem's structure.

SUBPLOT   A subordinate plot that parallels the main plot in a story or play. The subplot usually amplifies or complements the main plot in some way. Shakespeare routinely used subplots in his plays.

SYMBOL   Something that stands for something else, especially something concrete that stands for something abstract or immaterial. The meaning of a symbol is often complex and multiple, as opposed to that of a **sign,** which has a one-to-one relationship to what it stands for—a cross standing for Christianity, for example.

SYNECDOCHE   See **metonymy.**

TERZA RIMA   A verse form consisting of stanzas of three pentameter lines. The middle line of each triplet rhymes with the first and third lines of the following triplet.

Tetrameter A line of verse containing four metrical feet.

Theatricalization The process by which materials come to invite interpretation by being placed on stage.

Theme The central idea developed in a literary work.

Tragedy A dramatic work, or by extension any other literary work, that presents a protagonist engaged in a morally significant struggle and that ends in the protagonist's death or defeat. A key issue in differentiating types of tragedies is the degree of responsibility the protagonist bears for his or her fate. In **tragedy of character** the protagonist brings about his or her own defeat; in **tragedy of fate** the defeat is arbitrary and undeserved. The critic Northrop Frye distinguishes eight degrees of guilt and thus eight kinds of tragedy.

Tragicomedy Term used for a play, and by extension any narrative, that combines elements of tragedy and comedy. Most modern plays are of this mixed kind.

Trimeter A poetic line containing three metrical feet.

Trochee A metrical foot consisting of one stressed syllable followed by an unstressed one: ´˘.

Unreliable narrator A narrator whose account of the events of the story cannot be trusted, whether because of prejudice, ignorance, or lack of intelligence. Often, the disparity between the narrator's interpretation and the one that the reader surmises creates **dramatic irony.**

ACKNOWLEDGMENTS

ABBASI, TALAT. "Sari Petticoats" from *The Forbidden Stitch: An Asian American Women's Anthology*, edited by Shirley Geok-lin Lim et al., published by Calyx Books © 1989. Reprinted by permission of the author and the publisher.

ALGARIN, MIGUEL. "Always throw the first punch" and "Taos Pueblo Indians: 700 strong according to Bobbie's last census" from *On Call* by Miguel Algarin, published by Arte Publico Press, Houston, 1980. Reprinted by permission of Arte Publico Press.

ALLEN, PAULA GUNN. "Powwow 79, Durango" and "Los Angeles, 1980" from *Shadow Country* by Paula Gunn Allen, published by American Indian Studies Center, UCLA, 1982. Reprinted by permission of The Regents of the University of California, Los Angeles.

ALVAREZ, JULIA. "Daughter of Invention" reprinted from *How the Garcia Girls Lost Their Accents* by Julia Alvarez. Copyright © 1991 by Julia Alvarez. Reprinted by permission of Algonquin Books of Chapel Hill, a division of Workman Publishing Company, New York, NY.

ANGELOU, MAYA. "A Good Woman Feeling Bad" and "A Georgia Song" from *Shaker, Why Don't You Sing* by Maya Angelou. Copyright © 1983 by Maya Angelou. Reprinted by permission of Random House, Inc.

BACA, JIMMY SANTIAGO. "Ancestor" and "Immigrants in Our Own Land" from *Immigrants in Our Own Land* by Jimmy Santiago Baca. Copyright © Jimmy Santiago Baca. Reprinted by permission of the author.

BAMBARA, TONI CADE. "Medley" from *The Sea Birds Are Still Alive* by Toni Cade Bambara. Copyright © 1974, 1976, 1977 by Toni Cade Bambara. Reprinted by permission of Random House, Inc.

BARAKA, AMIRI. "Look for You Yesterday, Here You Come Today" and "Das Kapital" from *Selected Poems* by Amiri Baraka. Reprinted by permission of Sterling Lord Literistic, Inc. Copyright © 1975 by Amiri Baraka.

BEATTIE, ANN. "Weekend" from *Secrets and Surprises* by Ann Beattie. Copyright © 1976, 1977, 1978 by Ann Beattie. Reprinted by permission of Random House, Inc.

BELTON, DON. "My Soul Is a Witness" from *Breaking Ice: An Anthology of Contemporary African-American Fiction*. Copyright Don Belton. Reprinted by permission of the author, Don Belton.

BIDART, FRANK. "Another Life" and "Happy Birthday" from *In the Western Night, Collected Poems 1965–90* by Frank Bidart. Copyright © 1990 by Frank Bidart. Reprinted by permission of Farrar, Straus & Giroux, Inc.

BIRTHA, BECKY. "Johnnieruth" excerpted from *Lover's Choice* by Becky Birtha. Copyright © by Becky Birtha. Available from Seal Press, 3131 Western Avenue, #410, Seattle, WA 98121. 206-283-7844. Reprinted by permission of Seal Press.

BLUE CLOUD, PETER. "Stone Mountain Face" by Peter Blue Cloud. Reprinted by permission of the author.

BLUMENTHAL, MICHAEL. "Advice to My Students: How to Write a Poem" and "Against Romance" from *Against Romance* by Michael Blumenthal. Copyright © 1987 by Michael Blumenthal. Used by permission of Viking Penguin, a division of Penguin Books USA, Inc.

BORGES, JORGE LUIS. "The Garden of Forking Paths" from *Labyrinths* by Jorge Luis Borges. Copyright © 1962, 1964 by New Directions Publishing Corporation. Reprinted by permission of New Directions Publishing Corporation.

BROOKS, GWENDOLYN. "We Real Cool" and "A Bronzeville Mother Loiters in Mississippi. Meanwhile, a Mississippi Mother Burns Bacon" from *Blacks* by Gwendolyn Brooks. Copyright © 1987, published by The David Company, Chicago. Reprinted by permission of the author.

BROWN, JOESPH A., S. J. "Their Long Scars Touch Ours: A Reflection on the Poetry of Michael Harper" by Joseph A. Brown, S. J., from *Callaloo*, 9:1, Winter 1986, pp. 209–220. Reprinted by permission of The Johns Hopkins University Press.

BURNS, DIANE. "Gadoshkibos" and "Big Fun" reprinted from *Riding the One-Eyed Ford* by Diane Burns, Contact/II Publications, 1981. Reprinted by permission of the publisher.

CALLAHAN, JOHN F. "The Testifying Voice in Michael Harper's *Images of Kin*" by John F. Callahan. Reprinted from *Black American Literature Forum*, Volume 13, Number 3 (Fall 1979). Copyright © 1979 Indiana State University. Reprinted by permission of the publisher.

CARVER, RAYMOND. "What We Talk About When We Talk About Love" from *What We Talk About When We Talk About Love* by Raymond Carver. Copyright © 1981 by Raymond Carver. Reprinted by permission of Alfred A. Knopf, Inc.

CASTILLO, ANA. "Women Are Not Roses," "Napa, California," and "A Counter-Revolutionary Proposition" from *Women Are Not Roses*. Copyright © 1984 by Ana Castillo. Originally published by Arte Publico Press, Houston, 1984. Reprinted by permission of Susan Bergholz Literary Services, New York.

CERVANTES, LORNA DEE. "Uncle's First Rabbit" and "Visions of Mexico While at a Writing Symposium in Port Townsend, Washington" reprinted from *Explumada*, by Lorna Dee Cervantes, by permission of the University of Pittsburgh Press. © 1981 by Lorna Dee Cervantes.

CHAN, JEFFERY PAUL. Excerpt from "Introduction" to *The Big Aiiieeeee!* by Chan, Chin, Inada, and Wong. Copyright Jeffery Paul Chan. Reprinted by permission of Jeffery Paul Chan.

CHANG, DIANA. "The Oriental Contingent," "On Being in the Midwest," and "On the Fly" from *The Forbidden Stitch: An Asian American Women's Anthology*, edited by Shirley Geok-lin Lim and Mayumi Tsutakawa, published by Calyx Books, Inc., 1989. Copyright © Diana Chang. Reprinted by permission of the author.

CHERNOFF, MAXINE. "Bop" first appeared in *Bop* by Maxine Chernoff, Coffee House Press, 1986. Reprinted by permission of the publisher. Copyright © 1986 by Maxine Chernoff.

CHILDRESS, ALICE. *Wine in the Wilderness* by Alice Childress. Copyright © 1969 by Alice Childress. Used by permission of Flora Roberts, Inc.

CLAMPITT, AMY. "Stacking the Straw" from *Kingfisher* by Amy Clampitt. Copyright © 1979, 1980, 1981, 1982, 1983 by Amy Clampitt. Reprinted by permission of Alfred A. Knopf, Inc. "Iola, Kansas" from *Westward* by Amy Clampitt. Copyright © 1990 by Amy Clampitt. Reprinted by permission of Alfred A. Knopf, Inc.

CLIFF, MICHELLE. "If I Could Write This in Fire I Would Write This in Fire" from *The Land of Look Behind* by Michelle Cliff. Reprinted by permission of Firebrand Books, Ithaca, New York.

CLIFTON, LUCILLE. "Some Jesus," including "adam and eve," "cain," "moses," "solomon," "job," "daniel," "jonah," "john," "mary," "joseph," "the calling of the disciples," "the raising of lazarus," "palm sunday," "good friday," "easter sunday," and "spring song," reprinted from *Good Woman: Poems and a Memoir 1969–1980* by Lucille Clifton, copyright © 1987 by Lucille Clifton, with the permission of BOA Editions, Ltd., 92 Park Avenue, Brockport, NY 14420.

CODY, GABRIELLE. "David Hwang's *M. Butterfly:* Perpetuating the Misogynist Myth" by Gabrielle Cody from *Theater* 20:2, Spring 1989, pp. 24–27. © *Theater Magazine,* 1988. Reprinted by permission of the publisher.

COFER, JUDITH ORTIZ. "The Idea of Islands" from *Terms of Survival* by Judith Ortiz Cofer. Reprinted by permission of Arte Publico Press. "They Never Grow Old" from *The Latin Deli* by Judith Ortiz Cofer. Reprinted by permission of The University of Georgia Press.

CORBIN, STEVEN. "Upward Bound" from *Breaking Ice,* edited by Terry McMillan. Copyright 1990 by Steven Corbin. Reprinted by permission of the author.

CRUZ, VICTOR HERNANDEZ. "Today Is a Day of Great Joy" and "Going Uptown to Visit Miriam" from *Snaps* by Victor Hernandez Cruz. Copyright © 1968, 1969 by Victor Hernandez Cruz. Reprinted by permission of Random House, Inc. "Poem" from *Mainland* by Victor Hernandez Cruz. Copyright © 1973 by Victor Hernandez Cruz. Reprinted by permission of Random House, Inc.

DENT, THOMAS C. "Poem for Willie Mays" and "Secret Messages" from *Blue Lights and River Songs* by Tom Dent (Lotus Press, 1982). By permission of the author.

DICKINSON, EMILY. "Wild Nights—Wild Nights!," "My Life had stood—a Loaded Gun," and "To make a prairie it takes a clover and one bee." Poems #249, 754, and 1755 from *The Complete Poems of Emily Dickinson,* edited by Thomas H. Johnson. Copyright 1929 by Martha Dickinson Bianchi; Copyright © renewed 1957 by Mary L. Hampson. By permission of Little, Brown and Company. Reprinted by permission of the publishers and the Trustees of Amherst College from *The Poems of Emily Dickinson,* edited by Thomas H. Johnson, Cambridge, MA: The Belknap Press of Harvard University Press, Copyright 1951, © 1955, 1979, 1983 by the President and Fellows of Harvard College.

DOVE, RITA. "Geometry" reprinted from *The Yellow House on the Corner* by Rita Dove, by permission of Carnegie Mellon University Press. "Parsley" reprinted from *Museum* by Rita Dove, by permission of Carnegie Mellon University Press.

DYBEK, STUART. "Chopin in Winter" from *The Coast of Chicago* by Stuart Dybek. Copyright © 1990 by Stuart Dybek. Reprinted by permission of Alfred A. Knopf, Inc.

ELIOT, T. S. "The Love Song of J. Alfred Prufrock" from *Collected Poems, 1909–1962* by T. S. Eliot; copyright 1936 by Harcourt Brace & Company, copyright © 1964, 1963 by T. S. Eliot, reprinted by permission of the publisher.

ERDRICH, LOUISE. "American Horse" from *Earth Power Coming: Short Fiction in Native American Literature,* edited by Simon J. Ortiz. Copyright © 1983 by Louise Erdrich. Reprinted by permission of the author.

ESTEVES, SANDRA MARIA. "For Fidel Castro" and "Some People Are About Jam" © 1980 Sandra Maria Esteves, reprinted from *Yerba Buena;* Greenfield Review; Greenfield Center, New York; 1980. Reprinted by permission of the author.

EURIPIDES. *Medea* from *Medea and Other Plays* by Euripides, translated by Philip Vellacott (Penguin Classics, 1963) copyright © Philip Vellacott, 1963.

EVANS, MARI. "I Am a Black Woman" and "early in the mornin" from *I Am a Black Woman* by Mari Evans, published by William Morrow & Co., 1970, by permission of the author.

FAULKNER, WILLIAM. "Barn Burning" from *Collected Stories of William Faulkner* by William Faulkner. Copyright © 1950 by Random House, Inc. and renewed 1977 by Jill Faulkner Summers. Reprinted by permission of Random House, Inc.

FORCHÉ, CAROLYN. "Return" from *The Country Between Us* by Carolyn Forché. Copyright © 1980 by Carolyn Forché. Reprinted by permission of HarperCollins Publishers.

FORD, KAREN. "*The Yellow Wallpaper* and Women's Discourse" from *Tulsa Studies in Women's Literature,* Vol. 4, No. 2, Fall 1985. © 1985, The University of Tulsa. Reprinted by permission of the publisher.

FROST, ROBERT. "Mending Wall" and "The Road Not Taken" from *The Poetry of Robert Frost,* edited by Edward Connery Lathem. Copyright 1944, © 1958 by Robert Frost. Copyright © 1967 by Lesley Frost Ballantine. Copyright 1916, 1930, 1939, © 1969 by Henry Holt and Company, Inc. Reprinted by permission of Henry Holt and Company, Inc.

GLÜCK, LOUISE. "For My Mother," "Poem," and "The School Children" © 1971, 1972, 1973, 1974, 1975 by Louise Glück. From *The House on Marshland* by Louise Glück, published by The Ecco Press. Reprinted by permission.

GOLDBARTH, ALBERT. "Before" reprinted from *Faith* (New Rivers Press) by permission of the author. "A History of Civilization" © 1983 by Albert Goldbarth (reprinted from *Original Light: New and Selected Poems,* published by Ontario Review Press). Reprinted by permission of the author.

GRAHAM, JORIE. "Mind" from *Hybrids of Plants and of Ghosts* by Jorie Graham. Copyright © 1980 by Princeton University Press. Reprinted by permission of Princeton University Press. "My Garden, My Daylight" from *Erosion* by Jorie Graham. Copyright © 1983 by Princeton University Press. Reprinted by permission of Princeton University Press.

GRAHN, JUDY. "The Common Woman" from *The Work of a Common Woman* by Judy Grahn. Copyright © 1978 by Judy Grahn.

GREEN, RAYNA. "When I Cut My Hair" and "Cooseponakeesa (Mary Mathews Musgrove Bosomsworth), Leader of the Creeks, 1700–1783" from *That's What She Said: Contemporary Poetry and Fiction by Native American Women,* edited by Rayna Green. Copyright © Rayna Green. Reprinted by permission of the author.

GRIFFIN, SUSAN. "Grandmother" and "Grandfather" from *Like the Iris of an Eye* by Susan Griffin. Copyright © Susan Griffin. Reprinted by permission of the author.

H. D. (HILDA DOOLITTLE). "Sea Rose" and "Helen" from *Collected Poems 1912–1944* by Hilda Doolittle. Copyright © 1982 by The Estate of Hilda Doolittle. Reprinted by permission of New Directions Publishing Corp.

HACKER, MARILYN. "Feeling and Form" and "Conte" from *Taking Notice* by Marilyn Hacker. Copyright © 1976, 1978, 1979, 1980 by Marilyn Hacker. Reprinted by permission of Alfred A. Knopf, Inc.

HARJO, JOY. "Remember," "Your Phone Call at Eight A.M.," and "She Had Some Horses" from *She Had Some Horses* by Joy Harjo. Copyright © 1983 by Thunder's Mouth Press. Used by permission of the publisher, Thunder's Mouth Press.

HASLAM, GERALD. "Hawk's Flight: An American Fable" from *Hawk Flights: Visions of the West,* published by Seven Buffaloes Press, Big Timber, Montana, 1983. Originally published in *Blue Cloud Quarterly* and later in *Earth Power Coming: Short Fiction in Native American Literature,* edited by Simon J. Ortiz, published by Navajo Community College Press, Tsaile, Arizona, 1983.

HARPER, MICHAEL S. "American History," "Reuben, Reuben," "Dear John, Dear Coltrane," "Here Where Coltrane Is," "High Modes: Vision as Ritual: Confirmation," "Continuous Visit," "Nightmare Begins Responsibility," "Alice," and "A Narrative of the Life and Times of John Coltrane, Played by Himself" from *Dear John, Dear Coltrane* by Michael S. Harper. Copyright © Michael S. Harper, 1970, 1985. Reprinted by permission of the author. "My Poetic Technique and the Humanization of the American Audience" by Michael S. Harper from *Black American Literature and Humanism,* edited by R. Baxter Miller, pp. 27–32. Copyright © 1981 by The University Press of Kentucky. Used by permission of the publishers.

HEDGES, ELAINE R. "Afterword" to *The Yellow Wallpaper* by Charlotte Perkins Gilman. From the book *The Yellow Wallpaper* by Charlotte Perkins Gilman. Published by The Feminist Press at the City University of New York. All rights reserved. Copyright © 1973 by Elaine R. Hedges.

HEMINGWAY, ERNEST. "The Snows of Kilimanjaro" from *The Short Stories of Ernest Hemingway.* Reprinted with permission of Charles Scribner's and Sons, an imprint of Macmillan Publishing Company. Copyright 1936 by Ernest Hemingway; renewal copyright © 1964 by Mary Hemingway.

HENSON, LANCE. "warrior nation trilogy," "Five Poems for Coyote from Cheyenne Country," and "At the Ramada Inn" from *Selected Poems 1980–1983* by Lance Henson, The Greenfield Review Press.

HINOJOSA-SMITH, ROLANDO. "One of Those Things" from *The Valley* by Rolando Hinojosa-Smith. Published by Bilingual Press/Editorial Bilingue, Eastern Michigan University, Ypsilanti, 1983.

HOBSON, GEARY. "Deer Hunting" and "Central Highlands, Viet Nam, 1968" from *Deer Hunting and Other Poems* by Geary Hobson, Strawberry Press. Reprinted by permission of the publisher.

HOGAN, LINDA. "Aunt Moon's Young Man" reprinted from *Missouri Review* 11:1 (1988), pp. 186–204. Reprinted by permission of The Missouri Review. "Leaving" and "Song for My Name" from *Calling Myself Home* by Linda Hogan. Reprinted by permission of the author.

HONGO, GARRETT KAORU. "Ancestral Graves, Kahuku" and "The Cadence of Silk" from *The River of Heaven* by Garrett Hongo. Copyright © 1981, 1983, 1985, 1986, 1987, 1988 by Garrett Hongo. Reprinted by permission of Alfred A. Knopf, Inc.

HUGHES, LANGSTON. "The Negro Speaks of Rivers" from *Selected Poems of Langston Hughes* by Langston Hughes. Copyright 1926 by Alfred A. Knopf, Inc. and renewed 1954 by Langston Hughes. Reprinted by permission of Alfred A. Knopf, Inc. "Freedom Train" from *Montage of a Dream Deferred.* Reprinted by permission of Harold Ober Associates Incorporated. Copyright 1951 by Langston Hughes. Copyright renewed 1979 by George Houston Bass.

HWANG, DAVID HENRY. *M. Butterfly* and "Afterword" to *M. Butterfly* by David Henry Hwang. Copyright © 1986, 1987, 1988 by David Henry Hwang. Used by permission of New American Library, a division of Penguin Books USA, Inc.

JOHNSON, CHARLES. "China" from *The Sorcerer's Apprentice* by Charles Johnson. Reprinted with permission of Atheneum Publishers, an imprint of Macmillan Publishing Company, from *The Sorcerer's Apprentice* by Charles Johnson. Copyright © 1983 by Charles Johnson. First appeared in MSS, 1983.

JORDAN, JUNE. "Poem for Granville Ivanhoe Jordan, November 4, 1890–December 21, 1974," "Cameo No. I," and "Cameo No. II" from *I Do Things in the Dark* by June Jordan. Copyright © 1992 by June Jordan. Reprinted by permission of the author.

KELLY, BRIGIT PEGEEN. "Imagining Their Own Hymns" and "Young Wife's Lament" from *To the Place of Trumpets* by Brigit Pegeen Kelly. Copyright © 1988 by Brigit Pegeen Kelly. Reprinted by permission of Yale University Press.

KENNY, MAURICE. "North," "Land," and "mulleins are my arms" from *Between Two Rivers: Selected Poems 1956–1984* by Maurice Kenny. White Pine Press, Fredonia, NY, 1987. Reprinted by permission of the publisher.

KIM CHI-WŎN. "A Certain Beginning" excerpted from *Words of Farewell: Stories by Korean Women Writers.* Copyright © by Kim Chi-wŏn. Available from Seal Press, 3131 Western Avenue, #410, Seattle, WA 98121. 206-283-7844. Reprinted by permission of Seal Press.

KINGSTON, MAXINE HONG. "No Name Woman" from *The Woman Warrior: Memoirs of a Girlhood Among Ghosts* by Maxine Hong Kingston. Copyright © 1975, 1976 by Maxine Hong Kingston. Reprinted by permission of Alfred A. Knopf, Inc.

KINNELL, GALWAY. "First Song" from *What a Kingdom It Was* by Galway Kinnell. Copyright © 1960, renewed 1988 by Galway Kinnell. Reprinted by permission of Houghton Mifflin Company. All rights reserved. "The Porcupine" from *Body Rags* by Galway Kinnell. Copyright © 1965, 1966, 1967 by Galway Kinnell. Reprinted by permission of Houghton Mifflin Company. All rights reserved.

KNIGHT, ETHERIDGE. "The Idea of Ancestry" and "For Langston Hughes" reprinted from *The Essential Etheridge Knight* by Etheridge Knight, by permission of the University of Pittsburgh Press. © 1986 by Etheridge Knight.

KOGAWA, JOY. "Ancestors' Graves in Kurakawa," "Woodtick," and "Snakes" from *A Choice of Dreams* by Joy Kogawa. Copyright Joy Kogawa. Reprinted by permission of the author.

LAWRENCE, D. H. "The Horse Dealer's Daughter" copyright 1922 by Thomas B. Seltzer, Inc., renewed by Freida Lawrence, from *Complete Short Stories of D. H. Lawrence* by D. H. Lawrence. Used by permission of Viking Penguin, a division of Penguin Books USA, Inc.

LENZ, GÜNTHER H. Excerpt from "Black Poetry and Black Music: Michael Harper and John Coltrane" in *History and Tradition in Afro-American Culture,* edited by Günther H. Lenz, pp. 293–303. Published by Campus Press, University of Frankfurt.

LIU, STEPHEN SHU NING. "Night Sailing," "Home Thoughts," "The Wild Horse Star," and "At the King's Funeral" previously published in *Dream Journeys to China* by New World Press, Beijing, China in 1981. Reprinted by permission of New World Press, Beijing. China.

LORDE, AUDRE. "Stations" and "Call" reprinted from *Our Dead Behind Us,* Poems by Audre Lorde, by permission of W. W. Norton & Company, Inc. Copyright © 1986 by Audre Lorde.

MCPHERSON, JAMES ALAN. "A Loaf of Bread" from *Elbow Room* by James Alan McPherson. Copyright © 1972, 1973, 1974, 1975, 1977 by James Alan McPherson. By permission of Little, Brown and Company.

MADHUBUTI, HAKI R. "The Secrets of the Victors," "Safisha," and "Lady Day" from *Earthquakes and Sunrise Missions* by Haki R. Madhubuti, Third World Press, Chicago, IL. Reprinted by permission of the publisher.

MADONICK, MICHAEL. "Letter to My Ex-Wife Who Is Having Lunch with Harold Bloom Tomorrow" by Michael Madonick in *New Jersey Poetry Journal*, 4, 1985. Reprinted by permission of the author. "White Deer" by Michael Madonick from *Creeping Bent*, 6, 1988. Reprinted by permission of the author.

MARSHALL, PAULE. "Barbados" from *Reena and Other Stories*. Copyright © 1961, 1983 by Paule Marshall. From the book *Reena and Other Stories*. Published by The Feminist Press at The City University of New York. All rights reserved.

MARTINEZ-SERROS, HUGO. "Learn! Learn!" from *The Last Laugh and Other Stories,* published by Arte Publico Press, Houston, 1986. Reprinted by permission of Arte Publico Press.

MARTONE, MICHAEL. "Fort Wayne Is Seventh on Hitler's List" from *Fort Wayne Is Seventh on Hitler's List* by Michael Martone. First published in the *Minnesota Review*, No. 16, 1981. Copyright © 1981 by Michael Martone. Reprinted by permission of the author.

MILLAY, EDNA ST. VINCENT. "Love Is Not All" and "On Thought in Harness" by Edna St. Vincent Millay. From *Collected Poems*, HarperCollins. Copyright © 1931, 1934, 1958, 1962 by Edna St. Vincent Millay and Norma Millay Ellis. Reprinted by permission of Elizabeth Barnett, literary executor.

MIRIKITANI, JANICE. "Jade" and "Breaking Traditions" from *Shedding Silence* by Janice Mirikitani. Copyright © 1987 by Janice Mirikitani. Reprinted by permission of Celestial Arts, Berkeley, California.

MOLIÈRE. *Tartuffe* by Molière, translated by Richard Wilbur, copyright © 1963, 1962, 1961, and renewed 1989 by Richard Wilbur, reprinted by permission of Harcourt Brace Jovanovich, Inc. CAUTION: Professionals and amateurs are hereby warned that this translation, being fully protected under the copyright laws of the United States of America, the British Commonwealth, including Canada, and all other countries which are signatories to the Universal Copyright Convention and the International Copyright Union, are subject to royalty. All rights, including professional, amateur, motion picture, recitation, lecturing, public reading, radio broadcasting, and television, are strictly reserved. Particular emphasis is laid on the question of readings, permission for which must be secured from the author's agent in writing. Inquiries on professional rights (except for amateur rights) should be addressed to Curtis Brown Ltd., 10 Astor Place, New York, NY 10003. Inquiries on translation rights should be addressed to Harcourt Brace Jovanovich, Inc., Permissions Department, Orlando, Florida 32887.

MOMADAY, N. SCOTT. "Plainview: 1," "Plainview: 2," "Plainview: 3," and "Plainview: 4" from *The Gourd Dancer* by N. Scott Momaday. Reprinted by permission of the author.

MOORE, MARIANNE. "Poetry" reprinted with permission of Macmillan Publishing Company from *Collected Poems of Marianne Moore*. Copyright 1935 by Marianne Moore, renewed 1963 by Marianne Moore and T. S. Eliot. "Nevertheless" reprinted with permission of Macmillan Publishing Company from *Collected Poems of Marianne Moore*. Copyright 1944, and renewed 1972, by Marianne Moore.

MORALES, AURORA LEVINS. "Sugar Poem" and "Class Poem" from *Getting Home Alive* by Aurora Levins Morales and Rosario Morales. Reprinted by permission of Firebrand Books, Ithaca, New York.

MORALES, ROSARIO. "My Revolution" and "Old" from *Getting Home Alive* by Aurora Levins Morales and Rosario Morales. Reprinted by permission of Firebrand Books, Ithaca, New York.

MORI, TOSHIO. "Toshio Mori" from *Yokohama, California* by Toshio Mori. The Caxton Printers, Ltd., Caldwell, Idaho.

MUKHERJEE, BHARATI. "The Management of Grief" from *The Middleman and Other Stories* by Bharati Mukherjee. Copyright © 1988 by Bharati Mukherjee. Used by permission of Grove Press, Inc.

NEAL, LARRY. "Malcolm X—An Autobiography" and "Lady's Days" from *Hoodoo Hollerin' Bebop Ghosts* by Larry Neal. Copyright © 1986, 1974 by Larry Neal. Reprinted by permission of Howard University Press.

NEELY, CAROL THOMAS. "Alternative Women's Discourse" from *Tulsa Studies in Women's Literature*, Vol. 4, No. 2, Fall 1985. © 1985, The University of Tulsa. Reprinted by permission of the publisher.

NORMAN, MARSHA. *Getting Out* by Marsha Norman. *Getting Out* is fully protected under the copyright laws of the United States of America, and of all countries covered by the International Copyright Union. The play was originally produced at the Actors Theatre of Louisville. © 1978. Any inquiries should be directed to the Tantleff office, 375 Greenwich St., Suite 700, New York, NY 10013.

OATES, JOYCE CAROL. "Where Are You Going? Where Have You Been?" from *The Wheel of Love*. Copyright © 1966 by Joyce Carol Oates. Reprinted by permission of John Hawkins & Associates, Inc.

OKITA, DWIGHT. "In Response to Executive Order 9066: All Americans of Japanese Descent Must Report to Relocation Centers" and "Crossing with the Light" first printed by Greenfield Review Press in *Breaking Silence: An Anthology of Contemporary Asian American Poets,* edited by Joseph Bruchac. Reprinted by permission of the author © 1983 Dwight Okita.

OLSEN, TILLIE. "I Stand Here Ironing" from *Tell Me a Riddle* by Tillie Olsen. Copyright © 1956, 1957, 1960, 1961 by Tillie Olsen. Used by permission of Delacorte Press/Seymour Lawrence, a division of Bantam Doubleday Dell Publishing Group, Inc.

ORTIZ, SIMON J. "Kaiser and the War" from *Fightin': New and Collected Stories* by Simon J. Ortiz. Reprinted by permission of the author. "Two Women" and "Many Farms Notes" from *Going for the Rain* by Simon J. Ortiz. Reprinted by permission of the author, Simon J. Ortiz.

PIETRI, PEDRO. "Intermission from Monday," "Intermission from Friday," and "The Night Is Out of Sight" from *Traffic Violations* by Pedro Pietri. Copyright by Pedro Pietri and Waterfront Press.

PIÑERO, MIGUEL. "A Lower East Side Poem" and "La Bodega Sold Dreams" from *La Bodega Sold Dreams* by Miguel Piñero, published by Arte Publico Press, Houston, 1985. Reprinted by permission of Arte Publico Press.

REED, ISHMAEL. "I Am a Cowboy in the Boat of Ra," "Why I Often Allude to Osiris," and "Beware: Do Not Read This Poem" reprinted with permission of Atheneum Publishing Company, from *New and Collected Poems* by Ishmael Reed. Copyright © 1972 by Ishmael Reed.

REVARD, CARTER. "Support Your Local Police Dog" and "Driving in Oklahoma" from *Ponca War Dancers* by Carter Revard. Copyright © Carter Revard. Reprinted by permission of the author.

RICH, FRANK. "Review/Theater: *M. Butterfly,* A Story of a Strange Love, Conflict and Betrayal," by Frank Rich, Mar. 21, 1988. Copyright © 1988 by The New York Times Company. Reprinted by permission.

RIOS, ALBERTO ALVARO. "Johnny Ray" from *The Iguana Killer: Twelve Stories of the Heart* by Alberto Alvaro Rios. Blue Moon Press and Confluence Press, 1984. Reprinted with permission. "Mi Abuelo" and "Nani" from *Whispering to Fool the Wind* by Alberto Alvaro Rios. Copyright © 1982 by Alberto Alvaro Rios. Reprinted by permission of the author.

ROSE, WENDY. "Truganinny" and "Kitty" from *The Halfbreed Chronicles and Other Poems* by Wendy Rose. Copyright © 1985 by Wendy Rose.

RUSHIN, DONNA KATE. "The Bridge Poem" from *This Bridge Called My Back: Writings by Radical Women of Color*, edited by Cherrie Moraga and Gloria Anzaldua. "The Black Back-ups" from *Home Girls: A Black Feminist Anthology*, edited by Barbara Smith. Both selections copyright © 1983 by Kate Rushin, used by permission of Kitchen Table: Women of Color Press, P.O. Box 908, Latham, NY 12110.

SANCHEZ, SONIA. "A Song," "Blues," and "Poem No. 10" from the book *Homegirls and Grenades* by Sonia Sanchez. Copyright © 1984 by Sonia Sanchez. Used by permission of the publisher, Thunder's Mouth Press.

SHAKESPEARE, WILLIAM. *The Tempest* by William Shakespeare. Reprinted by permission of Macmillan Publishing Company from *The Living Shakespeare*, edited by Oscar James Campbell. Copyright 1949 by Macmillan Publishing Company, renewed 1976 by Robert F. Campbell, Est. of Eunice C. Goodale, and Emily F. C. Meyer.

SHEPARD, SAM. "True West" from *Seven Plays* by Sam Shepard. Copyright © 1979 by Sam Shepard. Used by permission of Bantam Books, a division of Bantam Doubleday Dell Publishing Group, Inc.

SILKO, LESLIE MARMON. "Yellow Woman," "Prayer to the Pacific," and "Deer Dance/For Your Return" from *Storyteller* by Leslie Marmon Silko. Reprinted by permission of the author.

SIMIC, CHARLES. "Summer Morning" and "My Shoes" from *Dismantling the Silence* by Charles Simic. Copyright © 1971 by Charles Simic. Reprinted by permission of George Braziller, Inc.

SMITH, R. T. "Goyathlay" by R. T. Smith. Reprinted by permission of TAMAQUA Press, 1992. Originally appeared in *TAMAQUA*, Vol II, Issue 2, Winter/Spring, 1991.

SNYDER, GARY. "Axe Handles" excerpted from *Axe Handles*, copyright © 1983 by Gary Snyder. Published by North Point Press and reprinted by permission. "Riprap" reprinted by permission of the author, Gary Snyder.

SONG, CATHY. "Lost Sister" and "The Seamstress" from *Picture Bride* by Cathy Song. Copyright © 1983 by Cathy Song. Reprinted by permission of Yale University Press.

SOTO, GARY. "Black Hair" and "Ode to the Yard Sale" reprinted from *Black Hair* by Gary Soto, by permission of the University of Pittsburgh Press. Copyright © 1985 by Gary Soto.

STEVENS, WALLACE. "The Snow Man" and "Of Modern Poetry" from *The Collected Poems of Wallace Stevens* by Wallace Stevens. Copyright 1923, 1942 by Wallace Stevens. Copyright renewed 1951 by Wallace Stevens and renewed 1970 by Holly Stevens. Reprinted by permission of Alfred A. Knopf, Inc.

STRAND, MARK. "Where Are the Waters of Childhood?" and "Keeping Things Whole" from *Selected Poems* by Mark Strand. Copyright © 1979, 1980 by Mark Strand. Reprinted by permission of Alfred A. Knopf, Inc.

TALLMOUNTAIN, MARY. "The Last Wolf" and "The Ivory Dog for My Sister" from *There Is No Word for Goodbye* by Mary TallMountain. Copyright 1981 by Mary TallMountain, published in *The Blue Cloud Quarterly*. "The Sinh of Niguudzagha" by Mary TallMountain from *Earth Power Coming: Short Fiction in Native American Literature*, edited by Simon J. Ortiz, published by Navajo Community College Press, Tsaile, Arizona, 1983.

TAN, AMY. "Two Kinds" from *The Joy Luck Club* by Amy Tan. Reprinted by permission of The Putnam Publishing Group for *The Joy Luck Club* by Amy Tan. Copyright © 1989 by Amy Tan.

TREICHLER, PAULA A. "Escaping the Sentence: Diagnosis and Discourse in *The Yellow Wallpaper*" from *Feminist Issues in Literary Scholarship*, edited by Shari Benstock, published by Indiana University Press, 1984. Reprinted by permission of the publisher. "The Wall Behind the Yellow Wallpaper" from *Tulsa Studies in Women's Literature*, Vol. 4, No. 2, Fall 1985. © 1985, The University of Tulsa. Reprinted by permission of the publisher.

VALDEZ, LUIS. "Los Venditos" by Luis Valdez is reprinted with permission of the publisher from *Luis Valdez—Early Works: Actos, Bernabe and Pensamiento Serpentino* (Houston: Arte Publico Press—University of Houston, 1990).

WHITEMAN, ROBERTA HILL. "The Long Parenthesis" and "Star Quilt" from *Star Quilt* by Roberta Hill Whiteman, Holy Cow! Press, 1984. Reprinted by permission of Holy Cow! Press.

WIDEMAN, JOHN EDGAR. "Rock River" from *Fever: Twelve Stories* by John Edgar Wideman. Copyright © 1989 by John Edgar Wideman. Reprinted by permission of Henry Holt and Company, Inc.

WILLIAMS, SHERLEY ANNE. "I Want Aretha to Set This to Music" and "you were never miss brown to me" from *Someone Sweet Angel Chile* by Sherley Anne Williams. Copyright © 1982 by Sherley Anne Williams. Reprinted by permission of Sandra Dijkstra Literary Agency.

VAN WALLEGHEN, MICHAEL. "More Trouble with the Obvious" and "The Honeymoon of the Muse" from *More Trouble with the Obvious* by Michael Van Walleghen. Copyright © 1981 by University of Illinois Press, Urbana. Reprinted by permission of the publisher.

WILLIAMS, WILLIAM CARLOS. "Spring and All" from *Collected Poems of William Carlos Williams, 1909–1939, vol. I*. Copyright 1938 by New Directions Publishing Corp. Reprinted by permission of New Directions Publishing Corp. "Burning the Christmas Greens" from *Collected Poems of William Carlos Williams, 1939–1962, vol. II*. Copyright 1944, 1948 by William Carlos Williams. Reprinted by permission of New Directions Publishing Corp.

WILSON, AUGUST. *Ma Rainey's Black Bottom* by August Wilson. Copyright © 1985 by August Wilson. Used by permission of New American Library, a division of Penguin Books USA, Inc.

WONG, NELLY. "Dreams in Harrison Railroad Park" and "Not from the Food" from *Dreams in Harrison Railroad Park* by Nelly Wong, Kelsey Street Press, 1977. Reprinted by permission of the publisher.

WONG, SHAWN. "Love Among Friends" and "Elegy for a Greenhouse" by Shawn Wong. Copyright © 1973, 1992 by Shawn Wong. Reprinted by permission of the author.

WOOLF, VIRGINIA. "An Unwritten Novel" from *A Haunted House and Other Short Stories* by Virginia Woolf, copyright 1944 and renewed 1972 by Harcourt Brace & Company, reprinted by permission of the publisher.

WRIGHT, JAY. "The Homecoming Singer" and "The Invention of a Garden" from *Selected Poems of Jay Wright,* edited by Robert B. Stepto. Copyright © 1987 by Princeton University Press. Reprinted by permission of Princeton University Press.

YAMADA, MITSUYE. "The Club" from *Desert Run: Poems and Stories* by Mitsuye Yamada. Copyright © 1988 by Mitsuye Yamada. Used by permission of Kitchen Table: Women of Color Press, P.O. Box 908, Latham, NY 12110.

YAMAUCHI, WAKAKO. "And the Soul Shall Dance" (the story and the play) by Wakako Yamauchi from *New Worlds of Literature,* edited by Jerome Beaty and J. Paul Hunter. Copyright © Wakako Yamauchi. Reprinted by permission of the author, Wakako Yamauchi.

YOUNG BEAR, RAY A. "The Reason Why I Am Afraid Even Though I Am a Fisherman" and "The Language of Weather" from *The Invisible Musician* by Ray A. Young Bear, Holy Cow! Press, 1990. Reprinted by permission of Holy Cow! Press.

INDEX OF AUTHORS AND TITLES

🙚🙠